W9-BOK-159

MIDDLE AND JUNIOR HIGH
CORE COLLECTION

TENTH EDITION

CORE COLLECTION SERIES

Formerly
STANDARD CATALOG SERIES
JOHN GREENFIELDT, GENERAL EDITOR

CHILDREN'S CORE COLLECTION

MIDDLE & JUNIOR HIGH CORE COLLECTION

SENIOR HIGH CORE COLLECTION

PUBLIC LIBRARY CORE COLLECTION: NONFICTION

FICTION CORE COLLECTION

MIDDLE AND JUNIOR HIGH CORE COLLECTION

TENTH EDITION

Former Title:

Middle and Junior High School Library Catalog

EDITED BY

ANNE PRICE

ASSISTED BY

MARGUERITA ROWLAND

NEW YORK • DUBLIN

THE H. W. WILSON COMPANY

2009

Printed in the United States of America

Abridged Dewey Decimal Classification and Relative Index, Edition 14 is © 2004-2009 OCLC Online Computer Library Center, Incorporated. Used with Permission. DDC, Dewey, and Dewey Decimal Classification are registered trademarks of OCLC.

ISBN 978-0-8242-1102-8

Library of Congress Cataloging-in-Publication Data

Middle and junior high core collection / edited by Anne Price. — 10th ed.
   p. cm. — (Core collection series)
Includes index.

ISBN 978-0-8242-1102-8 (alk. paper)

1. Young adult literature—Bibliography. 2. Junior high school libraries—United States—Book lists. I. Price, Anne, 1946-

Z1037.J854 2009
011.62'5—dc22

2009027506

Visit H.W. Wilson's Web site at: www.hwwilson.com

CONTENTS

CONTENTS

PREFACE

Middle and Junior High Core Collection is a selective list of fiction and nonfiction books recommended for young people in grades five through nine. In addition to this volume, the service unit comprises annual supplements for 2010, 2011, and 2012 without further charge.

New in This Edition

There are two features of the *Middle and Junior High Core Collection* that are new in this edition. In the past every book in the collection was deemed suitable for either the younger middle school or junior high school audience, or for both, with only a single indication of "7 and up" for the older audience. We now designate a specific range of grade levels for every title. This is expressed by a series of numbers representing the grades, such as "4 5 6 7," or "5 6 7 8," or "8 9 10 11 12." The book is deemed suitable for any grade listed on that book.

The second new feature is the identification of titles that are considered "most highly recommended." These titles constitute a short list, as it were, of the essential books in a given category or on a given subject. There are often a number of recommended titles on a single subject, such as biographies of Abraham Lincoln, and the Short List designation helps a user who wants only one or two. A star (*) after the price indicates that a book is a "most highly recommended" title.

This edition includes more than 8,000 book titles, over 2,000 more than the 9th edition. Of these 8,000 titles, over 6,000 are new since the 9th edition. There are broad revisions in the areas of crafts; terrorism and international security; environment and global warming; diseases and medicine; and religion. An expanded list of works for the librarian or media specialist includes bibliographies and other resources for the selection and evaluation of print and nonprint materials; library management and programming; library building design; and the use of the Internet in instruction.

Scope

All the books listed are published in the United States, or published in Canada or the United Kingdom and distributed in the United States. All titles were in print at the time of listing.

The Core collection excludes the following: non-English-language materials, with the exception of bilingual materials, dictionaries, and similar items; works of adult fiction other than books originally written for adults but read by young people or books widely used in the curriculum; textbooks; and books about individual computer programs or versions of programs, and other topics that quickly become outdated. Periodicals and electronic resources are no longer listed in this publication but have been incorporated among other nonbook materials in a new database on WilsonWeb, entitled *Nonbook Materials Core Collection*. This volume includes a generous selection of graphic novels, even though a more comprehensive collection of recommended graphic novels can be found in *Graphic Novels Core Collection* on WilsonWeb.

History

Junior High School Library Catalog, first published in 1965, was developed to address the unique needs of younger adolescents. It developed from the *Standard Catalog for High School Libraries*, which was subsequently modified in scope and retitled *Senior High School Library Catalog*. With the seventh edition in 1995 the title of the Catalog was changed from *Junior High School Library Catalog* to *Middle and Junior High School Library Catalog* to reflect the prevalence of middle school programs and the extension of coverage to grades five and six. With this edition the title is changed to *Middle and Junior High Core Collection* to emphasize the function of the database in establishing and maintaining the solid core of a library, which can then be expanded in many ways, according to the library's individual needs.

Preparation

An advisory committee of distinguished librarians assisted in the compilation of this Core Collection. The committee reaffirmed the selection policy, reevaluated titles from the previous edition of the Core Collection and its supplements, and proposed many new titles. The committee represents a diversity of backgrounds in librarianship for young people and a wealth of experience on national juries and American Library Association committees.

ACKNOWLEDGMENTS

This Core Collection could not have been published without the cooperative efforts of publishers and the library community. The H. W. Wilson Company is indebted to the publishers who generously supplied copies of their books, as well as information about editions and prices. The Company also acknowledges its gratitude to the librarians of its advisory committee, who gave so generously of their time and expertise in advising the editors in the choice of materials to include in the Collection.

Members of the Advisory Committee:

Kathie Fitch
Librarian
Rachel Carson Middle School
Hendron, Virginia

Melinda Greenblatt
Program Director
Library Connections
Archdiocese of New York
New York, New York

Mari J. Hardacre
Young Adults' Services Manager
Allen County Public Library
Fort Wayne, Indiana

Pam Spencer Holley
Library Consultant
Hallwood, Virginia

Richie Partington
Lecturer, Library and Information Science
San Jose State University
San Jose, California

ACKNOWLEDGMENTS

This Core Collection could not have been published without the cooperative efforts of publishers and the library community. The H. W. Wilson Company is indebted to the publishers who generously supplied copies of their books as well as information about editions and prices. The Company also acknowledges its gratitude to the librarians of its advisory committee, who gave so generously of their time and expertise in advising the editors in the choice of materials to include in the collection.

Members of the Advisory Committee:

Kathie Fish
Librarian
Rachel Carson Middle School
Herndon, Virginia

Mindi Harrison
Young Adult Services Manager
Allen County Public Library
Fort Wayne, Indiana

Amanda Donahian
Program Director
Library Consultant
Archdiocese of New York
New York, New York

Patti Spencer Hadley
Library Consultant
Hollywood, Virginia

Richie Partington
Instructor, Library and Information Science
San Jose State University
San Jose, California

DIRECTIONS FOR USE OF THE CORE COLLECTION

USES OF THE COLLECTION

Middle and Junior High Core Collection is designed to serve a number of purposes:

As an aid in purchasing. The Core Collection is designed to assist in the selection and ordering of titles. Annotations are provided for each title along with information concerning publisher, ISBN, price, and availability. Since Part 1, the Classified Collection, is arranged according to the Dewey Decimal Classification, the Core Collection may be used to identify parts of the library collection that should be updated or strengthened. In evaluating the suitability of a work each library will want to consider the special character of the school and community it serves.

As an aid to the reader's advisor. The work of the reader's advisor is furthered by the information about sequels and companion volumes and the descriptive and critical annotations in the Classified Collection, and by the subject access in the Index.

As an aid in verification of information. For this purpose full bibliographical data are provided in the Classified Collection. Entries also include recommended subject headings based upon *Sears List of Subject Headings* and a suggested classification derived from the *Abridged Dewey Decimal Classification and Relative Index*. Notes describe editions available, awards, publication history, and other titles in the series.

As an aid in curriculum support. The classified approach, subject indexing, and annotations are helpful in identifying materials appropriate for classroom use.

As an aid in collection maintenance. Information about the titles available on a subject facilitates decisions to rebind, replace, or discard items. If a book has been deleted from the Core Collection in this edition because it is no longer in print, that deletion is not intended as a sign that the book is no longer valuable or that it should necessarily be weeded from the collection.

As an instructional aid. The Core Collection is useful in courses that deal with literature and book selection for young people.

ORGANIZATION

The Core Collection consists of two parts: a Classified Collection, and an Author, Title, and Subject Index

The Classified Collection is arranged with the nonfiction books first, classified according to the Dewey Decimal Classification in numerical order from 000 to 999. Individual biographies are classed at 92 and follow the 920s (collective biography). Fiction books, denoted by the symbol "Fic," follow the nonfiction. Short story collections, denoted by "S C," follow fiction. The information supplied for each book includes bibliographic description, suggested subject headings, an annotation, and, frequently, an evaluation from a quoted source.

An Outline of Classification, which serves as a table of contents to the Classified Collection, is reproduced on page xv. It should be remembered that many subjects are treated in more than one discipline and so are found in various parts of the classification. If a particular title is not found where it might be expected, the Index should be consulted to determine if the work is classified elsewhere.

Within classes, books are arranged alphabetically under main entry, usually the author. An exception is made for works of individual biography, classed at 92, which are arranged alphabetically under the name of the person written about.

The following is an example of a typical entry and a description of its components:

> **Gourley, Catherine, 1950-**
> Flappers and the new American woman; perceptions of women from 1918 through the 1920s. Twenty-first Century Books 2008 144p il (Images and issues of women in the twentieth century) lib bdg $38.60 *
> Grades 7 8 9 10   **305.4**
> 1. Women—United States—History 2. United States—History—1919-1933
> ISBN 978-0-8225-6060-9; 0-8225-6060-7
>   LC 2001-8530
> This describes images of women in the United States from 1918- through the 1920s.
> "The sparkling and engaging [text is] generously expanded by numerous, well-paced black-and-white photographs and period reproductions. . . . Great for research or browsing." SLJ
> Includes bibliographical references

The name of the author, Catherine Gourley, is given in conformity with *Anglo-American Cataloguing Rules*, 2nd edition, 2002 revision. The title of the book is *Flappers and the new American woman; perceptions of women from 1918 through the 1920s*. The book was published by Twenty-first Century Books in 2008.

The book has 144 pages and contains illustrations. It is published in the "Images and issues of women in the twentieth century" series, in a library binding, and sells for $38.60. (Prices given were current when the Collection went to press.) The star following the price indicates that this is a "most highly recommended" title. The book is recommended for any of the following grade levels: 7 8 9 10.

At the end of the last line of type in the body of the entry is the figure 305.4 in bold face type. This is the classification number derived from the fourteenth edition of the *Abridged Dewey Decimal Classification*. The number 305.4 is the classification number for "Women."

The numbered terms "1. Women—United States—History" and "2. United States—History—1919-1933" are recommended subject headings for this book based on *Sears List of Subject Headings*.

The ISBN (International Standard Book Number) is included to facilitate ordering. The Library of Congress control number is provided when available.

Following are three notes supplying additional information about the book. The first is a description of the book's content. The second is a critical note from *School Library Journal*. Such annotations are useful in evaluating books for selection and in determining which of several books on the same subject is best suited for the individual reader. The final note describes special features, in this case a bibliography. Notes are also made to describe sequels and companion volumes, editions available, awards, and publication history.

Part 2. AUTHOR, TITLE, AND SUBJECT INDEX

This Index is a comprehensive key to the Classified Collection. Each book is entered under author, title (if distinctive), series, subject, and other added entries as necessary. Following the name of the series all the titles in that series are listed. The classification number in bold face type is the key to the location of the main entry of the book in the Classified Collection. Works classed at 92, individual biography, will be found under the name of the person written about.

Cross-references are made in the Index from variant forms of names, from terms not used as subject headings to the term that is used, and from terms used as subject headings to related or more specific headings.

The following are examples of Index entries for the book cited above:

Author **Gourley, Catherine, 1950-**
    Flappers and the new American woman   **305.4**

Title **Flappers** and the new American woman. Gourley, C. **305.4**

Subject **Women—United States—History**
    Gourley, C. Flappers and the new American woman
                  305.4

There are also entries for joint authors, for example:

Joint Author **Marston, Elsa**
    (jt.auth) Harik, Ramsay M. Women in the Middle East
                  305.4

Outline of Classification

Reproduced below is the Second Summary of the Dewey Decimal Classification. * It will serve as a table of contents for the nonfiction section of the Classified Collection. (Fiction and Story Collections follow the nonfiction.) Note that the inclusion of this outline is not intended as a substitute for consulting the Dewey Decimal Classification itself.

* Reproduced from Edition 14 of the Abridged Dewey Decimal Classification and Relative Index, published in 2004, by permission of OCLC Online Computer Library Center, Inc., owner of copyright.

MIDDLE & JUNIOR HIGH CORE COLLECTION

TENTH EDITION

CLASSIFIED COLLECTION

000 COMPUTER SCIENCE, KNOWLEDGE & SYSTEMS

001.4 Research; statistical methods

The **Nobel** book of answers; the Dalai Lama, Mikhail Gorbachev, Shimon Peres, and other Nobel Prize winners answer some of life's most intriguing questions for young people; edited by Bettina Stiekel; translated by Paul De Angelis and Elisabeth Kaestner. Atheneum Bks. for Young Readers 2003 254p $14.95

Grades: 5 6 7 8   **001.4**
1. Nobel Prizes 2. Questions and answers
ISBN 0-689-86310-1   LC 2003-8721
"Will I soon have a clone? Why are leaves green? Why are some people rich and others poor? Why does 1 + 1 = 2? Why is there war? What is love? Nobel Prize winners honored for their work for peace and in science, economics, medicine, and literature speak to children about elemental issues. . . . Most of these intellectuals do an amazing job of explaining complex ideas. . . . This will be especially welcome as a discussion opener in science and social studies classrooms." Booklist

Valenza, Joyce Kasman
Power research tools; learning activities & posters; illustrated by Emily Valenza. American Library Association 2003 113p il pa $55 *
Grades: Professional   **001.4**
1. Research 2. Internet resources 3. Internet searching 4. Report writing
ISBN 0-8389-0838-1   LC 2002-8972
Contents: Searching; Ethics; Evaluation; Organizing and communicating
A collection of "lessons, rubrics, graphic organizers, and curriculum designed to help students become successful users of information. Beginning with the first steps of research, the development of a thesis, the material progresses logically through the succeeding steps, covering Boolean operators; search tools and strategies; subject and keyword searching; ethics; plagiarism; documenting and citing resources; creating source and note cards; the process of writing the paper; and quoting, paraphrasing, and summarizing. . . . This is an invaluable resource for teaching information skills in any subject area, in middle school or high school." SLJ

001.9 Controversial knowledge

Allen, Judy
Unexplained. Kingfisher 2006 144p il $19.95
Grades: 5 6 7 8   **001.9**
1. Parapsychology 2. Curiosities and wonders
ISBN 978-0-7534-5950-8; 0-7534-5950-7
This addresses such topics as ghosts, psychic phenomena, superstitions, mysterious natural phenomena, alleged monsters, disappearances, secrets and mysteries of ancient history, and possible extraterrestrials.
"A seamless combination of absorbing fact-filled text and stunning visuals in an investigation of mysteries that continue to baffle, tantalize, and spark endless debate." SLJ
Includes glossary

Ape-men; Kelly Wand, book editor. Greenhaven Press/Thomson/Gale 2006 174p (Fact or fiction?) $29.95
Grades: 6 7 8 9   **001.9**
1. Monsters 2. Yeti 3. Sasquatch
ISBN 0-7377-1892-7; 978-0-7377-1892-8
                                       LC 2005046293
"Five essays offer proof of the existence of large ape-like creatures around the world, while another five refute it. In an epilogue, readers are guided through the process of analyzing the arguments critically. Materials for further research include a fairly good selection of monographs, periodical articles, and three annotated Web sites." SLJ
Includes bibliographical references

Bardhan-Quallen, Sudipta
The real monsters; written by Sudipta Bardhan-Quallen; illustrated by Josh Cochran. Sterling 2008 88p il (Mysteries unwrapped) pa $5.95
Grades: 5 6 7 8   **001.9**
1. Monsters 2. Ghosts
ISBN 978-1-4027-3776-3; 1-4027-3776-9
                                       LC 2009275635
Investigates whether ghosts, werewolves, vampires, mummies, zombies and other such monsters exist.
The book has "an ample number of clear black-and-white and full-color photographs and illustrations. . . . Perfect for libraries that need a boost or an update to their scary-story collections." SLJ
Includes bibliographical references

Blackwood, Gary L.
Extraordinary events and oddball occurrences.
Benchmark Bks. (Tarrytown) 1999 80p il (Secrets
of the unexplained) lib bdg $29.93
Grades: 6 7 8 9   **001.9**
1. Parapsychology 2. Curiosities and wonders
ISBN 0-7614-0748-0   LC 98-30261
Discusses the details and possible explanations of
mysterious events throughout human history, including
strange things falling out of the sky, the teleportation of
objects, and unexplained appearances and disappearances
Includes bibliographical references

Gee, Joshua, fl. 1725-1750
Encyclopedia horrifica; the terrifying truth!
about vampires, ghosts, monsters, and more.
Scholastic Inc. 2007 129p il $14.99
Grades: 4 5 6 7   **001.9**
1. Vampires 2. Ghosts 3. Monsters
ISBN 978-0-439-92255-5; 0-439-92255-0
LC 2007061733
A visual reference contains true stories of such crea-
tures as vampires, aliens, werewolves, and ghosts, ac-
companied by photographic evidence, eyewitness ac-
counts, and original interviews.
"Each topic is replete with color illustrations and photos and is accompanied by a light, readable text that tries
to separate fact from fiction." Voice Youth Advocates
Includes bibliographical references

Halls, Kelly Milner, 1957-
Tales of the cryptids; mysterious creatures that
may or may not exist; by Kelly Milner Halls, Rick
Spears, Roxyanne Young; [illustrated by Rick
Spears] Darby Creek 2006 72p il map $18.95 *
Grades: 4 5 6 7   **001.9**
1. Monsters
ISBN 1-58196-049-2
This considers the existance of creatures such as
Bigfoot, the Loch Ness Monster, Marozi of Kenya, the
Orang-pendek of Sumatra, and the Thylacine of Tasma-
nia.
"The conversational text makes for fun reading, and a
plethora of pictures . . . will prove enticing." SLJ

Nardo, Don, 1947-
Atlantis; by Don Nardo. Lucent Books 2004
112p il map (Mystery library) $28.70
Grades: 6 7 8 9   **001.9**
1. Atlantis
ISBN 1-59018-287-1   LC 2003-13854
Contents: Plato's original account of Atlantis; The
modern world rediscovers Atlantis; Searching for Atlantis
around the globe; The Atlantean empire and Minoan
Crete; Thera and the blast that shook history; Myths as
memories: the making of a legend
Discusses the mystery and theories surrounding Atlan-
tis, a legendary lost continent which Plato wrote about in
399 B.C.
"Although the mystery may never be solved, the story
of Atlantis will continue to be a source of fascination."
SLJ
Includes bibliographical references

Martians; by Don Nardo. KidHaven Press 2008
48p il (Monsters) lib bdg $26.20
Grades: 4 5 6 7   **001.9**
1. Extraterrestrial beings 2. Popular culture
ISBN 978-0-7377-3639-7; 0-7377-3639-9
LC 2007-30616
"Nardo walks readers through everything from early
astronautical observations of the Red Planet to Martians
in the movies and on television. His writing is clear, informative and often humorous." SLJ
Includes glossary and bibliographical references

Stewart, Gail, 1949-
UFOs; by Gail B. Stewart. ReferencePoint Press
2007 96p il (The mysterious & unknown) lib bdg
$24.95
Grades: 6 7 8 9   **001.9**
1. Unidentified flying objects
ISBN 978-1-60152-030-2; 1-60152-030-1
This book "combines numerous stories of [UFO]
sightings with historical and scientific details about investigations, providing a balanced view of a controversial
topic. . . . Colorful illustrations and appealing design
will encourage readers." SLJ
Includes bibliographical references

004   Data processing. Computer science

Billings, Charlene W., 1941-
Supercomputers; charting the future of
cybernetics; [by] Charlene W. Billings and Sean
M. Grady. New ed. Facts on File 2004 228p
$29.95
Grades: 7 8 9 10   **004**
1. Supercomputers
ISBN 0-8160-4730-8   LC 2003-3628
First published 1995
"Defining 'supercomputers' as 'usually . . . the
fastest, and most expensive, computers available at any
given time,' the authors present a thorough history of
data storage and manipulation devices, from ancient Sumerian clay tablets through Charles Babbage's 'Difference Engine' to ENIAC, the sexy-looking creation of
Seymour Cray, and the recent growth of multiple-unit
cluster systems—not to mention the Internet. The development of office machines in general and the many uses
to which computers have been put in business, science,
military pursuits, and film animation are also examined."
SLJ
Includes bibliographical references

De la Bédoyère, Guy
The first computers. World Almanac Library
2006 48p il (Milestones in modern science) $30
Grades: 6 7 8 9   **004**
1. Computers—History
ISBN 0-8368-5854-9
This is a history of the invention of computers and
how they developed into the computers of today.

De la Bédoyère, Guy—*Continued*
The text is "complete, detailed, and not difficult to follow. . . . The illustrations are adequate and plentiful, including lots of photos and diagrams." SLJ
Includes bibliographical references

DeAngelis, Gina
Computers; processing the data; [by] Gina DeAngelis and David J. Bianco. Oliver Press 2005 143p il (Innovators) lib bdg $24.95
Grades: 7 8 9 10   **004**
    1. Computers—History 2. Scientists
    ISBN 1-881508-87-0
"After a historical overview of early calculating machines designed by the likes of Leonardo da Vinci and Blaise Pascal, this . . . traces the development of the computer chiefly through biographical accounts of later inventors and engineers. Seven chapters look at pivotal figures . . . among them, Charles Babbage (the analytical engine), Jack Kilby and Robert Noyce (the integrated circuit), Steve Wozniak (the personal computer), and Tim Berners-Lee (the World Wide Web). The authors write clearly, explaining the technical aspects of each development and usually giving a sense of the subject as an individual." Booklist
Includes bibliographical references

McAlpine, Margaret
Working with computers; [by] Margaret McAlpine. Gareth Stevens Pub. 2005 64p il (My future career) lib bdg $26
Grades: 7 8 9 10   **004**
    1. Computer science 2. Vocational guidance
    ISBN 0-8368-4242-1   LC 2004-45227
This describes seven computer-related careers including basic responsibilities and qualifications, and offers examples of a real-life professionals workday.
This "excellent [book] will be attractive to browsers. . . . The writing is clear and interesting." SLJ
Includes bibliographical references

Otfinoski, Steven, 1949-
Computers; [by] Steven Otfinoski. Marshall Cavendish Benchmark 2007 112p il (Great inventions) lib bdg $27.95
Grades: 6 7 8 9   **004**
    1. Computers—History
    ISBN 978-0-7614-2597-7   LC 2006030372
"An examination of the origins, history, development, and societal impact of the computer." Publisher's note
"The book's illustrations, primarily of innovators and their hardware, are effective in dramatizing the rapid pace of technological change." Booklist
Includes glossary and bibliographical references

Rooney, Anne
Computers; faster, smaller, and smarter; [by] Anne Rooney. Heinemann Library 2006 56p il (The cutting edge) lib bdg $32.86 *
Grades: 5 6 7 8   **004**
    1. Computers
    ISBN 1-4034-7426-5   LC 2005018014

This "describes early machines and then looks at embedded computers, robotics, communication, imaging and simulation, viruses, spyware, hackers, and the future of computers. . . . Informative, fascinating, and useful for reports." SLJ
Includes glossary and bibliographical references

005   Computer programming, programs, data

The **Software** encyclopedia. Bowker 2v pa set $379
Grades: Professional   **005**
    1. Computer software
Annual. First published 1985
Contents: v1 Titles, publishers; v2 System compatibility/applications
A guide to currently available microcomputer software packages including publishing-related programs, word processing programs, database programs and spreadsheet programs
"This annually updated work is considered the most comprehensive and current list available." Nichols. Guide to Ref Books for Sch Media Cent. 4th edition

005.7   Data in computer systems

Smith, Susan S.
Web-based instruction; a guide for libraries; [by] Susan Sharpless Smith. 2nd ed. American Library Association 2006 263p il pa $52 *
Grades: Professional   **005.7**
    1. Bibliographic instruction 2. Computer-assisted instruction 3. Web sites 4. Library information networks
    ISBN 0-8389-0908-6   LC 2005-15011
First published 2001
"Throughout the book's eight chapters, which are organized to offer a step-by-step approach for planning and implementing Web-based instruction, the author discusses the design and development of different types of Web projects and instruction, project development tools, user interfaces, multimedia, interactivity, evaluation, testing, and assessment. . . . [This is] an excellent resource notable for its practical content, thoroughness, and high readability." Booklist
Includes bibliographical references

006.3   Artificial intelligence

Henderson, Harry, 1951-
Artificial intelligence; mirrors for the mind. Chelsea House 2007 190p il (Milestones in discovery and invention) $35
Grades: 7 8 9 10 11 12   **006.3**
    1. Artificial intelligence
    ISBN 0-8160-5749-4; 978-0-8160-5749-8
                       LC 2006-16639
This book includes "portraits of the men and women in the vanguard of this innovative field. Subjects include Alan Turing, who made the connection between mathe-

Henderson, Harry, 1951-—*Continued*

matical reasoning and computer operations; Allen Newell and Herbert Simon, who created a program that could reason like a human being; Pattie Maes, who developed computerized agents to help people with research and shopping; and Ray Kurzweil, who, besides inventing the flatbed scanner and a reading machine for the blind, has explored relationships between people and computers that may exceed human intelligence." Publisher's note

Includes glossary and bibliographical references

Margulies, Phillip

Artificial intelligence; written by Phillip Margulies. Blackbirch Press 2004 48p il (Science on the edge) $23.70

Grades: 5 6 7 8   **006.3**

  1. Artificial intelligence

  ISBN 1-56711-783-X   LC 2002-13160

  Contents: History of artificial intelligence; The quest for artificial intelligence; The future of artificial intelligence

Discusses the definition of artificial intelligence, the development of "thinking" machines, and what computers may be able to do in the future

Includes glossary and bibliographical references

006.6   Computer graphics

Souter, Gerry

Creating animation for your Web page; [by] Gerry, Janet and Allison Souter. Enslow Pubs. 2003 64p il (Internet library) $22.60

Grades: 4 5 6 7   **006.6**

  1. Computer animation 2. Web sites

  ISBN 0-7660-2083-5   LC 2002-152960

  Contents: Types of animation; GIF animations; Animating with GIF Construction Set; Animating with GifBuilder; Java Applets; JavaScript; Flash and QuickTime

The authors "explore the many options and possibilities in adding animation to a Web page. Instructions are provided . . . and software for both PCs and Macs is covered. The authors explore ways to borrow animation for free, as well as the different methods for creating your own animations, from the simple to the complex." Publisher's note

Includes glossary and bibliographical references

006.7   Multimedia systems

Selfridge, Benjamin

A teen's guide to creating Web pages and blogs; [by] Benjamin Selfridge, Peter Selfridge, and Jennifer Osburn. Prufrock Press 2009 148p il pa $16.95

Grades: 5 6 7 8 9 10   **006.7**

  1. Web sites—Design 2. Weblogs 3. Internet and teenagers

  ISBN 978-1-5936-3345-5; 1-5936-3345-9

                   LC 2008-40044

First published 2004 by Zephyr Press with title: Kid's guide to creating Web pages for home and school

"This guide begins with basic step-by-step information about HTML, fonts, images, lists, and tables. . . . The book's last half introduces more advanced techniques, such as JavaScript, functions, loops, and applications like Flash and Instant Messenger. . . . Illustrated, with references and a glossary, this attractive paperback has lots of practical content." Voice Youth Advocates

Includes glossary and bibliographical references

011   Bibliographies

Barr, Catherine, 1951-

Best new media, K-12; a guide to movies, subscription web sites, and educational software and games. Libraries Unlimited 2008 237p (Children's and young adult literature reference series) $50

Grades: Professional   **011**

  1. Libraries—Special collections 2. Libraries—Collection development

  ISBN 978-1-59158-467-4; 1-59158-467-1

                   LC 2008020191

This "guides readers to the best movies, educational software and games, and subscription Web sites for children and teens. Entries feature full bibliographic information (including grade level), a descriptive annotation, and review citations. An introduction addresses selection, acquisition, cataloging, shelving, and security of new media." Publisher's note

"The book is a convenient compilation of resources that are otherwise hard to identify, making it a desirable purchase, particularly for libraries that are just starting to build game collections." SLJ

Recommended reference books for small and medium-sized libraries and media centers; Shannon Graff Hysell, associate editor. Volume 28, 2008 ed. Libraries Unlimited 2008 xxi, 343p $70 *

Grades: Professional   **011**

  1. Reference books 2. Reference books—Bibliography 3. Reference books—Reviews

  ISSN 0277-5948

  ISBN 978-1-59158-692-0; 1-59158-692-5

  Annual. First published 1981

Each annual volume includes reviews of about 550 titles chosen by the editor as the most valuable reference titles published during the previous year.

"Where budget restrictions are a consideration, this is an invaluable asset; for small libraries, a superior selection/acquisitions tool. Highly recommended." Voice Youth Advocates

011.6 General bibliographies of works for specific kinds of users and libraries

Barnhouse, Rebecca, 1961-
The Middle Ages in literature for youth; a guide and resource book. Scarecrow Press 2004 183p (Literature for youth) pa $30
Grades: Professional   **011.6**
1. Reference books 2. Children's literature—Bibliography 3. Young adult literature—Bibliography 4. Middle Ages—Bibliography
ISBN 0-8108-4916-X   LC 2004-74
"Searchable by subject, title, location, or author, this is a comprehensive guide to books about the period. Each chapter presents a topic, such as Vikings or Crusades, and then gives annotated lists of both fiction and nonfiction titles. Added features include classroom activities such as creative-writing prompts, medieval measurements using tools from the time period, and math involving computations using Roman numerals. . . . Professional sources for educators round out this useful bibliography." SLJ

Best books for young adult readers; Stephen J. Calvert, editor. Bowker 1997 xx, 744p $63
Grades: Professional   **011.6**
1. Reference books 2. Best books 3. Young adult literature—Bibliography
ISBN 0-8352-3832-6   LC 97-478
Combines and updates Best books for Junior high readers and Best books for senior high readers
This volume lists and annotates about 6,500 titles published between 1990 and 1996. Each entry provides bibliographic information, awards, review citations, etc.

Children's catalog. 19th ed.; edited by Anne Price. H. W. Wilson Co. 2006 1670p (Core collections series) $195 *
Grades: Professional   **011.6**
1. Reference books 2. Children's literature—Bibliography 3. Classified catalogs 4. School libraries—Catalogs
ISBN 0-8242-1073-5; 978-0-8242-1073-1
Also available online
First published 1909
Kept up to date by annual supplements included in the price of main volume
This collection of recommended materials includes approximately 9,000 entries of books for children from preschool to grade six including fiction and nonfiction works, story collections, picture books, and graphic novels. Entries contain full bibliographic information, Dewey Decimal Classification number, subject headings, reading level, descriptive, and when possible, critical annotations. Also included are professional literature for the children's librarian, lists of recommended periodicals for children and for professionals, and of Web resources.
"This work as been a mainstay for almost 100 years . . . in supplying authoritative and dependable information on collection evaluation and development for children's libraries in elementary schools and public libraries. . . . An essential professional tool for all libraries serving children." Am Ref Book Annu, 2007

Gillespie, John Thomas, 1928-
The children's and young adult literature handbook; a research and reference guide. Libraries Unlimited 2005 393p (Children's and young adult literature reference series) $55 *
Grades: Professional   **011.6**
1. Reference books 2. Children's literature—Bibliography 3. Children's literature—History and criticism 4. Young adult literature—Bibliography 5. Young adult literature—History and criticism
ISBN 1-56308-949-1
This is "a selection guide and collection development aid for librarians, as well as a navigation tool for researchers. Describing and evaluating more than 1,000 publications, the book covers . . . general reference, bibliographies, and biographies to review sources, literary awards, professional organizations, and special library collections. Internet and other nonprint media are included, as are major English-language resources from Britain, Canada, Australia, and South Africa." Publisher's note
"This reference should meet the needs of librarians, teachers, and scholars." Choice

Classic teenplots; a booktalk guide to use with readers ages 12-18; [by] John T. Gillespie and Corinne J. Naden. Libraries Unlimited 2006 348p (Children's and young adult literature reference series) $55
Grades: Professional   **011.6**
1. Book talks 2. Young adult literature 3. Teenagers—Books and reading
ISBN 1-59158-312-8   LC 2006017624
"Prefaced by a brief guide to booktalking are one hundred entries for in-print classic titles for teens, taken from the out-of-print Juniorplots and Seniorplots series. Additional titles have been added to round out the eight theme/genre-based sections, which include topics such as Teenage Life and Concerns, Historical Fiction and Other Lands, and Important Nonfiction. . . . This excellent resource offers from sixteen to twenty titles per section. " Voice Youth Advocates
Includes bibliographical references

Hubert, Jennifer, 1973-
Reading rants; a guide to books that rock! Neal-Schuman Publishers 2007 265p (Teens @ the library series) pa $49.95
Grades: Professional   **011.6**
1. Reference books 2. Young adult literature—Bibliography
ISBN 978-1-55570-587-9; 1-55570-587-1
                                             LC 2006-102711
"Hubert suggests 100 recently published YA titles and arranges them by themes. . . . Each novel includes the following information: the story . . . ; the message . . . ; the most likely audience . . . ; why it rocks; likely titles to 'hook up with,' and citations for reviews. Any library wishing to expand its YA collection or booktalking catalog will want this valuable tool." SLJ

Matulka, Denise I.

Picture this; picture books for young adults: a curriculum-related annotated bibliography. Greenwood Press 1997 xx, 267p $39.95

Grades: Professional **011.6**

1. Reference books 2. Picture books for children—Bibliography 3. Teenagers—Books and reading 4. Young adult literature—Bibliography

ISBN 0-313-30182-4 LC 97-2234

"This bibliography introduces 424 titles. . . . It is organized according to curriculum-content areas—the arts, health, literature, mathematics, science, and social sciences and history. Each annotation lists bibliographic information, summarizes the book, discusses artistic style and mediums employed, suggests companion titles, and provides ideas for classroom use." SLJ

Includes bibliographical references

New York Public Library

Books for the teen age, 2008. New York Public Lib. il pa $10 *

Grades: Professional **011.6**

1. Reference books 2. Young adult literature—Bibliography 3. Best books

ISBN 978-0-87104-779-3; 0-87104-779-9

Also available online

Annual. First published 1929

A list of approximately 1,000 books of interest to teenagers arranged in broad categories. Many of the titles address current concerns.

Nieuwenhuizen, Agnes

Right book, right time; 500 great books for teenagers. Allen & Unwin 2008 355p il pa $19.95

Grades: 7 8 9 10 11 12 Professional

011.6

1. Reference books 2. Young adult literature—Bibliography 3. Teenagers—Books and reading

ISBN 978-1-74114-883-1; 1-74114-883-9

"This Australian reader's guide offers detailed annotations of 200 recent young adult and adult books divided into twelve thematic sections ranging from 'Actions, Adventure & Crime' to 'When You Want to Laugh.' . . . Titles from Australia intermingle with books from the UK and the U.S. . . . With its open format and direct address to the reader, this will be a useful reference for those YAs looking to expand their reading horizons, but enterprising YA librarians will also find this a useful new dimension for expanding or promoting a collection. Interspersed with the annotations are essays championing a variety of literatures ranging from graphic novels to chick-lit." Bull Cent Child Books

Includes bibliographical references

Schon, Isabel

The best of Latino heritage 1996-2002; a guide to the best juvenile books about Latino people and cultures. Scarecrow Press 2003 269p $45.50 *

Grades: Professional **011.6**

1. Reference books 2. Children's literature—Bibliography 3. Latin America—Bibliography

ISBN 0-8108-4669-1 LC 2002-154088

Companion volume to The best of Latino heritage, published 1997

Schon "identifies both fiction and nonfiction works useful in exposing K-12 students to Latino public figures, history, art, politics, social issues, and economics. . . . Each title receives a full bibliographic citation, suggested grade level, and a paragraph-long annotation. . . . Recommended books are in English or bilingual editions and are available from U.S. publishers. An excellent tool for collection development." Booklist

Includes bibliographical references

Senior high core collection; a selection guide; edited by Raymond W. Barber and Patrice Bartell. 17th ed. H.W. Wilson Co. 2007 1456p (Core Collections series) $245 *

Grades: Professional **011.6**

1. Reference books 2. Classified catalogs 3. High school libraries—Catalogs 4. Young adult literature—Bibliography

ISBN 978-0-8242-1086-1 LC 2007-31812

Also available online

First published 1926-28 with title: Standard catalog for high school libraries; previous edition published 2002 with title: Senior high school library catalog

Kept up to date by annual supplements included in price of main volume

This collection of recommended materials includes more than 6,200 titles and over 4,500 analytical entries of books for grades nine through twelve. Entries contain full bibliographic information, Abridged Dewey Decimal Classification number, subject headings, rosettes for most highly recommended titles, descriptive, and when available, critical annotations. Includes lists of recommended periodicals and electronic resources.

Wright, Cora M.

More hot links; linking literature with the middle school curriculum. Libraries Unlimited 2002 212p tab pa $33.95 *

Grades: Professional **011.6**

1. Reference books 2. Children's literature—Bibliography 3. Books and reading

ISBN 1-56308-942-4 LC 2002-11278

Companion to: Hot links

Contents: Biographies; English: classics; English: use of language; Fine arts; Greatest of the latest; Humor; Mathematics; Multicultural; Myths, folktales, and legends; Picture books for all ages; Poetry; Read alouds; Science; Series; Social studies: ancient and early cultures; Social studies: United States history; Sports and games; Unique presentations

"This companion to . . . Hot Links by the same author provides . . . annotations for an additional 300+ fiction and nonfiction books . . . that support and enhance the middle school curriculum." Publisher's note

Includes bibliographical references

York, Sherry, 1947-

Ethnic book awards; a directory of multicultural literature for young readers. Linworth Pub. 2005 157p pa $36.95 *

Grades: Professional **011.6**

1. Reference books 2. Children's literature—Bibliography 3. Young adult literature—Bibliography 4. Multiculturalism—Bibliography

ISBN 1-58683-187-9 LC 2005004332

"Part one provides basic background information and Web sites for the Sydney Taylor Book Award, the Coretta Scott King Award, the Carter G. Woodson Award, the Américas Award, the Tomás Rivera Mexican American Children's Literature Award, the Pura Belpré Award, and the Asian Pacific American Award for Literature. Part two, the bulk of the book, lists the books alphabetically by title, along with a one or two-sentence annotation and the honor citation(s). An extensive subject index is included, as is an index of authors, editors, illustrators, and translators." SLJ

Young Adult Library Services Association

The official YALSA awards guidebook; compiled and edited by Tina Frolund for the Young Adult Library Services Association. Neal-Schuman Publishers 2008 171p pa $55

Grades: Professional **011.6**

1. Reference books 2. Young adult literature—Awards 3. Young adult literature—Bibliography 4. Teenagers—Books and reading 5. Young adults' libraries

ISBN 978-1-55570-629-6; 1-55570-629-0 LC 2008-17584

Contents: Using award winners to build better young adult collections; Marketing award-winning books to teens; The Alex award; The Edwards award; The Printz award; Reproducible materials you can use to promote these great reads

This "volume offers one-stop shopping for an overview of the Alex, Printz, and Edwards awards. In addition to annotated bibliographies of winners and honor books, the title includes acceptance speeches for the Printz and Edwards awards and award interviews from YALSA starwarts Mary Arnold, Michael Cart, and Better Carter." Bull Cent Child Books

Includes bibliographical references

Your reading; an annotated booklist for middle school and junior high; Jean E. Brown and Elaine C. Stephens, editors, and the Committee on the Middle School and Junior High Booklist; foreword by Joan Bauer; afterword by Joyce Hansen. 11th ed. National Council of Teachers of English 2003 387p (NCTE bibliography series) pa $33.95 *

Grades: Professional **011.6**

1. Reference books 2. Children's literature—Bibliography 3. Young adult literature—Bibliography 4. Best books

ISBN 0-8141-5944-3

First published 1954

This booklist offers annotations of more than 1,200 fiction and non-fiction books recommended for young adults, grouped under 18 headings such as Families, Adventure and Survival, Mysteries and Suspense, Diversity, and Historical Fiction

015.73 Bibliographies and catalogs of works issued or printed in the United States

Books in print. Bowker 9v set $859

Grades: Professional **015.73**

1. Reference books 2. Bibliography

ISSN 0068-0214

Also available CD-ROM version and online

Annual. First published 1948

Updated by Books in print Supplement (3v) published annually in Spring, available at $459 (ISSN 0000-0310)

Contents: v1-4 Authors; v5-8 Titles; v9 Publishers

Lists titles available during the current year from American publishers, supplying such information as authors, co-authors, title, price, publisher, year of publication, and International Standard Book Numbers of cooperating publishers

Subject guide to Books in print. Bowker 6v set $550

Grades: Professional **015.73**

1. Reference books 2. Subject catalogs 3. Bibliography

ISSN 0000-0159

Annual. First published 1957

This companion publication to Books in print, lists titles currently available from United States publishers indexing them under LC subject headings

Subject guide to Children's books in print. Bowker $270

Grades: Professional **015.73**

1. Reference books 2. Children's literature—Bibliography 3. Subject catalogs

ISSN 0000-0167

Also available CD-ROM version

Annual. First published 1970

This publication provides a subject approach to its companion work: Children's books in print. The headings used are based on the Sears list of subject headings supplemented by headings from LC. Entries include author, title, publisher, year of publication, binding, price, ISBN, and, in some cases, grade level. A directory of publishers and distributors is included

016 Bibliographies and catalogs of works on specific subjects or in specific disciplines

Al-Hazza, Tami Craft
Books about the Middle East; selecting and using them with children and adolescents; [by] Tami Craft Al-Hazza and Katherine T. Bucher. Linworth Pub. 2008 168p pa $39.95 *

Grades: Professional   **016**
1. Reference books 2. Middle East—Bibliography 3. Children's literature—Bibliography 4. Young adult literature—Bibliography
ISBN 978-1-58683-285-8; 1-58683-285-9
    LC 2007-40149
"This book examines the body of literature about the diverse groups of people who inhabit the Middle East, and it also explores a variety of ways in which this literature can be used. . . . It fills a huge gap and should not be overlooked. This powerhouse book will be tremendously helpful to media specialists, educators, and public librarians." Voice Youth Advocates
Includes bibliographical references

016.02 Bibliographies of library science

Fraser, Elizabeth, 1970-
Reality rules! a guide to teen nonfiction reading interests. Libraries Unlimited 2008 246p (Genreflecting advisory series) $48

Grades: Professional   **016.02**
1. Reference books 2. Young adult literature—Bibliography 3. Teenagers—Books and reading
ISBN 978-1-59158-563-3   LC 2007-51063
"This guide focuses on titles created for teens and those with strong teen appeal. The author covers more than 500 titles published since 2000, also including benchmarks and perennial classics." Publisher's note
Includes bibliographical references

016.3 Bibliographies of the social sciences

Crew, Hilary S., 1942-
Women engaged in war in literature for youth; a guide to resources for children and young adults. Scarecrow Press 2007 303p (Literature for youth) pa $51

Grades: Professional   **016.3**
1. Reference books 2. War—Bibliography 3. Women—Bibliography 4. Children's literature—Bibliography 5. Young adult literature—Bibliography
ISBN 978-0-8108-4929-7; 0-8108-4929-1
    LC 2006-101112
"Crew's guide to print and online sources documents women's roles in wars over the centuries and throughout the world, divided by time periods. . . . This is a great

addition for libraries looking for a way to move Women's Studies beyond the month of March." SLJ
Includes bibliographical references

Mosley, Shelley, 1950-
The suffragists in literature for youth; the fight for the vote; [by] Shelley Mosley, John Charles. The Scarecrow Press, Inc. 2006 326p (Literature for youth) pa $45

Grades: Professional   **016.3**
1. Reference books 2. Women—Suffrage—Bibliography 3. Children's literature—Bibliography 4. Young adult literature—Bibliography
ISBN 978-0-8108-5372-0 (pa); 0-8108-5372-8 (pa)
    LC 2006-17542
"This book focuses on the American suffrage movement and its leaders from 1848, when the first Woman's Rights Convention was held in Seneca Falls, New York, to 1920, when the 19th Amendment was finally ratified. Resources—print, non-print, and electronic—are annotated, arranged by format, and listed by age group." Publisher's note
"This book would be a tremendous resource to any library or classroom collection." Voice Youth Advocates
Includes bibliographical references

Notable social studies trade books for young people. Children's Bk. Council * pa $2
Grades: Professional   **016.3**
1. Reference books 2. Social sciences—Bibliography 3. Best books 4. Children's literature—Bibliography 5. Young adult literature—Bibliography
An annual annotated list, reprinted from an issue of the periodical Social Education, of the preceding year's best trade books in the field of social studies of interest to children in grades K-8. Prepared by the Book Review Panel of the National Council for the Social Studies—Children's Book Council Joint Committee. Titles are selected for emphasis on human relations, originality, readability and, when appropriate, illustrations. General reading levels (primary, intermediate, advanced) are indicated

Walter, Virginia A.
War & peace; a guide to literature and new media, grades 4-8; [by] Virginia A. Walter. Libraries Unlimited 2007 276p (Children's and young adult literature reference series) pa $40 *

Grades: Professional   **016.3**
1. Reference books 2. War—Bibliography 3. Peace—Bibliography 4. Children's literature—Bibliography 5. Young adult literature—Bibliography
ISBN 1-59158-271-7 (pa); 978-1-59158-271-7 (pa)
    LC 2006030671
"Walter addresses the issue of war—and peace—by examining the information needs of children and how we as professionals can meet them. . . . The bulk of the book is the annotated listing of resources that is divided topically. . . . The well-annotated bibliography includes books, DVDs, Web sites, and CDs, as well as suggestions for using the materials. . . . This book should be a 'must purchase.'" SLJ
Includes bibliographical references

016.3058 Bibliographies of racial, ethnic, national groups

Garcha, Rajinder
The world of Islam in literature for youth; a selective annotated bibliography for K-12; [by] Rajinder Garcha, Patricia Yates Russell. Scarecrow Press 2006 xx, 221p (Literature for youth) pa $35
Grades: Professional   **016.3058**
1. Reference books 2. Islam—Bibliography 3. Children's literature—Bibliography 4. Young adult literature—Bibliography
ISBN 0-8108-5488-0; 978-0-8108-5488-8
     LC 2005-26645
"This annotated bibliography has more than 700 selected print and electronic resources. Each numbered entry includes complete bibliographic information, a recommended grade level, and a one-paragraph summary and critique." SLJ
"This highly useful bibliography fills a conspicuous gap in a much-needed cultural area." Voice Youth Advocates
Includes bibliographical references

016.3713 Bibliographies of instructional materials

El-hi textbooks and serials in print. Bowker 2v set $290
Grades: Professional   **016.3713**
1. Reference books 2. Textbooks—Bibliography 3. Periodicals—Bibliography
ISSN 0000-0825
Annual. Title varies
"Index to textbooks, dictionaries, encyclopedias, maps, atlases, professional books, teaching aids and auxiliary AV materials for grades K-12, plus adult and special education. Subject index contains grade and reading level; also author and title indexes and series index. Lists information not in 'Books in Print.'" N Y Public Libr. Ref Books for Child Collect. 2d edition

016.5 Bibliographies of science

Outstanding science trade books for students K-12. Children's Bk. Council * pa $2
Grades: Professional   **016.5**
1. Reference books 2. Science—Bibliography 3. Best books 4. Children's literature—Bibliography 5. Young adult literature—Bibliography
An annual annotated list, reprinted from an issue of the periodical Science and Children, of the preceding year's best trade books in the field of science of interest to children in grades K-8. Prepared by a Book Review Committee appointed by the National Science Teachers Association in cooperation with the Children's Book Council. Titles are selected for accuracy, readability and pleasing format. General reading levels (primary, intermediate, advanced) are indicated

016.7 Bibliographies of the arts

Pawuk, Michael G.
Graphic novels; a genre guide to comic books, manga, and more; foreword by Brian K. Vaughn. Libraries Unlimited 2007 xxxv, 633p il (Genreflecting advisory series) $65 *
Grades: Professional   **016.7**
1. Reference books 2. Graphic novels—Bibliography
ISBN 1-59158-132-X; 978-1-59158-132-1
     LC 2006-34156
"This guide is intended to help you start, update, or maintain a graphic novel collection and advise readers about the genre. It covers more than 2,400 titles, including series titles, and organizes them according to genre, subgenre, and theme—from super-heroes and adventure to crime, humor, and nonfiction. Reading levels, awards/recognition, and core titles are identified; and tie-ins with gaming, film, anime, and television are noted." Publisher's note
Includes bibliographical references

Weiner, Stephen
The 101 best graphic novels. NBM 2005 60p il $15.95; pa $9.95 *
Grades: Professional   **016.7**
1. Reference books 2. Graphic novels—Bibliography 3. Best books
ISBN 978-1-56163-443-9; 1-56163-443-3; 978-1-56163-444-6 (pa); 1-56163-444-1 (pa)
     LC 2005-932866
"The young adult category has been subdivided into ages 12-15 and 16-19. . . . The greats you'd expect to find (Frank Miller, Alan Moore, Will Eisner, Neil Gaiman) are here along with many newer authors. . . . [This] is a useful tool for librarians and graphic-novel fans alike." SLJ
Includes bibliographical references

016.8 Bibliographies of literature

Day, Frances Ann
Lesbian and gay voices; an annotated bibliography and guide to literature for children and young adults; foreword by Nancy Garden. Greenwood Press 2000 xxi, 268p $38.95 *
Grades: Professional   **016.8**
1. Reference books 2. Children's literature—Bibliography 3. Young adult literature—Bibliography 4. Homosexuality in literature—Bibliography
ISBN 0-313-31162-5   LC 00-21047
This reference "lists over 275 recommended books that incorporate various aspects of homosexuality. . . . Each chapter looks at a particular literary genre. Listed alphabetically by author, each entry includes complete bibliographic information, a detailed annotation, topics, age level specifications, mention of any strong language or explicit sex, a summary of pertinent criticism, and a listing of literary awards." Book Rep
A "much-needed, thorough guide. . . . this is an ex-

Day, Frances Ann—*Continued*
traordinary compilation that belongs in every collection."
SLJ

Includes bibliographical references

Fichtelberg, Susan
Encountering enchantment; a guide to speculative fiction for teens. Libraries Unlimited 2007 328p (Genreflecting advisory series) $48 *
Grades: Professional   **016.8**
1. Reference books 2. Fantasy fiction—Bibliography 3. Science fiction—Bibliography 4. Young adult literature—Bibliography
ISBN 1-59158-316-0; 978-1-59158-316-5
LC 2006-33739
"This guide organizes by genre, subgenre, and theme some 1,400 titles of fantasy, science fiction and paranormal titles, most published within the last decade. Chapters cover such subgenres as epic fantasy, wizardry, romance, and mystery, which are further broken down by subgenres and themes. Annotations offer bibliographic information, brief plot summaries, reading levels, alternative media formats (including large print and Braille), and awards information." Publisher's note
"This useful guide should be in every YA collection." SLJ

Includes bibliographical references

Gillespie, John Thomas, 1928-
Historical fiction for young readers (grades 4-8); an introduction. Libraries Unlimited 2008 489p $60
Grades: Professional   **016.8**
1. Children's literature—Bibliography 2. Young adult literature—Bibliography 3. Historical fiction—Bibliography
ISBN 978-1-59158-621-0; 1-59158-621-6
LC 2008031343
"Gillespie begins with chapters that suggest the criteria by which fiction, and historical fiction specifically, should be evaluated. He gives a detailed and enlightening look at the development of the genre that serves as a useful guide for building a collection of must-haves or classics. He also includes a generic chapter on how to bring books and children together. . . . The strength of the volume is the in-depth coverage of the 81 featured novels, organized geographically, and then chronologically. Historical background, information about the author, a lengthy synopsis, passages for booktalking, and discussions of themes are all provided." SLJ

Includes bibliographical references

Hall, Susan, 1940-
Using picture storybooks to teach literary devices; recommended books for children and young adults. v4. Libraries Unlimited 2007 282p (Using picture books to teach) pa $42
Grades: Professional   **016.8**
1. Literature—Study and teaching
ISBN 978-1-59158-493-3; 1-59158-493-0
Additional volumes published 1990, 1994, and 2002

"This fourth volume of the series, . . . gives teachers and librarians the . . . tool to teach literary devices in grades K–12. With this volume, the author has added: colloquialism; counterpoint; solecism; archetype; and others to the list of devices. The entries have been reorganized to include all the information under the book listing itself. Each entry includes an annotation, a listing of curricular tie-ins for the book and the art style used, and a listing and explanation of all the literary devices taught by that title." Publisher's note

Helbig, Alethea
Many peoples, one land; a guide to new multicultural literature for children and young adults; [by] Alethea K. Helbig, Agnes Regan Perkins. Greenwood Press 2001 431p $70.95
Grades: Professional   **016.8**
1. Reference books 2. Children's literature—Bibliography 3. Young adult literature—Bibliography 4. Minorities—Bibliography
ISBN 0-313-30967-1   LC 00-25111
Replaces This land is our land published 1994
"This volume contains 561 entries covering works of literature published from 1994 to 1999. It offers entries for African Americans, Asian Americans, Hispanic Americans, and Native-American Indians, which are then subdivided into separate sections for books of fiction, books of poetry, and oral tradition for audiences from preschool through high school. Each numbered entry includes author, title, illustrator, publisher, publication year, ISBN, price, number of pages, age level, and grade level. A brief description of each literary work contains the major themes, plot, characters, settings, and illustration style of each work." Book Rep
"An excellent tool for readers' advisory and collection building." SLJ

Includes bibliographical references

Herald, Diana Tixier
Teen genreflecting; a guide to reading interests. 2nd ed. Libraries Unlimited 2003 275p lib bdg $40
Grades: Professional   **016.8**
1. Reference books 2. Young adult literature—Bibliography 3. Teenagers—Books and reading
ISBN 1-56308-996-3   LC 2003-54610
First published 1997
"The first chapter offers an overview of teen readers' advisory services, and subsequent chapters focus on popular genres of young adult literature, including but not limited to suspense, adventure, fantasy, alternate formats (including graphic novels), and Christian fiction. Both recent and classic YA books are listed in their appropriate genres, and every entry contains the author, title, publication date, and age level of the book. . . . When appropriate, awards and any best lists on which a book might have appeared are cited. . . . In addition to its value as a readers' advisory guide, this book can serve as a key to building a core young adult fiction collection or as a guide to purchasing for a collection that is weak in some genres." Voice Youth Advocates

Includes bibliographical references

Leeper, Angela

Poetry in literature for youth. Scarecrow Press 2006 303p (Literature for youth) pa $40

Grades: Professional   **016.8**

1. Reference books 2. Poetry—Bibliography

ISBN 0-8108-5465-1   LC 2005030719

This "provides annotated listings of titles arranged by subjects. . . . More than 900 entries describe collections, anthologies, performance poetry, poet biographies, and more, for kindergarten through high school." Booklist

"This title is packed with innovative ways to integrate poetry into the K-12 curriculum." SLJ

Includes bibliographical references

Lynn, Ruth Nadelman, 1948-

Fantasy literature for children and young adults; a comprehensive guide. 5th ed. Libraries Unlimited 2005 1128p (Children's and young adult literature reference series) $65

Grades: Professional   **016.8**

1. Reference books 2. Fantasy fiction—Bibliography 3. Fairy tales—Bibliography

ISBN 1-59158-050-1

First published 1979 with title: Fantasy for children

This describes and categorizes "fantasy novels and story collections published between 1900 and 2004. More than 7,500 titles . . . for readers grades 3-12 are organized in chapters based on fantasy subgenres and themes, including animal, alternate worlds, time travel, witchcraft, and sorcery. Lynn provides complete bibliographic information, grade level, a brief annotation, and a list of review citations, and notes recommended titles." Publisher's note

"This is an excellent resource." Booklist

Steiner, Stanley F.

Promoting a global community through multicultural children's literature; illustrations by Peggy Hokom; foreword by Alma Flor Ada. Libraries Unlimited 2001 179p pa $35

Grades: Professional   **016.8**

1. Reference books 2. Minorities—Bibliography 3. Children's literature—Bibliography 4. Young adult literature—Bibliography

ISBN 1-56308-705-7   LC 00-50702

This guide to developing a children's multicultural book collection lists over 800 titles for kindergarten through eighth grade

"A timely and informative guide for educators who are trying to promote an understanding of world cultures and our interconnectedness." SLJ

Includes bibliographical references

Thomas, Rebecca L.

Popular series fiction for middle school and teen readers; a reading and selection guide; [by] Rebecca L. Thomas and Catherine Barr. 2nd ed. Libraries Unlimited 2009 710p (Children's and young adult literature reference series) $65

Grades: Professional   **016.8**

1. Reference books 2. Children's literature—Bibliography 3. Young adult literature—Bibliography

ISBN 978-1-59158-660-9   LC 2008-38125

First published 2005

"The authors have identified nearly 2,200 in-print series . . . (including manga, Cine-Manga, and illustrated novels) that will appeal to readers in grades 6-12. Entries are arranged by the series title and contain author, most recent publisher, grade level, notation for availability of accelerated-reader resources, genre, a descriptive three- to five-sentence annotation, and a list of individual titles in the series, arranged by publication date." Booklist

Includes bibliographic references

016.9 Bibliographies of geography and history

Adamson, Lynda G.

Literature connections to world history, 7-12; resources to enhance and entice. Libraries Unlimited 1998 511p pa $38.50

Grades: Professional   **016.9**

1. Reference books 2. History—Bibliography 3. Audiovisual materials—Catalogs 4. Young adult literature—Bibliography

ISBN 1-56308-505-4   LC 97-35953

Also available Literature connections to world history, K-6

Covers books, CD-ROMs, and videotapes; Includes indexes

This resource is divided "into two main sections. The first section lists authors and book titles in the categories of historical fiction, biography, collective biography, history trade book, CD-ROM, and videotape within specific time periods according to grade levels. The second section contains annotated bibliographies of titles listed in the first part: books, CD-ROMs, and videotapes." Introduction

Barancik, Sue, 1944-

Guide to collective biographies for children and young adults. Scarecrow Press 2005 447p pa $44.95

Grades: Professional   **016.9**

1. Reference books 2. Biography—Bibliography 3. Children's literature—Bibliography 4. Young adult literature—Bibliography

ISBN 0-8108-5033-8 (pa)   LC 2004-19560

"This text indexes 721 titles for children and young adults in order to provide access to 5,760 notable individuals from early to modern times. All of the referenced titles were published between 1988 and 2002." Booklist

"A current guide such as this one is essential. . . . A must-have for libraries serving grades 4 through 12." SLJ

Beck, Peggy, 1949-

GlobaLinks: resources for world studies, grades K-8. Linworth Pub. 2002 148p pa $39.95 *

Grades: Professional   **016.9**

1. Reference books 2. World history—Bibliography 3. Children's literature—Bibliography 4. Young adult literature—Bibliography

ISBN 1-58683-040-6   LC 2001-50718

Also available GlobaLinks: resources for Asian studies, grades K-8

Beck, Peggy, 1949-—*Continued*

This "annotated bibliography of books, videos, CD-ROMs and Web sites includes items selected on the basis of the 10 strands of social studies. . . . For each source, whether print, non-print, Web site, or key and pen pal project, complete bibliographic information is given, as well as two to four sentences about the source and its intended audience." Book Rep

"The author's strength . . . lies not only in her selections, but also in her consistently high-quality annotations. . . . This compilation is highly recommended for the professional collection of young adult sections and school media centers." Am Ref Books Annu, 2003

Wee, Patricia Hachten, 1948-

World War II in literature for youth; a guide and resource book; [by] Patricia Hachten Wee, Robert James Wee. Scarecrow Press 2004 391p (Literature for youth) pa $48

Grades: Professional **016.9**

1. Reference books 2. World War, 1939-1945—Bibliography 3. Children's literature—Bibliography 4. Young adult literature—Bibliography

ISBN 0-8108-5301-9 LC 2004-11087

This "offers more than 3,000 annotated bibliographies for resources on the Second World War. Entries are arranged according to well-thought-out subjects and cover multiple genres (biographies, memoirs, fiction, eyewitness accounts, technical reports, etc.) and formats (monographs, reference sets, periodicals, Web sites, CDs, videos, DVDs). Annotations are succinct but informative and include both positive and negative comments." Booklist

Includes bibliographical references

016.94053 Bibliographies of World War II, 1939-1945

Rosen, Philip, 1928-

Bearing witness; a resource guide to literature, poetry, art, music, and videos by Holocaust victims and survivors; [by] Philip Rosen and Nina Apfelbaum. Greenwood Press 2002 210p $52.95

Grades: Professional **016.94053**

1. Reference books 2. Holocaust, 1933-1945—Bibliography

ISBN 0-313-31076-9 LC 00-69153

This is a resource guide to "over 800 first-person accounts, fiction, poetry, art interpretations, and music by Holocaust victims and survivors, as well as videos relating the testimony and experiences of Holocaust survivors." Publisher's note

"This volume will be valuable to all who are researching the Holocaust. Its strength lies in the inclusion of materials not often found elsewhere." Booklist

Includes bibliographical references

016.973 Bibliographies of United States history

Stephens, Elaine C., 1943-

Learning about—the Civil War; literature and other resources for young people; [by] Elaine C. Stephens and Jean E. Brown. Linnet Professional Publs. 1998 259p $32; pa $25

Grades: Professional **016.973**

1. Reference books 2. United States—History—1861-1865, Civil War—Bibliography 3. Children's literature—Bibliography 4. Young adult literature—Bibliography

ISBN 0-208-02464-6; 0-208-02449-2 (pa)

LC 98-14569

"First discussing separately both the Civil War and the role of literature in the curriculum, the authors then discuss how literature can be used to teach about the Civil War. . . . Each of the following chapters focuses on one aspect of the Civil War, providing basic information and the significance of that aspect for those with little background. 'Focus Books' directly relating to that specific aspect are then listed. Each book is briefly summarized, then fully annotated with the appropriate grade level indicated." Voice Youth Advocates

020 Library & information sciences

McCain, Mary Maude

Dictionary for school library media specialists; a practical and comprehensive guide; [by] Mary Maude McCain and Martha Merrill. Libraries Unlimited 2001 219p pa $42

Grades: Professional **020**

1. Reference books 2. School libraries—Dictionaries

ISBN 1-56308-696-4 LC 01-16506

"The book defines more than 375 terms. There are two types of definitions—shorter glossary descriptions (*capital outlay, reboot*) and longer, more detailed treatments (*poetry, proximity operators*). *See* references (especially from acronyms and abbreviations) and *see also* references facilitate use." Booklist

Misakian, Jo Ellen Priest

The essential school library glossary; [by] Jo Ellen Priest Misakian. Linworth Pub. 2004 96p pa $36.95

Grades: Professional **020**

1. Reference books 2. School libraries—Dictionaries

ISBN 1-58683-150-X LC 2004-6746

"This useful compendium of terms from 'Abstract' to 'Online Computer Library Center' to 'W3C' is succinct and easy to read. . . . Misakian includes terms specific to library-media programs as well as those related to the whole school program. This is a valuable resource for school librarians at all stages in their career." SLJ

021.2 Relationships with the community

Gillespie, Kellie M., 1960-
Teen volunteer services in libraries. VOYA Books 2004 133p il (VOYA guides) pa $26.95
Grades: Professional **021.2**
1. Volunteer work 2. Libraries
ISBN 0-8108-4837-6 LC 2003-17932
Contents: Why teens as volunteers?; Getting started; Marketing, recruiting, and placement; Orientation and training; Recognition and retention; Supervising volunteers; Volunteer program variations; How do they do it?: interviews with teen volunteer managers; Successful teen volunteer programs
This offers "advice about starting and maintaining effective teen volunteer programs in school and public libraries. . . . [The author discusses] recruitment, orientation and training, recognition and retention, and supervision." Publisher's note
"If you are even considering starting a teen volunteer program, you must read this book. If you already have one in your library, this volume still has much to offer." SLJ
Includes bibliographical references

Langemack, Chapple
The author event primer; how to plan, execute and enjoy author events. Libraries Unlimited 2007 188p pa $35
Grades: Professional **021.2**
1. Libraries and community 2. Authors
ISBN 978-1-59158-302-8 (pa); 1-59158-302-0 (pa)
LC 2006032405
"Langemack gives practical guidance that will be useful to experienced and novice planners on how to host an author event. She covers everything, from reasons for having author visits to carrying off 'the really big do', with humor and experience. The text is supplemented with charts; sample event proposals, fact sheets, letters, forms, and emails. . . . This book will be an invaluable source." Libr Media Connect
Includes bibliographical references

021.7 Promotion of libraries, archives, information centers

Brown, Mary E.
Exhibits in libraries; a practical guide; [by] Mary E. Brown and Rebecca Power. McFarland & Co. 2006 250p il pa $45
Grades: Professional **021.7**
1. Libraries—Exhibitions
ISBN 0-7864-2352-8 LC 2005018508
This explains "what embodies an exhibit, types of exhibits, skills that a librarian needs to put an exhibit together, and the importance of exhibits. . . . This book is appropriate for all libraries thinking about exhibitions." Booklist
Includes bibliographical references

Flowers, Helen F., 1931-
Public relations for school library media programs; 500 ways to influence people and win friends for your school library media center. Neal-Schuman 1998 158p pa $49.95
Grades: Professional **021.7**
1. Libraries—Public relations 2. School libraries
ISBN 1-55570-320-8 LC 98-11470
The author recommends "techniques for promoting the use of the library media services by students, faculty, building administrators, and school support staff. Readers will also learn how to target administrators, the board of education, parents, community, and legislators to maintain and increase support for staff, materials, equipment, and space." Publisher's note
"Writing with a sense both of purpose and of humor, Flowers turns a book of excellent lists into a good, entertaining read." Voice Youth Advocates
Includes bibliographical references

Hill, Ann
Tooting your own horn; web-based public relations for the 21st century librarian; [by] Ann Hill and Julieta Dias Fisher. Linworth Pub. 2002 130p il pa $39.95 *
Grades: Professional **021.7**
1. Libraries—Public relations 2. Web sites 3. Internet
ISBN 1-58683-066-X LC 2002-32440
"Hill and Fisher offer a step-by-step approach to marketing the library program by using the Internet to provide information to students, teachers, administrators, parents, and the community. . . . Enlightening, engaging and chock-full of practical tips." Libr Media Connect
Includes glossary and bibliographical references

Imhoff, Kathleen R.
Library contests; a how-to-do-it manual; [by] Kathleen R.T. Imhoff, Ruthie Maslin. Neal-Schuman Publishers 2007 182p il (How-to-do-it manuals for librarians) pa $55
Grades: Professional **021.7**
1. Contests 2. Libraries—Public relations 3. Advertising—Libraries 4. Libraries and community
ISBN 1-55570-559-6 (pa); 978-1-55570-559-6 (pa)
LC 2006-33177
"This comprehensive book covers planning, implementing, and evaluating contests of all kinds, for all kinds of libraries. It addresses setting budgets and schedules, choosing prizes and judges, establishing rules, promoting the contest, and evaluating it once it is over. . . . The authors . . . cover potential negatives as well as positives in plain language. . . . The illustrations are informative." SLJ
Includes bibliographical references

Phillips, Susan P., 1945-
Great displays for your library step by step. McFarland & Co. 2008 234p il pa $45
Grades: Professional **021.7**
1. Libraries—Exhibitions
ISBN 978-0-7864-3164-9; 0-7864-3164-4
LC 2007-47450

Phillips, Susan P., 1945-—_Continued_

This volume is a "tool for designing . . . visual statements for library spaces. Each display includes a brief introduction to the subject; an explanation of the genesis of the idea; specifics regarding the information included and its source; step-by-step instructions for assembly; and ideas on how to customize the display to any available space." Publisher's note

"Phillip's enthusiasm, creativity, and breadth of personal interests are evident throughout this book. . . . This text will inspire readers to locate and showcase the treasures in their own collections." SLJ

Includes bibliographical references

022   Administration of physical plant

Bolan, Kimberly

Teen spaces; the step-by-step library makeover. 2nd ed. American Library Association 2009 225p il pa $40

Grades: Professional   **022**

1. Young adults' libraries

ISBN 978-0-8389-0969-0; 0-8389-0969-8

LC 2008-26621

First published 2003

"An essential guide for any library planning a teen-space project. . . . After an introductory chapter on teens and their needs within a library, all aspects of teen areas are explained. From the analysis and planning to design and decoration, Bolan outlines the steps to take and the pitfalls to avoid. . . . This book truly is a guide to step-by-step library makeovers." SLJ

Includes bibliographical references

025.04   Information storage and retrieval systems

Alcorn, Louise E., 1970-

Wireless networking; a how-to-do-it manual for librarians; [by] Louise E. Alcorn, Maryellen Mott Allen. Neal-Schuman Publishers 2006 201p (How-to-do-it manuals for librarians) pa $65

Grades: Professional   **025.04**

1. Wireless communication systems 2. Library information networks

ISBN 1-55570-478-6; 978-1-55570-478-0

LC 2004053760

"This practical reference provides timely, appropriate guidance on how and why libraries should go wireless. The authors present data and ideas on standards, transfer rates, equipment costs and options, planning and implementation, technical and project-management concerns, and site surveys. Common issues such as marketing, compatibility with existing networks, privacy and security options, and troubleshooting and maintenance are also covered." Booklist

Includes bibliographical references

Blowers, Helene

Weaving a library Web; a guide to developing children's websites; [by] Helene Blowers and Robin Bryan. American Library Association 2004 197p il pa $32 *

Grades: Professional   **025.04**

1. Web sites

ISBN 0-8389-0877-2   LC 2004-1806

"A detailed description of topics and issues involved in designing, implementing, and maintaining Web sites for children. . . . This book can be used as a beginner's first stop and as a webmaster's companion. It is uncomplicated and easy to read." SLJ

Includes bibliographical references

Braun, Linda W.

Hooking teens with the Net. Neal-Schuman 2003 133p (Teens @ the library series) pa $45

Grades: Professional   **025.04**

1. Internet resources 2. Internet searching—Study and teaching

ISBN 1-55570-457-3   LC 2002-45221

This is a "guide to integrating information-literacy skills into the curriculum via the Internet. Through the use of popular teen sites, the author suggests that students will make an easy transition to more traditional electronic tools. . . . Each chapter includes an overview and bulleted skills and technology requirements as well as skills taught and extension activities, and each one culminates with a resource list. . . . A detailed and useful teaching tool." SLJ

Includes bibliographical references

Diaz, Karen R.

IssueWeb: a guide and sourcebook for researching controversial issues on the Web; [by] Karen R. Diaz, Nancy O'Hanlon. Libraries Unlimited 2004 287p pa $30

Grades: Professional   **025.04**

1. Internet resources 2. Internet searching—Study and teaching

ISBN 1-59158-078-1   LC 2003-65946

The authors "open with an online research guide that concentrates on finding an appropriate topic, using the right terminology, and evaluating online research, considering bias, balance, and documentation. . . . Recommended Web sites follow, subdivided into reference, legal issues, news, data sources, and advocacy for and against." Choice

"A veritable gold mine of more than 40 well-organized, well-presented issues briefs follows three remarkably clear, concise chapters on finding, evaluating, and incorporating Internet resources." SLJ

Gordon, Rachel Singer

Teaching the Internet in libraries. American Library Association 2001 143p pa $38 *

Grades: Professional   **025.04**

1. Internet searching—Study and teaching 2. Computer networks

ISBN 0-8389-0799-7   LC 00-52564

Gordon, Rachel Singer—*Continued*

"Chapters cover the reasons and methods to initiate programs, including convincing others of the necessity of such training, the importance of choosing proper trainers and how to do so; techniques for reaching diverse audiences such as parents, senior citizens, and Hispanics; training techniques and considerations such as lists of popular searches requested by patrons; and criteria for evaluating the program. Each section of the book concludes with resources for further information." Book Rep

An "excellent and readable volume." Voice Youth Advocates

Includes bibliographical references

Managing the Internet controversy; edited by Mark L. Smith. Neal-Schuman 2000 226p (Neal-Schuman net-guide series) pa $49.95

Grades: Professional   **025.04**

1. Library information networks 2. Internet

ISBN 1-55570-395-X   LC 00-62516

This is a "compilation of 12 essays. . . . Topics range from the historical and philosophical underpinnings of intellectual freedom to strategies for building public support for library policies to handling media interviews. Although the core of the discussion is the Internet and the concerns raised by its widespread use in libraries, the end product is a seminar on the key issues of library management. . . . Thought-provoking analysis by respected library professionals coupled with practical tools for addressing difficult issues makes this a valuable resource for school and public librarians." Book Rep

Includes bibliographical references

McClure, Charles R.

Public libraries and internet service roles; measuring and maximizing Internet services; [by] Charles R. McClure and Paul T. Jaeger. American Library Association 2009 112p il map pa $65 *

Grades: Professional   **025.04**

1. Public libraries 2. Internet

ISBN 978-0-8389-3576-7; 0-8389-3576-1

     LC 2008-26622

The authors "summarize the existing research on the meanings of social roles and expectations of public libraries and the results of studies detailing those roles and expectations in relation to the Internet. . . . Their book raises our awareness of some very critical issues and is required reading for anyone who cares about public libraries." Booklist

Includes bibliographical references

Raatma, Lucia

Safety on the Internet. Child's World 2005 32p il (Living well) lib bdg $25.64 *

Grades: 4 5 6 7   **025.04**

1. Internet and children 2. Safety education

ISBN 1-59296-242-4   LC 2003-27212

Contents: Daniel's school report; Safe surfing; E-mail, IMS, and netiquette; Knowing to whom you are talking; Guarding your computer; When it's time to sign off; Glossary; Questions and answers about Internet safety; Helping a friend learn about Internet safety; Did you know?; How to learn more about Internet safety

This is an "overview of online safety, including choosing age-appropriate sites, e-mailing, instant messaging, netiquette, and maintaining one's privacy." SLJ

Includes glossary

Wan Guofang

Virtually true; questioning online media; by Guofang Wan. Fact Finders 2007 32p il (Media literacy) lib bdg $22.60; pa $7.95

Grades: 4 5 6 7   **025.04**

1. Internet 2. Information literacy

ISBN 978-0-7368-6767-2 (lib bdg); 0-7368-6767-8 (lib bdg); 978-0-7368-7863-0 (pa); 0-7368-7863-7 (pa)

     LC 2006021446

"Describes what media is, how the Internet is part of media, and encourages readers to question the medium's influential messages." Publisher's note

This is "written in a breezy style and [has] plenty of popping colors and photos. . . . Useful and attractive." SLJ

Includes bibliographical references

Wolinsky, Art

Internet power research using the Big6 approach. rev ed. Enslow Publishers 2005 64p il (Internet library) lib bdg $22.60; pa $11.93 *

Grades: Professional   **025.04**

1. Information systems 2. Research

ISBN 0-7660-1563-7 (lib bdg); 0-7660-1564-5 (pa)

     LC 2004-22185

First published 2002

Provides instructions for using the "Big6" research method and scenarios for applying the technique to research conducted on the Internet.

The information is presented in "a friendly, informal writing style. . . . This is a helpful resource for students who want to hone their research strategies." SLJ

Includes glossary and bibliographical references

025.1   Administration

Anderson, Cynthia, 1945-

Write grants, get money; [by] Cynthia Anderson and Kathi Knop. 2nd ed. Linworth Pub. 2008 128p pa $44.95

Grades: Professional   **025.1**

1. Grants-in-aid

ISBN 978-1-58683-303-9; 1-58683-303-0

     LC 2008-22038

First published 2002

"This practical, grant writing manual will prove invaluable to both novice and experienced grant writers. Written clearly and concisely, this title outlines the grant writing process step by step, from generating ideas to the nuts and bolts of writing an effective proposal. . . . Multiple appendices provide a plethora of supplemental information such as resources on grant writing, Web sites, awards and contests, listservs for media specialists, and a sample grant proposal format. . . . This book makes grant writing as simple as its title." Libr Media Connect

Includes glossary and bibliographical references

Curzon, Susan Carol

Managing change; a how-to-do-it manual for librarians. rev. ed. Neal-Schuman Publishers 2005 129p (How-to-do-it manuals for librarians) pa $55

Grades: Professional   **025.1**

1. Libraries—Administration

ISBN 1-55570-553-7   LC 2005-22846

First published 1989

The author "outlines the step-by-step processes and . . . instructions necessary for conceptualizing the issues; planning; preparing; decision-making; controlling resistance; and implementing changes. Practical guidance for dealing with technology's impact on libraries, applying the latest research in change management, and developing new strategies for coping with change are included." Publisher's note

"The real-world approach makes the book a valuable addition to the professional collection." Booklist

Includes bibliographical references

Grantsmanship for small libraries and school library media centers; [by] Sylvia D. Hall-Ellis [et al.]; edited by Frank W. Hoffmann. Libraries Unlimited 1999 173p pa $34

Grades: Professional   **025.1**

1. Grants-in-aid

ISBN 1-56308-484-8   LC 98-31247

This "guide outlines each step of the process for obtaining grants, providing examples and definitions along the way. . . . This helpful and easy-to-use handbook should be a part of every professional collection." SLJ

Includes bibliographical references

Hall-Ellis, Sylvia Dunn, 1949-

Grants for school libraries; [by] Sylvia D. Hall-Ellis and Ann Jerabek. Libraries Unlimited 2003 197p il pa $35 *

Grades: Professional   **025.1**

1. Grants-in-aid 2. School libraries

ISBN 1-59158-079-X   LC 2003-54630

"Hall-Ellis and Jerabek provide a systematic approach to every aspect of the grant process. Each section breaks down important concepts and is clearly supported by reproducible forms, examples, and lists. Two important segments address budget and personnel considerations. The project-evaluation section includes data-collection instruments and time lines, while a final chapter discusses practical suggestions such as publicity and writing letters of appreciation. . . . This surprisingly readable guide should be on every school library media specialist's professional shelf." SLJ

Includes bibliographical references

Hallam, Arlita

Managing budgets and finances; a how-to-do-it manual for librarians and information professionals. Neal-Schuman Publishers 2005 233p il (How-to-do-it manuals for librarians) pa $65 *

Grades: Professional   **025.1**

1. Library finance

ISBN 1-55570-519-7

"This budgeting manual . . . offers the new or seasoned library administrators, board members, department heads, or finance professionals a way to budget carefully and clearly by offering a variety of strategies, definitions, and suggestions. The manual is divided into three parts: basics for librarians, special topics in financial management for libraries, and alternative library funding." Booklist

Includes bibliographical references

Harvey, Carl A., II

No school library left behind; leadership, school improvement, and the media specialist; [by] Carl A. Harvey II. Linworth Pub. 2008 106p pa $39.95 *

Grades: Professional   **025.1**

1. School libraries 2. Libraries—Administration 3. Instructional materials centers

ISBN 978-1-58683-233-9; 1-58683-233-6

     LC 2007-42178

"The content [of this book] constitutes a crash course in school improvement, covering definitions, history, legislation, research, best practices, assessment, profiles of accreditation associations, and most importantly, a strong rationale for why media specialists should lead the way in school improvement efforts. . . . Of major interest to novice and seasoned practitioners, this guide is timely and relevant." Libr Media Connect

Includes bibliographical references

MacDonell, Colleen

Essential documents for school libraries; I've-got-it! answers to I-need-it-now! questions. Linworth Pub. 2004 132p il $44.95 *

Grades: Professional   **025.1**

1. Libraries—Administration

ISBN 1-58683-174-7   LC 2004-19392

Contents: Planning documents; Official reports; Publicity; Teaching documents; Programming documents; Procedure sheets and guides; Library rules and regulations; Interactive forms

"Each chapter begins with why the documents are needed, followed by practical advice for writing the documents, and examples of how the documents make an effective change in the library media program." Libr Media Connect

"An excellent addition for school librarians who always want to be prepared." SLJ

Includes bibliographical references

Miller, Ellen G. Wasby, 1939-

Library board strategic guide; going to the next level; [by] Ellen G. Miller, Patricia H. Fisher. Scarecrow Press 2007 222p il pa $35

Grades: Professional   **025.1**

1. Public libraries 2. Libraries—Administration 3. Library trustees

ISBN 978-0-8108-5689-9 (pa); 0-8108-5689-1 (pa)

     LC 2006036397

"The authors see library governance as a team sport that requires knowledge of the complex issues facing today's libraries, political skills to acquire resources, and willingness to become community leaders and library advocates. The book consists of five chapters, each of

Miller, Ellen G. Wasby, 1939-—*Continued*
which addresses a strategic issue that modern libraries
face. . . . The material is tightly written for busy readers
and includes current relevant data, real case histories,
practical tips, and useful quotes. The companion Web
site provides downloadable forms that can be custom-
ized." Booklist
Includes bibliographical references

Pugh, Lyndon
Managing 21st century libraries; [by] Lyndon
Pugh. Scarecrow Press 2005 211p pa $40 *
Grades: Professional   **025.1**
  1. Libraries—Administration
  ISBN 0-8108-5185-7   LC 2005014531
This "details ways library managers and staff can develop systems for managing contemporary library services while taking advantage of circumstances that provide innovative organization development in the library
services of today. Additionally, Lyndon Pugh specifically
relates important issues in personnel management to the
characteristics of libraries that deal significantly with
both digital and printed material." Publisher's note
"A valuable guide to creating an organization for the
e-future." Booklist
Includes bibliographical references

School library management; [edited by] Judi
Repman and Gail Dickinson. 6th ed. Linworth
Pub. 2007 200p il pa $44.95 *
Grades: Professional   **025.1**
  1. School libraries 2. Libraries—Administration
  ISBN 1-58683-296-4; 978-1-58683-296-4
                                        LC 2006-103468
"This collection of more than 35 articles written for
Library Media Connection from 2003 to 2006 is a virtual
treasure trove for library media specialists. . . . The
book covers the very practical everyday issues such as
scheduling and overdues, and also provides invaluable information on data gathering, facilities planning, professional development, the role of the library in the world
of standardized testing, the technological future of libraries, and much more." SLJ
Includes bibliographical references

Stueart, Robert D.
Library and information center management. 7th
ed. Libraries Unlimited 2007 xxviii, 492p (Library
and information science text series) $70; pa $50
Grades: Professional   **025.1**
  1. Libraries—Administration
  ISBN 978-1-59158-408-7; 978-1-59158-406-3 (pa)
                                        LC 2007-7922
This "covers all the essential functions involved in library management. New theories, concepts, and practices
currently being developed and used are included. . . .
Both novices and veteran managers will find this to be
a valuable tool." Booklist
Includes bibliographical references

The **whole** digital library handbook; edited by
Diane Kresh for the Council on Library and
Information Resources. American Library
Association 2007 416p il pa $55
Grades: Professional   **025.1**
  1. Digital libraries
  ISBN 0-8389-0926-4; 978-0-8389-0926-3
                                        LC 2006-27498
"Part 1 defines the digital library, e-reference, and the
digital library federation. Additional parts cover users,
tools, operations, and more. Besides librarians, other experts and commentators on the various technologies present their views on topics ranging from Google's digital
book project, to interpretations of NextGen demographic
data, to digital preservation. . . . [This] should engender
raucous discussions and debates." Booklist
Includes bibliographical references

025.2 Acquisitions and collection development

Baumbach, Donna
Less is more; a practical guide to weeding
school library collections. American Library
Association 2006 194p il pa $32 *
Grades: Professional   **025.2**
  1. Libraries—Collection development
  ISBN 0-8389-0919-1; 978-0-8389-0919-5
                                        LC 2006-7490
Contents: The role of weeding in collection develop-
ment (why less is more); General weeding guidelines;
Getting started and keeping on keeping on; Weeding
criteria by topic and Dewey number; What automation
hath wrought; What's next?
"This outstanding, easy-to-use guide makes weeding
realistic and achievable. . . . This is an indispensable resource for every school library." Booklist
Includes bibliographical references

Brenner, Robin E., 1977-
Understanding manga and anime. Libraries
Unlimited 2007 335p il $40 *
Grades: Professional   **025.2**
  1. Manga—Study and teaching 2. Anime
  3. Libraries—Special collections—Graphic novels
  4. Libraries—Collection development
  ISBN 978-1-59158-332-5   LC 2007-9773
Contents: Short history of manga and anime; Manga
and anime vocabulary; Culture clash: East meets West;
Adventures with ninjas and schoolgirls: humor and realism; Samurai and shogun: action, war, and historical fiction; Giant robots and nature spirits: science fiction, fantasy, and legends; Understanding fans and fan culture;
Draw in a crowd: promotion and programs; Collection
development
The author "provides thorough explanations of manga
and anime vocabulary, potential censorship issues because of cultural disparities, and typical Manga conventions. . . . No professional collection could possibly be
complete without this all-inclusive and exceptional
work." Voice Youth Advocates

Doll, Carol Ann

Managing and analyzing your collection; a practical guide for small libraries and school media centers; [by] Carol A. Doll, Pamela Petrick Barron. American Library Association 2002 93p il pa $30 *

Grades: Professional   025.2
  1. Libraries—Collection development
  ISBN 0-8389-0821-7   LC 2001-53747

This guide to collection development is divided into chapters covering management objectives, gathering and analyzing collection data, and weeding

This is a "book that librarians will actually read from cover to cover. . . . [It] isn't overwhelming and technical. Instead, it is rather chatty with solid, useful information." Book Rep

Includes bibliographical references

Greiner, Tony

Analyzing library collection use with Excel. American Library Association 2007 167p il pa $40 *

Grades: Professional   025.2
  1. Library circulation 2. Libraries—Collection development 3. Excel (Computer program)
  ISBN 0-8389-0933-7 (pa); 978-0-8389-0933-1
                      LC 2006-101539

The authors "show how to use Excel® to translate circulation and collection data into meaningful reports for making collection management decisions." Publisher's note

Includes bibliographical references

Hughes-Hassell, Sandra

Collection management for youth; responding to the needs of learners; [by] Sandra Hughes-Hassell, Jacqueline C. Mancall. ALA Editions 2005 103p il pa $35 *

Grades: Professional   025.2
  1. Libraries—Collection development 2. Instructional materials centers
  ISBN 0-8389-0894-2   LC 2004-26911

"The authors present 11 . . . tools for creating a learner-centered collection with suggestions on the best methods for easy implementation of these procedures. . . . Every library media specialist wanting a more practical approach to collection management would find this book an important addition to his or her professional development library." Libr Media Connect

Includes bibliographical references

Lukenbill, W. Bernard

Community resources in the school library media center; concepts and methods; [by] W. Bernard Lukenbill. Libraries Unlimited 2004 195p il $40

Grades: Professional   025.2
  1. School libraries 2. Libraries and community
  ISBN 1-59158-110-9   LC 2004-48926

"This text outlines organizational strategies for managing community resources. . . . Lukenbill includes information such as agency directories, telementoring numbers, historical documents, museum exhibits, photos, and volunteer pools. Expanding the concept of the vertical file, the author presents ideas for developing, managing, marketing, and accessing electronic photo archives, Web site links, school documents, and bulletin boards. One chapter addresses sensitive community information, censorship, privacy, and terrorism concerns. . . . A definitive tool for developing community-resource collections." SLJ

Lyga, Allyson A. W.

Graphic novels in your media center; a definitive guide; by Allyson A. W. Lyga with Barry Lyga. Libraries Unlimited 2004 180p il pa $35 *

Grades: Professional   025.2
  1. Graphic novels—Administration 2. Book selection 3. Books and reading
  ISBN 1-59158-142-7   LC 2004-46517

In the first section the authors "make cogent arguments for the inclusion of graphic novels. A second section introduces common terms and includes an extremely useful 'how to read' subsection, complete with sample pages. The remaining sections provide recommended titles for all ages, testimonials from teachers and comic book store proprietors, resource lists, and a set of 17 lesson plans." Booklist

"This indispensable, well-organized guide will provide school librarians with all of the necessary information for implementing and developing a graphic-novels collection." SLJ

Miller, Steve

Developing and promoting graphic novel collections. Neal-Schuman Publishers 2005 130p il (Teens @ the library series) pa $49.95 *

Grades: Professional   025.2
  1. Graphic novels—Administration 2. Book selection 3. Books and reading
  ISBN 1-55570-461-1   LC 2004-40159

This is an "overview of graphic novels and their use as reader development tools. Miller explores the evolution, categories, and genres of graphic novels; he then addresses the . . . details of collection development, acquisition, cataloging, and maintenance for this unique format. A special section shows how to promote graphic novels (include display ideas)." Publisher's note

"This volume is filled with practical information and savvy advice." SLJ

Includes bibliographical references

Reichman, Henry, 1947-

Censorship and selection; issues and answers for schools. 3rd ed. American Library Association 2001 223p pa $37 *

Grades: Professional   025.2
  1. Censorship 2. School libraries 3. Academic freedom
  ISBN 0-8389-0798-9   LC 00-67657
  First published 1988

The author "covers the different media (including books, school newspapers, and the Internet), the impor-

Reichman, Henry, 1947-—*Continued*

tant court cases (including recent litigations involving Harry Potter, the Internet, and Huck Finn), the issues in dispute (including violence, religion, and profanity), and how the laws on the books can be incorporated into selection policies." Publisher's note

"Reichman's manual provides sound practical advice on how to handle this complex and emotionally charged subject." Voice Youth Advocates

Includes bibliographical references

Slote, Stanley J.

Weeding library collections; library weeding methods. 4th ed. Libraries Unlimited 1997 xxi, 240p il $69

Grades: Professional   **025.2**
1. Libraries—Collection development
ISBN 1-56308-511-9   LC 96-54865
First published 1975

"The author demonstrates how weeding strengthens a collection and increases circulation. . . . Four weeding methods are presented: the book card method, the spine-marking method, the historical reconstruction method, and the computer-assisted method. Slote gives precise instructions for each method, enhanced with illustrations." Book Rep

Includes bibliographical references

Symons, Ann K.

Protecting the right to read; a how-to-do-it manual for school and public librarians; [by] Ann K. Symons, Charles Harmon; illustrations by Pat Race. Neal-Schuman 1995 211p il (How-to-do-it manuals for librarians) pa $55

Grades: Professional   **025.2**
1. Libraries—Censorship 2. Intellectual freedom
ISBN 1-55570-216-3   LC 95-42444

"The authors take readers from discussion of the policies and principles of intellectual freedom to considerations specific to school and public libraries to the protection of freedom on the Internet. . . . Appendixes consist of reprints of documents put out by the ALA and the Minnesota Coalition Against Censorship." Book Rep

"Intellectual freedom issues and guiding principles get a thorough and comprehensive treatment. . . . An essential book." Voice Youth Advocates

Includes bibliographical references

Walker, Barbara J.

Developing Christian fiction collections for children and adults; selection criteria and a core collection. Neal-Schuman 1998 224p pa $45

Grades: Professional   **025.2**
1. Reference books 2. Christian fiction—Bibliography
3. Children's literature—Bibliography 4. Young adult
literature—Bibliography
ISBN 1-55570-292-9   LC 98-5881

"Areas covered include an overview of Christian fiction, establishing a solid selection process, and promoting this category in your library. Detailed appendixes feature annotated bibliographies of recommended books for children, adults, and young adults; listings of the Gold Me-

dallion Fiction award winners from 1978 to present; biographies of prominent authors; and a selected, annotated videography on the best Christian videos." Publisher's note

Includes bibliographical references

025.3 Bibliographic analysis and control

Cataloging correctly for kids; an introduction to the tools; edited by Sheila S. Intner, Joanna F. Fountain, Jane E. Gilchrist; Association for Library Collections and Technical Services. 4th ed. American Library Association 2006 136p bibl il tab pa $32

Grades: Professional   **025.3**
1. Reference books 2. Cataloging
ISBN 0-8389-3559-1   LC 2005018838
First published 1989 by the Cataloging for Children's Materials Committee

Among the topics discussed are: guidelines fo standardized cataloging for children; how children search; using AACR2 and MARC 21; Sears List of Subject Headings; LC Children's headings; sources for Dewey numbers; cataloging nonbook materials; authority control; how the CIP program helps children; automating the children's catalog; vendors of cataloging for children's materials

Includes bibliographical references

Gorman, Michael, 1941-

The concise AACR2; prepared by Michael Gorman. 4th ed. American Library Association 2004 179p pa $40

Grades: Professional   **025.3**
1. Anglo-American cataloguing rules 2. Reference books 3. Cataloging
ISBN 0-8389-3548-6   LC 2004-16088
First published 1981

"This practical guidebook . . . [is] in concordance with AACR2, 2002 Revision 2004 Update. Michael Gorman . . . explains the more generally applicable AACR2 rules for cataloging library materials in simplified terms that make the rules more accessible and practical for practitioners and students who are in less complex library and bibliographic environments." Publisher's note

Intner, Sheila S., 1935-

Standard cataloging for school and public libraries; [by] Sheila S. Intner and Jean Weihs. 4th ed. Libraries Unlimited 2007 286p il pa $50 *

Grades: Professional   **025.3**
1. Reference books 2. Cataloging 3. Library classification
ISBN 978-1-59158-378-3; 1-59158-378-0
LC 2007-9009

First published 1990

This explains the Anglo-American Cataloging Rules (AACR2), Sears and Library of Congress subject headings, Dewey decimal and Library of Congress classifica-

Intner, Sheila S., 1935-—*Continued*
tion systems, MARC format, large computer networks, policy manuals, and how to manage a cataloging department.

Includes bibliographical references

Kaplan, Allison G.
Catalog it! [by] Allison G. Kaplan, Ann Marlow Riedling. 2nd ed. Linworth Publishing 2006 212p il $44.95 *
Grades: Professional   025.3
1. Reference books 2. Cataloging 3. School libraries 4. Instructional materials centers
ISBN 1-58683-197-6
"This practical, how-to manual provides a breakdown of the theories, rules, and issues that anyone cataloging school library materials needs to know. The first part . . . includes a condensed history of cataloging, basic tools for copy cataloging, and information on theory and the MARC record. The second part is devoted to application. . . . Using clear summaries and a nice variety of examples, this section also offers exercises. . . . This is a must for school libraries and academic libraries that have K-12 collections." Booklist

025.4 Subject analysis and control

Sears list of subject headings; Joseph Miller, editor; Barbara A. Bristow, associate editor. 19th ed. Wilson, H. W. 2007 li, 823p $145 *
Grades: Professional   025.4
1. Subject headings
ISBN 978-0-8242-1076-2
Also available Canadian companion. 6th edition published 2001
First published 1923 with title: List of subject headings for small libraries, by Minnie Earl Sears
This is "a standard authority list for subject cataloging in small and medium-sized libraries. It contains more than 8,000 established subject terms and . . . provisions for establishing further terms as needed. It also contains more than 500 authorized subdivisions with instructions in their application, scope notes, suggested cross-references, and suggestions for classification." Publisher's note

025.5 Services for users

Bell, Suzanne S.
Librarian's guide to online searching. 2nd ed. Libraries Unlimited 2009 287p il $45
Grades: Professional   025.5
1. Internet searching
ISBN 978-1-59158-763-7; 1-59158-763-8
                                       LC 2008-35924
First published 2006
This "online searching guide will be invaluable to anyone starting out or looking for a refresher course on this topic. In clear concise language, the author covers everything from Boolean searching to using specific topic-based databases. . . . This easy-to-use manual, written

with just a touch of humor and not a drop of condescension, is sure to be embraced by librarians of all skill levels." Voice Youth Advocates
Includes bibliographical references

Developing an information literacy program, K-12; a how-to-do-it manual and CD-ROM package; developed by the Iowa City Community School District; edited by Mary Jo Langhorne. 2nd ed. Neal-Schuman 2004 432p (How-to-do-it manuals for librarians) pa $89.95 *
Grades: Professional   025.5
1. Bibliographic instruction 2. School libraries 3. Library information networks
ISBN 1-55570-509-X   LC 2004-46046
First published 1998
"Over twenty lessons . . . cover keyword research, library and library materials organization, using nonfiction books, using the library catalog, using online databases, using the Internet, note-taking, creating bibliographies, and more. You will also find planning and assessment forms, checklists, tables, and worksheets for developing, implementing, and instructing your information literacy programs—all reproduced in the book and accompanying CD-ROM." Publisher's note

Duncan, Donna
I-search for success; a how-to-do-it manual for linking the I-search process with standards, assessment, tests, and evidence-based practice; [by] Donna Duncan and Laura Lockhart. Neal-Schuman Publishers 2005 xxi, 277p il (How-to-do-it manuals for librarians) pa $75
Grades: Professional   025.5
1. Research 2. Libraries
ISBN 1-55570-510-3   LC 2004-54665
"Extending the authors' previous book, *I-Search, You Search, We All Learn to Research* (Neal-Schuman, 2000), this title takes readers step-by-step through a unit for grades three and four, from planning to assessment. . . . Large boxed figures interspersed throughout the text include I-Search forms, worksheets, organizational tools, and lists of resources for further information. The accompanying CD-ROM contains the collaborative planning guide, the I-Search journal for students, and a PowerPoint presentation for professional development found in the book, with all of the figures incorporated for easy modification and printing. This is a valuable resource guide for teachers and librarians using, or planning to use, the I-Search method." Booklist
Includes bibliographical references

Farmer, Lesley S. Johnson, 1949-
Technology-infused instruction for the educational community; a guide for school library specialists; [by] Lesley S.J. Farmer. Scarecrow Press 2005 209p il pa $40 *
Grades: Professional   025.5
1. School libraries 2. Information technology
ISBN 0-8108-5118-0   LC 2004-18028
"Library media teachers who provide staff development would do well to read this concise manual, which

Farmer, Lesley S. Johnson, 1949-—*Continued*
provides a welcome shortcut for the training of teachers
and parents in the use of technology. . . . Farmer keeps
the information moving swiftly through an engaging text
that sparks ideas that readers can transfer smoothly into
practice. Useful checklists and worksheets that translate
into visuals abound." SLJ
Includes glossary and bibliographical references

Lanning, Scott
Essential reference services for today's school
media specialists; [by] Scott Lanning and John
Bryner. Libraries Unlimited 2004 129p il pa $40
Grades: Professional   025.5
  1. Reference services (Libraries) 2. School libraries
  ISBN 1-59158-137-0   LC 2004-40833
This book "covers not only how to develop a quality
reference section for school library media specialists, but
also how to complete a reference interview and work
with teachers to reach the most students. . . . All librarians will find something useful in this book." Libr Media
Connect
Includes bibliographical references

Lenburg, Jeff
The Facts On File guide to research; [by] Jeff
Lenburg. Facts on File 2005 xxxii, 560p $45; pa
$18.95
Grades: 8 9 10 11 12   025.5
  1. Research 2. Information resources
  ISBN 0-8160-5741-9; 0-8160-5742-7 (pa)
                              LC 2004-18941
This is "a nuts-and-bolts guide to research. Introductory chapters offer strategies to help students get started.
. . . Gathering Your Information is an overview of the
variety of sources that most libraries provide. . . . Evaluating Your Sources addresses timeliness, relevance, objectivity, accuracy, and more. This narrative section is
followed by lengthy chapters that list specific sources by
type of resource. . . . There is a chapter on search engines and how to use them. . . . A final chapter about
citing sources and avoiding plagiarism is followed by appendixes that show examples of APA, MLA, and Chicago Manual of Style bibliographic format. A no-frills, solid reference source." SLJ
Includes bibliographical references

Riedling, Ann Marlow, 1952-
Information literacy; what does it look like in
the school library media center. Libraries
Unlimited 2004 121p il pa $35 *
Grades: Professional   025.5
  1. Bibliographic instruction 2. School libraries
  3. Information networks
  ISBN 1-59158-201-6   LC 2004-48773
This "instructional manual is designed to teach school
library media specialists what information literacy 'looks
like' in general, in the school, in the classroom, in your
mind, in life, and in motion. . . . It discusses information literacy, research, independent learning, ethics and
more. . . . Annotated resources are provided within each
chapter, as are . . . related readings and Web sites."

Publisher's note
  This is "a worthwhile addition." SLJ
  Includes bibliographical references

Tallman, Julie I., 1944-
Making the writing and research connection
with the I-search process; a how-to-do-it manual;
[by] Julie I. Tallman, Marilyn Z. Joyce. 2nd ed.
Neal-Schuman Publishers 2006 xx, 167p il
(How-to-do-it manuals for librarians) pa $55
Grades: Professional   025.5
  1. Bibliographic instruction 2. Young adults' libraries
  3. Research 4. Report writing
  ISBN 1-55570-534-0; 978-1-55570-534-3
                              LC 2005-32473
First published 1997
Joyce's name appears first on the earlier edition
This volume "covers the I-Search process for middle
and high-school students and . . . includes a detailed explanation of I-Search in the context of content units. Although it is useful for the media specialist and teacher
who are familiar with I-Search, novices will also find
valuable information. . . . The accompanying CD-ROM
contains all of the figures found in the book (templates,
handouts, etc.), which can be reproduced and adapted."
Booklist
Includes bibliographical references

Yucht, Alice H.
Flip it! an information skills strategy for student
researchers. Linworth Pub. 1997 105p il
(Professional growth series) $29.95
Grades: Professional   025.5
  1. Bibliographic instruction 2. School libraries
  ISBN 0-938865-62-5   LC 97-3887
The author "presents a new information skills strategy
for librarians and teachers to use with students. . . .
FLIP IT is a mnemonic for research processes: Focus—
on the topic; Link—new information to what is already
known; Input—implement the information; Payoff—put it
all together (finished product)." Voice Youth Advocates
Includes bibliographical references

025.8   Maintenance and preservation of collections

Halsted, Deborah D.
Disaster planning; a how-to-do-it manual for
librarians with planning templates on CD-ROM.
Neal-Schuman Publishers 2005 xx, 247p il
(How-to-do-it manuals for librarians) pa $85
Grades: Professional   025.8
  1. Disaster relief 2. Accidents—Prevention 3. Library
  resources—Conservation and restoration
  ISBN 1-55570-486-7   LC 2003-65152
Includes CD-ROM
"Step-by-step instructions discuss creating a working
disaster team, establishing a communications strategy,
identifying relief and recovery agencies, developing response plans, and examining issues of cutting-edge library security. . . . This valuable resource is an important addition to most professional collections." Booklist
Includes bibliographical references

027   General libraries, archives, information centers

Trumble, Kelly
The Library of Alexandria; illustrated by Robina MacIntyre Marshall. Clarion Bks. 2003 72p il maps $17
Grades: 5 6 7 8   **027**
1. Alexandrian Library (Egypt) 2. Egypt—Civilization 3. Ancient civilization
ISBN 0-395-75832-7   LC 2003-150
Contents: A city of learning; Collecting books; Pergamum; Astronomy; Geography; Mathematics; Medicine; Decline and destruction; The fate of the Library of Alexandria
An introduction to the largest and most famous library in the ancient world, discussing its construction in Alexandria, Egypt, its vast collections, rivalry with the Pergamum Library, famous scholars, and destruction by fire
This is a "well-organized and thorough resource." SLJ
Includes glossary and bibliographical references

027.6   Libraries for special groups and organizations

Alire, Camila
Serving Latino communities; a how-to-do-it manual for librarians. 2nd ed. Neal-Schuman Publishers 2007 229p bibl il (How-to-do-it manuals for librarians) pa $59.95 *
Grades: Professional   **027.6**
1. Libraries and Hispanic Americans
ISBN 978-1-55570-606-7; 1-55570-606-1
LC 2007-7783
First published 1998
"The information covered helps library staff understand the needs of their library's Latino community; develop successful programs and services; obtain funding for projects and programs; prepare staff to work more effectively with Latinos; establish partnerships with relevant external agencies and organizations; improve collection development; and perform effective outreach and public relations. . . . There are few resources widely available on this topic and none as complete." Libr Media Connect
Includes bibliographical references

Byrd, Susannah Mississippi, 1971-
Bienvenidos! = Welcome! a handy resource guide for marketing your library to Latinos; foreword by Carol Brey-Casiano. American Library Association 2005 110p il pa $20 *
Grades: Professional   **027.6**
1. Libraries and Hispanic Americans
ISBN 0-8389-0902-7; 978-0-8389-0902-7
LC 2005-6315
This "guide covers everything from survey analysis to access and outreach to collection development, and offers practical solutions and suggestions. . . . Byrd includes resources, services, government agencies, projects, pro-

fessional organizations, etc., making this title a valuable addition to libraries and organizations that are initiating programs directed toward diverse Latino populations." SLJ
Includes bibliographical references

Lerch, Maureen T.
Serving homeschooled teens and their parents. Libraries Unlimited 2004 242p (Libraries Unlimited professional guides for young adult librarians) pa $39
Grades: Professional   **027.6**
1. Home schooling 2. Young adults' libraries
ISBN 0-313-32052-7   LC 2004-46518
"After introductory chapters that dispel many myths about homeschooling and delve into adolescent psychology, the two experts give sound advice and great examples for service plan creation, collection development, programming, and promotion of services." Libr Media Connect
Includes bibliographical references

027.62   Libraries for specific age groups

Alessio, Amy
A year of programs for teens. American Library Association 2007 159p il pa $35
Grades: Professional   **027.62**
1. Young adults' libraries 2. Teenagers—Books and reading
ISBN 0-8389-0903-5; 978-0-8389-0903-4
LC 2006-13758
"Following an overview of the planning component of successful teen programming, this guide is presented as a calendar of ideas for each month of the year. Each month offers three to four programs with the preparation time, the length of the program, the recommended number of teen participants, age range, a shopping list, the setup required, variations or extra activities, and resources. . . . Librarians working with teens will find plenty of fresh ideas here." Booklist
Includes bibliographical references

Anderson, Sheila B.
Extreme teens; library services to nontraditional young adults. Libraries Unlimited 2005 xxiii, 175p (Libraries Unlimited professional guides for young adult librarians) pa $36
Grades: Professional   **027.62**
1. Young adults' libraries 2. Teenagers—Books and reading
ISBN 1-59158-170-2   LC 2005016076
"This accessible manual offers practical advice on working with 'extreme teens,' young adults who, because of their sexuality, educational circumstances, or living situations, tend to be underserved by traditional public library services. Individual sections discuss definitions of various populations, service specifications for subgroups, collection development, and promotional programs. Additional features include statistics, scenarios, cited sources,

Anderson, Sheila B.—*Continued*
and lists of recommended print and electronic resources, both fiction and nonfiction." Booklist
Includes bibliographical references

Braun, Linda W.
Technically involved; technology-based youth participation activities for your library. American Library Association 2003 138p il pa $34
Grades: Professional   **027.62**
 1. Young adults' libraries
 ISBN 0-8389-0861-6   LC 2003-12021
Contents: Youth participation—the what and the why; Getting teens involved; On the road to greatness; Bringing generations together; Reading, writing, and youth participation; Getting things done at the library; Overcoming obstacles
In this "title, Braun encourages librarians to involve teens in technology-related activities and projects that will benefit them and others. She responds to questions regarding participation, benefits to patrons and libraries, and training. The author provides numerous suggestions for activities. . . . This excellent volume is a must for libraries with teen groups, and a consideration for those that don't have them." SLJ
Includes bibliographical references

Brehm-Heeger, Paula
Serving urban teens. Libraries Unlimited 2008 229p (Libraries Unlimited professional guides for young adult librarians) pa $40
Grades: Professional   **027.62**
 1. Young adults' libraries 2. Teenagers—Books and reading
 ISBN 978-1-59158-377-6; 1-59158-377-2
                                             LC 2007-45415
This book "begins with definitions and a brief history of library services to urban teens, followed by a description of issues concerning this special group. The remaining chapters detail every aspect of making positive connections with teens, from training staff—the entire library staff—to making space, developing the collection, designing programs, and developing partnerships within the community. . . . It is not only the mission of libraries but also in their self-interest to capture the minds and hearts of youth while they can. This book provides the tools to accomplish the job." Voice Youth Advocates
Includes bibliographical references

Burek Pierce, Jennifer
Sex, brains, and video games; a librarian's guide to teens in the twenty-first century. American Library Association 2008 130p pa $35
Grades: Professional   **027.62**
 1. Young adults' libraries 2. Adolescence 3. Teenagers—United States
 ISBN 978-0-8389-0951-5; 0-8389-0951-5
                                             LC 2007-21926
"This guide provides new and reevaluated ideas and insights about the sociological, neurological, emotional, and sexual perspectives of adolescence. The author's purpose is to assist librarians as they try to engage teens

through relevant and attractive responses to their recreational, informational, and technological needs and interests. . . . It is filled with a great deal of pertinent and thought-provoking advice and information." SLJ
Includes bibliographical references

Coleman, Tina
The hipster librarian's guide to teen craft projects; [by] Tina Coleman and Peggie Llanes; foreword by Heather Booth. American Library Association 2009 91p $40
Grades: Professional   **027.62**
 1. Young adults' libraries 2. Handicraft
 ISBN 978-0-8389-0971-3; 0-8389-0971-X
                                             LC 2008019988
"This book presents 12 different craft projects designed to appeal to teens. . . . The directions are straighforward, and black-and-white illustrations are featured throughout. . . . This would be a useful resource for anyone interested in increasing or expanding their teen programming." Booklist

Doyle, Miranda, 1972-
101+ great ideas for teen library Web sites. Neal-Schuman Publishers 2007 xx, 307p (Teens @ the library series) pa $65 *
Grades: Professional   **027.62**
 1. Web sites 2. Young adults' libraries
 ISBN 978-1-55570-593-0; 1-55570-593-6
                                             LC 2006-39132
"The theme is that teens are experienced tech users, and libraries need to make their online presence as inviting and informative as their physical space. To make this happen, Doyle provides excellent, inspiring ideas, many of which involve minimal knowledge or expense. . . . Clearly written and well presented, this book provides a variety of ways to provide interaction with young patrons and visibility for library services." Booklist
Includes bibliographical references

Farmer, Lesley S. Johnson, 1949-
Digital inclusion, teens, and your library. Libraries Unlimited 2005 176p (Libraries Unlimited professional guides for young adult librarians) $39
Grades: Professional   **027.62**
 1. Internet 2. Young adults' libraries
 ISBN 1-59158-128-1   LC 2004-63833
"This guide helps librarians to identify 'tech-nots'—technologically disadvantaged teens—in a community or school and to reach out and build information literacy in underserved teen populations." Publisher's note
Includes bibliographical references

Follos, Alison M. G.
Reviving reading; school library programming, author visits, and books that rock! [by] Alison M. G. Follos; foreword by Jack Gantos. Libraries Unlimited 2006 xx, 143p bibl pa $32
Grades: Professional   **027.62**
 1. Books and reading 2. Children's libraries 3. Young adults' libraries
 ISBN 1-59158-356-X   LC 2006017616

Follos, Alison M. G.—*Continued*

This is an "idea-packed manual on innovative literacy programs for elementary, middle, and high-school students. . . . Three sections address why, how, and what needs to be done to instill lifelong reading habits in children and young adults. . . . This realistic and reasonable guide is recommended for school and public library professional collections." Booklist

Includes bibliographical references

Gorman, Michele

Connecting young adults and libraries; a how-to-do-it manual; [by] Michele Gorman and Tricia Suellentrop. 4th ed. Neal-Schuman Publishers Inc. 2009 450p il (How-to-do it manuals) pa $85

Grades: Professional　　　　　　　**027.62**

1. Young adults' libraries 2. Young adult literature—Bibliography 3. Teenagers—Books and reading
ISBN 978-1-55570-665-4　　　　　LC 2009-17657

First published 1992 under the authorship of Patrick Jones

"Not only are the building blocks of library services such as collection development, outreach, programs, booktalking, and teen space included, but the authors also discuss why they are important and why they work. Peppered throughout are examples of libraries successfully connecting with teens. . . . An upbeat, well-organized must-have for anyone working with this audience." SLJ [review of 2004 edition]

Includes bibliographical references

Hardesty, Constance

The teen-centered writing club; bringing teens and words together. Libraries Unlimited 2008 174p il (Libraries Unlimited professional guides for young adult librarians) pa $40

Grades: Professional　　　　　　　**027.62**

1. Young adults' libraries 2. Creative writing 3. English language—Composition and exercises
ISBN 978-1-59158-548-0; 1-59158-548-1

　　　　　　　　　　　　　　　LC 2008-11519

"Hardesty encourages librarians to listen to teens and assist them in their search for identity through the written word. . . . From starting a club and the writing activities to share, to grand finales and how to evaluate the program's effectiveness, the author details all the information needed to create such a club. Particularly useful are chapters on the four roles of facilitators, creating a nonfiction writing club, and how to take your efforts online. Many handouts are included, a boon to any busy librarian. An appendix includes resources for publishing. All this information is laid out in a straightforward, positive manner. An essential resource for planning or presenting writing clubs." SLJ

Includes bibliographical references

Honnold, RoseMary, 1954-

101+ teen programs that work. Neal-Schuman 2003 xxi, 195p il (Teens @ the library series) pa $49.95

Grades: Professional　　　　　　　**027.62**

1. Young adults' libraries 2. School libraries—Activity projects 3. Teenagers—Books and reading
ISBN 1-55570-453-0　　　　　　LC 2002-29385

Program plans cover activities such as summer reading games, contests, crafts, coffeehouse style poetry and Mike nights.

"Those who work with teens will find plenty of year-round programming ideas in this useful volume. The author has incorporated tried-and-true activities complete with instructions on how to plan and present each one." SLJ

Includes bibliographical references

More teen programs that work. Neal-Schuman Publishers 2005 xxi, 245p il (Teens @ the library series) $49.95 *

Grades: Professional　　　　　　　**027.62**

1. Young adults' libraries 2. School libraries—Activity projects 3. Teenagers—Books and reading
ISBN 1-55570-529-4　　　　　　LC 2004-19032

Follow-up to: 101+ teen programs that work

Contents: Measuring unmeasurable outcomes; Summer reading and teen read week; More independent programs; More craft programs; Book themed programs; Food programs; More parties, games, and lock-ins; Programs for girls; Programs for boys; Programs for tweens; More programs for teens and adults and teens and children; Writing programs; Teens in the spotlight; School and life skills; Teen volunteer and fund raising projects

"Full of practical and excellent information, this is a definite choice for any library that wants to expand its programming for teens." SLJ

Includes bibliographical references

Information literacy skills, grades 7-12; Catherine M. Andronik, compiler. 3rd ed. Linworth Pub. 1999 315p pa $39.95

Grades: Professional　　　　　　　**027.62**

1. Young adults' libraries
ISBN 0-938865-82-6

First published 1990 with title: Library research skills workbook, grades 7-12

This is a compilation of articles "gathered from *The Book Report* and *Library Talk*. The 11 thematic chapters cover both practical and theoretical aspects of secondary librarianship, with topics ranging from research models and Internet skills, to assessment and literature." Booklist

Jones, Ella W.

Start-to-finish YA programs; hip-hop symposiums, summer reading programs, virtual tours, poetry slams, teen advisory boards, term paper clinics, and more! Neal-Schuman Publishers 2009 217p il pa $75

Grades: Professional　　　　　　　**027.62**

1. Cultural programs 2. Young adults' libraries
ISBN 978-1-55570-601-2; 1-55570-601-0

　　　　　　　　　　　　　　　LC 2008-50853

Includes CD-ROM

Jones, Ella W.—*Continued*
"Each of the 25 programs includes descriptions, goals, and a how-to-do it section, complete with book display and program-evaluation suggestions." SLJ

"Jones's creativity, twenty-five years of experience, and her genuine love for teenagers is obvious in the meticulous and creative programming ideas and materials. This valuable resource will be appreciated by librarians in public and school settings." Voice Youth Advocates
Includes bibliographical references

Jones, Patrick
Do it right! best practices for serving young adults in school and public libraries; [by] Patrick Jones and Joel Shoemaker. Neal-Schuman 2001 182p il (Teens @ the library series) pa $45
Grades: Professional   **027.62**
1. Young adults' libraries 2. Public libraries 3. School libraries
ISBN 1-55570-394-1   LC 2001-30718
"In the first half of the book, Shoemaker concentrates on turning the school library media center into 'library heaven,' while in the second half Jones addresses the challenges and rewards of working with young adults in the public library. . . . The book . . . provides plenty of training ideas, sample surveys, action plans, job descriptions, library policies, and interview questions." SLJ
Includes bibliographical references

Kan, Katharine
Sizzling summer reading programs for young adults; [by] Katharine L. Kan for the Young Adult Library Services Association. 2nd ed. American Library Association 2006 110p il pa $30 *
Grades: Professional   **027.62**
1. Young adults' libraries 2. Teenagers—Books and reading
ISBN 0-8389-3563-X
First published 1998
This "presents more than 50 summer reading programs that have been used successfully with preteens and teenagers. . . . Submissions represent a cross section of themes, incentives, activities and budgets. . . . Children and young adult services librarians will find a wealth of practical, hands-on information." Booklist

Koelling, Holly
Classic connections; turning teens on to great literature. Libraries Unlimited 2004 xxi, 405p (Libraries Unlimited professional guides for young adult librarians) pa $40
Grades: Professional   **027.62**
1. Teenagers—Books and reading
ISBN 1-59158-072-2   LC 2004-48644
"The book is divided into two sections: Laying the Groundwork and Making it Happen. The first section covers the essential elements that define a book as a classic, reviews adolescent development and reading habits, and discusses what types of classics have teen appeal. The second section contains a discussion of collection development, readers' advisory, programming, booktalking, and promotion of the classics. . . . It is a

valuable book for anyone trying to connect teens to classic literature." Voice Youth Advocates
Includes bibliographical references

Kunzel, Bonnie Lendermon
The teen-centered book club; readers into leaders; [by] Bonnie Kunzel and Constance Hardesty. Libraries Unlimited 2006 xxi, 211p (Libraries Unlimited professional guides for young adult librarians) pa $40
Grades: Professional   **027.62**
1. Young adults' libraries 2. Teenagers—Books and reading
ISBN 1-59158-193-1
"Two experienced youth-services librarians introduce the idea of teen-centered book clubs. . . . In clear prose supported by research, the authors cover every aspect of the program, from assessing the needs of the library and teens to conducting successful meetings to evaluating activities. . . . An excellent reference." SLJ
Includes bibliographical references

Mahood, Kristine
A passion for print; promoting reading and books to teens. Libraries Unlimited 2006 239p il (Libraries Unlimited professional guides for young adult librarians) pa $40
Grades: Professional   **027.62**
1. Young adults' libraries 2. Teenagers—Books and reading
ISBN 1-59158-146-X; 978-1-59158-146-8
                                           LC 2006-3716
"Beginning with research on reading, Mahood moves on to merchandising principles; developing teen collections, spaces, and Web sites; and finally to booktalking, readers' advisory, and events scheduling. The author's enthusiasm and experience, coupled with citing current studies, other professional books, articles, and Web sites, make her suggestions appealing and attainable. She provides everything from lists of YA genres to easy design principles for displays to suggestions for questions to ask for better readers' advisory." Booklist

Martin, Hillias J., Jr.
Serving lesbian, gay, bisexual, transgender, and questioning teens; a how-to-do-it manual for librarians; [by] Hillias J. Martin, Jr., James R. Murdock. Neal-Schuman Publishers 2007 267p (How-to-do-it manuals for librarians) pa $55 *
Grades: Professional   **027.62**
1. Young adults' libraries 2. Gay men 3. Lesbians 4. Transsexualism 5. Bisexuality
ISBN 978-1-55570-566-4; 1-55570-566-9
                                           LC 2006-39469
"This volume offers abundant useful guidance not only for reaching the target audience, but also for planning and promoting library services to teens in general. . . . The tone is friendly and largely free of jargon. . . . All librarians should turn to this book for pertinent insight on the needs of 5 to 10 percent of the teen population." SLJ
Includes bibliographical references

Miller, Donna P., 1948-
Crash course in teen services. Libraries Unlimited 2008 xi, 128p bibl (Crash course) $30
Grades: Professional   **027.62**
  1. Young adults' libraries
  ISBN 978-1-59158-565-7 (pa); 1-59158-565-1 (pa)
          LC 2007-32758
"Designed for public librarians new to teen service, the book offers advice on relating to teens and creating teen-friendly space as well as tips on teen-centered reference, collection development, readers' advisory, programming, and 'the three Ps': professional resources, professional development, and public relations." Booklist
Includes bibliographical references

Mondowney, JoAnn G.
Hold them in your heart; successful strategies for library services to at-risk teens. Neal-Schuman 2001 139p (Teens @ the library series) pa $45
Grades: Professional   **027.62**
  1. Young adults' libraries
  ISBN 1-55570-393-3   LC 00-58413
"This book focuses on specific services for teens. . . . It includes sections on gaining support, needs assessment, funding, and planning and evaluation." SLJ
Includes bibliographical references

New directions for library service to young adults; Young Adult Library Services Association with Patrick Jones; edited by Linda Waddle. American Library Association 2002 146p pa $32 *
Grades: Professional   **027.62**
  1. Young adults' libraries
  ISBN 0-8389-0827-6   LC 2002-3377
This "covers guidelines on planning, implementing, and evaluating services with youth involved in each step of the process. Twelve goal statements for YA services and ten core values upon which these goals are built are presented. . . . Besides his usual clear writing, ubiquitous lists, and deft editorial organization, Jones writes a manifesto for how services for young adults should be conceptualized." Voice Youth Advocates
Includes bibliographical references

O'Dell, Katie
Library materials and services for teen girls. Libraries Unlimited 2002 179p il (Libraries Unlimited professional guides for young adult librarians) pa $45
Grades: Professional   **027.62**
  1. Young adults' libraries 2. Libraries—Collection development 3. Girls—Books and reading
  ISBN 0-313-31554-X   LC 2002-7609
Contents: Girls in the spotlight: a short history; Collection development; Programming; Girls and technology; Volunteers; Collaboration; Outreach to teen girls
In this "guide to providing library services to teen girls in a public library setting, chapters cover such topics as collection development . . . programming; girls and technology; volunteers; collaboration; and outreach." Booklist

"This book will be useful to librarians with the very specific goal of attracting adolescent girls to the library." SLJ
Includes bibliographical references

Ott, Valerie A.
Teen programs with punch; a month-by-month guide. Libraries Unlimited 2006 282p il tab (Libraries Unlimited professional guides for young adult librarians) pa $40
Grades: Professional   **027.62**
  1. Young adults' libraries 2. Teenagers—Books and reading
  ISBN 1-59158-293-8   LC 2006012775
"Ott has gathered together less-than-conventional program ideas arranged by month. She provides clear instructions, lists of supplemental materials, promotional ideas, reading lists, costs, and suggested grade levels for each one. For librarians with limited budgets, and who may be pressed for time, there are quick and easy ideas that cost little or no money. . . . Many of the programs are designed to draw underserved populations, such as goths, GLBTQ teens, and vegetarians, into the library. . . . This highly informative guide would make a great addition to any YA librarian's professional collection." SLJ
Includes bibliographical references

Rankin, Virginia
The thoughtful researcher; teaching the research process to middle school students. Libraries Unlimited 1999 211p il (Information literacy series) $30.50 *
Grades: Professional   **027.62**
  1. School libraries 2. Bibliographic instruction 3. Research
  ISBN 1-56308-698-0   LC 98-55916
Rankin "offers concrete suggestions (and 16 reproducible handouts) for researching a topic, generating questions, planning a project, managing time, searching for information, evaluating sources, note taking, mastering thinking skills, selecting a presentation format, and assessing the product and the process. . . . A must-have resource for school libraries serving grades 5-9, this will be welcomed by classroom teachers and teacher-librarians." Booklist
Includes bibliographical references

Reid, Rob
Something funny happened at the library; how to create humorous programs for children and young adults. American Library Association 2003 163p $32
Grades: Professional   **027.62**
  1. Children's libraries 2. Young adults' libraries 3. Storytelling
  ISBN 0-8389-0836-5   ·   LC 2002-8970
Contents: Tricks of the trade; Humor programs for younger children: preschool and primary school age; Humor programs for intermediate school age children; Humor programs for middle and high school students; Reader's theater; Lively library tours & visits to schools; Raps and closings; The funniest books in the library; Two last treats

Reid, Rob—*Continued*

This is "an excellent resource for adding wit to your library repertoire." SLJ

Includes bibliographical references

Serving young teens and 'tweens; edited by Sheila B. Anderson; foreword by James M. Rosinia. Libraries Unlimited 2007 xxv, 158p (Libraries Unlimited professional guides for young adult librarians) pa $40

Grades: Professional   **027.62**

1. Reference books 2. Young adults' libraries 3. Teenagers—Books and reading 4. Young adult literature—Bibliography

ISBN 1-59158-259-8 (pa); 978-1-59158-259-5 (pa)
LC 2006030666

This "is aimed at librarians serving middle school, roughly ages 10-14. The book defines tweens developmentally and describes nonfiction and fiction resources, programming, and booktalking for this group. Well-qualified contributors provide practical ideas, balanced and specific examples, up-to-date book lists, and citations to research-oriented works." Booklist

Includes bibliographical references

Sima, Judy

Raising voices; creating youth storytelling groups and troupes; [by] Judy Sima, Kevin Cordi. Libraries Unlimited 2003 xxviii, 241p pa $32.50

Grades: Professional   **027.62**

1. Storytelling

ISBN 1-56308-919-X   LC 2003-47631

This offers a "blueprint for beginning and sustaining a successful group or troupe of storytellers from grades 4 to 12. . . . The book includes reproducible forms that will save a lot of work and lists of valuable resources. . . . Raising Voices is the complete, and essential, handbook for this special group of storytellers." SLJ

Includes bibliographical references

Simpson, Martha Seif, 1954-

Bringing classes into the public library; a handbook for librarians; [by] Martha Seif Simpson and Lucretia I. Duwel. McFarland & Co. 2007 175p il pa $45

Grades: Professional   **027.62**

1. Children's libraries 2. Young adults' libraries 3. Libraries and schools 4. Public libraries

ISBN 978-0-7864-2806-9 (pa); 0-7864-2806-6 (pa)
LC 2006037527

"This handbook articulates the reasons and defines a strategy for promoting a program of class visits to the public library, and provides . . . instructions and . . . templates to assist librarians in initiating an organized program of class visits." Publisher's note

Soltan, Rita

Reading raps; a book club guide for librarians, kids, and families; [by] Rita Soltan. Libraries Unlimited 2006 354p pa $35

Grades: Professional   **027.62**

1. Reference books 2. Children's libraries 3. Books and reading 4. Children's literature—Bibliography

ISBN 1-59158-234-2   LC 2005030842

"The author provides librarians with a guide to book discussion groups for children and adults, with plans for 100 books geared to grades 3-8. Ideas for forming groups and choosing titles, discussion questions, and icebreakers are included. Titles range from older classics to books published in 2004 and cover all fiction genres. . . . The novice group leader will find this book helpful, and the experienced facilitator will find many new ideas." Booklist

Includes bibliographical references

Welch, Rollie James, 1957-

The guy-friendly YA library; serving male teens. Libraries Unlimited 2007 xxi, 196p (Libraries Unlimited professional guides for young adult librarians) pa $40

Grades: Professional   **027.62**

1. Young adults' libraries 2. Boys—Books and reading 3. Teenagers—Books and reading

ISBN 978-1-59158-270-0; 1-59158-270-9
LC 2006-102882

"The first chapter offers key components for quality service for teen males, while the second chapter explains the characteristics and developmental issues of this population. The book emphasizes reading, with three chapters dedicated to male teen reading habits, topics of interest, and detailed genre coverage. . . . The sixth chapter deals with programming and also explains how the establish an effective teen advisory board. . . . The seventh chapter covers school visits and emphasizes the importance of booktalks. The eighth chapter discusses creating a teen area in the library." Booklist

Includes bibliographical references

027.8   School libraries

Adams, Helen R., 1943-

Ensuring intellectual freedom and access to information in the school library media program; foreword by Dianne McAfee Hopkins. Libraries Unlimited 2008 xxi, 254p il map pa $40 *

Grades: Professional   **027.8**

1. School libraries 2. Censorship 3. Freedom of information

ISBN 978-1-59158-539-8; 1-59158-539-2
LC 2008-16753

This is "an extremely helpful guide for dealing with intellectual-freedom and information-access issues. In chapters geared to school situations and covering topics including selection of resources, the First Amendment, privacy, challenges to resources, the Internet, and access for students with disabilities, Adams offers background on the topic and bulleted lists of strategies for dealing with the issue. . . . This is a book that every school librarian needs to keep handy and share with administrators, colleagues, and parents." Booklist

Includes bibliographical references

American Association of School Librarians

Information power; building partnerships for learning; prepared by the American Association of School Librarians [and] Association for Educational Communications and Technology. American Library Association 1998 205p il pa $37 *

Grades: Professional   **027.8**

1. School libraries 2. Instructional materials centers
ISBN 0-8389-3470-6   LC 98-23291
First published 1988

This resource "relates the library-media program to the entire educational infrastructure. The authors explicate their themes in terms of standards, indicators, levels of proficiency, goals, principles, and examples of student activities. The appendixes contain essential information on Library Power, AASL's ICON-nect project, the Library Bill of Rights, confidentiality, censorship, access equity, and ethics." SLJ

Includes bibliographical references

Baule, Steven M., 1966-

Facilities planning for school library and technology centers. 2nd ed. Linworth Pub. 2007 134p il pa $39.95

Grades: Professional   **027.8**

1. Instructional materials centers—Design and construction 2. School libraries—Design and construction
ISBN 1-58683-294-8; 978-1-58683-294-0
                         LC 2006-34179
First published 1992

The author "provides information on how to put together a planning team; how to perform a needs assessment for the library media center or technology lab; how to create bid documents and specification charts; how to develop time lines; and how to plan to move into the new facility once construction is complete. . . . Anyone who is going to build or renovate a facility will want this book." Booklist

Includes bibliographical references

Bishop, Kay, 1942-

The collection program in schools; concepts, practices, and information sources. 4th ed. Libraries Unlimited 2007 xx, 269p il (Library and information science text series) $65; pa $50

Grades: Professional   **027.8**

1. School libraries 2. Libraries—Collection development
ISBN   978-1-59158-583-1;   1-59158-583-X; 978-1-59158-360-8 (pa); 1-59158-360-8 (pa)
                         LC 2007-9005
First published 1988 under the authorship of Phyllis J. Van Orden

Contents: The collection; Collection development; Community analysis and needs assessment; The media center program; Policies and procedures; Selection; General selection criteria; Criteria by format; Acquisitions and processing; Maintenance and preservation; Circulation and promotion of the collection; Evaluation of the collection; Ethical issues and the collection; The curriculum; Special groups of students; Fiscal issues relating to the collection; Opening, moving, or closing the collection

"Media specialists who read this book will be renewed in their quest for excellence in their collections. . . . The book covers A-Z: Acquisitions, Evaluation, Ethical Issues, Inventory, Procedure Manual, Selection, Special Groups of Students, Weeding, etc. . . . This is a must purchase for every school library media center." Libr Media Connect

Includes bibliographical references

Church, Audrey P., 1957-

Leverage your library program to help raise test scores; a guide for library media specialists, principals, teachers, and parents. Linworth Pub. 2003 123p il pa $39.95 *

Grades: Professional   **027.8**

1. School libraries 2. Instructional materials centers
ISBN 1-58683-120-8   LC 2003-40080

"In chapter one, recent research on school libraries is provided and briefly explains the results in layman terms. This is followed by a chapter each for the administrators, teachers, and parents that describes what each needs to know about the library and librarian's roles. A chapter is included for the librarian on what they need to do. The final chapter pulls the book together with perspectives from principals and librarians . . . This book can serve as a means to start a dialog with the administration and at the same time as a reference book for the school librarian." Lib Media Connect

Includes bibliographical references

Craver, Kathleen W.

Creating cyber libraries; an instructional guide for school library media specialists. Libraries Unlimited 2002 xxvi, 222p (Greenwood professional guides in school librarianship) pa $40

Grades: Professional   **027.8**

1. Internet resources 2. School libraries
ISBN 0-313-32080-2   LC 2001-55619

"Nine chapters cover guidelines; policies to consider; Web-design issues; the use of portals; and strategies for maintaining, evaluating, and promoting a library Web site. Special-interest areas, such as providing a virtual reading room and online instruction, are also discussed. . . . This title is a one-stop-shopping bonanza of wonderful, useful ideas on how to create a cyber library that will meet the information needs of our patrons." Libr J

Includes bibliographical references

Curriculum connections through the library; edited by Barbara K. Stripling and Sandra Hughes-Hassell. Libraries Unlimited 2003 xxi, 229p (Principles and practice series) pa $37.50 *

Grades: Professional   **027.8**

1. School libraries
ISBN 1-56308-973-4   LC 2003-54628

The editors have chosen "essays that sample existing scholarship and direct professionals in ways to affect curriculum, collections, and collaboration across disciplines and to aid students who must perform under the scrutiny of the national standards movement. The book contains some suggestions for joint projects, but primarily promotes open-ended, inquiry-based learning. . . . The writ-

Curriculum connections through the library—
Continued
ing is clear and purposeful. . . . A stimulating choice for practicing librarians and students of library science." SLJ
Includes bibliographical references

Erikson, Rolf
Designing a school library media center for the future; [by] Rolf Erikson and Carolyn Markuson. 2nd ed. American Library Association 2007 117p il pa $45
Grades: Professional   **027.8**
    1. Instructional materials centers—Design and construction 2. School libraries—Design and construction
    ISBN 978-0-8389-0945-4; 0-8389-0945-0
                            LC 2006-37644
First published 2000
"The first chapter offers an overview of the various steps involved in any project. Succeeding chapters cover technology planning, space allocations, furniture and placement, lighting and acoustics, ADA requirements, specifications, and bids." Booklist
Includes bibliographical references

Everhart, Nancy
Evaluating the school library media center; analysis techniques and research practices. Libraries Unlimited 1998 262p pa $37
Grades: Professional   **027.8**
    1. School libraries 2. Instructional materials centers
    ISBN 1-56308-085-0   LC 98-6949
"The author describes qualitative and quantitative techniques for evaluating in areas of curriculum, personnel, facilities, collections, usage, and technology. She also provides step-by-step instructions on how to create in-house surveys, conduct interviews, and use observation to gather data." Publisher's note
Includes bibliographical references

Farmer, Lesley S. Johnson, 1949-
Collaborating with administrators and educational support staff; [by] Lesley S. J. Farmer. Neal-Schuman Publishers 2007 217p (Best practices for school library media professionals) pa $65
Grades: Professional   **027.8**
    1. School libraries 2. Instructional materials centers 3. Schools—Administration
    ISBN 1-55570-572-3; 978-1-55570-572-5
                            LC 2006-11171
"Farmer begins by exploring how schools work, the role of the library media specialist, and the background on collaboration. She then discusses, in some depth, how to work with different levels of administrators and key service personnel, such as technology directors, reading specialists, special-education educators, pupil services personnel, and physical health and co-curricular personnel. Farmer concludes with ways of measuring the impact of collaboration and improving literacy, and provides suggestions for becoming a collaborative leader. This book is a must for school districts and a school library media specialists' personal collections." SLJ
Includes bibliographical references

Student success and library media programs; a systems approach to research and best practice; [by] Lesley S. J. Farmer. Libraries Unlimited 2003 180p pa $45
Grades: Professional   **027.8**
    1. School libraries 2. Academic achievement
    ISBN 1-59158-058-7   LC 2003-53881
"Designed for school library media specialists, this book focuses on library media programs and examines the factors that influence student achievement." Publisher's note
This is a "comprehensive and thoroughly researched book. . . . An invaluable guide for media specialists." SLJ
Includes bibliographical references

Foundations for effective school library media programs; Ken Haycock, editor. Libraries Unlimited 1999 331p hardcover o.p. pa $52
Grades: Professional   **027.8**
    1. School libraries 2. Instructional materials centers 3. Bibliographic instruction
    ISBN 1-56308-720-0; 1-56308-368-X (pa)
                            LC 98-40343
Explores the role of library media specialists in school improvement, curriculum design, collaboration with teachers, and building information literacy. Articles discuss learning theories, flexible scheduling, new technologies, and thematic units
Includes bibliographical references

Grimes, Sharon
Reading is our business; how libraries can foster reading comprehension. American Library Association 2006 155p il pa $35 *
Grades: Professional   **027.8**
    1. School libraries 2. Books and reading 3. Reading comprehension
    ISBN 0-8389-0912-4   LC 2005028263
Grimes "led a school-wide research study with classroom teachers to transform the reading program at Lansdowne Elementary School in Baltimore. The study resulted in dramatic and measurable gains in student reading achievement. This book can be used as a toolkit to duplicate those results. Grimes's work is informed by solid educational research in the field of reading comprehension. The text is lively and clearly written, accessible to teachers and librarians." SLJ
Includes bibliographical references

Harada, Violet H.
Assessing learning; librarians and teachers as partners. Libraries Unlimited 2005 149p diag il tab pa $40 *
Grades: Professional   **027.8**
    1. School libraries 2. Instructional materials centers
    ISBN 1-59158-200-8
"After reviewing the topic of assessment, the authors look at library media centers to determine where and how students should be assessed and then examine assessment tools and explain a wide array of effective graphic organizers. . . . Close to 100 illustrations dem-

Harada, Violet H.—*Continued*

onstrate the many forms of assessment described. Chapters are well constructed and the writing is clear." SLJ
Includes bibliographical references

Hart, Thomas L.

The school library media facilities planner. Neal-Schuman Publishers 2006 253p diag il (Best practices for school library media professionals) pa $95 *

Grades: Professional   027.8
1. School libraries—Design and construction 2. Instructional materials centers—Design and construction
ISBN 1-55570-503-0   LC 2004047424
"This book presents timely information on designing, building, remodeling, and equipping library media centers. Chapters cover every phase of the process, from assessing needs, allocating space, selecting furniture, and working with the architect to moving into the new facility. . . . A CD 'view book' of several Florida libraries allows the user to see and hear librarians describe the pros and cons of their individual libraries." Booklist
Includes bibliographical references

Hughes-Hassell, Sandra

School reform and the school library media specialist; [by] Sandra Hughes-Hassell and Violet H. Harada. Libraries Unlimited 2007 xxiii, 204p il (Principles and practice series) pa $40

Grades: Professional   027.8
1. School libraries
ISBN 978-1-59158-427-8; 1-59158-427-2
                             LC 2007-16437
"This volume covers critical issues impacting school libraries today and offers practical solutions to meet these challenges. Written by leaders in the field such as Pam Berger, Carol Gordon, Barbara Stripling, and Ross Todd, the articles expound on implications of No Child Left Behind legislation, 21st-century literacy requirements, population diversity, and professional growth. . . . This volume will empower current and future school librarians as they embrace its guidelines." SLJ

The **Information-powered** school; [by] Public Education Network, American Association of School Librarians; edited by Sandra Hughes-Hassell, Anne Wheelock. American Library Association 2001 138p il pa $35

Grades: Professional   027.8
1. Library Power (Program) 2. School libraries 3. Instructional materials centers
ISBN 0-8389-3514-1   LC 2001-22561
"This volume presents a variety of articles highlighting various aspects and activities of Information Powered Schools and giving tips for putting the principles and practices to work. . . . Checklists, surveys, and planning forms are included to determine the status of current practices. The collaborative planning worksheets, request forms, unit evaluation and collaborative-unit evaluation forms will be of special interest to librarians already involved in this process." SLJ
Includes bibliographical references

Job, Amy G., 1942-

The school library media specialist as manager; a book of case studies; [by] Amy G. Job and Mary Kay W. Schnare. Scarecrow Press 1997 195p (School librarianship series) pa $29.95

Grades: Professional   027.8
1. School libraries 2. Instructional materials centers
ISBN 0-8108-3363-8   LC 97-20841
"Chapters are devoted to broad topics—leadership, planning, and management; personnel; resources and equipment; facilities; and district, regional, and state leadership—with specific scenarios for elementary, middle, and high school media centers. The most practical feature of this book is the appendix section, which contains the American Association of School Librarians' position statements on various subjects." SLJ
Includes bibliographical references

Jweid, Rosann, 1933-

The library-classroom partnership; teaching library media skills in middle and junior high school; [by] Rosann Jweid and Margaret Rizzo. 2nd ed. Scarecrow Press 1998 238p il pa $42.95 *

Grades: Professional   027.8
1. School libraries 2. Instructional materials centers 3. Bibliographic instruction
ISBN 0-8108-3476-6   LC 98-21206
First published 1988
The authors describe ways to coordinate library media skills with classroom subjects. English, mathematics, social studies, science, art, music, home economics, vocational guidance, physical education, technology and foreign language curricula are covered. Reading enrichment and accessing of information electronically are also discussed
Includes bibliographical references

Kearney, Carol A.

Curriculum partner; redefining the role of the library media specialist. Greenwood Press 2000 xxiv, 180p (Greenwood professional guides in school librarianship) $46.95

Grades: Professional   027.8
1. School libraries 2. Instructional materials centers
ISBN 0-313-31025-4   LC 99-462341
The author "includes chapters on leadership, change, vision, partnering, collaborative planning, staff development, and advocacy and provides examples from the experiences of practitioners to support her ideas." SLJ
Includes bibliographical references

Martin, Ann M.

7 steps to an award-winning school library program; [by] Ann M. Martin; foreword by Ruth Toor. Libraries Unlimited 2005 129p diag il tab pa $35 *

Grades: Professional   027.8
1. School libraries 2. Instructional materials centers
ISBN 1-59158-173-7
"The author's purpose in this book is to describe how to use *Information Power* effectively and how to achieve

Martin, Ann M.—*Continued*
the goal of winning a national award. . . . Her description of the process is organized in seven clearly explained steps. Appendixes contain helpful forms and policy statements. . . . [This is a] well-written, unique, and important book." Booklist

Mendrinos, Roxanne Baxter
Using educational technology with at-risk students; a guide for library media specialists and teachers. Greenwood Press 1997 227p il map $46.95
Grades: Professional   **027.8**
1. School libraries 2. Computer-assisted instruction 3. Instructional materials centers
ISBN 0-313-29369-4   LC 96-50290
"Mendrinos explores the uses and appeal of technology-based education in various subject areas, particularly in terms of reaching 'the average and below-average student who is in danger of dropping out, or who does not have the skills to enter and succeed in the information technology job market of today.' . . . Chapters focus on technology applications in library media centers, and in language arts, social studies, and science classrooms. Specific projects and Web sites are cited frequently." SLJ
Includes bibliographical references

Morris, Betty J.
Administering the school library media center. 4th ed, rev and expanded. Libraries Unlimited 2004 683p $70; pa $55 *
Grades: Professional   **027.8**
1. School libraries 2. Instructional materials centers
ISBN 0-313-32261-9; 1-59158-183-4 (pa)
                                LC 2004-41797
First published 1973 under the authorship of John T. Gillespie and Diana L. Spirt with title: Creating a school media program
"This volume covers library media center programming, facilities and technologies, student learning, policies and procedures, and library media specialist roles. . . . Highlights include budget planning and justification, library media job descriptions, and information on the bid process. The chapter on facilities contains infrequently found information on the psychology of color, URLs for Web sites with floor plans, and guidelines for space planning." Booklist

Ray, Virginia Lawrence
School wide book events; how to make them happen; [by] Virginia Lawrence Ray. Libraries Unlimited 2003 133p pa $25
Grades: Professional   **027.8**
1. School libraries 2. Books and reading
ISBN 1-59158-038-2   LC 2003-47724
"The author's intent is to present ideas on how to celebrate reading across grade levels and curriculum, involving teachers, administration, faculty, and students both in preparation and actual activities. She proposes that school libraries have a Book Event for the whole school. . . . All events require simple resources and are easy to follow even for school systems with extremely limited budgets." SLJ
Includes bibliographical references

Schuckett, Sandy
Political advocacy for school librarians; you have the power! Linworth Pub. 2004 128p pa $39.95
Grades: Professional   **027.8**
1. School libraries 2. Libraries and community 3. Lobbying
ISBN 1-58683-158-5   LC 2004-4869
"Schuckett motivates and explicitly details an exciting 'how-to' of political lobbying at all levels—from the school site and local board all the way to the national level. . . . School librarians need political clout, and Schuckett shows us how to get it." SLJ
Includes bibliographical references

Schultz-Jones, Barbara
An automation primer for school library media centers and small libraries. Linworth Pub. 2006 280p pa $39.95
Grades: Professional   **027.8**
1. School libraries—Automation 2. Instructional materials centers—Automation 3. Libraries—Automation
ISBN 1-58683-180-1   LC 2006005798
"This thorough guide to library automation provides an in-depth look at the many components and options available to school libraries. Topics discussed include defining automation systems, features of systems, Web access, technical considerations, and emerging technologies. In addition, the book outlines a step-by-step process of project planning, selection, and site preparation." Booklist
Includes bibliographical references

Skaggs, Gayle, 1952-
On display; 25 themes to promote reading. McFarland & Co. 1999 162p il pa $29.95
Grades: Professional   **027.8**
1. School libraries 2. Libraries—Exhibitions
ISBN 0-7864-0657-7   LC 98-54964
The emphasis is "on simple themes that will attract kids, such as rock and roll, basketball, and outer space. Along with the ideas there are directions for bulletin boards and simple displays: a jukebox, a freestanding basketball hoop, a bookworm." Booklist

Stephens, Claire Gatrell
Library 101; a handbook for the school library media specialist; [by] Claire Gatrell Stephens and Patricia Franklin. Libraries Unlimited 2007 233p il pa $35
Grades: Professional   **027.8**
1. School libraries 2. Instructional materials centers 3. Libraries—Handbooks, manuals, etc.
ISBN 978-1-59158-324-0; 1-59158-324-1
                                LC 2007-18420
"This handbook provides information for brand-new and inexperienced librarians preparing for a first job in

Stephens, Claire Gatrell—*Continued*

a school library media center. Articles are divided into four subcategories covering day-to-day operations (library organization, circulation policies, media management, scheduling, staffing, and media center arrangement); collaboration with teachers; collection development and management; and equipment." Booklist

Includes bibliographical references

Valenza, Joyce Kasman

Power tools recharged; 125+ essential forms and presentations for your school library information program; illustrated by Emily Valenza. American Library Association 2004 various paging il pa $55 *

Grades: Professional   **027.8**
1. School libraries 2. Libraries—Public relations
ISBN 0-8389-0880-2   LC 2004-5853
First published 1998 with title: Power tools
This offers a compilation of customizable, reproducible forms and handouts for school library administration and assessment, teaching information literacy, making presentations. Included are such items as templates for a gift book program, letters to parents and faculty members, a checklist of tasks, library equipment sign-out forms, and a reading interest survey.

Includes bibliographical references

Van Deusen, Jean Donham, 1946-

Enhancing teaching and learning; a leadership guide for school library media specialists; [by] Jean Donham. rev. ed. Neal-Schuman Publishers 2008 353p il pa $65
Grades: Professional   **027.8**
1. School libraries 2. Instructional materials centers
ISBN 978-1-55570-647-0; 1-55570-647-9
LC 2008-23321
First published 1998
This attempts to show "how to develop and implement an effective library media program by integrating it into the total education environment. Part One covers all aspects of the school environment: students, curriculum and instruction, principals, school district administrators, and the community. Part Two shows you how to use interaction and collaboration to make the school library media program integral to all of these communities." Publisher's note

Includes bibliographical references

The **Whole** school library handbook; edited by Blanche Woolls and David V. Loertscher. American Library Association 2005 448p pa $45 *

Grades: Professional   **027.8**
1. School libraries 2. Instructional materials centers
ISBN 0-8389-0883-7   LC 2004-20198
This reference resource to the school media center includes "facts, . . . articles, checklists, organization contact information, trivia, [and] advice from the field's experts. . . . [It also features] information on fundraising, grant writing, flexible scheduling, promoting the school library, and advocating its value in the school community." Publisher's note

Includes bibliographical references

Wilson, Patricia J. (Patricia Jane)

Center stage; library programs that inspire middle school patrons; [by] Patricia Potter Wilson and Roger Leslie. Libraries Unlimited 2002 xx, 204p il pa $35
Grades: Professional   **027.8**
1. School libraries 2. Instructional materials centers
ISBN 1-56308-796-0   LC 2002-3185
"Wilson and Leslie discuss the purpose and benefits of programming and carefully delineate the stages of planning, implementation, and evaluation and include bulleted lists, checklists, and evaluative handouts. . . . *Center Stage* is well organized and written in a way that is easy to understand and put into practice." SLJ

Includes bibliographical references

Woolls, E. Blanche

The school library media manager; [by] Blanche Woolls. 4th ed. Libraries Unlimited 2008 xiii, 279p il (Library and information science text series) $55; pa $45
Grades: Professional   **027.8**
1. School libraries 2. Instructional materials centers
ISBN   978-1-59158-648-7;   1-59158-648-8;
978-1-59158-643-2 (pa); 1-59158-643-7 (pa)
LC 2008-18081
First published 1994
Provides information "for teaching the administration of school library media centers. . . . Readers learn how to choose a credential program, how to find the requirements for working in each of the 50 states, what to do when looking for and choosing a job, and how to survive the first week in that new position. . . . Sections also cover: collaborating with teachers, how to write a proposal, and how to accept leadership responsibilities, including the role of a media specialist in the legislative process." Publisher's note

Includes bibliographical references

028   Reading and use of other information media

Ross, Val

You can't read this; forbidden books, lost writing, mistranslations, & codes. Tundra Books 2006 140p il $19.95
Grades: 7 8 9 10   **028**
1. Books and reading—History 2. Books—Censorship
ISBN 0-88776-732-X
The author "offers a unique historical survey based around a broadly interpreted theme: the power of reading. The chronologically arranged chapters touch on censorship, literacy, and the influence of political texts. . . . The accounts are fascinating, and Ross is an accomplished storyteller who brings history right into the present. Scattered black-and-white photos and art illustrate this timely, powerful text." Booklist

Includes bibliographical references

028.1   Reviews

Best books for young adults; edited by Holly Koelling; foreword by Betty Carter. 3rd ed. American Library Association 2007 346p il pa $42 *

Grades: Professional   **028.1**
1. Reference books 2. Teenagers—Books and reading 3. Best books 4. Young adult literature—Bibliography
ISBN 978-0-8389-3569-9; 0-8389-3569-9
                                        LC 2007-26009
First published 1994 under the editorship of Betty Carter

This "is a classic, standard resource for collection building and on-the-spot readers' advisory. . . . Absolutely indispensable for school and public libraries." Booklist

Includes bibliographical references

Dodson, Shireen
100 books for girls to grow on; lively descriptions of the most inspiring books for girls, terrific discussion questions to spark conversation, great ideas for book-inspired activities, crafts, and field trips. HarperCollins Pubs. 1998 334p pa $14
Grades: Professional   **028.1**
1. Girls—Books and reading 2. Children's literature—Bibliography 3. Young adult literature—Bibliography
ISBN 0-06-095718-2   LC 98-27606
The author summarizes "books that girls ages nine to thirteen might enjoy reading on their own or sharing in a book discussion group. . . . Organized alphabetically by title, each book is broken down into several categories including the summary, reading time, themes, discussion questions, information about the author, activities to do beyond the book, and recommended further reading." Voice Youth Advocates

Horning, Kathleen T.
From cover to cover; evaluating and reviewing children's books. HarperCollins Pubs. 1997 230p pa $14.99 hardcover o.p.
Grades: Professional   **028.1**
1. Books—Reviews 2. Children's literature—History and criticism
ISBN 0-06-446167-X (pa); 0-06-024519-0 (hc)
                                        LC 96-27281
The author "begins with an overview of how children's books are published in the United States, the physical parts of the book, and categories of children's books. The next six chapters are devoted to the definition and scope of those categories." Bull Cent Child Books
"Anyone entering the field of children's book reviewing, or indeed, the wider field of children's literature, will find *From Cover to Cover* an excellent guide to analyzing books and presenting clear, useful reviews." Booklist

Includes bibliographical references

Into focus; understanding and creating middle school readers; editors: Kylene Beers, Barbara G. Samuels. Christopher-Gordon Pubs. 1998 xx, 490p il pa $44.95 *
Grades: Professional   **028.1**

1. Reading 2. Literature—Study and teaching
ISBN 0-926842-64-1
In this "handbook, 24 experts from the fields of reading theory, library science, response theory, children's literature, and middle school philosophy present strategies, describe programs, and provide lists that foster academic success and a lifelong love of reading." SLJ

Includes bibliographical references

The **ultimate** teen book guide; editors, Daniel Hahn & Leonie Flynn; associate editor, Susan Reuben. Walker & Co. 2008 432p il $26.95; pa $16.95 *

Grades: 7 8 9 10 11 12 Professional
                                                       028.1
1. Young adult literature 2. Book reviews 3. Teenagers—Books and reading
ISBN   978-0-8027-9730-8;   0-8027-9730-X;
978-0-8027-9731-5 (pa); 0-8027-9731-8 (pa)
                                        LC 2007024238
First published 2006 in the United Kingdom
"This attractive volume includes reviews of more than 700 fiction titles, nonfiction, classics, and graphic novels that will be of interest to young adults. The reviewers/contributors are popular authors, librarians, and teens themselves. Brief entries of one half to one page per title are easy to read with black-and-white images of book covers, suggested ages, and additional recommendations included. . . . It's an excellent source for a variety of book reviews spanning time and genre." SLJ

028.5   Reading and use of other information media by young people

Baxter, Kathleen A.
Gotcha! nonfiction booktalks to get kids excited about reading; by Kathleen A. Baxter [and] Marcia Agness Kochel. Libraries Unlimited 1999 183p pa $28
Grades: Professional   **028.5**
1. Books and reading 2. Children's literature—Bibliography 3. Young adult literature—Bibliography 4. Book talks
ISBN 1-56308-683-2   LC 99-34279
This guide to booktalking discusses more than 350 titles for grades one through eight
The books are presented in a "conversational style that is extremely readable and entertaining; useful bibliographies following each section assign appropriate grade levels to the books. The authors also give general tips on organizing booktalks." SLJ

Includes bibliographical references

Gotcha again! more nonfiction booktalks to get kids excited about reading; [by] Kathleen A. Baxter, Marcia Agness Kochel. Libraries Unlimited/Teacher Ideas Press 2002 165p il pa $35
Grades: Professional   **028.5**
1. Books and reading 2. Children's literature—Bibliography 3. Young adult literature—Bibliography 4. Book talks
ISBN 1-56308-940-8   LC 2001-50859

Baxter, Kathleen A.—*Continued*

"This guide provides many ready-to-use booktalks, ranging in length from quick introductions to more detailed scripts. Loosely arranged by topic, . . . each chapter includes subgroups . . . comprised of approximately 10 titles for a total of nearly 350 books. Each section concludes with a bibliography that includes recommended grade levels from kindergarten through eighth grade. . . . Creative and well-organized, this valuable resource will be useful for booktalking or as a handy selection tool." SLJ

Includes bibliographical references

Gotcha for guys! nonfiction books to get boys excited about reading; [by] Kathleen A. Baxter and Marcia Agness Kochel. Libraries Unlimited 2007 269p il pa $35

Grades: Professional   **028.5**
1. Boys—Books and reading 2. Children's literature—Bibliography 3. Young adult literature—Bibliography
ISBN 1-59158-311-X (pa); 978-1-59158-311-0 (pa)
     LC 2006030667

This "focuses on nonfiction books to get boys excited about reading. There are citations for more than 1,100 books grouped by themes such as 'Prehistoric Creatures,' 'All Things Gross,' and 'Disasters and Unsolved Mysteries.' The last chapter, 'Hot Topics,' includes books on things such as riddles, games, and fascinating facts. With the exception of this last chapter, each chapter offers complete booktalks, short annotations and talks for additional books, and lists of titles that have been well reviewed. . . . This title is helpful for nonfiction collection development and can be used as a starting point for creating attractive, themed displays." Booklist

Includes bibliographical references

Gotcha good! nonfiction books to get kids excited about reading; [by] Kathleen A. Baxter and Marcia Agness Kochel. Libraries Unlimited 2008 259p pa $35

Grades: Professional   **028.5**
1. Books and reading 2. Children's literature—Bibliography 3. Young adult literature—Bibliography
ISBN 978-1-59158-654-8; 1-59158-654-2
     LC 2008010350

"In addition to annotations for over 1000 nonfiction titles, [the authors] profile eight prolific authors and provide fun top-10 features for the various subjects covered. . . . The titles chosen are truly high quality, relevant, and up-to-date, with suggested ages provided, most ranging from grades three through eight. . . . A must-have for all librarians who want to get kids excited about nonfiction." SLJ

Includes bibliographical references

Bilz, Rachelle Lasky

Life is tough; guys, growing up, and young adult literature; [by] Rachelle Lasky Bilz. Scarecrow Press 2004 xiii, 153p (Scarecrow studies in young adult literature) $45

Grades: Professional   **028.5**
1. Boys—Books and reading 2. Young adult literature—Bibliography
ISBN 0-8108-5055-9; 978-0-8108-5055-2
     LC 2004-8439

"Bilz focuses on books that can help boys mature into resourceful, well-adjusted young men. She begins with an overview of classic tales of heroism in which strong male protagonists like Robin Hood, King Arthur, and Robinson Crusoe not only exhibit their steely strengths, but share, too, their fears and doubts along the way. Her lists of contemporary treatments and read-alikes of each of these tales will be particularly helpful to educators seeking thematic bridges between old and new. . . . This is a useful bibliography for anyone who wants to place books in the paths of boys as beacons toward meaningful manhood." SLJ

Bodart, Joni Richards

Radical reads; 101 YA novels on the edge. Scarecrow Press 2002 376p pa $34.95

Grades: Professional   **028.5**
1. Teenagers—Books and reading 2. Young adult literature—Bibliography
ISBN 0-8108-4287-4   LC 2001-57705

This resource examines "the 'edgy, raw, and relevant' in contemporary YA literature. The entries, arranged alphabetically by title, include bibliographic information, suggested reading and interest levels, and an extensive list of keywords that helps describe each book's content. . . . Detailed booktalk and discussion tips and ideas, a well-written and informative booktalk, and excerpts from reviews are provided. . . . The 101 selections, dating from 1994 to 2001, offer a balanced depiction of the literature and its authors." SLJ

Includes bibliographical references

Booth, Heather, 1978-

Serving teens through readers' advisory. American Library Association 2007 159p (ALA readers' advisory series) pa $36 *

Grades: Professional   **028.5**
1. Teenagers—Books and reading 2. Young adult literature—Bibliography 3. Young adults' libraries
ISBN 0-8389-0930-2; 978-0-8389-0930-0
     LC 2006-36134

"The first few chapters discuss teen reading habits and why readers' advisory for this group is different and also provide 'tips for the generalist' who may not be an expert in teen fiction. Other chapters cover elements of the readers' advisory interaction . . . and survey the appropriate books. Two unique chapters offer well-thought-out and practical advice on making reading-related homework assignments less painful for staff and students as well as suggestions for providing readers' advisory services to teens through their parents or other adults. . . . Filled with excellent tips and great ideas. . . . [This] is essential reading for all readers' advisors and any library staff who work with teens." Booklist

Includes bibliographical references

Bromann, Jennifer

Booktalking that works. Neal-Schuman 2001 155p (Teens @ the library series) pa $35 *

Grades: Professional   **028.5**
1. Book talks 2. Young adults' libraries 3. Teenagers—Books and reading
ISBN 1-55570-403-4   LC 2001-18340

Bromann, Jennifer—*Continued*

This presents "a variety of booktalking techniques, selection tips for booktalk titles, and how to write and prepare for booktalks. The book begins by addressing who today's teenagers are, what they want, and what they need. There are specific magazines, catalogs, and on-line Web sites mentioned for selection." Book Rep

"Practical, smart, hip, and irreverent. . . . A fun read that will encourage you to find your own personal style." Booklist

Includes bibliographical references

More booktalking that works. Neal-Schuman 2005 145p (Teens @ the library series) pa $49.95
Grades: Professional   **028.5**
1. Book talks 2. Young adults' libraries 3. Teenagers—Books and reading
ISBN 1-55570-525-1   LC 2005-2326

"Bromann has expanded on her previous booktalking title, *Booktalking That Works* (Neal-Schuman, 2001), with additional practical advice based on added years of experience. . . . The first part of this book is arranged in a question-and-answer format covering various aspects of booktalking, from creating and presenting booktalks to choosing books and developing hooks for reluctant readers. This section includes a list of the top-20 types of books to booktalk and 10 very brief quick talks. The second section offers 200 booktalks of varying length and covering several fiction and nonfiction genres that she encourages librarians to adapt for personal use. . . . School and public librarians will find many helpful hints, whether they are novice or veteran booktalkers." Booklist

Children's books in children's hands; an introduction to their literature; [by] Charles Temple, Mariam Martinez, Junko Yokota; with contributions by Evelyn B. Freeman. 3rd ed. Pearson Allyn and Bacon 2006 xxv, 630p il $126.67
Grades: Professional   **028.5**
1. Children's literature—History and criticism 2. Books and reading
ISBN 0-205-42043-5; 978-0-205-42043-8
          LC 2006272616

First published 1998

Includes CD-ROM

Part I covers the intellectual development of children, literary elements of children's literature, and reader response criticism. Part II surveys the literature by genre. Part III shows how to create a literature-based classroom through activities, classroom libraries, and book discussions. Appendices list award-winning titles, professional organizations, publishers, children's periodicals and Web sites. This edition has been updated to include coverage of such topics as technology in the classroom, visual literacy, and the influence of the No Child Left Behind Act of 2000 on reading instruction in the public schools.

Includes bibliographical references

Closter, Kathryn, 1950-

Fiction, food, and fun; the original recipe for the Read 'n' Feed Program; [by] Kathryn Closer, Karen L. Sipes, and Vickie Thomas; foreword by Caroline B. Cooney. Libraries Unlimited 1998 xx, 224p il pa $30.95
Grades: Professional   **028.5**
1. Books and reading
ISBN 1-56308-519-4   LC 98-9511

This "resource provides detailed information—activities, publicity, discussion questions, author background, and more—for 10 titles. . . . The program is designed to introduce young people to quality literature, actively involve them in discussion, and encourage them to become lifelong readers. Each chapter includes bibliographic information, suggested interest level, plot summary, and a booktalk." SLJ

Includes bibliographical references

Collins, Joan, 1946-

Motivating readers in the middle grades; [by] Joan Collins. Linworth Pub. 2008 128p il pa $36.95
Grades: Professional   **028.5**
1. Youth—Books and reading 2. Middle schools
ISBN 978-1-58683-297-1; 1-58683-297-2
          LC 2007-51426

"This workbook describes three six-week projects for inciting reading motivation in grades six through eight, developed by Massachusetts middle school educators. . . . This resource is supremely teacher-friendly; projects are presented by grade with concise rationales, instructions, suggestions, and caveats. Suggested novels are annotated, varied, and age appropriate." Voice Youth Advocates

Includes bibliographical references

The **Coretta** Scott King awards, 1970-2009; edited by Henrietta M. Smith. 4th ed. American Library Association 2009 131p pa $50 *
Grades: Professional   **028.5**
1. Coretta Scott King Award 2. Children's literature—History and criticism 3. American literature—African American authors 4. African Americans in literature
ISBN 978-0-8389-3584-2 (pa); 0-8389-3584-2 (pa)
          LC 2009000628

First published 1994

This guide to the Coretta Scott King awards includes "comprehensive coverage of the award winning books; biographical profiles that introduce the creative artists and illustrators; color plates that give a . . . sense of the story and art; a subject index." Publisher's note

Includes bibliographical references

Cox Clark, Ruth E.

Tantalizing tidbits for middle schoolers; quick booktalks for the busy middle school and jr. high library media specialist; [by] Ruth E. Cox Clark. Linworth Pub. 2005 140p pa $36.95
Grades: Professional   **028.5**
1. Book talks 2. Books and reading 3. Children's literature—Bibliography 4. Young adult literature—Bibliography
ISBN 1-58683-195-X   LC 2005013159

Cox Clark, Ruth E.—*Continued*

"In the first sections, the author provides information on annual recommended reading lists and children's book awards and describes different booktalking techniques. Section 5, the heart of the book, offers 75 booktalk examples. For each, the author provides bibliographic information, subjects and genres, references to pertinent reading lists and awards, and interest levels. This information is followed by a brief annotation, a booktalk, a page reference for an excerpt to read, a curriculum connection, and a list of similar books. A list of themes and an index of the books and authors mentioned conclude the volume, which is highly recommended for librarians, teachers, and students." Booklist

Crossing boundaries with children's books; edited by Doris Gebel. Scarecrow Press 2006 431p il pa $40

Grades: Professional   **028.5**
1. Children—Books and reading 2. Children's literature—Bibliography
ISBN 0-8108-5203-9; 978-0-8108-5203-7
     LC 2005032774

"Sponsored by the United States Board on Books for Young People"

This "opens with several thoughtful essays that examine the complex issues related to international publishing and translations. . . . Part two is a carefully prepared, comprehensive, annotated bibliography organized by countries and regions of the world. . . . This is an important resource for all libraries to build and promote collections that reflect a global vision." SLJ

Includes bibliographical references

Dear author; letters of hope; edited by Joan F. Kaywell; with an introduction by Catherine Ryan Hyde. Philomel Books 2007 222p $14.99
*

Grades: 8 9 10 11 12   **028.5**
1. Teenagers—Books and reading 2. Authors, American
ISBN 978-0-399-23705-8; 0-399-23705-4
     LC 2006-21050

"Chris Lynch, Nancy Garden, and Christopher Paul Curtis and are just a few of the well-known authors who respond to real teens' letters in this powerful compilation. Not mere fan mail, the selections speak about teens' gravest concerns—bullying, derailed friendships, racism, date rape, incest, illness, divorce, and more—and they describe how the authors' books helped them face the heartaches. . . . For some readers, this dialogue between writers and readers will be inspiring; for those harboring their own wounding secrets, it may be lifesaving." Booklist

Includes bibliographical references

Embracing, evaluating, and examining African American children's and young adult literature; edited by Wanda M. Brooks, Jonda C. McNair; foreword by Rudine Sims Bishop. Scarecrow Press 2008 251p pa $45

Grades: Professional   **028.5**
1. American literature—African American authors—History and criticism 2. Children's literature—History and criticism 3. Young adult literature—History and criticism 4. Children—Books and reading 5. African Americans in literature
ISBN 978-0-8108-6027-8 (pa); 0-8108-6027-9 (pa)
     LC 2007025703

"Brooks and McNair have compiled 12 scholarly studies about the use of books by and about African-American children and young adults in classrooms across the United States. Selections include a detailed textual analysis of the work of Arna Bontemps and Langston Hughes; a sociolinguistic perspective on readers' response to books containing African-American Vernacular English; and a detailed study of the books used as classroom read-alouds by teachers in rural schools, which found that only three percent were about African Americans. While each study is complete in and of itself, the text as a whole gives a broad picture of what is currently being done in this field, both in K-12 classrooms and college classes that emphasize children's literature." SLJ

Includes bibliographical references

Gelman, Judy, 1962-
The kids' book club book; reading ideas, recipes, activities, and smart tips for organizing terrific kids' book clubs; [by] Judy Gelman and Vicki Levy Krupp. Penguin Group 2007 460p pa $16.95

Grades: Professional   **028.5**
1. Children—Books and reading 2. Teenagers—Books and reading 3. Children's literature—Bibliography 4. Young adult literature—Bibliography
ISBN 978-1-58542-559-4   LC 2006-101469

"Stellar advice on running book clubs is presented in a friendly format. . . . The first section covers types of clubs, recruitment, organization, location, and duration. . . . In the second part, comprising the bulk of the text, the authors describe the top 50 recommended books arranged by grade level." SLJ

Includes bibliographical references

Gillespie, John Thomas, 1928-
The Newbery/Printz companion; booktalk and related materials for award winners and honor books; [by] John T. Gillespie and Corinne J. Naden. 3rd ed. Libraries Unlimited 2006 503p (Children's and young adult literature reference series) $75 *

Grades: Professional   **028.5**
1. Newbery Medal 2. Michael L. Printz award 3. Children's literature—History and criticism 4. Authors 5. Book talks
ISBN 1-59158-313-6   LC 2006-14955

First published 1996 with title: The Newbery companion

Gillespie, John Thomas, 1928-——*Continued*

This guide to the "Newbery and Printz awards for children's and young adult literature provides information on each year's winners and honor books, as well as on the awards themselves and the librarians for whom they are named. For each award-winning book, there is a plot summary, list of characters and themes, background on the author, incidents for booktalking, related reads, and . . . ideas for introducing the book to young readers." Publisher's note

"This invaluable source should be in every school and public library." Booklist

Includes bibliographical references

Gilmore, Barry

Speaking volumes; how to get students discussing books, and much more. Heinemann 2006 128p pa $17.95 *

Grades: Professional   028.5
1. Books and reading
ISBN 0-325-00915-5; 978-0-325-00915-5
LC 2005-28371

"Gilmore provides practical, hands-on methods to involve students in oral and written classroom conversations that encourage reflection and ultimately polished, coherent expression. . . . Both new and seasoned discussion leaders will want a copy for repeated reference." Voice Youth Advocates

Includes bibliographical references

Honnold, RoseMary, 1954-

The teen reader's advisor. Neal-Schuman Publishers 2006 491p (Teens @ the library series) pa $75

Grades: Professional   028.5
1. Teenagers—Books and reading 2. Young adults' libraries 3. Young adult literature—Bibliography
ISBN 1-55570-551-0   LC 2006-12640

"The first part deals with the challenges of working with teens, from developing a rapport and dealing with the more conservative adults in their lives, to marketing a YA collection to its audience. The author's descriptions of the major awards and lists relating to the literature as well as the list of print and online reader's advisory resources are sure to be helpful. Part two consists of subject and genre lists. Each one has at least 10 titles. The annotations are excellent." SLJ

Includes bibliographical references

Jones, Patrick

Connecting with reluctant teen readers; tips, titles, and tools; [by] Patrick Jones, Maureen L. Hartman, Patricia Taylor. Neal-Schuman Publishers 2006 xxi, 314p $59.95 *

Grades: Professional   028.5
1. Teenagers—Books and reading 2. Young adults' libraries 3. Young adult literature—Bibliography
ISBN 1-55570-571-5; 978-1-55570-571-8
LC 2006-12355

"Well written and well researched, this practical hands-on guide to defining and wooing reluctant readers is a must-read for librarians and teachers who work with

adolescents. It is divided into three parts: 'Tips That Work,' 'Titles That Work,' and 'Tools That Work.'" SLJ

Includes bibliographical references

Jweid, Rosann, 1933-

Building character through literature; a guide for middle school readers; [by] Rosann Jweid, Margaret Rizzo. Scarecrow Press 2001 232p $34.50

Grades: Professional   028.5
1. Best books 2. Children's literature—Bibliography 3. Young adult literature—Bibliography 4. Characters and characteristics in literature
ISBN 0-8108-3951-2   LC 00-46401

"This book describes fifty young adult novels chosen for their protagonists' trials of character. The entry for each book includes awards, characters, setting, plot summary, discussion questions, supplemental projects, vocabulary lists, and author biography; sometimes there are comments from the author. The books span more than a century." Voice Youth Advocates

"This book is an invaluable tool for booktalks, book reports, and unit/lesson plans." Book Rep

Includes bibliographical references

Kajder, Sara B., 1975-

Bringing the outside in; visual ways to engage reluctant readers; [by] Sara B. Kajder; foreword by Linda Rief. Stenhouse Publishers 2006 105p il $18.50

Grades: Professional   028.5
1. Reading
ISBN 1-57110-401-1; 978-1-57110-401-4
LC 2005056415

The author "demonstrates myriad ways to employ students' outside talents in the classroom. . . . She shows how she adapts the curriculum to incorporate an expanded definition of literacy tools. Sara offers teachers guidance on how to extend their repertoire of teaching strategies, and help kids connect their natural curiosity and skills as readers and writers of both print and electronic texts." Publisher's note

"Teachers, especially those working with at-risk students, will be thankful for hands-on methods to engage teens through technology." Voice Youth Advocates

Includes bibliographical references

Keane, Nancy J.

The big book of teen reading lists; 100 great, ready-to-use book lists for educators, librarians, parents, and teens. Libraries Unlimited 2006 297p pa $35

Grades: Professional   028.5
1. Young adult literature—Bibliography 2. Teenagers—Books and reading
ISBN 1-59158-333-0; 978-1-59158-333-2
LC 2006-17627

"Listing fiction and nonfiction published mostly in the last 10 years, this volume is divided into six parts: 'Genres,' 'Characters,' 'Books about Self,' 'Setting,' 'Subjects,' and 'Audience.' . . . Each title entry contains a bibliographic reference and a brief annotation of one or

Keane, Nancy J.—*Continued*

two sentences. Following the six sections, the book provides some sample reproducible bookmarks suggesting further reading on specific topics." Booklist

"Keane has produced another great resource for teachers, librarians, and students, especially reluctant readers." SLJ

Includes bibliographical references

Booktalking across the curriculum: the middle years. Libraries Unlimited 2002 217p il pa $30 *

Grades: Professional   **028.5**

1. Books and reading 2. Children's literature 3. Book talks

ISBN 1-56308-937-8   LC 2002-12171

"More than 170 booktalks and an additional 330 suggested books for middle-school students are organized by subject. . . . Most of the books are fiction, but 10 percent are nonfiction. Brief booktalks are followed by learning extensions and suggestions for further reading." Booklist

"The booktalks are well written, easy to use, and encourage critical thinking." Libr Media Connect

Includes bibliographical references

Knowles, Elizabeth, 1946-

Boys and literacy; practical strategies for librarians, teachers, and parents; [by] Elizabeth Knowles and Martha Smith. Libraries Unlimited 2005 xxi, 164p il pa $35

Grades: Professional   **028.5**

1. Boys—Books and reading 2. Children's literature—Bibliography 3. Young adult literature—Bibliography

ISBN 1-59158-212-1

"Boys don't seem to like to read. . . . This book briefly explores the research about this situation, outlines strategies to reverse this trend, and lists books within genres that boys enjoy reading. . . . The best part of the book is the author section. . . . For each author covered, there is a complete list of books, contact information, . . . and Web sites. . . . This is a wonderful resource for teachers and parents to begin working on improving literacy with boys." Booklist

Reading rules! motivating teens to read; [by] Elizabeth Knowles, Martha Smith. Libraries Unlimited 2001 168p pa $33.50

Grades: Professional   **028.5**

1. Teenagers—Books and reading 2. Young adult literature—Bibliography

ISBN 1-56308-883-5   LC 2001-29738

"Some of the strategies discussed are literature circles, book clubs, booktalks, interdisciplinary and thematic units, and reading in the content areas. Each chapter has the same format: identification of the problem or strategy, professional development questions, practical application suggestions, annotated young adult literature titles, annotated professional journal articles, annotated professional books, and Web sites." Book Rep

Includes bibliographical references

Krashen, Stephen D.

The power of reading; insights from the research; by Stephen D. Krashen. 2nd ed. Libraries Unlimited 2004 199p bibl diag tab $25 *

Grades: Professional   **028.5**

1. Reading 2. Literacy

ISBN 1-59158-169-9 (pa)   LC 2004-44207

First published 1993

The author presents research for "the argument that free voluntary reading (FVR) is the most effective tool available for increasing literacy. . . . Some of the topics he explores include the research surrounding second language acquisition, reading rewards and incentives programs, and some of today's popular 'electronic reading products.'" Publisher's note

Includes bibliographical references

Langemack, Chapple

The booktalker's bible; how to talk about the books you love to any audience; [by] Chapple Langemack. Libraries Unlimited 2003 199p pa $30 *

Grades: Professional   **028.5**

1. Book talks

ISBN 1-56308-944-0   LC 2003-47543

"This book reminds readers that booktalks . . . are an effective way to present books and can be aimed at all types of settings . . . and age groups. It explains why booktalks are needed, tells how to hold one, and offers tips for a fail-safe presentation. Each chapter provides practical examples and closes with additional reading. Appendixes include sample talks and ideas for titles as well as other helpful resources." Booklist

Includes bibliographical references

Larson, Jeanette C.

Bringing mysteries alive for children and young adults; [by] Jeanette Larson. Linworth Pub. 2004 134p il pa $39.95

Grades: Professional   **028.5**

1. Children—Books and reading 2. Teenagers—Books and reading 3. Mystery fiction

ISBN 1-58683-012-0   LC 2003-22064

Contents: Introducing mystery; Defining mystery; Appreciating mysteries; Looking at series mysteries; Suggestions for integrating mysteries into the curriculum; Programming with mysteries

"The book has excellent ideas for beginning as well as seasoned professionals." SLJ

Includes bibliographical references

Lukenbill, W. Bernard

Biography in the lives of youth; culture, society, and information. Libraries Unlimited 2006 251p il pa $45

Grades: Professional   **028.5**

1. Children—Books and reading 2. Teenagers—Books and reading 3. Biography 4. Children's libraries 5. Young adults' libraries

ISBN 1-59158-284-9   LC 2006007466

Lukenbill, W. Bernard—*Continued*

"Reflecting on the different and varied uses of biography depending on the age, interests, and developmental needs of students, Lukenbill breaks the genre down into the different types of biographies and how they have changed over time. He includes author and literature suggestions throughout the text and concludes with an extensive bibliography of selection aids, including books and periodicals, for locating recommended titles." SLJ

Includes bibliographical references

McDaniel, Deanna

Gentle reads; great books to warm hearts and lift spirits, grades 5-9; [by] Deanna J. McDaniel. Libraries Unlimited 2008 318p (Children's and young adult literature reference series) $45

Grades: Professional   **028.5**

1. Children's literature—Bibliography 2. Young adult literature—Bibliography

ISBN 978-1-59158-491-9   LC 2008018878

This includes "500 recommended titles. Here readers will find books with divorce, drug use, attempted suicides, and more but they all meet the criteria the author has set by being either inspiring, heartwarming, or in some way uplifting. . . . Arranged by genres, the entries include full bibliographic information, an annotation, and a description of why the book fits the 'gentle criteria.'" SLJ

Includes bibliographical references

Nilsen, Alleen Pace

Literature for today's young adults; [by] Alleen Pace Nilsen, Kenneth L. Donelson. 8th ed. Allyn and Bacon/Pearson 2008 c2009 xx, 491p il $122.20 *

Grades: Professional   **028.5**

1. Young adult literature—History and criticism 2. Books and reading

ISBN 978-0-205-59323-1; 0-205-59323-2

     LC 2008-2625

First published 1980

Authors' names appear in reverse order in 7th ed.

This is an "introduction to young adult literature framed within a literary, historical, and social context. The authors provide teachers with criteria for evaluating books of all genres, from poetry and nonfiction to mysteries, science fiction, and graphic novels. . . . [It also includes coverage of] issues such as pop culture and mass media." Publisher's note

Includes bibliographical references

Pearl, Nancy

Book crush; for kids and teens; recommended reading for every mood, moment, and interest. Sasquatch Books 2007 288p $16.95 *

Grades: Professional   **028.5**

1. Books and reading 2. Best books

ISBN 1-57061-500-4; 978-1-57061-500-9

     LC 2007-13865

Presents lists of recommended book titles for children and teenagers divided into three age groups and then further subdivided into more than 118 categories, including animals, folktales, girl power, autobiographies, comic books, and many others.

"Librarians, parents, and young people will enjoy browsing this resource." Voice Youth Advocates

The **Pura** Belpré Awards; celebrating Latino authors and illustrators; Rose Zertuche Treviño, editor. American Lib. Assn. 2006 86p il pa $35 *

Grades: Professional   **028.5**

1. Pura Belpré award 2. American literature—Hispanic American authors—Bio-bibliography 3. Children's literature—Bibliography

ISBN 978-0-8389-3562-0; 0-8389-3562-1

Includes DVD

This reference explains the significance of Pura Belpré, her work, and the partnership that launched this honor for Latino children's literature. It covers the first ten years of the Pura Belpré Awards, from 1996 to 2006, and includes annotations of the winning titles, brief biographies of the winning authors and illustrators, program ideas, activities, and book talks.

"A well-crafted addition to any professional-reading shelf. . . . This superb guide will be valuable to librarians, teachers, and children's literature enthusiasts." SLJ

Schall, Lucy

Booktalks and beyond; promoting great genre reads to teens. Libraries Unlimited 2007 276p pa $40

Grades: Professional   **028.5**

1. Teenagers—Books and reading 2. Book talks 3. Young adult literature—Bibliography

ISBN 978-1-59158-466-7; 1-59158-466-3

     LC 2006-37492

"A selection of 101 teen-oriented titles published between 2001 and 2006 are organized into 7 genres. . . . Within each genre, titles are arranged into subject groupings. . . . The same information is provided for each book: publication data, reading levels, themes and topics, a description, at least 5 suggested passages for reading aloud, a complete (brief) booktalk, individual or group 'Learning Opportunities' and an annotated list of 5 or 6 related works. This volume will be most useful for librarians new to teen literature, as well as those needing a refresher on more recent titles." Booklist

Includes bibliographical references

Teen genre connections; from booktalking to booklearning. Libraries Unlimited 2005 318p $40

Grades: Professional   **028.5**

1. Young adult literature—Bibliography 2. Teenagers—Books and reading 3. Best books

ISBN 1-59158-229-6   LC 2005-14288

"The author organizes over 100 popular titles into subject groupings with explanations as to why specific titles are included. . . . She provides themes, summaries, booktalk ideas, discussion starters, and related titles for each book included. . . . This volume will help librarians develop collections in specific areas of teen interest such as personal challenges, survival, paranormal suspense, and fantasy. A well-rounded effort." SLJ

Includes bibliographical references

Silvey, Anita
500 great books for teens. Houghton Mifflin Co. 2006 397p $26
Grades: Professional **028.5**
1. Teenagers—Books and reading 2. Young adult literature—Bibliography
ISBN 978-0-618-61296-3; 0-618-61296-3
LC 2006003350
"A Frances Tenenbaum book"
"Silvey selects and annotates five hundred titles for young adults, arranging them loosely in twenty-one chapters by genre and/or area of interest, from 'Adventure and Survival' to 'War and Conflict.' Each book is coded for either younger (12-14) or older (14-18) teens and gets a couple hundred words or so. . . . The selections are both sturdy and wide-ranging." Horn Book
Includes bibliographical references

Sullivan, Edward T.
Reaching reluctant young adult readers; a handbook for librarians and teachers. Scarecrow Press 2002 121p $24.50
Grades: Professional **028.5**
1. Teenagers—Books and reading 2. Young adult literature—Bibliography
ISBN 0-8108-4343-9 LC 2002-21219
"Sullivan explains his concern over the preponderance of 'aliterate' (able to read, but choosing not to) young adults. He defines young adult readers as those between the ages of 10 and 15. . . . He places responsibility for the problem on teachers, librarians, and parents and then offers strategies to reverse the trend. The bulk of the book concentrates on overlooked resources including fiction series and short stories, comics and graphic novels, nonfiction, magazines, picture books, and audiobooks. . . . A bibliography of professional resources completes the practical information provided. . . . A valuable tool to combat the nonreader." Booklist
Includes bibliographical references

Sullivan, Michael, 1967-
Connecting boys with books 2; closing the reading gap. American Library Association 2009 119p il pa $40 *
Grades: Professional **028.5**
1. Boys—Books and reading 2. Children's libraries 3. Young adults' libraries 4. School libraries
ISBN 978-0-8389-0979-9; 0-8389-0979-5
LC 2008-34925
Sullivan "looks at developmental differences between boys and girls and how our culture views reading as a leisure activity. He also looks at materials that will attract male readers. His concern is not necessarily the boy who cannot read but the aliterate boy—the one who can read but chooses not to." Booklist
"A must-read for all librarians and media specialists." SLJ
Includes bibliographical references

Sutherland, Zena, 1915-2002
Children & books; [by] Zena Sutherland; cover, frontispiece, and part opening illustrations by Trina Schart Hyman. 9th ed. Longman 1997 720p $119
Grades: Professional **028.5**

1. Children's literature—History and criticism 2. Children—Books and reading
ISBN 0-673-99733-2
First edition by May Hill Arbuthnot published 1947 by Scott, Foresman
"This children's literature textbook emphasizes the best books and authors. The introductory sections about children and books in general are followed by genre overviews which emphasize the major authors in each category. A third section discusses ways to bring children and books together, while a final section covers issues such as censorship. Lavish color illustrations, viewpoint boxes, extensive bibliographies and useful appendices make this an attractive and stimulating work." Safford. Guide to Ref Materials for Sch Libr Media Cent. 5th edition

Trelease, Jim
The read-aloud handbook. 6th ed. Penguin Books 2006 xxvi, 340p il pa $15 *
Grades: Professional **028.5**
1. Books and reading 2. Children's literature—Bibliography
ISBN 0-14-303739-0 LC 2006-41773
First published 1982
This handbook explains the importance of reading aloud to children, offers guidance on how to set up a read-aloud atmosphere in the home or classroom and suggests 1,500 titles for reading aloud.
Includes bibliographical references

York, Sherry, 1947-
Children's and young adult literature by Latino writers; a guide for librarians, teachers, parents, and students. Linworth Pub. 2002 184p pa $36.95
Grades: Professional **028.5**
1. American literature—Hispanic American authors—Bibliography 2. Young adult literature—Bibliography 3. Children's literature—Bibliography 4. Books and reading
ISBN 1-58683-062-7 LC 2002-67112
This guide includes "bibliographic information for a variety of titles in various genres including novels, chapter books, short stories, folklore, drama, poetry, and nonfiction. A list of additional resource materials, as well as publisher information and an index, is also included." Publisher's note
"This publication fills a necessary void for professionals looking for all forms of Latino literature for primary grades through high school. . . . This book should provide the framework for building a solid collection." SLJ
Includes bibliographical references

Zbaracki, Matthew D.
Best books for boys; a resource for educators; foreward by Jon Scieszka. Libraries Unlimited 2008 189p il (Children's and young adult literature reference series) $45
Grades: Professional **028.5**
1. Boys—Books and reading 2. Best books 3. Children's literature—Bibliography 4. Young adult literature—Bibliography
ISBN 978-1-59158-599-2; 1-59158-599-6
LC 2007-51065

Zbaracki, Matthew D.—*Continued*

"This guide offers ideas for educators, librarians, and parents on fiction and nonfiction books that will interest boys in grades three to 10." Publisher's note

"Good source notes guide readers to additional writings on the topic and speak to the author's significant research in his field. Nicely indexed by author, title, and subject, this [is an] easy-to-navigate resource." Voice Youth Advocates

Includes bibliographical references

028.7 Use of books and other information media as sources of information

Callison, Daniel, 1948-

The blue book on information age inquiry, instruction and literacy; [by] Daniel Callison and Leslie Preddy. Libraries Unlimited 2006 643p il pa $45 *

Grades: Professional   028.7
  1. Information literacy
  ISBN 1-59158-325-X; 978-1-59158-325-7
                                        LC 2006-23645

A revised edition of Key Words, Concepts and Methods for Information Age Instruction, published 2003 by LMS Associates

"Part 1 introduces the concepts of information inquiry, providing foundational documents and exploring search and use models, information literacy, standards, the instructional role of library media specialists, online inquiry learning, and resource management. Part 2 offers concrete examples of inquiry applied to the middle-school student research process and supplies reproducible pages for classroom use. Part 3 discusses and defines 51 key terms. Entries here are several pages in length and include citations and references. Indispensable for all school media specialists, this book will also appeal to other readers, who will be impressed by its well-organized design, thoroughness, and practicality." Booklist

Includes bibliographical references

Riedling, Ann Marlow, 1952-

Learning to learn; a guide to becoming information literate; introduction by Michael Eisenberg. Neal-Schuman 2002 129p pa $24.95

Grades: Professional   028.7
  1. Research 2. Internet resources 3. Internet searching 4. Information literacy
  ISBN 1-55570-452-2   LC 2002-26532

This is a "guide to the research/learning process. Chapters lead researchers step-by-step through the information maze to find what they are looking for. Numerous URLs and exercises are included, as is material on copyright, plagiarism, and basic citation styles. . . . The section on evaluating Web sites is particularly valuable. As an added bonus, all mentioned sites are updated and hyperlinked at the publisher's Web site. This is a practical guide for all librarians, but particularly for those teaching research skills." SLJ

Includes bibliographical references

Taylor, Joie

Information literacy and the school library media center. Libraries Unlimited 2006 148p il (Libraries Unlimited professional guides in school librarianship) pa $35

Grades: Professional   028.7
  1. Information literacy 2. School libraries
  ISBN 0-313-32020-9

"Beginning with a description of what it means to be information literate, the author goes on to highlight how the American Association of School Librarians (AASL) and Association for Educational Communications and Technology (AECT) standards can be integrated into the curriculum in ways that complement state and district standards, giving specific examples from several states. She discusses how the library media specialist through flexible scheduling and curriculum mapping can facilitate an environment where students can hone their information literacy skills. . . . Two things make this book exceptional. First the chapter on collaboration is a refreshingly frank discussion of the value of working with classroom teachers that delineates the roles of the teacher and the library media specialist, while being realistic in realizing that barriers do exist to real collaboration. Second the extensive bibliography is filled with books, journal articles, and Web resources that will guide readers to the bestpractices in information literacy at the current time." Voice Youth Advocates

031 General encyclopedic works in American English

Britannica student encyclopedia. Encyclopedia Britannica 2007 11v il set $499 *

Grades: 3 4 5 6 7   031
  1. Encyclopedias and dictionaries 2. Reference books
  ISBN 1-59339-300-8; 978-1-59339-300-7

"With a clear grasp of the interests of the target audience, this attractive and engaging set is a delightful entry into the student-encyclopedia market and a much-needed addition for the age group. It provides just the right amount of information without overwhelming young researchers." Booklist

Hirsch, E. D. (Eric Donald), 1928-

The new dictionary of cultural literacy; [by] E.D. Hirsch, Joseph F. Kett, James Trefil. Completely rev and updated, 3rd ed. Houghton Mifflin 2002 647p il maps $29.95

Grades: 8 9 10 11 12 Adult   031
  1. Reference books 2. English language—Dictionaries
  ISBN 0-618-22647-8   LC 2002-27609

First published 1988 with title: The dictionary of cultural literacy

"The text is divided into sections by subject—e.g., fine arts, world politics, life sciences—each with a brief introduction; access is also aided by a thorough index. The entries themselves are complete, concise, and clearly written as well as extensively and effectively cross-referenced." Libr J

One million things; a visual encyclopedia; [by]
Kim Bryan ... [et al.] DK Publishing 2008 304p
il map $24.99
Grades: 5 6 7 8 9   **031**
1. Encyclopedias and dictionaries 2. Curiosities and
wonders 3. Science—Encyclopedias 4. Technology—
Encyclopedias 5. Art—Encyclopedias 6. Reference
books
ISBN 978-0-7566-3843-6; 0-7566-3843-7
     LC 2008-298840
"DK has put together a visual encyclopedia that runs
with the concept of cramming a million bits of information into one volume. . . . Arranged in sections from nature to nutrition, the human body to technology, people
and places to art and culture, the breadth of subject matter is impressive. Vital to the operation are the photographs. This may be the single largest collection of pictures kids have ever seen in one place, and each page
shows as much as it tells." SLJ

Scholastic children's encyclopedia. Scholastic
Reference 2004 710p il map $19.95
Grades: 4 5 6 7   **031**
1. Encyclopedias and dictionaries 2. Reference books
ISBN 0-439-43816-0   LC 2003-45591
"More than 600 entries are arranged alphabetically and
range in length from one-half page to just over four
pages. Entries are illustrated with more than 2,000 photographs, diagrams, charts, time lines, and maps. Longer
entries include subheadings that divide text into easy-to-
read sections. . . . Libraries serving younger students
will want multiple copies of this highly usable and user-
friendly tool." Booklist

The **World** Book encyclopedia. World Book 2009
22v il map set $1,009 *
Grades: 4 5 6 7 8 9 10 11 12 Adult
     031
1. Encyclopedias and dictionaries 2. Reference books
ISBN 978-0-7166-0109-8; 0-7166-0109-5
     LC 2008-28060
First published 1917-1918 by Field Enterprises. Frequently revised
Supplemented by: World Book's year in review; another available annual supplement is World Book's science year in review
"A 22-volume, highly illustrated, A-Z general encyclopedia for all ages, featuring sections on how to use
World Book, other research aids, pronunciation key, a
student guide to better writing, speaking, and research
skills, and comprehensive index." Publisher's note
Includes bibliographical references

031.02 American books of miscellaneous facts

Aronson, Marc
For boys only; the biggest, baddest book ever;
[by] Marc Aronson [and] H.P. Newquist. Feiwel
and Friends 2007 157p il map $14.95
Grades: 4 5 6 7   **031.02**
1. Curiosities and wonders 2. Boys
ISBN 978-0-312-37706-9; 0-312-37706-1
     LC 2007-32847

"In a tone both light and humorous, Newquist and
Aronson aim to please by assembling a tantalizing mis-
cellany—codes, puzzles, best lists, brief history and science facts, instructions for making fake blood and playing Ultimate Frisbee. . . . This offers lots of good fun."
Booklist

Ash, Russell
The top 10 of everything 2009. Hamlyn;
distributed by Sterling Publishing 2008 256p il
$24.94
Grades: 8 9 10 11 12   **031.02**
1. Curiosities and wonders
ISSN 1541-7697
ISBN 0-600-61739-4; 978-0-600-61739-6
Annual. First published 1994 by Dorling Kindersley
Ash "has amassed thousands of statistics on topics of
popular interest, listing the 10 most (or least) common,
popular, expensive, or best in each category. . . . The
wide range of categories reported spans from the natural
sciences (the Earth, universe, and human body), to entertainment (music, stage, radio, sports, and travel). Bright,
splashy, full-color photos enliven the columnar text, as
do relevant 'Did you know' sidebars. . . . A browser's
dream." SLJ

Encyclopaedia Britannica almanac, 2006.
Encyclopaedia Britannica 2005 pa $11.95
Grades: Professional   **031.02**
1. Almanacs 2. Statistics 3. United States—Statistics
4. Reference books
ISSN 1540-8868
ISBN 1-4022-0604-6; 978-1-4022-0604-7
2008 edition available as an e-book
Annual. First published 2002
"Features include biographies of notable figures, from
the past as well as the present; a lookup of thousands of
facts covering various branches of knowledge (e.g., science, business, history, entertainment, sports, and the
arts). . . . There are also entries for countries and their
leaders, with maps, flags, and various statistics; for
awards and award winners; for sporting events; and
much more." Libr J

Farndon, John
Do not open; written by John Farndon. DK
Publishing 2007 256p il $24.99
Grades: 4 5 6 7   **031.02**
1. Curiosities and wonders
ISBN 978-0-7566-3205-2; 0-7566-3205-6
     LC 2007300131
This encyclopedic tome catalogues "the mysterious
and unusual. . . . Flaps, foldout pages and varied styles
of illustration—from photomontage to digital cartoons
and more conventional line art—keep the book visually
fresh and ably complement the subject matter. . . . Taking in everything from weird weather like St. Elmo's fire
and raining frogs to possible locations of Atlantis, the
book incites curiosity—and expansively rewards it." Publ
Wkly

Iggulden, Conn, 1971-
The dangerous book for boys; [by] Conn Iggulden, Hal Iggulden. Collins 2007 270p il map $24.95
Grades: 4 5 6 7 8   **031.02**
1. Curiosities and wonders 2. Amusements 3. Recreation 4. Boys
ISBN 0-06-124358-2; 978-0-06-124358-5
LC 2006-491918
"This eclectic collection addresses the undeniable boy-appeal of certain facts and activities. Dozens of short chapters, in fairly random order, cover a wide range of topics in conversational prose. Simple instructions for coin tricks and paper airplanes alternate with excerpts from history such as Famous Battles and facts about ancient wonders of the world and astronomy. . . . Tongue-in-cheek humor emerges throughout." SLJ

Kane, Joseph Nathan, 1899-2002
Famous first facts; a record of first happenings, discoveries, and inventions in American history; [by] Joseph Nathan Kane, Steven Anzovin, & Janet Podell. 6th ed. H.W. Wilson 2006 1307p il $185
Grades: 5 6 7 8 9 10 11 12 Adult
031.02
1. Encyclopedias and dictionaries 2. United States—History—Dictionaries 3. Reference books
ISBN 978-0-8242-1065-6; 0-8242-1065-4
LC 2006-3096
Also available CD-ROM version and online
First published 1933
Over 7500 entries cover first occurences in American history, organized into 16 chapters each divided into sections. Sections are alphabetically organized, and individual entries are organized chronologically within each section. Includes five indexes: subject index, index by years, index by days, index to personal names, and geographical index.
"Besides serving as an essential ready-reference source, the book is also fun to read out loud to colleagues—when was bubble gum first manufactured in the U.S.? When was the spray can introduced?" Booklist

The **New** York Times 2008 almanac; edited by John W. Wright with editors and reporters of the Times. Penguin Reference 2007 1004p il map pa $11.95
Grades: 8 9 10 11 12 Adult   **031.02**
1. Almanacs 2. Statistics 3. United States—Statistics 4. Reference books
ISSN 1523-7079
ISBN 978-0-14-311233-4; 0-14-311233-3
Annual. First published 1997
On cover: The almanac of record
This almanac contains a "chronology of the year; major news stories of the year; U.S. history; U.S. presidential biographies; world history; world geography; economic and climate data; major awards in the arts, sciences, and sports; and a wide variety of U.S. demographic information. . . . It is well organized, the table layout is easy to read, and the typeface does not invite eye strain." Am Ref Books Annu, 1998

The **world** almanac and book of facts, 2008; [editorial director, C. Alan Joyce; managing editor, Elizabeth J. Lazzara; editor, Sarah Janssen] 140th anniversary ed. World Almanac Books 2008 1008p il map $32.99; pa $12.99
Grades: 6 7 8 9 10 11 12 Adult
031.02
1. Almanacs 2. Statistics 3. United States—Statistics 4. Reference books
ISSN 0084-1382
ISBN 978-1-60057-073-5; 978-1-60057-072-8 (pa)
Annual. First published 1868. Publisher varies
"This is the most comprehensive and well-known of almanacs. . . . Contains a chronology of the year's events, consumer information, historical anniversaries, annual climatological data, and forecasts. Color section has flags and maps. Includes detailed index." N Y Public Libr Book of How & Where to Look It Up

The **World** almanac for kids. World Almanac il maps $18.95; pa $10.95
Grades: 4 5 6 7   **031.02**
1. Reference books 2. Almanacs
Annual. First published 1995 for 1996
This volume contains information on animals, art, religion, sports, books, law, language, science and computers. Includes a section of full-color maps and flags. Illustrated throughout with pictures, diagrams, and charts

032.02 English books of miscellaneous facts

Guinness world records 2009. Guinness World Records 2008 287p il $28.95 *
Grades: 5 6 7 8 9 10 11 12 Adult
032.02
1. Curiosities and wonders
ISSN 1475-7419
ISBN 1-904994-37-7; 978-1-904994-37-4
Annual. First published 1955 in the United Kingdom; in the United States 1962. Variant titles: Guinness book of records; Guinness book of world records
"Ready reference for current record holders in all fields, some esoteric. Index provides access to information arranged in broad subject categories. Must be replaced annually." N Y Public Libr. Ref Books for Child Collect

050 Magazines, journals & serials

Botzakis, Stergios
Pretty in print; questioning magazines; by Stergios Botzakis. Fact Finders 2007 32p il (Media literacy) lib bdg $22.60; pa $7.95
Grades: 4 5 6 7   **050**
1. Periodicals 2. Publishers and publishing
ISBN 978-0-7368-6764-1 (lib bdg); 0-7368-6764-3 (lib bdg); 978-0-7368-7860-9 (pa); 0-7368-7860-2 (pa)
LC 2006021443
"Describes what media is, how magazines are part of media, and encourages readers to question the medium's

Botzakis, Stergios—*Continued*
influential messages." Publisher's note

This is "written in a breezy style and [has] plenty of popping colors and photos. . . . Useful and attractive." SLJ

Includes bibliographical references

051   General serial publications in American English

Abridged readers' guide to periodical literature. Wilson, H.W. $205 per year

Grades: 8 9 10 11 12 Adult   051

1. Periodicals—Indexes 2. Reference books

ISSN 0001-334X

First published July 1935. Monthly except June, July, and August (The indexing for these months is included in the September issue). Permanent bound annual cumulations

An index to over 80 periodicals of general interest which have been chosen by the subscribers to the index from the approximately 200 periodicals covered by the unabridged Readers' guide to periodical literature. The form of indexing is the same as that used in the unabridged Readers' guide

"Designed especially for school and small public libraries unable to afford the regular Readers' guide." Sheehy. Guide to Ref Books. 11th edition

070.1   Documentary media, educational media, news media

Garner, Joe
We interrupt this broadcast; the events that stopped our lives—from the Hindenburg explosion to the attacks of September 11. Updated 3rd ed. Sourcebooks 2002 178p il + 2 sound discs $49.95

Grades: 7 8 9 10 11 12 Adult   070.1

1. Television broadcasting of news 2. Broadcast journalism 3. Disasters

ISBN 1-57071-974-8   LC 2003-265013

First published 1998

"This book and double-CD set documents, in text, audio and black-and-white photographs, the moments when history, for better or for worse (though usually for worse), was made in an instant. . . . In addition to the CDs' reports and sound bites dramatically introduced and explained . . . each event gets about four pages of coverage, with an efficient summary and at least half a dozen photos. . . . These are the kinds of moments that still shock and amaze. This moving book is 'a tribute of sorts' to the events that defined eras, the journalists who reported on them and the media television, radio that made us all witnesses." Publ Wkly

070.4   Journalism

Bausum, Ann
Muckrakers; how Ida Tarbell, Upton Sinclair, and Lincoln Steffens helped expose scandal, inspire reform, and invent investigative journalism; by Ann Bausum; foreword by Daniel Schorr. National Geographic 2007 111p il $21.95; lib bdg $32.90 *

Grades: 6 7 8 9   070.4

1. Tarbell, Ida M., 1857-1944 2. Sinclair, Upton, 1878-1968 3. Steffens, Lincoln, 1866-1936 4. Journalism

ISBN   978-1-4263-0137-7;   1-4263-0137-5; 978-1-4263-0138-4 (lib bdg); 1-4263-0138-3 (lib bdg)

LC 2007-11391

This describes "muckrakers, 20th-century journalists who investigated corruption and called for reform. . . . The well-captioned, black-and-white illustrations, mainly photos, are sometimes reproduced with a sepia tone. . . . Clearly written, this offers a very readable and informative introduction to American muckrakers." Booklist

Includes bibliographical references

Gourley, Catherine, 1950-
War, women, and the news; how female journalists won the battle to cover World War II. Atheneum Books for Young Readers 2007 198p il $21.99

Grades: 7 8 9 10   070.4

1. World War, 1939-1945—Journalists 2. Women journalists

ISBN 978-0-689-87752-0; 0-689-87752-8

LC 2005-20269

This describes the work of women journalists before, during, and after World War II, including Margaret Bourke-White, who covered the battles in Russia; Lee Miller, who photographed the wounded in field hospitals in France; Shelley Mydans, who was a prisoner of war in the Philippines; and Marguerite Higgins, who reported at the liberation of Dachau.

"Rich in information, simply written, and easy to understand, this book offers valuable information about history and female journalists. . . . Black-and-white photographs richly enhance the text." Voice Youth Advocates

Reeves, Diane Lindsey, 1959-
TV journalist; [by] Diane Lindsey Reeves. Ferguson 2007 64p il (Virtual apprentice) $29.95

Grades: 6 7 8 9   070.4

1. Television broadcasting of news 2. Vocational guidance

ISBN 978-0-8160-6753-4; 0-8160-6753-8

LC 2006-36570

This book about becoming a TV journalist is "written with engaging language capable of drawing even reluctant readers into the prose. . . . Pop quizzes, information boxes, quotes from famous people in the field, and on-the-job description make these books highly attractive to the target audience." Libr Media Connect

Sullivan, George
Journalists at risk; reporting America's wars; [by] George Sullivan. Twenty-First Century Books 2006 128p il (People's history) lib bdg $26.60
Grades: 5 6 7 8   **070.4**
1. Journalism 2. War
ISBN 0-7613-2745-2   LC 2003015855
Discusses the role of reporters during war time, including the risks they take and the censorship they face, and how their jobs have changed with each conflict since the Civil War.
"As a case study in the fluidity of First Amendment rights in wartime, it's thought-provoking reading." Booklist
Includes bibliographical references

070.5   Publishing

Benini Pietromarchi, Sophie
The book book: a journey into bookmaking; written and illustrated by Sophie Benini Pietromarchi. Tara Publishing 2007 131p il $19.95
Grades: 4 5 6 7   **070.5**
1. Books 2. Handicraft 3. Authorship
ISBN 978-81-86211-24-3; 81-86211-24-1
This "offers a detailed enticement to young people to create their own literary works. The book includes a section devoted to the writing of the story . . . but most of the explanation is geared to encouraging a full sweep of visual creativity, from considering and repurposing found objects to constructing a cover to a 'feather book,' with feathery bundled strips of paper, to pop-up and shaped books." Bull Cent Child Books

Broderick, James F., 1963-
Consider the source; a critical guide to 100 prominent news and information sites on the web; [by] James F. Broderick and Darren W. Miller. CyberAge Books 2007 457p $24.95
Grades: 7 8 9 10 11 12   **070.5**
1. Weblogs—Directories 2. Web sites—Directories
ISBN 978-0-910965-77-4; 0-910965-77-3
LC 2007012463
"This accessible resource will be valuable in a wide variety of classes, including public speaking and journalism. Each entry includes an overview of the company behind the publication, what appears on the site, images, reasons to visit, and a rating of the content. Web site reviews on this topic are available from many online and print sources, but this one is the most concise and easiest to use." SLJ
Includes bibliographical references

Brookfield, Karen
Book; written by Karen Brookfield; photographed by Laurence Pordes. Dorling Kindersley 2000 63p il (DK eyewitness books) $15.95; lib bdg $19.99
Grades: 4 5 6 7   **070.5**
1. Books
ISBN 0-7894-5892-6; 0-7894-6597-3 (lib bdg)
First published 1993 by Knopf

Text and photographs trace the evolution of the written word, how the alphabet grew out of pictures, the development of papermaking, bookbinding, children's books, and more.

Todd, Mark
Whatcha mean, what's a zine? the art of making zines and mini comics; [by] Mark Todd + Esther Peal Watson; with contributions by more than 20 creators of Indie-comics and magazines. Houghton Mifflin 2006 110p il pa $12.99
Grades: 7 8 9 10   **070.5**
1. Zines 2. Desktop publishing 3. Comic books, strips, etc.
ISBN 978-0-618-56315-9; 0-618-56315-6
LC 2005-55026
"A zine is a mini-magazine or homemade comic about any topic of the creator's choice, designed for maximum creativity and expression. The authors present a history of self-publishing. . . . Other topics include ideas for zine subjects; copying, binding, and printing tips, including easy-to-understand silk-screening and gocco instruction. . . . Throughout, technical terms are deftly used and advice is dispensed in an accessible, rousing format that includes comics, drawings, and cut-and-paste zine techniques. This well-designed and entertaining resource is sure to find an audience among hip, artistic, and do-it-yourself enthusiasts." SLJ

100   PHILOSOPHY

130   Parapsychology & occultism

Steiger, Brad
Gale encyclopedia of the unusual and unexplained; [by] Brad E. Steiger and Sherry Hansen Steiger. Thomson/Gale 2003 3v il map set $205
Grades: 7 8 9 10 11   **130**
1. Occultism—Encyclopedias 2. Supernatural—Encyclopedias 3. Reference books
ISBN 0-7876-5382-9   LC 2003-3995
"These volumes cover broad concepts from 'Afterlife Mysteries' to 'Invaders from Outer Space.' . . . [This is] an encyclopedia for believers. The volumes are meant to 'explore and describe the research of those who take such phenomena seriously.'. . . The work covers material of interest to a large segment of the public in a way that is clear and readable." Booklist
Includes bibliographical references

133 Specific topics in parapsychology and occultism

Paranormal phenomena: opposing viewpoints; Mary E. Williams, book editor. Greenhaven Press/Thomson Gale 2003 205p il lib bdg $21.95; pa $14.96 *

Grades: 7 8 9 10 **133**

1. Parapsychology

ISBN 0-7377-1238-4 (lib bdg); 0-7377-1237-6 (pa)
LC 2002-66461

"Opposing viewpoints series"

Replaces the edition published 1997 under the editorship of Paul A. Winters

"Four chapters of four to six essays each offer opinions on the reality of ghosts, psychic ability, extraterrestrial life, UFO's, near-death experiences, reincarnation, and changing concepts of eternal life. Each essay is preceded by an introduction, which poses questions to be answered in the article." SLJ

Includes bibliographical references

133.1 Apparitions

Stefoff, Rebecca, 1951-
Ghosts and spirits; [by] Rebecca Stefoff. Marshall Cavendish Benchmark 2007 c2008 94p il (Secrets of the supernatural) lib bdg $32.79

Grades: 5 6 7 8 **133.1**

1. Ghosts

ISBN 978-0-7614-2634-9 (lib bdg); 0-7614-2634-5 (lib bdg) LC 2006031652

This is a history of beliefs in ghosts and spirits throughout the world, including haunted houses, spiritualism, hauxes, and investigations into paranormal phenomena.

"Nearly every other page has an illustration. . . . The text is accessible." Libr Media Connect

Includes glossary and bibliographical references

Wetzel, Charles
Haunted U.S.A.; written by Charles Wetzel; illustrated by Josh Cochran. Sterling 2008 86p il (Mysteries unwrapped) pa $5.95 **133.1**

1. Ghosts

ISBN 978-1-4027-3735-0; 1-4027-3735-1
LC 2007045905

"Wetzel tells stories of haunted America from the White House to Hollywood. Although some of the places and people mentioned, such as the Amityville house and Rudolph Valentino, might be unfamiliar to younger readers, the selections are still good ghost stories. . . . [The book has] an ample number of clear black-and-white and full-color photographs and illustrations. . . . Perfect for libraries that need a boost or an update to their scary-story collections." SLJ

Includes bibliographical references

133.3 Divinatory arts

Stefoff, Rebecca, 1951-
Prophets and prophecy; [by] Rebecca Stefoff. Marshall Cavendish Benchmark 2007 c2008 79p il (Secrets of the supernatural) lib bdg $32.79

Grades: 5 6 7 8 **133.3**

1. Prophets 2. Prophecies

ISBN 978-0-7614-2638-7 (lib bdg); 0-7614-2638-8 (lib bdg) LC 2007008779

This is a history of prophecy and fortune-telling from ancient times to the present, discussing such topics as tarot cards, the Oracle of Delphi, astrology, fate, Nostradamus, Jean Dixon, omens, and the *I Ching*.

"Nearly every other page has an illustration. . . . The text is accessible." Libr Media Connect

Includes glossary and bibliographical references

133.4 Demonology and witchcraft

Black magic and witches; Tamara L. Roleff, book editor. Greenhaven Press 2003 127p (Fact or fiction) $29.95; pa $21.20

Grades: 6 7 8 9 **133.4**

1. Witchcraft 2. Magic

ISBN 0-7377-1318-6; 0-7377-1319-4 (pa)
LC 2002-378

Explores both sides of the question of whether or not witchcraft is destructive, looking at issues related to the Harry Potter books, wiccans serving in the military, and the validity of magic

"This is a useful introduction to current debate over witchcraft." SLJ

Includes bibliographical references

Stefoff, Rebecca, 1951-
Magic; [by] Rebecca Stefoff. Marshall Cavendish Benchmark 2007 c2008 92p il (Secrets of the supernatural) lib bdg $32.79

Grades: 5 6 7 8 **133.4**

1. Magic

ISBN 978-0-7614-2636-3 (lib bdg); 0-7614-2636-1 (lib bdg) LC 2007006722

"A critical exploration of magic, its history, and practitioners." Publisher's note

"Nearly every other page has an illustration. . . . The text is accessible." Libr Media Connect

Includes glossary and bibliographical references

Witches and witchcraft; [by] Rebecca Stefoff. Marshall Cavendish Benchmark 2007 c2008 80p il (Secrets of the supernatural) lib bdg $32.79

Grades: 5 6 7 8 **133.4**

1. Witches 2. Witchcraft

ISBN 978-0-7614-2637-0 (lib bdg); 0-7614-2637-X (lib bdg) LC 2007013304

This is a history of beliefs in witches and witchcraft, including persecutions such as the Inquisition and the Salem witch trials, the depiction of witches in literature and popular culture, and modern-day Wiccans.

"Nearly every other page has an illustration. . . . The text is accessible." Libr Media Connect

Includes glossary and bibliographical references

150 Psychology

Gardner, Robert, 1929-
Health science projects about psychology; [by] Robert Gardner and Barbara Gardner Conklin. Enslow Pubs. 2002 112p il (Science projects) $26.60 *
Grades: 7 8 9 10   **150**
  1. Psychology 2. Science projects
  ISBN 0-7660-1439-8   LC 2001-3425
  Uses science projects to explore such areas of psychology as personality, emotions, perception, learning, memory, and parapsychology
  "Schools with psychology classes should find this title helpful as well as schools whose students participate in science fair competitions." Book Rep
  Includes bibliographical references

Kincher, Jonni, 1949-
Psychology for kids vol. 1: 40 fun tests that help you learn about yourself; [by] Jonni Kincher; [edited by Julie Bach and Pamela Espeland] updated ed. Free Spirit Pub. Inc. 2008 132p il pa $21.95
Grades: 6 7 8 9   **150**
  1. Psychological tests 2. Personality
  ISBN 978-1-57542-283-1   LC 2008020660
  First published 1990
  Includes CD-ROM
  "Are you an extrovert or an introvert? An optimist or a pessimist? Can you predict the future? Are you creative? Left-brained or right-brained? What body language do you speak? Do you have ESP? Based on . . . psychological concepts, these 40 . . . tests help kids explore their interests and abilities." Publisher's note
  Includes bibliographical references

Psychology for kids vol. 2: 40 fun experiments that help you learn about others. Free Spirit Pub. 2008 132p il pa $21.95
Grades: 6 7 8 9   **150**
  1. Psychology
  ISBN 978-1-57542-284-8   LC 2008020663
  First published 1995
  Includes CD-ROM
  "Are people more logical or emotional? How do people make judgments? Do males and females see things differently? Can we shape other people's behavior? Are we more alike or more different? Based on science and . . . psychological concepts and research, 40 . . . experiments make it fun for kids to learn about what makes people tick." Publisher's note
  Includes bibliographical references

152.1 Sensory perception

Jackson, Donna M., 1959-
Phenomena; secrets of the senses. Little, Brown and Company 2008 174p il $16.99
Grades: 6 7 8 9   **152.1**
  1. Senses and sensation
  ISBN 978-0-316-16649-2; 0-316-16649-9
                                LC 2008-31215
  "Students with an interest in the weird and unusual will find this book fascinating. It begins with an introduction to human senses and continues with chapters devoted to phenomena such as the 'sixth sense,' synethesia, and intuition. One of the most interesting sections discusses animals that use their senses in unusual ways. . . . The black-and-white illustrations and photographs are plentiful enough to make the text accessible to reluctant readers. Accurate, entertaining nonfiction." SLJ
  Includes glossary and bibliographical references

152.14 Visual perception

Wick, Walter, 1953-
Walter Wick's optical tricks; by Walter Wick. 10th anniversary edition. Cartwheel Books 2008 43p il $14.99 *
Grades: 4 5 6 7   **152.14**
  1. Optical illusions
  ISBN 978-0-439-85520-4; 0-439-85520-9
  First published 1998
  Presents a series of optical illusions and explains what is seen.
  The author "has produced a stunning picture book of optical illusions. With crystal-clear photographs, he creates a series of scenes that fool the eye and the brain." Booklist [review of 1998 ed.]

152.4 Emotions

Andrews, Linda Wasmer
Emotional intelligence. Franklin Watts 2004 80p il (Life balance) $19.50
Grades: 5 6 7 8 9   **152.4**
  1. Emotions
  ISBN 0-531-12335-9   LC 2003-19772
  Contents: Dealing with feeling; Name that emotion!; Understanding yourself; Handling Your emotions; Managing relationships
  "This book explains that the ability to manage one's emotions and to understand those of others is important for success in life. . . . This title will help young people to understand themselves and others better, and the tools for managing relationships and one's own emotions will promote maturity and development of social skills." SLJ
  Includes glossary and bibliographical references

Crist, James J.
What to do when you're scared & worried; a guide for kids; [by] James Crist. Free Spirit Pub. 2004 128p il pa $9.95 *
Grades: 5 6 7 8   **152.4**

Crist, James J.—Continued
1. Fear 2. Worry
ISBN 1-57542-153-4
"Part one deals with normal anxiety, offering detailed steps for developing 10 coping mechanisms. Expert help is needed to deal with the more serious problems discussed in Part two (e.g., phobias, separation anxiety, obsessive-compulsive disorder). Throughout, the author provides information, case histories, and coping skills in a manner that is both reassuring and encouraging. . . . Illustrations lighten the tone of the subject matter." SLJ
Includes bibliographical references

Tym, Kate
Coping with your emotions; [by] Kate Tym and Penny Worms. Raintree 2005 48p il (Get real) $29.93
Grades: 6 7 8 9   **152.4**
1. Emotions
ISBN 1-4109-0575-6   LC 2004-8069
Contents: Painfully shy; Feeling blue; Depression; Scaredy cats; Blow your top; Love bug; Lots to smile about
"Chapters consist of a spread presenting an overview of a topic such as depression . . . followed by three case studies about teens dealing with the problem. On the same page, three 'experts' . . . offer advice. . . . The advice of professionals lends credibility to the information presented. . . . Sure to appeal to readers looking for advice." SLJ
Inlcudes glossary and bibliographical references

153.1   Memory and learning

Hudmon, Andrew
Learning and memory. Chelsea House Publishers 2005 136p il (Gray matter) $32.95 *
Grades: 8 9 10 11 12   **153.1**
1. Psychology of learning 2. Memory 3. Brain
ISBN 0-7910-8638-0   LC 2005-11699
This "volume provides fascinating insights into various processes involved in how we learn different things in different ways. Particularly enlightening is the section differentiating explicit memory (learning facts) and implicit memory (learning processes) . . . The [book features] colorful historical photos and illustrations, process models, and shaded insets." SLJ
Includes bibliographical references

153.8   Will (Volition)

Bachel, Beverly K., 1957-
What do you really want? how to set a goal and go for it! A guide for teens. Free Spirit 2000 134p il pa $12.95 *
Grades: 7 8 9 10 11 12   **153.8**
1. Success 2. Motivation (Psychology)
ISBN 1-57542-085-6   LC 00-57286
The book discusses various ways for teenagers to set goals, build support networks, keep themselves motivated

in the process and reap the harvest of their successes
Bachel's "helpful advice is well supported by quotations from teens who have tried some of the techniques, and simple, appealing graphics keep things light. . . . Back matter includes goal-setting resources and some helpful organizations and Web sites." Booklist

153.9   Intelligence and aptitudes

Armstrong, Thomas
You're smarter than you think; a kid's guide to multiple intelligences; edited by Jennifer Brannen. Free Spirit 2003 186p il pa $15.95
Grades: 7 8 9 10 11 12   **153.9**
1. Intellect
ISBN 1-57542-113-5   LC 2002-2687
Contents: The many ways of being smart; Picture Smart, visualizing your artistic ways; Body Smart, displaying your physical fabulousness; Music Smart, singing out your melodic and rhythmic nature; People Smart, shining forth with your social graces; Self Smart, reflecting on your radiant personality; Nature Smart, exploring the wide world of the outdoors; Number Smart, calculating your math science expertise; Word Smart, verbalizing your literary gifts; Using all your smarts in school; Playing it smart eight ways outside of school; Being smart for the future; MI Pizza
The author "covers eight different intelligences—word, music, logic, picture, body, people, self, and nature—and talks about what they mean." Booklist
"A self-help book that's clear, concise, and fun to peruse." SLJ
Includes bibliographical references

155.9   Environmental psychology

Altman, Linda Jacobs, 1943-
Death: an introduction to medical-ethical dilemmas. Enslow Pubs. 2000 112p il (Issues in focus) lib bdg $26.60 *
Grades: 7 8 9 10 11 12   **155.9**
1. Death
ISBN 0-7660-1246-8   LC 99-32714
The author "addresses a variety of topics, including the actual physiology of dying, the ethics and legal issues involved in prolonging life, euthanasia, rituals surrounding death, and how various cultures perceive an afterlife. Scattered black-and-white illustrations, a Webliography, and a useful glossary round out the presentation." SLJ
Includes bibliographical references

Gootman, Marilyn E., 1944-
When a friend dies; a book for teens about grieving & healing; edited by Pamela Espeland. Rev. and updated ed. Free Spirit Pub. 2005 118p pa $9.95 *
Grades: 7 8 9 10   **155.9**
1. Death 2. Bereavement
ISBN 1-57542-170-4   LC 2005-447
First published 1994

Gootman, Marilyn E., 1944——*Continued*
This offers "information on subjects including: How can I stand the pain? How should I be acting? What is 'normal'? What if I can't handle my grief on my own? and How can I find a counselor or a therapist? Interspersed throughout the book . . . are quotes by teenagers who have experienced grief. . . . Quotes from well-known writers and philosophers give insight into the grieving process and healing." SLJ

Myers, Edward, 1950-
When will I stop hurting? teens, loss, and grief; illustrations by Kelly Adams. Scarecrow Press 2004 159p il (It happened to me) $34.50 *
Grades: 7 8 9 10   **155.9**
1. Bereavement 2. Loss (Psychology)
ISBN 0-8108-4921-6   LC 2003-23698
"Outlining the phases of the grieving process, Myers incorporates . . . personal accounts and quotes from young adults who have experienced the death of a family member into the text. He discusses the range of emotions young people may have from anger and fear to relief and sadness and assures readers that these feelings are normal." SLJ
This book "will be extremely helpful for teens struggling to understand their emotions following the loss of a loved one. Grieving is well explained and the individual nature of grief is stressed." Libr Media Connect
Includes bibliographical references

158   Applied psychology

Amblard, Odile
Friends forever? why your friendships are so important; by Odile Amblard; illustrated by Andree Prigent; edited by Andrea Bussell. Amulet Books 2008 112p il (Sunscreen) $9.95
Grades: 5 6 7 8   **158**
1. Friendship 2. Interpersonal relations
ISBN 978-0-8109-9480-5; 0-8109-9480-1
LC 2007-43138
"The importance of friendship is stressed in the opening of *Friends Forever?*, followed by brief discussions on the types of friendships and how they are formed and maintained. . . . The tone of the [book] is breezy and light without being flippant. The [author] never [talks] down to the teen reader." Voice Youth Advocates

Andrews, Linda Wasmer
Meditation; [by] Linda Wasmer Andrews. F. Watts 2004 79p (Life balance) $19.50; pa $6.95
Grades: 5 6 7 8   **158**
1. Meditation
ISBN 0-531-12219-0; 0-531-16609-0 (pa)
LC 2003-7153
Contents: Meditation myth-busters; The relaxation response; The mind/body/spirit link; Minding your mindfulness
"Andrews emphasizes that meditation is not a flaky practice, or a particularly religious one, but one that's designed to reduce stress and help individuals manage their

lives. Four chapters explain the why and how of meditating. . . . [This offers] solid, easy-to-understand information" SLJ
Includes bibliographical references

Auderset, Marie-Josée
Walking tall; how to build confidence and be the best you can be; by Marie-Jose Auderset; illustrated by Gaetan de Seguin; edited by N.B. Grace. Amulet Books 2008 112p il (Sunscreen) $9.95
Grades: 5 6 7 8   **158**
1. Self-confidence
ISBN 978-0-8109-9479-9; 0-8109-9479-8
LC 2007-43416
This "addresses issues of self-confidence and section one deals with feelings of high and low self-esteem, acceptance of oneself, and body image issues. It includes an exercise to help the reader realize her strengths and use that realization to build self-confidence. . . . The tone of the [book] is breezy and light without being flippant. The [author] never [talks] down to the teen reader." Voice Youth Advocates
Includes bibliographical references

Canfield, Jack, 1944-
Chicken soup for the teenage soul [I-IV]; [by] Jack Canfield, Mark Victor Hansen, Kimberly Kirberger. Health Communications 1997-2000 4v il hardcover o.p. v1 pa $14.95; v2 pa $9.99; v3 pa $14.95; v4 pa $14.95
Grades: 7 8 9 10 11 12   **158**
1. Interpersonal relations 2. Emotions
ISBN 1-55874-468-1 ([I]); 1-55874-463-0 ([I pa]); 1-55874-615-3 ([II]); 1-55874-616-1 ([II pa]); 1-55874-761-3 ([III]); 0-7573-0233-5 ([IV])
These books cover "teenage subjects running the gamut from love, family ties, and self-esteem to developing values and life crises, such as a death in the family. . . . Teenagers not only helped select the poems, stories, and accounts that have been included but also have written some of them . . . with a few contributions by well-known people, including Sandra Cisneros, Helen Keller, and Robert Fulghum. . . . This isn't a religious book, but it is an inspirational and motivational one, sometimes funny, sometimes poignant." Booklist [review of 1997 volume]
Includes bibliographical references

Chicken soup for the teenage soul's the real deal; school: cliques, classes, clubs, and more; [compiled by] Jack Canfield, Mark Victor Hansen, Deborah Reber. Health Communications 2005 292p pa $12.95
Grades: 7 8 9 10   **158**
1. Interpersonal relations 2. Emotions
ISBN 0-7573-0255-6   LC 2005046051
"The stories included here were submitted by students and are based on their own experiences. Almost every page includes a fun fact, a statistic, or a quiz." SLJ

Crist, James J.
What to do when you're sad & lonely; a guide
for kids; [by] James J. Crist. Free Spirit Pub. 2006
124p il pa $9.95
Grades: 4 5 6 7   **158**
  1. Depression (Psychology) 2. Solitude
  ISBN 978-1-57542-189-6 (pa); 1-57542-189-5 (pa)
                             LC 2005021794
"Advising his audience to read this book and work
through negative feelings with an adult, Crist describes
sad and lonely feelings, distinguishes them from more
serious conditions such as depression, and then suggests
'Blues Busters' and ways to ask for help. . . . Crist's
clear explanations and simple techniques . . . are relevant for both children and adults." Voice Youth Advocates
  Includes bibliographical references

Fox, Annie, 1950-
Be confident in who you are; [by] Annie Fox.
Free Spirit Pub. 2008 92p il (Middle school
confidential) pa $9.95
Grades: 5 6 7 8   **158**
  1. Self-confidence
  ISBN 978-1-57542-302-9; 1-57542-302-2
                             LC 2008-4754
"With the help of graphic-novel-style illustrations,
. . . [This] title . . . offers insider information on common middle school concerns and practical advice for being healthy, feeling good about who you are, and staying
in control of your feelings and actions." Publisher's note
  "The book contains quizzes, is chock-full of helpful
hints, and lists other resources to help readers increase
their self-esteem. Kindt's cartoons include several great
panels that move the teens' story forward. The graphic-
novel-like design will make this self-help tool stand out
and appeal to fans of that format." SLJ

Too stressed to think? a teen guide to staying
sane when life makes you crazy; by Annie Fox
and Ruth Kirschner; edited by Elizabeth Verdick.
Free Spirit Pub. 2005 163p il pa $14.95 *
Grades: 7 8 9 10   **158**
  1. Stress (Psychology)
  ISBN 1-57542-173-9   LC 2005018484
"This well-organized, upbeat book discusses what
stress is and how it affects the body and brain, talks
about tools to reduce and control it, and gives suggestions for recognizing the myriad situations that can trigger stress at home and at school and seeking help when
necessary. Best of all, each one of these scenarios includes information on how the situation might be addressed." SLJ
  Includes bibliographical references

Hantman, Clea
30 days to finding and keeping sassy sidekicks
and BFFs; a friendship manual; [by] Clea
Hantman. Delacorte Press 2009 176p pa $7.99
Grades: 8 9 10 11 12   **158**
  1. Friendship
  ISBN 978-0-385-73623-7; 0-385-873623-1
                             LC 2007-51599

"In an easy-to-read style, Hantman begins at the beginning with how to initiate a friendship and includes
ideas for parties, clubs, and just simple approachability
and kindness. . . . She addresses ways to work through
problems with female friends, whether the issue is boyfriend stealing, depression, or competition. . . .
Hantman's sense of humor and youthfulness will make
this book appealing to female readers. . . . This book
should prove very popular with its intended audience."
Voice Youth Advocates

30 days to getting over the dork you used to
call your boyfriend; a heartbreak handbook; by
Clea Hantman. Delacorte Press 2008 161p il pa
$7.99
Grades: 8 9 10 11 12   **158**
  1. Loss (Psychology)
  ISBN 978-0-385-73549-0 (pa); 0-385-73549-9 (pa)
                             LC 2007005945
"Hautman outlines a thirty-day process to help teens
get through the five stages of a break-up—denial, anger,
bargaining, depression, and acceptance. . . . Each day
involves exercises to help put events, one's ex, and oneself in perspective. Each day also has a song of the day,
which highlights the day's theme, and a bonus inspirational haiku. . . . The process and activities are helpful
and even fun." Voice Youth Advocates

Hernández, Roger E.
Teens & relationships; [by] Roger E. Hernández.
Mason Crest Publishers 2005 112p il (Gallup
Youth Survey, major issues and trends) $22.95
Grades: 7 8 9 10   **158**
  1. Interpersonal relations
  ISBN 1-59084-875-6   LC 2004-13751
This is "based on the findings of the Gallup Youth
Survey (a 20-year ongoing survey of teens). . . .
Hernández discusses attitudes toward parents, how di-
vorce changes family relationships, dating the opposite
sex (with a separate chapter on interracial and interfaith
relationships), and friendship. . . . [The book is] well
documented." SLJ
  Includes bibliographical references

Jones, Jami Biles
Bouncing back; dealing with the stuff life
throws at you; [by] Jami L. Jones. Franklin Watts
2007 112p il (Choices) lib bdg $22.50; pa $8.95
Grades: 6 7 8 9 10 11 12   **158**
  1. Problem solving 2. Personality
  ISBN 0-531-12404-5 (lib bdg); 978-0-531-12404-8 (lib
  bdg); 0-531-17730-0 (pa); 978-0-531-17730-3 (pa)
                             LC 2004018426
"The image of a bouncing ball is used effectively
throughout this book to discuss the concept of resiliency
in the context of adjusting to life's problems. Each chapter begins with a short vignette of a teen facing a stressful situation and ends by reminding readers of the story
and hypothesizing solutions. . . . The advice given is
psychologically sound, the writing is clear and easy to
read, the pages are visually appealing, and photos show
teens of both genders and various racial backgrounds."
SLJ
  Includes glossary and bibliographical references

Kreiner, Anna

Everything you need to know about creating your own support system. Rosen Pub. Group 1996 64p il (Need to know library) lib bdg $25.25
Grades: 7 8 9 10   **158**
1. Interpersonal relations
ISBN 0-8239-2215-4   LC 95-10753
Discusses how teenagers can create their own support system, a group of people in their lives to whom they feel connected and who can help them build skills and solve problems

This offers "valuable information in easily understood language, illustrated with appealing black-and-white and full-color photographs with a nice mix of genders and ethnic groups." SLJ

Includes glossary and bibliographical references

McIntyre, Thomas, 1952-

The behavior survival guide for kids; how to make good choices and stay out of trouble; [by] Thomas McIntyre. Free Spirit Pub. 2003 167p pa $14.95 *
Grades: 5 6 7 8   **158**
1. Interpersonal relations 2. Conduct of life
ISBN 1-57542-132-1   LC 2003-4565
"The author provides skills and activities to learn and practice so that new behaviors can replace those that have resulted in getting students into trouble. . . . Those motivated to make better choices for how they behave in school or with friends and family will find much to help them." Voice Youth Advocates

Perrier, Pascale

Flying solo; how to soar above your lonely feelings, make friends, and find the happiest you; by Pascale Perrier with Erin Zimring; illustrated by Klaas Verplancke. Amulet Books 2007 112p il pa $9.95
Grades: 5 6 7 8   **158**
1. Friendship 2. Solitude
ISBN 978-0-8109-9281-8 (pa); 0-8109-9281-7 (pa)
      LC 2006023609
"A self-help book with solid, practical advice. The text is divided into three sections or, as they are called here, phases: 'Why do I feel alone?,' 'How to stop feeling lonely,' and 'Finding solitude.' Each section has a series of subsections with quick discussions of mini-topics designed to hold readers' attention while imparting the necessary information. For the most part, the presentation is clear, understandable, and immediate. . . . The cartoon drawings are colorfully bright and match the text in its attempt to keep the tone light." SLJ

Piquemal, Michel, 1954-

When life stinks; how to deal with your bad moods, blues, and depression; [by] Michel Piquemal with Melissa Daly; illustrated by Olivier Tossan ; [translated by Jane Moseley] Amulet Books 2004 112p il pa $9.95
Grades: 7 8 9 10   **158**
1. Depression (Psychology)
ISBN 0-8109-4932-6   LC 2004-13001

This "book examines dark moods and mental illness, and gives young people tools for coping, plus advice on when, where, and how to get help." Publisher's note

"The pleasing use of blocks of color and cartoon illustrations enhances the text. . . . Using the common-sense suggestions provided, readers will more successfully navigate the turmoil of adolescence." SLJ

Includes bibliographical references

Romain, Trevor

Cliques, phonies & other baloney. Free Spirit 1998 129p il pa $9.95 *
Grades: 7 8 9 10   **158**
1. Social groups 2. Interpersonal relations 3. Friendship
ISBN 1-57542-045-7   LC 98-36248
Discusses cliques, what they are and their negative aspects, and gives advice on forming healthier relationships and friendships

"With a sense of ease and lighthearted humor . . . the author serves up solid advice in friendly, reassuring prose." SLJ

Includes bibliographical references

Taylor, Julie, 1971-

The girls' guide to friends; straight talk on making close pals, creating lasting ties, and being an all-around great friend. Three Rivers Press (NY) 2002 222p pa $12
Grades: 7 8 9 10   **158**
1. Friendship
ISBN 0-609-80857-5   LC 2002-18123
Explores the comforts and confusions of friendship, discussing the different kinds of friends, keeping in touch with friends, mixing romance and friendship, the impact of friendship, saving a friendship, and more

"In her practical guide, journalist Taylor maintains the format and bouncy voice of teen-oriented magazines, with slang, cutesy wordplay, and plenty of how-tos." Booklist

Wells, Donna Koren, 1951-

Live aware, not in fear; the 411 after 9-11: a book for teens; [by] Donna K. Wells, Bruce C. Morris. Health Communications 2002 160p il pa $9.95
Grades: 7 8 9 10   **158**
1. September 11 terrorist attacks, 2001 2. Terrorism 3. Stress (Psychology)
ISBN 0-7573-0013-8   LC 2002-19993
A collection of facts, concrete advice, and thought-provoking questions designed to help teens cope with the aftermath of the September 11th, 2001, terrorist attacks, as well as other dangers in today's world

"This book, which is divided into informative text and well-selected question and answers . . . fulfills its purpose." Booklist

170   Ethics

Robinson, Sharon, 1950-
Jackie's nine; Jackie Robinson's values to live
by; courage, determination, teamwork, persistence,
integrity, citizenship, justice, commitment,
excellence. Scholastic 2001 181p il $15.95; pa
$4.99
Grades: 6 7 8 9   **170**
    1. Robinson, Jackie, 1919-1972 2. Values
    ISBN 0-439-23764-5; 0-439-38550-4 (pa)
                            LC 2001-269598
"Written by Jackie Robinson's daughter, this book
contains nine sections, each focusing on one of nine values the ballplayer lived by (courage, determination, and
so on). Each section contains a scene from the author's
life, one from her father's (by various writers, including
Robinson himself), and a sketch of one of her heroes."
Horn Book Guide
"The glimpses into Robinson's life and that of her famous father are stirringly honest, and the hero stories are
thought provoking. . . . The short essays are readable,
and the generous number of photos enhances the collection nicely." Voice Youth Advocates
Includes bibliographical references

Weinstein, Bruce D.
    Is it still cheating if I don't get caught; [by]
Bruce Weinstein; illustrations by Harriet Russell.
Roaring Brook 2009 160p il pa $12.95 *
Grades: 8 9 10 11 12   **170**
    1. Ethics
    ISBN 978-1-59643-306-9 (pa); 1-59643-306-X (pa)
The author "addresses adolescent ethical dilemmas us-
ing a set of five 'Life Principles' (Do No Harm, Make
Things Better, Respect Others, Be Fair, Be Loving)."
Publ Wkly
"This appealing guide speaks to the ethical dilemmas
that all young people experience in their daily lives, and
it should prompt considerable conversation and reflec-
tion." Kirkus

174   Occupational ethics

Ethics in school librarianship; a reader; edited by
    Carol Simpson. Linworth Pub 2003 164p pa
    $44.95 *
    Grades: Professional   **174**
    1. School libraries 2. Librarians—Ethics
    ISBN 1-58683-084-8   LC 2003-7956
    Contents: An ethical dilemma by Carol Simpson; Ethi-
cal issues in collection development by Kay Bishop; Ethics in access by Mary Ann Bell; Confidentiality in the
school library by Harry Willems; Ethics in the use of
technology by Doug Johnson; Ethics and intellectual
freedom by Carrie Gardner; Ethics in intellectual property by Carol Simpson; Ethics in the administration of
school library media centers by Nancy Everhart; Ethics
in Internet use by Nancy Willard; Ethics in professional
realtionships by Frank Hoffman

This is a compilation of "articles dealing with the ethical aspects of collection development, access, confidentiality, technology, intellectual freedom, intellectual property, administration, Internet use, and professional relationships. . . . School librarians and administrators
would do well to have this thought and discussion-
provoking book on hand." SLJ
Includes bibliographical references

174.2   Occupational ethics—Medical professions

Altman, Linda Jacobs, 1943-
    Bioethics; who lives, who dies, and who
decides? Enslow Publishers 2006 112p il (Issues in
focus today) lib bdg $23.95 *
Grades: 7 8 9 10 11 12   **174.2**
    1. Bioethics
    ISBN 0-7660-2546-2; 978-0-7660-2546-2
                            LC 2006-07002
This "provides an overview of the big moral issues
brought about by breakthroughs in biotechnology.
Altman is fair to all sides, whether the passionate argument is about abortion, the cloning of animals, assisted
suicide, artificial life support, or organ transplants. . . .
The readable style and clear, abundantly illustrated de-
sign will stimulate debate." Booklist
Includes glossary and bibliographical references

Black, Laura
    The stem cell debate; the ethics and science
behind the research. Enslow Pubs. 2006 128p il
(Issues in focus today) $31.93 *
Grades: 7 8 9 10 11 12   **174.2**
    1. Stem cell research
    ISBN 0-7660-2545-4; 978-0-7660-2545-5
                            LC 2005-37880
The author "describes what stem cells are, how they
work, and what scientists are trying to make them do.
She explains the arguments on all sides of the stem cell
controversy so that young readers can form their own
opinions." Publisher's note
Includes bibliographical references

Boskey, Elizabeth
    America debates genetic DNA testing. Rosen
Central 2008 64p il (America debates) lib bdg
$29.25
Grades: 7 8 9 10   **174.2**
    1. Genetic screening
    ISBN 978-1-4042-1926-7 (lib bdg); 1-4042-1926-9 (lib
    bdg)   LC 2006-102516
This "book explains genetic testing and examines the
debate over prenatal and adult testing, and the effects
that genetic DNA testing can potentially have on soci-
ety." Publisher's note
The issues "are debated in a clear, concise manner.
. . . Color photographs and boxed information highlight-
ed in red break up the [text]." SLJ
Includes glossary and bibliographical references

Freedman, Jeri
America debates stem cell research. Rosen Central 2008 64p il map (America debates) lib bdg $29.25
Grades: 7 8 9 10   **174.2**
1. Stem cell research
ISBN 978-1-4042-1928-1 (lib bdg); 1-4042-1928-5 (lib bdg)   LC 2007-1036
This book is an "overview of the issues surrounding stem cells and their potential to revolutionize medicine and provide cures, with a focus on the use of embryonic stem cells. The ethical and moral debates over how cells are obtained, the definition of 'personhood,' and various religious perspectives are explored, as well as how politics play a part in the discussion of this issue. It includes a look at stem cell research around the world." Publisher's note
Includes glossary and bibliographical references

Lovegrove, Ray
Health; ethical debates in modern medicine. Black Rabbit Books 2008 c2009 46p il map (Dilemmas in modern science) lib bdg $34.25
Grades: 7 8 9 10   **174.2**
1. Medical ethics
ISBN 978-1-59920-095-8; 1-59920-095-3
                                                       LC 2007-35690
"Presents both sides of modern medical issues, including drug testing, organ transplants, genetic engineering, and stem cell research." Publisher's note
This title is "easy to navigate as evocative photographs, charts, and sidebars help break down complicated arguments into manageable parts for easy digestion." SLJ
Includes glossary and bibliographical references

Marzilli, Alan, 1970-
Stem cell research and cloning. Chelsea House 2007 144p il (Point/counterpoint) lib bdg $35
Grades: 7 8 9 10   **174.2**
1. Stem cell research 2. Cloning
ISBN 978-0-7910-9230-5 (lib bdg); 0-7910-9230-5 (lib bdg)   LC 2006017148
"This book explores the legal and political ramifications of the debates about [stem cell research and cloning], including federal funding for stem cell research, privately funded research, and the government's role in limiting scientific inquiry." Publisher's note
Includes bibliographical references

Uschan, Michael V., 1948-
Forty years of medical racism; the Tuskegee experiments. Lucent Books 2005 112p il map (Lucent library of Black history) lib bdg $28.70
Grades: 8 9 10 11 12   **174.2**
1. Human experimentation in medicine 2. Syphilis 3. African Americans—Health and hygiene
ISBN 1-59018-486-6
This is an account of "the Tuskegee Study of Untreated Syphilis in the Negro Male. . . . Halftone photographs of participants and of the persons who designed, conducted, or criticized the project supplement the text. Informational sidebars provide additional descriptions and

photographs of some of the damage done by untreated syphilis." SLJ
Includes bibliographical references

176   Ethics of sex and reproduction

Cloning; Louise I. Gerdes, book editor. Greenhaven Press 2006 141p il (Introducing issues with opposing viewpoints) $32.45 *
Grades: 7 8 9 10 11 12   **176**
1. Cloning
ISBN 0-7377-3220-2   LC 2005-46292
"In this compilation, authors debate some of the controversies surrounding the cloning of people and animals." Publisher's note
Includes bibliographical references

Cloning; William Dudley, book editor. Greenhaven Press 2005 c2006 112p il (Writing the critical essay) $26.20
Grades: 7 8 9 10   **176**
1. Cloning
ISBN 0-7377-3196-6
"An Opposing viewpoints guide"
This presents essays representing various points of view on the ethics of cloning and includes questions designed to aid the reader in analyzing each essay.
Includes bibliographical references

Perl, Lila
Cloning. Marshall Cavendish Benchmark 2005 c2006 140p il (Open for debate) $25.95
Grades: 7 8 9 10   **176**
1. Cloning
ISBN 0-7614-1884-9
Contents: A human clone in sheep's clothing?; Why create copies of ourselves?; Should human reproductive cloning be banned?; Should we clone human cells to cure illnesses?; Should we try to genetically engineer humans?; Should we continue to clone animals?; What is the future of the genetic revolution?
This discusses the ethics of cloning
Includes glossary and bibliographical references

178   Ethics of consumption

Kerr, Jim
Food; ethical debates on what we eat. Smart Apple Media 2009 46p il map (Dilemmas in modern science) lib bdg $34.25
Grades: 7 8 9 10   **178**
1. Food industry 2. Genetic engineering
ISBN 978-1-59920-094-1; 1-59920-094-5
                                                       LC 2007-39651
"Presents both sides of food production issues, including animal welfare, high-tech farming, genetically modified foods, organic farming, food distribution, and world hunger." Publisher's note
This title is "easy to navigate as evocative photographs, charts, and sidebars help break down complicated arguments into manageable parts for easy digestion." SLJ
Includes glossary and bibliographical references

179 Other ethical norms

Day, Nancy, 1953-
Animal experimentation; cruelty or science? rev ed. Enslow Pubs. 2000 128p il (Issues in focus) lib bdg $26.60
Grades: 7 8 9 10   **179**
1. Animal experimentation 2. Animal rights
ISBN 0-7660-1244-1   LC 99-49334
First published 1994
Discusses issues surrounding animal experimentation, including animal rights, medical breakthroughs, and alternatives to animal experimentaion
"Great for reports or debates." Voice Youth Advocates
Includes glossary and bibliographical references

Judson, Karen, 1941-
Animal testing. Marshall Cavendish Benchmark 2006 144p il (Open for debate) lib bdg $37.07 *
Grades: 7 8 9 10   **179**
1. Animal experimentation 2. Animal rights
ISBN 0-7614-1882-2
This presents a history of animal testing, arguments for and against the use of animals in product safety testing, biomedical research, and education, and describes animal rights organizations and alternatives to animal testing.

Ravilious, Kate
Power; ethical debates about resources and the environment. Black Rabbit Books 2009 46p il map (Dilemmas in modern science) lib bdg $29.25
Grades: 7 8 9   **179**
1. Natural resources—Management 2. Conservation of natural resources
ISBN 978-1-59920-096-5; 1-59920-096-1
                                       LC 2007-35691
"Presents both sides of environmental issues involving natural resources, including environmental ethics, power and energy, renewable resources, transportation and travel, and wood and water use." Publisher's note
This title is "easy to navigate as evocative photographs, charts, and sidebars help break down complicated arguments into manageable parts for easy digestion." SLJ
Includes glossary and bibliographical references

179.7 Respect and disrespect for human life

Death and dying; Jane Langwith, book editor. Greenhaven Press 2008 128p il (Introducing issues with opposing viewpoints) lib bdg $33.70
Grades: 7 8 9 10   **179.7**
1. Death 2. Right to die 3. Future life 4. Bereavement 5. Terminal care—Ethical aspects
ISBN 978-0-7377-3974-9; 0-7377-3974-6
Presents essays covering different viewpoints on death, including the role of religion in death, the possibility of the afterlife, and whether physicians should assist in the process of dying.
Includes bibliographical references

Euthanasia: opposing viewpoints; Carrie L. Snyder, book editor. Greenhaven Press 2006 269p il lib bdg $34.95; pa $23.70
Grades: 7 8 9 10   **179.7**
1. Euthanasia
ISBN 0-7377-2933-3 (lib bdg); 0-7377-2934-1 (pa)
                                       LC 2005-55110
"Opposing viewpoints series"
"The four chapters explore whether euthanasia is ethical, if it should be legalized, if legalization would lead to involuntary killing, and under what circumstances, if any, doctors should assist in suicide." Booklist [review of 2000 edition]
Includes bibliographical references

Rebman, Renee C., 1961-
Euthanasia and the "right to die"; a pro/con issue. Enslow Pubs. 2002 64p il (Hot pro/con issues) lib bdg $27.93
Grades: 7 8 9 10   **179.7**
1. Euthanasia 2. Right to die
ISBN 0-7660-1816-4   LC 2001-5251
The author discusses "the right to die by choice rather than by nature. . . . Rebman steps into the debate by asking what is a 'good death.' . . . She goes on to offer a variety of possible answers without bias, and she paints a historic picture of the controversy and how technology has complicated our definitions of life and death. . . . Objectivity makes this a good reference." Booklist
Includes bibliographical references

Stefoff, Rebecca, 1951-
The right to die. Marshall Cavendish Benchmark 2009 126p il (Open for debate) lib bdg $29.95
Grades: 7 8 9 10   **179.7**
1. Right to die 2. Euthanasia 3. Suicide 4. Medical ethics
ISBN 978-0-7614-2948-7 (lib bdg); 0-7614-2948-4 (lib bdg)   LC 2008000361
This presents arguments for and against euthanasia and assisted suicide in ancient and modern times
Includes bibliographical references

181 Eastern philosophy

Slavicek, Louise Chipley, 1956-
Confucianism. Lucent Bks. 2002 128p il maps (Religions of the world) $27.45
Grades: 6 7 8 9   **181**
1. Confucianism
ISBN 1-56006-984-8   LC 2001-5773
Discusses what Confucianism is, the life, times, and teachings of Confucius, and the spread and practice of Confucianism in modern times
"Informative and well organized. The writing is clear and the 'Works Consulted' lists include a healthy helping of Web sites." SLJ
Includes bibliographical references

Whitfield, Susan

Philosophy and writing. Sharpe Focus 2009 80p il map (Inside ancient China) $34.95

Grades: 7 8 9 10 **181**

1. Chinese philosophy 2. Chinese literature 3. China—Civilization

ISBN 978-0-7656-8168-3; 0-7656-8168-4

LC 2008031167

"Whitfield covers religion and philosophy [of ancient China] and how they have been passed down using various precursors to books and printing. . . . [This is illustrated with] fine and frequent color photographs and reproductions. Readers will be rewarded . . . with clear, accessible writing, peppered liberally with entertaining stories from history." SLJ

Includes glossary and bibliographical references

200 RELIGION

Breuilly, Elizabeth

Religions of the world; the illustrated guide to origins, beliefs, traditions & festivals; [by] Elizabeth Breuilly, Joanne O'Brien, Martin Palmer; consultant editor, Martin E. Marty. rev ed. Facts on File 2005 160p il map $29.95 *

Grades: 7 8 9 10 **200**

1. Religions

ISBN 0-8160-6258-7

LC 2005051101

First published 1997

This "looks at the key issues of faith as it exists today. It includes features on beliefs, traditions, festivals and practices of the major faiths and also looks at and discusses the differences within as well as between the faiths." Publisher's note

This "is a valuable resource, covering the beliefs and practices of 10 major religions and lavishly illustrated with color photos, maps, diagrams, and charts." SLJ

Includes bibliographical references

Buller, Laura

A faith like mine; a celebration of the world's religions . . . seen through the eyes of children. DK 2005 80p il maps $19.99

Grades: 4 5 6 7 **200**

1. Religions

ISBN 0-7566-1177-6

"Buller introduces Hinduism, Islam, Judaism, Christianity, Buddhism, and Sikhism through the eyes of children. . . . The amount of information is adequate and straightforward and focuses on aspects of the religion that would appeal to children. The clear, vibrant photographs are especially inviting." SLJ

Langley, Myrtle

Religion; written by Myrtle Langely; special photography by Ellen Howden . . . [et al.] Rev. ed. DK Pub. 2005 72p il (DK eyewitness books) $15.99; lib bdg $19.99

Grades: 4 5 6 7 **200**

1. Religion

ISBN 978-0-7566-1087-6; 0-7566-1087-7; 978-0-7566-1088-3 (lib bdg); 0-7566-1088-5 (lib bdg)

LC 2005-278287

First published 1996 by Knopf

Introduces the history, philosophies, and rituals of various world religions including Hinduism, Buddhism, Shintoism, Zoroastrianism, and Christianity.

"Text consists of comprehensive, elucidative captions for the eye-catching, full-color photographs, drawings, and reproductions of paintings clustered on the pages. . . . This is a superb, succinct overview of the founders, tenets, and ways of worship of the world's major religions." SLJ

Murphy, Larry

African-American faith in America; [by] Larry G. Murphy. Facts on File 2003 128p il (Faith in America) $30 *

Grades: 7 8 9 10 **200**

1. African Americans—Religion

ISBN 0-8160-4990-4

LC 2002-28593

"In-depth coverage of diverse religious worship practiced among African Americans is presented. Murphy examines popular Christian religions, but also explores Judaism, Islam, Buddhism, and more. The well-written account begins with the religious experiences of the first Africans in America, moves to the establishment of pioneer religious institutions, and culminates with a chapter on the current status of diverse congregations. . . . Students will find ample material on well-known historical figures and current leaders" SLJ

Includes bibliographical references

Osborne, Mary Pope, 1949-

One world, many religions; the ways we worship. Knopf 1996 86p il map $19.95 *

Grades: 4 5 6 7 **200**

1. Religions

ISBN 0-679-83930-5

LC 96-836

This is an "overview of major world religions—Judaism, Christianity, Islam, Hinduism, Buddhism, Confucianism, and Taoism. . . . Each of six essay-styled chapters addresses themes of religious tenets, deities, morality, and ritual only as they are pertinent to a particular faith." Bull Cent Child Books

"The presentation is notable for its respect to each group, succinctness, and clarity. . . . The artful, full-page, color and black-and-white photographs tell much of the story." SLJ

Includes glossary and bibliographical references

The **Wilson** chronology of the world's religions; edited by David Levinson with contributions from John Bowman [et al.] Wilson, H.W. 2000 688p $110

Grades: 8 9 10 11 12 Adult **200**

1. Religion—History—Chronology

ISBN 0-8242-0978-8

LC 99-52362

**The Wilson chronology of the world's reli-
gions**—*Continued*

"The entries cover religion in the prehistoric and ancient world; world religions, sects, and cults; religious
tolerance and intolerance; state religions; and many other
topics. The chronology is supplemented by 250 informational sidebars which provide coverage of religions and
sects, religious leaders, texts, and major events." Publisher's note

Includes bibliographical references

200.3   Religion—Encyclopedias and dictionaries

The **encyclopedia** of world religions; Robert S.
Ellwood, general editor; Gregory D. Alles,
associate editor. Rev. ed. Facts on File 2006
514p il map (Facts on File library of religion
and mythology) $50
Grades: 7 8 9 10 11 12   **200.3**
1. Religions—Encyclopedias 2. Reference books
ISBN 0-8160-6141-6; 978-0-8160-6141-9
LC 2005-56750
First published 1998

This encyclopedia "covers all the major and minor religions of the world, including the religions of the ancient world; the major religions practiced around the
world today; religions of contemporary indigenous peoples; definitions of religious symbols and ideas; key leaders and thinkers; and terms and definitions." Publisher's
note

Includes bibliographical references

200.9   Historical, geographic, persons treatment

Braude, Ann
Women and American religion; Jon Butler &
Harry S. Stout, general editors. Oxford University
Press 2000 141p il (Religion in American life) lib
bdg $28 *
Grades: 7 8 9 10   **200.9**
1. Women—Religious life 2. United States—Religion
ISBN 0-19-510676-8   LC 99-32968

Braude discusses "how women from various groups,
including African Americans, immigrants, and social cru-
saders, shaped the face of religion in the U.S. . . . Included are individuals such as colonist Margaret Winthrop and African American preacher Jarena Lee, as well
as religious leaders such as Mary Baker Eddy and Mother Elizabeth Seaton. Black-and-white illustrations and
historical engravings pepper the text." Booklist

Includes bibliographical references

Fridell, Ron, 1943-
Religious fundamentalism. Marshall Cavendish
Benchmark 2009 144p il (Open for debate) $29.95
Grades: 7 8 9 10   **200.9**
1. Religious fundamentalism 2. Christianity 3. Islam
ISBN 978-0-7614-2945-6; 0-7614-2945-X
LC 2008000364

This examines religious fundamentalism in Christianity
and Islam.

Includes bibliographical references

Religion in America: opposing viewpoints; Mary
E. Williams, book editor. Greenhaven Press
2006 224p il (Opposing viewpoints series) lib
bdg $34.95; pa $23.70 *
Grades: 7 8 9 10   **200.9**
1. United States—Religion
ISBN 0-7377-2957-0 (lib bdg); 0-7377-2958-9 (pa)
LC 2005-40386

Replaces the edition published 2002 under the
editorship of William Dudley

"Contributors provide . . . views on both the private
religious attitudes of Americans and the social signifi-
cance of religious belief in the following chapters: Is
America a Religious Nation? What Effect Does Religion
Have on American Society? What Should Be Done to
Accommodate Religious Freedom in America? What
Values Should Religious Americans Support?" Publish-
er's note

Includes bibliographical references

201   Religious mythology, general classes of religion, interreligious relations and attitudes, social theology

Glick, Susan
War and peace; by Susan Glick. Lucent Books
2004 112p il map (Discovering mythology) $28.70
Grades: 6 7 8 9   **201**
1. Mythology 2. War 3. Peace
ISBN 1-56006-903-1   LC 2004-6290

Contents: Ancient battles between the Babylonian
gods of creation; Power struggles in the Aegean; Warrior
magic and the Celtic otherworld; War and peace in the
wild land of the giants; Vishnu and other demon-fighters
of Hindu myth; The hero twins and their fight against
the forces of the darkness

This examines the meaning and cultural significance
behind the myths concerning war and peace in ancient
world cultures

Includes bibliographical references

Hamilton, Virginia, 1936-2002
In the beginning; creation stories from around
the world; told by Virginia Hamilton; illustrated
by Barry Moser. Harcourt Brace Jovanovich 1988
161p il hardcover o.p. pa $20 *
Grades: 5 6 7 8   **201**
1. Creation 2. Mythology
ISBN 0-15-238740-4; 0-15-238742-0 (pa)
LC 88-6211

"Hamilton has gathered 25 creation myths from various cultures and retold them in language true to the original. Images from the tales are captured in Moser's 42
full-page illustrations, tantalizing oil paintings that are
rich with somber colors and striking compositions. Included in the collection are the familiar stories (biblical

Hamilton, Virginia, 1936-2002—*Continued*
creation stories, Greek and Roman myths), and some that
are not so familiar (tales from the Australian aborigines,
various African and native American tribes, as well as
from countries like Russia, China, and Iceland). At the
end of each tale, Hamilton provides a brief commentary
on the story's origin and originators." Booklist
Includes bibliographical references

Kallen, Stuart A., 1955-
Shamans; by Stuart A. Kallen. Lucent Books
2004 112p il (Mystery library) $28.70
Grades: 6 7 8 9   201
1. Shamanism
ISBN 1-59018-628-1   LC 2004-12665
Contents: Introduction: The mystery of Shamanism;
An enduring tradition; Communicating with the spirits;
Shamanistic healing; Shamans who kill; Shamans in a
new age
"The methods employed by shamans to visit the realm
of spirits in order to learn how to effect cures are described in some detail. . . . Activities of Siberian and
North, Central, and South American shamans receive the
most attention. Chinese, Australian aboriginal, Green-
lander, ancient Greek, and a few other practitioners are
mentioned. . . . Halftone photographs make textual descriptions real while numerous shaded sidebars offer considerable supplementary material. . . . This title provides
a varied, understandable introduction to the spiritual side
of many human cultures." SLJ
Includes bibliographical references

Mass, Wendy, 1967-
Gods and goddesses. Lucent Bks. 2002 112p
(Discovering mythology) $27.45
Grades: 6 7 8 9   201
1. Gods and goddesses 2. Mythology
ISBN 1-56006-852-3   LC 2001-5775
Examines the origins and nature of Egyptian, Hindu,
Celtic, Greek, Roman, Viking, and Aztec gods and god-
desses as revealed in the mythologies of these cultures
"This is a good overview for study of mythology that
may spark interest in further study." Book Rep
Includes bibliographical references

McIntosh, Kenneth, 1959-
When religion & politics mix; how matters of
faith influence political policies; by Kenneth
McIntosh, M.Div., and Marsha McIntosh. Mason
Crest Publishers 2005 112p il (Religion and
modern culture) $22.95 *
Grades: 7 8 9 10   201
1. Church and state—United States 2. Religion and
politics
ISBN 1-59084-971-X; 978-1-59084-971-2
LC 2005-3057
This is an "overview of where U.S. voters stand on
the relevance of religion in their personal and public
lives. The book explores topics such as abortion, same-
sex marriage, and stem cell research, and it compares religious views in the U.S. with Canada's more secular
perspectives. . . . [The book provides] a lucid perspec-

tive on different beliefs within and beyond various religions." Booklist
Includes bibliographical references

Wilkinson, Philip, 1955-
Illustrated dictionary of mythology; heroes,
heroines, gods, and goddesses from around the
world; written by Philip Wilkinson; consultant,
Neil Philip. DK Pub. 1998 128p il map hardcover
o.p. pa $12.95
Grades: 7 8 9 10   201
1. Mythology—Dictionaries 2. Reference books
ISBN 0-7894-3413-X; 978-0-7566-2017-2 (pa)
LC 98-22992
This volume describes myths and deities from cultures
around the world divided into nine geographic regions
including Japan, North America, Australia, Greece and
Rome. 2000 illustrations accompany the text

World mythology; the illustrated guide; Roy
Willis, general editor. Oxford University Press
2006 311p il map pa $22.50
Grades: 8 9 10 11 12   201
1. Mythology
ISBN 0-19-530752-6; 978-0-19-530752-8
LC 2005-30779
First published 1993 by Holt & Co.
This book describes "the myths of Egypt, the Middle
East, India, China, Tibet, Mongolia, Japan, Greece,
Rome, the Celtic lands, Northern and Eastern Europe, the
Arctic, North and South America, Mesoamerica, Africa,
Australia, Oceania, and Southeast Asia." Libr J [review
of 1993 edition]
Includes bibliographical references

201.03   Religious mythology— Encyclopedias and dictionaries

UXL Encyclopedia of world mythology. UXL
2009 5v il set $314
Grades: 7 8 9 10 11 12   201.03
1. Mythology—Encyclopedias 2. Reference books
ISBN 978-1-41443-030-0; 1-41443-030-2
LC 2008-12696
"In A-Z format, the set provides more than 300 entries
for five content areas: characters, deities, myths, themes,
and cultures. . . . The entries generally range from three
to four pages. . . . Recommended for middle- and high-
school libraries." Booklist

204   Religious experience, life, practice

In the house of happiness; a book of prayers and
praise; selected by Neil Philip; illustrated by
Isabelle Brent. Clarion Bks. 2003 unp il $17 *
Grades: 6 7 8 9   204
1. Prayers
ISBN 0-618-23481-0   LC 2002-10269

In the house of happiness—*Continued*

A collection of short prayers from major religions—Christianity, Judaism, Hinduism, Buddhism, and Islam—along with tribal chants, folk rhymes, and poems of praise and devotion

"The beautiful art encourages readers to pick up the book. Brent, who was inspired by the *Book of Hours*, lavishly employs illumination to highlight her pictures of nature. . . . This book offers the opportunity for quiet moments of reflection in a lovely setting." Booklist

209   Sects and reform movements

Stein, Stephen J.

Alternative American religions. Oxford Univ. Press 1999 156p il (Religion in American life) lib bdg $28

Grades: 7 8 9 10   **209**

1. Sects 2. Cults 3. United States—Religion

ISBN 0-19-511196-6   LC 99-42370

Examines various alternative religions, or New Religious Movements, that have existed in the United States from colonial times through the twentieth century and from the perspectives of both insiders and outsiders

"The tone throughout is nonjudgmental and the emphasis is on people and their ideas. Black-and-white photos and reproductions add information and perspective to the presentation." SLJ

220   Bible

Brown, Alan

The Bible and Christianity; by Alan Brown. Smart Apple Media 2003 30p il (Sacred texts) $27.10

Grades: 5 6 7 8   **220**

1. Bible (as subject) 2. Christianity

ISBN 1-58340-243-8   LC 2003-41645

Explains how the Old and New Testaments came to be part of the Bible used by Christians and discusses some of the important messages found in the holy scriptures.

"Colorful strips of symbolic patterns adorn the pages and accent the informative text boxes. . . . The clear captioned . . . illustrations (photos and historical art) provide additional background." Horn Book Guide

Includes glossary

220.3   Bible—Encyclopedias and topical dictionaries

The **Oxford** companion to the Bible; edited by Bruce M. Metzger, Michael D. Coogan. Oxford Univ. Press 1993 xxi, 874p il map $70

Grades: 8 9 10 11 12 Adult   **220.3**

1. Bible (as subject)—Dictionaries 2. Reference books

ISBN 0-19-504645-5   LC 93-19315

This volume "contains more than 700 signed entries treating the formation, transmission, circulation, sociohistorical situation, interpretation, theology, uses,

and influence of the Bible." Libr J

"The many contributors read as a veritable who's who among biblical scholars. Although this companion is not meant to be an exhaustive reference, it is a highly reliable guide." Booklist

220.5   Bible—Modern versions and translations

Bible.

The Bible: Authorized King James Version; with an introduction and notes by Robert Carroll and Stephen Prickett. Oxford University Press 1998 lxxiv, 1039, 248, 445p il map (Oxford world's classics) pa $18.95

Grades: 5 6 7 8 9 10 11 12 Adult   **220.5**

ISBN 0-19-283525-4; 978-0-19-283525-3

LC 96-28858

"Reissued as an Oxford world's classics paperback 1998" Verso of title page

The authorized or King James Version originally published 1611

Includes bibliographical references

Good news Bible; today's English version. American Bible Soc. 2006 $10.99

Grades: 8 9 10 11 12 Adult   **220.5**

ISBN 978-1-58516-154-6; 1-58516-154-3

"Begun in 1964 with the Gospel of Mark, The New Testament was completed in 1966, with rev. eds. in 1971 and 1976. The whole Bible was published in 1976. An extremely popular, inexpensive translation using contemporary American English. . . . Especially useful for youth or lay Bible study as well as for private reading." Bollier. Lit of Theology

The **Holy** Bible; containing the Old and New Testaments with the Apocryphal/Deuterocanonical books: New Revised Standard Version. Oxford University Press 1989 xxi, 996, 298, 284p map $29.99

Grades: 5 6 7 8 9 10 11 12 Adult   **220.5**

ISBN 0-19-528330-9; 978-0-19-528330-3

LC 90-222105

"Intended for public reading, congregational worship, private study, instruction, and meditation, it attempts to be as literal as possible while following standard American English usage, avoids colloquialism, and prefers simple, direct terms and phrases." Sheehy. Guide to Ref Books. 10th edition. suppl

The **New** American Bible; translated from the original languages with critical use of all the ancient sources including the revised Psalms and the revised New Testament; authorized by the Board of Trustees of the Confraternity of Christian Doctrine and approved by the Administrative Committee Board of the National Conference of Catholic Bishops and the United States Catholic Conference. Oxford University Press 2006 c2005 xxiii, 1514p $39.99

Grades: 8 9 10 11 12 Adult   **220.5**

Bible.—*Continued*
ISBN 978-0-19-528900-8; 0-19-528900-5
First published 1970 by Kenedy
"Roman Catholic version based on modern English translations; replaces the Douay edition." N Y Public Libr Book of How & Where to Look It Up

The new Jerusalem Bible; [general editor: Henry Wansbrough] Doubleday 1985 2108p map $45; pa $29.95
Grades: 7 8 9 10 11 12 Adult   **220.5**
ISBN   0-385-14264-1;   978-0-385-14264-9;
0-385-24833-4 (pa); 978-0-385-24833-4 (pa)
LC 85-16070
First published in this format 1966 with title: The Jerusalem Bible
"Derives from the French version edited at the Dominican Ecole Biblique de Jerusalem and known as 'La Bible de Jerusalem.' The introductions and notes are 'a direct translation from the French, though revised and brought up to date in some places' but translation of the Biblical text goes back to the original languages." Guide to Ref Books. 11th edition

220.9   Bible—Geography, history, chronology, persons of Bible lands in Bible times

Daughters of the desert; stories of remarkable women from Christian, Jewish, and Muslim traditions; [by] Claire Rudolf Murphy . . . [et al.] SkyLight Paths Pub. 2003 178p $19.95 *
Grades: 7 8 9 10   **220.9**
1. Bible 2. Women in the Bible 3. Women in the Koran 4. Bible stories
ISBN 1-89336-172-1   LC 2002-153821
"Using sacred writings as their basis, the five women authors have reshaped the stories of such individuals as Sarah, Mary Magdalene, Eve, and Khadiji, the wife of Mohammed. . . . The stories are short and simply told, but they are intriguing and invite discussion." Booklist
Includes bibliographical references

Lottridge, Celia Barker
Stories from Adam and Eve to Ezekiel; retold from the Bible; by Celia Barker Lottridge; illustrated by Gary Clement. Douglas & McIntyre/Groundwood 2004 192p il $24.95
Grades: 4 5 6 7   **220.9**
1. Bible stories
ISBN 0-88899-490-7
"Lottridge uses her storyteller's ear to bring ancient stories from the Hebrew Bible to a young audience, tailoring them to make them more age appropriate. . . . The numerous, well-drawn ink-and-watercolor illustrations are reminiscent of Warwick Hutton's work. Some pictures . . . are quite spectacular." Booklist

Tubb, Jonathan N.
Bible lands. Dorling Kindersley 2000 63p il map (DK eyewitness books) $15.99; lib bdg $19.99
Grades: 4 5 6 7   **220.9**
1. Bible—Antiquities 2. Bible (as subject)—Antiquities
ISBN 0-7894-5770-9; 0-7694-6579-5 (lib bdg)
Photographs and text document life in Biblical times, surveying the clothing, food, and civilizations of a wide variety of cultures, including the Israelites, Babylonians, Persians, and Romans.

221.9   Bible. Old Testament— Geography, history, stories

Ward, Elaine M.
Old Testament women; [by] Elaine Ward. Enchanted Lion 2004 32p il (Art revelations) $18.95
Grades: 5 6 7 8   **221.9**
1. Women in the Bible 2. Bible stories
ISBN 1-59270-011-X
These Old Testament stories about women include "explanatory paragraphs, sidebars, and captions by the author. Art masterpieces . . . illustrate each story. . . . The captions provide background on the artist and the significance of each painting or mosaic. . . . The 18 women . . . include Rachel, Leah, Ruth, and Bathsheba. . . . Bosch, Botticelli, and Poussin are among the painters whose work appears here. . . . Visually stunning." SLJ

222   Historical books of Old Testament

Bible. O.T. Pentateuch.
The contemporary Torah; a gender-sensitive adaptation of the JPS translation; revising editor, David E.S. Stein; consulting editors, Adele Berlin, Ellen Frankel, and Carol L. Meyers. Jewish Publication Society 2006 xlii, 412p $28
Grades: 8 9 10 11 12 Adult   **222**
ISBN 0-8276-0796-2; 978-0-8276-0796-5
LC 2006-40608
A modern adaptation of the Jewish Publication Society's translation of the Torah. "In places where the ancient audience probably would not have construed gender as pertinent to the text's plain sense, the editors changed words into gender-neutral terms; where gender was probably understood to be at stake, they left the text as originally translated, or even introduced gendered language where none existed before. They made these changes regardless of whether words referred to God, angels, or human beings." Publisher's note

The Torah: the five books of Moses; a new translation of the Holy Scriptures according to the Masoretic text; first section. Jewish Publication Society 1963 393p $20; pa $15
Grades: 8 9 10 11 12 Adult   **222**

Bible. O.T. Pentateuch.—*Continued*

ISBN 0-8276-0015-1; 0-8276-0680-X (pa)

This "translation of Genesis, Exodus, Leviticus, Numbers, and Deuteronomy was prepared . . . to present a version of the Bible that takes into account modern insights and knowledge of ancient times. . . . Of chief value to persons of the Jewish religion but of interest to Bible scholars of any religion." Booklist

Feiler, Bruce S.

Walking the Bible; an illustrated journey for kids through the greatest stories ever told; by Bruce Feiler; illustrated by Sasha Meret. 1st ed. HarperCollinsPublishers 2004 108p il map $16.99; lib bdg $17.89 *

Grades: 5 6 7 8   **222**

1. Middle East 2. Bible (as subject)

ISBN 0-06-051117-6; 0-06-051118-4 (lib bdg)

LC 2003-15861

Contents: Walking the Bible; Creating the world; Noah's ark; Abraham; Abraham in the promised land; Abraham and Isaac; Joseph in Egypt; Moses parts the Red Sea; The burning bush; Climbing Mt. Sinai

The author describes his journey through places mentioned in the Old Testament

"In this version of his adult book with the same title (Morrow, 2001), Feiler largely succeeds in slimming rather than dumbing down his account of his trip across the 10,000-mile setting of the earliest Bible stories. The author's unpretentious . . . tone and astute pacing help make the volume accessible, and his sincerity is palpable." SLJ

Fischer, Chuck

In the beginning: the art of Genesis; a pop-up book; by Chuck Fischer. Little, Brown 2008 unp il $35 *

Grades: 5 6 7 8   **222**

1. Bible. O.T. Genesis 2. Bible stories 3. Pop-up books 4. Religious art

ISBN 978-0-316-11842-2; 0-316-11842-7

LC 2007045411

Fischer "presents an impressive, three-dimensional view of the Book of Genesis. . . . Fischer and his collaborators offer a Garden of Eden scene executed in an artistic style that recalls ancient tile work; a huge Noah's Ark landed atop a mountain; and a Tower of Babel impressively high. . . . The text, more commentary than story, is hidden in inset mini-books and is accompanied by reproductions of biblical masterpieces. . . . This book becomes more amazing as the pages are turned." Booklist

223 Poetic books of Old Testament

Bible. O.T. Ecclesiastes.

To every thing there is a season; verses from Ecclesiastes; illustrations by Leo and Diane Dillon. Blue Sky Press (NY) 1998 unp il $16.95 *

Grades: 4 5 6 7 8   **223**

ISBN 0-590-47887-7   LC 97-35124

Presents that selection from Ecclesiastes which relates that everything in life has its own time and season

"The Dillons compellingly convey the relevance of the Ecclesiastes verse throughout history, via a stunning array of artwork that embraces motifs from cultures the world over." Publ Wkly

226 Gospels and Acts

Connolly, Sean, 1956-

New Testament miracles. 1st American ed. Enchanted Lion Books 2004 32p il (Art revelations) $18.95

Grades: 7 8 9 10   **226**

1. Miracles—Christianity 2. Christian art

ISBN 1-59270-012-8   LC 2003-49414

"The 12 miracles discussed . . . include Jesus healing the man born blind, Jesus raising Lazarus from the dead, and the conversion of Paul. Each one is told from verses in the four Gospels or the Book of Acts, with explanatory paragraphs, sidebars, and captions by the author. Art masterpieces . . . illustrate each story. Works by El Greco, Rembrandt, Tintoretto, and Witz, among others, are featured. . . . Visually stunning." SLJ

230 Christianity & Christian theology

Lace, William W.

Christianity; by William W. Lace. Lucent Books 2004 128p il map (Religions of the world) $28.70

Grades: 6 7 8 9   **230**

1. Christianity

ISBN 1-59018-141-7   LC 2004-10844

Contents: Birth and growth; Persecution to prominence; Heresy and schism; Power and perversion; Reformation and counter reformation; Expansion and enlightenment; Beliefs and worship; Christianity in the new millennium

This offers a history of Christianity, outlining the life of Jesus, Saint Paul's role in spreading the faith, the rise of Christianity, persecutions, heresies, and schisms, the Reformation and Counter-Reformation, world expansion of the faith, beliefs and worship, and Christian faiths today.

Includes bibliographical references

Self, David

Christianity; [by] David Self. World Almanac Library 2005 48p il map (Religions of the world) lib bdg $30 *

Grades: 5 6 7 8   **230**

1. Christianity

ISBN 0-8368-5866-2   LC 2005041712

This is a summary of the Christian religion including history, beliefs, worship, festivals, practice, and current disagreements.

"Wonderfully colorful in images, language, and fact. . . . [This is] enumerated with full-color photographs on every page, charts, maps, and tables." SLJ

Includes bibliographical references

232.9 Family and life of Jesus

Lottridge, Celia Barker
Stories from the life of Jesus; retold from the Bible by Celia Barker Lottridge; illustrated by Linda Wolfsgruber. Doulgas & McIntyre 2004 140p il $24.95
Grades: 4 5 6 7   **232.9**
1. Jesus Christ 2. Bible stories
ISBN 0-88899-497-4
"A Groundwood book"
A retelling of selected events from the life of Christ based on biblical accounts
This is an "exceptional collection. . . . Each story is retold in three or four pages of clear, concise prose that is meant to be read aloud. . . . Each selection is enhanced by dramatic and atmospheric, mixed-media illustrations that are executed in warm earth tones." SLJ

274 Christian Church in Europe

Hinds, Kathryn, 1962-
The church. Benchmark Bks. 2004 95p il (Life in the Renaissance) lib bdg $20.95 *
Grades: 6 7 8 9   **274**
1. Reformation 2. Renaissance 3. Europe—Church history
ISBN 0-7614-1679-X   LC 2003-8258
Contents: Christian roots and branches; Power and protest; Community life; Men of God; Women and the church; Holy days and every day; Learning tolerance
A description of the religious controversies of the Renaissance and Reformation with a focus on what life was like for ordinary people, both Catholic and Protestant
"Informative and beautifully illustrated. . . . Quality period reproductions of paintings and clear, color photos appear throughout." SLJ
Includes glossary and bibliographical references

The church. Benchmark Books 2001 80p il (Life in the Middle Ages) lib bdg $32.79 *
Grades: 6 7 8 9   **274**
1. Middle Ages 2. Europe—Church history
ISBN 0-7614-1008-2   LC 00-37849
This "provides a brief overview of the tenets of Christianity and the organization of the Church, the parish, and the diocese and its governance. The hierarchy and training of the various roles within the Church are described for both men and women as are the daily routines and rules that regulated these lives. Heresies and religious intolerance are also mentioned. [The text is] enriched by excerpts from the literature of this era. Quality period reproductions of paintings and clear, color photos appear throughout." SLJ
Includes glossary and bibliographical references

The church; [by] Kathryn Hinds. Marshall Cavendish Benchmark 2007 80p il (Life in Elizabethan England) lib bdg $32.79 *
Grades: 6 7 8 9 10 11 12   **274**
1. Church of England 2. Great Britain—History—1485-1603, Tudors 3. Great Britain—Religion
ISBN 978-0-7614-2545-8   LC 2007-9392

This describes the role of the Church of England in Elizabethan society, discussing the church's role in the community, the roles of men and women in the church, the church's role in life stages, and holy days.
This offers "good-quality, full-color reproductions. . . . The attractive, open format and the engaging presentation of the subject matter, combined with documented primary-source quotations and sidebars . . . will appeal to both researchers and those who are just interested in learning more about this period." SLJ
Includes glossary and bibliographical references

280 Christian denominations

Brown, Stephen F.
Protestantism. 3rd ed. Chelsea House 2009 144p il map (World religions) $40
Grades: 7 8 9 10 11 12   **280**
1. Protestantism
ISBN 978-1-60413-112-3; 1-60413-112-8
                                          LC 2008029659
First published 1991 by Facts on File
This "explores the origins, customs, and history of Protestantism, from its beginnings in the Middle Ages to its role in today's world. Current issues, such as the development of new religious denominations, its stance on abortion, the ordination of gays and women, and the relationship between religion and politics, are explored within the framework of the fundamental moral tenets of the faith." Publisher's note
Includes bibliographical references

Noll, Mark A., 1946-
Protestants in America; general editors, Jon Butler and Harry S. Stout. Oxford University Press 2000 155p il (Religion in American life) lib bdg $28 *
Grades: 7 8 9 10   **280**
1. Protestant churches
ISBN 0-19-511034-X   LC 00-27271
Discusses the origins of Protestantism, the diversity of Protestant churches in the United States, and the role of Protestants in American life from colonial times to the present
"This volume is especially valuable for its discussion of the church in the African-American community and its coverage of smaller sects, like the Shakers. The many black-and-white photographs and reproduction add immensely to the text." SLJ
Includes bibliographical references

289.3 Latter-Day Saints (Mormons)

Bial, Raymond
Nauvoo; Mormon city on the Mississippi River; [by] Raymond Bial. Houghton Mifflin Co. 2006 44p il map $17
Grades: 5 6 7 8   **289.3**
1. Mormons 2. Church of Jesus Christ of Latter-day Saints 3. Illinois—History
ISBN 978-0-618-39685-6; 0-618-39685-3
                                          LC 2005027528

Bial, Raymond—*Continued*

"Bial introduces readers to a city that was established by the Church of Jesus Christ of Latter Day Saints in 1839. . . . This effectively written account provides a sympathetic but balanced introduction to Mormon beliefs. . . . Excellent color photographs grace almost every page." SLJ

Book of Mormon.

The Book of Mormon; another testament of Jesus Christ; [translated by Joseph Smith, Jr.] Doubleday 2004 586p $24.95 *

Grades: 8 9 10 11 12 Adult   **289.3**

1. Mormons 2. Church of Jesus Christ of Latter-day Saints

ISBN 0-385-51316-X   LC 2004-51982

Also available in other bindings and editions

First published 1830

"Based on golden plates which Joseph Smith claimed were revealed to him, and which he unearthed from Cumorah Hill, New York, this book is roughly similar in structure to the Bible. . . . Emphasized are the doctrines of pre-existence, perfection, the afterlife, and Christ's second coming." Haydn. Thesaurus of Book Dig

Bushman, Claudia L.

Mormons in America; [by] Claudia Lauper Bushman and Richard Lyman Bushman. Oxford Univ. Press 1998 142p il (Religion in American life) $28 *

Grades: 7 8 9 10   **289.3**

1. Mormons 2. Church of Jesus Christ of Latter-day Saints

ISBN 0-19-510677-6   LC 98-18605

Chronicles the history of the Church of Jesus Christ of Latter-Day Saints beginning in America in the early 1800s and continuing to the present day throughout the world

"A solid resource for libraries. Illustrated with historical material and black-and-white photos. Time line and bibliography appended." Booklist

Includes bibliographical references

292   Classical religion (Greek and Roman religion)

Fleischman, Paul

Dateline: Troy; [by] Paul Fleischman; collages by Gwen Frankfeldt & Glenn Morrow. new updated ed. Candlewick Press 2006 80p il $18.99 *

Grades: 7 8 9 10   **292**

1. Trojan War

ISBN 978-0-7636-3083-6; 0-7636-3083-7

First published 1996

A retelling of the story of the Trojan War illustrated with collages featuring newspaper clippings of modern events from World War I through the Iraq War

Hamilton, Edith, 1867-1963

Mythology; illustrated by Steele Savage. Little, Brown 1942 497p il $27.95; pa $13.95

Grades: 8 9 10 11 12 Adult   **292**

1. Classical mythology 2. Norse mythology

ISBN 0-316-34114-2; 0-316-34151-7 (pa)

Contents: The gods, the creation and the earliest heroes; Stories of love and adventure; Great heroes before the Trojan War; Heroes of the Trojan War; Great families of mythology; Less important myths; Mythology of the Norsemen; Genealogical tables

A retelling of Greek, Roman and Norse myths

Hinds, Kathryn, 1962-

Religion. Benchmark Books 2004 c2005 87p il (Life in the Roman empire) lib bdg $20.95

Grades: 6 7 8 9   **292**

1. Rome—Religion 2. Rome—Civilization

ISBN 0-7614-1657-9   LC 2004-8400

Contents: A world of gods and spirits; Beliefs and ceremonies; Sacred places; Religious roles for men; Women and worship; Through life's stages; Roman holiday; Conflict and tolerance

This considers the religion of the Roman empire, describing beliefs in gods and spirits, ceremonies and sacred places, religious roles of men and women, and religious conflict and tolerance.

Includes glossary and bibliographical references

McCaughrean, Geraldine, 1951-

Hercules; retold by Geraldine McCaughrean. Cricket Books 2005 142p il (Heroes) $16.95 *

Grades: 5 6 7 8   **292**

1. Hercules (Legendary character) 2. Classical mythology

ISBN 978-0-8126-2737-4; 0-8126-2737-7

     LC 2005004524

First published 2003 by Oxford University Press

This is a retelling of the twelve labors of Hercules including his battles with the Cretan Bull, the many-headed Hydra, the Nemean Lion, and the three-headed guardian of hell, Cerberus.

"This volume does a creditable job of making Hercules a dimensional character whose struggles against fate and the vindictiveness of the gods arouse readers' sympathy. . . . McCaughrean enlivens the familiar story with arresting imagery." SLJ

Odysseus; retold by Geraldine McCaughrean. 1st American ed. Cricket Books 2004 148p il (Heroes) $16.95 *

Grades: 5 6 7 8   **292**

1. Odysseus (Greek mythology) 2. Classical mythology

ISBN 978-0-8126-2721-3; 0-8126-2721-0

     LC 2004-10734

This is a retelling of the "adventures of Odysseus, including his encounters with the evil Cyclops, the monsters Scylla and Charybdis, the beautiful sorceress Circe, and . . . Poseidon." Publisher's note

"With mounting suspense, wild action, and simple, rhythmic prose, this dramatic retelling of Homer's classic makes a gripping read-aloud as well as an exciting introduction to the story." Booklist

McCaughrean, Geraldine, 1951-—Continued

Perseus; retold by Geraldine McCaughrean. Cricket Books 2005 118p (Heroes) $16.95 *
Grades: 5 6 7 8   292
   1. Perseus (Greek mythology) 2. Classical mythology
   ISBN 978-0-8126-2735-0; 0-8126-2735-0
This follows the story of "Perseus as he lives the fate the oracles have declared, an impossible quest to kill the hideous, snake-haired Medusa to save his mother from marriage to an evil king." Publisher's note
   This "makes a thrilling read-aloud. . . . McCaughrean blends the colloquial and contemporary into the heroic quest." Booklist

Nardo, Don, 1947-

The Greenhaven encyclopedia of Greek and Roman mythology; Don Nardo, author; Barbette Spaeth, consulting editor. Greenhaven Press 2002 304p il (Greenhaven encyclopedia of) lib bdg $76.20
Grades: 7 8 9 10   292
   1. Classical mythology
   ISBN 0-7377-0719-4   LC 2001-40864
This is an overview of classical mythology, its heroes, and its influence on the history of Western civilization
   Includes bibliographical references

Rylant, Cynthia

The beautiful stories of life; six Greek myths, retold; illustrated by Carson Ellis. Harcourt 2009 71p il $16
Grades: 5 6 7 8   292
   1. Classical mythology
   ISBN 978-0-15-206184-5; 0-15-206184-3
             LC 2007-34808
"Rylant retells the stories of Pandora, Persephone, Orpheus, Pygmalion, Narcissus, and Psyche in this trim, handsome book. Written in a modern style with an old-fashioned feel, the selections sit well with other titles in the genre. . . . Accompanied by full-page black-and-white illustrations and sprinkled with decorations, the whole package is nicely done." SLJ

Schomp, Virginia, 1953-

The ancient Greeks; [by] Virginia Schomp. Marshall Cavendish Benchmark 2007 c2008 96p il map (Myths of the world) lib bdg $22.95
Grades: 6 7 8 9   292
   1. Classical mythology 2. Greece—Civilization
   ISBN 978-0-7614-2547-2   LC 2006028375
"A retelling of several key ancient Greek myths, with background information describing the history, geography, belief systems, and customs of the ancient Greeks." Publisher's note
   "With [its] beautiful illustrations, high-quality production, and focus on source material, the [book] should whet the interest of readers." SLJ
   Includes glossary and bibliographical references

The ancient Romans; [by] Virginia Schomp. Marshall Cavendish Benchmark 2008 96p il map (Myths of the world) lib bdg $23.93
Grades: 6 7 8 9   292
   1. Classical mythology 2. Rome—Civilization
   ISBN 978-0-7614-3094-0; 0-7614-3094-6
             LC 2008007083
"A retelling of several key ancient Roman myths, with background information describing the history, geography, belief systems, and customs of ancient Rome." Publisher's note
   Includes glossary and bibliographical references

Smith, Charles R., 1969-

The mighty 12; superheroes of Greek myth; by Charles R. Smith, Jr.; illustrated by P. Craig Russell. 1st ed. Little, Brown 2008 48p il $16.99
Grades: 5 6 7 8   292
   1. Classical mythology 2. Gods and goddesses
   ISBN 978-0-316-01043-6; 0-316-01043-X
             LC 2007048729
"Future students of Homer get a handy checklist of musclebound Greek gods in this combo of mythology, comics and loose rhyme. . . . Smith and Russell make the pairing of classical material and a comics-like format look completely natural, with a gee-why-didn't-we-think-of-that simplicity." Publ Wkly
   Includes bibliographical references

293   Germanic religion

Porterfield, Jason

Scandinavian mythology; [by] Jason Porterfield. 1st ed. Rosen Pub. Group 2008 64p il map (Mythology around the world) lib bdg $29.95
Grades: 5 6 7 8   293
   1. Norse mythology 2. Scandinavia—Civilization
   ISBN 978-1-4042-0740-0 (lib bdg); 1-4042-0740-6 (lib bdg)   LC 2005037508
The author describes the history of "the Scandinavian nations, introducing concepts and characters central to Norse myths. . . . The most remarkable part of [this book] . . . is the respect [it shows] for the mythological customs, treating them throughout with the same care that writers of books on major religions might offer. The illustrations show both ancient and modern incarnations of the deities and heroes described in the [text]." SLJ
   Includes glossary and bibliographical references

Schomp, Virginia, 1953-

The Norsemen; [by] Virginia Schomp. Marshall Cavendish Benchmark 2007 c2008 96p il map (Myths of the world) lib bdg $22.95
Grades: 6 7 8 9   293
   1. Norse mythology 2. Scandinavia—Civilization
   ISBN 978-0-7614-2548-9   LC 2007002772
"A retelling of several key early Scandinavian myths, with backround information describing the history, geography, belief system, and customs of the Norse World." Publisher's note
   "With [its] beautiful illustrations, high-quality produc-

Schomp, Virginia, 1953-—_Continued_
tion, and focus on source material, the [book] should
whet the interest of readers." SLJ
Includes bibliographical references

294   Religions of Indic origin

Hoffman, Nancy, 1955-
Sikhism. Lucent Books 2006 128p il map
(Religions of the world) $28.70 *
Grades: 6 7 8 9 10   **294**
   1. Sikhism
   ISBN 1-59018-453-X
"Using a basic chronological scheme for organization,
this resource contains themed chapters that provide . . .
information for the general reader wishing to learn about
the basic history, development, and beliefs of [Sikhism]."
Voice Youth Advocates
   "The information is precise, statistics are accurate, and
the organization is excellent." SLJ
Includes bibliographical references

Mann, Gurinder Singh
Buddhists, Hindus, and Sikhs in America; [by]
Gurinder Singh Mann, Paul David Numrich &
Raymond B. Williams. Oxford University Press
2001 158p il (Religion in American life) lib bdg
$28
Grades: 7 8 9 10   **294**
   1. Buddhism 2. Hinduism 3. Sikhism 4. Asian Ameri-
cans—Religion
   ISBN 0-19-512442-1   LC 2001-45151
Presents the basic tenets of these three Asian religions
and discusses the religious history and experience of
their practitioners after immigration to the United States
   "Solid information, a large selection of historical and
contemporary photographs, interesting readings from primary sources, and accounts from school-age Buddhists,
Hindus, and Sikhs combine to make this is a valuable resource." Booklist
Includes bibliographical references

294.3   Buddhism

Demi, 1942-
Buddha. Holt & Co. 1996 unp il $21.95 *
Grades: 4 5 6   **294.3**
   1. Gautama Buddha
   ISBN 0-8050-4203-2   LC 95-16906
The author "tells the story of Siddhartha's birth and
the prophecies surrounding it, touches upon his childhood, and then follows his path to enlightenment."
Booklist
   Demi "uses clear, uncomplicated storytelling to present complex philosophical concepts. . . . The gilded illustrations (based, according to the jacket, on 'Indian,
Chinese, Japanese, Burmese, and Indonesian paintings,
sculptures, and sutra illustrations') are delicate, yet the
colors and composition are bold, with central figures and
action cascading beyond the careful borders." Bull Cent
Child Books

Ganeri, Anita, 1961-
Buddhism; [by] Anita Ganeri. World Almanac
Library 2006 48p il map (Religions of the world)
lib bdg $30.60 *
Grades: 5 6 7 8   **294.3**
   1. Buddhism
   ISBN 0-8368-5865-4   LC 2005041708
The author "presents a survey of Buddhist history, be-
liefs, sacred texts, festivals, and lifecycle events. . . .
There is discussion of the art and folk literature associat-
ed with the religious tradition. Colorful photographs, il-
lustrations, and art reproductions appear throughout." SLJ
Includes bibliographical references

Gedney, Mona
The life and times of Buddha. Mitchell Lane
Pubs. 2005 48p il map (Biography from ancient
civilizations) lib bdg $19.95 *
Grades: 5 6 7 8   **294.3**
   1. Gautama Buddha
   ISBN 1-58415-342-3
A biography of Siddhartha Gautama, who became
known as Buddha.
   This "offers a fluid and lively retelling of the basic
story, including insight into the broader context of the
times, an introduction to the teachings of [Buddha], and
a recounting of the facts that most believers would assent
to." SLJ
Includes bibliographical references

Lee, Jeanne M.
I once was a monkey; stories Buddha told.
Farrar, Straus & Giroux 1999 unp il $16
Grades: 4 5 6 7   **294.3**
   1. Jataka stories
   ISBN 0-374-33548-6   LC 98-17651
A retelling of six Jatakas, or birth stories, which illustrate some of the central tenets of Buddha's teachings,
such as compassion, honesty, and thinking clearly before
acting
   "The appealing character of the monkey will pull children into the tales, which convey lessons in a direct yet
gentle way that is never preachy. The accompanying li-
nocut illustrations are lovely." Booklist

Wangu, Madhu Bazaz
Buddhism. 4th ed. Chelsea House 2009 144p il
(World religions) $40
Grades: 7 8 9 10 11 12   **294.3**
   1. Buddhism
   ISBN 978-160413-105-5; 1-60413-105-5
   First published 1993 by Facts on File
This "tells the story of Buddhism's origins and its development into three major schools of thought—and
presents the particular beliefs and practices of those
schools of Buddhism. . . . This . . . title explores the
concept of the 'socially engaged Buddhist,' the growth
and practice of Buddhism in America, and the recent revival of Buddhism in Asia." Publisher's note
Includes glossary and bibliographical references

Wilkinson, Philip, 1955-
Buddhism; written by Philip Wilkinson; photographed by Steve Teague. DK Pub. 2003 64p il (DK eyewitness guides) $15.99; lib bdg $19.99
Grades: 4 5 6 7   **294.3**
1. Buddhism
ISBN 0-7894-9833-2; 0-7894-9834-0 (lib bdg)
LC 2003-51656
"This introduction to Buddhism presents a series of topics on double-page spreads, each with a paragraph of text and many excellent color photographs, accompanied by lengthy captions in small type. . . . The book provides a visually appealing introduction to Buddhism and is a good source of photos of Buddhist sites, art, and artifacts." Booklist

Winston, Diana
Wide awake: a Buddhist guide for teens. Perigee Bk. 2003 290p pa $13.95 *
Grades: 7 8 9 10 11 12   **294.3**
1. Buddhism
ISBN 0-399-52897-0   LC 2002-192666
"Switching between anecdotes of her own journey in Buddhism and advice on how teens can apply the Buddha's teachings to their lives, Winston offers a personal and thoughtful introduction to Buddhist thought and practice." Booklist

294.5   Hinduism

Ganeri, Anita, 1961-
The Ramayana and Hinduism. Smart Apple Media 2003 30p il (Sacred texts) $27.10
Grades: 5 6 7 8 9   **294.5**
1. Hinduism
ISBN 1-58340-242-X   LC 2003-42352
Contents: Origins; Texts and teaching; In daily life
Explains the history and practices of the religion of Hinduism, especially as revealed through its sacred book, the Ramayana

Plum-Ucci, Carol, 1957-
Celebrate Diwali; [by] Carol Plum-Ucci. Enslow Publishers 2008 128p il map (Celebrate holidays) $31.93
Grades: 5 6 7 8   **294.5**
1. Divali
ISBN 978-0-7660-2778-7; 0-7660-2778-3
LC 2006028106
This describes the history, cultural significance, customs, symbols and celebrations around the world of the Hindu holiday of Diwali.
"Captioned photographs, maps, drawings, and sidebars combine with accessible text to present a thorough discussion of [Diwali]. . . . This . . . is a useful resource." Horn Book Guide
Includes glossary and bibliographical references

Rasamandala Das
Hinduism. World Almanac Library 2006 48p il map (Religions of the world) $30.60 *
Grades: 5 6 7 8   **294.5**

1. Hinduism
ISBN 0-8368-5867-0
Hinduism is "explored in an accessible introductory manner, including information on [its] history, teachings, religious practices, culture and lifestyle, and the [faith's role] in today's global society. Vibrant full-color photographs are appropriately placed within the [text]. Ideal for . . . school reports or for general interest." SLJ
Includes bibliographical references

Wangu, Madhu Bazaz
Hinduism. 4th ed. Chelsea House 2009 144p il (World religions) $40
Grades: 7 8 9 10 11 12   **294.5**
1. Hinduism
ISBN 978-1-60413-108-6; 1-60413-108-X
LC 2008043047
First published 1991 by Facts on File
This describes the history of Hinduism, its customs, beliefs, and rites of passage, the Hindu nationalist movement in India, Hinduism and the interfaith movement, and Hinduism and the environmental movement.
Includes glossary and bibliographical references

296   Judaism

Buxbaum, Shelley M.
Jewish faith in America; [by] Shelley M. Buxbaum, Sara E. Karesh. Facts on File 2003 128p il (Faith in America) $30
Grades: 7 8 9 10   **296**
1. Judaism 2. Jews—United States 3. United States—Ethnic relations
ISBN 0-8160-4986-6   LC 2002-29392
This offers a history of the Jewish people in America "from the early days . . . and their participation in the Revolutionary and Civil Wars, to the impact of World War II and the Holocaust on Jewish life in America. . . . [It also covers] the various ways Judaism is practiced in the U.S. as well as the contributions Jews have made to American society." Publisher's note
"Thoroughly researched and heavily illustrated." Libr Media Connect
Includes glossary and bibliographical references

Fisher, Leonard Everett, 1924-
To bigotry, no sanction; the story of the oldest synagogue in America. Holiday House 1998 64p il $16.95
Grades: 4 5 6 7   **296**
1. Touro Synagogue (Newport, R.I.) 2. Jews—United States
ISBN 0-8234-1401-9   LC 98-12834
The author discusses "the history of the Jews in America in general and the building of the Touro Synagogue, the oldest in the U.S. in particular. Fisher does his usual excellent job of bringing history to life." Booklist
Includes bibliographical references

Keene, Michael

Judaism; [by] Michael Keene. World Almanac Library 2006 48p il map (Religions of the world) lib bdg $30.60 *

Grades: 5 6 7 8   **296**

1. Judaism

ISBN 0-8368-5869-7   LC 2005041734

This "volume presents fundamental beliefs and faith foundations, current status and practices of [Judaism] around the globe, and a time line of historically significant events. . . . The [book is] enumerated with full-color photographs on every page, charts, maps, and tables. . . . [This title] will enhance the education of diverse populations." SLJ

Includes bibliographical references

Morrison, M. A. (Martha A.), 1948-

Judaism; by Martha A. Morrison and Stephen F. Brown. 4th ed. Chelsea House 2009 144p il (World religions) $40

Grades: 7 8 9 10 11 12   **296**

1. Judaism

ISBN 978-1-60413-110-9; 1-60413-110-1

     LC 2008029657

First published 1991 by Facts on File under the authorship of Fay Carol Gates

This "presents the basic beliefs of the Jewish religious heritage and highlights the different manners in which these traditions can be upheld. Both Orthodox Judaism and the religious practices and movements within Reformed Judaism, including Reform Judaism, Conservative Judaism, and Reconstructionist Judaism, are explored." Publisher's note

Includes glossary and bibliographical references

296.03 Judaism—Encyclopedias and dictionaries

The **Oxford** dictionary of the Jewish religion; editors in chief, R.J. Zwi Werblowsky, Geoffrey Wigoder. Oxford University Press 1997 764p $125

Grades: 8 9 10 11 12 Adult   **296.03**

1. Judaism—Dictionaries 2. Reference books

ISBN 0-19-508605-8   LC 96-45517

"The 2400 entries in this dictionary include unsigned but revised articles from the editors' Encyclopedia of the Jewish Religion (1966), as well as . . . new signed articles covering [topics] . . . and biographies related to the Jewish religion and interfaith relations." Libr J

296.1 Judaism—Sources

Chaikin, Miriam, 1928-

Angels sweep the desert floor; Bible legends about Moses in the wilderness; illustrated by Alexander Koshkin. Clarion Bks. 2002 102p il $19 *

Grades: 4 5 6 7   **296.1**

1. Moses (Biblical figure) 2. Angels—Fiction 3. Jewish legends 4. Bible stories

ISBN 0-395-97825-4   LC 2001-47501

A collection of eighteen stories based on the Bible which tell how angels respond to God's commands to ease the way for Moses and the Israelites as they cross the wilderness after being freed from slavery in Egypt

"The full-page watercolor, tempera, and gouache illustrations have a fanciful formality that complements the narrative. Capable of exciting the creative, as well as the spiritual imagination, these wonderful stories make great read-alouds." SLJ

Includes bibliographical references

Pinsker, Marlee

In the days of sand and stars; illustrated by François Thisdale. Tundra Books 2006 87p il $22.95

Grades: 5 6 7 8   **296.1**

1. Jewish legends 2. Women in the Bible 3. Bible stories

ISBN 978-0-88776-724-1; 0-88776-724-9

This is a collection of stories from the Midrash about women including Eve, Naamah, Sarai, Sarah, Rebecca, Leah, Rachel, Dina, and Yocheved.

"Pinsker works like a musician, playing with words instead of notes, but the result is just as lilting and lyrical. The stories are matched by unusual illustrations. Thisdale blends traditional artwork with digital technology. Pieces of photographs mix with ancient elements, giving the pictures a fresh, compelling look." Booklist

296.4 Judaism—Traditions, rites, public services

Berger, Gilda

Celebrate! stories of the Jewish holidays; paintings by Peter Catalanotto. Scholastic 1998 114p il hardcover o.p. pa $8.99

Grades: 4 5 6 7   **296.4**

1. Jewish holidays

ISBN 0-439-43052-6; 0-590-93503-8 (pa)

     LC 97-40150

"Berger examines the history of the major holidays of the Jewish faith and the Bible story that lies behind the celebration of each, as well as the customs that make these special days. The lively writing coupled with Catalanotto's dramatic watercolors ensure that this volume will become a treasured family favorite." Publ Wkly

Kimmel, Eric A.

Wonders and miracles; a Passover companion; illustrated with art spanning three thousand years; written and compiled by Eric A. Kimmel. Scholastic Press 2004 136p il $18.95 *

Grades: 4 5 6 7   **296.4**

1. Passover

ISBN 0-439-07175-5   LC 2002-4732

Presents the steps performed in a traditional Passover Seder, plus stories, songs, poetry, and pictures that celebrate the historical significance of this holiday to Jews all over the world.

"The marvelous selection of art—paintings, photographs, artifacts, and illustrations from historical Hagga-

Kimmel, Eric A.—*Continued*
dahs—illuminates each step in the service. . . . Both the presentation of information and the overall design attest to the careful and loving attention given to every detail. This inviting, handsome, and informative compendium should find a place of honor in every library." SLJ
Includes bibliographical references

Metter, Bert
Bar mitzvah, bat mitzvah; the ceremony, the party, and how the day came to be; by Bert Metter; illustrated by Joan Reilly. Clarion Books 2007 unp il $16; pa $5.95
Grades: 4 5 6 7   **296.4**
1. Bar mitzvah 2. Bat mitzvah
ISBN   978-0-618-76772-4;   0-618-76772-X; 978-0-618-76773-1 (pa); 0-618-76773-8 (pa)
                                        LC 2006032942
"Portions of this text were originally published as Bar mitzvah, bat mitzvah: how Jewish boys and girls come of age, copyright (c) 1984 by Bert Metter"--T.p. verso.
The author "describes a typical ceremony and explains how this custom began for boys during the Middle Ages and how it was adapted for girls beginning in 1922. He also discusses the recent custom of adult bar and bat mitzvahs and celebratory parties. The writing is clear and concise; ink illustrations . . . help break up the text." Booklist
Includes bibliographical references

Schecter, Ellen
The family Haggadah; illustrated by Neil Waldman. Viking 1999 66p il music pa $13.99 *
Grades: 4 5 6 7   **296.4**
1. Passover
ISBN 0-670-88341-7   LC 98-28597
"This book interweaves original writing with traditional Haggadah, prayer book, and biblical texts, as well as with midrash (rabbinic stories and commentaries)." Verso of title page
"Although really intended for parents to use with their children at a family Passover seder, this attractive book may also be useful to children wanting to plan their own model celebration." Booklist

297   Islam, Babism, Bahai Faith

Alkouatli, Claire
Islam. Marshall Cavendish 2006 143p il (World religions) lib bdg $39.93
Grades: 7 8 9 10   **297**
1. Islam
ISBN 978-0-7614-2120-7 (lib bdg); 0-7614-2120-3 (lib bdg)   LC 2005026862
"Provides an overiew of the history and origins, basic tenets and beliefs, organization, traditions, customs, rites, societal and historical influences, and modern-day impact of Islam." Publisher's note
This offers a "fine, well-detailed overview of the second largest religion in the world." Booklist
Includes glossary and bibliographical references

Clark, Charles, 1949-
Islam. Lucent Bks. 2002 128p il (Religions of the world) lib bdg $27.45
Grades: 6 7 8 9   **297**
1. Islam
ISBN 1-56006-986-4   LC 2001-4872
Discusses the history, beliefs, popularity, practices, politics, and challenges of one of the world's major religions, Islam
Includes glossary and bibliographical references

Demi, 1942-
Muhammad; written and illustrated by Demi. Margaret K. McElderry Bks. 2003 unp il $19.95 *
Grades: 4 5 6 7   **297**
1. Muḥammad, d. 632 2. Islam
ISBN 0-689-85264-9   LC 2002-2985
"With dramatic scenes extending past the borders of the intricately patterned frames, the art will be a continual source of interest for young people. . . . [An] excellent retelling of the Prophet's life that combines beauty and scholarship." Booklist
Includes bibliographical references

Gordon, Matthew
Islam; by Matthew S. Gordon. 4th ed. Chelsea House 2009 144p il (World religions) $40
Grades: 7 8 9 10 11 12   **297**
1. Islam
ISBN 978-1-60413-109-3; 1-60413-109-8
                                        LC 2008035810
First published 1991 by Facts on File
This describes the founding of Islam and its spread,The Koran, Hadith, and Islamic law, branches of Islam and their basic beliefs, Muslim customs and rituals, the pattern of Islamic life, and the place of Islam in the modern world.
Includes glossary and bibliographical references

Hafiz, Dilara
The American Muslim teenager's handbook; by Dilara Hafiz, Imran Hafiz, and Yasmine Hafiz. [new ed.] Atheneum Books for Young Readers 2009 168p il pa $11.99
Grades: 7 8 9 10 11 12   **297**
1. Islam 2. Muslims—United States 3. Conduct of life 4. Teenagers—Religious life
ISBN 978-1-4169-8578-5; 1-4169-8578-6
"Ginee Seo books"
A revised edition of the title first published 2007 by Acacia Pub.
"Casual, colloquial, joking, contemporary, and passionate, this interactive handbook by two Arizona teens and their mom talks about their faith, about what it is like to be both proud Americans and proud Muslims, and about misunderstandings and stereotypes. . . . There are also step-by-step guides on how to pray, how to read the Qur an, and how to fast at Ramadan. Muslim and non-Muslim teens alike will be caught by the candor, the humor, and the call for interfaith dialogue and tolerance." Booklist
Includes bibliographical references

Hinds, Kathryn, 1962-

Faith; [by] Kathryn Hinds. Marshall Cavendish Benchmark 2008 c2009 96p il map (Life in the Medieval Muslim world) lib bdg $23.95 *

Grades: 6 7 8 9   **297**

1. Islam—History 2. Medieval civilization 3. Middle Ages 4. Islamic countries

ISBN 978-0-7614-3092-6 (lib bdg); 0-7614-3092-X (lib bdg)   LC 2008019268

"A social history of the Muslim world from the eighth through the mid-thirteenth century, with a focus on the religion of Islam." Publisher's note

Includes glossary and bibliographical references

Is Islam a religion of war or peace? Jann Einfeld, book editor. Greenhaven Press 2005 108p (At issue) lib bdg $28.70; pa $19.95

Grades: 7 8 9 10   **297**

1. Islam 2. Terrorism 3. War—Religious aspects

ISBN 0-7377-3099-4 (lib bdg); 0-7377-3100-1 (pa)   LC 2004-59678

"Eleven opinions are presented here. The book begins with Osama bin Laden's justification for his attacks on Americans. The portrayal of Islam as a predominantly peaceful religion by President George W. Bush is countered by evangelist Pat Robertson. Additional perspectives are offered by Islamic scholars, a former Muslim, a female Muslim reformer, and a rabbi who is an expert on Islam." SLJ

Includes bibliographical references

Islam in America; Laura K. Egendorf, book editor. Greenhaven Press 2006 112p (At issue) lib bdg $28.70; pa $19.95

Grades: 7 8 9 10 11 12   **297**

1. Islam 2. Muslims—United States

ISBN 0-7377-2727-6 (lib bdg); 0-7377-2728-4 (pa)   LC 2005046317

The selections in this collection "treat such subjects as whether American Muslims support terrorist groups and whether or not they experience discrimination. The pieces on African-American Muslims and the growing popularity of Islam among Hispanic Americans are particularly interesting." SLJ

Includes bibliographical references

Oliver, Marilyn Tower, 1935-

Muhammad. Lucent Bks. 2003 112p il maps (Importance of) lib bdg $27.45

Grades: 7 8 9 10   **297**

1. Muḥammad, d. 632 2. Muslims 3. Islam

ISBN 1-59018-232-4   LC 2002-11291

Contents: The beginning: before the revelations; A messenger for God; The early Muslims meet with opposition; Hijra, the flight to Yathrib (Medina); Raids and battles; The return to Mecca; The final years

Profiles the life of Muhammad and his founding of the religion known as Islam

"A solid and balanced look at the 'last prophet.'" SLJ

Includes glossary and bibliographical references

Siddiqui, Haroon

Being Muslim. Groundwood Books 2006 160p il (Groundwork guides) $15.95 *

Grades: 8 9 10 11 12   **297**

1. Islam 2. Muslims

ISBN 978-0-88899-785-2; 0-88899-785-X

"House of Anansi Press"

"In the wake of 9/11, 'Islam-bashing' bears all the symptoms of racism. . . . That's the argument of award-winning Canadian journalist Siddiqui. . . . His clear, passionate discussion confronts international issues that are in the news now. . . . This timely volume . . . is sure to spark debate." Booklist

Includes bibliographical references

Wormser, Richard, 1933-

American Islam; growing up Muslim in America. Walker & Co. 1994 130p il hardcover o.p. pa $8.95

Grades: 7 8 9 10   **297**

1. Islam

ISBN 0-8027-8343-0; 0-8027-7628-0 (pa)   LC 94-12335

"A portrait of Muslim American youth and their faith. Wormser describes the cultural, literary, and scientific heritage of Islamic civilization; their traditional tolerance of unbelievers; and the history of Muslim settlement in the Christian West. He also offers a concise summary of the religion's origins, its Sunni and Shia branches, and its basic beliefs." SLJ

"Although historical background is interlaced within the text, much of the information comes from interviews. This anecdotal method lends an immediacy that will appeal to young people." Book Rep

Includes bibliographical references

297.1   Sources of Islam

Koran.

The Koran *

Grades: 8 9 10 11 12 Adult   **297.1**

Available in various bindings and editions

"The sacred scripture of Islam, regarded by Muslims as the Word of God, and except in sūra I.—which is a prayer to God—and some few passages in which Muhammad or the angels speak in the first person, the speaker throughout is God." Ency Britannica

The meaning of the glorious Koran; an explanatory translation by Marmaduke Pickthall; with an introduction by William Montgomery Watt. A.A. Knopf 1992 xxiv, 693p il $22

Grades: 7 8 9 10 11 12 Adult   **297.1**

ISBN 0-679-41736-2; 978-0-679-41736-1   LC 92-52928

"Everyman's library"

This translation first published 1930

"The sacred scripture of Islam, regarded by Muslims as the Word of God, and except in sura I.—which is a prayer to God—and some few passages in which Muhammad or the angels speak in the first person, the speaker throughout is God." Ency Britannica

297.3 Islamic worship

Jeffrey, Laura S.
Celebrate Ramadan; [by] Laura S. Jeffrey. Enslow Publishers 2007 112p il (Celebrate holidays) lib bdg $31.93
Grades: 5 6 7 8   297.3
1. Ramadan 2. Id al-Adha 3. Islam
ISBN 978-0-7660-2774-9 (lib bdg); 0-7660-2774-0 (lib bdg)   LC 2006028107
"This book opens by introducing a contemporary Muslim, Bushra, who celebrated Ramadan as a girl growing up in England [and] later immigrated to the United States. . . . An informative chapter surveys the history, beliefs, and practices of Islam. . . . The remainder of the book offers a detailed discussion of Ramadan, prayer, and spiritual awareness, and of l'Id al Fitr. . . . Punctuated by sidebars and illustrated with color photos, this clearly written book offers a good overview of how the holidays of Islam are celebrated." Booklist
Includes glossary and bibliographical references

297.9 Babism and Bahai Faith

Hartz, Paula
Baha'i Faith. 3rd ed. Chelsea House 2009 144p il (World religions) $40
Grades: 7 8 9 10 11 12   297.9
1. Bahai Faith
ISBN 978-1-60413-104-8; 1-60413-104-7
                                               LC 2008043045
First published 2002 by Facts and File
This "explores all aspects of the Baha'i faith, from the original teachings of its founder, Baha'u'llah, to the modern-day communities that exist in 236 countries and territories throughout the world." Publisher's note
Includes glossary and bibliographical references

299 Religions not provided for elsewhere

Harpur, James, 1956-
Celtic myth; a treasury of legends, art, and history; [by] James Harpur. M.E. Sharpe 2008 96p il (The world of mythology) $35.95
Grades: 8 9 10 11 12   299
1. Celtic mythology 2. Celtic civilization
ISBN 978-0-7656-8102-7   LC 2007006015
"With lots of heroic adventures and exciting, sometimes gruesome detail, Harpur retells stories of the Irish and Welsh Celts and weaves in facts about their culture and the history of their struggle for dominence. The dense text is broken up with beautiful, color images on every page, including paintings and photos of the settings, sculptures, weapons, and other artifacts." Booklist
Includes glossary and bibliographical references

Hinds, Kathryn, 1962-
Religion. Marshall Cavendish Benchmark 2006 c2007 72p il map (Life in Ancient Egypt) lib bdg $32.79 *
Grades: 6 7 8 9   299
1. Egypt—Religion 2. Egypt—Civilization
ISBN 978-0-7614-2186-3; 0-7614-2186-6
"Describes the role of religion in ancient Egypt during the New Kingdom period, from about 1550 BCE to about 1070 BCE, including the diverse gods and goddesses the people worshipped, their creation myths, and the role of priesthood." Publisher's note
"Hinds supports the smoothly flowing text with illuminating details and excerpts from a variety of sources. Handsome color photos of Egyptian sites and artifacts greatly enhance the text." Booklist
Includes glossary and bibliographical references

Kramer, Ann, 1946-
Egyptian myth; a treasury of legends, art, and history. M. E. Sharpe 2008 96p il map (The world of mythology) $35.95
Grades: 5 6 7 8   299
1. Egyptian mythology 2. Egyptian art 3. Egypt—History
ISBN 978-0-7656-8105-8; 0-7656-8105-6
                                               LC 2007005876
This "handsomely designed [book is] illustrated with works of art from the culture. [It] is a well-organized presentation that includes information and tales about the gods and the pharoahs as well as magical stories and legends, providing an excellent introduction to this fascinating culture." SLJ
Includes glossary and bibliographical references

Matson, Gienna
Celtic mythology A to Z; [by] Gienna Matson. Facts on File 2004 114p il map (Mythology A to Z) $40
Grades: 8 9 10 11 12 Adult   299
1. Celtic mythology
ISBN 0-8160-4890-8   LC 2004-47111
This is an "illustrated guide to the characters, objects, and places that make up the mythic lore of the Celtic peoples." Publisher's note
"This title is an excellent introduction to the mythology of Celtic cultures and should be in most public and school libraries." Booklist
Includes bibliographical references

Schomp, Virginia, 1953-
The ancient Egyptians; [by] Virginia Schomp. Marshall Cavendish Benchmark 2007 c2008 95p il map (Myths of the world) lib bdg $22.95
Grades: 6 7 8 9   299
1. Egyptian mythology 2. Egypt—Civilization
ISBN 978-0-7614-2549-6   LC 2006037686
"A retelling of several key ancient Egyptian myths, with background information describing the history, geography, belief systems, and customs of the ancient Egypt." Publisher's note
"With [its] beautiful illustrations, high-quality produc-

Schomp, Virginia, 1953-—*Continued*
tion, and focus on source material, the [book] should whet the interest of readers." SLJ
Includes glossary and bibliographical references

299.5   Religions of East and Southeast Asian origin

Demi, 1942-
The legend of Lao Tzu and the Tao te ching. Margaret K. McElderry Books 2007 unp il $21.99
*
Grades: 4 5 6 7   **299.5**
1. Lao-tzu, 6th cent. B.C. 2. Taoism
ISBN 1-4169-1206-1; 978-1-4169-1206-4
      LC 2005029695
"This is the legend of Lao Tzu . . . who may or may not have founded Taoism, one of the greatest religions of the world. Demi's elegant picture-book introduction to the legendary Chinese philosopher . . . combines nuggets of his purported life with 20 verses from the Tao Te Ching. . . . The narrative and graceful paintings are contained in a gold circular frame on each parchment shaded page." SLJ

Hartz, Paula
Taoism; by Paula R. Hartz. Updated ed. Facts on File 2004 128p il (World religions) $30
Grades: 7 8 9 10 11 12   **299.5**
1. Taoism
ISBN 0-8160-5724-9   LC 2004-43224
First published 1993
This book "traces the progress of Taoist thought, from the great *Tao Te Ching* or 'The Book of the Way and Its Power,' by Laozi to the contemporary *Tao of Physics* by Fritjof Capra. It also examines the restoration of Taoism under China's religious freedom clause, the slow rebirth of Taoist monasticism, renewed interest in Taoism in China and abroad, and the impact of tourism on the monastic tradition." Publisher's note
Includes bibliographical references

Helft, Claude
Chinese mythology; stories of creation and invention; [by] Claude Helft; illustrations by Chen Jiang Hong; translated from the French by Michael Hariton and Claudia Bedrick. 1st American ed. Enchanted Lion Books 2007 78p il $14.95
Grades: 7 8 9 10   **299.5**
1. Chinese mythology
ISBN 978-1-59270-074-5; 1-59270-074-8
      LC 2007031297
"This slim book offers high visual interest along with concise introductions to an important body of myths. Helft deftly organizes what can be confusing anecdotes about gods who often occupy themselves with governing and making war. . . . Interleaved pages describe a dozen cultural items (jade, yin/yang, dragons, etc.). . . . Full-page and vignette illustrations in traditional style with strong ink lines emphasize vitality and movement. Chen's evocative and richly colored paintings add value to this compact collection." SLJ

Kallen, Stuart A., 1955-
Shinto. Lucent Bks. 2002 128p il map (Religions of the world) lib bdg $27.45
Grades: 6 7 8 9   **299.5**
1. Shinto
ISBN 1-56006-988-0   LC 2001-6120
Discusses historical origins, the teachings, practices, and the spread of Shinto into modern times
Includes glossary and bibliographical references

Levin, Judith, 1956-
Japanese mythology; [by] Judith Levin. 1st ed. The Rosen Pub. Group 2008 64p il map (Mythology around the world) $29.95
Grades: 5 6 7 8   **299.5**
1. Japanese mythology 2. Shinto 3. Buddhism 4. Japan—Civilization
ISBN 978-1-4042-0736-3; 1-4042-0736-8
      LC 2005035279
This "presents not only an introduction to Shinto and Buddhist beliefs, but also Japanese history and mythology in general. . . . The most remarkable part of [this book] . . . is the respect [it shows] for the mythological customs, treating them throughout with the same care that writers of books on major religions might offer. The illustrations show both ancient and modern incarnations of the deities and heroes." SLJ
Includes glossary and bibliographical references

Roberts, Jeremy, 1956-
Chinese mythology A to Z; a young reader's companion; by Jeremy Roberts. 1st ed. Facts on File 2004 160p il map (Mythology A to Z) $40
Grades: 7 8 9 10   **299.5**
1. Chinese mythology
ISBN 0-8160-4870-3   LC 2004-5341
"Alphabetically arranged entries describe [Chinese] historical and mythological figures, places, objects, themes, and story cycles. . . . The inviting [format features] generous white space and large headings plus numerous drawings, reproductions, and sharp halftone photographs. The clarity of wording, well-chosen bibliographic sources, and detailed [index makes this title an] excellent [resource]. " SLJ
Includes bibliographical references

299.6   Religions originating among Black Africans and people of Black African descent

Lynch, Patricia Ann
African mythology A to Z; [by] Patricia Ann Lynch. Facts on File 2004 xx, 137p il map (Mythology A to Z) $40
Grades: 7 8 9 10   **299.6**
1. African mythology
ISBN 0-8160-4892-4   LC 2004-47109
This is a "reference to the deities, places, events, animals, beliefs, and other subjects that appear in the myths of various African peoples." Publisher's note

Lynch, Patricia Ann—*Continued*
"This title is an excellent introduction to the mythologies of African cultures and should be in most public and school libraries." Booklist
Includes bibliographical references

Schomp, Virginia, 1953-
The ancient Africans; [by] Virginia Schomp. Marshall Cavendish Benchmark 2009 96p il map (Myths of the world) $23.95
Grades: 6 7 8 9   **299.6**
1. African mythology 2. Africa—Civilization
3. Ethnology—Africa
ISBN 978-0-7614-3099-5; 0-7614-3099-7
                                                     LC 2008011695
"A retelling of several ancient African myths, with background information describing the history, geography, belief systems, and customs of various peoples of Africa." Publisher's note
Includes bibliographical references

299.7   Religions of North American native origin

Hartz, Paula
Native American religions; [by] Paula R. Hartz. 3rd ed. Chelsea House 2009 144p il (World religions) $40
Grades: 7 8 9 10 11 12   **299.7**
1. Native Americans—Religion
ISBN 978-1-60413-111-6; 1-60413-111-X
                                                     LC 2008051197
First published 1997 by Facts on File
This "presents the history of the Native American religions, starting from their roots as tribal religions, and then details the detrimental effects of European colonization, the annihilation of the Native Americans that threatened the religions, and their sudden restoration in the 20th century." Publisher's note
Includes glossary and bibliographical references

Martin, Joel
Native American religion. Oxford University Press 1999 157p il (Religion in American life) $28 *
Grades: 7 8 9 10   **299.7**
1. Native Americans—Religion
ISBN 0-19-511035-8   LC 98-50155
An "examination of religious life and practices from ancient times through the Colonial period and the Western Expansion, and into the 20th century. Martin acknowledges the importance of religion in all aspects of Native American daily life and explores some of the differences among the various cultures. He also addresses the impact of the arrival of Europeans on spiritual life." SLJ
Includes bibliographical references

300   SOCIAL SCIENCES, SOCIOLOGY & ANTHROPOLOGY

301   Sociology and anthropology

Batten, Mary
Anthropologist: scientist of the people; with photographs by A. Magdalena Hurtado and Kim Hill. Houghton Mifflin 2001 64p il map (Scientists in the field) $16 *
Grades: 4 5 6 7   **301**
1. Hurtado, A. Magdalena 2. Hill, Kim
3. Anthropology 4. Guayaki Indians
ISBN 0-618-08368-5
This book "introduces readers to Magdalena [Hurtado] and Kim Hill, a husband-and-wife team who study the Aché of Paraguay. . . . Batten's graceful text covers basic science concepts (what an anthropologist really does; what evolutionary biology is) in accessible, clear language and examples just right for kids, offering fascinating hypotheses along the way." Booklist

302.2   Communication

Liungman, Carl G., 1938-
Dictionary of symbols. W.W. Norton 1994 596p il pa $21.95
Grades: 8 9 10 11 12 Adult   **302.2**
1. Signs and symbols 2. Picture writing 3. Reference books
ISBN 0-393-31236-4; 978-0-393-31236-2
Original Swedish edition, 1974
This dictionary groups "icons according to their graphical style rather than their meaning. For example, all symbols based upon the cross are included in one chapter, those based upon the triangle in another, and those based upon the circle in yet another. Each symbol is succinctly defined and a source of origin (if known) is given. To enhance access, both name and form indexes are provided. This work will certainly become one of the key sources for tracing symbols and their meanings." Am Libr
Includes bibliographical references

302.23   Media (Means of communication)

Ali, Dominic
Media madness; an insider's guide to media; written by Dominic Ali; illustrated by Michael Cho. Kids Can Press 2005 64p il hardcover o.p. pa $8.95
Grades: 4 5 6 7   **302.23**
1. Mass media
ISBN 1-55337-174-7; 1-55337-175-5 (pa)
Host Max McLoon gives pointers on how to analyze media, and takes readers behind the scenes to reveal me-

Ali, Dominic—*Continued*

dia workplaces in action. The book also includes activities for readers to further explore concepts or try their own media-making.

"The hip illustrations and wry sidebars prevent the book from coming off as goofy or childish, while the humorous treatment takes a bit of the edge off of otherwise 'heavy' issues like stereotypes, sexism, and violence. Light and loony, but enlightening, too." SLJ

Mass media: opposing viewpoints; William Dudley, book editor. Greenhaven Press 2005 218p il $33.70; pa $22.45

Grades: 8 9 10 11 12   **302.23**

1. Mass media

ISBN 0-7377-2242-8; 0-7377-2243-6 (pa)

LC 2004-42401

Replaces the 1999 edition under the editorship of Byron L. Stay

"Opposing viewpoints series"

Presents opposing viewpoints on various aspects of mass media including television's affect on society, whether or not advertising is harmful, the influence of media on politics, whether or not pornography on the Internet should be regulated, and the regulation of television for children

Includes bibliographical references

Streissguth, Thomas

Media bias. Marshall Cavendish Benchmark 2006 127p il (Open for debate) lib bdg $39.93

Grades: 7 8 9 10   **302.23**

1. Mass media

ISBN 978-0-7614-2296-9; 0-7614-2296-X

"Discusses bias in the American media, including its historical development and the effects of new technologies. Includes discussions of different types of bias, government regulations, politics, and public relations, and how they shape the media." Publisher's note

Includes bibliographical references

302.3   Social interaction within groups

Bullying; Beth Rosenthal, book editor. Greenhaven Press 2008 120p il (Introducing issues with opposing viewpoints) lib bdg $33.70

Grades: 7 8 9 10   **302.3**

1. Bullies

ISBN 978-0-7377-3801-8; 0-7377-3801-4

LC 2007-32382

"Topics covered in this book range from the causes of bullying, what role society plays in encouraging bullying, the roles of TV and/or video games in violence and bullying, the responsibility of parents, the value of anti-bullying programs, and the ways that the behavior can be reduced. . . . Articles are presented in a pro/con format; 'active reading' questions preface each viewpoint and are designed to help students focus on the main points and to read carefully. Full-color photos and other graphics appear throughout." SLJ

Includes bibliographical references

Kevorkian, Meline

101 facts about bullying; what everyone should know; [by] Meline Kevorkian and Robin D'Antona. Rowman & Littlefield Pub. 2008 148p $32.95

Grades: Professional   **302.3**

1. Bullies

ISBN 978-1-57886-849-0; 1-57886-849-1

This "is designed to break down what the research says about bullying and its effects, offering ideas for what can and should be done to minimize or reduce it. Meline Kevorkian . . . discusses topics ranging from relational bullying to cyber bullying to media and video violence to the legal ramifications of bullying." Publisher's note

"A user-friendly, accessible, and well-organized resource. . . . The format will lend itself well to group discussions and give teachers and others who work with young people a solid basis upon which to explore the issues surrounding this prevalent problem." SLJ

303.3   Coordination and control

Prejudice in the modern world reference library. UXL 2007 5v il set $247

Grades: 7 8 9 10 11 12   **303.3**

1. Prejudices

ISBN 978-1-4144-0204-8

Also available as separate volumes; contact publisher for more information

Contents: Almanac (2 volumes); Biographies; Primary Sources; Cumulative Index

This is an "examination of the historical and social ramifications of prejudice in several societies across the globe. Two *Almanac* volumes highlight the foundations, causes, and types of prejudices as well as specific case studies on prejudice in action in the modern world. *Biographies* highlights key activists, politicians, religious leaders, as well as ordinary citizens that have played important roles in cases of prejudice in the world, from Heinrich Himmler and Saddam Hussein to Rosa Parks and Cesar Chavez. *Primary Sources* uses documents, speeches, letters and other sources to explain events related to prejudice." Publisher's note

"This is an excellent adjunct to American and world history units and classes on government, intercultural heritage, the Holocaust, and law." Booklist

303.4   Social change

Hill, Laban Carrick

America dreaming; how youth changed America in the sixties. Little, Brown & Company 2007 165p il $19.99 *

Grades: 6 7 8 9   **303.4**

1. United States—History—1961-1974 2. Social change 3. Youth movement 4. Baby boom generation

ISBN 978-0-316-00904-1; 0-316-00904-0

LC 2006-27898

"Covering subjects such as the civil rights movement, hippie culture, black nationalism, and the feminist movement, Hill paints a . . . picture of life in the '60's and

Hill, Laban Carrick—*Continued*

shows how teenagers were on the forefront of the societal changes that occurred during this . . . decade." Publisher's note

"An excellent textbook for the children and, probably, grandchildren of baby boomers who want to know what the youth culture of the time as all about." NY Times Book Rev

Includes bibliographical references

The **Internet:** opposing viewpoints; James D. Torr, book editor. Greenhaven Press 2005 204p il lib bdg $34.95; pa $23.70

Grades: 8 9 10 11 12   **303.4**
1. Internet
ISBN 0-7377-2941-4 (lib bdg); 0-7377-2942-2 (pa)
LC 2004-59699

Replaces the edition published 2002 under the editorship of Helen Cothran

"Opposing viewpoints series"

"The authors in this volume examine the diverse effects of the Internet revolution—and suggest ways in which the technology can be harnessed for the better." Publisher's note

Includes bibliographical references

Kronenwetter, Michael

Protest! 21st Cent. Bks. (NY) 1996 126p il lib bdg $23.40

Grades: 7 8 9 10   **303.4**
1. Dissent 2. Demonstrations
ISBN 0-8050-4103-6   LC 96-9866

This is an "introduction to and overview of the history of protest in the U.S. and elsewhere. . . . Particularly attention-getting are the chapters on the birth of the women's rights movement and the persistence of the suffragists; on the heroism of Gandhi and his consistent practice of nonviolent protest throughout his long life; and on the role of unions and strikes within the labor movement." SLJ

Includes glossary and bibliographical references

Turney, Jon

Technology; ethical debates about the application of science. Smart Apple Media 2009 46p il (Dilemmas in modern science) $34.25

Grades: 7 8 9 10   **303.4**
1. Technology 2. Science—Ethical aspects
ISBN 978-1-59920-097-2; 1-59920-097-X
LC 2007-35692

"Presents both sides of issues arising from how we use technology, including Internet use, identity theft, technology and the military, nanotechnology, and robots and automation." Publisher's note

This title is "easy to navigate as evocative photographs, charts, and sidebars help break down complicated arguments into manageable parts for easy digestion." SLJ

Includes glossary and bibliographical references

Yount, Lisa

Biotechnology and genetic engineering. 3rd ed. Facts on File 2008 364p (Library in a book) $45

Grades: 8 9 10 11 12   **303.4**
1. Biotechnology 2. Genetic engineering
ISBN 978-0-8160-7217-0; 0-8160-7217-5
LC 2007041313

First published 2000

This "provides an overview of the history of [biotechnology and genetic engineering] and the opinions surrounding it, ranging from the study of fermentation by French chemist Louis Pasteur in the 1850s to the nascent field of synthetic biology. [It includes a] discussion of recent court cases such as *United States v. Kincade*, . . . [an] overview essay, capsule biographies, a large annotated bibliography, a chronology of significant events, organization and agency listings, and a glossary. . . . Coverage includes: Whether or not genetically modified food impacts the environment and health; How biotechnology has transformed the pharmaceutical industry; The legal implications of genetic testing and more." Publisher's note

303.6   Conflict and conflict resolution

Drew, Naomi

The kids' guide to working out conflicts; how to keep cool, stay safe, and get along; Naomi Drew. Free Spirit Pub. 2004 146p il pa $13.95 *

Grades: 6 7 8 9   **303.6**
1. Conflict management
ISBN 1-57542-150-X   LC 2003-21108

Describes common forms of conflict, the reasons behind conflicts, and various positive ways to deal with and defuse tough situations at school, at home, and in the community without getting physical.

"In clean, respectful language, [the author] offers youth a highly doable eight-step plan to overcome anger issues. . . . The thoughtful encouraging tone of this important book . . . embraces children all along the conflict spectrum, from tortured victims of bullying to those who endure sustained stress and from moderate levels of conflict to full-blown bullies. . . . Highly recommended." Voice Youth Advocates

Includes bibliographical references

Ellis, Deborah, 1960-

Off to war; voices of soldiers' children. Groundwood Books/House of Anansi Press 2008 175p il $15.95 *

Grades: 5 6 7 8   **303.6**
1. Children and war 2. Iraq War, 2003-
3. Afghanistan
ISBN 978-0-88899-894-1; 0-88899-894-5;
978-0-88899-895-8 (pa); 0-88899-895-3 (pa)

The wars in Iraq and Afghanistan have impacted the children of soldiers—men and women who have been called away from their families to fight in a faraway war. In their own words, some of these children describe how their experience has marked and shaped their lives.

"Accessible and utterly readable. . . . The book is an

Ellis, Deborah, 1960-—*Continued*
excellent resource for opening discussions about the current events." SLJ

Includes glossary and bibliographical references

Engle, Dawn
PeaceJam; a billion simple acts of peace; written
by Ivan Suvanjieff and Dawn Gifford Engle.
Puffin Books 2008 194p il pa $16.99
Grades: 5 6 7 8 9   **303.6**
    1. PeaceJam Foundation 2. Peace 3. Youth
    ISBN 978-0-14-241234-3; 0-14-241234-1
                                LC 2008-24865
    Includes DVD
"This visually impressive and well-organized book
would work well as a reference tool, how-to handbook,
or promotional device for classroom altruistic activities
or civil service clubs. Each stand-alone chapter uses a
Noble Peace Laureate as the catalyst for a particular crisis, introduces the reader to a courageous young person
who has been inspired to help with a specific problem,
and ends with a list of ten very 'doable' suggestions of
ways that every concerned citizen can help. The resources listed in the back of the book are extensive and
current. An excellent addition to the text is a snappy thir-
ty-minute DVD that could serve as a book talk, review
tool or promotional device." Voice Youth Advocates

Gelletly, LeeAnne
Violence in the media; by LeeAnne Gelletly.
Lucent Books 2005 112p il (Lucent Overview
series) $28.70
Grades: 7 8 9 10   **303.6**
    1. Violence 2. Mass media
    ISBN 1-56006-508-7   LC 2004-10692
    Contents: Violence in film and television; Violence in
music; Violence in interactive media; Linking media violence with real-life violence; Regulating the media
    Explores the issue of violence in television, films, mu-
sic, and other forms of media, with an examination of
the link between media violence and real-life violence
and discussion of the steps that have been taken to regu-
late violent media
    Includes bibliographical references

Gifford, Clive
Violence on the screen. Smart Apple Media
2006 48p il $31.35
Grades: 7 8 9 10 11 12   **303.6**
    1. Violence 2. Mass media
    ISBN 1-58340-985-5
"How harmful to young viewers is violence on TV, in
movies, computer games, and videos, and on the
Internet? Adult experts and kids debate the hot issue.
. . . The points Gifford raises will engage teens and
spark argument." Booklist
    Includes glossary and bibliographical references

Gottfried, Ted, 1928-
The fight for peace; a history of antiwar
movements in America. 21st Century Bks. 2006
136p il (People's history) $26.60 *
Grades: 7 8 9 10   **303.6**

    1. Pacifism 2. Peace 3. War
    ISBN 0-7613-2932-3
"Gottfried starts out by explaining that a group in
Connecticut rallied together in 2003 to peacefully protest
the war against Iraq. . . . Then the author discusses the
antiwar movement during the Civil War and proceeds
through history, beginning with the ancient Greek play
Lysistrata. . . . The pictures, political cartoons, and
quotes are an excellent addition. . . . This is a book that
can be read for general interest as well as for reports."
SLJ
    Includes bibliographical references

Gupta, Dipak K.
Who are the terrorists? Chelsea House 2006
116p il map (The roots of terrorism) lib bdg $35
*
Grades: 7 8 9 10   **303.6**
    1. Terrorism
    ISBN 0-7910-8306-3   LC 2005021627
This "volume discusses the world history as well as
the groups and individuals behind today's headlines. . . .
Gupta emphasizes that equating Islam with the barbaric
acts of a few terrorists is like making the burning crosses
of the Ku Klux Klan the essence of Christianity. He also
points out the role of the American invasion of Iraq and
the images from Abu Ghraib. . . . This is sure to spark
vehement group discussion." Booklist
    Includes bibliographical references

Innes, Brian, 1928-
International terrorism; by Brian Innes. Mason
Crest Publishers 2003 96p il (Crime and detection)
lib bdg $22.95; pa $9.95
Grades: 6 7 8 9   **303.6**
    1. Terrorism
    ISBN 1-59084-371-1 (lib bdg); 1-59084-592-7 (pa)
                                LC 2003-485
    Contents: Introduction; The rise of terrorism; The rise
of the PLO; Urban guerrillas; Terrorism and religion;
Osama bin Laden and al Qaeda; Counter-terrorist organi-
zations
    Includes bibliographical references

Judson, Karen, 1941-
Resolving conflicts; how to get along when you
don't get along. Enslow Pubs. 2005 112p il (Issues
in focus today) $31.93 *
Grades: 7 8 9 10 11 12   **303.6**
    1. Conflict management
    ISBN 0-7660-2359-1   LC 2004-28119
The author "describes different kinds of conflicts and
how they can be resolved, with a special focus on teens
and building their conflict-resolution skills and understanding." Publisher's note
    Includes bibliographical references

Levin, Jack, 1941-

Domestic terrorism; [by] Jack Levin. Chelsea House 2006 93p il (The roots of terrorism) lib bdg $30 *

Grades: 7 8 9 10   **303.6**

1. Terrorism

ISBN 0-7910-8683-6   LC 2006006020

This "chronicles the role of terrorism in American history, examing left-wing, right-wing, and single-issue terrorism. This book analyzes major American terrorist groups such as the Ku Klux Klan, the Weather Underground, ELF, and the Symbionese Army. It also includes a section on how to confront domestic terrorism." Publisher's note

"This series has a great deal of information. . . . The glossy pages show off an eye-pleasing color format with neat sections and well-placed pictures." Voice Youth Advocates

Includes bibliographical references

Moghadam, Assaf, 1974-

The roots of terrorism; [by] Assaf Moghadam. Chelsea House Publishers 2006 144p il (The roots of terrorism) lib bdg $35 *

Grades: 7 8 9 10   **303.6**

1. Terrorism

ISBN 0-7910-8307-1   LC 2005021625

"This focuses on from where terrorism itself stems from and whether the issues are psychological, organizational, or political. . . . This series has a great deal of information. . . . The glossy pages show off an eye-pleasing color format with neat sections and well-placed pictures." Voice Youth Advocates

Includes bibliographical references

O'Brien, Anne Sibley, 1952-

After Gandhi; one hundred years of nonviolent resistance; [by] Anne Sibley O'Brien and Perry Edmond O'Brien. Charlesbridge 2009 181p il map $15.95

Grades: 7 8 9 10   **303.6**

1. Passive resistance 2. Nonviolence

ISBN 978-1-58089-129-5; 1-58089-129-2

LC 2008-10660

"Using Gandhi as its starting point, this large-format book traces the history of nonviolent resistance by looking at significant adherents from 1908 to 2003 including Martin Luther King, Jr., Nelson Mandela, Charles Perkins, César Chávez, Aung San Suu Kyi, Vaclav Havel, and Wangari Maathi and groups such as the student activists of Tiananmen Square and the Madres de Plaza de Mayo (Mothers of the Disappeared) in Argentina. . . . The handsome design and striking black-and-white illustrations are strong visuals that complement the story of nonviolent resistance in action." Booklist

Includes bibliographical references

Perliger, Arie

Middle Eastern terrorism; [by] Arie Perliger. Chelsea House 2006 111p il map (The roots of terrorism) lib bdg $30 *

Grades: 7 8 9 10   **303.6**

1. Terrorism 2. Middle East

ISBN 0-7910-8309-8   LC 2006006019

After defining terrorism, this volume describes terrorism in Egypt and Syria and goes on to consider Palestinian terrorism, terrorism in Iran and Afghanistan, nationalism, religious fundamentalism, and such groups as Hezbollah and Al-Qaeda.

"This series has a great deal of information. . . . The glossy pages show off the eye-pleasing color format with neat sections and well-placed pictures." Voice Youth Advocates

Includes bibliographical references

Ross, Jeffrey Ian

Will terrorism end? [by] Jeffrey Ian Ross. Chelsea House 2006 112p il map (The roots of terrorism) lib bdg $35 *

Grades: 7 8 9 10   **303.6**

1. Terrorism

ISBN 0-7910-8310-1   LC 2006006021

This volume offers arguments for and against the end of terrorism, citing examples of terrorist groups which have disbanded or where decimated and those which still exist, and considers the idea that terrorism is cyclical.

"This series has a great deal of information. . . . The glossy pages show off an eye-pleasing color format with neat sections and well-placed photographs." Voice Youth Advocates

Includes bibliographical references

Taylor, Robert, 1948-

History of terrorism. Lucent Bks. 2002 96p il map (Terrorism library) $28.70 *

Grades: 7 8 9 10   **303.6**

1. Terrorism

ISBN 1-59018-206-5   LC 2002-1910

Contents: Zealots, assassins, and the reign of terror; Propaganda of the bomb; Anti-colonial terrorism; Terrorism and the Left; Separatist terrorism; Holy War

Examines the political agendas, actions, and religious beliefs of individuals and groups who, throughout history, have resorted to violent actions in order to generate fear and gain their objectives

This "is an excellent resource that demonstrates thorough research and opens up issues for discussion." Booklist

Includes bibliographical references

Weinberg, Leonard, 1939-

What is terrorism? [by] Leonard Weinberg and William Eubank. Chelsea House Publishers 2006 104p il (The roots of terrorism) lib bdg $35 *

Grades: 7 8 9 10   **303.6**

1. Terrorism

ISBN 0-7910-8305-5   LC 2005027569

Weinberg, Leonard, 1939- — *Continued*

This "gives a history of terrorism from its early beginnings through current events. This volume describes the actions and goals of numerous terrorist groups. . . . This . . . has a great deal of information. . . . The glossy pages show off an eye-pleasing color format with neat sections and well-placed pictures." Voice Youth Advocates

Includes bibliographical references

Woolf, Alex

Why are people terrorists? Raintree 2005 48p il (Exploring tough issues) lib bdg $31.43

Grades: 4 5 6 7   **303.6**
1. Terrorism
ISBN 0-7398-6686-9   LC 2003-11571

Contents: What is terrorism?; Why do people become terrorists?; What methods do terrorists use?; The supporters of terrorism; What can be done about terrorism?; What is the war on terrorism?

Explores issues related to terrorism, such as who becomes a terrorist and why, and options such as the "War Against Terrorism" for fighting against these acts of violence agains innocent people.

"Up-to-date information for young people who are concerned about security and want to learn more about important political issues." SLJ

304.2   Human ecology

Desonie, Dana

Polar regions; human impacts. Chelsea House 2008 202p il map (Our fragile planet) $35

Grades: 7 8 9 10   **304.2**
1. Polar regions 2. Human influence on nature
ISBN 978-0-8160-6218-8; 0-8160-6218-8

Describes the climate, weather, flora, and fauna of the Arctic and Antarctic and the effect of human beings on these fragile environments.

Includes glossary and bibliographical references

304.6   Population

Altman, Linda Jacobs, 1943-

Genocide; the systematic killing of a people. rev. and expanded. Enslow Publishers 2009 128p il map (Issues in focus today) lib bdg $31.93

Grades: 6 7 8 9   **304.6**
1. Genocide
ISBN 978-0-7660-3358-0 (lib bdg); 0-7660-3358-9 (lib bdg)   LC 2007050697
First published 1995

"Examines the history of genocide throughout the world, including the Holocaust, and explores the definition of the term, the importance of bearing witness, and the necessary steps to prevent genocide in the future." Publisher's note

This is written in "short accessible chapters." Horn Book Guide

Includes glossary and bibliographical references

January, Brendan, 1972-

Genocide; modern crimes against humanity. Twenty-First Century Books 2007 160p il map lib bdg $31.93 *

Grades: 8 9 10 11 12   **304.6**
1. Genocide
ISBN 978-0-7613-3421-7 (lib bdg); 0-7613-3421-1 (lib bdg)   LC 2005032850

"January gives young readers a sensitive, solid framework with which to comprehend multiple facets of genocide, from etymology of the term to acknowledging deniers of the Holocaust. The slim volume devotes chapters to separate examples of genocide, historic and contemporary: Armenians of the Ottoman Empire, European Jews, Cambodians, Tutsis of Rwanda, Muslims of Bosnia, and tribes of Darfur. . . . This outstanding book sparks thoughtful inquiry." Voice Youth Advocates

Includes bibliographical references

Sheehan, Sean, 1951-

Genocide; by Sean Sheehan. Raintree 2005 56p il (Face the facts)

Grades: 6 7 8 9   **304.6**
1. Genocide
ISBN 1-4109-1070-9   LC 2003-25691

Contents: What is genocide?; Genocide before the Nazis; The Holocaust; Recent holocausts; Seeking explanations; Traumatic times; Accusing others; Nationalism; Serb nationalism; Colonialism; Imperialism and genocide; The power of the state; The trouble with facts; What counts as genocide?; Who is to blame?; Willing executioners?; Is human nature to blame?; Genocide and the law; Genocide on trial; Racism; Ethics; Global ethics

The "author gives readers an unbiased view of [genocide] along with an overview of the topic. The full-color photos and graphics are well chosen . . . and the quotes sprinkled throughout personalize the accounts." SLJ

Includes bibliographical references

Springer, Jane

Genocide. Groundwood Books 2006 144p (Groundwork guides) $15.95 *

Grades: 8 9 10 11 12   **304.6**
1. Genocide
ISBN 978-0-88899-681-7; 0-88899-681-0

"This disturbing history of mass ethnic killings across the world examines the why, when, where, and how genocide takes place. . . . In a lucid, informal text, Springer ably documents particular crimes against humanity, including the transatlantic slave trade, the slaughter of America's Native peoples, the Turkish massacre of the Armenians, the Nanking massacre, the Holocaust, and the Khmer Rouge slaughter in Cambodia." Booklist

304.8 Movement of people

Andryszewski, Tricia, 1956-
Walking the earth; a history of human migration; [by] Tricia Andryszewski. Twenty-First Century Books 2007 80p il map lib bdg $27.23 *
Grades: 5 6 7 8   **304.8**
1. Immigration and emigration 2. Prehistoric peoples
3. Population
ISBN 978-0-7613-3458-3; 0-7613-3458-0
                                       LC 2005033430
"The long history of humankind from 150,000 years ago to the present is examined in terms of how populations spread slowly around the globe. Along the way, the book describes innovations in food, clothing, and shelter that enabled people to progress." Voice Youth Advocates
"Copious sepia-toned visuals, including drawings, photographs, maps, and charts, create an attractive and accessible presentation of complex material." SLJ
Includes bibliographical references

305.23 Young people

Brashich, Audrey
All made up; a girl's guide to seeing through celebrity hype and celebrating real beauty; [by] Audrey D. Brashich; illustrations by Shawn Banner. Walker & Co. 2006 147p il $16.95; pa $9.95 *
Grades: 6 7 8 9   **305.23**
1. Girls 2. Personal grooming 3. Celebrities
ISBN   978-0-8027-8074-4;   0-8027-8074-1;
978-0-8027-7744-7 (pa); 0-8027-7744-9 (pa)
                                       LC 2005-37183
"Brashich has created an accessible guide that explores the relationship between self-esteem and pop culture. . . . She challenges readers to feel good about themselves in spite of a culture that celebrates thinness and celebrity, and to see that beauty comes in many shapes and sizes. She shares personal experiences and incorporates quotes from teens." SLJ
Includes bibliographical references

Burton, Bonnie
Girls against girls; why we are mean to each other and how we can change. Zest Books 2009 128p il pa $12.95
Grades: 7 8 9 10   **305.23**
1. Girls—Psychology 2. Bullies
ISBN 978-0-97901-736-0; 0-97901-736-X
This guide for teenage girls explains why girls can sometimes be mean to each other, what to do if you are a victim of bullying, and the importance of treating other girls with respect.
This offers "excellent coping techniques. . . . Burton never talks down to her readers, nor does she pull her punches. Readers will respond to the author's clear respect for the painful nature of the problem." Booklist

The **Courage** to be yourself; true stories by teens about cliques, conflicts, and overcoming peer pressure; edited by Al Desetta with Educators for Social Responsibility. Free Spirit Pub. 2005 145p pa $13.95 *
Grades: 7 8 9 10 11 12   **305.23**
1. Teenagers 2. Conduct of life
ISBN 1-57542-185-2   LC 2005-5173
"In 26 first-person stories, real teens write about their lives." Publisher's note
"There is certainly some value in hearing teens of many ethnicities and orientations speaking plainly about being fat, or being from India in a school full of blond, blue-eyed folk, or being Arab after 9/11." Booklist
Includes bibliographical references

Dalton, David
Living in a refugee camp; Carbino's story. World Almanac Lib. 2005 48p il map (Children in crisis) $30
Grades: 6 7 8 9   **305.23**
1. Refugees 2. Sudan
ISBN 0-8368-5960-X
"Carbino was 11 when he left his Sudanese village to go to school in Ethiopia; 14 years passed before he returned. Now 28, he recounts the story of his life in his homeland, then being marched from one place to another, living in camps, making friends only to see them killed, and finally returning home, where he is a translator for Doctors Without Borders. . . . [This is] attractively designed. . . . Well written and informative." SLJ

Freedman, Russell
Children of the Great Depression. Clarion Books 2005 118p il lib bdg $20   **305.23**
1. Children—United States 2. Great Depression, 1929-1939 3. United States—Social conditions
ISBN 0-618-44630-3   LC 2005-06506
"Eight chapters cover the causes of the Great Depression, schooling, work life, migrant work, the lives of children who rode the rails, entertainment, and the economic resurgence of the early '40s." SLJ
"This stirring photo-essay combines . . . unforgettable personal details with a clear historical overview of the period and black-and-white photos by Dorothea Lange, Walker Evans, and many others." Booklist

Hartman, Holly
Girlwonder; every girl's guide to the fantastic feats, cool qualities, and remarkable abilities of women and girls; [by] Holly Hartman with the editors of Information Please. Houghton Mifflin 2003 234p il pa $9.95
Grades: 5 6 7 8   **305.23**
1. Women—United States 2. Girls 3. Teenagers
ISBN 0-618-31939-5
An updated and expanded edition of The Information Please girls' almanac by Margo McLoone and Alice Siegel, published 1995
"After opening with a day-by-day calendar of events in women's history, Hartman divides the information into

Hartman, Holly—_Continued_
topical sections, including chapters on American history, sports, literature, science, and careers. Famous women are highlighted throughout the pages. . . . There are also scattered bits of advice about health issues and relationships, as well as interesting tidbits about love and romance, mythological characters, and fashion trends. Readers will enjoy thumbing through this fact-packed text." SLJ

Howard, Helen, 1955-
Living as a refugee in America; Mohammed's story; text by Helen Howard; accompanied by interview in the words of Mohammed Nazari; interview conducted by Amy De Leal. World Almanac Library 2005 48p il map (Children in crisis) lib bdg $30.60
Grades: 6 7 8 9   **305.23**
1. Refugees 2. Afghan Americans
ISBN 0-8368-5959-6   LC 2005045251
"Mohammed, 15, is an Afghan who escaped the Taliban with his mother and two sisters; his father fled earlier. After briefly living in Iran and Turkey, they settled in St. Louis, MO. The teen remembers little of his early life as he was only six or seven when he left his homeland, but he describes his experiences before coming to America. . . . [This is] attractively designed. . . . Well written and informative." SLJ
Includes bibliographical references

Jukes, Mavis
The guy book; an owner's manual for teens: safety, maintenance, and operating instructions for teens. Crown 2002 152p il hardcover o.p. pa $12.95 *
Grades: 7 8 9 10   **305.23**
1. Boys 2. Adolescence 3. Sex education
ISBN 0-679-99028-3 (lib bdg); 0-679-89028-9 (pa)
LC 2001-47073
Provides information for boys on changes that occur in their bodies during puberty and offering advice on sexual topics, nutrition, drugs, girls, and more.
"In a jokey premise that will appeal to teens, the book follows the format of a car owner's manual with a retro look. . . . Much of this information is available in other sources, but the added sense of fun will make this a first choice for a lot of young men." Booklist
Includes bibliographical references

It's a girl thing; how to stay healthy, safe, and in charge; illustrations by Debbie Tilley. Knopf 1996 135p il hardcover o.p. pa $12 *
Grades: 7 8 9 10   **305.23**
1. Girls 2. Adolescence 3. Sex education
ISBN 0-679-94325-0; 0-679-87392-9 (pa)
LC 93-40296
"Jukes discusses a wide variety of subjects from buying a bra to sexual harassment and abuse. In a warm, conversational style, she covers body changes in both boys and girls, menstruation, general health, drinking and drugs, sexual feelings, pregnancy, contraceptives, and sexually transmitted diseases including AIDS. The text is sometimes humorous, but always conveys caring, respect,

and concern." SLJ
Includes bibliographical references

Making it home; real-life stories from children forced to flee; with an introduction by Beverley Naidoo. Dial Books 2005 c2004 117p $17.99; pa $6.99
Grades: 4 5 6 7   **305.23**
1. Refugees 2. Children and war
ISBN 0-8037-3083-7; 0-14-240455-1 (pa)
LC 2005045904
First published 2004 in the United Kingdom
This includes 20 "brief narratives by young people escaping their war-torn lands and lives. . . . Narrators from Kosovo, Bosnia, Afghanistan, Iraq, Congo, Liberia, Sudan, and Burundi reveal the injustices of their lives, forced by fate to have anything but normal childhoods. A short introduction precedes each narrative or set of narratives and gives the history of the country's conflict, providing much-needed background information. . . . A centerfold features full-color photos of several of the young people." SLJ

Muharrar, Aisha
More than a label; why what you wear and who you're with doesn't define who you are. Free Spirit 2002 144p il pa $13.95 *
Grades: 7 8 9 10   **305.23**
1. Adolescent psychology 2. Conduct of life
ISBN 1-57542-110-0   LC 2001-7386
Drawn from a survey of more than one thousand teenagers, first-person stories help to address the problems inherent in labeling people
"The enthusiastic, conversational tone will make the compassionate message very acceptable to teen readers." Booklist
Includes bibliographical references

Rimm, Sylvia B., 1935-
See Jane win for girls; a smart girl's guide to success; [by] Sylvia Rimm. Free Spirit 2003 131p il pa $13.95 *
Grades: 5 6 7 8   **305.23**
1. Girls 2. Success 3. Conduct of life
ISBN 1-57542-122-4   LC 2002-155780
Adapted from the author's title for adults See Jane win, published 1999 by Crown
Presents tips, quizzes, activities, and words of wisdom from successful women for girls trying to make positive changes and choices in all areas of their lives and develop confidence, inner strength, and the desire to learn
"The message is strong and simple, the advice is practical, and readers looking for guidance and direction will respond positively to the book's format. . . . A useful self-help book and practical guide to life." SLJ
Includes bibliographical references

Shandler, Sara
Ophelia speaks; adolescent girls write about their search for self. HarperPerennial 1999 285p pa $12.95
Grades: 7 8 9 10   **305.23**
1. Girls 2. Adolescence
ISBN 0-06-095297-0   LC 99-13534

Shandler, Sara—*Continued*

"Shandler collected writings from adolescent girls all over the country on topics that include sexuality, eating disorders, feminism, family dynamics, and friendship; their words, framed by Shandler's own reflections, are riveting and revealing." Libr J

Sherrow, Victoria

Encyclopedia of youth and war; young people as participants and victims. Oryx Press 2000 366p il $68.95

Grades: 8 9 10 11 12 Professional   **305.23**
1. Children and war
ISBN 1-57356-287-4   LC 99-43452

"Beginning with the Thirty-Year War in the mid-1600s, this single volume containing over three hundred individual entries addresses the impact of war on young people from the perspectives of both victim and participant. . . . Students will find valuable and interesting information on broad subjects such as volunteers, land mines, disease, or resistance movements as they relate specifically to children aged eighteen or younger." Voice Youth Advocates

Includes bibliographical references

Wilson, Janet, 1962-

One peace; true stories of young activists; written and illustrated by Janet Wilson. Orca Book Publishers 2008 43p il $19.95

Grades: 4 5 6 7   **305.23**
1. Children and war 2. Peace
ISBN 978-1-55143-892-4; 1-55143-892-5

"The stories of young people who have been refugees from war, injured by land mines, or learned about the consequences of violence through other means are interspersed with children's poems, quotes, artwork, and photographs. The brief, powerful accounts document how these children ages 8 to 15 worked for or became symbols of peace." SLJ

305.3   Men and women

Male/female roles: opposing viewpoints; Auriana Ojeda, book editor. Greenhaven Press 2005 219p il lib bdg $33.70; pa $22.45

Grades: 8 9 10 11 12   **305.3**
1. Sex role
ISBN 0-7377-2240-1 (lib bdg); 0-7377-2241-X (pa)
LC 2004-40605

Replaces the 2000 edition under the editorship of Laura K. Egendorf

"Opposing viewpoints series"

"Authors in this anthology debate whether gender is biological or culturally determined, if male and female roles have changed for the better, and how best to improve relationships between men and women." Publisher's note

Includes bibliographical references

305.4   Women

33 things every girl should know about women's history; from suffragettes to skirt lengths to the E.R.A.; edited by Tonya Bolden. Crown 2002 240p il hardcover o.p. pa $12.95 *

Grades: 5 6 7 8   **305.4**
1. Women—United States—History 2. Feminism
3. Women's rights
ISBN 0-375-91122-7; 0-375-81122-2 (pa)
LC 2001-47131

Uses poems, essays, letters, photographs and more to present the actions and achievements of women in the United States, from its beginnings up through the twentieth century

"This is a very strong, highly readable offering that gives context to the feminist movement." Booklist

Bausum, Ann

With courage and cloth; winning the fight for a woman's right to vote; by Ann Bausum. National Geographic 2004 111p il $21.95; lib bdg $32.90 *

Grades: 6 7 8 9   **305.4**
1. Women—Suffrage 2. Women—United States—History
ISBN 0-7922-7647-7; 0-7922-6996-9 (lib bdg)
LC 2004-1191

Contents: Introduction; Parade, 1913; Rights, 1848-1906; Momentum, 1906-1916; Protest, 1917; Prison, 1917; Action, 1918-1919; Victory, 1919-1920

This is a history of the movement for women's suffrage in the United States.

"Vintage photographs, some never before published, depict key figures in the movement speaking, protesting, parading, picketing, and going to jail. Bausum's careful research is evident throughout, with sources thoroughly cited and a text studded with original source quotations." SLJ

Coppens, Linda Miles, 1944-

What American women did, 1789-1920; a year-by-year reference. McFarland & Co. 2001 259p il $38.50 *

Grades: 7 8 9 10   **305.4**
1. Women—United States—History 2. Women—Social conditions
ISBN 0-7864-0899-5   LC 00-64010

"A chronological account of women's accomplishments in the areas of domesticity, work, education, religion, the arts, law and politics, and reform efforts. . . . This work will prove useful for students wishing to gain a better perspective of history, particularly social history, as it pertained to women." SLJ

Includes bibliographical references

Cullen-DuPont, Kathryn

Encyclopedia of women's history in America. 2nd ed. Facts on File 2000 418p il $71.50 *

Grades: 8 9 10 11 12 Adult   **305.4**
1. Women—United States—History 2. Feminism
3. Reference books
ISBN 0-8160-4100-8   LC 99-87498

Cullen-DuPont, Kathryn—*Continued*
First published 1996
This work highlights the lives and contributions of women in American history ranging from Pocahontas to Hillary Clinton and Madeleine Albright. Entries cover individuals, movements, court cases and women's issues from Colonial times to the present
"Well-written and informative. . . . An excellent quick reference source . . . recommended." Choice
Includes bibliographical references

Esherick, Joan
Women in the Arab world. Mason Crest Publishers 2005 112p il map (Women's issues, global trends) $22.95 *
Grades: 7 8 9 10   **305.4**
1. Women—Arab countries
ISBN 1-59084-861-6   LC 2004-12709
Contents: The modern Arab world: extremes for women; Arab women in ages past; Religion and Arab women; Arab women and the public world; Family life; Changing their world: Arab women who are making a difference; Unfinished business: issues and controversies facing Arab women today
This examines the roles of women in Arab countries.
This is "physically attractive, browsable, and up-to-date. . . . It is detailed and thorough, includes many charts and facts, and takes great care to differentiate between what most Arabs do or believe and what may occur in specific countries or among specific groups." SLJ
Includes bibliographical references

Gourley, Catherine, 1950-
Flappers and the new American woman; perceptions of women from 1918 through the 1920s. Twenty-First Century Books 2008 144p il (Images and issues of women in the twentieth century) lib bdg $38.60 *
Grades: 7 8 9 10   **305.4**
1. Women—United States—History 2. United States—History—1919-1933
ISBN 978-0-8225-6060-9; 0-8225-6060-7
               LC 2006-28983
This describes images of women in the United States from 1918 through the 1920s.
"The sparkling and engaging [text is] generously expanded by numerous, well-placed black-and-white photographs and period reproductions. . . . Great for research or browsing." SLJ
Includes bibliographical references

Gibson girls and suffragists; perceptions of women from the turn of the century through 1918. Twenty-First Century Books 2008 144p il (Images and issues of women in the twentieth century) lib bdg $38.60 *
Grades: 7 8 9 10   **305.4**
1. Women—United States—History 2. United States—History—1898-1919
ISBN 978-0-8225-7150-6; 0-8225-7150-1
               LC 2007-1689
This describes the images of women in United States at the beginning of the twentienth century.

"The sparkling and engaging [text is] generously expanded by numerous, well-placed black-and-white photographs and period reproductions. . . . Great for research or browsing." SLJ
Includes bibliographical references

Gidgets and women warriors; perceptions of women in the 1950s and 1960s; by Catherine Gourley. Twenty-First Century Books 2008 144p il (Images and issues of women in the twentieth century) $38.60 *
Grades: 7 8 9 10   **305.4**
1. Women—United States—History 2. United States—History—20th century
ISBN 978-0-8225-6805-6; 0-8225-6805-5
               LC 2006036103
This "examines women after World War II. Chapters explore varied aspects of the lives of white women as teens, consumers, wives, mothers, and burgeoning activists. . . . Most images and discussions of minority women are confined to the chapter on the Civil Rights movement. . . . Text is accessible and interesting for teens fascinated with women's history." Youth Voice Advocates
Includes bibliographical references

Rosie and Mrs. America; perceptions of women in the 1930s and 1940s. Twenty-First Century Books 2008 144p il (Images and issues of women in the twentieth century) lib bdg $38.60 *
Grades: 7 8 9 10   **305.4**
1. Women—United States—History 2. United States—History—20th century
ISBN 978-0-8225-6804-9; 0-8225-6804-7
               LC 2006-28984
This describes images of women in the United States in the 1930s and 1940's.
"The sparkling and engaging [text is] generously expanded by numerous, well-placed black-and-white photographs and period reproductions. . . . Great for research or browsing." SLJ
Includes bibliographical references

Harik, Ramsay M.
Women in the Middle East; tradition and change; [by] Ramsay M. Harik and Elsa Marston. rev ed. Watts 2003 192p il map lib bdg $29.50 *
Grades: 7 8 9 10 11 12   **305.4**
1. Women—Middle East
ISBN 0-531-12222-0   LC 2002-8510
First published 1996
Contents: The Middle East; Growing up; School days; Religion and tradition; Becoming a wife; Married life; Family and home: women's world; Veiling; Women's health; Women at work; Women in the arts and athletics; Women in public life; Is there a Middle Eastern women's movement?; A woman's later years; Afghanistan: the extremes of oppression; Looking toward tomorrow
Discusses the lives of women in the Middle East today including the traditions that shape these lives, the present day religious, social and political realities, and changing expectations
"A fine and timely revision. . . . A colorful and inviting new dust jacket along with a well-researched and

Harik, Ramsay M.—*Continued*
well-written text combine to make this an important purchase for general readers and student researchers alike."
SLJ
Includes bibliographical references

Macdonald, Fiona
Women in 19th-century Europe. Bedrick Bks.
1999 48p il (Other half of history) $17.95
Grades: 5 6 7 8   **305.4**
1. Women—Europe 2. Women—Social conditions
ISBN 0-87226-565-X   LC 98-42170
Examines the reality of women's lives in Europe dur-
ing the 1800s and how change slowly occurred
"The pages are a panorama of illustrations from black-
and-white woodcuts to line drawings and full-color re-
productions, each accompanied by a succinct caption.
. . . A delight to browse, and should lead readers to
more extensive exploration." SLJ
Includes glossary and bibliographical references

Matthews, Glenna
American women's history; a student
companion. Oxford Univ. Press 2000 368p il
(Oxford student companions to American history)
lib bdg $60
Grades: 7 8 9 10 11 12   **305.4**
1. Women—United States—History
ISBN 0-19-511317-9   LC 99-87245
Alphabetical articles on major events, documents, persons, social movements, and political and social concepts
connected with the history of women in America
"Articles vary in length and are easy to read. Many
articles are accompanied by a photograph. . . . This is
a helpful reference tool that will be useful to students
needing information about American women and their
contributions to U.S. history." Booklist
Includes bibliographical references

Miller, Brandon Marie
Good women of a well-blessed land; women's
lives in colonial America. Lerner Publs. 2003 96p
il (People's history) $31.93
Grades: 6 7 8 9   **305.4**
1. Women—United States—History 2. United States—
Social life and customs—1600-1775, Colonial period
ISBN 0-8225-0032-9   LC 2002-8902
Contents: The natural inhabitants; In this new discovered Virginia; Goodwives to New England; Weary, weary, weary, o; Up to their elbows in housewifery; Daughters of Eve; A changing world
A social history of the American colonial period with
a focus on the daily lives of women, including European
immigrants, Native Americans, and slaves
"The well-written account offers enough solid information to give readers a good sense of the period and
enough fascinating detail to keep them interested."
Booklist
Includes bibliographical references

Schomp, Virginia, 1953-
American voices from the women's movement.
Marshall Cavendish Benchmark 2007 138p il
(American voices from--) lib bdg $37.07 *
Grades: 6 7 8 9 10 11 12   **305.4**
1. Feminism 2. Women—United States—History
3. Women's rights
ISBN 978-0-7614-2171-9 (lib bdg); 0-7614-2171-8 (lib
bdg)   LC 2006-5800
"Describes the history of the women's rights movement in the United States, from colonial times to the
present day, through the use of primary resources such
as letters, diary entries, official government documents,
newspaper articles, historical art, and photographs." Publisher's note
Includes glossary and bibliographical references

Stearman, Kaye, 1951-
Feminism; [by] Kaye Stearman. Raintree 2004
64p il (Ideas of the modern world) lib bdg $32.79
Grades: 7 8 9 10   **305.4**
1. Feminism
ISBN 0-7398-6415-7   LC 2003-2068
Contents: What is feminism?; Raising the issues;
Campaigning for the vote; The forgotten years of feminism; Feminism becomes women's liberation; I'm not a
feminist but . . . ; Beijing and beyond
"Stearman discusses the history of women's rights
with connections made to other political movements such
as abolitionism and temperance. . . . The author looks at
new interpretations of feminism and issues such as
sweatshop labor, countries with controversial social laws
against women's rights, and female genital mutilation.
[This book has] a balance of ideas and nonjudgmental
language. Black-and-white and full-color photos appear
throughout." SLJ
Includes bibliographical references

Swisher, Clarice, 1933-
Women of the roaring twenties; [by] Clarice
Swisher. Lucent Books 2006 112p il (Women in
history) $28.70
Grades: 7 8 9 10   **305.4**
1. Women—United States—History 2. United States—
History—1919-1933
ISBN 1-59018-363-0   LC 2004-23410
Contents: The defiant spirit; Women performers; The
new woman; Women in business and the professions;
Working women; Political activists; Women writers
This "account draws on diaries, letters, and journals to
tell the story of women in the 1920s—coeds and house-
wives, laborers and professionals, writers and activists.
. . . The clear prose and occasional photos will hold
readers." Booklist
Includes bibliographical references

305.8   Ethnic and national groups

The **African** American almanac. Gale Res. 2007 il
$240 *
Grades: 8 9 10 11 12 Adult   **305.8**

The African American almanac—*Continued*
1. African Americans 2. Reference books
ISSN 1071-8710
ISBN 0-7876-4021-2; 978-0-7876-4021-7
First edition under the editorship of Harry A. Ploski published 1967 by Bellwether with title: The Negro almanac. Periodically revised. Editors vary
"Reference covering the cultural and political history of Black Americans. Includes generous amount of statistical information and biographies of Black Americans, both historical and contemporary." N Y Public Libr. Book of How & Where to Look It Up

African-American culture and history; a student's guide; Jack Salzman, editor-in-chief. Macmillan Ref. USA 2001 4v il set $415
Grades: 6 7 8 9   **305.8**
1. African Americans—Encyclopedias 2. Reference books
ISBN 0-02-865531-1   LC 00-61657
Adapted from the five-volume Encyclopedia of African American culture and history published by Macmillan in 1996; revised for a sixth- to seventh-grade, middle school audience
"The 852 alphabetically arranged articles include biographies of notable African-Americans, events, historical eras, legal cases, areas of cultural achievement, professions, sports, and places. . . . The final volume includes supplemental material such as a detailed chronology of African-American history from 1444 through 2000, a glossary; list of suggested resources, and comprehensive index." Book Rep
"This is a good choice for a comprehensive, readable resource about African American culture and history." Booklist

The Arabs; Jean Brodsky Schur, book editor. Greenhaven Press 2005 218p il map (Coming to America) lib bdg $34.95
Grades: 8 9 10 11 12   **305.8**
1. Arab Americans
ISBN 0-7377-2148-0   LC 2004-52356
"After a short introduction about Arab immigration, subsequent chapters discuss the various reasons Arabs chose to leave their home countries, the ways in which Arab Christians and Muslims adapted to American culture, and the types of discrimination and anti-Arab stereotyping faced by this group. . . . The selections are clearly written and informative." SLJ
Includes bibliographical references

Aronson, Marc
Race: a history beyond black and white. Atheneum Books for Young Readers 2007 322p il $18.99 *
Grades: 8 9 10 11 12   **305.8**
1. Race 2. Racism
ISBN 978-0-689-86554-1; 0-689-86554-6
                                            LC 2007-31912
"Ginee Seo Books"
This is a "history of racism and its antecedents, from ancient Sumer to the Rodney King beating and beyond, interspersed with personal vignettes tailored to a young audience. . . . The pictorial implementation increases the

impact of the text. . . . Clearly in evidence . . . are the complexity of race and the tenacity of racism." Horn Book

Birdseye, Debbie Holsclaw
Under our skin; kids talk about race; by Debbie Holsclaw Birdseye and Tom Birdseye; photographs by Robert Crum. Holiday House 1997 30p il $15.95
Grades: 4 5 6 7   **305.8**
1. United States—Race relations 2. Ethnic relations
ISBN 0-8234-1325-X   LC 97-9395
Six young people discuss their feelings about their own ethnic backgrounds and about their experiences with people of different races
"This book provides an excellent starting point for discussion. It gives readers a chance to see what life is like through someone else's eyes, and in someone else's skin." SLJ
Includes bibliographical references

Bolden, Tonya
Tell all the children our story; memories and mementos of being young and Black in America. Abrams 2001 128p il $24.95 *
Grades: 5 6 7 8   **305.8**
1. African American children 2. United States—Race relations
ISBN 0-8109-4496-0   LC 2001-1353
"This compilation of the African American experience, from colonial times through the twentieth century, reads and looks like a family scrapbook. . . . Photographs, excerpts from diaries and memoirs, and reproductions of artwork by black artists such as Charles Altson beautifully bring the story of each generation to life. Bolden vibrantly delivers her historical message through a contemporary perspective." Booklist
Includes bibliographical references

Byers, Ann
African-American history from emancipation to today; rising above the ashes of slavery; foreword by series advisor Henry Louis Gates. Enslow Publishers 2004 128p il map (Slavery in American history) lib bdg $26.60 *
Grades: 7 8 9 10   **305.8**
1. African Americans—History
ISBN 0-7660-2153-X   LC 2003-24558
Contents: Free at last?: 1865-1866; Free but not equal: 1865-1877; Equal but separate: 1877-1915; Separate but proud: 1915-1941; Equal rights: 1941-1965; Equal power: 1966-1972; Righting the wrongs
"Byers brings together the issues and their impact from 1865 to 2002 by discussing such topics as Reconstruction, sharecropping, Jim Crow, the Harlem Renaissance, Brown v. Board of Education, Malcolm X, Black Panthers, and reparation debates. . . . [This book] will be useful in American-history collections." SLJ
Includes bibliographical references

The **Chinese**; C.J. Shane, book editor. Greenhaven Press 2005 206p map (Coming to America) lib bdg $34.95
Grades: 8 9 10 11 12   **305.8**
1. Chinese Americans
ISBN 0-7377-2150-2   LC 2003-67533
This book focuses on the experiences of Chinese immigrants, including the prejudices they faced in America. Includes chronologies and profiles of prominent Chinese Americans.
Includes bibliographical references

Choi, Anne Soon
Korean Americans; [by] Anne Soon Choi. Chelsea House 2007 132p il map (The new immigrants) $27.95
Grades: 7 8 9 10 11 12   **305.8**
1. Korean Americans
ISBN 0-7910-8788-3   LC 2006019745
This is a history of immigration from Korea to North America which describes the achievements and challenges of Korean Americans.
Includes glossary and bibliographical references

The **Cubans**; Jacquelyn Landis, book editor. Greenhaven Press 2005 208p il (Coming to America) $34.50
Grades: 8 9 10 11 12   **305.8**
1. Cuban Americans
ISBN 0-7377-2763-2   LC 2004-60583
Traces the history of Cubans in the United States, discussing the impact of Castro's revolution and America's no-trade policy on immigration, the problems Cubans have faced in a new society, and their contributions to the culture of the country.

Diner, Hasia R.
Jews in America. Oxford Univ. Press 1999 158p il (Religion in American life) lib bdg $28
Grades: 7 8 9 10   **305.8**
1. Jews—United States
ISBN 0-19-510678-4   LC 98-17645
Examines the migration and background of those Jews who came to America, their adaptations to their new life, the rituals, traditions, and organizations of Jewish Americans, and their contemporary situation
"The coverage is brief, but the text is clear and lively. A host of archival photos and reproductions enhance the presentation." SLJ
Includes glossary and bibliographical references

Discrimination: opposing viewpoints; Jacqueline Langwith, book editor. Greenhaven Press 2008 247p il $36.20; pa $24.95
Grades: 8 9 10 11 12   **305.8**
1. Discrimination 2. Affirmative action programs 3. Minorities
ISBN   978-0-73773-739-4;   0-73773-739-5; 978-0-73773-740-0 (pa); 0-73773-740-9 (pa)
                            LC 2007-933224
"Opposing viewpoints series"
Replaces the edition published 1997 under the editorship of Mary E. Williams

This covers the topic of discrimination "in pro and con articles written by experts in the field or journalists with relevant experience. Clearly written, well researched, and far reaching, *Discrimination* explores the problem in its many forms." SLJ
Includes bibliographical references

Doak, Robin S., 1963-
Struggling to become American; [by] Robin Doak. Chelsea House 2007 106p il map (Latino American history) $35
Grades: 5 6 7 8   **305.8**
1. Hispanic Americans 2. Immigrants—United States
ISBN 0-8160-6443-1; 978-0-8160-6443-4
                            LC 2006017140
"Topics such as U.S. policy decisions regarding Puerto Rico and Cuba, racism experienced by immigrants and those who became American when the U.S. Mexican border shifted in 1848, Latino culture in the United States, and the repatriation of Mexicans during the Great Depression are covered in a reasonable amount of detail. Plenty of captioned photographs, political cartoons, and colorful subheads and informational sidebars keep the book visually interesting." SLJ
Includes bibliographical references

Frankel, Noralee, 1950-
Break those chains at last: African Americans, 1860-1880. Oxford Univ. Press 1996 143p il map (Young Oxford history of African Americans) lib bdg $25
Grades: 6 7 8 9   **305.8**
1. African Americans—History 2. Slavery—United States
ISBN 0-19-508798-4   LC 95-1848
After a chapter on the Civil War, this volume addresses such topics as suffrage and political participation; economic and educational opportunities; and marriage and family life of the newly freed slaves
"Frankel makes especially good use of quotations from interviews with former slaves done in the 1930s; Reconstruction Era pension examiners' interviews with Black Civil War widows; Freedmen's Bureau records, etc." SLJ
Includes bibliographical references

Gay, Kathlyn, 1930-
Cultural diversity; conflicts and challenges: the ultimate teen guide. Scarecrow Press 2003 121p (It happened to me) pa $25.95
Grades: 7 8 9 10   **305.8**
1. Multiculturalism 2. Prejudices 3. Racism 4. Toleration
ISBN 0-8108-4805-8   LC 2003-7709
Contents: Out of many, one?; Challenges in a diverse society; Prejudice and racism amidst diversity; Racist images and stereotypes; Religious diversity and conflicts; From intolerance to hatred to violence; Reducing bigotry, racism, and hate crimes; Respecting diversity; Speaking out
The author discusses prejudice, racism, religious intolerance, stereotypes, and hate crimes and how to reduce

Gay, Kathlyn, 1930——_Continued_

them

"The author does an outstanding job of tackling an emotionally charged topic and relates violent and destructive situations with grace and intelligence. Cultural Diversity should be in all libraries." SLJ

Includes bibliographical references

The **Germans**; Jacquelyn Landis, book editor. Greenhaven Press 2006 224p il (Coming to America) $34.95

Grades: 8 9 10 11 12   **305.8**
1. German Americans
ISBN 0-7377-2152-9   LC 2005-51268

In a series of essays, explores the experience of German immigrants in America, and their influence on American society.

Hall, Loretta

Arab American voices. U.X.L 2000 233p il $58

Grades: 7 8 9 10 11 12   **305.8**
1. Arab Americans
ISBN 0-7876-2956-1   LC 99-37500

Twenty primary source documents from speeches, memoirs, poems, novels, and autobiographies present the words of Americans with roots in Lebanon, Syria, Palestine, Iraq, Egypt, and other Arab nations

"The works selected, from Kahlil Gibran's 'Dead Are My People' to the text of the U.S. government's Antiterrorism and Effective Death Penalty Act of 1986, should provide many new openings for discussions with students." Booklist

Includes glossary and bibliographical references

Haskins, James, 1941-2005

Out of the darkness; the story of Blacks moving North, 1890-1940; by James Haskins and Kathleen Benson. Benchmark Bks. 2000 112p (Great journeys) lib bdg $32.79

Grades: 5 6 7 8   **305.8**
1. Bricktop, 1894-1984 2. Jones, Joe, 1896-1987 3. African Americans—History 4. United States—Race relations
ISBN 0-7614-0970-X   LC 99-19882

Uses the experiences of two individuals, Ada "Bricktop" Smith and Joe Jones, to present the story of the Great Migration of Southern Blacks to northern cities from the late 1800s to the years after World War I.

This "delivers a compelling account of the 'Great Migration' from the South to the North. . . . Black-and-white photos and quotes greatly enhance the narrative." SLJ

Includes bibliographical references

The rise of Jim Crow; by James Haskins and Kathleen Benson; with Virginia Schomp. Marshall Cavendish Benchmark 2008 80p il (Drama of African-American history) lib bdg $23.95 *

Grades: 5 6 7 8   **305.8**
1. African Americans—Segregation 2. African Americans—History 3. United States—Race relations
ISBN 978-0-7614-2640-0

"Provides a history of the decades of poverty, oppression, and terror that African Americans suffered under

the system of segregation in the United States, from the end of the Reconstruction era through the early decades of the twentieth century." Publisher's note

Includes glossary and bibliographical references

Hoobler, Dorothy

The Chinese American family album; [by] Dorothy and Thomas Hoobler; introduction by Bette Bao Lord. Oxford Univ. Press 1994 128p il map (American family albums) hardcover o.p. pa $16.95 *

Grades: 5 6 7 8 9   **305.8**
1. Chinese Americans
ISBN 0-19-509123-X; 0-19-512421-9 (pa)
       LC 93-11873

"This sourcebook on the Chinese immigrant experience is divided into six topics: the homeland, the voyage to America, arrival in America, first-generation life, the integration of . . . generations, and Chinese Americans today. The authors introduce each chapter with a summary essay, then let the immigrants and their descendents speak for themselves in excerpts from oral reminiscences, written histories, and fiction spanning the years from the Gold Rush to the 1980s. Period photographs and drawings, maps, and sidebars enhance the text. The result resembles a well-organized, handsomely designed scrapbook. . . . A valuable resource." SLJ

Includes bibliographical references

The German American family album; [by] Dorothy and Thomas Hoobler; introductions by Werner Klemperer. Oxford University Press 1996 127p il (American family albums) hardcover o.p. pa $16.95 *

Grades: 5 6 7 8   **305.8**
1. German Americans
ISBN 0-19-508133-1; 0-19-512422-7 (pa)
       LC 95-14448

Traces the history of German immigrants to the United States through letters, diaries and newspaper accounts

Includes bibliographical references

The Irish American family album; [by] Dorothy and Thomas Hoobler; introduction by Joseph P. Kennedy II. Oxford University Press 1995 128p il (American family albums) hardcover o.p. pa $16.95 *

Grades: 5 6 7 8   **305.8**
1. Irish Americans
ISBN 0-19-509461-1; 0-19-512418-7 (pa)
       LC 94-19569

"Selections from diaries, letters, interviews, newspaper and magazine articles, and books provide an arresting picture of what it has meant to be of Irish heritage in America. . . . Topics such as prejudice, working conditions and labor unions; politics; and the importance of family, friends, and the Catholic Church are touched upon." SLJ

Includes bibliographical references

Hoobler, Dorothy—*Continued*
The Italian American family album; [by] Dorothy and Thomas Hoobler; introduction by Governor Mario M. Cuomo. Oxford University Press 1994 127p il map (American family albums) hardcover o.p. pa $24.95 *
Grades: 5 6 7 8   **305.8**
    1. Italian Americans
    ISBN 0-19-509124-8; 0-19-512420-0 (pa)
                                           LC 93-46918
This volume includes selections from "diaries, letters, and oral histories. . . . Each of the six chapters begins with background information and then goes on to discuss life in the old country, coming to America, first impressions, working, forming a new life, and becoming a part of America." SLJ
Includes bibliographical references

The Japanese American family album; [by] Dorothy and Thomas Hoobler; introduction by George Takei. Oxford Univ. Press 1995 127p il map (American family albums) hardcover o.p. pa $16.95 *
Grades: 5 6 7 8   **305.8**
    1. Japanese Americans
    ISBN 0-19-508131-5; 0-19-512423-5 (pa)
                                           LC 94-43466
"Organized chronologically, this book captures the broad sweep of the Japanese-American experience. Each of the six chapters offers a succinct historical presentation followed by first-person accounts. Relying on oral histories and original documents, both pictorial and written, the Hooblers have truly humanized historical events." SLJ
Includes bibliographical references

Horst, Heather A.
Jamaican Americans; [by] Heather A. Horst and Andrew Garner; series editor, Robert D. Johnston. Chelsea House 2007 144p il map (The new immigrants) lib bdg $27.95
Grades: 7 8 9 10 11 12   **305.8**
    1. West Indian Americans 2. Immigrants—United States
    ISBN 0-7910-8790-5; 978-0-7910-8790-9
                                           LC 2006-25904
"Drawing on personal stories and historical fact, this . . . book focuses on [Jamaican Americans] and assesses their lasting impact." Publisher's note
The "chatty narrative style may engage readers." Horn Book Guide
Includes bibliographical references

Horton, James Oliver
Landmarks of African American history. Oxford University Press 2004 207p (American landmarks) $30
Grades: 8 9 10 11 12   **305.8**
    1. Historic sites 2. African Americans—History
    ISBN 0-19-514118-0   LC 2004-2798
"Published in association with the National Register of Historic Places, National Park Service, and the National Parks Foundation"--T.p. verso

"Horton discusses 13 historic places, beginning with Jamestown, VA, and ending with the Woolworth department store in Greensboro, NC, the site of the first student sit-in in 1960. Clearly written and well organized, the text enriches the study of African-American history, providing a context and a look at its artifacts. . . . Well-placed illustrations of archival and current photographs and maps make for an attractive presentation." SLJ
Includes bibliographical references

Interracial America: opposing viewpoints; Eleanor Stanford, book editor. Greenhaven Press 2006 205p il lib bdg $34.95; pa $23.70
Grades: 8 9 10 11 12   **305.8**
    1. United States—Race relations 2. Ethnic relations
    ISBN 0-7377-2943-0 (lib bdg); 0-7377-2944-9 (pa)
                                           LC 2005-54893
Replaces the edition published 2001 under the editorship of Mary E. Williams
"Opposing viewpoints series"
The question of racial and ethnic differences is addressed sociologically and politically. Attention is given to immigration, affirmative action, interracial marriage, biracial children, and transracial adoption.
"For social-studies classes wishing to delve into the matter of race, this volume should prove helpful when used in conjunction with other source materials. It will be a boon to debaters." SLJ
Includes bibliographical references

The **Irish**; Karen Price Hossell, book editor. Greenhaven Press 2005 207p il (Coming to America) lib bdg $34.95
Grades: 8 9 10 11 12   **305.8**
    1. Irish Americans
    ISBN 0-7377-2154-5   LC 2004-47582
"The contributors to this volume explore why the Irish left their homeland, the experiences of the immigrants and their descendants, and the achievements of notable Irish Americans." Publisher's note
Includes bibliographical references

The **Italians**; C.J. Shane, book editor. Greenhaven Press 2005 208p il (Coming to America) lib bdg $34.95
Grades: 8 9 10 11 12   **305.8**
    1. Italian Americans
    ISBN 0-7377-2765-9   LC 2004-54132
This book focuses on the experiences of Italian immigrants, including the ethnic stereotyping Italian Americans still face today. Includes chronologies and profiles of prominent Italian Americans.
Includes bibliographical references

The **Jews**; Adriane Ruggiero, book editor. Greenhaven Press 2006 199p il (Coming to America) $34.95
Grades: 8 9 10 11 12   **305.8**
    1. Jews—United States 2. Immigrants—United States 3. United States—Ethnic relations
    ISBN 0-7377-2767-5   LC 2005-44745
Presents essays on the experiences of Jews in the United States, discussing the successive waves of immigrants, the persecutions they have fled in their homelands, and issues of discrimination they contend with in American society.

Katz, William Loren

Black Indians; a hidden heritage. Atheneum Pubs. 1986 198p il $17.95; pa $10

Grades: 8 9 10 11 12   **305.8**

1. African Americans 2. Native Americans

ISBN 0-689-31196-6; 0-689-80901-8 (pa)

LC 85-28770

Traces the history of relations between blacks and American Indians, and the existence of black Indians, from the earliest foreign landings through pioneer days.

The author "has provided a valuable addition to titles on American Indians. Excellent for assignments, it contains important information many history instructors may be unaware of. His sections on black Indians and the Seminoles of Florida and their views about living together are particularly good." Child Book Rev Serv

Includes bibliographical references

Masoff, Joy, 1951-

The African American story; the events that shaped our nation—and the people that changed our lives. Five Ponds 2007 95p il map $26.50 *

Grades: 4 5 6 7   **305.8**

1. African Americans—History

ISBN 978-0-972715-69-0

This "covers the history of the African people in America from the 1400s to the present. Historical photographs, archival documents, maps, and a fact-filled time line provide a visually stimulating introduction to the subject. . . . Masoff provides a tremendous amount of material in an exciting, appealing title that is useful for browsing, introductory lessons, quick reference, and beginning research." SLJ

Includes bibliographical references

McClaurin, Irma

Facing the future; by Irma McClaurin with Virginia Schomp. Marshall Cavendish Benchmark 2008 il (Drama of African-American history) lib bdg $23.95 *

Grades: 5 6 7 8   **305.8**

1. African Americans—History 2. United States—Race relations

ISBN 978-0-7614-2644-8; 0-7614-2644-2

"Covers the struggle for racial equality from the end of the civil rights movement in the 1960s to the present day." Publisher's note

Includes glossary and bibliographical references

The **Mexicans**; C.J. Shane, book editor. Greenhaven Press 2005 221p il map (Coming to America) lib bdg $34.95

Grades: 8 9 10 11 12   **305.8**

1. Mexican Americans

ISBN 0-7377-2156-1   LC 2004-46078

This book focuses on the experiences of Mexican immigrants, including those who became Americans by default after the Mexican-American War of 1848 and those who are immigrating today. Includes chronologies and profiles of prominent Mexican Americans

Includes bibliographical references

Ochoa, George

Atlas of Hispanic-American history; [by] George Ochoa and Carter Smith. Rev ed. Facts on File 2008 c2009 250p il map (Facts on File library of American history) $95; pa $21.95

Grades: 7 8 9 10   **305.8**

1. Hispanic Americans—History 2. Reference books

ISBN 978-0-8160-7092-3; 978-0-8160-7736-6 (pa)

LC 2008-20664

First published 2001

This reference chronicles the "cultural, historical, political, and social experiences of Hispanic Americans through the years. . . . [It] examines Spanish, Native American, and African influences and how they combine in different ways to form the varied cultures of Hispanic America." Publisher's note

Includes bibliographical references

Perl, Lila

North across the border; the story of the Mexican Americans. Benchmark Bks. 2002 112p il (Great journeys) lib bdg $32.79

Grades: 6 7 8 9   **305.8**

1. Mexican Americans

ISBN 0-7614-1226-3   LC 00-57017

The author "begins by describing the monumental effect the arrival of Europeans had on Mexican civilizations. She then discusses the impact, on both countries, of the great migration to the U.S., which began in the twentieth century. . . . [This book is] filled with crisp, well-selected photographs and historical illustrations." Booklist

Includes bibliographical references

To the Golden Mountain; the story of the Chinese who built the transcontinental railroad. Benchmark Bks. 2002 112p il music (Great journeys) lib bdg $32.79   **305.8**

1. Chinese—United States 2. Railroads—United States 3. United States—Immigration and emigration

ISBN 0-7614-1324-3   LC 2001-6241

Contents: From the land of the celestials; Gold fields and Chinatowns; Working on the railroad; Blasting through the mountains; The race to the finish; The Chinese must go; The door to the Golden Mountain closes

"More than the story of Chinese workers' contributions to building the transcontinental railroad, this book is also a brief history of China's contacts with the West, focusing on the financial despair that drove many men to emigrate, beginning in the 1840s. The anti-Chinese sentiment that rose in California after their success in the gold rush is discussed, as is life in the Chinatowns that were established." SLJ

Includes bibliographical references

Petrillo, Valerie

A kid's guide to Latino history; more than 70 activities. Chicago Review Press 2009 il pa $14.95

Grades: 4 5 6 7   **305.8**

1. Hispanic Americans—History

ISBN 978-1-55652-771-5; 1-55652-771-3

LC 2008040433

Petrillo, Valerie—*Continued*

"This big, lively overview examines the history of Latinos in the U.S. . . . The chatty, informative text, presented in readable, spacious layouts, will draw kids with lots of fun, illustrated instructions for related activities. . . . The accessible facts and the individual portraits of notable authors, athletes, entertainers, and politicians portray Latinos' rich contribution to U.S. heritage, and kids will want to talk about the well-presented issues." Booklist

Includes bibliographical references

Race relations: opposing viewpoints; James D. Torr, book editor. Greenhaven Press 2005 208p il lib bdg $34.95; pa $23.70

Grades: 8 9 10 11 12   **305.8**

1. United States—Race relations

ISBN 0-7377-2955-4 (lib bdg); 0-7377-2956-2 (pa)
      LC 2004-59763

Replaces the edition published 2000 under the editorship of Mary E. Williams

"Opposing viewpoints series"

This book explores race-related "topics in the following chapters: What Is the State of Race Relations in America? Is Racism a Serious Problem? What Should the Government Do to Improve Race Relations? How Can Society Improve Race Relations?" Publisher's note

Includes bibliographical references

Racism: an opposing viewpoints guide; Lauri S. Friedman, book editor. Greenhaven Press 2006 104p il map (Writing the critical essay) lib bdg $26.20

Grades: 8 9 10 11 12   **305.8**

1. Racism 2. United States—Race relations 3. Authorship 4. Critical thinking

ISBN 0-7377-3464-7

"The publisher of the Opposing Viewpoints series has recycled its essays on racism and restructured the format to teach writing style and technique. Students are given an opportunity to read the essays presented, not merely for content but also for critical analysis. Through specific questions about each selection, they are guided in uncovering exactly why it is effective. They are then encouraged to write persuasive essays of their own." SLJ

Includes bibliographical references

Radzilowski, John, 1965-

Ukrainian Americans; [by] John Radzilowski. Chelsea House 2006 128p il map (The new immigrants) lib bdg $27.95

Grades: 7 8 9 10 11 12   **305.8**

1. Ukrainian Americans

ISBN 978-0-7910-8789-3 (lib bdg); 0-7910-8789-1 (lib bdg)   LC 2006-15644

"In addition to profiles on notable Ukrainian Americans, such as actor Jack Palance and Hall of Fame NHL goaltender Terry Sawchuk, . . . [this book provides an] introduction to the history, culture, religion, and experiences of this immigrant group." Publisher's note

Includes glossary and bibliographical references

Rangaswamy, Padma, 1945-

Indian Americans; [by] Padma Rangaswamy. Chelsea House 2007 158p il map (The new immigrants) lib bdg $27.95

Grades: 7 8 9 10 11 12   **305.8**

1. East Indian Americans 2. Immigrants—United States

ISBN 0-7910-8786-7   LC 2006-8384

The author traces the history of new immigrants from India "from the early days of the Punjabi pioneers in California to the triumphs of the 'dot-com generation.'" Publisher's note

Includes bibliographical references

Rubin, Susan Goldman, 1939-

L'chaim! to Jewish life in America! [by] Susan Goldman Rubin. Harry N. Abrams 2004 176p il map $24.95 *

Grades: 7 8 9 10   **305.8**

1. Jews—United States

ISBN 0-8109-5035-9   LC 2004-5848

"Rubin focuses on particular individuals to show how European immigrants have found ways to be both Jewish and American." SLJ

This is an "exceptionally attractive package, packed with quotes, personal stories, and photos of art from The Jewish Museum. . . . The art is gorgeous, and Rubin . . . writes with clarity and enthusiasm." Booklist

Includes bibliographical references

Schomp, Virginia, 1953-

Marching toward freedom; by Virginia Schomp. Marshall Cavendish Benchmark 2008 80p il (Drama of African-American history) lib bdg $23.95 *

Grades: 5 6 7 8   **305.8**

1. African Americans—History 2. United States—Race relations

ISBN 978-0-7614-2643-1

"Explores the period between 1929 and 1954 in African-American history, when the 'New Negro' emerged, proud of his or her racial heritage and determined to topple the barriers to black advancement." Publisher's note

Includes glossary and bibliographical references

Schroeder, Michael J.

Mexican Americans; [by] Michael J. Schroeder. Chelsea House 2007 150p il map (The new immigrants) lib bdg $27.95 *

Grades: 6 7 8 9   **305.8**

1. Mexican Americans 2. Immigrants—United States

ISBN 0-7910-8785-9   LC 2006008380

"Focused primarily on the achievements and hardships of Mexican American immigrants since the passage of the Immigration and Naturalization Services Act in 1965, this book . . . offers important historical understanding of how U.S. immigration issues and policies have evolved over the past few decades." Booklist

Includes bibliographical references

Sonneborn, Liz

Vietnamese Americans; [by] Liz Sonneborn. Chelsea House 2006 136p il map (The new immigrants) lib bdg $27.95

Grades: 7 8 9 10 11 12   **305.8**

1. Vietnamese Americans

ISBN 0-7910-8787-5; 978-0-7910-8787-9

LC 2006-8383

This book looks at the challenges faced by Vietnamese immigrants, many of whom came to the United States after the Vietnam War.

Includes glossary and bibliographical references

Sterngass, Jon, 1955-

Filipino Americans; [by] Jon Sterngass. Chelsea House 2006 144p il map (The new immigrants) lib bdg $27.95

Grades: 7 8 9 10 11 12   **305.8**

1. Filipino Americans 2. Immigrants—United States

ISBN 0-7910-8791-3   LC 2006015645

"This book examines the history and culture, as well as the trials and successes, of [Filipino Americans]." Publisher's note

Includes glossary and bibliographical references

Student almanac of African American history; Media Project, Inc. Greenwood Press 2003 2v il map (Middle school reference) set $80 *

Grades: 6 7 8 9   **305.8**

1. African Americans—History 2. Reference books

ISBN 0-313-32596-0   LC 2002-35332

Contents: v1 From slavery to freedom, 1492-1876; v2 From Reconstruction to today, 1877-present

"This basic overview covers the history of African Americans in the U.S. from 1492 to the present. Each straightforward chapter introduces a time period through a short narrative essay followed by an A-to-Z section outlining the important figures and terms." SLJ

"This attractive almanac provides information on topics of interest to users in middle school and up. . . . It will be a welcome addition to school and public libraries where there is a need for additional information about African Americans." Booklist

Includes bibliographical references

The **Vietnamese**; Michelle E. Houle, book editor. Greenhaven Press 2006 191p il (Coming to America) $34.95

Grades: 8 9 10 11 12   **305.8**

1. Vietnamese Americans 2. Immigrants—United States

ISBN 0-7377-2769-1   LC 2005-46131

Presents a series of essays on the experiences of Vietnamese who have migrated to the United States, discussing the effects of the Vietnam War on their troubled homeland, their problems in assimilation, and prominent countrymen who have achieved success in America.

What are you? voices of mixed-race young people; [edited by] Pearl Fuyo Gaskins. Holt & Co. 1999 273p il $18.95

Grades: 7 8 9 10   **305.8**

1. Racially mixed people 2. Teenagers 3. United States—Race relations

ISBN 0-8050-5968-7   LC 98-37381

Many young people of racially mixed backgrounds discuss their feelings about family relationships, prejudice, dating, personal identity, and other issues

"While underscoring the complexity of the mixed-race experience, these unadorned voices offer a genuine, poignant, enlightening and empowering message to all readers." SLJ

Includes bibliographical references

306   Culture and institutions

Bowling, beatniks, and bell-bottoms; pop culture of 20th-century America; Sara Pendergast and Tom Pendergast, editors. U.X.L 2002 5v il set $250

Grades: 8 9 10 11 12 Adult   **306**

1. Popular culture—United States 2. United States—Civilization

ISBN 0-7876-5675-5   LC 2002-1829

Contents: v1 1900s and 1910s; v2 1920s and 1930s; v3 1940s and 1950s; v4 1960s and 1970s; v5 1980s and 1990s

The editors "track trends in American popular culture through 750 entries arranged chronologically by decade over five volumes. Within decades, entries are divided into nine major areas: 'Commerce,' 'Fashion,' 'Film and Theater,' 'Food and Drink,' 'Music,' 'Print Culture,' 'Sports and Games,' Television and Radio,' and 'The Way We Lived. . . . Informative, entertaining, and clearly presented." Libr J

Includes bibliographical references

306.7   Sexual relations

Burningham, Sarah O'Leary

Boyology; a teen girl's crash course in all things boy; illustrations by Keri Smith. Chronicle Books 2009 167p il pa $12.99

Grades: 6 7 8 9   **306.7**

1. Boys—Psychology 2. Interpersonal relations 3. Dating (Social customs)

ISBN 978-0-8118-6436-7 (pa); 0-8118-6436-7 (pa)

LC 2008005277

"Adolescent girls seeking a deeper understanding of the opposite sex will appreciate this appealing, entertaining guide full of useful facts and sound advice. Burningham . . . explores a wide range of subjects, including how to determine which 'breed' of boy you're dealing with, first dates and the rules of the dating game, setting boundaries, peer conflicts and pressures, dealing with parents, the difference between having a boyfriend and boy friends and coping with the inevitable breakup." Kirkus

Forssberg, Manne, 1983-

Sex for guys; translated by Maria Lundin. Groundwood Books/House of Anansi 2007 142p il (Groundwork guides) $15.95; pa $9.95 *

Grades: 7 8 9 10 11 12   **306.7**

Forssberg, Manne, 1983-—*Continued*
1. Sex education 2. Men—Sexual behavior
ISBN 978-0-88899-770-8; 978-0-88899-771-5 (pa)

"Originally published in Sweden, this first person approach speaks directly to a primarily male audience. In a straightforward manner, the author tackles a broad range of sensitive topics such as male and female anatomy, masturbation, orgasm, intercourse, oral and gay sex, sexually transmitted diseases, pornography, and relationships. Facts, opinions, and testimonials by the author and other young adults are . . . presented." Libr Media Connect

This "will prove invaluable to guys bombarded with less sensitive and comprehensive media messages. . . . This is a witty, sane treatment of the things that drive guys crazy—a must read for teens with questions." Bull Cent Child Books

Includes bibliographical references

Sex: opposing viewpoints. Greenhaven Press 2006 208p il lib bdg $34.95; pa $23.70
Grades: 7 8 9 10 **306.7**
1. Sexual behavior
ISBN 0-7377-2959-7 (lib bdg); 0-7377-2960-0 (pa)
LC 2005-52578

Replaces the edition published 2000

"Opposing viewpoints series"

"Authors debate several issues such as premarital sex, gay marriage, and virginity pledges in this . . . anthology." Publisher's note

Includes bibliographical references

306.76 Sexual orientation

Alsenas, Linas
Gay America; struggle for equality. Amulet Books 2008 160p il $24.95 *
Grades: 7 8 9 10 **306.76**
1. Gay men—Civil rights 2. Lesbians—Civil rights 3. Gay liberation movement 4. Homosexuality
ISBN 978-0-8109-9487-4; 0-8109-9487-9
LC 2007-28066

"This eminently readable work highlights the history of gays and lesbians in the U.S. Beginning with the Victorian period and following with five more chapters covering the 20th and 21st centuries through 2006. . . . A good index, excellent notes, and a selected bibliography of resources, into which the author encourages readers to 'dig deeper,' only increase the usefulness of Gay America." SLJ

The **Full** spectrum; a new generation of writing about gay, lesbian, bisexual, transgender, questioning, and other identities; edited by David Levithan & Billy Merrell. Knopf 2006 272p il pa $9.95 *
Grades: 8 9 10 11 12 **306.76**
1. Gay men 2. Lesbians 3. Sex role 4. Homosexuality
ISBN 0-375-93290-9 LC 2005-23435

"The 40 contributions to this invaluable collection about personal identity have two things in common: all are nonfiction and all are by writers under the age of 23. Beyond that, diversity is the order of the day, and the result is a vivid demonstration of how extraordinarily broad the spectrum of sexual identity is among today's gay, lesbian, bisexual, transgender, and questioning youth. . . . Insightful, extraordinarily well written, and emotionally mature, the selections offer compelling, dramatic evidence that what is important is not *what* we are but *who* we are." Booklist

Hear me out: true stories of Teens Educating and Confronting Homophobia; a project of Planned Parenthood of Toronto; [edited by Frances Rooney] Second Story Press 2004 197p il pa $9.95 *
Grades: 8 9 10 11 12 **306.76**
1. Homosexuality 2. Transsexualism 3. Bisexuality
ISBN 1-896764-87-8

"A project of Planned Parenthood of Toronto, this collection of personal accounts of sexual self-discovery by volunteers in the organization's peer-based T.E.A.C.H. program (Teens Educating and Confronting Homophobia) is remarkable for the diversity of social, economic, ethnic, and racial backgrounds represented. The 20 stories included demonstrate the wide spectrum of gay, lesbian, queer, transgender, transsexual, and questioning young-adult experiences. . . . An important and emotionally powerful collection that is sure to encourage thought and discussion." Booklist

Homosexuality: opposing viewpoints; Cynthia A. Bily, book editor. Greenhaven Press 2009 242p il lib bdg $37.40; pa $25.95
Grades: 7 8 9 10 11 12 **306.76**
1. Homosexuality
ISBN 978-0-7377-4214-5 (lib bdg); 978-0-7377-4215-2 (pa) LC 2008-24132

Replaces the edition published 2004 under the editorship of Auriana Ojeda

"Opposing viewpoints series"

This anthology "presents arguments about the causes of same-sex preference before delving into some of . . . today's headlining issues." Booklist

Includes bibliographical references

Hudson, David L., 1969-
Gay rights; [by] David L. Hudson, Jr. Chelsea House 2004 114p (Point-counterpoint) $37.50
Grades: 7 8 9 10 **306.76**
1. Lesbians—Civil rights 2. Gay men—Civil rights
ISBN 0-7910-8094-3 LC 2004-13828

Contents: Point: same-sex couples have a fundamental right to marry; Counterpoint: marriage is between a man and a woman; Point: gays and lesbians should not face discrimination as parents; Counterpoint: states have the power to protect children by giving preference to heterosexual parents; Point: employers should not be able to discriminate against gays and lesbians; Counterpoint: gays and lesbians don't need special treatment in the workforce; Point: the military should end its discriminatory policy toward gays and lesbians; Counterpoint: the military can prohibit homosexual conduct in the military

"Gay marriage, adoption rights, workplace rights, and service in the armed forces are all argued pro and con in a clear, journalistic style. Both sides of an issue are reinforced with sidebars of pertinent U.S. court case de-

Hudson, David L., 1969—*Continued*

cisions and provocative questions. Well-organized footnotes and an index provide easy access to more specific perspectives on each argument, and a section on 'Beginning Legal Research' is also included." SLJ

Includes bibliographical references

Huegel, Kelly

GLBTQ (Gay, Lesbian, Bisexual, Transgender, Questioning); the survival guide for queer & questioning teens. Free Spirit 2003 224p il pa $15.95 *

Grades: 7 8 9 10 11 12   **306.76**
 1. Homosexuality 2. Transsexualism 3. Bisexuality
ISBN 1-57542-126-7   LC 2002-156692
 Contents: GLBTQ basics; Homophobia; Coming out; Life at school; GLBTQ friends; Dating and relationships; Sex; Your health; Drugs, alcohol and tobacco; Religion and culture; Work, college & beyond; Transgender teens
 Describes the challenges faced by gay, lesbian, bisexual, and transgendered teens, offers practical advice, real-life experiences, and accessible resources and support groups
 "Huegel has written an indispensable guide for gay, lesbian, bisexual, transgender, and questioning teens, as well as for their straight peers and parents." Booklist
 Includes bibliographical references

Kafka, Tina, 1950-

Gay rights. Lucent Books 2006 104p il map (Hot topics) lib bdg $31.20 *

Grades: 7 8 9 10   **306.76**
 1. Gay men—Civil rights 2. Lesbians—Civil rights
ISBN 1-59018-637-0   LC 2005005595
 This "provides excellent, well-balanced discussion about the gay rights struggle. A look at the American Psychiatric Association's landmark 1973 decision to remove homosexuality from its list of mental illnesses is followed by examination of contemporary issues—gay marriage, gay families, and gay rights in schools and in the workplace." Booklist
 Includes bibliographical references

Marcovitz, Hal

Teens & gay issues. Mason Crest Publishers 2005 112p il (Gallup Youth Survey) $22.95

Grades: 7 8 9 10   **306.76**
 1. Homosexuality 2. Gay men—Civil rights 3. Lesbians—Civil rights
ISBN 1-59084-873-X   LC 2004-13755
 "Marcovitz addresses the challenges affecting gay teens (like the decision to come out and homophobia in schools), as well as larger gay issues like the nature vs. nurture debate regarding whether sexual orientation is by choice or genetically assigned and recent controversies over gay marriage and adoption of children by gay and lesbian couples. . . . [This is] well documented." SLJ
 Includes bibliographical references

Marcus, Eric

What if someone I know is gay? answers to questions about what it means to be gay and lesbian. Rev. and updated, 1st Simon Pulse ed. Simon & Schuster 2007 183p pa $8.99

Grades: 7 8 9 10 11 12   **306.76**
 1. Homosexuality
ISBN 1-4169-4970-4; 978-1-4169-4970-1
 First published 2000 by Price/Stern/Sloan
 Contents: Basic stuff; Friends and family; Dating, marriage, and kids; Sex; God and religion; School; Parades, activism, and discrimination; For parents
 "The content . . . stands strong, and readers will appreciate Marcus's gentle tone and the careful candor that he uses to describe the sometimes-rocky LGB experience. Helpful information about gay-straight alliances and marriage and partnership issues are all addressed." SLJ
 Includes bibliographical references

306.8   Marriage and family

Andryszewski, Tricia, 1956-

Same-sex marriage; moral wrong or civil right? Twenty-First Century Books 2008 144p il lib bdg $38.60

Grades: 7 8 9 10 11 12   **306.8**
 1. Same-sex marriage 2. Gay couples—Legal status, laws, etc.
ISBN 978-0-8225-7176-6 (lib bdg); 0-8225-7176-5 (lib bdg)   LC 2007-10397
 This examines the legal and moral issues surrounding same-sex marriage.
 This is a "very detailed, in depth overview. . . . Throughout, quotes from all sides of the debate appear. . . . With lots of color, captioned photos . . . and sidebars . . . the book's design is sure to draw curious browser, as well as passionately engaged researchers." Booklist
 Includes bibliographical references

MacGregor, Cynthia

Jigsaw puzzle family; the stepkids' guide to fitting it together. Impact Pub. 2005 106p (RebuildingBooks, relationships, divorce and beyond) pa $12.95 *

Grades: 5 6 7 8   **306.8**
 1. Stepfamilies
ISBN 1-886230-63-3
 "MacGregor offers simple guidelines, practical advice, and lots of fictional examples about living with a new blended family. . . . This title offers healthy and helpful suggestions for resolving much of the conflict that arises when family situations change." SLJ
 Includes bibliographical references

The **sibling** slam book; what it's really like to have a brother or sister with special needs. Woodbine House 2005 152p il pa $15.95

Grades: 6 7 8 9   **306.8**

The sibling slam book—*Continued*
1. Handicapped children 2. Siblings
ISBN 1-890627-52-6
"This multifaceted vehicle for eliciting some unique and many universal emotions is designed specifically for siblings of special-needs children. An adolescent mainstay, the slam book is the chosen venue for encouraging the venting of opinions, hopes, fears, frustrations, and triumphs. Comments by 81 young people display the recurring theme of optimism, complicated by hard work, dedication, resentment, and fierce protection, all as byproducts of love." SLJ

Snow, Judith E.
How it feels to have a gay or lesbian parent; a book by kids for kids of all ages. Harrington Park Press 2004 110p $19.95; pa $12.95
Grades: 5 6 7 8 9 10   **306.8**
1. Gay parents 2. Parent-child relationship
ISBN 1-56023-419-9; 1-56023-420-2 (pa)
LC 2003-18008
In their own words, children of different ages talk about how and when they learned of their gay or lesbian parent's sexual orientation and the effect it has had on them.
"This inspirational, eye-opening title gives readers who have gay and lesbian parents a much-deserved voice." SLJ

Stefoff, Rebecca, 1951-
Marriage. Marshall Cavendish Benchmark 2006 143p il (Open for debate) lib bdg $39.93
Grades: 7 8 9 10   **306.8**
1. Marriage
ISBN 978-0-7614-2299-0; 0-7614-2299-4
"Focuses on the pros and cons of marriage in the United States—including covenant marriages, same-sex unions, and the effect of divorce on kids—through personal stories, opinions, and scholarly studies. Provides a historical look at marriage and includes . . . reports and statistics." Publisher's note
Includes bibliographical references

Trapani, Margi
Listen up! teenage mothers speak out. Rosen Pub. Group 1997 64p il (Teen pregnancy prevention library) lib bdg $17.95
Grades: 7 8 9 10   **306.8**
1. Teenage mothers 2. Teenage pregnancy
ISBN 0-8239-2254-5   LC 95-42449
"Seven young mothers describe the reality of their lives before and since the birth of their babies. None of them have maintained a relationship with their child's father. They all voice regret for lost youth and forgone opportunities." SLJ
Includes glossary and bibliographical references

Reality check; teenage fathers speak out. rev ed. Rosen Pub. Group 1999 64p il (Teen pregnancy prevention library) lib bdg $23.95
Grades: 7 8 9 10   **306.8**
1. Teenage fathers 2. Parenting
ISBN 0-8239-2995-7   LC 95-42450

First published 1997
Teenage fathers highlight the challenges of being a teen parent, discussing responsibility, economic hardship, and emotional issues involved in parenting at a young age
This book presents "a true picture of the hardships of being a teenage parent." Voice Youth Advocates [review of 1997 edition]
Includes glossary and bibliographical references

Winchester, Elizabeth, 1973-
Sisters and brothers; the ultimate guide to understanding your siblings and yourself; [by] Elizabeth Siris Winchester. Franklin Watts 2008 112p il (Scholastic choices) lib bdg $27; pa $8.95
Grades: 6 7 8 9 10   **306.8**
1. Siblings 2. Family
ISBN 978-0-531-13870-0 (lib bdg); 0-531-13870-4 (lib bdg); 978-0-531-20528-0 (pa); 0-531-20528-2 (pa)
LC 2007-51871
Real-life stories from teenagers about interacting with siblings, whether blood, adopted, foster, or step.
"Colorful and compact, with [an] attractive cover [and] . . . excellent black-and-white photographs of a diverse array of teens." SLJ
Includes glossary and bibliographical references

306.89 Separation and divorce

Bingham, Jane
Why do families break up? Raintree 2005 48p il (Exploring tough issues) lib bdg $31.43
Grades: 4 5 6 7   **306.89**
1. Divorce
ISBN 0-7398-6683-4   LC 2003-20285
Contents: Happily every after?; Getting along; When things go wrong; How it feels; Splitting up; Moving on
"This book looks at the reasons people divorce and discusses the stages a family goes through when a marriage breaks up. It also considers how different family members struggle with the painful effects, and the benefits of counseling. Case studies, quotes, and color photos personalize the issues, and fact boxes provide a few statistics. . . . Libraries needing self-help information for young people dealing with divorce will find Bingham's volume a useful addition." SLJ
Includes bibliographical references

Trueit, Trudi Strain
Surviving divorce; teens talk about what helps and what hurts; [by] Trudi Strain Trueit. 1st ed. Scholastic 2007 112p il (Choices) lib bdg $22.50; pa $8.95
Grades: 6 7 8 9   **306.89**
1. Divorce
ISBN 0-531-12368-5 (lib bdg); 978-0-531-12368-3 (lib bdg); 0-531-16726-7 (pa); 978-0-531-16726-7 (pa)
LC 2004018423
This "is an inviting guide to the facts and feelings of parental divorce. Personal stories and photos of kids begin each chapter, and frequent statistics and quizzes will

Trueit, Trudi Strain—*Continued*

help readers assess their feelings and put them into context. The solid advice is well presented, as are the messages that readers are not alone and that there are many ways to seek help." Booklist

Includes glossary and bibliographical references

The **truth** about divorce; Mark J. Kittleson, general editor; William Kane, advisor; Richelle Rennegarbe, advisor; Barry Youngerman, principal author. Facts on File 2005 180p il (Truth about series) $35 *

Grades: 8 9 10 11 12   **306.89**
1. Divorce 2. Marriage
ISBN 0-8160-5304-9   LC 2004-10236

Contents: Child support, spousal support; Children, psychological effects of divorce on; Communication and compromise in divorced families; Custody and visitation; Divorce, adjusting to the realities of; Divorce alternatives; Divorce in America; Divorce, the business side of; Divorce, the legal process of; Divorce, the psychological cost for spouses; Families, blended; Finances and divorce; Generational patterns and adult children of divorce; Help for troubled marriages; Love and marriage ; Marriage lifestyles, alternative; Media and divorce; Racially and culturally mixed marriages; Relationship after divorce, parents'; Relationship failure; Relationships, types of; Religion and divorce; Stress factors in marriage, external; Hotlines and helpsites

Includes glossary and bibliographical references

306.9   Institutions pertaining to death

Noyes, Deborah, 1965-
Encyclopedia of the end; mysterious death in fact, fancy, folklore, and more. Houghton Mifflin Co. 2008 143p il $25 *

Grades: 7 8 9 10 11 12   **306.9**
1. Death 2. Funeral rites and ceremonies 3. Reference books
ISBN 978-0-618-82362-8; 0-618-82362-X
LC 2008-1872

"This stylish A-to-Z encounter with all things related to death and dying shows Noyes . . . at her liveliest. . . . The author offers a broad illumination of spiritual, historical and biological aspects of death. Photos, paintings and engravings in homage to 'the end' make the book dynamic visually, too." Publ Wkly

307   Communities

Anderson, Judith
Looking at settlements; by Judith Anderson. Smart Apple Media 2007 il map (Geography skills) $22.95 *

Grades: 6 7 8 9   **307**
1. Human settlements
ISBN 978-1-59920-052-1; 1-59920-052-X
LC 2006036142

Contents: What is a settlement?; How settlements began; Changes over time; Where you live; Housing; Work; Shops; Water; Transport; Public services; Leisure; Links with other settlements; Seaside resort; Capital city; Growth; Pollution; Poverty; New settlements; Planning for the future

"The text is easy to follow. . . . The examples given in the text that involve places are almost always accompanied by excellent photographs. . . . Maps, block diagraoms, tables, and graphs are clearly presented and easy to interpret." Sci Books Films

Includes glossary and bibligraphical references

307.7   Specific kinds of communities

Collier, Christopher, 1930-
The rise of the cities, 1820-1920; [by] Christopher Collier, James Lincoln Collier. Benchmark Bks. (Tarrytown) 2001 95p il maps (Drama of American history) lib bdg $31.36

Grades: 6 7 8 9   **307.7**
1. Cities and towns—United States
ISBN 0-7614-1051-1   LC 99-38409

This "traces the development, problems, and increasing prominence of cities in America between 1820 and 1920. Illustrations, many in color, include period photographs and engravings as well as maps and charts. . . . Highly readable and informative." Booklist

Includes bibliographical references

Lorinc, John, 1963-
Cities. Groundwood Books/House of Anansi Press 2008 144p (Groundwork guides) $18.95; pa $10

Grades: 7 8 9 10 11 12   **307.7**
1. Cities and towns 2. Urbanization
ISBN   978-0-88899-820-0;   0-88899-820-1;
978-0-88899-819-4 (pa); 0-88899-819-8 (pa)

"This packed, highly readable [title] . . . does an excellent job of tracing urban history worldwide, raising the big social, political, and economic issues of poverty, migration, conservation, public health, crime, transportation, and much more, always rooted in specific examples of the problems and riches of city life." Booklist

Includes bibliographical references

310.5   General statistics—Serial publications

The **statesman's** yearbook 2009; the politics, cultures and economies of the world; edited by Barry Turner. Palgrave Macmillan 2008 xxxi, 1573p il $265

Grades: 8 9 10 11 12 Adult   **310.5**
1. Statistics 2. Political science 3. Reference books
ISSN 0081-4601
ISBN 978-1-4039-9278-9; 1-4039-9278-9
Also available online
Annual. First published 1864

The statesman's yearbook 2009—*Continued*
"Descriptive and statistical information about international organizations and countries of the world-brief history, area, political status, economy, etc." N Y Public Libr. Ref Books for Child Collect. 2d edition
Includes bibliographical references

317.3   General statistics of the United States

United States. Bureau of the Census
Statistical abstract of the United States, 2008; the national data book. 127th ed. U.S. Census Bureau 2007 994p il map $39; pa $35
Grades: 8 9 10 11 12 Adult   **317.3**
1. United States—Statistics 2. Reference books
ISBN   978-0-16-079584-8;   0-16-079584-2;
978-0-16-079581-7 (pa); 0-16-079581-8 (pa)
Also available online
Annual. First published for the year 1878
"Compendium of statistics on the social, political and economic organization of the U.S. presented in tables. Lists other sources of such information." N Y Public Libr. Ref Books for Child Collect. 2d edition

320   Political science

Zeinert, Karen, 1942-2002
Women in politics; in the running. 21st Cent. Bks. (Brookfield) 2002 112p il lib bdg $29.90
Grades: 6 7 8 9   **320**
1. Women in politics
ISBN 0-7613-2253-1   LC 2001-52253
Examines the contributions women have made at every level of American politics throughout the history of the United States, as well as the struggles they have encountered
"Zeinert does a solid job of introducing these pioneering women, and her overview makes a good starting point for research." Booklist
Includes bibliographical references

320.03   Political science—Encyclopedias and dictionaries

Encyclopedia of American government; consulting editor, Joseph M. Bessette; project editor, R. Kent Rasmussen. Salem Press 1998 4v il maps set $221
Grades: 8 9 10 11 12 Adult   **320.03**
1. United States—Politics and government—Encyclopedias 2. Reference books
ISBN 0-89356-117-7   LC 98-28986
Contents: v1 Accountability in government—criminal justice system; v2 Declaration of independence—juvenile justice; v3 Labor law—right to die; v4 School law—women in politics
"Two hundred alphabetically arranged essays make up this . . . set that covers the basics of American govern-

ment. Well-written, illuminating articles range from broad subjects such as Federalism to more specific topics such as 'Iron Triangles' and reflect an awareness for gender and minority issues." SLJ
Includes bibliographical references

320.5   Political ideologies

Fleming, Thomas, 1945-
Socialism. Marshall Cavendish Benchmark 2007 c2008 143p il (Political systems of the world) lib bdg $39.93
Grades: 7 8 9 10 11 12   **320.5**
1. Socialism
ISBN 978-0-7614-2632-5; 0-7614-2632-9
                                        LC 2006-33048
"Discusses socialism as a political system, and details the history of socialist governments throughout the world." Publisher's note
"There is solid information here." SLJ
Includes bibliographical references

Tames, Richard
Nationalism; [by] Richard Tames. Raintree 2004 64p il (Ideas of the modern world) $32.79
Grades: 7 8 9 10   **320.5**
1. Nationalism
ISBN 0-7398-6417-3   LC 2003-913
Contents: What is nationalism?; The birth of modern nationalism; Nations and empires; Empires into nations; Nationalism and communism; Beyond the nation-state; Nationalism : today and tomorrow
This "begins with a succinct definition of [nationalism] and includes historical examples to clarify it. . . . The American and French Revolutions, are discussed [as well as] the unification of Italy, Greek independence, and Scotland's evolution into a free, independent state. . . . Conflicts, such as those in East Timor, Sri Lanka, and Kurdistan, are part of the discussion. Pan-Slavism, Pan-Arabism, and Pan-Africanism are also included. The author has taken a complex subject, simplified it, and made it accessible to students." SLJ
Includes bibliographical references

321   Systems of governments and states

Perl, Lila
Theocracy. Marshall Cavendish Benchmark 2007 c2008 158p il (Political systems of the world) lib bdg $27.95
Grades: 7 8 9 10 11 12   **321**
1. Theocracy
ISBN 978-0-7614-2631-8   LC 2006-26055
"Gives an overview of theocracy as a political system, including and historical discussion of theocratic regimes throughout the world." Publisher's note
Includes bibliographical references

Stefoff, Rebecca, 1951-
Monarchy. Marshall Cavendish Benchmark 2007
c2008 143p il (Political systems of the world) lib
bdg $27.95
Grades: 7 8 9 10 11 12   321
1. Monarchy
ISBN 978-0-7614-2630-1   LC 2006-26384
"Discusses monarchies as a political system, and de-
tails the history of monarchies throughout the world."
Publisher's note
Includes bibliographical references

321.8 Democratic government

Lansford, Tom
Democracy. Marshall Cavendish Benchmark
2007 c2008 143p il (Political systems of the
world) lib bdg $27.95
Grades: 7 8 9 10 11 12   321.8
1. Democracy
ISBN 978-0-7614-2629-5   LC 2006-25351
"Gives an overview of democracy as a political system, including an historical discussion of democracies
throughout the world." Publisher's note
Includes bibliographical references

Laxer, James
Democracy. Groundwood Books 2009 143p
(Groundwork guides) $18.95; pa $10
Grades: 8 9 10 11 12   321.8
1. Democracy
ISBN   978-0-88899-912-2;   0-88899-912-7;
978-0-88899-913-9 (pa); 0-88899-913-5 (pa)
"House of Anansi Press"
This is an "overview of democracy from ancient
Greece and Rome through the American and French
Revolutions and on through modern movements for de-
mocracy in the developing world." Kirkus
"This dynamic . . . title . . . stands out for its acces-
sible introduction to historical and contemporary democ-
racy across the globe. Laxer skillfully supports his argu-
ments with examples and avoids pat definitions."
Booklist
Includes bibliographical references

321.9 Authoritarian government

Fridell, Ron, 1943-
Dictatorship. Marshall Cavendish Benchmark
2007 144p il (Political systems of the world) lib
bdg $27.95
Grades: 7 8 9 10 11 12   321.9
1. Dictators
ISBN 978-0-7614-2627-1   LC 2006-23121
"Discusses dictatorships as a political system, and de-
tails the history of dictatorships throughout the world."
Publisher's note
Includes bibliographical references

323 Civil and political rights

Altman, Linda Jacobs, 1943-
Human rights; issues for a new millennium.
Enslow Pubs. 2002 128p il (Issues in focus) lib
bdg $20.95
Grades: 7 8 9 10   323
1. Human rights
ISBN 0-7660-1689-7   LC 2002-6050
Partial contents: The foundations of human rights;
Rights and revolutions; The struggle against slavery; In
time of war; Human rights and civil disobedience; The
activist sixties
Explores the history of concern for human rights
around the world, looking particularly at the internation-
alism begun in the last quarter of the twentieth century
and its influence on human rights issues
"This book is a good introduction and overview of the
subject." BAYA Book Rev
Includes glossary and bibliographical references

Banks, Deena
Amnesty International; by Deena Banks. World
Almanac Library 2004 48p (International
organizations) $30; pa $15.93
Grades: 6 7 8 9   323
1. Amnesty International
ISBN 0-8368-5517-5; 0-8368-5526-4 (pa)
                              LC 2003-45030
Contents: Human rights: a vision; Goals and organiza-
tion to achieve them; How Amnesty International works;
Current campaigns and urgent actions; Success stories
This describes the history and goals of "Amnesty In-
ternational, which is dedicated to persuading govern-
ments around the world to free prisoners of conscience
or those who have been imprisoned for disagreeing with
their actions." Publisher's note
This provides "ample material for reports." SLJ
Includes bibliographical references

Civil liberties and war; edited by Andrea C.
Nayaka. Greenhaven Press/Thomson Gale 2006
78p il (Examining issues through political
cartoons) lib bdg $27.45
Grades: 7 8 9 10   323
1. Civil rights 2. War—Public opinion 3. Military policy—United States
ISBN 0-7377-2517-6
This "spotlights 16 cartoons related to the suspension
of civil liberties and human rights during America's
wars. The first chapter presents cartoons from the Civil
War to the War in Vietnam, while chapter two considers
'America's War on Terrorism' and chapter three, the current war in Iraq. . . . Each political cartoon is accompanied by a paragraph or two of commentary and a brief
note on the cartoonist. The book concludes with a bibliography and an excellent, varied list of 16 relevant organizations and government agencies, with descriptions and
contact information." Booklist
Includes bibliographical references

Civil liberties: opposing viewpoints; Auriana Ojeda, book editor. Greenhaven Press 2004 204p il $33.70; pa $22.45

Grades: 8 9 10 11 1 2 **323**

1. Civil rights

ISBN 0-7377-1675-4; 0-7377-1676-2 (pa)

LC 2003-59647

Replaces the edition published 1999 under the editorship of Tamara L. Roleff

"Opposing viewpoints series"

"This volume examines the pros and cons of such issues as regulation of hate speech, flag burning, banning of child pornography, posting of the Ten Commandments in public places, public surveillance cameras, the war on terrorism, and ethnic profiling. Twenty-two essays from contributors ranging from the ACLU to John Ashcroft and from such publications as the 'Humanist', the 'Seattle Times', and 'Midstream' offer arguments from a variety of perspectives. . . . This highly accessible book will prove useful for opinion and research papers." SLJ

Includes bibliographical references

Declare yourself; speak. connect. act. vote.: more than 50 celebrated Americans tell you why; foreward by Norman Lear, introduction by America Ferrara. Greenwillow Books 2008 325p il $16.99; pa $11.99

Grades: 7 8 9 10 11 12 **323**

1. United States—Politics and government 2. Youth—Political activity 3. Suffrage

ISBN 978-0-06-147332-6; 0-06-147332-4; 978-0-06-147316-6 (pa); 0-06-147316-2 (pa)

LC 2007049592

"Collection of celebrity testimonials to the importance of voting. . . . Teens are likely to find at least several contributors whose voices interest them: media stars (Tyra Banks, Rob Riggle), athletes (Mike James, Sasha Cohen), musicians (the members of Maroon 5, L'il Romeo), authors (Maya Angelou, Chris Crutcher), etc. . . . An appendix lists resources for further political engagement." Publ Wkly

Every human has rights; a photographic declaration for kids; based on the United Nations Universal Declaration of Human Rights; with poetry from the community; foreword by Mary Robinson. National Geographic 2009 il $26.90 *

Grades: 4 5 6 7 8 **323**

1. Human rights

ISBN 978-1-4263-0511-5; 1-4263-0511-7

"On the sixtieth anniversary of the Universal Declaration of Human Rights, this full-color photo-essay combines prize-winning poems by young people with beautiful photographs from all over the world. . . . The stirring pictures will stimulate classroom discussion about the declaration, which is quoted in full at the back." Booklist

Gillam, Scott

Civil liberties; [by] Scott Gillam. ABDO Pub. 2008 112p il (Essential viewpoints) $22.95

Grades: 7 8 9 10 **323**

1. Civil rights

ISBN 978-1-59928-858-1

LC 2007013878

This is a "balanced [overview] of [a] complex, divisive [issue]. Though not exhaustive, [this title includes] the topic's history and most salient points in an accessible and reader-friendly format. . . . [This] covers recent and historical limits in the name of national security; the First, Fourth, and Eighth Amendments; habeas corpus and due process; and the right to a speedy trial. . . . Color images enhance the [text], and charts and maps further clarify the content. Sidebars expand on related topics through quotes, primary-source snippets, and other salient information." SLJ

Includes glossary and bibliographical references

Human rights: opposing viewpoints; opposing viewpoints; Laura K. Egendorf, book editor. Greenhaven Press 2003 208p lib bdg $34.95; pa $23.70

Grades: 8 9 10 11 1 2 **323**

1. Human rights

ISBN 0-7377-1689-4 (lib bdg); 0-7377-1690-8 (pa)

LC 2002-192800

"Opposing viewpoints series"

"In this anthology, the authors address the definition of human rights, the state of these rights, and ways in which the United States and the rest of the world should respond to human rights abuses." Publisher's note

Includes bibliographical references

Spangenburg, Ray, 1939-

Civil liberties; [by] Ray Spangenburg and Kit Moser. Marshall Cavendish Benchmark 2006 143p il (Open for debate) lib bdg $37.07 *

Grades: 8 9 10 11 12 **323**

1. Civil rights

ISBN 0-7614-1886-5 LC 2005001165

This looks at civil liberties in the United States after September 11, 2001 discussing such issues as the Patriot Act, flag burning, freedom of speech, religious freedom and the rights to assembly, to bear arms, and to privacy. SLJ

"The content is outlined in a logical manner, beginning with a broad definition of the terms, followed by discussions of more specific topics. The writing is clear and factual and presents both sides of the arguments. Each chapter raises pertinent and difficult questions for readers to consider as they form their own opinions." SLJ

Includes bibliographical references

Stewart, Gail, 1949-

Human rights in the Middle East; by Gail B. Stewart. Lucent Books 2004 c2005 112p il map (Lucent library of conflict in the Middle East) $28.70

Grades: 6 7 8 9 **323**

1. Human rights 2. Middle East

ISBN 1-59018-488-2 LC 2004-10836

Contents: Introduction; Systems of injustice; Women and injustice; The right of expression; Children's rights; Persecution of minorities

This discusses such human rights issues in the Middle East as the forced labor of children, discrimination against women and ethnic minorities, torture and executions, and censorship.

Includes bibliographical references

323.1   Civil and political rights of nondominant groups

American civil rights: primary sources; [compiled by] Phillis Engelbert; edited by Betz Des Chenes. U.X.L 1999 xl, 200p il $58

Grades: 8 9 10 11 12   **323.1**
1. Civil rights
ISBN 0-7876-3170-1   LC 99-27167

Presents fifteen documents, including speeches, autobiographical texts, and proclamations, related to the civil rights movement and arranged by category under economic rights, desegregation, and human rights

"The uniqueness of this set lies in the range of people covered. Students will find it an excellent resource for reports and interesting reading." Booklist

Includes bibliographical references

Aretha, David
Freedom Summer. Morgan Reynolds Pub. 2007 128p (The civil rights movement) lib bdg $27.95

Grades: 7 8 9 10 11 12   **323.1**
1. Mississippi Freedom Project 2. African Americans—Civil rights 3. Mississippi—Race relations
ISBN 978-1-59935-059-2; 1-59935-059-9
     LC 2007-23815

This "discusses the collaborative strategies black and white Americans . . . devised to dismantle the restrictive, often violent measures used in the South to prevent most African Americans from voting. . . . [This title is] visually appealing with generous white space around the [text]. Throughout, mostly black-and-white historical photos . . . enhance the [narrative]. Also adding impact are numerous dramatic accounts by participants in the struggle." SLJ

Includes bibliographical references

Montgomery bus boycott. Morgan Reynolds Pub. 2009 128p il (Civil rights) $28.95

Grades: 7 8 9 10   **323.1**
1. Montgomery (Ala.)—Race relations 2. African Americans—Civil rights
ISBN 978-1-59935-020-2; 1-59935-020-3
     LC 2008-18679

"The wrenching consequences of Rosa Parks's decision that sparked the Civil Rights Movement are depicted in this well-written book. Descriptions of civil rights activism dating back to 1865 . . . provide historical context and a sense of the fervor surrounding discrimination and segregation. The facts of the boycott are documented with supportive news articles, relevant quotations, moving individual stories, and significant court cases. . . . Photographs . . . depict significant figures and document incidents such as meetings and carpooling to avoid buses." SLJ

Includes bibliographical references

Bausum, Ann
Freedom Riders; John Lewis and Jim Zwerg on the front lines of the civil rights movement; by Ann Bausum; forewords by Freedom Riders Congressman John Lewis and Jim Zwerg. National Geographic 2006 79p il por $18.95; lib bdg $28.90
*

Grades: 5 6 7 8   **323.1**
1. Lewis, John, 1940- 2. Zwerg, Jim, 1939- 3. African Americans—Civil rights 4. Southern States—Race relations
ISBN 0-7922-4173-8; 0-7922-4174-6 (lib bdg)
     LC 2005012947

"Eschewing a general overview of the 1961 Freedom Rides for specific, personal histories of real participants in the dangerous bus integration protests, Bausum focuses on two college students from strikingly different backgrounds: Jim Zwerg, a white Wisconsin native who became involved during an exchange visit to Nashville, and John Lewis, a black seminarian and student leader of the nonviolence movement." Booklist

"Bausum's narrative style, fresh, engrossing, and at times heart-stopping, brings the story of the turbulent and often violent dismantling of segregated travel alive in vivid detail. The language, presentation of material, and pacing will draw readers in and keep them captivated." SLJ

Includes bibliographical references

Boerst, William J., 1939-
Marching in Birmingham. Morgan Reynolds Pub. 2008 112p il map (The civil rights movement) $27.95

Grades: 7 8 9 10 11 12   **323.1**
1. King, Martin Luther, Jr., 1929-1968 2. African Americans—Civil rights 3. Birmingham (Ala.)—Race relations
ISBN 978-1-59935-055-4; 1-59935-055-6
     LC 2007-26640

This "focuses on Alabama and the organized efforts by both black and white Americans to end local-government-sanctioned segregation and inequality. [This title is] visually appealing with generous white space around the [text]. Throughout, mostly black-and-white historical photos . . . enhance the [narrative]. Also adding impact are numerous dramatic accounts by participants in the struggle." SLJ

Includes bibliographical references

Bullard, Sara
Free at last; a history of the Civil Rights Movement and those who died in the struggle; introduction by Julian Bond. Oxford Univ. Press 1993 112p il map $28; pa $12.95

Grades: 8 9 10 11 1 2   **323.1**
1. African Americans—Civil rights 2. United States—Race relations
ISBN 0-19-508381-4; 0-19-509450-6 (pa)
     LC 92-38174

An illustrated history of the civil rights movement, including a timeline and profiles of forty people who gave their lives in the movement

Includes bibliographical references

Civil rights; edited by Mary E. Williams. Greenhaven Press 2002 94p il (Examining issues through political cartoons) lib bdg $24.95; pa $16.20
Grades: 7 8 9 10 **323.1**
ISBN 0-7377-1100-0 (lib bdg); 0-7377-1099-3 (pa)
LC 2001-55743
The author provides "readers with an overview of African Americans' struggle for those rights enjoyed by other citizens and of the historical role of the political cartoon. . . . Four chapters ('The Struggle for Justice,' 'Has the Civil Rights Movement Benefited Minorities?' 'How Has Affirmative Action Affected Civil Rights?' and 'What Is the Legacy of the Civil Rights Movement?') examine three to six cartoons each. All are reproduced in the book, and information about the artist is provided." SLJ
"Facts, statistics, and historical perspectives are presented in easy-to-understand terms. . . . This title is an excellent resource for history, government, and debate classes." Book Rep
Includes bibliographical references

Civil rights; Jill Karson, book editor. Greenhaven Press 2003 238p il map (Great speeches in history series) lib bdg $33.70; pa $22.45
Grades: 7 8 9 10 **323.1**
1. African Americans—Civil rights 2. United States—Race relations 3. Speeches
ISBN 0-7377-1593-6 (lib bdg); 0-7377-1594-4 (pa)
LC 2002-32209
"A collection of the speeches of well-known individuals who participated in or supported the American Civil Rights Movement from early pioneers through the 1960s up until today. Selections from Frederick Douglass, Malcolm X, Fannie Lou Hamer, Jesse Jackson, and Nelson Mandela emphasize the power of oratory to inform, persuade, and make an impact." SLJ
Includes bibliographical references

Cooper, John, 1958-
Season of rage; Hugh Burnett and the struggle for civil rights; [by] John Cooper. Tundra Books 2005 71p il pa $9.95
Grades: 7 8 9 10 **323.1**
1. Burnett, Hugh, 1919-1991 2. Canada—Race relations 3. Race discrimination
ISBN 0-88776-700-1
"Cooper has chosen the small town of Dresden, Ontario, to paint a picture of what life was like for black Canadians in the middle of the last century. One Sunday in the early 1930s, when 12-year-old Hugh Burnett and his younger brother had a hankering for ice cream, they entered a restaurant. The boys were told that they would have to eat in the kitchen. . . . The event in the restaurant sparked a lifelong crusade for Burnett, who spearheaded the formation of the National Unity Association. . . . A number of archival photos enhance the text. . . . An eye-opening story." SLJ

Cruz, Bárbara
Triumphs and struggles for Latino civil rights. Enslow Pubs. 2008 128p il map (From many cultures, one history) lib bdg $31.93
Grades: 6 7 8 9 **323.1**
1. Hispanic Americans 2. Civil rights 3. United States—Ethnic relations
ISBN 978-0-7660-2804-3 (lib bdg); 0-7660-2804-6 (lib bdg)
The author "describes the long journey of Latinos in the United States, from the founding of the oldest city on the American mainland at St. Augustine, Florida, to the continued struggle for civil rights today." Publisher's note
Includes glossary and bibliographical references

Engelbert, Phillis
American civil rights: almanac. U.X.L 1999 2v il set $110
Grades: 7 8 9 10 **323.1**
1. Civil rights
ISBN 0-7876-3172-8 LC 98-52526
Contents: v1 African Americans, Asian Americans; v2 Hispanic Americans, Native Americans, selected immigrant groups, selected nonethnic groups
"The format of both volumes is identical. Following an introduction, a time line chronicles major events from the first signing of U.S. government and Native American treaties in 1778 to the April 20, 1999, award of the Congressional Gold Medal to Rosa Parks." Booklist
Includes bibliographical references

Finlayson, Reggie
We shall overcome; the history of the American civil rights movement. Lerner Publs. 2003 96p il (People's history) lib bdg $25.26
Grades: 6 7 8 9 **323.1**
1. African Americans—Civil rights 2. United States—Race relations
ISBN 0-8225-0647-5 LC 2002-954
Contents: We shall overcome; This little light; Ain't gonna ride; The walls come a tumblin' down; The fires of frustration and discord; On my way; Selma, Bloody Sunday; Solving the American problem; Timeline; In their own words
Uses the words of spirituals and other music of the time to frame a discussion of the civil rights movement in the United States, focusing on specific people, incidents, and court cases
The author "ably places events in their historical context and tells a linear, inspiring story of the crucial era. Compelling black-and-white photos . . . bring the events up close." Booklist
Includes bibliographical references

Freedman, Russell
Freedom walkers; the story of the Montgomery bus boycott. Holiday House 2006 114p il $18.95
*
Grades: 4 5 6 7 **323.1**
1. Montgomery (Ala.)—Race relations 2. African Americans—Civil rights
ISBN 978-0-8234-2031-5; 0-8234-2031-0
LC 2006-41148

Freedman, Russell—Continued

This account of the Montgomery bus boycott of 1955 focuses on Jo Ann Robinson, Claudette Colvin, Rosa Parks, Martin Luther King, and other participants.

This offers "expertly paced text, balanced but impassioned. . . . The narrative arc is compelling; well-captioned black-and-white photographs enhance the impact." Horn Book

Includes bibliographical references

George, Linda

Civil rights marches; [by] Linda and Charles George. Children's Press 1999 30p il (Cornerstones of freedom) lib bdg $21; pa $5.95

Grades: 4 5 6   **323.1**

1. African Americans—Civil rights 2. United States—Race relations

ISBN 0-516-21183-8 (lib bdg); 0-516-26516-4 (pa)

LC 98-41943

Describes the peaceful marches in the United States on behalf of civil rights for blacks from the 1950s to the 1990s, including the March on Washington and other important marches

Gold, Susan Dudley, 1949-

Korematsu v. United States; Japanese-American internment. Marshall Cavendish Benchmark 2005 c2006 159p il (Supreme Court milestones) lib bdg $39.93

Grades: 7 8 9 10   **323.1**

1. Korematsu, Fred, 1919-2005 2. Japanese Americans—Evacuation and relocation, 1942-1945 3. World War, 1939-1945—Reparations

ISBN 0-7614-1943-8   LC 2005-2534

Describes the historical context of the Korematsu versus United States Supreme Court Case in which a Japanese-American sought compensation for being sent to an internment camp during World War II.

Includes bibliographical references

Johnson, Troy R.

Red power; the Native American civil rights movement; [by] Troy R. Johnson. Chelsea House 2007 112p il (Landmark events in Native American history) lib bdg $35

Grades: 7 8 9 10   **323.1**

1. Native Americans—Civil rights 2. United States—Race relations

ISBN 978-0-7910-9341-2 (lib bdg); 0-7910-9341-7 (lib bdg)   LC 2006102264

This "describes and defines what has come to be known as the American Indian Movement. . . . Early resistance . . . is summarized briefly and includes a chapter on the massacre at Wounded Knee Creek in 1890. The remaining six chapters focus on pivotal events such as the murders at Pine Ridge Reservation, the occupations of Alcatraz in 1969 and Wounded Knee in 1973, and the subsequent changes in government policy toward Native self-governance. . . . [This book is an excellent [tool] for first-time researchers and history buffs alike." SLJ

Includes bibliographical references

Kallen, Stuart A., 1955-

Women of the civil rights movement; [by] Stuart A. Kallen. Lucent Books 2005 112p il map (Women in history) $28.70

Grades: 7 8 9 10   **323.1**

1. African Americans—Civil rights 2. Women—Biography

ISBN 1-59018-569-2   LC 2004023822

"Kallen spotlights the unsung women who played a significant role in the Civil Rights movement. Short chapters are divided into various aspects of the struggle, including organizations, protests, education, voting rights, political office, radicals, and creative expression. Upclose black-and-white photographs and vignettes highlight key people." SLJ

Includes bibliographical references

Kasher, Steven

The civil rights movement: a photographic history, 1954-68; [by] Steven Kasher; foreword by Myrlie Evers-Williams. Abbeville Press 1996 255p il $45; pa $29.95

Grades: 8 9 10 11 12 Adult   **323.1**

1. African Americans—Civil rights

ISBN 0-7892-0123-2; 0-7892-0656-0 (pa)

LC 96-4337

"This book contains images by more than 50 photographers, whose images were borrowed from photo agencies, galleries, and private collections. Ten accompanying essays break the Civil Rights movement into chronological periods. Kasher's research, writing, and photo selection are impeccable and engaging." Libr J

Includes bibliographical references

King, Martin Luther, Jr., 1929-1968

The words of Martin Luther King, Jr.; selected by Coretta Scott King. Newmarket Press 1983 112p il $15.95; pa $11.95

Grades: 8 9 10 11 12 Adult   **323.1**

1. African Americans—Civil rights 2. United States—Race relations

ISBN 0-937858-28-5; 1-55704-483-X (pa)

LC 83-17306

This "volume of selections from Dr. King's speeches and writings . . . focuses on seven areas of his concerns: 'The Community of Man, Racism, Civil Rights, Justice and Freedom, Faith and Religion, Nonviolence, and Peace'" Publisher's note

Includes bibliographical references

Linda Brown, you are not alone; the Brown v. Board of Education decision: a collection; edited by Joyce Carol Thomas; illustrations by Curtis James. Jump at the Sun/Hyperion Books for Children 2003 114p il $15.99

Grades: 5 6 7 8   **323.1**

1. School integration 2. African Americans—Civil rights 3. United States—Race relations

ISBN 0-7868-0821-7

A collection of personal reflections, stories and poems of 10 well-known children's authors, such as Jerry Spinelli, Eloise Greenfield, Lois Lowry, Michael Cart, and Katherine Paterson, who were themselves young

Linda Brown, you are not alone—*Continued*
people in 1954 when the Supreme Court handed down
the decision to desegregate public schools.

The authors' "personal reminiscences capture a spectrum of powerfully expressed emotions. . . . James's
closely focused, lifelike pastel illustrations feature striking portraits and memorable images." Publ Wkly

Living through the Civil Rights Movement;
Charles George, book editor. Greenhaven Press
2007 117p il (Living through the Cold War) lib
bdg $32.35
Grades: 7 8 9 10   323.1
1. African Americans—Civil rights 2. United States—
Race relations
ISBN 978-0-7377-2919-1 (lib bdg); 0-7377-2919-8 (lib
bdg)   LC 2006017184
"This title does an excellent job of chronicling the
movement by using primary-source documents. Excerpts
from speeches by government officials, such as Lyndon
Baines Johnson, George Wallace, and John F. Kennedy,
appear as well as speeches or statements from Malcolm
X, Martin Luther King, Jr., and Stokely Carmichael."
SLJ
Includes bibliographical references

Malaspina, Ann, 1957-
The ethnic and group identity movements;
earning recognition. Chelsea House 2007 176p il
map (Reform movements in American history) lib
bdg $30
Grades: 6 7 8 9 10   323.1
1. Minorities 2. Civil rights 3. Social movements
4. United States—Ethnic relations 5. Multiculturalism
ISBN 978-0-7910-9571-3; 0-7910-9571-1
                                                            LC 2007-21721
"Malaspina explains how leaders within the Asian,
disability, Chicano, senior, gay, American Indian, and
Muslim communities drew on models of the successful
civil and women's rights movements to build group identity and improve the political and social treatment of
their members. . . . Illustrations include black-and-white
and color photos and period art." SLJ
Includes bibliographical references

Mayer, Robert H., 1950-
When the children marched; the Birmingham
civil rights movement. Enslow Publishers 2008
176p il map (Prime) $34.60 *
Grades: 7 8 9 10   323.1
1. African Americans—Civil rights 2. Birmingham
(Ala.)—Race relations 3. African American children
ISBN 978-0-7660-2930-9; 0-7660-2930-1
                                                            LC 2007-25590
"Children played a significant role in Birmingham's
crucial civil rights struggle, and this stirring history of
the movement, with many photos, news reports, and
quotes from all sides, emphasizes the connections between the young people's power and that of the big leaders. . . . From the cover picture of police escorting African American children to jail, the numerous photos of
youth in nonviolent confrontation—marching, attacked by
dogs and fire hoses, crammed in prisons—will draw
readers with their gripping drama." Booklist
Includes glossary and bibliographical references

McClaurin, Irma
The civil rights movement; by Irma McClaurin.
Marshall Cavendish Benchmark 2008 80p il
(Drama of African-American history) lib bdg
$23.95 *
Grades: 5 6 7 8   323.1
1. African Americans—Civil rights 2. United States—
Race relations
ISBN 978-0-7614-2642-4
"Covers the struggle of African Americans to gain
their civil rights, from Brown v. Board of Education in
1954 through the turbulent Sixties." Publisher's note

McWhorter, Diane
A dream of freedom; the Civil Rights
Movement from 1954 to 1968; foreword by
Reverend Fred Shuttlesworth. Scholastic
Nonfiction 2004 160p il $19.95
Grades: 5 6 7 8   323.1
1. African Americans—Civil rights 2. United States—
Race relations
ISBN 0-439-57678-4
The author discusses "the national civil rights movement from Brown v. the Board of Education to the assassination of Martin Luther King Jr. . . . This account is
both factual and personal. She discusses her feelings as
a white child in the South, and she focuses in on the
many ways in which both white and black children were
involved in the movement. . . . The breadth and depth
of McWhorter's book is exemplary." Booklist

Sharp, Anne Wallace
A dream deferred; the Jim Crow era; [by] Anne
Wallace Sharp. Lucent Books 2005 112p il
(Lucent library of Black history) lib bdg $22.96
Grades: 7 8 9 10   323.1
1. African Americans—Civil rights 2. United States—
Race relations
ISBN 1-59018-700-8   LC 2005002799
This title "about the Jim Crow Era, organized
chronologically from Reconstruction through the *Brown
v. Board of Education* decision, emphasizes the devastating and demoralizing effect of Jim Crow laws on the
black community, and the eventual organized response
that became the birth of the civil rights movement. . . .
The black-and-white photographs and drawings that accompany the text are well captioned and clearly reproduced. This is a straightforward overview that will prove
invaluable for homework assignments on the origins of
the civil rights movement." Booklist
Includes bibliographical references

Sirimarco, Elizabeth, 1966-
American voices from the civil rights
movement. Benchmark Books 2004 xxi, 134p
(American voices from--) lib bdg $34.21 *
Grades: 6 7 8 9   323.1
1. African Americans—Civil rights 2. United States—
Race relations
ISBN 0-7614-1697-8   LC 2003-7952

Sirimarco, Elizabeth, 1966-—*Continued*
Presents the history of the civil rights movement in the United States, from Reconstruction to the late 1960s, through excerpts from letters, newspaper articles, speeches, songs, and poems of the time.

This "excellent [resource stands] out . . . because [it deals] strictly with primary sources, [contains] topnotch illustrations, and [enables] students to grasp the concepts without being overwhelmed." SLJ

Includes glossary and bibliographical references

Turck, Mary, 1950-
Freedom song; young voices and the struggle for civil rights; [by] Mary C. Turck. Chicago Review Press 2009 146p il pa $18.95 *
Grades: 7 8 9 10   323.1
1. Chicago Children's Choir 2. Freedom Singers (Musical group) 3. African Americans—Civil rights 4. African American music
ISBN 978-1-55652-773-9; 1-55652-773-X
LC 2008029673
"The book is divided into chapters that represent the history of the Civil Rights Movement. 'Sunday of Song,' 'Singing in the Churches,' and 'South Africa,' for example, contain information about the factual events while including how the evolution of the music captured the mood and sentiment of the time. The importance of music in the lives of African Americans is described in depth. . . . The accompanying CD allows students to internalize the words and their emotional impact as they listen. Overall, this informative and well-written book is an excellent addition to any collection." SLJ

Includes bibliographical references

Walsh, Frank
The Montgomery bus boycott. World Almanac Library 2003 48p il map (Landmark events in American history) lib bdg $26.60; pa $11.95
Grades: 5 6 7 8   323.1
1. African Americans—Civil rights 2. Montgomery (Ala.)—Race relations
ISBN 0-8368-5375-X (lib bdg); 0-8368-5403-9 (pa)
LC 2002-36020
Contents: Slavery in America; Segregation and racism; The spark; The boycott; The Civil Rights Movement
Describes how the black community of Montgomery, Alabama, staged the 1955 boycott to end segregation on public buses and discusses that struggle in the context of the Civil Rights Movement
"Brief but informative. . . . [The book is] heavily illustrated with well-chosen and carefully placed archival photographs and . . . reproductions of historical documents." SLJ

Includes glossary and bibliographical references

Wexler, Sanford
The civil rights movement; an eyewitness history; introduction by Julian Bond. Facts on File 1993 356p il maps (Eyewitness history series) $75
Grades: 7 8 9 10   323.1
1. African Americans—Civil rights 2. United States—Race relations
ISBN 0-8160-2748-X   LC 92-28674

Uses speeches, articles, and other writings of those involved to trace the history of the civil rights movement in the United States, primarily from 1954 to 1965

"This very readable source deserves a place in every public and middle and high school library, though it may fit better in the circulating collection." Booklist

Includes bibliographical references

Williams, Juan
Eyes on the prize: America's civil rights years, 1954-1965; [by] Juan Williams with the Eyes on the prize production team; introduction by Julian Bond. Viking 1987 300p il hardcover o.p. pa $20
Grades: 7 8 9 10   323.1
1. African Americans—Civil rights 2. United States—Race relations
ISBN 0-670-81412-1; 0-14-009653-1 (pa)
LC 86-40271
"A Robert Lavelle book"
"This companion volume to the PBS TV series of the same name is an . . . account of black America's struggle for social and political equality, covering the civil rights battle from the landmark Brown v. Board of Education decision in 1954 to the Selma protest marches, and Voting Rights Act of 1965." Libr J
"Highly recommended both as a socio-historical document and as a heartfelt, poignant remembrance of a movement and its activists." Booklist

Includes bibliographical references

323.3   Civil and political rights of other social groups

Biddle, Wendy
Immigrants' rights after 9/11; [by] Wendy E. Biddle. Chelsea House 2008 110p il (Point/counterpoint) lib bdg $32.95
Grades: 7 8 9 10   323.3
1. Immigrants—United States 2. United States—Immigration and emigration 3. Civil rights
ISBN 0-7910-8682-8; 978-0-7910-8682-7
LC 2006-17147
"An overview makes the point that the rules governing immigration issues such as indefinite detention and the right to an attorney have been tightened since 9/11. The debate centers around the question of whether these changes are necessary for the safety of U.S. citizens, or whether they infringe on the civil liberties that are afforded to all American residents, legal or not. . . . This solid work thoroughly presents both sides of the argument." SLJ

Includes bibliographical references

323.44   Freedom of action (Liberty)

Bridegam, Martha A.
The right to privacy. Chelsea House 2003 117p il (Point-counterpoint) lib bdg $26.95 *
Grades: 7 8 9 10   323.44
1. Right of privacy
ISBN 0-7910-7373-4   LC 2002-152056

Bridegam, Martha A.—*Continued*

Contents: Defining and valuing the rignt to privacy; Not everyone can be safely "let alone"; Too much official invasion of privacy harms the public interest; Civilized life requires the exchange of information; Institutions and businesses are exploiting personal information unfairly; A free society depends on the right to learn and share information; Some kinds of information should always be protected; Drawing lines

"This book explores the right to privacy from various perspectives, including the rights of criminal suspects, witnesses, and even those subjected to extra security measures regardless of whether or not they're suspected of a crime. Special emphasis has been given to the heightened debate over civil liberties in the post-9/11 United States." Publisher's note

Includes bibliographical references

Freedman, Jeri

America debates civil liberties and terrorism. Rosen Central 2008 64p il (America debates) lib bdg $29.25

Grades: 5 6 7 8 9 10 11 12   323.44

1. Civil rights 2. Terrorism

ISBN 978-1-4042-1927-4 (lib bdg); 1-4042-1927-7 (lib bdg)   LC 2007-8692

This "volume explores the crisis of the war on terror and the actions taken by the executive branch of government against civil liberties. The . . . issues surrounding the Patriot Act, the Abu Ghraib prison abuse scandal, and the suspension of the right of habeas corpus are discussed, as well as the debates over what has truly been gained by such recent acts and events." Publisher's note

The issues "are debated in a clear, concise manner. . . . Colorful photographs and boxed information highlighted in red break up the [text]." SLJ

Includes glossary and bibliographical references

America debates privacy versus security; [by] Jeri Freedman. Rosen Pub. Group, Inc. 2008 64p il (America debates) lib bdg $29.25

Grades: 5 6 7 8 9 10 11 12   323.44

1. Right of privacy 2. National security

ISBN 978-1-4042-1929-8 (lib bdg); 1-4042-1929-3 (lib bdg)   LC 2007-4749

This title is an "exploration of the debate on privacy versus security in post-9/11 America. An . . . examination of the Constitutional definition of the right to privacy is included, and scholars weigh in on the debate. Increased surveillance is discussed, with a look at whether it has paid off so far, and if it is worth the cost." Publisher's note

The issues "are debated in a clear, concise manner. . . . Colorful photographs and boxed information highlighted in red break up the [text]." SLJ

Includes glossary and bibliographical references

Intellectual freedom manual; compiled by the Office for Intellectual Freedom of the American Library Association. 7th ed. American Library Association 2006 xx, 521p pa $57 *

Grades: Professional   323.44

1. Intellectual freedom 2. Libraries—Censorship

ISBN 0-8389-3561-3; 978-0-8389-3561-3

LC 2005-22409

First published 1974

This guide to preserving intellectual freedom includes: ALA interpretations to the Library Bill of Rights; recommendations for special libraries and specific situations; information about legal decisions affecting school and public libraries; a section on the ALA's Intellectual Freedom Action Network.

"This manual details the professional standards to which librarians aspire and offers practical information about how to achieve those goals; it's a must for any librarian's professional library." Book Rep

Includes bibliographical references

Kuhn, Betsy

Prying eyes; privacy in the twenty-first century. Twenty-First Century Books 2008 160p lib bdg $38.60

Grades: 6 7 8 9 10   323.44

1. Right of privacy

ISBN 978-0-8225-7179-7   LC 2007-21247

"Kuhn examines the technology, the past and present legal and legislative landscapes, the benefits, and . . . the abuses of recent advances in aerial photography, biometrics, DNA testing, consumer data storage, and other challenges to privacy. . . . This cogent, clearly written assignment title is backed up by substantial source notes, annotated rosters of recent legal decisions, and multimedia resources." Booklist

Includes bibliographical references

Scales, Pat R.

Teaching banned books; 12 guides for young readers. American Library Association 2001 134p pa $28

Grades: Professional   323.44

1. Books—Censorship 2. Children's literature—Study and teaching 3. School libraries

ISBN 0-8389-0807-1   LC 01-22340

The author "offers twelve strategies for teaching books that have been challenged or censored in the United States. Designed to accompany teaching about the First Amendment, 'each strategy includes a summary of the novel, a pre-reading activity, discussion questions to encourage critical thinking, and activities to broaden students' knowledge of topics in the novel.'" Bull Cent Child Books

"Scales knows her material inside out. She also knows how to inspire others to take up this cause and gives them an effective handbook to do just that." Booklist

Includes bibliographical references

324   The political process

The **Election** of 2000 and the administration of George W. Bush; editor, Arthur M. Schlesinger, Jr.; associate editors, Fred L. Israel & Jonathan H. Mann. Mason Crest Publs. 2003 128p il (Major presidential elections and the administrations that followed) lib bdg $24.95

Grades: 7 8 9 10   324

1. Bush, George W. 2. Presidents—United States—Election—2000 3. United States—Politics and government—1989-

ISBN 1-59084-365-7   LC 2002-13397

The Election of 2000 and the administration of George W. Bush—*Continued*

A discussion of the presidential election of 2000 and the subsequent administration of George W. Bush, based on source documents

"An exemplary, evenhanded discussion of the election and of the Bush administration, through the Trade Bill of 2002." SLJ

Includes bibliographical references

Goodman, Susan, 1952-

See how they run; campaign dreams, election schemes, and the race to the White House; [by] Susan E. Goodman; illustrated by Elwood H. Smith. 1st U.S. ed. Bloomsbury Children's Books 2008 96p il lib bdg $16.95; pa $9.95

Grades: 4 5 6 7   **324**

1. Presidents—United States—Election

ISBN 978-1-59990-285-2 (lib bdg); 1-59990-285-0 (lib bdg); 978-1-59990-171-8 (pa); 1-59990-171-4 (pa)

LC 2007044452

"A lighthearted, fact-filled look at elections in the United States. The engaging conversational narrative and funny cartoons lend appealing irreverence to [the] topic. . . . The book covers a lot of ground and introduces concepts and personalities in ways that readers will understand and remember. Coverage includes the electoral college, campaigning, and many other aspects of elections. . . . Plentiful illustrations utilize humor to demonstrate content. . . . Informative, entertaining, and timely." SLJ

Includes bibliographical references

Morris-Lipsman, Arlene

Presidential races; the battle for power in the United States; [by] Arlene Morris-Lipsman. Twenty-First Century Books 2007 c2008 112p il (People's history) lib bdg $30.60

Grades: 5 6 7 8   **324**

1. Presidents—United States—Election

ISBN 978-0-8225-6783-7   LC 2006102637

Describes how election campaigns for the office of president of the United States have changed from the time of George Washington to the Bush vs. Kerry campaign of 2004.

"Political cartoons and photographs, all in black and white and accompanied by substantial captions, flesh out the text. . . . A timely and accessible book." SLJ

Includes bibliographical references

Steele, Philip

Vote. DK Pub. 2008 72p il (Eyewitness books) $15.99

Grades: 4 5 6 7 8   **324**

1. Elections

ISBN 978-0-7566-3382-0; 0-7566-3382-6

"Engaging visual material and a wealth of assorted facts trace the history of voting and its impact on human rights, politics, and other related areas. The first half moves chronologically from ancient Greece to modern times, with current information into the 21st century. Later sections look at political structures, election logis-

tics, and even nongovernmental elections (including trade unions, the Oscars, and Britain's Pop Idol). Several high-quality photographs and reproductions appear on each spread. . . . The book does a nice job of pulling together an impressive array of topics, events, and ideas within the broad concept of global suffrage. The book comes with a poster-size wall chart and a clip-art CD with downloadable images of many of the illustrations." SLJ

Wagner, Heather Lehr

How the president is elected; [by] Heather Lehr Wagner. Chelsea House 2007 95p il map (The U.S. government: how it works) lib bdg $30

Grades: 5 6 7 8   **324**

1. Presidents—United States—Election

ISBN 978-0-7910-9418-1 (lib bdg); 0-7910-9418-9 (lib bdg)   LC 2006102365

"Wagner opens with the controversial election of 2000 between George W. Bush and Al Gore, and uses it as a springboard to discuss how the Electoral College works. Subsequent chapters discuss the two-party system, presidential campaigns, and what types of qualifications presidential candidates need. . . . The writing is clear and concise, facts are easy to find, and the prose is fluid." SLJ

Includes glossary and bibliographical references

324.2   Political parties

Cox, Vicki

The history of the third parties; [by] Vicki Cox. Chelsea House 2007 125p (The U.S. government: how it works) lib bdg $30

Grades: 7 8 9 10   **324.2**

1. Third parties (United States politics) 2. United States—Politics and government

ISBN 978-0-7910-9421-1 (lib bdg); 0-7910-9421-9 (lib bdg)   LC 2006-100704

"Beginning with the Tertium Quids in 1806 and continuing to today's Green Party, . . . [this book] chronicles third parties and their increasing visibility in the American political system." Publisher's note

"Black-and-white photos and sidebars about government history and process enhance the neatly presented volume, which will find wide use in this coming election year. A glossary, bibliography, and suggested book and Web resources conclude." Booklist

Includes glossary and bibliographical references

324.6   Election systems and procedures; suffrage

Aretha, David

Selma and the Voting Rights Act. Morgan Reynolds Pub. 2007 128p il (The civil rights movement) lib bdg $27.95

Grades: 7 8 9 10 11 12   **324.6**

1. Voting Rights Act of 1965 2. African Americans—Civil rights 3. African Americans—Suffrage 4. Selma (Ala.)—Race relations

ISBN 978-1-59935-056-1; 1-59935-056-4

LC 2007-24655

Aretha, David—*Continued*

The author discusses "mid-1960s Alabama and the black struggle to exercise the constitutional right to vote. Even those who know the story of the famous protest marches will be interested in the details here. . . . There are quotes from and photos of the famous as well as the unknown, as well as excerpts from speeches and news photos." Booklist

Includes bibliographical references

Connolly, Sean, 1956-

The right to vote; [by] Sean Connolly. 1st ed. Smart Apple Media 2006 47p il (Campaigns for change) $24.77 *

Grades: 5 6 7 8   **324.6**

1. Suffrage

ISBN 1-58340-517-8   LC 2004051209

This "is a strong, historically based introduction to the role of democratic participation, beginning in Ancient Greece and continuing up to the international process found in the United Nations General Assembly." Voice Youth Advocates

Includes bibliographical references

Marzilli, Alan, 1970-

Election reform. Chelsea House 2004 123p il (Point-counterpoint) lib bdg $29.95

Grades: 7 8 9 10   **324.6**

1. Elections 2. Politics

ISBN 0-7910-7698-9   LC 2003-11607

"This volume addresses three important issues: voter fraud, campaign contributions, and political advertising. . . . An excellent resource for assignments." SLJ

Includes bibliographical references

Monroe, Judy

The Susan B. Anthony women's voting rights trial; a headline court case. Enslow Pubs. 2002 112p il (Headline court cases) lib bdg $26.60

Grades: 7 8 9 10   **324.6**

1. Anthony, Susan B., 1820-1906 2. Women—Suffrage

ISBN 0-7660-1759-1   LC 2001-4528

Examines the efforts to gain the right for women in the United States to vote, focusing on the trial of Susan B. Anthony for illegally voting in the presidential election in 1872

"Simple syntax, insightful quotes, and logical organization make the information easily accessible." SLJ

Includes glossary and bibliographical references

325.73 Immigration to the United States

Allport, Alan, 1970-

Immigration policy; by Alan Allport; [rev. by John E. Ferguson, Jr.] 2nd ed. Chelsea House 2009 146p (Point-counterpoint) $35

Grades: 7 8 9 10   **325.73**

1. United States—Immigration and emigration

ISBN 978-1-60413-126-0; 1-60413-126-8

     LC 2008-35049

First published 2005

"Presents . . . viewpoints on immigration and on making English the official language of the United States." Publisher's note

This is "well organized, clearly written, and [includes] a rich array of bibliographic resources." SLJ [review of 2005 edition]

Includes bibliographical references

Ambrosek, Renee

America debates United States policy on immigration; [by] Renee Ambrosek. Rosen Pub. Group 2007 64p il (America debates) lib bdg $29.25

Grades: 5 6 7 8 9 10 11 12   **325.73**

1. United States—Immigration and emigration 2. Immigrants—United States

ISBN 978-1-4042-1924-3 (lib bdg); 1-4042-1924-2 (lib bdg)   LC 2006-101215

This "book explores the economic, social services, global policy, and security and border debates in connection with the immigration policies of the United States. The arguments of the critics and supporters on each side of the issue are . . . presented." Publisher's note

The issues "are debated in a clear, concise manner. . . . Colorful photographs and boxed information highlighted in red break up the [text]." SLJ

Includes glossary and bibliographical references

Anderson, Dale, 1953-

Arriving at Ellis Island. World Almanac Library 2002 48p il map (Landmark events in American history) lib bdg $26.60; pa $11.95

Grades: 5 6 7 8   **325.73**

1. Ellis Island Immigration Station 2. United States—Immigration and emigration

ISBN 0-8368-5337-7 (lib bdg); 0-8368-5351-2 (pa)

     LC 2002-24627

Discusses immigration to the United States during the nineteenth and early twentieth centuries and describes the small island in New York harbor that served as the point of entry for millions of immigrants from 1892 to 1954

The "design is attractive, with drawings, maps, paintings, and photos; primary sources, such as excerpts from diaries, letters, and newspapers, support and enhance the [text]. . . . Informative, competently written." Booklist

Includes glossary and bibliographical references

Bausum, Ann

Denied, detained, deported; stories from the dark side of American immigration. National Geographic 2009 111p il $21.95; lib bdg $32.90 *

Grades: 6 7 8 9 10 11 12   **325.73**

1. Immigrants—United States 2. United States—Immigration and emigration

ISBN 978-1-4263-0332-6; 1-4263-0332-7; 978-1-4263-0333-3 (lib bdg); 1-4263-0333-5 (lib bdg)

"This volume deals frankly with the more troubling aspects of United States immigration policy. The author chose the stories of three immigrants. . . . Twelve-year-old German-Jew Herb Karliner was denied entry to the United States at the border when he attempted to escape

Bausum, Ann—*Continued*

Nazi Germany. Sixteen-year-old Japanese-American Mary Matsuda was detained with the rest of her family during World War II. Labor-activist Emma Goldman was deported for her 'un-American' views. . . . The themes of the three stories are unified by the introduction and conclusion, which deal with Chinese immigration during the late 19th century and the history of immigration across the southern border of the United States, respectively. Photographs throughout will help students relate to the narrative. . . . This is an interesting and readable book." SLJ

Includes bibliographical references

Bial, Raymond

Ellis Island; coming to the land of liberty. Houghton Mifflin Books for Children 2009 56p il $18

Grades: 4 5 6 7   **325.73**

1. Ellis Island Immigration Station 2. United States—Immigration and emigration

ISBN 978-0-618-99943-9; 0-618-99943-4

LC 2008036794

"Bial examines the history of the famed immigration station. . . . He looks at the socio-historical roots of the mass exodus to America and provides a detailed look at the immigrant experience from ship to shore, with Ellis Island in between. Primary-source quotes and period photos pair eloquently with the modern narrative voice and color photographs of the museum exhibits. . . . The generously sized period photos and Bial's museum shots tell a vivid and poignant tale." SLJ

Includes bibliographical references

Conway, Lorie, 1954-

Forgotten Ellis Island; the extraordinary story of America's immigrant hospital; [by] Lorie Conway. 1st Smithsonian Books ed. Smithsonian Books/Collins 2007 185p il map $26.95

Grades: 7 8 9 10 11 12   **325.73**

1. Ellis Island Immigration Station 2. Hospitals 3. United States—Immigration and emigration 4. Immigrants—Health and hygiene

ISBN 978-0-06-124196-3; 0-06-124196-2

LC 2007022913

"Conway details the medical inspection that immigrants went through after disembarking and shows how thousands of people were treated at the island's hospitals, sometimes against their will. . . . Each chapter contains dozens of interesting archival photographs and large blocks of quotes from doctors and immigrants. . . . [The book] will add depth to any report on U.S. immigration." SLJ

Includes bibliographical references

Daniels, Roger

American immigration; a student companion. Oxford Univ. Press 2000 303p (Oxford student companions to American history) lib bdg $60

Grades: 7 8 9 10   **325.73**

1. United States—Immigration and emigration 2. Immigrants—United States

ISBN 0-19-511316-0   LC 00-56673

"Following an essay that provides an overview of the book, students find immigration statistics, areas of settlement, major periods of immigration, and the predominant religion of the immigrant groups. Key pieces of legislation . . . are discussed. . . . The appendices cover important dates in immigration history; immigration, ethnic, and refugee organizations." Book Rep

"This resource would be ideal for young adults seeking brief overviews of particular ethnic groups." Voice Youth Advocates

Includes bibliographical references

I was dreaming to come to America; memories from the Ellis Island Oral History Project; selected and illustrated by Veronica Lawlor; foreword by Rudolph W. Giuliani. Viking 1995 38p il hardcover o.p. pa $6.99

Grades: 4 5 6 7   **325.73**

1. Ellis Island Immigration Station 2. United States—Immigration and emigration

ISBN 0-670-86164-2; 0-14-055622-2 (pa)

LC 95-1281

In their own words, coupled with hand-painted collage illustrations, immigrants recall their arrival in the United States. Includes brief biographies and facts about the Ellis Island Oral History Project

"There is a flavor of Chagall in the peasant figures dancing above the ship or hopping ashore near the turreted towers of the huge building on Ellis Island. The elegant rendering offers a timeless view of this significant journey that is at once personal and universal." Horn Book

Illegal immigration: opposing viewpoints; Margaret Haerens, book editor. Greenhaven Press 2007 212p il lib bdg $34.95; pa $23.70 *

Grades: 8 9 10 11 12   **325.73**

1. Illegal aliens 2. United States—Immigration and emigration

ISBN 0-7377-3356-X (lib bdg); 0-7377-3357-8 (pa)

LC 2005-55049

Replaces the edition published 2002 under the editorship of William Dudley

"Opposing viewpoints series"

"The writers present opposing perspectives on such topics as border-patrol efforts, immigration policy reform, racism, the development of a guest worker program, and the connection between illegal immigration and terrorism. . . . Even reluctant readers will find many compelling and inflammatory arguments to hold their interest." SLJ

Includes bibliographical references

Kenney, Karen Latchana, 1974-

Illegal immigration; by Karen Kenney. ABDO Publishing 2008 112p il map (Essential viewpoints) $22.95

Grades: 7 8 9 10   **325.73**

1. Illegal aliens 2. United States—Immigration and emigration

ISBN 978-1-59928-861-1; 1-59928-861-3

LC 2007013881

This is a "balanced [overview] of [a] complex, divisive [issue]. Though not exhaustive, [this title includes] the topic's history and most salient points in an accessi-

Kenney, Karen Latchana, 1974-—_Continued_
ble and reader-friendly format. . . . [This book's] opening chapter begins with 2006 Immigration and Customs
Enforcement raids and closes with questions about how
illegal immigration impacts the U.S. economy and culture. Subsequent chapters address the history of U.S. immigration, crime and drugs, costs, labor concerns, border
security, and proposals for reform. Color images enhance
the [text], and charts and maps further clarify the content. Sidebars expand on related topics through quotes,
primary-source snippets, and other salient information."
SLJ
    Includes bibliographical references

Masoff, Joy, 1951-
    We are all Americans; understanding diversity.
Five Ponds 2006 63p il $26.50
Grades: 4 5 6 7   **325.73**
    1. United States—Immigration and emigration
2. Multiculturalism
    ISBN 0-972715-62-2
    "Gloriously supported by photographs, diagrams, and
maps, this five-chapter overview offers information about
America's immigrants. 'In the Beginning' describes diversity and how it is created. 'A New Start' focuses on
the mechanisms in place for journeying from country to
country—passports and visas, Ellis Island and Angel Island. The most comprehensive section, 'Who Are We?,'
chronicles those who have come from Africa, Asia, Europe, North America, South America, and Oceania to
make a home in the United States. . . . 'Coming Together,' . . . features plants and animals, food, sports, games,
holidays, and music from myriad backgrounds that
Americans now enjoy. The last section, 'All Together
Now,' discusses the strengths of diversity, featuring significant Americans." SLJ

Meltzer, Milton, 1915-
    Bound for America; the story of the European
immigrants. Benchmark Bks. 2002 112p il (Great
journeys) $32.79 *
Grades: 5 6 7 8   **325.73**
    1. United States—Immigration and emigration
    ISBN 0-7614-1227-1   LC 00-51875
    This history of immigration to the United States focus-
es on Europeans who arrived in the late 19th and early
20th century
    Includes bibliographical references

Miller, Debra A.
    Illegal immigration. ReferencePoint Press 2007
110p il (Compact research) $24.95
Grades: 8 9 10 11 12   **325.73**
    1. Illegal aliens 2. United States—Immigration and
emigration
    ISBN 978-1-6015-2009-8; 1-6015-2009-3
                    LC 2006-32349
    "After the detailed overview, Miller discusses conflict-
ing opinions on assimilation, effects on the economy,
amnesty, border enforcement, guest worker programs,
and more. The design is highly readable, including extensive primary-source quotes, as well as facts and color
charts with each chapter. . . . The debate is balanced;
opposing sides have their say." Booklist

The **Newest** Americans. Greenwood Press 2003 5v
il maps (Middle school reference) set $200
Grades: 6 7 8 9   **325.73**
    1. United States—Immigration and emigration—Ency-
clopedias 2. Minorities—Encyclopedias 3. Reference
books
    ISBN 0-313-32553-7   LC 2002-35214
    Contents: v1 A-D, Afghans to Dominicans; v2 E-H,
Ecuadoreans to Hatians; v3 I-L, Indians to Laotians; v4
M-P, Mexicans to Puerto Ricans; v5 R-V, Russians to
Vietnamese
    Provides historical, social, political, and cultural infor-
mation about immigrant groups that have been changing
the face of the United States from 1960 to the present,
as well as facts about immigrants in general
    "These volumes present thorough and accessible infor-
mation. . . . A good choice for contemporary immigration assignments." SLJ

Sandler, Martin W.
    Island of hope; the story of Ellis Island and the
journey to America. Scholastic Nonfiction 2004
144p il $18.95
Grades: 5 6 7 8   **325.73**
    1. Ellis Island Immigration Station 2. United States—
Immigration and emigration
    ISBN 0-439-53082-2   LC 2003-54448
    Relates the story of immigration to America through
the voices and stories of those who passed through Ellis
Island, from its opening in 1892 to the release of the last
detainee in 1954.
    "This engagingly written, inspirational account will
give children, particularly immigrants or descendants of
immigrants, some sharp insight into the trials and triumphs of their predecessors." Booklist
    Includes bibliographical references

Stefoff, Rebecca, 1951-
    American voices from a century of immigration:
1820-1924. Marshall Cavendish Benchmark 2006
c2007 115p (American voices from--) lib bdg
$37.07 *
Grades: 6 7 8 9   **325.73**
    1. United States—Immigration and emigration
2. Immigrants—United States
    ISBN 978-0-7614-2172-6 (lib bdg); 0-7614-2172-6 (lib
bdg)   LC 2005035963
    "Describes the diverse peoples who came to the Unit-
ed States from 1820, when records began to be kept, to
1924, when the gates were nearly closed to immigrants.
The reactions of Americans to the new arrivals, laws that
were passed, and the experiences of the immigrants
themselves are covered through the use of primary
sources." Publisher's note
    Includes glossary and bibliographical references

Wepman, Dennis
    Immigration. Facts on File, Inc. 2008 476p il
map (American experience) $80
Grades: 7 8 9 10   **325.73**
    1. United States—Immigration and emigration
    ISBN 978-0-8160-6240-9; 0-8160-6240-4
                    LC 2007-29713

Wepman, Dennis—*Continued*

First published 2002 as a volume in the Eyewitness History series

"This volume covers the years between 1607 and June 2007. Each chapter is divided into three sections: an 18 to 25-page main body, a 'Chronicle of Events' by year, and well-documented 'Eyewitness Testimony.' . . . [The author] maintains a high quality of research and a clear writing style, and provides detailed source documentation." SLJ

Includes bibliographical references

326 Slavery and emancipation

Altman, Linda Jacobs, 1943-

The politics of slavery; fiery national debates fueled by the slave economy; foreword by series advisor Henry Louis Gates. Enslow 2004 128p il map (Slavery in American history) lib bdg $26.60

Grades: 7 8 9 10   **326**

1. Slavery—United States 2. United States—Politics and government 3. United States—Race relations

ISBN 0-7660-2150-5   LC 2003-26532

Contents: The beginnings of American slavery; From servants to slaves; Slavery and the founding freedoms; Compromise and the Constitution; Slavery in a growing nation; Missouri and the westward expansion; Slavery and manifest destiny; North and South: a clash of cultures; The road to disunion

"Altman relates the beginning of 'the peculiar institution' and the constitutional, historical, and political issues and figures surrounding it from 1619 to the ratification of the Thirteenth Amendment in 1865. . . . [This book] will be useful in American-history collections." SLJ

Bial, Raymond

The strength of these arms; life in the slave quarters. Houghton Mifflin 1997 40p il $16

Grades: 4 5 6 7   **326**

1. Slavery—United States 2. Plantation life 3. African Americans—Social life and customs

ISBN 0-395-77394-6   LC 96-39860

Describes how slaves were able to preserve some elements of their African heritage despite the often brutal treatment they experienced on Southern plantations

"This volume features clear, color photographs of plantation sites and artifacts, as well as a few early photos of people living under slavery. . . . This makes slavery in America more concrete than many other books on the subject." Booklist

Includes bibliographical references

The Underground Railroad. Houghton Mifflin 1995 48p il map hardcover o.p. pa $6.95

Grades: 4 5 6 7   **326**

1. Underground railroad 2. Slavery—United States

ISBN 0-395-69937-1; 0-395-97915-3 (pa)

LC 94-19614

Using first-person accounts, historical documents, and his own photographs, the author "focuses on the history of the Underground Railroad, building on the experiences of both riders and conductors as he outlines the political

climate and the moral beliefs that allowed slavery to thrive and those that helped bring about its downfall." Publ Wkly

"Although the text covers ground often trodden by other works on this popular subject, Bial's shots of places and things which now appear tidy and innocent conjure spirits of desperate freedom-seekers as handily as do more detailed narratives." Bull Cent Child Books

Includes bibliographical references

Cloud Tapper, Suzanne

Voices from slavery's past; yearning to be heard; foreword by series advisor Henry Louis Gates. Enslow Publishers 2004 128p il map (Slavery in American history) lib bdg $26.60

Grades: 7 8 9 10   **326**

1. Abolitionists 2. Slavery—United States

ISBN 0-7660-2157-2   LC 2003-25134

This profiles escaped slave Henry Bibb, slave trader John Newton, captured African Olauda Equiano, racist scientist Joseph Le Conte, slave mistress Letitia Burwell, escaped slave Harriet Jacobs, and abolitionists William Lloyd Garrison and Frederick Douglass

This title is "consistently solid, with many informative period photographs and drawings, excerpts from primary-source documents, and strong back matter." SLJ

Includes glossary and bibliographical references

The **Complete** history of American slavery; James Miller, book editor. Greenhaven Press 2001 642p il map (Complete history of) lib bdg $123.75

Grades: 7 8 9 10   **326**

1. Slavery—United States 2. African Americans—History

ISBN 0-7377-0424-1   LC 00-39332

This anthology includes more than 90 entries and "begins with the Atlantic slave trade and ends with the Civil War, with entries by Frederick Douglass, Nat Turner, Mary Chestnut, and many others. It is organized into 16 chapters on a number of topics, including a fascinating discussion of whether the Underground Railroad actually existed." Booklist

Includes bibliographical references

Currie, Stephen, 1960-

Slavery. Greenhaven Press 1999 111p il (Opposing viewpoints digests) lib bdg $29.95; pa $19.95

Grades: 7 8 9 10   **326**

1. Slavery—United States

ISBN 1-56510-881-7 (lib bdg); 1-56510-880-9 (pa)

LC 98-36198

Contributors discuss slavery in the United States from historical, political, economic and sociological perspectives

Includes bibliographical references

DeFord, Deborah H.

Life under slavery; [by] Deborah H. DeFord. Chelsea House 2006 112p il map (Slavery in the Americas) $35 *

Grades: 6 7 8 9   **326**

1. Slavery—United States

ISBN 978-0-8160-6135-8; 0-8160-6135-1

LC 2005034651

This describes the treatment of slaves in the United States, life expectancies, entertainments, and family lives of slaves, and the cultural elements introduced into the New World by enslaved Africans.

"Clearly written, accessible, and well organized . . . [this] is illustrated with black-and-white drawings, period photographs, and explanatory text boxes." SLJ

Includes bibliographical references

Edwards, Judith

Abolitionists and slave resistance; breaking the chains of slavery; foreword by Henry Louis Gates. Enslow Publishers 2004 128p il map (Slavery in American history) lib bdg $26.60

Grades: 7 8 9 10   **326**

1. Abolitionists 2. Slavery—United States

ISBN 0-7660-2155-6   LC 2003-13457

Contents: Events leading to abolition; Slavery and the Revolution; The anti-slavery movement gathers force; Abolitionists organize; The Amistad and the new decade; The rebels and the runaways; Escape from slavery; John Brown's raid; On the antislavery side; From slave to soldier

"Edwards examines the growth of the abolition movement and provides examples of some of the ways slaves themselves protested, including theft, work slowdowns, and destruction of property. Rebellions, runaways, and the Underground Railroad are also covered. The sensitive and respectful approach leads to an understanding of the social issues that remain as a legacy of slavery in American society today." SLJ

Includes bibliographical references

Eskridge, Ann E., 1949-

Slave uprisings and runaways; fighting for freedom and the Underground Railroad; foreword by series advisor Henry Louis Gates. Enslow 2004 128p il map (Slavery in American history) lib bdg $26.60   **326**

1. Slavery—United States 2. Underground railroad

ISBN 0-7660-2154-8   LC 2003-26533

This history of slave rebellions and escapes covers such topics as Nat Turner, John Brown, Harriet Tubman, Frederick Douglass, The Fugitive Slave Act, and The Underground Railroad.

Includes bibliographical references

Fradin, Dennis B.

Bound for the North Star; true stories of fugitive slaves; [by] Dennis Brindell Fradin. Clarion Bks. 2000 206p il $20

Grades: 7 8 9 10   **326**

1. Slavery—United States 2. Underground railroad 3. Abolitionists

ISBN 0-395-97017-2   LC 00-29052

"Fradin here draws on more than 16 slaves' personal experiences to show what slavery was like: the unrelenting racism; the physical brutality, including rape and flogging; the anguish of family separation. . . . The narrative is direct, with no rhetoric or cover-up. . . . This is painful reading about legal racist cruelty and those who resisted it." Booklist

Includes bibliographical references

Fradin, Judith Bloom

5,000 miles to freedom; Ellen and William Craft's flight from slavery; [by] Judith Bloom Fradin and Dennis Brindell Fradin. National Geographic 2006 96p il $19.95; lib bdg $29.90 *

Grades: 5 6 7 8 9 10   **326**

1. Craft, Ellen, 1826-1891 2. Craft, William, 19th cent. 3. Slavery—United States

ISBN 0-7922-7885-2; 0-7922-7886-0 (lib bdg)

"In 1848, light-skinned Ellen Craft, dressed in the clothing of a rich, white man, assumed the identity of Mr. William Johnson and, escorted by his black slave, William, traveled by railroad and boat to reach the North. With the passage of a more stringent Fugitive Slave Law in 1850, the couple . . . decided to travel to England. . . . In 1869, they returned to the United States, opening a school and operating a farm in Georgia. . . . This lively, well-written volume presents the events in their lives in an exciting, page-turner style that's sure to hold readers attention. Black-and-white photographs, illustrations, and reproductions enhance the text." SLJ

Includes bibliographical references

Gold, Susan Dudley, 1949-

United States v. Amistad; slave ship mutiny. Marshall Cavendish Benchmark 2006 c2007 144p il (Supreme Court milestones) lib bdg $39.93

Grades: 7 8 9 10   **326**

1. Amistad (Schooner) 2. Slavery—United States

ISBN 978-0-7614-2143-6; 0-7614-2143-2

This is an account of the 1841 Supreme Court case involving the mutiny aboard the slave ship Amistad and the circumstances which surrounded it.

Includes bibliographical references

Hulm, David

United States v. the Amistad; the question of slavery in a free country. Rosen Pub. Group 2004 64p il (Supreme Court cases through primary sources) lib bdg $29.25

Grades: 7 8 9 10   **326**

1. Amistad (Schooner) 2. Slavery—United States

ISBN 0-8239-4013-6   LC 2003-5938

Contents: A mutiny changes American history; Trials and tribulations; District Court and Circuit Court; Forged in the fires of adversity; Free, but not home

This is an account of the mutiny aboard the slave ship Amistad and the court cases which followed.

This "deserves a place in every library. . . . Copious and well-chosen primary source documents give extra value to this [book]. . . . Each document adds human drama to the already engaging text." Lib Media Connect

Includes glossary and bibliographical references

Jordan, Anne Devereaux, 1943-
Slavery and resistance; by Anne Devereaux Jordan; with Virginia Schomp. Marshall Cavendish Benchmark 2007 70p il (Drama of African-American history) lib bdg $23.95 *
Grades: 5 6 7 8   326
1. Slavery—United States
ISBN 978-0-7614-2178-8; 0-7614-2178-5
LC 2006012313
"Describes slavery in the United States from colonial times up to the Civil War." Publisher's note
This "is a standout, with elements both well done and well balanced. Foremost is the text, which is as engaging as it is solidly written. . . . The handsome art, which includes paintings and photos . . . is compelling." Booklist
Includes glossary and bibliographical references

Lester, Julius
From slave ship to freedom road; paintings by Rod Brown. Dial Bks. 1998 40p il $17.99; pa $6.99 *
Grades: 5 6 7 8   326
1. Slavery—United States
ISBN 0-8037-1893-4; 0-14-056669-4 (pa)
LC 96-44422
"Lester uses empathy-provoking exercises, open-ended questions, and the paintings of Rod Brown to help readers understand the experience of African-American slaves." Bull Cent Child Books
"Lester's impassioned questions grow from his visceral response to Brown's narrative paintings. . . . The combination of history, art, and commentary demands interaction." Booklist

McKissack, Patricia C., 1944-
Rebels against slavery; by Patricia C. McKissack and Fredrick McKissack. Scholastic 1996 181p il $15.95 *
Grades: 5 6 7 8   326
1. Slavery—United States
ISBN 0-590-45735-7   LC 94-41089
A Coretta Scott King honor book for text, 1997
The authors "explore slave revolts and the men and women who led them, weaving a tale of courage and defiance in the face of tremendous odds. Readers learn not only about Nat Turner and Denmark Vesey, but also about Cato, Gabriel Prosser, the maroons, and the relationship between escaped slaves and Seminole Indians. The activities of abolitionists are described as well. The authors' careful research, sensitivity, and evenhanded style reveal a sad, yet inspiring story of the will to be free." SLJ

McNeese, Tim
The rise and fall of American slavery; freedom denied, freedom gained; foreword by series advisor Dr. Henry Louis Gates, Jr. Enslow Publishers 2004 128p il map (Slavery in American history) lib bdg $26.60
Grades: 7 8 9 10   326
1. Slavery—United States
ISBN 0-7660-2156-4   LC 2003-13459

Contents: The story of Josiah Henson; The slave trade; Slavery in the colonies; Slavery and revolution; King Cotton; Abolition and emancipation
This is a history of American slavery from colonial times to emancipation.
"Drawing on personal slave narratives as well as the commentary and analysis of eminent scholars, [this title] . . . [brings] immediacy and depth to crucial events and [assesses] their lasting impact on America's economy, politics, and culture. . . . The documentation is exemplary." Booklist
Includes glossary and bibliographical references

Nardo, Don, 1947-
The Atlantic slave trade; [by] Don Nardo. Thomson/Gale 2008 104p il (Lucent library of black history) lib bdg $32.45
Grades: 6 7 8 9   326
1. Slave trade 2. Slavery
ISBN 978-1-4205-0007-3 (lib bdg); 1-4205-0007-4 (lib bdg)
LC 2007-22999
"Nardo examines [slave trade and] its impact on West Africa, its implication for the economic and social health of the entire African continent, the role that black Africans played in the sale of their countrymen, and the continuing shadow slavery still casts over this country's race relations. . . . Include[s] extensive bibliographies, period illustrations, and primary-source documents." SLJ
Includes bibliographical references

Sawyer, Kem Knapp
The underground railroad in American history. Enslow Pubs. 1997 128p il maps (In American history) lib bdg $26.60
Grades: 7 8 9 10   326
1. Underground railroad 2. Slavery—United States
ISBN 0-89490-885-5   LC 96-30901
Describes the Underground Railroad and the historical events surrounding it and presents the stories of some of its conductors
Includes bibliographical references

Sharp, S. Pearl
The slave trade and the middle passage; by S. Pearl Sharp with Virginia Schomp. Marshall Cavendish Benchmark 2007 70p il map (Drama of African-American history) lib bdg $34.21 *
Grades: 5 6 7 8   326
1. Slave trade 2. Slavery
ISBN 978-0-7614-2176-4 (lib bdg); 0-7614-2176-9 (lib bdg)
LC 2006005321
"Traces the history of the transatlantic slave trade and the development of slavery in the New World." Publisher's note
Includes glossary and bibliographical references

Sirimarco, Elizabeth, 1966-
American voices from the time of slavery.
Marshall Cavendish Benchmark 2007 114p
(American voices from--) lib bdg $37.07 *
Grades: 6 7 8 9   **326**
1. Slavery—United States 2. African Americans—History
ISBN 978-0-7614-2169-6 (lib bdg); 0-7614-2169-6 (lib
bdg)   LC 2005025854
"Describes the history of slavery in the United
States—from the landing of the first enslaved Africans to
the close of the Civil War—through various primary
source documents, such as slave narratives, advertisements, newspaper accounts, official documents and laws,
plus contemporary art and photos." Publisher's note
Includes glossary and bibliographical references

Slavery; James D. Torr, book editor. Greenhaven
Press 2004 240p map (Opposing viewpoints in
world history series) $33.70; pa $22.45
Grades: 8 9 10 11 12   **326**
1. Slavery—United States
ISBN 0-7377-1705-X; 0-7377-1706-8 (pa)
LC 2003-44812
This book offers "perspectives on American slavery
through a selection of primary sources. The excerpts, are
culled from speeches, pamphlets, and scholarly texts, are
divided into four sections that cover moral issues, slave
resistance, abolitionists, and events that led to the Civil
War. . . . The entries that are included . . . will greatly
enhance students' understanding of the issues. . . . An
important, useful addition to the high-school history curriculum." Booklist
Includes bibliographical references

Tackach, James, 1954-
The abolition of American slavery. Lucent Bks.
2002 112p il maps (World history series) lib bdg
$27.45 *
Grades: 7 8 9 10   **326**
1. Abolitionists 2. Slavery—United States
ISBN 1-59018-002-X   LC 2001-5301
Discusses the introduction of slaves into American society, the beginnings of the abolitionist movement, the
national conflict over slavery and the resulting Civil
War, emancipation of the slaves, and slavery's legacy
"There is a good deal of information packed into the
brief text and both report writers and general readers will
be well served. The book is illustrated with archival photographs and reproductions of prints and broadsides."
SLJ
Includes bibliographical references

Thomas, Velma Maia
Lest we forget; the passage from Africa to
slavery and emancipation. Crown 1997 32p il
$29.95
Grades: 7 8 9 10   **326**
1. Slavery—United States 2. African Americans—History 3. Slave trade
ISBN 0-609-60030-3   LC 96-54240
"A three-dimensional interactive book with photographs and documents from the Black Holocaust Exhibit." Title page

"By combining highly effective and readable text with
photographs, news clippings, drawings, and facsimilies of
documents, Thomas shares with her readers the details of
virtually every aspect of slave life. . . . Throughout the
assortment of pop-out and pull-out replicas, points are
raised that will lead to classroom discussion." SLJ

Worth, Richard, 1945-
Slave life on the plantation; prisons beneath the
sun. Enslow Publishers 2004 128p il (Slavery in
American history) lib bdg $26.60
Grades: 7 8 9 10   **326**
1. Slavery—United States 2. Plantation life
ISBN 0-7660-2152-1   LC 2003-24291
Contents: A slave's life; Slavery in the 1600s; Plantation life in 1700s; King Cotton; Relationships between
owners and slaves; African-American culture on the
plantation; Freedom
"Worth frames his account within the sweep of history, but his focus is on daily life—the work, the hardship
(especially the breakup of family life), punishment, and
resistance—and he discusses the relationship between
owners and slaves, the importance of cotton, and African
American culture. [This title includes] several stirring
page-long slave narratives as well as black-and-white
drawings and photos. The documentation is exemplary."
Booklist
Includes glossary and bibliographical references

The slave trade in America; cruel commerce;
foreword by series advisor Dr. Henry Louis Gates,
Jr. Enslow Publishers 2004 128p il map (Slavery
in American history) lib bdg $26.60
Grades: 7 8 9 10   **326**
1. Slave trade 2. Slavery—United States
ISBN 0-7660-2151-3   LC 2003-12079
Contents: Stories of the slave trade; Origins of the
slave trade; The slave trade in the 1600s; The slave trade
in the 1700s; The slave trade and the law; Slave trade
within the South; Major centers of internal slave trade;
End of the slave trade
This is a history of the slave trade in America from
colonial times to emancipation
This "clearly written, well-researched [book presents]
solid coverage of the subject." SLJ
Includes glossary and bibliographical references

327.1 Foreign policy and specific topics in international relations

Blohm, Craig E., 1948-
Weapons of peace; the nuclear arms race.
Lucent Bks. 2003 128p il map (American war
library, Cold War) $27.45
Grades: 6 7 8 9   **327.1**
1. Nuclear weapons 2. Arms race 3. Arms control
4. World politics—1945-
ISBN 1-59018-212-X   LC 2002-11035
Discusses the development of nuclear weapons, the
race for nuclear supremacy, deployment of these weapons during the Cold War, and disarmament
Includes bibliographical references

327.12 Espionage and subversion

Coleman, Janet Wyman

Secrets, lies, gizmos, and spies; a history of spies and espionage. Harry N. Abrams 2006 113p il $24.95

Grades: 6 7 8 9   **327.12**

1. Espionage

ISBN 0-8109-5756-6   LC 2005-27824

Published in association with the International Spy Museum

"Filled with historical and modern photos and reproductions and arranged loosely by topic, this quick read dives into the secret world of espionage. . . . The true tales describe disguises, ways of gathering information, snooping devices, codes, clandestine operations, and weapons. . . . The engrossing, readable text will hold the interest of even reluctant readers." SLJ

Includes bibliographical references

Fridell, Ron, 1943-

Spy technology. Lerner Publications Co. 2007 48p il (Cool science) lib bdg $27.93

Grades: 4 5 6 7   **327.12**

1. Espionage

ISBN 978-0-8225-5934-4 (lib bdg); 0-8225-5934-X (lib bdg)   LC 2005-33043

Readers of this book "will be delighted to learn that such ingenius gadgets as pistols in lipstick cases are just eh stuff of James Bond, but have been used by organizations like the CIA and the KGB. . . . This attractive book is an excellent introduction to the motivations of governments to look into the military and political secrets of enemy groups as well as within their own countries." SLJ

Includes bibliographical references

Keeley, Jennifer, 1974-

Espionage. Lucent Bks. 2003 112p il map (American war library, Cold War) $27.45

Grades: 6 7 8 9   **327.12**

1. Espionage 2. Cold war

ISBN 1-59018-210-3   LC 2002-2218

Discusses the agents, communications, technological advances, covert actions, and double agents during the Cold War

Includes bibliographical references

Kupperberg, Paul

Spy satellites. Rosen Pub. Group 2003 63p il (Library of satellites) lib bdg $26.50

Grades: 4 5 6 7   **327.12**

1. Espionage 2. Artificial satellites

ISBN 0-8239-3854-9   LC 2002-10747

Contents: A cold war in space; CORONA; Inside a spy satellite; Eyes in the sky

Examines the history, technology, and uses of spy satellites, looking especially at the various reconnaissance satellite programs of the United States, from the mid-twentieth century to the present

"Clear and topical photographs enliven the [presenta-

tion]. While packed with information, the [text is] easy to read." SLJ

Includes glossary and bibliographical references

327.73 United States—Foreign relations

Collier, Christopher, 1930-

The United States in the Cold War: 1945-1989; [by] Christopher Collier, James Lincoln Collier. Benchmark Bks. 2001 95p il maps (Drama of American history) $31.36 *

Grades: 6 7 8 9   **327.73**

1. Cold war 2. World politics—1945-1991 3. United States—Foreign relations—Soviet Union 4. Soviet Union—Foreign relations—United States

ISBN 0-7614-1317-0   LC 00-68010

The author discusses such topics as the Berlin Wall, the Korean and Vietnam Wars, the arms race, and other conflicts between the United States and the Soviet Union and other communist countries

This is written in "engaging narrative style . . . [and is] easy to read and informative." Book Rep

Includes bibliographical references

Renehan, Edward J., 1956-

The Monroe doctrine; the cornerstone of American foreign policy; [by] Edward J. Renehan Jr. Chelsea House 2007 122p il map (Milestones in American history) lib bdg $35

Grades: 7 8 9 10   **327.73**

1. Monroe Doctrine 2. United States—Foreign relations

ISBN 0-7910-9353-0 (lib bdg); 978-0-7910-9353-5 (lib bdg)   LC 2006034126

This description of the Monroe Doctrine is "accessible, lively. . . . Many quotations, sidebars, art reproductions, and maps support the [text]. Excerpts from primary source materials also help give readers a sense of time and place." Horn Book Guide

Includes bibliographical references

328 The legislative process

Horn, Geoffrey

The Congress; by Geoffrey M. Horn. World Almanac Library 2003 48p il (World Almanac Library of American government) lib bdg $30; pa $11.95

Grades: 5 6 7 8   **328**

1. United States. Congress

ISBN 0-8368-5457-8 (lib bdg); 0-8368-5462-4 (pa)   LC 2002-514111

Contents: Congress and the Capitol; What the Constitution says; Getting elected and reelected; House and Senate; How a bill becomes a law; Landmark legislation; Congress in the spotlight

This describes "how the Constitution gives different jobs to each chamber of Congress, the extent and limits

Horn, Geoffrey—*Continued*
of their powers, and the roles each performs in the making of federal laws. . . . [It also discusses] the important officials in Congress, the legislative process, and some important laws Congress has passed. Special sections explain concepts such as pork-barrel spending, lameduck sessions, and filibusters." Publisher's note
Includes bibliographical references

330.1   Systems, schools, theories

Grant, R. G. (Reg G.)
Protesting Capitalism. Raintree 2004 64p il (Ideas of the modern world) lib bdg $34.29
Grades: 7 8 9 10   330.1
1. Capitalism 2. Demonstrations 3. Social movements
ISBN 0-7398-6414-9   LC 2003-2066
Contents: Protest on the streets; The rise of capitalism; The alternative vision; Communism and social democracy; The third world and the new left; Opposing global capitalism; Into the twenty-first century
"After beginning with a description of the Seattle protest against the World Trade Organization in 1999, Grant moves on to define capitalism and discuss the Industrial Revolution. Utopian visions, communism, and socialism are explored as alternative visions to free enterprise. Also discussed are conflicts between developing and industrialized nations after World War II, the downfall of communism in Eastern bloc countries, globalization, and the connection between anticapitalism and the environmental movement. . . . [The book has] a balance of ideas and nonjudgmental language. Black-and-white and full-color photos appear throughout. While the [text is] clearly written, [it does] not shy away from complex ideas" SLJ
Includes glossary and bibliographical references

330.9   Economic situation and conditions

Arnold, James R., 1952-
The industrial revolution; [by] James R. Arnold and Roberta Weiner. Grolier 2005 10v il map set $299
Grades: 5 6 7 8   330.9
1. Industrial revolution 2. Reference books
ISBN 0-7172-6031-3   LC 2004-54243
Contents: v1 A turning point in history; v2 The industrial revolution begins; v3 The industrial revolution spreads; v4 The industrial revolution comes to America; v5 The growth of the industrial revolution in America; v6 The industrial revolution spreads through Europe; v7 The worldwide industrial revolution; v8 America's second industrial revolution; v9 The industrial revolution and the working class; v10 The industrial revolution and American society
"The Industrial Revolution spanned several centuries and continents, and this set covers developments and their impact in a well-organized fashion. . . . The set is copiously illustrated, with a variety of art reproductions, diagrams, and historical photographs. . . . With worldwide scope and coverage from the 18th century through the early 1900s, this is more comprehensive than single-

volume histories, while the logical structure and appealing layout make it accessible to a wide range of students." SLJ
Includes glossary and bibliographical references

Blumenthal, Karen
Six days in October; the stock market crash of 1929. Atheneum Bks. for Young Readers 2002 156p il $17.95
Grades: 7 8 9 10   330.9
1. New York Stock Exchange, Inc. 2. Great Depression, 1929-1939 3. United States—Economic conditions—1919-1933
ISBN 0-689-84276-7   LC 2001-46360
"A Wall Street Journal book"
A comprehensive review of the events, personalities, and mistakes behind the Stock Market Crash of 1929, featuring photographs, newspaper articles, and cartoons of the day
"This fast-paced, gripping . . . account of the market crash of October 1929 puts a human face on the crisis." Publ Wkly
Includes bibliographical references

Doak, Robin S., 1963-
Black Tuesday; prelude to the Great Depression; by Robin S. Doak. Compass Point Books 2008 96p il map (Snapshots in history) lib bdg $31.93
Grades: 6 7 8 9   330.9
1. Stock market crash, 1929 2. Great Depression, 1929-1939 3. United States—Economic conditions—1919-1933
ISBN 978-0-7565-3327-4 (lib bdg); 0-7565-3327-9 (lib bdg)   LC 2007004911
This "explains how the decade's economic boom and unregulated markets created the speculative bubble that burst when the stock market crashed in 1929. Doak concludes that growing investor panic and inadequate government response to the crash contributed to the Great Depression. . . . [The text incorporates] primary-source material and [includes] numerous period photos and political cartoons." SLJ

Lange, Brenda
The Stock Market Crash of 1929; the end of prosperity; [by] Brenda Lange. Chelsea House 2007 114p il (Milestones in American history) lib bdg $35
Grades: 7 8 9 10   330.9
1. Stock market crash, 1929 2. Great Depression, 1929-1939 3. United States—Economic conditions—1919-1933
ISBN 0-7910-9354-9 (lib bdg); 978-0-7910-9354-2 (lib bdg)   LC 2006038868
This describes the Stock Market Crash of October 29, 1929, also known as Black Tuesday, and its consequences.
This is "accessible, lively. . . . Many quotations, sidebars, art reproductions, and maps support the [text]. Excerpts from primary source materials also help give readers a sense of time and place." Horn Book Guide
Includes bibliographical references

Outman, James L., 1946-
Industrial Revolution: almanac; [by] James L. Outman, Elisabeth M. Outman. U.X.L 2003 242p il (Industrial revolution reference library) $55
Grades: 8 9 10 11 12 **330.9**
1. Industrial revolution 2. Reference books
ISBN 0-7876-6513-4 LC 2002-155422
Contents: Origins of the Industrial Revolution; The revolution begins: steam engines, railroads, steamboats; New machines and the factory system; The social and political impact of the Industrial Revolution, part 1; The age of petroleum and electricity; The new business models; The social and political impact of the Industrial Revolution, part 2; Globalization
"This is an excellent adjunct to American and world history units and classes on economics and labor movements." Booklist
Includes bibliographical references

Industrial Revolution: primary sources; [by] James L. Outman, Elisabeth M. Outman. U.X.L 2003 212p il (Industrial revolution reference library) $55
Grades: 8 9 10 11 12 **330.9**
1. Industrial revolution 2. Reference books
ISBN 0-7876-6515-0 LC 2002-155420
Contents: Economic theory; Adam Smith; The Wealth of Nations; Andrew Ure; The philosophy of manufacturers; Karl Marx; The Communist Manifesto; Andrew Carnegie; The gospel of wealth; Technological advances and criticisms; Thomas Savery; Uses of the fire engine; Leeds letters; Luddites; Samuel Morse; On the telegraph; J. Stillman; The last tie; The Industrial Revolution and working conditions; Sadler Report; Samuel Gompers; Germinal Zola and coal miners; Upton Sinclair; Excerpt from The Jungle; Triangle Shirtwaist fire; Jane Addams; Excerpt from Hull House; Carmen Teoli; Congressional testimony; Politics and law in the Industrial Revolution; United States Supreme Court; Northern Securities v. United States; Theodore Roosevelt; Progressive Party platform
"This is an excellent adjunct to American and world history units and classes on economics and labor movements." Booklist
Includes bibliographical references

331.1 Labor force and market

Ching, Jacqueline
Outsourcing U.S. jobs. Rosen Pub. 2009 64p il (In the news) lib bdg $21.95; pa $12.65
Grades: 7 8 9 10 **331.1**
1. Outsourcing 2. Labor supply
ISBN 978-1-4358-5039-2 (lib bdg); 1-4358-5039-4 (lib bdg); 978-1-4358-5367-6 (pa); 1-4358-5367-9 (pa)
LC 2008-16890
"Accessible and up-to-date. . . . The generally well-chosen color photos and diagrams add visual interest. . . . *Outsourcing U.S. Jobs* uses clear examples to discuss the global marketplace and the practical and ethical considerations that come with free trade. The specific details are geared toward kids' concerns." Booklist
Includes bibliographical references

Cosson, M. J.
Affirmative action; [by] M. J. Cosson. ABDO Pub. 2008 112p il (Essential viewpoints) $22.92
Grades: 7 8 9 10 **331.1**
1. Affirmative action programs 2. Minorities—Employment
ISBN 978-1-59928-857-4; 1-59928-857-5
LC 2007013877
This is a "balanced [overview] of [a] complex, divisive [issue]. Though not exhaustive, [this title includes] the topic's history and most salient points in an accessible and reader-friendly format. [This] discusses civil rights history and the controversies at the heart of today's affirmative action debate. . . . Color images enhance the [text], and charts and maps further clarify the content. Sidebars expand on related topics through quotes, primary-source snippets, and other salient information." SLJ
Includes glossary and bibliographical references

Kowalski, Kathiann M., 1955-
Affirmative action. Marshall Cavendish Benchmark 2006 143p (Open for debate) lib bdg $39.93
Grades: 7 8 9 10 **331.1**
1. Affirmative action programs 2. Discrimination in education 3. Discrimination in employment
ISBN 978-0-7614-2300-3 (lib bdg); 0-7614-2300-1 (lib bdg)
This offers arguments for and against Affirmative Action programs aimed at ending discrimination in employment and education.
This is "well organized and . . . clearly and plainly written." SLJ

331.3 Workers by age group

Bartoletti, Susan Campbell, 1958-
Growing up in coal country. Houghton Mifflin 1996 127p il $17; pa $7.95 *
Grades: 5 6 7 8 **331.3**
1. Child labor 2. Coal mines and mining
ISBN 0-395-77847-6; 0-395-97914-5 (pa)
LC 96-3142
This is an "account of working and living conditions in Pennsylvania coal towns. The first half of the volume details various duties in the mines, from jobs performed by the youngest boys to the tasks of adult miners, while the second half describes the company village, common customs and recreational activities, and the accidents and diseases that frequently beset the workers." Horn Book
"With compelling black-and-white photographs of children at work in the coal mines of northeastern Pennsylvania about 100 years ago, this handsome, spacious photo-essay will draw browsers as well as students doing research on labor and immigrant history." Booklist
Includes bibliographical references

Chambers, Catherine, 1954-
Living as a child laborer; Mehboob's story; by Catherine Chambers. World Almanac Library 2006 48p il (Children in crisis) lib bdg $30
Grades: 6 7 8 9   331.3
1. Child labor 2. Poverty 3. India—Social conditions
ISBN 0-8368-5958-8   LC 2005045250
This focuses on a young Indian boy named Mehboob subjected to child labor.
This includes "numerous full-color photographs. . . . The material is basically accurate, clearly written, and thought provoking." SLJ
Includes bibliographical references

Freedman, Russell
Kids at work; Lewis Hine and the crusade against child labor; with photographs by Lewis Hine. Clarion Bks. 1994 104p il $20; pa $9.95 *
Grades: 5 6 7 8   331.3
1. Hine, Lewis Wickes, 1874-1940 2. Child labor
ISBN 0-395-58703-4; 0-395-79726-8 (pa)
LC 93-5989
"Using the photographer's work throughout, Freedman provides a documentary account of child labor in America during the early 1900s and the role Lewis Hine played in the crusade against it. He offers a look at the man behind the camera, his involvement with the National Child Labor Committee, and the dangers he faced trying to document unjust labor conditions." SLJ
Freedman "does an outstanding job of integrating historical photographs with meticulously researched and highly readable prose." Publ Wkly
Includes bibliographical references

Herumin, Wendy
Child labor today; a human rights issue. Enslow Publishers 2007 112p il (Issues in focus today) $23.95 *
Grades: 7 8 9 10 11 12   331.3
1. Child labor 2. Human rights
ISBN 978-0-7660-2682-7; 0-7660-2682-5
LC 2007010625
"An estimated 218 million children world-wide work in terrible conditions, and this powerful title . . . combines up-to-date facts with moving portraits of individual children who toil in mines, factories, the sex trade; on farms; as domestics, soldiers, and more. . . . Many full-color photos of contemporary young people trapped in harsh workplaces are included." Booklist
Includes bibliographical references

Springer, Jane
Listen to us; the world's working children. Douglas & McIntyre 1997 96p il $24.95; pa $16.95
Grades: 7 8 9 10   331.3
1. Child labor
ISBN 0-88899-291-2; 0-88899-307-2 (pa)
This "photo-essay looks at the hazardous work children do in developing and industrialized countries, in agriculture, industry, the home, the military, on the street, and in sex work. . . . There are easy-to-read sidebars,

charts, and maps, but it is the personal accounts that have the most authority. The pictures of small brickmakers, garbage pickers, migrant workers, and bonded laborers are heartbreaking, and the voices are authentic." Booklist
Includes glossary and bibliographical references

331.4 Women workers

Colman, Penny
Rosie the riveter; women working on the home front in World War II. Crown 1995 120p il hardcover o.p. pa $10.99 *
Grades: 5 6 7 8   331.4
1. Women—Employment 2. World War, 1939-1945—United States
ISBN 0-517-88567-0; 0-517-59790-X (pa)
LC 94-3614
This is an account of women's employment in wartime industry during the Second World War. "Colman looks at the jobs women took, the impact women had on the workplace, and what happened to working women at war's end. . . . [She also discusses] the public relations campaign that not only 'wooed' women into the workplace, but also sought to change firmly entrenched attitudes about women's role in society." Booklist
"A thoughtfully prepared look at women's history and wartime society, this dynamic book is characterized by extensive research." Horn Book
Includes bibliographical references

Reber, Deborah
In their shoes; extraordinary women describe their amazing careers. Simon Pulse 2007 411p il pa $12.99
Grades: 8 9 10 11 12   331.4
1. Women—Employment 2. Occupations 3. Vocational guidance
ISBN 978-1-4169-2578-1; 1-4169-2578-3
LC 2006-34801
"Each chapter contains an interview with its subject . . . as well as sidebars and lists on what to do now to prepare, what the person's day is like, and a time line of how her career took shape over the years. Concrete details about the women's current lives and about how they attained their goals are included. . . . A fine addition to any collection." SLJ

331.5 Special categories of workers other than by age or sex

Atkin, S. Beth
Voices from the fields; children of migrant farmworkers tell their stories; interviews and photographs by S. Beth Atkin. Little, Brown 1993 96p il $18.95; pa $13.99
Grades: 5 6 7 8   331.5
1. Migrant labor 2. Agricultural laborers 3. Mexican Americans 4. Children's writings
ISBN 0-316-05633-2; 978-0-316-05620-5 (pa)
LC 92-32248

Atkin, S. Beth—*Continued*
"Joy Street books"

Photographs, poems in Spanish and English, and interviews with children reveal the hardships and hopes of Mexican American migrant farm workers and their families

"The Spanish is accurate, the English expressive, and the whole is a thoughtful tribute to the migrant experience. The black-and-white photographs are crisp and clear, frequently transcending the representational to achieve art." SLJ

Includes bibliographical references

331.6 Categories of workers by ethnic and national origin

Ouellette, Jeannine
A day without immigrants; rallying behind America's newcomers; by Jeannine Ouellette. Compass Point Books 2008 96p il map (Snapshots in history) $31.93
Grades: 6 7 8 9   **331.6**
1. Migrant labor 2. Immigrants—United States 3. Illegal aliens
ISBN 978-0-7565-2498-2 (lib bdg); 0-7565-2498-9 (lib bdg)   LC 2007004679
This book "uses the rallies of May 1, 2006 to address issues about immigration, both legal and illegal. . . . [This] volume includes a minimal glossary, a helpful time line, and suggestions for further reading." Voice Youth Advocates
Includes glossary and bibliographical references

331.7 Labor by industry and occupation

Barter, James, 1946-
A worker on the transcontinental railroad. Lucent Bks. 2003 112p il map (Working life) $27.45
Grades: 6 7 8 9   **331.7**
1. Railroad engineering 2. Railroads—History
ISBN 1-59018-247-2   LC 2002-9883
This presents a history of the construction of the Union Pacific and Central Pacific railroads focusing on the lives and labor of the construction workers
Includes bibliographical references

Career discovery encyclopedia. 6th ed. Ferguson 2007 8v il set $225 *
Grades: 6 7 8 9   **331.7**
1. Vocational guidance 2. Occupations 3. Reference books
ISBN 0-8160-6696-5; 978-0-8160-6696-4
                                        LC 2006005575
Replaces the edition published 2003
First published 1990
This set presents articles describing over 650 jobs or career fields, discussing personal, educational, and professional requirements; ways of exploring the career; sal-

ary statistics; job outlook; and how to obtain more information about the career.
This is a "reliable and succinct source." SLJ
Includes bibliographical references

Encyclopedia of careers and vocational guidance. 14th ed. Ferguson 2008 5v il set $249.95
Grades: 8 9 10 11 12 Adult   **331.7**
1. Occupations 2. Vocational guidance 3. Reference books
ISBN 978-0-8160-7066-4; 0-8160-7066-0
                                        LC 2006-101604
First published 1967
"These five volumes contain more than 700 . . . [articles] on careers in nearly 100 industries. Each three- to five-page entry provides a concise and engaging profile of fields like accounting, animal care, computers, the environment, publishing, sales, and the visual arts. Included in each job entry are an overview, a history, a description, requirements, employers, advancement, earnings, work environment, outlook, and more." Libr J
Includes bibliographical references

Hopkinson, Deborah
Up before daybreak; cotton and people in America. Scholastic Nonfiction 2005 120p il $18.99 *
Grades: 5 6 7 8   **331.7**
1. Cotton 2. Textile industry—History 3. Working class
ISBN 0-439-63901-8   LC 2005-8128
"From the industrial revolution to the 1950s demise of the Lowell cotton mills, Hopkinson discusses the history and sociology of king cotton, frequently emphasizing the children who labored under slave masters, endured dead-end mill jobs, or helped sharecropping parents claw out a living. . . . Stories of real people . . . sharply focus the dramatic history, as do arresting archival photos of stern youngsters manipulating hoes, cotton sags, or bobbins." Booklist

Reeves, Diane Lindsey, 1959-
Career ideas for teens in education and training; [by] Diane Lindsey Reeves with Gail Karlitz. Ferguson 2005 183p il (Career ideas for teens) $40; pa $16.95
Grades: 7 8 9 10   **331.7**
1. Teaching 2. Education 3. Vocational guidance
ISBN 0-8160-5295-6; 0-8160-6919-0 (pa)
                                        LC 2004024220
This book explorers 35 occupations in education and training. "Information for each job includes education requirements, relevant Web sites, and median salaries. . . . [It] also covers volunteer opportunities; lists entry-level jobs within the field; provides interview tips and sample questions. . . . [It offers a] lively style and variety of engaging activities." SLJ

Unger, Harlow G., 1931-
But what if I don't want to go to college? a guide to success through alternative education. 3rd ed. Ferguson 2006 246p $34.95; pa $16.95 *
Grades: 8 9 10 11 12   331.7
1. Occupational training 2. Vocational education 3. Vocational guidance
ISBN 0-8160-6557-8; 0-8160-6558-6 (pa)
LC 2005-55521
First published 1992
This "volume examines careers in 16 industry categories and describes the skills and experiences required for each. It also offers guidance for self-assessment and determining what essential employment skills readers already possess." Publisher's note

United States. Bureau of Labor Statistics
Occupational outlook handbook 2008-2009; U.S. Department of Labor, U.S. Bureau of Labor Statistics. 2008-09 library ed. Claitor's Publishing Division 2008 890p il (Bulletin of the United States Bureau of Labor Statistics) $39
Grades: 8 9 10 11 12 Adult   331.7
1. Occupations 2. Vocational guidance 3. Reference books
ISBN 978-1-59804-410-2; 1-59804-410-9
Also available in paperback from JIST Works and from McGraw-Hill
Biennial. First published 1949. Supplemented by Occupational Outlook Quarterly, subscription $15
"Gives information on employment trends and outlook in more than 800 occupations. Indicates nature of work, qualifications, earnings and working conditions, how to enter, where to go for more information, etc." Guide to Ref Books. 11th edition

Young person's occupational outlook handbook. 5th ed. Jist Works 2005 319p il $19.95
Grades: 6 7 8 9   331.7
1. Occupations 2. Vocational guidance 3. Reference books
ISBN 1-59357-125-9   LC 2004-13091
This "career reference includes 277 jobs employing 88 percent of the workforce. . . . Each entry includes a short description of duties and working conditions; suggested academic preparation; hands-on activites simulating actual job aspects; related personal habits and preferences or sources for further investigation; and additional related jobs. . . . The book is a strong starting point for student research." Voice Youth Advocates

331.8 Labor unions, labor-management bargaining and disputes

Baker, Julie, 1967-
The Bread and Roses strike of 1912. Morgan Reynolds Pub. 2007 160p il (American workers) $27.95
Grades: 6 7 8 9 10   331.8
1. Strikes 2. Textile industry—History 3. Lawrence (Mass.)—History
ISBN 978-1-59935-044-8; 1-59935-044-0
LC 2006101826
A history of the 1912 strike of textile workers in Lawrence, Massachusetts.
"Baker's style is readable, and the well-chosen, well-reproduced photos make the subject all the more real." SLJ
Includes bibliographical references

Bartoletti, Susan Campbell, 1958-
Kids on strike! Houghton Mifflin 1999 208p il $20; pa $8.95 *
Grades: 5 6 7 8   331.8
1. Jones, Mother, 1830-1930 2. Strikes 3. Child labor
ISBN 0-395-88892-1; 0-618-36923-6 (pa)
LC 98-50575
Describes the conditions and treatment that drove workers, including many children, to various strikes, from the mill workers strikes in 1828 and 1836 and the coal strikes at the turn of the century to the work of Mother Jones on behalf of child workers
"This well-researched and well-illustrated account creates a vivid portrait of the working conditions of many American children in the 19th and early 20th centuries." SLJ
Includes bibliographical references

Laughlin, Rosemary, 1941-
The Ludlow massacre of 1913-14; [by] Rosemary Laughlin. 1st ed. Morgan Reynolds Pub. 2006 144p il (American workers) lib bdg $27.95
Grades: 6 7 8 9   331.8
1. Strikes 2. Coal mines and mining 3. Labor movement—History
ISBN 978-1-931798-86-0; 1-931798-86-9
LC 2005030050
"In the autumn of 1913, coal miners working for the Colorado Fuel and Iron Company walked off the job, demanding recognition of their union. This . . . chronicles the long strike that frequently erupted into armed combat between the Colorado state militia and the miners. Vivid portraits are presented of the protagonists in the struggle. . . . Laughlin presents the facts with a storyteller's flair, supplemented by frequent quotes, period photographs, and engravings that show what life was like for the miners." Booklist
Includes bibliographical references

Laughlin, Rosemary, 1941-—*Continued*

The Pullman strike of 1894; [by] Rosemary Laughlin. Morgan Reynolds Pub. 2006 144p il (American workers) lib bdg $27.95

Grades: 6 7 8 9   **331.8**

1. Strikes 2. Railroads—History 3. Labor movement—History

ISBN 978-1-931798-89-1; 1-931798-89-3

LC 2005028637

First published 2000 in the series Great events

This "tells the story of the strike and explains its long-term effects on the labor movement and the nation. The author examines the arguments made by labor and management and explains how the strike affected all of those involved. . . . [This is] a good choice for report material on industrialization, labor history, or the Gilded Age." SLJ

Includes bibliographical references

Skurzynski, Gloria, 1930-

Sweat and blood; a history of U.S. labor unions. Twenty-First Century Books 2008 112p il (People's history) lib bdg $31.93

Grades: 7 8 9 10   **331.8**

1. Labor unions 2. Working class

ISBN 978-0-8225-7594-8; 0-8225-7594-9

LC 2007-50270

This "begins with the roots of unionization in colonial America, cruises through the frenzy of industrialization in the twentieth century, and ends in the present day. . . . The period prints and photographs are well chosen to highlight and comment on the text. Classes studying any part of the industrial or social history of this country will be well served by this valuable resource." Booklist

Includes bibliographical references

Whitelaw, Nancy

The Homestead Steel Strike of 1892; [by] Nancy Whitelaw. 1st ed. Morgan Reynolds Pub. 2006 144p il (American workers) lib bdg $27.95

Grades: 6 7 8 9   **331.8**

1. Carnegie, Andrew, 1835-1919 2. Frick, Henry Clay, 1849-1919 3. Steel industry 4. Homestead Strike, 1892 5. Strikes 6. Labor movement—History

ISBN 978-1-931798-88-4; 1-931798-88-5

LC 2005027113

This is the story of the 1892 strike against the Homestead Steel company owned by Andrew Carnegie and Henry Clay Frick which led to bloodshed and a breaking of the union.

"This is a riveting story told in 11 well-written, lively chapters, with well-placed, good-quality reproductions and drawings throughout the text." SLJ

Includes bibliographical references

332.024   Personal finance

Blatt, Jessica

The teen girl's gotta-have-it guide to money; getting smart about making it, saving it, and spending it; by Jessica Blatt with Variny Paladino; illustrated by Cynthia Frenette. Watson-Guptill Publications 2008 96p il pa $8.95

Grades: 7 8 9 10   **332.024**

1. Personal finance 2. Teenagers—Employment

ISBN 978-0-8230-1727-0; 0-8230-1727-3

LC 2007-25948

Explains to teenage girls how to budget their money, save, invest and create business plans.

"This is a great little reference guide for teenage girls to peruse and learn about money matters. . . . This is an important addition to any collection." KLIATT

Bochner, Arthur Berg

The new totally awesome money book for kids (and their parents); [by] Arthur Bochner & Rose Bochner; foreword by Adriane G. Berg. 3rd ed., rev & updated. Newmarket Press 2007 189p il pa $9.95

Grades: 4 5 6 7   **332.024**

1. Personal finance

ISBN 978-1-55704-738-0   LC 2006038930

First published 1993 with title: The totally awesome money book for kids (and their parents)

An introduction to money for kids including the basics of saving, investing, working, and taxes.

"Using an easy and comfortable style that young people will find unthreatening, the book presents a wealth of information. . . . The cute illustrations are also fun." Voice Youth Advocates

Includes bibliographical references

Hall, Alvin

Show me the money; [by] Alvin Hall. DK 2008 96p il $15.99 *

Grades: 4 5 6   **332.024**

1. Personal finance 2. Money

ISBN 978-0-7566-3762-0; 0-7566-3762-7

"Four main sections cover the history of money, expenses/income, the basics of economics, and the world of work and business. Brief profiles of eight wealthy entrepreneurs and their paths to prosperity and eight significant economists and their theories are included. The lively writing features real-life examples that will be meaningful to students and is presented in a balanced, nonjudgmental style that encourages them to decide for themselves among the various ideas concerning economic policies. . . . Color photos and graphics excel at conveying the concepts presented and represent diversity well." SLJ

Includes glossary

Holyoke, Nancy

A smart girl's guide to money; how to make it, save it, and spend it; illustrated by Ali Douglass. Pleasant Co. 2006 95p il pa $9.95

Grades: 4 5 6 7   **332.024**

Holyoke, Nancy—Continued
1. Personal finance
ISBN 1-59369-103-3
"American Girl"
This "offers advice on earning, saving, and spending money. Holyoke addresses topics such as feelings about money, launching a business, becoming a smart shopper, and investing. . . . The text is upbeat and informal. . . . This book is an engaging introduction to personal economics." Booklist

Menhard, Francha Roffe
Teen consumer smarts; shop, save, and steer clear of scams. Enslow Pubs. 2002 64p il (Teen issues) lib bdg $22.60 *
Grades: 7 8 9 10   **332.024**
1. Consumer education
ISBN 0-7660-1667-6   LC 2001-3675
Provides advice on developing good financial and consumer skills
This "is a basic primer that may well lead interested teens to seek out further information on investment or financial management." SLJ
Includes glossary and bibliographical references

Roderick, Stacey
Centsibility; the Planet Girl guide to money; [by] Stacey Roderick and Ellen Warwick; illustrated by Monika Melnychuk. Kids Can Press 2008 80p il (Planet girl) $12.95
Grades: 5 6 7 8   **332.024**
1. Personal finance
ISBN 978-1-55453-208-7
"This book presents handy methods for managing money. . . . Chapters are broken down into subsections . . . which are peppered with quizzes and craft projects to keep readers engaged. . . . The book's sound advice is both practical and approachable." Horn Book Guide

332.4 Money

Cribb, Joe
Money; written by Joe Cribb. rev ed. DK Pub. 2005 72p il (DK eyewitness books) $15.99 hardcover o.p. *
Grades: 4 5 6 7   **332.4**
1. Money
ISBN 0-7566-1389-2; 0-7566-1398-1
First published 1990 by Knopf
Examines, in text and photographs, the symbolic and material meaning of money, from shekels, shells, and beads to gold, silver, checks, and credit cards. Also discusses how coins and banknotes are made, the value of money during wartime, and how to collect coins

Kummer, Patricia K.
Currency; [by] Patricia K. Kummer. Franklin Watts 2004 80p il (Inventions that shaped the world) lib bdg $30.50; pa $9.95
Grades: 4 5 6 7   **332.4**
1. Money
ISBN 0-531-12341-3 (lib bdg); 0-531-16734-8 (pa)
LC 2003-16309
Contents: What is currency?; Barter and early currency; Important developers of modern currency; Development of modern currency: coins and paper money; Role of currency in daily life and in the life of countries
"Kummer covers the history of currency around the world, how money is made, and its prospective use in the future. Information about early barter systems and the role that currency plays in modern society are also included. . . . [The book has] appropriate color and black-and-white photographs, reproductions, and/or diagrams on virtually every spread. [This offering is an] excellent [resource] for reports and should also appeal to readers." SLJ

332.6 Investment

McGowan, Eileen Nixon
Stock market smart; [by] Eileen Nixon McGowan & Nancy Lagow Dumas. Millbrook Press 2002 64p lib bdg $23.90 *
Grades: 5 6 7 8   **332.6**
1. Investments 2. Stocks
ISBN 0-7613-2113-6   LC 2001-32694
"Short chapters in a question-and-answer format discuss 'Setting Up a Portfolio,' 'Buying and Selling Stocks,' 'Piggy Banks to Government Bonds,' and other related topics. . . . Clear, color photos, varied fonts in different colors, and plenty of white space result in an attractive presentation. This well-organized book will be welcome in collections needing material on the topic." SLJ
Includes glossary and bibliographical references

333.7 Land, recreational and wilderness areas, energy

Conserving the environment; John Woodward and Jennifer Skancke, book editors. Greenhaven Press 2007 c2006 248p il (Current controversies) lib bdg $32.20; pa $24.95
Grades: 7 8 9 10 11 12   **333.7**
1. Environmental protection 2. Biological diversity
ISBN 978-0-7377-2476-9 (lib bdg); 0-7377-2476-5 (lib bdg); 978-0-7377-2477-6 (pa); 0-7377-2477-3 (pa)
LC 2005055071
"This volume examines the degree to which the environment is in jeopardy, whether global warming should be addressed, the role of the government vis-à-vis conservation, and how society can protect the environment. The first two chapters present affirmative and negative responsive essays. Chapters three and four invoke timely topics such as the Clear Skies Act, drilling in the Arctic National Wildlife Refuge, renewal of the Endangered Species Act, the cost of renewable energy, organic farm-

Conserving the environment—*Continued*
ing, and fuel-efficient vehicles vs. SUVs. . . . The essays are accessible, divided into subtopics, and useful for reports and debates." SLJ

Includes bibliographical references

Fridell, Ron, 1943-
Environmental issues; handle with care! Marshall Cavendish Benchmark 2005 c2006 144p il (Open for debate) lib bdg $37.07 *
Grades: 7 8 9 10   **333.7**
1. Environmental policy 2. Economic policy—United States
ISBN 0-7614-1885-7
Contents: Master of the planet; Agents of change; Wealth and wild places; Land and food; Precious water; Power for sale; Produce and consume; Warming the globe

333.71   General topics of natural resources and energy

Global resources: opposing viewpoints; Clare Hanrahan, book editor. Greenhaven Press 2008 233p il $37.40; pa $25.95
Grades: 8 9 10 11 12   **333.71**
1. Natural resources—Management 2. Conservation of natural resources
ISBN   978-0-7377-3743-1;   0-7377-3743-3; 978-0-7377-3744-8 (pa); 0-7377-3744-1 (pa)
           LC 2007038577
"Opposing viewpoints series"
Replaces the edition published 2004 under the editorship of Helen Cothran
This is a collection of essays representing various viewpoints about the following topics: the depletion of oil reserves, food, and water; agricultural policies toward organic farming, genetically modified foods, and fish farming; solar energy, wind power, and biofuels; sustainable development, free-trade agreements, and the sharing of resources.
Includes bibliographical references

333.72   Conservation and protection

Anderson, Tom, 1970-
MySpace/OurPlanet; change is possible; by Tom Anderson, MySpace friends, and Jeca Taudte. Collins 2008 166p il $12.99
Grades: 8 9 10 11 12   **333.72**
1. MySpace (Web site) 2. Conservation of natural resources 3. Internet and teenagers
ISBN 978-0-06-156204-4; 0-06-156204-1
           LC 2007049877
"Printed on post-consumer-waste recycled paper with vegetable-oil-based inks, this guide to saving the planet practices what it preaches as it encourages teens to adopt green habits. . . . The presentation here, impressing readers with the need to think through the environmental impact of their actions, uses the examples of MySpace peers to encourage compliance." Publ Wkly

Malaspina, Ann, 1957-
Saving the American wilderness. Lucent Bks. 1999 96p il (Our endangered planet) lib bdg $28.70
Grades: 5 6 7 8   **333.72**
1. Wilderness areas 2. Conservation of natural resources
ISBN 1-56006-505-2   LC 98-31959
Discusses saving the American wilderness, including preservation and conservation, environmental activism, recreation in the wilderness, and the future of wilderness management
Includes bibliographical references
•

Nagle, Jeanne M.
Living green; [by] Jeanne Nagle. Rosen Pub. 2009 il (In the news) lib bdg $21.95
Grades: 7 8 9 10   **333.72**
1. Environmental protection
ISBN 978-1-43585037-8; 1-435-85037-8
"Accessible and up-to-date. . . . *Living Green* presents theories of climate change and short biographies of green pioneers before examining the role of government and NGOs in environmental protection, as well as basic, earth-friendly lifestyle changes that individuals can make. Throughout, Nagle addresses the controversies that surround issues, encouraging readers to take a wide, nuanced view." Booklist

Rapp, Valerie
Protecting Earth's land; by Valerie Rapp. Lerner Publications 2009 72p il map (Saving our living Earth) lib bdg $30.60
Grades: 5 6 7 8   **333.72**
1. Environmental protection
ISBN 978-0-8225-7559-7; 0-8225-7559-0
           LC 2008-3549
"Provides a thorough, interesting discussion of multiple aspects of [land protection], including historical origins, the current situation, and potential solutions. . . . Photos from around the world accompany discussions. . . . [This is a] solid choice to replace outdated books." SLJ
Includes glossary and bibliographical references

Sivertsen, Linda, 1964-
Generation green; the ultimate teen guide to living an eco-friendly life; written by Linda Sivertsen and Tosh Sivertsen. Simon Pulse 2008 248p pa $10.99
Grades: 5 6 7 8   **333.72**
1. Environmental movement
ISBN 978-1-4169-6122-2; 1-4169-6122-4
"A thorough yet accessible manual on green living. . . . The book's incisive voice, using teen idioms, is accessible to those who have little or no background in environmental issues, yet the standards within will likewise engage readers already committed to being green. . . . [This book is] unique, for its central focus is not to explain the science behind current environmental challenges, but rather to reveal how young people can work to solve those problems in their everyday lives." SLJ
Includes bibliographical references

333.73 Land

Casper, Julie Kerr
Lands; taming the wilds. Chelsea House 2007
226p il (Natural resources) $39.50
Grades: 8 9 10 11 12   **333.73**
1. Land use
ISBN 978-0-8160-6356-7; 0-8160-6356-7
LC 2006-37262
This "addresses human impacts on all types of land-
scapes and how people can become responsible caretak-
ers of these vital repositories of nature's bounty." Pub-
lisher's note
Includes bibliographical references

Desonie, Dana
Geosphere; the land and its uses. Chelsea House
2008 200p il map (Our fragile planet) $35
Grades: 7 8 9 10   **333.73**
1. Land use 2. Human influence on nature
ISBN 978-0-8160-6217-1; 0-8160-6217-X
LC 2007-25453
Outlines the causes and effects of the human impact
on the environment, discussing such topics as agriculture,
mining, energy production, urbanization, and overpopulation, and describes ways to achieve sustainable environmental practices.
Includes glossary and bibliographical references

333.75 Forest lands

Casper, Julie Kerr
Forests; more than just trees. Chelsea House
Publishers 2007 194p il map (Natural resources)
$39.50
Grades: 8 9 10 11 12   **333.75**
1. Forests and forestry
ISBN 978-0-8160-6355-0; 0-8160-6355-9
LC 2006100042
This "focuses on the importance of all types of for-
ests, why it is necessary to protect and conserve these
natural resources, and what people can do to maintain
healthy forest ecosystems." Publisher's note
Includes bibliographical references

333.79 Energy

Alternative energy; Neil Schlager and Jayne
Weisblatt, editors. UXL 2006 3v il map set
$165
Grades: 6 7 8 9 10   **333.79**
1. Renewable energy resources
ISBN 0-7876-9440-1; 978-0-7876-9440-1
LC 2006-3763
"This set objectively presents many of the issues and
challenges involved in using new and existing energy
sources. . . . The set is well-organized and clearly writ-
ten." Booklist
Includes bibliographical references

Ballard, Carol
From steam engines to nuclear fusion;
discovering energy; [by] Carol Ballard. Heinemann
Library 2007 64p il (Chain reactions) lib bdg
$34.29
Grades: 6 7 8 9   **333.79**
1. Energy resources
ISBN 1-4034-9554-8 (lib bdg); 978-1-4034-9554-9 (lib
bdg)   LC 2006049785
"Ballard traces the history of the scientific community's understanding of energy and how that has been applied to everyday life. Beginning with an explanation of
what energy is, the discussion touches on topics such as
steam power, electricity, radioactivity, quantum theory,
relativity, and nuclear power. . . . Illustrations, many in
color, include period portraits of scientists and photos of
equipment, as well as a few diagrams." Booklist
Includes glossary and bibliographical references

Bowden, Rob
Energy; by Rob Bowden. KidHaven Press 2004
48p (Sustainable world) $23.70 *
Grades: 5 6 7 8   **333.79**
1. Renewable energy resources 2. Energy development
ISBN 0-7377-1897-8   LC 2003-52953
This "briefly introduces various forms of sustainable
energy—water, wind, sun, geothermal sources—and takes
a look at where sustainable technology is headed. . . .
Bowden writes with admirable simplicity about complicated subjects, and he's careful to separate facts from
opinions when he quotes others. [This book includes] excellent color photos . . . and gripping statistics."
Booklist
Includes glossary and bibliographical references

Casper, Julie Kerr
Energy; powering the past, present, and future.
Chelsea House Publishers 2007 210p il map
(Natural resources) $39.50
Grades: 8 9 10 11 12   **333.79**
1. Energy resources
ISBN 978-0-8160-6354-3; 0-8160-6354-0
LC 2006034847
"Casper presents an overview of the history of energy,
renewable and nonrenewable resources, energy develop-
ment, as well as information on management and conser-
vation. A few full-color photographs, diagrams, and
sidebars break up the large blocks of plain text." SLJ
Includes bibliographical references

Fridell, Ron, 1943-
Earth-friendly energy; by Ron Fridell. Lerner
Publications 2009 72p il map (Saving our living
earth) lib bdg $30.60
Grades: 5 6 7 8   **333.79**
1. Renewable energy resources 2. Environmental
movement
ISBN 978-0-8225-7563-4 (lib bdg); 0-8225-7563-9 (lib
bdg)   LC 2007-35923
"Provides a thorough, interesting discussion of multiple aspects of [Earth-friendly energy], including historical
origins, the current situation, and potential solutions. . . .

Fridell, Ron, 1943-—*Continued*
Photos from around the world accompany discussions.
. . . [This is a] solid choice to replace outdated books."
SLJ
Includes glossary and bibliographical references

Hirschmann, Kris, 1967-
Solar energy. KidHaven Press 2006 48p il (Our
environment) lib bdg $23.70
Grades: 5 6 7 8   **333.79**
1. Solar energy
ISBN 0-7377-3049-8
"This book examines all aspects of the solar energy
question-how solar energy works, its problems and potential, where it is being used today and more." Publisher's note

Juettner, Bonnie, 1968-
Energy; by Bonnie Juettner. KidHaven Press
2004 48p il map (Our environment) $23.70
Grades: 5 6 7 8   **333.79**
1. Energy resources
ISBN 0-7377-1821-8   LC 2003-876
Contents: What does the world use for energy?; How
is energy managed?; Are we running out of energy?;
What will happen in the future?
"The liberal use of vibrant colors, the inclusion of a
photograph or diagram on most pages, and the generous
print size will appeal to reluctant readers. [This title] will
help students examine cause and effect (and possible solutions), and challenge them to live green." SLJ
Includes glossary and bibliographical references

McNamee, Gregory
Careers in renewable energy; get a green energy
job. PixyJack Press 2008 190p il map pa $20
Grades: 6 7 8 9 10   **333.79**
1. Renewable energy resources 2. Environmental sciences 3. Vocational guidance
ISBN 978-0-9773724-3-0; 0-9773724-3-X
LC 2007-50090
"This handy text reviews careers in solar, wind, geothermal, and hydroelectric energy, hydrogen energy and
fuel cells, and nuclear energy as well as employment in
green building, management, and transportation. . . . Edifying and accessible, this volume will be a welcome addition for career centers and environmental collections."
SLJ

Morgan, Sally
From windmills to hydrogen fuel cells;
discovering alternative energy. Heinemann Library
2007 64p il (Chain reactions) lib bdg $34.29
Grades: 6 7 8 9   **333.79**
1. Renewable energy resources
ISBN 978-1-4034-9555-6 (lib bdg); 1-4034-9555-6 (lib
bdg)   LC 2006-46853
The author "focuses on alternative energy sources and
includes wind, solar, water, nuclear, geothermal,
biopower, and fuel-cell technologies. Archival and full-
color photos are reproductions appear on nearly every
page." SLJ
Includes glossary and bibliographical references

Nakaya, Andrea C., 1976-
Energy alternatives. ReferencePoint Press, Inc.
2008 112p il map (Compact research) lib bdg
$24.95
Grades: 8 9 10 11 12   **333.79**
1. Renewable energy resources
ISBN 978-1-60152-017-3; 1-60152-017-4
LC 2007-18025
This "provides a variety of possible alternatives to fossil fuels. Wind, solar, nuclear, hydro, ocean, and geothermal power are examined with the possible benefits and
problems associated with each. . . . [This book] will be
helpful to students looking for a one-stop information
source." SLJ
Includes bibliographical references

Povey, Karen D., 1962-
Energy alternatives; by Karen D. Povey. Lucent
2007 112p il (Hot topics) lib bdg $32.45
Grades: 7 8 9 10   **333.79**
1. Energy resources
ISBN 978-1-59018-980-1 (lib bdg); 1-59018-980-9 (lib
bdg)   LC 2007007782
Examines the problems caused by the use of traditional fossil fuels and looks at alternatives such wind, solar,
and nuclear energy.
"Povey's writing is solid, and readers predisposed to
the topic will find the book useful. Charts, sidebars, and
relevant photos appear throughout." Horn Book Guide
Includes bibliographical references

Woodford, Chris, 1943-
Energy; written by Chris Woodford. DK 2007
64p il (See for yourself) $14.99
Grades: 4 5 6 7   **333.79**
1. Energy resources 2. Force and energy
ISBN 978-0-7566-2561-0
The author "defines energy, giving examples of both
potential and kinetic forms; explains how energy is released and travels; and provides detailed discussions of
many energy sources. Chapters are composed of heavily
illustrated double-page spreads that offer a main text and
several sidebar comments. Most illustrations are full-
color photographs, but captioned diagrams . . . offer
much detail for readers to ponder." Booklist

333.8 Subsurface resources

Gorman, Jacqueline Laks, 1955-
Fossil fuels; by Jacqueline Laks Gorman. Gareth
Stevens Pub. 2009 il (What if we do nothing?) lib
bdg $31
Grades: 5 6 7 8   **333.8**
1. Petroleum 2. Coal 3. Environmental protection
ISBN 978-1-4339-0087-7; 1-4339-0087-4
LC 2008029214
This "examines a potential crisis, its historical causes,
scientific background, and possible outcome if no action
is taken. . . . [The book] makes the connection between
climate change and the use of polluting energy sources,
and the Kyoto Protocol's plans for the reduction of

Gorman, Jacqueline Laks, 1955-—*Continued*
globe-warming emissions are considered. . . . Full-color
photographs, charts, and maps help illustrate some of the
ideas and problems." SLJ
Includes glossary and bibliographical references

Oil; Crystal McCage, book editor. Greenhaven
Press 2007 138p il map (Fueling the future)
$34.95
Grades: 7 8 9   **333.8**
1. Petroleum 2. Renewable energy resources
ISBN 978-0-7377-3588-8; 0-7377-3588-0
LC 2006-27870
Discusses the advantages and disadvantages of using
oil and it's derivatives as sources of energy.
Includes bibliographical references

333.91   Water and lands adjoining bodies of water

Vogel, Carole Garbuny
Human impact; [by] Carole G. Vogel. F. Watts
2003 95p il (Restless sea) $29.59 paperback o.p.
Grades: 5 6 7 8   **333.91**
1. Marine pollution 2. Human influence on nature
ISBN 0-531-12323-5; 0-531-16680-5
LC 2003-5301
Contents: Troubled waters; Sea sick; Too many fisher-
men; The impact of global warming; The human foot-
print
This "provides a detailed description of the results of
population growth, global warming, and the development
of coastal areas. The devastation to marine life resulting
from occurrences such as oil spills and the dead zones
caused by oxygen-depleted water are described through
both heart-wrenching photographs and informative text."
SLJ
Includes bibliographical references

333.95   Biological resources

Bortolotti, Dan
Tiger rescue; changing the future for endangered
wildlife. Firefly 2003 64p il map lib bdg $19.95;
pa $9.95
Grades: 4 5 6 7   **333.95**
1. Tigers 2. Wildlife conservation
ISBN 1-55297-599-1 (lib bdg); 1-55297-558-4 (pa)
This describes the tiger's "natural habitat, habits,
physiology, and behavior in captivity. [It also includes]
a time line of conservation efforts, profiles of conservationists in the field, and forecasts of the animals' future.
Throughout, the author makes clear the factors that can
threaten animal populations, and discusses human attitudes toward the animals throughout history. . . . Written in accessible, lively language and nicely illustrated
with exciting color photos, [this] will be useful for reports and browsing." Booklist

Burnie, David
Endangered planet; [by] David Burnie. 1st ed.
Kingfisher 2004 63p il maps (Kingfisher
knowledge) $11.95; pa $8.99 *
Grades: 5 6 7 8   **333.95**
1. Human influence on nature 2. Environmental degradation
ISBN 0-7534-5776-8; 0-7534-6160-9 (pa)
LC 2004-478
This "explores the delicate web of natural cycles that
supports millions of species . . . and reveals how our
ever-growing demand for food, fuel, and living space
threatens to damage Earth's habitats beyond repair." Publisher's note
"Children will be immediately drawn to the high-
quality graphics artfully laid out on brightly colored
spreads. . . . The [narrative is] logically arranged into
three chapters, each containing a broad overview as well
as more detailed subtopics." SLJ
Includes glossary

Endangered oceans: opposing viewpoints; Louise
I. Gerdes, book editor. Greenhaven Press 2004
220p il lib bdg $34.95; pa $23.70
Grades: 7 8 9 10   **333.95**
1. Marine ecology 2. Environmental policy 3. Marine
pollution
ISBN 0-7377-2274-6 (lib bdg); 0-7377-2275-4 (pa)
LC 2003-54015
Replaces the edition published 1999 under the
editorship of William Dudley
"Opposing viewpoints series"
"The collection includes views of scientists,
policymakers, and other experts debating the future of
the world's oceans." Publisher's note
Includes bibliographical references

Endangered species; Cynthia A. Bily, book editor.
Greenhaven Press 2008 128p il map
(Introducing issues with opposing viewpoints)
lib bdg $33.70
Grades: 6 7 8 9 10   **333.95**
1. Endangered species 2. Nature conservation
ISBN 978-0-7377-3849-0; 0-7377-3849-9
LC 2007-31324
"This book exposes readers to diametrically opposed
views. . . . The articles were written by various experts
and . . . the color photographs, graphs, and maps add
substantially to the visual appeal and content. . . . An illuminating presentation that will improve critical-thinking
skills." SLJ
Includes glossary and bibliographical references

Gallant, Roy A.
The wonders of biodiversity. Benchmark Bks.
2003 80p il maps (Story of science) lib bdg
$19.95 *
Grades: 5 6 7 8   **333.95**
1. Biological diversity
ISBN 0-7614-1427-4   LC 2002-916
Partial contents: Beetles, bacteria, and biodiversity;
Critters galore, what they are; Critters galore, where they
live; Major ecosystems; Tragedy of the rain forests; Gaia

Gallant, Roy A.—*Continued*

Discusses the many different life forms that have existed on Earth, their importance, and how they have changed over time

"Readers will find accurate, readable explanations for the scientific principles here addressed. . . . Up-to-date controversies and predictions conclude the [book] . . . illustrated with well-captioned photos." Horn Book Guide

Includes glossary and bibliographical references

Mackay, Richard

The atlas of endangered species. Rev and updated. University of California Press 2009 128p il map pa $19.95

Grades: 6 7 8 9   **333.95**

1. Endangered species

ISBN 978-0-520-25862-4 (pa); 0-520-25862-2 (pa)

First published 2002 in the United Kingdom

Catalogs the inhabitants of a wide variety of ecosystems, including forests, mangroves, and coral reefs. It examines the major threats to biodiversity, from loss of habitat to hunting, and describes the steps being taken toward conservation.

"More than 40 topics, among them 'Human Environmental Impact,' 'Temperate Forests,' 'Dolphins and Whales,' and 'Conserving Domestic Breeds,' are presented on double-page spreads containing full-color maps, charts, graphs, small photographs, and text. The presentation is clear and attractive." Booklist

Includes bibliographical references

Mills, Andrea

Animals like us; written and edited by Andrea Mills. DK Pub. 2005 79p il map $19.99

Grades: 5 6 7 8   **333.95**

1. Endangered species 2. Rare animals 3. Wildlife conservation

ISBN 978-0-7566-1008-1; 0-7566-1008-7

           LC 2005299478

"In association with ARKive"

Colorful introduction to animals around the world details physical attributes, geographic distribution, and habitat.

"Captivating digital photo layouts are interspersed with 'fact files' that point out loss of habitat and dwindling animal populations." Horn Book Guide

Salmansohn, Pete, 1947-

Saving birds; heroes around the world; [by] Pete Salmansohn and Stephen W. Kress. Tilbury House 2003 39p il $16.95; pa $7.95

Grades: 5 6 7 8   **333.95**

1. Birds—Protection 2. Wildlife conservation 3. Endangered species

ISBN 0-88448-237-5; 0-88448-276-6 (pa)

           LC 2002-6710

Profiles adults and children working in six habitats around the world to save wild birds, some of which are on the brink of extinction.

"As a teaching aid, this volume is an exceptional supplement. The six articles relating the heroic rescue of the endangered birds are accurate and enhanced by appropriate color photographs." Sci Books Films

Sheehan, Sean, 1951-

Endangered species; by Sean Sheehan. Gareth Stevens Pub. 2009 48p il map (What if we do nothing?) lib bdg $31

Grades: 5 6 7 8   **333.95**

1. Endangered species

ISBN 978-1-4339-0086-0 (lib bdg); 1-4339-0086-6 (lib bdg)   LC 2008029167

"Some scientists predict that, if we do nothing, half of all species alive today will be extinct by 2100. This book looks at the many animals and plants that have become endangered through hunting, poaching, pollution, habitat loss, and climate change. It also discusses the steps conservationists are taking to protect threatened species." Publisher's note

"Using intelligent, focused text; an open design; vivid photos; and excellent maps, [this] book demands attention." Booklist

Includes bibliographical references

Should drilling be permitted in the Arctic National Wildlife Refuge? David M. Haugen, book editor. Greenhaven Press 2008 92p (At issue) lib bdg $29.95; pa $21.20

Grades: 7 8 9 10 11 12   **333.95**

1. Oil well drilling 2. Arctic National Wildlife Refuge (Alaska)

ISBN 978-0-7377-3930-5 (lib bdg); 0-7377-3930-4 (lib bdg); 978-0-7377-3931-2 (pa); 0-7377-3931-2 (pa)

           LC 2007-51383

"This collection of essays, . . . examines the current issue of drilling for oil in the Arctic National Wildlife Refuge (ANWR). . . . Having these essays collected into one volume makes this book a valuable option for young adults in speech and debate activities. Additional strengths are the list of organizations to contact and a bibliography of recent books and articles on this hot topic." Booklist

Includes bibliographical references

Spilsbury, Louise, 1963-

Animals under threat; [by] Louise and Richard Spilsbury. Heinemann Library 2007 48p il map (Planet under pressure) lib bdg $31.43

Grades: 6 7 8 9   **333.95**

1. Endangered species 2. Wildlife conservation

ISBN 978-1-4034-8217-4; 1-4034-8217-9

           LC 2006017850

"This book examines the issues surrounding animals and helps students learn how to protect endangered animals." Publisher's note

Includes bibliographical references

Swinburne, Stephen R.

Once a wolf; how wildlife biologists fought to bring back the gray wolf; with photographs by Jim Brandenburg. Houghton Mifflin 1999 48p il $16

Grades: 4 5 6 7   **333.95**

1. Wolves 2. Wildlife conservation

ISBN 0-395-89827-7   LC 98-16865

Surveys the history of the troubled relationship between wolves and humans, examines the view that these predators are a valuable part of the ecosystem, and de-

Swinburne, Stephen R.—*Continued*
scribes the conservation movement to restore them to the
wild

The "crisp color photographs showing wolves in their
natural environment are exceptional. Swinburne's text
adds suspense and excitement to the story. . . . This is
an involving study . . . which makes fascinating reading." Bull Cent Child Books

Includes bibliographical references

Thomas, Peggy
Big cat conservation. 21st Cent. Bks.
(Brookfield) 2000 64p il (Science of saving
animals) lib bdg $25.90
Grades: 6 7 8 9   **333.95**
1. Wild cats 2. Wildlife conservation
ISBN 0-7613-3231-6   LC 99-37434
Examines how scientists and zoos around the world
are managing wild and captive big cats like panthers,
cheetahs, tigers, and lions by radio tracking, scat examination, zoo breeding programs, and habitat conservation

This offers "well-written {text}; open, easy-to-read
page design; and attractive, good-quality, full-color photographs of wildlife and scientists conducting fieldwork."
SLJ

Includes bibliographical references

Bird alert. 21st Cent. Bks. (Brookfield) 2000
64p il (Science of saving animals) lib bdg $25.90
Grades: 6 7 8 9   **333.95**
1. Birds 2. Wildlife conservation
ISBN 0-7613-1457-1   LC 00-25028
Surveys programs and individuals dedicated to preserving birds and bird habitats.

"The text is highly readable. . . . Good-quality, color
photographs are well integrated with text." SLJ

Includes glossary and bibliographical references

Turner, Pamela S.
Gorilla doctors; saving endangered great apes.
Houghton Mifflin 2005 64p il map (Scientists in
the field) $17
Grades: 5 6 7 8   **333.95**
1. Gorillas 2. Wildlife conservation
ISBN 0-618-44555-2   LC 2004-9213
This describes The Mountain Gorilla Veterinary Proj-
ect which works to save the mountain gorilla population
in Rwanda and Uganda.

This offers "readable text . . . accompanied by striking, full-color photographs." SLJ

Includes bibliographical references

Walker, Niki, 1972-
Biomass; fueling change; [by] Niki Walker.
Crabtree Pub. 2007 32p il (Energy revolution) lib
bdg $19.95; pa $8.95
Grades: 5 6 7 8   **333.95**
1. Biomass energy
ISBN 978-0-7787-2914-3 (lib bdg); 0-7787-2914-1 (lib
bdg); 978-0-7787-2928-0 (pa); 0-7787-2928-1 (pa)
                                      LC 2006016035

This "book presents a range of historical uses of the
various forms of biomass, from charcoal smelters in ancient Egypt to ethanol-fueled lanterns in the 19th century
and gasifiers during World War II. Vivid color photographs with informative captions extend the [text]." SLJ

Includes glossary

335.4   Marxian systems

Lansford, Tom
Communism. Marshall Cavendish Benchmark
2007 143p il map (Political systems of the world)
lib bdg $27.95
Grades: 7 8 9 10   **335.4**
1. Communism
ISBN 978-0-7614-2628-8   LC 2006-25349
"Gives an overview of communism as a political system, including an historical discussion of communist regimes throughout the world." Publisher's note

Includes bibliographical references

336.2   Taxes

Kowalski, Kathiann M., 1955-
Taxes; [by] Kathiann M. Kowalski. Marshall
Cavendish Benchmark 2006 139p il (Open for
debate) lib bdg $37.07
Grades: 7 8 9 10   **336.2**
1. Taxation—United States
ISBN 0-7614-1887-3   LC 2005003073
This discusses the history of taxes in the United
States, the federal income system, problems with and al-
ternatives to federal income tax.

Includes bibliographical references

336.3   Public debt and expenditures

Garlake, Teresa
Global debt. Raintree 2003 64p il (21st century
debates) lib bdg $28.56
Grades: 7 8 9 10   **336.3**
1. Public debts 2. Developing countries—Economic
conditions
ISBN 0-7398-6035-6   LC 2002-15214
Contents: What is debt?; How did the debt problem
start?; The effects of debt on education; The effects of
debt on health; The debt boomerang; Is aid the answer?;
Debt and trade; Debt relief

"Garlake describes the relationship between global
debt and the quality of life of ordinary people. . . .
[She] examines the issues involved in giving aid to debt-
ridden countries, and concludes with a look to the future.
[The title has] many well-placed sidebars with facts, debates, and viewpoints [and] . . . good-quality color photographs." SLJ

Includes bibliographical references

338.2　Extraction of minerals

Gunderson, Cory Gideon
The need for oil; [by] Cory Gunderson. Abdo
Pub 2004 48p il map (World in conflict, Middle
East) $25.65 *
Grades: 6 7 8 9　　　　　　　　　　　　**338.2**
　　1. Petroleum industry 2. World politics—1991-
3. Middle East—Politics and government
　　ISBN 1-59197-417-8　　　　　LC 2003-44376
　　Contents: An overview of oil; Who has oil?; Who
needs oil?; Organization of Petroleum Exporting Countries (OPEC); Middle East conflicts and oil; The future
of oil
　　Examines the importance of oil, how it is formed and
obtained, the dependence of industrialized nations on oil,
and why it has become a bargaining chip between Middle Eastern and Western nations.
　　This title offers "current, factual information in an
eye-catching, hi/lo format. Although chapters and sentences are brief, the [text is] politically balanced. Maps
and photographs are clear, colorful, and up-to-date." SLJ
　　Includes glossary and bibliographical references

338.9　Economic development and growth

Belmont, Helen
Planning for a sustainable future; [by] Helen
Belmont. Smart Apple Media 2008 46p il map
(Geography skills) $22.95 *
Grades: 6 7 8 9　　　　　　　　　　　　**338.9**
　　1. City planning 2. Human ecology
　　ISBN 978-1-59920-051-4; 1-59920-051-1
　　　　　　　　　　　　　　LC 2006100028
　　Contents: Planning for the future; What is
sustainability?; Water: a key resource; River planning;
Coastal defense; Forests of the future; How to use ener-
gy; Climate change; Earthquakes; Reduce, reuse, recycle;
Overpopulation; Underpopulation; Settlements in the fu-
ture; Fair trade; City transportation; Controlling tourism;
Our food; Breaking out of poverty; Reducing the Digital
Divide
　　"The text is easy to follow. . . . The examples given
in the text that involve places are almost always accompanied by excellent photographs. . . . Maps, block diagrams, tables, and graphs are clearly presented and easy
to interpret." Sci Books Films
　　Includes glossary and bibliographical references

339.4　Factors affecting income and wealth

Poverty: opposing viewpoints; Viqi Wagner, book
editor. Greenhaven Press 2008 279p il lib bdg
$37.40; pa $25.95
Grades: 8 9 10 11 12　　　　　　　　　**339.4**
　　1. Poverty
　　ISBN 978-0-7377-3747-9 (lib bdg); 0-7377-3747-6 (lib
bdg); 978-0-7377-3748-6 (pa); 0-7377-3748-4 (pa)
　　"Opposing viewpoints series"

　　"After an introduction that raises the idea of how poverty is portrayed in the media, the book provides previously published material debating the various issues.
While chapters one through three feature articles that debate the causes and possible solutions to U.S. deprivation, chapter four discusses the issue from a global perspective. . . . This title should be in demand in many libraries." SLJ
　　Includes bibliographical references

341.23　United Nations

Ross, Stewart
The United Nations. Heinemann Lib. 2003 48p
il maps (20th-century perspectives) lib bdg $25.64
Grades: 7 8 9 10　　　　　　　　　　　**341.23**
　　1. United Nations
　　ISBN 1-4034-0152-7　　　　　LC 2002-4550
　　Contents: What is the United Nations?; The League of
Nations; A new beginning; A world parliament; Struggling secretaries; International law and justice; The Security Council; Working for peace; Enforcement; The
blue helmets; The Gulf War; Disarmament and arms lim-
itation; Closing the economic gap; World health; Emergency!; Human rights; The rights of women; The environment; Kyoto; Past and future; Timeline
　　Discusses the establishment of the United Nations, its
function in preventing war and eliminating poverty, and
its role in various international conflicts
　　This is a "timely overview. . . . Black-and-white and
clear color photographs of the U.N. peacekeeping troops
and relief workers throughout its history will provide students with a sense of those places in which the organization has been and is an active presence." SLJ
　　Includes glossary and bibliographical references

342　Constitutional and administrative law

Alonso, Karen
Schenck v. United States; restrictions on free
speech. Enslow Pubs. 1999 128p il (Landmark
Supreme Court cases) lib bdg $26.60
Grades: 7 8 9 10　　　　　　　　　　　**342**
　　1. Schenck, Charles 2. Freedom of speech
　　ISBN 0-7660-1089-9　　　　　LC 98-34010
　　Describes the landmark case which limited free speech
in cases of "clear and present danger" to national securi-
ty, as well as later cases which continued working out
the limits of freedom of speech
　　Includes glossary and bibliographical references

Anderson, Wayne, 1966-
Plessy v. Ferguson; legalizing segregation.
Rosen Pub. Group 2004 64p il (Supreme Court
cases through primary sources) lib bdg $29.25
Grades: 6 7 8 9　　　　　　　　　　　　**342**
　　1. Plessy, Homer 2. Discrimination in public accommodations 3. Segregation—Law and legislation
4. United States—Race relations
　　ISBN 0-8239-4011-X　　　　　LC 2002-154574

Anderson, Wayne, 1966—*Continued*
Contents: The social environment; A ride into history; The case for Plessy; The case for Louisiana; The decision; The aftermath

This examines the Supreme Court case that challenged a state's right to allow separate but equal railroad accommodations for different races.

This "deserves a place in every library. . . . Copious and well-chosen primary source documents give extra value to this [book]. . . . Each document adds human drama to the already engaging text." Lib Media Connect

Includes glossary and bibliographical references

Axelrod-Contrada, Joan
Plessy v. Ferguson; separate but unequal. Marshall Cavendish Benchmark 2009 143p il (Supreme Court milestones) $29.95
Grades: 7 8 9 10   **342**
1. Plessy, Homer 2. Discrimination in public accommodations 3. Segregation—Law and legislation 4. United States—Race relations
ISBN 978-0-7614-2951-7; 0-7614-2951-4
          LC 2007031606
Looks at the 1896 Supreme Court case that tested the constitutionality of laws in the South that enforced racial segregation in train travel, and discusses the impact of the verdict which provided a legal cover for racial discrimination throughout the United States.
Includes bibliographical references

Civil liberties; Andrea C. Nakaya, book editor. Greenhaven Press 2006 142p il (Introducing issues with opposing viewpoints) lib bdg $32.45
Grades: 7 8 9 10 11 12   **342**
1. Civil rights
ISBN 0-7377-3387-X   LC 2005-46144
The articles in this anthology "debate issues such as flag burning, Internet filters in public libraries, racial profiling, and the Patriot Act. Authors as disparate as NASCAR driver John Andretti and former U.S. Attorney General John Ashcroft trade arguments about civil liberties in essays that address issues such as media censorship and the treatment of immigrants during the war on terror. . . . A solid resource for research." SLJ
Includes bibliographical references

Collier, Christopher, 1930-
Creating the Constitution, 1787; [by] Christopher Collier, James Lincoln Collier. Benchmark Bks. (Tarrytown) 1999 95p il map (Drama of American history) lib bdg $31.36
Grades: 6 7 8 9   **342**
1. United States. Constitutional Convention (1787) 2. Constitutional history—United States 3. United States—Politics and government—1783-1809
ISBN 0-7614-0776-6   LC 97-1788
Examines the events and personalities involved in creating the Constitution of the United States in 1787, a document which has been the foundation of American democracy for over 200 years

"Most spreads are brightened by at least one illustration, a painting or print from the period, a photo of a site or artifact, or a map. Useful for school reports and surprisingly readable." Booklist
Includes bibliographical references

The **Constitutional** Convention; Richard Haesly, book editor. Greenhaven Press 2002 240p il maps (History firsthand) lib bdg $34.95; pa $23.70
Grades: 7 8 9 10   **342**
1. Constitutional history—United States
ISBN 0-7377-1072-1 (lib bdg); 0-7377-1071-3 (pa)
          LC 2001-23832
This is a "study of the historical and political events that led up to the ratification of the U.S. Constitution. Using accounts and opinions by actual delegates and other prominent figures such as Patrick Henry and Thomas Jefferson, Haesly outlines the concepts of the Declaration of Independence, the Articles of Confederation, and the Constitution/Bill of Rights. The volume is enlivened by personal stories of those who lived through and influenced the events depicted, and includes discussions on slavery and the nature of the presidency. . . . Well suited for reports." SLJ
Includes bibliographical references

Feinberg, Barbara Silberdick, 1938-
The Articles of Confederation; the first constitution of the United States. 21st Cent. Bks. (Brookfield) 2002 110p il maps lib bdg $24.90
Grades: 7 8 9 10   **342**
1. United States. Articles of Confederation 2. Constitutional history—United States 3. United States—Politics and government—1775-1783, Revolution
ISBN 0-7613-2114-4   LC 2001-27441
"Feinberg introduces the history and text of 'The Articles of Confederation and Perpetual Union,' the constitution that guided the U.S. government from 1776 to 1787. . . . Attractively laid out, this solid choice includes many black-and-white illustrations, including portrait paintings, engravings, and maps." Booklist
Includes bibliographical references

Finkelman, Paul, 1949-
The Constitution. National Geographic 2006 32p il (American documents) $15.95; lib bdg $23.90 *
Grades: 4 5 6 7   **342**
1. United States. Constitution 2. Constitutional history
ISBN 0-7922-7937-9; 0-7922-7975-1 (lib bdg)
An introduction to the American Constitution, including why and how it was written and how it is amended.
This title is "clear and concise. . . . The superior layout and illustrations enhance and reinforce the [text] through a combination of high-quality reproductions, photographs, artwork, and biographical sidebars." SLJ
Includes glossary

Fireside, Harvey, 1929-
New York Times v. Sullivan; affirming freedom of the press. Enslow Pubs. 1999 128p il (Landmark Supreme Court cases) lib bdg $26.60
Grades: 7 8 9 10   **342**
1. Sullivan, L. B. 2. New York Times Company 3. Freedom of the press
ISBN 0-7660-1085-6   LC 98-36959

Fireside, Harvey, 1929—*Continued*
Describes the Supreme Court decision in the case of
New York Times v. Sullivan, preventing public officials
from receiving damages for false statements unless they
can prove actual malice
Includes glossary and bibliographical references

Free speech; John Boaz, book editor. Greenhaven
Press 2006 221p (Current controversies) lib bdg
$34.95; pa $23.70 *
Grades: 8 9 10 11 1 2   **342**
1. Freedom of speech
ISBN 0-7377-2204-5 (lib bdg); 978-0-7377-2204-8 (lib
bdg); 0-7377-2205-3 (pa)   LC 2005-46225
Replaces the edition published 2000 under the
editorship of Scott Barbour
"This volume explores the challenges facing free
speech post September 11, 2001, including the Patriot
Act, commercial free speech, and consolidation of the
media." Publisher's note
Includes bibliographical references

Freedman, Russell
In defense of liberty; the story of America's Bill
of Rights. Holiday House 2003 196p il $24.95 *
Grades: 5 6 7 8 9   **342**
1. United States. Constitution. 1st-10th amendments
2. Civil rights
ISBN 0-8234-1585-6   LC 2002-191918
Describes the origins, applications of, and challenges
to the ten amendments to the United States Constitution
that comprise the Bill of Rights
"This excellent study of the continually evolving
meaning and interpretation of the Bill of Rights . . . is
an essential purchase for all libraries." SLJ
Includes bibliographical references

Fridell, Ron, 1943-
Privacy vs. security; your rights in conflict; Ron
Fridell. Enslow Publishers 2004 128p il (Issues in
focus) lib bdg $26.60
Grades: 8 9 10 11 12   **342**
1. Right of privacy
ISBN 0-7660-2161-0   LC 2003-14755
Contents: Privacy's widening scope; Watchers and lis-
teners; Searches and seizures; Intrusions and exposures;
Students: a special case; Privacy for sale; Privacy stolen;
Privacy and terrorism
This is an "overview of specific topics like searches
and seizures, credit-card fraud, identity theft, student re-
cords, drug testing, medical records, and library records.
There are warnings about protecting personal informa-
tion, and case studies regarding challenges to students'
rights in high schools." SLJ
Includes glossary and bibliographical references

U.S. v. Eichman; flag burning and free speech.
Marshall Cavendish Benchmark 2009 144p il
(Supreme Court milestones) $29.95
Grades: 7 8 9 10   **342**
1. Eichman, Shawn—Trials, litigation, etc. 2. John-
son, Gregory Lee—Trials, litigation, etc. 3. Flags—
Law and legislation 4. Freedom of speech
ISBN 978-0-7614-2953-1; 0-7614-2953-0
LC 2007022595

This examines the Supreme Court case regarding the
Flag Protection Act of 1989.
Includes bibliographical references

Friedman, Ian C.
Freedom of speech and the press. Facts on File
2005 128p il map (American rights) $35
Grades: 7 8 9 10   **342**
1. Freedom of speech 2. Freedom of the press
ISBN 0-8160-5662-5   LC 2004-21003
Contents: Foundations of free speech and press; Defin-
ing free speech and press in a new nation; Influencing
American society in the 19th century; Evolving roles in
the early 20th century; Engaging patriotism, decency, and
race; Vietnam and Watergate; Battles over hateful words;
The present and future of free speech and press
Includes bibliographical references

Gold, Susan Dudley, 1949-
New York Times Co. v. Sullivan; freedom of
the press or libel? [by] Susan Dudley Gold.
Marshall Cavendish Benchmark 2006 144p il
(Supreme Court milestones) lib bdg $39.93
Grades: 7 8 9 10   **342**
1. Sullivan, L. B. 2. New York Times Company
3. Freedom of the press
ISBN 978-0-7614-2145-0; 0-7614-2145-9
LC 2005033983
This is an account of the 1960 Supreme Court case in-
volving a libel suit against the New York Times by Ala-
bama politician L. B. Sullivan claiming false statements
were made about police treatment of civil rights protest-
ers.
Includes bibliographical references

The Pentagon papers; national security or the
right to know; by Susan Dudley Gold. Benchmark
Books 2004 144p il lib bdg $25.95
Grades: 7 8 9 10   **342**
1. New York Times Company v. United States
2. Pentagon Papers 3. Freedom of the press
ISBN 0-7614-1843-1   LC 2004-8583
Contents: The Pentagon study; The leak; Prior restraint: censorship versus censure; *The New York Times*
goes to press; *The Washington Post:* keeping up the momentum; Before the Supreme Court; The decision; Aftermath
An examination of the Supreme Court decision regarding the New York Times decision to publish articles
about United States government's "secret war" in Cambodia and Vietnam
"The format of the [book] makes [it] easy to read and
understand. [A] valuable [resource] for reports." SLJ
Includes bibliographical references

Roberts v. Jaycees; women's rights. Marshall
Cavendish Benchmark 2009 144p il (Supreme
Court milestones) $29.95
Grades: 7 8 9 10   **342**
1. Sex discrimination
ISBN 978-0-7614-2952-4; 0-7614-2952-2
LC 2007043021
First published 1984 by Twenty-First Century Books
with title: Roberts v. U.S. Jaycees

Gold, Susan Dudley, 1949-—*Continued*

This examines the Supreme Court case regarding sex discrimination against women members of the the Jaycees organization.

Includes bibliographical references

Tinker v. Des Moines; free speech for students; [by] Susan Dudley Gold. Marshall Cavendish Benchmark 2006 143p il (Supreme Court milestones) lib bdg $39.93

Grades: 7 8 9 10   **342**

1. Tinker, John Frederick 2. Des Moines Independent Community School District 3. Freedom of speech 4. Vietnam War, 1961-1975—Protest movements

ISBN 978-0-7614-2142-9; 0-7614-2142-4

LC 2005029838

This is an account of the Supreme Court case which dealt with the rights of students to protest against the U.S. involvement in the Vietnam War.

Includes bibliographical references

Worcester v. Georgia; American Indian rights. Marshall Cavendish Benchmark 2009 144p il (Supreme Court milestones) $29.95

Grades: 7 8 9 10   **342**

1. Worcester, Samuel Austin, 1798-1859 2. Cherokee Indians 3. Native Americans—Civil rights

ISBN 978-0-7614-2956-2; 0-7614-2956-5

LC 2007050437

This describes the 1832 Supreme Court case of missionary Samuel Worcester against the State of Georgia, which arrested him for not obtaining a permit to work on Cherokee Indian tribal lands, and discusses the history of Cherokee relations with the U.S. government, including the Trail of Tears.

Includes bibliographical references

Haynes, Charles C.

First freedoms; a documentary history of the First Amendment Rights in America; [by] Charles C. Haynes, Sam Chaltain, Susan M. Glisson. Oxford University Press 2005 255p il $40

Grades: 8 9 10 11 12   **342**

1. United States. Constitution. 1st-10th amendments 2. Constitutional history—United States

ISBN 978-0-19-515750-5; 0-19-515750-8

LC 2005-31880

This book features "information and primary documents concerning the origins and attacks on the First Amendment. The various documents go from the Charter of Rhode Island and Providence Plantations in 1663 through the Patriot Act of 2001." Libr Media Connect

This is "an excellent resource for all libraries, as well as enjoyable reading for history buffs." SLJ

Head, Tom

Freedom of religion. Facts on File 2005 146p il map (American rights) $35

Grades: 7 8 9 10   **342**

1. Freedom of religion 2. United States—Religion

ISBN 0-8160-5664-1   LC 2004-20547

Contents: Religious freedom in the American colonies; The freedom of conscience; A diverse religious nation; Religious expression and the law; Conscientious objectors and the draft; Religion in public schools; Freedom from religion?; Religious liberty around the world; The future of religious freedom in America

"This solid, readable volume walks readers through the part religion played in the formation of the colonies and looks at how faith informed the people's lives and the tensions among various religions." Booklist

Includes bibliographical references

Icenoggle, Jodi, 1967-

Schenck v. United States and the freedom of speech debate. Enslow Pubs. 2005 128p il (Debating Supreme Court decisions) lib bdg $26.60

Grades: 7 8 9 10   **342**

1. Schenck, Charles 2. Freedom of speech

ISBN 0-7660-2392-3

In the "case of *Schenck v. United States,* the Supreme Court held that people who opposed World War I were not allowed to use their free speech rights to interfere with the draft. . . . [In this book the author] explains the different arguments that have been used for and against free speech." Publisher's note

Includes glossary and bibliographical references

Johnson, Terry, 1961-

Legal rights. Facts on File 2005 152p il map (American rights) $35

Grades: 7 8 9 10   **342**

1. Civil rights

ISBN 0-8160-5665-X   LC 2004-23350

Contents: Origins of American legal rights; The right against unreasonable searches and seizures; The right to fair treatment; The right to a fair trial; The right against excessive or cruel and unusual punishments; Legal rights and the war on terrorism; The USA Patriot Act and the future of American legal rights

"The content is well organized, beginning with the origins and foundations of the rights, and proceeding with a clear discussion of the challenges they face even today. . . . Black-and-white maps, charts and graphs, photos, reproductions, and political cartoons contribute useful information." SLJ

Includes bibliographical references

Krull, Kathleen, 1952-

A kid's guide to America's Bill of Rights; curfews, censorship, and the 100-pound giant; illustrated by Anna DiVito. Avon Bks. 1999 226p il $15.99

Grades: 4 5 6 7   **342**

1. United States. Constitution. 1st-10th amendments 2. Civil rights

ISBN 0-380-97497-5   LC 99-17324

"After describing how the first 10 amendments came to be added to the Constitution, the book considers each one from a historical point of view, examining Supreme Court cases and famous challenges, and explaining in what ways each amendment applies to children and

Krull, Kathleen, 1952-—*Continued*
teenagers. Anna Divito's cartoonlike drawings add a visually appealing touch." Booklist
Includes bibliographical references

McKissack, Patricia C., 1944-
To establish justice; citizenship and the Constitution; [by] Patricia McKissack and Arlene Zarembka. Alfred A. Knopf 2004 154p il map $18.95; lib bdg $22.99
Grades: 7 8 9 10   **342**
   1. Discrimination—Law and legislation
   ISBN 0-679-89308-3; 0-679-99308-8 (lib bdg)
                         LC 2003-27929
The authors "examine issues of justice and equality in American history by focusing on the Supreme Court's role in defining rights of minority groups and citizens. . . . This book covers a broad spectrum of cases, and the authors do a fine job of providing the history, background, and events surrounding each Supreme Court decision." SLJ

Naden, Corinne J.
Dred Scott; person or property? [by] Corinne J. Naden and Rose Blue. Benchmark Books 2004 128p il (Supreme Court milestones) lib bdg $25.95
Grades: 7 8 9 10   **342**
   1. Scott, Dred, ca. 1795-1858 2. Slavery—United States
   ISBN 0-7614-1841-5   LC 2003-25568
Contents: A slave asks for freedom; The way it was; A case for judicial restraint; The "worst" decision; The long, bloody path to justice
The is an account of the 1857 Supreme Court decision regarding Dred Scott, who sued for his freedom from slavery
The authors "sandwich a clear account of the case's course, arguments, and participants between summaries of prior and subsequent historical events and an analysis of the decision's place in Supreme Court history. Illustrated with images of documents and oil portraits and supplemented by boxed essays." Booklist
Includes bibliographical references

Patrick, John J.
The Bill of Rights; a history in documents. Oxford Univ. Press 2003 205p il map (Pages from history) lib bdg $32.95
Grades: 7 8 9 10   **342**
   1. United States. Constitution. 1st-10th amendments 2. Civil rights
   ISBN 0-19-510354-8   LC 2002-6294
Contents: The roots of American rights; Rights revolution and in America; The birth of the Bill of Rights; The Bill of Rights marginalized; Rights renewed and denied; A resurgence of rights; Nationalization of the Bill of Rights; Political cartoons on the right to bear arms; Consensus and controversy
Uses contemporary documents to explore the history of the first ten amendments to the U.S. Constitution, the British traditions on which they were based, and their impact on American society

"This attractive and informative volume will be a valuable resource for most collections." SLJ
Includes bibliographical references

Pendergast, Tom, 1964-
Constitutional amendments: from freedom of speech to flag burning; [by] Tom Pendergast, Sara Pendergast, and John Sousanis; Elizabeth Shaw Grunow, editor. U.X.L 2001 3v set $165
Grades: 7 8 9 10   **342**
   1. United States. Constitution. 1st-10th amendments 2. Constitutional law—United States 3. Civil rights
   ISBN 0-7876-4865-5   LC 00-67236
"Covering each of the 27 amendments, this 3-vol. resource provides the history and social context of the amendment process. Entries range in length from 10 to 15 pages and begin with the full text of the amendment followed by an essay on the social and political climate that gave rise to its proposal." Publisher's note
"Presentation is very clear. . . . This is definitely a set that belongs in school and public libraries." Booklist
Includes glossary and bibliographical references

Phillips, Tracy A.
Hazelwood v. Kuhlmeier and the school newspaper censorship debate; debating Supreme Court decisions. Enslow Publishers 2006 112p il (Debating Supreme Court decisions) lib bdg $26.60
Grades: 7 8 9 10   **342**
   1. Hazelwood School District v. Kuhlmeier 2. Censorship 3. Freedom of the press 4. Students—Law and legislation
   ISBN 0-7660-2394-X   LC 2005034655
This discusses the Supreme Court case involving the censorship of a high school newspaper in Hazelwood Missouri.
This is "objectively and clearly written and would be useful for reports." SLJ
Includes bibliographical references

Racial discrimination; Mitchell Young, book editor. Greenhaven Press 2006 183p il (Issues on trial) lib bdg $34.95
Grades: 8 9 10 11 12   **342**
   1. Race discrimination
   ISBN 0-7377-2787-X (lib bdg); 978-0-7377-2787-6 (lib bdg)   LC 2005-55092
This anthology examines four major court cases involving racial discrimination: Plessy v. Ferguson (1896), Brown v. Board of Education (1954), Wisconsin v. Mitchell (1993), and Grutter v. Bollinger (2003).
Includes bibliographical references

Ritchie, Donald A., 1945-
Our Constitution. Oxford University Press 2006 255p il map $40 *
Grades: 7 8 9 10   **342**
   1. United States. Constitution 2. Constitutional history—United States
   ISBN 978-0-19-522385-9; 0-19-522385-3
                       LC 2005031885

Ritchie, Donald A., 1945-—*Continued*

This "volume begins with five chapters of background (Why have a constitution? How has it changed?) and then goes on to discuss the preamble, articles, and amendments, using a What It Says (word for word) and What It Means format. Every spread contains photos, reproductions, and sidebars, all of which invite students to read and understand this living document. . . . This is an excellent, well-documented addition for most libraries." SLJ

Includes glossary and bibliographical references

Sergis, Diana K.

Bush v. Gore; controversial presidential election case; Diana K. Sergis. Enslow Publishers 2003 128p il (Landmark Supreme Court cases) $26.60
Grades: 7 8 9 10   342
  1. Bush, George W. 2. Gore, Al, 1948-
3. Presidents—United States—Election—2000
  ISBN 0-7660-2095-9   LC 2002-154646
  Contents: Building a case; Electing a president as set by the constitution; The road to the Supreme Court; The case for George W. Bush; The case for Al Gore; The decision; Where do we stand today?
  An account of the Supreme Court decision which decided the outcome of the 2000 presidential election.
  "Hewing closely to the legal aspects of the contest, the book nevertheless gives some of the atmosphere surrounding the decision, maintaining a balanced tone without avoiding the tough questions." Horn Book Guide
  Includes bibliographical references

Stefoff, Rebecca, 1951-

U.S. v. Nixon; the limits of presidential privilege. Marshall Cavendish Benchmark 2009 127p il (Supreme Court milestones) lib bdg $29.95
Grades: 7 8 9 10   342
  1. Nixon, Richard M. (Richard Milhous), 1913-1994
2. Watergate Affair, 1972-1974
  ISBN 978-0-7614-2955-5 (lib bdg); 0-7614-2955-7 (lib bdg)   LC 2007031607
  This examines the Supreme Court regarding the Watergate scandal.
  Includes bibliographical references

Vile, John R.

The United States Constitution; questions and answers. Greenwood Press 1998 316p il $39.95
Grades: 8 9 10 11 12   342
  1. United States. Constitution 2. Constitutional law—United States
  ISBN 0-313-30643-5   LC 97-32008
  The author examines each section of the U.S. Constitution "and provides a question-and-answer format that allows for easy explanation of a complicated document. The amendments are addressed in detail. . . . The book is easy to read and well laid out." Book Rep
  Includes bibliographical references

343 Military, defense, public property, public finance, tax, commerce (trade), industrial law

Streissguth, Thomas

Clay v. United States and how Muhammad Ali fought the draft; [by] Tom Streissguth. Enslow Pubs. 2006 112p il (Debating Supreme Court decisions) lib bdg $26.60
Grades: 7 8 9 10   343
  1. Ali, Muhammad, 1942- 2. Draft—Law and legislation
  ISBN 0-7660-2393-1
  Describes the trial of Muhammad Ali, the first three-time boxing Heavyweight Champion of the world, for refusing to serve in the Vietnam War.

344 Labor, social service, education, cultural law

Anderson, Wayne, 1966-

Brown v. Board of Education; the case against school segregation. Rosen Pub. Group 2004 64p il (Supreme Court cases through primary sources) lib bdg $29.95 *
Grades: 6 7 8 9   344
  1. Brown, Oliver, 1919-1961 2. Topeka (Kan.). Board of Education 3. Segregation in education
  ISBN 0-8239-4009-8   LC 2003-219
  Contents: Jim Crow; The NAACP challenges segregation; The NAACP's case against segregation; The case for the states; Rearguments and a decision; Implementation and impact
  This is a discussion of the Supreme Court decision which ended racial segregation in public schools.
  This "deserves a place in every library. . . . Copious and well-chosen primary source documents give extra value to this [book]. . . . Each document adds human drama to the already engaging text." Lib Media Connect
  Includes glossary and bibliographical references

Andryszewski, Tricia, 1956-

School prayer; a history of the debate. Enslow Pubs. 1997 104p il (Issues in focus) lib bdg $19.95 *
Grades: 7 8 9 10   344
  1. Religion in the public schools 2. Church and state
  ISBN 0-89490-904-5   LC 96-51951
  "Issues in focus."
  "Beginning with a discussion of the concept of separation of church and state, the author discusses the Supreme Court cases and laws dealing with school prayer." Horn Book Guide
  "With clear, concise language, difficult and often ambiguous concepts, such as tolerance, equal access, and separation of church and state, are delineated and elucidated." Voice Youth Advocates
  Includes bibliographical references

Axelrod-Contrada, Joan
Reno v. ACLU; internet censorship. Marshall Cavendish Benchmark 2006 144p il (Supreme Court milestones) lib bdg $39.93
Grades: 7 8 9 10   **344**
   1. American Civil Liberties Union 2. Internet—Law and legislation 3. Obscenity (Law) 4. Freedom of speech
   ISBN 978-0-7614-2144-3; 0-7614-2144-0
This is an account of the 1996 Supreme Court case in which the American Civil Liberties Union challenged the law which made it a crime to send "patently offensive" material over the internet to anyone under the age of 18.
Includes bibliographical references

Chmara, Theresa
Privacy and confidentiality issues; a guide for libraries and their lawyers. American Library Association 2009 98p pa $40
Grades: Professional   **344**
   1. Libraries—Law and legislation 2. Right of privacy 3. Library services
   ISBN 978-0-8389-0970-6; 0-8389-0970-1
                                  LC 2008-34902
"This slim title is a must read. Chmara, a First Amendment attorney and litigation expert, clarifies privacy and confidentiality issues such as requests or subpoenas for patron-use records (both book and Internet), hostile-work-environment issues, state and federal privacy and confidentiality statutes, and minors' First Amendment rights and rights to privacy." Booklist
Includes bibliographical references

Donnelly, Karen J.
Cruzan v. Missouri; the right to die; by Karen Donnelly. Rosen Pub. Group 2004 64p il (Supreme Court cases through primary sources) lib bdg $29.25
Grades: 6 7 8 9   **344**
1. Cruzan, Nancy 2. Cruzan, Joe, d. 1996 3. Right to die—Law and legislation
   ISBN 0-8239-4014-4   LC 2002-156162
   Contents: The accident; The history behind the case; The Cruzans argue their case; Missouri's case; Appealing the decision; The Supreme Court; After the decision
"Donnelly covers the . . . right-to-die trials of the Cruzan family, whose adult daughter lingered in a vegetative state for many years before she was taken off life support." SLJ
This "deserves a place in every library. . . . Copious and well-chosen primary source documents give extra value to this [book]. . . . Each document adds human drama to the already engaging text." Lib Media Connect
Includes glossary and bibliographical references

Dudley, Mark E.
Engel v. Vitale (1962); religion in the schools. 21st Cent. Bks. (NY) 1995 96p il (Supreme Court decisions) $18.90
Grades: 7 8 9 10   **344**
   1. Engel, Stephen 2. Vitale, William J. 3. Religion in the public schools 4. Church and state
   ISBN 0-8050-3916-3   LC 95-19435

The author points out that although a 1962 Supreme Court case decided that official prayers in public schools are unconstitutional, the issue of separation of church and state remains.
This volume is "clearly written and well organized." SLJ
Includes bibliographical references

Fridell, Ron, 1943-
Cruzan v. Missouri and the right to die debate; debating Supreme Court decisions. Enslow Publishers 2005 128p il (Debating Supreme Court decisions) lib bdg $26.60
Grades: 7 8 9 10   **344**
   1. Cruzan, Nancy 2. Cruzan, Joe, d. 1996 3. Right to die—Law and legislation
   ISBN 0-7660-2356-7   LC 2004-20028
   Contents: Legal questions; The changing face of death; Through supporters' eyes; Through opponents' eyes; Right to die laws; Lower court cases; U.S. Supreme Court cases; The issues today; Debating the issues
This examines both sides of the debate concerning assisted suicide and related Supreme Court decisions.
Includes glossary and bibliographical references

Gold, Susan Dudley, 1949-
Brown v. Board of Education; separate but equal? by Susan Dudley Gold. Benchmark Books 2004 c2005 143p il (Supreme Court milestones) lib bdg $25.95
Grades: 6 7 8 9   **344**
   1. Brown, Oliver, 1919-1961 2. Topeka (Kan.). Board of Education 3. Segregation in education
   ISBN 0-7614-1842-3   LC 2004-5866
   Contents: A girl and a dream; Civil War legacy; Separate but not equal; Through the court system; To the Supreme Court; A momentous decision; A new day; Darkness and light
An overview of the Supreme Court decision which struck down racial segregation in schools.
"The format of the [book] makes [it] easy to read and understand. [A] valuable [resource] for reports." SLJ

Engel v. Vitale; prayer in the schools. Marshall Cavendish Benchmark 2005 c2006 160p il (Supreme Court milestones) lib bdg $37.07
Grades: 7 8 9 10   **344**
   1. Engel, Stephen 2. Vitale, William J. 3. Religion in the public schools 4. Church and state
   ISBN 0-7614-1940-3
   Contents: The regents' prayer; A constitution and a bill of rights; First Amendment on trial; A prayer goes to court; Before the Supreme Court; A landmark decision; Politics and religion: a potent mix
"Describes the historical context of the Engel versus Vitale Supreme Court case, detailing the claims made by both sides as well as the outcome, and including excerpts from the Supreme Court justices' decisions and relevant sidebars." Publisher's note

Gold, Susan Dudley, 1949-—*Continued*
Roe v. Wade; a woman's choice? by Susan
Dudley Gold. Benchmark Books 2004 144p il
(Supreme Court milestones) lib bdg $25.95
Grades: 6 7 8 9   **344**
  1. McCorvey, Norma 2. Wade, Henry, 1914-2001
  3. Abortion—Law and legislation
  ISBN 0-7614-1839-3   LC 2003-25567
Contents: A fundamental right; Two women's stories;
Bans on abortion; A case and a plaintiff; Filing suit;
Making a case for abortion; Supreme Court arguments;
A momentous decision
An overview of the Supreme Court decision which
made abortion legal.
"The format of the [book] makes [it] easy to read and
understand. [A] valuable [resource] for reports." SLJ
Includes bibliographical references

Vernonia School District v. Acton; drug testing
in the schools. Marshall Cavendish Benchmark
2005 c2006 141p il (Supreme Court milestones)
lib bdg $37.07
Grades: 7 8 9 10   **344**
  1. Acton, James 2. Vernonia School District 47J (Or.)
  3. Drug testing 4. Students—Law and legislation
  ISBN 0-7614-1941-1
"Describes the historical context of the Vernonia
School District versus Acton case, detailing the claims
made by both sides and the outcome and including excerpts from the Supreme Court justices' decisions and
revelant sidebars." Publisher's note
Includes bibliographical references

Gonzales, Doreen
A look at the Second Amendment; to keep and
bear arms; [by] Doreen Gonzales. Enslow
Publishers 2008 128p il (The Constitution of the
United States) $33.27
Grades: 6 7 8 9   **344**
  1. Gun control
  ISBN 978-1-59845-061-3; 1-59845-061-1
                  LC 2006022411
"Gonzales expertly traces the history of the Second
Amendment, along with important court decisions over
the last 200 years. Also highlighted is the debate of
whether it is an individual or a collective right. . . .
[The book has] numerous, well-captioned photographs
and illustrations and [provides] access to
MyReportLinks.com, containing updated and relevant
Internet sites for further research on the topics. Solid."
SLJ
Includes bibliographical references

Kowalski, Kathiann M., 1955-
The Earls case and the student drug testing
debate; debating Supreme Court decisions. Enslow
Publishers 2006 128p il (Debating Supreme Court
decisions) lib bdg $26.60
Grades: 7 8 9 10   **344**
  1. Earls, Lindsay 2. Students—Law and legislation
  3. Drug testing
  ISBN 0-7660-2478-4   LC 2005034654

This is an account of the Supreme Court case involving Lindsay Earls, a high school student in Oklahoma
who was subjected to a random drug test.
This is "objectively and clearly written and would be
useful for reports." SLJ
Includes glossary and bibliographical references

McPherson, Stephanie Sammartino
The Bakke case and the affirmative action
debate. Enslow Pubs. 2005 128p il (Debating
Supreme Court decisions) lib bdg $26.60
Grades: 7 8 9 10   **344**
  1. Bakke, Allan Paul 2. Affirmative action programs
  ISBN 0-7660-2526-8
"In 1973, [Allan] Bakke applied to medical school.
. . . He was not admitted. When he found out that the
medical school class reserved some positions for members of minority groups, he took the university to court,
charging discrimination. His case went . . . to the Supreme Court. Is affirmative action an effort to 'level the
playing field,' or is it unfair preferential treatment to minorities? . . . [This] explores both sides of the argument
as well as related court cases and laws." Publisher's note

Mountjoy, Shane, 1967-
Engel v. Vitale; school prayer and the
establishment clause. Chelsea House 2007 128p il
(Great Supreme Court decisions) lib bdg $30
Grades: 7 8 9 10   **344**
  1. Engel, Stephen 2. Vitale, William J. 3. Religion in
  the public schools 4. Church and state
  ISBN 0-7910-9241-0; 978-0-7910-9241-5
                  LC 2006-7328
This describes the 1962 Supreme Court case which
ruled that official prayers in public schools were uncon-
stitutional.
"Excellent period photos, magazine covers, and por-
traits of historical figures are closely cued to the [text].
. . . Handsomely packaged, accessible." SLJ
Includes glossary and bibliographical references

Payment, Simone
Roe v. Wade; the right to choose. Rosen Pub.
Group 2004 64p il (Supreme Court cases through
primary sources) lib bdg $29.25 *
Grades: 7 8 9 10   **344**
  1. McCorvey, Norma 2. Wade, Henry, 1914-2001
  3. Abortion—Law and legislation
  ISBN 0-8239-4012-8   LC 2002-155346
Contents: A historic case begins in Texas; Abortion
goes on trial; Next stop: Supreme Court; Another trip to
the Supreme Court; Finally, a decision; After Roe v.
Wade
This examines the Supreme Court decision which legalized abortion.
This "deserves a place in every library. . . . Copious
and well-chosen primary source documents give extra
value to this [book]. . . . Each document adds human
drama to the already engaging text." Lib Media Connect
Includes glossary and bibliographical references

Perl, Lila

Cruzan v. Missouri; the right to die? Marshall Cavendish Benchmark 2007 143p il (Supreme Court milestones) $27.95

Grades: 7 8 9 10   **344**

1. Cruzan, Nancy 2. Cruzan, Joe, d. 1996 3. Right to die—Law and legislation

ISBN 978-0-7614-2581-6; 0-7614-258-0

LC 2006-25740

"Perl discusses Nancy Cruzan's parents quest for her right to die following an auto accident and her resulting vegetative state. Highlights include the discussion of religious arguments, physician-assisted suicide, and the cases of Karen Ann Quinlan and Terry Schiavo. . . . Additional information is presented in sidebars. Occasional black-and-white photos add interest." SLJ

Includes bibliographical references

Somervill, Barbara A., 1948-

Brown v. Board of Education; the battle for equal education. Child's World 2005 40p il (Journey to freedom) lib bdg $28.50

Grades: 5 6 7 8   **344**

1. Brown, Oliver, 1919-1961 2. Topeka (Kan.). Board of Education 3. Segregation in education

ISBN 1-59296-229-7   LC 2003-27079

Contents: A long walk to school; Separate . . . not equal; Brown v. Board of Education; Desegregation; Linda Brown's legacy; Timeline

This book provides an account of the famous Supreme Court case which led to the outlawing of racial segregation in public schools

A "quality [title] both in content and design. . . . Excellent historical and current photos enhance the easy-to-read [text] on every spread." SLJ

Includes bibliographical references

Stefoff, Rebecca, 1951-

The Bakke case; challenging affirmative action. Marshall Cavendish Benchmark 2005 c2006 143p il (Supreme Court milestones) lib bdg $37.07

Grades: 7 8 9 10   **344**

1. Bakke, Allan Paul 2. Discrimination in education—Law and legislation

ISBN 0-7614-1939-X

"Describes the historical context of the case, University of California Regents v. Bakke, and details the claims made by both sides as well as the outcome, including excerpts from the Supreme Court justices decisions." Publisher's note

Includes bibliographical references

Telgen, Diane

Brown v. Board of Education. Omnigraphics 2005 xxxiv, 246p il (Defining moments) lib bdg $38 *

Grades: 7 8 9 10   **344**

1. Brown, Oliver, 1919-1961 2. Topeka (Kan.). Board of Education 3. Segregation in education

ISBN 0-7808-0775-8

This "opens with an 'Important People, Places, and Terms' section and a detailed chronology that takes read-

ers from an 1849 school-segregation case to the 2003 University of Michigan rulings on student diversity. The book includes a narrative overview, biographies of individuals involved, and primary sources. This latter, impressive section gives this treatment of Brown v. Board of Education depth and promotes a greater empathy from readers. . . . Telgen has done a fine job of making this topic accessible to and engaging for today's students." SLJ

Includes bibliographical references

Torrans, Lee Ann, 1952-

Law for K-12 libraries and librarians. Libraries Unlimited 2003 250p pa $25 *

Grades: Professional   **344**

1. Libraries—Law and legislation 2. School libraries

ISBN 1-59158-036-6   LC 2003-2592

Contents: Copyright; The scope of copyright; The fair use of material protected by copyright in education; Library archiving and section 108 of the DMCA; Tracing copyright; Library bibliographies criteria for selection and the legal implications and limitations of linking; Faculty created web sites: who owns them?; Patron privacy and filtering in the school library: guarding outgoing data, monitoring incoming data; Library bibliographies: student web pages, metatags in websites and the law; Licensing in the library; Americans with disabilities and the school library; Employment in the library; Policies and procedures: a difference with significance

"Advice and regulations addressing what can be copied, taped, and used on school Web sites will be helpful for both media specialists and teachers. Comprehensive yet readable, this guide is logically organized and solidly supported by examples and references. An indispensable resource." SLJ

Includes bibliographical references

345   Criminal law

Aaseng, Nathan, 1953-

You are the juror. Oliver Press (Minneapolis) 1997 160p (Great decisions) lib bdg $18.95

Grades: 6 7 8 9   **345**

1. Trials 2. Jury

ISBN 1-88150-840-4   LC 96-53046

The reader assumes the role of a juror in eight famous trials of the twentieth century: the Lindbergh kidnapping, Sullivan v. New York Times, the Chicago Seven, Patty Hearst's trial for armed robbery, and others

"For each case, the author presents just enough information for readers to assume the role of juror, with three options from which to choose. He then reveals the actual results and analyzes the consequences. This format balances the passions of those on all sides of these cases and allows Aaseng to present controversial views in a palatable way." SLJ

Includes bibliographical references

Aretha, David
The trial of the Scottsboro boys. Morgan Reynolds Pub. 2007 128p il (The civil rights movement) lib bdg $27.95
Grades: 7 8 9 10 11 12   **345**
1. Scottsboro case 2. Trials 3. African Americans—Civil rights
ISBN 978-1-59935-058-5; 1-59935-058-0
                         LC 2007-23818
This describes the case of nine young black men between the ages of 13 and 20 who were accused of rape in the 1930s in Alabama by two white women and were sentenced to death.
"Aretha writes clearly, with objectivity and compassion." SLJ
Includes bibliographical references

Cohen, Laura
The Gault case and young people's rights; debating Supreme Court decisions. Enslow Publishers, Inc. 2006 128p il (Debating Supreme Court decisions) lib bdg $26.60
Grades: 7 8 9 10   **345**
1. Gault, Gerald 2. Juvenile courts 3. Children—Law and legislation
ISBN 0-7660-2476-8   LC 2006001741
Examines the 1967 Supreme Court Case in which the court ruled that juvenile courts cannot deprive children of certain rights guaranteed by the Constitution.
This is "objectively and clearly written and would be useful for reports." SLJ
Includes bibliographical references

Crewe, Sabrina
The Scottsboro case; [by] Sabrina Crewe and Michael V. Uschan. Gareth Stevens Pub. 2005 32p il map (Events that shaped America) lib bdg $24.67; pa $11.95
Grades: 4 5 6 7   **345**
1. Scottsboro case 2. Trials 3. African Americans—Civil rights
ISBN 0-8368-3407-0 (lib bdg); 0-8368-5416-0 (pa)
                         LC 2004-44240
An account of the 1931 court case in which nine African American youths were charged with rape
"The authors do a good job of a taking a subject that is rife with conflict, duplicity, and ugly words and actions . . . and shaping it into a useful, informative book for middle-graders. . . . [It] is attractively designed with plenty of crisply reproduced, black-and-white photos, and historical art, such as posters, in color. The writing is clear and the text doesn't pull punches." Booklist
Includes bibliographical references

Fridell, Ron, 1943-
Gideon v. Wainwright; the right to free counsel. Marshall Cavendish Benchmark 2006 144p il (Supreme Court milestones) lib bdg $39.93
Grades: 7 8 9 10   **345**

1. Gideon, Clarence Earl 2. Wainwright, Louie L. 3. Legal aid
ISBN 978-0-7614-2146-7; 0-7614-2146-7
This describes the Supreme Court case which established the right to free counsel.
Includes bibliographical references

Miranda law; the right to remain silent; [by] Ron Fridell. 1st ed. Marshall Cavendish Benchmark 2006 144p il (Supreme Court milestones) lib bdg $37.07
Grades: 7 8 9 10   **345**
1. Miranda, Ernesto 2. Right to counsel
ISBN 0-7614-1942-X   LC 2005001156
"Describes the historical context of the Miranda versus Arizona Supreme Court case, detailing the claims made by both sides as well as the outcome, and including excerpts from the Supreme Court justices' decisions and relevant sidebars." Publisher's note
Includes bibliographical references

Herda, D. J., 1948-
Furman v. Georgia; the death penalty case. Enslow Pubs. 1994 104p il (Landmark Supreme Court cases) lib bdg $26.60
Grades: 7 8 9 10   **345**
1. Furman, William Henry 2. Capital punishment
ISBN 0-89490-489-2   LC 93-37512
Herda presents "the account of William Furman—convicted in 1967 and sentenced with the death penalty—and his legal attempts to appeal. The story highlights the author's goal of dealing with the issue of capital punishment in the United States, including the history of capital punishment and suspected bias according to race." Sci Books Films
Includes bibliographical references

Hile, Kevin S.
The trial of juveniles as adults; [by] Kevin Hile. Chelsea House 2003 128p il (Point-counterpoint) lib bdg $25.95; pa $11.95
Grades: 7 8 9 10   **345**
1. Administration of criminal justice 2. Juvenile delinquency
ISBN 0-7910-7374-2 (lib bdg); 0-7910-7506-0 (pa)
                         LC 2002-15638
This gives a brief history of the juvenile justice system, and offers arguments for and against trying juveniles as adults.
Includes bibliographical references

Hinds, Maurene J.
Furman v. Georgia and the death penalty debate; [by] Maurene J. Hinds. Enslow Publishers 2005 128p il (Debating Supreme Court decisions) lib bdg $26.60
Grades: 7 8 9 10   **345**
1. Capital punishment
ISBN 0-7660-2390-7   LC 2004-18943
Contents: The controversy over capital punishment: the Karla Faye Tucker case; History of the death penalty;

Hinds, Maurene J.—*Continued*

Arguments for the death penalty; Arguments against the death penalty; Laws; Significant court cases; Supreme Court cases; The issue today; How to conduct a mock trial

The author "examines the arguments on both sides of the [death penalty] debate, and she shows how the courts—especially the Supreme Court—have played a part in the evolution of capital punishment in the United States." Publisher's note

Includes glossary and bibliographical references

Jacobs, Thomas A.

They broke the law, you be the judge; true cases of teen crime; edited by Al Desetta. Free Spirit Pub. 2003 213p il pa $15.95 *

Grades: 7 8 9 10   345

1. Administration of criminal justice 2. Juvenile courts

ISBN 1-57542-134-8   LC 2003-4814

"This book details 21 cases ranging from truancy to auto theft. Following a description of events leading up to and including the crime itself, readers are given background about the individual, sentencing options, and questions to consider before sentencing, and then asked to make a decision about the case." SLJ

"An excellent introduction to how juvenile justice works, this will be a great resource for classroom and group discussions." Booklist

Includes bibliographical references

Jarrow, Gail, 1952-

The printer's trial; the case of John Peter Zenger and the fight for a free press; [by] Gail Jarrow. 1st ed. Calkins Creek Books 2006 102p il $18.95

Grades: 7 8 9 10   345

1. Zenger, John Peter, 1697-1746 2. Freedom of the press 3. Trials

ISBN 978-1-59078-432-7; 1-59078-432-4

     LC 2006000772

"This volume presents the 1735 trial of New York printer John Peter Zenger. The discussion begins with a good summary of Zenger's legal battle and why it matters, followed by a helpful, annotated list of participants and an intelligent discussion that acknowledges the limits of research based on those printed records that have survived." Booklist

Includes bibliographical references

Kelly-Gangi, Carol

Miranda v. Arizona and the rights of the accused; debating Supreme Court decisions; [by] Carol Kelly-Gangi. Enslow Publishers 2006 128p il (Debating Supreme Court decisions) lib bdg $26.60

Grades: 7 8 9 10   345

1. Miranda, Ernesto 2. Right to counsel

ISBN 0-7660-2477-6   LC 2006011737

This discusses the Supreme Court case involving a suspect's rights while being questioned by police.

Includes bibliographical references

Margulies, Phillip, 1952-

The devil on trial; witches, anarchists, atheists, communists, and terrorists in America's courtrooms; by Phillip Marguiles and Maxine Rosaler. Houghton Mifflin Co. 2008 218p il $22 *

Grades: 7 8 9 10 11 12   345

1. Trials 2. Administration of criminal justice

ISBN 978-0-618-71717-0; 0-618-71717-X

     LC 2008-1870

The authors "examine five highly emotional court cases, each of which served as a litmus test for the health of America's justice system at the time it occurred. . . . Each chapter gives historical context of the court proceeding, describes its progression in some detail, and comments on the political and intellectual aftermath. . . . [This is] a highly relevant and riveting book." SLJ

Includes glossary and bibliographical references

Miller, Debra A.

The Patriot Act. Lucent Books 2007 112p il (Hot topics) $32.45

Grades: 7 8 9 10 11 12   345

1. USA Patriot Act of 2001 2. Terrorism 3. National security 4. Civil rights 5. War on terrorism

ISBN 978-1-59018-981-8; 1-59018-981-7

     LC 2007-7799

This "defines [The Patriot Act] and explores the tension between balancing national security with civil liberties. . . . Miller knows her [subject] and offers enough intrigue to hold readers' attention. Sidebars and relevant photos appear throughout." Horn Book Guide

Includes bibliographical references

Olson, Steven P.

The trial of John T. Scopes; a primary source account; by Steven P. Olson. Rosen Pub. Group 2004 64p il (Great trials of the 20th century) lib bdg $29.25 *

Grades: 5 6 7 8   345

1. Scopes, John Thomas 2. Evolution—Study and teaching

ISBN 0-8239-3974-X   LC 2002-153354

Contents: The meeting at the drugstore; Evolution vs. creation; The nation takes sides; The trial begins; The prosecution; The defense; Darrow vs. Bryan; The meaning of the Scopes trial

An account of the trial of John T. Scopes, prosecuted in 1925 for teaching evolution.

This title utilizes "photographs, copies of original transcripts, political cartoons, and quotations from those involved. [This] is written with respectful attention to the issues of evolution and creationism, the separation of church and state, and the power of the government. Readers interested in the law will be captivated by the complexities of the arguments." SLJ

Includes bibliographical references

Pellowski, Michael, 1949-

The O.J. Simpson murder trial; a headline court case; [by] Michael J. Pellowski. Enslow Pubs. 2001 112p il (Headline court cases) lib bdg $26.60

Grades: 6 7 8 9   **345**

1. Simpson, O. J., 1947- 2. Trials (Homicide)

ISBN 0-7660-1480-0   LC 00-11907

"This book provides background information, the cases for the prosecution and for the defense, and a follow-up to one of the most controversial murder trials of all time. . . . The author presents the elements of the investigation in an objective manner. . . . Excerpts of public opinion and legal analysis are included as well as a page of questions to be used as springboard for discussion. . . . Well done and worthy of shelf space." SLJ

Includes glossary and bibliographical references

Ruschmann, Paul

Legalizing marijuana. Chelsea House 2004 129p il (Point-counterpoint) $25.95

Grades: 7 8 9 10   **345**

1. Marijuana 2. Drugs—Law and legislation

ISBN 0-7910-7483-8   LC 2003-9497

Contents: Marijuana and prohibition; Marijuana use is harmless enough to be considered a personal choice; Laws are needed to protect uninformed people from the dangers of marijuana; Enforcement of marijuana laws is uneven, ineffective, and wasteful; Marijuana laws should be strictly enforced; Heavily regulated marijuana is a better alternative than the black market; Relaxing marijuana laws would lead to too many problems; The future of marijuana policy

This presents arguments for and against legalization of marijuana, including whether or not the drug is dangerous, how marijuana laws are enforced, and whether or not relaxing the laws would be good for society.

Includes bibliographical references

Sherrow, Victoria

Gideon v. Wainwright; free legal counsel. Enslow Pubs. 1995 104p il (Landmark Supreme Court cases) lib bdg $18.95

Grades: 7 8 9 10   **345**

1. Gideon, Clarence Earl 2. Wainwright, Louie L. 3. Legal aid

ISBN 0-89490-507-4   LC 93-45981

This "volume details the genesis of the case that established the right to free legal counsel, the Supreme Court decision, and the arguments presented by the lawyers for each side. A fine addition to the thought-provoking series." Horn Book Guide

Includes bibliographical references

Sonneborn, Liz

Miranda v. Arizona. Rosen Pub. Group 2004 64p il (Supreme Court cases through primary sources) lib bdg $29.95

Grades: 8 9 10 11 12   **345**

1. Miranda, Ernesto 2. Right to counsel

ISBN 0-8239-4010-1   LC 2002-154575

Contents: A rape in Arizona; Confessing to the crime; The rights of the accused; Making a case; The Supreme Court decision; The legacy of Miranda

This discusses the case in which the Supreme Court ruled that suspects must be informed of their rights to remain silent and the right to counsel when they they are being questioned by the police.

This "deserves a place in every library. . . . Copious and well-chosen primary source documents give extra value to this [book]. . . . Each document adds human drama to the already engaging text." Libr Media Connect

Includes glossary and bibliographical references

Sorensen, Lita

The Scottsboro Boys Trial; a primary source account. Rosen Pub. Group 2004 64p il (Great trials of the 20th century) lib bdg $29.25

Grades: 8 9 10 11 12   **345**

1. Scottsboro case 2. Trials 3. African Americans—Civil rights

ISBN 0-8239-3975-8   LC 2002-153356

Contents: Background: a journey interrupted; The story of two white girls; A court in the Old South; The role of the NAACP and the ILD; Appeals, outcomes, and a landmark decision; A long road to justice; Impact of the Scottsboro Boys Trial in American history

An account of the 1931 trial in which African American youths were charged with rape.

This is "packed with information. . . . [An] attractive, intelligent offering." SLJ

Includes bibliographical references

Stefoff, Rebecca, 1951-

Furman v. Georgia; debating the death penalty. Marshall Cavendish Benchmark 2007 127p il (Supreme Court milestones) lib bdg $27.95

Grades: 7 8 9 10   **345**

1. Furman, William Henry 2. Capital punishment

ISBN 978-0-7614-2583-0; 0-7614-2583-7

LC 2007-582

"Stefoff shows how Furman's murder case, guilty verdict, and death sentence went through the process of appeals to the final decision. Discussions of the history of the death penalty and the use of the electric chair, gas chamber, and lethal injection contribute insight into the controversy and complexities of the case. . . . Additional information is presented in sidebars. Occasional black-and-white and color photos add interest." SLJ

Includes bibliographical references

Torr, James D., 1974-

The Patriot Act; [by] James D. Torr. Lucent Books 2006 96p il map (Lucent terrorism library) $28.70 *

Grades: 7 8 9 10   **345**

1. USA Patriot Act of 2001 2. National security 3. War on terrorism 4. Civil rights

ISBN 1-59018-774-1   LC 2005009043

"The introduction focuses on the question posed by free-speech advocates and the government regarding the Patriot Act: how do we balance security and liberty? The first chapter discusses how the act was negotiated and how it became law. . . . Following chapters raise issues related to government wiretapping, Internet surveillance, and secret searches, and discuss snooping through library

Torr, James D., 1974—_Continued_
records, government limitations on rights of immigrants, and detention of noncitizens. . . . The organization of the text is logical, with bulleted subtopics and occasional boxed information. The material is clear and unbiased." SLJ
Includes bibliographical references

VanMeter, Larry A.
Miranda v. Arizona; the rights of the accused. Chelsea House 2007 112p il (Great Supreme Court decisions) lib bdg $30
Grades: 7 8 9 10   **345**
1. Miranda, Ernesto 2. Right to counsel
ISBN 0-7910-9259-3; 978-0-7910-9259-0
               LC 2006-7578
This discusses the case in which the Supreme Court ruled that suspects must be informed of their rights to remain silent and the right to counsel when they are being questioned by the police.
"Excellent period photos, magazine covers, and portraits of historical figures are closely cued to the [text]. Reproductions of primary documents, including Ernesto Miranda's signed confession, greatly enhance the presentation of the [case]. . . . Handsomely packaged, accessible." SLJ
Includes glossary and bibliographical references

Wormser, Richard, 1933-
Defending the accused; stories from the courtroom. Watts 2001 127p $25
Grades: 7 8 9 10   **345**
1. Criminal procedure 2. Administration of criminal justice 3. Lawyers
ISBN 0-531-11378-7   LC 00-33036
Presents case histories that illustrate the role of and techniques used by defense lawyers in the American judicial system
"The writing is lively and accessible. . . . This solid introduction to the subject will stimulate class discussion." SLJ
Includes glossary and bibliographical references

346   Private law

Gold, Susan Dudley, 1949-
Loving v. Virginia; lifting the ban against interracial marriage. Marshall Cavendish Benchmark 2007 143p il (Supreme Court milestones) lib bdg $27.95
Grades: 7 8 9 10   **346**
1. Loving, Richard 2. Loving, Mildred Jeter 3. Interracial marriage—Law and legislation
ISBN 978-0-7614-2586-1 (lib bdg); 0-7614-2586-1 (lib bdg)   LC 2006-35955
"Gold looks at the issue of interracial marriage, brought to the forefront in 1958 with the arrest of a couple living in Virginia. She discusses the history of interracial-marriage laws, the impact of the 14th amendment, civil rights issues, and the couple's struggle to have their case heard in the Supreme Court. . . . Additional infor-

mation is presented in sidebars. Occasional black-and-white and color photos add interest." SLJ
Includes bibliographical references

Jacobs, Thomas A.
What are my rights? 95 questions and answers about teens and the law; by Thomas A. Jacobs. rev. ed. Free Spirit Pub. 2006 199p il pa $14.95
Grades: 7 8 9 10 11 12   **346**
1. Youth—Law and legislation
ISBN 1-57542-028-7   LC 97-8599
First published 1997
This "presents answers to questions about laws that affect teens, encouraging youths to understand both their rights and responsibilities in order to make sound decisions. The book is organized into chapters on family, school, work, teens and their bodies, growing up, criminal behavior, and the legal system. . . . An accessible, current resource." SLJ
Includes bibliographical references

346.03   Torts (Delicts)

Sergis, Diana K.
Cipollone v. Liggett Group; suing tobacco companies. Enslow Pubs. 2001 128p (Landmark Supreme Court cases) lib bdg $26.60
Grades: 7 8 9 10   **346.03**
1. Cipollone, Rose, d. 1984 2. Liggett & Myers Tobacco Company 3. Trials 4. Liability (Law) 5. Tobacco industry
ISBN 0-7660-1343-X   LC 00-9787
"This volume focuses on the Supreme Court case concerning whether or not cigarette companies are protected from litigation by warning labels mandated by federal law. The text contains clear and useful background information on previous cases, explanations of the legal issues, and a discussion of repercussions of the case." Horn Book Guide
Includes glossary and bibliographical references

346.04   Property

Butler, Rebecca P.
Copyright for teachers and librarians. Neal-Schuman Publishers 2004 248p il pa $59.95
*
Grades: Professional   **346.04**
1. Copyright 2. Fair use (Copyright)
ISBN 1-55570-500-6   LC 2004-46013
"The five chapters in Part I are . . . reviews of copyright law, the concept of fair use, determining what is in public domain, how to obtain permissions, and other general guidelines on such topics as licensing, loaning, penalties, plagiarism, and exemptions. The bulk of the book is in Part II, which deals with specific applications, such as Internet and public access, videos and DVDs, television, software, music, multimedia, distance learning and—oh, yes!—print! . . . An indispensable addition." SLJ
Includes bibliographical references

Complete copyright; an everyday guide for librarians; Carrie Russell, editor. American Library Association 2004 262p il spiral bdg $50

Grades: Professional   **346.04**
1. Copyright
ISBN 0-8389-3543-5   LC 2004-7681

Russell provides "guidance for both common copyright issues and latest trends, including the intricacies of copyright in the digital world. Through real-life examples, she also illustrates how librarians can be advocates for a fair and balanced copyright law." Publisher's note

Crews, Kenneth D.

Copyright law for librarians and educators; creative strategies and practical solutions; with contributions from Dwayne K. Buttler . . . [et al.] 2nd ed. American Library Association 2006 141p il pa $45 *

Grades: Professional   **346.04**
1. Copyright
ISBN 0-8389-0906-X   LC 2005-13804

First published 2000 with title: Copyright essentials for librarians and educators

The author "addresses 18 areas of copyright in 5 parts. He begins with the scope of protectable works as well as works without copyright protection. Next, he discusses the rights of ownership, including duration and exceptions. He then explains fair use and its related guidelines. Part 4 focuses on the TEACH Act, Section 108, and responsibilities and liabilities. Lastly, Crews examines special issues such as the Digital Millennium Copyright Act." Booklist

Includes bibliographical references

Gordon, Sherri Mabry

Downloading copyrighted stuff from the Internet; stealing or fair use? Enslow Publishers 2005 104p il (Issues in focus today) lib bdg $31.93 *

Grades: 7 8 9 10   **346.04**
1. Copyright 2. Internet
ISBN 0-7660-2164-5   LC 2004-9954

Contents: Downloading: a history; Tools of the underground Internet; The underground Internet today; Free speech? The argument for the underground Internet; Copyright infringement? the argument against the underground Internet;Underground Internet lawsuits and their outcomes; What's next? the future of the underground Internet

This presents "two sides of the ongoing controversy surrounding the use of the Internet to download copyrighted material. . . . The author presents specific legal action and instances to support each side of the debate. . . . Clearly written, this is an accessible treatment of a complex topic." SLJ

Includes glossary and bibliographical references

347   Civil procedure and courts

Brannen, Daniel E., 1968-

Supreme Court drama; cases that changed America; [by] Daniel E. Brannen & Richard Clay Hanes; Elizabeth M. Shaw, editor. U.X.L 2001 4v il set $215 *

Grades: 7 8 9 10   **347**
1. United States. Supreme Court 2. Constitutional law—United States
ISBN 0-7876-4877-9   LC 00-56380

"The 159 cases included span the years 1803 to 2000 and are organized under major legal topics such as 'Individual Liberties' and 'Equal Protection and Civil Rights.' Each entry, ranging from three to five pages, is introduced by a profile listing the appellant and appellee or petitioner and respondent, attorneys, and justices along with a brief description of the case and its significance. . . . Each volume contains alphabetical and chronological lists of the cases, a guide to how the Supreme Court works, a list of Supreme Court Justices, and the text of the U.S. Constitution." SLJ

"This set will be an especially useful reference when students need to retrieve concise information on Supreme Court cases." Book Rep

Includes glossary and bibliographical references

DeVillers, David

Marbury v. Madison; powers of the Supreme Court. Enslow Pubs. 1998 112p il (Landmark Supreme Court cases) lib bdg $19.95

Grades: 7 8 9 10   **347**
1. Marbury, William, 1761?-1835 2. Madison, James, 1751-1836 3. United States. Supreme Court
ISBN 0-89490-967-3   LC 97-24865

Discusses the case Marbury v. Madison in which the idea of judicial review became part of the federal government's system of checks and balances.

Includes glossary and bibliographical references

Fireside, Harvey, 1929-

The Fifth Amendment; the right to remain silent. Enslow Pubs. 1998 128p il (Constitution) lib bdg $19.95

Grades: 7 8 9 10   **347**
1. Criminal procedure
ISBN 0-89490-894-4   LC 97-33476

An overview of the Fifth Amendment of the United States Constitution, which defines and protects a citizen's rights within the legal system

Includes glossary and bibliographical references

Horn, Geoffrey

The Supreme Court; by Geoffrey M. Horn. World Almanac Library 2003 48p il (World Almanac Library of American government) lib bdg $30; pa $11.95

Grades: 5 6 7 8   **347**
ISBN 0-8368-5459-4 (lib bdg); 0-8368-5464-0 (pa)
                                LC 2002-38091

Horn, Geoffrey—*Continued*

Contents: First Monday in October; What the Constitution says; Getting Confirmed; Arguing a case; The Chief Justices; Great dissenters; Finding a balance

This describes "the organization of the Court, the extent and limits of its powers, and how it checks and balances the president and Congress. . . . the history of the Court, how a person becomes a Supreme Court justice, how cases come before the Court, the role of the chief justice, and the importance of dissenting opinions." Publisher's note

"An amazing array of historical photos, statistics, primary-source documents, tables, graphs, and case studies supports the [text]." SLJ

Includes bibliographical references

Jost, Kenneth

The Supreme Court A to Z. 4th ed. CQ Press 2007 622p il (CQ's American government A to Z series) $85 *

Grades: 8 9 10 11 12 Adult   **347**

1. United States. Supreme Court

ISBN 0-87289-335-9; 978-0-87289-335-1

LC 2006-38701

First published 1993

This book "provides biographies of past and present justices, the history of important cases, and explanations of constitutional principles and legal concepts." Publisher's note

Includes bibliographical references

Panchyk, Richard, 1970-

Our Supreme Court; a history with 14 activities. Chicago Review Press 2006 195p il $16.95

Grades: 7 8 9 10   **347**

1. United States. Supreme Court 2. Constitutional law—United States

ISBN 978-1-55652-607-7; 1-55652-607-5

LC 2006009018

"The history and evolution of the court and how it works are discussed in the first chapter. Thematic sections follow, covering such topics as free speech, privacy, and civil rights, with significant decisions included. . . . This a solid work that makes a complex and important subject accessible to students." SLJ

Includes bibliographical references

352.2   Organization of administration

United States government manual 2007-2008; Office of the Federal Register, National Archives and Records Service, General Services Administration. Claitor's Law Bks. 2007 pa $27

Grades: 8 9 10 11 12 Adult   **352.2**

1. United States—Politics and government—Handbooks, manuals, etc.

ISBN 1-59804-377-3; 978-1-59804-377-8

Annual. First published 1935. Variant title: United States government organization manual

"Official handbook of the Federal government describing the purposes and programs of most Government agencies and listing the top personnel." N Y Public Libr. Ref Books for Child Collect. 2d edition

352.23   Chief executives

The **presidency** A to Z; Gerhard Peters, editor; John T. Woolley, editor; Michael Nelson, advisory editor. 4th ed. CQ Press 2008 675p il map (CQ's American government A to Z series) $85 *

Grades: 8 9 10 11 12 Adult   **352.23**

1. Reference books 2. Presidents—United States—Encyclopedias

ISBN 978-0-87289-367-2; 0-87289-367-7

LC 2007-31322

First published 1992 with Michael Nelson's name appearing first

"Volume 1 traces the history of the office from the creation of the United States Constitution to present-day duties and responsibilities. . . . Volume 2 examines the interaction between the President and the other branches of government. It also includes biographies of Presidents, Vice Presidents, and First Ladies and concludes with tables listing the popular and electoral votes in presidential elections, party nominees for President, and cabinet members. . . . Students of history, political science, and public policy will find it useful when looking for background information about the office of the President." Libr J

Includes bibliographical references

352.24   Cabinets and cabinet-level committees

Feinberg, Barbara Silberdick, 1938-

The cabinet. 21st Cent. Bks. (NY) 1995 64p il (Inside government) $18.90

Grades: 5 6 7 8   **352.24**

1. Cabinet officers

ISBN 0-8050-3421-8   LC 94-41760

Provides a historical perspective for the development of the cabinet with heads of executive departments of government as advisers to the president

"Excellent-quality black-and-white and full-color photographs and reproductions accompany the interesting and lively text." SLJ

Includes bibliographical references

355   Military science

Ashabranner, Brent K., 1921-

A date with destiny; the Women in Military Service for America Memorial; [by] Brent Ashabranner; photographs by Jennifer Ashabranner. 21st Cent. Bks. (Brookfield) 2000 64p il lib bdg $25.90

Grades: 6 7 8 9   **355**

1. Women in Military Service for America Memorial (Arlington, Va.) 2. Women in the armed forces

ISBN 0-7613-1472-5   LC 99-36384

Describes the planning and creation of the Women in Military Service for America Memorial, profiles some of the servicewomen involved, and presents a general histo-

Ashabranner, Brent K., 1921-—*Continued*
ry of women in military service

"The excellent, full-color photographs include many images featuring the memorial as well as others showing related exhibits and events. A good, readable introduction to a subject barely represented in library collections." Booklist

Includes bibliographical references

Brownlie, Ali

Why do people fight wars? [by] Ali Brownlie & Chris Mason. Raintree Steck-Vaughn Pubs. 2002 48p il (Exploring tough issues) lib bdg $25.69
Grades: 6 7 8 9   355
1. War 2. Military history
ISBN 0-7398-4961-1   LC 2001-48372

Explores issues related to war, such as causes, types, results, and peacekeeping efforts, illustrated by examples of armed conflicts throughout history and throughout the world

This "does an excellent job of giving students a solid background and well-written explanation of [the subject]." Voice Youth Advocates

Includes glossary and bibliographical references

Chapman, Caroline, 1941-

Battles & weapons: exploring history through art; [by] Caroline Chapman. Two-Can 2007 64p il (Picture that!) $19.95 *
Grades: 5 6 7 8   355
1. Military art and science 2. Military history 3. War in art
ISBN 978-1-58728-588-2   LC 2006033229

"Period paintings from ancient times through World War II are used as a vehicle for introducing battles and weapons and discussing how they have changed over the centuries." Publisher's note

"High quality reproductions of paintings, murals, sculptures, and artifacts show military customs and equipment over the centuries. . . . The lively, informative text creates a 'you are there' sense that will engage even reluctant readers." SLJ

Includes bibliographical references

Chrisp, Peter

Warfare; by Peter Chrisp. Lucent Books 2004 48p il map (Medieval realms) $28.70
Grades: 6 7 8 9   355
1. Military history 2. Medieval civilization 3. Knights and knighthood
ISBN 1-59018-537-4   LC 2003-18308

Contents: 1. Warrior nobles; War and the Church; The Normans; 1066: the year of three battles; Castles; 2. Holy war; Siege warfare; Warrior Monks of Outremer; Muslim holy war; Chivalry; The dead of Visby; 3. The Hundred Years War; English victory; The Campaign of Crecy; 4. The Black Prince's War, Chivalry in Decline; 5. Joan of Arc; Gunpowder; Swiss footsoldiers; 6. The Wars of the Roses; New armies

This briefly describes wars and warfare in the Middle Ages, including the Norman invasions, the Crusades, knighthood and chivalry, the Hundred Years War, the campaign of Crécy, the Black Prince's War, and the Wars of the Roses

Inlcudes glossary and bibliographical references

Clinton, Catherine, 1952-

The Black soldier; 1492 to the present. Houghton Mifflin 2000 117p il $17
Grades: 5 6 7 8   355
1. African American soldiers
ISBN 0-395-67722-X   LC 99-48935

Chronicles the military accomplishments of African Americans who fought for the independence and preservation of the United States while struggling to be treated as equals and recognized for their valor and achievement

"Numerous black-and-white archival photographs and reproductions appear throughout this well-organized, readable resource." SLJ

Includes bibliographical references

Friedman, Lauri S.

Nuclear weapons and security. ReferencePoint Press 2008 112p il map (Compact research) lib bdg $24.95
Grades: 8 9 10 11 12   355
1. Nuclear weapons 2. Terrorism
ISBN 978-1-60152-021-0; 1-60152-021-2
                              LC 2007-16581

"Friedman gives a short history of nuclear arms and describes the current proliferation of such arms. A section on world survival after a nuclear war discusses the devastating consequences of such an event. . . . [This book] will be helpful to students looking for a one-stop information source." SLJ

Includes bibliographical references

Graham, Ian, 1953-

Military technology; [by] Ian Graham. Black Rabbit Books 2008 46p il (New technology) lib bdg $22.95
Grades: 7 8 9 10   355
1. United States—Armed forces 2. Weapons 3. Military art and science
ISBN 978-1-59920-165-8 (lib bdg); 1-59920-165-8 (lib bdg)   LC 2008000441

"Describes new technologies that are helping make military aviation, land warfare, warships and submarines, intelligence, non-lethal weapons, and space weapons more efficient and discusses the implications these technologies have on current and future warfare." Publisher's note

"The brevity of the text and the vivid visual design will make [this book] especially appealing to reluctant readers." Booklist

Includes glossary and bibliographical references

Gravett, Christopher

Going to war in Viking times. Watts 2001 32p il (Armies of the past) lib bdg $24.50; pa $6.95
Grades: 4 5 6   355
1. Vikings 2. Military history 3. Naval art and science
ISBN 0-531-14592-1 (lib bdg); 0-531-16353-9 (pa)
                              LC 00-42642

Gravett, Christopher—*Continued*

This describes the weaponry, dress, transportation, and military and naval strategies of Viking times

This volume is "wonderfully attractive, highly visual, and historically accurate." Book Rep

Includes glossary

Kallen, Stuart A., 1955-

National security. ReferencePoint Press 2008 112p il map (Compact research) lib bdg $24.95

Grades: 7 8 9 10 11 12   **355**

1. National security 2. Terrorism

ISBN 978-1-60152-020-3; 1-60152-020-4

    LC 2007-1567

This "includes information on the effect of security concerns on privacy, American foreign policy, and the Iraq War. . . . [The] volume includes people and groups associated with the issue, a chronology of events, related organizations, and suggestions for further research. Chapters open and end with an array of quotes that argue for or against a particular argument or aspect of the issue, complete with full citation." SLJ

Includes bibliographical references

Nathan, Amy

Count on us; American women in the military. National Geographic 2004 89p il $21.95 *

Grades: 6 7 8 9   **355**

1. Women in the armed forces

ISBN 0-7922-6330-8   LC 2003-14189

Reviews the history of American women's involvement in the Armed Forces from the Revolutionary War to the present

This is a "clearly written, well-organized book. . . . Readers will find this book valuable for research and interesting for browsing." SLJ

Inlcudes bibiographical references

War: opposing viewpoints; Louise Gerdes, book editor. Greenhaven Press 2005 239p il lib bdg $34.95; pa $23.70

Grades: 8 9 10 11 12   **355**

1. War

ISBN 0-7377-2591-5 (lib bdg); 0-7377-2592-3 (pa)

    LC 2004-54283

Replaces the edition published 1999 under the editorship of Tamara L. Roleff

"Opposing viewpoints series"

In this anthology the authors "debate controversies surrounding the causes and conduct of war, including under what circumstances war is justified, how prisoners and civilians should be treated, and what measures, if any, will prevent wars." Publisher's note

Includes bibliographical references

355.3   Organization and personnel of military forces

Rice, Earle

The U.S. Army and military careers; [by] Earle Rice Jr. Enslow Publishers 2006 128p il map (The U.S. Armed Forces and military careers) lib bdg $31.93

Grades: 6 7 8 9   **355.3**

1. United States. Army 2. Vocational guidance

ISBN 0-7660-2699-X   LC 2006011736

"This book takes the reader inside the Army—revealing its history, describing its current operations and structure, exploring the career paths it offers, and spotlighting the equipment and the soldiers of the American force." Publisher's note

Includes glossary and bibliographical references

355.7   Military installations

Adams, Simon

Castles & forts; foreword by Clifford J. Rogers. Kingfisher (NY) 2003 63p il (Kingfisher knowledge) hardcover o.p. pa $8.95

Grades: 5 6 7 8   **355.7**

1. Fortification 2. Castles

ISBN 978-0-7534-5620-0; 0-7534-5620-6; 978-0-7534-6119-8 (pa); 0-7534-6119-6 (pa)

    LC 2003-44631

An illustrated exploration of a wide array of castles and fortifications throughout the world, from Norman mottes to Maori forts, including how and why they were built and their importance in history

This title includes "stunning, captioned photos and illustrations that emphasize the many intriguing factual details in the text." SLJ

Includes glossary

355.8   Military equipment and supplies (Matériel)

Byam, Michèle

Arms & armor; written by Michéle Byam. rev ed. DK Pub. 2004 72p il (DK eyewitness books) $15.99 hardcover o.p.

Grades: 4 5 6 7   **355.8**

1. Weapons 2. Armor

ISBN 0-7566-0654-3; 0-7566-0653-5 (lib bdg)

    LC 2004-558979

First published 1988 by Knopf

A photo essay examining the design, construction, and uses of hand weapons and armor from a Stone Age axe to the revolvers and rifles of the Wild West.

Making and using the atomic bomb; Mark McKain, book editor. Greenhaven Press 2003 240p (History firsthand) lib bdg $25.96; pa $16.96 *

Grades: 7 8 9 10   355.8

1. Manhattan Project 2. Atomic bomb

ISBN 0-7377-1412-3 (lib bdg); 0-7377-1413-1 (pa)

LC 2002-27880

"This collection of writings surveys the history of the atomic bomb, its use, and its destructive capability. . . . The volume is divided into four chapters—'Discovery of Fission,' 'The Manhattan Project,' 'Using the Bomb,' and 'The Aftermath'—with several contemporary narratives and reminiscences in each." SLJ

Includes bibliographical references

Sullivan, Edward T., 1966-

The ultimate weapon; the race to develop the atomic bomb. Holiday House 2007 182p il $24.95

Grades: 6 7 8 9   355.8

1. Manhattan Project 2. Atomic bomb

ISBN 978-0-8234-1855-8; 0-8234-1855-3

LC 2005-50330

This history of the Manhattan Project "effectively distills the science behind the development of the atomic bomb into understandable terms that turns the human story behind the project into compelling drama." Booklist

Includes bibliographical references

356 Foot forces and warfare

Haney, Eric L.

Inside Delta Force; the story of America's elite counterterrorist unit. Delacorte Press 2006 246p il $15.95; lib bdg $17.99

Grades: 8 9 10 11 12   356

1. United States. Army. Delta Force

ISBN 0-385-73251-1; 0-385-90273-5 (lib bdg)

LC 2004-30945

"In this adaptation of an adult book, Retired Command Sergeant Major Haney relates a . . . story of the 1977 founding of the ultrasecret counterterrorist unit of the U.S. Army known as Delta Force. . . . Better stock up on copies; you won't want to ration this one." Booklist

358 Air and other specialized forces and warfare; engineering and related services

Gay, Kathlyn, 1930-

Silent death; the threat of chemical and biological terrorism. 21st Cent. Bks. (Brookfield) 2001 128p il lib bdg $24.90

Grades: 7 8 9 10   358

1. Chemical warfare 2. Biological warfare 3. Terrorism

ISBN 0-7613-1401-6   LC 00-41807

"Citing examples of military and civilian persons exposed to chemical-biological agents, primarily from World War I to the Persian Gulf War, Gay argues for the need to understand and curtail the use of agents that often cannot be detected until the damage is done. . . . Relevant, engrossing." Booklist

Includes bibliographical references

Judson, Karen, 1941-

Chemical and biological warfare. Benchmark Bks. 2004 144p il (Open for debate) lib bdg $25.95

Grades: 7 8 9 10   358

1. Biological warfare 2. Chemical warfare

ISBN 0-7614-1585-8   LC 2003-7768

This describes various types of biological and chemical weapons, their histories and effects, and their development, testing, and control, and their effects on current events and policies.

"Well-organized and informative." SLJ

Includes bibliographical references

Weapons of mass destruction: opposing viewpoints; James D. Torr, book editor. Greenhaven Press 2005 207p il lib bdg $33.70; pa $22.45

Grades: 8 9 10 11 12   358

1. Weapons

ISBN 0-7377-2250-9 (lib bdg); 0-7377-2251-7 (pa)

LC 2004-47587

Replaces the 1999 edition under the editorship of Jennifer A. Hurley

"Opposing viewpoints series"

"The viewpoints in the volume examine WMD threats from terrorist groups and 'axis of evil' nations in the following chapters: How Likely Is an Attack Involving Weapons of Mass Destruction? How Should the United States Deal with Countries that Threaten to Develop Weapons of Mass Destruction? What Policies Should the United States Adopt Toward Nuclear Weapons? How Can the United States Defend Itself Against Weapons of Mass Destruction?" Publisher's note

Includes bibliographical references

Wolny, Philip

Weapons satellites. Rosen Pub. Group 2003 63p il (Library of satellites) lib bdg $26.50

Grades: 4 5 6 7   358

1. Space warfare 2. Space weapons 3. Artificial satellites

ISBN 0-8239-3855-7   LC 2002-10746

Contents: From space race to arms race and back again; The high ground and its perils; Inside weapons satellites; The future

Examines the development of weapons satellites which are not yet in use but which, when deployed, can use laser beams to attack large targets, disrupt the weather, or eliminate nuclear missiles in flight

"Clear and topical photographs enliven the [presentation]. While packed with information, the [text is] easy to read." SLJ

Includes glossary and bibliographical references

358.4   Air forces and warfare

Camelo, Wilson
The U.S. Air Force and military careers. Enslow
Pubs. 2006 128p il (The U.S. Armed Forces and
military careers) lib bdg $31.93
Grades: 6 7 8 9   **358.4**
1. United States. Air Force 2. Vocational guidance
ISBN 0-7660-2524-1
This offers a history of the U.S. Air Force, describes
what the Air Force does and outlines career opportuni-
ties.
"This volume . . . does a fine job of tracing [Air
Force] history. . . . Attractively formatted with color
photos, the book will make a fine library acquisition."
Booklist
Includes glossary and bibliographical references

359   Sea forces and warfare

Kiland, Taylor Baldwin, 1966-
The U.S. Navy and military careers; [by] Taylor
Baldwin Kiland. Enslow Publishers 2006 128p il
(The U.S. Armed Forces and military careers) lib
bdg $31.93
Grades: 6 7 8 9   **359**
1. United States. Navy 2. Vocational guidance
ISBN 0-7660-2523-3   LC 2006001745
"Kiland begins with action in the Persian Gulf before
devoting two chapters to the history and development of
the U.S. Navy. . . . The remaining . . . chapters . . .
describe the roles of [The Navy] in defending our nation.
Considerable space is devoted to personnel requirements,
expectations, duties, and qualifications. . . . Generously
illustrated with numerous high-quality, color photos."
SLJ
Includes glossary and bibliographical references

359.8   Naval equipment and supplies (Naval matériel)

Myers, Walter Dean, 1937-
USS Constellation; pride of the American navy.
Holiday House 2004 86p il $16.95
Grades: 5 6 7 8   **359.8**
1. Constellation (Frigate)
ISBN 0-8234-1816-2   LC 2003-56764
This "book traces the history of the USS Constellation, which was built as a frigate, launched in 1797, and
initially charged with battling privateers that threatened
U.S. trade with Europe. She was rebuilt as a sloop in
1854 and, in 1999, restored to her 1854 glory and
docked in Baltimore Harbor. . . . The volume features
an attractive design and many black-and-white reproductions of period photographs, drawings, paintings, and
documents. . . . A unique addition to American history
collections." Booklist
Includes glossary and bibliographical references

359.9   Specialized combat forces; engineering and related services

Gray, Judy Silverstein
The U.S. Coast Guard and military careers; [by]
Judy Silverstein Gray. Enslow Publishers 2007
c2008 128p il (The U.S. Armed Forces and
military careers) lib bdg $31.93
Grades: 6 7 8 9   **359.9**
1. United States. Coast Guard 2. Vocational guidance
ISBN 978-0-7660-2493-9 (lib bdg); 0-7660-2493-8 (lib
bdg)   LC 2006001744
This offers a history of the U.S. Coast Guard, describes what the Coast Guard does and outlines career
opportunities.
Includes glossary and bibliographical references

Stein, R. Conrad, 1937-
The U.S. Marine Corps and military careers;
[by] R. Conrad Stein. Enslow Publishers 2006
128p il (The U.S. Armed Forces and military
careers) lib bdg $31.93
Grades: 6 7 8 9   **359.9**
1. United States. Marine Corps 2. Vocational guidance
ISBN 0-7660-2521-7   LC 2005037881
"Stein opens with 9/11, followed by a compact history
of the Corps from 1775 to 1918. Chapter three is an
overview of World War II to the present. The remaining
five or six chapters . . . describe the roles of [The Marine Corps] in defending our nation. Considerable space
is devoted to personnel requirements, expectations, duties, and qualifications. Dangers are honestly dealt with.
Charts present the various pay scales. . . . Generously illustrated with numerous high-quality, color photos." SLJ
Includes glossary and bibliographical references

361.2   Social action

Halpin, Mikki
It's your world—if you don't like it, change it;
activism for teenagers. Simon Pulse 2004 305p pa
$8.99 *
Grades: 7 8 9 10   **361.2**
1. Social action
ISBN 0-689-87448-0
"Animal rights, racism, war protest, AIDS, school violence and bullying, women's rights, and promoting tolerance are among the topics covered here. Halpin provides
basic information about each one and then makes myriad
suggestions for action at home, in the community, the
'five-minute activist,' etc. The ideas are easy to implement. . . .This is an important book that will empower
any young adult who would like to make a difference."
SLJ
Includes bibliographical references

Zeiler, Freddi
A kid's guide to giving; illustrated by Ward
Schumaker. InnovativeKids 2006 205p il pa $9.99
Grades: 7 8 9 10   **361.2**

Zeiler, Freddi—*Continued*
1. Charity
ISBN 1-58476-489-9
"In this inspiring and motivating book, Zeiler challenges teens to make a difference by contributing to charitable causes. Her enthusiastic, personal appeal offers advice on selecting a charity and deciding whether to donate money, useful items, or time." SLJ

361.3 Social work

Gay, Kathlyn, 1930-
Volunteering; the ultimate teen guide. Scarecrow Press 2004 127p il (It happened to me) $37.50; pa $14.95 *
Grades: 7 8 9 10   361.3
1. Volunteer work
ISBN   0-8108-4922-4;   978-0-8108-4922-8;
0-8108-5833-9 (pa); 978-0-8108-5833-6 (pa)
LC 2004-8174
Contents: Being a volunteer; Building and repairing; Closing the generation gap; Helping with health care; Helping the homeless, feeding the hungry; Protecting the environment and animals; Preserving the past; Counseling, teaching, and tutoring; Reducing bigotry, prejudice, and racism; Campaigning, communicating, and collecting; Getting started, reaping rewards
"This is a useful tool in that it provides a one-stop resource for teens interested in locating volunteer opportunities." SLJ
Includes bibliographical references

Karnes, Frances A.
Empowered girls; a girl's guide to positive activism, volunteering, and philanthropy; [by] Frances Karnes A. & Kristen R. Stephens. Prufrock Press 2005 191p pa $14.95
Grades: 6 7 8 9   361.3
1. Volunteer work 2. Social action 3. Charity organization
ISBN 1-59363-163-4
This "book seeks to inspire young women to recognize their potential to have an impact on their schools and communities by offering their time and talents. . . . It serves as both an instruction book that defines the concepts of positive activism, volunteering, and philanthropy while providing true-life stories of contemporary teens who can testify to the numerous benefits of getting involved in a cause in which one believes." Voice Youth Advocates
"Those looking to get involved in service projects will find this an inspiring and motivational guide." SLJ
Includes bibliographical references

Marcovitz, Hal
Teens & volunteerism. Mason Crest 2005 112p il (Gallup Youth Survey) $22.95
Grades: 7 8 9 10   361.3
1. Volunteer work
ISBN 1-59084-877-2   LC 2004004827

This is "based on the findings of the Gallup Youth Survey (a 20-year ongoing survey of teens). . . . [It] covers the gamut of issues surrounding [volunteerism and youth], focusing on mandatory vs. optional community service in high school and college, military service, political community service, and activism. [The book is] well documented." SLJ
Includes bibliographical references

362.1 Physical illness

Fleischman, John
Phineas Gage: a gruesome but true story about brain science. Houghton Mifflin 2002 86p il $16; pa $8.95 *
Grades: 5 6 7 8 9   362.1
1. Gage, Phineas P., d. 1861 2. Brain—Wounds and injuries
ISBN 0-618-05252-6; 0-618-49478-2 (pa)
LC 2001-39253
"Phineas, a railroad construction foreman, was blasting rock near Cavendish, Vermont, in 1848 when a thirteen-pound iron rod was shot through his brain. Miraculously, he survived to live another eleven years and become a textbook case in brain science." Publisher's note
"The author deftly introduces readers to a diverse range of relevant scientific history as well as more specific beliefs that influenced the medical establishment's understanding of Gage, then goes on to examine subsequent neurological discoveries that have changed and enhanced our understanding of Gage's fate. The book's present-tense narrative is inviting and intimate, and the text is crisp and lucid." Bull Cent Child Books
Includes glossary and bibliographical references

Foley, Ronan
World health; the impact on our lives. Raintree Steck-Vaughn Pubs. 2003 64p il map (21st century debates) lib bdg $28.56
Grades: 7 8 9 10   362.1
1. World Health Organization 2. Health 3. Public health
ISBN 0-7398-5507-7   LC 2002-151937
Contents: A healthy world?; Measuring health; World diseases; The HIV/AIDS crisis; Health inequalities around the world; Health and environment; Food, poverty, development, and health; The future of world health
Provides an overview of global health issues, as well as the health problems that arise from economic and social situations in particular parts of the world, and explores the work of the World Health Organization
This title has "many well-placed sidebars with facts, debates, and viewpoints . . . [and] good-quality color photographs." SLJ
Includes bibliographical references

Gray, Susan Heinrichs
Living with cerebral palsy. Child's World 2003 32p il (Living well) lib bdg $25.64
Grades: 4 5 6 7   362.1
1. Cerebral palsy
ISBN 1-56766-101-7   LC 2002-2865

Gray, Susan Heinrichs—*Continued*

This title "leads off with an introduction to a young person who has [cerebral palsy]. Subsequent chapters explain the physiology of the illness, what causes it, and what it's like to live with it. [The concluding section looks] at possible treatments and potential cures. The [text is] clear and simple, double spaced, and punctuated by colorful exemplary photos of kids dealing with the disease. Gray provides a surprising amount of information and develops considerable empathy in readers." SLJ

Includes glossary and bibliographical references

Libal, Autumn

Social discrimination and body size; too big to fit? Mason Crest Publishers 2006 104p il (Obesity: modern-day epidemic) $23.95

Grades: 7 8 9 10   **362.1**

1. Obesity 2. Body image 3. Discrimination
ISBN 978-1-59084-949-1; 1-59084-949-3

LC 2004-27863

Explains "the effects social discrimination based on body size have on individuals and society." Publisher's note

Includes bibliographical references

Mintzer, Richard

The National Institutes of Health; [by]} Rich Mintzer. Chelsea House 2002 64p il (Your government—how it works) lib bdg $20.75

Grades: 6 7 8 9   **362.1**

1. National Institutes of Health (U.S.)
ISBN 0-7910-6793-9   LC 2002-43

Presents an overview of the history of infectious disease epidemics in the United States, as well as the history of the National Institutes of Health, the structure and role of that institution, and current major health concerns that are its focus

"This is a complete and fascinating overview of not just a government agency but also a complex organization that plays an important role in all of our lives." SLJ

Includes glossary and bibliographical references

Naden, Corinne J.

Patients' rights; [by] Corinne Naden. Marshall Cavendish Benchmark 2008 144p il (Open for debate) lib bdg $27.95

Grades: 7 8 9 10   **362.1**

1. Medical care
ISBN 978-0-7614-2576-2; 0-7614-2576-4

LC 2006-21786

"Discusses patients' rights, including the issues surrounding physician-assisted suicide, HMOs, the rights of children, abortion, stem cell research, and the difference between public and private rights." Publisher's note

This book maintains a "balanced tone while providing an abundance of examples and factual information. Many captioned color photos enhance the text." SLJ

Includes bibliographical references

Parks, Peggy J., 1951-

HPV. ReferencePoint Press 2009 104p il map (Compact research. Diseases and disorders) $25.95

Grades: 7 8 9 10 11 12   **362.1**

1. Papillomaviruses
ISBN 978-1-60152-070-8; 1-60152-070-0

LC 2008-44026

Presents an overview of the causes, symptoms, and various types of the Human Papillomavirus; and provides information on available vaccines, health risks of genital HPV, and organizations and advocacy groups.

This book "is a timely overview of the most prevalent sexually transmitted disease among female teens today." Booklist

Includes bibliographical references

Terminal illness: opposing viewpoints; Andrea C. Nakaya, book editor. Greenhaven Press 2005 204p il lib bdg $34.95; pa $23.70

Grades: 8 9 10 11 12   **362.1**

1. Terminal care
ISBN 0-7377-2963-5 (lib bdg); 0-7377-2964-3 (pa)

LC 2004-60595

Replaces the edition published 2001 under the editorship of Mary E. Williams

"Opposing viewpoints series"

"The authors of this anthology present various opinions on the best way to care for the terminally ill and their friends and family, including a debate on the role of euthanasia." Publisher's note

Includes bibliographical references

What can I do now?: Health care. Ferguson 2007 222p $29.95

Grades: 8 9 10 11 12   **362.1**

1. Medicine 2. Vocational guidance
ISBN 0-8160-6031-2; 978-0-8160-603-1

LC 2006030410

"This volume offers an overview of the health-care industry, a look at different careers, ideas for getting experience, and additional resources. . . . The layout is attractive, the font a good size, and the information accessible. . . . An excellent addition." SLJ

Winick, Judd, 1970-

Pedro and me; friendship, loss, and what I learned. Holt & Co. 2000 187p il pa $16

Grades: 7 8 9 10 11 12   **362.1**

1. Zamora, Pedro, 1972-1994 2. Real world (Television program) 3. AIDS (Disease)—Graphic novels 4. Friendship—Graphic novels 5. Graphic novels 6. Biographical graphic novels
ISBN 0-8050-6403-6   LC 99-40729

In this "volume—part graphic novel, part memoir—professional cartoonist Winick pays tribute to his *Real World* housemate and friend Pedro Zamora, an AIDS activist who died of the disease in 1994." Publ Wkly

"The author does a stellar job of marrying image to word to form a flowing narrative. . . . This is an important book for teens and the adults who care about them. Winick handles his topics with both sensitivity and a thoroughness that rarely coexist so seamlessly." SLJ

362.2 Mental and emotional illnesses and disturbances

Mental illness: opposing viewpoints; Mary E. Williams, book editor. Greenhaven Press 2007 238p lib bdg $36.20; pa $24.95
Grades: 8 9 10 11 12   362.2
1. Mental illness
ISBN 0-7377-2947-3 (lib bdg); 978-0-7377-2947-4 (lib bdg); 0-7377-2948-1 (pa); 978-0-7377-2948-1 (pa)
LC 2006-20106
Replaces the edition published 2000 under the editorship of Tamara L. Roleff and Laura K. Egendorf
"Opposing viewpoints series"
"This collections of articles, written by individuals with differing opinions and from varying backgrounds, analyzes issues relevant to mental health and public policy." SLJ
Includes bibliographical references

362.28 Suicide

Nelson, Richard E.
The power to prevent suicide; a guide for teens helping teens; [by] Richard E. Nelson, Judith C. Galas; foreword by Bev Cobain; edited by Pamela Espeland. Updated ed. Free Spirit 2006 115p pa $13.95 *
Grades: 7 8 9 10 11 12   362.28
1. Suicide
ISBN 1-57542-206-9; 978-1-57542-206-0
First published 1994
"The authors' premise is that, as trusted and caring friends, YAs have a special role in the prevention of suicide among their peers, and discuss what to do if they observe the danger signals. . . . This book provides clear, practical information and advice." SLJ

Suicide: opposing viewpoints; Roman Espejo, book editor. Greenhaven Press 2003 207p il lib bdg $34.95; pa $23.70
Grades: 8 9 10 11 12   362.28
1. Suicide
ISBN 0-7377-1242-2 (lib bdg); 0-7377-1241-1 (pa)
LC 2002-32214
Replaces the edition published 1998 under the editorship of Tamara L. Roleff
"Opposing viewpoints series"
In this "anthology, authors debate the causes and possible solutions to this problem in the following chapters: Is Suicide Ever Acceptable? What are the Causes of Teen Suicide? Should Assisted Suicide Be Legalized? How Can Suicide Be Prevented?" Publisher's note
Includes bibliographical references

362.29 Substance abuse

Addiction: opposing viewpoints; Louise I. Gerdes, book editor. Greenhaven Press 2005 189p il $33.70; pa $22.45
Grades: 8 9 10 11 12   362.29
1. Drug abuse 2. Alcoholism 3. Tobacco habit
ISBN 0-7377-2216-9; 0-7377-2217-7 (pa)
LC 2003-67520
Replaces the 2000 edition under the editorship of Jennifer A. Hurley
"Opposing viewpoints series"
"Authors in this . . . anthology debate controversies surrounding the concept of addiction, including what behaviors should be considered addictive, what causes addiction, what treatments are most effective, and whether the government should intervene to reduce the costs associated with addiction." Publisher's note
Includes bibliographical references

Axelrod-Contrada, Joan
The facts about drugs and society. Marshall Cavendish Benchmark 2008 143p il (Drugs) $27.95
Grades: 7 8 9 10 11 12   362.29
1. Drugs
ISBN 978-0-7614-2674-5
This discusses drugs in relation to history, pop culture, risk factors, gender, the brain, the law, treatment and prevention.
This is "well-organized, attractively illustrated, current, and highly informative." Sci Books Films

Barter, James, 1946-
Hallucinogens. Lucent Bks. 2002 112p il (Drug education library) lib bdg $27.45
Grades: 7 8 9 10   362.29
1. Hallucinogens 2. Drug abuse
ISBN 1-56006-915-5   LC 2001-5776
Discusses the development of hallucinogens, their use for spiritual, medicinal, and recreational purposes, and the laws governing their use
"This intelligently written, objective title provides students with detailed information." SLJ
Includes bibliographical references

Berne, Emma Carlson
Methamphetamine. ReferencePoint Press 2007 102p il map (Compact research) $24.95
Grades: 8 9 10 11 12   362.29
1. Methamphetamine 2. Drug abuse
ISBN 978-1-60152-004-3; 1-60152-004-2
LC 2006032206
"Berne explores whether methamphetamine usage in the U.S. has reached epidemic proportions, its dangers, the link between addiction and crime, and abuse prevention." SLJ
Includes bibliographical references

Breguet, Amy
Vicodin, OxyContin, and other pain relievers; [by] Amy E. Breguet. Chelsea House 2008 112p il (Junior drug awareness) $30
Grades: 6 7 8 9   **362.29**
1. Narcotics 2. Analgesics 3. Drug abuse
ISBN 978-0-7910-9700-7; 0-7910-9700-5
LC 2007032350
This describes the effects of Vicodin and OxyContin and other pain relievers, how they are used and abused, and how to get help for addiction.
Includes glossary and bibliographical references

Drug abuse: opposing viewpoints; Tamara L. Roleff, book editor. Greenhaven Press 2005 221p il lib bdg $33.70; pa $22.45
Grades: 8 9 10 11 12   **362.29**
1. Drug abuse
ISBN 0-7377-2226-6 (lib bdg); 0-7377-2227-4 (pa)
LC 2004-42406
Replaces the 1999 edition under the editorship of James D. Torr
A collection of articles and speeches, book excerpts and quotations on various aspects of the drug abuse problem
Includes bibliographical references

Drugs, alcohol, and tobacco; learning about addictive behavior; Rosalyn Carson-DeWitt, editor in chief. Macmillan Ref. USA 2003 3v set $295
Grades: 7 8 9 10   **362.29**
1. Reference books 2. Drug abuse—Encyclopedias
ISBN 0-02-865756-X   LC 2002-9270
Based on the Encyclopedia of drugs, alcohol & addictive behavior, 2nd edition, published 2001
"The 190 alphabetically arranged articles range from one to six pages in length and yield a comprehensive look at the nature of, treatments for, and social issues surrounding addictive substances and behaviors. Topics include specific drugs, diagnoses, treatments, legal and social implications, drug trafficking, cultural pressures, and related compulsive behaviors." SLJ
Includes bibliographical references

Egendorf, Laura K., 1973-
Performance-enhancing drugs. Reference point 2007 96p il (Compact research) lib bdg $24.95
Grades: 8 9 10 11 12   **362.29**
1. Drugs 2. Athletes—Drug use
ISBN 978-1-60152-003-6 (lib bdg); 1-60152-003-4 (lib bdg)
This "well-organized [volume presens] general information that report writers, particularly reluctant readers, will find useful. Brightly colored illustrated facts and statistics charts invite perusal. Thought-provoking questions introduce most of the chapters. . . . [This book] covers ethical issues and dangers in usage, effectiveness of testing, and prevention. . . . Primary-source quotes are well documented." SLJ

Gottfried, Ted, 1928-
The facts about marijuana. Benchmark Books 2004 c2005 109p il (Drugs) lib bdg $37.07 *
Grades: 6 7 8 9   **362.29**
1. Marijuana
ISBN 0-7614-1806-7   LC 2004-5578
Contents: What is marijuana?; Highs and lows; Go directly to jail; Pot, pain and punishment; Tests that count!
The author describes the effects of marijuana use, varying opinions about legalization, marijuana laws, and drug testing in schools.
Includes glossary and bibliographical references

Ingram, Scott, 1948-
Marijuana; [by] W. Scott Ingram. Chelsea House 2008 110p il (Junior drug awareness) lib bdg $30
Grades: 6 7 8 9   **362.29**
1. Marijuana 2. Drug abuse
ISBN 978-0-7910-9695-6 (lib bdg); 0-7910-9695-5
LC 2007-24826
"Marijuana traces the history of this controversial drug, describes both the positive and negative effects it can have on the body and mind, and explains why it currently is illegal." Publisher's note
This "provides useful, balanced, and comprehensive information." Horn Book Guide
Includes glossary and bibliographical references

Klosterman, Lorrie
The facts about drug dependence to treatment. Marshall Cavendish Benchmark 2008 126p il (Drugs) lib bdg $31.94
Grades: 7 8 9 10 11 12   **362.29**
1. Drug abuse
ISBN 978-0-7614-2676-9   LC 2007-8780
This discusses the beginnings of drug dependence, its costs, first steps to recovery, rehabilitation, and lifetime freedom from drugs.
This is "well-organized, attractively illustrated, current, and highly informative." Sci Books Films
Includes glossary and bibliographical references

Koellhoffer, Tara
Ecstasy and other club drugs; [by] Tara Koellhoffer. Chelsea House 2008 120p il (Junior drug awareness) $30
Grades: 6 7 8 9   **362.29**
1. Ecstasy (Drug) 2. Drug abuse
ISBN 978-0-7910-9697-0; 0-7910-9697-1
LC 2007017789
This describes the effects of Ecstasy (MDMA), GHB, Rohypnol, Ketamine, LSD, and other drugs, why people take them, and addiction and treatment.
This "provides useful, balanced, and comprehensive information." Horn Book Guide
Includes glossary and bibliographical references

Koellhoffer, Tara—*Continued*

Inhalants and solvents; [by] Tara Koellhoffer. Chelsea House 2008 112p il (Junior drug awareness) lib bdg $30

Grades: 6 7 8 9 **362.29**
1. Inhalant abuse
ISBN 978-0-7910-9698-7 (lib bdg); 0-7910-9698-X (lib bdg)   LC 2007024824

This "examines the many household products—approximately 1,400 of them in all—that can be abused and explains the damage they can do to the brain and body." Publisher's note

This "provides useful, balanced, and comprehensive information." Horn Book Guide

Includes glossary and bibliographical references

Kreske, Damian P.

How to say no to drugs. Chelsea House Publishers 2008 112p il (Junior drug awareness) lib bdg $30

Grades: 6 7 8 9 **362.29**
1. Drug abuse
ISBN 978-0-7910-9699-4 (l); 0-7910-9699-8
LC 2007043664

This "explains how drug use affects the body and can lead to addiction, as well as how young people can avoid peer pressure to use drugs. The book also includes the personal stories of teenagers who have gone through treatment to repair the damage their drug use did." Publisher's note

Includes glossary and bibliographical references

Landau, Elaine

Meth; America's drug epidemic; [by] Elaine Landau. Twenty-First Century Books 2007 120p il lib bdg $30.60

Grades: 7 8 9 10 **362.29**
1. Methamphetamine 2. Drug abuse
ISBN 978-0-8225-6808-7   LC 2006030923

"This excellent exposé explains the facts about methamphetamine: its effects upon addicts, the impact of the drug's widespread manufacture and use upon society as a whole, and the efforts of government and law enforcement to curtail its spread." Booklist

Includes bibliographical references

Let's clear the air: 10 reasons not to start smoking; with a foreword by Christy Turlington; [illustrations by Deanne Staffo] Lobster Press 2007 192p il pa $14.95

Grades: 5 6 7 8 **362.29**
1. Smoking
ISBN 978-1-897073-66-7; 1-897073-66-6

"Young people ranging in ages from 9 to 14 offer sound arguments for not taking up cigarettes. . . . Interspersed throughout the accessible text are boxes and sidebars with facts and statistics, photos, and spot art. . . . The antismoking message here is all the more effective coming directly from a diverse group of young people." Booklist

LeVert, Suzanne

The facts about cocaine; [by] Suzanne LeVert. Marshall Cavendish Benchmark 2005 c2006 96p il map (Drugs) lib bdg $42.79; pa $6.99 *

Grades: 7 8 9 10 **362.29**
1. Cocaine 2. Drug abuse
ISBN 978-0-7614-1973-0 (lib bdg); 0-7614-1973-X (lib bdg); 978-0-7614-3593-8 (pa); 0-7614-3593-X (pa)   LC 2005-1313

Describes how cocaine affects the mind and body, the dangers of cocaine abuse, cocaine and the law, and how to deal with addiction.

Includes glossary and bibliographical references

The facts about ecstasy; [by] Suzanne LeVert. Benchmark Books 2004 c2005 96p il (Drugs) lib bdg $$2.79; pa $6.99 *

Grades: 6 7 8 9 **362.29**
1. Ecstasy (Drug)
ISBN 978-0-7614-1807-8 (lib bdg); 0-7614-1807-5 (lib bdg); 978-0-7614-3588-4 (pa); 0-7614-3588-3 (pa)
LC 2004-9341

Contents: Ecstasy: number one club drug; Drugs by design; Risky business: the body and brain on X; Ecstasy and the law; Designing a drug-free life

The author describes the drug MDMA, commonly known as ecstasy, and how it is abused, its health risks, the laws against it, and how to recover from the habit

Inlcudes glossary and bibliographical references

The facts about heroin; [by] Suzanne LeVert. Marshall Cavendish Benchmark 2005 c2006 95p il (Drugs) lib bdg $42.79; pa $6.99 *

Grades: 7 8 9 10 **362.29**
1. Heroin 2. Drug abuse
ISBN 978-0-7614-1975-4 (lib bdg); 0-7614-1975-6 (lib bdg); 978-0-7614-3595-2 (pa); 0-7614-3595-6 (pa)
LC 2005001728

"Describes the history, characteristics, legal status, and abuse of the drug Heroin." Publisher's note

Includes glossary and bibliographical references

The facts about LSD and other hallucinogens; [by] Suzanne LeVert. Marshall Cavendish Benchmark 2005 c2006 96p il (Drugs) lib bdg $42.79; pa $6.99 *

Grades: 7 8 9 10 **362.29**
1. LSD (Drug) 2. Hallucinogens 3. Drug abuse
ISBN 978-0-7614-1974-7 (lib bdg); 0-7614-1974-8 (lib bdg); 978-0-7614-3596-9 (pa); 0-7614-3596-4 (pa)
LC 2005-3948

"Describes the history, characteristics, legal status, and abuse of LSD." Publisher's note

This "useful [volume is] attractively packaged and will be of interest to report writers and general readers. [Text] and photos do an excellent job of showing how [this] group of drugs affects the body." SLJ

Includes glossary and bibliographical references

LeVert, Suzanne—*Continued*

The facts about nicotine; [by] Suzanne LeVert. Marshall Cavendish Benchmark 2007 112p il (Drugs) lib bdg $42.79 *

Grades: 6 7 8 9   362.29

1. Smoking 2. Tobacco

ISBN 978-0-7614-2244-0 (lib bdg); 0-7614-2244-7 (lib bdg)   LC 2006002405

This describes the effects of nicotine and smoking on the mind and body, the tobacco industry and the law, and how live free of smoke and nicotine.

Includes glossary and bibliographical references

The facts about steroids; [by] Suzanne LeVert. Benchmark Books 2004 c2005 96p il (Drugs) lib bdg $42.79 *

Grades: 6 7 8 9   362.29

1. Steroids 2. Athletes—Drug use

ISBN 978-0-7614-1808-5 (lib bdg); 0-7614-1808-3 (lib bdg)   LC 2004-11852

Contents: The game of steroids; Steroids and your body; The health risks of taking steroids; Steroids and the law; Treatment, prevention, and healthy fitness

The author "discusses the effects of steroids on the body, health risks, the law, prevention, and treatment. The medicinal use of steroids is very briefly mentioned. . . . [This title has a] readable, well-organized [text], and good use of color, graphics, photographs, tables, diagrams, and labels helps to spark readers' interest." SLJ

Includes glossary and bibliographical references

Menhard, Francha Roffe

The facts about amphetamines; [by] Francha Roffé Menhard. 1st ed. Marshall Cavendish Benchmark 2005 c2006 96p il (Drugs) lib bdg $42.79 *

Grades: 7 8 9 10   362.29

1. Amphetamines 2. Drug abuse

ISBN 978-0-7614-1972-3 (lib bdg); 0-7614-1972-1 (lib bdg)   LC 2005001142

"Describes the history, characteristics, legal status, and abuse of amphetamines and methamphetamines." Publisher's note

This "useful [volume is] attractively packaged and will be of interest to report writers and general readers. [Text] and photos do an excellent job of showing how [this] group of drugs affects the body." SLJ

Includes glossary and bibliographical references

The facts about inhalants; [by] Francha Roffe Menhard. Benchmark Books 2004 c2005 92p il (Drugs) lib bdg $$42.79 *

Grades: 6 7 8 9   362.29

1. Solvent abuse

ISBN 978-0-7614-1809-2 (lib bdg); 0-7614-1809-1 (lib bdg)   LC 2004-11858

Contents: Introduction; What are inhalants?; A history of inhalant abuse; The dangers of inhalant abuse; Help for inhalant abusers; Inhalants and the law

The author "addresses the types of inhalants, the history, dangers, effects, available help for abuse of these drugs, and the laws regulating them. . . . [This title has a] readable, well-organized [text], and good use of color,

graphics, photographs, tables, diagrams, and labels helps to spark readers' interest." SLJ

Includes glossary and bibliographical references

Mezinski, Pierre, 1950-

Drugs explained; the real deal on alcohol, pot, ecstasy, and more; [by] Pierre Mezinski, with Melissa Daly and Françoise Jaud; illustrated by Redge. Amulet Books 2004 111p (Sunscreen) pa $9.95

Grades: 7 8 9 10   362.29

1. Drug abuse

ISBN 0-8109-4931-8   LC 2004-12563

"Combining the diary of a girl tempted by drugs and sections of factual information, this is a . . . look at the most prevalent drugs and the social situations in which young people might be invited to use them. . . . This book answers teens' and preteens' questions about what drugs really do, how to say no, and how to help a friend in trouble." Publisher's note

"This book offers solid information and advice in a friendly, conversational style. . . . Colorful and at times humorous paintings combine with a supportive, upbeat text." SLJ

Includes bibliographical references

Naff, Clay Farris

Nicotine and tobacco; by Clay Farris Naff. ReferencePoint Press, Inc. 2007 110p il (Compact research) $24.95

Grades: 8 9 10 11 12   362.29

1. Smoking 2. Tobacco habit

ISBN 978-1-60152-006-7; 1-60152-006-9

LC 2006033962

This "well-organized [volume presents] general information that report writers, particularly reluctant readers, will find useful. Brightly colored illustrated facts and statistics charts invite perusal. Thought-provoking questions introduce most of the chapters. . . . [This book] addresses the dangers of smoking and chewing tobacco and of exposure to secondhand smoke, why young people use tobacco, and how numbers can be reduced. Primary-source quotes are well documented." SLJ

Includes bibliographical references

Porterfield, Jason

Doping; athletes and drugs; [by] Jason Porterfield. 1st ed. Rosen Pub. 2008 64p il (In the news) $29.95

Grades: 5 6 7 8   362.29

1. Steroids 2. Drug abuse 3. Athletes—Drug use

ISBN 978-1-4042-1917-5; 1-4042-1917-X

LC 2007015919

"Overview of the sports and sports figures most often connected with drug scandals, why athletes resort to drug use, the different types of drugs used for physical enhancement, and the methods used to police doping. . . . [This] short [volume is] packed full of information." Voice Youth Advocates

Includes glossary and bibliographical references

Powell, Jillian
Alcohol and drug abuse; by Jillian Powell; health consultant, John G. Samanich. Gareth Stevens Pub. 2009 48p il (Emotional health issues) lib bdg $31
Grades: 6 7 8 9   **362.29**
1. Alcoholism 2. Drug abuse
ISBN 978-0-8368-9199-7; 0-8368-9199-6
LC 2008-5459
First published 2008 in the United Kingdom
This book about alcohol and drug abuse has "clear language and explanations. . . . [It is] suitable for fact-finding missions, but the abundant graphics and case studies are likely to draw in browsers as well. Throughout, unfamiliar vocabulary is highlighted in bold and explained in context and in the glossary. . . . Fact boxes and case study sidebars add information." SLJ
Includes glossary and bibliographical references

Smoking; Laurie S. Friedman, book editor. Greenhaven Press 2006 126p il (Introducing issues with opposing viewpoints) lib bdg $32.45
Grades: 8 9 10 11 12   **362.29**
1. Smoking 2. Tobacco habit
ISBN 0-7377-3342-X   LC 2005-46140
"The articles in this anthology expose multiple sides of . . . [the smoking] debate." Publisher's note
Includes bibliographical references

Tobacco information for teens; edited by Karen Bellenir. Omnigraphics 2007 440p il (Teen health series) $65
Grades: 7 8 9 10 11 12   **362.29**
1. Smoking 2. Tobacco habit
ISBN 978-0-7808-0976-5; 0-7808-0976-9
LC 2006-37072
"Health tips about the hazards of using cigarettes, smokeless tobacco, and other nicotine products: including facts about nicotine addiction, immediate and long-term health effects of tobacco use, related cancers, smoking cessation, tobacco use prevention, and tobacco use statistics." Title page
"A comprehensive resource." SLJ
Includes bibliographical references

Warburton, Lianne
Amphetamines and other stimulants; [by] Lianne Warburton and Diana Callfas. Chelsea House 2008 120p il (Junior drug awareness) lib bdg $30
Grades: 6 7 8 9   **362.29**
1. Amphetamines 2. Stimulants 3. Drug abuse
ISBN 978-0-7910-9712-0 (lib bdg); 0-7910-9712-9 (lib bdg)   LC 2007018860
This "explores the science and history behind commonly used stimulants, and provides information about addiction and treatment options." Publisher's note
This "provides useful, balanced, and comprehensive information." Horn Book Guide
Includes glossary and bibliographical references

West, Krista
Cocaine and crack; [by] Krista West. Chelsea House Publishers 2008 119p il map (Junior drug awareness) lib bdg $30
Grades: 6 7 8 9   **362.29**
1. Cocaine 2. Crack (Drug) 3. Drug abuse
ISBN 978-0-7910-9704-5 (lib bdg); 0-7910-9704-8 (lib bdg)   LC 2007024971
This "examines how cocaine became an illegal drug after many years of legal use in commercial products, and explains why crack was formulated in the 1980s to make a cheaper and more powerful version of the addictive drug. Information about these drugs' effects on the body and mind and advice on how to overcome addiction to them are also included." Publisher's note
This "provides useful, balanced, and comprehensive information." Horn Book Guide
Includes glossary and bibliographical references

362.292   Alcohol

Alcoholism; James D. Torr, book editor. Greenhaven Press 2000 202p (Current controversies) lib bdg $33.70; pa $22.45
Grades: 8 9 10 11 12   **362.292**
1. Alcoholism
ISBN 0-7377-0139-0 (lib bdg); 0-7377-0138-2 (pa)
LC 99-37265
This "selection of primary source materials . . . is used to debate such topics as the effectiveness of Alcoholics Anonymous and the alcohol industry's responsibility for its marketing program. . . . A solid, invaluable resource on its subject." Booklist
Includes bibliographical references

Aretha, David
On the rocks; teens and alcohol; by David Aretha. Franklin Watts 2007 144p il pa $17.95
Grades: 6 7 8 9   **362.292**
1. Teenagers—Alcohol use 2. Alcoholism
ISBN 0-531-16792-5 (pa); 978-0-531-16792-2 (pa)
LC 2005024291
"Basic facts about drinking in America, teen usage, and warning signs of alcoholism are presented in this readable, unbiased text. The effects of alcoholism on families, the dangers of binge drinking, and the successes and failures of solutions and strategies to solve these issues are discussed." SLJ
Includes bibliographical references

Gottfried, Ted, 1928-
The facts about alcohol; [by] Ted Gottfried. Benchmark Books 2004 c2005 111p il (Drugs) lib bdg $$2.79; pa $6.99 *
Grades: 6 7 8 9   **362.292**
1. Drinking of alcoholic beverages 2. Alcoholism 3. Teenagers—Alcohol use
ISBN 978-0-7614-1805-4 (lib bdg); 0-7614-1805-9 (lib bdg); 978-0-7614-3587-7 (pa); 0-7614-3587-5 (pa)
LC 2004-5388
Contents: What's in a drink?; The noble experiment; Liquor: lobbies and laws; A problem in the family; Help, hope, and healing

Gottfried, Ted, 1928—*Continued*
The author "includes historical aspects of alcohol and society, including humans' first experimentations with fermentation, Prohibition, and the temperance movement; related laws and legislation; and definition, causes, treatment, and effects. . . . [This title has a] readable, well-organized [text], and good use of color, graphics, photographs, tables, diagrams, and labels helps to spark readers' interest." SLJ
Includes glossary and bibliographical references

Teen alcoholism; Laura K. Egendorf, book editor. Greenhaven Press 2001 138p (Contemporary issues companion) lib bdg $22.96; pa $14.96 *
Grades: 8 9 10 11 12   **362.292**
1. Teenagers—Alcohol use 2. Alcoholism
ISBN 0-7377-0683-X (lib bdg); 0-7377-0682-1 (pa)
LC 00-68181
A collection of essays on such topics as the risk factors of teen alcoholism, the effects of parental drinking, social pressures, and advertising on teen drinking, and the dangers of alcohol abuse
The editor includes "an entire chapter of personal essays from people who have actually struggled with teen alcoholism or seen effects on a friend or family member. This chapter alone is worth the entire volume. . . . The rest of the book, which includes charts and sometimes staggering facts, will help in standard research." Booklist
Includes bibliographical references

The **Truth** about alcohol; Mark J. Kittleson, general editor; William Kane, adviser; Richelle Rennegarbe, adviser; Barry Youngerman, principal author. Facts on File 2004 196p (Truth about series) $35
Grades: 8 9 10 11 1 2   **362.292**
1. Teenagers—Alcohol use 2. Alcoholism
ISBN 0-8160-5298-0   LC 2004-509
This discusses such topics as binge drinking, underage drinking, the prevalence of drinking on college campuses, drunken driving, dealing with alcohol abuse in the family, alcohol advertising and counter-advertising, and seeking help for an alcohol problem.
This title does "an excellent job of providing accurate information for teens. For reports or for self-help, [it belongs] in any library serving young adults." SLJ
Includes glossary and bibliographical references

362.3   Mental retardation

Libal, Autumn
My name is not Slow; youth with mental retardation. Mason Crest Publishers, Inc. 2004 127p il (Youth with special needs) $24.95
Grades: 7 8 9 10   **362.3**
1. Mental retardation 2. Down syndrome
ISBN 1-59084-731-8   LC 2003-18435
Through the story of Penelope, a girl growing up with Down's syndrome, this book discusses "mental retardation, the special needs of individuals living with this form of disability, and the support systems available to help people with mental retardation acquire independence and success." Publisher's note
Includes glossary and bibliographical references

362.4   Problems of and services to people with physical disabilities

Thornton, Denise, 1949-
Physical disabilities; the ultimate teen guide. Scarecrow Press 2007 162p il (It happened to me) $42
Grades: 7 8 9 10 11 12   **362.4**
1. Physically handicapped
ISBN 978-0-8108-5300-3; 0-8108-5300-0
LC 2006-29235
"Thornton interviewed hundreds of young people to help readers understand disabilities from a personal viewpoint. She divides this very broad subject into eight areas—school, technologies and tools, getting around, sports, the arts, relationships, independence, and advocacy. In each section, she includes personal stories plus essential information helpful to the disabled. . . . Well-organized and helpful." SLJ
Includes bibliographical references

362.5   Problems of and services to poor people

The **Homeless:** opposing viewpoints; Jennifer A. Hurley, book editor. Greenhaven Press 2002 186p lib bdg $34.95; pa $23.70
Grades: 8 9 10 11 1 2   **362.5**
1. Homeless persons
ISBN 0-7377-0750-X (lib bdg); 0-7377-0749-6 (pa)
LC 2001-23916
"Opposing viewpoints series"
Replaces the edition published 1995 under the editorship of Tamara L. Roleff
This collection of essays addresses the causes and seriousness of homelessness and possible remedies
Includes bibliographical references

Inner-city poverty; Tamara L. Roleff, book editor. Greenhaven Press 2002 176p (Contemporary issues companion) $22.45; pa $16.96
Grades: 8 9 10 11 12   **362.5**
1. Poverty 2. Poor—United States 3. Public welfare 4. Inner cities
ISBN 0-7377-0841-7; 0-7377-0840-9 (pa)
LC 2002-23639
"A number of writers contributed to this collection of articles about the severity of the urban poverty dilemma. All aspects of the problem are clearly presented. Proposed solutions are suggested. The effectiveness of these solutions in dealing with the urban poor is discussed. Several personal accounts shed illuminating perspectives on living the life of the inner city poor." Libr Media Connect
Includes bibliographical references

Kowalski, Kathiann M., 1955-
Poverty in America; causes and issues. Enslow Pubs. 2003 128p il (Issues in focus) lib bdg $26.60 *

Grades: 8 9 10 11 12 **362.5**
1. Poverty 2. Poor—United States
 ISBN 0-7660-1945-4 LC 2002-156034
 Contents: Unequal wealth; Who are the poor?; What has America done about poverty?; The war over welfare; Homelessness and housing issues; Help for low-income workers; The bigger picture
 Explores the issues of poverty in the United States through real-life stories of poor people and the agencies and organizations available to help them
 "Kowalski tackles a tough topic and makes balanced sense of it. . . . Well organized, this book provides fundamental information and perspectives for vital classroom discussion." SLJ
 Includes bibliographical references

Mason, Paul, 1967-
Poverty; [by] Paul Mason. Heinemann Library 2006 48p il map (Planet under pressure) lib bdg $31.43 *

Grades: 4 5 6 7 **362.5**
1. Poverty
 ISBN 1-4034-7743-4 LC 2005017166
 "Mason presents common factors for poverty worldwide, such as lack of money and education, as well as natural disasters. He also addresses the effects of outsourcing jobs from wealthier countries to poorer ones and how poverty affects environment. The book should make the global situation clearer. [This has] numerous quality color visuals, and sidebars. Up-to-date and informative." SLJ
 Includes bibliographical references

Poverty; David M. Haugen and Matthew J. Box, book editors. Greenhaven Press 2006 108p il (Social issues firsthand) lib bdg $28.70
 Grades: 8 9 10 11 12 **362.5**
1. Poverty 2. Poor—United States
 ISBN 0-7377-2899-X LC 2005-45120
 "Collecting intimate stories of individuals living in poverty and those helping them, this anthology includes personal narratives of poor people struggling to survive on little or no income, and also writings that convey the thoughts and deeds of people trying to alleviate the plight of the impoverished." Publisher's note
 These "16 accounts from poverty's gritty trenches evaporate easy assumptions about the poor, and reveal the obstacles faced by stricken individuals and families hampered by catch-22 social policies, entrenched racial inequities, and logistics such as cleaning up for an interview." Booklist
 Includes bibliographical references

Senker, Cath
Poverty; [by] Cath Senker. World Almanac Library 2007 48p il (What if we do nothing?) lib bdg $30.60; pa $11.95

Grades: 5 6 7 8 **362.5**
1. Poverty 2. Poor
 ISBN 978-0-8368-7757-1 (lib bdg); 978-0-8368-8157-8 (pa) LC 2006030447
 "After discussing patterns of poverty, each chapter raises specific 'What would you do?' questions, with brief suggested answers at the back of the book. Whether the issue is increased taxation of the wealthy, cancellation of unpayable debts, improving primary health care, or more, student activists will want to talk about it, and social-studies teachers will find this a strong curriculum title." Booklist
 Includes bibliographical references

362.7 Problems of and services to young people

Adoption; David M. Haugen and Matthew J. Box, book editors. Greenhaven Press 2005 108p (Social issues firsthand) lib bdg $28.70 *
 Grades: 8 9 10 11 12 **362.7**
1. Adoption
 ISBN 0-7377-2881-7 LC 2005-46075
 "The book explores such diverse issues as gay adoptive parents, open and transracial adoptions, the search for and reunion with birthparents, custody battles, and more. The editors have done an excellent job of selecting 16 lively, articulate, and poignant essays by birthparents, adoptive parents, and adoptees, all offering different perspectives on the process." SLJ
 Includes bibliographical references

Adoption: opposing viewpoints; Mary E. Williams, book editor. Greenhaven Press 2006 226p il lib bdg $34.95; pa $23.70
 Grades: 7 8 9 10 **362.7**
1. Adoption
 ISBN 0-7377-3301-2 (lib bdg); 978-0-7377-3301-3 (lib bdg); 0-7377-3302-0 (pa); 978-0-7377-3302-0 (pa)
  LC 2006-43350
 Replaces the edition published 2002 under the editorship of Roman Espejo
 "Opposing viewpoints series"
 This anthology addresses such topics as "whether adoption should be encouraged; conflicting views on transracial, international, and gay parent adoptions; whose rights are most in need of protection—adoptive or birth parents or those of adoptees; as well as what government policies should be implemented." SLJ
 Includes bibliographical references

Bode, Janet
Kids still having kids; talking about teen pregnancy; art by Stan Mack and Ida Marx Blue Spruce. rev ed. Watts 1999 159p il lib bdg $23; pa $9.95
 Grades: 8 9 10 11 12 **362.7**
1. Teenage pregnancy 2. Teenage mothers
 ISBN 0-531-11588-7 (lib bdg); 0-531-11593-6 (pa)
  LC 98-45477

Bode, Janet—*Continued*

First published 1992

Presents interviews with teenage mothers and provides information about adoption, parenting, abortion, and foster care

"Bode provides a valuable resource for young adults making decisions about pregnancy, as well as those researching the issue for school projects. . . . A lively design, which includes cartoon strips and snippets from current newspaper and magazine articles, adds to the dynamic presentation." Horn Book Guide

Includes bibliographical references

Child and youth security sourcebook; edited by Chad T. Kimball. Omnigraphics 2003 646p il (Security reference series) $68 *

Grades: 8 9 10 11 12   **362.7**

1. Safety education 2. Youth—Health and hygiene
3. School violence
ISBN 0-7808-0613-1   LC 2002-45010

This is an "examination of safety and security issues in the lives of children and teenagers geared toward parents, teachers, and students. . . . The nine sections discuss how to protect young people from school crime and violence, physical/sexual/emotional abuse and neglect, drug use and abuse, gangs, Internet sex offenders, and mental and emotional health risks. . . . This successful blend of clear writing, quality research, and meticulous attention to detail conveys much of the information through user-friendly outlines, checklists, and lists of key points. . . . An essential purchase for all libraries serving youth." SLJ

Includes bibliographical references

Dean, Ruth, 1947-

Teen prostitution; by Ruth Dean and Melissa Thomson. Lucent Bks. 1998 96p il (Teen issues) lib bdg $22.45 *

Grades: 7 8 9 10   **362.7**

1. Juvenile prostitution
ISBN 1-56006-512-5   LC 97-27452

Presents an overview of the problem of teenage prostitutes, including some of the causes and consequences of this phenomenon and what can be done to prevent it

Includes glossary and bibliographical references

Ellis, Deborah, 1960-

Our stories, our songs; African children talk about AIDS. Fitzhenry & Whiteside 2005 104p il $18.95

Grades: 6 7 8 9   **362.7**

1. AIDS (Disease) 2. Orphans 3. Tanzania 4. Malawi
ISBN 1-55041-913-7

"In the summer of 2003, Ellis traveled to Malawi and Zambia and met with children and teens whose lives have been touched by AIDS. In short, autobiographical vignettes, the young people, many of whom are orphans or living on the street, discuss their families, their favorite pastimes, their fears, and their dreams. . . . Ellis presents the stories in a matter-of-fact and compassionate manner that maintains the children's dignity. . . . An impressive offering whose chilling accounts remain with readers long after the book is finished." SLJ

Gordon, Sherri Mabry

Beyond bruises; the truth about teens and abuse. Enslow 2009 128p il (Issues in focus today) lib bdg $31.93

Grades: 7 8 9 10   **362.7**

1. Child abuse 2. Domestic violence 3. Date rape
4. Invective
ISBN 978-0-7660-3064-0; 0-7660-3064-4
       LC 2008-12273

"Discusses the various types of abuse teenagers face, including both domestic and dating abuse, the impact abuse has on teens, and several ways to help teens who suffer from some form of abuse." Publisher's note

"Bolstered with well-integrated quotes and relevant statistics, [this book offers] an excellent starting point for students seeking [a] broad, thoroughly researched [introduction] to [the issue of abuse]. . . . Illuminating case studies, enhanced with multiple viewpoints, personalize the facts and place them in broader context." Booklist

Includes glossary and bibliographical references

Hurley, Jennifer A., 1973-

Teen pregnancy. Greenhaven Press 2000 96p il (Opposing viewpoints digests) lib bdg $28.70; pa $18.70 *

Grades: 8 9 10 11 12   **362.7**

1. Teenage pregnancy
ISBN 0-7377-0366-0 (lib bdg); 0-7377-0365-2 (pa)
       LC 00-37135

Examines the differing viewpoints on issues related to teen pregnancy, including factors that contribute to this problem, its effects on teenagers' lives, and possible ways to prevent teen pregnancy

"Debaters will find this a useful tool, both for its concise summations of differing views, and its occasional inclusion of an unpopular viewpoint." Booklist

Includes bibliographical references

Hynson, Colin

Living on the street; Hamilton's story; [by] Colin Hynson. World Almanac Library 2006 48p il (Children in crisis) lib bdg $30

Grades: 6 7 8 9   **362.7**

1. Homeless persons 2. Brazil
ISBN 0-8368-5961-8   LC 2005047521

This is the story of a homeless boy in Rio, Brazil named Hamilton Correia Rodrigues

"The material is basically accurate, clearly written, and thought provoking." SLJ

Includes bibliographical references

Jocelyn, Marthe, 1956-

A home for foundlings. Tundra Books 2005 128p il pa $15.95

Grades: 7 8 9 10   **362.7**

1. Foundling Hospital (London, England)
2. Abandoned children
ISBN 0-88776-709-5

"A Lord Museum book"

"Published in cooperation with Foundling Museum and LORD Cultural Resources Planning and Management."

Jocelyn, Marthe, 1956-—*Continued*
A "history of Foundling Hospital, a London orphanage that took in more than 27,000 children from the time it was established in the eighteenth century as a home for abandoned babies." Booklist
"Black-and-white reproductions of early admission documents and ledgers as well as period photographs and engravings appear throughout. This is a useful resource." SLJ

Kaminker, Laura
Everything you need to know about being adopted. Rosen Pub. Group 1999 64p il (Need to know library) $23.95
Grades: 7 8 9 10   362.7
1. Adoption
ISBN 0-8239-2834-9   LC 98-45629
"Kaminker gives legal facts about adoption and brings up many of the problems adolescent adoptees face. . . . The author's suggestions are sensible." SLJ
Includes glossary and bibliographical references

Kim, Henny H., 1968-
Child abuse. Greenhaven Press 2000 144p il (Opposing viewpoints digests) lib bdg $28.70; pa $18.70
Grades: 8 9 10 11 12   362.7
1. Child abuse
ISBN 1-56510-867-1 (lib bdg); 1-56510-866-3 (pa)
                                       LC 99-47464
Presents differing views on various aspects of the topic of child abuse, including defining what child abuse is, the seriousness of the problem, and ways to handle and prevent it
Includes bibliographical references

Lanchon, Anne
All about adoption; how to deal with the questions of your past; illustrated by Monike Czarnecki; edited by Tucker Shaw. Abrams/Amulet 2006 104p il (Sunscreen) pa $9.95
Grades: 7 8 9 10   362.7
1. Adoption
ISBN 0-8109-9227-2
"This guide covers an adopted child's traditional worries and concerns, such as establishing identity and living with overprotective parents. It also addresses such squirm-worthy issues as the fear of abandonment, racist comments, and discussing birth parents with adoptive parents. . . . Originally published in France, this handsomely designed self-help title . . . provides practical advice and reassurance for adopted teens and their families." Booklist
Includes bibliographical references

McAlpine, Margaret
Working with children. Gareth Stevens Pub 2005 64p il (My future career) lib bdg $26
Grades: 6 7 8 9   362.7
1. Child care 2. Teaching 3. Child development 4. Vocational guidance
ISBN 0-8368-4241-3   LC 2004-45226

This describes seven occupations related to children, including a description of the job and the responsibilities, qualifications, and best personality type for each one.
"The writing is clear and interesting, and the [book is] visually well organized." SLJ
Includes bibliographical references

Medina, Sarah, 1960-
Abuse and neglect; by Sarah Medina; health consultant, John G. Samanich. G. Stevens Pub. 2009 48p il (Emotional health issues) lib bdg $31
Grades: 6 7 8 9   362.7
1. Child abuse 2. Child sexual abuse
ISBN 978-0-8368-9198-0 (lib bdg); 0-8368-9198-8 (lib bdg)   LC 2008-5458
First published 2008 in the United Kingdom
This book about abuse has "clear language and explanations. . . . [It is] suitable for fact-finding missions, but the abundant graphics and case studies are likely to draw in browsers as well. Throughout, unfamiliar vocabulary is highlighted in bold and explained in context and in the glossary. . . . Fact boxes and case study sidebars add information." SLJ
Includes glossary and bibliographical references

Pregnancy; William Dudley, book editor. Greenhaven Press 2001 191p il (Teen decisions) lib bdg $33.70; pa $22.45
Grades: 7 8 9 10   362.7
1. Teenage pregnancy 2. Youth—Sexual behavior
ISBN 0-7377-0492-6 (lib bdg); 0-7377-0491-8 (pa)
                                       LC 00-32162
"This volume features the stories of teens who chose adoption, abortion, or parenthood, and the advice they offer to others." Publisher's note
Includes bibliographical references

Reef, Catherine
Alone in the world; orphans and orphanages in America; by Catherine Reef. Clarion Books 2005 135p il $18
Grades: 6 7 8 9   362.7
1. Orphanages 2. Orphans
ISBN 0-618-35670-3   LC 2004-20179
Contents: Thrown upon the world; Asylum children; Saving youthful hearts; Let society beware!; Soldiers' orphans; Everyone's business; This army of children; Afterword: where life led some of the children who appeared in this book
This is a history of orphanages "in the U.S. beginning in 1729, when a place for girls was founded in New Orleans. . . . [The author] ends with a discussion of the challenges the U.S. faces today in caring for growing numbers of homeless, abused, or neglected children. Illustrated with archival photographs and reproductions." SLJ
Includes bibliographical references

Strong at the heart; how it feels to heal from sexual abuse; [compiled] by Carolyn Lehman. Farrar, Straus & Giroux 2005 156p il $18 *
Grades: 8 9 10 11 12   362.7
1. Child sexual abuse 2. Incest 3. Rape
ISBN 0-374-37282-9   LC 2004-56280

Strong at the heart—*Continued*

"Melanie Kroupa Books"

This "gathers 11 personal stories by young men and women who experienced rape, molestation, or incest and found healing through speaking out about their abuse. . . . Clearly and candidly written, the narratives recounted here include sufficient details of abuse to be authentic, but never titillating. . . . An attractive, accessible format and black-and-white portraits throughout personalize the presentation." SLJ

Teens at risk: opposing viewpoints; Laura K. Egendorf, book editor; Jennifer A. Hurley, book editor. Greenhaven Press 1999 190p il lib bdg $31.20; pa $19.95

Grades: 8 9 10 11 12   **362.7**

1. Teenagers

ISBN 1-56510-949-X (lib bdg); 1-56510-948-1 (pa)

LC 98-23191

"Opposing viewpoints series"

This collection of articles presents differing viewpoints about the causes, possible prevention, and remedies for such problems as teenage crime, pregnancy, and drug use

Includes bibliographical references

Veladota, Christina

Teen runaways; by Christina Veladota. Lucent Books 2004 112p il (Teen issues) $28.70

Grades: 7 8 9 10   **362.7**

1. Runaway teenagers

ISBN 1-56006-780-2   LC 2003-2057

Contents: Who runs away and why do they run?; Life on the streets; Runaways face serious health risks; Runaways and the law; Help for runaways; Alternatives and prevention

"Who are teen runaways and why do they run? What risks do they face on the streets? What happens to runaways when the law gets involved? These questions, along with facts about prevention and alternatives to running away, are explored." Publisher's note

Includes bibliographical references

Warren, Andrea

Orphan train rider; one boy's true story. Houghton Mifflin 1996 80p il hardcover o.p. pa $7.95

Grades: 4 5 6 7   **362.7**

1. Nailling, Lee, 1917- 2. Orphans 3. Adoption

ISBN 0-395-69822-7; 0-395-91362-4 (pa)

LC 94-43688

"From 1854 to 1930, the orphan trains took homeless children from cities in the East to new homes in the West, the Midwest, and the South. In Warren's book, one man's memories of his childhood abandonment and adoption give a personal slant on the subject. Chapters telling the story of Lee Nailing, who took an orphan train west in 1926, alternate with chapters filling in background information about the trains and the experiences of other children who rode them to their destinies." Booklist

"An excellent introduction to researching or discussing children-at-risk in an earlier generation. The book is clearly written and illustrated with numerous black-and-white photographs and reproductions." SLJ

Includes bibliographical references

We rode the orphan trains. Houghton Mifflin 2001 132p il $18; pa $8.95

Grades: 4 5 6 7   **362.7**

1. Orphans

ISBN 0-618-11712-1; 0-618-11712-1 (pa)

LC 00-47279

The author "interviews eight orphan train riders concerning their childhood experiences during 'the largest children's migration in history' between 1854 and 1929 as part of a 'placing out' program run by the Children's Aid Society of New York City." Publ Wkly

"This is powerful nonfiction for classroom and personal reading and for discussion." Booklist

Includes bibliographical references

Weiss, Ann E., 1943-

Adoptions today; questions and controversies. 21st Cent. Bks. (Brookfield) 2001 144p il lib bdg $24.90

Grades: 7 8 9 10   **362.7**

1. Adoption

ISBN 0-7613-1914-X   LC 00-53633

"Following a brief history of adoption, Weiss discusses nontraditional adoption (interracial, interfaith, gay and lesbian), international adoption, and changing attitudes on such aspects as open adoption and searches for birth parents. Her perspective on adoption is overwhelmingly positive . . . but she does offer information on the adoption black market and the problems of Internet adoptions." Booklist

Includes bibliographical references

362.82   Problems of and services to families

Battered women; Lane E. Volpe, book editor. Greenhaven Press 2004 138p (Contemporary issues companion) hardcover o.p. pa $22.45

Grades: 8 9 10 11 12   **362.82**

1. Domestic violence 2. Abused women

ISBN 0-7377-1617-7; 0-7377-1618-5 (pa)

LC 2003-56877

Replaces the edition published 1999 under the editorship of Louise Gerdes

"Contributors to this . . . anthology investigate the nature of domestic violence and examine various measures that can protect battered women. Personal profiles of individuals whose lives have been touched by domestic violence round out this look at a disturbing but important issue." Publisher's note

Includes bibliographical references

Domestic violence: opposing viewpoints; David M. Haugen, book editor. Greenhaven Press 2005 186p il lib bdg $33.70; pa $22.45 *

Grades: 8 9 10 11 12   **362.82**

1. Domestic violence

ISBN 0-7377-2224-X (lib bdg); 0-7377-2225-8 (pa)

LC 2004-41168

Replaces the 2000 edition under the editorship of Tamara L. Roleff

"Opposing viewpoints series"

Domestic violence: opposing viewpoints—*Continued*

"This volume examines the prevalence of domestic violence in America, its causes, and its remedies." Publisher's note

Includes bibliographical references

Family violence; J. D. Lloyd, book editor. Greenhaven Press 2000 138p (Current controversies) lib bdg $33.70; pa $22.45
Grades: 8 9 10 11 12   **362.82**
1. Domestic violence
ISBN 0-7377-0452-7 (lib bdg); 0-7377-0451-9 (pa)
LC 00-27984

This "title examines violence in the home, mainly against spouses and children, but also against the elderly and gay and lesbian partners. . . . The 19 selections, mainly magazine articles and book excerpts . . . do justice to the complexity of the issues. A helpful resource for students." Booklist

362.87   Problems of and services to victims of oppression

Gay, Kathlyn, 1930-
Leaving Cuba; from Operation Pedro Pan to Elian. 21st Cent. Bks. (Brookfield) 2000 144p il maps lib bdg $24.90
Grades: 7 8 9 10   **362.87**
1. Cuban Americans 2. Cuban refugees
ISBN 0-7613-1466-0   LC 99-462149

Considers the various ways children have escaped from Communist Cuba and found refuge in the United States through different plans set up to help them, from the early 1960s to the present

The author "uses biographical sketches to put a human face on the agonies of family separation as well as the readjustment to life in a new country and culture. The book concludes with an unbiased reporting of the Elian Gonzalez case." SLJ

Includes bibliographical references

362.88   Problems of and services to victims of crimes

Bode, Janet
Voices of rape. rev ed. Watts 1998 160p il lib bdg $25; pa $9.95 *
Grades: 8 9 10 11 12   **362.88**
1. Rape
ISBN 0-531-11518-6; 0-531-15932-9 (0a)
LC 97-41225

First published 1990

This volume includes "first-person accounts by rape victims, counselors, health-care providers, law-enforcement officials, and offenders. . . . The author offers her interviewees' statements with little editorial comment. . . . While valuable information is provided in addition to the interviews (sections on crisis centers and emergency-room procedures are particularly noteworthy),

it is the words of the people directly involved that carry the greatest power." SLJ

Includes bibliographical references

Faherty, Sara
Victims and victims' rights. Chelsea House 1999 111p il (Crime, justice, and punishment) lib bdg $19.95
Grades: 7 8 9 10   **362.88**
1. Victims of crimes
ISBN 0-7910-4308-8   LC 98-36531

Explores victims and victims' rights from various perspectives, including the psychological consequences of victimization, the divergent responses of victims seeking justice and emotional healing, and the tension between granting the wishes of victims and protecting the rights of criminal defendants

Includes bibliographical references

Landau, Elaine
Date violence; [by] Elaine Landau. Franklin Watts 2004 80p (Life balance) $20.50; pa $6.95 *
Grades: 5 6 7 8   **362.88**
1. Dating (Social customs) 2. Date rape 3. Violence
ISBN 0-531-12214-X; 0-531-16613-9 (pa)
LC 2003-19480

Contetnts: When love turns ugly; A pattern of abuse; Date rape; Surviving date violence

"Landau helps those who are new to dating to distinguish between healthy and unhealthy relationships by providing understandable warning signs of emotional, physical, and sexual abuse. . . . This book will help young people make informed decisions and more wisely navigate the emotionally charged, confusing issues associated with adolescent relationships." SLJ

Includes glossary and bibliographical references

363.1   Public safety programs

Bennie, Paul
The great Chicago fire of 1871; [by] Paul Bennie. Chelsea House 2008 128p il (Great historic disasters) $35
Grades: 7 8 9 10   **363.1**
1. Fires—Chicago (Ill.)
ISBN 978-0-7910-9638-3; 0-7910-9638-6
LC 2007-36550

"On October 8, 1871, a fire started in the O'Learys' barn in Chicago. . . . [This occurence] brought about lasting changes in fire prevention and building codes. . . . [This book], which [describes] the [disaster] and [its] aftermath in detail, [is] well written and informative. . . . [This is] first-rate for reports and general browsing." SLJ

Includes bibliographical references

Drunk driving; Christine Van Tuyl, book editor. Greenhaven Press 2007 136p il map (Issues that concern you) $32.45
Grades: 8 9 10 11 12   **363.1**

Drunk driving—*Continued*
1. Drunk driving
ISBN 0-7377-3239-3

A selection of "articles, culled from periodicals as disparate as *The FBI Law Enforcement Bulletin, The Wall Street Journal,* and *Traffic Safety Facts,* debate issues surrounding drunk driving, such as setting a legal drinking age and determining blood-alcohol levels, effectively addressing the problems as well as the moral and legal questions surrounding the apprehension and punishment of drunk drivers. Clearly presented and organized and illustrated with photos and charts, this useful title should be a staple in YA collections." Booklist

Lace, William W.
The Hindenburg disaster of 1937. Chelsea House Publishers 2008 120p il (Great historic disasters) lib bdg $35
Grades: 6 7 8 9 10   **363.1**
1. Hindenburg (Airship) 2. Aircraft accidents
ISBN 978-0-7910-9739-7; 0-7910-9739-0
                 LC 2008004890
On May 6, 1937, the celebrated airship Hindenburg caught fire during its landing in Lakehurst, New Jersey, killing 36 people. This describes the disaster and its aftermath.

The book covers its topic "thoroughly and [includes] high-quality photographs and occasional sidebars. Lace's account of the airship has a good deal of intrigue and drama and could be useful for reports or recreational reading." SLJ
Includes glossary and bibliographical references

Mayell, Mark
Tragedies of space exploration. Lucent Books 2004 112p il (Manmade disasters) $27.45
Grades: 5 6 7 8   **363.1**
1. Space vehicle accidents 2. Astronautics
ISBN 1-59018-508-0   LC 2003-15618
Contents: Into the dead zone; A pair of shuttle disasters; Rescue efforts; Challenging investigations; Preventing future accidents
Analyzes the inherent risks and dangers of human space exploration, from those that affect the health of astronauts to those that result in shuttle explosions, and examines ways of reducing safety-related incidents.
"Behind-the-headlines details are fresh and thought-provoking. . . . Halftone photographs and clear drawings speak to the reality of these events. . . . [This is] rich in content and detail." SLJ
Includes bibliographical references

Mintzer, Richard
The National Transportation Safety Board; {by} Rich Mintzer. Chelsea House 2002 64p il (Your government—how it works) lib bdg $20.75
Grades: 6 7 8 9   **363.1**
1. United States. National Transportation Safety Board 2. Traffic accidents
ISBN 0-7910-6794-7   LC 2002-44
Contents: The early growth of transportation in America; The need for safer transportation; The National

Transportation Safety Board: how it works; Investigating accidents: the go-team; Investigating Flight 587; Making safety recommendations; Safety concerns of the future
Describes the workings and history of the National Transportation Safety Board as part of the United States government, including how it investigates transportation accidents and makes safety recommendations
Includes glossary and bibliographical references

Vogt, Gregory
Disasters in space exploration; [[by] Gregory L. Vogt. rev ed. Millbrook Press 2003 79p il lib bdg $25.90
Grades: 6 7 8 9   **363.1**
1. Space vehicle accidents
ISBN 0-7613-2895-5   LC 2003-10864
First published 2001
Examines the failed missions, accidents, and destroyed vehicles of various world space programs, including the explosion of the space shuttle Columbia in 2003
"The writing is interesting and succinct without leaving out any of the details. Brimming with clearly reproduced full-color and black-and-white photographs." SLJ
Includes bibliographical references

363.2   Police services

Allman, Toney, 1947-
The medical examiner. Gale 2006 104p il (Crime scene investigations) lib bdg $31.20 *
Grades: 7 8 9 10   **363.2**
1. Forensic sciences 2. Medical jurisprudence
ISBN 1-59018-912-4
Contents: At the death scene; Autopsy; Poison, blood, and DNA; Decomposition; Getting the story right
Discusses what medical examiners do.
This "book has fascinating, factual information and quotes taken from interviews with professionals. . . . [This] well-organized [title has] clear subheadings, tables of statistics, and well-chosen color photos." SLJ

Bell, Suzanne
Encyclopedia of forensic science; foreword by Barry A.J. Fisher; preface by Robert C. Shaler. rev ed. Facts on File 2008 402p il (Facts on File science library) $85
Grades: 8 9 10 11 12 Adult   **363.2**
1. Forensic sciences—Encyclopedias 2. Reference books
ISBN 978-0-8160-6799-2; 0-8160-6799-6
                 LC 2008-5862
First published 2003
"In addition to explaining the science of forensics, Bell . . . reviews various disciplines related to forensic science, among them entomology, odontology, and psychology. Other entries cover professional organizations, government agencies, famous names in the field of forensics, evidence, and legal issues. . . . With its clear language and brief entries [this] volume will provide readers with a nuts-and-bolts understanding of the real world of forensic science." Booklist [review of 2003 edition]
Includes bibliographical references

Bell, Suzanne—*Continued*

Fakes and forgeries. Facts On File 2008 108p il (Essentials of forensic science) $35
Grades: 7 8 9 10 11 12   **363.2**
1. Forgery 2. Fraud
ISBN 978-0-8160-5514-2; 0-8160-5514-9
LC 2008-4502

This is a "fascinating introduction to how scientists identify fraudulent copies, from signatures to oil paintings. . . . Bell moves from examples of the crime that date back to ancient Mesopotamian civilizations all the way through to today's high-tech counterfeiting cases." Booklist

Includes glossary and bibliographical references

Denega, Danielle, 1978-

Gut-eating bugs; maggots reveal the time of death! by Danielle Denega. Franklin Watts 2007 64p il map (24/7, science behind the scenes) $26
Grades: 5 6 7 8   **363.2**
1. Forensic sciences 2. Death 3. Insects 4. Criminal investigation
ISBN 0-531-11824-X; 978-0-531-11824-5
LC 2006020871

"Denega shows how forensic entomologists use insect evidence to narrow down the times of criminal and other deaths. . . . [This] will both rivet and inform true-crime fans." SLJ

Includes glossary and bibliographical references

Have you seen this face? the work of forensic artists; [by] Danielle Denega. Franklin Watts 2007 64p il map (24/7, science behind the scenes) lib bdg $26; pa $7.95
Grades: 5 6 7 8   **363.2**
1. Drawing 2. Forensic sciences 3. Criminal investigation
ISBN 978-0-531-11823-8 (lib bdg); 0-531-11823-1 (lib bdg); 978-0-531-15458-8 (pa); 0-531-15458-0 (pa)
LC 2006020870

"A forensic artist uses her talent to construct a lifelike replica of a murder victim found in New York. This book focuses on the process of reconstruction. . . . Further sections highlight important advances in forensic art such as the introduction of computers to the field and offer examples of how forensic artists can use their skills." Voice Youth Advocates

"Concise and interesting." SLJ

Includes glossary and bibliographical references

Skulls and skeletons; true life stories of bone detectives. Franklin Watts 2007 64p il map (24/7: Science behind the scenes) lib bdg $26; pa $7.95
Grades: 6 7 8 9   **363.2**
1. Forensic anthropology 2. Forensic sciences
ISBN 978-0-531-12064-4 (lib bdg); 0-531-12064-3 (lib bdg); 978-0-531-17527-9 (pa); 0-531-17527-8 (pa)
LC 2006-21229

Explains how forensic anthropologists figure out a victim's profile and examines three case studies in which forensic anthropologists help identify the victims.

Includes glossary and bibliographical references

Fridell, Ron, 1943-

Forensic science. Lerner Publications Co. 2007 48p il (Cool science) lib bdg $26.60
Grades: 4 5 6 7   **363.2**
1. Forensic sciences 2. Criminal investigation
ISBN 978-0-8225-5935-1 (lib bdg); 0-8225-5935-8 (lib bdg)
LC 2005-33039

This is a "history of forensic science, from its beginnings in 1910 through the present. Examples of investigations abound and are brought to life by photos. Most riveting are the descriptions of professionals involved in a murder case, including a medical examiner who dissects corpses and a forensic entomologist who examines dead flesh." SLJ

Includes bibliographical references

Gardner, Robert, 1929-

Forensic science projects with a crime lab you can build; [by] Robert Gardner. Enslow Publishers 2007 c2008 128p il (Build-a-lab! science experiments) $23.95
Grades: 6 7 8 9   **363.2**
1. Forensic sciences 2. Criminal investigation 3. Science projects
ISBN 978-0-7660-2806-7; 0-7660-2806-2
LC 2006039026

Describes how to build a crime lab out of everyday materials so that things like fingerprints and handwriting can be analyzed.

"Gardner creatively handles the challenging task of assembling activities that connect strongly with his often grisly theme. . . . While the forensics information will draw students' interest, the potential dangers may lead some recommenders to set this aside for use in classrooms, where adult supervision can be ensured." Booklist

Includes bibliographical references

Harris, Elizabeth Snoke, 1973-

Crime scene science fair projects. Lark Books 2006 112p il $25.95 *
Grades: 6 7 8 9 10   **363.2**
1. Forensic sciences 2. Criminal investigation 3. Science projects
ISBN 1-57990-765-2   LC 2006-16803

"Harris begins with an explanation of forensic science and how it's applied in the everyday world, followed by a discussion of how to plan for a successful project. The projects involve lie detection, lifting fingerprints, recovering data from burned documents, and so on. . . . The author's concise, lively style will even engage students who aren't fond of reading nonfiction." SLJ

Hunter, William, 1971-

DNA analysis. Mason Crest Publishers 2006 112p il (Forensics, the science of crime-solving) $22.95
Grades: 7 8 9 10   **363.2**
1. Forensic sciences 2. DNA fingerprinting 3. Medical jurisprudence
ISBN 978-1-4222-0026-1; 1-4222-0026-4
LC 2005-10082

Hunter, William, 1971-—*Continued*

Introduces DNA and DNA profiling, examines how investigators collect genetic evidence, and discusses how DNA has altered crime-solving.

"The text is interspersed with examples of how . . . [DNA analysis] . . . is used to solve criminal and civil cases. The layout is appealing, with colorful photographs or illustrations on nearly every page." Libr Media Connect

Includes glossary and bibliographical references

Innes, Brian, 1928-

DNA and body evidence. Sharpe Focus 2008 96p il (Forensic evidence) $39.95

Grades: 7 8 9 10 11 12   **363.2**

1. DNA fingerprinting 2. Forensic sciences 3. Criminal investigation

ISBN 978-0-7656-8115-7   LC 2007-6749

This "book begins with the history of DNA and fluid analysis, continues with DNA fingerprinting and gathering evidence, and highlights landmark usage of DNA evidence as well as its routine uses in both the judicial and penal systems. . . . The [book is] comprehensive enough for students with prior knowledge of forensics but approachable for beginners. . . . [It weaves] technical terms and anecdotal evidence into a seamless presentation." SLJ

Includes glossary and bibliographical references

Fingerprints and impressions. Sharpe Focus 2008 96p il (Forensic evidence) $39.95

Grades: 7 8 9 10 11 12   **363.2**

1. Fingerprints 2. Criminal investigation 3. Forensic sciences

ISBN 978-0-7656-8114-0   LC 2007-6751

This "covers the origins of fingerprinting and the analysis and usage of fingerprinting data and concludes with its use as admissible evidence in court. . . . [The book is] comprehensive enough for students with prior knowledge of forensics but approachable for beginners. . . . [It weaves] technical terms and anecdotal evidence into a seamless presentation." SLJ

Includes glossary and bibliographical references

Forensic science. Mason Crest Publs. 2003 96p il (Crime and detection) lib bdg $22.95

Grades: 7 8 9 10   **363.2**

1. Forensic sciences 2. Criminal investigation

ISBN 1-59084-373-8   LC 2003-479

Contents: Every contact leaves a trace; Finger of fate; Deadly poison; Telltale blood; The smoking gun; Fragments of evidence

"The minute details of crime-scene investigation and painstaking laboratory examination of evidence are described. . . . The large format allows clear views of fingerprinting, bloody footprints, and police examining the scene of a bombing. The features that separate this treatment from earlier titles . . . are the abundance of color photographs and the international scope. . . . This is a detailed and thorough package." SLJ

Includes bibliographical references

Joyce, Jaime, 1971-

Bullet proof! the evidence that guns leave behind; [by] Jaime Joyce. Franklin Watts 2007 64p il map (24/7, science behind the scenes) lib bdg $26; pa $7.95

Grades: 5 6 7 8   **363.2**

1. Forensic sciences 2. Firearms 3. Criminal investigation

ISBN 0-531-11820-7 (lib bdg); 978-0-531-11820-7 (lib bdg); 0-531-15455-6 (pa); 978-0-531-15455-7 (pa)

LC 2006005718

"Joyce explores the field of forensic firearms analysis, including the facts and figures behind the science of ballistics, real-life case studies of historical and contemporary crimes involving gun violence, and information for young people interested in pursuing ballistics as a career path. . . . Photographs, sidebars, maps, and other graphic elements are used liberally to enliven and build upon the narrative." SLJ

Includes glossary and bibliographical references

Kops, Deborah

Racial profiling. Marshall Cavendish Benchmark 2006 127p il (Open for debate) lib bdg $39.93 *

Grades: 7 8 9 10   **363.2**

1. Racial profiling 2. Law enforcement

ISBN 978-0-7614-2298-3; 0-7614-2298-6

"Focuses on the debate surrounding racial profiling in the United States—including a historial look at criminal profiles and U.S. government intitiatives like Japanese-American internment during World War II through to the modern anti-terrorist age—through scholarly opinions, statistics, and studies." Publisher's note

This is "well organized and . . . clearly and plainly written." SLJ

Includes bibliographical references

Owen, David, 1939-

Police lab; how forensic science tracks down and convicts criminals. Firefly Bks. 2002 128p il $19.95; pa $9.95

Grades: 7 8 9 10   **363.2**

1. Forensic sciences 2. Criminal investigation

ISBN 1-55297-620-3; 1-55297-619-X (pa)

LC 2002-512986

The author explains "how forensics experts gather, analyze, and assess data on forgery, poisoning, suicides, explosions, and murder by fire, water, suffocation, and various weapons. Detailed descriptions of the forensics process are always put into historical context, with brief, gripping summaries of many famous cases and historical events. . . . An exciting, enlightening read." Booklist

Includes glossary

Platt, Richard, 1953-

Crime scene; the ultimate guide to forensic science. DK Publishing 2003 144p il $25; pa $16.95

Grades: 8 9 10 11 12   **363.2**

1. Forensic sciences 2. Criminal investigation

ISBN 0-7894-8891-4; 0-7566-1896-7 (pa)

LC 2003-271170

Platt, Richard, 1953-—*Continued*

"Techniques such as fingerprint analysis, shoe prints and tire tracks, tool marks and fabric prints, insect analysis, nuclear and mitochondrial DNA evidence, and other tools used by scene-of-the crime investigators are described; details of the collaborative roles of the medical examiner, law enforcement officers, and officers of the court are also included." Sci Books Films

"This is a solid, thorough, well-organized, and beautifully illustrated treatment of the subject of forensic science . . . This book would be invaluable for law classes and reports, as well as for mystery readers and writers." Libr Media Connect

Forensics. Kingfisher 2005 63p il (Kingfisher knowledge) $12.95

Grades: 5 6 7 8   **363.2**
    1. Forensic sciences 2. Criminal investigation
    ISBN 0-7534-5862-4

"This book looks at the . . . topic of collecting and analyzing evidence. Each spread focuses on a subtopic under the categories Signs of the Crime, Who Is It? and Crime Lab. Abundant, closeup color photographs illustrate everything from ballistics to counterfeit money. . . . This visually appealing book gives a basic overview of everything that goes into investigating a crime and is good for browsing." SLJ

Includes glossary

Police brutality: opposing viewpoints; Helen Cothran, book editor. Greenhaven Press 2001 154p il lib bdg $34.95; pa $23.70

Grades: 8 9 10 11 12   **363.2**
    1. Police brutality 2. Race discrimination
    ISBN 0-7377-0516-7 (lib bdg); 0-7377-0515-9 (pa)
                                        LC 00-32996

"Opposing viewpoints series"

"Citing examples overwhelmingly from Los Angeles and New York City, the various contributors to this volume . . . argue heatedly about issues concerning police brutality, especially in relation to alleged abuse of teen suspects. Four chapters explore whether or not police misconduct truly is a serious problem, what factors cause police brutality, whether modern police methods cause police misconduct, and who should police the police." Booklist

Includes bibliographical references

Rainis, Kenneth G.

Blood & DNA evidence; crime-solving science experiments; science consultant, Brian Gestring. Enslow Publishers 2006 104p il (Forensic science projects) lib bdg $31.93 *

Grades: 7 8 9 10   **363.2**
    1. Forensic sciences 2. DNA fingerprinting
    ISBN 0-7660-1958-6   LC 2005029214

This "invites readers to complete scientific experiments that emulate the solution to actual murders. . . . Following each real-life scenario, the book provides a checklist of materials and a step-by-step experiment to get the same results as the detectives. . . . The format is easy to follow, the scenarios intriguing, and the experiments complex enough for real science buffs to feel challenged." Booklist

Includes glossary and bibliographical references

Fingerprints; crime-solving science experiments. Enslow Publishers, Inc. 2006 128p il (Forensic science projects) lib bdg $31.93 *

Grades: 7 8 9 10   **363.2**
    1. Fingerprints 2. Forensic sciences
    ISBN 0-7660-1960-8   LC 2005036760

This describes how fingerprints are used in solving crimes and offers activities.

Includes glossary and bibliographical references

Forgery; crime-solving science experiments. Enslow Pub, Inc. 2006 128p il (Forensic science projects) lib bdg $31.93 *

Grades: 7 8 9 10   **363.2**
    1. Forgery 2. Forensic sciences
    ISBN 0-7660-1961-6   LC 2005029212

This describes how forgeries are detected and offers activities

Includes glossary and bibliographical references

Hair, clothing and tire track evidence; crime-solving science experiments; [by] Kenneth G. Rainis. Enslow Publishers, Inc. 2006 128p il (Forensic science projects) lib bdg $31.93 *

Grades: 7 8 9 10   **363.2**
    1. Forensic sciences
    ISBN 0-7660-2729-5   LC 2005037399

This describes how hair, clothing and tire tracks are used in solving crimes and offers activities in forensic science.

Includes glossary and bibliographical references

Stewart, Gail, 1949-

Bombings; by Gail B. Stewart. Thomson/Gale 2006 104p il (Crime scene investigations series) $28.70

Grades: 7 8 9 10   **363.2**
    1. Bombings 2. Criminal investigation
    ISBN 1-59018-620-6   LC 2005026125

An examination of criminal investigations of bombings.

This scrutinizes "current, highly publicized criminal cases that young readers will recognize. . . . Case studies are accompanied by actual, clearly labeled, color case photos showing just enough to fascinate the reader without unneeded gore." Voice Youth Advocates

Includes bibliographical references

Police brutality; by Gail B. Stewart. Lucent Books 2005 112p il (Lucent overview series) $28.70 *

Grades: 7 8 9 10   **363.2**
    1. Police brutality
    ISBN 1-59018-190-5   LC 2004-21489

Contents: Introduction; The crossed line; What causes police brutality?; The undercurrent of racism; The effects of police brutality; Tackling the problem

This discusses the use of force by police, the causes and effects of police brutality, racism and the police, and possible solutions to the problem.

Includes bibliographical references

Webber, Diane, 1932-
Do you read me? famous cases solved by handwriting analysis! [by] Diane Webber. Franklin Watts 2007 64p il map (24/7, science behind the scenes) lib bdg $26; pa $7.95
Grades: 5 6 7 8   **363.2**
1. Graphology 2. Forensic sciences
ISBN 978-0-531-12066-8 (lib bdg); 0-531-12066-X (lib bdg); 978-0-531-15456-4 (pa); 0-531-15456-4 (pa)
LC 2006006797
"Cases such as the infamous Lindbergh kidnapping and the discovery of Hitler's lost diaries are used to explore how handwriting can be used to solve a mystery. Subsequent sections tackle questions such as the validity of handwriting analysis as well as explore some of the nuances of the science." Voice Youth Advocates
Includes glossary and bibliographical references

Yancey, Diane
Tracking serial killers; by Diane Yancey. Thomson/Gale 2007 104p il (Crime scene investigations) $32.45
Grades: 7 8 9 10   **363.2**
1. Criminal investigation 2. Homicide 3. Forensic sciences
ISBN 978-1-59018-985-6; 1-59018-985-X
LC 2007006813
Presents the forensic techniques that are used in the investigations of serial killers and that aid in their apprehension, including such processes as psychological and DNA profiling, analyses of biological evidence, and the coordinated use of national databases.
"Reluctant readers will be fascinated." SLJ
Includes bibliographical references

Yount, Lisa
Forensic science; from fibers to fingerprints. Facts on File 2007 206p il (Milestones in discovery and invention) $35
Grades: 7 8 9 10 11 12   **363.2**
1. Forensic sciences 2. Criminal investigation
ISBN 0-8160-5751-6; 978-0-8160-5751-1
LC 2006-1748
This book "profiles key figures in this newsmaking field, both pioneers and today's top forensics experts." Publisher's note
Includes glossary and bibliographical references

363.3   Other aspects of public safety

Campbell, Geoffrey A.
A vulnerable America; an overview of national security; by Geoffrey A. Campbell. Lucent Books 2004 112p il (Lucent library of homeland security) $28.70
Grades: 7 8 9 10   **363.3**
1. Civil defense 2. Terrorism 3. National security
ISBN 1-59018-383-5   LC 2003-8150
Contents: Safeguarding the nation's transportation system; Bracing for bioterrorism and other weapons; Racial profiling and the battle against terrorism; A consolidation of power; A changing way of life.

"Campbell examines America's response to the terrorist attacks of September 11, 2001, and explores the measures taken to increase security and the new challenges to our personal freedoms." SLJ
"Current, informative, and well researched." Booklist
Includes bibliographical references

Media violence: opposing viewpoints; David Haugen and Susan Musser, book editors. Greenhaven Press 2009 232p il lib bdg $37.40; pa $25.95
Grades: 8 9 10 11 12   **363.3**
1. Violence 2. Mass media
ISBN   978-0-7377-4218-3   (lib   bdg); 978-0-7377-4219-0 (pa)   LC 2008-30355
Replaces the edition published 2004 under the editorship of Louise I. Gerdes
"Opposing viewpoints series"
This anthology "begins with articles that probe the scope and severity of the phenomenon and then moves on to sections about how violence in the media should be regulated, the effects of violence in the news, and cyberbullying." Booklist
Includes bibliographical references

363.31   Censorship

Gottfried, Ted, 1928-
Censorship. Benchmark Books 2005 c2006 143p il (Open for debate) $37.07 *
Grades: 7 8 9 10   **363.31**
1. Censorship
ISBN 0-7614-1883-0
Contents: Restricting the internet; Morality or prudery?; See-saw: smut and the law; That's entertainment!; The rules of war; Words and deeds; Around the world; Protecting the young
This discusses censorship issues in regard to such topics as pornography, the internet, motion pictures, politics, and literature.
Includes bibliographical references

Steffens, Bradley, 1956-
Censorship; by Bradley Steffens. Lucent Books 2004 112p il (Lucent overview series) $27.45 *
Grades: 7 8 9 10   **363.31**
1. Censorship
ISBN 1-59018-187-5   LC 2004-10852
Discusses the history of censorship, what is and is not protected under the First Amendment, and regulations and standards for the Internet
"Interestingly written chapters are short but comprehensive. Well-chosen illustrations add visual interest and provide additional information." SLJ
Includes bibliographical references

363.32 Control of violence and terrorism

Can the War on Terrorism be won? David Haugen and Susan Musser, book editors. Greenhaven Press 2007 109p (At issue: National security) $29.95; pa $21.20
Grades: 6 7 8 9   **363.32**
1. War on terrorism 2. Terrorism
ISBN 978-0-7377-1973-4; 978-0-7377-1974-1 (pa)
LC 2006039099
This "gathers 13 excerpted articles and speeches. . . . Readers encounter a spectrum of opinions about the War on Terror. . . . Each extract is headed with a straightforward title . . . and prefaced with a helpful abstract. Capped by an extensive reading list and annotated list of organizations, this is a strong option for assignment or debate-team research." Booklist
Includes bibliographical references

Friedman, Lauri S.
Terrorist attacks. ReferencePoint Press 2008 128p il map (Compact research) lib bdg $24.95
Grades: 7 8 9 10 11 12   **363.32**
1. Terrorism
ISBN 978-1-60152-022-7; 1-60152-022-0
LC 2007-9907
This "introduces theories as to why people carry out terrorist attacks, how they are executed, and how the attacks might be prevented. . . . [The] volume includes people and groups associated with the issue, a chronology of events, related organizations, and suggestions for further research. Chapters open and end with an array of quotes that argue for or against a particular argument or aspect of the issue, complete with full citation." SLJ
Includes glossary and bibliographical references

Katz, Samuel M., 1963-
Against all odds; counterterrorist hostage rescues; by Samuel M. Katz. Lerner Publications 2005 72p il (Terrorist dossiers) lib bdg $26.60
Grades: 7 8 9 10   **363.32**
1. Hostages 2. Terrorism 3. Police
ISBN 0-8225-1567-9   LC 2004-6215
Contents: Operation Isotope 1; Deadline in Djibouti; The Mother of all operations; The virtue of patience; Operation Magic Fire; Operation Nimrod; The rescue of Bridadier General James A. Dozier; Merry Christmas Marseilles; The tunnel rats of Lima; Lose small or lose big
"Katz presents the history and politics behind high-profile hostage rescues and highlights the work of groups such as the Sayeret Mat'kal of Israel, the Groupe d' Intervention de la Gendarmerie Nationale (GIGN) in France, the Dutch Bijzondere Bijstands Eenheid (BBE) and Grenzschutzgruppe 9 (GSG-9) of Germany, Britain's Special Air Service (SAS), Italy's Nucleo Operativo Centrale di Sicurezza (NOCS), Fuerza de Operaciones Especiales (FOE) in Peru, and Russia's Alpha Group. . . . A useful addition for reports." SLJ
Includes bibliographical references

Landau, Elaine
Suicide bombers; foot soldiers of the terrorist movement. Twenty-First Century Books 2007 120p lib bdg $31.93 *
Grades: 7 8 9 10   **363.32**
1. Suicide bombers 2. Terrorism
ISBN 978-0-7613-3470-5; 0-7613-3470-X
LC 2005033422
"The author studies several individual examples of young people who are recruited into or choose to become human sacrifices, and the convoluted path that leads them to their final, grisly end. Landau . . . does an excellent job of dissecting the complex history, motives, and philosophies that feed the culture of the suicide bomber. . . . Compelling and easy to follow." Voice Youth Advocates
Includes bibliographical references

Terrorism; an opposing viewpoints guide; Stephen Currie, book editor. Greenhaven Press 2006 111p il (Writing the critical essay) lib bdg $36.20
Grades: 8 9 10 11 12   **363.32**
1. Terrorism 2. Authorship
ISBN 0-7377-3206-7   LC 2005049314
"Opposing viewpoints series"
This title "makes use of the . . . Opposing Viewpoints format (with selections that argue crucial issues from many sides), adding exercises, suggestions, and models for students' writing. More than half the book is published articles from alternative viewpoints, and the vital contemporary questions (Are terrorist attacks inevitable? Is the threat of terrorism exaggerated? etc.) will spark debate and discussion." Booklist
Includes bibliographical references

363.33 Control of explosives and firearms

Atkin, S. Beth
Gunstories; life-changing experiences with guns; interviews and photographs by S. Beth Atkin. HarperCollins Publishers 2006 245p il $16.99; lib bdg $17.89 *
Grades: 7 8 9 10 11 12   **363.33**
1. Firearms
ISBN 0-06-052659-9; 0-06-052660-2 (lib bdg)
LC 2005-2076
The author "gathers testimonials addressing how guns are an integral part of teens' lives. Situated between oral testimonials, and figuratively placing an exclamation mark on the topic, are summaries of thirty-four school shootings occurring between 1995 and 2005." Voice Youth Advocates
"This book should be useful for students involved in the debate about guns in our culture as well as for those with a general interest in the subject." SLJ

Guns and violence; Laura K. Egendorf, book editor. Greenhaven Press 2005 202p (Current controversies) lib bdg $34.95; pa $23.70 *
Grades: 8 9 10 11 12   363.33
1. Gun control 2. Violence
ISBN 0-7377-2206-1 (lib bdg); 0-7377-2207-X (pa)
                                                LC 2004-52287
Replaces the edition published 1999 under the editorship of Henny H. Kim
Presents differing viewpoints on the seriousness of gun violence, whether or not gun control reduces crime and its constitutionality, the effectiveness of gun ownership as self defense, and what measures would reduce gun violence
Includes bibliographical references

363.34 Disasters

Barnard, Bryn
Dangerous planet; natural disasters that changed history; written and illustrated by Bryn Barnard. Crown Pubs. 2003 48p il map $17.95; lib bdg $19.99 *
Grades: 5 6 7 8   363.34
1. Natural disasters
ISBN 0-375-82249-6; 0-375-92249-0 (lib bdg)
                                                LC 2002-17545
Describes specific occurrences of natural disasters such as meteor impacts, landslides, typhoons, volcanic eruptions, and earthquakes, and their impact on human history
This is "an absorbing narrative that includes touches of humor. . . . Teachers will find many uses for this, but the book is so engaging it will also attract browsers—and hold them." Booklist
Includes bibliographical references

Butts, Edward, 1951-
SOS: stories of survival; true tales of disaster, tragedy, and courage; by Ed Butts. Tundra Books 2007 119p il pa $12.95
Grades: 6 7 8 9   363.34
1. Disasters
ISBN 978-0-88776-786-9 (pa)
"Butts writes with taut excitement about 13 devastating events—floods, fires, explosions, mountain slides, and more—from the 1891 Canadian Springhill Mine Disaster and the Triangle Shirtwaist Fire to Chernobyl, the Tsunami of 2004, and Hurricaine Katrina. . . . The personal eyewitness accounts and occasional archival photos dramatize the cataclysmic events." Booklist
Includes bibliographical references

Engelbert, Phillis
Dangerous planet; the science of natural disasters. U.X.L 2001 3v il maps set $165
Grades: 6 7 8 9   363.34
1. Natural disasters
ISBN 0-7876-2848-4   LC 98-54422
Contents: v1 Avalanche to El Niño; v2 Flow to mud flow; v3 Tornado to volcano

This set "explains the science behind earthquakes, volcanoes, tornadoes, avalanches, mudslides and other devastating natural disasters. Alphabetically arranged entries typically include a definition of the type of disaster; a summary, including coverage of particularly well-known or destructive occurrences; a discussion of the causes of the disaster; technology's role in predicting and measuring a disaster; [and] a list of further reading." Publisher's note
"The science is accurate, and the technical terms are explained well. The illustrations are clear and well placed." Booklist
Includes bibliographical references

Fradin, Judith Bloom
Droughts; [by] Judy & Dennis Fradin. National Geographic 2008 48p il map (Witness to disaster) $16.95; lib bdg $20.90 *
Grades: 4 5 6 7   363.34
1. Droughts
ISBN   978-1-4263-0339-5;   1-4263-0339-4;
978-1-4263-0340-1 (lib bdg); 1-4263-0340-8 (lib bdg)
                                                LC 2008020424
"This book examines the lessons from the Dust Bowl droughts for farmers, including the importance of topsoil. The history of droughts around the world compares impacts on a wide variety of societies. The final chapter looks at the latest tools and technologies developed to help us survive future droughts." Publisher's note
Includes glossary and bibliographical references

Karwoski, Gail, 1949-
Tsunami; the true story of an April Fools' Day disaster; [by] Gail Langer Karwoski; illustrated by John MacDonald. Darby Creek Pub. 2006 64p il $17.95
Grades: 4 5 6 7   363.34
1. Tsunamis 2. Hawaii
ISBN 1-58196-944-1
The author "opens with a description of the tsunami waves that struck the northern coast of the Hawaiian Islands in 1946, destroying a school and sweeping many children and adults out to sea. The book goes on to provide broader information about tsunamis, from scientific understanding of how they occur to ongoing efforts at early warning systems. . . . Clearly written and informative." Booklist

Langley, Andrew
Hurricanes, tsunamis, and other natural disasters; [by] Andrew Langley. Kingfisher 2006 63p il map (Kingfisher knowledge) $12.95
Grades: 5 6 7 8   363.34
1. Natural disasters
ISBN 978-0-7534-5975-1; 0-7534-5975-2
                                                LC 2005027200
This briefly describes such natural disasters as hurricanes, tsunamis, avalanches, brush fires, earthquakes, floods, tornadoes, drought and famine, pandemics, with many color illustrations and maps
"This book presents a high-interest topic in an attractively designed format that features colorful, eye-catching graphics and a solidly written text." Booklist
Includes glossary and bibliographical references

Markle, Sandra, 1946-
Rescues! Millbrook Press 2006 88p il map lib bdg $25.26
Grades: 4 5 6 7 **363.34**
  1. Rescue work 2. Survival after airplane accidents, shipwrecks, etc.
  ISBN 978-0-8225-3413-6; 0-8225-3413-4
  LC 2005-09707
"From the collapse of a Pennsylvania coal mine in 2002 to the tsunami that struck 11 countries in 2004 to Hurricane Katrina in 2005, the 11 disasters Markle describes are straight from news headlines. In this full-color photo-essay, she uses individual experiences of rescue and survival to bring each drama close." Booklist
  Includes bibliographical references

Miller, Debra A.
Hurricane Katrina; devastation on the Gulf Coast; by Debra A. Miller. Lucent Books 2006 104p il map (Overview series) $28.70
Grades: 7 8 9 10 **363.34**
  1. Hurricane Katrina, 2005
  ISBN 1-59018-936-1 LC 2005030656
"This readable account of the hurricane and the subsequent flood stresses the effect of the disaster on the survivors, quoting them frequently. In addition to the storm itself, the author covers the response, the damage, the hurricanes effect on New Orleans's residents, and prospects for their future, including the cost, responsibility, and viability of rebuilding." SLJ
  Includes bibliographical references

Miller, Mara, 1968-
Hurricane Katrina strikes the Gulf Coast; disaster & survival; [by] Mara Miller. Enslow Publishers 2006 48p il map (Deadly disasters) $23.93
Grades: 4 5 6 7 **363.34**
  1. Hurricane Katrina, 2005 2. Hurricanes 3. Rescue work
  ISBN 0-7660-2803-8 LC 2005030989
Contents: Katrina gains strength; What is a hurricane?; Katrina strikes; New Orleans floods; After Katrina; The next hurricane
"Miller begins with an account of the development of Hurricane Katrina as it struck Florida and then threatened the Gulf Coast. She discusses the subsequent flooding of New Orleans, the damage it caused, rescue and recovery attempts, and planning for the aftermath of future hurricanes. The author includes a clear scientific description of hurricanes, defining key terms. Color photos and graphics help explain concepts such as the structure of a hurricane, Katrina's path, and the conditions endured by the victims." SLJ
  Includes glossary and bibliographical references

Palser, Barb
Hurricane Katrina; aftermath of disaster. Compass Point Books 2007 96p il map (Snapshots in history) lib bdg $31.93 *
Grades: 7 8 9 10 **363.34**
  1. Hurricane Katrina, 2005 2. Hurricanes 3. Disaster relief
  ISBN 978-0-7565-2101-1 (lib bdg); 0-7565-2101-7 (lib bdg) LC 2006009119
This describes the impact of the hurricane which struck New Orleans and the Gulf coast in 2005 and subsequent relief and rebuilding efforts
"An unusually handsome design and a brisk, information-packed narrative make this . . . volume . . . an outstanding acquisition for libraries." Booklist
  Includes glossary and bibliographical references

Pietras, Jamie
Hurricane Katrina; [by] Jamie Pietras. Chelsea House 2008 128p il map (Great historic disasters) $35
Grades: 7 8 9 10 **363.34**
  1. Hurricane Katrina, 2005
  ISBN 978-0-7910-9639-0; 0-7910-9639-4
  LC 2007036551
"This book details the meteorological, political, and social circumstances that came together so fatally during 2005's Hurricane Katrina. Mostly objective, the writing is occasionally peppered with commentary on the local and federal governments' missteps and inaction following the storm and ensuing floods. Gripping photographs support the text." Horn Book Guide
  Includes glossary and bibliographical references

363.4 Controversies related to public morals and customs

Hill, Jeff
Prohibition. Omnigraphics 2004 xxv, 201p il (Defining moments) $38
Grades: 7 8 9 10 **363.4**
  1. Prohibition
  ISBN 0-7808-0768-5 LC 2004-22643
This book provides an "historical analysis of the Prohibition era (1920-33), including the politics of the Eighteenth Amendment; the Mob wars; the roles played by important public figures, from mobster Al Capone to Prohibition activist Carry Nation to President Warren Harding; and much more. . . . With a detailed glossary, a chronology, and an annotated bibliography, this is an important curriculum resource on the social and political history of an era." Booklist
  Includes bibliographical references

Pornography: opposing viewpoints; Helen Cothran, book editor. Greenhaven Press 2002 186p il lib bdg $34.95; pa $23.70
Grades: 8 9 10 11 1 2 **363.4**
  1. Pornography
  ISBN 0-7377-0761-5 (lib bdg); 0-7377-0760-7 (pa)
  LC 2001-16036
Replaces the edition published 1997 under the editorship of Carol Wekesser

Pornography: opposing viewpoints—*Continued*

"Opposing viewpoints series"

This collection of essays "addresses both sides of the following questions: 'Is Pornography Harmful?' 'Should Pornography Be Censored?' 'How Should Internet Pornography Be Regulated?' 'What Should Be the Feminist Stance on Pornography?'" SLJ

Includes bibliographical references

Smoking; Auriana Ojeda, book editor. Greenhaven Press 2002 175p (Current controversies) lib bdg $31.20; pa $19.95

Grades: 8 9 10 11 12   **363.4**

1. Smoking

ISBN 0-7377-0857-3 (lib bdg); 0-7377-0856-5 (pa)
                                     LC 2001-51247

"Selections debate whether the health risks of smoking are exaggerated, consider the impact of advertising by tobacco companies, look at government regulation, and more. . . . Researchers will appreciate the bibliography and the extensive, annotated list of organizations." Booklist

Includes bibliographical references

The war on drugs: opposing viewpoints; Tamara L. Roleff, book editor. Greenhaven Press 2004 222p il lib bdg $34.95; pa $23.70

Grades: 8 9 10 11 12   **363.4**

1. Drug abuse

ISBN 0-7377-2284-3 (lib bdg); 0-7377-2285-1 (pa)
                                     LC 2003-63063

"Opposing viewpoints series"

"Chapters in this . . . anthology include Is the War on Drugs Succeeding? Is There a Link Between the War on Drugs and Terrorism? Which Policies Are Working in the War on Drugs? [and] Should Illegal Drugs Be Legalized?" Publisher's note

Includes bibliographical references

363.46   Abortion

The abortion controversy; Lucinda Almond, book editor. Greenhaven Press 2007 199p (Current controversies) $36.20; pa $24.95

Grades: 8 9 10 11 12   **363.46**

1. Abortion

ISBN   978-0-7377-3273-3;   0-7377-3273-3;
978-0-7377-3274-0 (pa); 0-7377-3274-1 (pa)
                                     LC 2007-4509

Replaces the edition published 2001 under the editorship of Lynette Knapp

"With vehement arguments from all sides of th abortion debate this . . . includes essays by a range of today's writers and activists. . . . The range of viewpoints represented here will spark passionate responses from teens." Booklist

Includes bibliographical references

Abortion: opposing viewpoints; James D. Torr, book editor. Greenhaven Press 2006 192p il lib bdg $34.95; pa $23.70 *

Grades: 8 9 10 11 12   **363.46**

1. Abortion

ISBN 0-7377-2921-X (lib bdg); 0-7377-2922-8 (pa)
                                     LC 2005-46396

Replaces the edition published 2001 under the editorship of Mary E. Williams

"Opposing viewpoints series"

"The viewpoints in this anthology debate Roe v. Wade, the ethics of abortion, and related issues in the following chapters: Is Abortion Immoral? How Does Abortion Affect Women? Should Abortion Rights Be Restricted? How Are Controversies Over Embryo Testing and Research Related to the Abortion Debate?" Publisher's note

Includes bibliographical references

Haney, Johannah

The abortion debate; understanding the issues. Enslow Publishers 2009 112p il (Issues in focus today) lib bdg $31.93

Grades: 6 7 8 9   **363.46**

1. Abortion

ISBN 978-0-7660-2916-3 (lib bdg); 0-7660-2916-6 (lib bdg)   LC 2008013900

"Examines the debate over abortion, discussing both the pro-life and pro-choice sides of the argument, the history and laws on abortion in the United States, and finding a middle ground on the issue." Publisher's note

Includes bibliographical references

Naden, Corinne J.

Abortion. Marshall Cavendish Benchmark 2008 143p il (Open for debate) lib bdg $27.95

Grades: 7 8 9 10   **363.46**

1. Abortion—Law and legislation

ISBN 978-0-7614-2573-1; 0-7614-2573-X
                                     LC 2006-28525

This book about abortion "features chapters on the history of the debate, the politics surrounding the subject, rape and incest, and medical issues. . . . Many captioned color photos enhance the text." SLJ

Includes bibliographical references

363.6   Public utilities and related services

Bowden, Rob

Water supply; our impact on the planet. Raintree Steck-Vaughn Pubs. 2003 64p il (21st century debates) lib bdg $28.56

Grades: 6 7 8 9   **363.6**

1. Water supply

ISBN 0-7398-5506-9   LC 2002-151938

Contents: A thirsty world; Water as a resource; Water is life; The well runs dry; Polluted water; Water conservation; Water conflicts; A new water economy; Water for tomorrow

This title "looks at the problem of water scarcity, how we use and misuse this precious resource, and what can be done to conserve it, both now and in the future." Publisher's note

The author packs "in a dense amount of data, made accessible by the attractive page design, full-color photos, sidebars, and boxes that extend the scope of {the} volume." Booklist

Includes bibliographical references

363.7 Environmental problems

Berne, Emma Carlson
Global warming and climate change. ReferencePoint Press 2008 112p il (Compact research) $24.95
Grades: 8 9 10 11 12 **363.7**
1. Greenhouse effect 2. Climate—Environmental aspects
ISBN 978-1-60152-019-7; 1-60152-019-0
LC 2007-8371
This discusses global warming and climate change, its consequences and controversies and possible solutions.
"Useful for reports. . . . [This] presents pertinent questions with appropriate and well-documented quotations from a variety of viewpoints and basic facts and diagrams." SLJ
Includes bibliographical references

Bowden, Rob
Waste; by Rob Bowden. KidHaven Press 2004 48p il (Sustainable world) lib bdg $23.70
Grades: 5 6 7 8 **363.7**
1. Refuse and refuse disposal
ISBN 0-7377-1902-8 LC 2003-52951
This "discusses innovations in reuse and recycling, ingenious ways to use what would be discarded, and changes in taxation policy. The many full-color photographs clarify the [text]. [This] will be highly useful for both reports and in classroom discussions." SLJ
Includes bibliographical references

Bryan, Nichol, 1958-
Bhopal; chemical plant accident. World Almanac Library 2004 48p il map (Environmental disasters) lib bdg $29.27 paperback o.p.
Grades: 5 6 7 8 **363.7**
1. Chemical industry—Accidents 2. Bhopal Union Carbide Plant Disaster, Bhopal, India, 1984
ISBN 0-8368-5503-5 (lib bdg); 0-8368-5510-8 (pa)
LC 2003-49718
Presents an account of the 1984 chemical accident at the Union Carbide plant in Bhopal, India, and its aftermath
Includes glossary and bibliographical references

Chernobyl; nuclear disaster. World Almanac Library 2004 48p il map (Environmental disasters) lib bdg $29.27 paperback o.p.
Grades: 5 6 7 8 **363.7**
1. Chernobyl Nuclear Accident, Chernobyl, Ukraine, 1986 2. Nuclear power plants—Environmental aspects
ISBN 0-8368-5504-3 (lib bdg); 0-8368-5511-6 (pa)
LC 2003-42291
Discusses the disastrous 1986 accident at the Chernobyl nuclear power plant in the Ukraine.
Includes glossary and bibliographical references

Danube; cyanide spill; by Nichol Bryan. World Almanac Library 2004 48p il map (Environmental disasters) lib bdg $29.27; pa $11.95
Grades: 5 6 7 8 **363.7**
1. Chemical spills 2. Water pollution
ISBN 0-8368-5505-1 (lib bdg); 0-8368-5512-4 (pa)
LC 2003-57694
Discusses the disastrous year 2000 overflow of a Romanian reservoir that held heavy metals and cyanide, pouring the deadly mix into rivers that feed the Danube and killing all living creatures in its path.
Includes glossary and bibliographical references

Exxon Valdez oil spill. World Almanac Library 2004 48p il map (Environmental disasters) lib bdg $29.27 paperback o.p.
Grades: 5 6 7 8 **363.7**
1. Exxon Valdez (Ship) 2. Oil spills
ISBN 0-8368-5506-X (lib bdg); 0-8368-5513-2 (pa)
LC 2003-47991
Describes the oil tanker Exxon Valdez, the events that led up to its disastrous oil spill in 1989, and the effects of the spill on the Alaskan environment.
This is "well-illustrated. . . . [It does] a fine job of placing [the] disaster within a larger context by including detailed background about America's industrial and environmental history; quotes from eyewitnesses, politicians, and journalists; and clear explanations of the changes in policy that [the] disaster instigated." Booklist
Includes glossary and bibliographical references

Love Canal; pollution crisis. World Almanac Library 2004 48p il map (Environmental disasters) lib bdg $29.27 paperback o.p.
Grades: 5 6 7 8 **363.7**
1. Love Canal Chemical Waste Landfill (Niagara Falls, N.Y.) 2. Pollution
ISBN 0-8368-5508-6 (lib bdg); 0-8368-5515-9 (pa)
LC 2003-57162
Traces the history and eventual cleanup of the ecological disaster known as Love Canal, which resulted from building a neighborhood over a chemical dumpsite that poisoned the environment and endangered the health of residents.
This is "well-illustrated. . . . [It does] a fine job of placing [the] disaster within a larger context by including detailed background about America's industrial and environmental history; quotes from eyewitnesses, politicians, and journalists; and clear explanations of the changes in policy that [the] disaster instigated." Booklist
Includes glossary and bibliographical references

Cherry, Lynne, 1952-
How we know what we know about our changing climate; scientists and kids explore global warming; by Lynne Cherry and Gary Braasch; photographs by Gary Braasch. Dawn Publications 2008 66p il $17.95 *
Grades: 4 5 6 7 **363.7**
1. Greenhouse effect 2. Climate—Environmental aspects
ISBN 978-1-58469-103-7; 0-1-58469-103-4
LC 2007-37255

Cherry, Lynne, 1952-—*Continued*

"This volume describes where scientists look to find evidence of climate change—from changes in bird migration patterns and fruit blossom dates, to obtaining tree rings and mud cores—and especially how students and other citizen-scientists are assisting to monitor climate change, as well as what can be done to mitigate global warming." Publisher's note

"The can-do emphasis helps to make the topic less depressing, and the intriguing color photographs are thoughtful and upbeat." Booklist

David, Laurie

The down-to-earth guide to global warming; [by] Laurie David and Cambria Gordon. Orchard Books 2007 112p il map pa $15.99 *

Grades: 4 5 6 7   **363.7**

1. Greenhouse effect 2. Climate—Environmental aspects

ISBN 978-0-439-02494-5 (pa); 0-439-02494-3 (pa)

LC 2006-35705

The authors "put forth the basics on global warming, climate change, and how readers can green up the environment. They temper the book's often troubling subject matter with kid-friendly humor, some celebrity shout-outs, and explanations of the scientific underpinnings. An amply illustrated layout, featuring attention-grabbing sidebars, dramatic photos, and diagrams, will sustain reader interest." Booklist

Includes bibliographical references

Delano, Marfe Ferguson

Earth in the hot seat; bulletins from a warming world. National Geographic 2009 63p il (Preserve our planet) $19.95; lib bdg $28.90 *

Grades: 5 6 7 8   **363.7**

1. Greenhouse effect 2. Climate—Environmental aspects

ISBN 978-1-4263-0434-7; 1-4263-0434-X; 978-1-4263-0435-4 (lib bdg); 1-4263-0435-8 (lib bdg)

LC 2008029317

"This book lays out . . . the evidence for global warming and the part that human activity plays in it. Five chapters lay out the signs and evidences of a warming world. . . . Subsequent chapters of the book are devoted to what humankind can expect in a warming world and steps that must be taken to avert catastrophe for humans and the planet. . . . The illustrative photos are fully up to National Geographic high standards. This [is a] fine book, reasonably priced and carefully researched." Voice Youth Advocates

Includes bibliographical references

The **Environment** encyclopedia; acid rain—zoning; edited by Ruth A. Eblen, William R. Eblen. Marshall Cavendish 2000 11v il maps set $459.95

Grades: 6 7 8 9   **363.7**

1. Environmental sciences—Encyclopedias 2. Ecology—Encyclopedias 3. Earth sciences—Encyclopedias 4. Reference books

ISBN 0-7614-7182-0   LC 99-86986

Replaces The encyclopedia of the environment published 1994 by Houghton Mifflin

This reference includes 400 articles and over 1,400 color photographs covering such subjects as "natural ecosystems; cultural ecosystems; the history of environmentalism; law, government and education; art, literature and ethics; and biographies." Publisher's note

"This is an attractive, useful set that's sure to hold readers' attention." SLJ

The **Environment**: opposing viewpoints; Laura K. Egendorf, book editor. Greenhaven Press 2005 202p il (Opposing viewpoints series) $33.70; pa $26.20

Grades: 8 9 10 11 12   **363.7**

1. Pollution 2. Human ecology 3. Environmental policy—United States

ISBN 0-7377-2230-4; 0-7377-2231-2 (pa)

LC 2004-49292

Replaces the 2001 edition under the editorship of William Dudley

"Opposing viewpoints series"

This collection of essays offers varying viewpoints on environmental pollution and protection

Includes bibliographical references

Evans, Kate, 1972-

Weird weather; everything you didn't want to know about climate change but probably should find out; [with an introduction by George Monbiot] Groundwood Books 2007 95p il $15.95

Grades: 8 9 10 11 12   **363.7**

1. Graphic novels 2. Greenhouse effect—Graphic novels 3. Climate—Environmental aspects—Graphic novels 4. Weather—Graphic novels

ISBN 978-0-88899-838-5

First published 2006 in the United Kingdom with title: Funny weather

This book, in graphic novel format, presents "the history of global warming, likely outcomes of current pollution patterns, and what can be done if we hope to survive as a species. Cleverly, the narrative unfolds through the voices of three main characters: an outraged young idealist, a scientist fascinated by the challenges of the situation, and a greedy consumer who is only interested in himself. Accessible and entertaining, this book will be adored by science teachers. . . . Important reading for secondary students and adults." SLJ

Includes bibliographical references

Fridell, Ron, 1943-

Protecting Earth's water supply; by Ron Fridell. Lerner Publications Co. 2009 72p il (Saving our living Earth) lib bdg $30.60

Grades: 5 6 7 8   **363.7**

1. Water pollution 2. Water conservation

ISBN 978-0-8225-7557-3; 0-8225-7557-4

LC 2007-35924

"Provides a thorough, interesting discussion of multiple aspects of [water supply protection], including historical origins, the current situation, and potential solutions. . . . Photos from around the world accompany discussions. . . . [This is a] solid choice to replace outdated books." SLJ

Includes glossary and bibliographical references

Gardner, Robert, 1929-
Science projects about the environment and ecology. Enslow Pubs. 1999 112p il (Science projects) lib bdg $20.95
Grades: 7 8 9 10   **363.7**
1. Environmental protection 2. Ecology 3. Science—Experiments 4. Science projects
ISBN 0-89490-951-7   LC 98-35049
Presents experiments and projects suitable for science fairs, dealing with such aspects of the environment and ecology as the atmosphere, soil, water, plants, animals, and climate
"Each project is clearly outlined with a list of generally available supplies. The text [is] concise and informative." SLJ
Includes bibliographical references

Gifford, Clive
Pollution; [by] Clive Gifford. Heinemann Library 2006 48p il map (Planet under pressure) lib bdg $31.43
Grades: 4 5 6 7   **363.7**
1. Pollution
ISBN 1-4034-7742-6   LC 2005017064
"Gifford discusses the many types of pollution, global warming and the greenhouse effect, the worldwide impact on human lives and well-being, and possible solutions. . . . [This has] numerous quality color visuals, and sidebars. Up-to-date and informative." SLJ
Includes bibliographical references

Global warming; Mary E. Williams, book editor. Greenhaven Press 2006 96p il map (Writing the critical essay) lib bdg $26.20
Grades: 8 9 10 11 12   **363.7**
1. Greenhouse effect 2. Authorship 3. Essays
ISBN 0-7377-3210-5   LC 2005055066
"Section one presents five opposing excerpts from recent periodicals, each one beginning with a short summary and questions for readers to consider and including relevant illustrations, political cartoons, and color photographs. Section two offers information on essay writing and includes annotated examples. . . . This volume provides a useful way for English composition, science, and social science teachers to integrate library research into their classrooms." SLJ
Includes bibliographical references

Global warming; Debra A. Miller, book editor. Greenhaven Press 2008 189p (Current controversies) $37.40; pa $25.95
Grades: 8 9 10 11 12   **363.7**
1. Greenhouse effect
ISBN   978-0-7377-4070-7;   0-7377-4070-1;
978-0-7377-4071-4 (pa); 0-7377-4071-X (pa)
LC 2008-1004
"Controversies covered in this volume include . . . [global warming's] causes, potential threats, and the possible actions society can take to reduce its effects. For each question considered, opposing opinions are showcased in the form of articles, reports, and essays authored by a variety of individuals including journalists, scientists, and policymakers. . . . This book will be an excellent choice for teens writing a pro/con paper, as both

sides of the issues are clearly delineated." SLJ
Includes bibliographical references

Global warming: opposing viewpoints; Cynthia A. Bily, book editor. Greenhaven Press 2006 208p il lib bdg $34.95; pa $23.70 *
Grades: 8 9 10 11 12   **363.7**
1. Greenhouse effect
ISBN 0-7377-2935-X (lib bdg); 0-7377-2936-8 (pa)
LC 2005-52779
Replaces the edition published 2002 under the editorship of James Haley
"Opposing viewpoints series"
"The essays address and assess the magnitude of the threat of global warming, its causes and effects, and the measures to be taken to combat it. The discussions range from SUVs to power plants to the Kyoto Protocol and solar flares. The points of view are radically divergent and promote excellent classroom discussion." SLJ
Includes bibliographical references

Gore, Al, Jr., 1948-
An inconvenient truth; the crisis of global warming; adapted for young readers by Jane O'Connor. rev ed. Viking 2007 191p il map $23; pa $16 *
Grades: 5 6 7 8   **363.7**
1. Greenhouse effect 2. Climate—Environmental aspects
ISBN 978-0-670-06271-3; 978-0-670-06272-0 (pa)
Adapted from the title for adults published 2006 by Rodale Press
This explains what global warming is, what causes it, and explains how to take action to stop this crisis.
This is illustrated with "easy-to-grasp graphics and revealing before-and-after photos. . . . O'Connor rephrases Gore's arguments in briefer, simpler language without compromising their flow." SLJ

Hall, Eleanor J.
Recycling. KidHaven Press 2004 c2005 48p il (Our environment) $23.70 *
Grades: 5 6 7 8   **363.7**
1. Recycling
ISBN 0-7377-1517-0   LC 2003-21682
Contents: What is recycling?; The challenges of recycling; The benefits of recycling; What does the future hold?
"The liberal use of vibrant colors, the inclusion of a photograph or diagram on most pages, and the generous print size will appeal to reluctant readers. [This title] will help students examine cause and effect (and possible solutions), and challenge them to live green." SLJ
Includes glossary and bibliographical references

Hirschmann, Kris, 1967-
Pollution. Kidhaven Press 2004 c2005 48p il (Our environment) $23.70
Grades: 5 6 7 8   **363.7**
1. Pollution
ISBN 0-7377-1563-4
Contents: What is pollution?; Air pollution; Water pollution; Garbage

Hirschmann, Kris, 1967-—*Continued*
This briefly describes the sources and effects of air and water pollution and refuse disposal and suggests possible solutions.
Includes glossary and bibliographical references

Johnson, Rebecca L., 1956-
Understanding global warming; by Rebecca L. Johnson. Lerner Publications 2009 72p il map (Saving our living Earth) lib bdg $30.60
Grades: 5 6 7 8   **363.7**
1. Greenhouse effect 2. Climate—Environmental aspects
ISBN 978-0-8225-7561-0 (lib bdg); 0-8225-7561-2 (lib bdg)   LC 2007-48358
"Provides a thorough, interesting discussion of multiple aspects of [global warming], including historical origins, the current situation, and potential solutions. . . . Photos from around the world accompany discussions. . . . [This is a] solid choice to replace outdated books." SLJ
Includes glossary and bibliographical references

Morris, Neil, 1946-
Global warming. World Almanac Library 2007 48p il (What if we do nothing?) lib bdg $22.95; pa $11.95 *
Grades: 5 6 7 8   **363.7**
1. Greenhouse effect 2. Climate—Environmental aspects
ISBN 0-8368-7755-1 (lib bdg); 978-0-8368-755-7 (lib bdg); 978-0-8368-155-4 (pa); 0-8368-8155-9 (pa)   LC 2006-30444
This "explains how we can measure [global warming] and what is likely to happen to our world as a result of warming. It discusses both human activity and natural cycles that contribute to global warming, and it urges the reader to think about what we can do to preserve: Land from being lost, Human health, Endangered species." Publisher's note
This "boasts an attractive format, with large pages that allow room for pictures, excellent charts and graphs, as well as a thoughtful, clear discussion of the topic." Booklist
Includes bibliographical references

Nardo, Don, 1947-
Climate crisis; the science of global warming; by Don Nardo. Compass Point Books 2009 47p il map (Headline science) lib bdg $27.93; pa $7.95
Grades: 5 6 7   **363.7**
1. Greenhouse effect 2. Climate—Environmental aspects
ISBN 978-0-7565-3571-1 (lib bdg); 0-7565-3571-9 (lib bdg); 978-0-7565-3948-1 (pa); 0-7565-3948-X (pa)   LC 2008-7259
"Presents an introduction to global warming, discussing the impact of rising temperatures, melting ice, water shortages, increased rate of animal extinctions, and the current human efforts underway to lessen the effects." Publisher's note
"Color photos and graphics provide visual informa-

tion; a timeline is helpful to find fast facts, and the Facthound Web site provides students with additional information." Libr Media Connect
Includes glossary and bibliographical references

Parks, Peggy J., 1951-
Global warming. KidHaven Press 2004 48p il (Our environment) $23.70
Grades: 5 6 7 8   **363.7**
1. Greenhouse effect 2. Climate—Environmental aspects
ISBN 0-7377-1822-6   LC 2002-156050
Contents: What is global warming?; Caused by humans or caused by nature?; Signs and effects of global warming; What can be done?
"The liberal use of vibrant colors, the inclusion of a photograph or diagram on most pages, and the generous print size will appeal to reluctant readers. [This title] will help students examine cause and effect (and possible solutions), and challenge them to live green." SLJ
Includes glossary and bibliographical references

Pollution: opposing viewpoints; Louise I. Gerdes, book editor. Greenhaven Press 2006 221p il lib bdg $34.95; pa $23.70
Grades: 8 9 10 11 12   **363.7**
1. Pollution
ISBN 0-7377-2949-X (lib bdg); 0-7377-2950-3 (pa)   LC 2005-45983
Replaces the edition published 2000 under the editorship of Tamara L. Roleff
"Opposing viewpoints series"
"The authors in this . . . anthology debate several controversial questions, including whether various forms of pollution continue to be a serious problem, whether pollution poses a public health threat, and what policies and programs will best reduce pollution." Publisher's note
Includes bibliographical references

Rapp, Valerie
Protecting Earth's air quality; by Valerie Rapp. Lerner Publications 2009 72p il map (Saving our living Earth) lib bdg $30.60
Grades: 5 6 7 8   **363.7**
1. Air pollution
ISBN 978-0-8225-7558-0; 0-8225-7558-2
         LC 2008-907
"Provides a thorough, interesting discussion of multiple aspects of [protecting Earth's air quality], including historical origins, the current situation, and potential solutions. . . . Photos from around the world accompany discussions. . . . [This is a] solid choice to replace outdated books." SLJ
Includes glossary and bibliographical references

Reilly, Kathleen M.
Planet Earth; 25 environmental projects you can build yourself; by Kathleen M. Reilly. Nomad Press 2008 122p il (Projects you can build yourself) $21.95; pa $14.95
Grades: 4 5 6 7   **363.7**

Reilly, Kathleen M.—*Continued*
1. Environmental sciences 2. Science projects
ISBN 978-1-934670-05-7; 1-934670-05-7;
978-1-934670-04-0 (pa); 1-934670-04-9 (pa)
"Both comprehensive and approachable, this title . . . combines explanations of science concepts and environmental issues with hands-on projects. . . . Elementary- and middle-school students will find the succinct overview of the facts very useful, and they'll welcome the clearly presented projects." Booklist

Robinson, Matthew, 1971-
America debates global warming; crisis or myth? Rosen Central 2008 64p il (America debates) lib bdg $29.25
Grades: 5 6 7 8 9 10 11 12   363.7
1. Greenhouse effect 2. Climate—Environmental aspects
ISBN 978-1-4042-1925-0 (lib bdg); 1-4042-1925-0 (lib bdg)   LC 2007-10931
This is a "presentation of the debate on global warming. . . . Scientists, world leaders, and political leaders weigh in." Publisher's note
This "is especially effective in laying out the information in a simple, logical format." SLJ
Includes glossary and bibliographical references

Scarborough, Kate
Nuclear waste. Bridgestone Bks. 2003 32p il (Our planet in peril) lib bdg $22.60 *
Grades: 5 6 7 8   363.7
1. Radioactive waste disposal 2. Nuclear energy
ISBN 0-7368-1362-4   LC 2002-10139
Contents: What is nuclear waste?; The world's energy needs; Fossil fuels; Nuclear energy; Background radiation; Nuclear power stations; Nuclear waste; Low level and intermediate waste; High level waste; Further research; Nuclear fusion; Public concerns; The future of nuclear power
"Chapters introduce topics such as . . . 'What is nuclear power?' through brief paragraphs of information. Numerous colorful photographs, graphs, and diagrams with informative captions add details on each spread." SLJ
Includes glossary and bibliographical references

Silverstein, Alvin
Global warming; by Alvin Silverstein, Virginia Silverstein, Laura Silverstein Nunn. rev. ed. Twenty-First Century Books 2009 112p il (Science concepts, second series) $31.93
Grades: 5 6 7 8   363.7
1. Greenhouse effect 2. Climate—Environmental aspects
ISBN 978-0-7613-3935-9; 0-7613-3935-3
First published 2003
Contents: Heating up; Our planet Earth; The greenhouse effect; Our changing climate; Is global warming for real?; The effects of global warming; Can global warming be stopped?
Includes bibliographical references

Sohn, Emily
The environment; series editor, Tara Koellhoffer; with a foreword by Emily Sohn. Chelsea Clubhouse 2006 122p il (Science news for kids) $22.50 *
Grades: 4 5 6 7   363.7
1. Environmental sciences
ISBN 0-7910-9123-6   LC 2005037548
Articles written chiefly by Emily Sohn
"Lively writing style, good organization, an attractive design, and thought-provoking study questions help introduce the interwoven topics relating to the environment and global warming. Succinct overviews prefacing each section and plenty of color photographs make for an accessible presentation." Booklist
Includes bibliographical references

Stille, Darlene R., 1942-
The greenhouse effect; warming the planet. Compass Point Books 2006 c2007 48p il map (Exploring science) $26.60
Grades: 7 8 9 10   363.7
1. Greenhouse effect 2. Climate—Environmental aspects
ISBN 978-0-7565-1956-8; 0-7565-1956-X
                                              LC 2006-06763
"The book provides a brief, yet thorough, explanation and overview of the greenhouse effect. . . . The text . . . is straightforward and clearly written. The illustrations and diagrams . . . further clarify the explanations in the text." Sci Books Films
Includes glossary and bibliographical references

Tanaka, Shelley
Climate change. Groundwood Books 2006 144p il (Groundwork guides) $15.95 *
Grades: 8 9 10 11 12   363.7
1. Greenhouse effect 2. Climate—Environmental aspects
ISBN 978-0-88899-783-8; 0-88899-783-3
"House of Anansi Press"
This "presents background on Earth's climate and about how, primarily through humankind's carelessness, global warming has escalated to a point of major concern. . . . The book also considers strategies people and nations might take to reverse the destructive trends. . . . Many students needing material for reports or debates will want this for the well-documented information and handy, backpack-friendly size." Booklist
Includes glossary and bibliographical references

Townsend, John, 1955-
Predicting the effects of climate change. Heinemann Library 2009 56p il map (Why science matters) $31.43; pa $9.49
Grades: 6 7 8 9   363.7
1. Greenhouse effect 2. Climate—Environmental aspects
ISBN 978-1-4329-1839-2; 1-4329-1839-7;
978-1-4329-1852-1 (pa); 1-4329-1852-4 (pa)
                                              LC 2008-14309

Townsend, John, 1955-—_Continued_

Provides an overview of climate change, discussing evidence, causes, and effects, and examines what can be done to stop its progression.

This book "would be a good addition to middle school libraries." Sci Books Films

Includes filmography, glossary and bibliographical references

Wilcox, Charlotte

Earth-friendly waste management; by Charlotte Wilcox. Lerner 2009 72p il (Saving our living Earth) lib bdg $30.60

Grades: 5 6 7 8   **363.7**

1. Refuse and refuse disposal 2. Recycling

ISBN 978-0-8225-7560-3 (lib bdg); 0-8225-7560-4 (lib bdg)   LC 2008-1883

"Provides a thorough, interesting discussion of multiple aspects of [waste management], including historical origins, the current situation, and potential solutions. . . . Photos from around the world accompany discussions. . . . [This is a] solid choice to replace outdated books." SLJ

Includes glossary and bibliographical references

Recycling. Lerner Publications 2008 48p il (Cool science) lib bdg $26.60

Grades: 4 5 6   **363.7**

1. Salvage 2. Recycling

ISBN 978-0-8225-6768-4 (lib bdg); 0-8225-6768-7 (lib bdg)   LC 2006102423

"This book explains the many amazing ways people use science to recycle garbage into great things." Publisher's note

Includes glossary and bibliographical references

363.8   Food supply

Bowden, Rob

Food and farming; by Rob Bowden. KidHaven Press 2004 il map (Sustainable world) lib bdg $23.70

Grades: 5 6 7 8   **363.8**

1. Food 2. Agriculture

ISBN 0-7377-1899-4   LC 2003-52952

This "first presents conventional techniques of food production, but focuses primarily on sustainable agriculture methods. . . . Bowden writes with admirable simplicity about complicated subjects, and he's careful to separate facts from opinions when he quotes others. . . . [The book includes] excellent color photos, and gripping statistics." Booklist

Includes glossary and bibliographical references

Morris, Neil, 1946-

Do you know where your food comes from? [by] Neil Morris. Heinemann Library 2006 56p il (Making healthy food choices) $32.86; pa $9.49

Grades: 6 7 8 9   **363.8**

1. Nutrition 2. Food industry

ISBN   978-1-4034-8575-5;   1-4034-8575-5; 978-1-4034-8581-6 (pa); 1-4034-8581-X (pa)

LC 2006003973

This "not only teaches adolescents about how and where food is produced but also about how to make sensible food choices. Also addressed are issues that move beyond personal health (such as the environmental impact of limiting 'food miles,' the distance foods travel from where they are produced to where they are consumed). Straightforward paragraphs are nicely supported by colorful fact boxes and sidebars, covering information as diverse as the world's top producers of milk and the omega-3 content of various fish. An attractive layout and full-color photos enhance the content." Booklist

363.9   Population problems

Mason, Paul, 1967-

Population; [by] Paul Mason. Heinemann Library 2006 48p il map (Planet under pressure) lib bdg $31.43 *

Grades: 4 5 6 7   **363.9**

1. Population 2. Human ecology

ISBN 1-4034-7741-8   LC 2005017063

"Mason describes the many factors that cause population levels to increase or decline; the impact of overpopulation, such as the depletion of food and clean-water supplies; current population figures; future forecasts; and more. Facts and figures show that overpopulation is affecting both rich and poor countries. The ethical question of whether societies and governments have the right to control personal choices is also addressed. . . . [This title has] numerous quality color visuals, and sidebars. Up-to-date and informative." SLJ

Includes bibliographical references

McLeish, Ewan, 1950-

Overcrowded world. Gareth Stevens Pub. 2009 48p il map (What if we do nothing?) lib bdg $31

Grades: 5 6 7 8   **363.9**

1. Overpopulation

ISBN 978-1-4339-0088-4; 1-4339-0088-2

LC 2008029182

"This book looks at the issue of overpopulation, its causes, and its impact on people and the environment. It also discusses the strategies adopted by different governments to deal with the problem." Publisher's note

"Using intelligent, focused text; an open design; vivid photos; and excellent maps, [this] book demands attention." Booklist

Includes bibliographical references

364   Criminology

Lane, Brian

Crime and detection; written by Brian Lane. Dorling Kindersley 2005 61p il (DK eyewitness books) $15.99   **364**

1. Crime 2. Forensic sciences 3. Criminal investigation

ISBN 0-7566-1386-8

First published 1998 by Knopf

Explores the many different methods used to solve crimes, covering such topics as criminal, detectives, and forensics.

Townsend, John, 1955-
Crime through time. Raintree 2006 48p il (Painful history of crime) lib bdg $31.43
Grades: 6 7 8 9   **364**
1. Crime—History
ISBN 1-4109-2051-8
"Raintree freestyle"
This "looks at violations of the law from ancient times to the present, giving insight into criminals, types of crime, and methods of solving it. . . . The subject, format, and presentation of material in [this book] will inform students, including reluctant readers." SLJ
Includes bibliographical references

364.1   Criminal offenses

Allman, Toney, 1947-
Internet predators. Erickson 2007 64p (Ripped from the headlines) $23.95
Grades: 7 8 9 10   **364.1**
1. Computer crimes 2. Safety education 3. Sex crimes
ISBN 978-1-60217-000-1; 1-60217-000-2
"Allman pulls no punches about the dangers of sexual predators on many Web sites and chat rooms. . . . He offers closeup profiles and full-color photos of real criminals and the tricks they use, of young victims and survivors and what happened to them, and of ongoing sting operations to catch the criminals online. The prose is terse, and lots of screen shots supply detailed advice and safety tips." Booklist

Aretha, David
The murder of Emmett Till. Morgan Reynolds Pub. 2007 160p il (The civil rights movement) lib bdg $27.95
Grades: 7 8 9 10 11 12   **364.1**
1. Till, Emmett 2. Lynching 3. African Americans—Civil rights 4. Mississippi—Race relations
ISBN 978-1-59935-057-8; 1-59935-057-2
                                    LC 2007-26250
"The heinous murder of Emmett Till galvanized the civil rights movement and raised the nation's awareness of the extreme racism in the South. . . . This title . . . details the events surrounding Till's murder, the trial and acquittal of his killers, and the nation's racial climate before and after this milestone in civil rights history." Booklist
Includes bibliographical references

Blackwood, Gary L.
Gangsters. Benchmark Bks. 2002 72p il (Bad guys) lib bdg $29.93
Grades: 4 5 6   **364.1**
1. Criminals
ISBN 0-7614-1016-3   LC 00-57154
This profiles Monk Eastman, James Colosimo, Al Capone, Clyde Barrow, John Dillinger, and Alvin Karpis
"Useful for research and pleasure reading. . . . There is an attractive mix of illustrations, photos, maps, and reproductions." Book Rep
Includes glossary and bibliographical references

Highwaymen. Benchmark Bks. 2002 72p il (Bad guys) lib bdg $29.93
Grades: 4 5 6   **364.1**
1. Thieves
ISBN 0-7614-1017-1   LC 99-86663
Describes the lives and careers of such European and American highwaymen as Claude Duval, Mary Frith, and Joseph Thompson Hare
"Well written and well designed. . . . {This book is} illustrated with reproductions of period artwork, documents, and photographs." Booklist
Includes glossary and bibliographical references

Outlaws. Benchmark Bks. 2002 72p il (Bad guys) lib bdg $29.93
Grades: 4 5 6   **364.1**
1. Thieves 2. West (U.S.)—History
ISBN 0-7614-1015-5   LC 00-57161
This profiles seven outlaws of the Old West including Joaquin Murieta, Jesse James, John Wesley Hardin, Billy the Kid, Black Bart, Pearl Hart, and Henry Starr
"Vivid photographs, reproductions, and illustrations effectively complement the text. . . . Entertaining and informative reading." SLJ
Includes glossary and bibliographical references

Swindlers. Benchmark Bks. 2002 72p il (Bad guys) lib bdg $29.93
Grades: 4 5 6   **364.1**
1. Swindlers and swindling
ISBN 0-7614-1031-7   LC 00-57153
"*Swindlers* traces the concept of cheating to the biblical story of Jacob and Esau but focuses on historical personages such as William Henry Ireland, an English forger of Shakespearean plays; Soapy Smith, a con artist of the American West; and Joseph 'Yellow Kid' Weil, a swindler on a grand scale. Well written and well designed. . . . Illustrated with reproductions of period artwork, documents, and photographs." Booklist
Includes glossary and bibliographical references

Crowe, Chris
Getting away with murder: the true story of the Emmett Till case. Phyllis Fogelman Bks. 2003 128p il map $18.99
Grades: 7 8 9 10   **364.1**
1. Till, Emmett 2. Lynching 3. Racism 4. Trials (Homicide) 5. Mississippi—Race relations
ISBN 0-8037-2804-2   LC 2002-5736
Contents: The boy who triggered the civil rights movement; Kicking the hornets' nest; The boy from Chicago; The wolf whistle; Setting the stage; Getting away with murder; Aftershocks
This is the story of "the black 14-year-old from Chicago who was brutally murdered while visiting relatives in the Mississippi Delta in 1954. . . . The gruesome, racially motivated crime and the court's failure to convict the white murderers was a powerful national catalyst for the civil rights movement. . . . Crowe's powerful, terrifying account does justice to its subject in bold, direct telling, supported by numerous archival photos and quotes from those who remember." Booklist
Includes bibliographical references

Fooks, Louie

The drug trade; the impact on our lives; [by] Louie Fooks. Raintree 2003 64p il (21st century debates) lib bdg $32.79

Grades: 6 7 8 9   **364.1**

1. Drug traffic 2. Drugs and crime

ISBN 0-7398-6033-X   LC 2003-3593

Contents: The global drug trade; Illegal drugs; Production of illegal drugs; Traffic!; Who uses illegal drugs?; Looking toward solutions; What else can be done?

This "looks at global drug production and trafficking, types of illegal drugs, who uses them, and possible solutions. The book includes information about drug crops and the economic implications that make it difficult for governments around the world to control their sale and abuse. . . . Color photographs are plentiful and color-keyed boxes include opposing viewpoints, facts, and topics to debate." SLJ

Gangs; Scott Barbour, book editor. Greenhaven Press 2006 128p il map (Introducing issues with opposing viewpoints) $32.45 *

Grades: 8 9 10 11 12   **364.1**

1. Gangs

ISBN 0-7377-3221-0   LC 2005-40395

"In such chapters as, How Can Gang Violence Be Reduced? the issue is presented viewpoint by viewpoint, with an introduction and the author's credentials provided for each essay. Thought-provoking queries are given. . . . Fast Facts are also included. The book is heavily illustrated with color photos, cartoons, and tables. This informative book encourages active reading and makes research accessible for less-able students who are learning critical reading and research skills. A top resource for every library." SLJ

Hate groups: opposing viewpoints; Mary E. Williams, editor. Greenhaven Press 2004 192p il lib bdg $34.95; pa $23.70

Grades: 8 9 10 11 12   **364.1**

1. Hate crimes

ISBN 0-7377-2280-0 (lib bdg); 0-7377-2281-9 (pa)

LC 2003-54324

Replaces the edition published 1999 under the editorship of Tamara L. Roleff

"Opposing viewpoints series"

"Contributors debate whether hate groups pose a serious threat and whether extra penalties should be applied to hate crimes." Publisher's note

Includes bibliographical references

Johnson, Julie

Why do people join gangs? Raintree Steck-Vaughn Pubs. 2001 48p il (Exploring tough issues) lib bdg $29.93

Grades: 6 7 8 9   **364.1**

1. Gangs

ISBN 0-7398-3236-0   LC 00-51750

This attempts to explain the attraction of gangs with sections on bullying, rites and rituals, gang mentality, and drug and protection rackets

"Concise and well written, this book provides an overview of the problem, focusing on the United States, but discussing other countries as well." SLJ

Includes glossary and bibliographical references

Kaminker, Laura

Everything you need to know about dealing with sexual assault. Rosen Pub. Group 1998 64p il (Need to know library) lib bdg $17.95

Grades: 6 7 8 9   **364.1**

1. Rape

ISBN 0-8239-2837-3   LC 98-7048

Discusses the myths and facts surrounding sexual assault and rape, the physical and psychological consequences, suggests ways to stay safe, and explains what to do if sexually assaulted

Includes glossary and bibliographical references

Miller, Debra A.

Political corruption; by Debra A. Miller. Lucent Books 2007 112p il (Hot topics) $32.45

Grades: 7 8 9 10   **364.1**

1. Political corruption

ISBN 978-1-59018-982-5; 1-59018-982-5

LC 2007007793

This "offers a historical overview of political misdeeds and current efforts to curb them. Miller knows her [subject] and offers enough intrigue to hold readers' attention. Sidebars and relevant photos appear throughout." Horn Book Guide

Includes bibliographical references

Roleff, Tamara L., 1959-

Hate groups; by Tami Roleff. Greenhaven Press 2001 112p il (Opposing viewpoints digests) $29.95; pa $19.95

Grades: 8 9 10 11 12   **364.1**

1. Hate crimes

ISBN 0-7377-0677-5; 0-7377-0676-7 (pa)

LC 00-12170

This book "poses three basic questions about hate groups and hate speech (Are these groups a problem? Should hate speech be restricted? Are hate crimes laws necessary?) before unveiling documented pro and con essays that explore each question's complexities. Roleff's crisp, journalistic writing combines anecdotes and facts in a dense, but easily readable style." Booklist

Includes bibliographical references

Schroeder, Andreas, 1946-

Scams! ten stories that explore some of the most outrageous swindlers and tricksters of all time. Annick Press 2004 154p (True stories from the edge) $18.95; pa $7.95 *

Grades: 5 6 7 8   **364.1**

1. Fraud 2. Swindlers and swindling

ISBN 1-55037-853-8; 1-55037-852-X (pa)

This is a "collection of stories about forgers, con artists, and other individuals who duped the public for fame, money, love, or power. . . . Schroeder's lively narration with undocumented dialogue breathes life into characters whom readers can't help but marvel at for their sheer ingenuity. . . . Schroeder's page-turning stories are suspenseful." SLJ

Includes bibliographical references

Sherrow, Victoria

The Oklahoma City bombing; terror in the heartland. Enslow Pubs. 1998 48p il (American disasters) lib bdg $18.95

Grades: 4 5 6 7   364.1

1. Oklahoma City (Okla.) bombing, 1995 2. Terrorism

ISBN 0-7660-1061-9   LC 97-45750

Details the events surrounding the 1995 terrorist bombing of the federal building in Oklahoma City, as well as the investigation and trial of those responsible for the blast

"A vivid accounting. . . . Chapters are brief and punctuated with photographs, which, though not gory, bring the disaster to life in horrifying color." Booklist

Includes glossary and bibliographical references

St. George, Judith, 1931-

In the line of fire; presidents' lives at stake. Holiday House 1999 144p il lib bdg $22.95

Grades: 4 5 6 7   364.1

1. Presidents—United States—Assassination

ISBN 0-8234-1428-0   LC 98-39030

"The first of the two main sections concerns the four slain U.S. presidents as well as their respective assassins, and also discusses the effects of these fatal events on the country. Each chapter preface relays the day's events preceding the murder in a dramatic fashion. The second half concerns the assassination attempts on six presidents and their would-be assassins. St. George includes intriguing anecdotes. . . . Nicely placed illustrations and photos add power to the text." SLJ

Includes bibliographical references

Uschan, Michael V., 1948-

Lynching and murder in the deep South; [by] Michael V. Uschan. Lucent Books 2007 104p il map (Lucent library of Black history) $32.45

Grades: 8 9 10 11 12   364.1

1. Lynching 2. African Americans—Civil rights 3. Southern States—Race relations

ISBN 1-59018-845-4   LC 2005037807

"Uschan deals honestly with this important historical topic . . . that occurred from the end of Reconstruction through the 1920s, '30s, and into the '40s and '50s. Writing in clear and telling prose, the author chronicles the horrific history of this practice in the South, why it was so pervasive, and how it was eventually brought to an end. This is a book that fills a gap. . . . Black-and-white photos and reproductions appear throughout." SLJ

Includes bibliographical references

What is a hate crime? Roman Espejo, book editor. Greenhaven Press 2002 106p (At issue) lib bdg $28.70; pa $19.95

Grades: 7 8 9 10   364.1

1. Hate crimes

ISBN 0-7377-0813-1 (lib bdg); 0-7377-0812-3 (pa)

LC 2001-23817

This presents a range of opinions about hate crimes from a variety of sources

Includes bibliographical references

Worth, Richard, 1945-

Massacre at Virginia Tech; disaster & survival; [by] Richard Worth. Enslow Publishers 2008 48p il map (Deadly disasters) $23.93

Grades: 4 5 6 7   364.1

1. Cho, Seung-Hui, 1984-2007 2. Virginia Polytechnic Institute and State University 3. Virginia Tech (Blacksburg, Va.) shootings, 2007 4. School violence

ISBN 978-0-7660-3274-3; 0-7660-3274-4

LC 2007025592

Examines the tragic school shooting at Virginia Tech University, detailing the horrifying massacre, the lives of the killer and victims, and the sociological problems surrounding school shootings.

"The sequence of events, profiles of pertinent figures, and related topics such as gun control are all discussed. Photographs of the killer, victims, and survivors lend chilling immediacy." Horn Book Guide

Includes glossary and bibliographical references

364.36 Juvenile delinquents

Youth violence; Henny H. Kim, book editor. Greenhaven Press 1998 204p (Current controversies) lib bdg $34.95

Grades: 8 9 10 11 12   364.36

1. Juvenile delinquency 2. Violence

ISBN 1-56510-811-6   LC 98-5784

Replaces the edition published 1992 under the editorship of Michael D. Biskup and Charles P. Cozic

This collection of articles "examines the problem of violence among the nation's young people. Chapters include: Is youth violence a serious problem? What causes youth violence? How can youth violence be reduced? Should violent youths receive harsh punishment?" Publisher's note

Includes bibliographical references

364.6 Penology

Kerrigan, Michael

The history of punishment; [by] Michael Kerrigan. Mason Crest Publishers 2003 96p il (Crime and detection) $22.95

Grades: 7 8 9 10   364.6

1. Punishment

ISBN 1-59084-386-X   LC 2003-488

Contents: Introduction; The wages of sin; A debt to society; Corporal punishment; Capital punishment; The rise of rehabilitation

This covers punishment "from the beginning of time, taking into account secular and religious laws and rules of conduct, and the various means people have employed to punish those who violate the laws, including corporal punishment, imprisonment, capital punishment, and rehabilitation efforts. . . . [This book provides] no-nonsense, straightforward, gritty information, accompanied by good-quality, full-color photos, reproductions, and illustrations." SLJ

Townsend, John, 1955-

Punishment and pain; [by] John Townsend. Raintree 2006 48p il (Painful history of crime) lib bdg $31.43; pa $8.90

Grades: 6 7 8 9   **364.6**

1. Punishment

ISBN 1-4109-2054-2 (lib bdg); 1-4109-2059-3 (pa)

LC 2005012517

"Raintree freestyle"

This "shows the painful consequences of crime through torture and death, from the 1500s to the present. . . . The subject, format, and presentation of material in [this book] will inform students, including reluctant readers." SLJ

Includes bibliographical references

364.66   Capital punishment

The **death** penalty: opposing viewpoints; Diane Andrews Henningfeld, book editor; Bonnie Szumski, publisher; Helen Cothran, managing editor. Greenhaven Press 2006 223p il $34.95; pa $23.70

Grades: 8 9 10 11 12   **364.66**

1. Capital punishment

ISBN 0-7377-2929-5; 0-7377-2930-9 (pa)

LC 2005052743

Replaces the edition published 2001 under the editorship of Mary E. Williams

"Opposing viewpoints series"

"Powerful people and organizations contribute essays to the death-penalty debate. Supreme Court Justice Antonin Scala argues that the death penalty is just, and his former colleague, Sandra Day O'Connor, debates whether juveniles should be exempt from it. This nonbiased, comprehensive look at one of today's most difficult issues will be helpful for students writing persuasive essays and for debate groups." SLJ

Includes bibliographical references

Kuklin, Susan

No choirboy; murder, violence, and teenagers on death row. Henry Holt and Co. 2008 212p il $17.95 *

Grades: 8 9 10 11 12   **364.66**

1. Capital punishment 2. Juvenile delinquency

ISBN 978-0-8050-7950-0; 0-8050-7950-5

LC 2007-46940

"The book opens with candid interviews that introduce three inmates, all of them teenagers when they committed their crimes. . . . This eye-opening account will likely open minds. . . . The book concludes with solid back matter—notes, glossary, bibliography, and index." Horn Book

Includes glossary and bibliographical references

365   Penal and related institutions

America's prisons: opposing viewpoints; Clare Hanrahan, book editor. Greenhaven Press 2006 203p il map lib bdg $34.95; pa $23.70

Grades: 8 9 10 11 12   **365**

1. Prisons—United States

ISBN 0-7377-3344-6 (lib bdg); 0-7377-3345-4 (pa)

LC 2005-52659

Replaces the edition published 2002 under the editorship of Roman Espejo

"Opposing viewpoints series"

"This collection of opposing viewpoints provides students an opportunity to weigh the merits of arguments that support or oppose the operation of America's prisons." Publisher's note

Includes bibliographical references

Edge, Laura Bufano, 1953-

Locked up; a history of the U.S. prison system; by Laura B. Edge. Twenty-First Century Books 2009 112p il (People's history) lib bdg $31.93

Grades: 6 7 8 9 10   **365**

1. Prisons—United States

ISBN 978-0-8225-8750-7; 0-8225-8750-5

LC 2008-26883

"Using primary resources, photographs, and solid research, Edge has written a well-organized and engaging history of our prison system. . . . This book can serve as an excellent resource for reports." SLJ

Includes bibliographical references

Lock, Joan

Famous prisons; [by] Joan Lock. Mason Crest Publishers 2003 96p il (Crime and detection) $22.95

Grades: 7 8 9 10   **365**

1. Prisons

ISBN 1-59084-380-0   LC 2003-477

Contents: Alcatraz Federal Penitentiary, California; Up river: Sing Sing Prison, New York State; Halfway to Hell: Dartmoor Prison; The big house: San Quentin State Penitentiary, California; Ireland's model prison: Mountjoy, Dublin; Going around in circles: Stateville Penitentiary, Joliet, Illinois

"Lock takes readers on a tour of famous U.S. prisons . . . as well as one in England . . . and another in Ireland. . . . She includes a history of each one, and the conditions over time, as well as interesting stories about each prison, and some of its famous inmates. . . . [The book provides] no-nonsense, straightforward, gritty information, accompanied by good-quality, full-color photos, reproductions, and illustrations." SLJ

Includes bibliographical references

Rabiger, Joanna

Daily prison life; [by] Joanna Rabiger. Mason Crest Publishers 2003 96p il (Crime and detection) $22.95

Grades: 7 8 9 10   **365**

1. Prisons 2. Prisoners

ISBN 1-59084-384-3   LC 2003-364

Rabiger, Joanna—*Continued*

"Rabiger concentrates on the U.S. prison system and gives readers a closeup and grimly realistic view of living in one. . . . [This book provides] no-nonsense, straightforward, gritty information, accompanied by good-quality, full-color photos, reproductions, and illustrations." SLJ

Includes bibliographical references

Townsend, John, 1955-

Prisons and prisoners; [by] John Townsend. Raintree 2006 48p il (Painful history of crime) lib bdg $31.45; pa $8.90

Grades: 6 7 8 9   **365**

1. Prisons 2. Prisoners

ISBN 1-4109-2053-4 (lib bdg); 1-4109-2058-5 (pa)

LC 2005012516

"Raintree freestyle"

This "looks at the history of [prisons] and the reforms that have taken place over the years from the days of the medieval castle dungeon to modern Supermax prisons. . . . The subject, format, and presentation of material in [this book] will inform students, including reluctant readers." SLJ

Includes bibliographical references

370.15   Educational psychology

Wilson, David, 1974-

Strategies for evaluation; forming judgments about information for classroom, homework, and test success; [by] David Wilson. 1st ed. Rosen Pub. Group 2006 48p il (The library of higher order thinking skills) lib bdg $25.25; pa $11.95 *

Grades: 5 6 7 8   **370.15**

1. Critical thinking 2. Evaluation

ISBN 1-4042-0473-3 (lib bdg); 1-4042-0656-6 (pa)

LC 2004030620

"In an effort to help students improve their ability to think critically, this slim, colorful volume discusses how to evaluate and form judgments about information so that one can be successful in the classroom, with homework, and on tests. . . . While the information is basic, the book is easy to read for students who need some help learning how to tap into those higher-order thinking skills." SLJ

Includes bibliographical references

370.25   Education—Directories

The **Handbook** of private schools; an annual descriptive survey of independent education. 89th ed. Sargent Pubs. 2008 1296p il map $99

Grades: Professional   **370.25**

1. Reference books 2. Private schools—Directories 3. Education—United States—Directories

ISSN 0072-9884

ISBN 978-0-87558-165-1; 0-87558-165-X

Annual. First published 1915 with title: Handbook of the best private schools of the United States and Canada

"Describes more than 1,700 boarding and day schools, providing information on age and grade ranges, whether co-educational or for boys or girls, enrollment, faculty size and background, academic orientation and curriculum, and where graduates attend college. 'Features classified' section lists institutions offering military programs, elementary boarding divisions, programs for students with learning differences, international and bilingual schools, and schools with more than 500 or fewer than 100 students." Guide to Ref Books. 11th edition

371.1   Teachers and teaching, and related activities

Harada, Violet H.

Inquiry learning through librarian-teacher partnerships; [by] Violet H. Harada and Joan M. Yoshina. Linworth Pub 2004 172p il pa $39.95

Grades: Professional   **371.1**

1. Teaching teams 2. School libraries

ISBN 1-58683-134-8   LC 2004-662

"The authors describe what happens in an inquiry-based classroom and library media center and show teachers/librarians how to develop a curriculum that incorporates essential questions and important habits of mind, all aligned with content standards. . . . The volume contains everything a teacher-librarian team would need to create, teach, research, and assess major interdisciplinary units." SLJ

Includes bibliographical references

371.3   Methods of instruction and study

Bell, Ann, 1945-

Handheld computers in schools and media centers; [by] Ann Bell. Linworth Pub. 2007 134p il pa $39.95

Grades: Professional   **371.3**

1. Computer-assisted instruction 2. Wireless communication systems 3. School libraries—Automation 4. Instructional materials centers

ISBN 1-58683-212-3   LC 2006025691

"This guide will be a tremendous resource for students and teachers who are using handheld devices. Thoroughly indexed and easy to read and follow, it will give teachers and media specialists a means to integrate handheld computers into their curricula and library-media programs. Bell discusses using the devices to meet national and state academic standards and curriculum integration; selecting appropriate hardware and software; finding, assimilating, circulating, and designing digital media, like e-books and e-audiobooks; and common copyright issues with this format." SLJ

Includes bibliographical references

Braun, Linda W.

Listen up! podcasting for schools and libraries. Information Today, Inc. 2007 97p il pa $29.50 *

Grades: Professional   **371.3**

1. Podcasting

ISBN 978-1-57387-304-8   LC 2007-23650

Braun, Linda W.—*Continued*

"In six conversational chapters, Braun explains podcasting's technical terms, ongoing development, necessary components such as an RSS feed and a feed reader, creating subscriptions, and methods of distribution." SLJ

"This is a valuable resource for those interested in learning more about podcasting and utilizing the technology to improve their programming and outreach." Booklist

Includes bibliographical references

Crane, Beverley E.

Using WEB 2.0 tools in the K-12 classroom. Neal-Schuman Publishers 2009 189p il pa $59.95

Grades: Professional   **371.3**

1. Internet in education 2. Education—Curricula 3. Web 2.0

ISBN 978-1-55570-653-1; 1-55570-653-3

LC 2008-46167

"In this extensive resource, teachers will find a wealth of suggestions, ideas, unit plans, and answers to questions pertaining to how to integrate and use Web 2.0 tools throughout the curriculum." SLJ

"This excellent resource should be widely appealing to teachers, librarians, and school media specialists." Voice Youth Advocates

Includes glossary and bibliographical references

Fontichiaro, Kristin

Podcasting at school; foreword by Diane R. Chen. Libraries Unlimited 2008 170p il pa $30 *

Grades: Professional   **371.3**

1. Podcasting

ISBN 978-1-59158-587-9; 1-59158-587-2

LC 2007-35040

"This book takes [a] . . . look at several podcasting tools . . . that can be used by educators to create podcasts. After building a . . . technical foundation, the book introduces readers to . . . lesson plans that motivate students and stretch their higher-order thinking. Discussion of student privacy issues is interwoven throughout." Publisher's note

"The book provides simple, clear explanations of podcasting terms, procedures, and protocols. . . . This book is an essential purchase for professional development collections." Libr Media Connect

Includes bibliographical references

Fox, Janet S.

Get organized without losing it; by Janet S. Fox; edited by Pamela Espeland. Free Spirit Pub. 2006 105p il (Laugh & learn) pa $8.95 *

Grades: 5 6 7 8   **371.3**

1. Study skills 2. Time management 3. Life skills

ISBN 1-57542-193-3; 978-1-57542-193-3

LC 2005032809

"In this handbook for students, Fox uses humor to provide practical, easy-to-follow ideas for organizing desks, backpacks, and lockers; managing time for homework and after school activities; planning long-term projects; and taking better notes. . . . Fox writes in a con-versational style. . . . Humorous illustrations complement the text." Voice Youth Advocates

Includes bibliographical references

Technologies for education; a practical guide; [by] Ann E. Barron . . . [et al.] 5th ed. Libraries Unlimited 2006 189p il pa $48

Grades: Professional   **371.3**

1. Teaching—Aids and devices

ISBN 1-59158-250-4 (pa); 978-1-59158-250-2 (pa)

LC 2006012708

This offers an "overview of the technologies that are impacting education. . . . [It includes] information on a variety of educational technology topics (with a . . . chapter featuring PDAs) and demonstrates how technologies can best be applied in educational settings. . . . Chapters include: Teaching With Technology; Digital Audio; Digital Video; Computer Graphics; Telecommunications; Distance Learning and others." Publisher's note

Includes bibliographical references

371.5   School discipline and related activities

Beaudoin, Marie-Nathalie

Responding to the culture of bullying and disrespect; new perspectives on collaboration, compassion, and responsibility; [by] Marie-Nathalie Beaudoin, Maureen Taylor. rev. 2nd ed. Corwin Press 2009 281p il $76.95; pa $36.95

Grades: Professional   **371.5**

1. Bullies 2. School discipline

ISBN 978-1-4129-6853-9; 1-4129-6853-4; 978-1-4129-6854-6 (pa); 1-4129-6854-2 (pa)

LC 2008-55933

First published 2004 with title: Breaking the culture of bullying and disrespect

"This profound resource explores the behaviors that cultivate a culture of bullying and disrespect. . . . Concrete solutions to issues are offered, and the authors make sure to load this title with practical suggestions for affecting change. They delve into ways to work directly with young people to better address their concerns. . . . This purchase is essential for any educator, counselor, or parent. It should be a staple of the school library reference collection because the information provided should be used daily. It will be a title that can be referenced for years to come and will help with adults struggling to overcome bullying." Voice Youth Advocates

Includes glossary and bibliographical references

Bott, C. J., 1947-

The bully in the book and in the classroom; [by] C. J. Bott. Scarecrow Press 2004 185p il pa $30

Grades: Professional   **371.5**

1. Reference books 2. Bullies 3. Children's literature—Bibliography 4. Young adult literature—Bibliography

ISBN 0-8108-5048-6   LC 2004-8536

This "was written to address the . . . problem of bullying in the halls, offices, and classrooms of our schools

Bott, C. J., 1947-—*Continued*
and to help educators know what to look for and how to react when they witness harassment. . . . Bott also reviews books recommended for each reading level. . . . Each review contains . . . [a] summary, activities, and quotes from the book." Publisher's note

"The volume may be useful as a beginning effort in dealing with this very real and pervasive problem." SLJ

Includes bibliographical references

Winkler, Kathleen
Bullying; how to deal with taunting, teasing, and tormenting. Enslow Pubs. 2005 104p il (Issues in focus today) lib bdg $31.93 *

Grades: 5 6 7 8   **371.5**
1. Bullies
ISBN 0-7660-2355-9

"Winkler examines the impact of bullying on both the victim and the victimizer. In straightforward and clear language, she uses conversations with teens, quotes from magazine and newspaper articles, interviews with professional therapists and school officials, plus excerpts from titles such as Rachel Simmons's *Odd Girl Out: The Hidden Culture of Aggression in Girls* (Harcourt, 2002) to provide a readable discussion of what bullying is, why bullies do what they do, and why victims take it." SLJ

Includes glossary and bibliographical references

371.7   Student welfare

Hester, Joseph P.
Public school safety; a handbook, with a resource guide. McFarland & Co. 2003 200p pa $35 *

Grades: Professional   **371.7**
1. School violence 2. Education—Government policy
ISBN 0-7864-1483-9   LC 2003-2511

Contents: The state of youth violence and its roots; Public school safety, government initiatives; Strategies for building a school safety program; Measures to ensure school safety, model programs; Building a leadership culture; National resources for safe school programs; Resources for the Surgeon General's report

This "begins by discussing a number of important government reports that have identified the problems and causes of youth violence and some ideas for combating it. . . . The myriad strategies involving the community, parents, and teachers are discussed and both ineffective and effective programs are evaluated. . . . This is a solid and thorough guide." SLJ

Includes bibliographical references

Orr, Tamra
Violence in our schools; halls of hope, halls of fear. Franklin Watts 2003 192p il $29.50 *

Grades: 7 8 9 10   **371.7**
1. School violence
ISBN 0-531-12268-9   LC 2003-104

Chronicles school violence and discusses its causes, perpetrators, and solutions, including "Questions to ponder" and specific advice for individual action

"This book takes an evenhanded, enlightening look at the problem of, and possible solutions for, school violence. . . . For students doing research, the book offers succinct summaries of incidents of school violence dating back to the 1920s, and it includes an overview of the Columbine tragedy. . . . For sociology research and for schools seeking proactive ideas for creating safe and inclusive campuses, this is an excellent resource." Booklist

Includes bibliographical references

Parks, Peggy J., 1951-
School violence. ReferencePoint Press 2008 104p il map (Compact research) $25.95

Grades: 8 9 10 11 12   **371.7**
1. School violence
ISBN 978-1-60152-057-9; 1-60152-057-3
                                              LC 2008-18372

The introduction "looks at the prevalence of [school violence]; causes such as bullying and gangs; the influence of the media, including online sources, on behavior; and the roles of alcohol and drugs, etc. The '. . . at a glance' spread and 'Overview' prepare readers for the more detailed information to come and provide facts about safety issues. Each of four chapters then addresses both sides of a question, followed by four pages of quotes and a section of colorful graphs, charts, and illustrations. . . . The accessible and objective [presentation] and lists of key people and advocacy groups make [this a] useful [resource] for research." SLJ

Includes bibliographical references

Student drug testing; Patty Jo Sawvel, book editor. Greenhaven Press 2007 136p il (Issues that concern you) lib bdg $33.70

Grades: 7 8 9 10 11 12   **371.7**
1. Drug testing 2. Students—Civil rights 3. Youth—Drug use
ISBN 0-7377-2424-2 (lib bdg); 978-0-7377-2424-0 (lib bdg)   LC 2006043352

"This title compiles articles and essays that take opposing viewpoints on the issues of teen drug testing. A range of opinions is introduced, from students and educators to journalists, government officials, and experts specializing in this topic. . . . Color illustrations are attractive and effective in emphasizing points, and cartoons add humor and interest. . . . A well-rounded presentation." SLJ

Includes bibliographical references

371.8   Students

Tym, Kate
School survival; a guide to taking control of your life; [by] Kate Tym and Penny Worms. Raintree 2005 48p il (Get real) $29.93

Grades: 7 8 9 10   **371.8**
1. Socialization 2. Schools 3. Peer pressure
ISBN 1-4109-0577-2   LC 2004-8070

Contents: It's what I go to school for; A friend in need; Peer pressure; Misfit city; Bully boys and girls; I'm in trouble; Moving on

Tym, Kate—*Continued*

"Chapters consist of a spread presenting an overview of a topic such as . . . peer pressure, followed by three case studies about teens dealing with the problem. On the same page, three 'experts' . . . offer advice. . . . The advice of professionals lends credibility to the information presented. . . . [This volume is] sure to appeal to readers looking for advice." SLJ

371.9   Special education

Brinkerhoff, Shirley

Why can't I learn like everyone else? youth with learning disabilities; by Shirley Brinkerhoff. Mason Crest Publishers 2004 127p il (Youth with special needs) $24.95; pa $14.95

Grades: 5 6 7 8   **371.9**
    1. Learning disabilities
    ISBN 1-59084-730-X; 1-42220-432-0 (pa)
                          LC 2003-18438
    Contents: Changes; Learning to get by; Anger; Another world; Conflicts; Tensions; The power of persistence; Hope

"Charlie Begay, an eighth-grade Navajo student in New Mexico who cannot read due to dyslexia, describes his personal journey of embarrassment, frustration, and low self-esteem. Following the fictional narrative is factual material about learning disabilities, covering terminology, possible signs, diagnosis, the law, coping strategies, and success stories." SLJ

"The writing is straightforward but not simplistic and liberally illustrated with photographs and occasional diagrams." Voice Youth Advocates

Includes bibliographical references

Kent, Deborah, 1948-

Athletes with disabilities. Watts 2003 63p il lib bdg $24 paperback o.p.

Grades: 4 5 6 7   **371.9**
    1. Sports for the handicapped
    ISBN 0-531-12019-8 (lib bdg); 0-531-16664-3 (pa)
                          LC 2002-8883
    "Watts library"
    Contents: The love of the game; Beating the odds; Brave in the attempt; Going for the Gold; A level playing field

Explores the people and events involved in sports competitions for people with disabilities and discusses people with disabilities who play professional sports

"Information is effectively conveyed through clear, straightforward prose and accounts of individual athletes. . . . [This is] informative, often inspirational and thought-provoking." Booklist

Includes bibliographical references

Paquette, Penny Hutchins

Learning disabilities; the ultimate teen guide; [by] Penny Hutchins Paquette, Cheryl Gerson Tuttle. Scarecrow Press 2003 301p il (It happened to me) lib bdg $32.50; pa $17.95 *

Grades: 7 8 9 10   **371.9**
    1. Learning disabilities
    ISBN 0-8108-4261-0 (lib bdg); 0-8108-5643-3 (pa)
                          LC 2002-17588

This provides an "overview of the most common disabilities. . . . The book also teaches students how to advocate for themselves, informing them of their rights under law both during the school years and after high school graduation. . . . Assistive technology that can help students improve their learning abilities such as Optical Character Recognition (OCR) systems, screen reading software, books on tape, electronic notebooks, and other tools that aid student learning are covered." Publisher's note

"Far more detailed than similiar books from other publishers." Voice Youth Advocates

Includes bibliographical references

Stanley, Jerry, 1941-

Children of the Dust Bowl; the true story of the school at Weedpatch Camp. Crown 1992 85p il map hardcover o.p. pa $9.95

Grades: 5 6 7 8   **371.9**
    1. Migrant labor 2. Great Depression, 1929-1939 3. Education—Social aspects
    ISBN 0-517-88094-6; 0-517-58782-3 (pa)
                          LC 92-393

Describes the plight of the migrant workers who traveled from the Dust Bowl to California during the Depression and were forced to live in a federal labor camp and discusses the school that was built for their children

"Stanley's text is a compelling document. . . . The story is inspiring and disturbing, and Stanley has recorded the details with passion and dignity." Booklist

Includes bibliographical references

371.95   Gifted students

Karnes, Frances A.

Competitions for talented kids; win scholarships, big prize money, and recognition; [by] Frances A. Karnes & Tracy L. Riley. Prufrock Press 2005 245p il $17.95 *

Grades: 7 8 9 10 11 12   **371.95**
    1. Contests 2. Gifted children
    ISBN 1-59363-156-1

"Featuring more than 140 competitions focused on a wide range of academic subjects, studio arts, performing arts, leadership, and service learning, this volume encourages students to seek scholarships, prize money, and recognition for their talents." Booklist

Includes bibliographical references

372 Elementary education

Mackey, Bonnie
A librarian's guide to cultivating an elementary school garden; [by] Bonnie Mackey and Jennifer Mackey Stewart. Linworth Pub. 2009 124p il pa $39.95
Grades: Professional   372
1. School libraries—Activity projects 2. Gardening
ISBN 978-1-58683-328-2; 1-58683-328-6
         LC 2008-34963
"In this comprehensive guide to designing and implementing a school garden, Mackay and Stewart offer practical advice on acquiring funding sources and developing community partnerships, as well as specific instructions for developing various types of gardens: vegetable, butterfly, natural habitat, etc. A wide variety of activities is included, each one linked to the National Science Standards. Annotated book lists and webliographies of appropriate material for both students and faculty are presented throughout." SLJ
"Its unusual topic makes this book a standout." Libr Media Connect
Includes bibliographical references

372.4 Reading

Bouchard, Dave
The gift of reading; [by] David Bouchard, with Wendy Sutton. Orca Bk. Pubs. 2001 158p il pa $16.95
Grades: Professional   372.4
1. Reading 2. Books and reading
ISBN 1-55143-214-5   LC 2001-92682
This "overview of what young people need to become independent readers . . . targets families, teachers, and school administrators, claiming that nothing extravagant is required to promote reading. . . . All groups will find the grade-level reading lists and abundant literacy strategies helpful." Voice Youth Advocates

Knowles, Elizabeth, 1946-
Talk about books! a guide for book clubs, literature circles, and discussion groups, grades 4-8. Libraries Unlimited 2003 147p il pa $30 *
Grades: Professional   372.4
1. Books and reading
ISBN 1-59158-023-4   LC 2003-51582
"Each of the fifteen chapters focuses on a different book that serves as a prototype for a particular subject or genre. . . . Each focal book is briefly summarized, followed by a bit of biographical information about its author. Then a list of discussion questions is offered. . . . The questions nicely probe both concrete and abstract understanding of the book. . . . In addition, each chapter includes activities for all areas of the curriculum, an annotated list of related books, an annotated list of the author's other works, dozens of Web site suggestions, and the publisher's information." Voice Youth Advocates
Includes bibliographical references

Moreillon, Judi
Collaborative strategies for teaching reading comprehension; maximizing your impact; [by] Judi Moreillon. American Library Association 2007 170p il $38
Grades: Professional   372.4
1. Reading comprehension
ISBN 978-0-8389-0929-4; 0-8389-0929-9
         LC 2006036132
This "begins by emphasizing the importance of collaboration between classroom teachers and teacher-librarians. . . . The bulk of the book focuses on seven reading comprehension strategies and how to teach them. . . . Overall this book is a cut above other 'how-to' books with its plethora of suggestions and resources for teachers and librarians." Voice Youth Advocates
Includes glossary and bibliographical references

372.6 Language arts (Communication skills)

Ellis, Sarah, 1952-
From reader to writer; teaching writing through classic children's books. Douglas & McIntyre 2000 176p hardcover o.p. pa $14.95
Grades: Professional   372.6
1. Rhetoric—Study and teaching 2. Children's literature—Study and teaching
ISBN 0-88899-372-2; 0-88899-440-0 (pa)
"A Groundwood book"
The author discusses the work of seventeen British, Canadian and American authors of children's literature. "With each classic book, there's a 'sneak preview' (i.e., booktalk), a suggested read-aloud, exercises to help students and adult writers find their own stories, and a short annotated bibliography of related children's books." Booklist

Hamilton, Martha
Children tell stories; teaching and using storytelling in the classroom; [by] Martha Hamilton and Mitch Weiss. 2nd ed. Richard C. Owen Publishers 2005 xx, 264p il pa $29.95
Grades: Professional   372.6
1. Storytelling
ISBN 978-1-57274-663-3; 1-57274-663-7
         LC 2005021667
First published 1990
"Presents concrete methods of incorporating storytelling by students of all ages into classroom practice to help teachers meet U.S. education standards of reading, writing, speaking, listening, viewing, and visually representing." Publisher's note
"Combining enthusiasm and inspiration with practical tips, handouts, and resources, Hamilton and Weiss offer a comprehensive second edition that will be useful to both novice and experienced tellers. . . . The accompanying high-quality DVD shows children and adults telling stories, gives Web links, and includes 25 stories to download and print." SLJ
Includes bibliographical references

Hopkins, Lee Bennett, 1938-
Pass the poetry, please! 3rd ed. HarperCollins
Pubs. 1998 277p $25; pa $5.99 *
Grades: Professional   **372.6**
1. Poetry—Study and teaching
ISBN 0-06-027746-7; 0-06-446199-8 (pa)
LC 98-19617
First published 1972
"Written for teachers and librarians seeking ways of
getting poetry into the lives of children. . . . Through-
out, many poets are cited, from Langston Hughes to
Nikki Giovanni and from Jack Prelutsky to Robert
Frost." Booklist
"This a must-purchase." SLJ
Includes bibliographical references

Miller, Donalyn, 1967-
The book whisperer; awakening the inner reader
in every child; [by] Donalyn Miller; foreword by
Jeff Anderson. 1st ed. Jossey-Bass 2009 227p
$22.95 *
Grades: Professional   **372.6**
1. Books and reading
ISBN 978-0-4703-7227-2; 0-4703-7227-3
LC 2008055666
Donalyn Miller's approach to reading promotion "is
simple yet provocative: affirm the reader in every student, allow students to choose their own books, carve out
extra reading time, model authentic reading behaviors,
discard time-worn reading assignments such as book reports and comprehension worksheets, and develop a
classroom library filled with high-interest books. . . .
Miller provides many tips for teachers and parents and
includes a useful list of ultimate reading suggestions
picked by her students. This outstanding contribution to
the literature is highly recommended." Libr J
Includes bibliographical references

Pellowski, Anne, 1933-
The storytelling handbook; a young people's
collection of unusual tales and helpful hints on
how to tell them; illustrated by Martha Stoberock.
Simon & Schuster Bks. for Young Readers 1995
129p il hardcover o.p. pa $7.99
Grades: 4 5 6 7   **372.6**
1. Storytelling
ISBN 0-689-80311-7; 978-1-4169-7598-4 (pa);
1-4169-7598-5 (pa)   LC 95-2991
This work "addresses the young person who wants to
tell stories in a public setting. It is similar in format to
many adult books on storytelling how-tos, with sections
on getting started and selecting and preparing stories, as
well as a selection of sample tales. Pellowski's notes are
extensive and will be very useful to novices looking for
ways to research stories." Booklist
Includes bibliographical references

Roth, Rita
The story road to literacy; [by] Rita Roth.
Teacher Ideas Press 2006 176p il pa $30
Grades: Professional   **372.6**
1. English language—Study and teaching
2. Language arts 3. Children of immigrants
ISBN 1-59158-323-3   LC 2005030835

"Roth advances the idea that using traditional literature with students who are learning English will help
them acquire critical communication skills while tying
unfamiliar new places to familiar elements of their own
heritages. The author provides practical, ready-to-use lesson plans, story samples, and suggested activities." SLJ
Includes bibliographical references

373.1 Organization and activities in
secondary education

Bluestein, Jane
High school's not forever; [by] Jane Bluestein
and Eric Katz. HCI Teens 2005 302p il pa $12.95
Grades: 7 8 9 10 11 12   **373.1**
1. High school students
ISBN 0-7573-0256-4   LC 2005-50232
"Culled from the responses of some 2000 high and
post-high school students, this title gives voice to young
people who have lived through the experience and who
offer both affirming and cautionary tales as they attempted to navigate the uncertain seas of friendship, depression, academic achievement, drugs, and sexuality. . . .
There is no question that this book will enhance most
YA collections." SLJ
Includes bibliographical references

Braun, Linda W.
Teens, technology, and literacy; or, Why bad
grammar isn't always bad. Libraries Unlimited
2007 105p il pa $30 *
Grades: Professional   **373.1**
1. Literacy 2. Teenagers—Books and reading
3. Bibliographic instruction 4. Computer-assisted instruction 5. Information technology
ISBN 1-59158-368-3; 978-1-59158-368-4
LC 2006-31714
"Braun shows teachers, administrators, and librarians
how to incorporate today's technologies into the development of literacy skills. The author backs up the grammar
used in IMs and text messaging by explaining how these
technologies promote better literacy in the classroom.
. . . This book is a must for most collections." SLJ
Includes bibliographical references

Elliott, Kathleen
How to prepare for the SSAT/ISEE, Secondary
School Admissions Test/Independent School
Entrance Exam. Barron's 2005 358p pa $16.95
Grades: 6 7 8 9   **373.1**
1. High schools—Entrance requirements
ISBN 0-76412-900-7 (pa); 978-0-76412-900-1 (pa)
LC 2004061121
This "manual prepares students to pass either the Secondary School Admissions Test or the Independent
School Entrance Exam, tests that are nationally adminis-
tered as admission requirements by many private secondary schools. Students will find practice and review exercises in verbal skills, reading comprehension, analogies,
essay writing, and mathematics, with review material designed to help students pinpoint areas where they need
more intensive study. Two practice SSAT exams and two
practice ISEE exams are included." Publisher's note

Erlbach, Arlene
The middle school survival guide; illustrations by Helen Flook. Walker & Co. 2003 150p il pa $8.95
Grades: 5 6 7 8   **373.1**
1. Life skills 2. Middle schools 3. Teenagers
ISBN 0-8027-8852-1   LC 2002-34784
Contents: A new school, a new environment; Teachers; Academics; Peers; The opposite sex; Home life; Puberty; Really serious stuff; Being yourself
A guidebook to help deal with changes in school, families, social lives, and bodies that come during the middle school years, with specific advice for a variety of situations
"Erlbach's advice is sound, but the real gems are the quotes from kids. There are some explicit content and frank discussion, with Erlbach using the same nononsense language whether covering drugs, sexual harassment, crushes, cheating, oral sex, or pregnancy. . . . Strong, and well-delivered, often necessary medicine." Booklist

Farrell, Juliana
Middle school, the real deal; from cafeteria food to combination locks; [by] Juliana Farrell, Beth Mayall. rev. ed. Collins 2007 167p il pa $7.99 *
Grades: 4 5 6 7   **373.1**
1. Middle schools
ISBN 978-0-06-122742-4 (pa); 0-06-122742-0 (pa)
                                    LC 2006102931
First published 2001
"New middle school students are given advice about living through the first day of school, handling the changing classroom schedule after being in a single elementary classroom, the benefits of extracurricular activities, making and keeping friends, and how to get along with parents." Voice Youth Advocates [review of 2001 ed.]

Middle school: how to deal; by Sara Borden . . . [et al.]; illustrated by Yuki Hatori; with a foreword by Karen Bokram. Chronicle Books 2005 lib bdg $15.50; pa $9.95 *
Grades: 4 5 6 7   **373.1**
1. Middle schools
ISBN 0-8118-4845-0 (lib bdg); 0-8118-4497-8 (pa)
Five middle school girls write about how to navigate middle school and deal with the changes in your life.
"The writing style is reassuring and casual. . . . The majority of rising middle-school readers will find much good advice here." Booklist

Pipkin, Gloria
At the schoolhouse gate; lessons in intellectual freedom; [by] Gloria Pipkin and ReLeah Cossett Lent; foreword by Susan Ohanian. Heinemann (Portsmouth) 2002 xx, 235p pa $21
Grades: Professional   **373.1**
1. Academic freedom 2. Censorship 3. Public schools
ISBN 0-325-00395-5   LC 2001-39909
"Two English teachers share their . . . personal battle to support students intellectual rights in the Bay County

School District in Florida in the 1980s when censorship cases were looming in schools throughout the nation. . . . This book is one of inspiration, and teachers, librarians, and school administrators may find it encouraging as they face similar battles." SLJ
Includes bibliographical references

Serritella, Judy, 1948-
Look again! appealing bulletin board ideas for secondary students. Linworth Pub. 2002 160p pa $36.95
Grades: Professional   **373.1**
1. Bulletin boards 2. Teenagers—Books and reading
ISBN 1-58683-053-8   LC 2002-16181
"Basic practical tips suggest ways to liven up board displays, for example, by using three-dimensional materials such as corrugated cardboard or wallpaper. Ideas focus on providing students with information they need, as well as on promoting reading and library services." Book Rep
Includes bibliographical references

375 Curricula

Managing curriculum and assessment; a practitioner's guide; [by] Beverly Nichols . . . [et al.] Linworth Publishing 2006 170p pa $49.95
Grades: Professional   **375**
1. Education—Curricula 2. Evaluation
ISBN 1-58683-216-6   LC 2006003202
"This is a guide by practitioners who give advice on how to respond to the laws and requirements of No Child Left Behind. It is an invaluable resource that provides new insights. . . . There are three sections to the guide with an accompanying CD that contains everything in the book and more. . . . This guide is loaded with examples and is a must have for your professional library." Libr Media Connect
Includes bibliographical references

379 Public policy issues in education

Haskins, James, 1941-2005
Separate, but not equal; the dream and the struggle. Scholastic 1998 184p il hardcover o.p. pa $4.99
Grades: 5 6 7 8   **379**
1. African Americans—Education 2. School integration 3. Segregation in education
ISBN 0-590-45911-2; 0-590-45910-4 (pa)
                                    LC 96-51507
The author traces "the history of the African American struggle for equal rights to education, from the enforced illiteracy of slavery times to the present debate about affirmative action." Booklist
"With his knack for blending historical facts and thoughtful interpretation, Haskins offers an informative, closeup look at the course of black education in America." SLJ
Includes bibliographical references

Miller, Mara, 1968-
School desegregation and the story of the Little
Rock Nine; [by] Mara Miller. Enslow Publishers
2008 128p il map (From many cultures, one
history) lib bdg $31.93
Grades: 6 7 8 9   379
1. Central High School (Little Rock, Ark.) 2. School
integration 3. Segregation in education 4. African
Americans—Education 5. Arkansas—Race relations
ISBN 978-0-7660-2835-7; 0-7660-2835-6 (lib bdg)
LC 2007023376
"Through the 1950s, segregation was a way of life in
the Deep South. But in 1957, after the U.S. Supreme
Court ruling in the case of Brown v. Board of Education,
nine courageous African-American students, the Little
Rock Nine, prepared to integrate Central High School in
Little Rock, Arkansas." Publisher's note
Includes glossary and bibliographical references

Sharp, Anne Wallace
Separate but equal; the desegregation of
America's schools; [by] Anne Wallace Sharp.
Lucent Books 2007 104p il (Lucent library of
black history) $28.70
Grades: 7 8 9 10   379
1. School integration 2. Segregation in education
3. African Americans—Education
ISBN 1-59018-953-1; 978-1-59018-953-5
LC 2006008269
"This simple and direct overview begins with the ban
against educating slaves and the efforts of Prudence
Crandall to provide black girls with schooling in Connecticut in 1832. Following a history of segregation, the
major battles to desegregate public schools in the North
and in the South, as well as those to desegregate univer-
sities and colleges, are highlighted. The violent white
backlash that occurred in both Southern and Northern
states in the 1960s and '70s is also covered." SLJ
Includes bibliographical references

Somerlott, Robert, 1928-
The Little Rock school desegregation crisis in
American history. Enslow Pubs. 2001 128p il (In
American history) lib bdg $26.60
Grades: 7 8 9 10   379
1. Central High School (Little Rock, Ark.) 2. School
integration 3. Segregation in education 4. African
Americans—Education 5. Arkansas—Race relations
ISBN 0-7660-1298-0   LC 00-11444
This book discusses the desegregation of Central High
School in Little Rock Arkansas in 1957
This is a "well-researched and well-documented ac-
count. . . . Somerlott clearly captures the courage of the
students and their families in the face of violent threats.
He also presents a broader view of the impact of this
event on the city of Little Rock, the state of Arkansas,
and the nation." SLJ
Includes bibliographical references

Stokes, John, 1931-
Students on strike; Jim Crow, civil rights,
Brown, and me; a memoir; by John A. Stokes with
Lois Wolfe, and Herman J. Viola. National
Geographic 2008 127p il $15.95; lib bdg $23.90 *
Grades: 4 5 6 7   379
1. Segregation in education 2. African Americans—
Education
ISBN 978-1-4263-0153-7;   1-4263-0153-7;
978-1-4263-0154-4 (lib bdg); 1-4263-0154-5 (lib bdg)
"In 1951, a group of African-American high school
students in Prince Edward County, VA, went on strike to
protest the substandard conditions in their segregated
schools. They eventually became plaintiffs in a lawsuit
that was one of the five that were part of the 1954
Brown decision . . . Fear of retribution and lingering
bitterness has kept the strike leaders silent, but Stokes,
who was among them, has decided that the story of the
strike and its aftermath need to be told. . . . Stoke's inspiring story reveals an almost completely unreported
part of one of the most important court cases of the 20th
century." SLJ

Walker, Paul Robert
Remember Little Rock; the time, the people, the
stories; by Paul Robert Walker. National
Geographic 2008 61p il map $17.95; lib bdg
$27.90 *
Grades: 5 6 7 8 9   379
1. Central High School (Little Rock, Ark.) 2. School
integration 3. Segregation in education 4. African
Americans—Education 5. Arkansas—Race relations
ISBN 978-1-4263-0402-6;   1-4263-0402-1;
978-1-4263-0403-3 (lib bdg); 1-4263-0403-X (lib bdg)
LC 2008-24959
"The story of the battle to integrate Central High
School in 1957 Little Rock, Arkansas, is presented
through photographs and firsthand accounts from those
who were there. . . . The multitude of eyewitness accounts, the poignant photographs, and the contextual
background make this text a must-have addition to any
classroom or library." Voice Youth Advocates
Includes bibliographical references

382   International commerce (Foreign trade)

Gifford, Clive
The arms trade. Chrysalis Education 2004 61p
il (World issues) $29.95
Grades: 7 8 9 10   382
1. Firearms industry 2. Defense industry
ISBN 1-59389-154-7
"This book examines . . . questions surrounding the
arms trade today. What is the arms trade? Is the arms
trade legal? What are weapons of mass destruction? Are
there benefits from the arms trade? Will the arms trade
ever stop?" Publisher's note
"This book packs in copious information from a well-
rounded perspective. . . . Very effective color photos
. . . add a startling and engrossing element." Booklist
Includes glossary and bibliographical references

384 Communications
Telecommunication

Henderson, Harry, 1951-
Communications and broadcasting; from wired words to wireless Web. rev ed. Facts on File 2006 201p il (Milestones in discovery and invention) $35 *
Grades: 7 8 9 10 11 12   **384**
   1. Telecommunication
   ISBN 0-8160-5748-6; 978-0-8160-5748-1
                          LC 2006-5577
First published 1997
This is a "look at the development and interconnection of [the following] scientific ideas: electromagnetism, leading to the telegraph and telephone; Maxwell's wave theory, leading to radio and television; and communications and information theory, from Claude Shannon to the World Wide Web and beyond. In addition, there are . . . portraits of the inventors themselves." Publisher's note
Includes glossary and bibliographical references

384.5 Wireless communication

Byers, Ann
Communications satellites. Rosen Pub. Group 2003 58p il (Library of satellites) lib bdg $26.50
Grades: 4 5 6 7   **384.5**
   1. Artificial satellites in telecommunication
   ISBN 0-8239-3851-4   LC 2002-7527
Contents: How satellites work; The "global village"; The business of satellite communication; What comes next?
This discusses the history, development, and applications of communications satellites
"Clear and topical photographs enliven the [presentation]. While packed with information, the [text is] easy to read." SLJ
Includes bibliographical references

384.55 Television

Wan Guofang
TV takeover; questioning television; by Guofang Wan. Fact Finders 2007 32p il (Media literacy) lib bdg $22.90; pa $7.95
Grades: 4 5 6 7   **384.55**
   1. Television broadcasting
   ISBN 978-0-7368-6763-4 (lib bdg); 0-7368-6763-5 (lib bdg); 978-0-7368-7859-3 (pa); 0-7368-7859-9 (pa)
                          LC 2006021442
"Describes what media is, how television is part of media, and encourages readers to question the medium's influencial messages." Publisher's note
This is "written in a breezy style and [has] plenty of popping colors and photos. . . . Useful and attractive." SLJ
Includes bibliographical references

385 Railroad transportation

Zimmermann, Karl R.
All aboard! passenger trains around the world; [by] Karl Zimmermann; photography by the author. Boyds Mills Press 2006 48p il $19.95 *
Grades: 5 6 7 8   **385**
   1. Railroads
   ISBN 1-59078-325-5   LC 2005-24990
"Zimmerman has traveled by train across six continents, and his beautiful, big color photos appear on every double-page spread of this enthusiastic account, which blends history, geography, business, and engineering with his personal focus." Booklist

Steam locomotives; whistling, chugging, smoking iron horses of the past. Boyds Mills Press 2004 48p il $19.95 *
Grades: 4 5 6 7   **385**
   1. Locomotives 2. Steam engines
   ISBN 1-59078-165-1
"In this photo-essay, Zimmermann shares his excitement for steam locomotives with young readers, tracing the development of the early engines and their impact on the history of the U.S. He includes a clear explanation . . . of how a steam engine works. The photographs, some archival and some from the present day, are excellent. . . . The engaging text clearly imparts the author's enthusiasm and love for the subject." SLJ
Includes glossary

385.09 Railroad transportation— Historical and geographic treatment

Landau, Elaine
The transcontinental railroad; [by] Elaine Landau. Franklin Watts 2005 63p il $25.50
Grades: 5 6 7 8   **385.09**
   1. Central Pacific Railroad 2. Union Pacific Railroad Company 3. Railroads—History 4. West (U.S.)—History
   ISBN 0-531-12326-X   LC 2005000914
"Watts library"
"Landau describes how people traveled prior to the building of the railroads and how the concept of Manifest Destiny influenced the development of the railroads. . . . Black-and-white and color illustrations, maps, sidebars, and time lines enhance the well-organized [text]." SLJ
Includes bibliographical references

Meltzer, Milton, 1915-
Hear that train whistle blow! how the railroad changed the world. Random House 2004 157p il hardcover o.p. pa $8.95 *
Grades: 5 6 7 8   **385.09**
   1. Railroads—History
   ISBN 0-375-81563-5; 0-375-91563-X (lib bdg); 0-375-82922-9 (pa)   LC 2003-13255
"Landmark books"

Meltzer, Milton, 1915- —*Continued*

Takes a look at the history of rail transportation, focussing on how it transformed societies from isolated communities which rarely communicated or traded into unified nations

"Illustrated with numerous archival photographs, this excellent, comprehensive history will be a welcome addition." SLJ

Renehan, Edward J., 1956-

The Transcontinental Railroad; the gateway to the West; [by] Edward J. Renehan, Jr. Chelsea House 2007 120p il (Milestones in American history) lib bdg $35

Grades: 7 8 9 10   **385.09**

1. Central Pacific Railroad 2. Union Pacific Railroad Company 3. Railroads—History 4. West (U.S.)—History

ISBN 0-7910-9351-4 (lib bdg); 978-0-7910-9351-1 (lib bdg)   LC 2006-38870

This history of the transcontinental railroad is "accessible, lively. . . . Many quotations, sidebars, art reproductions, and maps support the [text]. Excerpts from primary source materials also help give readers a sense of time and place." Horn Book Guide

Includes bibliographical references

386   Inland waterway and ferry transportation

Bial, Raymond

The canals. Benchmark Bks. 2002 56p il map (Building America) lib bdg $27.07

Grades: 6 7 8 9   **386**

1. Canals

ISBN 0-7614-1336-7   LC 00-65078

This describes the history of canals in America from colonial times to the 19th century

This book is "marked by strong research, clear writing, good organization, and very handsome color photographs." Booklist

Includes glossary and bibliographical references

Coleman, Wim

The amazing Erie Canal and how a big ditch opened up the West; [by] Wim Coleman & Pat Perrin. MyReportLinks.com Books 2006 128p il map (The wild history of the American West) lib bdg $33.27

Grades: 6 7 8 9   **386**

1. Erie Canal (N.Y.)

ISBN 1-59845-017-4   LC 2005029389

This book "shares a brief, informative history of canals; the geographic need for the Erie Canal; and an explanation of how its creation impacted American commerce and history. . . . Throughout the text, illustrations of Web pages invite readers to search online for more detailed information. The book's text is clear, and the format is attractive, with excellent black-and-white photos and color illustrations on nearly every page." Booklist

Includes bibliographical references

Roop, Peter, 1951-

River roads west; America's first highways; [by] Peter and Connie Roop. Calkins Creek 2007 64p il map $19.95

Grades: 6 7 8 9   **386**

1. Rivers 2. Canals 3. Transportation—History 4. United States—History

ISBN 1-59078-430-8; 978-1-59078-430-3

"The role of transportation in national history has seldom been more clearly delineated than in this meticulous treatment. Spanning prehistory to the 19th century, the sparkling text, inflected with wry humor, focuses sequentially on the Hudson River and Erie Canal, the Ohio, Mississippi, Missouri, Rio Grande, and the Colorado Rivers, and the Columbia River." SLJ

Includes bibliographical references

387.1   Ports

House, Katherine L.

Lighthouses for kids; history, science, and lore with 21 activities; [by] Katherine L. House. Chicago Review Press 2008 118p il pa $14.95

Grades: 4 5 6 7 8   **387.1**

1. Lighthouses

ISBN 978-1-55652-720-3; 1-55652-720-9
                    LC 2007-27093

"This book is noteworthy for the way in which the activities are related to the information in the text. . . . Readers learn about the challenges of building . . . [lighthouses], inventions to make them more reliable, and how lighthouses function as historical relics today." SLJ

Includes glossary and bibliographical references

Plisson, Philip

Lighthouses; photographs by Philip Plisson; text by Francis Dreyer; drawings by Daniel Dufour. Harry N. Abrams 2005 78p il $18.95 *

Grades: 4 5 6 7   **387.1**

1. Lighthouses

ISBN 0-8109-5958-5   LC 2005011781

"Plisson's magnificent color photos will draw young people to this introduction to lighthouses and the work of tending them. Each spread in the oversize volume introduces a different aspect of the history and technology of the structures or the work of maintaining them, from the lighthouses of ancient Egypt to the automated towers of today. Dreyer's engaging text . . . will pull readers to the facts through anecdotes about lighthouse keepers' lives." Booklist

387.2   Ships

Kentley, Eric

Boat; written by Eric Kentley; [special photography, James Stevenson and Tina Chambers] Dorling Kindersley 2000 63p il (DK eyewitness books) $15.99; lib bdg $19.99

Grades: 4 5 6 7   **387.2**

1. Ships 2. Boats and boating

ISBN 0-7894-5758-X; 0-7894-6585-X (lib bdg)

First published 1992 by Knopf

Kentley, Eric—*Continued*
A history of the development and uses of boats, ships, and rafts, from birch-bark canoes to luxury liners.

Macaulay, David, 1946-
Ship. Houghton Mifflin 1993 96p il $19.95; pa $12.95 *
Grades: 4 5 6 7 8 9   **387.2**
1. Shipwrecks 2. Underwater exploration 3. Caribbean region—Antiquities
ISBN 0-395-52439-3; 0-395-74518-7 (pa)
LC 92-1346
This book "opens with an underwater find in the Caribbean and, in story and illustration, follows the work of marine archeologists in studying the wreck. As part of the background research in Spain, one of the team finds a diary recording the building of a caravel in 1504. The rest of the book contains a 'translation' of the diary with accompanying illustrations. Though a fictional account, the narrative gives a good feel for the maritime technology of the early 16th century." Sci Books Films

Sandler, Martin W.
On the waters of the USA; ships and boats in American life. Oxford Univ. Press 2004 63p il (Transportation in America) $19.95
Grades: 5 6 7 8   **387.2**
1. Shipping—United States 2. Ships 3. Boats and boating
ISBN 0-19-513227-0
Explores the evolving role of boats and ships in American history, from the dugout and birchbark canoes of Native Americans to twenty-first century container ships and supertankers.
This is a "fascinating account. . . . Drawings, maps, and photographs are well placed and fully captioned. . . . The large type is reader friendly, and the writing is clear and engaging." SLJ
Includes bibliographical references

388   Transportation Ground transportation

Herbst, Judith
The history of transportation; [by] Judith Herbst. Twenty-First Century Books 2006 56p il (Major inventions through history) lib bdg $26.60
Grades: 5 6 7 8   **388**
1. Transportation—History
ISBN 0-8225-2496-1   LC 2004-23020
Contents: The wheel; Boats; The steam engine; The internal combustion engine; Air travel; Timeline
This history of transportation "covers the wheel, sail, steam engine, internal combustion engine, and airplane. . . . The text . . . is breezy but informative; unfamiliar terms are defined. Illustrations are a mixture of period black-and-white and color photos." SLJ
Includes bibliographical references

388.4   Local transportation

DuTemple, Lesley A., 1952-
The New York subways. Lerner Publs. 2003 80p il (Great building feats) lib bdg $27.93
Grades: 5 6 7 8   **388.4**
1. Subways 2. New York (N.Y.)—History
ISBN 0-8225-0378-6   LC 2001-6143
Traces the history of the underground transportation system in New York City, discussing the politics involved, how it was financed, the men who built it, and the construction techniques
"DuTemple does a fine job. . . . [Photos] sidebars, maps, and archival material work beautifully together to supplement the information." Booklist
Includes bibliographical references

Sandler, Martin W.
Secret subway; the fascinating tale of an amazing feat of engineering. National Geographic 2009 96p il $17.95; lib bdg $26.90
Grades: 5 6 7 8   **388.4**
1. Subways 2. New York (N.Y.)—History
ISBN   978-1-4263-0462-0;   1-4263-0462-5; 978-1-4263-0463-7 (lib bdg); 1-4263-0463-3 (lib bdg)
LC 2008-39831
"Sandler takes an in-depth look at the building of New York's first subway. . . . [He] writes about the subway in a well-put-together book with interesting information, great pictures, and a compelling true story." Voice Youth Advocates
Includes bibliographical references

391   Costume and personal appearance

Fashions of a decade [series] Chelsea House Publishers 2006 8v il set $280 *
Grades: 7 8 9 10 11 12   **391**
1. Costume
ISBN 0-8160-7059-8; 978-0-8160-7059-6
Volumes also available separately ea $35
First published 1991-1992
Contents: The 1920s by Jacqueline Herald; The 1930s by Maria Constantino; The 1940s by Patricia Baker; The 1950s by Patricia Baker; The 1960s by Yvonne Connikie; The 1970s by Jacqueline Herald; The 1980s by Vicky Carnegy; The 1990s by Anne McEvoy
This set describes clothing styles of the 20th century in the context of world events, social movements, and cultural movements of each decade.
"These titles provide colorful and fascinating information. . . . Attractive black-and-white illustrations, color photos, reproductions, sketches from magazines and newspapers, and fact boxes enhance and bring to life these lively and accessible texts." SLJ

Finley, Carol

The art of African masks; exploring cultural traditions. Lerner Publs. 1999 64p il map (Art around the world) $23.93

Grades: 5 6 7 8   391

1. Masks (Facial) 2. African art

ISBN 0-8225-2078-8   LC 98-10570

Describes how different types of masks are made and used in Africa and how they reflect the culture of their ethnic groups

"Clear, sharp full-color photographs of museum artifacts are well placed on the pages. . . . Pictures of modern members of still-existing cultures add to the attractiveness of this volume." SLJ

Includes bibliographical references

Graydon, Shari

In your face; the culture of beauty and you. Annick 2004 176p il $24.94; pa $14.95

Grades: 7 8 9 10   391

1. Personal appearance

ISBN 1-55037-857-0; 1-55037-856-2 (pa)

The author "looks at fashion across time and cultures, and analyzes the underlying messages in today's focus . . . on thinness, long nails, and high heels. Along the way, she warns both young men and women of the very real dangers of eating disorders, plastic surgery, liposuction, and other body-image 'solutions.' . . . Graydon will make readers laugh as well as think about the issues." Booklist

Includes bibliographical references

Kyi, Tanya Lloyd, 1973-

The blue jean book; the story behind the seams. Annick Press 2005 79p il $24.95; pa $12.95 *

391

1. Jeans (Clothing)

ISBN 1-55037-917-8; 1-55037-916-X (pa)

"Kyi traces the history of these pants from the early life of Levi Strauss and the patented riveted pocket to the stiff competition and controversy of production in our modern world. . . . History and social issues are intertwined to show how activities, jobs, and the economy influence the development and production of clothing. . . . This is an enjoyable read for anyone wishing to know more about this fashion item and an excellent resource for an introduction to product development and economy." SLJ

Mason, Paul, 1967-

Body piercing and tattooing. Heinemann Lib. 2003 56p il (Just the facts) lib bdg $25.64 *

Grades: 6 7 8 9   391

1. Tattooing 2. Body piercing

ISBN 1-4034-0817-3   LC 2002-10936

Describes the history of body piercing and tattooing, as well as what motivates people to get a piercing or a tattoo, how to care for them, problems that can arise, and legal issues surrounding them

"The writing is clear and frank. . . . Students will find much to like and make use of in [this book]." Libr Media Connect

Includes glossary and bibliographical references

Pendergast, Sara

Fashion, costume, and culture; clothing, headwear, body decoration, and footwear through the ages; [by] Sara Pendergast and Tom Pendergast. U.X.L 2004 5v il set $275

Grades: 6 7 8 9   391

1. Costume—History 2. Clothing and dress 3. Fashion

ISBN 0-7876-5417-5

This set "surveys how people have covered and adorned themselves through the ages and around the world. . . . There are 430 entries in all, ranging from a paragraph or two to a page. . . . The work is notable for its organization, breadth of coverage, and attractive design. Strongly recommended for school and public libraries." Booklist

Platt, Richard, 1953-

They wore what?! the weird history of fashion and beauty; [by] Richard Platt. Two-Can 2007 48p il $16.95; pa $9.95

Grades: 4 5 6   391

1. Fashion—History 2. Personal appearance

ISBN   978-1-58728-582-0;   1-58728-582-7; 978-1-58728-584-4 (pa); 1-58728-584-3 (pa)

LC 2006039159

Published in the United Kingdom with title: Would you believe in 1500, platform shoes were outlawed?

"Busy, colorful pages recount the historical, social, and political sides of clothing, hair, hats, and shoes, from legal and moral issues such as wearing fur to dangerous practices like cinched waists and bound feet. . . . Ever-fluctuating ideas of beauty and body image are also explored." Horn Book Guide

Includes glossary and bibliographical references

Rowland-Warne, L.

Costume; written by L. Rowland-Warne; [special photography, Liz McAulay] Dorling Kindersley 2000 63p il (DK eyewitness books) $15.99; lib bdg $19.99

Grades: 4 5 6 7   391

1. Costume 2. Clothing and dress 3. Fashion—History

ISBN 0-7894-5586-2; 0-7894-6584-1 (lib bdg)

First published 1992 by Knopf

Photographs and text document the history and meaning of clothing, from loincloths to modern children's clothes.

Shaskan, Kathy

How underwear got under there; a brief history; illustrated by Regan Dunnick. Dutton 2007 47p il $16.99

Grades: 4 5 6   391

1. Underwear 2. Fashion—History

ISBN 978-0-525-47178-3; 0-525-47178-2

A humorous look at the science, fashion, and social ramifications of underwear throughout history.

This is a "lighthearted but thoughtful discourse on dainties. . . . [Illustrated with] Dunnick's watercolor cartoons." Bull Cent Child Books

Sills, Leslie

From rags to riches; a history of girls' clothing in America; [by] Leslie Sills. 1st ed. Holiday House 2005 48p il $16.95; pa $6.95

Grades: 5 6 7 8   **391**

1. Children's clothing 2. Girls 3. Fashion—History
ISBN 0-8234-1708-5; 0-8234-2048-5 (pa)
LC 2003-67600

A history of the clothing of American girls from colonial times to the present.

"The sparkling design of Sills' overview makes this a pleasure to page through. . . . A marvelous collection of paintings and photographs show off the apparel." Booklist

Includes glossary and bibliographical references

393   Death customs

Colman, Penny

Corpses, coffins, and crypts; a history of burial. Holt & Co. 1997 212p il $17.95 *

Grades: 7 8 9 10   **393**

1. Funeral rites and ceremonies 2. Burial
ISBN 0-8050-5066-3   LC 97-7842

Documents the burial process throughout the centuries and in different cultures.

The author "is both candid and detailed in her handling of the gruesome nitty-gritty. . . . Many of the photographs in the liberally illustrated text are from her own explorations, and all are captioned, some in great detail. . . . She's filled her sensitive, solid book with answers to questions people often need and want to know but are too reluctant to ask." Booklist

Includes glossary and bibliographical references

Greene, Meg

Rest in peace; a history of American cemeteries. Twenty-First Century Books 2008 112p il map (People's history) lib bdg $30.60

Grades: 8 9 10 11 12   **393**

1. Cemeteries 2. Burial 3. United States—Social life and customs
ISBN 978-0-8225-3414-3 (lib bdg); 0-8225-3414-2 (lib bdg)   LC 2007022093

"This account of cemeteries in the U.S. offers a sweeping history . . . as well as plenty of noteworthy details, illustrated throughout with black-and-white photos shaded in sepia tones. . . . This book . . . presents many aspects of an unusual topic." Booklist

Includes bibliographical references

Halls, Kelly Milner, 1957-

Mysteries of the mummy kids. Darby Creek Pub. 2007 72p il map $18.95

Grades: 4 5 6 7   **393**

1. Mummies
ISBN 978-1-58196-059-4; 1-58196-059-X

"Halls presents an eerily fascinating exploration of mummified children and teens found in South and North America, Europe, and Asia. . . . The writing style is plain yet absorbing, presenting scientific and historical information in simple terms." Voice Youth Advocates

Includes bibliographical references

Malam, John, 1957-

Mummies; foreword by Ron Beckett and Gerald Conlogue. Kingfisher 2003 63p il (Kingfisher knowledge) $11.95

Grades: 5 6 7 8   **393**

1. Mummies
ISBN 0-7534-5623-0   LC 2003-44630

Contents: Two ways to make a mummy; Egypt, the land of mummies; Mummy world; Mummies today

"Malam covers Egyptian mummies; the discovery of a variety of preserved bodies throughout history and the world in bogs, deserts, and ice; animal mummies; and mummies today. [The title includes] stunning, captioned photos and illustrations that emphasize the many intriguing factual details in the text." SLJ

Includes glossary and bibliographical references

Markle, Sandra, 1946-

Outside and inside mummies. Walker & Co. 2005 40p il $17.95; lib bdg $18.85 *

Grades: 4 5 6 7   **393**

1. Mummies
ISBN 0-8027-8966-8; 0-8027-8967-6 (lib bdg)
LC 2004-66128

"Markle explores a global smorgasbord of mummy varieties, both those created by human procedures and those caused by nature. Crisp (if gruesome) color photos accompany the readable, informative text, which discusses not only the mummification process, but also the cutting-edge technologies used by forensic anthropologists and others to study the mummies themselves." SLJ

Includes glossary

Perl, Lila

Mummies, tombs, and treasure; secrets of ancient Egypt; drawings by Erika Weihs. Clarion Bks. 1987 120p il lib bdg $16; pa $8.95

Grades: 4 5 6 7   **393**

1. Mummies 2. Funeral rites and ceremonies 3. Egypt—Antiquities
ISBN 0-89919-407-9 (lib bdg); 0-395-54796-2 (pa)
LC 86-17646

The author incorporates "information on burial customs, religious beliefs, and historical background along with specifics of the mummification process and the archeological finds that have kept the study of the dead a dynamic one." Bull Cent Child Books

This "book is attractive, readable, plentifully illustrated with drawings and black-and-white photographs. . . . Phonetic pronunciations throughout make this easily accessible." Appraisal

Includes bibliographical references

Sloan, Christopher

Bury the dead; tombs, corpses, mummies, skeletons, & rituals; foreword by Bruno Frohlich. National Geographic Soc. 2002 64p il $18.95 *

Grades: 5 6 7 8   **393**

1. Funeral rites and ceremonies 2. Burial
ISBN 0-7922-7192-0   LC 2001-7507

Examines the customs and practices related to burial that have existed from ancient times to the present

Sloan, Christopher—*Continued*

The author "does a terrific job of providing an intriguing, reader-friendly text that is not overshadowed by the fabulous color photographs." Booklist

Includes bibliographical references

Tanaka, Shelley

Mummies; the newest, coolest, and creepiest from around the world; archaeological consultation by Paul Bahn. Harry N. Abrams 2005 48p il map $16.95

Grades: 4 5 6 7   393

1. Mummies

ISBN 0-8109-5797-3   LC 2005-00984

"After a brief discussion of mummification and the sorts of places in which mummified bodies have been found, Tanaka organizes her text by continent. Simple outlined and colored maps display the countries featured, supplementing the author's descriptions of the local conditions. . . . The main text for each mummy or cache of mummies is generally a few paragraphs, often supported by a shorter text, both of which are illustrated by photographs or reproductions." SLJ

"Not for the squeamish, the descriptions are graphic, and, like the riveting photos, they will draw kids right into the science." Booklist

Includes bibliographical references

394.1   Eating, drinking; using drugs

Schlosser, Eric

Chew on this; everything you don't want to know about fast food; by Eric Schlosser and Charles Wilson. Houghton Mifflin Co. 2006 304p il $16 *

Grades: 6 7 8 9   394.1

1. Eating habits 2. Convenience foods 3. Food industry

ISBN 0-618-71031-0   LC 2005027527

"An adaptation of Schlosser's *Fast Food Nation* (Houghton, 2001), *Chew on This* covers the history of the fast-food industry and delves into the agribusiness and animal husbandry methods that support it. . . . Equally disturbing is his revelation of the way that the fast-food giants have studied childhood behavior and geared their commercials and free toy inclusions to hook the youngest consumers. The text is written in a lively, layout-the-facts manner. Occasional photographs add bits of visual interest." SLJ

Whitman, Sylvia, 1961-

What's cooking? the history of American food. Lerner Publs. 2001 88p il (People's history) lib bdg $22.60

Grades: 5 6 7 8   394.1

1. Food—History 2. United States—Social life and customs

ISBN 0-8225-1732-9   LC 00-9168

A look at food in the United States from colonial times to the present, describing what we have eaten, where it came from, and how it reflected events in

American history

"The text is very accessible, and there are many interesting black-and-white photographs. . . . Intriguing as well as informative." Booklist

Includes bibliographical references

394.2   Special occasions

Heath, Alan

Windows on the world; multicultural festivals for schools and libraries. Scarecrow Press 1995 392p il hardcover o.p. pa $47.95

Grades: Professional   394.2

1. Festivals 2. Multiculturalism

ISBN 0-8108-2880-4; 0-8108-3958-X (pa)

LC 94-10032

This guide "promotes reading through thematic festive activities centered around diverse cultural celebrations. Students explore varied art forms, from sculpture, printmaking, batik, and puppetry to drama, music, dancing, cooking, and writing. . . . The book is profusely illustrated with photographs, diagrams, activity sheets, maps, bulletin board ideas, and . . . instructions for arts and crafts projects." Publisher's note

Includes bibliographical references

394.26   Holidays

Altman, Linda Jacobs, 1943-

Celebrate Kwanzaa; [by] Linda Jacobs Altman. Enslow Pub. 2008 104p il map (Celebrate holidays) lib bdg $31.93

Grades: 5 6 7 8   394.26

1. Kwanzaa 2. African Americans—Social life and customs

ISBN 978-07660-2862-3 (lib bdg); 0-7660-2862-3 (lib bdg)   LC 2007002421

This offers an introduction to harvest festivals around the world, outlines the life of Ronald Everett, who changed his name to Maulana Karenga and started the African American celebration of Kwanzaa in 1966, and describes how Kwanzaa is celebrated today.

"This is a useful look at the origins and greater context of Kwanzaa." SLJ

Includes glossary and bibliographical references

The **American** book of days; compiled and edited by Stephen G. Christianson. 4th ed. Wilson, H.W. 2000 xxvi, 945p $140 *

Grades: 8 9 10 11 12 Adult   394.26

1. Holidays 2. Festivals

ISBN 0-8242-0954-0   LC 99-86611

First published 1937 under the authorship of George William Douglas

This work "consists of essays that are a day-to-day recounting of selective American historic events, including those of festivals and celebrations. . . . The topics of these essays vary, with the editor highlighting notable activities from military, scientific, ethnic, political, and cultural occurrences. Not limited strictly to events, essays are also devoted to individuals who played a significant

The American book of days—*Continued*
role in American history. . . . A comprehensive index
and table of contents provide excellent means for finding
specific topics." Am Ref Books Annu, 2001

Bowler, Gerald, 1948-
The world encyclopedia of Christmas; [by]
Gerry Bowler. McClelland & Stewart 2000 257p
il hardcover o.p. pa $12.95
Grades: 8 9 10 11 12   **394.26**
  1. Christmas—Encyclopedias 2. Reference books
  ISBN 0-7710-1531-3; 0-7710-1535-6 (pa)
  This "provides more than 1,000 entries on worldwide
secular and religious Christmas practices expressed in
song, literature, events, film, arts, and trivia and is aimed
at young adult and adult readers as well as researchers.
Entries are primarily descriptive, but a number of them,
especially those on films, contain critical commentary.
. . . The book is enticing reading with its many descriptions of exotic customs and its blend of the ancient and
the modern. It is written well and concisely." Booklist

Breuilly, Elizabeth
  Festivals of the world; the illustrated guide to
celebrations, customs, events, and holidays; [by]
Elizabeth Breuilly, Joanne O'Brien, Martin Palmer.
Checkmark Bks. 2002 160p il maps $29.95
Grades: 6 7 8 9   **394.26**
  1. Festivals 2. Religious holidays 3. Reference books
  ISBN 0-8160-4481-3   LC 2001-59876
  The religions featured include Judaism, Christianity,
Islam, Hinduism, Buddhism, Sikhism, Taoism, and Zoroastrianism
  "A unique approach to holidays, organized by religion
rather than alphabet, marks this thoughtful reference
book. The introduction relates world festivals to the universal human search for meaning, and offers thematic relationships between seemingly disparate events. . . .
Beautiful full-color photographs, diagrams, and maps
bring the celebrations to life, and informative text boxes
offer additional facts. . . . This book deserves to be in
every reference collection." SLJ
  Includes glossary and bibliographical references

Colman, Penny
  Thanksgiving; the true story; [by] Penny
Colman. Henry Holt 2008 149p il $18.95
Grades: 5 6 7 8   **394.26**
  1. Thanksgiving Day 2. United States—Social life and
customs
  ISBN 978-0-8050-8229-6; 0-8050-8229-8
                LC 2007046943
  "Drawing on historical research and the results of a
written questionaire, Colman first retraces the growth of
Thanksgiving as a national holiday and then surveys the
wide range of customs and mouthwatering comestibles
associated with the celebration. Both tracks are illuminating. . . . A selection of old photos and prints illustrate
this engagingly presented [title]." Booklist
  Includes bibliographical references

Henderson, Helene, 1963-
  Patriotic holidays of the United States; an
introduction to the history, symbols, and traditions
behind the major holidays and days of observance;
by Helene Henderson; foreword by Matthew
Dennis. Omnigraphics 2006 408p il map $63
Grades: 7 8 9 10 11 12   **394.26**
  1. Holidays 2. Patriotism 3. United States—Social life
and customs
  ISBN 0-7808-0733-2   LC 2005024870
  "Henderson defines patriotic holidays as those dealing
with aspects of democratic civic rights, responsibilities,
and values consistent with the ideals laid out in the nation's founding documents. . . . The book begins with a
fascinating look at patriotism. Along with several definitions and views on it, the author explores different symbols of the U.S., including those of political parties, the
cornucopia, the eagle, and the flag. She then considers
each holiday in alphabetical order, describing any customs, songs, and foods associated with it; the history behind the observance; and a sampling of activities and observances around the country. . . . The volume also contains almost 100 pages of useful primary documents related to holidays, including The Mayflower Compact;
The Declaration of Independence; flag laws; and excerpts
from diaries, letters, and speeches." SLJ
  Includes bibliographical references

Holidays, festivals, and celebrations of the world
dictionary. 3rd ed. Omnigraphics 2005 xxxv,
906p $110 *
Grades: 8 9 10 11 12 Adult   **394.26**
  1. Holidays 2. Festivals
  ISBN 0-7808-0422-8   LC 2004-25017
  First edition published 1994 compiled by Sue Ellen
Thompson and Barbara W. Carlson
  "Contains information about nearly 2,500 holidays,
festivals, holy days, feasts and fasts, and other obser-
vances, including popular, secular, and religious celebra-
tions for more than 100 countries and every state of the
United States"—Title page. New edition in preparation
  "From Labor Day in the United States to Kallemooi
in the North Coast Islands of the Netherlands, the work
covers a wide range of religious and political festivities."
Libr J
  Includes bibliographical references

Jeffrey, Laura S.
  Celebrate Martin Luther King, Jr., Day; [by]
Laura S. Jeffrey. Enslow 2006 104p il (Celebrate
holidays) lib bdg $31.93
Grades: 5 6 7 8   **394.26**
  1. King, Martin Luther, Jr., 1929-1968 2. Martin Lu-
ther King Day 3. African Americans—Civil rights
  ISBN 0-7660-2492-X   LC 2005028110
  This offers a brief introduction to the life of Martin
Luther King and the Civil Rights movement in the Unit-
ed States and how Martin Luther King Day became a
holiday and is celebrated.
  Includes glossary and bibliographical references

Jeffrey, Laura S.—*Continued*

Celebrate Tet; [by] Laura S. Jeffrey. Enslow Publishers 2008 104p il map (Celebrate holidays) lib bdg $31.93

Grades: 5 6 7 8 **394.26**
1. Vietnamese New Year
ISBN 978-0-7660-2775-6 (lib bdg); 0-7660-2775-9 (lib bdg)　　　　　　LC 2006031922

"Captioned photographs, maps, drawings, and sidebars combine with an accessible text to present a thorough discussion of the Vietnamese New Year celebration. Jeffrey discusses the holiday's legendary origins and ancient traditions along with people's modern-day observances." Horn Book Guide

Includes glossary and bibliographical references

Junior Worldmark encyclopedia of world holidays; [edited by Robert Griffin and Ann H. Shurgin] U.X.L 2000 4v il set $185

Grades: 6 7 8 9 **394.26**
1. Holidays 2. Festivals 3. Reference books
ISBN 0-7876-3927-3　　　　　　LC 00-23425

Alphabetically arranged entries provide descriptions of celebrations around the world of some thirty holidays and festivals, including national and cultural holidays, such as Independence Day and New Year's Day, which are commemorated on different days for different reasons in a number of countries

Includes bibliographical references

Kule, Elaine A.

Celebrate Chinese New Year; [by] Elaine A. Kule. Enslow Publishers 2006 112p il map (Celebrate holidays) lib bdg $31.93

Grades: 5 6 7 8 **394.26**
1. Chinese New Year
ISBN 0-7660-2577-2　　　　　　LC 2005028106

This describes the history of Chinese New Year, its cultural significance and traditions, and its signs and symbols, and includes instructions for making a paper lantern.

Includes glossary and bibliographical references

Marks, Diana F.

Let's celebrate today; calendars, events, and holidays; illustrated by Donna L. Farrell. 2nd ed. Libraries Unlimited 2003 340p il pa $38.95

Grades: Professional **394.26**
1. Holidays 2. Festivals 3. Calendars
ISBN 1-59158-060-9　　　　　　LC 2003-47723
First published 1998

This is a "day-by-day calendar . . . for planning . . . activities and classroom units based on national and international holidays, multicultural and historic events, famous firsts, inventions, birthdays of important individuals (including authors), and more. The entries are annotated and include contact information and Web site addresses to facilitate further research and learning. In addition, three suggested learning activities are provided for each day of the year." Publisher's note

Includes bibliographical references

Mattern, Joanne, 1963-

Celebrate Christmas; [by] Joanne Mattern. Enslow Publishers 2007 112p il (Celebrate holidays) lib bdg $31.93

Grades: 5 6 7 8 **394.26**
1. Christmas
ISBN 978-0-7660-2776-3 (lib bdg); 0-7660-2776-7 (lib bdg)　　　　　　LC 2006025258

The author "devotes several pages to the origins of Christmas, first as a pagan holiday, then as a celebration of Jesus' birth, and its evolution into the holiday as it is observed today. Symbols of Christmas, important people, and traditions from around the world are explored, and there is a fair amount of discussion about the commercialization of the holiday. . . . Full-color photos and reproductions appear throughout. There is plenty here for reports." SLJ

Includes glossary and bibliographical references

Celebrate Cinco de Mayo; [by] Joanne Mattern. Enslow Pub. 2006 104p il map (Celebrate holidays) lib bdg $31.93

Grades: 5 6 7 8 **394.26**
1. Cinco de Mayo 2. Mexico—History 3. Mexico—Social life and customs
ISBN 0-7660-2579-9　　　　　　LC 2005028107

This describes the history of Cinco de Mayo and how it is celebrated.

Includes glossary and bibliographical references

Matthew, Kathryn I.

Neal-Schuman guide to celebrations & holidays around the world; [by] Kathryn I. Matthew, Joy L. Lowe. Neal-Schuman Publishers 2004 xx, 452p il pa $65

Grades: Professional **394.26**
1. Holidays—Bibliography 2. Festivals—Bibliography 3. Children's literature—Bibliography 4. Reference books
ISBN 1-55570-479-4　　　　　　LC 2003-59940

"The first section provides bibliographic information and suggested grade levels for titles on specific days. Sections that follow offer longer, more detailed explanations of the meaning and significance of a holiday and a . . . description of the content of each recommended book or media choice. 'Explorations,' or activities for sharing specific titles with students, are included." SLJ

"Selecting books that represent favorite authors who will appeal to children, the authors have designed a work that will be useful to elementary librarians and teachers looking for culturally sensitive resources and activities to teach K-8 students about more than 80 holidays." Booklist

Includes bibliographical references

Rajtar, Steve, 1951-

United States holidays and observances; by date, jurisdiction, and subject, fully indexed. McFarland & Co. 2003 165p $45

Grades: Professional **394.26**
1. Holidays 2. Festivals
ISBN 0-7864-1446-4　　　　　　LC 2002-154293

Rajtar, Steve, 1951-—*Continued*

This "concentrates on observances and holidays established by statute in the U.S. and American Samoa, District of Columbia, Guam, the Northern Mariana Islands, Puerto Rico, and the U.S. Virgin Islands. In addition, UN-designated holidays are included. . . . The text is arranged by month, and chapters for each month are divided into 'Observances with Variable Dates' and 'Observances with Fixed Dates.' Each entry identifies the observance as federal or specific to a state and offers a description that ranges in length from three or four lines to a quarter page. . . . [This] would be a good addition to ready-reference desks in public libraries and information centers in schools." Booklist

395 Etiquette (Manners)

Dougherty, Karla

The rules to be cool; etiquette and netiquette. Enslow Pubs. 2001 64p il (Teen issues) lib bdg $22.60 *

Grades: 7 8 9 10   395

1. Etiquette

ISBN 0-7660-1607-2   LC 00-10311

"Dougherty approaches good manners as a means of showing respect and consideration for others, thereby prompting reciprocation and easing social relationships and situations. . . . Always practical and low-key, the tips and attitudes emphasize kindness and courtesy as a way of life." SLJ

Includes bibliographical references

Packer, Alex J., 1951-

How rude! the teenagers' guide to good manners, proper behavior, and not grossing people out. Free Spirit 1997 465p il pa $19.95 *

Grades: 7 8 9 10   395

1. Etiquette

ISBN 1-57542-024-4   LC 97-13015

This guide to etiquette for teenagers covers such areas as sex etiquette, toilet etiquette, net etiquette (cyberspace behavior) as well as the correct way to answer invitations and standard protocols for life in a "proper" society

"This volume not only uses humor to make the subject palatable but also makes good sense in terms of most young poeple's everyday lives." Booklist

Includes bibliographical references

Post, Peggy, 1945-

Emily Post's table manners for kids. Collins 2009 96p $15.99

Grades: 4 5 6 7   395

1. Etiquette

ISBN 978-0-06-111709-1; 0-06-111709-9

LC 2008010655

"This deceptively slim guide teems with advice about everything from meal courses to table settings, from the art of conversation to dining out. The tone is measured and mildly proscriptive, offset by Bjorkman's amusing cartoons. . . . A strength: the excellent troubleshooting for specific concerns, such as eating fondue and using chopsticks." Kirkus

Emily Post's The guide to good manners for kids; by Peggy Post & Cindy Post Senning. HarperCollins 2004 144p il $15.99; lib bdg $16.89

Grades: 4 5 6 7   395

1. Etiquette

ISBN 0-06-057196-9; 0-06-057197-7 (lib bdg)

LC 2003-26426

This offers advice on etiquette at home, at school, and other places, including letter writing and on-line communication, table manners, phone answering, and behavior at social gatherings, and public places.

"The writing is clear, friendly, and sometimes clever. . . . The advice is consistently practical and simple." SLJ

Senning, Cindy Post

Teen manners; from malls to meals to messaging and beyond; by Cindy Post Senning and Peggy Post. 1st ed. Collins 2007 134p il $15.99; lib bdg $16.89

Grades: 7 8 9 10   395

1. Etiquette

ISBN   978-0-06-088198-6;   0-06-088198-4; 978-0-06-088199-3 (lib bdg); 0-06-088199-2 (lib bdg)

LC 2007010991

This offers advice on etiquette in personal relationships, in communication, dining, school, getting a job or getting into college, parties and dating, and other social situations.

398 Folklore

Allen, Judy

Fantasy encyclopedia. 1st ed. Kingfisher 2005 144p il $19.95

Grades: 4 5 6 7   398

1. Fairies 2. Mythical animals

ISBN 0-7534-5847-0   LC 2004-29475

"This highly visual presentation introduces readers to fantasy characters within their habitats and genres. . . . More than 50 types of characters are arranged in nine chapters covering topics such as 'The Little People,' 'Mysterious Animals,' and 'Ghosts and Spirits.' . . . Student fans of the fantasy genre will find this tool exceedingly browsable, and school and public libraries will want to purchase reference and circulating copies." Booklist

Includes glossary

The **Dictionary** of folklore; David Adams Leeming, general editor. Watts 2002 128p il $35

Grades: 4 5 6 7   398

1. Folklore—Dictionaries 2. Reference books

ISBN 0-531-11985-8   LC 2001-22034

This work answers such questions as "Why was Abraham Lincoln known as 'Honest Abe?' Did George Washington really cut down his father's cherry tree? How much truth is there to the tall tale of John Henry, the 'natural-born steel-driving man,' or Paul Bunyon and Babe the Blue Ox?" Publisher's note

"The layout of the book is pleasing. It is organized in alphabetical order and the content is understandable with

The Dictionary of folklore—*Continued*

many cross-references. The illustrations complement the text. . . . Leeming does an excellent job of enticing the reader to be curious." Book Rep

Includes bibliographical references

Myths and legends. Macmillan Lib. Ref. USA 2000 436p (Macmillan profiles) $95

Grades: 7 8 9 10   **398**

1. Folklore—Dictionaries 2. Mythology—Dictionaries 3. Reference books

ISBN 0-02-865376-9   LC 99-51558

Entries in this volume "are drawn from the mythologies of numerous cultures, ranging from antiquity (*Astarte*) to more modern times (*Paul Bunyan*). Some articles focus on groups: *Centaurs Leprechauns, Mermaids*. Some profile real-life heroes: *Casey Jones* and *Davy Crockett* among others. More than 40 of the articles cover classical Greek and Roman mythology." Booklist

This volume "contains informative, accurate, and detailed information." SLJ

Nigg, Joe

Wonder beasts; tales and lore of the phoenix, the griffin, the unicorn, and the dragon. Libraries Unlimited 1995 160p il $27.50

Grades: 7 8 9 10   **398**

1. Animals—Folklore

ISBN 1-56308-242-X   LC 94-46797

The author "has compiled material ranging from Herodotus, Ovid, Pliny the Elder, to Chinese and Native American folk tales, and fantasies by Edith Nesbit. Each entry is carefully documented and a reference list at the end provides dozens of full citations for those who'd like to delve deeper. Wonder Beasts will be useful to students who are researching myth and folklore, and to librarians and scholars who are looking for a comprehensive source list on the topic." Voice Youth Advocates

Stefoff, Rebecca, 1951-

Vampires, zombies, and shape-shifters; [by] Rebecca Stefoff. Marshall Cavendish Benchmark 2007 c2008 79p il (Secrets of the supernatural) lib bdg $32.79

Grades: 5 6 7 8   **398**

1. Vampires 2. Zombies 3. Werewolves

ISBN 978-0-7614-2635-6 (lib bdg); 0-7614-2635-3 (lib bdg)   LC 2007008477

This is a history of beliefs in vampires, zombies, werewolves, and other shape-shifters, including Haitian voodoo, Count Dracula, and depictions of such creatures in literature, movies, and popular culture.

"Nearly every other page has an illustration, whether a drawing, photograph, or some scene from a movie. . . . The text is accessible." Libr Media Connect

Includes glossary and bibliographical references

398.2   Folk literature

Sagas, romances, legends, ballads, and fables in prose form, and fairy tales, folk tales, and tall tales are included here, instead of with the literature of the country of origin, to keep the traditional material together and to make it more readily accessible. Modern fairy tales are classified with Fiction, Story collections (SC)

African folktales; traditional stories of the black world; selected and retold by Roger D. Abrahams. Pantheon Bks. 1983 354p il (Pantheon fairy tale & folklore library) pa $18 hardcover o.p.

Grades: 8 9 10 11 12 Adult   **398.2**

1. Folklore—Africa

ISBN 0-394-72117-9 (pa)   LC 83-2474

This collection contains almost one hundred tales gleaned from the storytelling traditions of Africa, south of the Sahara

Includes bibliographical references

American Indian myths and legends; selected and edited by Richard Erdoes and Alfonso Ortiz. Pantheon Bks. 1984 527p il pa $18 hardcover o.p.

Grades: 8 9 10 11 12 Adult   **398.2**

1. Native Americans—Folklore 2. Native Americans—Religion

ISBN 0-394-74018-1   LC 84-42669

"This volume comprises 160 tales of native folklore and myth ranging from one geographical end of our continent to the other. The book is organized according to type of myth. . . . Erdoes and Ortiz seek to keep Indian myth intact and pure through their retellings, using, as often as possible, primary sources." Booklist

Includes bibliographical references

Baynes, Pauline, 1922-2008

Questionable creatures; a bestiary; [by] Pauline Baynes. Eerdmans Books for Young Readers 2006 47p il $18

Grades: 4 5 6 7   **398.2**

1. Mythical animals 2. Bestiaries

ISBN 978-0-8028-5284-7; 0-8028-5284-X

     LC 2005033658

"Baynes introduces readers to the creatures and myths found in medieval bestiaries and explains how the books were made and how they were viewed by the general public. The rest of the volume details the commonly held beliefs that both peasants and scholars embraced about specific animals. . . . Baynes's detailed gouache and colored-pencil illustrations . . . are done in the style of medieval illuminations. . . . The artist shows great respect for the early bestiary creators while also giving the stories relevance for modern readers." SLJ

Includes bibliographical references

Bedard, Michael, 1949-

The painted wall and other strange tales; selected and adapted from the Liao-chai of Pu Sung-ling by Michael Bedard. Tundra Books 2003 109p $16.95

Grades: 7 8 9 10   **398.2**

Bedard, Michael, 1949——*Continued*
   1. Folklore—China
   ISBN 0-88776-652-8
   Contents: Planting a pear tree; Tiger of Chao-cheng; Princess Lily; Missing silver; Wonderful stone; Taoist priest of Lao Shan; Pianpian, the leaf fairy; Past lives; Paper robes; Jen Shui, the gambler; Invisible priest; Man who was changed into a crow; Glass eyes; Two friends; Talking eye pupils; Theft of the peach; Assistant to the Thunder God; Case of possession; Supernatural wife; Pigeon collector; Arrival of the Buddhist monks; Magic path; Painted wall
   "Known as the Liao-chai, these . . . stories were first collected by a scholar named Pu Sung-ling. . . . Wildly popular in China but little known in the West, they draw on the supernatural or unusual to cast their spell. . . . The stories are short and accessible to reluctant readers." SLJ

Blackwood, Gary L.
   Legends or lies? Marshall Cavendish Benchmark 2006 72p il (Unsolved history) lib bdg $29.93
   Grades: 4 5 6 7   **398.2**
   1. Legends
   ISBN 0-7614-1891-1
   Describes several legends that have intrigued people for centuries: the lost civilization of Atlantis, the Amazons, King Arthur, St Brendon, Pope Joan, and El Dorado
   This collection of "of tidbits about lingering mysteries of the past . . . [offers] more substance than most. . . . [It offers] a full-page illustration opening each chapter; reproductions, many in color; and a generously spaced format." SLJ
   Includes glossary and bibliographical references

Boughn, Michael
   Into the world of the dead; astonishing adventures in the underworld. Annick Press 2006 56p il lib bdg $24.95; pa $12.95
   Grades: 5 6 7 8   **398.2**
   1. Death—Folklore 2. Future life—Folklore
   ISBN 1-55037-959-3 (lib bdg); 1-55037-958-5 (pa)
   "Boughn retells stories from many cultures on every continent except South America, including quite a few from Mesoamerica, Asia, Africa, and Oceania. Readers will find heroes who have traveled to and returned from the underworld as well as the gods and monsters who dwell there. Full-color and black-and-white illustrations, including reproductions, photos, and plenty of graphics of skulls, appear on every page. . . . This is a book that many young people may find appealing." SLJ

Brown, Dee Alexander
   Dee Brown's folktales of the Native American; retold for our times. Holt & Co. 1993 174p pa $12
   Grades: 7 8 9 10   **398.2**
   1. Native Americans—Folklore
   ISBN 0-8050-2607-X   LC 93-12449
   "An Owl book"
   First published 1979 by Holt, Rinehart & Winston with title: Teepee tales of the American Indian

   Contents: The Rooster, the Mockingbird and the maiden; The bear man; How Antelope Carrier saved the Thunderbirds; Why dogs have long tongues; The great shell of Kintyel; The girl who climbed to the sky; The Cheyenne prophet; The deeds and prophecies of Old Man; How day and night were divided; How the buffalo were released on earth; How corn came to the earth; How Rabbit brought fire to the people; Godasiyo the woman chief; The return of Ice Man; Ice Man and the messenger of springtime; How Ioscoda and his friends met the white men from the east and journeyed across the great waters; Katlian and the Iron People; How the first white men came to the Cheyennes; How a Piegan warrior found the first horses; Water Spirit's gift of horses; How Rabbit fooled Wolf; Coyote and the rolling rock; Skunk outwits Coyote; Nihancan and the dwarf's arrow; Swift-Runner and the trickster Tarantula; Buffalo Woman, a story of magic; The hunter and the Dakwa; The prisoners of Court House Rock; Red Shield and Running Wolf; The bluebird and the Coyote; The story of the Bat; Crow and Hawk; Why Coyote stopped imitating his friends; The lame warrior and the skeleton; Heavy Collar and the ghost woman; The Sioux who wrestled with a ghost
   This is a collection of 36 folktales from Native American tribes, including the Seneca, Hopi, Navaho, Creek, Cheyenne, Cherokee, and Blackfoot, grouped by themes such as tricksters and magicians, heroes and heroines, and ghost stories
   Includes bibliographical references

Bryan, Ashley, 1923-
   Ashley Bryan's African tales, uh-huh. Atheneum Bks. for Young Readers 1998 198p $22 *
   Grades: 4 5 6   **398.2**
   1. Folklore—Africa
   ISBN 0-689-82076-3   LC 97-77743
   This volume combines three previously published titles: The ox of the wonderful horns and other African folktales (1971), Beat the story-drum, pum-pum (1980), Lion and the ostrich chicks and other African folktales (1986)
   This collection of African folktales is "told with Bryan's distinctive rhythmic word patterns and filled with humor, life lessons, and the antics of trickster Ananse. . . . Quality reproductions of the original woodcuts enrich this handsome volume." Horn Book Guide

Burns, Batt
   The king with horse's ears and other Irish folktales; [by] Batt Burns; illustrated by Igor Oleynikov. Sterling Pub. Co. 2009 96p il (Folktales of the world) $14.95 *
   Grades: 4 5 6 7   **398.2**
   1. Fairy tales 2. Folklore—Ireland
   ISBN 978-1-4027-3772-5; 1-4027-3772-6
      LC 2007035258
   Contents: The king with horse's ears; Fionn Mac Cumhail and the Fianna of Ireland; The greedy barber; The charm setter; A famous thief; Back from the fairies; Oisin in the Land of the Ever Young; Just one choice; Paying the rent; The naming of Cuchulainn; The boy and the Pooka; A strange night; A clever leprechaun; The Lost Island of Lonesome Seals

Burns, Batt—*Continued*

"These 13 Irish tales retold by storyteller Burns follow fairies and warriors, heroes and clever thieves. . . . The stories are cleanly retold in contemporary, accessible language, and each is introduced with a short paragraph providing cultural or other information. . . . Oleynikov's paintings have a rough texture that suits the energy of the retellings and adds to the lively tone. This is a hearty collection, handsomely produced with Celtic-knot borders and gouache full-page and spot illustrations." Booklist

Includes glossary

Curry, Jane Louise, 1932-

Hold up the sky: and other Native American tales from Texas and the Southern Plains; illustrated by James Watts. Margaret K. McElderry Bks. 2003 159p il $17.95

Grades: 4 5 6 7   **398.2**

1. Native Americans—Folklore 2. Folklore—Southern States

ISBN 0-689-85287-8   LC 2002-16519

Contents: The beginning of the world; Coyote makes the sun; Why Bear waddles when he walks; The quarrel between Wind and Thunder; Thunderbird Woman, Skiwis, and Little Big-Belly Boy; The monsters and the flood; Coyote and the seven brothers; Slaying the monsters; Hold up the sky; Coyote and Mouse; Coyote and the smallest snake; Coyote flies with the geese; Coyote frees the buffalo; The great meatball; The fight between the animals and insects; How Rabbit stole Mountain Lion's teeth; Fox and Possum; Sendeh sings to the prairies dogs; The deserted children; Mountain lion and the four sisters; How Poor Boy won his wife; The ghost woman; The boy who killed the hill; White Fox; The tonkawa and the bear; Young Boy Chief and his sister

Retells twenty-six tales from Native Americans whose traditional lands were in Texas and the Southern Plains, and provides a brief introduction to the history of each tribe

"Curry has carefully researched and sensitively retold tales from fourteen Native American nations. Attractive pencil drawings enhance the stories." Horn Book Guide

Includes bibliographical references

Delacre, Lulu, 1957-

Golden tales; myths, legends, and folktales from Latin America; [retold by] Lulu Delacre. Scholastic 1996 73p pa $5.99 hardcover o.p.

Grades: 5 6 7 8   **398.2**

1. Folklore—Latin America 2. Native Americans—Folklore

ISBN 0-439-24398-X (pa)   LC 94-36724

Contents: How the sea was born; Guanina; The eleven thousand Virgins; The laughing skull; Sención, the Indian girl; When the sun and the moon were children; How the rainbow was born; The miracle of Our Lady of Guadalupe; El Dorado; Manco Capac and the rod of gold; Kákuy; The courier

This includes 12 "stories from four native cultures (Taino, Zapotec, Muisca, and Quechua), including *pourquoi* tales, legends of the conquistadores, and folktales from before and after the age of Columbus. . . . [The author's] . . . retellings are done in a clear and confident voice and are accompanied by her robust, col-

orful oil paintings. . . . This impressively presented and referenced collection will inspire readers and tellers alike." Booklist

Includes bibliographical references

English folktales; edited by Dan Keding and Amy Douglas. Libraries Unlimited 2005 231p il map (World folklore series) $35

Grades: Professional   **398.2**

1. Folklore—Great Britain

ISBN 1-59158-260-1   LC 2005016075

"This collection of more than 50 English folktales contains a variety of stories arranged by common themes: The Fool in All His Glory, Wily Wagers and Tall Tales, Dragons and Devils, etc. The work of 22 storytellers is represented and their tellings are lively and inflected with the rhythms and speech of the regions from which their stories emanate. It is a delightful compendium for storytellers." SLJ

Forest, Heather

Wisdom tales from around the world; retold by Heather Forest. August House 1996 156p $28; pa $17.95

Grades: 7 8 9 10   **398.2**

1. Folklore

ISBN 0-87483-478-3; 0-87483-479-1 (pa)

                 LC 96-31141

A collection of traditional stories from around the world, reflecting the cumulative wisdom of Sufi, Zen, Taoist, Buddhist, Jewish, Christian, African, and Native American cultures

"Forest retells folktales, proverbs, and parables in a thoughtful and satisfying style that amuses as it deftly imparts lessons for living." SLJ

Includes bibliographical references

Hamilton, Virginia, 1936-2002

The people could fly: American Black folktales; told by Virginia Hamilton; illustrated by Leo and Diane Dillon 2009 c1985 178p il $24.99; pa $13 *

Grades: 5 6 7 8   **398.2**

1. African Americans—Folklore

ISBN   978-0-394-86925-4;   0-394-86925-7; 978-0-679-84336-8 (pa); 0-679-84336-1 (pa)

A reissue of the title first published 1985

"Hamilton retells 24 representative black folktales. . . . The stories are organized into four sections: tales of animals; the supernatural; the real, extravagent, and fanciful; and freedom tales." Booklist

The author "has been successful in her efforts to write these tales in the Black English of the slave storytellers. Her scholarship is unobtrusive and intelligible. She has provided a glossary and notes concerning the origins of the tales and the different versions in other cultures. Handsomely illustrated." NY Times Book Rev

Includes bibliographical references

Harris, John, 1950 July 7-
Strong stuff; Herakles and his labors; fierce words by John Harris; powerful art by Gary Baseman. J. Paul Getty Museum 2005 unp il map $16.95
Grades: 4 5 6 7   **398.2**
   1. Hercules (Legendary character)
   ISBN 0-89236-784-9   LC 2004-7904
   This is a "simplified version of the 12 labors of Hercules (Herakles as the Greeks called him). . . . Each labor is allotted a spread with bright and bold illustrations featuring Herakles locked in mortal combat with the monster of the moment, accompanied by a chatty, humorous commentary." SLJ

Hausman, Gerald
   Horses of myth; [by] Gerald and Loretta Hausman; pictures by Robert Florczak. 1st ed. Dutton Children's Books 2004 100p il $19.99
Grades: 4 5 6 7   **398.2**
   1. Horses—Folklore 2. Folklore
   ISBN 0-525-46964-8   LC 2002-40809
   Contents: The Arabian: Abjer, the horse of the Saharan sands; The Mustang: Snail, the horse of the American plains; The Mongolian pony: Humpy, the horse of the Russian steppes; The Timor: Ghost Chaser, the horse of the Tahitian shadows; The Karabair: Kourkig Jelaly, the horse of the Armenian Highlands
   "These five tales each feature a different type of horse, remarkable for both its individuality and the qualities representative of its breed. . . . Florczak's illustrations adapt characteristics appropriate to the locations and time periods of each selection's origins. . . . This is an attractive volume, useful to teachers and librarians for read-alouds and of interest to horse-loving youngsters." SLJ

Hayes, Joe, 1945-
   Dance, Nana, dance; Cuban folktales in English and Spanish; retold by Joe Hayes; illustrated by Mauricio Trenard Sayago. Cinco Puntos Press 2008 128p il $20.95
Grades: 5 6 7 8 9   **398.2**
   1. Folklore—Cuba 2. Bilingual books—English-Spanish
   ISBN 978-1-933693-17-0; 1-933693-17-7
                                  LC 2007-38295
   A collection of stories from Cuban folklore, representing the cultures of Spain, Africa, and the Caribbean.
   "Each tale is accompanied by a full-page illustration that is colorful and contributes to the text. This book is a great addition to folktale and Spanish language collections. Students will enjoy these stories that could easily be incorporated into the curriculum." Libr Media Connect

Hearne, Betsy Gould, 1942-
   Beauties and beasts; by Betsy Hearne; illustrated by Joanne Caroselli. Oryx Press 1993 179p il (Oryx multicultural folktale series) pa $33.95
Grades: 8 9 10 11 12 Adult   **398.2**
   1. Fairy tales 2. Folklore 3. Mythology
   ISBN 0-89774-729-1   LC 93-16

   "The theme of a lonely beast who is transformed by the magic of human love is threaded throughout worldwide variations of the 'Beauty and the Beast' folktale. Author Betsy G. Hearne presents 28 versions of the beloved fable with minimal adaptations from around the world." Publisher's note
   "Professionals will be very grateful for this sensitively written, thoughtful, and accessible interpretive collection." J Youth Serv Libr
   Includes bibliographical references

Helbig, Alethea
   Myths and hero tales; a cross-cultural guide to literature for children and young adults; [by] Alethea K. Helbig and Agnes Regan Perkins. Greenwood Press 1997 288p $49.95
Grades: 8 9 10 11 12 Adult   **398.2**
   1. Mythology—Bibliography 2. Reference books
   ISBN 0-313-29935-8   LC 97-8778
   "Brief, incisive critical reviews of 189 books, published between 1985 and 1996, that contain 1455 myths and hero tales form the heart of this . . . sourcebook. Scholarly accuracy and literary quality are the authors' chief criteria for inclusion, but they also comment trenchantly on illustrations. Indexes list stories by writer, tale type, culture, character and place name, grade level, title, or illustrator." SLJ

Houston, James A., 1921-2005
   James Houston's Treasury of Inuit legends. Harcourt 2006 268p $18; pa $8.95
Grades: 5 6 7 8   **398.2**
   1. Inuit—Folklore
   ISBN 978-0-15-205924-8; 978-0-15-205930-9 (pa)
                                    LC 2006043577
   "An Odyssey Harcourt young classic"
   "This collection includes four previously published stories: 'Tiktaliktak' (1965), 'The White Archer' (1967), 'Akavak' (1968), and 'Wolf Run' (1971). Noted artist Houston lived among the Inuit people for fourteen years and brought their culture to life through his books and artwork." Horn Book Guide

Index to fairy tales; including folklore, legends, and myths in collections. Scarecrow Press 1985-1994 4v *
Grades: Professional   **398.2**
   1. Folklore—Indexes 2. Fairy tales 3. Legends—Indexes 4. Reference books 5. Mythology—Indexes
   Volumes covering 1949-1972 and 1973-1977 first published by Faxon 1973 and 1979 respectively
   A continuation of Index to fairy tales, myths and legends and its two supplements, compiled by Mary Huse Eastman, published 1926-1952 by Faxon (o.p.)
   Volume covering 1949-1972 compiled by Norma Olin Ireland $85 (ISBN 0-8108-2011-0); volume covering 1973-1977 compiled by Norma Olin Ireland (o.p) (ISBN 0-8108-1855-8); volume covering 1978-1986 compiled by Norma Olin Ireland and Joseph W. Sprug $95 (ISBN 0-8108-2194-X); volume covering 1987-1992 compiled by Joseph W. Sprug $95 (ISBN 0-8108-2750-6)
   "Although this is an essential reference book for the children's department, it is also a valuable source for the

Index to fairy tales—*Continued*
location of much folklore and fairy-tale material and
should be available in adult book collections as well."
Ref Sources for Small & Medium-sized Libr. 6th edition

Jaffe, Nina
The cow of no color: riddle stories and justice
tales from around the world; [by] Nina Jaffe and
Steve Zeitlin; pictures by Whitney Sherman. Holt
& Co. 1998 159p il $17
Grades: 4 5 6 7　　　　　　　　　　　　　　**398.2**
　1. Folklore
　ISBN 0-8050-3736-5　　　　　　　　LC 98-14167
　Contents: The cow of no color; The sound of work;
Ximen Bao and the river spirit; The cloak; The thief and
the pig; The testimony of the fly; Susannah and the el-
ders; The jury; The magic seed; The bird lovers; An
ounce of mud; The dance of Elegba; The three wives of
Nenpetro; The flask; Kim Son Dal and the water-carriers;
The land; Sharing the soup; A higher truth; The walnut
and the pumpkin; The wise king; Josephus in the cave;
The water pot and the necklace; The test
　In each of these stories, collected from around the
world, a character faces a problem situation which requires that he make a decision about what is fair or just
　"Sherman's black-and-white line drawings have a
stark gracefulness that complements the tales' form and
structure; the tales themselves are simply told with little
embellishment." Bull Cent Child Books
　Includes bibliographical references

Krasno, Rena, 1923-
Cloud weavers; ancient Chinese legends; [by]
Rena Krasno and Yeng-Fong Chiang; illustrations
from the collection of Yeng-Fong Chiang. Pacific
View Press 2003 96p il $22.95
Grades: 5 6 7 8　　　　　　　　　　　　　　**398.2**
　1. Folklore—China
　ISBN 1-881896-26-9　　　　　　　LC 2002-35911
　Presents legends and tales from China, including ancient folktales, stories that reflect Chinese traditions and
virtues, historical tales, and selections from literature
　This collection "provides a showcase for some remarkable pieces of Chinese calendar art and advertising
posters from the 1920s and 1930s. . . . Prefaces provide
cultural insight for some stories, and the brisk retellings
weave important background unobtrusively into the narrative." Booklist

Lester, Julius
Uncle Remus, the complete tales; with a new
introduction; as told by Julius Lester; illustrated by
Jerry Pinkney 1999 xxi, 686p lib bdg $35 *
Grades: 4 5 6　　　　　　　　　　　　　　　**398.2**
　1. African Americans—Folklore 2. Animals—Folklore
　ISBN 0-8037-2451-9　　　　　　　　LC 99-17121
　Reprint in one volume of works originally published
separately, 1987-1994
　Contents: book 1. The tales of Uncle Remus; book 2.
More tales of Uncle Remus; book 3. Further tales of Un-
cle Remus; book 4. The last tales of Uncle Remus

Lester retells stories of the trickster rabbit from African American folklore collected by Joel Chandler Harris.
　"This is a landmark collection. . . . Lester's retellings
are sharp and flavorful and grounded in the here and
now." [review of book 1] Booklist

Livo, Norma J., 1929-
Folk stories of the Hmong; peoples of Laos,
Thailand, and Vietnam; [by] Norma J. Livo and
Dia Cha. Libraries Unlimited 1991 135p il $26
Grades: 8 9 10 11 12 Adult　　　　　　　　**398.2**
　1. Hmong Americans
　ISBN 0-87287-854-6　　　　　　　　LC 91-370
　Includes the following stories: The beginning of the
world; Legend of the rice seed; How seeds came again
into the world and why dogs eat feces droppings; The
origin of the shaman; Another age of happiness; Creation, flood, naming story; Why monkey and man do not
live together; Why animals cannot talk; Why people eat
three meals a day and why doodle bugs roll balls of
dung; Why farmers have to work so hard; Why birds are
never hungry; Why Hmong are forbidden to drink mother's milk; Why the Hmong live on mountains; Shoa and
his fire; The story of the owl; A bird couple's vow; The
monkeys and the grasshoppers; Sister-in-law Yer and the
tiger: how a wise woman tricked the tiger; Zeej Choj
Kim, the lazy man; Pumpkin seed and the snake; The
handsome husband; Ngao Nao and Shee Na; The tiger
steals Nkauj Ncoom; The orphan and the monkeys; The
orphan boy and his wife; The tigers steal Nou Plai's
wife, Ntxawm; Gwa and Uo and their two fish wives
　This is a collection of folktales of the Hmong people
of Asia which also includes a description of Hmong history and culture, with 16 pages of color photographs of
Hmong dress and needlework
　Includes bibliographical references

Marshall, James Vance, 1924-
Stories from the Billabong; retold by James
Vance Marshall; illustrated by Francis Firebrace.
Frances Lincoln Children's Books 2009 61p il
$19.95
Grades: 3 4 5 6　　　　　　　　　　　　　**398.2**
　1. Aboriginal Australians—Folklore
　ISBN 978-1-84507-704-4; 1-84507-704-0
　"With the help of Aboriginal storytellers who have
collected the tales and myths of their people, Marshall
has assembled 10 fascinating stories of the Dreamtime.
. . . Each selection is beautifully told and is illustrated
by a traditional artist who uses the distinctive symbols
and colors of the Aboriginal people. . . . This is an engaging, colorful book that belongs in most libraries." SLJ

Martin, Rafe, 1946-
The world before this one; a novel told in
legend; with paper sculpture by Calvin Nicholls.
Levine Bks. 2002 195p il hardcover o.p. pa $5.99
*
Grades: 4 5 6 7　　　　　　　　　　　　　**398.2**
　1. Seneca Indians—Folklore
　ISBN 0-590-37976-3; 978-0-590-37980-9 (pa);
　0-590-37980-1 (pa)　　　　　　　LC 2001-23403

Martin, Rafe, 1946——_Continued_

Contents: Dangers; Moving; Gaqka, crow; The bow; The rock; Questions; New day; Two boys; Allies; Men's tales; Dream; Stories; The council; The people and the stone; Farewell

"Written in the style of a novel, this collection of 14 Seneca tales is presented through the retelling of one central story into which all of the others are artfully woven. . . . Martin offers sources for the tales along with an introductory note by Seneca Elder Peter Jemison. Each chapter includes a painstakingly detailed white paper sculpture of a character (often an animal) from one of the stories." SLJ

McCaughrean, Geraldine, 1951-

The epic of Gilgamesh; retold by Geraldine McCaughrean; illustrated by David Parkins. Eerdmans Bks. for Young Readers 2003 c2002 95p il $18 *

Grades: 5 6 7 8   398.2

1. Gilgamesh 2. Folklore—Iraq
ISBN 0-8028-5262-9   LC 2003-1086

Cover title: Gilgamesh the hero

A retelling, based on seventh-century B.C. Assyrian clay tablets, of the wanderings and adventures of the god king, Gilgamesh, who ruled in ancient Mesopotamia (now Iraq) in about 2700 B.C., and of his faithful companion, Enkidu

This is "clearly a telling for our time, but one that honors its source. Parkins captures the epic's primitive power and universal emotions in rough, broadly rendered portraits." Horn Book

McKinley, Robin

The outlaws of Sherwood. Greenwillow Bks. 1988 282p hardcover o.p. pa $14 *

Grades: 8 9 10 11 12   398.2

1. Robin Hood (Legendary character)
ISBN 0-688-07178-3; 0-441-01325-2 (pa)
                                                LC 88-45227

"McKinley takes a fresh look at a classic, changing some of the events or deviating from standard characterization to gain new dimensions. Her afterword explains her artistic compromise with myth and history, her wish to write a version that is 'historically unembarrassing.' With a few exceptions, she has done that admirably, creating a story that has pace and substance and style, and that is given nuance and depth by the characterization." Bull Cent Child Books

Menchú, Rigoberta

The secret legacy; [by] Rigoberta Menchu with Dante Liano; pictures by Domi; translated by David Unger. Groundwood Books/House of Anansi Press 2008 64p il $19.95

Grades: 4 5 6 7 8   398.2

1. Mayas—Folklore 2. Folklore—Guatemala
ISBN 978-0-88899-896-5; 0-88899-896-1

"On her first day watching over her Mayan grandfather's cornfields, young Ixkem is invited by the _b'e'n_, spirits in the form of small humans, to visit them underground. They feed her generously and she tells them stories that explain Mayan customs and include bits of folklore. . . . The Mexican artist Domi has provided bright paintings in a naturalistic, folk-art style. The lyrical translation preserves the storyteller's voice." SLJ

Morpurgo, Michael

Beowulf; illustrated by Michael Foreman. Candlewick Press 2006 92p il $17.99 *

Grades: 5 6 7 8   398.2

1. Beowulf 2. Monsters—Folklore 3. Folklore—Europe
ISBN 978-0-7636-3206-9; 0-7636-3206-6

"Morpurgo retells the classic story of the courageous young warrior . . . who used his brute strength to save the neighboring Danes, then his own kinsmen, by slaying two horrible monsters, a sea serpent, and a massive dragon. . . . Many attractive full-page watercolor and pastel paintings illustrate important action-filled scenes. . . . This is a fine retelling." SLJ

Sir Gawain and the Green Knight; as told by Michael Morpurgo; illustrated by Michael Foreman. Candlewick Press 2004 114p il $18.99

Grades: 5 6 7 8   398.2

1. Arthurian romances 2. Gawain (Legendary character)
ISBN 0-7636-2519-1   LC 2003-65527

The quest of Sir Gawain for the Green Knight teaches him a lesson in pride, humility, and honor

"Morpurgo's sprightly writing brings out all the humor as well as the horror of the original tale, and Foreman's profuse, evocative watercolor-and-pastel illustrations highlight the drama in each scene." SLJ

Norman, Howard

Between heaven and earth; bird tales from around the world; illustrated by Leo & Diane Dillon. Harcourt 2004 78p il lib bdg $22 *

Grades: 4 5 6 7   398.2

1. Folklore 2. Birds—Folklore
ISBN 0-15-201982-0   LC 2003-7874

"Gulliver books"

A collection of folktales from around the world, all of which have a bird as a main character.

This is "a collection of stories that are rich in cultural references from the lands of their origins. . . . The Dillons' luminous watercolor-and-pencil illustrations, detailed with patterns drawn from each tale's culture of origin, will draw readers and listeners back to the stories." Booklist

Oberman, Sheldon, 1949-2004

Solomon and the ant; and other Jewish folktales; retold by Sheldon Oberman; introduction and commentary by Peninnah Schram. 1st ed. Boyds Mills Press 2006 165p $19.95 *

Grades: 5 6 7 8   398.2

1. Jews—Folklore
ISBN 1-59078-307-7   LC 2005020115

"This collection of 43 traditional Jewish stories is authoritative as well as immensely entertaining. . . . The

Oberman, Sheldon, 1949-2004—*Continued*
stories, from both Ashkenazi and Sephardic traditions, are arranged more or less chronologically—from biblical days through the talmudic period to more contemporary times. There are legends, medieval fables, trickster tales, and more. . . . The stories, wonderful for storytelling and sharing, are accessible even to listeners younger than the target audience, and the notes and commentary will provide older children with context and history." Booklist
Includes bibliographical references

Olson, Arielle North, 1932-
Ask the bones: scary stories from around the world; selected and retold by Arielle North Olson and Howard Schwartz; illustrated by David Linn. Viking 1999 145p il $15.99; pa $5.99
Grades: 4 5 6 7 **398.2**
1. Folklore
ISBN 0-670-87581-3; 0-14-230140-X (pa)
LC 98-19108
Contents: The haunted forest; The murky secret; Next-of-kin; The bloody fangs; Ask the bones; The four-footed horror; Beginning with the ears; Fiddling with fire; The Laplander's drum; A night of terror; Nowhere to hide; The handkerchief; The mousetrap; The speaking head; The dripping cutlass; The black snake; The hand of death; The invisible guest; A trace of blood; The bridal gown; The greedy man and the goat; The evil eye
A collection of scary folktales from countries around the world including China, Russia, Spain, and the United States
"David Linn's bone-chilling black-and-white illustrations . . . will stay with the reader long after the book is closed. Excellent for reading aloud, this collection will satisfy even jaded genre fans." Booklist
Includes bibliographical references

More bones; scary stories from around the world; selected and retold by Arielle North Olson and Howard Schwartz; illustrated by E.M. Gist. Viking 2008 162p il $15.99
Grades: 4 5 6 7 **398.2**
1. Folklore
ISBN 978-0-670-06339-0; 0-670-06339-8
"This tour of the world's shadowy corners is full of dark wizards, unkind witches, and other untrustworthy creatures. . . . The 22 tales, as retold by Olson and Schwartz, give a vivid glimpse into unfamiliar, unnerving territory. . . . The atmospheric illustrations, while not intricately detailed, are somewhat startling in their imagery." Booklist

Perkins, John, 1939-
Perceval; King Arthur's Knight of the Holy Grail; retold by John Perkins; illustrated by Gennady Spirin. Marshall Cavendish 2007 36p il $16.99 *
Grades: 5 6 7 8 **398.2**
1. Perceval (Legendary character) 2. Arthurian romances
ISBN 978-0-7614-5339-0
Retells the Arthurian legend of Perceval, a foolish and impatient boy who realizes his dream of becoming a great knight, but meets with misfortune when he forgets to pray and serve God.
"Younger readers will need help navigating the more oblique parts of the story . . . but there are still plenty of straightforward heroics to keep the pages turning. Spirin's intricate full-color paintings, done in the gesso technique used by medieval and Renaissance painters, display a range of passions and action." Booklist

Philip, Neil
Celtic fairy tales; retold with an introduction by Neil Philip; illustrated by Isabelle Brent. Viking 1999 137p il $21.99 *
Grades: 4 5 6 7 **398.2**
1. Fairy tales 2. Celts—Folklore 3. Folklore—Great Britain
ISBN 0-670-88387-5 LC 98-50081
Contents: The battle of the birds; Fair, Brown, and Trembling; The brown bear of the Green Glen; The King of Ireland's son; The three blows; Rory the fox; Lutey and the mermaid; Give me a crab, John; The black bull of Norroway; Finn MacCool and the Scottish giant; Duffy and the devil; Molly Whuppie; The black cat; The king and the workman's daughter; The soul cages; The fiddler in the cave; The well at the world's end; The ship that went to America; The little bird; The tail
An illustrated collection of twenty stories from many Celtic regions, including "The Battle of the Birds," "Finn MacCool and the Scotch Giant," and "The Ship that Went to America."
"There's a mix of the almost familiar and nicely exotic in this collection, which is lavishly illustrated with a glowing full-page painting for each tale and Celtic motifs on every page." Booklist

Pyle, Howard, 1853-1911
The merry adventures of Robin Hood; [by] Howard Pyle; illustrated by Scott McKowen. Sterling Pub. 2004 335p il (Sterling unabridged classics) $9.95
Grades: 8 9 10 11 12 **398.2**
1. Robin Hood (Legendary character) 2. Folklore—Great Britain
ISBN 978-1-4027-1456-6; 1-4027-1456-4
LC 2004016213
Recounts the legend of Robin Hood, who plundered the king's purse and poached his deer and whose generosity endeared him to the poor.

The story of King Arthur and his knights; written and illustrated by Howard Pyle. Scribner 1984 312p il $22.95
Grades: 8 9 10 11 1 2 **398.2**
1. Arthur, King 2. Arthurian romances
ISBN 0-684-14814-5 LC 84-50167
Also available in paperback from Dover Publs. and Signet Classics
A reissue of the title first published 1903
The first of a four-volume series retelling the Arthurian legends
This is an account of the times "when Arthur, son of Uther-Pendragon, was Overlord of Britain and Merlin was a powerful enchanter, when the sword Excalibur was forged and won, when the Round Table came into being." Publisher's note

Pyle, Howard, 1853-1911—*Continued*

The story of Sir Launcelot and his companions. Dover Publications 1991 340p il pa $13.95

Grades: 8 9 10 11 12 **398.2**
1. Lancelot (Legendary character) 2. Arthurian romances
ISBN 0-486-26701-6   LC 90-22326

A reissue of the title first published 1907 by Scribner

This third book of the series follows "Sir Launcelot's adventures as he rescues Queen Guinevere from the clutches of Sir Mellegrans, does battle with the Worm of Corbin, wanders as a madman in the forest and is finally returned to health by the Lady Elaine." Best Sellers

The story of the champions of the Round Table; written and illustrated by Howard Pyle. Dover Publications 1968 328p il pa $11.95

Grades: 8 9 10 11 12 **398.2**
1. Arthurian romances
ISBN 0-486-21883-X

A reissue of the title first published 1905 by Scribner

Contents: The story of Launcelot; The book of Sir Tristram; The book of Sir Percival

"Pyle's second volume of Arthurian legends will be of interest to motivated students of literature and history, as well as useful in professional collections for comparisons and source work. In spite of the archaic language . . . the narrative depth and graphic force . . . will draw in readers." Booklist

The story of the Grail and the passing of Arthur. Dover Publications 1992 258p il pa $12.95

Grades: 8 9 10 11 12 **398.2**
1. Arthur, King 2. Arthurian romances 3. Grail—Fiction
ISBN 0-486-27361-X   LC 92-29058

A reissue of the title first published 1910 by Scribner

This fourth volume of the series follows the adventures of Sir Geraint, Galahad's quest for the holy Grail, the battle between Launcelot and Gawaine, and the slaying of Mordred

Rapunzel and other magic fairy tales; selected and illustrated by Henriette Sauvant; translated by Anthea Bell. Trafalgar Square 2008 157p il $15.95

Grades: 5 6 7 8 **398.2**
1. Fairy tales 2. Folklore
ISBN 1-4052-2702-8

Contents: Rapunzel; Jack and the beanstalk; The master cat, or Puss in boots; The sea rabbit; The iron stove; Cinderella, or The little glass slipper; The Bremen town band; The girl with no hands; The drummer; Mother Holle; The wishing-table, the gold-donkey and the cudgel in the sack; The frog king, or Iron Henry; The goosegirl; Hansel and Gretel

"Sauvant has selected 14 tales of German, English, and French origin, many of them written down by the Grimm brothers. While most of them are familiar . . . others will be unknown to most readers. . . . The illustrations, which range in size from tiny fillers to full-page and double-page pictures, appear to be painted in watercolor or acrylic on a textured surface. While some are painted in classic fairy-tale style, others are best de-scribed as surreal. . . . The sophistication of both stories and artwork makes this collection most suitable for older readers." SLJ

Raven, Nicky

Beowulf; a tale of blood, heat, and ashes; retold by Nicky Raven; illustrated by John Howe. 1st U.S. ed. Candlewick Press 2007 72p il $18.99 *

Grades: 7 8 9 10 11 12 **398.2**
1. Beowulf 2. Monsters—Folklore 3. Folklore—Europe
ISBN 978-0-7636-3647-0; 0-7636-3647-9   LC 2007027094

A modern, illustrated retelling of the Anglo-Saxon epic about the heroic efforts of Beowulf, son of Ecgtheow, to save the people of Heorot Hall from the terrible monster, Grendel.

This is "a gripping rendition of the Anglo-Saxon epic. . . . Raven takes some liberties that add welcome nuance to the story. . . . Howe's artwork . . . is . . . spectacular, easily capturing the heroic grandeur and horrific gruesomeness of the tale." Booklist

Rogasky, Barbara, 1933-

The golem; a version; illustrated by Trina Schart Hyman. Holiday House 1996 96p il $18.95 *

Grades: 4 5 6 7 **398.2**
1. Jews—Folklore 2. Monsters—Folklore
ISBN 0-8234-0964-3   LC 94-13040

This is "the legend of the golem—a monster created of clay—who, under the guidance of the chief rabbi of Prague, rescued the Jews from persecution by anti-Semitic Christians in the late 16th century. Rogasky's strong storytelling skills are evident. . . . Hyman's colorful, fairy tale-like illustrations bring the story to life." SLJ

Rumford, James, 1948-

Beowulf; a hero's tale retold. Houghton Mifflin Company 2007 unp il $17 *

Grades: 4 5 6 7 **398.2**
1. Beowulf 2. Monsters—Folklore 3. Folklore—Europe
ISBN 0-618-75637-X; 978-0-618-75637-7

A simplified and illustrated retelling of the exploits of the Anglo-Saxon warrior, Beowulf, and how he came to defeat the monster Grendel, Grendel's mother, and a dragon that threatened the kingdom.

"Superb on all counts—from the elegant bookmaking to the vigorous, evocative prose . . . to the pen-and-ink and watercolor illustrations that strikingly recall the work of Edmund Dulac." Horn Book

San Souci, Robert, 1946-

Cut from the same cloth; American women of myth, legend, and tall tale; collected and told by Robert D. San Souci; illustrated by Brian Pinkney; introduction by Jane Yolen. Philomel Bks. 1993 140p il $21.99; pa $6.99 *

Grades: 4 5 6 7   **398.2**

1. Folklore—United States 2. Tall tales 3. Women—Folklore

ISBN 0-399-21987-0; 0-698-11811-1 (pa)

                     LC 92-5233

Contents: The Star Maiden; Bess Call; Drop Star; Molly Cottontail; Annie Christmas; Susanna and Simon; Sal Fink; Sweet Betsey from Pike; Old Sally Cato; Pale-Face Lightning; Pohaha; Sister Fox and Brother Coyote; Hekeke; Otoonah; Hiiaka

A collection of fifteen stories about legendary American women from Anglo-American, African American, and Native American folklore

"San Souci's language is vigorous and action verbs abound; Pinkney's black-and-white block prints match the strength of the telling. The inclusion of notes on the sources and a general bibliography make this an academic resource as well as a good collection of rolicking stories." Child Book Rev Serv

A terrifying taste of short & shivery; thirty creepy tales; retold by Robert D. San Souci; illustrated by Lenny Wooden. Delacorte Press 1998 159p il $14.95; pa $10.95 *

Grades: 4 5 6 7   **398.2**

1. Ghost stories 2. Folklore

ISBN 0-385-32635-1; 0-385-32255-0 (pa)

                     LC 98-5551

Contents: Crooker waits; Yara-ma-yha-who; The fata; The fiddler; Land-otter; A fish story; Apparitions; The bijli; The lutin; The hundredth skull; The ogre's arm; The hairy hands; The snow husband; The zimwi; Witchbirds; Dangerous hill; The witch's head; Dinkins is dead; Old Nan's ghost; The interrupted wedding; The mulombe; The haunted grove; The tiger woman; Peacock's ghost; Israel and the werewolf; Hoichi the earless; A snap of the fingers; Narrow escape; The black fox; The mother and death

"Drawing on urban legends, myths, folktales, and ghost stories from around the world and across time, the reteller serves up 30 tales of the supernatural that range from eerie to downright scary. . . . Suspenseful, accessible, and energetic, the tales are uniformly brief and gripping." SLJ

Includes bibliographical references

Sanna, Ellyn, 1957-

Latino folklore and culture; stories of family, traditions of pride; [by] Ellyn Sanna. Mason Crest Publishers 2005 112p il (Hispanic heritage) $22.95 *

Grades: 7 8 9 10   **398.2**

1. Folklore—Latin America 2. Latin Americans—Social life and customs

ISBN 1-59084-932-9   LC 2004024248

This "book begins with a description of the place of folklore in culture and the differences between the terms Latino and Hispanic. Specific folktales, such as the many

versions of 'La Llorona,' and dominant themes, such as machismo, strong women, and religion, are described in subsequent chapters. . . . [This is] an excellent resource both for students researching Latino arts for reports and for general readers." SLJ

Includes bibliographical references

Schwartz, Alvin, 1927-1992

More scary stories to tell in the dark; collected & retold from folklore by Alvin Schwartz; drawings by Stephen Gammell. Lippincott 1984 100p il $15.99; lib bdg $16.89; pa $5.99 *

Grades: 4 5 6 7   **398.2**

1. Ghost stories 2. Horror fiction 3. Folklore—United States

ISBN 0-397-32081-7; 0-397-32082-5 (lib bdg); 0-06-440177-4 (pa)   LC 83-49494

This volume contains stories of ghosts, murders, graveyards and other horrors

"The stories are all short and lively, very tellable, and greatly enhanced by the gray, ghoulish, horrifying illustrations of dismembered bodies, hideous creatures, and mysterious lights. A fine compendium by a well-known collector, easily accessible to young readers." Horn Book

Includes bibliographical references

Scary stories 3; more tales to chill your bones; collected from folklore and retold by Alvin Schwartz; drawings by Stephen Gammell. HarperCollins Pubs. 1991 115p il music $15.99; lib bdg $16.89; pa $5.99 *

Grades: 4 5 6 7   **398.2**

1. Ghost stories 2. Horror fiction 3. Folklore—United States

ISBN 0-06-021794-4; 0-06-021795-2 (lib bdg); 0-06-440418-8 (pa)   LC 90-47474

Traditional and modern-day stories of ghosts, haunts, superstitions, monsters, and horrible scary things

"The book is well paced and continually captivates, surprises, and entices audiences into reading just one more page. Gammell's gauzy, cobwebby, black-and-white pen-and-ink drawings help to sustain the overall creepy mood." SLJ

Includes bibliographical references

Scary stories to tell in the dark; collected from American folklore by Alvin Schwartz; with drawings by Stephen Gammell. Lippincott 1981 111p il $15.99; lib bdg $16.89; pa $5.99 *

Grades: 4 5 6 7   **398.2**

1. Ghost stories 2. Horror fiction 3. Folklore—United States

ISBN 0-397-31926-6; 0-397-31927-4 (lib bdg); 0-06-440170-7 (pa)   LC 80-8728

"A collection of scary, semi-scary, and humorous stories about ghosts and witches collected from American folklore. Most of the stories (poems and songs also) are very short and range from the traditional to the modern. The author includes suggestions on how to tell scary stories effectively." Bull Cent Child Books

"The scholarship in the source notes and bibliography will be useful to serious literature students." SLJ

Schwartz, Howard, 1945-

The day the Rabbi disappeared: Jewish holiday tales of magic; retold by Howard Schwartz; illustrated by Monique Passicot. Viking 2000 80p il hardcover o.p. pa $9.95

Grades: 4 5 6 7   398.2

1. Jews—Folklore 2. Jewish holidays—Fiction
ISBN 0-670-88733-1; 0-8276-0757-1 (pa)

LC 99-42061

Contents: A flock of angels; Drawing the wind; The cottage of candles; Four who entered paradise; The flying shoe; The enchanted menorah; The souls of trees; The angel of dreams; The magic wine cup; The dream of the Rabbi's daughter; A gift for Jerusalem; The day the Rabbi disappeared

Retellings of twelve traditional tales from Jewish folklore featuring elements of magic and relating to holidays, including Rosh Hodesh, Sukkot, Tu bi-Shevat, and Shabbat

"Schwartz follows these brief, clear, and simply told tales with rich and highly readable notes about the history of the holiday, the importance of the rabbi, and the sources of the story." Horn Book

Shelby, Anne

The adventures of Molly Whuppie and other Appalachian folktales; [by] Anne Shelby; illustrations by Paula McArdle. The University of North Carolina Press 2007 88p il $14.95

Grades: 4 5 6 7   398.2

1. Folklore—Appalachian Mountains
ISBN 978-0-8078-3163-2   LC 2007013789

A collection of Appalachian folktales featuring Molly Whuppie and her adventures.

"Shelby has captured the language of Appalachia. . . . Her adaptations are true to the traditional folktales. . . . Young readers and listeners will make these stories their own and enjoy retelling them." SLJ

Includes bibliographical references

Spencer, Ann, 1955-

And round me rings; bell tales and folklore; Illustrated by Lindsay Grater. Tundra 2003 225p il pa $11.95

Grades: 7 8 9 10   398.2

1. Folklore 2. Bells—Folklore
ISBN 0-88776-597-1

"Spencer assembles a variety of traditional tales, true accounts, and poetry about bells. The selections are arranged by broad themes, such as bells used to herald nature, those related to the performing of miracles, those that ring away evil, and those that reflect the rhythm of life." SLJ

"Spencer's smooth writing style brings continuity to the dozens of entries. . . . The variety of material and its attractive presentation make this well-rounded volume a good source for storytelling as well as individual reading." Booklist

Talk that talk: an anthology of African-American storytelling; edited by Linda Goss & Marian E. Barnes. Simon & Schuster 1989 521p hardcover o.p. pa $32.95

Grades: 8 9 10 11 12 Adult   398.2

1. African Americans—Folklore
ISBN 0-671-67167-7; 0-671-67168-5 (pa)

LC 89-10582

The selections included range "from slave stories and the animal legends of Brer Rabbit and Brer Fox to the comedy monologues of Dick Gregory and rap routines. . . . Interspersed throughout are brief sections of commentary and analysis." Booklist

Includes bibliographical references

Taylor, C. J. (Carrie J.), 1952-

Peace walker; the legend of Hiawatha and Tekanawita. Tundra Books 2004 45p il $15.95

Grades: 6 7 8 9   398.2

1. Iroquois Indians—Folklore
ISBN 0-88776-547-5

"The events surrounding the collaboration of two chiefs, the Onondaga Hiawatha and Tekanawita of the Mohawk, to upset the tyrant Atotarho are related simply and abound with graphic details of Native life. . . . Each chapter includes one full-page illustration done in acrylic on canvas in a slightly naive style. . . . The writing is eloquent and poetically rhythmic." SLJ

Tchana, Katrin Hyman, 1963-

Changing Woman and her sisters; stories of goddesses from around the world; retold by Katrin Hyman Tchana; illustrated by Trina Schart Hyman. Holiday House 2006 80p il $18.95 *

Grades: 5 6 7 8   398.2

1. Gods and goddesses 2. Folklore
ISBN 0-8234-1999-1; 978-0-8234-1999-9

LC 2005-52504

An illustrated collection of traditional tales which feature goddesses from different cultures, including Navajo, Mayan, and Fon. Notes explain each goddess's place in her culture, the reason for the book, and how the illustrations were developed.

"This large, handsome volume assembles well-chosen, well-told stories. . . . Hyman . . . contributed distinctive portrayals of the goddesses using a technique that melded photographs and found materials into full-page ink and acrylic paintings." Booklist

Includes bibliographical references

The serpent slayer: and other stories of strong women; retold by Katrin Tchana; illustrated by Trina Schart Hyman. Little, Brown 2000 113p il $22.99 *

Grades: 4 5 6 7   398.2

1. Women—Folklore
ISBN 0-316-38701-0   LC 95-35077

Contents: The serpent slayer; The barber's wife; Nesoowa and the Chenoo; Clever Marcela; Sister Lace; The rebel princess; Beebyeebyee and the Water God; Kate Crackernuts; The old woman and the Devil; The magic lake; Grandmother's skull; Three whiskers from a

Tchana, Katrin Hyman, 1963-—_Continued_
lion's chin; Duffy the Lady; Sun-Girl and Dragon-Prince; Staver and Vassilissa; Tokoyo; The lord's daughter and the blacksmith's son; The marriage of two masters

"These 18 folktales emphasize feminine strength, courage, and wit. . . . The selections come from places as diverse as China, Scotland, and the Gambia." SLJ

"Tchana offers solid retellings of the oft-anthologized ('Kate Crackernuts') and the not oft-anthologized ('Sister Lace'). . . . The thematic variety of the stories provides something for everyone. . . . Humor, suspense, romance, and horror are reflected through the medium of Hyman's powerful art." Bull Cent Child Books

Includes bibliographical references

Thomas, Joyce Carol
The skull talks back and other haunting tales; collected by Zora Neale Hurston; adapted by Joyce Carol Thomas; illustrated by Leonard Jenkins. 1st ed. HarperCollins 2004 56p $15.99; lib bdg $16.89 *

Grades: 4 5 6 7   **398.2**
1. Hurston, Zora Neale, 1891-1960—Adaptations 2. Horror fiction 3. African Americans—Folklore
ISBN 0-06-000631-5; 0-06-000634-X (lib bdg)
                                    LC 2003-22215
Contents: Big, bad Sixteen; Bill, the talking mule; High Walker; The witch who could slip off her skin; The skull talks back; The haunted house

"Thomas retells six supernatural folktales selected from Hurston's Every Tongue Got to Confess" SLJ

"Using a direct style that loses none of the colloquial immediacy of the original voices, Thomas has done a great job of retelling six of Hurston's supernatural tales, and Jenkins' monochromatic collages and silhouettes capture the delicious, shivery glow of skeletons and graveyards." Booklist

Tingle, Tim
Spirits dark and light; supernatural tales from the five civilized tribes; [by] Tim Tingle. August House 2006 192p $15.95
Grades: 6 7 8 9   **398.2**
1. Native Americans—Folklore 2. Supernatural—Fiction
ISBN 0-87483-778-2   LC 2006042709
"Choctaw storyteller Tingle tells 25 deliciously scary tales collected from the five major Native American tribes of the southeastern U.S.the Cherokee, Chickasaw, Choctaw, Creek, and Seminole. . . . For each tribe, Tingle begins with background on history, culture, and folklore. The language is clear and informal, and the dialogue is immediate." Booklist

Walking the Choctaw road. Cinco Puntos Press 2003 142p il $24.95; pa $10.95
Grades: 7 8 9 10   **398.2**
1. Choctaw Indians—Folklore 2. Folklore—Southern States
ISBN 0-938317-74-1; 0-938317-73-3 (pa)
                                    LC 2003-1069
A collection of stories of the Choctaw people, including traditional lore arising from beliefs and myths, histor-

ical tales passed down through generations, and personal stories of contemporary life

"Sophisticated narrative devices and some subtle character nuances give these stories a literary cast, but the author's evocative language, expert pacing, and absorbing subject matter will rivet readers and listeners both." Booklist

Yep, Laurence
The rainbow people; [retold by] Laurence Yep; illustrated by David Wiesner. Harper & Row 1989 194p il hardcover o.p. pa $6.99 *
Grades: 4 5 6 7   **398.2**
1. Folklore—China
ISBN 0-06-026760-7; 0-06-026761-5; 0-06-440441-2 (pa)   LC 88-21203
"Twenty Chinese folktales, selected and retold by Yep from those collected in the 1930s in the Oakland Chinatown as part of a WPA project. . . . The tales, while drawn from the depicting Chinese culture, present a variety of familiar motifs and types: wizards and saints, shape changing and magical objects, pourquoi tales and lessons. An 'Afterword' provides suggestions for further reading on Chinese folktales. This is an excellent introduction to Chinese and Chinese-American folklore." SLJ

Includes bibliographical references

Yolen, Jane
Mightier than the sword; world folktales for strong boys; collected and told by Jane Yolen; with illustrations by Raul Colón. Silver Whistle/Harcourt 2003 112p il $19 *
Grades: 4 5 6 7   **398.2**
1. Folklore
ISBN 0-15-216391-3   LC 2002-9886
Contents: The magic brocade; The young man protected by the river; The devil with the three golden hairs; Eating with trolls; Knee-high man; Language of the birds; Thick-head; The fisherman and the chamberlain; Jack and his companions; The truthful shepherd; And who cured the princess?; The false knight on the road; Hired hands; Mighty mikko

A collection of folktales from around the world which demonstrate the triumph of brains over brawn

Yolen's "versions of these stories are lively, expressively written, ready for reading aloud or telling, and illustrative of her point." SLJ

Includes bibliographical references

400 LANGUAGE

411 Writing systems of standard forms of languages

Donoughue, Carol, 1935-
The story of writing; [by] Carol Donoughue. Firefly Books 2007 48p il map $19.95
Grades: 4 5 6 7   **411**

Donoughue, Carol, 1935—*Continued*
1. Alphabet—History 2. Writing—History
ISBN 978-1-55407-306-1; 1-55407-306-5
This is an "introduction to the history of the Roman alphabet. . . . Beginning sections about early civilizations' alphabets, starting with Sumerian cuniforms, include a you-are-there narrative. . . . Later spreads cover European illuminated manuscripts and the development of printing technology. A final section [covers] Chinese characters. . . . Numerous carefully chosen color photos of artifacts . . . greatly enhance the book's appeal." Booklist
Includes bibliographical references

Robb, Don
Ox, house, stick; the history of our alphabet; illustrated by Anne Smith. Charlesbridge 2007 48p il $16.95 *
Grades: 4 5 6 7   **411**
1. Alphabet—History 2. Writing—History
ISBN 978-1-57091-609-0; 978-1-57091-610-6 (pa)
LC 2005-06015
"Robb traces the history of each letter from its origin to its modern appearance in the Roman alphabet. He explains the birth of writing in pictogram form and the eventual transition to written symbols that stand for sounds. . . . Smith's whimsical paintings are a fitting companion to Robb's lighthearted text." SLJ

419   Sign languages

Butterworth, Rod R.
The Perigee visual dictionary of signing; an A-to-Z guide to over 1,350 signs of American Sign Language; [by] Rod R. Butterworth and Mickey Flodin. rev & expanded 3rd ed. Berkley Pub. Group 1995 478p il pa $15.95
Grades: 8 9 10 11 12 Adult   **419**
1. Sign language—Dictionaries 2. Reference books
ISBN 0-399-51952-1   LC 95-1380
"A Perigee book"
First published 1983
This guide to American Sign Language features more than 1,350 alphabetically arranged signs with directions on how to form them. Illustrations show precise hand positions and movements. Includes memory aids

The **Comprehensive** signed English dictionary; edited by Harry Bornstein, Karen L. Saulnier, Lillian B. Hamilton; illustrated by Ralph R. Miller, Sr. Gallaudet College Press 1983 456p il $39.95 *
Grades: 8 9 10 11 12 Adult   **419**
1. Sign language—Dictionaries 2. Reference books
ISBN 0-913580-81-3   LC 82-82830
"An introductory essay about learning Signed English is followed by 3,100 words and 14 markers representing English usage. The words are arranged in alphabetical order with illustrations and descriptions." Safford Guide to Ref Materials for Sch Libr Media Cent. 5th edition
Includes bibliographical references

Costello, Elaine
Random House Webster's American Sign Language dictionary: unabridged. Random House Reference 2008 xxxii, 1200p $55
Grades: 8 9 10 11 12 Adult   **419**
1. Sign language—Dictionaries 2. Reference books
ISBN 978-0-375-42616-2; 0-375-42616-7
Also available Random House Webster's American Sign Language dictionary: compact edition pa $21.95 (ISBN 978-0-375-72277-6; 0-375-72277-7)
First published 1994 with title: Random House American Sign Language dictionary
This dictionary includes "over 5,600 signs for the novice and experienced user alike. It includes complete descriptions of each sign, plus full-torso illustrations. There is also a subject index for easy reference as well as alternate signs for the same meaning." Publisher's note

The **Gallaudet** dictionary of American Sign Language; Clayton Valli, editor in chief; illustrated by Peggy Swartzel Lott, Daniel Renner, and Rob Hills. Gallaudet University Press 2005 xli, 558p il $49.95 *
Grades: 8 9 10 11 12 Adult   **419**
1. Sign language—Dictionaries 2. Reference books
ISBN 1-56368-282-6; 978-1-56368-282-7
LC 2005-51129
This "reference work is composed of approximately 3000 illustrated entries, each showing the American Sign Language equivalent for an English word. The entries are arranged alphabetically and include synonyms where appropriate." Libr J
"This is a very valuable language resource for parents, students, and teachers learning ASL as a first language and as a second language." Choice
Includes bibliographical references

Sternberg, Martin L. A.
American Sign Language; a comprehensive dictionary; illustrated by Herbert Rogoff. Unabridged. HarperCollins Pubs. 1998 xxi, 983p il $60; pa $24 *
Grades: 8 9 10 11 12 Adult   **419**
1. Sign language—Dictionaries 2. Reference books
ISBN 0-06-271608-5; 0-06-273634-5 (pa)
LC 98-26649
Also available American sign language concise dictionary pa $12 (ISBN 0-06-274010-5)
First published 1981
Arranged alphabetically, this dictionary features 7,000 sign entries, with cross-references and more than 12,000 illustrations
Includes bibliographical references

Warner, Penny
Signing fun; American sign language vocabulary, phrases, games & activities; illustrated by Paula Gray. Gallaudet Univ. Press 2006 225p il pa $19.95
Grades: 4 5 6 7 8   **419**

Warner, Penny—*Continued*
1. Sign language
ISBN 1-56368-292-3

This "offers 441 . . . signs on a variety of favorite topics. . . . Each chapter includes practice sentences using everyday phrases. . . . *Signing Fun* provides dozens of . . . games and activities, too." Publisher's note

"This book is a great resource for readers who want to learn more signs, or for teachers and librarians looking for fun ways to share them with kids." SLJ

422   Etymology of standard English

Baker, Rosalie F.
In a word; 750 words and their fascinating stories and origins; by Rosalie Baker; illustrated by Tom Lopes. 1st American ed. Cobblestone Pub. 2003 221p il $17.95
Grades: 5 6 7 8   **422**
1. English language—Etymology
ISBN 0-8126-2710-5   LC 2003-25582

Contents: Cultural creations; Worldly words & power people; Math magic & science synergy; Religious rituals, fabulous folklore, & marvelous myths; Exceptional expressions; Clothing collection; Glorious gizmos & great grub; Spectacular sports; Joyful journeys; Natural necessities; Awesome archaeology; Political powerhouse; Military madness; Tantalizing tidbits; Fickle finances; Fantastic foreigners

"The entries in this book discuss the meanings and derivations of 750 words and phrases. . . . While exploring word origins, Baker also touches on interesting facets of European history and Greek mythology. The jaunty illustrations are reproduced in black and shades of gray. . . . This informative book fosters an appreciation for the richness of the English language." Booklist

Hitchings, Henry, 1974-
The secret life of words; how English became English. Farrar, Straus and Giroux 2008 440p $27
Grades: 8 9 10 11 12 Adult   **422**
1. English language—Etymology
ISBN 978-0-374-25410-0; 0-374-25410-9
                 LC 2008026055

"Hitchings here provides a colorful, thematic history of the English language. Treating borrowings and coinages as psychological windows to history, the author takes the reader on a tour of the lexicon from Anglo-Saxon to the present day and shows how new words answer linguistic needs. . . . Hitchings treats the reader to some 3,000 word histories. . . . With 90-plus pages of notes, sources, and useful indexes, this is a fine choice for libraries and a 'smorgasbord' for language aficionados." Choice

Includes bibliographical references

422.03   Etymology of standard English—Dictionaries

The **Barnhart** dictionary of etymology; Robert K. Barnhart, editor; Sol Steinmetz, managing editor. Wilson, H.W. 1988 xxvii, 1284p $115 *
Grades: 8 9 10 11 12 Adult   **422.03**
1. English language—Etymology 2. Reference books
ISBN 0-8242-0745-9   LC 87-27994

Also available The Barnhart concise dictionary of etymology (HarperCollins Pubs. 1995)

This dictionary "focuses on words used in contemporary American English and words of American origin and incorporates current American scholarship. Entries give spelling variations, pronunciation for difficult words, part of speech, definition, and information on word origins. Written for a wide audience, this is a very attractive, readable work suited for most library users." Ref Sources for Small & Medium-sized Libr. 6th edition

More word histories and mysteries; from aardvark to zombie; from the editors of the American Heritage dictionaries. Houghton Mifflin 2006 288p il pa $12.95
Grades: 8 9 10 11 12 Adult   **422.03**
1. English language—Etymology 2. Reference books
ISBN 978-0-618-71681-4; 0-618-71681-5
                 LC 2006020835

This "emphasizes the huge number of source languages from which English draws its vast vocabulary—from Sanskrit to French and beyond. The introductory pages give the reader a brief overview of the methods and aims of etymology and a potted history of the origins of English. . . . The editors then present an alphabetical listing of words and their etymology. Each of the 300-plus entries is about half a page to a page long and briefly outlines the origins of the word, its use, and the evolution of its meaning. . . . The book's informative yet informal writing style would appeal to the amateur enthusiast, and accessibility is further enhanced by a useful glossary of linguistic terms." Libr J

Morris, William, 1913-1994
Morris dictionary of word and phrase origins; [by] William and Mary Morris; foreword by Isaac Asimov. 2nd ed. Harper & Row 1988 669p $38
Grades: 8 9 10 11 12 Adult   **422.03**
1. English language—Etymology 2. English language—Terms and phrases
ISBN 0-06-015862-X   LC 87-45651

Original three volume edition published 1962-1971; one volume edition first published 1977

"Traces the origins of several thousand words and phrases commonly used in the English language, including slang terms and clichés not usually found in more formal works. Entries are listed alphabetically by the first word in the phrase, with an index at the end." Ref Sources for Small & Medium-sized Libr. 6th edition

Word histories and mysteries; from abracadabra to Zeus; from the editors of the American Heritage dictionaries. Houghton Mifflin Co. 2004 xvi, 348p il pa $12.95

    Grades: 8 9 10 11 12 Adult   **422.03**
    1. English language—Etymology 2. Reference books
    ISBN 978-0-618-45450-1; 0-618-45450-0
    LC 2004014798

    "The 400 alphabetically arranged entries here illustrate the diversity from which the English language draws its vocabulary, particularly from the prehistoric base that linguists call Proto-Indo-European. As a result, the editors aim to demonstrate links between the ancient base and modern English. . . . An overall quality resource." Libr J

423   Dictionaries of standard English

The **American** Heritage student dictionary. Updated ed. Houghton Mifflin 2007 xx, 1068p il $19.95 *

    Grades: 6 7 8 9   **423**
    1. English language—Dictionaries 2. Reference books
    ISBN 978-0-618-70149-0; 0-618-70149-4
    LC 2006277388

    First published 1977 with title: The American Heritage school dictionary

    Contains more than 65,000 entries, including hundreds of notes on usage, word histories, accompanied by 2000 color photo and illustrations.

Bartlett's Roget's thesaurus. Little, Brown 1996 xxxii, 1415p $21.95; pa $16.95 *

    Grades: 8 9 10 11 12 Adult   **423**
    1. English language—Synonyms and antonyms 2. Americanisms 3. Reference books
    ISBN 0-316-10138-9; 0-316-73587-6 (pa)
    LC 96-18343

    This thesaurus "reflects the current state of American English, including terminology from the worlds of composers and television, with such sub-categories as 'Living Things,' 'The Arts,' 'Feelings.' But what really makes the book a joy to use is the tremendously useful lists— everything from phobias to styles and periods of furniture." Am Libr

Hellweg, Paul
    The American Heritage children's thesaurus; by Paul Hellweg with the editors of American Heritage dictionaries. Houghton Mifflin 2006 280p $17.95 *

    Grades: 4 5 6   **423**
    1. English language—Synonyms and antonyms 2. Reference books
    ISBN 0-618-70166-4
    Replaces the edition published 2003
    First published 1997

    Presents over than 4,000 alphabetically arranged words with several synoyms and an illustrative sentence for each

McCutcheon, Marc
    The Facts on File student's thesaurus. Facts on File 2005 592p $60 *

    Grades: 6 7 8 9   **423**
    1. English language—Synonyms and antonyms 2. Reference books
    ISBN 0-8160-6038-X   LC 2004061966

    This provides synonyms and antonyms for more than 9,000 words listed in alphabetical order

Merriam-Webster's dictionary of synonyms; a dictionary of discriminated synonyms with antonyms and analogous and contrasted words. Merriam-Webster 1984 909p $22.95

    Grades: 8 9 10 11 12 Adult   **423**
    1. English language—Synonyms and antonyms
    ISBN 0-87779-341-7

    Also available in paperback with title: The Merriam-Webster dictionary of synonyms and antonyms

    First published 1942 with title: Webster's dictionary of synonyms

    "This synonym dictionary is an outstanding work. . . . Synonyms and similar words, alphabetically arranged, are carefully defined, discriminated, and illustrated with thousands of quotations. The entries also include antonyms and analogous words." Nichols. Guide to Ref Books for Sch Media Cent. 4th edition

Merriam-Webster's intermediate dictionary. Merriam-Webster 2004 18a, 1005p il $17.95 *

    Grades: 5 6 7 8   **423**
    1. English language—Dictionaries 2. Reference books
    ISBN 0-87779-579-7   LC 2004-45792

    First published 1994 as a replacement for Webster's intermediate dictionary (1986)

    This dictionary includes over 70,000 words and more than 1,000 illustrations, providing definitions, pronunciation, etymology, part of speech designation, and other appropriate information.

Merriam-Webster's school thesaurus. Merriam-Webster 1994 690p $15.95

    Grades: 7 8 9 10   **423**
    1. English language—Synonyms and antonyms 2. Reference books
    ISBN 0-87779-178-3

    First published 1978 with title: Webster's student thesaurus

    This alphabetically arranged volume includes more than 43,000 synonyms, antonyms, idiomatic phrases, related words, and contrasted words

Random House Webster's unabridged dictionary. 2nd ed. Random House 2005 xxvi, 2230p il map $59.95 *

    Grades: 8 9 10 11 12 Adult   **423**
    1. English language—Dictionaries 2. Reference books
    ISBN 0-375-42599-3

    A reissue of the edition published 2001

    First published 1966 with title: The Random House dictionary of the English language

    This dictionary contains over 315,000 entries. A new-words section and an essay on the growth of English are included. 2,400 spot maps and illustrations complement the text

Roget's 21st century thesaurus in dictionary form; the essential reference for home, school, or office; edited by the Princeton Language Institute; Barbara Ann Kipfer, head lexicographer. 3rd ed. Bantam Dell 2005 962p $15; pa $5.99

Grades: 8 9 10 11 12 Adult **423**
1. English language—Synonyms and antonyms 2. Reference books
ISBN 0-385-33895-3; 0-440-24269-X (pa)
"A Delta book"
First published 1992
"Produced by the Philip Lief Group, Inc."
This thesaurus, cross referencing each word with the same concept, provides 500,000 synonyms and antonyms in a dictionary format and includes recently coined and common slang terms and commonly used foreign terms.

Roget's II; the new thesaurus. Houghton Mifflin 2003 1200p $21

Grades: 8 9 10 11 12 Adult **423**
1. English language—Synonyms and antonyms 2. Reference books
ISBN 0-618-25414-5
Also available online
First published 1980
The work uses a dictionary format, with words and numbered definitions on the left column of a page, and corresponding numbered synonyms, near-synonyms, antonyms and near-antonyms on the right column.

Roget's international thesaurus. 6th ed, edited by Barbara Ann Kipfer; Robert L. Chapman, consulting editor. HarperResource 2001 xxv, 1248p $20.95; pa $16.95

Grades: 8 9 10 11 12 Adult **423**
1. English language—Synonyms and antonyms 2. Reference books
ISBN 0-06-273693-0; 0-06-093544-8 (pa)
LC 2002-276277
Also available thumb-indexed edition
First copyright edition published 1911 with title: The standard thesaurus of English words and phrases classified and arranged so as to facilitate the expression of ideas and assist in literary composition
This edition includes 330,000 words and phrases organized into 1,075 categories and a pinpoint reference system that directs the user from a comprehensive index to the numbered category of the right word. Cross-references throughout lead to other categories. Also included are supplemental word lists that supply the names of things which have no synonyms (measurements, wines, state mottoes) as well as quotations that amplify the meanings of selected words

Scholastic dictionary of synonyms, antonyms, and homonyms. Scholastic Reference 2001 220p pa $5.99

Grades: 7 8 9 10 11 12 **423**
1. English language—Synonyms and antonyms 2. English language—Homonyms 3. Reference books
ISBN 0-439-25415-9 LC 2001-278627
A revised edition of Webster's synonyms, antonyms, homonyms, published 1962

"Most of the book is dedicated to the dictionary of synonyms and antonyms; the final 25 pages or so list homonyms. This is good for browsing or for a writer's quick reference." KLIATT

Simon & Schuster thesaurus for children; [edited by] Jonathan P. Latimer and Karen Stray Nolting. Simon & Schuster Bks. for Young Readers 2001 288p $16.95

Grades: 4 5 6 **423**
1. English language—Synonyms and antonyms 2. Reference books
ISBN 0-689-84322-4 LC 2001-31083
"This volume offers cross-references leading to a number of related terms. The main entries generally focus on one thread of meaning; for example, for 'correct,' the entry lists 'adjust' and 'revise' as synonyms with a see-also for 'change' and 'fix.' Each main entry word and synonym are separately defined and include a sample sentence. . . . Different colors highlight sidebars and distinguish main-entry words from synonyms. There is a useful 23-page index. Clear print and an easy-to-use format make this serviceable resource a good choice for novices." SLJ

Terban, Marvin
Scholastic dictionary of idioms. new & updated. Scholastic 2006 298p il pa $19.85 *

Grades: 4 5 6 7 **423**
1. English language—Idioms 2. Reference books
ISBN 978-0-4397-7083-5; 0-4397-7083-1
First published 1996
This "introduction to American slang and phrase origins identifies and defines more than six hundred commonly used idioms, complementing the entries with . . . sample sentences and . . . illustrations." Publisher's note

Webster's third new international dictionary of the English language, unabridged; editor in chief, Philip Babcock Gove and the Merriam-Webster editorial staff. Merriam-Webster 2002 144a, 2662p il $129

Grades: 8 9 10 11 12 Adult **423**
1. English language—Dictionaries 2. Reference books
ISBN 0-87779-201-1 LC 2003-272164
Prices vary according to binding; Also available online
Original edition by Noah Webster published 1828 with title: An American dictionary of the English language. Has also appeared under various other titles. First published with present title 1961
"Clear, accurate definitions are given in historical order. Outstanding for its numerous illustrative quotations, impeccable authority, and etymologies, Webster's third is regarded as the most reliable, comprehensive general unabridged dictionary." Ref Sources for Small & Medium-sized Libr. 6th edition

427 Historical and geographic variations, modern nongeographic variations

Dictionary of American slang; Barbara Ann Kipfer, editor; Robert L. Chapman, founding editor. 4th ed., fully rev. and updated. Collins 2007 592p $45

Grades: 8 9 10 11 12 Adult   **427**
1. English language—Slang—Dictionaries 2. Americanisms 3. Reference books
ISBN 978-0-06-117646-3; 0-06-117646-X

First published 1960 by Crowell. Variant title: New dictionary of American slang

This dictionary of American slang terms "features pronunciation guides, word origins, examples of appropriate usage as well as a . . . highlighting system that lets you know which terms should be used with caution, and never in polite company." Publisher's note

428 Standard English usage (Prescriptive linguistics) Applied linguistics

L is for lollygag; quirky words for a clever tongue. Chronicle Books 2008 125p $12.99

Grades: 4 5 6 7   **428**
1. Vocabulary
ISBN 978-0-8118-6021-5; 0-8118-6021-3
    LC 2007021061

"Budding and accomplished wordsmiths will delight in this specialized dictionary showcasing oft-overlooked gems of the English language. . . . Each definition is related with humor, sometimes including word origination and listing equally interesting synonyms. . . . Black-and-white engravings juxtaposed with cartoons in Picassoesque profile give an old-fashioned yet offbeat air to this unusual compendium." SLJ

Includes bibliographical references

O'Conner, Patricia T.

Woe is I Jr; the junior grammarphobes' guide to better English in plain English; [by] Patricia O'Conner; drawings by Tom Stiglich. G.P. Putnam's Sons 2007 152p il $16.99

Grades: 4 5 6 7 8   **428**
1. English language—Grammar 2. English language—Usage
ISBN 978-0-399-24331-8   LC 2006020575

An adaptation of Woe is I, published 2003 for adults by Riverhead Books

The author "covers pronouns, plurals, possessives, verb usage, subject-verb agreement, capitalization, and punctuation with jargon-free explanations and entertaining examples. . . . She knows her subject, can convey her message with wit and ease, and does it all in a compact, easy-to-read format." SLJ

Ostler, Rosemarie

Dewdroppers, waldos, and slackers; a decade-by-decade guide to the vanishing vocabulary of the twentieth century. Oxford University Press 2003 239p il hardcover o.p. pa $23

Grades: 8 9 10 11 12   **428**
1. English language—Slang 2. Reference books
ISBN 978-0-19-516146-5; 0-19-516146-7; 978-0-19-518254-5 (pa); 0-19-518254-5 (pa)
    LC 2003-8302

"This reference work is not simply a slang dictionary. Along with definitions . . . Ostler includes in each decade's chapter both brief discussions of relevant cultural topics and a few photos. These short, often humorous essays are a way to provide examples for the terms defined. . . . Ostler's work is fun for browsing; it offers a unique presentation of recent cultural history." Libr J

Includes bibliographical references

Terban, Marvin

Scholastic dictionary of spelling; over 15,000 words. Scholastic Ref. 1998 223p il hardcover o.p. pa $9.99

Grades: 4 5 6   **428**
1. Spellers 2. Reference books
ISBN 0-590-30697-9; 0-439-14496-5 (pa)
    LC 97-18020

The words in this speller are "arranged alphabetically (i.e., ladies comes before lady) broken into syllables with the accented syllables in boldface, on attractively laid-out pages, with occasional cartoonish illustrations. Homophones include pronunciation help, and a parenthetical sentence illustrates proper use. The first 26 pages are a treasure trove of helpful hints. . . . The book concludes with the 'Misspeller's Dictionary,' 600 words with tricky beginnngs listed in matched pairs of the common misspelling and the correct one." Book Rep

Truss, Lynne

Eats, shoots & leaves; the zero tolerance approach to punctuation. Gotham Books 2004 xxvii, 209p $19.95; pa $12

Grades: 8 9 10 11 12 Adult   **428**
1. Punctuation
ISBN 1-59240-087-6; 1-59240-203-8 (pa)
    LC 2004-40646

First published 2003 in the United Kingdom

The author "dissects common errors that grammar mavens have long deplored (often, as she readily points out, in isolation) and makes . . . arguments for increased attention to punctuation correctness. . . . Truss serves up delightful, unabashedly strict and sometimes snobby little book, with cheery Britishisms ('Lawks-a-mussy!') dotting pages that express a more international righteous indignation." Publ Wkly

Includes bibliographical references

433 Dictionaries of standard German

Cassell's German-English, English-German dictionary; completely revised by Harold T. Betteridge. Macmillan 2v in 1 thumb-indexed $27
Grades: 8 9 10 11 12 Adult   **433**
1. German language—Dictionaries 2. Reference books
First compiled 1888 by Elizabeth Weir and published by Heath. Periodically revised. Previous American editions published by Funk & Wagnalls with title: The New Cassell's German dictionary

This dictionary incorporates "many new words and usages. Gives phonetic transcriptions of headwords. One of the most useful bilingual dictionaries." Guide to Ref Books. 11th edition

443 Dictionaries of standard French

Cassell's French dictionary; French-English, English-French; completely revised by Denis Girard with the assistance of Gaston Dulong, Oliver Van Oss, and Charles Guinness. Wiley 2002 762, 655p thumb-indexed $24.95
Grades: 8 9 10 11 12 Adult   **443**
1. French language—Dictionaries 2. Reference books
ISBN 0-02-522620-7
First published 1920 with title: Cassell's French-English, English-French dictionary. Previous American editions published by Funk & Wagnalls with title: The New Cassell's French dictionary

"New words including colloquialisms, slang, American English and French-Canadian terms [are included]. . . . There are also sections on French verbs and French and English abbreviations. Reliable, standard dictionary. A first choice." N Y Public Libr. Ref Books for Child Collect. 2d edition

453 Dictionaries of standard Italian

Cassell's Italian dictionary; Italian-English, English-Italian; compiled by Piero Rebora, with the assistance of Francis M. Guercio and Arthur L. Hayward. Wiley 2002 xxi, 1128p thumb-indexed $24.95
Grades: 8 9 10 11 12 Adult   **453**
1. Italian language—Dictionaries 2. Reference books
ISBN 0-02-522540-5
First published 1958 in the United Kingdom with title: Cassell's Italian-English, English-Italian dictionary. Previous United States editions published by Funk & Wagnalls

"A general dictionary of the Italian language as currently written and spoken." Ref Sources for Small & Medium-sized Libr. 5th edition

463 Dictionaries of standard Spanish

Cassell's Spanish-English, English-Spanish dictionary; completely revised by Anthony Gooch, Angel Garcia de Paredes. Wiley 2002 xxv, 1109p $22.95
Grades: 8 9 10 11 12 Adult   **463**
1. Reference books 2. Spanish language—Dictionaries
ISBN 0-02-522910-9
Also available in a concise edition for $13 (ISBN 0-02-522660-6)
Previously published in 1978 by Macmillan
This dictionary emphasizes the Spanish of Latin America, and includes both classical and literary Spanish as well as the language of the modern Spanish-speaking world.

Corbeil, Jean-Claude
The Firefly Spanish/English junior visual dictionary; [by] Jean-Claude Corbeil; Ariane Archambault. Firefly Books 2006 368p il $19.95
*
Grades: 5 6 7 8 9 10 11 12   **463**
1. Spanish language—Dictionaries 2. Picture dictionaries 3. Reference books
ISBN 978-1-55407-190-6; 1-55407-190-9
"Items are arranged under 22 broad topics such as 'Astronomy,' 'Music,' and 'Transportation.' . . . In the labels, the Spanish word appears under the English word. . . . There are 12,000 terms and 2,000 illustrations for everyday objects like suitcases, airplanes, and different kinds of gloves." Booklist

473 Dictionaries of classical Latin

Cassell's Latin dictionary; Latin-English, English-Latin; by D. P. Simpson. Macmillan 1977 c1959 883p thumb-indexed $24.95
Grades: 8 9 10 11 12 Adult   **473**
1. Latin language—Dictionaries 2. Reference books
ISBN 0-02-522580-4   LC 77-7670
Also available in a concise paperback edition for $7.99 (ISBN 0-02-013340-5; ISBN-13: 978-0-02-013340-7)
First published 1854. This edition first published 1959. Previous United States editions published by Funk & Wagnalls with title: Cassell's New Latin dictionary

"Cassell's incorporates current English idiom and Latin spelling into the traditional presentation of classical Latin. The 30,000 entries include generic terms, geographical and proper nouns. Etymological notes and illustrative quotations are provided within entries." Wynar. Guide to Ref Books for Sch Media Cent. 3d edition

493 Non-Semitic Afro-Asiatic languages

Giblin, James, 1933-
The riddle of the Rosetta Stone; key to ancient Egypt; [by] James Cross Giblin. Crowell 1990 85p il pa $7.99 hardcover o.p.
Grades: 5 6 7 8 **493**
1. Rosetta stone 2. Egyptian language 3. Hieroglyphics
ISBN 0-06-446137-8 (pa) LC 89-29289
Describes how the discovery and deciphering of the Rosetta Stone unlocked the secret of Egyptian hieroglyphics
"Suspense keeps the reader glued to this fine piece of nonfiction as the mystery of hieroglyphs is slowly unraveled. . . . The author has done a masterful job of distilling information, citing the highlights, and fitting it all together in an interesting and enlightening look at a puzzling subject." Horn Book
Includes bibliographical references

495.1 Chinese

Oxford Chinese dictionary; English-Chinese, Chinese-English = [Ying Han, Han Ying]; monolingual English text edited by Martin H. Manser; English-Chinese dictionary edited and translated by Zhu Yuan, Wang Liangbi, Ren Yongchang; Chinese-English dictionary edited by Wu Jingrong . . . [et al.] Oxford University Press 2003 various paging $39.95
Grades: 8 9 10 11 12 Adult **495.1**
1. Reference books 2. Chinese language—Dictionaries
ISBN 978-0-19-596459-2; 0-19-596459-4
LC 2005-295454
This Chinese dictionary contains "88,000 words and phrases,130,000 translations, an index system of radicals, Pinyin romanizations, a CD-ROM, and full audio of Mandarin pronunciations of 22,000 single-character dictionary entries." Publisher's note

495.6 Japanese

Basic Japanese-English dictionary. 2nd ed. Oxford University Press, Bonjinsha 2004 1000p pa $19.95
Grades: 8 9 10 11 12 Adult **495.6**
1. Japanese language—Dictionaries 2. Reference books
ISBN 0-19-860859-4 LC 2004-54786
First published 1986 in Japan; 1989 by Oxford University Press
This "dictionary contains over 3,000 entries which, along with providing basic meanings and grammatical information, also distinguish between senses, list compounds, and give sample sentences and idiomatic expressions. . . . It presents all the Japanese words and phrases in roman script with standard Japanese script alongside. . . . Cross-references direct the user to words of contrasting or related meaning, and, where necessary, the dictionary provides notes on special usage. It also includes [an] appendix which gives an introduction to Japanese grammar." Publisher's note

495.7 Korean

Shapiro, Norma
The Oxford picture dictionary, English-Korean; [by] Norma Shapiro and Jayme Adelson-Goldstein; translated by Techno-Graphics & Translations, Inc. Oxford Univ. Press 1998 228p pa $13.95
Grades: 8 9 10 11 12 Adult **495.7**
1. Korean language—Dictionaries 2. Picture dictionaries 3. Reference books
ISBN 0-19-435191-2 LC 98-10947
Over 3,700 words are defined in labeled illustrations grouped into 12 thematic areas. Exercises and a pronunciation guide are provided.

500 SCIENCE

Murphy, Glenn
Why is snot green; and other extremely important questions (and answers). Roaring Brook Press 2009 236p il pa $9.95
Grades: 4 5 6 7 **500**
1. Science 2. Technology
ISBN 978-1-59643-500-1 (pa); 1-59643-500-3 (pa)
"Conservation, evolution, technology, animal life, space travel, physics, and much more are discussed in this lively science book. . . . [This offers] chatty questions and answers . . . with text that is compelling, never intimidating, and sometimes deliberately outrageous. . . . Children will have fun browsing the spacious pages and sharing what they read with adults." Booklist

Sussman, Art, 1944-
Dr. Art's guide to science; connecting atoms, galaxies, and everything in between. Jossey-Bass in partnership with WestEd 2006 246p $22.95
Grades: 6 7 8 9 **500**
1. Science
ISBN 978-0-7879-8326-0; 0-7879-8326-8
LC 2005-57876
"Sussman uses a personable writing style to make a case for the importance of science. With humorous references to pop culture and questions designed to encourage critical thinking, he makes scientific fundamentals accessible. . . . Profuse color visuals help to summarize and clarify concepts." SLJ

Thimmesh, Catherine
The sky's the limit; stories of discovery by women and girls; illustrated by Melissa Sweet. Houghton Mifflin 2002 73p il $16; pa $7.95
Grades: 5 6 7 8 **500**
1. Science 2. Women scientists
ISBN 0-618-07698-0; 0-618-49489-8 (pa)
LC 2001-39111
"This collection highlights a variety of women discoverers from the well known, including Jane Goodall and Mary Leakey, to budding pioneers, such as eleven-year-

Thimmesh, Catherine—_Continued_

old science-lover Katie Murray." Voice Youth Advocates

"The lively design and the mixed-media collage artwork is a creative delight, and the intricate ink-and-watercolor borders, inventive paintings, and childlike pictures will draw readers in. The best thing about the book, however, is Thimmesh's sparkling writing style. . . . Report writers will appreciate this, but the book will also charm browsers." Booklist

Includes bibliographical references

Wollard, Kathy

How come? in the neighborhood; illustrated by Debra Solomon. Workman Pub. 2007 292p il pa $12.95

Grades: 5 6 7   **500**
1. Science
ISBN 978-0-7611-4429-8

"Wollard explains hundreds of phenomena commonly encountered at home, at school, or in the yard—from boiling water to blushing, from why a yo-yo comes back to how the body makes and uses fat. Even taking on such knotty issues as whether the chicken or the egg came first, she answers each query with a specific, closely reasoned answer, animated by lively turns of phrase and intriguing observations. . . . Decorated with small, comical line drawings and supplemented by a healthy list of relevant Web sites, this volume will draw both browsers and serious-minded students like bugs to a porch light." Booklist

500.5   Space sciences

Space sciences; Pat Dasch, editor in chief. Macmillan Ref. USA 2002 4v il set $395

Grades: 8 9 10 11 12   **500.5**
1. Space sciences 2. Reference books
ISBN 0-02-865546-X   LC 2002-1707

"The Macmillan science library." On cover

Contents: v1 Space business; v2 Planetary science and astronomy; v3 Humans in space; v4 Our future in space

"The entries in each volume are in alphabetical order and range from a single paragraph to several pages in length, with most being one or two pages long. The front and back matter are the same in each volume and include a few pages of reference tables such as conversion charts, time lines of milestones in space history and human achievements in space, a list of contributors, a table of contents for the set, and a glossary." Booklist

"A comprehensive and usable survey of space exploration, this marvelous encyclopedia works equally well as a multivolume set and as four standalone volumes. . . . The photographs are excellent." Libr J

Includes bibliographical references

502   Miscellany

Ochoa, George

The Wilson chronology of science and technology; [by] George Ochoa and Melinda Corey. Wilson, H.W. 1997 440p $105

Grades: 8 9 10 11 12 Adult   **502**
1. Science—History 2. Technology—History 3. Reference books
ISBN 0-8242-0933-8   LC 97-22060

This chronology begins in 2,500,000 B.C. and continues into 1997. "Within each year, entries are arranged alphabetically according to one of 13 categories: archaeology; astronomy, space science, and space exploration; biology, biochemistry, agriculture, and ecology; chemistry; earth sciences (geology, oceanography, meteorology) and earth exploration; mathematics; medicine; miscellaneous; paleontology; physics; psychology, neuroscience, and artificial intelligence; social sciences (anthropology, sociology, economics, political science) and linguistics; and technology and engineering." Publisher's note

Includes bibliographical references

502.8   Auxiliary techniques and procedures; apparatus, equipment, materials

Kramer, Stephen

Hidden worlds: looking through a scientist's microscope; photographs by Dennis Kunkel. Houghton Mifflin 2001 57p il (Scientists in the field) $16; pa $5.95 *

Grades: 4 5 6 7   **502.8**
1. Kunkel, Dennis 2. Microscopes
ISBN 0-618-05546-0; 0-618-35405-0 (pa)
            LC 00-58083

This book takes a "look at the work of a microscopist. Kunkel works with microscopes to explore science. . . . This book contains many of his photos, most taken with electron microscopes. . . . Several opening pages, along with the front and back endpapers, are visually dazzling. The heart of the book, though, is what readers learn about how Kunkel produces these images, and to what uses scientists put them. . . . This title offers a wealth of scientific information along with an insightful look at the world of an individual scientist." SLJ

Includes bibliographical references

Levine, Shar, 1953-

The ultimate guide to your microscope; [by] Shar Levine & Leslie Johnstone. Sterling Pub. 2008 143p il pa $9.95 *

Grades: 5 6 7 8 9   **502.8**
1. Microscopes
ISBN 978-1-4027-4329-0 (pa); 1-4027-4329-7 (pa)
            LC 2006-100967

"Through this fun and inviting book, readers can begin to explore the world using a microscope. Students are encouraged to learn the basics in the two first chapters and then undertake the 41 hands-on activities in the next eight chapters. Activities are presented in manageable one or two-page uniformly formatted modules." SLJ

Petersen, Christine
The microscope; [by] Christine Petersen. Franklin Watts 2006 80p il (Inventions that shaped the world) $30.50
Grades: 5 6 7 8 **502.8**
1. Microscopes
ISBN 978-0-5311-2408-6; 0-5311-2408-8
LC 2005007257
Describes early developments in magnification, the invention and improvement of the microscope, and the discoveries about germs, illness, and disease that the advent of the microscope made possible.
Includes bibliographical references

Stefoff, Rebecca, 1951-
Microscopes and telescopes. Marshall Cavendish Benchmark 2006 128p il (Great inventions) lib bdg $39.93
Grades: 7 8 9 10 **502.8**
1. Microscopes 2. Telescopes
ISBN 978-0-7614-2230-3; 0-7614-2230-7
LC 2005-37558
"An exploration of the origins, history, development, and societal impact of the microscope and the telescope." Publisher's note
Includes glossary and bibliographical references

503 Dictionaries, encyclopedias, concordances

The **American** Heritage science dictionary. [rev. ed] Houghton Mifflin Harcourt 2008 695p il $21.95 *
Grades: 8 9 10 11 12 Adult **503**
1. Science—Dictionaries 2. Reference books
ISBN 978-0-618-88274-8; 0-618-88274-X
LC 2008-276195
First published 2005
This science dictionary has 8,500 entries in all areas of science and includes biographical entries, cross-references, photographs, drawings, tables, and charts.

Britannica illustrated science library. Encyclopaedia Britannica 2008 16v il map set $425 *
Grades: 5 6 7 8 9 **503**
1. Science—Encyclopedias 2. Reference books
ISBN 978-1-59339-382-3 (set); 1-59339-382-2 (set)
These "volumes cover a wide range of topics correlating nicely with science curriculums in the fields of the earth sciences, the life sciences, and the physical sciences. Each topic is addressed in no more than two pages with well-organized information and simple language. The editors have carefully linked their scientific explanations to topics of interest and the student's experience. . . . These volumes contain more than 10,000 engaging pictures and illustrations that fill an entire page and help the reader grasp complex scientific topics." Libr J

Growing up with science. 3rd ed. Marshall Cavendish 2006 17v il set $429.95
Grades: 5 6 7 8 **503**
1. Science—Encyclopedias 2. Technology—Encyclopedias 3. Reference books
ISBN 0-7614-7505-2 LC 2004049962
First published 1987
This set "explains many of the most complicated aspects of science and technology, such as how laser disks and computers work, in clear and precise language with the help of beautiful color photographs and drawings. . . . More than 500 articles are arranged in alphabetical order. . . . What is covered is important, current, and well presented." Booklist

The **new** book of popular science. Scholastic Library Pub. 2008 6v il set $399
Grades: 7 8 9 10 11 12 **503**
1. Science—Encyclopedias 2. Technology—Encyclopedias 3. Reference books
ISBN 978-0-7172-1226-2 LC 2007-41858
First published 1924 with title: The book of popular science. Frequently revised
Contents: v1 Astronomy, space science, mathematics, past and future; v2 Earth sciences, energy, environmental sciences; v3 Chemistry, physics, biology; v4 Plant life, animal life; v5 Mammals, human sciences; v6 Technology
The information in this set is classified under such broad categories as astronomy and space science, computers and mathematics, earth sciences, energy, environmental sciences, physical sciences, general biology, plant life, animal life, mammals, human sciences and technology.
Includes bibliographical references

U.X.L encyclopedia of science. 2nd ed, Rob Nagel, editor. U.X.L 2002 10v il maps set $395
Grades: 9 10 11 12 **503**
1. Science—Encyclopedias 2. Reference books
ISBN 0-7876-5432-9 LC 2001-35562
First published 1997
Includes 600 topics in the life, earth, and physical sciences as well as in engineering, technology, math, environmental science, and psychology
It's "difficult to find fault with this clearly written resource that uses simple, nontechnical terms to explain scientific concepts at a basic level." Booklist

The **World** Book student discovery science encyclopedia. World Book 2005 c2006 13v il map Set$399
Grades: 4 5 6 7 **503**
1. Science—Encyclopedias 2. Reference books
ISBN 978-0-7199-7414-6
"This work has more than 2,100 short entries in a single alphabetical arrangement. There are entries for kinds of science . . . as well as for tools, concepts, discoveries, and people. Each entry has at least one large color illustration. Spread throught the volumes are more than 60 simple science experiments that might also be used as the basis for science-fair projects." Booklist

507.8   Use of apparatus and equipment in study and teaching

Bardhan-Quallen, Sudipta

Last-minute science fair projects; when your Bunsen's not burning but the clock's really ticking. Sterling Pub. 2006 112p il $19.95

Grades: 5 6 7 8   **507.8**

1. Science projects 2. Science—Experiments

ISBN 978-1-4027-1690-4; 1-4027-1690-7

                         LC 2005-34455

"The introduction goes through a stripped-down summary of things to consider in choosing a project . . . a description of what to include in the project report, and some tips on presentation. . . . The description of each project is succinct and specific, with question, hypothesis, materials, and procedures clearly outlined." Sci Books Films

Bochinski, Julianne Blair, 1966-

The complete handbook of science fair projects; illustrated by Judy DiBiase. Newly rev and updated. J. Wiley 2004 228p il hardcover o.p. pa $14.95

Grades: 8 9 10 11 12   **507.8**

1. Science projects

ISBN 0-471-45767-1; 0-471-46043-5 (pa)

                         LC 2003-19494

First published 1991

Discusses various aspects of science fair projects including advice on choosing a topic, doing research, developing experiments, organizing data results, and presenting a project to the judges

"An excellent resource for students looking for ideas." Booklist

More award-winning science fair projects; illustrated by Judy J. Bochinski-DiBiase. J. Wiley 2004 228p il $29.95; pa $14.95 *

Grades: 7 8 9 10   **507.8**

1. Science projects 2. Science—Experiments

ISBN 0-471-27338-4; 0-471-27337-6 (pa)

                         LC 2003-9477

Presents forty award-winning science fair projects, a section on how to do a science fair project, updates to science fair rules and science supply resources, as well as new material on useful web sites.

Bonnet, Robert L.

46 science fair projects for the evil genius. McGraw-Hill 2009 194p il (Evil genius series) pa $19.95

Grades: 6 7 8 9   **507.8**

1. Science projects 2. Science—Experiments

ISBN 978-0-07-160027-9; 0-07-160027-2

                         LC 2008008078

Provides instructions and plans for science projects across various disciplines, including physics, astronomy, energy, environmental science and economics.

Cobb, Vicki, 1938-

We dare you! hundreds of science bets, challenges, and experiments you can do at home; [by] Vicki Cobb and Kathy Darling. Skyhorse Pub. 2007 321p il $19.95 *

Grades: 4 5 6 7   **507.8**

1. Science—Experiments

ISBN 978-1-60239-225-0; 1-60239-225-0

                         LC 2007-51236

"Divided into chapters with titles such as 'The Human Wonder,' 'Fluid Feats,' 'Energy Entrapments,' and 'Mathematical Duplicity,' this volume has more than 200 experiments with clear how-to instructions. All of the projects are doable and the science behind them is explained in a kid-accessible manner. . . . Black-and-white line drawings add humor and clarify instructions. This is a great resource for teachers, parents, and budding scientists—and for any youngster who can't resist a challenge." SLJ

Includes bibliographical references

Gardner, Robert, 1929-

Light, sound, and waves science fair projects; using sunglasses, guitars, CDs, and other stuff. Enslow Publishers 2004 128p il (Physics! best science projects) lib bdg $20.95

Grades: 7 8 9 10   **507.8**

1. Light 2. Sound 3. Science projects 4. Science—Experiments

ISBN 0-7660-2126-2   LC 2003-13713

Contents: Some properties of sound and waves; Some properties of light; Light, sound, and reflection; Light, sound, and refraction; Dispersion, light, and color; Sound, light, and waves; Transverse waves and polarized light

These science fair projects attempt to answer such questions as "why dogs can hear things that humans cannot? Why a flame gives off light? Why certain mirrors make you look shorter or taller?"

"This is a very good book, as both a practical and a reference resource." Sci Books Films

Includes glossary and bibliographical references

Planet Earth science fair projects using the moon, stars, beach balls, frisbees, and other far-out stuff; [by] Robert Gardner. Enslow Publishers 2005 128p il (Earth science! best science projects) lib bdg $26.60

Grades: 7 8 9 10   **507.8**

1. Science—Experiments 2. Science projects

ISBN 0-7660-2362-1   LC 2004-10733

This "includes experiments on Earth's relationship to space, the Moon, water and the planet's ever-changing features, the greenhouse effect and global warming, and how to make accurate maps. A helpful listing of the names, mailing addresses, toll-free numbers, and Internet addresses of science supply companies is appended." SLJ

Includes bibliographical references

Goodstein, Madeline

Plastics and polymers science fair projects; using hair gel, soda bottles, and slimy stuff. Enslow Publishers 2004 128p il (Chemistry! best science projects) lib bdg $20.95

Grades: 7 8 9 10   **507.8**

1. Plastics 2. Polymers 3. Science projects 4. Science—Experiments

ISBN 0-7660-2123-8   LC 2003-12825

Contents: Plastics and polymers are all around us; Some properties of polymers; Testing plastics; The mysterious case of natural rubber

This "is a compilation of 20 hands-on activities having to do with the chemical compositon of plastics and common polymers. . . . The directions for the activities are clear and concise while addressing key safety considerations. . . . The book is an excellent example of cross-disciplinary science." Sci Books Films

Includes glossary and bibliographical references

Haduch, Bill

Science fair success secrets; how to win prizes, have fun, and think like a scientist; illustrated by Philip Scheuer. Dutton 2002 134p il pa $10.99

Grades: 5 6 7 8   **507.8**

1. Science projects 2. Science—Experiments

ISBN 0-525-46534-0   LC 2002-23536

Explains the scientific method and describes a variety of actual science fair projects in such fields as engineering, botany, behavioral science, and chemistry

"The often jaunty tone of the text and the cartoon-style drawings make this an unusually appealing book on the topic, while the respect for science and the solid presentation make it a highly useful book as well." Booklist

Includes bibliographical references

Harris, Elizabeth Snoke, 1973-

Save the Earth science experiments; science fair projects for eco-kids; [illustrator, Orrin Lundgren] 1st ed. Lark Books 2008 112p il $19.95

Grades: 4 5 6   **507.8**

1. Science projects 2. Science—Experiments 3. Environmental protection

ISBN 978-1-60059-322-2; 1-60059-322-4

LC 2008017826

Contents: Save the Earth with your science fair project!; How to make a great science fair project; Rethinking energy; Alternative oils; Power plants; A bright idea; Running on air; The sun solution; Methane madness; Blowing in the wind; Putting the sun to work; Out the window; Rethinking garbage; Garbage diet; Recycled paper; Is bulk better?; Disappearing waste; Rethinking pollution; Heating up; No-zone; Lights out!; Clean up your act; Rethinking water; Down the drain; Water power; Not so fast grass; Solar still; Deadly fertilizers

This describes science fair projects such as how to harness energy with windmills, make a biogas generator, create alternative fuels, and recycle paper.

Newcomb, Rain

Smash it! crash it! launch it! 50 mind-blowing, eye-popping science experiments; [by] Rain Newcomb & Bobby Mercer. Lark Books 2006 80p il $14.95

Grades: 4 5 6 7   **507.8**

1. Science—Experiments

ISBN 978-1-57990-795-2; 1-57990-795-4

LC 2006-05518

"Science teachers will find entertaining ways to impress their students with Newton's laws if they're willing to break a few eggs as described in this engaging book. The study of physics becomes appealing when combined with marshmallow catapults, potato popguns, and water-balloon launchers. The authors provide a brief explanation of the physical principles involved and emphasize that cleanup is required on some of the messier projects. . . . Humorous cartoon illustrations and sketchy templates supplement the descriptions of how to set up the projects. Typical household ingredients like straws, pop bottles, fruits, and lots of eggs are the materials required." SLJ

Pilger, Mary Anne

Science experiments index for young people. 4th ed. Libraries Unlimited 2005 184p $60

Grades: Professional   **507.8**

1. Science—Experiments—Indexes 2. Reference books

ISBN 1-59158-237-7

This is a guide to science books that contain elementary and intermediate-level projects and experiments. Organized alphabetically by subject and including a list of headings, the book has 7000 entries that consist of a brief description, book and page numbers, and cross-references.

Rosner, Marc Alan

Science fair success using the Internet. rev. and updated. Enslow Publishers 2006 112p il (Science fair success) lib bdg $26.60 *

Grades: 7 8 9 10   **507.8**

1. Science projects 2. Science—Experiments 3. Internet

ISBN 0-7660-2425-3 (lib bdg)   LC 2005-06749

First published 1999

Explains how to use Internet resources, including e-mailing experts and using search engines, to enhance science projects, with sample projects in biology, chemistry, physics, environment and earth science, and astronomy.

Includes bibliographical references

Science activities for **all** students; edited by Aviva Ebner. Facts on File 2009 2v various paging il loose-leaf $296

Grades: Professional   **507.8**

1. Science—Experiments 2. Science projects

ISBN 978-0-8160-7396-2; 0-8160-7396-1

LC 2008043827

Replaces *Science Projects for All Students* and *More Science Projects for All Students*, published 1998 and 2002 respectively

These "binders enable students in grades 4 through 9 with developmental or physical challenges to join their

Science activities for all students—*Continued*
classmates in . . . hands-on [science] activities. There
are 60 experiments in each binder—designed to be as inclusive as possible—in the areas of basic skills, Earth
science, weather, space science, life science, and physical
science. Each binder is also enhanced by approximately
250 black-and-white line illustrations." Publisher's note
Includes glossary and bibliographical references

VanCleave, Janice Pratt
Janice VanCleave's engineering for every kid;
easy activities that make learning science fun.
Jossey-Bass 2007 205p il (Science for every kid
series) pa $14.95
Grades: 4 5 6 7   **507.8**
1. Engineering 2. Science projects 3. Science—Experiments
ISBN 978-0-471-47182-0; 0-471-47182-8
                   LC 2006-10540
Explains some of the basic physical principles of engineering, accompanied by activities that illustrate those
principles.

Janice VanCleave's guide to more of the best
science fair projects. Wiley 2000 156p il pa
$14.95 *
Grades: 5 6 7 8   **507.8**
1. Science projects 2. Science—Experiments
ISBN 0-471-32627-5   LC 99-25575
Companion volume to Janice VanCleave's guide to
the best science fair projects
This volume includes "fifty experiments . . . in the
areas of astronomy, biology, earth science, engineering,
physical science, and mathematics. . . . A valuable addition to science collections." SLJ
Includes bibliographical references

Walker, Pamela, 1958-
Science experiments on file; [by] Pamela
Walker and Elaine Wood. Facts on File 2004-2005
2v unp il loose-leaf ea $185
Grades: Professional   **507.8**
ISBN 0-8160-5734-6   LC 2004-47230
Also available CD-ROM version
First published 1988
This offers 120 science experiments with over 250 il-
lustrations, tables, and diagrams, listing time required,
safety precautions, materials, procedure, principles illus-
trated, data tables, connections, and additional activities,
which may be reproduced for classroom use
Includes glossaries and bibliographical references

508 Natural history

Art, Henry Warren
Woodswalk; peepers, pikas, and exploding puff
balls; [by] Henry W. Art and Michael W. Robbins.
Storey Books 2003 122p il map $21.95; pa $14.95
Grades: 4 5 6   **508**

1. Forest animals 2. Forest plants 3. Nature study
4. Seasons
ISBN 1-58017-477-9; 1-58017-452-3 (pa)
"This inviting introduction to forests describes the
sights, sounds, and smells that await young explorers.
The accessible text details the wonders of each season in
both eastern and western locales, while full-color photos
depict the flora and fauna that inhabit these intriguing
environments." SLJ

Lynch, Wayne
The Everglades; text and photographs by Wayne
Lynch. NorthWord Books for Young Readers 2007
64p il (Our wild world: ecosystems) $16.95; pa
$8.95
Grades: 4 5 6 7   **508**
1. Everglades (Fla.) 2. Natural history—Florida
ISBN   978-1-55971-970-4;   1-55971-970-2;
978-1-55971-971-1 (pa); 1-55971-971-0 (pa)
                  LC 2006-101497
This "provides an up-close look at the fascinating flo-
ra and fauna of the world-famous Everglades. . . .
Lynch . . . smoothly pairs engaging prose with numerous color photographs that capture the beauty of the region in both sweeping panorama and close-up detail."
Booklist

Weber, Sandra, 1961-
Two in the wilderness; adventures of a mother
and daughter in the Adirondack Mountains;
photographs by Carl E. Heilman II. Boyds Mills
Press 2005 48p lib bdg $19.95
Grades: 4 5 6 7   **508**
1. Natural history—New York (State) 2. Adirondack
Mountains (N.Y.) 3. Hiking 4. Outdoor life
ISBN 1-59078-182-1
The author "recounts with vivid detail a 12-day journey with her 11-year-old daughter, Marcy, in the Adirondack Mountains. . . . The narrative weaves together the
history of the mountains, both geological and cultural,
with a here-and-now account of their ups and downs
through this rugged landscape. . . . Sidebars from Marcy's own journal of the trip offer up a humorous counterpoint to her mother's poetic descriptions of the environment. Color photographs . . . document most of the
outing." SLJ

Woods, Michael, 1946-
Seven natural wonders of Africa; by Michael
Woods and Mary B. Woods. Twenty-First Century
Books 2009 80p il map (Seven natural wonders)
lib bdg $33.26
Grades: 5 6 7 8   **508**
1. Natural history—Africa 2. Africa 3. Curiosities and
wonders
ISBN 978-0-8225-9071-2; 0-8225-9071-9
                  LC 2008-21867
This book "takes seven noteworthy wonders in [Afri-
ca] and spotlights them in separate chapters. The text introduces each one from a historical perspective, and
beautiful color photographs offer inviting views, while
maps, sidebars, and featured quotes add variety to the

Woods, Michael, 1946-—*Continued*
pages. [This book] looks at mountain gorillas, the Nile,
Victoria Falls, the Sahara Desert, Mount Kilimanjaro, the
Seychelles Islands and the Serengeti Plain." Booklist
Includes bibliographical references

Seven natural wonders of Asia and the Middle
East; by Michael Woods and Mary B. Woods.
Twenty-First Century Books 2009 80p il (Seven
natural wonders) lib bdg $33.26
Grades: 5 6 7 8   **508**
1. Natural history—Asia 2. Natural history—Middle
East 3. Asia 4. Middle East 5. Curiosities and wonders
ISBN 978-0-8225-9073-6; 0-8225-9073-5
LC 2008027605
Chapters in this book describe Mount Everest, the
Gobi Desert, Mount Fuji, Sumatra rain forests, the Dead
Sea, Cappadocia, and the Chocolate Hills, including his-
torical perspectives and color photographs.
Includes bibliographical references

Seven natural wonders of Australia and Oceania;
by Michael Woods and Mary B. Woods.
Twenty-First Century Books 2009 il (Seven natural
wonders) lib bdg $33.26
Grades: 5 6 7 8   **508**
1. Natural history—Australia 2. Australia
3. Curiosities and wonders
ISBN 978-0-8225-9074-3; 0-8225-9074-3
LC 2008014003
Chapters in this book describe the Australian outback,
Aoraki/Mount Cook, Mount Kilauea, the Bungle Bun-
gles, the Tasmanian wilderness, Bora Bora, and New
Caledonia, including historical perspectives and color
photographs.
Includes bibliographical references

Seven natural wonders of Central and South
America; by Michael Woods and Mary B. Woods.
Twenty-First Century Books 2009 il map (Seven
natural wonders) lib bdg $33.26
Grades: 5 6 7 8   **508**
1. Natural history—South America 2. Natural history—Central America 3. Curiosities and wonders
ISBN 978-0-8225-9070-5; 0-8225-9070-0
LC 2008027203
This book "takes seven noteworthy wonders in [Cen-
tral and South America] . . . and spotlights them in separate chapters. The text introduces each one from a historical perspective, and beautiful color photographs offer
inviting views, while maps, sidebars, and featured quotes
add variety to the pages. . . . [This book] discusses Angel Falls, the Amazon River, the Atacama Desert, the
Galápagos Islands, the Montecristo Cloud Forest, Poás
Volcano, and the Andes Mountains." Booklist
Includes glossary and bibliographical references

Seven natural wonders of Europe; by Michael
Woods and Mary B. Woods. Twenty-First Century
Books 2009 il (Seven natural wonders) lib bdg
$33.26
Grades: 5 6 7 8   **508**
1. Natural history—Europe 2. Europe—Description
and travel 3. Curiosities and wonders
ISBN 978-0-8225-9072-9; 0-8225-9072-7
LC 2008027604

Chapters in this book describe Loch Ness, Westmann
Islands, Lake Baikal, Black Forest, Mons Klint, Fjords of
Norway, and The Alps, including historical perspectives
and color photographs.
Includes bibliographical references

Seven natural wonders of North America; by
Michael Woods and Mary B. Woods. Twenty-First
Century Books 2009 80p il map (Seven natural
wonders) lib bdg $33.26
Grades: 5 6 7 8   **508**
1. Natural history—North America 2. North America
3. Curiosities and wonders
ISBN 978-0-8225-9069-9; 0-8225-9069-7
LC 2008021864
This book "takes seven noteworthy wonders in [North
America] . . . and spotlights them in separate chapters.
The text introduces each one from a historical perspec-
tive, and beautiful color photographs offer inviting views,
while maps, sidebars, and featured quotes add variety to
the pages. . . . [This book] takes readers to Dinosaur
Provincial Park, Pacific Rim National Park, the redwood
forests, Niagara Falls, the Grand Canyon, Yellowstone
National Park, and the Paricutin Volcano." Booklist
Includes glossary and bibliographical references

509 Historical, geographic, persons treatment

Fradin, Dennis B.
With a little luck; surprising stories of amazing
discoveries; [by] Dennis Brindell Fradin. 1st ed.
Dutton Children's Books 2006 183p il $17.99 *
Grades: 5 6 7 8   **509**
1. Science—History
ISBN 0-525-47196-0   LC 2005-04798
This describes 11 scientific discoveries, including
gravity, fossils, rubber, anesthesia, hygienic medicine,
prehistoric cave paintings, penicillin, the planet Pluto, nuclear fission, the Dead Sea Scrolls, and pulsars.
The author "smoothly combines personal stories . . .
with fascinating science, technology, and history. His
style is open and chatty, and the book design is very attractive." Booklist
Includes bibliographical references

Hakim, Joy
The story of science: Aristotle leads the way.
Smithsonian Books 2004 282p (Story of science)
$24.95 *
Grades: 8 9 10 11 12   **509**
1. Science—History 2. Ancient civilization
ISBN 1-58834-160-7
This "invites readers . . . to meet the forebearers of
modern science—Thales, Pythagoras, Archimedes, Aris-
totle, Arab and Chinese thinkers, Thomas Aquinas, Roger
Bacon, and many others—and share in their . . . discov-
eries in astronomy, math, and physics." Publisher's note
"Hakim has interwoven creation myths, history, physics, and mathematics to present a seamless, multifaceted
view of the foundation of modern science. . . . The entire volume is beautifully organized." SLJ
Includes bibliographical references

Hakim, Joy—*Continued*

The story of science: Einstein adds a new dimension. Smithsonian Books 2007 468p il (Story of science) $27.95 *

Grades: 8 9 10 11 12   **509**

1. Science—History 2. Cosmology 3. Quantum theory
ISBN 978-1-58834-162-4; 1-58834-162-3
LC 2007-14096

Hakim delivers a "brisk, intellectually challenging account of the development of quantum theory and modern cosmology. . . . She introduces a teeming cast of deep thinkers who . . . delivered a series of brilliant experiments and insights. . . . Supplemented by a digestible resource list and a generous assortment of illustrations." Booklist

Includes bibliographical references

The story of science: Newton at the center. Smithsonian Books 2005 463p (Story of science) $24.95 *

Grades: 8 9 10 11 12   **509**

1. Science—History 2. Astronomy 3. Physics
ISBN 1-58834-161-5   LC 2004-58465

This "is an account of the history of astronomy and physics from c.1500 to 1900."

"Teachers will find anecdotal information to enliven their lessons; browsers will be fascinated by the sidebars and captioned illustrations that enhance the text or show related information." SLJ

Includes bibliographical references

Hatt, Christine

Scientists and their discoveries. Watts 2001 62p il (Documenting history) lib bdg $23.50

Grades: 7 8 9 10   **509**

1. Scientists 2. Science—History
ISBN 0-531-14614-6   LC 2001-17574

This "highlights an assortment of astronomers, chemists, physicists, geologists, and biologists, profiling their lives and contributions and explaining the basics of their theories and discoveries." Booklist

Jackson, Donna M., 1959-

Extreme scientists; exploring nature's mysteries from perilous places. Houghton Mifflin Harcourt 2009 63p il (Scientists in the field) $18 *

Grades: 5 6 7 8   **509**

1. Barton, Hazel 2. Sillett, Steve 3. Flaherty, Paul 4. Scientists 5. Explorers
ISBN 978-0-618-77706-8; 0-618-77706-7
LC 2008-36796

This volume "profiles three scientists working far out in the field. Hurricane hunter Paul Flaherty, . . . Hazel Barton, a microbiologist specializing in single-cell organisms living in extreme conditions, . . . [and] ecologist and college professor Steve Sillett, who . . . climbs into the canopies to study redwoods. While the clearly written text includes vivid passages about the dangers these scientists face, it goes on to discuss what drives them to pursue their subjects and what they have discovered along the way. . . . The many excellent color photos

portray these adventures as scientists intently focused on their work." Booklist

Includes glossary and bibliographical references

Spangenburg, Ray, 1939-

The history of science; [by] Ray Spangenburg and Diane Kit Moser. Facts on File 2004 5v set $200

Grades: 7 8 9 10 11 12   **509**

1. Science—History
ISBN 0-8160-4850-9

First published 1993-1994 with title: On the shoulders of giants

Volumes also available separately ea $40

Contents: The birth of science: ancient times to 1699; The rise of reason: 1700-1799; The age of synthesis: 1800-1895; Modern science, 1896-1945; Science frontiers, 1946 to the present

This set discusses major scientists and the scientific issues and discoveries for which they are known.

Includes glossary and bibliographical references

510   Mathematics

Bazin, Maurice

Math and science across cultures; activities and investigations from the Exploratorium; [by] Maurice Bazin, Modesto Tamez, and the Exploratorium Teacher Institute. New Press 2002 176p il maps pa $19.95 *

Grades: Professional   **510**

1. Mathematics 2. Science
ISBN 1-56584-541-2   LC 00-136455

This book provides "activities that integrate geography, math, and science into a multicultural curriculum. . . . Each topic provides a hands-on, minds-on activity that enriches thinking skills and the application-research-based process." Sci Books Films

Includes bibliographical references

Henderson, Harry, 1951-

Mathematics: powerful patterns in nature and society. Facts on File 2007 170p il (Milestones in discovery and invention) $35

Grades: 7 8 9 10 11 12   **510**

1. Mathematics
ISBN 0-8160-5750-8; 978-0-8160-5750-4
LC 2006-24680

"Some mathematicians have discovered relatively simple yet exceedingly powerful patterns that yield insight into aspects of natural and human behavior. . . . [This book] presents 10 essays that profile the minds behind such patterns, many of which have surfaced in recent popular culture." Publisher's note

Includes glossary and bibliographical references

Lee, Cora

The great number rumble; [by] Cora Lee & Gillian O'Reilly; illustrations by Viginia Gray. Annick Press 104p il $24.95; pa $14.95

Grades: 4 5 6   **510**

Lee, Cora—*Continued*
1. Mathematics
ISBN 978-1-55451-032-0; 1-55451-032-5;
978-1-55451-031-3 (pa); 1-55451-031-7 (pa)

When his school district cuts math from the curriculum, saying it causes too much stress for students, one student, a self-proclaimed "mathnik," sets out to prove that math is everywhere, necessary, and not as hard as everyone thinks, in a story that includes real mathematical facts, problems, and solutions.

"Interspersed with the story line are one-page biographies of Pythagoras, Archimedes, Hypatia of Alexandria, Sophie Germain, Charles Ludwig Dodgson, Srinivasa Ramanujan, and Andrew Wiles. Sidebars with Jeremy's thoughts on chaos theory, cash prizes for new prime numbers, laws of probability, and palindrome numbers add to the information. Full-color cartoons, diagrams, and photos appear throughout." SLJ

Mathematics; Barry Max Brandenberger, Jr., editor in chief. Macmillan Ref. USA 2002 4v set $395
Grades: 8 9 10 11 12 **510**
1. Mathematics—Encyclopedias 2. Reference books
ISBN 0-02-865561-3 LC 00-45593

This alphabetically arranged encyclopedia includes "articles about the history of mathematics, prominent scientists from Hypatia to Grace Hopper, technology, and mathematics-related careers, as well as such everyday applications as culinary math." SLJ

This reference "meets its goal of presenting mathematics in a realistic, practical manner." Booklist

Includes bibliographical references

McKellar, Danica
Math doesn't suck; how to survive middle school math without losing your mind or breaking a nail; [by] Danica McKellar. Hudson Street Press 2007 297p il $23.95 *
Grades: 5 6 7 8 **510**
1. Mathematics
ISBN 978-1-59463-039-2; 1-59463-039-9
LC 2007017091

This "covers some of the most basic ideas of middle-grade math, including concepts relating to fractions, decimals, and ratios, making each comprehensible, interesting, and fun. Using real-world constructions, such as tangled necklaces, boyfriends, and pizza, concepts are thoroughly explained." Voice Youth Advocates

510.7 Education and related topics

Salvadori, Mario George, 1907-1997
Math games for middle school; challenges and skill-builders for students at every level; [by] Mario Salvadori and Joseph P. Wright. Chicago Review Press 1998 168p il pa $16.95 *
Grades: 6 7 8 9 **510.7**
1. Mathematics—Study and teaching
ISBN 1-55652-288-6 LC 97-51422

Uses explanations, word problems, and games to cover some mathematical topics that middle school students

need to know, including the invention of numerical notations, basic arithmatical operations, measurements, geometry, graphs, and probability

513 Arithmetic

Julius, Edward H., 1952-
Arithmetricks; 50 easy ways to add, subtract, multiply, and divide without a calculator; illustrations by Dale M. Gladstone. Wiley 1995 142p il pa $12.95
Grades: 7 8 9 10 **513**
1. Arithmetic
ISBN 0-471-10639-9 LC 94-41836

This book "offers fifty ways to do simple arithmetic calculations in one's head. . . . Each trick is covered on two facing pages. The first page presents the problem and gives two examples of how to use the trick. The facing page has a black and white cartoon and extra exercises to practice. The correct answers are given at the end of the book. This would be a fun book for mathematically inclined Middle-Schoolers and up. Math teachers will enjoy using this book for extra-curricular activities." Appraisal

516 Geometry

Sullivan, Navin
Area, distance, and volume; [by] Navin Sullivan. Marshall Cavendish Benchmark 2007 44p il (Measure up!) lib bdg $20.95
Grades: 4 5 6 7 **516**
1. Measurement 2. Geometry
ISBN 978-0-7614-2323-2 (lib bdg); 0-7614-2323-0 (lib bdg) LC 2006026394

"This book opens with a chapter on the history of customary measurement and the metric system. After introducing a few physical and conceptual tools used in measuring, Sullivan explains how to determine distances, . . . areas of common two-dimensional geometric shapes, and volumes of three-dimensional objects." Booklist

An "engaging and informative [title]. . . . An excellent blend of photographs, charts, and diagrams complements the [text]." SLJ

Includes glossary and bibliographical references

516.2 Euclidean geometry

Blatner, David
Joy of [pi] Walker and Co. 1997 129p il hardcover o.p. pa $12 *
Grades: 8 9 10 11 12 **516.2**
1. Geometry 2. Numbers
ISBN 0-8027-1332-7; 0-8027-7562-4 (pa)

"Why does an irrational number impel rational people to do irrational things—like calculating pi to several billion digits? That's what's happening with a pair of characters in Blatner's delightful excursion through the history of pi. . . . Even numerically challenged readers will

Blatner, David—*Continued*

find Blatner's tale immensely appealing, both for the graphic layout, in day-glo colors, no less, and for the amusing and informative anecdotes Blatner relates." Booklist

520   Astronomy

Aguilar, David A.

Planets, stars, and galaxies; a visual encyclopedia of our universe; written and illustrated by David A. Aguilar; contributing writers Christine Pulliam & Patricia Daniels. National Geographic 2007 191p il $24.95; lib bdg $38.90 *

Grades: 5 6 7 8 9 10 11 12   520
    1. Solar system 2. Galaxies 3. Astronomy
    ISBN   978-1-4263-0170-4;   1-4263-0170-7;
978-1-4263-0171-1 (lib bdg); 1-4263-0171-5 (lib bdg)
                      LC 2007061234

"This text introduces readers to the most current information available about the universe. Informatiion is presented is a clear and easy-to-understand manner. . . . The book features bright, eye-catching illustrations that Aguilar created on his computer. In addition, there are many vibrant photographs in the book that were taken by cameras here on Earth as well as by satellites and telescopes." Booklist

Includes glossary and bibliographical references

Lippincott, Kristen, 1954-

Astronomy; written by Kristen Lippincott. rev. ed. DK Pub. 2008 72p il map (DK eyewitness books) $15.99

Grades: 4 5 6 7   520
    1. Astronomy
    ISBN 978-0-7566-3767-5; 0-7566-3767-8
                      LC 2008-276037

First published 1994

Includes CD-Rom

This covers a history of astronomy and telescopes, the planets and stars, galaxies, and modern research.

NightWatch: a practical guide to viewing the universe; foreword by Timothy Ferris; illustrations by Adolf Schaller, Victor Costanzo, Roberta Cooke, Glenn LeDrew; principal photography by Terence Dickinson. 4th ed. Firefly Books 2006 192p il $35 *

Grades: 8 9 10 11 12   520
    1. Astronomy
    ISBN 978-1-55407-147-0; 1-55407-147-X
                      LC 2006-491527

First published 1983

This "handbook for amateur astronomers combines a text both meaty and hard to put down with a great array of charts, boxes, tables, and dazzling full-color photos of the sky." SLJ [review of 1998 edition]

Includes bibliographical references

Reed, George, 1939-

Eyes on the universe. Benchmark Bks. 2001 80p il (Story of science) lib bdg $29.93

Grades: 5 6 7 8   520
    1. Astronomy
    ISBN 0-7614-1150-X   LC 00-31527

This survey examines the history of astronomy from ancient times to the present. Aristotle, Ptolemy, Galileo, Newton, Copernicus, William Hubble and Karl Jansky are among the major figures discussed

Includes glossary and bibliographical references

Rhatigan, Joe

Out-of-this-world astronomy; 50 amazing activities & projects; [by] Joe Rhatigan & Rain Newcomb; with Gregg Doppmann, special consultant. Lark Books 2003 128p il hardcover o.p. pa $12.95 *

Grades: 5 6 7 8   520
    1. Astronomy
    ISBN 1-57990-410-6; 1-57990-675-3 (pa)
                      LC 2003-5196

Contents: The view from here; The Moon; The Sun; The solar system; The stars and beyond

Introduces the study of "stuff in space," providing statistics, quizzes, activities, and experiments about the stars and planets

"An excellent introduction to astronomy. . . . Most [of the projects] are interesting, informative, and well within the abilities of the intended audience. . . . Spectacular color photos and other graphics, useful charts, and graphs augment the text." SLJ

Includes glossary

Ridpath, Ian

Facts on File stars & planets atlas; [by] Ian Ridpath. 4th ed. Facts on File 80p il map $18.95

Grades: 6 7 8 9   520
    1. Astronomy 2. Stars 3. Planets
    ISBN 978-0-8160-6294-2; 0-8160-6294-3

First published 1992 in the United Kingdom; first U. S. edition, 1993

An overview of the solar system, including such topics as the earth and other planets, the sun, moon, asteroids, comets, meteors, and black holes.

Silverstein, Alvin

The universe; by Alvin & Virginia Silverstein & Laura Silverstein Nunn. rev. ed. Twenty-First Century Books 2009 112p il (Science concepts, second series) lib bdg $31.93 *

Grades: 6 7 8 9   520
    1. Astronomy 2. Universe
    ISBN 978-0-7613-3937-3; 0-7613-3937-X
                      LC 2007052245

First published 2003

This book explores the universe and its elements, including the Milky Way, the solar system, the stars, and other astronomical bodies.

"Authoritative, objective, and broadly based. . . . Beautifully designed and well illustrated." SLJ [review of 2003 edition]

Includes bibliographical references

VanCleave, Janice Pratt
Janice VanCleave's A+ projects in astronomy; winning experiments for science fairs and extra credit. Wiley 2002 216p il $32.50; pa $12.95
Grades: 7 8 9 10 **520**
1. Astronomy 2. Science projects 3. Science—Experiments
ISBN 0-471-32816-2; 0-471-32820-0 (pa)
LC 2001-24708
This "has seven sections: Measurements, Optical Instruments, the Sun, the Planets, Moons, and Stars, Meteors, and Artificial Satellites. Project descriptions include purpose, needed materials, procedure, results, and a 'Why?' section. . . . The materials needed are all readily available." Book Rep

Yount, Lisa
Modern astronomy; expanding the universe. Facts on File 2006 204p il (Milestones in discovery and invention) $35
Grades: 7 8 9 10 11 12 **520**
1. Astronomy
ISBN 0-8160-5746-X; 978-0-8160-5746-7
LC 2005-25113
This book profiles "12 men and women whose research and work in new technologies brought about a revolution in the understanding of time and space during the 20th century." Publisher's note
Includes glossary and bibliographical references

520.3 Astronomy—Encyclopedias and dictionaries

The **Facts** on File dictionary of astronomy; edited by John Daintith, William Gould. 5th ed. Facts on File 2006 550p il (Facts on File science library) $59.50
Grades: 7 8 9 10 11 12 **520.3**
1. Astronomy—Dictionaries 2. Reference books
ISBN 0-8160-5998-5; 978-0-8160-5998-0
LC 2006-40860
First published 1979 under the editorship of Valerie Illingworth
This dictionary includes "more than 3,700 entries . . . that reflect all aspects of astronomy, together with associated terms in spectroscopy, photometry, and particle physics." Publisher's note
Includes bibliographical references

522 Techniques, procedures, apparatus, equipment, materials

Cole, Michael D.
Hubble Space Telescope; exploring the universe. Enslow Pubs. 1999 48p il (Countdown to space) lib bdg $23.93
Grades: 4 5 6 7 **522**
1. Astronomy 2. Hubble Space Telescope 3. Astronautics
ISBN 0-7660-1120-8 LC 98-3298

Details the initiation of the Hubble Space Telescope in April 1990 and the repair and servicing missions which followed; explains the telescope's role in answering questions about the universe
"Illustrated with color photographs, the book provides solid basic information." Horn Book
Includes glossary and bibliographical references

DeVorkin, David H., 1944-
Hubble imaging space and time; [by] David Devorkin & Robert W. Smith. Smithsonian National Air and Space Museum in association with National Geographic 2008 223p il $50
Grades: 8 9 10 11 12 Adult **522**
1. Hubble Space Telescope 2. Astronomy
ISBN 978-1-4262-0322-0; 1-4262-0322-5
LC 2008018242
"This handsome volume celebrates the technological and scientific breakthroughs that have made the Hubble such a resounding success. The full, up-to-date story is told in glorious photographs and the equally sparkling commentary of Hubble experts DeVorkin and Smith. . . . The authors cover the people, science, and aesthetics of the stellar Hubble era. Not only are the telescope's contributions to science beyond quantification, DeVorkin and Smith aver, the images the Hubble has gathered have also had profound effects on our imagination and spiritual growth." Booklist
Includes bibliographical references

Gardner, Robert, 1929-
Astronomy projects with an observatory you can build; [by] Robert Gardner. Enslow Publishers 2007 c2008 128p il (Build-a-lab! science experiments) lib bdg $31.93
Grades: 7 8 9 10 **522**
1. Astronomy 2. Science—Experiments 3. Science projects
ISBN 978-0-7660-2808-1 (lib bdg); 0-7660-2808-9 (lib bdg) LC 2006032807
This describes the scientific method and offers instructions in building an observatory and projects in observing Earth, the moon, the sun, the stars, and the planets.
"The digitally rendered diagrams are helpful in clarifying the written directions. [This volume is] involving and entertaining." SLJ
Includes bibliographical references

Matloff, Gregory L.
More telescope power; all new activities and projects for young astronomers; with drawings by C. Bangs. Wiley 2002 118p il pa $12.95
522
1. Telescopes 2. Astronomy 3. Science—Experiments
ISBN 0-471-40985-5 LC 2001-46738
Presents various astronomy activities using a telescope, including constructing a simple telescope, tracking satellites, and sketching details of the moon
This "book is well-written, interesting, and suitable for anyone who wants to learn more about astronomy." Book Rep
Includes glossary and bibliographical references

219

Simon, Seymour, 1931-
Destination: space. HarperCollins Pubs. 2002
unp il $15.99; lib bdg $16.89; pa $6.99 *
Grades: 4 5 6 7   522
1. Astronomy 2. Hubble Space Telescope
ISBN 0-688-16289-4; 0-688-16290-8 (lib bdg);
0-06-059681-3 (pa)   LC 2001-24773
Explains new discoveries about the universe made
possible by the Hubble Telescope
This book is "handsome and fascinating. . . . On each
spread, the large-print, easy-to-understand text is supported by a stunning, full-page color photograph. The author explains what discovery each image produced and
how the information fits into our existing knowledge. His
enthusiastic descriptions create vivid pictures in and of
themselves." SLJ

Spangenburg, Ray, 1939-
The Hubble Space Telescope; [by] Ray
Spangenburg and Kit Moser. Watts 2002 128p il
(Out of this world) lib bdg $33.50; pa $14.95 *
Grades: 6 7 8 9   522
1. Astronomy 2. Hubble Space Telescope
ISBN 0-531-11894-0 (lib bdg); 0-531-15565-X (pa)
                                LC 2001-17563
This "begins by tracing the origins of stargazing and
the development of the first telescopes. Eventually, after
great technological advances and a few setbacks, the
Hubble is completed and put into place. Dramatic photos
of faraway galaxies underline the significant contributions that it has made to understanding the universe. The
book includes the telescope's specifications and brief biographies of historical figures and present-day scientists,
as well as a time line of discoveries and achievements
that led to its creation." Voice Youth Advocates
Includes bibliographical references

523   Specific celestial bodies and phenomena

Chartrand, Mark R.
The Audubon Society field guide to the night
sky; astronomical charts by Wil Tirion. Knopf
1991 714p il map $19.95
Grades: 8 9 10 11 12 Adult   523
1. Astronomy 2. Stars
ISBN 0-679-40852-5   LC 91-52708
"A Chanticleer Press edition. The Audubon Society
field guide series"
This guide "begins with monthly star charts and constellation star charts . . . then gives photographs of the
constellations; and finally, provides detailed information
on each constellation including stars, galaxies, and nebulae. . . . Other information includes hints on observing
ther sky; dates of solar and lunar eclipses, meteor showers, and comets, and the Messier catalog. . . . Students
interested in astronomy will find lots of observing tips
and information." Voice Youth Advocates
Includes bibliographical references

Pasachoff, Jay M.
A field guide to the stars and planets. 4th ed,
Jay M. Pasachoff; with monthly star maps and
atlas charts by Wil Tirion. Houghton Mifflin 2000
578p il map (Peterson field guide series) $30; pa
$19
Grades: 8 9 10 11 12 Adult   523
1. Astronomy 2. Stars
ISBN 0-395-93432-X; 0-395-93431-1 (pa)
                                LC 99-27354
First published 1964 under the authorship of Donald
H. Menzel and Jay M. Pasachoff
This guide contains 24 monthly sky maps, 54 atlas
charts, information and numerous color photographs from
NASA and other sources, and time-sensitive material
through 2010
Includes bibliographical references

Ridpath, Ian
The monthly sky guide; [by] Ian Ridpath;
illustrated by Wil Tirion. 7th ed. Cambridge
University Press 2006 63p il $16
Grades: 8 9 10 11 12 Adult   523
1. Astronomy 2. Stars
ISBN 978-0-52168-435-4; 0-52168-435-8
"In full colour throughout, the seventh edition of Ian
Ridpath and Wil Tirion's . . . guide to the night sky is
fully revised and updated for planet positions and forth-
coming eclipses up to the end of the year 2011. The
book contains a chapter on the main sights visible in
each month of the year. . . . It will help you to identify
prominent stars, constellations, star clusters, nebulae and
galaxies, to watch out for meteor showers, and to follow
the movement of the four brightest planets." Publisher's
note

Simon, Seymour, 1931-
The universe. Morrow Junior Bks. 1998 unp il
$16.95; pa $6.99 *
Grades: 4 5 6 7   523
1. Cosmology
ISBN 0-688-15301-1; 0-06-443752-3 (pa)
                                LC 97-20489
"Matching full-color, full- and double-page-spread-
sized light and radio photographs of nebulas, galaxies,
and sundry deep-space phenomena with two or three
paragraphs of explanatory text [Simon] covers a wide
range of topics, from the Big Bang to quasars, from star
formation to extrasolar planets. . . . The choice of detail
is guaranteed to whet youngster's appetites for a more
thorough, narrowly focused treatment." SLJ

523.1   The universe, galaxies, quasars

Fleisher, Paul
The big bang; by Paul Fleisher. Twenty-First
Century Books 2006 80p il (Great ideas of
science) lib bdg $27.93 *
Grades: 6 7 8 9   523.1
1. Big bang theory
ISBN 0-8225-2133-4   LC 2005001234

Fleisher, Paul—*Continued*

Explains how scientists' observations of the stars led to the development of the big bang theory, a theory of how our universe was formed.

"The book offers a few interesting analogies and includes 22 color diagrams, photos, and informational sidebars. A solid addition for introductory reports." SLJ

Includes bibliographical references

Solway, Andrew

What's inside a black hole? deep space objects and mysteries. Heinemann Library 2006 48p il (Stargazers' guides) lib bdg $22

Grades: 4 5 6   **523.1**

1. Cosmology 2. Astronomy 3. Stars 4. Black holes (Astronomy)

ISBN 1-4034-7710-8 (lib bdg); 1-4034-7717-5 (pa)
LC 2005029113

Contents: The universe in the sky; Shapes in the sky; Looking into the past; Types of stars; A star is born; Black holes and wormholes; Gas and dust; Galaxies; Quasars and red shift; Rewinding the tape; What's next?; Timeline of the universe; Ten brightest stars

Includes bibliographical references

523.2 Planetary systems

Benson, Michael

Beyond; a solar system voyage. Abrams Books for Young Readers 2009 121p il $19.95

Grades: 5 6 7 8 9 10   **523.2**

1. Solar system 2. Astronomy

ISBN 978-0-8109-8322-9; 0-8109-8322-2
LC 2008-22297

"The book's focus is the exploration of the solar system by space probes, with many full-page photos. . . . The author skillfully blends lively narrative with the photos to contribute to the excitement of the explorations. . . . It is an inexpensive but valuable addition for any library." Voice Youth Advocates

Includes glossary and bibliographical references

Carson, Mary Kay, 1964-

Exploring the solar system; a history with 22 activities; [by] Mary Kay Carson. 1st ed. Chicago Review Press 2006 168p il pa $17.95 *

Grades: 5 6 7 8   **523.2**

1. Solar system 2. Astronomy 3. Outer space—Exploration

ISBN 1-55652-593-1   LC 2005028284

This "traces the history of human exploration of the solar system, and, even better, conveys a sense of the enthusiasm that often drives astronomers, engineers, and others involved in the process. . . . Carson highlights the achievements of historical figures as well as contemporary space scientists, and each chapter includes a few simple activities. . . . Excellent color photos and clear drawings and diagrams appear throughout the book." Booklist

Includes bibliographical references

VanCleave, Janice Pratt

Janice VanCleave's solar system; mind-boggling experiments you can turn into science fair projects. Wiley 2000 90p il map pa $10.95

Grades: 4 5 6 7   **523.2**

1. Solar system 2. Science projects 3. Science—Experiments

ISBN 0-471-32204-0   LC 99-15479

Provides instructions for a variety of experiments and science fair projects exploring the solar system, including the sun, moon, planets, comets, and meteorites

"Welcome and valuable." SLJ

Includes glossary

523.3 Moon

Carlowicz, Michael J.

The moon; [by] Michael Carlowicz. Abrams 2007 240p il $19.95

Grades: 8 9 10 11 1 2   **523.3**

1. Moon

ISBN 978-0-8109-9307-5; 0-8109-9307-4
LC 2006102611

A collection of photographs celebrate the moon, its influence on Earth and society, and the scientific expeditions to the satellite

Includes bibliographical references

Simon, Seymour, 1931-

The moon. [rev ed] Simon & Schuster Bks. for Young Readers 2003 unp il $17.95 *

Grades: 4 5 6 7   **523.3**

1. Moon

ISBN 0-689-83563-9   LC 2001-31303

First published 1984 by Four Winds Press

A basic introduction to Earth's closest neighbor, its composition, and man's missions to it

"The digitally remastered color photographs in this update are incredible. . . . The text has undergone minimal change. . . . The facts remain true and relevant, and the writing reflects the graphics: beautiful. This is a must-have for astronomy sections." SLJ

523.4 Planets

Aguilar, David A.

11 planets; a new view of the solar system. National Geographic 2008 47p il $16.95; lib bdg $25.90 *

Grades: 5 6 7 8   **523.4**

1. Planets 2. Solar system

ISBN 978-1-4263-0236-7; 1-4263-0236-3; 978-1-4263-0237-4 (lib bdg); 1-4263-0237-1 (lib bdg)

"Aguilar uses the classification by the International Astronomical Union (which demoted Pluto to dwarf status in 2006). In addition to the eight full-fledged planets, the group of 11 includes the three dwarf planets, Ceres . . . and Eris. . . . The book offers a visually impressive tour of major objects in the solar system. . . . An attractive and timely addition to astronomy collections." Booklist

Includes glossary and bibliographical references

Bortolotti, Dan

Exploring Saturn. Firefly Bks. 2003 64p il
$19.95; pa $9.95

Grades: 5 6 7 8   **523.4**

1. Saturn (Planet)

ISBN 1-55297-766-8; 1-55297-765-X (pa)

This "introduction to the sixth planet [describes] . . .
what we know, don't know, and hope to find out soon.
The author . . . lays out Saturn's probable origins and
inner structure, provides . . . glimpses of [its] rings, and
describes each moon in turn—including one, as yet
unnamed, discovered in 2003. He then covers the
Cassini-Huygens mission in detail." SLJ

"This appealing presentation features a well-organized
and engaging text as well as many exceptionally clear,
colorful illustrations: photographs, space-telescope images, paintings, and drawings." Booklist

Croswell, Ken

Ten worlds; everything that orbits the sun. 1st
ed. Boyds Mills Press 2006 56p il $19.95 *

Grades: 5 6 7 8   **523.4**

1. Planets 2. Solar system

ISBN 1-59078-423-5   LC 2005-35316

This describes the planets of our solar system and
their moons, plus comets, meteors, and asteroids.

"On the basis of its striking design and photographs,
this handsome, large-format volume is well worthy of
praise. And astronomer Croswell's . . . concise yet conversational, information-packed text wins it sky-high ac-
colades in the narrative sphere as well." Publ Wkly

Miller, Ron, 1947-

Jupiter. 21st Cent. Bks. (Brookfield) 2002 72p
il (Worlds beyond) lib bdg $27.90

Grades: 5 6 7 8   **523.4**

1. Jupiter (Planet)

ISBN 0-7613-2356-2   LC 2001-36790

Chronicles the discovery and explorations of the planet Jupiter and discusses each of its moons, its place in
the solar system, and more

Illustrated "with a mix of NASA photos and big,
amazingly realistic, digitally produced, color images."
SLJ

Includes glossary and bibliographical references

Mars; [by] Ron Miller. Twenty-First Century
Books 2006 95p il (Worlds beyond) lib bdg
$27.90

Grades: 7 8 9 10   **523.4**

1. Mars (Planet)

ISBN 0-7613-2362-7   LC 2003-10139

Contents: The red planet; The men of Mars; The exploration of Mars; The biography of a planet; A Martian
weather report; Blue Mars?; A tour of Mars; The moons;
Life on Mars?; Future Mars

Chronicles the discovery and explorations of the planet Mars and discusses each of its moons, its place in the
solar system, and more.

"Chock full of stunning photographs and illustrations.
. . . Written clearly and concisely. . . . A valuable resource." Voice Youth Advocates

Includes bibliographical references

Saturn. Twenty-First Century Books 2003 80p il
(Worlds beyond) lib bdg $27.90

Grades: 5 6 7 8   **523.4**

1. Saturn (Planet)

ISBN 0-7613-2360-0   LC 2002-14098

Contents: Lord of the rings; Exploring Saturn; The
crown jewel of the solar system; Moons, moons, and
more moons; The future of Saturn

Chronicles the discovery and exploration of the planet
Saturn and discusses its rings and moons, its place in the
solar system, and more.

"Concepts are explained clearly, and helpful diagrams
and carefully chosen illustrations assist understanding."
SLJ

Includes bibliographical references

Schwabacher, Martin

Jupiter. Benchmark Bks. 2001 c2002 64p il
(Blastoff!) lib bdg $28.50

Grades: 5 6 7 8   **523.4**

1. Jupiter (Planet)

ISBN 0-7614-1236-0   LC 2001-25640

This describes astronomers' present knowledge of the
planet Jupiter "with considerable attention given to the
sources of information (visiting spacecraft, the Hubble
telescope, ground-based observation, mathematical inference. . . . [It includes] many well-captioned photos, illustrations, and diagrams." Horn Book Guide

Includes glossary and bibliographical references

Scott, Elaine, 1940-

When is a planet not a planet? the story of
Pluto. Clarion Books 2007 43p il $17

Grades: 3 4 5 6   **523.4**

1. Planets

ISBN 978-0-618-89832-9; 0-618-89832-8

"Scott takes the 2006 downgrading of Pluto from
planet to dwarf planet as a teachable moment for discussing questions such as how the number of planets has
changed through the centuries, what can be called a planet, and how scientists come to conclusions—and occasionally change their minds. . . . Beautifully designed,
the book includes many well-captioned, color illustrations, from period portraits to NASA images to artist's
conceptions." Booklist

Simon, Seymour, 1931-

Destination: Jupiter. rev ed. Morrow Junior Bks.
1998 unp il $16.89; pa $6.99

Grades: 3 4 5 6   **523.4**

1. Jupiter (Planet)

ISBN 0-688-15620-7; 0-06-443759-0 (pa)

LC 97-20488

First published 1985 with title: Jupiter

This is a "guide to the planet and its four Galilean
moons, Io, Europa, Ganymede, and Callisto. The complete planetary portrait is achieved by combining classic
Voyager spacecraft images and more recent *Galileo* mission photographs." Horn Book Guide

"Expertly balancing the verbal and visual presentation,
Simon . . . demonstrates his ability to inform and entertain simultaneously." SLJ

Skurzynski, Gloria, 1930-
Discover Mars. National Geographic Soc. 1998
44p il $17.95
Grades: 4 5 6 **523.4**
  1. Mars (Planet)
  ISBN 0-7922-7099-1   LC 98-13190
  Includes two pairs of 3-D glasses
Reviews results from the study of Mars, from Copernicus through the Viking and Pathfinder missions, and speculates on a future human landing
"Scattered throughout this thoroughly illustrated report are specially printed photos that, when viewed through cardboard 'anaglyph' glasses, appear as 3-D. . . . The book makes an inviting package, with plenty of big, bright photographs and artists' conceptions for standard illustrations, a concise but specific summary of what is now known about Mars, and a generous selection of Web sites at the end." SLJ

Spangenburg, Ray, 1939-
A look at Mercury; [by] Ray Spangenburg and Kit Moser. Watts 2003 110p il map (Out of this world) lib bdg $33.50; pa $14.95
Grades: 6 7 8 9 **523.4**
  1. Mercury (Planet)
  ISBN 0-531-11928-9 (lib bdg); 0-531-16673-2 (pa)
    LC 2002-8508
Describes the discovery and observation of the planet nearest the sun, Mercury, including the findings of the Mariner 10 fly-by mission of 1974-75
  Includes glossary and bibliographical references

Stefoff, Rebecca, 1951-
Neptune. Benchmark Bks. 2001 c2002 64p il (Blastoff!) lib bdg $28.50
Grades: 5 6 7 8 **523.4**
  1. Neptune (Planet)
  ISBN 0-7614-1232-X   LC 00-59643
This is a study of the planet Neptune from its discovery in 1846 to recent and future space probes
"Students will find {this book} useful for science projects and gathering information for class presentations." Book Rep
  Includes glossary and bibliographical references

Stone, Tanya Lee
Mars. Benchmark Bks. 2001 c2002 64p il (Blastoff!) lib bdg $28.50
Grades: 5 6 7 8 **523.4**
  1. Mars (Planet)
  ISBN 0-7614-1233-6   LC 00-46775
This is a study of the planet Mars from ancient times to the present that also discusses future space missions
"Students will find [this book] useful for science projects and gathering information for class presentations." Book Rep
  Includes glossary and bibliographical references

Saturn. Benchmark Bks. 2001 c2002 64p il (Blastoff!) lib bdg $28.50
Grades: 5 6 7 8 **523.4**

  1. Saturn (Planet)
  ISBN 0-7614-1234-4
This is a study of the planet Saturn and its moons from early astronomers such as Galileo, Huygens, and Cassini to recent space probes
"Students will find [this book] useful for science projects and gathering information for class presentations." Book Rep
  Includes glossary and bibliographical references

Tabak, John
A look at Neptune. Watts 2003 107p il (Out of this world) lib bdg $33.50; pa $14.95
Grades: 6 7 8 9 **523.4**
  1. Neptune (Planet)
  ISBN 0-531-12267-0 (lib bdg); 0-531-15584-6 (pa)
    LC 2002-2023
Describes the discovery and observation of the planet Neptune and what has been learned about it, particularly from the Voyager spacecraft mission
Overall this "conveys the material well. Outstanding color photos contribute to the content." SLJ
  Includes glossary and bibliographical references

Tocci, Salvatore
A look at Uranus. Watts 2003 109p il (Out of this world) lib bdg $33.50; pa $14.95
Grades: 6 7 8 9 **523.4**
  1. Uranus (Planet)
  ISBN 0-531-12250-6 (lib bdg); 0-531-15570-6 (pa)
    LC 2002-156020
Looks at the history and discovery of the planet Uranus
This "does everything it should to be both interesting to young people and informative. . . . The graphic material is excellent." Sci Books Films
  Includes glossary and bibliographical references

Tyson, Neil De Grasse
The Pluto files; the rise and fall of America's favorite planet. W.W. Norton 2009 194p il $23.95
Grades: 8 9 10 11 12 Adult **523.4**
  1. Pluto (Planet)
  ISBN 978-0-393-06520-6; 0-393-06520-0
    LC 2008-40436
An exploration of the controversy surrounding Pluto and its planet status from an astrophysicist at the heart of the controversy.
The author "uses an engaging mix of facts, photographs, cartoons, illustrations, songs, e-mails, and humor to explain what's up (and down) with Pluto." Christ Sci Monit
  Includes bibliographical references

Ward, David J. (David John)
Exploring Mars; [by] D. J. Ward. Lerner Publications Co. 2007 48p il (Cool science) $27.93
Grades: 4 5 6 **523.4**
  1. Mars (Planet)
  ISBN 978-0-8225-5936-8; 0-8225-5936-6
    LC 2005032346

Ward, David J. (David John)—*Continued*

This describes what is known about the planet Mars and its moons, the possiblity of life on Mars, and past and possible future missions to the planet.

Includes glossary and bibliographical references

523.5   Meteors, solar wind, zodiacal light

Koppes, Steven N.

Killer rocks from outer space; asteroids, comets, and meteorites. Lerner Publications Co. 2004 112p il (Discovery!) $26.60

Grades: 6 7 8 9   **523.5**

1. Asteroids 2. Comets 3. Meteorites

ISBN 0-8225-2861-4   LC 2003-10077

Describes the role that collisions with meteors, comets, and asteroids have played in the history of Earth and other planets in the solar system and examines what is being done to protect Earth from future collisions

"A catchy title, colorful cover, and well-written and interesting information combine to make this unusual science book one that students will find to be very readable and extremely useful for research projects. . . . This book will find many readers and should inspire students to further study astronomy." Lib Media Connect

Includes bibliographical references

Miller, Ron, 1947-

Asteroids, comets, and meteors; [by] Ron Miller. Twenty-First Century Books 2006 80p il (Worlds beyond) lib bdg $27.90 *

Grades: 7 8 9 10   **523.5**

1. Asteroids 2. Comets 3. Meteors

ISBN 0-7613-2363-5   LC 2003-10410

Contents: Building a solar system; Miniature worlds; The asteroid belt; Exploring asteroids; Comets; Meteors

Chronicles the formation of the solar system, particularly how asteroids, comets, and meteors were formed, and relates how astronomers learn about the existence and characteristics of these bodies.

This combines a "clear, extended [exposition] with a vivid mix of colorful space photos, well-designed diagrams, and dramatic paintings." SLJ

Includes bibliographical references

Spangenburg, Ray, 1939-

Meteors, meteorites, and meteoroids; [by] Ray Spangenburg and Kit Moser. Watts 2002 112p il (Out of this world) $33.50; pa $14.95

Grades: 6 7 8 9   **523.5**

1. Meteors 2. Meteorites

ISBN 0-531-11925-4; 0-531-15567-6 (pa)

LC 2002-17

Contents: Space rocks!; Meteors: nature's fireworks; Meteorites: rocks from the sky; The great hunt; Big impacts and earth's scars; Meteoroids: source material; Keeping watch; Clues to the universe

Explores the mysteries of rocks that travel vast distances through space, sometimes passing through Earth's atmosphere and sometimes landing on the surface

This "includes scientific facts and personal touches that give the text warmth. The conversational style makes for easy reading and high interest. The illustrations are accurate and colorful and significantly provide understanding to the text." Book Rep

Includes glossary and bibliographical references

523.6   Comets

Cole, Michael D.

Comets and asteroids; ice and rocks in space. Enslow Pubs. 2003 48p il (Countdown to space) lib bdg $18.95

Grades: 4 5 6 7   **523.6**

1. Comets

ISBN 0-7660-1954-3   LC 2002-8520

Explores what comets and asteroids are, how scientists have studied them throughout history, and the effects of space debris on the Earth when it enters our atmosphere

Includes glossary and bibliographical references

523.7   Sun

Miller, Ron, 1947-

The sun. 21st Cent. Bks. (Brookfield) 2002 64p il (Worlds beyond) lib bdg $27.90 *

Grades: 5 6 7 8   **523.7**

1. Sun

ISBN 0-7613-2355-4   LC 2001-35811

Presents information about the sun's origins, characteristics, future, and importance to the earth

"Both the writing and the visuals go beyond stating the facts to help readers imagine the ideas and processes described. Some of the colorful, well-reproduced illustrations are images from NASA, but others are original art created by Miller. The diagrams are usually clear and attractive." Booklist

Includes bibliographical references

Spangenburg, Ray, 1939-

The sun; [by] Ray Spangenburg and Kit Moser. Watts 2001 63p il map $24.50; pa $8.95

Grades: 4 5 6   **523.7**

1. Sun

ISBN 0-531-11767-7; 0-531-13991-3 (pa)

LC 00-39924

"Watts library"

This describes the sun "beginning with a historical account of its formation and discovery. About half of [the] book focuses on modern exploration . . . using earth-based and space-based telescopes and spacecraft. . . . [This book is] well illustrated with both diagrams and photographs . . . [and] difficult concepts are presented in an easy-to-understand fashion." Sci Books Films

Includes glossary and bibliographical references

523.8   Stars

525   Earth (Astronomical geography)

Jackson, Ellen B., 1943-
The mysterious universe; supernovae, dark energy, and black holes; text by Ellen Jackson; photographs and illustrations by Nic Bishop. Houghton Mifflin 2008 60p il (Scientists in the field) $18 *
Grades: 5 6 7 8   523.8
  1. Filippenko, Alexei V. 2. Supernovas 3. Black holes (Astronomy)
  ISBN 978-0-618-56325-8; 0-618-56325-3
                      LC 2007-41165
This "follows prominent astronomer Alex Filippenko and associates from the Keck Observatory in Hawaii to the Lick Observatory in California on a hunt for supernovae and related large-scale astronomical phenomena. . . . Along with depicting the scientists, the images also include massive telescopes and photos or digital simulations of galaxies, exploding stars, and other astronomical phenomena." SLJ
Includes glossary and bibliographical references

Kerrod, Robin, 1938-
The star guide; learn how to read the night sky star by star. 2nd ed. Wiley 2005 160p il $29.95
Grades: 8 9 10 11 12 Adult   523.8
  1. Stars—Atlases 2. Reference books
  ISBN 0-471-70617-5   LC 2004-22953
  First published 1993
The presentation for this instructional guide to stargazing "is structured around monthly star maps (for midlatitude observers) in two-page spreads, with a follow-up feature on that month's outstanding constellation. . . . Photos featuring Hubble Space Telescope spectaculars, supplemented by tips for viewing the sun, moon, and planets, round out this attractive book on basic astronomy." Booklist

Miller, Ron, 1947-
Stars and galaxies. Twenty-First Century Books 2006 96p il (Worlds beyond) lib bdg $27.93 *
Grades: 7 8 9 10   523.8
  1. Stars 2. Galaxies
  ISBN 0-7613-3466-1   LC 2004-30813
"A cursory description of how the ancients observed and measured the stars leads into chapters about the sun, varieties of stars and the spaces between them, the Milky Way and surrounding galaxies, and theories about how the universe began and how it will end. Miller's text is thorough and substantial, yet his clear examples make the concepts accessible. . . . Miller's own original artwork mixes with stunning NASA photos." Booklist
Includes bibliographical references

Bell, Trudy E.
Earth's journey through space; by Trudy E. Bell. Chelsea House Publishers 2008 80p il (Scientific American) lib bdg $30
Grades: 5 6 7 8   525
  1. Earth 2. Astronomy 3. Solar system
  ISBN 978-0-7910-9050-3 (lib bdg); 0-7910-9050-7 (lib bdg)   LC 2007032351
The author "describes in some detail just how our planet's axial tilt, rotation, and orbital path were discovered and measured, as well as how external forces affect all three. She then goes on to explain how scientists use parallax and other physical effects to determine distances and movements in our galaxy and the universe at large. . . . In general, the old prints, modern space photos, and clear digital images are well chosen to clarify and enhance the presentation." SLJ
Includes bibliographical references

Miller, Ron, 1947-
Earth and the moon. 21st Cent. Bks. (Brookfield) 2003 96p il (Worlds beyond) lib bdg $25.90
Grades: 5 6 7 8   525
  1. Earth 2. Moon
  ISBN 0-7613-2358-9   LC 2001-8479
  Contents: Discovering a planet; The beginning; The story of the moon; Earth, air, fire, and water; The birth of life; The first animals; Earth takes shape; The rise and fall of the dinosaurs; Earth today; Earth around us; A planet on the move; A visit to the moon; The end of the world
Chronicles the origin, evolution, and exploration of the Earth and the Moon, and discusses their composition, their place in our solar system, and more
This is illustrated "with a mix of NASA photos and wide-angle, computer-generated art. . . . Students with a serious interest in the physical history of the Earth and its moon will be engrossed by his account of our planet's first few billion years, the Moon's probable origin, and the rise of life." SLJ
Includes glossary and bibliographical references

Simon, Seymour, 1931-
Earth: our planet in space. [rev ed] Simon & Schuster Bks. for Young Readers 2003 unp il $17.95 *
Grades: 4 5 6 7   525
  1. Earth
  ISBN 0-689-83562-0   LC 2001-31304
  First published 1984 by Four Winds Press
This describes the relationship between the Earth, the sun, and the moon and explains the seasons, day and night, the atmosphere, and changes in the planet's surface. Illustrated with photographs taken from space

526.9   Surveying

Anderson, Judith
Ways to do surveys; [by] Judith Anderson.
Smart Apple Media 2008 32p il map (Geography
skills) $22.95 *
Grades: 6 7 8 9   **526.9**
1. Surveying
ISBN 978-1-59920-053-8; 1-59920-053-8
         LC 2006036140
Contents: What is a survey?; Starting out; Traffic survey; The journey to school; Shopping habits; Collecting
local opinions; Transporting food; International perspectives; Improving disabled access; Surveying a stream;
Using a river; Garbage at a glance; Water watch; Forest
habitats; Weather watch; Investigating climates; Entertainment expense; Tourism; A growing population
"The text is easy to follow. . . . The examples . . .
are almost always accompanied by excellent photographs.
. . . Maps, block diagrams, tables, and graphs are clearly
presented and easy to interpret." Sci Books Films
Includes glossary and bibliographical references

529   Chronology

Farndon, John
Time. Benchmark Bks. 2003 32p il (Science
experiments) lib bdg $24.21
Grades: 5 6 7 8   **529**
1. Time 2. Science—Experiments
ISBN 0-7614-1470-3   LC 2002-4846
Contents: What is time?; Dividing the day; Solar time;
Sun clock; Clocks; Beating time; Calendars; Seasons;
Months; Standard time; Time zones and the date line;
Life times; Time and space; Experiments in science
Includes glossary

Kummer, Patricia K.
The calendar; by Patricia K. Kummer. Franklin
Watts 2005 80p il (Inventions that shaped the
world) $30.50; pa $9.95 *
Grades: 4 5 6 7   **529**
1. Calendars
ISBN 0-531-12340-5; 0-531-16720-8 (pa)
        LC 2004-6914
This "book presents the origins and history of the cal-
endar. . . . The illustrations include clear reproductions
of period paintings, engravings, and drawings as well as
photos of artifacts, sculpture, and contemporary scenes.
. . . A good basic introduction." Booklist
Includes bibliographical references

Sullivan, Navin
Time; [by] Navin Sullivan. Marshall Cavendish
Benchmark 2007 48p il (Measure up!) lib bdg
$20.95
Grades: 4 5 6 7   **529**

1. Time 2. Clocks and watches 3. Calendars
ISBN 978-0-7614-2321-8 (lib bdg); 0-7614-2321-4 (lib
bdg)
"Since the beginning of human history, people have
found different ways to mark time by using the stars, the
Sun, and the seasons, or by creating clocks made of water, sand, and mechanical parts. *Time* explores these inventions and discusses time-related concepts such as leap
years, Daylight Saving Time, time zones, radiocarbon
dating, clocks found in nature, and much more." Publisher's note
This is "engaging and informative. . . . The excellent
blend of photographs, charts, and diagrams complements
the [text]." SLJ
Includes glossary and bibliographical references

530   Physics

The **Facts** on File physics handbook; the Diagram
Group. rev ed. Facts on File 2006 272p il (Facts
on File science library) $35 *
Grades: 8 9 10 11 12   **530**
1. Physics
ISBN 0-8160-5880-6   LC 2004-59265
First published 2000
Also covering mathematics and computer science, this
reference "contains, in separate sections, a dictionary of
around 1500 entries; 250-400 thumbnail biographies; a
multipage chronology; and an array of field-specific
charts, tables, and diagrams." SLJ [review of 2000 edi-
tion]
Includes bibliographical references

Farndon, John
Experimenting with physics. Marshall Cavendish
Benchmark 2009 112p il (Experimenting with
science) $35.64
Grades: 7 8 9 10   **530**
1. Physics 2. Science—Experiments
ISBN 978-0-7614-3929-5; 0-7614-3929-3
        LC 2008017568
"Explores and explains physics concepts—including
energy, motion, simple machines, gravity, flight, electricity, and magnetism—and provides experiments to aid in
understanding physics." Publisher's note

Gardner, Robert, 1929-
Physics projects with a light box you can build;
[by] Robert Gardner. Enslow Publishers 2008 128p
il (Build-a-lab! science experiments) lib bdg
$31.93
Grades: 6 7 8 9   **530**
1. Physics 2. Light 3. Color 4. Science projects
5. Science—Experiments
ISBN 978-0-7660-2810-4 (lib bdg); 0-7660-2810-0 (lib
bdg)   LC 2006100566
This describes experiments and projects on such topics
as light, images, shadows, refraction and lenses, light and
color.
"The detailed instructions, accompanied by helpful diagrams, color photographs, and suggestions for science
fair projects, allow science-minded readers to form their
own conclusions." Horn Book Guide
Includes bibliographical references

Gardner, Robert, 1929- —_Continued_

Science projects about physics in the home. Enslow Pubs. 1999 112p il (Science projects) lib bdg $26.60

Grades: 5 6 7 8   **530**

1. Physics 2. Science—Experiments 3. Science projects

ISBN 0-89490-948-7   LC 98-6822

Presents instructions for physics projects and experiments that can be done at home and exhibited at science fairs

"This volume is well organized with lots of hands-on activities that use relatively simple pieces of equipment. . . . A good starting point in the understanding of the physics of objects and events in our daily life." Sci Books Films

Includes bibliographical references

Green, Dan

Physics; why matter matters! [by] Dan Green; Simon Basher, illustrator. Kingfisher 2008 128p il pa $8.95

Grades: 5 6 7 8   **530**

1. Physics

ISBN 978-0-7534-6214-0; 0-7534-6214-1

     LC 2007-31805

This "introduces the elements of physics as anthropomorphic, cartoon-style characters. . . . Each of the groupings begins with an introduction and each concept is given its own spread that shows the cartoon figure and describes its 'personality.' The information is presented in a chatty and conversational tone. . . . Along with the narrative, which is written in the first person from the concept's point of view, other key facts are presented. This book would be handy as a supplement to a physics curriculum." SLJ

Includes glossary

Hammond, Richard, 1969-

Can you feel the force? [by] Richard Hammond. 1st American ed. DK Pub. 2006 96p il $15.99 *

Grades: 5 6 7 8   **530**

1. Physics

ISBN 978-0-7566-2033-2; 0-7566-2033-3

     LC 2006-16429

This "book includes information, experiments, and questions and answers about physics, in four sections. In the beginning presents a historical overview of human understanding of the topic; Can you feel the force? defines some terms and explains Newton's laws. What's the matter? explores atomic makeup, magnets, and the states of matter; and Can you see the light? looks at particle theory, color, electromagnetic rays, and the speed of light. . . . The format includes eye-catching photos and graphics on every spread. . . . Hammond's lively style and kid-centric examples provide an effective introduction to the basic concepts of physics and the scientists who discovered them." SLJ

Morgan, Sally

From Greek atoms to quarks; discovering atoms; by Sally Morgan. Heinemann Library 2007 64p il (Chain reactions) lib bdg $34.29

Grades: 6 7 8 9   **530**

1. Atoms 2. Matter

ISBN 978-1-4034-9551-8 (lib bdg); 1-4034-9551-3 (lib bdg)   LC 2006037044

"Morgan tells the story of the atom, including its discovery, structure, power, and future in subatomic particles. . . . Archival and full-color photos and reproductions appear on nearly every page." SLJ

Includes glossary and bibliographical references

Silverstein, Alvin

Matter; by Alvin Silverstein, Virginia Silverstein, Laura Silverstein Nunn. Twenty-First Century Books 2009 112p il (Science concepts) lib bdg $31.93

Grades: 5 6 7 8   **530**

1. Matter

ISBN 978-0-8225-7515-3; 0-8225-7515-9

     LC 2007049493

This is a "simple and straightforward [discussion] of the [subject]. The layout . . . is attractive and inviting, with full-color photographs and/or diagrams on almost every spread. In addition, the authors make good use of fact boxes. . . . [This] discusses the states of matter, the elements, chemical reactions, and more. [This title] will interest browsers and provide ample information for reports." SLJ

Includes glossary and bibliographical references

Stille, Darlene R., 1942-

Physical change; reshaping matter; by Darlene R. Stille. Compass Point Books 2006 48p il (Exploring science) $25.27 *

Grades: 6 7 8 9   **530**

1. Matter

ISBN 0-7565-1257-3   LC 2005002476

This "discusses physical change and molecules; the changing states of matter; mixing and separating solids, liquids, and gases; and physical change in nature. . . . Full-color photographs, illustrations, or diagrams appear on almost every page, accompanied by captions that complement the text." SLJ

Includes glossary and bibliographical references

Townsend, John, 1955-

Foolish physics. Raintree 2007 56p il map (Weird history of science) lib bdg $23; pa $9.49

Grades: 4 5 6 7   **530**

1. Physics

ISBN 978-1-4109-2377-6 (lib bdg); 1-4109-2377-0 (lib bdg); 978-1-4109-2382-0 (pa); 1-4109-2382-7 (pa)

     LC 2006-07739

Describes how some of the most important, and sometimes the strangest, theories of physics were arrived at or proven.

Includes bibliographical references

530.4   States of matter

Claybourne, Anna
The nature of matter; [by] Anna Claybourne.
Gareth Stevens Pub. 2007 48p il (Gareth Stevens
vital science: physical science) lib bdg $26.60; pa
$11.95
Grades: 4 5 6 7   **530.4**
   1. Matter
   ISBN   978-0-8368-8088-5   (lib   bdg);
978-0-8368-8097-7 (pa)   LC 2006033732
This describes uses for matter and what happens when
it changes from one form to another, the basic physical
laws and properties of matter, and the various ways in
which we control how matter behaves.
This is "straightforward and clear. . . . The layout is
bright and colorful, with photographs and illustrations on
almost every page." SLJ
Includes glossary and bibliographical references

Farndon, John
Solids, liquids, and gases. Benchmark Bks. 2001
32p il (Science experiments) lib bdg $25.64
Grades: 5 6 7 8   **530.4**
   1. Matter 2. Science—Experiments
   ISBN 0-7614-1338-3   LC 00-68017
This presents six experiments involving melting
points, crystals, hydraulic power, gases and volume,
freezing, and solutions
Includes glossary

Oxlade, Chris
States of matter; [by] Chris Oxlade. rev. and
updated. Heimemann Library 2007 48p il
(Chemicals in action) lib bdg $31.43; pa $8.95
Grades: 6 7 8 9   **530.4**
   1. Matter
   ISBN   978-1-4329-0055-7   (lib   bdg);
978-1-4329-0062-5 (pa)
First published 2002
"This title explores how elements change from one
state to another, how the water cycle works, and how
changes of state are used in our everyday lives. [It also
includes] several experiments that can be done at home."
Publisher's note
"Explanations are concise and clear without being
oversimplified, and the arrangement is attractive and
open. Colorful diagrams, drawings, and photographs appear on every page." SLJ
Includes glossary and bibliographical references

531   Classical mechanics. Solid mechanics

Farndon, John
Energy. Benchmark Bks. 2003 32p il (Science
experiments) lib bdg $$28.50
Grades: 5 6 7 8   **531**
   1. Force and energy 2. Power (Mechanics)
3. Science—Experiments
   ISBN 978-0-7614-1469-8 (lib bdg); 0-7614-1469-X
(lib bdg)   LC 2002-4631
Contents: What is energy?; Kinds of energy; Stored
energy; Movement energy; Energy changes; Putting ener-
gy to work; Conserving energy; Losing energy; Energy
sources; Solar energy; Human energy; Nuclear energy;
Alternative energy; Experiments in science
Includes glossary

Gravity. Benchmark Bks. 2002 32p il (Science
experiments) lib bdg $29.93
Grades: 5 6 7 8   **531**
   1. Gravitation 2. Science—Experiments
   ISBN 978-0-7614-1340-0 (lib bdg); 0-7614-1340-5 (lib
bdg)   LC 2001-25965
This presents six experiments titled Falling first, Fall-
ing faster, Fighting gravity, Up and down, Centrifugal
force, and Tides
Includes glossary

Motion. Benchmark Bks. 2003 32p il (Science
experiments) lib bdg $28.50
Grades: 5 6 7 8   **531**
   1. Motion 2. Science—Experiments
   ISBN 978-0-7614-1471-1 (lib bdg); 0-7614-1471-1
          LC 2002-5010
Contents: What is motion?; How fast?; Measuring
speed; Getting faster; Understanding acceleration; Start-
ing to move; Beating inertia; Force and acceleration;
Friction; Rough and smooth; Action and reaction; Reac-
tion rockets; High speed motion; Experiments in science
Includes glossary

Gardner, Robert, 1929-
Bicycle science projects; physics on wheels.
Enslow Publishers 2004 112p il (Science fair
success) lib bdg $26.60
Grades: 6 7 8 9   **531**
   1. Physics 2. Bicycles 3. Cycling 4. Science—Experi-
ments 5. Science projects
   ISBN 0-7660-1630-7   LC 2003-26961
Contents: The emergence of bicycles; Bikes, gears,
and speed; Using your bicycle to measure distance and
speed; Forces every cyclist must overcome or apply;
Working on your bicycle
"Gardner demonstrates the principles of physics
through 22 projects and many related activities using bi-
cycles. An introductory chapter, which features advice
about experiments, science fairs, and safety, is followed
by a brief section on bicycle history. Gardner then clear-
ly explains a series of progressively more difficult proj-
ects. . . . The black-and-white drawings that illustrate
the projects are unusually clear, accurate, and expres-
sive." Booklist
Includes bibliographical references

Gardner, Robert, 1929—*Continued*

Forces and motion science fair projects; using water balloons, pulleys, and other stuff. Enslow Publishers 2004 128p il (Physics! best science projects) lib bdg $20.95

Grades: 6 7 8 9   **531**

1. Motion 2. Force and energy 3. Science—Experiments 4. Science projects

ISBN 0-7660-2129-7   LC 2003-11107

Motion: measuring distance and time— Forces and motion—Pendulums and springs: oscillating motion—Motions that curve or circle—Forces, machines, and muscles

This describes experiments for science fairs which attempt to answer such questions as "Why don't you fall out of a roller coaster when it goes upside down? Which is stronger—your arms or your legs? Why do skydivers spread out their bodies when they jump from a plane?" Publisher's note

Includes bibliographical references

Nardo, Don, 1947-

Force and motion; laws of movement; by Don Nardo. Compass Point Books 2008 48p il (Exploring science) lib bdg $26.60

Grades: 7 8 9 10   **531**

1. Force and energy 2. Motion

ISBN 978-0-7565-3264-2 (lib bdg); 0-7565-3264-7 (lib bdg)   LC 2007004604

Contents: Mass and weight; Gravity and other universal forces; The laws of motion; Energy and speed; Pressure and floating bodies; Simple and complex machines

Includes glossary and bibliographical references

Parker, Barry R.

The mystery of gravity. Benchmark Bks. 2003 78p il (Story of science) lib bdg $28.50

Grades: 5 6 7 8   **531**

1. Gravitation

ISBN 0-7614-1428-2   LC 2002-970

Defines gravity and discusses how our knowledge of the natural force has broadened and evolved

"Readers will find accurate, readable explanations for the phenomenon of gravity. The text moves from classical attempts to understand why and how objects fall to the work of Kepler, Galileo, Newton, and Einstein's general theory of relativity. The book is ably illustrated by well-captioned photos and clear diagrams, such as the wormhole of a black hole." Horn Book Guide

Includes glossary and bibliographical references

Phelan, Glen

Invisible force; the quest to define the laws of motion; [by] Glen Phelan. National Geographic 2006 59p il (Science quest) $17.95; lib bdg $25.90

Grades: 5 6 7 8   **531**

1. Motion 2. Gravity

ISBN 0-7922-5539-9; 0-7922-5540-2 (lib bdg)   LC 2005027350

This "traces the historical and scientific path to man's understanding of motion and gravity." Publisher's note

Includes glossary and bibliographical references

Pinna, Simon de

Transfer of energy; by Simon de Pinna. Gareth Stevens Pub. 2007 48p il (Gareth Stevens vital science: physical science) lib bdg $26.60; pa $11.95

Grades: 4 5 6 7   **531**

1. Force and energy

ISBN 978-0-8368-8091-5   (lib bdg); 978-0-8368-8100-4 (pa)   LC 2006033733

This explains such terms and concepts as kinetic and potential energy, chain reactions, energy pyramid, and power grid; the uses for the varying wavelengths of the electromagnetic spectrum; the ways that plants and animals use energy; and concepts such as conduction, convection, reflection, and transmission.

This is "straightforward and clear. . . . The layout is bright and colorful, with photographs and illustrations on almost every page." SLJ

Includes bibliographical references

Silverstein, Alvin

Forces and motion; [by Alvin & Virginia Silverstein & Laura Silverstein Nunn] Twenty-First Century Books 2008 c2009 112p il (Science concepts) lib bdg $31.93

Grades: 5 6 7 8   **531**

1. Force and energy 2. Motion

ISBN 978-0-8225-7514-6 (lib bdg); 0-8225-7514-0 (lib bdg)   LC 2007-48826

"The breadth of material the authors cover in this volume is impressive. They discuss energy (kenetic and potential), forces (friction, gravity, electricity, and magnetism), simple machines (lever, wheel, pulley, ramp, and wedge), motion in fluids, and Newton's laws of motion. . . . [This offers] simple writing, many colorful pictures, and lots of examples." Sci Books Films

Includes glossary and bibliographical references

Snedden, Robert

Forces and motion; by Robert Snedden. Gareth Stevens Pub. 2007 48p il (Gareth Stevens vital science: physical science) lib bdg $26.60; pa $11.95

Grades: 4 5 6 7   **531**

1. Force and energy 2. Motion

ISBN 978-0-8368-8087-8   (lib bdg); 978-0-8368-8096-0 (pa)   LC 2006033731

This explains speed and acceleration, force and Newton's laws, balanced and unbalanced forces, gravity, friction pressure, squashing and stretching, and machines

This is "straightforward and clear. . . . The layout is bright and colorful, with photographs and illustrations on almost every page." SLJ

Includes glossary and bibliographical references

Solway, Andrew

Exploring forces and motion. Rosen Central 2008 48p il (Exploring physical science) lib bdg $26.50

Grades: 5 6 7 8   **531**

1. Force and energy 2. Motion

ISBN 978-1-4042-3747-6; 1-4042-3747-X   LC 2006036680

Solway, Andrew—*Continued*

Contents: What is a force?; Speed and direction; Moving forces; Resisting movement; The force of gravity; Balanced and unbalanced forces; Moving the earth; The future of forces

Includes glossary and bibliographical references

Stille, Darlene R., 1942-

Waves; energy on the move; by Darlene R. Stille. Compass Point Books 2006 48p il map (Exploring science) $25.27 *

Grades: 6 7 8 9   **531**

1. Waves

ISBN 0-7565-1259-X   LC 2005002477

This decribes water waves, sound waves, light waves, radio waves, and earthquake waves.

This "provides a straightforward and clear discussion of its topic. . . . Full-color photographs, illustrations, or diagrams appear on almost every page, accompanied by captions that complement the text." SLJ

Includes glossary and bibliographical references

Sullivan, Navin

Speed. Marshall Cavendish Benchmark 2007 48p il (Measure up!) lib bdg $20.90

Grades: 4 5 6 7   **531**

1. Speed 2. Measurement

ISBN 978-0-7614-2325-6 (lib bdg); 0-7614-2325-7 (lib bdg)

"Have you ever wondered how we measure different speeds? How do we know how fast an airplane travels or how much speed a shuttle needs to travel to outer space? What does speed have to do with satellites? How does the speed of light compare with the speed of sound? *Speed* answers these questions and explores the history of humankind's discoveries about speed." Publisher's note

Includes glossary and bibliographical references

Weight. Marshall Cavendish Benchmark 2007 48p il (Measure up!) lib bdg $20.90

Grades: 4 5 6 7   **531**

1. Gravity 2. Weights and measures

ISBN 978-0-7614-2324-9 (lib bdg); 0-7614-2324-9 (lib bdg)

This "explains concepts such as how gravity affects weight on Earth and in space, the relationship between volume and density, and why some objects float better than others." Publisher's note

"Examples using familiar objects and excellent full-color graphics help to bring concepts to life." SLJ

Includes glossary and bibliographical references

VanCleave, Janice Pratt

Janice VanCleave's energy for every kid; [by] Janice VanCleave. J. Wiley & Sons 2006 221p il (Science for every kid series) pa $12.95

Grades: 4 5 6 7   **531**

1. Force and energy 2. Energy resources 3. Science projects 4. Science—Experiments

ISBN 978-0-471-33099-8; 0-471-33099-X

     LC 2004-27114

Presents problems and experiments that introduce the different types of energy.

Viegas, Jennifer

Kinetic and potential energy; understanding changes within physical systems; [by] Jennifer Viegas. 1st ed. Rosen Pub. Group 2005 48p il (Library of physics) lib bdg $25.25 *

Grades: 7 8 9 10   **531**

1. Force and energy 2. Dynamics

ISBN 1-4042-0333-8   LC 2004019126

"Viegas begins by explaining kinetic and potential energy and the history of their discoveries. Mechanical energy, momentum, and the laws of energy are also presented. . . . The [layout is] open and appealing and [includes] well-captioned photographs and simple diagrams." SLJ

Includes bibliographical references

532   Fluid mechanics Liquid mechanics

Meiani, Antonella

Water. Lerner Publs. 2003 40p il (Experimenting with science) lib bdg $23.93

Grades: 4 5 6 7   **532**

1. Water 2. Science—Experiments

ISBN 0-8225-0083-3   LC 2001-50773

Contents: The force of water; To float or not to float?; The transformation of water; Water solutions; The force of water; Fact finder; Metric conversion chart

Describes experiments with water which answer such questions as "Why are water droplets round?" and "Why do some things, like salt, dissolve in water and other things, like fish, don't?"

This offers "straightforward, well-designed experiments. . . . Numerous clear diagrams, some photos, and occasional historical sidebars extend this material, which is notable for its substance." Horn Book Guide

Includes glossary and bibliographical references

Parker, Steve

The science of water; projects with experiments with water and power; [by] Steve Parker. Heinemann Library 2005 32p il (Tabletop scientist) lib bdg $29.29; pa $7.85

Grades: 4 5 6 7   **532**

1. Water 2. Science—Experiments

ISBN 1-4034-7282-3 (lib bdg); 1-4034-7289-0 (pa)

     LC 2005007027

This "has experiments on the water cycle, water density, water as a solvent, surface tension, capillary action, buoyancy, water power, and water propulsion. . . . The colorful illustrations, organization, and ease of use of [this title makes it an] excellent [addition]." SLJ

Includes glossary

533   Pneumatics (Gas mechanics)

Meiani, Antonella

Air. Lerner Publs. 2003 40p il (Experimenting with science) lib bdg $23.93

Grades: 4 5 6 7   **533**

1. Air 2. Science—Experiments

ISBN 0-8225-0082-5   LC 2001-37730

Meiani, Antonella—*Continued*

Explains the properties of air through experiments which feature such topics as what air is, how much force wind has, what shape is best for flying, and how sound travels

This offers "straightforward, well-designed experiments. . . . Numerous clear diagrams, some photos, and occasional historical sidebars extend this material, which is notable for its substance." Horn Book Guide

Includes glossary and bibliographical references

Parker, Steve

The science of air; projects and experiments on air and flight; [by] Steve Parker. Heinemann Library 2005 32p il (Tabletop scientist) lib bdg $29.29; pa $7.85

Grades: 4 5 6 7   **533**

1. Air 2. Science—Experiments

ISBN 1-4034-7280-7 (lib bdg); 1-4034-7287-4 (pa)

LC 2005006940

"The 12 experiments in [this] book have a materials list and step-by-step photo instructions. Boxed text explains the scientific ideas in each project and the processes that make it work, and offer ideas for further experimentation. The activities are followed by a history of the topic. . . . [This] title introduces air movement, air pressure, wind resistance, lift, flight, and energy from the wind. . . . The colorful illustrations, organization, and ease of use [this title makes it an] excellent [addition]." SLJ

Includes glossary

534   Sound and related vibrations

Gardner, Robert, 1929-

Sound projects with a music lab you can build. Enslow Publishers 2008 128p il (Build-a-lab! science experiments) lib bdg $31.93 *

Grades: 6 7 8 9   **534**

1. Sound 2. Music 3. Science—Experiments 4. Science projects

ISBN 978-0-7660-2809-8 (lib bdg); 0-7660-2809-7 (lib bdg)

LC 2007-19458

This describes science experiments and projects about music and sound such as making a washtub bass, a two-string bottle banjo, a shoe-box guitar, or pan pipes.

"The author does an excellent job presenting a balance of open-ended questions and supporting information that provide a solid foundation for successful experimentation." Sci Books Films

Includes bibliographical references

Parker, Steve

The science of sound; projects with experiments with music and sound waves; [by] Steve Parker. Heinemann Library 2005 32p il (Tabletop scientist) lib bdg $29.29; pa $7.85

Grades: 4 5 6 7   **534**

1. Sound 2. Music 3. Science—Experiments

ISBN 1-4034-7281-5 (lib bdg); 1-4034-7288-2 (pa)

LC 2005006960

This book of experiments "covers sound waves as they travel through air and underwater, high and low sounds, how we hear, the Doppler effect, soundproofing, and recorded sound. . . . The colorful illustrations, organization, and ease of use of [this title makes it an] excellent [addition]." SLJ

Includes glossary

535   Light and infrared and ultraviolet phenomena

Burnie, David

Light. Dorling Kindersley 1992 64p il (Eyewitness science) $15.95; lib bdg $19.99

Grades: 6 7 8 9   **535**

1. Light

ISBN 0-7894-4885-8; 0-7894-6709-7 (lib bdg)

LC 92-7661

A guide to the origins, principles, and historical study of light

"Each double-page spread is lavishly illustrated with full-color photographs and diagrams, and each contains a wealth of information." Booklist

Meiani, Antonella

Light. Lerner Publs. 2003 40p il (Experimenting with science) lib bdg $23.93

Grades: 4 5 6 7   **535**

1. Light 2. Science—Experiments

ISBN 0-8225-0084-1   LC 2001-38947

Experiments with light explain shadows and colors, and demonstrate such concepts as reflection and refraction

This offers "straightforward, well-designed experiments. . . . Numerous clear diagrams, some photos, and occasional historical sidebars extend this material, which is notable for its substance." Horn Book Guide

Includes glossary and bibliographical references

Stille, Darlene R., 1942-

Manipulating light; reflection, refraction, and absorption; by Darlene R. Stille. Compass Point Books 2006 48p il (Exploring science) $25.27 *

Grades: 6 7 8 9   **535**

1. Light

ISBN 0-7565-1258-1   LC 2005003903

This "book examines how light behaves, the law of reflection, mirrors, refraction, and absorption. . . . Full-color photographs, illustrations, or diagrams appear on almost every page, accompanied by captions that complement the text." SLJ

Includes glossary and bibliographical references

536 Heat

Gardner, Robert, 1929-
Science projects about temperature and heat; {by} Robert Gardner and Eric Kemer. Enslow Pubs. 1994 128p il lib bdg $26.60
Grades: 7 8 9 10   **536**
1. Temperature 2. Heat 3. Science—Experiments
ISBN 0-89490-534-1   LC 93-48800
The authors suggest "investigations about heat and how it is measured as temperature. Some of the experiments cover the rules of temperature change, how different materials conduct heat, and how heat is made by friction." Publisher's note
Includes bibliographical references

Sullivan, Navin
Temperature; [by] Navin Sullivan. Marshall Cavendish Benchmark 2007 48p il (Measure up!) lib bdg $20.90
Grades: 4 5 6 7   **536**
1. Heat 2. Thermometers 3. Temperature
ISBN 978-0-7614-2322-5 (lib bdg); 0-7614-2322-2 (lib bdg)   LC 2006011981
This "explains how molecules react to heat, how different types of thermometers measure heat energy, and shows the immense impact temperature has on every part of our lives." Publisher's note
This is "engaging and informative. . . . The excellent blend of photographs, charts, and diagrams complements the [text]." SLJ
Includes glossary and bibliographical references

537 Electricity and electronics

Dreier, David Louis
Electrical circuits; harnessing electricity; by David Dreier; illustrator Ashlee Schultz. Compass Point Books 2007 48p il (Exploring science: physical science) lib bdg $19.95
Grades: 6 7 8 9   **537**
1. Electric circuits 2. Electricity
ISBN 978-0-7565-3267-3 (lib bdg); 0-7565-3267-1 (lib bdg)   LC 2007004603
"This straightforward introduction to electricity . . . covers all the bases. It begins with what electricity is, how it appears in nature, and how it has been harnessed for public use. Atoms, the concept of electric charge, and magnetism are explained clearly. . . . Dreier tries to make a complex subject more understandable by using familiar examples. . . . This helps, as does the book's clean format, illustrated with sharp, bright color photographs." Booklist
Includes glossary and bibliographical references

Gardner, Robert, 1929-
Easy genius science projects with light; great experiments and ideas; [by] Robert Gardner. Enslow Publishers 2008 c2009 128p il (Easy genius science projects) lib bdg $31.93
Grades: 6 7 8 9   **537**
1. Light 2. Science projects 3. Science—Experiments
ISBN 978-0-7660-2926-2; 0-7660-2926-3
     LC 2007-38468
This includes science projects and experiments about such light-related topics as colors, lenses, mirages, reflections, refraction, particle theory, polarization, and after images.
"The physics involved are . . . fascinating and will grab curious readers. . . . The inviting and chatty text for each project includes a boxed list of 'things you will need,' all of them commonly available, followed by detailed step-by-step instructions with clear diagrams." Booklist
Includes glossary and bibliographical references

Parker, Steve
Electricity; written by Steve Parker. rev ed. DK Pub. 2005 64p il (DK eyewitness books) $15.99
Grades: 4 5 6 7   **537**
1. Electricity
ISBN 0-7566-1388-4
First published 1992
Discusses the properties of electricity and describes how it is made and used

Electricity and magnetism; [by] Steve Parker. Gareth Stevens Pub. 2007 48p il (Gareth Stevens vital science: physical science) lib bdg $26.60; pa $11.95
Grades: 4 5 6 7   **537**
1. Electricity 2. Magnetism
ISBN   978-0-8368-8085-4   (lib   bdg); 978-0-8368-8094-6 (pa)   LC 2006034188
This explains "terms and concepts such as superconductor, static electricity, magnetic repulsion, and the piezoelectric effect; [the use of] electricity and magnetism [in] electrolysis, electromagnetic induction, and medical diagnostics and imaging; . . . lightning, auroras, St. Elmo's fire, animal navigation, and other electromagnetic phenomena." Publisher's note
This is "straightforward and clear. . . . The layout is bright and colorful, with photographs and illustrations on almost every page." SLJ
Includes glossary and bibliographical references

Sonneborn, Liz
Forces in nature; understanding gravitational, electrical, and magnetic force; [by] Liz Sonneborn. Rosen Pub. Group 2005 48p il (Library of physics) lib bdg $25.25 *
Grades: 7 8 9 10   **537**
1. Electromagnetism 2. Gravitation
ISBN 1-4042-0332-X   LC 2004-11072
Contents: The forces around us; The gravitational force; The electromagnetic force; Electromagnetism at work; The strong and weak forces; The unification of forces

Sonneborn, Liz—*Continued*

"Sonneborn covers gravitational force, electromagnetic force, electromagnetism at work, and strong and weak forces. The writing is clear and easy to read. A final chapter discusses the unification of forces. . . . [This title provides a] basic [introduction] to [its topic] and [is] especially useful for reluctant readers or those new to the [topic]. The [layout is] open and appealing and [includes] well-captioned photographs and simple diagrams." SLJ

Includes bibliographical references

Tomecek, Steve

Electromagnetism, and how it works; [by] Stephen M. Tomecek. Chelsea House 2007 72p il (Scientific American) $30

Grades: 6 7 8 9   **537**

1. Electromagnetism

ISBN 978-0-7910-9052-7; 0-7910-9052-3

          LC 2007-17744

Contents: The magic of magnets; Current electricity and electromagnetism; Magnets on the move; Communicating with electromagnets; The electromagnetic spectrum; Modern electromagnetic marvels

This describes the history of magnets including the discoveries of such scientists as Gilbert, Volta, Sturgeon, Edison, Westinghouse, and Tesla. It discusses inventions which depended on the understanding of magnets and electricity such as the telegraph, Morse Code, the telephone, the wireless radio, radar, the microwave, x-rays, and MRIs. The author explains how magnets work and how they can be used to create electricity.

Includes glossary and bibliographical references

Woodford, Chris, 1943-

Electricity; [by] Chris Woodford. Blackbirch Press 2004 40p il (Routes of science) $23.70; pa $18.70

Grades: 5 6 7 8   **537**

1. Electricity

ISBN 1-4103-0165-6; 1-4103-0304-7 (pa)

          LC 2004-301790

Contents: The mysteries of electric fluid; From frogs' legs to batteries; Electricity meets magnetism; The power of electricity; Electricity makes waves; The electronic age; Into the future

"This book traces the history of electrical discovery from ancient Greek experiments with static electricity to Benjamin Franklin's famous kite experiment to today's work with superconductivity." Publisher's note

This "volume contains color photographs, illustrations, and diagrams to help explain the important concepts and discoveries. [This volume] would be [an] excellent [supplement] to the science curriculum." SLJ

Includes glossary and bibliographical references

538   Magnetism

Meiani, Antonella

Magnetism. Lerner Publs. 2003 40p il (Experimenting with science) lib bdg $23.93

Grades: 4 5 6 7   **538**

1. Magnetism 2. Science—Experiments

ISBN 0-8225-0085-X   LC 2001-50464

Describes a variety of experiments that explore the world of magnets and magnetism, arranged in the categories "Magnets," "Magnetic Poles," "Magnetic Force," and "Magnetism and Electricity"

This offers "straightforward, well-designed experiments. . . . Numerous clear diagrams, some photos, and occasional historical sidebars extend this material, which is notable for its substance." Horn Book Guide

Includes glossary and bibliographical references

539   Modern physics

Willett, Edward, 1959-

The basics of quantum physics; understanding the photoelectric effect and line spectra. Rosen Pub. Group 2005 48p il (Library of physics) lib bdg $25.25

Grades: 7 8 9 10   **539**

1. Quantum theory 2. Spectrum analysis

ISBN 1-4042-0334-6

"Willett introduces readers to the nature of light and of the atom. The ultraviolet catastrophe, the photoelectric effect, and line spectra are also addressed. [This title is] especially useful for reluctant readers or those new to the [topic]. The [layout is] open and appealing and [includes] well-captioned photographs and simple diagrams." SLJ

Includes bibliographical references

539.7   Atomic and nuclear physics

Cregan, Elizabeth R.

The atom. Compass Point Books 2009 40p il (Mission: science) lib bdg $26.60

Grades: 4 5 6   **539.7**

1. Atoms 2. Atomic theory 3. Nuclear energy

ISBN 978-0-7565-3953-5 (lib bdg); 0-7565-3953-6 (lib bdg)   LC 2008007724

"Cregan discusses the structure of the atom, key scientists, cathode rays and electrons, radioactivity, and atom smashers. . . . The [book has an] open [layout] and large, easy-to-read type. . . . Large eye-catching and colorful photographs and illustrations appear on every page. The [book] includes a simple activity." SLJ

Includes glossary and bibliographical references

Henderson, Harry, 1951-

Nuclear physics. Facts on File 1998 132p il (Milestones in discovery and invention) $25

Grades: 7 8 9 10   **539.7**

1. Nuclear physics 2. Physicists

ISBN 0-8160-3567-9   LC 97-17380

This book profiles physicists Marie and Pierre Curie, Ernest Rutherford, Niels Bohr, Lise Meitner, Richard Feynman, and Murray Gell-Mann, explains their scientific discoveries, and outlines questions in current physics research.

Includes bibliographical references

Jerome, Kate Boehm

Atomic universe; the quest to discover radioactivity; by Kate Boehm Jerome. National Geographic 2006 59p il (Science quest) $17.95; lib bdg $25.90

Grades: 5 6 7 8	**539.7**

1. Nuclear physics 2. Radioactivity

ISBN 0-7922-5543-7; 0-7922-5544-5 (lib bdg)

LC 2006001316

This "traces the path to the discovery of radioactivity and places this major scientific breakthrough in the context of history." Publisher's note

The text offers "key concepts in a pleasing and readable format that would appeal to reluctant readers." SLJ

Includes glossary and bibliographical references

Manning, Phillip, 1936-

Atoms, molecules, and compounds. Chelsea House 2008 137p il (Essential chemistry) $35 *

Grades: 7 8 9 10	**539.7**

1. Atoms 2. Molecules 3. Matter 4. Chemical reactions

ISBN 978-0-7910-9534-8; 0-7910-9534-7

LC 2007-11403

This book "explores the reactions between atoms and shows how the characteristics of the reacting atoms determine the type of molecule produced." Publisher's note

"In relatively few pages, and with lots of colorful, clear illustrations, Manning takes us from Thompson's plum-pudding model of the atom to Rutherford's model to the quantum model, and through the discovery of atomic particles and the teasing out of atomic forces, in a very clear, compelling path. . . . The clear linkages he makes between the different types of chemical bonds and the nature of various materials will remain with the reader." Sci Books Films

Includes glossary and bibliographical references

Oxlade, Chris

Atoms; [by] Chris Oxlade. rev and updated. Heinemann Library 2007 48p il (Chemicals in action) lib bdg $31.43; pa $8.99

Grades: 6 7 8 9	**539.7**

1. Atoms 2. Atomic theory 3. Matter

ISBN	978-1-4329-0051-9	(lib	bdg); 978-1-4329-0058-8 (pa)

First published 2002

"This title explores what atoms are like, how they combine with each other, and how they form the building blocks of everything on Earth. [It also includes] several experiments that can be done at home." Publisher's note

"Explanations are concise and clear without being oversimplified, and the arrangement is attractive and open. Colorful diagrams, drawings, and photographs appear on every page." SLJ

Includes glossary and bibliographical references

540 Chemistry

Chemistry matters! Grolier 2007 10v set $389 *

Grades: 7 8 9 10	**540**

1. Chemistry—Encyclopedias 2. Reference books

ISBN 0-7172-6194-8	LC 2006026209

Contents: v1 Atoms and molecules; v2 States of matter; v3 Chemical reactions; v4 Energy and reactions; v5 The periodic table; v6 Metals and metalloids; v7 Nonmetals; v8 Organic chemistry; v9 Biochemistry; v10 Chemistry in action

"These volumes cover a broad range of topics. . . . Each 80 page volume could serve as a stand-alone title, introducing its subject and covering many aspects of its current study and applications." Booklist

Includes bibliographical references

The **Facts** on File chemistry handbook; the Diagram Group. Rev. ed. Facts on File 2006 272p il (Facts on File science library) $35 *

Grades: 8 9 10 11 12	**540**

1. Chemistry

ISBN 0-8160-5878-4	LC 2005-55496

First published 2000

In addition to a dictionary of around 1500 entries, this source also includes hundreds of thumbnail biographies and an extensive chronology. Charts, tables, and diagrams are included.

Includes bibliographical references

Farndon, John

Experimenting with chemistry. Marshall Cavendish Benchmark 2009 104p il (Experimenting with science) $35.64

Grades: 7 8 9 10	**540**

1. Chemistry 2. Science—Experiments

ISBN 978-0-7614-3928-8; 0-7614-3928-5

LC 2008017570

"Explores and explains chemistry concepts and provides experiments to aid in understanding chemistry." Publisher's note

Gardner, Robert, 1929-

Chemistry projects with a laboratory you can build. Enslow Publishers 2007 128p il (Build-a-lab! science experiments) $23.95

Grades: 6 7 8 9	**540**

1. Chemistry 2. Science—Experiments

ISBN 978-0-7660-2805-0; 0-7660-2805-4

LC 2006-21071

This "is a guide to creating an at-home laboratory for conducting chemistry experiments. . . . Safety rules and ample warnings are provided. . . . The book describes 28 experiments, organized into four chapters. . . . The experiments are ongoing and would be fun activities for children who are curious about science." Sci Books Films

Includes bibliographical references

Chemistry science fair projects using acids, bases, metals, salts, and inorganic stuff; [by] Robert Gardner. Enslow Publishers 2004 128p il (Chemistry! best science projects) lib bdg $26.60

Grades: 7 8 9 10	**540**

1. Chemistry 2. Science—Experiments 3. Science projects

ISBN 0-7660-2210-2	LC 2003-27476

Gardner, Robert, 1929-—*Continued*

Contents: Identifying substances; Conservation of matter; Some chemical reactions and their reaction speeds; Energy in chemical and physical changes; Acids, bases, ions, and an electric cell

"An introduction offers a short explanation of inorganic chemistry and then discusses the materials required for the more than 25 experiments presented. . . . The text is clear and concise and includes many questions to be considered for further research. Simple black-and-white illustrations accompany the text. A solid addition to any collection." SLJ

Includes bibliographical references

Newmark, Ann

Chemistry; written by Ann Newmark. rev ed. DK Pub. 2005 72p il (DK eyewitness books) $15.99

Grades: 4 5 6 7   540

1. Chemistry
   ISBN 0-7566-1385-X
   First published 1993

Explores the world of chemical reactions and shows the role that chemistry plays in our world.

Oxlade, Chris

Material changes and reactions; [by] Chris Oxlade. rev. and updated. Heinemann Library 2007 48p il (Chemicals in action) lib bdg $31.43; pa $8.99

Grades: 6 7 8 9   540

1. Chemical reactions
   ISBN   978-1-4329-0053-3   (lib   bdg); 978-1-4329-0053-3 (pa)
   First published 2002

"This title explores how elements melt, boil, and freeze; how they combine with each other to make new substances; and how chemical reactions take place every day in factories and in your home. [It also includes] several experiments that can be done at home." Publisher's note

Includes glossary and bibliographical references

Townsend, John, 1955-

Crazy chemistry. Raintree 2007 56p il (Weird history of science) lib bdg $23; pa $9.49

Grades: 4 5 6 7   540

1. Chemistry
   ISBN   978-1-4109-2378-3   (lib   bdg); 978-1-4109-2383-7 (pa)   LC 2006-07031

"This book shows how chemists through the ages risked their lives with poison gases, lethal liquids and dangerous reactions. Read how they tried to turn ordinary metals into gold, how urine was made into a glow-in-the-dark explosive, and how chemistry can catch murderers." Publisher's note

"This is an unusual book that gets its message across very effectively." Sci Books Films

Includes bibliographical references

Van Gorp, Lynn

Elements. Compass Point Books 2009 40p il (Mission: science) lib bdg $26.60

Grades: 4 5 6   540

1. Chemical elements
   ISBN 978-0-7565-3951-1 (lib bdg); 0-7565-3951-X (lib bdg)   LC 2008007284

"Van Gorp provides an overview of matter and the elements and how the latter combine to form compounds; ionic and covalent bonds; the periodic table of the elements; reactions; and mixtures and solutions. The [book has an] open [layout] and large, easy-to-read type. . . . Large eye-catching and colorful photographs and illustrations appear on every page. . . .The [book] includes a simple activity." SLJ

Includes glossary and bibliographical references

Woodford, Chris, 1943-

Atoms and molecules; [by] Chris Woodford [and] Martin Clowes. Blackbirch Press 2004 40p il (Routes of science) $23.70; pa $18.70 *

Grades: 5 6 7 8   540

1. Atoms 2. Molecules
   ISBN 1-4103-0295-4; 1-4103-0324-1 (pa)

Contents: Philosophers and alchemists; Discovering the elements; The periodic table; Molecules, matter, and motion; Inside the atom; Into the future

"This book traces the history of atomic discovery from ancient Greek theories about four basic elements to today's research into nanotechnology." Publisher's note

This "volume contains color photographs, illustrations, and diagrams to help explain the important concepts and discoveries. [This] up-to-date [volume] would be [an] excellent [supplement] to the science curriculum." SLJ

540.7   Chemistry—Education and related topics

Farndon, John

Chemicals. Benchmark Bks. 2003 32p il (Science experiments) lib bdg $25.64

Grades: 5 6 7 8   540.7

1. Chemistry 2. Science—Experiments
   ISBN 0-7614-1466-5   LC 2002-108284

Presents information on chemicals and chemistry, providing instructions for relevant scientific experiments

Includes glossary

Gardner, Robert, 1929-

Easy genius science projects with chemistry; great experiments and ideas. Enslow Publishers 2009 112p il (Easy genius science projects) lib bdg $31.93 *

Grades: 7 8 9 10   540.7

1. Chemistry 2. Science—Experiments
   ISBN 978-0-7660-2925-5 (lib bdg); 0-7660-2925-5 (lib bdg)   LC 2007-38469

This book offers science projects and experiments about chemistry divided into the following chapters: atoms, molecules, elements, and compounds; chemical

Gardner, Robert, 1929——_Continued_
reactions; oxygen and oxidation; separating and testing
substances.

"Illustrations are bright and useful in explaining the
techniques presented. . . . An excellent resource." Sci
Books Films

Includes glossary and bibliographical references

Science project ideas about kitchen chemistry.
rev ed. Enslow Publishers 2002 128p il lib bdg
$26.60

Grades: 7 8 9 10   **540.7**
1. Chemistry 2. Science projects 3. Science—Experiments

ISBN 0-7660-1706-0   LC 2001-704

First published 1988 with title: Kitchen chemistry

Presents experiments suitable for science fair projects,
dealing with the chemistry involved with foods and activities related to the kitchen

Includes bibliographical references

Meiani, Antonella
Chemistry. Lerner Publs. 2003 40p il
(Experimenting with science) lib bdg $23.93
Grades: 4 5 6 7   **540.7**
1. Chemistry 2. Science—Experiments
ISBN 0-8225-0087-6   LC 2001-50503
Uses experiments to explore such topics as how heat
changes a substance, the purpose of chemical analysis,
and how the human stomach digests food

"This book makes chemistry both accessible and exciting." Sci Books Films

Includes glossary and bibliographical references

Oxlade, Chris
Chemistry; photography by Chris Fairclough.
Raintree Steck-Vaughn Pubs. 1999 48p il (Science
projects) $29.93
Grades: 4 5 6 7   **540.7**
1. Chemistry 2. Science projects 3. Science—Experiments
ISBN 0-8172-4948-6   LC 97-46796
Introduces basic concepts of chemistry through a variety of experiments, exploring such topics as changes of
state, distillation, and catalysts

"A colorful and commonsensical introduction to major
topics in chemistry." Sci Books Films

Includes glossary and bibliographical references

546 Inorganic chemistry

Dingle, Adrian
The periodic table; elements with style! [created
by Simon Basher; written by Adrian Dingle]
Kingfisher 2007 128p il pa $8.95 *
Grades: 4 5 6 7   **546**
1. Chemical elements
ISBN 978-0-7534-6085-6 (pa); 0-7534-6085-8 (pa)
      LC 2006022515

"After a brief introduction to Mendeleev's famous table
and a spread on the chart-topping loner, hydrogen,
Dingle presents the elements by group. . . . Data on featured elements includes symbol, atomic number and
weight, color, standard state, classification, density, boiling and melting points, . . . a diagram of the position in
the periodic table, a full-page original anime-styled icon,
. . . and descriptive paragraphs that rise from informative all the way to entertaining." Bull Cent Child Books

The **Elements**. Benchmark Bks. 1999-2007 40v il
* ea $25.64
Grades: 5 6 7 8   **546**
1. Chemical elements
Contents: Aluminum, by J. Farndon; Arsenic by C.
Cooper; Boron by R. Beatty; Bromine by Krista West;
Cadmium by Allan Cobb; Calcium, by J. Farndon; Carbon, by G. Sparrow; Chlorine, by S. Watt; Chromium,
by N. Lepora; Cobalt by S. Watt; Copper, by R. Beatty;
Fluorine by T. Jackson; Gold, by S. Angliss; Hydrogen,
by J. Farndon; Iodine by L. Gray; Iron, by G. Sparrow;
The Lanthanides by Richard Beatty; Lead by S. Watt;
Lithium by T. Jackson; Magnesium, by C. Uttley; Manganese by R. Beatty; Mercury by Susan Watt; Molybdenum by N. Lepora; Nickel by G. Sparrow; Nitrogen, by
J. Farndon; Noble gases, by J. Thomas; Oxygen, by J.
Farndon; Phosphorus, by R. Beatty; Platinum by I.
Wood; Potassium, by C. Woodford; Radioactive elements
by T. Jackson; Silicon, by J Thomas; Silver, by S. Watt;
Sodium, by A. O'Daly; Sulfur, by R. Beatty; Tin, by L.
Gray; Titanium, by C. Woodford; Tungsten by K.
Turrell; Zinc by L. Gray; Zirconium by Susan Watt

These "titles cover where these substances are found,
how they were discovered, their characteristics and reactions, and their importance in the human body and the
environment. Each volume includes a double-page spread
on the element's position in the periodic table. The captioned, full-color drawings, photographs, and diagrams
clarify the text while boxed 'Did you Know?' items offer
interesting extensions to it. . . . Informative, accessible
science books that will be of interest for both general
reading and report writing." SLJ

Includes glossaries

Hasan, Heather
Iron; by Heather Hasan. Rosen Pub. Group 2004
48p il (Understanding the elements of the periodic
table) lib bdg $26.50
Grades: 5 6 7 8   **546**
1. Iron 2. Periodic law
ISBN 978-1-4042-0157-6; 1-4042-0157-2
      LC 2003-22262
Explains the characteristics of iron, where it is found,
how it is used by humans, and its relationship to other
elements found in the periodic table

Includes bibliographical references

Just add water; science projects you can sink,
squirt, splash & sail. Children's Press 2008 32p
il (Experiment with science) lib bdg $25; pa
$7.95 *
Grades: 5 6 7 8   **546**
1. Water 2. Science—Experiments
ISBN 978-0-531-18545-2 (lib bdg); 0-531-18545-1 (lib
bdg); 978-0-531-18762-3 (pa); 0-531-18762-4 (pa)
      LC 2007-21682

Just add water—*Continued*

"The book consists of nine hands-on activities that target physical science concepts inherent in water (e.g. density, buoyancy, and hardness.) . . . Students . . . will likely find the age-appropriate activities engaging and purposeful. . . . The colorful photos augment the narrative and the science is sound." Sci Books Films

Includes glossary and bibliographical references

Lew, Kristi, 1968-

Acids and bases. Chelsea House 2008 124p il (Essential chemistry) $35

Grades: 7 8 9 10   546

1. Acids 2. Bases (Chemistry)

ISBN 978-0-7910-9783-0; 0-7910-9783-8

LC 2008-24015

"Introduces acids and bases in nature and everyday life and describes their properties and how they react." Publisher's note

"Annotated, colorful photographs and illustrations appear on most spreads, and boxed areas and sidebars highlight specific subjects and areas. The explanations are clear and detailed." SLJ

Includes glossary and bibliographical references

Miller, Ron, 1947-

The elements. Twenty-First Century Books 2006 135p il lib bdg $28.90 *

Grades: 8 9 10 11 12   546

1. Chemical elements

ISBN 0-7613-2794-0   LC 2003-20874

Discusses the history of the periodic table of the elements, includes biographies of major figures in the field of chemistry, and provides information on each element.

"A useful overview." SLJ

Includes bibliographical references

Oxlade, Chris

Acids and bases; [by] Chris Oxlade. rev. and updated. Heinemann Library 2007 48p il (Chemicals in action) lib bdg $31.43; pa $8.99

Grades: 6 7 8 9   546

1. Acids 2. Bases (Chemistry)

ISBN   978-1-4329-0050-2   (lib   bdg); 978-1-4329-0057-1 (pa)

First published 2002

This explains "what gives acids and bases their properties, how they react with each other, and how we use them in our everyday lives. [It also includes] several experiments that can be done at home." Publisher's note

"Explanations are concise and clear without being oversimplified, and the arrangement is attractive and open. Colorful diagrams, drawings, and photographs appear on every page." SLJ

Includes glossary and bibliographical references

Elements and compounds; [by] Chris Oxlade. rev. and updated. Heinemann Library 2007 48p il (Chemicals in action) lib bdg $31.43; pa $8.99

Grades: 6 7 8 9   546

1. Chemical elements

ISBN   978-1-4329-0052-6   (lib   bdg); 978-1-4329-0059-5 (pa)

First published 2002

"This title explores how atoms and molecules combine to form elements and compounds, why they are given the names that they have, and how they are used in our everyday lives. [It also includes] several experiments that can be done at home." Publisher's note

"Explanations are concise and clear without being oversimplified, and the arrangement is attractive and open. Colorful diagrams, drawings, and photographs appear on every page." SLJ

Includes glossary and bibliographical references

Metals; [by] Chris Oxlade. rev. and updated. Heinemann Library 2007 48p il (Chemicals in action) lib bdg $31.43; pa $8.99

Grades: 6 7 8 9   546

1. Metals

ISBN   978-1-4329-0054-0   (lib   bdg); 978-1-4329-0061-8 (pa)

First published 2002

"This title explores what metals are like, how they are mixed with each other to form alloys, and how they are used to make everything from paper clips to skyscrapers. [It also includes] several experiments that can be done at home." Publisher's note

Includes glossary and bibliographical references

West, Krista

Carbon chemistry. Chelsea House 2008 117p il (Essential chemistry) $35

Grades: 7 8 9 10   546

1. Carbon

ISBN 978-0-7910-9708-3; 0-7910-9708-0

LC 2007-51318

Explains how carbon is integrated into all facets of life as we know it and discusses the unique properties of this essential element.

"Annotated, colorful photographs and illustrations appear on most spreads, and boxed areas and sidebars highlight specific subjects and areas. The explanations are clear and detailed." SLJ

Includes glossary and bibliographical references

Winston, Robert M. L.

It's elementary! how chemistry rocks our world. DK 2007 95p il $15.99 *

Grades: 5 6 7 8   546

1. Chemical elements

ISBN 978-0-7566-2666-2; 0-7566-2666-8

LC 2007-298755

A comprehensive look at the elements describes the history of how they were discovered, what they are made of, their properties, where they are found, and their various applications.

547   Organic chemistry

Gardner, Robert, 1929-
Chemistry science fair projects using french fries, gumdrops, soap, and other organic stuff; [by] Robert Gardner and Barbara Gardner Conklin. Enslow Publishers 2004 128p il (Chemistry! best science projects) lib bdg $26.60
Grades: 7 8 9 10   **547**
   1. Chemistry 2. Science—Experiments 3. Science projects
   ISBN 0-7660-2211-0   LC 2004-2465
Contents: Organic chemistry in your life; Compounds of carbon; Polar and nonpolar compounds; Food: organic compounds; Baking: organic chemistry in the kitchen
"How does invisible ink work? Why does detergent remove dirt from your clothing? How much fat is in a French fry? What makes bread rise? This book is filled with experiments to help you discover the world of organic chemistry." Publisher's note
"Simple black-and-white drawings complement the text, and illustrations of chemical structures help to demonstrate reactions. A sound addition to science collections." SLJ
Includes bibliographical references

548   Crystallography

Symes, R. F.
Crystal & gem; written by R.F. Symes and R.R. Harding. Rev. ed. DK Pub. 2007 72p il (DK eyewitness books) $15.99
Grades: 4 5 6 7   **548**
   1. Crystals 2. Precious stones
   ISBN 978-0-7566-3001-0; 0-7566-3001-0
                  LC 2007-277721
First published 1991
Includes CD-Rom
Describes the seven basic shapes of crystals and other aspects of crystallography, including how they form in nature and how crystals are studied and identified.

549   Mineralogy

Casper, Julie Kerr
Minerals; gifts from the Earth. Chelsea House 2007 194p il map (Natural resources) $39.50
Grades: 8 9 10 11 12   **549**
   1. Minerals 2. Mines and mineral resources
   ISBN 978-0-8160-6357-4; 0-8160-6357-5
                  LC 2006102275
Explains how minerals and formed and how they are used in technology.
Includes bibliographical references

Chesterman, Charles W.
The Audubon Society field guide to North American rocks and minerals; scientific consultant, Kurt E. Lowe. Knopf 1979 c1978 850p il $19.95
Grades: 8 9 10 11 12 Adult   **549**
   1. Minerals 2. Rocks
   ISBN 0-394-50269-8   LC 78-54893
"Pocket guide providing color photos and descriptions of some 232 mineral species and forty types of rocks. Includes guide to mineral environments, glossary, bibliography, and indexes by name and locality." Ref Sources for Small & Medium-sized Libr. 5th edition

Farndon, John
Rocks and minerals. Benchmark Bks. 2003 32p il (Science experiments) lib bdg $25.64
Grades: 5 6 7 8   **549**
   1. Rocks 2. Minerals 3. Science—Experiments
   ISBN 0-7614-1468-1   LC 2002-908
Discusses the physical properties of various rocks and minerals and gives instructions for experiments that identify their unique characteristics
Includes glossary

Pellant, Chris
Rocks and minerals; Helen Pellant, editorial consultant; photography by Harry Taylor. 2nd American ed. Dorling Kindersley 2002 256p il (Smithsonian handbooks) pa $20
Grades: 11 12 Adult   **549**
   1. Rocks 2. Minerals
   ISBN 0-7894-9106-0; 978-0-7894-9106-0
First published 1992 as part of the Eyewitness handbooks series
This field guide to identification of rocks and minerals includes techniques for collection and classification, and facts about physical and chemical composition and formation.

Pough, Frederick H., 1906-2006
A field guide to rocks and minerals; photographs by Jeff Scovil. 5th ed. Houghton Mifflin 1996 396p il hardcover o.p. pa $20
Grades: 8 9 10 11 12   **549**
   1. Minerals 2. Rocks
   ISBN 0-395-72778-2; 0-395-91096-X (pa)
                  LC 94-49005
"The Peterson field guide series"
First published 1953
"Sponsored by the National Audubon Society, the National Wildlife Federation, and the Roger Tory Peterson Institute"
This illustrated guide utilizes traditional identification methods and includes discussions of crystallography, mineralogy and home laboratory techniques.
Includes bibliographical references

Simon and Schuster's guide to rocks and minerals; edited by Martin Prinz, George Harlow, and Joseph Peters. Simon & Schuster 1978 607p il pa $17 hardcover o.p.
Grades: 8 9 10 11 12 Adult   **549**
   1. Minerals 2. Rocks
   ISBN 0-671-24417-5 (pa)   LC 78-8610

Simon and Schuster's guide to rocks and minerals—*Continued*

Original Italian edition, 1977

"Half of this book consists of color plates; the other half is an authoritative text which describes the elements of mineralogy and petrology. Crystal system or family, physical and chemical properties, occurrence, uses, and rarity are included for each species." Libr J

Symes, R. F.

Eyewitness rocks & minerals; written by R. F. Symes and the staff of the Natural History Museum, London. rev ed. DK Pub. 2004 72p il (DK eyewitness books) $15.99

Grades: 4 5 6 7   **549**

1. Rocks 2. Minerals

ISBN 0-756-0719-1

First published 1988

Text and photographs examine the creation, importance, erosion, mining, and uses of rocks and minerals

550   Earth sciences & geology

Allaby, Michael, 1933-

Visual encyclopedia of earth. National Geographic 2008 256p il map $24.95; lib bdg $32.90 *

Grades: 7 8 9 10   **550**

1. Earth sciences—Encyclopedias 2. Reference books

ISBN   978-1-4263-0366-1;   1-4263-0366-1; 978-1-4263-0367-8 (lib bdg); 1-4263-0367-X (lib bdg)

LC 2008-301484

"This overview of the earth . . . cover[s] all aspects of earth science. . . . [This] is a feast for the eyes and an exceptional introduction to earth science. It will be a useful resource for science teachers who want to engage their students in this subject matter." Libr Media Connect

Calhoun, Yael

Earth science fair projects using rocks, minerals, magnets, mud, and more. Enslow Publishers 2005 128p il (Earth science! best science projects) lib bdg $26.60

Grades: 7 8 9 10   **550**

1. Earth sciences 2. Science projects 3. Science—Experiments

ISBN 0-7660-2363-X   LC 2004-15723

"This book explores geological topics such as continental drift, earthquakes, volcanoes, watersheds, types of erosion, and the formation of igneous, sedimentary, and metamorphic rocks. After an introduction to the scientific method and a list of safety rules, the presentation offers 23 experiments. . . . A useful source of ideas for worthwhile science fair projects." Booklist

Includes glossary and bibliographical references

Day, Trevor, 1955-

DK guide to savage Earth. DK Pub. 2001 64p $15.95

Grades: 4 5 6   **550**

1. Earth 2. Natural disasters

ISBN 0-7894-7919-2   LC 2001-275872

The author takes us on a "journey from Earth's violent beginnings to possible future destruction from such forces as asteroid strikes and other natural disasters, global warming, or a depletion of the forests and fisheries of the world. Each chapter focuses on one force of nature, discussing how and why it has shaped the Earth in the past and how it is changing the shape of the Earth in the present. . . . The text is concise, authoritative, and very interesting and easy to read." Book Rep

Includes glossary

Earth; editor-in-chief, James F. Luhr. Compact ed. DK Pub. 2007 520p il map pa $24.95

Grades: 8 9 10 11 12 Adult   **550**

1. Earth

ISBN 978-0-7566-3332-5; 0-7566-3332-X

LC 2007282646

Presents an overview of the Earth, discussing its internal structure, the major features of its lands, mountains, and oceans, its climate, weather, and place in the universe.

The **Facts** on File Earth science handbook; [by] the Diagram Group. Rev. ed. Facts on File 2006 272p il (Facts on File science library) $35 *

Grades: 8 9 10 11 12   **550**

1. Earth sciences

ISBN 0-8160-5879-2   LC 2005-44692

First published 2000

This guide to earth sciences contains a dictionary with around 1400 entries, a chronology, thumbnail biographies, an A to Z list of over 150 advances in earth science, and a list of Tyler Prize winners.

Includes bibliographical references

Patent, Dorothy Hinshaw

Shaping the earth; photographs by William Muñoz. Clarion Bks. 2000 88p il maps $18 *

Grades: 4 5 6 7   **550**

1. Geology

ISBN 0-395-85691-4   LC 99-37093

Explains the forces that have created the geological features on the earth's surface

"This concise, attractive volume succeeds in a daunting task—to present the history of Earth in 88 pages of compelling, age-appropriate text. . . . William Muñoz's full-color photographs, well-chosen and reproduced, will draw young readers into the text. . . . A glossary and a list of further references, including Web sites, are appended." Booklist

Includes bibliographical references

Stefoff, Rebecca, 1951-

Earth and the moon. Benchmark Bks. 2001 c2002 64p il (Blastoff!) lib bdg $28.50

Grades: 4 5 6   **550**

1. Earth 2. Moon

ISBN 0-7614-1235-2   LC 00-54710

This describes astronomers' present knowledge of the planet Earth "and Earth's moon, with considerable attention given to the sources of information (visiting spacecraft, the Hubble telescope, ground-based observations, mathematical inference). . . . [It includes] many well-

Stefoff, Rebecca, 1951--—*Continued*
captioned photos, illustrations, and diagrams." Horn
Book Guide
Includes glossary and bibliographical references

Tabak, John
A look at earth. Watts 2003 109p il map (Out
of this world) lib bdg $33.50; pa $14.95
Grades: 5 6 7 8   **550**
1. Earth
ISBN 0-531-12266-2 (lib bdg); 0-531-15583-8 (pa)
LC 2002-1728
An in-depth look at the Earth's composition, environ-
ment, and biomes
Includes glossary and bibliographical references

VanCleave, Janice Pratt
Janice VanCleave's A+ projects in earth science;
winning experiments for science fairs and extra
credit. Wiley 1999 234p $32.50; pa $12.95
Grades: 7 8 9 10   **550**
1. Earth sciences 2. Science projects 3. Science—Experiments
ISBN 0-471-17769-5; 0-471-17770-9 (pa)
LC 98-14795
Presents thirty sample science projects as well as ideas
for small changes to the original experiments thereby encouraging creativity and increased learning
"Students will appreciate the clear, organized instructions and the fact that most of the projects use such ordinary household items as soda bottles, kitchen utensils,
rulers, and strings. . . . A rock-solid addition to library
collections." SLJ
Includes glossary

551   Geology, hydrology, meteorology

Cobb, Allan B.
Earth chemistry. Chelsea House 2008 130p il
map (Essential chemistry) $35
Grades: 7 8 9 10   **551**
1. Environmental sciences 2. Chemistry
ISBN 978-0-7910-9677-2; 0-7910-9677-7
LC 2007-51317
This book explains "chemical or physical changes on
Earth, exploring how the atmosphere, hydrosphere,
lithosphere, and biosphere relate to and interact with one
another." Publisher's note
"Annotated, colorful photographs and illustrations ap-
pear on most spreads, and boxed areas and sidebars high-
light specific subjects and areas. The explanations are
clear and detailed." SLJ
Includes glossary and bibliographical references

Kelly, Erica
Evolving planet; [by] Erica Kelly & Richard
Kissel. Harry N. Abrams 2008 136p il map $19.95
*
Grades: 5 6 7 8   **551**
1. Field Museum of Natural History 2. Earth
3. Evolution
ISBN 978-0-8109-9486-7; 0-8109-9486-0
LC 2007-36342
"Published in association with The Field Museum,
Chicago."
"Based on a exhibit at Chicago's Field Museum, this
big spacious volume packs in a wealth of information
about evolution over four billion years. . . . There are
detailed, beautiful photographs and glorious paintings on
every double-page spread and the chatty text is accessible for grade-schoolers." Booklist
Includes glossary and bibliographical references

551.1   Gross structure and properties of the earth

Gallant, Roy A.
Dance of the continents. Benchmark Bks. 2000
80p il (Story of science) lib bdg $29.93
Grades: 5 6 7 8   **551.1**
1. Plate tectonics 2. Geology
ISBN 0-7614-0962-9   LC 98-28046
Describes the development of geological theory from
the ancient Greek philosophers to the discovery of plate
tectonics, which explains the forming of geological struc-
tures
"This book is a good brief description of continental
drift as it is now perceived by most geologists." Sci
Books Films
Includes glossary and bibliographical references

Plates; restless earth. Benchmark Bks. 2002
c2003 80p il map (Earthworks) lib bdg $29.93
Grades: 5 6 7 8   **551.1**
1. Plate tectonics
ISBN 0-7614-1370-7   LC 2002-915
Discusses plate tectonics, the theory that the surface of
the earth is always moving, and the connection of this
phenomenon to earthquakes and volcanoes
Includes glossary and bibliographical references

Silverstein, Alvin
Plate tectonics; by Alvin & Virginia Silverstein
& Laura Silverstein Nunn. rev. ed. Twenty-First
Century Books 2009 120p il map (Science
concepts, second series) lib bdg $31.93
Grades: 6 7 8 9   **551.1**
1. Plate tectonics
ISBN 978-0-7613-3936-6; 0-7613-3936-1
LC 2007051039
First published 1998
The authors "explain the theory of plate tectonics and
how moving plates can cause . . . natural disasters:
earthquakes, volcanoes, and tsunamis. The authors also
explore how plate tectonics are changing our planet, and

Silverstein, Alvin—*Continued*
how they could affect our future on Earth." Publisher's note

Includes glossary and bibliographical references

Stille, Darlene R., 1942-
Plate tectonics; earth's moving crust. Compass Point Books 2006 48p il (Exploring science) $26.60 *
Grades: 7 8 9 10   **551.1**
1. Plate tectonics
ISBN 978-0-7565-1957-5; 0-7565-1957-8
                                                LC 2006-06764
This describes the shifting of the earth's crust and its consequences.
Includes glossary and bibliographical references

Vogt, Gregory
Earth's core and mantle; heavy metal, moving rock; by Gregory L. Vogt. Twenty-First Century Books 2007 80p il map (Earth's spheres) lib bdg $29.27
Grades: 6 7 8 9   **551.1**
1. Earth—Internal structure
ISBN 978-0-7613-2837-7 (lib bdg); 0-7613-2837-8 (lib bdg)   LC 2003-23969
This "explores the makeup of the universe, the origin of the planet and its moon, and the layers under Earth's surface. . . . Each of these complex topics is made understandable by the use of colorful photographs, graphs, charts, and other illustrations. Captions include new and useful information, and the sidebars and fact pages are helpful." SLJ
Includes bibliographical references

The lithosphere; Earth's crust; by Gregory L. Vogt. Twenty-First Century Books 2007 80p il map (Earth's spheres) lib bdg $29.27
Grades: 6 7 8 9   **551.1**
1. Earth—Crust
ISBN 978-0-7613-2838-4 (lib bdg); 0-7613-2838-6 (lib bdg)   LC 2006-14882
This "explains the [Earth's] crust and how land is built and eroded, covering such subjects as plate tectonics, volcanoes, and geysers. Each of these complex topics is made understandable by the use of colorful photographs, graphs, charts, and other illustrations. Captions include new and useful information, and the sidebars and fact pages are helpful." SLJ
Includes bibliographical references

551.2   Volcanoes, earthquakes, thermal waters and gases

Burleigh, Robert, 1936-
Volcanoes; journey to the crater's edge; photographs by Philippe Bourseiller; adapted by Robert Burleigh; text by Helene Montardre; drawings by David Giraudon. H.N. Abrams 2003 75p il map $14.95 *
Grades: 4 5 6 7   **551.2**
1. Volcanoes
ISBN 0-8109-4590-8   LC 2003-971
Over thirty photographs and accompanying text reveal the facts about the world's volcanoes
"Photographer Bourseiller takes young readers to the crater's edge with truly spectacular full-color photographs. . . . The book does an excellent job of documenting the effect of volcanoes on the lives of those who live close to them, and small watercolor paintings further enliven the sense of human history." Booklist

Fradin, Judith Bloom
Earthquakes; witness to disaster; by Judy and Dennis Fradin. National Geographic 2008 48p map (Witness to disaster) $16.95; lib bdg $26.90 *
Grades: 4 5 6 7   **551.2**
1. Earthquakes
ISBN   978-1-4263-0211-4;   1-4263-0211-8; 978-1-4263-0212-1 (lib bdg); 1-4263-0212-6 (lib bdg)
                                                LC 2007044164
"The first chapter documents the 1964 Alaskan quake that shook Prince William Sound with a 9.2 magnitude force, and set off a tsunami that ultimately caused most of the deaths attributed to this frightening act of nature. The following chapters explore the deadly history of earthquakes and the seismic and geological science of this phenomenon." Publisher's note
"The combination of good writing and excellent graphics paired with archival and personal perspectives makes this book a valuable addition." SLJ
Includes glossary and bibliographical references

Volcanoes; by Judy and Dennis Fradin. National Geographic 2007 48p il map (Witness to disaster) $16.95; lib bdg $26.90 *
Grades: 4 5 6   **551.2**
1. Volcanoes
ISBN   978-0-7922-5376-1;   0-7922-5376-0; 978-0-7922-5377-8 (lib bdg); 0-7922-5377-9 (lib bdg)
                                                LC 2006-102817
This "introduces readers to these violent eruptions, using eyewitness accounts to explain the history and science involved. They begin with a report of the 1943 birth of a volcano in Paricutín, Mexico. . . . Subsequent chapters describe other celebrated volcanoes, explain their causes and types, note the benefits of these eruptions, and clarify how they are currently predicted. . . . Numerous clear, well-chosen photographs and diagrams help to convey the great power of volcanic activity and the consequences to humans. . . . This will be useful for report writers, and a fascinating pick for browsers." Booklist
Includes bibliographical references

Grace, Catherine O'Neill, 1950-

Forces of nature; the awesome power of volcanoes, earthquakes, and tornadoes; by Catherine O'Neill Grace. National Geographic Society 2004 62p il $17.95 *

Grades: 4 5 6 7   551.2

1. Stein, Ross S. 2. Wurman, Joshua 3. Edmonds, Marie 4. Herd, Richard 5. Volcanoes 6. Earthquakes 7. Tornadoes

ISBN 0-7922-6328-6   LC 2003-18929

Contents: On the rim of a volcano; In an earthquake zone; In the path of a storm

"A companion volume to the National Geographic film of the same title, this book presents the basics of these phenomena with a focus on the work of four scientists who study them: Richard Herd, Marie Edmonds, Ross Stein, and Joshua Wurman. . . . Outstanding color and black-and-white photos and diagrams augment the very readable text." SLJ

Levy, Matthys

Earthquakes, volcanoes, and tsunamis; projects and principles for beginning geologists; [by] Matthys Levy and Mario Salvadori. Chicago Review Press 2009 136p il pa $14.95

Grades: 5 6 7 8   551.2

1. Earthquakes 2. Volcanoes 3. Tsunamis

ISBN 978-1-55652-801-9; 1-55652-801-9

LC 2008040143

This "is an excellent introduction for young minds to the subject of earthquakes, volcanoes, and related phenomena. . . . The book is filled with projects to help young people understand the occurrence and consequences of earthquakes, volcanoes, and tsunamis." Sci Books Films

Lindop, Laurie

Probing volcanoes. Twenty-First Century Books 2003 80p il map (Science on the edge) lib bdg $26.90

Grades: 5 6 7 8   551.2

1. Volcanoes

ISBN 0-7613-2700-2   LC 2002-14251

Contents: Predicting eruptions; Eruption! Volcanologists on the edge; History of volcano monitoring; Looking to the future; Becoming a volcanologist

This "examines the work of volcanologists, whose main goal is to determine how to predict volcanic eruptions. A great deal of scientific information is included, beginning with a basic explanation of the subject and what the scientists are trying to discover. . . . [The book is] profusely illustrated with well-placed color photographs." SLJ

Includes bibliographical references

McCollum, Sean, 1963-

Volcanic eruptions, earthquakes, and tsunamis. Chelsea House 2007 80p il (Scientific American) lib bdg $30

Grades: 5 6 7 8   551.2

1. Earthquakes 2. Tsunamis 3. Volcanoes

ISBN 978-0-7910-9047-3; 0-7910-9047-7

LC 2007017740

"Following an introduction that focuses on the formation of a volcano off the coast of Iceland in 1963 and presents the principles of seismology, geology, and the structure of the Earth, individual chapters on volcanoes, earthquakes, and tsunamis describe these phenomena, how they happen, and their characteristics. . . . The workmanlike writing is clear, with glossary terms highlighted in the text. Major events, such as Mount St. Helens, the 2004 tsunami, and the 1906 San Francisco earthquake, are used as examples, while good color diagrams and photos effectively illustrate ideas presented." SLJ

Includes bibliographical references

Reed, Jennifer

Earthquakes; disaster & survival; [by] Jennifer Bond Reed. Enslow Publishers 2004 48p il map (Deadly disasters) $23.93 *

Grades: 4 5 6 7   551.2

1. Earthquakes

ISBN 0-7660-2381-8   LC 2004-11698

Contents: Living dangerously; What is an earthquake?; Devastation in Central and South America; Asia and the Middle East; On shaky ground: North America; Saving lives; Top ten deadliest earthquakes ever

This explains the causes of earthquakes, tells stories of survivors and rescuers, and offers safety advice

This is an "attractive and straightforward volume. . . . Illustrations include dramatic full-color photos, as well as maps and diagrams." SLJ

Includes glossary and bibliographical references

Stille, Darlene R., 1942-

Great shakes; the science of earthquakes. Compass Point Books 2009 43p il map (Headline science) lib bdg $27.93; pa $7.95

Grades: 5 6 7 8   551.2

1. Earthquakes

ISBN 978-0-7565-3947-4 (lib bdg); 0-7565-3947-1 (lib bdg); 978-0-7565-3368-7 (pa); 0-7565-3368-6 (pa)

LC 2008-05739

This "is an accessible, technically accurate introduction to [earthquakes]. . . . In addition to the ludic writing, this slim volume offers . . . readers comprehensive coverage of the fundamentals of earthquakes, including the effects, plate tectonics, fault systems, seismic waves, forecasting, and safer building designs. . . . The many charts and graphs enrich the volume and clarify technical issues." Sci Books Films

Includes glossary and bibliographical references

Trueit, Trudi Strain

Earthquakes. Watts 2003 63p il map $24; pa $8.95

Grades: 4 5 6   551.2

1. Earthquakes

ISBN 0-531-12197-6; 0-531-16243-5 (pa)

LC 2002-6150

"Watts library"

Contents: Moment of terror; On shaky ground; Sizing up shocks; Triggering disaster; Predicting and preparing

This describes earthquakes including their measurement on the Mercalli and Richter scales and by move-

Trueit, Trudi Strain—*Continued*

ment magnitude and includes a brief description of the work of a woman seismologist

This includes "attention-grabbing photography, excellent charts and diagrams, short articles with or without photographs, and vocabulary terms that appear in bold and are explained in context." Sci Books Films

Includes glossary and bibliographical references

Volcanoes. Watts 2003 63p il map $24; pa $8.95

Grades: 4 5 6   **551.2**

1. Volcanoes

ISBN 0-531-12198-4; 0-531-16244-3 (pa)

LC 2002-11647

"Watts library"

Discusses the formation and characteristics of volcanoes, the causes and effects of their eruption, and describes specific volcanic eruptions such as that of Mount St. Helen's in 1980

This includes "attention-grabbing photography, excellent charts and diagrams, short articles with or without photographs, and vocabulary terms that appear in bold and are explained in context." Sci Books Films

Includes bibliographical references

Winchester, Simon

The day the world exploded; the earthshaking catastrophe at Krakatoa; adaptation by Dwight Jon Zimmerman; illustrated by Jason Chin. Collins 2008 96p il map $22.99; lib bdg $23.89

Grades: 5 6 7 8   **551.2**

1. Volcanoes

ISBN   978-0-06-123982-3;   0-06-123982-8; 978-0-06-123983-0 (lib bdg); 0-06-123983-6 (lib bdg)

Adapted from: Krakatoa: the day the world exploded, August 27, 1883, published 2003 for adults

This presents an account of the catastrophic eruption off the coast of Java of the volcano-island of Krakatoa in 1883 and its effects.

"Chin's full-color cartoon illustrations enhance the many archival and contemporary photographs, historical illustrations, and maps that accompany the text. . . . In addition to this work's educational and reference potential, it lends a human face to a natural disaster and will attract general readers as well." SLJ

Includes glossary and bibliographical references

551.3 Surface and exogenous processes and their agents

Stille, Darlene R., 1942-

Erosion; how land forms, how it changes; by Darlene R. Stille. Compass Point Books 2005 48p il map (Exploring science) $25.27 *

Grades: 6 7 8 9   **551.3**

ISBN 0-7565-0854-1   LC 2004-23077

Contents: The power of erosion; The erosion process; How does water cause erosion?; How does wind cause erosion?; How do glaciers cause erosion?; Controlling erosion

Examines the dangers, causes, and control of erosion. "A few maps and many clear, color photos illustrate the book." Booklist

Includes glossary and bibliographical references

551.4 Geomorphology and hydrosphere

Aleshire, Peter

Deserts. Chelsea House 178p il map (The extreme Earth) $35

Grades: 8 9 10 11 12   **551.4**

1. Deserts

ISBN 978-0-8160-6434-2; 0-8160-6434-2

This describes desert locations, their plants and animals, their indigenous peoples, ecology, and history.

Mountains; foreword by Geoffrey H. Nash. Chelsea House Publishers 2008 144p il map (The extreme Earth) $35

Grades: 8 9 10 11 12   **551.4**

1. Mountains

ISBN 978-0-8160-5918-8; 0-8160-5918-7

LC 2007020692

This describes how mountains were formed, how they have changed over the span of geologic time, and their contributions to the environment, and goes on to describe specific mountains and mountain ranges including Mount Everest, the Appalachians, the Alps, the Mid-Atlantic Ridge of North America, the Sierra Nevadas, the Andes, Mauna Kea in Hawaii, Mount Saint Helens, Mount Kilimanjaro, and Humphreys Peak, in the southwestern United States.

Includes bibliographical references

Erickson, Jon, 1948-

Making of the earth; geologic forces that shape our planet; foreword by Donald R. Coates. Facts on File 2000 257p il map (Living earth) $55 *

Grades: 7 8 9 10   **551.4**

1. Geology

ISBN 0-8160-4276-4   LC 00-39343

The author provides an "overview of geomorphology, the branch of geology that focuses on landforms, the structures that endow the earth with its myriad landscapes. . . . Charts, maps, photographs, a glossary, and bibliography make this enjoyable read an extremely useful resource." Booklist

Includes bibliographical references

Hanson, Erik A.

Canyons; [by] Erik Hanson; foreword by Geoffrey H. Nash. Chelsea House 2007 206p il map (The extreme Earth) $35

Grades: 8 9 10 11 12   **551.4**

1. Canyons 2. Plate tectonics

ISBN 0-8160-6435-0; 978-0-8160-6435-9

LC 2006-15810

Profiles canyons around the world including the Grand Canyon, the Columbia River Gorge, Fish River Canyon,

Hanson, Erik A.—*Continued*
and Monterey Canyon; and describes how and when they
were formed, how the landscape has changed over time,
and the contribution of each to the environment.

"The story in this book may generate a longing within
the reader to visit vistas and hike into canyons for an intimate view of earth history." Sci Books Films

Includes glossary and bibliographical references

Hanson, Jeanne K.
Caves; foreword by Geoffrey H. Nash. Chelsea
House 2007 142p il map (The extreme Earth)
Grades: 8 9 10 11 12   **551.4**
    1. Caves
    ISBN 0-8160-5917-9   LC 2006-11718

The describes types of caves and how they are
formed, their exploration, and some specific caves including Mammoth Cave of Kentucky; the caves of Yuca-
tan, Mexico; Lascaux Cave of southwestern France;
Lubang Nasib Bagus and the Sarawak Chamber of Bor-
neo, Malaysia; Kazumura Cave of Hawaii; Waitomo
Cave of New Zealand; and Wind Cave of South Dakota.

Includes bibliographical references

Lindop, Laurie
Cave sleuths. Twenty-First Century Books 2006
80p il (Science on the edge) lib bdg $26.90
Grades: 5 6 7 8   **551.4**
    1. Caves
    ISBN 0-7613-2702-9   LC 2003-16946

Discusses the science of speleology and what scientists have learned about caves, how they are formed, and
what lives in them.

"The science is intriguing here. . . . The photos . . .
are all intriguing and lend interest." Voice Youth Advocates

Includes glossary and bibliographical references

Simon, Seymour, 1931-
Mountains. Morrow Junior Bks. 1994 unp il pa
$6.99 hardcover o.p. *
Grades: 4 5 6 7   **551.4**
    1. Mountains
    ISBN 0-688-15477-8 (pa)   LC 93-11398

Introduces various mountain ranges, how they are
formed and shaped, and how they affect vegetation and
animals, including humans

"The striking color photographs work well with the
clear text to illustrate key points and highlight the diversity among the Earth's mountain ranges." Horn Book
Guide

Taylor, Barbara, 1954-
Understanding landforms; [by] Barbara Taylor.
Smart Apple Media 2008 46p il (Geography skills)
$22.95 *
Grades: 6 7 8 9   **551.4**
    1. Landforms 2. Physical geography
    ISBN 1-59920-049-X; 978-1-59920-049-1
                 LC 2006036141

Contents: What shapes the land?; Earth's jigsaw; Volcanoes; Mountains; Earthquakes; Rocks; Weathering;
Erosion; Deserts; Limestone landscapes; Rivers at work;
The upper river; The middle and lower river; River
flooding; Ice at work; Shaping the coast; Wearing away
coasts; Building coasts; Managing coasts

This describes how to identify the distinguishing features of landscapes and how they were formed.

"The text is easy to follow. . . . The examples given
in the text that involve places are almost always accompanied by excellent photographs. . . . Maps, block diagrams, tables, and graphs are clearly presented and easy
to interpret." Sci Books Films

Includes glossary and bibliographical references

Waltham, A. C. (Antony Clive), 1942-
Great caves of the world. Firefly Books 2008
112p il $29.95
Grades: 8 9 10 11 12 Adult   **551.4**
    1. Caves
    ISBN 978-1-55407-413-6; 1-55407-413-4
                 LC 2009277166

More than twenty-five caves around the world are examined, including Kentucky's Mammoth Cave and New
Zealand's Waitomo Cave, in a colorfully illustrated tour
of their environments, special features, unique inhabitants, and geological histories.

Includes bibliographical references

551.46   Hydrosphere and submarine geology. Oceanography

Aleshire, Peter
Ocean ridges and trenches; foreword by
Geoffrey H. Nash. Chelsea House 2007 148p il
map (The extreme Earth) $35
Grades: 8 9 10 11 12   **551.46**
    1. Ocean bottom 2. Marine ecology
    ISBN 978-0-8160-5919-5; 0-8160-5919-5
                 LC 2006032058

Provides information about the formation of ocean
ridges and trenches. Includes ten examples of ridges and
trenches from around the world.

Includes bibliographical references

Burns, Loree Griffin
Tracking trash; flotsam, jetsam, and the science
of ocean motion. Houghton Mifflin 2007 56p il
map (Scientists in the field) $18 *
Grades: 5 6 7 8   **551.46**
    1. Ocean currents 2. Pollution
    ISBN 978-0-618-58131-3; 0-618-58131-6
                 LC 2006-11534

"The book profiles two oceanographers who devised
experiments using computer-modeling programs of ocean
surface current movement to predict the landfall of . . .
drifting objects. . . . Spacious layout, exceptionally fine
color photos, and handsome maps give this book an inviting look. . . . A unique and often fascinating book."
Booklist

Includes glossary and bibliographical references

Carson, Rachel, 1907-1964

The sea around us; [by] Rachel L. Carson; introduction by Ann H. Zwinger; afterword by Jeffrey S. Levinton. Oxford University Press 1989 xxvii, 250p hardcover o.p. pa $15.95

Grades: 8 9 10 11 12 Adult   **551.46**
1. Ocean
ISBN 0-19-506186-1; 0-19-506997-8 (pa)
                                        LC 89-16333

First published 1951; revised edition published 1961; this is a reissue of the 1979 edition which added the introduction and afterword

Beginning with a description of how the earth acquired its oceans, the book covers such topics as how life began in the primeval sea, the hidden lands, the life discovered in the abyss by highly delicate sounding apparatus, currents and tides, the formation of volcanic islands, and mineral resources

Includes bibliographical references

Day, Trevor, 1955-

Oceans; illustrations by Richard Garratt. rev ed. Facts on File 2008 318p il map (Ecosystem) $70

Grades: 8 9 10 11 12 Adult   **551.46**
1. Ocean 2. Oceanography
ISBN 0-8160-5932-2; 978-0-8160-5932-4
                                        LC 2006-100769

First published 1999

This volume describes the oceans of the world with regard to their geography, geology, history, chemistry, biology, ecology, exploration, relationship to the atmosphere, economic resources, and management.

Includes glossary and bibliographical references

Desonie, Dana

Oceans; how we use the seas. Chelsea House 2007 215p il map (Our fragile planet) $35

Grades: 8 9 10 11 12   **551.46**
1. Ocean 2. Oceanography 3. Marine ecology
ISBN 978-0-8160-6216-4; 0-8160-6216-1
                                        LC 2007-13560

An introduction to how life in our oceans works, and how we are threatening it with pollution and depletion of fisheries.

The author "offers a comprehensive, detailed introduction to ocean science and conservation in this amply illustrated volume." Booklist

Includes glossary and bibliographical references

Erickson, Jon, 1948-

Marine geology; exploring the new frontiers of the ocean; foreword by Timothy Kusky. rev ed. Facts on File 2003 317p il (Living earth) $55

Grades: 7 8 9 10   **551.46**
1. Submarine geology 2. Marine biology
ISBN 0-8160-4874-6   LC 2002-1295

Replaces the edition published 1996 in the Changing earth series

"Facts on File science library"

First published 1996

This "examines the interrelationship between water and its life forms and geologic structures. It looks at several ideas for the origins of the Earth, continents and oceans, and how these processes fit into the origin of the universe." Publisher's note

Includes glossary and bibliographical references

Fradin, Judith Bloom

Tsunamis; witness to disaster; [by] Judy & Dennis Fradin. National Geographic 2008 48p il map (Witness to disaster) $16.95; lib bdg $20.90 *

Grades: 4 5 6 7   **551.46**
1. Tsunamis
ISBN   978-0-7922-5380-8;   0-7922-5380-9;
978-0-7922-5381-5 (lib bdg); 0-7922-5381-7 (lib bdg)
                                        LC 2008010536

This "explores the science, history, and personal experience of tsunamis and shows kids what scientists are doing to develop early warning systems so we can survive such disasters in the future." Publisher's note

Includes glossary and bibliographical references

Kusky, Timothy M.

Tsunamis; giant waves from the sea; [by] Timothy Kusky. Facts on File 2008 134p il (The hazardous Earth) $39.50

Grades: 8 9 10 11 12   **551.46**
1. Tsunamis
ISBN 978-0-8160-6464-9; 0-8160-6464-4
                                        LC 2007023477

"This detailed study of the causes and physics of massive waves covers not only the oceanic sort but also similar phenomena, 'seiches,' that occur in closed bodies of water. . . . After analyzing tsunamis' various forms and behaviors, Kusky delivers harrowing accounts of over a dozen disasters, from those centuries past to the devastating Indian Ocean tsunami in 2004. He then closes with a discussion of early-warning systems. Occasional photos capture the devastation of which these waves are capable." Booklist

Includes bibliographical references

Lindop, Laurie

Venturing the deep sea. Twenty-First Century Books 2006 80p il map (Science on the edge) lib bdg $27.93 *

Grades: 5 6 7 8   **551.46**
1. Ocean bottom 2. Underwater exploration
ISBN 0-7613-2701-0   LC 2004-29729

"Comparing exploration of the ocean with that of outer space, Lindop covers the equipment used and knowledge sought by underwater biologists and geologists. She presents the different zones of the sea, traces the development of diving equipment, and describes a typical dive. Topics include the mid-ocean ridge, plate tectonics, and continental drift; hydrothermal vents; bioluminescence; underwater cameras; and deep-sea remotely operated robot explorers." SLJ

"The science is intriguing here. . . . The photos of undersea projects, creatures, weird cave and underwater tube formations are all intriguing." Voice Youth Advocates

Includes bibliographical references

Mallory, Kenneth

Diving to a deep-sea volcano. Houghton Mifflin Company 2006 60p il map (Scientists in the field) $17 *

Grades: 5 6 7 8   551.46

1. Lutz, Richard A. 2. Ocean bottom 3. Underwater exploration 4. Marine biology

ISBN 978-0-618-33205-2; 0-618-33205-7

LC 2005-25449

This describes the exploration by marine biologist Rich Lutz and his crew of deep sea hydrothermal vents and the creatures that survive there.

"The profile of an enthusiastic scientist injects excitement into even unassuming facts." Booklist

Includes glossary and bibliographical references

Matsen, Bradford

The incredible record-setting deep-sea dive of the bathysphere; [by] Brad Matsen. Enslow Pubs. 2003 48p il map (Incredible deep-sea adventures) lib bdg $18.95

Grades: 4 5 6 7   551.46

1. Beebe, William, 1877-1962 2. Barton, Otis 3. Underwater exploration 4. Ocean bottom

ISBN 0-7660-2188-2   LC 2002-13822

Contents: Heroes of the deep; The voyage into the depths; A record is broken, a record is set; Explorers of the abyss; The ultimate dive to the bottom of the sea

Describes the 1934 dive of a bathysphere, or "sphere of the deep," in which two explorers, William Beebe and Otia Barton, set the world depth record and saw mysterious creatures of the deep ocean

"Attractive color photos contribute to the content." SLJ

Includes glossary and bibliographical references

McMillan, Beverly

Oceans; [by] Beverly McMillan and John N. Musick. Simon & Schuster Books for Young Readers 2007 64p il map (Insiders) $16.99

Grades: 4 5 6 7   551.46

1. Ocean 2. Marine ecology 3. Marine biology

ISBN 978-1-4169-3859-0; 1-4169-3859-1

LC 2007-61730

"This first half of this richly illustrated guide introduces general concepts: how the ocean was formed, what lives in it, and how scientists have collected this information. The book then focuses on the various bio-zones and ecosystems supported by and within the ocean." Horn Book

This book will "assault the reader with vibrant colors and eye-popping graphics. The illustrations range in size from full-page background art to thumbnails. Even the smallest pictures are clear, with easy to distinguish details; all are either labeled or captioned. . . . You may want to purchase more than one copy." Libr Media Connect

Includes glossary

Morrison, Taylor, 1971-

Tsunami warning. Houghton Mifflin 2007 32p il map $17

Grades: 4 5 6   551.46

1. Tsunamis 2. Weather forecasting

ISBN 978-0-618-73463-4; 0-618-73463-5

LC 2006035640

"With particular reference to the tsunamis that struck Hawaii in 1946 and 1957, Morrison explains the creation of an earthquake warning system around the eastern edge of the Pacific Ocean." Booklist

"The text is brief and could use more elaboration in spots, but it is nonetheless effective. Attractive paintings help tell the story and demonstrate the technology involved." SLJ

Includes glossary and bibliographical references

Yount, Lisa

Modern marine science; exploring the deep. Chelsea House 2006 204p il map (Milestones in discovery and invention) $35

Grades: 7 8 9 10 11 12   551.46

1. Marine sciences

ISBN 0-8160-5747-8   LC 2005-30562

This book "profiles 12 men and women who led the way into the oceans' deepest waters through research and new technologies. From Charles Darwin to Henry Stommel to Robert Ballard, this volume explores the lives and accomplishments of these scientific revolutionaries." Publisher's note

Includes glossary and bibliographical references

551.48   Hydrology

Allaby, Michael, 1933-

Floods; [by] Michael Allaby; illustrations by Richard Garratt. rev ed. Facts on File 2003 196p il map (Dangerous weather) $40

Grades: 7 8 9 10   551.48

1. Floods

ISBN 0-8160-4794-4   LC 2002-153845

First published 1998

The author describes: floodplains and meanders; aquifers, springs, and wells; natural drainage; floods and agriculture; latent heat and dewpoint; tsunamis; tidal surges; coastal erosion; prevention, warning, and survival. Illustrated with black-and-white photographs, drawings, charts and graphs

Includes bibliographical references

Burnham, Laurie

Rivers; foreword by Geoffrey H. Nash. Chelsea House 2007 176p il map (The extreme Earth) $35

Grades: 8 9 10 11 12   551.48

1. Rivers

ISBN 0-8160-5916-0; 978-0-8160-5916-4

LC 2006-31302

This is a "portrait of 10 of the most unusual rivers that examines what was on-site before the river, how it was formed, how and why it has changed over time, and its contributions to the environment." Publisher's note

Includes glossary and bibliographical references

Carrigan, Patricia
Waterfalls. Chelsea House 2007 146p il (The extreme Earth) $35
Grades: 8 9 10 11 12   **551.48**
1. Waterfalls
ISBN 978-0-8160-6436-6; 0-8160-6436-9
Presents an introduction to waterfalls, describing how they develop and how they are used to generate power, and providing the history and current formation of ten of the world's most famous waterfalls

Desonie, Dana
Hydrosphere; freshwater systems and pollution. Chelsea House 2008 194p il map (Our fragile planet) $35
Grades: 7 8 9 10   **551.48**
1. Water pollution 2. Water purification
ISBN 978-0-8160-6215-7; 0-8160-6215-3
       LC 2007-22398
"Looks at the environmental and health effects of water pollution." Publisher's note
Includes glossary and bibliographical references

Hanson, Jeanne K.
Lakes; foreword, Geoffrey H. Nash. Facts on File 2007 146p il map (The extreme Earth) $35
Grades: 8 9 10 11 12   **551.48**
1. Lakes
ISBN 978-0-8160-5914-0; 0-8160-5914-4
       LC 2005-34327
This describes how lakes are formed, the current environmental health of the lakes and their future prognosis, and some specific bodies of water including the Caspian Sea in the Middle East, the Aral Sea in Western Asia, Lake Superior in North America, Lake Baikal in Central Asia, and Lake Titicaca in South America.
Includes bibliographical references

551.5   Meteorology

Banqueri, Eduardo, 1966-
Weather. Enchanted Lion Books 2006 33p il (Field guides) $16.95
Grades: 4 5 6 7   **551.5**
1. Weather
ISBN 1-59270-059-4   LC 2006-42864
This "book is filled with information about all aspects of weather, from why there are seasons to predicting the weather. Complementing the scientifically accurate text is an excellent mix of drawings and photographs." Sci Books and Films

Carson, Mary Kay, 1964-
Weather projects for young scientists; experiments and science fair ideas. Chicago Review Press 2007 134p il $14.95
Grades: 4 5 6 7   **551.5**
1. Weather 2. Science—Experiments
ISBN 978-1-55652-629-9; 1-55652-629-6
       LC 2006-16430

This covers "fundamentals about the water cycle and seasons as well as more sophisticated topics, such as pressure systems, greenhouse gases, and forecasting. The information alternates with more than 40 activities." Booklist
This "presents difficult concepts in a very concrete, basic manner." Sci Books Films

Cosgrove, Brian, 1926-
Weather; written by Brian Cosgrove. rev ed. DK Publishing 2007 72p il map (DK eyewitness books) $15.99; lib bdg $19.99
Grades: 4 5 6 7   **551.5**
1. Weather 2. Climate 3. Atmosphere
ISBN   978-0-7566-3006-5;   0-7566-3006-1; 978-0-7566-0737-1 (lib bdg); 0-7566-0737-X (lib bdg)
       LC 2007-281112
First published 1991 by Knopf
"Discover the world's weather—from heat waves and droughts to blizzards and floods"—Cover. Includes discussion of why the climate may change in the future.
"Accompanying the book are a poster, additional images on CD-ROM, and a useful glossary. Altogether, this book and its supplements are well crafted to motivate young learners about the importance of weather, to deepen their conceptual understanding of it, and to pique their interest in participating in its study." Sci Books Films
Includes glossary

Farndon, John
Extreme weather; written by John Farndon. 1st American ed. DK 2007 65p il map $15.99
Grades: 6 7 8 9   **551.5**
1. Weather
ISBN 978-0-7566-2837-6; 0-7566-2837-7
       LC 2007279512
Describes a wide variety of extreme weather such as tornadoes, droughts, storms, and extreme hot and cold temperatures.

Gardner, Robert, 1929-
Meteorology projects with a weather station you can build; by Robert Gardner. Enslow Publishers 2008 128p il (Build-a-lab! science experiments) lib bdg $31.93
Grades: 6 7 8 9   **551.5**
1. Meteorology 2. Weather forecasting 3. Science— Experiments 4. Science projects
ISBN 978-0-7660-2807-4 (lib bdg); 0-7660-2807-0 (lib bdg)   LC 2007010614
This describes science experiments and projects on such topics as wind, temperature, rain, clouds, climate and other aspects of weather.
Includes bibliographical references

Silverstein, Alvin

Weather and climate; [by] Alvin Silverstein, Virginia Silverstein, and Laura Silverstein Nunn. rev ed. Twenty-First Century Books 2008 96p il map (Science concepts, second series) lib bdg $31.93

Grades: 6 7 8 9   **551.5**

1. Weather 2. Meteorology 3. Climate

ISBN 978-0-8225-6796-7; 0-8225-6796-2

LC 2007003188

First published 1998

Examines the changes in the atmosphere that produce various weather phenomena and how weather patterns over a period of time determine the climates of the Earth's various regions.

Includes bibliographical references

Vogt, Gregory

The atmosphere; planetary heat engine; by Gregory L. Vogt. Twenty-First Century Books 2007 80p il map (Earth spheres) lib bdg $29.27

Grades: 6 7 8 9   **551.5**

1. Atmosphere 2. Weather

ISBN 978-0-76132-841-4 (lib bdg); 0-76132-841-6 (lib bdg)

LC 2006-07391

"The book covers a wide range of topics, including air currents, the water cycle, . . . meteorology, and climate change, and explores how they affect our daily lives. A good deal of discussion is devoted to scientists' use of satellites and other high-tech tools to study the atmosphere. Color graphs, photographs, and sidebars . . . supplement the accessible text." Booklist

Includes bibliographical references

551.51 Composition, regions, dynamics of atmosphere

Friend, Sandra

Earth's wild winds. 21st Cent. Bks. (Brookfield) 2002 32p il maps (Exploring planet earth) lib bdg $24.90

Grades: 5 6 7 8   **551.51**

1. Winds

ISBN 0-7613-2673-1   LC 2001-6515

Examines different aspects of the wind, including its measurement, effects on weather, potential destructiveness, and uses

"This attractive and fact-filled book will be useful for earth-science reports. . . . The full-color charts, maps, and photos contribute immeasurably to the success of the presentation." SLJ

Includes bibliographical references

Gallant, Roy A.

Atmosphere; sea of air. Benchmark Bks. 2002 79p il (Earthworks) lib bdg $19.95

Grades: 5 6 7 8   **551.51**

1. Atmosphere 2. Meteorology

ISBN 0-7614-1366-9   LC 2001-43301

Describes the atmosphere which makes life on earth possible, explores its effects on weather and climate, and examines what causes air pollution and what can be done it

"Gallant's prose is nearly conversational in its easy delivery, but his facts are always thorough and his ideas clearly explained. . . . Crisp graphs, maps, and excellent color photos illustrate [this] fine [volume]." Booklist

Includes glossary and bibliographical references

551.55 Atmospheric disturbances and formations

Ceban, Bonnie J.

Hurricanes, typhoons, and cyclones; disaster & survival; [by] Bonnie J. Ceban. Enslow Pubs. 2005 48p il map (Deadly disasters) lib bdg $31.93

Grades: 4 5 6 7   **551.55**

1. Hurricanes 2. Typhoons 3. Cyclones

ISBN 0-7660-2388-5

This briefly explains the science of hurricanes, typhoons, and cyclones; describes Cyclone Tracy in Australia in 1974, Hurricanes Andrew and Floyd in Florida in 1991 and 1999 respectively, and Typhoon Tokage in Japan in 2004; and suggests safety precautions.

Includes glossary and bibliographical references

Tornadoes; disaster & survival; [by] Bonnie J. Ceban. Enslow Publishers 2005 48p il map (Deadly disasters) $23.93

Grades: 4 5 6 7   **551.55**

1. Tornadoes

ISBN 0-7660-2383-4   LC 2004-11700

This explores the causes of tornadoes, how people survive these storms, and how they are predicted.

Includes glossary and bibliographical references

Fradin, Judith Bloom

Hurricanes; by Judy and Dennis Fradin. National Geographic 2007 48p il (Witness to disaster) $16.95; lib bdg $26.90 *

Grades: 4 5 6 7   **551.55**

1. Hurricanes

ISBN 978-1-4262-0111-0; 1-4262-0111-7; 978-1-4262-0112-7 (lib bdg); 1-4262-0112-5 (lib bdg)

LC 2006-103003

This describes Hurricane Katrina, the science of hurricanes, some hurricanes of the past, and the prediction of hurricanes.

This offers "dramatic first-person quotes and an array of impressive photographs." Horn Book Guide

Includes glossary and bibliographical references

Harris, Caroline, 1964-

Wild weather. Kingfisher 2005 53p il map (Kingfisher voyages) $14.95

Grades: 4 5 6 7   **551.55**

1. Storms 2. Weather

ISBN 0-7534-5931-0; 978-0-7534-5911-9

This describes weather phenomena such as monsoons, tsunamis, blizzards, tornadoes, cyclones, mirages, and El

Harris, Caroline, 1964-—Continued

Niño.

This "book has bright and exciting pictures. . . . The organization . . . is great, and the text is easy to read." Sci Books Films

Includes glossary

Lindop, Laurie

Chasing tornadoes. Twenty-First Century Books 2003 80p il map (Science on the edge) lib bdg $26.90

Grades: 7 8 9 10   551.55

1. Tornadoes

ISBN 0-7613-2703-7   LC 2002-14250

Contents: Tornado!; Tornado research; Project Vortex; History of tornado science; When a tornado strikes

In this title "researchers chase tornadoes and waterspouts using many different modes of transportation in order to document the weather conditions that cause these deadly storms. . . . A great deal of scientific information is included. . . . [The book is] profusely illustrated with well-placed color photographs." SLJ

Includes bibliographical references

Longshore, David

Encyclopedia of hurricanes, typhoons, and cyclones. New ed. Facts on File 2008 468p il map (Facts on File science library) $75

Grades: 8 9 10 11 12 Adult   551.55

1. Hurricanes—Encyclopedias 2. Typhoons—Encyclopedias 3. Cyclones—Encyclopedias 4. Reference books

ISBN 978-0-8160-6295-9; 0-8160-6295-1

LC 2007-32336

First published 1998

This encyclopedia describes named hurricanes, typhoons and cyclones, explains meteorological terms and instruments, and includes biographical data, a chronology, and a list of hurricane safety procedures.

"This is an excellent basic reference work that belongs in all school, public, and academic libraries." Sci Books Films

Includes bibliographical references

Prokos, Anna

Tornadoes; by Anna Prokos. Gareth Stevens Pub. 2009 48p il map (The ultimate 10. Natural disasters) lib bdg $31

Grades: 5 6 7 8   551.55

1. Tornadoes

ISBN 978-0-8368-9153-9; 0-8368-9153-8

LC 2008-18949

Explains how tornadoes "happen, what damage they cause, and how to stay safe from one." Publisher's note

Tornadoes "are described, while color photos illustrate the resulting damage, conveying a significant part of the information through their captions. . . . Explanations of weather terms . . . are included; additional facts are boxed off from the text; and preparation/safety tips are appended. . . . An especially useful book." SLJ

Includes glossary and bibliographical references

Ryback, Carol

Hurricanes; by Carol Ryback and Jayne Keedle. Gareth Stevens Pub. 2009 48p il map (The ultimate 10. Natural disasters) lib bdg $31

Grades: 5 6 7 8   551.55

1. Hurricanes

ISBN 978-0-8368-9152-2 (lib bdg); 0-8368-9152-X (lib bdg)   LC 2008-24628

"A look at how hurricanes form, the destruction they cause, and what to do if one strikes your area." Publisher's note

Hurricanes "are described, while color photos illustrate the resulting damage, conveying a significant part of the information through their captions. . . . Explanations of weather terms . . . are included; additional facts are boxed off from the text; and preparation/safety tips are appended. . . . An especially useful book." SLJ

Includes glossary and bibliographical references

Simon, Seymour, 1931-

Tornadoes. Morrow Junior Bks. 1999 unp il map $16.95; pa $6.99 *

Grades: 4 5 6 7   551.55

1. Tornadoes

ISBN 0-688-14646-5; 0-06-443791-4 (pa)

LC 98-27953

Describes the location, nature, development, measurement, and destructive effects of tornadoes, as well as how to stay out of danger from them

"Incredible full-color photographs and diagrams, clearly portraying the different formations and devastating power of the windstorms, complement the text perfectly." Booklist

Stewart, Mark

Blizzards and winter storms; by Mark Stewart. Gareth Stevens Pub. 2009 48p il map (The ultimate 10. Natural disasters) lib bdg $31

Grades: 5 6 7 8   551.55

1. Blizzards 2. Storms

ISBN 978-0-8368-9150-8; 0-8368-9150-3

LC 2008-28230

A "look at how winter storms form and how they wreak havoc in different parts of the world." Publisher's note

Blizzards and winter storms "are described, while color photos illustrate the resulting damage, conveying a significant part of the information through their captions. . . . An especially useful book." SLJ

Includes glossary and bibliographical references

Treaster, Joseph B.

Hurricane force; in the path of America's deadliest storms. Kingfisher 2007 128p il map $16.95 *

Grades: 4 5 6 7 8   551.55

1. Hurricanes 2. Storms

ISBN 978-0-7534-6086-3   LC 2006-22517

Describes how violent storms and hurricanes are formed and notes some of history's greatest storms to hit the U.S. such as Hurricane Katrina.

This is a "gripping photo-essay. . . . There are lots of

Treaster, Joseph B.—*Continued*

full-color photographs that bring close the high winds and surging seas of hurricanes, the shattered homes, and pictures of people rescued or lost. The extensive back matter is an integral part of the book." Booklist

Includes bibliographical references

551.56 Atmospheric electricity and optics

Simon, Seymour, 1931-

Lightning. Morrow Junior Bks. 1997 unp il hardcover o.p. pa $6.99 *

Grades: 4 5 6 7   **551.56**

1. Lightning

ISBN 0-688-14638-4; 0-06-088435-5 (pa)

LC 96-16962

Photographs and text explore the natural phenomenon of lightning

"The subject is exciting, the information is amazing, and the full-color photographs are riveting. . . . Simon's explanations are concise but thorough." Booklist

551.57 Hydrometeorology

Allaby, Michael, 1933-

Droughts; illustrations by Richard Garratt. rev ed. Facts on File 2003 212p il map (Dangerous weather) $35 *

Grades: 7 8 9 10   **551.57**

1. Droughts

ISBN 0-8160-4793-6   LC 2002-13035

First published 1997

This examination of droughts and their impact includes "coverage of topics such as the geography of deserts; climate cycles and oscillations. . . . [Sidebars explain concepts] from atmospheric science, such as adiabatic cooling and warming, potential temperature, lapse rates, and the intertropical convergence and equatorial trough, as well as biological processes." Publisher's note

Gardner, Robert, 1929-

Science project ideas about rain. Enslow Pubs. 1997 96p il (Science project ideas) lib bdg $25.26

Grades: 7 8 9 10   **551.57**

1. Rain 2. Clouds 3. Science projects 4. Science—Experiments

ISBN 0-89490-843-X   LC 96-42411

Uses experiments to illustrate the properties of rain as well as the reasons that water is such an important part of life

"This useful collection of demonstrations, experiments, and information . . . is clearly written and well illustrated with charts and diagrams that assist in the understanding of the text." Voice Youth Advocates

Includes bibliographical references

551.6 Climatology and weather

Arnold, Caroline, 1944-

El Niño; stormy weather for people and wildlife. Clarion Bks. 1998 48p il $16; pa $5.95 *

Grades: 4 5 6 7   **551.6**

1. El Niño Current 2. Climate

ISBN 0-395-77602-3; 0-618-55110-7 (pa)

LC 98-4826

Explores the nature of the El Niño current and its effects on people and wildlife

This book has a "readable, informative text. . . . Full-color photos, a computer-image series, diagrams, and Internet sources bolster the narrative." SLJ

Includes glossary and bibliographical references

Christie, Peter, 1962-

The curse of Akkad; climate upheavals that rocked human history. Annick Press 2008 144p il map $19.95; pa $11.95

Grades: 6 7 8 9   **551.6**

1. Climate 2. World history

ISBN   978-1-55451-119-8;   1-55451-119-4; 978-1-55451-118-1 (pa); 1-55451-118-6 (pa)

"Christie discusses the ways in which environmental conditions have shaped human history. The chapters, each discussing a different aspect of climate change, are arranged in loose chronological order. Every section opens with a fictionalized account featuring either an imagined or a real historical figure. The author then explains how climate change caused the events to occur. . . . The book is well researched. . . . The text is readable." SLJ

Includes bibliographical references

Desonie, Dana

Climate; causes and effects of climate change. Chelsea House 2008 199p il map (Our fragile planet) $35

Grades: 7 8 9 10   **551.6**

1. Greenhouse effect 2. Climate—Environmental aspects

ISBN 978-0-8160-6214-0; 0-8160-6214-5

LC 2007-27825

"Discusses how human-related activities are contributing to the warming of the Earth's climate, describes the effects of climate change on people and the environment, and outlines measures that can be taken to help manage the problem." Publisher's note

Includes glossary and bibliographical references

Johnson, Rebecca L., 1956-

Investigating climate change; scientists' search for answers in a warming world; by Rebecca L. Johnson. Twenty-First Century Books 2008 c2009 111p il map (Discovery) lib bdg $30.60

Grades: 7 8 9 10   **551.6**

1. Greenhouse effect 2. Climate—Environmental aspects

ISBN 978-0-8225-6792-9; 0-8225-6792-X

LC 2007-38566

Johnson, Rebecca L., 1956-—*Continued*
This "presents contemporary scientific research into the causes of climate change. . . . Johnson . . . lays out complex scientific data and theories in an engaging, straightforward narrative that will not overwhelm readers. Complementing the text are numerous color diagrams, graphs, maps, and photographs." Booklist
Includes bibliographical references

Simpson, Kathleen
Extreme weather; science tackles global warming and climate change; by Kathleen Simpson; Jonathan D.W. Kahl, consultant. National Geographic 2008 64p il map (National Geographic investigates) $17.95; lib bdg $27.90 *
Grades: 4 5 6 7   **551.6**
1. Greenhouse effect 2. Climate—Environmental aspects
ISBN   978-1-4263-0359-3;   1-4263-0359-9;
978-1-4263-0281-7 (lib bdg); 1-4263-0281-9 (lib bdg)
"An exploration of extreme weather explains how weather is created, shows how hurricanes and tornadoes form and are rated, covers types of clouds and precipitation, and looks at the link between climate and weather." Publisher's note
This "is a well-written and engaging book. . . . Excellent descriptions of how and why these various weather patterns occur are presented. The book includes dramatic photographs and clear diagrams." Sci Books Films
Includes glossary and bibliographical references

Weather almanac. Gale Res. il maps * $165
Grades: 8 9 10 11 12 Adult   **551.6**
1. United States—Climate—Statistics 2. Weather—Statistics 3. Reference books
First published 1974. (11th edition 2003) Periodically revised
Editors vary
"Definitions and articles on major weather events and meteorological issues. Includes layperson's guide to 'weather fundamentals' and a glossary. Provides meteorological and climatological information and statistics for major U.S. and world cities." N Y Public Libr Book of How & Where to Look It Up

551.7   Historical geology

Gallant, Roy A.
History; journey through time. Benchmark Bks. 2002 c2003 80p il (Earthworks) lib bdg $19.95
Grades: 5 6 7 8   **551.7**
1. Stratigraphic geology
ISBN 0-7614-1367-7   LC 2001-43253
An overview of the history of the Earth, the life that evolved on it, and known periods of mass extinctions, from the planet's origin to the present
Includes glossary and bibliographical references

552   Petrology

Extreme rocks & minerals! Q & A. Collins 2007 47p il $17.99; pa $6.99
Grades: 4 5 6   **552**
1. Rocks 2. Minerals
ISBN   978-0-06-089982-0;   0-06-089982-4;
978-0-06-089981-3 (pa); 0-06-089981-6 (pa)
LC 2007001760
This describes types of rocks and minerals, how they are formed, and how people use them.
"It's hard to beat this title for a clear, accurate, and appealing survey. Illustrations are key to this subject, and the range of crisp photos is excellent." SLJ
Includes bibliographical references

Hynes, Margaret, 1970-
Rocks & fossils; foreword by Jack Horner. Kingfisher 2006 63p il (Kingfisher knowledge) $12.95
Grades: 5 6 7 8   **552**
1. Rocks 2. Fossils
ISBN 978-0-7534-5974-4; 0-7534-5974-4
LC 2005-23897
This covers "the history of rock, . . . the minerals that make them, and . . . their different uses, from building materials to pigments for paints and dyes. The formation of fossils is also explained." Publisher's note
This is a "lavishly illustrated book. . . . The well-written text is pithy and comprehensible." Voice Youth Advocates
Includes glossary and bibliographical references

Trueit, Trudi Strain
Rocks, gems, and minerals. Watts 2003 63p il $24; pa $8.95
Grades: 4 5 6 7   **552**
1. Rocks 2. Minerals 3. Precious stones
ISBN 0-531-12195-X; 0-531-16241-9 (pa)
LC 2001-7222
"Watts library"
Contents: World of wonders; Mineral magic; The circle of stone; A rocky road; Where do you stand?
"The formation of basic rocks— sedimentary, igneous, and metamorphic—are covered, as are rock crystals and crystallization. Chemical symbols for elements, charts such as the Mohs scale and the geographic location of major gem finds, and fun facts are included." SLJ
This includes "attention-grabbing photography, excellent charts and diagrams, short articles with or without photographs, and vocabulary terms that appear in bold and are explained in context." Sci Books Films
Includes glossary and bibliographical references

553.7   Water

Casper, Julie Kerr

Water and atmosphere; the lifeblood of natural systems. Chelsea House 2007 207p il map (Natural resources) $39.50

Grades: 8 9 10 11 12   **553.7**

1. Water supply 2. Atmosphere

ISBN 978-0-8160-6359-8; 0-8160-6359-1

LC 2007-261

This covers such topics as the roles of water and atmospheric resources in exploration and trade; climate change and global warming; renewable and nonrenewable resources; surface and ground water, aquifers, and other natural water reservoirs; management and environmental issues; effects on endangered species; future issues and the importance of public education; and marine exploration.

Includes bibliographical references

Gallant, Roy A.

Water; our precious resource. Benchmark Bks. 2002 c2003 79p il map (Earthworks) lib bdg $29.93

Grades: 5 6 7 8   **553.7**

1. Water

ISBN 0-7614-1365-0   LC 2001-43290

Contents: What is water?; Some properties of water; Where is all the water?; Our needs for water; Water pollution and purification; Whose water is it?

An in-depth look at Earth's waters and mankind's uses of water throughout history which includes ideas about planning better use of this critical resource in the future

"Gallant's prose is nearly conversational in its easy delivery, but his facts are always thorough and his ideas clearly explained. Best of all, he raises informed points that will help readers rethink their habits and realize the complexity of the issues. . . . Crisp graphs, maps, and excellent color photos illustrate [this] fine [volume]." Booklist

Includes glossary and bibliographical references

Woodward, John, 1954-

Water; written by John Woodward. DK Pub. 2009 72p il (DK eyewitness books) $16.99; lib bdg $19.99

Grades: 4 5 6 7   **553.7**

1. Water

ISBN 978-0-7566-4537-3; 0-7566-4537-9; 978-0-7566-4538-0 (lib bdg); 0-7566-4538-7 (lib bdg)

Includes CD-ROM

Takes a look at the role of water in our bodies, our cultures, and our world.

557   Earth sciences of North America

Collier, Michael, 1950-

Over the mountains; an aerial view of geology; foreword by John S. Shelton. Mikaya Press 2007 unp il map $29.95 *

Grades: 8 9 10 11 12   **557**

1. Geology—North America 2. Mountains 3. Aerial photography

ISBN 1-931414-18-1; 978-1-931414-18-0

LC 2006-47151

The author "expresses his passion for geology through awe-inspiring aerial photographs that reveal how mountains were formed and modified across the eons of time. . . . The four sections of this book explore what mountains are, why some are peaked and others rounded, and why they are often strung together in ranges. . . . Collier's love for the land is contagious, and his flying field trips over the mountains are thrilling." Voice Youth Advocates

Includes bibliographical references

560   Fossils & prehistoric life

Bradley, Timothy J.

Paleo bugs; survival of the creepiest; written and illustrated by Timothy J. Bradley. Chronicle Books 2008 44p il $15.99 *

Grades: 4 5 6 7   **560**

1. Insects 2. Fossils 3. Prehistoric animals

ISBN 978-0-8118-6022-2; 0-8118-6022-1

LC 2007-18174

This offers an "eye-widening gallery of extinct arthropods, from the mayfly-like heptagenia to a seven-foot-long arthropleura. . . . Bradley decks out each of his painted figures in bright hues, poses them in natural settings . . . and sets them aside a human hand or body in silhouette to suggest scale. . . . Readers will . . . pore over the pictures and come away knowing more about both these extinct animals and their modern descendants." Booklist

Includes glossary and bibliographical references

Harrison, David Lee, 1937-

Cave detectives; unraveling the mystery of an Ice Age cave; written by David L. Harrison; illustrated by Ashley Mims; cave photographs by Edward Biamonte. Chronicle Books 2007 47p il $15.95 *

Grades: 4 5 6 7   **560**

1. Caves 2. Prehistoric animals 3. Fossils 4. Ice Age

ISBN 978-0-8118-5006-3; 0-8118-5006-4

LC 2005-30067

This "documents the discovery of a cave found in Greene County, Missouri, in 2001. . . . The book focuses on the investigations of a team of scientists . . . to map and explore the cave's many mysteries and wonders. . . . [The book] does a nice job explaining the ice age and how caves are formed and fossils created. It includes illustrations of animals and fossils found in or around Riverbluff Cave." Sci Books Films

Kimmel, Elizabeth Cody

Dinosaur bone war; Cope and Marsh's fossil feud. Random House 2006 118p il lib bdg $11; pa $5.99

Grades: 4 5 6   **560**

1. Cope, E. D. (Edward Drinker), 1840-1897 2. Marsh, Othniel Charles, 1831-1899 3. Fossils

ISBN 0-375-91349-1 (lib bdg); 0-375-81349-7 (pa)

"Writing in a lively style, Kimmel provides a solid introduction to the story of Edward Cope and Charlie Marsh, whose rivalry energized a new field of science, paleontology. . . . Black-and-white photographs and historical documents add to the book's pleasing accessibility." Booklist

Includes bibliographical references

Larson, Peter L.

Bones rock! everything you need to know to be a paleontologist; [by] Peter Larson and Kristin Donnan. 1st ed. Invisible Cities Press 2004 204p il pa $19.95

Grades: 5 6 7 8   **560**

1. Fossils

ISBN 1-93122-935-X   LC 2004-413

"Revealing true stories about kids who have made paleo-discoveries and providing young readers with the tools necessary to make the next big discovery, this book shows kids how to collect, clean, and study fossil samples in order to develop and further their own research interests." Publisher's note

"Illustrations include high-quality color photographs and helpful diagrams and drawings. There's fascinating information here, and Larson's enthusiasm and sound advice give plenty of encouragement to young scientists." SLJ

Includes bibliographical references

Sabuda, Robert

Sharks and other sea monsters; [by] Robert Sabuda & Matthew Reinhart. Candlewick Press 2006 unp il (Encyclopedia prehistorica) $27.99 *

Grades: 3 4 5 6 7   **560**

1. Prehistoric animals 2. Pop-up books

ISBN 0-7636-2229-X   LC 2005-44866

This pop-up book introduces such prehistoric creatures as giant sharks, sea scorpions, and squids.

"Gatefolds and inset minibooks expand the capacity of the book's seven spreads. . . . The sheer wonder generated by the collaborators' dimensional sleight-of-hand will more than justify purchase." Booklist

Taylor, Paul D., 1953-

Fossil; written by Paul D. Taylor. rev ed. DK Pub. 2004 72p il map (DK eyewitness books) $15.99; lib bdg $19.99 *

Grades: 4 5 6 7   **560**

1. Fossils

ISBN 0-7566-0682-9; 0-7566-0681-0 (lib bdg)

First published 1990 by Knopf

This book describes different types of fossils, from algae to birds and mammals.

Trueit, Trudi Strain

Fossils. Watts 2003 63p il $24; pa $8.95

Grades: 4 5 6   **560**

1. Fossils

ISBN 0-531-12196-8; 0-531-16242-7 (pa)

     LC 2001-8285

"Watts library"

Contents: Yesterday's world; Fossils forever; Digging into the past; Fascinating fossils; Dinosaurs and beyond; Treasure hunters

Presents information on fossils, including how different types are formed, how they have been used to date periods in Earth's history, and major areas of the world where fossil hunting is going on today

This includes "attention-grabbing photography, excellent charts and diagrams, short articles with or without photographs, and vocabulary terms that appear in bold and are explained in context." Sci Books Films

Includes glossary and bibliographical references

567   Fossil cold-blooded vertebrates Fossil Pisces (fishes)

Bradley, Timothy J.

Paleo sharks; survival of the strangest; written and illustrated by Timothy J. Bradley. Chronicle Books 2007 46p il $15.95

Grades: 4 5 6 7   **567**

1. Sharks 2. Fossils

ISBN 978-0-8118-4878-7; 0-8118-4878-7

     LC 2006-11652

This is "an intelligent, handsomely designed look at the ancient fish that are the forerunners of today's efficient predator, the shark. . . . Bradley uses bright colors and hard edges to delineate the best informed guesses as to what these sharks might have looked like." Booklist

Includes glossary and bibliographical references

Holmes, Thom

The first vertebrates; oceans of the Paleozoic era; [by] Thom Holmes. Chelsea House 2008 188p il (The prehistoric Earth) $35

Grades: 7 8 9 10   **567**

1. Fossils 2. Vertebrates

ISBN 978-0-8160-5958-4; 0-8160-5958-6

     LC 2007-45329

Describes the first instances of vertebrate life in the oceans of the Paleozoic Era, tracing the development of early fish from jawless species to sharks and bony fish.

This "is a comprehensive, well-written, and easily readable text. . . . The chapters are well-organized." Sci Books Films

Includes glossary and bibliographical references

567.9 Reptilia

Barrett, Paul M.

National Geographic dinosaurs; illustrated by Raul Martin; introduction by Kevin Padian. National Geographic Soc. 2001 192p il $29.95 *
Grades: 6 7 8 9   **567.9**
1. Dinosaurs
ISBN 0-7922-8224-8   LC 00-45263

"The opening chapters offer a chronology of the age of dinosaurs, a brief history of key discoveries, and . . . information about the creatures' habits and characteristics in general. The heart of the book is the 50 or so profiles of individual dinosaur genera, divided into the two major groups (bird-hipped and lizard-hipped)." SLJ

"Clearly distinguishing fact from theory, this book provides an exciting guide to the life and times of the dinosaurs." Sci Child

Includes glossary

Berkowitz, Jacob

Jurassic poop; what dinosaurs (and others) left behind; written by Jacob Berkowitz; illustrated by Steve Mack. Kids Can Press 2006 40p il $14.95; pa $7.95 *
Grades: 4 5 6 7   **567.9**
1. Fossils 2. Feces
ISBN   978-1-55337-860-0;   1-55337-860-1;
978-1-55337-867-9 (pa); 1-55337-867-9 (pa)

This describes fossilized feces, or coprolites, and what we can learn from them.

"Berkowitz' style is goofy and lighthearted, but there's plenty of real information. . . . The browsable format combines cartoony digital art, photographs . . . and design elements such a spiky borders and background shading." Bull Cent Child Books

Includes glossary

Collard, Sneed B., III

Reign of the sea dragons; illustrated by Andrew Plant. Charlesbridge 2008 61p il $17.95; pa $8.95 *
Grades: 5 6 7 8 9   **567.9**
1. Marine animals 2. Prehistoric animals
ISBN 978-1-58089-124-0; 978-1-58089-125-7 (pa)
                                    LC 2007-26201

"An arresting dust jacket depicting a humongous pliosaur snapping huge toothy jaws at a small, long-necked plesiosaur is an attention-grabber, but it is the informative text that brings these real sea monsters to life. Collard follows his usual pattern of careful organization, with a readable text and up-to-date information. . . . Plant has provided five full-color paintings, but it is his numerous black-and-white drawings that lend sturdy anatomical and physical information. . . . Collard's discussion on extinction theories is cogent." SLJ

Includes glossary, bibliographical references, and websites

Dingus, Lowell

Dinosaur eggs discovered! unscrambling the clues; [by] Lowell Dingus, Luis M. Chiappe [and] Rodolfo Coria. Twenty-First Century Books 2008 112p il map (Discovery!) lib bdg $30.60 *
Grades: 8 9 10 11 12   **567.9**
1. Dinosaurs 2. Fossils 3. Eggs
ISBN 978-0-8225-6791-2 (lib bdg); 0-8225-6791-1 (lib bdg)   LC 2006-102636

Recounts the discovery of a dinosaur nesting field containing a large number of eggs, describing the field work done to classify them, calculate the period of prehistory they came from, and identify the reasons why many of them never hatched.

This is "a valuable, unusually authoritative presentation for serious students of prehistoric life." Booklist

Includes glossary and bibliographical references

Dixon, Dougal, 1947-

Dougal Dixon's dinosaurs; [by] Dougal Dixon. 3rd ed. Boyds Mills Press 2007 160p il $19.95
Grades: 4 5 6 7   **567.9**
1. Dinosaurs
ISBN 978-1-59078-470-9   LC 2006037876
First published 1993

The life and times of dinosaurs, from their evolution to the present-day discovery of their fossils.

Includes glossary

Everhart, Michael J.

Sea monsters; prehistoric creatures of the deep; [by] Mike Everhart. National Geographic 2007 191p il map $30   **567.9**
1. Fossils 2. Marine animals 3. Prehistoric animals
ISBN 978-1-4262-0085-4; 1-4262-0085-4
                                    LC 2007-18671

Featuring "computer-generated images and 3D film clips—with 3D glasses—field photography by National Geographic cameramen, and much more, the book interweaves dramatic scenes of the far, far distant past; up-to-the-minute scientific profiles of nearly two dozen sea monsters; and a group portrait of the eccentric Sternberg family, Kansas-bred pioneers of marine paleontology." Publisher's note

Funston, Sylvia

Dino–why? the dinosaur question and answer book. Updated and rev. Maple Tree Press 2008 64p il $22.95; pa $10.95 *
Grades: 4 5 6 7   **567.9**
1. Dinosaurs
ISBN   978-1-897349-24-3;   1-897349-24-6;
978-1-897349-25-0 (pa); 1-897349-25-4 (pa)
                                    LC 2007-939082
First published 1992 by Joy Street Books with title: The dinosaur question and answer book

"This book is an excellent and highly readable introduction to dinosaurs. . . . The questions are well conceived, and the answers . . . are scientifically sound and up to date. . . . The illustrations, a few of them cartoon-like, are nicely drawn and useful." Sci Books Films

Halls, Kelly Milner, 1957-
Dinosaur mummies; beyond bare-bone fossils; illustrated by Rick Spears. Darby Creek 2003 48p il $17.95
Grades: 5 6 7 8   **567.9**
  1. Dinosaurs 2. Fossils
  ISBN 1-58196-000-X
After "explaining the fossilization process, the book spotlights six significant dinosaur mummies. . . . Halls' enthusiasm shines through in this well-researched and clearly written book. Drawings washed with color show how the dinosaurs might have looked, while many excellent color photos illustrate the fossilized finds, and dinosaur diggers and paleontologists at work." Booklist
Includes bibliographical references

Holtz, Thomas R., 1965-
Dinosaurs; the most complete, up-to-date encyclopedia for dinosaur lovers of all ages; by Dr. Thomas R. Holtz, Jr.; illustrated by Luis V. Rey. Random House 2007 427p il $34.99; lib bdg $37.99 *
Grades: 7 8 9 10   **567.9**
  1. Dinosaurs
  ISBN   978-0-375-82419-7;   0-375-82419-7; 978-0-375-92419-4 (lib bdg); 0-375-92419-1 (lib bdg)
                                LC 2006-102491
This "covers everything from dinosaur eggs to taxonomy and cladistics to the history of paleontology, glued together with chapters on the dinosaurs themselves. . . . The illustrations range from small photos to larger sepia-toned drawings to even larger full-color paintings. . . . This eye-catching imagination grabber will be enjoyed (on different levels) by dinophiles of all ages." SLJ
Includes glossary

Kelsey, Elin
Canadian dinosaurs. Maple Tree Press 2004 96p il $29.95; pa $19.95
Grades: 4 5 6   **567.9**
  1. Dinosaurs
  ISBN 1-894379-55-1; 1-894379-56-X (pa)
  "A Wow Canada! book"
"The main text discusses topics such as the types of dinosaurs that lived in Canada, recent discoveries as well as the country's history of paleontology, and the art of creating dinosaur exhibits. The many sidebars introduce individual researchers, events, and information of special interest. The colorful pages feature many excellent photos of fossils and sites as well as images of how the dinosaurs may have looked. . . . A treasure trove for . . . dinosaur fans." Booklist
  Includes glossary

Lambert, David, 1932-
DK guide to dinosaurs. DK Pub. 2000 64p il maps $19.95
Grades: 6 7 8 9   **567.9**
  1. Dinosaurs
  ISBN 0-7894-5237-5   LC 99-39207
  Depicts how dinosaurs lived and died, covering such topics as habitats, size, hunting techniques, self-defense, courtship, and family life

Long, John A., 1957-
Dinosaurs; [by] John Long. Simon & Schuster Books for Young Readers 2007 64p il (Insiders) lib bdg $16.99 *
Grades: 4 5 6 7   **567.9**
  1. Dinosaurs
  ISBN 978-1-4169-3857-6 (lib bdg); 1-4169-3857-5 (lib bdg)   LC 2007-61735
"The first section includes paleontological periods, extinction theories, and a . . . pictorial time line tracing the first bird archaeopteryx to the earliest feathered dinosaurs. The second section contains profiles of a diverse selection of species." Booklist
"Richly hued, crisp computer-generated art and 3D model imagery serve as a stunning and sophisticated graphic counterpoint to the educational text." Publ Wkly
  Includes glossary

Feathered dinosaurs; the origin of birds; foreword by Luis M. Chiappe. Oxford University Press 2008 193p il $39.95
Grades: 7 8 9 10   **567.9**
  1. Dinosaurs 2. Birds 3. Fossils
  ISBN 978-0-19-537266-3; 0-19-537266-2
                                LC 2008-1232
A "record of feathered dinosaurs illuminates the evolutionary march from these . . . prehistoric creatures through to the first true flying birds and includes . . . text that places these feathered dinosaurs within the larger family of dinosaurs." Publisher's note
  Includes bibliographical references

Malam, John, 1957-
Dinosaur atlas; authors, John Malam and John Woodward; consultant Michael Benton. Dorling Kindersley 2006 96p il map $19.99
Grades: 5 6 7 8   **567.9**
  1. Dinosaurs
  ISBN 0-7566-2235-2; 978-0-7566-2235-0
                                LC 2006-285529
  Includes CD-ROM
"The atlas is organized by continent. Each section is prefaced with a large map showing where various species are found, with a picture and a brief synopsis of each species on the facing page. . . . Each introductory map is followed by several regional maps, surveying important local fossil sites and formations. Each section provides attractive diorama snapshots for a wide range of periods and locations." Sci Books Films
  Includes glossary

Manning, Phillip Lars, 1967-
Dinomummy; the life, death, and discovery of Dakota, a dinosaur from Hell Creek; foreword by Tyler Lyson. Kingfisher 2007 64p il map $18.95 *
Grades: 4 5 6 7   **567.9**
  1. Dinosaurs 2. North Dakota
  ISBN 978-0-7534-6047-4; 0-7534-6047-5
                                LC 2007-02878
Tells about the discovery of the fossil remains of a hadrosaur in the hills of the Hell Creek Formation in

Manning, Phillip Lars, 1967—*Continued*
North Dakota.

"The color photographs and simple text offer a detailed account of carefully unearthing the fossil and transporting it safely to the laboratory, where many tests were performed. Dinosaurs buffs and young scientists will love this book. It is a thrilling story that is part narrative, part mystery, and part science lesson." Voice Youth Advocates

Relf, Patricia

A dinosaur named Sue: the story of the colossal fossil: the world's most complete T. rex; by Pat Relf; with the sue Science Team of the Field Museum. Scholastic 2000 64p il $15.95

Grades: 5 6 7 8   **567.9**
1. Fossils 2. Dinosaurs
ISBN 0-439-09985-4   LC 00-38038

"Sue, named after discoverer Susan Hendrickson, is the most complete *Tyrannosaurus Rex* in existence. The reader follows the scientific journey from the fossil excavation in 1990 to its display at Chicago's Field Museum." Sci Child

"Readers will get a real sense of the team effort that science can be. . . . Many color photographs, as well as diagrams and paintings, appear throughout the book." Booklist

Sabuda, Robert

Dinosaurs; by Robert Sabuda and Matthew Reinhart. 1st ed. Candlewick Press 2005 unp il (Encyclopedia prehistorica) $26.99 *

Grades: 3 4 5 6 7   **567.9**
1. Dinosaurs 2. Pop-up books
ISBN 0-7636-2228-1   LC 2004-51899

"With Sabuda lending deft paper engineering to artwork rendered by Reinhart, who also wrote this book's text, the Mesozoic's major players leap into three dimensions. Pop-ups featured on the six spreads include a gargantuan brachiosaurus; an anklyosaurus studded with paper spikes; and, perhaps most impressive from a technical standpoint, a minutely detailed T. rex skeleton." Booklist

Sloan, Christopher

Bizarre dinosaurs; some very strange creatures and why we think they got that way; [by] Christopher Sloan; with a foreword by James Clark and Cathy Forster. National Geographic 2008 31p il $16.95; lib bdg $25.90

Grades: 4 5 6 7   **567.9**
1. Dinosaurs
ISBN   978-1-4263-0330-2;   1-4263-0330-0; 978-1-4263-0331-9 (lib bdg); 1-4263-0331-9 (lib bdg)

This "book should engage children of all ages who are fascinated by dinosaurs. . . . The illustrations are of uniformly high quality. . . . Each species gets two pages of text, including a full-page illustration; an inset with basic facts such as range, diet, and geological period in which it lived; a silhouette comparing their size with that of humans; and a paragraph of text." Sci Books Films

Feathered dinosaurs; introduction by Philip J. Currie. National Geographic Soc. 2000 64p il $17.95

Grades: 5 6 7 8   **567.9**
1. Dinosaurs 2. Birds 3. Fossils
ISBN 0-7922-7219-6   LC 00-27001

Looks at the evidence of dinosaurs with skeletal structures and feathers so similar to birds and why that is convincing many scientists that birds evolved from dinosaurs

"This exciting title combines an accurate, readable text and excellent drawings, photos, and diagrams." SLJ

How dinosaurs took flight; the fossils, the science, what we think we know, and the mysteries yet unsolved; foreword by Dr. Xu Xing. National Geographic 2005 64p il $17.95 *

Grades: 5 6 7 8   **567.9**
1. Dinosaurs 2. Birds 3. Fossils
ISBN 0-7922-7298-6

This explains the evolutionary relationships between dinosaurs and birds, based on fossils and the latest research.

Includes glossary and bibliographical references

Supercroc and the origin of crocodiles; introduction by Paul Sereno. National Geographic Soc. 2002 55p il map $18.95

Grades: 5 6 7 8   **567.9**
1. Fossil reptiles 2. Crocodiles
ISBN 0-7922-6691-9   LC 2001-3976

Discusses prehistoric crocodiles, including the discovery of SuperCroc in the Sahara Desert, and the lifestyles, habitats, and conservation of modern crocodiles

"Fans of paleontology or of crocodiles will find a great deal of information clearly explained. The illustrations are up to the high National Geographic standard." Booklist

Includes glossary

Zoehfeld, Kathleen Weidner

Dinosaur parents, dinosaur young; uncovering the mystery of dinosaur families; with full-color paintings by Paul Carrick and line drawings by Bruce Shillinglaw. Clarion Bks. 2001 58p il map $17

Grades: 4 5 6 7   **567.9**
1. Dinosaurs 2. Fossils
ISBN 0-395-91338-1   LC 00-43101

The author "guides readers through the complex historical trail of evidence collection and theory development that make up what we currently believe we know about dinosaur family life." Horn Book Guide

"High-quality, color photographs of fossils of eggs and embryos and of paleontologists at work as well as line drawings and full-color paintings add to this inviting, thought-provoking book." SLJ

Includes glossary and bibliographical references

569 Fossil mammalia

Agenbroad, Larry D.
Mammoths; ice-age giants; [by] Larry D. Agenbroad and Lisa Nelson. Lerner Publs. 2002 120p il (Discovery!) lib bdg $27.93; pa $7.95
Grades: 5 6 7 8   **569**
1. Mammoths
ISBN 0-8225-2862-2 (lib bdg); 0-8225-0470-7 (pa)
LC 2001-1147
"Chapters discuss what is currently known about [mammoths] . . . when and where they lived, and the discovery of remains. The authors present several theories as to why mammoths might have died out. The book is well documented, and the many photos and drawings add clarity to the text." Horn Book Guide
Includes glossary and bibliographical references

Giblin, James, 1933-
The mystery of the mammoth bones; and how it was solved. HarperCollins Pubs. 1999 97p il lib bdg $16.89 *
Grades: 4 5 6 7   **569**
1. Peale, Charles Willson, 1741-1827 2. Mastodon 3. Mammoths 4. Fossil mammals
ISBN 0-06-027494-8   LC 98-6701
Describes the efforts of the artist, museum curator, and self-taught paleontologist, Charles Willson Peale, to excavate, study, and display the bones of a prehistoric creature that is later named "mastodon"
"Giblin's research is superb, and he turns to Peale's actual notes for details. He also includes recent information about the mammoth (and mastodon)." SLJ
Includes bibliographical references

Sabuda, Robert
Mega beasts; [by] Robert Sabuda & Matthew Reinhart. 1st ed. Candlewick Press 2007 unp il (Encyclopedia prehistorica) $27.99 *
Grades: 3 4 5 6 7   **569**
1. Prehistoric animals 2. Pop-up books
ISBN 978-0-7636-2230-5; 0-7636-2230-3
LC 2006052791
Pop-up illustrations and text about such prehistoric creatures as quetzalcoatlus, therapsids, megatherium, saber-toothed tiger, and wooly mammoth.
"Thick with layers of carefully painted, cut, folded, and glued papers, this book is designed to amaze, and so it does." Booklist

Turner, Alan, 1947-
National Geographic prehistoric mammals; illustrated by Mauricio Antón. National Geographic 2004 192p il map $29.95; lib bdg $49.90 *
Grades: 5 6 7 8   **569**
1. Fossil mammals
ISBN 0-7922-7134-3; 0-7922-6997-7 (lib bdg)
LC 2004-1189

This describes the Age of Mammals and profiles over 100 prehistoric mammals, including time lines, fact boxes, distribution maps, photos of fossils, and illustrations
"Dramatic full-color pictures . . . and captions enhance the brief, informative text." SLJ

570 Life sciences; biology

Biology; Richard Robinson, editor in chief. Macmillan Ref. USA 2002 4v set $395
Grades: 8 9 10 11 12 Adult   **570**
1. Biology 2. Reference books
ISBN 0-02-865551-6   LC 2001-40211
This set "provides 432 signed entries on a broad range of topics pertaining to biology, including basic concepts . . . history of the science . . . related fields . . . and issues . . . as well as topics of interest to young adults, such as smoking, birth control, alcohol, and STDs. . . . The eye-pleasing layout features many colorful photographs and diagrams that will appeal to casual browsers and the articles contain more than enough information to meet the needs of students. This informative set is highly recommended." Booklist
Includes bibliographical references

Biology matters! Grolier 2004 10v il set $389 *
Grades: 5 6 7 8 9 10   **570**
1. Biology 2. Reference books
ISBN 0-7172-5979-X   LC 2003-56942
Contents: v1 Introduction to biology; v2 Cell biology; v3 Genetics; v4 Microorganisms; v5 Plants; v6 Animals; v7 The human body; v8 Reproduction; v9 Evolution; v10 Ecology
"This set presents the fundamentals of the life sciences in a clear format. . . . Volumes contain between six and eight articles in 80 pages . . . introducing its subject, presenting a brief history, and covering many aspects of its current study and applications. . . . The text is large and easy to read, and the writing is straightforward. . . . This title . . . would be a useful addition for public and school libraries." Booklist

Calhoun, Yael
Plant and animal science fair projects; using beetles, weeds, seeds, and more. Enslow Pubs. 2005 128p il (Biology! best science projects) lib bdg $26.60
Grades: 7 8 9 10   **570**
1. Natural history 2. Science projects 3. Science—Experiments
ISBN 0-7660-2368-0   LC 2004-25172
This offers instructions for science fair projects covering such topics as biological diversity, plant growth, exercise and muscle growth, seed dispersal, and bird bills and food gathering.
Includes glossary and bibliographical references

The **Facts** on File biology handbook; [by] The Diagram Group. rev ed. Facts on File 2006 272p il (Facts on File science library) $35 *
Grades: 8 9 10 11 12   **570**
1. Biology
ISBN 0-8160-5877-6   LC 2004-59270

The Facts on File biology handbook—*Continued*
First published 2000

Topics covered include: amniocentesis, synthesis, hormones, glands, embryo, ventricle, and zygote. Francis Bacon, Edwin Hubble, and Linus Pauling are among the 400 scientists profiled. Includes a chronology of significant developments and discoveries from ancient Greece to the present day. Illustrated with tables, charts, and diagrams.

Includes bibliographical references

571.3   Anatomy and morphology

Animal anatomy on file; [by] the Diagram Group. New ed. Facts on File 2003 various paging il loose-leaf $185

Grades: Professional   **571.3**
1. Comparative anatomy
ISBN 0-8160-5102-X   LC 2003-49145
Replaces the edition published 1999
Also available CD-ROM version
First published 1990

This looseleaf volume offers 270 labeled photocopiable charts and diagrams of the internal and external anatomy of animals, divided into the following categories: lower groups; annelids and mollusks; anthropods and echinoderms; lower chordates and fish; amphibians and reptiles; birds; mammals

Includes glossary and bibliographical references

571.4   Biophysics

Winner, Cherie
Cryobiology. Lerner Publications Co. 2006 48p il (Cool science) lib bdg $26.60

Grades: 4 5 6   **571.4**
1. Cryobiology
ISBN 978-0-8225-2907-1; 0-8225-2907-6
      LC 2005006158

This book "discusses how different life forms survive low temperatures, e.g., hibernating animals. . . . [The book provides] clear explanations of the science and [covers] possible benefits to humans. A variety of photos and information boxes provide an eye-catching . . . layout." Horn Book Guide

Includes glossary and bibliographical references

571.6   Cell biology

Lee, Kimberly Fekany
Cells. Compass Point Books 2009 40p il (Mission: science) lib bdg $26.60

Grades: 4 5 6   **571.6**
1. Cells
ISBN 978-0-7565-3954-2 (lib bdg); 0-7565-3954-4 (lib bdg)   LC 2008007719

"Lee describes the difference between plant and animal cells, and their contents; diffusion; and cell storage, movement, and reproduction. . . . Large eye-catching and colorful photographs and illustrations appear on every page. . . . The [book] includes a simple activity." SLJ

Includes glossary and bibliographical references

Rainis, Kenneth G.
Cell and microbe science fair projects using microscopes, mold, and more; Kenneth G. Rainis. Enslow Pub. 2005 128p il (Biology! best science projects) lib bdg $26.60

Grades: 7 8 9 10   **571.6**
1. Cells 2. Microbiology 3. Science projects
ISBN 0-7660-2369-9 (lib bdg)   LC 2004-15720

"An introduction to the study of cells and microbes within the parameters of scientific inquiry. A brief but informative chapter on the history of cell experimentation leads into an instructive discussion of the scientific method. The author then outlines several experiments. . . . This is a valuable title for readers serious about science and interested in the study of microorganisms." SLJ

Includes bibliographical references

Silverstein, Alvin
Cells; by Alvin & Virginia Silverstein and Laura Silverstein Nunn. Twenty-First Century Books 2009 112p il (Science concepts, second series) lib bdg $31.93

Grades: 6 7 8 9   **571.6**
1. Cells
ISBN 978-0-7613-3934-2; 0-7613-3934-5
      LC 2007051038

A presentation of the structure and function of different types of cells and of research into developing technologies such as cloning and the use of stem cells.

Includes glossary and bibliographical references

Stewart, Melissa, 1968-
Cell biology. Twenty-First Century Books 2008 80p il (Great ideas of science) lib bdg $27.93

Grades: 5 6 7 8   **571.6**
1. Cells
ISBN 978-0-8225-6603-8; 0-8225-6603-6
      LC 2006-28542

Describes how the field of cytology began, discusses how this field has enhanced others, and explores how the use of technology has impacted the field.

Includes bibliographical references

571.8   Reproduction, development, growth

Morgan, Sally
From sea urchins to dolly the sheep; discovering cloning; [by] Sally Morgan. Heinemann Library 2006 64p il (Chain reactions) $34.29

Grades: 6 7 8 9   **571.8**
1. Cloning
ISBN 1-4034-8838-X   LC 2006009962

This "addresses cloning, from its beginnings in the 1890s to Dolly the sheep in 2003. The [book features]

Morgan, Sally—*Continued*
clear, straightforward writing and [a] bright and open [layout] with colorful photographs and illustrations on every spread." SLJ
Includes bibliographical references

Silverstein, Alvin
Growth and development; by Alvin Silverstein, Virginia Silverstein, and Laura Silverstein Nunn. Twenty-First Century Books 2008 112p il (Science concepts) lib bdg $31.93 *
Grades: 4 5 6 7   **571.8**
1. Growth 2. Biology
ISBN 978-0-8225-6057-9 (lib bdg); 0-8225-6057-7 (lib bdg)   LC 2006030299
This "considers the growth process, animals with and without skeletons, human and plant growth, and future trends as a result of medical technology. Clear organization, engaging anecdotes, and generally good photos and diagrams are strengths of the [volume]." Horn Book Guide
Includes glossary and bibliographical references

Spilsbury, Richard, 1963-
Plant growth; [by] Richard & Louise Spilsbury. Rev. and updated. Heinemann Library 2008 48p il (The life of plants) $27.50; pa $7.99
Grades: 5 6 7 8   **571.8**
1. Plants—Growth
ISBN   978-1-4329-1500-1;   1-4329-1500-2; 978-1-4329-1507-0 (pa); 1-4329-1507-X (pa)
LC 2008275394
First published 2003
Describes plant growth and development.
This book "contains many bright and colorful photographs and diagrams to support the text, boldface vocabulary terms, a series of experiments and activities to provide further investigation, a complete glossary, an index, and a list of sources for additional information. . . . [This] volume is a complete and well-rounded unit." Sci Books Films
Includes glossary and bibliographical references

572 Biochemistry

Silverstein, Alvin
Photosynthesis; [by] Alvin Silverstein, Virginia Silverstein, and Laura Silverstein Nunn. rev ed. Twenty-First Century Books 2008 79p il (Science concepts, second series) lib bdg $31.93
Grades: 6 7 8 9   **572**
1. Photosynthesis
ISBN 978-0-8225-6798-1; 0-8225-6798-9
LC 2006022566
First published 1998
"Photosynthesis explains the process; the history of discoveries leading to current understanding of photosynthesis; and related issues such as acid rain, the greenhouse effect, and the use of basic materials that are directly or indirectly dependent on photosynthesis. . . . [This book is] well researched and interesting and the

format is inviting for both general-interest reading and research. . . . The high-quality, full-color photographs have informative captions." SLJ
Includes glossary and bibliographical references

Sitarski, Anita
Cold light; creatures, discoveries, and inventions that glow. Boyds Mills Press 2007 48p il $16.95 *
Grades: 5 6 7 8   **572**
1. Bioluminescence 2. Light
ISBN 1-59078-468-5; 978-1-59078-468-6
"A clearly written, chatty text not only discusses the expected bioluminescent critters (think fireflies), but delves into the realms of chemiluminescence, photoluminescence, and LEDs (light-emitting diodes) as well. . . . The text lays out the historical hows and whys of cold light, its success in the natural world, and its application in medicine and domestic/industrial illumination. Clear color photos and information boxes abound." SLJ

572.8 Biochemical genetics

De la Bédoyère, Camilla
The discovery of DNA. World Almanac Library 2006 48p il (Milestones in modern science) $30
Grades: 6 7 8 9   **572.8**
1. DNA 2. Genetics
ISBN 0-8368-5851-4
This is an examination of the discovery of DNA, what work led to its discovery, and how that knowledge is being used today.
The text is "complete, detailed, and not difficult to follow. . . . The illustrations are adequate and plentiful, including lots of photos and diagrams." SLJ
Includes glossary and bibliographical references

Johnson, Rebecca L., 1956-
Amazing DNA; [by] Rebecca L. Johnson; illustrations by Jack Desrocher; diagrams by Jennifer E. Fairman. Millbrook Press 2008 48p il (Microquests) lib bdg $29.27
Grades: 4 5 6   **572.8**
1. DNA 2. Genetics
ISBN 978-0-8225-7139-1 (lib bdg); 0-8225-7139-0 (lib bdg)   LC 2006-102324
This describes DNA structure, cell replication and genetic transmission.
"Johnson builds one scientific concept at a time using authentic terminology and connecting new information to familiar things. . . . Full-color microscope images, drawings, and cartoons appear in a clean, uncluttered format, combining solid science with humor." Horn Book Guide
Includes glossary and bibliographical references

Phelan, Glen
Double helix; the quest to uncover the structure of DNA. National Geographic 2006 59p il (Science quest) $17.95 *
Grades: 5 6 7 8   **572.8**

Phelan, Glen—*Continued*
1. DNA 2. Genetics
ISBN 0-7922-5541-0
This "offers a brief but informative overview of the quest to understand heredity. The book focuses on the accomplishments of Francis Crick and James Watson, who eventually uncovered the structure of DNA, but begins with Gregor Mendel's experiments, which were used as the foundation of modern genetic research. . . . Attractively designed and abundantly illustrated." Booklist
Includes glossary and bibliographical references

Silverstein, Alvin
DNA; by Alvin Silverstein, Virginia Silverstein, Laura Silverstein Nunn. rev ed. Twenty-First Century Books 2009 104p il (Science concepts, second series) lib bdg $31.93
Grades: 6 7 8 9   **572.8**
1. DNA 2. Genetics
ISBN 978-0-8225-8654-8; 0-8225-8654-1
                                              LC 2007048819
First published 2002
Introduces DNA and discusses such topics as how heredity works, what can happen when the code goes wrong, and the science and technology that is being developed based on cells and DNA, including gene therapy and cloning.
Includes glossary and bibliographical references

Stille, Darlene R., 1942-
DNA; the master molecule of life. Compass Point Books 2006 48p il (Exploring science) lib bdg $27.93; pa $7.95
Grades: 7 8 9 10   **572.8**
1. DNA 2. Genetics
ISBN 978-0-7565-1617-8 (lib bdg); 0-7565-1617-X (lib bdg); 978-0-7565-1762-5 (pa); 0-7565-1762-1 (pa)
                                              LC 2005-25061
Find out where DNA is located and how it helps determine our individual traits.
"The writing is concise yet very informative and . . . [the book] includes charts and diagrams, career information, and additional resources." Libr Media Connect
Includes glossary and bibliographical references

575.6   Reproductive organs Flowers

Spilsbury, Richard, 1963-
Plant reproduction; [by] Richard & Louise Spilsbury. Rev. and updated. Heinemann Library 2008 48p il (Life of plants) $27.50; pa $7.99
Grades: 5 6 7 8   **575.6**
1. Plants
ISBN   978-1-4329-1501-8;   1-4329-1501-0; 978-1-4329-1508-7 (pa); 1-4329-1508-8 (pa)
                                              LC 2008275393
First published 2003
Discusses the different ways that plants reproduce, including pollination and spores.
This book "contains many bright and colorful photographs and diagrams to support the text, boldface vocab-

ulary terms, a series of experiments and activities to provide further investigation, a complete glossary, an index, and a list of sources for additional information . . . . [This] volume is a complete and well-rounded unit." Sci Books Films
Includes glossary and bibliographical references

576   Genetics and evolution

Gardner, Robert, 1929-
Genetics and evolution science fair projects; using skeletons, cereal, earthworms, and more. Enslow Pubs. 2005 128p il (Biology! best science projects) lib bdg $26.60
Grades: 7 8 9 10   **576**
1. Evolution 2. Genetics 3. Science projects 4. Science—Experiments
ISBN 0-7660-1175-5 (lib bdg)   LC 2004-28871
This offers instructions for science fair projects covering such topics as classification of plants and animals, Darwin's study of the beaks of finches, Mendel's experiments with heredity, and DNA
Includes bibliographical references

Walker, Denise
Inheritance and evolution. Smart Apple Media 2007 48p il (Basic biology) $34.25
Grades: 8 9 10 11 12   **576**
1. Genetics 2. Evolution
ISBN 978-1-58340-989-3   LC 2006000346
This explains genetics, DNA, natural selection and cloning, and the process of extinction.
This "is well written and visually appealing enough to entice a few kids who aren't normally interested in science. There's plenty of information, supported by excellent, full-color photos, charts, and graphs, as well as numerous examples that clarify facts." Booklist

576.5   Genetics

Day, Trevor, 1955-
Genetics; by Trevor Day. Blackbirch Press 2004 40p il (Routes of science) $23.70; pa $18.70
Grades: 5 6 7 8   **576.5**
1. Genetics
ISBN 1-4103-0301-2; 1-4103-0300-4 (pa)
                                              LC 2003-15949
Contents: Early ideas about inheritance; Genetics is born; From peas to fruit flies to people; The DNA story; Genetics goes molecular; Genes helping people; Into the future
"This book traces the history of genetic discoveries from ancient beliefs about spontaneous generation to modern-day advances in cloning." Publisher's note
This "volume contains color photographs, illustrations, and diagrams to help explain the important concepts and discoveries. [This] up-to-date [volume] would be [an] excellent [supplement] to the science curriculum." SLJ
Includes glossary and bibliographical references

Fridell, Ron, 1943-
Decoding life; unraveling the mysteries of the genome; written by Ron Fridell. Lerner Publications 2005 112p il (Discovery!) lib bdg $27.93 *
Grades: 6 7 8 9   576.5
1. Genetics
ISBN 0-8225-1196-7   LC 2004-4710
Contents: Exploring the unknown; Searching for damaged genes; Repairing damaged genes; Stems and snips; Living longer; Engineering ourselves; How far should we go?; Privacy and justice; Engineering nature
This offers an overview of modern genetics from Gregor Mendel to genetic engineering, and discusses the Human Genome Project.
Includes bibliographical references

Johnson, Rebecca L., 1956-
Genetics. Twenty-First Century Books 2005 80p il (Great ideas of science) $27.93
Grades: 5 6 7 8   576.5
1. Genetics
ISBN 0-8225-2910-6   LC 2004-28212
"The history of genetics is introduced, beginning with Gregor Mendel's studies of pea-plant cross-pollination. The book skillfully explains the discovery of DNA and the emergence of modern biotechnology, including how DNA is replicated, how genes are expressed and translated as cell proteins, and how the human genome is being mapped. Thirty color photos, informational sidebars, and detailed diagrams complement the text." SLJ
Includes bibliographical references

Kidd, J. S. (Jerry S.)
New genetics; the study of life lines; [by] J.S. Kidd and Renee A. Kidd. Chelsea House 2006 210p (Science and society) $35 *
Grades: 7 8 9 10   576.5
1. Genetics
ISBN 0-8160-5604-8   LC 2005-40141
First published 1999 with title: Life lines: the story of the new genetics
This "introduces readers to the history of genetics, including Gregor Mendel's studies of plant cross-pollination, Thomas Hunt Morgan's research with fruit flies, and Watson and Crick's discovery of the structure of DNA, and continuing with Nobel Prizewinning research of the 1980s and earlier. . . . The text discusses a few recent advances, such as the mapping of the human genome, cloning, and genetically modified crops and animals." SLJ
Includes bibliographical references

Morgan, Sally
From Mendel's peas to genetic fingerprinting; discovering inheritance. Heinemann Library 2007 64p il (Chain reactions) $34.29
Grades: 6 7 8 9   576.5
1. Genetics 2. Heredity
ISBN 1-4034-8837-1; 978-1-4034-8837-4
                                        LC 2006-11043

This book "informs students about genetics and its many applications, including the Human Genome Project and genetic fingerprinting. . . . The [book features] clear, straightforward writing and [a] bright and open [layout] with colorful photographs and illustrations on every spread." SLJ
Includes bibliographical references

Schacter, Bernice Zeldin, 1943-2008
Genetics in the news; [by] Bernice Schacter. Chelsea House 2007 102p il (Science news flash) $31.95
Grades: 7 8 9 10   576.5
1. Genetics
ISBN 978-0-7910-9255-2; 0-7910-9255-0
                                        LC 2007-6343
Discusses "modifying plant and human genes for specific purposes . . . then move[s] on to the science enabling such . . . [an] . . . activity, followed by its history, then current issues and future considerations. . . . Illustrations help clarify the information." Horn Book Guide
Includes glossary and bibliographical references

Simpson, Kathleen
Genetics; from DNA to designer dogs; by Kathleen Simpson; Sarah Tishkoff, consultant. National Geographic 2008 64p il map (National Geographic investigates) $27.90 *
Grades: 4 5 6 7   576.5
1. Genetics
ISBN 978-1-4263-0361-6; 1-4263-0361-0
This discusses topics in genetics such as the identification of an Egyptian mummy by DNA testing, the genetics of pea plants studied by Gregor Mendel, cloning, the Human Genome Project, and stem cell research.
"The content is fairly exciting and should grab the attention of its target audience. . . . The photographs throughout are of high quality. . . . An engaging look at a complex topic." Booklist

Yount, Lisa
Modern genetics; engineering life. rev ed. Facts on File 2006 204p il map (Milestones in discovery and invention) $35
Grades: 7 8 9 10 11 12   576.5
1. Genetics 2. Genetic engineering
ISBN 0-8160-5744-3; 978-0-8160-5744-3
                                        LC 2005-18152
First published 1997 with title: Genetics and genetic engineering
This book "profiles 14 men and women who were among the leaders in making important genetic discoveries in research and new technologies. Profiles include James Watson, Francis Crick, Herbert Boyer, Stanley N. Cohen, Michael Bishop, and Harold Varmus." Publisher's note
Includes glossary and bibliographical references

576.8   Evolution

Andryszewski, Tricia, 1956-
Mass extinction; examining the current crisis.
Twenty-First Century Books 2008 111p il lib bdg
$30.60
Grades: 7 8 9 10 11 12   **576.8**
    1. Mass extinction of species
    ISBN 978-0-8225-7523-8; 0-8225-7523-X
                   LC 2007-25620
"After noting the natural causes of previous mass extinctions, this book focuses on the human element of environment destruction, especially in North America. The
earnest writing is convincing and accessible. . . . Vibrant
photographs, illustrations, and sidebars supplement the
text." Horn Book Guide
    Includes glossary and bibliographical references

Bortz, Alfred B., 1944-
Astrobiology. Lerner Publications 2008 48p il
map (Cool science) lib bdg $26.60
Grades: 4 5 6   **576.8**
    1. Space biology 2. Life on other planets
    ISBN 978-0-8225-6771-4; 0-8225-6771-7
                   LC 2006033268
This describes "the search for life in the universe.
Astrobiologists compare life on Earth to signs of life on
other planets. They test meteorites for evidence of alien
bacteria. They collect soil and atmospheric samples from
other planets. They study photographs taken on space
missions. And they listen for signals from alien civilizations on enormous radio dishes." Publisher's note
    Includes bibliographical references

Evolution; Clay Farris Naff, book editor.
    Greenhaven Press 2005 222p (Exploring science
    and medical discoveries) lib bdg $34.95 *
Grades: 8 9 10 11 12   **576.8**
    1. Evolution
    ISBN 0-7377-2823-X   LC 2004-60590
In this anthology, "nineteen selections are arranged in
roughly chronological order, beginning with ancient
Greek philosophers whose ideas about nature hinted at
evolutionary theories to come. . . . This solid survey
provides a good overview with manageable amounts of
primary-source materials that would be dauntingly difficult to comprehend in their entirety." SLJ
    Includes bibliographical references

Fleisher, Paul
Evolution. Twenty-First Century Books 2006
80p il map (Great ideas of science) $27.93 *
Grades: 5 6 7 8   **576.8**
    1. Evolution
    ISBN 0-8225-2134-2   LC 2004-28897
"Fleisher summarizes some of the ideas about evolution before Darwin's *Origin of Species*. He goes on to
describe the observations Darwin made while on his famous Beagle voyage. . . . Objections to Darwin's theory
in the 1800s and developments and discoveries in the
field since then lead to a step-by-step description of how

life may have come about and changed through billions
of years. The final chapter touches on how principles of
evolution have been used to justify eugenics and led to
the advancement of genetic engineering and cloning in
recent years. Creation science and intelligent design are
mentioned as religious teachings rather than scientific
theories." SLJ

Gordon, Sherri Mabry
The evolution debate; Darwinism vs. intelligent
design. Enslow Publishers 2009 128p il (Issues in
focus today) lib bdg $31.93
Grades: 7 8 9 10   **576.8**
    1. Evolution 2. Intelligent design theory
    ISBN 978-0-7660-2911-8 (lib bdg); 0-7660-2911-5 (lib
bdg)   LC 2008-17416
"Discusses the debate between teaching evolution and
intelligent design in schools, including the history of
teaching Darwinism in science classes, and the arguments
from both sides of the issue." Publisher's note
    "This book is most notable for its unbiased presenta-
tion of the arguments on each side of this contentious
debate." SLJ
    Includes glossary and bibliographical references

Jackson, Ellen B., 1943-
Looking for life in the universe; the search for
extraterrestrial intelligence; by Ellen Jackson; with
photographs by Nic Bishop. Houghton Mifflin
2002 57p il (Scientists in the field) $16
Grades: 4 5 6 7   **576.8**
    1. Tarter, Jill Cornell, 1944- 2. Life on other planets
    ISBN 0-618-12894-8   LC 2001-51312
Investigates how scientists, particularly Jill Tarter, Director of the SETI Institute in Mountain View, California, use twenty-first century technology to investigate
whether life exists on other planets
    "An exciting, visually awesome look at frontier sci-
ence." SLJ
    Includes glossary and bibliographical references

Mehling, Randi
Great extinctions of the past; by Randi Mehling.
Chelsea House 2007 72p il (Scientific American)
lib bdg $30
Grades: 5 6 7 8   **576.8**
    1. Mass extinction of species
    ISBN 978-0-7910-9049-7 (lib bdg); 0-7910-9049-3 (lib
bdg)   LC 2006014851
Examines extinctions of prehistoric species including
the dinosaurs, looks at the five largest extinctions ever,
and explores the idea of a future mass extinction.
    "The ideas in this book are . . . clearly explained.
. . . [The book has] captioned color photos thoughout."
SLJ
    Includes glossary and bibliographical references

Scott, Elaine, 1940-
Mars and the search for life. Clarion Books 2008 60p il $17 *
Grades: 4 5 6 7   **576.8**
1. Mars (Planet) 2. Life on other planets
ISBN 978-0-618-76695-6; 0-618-76695-2
LC 2008-07243
The author discusses "the Mars Exploration Rover (MER) and tantalizing findings that suggest that conditions on the red planet may once have been hospitable to life. . . . Illustrations are arresting and clearly captioned." Bull Cent Child Books
Includes glossary and bibliographical references

Skurzynski, Gloria, 1930-
Are we alone? scientists search for life in space. National Geographic Society 2004 92p il $18.95 *
Grades: 5 6 7 8   **576.8**
1. Life on other planets
ISBN 0-7922-6567-X   LC 2003-17732
The author begins with a "history of how the idea of flying saucers and extraterrestrials became part of the American consciousness. Later chapters trace specific quests . . . for signs of life beyond earth. . . . The text remains readable even while explaining intricate scientific concepts and complex . . . ideas. The vibrant full-color photos enhance the work impressively." Booklist
Includes glossary and bibliographical references

Turner, Pamela S.
Life on earth—and beyond; an astrobiologist's quest. Charlesbridge 2008 109p il map lib bdg $19.95; pa $11.95 *
Grades: 5 6 7 8   **576.8**
1. McKay, Christopher P. 2. Life on other planets 3. Space biology
ISBN 978-1-58089-133-2 (lib bdg); 1-58089-133-0 (lib bdg); 978-1-58089-134-9 (pa); 1-58089-134-9 (pa)
LC 2007-01475
"Astrobiologists look outward from the Earth seeking evidence of life elsewhere in the universe. But, as this fascinating book shows, they also travel to places on Earth where extreme conditions may be similar to those on distant worlds. Turner follows astrobiologist Chris McKay as he looks for life in apparently hostile environments. . . . Illustrated with many excellent color photos and other images." Booklist
Includes bibliographical references

Winston, Robert M. L.
Evolution revolution; [by] Robert Wilson. DK Pub. 2009 96p il $16.99 *
Grades: 5 6 7 8   **576.8**
1. Evolution
ISBN 978-0-7566-45243-; 0-7566-4524-7
"The first two thirds of the book are devoted to the history of thought and research on evolution, from stories of Creation, through Darwin, to genetics. The last third looks at 'Evolution in Action.' Information on the fetuses of related species rubs shoulders with variations within species and a time line of the Earth. Visually, the book snaps with colored backgrounds, cool graphics, topflight photos, and clever word balloons coming from vintage black-and-white reproductions." SLJ

577 Ecology

Habitats of the world. Marshall Cavendish 2005 c2006 11v il map set $329.95
Grades: 5 6 7 8   **577**
1. Habitat (Ecology) 2. Reference books
ISBN 0-7614-7523-0   LC 2004-52782
Contents: v1 Abbey-Badlands; v2 Baikal-coral reef; v3 Cousteau-estuary and delta; v4 Etosha-Great Barrier Reef; v5 Habitat-island; v6 Kilimanjaro-Muir; v7 Nile River-pollution; v8 Pond-severe weather; v9 Shrubland-tree; v10 Tropical ocean-Yellowstone National Park; v11 Index
"This encyclopedia informs students about ecology and the connections between people and the natural environment. Emphasizing how humans make a difference, articles on particular habitats draw attention to the threat of species extinction, the promise of sustainability, and personal responsibilities for stewardship of the earth. Biographies of ecologists and articles discussing broad environmental concerns contribute to students' knowledge of concepts central to the science curriculum." Publisher's note

Pollock, Steve
Ecology; written by Steve Pollock. rev ed. DK Pub. 2005 72p il (DK eyewitness books) $15.99; lib bdg $19.99
Grades: 4 5 6 7   **577**
1. Ecology
ISBN 0-7556-1387-6; 0-7556-1396-5 (lib bdg)
First published 1993
Illustrations and text provide information about ecology in general, specific ecosystems, and our changing understanding of life around us.

Rompella, Natalie
Ecosystems; [by] Natalie Rompella. 1st ed. Heinemann Library 2008 48p il (Science fair projects) $30
Grades: 5 6 7 8   **577**
1. Ecology 2. Science—Experiments 3. Science projects
ISBN 978-1-4034-7915-0   LC 2006039543
This "describes 10 inquiry-based science projects related to life science and ecosystems. . . . Students from mid-elementary through middle school would find little difficulty following the clearly written instructions and suggestions. . . . The illustrations consist of colorful photographs and well-labeled diagrams." Sci Books Films
Includes bibliographical references

Rybolt, Thomas R.
Environmental science fair projects; using water, feathers, sunlight, balloons, and more; [by] Thomas R. Rybolt and Robert C. Mebane. Enslow Pubs. 2005 128p il (Earth science! best science projects) lib bdg $26.60
Grades: 7 8 9 10   **577**
1. Environmental sciences 2. Science projects 3. Science—Experiments
ISBN 0-7660-2364-8 (lib bdg)   LC 2004-27016

Rybolt, Thomas R.—*Continued*

This offers instructions for science projects covering such topics as removing dust from the air, purifying water, soil acidity and erosion, plants and acid rain, and solar energy.

Includes bibliographical references

Silverstein, Alvin

Food chains; [by] Alvin Silverstein, Virginia Silverstein, and Laura Silverstein Nunn. rev ed. Twenty-First Century Books 2008 96p il (Science concepts, second series) $31.93

Grades: 6 7 8 9   **577**

1. Food chains (Ecology)

ISBN 978-0-8225-6797-4; 0-8225-6797-0

First published 1998

Explains various components of a food chain and discusses energy flows, food webs, food pyramids, recycling in nature, and the effect of humans on food chains.

Somervill, Barbara A., 1948-

Our living world; earth's biomes. Tradition 2006 7v il map set $350 *

Grades: 5 6 7 8   **577**

1. Ecology 2. Reference books

ISBN 1-59187-052-6

"Seven volumes . . . examine the biomes: Oceans, Seas, and Reefs; Tundra; Rivers, Streams, Lakes, and Ponds; Wetlands; Deserts; Grasslands; and Forests. Each is truly a visual and informational feast for the intermediate-grades researcher. Following a solid definition of the pertinent ecosystem, eight chapters of readable text describe the indigenous animals and plants. Chapters include discussions on the key species, predators, prey, flora, herbivores, and life cycle. . . . All entries contain vibrant color photographs and maps, colored sidebars, and a variety of boxed supplemental reference features." Booklist

Stille, Darlene R., 1942-

Nature interrupted; the science of environmental chain reactions. Compass Point Books 2009 48p il map (Headline science) lib bdg $27.93

Grades: 5 6 7 8   **577**

1. Ecology   2. Food chains (Ecology) 3. Environmental degradation

ISBN 978-0-7565-3949-8; 0-7565-3949-8

LC 2008007282

This "reviews the importance of subtle links in the environmental chain and the far-reaching consequences of its disruption. The possible harm to the food chain caused by the use of antibacterial soap is one case study. The flow of energy from one organism to the next in the food web and the unexpected results when this relationship is disrupted are shown in examinations of monarch butterflies, zebra mussels, and algal blooms. The color illustrations and charts . . . are clear and helpful, and the text, although information rich, is not overly difficult." SLJ

Includes glossary and bibliographical references

Walker, Pamela, 1958-

Ecosystem science fair projects using worms, leaves, crickets, and other stuff; [by] Pam Walker and Elaine Wood. Enslow Publishers 2005 128p il (Biology! best science projects) lib bdg $26.60

Grades: 7 8 9 10   **577**

1. Ecology 2. Science—Experiments 3. Science projects

ISBN 0-7660-2367-2   LC 2004-8355

Contents: Ecosystems; Nonliving factors affect ecosystems; Living factors affect ecosystems; Humans affect ecosystems.

This "includes experiments on ecosystems, how nonliving and living factors affect them, pollution, and acid rain. . . . Even though there are many science-fair-project books on the market, [this one] would be [a] good [addition] to libraries needing to update their collections." SLJ

Includes glossary and bibliographical references

Wallace, Holly, 1961-

Food chains and webs; Holly Wallace. rev. and updated. Heinemann Library 2006 32p il (Life processes) $29.29

Grades: 4 5 6 7   **577**

1. Food chains (Ecology)

ISBN 1-40348-846-0; 1-40348-853-3 (pa)

LC 2006284908

First published 2000 with title: Food chains

This describes how plants and animals in a particular habitat are linked together by what they eat, the processes that keep animals and plants alive, and how people study them.

Includes glossary and bibliographical references

577.2 Specific factors affecting ecology

Simon, Seymour, 1931-

Wildfires. Morrow Junior Bks. 1996 unp il pa $6.99 hardcover o.p. *

Grades: 4 5 6 7   **577.2**

1. Forest fires 2. Forest ecology

ISBN 0-688-17530-9 (pa)   LC 95-12653

"Exploring the place of fire in nature, Simon explains that . . . forest fires have important functions in the ecosystem. With a brilliantly clear and colorful photograph facing each page of text, the book describes the causes and the progression of the wildfires that burned areas of Yellowstone National Park in 1988, explains how the fires were beneficial in many ways. . . . Lucid writing and excellent book design." Booklist

577.3 Forest ecology

Allaby, Michael, 1933-
Temperate forests; illustrations by Richard Garratt. rev ed. Facts on File 2008 336p il map (Ecosystem) $70
Grades: 7 8 9 10   **577.3**
1. Forest ecology 2. Forests and forestry
ISBN 0-8160-5930-6; 978-0-8160-5930-0
LC 2006-28859
First published 1999
This book "explores the evolution and contributions of this unique environment and how society can and must preserve it." Publisher's note
"Those who are curious about or who are studying the environment and ecosystems . . . will find this book both fascinating and enlightening." Sci Books Films
Includes glossary and bibliographical references

Burnie, David
Shrublands. Raintree Steck-Vaughn Pubs. 2003 64p il map (Biomes atlases) lib bdg $31.42
Grades: 5 6 7 8   **577.3**
1. Forest ecology
ISBN 0-7398-5514-X   LC 2002-68093
A comprehensive look at the shrubland biome, describing the climate, plants, animals, people, and future of these areas, and providing detailed views of some major shrubland regions
"Especially effective are the maps. Brief notes for 10 to 12 highlights appear on each one, commenting on the diversity of flora, fauna, and landforms that occurs. . . . [The book includes] excellent-quality, full-color photographs and related sidebars." SLJ
Includes glossary and bibliographical references

Castner, James L.
Layers of life. Benchmark Bks. 2002 64p il (Deep in the Amazon) lib bdg $28.50 *
Grades: 6 7 8 9   **577.3**
1. Rain forest ecology 2. Amazon River valley
ISBN 0-7614-1130-5   LC 2001-25472
"Castner discusses the many parts of the [Amazon] forest and their complex connections, from the litter on the ground to the canopy high above, conveying excitement about the spectacular things he has seen. . . . [This title is] attractive and informative." Booklist
Includes glossary and bibliographical references

Partners and rivals. Benchmark Bks. 2002 64p il (Deep in the Amazon) lib bdg $28.50 *
Grades: 6 7 8 9   **577.3**
1. Rain forest ecology 2. Amazon River valley
ISBN 0-7614-1131-3   LC 2001-25977
This account of the ecology of the Amazon River valley "provides illustrations of commensalism, mutualism, and parasitism by discussing the fascinating relationships among species. . . . The interesting accounts of plant and animal life will keep most readers involved beyond a mere search for facts to add to reports." SLJ
Includes glossary and bibliographical references

Fielding, Eileen
The Eastern forest. Benchmark Bks. (Tarrytown) 1999 64p il (Ecosystems of North America) lib bdg $28.50
Grades: 6 7 8 9   **577.3**
1. Forest ecology
ISBN 0-7614-0895-9   LC 97-33115
Examines the forests of eastern North America, their ecosystems, and their responses to temperature and weather
Includes glossary and bibliographical references

Greenaway, Theresa, 1947-
Jungle; written by Theresa Greenaway; photographed by Geoff Dann. rev ed. DK Pub. 2004 71p il map (DK eyewitness books) $15.99
Grades: 4 5 6 7   **577.3**
1. Rain forest ecology
ISBN 0-7566-0694-2   LC 2004558978
First published 1994
Color photographs, drawings, and brief text describe the animals, plants, and ecology of tropical forests of the world

Jackson, Kay, 1959-
Rain forests; by Kay Jackson. KidHaven Press 2007 48p il (Our environment) lib bdg $23.70
Grades: 5 6 7 8   **577.3**
1. Rain forests 2. Rain forest ecology
ISBN 978-0-7377-3624-3   LC 2007006892
"Jackson defines rain forests. . . . She explains why rain forests are important, . . . the causes of rain forest destruction, and current efforts to save diverse ecosystems. The writing is clear and succinct. . . . Full-color, captioned photographs and drawings appear on nearly every page." Booklist
Includes bibliographical references

Jackson, Tom, 1972-
Tropical forests. Raintree Steck-Vaughn Pubs. 2003 64p il map (Biomes atlases) lib bdg $31.42
Grades: 5 6 7 8   **577.3**
1. Rain forest ecology
ISBN 0-7398-5250-7   LC 2002-68094
A comprehensive look at the tropical forest biome, examining its climate, plants, animals, people, and future, plus detailed views of some particular tropical forest locations
"Especially effective are the maps. Brief notes for 10 to 12 highlights appear on each one, commenting on the diversity of flora, fauna, and landforms that occurs. . . . [The book includes] excellent-quality, full-color photographs and related sidebars." SLJ
Includes glossary and bibliographical references

Lasky, Kathryn

The most beautiful roof in the world; exploring the rainforest canopy; photographs by Christopher G. Knight. Harcourt Brace & Co. 1997 unp il $18; pa $9

Grades: 4 5 6 7   **577.3**

1. Lowman, Margaret 2. Rain forest ecology
ISBN 0-15-200893-4; 0-15-200897-7 (pa)
     LC 95-48193

"Gulliver Green"

Describes the work of Meg Lowman in the rainforest canopy, an area unexplored until the last ten years and home to previously unknown species of plants and animals

"Fresh in out-look and intriguing in details, this memorable book features colorful photographs that reflect the you-are-there quality of the text." Booklist

Includes glossary

Martin, Patricia A. Fink, 1955-

Woods and forests; illustrations by Bob Italiano and Steve Savage. Watts 2000 143p il (Exploring ecosystems) lib bdg $24

Grades: 7 8 9 10   **577.3**

1. Forest ecology 2. Science—Experiments
ISBN 0-531-11697-2 (lib bdg)   LC 99-33044

"In six chapters with 20 projects and 13 investigations, Martin starts students on a journey of understanding and appreciating our woods and forests. Topics in this book include tree identification, forest wildlife, and life cycles in the forest. . . . Appended are a glossary, an index, and a listing of books, videos, organizations, Web sites, and equipment suppliers." Book Rep

Includes bibliographical references

Miller-Schroeder, Patricia

Boreal forests; [by] Patricia Miller-Schroeder. Weigl Publishers 2005 32p il map (Biomes) $26; pa $7.99

Grades: 4 5 6 7   **577.3**

1. Forest ecology
ISBN 1-59036-345-0; 1-59036-351-5 (pa)
     LC 2005005436

This discusses the ecosystem of "the northern, coniferous forests or taigas. . . . The [volume contains] succinct text and [is] full of pictures, maps, graphs, and sidebars of interesting facts." Voice Youth Advocates

Includes bibliographical references

Quinlan, Susan E., 1954-

The case of the monkeys that fell from the trees; and other mysteries in tropical nature. Boyds Mills Press 2003 171p il map $15.95

Grades: 6 7 8 9   **577.3**

1. Rain forest ecology 2. Natural history
ISBN 1-56397-902-0   LC 2002-108914

This "presents a number of questions or 'mysteries' concerning plants and animals in the tropical forests of South and Central America and explains how scientists answered those questions." Booklist

"Quinlan's book is well organized and clearly written. . . . Besides presenting some fascinating case studies in a style that conveys the thrill of the scientific chase, it also provides information on the different kinds of tropical forests and how they function." SLJ

Includes bibliographical references

Sayre, April Pulley

Taiga. 21st Cent. Bks. (NY) 1994 64p il maps (Exploring Earth's biomes) lib bdg $25.90

Grades: 5 6 7 8   **577.3**

1. Forest ecology
ISBN 0-8050-2830-7   LC 94-19388

The author describes the taiga environments of open lichen woodland and closed forests, including weather and climate, geology, plants and animals, and the effects of human habitation. Includes experiments

"An excellent resource book. . . . Appropriately illustrated with color photos and sketches and written in a refreshing style, the pages are loaded with information about the taiga biome." Sci Books Films

Includes glossary and bibliographical references

Staub, Frank J.

America's forests; written and photographed by Frank Staub. Carolrhoda Bks. 1998 48p il map (Carolrhoda earth watch book) lib bdg $21.27 *

Grades: 4 5 6 7   **577.3**

1. Forests and forestry 2. Forest ecology
ISBN 1-57505-265-2   LC 98-7291

Examines the growth and changing nature of forests, the plants and animals living there, and the uses to which these lands are put

"Solid, accessible information presented in an attractive format. . . . Even students with little interest in nature will be drawn to the numerous full-color photographs that depict the beauty and variety of our country's woodlands." SLJ

Includes glossary

Tocci, Salvatore

The chaparral; life on the scrubby coast. Franklin Watts 2003 63p il map (Biomes and habitats) $25.50; pa $8.95

Grades: 4 5 6 7   **577.3**

1. Chaparral ecology
ISBN 0-531-12303-0; 0-531-16671-6 (pa)
     LC 2003-16574

"Watts library"

A look at the plants, animals, locations, and various habitats that make up the chaparral ecosystems of the world.

Life in the temperate forests. Franklin Watts 2005 63p il map (Biomes and habitats) $25.50

Grades: 4 5 6 7   **577.3**

1. Forest ecology
ISBN 0-531-12363-4   LC 2004027303

"Watts library"

Describes the plants and animals that live in temperate forests and the threats facing them.

Includes glossary and bibliographical references

Tocci, Salvatore—*Continued*

Life in the tropical forests. Franklin Watts 2005
63p il map (Biomes and habitats) $25.50
Grades: 4 5 6 7   **577.3**
   1. Rain forest ecology
   ISBN 0-531-12364-2   LC 2004027054
"Watts library"
Describes the animals, plants, and people that live in
rainforests and the threats to their existence.

Includes glossary and bibliographical references

Vogt, Richard Carl

Rain forests. Simon & Schuster Books for
Young Readers 2009 64p il (Insiders) $16.99
Grades: 4 5 6 7   **577.3**
   1. Rain forests
   ISBN 978-1-4169-3866-8; 1-4169-3866-4
                                LC 2008061111
"The layers of a rain forest are drawn with exacting
detail in every imaginable shade of green, while circular
inserts zoom in on flora with accompanying stats. Running down the length of the spread are markers
delineating the cutoff points for each layer—emergent,
canopy, and so on. The rest of the book is similarly fine,
bringing animals, reptiles, and insects into the mix. . . .
Some photographs join the mostly hand-illustrated affair.
. . . What will grab browsers are the 3D cover and vivid
drawings on thick, oversize pages, but what will keep
them reading is a cumulative sense of the rain forest as
a verdant universe nearly festering with life." Booklist

Warhol, Tom

Chaparral and scrub; [by] Tom Warhol.
Marshall Cavendish Benchmark 2006 c2007 80p il
(Earth's biomes) lib bdg $32.79
Grades: 6 7 8 9   **577.3**
   1. Chaparral ecology 2. Forests and forestry
   ISBN 978-0-7614-2195-5 (lib bdg); 0-7614-2195-5 (lib
   bdg)   LC 2006015824
"Explores chaparral and scrub biomes and covers
where they are located as well as the plants and animals
that inhabit them." Publisher's note
Includes glossary and bibliographical references

Forest; [by] Tom Warhol. Marshall Cavendish
Benchmark 2006 c2007 80p il (Earth's biomes) lib
bdg $32.79
Grades: 6 7 8 9   **577.3**
   1. Forest ecology 2. Forests and forestry
   ISBN 978-0-7614-2189-4 (lib bdg); 0-7614-2189-0 (lib
   bdg)   LC 2006015821
"Explores forest biomes and covers where they are located as well as the plants and animals that inhabit
them." Publisher's note
"The clarity of the narrative and the spectacular photography . . . make this . . . an appealing, useful addition to the . . . library." Voice Youth Advocates

Includes glossary and bibliographical references

Welsbacher, Anne, 1955-

Protecting Earth's rain forests; by Anne
Welsbacher. Lerner Publications 2009 72p il map
(Saving our living Earth) lib bdg $30.60
Grades: 5 6 7 8   **577.3**
   1. Rain forests 2. Environmental protection
   ISBN 978-0-8225-7562-7; 0-8225-7562-0
                                LC 2007-38859
"Provides a thorough, interesting discussion of multi-
ple aspects of [rain forest protection], including historical
origins, the current situation, and potential solutions. . . .
Photos from around the world accompany discussions.
. . . Solid choice to replace outdated books." SLJ

Includes glossary and bibliographical references

577.4   Grassland ecology

Collard, Sneed B., III

The prairie builders; reconstructing America's
lost grasslands; written and photographed by Sneed
B. Collard III. Houghton Mifflin Co. 2005 66p il
(Scientists in the field) $17; pa $8.95 *
Grades: 4 5 6 7   **577.4**
   1. Prairies 2. Nature conservation
   ISBN   0-618-39687-X;   978-0-618-39687-0;
   978-0-547-01441-8 (pa); 0-547-01441-4 (pa)
                                LC 2004-13201
This describes an effort to restore part of the native
tallgrass prairie in the the 8,000-acre Neal Smith National Wildlife Refuge in Iowa.
"The engaging text is accompanied by large, inviting
color photographs. . . . An essential purchase for libraries in prairie regions and a worthwhile choice for
others." SLJ

Includes bibliographical references

Hoare, Ben

Temperate grasslands. Raintree Steck-Vaughn
Pubs. 2003 64p il map (Biomes atlases) lib bdg
$31.42
Grades: 5 6 7 8   **577.4**
   1. Grassland ecology
   ISBN 0-7398-5249-3   LC 2002-12818
Contents: Biomes of the world; Temperate grasslands
of the world; Grassland climate; Grassland plants; Grassland animals; People and grasslands; The future
This offers a look at temperate grasslands of the world
describing their climate, plants, animals, people, and future
"Especially effective are the maps. Brief notes for 10
to 12 highlights appear on each one, commenting on the
diversity of flora, fauna, and landforms that occurs. . . .
[The book includes] excellent-quality, full-color photographs and related sidebars." SLJ

Includes glossary and bibliographical references

Lynch, Wayne

Rocky Mountains; text and photographs by Wayne Lynch; assisted by Aubrey Lang. NorthWord Books for Young Readers 2006 64p il map (Our wild world ecosystems) $16.95; pa $8.95

Grades: 6 7 8 9　　**577.4**

1. Mountain ecology 2. Natural history—Rocky Mountains 3. Rocky Mountains

ISBN 1-55971-948-6; 1-55971-949-4 (pa)

LC 2005-38014

"Introductory chapters explain the physical science that forms mountains and their weather. Each subsequent chapter zeros in on different mountain habitats (rivers and lakes, meadows and forests, and so on), introducing facts about the animals and plants in each. The authors . . . write in vivid, clear prose that, together with the quality of the beautiful images, sets this title apart from other . . . books on the topic." Booklist

Includes bibliographical references

Martin, Patricia A. Fink, 1955-

Prairies, fields, and meadows. Watts 2002 144p il map (Exploring ecosystems) lib bdg $24.50; pa $6.95

Grades: 7 8 9 10　　**577.4**

1. Prairie ecology 2. Grassland ecology

ISBN 978-0-531-11859-7; 0-531-11859-2 (lib bdg); 978-0-531-16604-8 (pa); 0-531-16604-X (pa)

LC 2001-17570

"Martin follows theories about how the prairies formed with an overview of plants and animals, including species and anatomy, and a consideration of the types of grasslands, how species coexist, and conservation efforts. Throughout, the author suggests activities." Booklist

"One can glean a great deal of useful information from this text." Libr Media Connect

Includes glossary and bibliographical references

Toupin, Laurie, 1963-

Life in the temperate grasslands; [by] Laurie Peach Toupin. 1st ed. Franklin Watts 2005 63p il map (Biomes and habitats) $25.50 *

Grades: 4 5 6 7　　**577.4**

1. Grassland ecology

ISBN 0-531-12385-5　　LC 2004-13282

"Watts library"

Contents: No trees, no problem; Tough as grass; Grazers big and small; Predators feathery, furry, and slippery; Giving mother nature a hand; In your hands

This describes the ecology of grasslands such as the North American prairie, the South American pampas, the African veldt and the European steppes.

This is "written in an accessible and interesting, conversational style. The [author conveys] a good deal of information about topics such as adaptation, environmental threats, seasonal changes, and other essentials important to report writers and general readers." SLJ

Includes bibliographical references

Savannas; life in the tropical grasslands; [by] Laurie Peach Toupin. 1st ed. Franklin Watts 2005 63p il map (Biomes and habitats) $25.50 *

Grades: 4 5 6 7　　**577.4**

1. Grassland ecology

ISBN 0-531-12386-3　　LC 2004-13281

"Watts library"

Contents: Too dry, too wet . . . ah, home!; Grasses rule; Landscapers and gardeners; Hoofed vegetarians; Tooth and claw; People and the grasslands

This introduces "readers to the climate characteristics as well as plants and animals of [tropical grasslands. It is] written in an accessible and interesting, conversational style. The authors convey a good deal of information about topics such as adaptation, environmental threats, seasonal changes, and other essentials important to report writers and general readers." SLJ

Includes bibliographical references

Warhol, Tom

Grassland; [by] Tom Warhol. Marshall Cavendish Benchmark 2006 c2007 80p il (Earth's biomes) lib bdg $32.79

Grades: 6 7 8 9　　**577.4**

1. Grassland ecology 2. Grasslands

ISBN 978-0-7614-2196-2 (lib bdg); 0-7614-2196-3 (lib bdg)　　LC 2006015820

"Explores grassland biomes and covers where they are located as well as the plants and animals that inhabit them." Publisher's note

Includes glossary and bibliographical references

577.5　Ecology of miscellaneous environments

Allaby, Michael, 1933-

Deserts; illustrations by Richard Garratt. rev ed. Facts on File 2008 320p il map (Ecosystem) $70 *

Grades: 7 8 9 10　　**577.5**

1. Desert ecology 2. Deserts

ISBN 0-8160-5929-2; 978-0-8160-5929-4

LC 2007-00477

First published 2001

This book provides "information on the climatic conditions that produce deserts and the climate cycles that make them expand and contract. . . . [It] also explores the locations and general types of deserts, and provides detailed accounts of the most important deserts." Publisher's note

"This book is a good mix of text, excellent maps, photographs, and scientific information." Sci Books Films

Includes glossary and bibliographical references

Fridell, Ron, 1943-

Life in the desert. Franklin Watts 2005 63p il map (Biomes and habitats) $25.50

Grades: 4 5 6 7　　**577.5**

1. Desert ecology 2. Deserts

ISBN 0-531-12384-7　　LC 2004027254

Fridell, Ron, 1943-—*Continued*
"Watts library"
Presents an introduction to desert environments, in simple text with illustrations, providing information on its average temperature, climate, plant and animal life, and people.
Includes glossary and bibliographical references

Moore, Peter D. (Peter Dale)
Tundra; [by] Peter D. Moore; illustrations by Richard Garratt. Facts on File 2006 xx, 220p il (Ecosystem) $39.50
Grades: 7 8 9 10   **577.5**
1. Tundra ecology
ISBN 0-8160-5325-1; 978-0-8160-5933-1
LC 2005-35618
This discusses "the geography, geology, ecology, economic uses, and future of [tundras]. . . . [It] includes both the polar regions and the peaks of the Earth's highest mountains. . . . [The text is] well organized. . . . Numerous sidebars; captioned maps, diagrams, and scattered charts; and high-quality color photographs of plant and animal life are included." SLJ
Includes bibliographical references

Tocci, Salvatore
Alpine tundra; life on the tallest mountain; [by] Salvatore Tocci. 1st ed. Franklin Watts 2005 63p il (Biomes and habitats) lib bdg $25.50 *
Grades: 4 5 6 7   **577.5**
1. Tundra ecology
ISBN 978-0-531-12365-2 (lib bdg); 0-531-12365-0 (lib bdg)   LC 2004-13583
"Watts library"
Contents: A land high up; The season to grow; The season to prepare; The season to hide; The season to reappear; People of the tundra
This introduces "readers to the climate characteristics as well as plants and animals of [the Alpine tundra. It is] written in an accessible and interesting, conversational style. The authors convey a good deal of information about topics such as adaptation, environmental threats, seasonal changes, and other essentials important to report writers and general readers." SLJ
Includes bibliographical references

Arctic tundra; life at the North Pole; [by] Salvatore Tocci. 1st ed. Franklin Watts 2005 63p il map (Biomes and habitats) lib bdg $25.50
Grades: 4 5 6 7   **577.5**
1. Tundra ecology
ISBN 978-0-531-12366-9 (lib bdg); 0-531-12366-9 (lib bdg)   LC 2004-13283
"Watts library"
This introduces "readers to the climate characteristics as well as plants and animals of [the Arctic tundra. It is] written in an accessible and interesting, conversational style. The authors convey a good deal of information about topics such as adaptation, environmental threats, seasonal changes, and other essentials important to report writers and general readers." SLJ
Includes bibliographical references

Warhol, Tom
Desert; [by] Tom Warhol. Marshall Cavendish Benchmark 2006 c2007 80p il (Earth's biomes) lib bdg $34.21
Grades: 6 7 8 9   **577.5**
1. Desert ecology 2. Deserts
ISBN 978-0-7614-2194-8 (lib bdg); 0-7614-2194-7 (lib bdg)   LC 2006015823
"Explores desert biomes and covers where they are located as well as the plants and animals that inhabit them." Publisher's note
Includes glossary and bibliographical references

Tundra; [by] Tom Warhol. Marshall Cavendish Benchmark 2006 c2007 80p il (Earth's biomes) lib bdg $34.21
Grades: 6 7 8 9   **577.5**
1. Tundra ecology
ISBN 978-0-7614-2193-1 (lib bdg); 0-7614-2193-9 (lib bdg)   LC 2006015822
"Explores tundra biomes and covers where they are located as well as the plants and animals that inhabit them." Publisher's note
"The clarity of the narrative and the spectacular photographs . . . make this . . . an appealing, useful addition to the . . . school." Voice of Youth Advocates
Includes glossary and bibliographical references

577.6   Aquatic ecology Freshwater ecology

Castner, James L.
River life. Benchmark Bks. 2002 64p il (Deep in the Amazon) lib bdg $28.50
Grades: 6 7 8 9   **577.6**
1. Amazon River 2. River ecology
ISBN 0-7614-1127-5   LC 99-57015
Describes the geology, topography, and fishes of the Amazon River Region
"Attractive and informative." Booklist
Includes glossary and bibliographical references

Josephs, David
Lakes, ponds, and temporary pools. Watts 2000 127p il (Exploring ecosystems) lib bdg $24; pa $6.95
Grades: 7 8 9 10   **577.6**
1. Lake ecology 2. Pond ecology
ISBN 0-531-11698-0 (lib bdg); 0-531-16506-X (pa)
LC 99-57578
Explains the importance of preserving and protecting slow-moving water habitats and provides instructions for related projects and activities
Includes bibliographical references

Moore, Peter D. (Peter Dale)
Wetlands; illustrations by Richard Garratt. rev
ed. Facts on File 2008 270p il map (Ecosystem)
$70
Grades: 7 8 9 10   **577.6**
1. Wetlands
ISBN 0-8160-5931-4; 978-0-8160-5931-7
LC 2006-37399
First published 2000
This book "examines the diversity of wetlands in the
past, present, and future, how they work, and how they
can be conserved." Publisher's note
Includes glossary and bibliographical references

Sayre, April Pulley
Lake and pond. 21st Cent. Bks. (NY) 1996 78p
il (Exploring Earth's biomes) lib bdg $25.90
Grades: 5 6 7 8   **577.6**
1. Lake ecology 2. Pond ecology
ISBN 0-8050-4089-7   LC 95-36228
Discusses the lake and pond biomes and how each is
affected by the environment and people
"The writing style, lively and precise, makes this . . .
unusually readable." Booklist

River and stream. 21st Cent. Bks. (NY) 1996
80p il (Exploring Earth's biomes) lib bdg $25.90
Grades: 5 6 7 8   **577.6**
1. River ecology
ISBN 0-8050-4088-9   LC 95-34458
Describes aquatic biomes, focusing on life in rivers
and streams, and explains the effect of pollution on these
biotic communities and on the lives of people everywhere
"Exceptionally well-focused, well-organized." SLJ

Toupin, Laurie, 1963-
Freshwater habitats; life in freshwater
ecosystems; [by] Laurie Peach Toupin. F. Watts
2005 63p il map (Biomes and habitats) $25.50; pa
$8.95
Grades: 4 5 6 7   **577.6**
1. Freshwater ecology
ISBN 0-531-12305-7; 0-531-16675-9 (pa)
LC 2003-16572
"Watts library"
A look at the plants, animals, locations, and various
habitats that make up the freshwater ecosystems of the
world.

Warhol, Tom
Water; [by] Tom Warhol. Marshall Cavendish
Benchmark 2006 c2007 80p il (Earth's biomes) lib
bdg $34.21
Grades: 6 7 8 9   **577.6**
1. Marine ecology 2. Freshwater biology
ISBN 978-0-7614-2192-4 (lib bdg); 0-7614-2192-0 (lib
bdg)   LC 2006011979
"Explores water biomes and covers where they are lo-
cated as well as the plants and animals that inhabit
them." Publisher's note
Includes glossary and bibliographical references

577.7   Marine ecology

Carson, Rachel, 1907-1964
The edge of the sea; with illustrations by Bob
Hines. Houghton Mifflin 1955 276p il pa $14
hardcover o.p.
Grades: 7 8 9 10 11 12 Adult   **577.7**
1. Marine biology 2. Seashore
ISBN 0-395-92496-0 (pa)
"The seashores of the world may be divided into three
basic types: the rugged shores of rock, the sand beaches,
and the coral reefs and all their associated features. Each
has its typical community of plants and animals. The Atlantic coast of the United States [provides] clear examples of each of these types. I have chosen it as the setting for my pictures of shore life." Preface

Collard, Sneed B., III
Lizard Island; science and scientists on
Australia's Great Barrier Reef. Watts 2000 143p il
$25; pa $12.95
Grades: 6 7 8 9   **577.7**
1. Coral reefs and islands 2. Marine ecology 3. Great
Barrier Reef (Australia)
ISBN 0-531-11719-7; 0-531-1619-1 (pa)
LC 99-55149
Describes the biologists who manage the Lizard Island
Research Station and their activities studying and protect-
ing the Great Barrier Reef
"The author ends with an ominous account of the
tragic destruction of many of the world's coral reefs and
a direct plea for more ecologically responsible behavior.
. . . This is a readable, enthusiastic visit with the prac-
ticing scientists in the field." Booklist
Includes bibliographical references

Gowell, Elizabeth Tayntor
Fountains of life; the story of deep sea vents.
Watts 1998 63p il $23; pa $6.95
Grades: 4 5 6   **577.7**
1. Ocean bottom 2. Marine ecology
ISBN 0-531-20369-7; 0-531-15908-6 (pa)
LC 97-10924
"A First book"
Discusses the formation and discovery of hydrother-
mal vents and the unusual animals and plants that can be
found near them
"Color diagrams of the formation of new sea floor and
tectonic plates are clear and understandable, and the
computer-generated map of the ocean floor pulsates in
vibrant color. Full-color illustrations amplify the descriptions, definitions, and explanations." SLJ
Includes glossary and bibliographical references

Kricher, John C.
Peterson first guide to seashores; [by] John
Kricher; illustrated by Gordon Morrison. Houghton
Mifflin 1992 128p il *
Grades: 6 7 8 9   **577.7**
1. Seashore 2. Marine biology
LC 91-38829

Kricher, John C.—*Continued*

Available 1998 edition with title: Peterson first guide to the seashore $5.95 (ISBN 0-395-91180-X)

This is a guide to identification of plants and animals found at the seashore

This is "sure to satisfy the curiosity of novices and inspire a deeper interest in nature. . . . The selections, grouped geographically and by habitat, are limited to those most commonly discovered by hikers or beachcombers. The clear, full-color pictures are simply labeled for easy identification." SLJ

Parker, Steve

Seashore; written by Steve Parker. rev ed. DK Pub. 2004 72p il (DK eyewitness books) $15.99; lib bdg $19.99 *

Grades: 4 5 6 7   **577.7**

1. Seashore 2. Marine animals 3. Marine plants

ISBN 0-7566-0721-3; 0-7566-0720-5 (lib bdg)

First published 1989 by Knopf

Brief text and photos introduce the animal inhabitants of the seashore, including fish, crustaceans, snails, and shorebirds.

Tocci, Salvatore

Coral reefs; life below the sea. Franklin Watts 2003 63p il map (Biomes and habitats) $25.50; pa $8.95

Grades: 4 5 6 7   **577.7**

1. Coral reefs and islands 2. Ecology

ISBN 0-531-12304-9; 0-531-16669-4 (pa)

LC 2003-16566

"Watts library"

Explores coral reefs, ridges of rocky materials just below the ocean's surface, which are inhabited by thousands of diverse organisms.

Includes glossary and bibliographical references

Walker, Pamela, 1958-

The coral reef; [by] Pam Walker and Elaine Wood. Facts on File 2005 140p (Life in the sea) $35 *

Grades: 6 7 8 9   **577.7**

1. Coral reefs and islands

ISBN 0-8160-5703-6

"An opening chapter gives detailed coverage of how reefs are formed. Later chapters examine the reefs' inhabitants, from essential microbes to the larger, showier fish, reptiles, and other animals. The final chapter . . . mentions environmental hazards and conservation efforts. . . . The range and depth of information . . . make this a fine addition for science collections." Booklist

577.8 Synecology and population biology

Silverstein, Alvin

Symbiosis; [by] Alvin Silverstein, Virginia Silverstein, and Laura Silverstein Nunn. rev ed. Twenty-First Century Books 2008 96p il (Science concepts, second series) lib bdg $31.93 *

Grades: 6 7 8 9   **577.8**

1. Symbiosis

ISBN 978-0-8225-6799-8 (lib bdg); 0-8225-6799-7 (lib bdg)   LC 2007003184

First published 1998

Discusses the three kinds of symbiosis—mutualism, commensalism, and parasitism—and describes examples of these relationships.

"Well researched and interesting and the format is inviting for both general-interest reading and research." SLJ [review of 1998 edition]

Includes bibliographical references

U.X.L encyclopedia of biomes; Marlene Weigel, Julie L. Carnagie, editor. U.X.L 1999 3v set $165

Grades: 7 8 9 10   **577.8**

1. Ecology—Encyclopedias 2. Reference books

ISBN 0-7876-3732-7   LC 99-23395

Contents: v1 Coniferous forests, continental margins, deciduous forests, and deserts; v2 Grasslands, lakes and ponds, oceans, and rainforests; v3 Rivers, seashores, tundras, and wetlands

"Alphabetically arranged entries on land biomes and water biomes range from 35 to 45 pages each and cover climate, elevation, soil water bodies, vegetation, animal life, food web, plant and animal adaptations, endangered species, human effects on the biome and the effects of the environment on humans' culture and economy." Publisher's note

Includes bibliographical references

578 Natural history of organisms and related subjects

Kelsey, Elin

Strange new species; astonishing discoveries of life on earth. Maple Tree Press 2005 96p il $24.95 *

Grades: 5 6 7 8   **578**

1. Natural history 2. Biology 3. Scientists

ISBN 1-897066-31-7; 1-897066-32-5 (pa)

"This large-format book showcases new species . . . and the scientists who have discovered them. . . . The discussion ends with information on cloning, genetically modified food, and the future of life. . . . With many excellent photos, this introductory book on new species will be an intriguing addition to classroom units on classification or biology." Booklist

Wildlife and plants. 3rd ed. Marshall Cavendish 2007 20v il set $359.95

Grades: 4 5 6 7   **578**

Wildlife and plants—*Continued*
1. Animals—Encyclopedias 2. Plants—Encyclopedias
3. Reference books
ISBN 978-0-76147693-1
First published 1994 with title: Wildlife and plants of the world

This set includes "more than 500 entries covering animals, plants, microorganisms, fungi, habitats, biomes, and overviews. . . . Entries provide a concise introduction followed by more detailed information including behavior, reproduction, characteristics, and survival tactics. . . . With its captivating information and photographs, students are sure to come to this easy-to-use set again and again." Booklist

578.4　Adaptation

Fullick, Ann
Adaptation and competition; [by] Ann Fullick. Heinemann Library 2006 64p il map (Life science in depth) lib bdg $34.29; pa $9.90 *
Grades: 6 7 8 9　　　　　　　　　　578.4
1. Adaptation (Biology) 2. Heredity
ISBN 1-4034-7518-0 (lib bdg); 1-4034-7526-1 (pa)
LC 2005023560
This "provides a detailed overview of how living organisms compete with one another to survive and how they adapt to climate and habitat. The style makes some complex science accessible, and the attractive book design breaks up the dense text. . . . The examples are lively." Booklist
Includes bibliographical references

Silverstein, Alvin
Adaptation; by Alvin Silverstein, Virginia Silverstein, and Laura Silverstein Nunn. Twenty-First Century Books 2008 112p il (Science concepts) lib bdg $31.93 *
Grades: 4 5 6 7　　　　　　　　　　578.4
1. Adaptation (Biology)
ISBN 978-0-8225-3434-1 (lib bdg); 0-8225-3434-7 (lib bdg)
LC 2007-02862
This "provides an accessible introduction to how living beings adapt to survive in diverse habitats. . . . The narrative gains clarity from abundant examples, colorful photos and diagrams, and fascinating sidebars." Booklist
Includes bibliographical references

578.6　Miscellaneous nontaxonomic kinds of organisms

Collard, Sneed B., III
Science warriors; the battle against invasive species; written by Sneed B. Collard III. Houghton Mifflin 2008 48p il (Scientists in the field) $17
Grades: 5 6 7 8　　　　　　　　　　578.6
1. Nonindigenous pests 2. Biological invasions
ISBN 978-0-618-75636-0; 0-618-75636-1
LC 2008-01867

"Collard focuses on four major invader species in the U.S.: the brown tree snake, . . . the red imported fire ant, . . . the melaleuca tree, . . . and the zebra mussel. . . . These are useful and thought-provoking case studies of a very large problem." Bull Cent Child Books
Includes glossary and bibliographical references

Fleisher, Paul
Parasites; latching on to a free lunch. Twenty-First Century Books 2006 112p il (Discovery!) lib bdg $29.27 *
Grades: 7 8 9 10　　　　　　　　　　578.6
1. Parasites
ISBN 978-0-8225-3415-0; 0-8225-3415-0
LC 2005-10521
This book describes "all sorts of unpleasant creatures that can feed on your body—head lice, fleas, ticks, tapeworms, and fungi—as well as the huge variety of parasites that feed on animals and plants all around you." Publisher's note
This is "well organized and quite up to date. The photos . . . are plentiful, colorful, and excellent. . . . Clear, concise, and interesting." Voice Youth Advocates
Includes bibliographical references

578.68　Rare and endangered species

Endangered species: opposing viewpoints; Helen Cothran, book editor. Greenhaven Press 2000 156p il lib bdg $34.95; pa $23.70
Grades: 8 9 10 11 12　　　　　　　　578.68
1. Endangered species
ISBN 0-7377-0506-X (lib bdg); 0-7377-0505-1 (pa)
LC 99-85752
Replaces the edition published 1995 under the editorship of Brenda Stalcup
"Opposing viewpoints series"
This collection of articles offers varying viewpoints on extinction, preservation, property rights, and international cooperation.
Includes bibliographical references

McGavin, George
Endangered; wildlife on the brink of extinction. Firefly Books 2006 192p il map $35 *
Grades: 7 8 9 10 11 12 Adult　　　　　578.68
1. Endangered species 2. Rare animals
ISBN 1-55407-183-6; 978-1-55407-183-8
LC 2007-271504
"Featuring more than 400 photographs, this book details the plant and animal species that are either endangered or so severely threatened that they soon will be." Publisher's note
"Written in simple, nonscientific prose and fully illustrated with color photographs, maps, and many sidebars, the book is visually appealing as well as intellectually stimulating." Voice Youth Advocates

Pobst, Sandy, 1959-

Animals on the edge; science races to save species threatened with extinction; by Sandra Pobst; Todd K. Fuller, consultant. National Geographic 2008 64p il (National Geographic investigates) $17.95; lib bdg $27.90 *

Grades: 4 5 6 7   **578.68**

1. Endangered species 2. Wildlife conservation

ISBN   978-1-4263-0358-6;   1-4263-0358-0;
978-1-4263-0265-7 (lib bdg); 1-4263-0265-7 (lib bdg)

This "examines numerous threats to animals in the wild, raising awareness of each species, and detailing the extent and urgency of the problem. The book also encourages young animal lovers to take an active role in the preservation of creatures great and small." Publisher's note

This "eye-catching [title features] full-color photographs. . . . The approach is to understand the challenges to protecting endangered animals, including global warming, destruction of habitat, tagging and tracking, poaching, captive breeding, and cloning." Voice Youth Advocates

Includes glossary and bibliographical references

578.7 Organisms characteristic of specific kinds of environments

Conlan, Kathy

Under the ice. Kids Can Press 2002 55p il $16.95; pa $8.95

Grades: 4 5 6 7   **578.7**

1. Marine biology 2. Marine pollution 3. Polar regions

ISBN 1-55337-001-5; 1-55337-060-0 (pa)

"A Canadian Museum of Nature book."

"In this photo-essay, Conlan details her three-month stay in Antarctica, highlighting some of her experiences and her involvement in ongoing experiments relating to the effects of human waste on marine life." SLJ

"The first-person text creates a feeling of immediacy. . . . Well-captioned, color photos appear throughout the book. . . . Conlan . . . offers readers an engaging account of her adventurous career in scientific field research." Booklist

Ferrari, Andrea

Reef life; [by] Andrea and Antonella Ferrari. Firefly Books 2002 287p il (A firefly guide) pa $24.95

Grades: 6 7 8 9   **578.7**

1. Coral reefs and islands 2. Marine biology

ISBN 978-1-55209-625-3; 1-55209-625-4
                                     LC 2002-277856

Orginal Italian edition, 1999

Describes four hundred species living among coral reefs, covering the range, habitat, behavior, appearance, and size of each animal.

Includes bibliographical references

Kummer, Patricia K.

The Great Barrier Reef; by Patricia K. Kummer. Marshall Cavendish Benchmark 2008 c2009 96p il map (Nature's wonders) lib bdg $24.95

Grades: 5 6 7 8   **578.7**

1. Coral reefs and islands 2. Great Barrier Reef (Australia)

ISBN 978-0-7614-2852-7 (lib bdg); 0-7614-2852-6 (lib bdg)   LC 2007026661

"Provides comprehensive information on the geography, history, wildlife, peoples, and environmental issues of the Great Barrier Reef." Publisher's note

Includes glossary and bibliographical references

Walker, Pamela, 1958-

The continental shelf; [by] Pam Walker & Elaine Wood. Facts on File 2005 142p (Life in the sea) $35 *

Grades: 6 7 8 9   **578.7**

1. Marine biology 2. Continental shelf

ISBN 0-8160-5704-4

This "title presents a comprehensive discussion of the physical aspects of the continental shelf; the variety of life beneath, on, and above the waters; and the many dangers to the health of these realms. . . . [This title has] helpful color photos and black-and-white charts and drawings. [This] important [work is] accessible to a variety of student abilities and should be considered for all collections." SLJ

Includes bibliographical references

The open ocean; [by] Pam Walker and Elaine Wood. Facts on File 2005 132p il (Life in the sea) $35 *

Grades: 6 7 8 9   **578.7**

1.   Marine   animals   2.   Marine   ecology
3. Oceanography

ISBN 0-8160-5705-2   LC 2004-24228

In this title "the areas beyond the continental shelf are profiled, and food chains, the diversity of life forms, and the anatomy of sea animals are discussed. . . . [This book includes] helpful color photos and black-and-white charts and drawings. [This] important [work is] accessible to a variety of student abilities and should be considered for all collections." SLJ

Includes bibliographical references

Wechsler, Doug

Marvels in the muck; life in the salt marshes. 1st ed. Boyds Mills Press 2008 48p il $17.95

Grades: 4 5 6 7   **578.7**

1. Salt marshes 2. Marsh ecology

ISBN 978-1-59078-588-1   LC 2007052583

"A season-by-season look at the ecology of an oft-overlooked habitat. Wechsler's lucid text introduces the insects, birds, reptiles, crustaceans, and other critters that claim this salty expanse as home. . . . Clear color photos present species mentioned in the text." SLJ

Includes glossary and bibliographical references

Winner, Cherie

Life on the edge. Lerner Publications Co. 2006 48p il (Cool science) lib bdg $26.60

Grades: 4 5 6   **578.7**

1. Adaptation (Biology)

ISBN 978-0-8225-2499-1; 0-8225-2499-6

LC 2005011071

This book "introduces creatures in extreme conditions such as thermal pools, Antarctica, and the deep sea. [The book provides] clear explanations of the science and [covers] possible benefits to humans. A variety of photos and information boxes provide an eye-catching . . . layout." Horn Book Guide

Includes glossary and bibliographical references

579   Microorganisms, fungi, algae

Farrell, Jeanette

Invisible allies; microbes that shape our lives. Farrar, Straus & Giroux 2005 165p il lib bdg $17

Grades: 8 9 10 11 12   **579**

1. Microorganisms

ISBN 0-374-33608-3 (lib bdg)   LC 2004-53750

This describes the roles of microbes in the making of cheese, bread, and chocolate, in digestion and killing harmful microbes, and in decomposition for waste treatment.

This is "a fascinating, broad-ranging and imminently readable book. . . . Illustrations include photos as well as interesting archival material." Booklist

Includes glossary and bibliographical references

Latta, Sara L.

The good, the bad, the slimy; the secret life of microbes; [by] Sara Latta; photographs by Dennis Kunkel. Enslow Publishers 2006 128p il lib bdg $31.93 *

Grades: 5 6 7 8 9   **579**

1. Microorganisms

ISBN 0-7660-1294-8 (lib bdg)   LC 2005-35405

This describes how bacteria, viruses, fungi and other microbes "live in and on our bodies, help make food, live in extreme environments, and even change history." Publisher's note

"Explanations are simple and clear, and the layout is appeling, open, and colorful." SLJ

Includes glossary and bibliographical references

May, Suellen

Invasive microbes. Chelsea House 2007 112p il (Invasive species) $30

Grades: 8 9 10 11 12   **579**

1. Microorganisms 2. Biological invasions

ISBN 0-7910-9131-7; 978-0-7910-9131-9

LC 2006011031

"An increase in global transportation has helped even the tiniest of organisms—microbes—find their way to new environments. . . . This . . . resource . . . [explains] the . . . impact . . . of invasive viruses, bacteria, protists, and fungi. This book evaluates scenarios for success in the escalating battle for containment." Publisher's note

Includes glossary and bibliographical references

Stefoff, Rebecca, 1951-

The Moneran kingdom; by Rebecca Stefoff. Marshall Cavendish Benchmark 2008 96p il (Family trees) $23.95

Grades: 6 7 8 9   **579**

1. Microorganisms

ISBN 978-0-7614-3076-6; 0-7614-3076-8

LC 2008-23210

"Explores the habitats, life cycles, and other characteristics of organisms in the Moneran kingdom." Publisher's note

Includes bibliographical references

Walker, Richard, 1951-

Microscopic life; [by] Richard Walker; foreword by Peter C. Doherty. 1st ed. Kingfisher 2004 63p il (Kingfisher knowledge) $12.95

Grades: 4 5 6 7   **579**

1. Microorganisms

ISBN 0-7534-5778-4   LC 2004-1321

"Double-page spreads introduce viruses, bacteria, 'mini animals' (e.g., Hydra and dust mites), and other microorganisms and explain how these unseen entities affect humanity in both harmful and helpful ways. The accompanying photographic enlargements . . . are fascinating." Horn Book Guide

Zabludoff, Marc

The protoctist kingdom. Benchmark Books 2006 95p il (Family trees) lib bdg $29.92 *

Grades: 5 6 7 8   **579**

1. Protoctista

ISBN 0-7614-1818-0   LC 2004-21821

This examines the physical traits, adaptations, diets, habitats, and life cycles of such life forms as bacteria, amoebas, slime nets, molds, algae, coccoliths, forams, and diatoms.

"Fact-filled, yet surprisingly readable. . . . [This] title contains a wide variety of excellent-quality, full-color photographs; interesting sidebars; and diagrams." SLJ

579.5   Fungi Eumycophyta (True fungi)

Souza, D. M. (Dorothy M.)

What is a fungus? Watts 2002 63p il lib bdg $24.50; pa $8.95

Grades: 5 6 7 8   **579.5**

1. Fungi

ISBN 0-531-11979-3 (lib bdg); 0-531-16223-0 (pa)

LC 2001-17565

"Watts library"

This explains "how a fungus lives, what it eats, and how it reproduces. The writing is accessible and entertaining enough to keep readers engaged." SLJ

Includes glossary and bibliographical references

Stefoff, Rebecca, 1951-
The fungus kingdom. Marshall Cavendish Benchmark 2008 95p il (Family trees) lib bdg $32.79
Grades: 6 7 8 9   **579.5**
1. Fungi
ISBN 978-0-7614-2696-7; 0-7614-2696-5
LC 2007003485
"Explores the habitats, life cycles, and other characteristics of organisms in the Fungus Kingdom." Publisher's note
Includes bibliographical references

579.6 Mushrooms

Lincoff, Gary
The Audubon Society field guide to North American mushrooms; [by] Gary H. Lincoff; visual key by Carol Nehring. Knopf 1981 926p il flexible bdg $19.95 *
Grades: 7 8 9 10 11 12 Adult   **579.6**
1. Mushrooms
ISBN 0-394-51992-2   LC 81-80827
"A Chanticleer Press edition. The Audubon Society field guide series"
This guide to 703 species of common mushrooms provides 762 color photographs and descriptions as keys to identifying these plants.
"The author is an expert on mushroom toxins and instills responsible cautions. The photos are uncommonly beautiful." SLJ

580 Plants (Botany)

Casper, Julie Kerr
Plants; life from the earth. Chelsea House 2007 194p il (Natural resources) $39.50
Grades: 8 9 10 11 12   **580**
1. Plants 2. Botany
ISBN 978-0-8160-6358-1; 0-8160-6358-3
LC 2006-28965
This "examines the many plants that exist and the role they play in biodiversity. It focuses on key preservation issues affecting plant life, and the ways everyone can become a 'backyard conservationist.'" Publisher's note
Includes bibliographical references

Gibson, J. Phil
Plant diversity; [by] J. Phil Gibson and Terri R. Gibson. Chelsea House 2006 2007 136p il (The green world) $37.50
Grades: 7 8 9 10 11 12   **580**
1. Plants
ISBN 0-7910-8960-6; 978-0-7910-8960-6
LC 2006-23234
Explores the diversity and natural history of green plants throughout the world.
This book is "lavishly illustrated with full-color photographs and illustrative diagrams . . . written in a clear but not condescending style. . . . An excellent series of

sidebars presents questions and then supports the reader in reasoning to the answers. . . . [It is] well worth the investment." Libr Media Connect
Includes glossary and bibliographical references

Plant sciences; Richard Robinson, editor in chief. Macmillan Ref. USA 2001 4v il set $415
Grades: 7 8 9 10   **580**
1. Botany 2. Plants 3. Reference books
ISBN 0-02-865434-X   LC 00-46064
This set covers "plant-related topics from acid rain to wood products. While this set includes complex information . . . it also offers basic facts on biomes, leaves, cells, individual scientists, related careers, and other subjects. The writing is clear and well organized, and depending on the topic, it's concise or very detailed." SLJ
Includes bibliographical references

Stefoff, Rebecca, 1951-
The flowering plant division. Benchmark Books 2006 91p il (Family trees) $20.95 *
Grades: 6 7 8 9   **580**
1. Plants
ISBN 0-7614-1817-2
This examines the physical traits, adaptations, habitats, and life cycles of flowering plants.
Includes glossary and bibliographical references

580.7 Education, research, related topics

Gardner, Robert, 1929-
Science projects about plants. Enslow Pubs. 1999 112p il (Science projects) lib bdg $26.60
Grades: 7 8 9 10   **580.7**
1. Plants 2. Science projects 3. Science—Experiments
ISBN 0-89490-952-5   LC 98-6821
Provides instructions for over thirty experiments appropriate for science fairs, involving plant physiology, reproduction, and growth
"The book offers solid ideas for projects." Booklist
Includes bibliographical references

VanCleave, Janice Pratt
Janice VanCleave's plants; mind-boggling experiments you can turn into science fair projects. Wiley 1997 90p il (Spectacular science projects series) pa $10.95
Grades: 5 6 7 8   **580.7**
1. Botany 2. Plants 3. Science projects 4. Science—Experiments
ISBN 0-471-14687-0   LC 96-2744
Presents facts about plants and includes experiments, projects, and activities related to each topic
This book "is inspiring without being flashy. . . . The black-and-white line drawings are sketchy but helpful. . . . This is a fine example of helpful information that is neither academically dry nor ingratiatingly slangy." SLJ
Includes glossary

Whitehouse, Patricia, 1958-
Plants; [by] Patricia Whitehouse. 1st ed. Heinemann Library 2008 48p il (Science fair projects) $30
Grades: 5 6 7 8   **580.7**
1. Plants 2. Science—Experiments 3. Science projects
ISBN 978-1-4034-7918-1   LC 2006039547
This guide to science fair projects about plants "is one of the better 'how-to-do-a-science-fair project' books on the market. . . . [It] guides students with initial concrete suggestions and ideas for projects, but continues to challenge students to extend their investigations. . . . The content is presented in a colorful and engaging format." Sci Books Films
Includes glossary and bibliographical references

581.6   Miscellaneous nontaxonomic kinds of plants

Young, Kim J.
Ethnobotany; series editor William G. Hopkins. Chelsea House 2006 c2007 112p il (The green world) lib bdg $37.50
Grades: 7 8 9 10   **581.6**
1. Ethnobotany 2. Economic botany
ISBN 0-7910-8963-0 (lib bdg)
This is "a primer on plant and human relationships and interactions. . . . The reader is given insight into the importance of plants to both ancient and modern cultures and into how people's of particular cultures make use of plants." Sci Books Films
Includes glossary and bibliographical references

581.7   Plant ecology, plants characteristic of specific environments

Johnson, Rebecca L., 1956-
Powerful plant cells; [by] Rebecca L. Johnson; illustrations by Jack Desrocher; diagrams by Jennifer E. Fairman. Millbrook Press 2008 48p il (Microquests) lib bdg $29.27
Grades: 5 6 7 8   **581.7**
1. Plants 2. Cells
ISBN 978-0-8225-7141-4; 0-8225-7141-2
                              LC 2006-36387
Explains what plant cells are, how they were discovered, their components, how they divide, different kinds, and what they do.
Includes bibliographical references

Spilsbury, Richard, 1963-
Plant habitats; Richard & Louise Spilsbury. Rev. and updated. Heinemann Library 2008 48p il (Life of plants) $27.50; pa $7.99
Grades: 5 6 7 8   **581.7**
1. Plants 2. Plant ecology
ISBN   978-1-4329-1502-5;   1-4329-1502-9; 978-1-4329-1509-4 (pa); 1-4329-1509-6 (pa)
                              LC 2008275392

First published 2003
Explains the different ways plants adapt to their environment in order to survive in a particular habitat.
This book "contains many bright and colorful photographs and diagrams to support the text, boldface vocabulary terms, a series of experiments and activities to provide further investigation, a complete glossary, an index, and a list of sources for additional information. . . . [This] volume is a complete and well-rounded unit." Sci Books Films
Includes glossary and bibliographical references

582.13   Plants noted for their flowers

Duncan, Wilbur Howard, 1910-
Wildflowers of the eastern United States; by Wilbur H. Duncan and Marion B. Duncan. University of Georgia Press 1999 380p il $34.95; pa $24.95
Grades: 7 8 9 10 11 12 Adult   **582.13**
1. Wild flowers
ISBN   978-0-8203-2107-3;   0-8203-2107-9; 978-0-8203-2747-1 (pa); 0-8203-2747-6 (pa)
                              LC 98-43314
"The eastern deciduous forest biome, . . . contains a variety of habitats supporting several thousand species of wildflowers. . . . The Duncans . . . have compiled a useful guide to more than 1,000 species. . . . A strength of the book is the photography, and although priority was given to showing diagnostic features, most photos are also very appealing visually. The 20-page introductory section includes a fine glossary and illustrations of necessary terminology." Choice

Niehaus, Theodore F.
A field guide to Pacific states wildflowers; illustrated by Charles L. Ripper. Houghton Mifflin 1976 xxxii, 432p il map (The Peterson field guide) hardcover o.p. pa $19 *
Grades: 7 8 9 10 11 12 Adult   **582.13**
1. Wild flowers
ISBN 0-395-21624-9; 0-395-91095-1 (pa)
                              LC 76-5873
"Sponsored by the National Audubon Society and National Wildlife Federation"
"Field marks of species found in Washington, Oregon, California and adjacent areas; a visual approach arranged by color, form, and detail." Title page
"This offering identifies 1492 common wildflowers. . . . Common and scientific name, habitat, and recognition features are given for each plant." Libr J

Ryden, Hope
Wildflowers around the year; photographs and text by Hope Ryden. Clarion Bks. 2001 90p il $17
Grades: 5 6 7 8   **582.13**
1. Wild flowers
ISBN 0-395-85814-3   LC 00-43011
"Ryden introduces the reader to 38 species of wildflowers. . . . The flowers are identified by both their

Ryden, Hope—*Continued*
common names and the genus-species nomenclature. The months during which they are expected to be in full bloom are given as well." Sci Books Films

"Accompanied by exquisite, sharply focused photos. . . . Filled with interesting tidbits, Ryden's lyrical text meanders appealingly through moments of wonder, experience, explanation, and speculation." Horn Book Guide

Includes bibliographical references

Souza, D. M. (Dorothy M.)
Freaky flowers. Watts 2002 63p il lib bdg $24.50; pa $8.95
Grades: 5 6 7 8   582.13
  1. Flowers
  ISBN 0-531-11981-5 (lib bdg); 0-531-16221-4 (pa)
                                    LC 2001-17573

"Watts library"

"The book begins with a short course in botany that stresses vocabulary and processes. Subsequent chapters discuss different ways plants attract pollinators through colors, odors, and habitats. The last chapter acts as a warning that many plants are endangered because their pollinators are threatened, emphasizing the balance of nature. The outstanding full-color photos feature some of the most spectacular flowers found anywhere. Small sidebars offer interesting bits of trivia about similar plants. The text is packed with biological information and pertinent vocabulary." SLJ

Includes bibliographical references

Spellenberg, Richard
National Audubon Society field guide to North American wildflowers, western region. 2nd ed rev. Knopf 2001 862p il map $19.95 *
Grades: 7 8 9 10 11 12 Adult   582.13
  1. Wild flowers
  ISBN 0-375-40233-0   LC 2001-269242

"A Chanticleer Press edition"

First published 1979

"More than 940 . . . full-color images show the wildflowers of western North America close-up and in their natural habitats. . . . Images are grouped by flower color and shape and keyed to . . . descriptions that reflect current taxonomy." Publisher's note

Thieret, John W., 1926-2005
National Audubon Society field guide to North American wildflowers: eastern region; revising author, John W. Thieret; original authors, William A. Niering and Nancy C. Olmstead. Knopf 2001 879p il map (National Audubon Society field guide series) $19.95 *
Grades: 7 8 9 10 11 12 Adult   582.13
  1. Wild flowers
  ISBN 0-375-40232-2   LC 2001-269241

"A Chanticleer Press edition"

First published 1979 under the authorship of William A. Niering and Nancy C. Olmstead

Spine title: Field guide to wildflowers, eastern region

"Covers the area east of the Rockies and east of the Big Bend area of Texas to the Atlantic. Color photo-graphs together with family and species descriptions make this a most useful field guide." Sci News {review of 1979 edition}

Venning, Frank D.
Wildflowers of North America; a guide to field identification; illustrated by Manabu C. Saito. rev ed. St. Martin's Press 2001 340p il (Golden field guides) pa $14.95
Grades: 8 9 10 11 12 Adult   582.13
  1. Wild flowers
  ISBN 978-1-58238-127-5; 1-58238-127-5
  First published 1984 by Golden Press

Accurate information on size, appearance, habitat, and known ranges and full-color illustrations constitute a guide to more than fifteen hundred native and naturalized species.

Includes bibliographical references

582.16   Trees

Brockman, C. Frank (Christian Frank), 1902-
Trees of North America; a field guide to the major native and introduced species north of Mexico; by C. Frank Brockman; illustrated by Rebecca Merrilees; revised by Jonathan P. Latimer and Karen Stray Nolting with David Challinor. rev and updated ed. St. Martin's Press 2001 280p il map (Golden field guides) pa $14.95
Grades: 8 9 10 11 12 Adult   582.16
  1. Trees—North America
  ISBN 978-1-58238-092-6 (pa); 1-58238-092-9 (pa)
                                    LC 2001272405
  First published 1968 by Golden Press

This "field guide features . . . characteristics—tree shape, bark, leaf, flower, fruit and twig—for quick identification. . . . [It includes] over 730 species in 76 families and 160 range maps." Publisher's note

Includes bibliographical references

Burnie, David
Tree; written by David Burnie. rev ed. DK Pub. 2005 72p il (DK eyewitness books) $15.99; lib bdg $19.99
Grades: 4 5 6 7   582.16
  1. Trees
  ISBN 0-7566-1094-X; 0-7566-1093-1 (lib bdg)
  First published 1988 by Knopf

Photographs and text explore the anatomy and life cycle of trees, examining the different kinds of bark, seeds, and leaves, the commercial processing of trees to make lumber, and the creatures that live in trees.

Gardner, Robert, 1929-
Science project ideas about trees. Enslow Pubs. 1997 96p il (Science project ideas) lib bdg $25.26
Grades: 5 6 7 8   582.16
  1. Trees 2. Science projects 3. Science—Experiments
  ISBN 978-0-89490-846-0 (lib bdg); 0-89490-846-4 (lib bdg)
                                    LC 97-6515

Gardner, Robert, 1929-—*Continued*

Contains many experiments introducing the processes that take place in plants and trees

The directions "are easy to understand, and the vocabulary is fairly accessible. The accompanying diagrams are particularly sharp and clear." SLJ

Includes bibliographical references

Petrides, George A.

A field guide to trees and shrubs; northeastern and north-central United States and southeastern and south-central Canada; illustrations by George A. Petrides, Roger Tory Peterson. 2nd ed. Houghton Mifflin 1986 xxxii, 428p il (The Peterson field guide) pa $19 hardcover o.p. *

Grades: 7 8 9 10 11 12 Adult   **582.16**
1. Trees—North America 2. Shrubs 3. Climbing plants
ISBN 0-395-35370-X   LC 76-157132
First published 1958

"Field marks of all trees, shrubs, and woody vines that grow wild in the northeastern and north-central United States and in southeastern and south-central Canada." Title page

"Descriptions and clear drawings compare similar species. Includes silhouettes showing typical branching of many of the trees." AAAS. Sci Book List. 3d edition

A field guide to western trees; eastern [i.e. western] United States and Canada; illustrated by Olivia Petrides. 1st ed., expanded. Houghton Mifflin 1998 428p il map (The Peterson field guide) pa $20

Grades: 7 8 9 10 11 12 Adult   **582.16**
1. Trees—North America
ISBN 978-0-395-90454-1 (pa); 0-395-90454-4 (pa)
          LC 98013624
First published 1992

Sponsored by the National Audubon Society, the National Wildlife Federation, and the Roger Tory Peterson Institute

This "guide features detailed descriptions of 387 species, arranged in six major groups by visual similarity." Publisher's note

Includes bibliographical references

Ridsdale, Colin

Trees; [by] Colin Ridsdale, John White, Carol Usher; foreword by David Mabberley. DK 2005 360p il (Eyewitness companions) pa $25

Grades: 7 8 9 10   **582.16**
1. Trees
ISBN 978-0-7566-1359-4; 0-7566-1359-0
          LC 2005296635

"From identification and anatomy to commercial exploitation and conservation, this is [a] . . . guide to more than 500 species of trees from around the world." Publisher's note

Williams, Michael D.

Identifying trees; an all-season guide to Eastern North America. Stackpole Books 2007 406p il pa $29.95

Grades: 7 8 9   **582.16**
1. Trees—North America
ISBN 978-0-8117-3360-1; 0-8117-3360-2
          LC 2006-10857

"Describes common locations and identifying characteristics [of trees]. . . . Covers every common tree in eastern North America." Publisher's note

583   Magnoliopsida (Dicotyledons)

Pascoe, Elaine

Carnivorous plants; text by Elaine Pascoe; photographs by Dwight Kuhn. Blackbirch Press 2005 48p il (Nature close-up) $23.70

Grades: 4 5 6 7   **583**
1. Carnivorous plants
ISBN 1-4103-0309-8   LC 2005-276141

This describes such plants as venus flytraps, pitcher plants, cobra plants, and blatterworts, with instructions for growing and investigating them.

Includes glossary and bibliographical references

584   Liliopsida (Monocotyledons)

Brown, Lauren

Grasses, an identification guide; written & illustrated by Lauren Brown. Houghton Mifflin 1979 240p il (Peterson nature library) hardcover o.p. pa $16

Grades: 7 8 910 11 12 Adult   **584**
1. Grasses
ISBN   978-0-395-27624-2;   0-395-27624-1;
978-0-395-62881-2 (pa); 0-395-62881-4 (pa)
          LC 78-24545

Identifies "135 of the most common species of North American grasses, sedges, and rushes, with their economic and ecological importance. " Publisher's note

Includes bibliographical references

585   Pinophyta (Gymnosperms) Coniferales (Conifers)

Stefoff, Rebecca, 1951-

The conifer division; [by] Rebecca Stefoff. Marshall Cavendish Benchmark 2008 96p il (Family trees) $23.95

Grades: 6 7 8 9   **585**
1. Evergreens 2. Biology—Classification
ISBN 978-0-7614-3077-3; 0-7614-3077-6
          LC 2008-23373

"Explores the life cycles and other characteristics of plants, trees, and shrubs in the Conifer division." Publisher's note

Includes glossary and bibliographical references

590   Animals (Zoology)

Casper, Julie Kerr
Animals; creatures that roam the planet. Chelsea House Publishers 2007 179p il map (Natural resources) $39.50
Grades: 8 9 10 11 12   **590**
  1. Animals
  ISBN 978-0-8160-6353-6; 0-8160-6353-2
                     LC 2006030227
This describes how animals have adapted to various environments on Earth and how they have evolved, the causes of animal extinctions in the past and the present, the importance of animals to humans, and the conservation of animal resources.
  Includes bibliographical references

Davies, Nicola, 1958-
Extreme animals; the toughest creatures on Earth; illustrated by Neal Layton. Candlewick Press 2006 61p il $12.99; pa $7.99
Grades: 3 4 5 6   **590**
  1. Animals 2. Adaptation (Biology)
  ISBN   978-0-7636-3067-6;   0-7636-3067-5;
  978-0-7636-4127-6 (pa); 0-7636-4127-8 (pa)
                     LC 2005-43544
"There is life everywhere on Earth . . . and much of that life thrives in conditions that humans could not endure for five minutes or less. This funny and appealing little book describes who these amazing life-forms are and how they manage to survive. Simple and inviting cartoon drawings enliven the text and convey the types of extremes in an easy-to-understand manner." SLJ
  Includes glossary

Johnson, Jinny
Animal tracks & signs. National Geographic Society 2008 192p il $24.95 *
Grades: 5 6 7 8   **590**
  1. Animal tracks 2. Animals 3. Tracking and trailing
  ISBN 978-1-4263-0253-4; 1-4264-0253-3
"This attractive book describes the tracks (paw prints, bird claw prints, slimy trails) and signs (molted skin, food remains, scat, tree markings) that animals leave in their wake. . . . A typical two-page layout includes a photo and short paragraph about the animal category, three or four colored boxes containing a photo or drawing of a specific animal (serval, bobcat), and a description of its size, geographic range, habitat, food, tracks and signs, and comments. . . . The beautiful photos vary from action . . . to informational. . . . The language is simple and readable." Voice Youth Advocates
  Includes glossary and bibliographical references

Lewin, Ted, 1935-
Tooth and claw; animal adventures in the wild. HarperCollins Pubs. 2003 97p il maps $15.99; lib bdg $16.89 *
Grades: 4 5 6 7   **590**
  1. Wildlife 2. Dangerous animals
  ISBN 0-688-14105-6; 0-688-14106-4 (lib bdg)
                     LC 2002-4588

Contents: Beach master; Grizzly; Macaco meojor; Waiting for puff adder; Bears, bears, bears; Roar; The meat eaters of Kibale; Barnstorming; Sleeping with bison; Rattler; Deputy Dawg; Downwind of a dung beetle; The joker; Garbage elephants
  Author/illustrator Ted Lewin relates fourteen of his experiences with wild animals while travelling the world, following each anecdote with facts about the featured animal and its habitat
  "This is outstanding nature storytelling, related in a distinctive voice imbued with humor and personality; it's even better when read aloud." Horn Book
  Includes glossary

Myers, Jack
On the trail of the Komodo dragon and other explorations of science in action; scientists probe 11 animal mysteries; illustrated by John Rice. Boyds Mills Press 1999 63p il $17.95; pa $9.95
Grades: 4 5 6 7   **590**
  1. Animals
  ISBN 1-56397-761-3; 1-59078-279-8 (pa)
  Based on science reporting columns published in Highlights for Children
  "Each article answers an intriguing question about a particular animal: How do horses sleep? Why do snakes flick their tongues? What helps cats fall safely? Information is clearly presented in succinct chapters; frequent illustrations, sidebars, and section titles further break up the text." Booklist
  Includes bibliographical references

Noyes, Deborah, 1965-
One kingdom; our lives with animals—the human-animal bond in myth, history, science, and story. Houghton Mifflin Company 2006 128p il $18 *
Grades: 7 8 9 10   **590**
  1. Animals
  ISBN 0-618-49914-8   LC 2005-25446
  In this "photo-essay, Noyes examines the ways that human lives have overlapped with animals and how our beliefs, culture, and science have been impacted throught history by the essential but frequently paradoxical human-animal connection. . . . Readers will find the provocative questions Noyes raises compelling and challenging, and the lyrical, urgent prose, along with beautiful black-and-white photos of the animals up close, will draw serious students and browsers alike." Booklist
  Includes bibliographical references

Staub, Frank J.
The signs animals leave; [by] Frank Staub. Watts 2001 63p il $24.50; pa $8.95 *
Grades: 4 5 6   **590**
  1. Animal behavior 2. Animal tracks
  ISBN 0-531-11863-0; 0-531-16575-2 (pa)
                     LC 00-43603
  "Watts library"
  This describes traces left by animals which reveal their behavior including tracks and scents
  Includes bibliographical references

590.3 Encyclopedias and dictionaries

Amazing animals of the world 1. Grolier 2008
10v il map set $199
  Grades: 6 7 8 9   590.3
  1. Animals—Encyclopedias 2. Reference books
  ISBN 978-0-7172-6225-0 (set); 0-7172-6225-1 (set)
                                         LC 2007012982
This "is a 10-volume set featuring 400 animals from
around the globe. Each page highlights one animal with
an interesting description and full-color picture. The pictures are beautiful and visually engaging. . . . The information is concise and appealing enough for reading for
personal information or for use in basic research." Sci
Books Films
  Includes glossary and bibliographical references

Animal; editors-in-chief, David Burnie & Don E.
  Wilson. DK Pub. 2001 624p il map hardcover
  o.p. pa $25
  Grades: 8 9 10 11 12 Adult   590.3
  1. Animals—Encyclopedias 2. Reference books
  ISBN 0-7894-7764-5; 0-7566-1634-4 (pa)
                                         LC 2001-28346
"The book is divided into three sections. The first is
a general introduction to animals and their lives. The
second looks at animal habitats, describing each habitat
in terms of its climate, plant life, and the animals found
there. The main part of the book profiles over 2000 species of animals, from the familiar to the extremely rare,
and includes some newly recognized species. . . . Each
individual listing gives the animal's range, habitat, size,
and social unit and includes a full-color illustration and
descriptive paragraph. . . . An outstanding publication
appropriate for all types of libraries. . . . This is unique
for its comprehensiveness and its coverage of animal
habitats and major evolutionary developments." Libr J

Animals; a children's encyclopedia. DK Pub. 2008
  304p il map $29.99 *
  Grades: 4 5 6 7   590.3
  1. Animals—Encyclopedias 2. Reference books
  ISBN 978-0-7566-4027-9; 0-7566-4027-X
                                         LC 2008-04654
"A visual encyclopedia of the major animal groups.
. . . Succinct but important details are provided for each
animal including size, location, life span, habitat, and
conservation status, using special colored icons. . . .
This is a true children's encyclopedia and a must-have
reference for every library." Libr Media Connect

The **encyclopedia** of animals; a complete visual
  guide; [text, Jenni Bruce . . . et al.] University
  of California Press 2004 608p il map $39.95
  Grades: 7 8 9 10 11 12   590.3
  1. Animals—Encyclopedias 2. Reference books
  ISBN 0-520-24406-0   LC 2004-303646
"The book starts with an introduction to animal evolution, biology, behavior, classification, habitats, and current conservation issues. This is followed by a survey of
animals, divided into the standard taxonomic classifications of mammals, birds, reptiles, amphibians, fishes, and
invertebrates. . . . Icons and symbols indicate habitat,

size, weight, and social and reproductive habits of the
various species." Libr J
  "This lavishly illustrated chronicle of Earth's
biodiversity is a visual delight." Booklist

McGhee, Karen
  Encyclopedia of animals; [by] Karen McGhee,
  George McKay. National Geographic 2007 192p il
  map $24.95; lib bdg $38.90 *
  Grades: 4 5 6 7 8   590.3
  1. Animals—Encyclopedias 2. Reference books
  ISBN 0-7922-5936-X; 0-7922-5937-8 (lib bdg)
                                         LC 2006299476
"This lavish, ambitious volume contains full-color illustrations of more than 1500 species. Each brief entry
includes common and scientific names and mention of an
interesting physical or behavioral trait. Range maps show
where each animal is found, and conservation data notes
which species are extinct, endangered, or vulnerable. In
addition to the realistic drawings, there are dramatic photos of animals in their habitats." SLJ

590.73 Collections and exhibits of living animals

Zoehfeld, Kathleen Weidner
  Wild lives; a history of the people & animals of
  the Bronx Zoo; with photographs from the
  Wildlife Conservation Society. Alfred A. Knopf
  2006 86p il $18.95; lib bdg $20.99
  Grades: 5 6 7 8   590.73
  1. Bronx Zoo 2. Zoos 3. Animals
  ISBN 0-375-80630-X; 0-375-90630-4 (lib bdg)
                                         LC 2005-18943
"Zoehfeld tells the story of the Bronx Zoo, from the
preparations for its opening in 1899 to its current efforts
in the areas of conservation and education. Along with
information on the zoo, she discusses trends in thinking
about wildlife, the ethics of removing animals from their
habitats for their safety or for public display, and ongoing threats to the existence of many species. . . . The
many photos, attractive layout, and use of color contribute to the visual appeal of this informative zoo story."
Booklist
  Includes bibliographical references

591.3 Genetics, evolution, young animals

Eamer, Claire
  Super crocs & monster wings; modern animals'
  ancient past; [by] Claire Eamer. Annick Press
  2008 93p il $19.95; pa $9.95
  Grades: 4 5 6 7   591.3
  1. Animals 2. Evolution 3. Prehistoric animals
  ISBN   978-1-55451-130-3;   1-55451-130-5;
  978-1-55451-129-7 (pa); 1-55451-129-1 (pa)
"The author's conversational and often-humorous
voice slides readers effortlessly through a great deal of

Eamer, Claire—*Continued*
fascinating scientific information in this title on animal evolution. After a brief but clear introduction to geologic time and Linnaean taxonomy, six chapters compare ancient and modern dragonflies, crocodilians, camelids, sloths, glyptodonts (armadillos), and beavers. . . . Jazzy fonts; crisp photos and paintings; and tilted illustrations, titles, and captions create an up-to-the-minute feel." SLJ

591.5   Behavior

Hirschi, Ron
Lions, tigers, and bears; why are big predators so rare? [by] Ron Hirschi; photographs by Thomas D. Mangelsen. Boyds Mills Press 2007 40p il $16.95
Grades: 3 4 5 6   **591.5**
1. Predatory animals 2. Wildlife conservation
ISBN 978-1-59078-435-8; 1-59078-435-9
                                        LC 2006037956
"Cougars, polar bears, lions, cheetahs, tigers, grizzly bears, and killer whales are nature's threatened giants. Each one gets its due in this important book. Hirschi's approach is gentle and engaging, but the urgency of his message is not lost—these animals need human help. . . . The text is clear and easy to follow, and the problems are balanced with hope. . . . Mangelsen's crisp color photographs are beautifully composed and heart-grabbing." SLJ
Includes bibliographical references

Settel, Joanne
Exploding ants; amazing facts about how animals adapt. Atheneum Bks. for Young Readers 1999 40p il $16.95
Grades: 4 5 6 7   **591.5**
1. Animal behavior
ISBN 0-689-81739-8   LC 97-35395
Describes examples of animal behavior that may strike humans as disgusting, including the "gross" ways animals find food, shelter, and safety in the natural world
"This attractive volume presents its material as wondrous science instead of sensational effect." Booklist
Includes glossary and bibliographical references

591.56   Behavior relating to life cycle

Perry, Phyllis J., 1933-
Animals that hibernate. Watts 2001 63p il lib bdg $24.50
Grades: 4 5 6   **591.56**
1. Hibernation
ISBN 0-531-11864-9   LC 00-43511
"Watts library"
This describes the hibernation habits of a variety of animals including gray bats and grizzly bears
Includes bibliographical references

Animals under the ground; [by] Phyllis Perry. Watts 2001 63p il lib bdg $24.50
Grades: 4 5 6   **591.56**
1. Animal behavior
ISBN 0-531-11759-6   LC 00-43601
"Watts library"
This describes the behavior and adaptations of animals that go underground including moles, pocket gophers, kangaroo rats, prairie dogs, and badgers
Includes bibliographical references

591.59   Communication

Sayre, April Pulley
Secrets of sound; studying the calls and songs of whales, elephants, and birds. Houghton Mifflin 2002 63p il (Scientists in the field) $16 *
Grades: 4 5 6 7   **591.59**
1. Animal communication
ISBN 0-618-01514-0   LC 2001-51877
Examines the work of several bioacousticians, scientists who study the sounds made by living creatures, discussing the results and importance of their research
"This fascinating title shows the thrill of scientific discovery up close. . . . Lots of well-edited quotes from the scientists convey their contagious enthusiasm for what they do, and sharp color photos, sound charts, and activity boxes break up the text, making it even more readable." Booklist
Includes glossary and bibliographical references

591.6   Miscellaneous nontaxonomic kinds of animals

Singer, Marilyn, 1948-
Venom. Darby Creek 2007 96p il $19.95 *
Grades: 5 6 7 8   **591.6**
1. Poisonous animals
ISBN 978-1-58196-043-3; 1-58196-043-3
"Singer introduces a teeming menagerie of creatures . . . that use venom for attack, defense, or, commonly, both. . . . The close-up, color photos . . . include not only views of many creepy crawlies but also such arresting scenes as wood ants spraying formic acid. . . . Browsers and dedicated young naturalists alike will enthusiastically dig their teeth into this substantial survey." Booklist

Wilkes, Angela
Dangerous creatures; foreword by Steve Leonard. Kingfisher 2003 63p il (Kingfisher knowledge) $11.95
Grades: 5 6 7 8   **591.6**
1. Dangerous animals
ISBN 0-7534-5622-2   LC 2003-40063
Describes various kinds of dangerous animals, such as lions, piranhas, killer bees, and vampire bats

591.68 Rare and endangered animals

Miles, Victoria, 1966-
Wild science; amazing encounters between animals and people who study them. Raincoast Books 2004 168p il pa $18.95
Grades: 5 6 7 8   **591.68**
1. Zoologists 2. Endangered species
ISBN 1-55192-618-0
This offers a "look at 10 wildlife biologists and their work. Each chapter contains sections describing a field experience, biographical data on the scientist, goals set and procedures followed, and pertinent facts on the animals themselves (including classification, habitat, food, and so on). . . . The readable text is conversational in tone, with frequent quotes from the scientists themselves, and is spiced with full-color photos of both animals and biologists." SLJ

591.7 Animal ecology, animals characteristic of specific environments

The **Deep**; Claire Nouvian [editor] University of Chicago Press 2007 252p il $60
Grades: 8 9 10 11 12 Adult   **591.7**
1. Marine animals 2. Marine ecology
ISBN 978-0-226-59566-5; 0-226-59566-8
LC 2006-26921
"The Deep takes readers . . . into the darkest realms of the ocean . . . revealing nature's oddest and most mesmerizing creatures." Publisher's note
"Readers will pick up science journalist Nouvian's book for its stunning, 200-plus full-page color photographs of dumbo octopi, vampire squid, frilled sharks, and hydrothermal vent worms; they will hang on to it for the well-written, extremely informative text. . . . Highly recommended for all types and sizes of libraries." Libr J

Includes bibliographical references

Exploring the world of aquatic life. Chelsea House Publishers 2009 6v il lib bdg set $210
Grades: 5 6 7 8   **591.7**
1. Marine animals—Encyclopedias 2. Reference books
ISBN 978-1-60413-255-7; 1-60413-255-8
LC 2008030416
This set "offers an introduction to the diversity of animals that inhabit oceans, rivers, and lakes. . . . Entries are arranged alphabetically. . . . [The set includes] more than 100 articles. . . . Large photographs and illustrations appear on every two-page spread. . . . With its large typeface, clear explanations, and open layout, this set will appeal to younger students and would be a useful addition to school and public libraries." Booklist

Includes bibliographical references

Johnson, Jinny
Simon & Schuster children's guide to sea creatures. Simon & Schuster Bks. for Young Readers 1998 80p il $21.95
Grades: 4 5 6 7   **591.7**
1. Marine animals
ISBN 0-689-81534-4   LC 97-8227
Describes the major groups of marine animals, including fish, birds, mammals, and crustaceans
"A beautifully illustrated guide, with a full-color drawing of each animal. . . . The book has enough information to be a useful research tool in the library. The organization, by habitat, is outstanding." Book Rep
Includes glossary

Swinburne, Stephen R.
The woods scientist; with photographs by Susan C. Morse. Houghton Mifflin 2002 41p il map (Scientists in the field) $16 *
Grades: 4 5 6 7   **591.7**
1. Morse, Susan 2. Forest animals
ISBN 0-618-04602-X   LC 2002-302
A devoted nature lover and animal tracker, Sue Morse shares her knowledge and love of some of the creatures that inhabit America's woodlands
"The language is immediate, clear, and filled with moment-by-moment observations and well-presented facts. . . . Readers will come away with a much more informed view of wildlife at risk, enriched by Morse's superb color photographs." Booklist
Includes glossary and bibliographical references

Vogel, Carole Garbuny
Ocean wildlife. Franklin Watts 2003 95p il $29.50; pa $12.95
Grades: 5 6 7 8   **591.7**
1. Marine animals
ISBN 0-531-12324-3; 0-531-16681-3 (pa)
LC 2003-5302
Discusses how various underwater creatures have adapted to their environment in order to keep themselves safe from dangerous predators
This offers "magnificent, full-color photographs. . . . The clearly written narrative introduces the many creatures that have adapted to the harsh conditions of the ocean. The disastrous effects of overfishing, contamination, and pollution are briefly examined." SLJ

592 Invertebrates

Cerullo, Mary M., 1949-
Sea soup: zooplankton; [by] Mary M. Cerullo; photography by Bill Curtsinger. Tilbury House 2001 39p il $16.95 *
Grades: 5 6 7 8   **592**
1. Zooplankton
ISBN 0-88448-219-7   LC 00-46721
This book "opens a pellucid window into the drifting world of mostly minute animals that, along with phytoplankton, form an aqueous 'soup' that nourishes a wide variety of sea creatures. . . . Curtsinger's often extraor-

Cerullo, Mary M., 1949-—*Continued*
dinary color photos allow readers to envision the often microscopically small creatures delineated in the text. . . . This is a fascinating look at a watery zoo of creatures whose ecological importance is far beyond the measure of their size." SLJ

Includes glossary and bibliographical references

Meinkoth, Norman August, 1913-
The Audubon Society field guide to North American seashore creatures; [by] Norman A. Meinkoth. Knopf 1981 799p il maps flexible bdg $19.95 *
Grades: 7 8 9 10 11 12 Adult   **592**
  1. Invertebrates 2. Marine biology
  ISBN 0-394-51993-0   LC 81-80828
"A Chanticleer Press edition. The Audubon Society field guide series"
This "unique field guide covers some 850 marine invertebrate animals living in or around the shallow waters of the temperate seacoasts of the United States and Canada. Excellent color photographs are grouped at the beginning of the book, followed by text that gives, for each animal, a short description, common and scientific names, habitat, range, and comments." Malinowsky. Best Sci & Technol Ref Books for Young People

594   Mollusca and Molluscoidea

Arthur, Alex
Shell; written by Alex Arthur; [special photography, Andreas von Einsiedel, Dave King, Colin Keates] Dorling Kindersley 2005 62p il (DK eyewitness books) $15.99; lib bdg $19.99
Grades: 4 5 6 7   **594**
  1. Shells
  ISBN 0-7894-5830-6; 0-7894-6558-2 (lib bdg)
First published 1989 by Knopf
Photographs and text examine different types of shells, including seashells, eggshells, and fossil shells, focusing on such aspects as how shells camouflage themselves and how they may be collected.

Douglass, Jackie Leatherbury
Peterson first guide to shells of North America; illustrations by John Douglass. Houghton Mifflin 1989 128p il pa $5.95 *
Grades: 7 8 9 10 11 12 Adult   **594**
  1. Shells
  ISBN 0-395-91182-6   LC 88-32884
"Shell collectors will enjoy the basic descriptions of shell types. Douglass has included the 'most colorful, not necessarily the most common, shells.' . . . Filled with precise color drawings and concise identification information." Booklist

595.3   Crustacea

Lassieur, Allison
Crabs, lobsters, and shrimps. Watts 2003 47p il (Animals in order) $25
Grades: 4 5 6   **595.3**
  1. Crustaceans
  ISBN 0-531-12265-4   LC 2002-11293
Explores the relationship between members of the decapoda order, including descriptions of several types of lobsters, crabs, and shrimp
This book makes "for fascinating reading. . . . Photographs are glorious." Libr Media Connect
Includes glossary and bibliographical references

595.4   Chelicerata Arachnida

Montgomery, Sy
The tarantula scientist; text by Sy Montgomery; photographs by Nic Bishop. Houghton Mifflin Co. 2004 80p il map (Scientists in the field) $18 *
Grades: 4 5 6 7   **595.4**
  1. Marshall, Samuel D. 2. Tarantulas
  ISBN 0-618-14799-3   LC 2003-20125
Describes the research that Samuel Marshall and his students are doing on tarantulas, including the largest spider on earth, the Goliath birdeating tarantula
"Enthusiasm for the subject and respect for both Marshall and his eight-legged subjects come through on every page of the clear, informative, and even occasionally humorous text. Bishop's full-color photos . . . are amazing." Booklist
Includes glossary and bibliographical references

Stefoff, Rebecca, 1951-
The arachnid class. Marshall Cavendish Benchmark 2008 96p il (Family trees) $23.95
Grades: 6 7 8 9   **595.4**
  1. Spiders
  ISBN 978-0-7614-3075-9; 0-7614-3075-X
             LC 2008017561
"Explores the habitats, life cycles, and other characteristics of arachnids, such as spiders, scorpions, mites, and ticks."
Includes glossary and bibliographical references

Zabludoff, Marc
Spiders; [by] Marc Zabludoff. Marshall Cavendish Benchmark 2006 112p il (Animalways) lib bdg $31.36 *
Grades: 7 8 9 10   **595.4**
  1. Spiders
  ISBN 0-7614-1747-8   LC 2004-16681
This discusses the evolution of spiders, their places in human culture, their life cycles, anatomy, and behavior
"Strong writing melds well with well-selected photos, all of which are clearly produced and of high quality. Some of the images are stunning." SLJ
Includes glossary and bibliographical references

595.7   Insecta (Insects)

Dixon, Norma

Focus on flies. Fitzhenry & Whiteside 2008 32p il $18.95

Grades: 4 5 6 7   **595.7**

1. Flies

ISBN 978-1-55005-128-5; 1-55005-128-8

This "chatty, informative title, illustrated with many clear color photos and diagrams, will hook readers with its fascinating view of a fly's 'creepy cool world.' . . . The gross details will appeal to middle-grade readers, who will then go on to learn about anatomy, metamorphosis, adaptation, diversity, classification, and flies' roles in plant pollination." Booklist

Includes bibliographical references

Evans, Arthur V.

National Wildlife Federation field guide to insects and spiders & related species of North America; written by Arthur Evans; foreword by Craig Tufts. Sterling Pub. 2007 496p il map pa $19.95

Grades: 8 9 10 11 12 Adult   **595.7**

1. Insects 2. Spiders

ISBN 978-1-4027-4153-1; 1-4027-4153-7

LC 2006-19491

"This guide presents a glimpse of the incredible array of colors, shapes, and forms found within the phylum Arthropoda. . . . Over 380 pages of color photographs follow, most showing two or three different species. . . . This is a very good guide that will find a wide audience." Choice

Includes bibliographical references

Jackson, Donna M., 1959-

The bug scientists; by Donna M. Jackson. Houghton Mifflin 2002 48p il (Scientists in the field) $16 *

Grades: 4 5 6 7   **595.7**

1. Insects

ISBN 0-618-10868-8   LC 2001-39256

Bug scientists, called entomologists, present information on insects and explain how they use that information in their work

"The much-maligned world of insects becomes fascinating in this . . . entry in the excellent Scientists in the Field series. . . . The highly readable text weaves in plenty of science. . . . With its crisp photos and lively story angles and language, this is sure to attract young readers." Booklist

Includes glossary and bibliographical references

Landau, Elaine

Killer bees. Enslow Publishers 2003 48p il map (Fearsome, scary, and creepy animals) lib bdg $23.93

Grades: 4 5 6   **595.7**

1. Bees

ISBN 978-0-7660-2061-0; 0-7660-2061-4

LC 2002-6937

Introduces Africanized, or killer, bees and why they sometimes attack humans, and tells of some real-life bee attacks.

The text is "spiced with dramatic anecdotes and embellished with diagrams, maps, and color photos." SLJ

Lasky, Kathryn

Monarchs; photographs by Christopher G. Knight. Harcourt Brace & Co. 1993 63p il pa $12 hardcover o.p. *

Grades: 4 5 6 7   **595.7**

1. Butterflies 2. Wildlife conservation

ISBN 978-0-15-255297-8 (pa); 0-15-255297-9 (pa)

LC 92-33972

"A Gulliver Green book"

Describes the life cycle and winter migrations of the eastern and western monarch butterflies and towns that protect their winter habitats including Pacific Grove, California and El Rosario, Mexico

"Vibrant description melds with fascinating full-color photographs in a book that strikes a perfect balance between science and humanity." SLJ

Latimer, Jonathan P.

Butterflies; [by] Jonathan P. Latimer, Karen Stray Nolting; illustrations by Amy Bartlett Wright; foreword by Virginia Marie Peterson. Houghton Mifflin 2000 48p il (Peterson field guides for young naturalists) $15; pa $5.95

Grades: 4 5 6 7   **595.7**

1. Butterflies

ISBN 0-395-97943-9; 0-395-97944-7 (pa)

LC 99-38605

A guide to help identify various butterflies, using the Peterson System of identification

Caterpillars; [by] Jonathan P. Latimer, Karen Stray Nolting; illustrations by Amy Bartlett Wright; foreword by Virginia Marie Peterson. Houghton Mifflin 2000 48p il (Peterson field guides for young naturalists) $15; pa $5.95

Grades: 4 5 6 7   **595.7**

1. Caterpillars

ISBN 0-395-97942-0; 0-395-97945-5 (pa)

LC 99-38944

Describes the physical characteristics, behavior, and habitat of a variety of caterpillars, arranged by the categories "Smooth," "Bumpy," "Sluglike," "Horned," "Hairy," "Bristly," and "Spiny"

Milne, Lorus Johnson, 1912-

The Audubon Society field guide to North American insects and spiders; [by] Lorus and Margery Milne; visual key by Susan Rayfield. Knopf 1980 989p il $19.95 *

Grades: 7 8 9 10 11 12 Adult   **595.7**

1. Insects 2. Spiders

ISBN 0-394-50763-0   LC 80-7620

"A Chanticleer Press edition. The Audubon Society field guide series"

Milne, Lorus Johnson, 1912-—*Continued*
The authors "have based their field guide on 702 excellent color photographs (75 of which are of spiders and other arachnids). In addition to some general information, the text (two thirds of the book) is made up of brief comments on each kind of arthropod pictured." Choice
Includes glossary

Pascoe, Elaine
Beetles; text by Elaine Pascoe; photographs by Dwight Kuhn. Blackbirch Press 2000 48p il (Nature close-up) lib bdg $23.70
Grades: 4 5 6   595.7
1. Beetles
ISBN 1-56711-175-0   LC 99-53770
Explains the characteristics, habits, life cycle, and appearance of the many species of beetles. Includes experiments
This book is "well organized and clearly written." SLJ
Includes glossary and bibliographical references

Flies; text by Elaine Pascoe; photographs by Dwight Kuhn. Blackbirch Press 2000 48p il (Nature close-up) lib bdg $23.70
Grades: 4 5 6   595.7
1. Flies
ISBN 1-56711-149-1   LC 99-53769
Explains the characteristics, habits, life cycle, and appearance of the many species of flies. Includes experiments
This book is "well organized and clearly written." SLJ
Includes glossary and bibliographical references

Pyle, Robert Michael
The Audubon Society field guide to North American butterflies; visual key by Carol Nehring and Jane Opper. Knopf 1981 916p il $19.95 *
Grades: 7 8 9 10 11 12 Adult   595.7
1. Butterflies
ISBN 0-394-51914-0   LC 80-84240
"A Chanticleer Press edition. The Audubon Society field guide series"
This guide "introduces more than 600 species of North American butterfly, including those native to the Hawaiian Islands. A section of brilliant color plates (more than 1,000 of them) featuring butterflies in their natural habitats, follows a general introduction and notes on text organization and use." Booklist

Rodriguez, Ana Maria, 1958-
Secret of the plant-killing ants . . . and more! Enslow Publishers 2008 c2009 48p il (Animal secrets revealed!) lib bdg $23.93
Grades: 5 6 7 8   595.7
1. Insects 2. Ants
ISBN 978-0-7660-2953-8 (lib bdg); 0-7660-2953-0 (lib bdg)   LC 2007039494
"Explains why ants in the Amazon rainforest kill all but one species of plant and details other strange abilities of different types of animals." Publisher's note
Includes glossary and bibliographical references

Schlaepfer, Gloria G.
Butterflies. Marshall Cavendish Benchmark 2006 112p il (Animalways) lib bdg $31.36
Grades: 6 7 8 9   595.7
1. Butterflies
ISBN 0-7614-1745-1   LC 2004-16682
This discusses the evolution of butterflies, their places in human culture, their life cycles, anatomy, and behavior
"Strong writing melds well with well-selected photos, all of which are clearly produced and of high quality. Some of the images are stunning." SLJ
Includes glossary and bibliographical references

Schwabacher, Martin
Bees. Benchmark Bks. 2002 c2003 112p il map (Animalways) lib bdg $35.64
Grades: 6 7 8 9   595.7
1. Bees
ISBN 978-0-7614-1392-9 (lib bdg); 0-7614-1392-8 (lib bdg)   LC 2002-909
Describes the physical characteristics, behavior, habitat, and life cycle of various types of bees
Includes glossary and bibliographical references

Whalley, Paul Ernest Sutton
Butterfly & moth; written by Paul Whalley; [special photography, Colin Keates, Kim Taylor, and Dave King] Dorling Kindersley 2000 63p il (DK eyewitness books) $15.99
Grades: 4 5 6 7   595.7
1. Butterflies 2. Moths
ISBN 0-7894-5832-2
First published 1988 by Knopf
Photographs and text explore the behavior and life cycles of butterflies and moths, examining mating rituals, camouflage, habitat, growth from pupa to larva to adult, and other aspects.

Wilkes, Sarah, 1964-
Insects; [by] Sarah Wilkes. World Almanac Library 2006 48p il (World Almanac Library of the animal kingdom) lib bdg $30.60
Grades: 5 6 7 8   595.7
1. Insects
ISBN 0-8368-6211-2 (lib bdg); 978-0-8368-6211-9 (lib bdg)   LC 2005052629
This "discusses a range of insects that help keep the natural world in balance. . . . [It describes] the common physical and behavioral traits of this . . . animal category . . . [and] what makes each species unique and how it fits into the natural world." Publisher's note
"One or two fine-quality, color close-up photos of representative species accompany the text on almost every page. . . . [This title is] precisely written, with unusual scientific terms defined as they appear." SLJ
Includes bibliographical references

Zabludoff, Marc

Beetles; by Marc Zabludoff. Marshall Cavendish Benchmark 2007 112p il (Animalways) lib bdg $34.21

Grades: 6 7 8 9　　　　　　　　　　　　**595.7**
1. Beetles
ISBN 978-0-7614-2532-8　　　　LC 2006038518
This describes the place of beetles in the animal kingdom, their evolution, anatomy, physiology, life cycle, diversity, and relationship to humans.

Includes glossary and bibliographical references

The insect class. Benchmark Books 2006 95p il (Family trees) lib bdg $29.93 *

Grades: 6 7 8 9　　　　　　　　　　　　**595.7**
1. Insects
ISBN 0-7614-1819-9 (lib bdg)　　　LC 2004-21819
This examines physical traits, adaptations, diets, habitats, and life cycles of insects.

"Fact-filled, yet surprisingly readable. . . . [This] title contains a wide variety of excellent-quality, full-color photographs; interesting sidebars; and diagrams." SLJ

Includes glossary and bibliographical references

596　Chordata

Silverstein, Alvin

Vertebrates; {by} Alvin, Virginia, and Robert Silverstein. 21st Cent. Bks. (NY) 1996 64p il (Kingdoms of life) lib bdg $25.90

Grades: 5 6 7 8　　　　　　　　　　　　**596**
1. Vertebrates
ISBN 0-8050-3517-6　　　　　　LC 95-45672
"Using a minimal amount of scientific terminology, the authors . . . provide a successful introduction for young readers to the basic principles of the taxonomy of vertebrates. . . . Color photographs that are suitably placed throughout the text aid in making the subject matter clear." Sci Books Films

Includes glossary

597　Cold-blooded vertebrates Pisces (Fishes)

Benchley, Peter, 1940-2006

Shark life; true stories about sharks & the sea; adapted for young people by Karen Wojtyla. Delacorte 2005 193p il $15.95, lib bdg $17.99

Grades: 5 6 7 8　　　　　　　　　　　　**597**
1. Sharks 2. Dangerous animals
ISBN 0-385-73109-4; 0-385-90135-6 (lib bdg)
Adapted from the adult's title for adults, Shark trouble
"Benchley writes about his personal experiences with sharks as well as a variety of other sea creatures considered dangerous to humans." SLJ

This "is an engaging, frequently exciting recounting of one man's fascinating adventures in the ocean." Booklist

Includes glossary

Buttfield, Helen

The secret life of fishes; from angels to zebras on the coral reef; watercolors & text by Helen Buttfield. Abrams 1999 72p il map $19.95

Grades: 5 6 7 8　　　　　　　　　　　　**597**
1. Fishes 2. Coral reefs and islands
ISBN 0-8109-3933-9　　　　　　LC 99-10892
Alphabetical entries introduce more than 250 fishes native to coral reefs around the world. Behavior, mating, and feeding habits are discussed. Illustrated with full-color photographs

Capuzzo, Mike

Close to shore; the terrifying shark attacks of 1916. Crown 2003 140p il $16.95; lib bdg $18.99

Grades: 6 7 8 9　　　　　　　　　　　　**597**
1. Sharks
ISBN 0-375-82231-3; 0-375-92231-8 (lib bdg)
　　　　　　　　　　　　　　LC 2002-29918
An adaptation of the title for adults published 2001 by Broadway Bks.

Details the first documented cases in American history of sharks attacking swimmers, which occured along the Atlantic coast of New Jersey in 1916

"This book has a rich assortment of photos and news clippings. . . . Capuzzo reconstructs events with a novelist's flair and a scientist's attention to detail, and his pacing is relentless." Booklist

Includes bibliographical references

Cerullo, Mary M., 1949-

The truth about great white sharks; written by Mary M. Cerullo; photographs by Jeffrey L. Rotman; illustrations by Michael Wertz. Chronicle Bks. 2000 48p il $14.95 *

Grades: 4 5 6 7　　　　　　　　　　　　**597**
1. Sharks
ISBN 0-8118-2467-5　　　　　　LC 00-31506
This provides information "about shark anatomy, senses, eating habits, and their relationships with humans. . . . The book also contains unusual information such as how these fish are measured and photographed and why they are not able to survive in an aquarium. The attractive layout blends line drawings, full-color photographs, varied typefaces, and eye-catching graphics. Rotman's pictures are clear and informative. . . . This title will be accessible to reluctant readers and is a must for most collections." SLJ

Includes bibliographical references

Gilbert, Carter Rowell, 1930-

National Audubon Society field guide to fishes, North America; [by] Carter R. Gilbert, James D. Williams. rev ed, 2nd ed, fully rev. Alfred A. Knopf 2002 607p il maps pa $19.95

Grades: 7 8 9 10 11 12 Adult　　　　　　**597**
1. Fishes—North America
ISBN 0-375-41224-7　　　　　　LC 2002-20773
"A Chanticleer Press edition"
First published 1983 with title: The Audubon Society field guide to North American fishes, whales, and dolphins

This guide covers over 600 freshwater and saltwater species in detail, with notes on 771 more species.

Macquitty, Miranda

Shark; written by Miranda MacQuitty. rev ed. DK Pub. 2004 72p il (DK eyewitness books) $15.99; lib bdg $19.99

Grades: 4 5 6 7   597

1. Sharks

ISBN 0-7566-0725-6; 0-7566-0724-8 (lib bdg)

First published 1992 by Knopf

Describes, in text and photographs, the physical characteristics, behavior, and life cycle of various types of sharks.

Mallory, Kenneth

Swimming with hammerhead sharks. Houghton Mifflin 2001 48p il (Scientists in the field) $16 *

Grades: 4 5 6 7   597

1. Klimley, A. Peter 2. Sharks

ISBN 0-618-05543-6   LC 00-61401

"A New England Aquarium book"

Published "in association with the New England Aquarium."

This book follows "marine biologist Pete Klimley and an IMAX film team to seamounts off Cocos Island in the Pacific Ocean to observe and film schooling hammerhead sharks. . . . A fascinating record of research and investigation, this inviting book is larded with numerous dramatic color photos." SLJ

Includes bibliographical references

Page, Lawrence M.

A field guide to freshwater fishes: North America north of Mexico; [by] Lawrence M. Page, Brooks M. Burr; illustrations by Eugene C. Beckham III, John Parker Sherrod, Craig W. Ronto. Houghton Mifflin 1991 432p il maps (The Peterson field guide) pa $19 hardcover o.p. *

Grades: 7 8 9 10 11 12 Adult   597

1. Fishes—North America

ISBN 0-395-91091-9 (pa)   LC 90-42049

"Sponsored by the National Audubon Society, the National Wildlife Federation, and the Roger Tory Peterson Institute"

This guide "covers all 790 species known in North America north of Mexico. Over 700 illustrations, most in color, show identifying marks. Also includes 377 distribution maps and additional line drawings of key details." Publisher's note

Includes bibliographical references

Rodriguez, Ana Maria, 1958-

Secret of the suffocating slime trap . . . and more! Enslow Publishers 2008 c2009 48p il (Animal secrets revealed!) lib bdg $23.93

Grades: 5 6 7 8   597

1. Fishes

ISBN 978-0-7660-2954-5; 0-7660-2954-9

LC 2007039493

"Explains how hagfish excrete slime to evade predators and details other strange abilities of different types of animals." Publisher's note

This book offers "fascinating accounts of how scientists systematically analyzed, tested, and proved their theories or how their findings led to other, serendipitous discoveries. . . . Science experiments are thoughtfully placed to inspire exploration, and captioned, full-color photos appear throughout." SLJ

Includes glossary and bibliographical references

Stefoff, Rebecca, 1951-

The fish classes; [by] Rebecca Stefoff. Marshall Cavendish Benchmark 2008 96p il (Family trees) $22.95 *

Grades: 6 7 8 9   597

1. Fishes

ISBN 978-0-7614-2695-0; 0-7614-2695-7

LC 2007003483

"Explores the habitats, life cycles, and other characteristics of animals in the Fish classes." Publisher's note

"Skillful weaving of engaging text and superb illustrations will incite interest." Voice Youth Advocates

Includes glossary and bibliographical references

Walker, Sally M.

Fossil fish found alive; discovering the coelacanth. Carolrhoda Bks. 2002 72p il map lib bdg $17.95 *

Grades: 5 6 7 8   597

1. Coelacanth

ISBN 1-57505-536-8   LC 2001-3815

Describes the 1938 discovery of the coelacanth, a fish previously believed to be extinct, and subsequent research about it

"Walker writes well, making this relatively unknown area of science history an exciting story of exploration and discovery. Excellent, full-color photos illustrate the text." Booklist

Includes bibliographical references

Wilkes, Sarah, 1964-

Fish; [by] Sarah Wilkes. World Almanac Library 2006 48p il (World Almanac Library of the animal kingdom) lib bdg $30.60

Grades: 5 6 7 8   597

1. Fishes

ISBN 0-8368-6210-4 (lib bdg); 978-0-8368-6210-2 (lib bdg)   LC 2005051693

This "introduces a wide range of aquatic creatures that contribute to the diversity of Earth's oceans and lakes. [It describes] the common physical and behavioral traits of this . . . animal category . . . [and] what makes each species unique and how it fits into the natural world." Publisher's note

"One or two fine-quality, color close-up photos of representative species accompany the text on almost every page. . . . [This title is] precisely written, with unusual scientific terms defined as they appear." SLJ

Includes bibliographical references

597.8   Amphibia (Amphibians)

Behler, John L.
Frogs; a chorus of colors; [by] John L Behler, Deborah A. Behler; foreword by Clyde and Chad Peeling. Sterling Publishing 2005 159p il $19.95; pa $14.95
Grades: 6 7 8 9   **597.8**
1. Frogs
ISBN   978-1-4027-2814-3;   1-4027-2814-X; 978-1-4027-5779-2 (pa); 1-4027-5779-4 (pa)
A colorful exploration of the world of frogs examines and illustrates their diversity of form, behavioral characteristics, and ecology.
"Sidebars throughout the text provide more information, and 'frogfacts' in each section furnish fun trivia. Lavishly illustrated." Booklist
Includes bibliographical references

Clarke, Barry
Amphibian; written by Barry Clarke; photographed by Geoff Brightling and Frank Greenaway. rev ed. DK Pub. 2005 72p il (DK eyewitness books) $15.99; lib bdg $19.99
Grades: 4 5 6 7   **597.8**
1. Amphibians
ISBN 0-7566-1380-9; 0-7566-1381-7 (lib bdg)
First published 1993
Examines the evolution, behavior, physical characteristics, and life cycle of various types of amphibians.

Fridell, Ron, 1943-
The search for poison-dart frogs. Watts 2001 48p il map lib bdg $23.50; pa $6.95
Grades: 4 5 6   **597.8**
1. Frogs 2. Wildlife conservation 3. Suriname
ISBN 0-531-11888-6 (lib bdg); 0-531-16570-1 (pa)
LC 00-36507
"Wildlife Conservation Society books"
This describes a scientific "expedition as a team travels to Suriname to study the electric blue amphibians. Written with vivid detail, the text explains environmental issues and shows why preservation of the area is so crucial." Booklist
Includes glossary and bibliographical references

Hamilton, Garry, 1962-
Frog rescue; changing the future for endangered wildlife. Firefly Books 2004 64p il (Firefly animal rescue series) $19.95; pa $9.95
Grades: 5 6 7 8   **597.8**
1. Frogs 2. Endangered species 3. Wildlife conservation
ISBN 1-55297-597-5; 1-55297-506-7 (pa)
This describes endangered species of frogs, how and why they are in danger, and explains what efforts are being made to protect them.
This is "well-written. . . . Stunning, full-color photographs bring each species to life and depict a number of individuals in the field and laboratory working to save these animals." SLJ

Miller, Sara Swan
Amazing amphibians. Watts 2001 63p il lib bdg $24.50; pa $8.95
Grades: 4 5 6   **597.8**
1. Amphibians
ISBN 0-531-11793-6 (lib bdg); 0-531-13980-8 (pa)
LC 99-57309
"Watts library"
Portrays several amphibian species with unusual appearances, habitats, or behaviors, including caecilians, tomato frogs, and midwife toads
Includes bibliographical references

Stefoff, Rebecca, 1951-
The amphibian class; [by] Rebecca Stefoff. Marshall Cavendish Benchmark 2008 96p il (Family trees) lib bdg $22.95 *
Grades: 6 7 8 9   **597.8**
1. Amphibians
ISSN lib bdg
ISBN 978-0-7614-2692-9 (lib bdg); 0-7614-2692-2
LC 2007003487
"Explores the habitats, life cycles, and other characteristics of animals in the Amphibian class." Publisher's note
This is "meticulously detailed. . . . Sharp color photographs appear on about every other page. Other illustrations consist of classification charts and anatomical diagrams. . . . [This is] well-organized and clearly written." SLJ
Includes glossary and bibliographical references

Wilkes, Sarah, 1964-
Amphibians; [by] Sarah Wilkes. World Almanac Library 2006 48p il (World Almanac library of the animal kingdom) lib bdg $25.78
Grades: 6 7 8 9   **597.8**
1. Amphibians
ISBN 0-8368-6208-2 (lib bdg); 0-8368-6227-9 (pa)
LC 2005052624
This describes the characteristics of amphibians and "briefly discusses threats to the . . . animals' survival and conservation efforts. . . . One or two fine-quality, color close-up photos of representative species accompany the text on almost every page, and extended captions identify most species by both common and scientific names." SLJ
Includes bibliographical references

597.9   Reptilia (Reptiles)

Conant, Roger, 1909-
A field guide to reptiles & amphibians; eastern and central North America; [by] Roger Conant and Joseph T. Collins; illustrated by Isabelle Hunt Conant and Tom R. Johnson. 3rd ed, expanded. Houghton Mifflin 1998 616p il map (Peterson field guide series) $21
Grades: 7 8 9 10 11 12 Adult   **597.9**
1. Reptiles 2. Amphibians
ISBN 0-395-90452-8   LC 98-13622

Conant, Roger, 1909-—_Continued_

First published 1958 with title: A field guide to reptiles and amphibians of the United States and Canada east of the 100th meridian

"Sponsored by the National Audubon Society, the National Wildlife Federation, and the Roger Tory Peterson Institute"

This guide describes 595 species and subspecies, featuring color photos, black and white drawings, and color distribution maps of reptiles and amphibians of the region. Also includes information on transporting live reptiles and amphibians

Includes glossary and bibliographical references

McCarthy, Colin, 1951-

Reptile; written by Colin McCarthy; [special photography, Karl Shone . . . [et al.]] Dorling Kindersley 2000 63p il (DK eyewitness books) $15.99; lib bdg $19.99

Grades: 4 5 6 7   **597.9**

1. Reptiles

ISBN 0-7894-5786-5; 0-7894-6575-2 (lib bdg)

First published 1991 by Knopf

Photographs and text depict the many different kinds of reptiles, their similarities and differences, habitats, and behavior.

Miller, Sara Swan

Radical reptiles. Watts 2001 63p il lib bdg $24.50; pa $8.95

Grades: 4 5 6   **597.9**

1. Reptiles

ISBN 0-531-11794-4 (lib bdg); 0-531-13989-1 (pa)   LC 99-57020

"Watts library"

Describes several species of reptiles that have unusual appearances, habitats, or behaviors

This is "well-organized . . . [and] includes numerous, well-placed color photographs." SLJ

Includes glossary and bibliographical references

Rodriguez, Ana Maria, 1958-

Secret of the puking penguins . . . and more! [by] Ana Maria Rodriguez. Enslow Publishers 2008 c2009 48p il (Animal secrets revealed!) lib bdg $23.93

Grades: 5 6 7 8   **597.9**

1. Reptiles 2. Birds

ISBN 978-0-7660-2955-2 (lib bdg); 0-7660-2955-7 (lib bdg)   LC 2007-39490

"Explains how King penguin fathers preserve food in their stomachs for their chicks and details other strange abilities of different types of animals." Publisher's note

"The methodology used by each scientist or team of scientists to make the discoveries is carefully explained is a lively and accessible manner. . . . The photo illustrations . . . are of excellent quality, well placed, and helpful." Booklist

Includes glossary and bibliographical references

Stebbins, Robert C. (Robert Cyril), 1915-

A field guide to Western reptiles and amphibians; text and illustrations by Robert C. Stebbins. 3rd ed newly rev. Houghton Mifflin 2003 533p il maps (The Peterson field guide) $22 *

Grades: 7 8 9 10 11 12 Adult   **597.9**

1. Reptiles 2. Amphibians

ISBN 0-395-98272-3   LC 2002-27561

First published 1966

"Sponsored by The National Wildlife Federation and the Roger Tory Peterson Institute"

This "covers all the species of reptiles and amphibians found in western North America. More than 650 full-color paintings and photographs show key details for making accurate identifications. . . . Color range maps give species' distributions. . . . [Includes] information on conservation efforts and survival status." Publisher's note

Includes bibliographical references

Zabludoff, Marc

The reptile class. Benchmark Books 2005 95p il (Family trees) lib bdg $29.92 *

Grades: 6 7 8 9   **597.9**

1. Reptiles

ISBN 0-7614-1820-2   LC 2004-21820

This examines physical traits, adaptations, diets, habitats, and life cycles of reptiles.

"Fact-filled, yet surprisingly readable. . . . [This] title contains a wide variety of excellent-quality, full-color photos; interesting sidebars; and diagrams." SLJ

597.92   Chelonia

Ferri, Vincenzo

Tortoises and turtles. Firefly Bks. 2002 c1999 255p il pa $24.95

Grades: 8 9 10 11 12 Adult   **597.92**

1. Turtles

ISBN 978-1-55209-631-4; 1-55209-631-9

Original Italian edition, 1999

An "illustrated guide to 190 land, marine and freshwater turtles and tortoises . . . describing the physical and biological characteristics of the majority of species." Publisher's note

"Turtle enthusiasts and students writing papers will find this guide and the additional resources it cites invaluable." Voice Youth Advocates

Includes glossary and bibliographical references

Hickman, Pamela M., 1958-

Turtle rescue; changing the future for endangered wildlife. Firefly 2005 64p il map (Firefly animal rescue) $19.95; pa $9.95

Grades: 5 6 7 8   **597.92**

1. Turtles 2. Endangered species 3. Wildlife conservation

ISBN 1-55297-916-4; 1-55297-915-6 (pa)

This "overview of the plight of the world's turtles and tortoises describes the general problems that all turtles face and then explains what is being done to rescue cer-

Hickman, Pamela M., 1958——*Continued*
tain species from near extinction. . . . The book is illustrated with excellent-quality photographs that are closely
tied to the text. Maps and charts are useful. . . . Other
books on the topic cannot match this one for its thorough
approach as well as the current information." SLJ

Lockwood, Sophie
Sea turtles; by Sophie Lockwood. Child's World
2006 40p il map (World of reptiles) lib bdg
$29.93
Grades: 4 5 6   **597.92**
1. Sea turtles
ISBN 1-59296-550-4   LC 2005024792
"Conservation is the dominant theme of this attractive
photo-essay. . . . which has beautiful full-page color
photos that bring readers close to the subject. Fast-fact
boxes focus on particular species, providing spot statistics on weight, length, color, habitat, threatened or endangered status, and more." Booklist
Includes glossary and bibliographical references

Stefoff, Rebecca, 1951-
Turtles; [by] Rebecca Stefoff. Marshall
Cavendish Benchmark 2007 110p il (Animalways)
lib bdg $34.21
Grades: 6 7 8 9   **597.92**
1. Turtles
ISBN 978-0-7614-2539-7   LC 2007013178
This describes the place of turtles in the animal king-
dom, their evolution, anatomy, physiology, diversity, life
cycle, and relationship to humans.
Includes glossary and bibliographical references

597.95   Sauria (Lizards)

Greenberg, Daniel A.
Lizards; [by] Dan Greenberg. Benchmark Bks.
2003 112p il (Animalways) lib bdg $21.95
Grades: 6 7 8 9   **597.95**
1. Lizards
ISBN 0-7614-1580-7   LC 2003-2566
Contents: All sizes and shapes; What is a lizard?; The
lizard body; Lizards in action; Getting to know lizards;
Reproduction; Lizards, today and tomorrow
This provides information on the physical characteris-
tics, behavior, and habitats of lizard species
Includes glossary and bibliographical references

597.96   Serpentes (Snakes)

Mattison, Christopher
Snake; by Chris Mattison. DK Pub. 1999 192p
il hardcover o.p. pa $12.99
Grades: 7 8 9 10 11 12 Adult   **597.96**
1. Snakes
ISBN 0-7894-4660-X; 0-7566-1365-5 (pa)
LC 99-19957

An illustrated guide to "more than 60 types of snakes,
ranging from adders to yellow anacondas. This richly
formatted book features each snake in detailed entries
with informative, readable text." Sci Child
Includes glossary

Menon, Sujatha
Discover snakes. Enslow Publishers 2008 47p il
(Discover animals) lib bdg $23.93
Grades: 4 5 6 7   **597.96**
1. Snakes
ISBN 978-0-7660-3471-6 (lib bdg); 0-7660-3471-2 (lib
bdg)   LC 2008013867
First published 2005 in the United Kingdom
This "introduces readers to a variety of snakes, from
pythons to boa constrictors and cobras. . . . Images and
text explain about a snake's fangs, life cycle, senses, and
how they fight and move. The book also discusses the
different snake families and the hunting styles of each."
Publisher's note
Includes glossary and bibliographical references

Montgomery, Sy
The snake scientist; photographs by Nic Bishop.
Houghton Mifflin 1999 48p il map $16; pa $5.95
*
Grades: 4 5 6 7   **597.96**
1. Mason, Bob 2. Snakes
ISBN 0-395-87169-7; 0-618-11119-0 (pa)
LC 98-6124
Discusses the work of Bob Mason and his efforts to
study and protect snakes, particularly red-sided garter
snakes
"The lively text communicates both the meticulous
measurements required in this kind of work and the thrill
of new discoveries. Large, full-color photos of the zoologist and young students at work, and lots of wriggly
snakes, pull readers into the presentation." SLJ
Includes bibliographical references

Pringle, Laurence P.
Snakes! strange and wonderful; by Laurence
Pringle; illustrated by Meryl Henderson. Boyds
Mills Press 2004 31p il $15.95
Grades: 3 4 5 6   **597.96**
1. Snakes
ISBN 1-59078-003-5   LC 2003-26418
"Short paragraphs describe [snakes'] major physical
and behavioral characteristics and highlight some distinctive traits of several different species. . . . More than
three dozen species from around the world are depicted
in the realistic watercolors. . . . The narrative is well organized and clearly written." SLJ

The **Snake** book; photography by Frank
Greenaway and Dave King. DK Pub. 1997 unp
il $12.99; pa $8.99
Grades: 4 5 6   **597.96**
1. Snakes
ISBN 0-7894-1526-7; 0-7894-6068-8 (pa)
LC 96-38294
Written and edited by Mary Ling and Mary Atkinson

The Snake book—*Continued*

The "creators of the book have used a stark white box as a background for some stark life-size photographs of 12 varieties of snakes. . . . Text containing very basic information about each snake sweeps around and inside the reptiles' coils, with the font varying in size from large to very small." Booklist

597.98 Crocodilia (Crocodilians)

Jango-Cohen, Judith

Crocodiles. Benchmark Bks. 2001 47p il map (Animalways) $34.21

Grades: 6 7 8 9   **597.98**

1. Crocodiles

ISBN 978-0-7614-1446-9; 0-7614-1136-4

LC 99-58363

Describes the evolution, physical characteristics, behavior, habitat, and folklore of crocodiles and examines various species and related crocodilians

"Striking, full-page photos and useful range maps, accompanied by clear, short sentences and easily found definitions, provide budding naturalists or young report writers with solid introductory resources." SLJ

Includes bibliographical references

Simon, Seymour, 1931-

Crocodiles & alligators. HarperCollins Pubs. 1999 unp il $15.95; lib bdg $16.89; pa $6.99 *

Grades: 4 5 6 7   **597.98**

1. Crocodiles 2. Alligators

ISBN 0-06-027473-5; 0-06-027474-3 (lib bdg); 0-06-443829-5 (pa)   LC 98-34705

Describes the physical characteristics and behavior of various members of the family of animals known as crocodilians

"The book is filled with interesting information, and the vivid, well-composed, full-color photographs and entertaining text will draw in browsers." SLJ

Snyder, Trish

Alligator & crocodile rescue; changing the future for endangered wildlife. Firefly Books 2006 64p il (Firefly animal rescue) lib bdg $19.95; pa $9.95

Grades: 5 6 7 8   **597.98**

1. Alligators 2. Crocodiles 3. Wildlife conservation

ISBN 1-55297-920-2 (lib bdg); 1-55297-919-9 (pa)

This "outlines the various threats to survival of [alligators and crocodiles] and introduces readers to organizations and individuals trying to save them. . . . Numerous photographs document the work of scientists, conservationists, educators, and other people around the world who are committed to wildlife preservation." SLJ

598 Aves (Birds)

Aziz, Laurel

Hummingbirds; a beginner's guide. Firefly Bks. (Buffalo) 2002 64p il lib bdg $19.95; pa $9.95

Grades: 6 7 8 9   **598**

1. Hummingbirds

ISBN 978-1-55209-487-7 (lib bdg); 1-55209-487-1 (lib bdg); 978-1-55209-372-6 (pa); 1-55209-372-7 (pa)

"This colorful, large-format book surveys the habits of hummingbirds. . . . The book offers a good deal of information illustrated with many clearly reproduced, brightly colored photos from many sources. Topics of discussion include the birds' metabolism, bills, vision, feathers, flight, migration, nesting, and hazards." Booklist

Birds of the world. Marshall Cavendish Reference 2008 11v il map set$359.95

Grades: 6 7 8 9   **598**

1. Birds—Encyclopedias 2. Reference books

ISBN 978-0-7614-7775-4; 0-7614-7775-6

LC 2008062300

"This encyclopedia, designed to introduce birds in all their varieties, contributes to and encourages student research. Nearly 140 . . . articles are arranged alphbetically. . . . Articles range in length from two to eight pages and include numerous full-color photographs, diagrams, and maps. . . . Clear and concise information is provided in an appealing layout most appropriate for upper-elementary through middle-school users." Booklist

Bull, John L.

The National Audubon Society field guide to North American birds, Eastern region; [by] John Bull and John Farrand, Jr.; revised by John Farrand, Jr.; visual key by Amanda Wilson and Lori Hogan. rev ed. Knopf 1994 797p il maps pa $19.95 *

Grades: 7 8 9 10 11 12 Adult   **598**

1. Birds—North America

ISBN 0-679-42852-6   LC 94-7768

Companion volume to National Audubon Society field guide to North American birds, Western region, by Miklos D. F. Udvardy

"A Chanticleer Press edition"

First published 1977

This pictorial guide to 508 eastern species arranges birds by color and shape to simplify identification. It also includes information on bird-watching and conservation status

Includes bibliographical references

Burnie, David

Bird; written by David Burnie. rev ed. DK Pub. 2008 72p il (DK eyewitness books) $15.99

Grades: 4 5 6 7   **598**

1. Birds

ISBN 978-0-7566-3768-2; 0-7566-3768-6

First published 1988 by Knopf

Includes CD-ROM

A photo essay on the world of birds examining such topics as body construction, feathers and flight, the adaptation of beaks and feet, feeding habits, courtship, nests and eggs, and bird watching.

Includes glossary

Chu, Miyoko

Birdscapes; A pop-up celebration of birdsongs in stereo sound; by Miyoko Chu, with the Cornell Lab of Ornithology; paper engineering by Gene Vosough, Renee Jablow, and Andy Baron; illustrations by Julia Hargreaves. Chronicle Books 2008 unp il $60

Grades: 5 6 7 8   **598**

1. Birds 2. Pop-up books

ISBN 978-0-8118-6428-2; 0-8118-6428-6

"With marvelously detailed pop-up spreads and high-quality sound, this look at various avian ecosystems is absolutely spectacular. Double-page sections depict the environmental characteristics and native species of the following North American habitats: the Sonoran Desert; a Pacific seabird colony; an eastern deciduous forest; the Arctic tundra; a cypress swamp; grasslands; and the Pacific rain forest. The paper sculptures, filled with colorful and realistic renderings of flora and local birdlife, are accompanied by a soundtrack of the species' calls and songs recorded . . . from the Cornell Lab of Ornithology's Macaulay Library collection." SLJ

Collard, Sneed B., III

Birds of prey; a look at daytime raptors; [by] Sneed B. Collard III. Watts 1999 64p il lib bdg $24.50; pa $8.95

Grades: 4 5 6   **598**

1. Birds of prey

ISBN 0-531-20363-8; 0-531-16419-5 (pa)

LC 98-38196

Discusses the physical features and behavior of daytime raptors, including eagles, harriers, kites, Old World vultures, caracaras, and falcons

"Illustrated with many color photographs and designed with fairly large type and generous use of white space, the book provides an attractive, clearly written overview." Booklist

Includes bibliographical references

Dubois, Philippe J.

Birds; photographs by Gilles Martin; text by Philippe J. Dubois and Valerie Guidoux; drawings by Jean Chevallier. H.N. Abrams 2005 70p il $18.95

Grades: 5 6 7 8   **598**

1. Birds

ISBN 0-8109-5878-3   LC 2004-22214

"This oversize album centers on Martin's knockout color photographs, enhanced by smaller watercolor sketches and illuminating commentary contributed by Philippe Dubois and Valerie Guidoux. . . . Martin not only captures such rare moments as egg laying in the wild and a face-off between a jackal and a nesting crane but also shows a gift for making even the most inconspicuous of birds as visually arresting as their more spectacular tropical cousins." Booklist

The **encyclopedia** of birds; edited by International Masters Publishers. Facts on File 2007 6v il set$425 *

Grades: 6 7 8 9 10 11 12   **598**

1. Birds—Encyclopedias 2. Reference books

ISBN 0-8160-5904-7; 978-0-8160-5904-1

LC 2006-49526

"Each volume begins with the same general introduction, followed by a comprehensive list of the 250 species included. Entries feature several . . . closeup photographs of the bird and its home, and data on breeding, status, food, and habitat. A panel provides information on length and weight, wingspan, number of eggs, lifespan, and more. . . . Both browsers and budding ornithologists will enjoy learning about some intriguing creatures." SLJ

Includes glossary and bibliographical references

Griggs, Jack L.

All the birds of North America; American Bird Conservancy's field guide; concept and design by Jack L. Griggs. HarperPerennial 1997 172p il maps pa $19.95 *

Grades: 7 8 9 10 11 12 Adult   **598**

1. Birds—North America

ISBN 0-06-52770-6   LC 96-49679

This identification guide to North American birds uses a system based on how and where birds collect food, with icons, color bars, key numbers, and color illustrations

Hickman, Pamela M., 1958-

Birds of prey rescue; changing the future for endangered wildlife. Firefly Books 2006 64p il (Firefly animal rescue) $19.95; pa $9.95

Grades: 5 6 7   **598**

1. Birds of prey 2. Endangered species 3. Wildlife conservation

ISBN   978-1-55407-145-6;   1-55407-145-3; 978-1-55407-144-9 (pa); 1-55407-144-5 (pa)

LC 2007271465

Provides details about birds of prey from around the world, their endangerment, and conservation programs designed to save them.

Hoose, Phillip M., 1947-

The race to save the Lord God Bird; [by] Phillip Hoose. Farrar, Straus and Giroux 2004 196p il map $20 *

Grades: 7 8 9 10   **598**

1. Woodpeckers 2. Endangered species

ISBN 0-374-36173-8

Tells the story of the ivory-billed woodpecker's extinction in the United States, describing the encounters between this species and humans, and discussing what these encounters have taught us about preserving endangered creatures

"Sharp, clear, black-and-white archival photos and reproductions appear throughout. The author's passion for his subject and high standards for excellence result in readable, compelling nonfiction." SLJ

Includes glossary and bibliographical references

Jacquet, Luc

March of the penguins; from the film by Luc Jacquet; narration written by Jordan Roberts; photographs by Jérôme Maison. National Geographic 2006 unp il $30

Grades: 8 9 10 11 12   **598**
1. Penguins
ISBN 0-7922-6182-8; 978-0-7922-6182-7
LC 2006-295371

"The book delves further than the hit movie into the lives of these remarkable penguins and their story of survival, and it also covers the conditions endured by the film crew to get the footage." Publisher's note

"This fine book works as a stand-alone volume, thanks to its charming photographs and revealing text." Publ Wkly

Kenyon, Linda, 1956-

Rainforest bird rescue; changing the future for endangered wildlife. Firefly Books 2006 64p il (Firefly animal rescue) $19.95; pa $9.95

Grades: 5 6 7 8   **598**
1. Birds 2. Rain forest animals 3. Wildlife conservation
ISBN 1-55407-153-4; 1-55407-152-6 (pa)

Provides details and facts about rainforest birds from around the world, their endangerment and a range of conservation programs to save them, including profiles of individual conservationists and rainforest bird species.

Latimer, Jonathan P.

Backyard birds; [by] Jonathan P. Latimer, Karen Stray Nolting; illustrations by Roger Tory Peterson; foreword by Virginia Marie Peterson. Houghton Mifflin 1999 48p il (Peterson field guides for young naturalists) pa $5.95 hardcover o.p.

Grades: 4 5 6 7   **598**
1. Birds
ISBN 0-395-92276-3   LC 98-35509

This is an identification guide to birds "'you are likely to see where you live.' . . . [It] includes a . . . selection of about 20 creatures . . . grouped by color. . . . Bright, full-color photographs and drawings clearly indicate distinguishing features. Useful, accessible." SLJ

Birds of prey; [by] Jonathan P. Latimer, Karen Stray Nolting; illustrations by Roger Tory Peterson; foreword by Virginia Marie Peterson. Houghton Mifflin 1999 48p il (Peterson field guides for young naturalists) $15; pa $5.95

Grades: 4 5 6 7   **598**
1. Birds of prey
ISBN 0-395-95211-5; 0-395-92277-1 (pa)
LC 98-35516

This illustrated volume introduces the physical characteristics, behavior, and habitats of such birds of prey as eagles, hawks, falcons, and owls.

Bizarre birds; [by] Jonathan P. Latimer, Karen Stray Nolting; illustrations by Roger Tory Peterson; foreword by Virginia Marie Peterson. Houghton Mifflin 1999 48p il (Peterson field guides for young naturalists) $15; pa $5.95

Grades: 4 5 6 7   **598**
1. Birds
ISBN 0-395-95213-1; 0-395-92279-8 (pa)
LC 98-35512

A field guide to odd birds such as roseate spoonbills, snail kites, anhimas, burrowing owls, and greater prairie chickens.

"Bright, full-color photographs and drawings clearly indicate distinguishing features. Useful, accessible." SLJ

Shorebirds; [by] Jonathan P. Latimer, Karen Stray Nolting; illustrations by Roger Tory Peterson; foreword by Virginia Marie Peterson. Houghton Mifflin 1999 48p il (Peterson field guides for young naturalists) $15; pa $5.95

Grades: 4 5 6 7   **598**
1. Birds
ISBN 0-395-95212-3; 0-395-92278-X (pa)
LC 98-35510

This is an illustrated field guide to shorebirds, including gulls, coots, sandpipers, and egrets.

"Bright, full-color photographs and drawings clearly indicate distinguishing features. Useful, accessible." SLJ

Songbirds; [by] Jonathan P. Latimer, Karen Stray Nolting; illustrations by Roger Tory Peterson; foreword by Virginia Marie Peterson. Houghton Mifflin 2000 48p il (Peterson field guides for young naturalists) $15; pa $5.95

Grades: 4 5 6 7   **598**
1. Birds 2. Birdsongs
ISBN 0-395-97941-2; 0-395-97946-3 (pa)
LC 99-38293

Describes the physical characteristics, habitats, feeding habits, and voices of a variety of songbirds, arranged under the categories "Simple Songs," "Complex Songs," "Whistling Songs," "Warbling Songs," "Trilling Songs," "Name-sayers," and "Mimics"

Laubach, Christyna M.

Raptor! a kid's guide to birds of prey; by Christyna & René Laubach and Charles W.G. Smith. Storey Bks. 2002 118p il maps $21.95; pa $14.95

Grades: 4 5 6 7   **598**
1. Birds of prey
ISBN 1-58017-475-2; 1-58017-445-0 (pa)
LC 2001-54980

This is an "overview of North American raptors. . . . After describing their characteristics and behavior, the book introduces individual species within family groups: vultures, hawks, falcons, barn owls, and true owls. . . . There is also advice on bird-watching and efforts to save endangered species. Well-designed projects . . . are followed by a glossary and extensive lists of hawk-watching sites, raptor centers, banding demonstration sites, books, videos, organizations, and Web sites related to birds in general and raptors in particular." Booklist

Osborn, Elinor, 1939-

Project UltraSwan; written and photographed by Elinor Osborn. Houghton Mifflin 2002 64p il map (Scientists in the field) $16 *

Grades: 4 5 6 7   598
   1. Swans
   ISBN 0-618-14528-1   LC 2002-223

Describes the life of large trumpeter swans, how they nearly became extinct, and efforts to reintroduce them to the Northeastern United States and to help them relearn migration routes

"Beautifully illustrated with crisp, colorful photographs and maps, *Project UltraSwan* describes in clear, succinct language all that the scientists must take into account in their work, as well as what they have learned about their subject so far." Booklist

Patent, Dorothy Hinshaw

The bald eagle returns; [by] Dorothy Hinshaw Patent; [photographs by] William Muñoz. Clarion Bks. 2000 68p il map $15 *

Grades: 4 5 6 7   598
   1. Bald eagle 2. Birds—Protection
   ISBN 0-395-91416-7   LC 00-21751

"A revised version of the author's and photographer's earlier book *Where the Bald Eagles Gather.*" Title page

Describes how bald eagles have recovered from the threat of extinction, how they raise their families, and why they are the national bird of the United States

This offers "exciting new information about the status of our national bird; and crisp, beautiful, full-color photos." SLJ

Peterson, Roger Tory, 1908-1996

Peterson field guide to birds of North America; with contributions from Michael DiGiorgio . . . [et al.] Houghton Mifflin Co. 2008 527p il map (Peterson field guide series) $26 *

Grades: 5 6 7 8 9 10 11 12 Adult   598
   1. Birds—North America
   ISBN 978-0-618-96614-1; 0-618-96614-5
                 LC 2007-39803

First published 1934 with title: A field guide to the birds. Previously published in two separate parts as A field guide to western birds (1990) and A field guide to the birds of eastern and central North America (2002)

This guide to birds found in North America contains colored illustrations painted by the author, with a description of each species on the facing page. Views of young birds and seasonal variations in plumage are included. The book also includes a URL to video podcasts.

"This field guide is of high quality and should be in millions of birders' and other nature lovers' backpacks." Sci Books Films

Rauzon, Mark J.

Hummingbirds. Watts 1997 63p il pa $6.95 hardcover o.p.

Grades: 4 5 6   598
   1. Hummingbirds
   ISBN 0-531-15849-7 (pa)   LC 96-36156

Describes the physical characteristics, behavior, and habitat of the smallest bird in the world

"The book is scientifically accurate, well written, and well illustrated." Sci Books Films

Includes glossary and bibliographical references

Vultures. Watts 1997 63p il pa $6.95 hardcover o.p.

Grades: 4 5 6   598
   1. Vultures
   ISBN 0-531-15853-5 (pa)   LC 96-31019
   "A First book"

Describes the physical characteristics, behavior, and different species of these scavenger birds

This "is well written and illustrated and contains much good science." Sci Books Films

Includes glossary and bibliographical references

Robbins, Chandler S., 1918-

Birds of North America; a guide to field identification; by Chandler S. Robbins, Bertel Bruun, and Herbert S. Zim; revised by Jonathan P. Latimer and Karen Stray Nolting and James Coe; illustrated by Arthur Singer. rev and updated. St. Martin's Press 2001 359p il maps $19.95; pa $15.95

Grades: 8 9 10 11 12 Adult   598
   1. Birds—North America
   ISBN 1-58238-091-0; 1-58238-090-2 (pa)
                 LC 2001-271739

"A Golden field guide"

First published 1966

This resource includes over 800 species and 600 range maps; illustrations featuring male, female, and juvenile plumage; and sonograms picturing sound for song recognition. Feeding habits, migration routes, and characteristic flight patterns as well as American Ornithologists' classifications are also provided.

Sattler, Helen Roney

The book of North American owls; illustrated by Jean Day Zallinger. Clarion Bks. 1995 64p il maps $17; pa $7.95

Grades: 4 5 6 7   598
   1. Owls
   ISBN 0-395-60524-5; 0-395-90017-4 (pa)
                 LC 91-43626

This volume "includes owl classification and history, hunting and habitat, courtship and nesting, and the complex relationship between owls and humans. The comprehensive glossary includes all of the 21 North American species." Sci Child

This "is a superb ornithological primer. . . . The book is lavishly illustrated." Appraisal

Includes bibliographical references

Stefoff, Rebecca, 1951-
The bird class; [by] Rebecca Stefoff. 1st ed. Marshall Cavendish Benchmark 2008 96p il (Family trees) $22.95 *
Grades: 6 7 8 9   **598**
1. Birds
ISBN 978-0-7614-2693-6; 0-7614-2693-0
LC 2007007706
"Explores the habitats, life cycles, and other characteristics of organisms in the bird class." Publisher's note
"Skillful weaving of engaging text and superb illustrations will incite interest." Voice Youth Advocates
Includes glossary and bibliographical references

Penguins. Marshall Cavendish Benchmark 2005 112p il (Animalways) lib bdg $31.36
Grades: 6 7 8 9   **598**
1. Penguins
ISBN 0-7614-1743-5   LC 2003-22113
Discusses the evolution, biology, life cycle, and social and mating behavior of penguins.
Includes glossary and bibliographical references

Thompson, Bill, III, 1962-
The young birder's guide to birds of eastern North America; [by] Bill Thompson III; illustrations by Julie Zickefoose. Houghton Mifflin Co. 2008 256p il map (Peterson field guide series) $14.95
Grades: 3 4 5 6   **598**
1. Birds 2. Bird watching
ISBN 978-0-547-11934-2; 0-547-11934-8
LC 2007-43904
This describes 200 species of birds of eastern North America, with color photos, black & white drawings, and range maps.
Includes glossary and bibliographical references

Udvardy, Miklos D. F., 1919-1998
National Audubon Society field guide to North American birds, Western region; revised by John Farrand, Jr.; visual key by Amanda Wilson and Lori Hogan. rev ed. Knopf 1994 822p il maps pa $19.95 *
Grades: 6 7 8 9 10 11 12 Adult   **598**
1. Birds—North America
ISBN 0-679-42851-8   LC 94-7415
Companion volume to National Audubon Society field guide to North American birds, Eastern region by John L. Bull
"A Chanticleer Press edition"
First published 1977
This pictorial guide to 544 western species arranges birds by color and shape to simplify identification. It also includes information on bird-watching and conservation status
Includes bibliographical references

Warhol, Tom
Eagles; [by] Tom Warhol and Chris Reiter. Benchmark Bks. 2004 112p il map (Animalways) lib bdg $31.36
Grades: 6 7 8 9   **598**
1. Eagles
ISBN 0-7614-1578-5   LC 2002-155814
Contents: Eagles, honored and feared; Eagle origins; The family of eagles; How eagles work; Flight, hunting, and migration; The life cycle; The fate of eagles
This discusses the evolution of eagles, their places in human culture, their life cycles, anatomy, and protection
Includes glossary and bibliographical references

Hawks; [by] Tom Warhol. Marshall Cavendish Benchmark 2005 112p il (Animalways) lib bdg $31.36 *
Grades: 6 7 8 9   **598**
1. Hawks
ISBN 0-7614-1744-3   LC 2003-22138
This describes the place of hawks in human culture and history, their evolution, anatomy, habits, life cycle, and protection.
Includes glossary and bibliographical references

Owls; [by] Tom Warhol. Marshall Cavendish Benchmark 2007 111p il (Animalways) lib bdg $34.21
Grades: 6 7 8 9   **598**
1. Owls
ISBN 978-0-7614-2537-3   LC 2006019708
This describes the place of owls in the animal kingdom, owl lore and legend, owls' evolution, diversity, anatomy and behavior, life cycle, and endangered status.
This "will pique readers' curiosity, and the content will keep them hooked. Vivid color photographs and illustrations and a clear font make [this work] stand out." SLJ
Includes glossary and bibliographical references

Webb, Sophie, 1958-
Looking for seabirds; journal from an Alaskan voyage. Houghton Mifflin Co. 2004 48p il $16
Grades: 4 5 6 7   **598**
1. Birds 2. Alaska
ISBN 0-618-21235-3   LC 2003-12420
A journal of the author's observations and adventures while working on a research vessel counting seabirds through Alaska's Aleutian Island chain.
The "immediacy of the narrative . . . and the clear and colorful watercolor-and-gouache landscapes and drawings of the birds form an appealing travelogue that is as exciting as it is informative." SLJ

My season with penguins; an Antarctic journal. Houghton Mifflin 2000 48p il map $15; pa $5.95 *
Grades: 4 5 6 7   **598**
1. Penguins 2. Antarctica
ISBN 0-395-92291-7; 0-618-43234-5 (pa)
LC 99-54781
Describes the author's two-month stay in Antarctica to study and draw penguins

Webb, Sophie, 1958-—*Continued*
"Webb presents a great deal of scientific information through an effective blend of journal entries and illustrations. . . . Done in gouache and watercolor, the paintings range from scenes of mountains and moving ice to depictions of penguins engaged in typical behaviors. . . . Webb offers a fine look at the scientific method in action." SLJ
Includes glossary

599   Mammalia (Mammals)

Exploring mammals. Marshall Cavendish 2007
20v il map set $399.95 *
Grades: 5 6 7 8 9 10   **599**
1. Mammals—Encyclopedias 2. Reference books
ISBN 978-0-76147-719-8   LC 2007060864
"About 90 animals . . . are described in these volumes. Each article includes . . . a 'Profile,' with introductory information; a discussion of anatomy, with diagrams; a discussion of habitat; descriptions of various behaviors; and a consideration of factors determining survival. Each article also has numerous boxed sections . . . as well as many color photographs and other illustrations. . . . This set has just about everything a student requires." Booklist
Includes bibliographical references

Exploring the world of mammals; [edited by Nancy Simmons, Richard Beatty, Amy Jane Beer] 1st ed. Chelsea House 2008 6v il map set $210 *
Grades: 5 6 7 8   **599**
1. Mammals—Encyclopedias 2. Reference books
ISBN 978-0-7910-9651-2 (set); 0-7910-9651-3 (set)
LC 2007028223
"This colorful and appealing set offers an introduction to the world of mammals. Most of entries are 2 to 4 pages in length. Sidebars offer extra details, and bright photographs and illustrations appear on every 2-page spread." Booklist

Hare, Tony
Animal fact-file; head-to-tail profiles of more than 100 mammals. Facts on File 1999 191p il $40
Grades: 4 5 6 7   **599**
1. Mammals
ISBN 0-8160-3921-6   LC 98-42092
This is "an alphabetical guide to mammals from aardvarks to wombats. The full-color illustrations are excellent. Pictures show external and internal views of the animals as a whole and highlight distinctive body parts. Interesting comparison drawings abound. . . . And there is, for every entry, an easy reference chart giving the mammal's classification, size, coloration, and features. . . . The book provides a lot of easily accessed information in digestible bits." SLJ

Rodriguez, Ana Maria, 1958-
Secret of the singing mice . . . and more! [by] Ana Maria Rodriguez. Enslow Publishers 2008 c2009 48p il (Animal secrets revealed!) lib bdg $23.93
Grades: 5 6 7 8   **599**
1. Mammals
ISBN 978-0-7660-2956-9; 0-7660-2956-5
LC 2007-39495
"Explains how mice use ultrasonic vocalizations to attract mates and details other strange abilities of different types of animals." Publisher's note
This book offers "fascinating accounts of how scientists systematically analyzed, tested and proved their theories or how their findings led to other, serendipitous discoveries. . . . Science experiments are thoughtfully placed to inspire exploration, and captioned, full-color photos appear throughout." SLJ
Includes glossary and bibliographical references

Whitaker, John O., Jr.
National Audubon Society field guide to North American mammals. rev ed. Knopf 1996 937p il maps pa $19.95 *
Grades: 6 7 8 9 10 11 12 Adult   **599**
1. Mammals
ISBN 0-679-44631-1   LC 95-81456
First published 1980
This field guide describes 390 species of mammals of North America and includes keys for identification, range maps, information on tracks and anatomy, and 375 color photos

599.2   Marsupialia and monotremata

Collard, Sneed B., III
Pocket babies and other amazing marsupials. Darby Creek 2007 72p il map $18.95 *
Grades: 4 5 6 7   **599.2**
1. Marsupials
ISBN 978-1-58196-046-4; 1-58196-046-8
"This large-format book provides an attractive introduction to marsupials around the world. . . . Attractive, informative side-bars, excellent maps, and many-clear, color photos appear throughout the book. . . . This handsomely designed volume introduces marsupials with panache." Booklist
Includes glossary and bibliographical references

Montgomery, Sy
Quest for the tree kangaroo; an expedition to the cloud forest of New Guinea; text by Sy Montgomery; photographs by Nic Bishop. Houghton Mifflin 2006 79p il map (Scientists in the field) $18 *
Grades: 5 6 7 8   **599.2**
1. Dabek, Lisa 2. Tree kangaroos 3. New Guinea
ISBN 0-618-49641-6   LC 2005-34849

Montgomery, Sy—*Continued*

"The writer and photographer of this exemplary description of science field work accompanied researcher Lisa Dabek on an expedition high in New Guinea's mountains to study tree kangaroos and promote the conservation of this elusive and endangered species. . . . Montgomery . . . paces her narrative well . . . keeping the reader engaged and concerned. . . . Bishop's photographs . . . are beautifully reproduced." Publ Wkly

Stefoff, Rebecca, 1951-

The marsupial order; [by] Rebecca Stefoff. Marshall Cavendish Benchmark 2008 96p il (Family trees) lib bdg $22.95 *

Grades: 6 7 8 9   **599.2**

1. Marsupials

ISBN 978-0-7614-2697-4 (lib bdg); 0-7614-2697-3 (lib bdg)   LC 2007007240

"Explores the habitats, life cycles, and other characteristics of organisms in the Marsupial Order." Publisher's note

This is "meticulously detailed. . . . Sharp color photographs appear on about every other page. Other illustrations consist of classification charts and anatomical diagrams. . . . [This is] well-organized and clearly written. . . . In addition to discussing such well-known animals as kangaroos, koalas, and opossums, [this book] includes material on less-familiar species 'marsupial mice,' quolls, bandicoots, and bilbies. . . . [The book is] well-researched." SLJ

Includes glossary and bibliographical references

599.3 Miscellaneous orders of Eutheria (placental mammals)

Lorbiecki, Marybeth

Prairie dogs; illustrations by Wayne Ford. NorthWord Press 2004 47p il map (Our wild world series) hardcover o.p. pa $7.95

Grades: 4 5 6   **599.3**

1. Prairie dogs

ISBN 978-1-55971-883-7; 1-55971-883-8; 978-1-55971-884-4 (pa); 1-55971-884-6 (pa)
                    LC 2003-59993

Discusses the physical characteristics, behavior, habitat, and life cycle of prairie dogs

Lorbiecki "offers a thorough discussion of the rodents' complex communication system of chirps and whistles. . . . Clear, full-color photos provide visual appeal. . . . The text[s] . . . [is] clearly written." SLJ

Markle, Sandra, 1946-

Prairie dogs. Lerner Publications Company 2007 39p il map (Animal prey) lib bdg $25.26; pa $7.95

Grades: 4 5 6   **599.3**

1. Prairie dogs

ISBN 978-0-8225-6438-6 (lib bdg); 0-8225-6438-6 (lib bdg); 978-0-8225-6441-6 (pa); 0-8225-6441-6 (pa)
                    LC 2006-598

Describes the behavior of prairie dogs in their native habitat, where they are the prey of larger animals and birds and where they must work together as a colony to create burrows and warning systems to protect themselves and their young.

Includes glosary and bibliographical references

599.35 Rodents

Marrin, Albert, 1936-

Oh, rats! the story of rats and people; illustrated by C.B. Mordan. Dutton Children's Books 2006 48p il $16.99

Grades: 3 4 5 6   **599.35**

1. Rats

ISBN 0-525-47439-0   LC 2004-24512

"Along with portraying rats in many roles, from pests to pets, Marrin . . . introduces rodent relatives and provides glimpses of rats' habits and innate intelligence, as well as their history as disease carriers, lab animals, predators, and . . . even entrees." Booklist

This is "lively and informative. . . . The nine short chapters are set in a handsome slim book with striking black-and-white scratchboard illustrations and muted red framing on many pages." SLJ

Includes bibliographical references

Stefoff, Rebecca, 1951-

The rodent order; by Rebecca Stefoff. Marshall Cavendish Benchmark 2008 96p il (Family trees) $23.95

Grades: 6 7 8 9   **599.35**

1. Rodents

ISBN 978-0-7614-3073-5; 0-7614-3073-3
                    LC 2008-17555

"Explores the habitats, life cycles, and other characteristics of rodents." Publisher's note

Includes glossary and bibliographical references

599.4 Chiroptera (Bats)

Lockwood, Sophie

Bats; by Sophie Lockwood. Child's World 2008 40p il map (World of mammals) lib bdg $29.93

Grades: 4 5 6   **599.4**

1. Bats

ISBN 978-1-59296-926-5 (lib bdg); 1-59296-926-7 (lib bdg)   LC 2007013565

This book about bats provides "all the basics for reports: an introduction to the creatures' challenges, the role humans play, physical traits and behaviors, habitats, and struggles for survival. Every part of their life [cycle], including sexual maturity, birth, and family relationships, is explained. . . . Clear bright photographs pump up the content. . . . The detail that Lockwood imparts is startlingly high. The [text is] written in a dynamic and engaging style." SLJ

Includes glossary and bibliographical references

Stokes beginner's guide to bats; [by] Kim Williams . . . [et al.] Little, Brown, and Co. 2002 159p il map $9.99
Grades: 6 7 8 9   599.4
1. Bats
ISBN 978-0-316-81658-8; 0-316-81658-2
LC 2001-38112
This book about bats gives "identification and behavior information in a portable pocket-sized format." Publisher's note

599.5   Cetacea and Sirenia

Greenberg, Daniel A.
Dolphins; [by] Dan Greenberg. Benchmark Bks. 2003 112p il (Animalways) lib bdg $21.95 *
Grades: 6 7 8 9   599.5
1. Dolphins
ISBN 0-7614-1576-9   LC 2002-155246
Contents: Mysterious travelers; What is a dolphin?; Dolphin habitats; Dolphins up close; Dolphins in action; The life of a dolphin; Dolphins, today and tomorrow
This provides information on the physical characteristics, behavior, and habitats of dolphin species
Includes glossary and bibliographical references

Whales; [by] Dan Greenberg. Benchmark Bks. 2002 110p il (Animalways) lib bdg $21.95 *
Grades: 6 7 8 9   599.5
1. Whales
ISBN 0-7614-1389-8   LC 2001-43883
Describes in detail the physical characteristics, behavior, and migration and life cycle of various kinds of whales, among the largest creatures ever known to have lived on Earth, and discusses the history of human interaction with these animals
"Written in engaging language. . . . Sharp color photos of the animals in the wild mix with archival images, helpful charts, and artists' renderings." Booklist
Includes glossary and bibliographical references

Hall, Howard
A charm of dolphins; the threatened life of a flippered friend. 2nd ed. London Town Press 2007 48p il map (Jean-Michel Cousteau presents) $8.95
Grades: 5 6 7 8   599.5
1. Dolphins
ISBN 978-0-9766134-8-0; 0-9766134-8-4
First published 1994 by Silver Burdett Press
Shows and describes species of dolphins around the world, depicts dolphin characteristics and behavior, and discusses the threats that human beings pose to the animals.
This "book covers the characteristics and unique traits of the . . . [dolphin] and includes colorful, awe-inspiring photos and immediate first-person narratives." SLJ
Includes glossary and bibliographical references

Hodgkins, Fran, 1964-
The whale scientists; solving the mystery of whale strandings. Houghton Mifflin Co. 2007 63p il map (Scientists in the field) $18 *
Grades: 5 6 7 8   599.5
1. Whales
ISBN 978-0-618-55673-1; 0-618-55673-7
LC 2006-34634
This describes the evolution of whales and their relationship to humans and offers various scientific theories about their strandings.
"Hodgkins packs her text with an impressive amount of information. . . . Well-chosen color photographs amply illustrate the well-organized discussion." SLJ
Includes glossary and bibliographical references

Hoyt, Erich, 1950-
Whale rescue; changing the future for endangered wildlife. Firefly 2005 64p il $19.95; pa $9.95
Grades: 5 6 7 8   599.5
1. Whales 2. Wildlife conservation
ISBN 1-55297-601-7; 1-55297-600-9 (pa)
"Hoyt examines the impact of commercial whaling on global whale populations and the efforts being made by scientists, environmentalists, and some governments to protect these endangered mammals. Crisp, color photos portray these leviathans in their natural habitat and also show scientists hard at work on cetacean projects, whaling ships and their harvest on the high seas, and seagoing environmentalists in action." SLJ

León, Vicki, 1942-
A pod of killer whales; the mysterious life of the intelligent orca. 2nd ed. London Town Press 2007 48p il (Jean-Michel Cousteau presents) pa $8.95
Grades: 5 6 7 8   599.5
1. Whales
ISBN 978-0-9766134-7-3; 0-9766134-7-6
First published 1995 by Silver Burdett Press
Introduces killer whales, describing their social structure, eating habits, communication and hunting methods, and threats to their way of life.
This "book covers the characteristics and unique traits of . . . [killer whales] and includes colorful, awe-inspiring photos and immediate first-person narratives." SLJ
Includes bibliographical references

Lockwood, Sophie
Whales; by Sophie Lockwood. Child's World 2008 40p il map (World of mammals) lib bdg $29.93
Grades: 4 5 6   599.5
1. Whales
ISBN 978-1-59296-930-2 (lib bdg); 1-59296-930-5 (lib bdg)
LC 2007020890
This book about whales presents "all the basics for reports: an introduction to the creatures' challenges, the role humans play, physical traits and behaviors, habitats, and struggles for survival. Every part of their life [cycle],

Lockwood, Sophie—*Continued*
including sexual maturity, birth, and family relationships, is explained. . . . Clear bright photographs pump up the content. . . . The detail that Lockwood imparts is startlingly high. The [text is] written in a dynamic and engaging style." SLJ
Includes glossary and bibliographical references

Montgomery, Sy
Encantado; pink dolphin of the Amazon; with photographs by Dianne Taylor-Snow. Houghton Mifflin 2002 73p il $18
Grades: 4 5 6 7   **599.5**
    1. Dolphins 2. Amazon River valley
    ISBN 0-618-13103-5   LC 2001-39251
Introduces the world of the freshwater dolphins called Encantados, or Enchanted, by the people who live near them in the region of the Amazon and Orinoco rivers in South America
"The book contains remarkable descriptions and color photos of the Amazonian rainforest and its inhabitants." Horn Book Guide
Includes bibliographical references

Rodriguez, Ana Maria, 1958-
Secret of the sleepless whales . . . and more! by Ana Maria Rodriguez. Enslow Publishers 2008 c2009 48p il (Animal secrets revealed!) lib bdg $23.93
Grades: 5 6 7 8   **599.5**
    1. Marine mammals
    ISBN 978-0-7660-2957-6 (lib bdg); 0-7660-2957-3 (lib bdg)   LC 2007039479
This book "does a thorough job of explaining the behaviors of some marine mammals and the scientific methods used to investigate them. . . . The team that worked on the specific issue is identified, and the methodology they used to answer their scientific inquiry is described in detail. . . . The full-color photos are interesting. . . . The content is solid with seamless explanations of terms, and it's fun to read." SLJ
Includes glossary and bibliographical references

Stefoff, Rebecca, 1951-
Sea mammals; by Rebecca Stefoff. Marshall Cavendish Benchmark 2008 96p il (Family trees) $23.95
Grades: 6 7 8 9   **599.5**
    1. Marine animals
    ISBN 978-0-7614-3072-8; 0-7614-3072-5
                                    LC 2008-11452
"Explores the habitats, life cycles, and other characteristics of sea mammals." Publisher's note
Includes glossary and bibliographical references

Swinburne, Stephen R.
Saving manatees; [by] Stephen Swinburne. Boyds Mills Press 2006 40p il map $16.95
Grades: 4 5 6 7   **599.5**
    1. Manatees
    ISBN 978-1-59078-319-1; 1-59078-319-0
                                    LC 2006000523

"In each chapter, Swinburne describes a different visit to a national wildlife refuge or other area in Florida's 'manatee country,' where he consults with biologists and park rangers and joins a field trip of fourth-graders as they swim with the animals. . . . Swinburne weaves a great deal of information into his personal narrative, and his enthusiastic descriptions of his experiences with the animals are contagious and will draw children right into the subject, as will the many large color photos." Booklist
Includes bibliographical references

599.63 Artiodactyla (Even-toed ungulates)

Lockwood, Sophie
Giraffes. Child's World 2006 40p il map (World of mammals) lib bdg $29.93
Grades: 4 5 6   **599.63**
    1. Giraffes
    ISBN 978-1-59296-496-3; 1-59296-496-6
                                    LC 2005-538
Explores the physical and behavioral characteristics of giraffes, examines their habitat and natural history, and discusses the role of humans in ensuring the continued survival of the species.
Includes glossary and bibliographical references

599.64 Bovidae

Marrin, Albert, 1936-
Saving the buffalo. Scholastic Nonfiction 2006 128p il $18.99 *
Grades: 4 5 6 7   **599.64**
    1. Bison
    ISBN 0-439-71854-6   LC 2005-51827
"In characteristically robust prose, Marrin retraces the American bison's roller-coaster ride from Lord of the Great Plains to near extinction at the end of the 19th century, and slow recovery. Along with showing how the buffalo fit into the habitat's complex, interdependent ecology, he describes in vivid detail how the animals were hunted and utilized by indigenous peoples. . . . A generous array of accompanying illustrations includes crisply reproduced photos, both new and old; prints; paintings; and pictures of artifacts." SLJ
Includes glossary and bibliographical references

599.65 Cervidae (Deer)

Heuer, Karsten
Being caribou; five months on foot with a caribou herd. Walker & Co. 2007 48p il map $17.95; lib bdg $18.95 *
Grades: 4 5 6 7   **599.65**
    1. Caribou 2. Arctic regions
    ISBN   978-0-8027-9565-6;   0-8027-9565-X;
    978-0-8027-9566-3 (lib bdg); 0-8027-9566-8 (lib bdg)
                                    LC 2006-27651
This is an adaptation of an adult title by the same name, published 2005 by Mountaineers Books

Heuer, Karsten—*Continued*

"Heuer recounts in short chapters of text and handsome color photographs a venture with his wife to follow on foot a herd of female caribou on their summer trek to their Arctic birthing grounds." SLJ

"The caribou calving grounds in the Arctic National Wildlife Refuge are being threatened by oil exploration. [This title] will help make kids aware of what is at stake and give them a glimpse of an extraordinary part of the world and the lengths the caribou go to traverse it. It is an important book." Quill Quire

Includes bibliographical references

Stefoff, Rebecca, 1951-

Deer; [by] Rebecca Stefoff. Marshall Cavendish Benchmark 2007 108p il (Animalways) lib bdg $34.21

Grades: 6 7 8 9   **599.65**
1. Deer
ISBN 978-0-7614-2534-2   LC 2007016932

This describes the place of deer in the animal kingdom, their evolution, anatomy, life cycle, diversity, and relationship to humans.

This "will pique readers' curiosity, and the content will keep them hooked. Vivid color photographs and illustrations and a clear font make [this work] stand out." SLJ

Includes glossary and bibliographical references

599.66   Perissodactyla (Odd-toed ungulates)

Carson, Mary Kay, 1964-

Emi and the rhino scientist; [by] Mary Kay Carson; with photographs by Tom Uhlman. Houghton Mifflin Company 2007 57p il (Scientists in the field) $18 *

Grades: 5 6 7 8   **599.66**
1. Roth, Terri 2. Rhinoceros
ISBN 978-0-618-64639-5; 0-618-64639-6
     LC 2006-34517

This describes "how Terri Roth, an expert in endangered-species reproduction at the Cincinnati Zoo, helped Emi to give birth to the first Sumatran rhino born in captivity in more than 100 years. . . . The text is full of important details, and the photographs are unfailingly crisp, bright, and full of variety." SLJ

Halls, Kelly Milner, 1957-

Wild horses; galloping through time; [by] Kelly Milner Halls; with illustrations by Mark Hallett. Darby Creek Pub. 2008 72p il $18.95

Grades: 3 4 5 6 7   **599.66**
1. Horses
ISBN 978-1-58196-065-5; 1-58196-065-4

Introduces the horse family tree including the relatives of today's modern horse that are now extinct, as well as the species of zebras and asses that still live in the wild.

"Colorful illustrations of prehistoric horses, and descriptions of differences from modern horses in terms of their size and number of toes, will intrigue readers. . . . A visual and informational blue-ribbon winner." SLJ

Includes bibliographical references

Hamilton, Garry, 1962-

Rhino rescue. Firefly Books 2006 64p il map (Firefly animal rescue) $19.95; pa $9.95

Grades: 5 6 7   **599.66**
1. Rhinoceros 2. Endangered species 3. Wildlife conservation
ISBN 978-1-55297-912-9; 1-55297-912-1; 978-1-55297-910-5 (pa); 1-55297-910-5 (pa)
     LC 2006275760

Provides details about rhinoceroses from Africa and Asia, their endangerment, and conservation programs designed to save them.

Lockwood, Sophie

Zebras; by Sophie Lockwood. Child's World 2008 40p il map (World of mammals) lib bdg $29.93

Grades: 4 5 6   **599.66**
1. Zebras
ISBN 978-1-59296-931-9; 1-59296-931-3
     LC 2007-21689

This book about Zebras looks "at all aspects of the mammal's life including where they live, how they live, and their unique habits. . . . Detailed and labeled color photographs enhance the information provided. Enjoyable and full of information." Libr Media Connect

Includes glossary and bibliographical references

599.67   Proboscidea (Elephants)

Lockwood, Sophie

Elephants. Child's World 2008 40p il map (World of mammals) lib bdg $29.93

Grades: 4 5 6   **599.67**
1. Elephants
ISBN 978-1-59296-928-9; 1-59296-928-3
     LC 2007-21942

Explores the physical and behavioral characteristics of elephants, examines their habitat and natural history, and discusses the role of humans in ensuring the continued survival of the species.

Includes glossary and bibliographical references

Redmond, Ian

Elephant; written by Ian Redmond; photographed by Dave King. Dorling Kindersley 2000 63p il (DK eyewitness books) $15.99; lib bdg $19.99

Grades: 4 5 6 7   **599.67**
1. Elephants
ISBN 0-7894-6591-4; 0-7894-6591-4 (lib bdg)
First published 1993 by Knopf

Discusses elephants, their physiology, behavior, evolution, relatives, uses by humans, and conservation

Schlaepfer, Gloria G.

Elephants; [by] Gloria Schlaepfer. Benchmark Bks. 2002 112p il (Animalways) lib bdg $21.95 *

Grades: 6 7 8 9   **599.67**
1. Elephants
ISBN 0-7614-1390-1   LC 2001-5592

Schlaepfer, Gloria G.—*Continued*

Contents: The world of elephants; Elephant ancestors; The remarkable nature of elephants; Elephant behavior; Special characteristics; The cycle of life; Conservation

"Written in engaging language. . . . Sharp color photos of the animals in the wild mix with archival images, helpful charts, and artists' renderings." Booklist

Includes glossary and bibliographical references

599.7 Carnivora Fissipedia (Land carnivores)

Lockwood, Sophie

Sea otters. Child's World 2006 40p il map (World of mammals) lib bdg $29.93

Grades: 4 5 6   599.7

1. Otters

ISBN 978-1-59296-500-7; 1-59296-500-8

LC 2005-568

Explores the physical and behavioral characteristics of sea otters, examines their habitat and natural history, and discusses the role of humans in ensuring the continued survival of the species.

Includes glossary and bibliographical references

Skunks; by Sophie Lockwood. Child's World 2008 40p il map (World of mammals) lib bdg $29.93

Grades: 4 5 6   599.7

1. Skunks

ISBN 978-1-59296-929-6 (lib bdg); 1-59296-929-1 (lib bdg)   LC 2007022219

This book about skunks presents "all the basics for reports: an introduction to the creatures' challenges, the role humans play, physical traits and behaviors, habitats, and struggles for survival. Every part of their life [cycle], including sexual maturity, birth, and family relationships, is explained. . . . Clear bright photographs pump up the content. . . . The detail that Lockwood imparts is startlingly high. The [text is] written in a dynamic and engaging style." SLJ

Includes glossary and bibliographical references

599.75 Felidae (Cat family)

Alderton, David

Wild cats of the world; photographs by Bruce Tanner. Facts on File 2002 192p il map $35

Grades: 7 8 9 10   599.75

1. Wild cats

ISBN 0-8160-5217-4   LC 2002-34736

First published 1993

This "volume explores the development and behavior of wild cats, with chapters covering form and function, evolution, and distribution. It also examines each species in detail, providing information on distinctive features such as sight, hearing, hunting techniques, and locomotion." Publisher's note

Includes bibliographical references

Becker, John E., 1942-

Wild cats: past & present; illustrations by Mark Hallett. Darby Creek 2008 80p il $18.95 *

Grades: 5 6 7 8   599.75

1. Wild cats

ISBN 978-1-58196-052-5; 1-58196-052-2

"Becker provides an informative introduction to wild cats, including an account of their ancient ancestors, an overview of the family Felidae and its subdivisions, accounts of wild cats alive in the world today, and woven throughout, discussions of the endangered status of many species. . . . Clearly written and well organized, the text is enhanced by many side-bars, maps, photos, and paintings." Booklist

Bonar, Samantha

Small wildcats. Watts 2002 63p il $24; pa $8.95

Grades: 4 5 6   599.75

1. Wild cats

ISBN 0-531-11965-3; 0-531-16632-5 (pa)

LC 2001-17581

"Watts library"

In this title "the reader learns terms, including species and genus, with various species examined more closely in chapters devoted to a particular region such as Africa, Europe and Asia, and the Americas. In addition, this book also provides conservation facts and ways in which the reader can help the endangered cats of the world." Libr Media Connect

Includes glossary and bibliographical references

Gamble, Cyndi

Leopards; natural history & conservation; text by Cyndi Gamble; photography by Rodney Griffiths. Voyageur Press 2004 48p il map (World life library) pa $12.95

Grades: 7 8 9 10   599.75

1. Leopards

ISBN 0-89658-656-1   LC 2004-14316

"The text offers a comprehensive look at these endangered animals and raises awareness of various efforts to preserve their habitats and to save them from extinction. Excellent-quality photographs appear throughout. . . . An attractive and informative addition." SLJ

Inlcudes bibliographical references

Lockwood, Sophie

Lions; by Sophie Lockwood. Child's World 2008 40p il map (World of mammals) lib bdg $29.93

Grades: 4 5 6   599.75

1. Lions

ISBN 978-1-59296-933-3 (lib bdg); 1-59296-933-X

LC 2007013567

This book about lions presents "all the basics for reports: an introduction to the creatures' challenges, the role humans play, physical traits and behaviors, habitats, and struggles for survival. Every part of their life [cycle], including sexual maturity, birth, and family relationships, is explained. . . . Clear bright photographs pump up the content. . . . The detail that Lockwood imparts is startlingly high. The [text is] written in a dynamic and engaging style." SLJ

Includes glossary and bibliographical references

Montgomery, Sy

The man-eating tigers of Sundarbans; with photographs by Eleanor Briggs. Houghton Mifflin 2001 57p il map hardcover o.p. pa $6.95 *

Grades: 4 5 6 7   **599.75**
1. Tigers
ISBN 0-618-07704-9; 0-618-49490-1 (pa)
LC 00-32031

"The author introduces readers to the geography of India and the ecology of Sundarbans, gives a brief overview of tiger behavior . . . discusses the man-eating habits of the tigers of Sundarbans, and puts forth some possible explanations for their unusual behavior." Bull Cent Child Books

"To draw readers into this scientific puzzle, Montgomery integrates science, storytelling, anthropology, and adventure in a unique treatment, illustrated with excellent color photos and diagrams." Horn Book Guide

Includes bibliographical references

Saign, Geoffrey, 1955-

The African cats. Watts 1999 64p il lib bdg $23

Grades: 4 5 6   **599.75**
1. Wild cats 2. Animals—Africa
ISBN 0-531-20365-4   LC 97-41629
"A First book"

Describes the physical characteristics and behavior patterns of ten types of cats found in Africa

"This combines dramatic wildlife color photographs with a lively, informative text." Booklist

Includes glossary and bibliographical references

Stefoff, Rebecca, 1951-

Lions. Marshall Cavendish Benchmark 2006 112p il map (Animalways) lib bdg $31.36 *

Grades: 6 7 8 9   **599.75**
1. Lions
ISBN 0-7614-1746-X   LC 2004-11466

This describes the place of lions in human history and culture, their evolution, anatomy, habits, life cycle and possible future.

Includes glossary and bibliographical references

Thompson, Sharon Elaine, 1952-

Built for speed; the extraordinary, enigmatic cheetah. Lerner Publs. 1998 88p il lib bdg $27.93

Grades: 5 6 7 8   **599.75**
1. Cheetahs
ISBN 0-8225-2854-1   LC 96-51094

Describes the habitat, physical characteristics, and behavior of the cheetah, as well as efforts to ensure the continued existence of this fastest land mammal

This "includes and explains many fascinating details of the animals' lives in a comprehensive, well-organized, and attractive way." Sci Books Films

Includes glossary and bibliographical references

599.77   Canidae (Dog family)

Halls, Kelly Milner, 1957-

Wild dogs; past and present. Darby Creek Pub. 2005 64p il (World of animals) $18.95

Grades: 5 6 7 8   **599.77**
1. Wild dogs
ISBN 1-58196-027-1

This "book explains how fossils and DNA are used to show the evolutionary lines from prehistoric canids to the dogs we live with today. . . . The author presents a wealth of detail through the accessible text; the informative captions, charts, sidebars; and the simple but clear maps." SLJ

Includes bibliographical references

Imbriaco, Alison

The red wolf; help save this endangered species! MyReportLinks.com Books 2008 128p $33.27

Grades: 4 5 6 7   **599.77**
1. Wolves 2. Endangered species
ISBN 978-1-59845-038-5; 1-59845-038-7
LC 2006020825

This describes the red wolf "and the reasons for its decline, along with the steps being taken to reverse possible extinction. . . . The [book is a] strong research [tool] on [its] own, but the addition of vetted, linked Internet sites that are recommended throughout the text makes [it] even more valuable." Voice Youth Advocates

Includes glossary and bibliographical references

Lockwood, Sophie

Foxes. Child's World 2008 40p il map (World of mammals) lib bdg $29.93

Grades: 4 5 6   **599.77**
1. Foxes
ISBN 978-1-59296-932-6; 1-59296-932-1
LC 2007-21943

Explores the physical and behavioral characteristics of foxes.

Includes glossary and bibliographical references

599.78   Ursidae (Bears)

Bortolotti, Dan

Panda rescue; changing the future for endangered wildlife. Firefly 2003 64p il map lib bdg $19.95; pa $9.95

Grades: 4 5 6 7   **599.78**
1. Giant panda 2. Wildlife conservation
ISBN 1-55297-598-3 (lib bdg); 1-55297-557-6 (pa)

This describes the panda's "natural habitat, habits, physiology, and behavior in captivity. [It also includes] a time line of conservation efforts, profiles of conservationists in the field, and forecasts of the animals' future. Throughout, the author makes clear the factors that can threaten animal populations, and discusses human attitudes toward the animals throughout history. . . . Written in accessible, lively language and nicely illustrated with exciting color photos, [this] will be useful for reports and browsing." Booklist

Hunt, Joni Phelps, 1956-

A band of bears; the rambling life of a lovable loner. London Town Press 2007 48p il (Jean-Michel Cousteau presents) pa $8.95

Grades: 5 6 7 8   599.78

1. Bears

ISBN 978-0-9766134-5-9; 0-9766134-5-X

Offers an in-depth look at the survival and social skills of these creatures as they live, play, and raise their families in their natural habitats, featuring grizzlies, black bears, and polar bears.

This "book covers the characteristics and unique traits of . . . [bears] and includes colorful, awe-inspiring photos and immediate first-person narratives." SLJ

Includes bibliographical references

Lockwood, Sophie

Polar Bears. Child's World 2005 40p il (World of mammals) lib bdg $29.93

Grades: 4 5 6   599.78

1. Polar bear

ISBN 1-59296-501-6

"The first chapter of Polar Bears discusses the bond between the animal and the Inuit people, who have depended on hunting the bears for survival. Then the discussion turns to the bears themselves: their physical features, behaviors, and relatives as well as the threats to their survival." Booklist

Includes glossary and bibliographical references

Montgomery, Sy

Search for the golden moon bear; science and adventure in the Asian tropics. Houghton Mifflin 2004 80p il $17 *

Grades: 5 6 7 8   599.78

1. Bears

ISBN 0-618-35650-9   LC 2004-5236

The author reports on an expedition into Laos and Thailand in search of a rare species of bear

"The exciting narrative is complemented by an array of full-color photos. . . . This attractive and informative offering is an intelligent reportage of science as it happens." SLJ

Includes bibliographical references

Ovsyanikov, Nikita

Polar bears. Voyageur Press 1998 72p il maps (World life library) pa $17.95

Grades: 7 8 9 10   599.78

1. Polar bear

ISBN 0-89658-358-9; 978-0-89658-358-0

LC 98-3431

This describes the polar bear's habits, behavior, and biology

"Approachable. . . . Written by an expert on the species. . . . Well illustrated with many excellent photos." Booklist

Includes bibliographical references

Patent, Dorothy Hinshaw

A polar bear biologist at work. Watts 2001 48p il map lib bdg $24.50 *

Grades: 4 5 6 7   599.78

1. Jonkel, Charles 2. Polar bear

ISBN 0-531-11850-9   LC 00-38151

"A Wildlife Conservation Society book"

Describes the work of Charles Jonkel, a biologist who studied polar bears in the Arctic and primarily in Churchill, Manitoba

"Patent's lucid text is brimming with enough data on habitat, physiology, and behavior to satisfy the needs of report writers. . . . Patent's book is important not only for the basic 'critter data' it contains, but also for its picture of a scientist at work in the field. . . . Approachable and appealing." SLJ

Includes glossary and bibliographical references

Stefoff, Rebecca, 1951-

Bears. Benchmark Bks. 2001 112p il map (Animalways) $34.21

Grades: 6 7 8 9   599.78

1. Bears

ISBN 978-0-7614-1268-7; 0-7614-1268-9

LC 00-54668

Discusses the life cycles, behaviors, and position within the animal kingdom of various types of bears.

This book about bears is "informative and full of details. The conversational tone and eye-catching photographs will appeal to those interested in . . . [bears] as well as to report researchers." Horn Book Guide

Includes bibliographical references

Thomas, Keltie

Bear rescue; changing the future for endangered wildlife. Firefly Books 2006 64p il (Firefly animal rescue series) $19.95

Grades: 5 6 7 8   599.78

1. Bears 2. Endangered species 3. Wildlife conservation

ISBN 1-55297-922-9

Provides details and facts about bears from around the world, their endangerment and a range of conservation programs to save them, including profiles of individual conservationsists and bear species

Ward, Paul, 1959-

Bears of the world; [by] Paul Ward & Suzanne Kynaston. Facts on File 2002 191p il map $35 *

Grades: 6 7 8 9   599.78

1. Bears

ISBN 0-8160-5208-5   LC 2002034739

A revised edition of Wild bears of the world, published 1995

This "explains why bears have meant so much to humans, from early in evolutionary history to the present. It looks at how bears were depicted in ancient mythology and religion. . . . The primary focus is on introducing the living species; charting their evolutionary history; and showing how they live, what they eat, how they behave, and how they cope with their habitats." Publisher's note

Includes bibliographical references

599.8 Primates

Bow, Patricia
Chimpanzee rescue; changing the future for endangered wildlife. Firefly Books 2004 64p il (Firefly animal rescue series) $19.95; pa $9.95
Grades: 5 6 7 8   **599.8**
1. Chimpanzees 2. Wildlife conservation
ISBN 1-55297-909-1; 1-55297-908-3 (pa)
This introduces chimpanzees, how and why they are in danger, and explains what efforts are being made to protect them.
This is "well-written. . . . Stunning, full-color photographs bring [this] species to life and depict a number of individuals in the field and laboratory working to save these animals." SLJ

Feinstein, Stephen
The chimpanzee; help save this endangered species! [by] Stephen Feinstein. MyReportLinks.com Books 2007 128p il (Saving endangered species) $33.27
Grades: 5 6 7 8   **599.8**
1. Chimpanzees 2. Endangered species
ISBN 978-1-59845-039-2; 1-59845-039-5
LC 2006028079
"Focuses on the study of the primates, demonstrating how similar they are to humans and why they should be preserved. . . . Provide[s] an excellent tool for teaching students to do research using both books and legitimate online sources." Voice Youth Advocates
Includes glossary and bibliographical references

Goodall, Jane, 1934-
The chimpanzees I love; saving their world and ours. Scholastic Press 2001 80p il map $17.95 *
Grades: 4 5 6 7   **599.8**
1. Chimpanzees
ISBN 0-439-21310-X   LC 00-47080
"A Byron Preiss book"
"Goodall presents her long involvement with the chimpanzees of Gombe, describing the amazing discoveries she has made over 40 years." SLJ
"Striking an admirable balance between scientific reporting and deep affection, Goodall's . . . impassioned introduction to the creatures to whom she's dedicated her life's work may well ignite in readers a similar appreciation." Publ Wkly
Includes bibliographical references

Lockwood, Sophie
Baboons. Child's World 2006 40p il map (World of mammals) lib bdg $29.93
Grades: 4 5 6   **599.8**
1. Baboons
ISBN 978-1-59296-497-0; 1-59296-497-4
LC 2005-533
Explores the physical and behavioral characteristics of baboons, examines their habitat and natural history, and discusses the role of humans in ensuring the continued survival of the species.
"Lockwood's dynamic and engaging style and intriguing insight . . . [make the] book shine. . . . Will give children solid information for reports." SLJ
Includes glossary and bibliographical references

Chimpanzees; by Sophie Lockwood. Child's World 2008 40p il map (World of mammals) lib bdg $29.93
Grades: 4 5 6   **599.8**
1. Chimpanzees
ISBN 978-1-59296-927-2; 1-59296-927-5
LC 2007-20870
This book about chimpanzees looks "at all aspects of the mammal's life including where they live, how they live, and their unique habits. . . . Detailed and labeled color photographs enhance the information provided. Enjoyable and full of information." Libr Media Connect
Includes glossary and bibliographical references

Redmond, Ian
Gorilla, monkey & ape; written by Ian Redmond; photographed by Peter Anderson & Geoff Brightling. Dorling Kindersley 2000 63p il (DK eyewitness books) $15.99; lib bdg $19.99
Grades: 4 5 6 7   **599.8**
1. Primates
ISBN 0-7894-6036-X; 0-7894-6613-9 (lib bdg)
First published 1995 by Knopf with title: Gorilla
An illustrated look at primates, including lemurs, monkeys, and apes.

Russon, Anne E.
Orangutans: wizards of the rainforest. rev ed. Firefly Books 2004 240p il map pa $24.95
Grades: 8 9 10 11 12   **599.8**
1. Orangutan
ISBN 1-55297-998-9   LC 2005-357221
First published 1999 in the United Kingdom
A firsthand account of the lives of orangutans including a scientific history of orangutans, a description of orangutans and their natural habitat, their behavior patterns, rehabilitation operations, the politics of orangutan rescue work, and a look at orangutans released back into the forest.
Includes bibliographical references

Saign, Geoffrey, 1955-
The great apes; [by] Geoffrey C. Saign. Watts 1998 63p il pa $6.95 hardcover o.p.
Grades: 4 5 6   **599.8**
1. Apes
ISBN 0-531-15902-7 (pa)   LC 97-1189
"A First book"
Describes and compares the four great apes: chimpanzees, bonobos, orangutans, and gorillas through a discussion of their physical, intellectual, emotional, and social characteristics
This is an "appealing, involving introduction. . . . The many color photographs are well chosen for their clarity and sensitivity as well as for their clear illustration of the text." Booklist
Includes glossary and bibliographical references

Sobol, Richard

Breakfast in the rainforest; a visit with mountain gorillas; with an afterword by Leonardo DiCaprio. Candlewick 2008 40p il map $18.99

Grades: 3 4 5 6   **599.8**

1. Gorillas 2. Rain forest ecology 3. Uganda

ISBN 978-0-7636-2281-7; 0-7636-2281-8

"Wildlife photographer Sobol recounts his travels to Uganda to observe gorillas living in the Virunga Mountains. In his personable text, he also touches on the creatures' habits, diet, and threats. Closeup photographs of the gorillas in addition to many pictures of the surrounding countryside and villagers help round out an understanding of the endangered animals' homeland." Horn Book Guide

Stefoff, Rebecca, 1951-

The primate order. Benchmark Books 2005 92p il (Family trees) lib bdg $29.93 *

Grades: 6 7 8 9   **599.8**

1. Primates

ISBN 0-7614-1816-4   LC 2004-21404

This examines physical traits, adaptations, diets, habitats, and life cycles of primates.

"Fact-filled, yet suprisingly readable. . . . [This] title contains a wide variety of excellent-quality, full-color photographs; interesting sidebars; and diagrams." SLJ

Zabludoff, Marc

Monkeys; by Marc Zabludoff. Marshall Cavendish Benchmark 2007 108p il (Animalways) lib bdg $34.21

Grades: 6 7 8 9   **599.8**

1. Monkeys

ISBN 978-0-7614-2535-9   LC 2007013172

This describes the place of monkeys in the animal kingdom, their evolution, anatomy, life cycle, behavior, diversity, and relationship to humans.

This "will pique readers' curiosity, and the content will keep them hooked. Vivid color photographs and illustrations and a clear font make [this work] stand out." SLJ

Includes glossary and bibliographical references

599.9   Hominidae Homo sapiens

Deem, James M.

Bodies from the ice; melting glaciers and the recovery of the past. Houghton Mifflin 2008 58p il map $17 *

Grades: 5 6 7 8 9 10   **599.9**

1. Mummies 2. Glaciers

ISBN 978-0-618-80045-2; 0-618-80045-X

LC 2008-01868

This describes the discovery of human remains preserved in glaciers in the Alps, the Andes, The Himalayas, and other places around the world and what can be learned from them.

"Full-color photographs, reproductions, and maps are clearly captioned; grand images of glaciated mountain peaks span entire pages, and detailed pictures of recov-

ered objects . . . are presented. . . . [This] is a fantastic resource. Deem superbly weaves diverse geographical settings, time periods, and climate issues into a readable work that reveals the increasing interdisciplinary dimensions of the sciences." SLJ

Includes bibliographical references

599.93   Genetics, sex and age characteristics, evolution

Anderson, Dale, 1953-

How do we know the nature of human origins. Rosen Pub. Group 2005 112p il (Great scientific questions and the scientists who answered them) lib bdg $31.95

Grades: 7 8 9 10   **599.93**

1. Human origins 2. Evolution 3. Fossil hominids

ISBN 978-1-4042-0077-7; 1-4042-0077-0

LC 2003-27875

Examines what is known about humankind's origins, and the scientists who have studied the topic

Anderson "enlivens the text by giving a little background information on the scientists involved. His presentation of controversies is quite well balanced [and] . . . the black-and-white photographs and charts are well chosen and well keyed to the text." SLJ

Includes bibliographical references

Boon, Kevin A.

The human genome project; what does decoding DNA mean for us? [by] Kevin Alexander Boon. Enslow Pubs. 2002 128p il (Issues in focus) lib bdg $26.60 *

Grades: 8 9 10 11 12   **599.93**

1. Human Genome Project 2. DNA 3. Genetics

ISBN 0-7660-1685-4   LC 2001-3388

Discusses genes, genetics, and the legal and ethical issues involved in mapping DNA in the human body

"Opposing viewpoints are presented and a great deal of well-documented information that could be used by debate teams is included. . . . A good update for science shelves." SLJ

Includes glossary and bibliographical references

Goldenberg, Linda, 1941-

Little people and a lost world; an anthropological mystery. Twenty-First Century Books 2007 112p il (Discovery!) lib bdg $29.27 *

Grades: 5 6 7 8   **599.93**

1. Fossil hominids 2. Excavations (Archeology)—Indonesia 3. Pygmies

ISBN 978-0-8225-5983-2; 0-8225-5983-8

LC 2005-33431

This is an account of the 2003 discovery of small fossil hominids on Flores Island, Indonesia.

"This will add important insights to the study of early humans as well as, more broadly, how science and politics interact." Booklist

Includes bibliographical references

La Pierre, Yvette

Neandertals; a prehistoric puzzle. Twenty-First Century Books 2008 112p il (Discovery!) lib bdg $30.60

Grades: 6 7 8 9   **599.93**

1. Neanderthals 2. Fossil hominids 3. Prehistoric peoples

ISBN 978-0-8225-7524-5; 0-8225-7524-8

LC 2007-22066

When the first Neanderthal skeleton was discovered nearly 150 years ago, scientists presented the race as barely developed brutes. But recent findings indicate that Neanderthals made complex tools, organized group hunts, cared for their sick and injured, and buried their dead.

"Several theories about these prehistoric humans are discussed, including evolution, creationism, linear evolution, and natural selection. This balanced presentation is a valuable aspect of this well–formatted and visually appealing book." Voice Youth Advocates

Includes glossary and bibliographical references

Robertshaw, Peter

The early human world; by Peter Robertshaw and Jill Rubalcaba. Oxford University Press 2005 c2004 173p il map (World in ancient times) lib bdg $32.95 *

Grades: 7 8 9 10   **599.93**

1. Human origins 2. Fossil hominids 3. Prehistoric peoples

ISBN 0-19-516157-2   LC 2004-9732

The author presents "information on human evolution as well as on early humanity in the New World. The text is matched with a great deal of supporting matter including time lines, maps, dramatis personae, high-quality photos, and artists' renderings." SLJ

Includes bibliographical references

Sloan, Christopher

The human story; our evolution from prehistoric ancestors to today; foreword by Meave Leakey and Louise Leakey; photographs by Kenneth L. Garrett; art by Kennis and Kennis. National Geographic Society 2004 80p il $21.95

Grades: 7 8 9 10   **599.93**

1. Evolution 2. Human origins

ISBN 0-7922-6325-1   LC 2003-13978

Contents: Of bones and genes; Our next of kin; Out of Africa; Becoming modern; Being human today

Explores the origins of humans, including how such developments as Linnaeus' classification system and recent understanding of the human genome have improved scientists' comprehension of evolution

"What many . . . readers will find most exciting is how today's cutting-edge technology helps us learn about the prehistoric connections all humans share. Great for classroom discussion." Booklist

Includes glossary and bibliographical references

Tattersall, Ian

Bones, brains and DNA; the human genome and human evolution; by Ian Tattersall & Rob DeSalle; illustrated by Patricia J. Wynne. Bunker Hill Pub., Inc. 2007 47p il $16.95 *

Grades: 5 6 7 8   **599.93**

1. Human origins 2. Evolution 3. Genetics

ISBN 978-1-59373-056-7; 1-59373-056-X

LC 2006931578

The "text follows the trail of human evolution, basing its factual content on current data exhibited in the New Hall of Human Origins in New York City's American Museum of Natural History. Using the skills of anthropologists, archaeologists, and paleontologists, the authors track clues laid down in the fossil record, and, more importantly, in our DNA. . . . The very unsimple concepts are presented clearly, in an attractive format, with splashings of small photos, colorful artwork, diagrams, and maps to attract the eye and elucidate the text." SLJ

Thimmesh, Catherine

Lucy long ago; uncovering the mystery of where we came from. Houghton Mifflin Harcourt 2009 63p il $18 *

Grades: 4 5 6 7   **599.93**

1. Human origins 2. Fossil hominids

ISBN 978-0-547-05199-4; 0-547-05199-9

LC 2008-36761

"The 1974 discovery of the fossilized partial skeleton of a small-brained primate who apparently walked upright 3.2 million years ago in what is now Ethiopia significantly changed accepted theories about human origins. Step by step, Thimmesh presents the questions the newly discovered bones raised and how they were answered. . . . Extensive research, clear organization and writing, appropriate pacing for new ideas and intriguing graphics all contribute to this exceptionally accessible introduction to the mystery of human origins." Kirkus

600 TECHNOLOGY

Macaulay, David, 1946-

The new way things work; [by] David Macaulay with Neil Ardley. Houghton Mifflin 1998 400p il $35 *

Grades: 4 5 6 7 8 9 10 11 12 Adult   **600**

1. Technology 2. Machinery 3. Inventions

ISBN 0-395-93847-3   LC 98-14224

First published 1988 with title: The way things work

Arranged in five sections this volume provides information on "the workings of hundreds of machines and devices—holograms, helicopters, airplanes, mobile phones, compact disks, hard disks, bits and bytes, cash machines. . . . Explanations [are also given] of the scientific principles behind each machine—how gears make work easier, why jumbo jets are able to fly, how computers actually compute." Publisher's note

Woodford, Chris, 1943-
Cool Stuff 2.0 and how it works; written by Chris Woodford and Jon Woodcock. DK Pub. 2007 256p il $24.99 *
Grades: 5 6 7 8   **600**
  1. Inventions 2. Technology
  ISBN 978-0-7566-3207-6; 0-7566-3207-2
                LC 2007-299442
"More than 100 entries present a wide variety of topics with high child appeal, from robot cars to high-tech toilets. . . . Full but uncluttered layouts mix photos, text boxes, diagrams, and captions to highlight key elements. . . . Readers should have an easy time understanding the basics of what each item does, how it is used, and how it works. Along with up-to-date scientific information on high-interest topics, this title has very strong browsing appeal and great booktalk potential." SLJ

609 Historical, geographic, persons treatment

Bender, Lionel
Invention; written by Lionel Bender. rev ed. DK Pub. 2005 72p il (DK eyewitness books) $15.99; lib bdg $19.99
Grades: 4 5 6 7   **609**
  1. Inventions
  ISBN 0-7566-1076-1; 0-7566-1075-3 (lib bdg)
  First published 1991 by Knopf
Photographs and text explore such inventions as the wheel, gears, levers, clocks, telephones, and rocket engines.

Bridgman, Roger Francis, 1940-
1,000 inventions & discoveries; written by Roger Bridgman. DK Pub. 2002 256p il hardcover o.p. pa $14.99
Grades: 5 6 7 8   **609**
  1. Inventions—History
  ISBN 0-7894-8826-4; 978-0-7566-1705-9 (pa); 0-7566-1705-7 (pa)   LC 2002-23742
  Summarizes 1000 notable inventions and discoveries of ancient and modern times, from 3,000,000 B.C. to the beginning of the twenty-first century A.D
  This offers "color photos, highly informative and readable text, and easy-to-read layouts." ALAN

Cole, D. J. (David J.), 1938-
Encyclopedia of modern everyday inventions; [by] David J. Cole, Eve Browning, and Fred E.H. Schroeder. Greenwood Press 2003 285p il $57.95
Grades: 7 8 9 10 11 12 Adult   **609**
  1. Inventions—History 2. Reference books
  ISBN 0-313-31345-8   LC 2002-69620
"Profiles of approximately 150 20th-century inventions, from Post-Its to Murphy beds, gumball machines to the Internet. . . . The articles include specific but non-technical discussions of the invention's development, principles, and components, and conclude with a short list of both print and electronic resources." SLJ

"The analysis of each invention is thorough and lively. . . . This book . . . would make an excellent addition to any school or public library needing books on technology and inventions in the modern world." Voice Youth Advocates
Includes bibliographical references

Historical inventions on file; [by] the Diagram Group. Facts on File 1994 various paging il loose-leaf $185
Grades: Professional   **609**
  1. Inventions—History
  ISBN 0-8160-2911-3   LC 94-7098
This work contains "65 experiments re-creating famous inventions. The purpose of these re-creations is to assist students in understanding important concepts and innovations in science. Intended for grades 6-12, the work is multidisciplinary in approach, making use of history, science, mathematics, and abstract and applied thinking. . . . This will be a useful source for middle- and high-school students and teachers doing science projects and experiments." Booklist

Horne, Richard, 1973-
101 things you wish you'd invented—and some you wish no one had; designed and illustrated by Richard Horne; written by Tracey Turner and Richard Horne. Walker & Co. 2008 unp il pa $11.99
Grades: 6 7 8 9   **609**
  1. Inventions
  ISBN 978-0-80279-788-9; 0-80279-788-1
                LC 2008-4990
"Offers explanations of how an array of both curious and common things came into existence in this . . . interactive book with checklists, adhesive stars, and activities." Publisher's note
"The authors have chosen interesting subjects and written concise and engaging histories and trivia. The quality of the book is quite impressive. With an appearance much like a field guide, this well-bound book is made with quality paper and has a very eye-catching layout." Voice Youth Advocates

Inventors and inventions. Marshall Cavendish 2008 5v il set$399.95 *
Grades: 6 7 8 9 10   **609**
  1. Inventions—History 2. Technology—History 3. Inventors 4. Reference books
  ISBN 978-0-7614-7761-7   LC 2007-60868
"*Inventions and Inventors* is designed to introduce students to an array of inventors from the past and present while encouraging 'interest in and knowledge of science' by exploring the history, development, and utility of a wide variety of inventions. This set contains 172 alphabetically arranged articles on a range of inventors as well as 21 overview articles. . . . The choice of inventors, the inclusion of more than 1,000 full-color illustrations, and the highly readable and engaging text all create a valuable reference for students and browsers alike." Booklist
Includes bibliographical references

Jedicke, Peter

Great inventions of the 20th century; by Peter Jedicke. Chelsea House 2007 72p il (Scientific American) $30

Grades: 5 6 7 8   **609**

1. Inventions—History 2. Technology—History
ISBN 978-0-7910-9048-0; 0-7910-9048-5

LC 2006014773

This "presents a celebration of the inventors and inventions that transformed the world during the age of technology. Topics presented include cellophane, the microwave oven, liquid-filled rockets, ultrasound, and robotic machines, among many others." Publisher's note

"The text is simple, clear, and concise. . . . [The book has] captioned color photos throughout." SLJ

Includes glossary and bibliographical references

Landau, Elaine

The history of everyday life. 21st Century Bks. 2005 56p il (Major inventions through history) $26.60

Grades: 5 6 7 8   **609**

1. Inventions—History
ISBN 0-8225-3808-3

This "explores fireplaces and central heating, indoor plumbing, the washing machine, food and clothing production, and microwave ovens. . . . [It] presents information about daily living from ancient times to the present. . . . The text . . . is breezy but informative. . . . Illustrations are a mixture of period black-and-white and color photos." SLJ

Includes bibligraphical references

MacLeod, Jilly

How nearly everything was invented . . . by the Brainwaves; illustrated by Lisa Swerling and Ralph Lazar; written by Jilly MacLeod. DK Pub. 2006 61p il $19.99

Grades: 4 5 6   **609**

1. Inventions—History 2. Technology—History
ISBN 0-7566-2077-5   LC 2006-10607

"Creatively designed and playfully illustrated, this large-format volume rounds up a wide range of information and covers more than 300 inventions. Energetic hooded characters called Brainwaves usher readers through the labyrinthine pages and provide an ongoing, amusing commentary." Publ Wkly

Robinson, James

Inventions; foreword by James Dyson. Kingfisher 2006 63p il (Kingfisher knowledge) $12.95

Grades: 5 6 7 8   **609**

1. Inventions—History 2. Technology—History
ISBN 978-0-7534-5973-7; 0-7534-5973-6

This "examines the ideas, machines, and technology that have shaped the modern age. Divided into four chapters—Communication, Inventions in the Home, Transportation, and Microtechnology—it charts the developments that led to the cell phone revolution and reveals the incredible growth of the information superhighway." Publisher's note

"A slim, colorful overview of inventions." Kirkus

Includes glossary

Rossi, Ann

Bright ideas; the age of invention in America, 1870-1910; [by] Ann Rossi. National Geographic 2005 40p il (Crossroads America) $12.95 *

Grades: 4 5 6   **609**

1. Inventions—History
ISBN 0-7922-8276-0   LC 2003-19834

This describes the history of late 19th and early 20th century inventions such as the light bulb, the telegraph, the telephone, and the automobile.

This "solid [title] for report writers may even pull in a few curious browsers because of [its] plentiful, full-color photos and reproductions. The [layout is] inviting, and the [text is] clear, informative, and readable." SLJ

Includes glossary

Sandler, Martin W.

Inventors; a Library of Congress book; introduction by James H. Billington. HarperCollins Pubs. 1996 93p il pa $10.99 hardcover o.p.

Grades: 5 6 7 8   **609**

1. Inventions—History 2. Inventors
ISBN 0-06-446746-5 (pa)   LC 95-944

"Composed mainly of historical photographs, reproductions, and period writing culled from the Library of Congress archives, the volume presents an intriguing montage of the inventors, technology, and ingenuity that flourished around the turn of the twentieth century. The brief present tense narrative is informative; the illustrative material is hugely appealing." Horn Book

Strapp, James

Science and technology. Sharpe Focus 2009 80p il (Inside ancient China) $31.45

Grades: 7 8 9 10   **609**

1. Science—China 2. Technology—History
3. Science and civilization
ISBN 978-0-7656-8169-0; 0-7656-8169-2

LC 2008-31168

"This colorful book surveys science and technology developed by the ancient Chinese. Strapp discusses early compasses and mapmaking, the building of canals, and the invention of . . . the wheelbarrow, water clocks, gunpowder, and the harness. The last chapter looks at Chinese medicine and feng shui. . . . The writing is clear and the format is inviting, with many sidebars and pictures. Illustrations include photos of artifacts and maps as well as period artwork and line-and-wash pictures." Booklist

Includes bibliographical references

Tomecek, Steve

What a great idea! inventions that changed the world; [by] Stephen M. Tomecek; illustrated by Dan Stuckenschneider. Scholastic Ref. 2003 112p il $22.99 *

Grades: 4 5 6 7   **609**

1. Inventions—History
ISBN 0-590-68144-3   LC 2001-20937

"Tomecek puts significant inventions and discoveries in a historical context. Dividing the text into five broad time periods, he offers a series of essays on important

Tomecek, Steve—*Continued*
advances that occurred in each 'age'. . . . What emerges is a sense of interconnectedness that other books often lack. . . . Full-color diagrams and illustrations are well integrated into each spread." SLJ
Includes bibliographical references

Tucker, Tom, 1944-
Brainstorm! the stories of twenty American kid inventors; with drawings by Richard Loehle. Farrar, Straus & Giroux 1995 148p il pa $6.95 hardcover o.p.
Grades: 5 6 7 8   609
1. Inventors 2. Inventions
ISBN 0-374-40928-5 (pa)   LC 94-38780
The author looks at inventions devised by children since the 18th century. Ear muffs, water skis, the popsicle, colored car wax and the electronic television are among the products discussed. Includes a discussion of how the Patent Office works
Includes glossary and bibliographical references

610   Medicine & health

Auden, Scott
Medical mysteries; science researches conditions from bizarre to deadly; by Scott Auden; Elizabeth Brownell, consultant. National Geographic 2008 64p il (National Geographic investigates) $17.95; lib bdg $27.90
Grades: 4 5 6 7   610
1. Medicine—Research 2. Diseases
ISBN   978-1-4263-0356-2;   1-4263-0356-4; 978-1-4263-0261-9 (lib bdg); 1-4263-0261-4 (lib bdg)
This title features "full-color photographs that readers have come to expect from this publisher. . . . [It] focuses on diseases that are regarded as bizarre and are often deadly, including Creutzfeldt-Jakob, Progeria, and Morgellons. The approach is to examine the way in which these mysterious diseases were discovered and how they are being studied to find a cure. . . . [This book offers] explanations simple enough for middle school students but with enough content to make them a useful resource for high school students as well." Voice Youth Advocates
Includes glossary and bibliographical references

Goldsmith, Connie, 1945-
Cutting-edge medicine. Lerner Publications Co. 2008 48p il (Cool science) lib bdg $26.60
Grades: 4 5 6   610
1. Medicine
ISBN 978-0-8225-6770-7; 0-8225-6770-9
LC 2007001946
"This book explains the many amazing ways new medical techniques are helping people live longer, healthier lives." Publisher's note
Includes glossary and bibliographical references

Morley, David
Healing our world. Fitzhenry & Whiteside 2007 121p il map $18.95 *
Grades: 6 7 8 9 10 11 12   610
1. Médecins Sans Frontières (Organization) 2. Medical assistance 3. War relief 4. Disaster relief
ISBN 978-1-55041-565-0
"Morley is a former executive director of the Canadian section of Doctors Without Borders, a humanitarian organization known throughout most of world as Medecins Sans Frontieres (MSF). With clarity and passion, he introduces the organization's history, charter, and current efforts to provide health care where it is needed most." Booklist

610.69   Medical personnel and relationships

Reeves, Diane Lindsey, 1959-
Career ideas for teens in health science; [by] Diane Lindsey Reeves with Gail Karlitz and Anna Prokos. Ferguson 2005 184p il (Career ideas for teens) $40; pa $16.95
Grades: 7 8 9 10   610.69
1. Medicine 2. Vocational guidance
ISBN 0-8160-5290-5; 0-8160-6920-4 (pa)
LC 2004-15040
The careers covered in this book include home health aide, chiropractor, dietician, biochemist, and pharmacist.

610.9   Medical sciences—Historical and geographic treatment

Davis, Lucile
Medicine in the American West. Children's Press 2001 30p il (Cornerstones of freedom) lib bdg $21 *
Grades: 4 5 6   610.9
1. Medicine—History 2. West (U.S.)—History
ISBN 0-516-22004-7   LC 00-31608
The author provides an "overview of medical practices at the time Lewis and Clark set out, and builds from there to include the importance of Native American herbals, wagon-train surgeries, traveling elixir salesmen, continuing to the introduction of ether to anesthetize patients in surgery. . . . High-quality, full-color illustrations add variety to the page layout." SLJ
Includes glossary

Dawson, Ian
Renaissance medicine. Enchanted Lion Books 2005 64p il (History of medicine) lib bdg $19.95 *
Grades: 6 7 8 9   610.9
1. Medicine—History 2. Renaissance
ISBN 1-59270-038-1
This "offers a concise overview of the fascinating advancements in European medicine between 1450 and 1750. . . . Dawson carefully shows how inventions such

Dawson, Ian—*Continued*

as the printing press and microscope and the work of artists such as da Vinci influenced medical knowledge. Quotes from primary sources enhance the plainspoken language, and numerous reproductions of paintings and engravings vividly evoke the realities of surgery, leech treatments, and the horrors of the plague." Booklist

Includes glossary and bibliographical references

Woolf, Alex

Death and disease; [by] Alex Woolf. Lucent Books 2004 48p il map (Medieval realms) $29.95 *

Grades: 5 6 7 8   **610.9**
1. Medicine—History 2. Medieval civilization
ISBN 1-59018-533-1   LC 2003-61797

This "discusses topics such as medieval theories about the body and disease, the influence of the Church on health practices, the causes and effects of bubonic plague, and the emergence of modern medicine as the medieval era drew to an end." Booklist

"Clear, well-organized [text] along with full-color reproductions of art and artifacts and photos of period structures immerse readers in . . . medieval life and offer sufficient information for reports." SLJ

Includes glossary and bibliographical references

611   Human anatomy, cytology, histology

Haywood, Karen Diane

Skeletal system; [by] Karen Haywood. Marshall Cavendish Benchmark 2009 80p il (The amazing human body) lib bdg $34.21

Grades: 6 7 8 9   **611**
1. Skeleton
ISBN 978-0-7614-3056-8; 0-7614-3056-3
     LC 2008-17574

"Discusses the parts that make up the human skeletal system, what can go wrong, how to treat those illnesses and diseases, and how to stay healthy." Publisher's note

Includes glossary and bibliographical references

Human anatomy on file; [by] The Diagram Group. New ed. Facts on File 2003 unp il loose-leaf $185

Grades: Professional   **611**
1. Human anatomy
ISBN 0-8160-5103-8   LC 2003-44821

Also available CD-ROM version

Companion volume to Human physiology on file

First published 1983 with title: The human body

This loose-leaf volume includes approximately 1500 labelled anatomical drawings and charts which may be reproduced for classroom use

Includes glossary and bibliographical references

Morgan, Jennifer, 1955-

Cells of the nervous system; [by] Jennifer R. Morgan and Ona Bloom. Chelsea House Publishers 2006 147p il (Gray matter) lib bdg $35

Grades: 8 9 10 11 12   **611**
1. Cells 2. Nervous system
ISBN 978-0-7910-8512-7; 0-7910-8512-0
     LC 2005-11690

An introduction to the human brain discusses how the nervous system relates and processes information, and how its parts can be damaged and repaired.

"Valuable addition[s] to an area where little is written for high school students." Libr Media Connect

Includes bibliographical references

Walker, Richard, 1951-

Body. DK Pub. 2005 96p il $19.99 *

Grades: 4 5 6 7   **611**
1. Human anatomy
ISBN 0-7566-1371-X

Subtitle on cover: an amazing tour of human anatomy

"This book features eye-catching views of the human body. The computer-generated, three-dimensional images were created by scanning successive horizontal slices of a specially treated human cadaver. . . . The accompanying CD allows users to examine interactive, 360-degree animations of the images. Suitable as a ready-reference source as well as for casual browsers, this informative title does a magnificent job of showing just how complicated and elaborate the human body is." SLJ

612   Human physiology

Being human; edited by Derek Hall. Grolier Educ. 2000 8v set $229

Grades: 5 6 7 8   **612**
1. Human beings 2. Reference books
ISBN 0-7172-9419-6   LC 99-34157

Contents: v1 The human body, by D. Hall; v2 The brain and senses, by D. Hall; v3 Health and illness, by M. Whiteside; v4 Keeping safe, by B. Collyer; v5 Personality and behavior, by P. Carmichael; v6 Communication, by B. Medlam; v7 Relationships, by S. Benson; v8 The human race, by P. Steele

"Within each volume, 16 topics are addressed in two-page presentations. . . . Full-color illustrations are copious and top quality, and both text and pictures are multicultural and gender inclusive." Booklist

Calabresi, Linda

Human body. Simon & Schuster Books for Young Readers 2008 unp il (Insiders) $16.99

Grades: 4 5 6 7   **612**
1. Physiology 2. Human body
ISBN 978-1-4169-3861-3; 1-4169-3861-3
     LC 2007-61744

This volume "offers excellent pictures of systems, organs, and even individual cells in the human body. . . . A visually dynamic introduction to the human package." Booklist

Ganeri, Anita, 1961-
Alive; the living, breathing human body book; [written by Anita Ganeri; paper engineering: Iain Smyth] DK Publishing 2007 unp il $24.99
Grades: 5 6 7   **612**
1. Human body 2. Pop-up books
ISBN 978-0-7566-3211-3; 0-7566-3211-0
This "riveting pop-up tour of human anatomy . . . kicks off with two glitzy special effects—a cutaway brain with a pushbutton cascade of sparkles on the cover, then the sound of a beating heart triggered by fully opening the first spread—and goes on for a seven-spread survey of the body's systems and cell biology. . . . A sure thing for display, for casual browsing, and to crank science units up a notch." SLJ

Gardner, Robert, 1929-
Easy genius science projects with the human body; great experiments and ideas. Enslow Publishers 2009 112p il (Easy genius science projects) lib bdg $31.93
Grades: 7 8 9 10   **612**
1. Human body 2. Science—Experiments
ISBN 978-0-7660-2927-9 (lib bdg); 0-7660-2927-1 (lib bdg)   LC 2007-32315
"Both simple and complex science experiments involving the human body are included in this guide for young scientists. An introduction reviews the issues of safety and adult supervision, plus a quick review of the scientific method is included. . . . The high level vocabulary indicates that this is a book for more advanced science students. This would be a great book to put in the hands of a highly motivated student needing fresh ideas for a science fair." Libr Media Connect

Human physiology on file; [by] The Diagram Group. New ed. Facts on File 2003 unp il loose-leaf $185
Grades: Professional   **612**
1. Physiology
ISBN 0-8160-5104-6   LC 2003-44822
Replaces Human body on file: physiology, published 1996
Also available CD-ROM version
Companion volume to Human anatomy on file
Previously published as: Human body on file : physiology. New York : Facts On File, 1996
This loose-leaf volume includes labelled diagrams illustrating physiological functions and body systems which may be reproduced for classroom use
Includes glossary and bibliographical references

Johnson, Rebecca L., 1956-
Ultra-organized cell systems; by Rebecca L. Johnson; illustrations by Jack Desrocher; diagrams by Jennifer Fairman. Millbrook Press 2008 48p il (Microquests) lib bdg $29.27 *
Grades: 5 6 7 8   **612**
1. Human body 2. Tissues
ISBN 978-0-8225-7138-4   LC 2006036395
This "is an introductory anatomy and physiology book. . . . The book contains a wealth of accurate information presented clearly in a logical arrangement. Clever cartoon diagrams . . . are fun and add to the understanding of the concepts illustrated. . . . The organization of cells into tissues, tissues into organs, and organs into organ systems is explained clearly and concisely." Sci Books Films
Includes glossary and bibliographical references

Macaulay, David, 1946-
The way we work; getting to know the amazing human body; [by] David Macaulay, with Richard Walker. Houghton Mifflin 2008 336p il $35 *
Grades: 6 7 8 9 10   **612**
1. Human body
ISBN 978-0-618-23378-6; 0-618-23378-4
      LC 2008-25109
"Walter Lorraine books"
"The opening chapter introduces basic concepts of biology and chemistry at the cellular level while subsequent chapters take us through the various systems of the body. . . . [Humor] occasionally leavens the information, which, though often complex and technical, is clearly and succintly presented in double-page spreads, accompanied by an illuminating array of illustrations." Horn Book

Nagel, Rob
Body by design; from the digestive system to the skeleton. U.X.L 2000 2v set $126 *
Grades: 7 8 9 10   **612**
1. Physiology 2. Human anatomy
ISBN 0-7876-3897-8   LC 99-14642
Contents: v1 Cardiovascular system; Digestive system; Endocrine system; Integumentary system; Lymphatic system; Muscular system; v2 Nervous system; Reproductive system; Respiratory system; Skeletal system; Urinary system; Special senses
"Each chapter examines one of the 11 organ systems of the body; the final chapter focuses on the senses. In addition to describing each system's structure and function, the diseases commonly associated with it and suggestions for keeping it healthy are also discussed." SLJ
"Black-and-white and color photographs are plentiful, and color is used throughout to highlight headings and subheadings, sidebars, and other features." Booklist
Includes bibliographical references

Parker, Steve
The human body book; [by] Steve Parker; foreword by Robert Winston. DK 2007 256p il $35 *
Grades: 6 7 8 9   **612**
1. Human body
ISBN 978-0-7566-2856-9
"This coffee-table quarto combines jaw-dropping illustrations with meaty captions and commentary to give . . . a mesmerizing tour of the body's parts and common diseases. . . . Packaged with a CD that contains interactive and animated versions of many illustrations." SLJ
Includes glossary

Redd, Nancy Amanda

Body drama; real girls, real bodies, real issues, real answers. Gotham 2008 271p pa $20

Grades: 6 7 8 9 10   612

1. Human body 2. Physiology 3. Girls—Health and hygiene 4. Puberty

ISBN 978-1-59240-326-4; 1-59240-326-3

Information for teenage girls about various issues pertaining to their changing physiology

"The author covers a myriad of physical as well as mental health issues, including cutting and depression. . . . It is likely to be a read-and-pass-along book not only for the helpful advice and accurate information but also for the gross-out pictures of head lice, warts, and keloid scars." Voice Youth Advocates

Includes bibliographical references

Reilly, Kathleen M.

The human body; 25 fantastic projects illuminate how the body works; illustrated by Shawn Braley. Nomad Press 2008 120p il $21.95; pa $15.95

Grades: 5 6 7 8   612

1. Human body

ISBN 978-1-934670-25-5; 1-934670-25-1; 978-1-934670-24-8 (pa); 1-934670-24-3 (pa)

"The workings of the human body are expertly summarized in 11 tidy chapters, which include experiments that explain how the body works by creating models that either imitate or test its functions. . . . Many of the activities require adult supervision due to the materials required. . . . Simple drawings and cartoons enliven and illuminate the text. . . . The scientific explanations are superb." SLJ

Somervill, Barbara A., 1948-

The human body. Gareth Stevens Pub. 2008 48p il (Gareth Stevens vital science: life science) lib bdg $26.60; pa $11.95 *

Grades: 5 6 7 8   612

1. Human body

ISBN 978-0-8368-8441-8 (lib bdg); 978-0-8368-8450-0 (pa)   LC 2007-16175

First published 2006 in the United Kingdom

This describes "human anatomy and physiology. . . . Factoids are scattered throughout the text in a fashion that captures the reader's attention and interest. . . . [The book offers] excellent graphics, namely photos and diagrams. The artwork complements and enhances the written content." Sci Books Films

Includes glossary and bibliographical references

Walker, Richard, 1951-

Dr. Frankenstein's human body book; the monstrous truth about how your body works; [author, Richard Walker; artist, Nick Abadzis] DK Pub. 2008 93p il $24.99 *

Grades: 4 5 6 7   612

1. Human body

ISBN 978-0-7566-4091-0; 0-7566-4091-1

"This anatomy book is as engrossing as any science fiction. Dr. Frankenstein, shown in a sepia photograph

standing in a laboratory, gazing at a skull he holds in one hand, invites readers to join him as he creates a human being. . . . The story line is sustained with brief, pun-happy journal entries. . . . Gothic fonts and engraved illustrations and vignettes (in red and black and also hand-colored) blend with state-of-the-art images from MEG scans, gamma scans and other advanced technology. Clear explanations broken into easily assimilable captions and text blocks encourage the reader." Publ Wkly

Includes glossary

Human body; written by Richard Walker. DK 2009 72p il (DK eyewitness books) $16.99; lib bdg $19.95

Grades: 4 5 6 7   612

1. Human body

ISBN 978-0-75664-545-8; 0-75664-545-X; 978-0-75664-545-8 (lib bdg); 0-75664-533-6 (lib bdg)   LC 2009419529

Includes CD-ROM

In this book, text and illustrations present information on the parts of the body and how they work.

Includes glossary and bibliographical references

Ouch! how your body makes it through a very bad day; written by Richard Walker. DK Pub. 2007 71p il $16.99

Grades: 4 5 6 7   612

1. Human body

ISBN 978-0-7566-2536-8; 0-7566-2536-X

"Tag along on a rotten day as a body copes with sneezing, getting cut, being stung by a bee, and vomiting, as well as performing more mundane actions such as urinating, tapping into its melanin supply, acting reflexively, and sweating. . . . Dramatic color graphics, both large and small, are accompanied by a multitude of informative captions. Researchers who find the information on the busy pages hard to grasp can pop in the accompanying CD-ROM and catch a ride up the esophagus on a wave of vomit. . . . Eye-catching, highly pictorial, informative, and with a megadose of ick! factor." SLJ

Includes glossary

World Book's human body works. World Book 2007 6v il set$139

Grades: 5 6 7 8   612

1. Human body 2. Reference books

ISBN 978-0-7166-4425-5

Contents: The circulatory system; The digestive system, the urinary system; The endocrine system, the reproductive system, human development; The nervous system, the skin, the senses; The respiratory system; The skeletal system, the muscular system

"These slim volumes, each corresponding to one of the body's pivotal systems, are clearly written and contain high-quality color photographs . . . and outstanding bright diagrams." SLJ

612.1 Blood and circulation

Bjorklund, Ruth
Circulatory system. Marshall Cavendish Benchmark 2009 80p il (The amazing human body) lib bdg $34.21
Grades: 6 7 8 9   **612.1**
1. Cardiovascular system
ISBN 978-0-7614-3053-7; 0-7614-3053-9
LC 2007-50436
"Discusses the parts that make up the human circulatory system, what can go wrong, how to treat those illnesses and diseases, and how to stay healthy." Publisher's note
Includes glossary and bibliographical references

Brynie, Faith Hickman, 1946-
101 questions about blood and circulation, with answers straight from the heart. 21st Cent. Bks. (Brookfield) 2001 176p il lib bdg $30.60
Grades: 8 9 10 11 1 2   **612.1**
1. Cardiovascular system 2. Blood 3. Heart
ISBN 0-7613-1455-5   LC 00-32570
"The book is divided into five chapters in a question-and-answer format: 'That Should Come First' (on the structure and function of the circulatory system), 'The Heart,' 'Blood', 'When Things Go Wrong'. . . and 'Your Healthy Heart'. . . . Comprehensive, informative, and highly instructional. . . . The reader will appreciate the many graphs, diagrams, tables, and photomicrographs." Sci Books Films
Includes bibliographical references

Parker, Steve
Heart, blood, and lungs. Gareth Stevens Pub. 2005 32p il (Understanding the human body) lib bdg $26
Grades: 7 8 9 10   **612.1**
1. Cardiovascular system 2. Heart 3. Respiratory system
ISBN 0-8368-4206-5   LC 2004-45328
This describes the anatomy and physiology of the human cardio-pulmonary system.
"Entertaining and informative. . . . Full-color photos and diagrams, computer-generated images, microscopic pictures, posed skeletons, X rays, and PET scans appear throughout." SLJ

Simon, Seymour, 1931-
The heart; our circulatory system; [by] Seymour Simon. rev ed. Collins 2006 30p il $16.99; pa $6.99 *
Grades: 4 5 6 7   **612.1**
1. Cardiovascular system 2. Cardiovascular system 3. Heart
ISBN 978-0-06-087720-0; 0-06-087720-0; 978-0-06-087721-7 (pa); 0-06-087721-9 (pa)
LC 2006-279215
First published 1996

Describes the heart, blood, and other parts of the body's circulatory system and explains how each component functions
"The text is succinct and direct, making the details understandable without losing the sense that the whole process of circulation is 'strange and wonderful.' . . . The often striking pictures include many computer-enhanced photographs as well as diagrams and highly enlarged images made possible by electron microscopes. Handsome and well-conceived in every way." Booklist [review of 1996 edition]

612.2 Respiration

Silverstein, Alvin
The respiratory system; [by] Alvin, Virginia and Robert Silverstein. 21st Cent. Bks. (NY) 1994 96p il (Human body systems) lib bdg $29.90
Grades: 5 6 7 8   **612.2**
1. Respiratory system
ISBN 0-8050-2831-5   LC 94-21422
This illustrated introduction to the morphology and physiology of the respiratory system also discusses respiratory diseases and their treatments
Includes glossary

Siy, Alexandra
Sneeze! [by] Alexandra Siy and Dennis Kunkel. Charlesbridge 2007 45p il lib bdg $16.95; pa $6.95 *
Grades: 4 5 6 7   **612.2**
1. Sneezing
ISBN 978-1-57091-653-3 (lib bdg); 978-157091-654-0 (pa)   LC 2005-27567
This describes some causes of sneezing, including "air-pollen, dust mites, mold spores, dust, goose down, cat hair, pepper, flu viruses, and bright light." Publisher's note
"Kunkel's big, clear, beautiful color electron micrographs on every double-page spead show everything from dust mites, mildew, and pollen to the influenza A virus." Booklist
Includes glossary and bibliographical references

612.3 Digestion

Brynie, Faith Hickman, 1946-
101 questions about food and digestion that have been eating at you . . . until now. 21st Cent. Bks. (Brookfield) 2002 176p il lib bdg $30.60
Grades: 8 9 10 11 12   **612.3**
1. Digestion 2. Nutrition
ISBN 0-7613-2309-0   LC 2001-52250
Questions and answers explain the human digestive system and how it uses food for nutrition
"Presenting solid research with a lively writing style, this book provides a great deal of information and sound advice on the topic." Booklist
Includes glossary and bibliographical references

Hoffmann, Gretchen
Digestive system. Marshall Cavendish Benchmark 2009 80p il (The amazing human body) lib bdg $34.21
Grades: 6 7 8 9   **612.3**
1. Digestion
ISBN 978-0-7614-3058-2; 0-7614-3058-X
       LC 2008-17573
"Discusses the parts that make up the human digestive system, what can go wrong, how to treat those illnesses and diseases, and how to stay healthy." Publisher's note
Includes glossary and bibliographical references

Parker, Steve
Digestion and reproduction. Gareth Stevens Pub. 2004 32p il (Understanding the human body) lib bdg $26
Grades: 7 8 9 10   **612.3**
1. Digestion 2. Reproductive system
ISBN 0-8368-4205-7   LC 2004-45329
This describes the anatomy and physiology of the human digestive and reproductive systems
"Entertaining and informative. . . . Full-color photos and diagrams, computer-generated images, microscopic pictures, posed skeletons, X rays, and PET scans appear throughout." SLJ

Simon, Seymour, 1931-
Guts; our digestive system; [by] Seymour Simon. 1st ed. HarperCollins 2005 unp il $16.99; lib bdg $17.89 *
Grades: 4 5 6 7   **612.3**
1. Digestion
ISBN 0-06-054651-4; 0-06-054652-2 (lib bdg)
       LC 2004-14508
This "explains how the digestive system works. . . . [The author] describes the complex facts and processes of the physiology, from the time food enters the mouth until all the various organs transform it into energy, nutrients, and waste." Booklist
"Simon's specialty of drawing in readers through large, detailed, breathtaking photos and then entertaining them with facts is again in evidence. . . . The text is enhanced with detailed colored X rays, computer-generated pictures, and microscopic photos." SLJ

612.4   Hematopoietic, lymphatic, glandular, urinary systems

Klosterman, Lorrie
Endocrine system. Marshall Cavendish Benchmark 2009 79p il (The amazing human body) lib bdg $34.21
Grades: 6 7 8 9   **612.4**
1. Endocrine glands
ISBN 978-0-7614-3055-1; 0-7614-3055-5
       LC 2007-50444
"Discusses the parts that make up the human endocrine system, what can go wrong, how to treat those illnesses and diseases, and how to stay healthy." Publisher's note
Includes glossary and bibliographical references

612.6   Reproduction, development, maturation

Bailey, Jacqui
Sex, puberty, and all that stuff; a guide to growing up; illustrated by Jan McCafferty. Barron's 2004 112p il pa $12.95
Grades: 5 6 7 8   **612.6**
1. Sex education 2. Adolescence 3. Puberty
ISBN 0-7641-2992-9
"Bailey describes the bodily and hormonal aspects of puberty and dispels myths such as the perils of too much masturbation. Also covered are same-sex attraction, managing a good relationship and contraception." Publ Wkly
"A large helping of straightforward, up-to-date information peppered with humor and bright, graphic illustrations make this book one of the best texts about sex for developing adolescents." Voice Youth Advocates
Includes bibliographical references

Brynie, Faith Hickman, 1946-
101 questions about reproduction; or how 1 + 1 = 3 or 4 or more. Twenty-First Century Books 2006 176p il lib bdg $27.90 *
Grades: 8 9 10 11 1 2   **612.6**
1. Pregnancy 2. Childbirth 3. Sex education
ISBN 0-7613-2311-2   LC 2003-16350
Uses a question-and-answer format to present information about physical, medical, and social issues surrounding human reproduction, including birth control, pregnancy, and childbirth.
"This is a splendid companion to Brynie's 101 Questions about Sex and Sexuality (21st Century Bks, 2003); together the books present informative, complementary coverage for browsers and researchers." SLJ
Includes bibliographical references

Gravelle, Karen
The period book; everything you don't want to ask (but need to know); by Karen Gravelle & Jennifer Gravelle; illustrations by Debbie Palen. Updated ed. Walker & Co. 2006 126p il $16.95
Grades: 4 5 6 7   **612.6**
1. Menstruation
ISBN 978-0-8027-8072-0; 0-8027-8072-5
       LC 2008270981
First published 1996
Explains what happens at the onset of menstruation, discussing what to wear, going to the gynecologist, and how to handle various problems
"The cartoonlike illustrations and conversational tone make this updated edition a friendly, reassuring resource as well as a thorough one." Horn Book Guide

Jukes, Mavis
Growing up: it's a girl thing; straight talk about first bras, first periods, and your changing body; illustrations by Debbie Tilley. Knopf 1998 72p il pa $10 hardcover o.p. *
Grades: 4 5 6 7   **612.6**
1. Adolescence 2. Girls 3. Menstruation
ISBN 0-679-89027-0 (pa)   LC 98-18113

Jukes, Mavis—*Continued*

This is a slightly revised version of chapters from the author's It's a girl thing

This "covers body hair and shaving, perspiration and deodorant, and how to buy your first bra. The second half of the book is devoted to what to expect and how to plan for your first period. . . . The narration has an easy, comfortable voice and imparts accurate and important information." SLJ

Movsessian, Shushann

Puberty girl. Allen & Unwin 2005 128p $15.95

Grades: 4 5 6 7   612.6

1. Puberty 2. Girls

ISBN 1-74114-104-4

"In addition to chapters about the basic body changes during female puberty, including one about menstruation and the necessary equipment, the author offers helpful suggestions for conflict resolution, listening to one's feelings, and understanding personal boundaries (and when they are breached). She also includes a brief list of boys' puberty changes, and a closing chapter mentions homosexuality. The glossy, girl-magazine design, with lots of color photos of attractive preteens, is matched by the bubbly, girl-power tone." Booklist

Parker, Steve

Reproduction. Raintree 2004 48p il (Our bodies) lib bdg $31.43

Grades: 5 6 7 8   612.6

1. Reproduction 2. Sex education 3. Growth

ISBN 0-7398-6623-0   LC 2003-10547

Contents: Female reproductive organs; The menstrual cycle; Egg production; Male reproductive organs; Sperm production; The reproductive process; The first week; Reproductive problems; The early embryo; Growth in the uterus; Life support in the uterus; Toward birth; The day of birth; A new baby; Birth problems; Growing up; The young child; The older child; Child to adult; The next generation

This "discusses the male and female reproductive organs and how they work, the process of fertilization, growth of the embryo and fetus, birth, and stages of life from infancy to adulthood. . . . The anatomy is accurate, and the format, with plenty of pictures, diagrams, and magnified photos, is very accessible. There are also lots of lively boxed facts." Booklist

Includes bibliographical references

The reproductive system. Heinemann Lib. 2003 48p il (Body focus: injury, illness and health) lib bdg $29.93; pa $8.50

Grades: 6 7 8 9   612.6

1. Reproduction 2. Sex education

ISBN 1-4034-0199-3 (lib bdg); 1-4034-0455-0 (pa)

LC 2002-14431

Contents: Reproduction; Female reproductive organs; Female cycle; Production of egg cells; Menstrual problems; Other female reproductive problems; Male reproductive organs; Production of sperm cells; Male reproductive system problems; Reproductive infections; Reproductive health; Sperm and egg; Embryo and fetus; Childbirth; Infancy and childhood; Adolescence and puberty; Fertility problems; Fertility control; Assisted reproduction; Reproduction and genetics

"Explains the parts of the reproductive system and their functions and provides an overview of human development from birth through adolescence." Publisher's note

This is "well organized and well written. The full-color photos, diagrams, and illustrations are clear and complement the text." SLJ

Includes bibliographical references

Price, Geoff

Puberty boy. Allen & Unwin 2006 122p il pa $15.95

Grades: 4 5 6 7   612.6

1. Puberty 2. Boys

ISBN 1-74114-563-5   LC 2006-482082

This "is a frank, reassuring discussion of male adolescence. Chapters on physiology present information clearly, in a colloquial voice that is never stuffy or condescending, and the questions that are asked and answered seem straight from kids. . . . The mechanics of sex aren't addressed, but there is some discussion of STDs and the emotional maturity intimacy requires. The book's unusual holistic approach includes coverage of the emotional changes, independence, and responsibility that come with puberty. There are also excellent suggestions to help boys connect respectfully with girls, find a mentor, develop emotional intelligence, and distinguish between 'boy thinking' and 'young man thinking.'" Booklist

Includes glossary and bibliographical references

Teen dreams; Elaine Pascoe, book editor. Blackbirch Press 2004 48p il (Body story) $23.70; pa $9.95

Grades: 7 8 9 10 11   612.6

1. Puberty 2. Adolescence

ISBN 1-4103-0061-7; 1-4103-0182-6 (pa)

LC 2003-9640

Contents: Puberty waits; Aggression; Sexual attraction

Next-door neighbors Natalie and Darren discover the effects that gonadotrophins, testosterone, and estrogen have on their bodies and minds as they enter puberty.

This volume is "bubbling over with informative, full-color photographs. . . . The [text is] amazingly concise and [takes] extraordinarily complex processes and [makes] them clearly understandable to the intended audience." SLJ

Includes bibliographical references

Waters, Sophie

The female reproductive system. Rosen Central 2008 48p il (Girls' health) lib bdg $26.50

Grades: 7 8 9   612.6

1. Reproductive system 2. Pregnancy 3. Birth control

ISBN 978-1-4042-1950-2; 1-4042-1950-1

LC 2006101218

Describes the parts of the female reproductive system, explains how pregnancy occurs and the steps in embryo development, and discusses various forms of birth control

"Generously interspersed with color photographs and diagrams . . . [this book will] offer girls a safe, comfortable place to get straight, honest answers about their personal health issues." Libr Media Connect

Includes glossary and bibliographical references

612.7 Musculoskeletal system, integument

Brynie, Faith Hickman, 1946-
101 questions about muscles to stretch your mind and flex your brain; by Faith Hickman Brynie. Twenty-First Century Books 2008 176p il (101 questions) lib bdg $30.60 *
Grades: 8 9 10 11 12   **612.7**
1. Muscles
ISBN 978-0-8225-6380-8; 0-8225-6380-0
                                LC 2006-37041
This answers such questions as "What do tendons do? What causes muscle cramps? . . . This . . . makes human physiology accessible, with questions everyone has always wondered about and up-to-date, detailed answers that discuss the complex science in chatty but never condescending style. Like the text, the clear diagrams and photographs deal with everything from basic information . . . to the more advanced." Booklist
Includes glossary and bibliographical references

Gold, Susan Dudley, 1949-
The musculoskeletal system and the skin. Enslow Pubs. 2003 48p il (Human body library) lib bdg $23.93
Grades: 7 8 9 10   **612.7**
1. Musculoskeletal system 2. Skin
ISBN 0-7660-2023-1   LC 2002-151081
Contents: What is the musculoskeletal system?; Who is on the team?; How does the system work?; Wear and tear; Staying healthy; Amazing but true
The author "examines the biology amd overall health of the musculoskeletal system. She explains what the musculoskeletal system is, how it works, and what parts of the body are involved. She also offers advice for ways to stay fit and healthy and interesting facts about this body system." Publisher's note
"The design is open and uncluttered, interspersed with occasional small, helpful, full-color diagrams. . . . A non-intimidating start to some fascinating science." Booklist
Includes bibliographical references

Hall, Margaret, 1947-
Skin deep. Raintree 2007 32p il (Raintree fusion) lib bdg $28.21; pa $7.99
Grades: 5 6 7 8   **612.7**
1. Skin
ISBN 978-1-4109-2582-4 (lib bdg); 1-4109-2582-X (lib bdg); 978-1-4109-2611-1 (pa); 1-4109-2611-7 (pa)
                                 LC 2006-8771
Explains what skin is and why it is important, including protecting the body from germs, helping cool down the body when it gets too hot, and absorbing Vitamin D from sunlight.
Includes glossary and bibliographical references

Klosterman, Lorrie
Skin. Marshall Cavendish Benchmark 2009 79p il (The amazing human body) lib bdg $34.21
Grades: 6 7 8 9   **612.7**
1. Skin
ISBN 978-0-7614-3057-5; 0-7614-3057-1
                                LC 2008-17580
"Discusses the parts that make up human skin, what can go wrong, how to treat those illnesses and diseases, and how to stay healthy." Publisher's note
Includes glossary and bibliographical references

Parker, Steve
The skeleton and muscles; [by] Steve Parker. Raintree 2004 48p il (Our bodies) lib bdg $29.93
Grades: 5 6 7 8   **612.7**
1. Musculoskeletal system
ISBN 0-7398-6622-2   LC 2003-6594
This "takes a look at bones, muscles, and joints; how they are connected and function; and how to keep them healthy. The anatomy is accurate, and the format, with plenty of pictures, diagrams, and magnified photos, is very accessible. There are also lots of lively boxed facts." Booklist
Includes bibliographical references

Skin, muscles, and bones. Gareth Stevens Pub. 2004 32p il (Understanding the human body) lib bdg $26
Grades: 7 8 9 10   **612.7**
1. Musculoskeletal system 2. Skin
ISBN 0-8368-4207-3   LC 2004-45327
This describes the anatomy and physiology of the human musculoskeletal system and skin
"Entertaining and informative. . . . Full-color photos and diagrams, computer-generated images, microscopic pictures, posed skeletons, X rays, and PET scans appear throughout." SLJ

612.8 Nervous system. Sensory functions

Bangalore, Lakshmi
Brain development; series editor, Eric H. Chudler. Chelsea House Publishers 2007 103p il (Gray matter) $32.95
Grades: 8 9 10 11 12   **612.8**
1. Brain
ISBN 978-0-7910-8954-5; 0-7910-8954-1
                                LC 2006-32428
This book "introduces basic brain anatomy and brain development to high school students. It discusses the molecular basis of central nervous system specification, starting from neural induction and pattern formation to neural migration, axon guidance, and synapse formation." Publisher's note
Includes glossary and bibliographical references

Brynie, Faith Hickman, 1946-

101 questions about sleep and dreams that kept you awake nights . . . until now. Twenty-First Century Books 2006 176p il lib bdg $27.93 *
Grades: 8 9 10 11 12   **612.8**
  1. Sleep 2. Dreams
  ISBN 978-0-7613-2312-9; 0-7613-2312-0
                  LC 2005-17276

This book describes the physical and psychological aspects of sleep and dreams.

The author "presents sometimes rather complicated scientific material in a way that is not only easily understood, but also thoroughly enjoyable." Sci Books Films
Includes bibliographical references

Evans-Martin, Fay

Emotion and stress; [by] F. Fay Evans-Martin. Chelsea House 2007 146p il (Gray matter) lib bdg $35
Grades: 8 9 10 11 12   **612.8**
  1. Emotions 2. Stress (Psychology) 3. Brain
  ISBN 978-0-7910-9491-4; 0-7910-9491-X
                  LC 2006101334

Discusses how the brain and body work together to create, express, and manage emotions and stress, focusing on the physical processes that occur in various parts of the brain during emotional and stressful situations.
Includes glossary and bibliographical references

May, Mike

Sensation and perception. Chelsea House Publishers 2007 120p il (Gray matter) lib bdg $35
Grades: 8 9 10 11 12   **612.8**
  1. Senses and sensation 2. Perception
  ISBN 978-0-7910-8958-3; 0-7910-8958-4
                  LC 2006-38552

This book focuses on how sensory "work, from the mechanics of individual cells to the interactions of thousands of cells in the brain. This book also delves into how our sensory capabilities change with age or damage." Publisher's note
Includes glossary and bibliographical references

Morgan, Michael, 1960-

The midbrain. Chelsea House 2006 114p il (Gray matter) $32.95
Grades: 8 9 10 11 12   **612.8**
  1. Brain
  ISBN 0-7910-8637-2   LC 2005-11988

This "stars the least flashy, less-well-researched part of the brain responsible for various movements (including Parkinson's problems), vision, hearing, sensuality, defense, and complex eye movements. . . . [This book proceeds] from a physiological model of the brain and address structure and behavior in various species while focusing on humans." SLJ
Includes bibliographical references

Newquist, H. P. (Harvey P.)

The great brain book; an inside look at the inside of your head; illustrations by Keith Kasnot and Eric Brace. Scholastic Reference 2005 c2004 160p il $18.95 *
Grades: 5 6 7 8   **612.8**
  1. Brain
  ISBN 0-439-45895-1   LC 2004-42955

This describes the anatomy and physiology of the brain and covers such topics as the history of brain research, neurons, learning and memory, brain diseases and mental illness, and the possible future of brain research.

"With an appealing, colorful design and a flashy cover, this in-depth introduction to the human brain and its remarkable powers will attract browsers, but strong readers are its best audience. . . . The clever, kid-friendly anecdotes amid the anatomy lessons . . . enhance accessibility." Booklist

Out of control; brain function and immune reactions; Elaine Pascoe, book editor. Blackbirch Press 2004 48p il (Body story) lib bdg $24.95; pa $9.95
Grades: 7 8 9 10   **612.8**
  1. Brain 2. Allergy
  ISBN 1-4103-0063-3 (lib bdg); 1-4103-0184-2 (pa)
                  LC 2003-9639

Contents: The brain; Signals; Allergic reactions

Explores how baby Robert's brain functions at birth and how the cerebral cortex develops to control his body, then looks at what happens to Phoebe's body when her brain cannot control an allergic reaction.

This volume is "bubbling over with informative, full-color photographs. . . . [The text is] amazingly concise and [takes] extraordinarily complex processes and [makes] them clearly understandable to the intended audience." SLJ
Includes bibliographical references

Parker, Steve

Brain, nerves, and senses. Gareth Stevens Pub. 2005 32p il (Understanding the human body) lib bdg $26
Grades: 7 8 9 10   **612.8**
  1. Nervous system 2. Brain 3. Senses and sensation
  ISBN 0-8368-4204-9   LC 2004-45330

The describes the anatomy and physiology of the human nervous system.

"Entertaining and informative. . . . Full-color photos and diagrams, computer-generated images, microscopic pictures, posed skeletons, X rays, and PET scans appear throughout." SLJ

Rosen, Marvin

Sleep and dreaming; [by] Marvin Rosen. Chelsea House Publishers 2006 159p il (Gray matter) $32.95
Grades: 8 9 10 11 12   **612.8**
  1. Sleep 2. Dreams
  ISBN 0-7910-8639-9   LC 2005011689

This "title covers normal processes, such as REM sleep, as well as developmental disorders and other ab-

Rosen, Marvin—*Continued*

normalities, such as snoring, sleepwalking, and night terrors. Different perspectives about the meaning of dreams are also included, ranging from the theories of Freud and Jung to current research. Color photos, numerous sidebars, and a variety of quotations from history and literature are included." SLJ

Includes bibliographical references

Saab, Carl Y.

The hindbrain. Chelsea House 2006 85p il (Gray matter) lib bdg $35

Grades: 8 9 10 11 12   **612.8**
1. Brain
ISBN 978-0-7910-8510-3; 0-7910-8510-4
        LC 2005-11687

Explains the structures and functions of the hindbrain, and explores the purposes of the cerebellum, the medulla, and pons.

A "valuable addition[s] to an area where little is written for high school students." Libr Media Connect

Includes glossary and bibliographical references

The spinal cord; [by] Carl Y. Saab. Chelsea House Publishers 2006 93p il (Gray matter) $32.95

Grades: 8 9 10 11 12   **612.8**
1. Spinal cord
ISBN 0-7910-8511-2   LC 2005011706

This "begins with a tribute to Christopher Reeve, moves on to the anatomy and physiology of the spinal cord, and concludes with personal stories and the status of research on spinal cord injuries. Colored images, photos, and figures illustrate key concepts. The volumes in this series are written by neuroscientists and provide in-depth explanations suitable for teachers or highly motivated students. But there is also enough story and personal information to be useful to the more casual reader." Voice Youth Advocates

Includes bibliographical references

Scott, Elaine, 1940-

All about sleep from A to ZZZZ; by Elaine Scott; illustrated by John O'Brien. Viking 2008 58p il $17.99

Grades: 5 6 7 8 9 10   **612.8**
1. Sleep
ISBN 978-0-670-06188-4; 0-670-06188-3
        LC 2008-6074

"The book covers a range of topics, including circadian rhythms, dreams, and the functions and stages of sleep." Booklist

"This excellent overview is packed with interesting tidbits. . . . Scott is careful to point out which information is factual and which is theory, an important distinction. . . . The fanciful cartoon illustrations add to the book's appeal. . . . It is interesting, highly engaging, and fun to read." SLJ

Silverstein, Alvin

Senses and sensors [series]; by Alvin Silverstein, Virginia Silverstein, and Laura Silverstein Nunn. 21st Century Books 2001-2002 4v lib bdg ea $25.90 *

Grades: 6 7 8 9   **612.8**

1. Senses and sensation
ISBN 0-7613-1666-3 (Hearing); 0-7613-1663-9 (Seeing); 0-7613-1667-1 (Smelling and tasting); 0-7613-1668-X (Touching and feeling)

Contents: Hearing; Seeing; Smelling and tasting; Touching and feeling

These volumes explain the anatomy and physiology of the senses and the ways technology is being used to repair or enhance them

"Color photographs, diagrams, and other images enhance the interesting, clearly presented text." Booklist

Simon, Seymour, 1931-

The brain; our nervous system; [by] Seymour Simon. rev ed. Collins 2006 30p il $17.99; pa $6.99 *

Grades: 4 5 6 7   **612.8**
1. Brain 2. Nervous system
ISBN   978-0-06-087718-7;   0-06-087718-9; 978-0-06-087719-4 (pa); 0-06-087719-7 (pa)
        LC 2007-272349

First published 1997

Describes the various parts of the brain and the nervous system and how they function to enable us to think, feel, move, and remember.

Simon's "clear, concise writing style is complemented by stunning color images taken with radiological scanners, such as CAT scans, MRIs, and SEMs (scanning electron microscopes.)" SLJ [review of 1997 edition]

Includes bibliographical references

Eyes and ears. HarperCollins Pubs. 2003 unp il hardcover o.p. pa $6.99 *

Grades: 4 5 6 7   **612.8**
1. Eye 2. Ear 3. Vision 4. Hearing
ISBN   0-688-15303-8;   978-0-06-073302-5   (pa); 0-06-073302-0 (pa)   LC 2002-19060

Describes the anatomy of the eye and ear, how those organs function and some ways in which they may malfunction, and how the brain is also involved in our seeing and hearing

"Simon is at his very best here. . . . The large, exquisitely reproduced photographs from a number of sources look like fiery planets, galaxies, and monster creatures. . . . The anatomy and physiology are detailed and accurate, with clear diagrams." Booklist

Tully, Elizabeth

The forebrain. Chelsea House 2006 93p il (Gray matter) lib bdg $35

Grades: 8 9 10 11 12   **612.8**
1. Brain
ISBN 978-0-7910-8509-7; 0-7910-8509-0
        LC 2005-11688

Examines the parts and functions of the frontal lobe of the brain.

"Valuable addition[s] to an area where little is written for high school students." Libr Media Connect

Includes glossary and bibliographical references

Vera-Portocarrero, Louis

Brain facts; series editor, Eric H. Chudler. Chelsea House 2007 106p il (Gray matter) lib bdg $35

Grades: 8 9 10 11 1 2　　　　　　　**612.8**

1. Brain

ISBN 978-0-7910-8956-9; 0-7910-8956-8

LC 2006-14243

An introduction to the brain describes how neurons work, how the brain develops, how it controls movement and perceives the senses, what happens during sleep, and how language, learning, and memory are developed.

"Researchers may find useful information here. Abundant endmatter concludes, and colorful illustrations and diagrams help to elucidate the complicated material." Booklist

Includes glossary and bibliographical references

Viegas, Jennifer

The revolution in healing the brain. Rosen Pub. Group 2003 64p il (Library of future medicine) lib bdg $29.25 *

Grades: 7 8 9 10　　　　　　　　　　**612.8**

1. Nervous system

ISBN 0-8239-3668-6　　　　　　　LC 2001-6721

Contents: Anatomy of the brain; Brain cells; Learning and intelligence; Sleep and dreams; Sensory awareness; Brain healing in the future

The author provides "basic information on the brain and its functions before describing various disorders and the . . . research involved in treating them. Chapters on learning and intelligence, sleep and dreaming, and sensory awareness are included. The book cites functional magnetic resonance imaging, high-powered microscopes, stem-cell research, and better pharmaceuticals as tools for healing the brain. . . . [The book is] well illustrated with well-positioned and captioned diagrams, drawings, photographs, and color-enhanced images." SLJ

Includes glossary and bibliographical references

613　Personal health and safety

American Medical Assocation boy's guide to becoming a teen. Jossey-Bass 2006 128p il pa $12.95 *

Grades: 4 5 6 7　　　　　　　　　　**613**

1. Boys—Health and hygiene 2. Puberty 3. Adolescence

ISBN 0-7879-8343-8

Contents: Welcome to puberty; Eating, exercise, and a healthy weight; Your height; Your skin, teeth, and hair; Your reproductive system-inside and out; Erections, wet dreams, and masturbation; Your feelings; Relationships; What about sex?

"This guide addresses puberty's changes clearly. . . . The text's approach is straightforward, accessible, and nonjudgmental, whether the topic is same-sex attraction or divorcing parents. The volume closes with an extensive resource section, including hotlines." Booklist

Includes bibliographical references

American Medical Association girl's guide to becoming a teen. Jossey-Bass 2006 128p pa $12.95 *

Grades: 4 5 6 7　　　　　　　　　　**613**

1. Girls—Health and hygiene 2. Puberty 3. Adolescence

ISBN 0-7879-8344-6

Contents: What is puberty?; Eating, exercise, and a healthy weight; Your height; Your skin and teeth; Your hair; Your changing body; Menstruation; Your emotions; Relationships; For more information

This "covers the physical and emotional changes that puberty brings, along with solid tips about grooming, diet, exercise, and other health issues, such as eating disorders. . . . The clear text communicates concepts clearly . . . and girls will find plenty of useful information." Booklist

Includes bibliographical references

Cheung, Lilian W. Y., 1951-

Be healthy! it's a girl thing; food, fitness, and feeling great; [by] Lilian Cheung and Mavis Jukes. Crown Publishers 2003 117p il lib bdg $18.99; pa $12.95 *

Grades: 5 6 7 8　　　　　　　　　　**613**

1. Girls—Health and hygiene 2. Nutrition 3. Physical fitness

ISBN 0-679-99029-1 (lib bdg); 0-679-89029-7 (pa)

LC 2003-10114

This "offers girls going through puberty advice on nutrition, fitness, self-image, and appearance." SLJ

"Given the alarmingly high rates of eating disorders, girls definitely need to hear some of the straight talk more often. . . . A chapter devoted to advertising is also helpful in countering the unrealistic images portrayed in the media." Booklist

Crump, Marguerite, 1955-

No B.O.! the head-to-toe book of hygiene for preteens; edited by Elizabeth Verdick. Free Spirit Pub. 2005 118p il pa $12.95

Grades: 5 6 7 8　　　　　　　　　　**613**

1. Youth—Health and hygiene 2. Adolescence

ISBN 978-1-57542-175-9; 1-57542-175-5

LC 2005-8376

First published 2002 with title: Don't sweat it

Presents advice for preteens on handling the many changes that come with puberty, including bad hair days, skin breakouts, and body odor.

"The author doesn't mince words but remains empathetic throughout, and the medical information behind personal hygiene practice is accurate and up-to-date. Sidebars present interesting facts, trivia, and humorous asides." SLJ [review of 2002 edition]

Includes bibliographical references

Dunham, Kelli

The girl's body book; everything you need to know for growing up you! illustrated by Laura Tallardy. Applesauce Press 2008 115p il pa $9.95

Grades: 4 5 6 7　　　　　　　　　　**613**

Dunham, Kelli—*Continued*
1. Girls—Health and hygiene 2. Puberty
3. Adolescence
ISBN 978-1-60433-004-5; 1-60433-004-X
"Girls will find solid answers to questions about their changing bodies and emotions while learning how to deal with friends, parents, and siblings. . . . Includes answers to common questions about puberty, first gynecological exam, emotions, eating disorders, and how to make and keep friends." Libr Media Connect

"The book's tone and lively cartoon illustrations are friendly and nonthreatening. . . . A solid choice for basic information about puberty." SLJ

Includes bibliographical references

Health matters! general editor William M. Kane. Grolier Educ. 2002 8v il set $459 *
Grades: 6 7 8 9　　　　　　　　　　　　613
1. Health 2. Reference books
ISBN 0-7172-5575-1　　　　　LC 2001-40248
Contents: v1 Addiction: tobacco, alcohol, and other drugs; v2 Mental health: depression, suicide, and other issues; v3 Sexuality and pregnancy; v4 Physical activity, weight, and eating disorders; v5 Injuries and violence; v6 Environmental poisoning; v7 HIV infections, AIDS, and STDs; v8 Diseases and disabling conditions

"This set serves two purposes: it is a means of answering young adults' questions about their health and empowering them to make sound decisions and also a reference source for school reports pertaining to health topics. . . . A useful addition to high-school or public libraries." Booklist

Klosterman, Lorrie
The facts about caffeine; [by] Lorrie Klosterman. Marshall Cavendish Benchmark 2007 111p il (Drugs) lib bdg $39.93
Grades: 6 7 8 9　　　　　　　　　　　　613
1. Caffeine
ISBN 978-0-7614-2242-6; 0-7614-2242-0
　　　　　　　　　　　　　　　　　LC 2005037351
This describes the history of caffeine use, its sources and effects on the body.
Includes glossary and bibliographical references

Libal, Autumn
Can I change the way I look? a teen's guide to the health implications of cosmetic surgery, makeovers, and beyond. Mason Crest Publishers 2005 128p il (Science of health) $24.95 *
Grades: 7 8 9 10　　　　　　　　　　　　613
1. Teenagers—Health and hygiene 2. Personal grooming
ISBN 1-59084-843-8　　　　　　LC 2004-1883
"Framing her discussion within an examination of the media influence on our culture's definition of beauty, Libal does an excellent job of discussing the risks and benefits of cosmetics, piercing and tattooing, diet, exercise, and cosmetic surgery. . . . The author also considers, in some detail, the dangers of anorexia nervosa, bulimia, and steroid use." SLJ
Includes bibliographical references

McCoy, Kathleen, 1945-
The teenage body book; [by] Kathy McCoy and Charles Wibbelsman; illustrations by Bob Stover and Kelly Grady. Rev and updated. Hatherleigh 2008 300p il pa $17.95
Grades: 7 8 9 10 11 12　　　　　　　　613
1. Teenagers—Health and hygiene 2. Adolescence
3. Sex education
ISBN 978-1-57826-277-9 (pa)　　LC 2009-368424
First published 1979 by Pocket Bks. with authors' names in reverse order

A handbook for teenagers discussing nutrition, health, fitness, emotions, and sexuality, including such topics as body image, drugs, STDs, fad diets and hazards and benefits of the Internet.

"This highly informative book . . . is at the same time easily readable, nonpreachy, and comprehensive. . . . This book should be not only in the library of every middle and high school, but also in the hands of every student and in health education classes." Sci Books Films

Reber, Deborah
Chill; stress-reducing techniques for a more balanced, peaceful you. Simon Pulse 2008 196p il pa $9.99
Grades: 8 9 10 11 12　　　　　　　　　613
1. Stress (Psychology) 2. Girls—Health and hygiene
ISBN 978-1-4169-5526-9 (pa); 1-4169-5526-7 (pa)
"This book has just the right combination of smart wit, know-it-all bravado, and advice from a pseudo big sister. The pages speed by, moving from topic to topic: time management, support systems, self-help therapy, exercise, nutrition, and more. Advice is free-flowing, complete with examples, exercises, and quizzes. . . . This helpful resource will appeal to a wide variety of young women." SLJ

613.2　Dietetics

Ballard, Carol
Food for feeling healthy; [by] Carol Ballard. Heinemann Library 2006 56p il (Making healthy food choices) $32.86; pa $9.49
Grades: 7 8 9 10　　　　　　　　　　　613.2
1. Nutrition
ISBN 978-1-4034-8571-7; 1-4034-8571-2; 978-1-4034-8577-9 (pa); 1-4034-8577-1 (pa)
　　　　　　　　　　　　　　　　LC 2006003970
"Ballard incorporates the new food pyramid into a discussion of basic nutritional requirements. She considers obesity, malnutrition, and eating disorders and comments on various factors that influence eating choices, such as advertising and peer pressure. After helping readers decipher food labels, she provides a week's worth of menus." SLJ

Includes bibliographical references

Bartell, Susan S.
Dr. Susan's girls-only weight loss guide; the easy, fun way to look and feel good! [by] Susan S. Bartell. Parent Positive Press 2006 270p il pa $14.95
Grades: 6 7 8 9　　　　　　　　　　　613.2

Bartell, Susan S.—*Continued*
1. Nutrition 2. Girls—Health and hygiene 3. Weight loss
ISBN 0-9721502-0-X
Offers tools to help teenage girls recognize and break away from unhealthy eating patterns, explains how depression, anger, and low self-esteem can translate into eating and weight gain, and tells how to find healthier, less destructive ways of coping.
"The book is effective without being read from cover to cover. Still, teens may end up doing just that as they experience a discussion that speaks to them with honesty and authenticity." SLJ

Bauchner, Elizabeth, 1970-
What do I have to lose? a teen's guide to weight management. Mason Crest Publishers 2005 128p il (The science of health) $24.95
Grades: 7 8 9 10   613.2
1. Weight loss
ISBN 978-1-59084-855-5; 1-59084-855-1
LC 2004-13222
Provides information on how to attain and maintain a healthy weight.
Includes bibliographical references

Can diets be harmful? Ron Lankford, book editor. Greenhaven Press 2007 115p (At issue: Health) lib bdg $28.70; pa $19.95
Grades: 8 9 10 11 12   613.2
1. Weight loss 2. Diet in disease
ISBN   978-0-7377-3397-6   (lib   bdg); 978-0-7377-3398-3 (pa)   LC 2007002993
"The selections, excerpted from articles by educators, journalists, and nutritionists, examine a wide range of issues, including the problems with crash and fad diets, commonly held myths about dieting, and the links between dieting obsession and eating disorders. . . . Whether driven by personal health concerns or assignment research, students who find this title will gain a broad, balanced overview." Booklist
Includes bibliographical references

Diet information for teens; edited by Karen Bellenir. 2nd ed. Omnigraphics 2006 432p (Teen health series) $58 *
Grades: 8 9 10 11 12   613.2
1. Nutrition 2. Teenagers—Health and hygiene
ISBN 0-7808-0820-7   LC 2006-4413
First published 2000
"Health tips about diet and nutrition including facts about dietary guidelines, food groups, nutrients, healthy meals, snacks, weight control, medical concerns related to diet, and more." Title page
This "is a compilation of articles on all facets of nutrition, drawn mainly from FDA documents. The information is presented in a straightforward, plainspoken manner." SLJ [review of 2000 edition]
Includes bibliographical references

Dieting; Claire Kreger Boaz, book editor. Greenhaven Press 2008 117p il (Issues that concern you) lib bdg $33.70
Grades: 8 9 10 11 12   613.2
1. Weight loss
ISBN 978-0-7377-3644-1 (lib bdg); 0-7377-3644-5 (lib bdg)   LC 2007-35368
This title presents various views on dieting and weight loss.
Includes bibliographical references

Doeden, Matt, 1974-
Eat right! how you can make good food choices; [by] Matt Doeden; illustrations by Jack Desrocher. Lerner Publications 2008 64p il (Health zone) lib bdg $30.60
Grades: 4 5 6 7   613.2
1. Nutrition
ISBN 978-0-8225-7552-8; 0-8225-7552-3
LC 2007043322
"This offers a highly readable, never preachy exploration into the benefits of providing quality fuel for your body. It opens with an anecdote of a kid who snacks on soda and chips while playing volleyball. A friend challenges him to to eat better for a week, and he comes back with more sustained energy and a fresh outlook. . . . The following chapters do a great job of detailing everything from the food pyramid and benefits of different nutrients to warnings against following the faddish, ineffective diets." Booklist
Includes bibliographical references

Favor, Lesli J.
Weighing in; nutrition and weight management. Marshall Cavendish Benchmark 2007 128p il (Food and fitness) lib bdg $25.95
Grades: 7 8 9 10   613.2
1. Weight loss 2. Nutrition
ISBN 978-0-7614-2555-7; 0-7614-2555-1
LC 2006-101930
This "offers an in-depth look at issues related to body weight. Chapters . . . discuss determining one's ideal weight; health risks associated with weight, from diabetes to anorexia; nutrition and wellness; teen dietary requirements and meal planning; and weight-loss strategies, with possible dangers highlighted. . . . Teens will find this a useful, often thought-provoking resource for personal or class research." Booklist
Includes bibliographical references

Ford, Jean
The truth about diets; the pros and cons; by Jean Ford with Autumn Libal. Mason Crest 2006 104p il (Obesity: modern-day epidemic) $23.95
Grades: 7 8 9 10   613.2
1. Weight loss 2. Diet
ISBN 978-1-59084-946-0; 1-59084-946-9
LC 2004-26244
This focuses on "the diet industry . . . [and] why individuals' focus should be on good health, not weight loss." Publisher's note
Includes bibliographical references

Gay, Kathlyn, 1930-

The scoop on what to eat; what you should know about diet and nutrition. Enslow Publishers 2009 112p il (Issues in focus today) lib bdg $31.93

Grades: 7 8 9 10   **613.2**
1. Nutrition
ISBN 978-0-7660-3066-4; 0-7660-3066-0
LC 2008-40382

"Discusses diet and nutrition for young people, including ideas for a well-balanced diet, good and bad foods to eat, the importance of exercise, and eating disorders." Publisher's note

"Bolstered with well-integrated quotes and relevant statistics, [this book offers] an excellent starting point for students seeking [a] broad, thoroughly researched [introduction] to [diet and nutrition]. . . . Illuminating case studies, enhanced with multiple viewpoints, personalize the facts and place them in boarder context." Booklist

Includes glossary and bibliographical references

Heller, Tania, 1958-

Overweight; a handbook for teens and parents; [by] Tania Heller; foreword by Mohsen Ziai. McFarland & Company 2005 180p pa $29.95

Grades: 7 8 9 10   **613.2**
1. Obesity 2. Weight loss 3. Teenagers—Health and hygiene
ISBN 0-7864-2082-0   LC 2005004360

"This work covers the causes and effects of the rise in childhood obesity while presenting . . . guidelines and recommendations for getting assessed and treated. Information is provided on healthy nutrition and physical activity for young people, tools for self-monitoring and medical conditions associated with weight gain." Publisher's note

"Heller balances her knack for clarification with a candid, proactive approach to deliver one of the best books available on adolescent weight management." Voice Youth Advocates

Includes glossary and bibliographical references

Ingram, Scott, 1948-

Want fries with that? obesity and the supersizing of America. Franklin Watts 2006 128p il $26

Grades: 7 8 9 10   **613.2**
1. Obesity 2. Convenience foods 3. Eating customs
ISBN 0-531-16756-9   LC 2005-5619

This is an "exploration of the physical phenomenon of obesity and its emotional and social ramifications. The text is packed with information on specific dangers such as increased risks of diabetes, cancer, and other health problems. The author casts a critical eye on the effect of advertising and the availability of fast food, both in and out of school, and covers recent state legislation seeking to inform parents of diagnoses of obesity in their children." SLJ

Includes glossary and bibliographical references

Libal, Autumn

Fats, sugars, and empty calories; the fast food habit. Mason Crest Publishers 2006 104p il (Obesity: modern day epidemic) $23.95

Grades: 7 8 9 10   **613.2**
1. Nutrition 2. Obesity 3. Health
ISBN 978-1-59084-943-9; 1-59084-943-4
LC 2004-15660

Discusses the dangers of fast food.
Includes glossary and bibliographical references

Morris, Neil, 1946-

Food for sports; [by] Neil Morris. Heinemann Library 2006 56p il (Making healthy food choices) $32.86; pa $9.49

Grades: 7 8 9 10   **613.2**
1. Nutrition 2. Sports
ISBN   978-1-4034-8573-1;   1-4034-8573-9;
978-1-4034-8579-3 (pa); 1-4034-8579-8 (pa)
LC 2006003971

This "talks about the types of foods that help athletes maximize their energy level. The information on sensible eating choices and calorie intake can help even non-athletes manage their health and weight. . . . [This is] well written. . . . There aren't many books out there that examine all aspects of food in such detail." SLJ

Includes bibliographical references

Platkin, Charles Stuart

Lighten up; stay sane, eat great, lose weight; by Charles Stuart Platkin. Razorbill 2005 216p pa $7.99 *

Grades: 7 8 9 10   **613.2**
1. Weight loss 2. Physical fitness 3. Teenagers—Health and hygiene
ISBN 1-59514-065-4   LC 2005023907

The author "outlines a step-by-step approach to . . . lifestyle changes that lead to permanent weight loss, targeted specifically to the diet needs of young people. He gives . . . advice on topics such as smarter options at the most common teen hangout spots; how to eat better in the school cafeteria; how to lose weight when your parents control the food in your house; how to find satisfying 'Calorie Bargains' to swap for high-calorie favorites; how to defeat your 'Eating Alarm Times.'" Publisher's note

Sanna, Ellyn, 1957-

America's unhealthy lifestyle; supersize it! Mason Crest Publishers 2006 104p il map (Obesity: modern-day epidemic) $23.95

Grades: 7 8 9 10   **613.2**
1. Nutrition 2. Eating customs 3. Convenience foods 4. Obesity
ISBN 978-1-59084-942-2; 1-59084-942-6
LC 2004-28650

Examines the ways in which Americans' cultural behaviors and eating habits have changed over the years, leading to an increase in weight, a decrease in physical activity, and the rise in obesity, diabetes, heart disease, and other problems.

"Visually appealing and easy to read, this . . . [book]

Sanna, Ellyn, 1957-—*Continued*
provides useful and current information in an attractive format." Voice Youth Advocates
Includes glossary and bibliograpical references

Schwartz, Ellen, 1949-
I'm a vegetarian; amazing facts and ideas for healthy vegetarians; illustrated by Farida Zaman. Tundra Bks. 2002 112p il pa $9.95
Grades: 6 7 8 9   **613.2**
1. Vegetarianism
ISBN 0-88776-588-2   LC 2001-95376
"The author opens with an overview of the different types of vegetarians and the rationale behind their decisions, then moves into advice on handling parental concerns and sticky social situations that are sure to arise. A consideration of nutrition and how to achieve a healthy diet that provides all necessary nutrients follows, ending with a smattering of suggested menus and recipes. . . . She writes in a light, chatty tone, using a question-and-answer format, bulleted facts and lists, boxed information, and humor. Black-and-white drawings throughout add to the book's appeal." SLJ
Includes glossary and bibliographical references

Shryer, Donna
Body fuel; a guide to good nutrition; [by] Donna Shryer. Marshall Cavendish Benchmark 2008 139p il (Food and fitness) $25.95
Grades: 7 8 9 10   **613.2**
1. Nutrition 2. Food
ISBN 978-0-7614-2552-6; 0-7614-2552-7
                                    LC 2007002270
"Provides a basic, comprehensive introduction to human nutrition, including information on how nutrients fuel the body, with a review of the food pyramid and how to read labels to make healthy food choices." Publisher's note
This "visually appealing and easy-to-read [volume is] definitely worth having. The information is up-to-date and the format is attractive." SLJ
Includes bibliographical references

Zahensky, Barbara A.
Diet fads. Rosen 2007 64p il (Danger zone: dieting and eating disorders) lib bdg $27.95
Grades: 4 5 6 7 8   **613.2**
1. Weight loss 2. Obesity
ISBN 978-1-4042-1999-1
"This clearly written overview emphasizes the impact of super-thin celebrity images on general self-esteem. . . . Zahensky considers the reasons people overeat and walks readers through practical steps to recognizing true hunger, making a weight-loss plan, and establishing good diet and exercise habits. She examines different types of fad and crash diets, pointing out their inherent dangers." SLJ

613.6 Personal safety and special topics of health

Orndorff, John
Terrorists, tornadoes, and tsunamis; how to prepare for life's danger zones; by John C. Orndorff and Suzanne Harper; [illustrations by Joana Penna] Abrams Books for Young Readers 2007 144p il map $16.95
Grades: 6 7 8 9   **613.6**
1. Safety education 2. Disasters
ISBN 978-0-8109-5767-1; 0-8109-5767-1
                                    LC 2006014837
"Orndorff and Harper describe several disasters and offer tips on preparing for, avoiding, and staying safe during each one. Chapters devoted to terrorism, crime, hurricanes, tornadoes, floods, earthquakes, and winter storms include briefing notes, or descriptions of the events, and a stay safe guide with suggested precautions in specific situations. . . . An added chapter includes briefer information on lightning, mudslides, avalanches, wildfires, tsunamis, and volcanoes. In general, the suggestions are sensible and practical." SLJ
Includes bibliographical references

Raatma, Lucia
Safety in your neighborhood. Child's World 2005 32p il (Living well) lib bdg $25.64
Grades: 4 5 6 7   **613.6**
1. Crime prevention 2. Safety education
ISBN 1-59296-240-8   LC 2003-27214
Contents: Who is that man?; Your home and neighborhood; Knowing your neighbors; Strangers on your street; Someone's at your door; Keeping your neighborhood safe; Glossary; Questions and answers about neighborhood safety; Helping a friend learn about neighborhood safety; Did you know?; How to learn more about neighborhood safety
This book teaches young readers how to keep their neighborhood a safe place and what to do if that safety is compromised.
This "clearly written [title has] an appealing layout with plenty of full-color photos and a triple-spaced text. . . . [It] provides solid tips." SLJ
Includes glossary and bibliographical references

Wiloch, Thomas
Everything you need to know about protecting yourself and others from abduction. Rosen Pub. Group 1998 64p il (Need to know library) $25.25
Grades: 6 7 8 9   **613.6**
1. Kidnapping 2. Safety education
ISBN 0-8239-2553-6   LC 97-44784
"This title calls attention to the increasing number of abductions of teens and children. While it categorizes the different types of abductions, it focuses on those committed by strangers. . . . Preventive measures as well as strategies for escaping attempted kidnappings are described. Chapters are devoted to precautions to take at home, and while babysitting, jogging, bicycling, using the Internet, etc. The author addresses teens although

Wiloch, Thomas—*Continued*

there is some discussion of the vulnerability of children. Most suggestions are intelligent, practical, and easy to follow." SLJ

Includes bibliographical references

613.7 Physical fitness

Birkemoe, Karen, 1974-

Strike a pose; the Planet Girl guide to yoga; written by Karen Birkemoe; illustrated by Heather Collett. Kids Can Press 2007 96p il (Planet girl) spiral $12.95 *

Grades: 5 6 7 8 **613.7**

1. Yoga 2. Girls—Health and hygiene

ISBN 978-1-55337-004-8

"This compact book offers a well-rounded overview of Hatha yoga. Using an easy conversational tone, Birkemoe relates the general practice and specific poses to reader's lives. The simple line drawings and color illustrations partner effectively with text to explain each move." SLJ

Includes glossary

Fitness information for teens; edited by Lisa Bakewell. 2nd ed. Omnigraphics 2009 432p (Teen health series) $65

Grades: 7 8 9 10 11 12 **613.7**

1. Physical fitness

ISBN 978-0-7808-1045-7; 0-7808-1045-7

LC 2008-31334

First published 2004

"Health tips about exercise, physical wellbeing, and health maintenance including facts about conditioning, stretching, strength training, body shape and body image, sports nutrition, and specific activities for athletes and non-athletes" Title page

"Provides basic consumer health information for teens on maintaining health through physical activity. Includes index, resource information and recommendations for further reading." Publisher's note

"This no-nonsense guide packs a great deal into its pages. . . . The text is written in a conversational tone that pairs well with the topic." SLJ

Includes bibliographical references

Gedatus, Gus

Exercise for weight management. LifeMatters 2001 64p il (Nutrition and fitness) lib bdg $23.93

Grades: 7 8 9 10 **613.7**

1. Exercise 2. Physical fitness

ISBN 0-7368-0706-3 LC 00-34899

This offers information on physical fitness and setting up a healthy exercise plan

"This brief, well-designed title delivers informative and relevant material for the serious teen reader." Sci Books Films

Includes glossary and bibliographical references

Hovius, Christopher

The best you can be; a teen's guide to fitness and nutrition. Mason Crest Publishers 2005 128p il (The science of health) $24.95

Grades: 7 8 9 10 **613.7**

1. Physical fitness 2. Nutrition

ISBN 978-1-590848-487; 1-59084-848-9

LC 2004-12715

Discusses the importance of good nutrition and adequate exercise for teens.

Includes bibliographical references

Libal, Autumn

The importance of physical activity and exercise; the fitness factor. Mason Crest Publishers 2006 104p il (Obesity: modern-day epidemic) $23.95

Grades: 7 8 9 10 **613.7**

1. Physical fitness 2. Exercise

ISBN 978-1-59084-945-3; 1-59084-945-0

LC 200425293

This book argues "that America is experiencing a fitness crisis. . . . Suggestions on how individuals can immediately get started on a path to better health and fitness are offered, along with information about avoiding body image problems and eating disorders.Visually appealing and easy to read, this . . . [book] provides useful and current information in an attractive format." Voice Youth Advocates

Includes bibliographical references

Porter, David, 1960-

Winning weight training for girls; fitness and conditioning for sports; foreword by Gerard K. Green. Facts on File 2004 205p il $35; pa $16.95

Grades: 7 8 9 10 **613.7**

1. Weight lifting 2. Physical fitness

ISBN 0-8160-5185-2; 0-8160-5186-0 (pa)

LC 2003-3500

"A Mountain Lion Book"

"The book describes the benefits of weight training, the muscles of the body and how they interact, biomechanics, anaerobic versus aerobic exercises, proper use of equipment, circuit programs for different levels of ability, training for performance or injury recovery, controlling weight, and much more." Publisher's note

This is "detailed yet easy to read. . . . Safety and proper technique are stressed throughout." SLJ

Includes bibliographical references

Purperhart, Helen

Yoga exercises for teens; developing a calmer mind and a stronger body; translated by Amina Marix Evans; illustrated by Barbara van Amelsfort. Hunter House Publishers 2008 160p il pa $14.95

Grades: 7 8 9 10 **613.7**

1. Yoga 2. Physical fitness 3. Teenagers—Health and hygiene

ISBN 978-0-8979-3503-6; 0-8979-3503-9

LC 2008-24262

This book about yoga "includes the eight yoga rules for life, the five precepts, and the five yoga abstinences." Publisher's note

Includes bibliographical references

Vedral, Joyce L.
Toning for teens; the 20-minute workout that makes you look good and feel great! Warner Bks. 2002 165p il pa $15.95
Grades: 7 8 9 10   **613.7**
1. Exercise 2. Physical fitness 3. Teenagers—Health and hygiene
ISBN 0-446-67815-5   LC 2002-101020
The author offers a "workout specifically aimed at helping adolescent girls tone and firm their muscles using free weights. . . . The author emphasizes sound nutrition and exercise information. . . . The exercises are clearly described, and illustrated with photos of teens performing the routines." SLJ

613.9   Birth control, reproductive technology, sex hygiene

Bell, Ruth
Changing bodies, changing lives; a book for teens on sex and relationships; [by] Ruth Bell and other co-authors of Our bodies, ourselves and Ourselves and our children, together with members of the Teen Book Project. expanded 3rd ed. Times Bks. 1998 411p il pa $24.95
Grades: 7 8 9 10 11 12   **613.9**
1. Sex education
ISBN 0-8129-2990-X   LC 97-29249
First published 1980
This is a "book on sex, physical and emotional health, and personal relationships. . . . Readers . . . will find emotional support as well as specific answers to most of their questions in this nonjudgmental resource." Booklist

Brynie, Faith Hickman, 1946-
101 questions about sex and sexuality—; with answers for the curious, cautious, and confused. Twenty-First Century Books 2003 176p il lib bdg $30.60
Grades: 8 9 10 11 12   **613.9**
1. Sex education
ISBN 0-7613-2310-4   LC 2002-11209
Uses a question-and-answer format to present information about the physical, emotional, and social topics surrounding sex and sexuality
"Brynie emphasizes abstinence as the only sure way of avoiding STDs and pregnancies, but also gives detailed information on contraception. . . . The matter-of-fact style is never condescending or alarmist in tone. . . . Explicit black-and-white illustrations lend an almost clinical touch. . . . The glossary; resource list of books, articles, and Web sites; and extensive citations make Brynie's title good for reports, while the directness of the presentation will appeal to general readers." SLJ
Includes bibliographical references

Harris, Robie H.
It's perfectly normal; a book about changing bodies, growing up, sex, and sexual health; illustrated by Michael Emberley. 10th anniversary edition. Candlewick Press 2004 89p il $22.99; pa $12.99 *
Grades: 4 5 6 7   **613.9**
1. Sex education
ISBN 0-7636-2610-4; 0-7636-2433-0 (pa)
First published 1994
The author "explains the physical, psychological, emotional and social changes that occur during puberty—and the implications of these changes." Publ Wkly
"This caring, conscientious, and well-crafted book will be a fine library resource as well as a marvelous adjunct to the middle-school sex-education curriculum. . . . The bold color cartoon drawings are very candid: a double-page spread of nudes, which beautifully demonstrates the varied shapes and sizes humans come in; a picture of a couple making love; one of a boy masturbating as he sits on his bed; another of a girl examining her genitals with a mirror. . . . Harris' text, as forthright as Emberley's art, encompasses . . . (the structure of the reproductive system and puberty) . . . intercourse, birth, abortion, sexual responsibility and respect." Booklist

Madaras, Lynda, 1947-
The "what's happening to my body?" book for boys; [by] Lynda Madaras with Area Madaras; drawings by Simon Sullivan. 3rd rev ed. Newmarket Press 2007 xx, 233p il $24.95; pa $12.95
Grades: 4 5 6 7   **613.9**
1. Adolescence 2. Puberty 3. Sex education 4. Boys—Health and hygiene
ISBN   978-1-55704-769-4;   1-55704-769-3; 978-1-55704-765-6 (pa); 1-55704-765-0 (pa)
LC 2007009874
First published 1984
Discusses the changes that take place in a boy's body during puberty, including information on the body's changing size and shape, the growth spurt, reproductive organs, pubic hair, beards, pimples, voice changes, wet dreams, and puberty in girls.
Includes bibliographical references

The "what's happening to my body?" book for girls; [by] Lynda Madaras with Area Madaras; drawings by Simon Sullivan. 3rd rev. ed. Newmarket Press 2007 xxvi, 259p il $24.95; pa $12.95
Grades: 4 5 6 7   **613.9**
1. Adolescence 2. Puberty 3. Sex education 4. Girls—Health and hygiene
ISBN   978-1-55704-768-7;   1-55704-768-5; 978-1-55704-764-9 (pa); 1-55704-764-2 (pa)
LC 2007009862
Discusses the changes that take place in a girl's body during puberty, including information on the body's changing size and shape, pubic hair, breasts, reproductive organs, the menstrual cycle, and puberty in boys.
Includes bibliographical references

Pardes, Bronwen

Doing it right. Simon & Schuster 2007 143p il pa $14.99

Grades: 7 8 9 10 11 12   **613.9**

1. Sex education

ISBN 978-1-4169-1823-X; 1-4169-1823-X

LC 2006-928450

On cover: making smart, safe, and satisfying choices about sex

The author "tackles the tough questions about sexual orientation, size, abuse, orgasm, pregnancy, STDs, and masturbation among others." Voice Youth Advocates

Pardes "strives to give teens the information they need, without judgment, to make their own decisions. She freely discusses sex without love, reproductive anatomy, transitioning as a transsexual, and sexually transmitted diseases. . . . The openness of this book will be a boon to teens looking for frank discussions of sexuality and making choices." SLJ

Includes bibliographical references

Sexual health information for teens; health tips about sexual development, reproduction, contraception, and sexually transmitted infections including facts about puberty, sexuality, birth control, chlamydia, gonorrhea, herpes, human papillomavirus, syphilis, and more; edited by Sandra Augustyn Lawton. 2nd ed. Omnigraphics 2008 430p il (Teen health series) $69 *

Grades: 7 8 9 10 11 12   **613.9**

1. Teenagers—Health and hygiene 2. Sex education

ISBN 978-0-7808-1010-5; 0-7808-1010-4

LC 2007052454

First published 2003

"Provides basic consumer health information for teens about puberty, sexuality, reproductive health, contraception, and disease prevention." Publisher's note

"This offering represents the most up-to-date information available on an array of topics. . . . The range of coverage . . . is thorough and extensive. Each chapter includes a bibliographic citation, and the three back sections containing additional resources, further reading, and the index are all first-rate. The few illustrations and diagrams range in quality from good to excellent." SLJ

Includes bibliographical references

614   Forensic medicine; incidence of injuries, wounds, disease; public preventive medicine

Fridell, Ron, 1943-

DNA fingerprinting; the ultimate identity. Watts 2001 112p il lib bdg $26

Grades: 7 8 9 10   **614**

1. DNA fingerprinting 2. Forensic sciences

ISBN 0-531-11858-4   LC 00-26925

Discusses the discovery of DNA fingerprinting, the processes involved, its initial use, and its past and present role in forensic identification, conservation biology, and human genetics

"Fridell consistently gets right to the heart of his sub-

ject, melding scientific, forensic, and historic information in an easy-to-grasp, often eye-opening fashion." Booklist

Includes bibliographical references

Jackson, Donna M., 1959-

The bone detectives; how forensic anthropologists solve crimes and uncover mysteries of the dead; by Donna M. Jackson; photographs by Charlie Fellenbaum. Little, Brown 1996 48p il lib bdg $17.99 *

Grades: 5 6 7 8   **614**

1. Forensic sciences 2. Criminal investigation

ISBN 0-316-82935-8   LC 95-19051

"Jackson follows forensic anthropologist Dr. Michael Charney and his colleagues as they solve an actual case by developing a physical profile from bones and teeth, reconstructing the victim's skull, and using clues from fibers and other material to make further identification." Booklist

"Laced with eye-catching full-color photos, this readable book is a fine example of the application of scientific knowledge to the 'real' world." SLJ

Includes glossary

Nardo, Don, 1947-

DNA evidence. Lucent Books 2008 104p il (Crime scene investigations) lib bdg $32.45

Grades: 7 8 9 10   **614**

1. DNA fingerprinting 2. Forensic sciences

ISBN 978-1-59018-951-1; 1-59018-951-5

LC 2007-21910

Describes the origins of DNA profiling, its use in solving criminal cases, exonerating the innocent, and identifying the dead and missing, and related issues of privacy and discrimination.

"Sidebars and photographs combine with an attention-grabbing text to highlight evidence gathering and interpretation, notable cases, career information, and statistics. Readers with an interest in criminal justice will appreciate the level of detail." Horn Book Guide

Includes glossary and bibliographical references

Walker, Sally M.

Written in bone; buried lives of Jamestown and Colonial Maryland. Carolrhoda Books 2009 144p il map $22.95 *

Grades: 6 7 8 9 10   **614**

1. Forensic sciences 2. Maryland—History 3. Jamestown (Va.)—History 4. United States—History—1600-1775, Colonial period 5. Excavations (Archeology)—United States

ISBN 978-0-8225-7135-3; 0-8225-7135-8

LC 2007-10768

"Walker takes readers on an archaeological investigation of human and material remains from 17th- and 18th-century Jamestown and colonial Maryland, while addressing relevant topics in forensic anthropology, history, and archaeology. . . . The text succinctly explains complex forensic concepts. . . . Captioned, full-color photographs of skeletal, dental, and artifactual remains shed light on colonial life. Historical documents, illustrated maps, and anatomical drawings complement images of

Walker, Sally M.—*Continued*
various specialists at work in the field. Photographs of reenactors performing period tasks . . . provide insight into the daily life of the recovered individuals." SLJ

Includes bibliographical references

614.4 Incidence of and public measures to prevent disease

Barnard, Bryn
Outbreak; plagues that changed history; written and illustrated by Bryn Barnard. Crown Publishers 2005 47p il maps $17.95 *
Grades: 5 6 7 8   **614.4**
1. Epidemics 2. Diseases
ISBN 0-375-82986-5   LC 2005-15086
This "volume explores specific plagues that have impacted society. Barnard begins with an introduction to microbes and the positive and negative effects that they can have on humans. A history of the study of microorganisms follows. The bulk of the book then focuses on specific plagues with a chapter devoted to each, including the Black Death, smallpox, yellow fever, cholera, tuberculosis, and influenza. The final chapter discusses the modern struggle against disease. . . . The evocative paintings help to clarify the text. Browsers and report writers alike will find this to be a fascinating and informative resource." SLJ

Brownlee, Christen, 1977-
Cute, furry, and deadly; diseases you can catch from your pet! [by] Christen Brownlee. Franklin Watts 2008 64p il map (24/7, science behind the scenes) lib bdg $26
Grades: 6 7 8 9 10   **614.4**
1. Communicable diseases 2. Pets—Health and hygiene
ISBN 0-531-12072-4 (lib bdg); 978-0-531-12072-9 (lib bdg)   LC 2006-21230
Hopefully, the worst thing your pet ever comes home with is bad breath. But some furry friends can carry nasty germs, and that's where zoonotic disease researchers come in and investigate and stop animal diseases before they get you!
"This series is a great pick for reluctant readers, busy teens, and anyone looking for a fun (if somewhat frightening) nonfiction read." Voice Youth Advocates
Includes glossary and bibliographical references

Epidemics: opposing viewpoints; Mary E. Williams, book editor. Greenhaven Press 2005 208p il lib bdg $37.40; pa $25.95
Grades: 8 9 10 11 12   **614.4**
1. Epidemics
ISBN 0-7377-2282-7 (lib bdg); 0-7377-2283-5 (pa)
                                       LC 2004-61657
Replaces the edition published 1999 under the editorship of William Dudley
"Opposing viewpoints series"
In this "anthology, authors examine the resurgent problem of infectious disease around the world and dis-

cuss how governments and individuals should respond to the threats posed by epidemics." Publisher's note

Includes bibliographical references

Farrell, Jeanette
Invisible enemies; stories of infectious diseases. 2nd ed. Farrar, Straus & Giroux 2005 272p il $18
Grades: 7 8 9 10   **614.4**
1. Communicable diseases
ISBN 0-374-33607-5   LC 2004-57668
First published 1998
The author "focuses on seven dreaded human diseases: smallpox, leprosy, plague, tuberculosis, malaria, cholera, and AIDS. Each chapter provides a description of the physical and psychological effects of the disease on its victims, early theories about its causes, and efforts made to avoid or cure it. Then the methods of research that revealed its cause and developed the means to control its spread are explained in fascinating detail. . . . If every science book for nonspecialists were written with such flair and attention to detail, science would soon become every student's favorite subject." SLJ
Includes glossary and bibliographical references

Friedlander, Mark P.
Outbreak; disease detectives at work; by Mark P. Friedlander Jr. [Updated and rev. ed.] Twenty-First Century Books 2009 128p il lib bdg $31.93 *
Grades: 6 7 8 9   **614.4**
1. Epidemiology 2. Diseases
ISBN 978-0-8225-9039-2; 0-8225-9039-5
                                       LC 2008025277
First published 2000
Describes the field of epidemiology and its history, presenting historical and modern case studies and biological explanations of some diseases and a discussion of the microbes most likely to be used by bioterrorists.
"This is a readable, intriguing overview of the destructive power of epidemics and the critical work of public health professionals." SLJ [review of 2003 edition]
Includes bibliographical references

Goldsmith, Connie, 1945-
Invisible invaders; new and dangerous infectious diseases. Twenty-First Century Books 2006 111p il (Discovery!) lib bdg $29.27 *
Grades: 7 8 9 10   **614.4**
1. Communicable diseases
ISBN 978-0-8225-3416-7; 0-8225-3416-9
                                       LC 2005-17271
This book covers "topics associated with current infectious diseases." Sci Books Films
"This title is a thorough, understandable, and accessible source of current information and medical definitions, and a trail to further research." SLJ
Includes bibliographical references

Grady, Denise
Deadly invaders; virus outbreaks around the world, from Marburg fever to avian flu. Kingfisher 2006 128p il map $16.95 *
Grades: 7 8 9 10   **614.4**
1. Communicable diseases 2. Viruses
ISBN 978-0-7534-5995-9; 0-7534-5995-7
LC 2006004441
"A New York Times book"
"In the first half of the book . . . Grady discusses the Marburg virus, the incurable disease it causes, and its effects on individuals and communities, as seen through the lens of her personal experiences in Angola. . . . Next she offers a short . . . chapter on each of seven deadly diseases: Marburg fever, avian flu, HIV/AIDS, Hantavirus pulmonary syndrome, West Nile disease, SARS, and monkeypox." Booklist
The "writing is informative and compelling. . . . The layout is appealing and includes good-quality, full-color, relevant photographs on almost every spread. . . . A fast-paced, timely, and important book." SLJ
Includes bibliographical references

Miller, Debra A.
Pandemics; [by] Debra A. Miller. Lucent Books 2006 unp (Hot topics) $32.45
Grades: 7 8 9 10   **614.4**
1. Communicable diseases 2. Epidemics
ISBN 1-59018-965-5; 978-1-59018-965-8
LC 2006007057
"This comprehensive and well-organized book covers potential threats; the control and prevention of pandemics; and factors that may facilitate the outbreak and transmission of diseases, such as pollution, poverty, overpopulation, and globalization. Teens will appreciate the interesting sidebars, quotations, diagrams, and full-color photos that are integrated throughout the text and will find the annotated lists of organizations and further-reading suggestions useful." SLJ
Includes bibliographical references

Piddock, Charles
Outbreak; science seeks safeguards for global health; [Caryn Oryniak, consultant] National Geographic 2008 64p il (National Geographic investigates) $17.95; lib bdg $27.90 *
Grades: 4 5 6 7   **614.4**
1. Epidemics 2. Diseases 3. Medicine—Research
ISBN   978-1-4263-0357-9;   1-4263-0357-2;
978-1-4263-0263-3 (lib bdg); 1-4263-0263-0 (lib bdg)
LC 2009-275290
This is an "introduction to the fight against infectious diseases, including scientists who discovered various viruses and bacteria. The text outlines how we have learned to fight nature's harmful strains and to use others to our advantage; it also provides the latest findings on bird flu and SARS, Ebola and AIDS, and highly resistant strains of tuberculosis." Publisher's note

Tilden, Thomasine E. Lewis, 1958-
Help! What's eating my flesh? runaway staph and strep infections! [by] Thomasine E. Lewis Tilden. Franklin Watts 2008 64p il map (24/7, science behind the scenes) lib bdg $26
Grades: 6 7 8 9 10   **614.4**
1. Communicable diseases
ISBN 0-531-12073-2; 978-0-531-12073-6
LC 2006-5871
This describes "how germs can invade your body; how a visit to the hospital turned deadly; the tools and equipment health-care workers use to fight the war on germs; and whether becoming an infectious disease specialist is the right career for you." Publisher's note
"A splashy tabloid-style presentation, including gross and disgusting photographs, will attract curious young teens who will be unable to resist. . . . [This] book also includes career information, resources (including Web sites and books), a historical section with key dates, and an author's note." Voice Youth Advoctaes
Includes glossary and bibliographical references

Walker, Richard, 1951-
Epidemics & plagues; foreword by Denise Grady. Kingfisher 2006 63p il (Kingfisher knowledge) $12.95; pa $8.95
Grades: 4 5 6 7   **614.4**
1. Epidemics 2. Diseases
ISBN   978-0-7534-6035-1;   0-7534-6035-1;
978-0-7534-6161-7 (pa); 0-7534-6161-7 (pa)
Discusses the spread of infectious diseases and their impact on human populations, from the Black Death in medieval Europe to such modern diseases as AIDS and West Nile virus, as well as efforts to stop the spread of these diseases.
Includes glossary

Ward, Brian R.
Epidemic; by Brian Ward. Dorling Kindersley 2000 64p il (DK eyewitness books) $15.99; lib bdg $19.99
Grades: 4 5 6 7   **614.4**
1. Epidemics
ISBN 0-7894-6296-6; 0-7894-6989-8 (lib bdg)
LC 00-27948
Discusses what an epidemic is, how it evolves, various causes and carriers, and efforts to prevent epidemics

614.5 Incidence of and public measures to prevent specific diseases and kinds of diseases

Ballard, Carol
AIDS and other epidemics. Gareth Stevens Pub. 2008 48p il map (What if we do nothing?) lib bdg $31
Grades: 5 6 7 8   **614.5**
1. AIDS (Disease) 2. Epidemics 3. Communicable diseases
ISBN 978-1-4339-0085-3 (lib bdg); 1-4339-0085-8 (lib bdg)
LC 2008029189

Ballard, Carol—*Continued*
"This book looks at the causes of major infectious diseases, how they spread, and how they can be treated. It also discusses different steps that governments and health organizations can take to handle and prevent epidemics and pandemics." Publisher's note
"Using intelligent, focused text; an open design; vivid photos; and excellent maps, [this] book demands attention." Booklist
Includes bibliographical references

Currie-McGhee, L. K., 1971-
Sexually transmitted diseases; [by] Leanne Currie-McGhee. ReferencePoint Press 2009 104p il map (Compact research. Diseases and disorders) lib bdg $25.95
Grades: 8 9 10   614.5
  1. Sexually transmitted diseases
  ISBN 978-1-60152-045-6; 1-60152-045-X
                                   LC 2008-12554
Presents information on sexually transmitted diseases through essays, quotations, statistics, and suggestions for further research.
"Sobering, enlightening, and up-to-date, this title . . . uses an effective blend of primary sources, diagrams, and thorough text to bring the latest facts about STDs to young readers. . . . A time line and lists of key advocacy groups and further reading close this valuable resource for teens." Booklist
Includes bibliographical references

Goldsmith, Connie, 1945-
Influenza: the next pandemic? Twenty-First Century Books 2007 112p il (Twenty-first century medical library) lib bdg $27.93
Grades: 6 7 8 9 10   614.5
  1. Influenza
  ISBN 978-0-7613-9457-0 (lib bdg); 0-7613-9457-5 (lib bdg)   LC 2005-23588
The author "traces the history of the flu, giving attention to past outbreaks and epidemics. She also describes flu viruses of today, explains treatments, and details health officials' concerns about bird flu. . . . Good for reports, and a worthy source to update collections." SLJ
Includes bibliographical references

Grady, Sean M., 1965-
Biohazards; humanity's battle with infectious disease; [by] Sean M. Grady and John Tabak. Facts on File 2006 194p il map (Science & technology in focus) $35 *
Grades: 7 8 9 10   614.5
  1. Communicable diseases
  ISBN 0-8160-4687-5   LC 2005-5610
This "work . . . examines the bacteria and viruses that make up a significant part of our world. The threat of bioterrorism; the risks of international travel; the spread, control, and treatment of such newly important diseases as anthrax, hantavirus, and HIV/AIDS, as well as historical ones like the Black Plague and smallpox, are clearly discussed." SLJ
Includes bibliographical references

Kupperberg, Paul
The influenza pandemic of 1918-1919. Chelsea House 2008 120p il map (Great historic disasters) $35
Grades: 7 8 9 10   614.5
  1. Influenza 2. Epidemics
  ISBN 978-0-7910-9640-6; 0-7910-9640-8
This "covers the history of the influenza outbreak and medical advances made over the last century to prevent future pandemics." Horn Book Guide
This is "well written and informative. . . . The inclusion of black-and-white and color photographs and drawings and sidebars help to make [this book] first-rate for reports and general browsing." SLJ

Marrin, Albert, 1936-
Dr. Jenner and the speckled monster; the search for the smallpox vaccine. Dutton Children's Bks. 2002 120p il $19.99 *
Grades: 5 6 7 8   614.5
  1. Jenner, Edward, 1749-1823 2. Smallpox
  ISBN 0-525-46922-2   LC 2002-2698
This is a "social history of smallpox, with an emphasis on Dr. Edward Jenner's contributions to eradicate the disease. . . . Marrin's writing is direct and succinct, and his scientific explanations are lucid and well detailed. Numerous black-and-white period illustrations (some appropriately gruesome) appear in most chapters, adding interest to the text." Booklist
Includes bibliographical references

Murphy, Jim, 1947-
An American plague; the true and terrifying story of the yellow fever epidemic of 1793. Clarion Bks. 2003 165p il map $18 *
Grades: 5 6 7 8   614.5
  1. Yellow fever
  ISBN 0-395-77608-2   LC 2002-151355
A Newbery Medal honor book, 2004
Contents: No one noticed; "All was not right;" Church bells tolling; Confusion, distress, and utter desolation; "It was our duty;" The prince of bleeders; "By twelve only;" "This unmerciful enemy;" "A delicate situation;" Improvements and the public gratitude; "A modern-day time bomb"
"Murphy culls from a number of historical records the story of the yellow fever epidemic that swept Philadelphia in 1793, skillfully drawing out from these sources the fear and drama of the time and making them immediate to modern readers. . . . Thoroughly documented, with an annotated source list, the work is both rigorous and inviting." Horn Book

Peters, Stephanie True, 1965-
The battle against polio. Benchmark Books 2004 c2005 69p il (Epidemic!) lib bdg $32.79 *
Grades: 4 5 6 7 8   614.5
  1. Poliomyelitis
  ISBN 0-7614-1635-8   LC 2004-3408
This is a history of the polio epidemic, early research into the disease, and the development of the polio vaccine.

Peters, Stephanie True, 1965-—*Continued*
"Peters makes both the science and the social history compelling in this title. . . . The book design is appealing, with wide margins and well-placed, mostly two-tone, photos. The exemplary back matter . . . includes an annotated bibliography, Web sites, and full notes for quotes." Booklist
Includes glossary

The Black Death. Benchmark Books 2004 c2005 69p il map (Epidemic!) lib bdg $32.79 *
Grades: 4 5 6 7 8   **614.5**
1. Plague 2. Middle Ages
ISBN 0-7614-1633-1   LC 2003-743
Describes the 1347 - 1351 outbreak of plague in Europe, known as the Black Death, which killed one out of three people and changed the course of European history.
Includes glossary and bibliographical references

Cholera; curse of the nineteenth century. Benchmark Books 2004 c2005 69p il (Epidemic!) lib bdg $32.79 *
Grades: 4 5 6 7 8   **614.5**
1. Cholera
ISBN 0-7614-1634-X   LC 2004-844
This is a history of cholera, including the effects of the Industrial Revolution, the epidemics of the 19th century, and the continued existance of the disease in the world today.
Includes bibliographical references

Smallpox in the new world. Benchmark Books 2004 c2005 69p il (Epidemic!) lib bdg $32.79 *
Grades: 4 5 6 7 8   **614.5**
1. Smallpox
ISBN 0-7614-1637-4   LC 2003-2646
Describes the history of smallpox in the Americas, covering the arrival of the Spanish as carriers, its spread throughout the New World, the development of the smallpox vaccine, the elimination of the disease, and its potential use as a terrorist weapon.
Includes glossary and bibliographical references

Slavicek, Louise Chipley, 1956-
The Black Death. Chelsea House Publishers 2008 127p il (Great historic disasters) lib bdg $35
Grades: 6 7 8 9 10   **614.5**
1. Plague 2. Middle Ages
ISBN 978-0-7910-9649-9; 0-7910-9649-1
                                    LC 2008004887
This describes the Plague epidemic and it's effects on Europe in the Middle Ages
Includes glossary and bibliographical references

Zahler, Diane
The Black Death. Twenty-First Century Books 2009 160p il map (Pivotal moments in history) lib bdg $38.60
Grades: 7 8 9 10   **614.5**
1. Plague 2. Middle Ages
ISBN 978-0-8225-9076-7; 0-8225-9076-X
                                    LC 2008-26878

This book discusses the pivotal moment in history when one out of three people died and changed the course of world history, the Black Death.
"This is a well-written and well-researched volume. Full-color illustrations, a note explaining the value of primary sources, a who's who, and careful source notes make this book a valuable addition to history collections." SLJ
Includes glossary and bibliographical references

615   Pharmacology and therapeutics

Collier, James Lincoln, 1928-
Vaccines. Benchmark Bks. 2003 127p il (Great inventions) lib bdg $39.93 *
Grades: 6 7 8 9 10   **615**
1. Vaccination
ISBN 0-7614-1539-4   LC 2002-156287
Contents: "And no bells tolled;" Doctor Jenner's milkhands; Death invisible; Cleaning up the cities; The forgotten plague; The great crippler; The future
Explains the diseases that led to the discovery of vaccines, how vaccines work, and how that has changed the history of medicine
"The writing is clear, and color and black-and-white illustrations appear throughout." SLJ
Includes bibliographical references

De la Bédoyère, Guy
The discovery of penicillin. World Almanac Library 2005 48p il (Milestones in modern science) $30 *
Grades: 6 7 8 9   **615**
1. Penicillin
ISBN 0-8368-5852-2
This is a history of the discovery of penicillin and the developments which led to its use in medicine today.
The text is "complete, detailed, and not difficult to follow. . . . The illustrations are adequate and plentiful, including lots of photos and diagrams." SLJ
Includes bibliographical references

The first polio vaccine. World Almanac Library 2006 48p il map (Milestones in modern science) $30 *
Grades: 6 7 8 9   **615**
1. Poliomyelitis vaccine
ISBN 0-8368-5855-7
This is an examination of the discovery of the first polio vaccine and what further work led to the vaccine used today.
The text is "complete, detailed, and not difficult to follow. . . . The illustrations are adequate and plentiful, including lots of photos and diagrams." SLJ

Durham, Michael, 1952-
Painkillers and tranquilizers. Heinemann Lib. 2003 56p il (Just the facts) $25.64
Grades: 6 7 8 9   **615**
1. Psychotropic drugs 2. Analgesics
ISBN 1-4034-0821-1   LC 2002-10941

Durham, Michael, 1952-—_Continued_

Contents: What are painkillers and tranquilizers?; Painkillers and tranquilizers; Some history; Why do we need painkillers?; Pain relief drugs today; What are anxiety & depression?; Tranquilizers and antidepressants today; The difference between painkillers and tranquilizers; How tranquilizers and antidepressants work; How drugs can help; Side effects; What is drug dependence?; Recognizing tranquilizer dependence; Effects of long-term dependence; Getting help; Alternatives; Legal matters; Treatment and counseling; People to talk to

Offers a description of drugs used to treat pain, anxiety, and depression, and discusses how these drugs work, possible side effects, long-term effects, and how to deal with dependency or addiction to them

This provides "well-organized information. . . . The writing is clear and frank." Libr Media Connect

Includes glossary and bibliographical references

Facklam, Margery, 1927-

Modern medicines; the discovery and development of healing drugs; Margery Facklam, Howard Facklam, and Sean M. Grady. rev ed. Facts on File 2004 226p il (Science & technology in focus) $35

Grades: 7 8 9 10   615
1. Pharmacology 2. Drugs
ISBN 0-8160-4706-5   LC 2003-11489

First published 1992 with title: Healing drugs: the history of pharmacology

Contents: Ancient remedies; A garden of simples; Patent cures and medicine shows; Formalizing pharmacology; A world of wonder drugs; Preemptive strikes; Biological systems management; Miracles in the medicine cabinet; From the laboratory to the pharmacy; Producing modern pills and potions; New uses for old drugs; When drugs go wrong; Back to the Garden?; Herbalists and scientists; Warning signs; Drug-resistant germs; The perils of medicine; Distribution woes; Future trends in pharmacology

"Straightforward, sensibly organized, and well researched, this volume . . . is an excellent introduction." Booklist

Goldsmith, Connie, 1945-

Superbugs strike back; when antibiotics fail. Twenty-First Century Books 2007 112p il (Discovery!) lib bdg $29.27 *

Grades: 7 8 9 10   615
1. Drug resistance 2. Bacteria 3. Antibiotics
ISBN 978-0-8225-6607-6; 0-8225-6607-9
                                            LC 2006-10726

"The emergence of 'superbugs'—antibiotic resistant bacteria—and the threat they pose to public health are examined in this detailed introduction. . . . Full-color tables, sidebars, diagrams, and good-quality photos and micrographs are interspersed throughout. The text is meticulous without being tedious." SLJ

Includes glossary and bibliographical references

Gordon, Melanie Apel

Drug interactions; protecting yourself from dangerous drug, medication, and food combinations; [by] Melanie Gordon. Rosen Pub. Group 1999 63p il (Drug abuse prevention library) $25.25

Grades: 6 7 8 9   615
1. Drugs
ISBN 0-8239-2825-X   LC 98-44974

Discusses illegal and legal drugs (both over-the-counter and prescription), alcohol, and food and explains how to prevent dangerous interactions among these substances

Includes bibliographical references

Henn, Debra

Diet pills; [by] Debra Henn and Deborah DeEugenio. Chelsea House 2005 120p il map (Drugs, the straight facts) $30; pa $13.95

Grades: 6 7 8 9   615
1. Appetite depressants
ISBN 0-7910-8198-2; 0-7910-8342-X (pa)
                                            LC 2004024766

"The authors explain how diet pills work, the FDA's rules regarding them, dietary supplements for weight loss, and the increasing rate of diet-pill addiction. Healthy ways to lose and maintain weight are suggested. . . . High-quality diagrams, color photos, and relevant case studies are included. The writing is clear, and no previous background is necessary to comprehend [this] well-organized [book]." SLJ

Includes bibliographical references

Kidd, J. S. (Jerry S.)

Potent natural medicines; Mother Nature's pharmacy; [by] J.S. Kidd and Renee A. Kidd. rev ed. Chelsea House 2006 212p il (Science and society) $35 *

Grades: 7 8 9 10   615
1. Pharmacology 2. Medical botany
ISBN 0-8160-5607-2   LC 2005041741

First published 1998 with title: Mother Nature's pharmacy

This introduces "plants' medicinal properties, pioneers who hunted for sources of and applications for botanical treatments, and the ways phytochemical nutrients prevent disease. . . . [Also included] are chapters about recent research, including investigation into animal sources for medicine; the impact of field research on native peoples; and the federal regulation of herb and plant supplements. . . . This [is] a good choice to support research and debate projects." Booklist

Includes bibliographical references

Klosterman, Lorrie

The facts about depressants; [by] Lorrie Klosterman. Marshall Cavendish Benchmark 2005 c2006 96p il (Drugs) lib bdg $42.79; pa $6.99

Grades: 7 8 9 10   615
1. Tranquilizing drugs 2. Drug abuse
ISBN 0-7614-1976-4 (lib bdg); 0-7614-1976-4 (lib bdg); 978-0-7614-3594-5 (pa); 0-7614-3594-8 (pa)
                                            LC 2005001729

Klosterman, Lorrie—*Continued*
"Describes the history, characteristics, legal status, and abuse of the tranquilizers and downers (depressants)" Publisher's note
This "useful [volume is] attractively packaged and will be of interest to report writers and general readers. [Text] and photos do an excellent job of showing how [this] group of drugs affects the body." SLJ
Includes glossary and bibliographical references

The facts about drugs and the body. Marshall Cavendish Benchmark 2006 143p il (Drugs) lib bdg $42.79
Grades: 7 8 9 10 11 12   615
1. Drugs
ISBN 978-0-7614-2675-2 (lib bdg); 0-7614-2675-2 (lib bdg)   LC 2007-2260
This discusses the effects of various drugs on the nervous, cardiovascular, respiratory, digestive, and reproductive systems of the body.
"Klosterman has done an excellent job of demonstrating how drugs affect the body functions. The illustrations and captions enhance the information to make it more understandable." SLJ
Includes glossary and bibliographical references

The facts about over-the-counter drugs; [by] Lorrie Klosterman. Marshall Cavendish Benchmark 2006 110p il (Drugs) lib bdg $$2.79
Grades: 6 7 8 9   615
1. Drugs 2. Pharmacology
ISBN 978-0-7614-2246-4 (lib bdg); 0-7614-2246-3 (lib bdg)   LC 2005037349
This offers a history of drug products in the United States and describes drugs sold over the counter, their safe use, and concerns about their use
Includes glossary and bibliographical references

LeVert, Suzanne
The facts about antidepressants; [by] Suzanne LeVert. Marshall Cavendish Benchmark 2007 112p il (Drugs) lib bdg $42.79
Grades: 6 7 8 9   615
1. Antidepressants
ISBN 978-0-7614-2241-9 (lib bdg); 0-7614-2241-2 (lib bdg)   LC 2006002403
This describes the benefits and risks of antidepressant drugs in the treatment of depression
Includes glossary and bibliographical references

Menhard, Francha Roffe
The facts about ritalin. Marshall Cavendish Benchmark 2006 c2007 112p il (Drugs) lib bdg $42.79
Grades: 6 7 8 9   615
1. Ritalin 2. Attention deficit disorder
ISBN 978-0-7614-2245-7 (lib bdg); 0-7614-2245-5 (lib bdg)
This describes the use and abuse of ritalin in the treatment of Attention Deficit Hyperactivity Disorder and the debate surrounding it
Includes glossary and bibliographical references

Naden, Corinne J.
The facts about the A-Z of drugs; [by] Corinne Naden. Marshall Cavendish Benchmark 2007 c2008 156p il (Drugs) lib bdg $42.79
Grades: 7 8 9 10 11 12   615
1. Drugs
ISBN 978-0-7614-2673-8 (lib bdg); 0-7614-2673-6 (lib bdg)   LC 2007-2267
This discusses drug classifications such as depressants, hallucinogens, inhalants, narcotics, and stimulants, and includes an alphabetically arranged description of various drugs.
This is "well-organized, attractively illustrated, current, and highly informative." Sci Books Films
Includes glossary and bibliographical references

Nardo, Don, 1947-
Vaccines. Lucent Bks. 2002 128p il (Great medical discoveries) lib bdg $27.45
Grades: 7 8 9 10   615
1. Vaccination
ISBN 1-56006-932-5   LC 2001-3198
Discusses the impact of vaccines on diseases, their history and development, current challenges in the field, and future research
This work is "refreshingly readable yet thorough. . . . Many halftone photographs, crisp diagrams, and shaded sidebars offer supplementary information in eye-appealing forms." SLJ
Includes bibliographical references

Olive, M. Foster
Prescription pain relievers; [by] M. Foster Olive; consulting editor, David J. Triggle. Chelsea House Publishers 2005 112p il (Drugs, the straight facts) $30; pa $13.95
Grades: 6 7 8 9   615
1. Analgesics
ISBN 0-7910-8199-0; 0-7910-8375-6 (pa)
                                         LC 2004024372
This "book describes what pain is and how it works, as well as the many types of drugs available to alleviate it, potential side effects, and the possibility of addiction. The plethora of herbal remedies is also discussed, as is the fact that many of them are not scientifically tested. High-quality diagrams, color photos, and relevant case studies are included. The writing is clear, and no previous background is necessary to comprehend [this] well-organized [book]." SLJ

Phelan, Glen
Killing germs, saving lives; the quest for the first vaccines. National Geographic 2006 59p il (Science quest) $17.95; lib bdg $25.90
Grades: 5 6 7 8   615
1. Vaccination
ISBN   0-7922-5537-2;   978-0-7922-5537-6; 0-7922-5538-0 (lib bdg); 978-0-7922-5538-3 (lib bdg)
                                          LC 2005-22143
This "traces the path to the creation of the vaccines that revolutionized modern medicine. [It includes] profiles [of such] figures [as] Louis Pasteur, Joseph Lister, and Florence Nightingale." Publisher's note
Includes glossary and bibliographical references

Townsend, John, 1955-
Pills, powders & potions; a history of medication. Raintree 2005 c2006 56p il (Painful history of medicine) lib bdg $32.86; pa $9.90
Grades: 6 7 8 9   **615**
1. Drugs 2. Pharmacology 3. Therapeutics
ISBN 1-4109-1335-X (lib bdg); 1-4109-1340-6 (pa)
LC 2004-14387
"Raintree freestyle"
Contents: Magic pills; Ancient times; The Middle Ages; Good for business; Mixtures from the 1800s; Wonder drugs; Modern times
A history of medication from ancient times to the present
"Each page is dominated by . . . photographs or illustrations, often graphically gross. . . . A photo of an exceedingly ugly wart accompanies mention of an ancient cure. . . . This . . . is certain to attract browsers. . . . Basic facts are presented plainly, making the titles accessible to a wide range of researchers as well." SLJ
Includes glossary and bibliographical references

Winner, Cherie
Circulating life; blood transfusion from ancient superstition to modern medicine. Twenty-First Century Books 2007 112p il (Discovery!) $30.60 *
Grades: 7 8 9 10   **615**
1. Blood—Transfusion
ISBN 978-0-8225-6606-9; 0-8225-6606-0
LC 2006-29921
Contents: A fine humor: early ideas about blood—A closer look at blood—The first transfusions—Answers at last—Taking blood apart—Old fears, new dangers—Twenty-first century blood transfusion—The future of transfusion
This "compendium is both a history of the art of transfusions and a scientific discourse on the chemistry of blood. From early 'bleeding treatments' to the discovery of the circulatory system; from the earliest attempts at transfusions to Charles Drew's heroic work with plasma in World War II, Winner's clear text takes readers on an epic trip." SLJ
Includes bibliographical references

615.5 Therapeutics

Billitteri, Thomas J.
Alternative medicine. 21st Cent. Bks. (Brookfield) 2001 112p il (Twenty-first century medical library) lib bdg $26.90 *
Grades: 7 8 9 10   **615.5**
1. Alternative medicine
ISBN 0-7613-0965-9   LC 00-57707
"Among the topics covered are homeopathic medicine, hypnosis, chiropractic touch therapy, and acupuncture. . . . This book is a solid choice for general information and for reports." SLJ
Includes bibliographical references

Complementary and alternative medicine information for teens; edited by Sandra Augustyn Lawton. Omnigraphics 2007 408p (Teen health series) $65
Grades: 7 8 9 10 11 12   **615.5**
1. Alternative medicine
ISBN 0-7808-0966-1   LC 2006-27704
"Health tips about nontraditional and nonwestern medical practices including information about acupuncture, chiropractic medicine, dietary and herbal supplements, hypnosis, massage therapy, prayer and spirituality, reflexology, yoga, and more." Title page
"This is a useful resource." SLJ
Includes bibliographical references

615.8 Specific therapies and kinds of therapies

West, Krista
Biofeedback. Chelsea House 2007 98p il (Gray matter) lib bdg $32.95
Grades: 8 9 10 11 12   **615.8**
1. Biofeedback training 2. Brain
ISBN 978-0-7910-9436-5 (lib bdg); 0-7910-9436-7 (lib bdg)
LC 2006-101019
"Highlights the uses of this treatment for physical and mental conditions. Brain-wave instruments are explored, studies are noted, and careers in the field are identified. . . . Highly recommended for curriculum support for middle school and high school students who will easily absorb the material presented." Voice Youth Advocates
Includes glossary and bibliographical references

615.9 Toxicology

Bjorklund, Ruth
Food-borne illnesses. Marshall Cavendish Benchmark 2006 64p il (Health alert) $19.95 *
Grades: 4 5 6 7   **615.9**
1. Food contamination 2. Diseases
ISBN 0-7614-1917-9
"Discusses food-borne illnesses and their effects on people and society." Publisher's note
"Children seeking up-to-date and reliable information about the many kinds of food-borne illnesses, treatments, preventions, and coping strategies, as well as a historical overview of food-safety efforts in the United States, will appreciate this easy-to-use and information-rich resource. . . . Useful features include color photos, diagrams, and sidebars." SLJ
Includes glossary and bibliographical references

Brands, Danielle A.
Salmonella. Chelsea House 2005 102p il (Deadly diseases and epidemics) $31.95
Grades: 7 8 9 10   **615.9**
1. Salmonellosis
ISBN 0-7910-8500-7   LC 2005-5348

Brands, Danielle A.—*Continued*

Contents: Salmonella strikes at the senior prom; Salmonella and food-borne illness; Hosts, sources, and carriers; Salmonella in the body; Treating salmonellosis; Salmonella outbreaks and current research; Other bacteria that cause food poisoning; Preventing salmonellosis

Includes glossary and bibliographical references

Silverstein, Alvin

The food poisoning update; [by] Alvin and Virginia Silverstein and Laura Silverstein Nunn. Enslow Publishers 2007 128p il (Disease update) lib bdg $31.93

Grades: 5 6 7 8   **615.9**

1. Food poisoning

ISBN 978-0-7660-2748-0 (lib bdg); 0-7660-2748-1 (lib bdg)   LC 2006032822

This describes the history of food poisoning, its causes, detection, treatment and prevention.

"This timely, well-written title . . . combines practical food-safety tips with clear science facts and concise, historical survey of foodborne illnesses." Booklist

Includes glossary and bibliographical references

616   Diseases

Calamandrei, Camilla

Fever; by Camilla Calamandrei. Marshall Cavendish Benchmark 2009 64p il (Health alert) $22.95

Grades: 4 5 6 7   **616**

1. Fever

ISBN 978-0-7614-2915-9; 0-7614-2915-8

LC 2007-26002

"Provides comprehensive information on the causes, treatment, and history of fever." Publisher's note

Includes glossary

Dendy, Leslie A., 1946-

Guinea pig scientists; bold self-experimenters in science and medicine; [by] Leslie Dendy and Mel Boring; with illustrations by C. B. Mordan. Henry Holt & Co. 2005 213p il $19.95 *

Grades: 5 6 7 8   **616**

1. Medicine—Research 2. Scientists

ISBN 0-8050-7316-7   LC 2004-52364

"The authors offer 10 . . . case studies of scientists from the past several centuries who became their own test subjects. . . . The accounts are lively, compelling, and not always for the squeamish. . . . The authors cogently discuss each experiment's significance in advancing our understanding of science and medicine. Illustrated with a mix of period black-and-white photos and Mordan's nineteenth-century-style portraits . . . the episodes make riveting reading." Booklist

Includes bibliographical references

Diseases; Bryan Bunch and Jenny Tesar, editors. 3rd rev ed. Scholastic Library Pub. 2006 8v il set$349

Grades: 6 7 8 9 10   **616**

1. Diseases—Encyclopedias 2. Reference books

ISBN 0-7172-6205-7   LC 2006-7986

First published 1997

Alphabetically arranged articles presenting medical information on more than 500 diseases, discussing causes, symptoms, stages of the disease, its likelihood of striking, treatments, prevention, and long-term effects.

"Students will find a goldmine of basic reference information in these attractive . . . volumes." SLJ

Includes bibliographical references

Hains, Bryan C.

Pain; series editor, Eric H. Chudler. Chelsea House Publishers 2006 121p il (Gray matter) lib bdg $32.95

Grades: 8 9 10 11 12   **616**

1. Pain 2. Brain

ISBN 0-7910-8951-7 (lib bdg); 978-0-7910-8951-4 (lib bdg)   LC 2006-15133

This book "explores the workings of the somatosensory and pain systems, how disorders can affect how we process information with these systems, and how pain can be treated." Publisher's note

Includes glossary and bibliographical references

Herbst, Judith

Germ theory. Twenty-First Century Books 2008 80p il (Great ideas of science) lib bdg $27.93

Grades: 5 6 7 8   **616**

1. Germ theory of disease 2. Life—Origin

ISBN 978-0-8225-2909-5 (lib bdg); 0-8225-2909-2 (lib bdg)   LC 2005-08809

Discusses how the germ theory of disease came about, how it was applied to various illnesses throughout the years, and why this theory has become so important in the field of medicine

Includes glossary and bibliographical references

Morgan, Sally

From microscopes to stem cell research; discovering regenerative medicine; [by] Sally Morgan. Heinemann Library 2006 64p il (Chain reactions) $34.29

Grades: 6 7 8 9   **616**

1. Stem cell research 2. Transplantation of organs, tissues, etc.

ISBN 1-4034-8836-3   LC 2006009973

This "provides information on stem cells and their uses, as well as some of the controversies surrounding them. Morgan begins with the discovery of cells by Robert Hooke in the early 1660s and concludes with an explanation of regenerative medicine and how stem-cell research has transformed the medical field. . . . The [book features] clear, straightforward writing and [a] bright and open [layout] with colorful photographs and illustrations on every spread." SLJ

Includes bibliographical references

Nardo, Don, 1947-
Cure quest; the science of stem cell research; by Don Nardo. Compass Point Books 2009 48p il (Headline science) lib bdg $27.93; pa $7.95
Grades: 5 6 7   **616**
1. Stem cell research
ISBN 978-0-7565-3371-7 (lib bdg); 0-7565-3371-6 (lib bdg); 978-0-7565-3374-8 (pa); 0-7565-3374-0 (pa)
         LC 2008-5738
Explains the science behind stem cell research.
"Color photos and graphics provide visual information; a timeline is helpful to find fast facts, and the Facthound Web site provides student with additional information." Libr Media Connect
Includes glossary and bibliographical references

Townsend, John, 1955-
Pox, pus & plague; a history of disease and infection; [by] John Townsend. Raintree 2005 c2006 56p il (Painful history of medicine) lib bdg $32.86; pa $9.90
Grades: 6 7 8 9   **616**
1. Diseases 2. Medicine—History 3. Epidemics
ISBN 1-4109-1333-3 (lib bdg); 1-4109-1338-4 (pa)
         LC 2004-14249
"Raintree freestyle"
Contents: Under attack; Ancient times; The Middle Ages; Epidemic; Secrets in the water; Great discoveries; Up to date
A history of disease and medicine from ancient times to the present
"Each page is dominated by black-and-white and color photographs or illustrations, often graphically gross. . . . This . . . is certain to attract browsers. . . . Basic facts are presented plainly, making the titles accessible to a wide range of researchers as well." SLJ
Includes glossary and bibliographical references

616.07   Pathology

Klosterman, Lorrie
Immune system; by Lorrie Klosterman. Marshall Cavendish Benchmark 2009 80p il (The amazing human body) $23.95
Grades: 6 7 8 9   **616.07**
1. Immune system
ISBN 978-0-7614-3054-4; 0-7614-3054-7
         LC 2007050439
"Illustrated with small but relatively revealing micro- and macro-photographs . . . this will inform upper middle-grade students on a wide range of biological topics." Booklist
Includes bibliographical references

McClafferty, Carla Killough, 1958-
The head bone's connected to the neck bone; the weird, wacky, and wonderful x-ray. Farrar, Straus & Giroux 2001 135p il $17
Grades: 7 8 9 10   **616.07**
1. X-rays
ISBN 0-374-32908-7   LC 00-140218

"Beginning with Roentgen's radiation experiments and concluding with high-tech potential for the future, this volume chronicles the history of X-rays. While reading like a novel, it is filled with excellent reference material as well." Sci Child
Includes glossary and bibliographical references

Sherrow, Victoria
Medical imaging; [by] Victoria Sherrow. Marshall Cavendish Benchmark 2007 127p il (Great inventions) lib bdg $39.93
Grades: 7 8 9 10   **616.07**
1. Diagnostic imaging
ISBN 978-0-7614-2231-0; 0-7614-2231-5
         LC 2006003229
"An examination of the origins, history, development, and societal impact of various medical-imaging devices, from X-rays to the MRI" Publisher's note
Includes glossary and bibliographical references

616.1   Diseases of cardiovascular system

Baldwin, Carol
Sickle cell disease. Heinemann Lib. 2003 32p il (Health matters) lib bdg $22.79
Grades: 4 5 6   **616.1**
1. Sickle cell anemia
ISBN 1-4034-0252-3   LC 2001-7975
Contents: What is sickle cell disease?; What causes sickle cell disease?; Diagnosing sickle cell disease; Treating sickle cell disease; Classmates with sickle cell disease; How you can help; Visiting friends with sickle cell disease; Sickle cell success stories
This "inviting, colorful [book] will attract students who need a clear, readable introduction to [sickle cell disease]." SLJ
Includes glossary and bibliographical references

Haney, Johannah
Heart disease. Benchmark Books 2005 63p il (Health alert) $31.36
Grades: 4 5 6 7   **616.1**
1. Heart diseases
ISBN 978-0-7614-1801-6; 0-7614-1801-6
         LC 2004-5974
Discusses heart disease, including what it is like to have the disease, the history and research, and how people live with it.
"Clear archival black-and-white and color photos and photomicrographs support and extend the text." Horn Book Guide
Includes glossary and bibliographical references

Jones, Phill, 1953-
Sickle cell disease; [by] Phill Jones. Chelsea House Pubs. 2008 143p il (Genes & disease) $35
Grades: 7 8 9 10   **616.1**
1. Sickle cell anemia
ISBN 978-0-7910-9587-4; 0-7910-9587-8
         LC 2008-4959

Jones, Phill, 1953-—*Continued*

Opens "with accounts of people who have [Sickle cell] disease . . . followed by information on history, symptoms, variations, diagnosis, treatments, and research. . . . Chapters devoted to current genetic research and therapies can become dense as they introduce complex topics but photos, diagrams and charts help to clarify the details. . . . Controversial issues . . . are introduced fairly." SLJ

Includes glossary and bibliographical references

Raabe, Michelle

Hemophilia. Chelsea House Publishers 2008 133p il (Genes & disease) lib bdg $35

Grades: 7 8 9 10   **616.1**

1. Hemophilia

ISBN 978-0-7910-9648-2 (lib bdg); 0-7910-9648-3 (lib bdg)   LC 2008-4897

This book opens "with accounts of people who have [Hemophilia] . . . followed by information on history, symptoms, variations, diagnosis, treatments, and research. . . . Chapters devoted to current genetic research and therapies can become dense as they introduce complex topics but photos, diagrams and charts help to clarify the details. . . . Controversial issues . . . are introduced fairly." SLJ

Includes glossary and bibliographical references

Silverstein, Alvin

Heart disease; [by] Alvin & Virginia Silverstein & Laura Silverstein Nunn. Twenty-First Century Books 2006 112p il (Twenty-first century medical library) lib bdg $27.93 *

Grades: 8 9 10 11 12   **616.1**

1. Heart diseases

ISBN 0-7613-3420-3   LC 2005-04161

"The authors explain the causes, methods of prevention, and treatment of heart disease in an accessible and interesting way. Terms and procedures are clearly explained. Various chapters deal effectively with everything from how the heart works to current repairs for broken hearts to the future of cardiology." SLJ

Includes bibliographical references

The sickle cell anemia update; [by] Alvin and Virginia Silverstein, and Laura Silverstein Nunn. Enslow Publishers 2006 112p il (Disease update) lib bdg $31.93 *

Grades: 5 6 7 8   **616.1**

1. Sickle cell anemia

ISBN 0-7660-2479-2   LC 2005018727

This describes the history, diagnosis, treatment, prevention, and future of sickle cell anemia.

Includes glossary and bibliographical references

616.2   Diseases of respiratory system

Asthma information for teens; edited by Karen Bellenir. Omnigraphics 2005 386p il (Teen health series) $65 *

Grades: 7 8 9 10 11 12   **616.2**

1. Asthma

ISBN 0-7808-0770-7

"Health tips about managing asthma and related concerns including facts about asthma causes, triggers, symptoms, diagnosis, and treatment." Title page

"Although this volume is nearly 400 pages long, it is so clearly written and well organized that even hesitant readers will be able to find the facts they need, whether for reports or for personal information. . . . A succinct but complete resource." SLJ

Berger, William E.

Living with asthma; by William E. Berger. Facts on File 2007 183p (Teen's guides) lib bdg $34.95; pa $14.95

Grades: 7 8 9 10 11   **616.2**

1. Asthma

ISBN 978-0-8160-6483-0 (lib bdg); 0-8160-6483-0 (lib bdg); 978-0-8160-7560-7 (pa); 0-8160-7560-3 (pa)   LC 2007003664

Examines asthma and provides teens with the information they need to understand it.

"There is a great directory of referral and online resources in the appendix. Although there are no illustrations, the text is appealing, well-organized, and accessible for the teen reader." Voice Youth Advocates

Includes glossary

Bjorklund, Ruth

Asthma. Benchmark Books 2005 64p il (Health alert) $28.50 *

Grades: 4 5 6 7   **616.2**

1. Asthma

ISBN 0-7614-1803-2   LC 2004-5976

The author explains "the causes, physiology, treatments, and complications associated with [asthma]. The [book is] well organized. . . . The photos are colorful and . . . some are startling." SLJ

Includes bibliographical references

Hicks, Terry Allan

The common cold. Marshall Cavendish Benchmark 2005 64p il (Health alert) $31.36

Grades: 4 5 6 7   **616.2**

1. Cold (Disease)

ISBN 978-0-7614-1913-6; 0-7614-1913-6   LC 2005-4999

"Discusses the common cold and its effects on people and society." Publisher's note

"Clear archival photos and photomicrographs support the text." Horn Book Guide

Includes glossary and bibliographical references

Hoffmann, Gretchen

The flu; [by] Gretchen Hoffmann. Marshall Cavendish Benchmark 2007 64p il (Health alert) lib bdg $31.36

Grades: 4 5 6 7   **616.2**

1. Influenza

ISBN 978-0-7614-2208-2; 0-7614-2208-0   LC 2006011980

Hoffmann, Gretchen—*Continued*
"Explores the history, causes, symptoms, treatments, and future of different types of influenza." Publisher's note
Includes glossary and bibliographical references

Silverstein, Alvin
The asthma update; [by] Alvin and Virginia Silverstein, and Laura Silverstein Nunn. Enslow Publishers 2006 128p il (Disease update) lib bdg $31.93 *
Grades: 5 6 7 8   **616.2**
  1. Asthma
  ISBN 0-7660-2482-2   LC 2005-18728
This describes the history, causes, diagnosis, treatment, prevention, and future of asthma.
This "provides a clearly written, well-organized, and well-documented account of a disease that is increasingly prevalent among young people." Booklist
Includes glossary and bibliographical references

The flu and pneumonia update; [by] Alvin and Virginia Silverstein, and Laura Silverstein Nunn. 1st ed. Enslow Publishers 2006 104p il (Disease update) lib bdg $31.93 *
Grades: 5 6 7 8   **616.2**
  1. Influenza 2. Pneumonia
  ISBN 0-7660-2480-6   LC 2005005988
This "provides a clear idea of the etiology, common symptoms, and treatment of both influenza and its secondary bacterial infection, pneumonia. The tone is serious but reassuring as the authors discuss the great flu epidemic of 1918, then go on to consider the nature of both illnesses and what readers can do to prevent or minimize effects." Booklist
Includes glossary and bibliographical references

The tuberculosis update; [by] Alvin and Virginia Silverstein, and Laura Silverstein Nunn. Enslow Elementary 2006 112p il (Disease update) $31.93 *
Grades: 5 6 7 8   **616.2**
  1. Tuberculosis
  ISBN 0-7660-2481-4   LC 2005-05989
This covers the "history, transmission, symptoms, diagnosis, treatment, current advances, and potential outbreaks [of tuberculosis]. . . . [It includes] numerous high-quality color illustrations and diagrams, informational sidebars highlighting important facts and statistics." SLJ
Includes bibliographical references

Smith, Terry L., 1944-
Asthma; [by] Terry L. Smith. Chelsea House 2008 128p il (Genes & disease) lib bdg $35
Grades: 7 8 9 10   **616.2**
  1. Asthma
  ISBN 978-0-7910-9663-5 (lib bdg); 0-7910-9663-7 (lib bdg)   LC 2008-44774
This book opens "with accounts of people who have [asthma] . . . followed by information on history, symptoms, variations, diagnosis, treatments, and research. . . .

Chapters devoted to current genetic research and therapies can become dense as they introduce complex topics but photos, diagrams and charts help to clarify the details. . . . Controversial issues . . . are introduced fairly." SLJ
Includes glossary and bibliographical references

Yancey, Diane
Tuberculosis. rev ed. Twenty-First Century Books 2008 128p il (Twenty-first century medical library) lib bdg $30.60
Grades: 8 9 10 11 1 2   **616.2**
  1. Tuberculosis
  ISBN 978-0-8225-9190-0 (lib bdg); 0-8225-9190-1 (lib bdg)   LC 2007-30486
The author begins this book with a history of tuberculosis, "tracing evidence of it back to the Neolithic Age and then explores the variety of treatments used to combat it. . . . The three personal cases related are from three different socioeconomic situations. Good-quality, black-and-white photos appear throughout." SLJ [review of 2001 edition]
Includes bibliographical references

Zonderman, Jon
Legionnaires' disease; [by] Jon Zonderman and Laurel Shader. Chelsea House Publishers 2006 79p il (Deadly diseases and epidemics) $31.95
Grades: 7 8 9 10   **616.2**
  1. Legionnaires' disease
  ISBN 0-7910-8885-5   LC 2005026622
This describes the history, diagnosis and treatment of Legionnaire's disease.
Includes glossary and bibliographical references

616.3   Diseases of digestive system

Bjorklund, Ruth
Cystic fibrosis; by Ruth Bjorklund. Marshall Cavendish Benchmark 2009 64p il (Health alert) $22.95
Grades: 4 5 6 7   **616.3**
  1. Cystic fibrosis
  ISBN 978-0-7614-2912-8; 0-7614-2912-3   LC 2007-46674
"Provides comprehensive information on the causes, treatment, and history of cystic fibrosis." Publisher's note

Ford, Jean
Diseases and disabilities caused by weight problems; the overloaded body. Mason Crest 2006 104p il (Obesity: modern-day epidemic) $23.95
Grades: 7 8 9 10   **616.3**
  1. Obesity
  ISBN 978-1-59084-944-6; 1-59084-944-2   LC 2004-26240
This describes the many health risks obesity and how its health complications are adding up for our society.
Includes glossary and bibliographical references

Fredericks, Carrie
Obesity. Reference Point Press 2008 104p il map (Compact research) lib bdg $24.95
Grades: 8 9 10 11 12   616.3
1. Obesity
ISBN 978-1-60152-040-1 (lib bdg); 1-60152-040-9 (lib bdg)   LC 2007-42183
Examines the topic of obesity in a format with objective overviews, primary source quotes, illustrated facts, and statistics.
"Both general readers and serious researchers will find something useful in this volume. It facilitates research for less-motivated students and supplies excellent information for better researchers." SLJ
Includes bibliographical references

Giddings, Sharon
Cystic fibrosis; [by] Sharon Giddings. Chelsea House 2009 128p il (Genes & disease) lib bdg $35
Grades: 7 8 9 10   616.3
1. Cystic fibrosis
ISBN 978-0-7910-9694-9 (lib bdg); 0-7910-9694-7 (lib bdg)   LC 2008-44771
This book opens "with accounts of people who have [Cystic fibrosis] . . . followed by information on history, symptoms, variations, diagnosis, treatments, and research. . . . Chapters devoted to current genetic research and therapies can become dense as they introduce complex topics but photos, diagrams and charts help to clarify the details. . . . Controversial issues . . . are introduced fairly." SLJ
Includes glossary and bibliographical references

Hicks, Terry Allan
Obesity; by Terry Allan Hicks. Marshall Cavendish Benchmark 2009 63p il (Health alert) $22.95
Grades: 4 5 6 7   616.3
1. Obesity
ISBN 978-0-7614-2911-1; 0-7614-2911-5
                                LC 2007-31246
"Provides comprehensive information on the causes, treatment, and history of obesity." Publisher's note
Includes glossary

Monroe, Judy
Cystic fibrosis. LifeMatters 2002 64p il (Perspectives on disease and illness) lib bdg $23.93
Grades: 7 8 9 10   616.3
1. Cystic fibrosis
ISBN 0-7368-1026-9   LC 00-12612
This defines cystic fibrosis and discusses how it affects the body, its diagnosis and treatment and living with the disease
"Simple and well-organized." Book Rep
Includes glossary and bibliographical references

Obesity; Eric Dillon, book editor. Greenhaven Press 2006 c2007 128p il (Issues that concern you) lib bdg $33.70
Grades: 7 8 9 10 11 12   616.3
1. Obesity
ISBN 0-7377-2194-4 (lib bdg); 978-0-7377-2194-2 (lib bdg)   LC 2006041071
"This title looks at obesity and presents various views on the health risks, causes, and severity of the problem. Colorful photos of real people help to intensify the reality of the issue. . . . This is a well-written, high-quality resource." SLJ
Includes bibliographical references

Obesity; Tom and Gena Metcalf, editors. 1st ed. Thomson / Gale 2008 136p il (Perspectives on diseases & disorders) lib bdg $34.95
Grades: 7 8 9 10   616.3
1. Obesity
ISBN 978-0-7377-3873-5 (lib bdg); 0-7377-3873-1 (lib bdg)   LC 2007037470
"This book explains what obesity is, provides insight into its causes, and takes a serious look at why it's becoming such an epidemic. Accounts by people who have firsthand experience dealing with being overweight add value to the book. The controversial side of the topic is also touched upon. . . . 'Fast Fact' sections, photographs, diagrams, charts, and graphs make the information easy to digest." SLJ
Includes bibliographical references

616.4 Diseases of hematopoietic, lymphatic, glandular systems Diseases of endocrine system

Allman, Toney, 1947-
Diabetes. Chelsea House Pubs. 2008 136p il (Genes & disease) lib bdg $35
Grades: 7 8 9 10   616.4
1. Diabetes
ISBN 978-0-7910-9585-0 (lib bdg); 0-7910-9585-1 (lib bdg)   LC 2008-01195
This "well-written book . . . [discusses] diabetes, its treatments, genetic variations contributing to the disease, and the prospects for a cure. The narrative starts with the diagnosis of diabetes and follows with seven chapters." Sci Books Films
Includes glossary and bibliographical references

Diabetes information for teens; edited by Sandra Augustyn Lawton. Omnigraphics 2006 410p il (Teen health series) $65 *
Grades: 8 9 10 11 12   616.4
1. Diabetes
ISBN 0-7808-0811-8   LC 2005036597
"Health tips about managing diabetes and preventing related complications including information about insulin, glucose control, healthy eating, physical activity, and learning to live with diabetes." Title page
"Students dealing with their own diabetes or that of a friend or family member or those writing reports on the topic will find this a valuable resource." SLJ
Includes bibliographical references

Haney, Johannah
Juvenile diabetes. Benchmark Books 2005 63p
il (Health alert) lib bdg $28.50
Grades: 4 5 6 7   **616.4**
1. Diabetes
ISBN 0-7614-1798-2   LC 2004-5969
The author explains "the causes, physiology, treatments, and complications associated with [juvenile diabetes]. The [book is] well organized. . . . The photos are colorful and . . . some are startling." SLJ
Includes bibliographical references

Hyde, Margaret Oldroyd, 1917-
Diabetes; [by] Margaret O. Hyde & Elizabeth
H. Forsyth. Franklin Watts 2003 96p il lib bdg
$25
Grades: 7 8 9 10   **616.4**
1. Diabetes
ISBN 0-531-12209-3   LC 2002-38033
Discusses the causes of diabetes, who is likely to have this condition, how to prevent diabetic problems, and the search for a cure
"A useful, well-written resource." SLJ
Includes glossary and bibliographical references

Sheen, Barbara, 1949-
Diabetes. Lucent Bks. 2003 112p il (Diseases
and disorders) lib bdg $27.45
Grades: 7 8 9 10   **616.4**
1. Diabetes
ISBN 1-59018-244-8   LC 2002-13620
Contents: What is diabetes?; Diagnosis and treatment; Alternative and complementary treatment; Living with diabetes; What the future holds
This explains what diabetes is, its diagnosis and treatment, living with the disease, and prospects for the future
This is "well written and well organized." SLJ
Includes glossary and bibliographical references

Silverstein, Alvin
The diabetes update; [by] Alvin and Virginia
Silverstein, and Laura Silverstein Nunn. 1st ed.
Enslow Publishers 2006 128p il (Disease update)
lib bdg $31.93 *
Grades: 5 6 7 8   **616.4**
1. Diabetes
ISBN 0-7660-2483-0   LC 2005-05991
This describes the symptoms and causes of diabetes, the history of the disease, diagnosis and treatments, and future possibilities.
Includes glossary and bibliographical references

616.5 Diseases of integument

Skin health information for teens; health tips about
dermatological concerns and skin cancer risks;
edited by Robert Aquinas McNally.
Omnigraphics 2003 429p il (Teen health series)
$58 *
Grades: 7 8 9 10 11 12   **616.5**
ISBN 0-7808-0446-5   LC 2003-53631

"Including facts about acne, warts, hives, and other conditions and lifestyle choices, such as tanning, tattooing, and piercing, that affect the skin, nails, scalp, and hair." Title page
"This volume bridges the gap between books with fashion-magazine appeal and serious medical reference works. . . . Well organized and comprehensive in coverage." SLJ

616.7 Diseases of musculoskeletal system

Gray, Susan Heinrichs
Living with juvenile rheumatoid arthritis.
Child's World 2003 32p il (Living well) lib bdg
$25.64
Grades: 5 6 7 8   **616.7**
1. Arthritis
ISBN 1-56766-104-1   LC 2002-2870
This title "leads off with an introduction to a young person who has [juvenile rheumatoid arthritis]. Subsequent chapters explain the physiology of the illness, what causes it, and what it's like to live with it. [The concluding section looks] at possible treatments and potential cures. [The text is] clear and simple, double spaced, and punctuated by colorful exemplary photos of kids dealing with the disease." SLJ
Includes glossary and bibliographical references

Hoffmann, Gretchen
Osteoporosis; [by] Gretchen Hoffmann. Marshall
Cavendish Benchmark 2007 c2008 64p il (Health
alert) lib bdg $21.95
Grades: 4 5 6 7   **616.7**
1. Osteoporosis
ISBN 978-0-7614-2702-5   LC 2007008787
This describes what it is like to have osteoporosis, what it is, its history and its diagnosis and treatment
Includes glossary and bibliographical references

616.8 Diseases of nervous system and mental disorders

Abramovitz, Melissa
Lou Gehrig's disease. Gale 2006 112p il
(Diseases and disorders) $31.20
Grades: 7 8 9 10   **616.8**
1. Amyotrophic lateral sclerosis
ISBN 1-59018-676-1
"A look at the degenerative and devastating affliction, amyotrophic lateral sclerosis (ALS), commonly known as Lou Gehrig's disease. The book answers important questions about causes, symptoms, diagnosis, and advances in treatment." SLJ
Includes bibliographical references

Bjorklund, Ruth
Cerebral palsy. Marshall Cavendish Benchmark
2007 64p il (Health alert) lib bdg $31.36 *
Grades: 4 5 6 7   **616.8**
1. Cerebral palsy
ISBN 978-0-7614-2209-9; 0-7614-2209-9 (lib bdg)
LC 2006-15818
"Explores the history, causes, symptoms, treatments,
and future of cerebral palsy." Publisher's note
Includes glossary and bibliographical references

Epilepsy. Marshall Cavendish Benchmark 2007
63p il (Health alert) lib bdg $21.95 *
Grades: 4 5 6 7   **616.8**
1. Epilepsy
ISBN 978-0-7614-2206-8; 0-7614-2206-4 (lib bdg)
LC 2006-15816
"Explores the history, causes, symptoms, treatments,
and future of epilepsy and seizure disorders." Publisher's
note
Includes glossary and bibliographical references

Borda, Cynthia
Alzheimer's disease and memory drugs. Chelsea
House Publishers 2006 96p il (Drugs, the straight
facts) lib bdg $30
Grades: 8 9 10 11 12   **616.8**
1. Alzheimer's disease
ISBN 0-7910-8555-4   LC 2005-32189
This "covers the history of [Alzheimer's disease], the
symptoms that distinguish it from normal memory loss,
diagnosis, and treatment of the disease. Details of the
current drug treatments available are provided, followed
by descriptions of potential future treatments." Publisher's note
Includes glossary and bibliographical references

Brill, Marlene Targ, 1945-
Alzheimer's disease. Benchmark Books 2005
64p il (Health alert) $28.50
Grades: 4 5 6 7   **616.8**
1. Alzheimer's disease
ISBN 0-7614-1799-0   LC 2004-6528
Contents: What is it like to have Alzheimer's disease;
Defining the disease; The history of Alzheimer's disease;
Coping with Alzheimer's disease; What treatments help
slow Alzheimer's disease
The author explains "the causes, physiology, treat-
ments, and complications associated with [Alzheimer's
disease]. The [book is] well organized. . . . The photos
are colorful and . . . some are startling, including the
brain scans of a patient with Alzheimer's." SLJ
Includes bibliographical references

Multiple sclerosis; [by] Marlene Targ Brill.
Marshall Cavendish Benchmark 2007 c2008 64p il
(Health alert) lib bdg $21.95
Grades: 4 5 6 7   **616.8**
1. Multiple sclerosis
ISBN 978-0-7614-2699-8   LC 2007008789
This describes what it is like to have mulitiple sclero-
sis, what it is, its history, and living with the disease.
Includes glossary and bibliographical references

Tourette syndrome. 21st Cent. Bks. (Brookfield)
2002 112p il (Twenty-first century medical library)
lib bdg $26.90 *
Grades: 8 9 10 11 12   **616.8**
1. Tourette syndrome
ISBN 0-7613-2101-2   LC 2001-41747
Examines the tic disorder known as Tourette syndrome, its symptoms and manifestations, how it can be
controlled and treated, and, through case studies, what it
is like to live with Tourette's
The author covers "most of the information report
writers would be seeking and a section about home and
school is especially helpful to anyone trying to understand the problems faced by a person with this disorder."
Book Rep
Includes glossary and bibliographical references

Burnfield, Alexander
Multiple sclerosis; [by] Alexander Burnfield.
Heinemann Library 2003 56p il (Just the facts) lib
bdg $31.36 *
Grades: 5 6 7 8   **616.8**
1. Multiple sclerosis
ISBN 1-4034-4602-4   LC 2003-10913
Contents: Multiple sclerosis; What is MS?; History of
MS; Types of MS; Diagnosis and investigations; Symp-
toms of MS; Who gets MS?; How does MS develop?;
Managing MS; Treating MS; Living with MS; MS fa-
tigue; Other problems; MS and the family; MS and society; Will a cure be found?; Information and advice
Describes the different types of MS, their symptoms,
why this disease can be difficult to diagnose, various
types of treatment, and other issues related to multiple
sclerosis.
This is "well written and organized, and [includes]
factual information without overwhelming readers." SLJ
Includes bibliographical references

Colligan, L. H.
Sleep disorders; by L.H. Colligan. Marshall
Cavendish Benchmark 2009 64p il (Health alert)
$22.95
Grades: 4 5 6 7   **616.8**
1. Sleep disorders
ISBN 978-0-7614-2913-5; 0-7614-2913-1
"Provides comprehensive information on the causes,
treatment, and history of sleep disorders." Publisher's
note
Includes glossary

Elliot-Wright, Susan
Epilepsy. Raintree 2004 64p il (Health issues)
lib bdg $28.56
Grades: 7 8 9 10   **616.8**
1. Epilepsy
ISBN 0-7398-6423-8
Examines the causes, symptoms, and treatment of epilepsy, a neurological condition that can lead to seizures.
"Filled with color photos, text boxes, and sidebars,
[this volume is] likely to attract browsers. . . . Students
writing short reports will find [this title] useful." SLJ

Esherick, Joan
The journey toward recovery; youth with brain injury. Mason Crest Publishers 2004 127p il (Youth with special needs) $24.95
Grades: 7 8 9 10   **616.8**
1. Brain damaged children
ISBN 1-59084-734-2   LC 2003-18640
Through the story of Jerome, a teenager who suffers a traumatic brain injury from a bike accident, this book discusses different "forms of brain injury; how these injuries affect people's lives; and how schools, doctors, and lawmakers are helping youth with this form of special need." Publisher's note
Includes glossary and bibliographical references

Freedman, Jeri
Tay-Sachs disease; [by] Jeri Freedman. Chelsea House 2009 128p il (Genes & disease) lib bdg $35
Grades: 7 8 9 10   **616.8**
1. Tay-Sachs disease
ISBN 978-0-7910-9634-5 (lib bdg); 0-7910-9634-3 (lib bdg)   LC 2008-44770
This book opens "with accounts of people who have [Tay-Sachs] disease . . . followed by information on history, symptoms, variations, diagnosis, treatments, and research. . . . Chapters devoted to current genetic research and therapies can become dense as they introduce complex topics but photos, diagrams and charts help to clarify the details. . . . Controversial issues . . . are introduced fairly." SLJ
Includes glossary and bibliographical references

Gay, Kathlyn, 1930-
Epilepsy; the ultimate teen guide; [by] Kathlyn Gay and Sean McGarrahan. Scarecrow Press 2002 103p il (It happened to me) lib bdg $32.50; pa $12.95 *
Grades: 7 8 9 10 11 12   **616.8**
1. Epilepsy
ISBN 0-8108-4339-0 (lib bdg); 978-0-8108-4339-4 (lib bdg); 978-0-8108-5835-0 (pa); 0-8108-5835-5 (pa)
LC 2002-4718
Contents: What's epilepsy; Fact or folklore?; What's happening?; Diagnosis and treatment; Surgery for epilepsy; Living with epilepsy; School and job issues; Sports and recreation; The female factor; Finding a cure
The authors explain the various forms epilepsy takes, the history of the disease, folklore about it, and its diagnosis and treatment
"An excellent look at epilepsy and its impact on diagnosed teens, their families, friends, and communities. . . . Readable, well organized, and well documented." SLJ
Includes glossary and bibliographical references

Goldstein, Natalie
Parkinson's disease. Chelsea House 2008 128p il (Genes & diseases) lib bdg $35
Grades: 7 8 9 10   **616.8**
1. Parkinson's disease
ISBN 978-0-7910-9584-3; 0-7910-9584-3
LC 2008-10494

This book opens "with accounts of people who have [Parkinson's] disease . . . followed by information on history, symptoms, variations, diagnosis, treatments, and research. . . . Chapters devoted to current genetic research and therapies can become dense as they introduce complex topics but photos, diagrams and charts help to clarify the details. . . . Controversial issues . . . are introduced fairly." SLJ
Includes glossary and bibliographical references

Goodfellow, Gregory
Epilepsy. Lucent Bks. 2001 95p il (Diseases and disorders) lib bdg $27.45
Grades: 7 8 9 10 11 12   **616.8**
1. Epilepsy
ISBN 1-56006-701-2   LC 00-8657
Discusses the causes, diagnosis, and treatment of epilepsy, the types of seizures, and the challenges of living with the disease
Includes bibliographical references

Hains, Bryan C.
Brain disorders; [by] Bryan Hains. Chelsea House Publishers 2006 122p il (Gray matter) $32.95
Grades: 8 9 10 11 12   **616.8**
1. Brain—Diseases
ISBN 0-7910-8513-9   LC 2005015851
This "begins with a chapter on Alzheimer's disease. The book includes the first description of the symptoms by Alois Alzheimer, the anatomy and physiology associated with the disorder, and current understandings of Alzheimer's. Other chapters on Parkinson's, Huntington's, multiple sclerosis, stroke, migraine, and brain tumors follow a similar pattern. The volumes in this series are written by neuroscientists and provide in-depth explanations suitable for teachers or highly motivated students. But there is also enough story and personal information to be useful to the more casual reader." Voice Youth Advocates
Includes glossary and bibliographical references

Kelly, Evelyn B.
Alzheimer's disease. Chelsea House Publishers 2008 126p il (Genes & disease) lib bdg $35
Grades: 7 8 9 10   **616.8**
1. Alzheimer's disease
ISBN 978-0-7910-9588-1; 0-7910-9588-6
LC 2007-51319
This book opens "with accounts of people who have [Alzheimer's] disease . . . followed by information on history, symptoms, variations, diagnosis, treatments, and research. . . . Chapters devoted to current genetic research and therapies can become dense as they introduce complex topics but photos, diagrams and charts help to clarify the details. . . . Controversial issues . . . are introduced fairly." SLJ
Includes glossary and bibliographical references

Klosterman, Lorrie

Meningitis; [by] Lorrie Klosterman. Marshall
Cavendish Benchmark 2007 64p il (Health alert)
lib bdg $31.36 *

Grades: 4 5 6 7   **616.8**
1. Meningitis
ISBN 978-0-7614-2211-2; 0-7614-2211-0
LC 2006015819

"Explores the history, causes, symptoms, treatments,
and future of different types of meningitis." Publisher's
note

Includes glossary and bibliographical references

Landau, Elaine

Alzheimer's disease; a forgotten life. Franklin
Watts 2005 112p il (Health and human disease)
$26 *

Grades: 7 8 9 10   **616.8**
1. Alzheimer's disease
ISBN 0-531-16755-0   LC 2005-01736

"Landau offers a well-researched, clearly written presentation on Alzheimer's and its effects. Topics discussed
include diagnostic tools, possible causes, symptoms,
stages, medications, research, and the problems faced by
caregivers." Booklist

Includes glossary and bibliographical references

Petreycik, Rick

Headaches; [by] Rick Petreycik. Marshall
Cavendish Benchmark 2007 64p il (Health alert)
lib bdg $31.36 *

Grades: 4 5 6 7   **616.8**
1. Headache
ISBN 978-0-7614-2210-5; 0-7614-2210-2
LC 2006015815

"Explores the history, causes, symptoms, treatments,
and future of different types of headaches." Publisher's
note

Includes glossary and bibliographical references

Routh, Kristina, 1961-

Meningitis; [by] Kristina Routh. Heinemann
Library 2004 56p il (Just the facts) $23

Grades: 5 6 7 8   **616.8**
1. Meningitis
ISBN 1-4034-5146-X   LC 2003-22569

Provides an overview of meningitis, describing what it
is, the history of the disease, what it is like to live with
meningitis, and some of the available treatments.

This is "well written and substantive without being
overly technical." SLJ

Includes bibliographical references

Silverstein, Alvin

Parkinson's disease; [by] Alvin and Virginia
Silverstein and Laura Silverstein Nunn. Enslow
Pubs. 2001 128p il (Diseases and people) lib bdg
$26.60 *

Grades: 7 8 9 10   **616.8**
1. Parkinson's disease
ISBN 0-7660-1593-9   LC 00-12073

This describes the history of Parkinson's disease, its
causes, symptoms, diagnosis and treatment, the disease
and society, and research

Includes glossary and bibliographical references

616.85 Miscellaneous diseases of nervous system and mental disorders

Anorexia; Karen F. Balkin, book editor.
Greenhaven Press 2005 110p (At issue) lib bdg
$28.70; pa $19.95

Grades: 8 9 10 11 12   **616.85**
1. Anorexia nervosa
ISBN 0-7377-2178-2 (lib bdg); 0-7377-2179-0 (pa)
LC 2004-61693

Replaces the edition published 2001 under the
editorship of Daniel A. Leone

This book "considers the physical, social, and psychological aspects of this puzzling disorder and includes
. . . viewpoints exploring anorexia in men, older women,
and women throughout the world." Publisher's note

Includes bibliographical references

Bingham, Jane

Eating disorders; by Jane Bingham. Gareth
Stevens Pub. 2009 48p il (Emotional health issues)
lib bdg $31

Grades: 6 7 8 9   **616.85**
1. Eating disorders
ISBN 978-0-8368-9200-0; 0-8368-9200-3
LC 2008-825

First published 2008 in the United Kingdom

This book about eating disorders has "clear language
and explanations. . . . [It is] suitable for fact-finding
missions, but the abundant graphics and case studies are
likely to draw in browsers as well. Throughout, unfamiliar vocabulary is highlighted in bold and explained in
context and in the glossary. . . . Fact boxes and case
study sidebars add information." SLJ

Includes glossary and bibliographical references

Stress and depression; [by] Jane Bingham.
Gareth Stevens 2009 48p il (Emotional health
issues) lib bdg $31

Grades: 6 7 8 9   **616.85**
1. Stress (Psychology) 2. Depression (Psychology)
ISBN 978-0-8368-9203-1 (lib bdg); 0-8368-9203-8 (lib
bdg)   LC 2008-5237

First published 2008 in the United Kingdom

This book about stress and depression has "clear language and explanations. . . . [It is] suitable for fact-
finding missions, but the abundant graphics and case
studies are likely to draw in browsers as well. Throughout, unfamiliar vocabulary is highlighted in bold and explained in context and in the glossary. . . . Fact boxes
and case study sidebars add information." SLJ

Includes glossary and bibliographical references

Bjorklund, Ruth

Eating disorders. Marshall Cavendish Benchmark 2005 c2006 64p il (Health alert) $31.36

Grades: 4 5 6 7 **616.85**

1. Eating disorders

ISBN 978-0-7614-1914-3; 0-7614-1914-4

"Discusses eating disorders and their effects on people and society." Publisher's note

"Clear archival photos and photomicrographs support the text." Horn Book Guide

Includes glossary and bibliographical references

Brill, Marlene Targ, 1945-

Autism; [by] Marlene Targ Brill. Marshall Cavendish Benchmark 2007 c2008 64p il (Health alert) lib bdg $21.95

Grades: 4 5 6 7 **616.85**

1. Autism

ISBN 978-0-7614-2700-1 LC 2007008786

This describes what it is like to have autism, what it is, its history, and living with the disease.

Includes glossary and bibliographical references

Down syndrome. Marshall Cavendish Benchmark 2007 64p il (Health alert) lib bdg $31.36 *

Grades: 4 5 6 7 **616.85**

1. Down syndrome

ISBN 978-0-7614-2207-5; 0-7614-2207-2 (lib bdg)

LC 2006-15817

"Explores the history, causes, symptoms, treatments, and future of Down syndrome." Publisher's note

Includes glossary and bibliographical references

Capaccio, George

ADD and ADHD; [by] George Capaccio. Marshall Cavendish Benchmark 2007 c2008 64p il (Health alert) lib bdg $21.95

Grades: 4 5 6 7 **616.85**

1. Attention deficit disorder

ISBN 978-0-7614-2705-6 LC 2007008790

This describes what it is like to have Attention Deficit Disorder or Attention Deficit Hyperactivity Disorder, what they are, their history, and living with the disorders.

Includes glossary and bibliographical references

Cobain, Bev, 1940-

When nothing matters anymore; a survival guide for depressed teens; edited by Elizabeth Verdick. rev and updated ed. Free Spirit Pub. 2007 146p il pa $14.95

Grades: 7 8 9 10 **616.85**

1. Depression (Psychology)

ISBN 978-1-57542-235-0 (pa); 1-57542-235-2 (pa)

LC 2006-36325

First published 1998

This book written for teens defines depression, describes the symptoms, and explains that depression is treatable

"This practical, reassuring book should be made available to all teens." Voice Youth Advocates

Includes bibliographical references

Connolly, Sucheta

Anxiety disorders; [by] Sucheta Connolly, David Simpson, Cynthia Petty. Chelsea House 2006 132p il (Psychological disorders) lib bdg $37.50 *

Grades: 8 9 10 11 12 **616.85**

1. Anxiety 2. Panic disorders 3. Phobias 4. Post-traumatic stress disorder

ISBN 0-7910-8543-0 LC 2006-4996

This describes the development, evaluation, and treatment of anxiety disorders including generalized anxiety, separation anxiety, social phobia, specific phobias, panic attacks, obsessive-compulsive disorder, and post-traumatic stress disorder.

"This book will be quite useful in helping adolescents deal with their anxieties." Sci Books Films

Includes glossary and bibliographical references

Corman, Catherine A.

Positively ADD; real success stories to inspire your dreams; [by] Catherine A. Corman and Edward M. Hallowell. Walker 2006 172p il $16.95; lib bdg $17.85 *

Grades: 8 9 10 11 12 **616.85**

1. Attention deficit disorder

ISBN 978-0-8027-8988-4; 0-8027-8988-9; 978-0-8027-8071-3 (lib bdg); 0-8027-8071-7 (lib bdg)

LC 2005037184

This "profiles 17 adults who began dealing with attention deficit disorder in childhood. Along with political strategist [James] Carville, subjects include a Pulitzer Prizewinning photographer, a major league pitcher, and a young Rhodes scholar. . . . [This is] an encouraging, helpful book for teens with ADD as well as for their parents, teachers, and friends." Booklist

Includes bibliographical references

Depression; Emma Carlson Berne, book editor. Greenhaven 2007 184p (Contemporary issues companion) $36.20; pa $24.95

Grades: 8 9 10 11 12 **616.85**

1. Depression (Psychology)

ISBN 978-0-7377-3645-8; 0-7377-3645-3; 978-0-7377-2451-6 (pa); 0-7377-2451-X (pa)

LC 2007-19643

First published 1999 under the editorship of Henny H. Kim

"Eighteen field specialists have each contributed an essay on topics as diverse as deep brain stimulation and alternative therapies. A chapter on antidepressants and their heavily debated effects concludes the book. Thoughtfully composed, this excellent introduction to a widely recognized condition contains an extensive bibliography and support organization contact list." Libr J

Includes bibliographical references

Eating disorders; Shasta Gaughen, book editor. Greenhaven Press 2004 154p (Contemporary issues companion) lib bdg $37.40; pa $25.95

Grades: 8 9 10 11 12 **616.85**

1. Eating disorders

ISBN 978-0-7377-1619-1 (lib bdg); 0-7377-1619-3 (lib bdg); 978-0-7377-1620-7 (pa); 0-7377-1620-7 (pa)

LC 2003-55107

First published 1999 under the editorship of Myra H. Immell

Eating disorders—*Continued*

This "anthology explores issues related to anorexia nervosa, bulimia, compulsive overeating, and other eating disorders. Contributing authors discuss the causes, effects, and available treatments for eating disorders." Publisher's note

Includes bibliographical references

Eating disorders information for teens; edited by Sandra Augustyn Lawton. 2nd ed. Omnigraphics 2009 377p il (Teen health series) $84 *

Grades: 8 9 10 11 12   **616.85**

1. Eating disorders

ISBN 978-0-7808-1044-0; 0-7808-1044-9

         LC 2008-49387

First published 2005

"Health tips about anorexia, bulimia, binge eating, and other eating disorders including information about risk factors, prevention, diagnosis, treatment, health consequences, and other related issues." Title page

"Provides basic consumer health information for teens about causes, prevention, and treatment of eating disorders, along with healthy eating tips. Includes index, resource information and recommendations for further reading." Publisher's note

"A solid addition for any nonfiction or reference collection." SLJ [review of 2005 edition]

Includes bibliographical references

Eating disorders: opposing viewpoints; Viqi Wagner, book editor. Greenhaven 2007 244p il lib bdg $36.20; pa $24.95

Grades: 8 9 10 11 12   **616.85**

1. Eating disorders

ISBN   978-0-7377-3348-8   (lib   bdg); 978-0-7377-3349-5 (pa)   LC 2007-7382

Replaces the edition published 2001 under the editorship of Jennifer A. Hurley

"Opposing viewpoints series"

This collection of essays offers various points of view about eating disorders.

Includes bibliographical references

Esherick, Joan

Diet and your emotions; the comfort food falsehood. Mason Crest Publishers 2006 104p il (Obesity: modern-day epidemic) $23.95

Grades: 7 8 9 10   **616.85**

1. Eating disorders 2. Weight loss 3. Body image

ISBN 978-1-59084-950-7; 1-59084-950-7

         LC 2004-19289

Discusses why people form certain relationships with food and what the consequences can be, what your body really needs to be healthy, and how to reevaluate food's role in your life to achieve nutritional and emotional balance.

Includes bibliographical references

Evans-Martin, Fay

Down syndrome; [by] F. Fay Evans-Martin. Chelsea House 2008 128p il (Genes & disease) lib bdg $35

Grades: 7 8 9 10   **616.85**

1. Down syndrome

ISBN 978-0-7910-9644-4 (lib bdg); 0-7910-9644-0 (lib bdg)   LC 2008-44773

This book opens "with accounts of people who have [Down syndrome] . . . followed by information on history, symptoms, variations, diagnosis, treatments, and research. . . . Chapters devoted to current genetic research and therapies can become dense as they introduce complex topics but photos, diagrams and charts help to clarify the details. . . . Controversial issues . . . are introduced fairly." SLJ

Includes glossary and bibliographical references

Favor, Lesli J.

Food as foe; nutrition and eating disorders. Marshall Cavendish Benchmark 2007 127p (Food and fitness) lib bdg $25.95

Grades: 7 8 9 10   **616.85**

1. Eating disorders 2. Nutrition

ISBN 978-0-7614-2553-3 (lib bdg); 0-7614-2553-5 (lib bdg)   LC 2006-101931

"Provides a basic, comprehensive introduction to eating disorders, including anorexia, bulimia, and binge eating, with a review of where to find help and how to make wise food choices to become healthy." Publisher's note

This "visually appealing and easy-to-read [volume is] definitely worth having. The information is up-to-date and the format is attractive." SLJ

Includes bibliographical references

Ford, Emily, 1979-

What you must think of me; a firsthand account of one teenager's experience with social anxiety disorder; by Emily Ford with Michael R. Liebowitz and Linda Wasmer Andrews. Oxford University Press 2007 xxi, 152p (Annenberg Foundation Trust at Sunnylands' adolescent mental health initiative) $30; pa $9.95 *

Grades: 7 8 9 10 11 12   **616.85**

1. Social phobia

ISBN   978-0-19-531302-4;   0-19-531302-X; 978-0-19-531303-1 (pa); 0-19-531303-8 (pa)

         LC 2006102285

"A professor of clinical psychiatry and a woman whose life has been adversely impacted by social anxiety disorder provide a unique view of the condition and its treatment in this slim volume. . . . Readers will find helpful charts throughout the book and an appendix loaded with further reading and contact information for advocacy groups. Thanks to its informative guide to diagnosis, suggestions for treatment and tips on dealing with the health care system, this is a must read for anyone who suffers from the disorder." Publ Wkly

Includes bibliographical references

Hyde, Margaret Oldroyd, 1917-

Stress 101; an overview for teens; by Margaret O. Hyde and Elizabeth H. Forsyth. TwentyFirst Century Books 2008 120p il (Teen overviews) lib bdg $26.60

Grades: 8 9 10 11 12 **616.85**

1. Stress (Psychology)

ISBN 978-0-82256-788-2 (lib bdg); 0-82256-788-1 (lib bdg) LC 2007027631

"Beginning with a brief history of stress from the time it was first identified, Hyde and Forsyth detail its effects on a young person's brain, heart, and immune system. . . . The writing is clear and informative. Interspersed with personal vignettes, the factual information is well organized and presented in small increments." SLJ

Includes bibliographical references

Hyman, Bruce M.

Obsessive-compulsive disorder; by Bruce M. Hyman and Cherry Pedrick. Twenty-First Century Books 2003 96p (The Twenty-first century medical library) $26.90 *

Grades: 7 8 9 10 **616.85**

1. Obsessive-compulsive disorder

ISBN 0-7613-2758-4 LC 2002-14252

Contents: What is OCD?; The symptoms of OCD; Treatment of OCD; The impact on family and friends; Living with OCD

Examines the anxiety disorder known as OCD, its symptoms and manifestations, how it can be controlled and treated, and, through case studies, what it is like to live with obsessive-compulsive disorder

"With little else written specifically for young adults on this topic—which has risen to prominence recently in the popular media—this will be useful to report writers as well as to those concerned about their own anxieties." Booklist

Includes glossary and bibliographical references

Landau, Elaine

Dyslexia; by Elaine Landau. Franklin Watts 2004 79p (Life balance) lib bdg $19.50; pa $6.95 *

Grades: 5 6 7 8 **616.85**

1. Dyslexia

ISBN 0-531-12217-4 (lib bdg); 0-531-16612-0 (pa) LC 2003-7142

Contents: Being dyslexic; Dyslexia; Getting help; Questions and answers about dyslexia

"Narration by dyslexics combines with an overview of the disorder to give readers an informative and thought-provoking look at this often misunderstood condition. Beginning with the struggles of a young student to cover for his difficulties, the book goes on to describe the various manifestations of dyslexia, therapies, and outcomes." SLJ

Includes glossary and bibliographical references

Levin, Judith, 1956-

Anxiety and panic attacks; [by] Judith Levin. Rosen Pub. 2008 48p il (Teen mental health) lib bdg $19.95

Grades: 7 8 9 10 **616.85**

1. Anxiety 2. Panic disorders

ISBN 978-1-4042-1797-3; 1-4042-1797-5 LC 2008-7144

This "volume offers a succinct discussion of mental disorders related to anxiety. . . . A vivid description of the causes and symptoms of panic attacks is followed up with a chapter suggesting ways to deal with these troubling events. . . . Color photos brighten this clearly written presentation." Booklist

Includes glossary and bibliographical references

Lynette, Rachel

Anorexia. Kidhaven Press 2006 48p il (Understanding diseases and disorders) $23.70

Grades: 4 5 6 **616.85**

1. Anorexia nervosa

ISBN 0-7377-3176-1

This book explains who is at risk for developing anorexia, possible causes, the physical and psychological effects of the disorder and how it is treated.

Includes glossary and bibliographical references

Miller, Allen R.

Living with anxiety disorders. Facts on File 2007 202p (Teen's guides) $34.95; pa $14.95

Grades: 7 8 9 10 **616.85**

1. Anxiety 2. Panic disorders 3. Phobias 4. Post-traumatic stress disorder

ISBN 978-0-8160-6344-4; 0-8160-6344-3; 978-0-8160-7559-1 (pa); 0-8160-7559-X (pa) LC 2007-553

This book "delineates the difference between an anxiety disorder and fear, suggests avenues for evaluation, describes therapies, and devotes a chapter each to social phobia, post-traumatic stress, generalized anxiety disorder, panic disorder, and specific phobias." Libr Media Connect

Includes glossary and bibliographical references

Living with depression. Facts on File 2007 202p (Teen's guides) lib bdg $34.95; pa $14.95

Grades: 7 8 9 10 **616.85**

1. Depression (Psychology)

ISBN 978-0-8160-6345-1 (lib bdg); 0-8160-6345-1 (lib bdg); 978-0-8160-7562-1 (pa); 0-8160-7562-X (pa) LC 2007-554

This "offers young adults concise information about depression and its treatments. . . . Chapters on treatments offer detailed information on psychotherapy, antidepressants, and self-help approaches such as diet, exercise, and stress management. . . . This book is a timely, useful resource." Booklist

Moragne, Wendy

Depression. 21st Cent. Bks. (Brookfield) 2001 112p il (Twenty-first century medical library) lib bdg $26.90

Grades: 7 8 9 10   **616.85**

1. Depression (Psychology)

ISBN 0-7613-1774-0   LC 00-36424

"Moragne presents the stories of seven teens diagnosed with different forms of depression, following the kids from the onset of their condition to successful treatment. Her profiles are respectful as well as thorough, including a surprising amount of information about symptoms, kinds of depression, causative factors, treatment . . . and the impact on one's self-esteem and personal relationships. . . . Difficult medical information . . . is presented clearly and without condescension." Booklist

Includes glossary and bibliographical references

Orr, Tamra

When the mirror lies; anorexia, bulimia, and other eating disorders. Franklin Watts 2007 144p il pa $17.95

Grades: 7 8 9 10   **616.85**

1. Eating disorders

ISBN 0-531-16791-7   LC 2005-25571

This "guide to the symptoms and effects of eating disorders also includes numerous case studies of various individuals who have experienced living with these challenging conditions. . . . Written in a reader-friendly tone, the book does a good job of presenting the psychological aspects of these diseases and of sympathizing with the young people who are wrestling with them." SLJ

Includes bibliographical references

Parks, Peggy J., 1951-

Down syndrome. ReferencePoint Press 2009 104p il (Compact research. Diseases and disorders) $25.95

Grades: 7 8 9 10 11 12   **616.85**

1. Down syndrome

ISBN 978-1-60152-065-4; 1-60152-065-4

LC 2008036644

"This up-to-date, excellent overview of Down syndrome addresses controversies and ethical issues associated with this genetic disorder. Parks also reports on current and potential scientific advances that may prevent it in the future and offer a better quality of life and opportunities for those born with it." SLJ

Includes bibliographical references

Pigache, Philippa

ADHD; [by] Philippa Pigache. Heinemann Library 2004 56p il (Just the facts) $23

Grades: 5 6 7 8   **616.85**

1. Attention deficit disorder

ISBN 1-4034-5142-7   LC 2003-22566

Provides an overview of attention-deficit hyperactivity disorder, describing what it is, the history of the disorder, what it is like to live with ADHD, and some of the available treatments.

"The well-organized information provides a good overview and a hopeful outlook." SLJ

Includes bibliographical references

Powell, Jillian

Self-harm and suicide; by Jillian Powell. Gareth Stevens 2009 48p il (Emotional health issues) lib bdg $31

Grades: 6 7 8 9   **616.85**

1. Self-mutilation 2. Suicide

ISBN 978-0-8368-9202-4; 0-8368-9202-X

LC 2008-4276

First published 2008 in the United Kingdom

This book about self-destructive behavior has "clear language and explanations. . . . [It is] suitable for fact-finding missions, but the abundant graphics and case studies are likely to draw in browsers as well. Throughout, unfamiliar vocabulary is highlighted in bold and explained in context and in the glossary. . . . Fact boxes and case study sidebars add information." SLJ

Includes glossary and bibliographical references

Routh, Kristina, 1961-

Down syndrome; [by] Kristina Routh. Heinemann Library 2004 56p il (Just the facts) $23

Grades: 5 6 7 8   **616.85**

1. Down syndrome

ISBN 1-4034-5145-1   LC 2003-22568

Provides an overview of Down's syndrome, describing what it is, the history of this disorder, what it is like to live with Down's syndrome, and some of the available treatments

This is "well written and substantive without being overly technical." SLJ

Roy, Jennifer Rozines

Depression. Benchmark Books 2005 64p il (Health alert) lib bdg $28.50 *

Grades: 4 5 6 7   **616.85**

1. Depression (Psychology)

ISBN 0-7614-1800-8   LC 2004-5970

Contents: What depression is like; Defining the disease; The history of depression; Living with depression; Coping with depression; Conclusion

The author explains "the causes, physiology, treatments, and complications associated with [depression]. The [book is] well organized. . . . The photos are colorful and . . . some are startling, including the brain scans of a patient . . . who suffers from depression." SLJ

Includes bibliographical references

Salomon, Ron

Suicide; [by] Ron Salomon; consulting editor, Christine Collins; foreword by Pat Levitt. Chelsea House 2007 109p il (Psychological disorders) lib bdg $37.50

Grades: 7 8 9 10 11 12   **616.85**

1. Suicide

ISBN 978-0-7910-9007-7 (lib bdg); 0-7910-9007-8 (lib bdg)   LC 2007010992

The book provides "thorough, scientifically based coverage of the symptoms, causes, and treatments of [suicide], as well as related brain chemistry. The [author] sensitively [explores] issues, carefully describing cases and using straightforward, nonjudgmental language." Horn Book Guide

Includes glossary and bibliographical references

Scowen, Kate

My kind of sad; what it's like to be young and depressed; [by] Kate Scowen; art by Jeff Szuc. Annick Press 2006 168p il $19.95; pa $10.95
Grades: 7 8 9 10   **616.85**
1. Depression (Psychology)
ISBN 1-55037-941-0; 1-55037-940-2 (pa)
"The book discusses the history of depression, adolescence and depression, and treatment options. Scowen's focus is on understanding the difference between simply being sad and suffering from depression. Topics such as bipolar disorder, self-mutilation, anorexia, and suicide are also discussed. . . . Scowen's book is well-written, easy to read and use, and quite informative." Voice Youth Advocates
Includes bibliographical references

Silverstein, Alvin

The ADHD update; understanding attention-deficit/hyperactivity disorder; [by] Alvin and Virginia Silverstein and Laura Silverstein Nunn. Enslow Publishers 2008 112p il (Disease update) lib bdg $31.93 *
Grades: 5 6 7 8   **616.85**
1. Attention deficit disorder
ISBN 978-0-7660-2800-5 (lib bdg); 0-7660-2800-3 (lib bdg)   LC 2007-13853
This describes Attention-deficit hyperactivity disorder (ADHD) and its history, diagnosis and treatment, living with it, and its future
"This book is an excellent primer on AD/HD." Sci Books Films
Includes glossary and bibliographical references

The eating disorders update; understanding anorexia, bulimia, and binge eating; [by] Alvin and Virginia Silverstein and Laura Silverstein Nunn. Enslow Publishers 2008 128p il (Disease update) lib bdg $31.93 *
Grades: 5 6 7 8   **616.85**
1. Eating disorders 2. Anorexia nervosa 3. Bulimia
ISBN 978-0-7660-2802-9 (lib bdg); 0-7660-2802-X (lib bdg)   LC 2007013985
"An introduction to the history and most up-to-date research and treatment of eating disorders." Publisher's note
Includes glossary and bibliographical references

Stewart, Gail, 1949-

Phobias; by Gail B. Stewart. Lucent Bks. 2001 96p il (Diseases and disorders) lib bdg $27.45
Grades: 7 8 9 10 11 12   **616.85**
1. Phobias
ISBN 1-56006-726-8   LC 00-10223
The author discusses the history, symptoms, and treatment of phobias
"A solid addition to mental-health sections." SLJ
Includes bibliographical references

Trueit, Trudi Strain

ADHD. Franklin Watts 2004 79p il (Life balance) $19.55
Grades: 5 6 7 8   **616.85**
1. Attention deficit disorder
ISBN 0-531-12261-1   LC 2003-7154
The author "examines the controversy surrounding ADHD, as well as the symptoms, possible causes, and methods of treatment." Publisher's note
"Trueit explains ADHD well. . . . [This book offers] solid, easy-to-understand information." SLJ

The **Truth** about eating disorders; Mark J. Kittleson, general editor; William Kane, adviser; Richelle Rennegarbe, adviser; Gerri Freid Kramer, principal author. Facts on File 2004 166p il (Truth about series) $35 *
Grades: 7 8 9 10   **616.85**
1. Eating disorders
ISBN 0-8160-5300-6   LC 2004-6389
This discusses anorexia, bulimia, fad diets, and laxative abuse, the causes of eating disorders, how to recognize the disorders, the portrayal of eating disorders in the media, and obesity and weight control.
This title does "an excellent job of providing accurate information for teens. For reports or for self-help, [it belongs] in any library serving young adults." SLJ
Includes glossary and bibliographical references

The **Truth** about fear and depression; Mark J. Kittleson, general editor; William Kane, adviser; Richelle Rennegarbe, adviser; Heather Denkmire, principal author. Facts on File 2004 164p il (Truth about series) $35 *
Grades: 7 8 9 10   **616.85**
1. Depression (Psychology) 2. Anxiety
ISBN 0-8160-5301-4   LC 2004-7364
This "title includes discussions of anxiety disorders and their treatment, causes of depression, and defense mechanisms. . . . [This title does] an excellent job of providing accurate information for teens. For reports or for self-help, [it belongs] in any library serving young adults." SLJ
Includes glossary and bibliographical references

616.86   Substance abuse (Drug abuse)

Alcohol information for teens; edited by Joyce Brennfleck Shannon. Omnigraphics 2005 370p (Teen health series) $65 *
Grades: 7 8 9 10 11 12   **616.86**
1. Teenagers—Alcohol use 2. Alcoholism 3. Alcohol—Physiological effect 4. Children of alcoholics
ISBN 0-7808-0741-3
"Health tips about alcohol and alcoholism: including facts about underage drinking, preventing teen alcohol use, alcohol's effects on the brain and the body, alcohol abuse treatment, help for children of alcoholics, and more." Title page
"This comprehensive resource presents clear facts, accurate information, and thoughtful advice." SLJ

Drug information for teens; health tips about the physical and mental effects of substance abuse; edited by Sandra Augustyn Lawton. 2nd ed. Omnigraphics 2006 468p (Teen health series) $65 *

Grades: 7 8 9 10 11 12   **616.86**
1. Drug abuse 2. Teenagers—Health and hygiene
ISBN 0-7808-0862-2   LC 2006012181
First published 2002

"Including information about marijuana, inhalants, club drugs, stimulants, hallucinogens, opiates, prescription and over-the-counter drugs, herbal products, tobacco, alcohol, and more." Title page

"Solid, thoughtful advice is given about how to handle peer pressure, drug-related health concerns, and treatment strategies. Articles are fully cited and are gathered from government agencies such as National Institutes of Health (NIH) and National Institute on Drug Abuse (NIDA), and a variety of other organizations." SLJ

Includes bibliographical references

Esherick, Joan
Dying for acceptance; a teen's guide to drug- and alcohol-related health issues. Mason Crest Publishers 2005 128p il (The science of health) $24.95

Grades: 7 8 9 10   **616.86**
1. Teenagers—Drug use 2. Teenagers—Alcohol use 3. Drugs—Physiological effect 4. Alcohol—Physiological effect
ISBN 978-1-59084-847-0; 1-59084-847-0
LC 2004-12125

Provides teenagers with information on drug and alcohol use, discussing types of drugs, reasons for using, and the dangers of using chemical substances

No more butts; kicking the tobacco habit. Mason Crest 2009 112p il (Tobacco: the deadly drug) lib bdg $26.95

Grades: 6 7 8 9   **616.86**
1. Smoking cessation programs
ISBN 978-1-4222-0236-4 (lib bdg); 1-4222-0236-4 (lib bdg)   LC 2008-13215

Explains how difficult smoking cessation can be and offers tips on how to quit for good.

"The writing is professional but not at a level that causes readers to struggle. The information is made relevant to the everyday reader . . . [and] . . . it would be a strong addition to the nonfiction section of any library and is appropriate for a broad age level." Voice Youth Advocates

Includes glossary and bibliographical references

Hunter, David, 1947-
Born to smoke; nicotine and genetics. Mason Crest 2009 112p il (Tobacco: the deadly drug) lib bdg $26.95

Grades: 6 7 8 9   **616.86**
1. Tobacco habit 2. Smoking 3. Behavior genetics
ISBN 978-1-4222-0243-2; 1-4222-0243-7
LC 2008-13218

Explains how genetics may affect an individual's susceptibility to nicotine addiction, and discusses the debate over genetic predisposition to nicotine addiction versus a person's upbringing.

"The writing is professional but not at a level that causes readers to struggle. The information is made relevant to the everyday reader . . . [and] . . . it would be a strong addition to the nonfiction section of any library and is appropriate for a broad age level." Voice Youth Advocates

Includes glossary and bibliographical references

Hyde, Margaret Oldroyd, 1917-
Smoking 101; an overview for teens; [by] Margaret O. Hyde, John F. Setaro. Twenty-First Century Books 2006 128p il lib bdg $26.60 *

Grades: 8 9 10 11 12   **616.86**
1. Smoking 2. Tobacco
ISBN 0-7613-2835-1   LC 2004-22757

Contents: The first cigarette won't kill me; Nicotine: the addiction culprit; I'll get my tobacco elsewhere; My smoking and my body: the physiology of smoking; My smoking and your body: second hand smoke; Ads: a reality check; The global view: what's happening with tobacco in the rest of the world?; The corporate view: what tobacco companies do; Now that I'm informed . . . some ideas for quitting

"The message is clear, the facts are well-presented, and the tone is insightful. These authors understand the teen audience and how to reach it." SLJ

Includes bibliographical references

Price, Sean, 1963-
Nicotine; [by] Sean Price. Chelsea House 2008 120p il (Junior drug awareness) lib bdg $30

Grades: 6 7 8 9   **616.86**
1. Tobacco habit 2. Smoking
ISBN 978-0-7910-9696-3 (lib bdg); 0-7910-9696-3 (lib bdg)   LC 2007024829

This "provides the facts about tobacco use among teenagers and offers young readers the facts about one of the most prevalent and addictive drugs in the United States." Publisher's note

Includes glossary and bibliographical references

Stoehr, James D.
The neurobiology of addiction. Chelsea House 2006 106p il (Gray matter) lib bdg $35

Grades: 8 9 10 11 12   **616.86**
1. Drug abuse 2. Brain
ISBN 978-0-7910-8574-5; 0-7910-8574-0
LC 2005-11989

This book "looks at the effects of different types of chemicals on the brain and the role they play in addiction." Libr Media Connect

Includes glossary and bibliographical references

616.89 Mental disorders

Baldwin, Carol
Autism. Heinemann Lib. 2003 32p il (Health matters) lib bdg $22.79 *
Grades: 4 5 6   616.89
1. Autism
ISBN 1-4034-0250-7   LC 2001-7973
Contents: What is autism?; What causes autism?; Diagnosing autism; Treating autism; Classmates with autism; How you can help; Visiting friends with autism; Autism success stories
This "inviting, colorful [book] will attract students who need a clear, readable introduction to [autism]." SLJ
Includes glossary and bibliographical references

Kent, Deborah, 1948-
Snake pits, talking cures, & magic bullets; a history of mental illness. 21st Cent. Bks. (Brookfield) 2003 160p il lib bdg $26.90 *
Grades: 6 7 8 9   616.89
1. Mental illness
ISBN 0-7613-2704-5   LC 2002-11208
Looks at how the mentally ill have been treated throughout history, focusing on advances made in the 19th and 20th centuries regarding mental hospitals, medications, and social acceptance
"An excellent history peppered with fascinating accounts. . . . Black-and-white archival photographs and reproductions appear throughout. . . . This is a fine treatment of a topic not heavily covered for this audience." SLJ
Includes glossary and bibliographical references

Mental health information for teens; health tips about mental wellness and mental illness; edited by Karen Bellenir. 2nd ed. Omnigraphics 2006 425p (Teen health series) $65 *
Grades: 7 8 9 10 11 12   616.89
1. Mental health 2. Teenagers—Health and hygiene
ISBN 0-7808-0863-0   LC 2006016689
First published 2001
"Including facts about mental and emotional health, depression and other mood disorders, anxiety disorders, behavior disorders, self-injury, psychosis, schizophrenia, and more." Title page
"Due to the book's valuable content, it is an excellent resource." SLJ
Includes bibliographical references

Silverstein, Alvin
The depression and bipolar disorder update; [by] Alvin and Virginia Silverstein and Laura Silverstein Nunn. Enslow Publishers 2008 128p il (Disease update) $31.93 *
Grades: 6 7 8 9   616.89
1. Depression (Psychology) 2. Manic-depressive illness
ISBN 978-0-7660-2801-2; 0-7660-2801-1
LC 2007-13854
"An introduction to the history . . . research and treatment of depression and bipolar disorder." Publisher's note
Includes bibliographical references

Stewart, Gail, 1949-
People with mental illness; by Gail B. Stewart; photographs by Carl Franzén. Lucent Bks. 2003 96p il (Other America) lib bdg $21.96
Grades: 7 8 9 10   616.89
1. Mental illness
ISBN 1-59018-237-5   LC 2002-7602
Presents the personal stories of four people with mental illness, discussing how each handles the daily demands of family, education, social life, and medical treatment and finds the strength and courage to continue the battle against this common debilitating condition
"An approachable, excellent resource." SLJ
Includes bibliographical references

A **student's** guide to mental health & wellness; [by] Creative Media Applications. Greenwood Press 2004 4v set $160
Grades: 7 8 9 10 11 12   616.89
1. Psychology 2. Mental health 3. Mental illness 4. Reference books
ISBN 0-313-32548-0   LC 2003-44817
Contents: v1 Words and terms; v2 Important people; v3 Debatable issues; v4 Disorders, diseases and treatments
This "set examines the evolution of psychology from its earliest roots to its contemporary view as a well-established and respected science. The first volume, Words and Terms, is a well-organized collection of lucid and relevant definitions. . . . Important People describes the intriguing history of psychology; research methods; types of therapy; and the pioneering work of psychologists such as Sigmund Freud, Karen Horney, William James, Jean Piaget, and B. F. Skinner. In Debatable Issues, contemporary controversial topics, such as the ethics of animal experimentation, the relationship of violence in children and the media, and the prevalence of the ADHD diagnosis, are discussed. The last volume, Disorders, Diseases, and Treatments, covers mental illnesses such as depression, anxiety disorders, conduct disorders, and schizophrenia, and provides useful material about their symptoms, diagnosis, and treatment options." SLJ
Includes bibliographical references

Szabo, Ross
Behind happy faces; taking charge of your mental health, a guide for young adults; [by] Ross Szabo, Melanie Hall. Volt Press 2007 263p pa $14.95
Grades: 7 8 9 10 11 12   616.89
1. Mental health 2. Mental illness
ISBN 978-1-56625-305-5; 1-56625-305-5
LC 2007013703
"Information about mental illness is interspersed with first-person narratives, including the story of Szabo's own bipolar disorder, from a 'rock bottom' experience to diagnosis, treatment, struggle, and his eventual ability not only to live with his condition, but also to thrive. The book discusses the symptoms of common disorders, resistance to seeking help, the role of friends and family, understanding and maintaining oneself, and more." SLJ
Includes bibliographical references

Veague, Heather Barnett

Schizophrenia; [by] Heather Barnett Veague; foreword by Pat Levitt. Chelsea House 2007 114p il (Psychological disorders) lib bdg $37.50

Grades: 7 8 9 10 11 12   **616.89**

1. Schizophrenia

ISBN 978-0-7910-8544-8 (lib bdg); 0-7910-8544-9 (lib bdg)   LC 2007010057

The book provides "thorough, scientifically based coverage of the symptoms, causes, and treatments of [schizophrenia], as well as related brain chemistry. The [author] sensitively [explores] issues, carefully describing cases and using straightforward, nonjudgmental language." Horn Book Guide

Includes glossary and bibliographical references

616.9   Other diseases

Abrams, Liesa

Chronic fatigue syndrome. Lucent Bks. 2003 96p il (Diseases and disorders) lib bdg $27.45

Grades: 7 8 9 10   **616.9**

1. Chronic fatigue syndrome

ISBN 1-59018-039-9   LC 2002-9459

Examines the symptoms, treatment options, and mystery of chronic fatigue syndrome, ongoing research into its causes, and how to live with this disease

This title is "well written and well organized." SLJ

Includes bibliographical references

Colligan, L. H.

Tick-borne illnesses; by L.H. Colligan. Marshall Cavendish Benchmark 2009 64p il (Health alert) $22.95

Grades: 4 5 6 7   **616.9**

1. Tick-borne diseases

ISBN 978-0-7614-2914-2; 0-7614-2914-X   LC 2007-38517

"Provides comprehensive information on the causes, treatment, and history of tick-borne illnesses." Publisher's note

Includes glossary

Emmeluth, Donald

Botulism; [by] Don Emmeluth. Chelsea House 2005 136p il (Deadly diseases and epidemics) $31.95

Grades: 7 8 9 10   **616.9**

1. Botulism

ISBN 0-7910-8674-7; 0-7910-8674-7   LC 2005-16673

Contents: Historical perspective; Causes of botulism; Transmission of botulism; Diagnosis of botulism; Botulism and the nervous system; Treating botulism; Preventing botulism; Concerns for the future; Hopes for the future

Includes glossary and bibliographical references

Hoffmann, Gretchen

Chicken pox; by Gretchen Hoffmann. Marshall Cavendish Benchmark 2009 62p il (Health alert) $22.95

Grades: 4 5 6 7   **616.9**

1. Chickenpox

ISBN 978-0-7614-2916-6; 0-7614-2916-6

"Provides comprehensive information on the causes, treatment, and history of chickenpox." Publisher's note

Includes glossary

Mononucleosis; [by] Gretchen Hoffmann. Marshall Cavendish Benchmark 2006 64p il (Health alert) lib bdg $28.50 *

Grades: 4 5 6 7   **616.9**

1. Mononucleosis

ISBN 0-7614-1915-2   LC 2005005001

This describes the symptoms and causes of mononucleosis, its history, diagnosis and treatment.

This is "well-designed and easy-to-use . . . with accurate and reliable information. Colorful photos, micrographs, and sidebars appear throughout." SLJ

Includes glossary and bibliographical references

Klosterman, Lorrie

Rabies; [by] Lorrie Klosterman. Marshall Cavendish Benchmark 2007 c2008 64p il (Health alert) lib bdg $21.95

Grades: 4 5 6 7   **616.9**

1. Rabies

ISBN 978-0-7614-2704-9   LC 2007008788

This describes what it is like to have rabies, what it is, its history, and its prevention, diagnosis, and treatment.

Includes glossary and bibliographical references

Lynette, Rachel

Leprosy; [by] Rachel Lynette. KidHaven Press 2006 48p il (Understanding diseases and disorders) $23.70

Grades: 4 5 6   **616.9**

1. Leprosy

ISBN 0-7377-3172-9   LC 2005012168

This describes the history, causes, diagnosis, and treatment of leprosy.

"A solid, up-to-date examination of the disease. . . . Lucid text . . . presents the factual material in an understandable style that is unburdened by medical jargon." SLJ

Includes bibliographical references

Silverstein, Alvin

Chickenpox and shingles; [by] Alvin and Virginia Silverstein and Laura Silverstein Nunn. Enslow Pubs. 1998 128p il (Diseases and people) lib bdg $26.60 *

Grades: 7 8 9 10   **616.9**

1. Chickenpox 2. Shingles (Disease)

ISBN 0-89490-715-8   LC 97-34041

"The book begins with a general profile of the two diseases mentioned in the title—their causes, transmis-

Silverstein, Alvin—*Continued*

sion, symptoms, treatment, and prevention. In subsequent chapters, each disease is described in greater detail. The relationship between these two viral infections is discussed, and how one may develop immunity to them is examined." Sci Books Films

Includes bibliographical references

Lyme disease; [by] Alvin Silverstein, Virginia Silverstein, Laura Silverstein Nunn. Watts 2000 63p il lib bdg $24.50; pa $8.95 *

Grades: 7 8 9 10   **616.9**

1. Lyme disease

ISBN 0-531-11751-0 (lib bdg); 0-531-11751-0 (pa)

LC 99-42674

"Watts library"

Discusses the causes, symptoms, and treatment of Lyme disease, as well as ways to protect against it

This "will be helpful for reports as well as for answering medical questions." Booklist

Includes bibliographical references

Smith, Tara C., 1976-

Ebola. Chelsea House 2005 104p il (Deadly diseases and epidemics) $31.95

Grades: 7 8 9 10   **616.9**

1. Ebola virus

ISBN 0-7910-8505-8   LC 2005-6515

Contents: A modern plague; Ebola in Africa; Ebola hits close to home; General characteristics of the virus; Ecology of the virus; Immunological methods of detection; Developing a vaccine; Other hemorrhagic fevers

Includes glossary and bibliographical references

Willett, Edward, 1959-

Ebola virus. Enslow Pubs. 2003 112p il map (Diseases and people) $26.60

Grades: 7 8 9 10   **616.9**

1. Ebola virus

ISBN 0-7660-1595-5   LC 2002-10149

Contents: Profile; A terrifying killer; The history of ebola; What is ebola hemorrhagic fever?; Diagnosing ebola hemorrhagic fever; Treatment of ebola hemorrhagic fever; Social implications of ebola hemorrhagic fever; Preventing ebola hemorrhagic fever; Research and future prospects; Q&A; Ebola hemorrhagic fever timeline

The author "explores the history and symptoms of the Ebola virus, from how it was first discovered to treatment options available for those who may contract this extremely rare—but deadly—disease. He also addresses the media attention and social factors that may add to the fear and stigma related to this virus." Publisher's note

Includes bibliographical references

616.95   Sexually transmitted diseases

Curran, Christine Perdan

Sexually transmitted diseases. Enslow Pubs. 1998 128p il (Diseases and people) lib bdg $26.60

Grades: 7 8 9 10   **616.95**

1. Sexually transmitted diseases

ISBN 0-7660-1050-3   LC 97-44140

Examines the history, symptoms, treatment, and prevention of such sexually transmitted diseases as syphilis, gonorrhea, herpes, AIDS, and hepatitis

Includes glossary and bibliographical references

Silverstein, Alvin

The STDs update; [by] Alvin and Virginia Silverstein and Laura Silverstein Nunn. Enslow Elementary 2006 128p il (Disease update) $31.93 *

Grades: 6 7 8 9   **616.95**

1. Sexually transmitted diseases

ISBN 0-7660-2484-9; 978-0-7660-2484-7

LC 2005-05990

This covers the "history, transmission, symptoms, diagnosis, treatment, current advances, and potential outbreaks . . . [of] such diseases as AIDS, chlamydia, genital warts, gonorrhea, hepatitis B, herpes, pubic lice, syphilis, and trichomoniasis. . . . [It includes] numerous high-quality color illustrations and diagrams, informational sidebars highlighting important facts and statistics." SLJ

Includes bibliographical references

616.97   Diseases of immune system

AIDS; Katherine Macfarlane, book editor. Greenhaven Press 2008 144p il (Perspectives on diseases and disorders) lib bdg $34.95

Grades: 8 9 10 11 12   **616.97**

1. AIDS (Disease)

ISBN 978-0-7377-3868-1 (lib bdg); 0-7377-3868-5 (lib bdg)   LC 2007-37471

Features a collection of essays on HIV and AIDS, discussing such topics as causes of the disease, current treatments, and the importance of HIV testing, and contains profiles of three individuals with the disease.

"The information is up-to-date and presented in a clearly organized fashion. . . . [This is] an excellent tool for research." Libr Media Connect

Includes glossary and bibliographical references

Allergy information for teens; edited by Karen Bellenir. 1st ed. Omnigraphics 2006 410p il (Teen health series) $58 *

Grades: 8 9 10 11 12   **616.97**

1. Allergy

ISBN 0-7808-0799-5   LC 2005031765

"Health tips about allergic reactions such as anaphylaxis, respiratory problems, and rashes, including facts about identifying and managing allergies to food, pollen, mold, animals, chemicals, drugs, and other substances." Title page

"This authoritative and useful self-help title is a solid addition to YA collections, whether for personal interest or reports." SLJ

Includes bibliographical references

Ehrlich, Paul

Living with allergies; [by] Paul M. Ehrlich, with
Elizabeth Shimer Bowers. Facts On File 2009
168p (Teen's guides) $34.95; pa $14.95

Grades: 7 8 9 10 11 12 **616.97**
1. Allergy
ISBN 978-0-8160-7327-6; 0-8160-7327-9;
978-0-8160-7742-7 (pa); 0-8160-7742-8 (pa)
LC 2008-34352

This "book addresses allergy triggers, preventing allergic reactions, what to expect from treatment, paying for
care, and how to help yourself, friends, or family members who may have allergies." Publisher's note

This is a "solid volume." SLJ

Includes glossary and bibliographical references

Gordon, Sherri Mabry

Peanut butter, milk, and other deadly threats;
what you should know about food allergies.
Enslow Publishers 2006 112p il (Issues in focus
today) $31.93 *

Grades: 8 9 10 11 12 **616.97**
1. Food allergy
ISBN 0-7660-2529-2 LC 2005-29219

Discusses what it is like to live with food allergies,
how teens and their families cope with them, the causes
of food allergies, and the research being done to prevent
and control them

"The format is open, with plenty of white space, making the book accessible to reluctant readers. Full-color
photos, helpful case studies, and a list of reputable organizations to contact for further information are included."
SLJ

Includes glossary and bibliographical references

Hicks, Terry Allan

Allergies. Marshall Cavendish Benchmark 2006
64p il (Health alert) lib bdg $28.50 *

Grades: 4 5 6 7 **616.97**
1. Allergy
ISBN 0-7614-1918-7 LC 2005-05000

This describes the causes of allergies, their history,
and how to live with them.

This is "well-designed and easy-to-use . . . with accurate and reliable information. Colorful photos, micrographs, and sidebars appear throughout." SLJ

Includes glossary and bibliographical references

Parker, Steve

Allergies; [by] Steve Parker. Heinemann Library
2004 56p il (Just the facts) lib bdg $32.86

Grades: 5 6 7 8 **616.97**
1. Allergy
ISBN 1-4034-4598-2 LC 2003-10872

Contents: Allergies; Early history of allergies; Recent
history of allergies; What is an allergy?; Different types
of allergies; Who is affected?; More and more allergies;
Allergies in the nose; Hay fever and similar allergies;
Skin allergies; Food allergies; Drug and microbe allergies; Allergies to bites and stings; Allergy can be
deadly=anaphylaxis; Is it an allergy?; Tackling an allergy; Living with an allergy; Allergy out and about; Pre-

vention and treatment; Medical science and allergies;
Complementary therapies; Can allergies be cured?; Hopes
for the future; Allergies: same but different

Defines what an allergy is, various types of allergies,
some prevention and treatment methods, and other issues
related to allergic conditions

This is "well written and organized." SLJ

Includes bibliographical references

Silverstein, Alvin

The AIDS update; [by] Alvin and Virginia
Silverstein and Laura Silverstein Nunn. Enslow
Publishers 2007 c2008 128p il (Disease update) lib
bdg $31.93 *

Grades: 5 6 7 8 **616.97**
1. AIDS (Disease)
ISBN 978-0-7660-2746-6 (lib bdg); 0-7660-2746-5 (lib
bdg) LC 2006100475

"Discusses the causes, diagnoses, treatment methods,
and future of AIDS." Publisher's note

Includes glossary and bibliographical references

616.99 Tumors and miscellaneous communicable diseases

Brill, Marlene Targ, 1945-

Lung cancer. Benchmark Books 2005 64p il
(Health alert) $31.36

Grades: 4 5 6 7 **616.99**
1. Lung cancer
ISBN 978-0-7614-1802-3; 0-7614-1802-4
LC 2004-5971

Discusses lung cancer, including what it is like to
have the disease, the history and research, and treatment.

"Clear archival black-and-white and color photos and
photomicrographs support and extend the text." Horn
Book Guide

Includes glossary and bibliographical references

Buckmaster, Marjorie L.

Skin cancer; [by] Marjorie L. Buckmaster.
Marshall Cavendish Benchmark 2007 c2008 60p il
(Health alert) lib bdg $21.95

Grades: 4 5 6 7 **616.99**
1. Cancer 2. Skin—Diseases
ISBN 978-0-7614-2703-2 LC 2007024623

This describes what it is like to have skin cancer,
what it is, its history, and diagnosing and treating skin
cancer.

Includes glossary and bibliographical references

Gillie, Oliver

Cancer; [by] Oliver Gillie. Heinemann Library
2004 56p il (Just the facts) $23

Grades: 5 6 7 8 **616.99**
1. Cancer
ISBN 1-4034-5144-3 LC 2003-22508

Provides an overview of cancer, describing what it is,
what the various forms are that it takes, what it is like

Gillie, Oliver—*Continued*
to live with this disease, and some of the available treatments
This is "well written and substantive without being overly technical." SLJ
Includes bibligraphical references

Klosterman, Lorrie
Leukemia. Marshall Cavendish Benchmark 2005 64p il (Health alert) $31.36
Grades: 4 5 6 7   **616.99**
1. Leukemia
ISBN 978-0-7614-1916-7; 0-7614-1916-0
     LC 2005-5002
"Discusses leukemia and its effects on people and society." Publisher's note
"Clear archival photos and photomicrographs support the text." Horn Book Guide
Includes glossary and bibliographical references

McKinnell, Robert Gilmore
Prevention of cancer; [by] Robert G. McKinnell; consulting editor, Donna M. Bozzone. Chelsea House 2008 144p il (Biology of cancer) lib bdg $31.95 *
Grades: 8 9 10 11 12   **616.99**
1. Cancer
ISBN 978-0-7910-8827-2 (lib bdg); 0-7910-8827-8 (lib bdg)
     LC 2007-34259
This book is "highly readable with interesting anecdotes as well as key scientific information to enable students to make informed choices in lifestyle to lower their risk of cancer. . . . [It] focuses on cancers of the skin, uterus, breast, and lung, emphasizing that at least half of cancers are preventable if people avoid risk factors and maintain healthy life styles. . . . The positive and non-preachy tone . . . empowers students to assume responsibility to reduce their risk to cancer rather than to accept cancer as part of our lives." Voice Youth Advocates
Includes glossary and bibliographical references

Peacock, Judith, 1942-
Breast cancer. LifeMatters 2001 64p il (Perspectives on disease and illness) lib bdg $26.26
Grades: 7 8 9 10   **616.99**
1. Breast cancer
ISBN 978-0-7368-1028-9 (lib bdg); 0-7368-1028-5 (lib bdg)
     LC 00-12364
This discusses breast cancer and its types, diagnosis, and treatment
"Simple and well-organized." Book Rep
Includes glossary and bibliographical references

Hodgkin's disease. LifeMatters 2001 64p il (Perspectives on disease and illness) lib bdg $25.26
Grades: 7 8 9 10   **616.99**
1. Hodgkin's disease
ISBN 978-0-7368-1027-2 (lib bdg); 0-7368-1027-7 (lib bdg)
     LC 00-12614

This offers information on the definition, diagnosis, and treatment of Hodgkin's disease and on living with the disease
The information is "simple and well-organized." Book Rep
Includes glossary and bibliographical references

Silverstein, Alvin
The breast cancer update; [by] Alvin and Virginia Silverstein and Laura Silverstein Nunn. Enslow Publishers 2008 128p il (Disease update) lib bdg $31.93 *
Grades: 5 6 7 8   **616.99**
1. Breast cancer
ISBN 978-0-7660-2747-3 (lib bdg); 0-7660-2747-3 (lib bdg)
     LC 2006-32821
This offers a history of breast cancer, a definition of it, and describes its diagnosis and treatment, prevention, and future
Includes glossary and bibliographical references

Smith, Terry L., 1944-
Breast cancer; current and emerging trends in detection and treatment; [by] Terry L. Smith. Rosen Pub. Group 2006 64p il (Cancer and modern science) lib bdg $29.25
Grades: 7 8 9 10   **616.99**
1. Breast cancer
ISBN 1-4042-0386-9   LC 2005000130
Contents: Breast cancer throughout history; What is breast cancer?; Who gets breast cancer?; Treatment for breast cancer; Can we prevent breast cancer?; The promise of research
"Photographs, diagrams, multihued headings, and spotlighted insets are plentiful. . . . [This is a] solid [overview] of the current understanding of [this condition]." SLJ
Includes bibliographical references

Stokes, Mark
Colon cancer; current and emerging trends in detection and treatment; [by] Mark Stokes. 1st ed. Rosen Pub. Group 2006 64p il (Cancer and modern science) lib bdg $29.25
Grades: 7 8 9 10   **616.99**
1. Colon cancer
ISBN 1-4042-0387-7   LC 2005003626
Contents: What is cancer?; Colon cancer screening and staging; Treating colon cancer; The future of colon cancer treatment; Prevention: the best cure
"Photographs, diagrams, multihued headings, and spotlighted insets are plentiful. . . . [This is a] solid [overview] of the current understanding of [this condition]." SLJ
Includes bibliographical references

Prostate cancer; current and emerging trends in detection and treatment; [by] Mark Stokes. 1st ed. Rosen Pub. Group 2006 64p il (Cancer and modern science) lib bdg $29.25
Grades: 7 8 9 10   **616.99**
1. Prostate gland—Cancer
ISBN 1-4042-0391-5   LC 2005003628

Stokes, Mark—*Continued*

Contents: The prostate: anatomy, physiology, and pathology; Screening and diagnosing prostate cancer; Traditional and new treatments; Emerging technologies in prostate cancer treatment

"Photographs, diagrams, multihued headings, and spotlighted insets are plentiful. . . . [This is a] solid [overview] of the current understanding of [this condition]." SLJ

Includes bibliographical references

617 Miscellaneous branches of medicine. Surgery

Giddens, Sandra

Future techniques in surgery; [by] Sandra and Owen Giddens. Rosen Pub. Group 2003 64p il (Library of future medicine) lib bdg $26.50

Grades: 6 7 8 9   617

1. Surgery

ISBN 0-8239-3667-8   LC 2001-5598

Contents: Surgery past; Surgery present; The future of surgery

Reviews the evolution of medical surgery during two hundred years and predicts new procedures that may lead to greater safety and efficacy

This "is a competent overview of the topic supported with colorful illustrations and many photos." Libr Media Connect

Includes glossary and bibliographical references

Townsend, John, 1955-

Scalpels, stitches & scars; a history of surgery. Raintree 2005 c2006 56p il (Painful history of medicine) lib bdg $32.86; pa $9.90 *

Grades: 6 7 8 9   617

1. Surgery

ISBN 1-4109-1332-5 (lib bdg); 1-4109-1337-6 (pa)
LC 2004-14248

"Raintree freestyle"

Contents: Cutting open; Ancient times; The Middle Ages; Blood, boils, and burns; Ground breaking; In the wars; Modern times

A history of surgery from ancient times to the present

This is "packed with grisly facts and gory images. . . . But the science is accurate, and many readers will be intrigued by the medical drama. . . . The design, with lots of color pictures, captions, and boxes, will grab browsers, and the cover art is a thrilling story in itself." Booklist

Includes glossary and bibliographical references

617.1 Injuries and wounds

Crash; the body in crisis; Elaine Pascoe, book editor. Blackbirch Press 2004 48p il (Body story) $23.70; pa $9.95

Grades: 7 8 9 10   617.1

1. Wounds and injuries 2. Traffic accidents

ISBN 1-4103-0062-5; 1-4103-0183-4 (pa)
LC 2003-12035

Contents: Brain power; Rushed to surgery; Laura's collapse

Describes what happens when David and Laura are in a car accident and suffer serious injuries, ranging from a ruptured blood vessel near Laura's spleen to a major artery that bursts in David's brain.

This volume is "bubbling over with informative, full-color photographs. . . . The [text is] amazingly concise and [takes] extraordinarily complex processes and [makes] them clearly understandable to the intended audience." SLJ

Includes bibliographical references

Shryer, Donna

Peak performance; sports nutrition. Marshall Cavendish Benchmark 2007 142p il (Food and fitness) $37.07

Grades: 7 8 9 10   617.1

1. Athletes—Nutrition 2. Sports medicine 3. Physical fitness

ISBN 978-0-7614-2554-0; 0-7614-2554-3
LC 2007-2271

"Provides a basic, comprehensive introduction to sports nutrition, including information on how nutrients help the athlete reach peak performance, with a review of the food pyramid and how to read labels to make healthy food choices." Publisher's note

This is "timely, well written, and appealing. . . . Charts and graphs highlight the textual information and enhance the usability of [this book]." Libr Media Connect

Includes glossary and bibliographical references

Sports injuries information for teens; health tips about acute, traumatic, and chronic injuries in adolescent athletes including facts about sprains, fractures, and overuse injuries, treatment, rehabilitation, sport-specific safety guidelines, fitness suggestions, and more; edited by Karen Bellenir. 2nd ed. Omnigraphics 2008 429p il (Teen health) $62 *

Grades: 7 8 9 10 11 12   617.1

1. Sports medicine 2. Wounds and injuries

ISBN 978-0-7808-1011-2; 0-7808-1011-2
LC 2008-9793

First published 2004

"Provides updated basic consumer health information for teens on sports-related injuries, treatment, and rehabilitation, along with safety guidelines and prevention tips. Includes index, and resource information." Publisher's note

"Along with physiological information about injuries and treatments, the special needs of teen athletes are considered in this comprehensive overview. . . . The information presented is copious and concise." SLJ [review of 2004 edition]

Includes bibliographical references

617.9 Operative surgery and special fields of surgery

Fullick, Ann
Rebuilding the body; organ transplantation. Heinemann Lib. 2002 64p il (Science at the edge) lib bdg $32.79; pa $9.50
Grades: 5 6 7 8   **617.9**
1. Transplantation of organs, tissues, etc.
ISBN 1-58810-700-0 (lib bdg); 1-4034-4122-7 (pa)
LC 2001-6082
Contents: The organs of the body; Organ failure; New parts for old; How is it done?; Rejection; Life from death; Lucy's story; Pushing the boundaries; Xenotransplantation; The cutting edge; Stem cell research
This "sets the stage for understanding complex transplant procedures by first explaining how the major organs function and some of the causes of organ failure, then discussing issues related to compatibility, organ preservation, rejection, and the ethics of organ donation and transplant research. . . . [This title is] nicely written, well organized, and filled with lots of visuals." Booklist
Includes glossary and bibliographical references

Jango-Cohen, Judith
Bionics; [by] Judith Jango-Cohen. Lerner Publications Co. 2007 48p il (Cool science) lib bdg $26.60
Grades: 4 5 6 7   **617.9**
1. Bionics 2. Artificial organs
ISBN 978-0-8225-5937-5 (lib bdg); 0-8225-5937-4 (lib bdg)
LC 2005032221
This "introduction to the field of bionics is divided into four chapters: 'Replacing Parts,' 'Fixing Malfunctions,' 'Assisting the Senses,' and 'Facing the Future.' Jango-Cohen uses a number of personal stories and references to pop culture to engage readers. . . . The explanations are clearly written and easily understood. Colorful photographs and illustrations are featured throughout the text." SLJ
Includes bibliographical references

McClellan, Marilyn
Organ and tissue transplants; medical miracles and challenges. Enslow Pubs. 2003 128p il (Issues in focus) lib bdg $20.95
Grades: 7 8 9 10   **617.9**
1. Transplantation of organs, tissues, etc. 2. Artificial organs
ISBN 0-7660-1943-8   LC 2002-8401
Explores the history of organ transplantation, as well as its medical, ethical, financial, and personal aspects, providing insights into the latter through stories of organ donors and recipients
"With its useful black-and-white photos, anatomical diagram, pie chart, and statistics, this book is equally approachable for curious readers and report writers." SLJ
Includes glossary and bibliographical references

Rosaler, Maxine
Bionics. Blackbirch Press 2003 48p il (Science on the edge) lib bdg $23.70
Grades: 5 6 7 8   **617.9**
1. Bionics
ISBN 1-56711-784-8   LC 2002-15970
Discusses the history of replacement body parts, current accomplishments in the field, and visions of future technology.
Includes glossary and bibliographical references

Schwartz, Tina P., 1969-
Organ transplants; a survival guide for the entire family: the ultimate teen guide. Scarecrow Press 2005 243p il (It happened to me) $36.50
Grades: 7 8 9 10   **617.9**
1. Transplantation of organs, tissues, etc.
ISBN 0-8108-4924-0   LC 2004-21563
"The 13 chapters, written in a question-and-answer format, detail the steps involved from diagnosis and being placed on a waiting list to pre and post-surgery. . . .The well-written text is complemented by a comprehensive section of suggestions for additional information. . . . Texts with this breadth of coverage are rare." SLJ
Includes bibliographical references

618.1 Gynecology

Fullick, Ann
Test tube babies; in-vitro fertilization. Heinemann Lib. 2002 64p il (Science at the edge) lib bdg $27.86; pa $9.99
Grades: 7 8 9 10   **618.1**
1. Fertilization in vitro 2. Infertility 3. Reproduction
ISBN 1-58810-703-5 (lib bdg); 978-1-40344-124-9 (pa); 1-40344-124-3 (pa)   LC 2001-6080
Contents: An everyday miracle; What causes infertility?; Treating infertility; The IVF story; How does IVF work?; The price of success; Doriver's story; Beyond IVF; Ethics, issues, and the law; Where do we go from here?
This "discusses the causes of infertility, the treatments, and ethical issues. The views of major religions are identified, as are laws that have been passed to deal with fertility issues. . . . [This title is] first-rate." SLJ
Includes bibliographical references

Orr, Tamra
Test tube babies; written by Tamra B. Orr. Blackbirch Press 2003 48p il (Science on the edge) lib bdg $23.70
Grades: 5 6 7 8   **618.1**
1. Fertilization in vitro 2. Infertility 3. Reproduction
ISBN 1-56711-788-0   LC 2002-11928
Contents: In the beginning; The current picture; A future of possibilities
Examines the causes of infertility, the history of in vitro fertilization, the steps involved in creating a 'test tube baby,' and ethical questions the technology has raised
Includes bibliographical references

Waters, Sophie
Seeing the gynecologist. Rosen Pub. Group 2007 47p il (Girls' health) $19.95
Grades: 7 8 9 10 11 12   **618.1**
1. Women—Health and hygiene 2. Girls—Health and hygiene
ISBN 978-1-4042-1948-9; 1-4042-1948-X
     LC 2007-1633
"Introductory chapters include a brief introduction to the physiology of women's reproduction and menstruation, but the majority of the book covers the specifics of a gynecological visit, from choosing a doctor and insurance concerns to what happens during a pelvic exam. . . . The accessible text is informative and supportive." Booklist
Includes bibliographical references

Winkler, Kathleen
High-tech babies; the debate over assisted reproductive technology; [by] Kathleen Winkler. Enslow Publishers 2006 58p il (Issues in focus today) lib bdg $31.93 *
Grades: 7 8 9 10 11 12   **618.1**
1. Infertility 2. Fertilization in vitro 3. Medical ethics
ISBN 0-7660-2528-4   LC 2005-34656
This discusses infertility and how it is diagnosed, assisted reproductive technologies such as intrauterine insemination (IUI) and in vitro fertilization (IVF), and the ethics of those technologies.
Includes glossary and bibliographical references

620 Engineering

Johnson, Rebecca L., 1956-
Nanotechnology. Lerner Publications 2006 48p il (Cool science) $25.26
Grades: 4 5 6   **620**
1. Nanotechnology
ISBN 978-0-8225-2111-2; 0-8225-2111-3
     LC 2005008791
"From clear sunscreen to space elevators, nanotechnology promises big changes in our daily lives. . . . Pointing to recent advances in sports equipment, stain resistant fabrics and moving parts for dolls that are but harbingers of revolutionary new developments in science, medicine and the whole approach to manufacturing things. In a final chapter, 'Nanobots and Beyond,' [the author] considers the potential—and . . . the dangers—of submicroscopic self-replicating machines." Kirkus
Includes glossary and bibliographical references

620.1 Engineering mechanics and materials

Finkelstein, Norman H., 1941-
Plastics; [by] Norman H. Finkelstein. Marshall Cavendish Benchmark 2007 c2008 144p il (Great inventions) lib bdg $27.95
Grades: 6 7 8 9   **620.1**
1. Plastics
ISBN 978-0-7614-2600-4   LC 2006020909

"An examination of the origin, history, development, and societal impact of the development of plastics." Publisher's note
Includes glossary and bibliographical references

Kassinger, Ruth
Glass; from Cinderella's slippers to fiber optics; [by] Ruth G. Kassinger. Twenty-First Century Bks. 2003 80p il lib bdg $25.90
Grades: 7 8 9 10   **620.1**
1. Glass
ISBN 0-7613-2109-8   LC 2002-5329
Describes the physical composition and characteristics of glass, and presents glassmaking techniques and the various uses made of glass throughout history
This "will catch the interest of a wide variety of readers. The color photographs are clear, interesting, and self-explanatory." Libr Media Connect
Includes bibliographical references

Knapp, Brian J.
Materials science. Grolier 2003 9v il set$319
Grades: 7 8 9 10   **620.1**
1. Materials 2. Reference books
ISBN 0-7172-5697-9   LC 2002-44537
Contents: v1 Plastics; v2 Metals; v3 Wood and paper; v4 Ceramics; v5 Glass; v6 Dyes, paints, and adhesives; v7 Fibers; v8 Water; v9 Air
Presents the main scientific properties of materials and how they are determined, as well as how substances can be manipulated or modified to produce a wide array of materials with an equally wide array of applications
"The volumes are generously enhanced with photographs and appropriate illustrative figures. . . . The written presentations are all brief, but clear and understandable for anyone who has had a general science background." Sci Books Films

Ward, David J. (David John)
Materials science; by D. J. Ward. Lerner Publications 2009 47p il (Cool science) lib bdg $26.60
Grades: 4 5 6   **620.1**
1. Materials
ISBN 978-0-8225-7588-7; 0-8225-7588-4 (lib bdg)
     LC 2007042176
This describes how scientists study the microscopic parts of materials such as plastic, glass, or stainless steel, how they learn how each part makes something hard or soft, strong or weak, or good or bad at carrying heat, and how they use that knowledge to create supermaterials to help make better sports equipment, tinier computer chips, and more.
Includes glossary and bibliographical references

621 Applied physics

Silverstein, Alvin
Energy; [by] Alvin Silverstein, Virginia Silverstein, Laura Silverstein Nunn. rev ed. Twenty-First Century Books 2008 128p il (Science concepts, second series) lib bdg $31.93
Grades: 6 7 8 9   **621**
1. Energy resources
ISBN 978-0-8225-8655-5 (lib bdg); 0-8225-8655-X (lib bdg)   LC 2007049535
First published 1998
Discusses the sources and uses of different types of energy, both natural and manmade, including electrical, magnetic, light, heat, sound, and nuclear energy
Includes glossary and bibliographical references

621.1 Steam engineering

Collier, James Lincoln, 1928-
The steam engine. Marshall Cavendish Benchmark 2006 112p il (Great inventions) lib bdg $37.07 *
Grades: 7 8 9 10   **621.1**
1. Steam engines
ISBN 0-7614-1880-6
This is a history of the steam engine and its influence on American history and culture.
This is presented "thoughfully yet conversationally. . . . [It] will reward steady reading." Horn Book Guide
Includes glossary and bibliographical references

621.31 Generation, modification, storage, transmission of electric power

Lew, Kristi, 1968-
Goodbye, gasoline; the science of fuel cells. Compass Point Books 2009 48p il (Headline science) lib bdg $27.93
Grades: 5 6 7 8   **621.31**
1. Fuel cells
ISBN 978-0-7565-3521-6; 0-7565-3521-2
                                    LC 2008011729
This "clearly examines the history and technology of hydrogen fuel cells, including the various types such as proton exchange membrane and alkaline cells. An excellent description of how the technology works gives readers an understanding of both the successes and problems relating to these promising energy sources. . . . The color illustrations and charts . . . are clear and helpful, and the text, although information rich, is not overly difficult." SLJ

621.32 Lighting

Collier, James Lincoln, 1928-
Electricity and the light bulb; [by] James Lincoln Collier. Marshall Cavendish Benchmark 2006 112p il (Great inventions) lib bdg $37.07 *
Grades: 7 8 9 10   **621.32**
1. Electric lighting 2. Electric power
ISBN 0-7614-1878-4   LC 2004-21623
This is a history of electric power and the invention of the light bulb and their influence on American history and culture.
This is presented "thoughfully yet conversationally. . . . [It] will reward steady reading." Horn Book Guide
Includes glossary and bibliographical references

Matthews, John R., 1937-
The light bulb. F. Watts 2005 80p il (Inventions that shaped the world) lib bdg $30.50
Grades: 6 7 8 9 10   **621.32**
1. Electric lighting
ISBN 978-0-531-12334-8 (lib bdg); 0-531-12334-0 (lib bdg)   LC 2004001673
An exploration of the scientific processes and discoveries that led to one of the world's most significant inventions
Includes bibliographical references

Sonneborn, Liz
The electric light; Thomas Edison's illuminating invention. Chelsea House 2007 120p il (Milestones in American history) lib bdg $35
Grades: 7 8 9 10   **621.32**
1. Edison, Thomas A. (Thomas Alva), 1847-1931
2. Electric lighting
ISBN 978-0-7910-9350-4 (lib bdg); 0-7910-9350-6 (lib bdg)   LC 2006-34432
This "accessible [volume captures] the hard work, perseverance, and natural talent of Edison. . . . The [text explores] the [man's life] along with providing information about the genesis and development of [electric light]. Many photographs, reproductions, and sidebars contribute to a clean design and help clarify topics." Horn Book Guide
Includes bibliographical references

621.381 Electronics

Oxlade, Chris
Electronics; MP3s, TVs, and DVDs; [by] Chris Oxlade. Heinemann Library 2006 56p il (The cutting edge) $32.86; pa $8.99 *
Grades: 5 6 7 8   **621.381**
1. Electronics
ISBN 1-4034-7427-3; 1-4034-7433-8 (pa)
                                    LC 2005018017
This "looks at the development of popular devices from conception to implementation. The introductory chapter describes how the valve gave way to the

Oxlade, Chris—*Continued*

microchip, how analog and digital signals differ, the many advantages of a digital signal, and the ability to store large amounts of information in the digital format. Following chapters examine cell phones, radio, music, cameras, television, video, and electronic games. A look into the future envisions cellular television and cellular teeth. . . . Informative, fascinating, and useful for reports." SLJ

Includes bibliographical references

Woodford, Chris, 1943-

Digital technology; [by] Chris Woodford. Chelsea House 2006 47p il (Science in focus) $27 *

Grades: 4 5 6 7   **621.381**

1. Electronics 2. Information technology

ISBN 0-7910-8861-8   LC 2006041011

"Packed with diverse and interesting bits of information that is divided into manageably small chunks, the book covers, among many other topics, the binary system, digital transmission and music, smart cards, imaging, computer-aided design, animation, mobile phones, the Internet, and broadcasting. . . . Eye-catching pages provide much to consider, digest, and relish." Booklist

Includes glossary and bibliographical references

621.383   Telegraphy

Coe, Lewis, 1911-

The telegraph; a history of Morse's invention and its predecessors in the United States. McFarland & Co. 1993 184p il pa $29.95 hardcover o.p.

Grades: 7 8 9 10   **621.383**

1. Morse, Samuel Finley Breese, 1791-1872 2. Telegraph

ISBN 0-7864-1808-7 (pa)   LC 92-53597

This study of the development of the telegraph includes brief biographical sketches of Samuel Morse and other inventors

Includes bibliographical references

621.384   Radio and radar

Firestone, Mary, 1951-

Wireless technology. Lerner Publications 2009 48p il (Cool science) lib bdg $27.93

Grades: 4 5 6   **621.384**

1. Wireless communication systems

ISBN 978-0-8225-7590-0 (lib bdg); 0-8225-7590-6 (lib bdg)   LC 2007041102

This describes "how cutting-edge science helps people communicate better, live healthier, and have more fun!" Publisher's note

Includes glossary and bibliographical references

621.385   Telephony

Kummer, Patricia K.

The telephone. Franklin Watts 2006 80p il (Inventions that shaped the world) lib bdg $30.50

Grades: 6 7 8 9   **621.385**

1. Telephone

ISBN 978-0-531-12407-9 (lib bdg); 0-531-12407-X (lib bdg)   LC 2005-9958

"Describes the evolution of communication from smoke signals to e-mail, focusing on the invention of the telephone by Alexander Graham Bell in 1876, and explains how this technology changed America's economy and environment." Publisher's note

Includes bibliographical references

Stefoff, Rebecca, 1951-

The telephone; by Rebecca Stefoff. Marshall Cavendish Benchmark 2006 127p il (Great inventions) lib bdg $37.07 *

Grades: 7 8 9 10   **621.385**

1. Telephone

ISBN 0-7614-1879-2   LC 2004-22108

This is a history of the telephone, from Alexander Graham Bell to today's cell phones.

This is presented "thoughtfully yet conversationally. . . . [It] will reward steady reading." Horn Book Guide

Includes glossary and bibliographical references

621.388   Television

Otfinoski, Steven, 1949-

Television; [by] Steven Otfinoski. 1st ed. Marshall Cavendish Benchmark 2007 111p il (Great inventions) lib bdg $42.79

Grades: 7 8 9 10   **621.388**

1. Television

ISBN 978-0-7614-2228-0 (lib bdg); 0-7614-2228-5 (lib bdg)   LC 2005026787

"An examination of the origin, history, development, and societal impact of television." Publisher's note

Includes glossary and bibliographical references

621.4   Prime movers and heat engineering

Walker, Niki, 1972-

Generating wind power; [by] Niki Walker. Crabtree Pub. 2007 32p il (Energy revolution) lib bdg $25.20; pa $8.95

Grades: 5 6 7 8   **621.4**

1. Wind power

ISBN 978-0-7787-2913-6 (lib bdg); 0-7787-2913-3 (lib bdg); 978-0-7787-2927-3 (pa); 0-7787-2927-3 (pa)   LC 2006014370

This describes various ways of gathering and using wind power, and offers a brief history of wind power and energy conservation tips.

Walker, Niki, 1972-—*Continued*
"Vivid color photographs with informative captions extend the [text], showing diverse people and applications." SLJ
Includes glossary

621.43   Internal-combustion engines

Miller, Ron, 1947-
Rockets. Lerner 2008 112p il (Space innovations) lib bdg $31.93
Grades: 7 8 9 10   **621.43**
  1. Rockets (Aeronautics) 2. Rocketry
  ISBN 978-0-8225-7153-7; 0-8225-7153-6
                                      LC 2006-21220
The author "describes the history of rocket science, beginning in ancient China, where saltpeter, sulfur, and charcoal were first combined to create gunpowder. . . . The stories of the development of rockets through time are complemented by short biographies of important scientists such as Robert Goddard, stories of young model rocket makers, and sidebars explaining the science that makes rockets work. . . . It is a good choice for high school libraries, as well as for boys who are interested in science and nonfiction." Voice Youth Advocates
Includes bibliographical references

Otfinoski, Steven, 1949-
Rockets; [by] Steven Otfinoski. Marshall Cavendish Benchmark 2007 111p il (Great inventions) lib bdg $42.79
Grades: 7 8 9 10   **621.43**
  1. Rockets (Aeronautics) 2. Rocketry
  ISBN 978-0-7614-2232-7 (lib bdg); 0-7614-2232-3 (lib bdg)   LC 2005034205
"An examination of the origins, history, development, and impact of rockets and rocketry science." Publisher's note
Includes glossary and bibliographical references

621.47   Solar-energy engineering

Walker, Niki, 1972-
Harnessing power from the sun; [by] Niki Walker. Crabtree Pub. Co. 2007 32p il map (Energy revolution) lib bdg $23.93; pa $8.95
Grades: 5 6 7 8   **621.47**
  1. Solar energy
  ISBN 978-0-7787-2912-9 (lib bdg); 0-7787-2912-5 (lib bdg); 978-0-7787-2926-6 (pa); 0-7787-2926-5 (pa)
                                      LC 2006014368
This describes various ways of gathering and distributing solar energy, and includes a brief history of solar power, and tips on energy conservation.
"Vivid color photographs with informative captions extend the [text], showing diverse people and applications." SLJ
Includes glossary

621.48   Nuclear engineering

Kidd, J. S. (Jerry S.)
Nuclear power; the study of quarks and sparks; [by] J.S. Kidd and Renee A. Kidd. rev ed. Chelsea House 2006 208p il (Science and society) $35 *
Grades: 7 8 9 10   **621.48**
  1. Nuclear energy
  ISBN 978-0-8160-5606-4; 0-8160-5606-4
                                      LC 2005-52872
First published 1999 with title: Quarks and sparks: the story of nuclear power
Examines the people, events, and motivations leading up to modern-day discoveries and advances in nuclear physics
"Extensive scientific explanations are kept manageable, thanks to consistent references to their historical context; and descriptions of the nuclear race during the Second World War are especially riveting." Booklist [review of 1999 edition]
Includes bibliographical references

623.4   Ordnance

Collier, James Lincoln, 1928-
Gunpowder and weaponry. Benchmark Bks. 2004 124p il (Great inventions) lib bdg $37.07 *
Grades: 6 7 8 9   **623.4**
  1. Military art and science 2. Firearms 3. Gunpowder
  ISBN 0-7614-1540-8   LC 2002-156289
Contents: Warfare before gunpowder; Gunpowder changes the ways of war; The rise of the professional army; Europeans export their weapons; The beginnings of the modern army; The Industrial Revolution in weapons; The bloody century; What does it all mean?
This is a history of warfare and weaponry with emphasis on the significance of the invention of gunpowder
Includes bibliographical references

Fridell, Ron, 1943-
Military technology. Lerner Publications Co. 2008 48p il (Cool science) lib bdg $27.93
Grades: 4 5 6   **623.4**
  1. Weapons 2. Military art and science
  ISBN 978-0-8225-6769-1 (lib bdg); 0-8225-6769-5 (lib bdg)   LC 2006019404
A history of military technology from ancient to modern times
Includes glossary and bibliographical references

Gurstelle, William
The art of the catapult; build Greek ballistae, Roman onagers, English trebuchets, and more ancient artillery. Chicago Review Press 2004 172p il map $16.95
Grades: 5 6 7 8   **623.4**
  1. Catapult
  ISBN 1-55652-526-5
"This collection of 10 working catapult projects offers a fascinating look at world history, military strategy, and

Gurstelle, William—*Continued*
physics, related with an engaging yet lighthearted touch.
. . . Instructions are clear, with full materials lists, helpful diagrams, and no skipped steps. . . . There's excellent booktalk potential here, and lively reading even for
those who never get around to constructing a catapult."
SLJ
Includes bibliographical references

Hamilton, John, 1959-
Weapons of war. Abdo & Daughters 2002 48p
(War on terrorism) lib bdg $25.65
Grades: 7 8 9 10   623.4
1. Military weapons
ISBN 1-57765-673-3   LC 2001-55991
Briefly describes the history and gives examples of
military weapons and technology including various types
of ships, guns, missiles, planes, tanks, and weapons of
mass destruction
"Clear and well focused, this highly accessible text
delivers the basic facts and the advantages of various
craft. Excellent color photos show more than a dozen
different planes, as well as five helicopters and other major weapons in use." Booklist

The **new** weapons of the world encyclopedia; an
international encyclopedia from 5000 B.C. to the
21st century; [by] the Diagram Group. rev ed.
St Martin's Press 2007 368p il pa $24.95
Grades: 8 9 10 11 12 Adult   623.4
1. Weapons—History 2. Reference books
ISBN 978-0-312-36832-6 (pa); 0-312-36832-1 (pa)
First published 1980 with title: Weapons: an international encyclopedia from 5000 B.C. to 2000 A.D
This "guide covers the entire history of weapons, from
the earliest, most primitive instruments up to remarkable
advances in modern defense and warfare. . . . Includes
weapons used in Kosovo, Afghanistan, Iraq and the Isra-
el-Lebanon conflict. . . . [This book is] illustrated, with
hundreds of color diagrams, charts [and] photographs."
Publisher's note
Includes bibliographical references

Trueit, Trudi Strain
Gunpowder. Franklin Watts 2005 80p il
(Inventions that shaped the world) $30.50
Grades: 6 7 8 9   623.4
1. Gunpowder
ISBN 978-0-531-12371-3; 0-531-12371-5
LC 2004030437
Describes the invention of gunpowder, the impact it
has had on modern culture, and patterns of change that
resulted from its use
Includes bibliographical references

623.82   Nautical craft

Stefoff, Rebecca, 1951-
Submarines; [by] Rebecca Stefoff. Marshall
Cavendish Benchmark 2006 127p il (Great
inventions) lib bdg $39.93
Grades: 7 8 9 10   623.82
1. Submarines
ISBN 978-0-7614-2229-7 (lib bdg); 0-7614-2229-3 (lib
bdg)   LC 2005033984
"An examination of the origin, history, development,
and impact of the submarine and related underwater ex-
ploration and transport technology." Publisher's note
Includes glossary and bibliographical references

623.89   Navigation

Morrison, Taylor, 1971-
The coast mappers. Houghton Mifflin Co. 2004
45p il map $16
Grades: 5 6 7 8   623.89
1. Davidson, George 2. Maps 3. Surveying 4. Pacific
Coast (North America)
ISBN 0-618-25408-0   LC 2003-13534
Chronicles the difficulties encountered by George Davidson and others as they attempted to create nautical
charts to complete the U.S. Coast Survey of the West
Coast in the mid-nineteenth century
"Cartographic methods are clearly explained through
both the carefully researched text and the precise illustrations. . . . The artwork clarifies the text, depicts the
breathtaking beauty of the coastline, and adds a sense of
adventure." SLJ
Includes glossary and bibliographical references

Williams, Linda D., 1958-
Navigational aids; [by] Linda Williams.
Marshall Cavendish Benchmark 2007 c2008 128p
il (Great inventions) lib bdg $27.95
Grades: 6 7 8 9   623.89
1. Navigation
ISBN 978-0-7614-2599-1   LC 2006028959
"An examination of the origins, history, development,
and impact of the various navigational aids humans have
used through the centuries." Publisher's note
Includes glossary and bibliographical references

Young, Karen Romano, 1959-
Across the wide ocean; the why, how, and
where of navigation for humans and animals at
sea. Greenwillow Books 2007 78p il $18.99; lib
bdg $19.89
Grades: 4 5 6 7   623.89
1. Navigation 2. Ocean 3. Marine animals
ISBN   978-0-06-009086-9;   0-06-009086-3;
978-0-06-009087-6 (lib bdg); 0-06-009087-1 (lib bdg)
LC 2005-46146
"Readers follow such disparate entities as a logger-
head sea turtle, a nuclear submarine, and a sailboat crew

Young, Karen Romano, 1959-—*Continued*
seeking scientific sightings of North Atlantic right whales
as Young explores the concept of navigation. . . .
Larded with photos, diagrams, and maps. . . . Deceptively simple in appearance, the informative text can push
some intense mental activity." SLJ

624   Civil engineering

Aaseng, Nathan, 1953-
Construction: building the impossible. Oliver
Press (Minneapolis) 2000 144p il (Innovators)
$21.95
Grades: 6 7 8 9   **624**
1. Civil engineering
ISBN 1-88150-859-5   LC 98-51815
Profiles eight builders and their famous construction
projects, including Imhotep and the Step Pyramid,
Alexandre Eiffel and the Eiffel Tower, and William
Lamb and the Empire State Building
"The prose is clear and engaging, with a layperson's
approach to technical information. Sidebars feature relat-
ed anecdotes, fun facts, and word definitions. Historical
photos, drawings, and diagrams are fascinating and well
chosen." Booklist
Includes glossary and bibliographical references

Caney, Steven
Steven Caney's ultimate building book. Running
Press 2006 596p il $29.95 *
Grades: 4 5 6 7 8   **624**
1. Civil engineering 2. Building
ISBN 0-7624-0409-4
"Caney examines 'building' in its broadest sense, en-
compassing everything from skyscrapers and bridges to
bird feeders and peanut-shell 'bricks.' Opening sections
investigate the history and techniques of construction,
with clearly written explanations supported by black-and-
white photographs and diagrams. . . . The author reinforces important concepts of design in a way that is fascinating and effective." SLJ

Fantastic feats and failures; by the editors of YES
magazine. Kids Can Press 2004 52p il hardcover
o.p. pa $7.95
Grades: 4 5 6 7   **624**
1. Civil engineering
ISBN 1-55337-633-1; 1-55337-634-X (pa)
This "book spotlights 20 notable highs and lows in
engineering. The 'feats' celebrated include the Sydney
Opera House, the Brooklyn Bridge, and Canadarm (a
huge, Canadian-built robotic arm used for repairs in
space). Among the 'failures' are the space shuttle Challenger, the Tacoma Narrows Bridge, and the Chernobyl
nuclear power plant. . . . Well organized and engagingly
written. . . . Excellent photos . . . illustrate the places
and events discussed, while colorful drawings visually
represent concepts." Booklist

Levy, Matthys
Engineering the city; how infrastructure works:
projects and principles for beginners; [by] Matthys
Levy and Richard Panchyk. Chicago Review Press
2000 129p pa $14.95
Grades: 6 7 8 9   **624**
1. Civil engineering 2. Municipal engineering
ISBN 1-55652-419-6   LC 00-31774
"Combining a study of urban infrastructure with the
history of human development, the authors examine the
topics of water, transportation, waste and garbage disposal, and pollution. A wide variety of projects include scientific experiments and extension activities. . . . Containing scientific and historical information, this book
will serve as a springboard for cross-curricular projects
in history and science, with connections to math and language arts." Book Rep
Includes glossary and bibliographical references

Macaulay, David, 1946-
Underground. Houghton Mifflin 1976 109p il
$19; pa $9.95 *
Grades: 5 6 7 8 9   **624**
1. Civil engineering
ISBN 0-395-24739-X; 0-395-34065-9 (pa)
In this "examination of the intricate support systems
that lie beneath the street levels of our cities, Macaulay
explains the ways in which foundations for buildings are
laid or reinforced, and how the various utilities or transportation services are constructed." Bull Cent Child
Books
"Introduced by a visual index—a bird's eye view of
a busy, hypothetical intersection with colored indicators
marking the specific locations analyzed in subsequent
pages—detailed illustrations are combined with a clear,
precise narrative to make the subject comprehenssible
and fascinating." Horn Book
Includes glossary

Malam, John, 1957-
Super structures; written by John Malam;
illustrated by Mark Bergin; created and designed
by David Salariya. Watts 2000 32p il (Fast
forward) lib bdg $28 paperback o.p.
Grades: 4 5 6   **624**
1. Buildings 2. Structural engineering 3. Architecture
ISBN 0-531-11875-4 (lib bdg); 0-531-16441-1 (pa)
                                            LC 00-27640
Explores world-famous man-made structures of the ancient and modern world, discussing how they were built,
why they are important, and how architecture may
change in the future

Reeves, Diane Lindsey, 1959-
Career ideas for teens in architecture and
construction; [by] Diane Lindsey Reeves with Gail
Karlitz and Don Rauf. Ferguson 2005 170p il
(Career ideas for teens) $40
Grades: 7 8 9 10   **624**
1. Architecture 2. Building 3. Engineering
4. Vocational guidance
ISBN 0-8160-5289-1   LC 2004-20030

Reeves, Diane Lindsey, 1959-—*Continued*
The careers described in this book include architect,
carpenter, electrician, interior designer, and urban planner

Sullivan, George
Built to last; building America's amazing
bridges, dams, tunnels, and skyscrapers. Scholastic
Nonfiction 2005 128p il map $18.99 *
Grades: 5 6 7 8   624
1. Civil engineering
ISBN 0-439-51737-0   LC 2004-60996
This is a "survey of American building—from the Erie
Canal to Boston's current 'Big Dig.' Chronological chapters describe the historical forces that helped drive each
project as well as the specific technological feats linked
to each pioneering structure. . . . The wide selection of
captivating illustrations includes archival photos and engravings, architectural drawings, and color photos. . . .
Sullivan's skillful integration of social and economic history distinguishes this clear, well-designed title." Booklist

627   Hydraulic engineering

DuTemple, Lesley A., 1952-
The Hoover Dam. Lerner Publications Co. 2003
96p il map (Great building feats) lib bdg $27.93
Grades: 5 6 7 8   627
1. Hoover Dam (Ariz. and Nev.)
ISBN 978-0-8225-4691-7 (lib bdg); 0-8225-4691-4 (lib
bdg)   LC 2002-13951
The construction history Hoover Dam is presented
"A fascinating and well-thought-out portrayal of one
of the United States's most incredible engineering accomplishments. . . . The story is intriguing and the writing is engaging. Many black-and-white photographs, reproductions, and diagrams supplement the text nicely."
SLJ
Includes bibliographical references

Mann, Elizabeth, 1948-
Hoover Dam; with illustrations by Alan
Witschonke. Mikaya Press 2001 44p il (Wonders
of the world) $19.95; pa $9.95
Grades: 4 5 6 7   627
1. Hoover Dam (Ariz. and Nev.)
ISBN   978-1-931414-02-9;   1-931414-02-5;
978-1-931414-13-5 (pa); 1-931414-13-0 (pa)
                              LC 2001-34520
Describes the engineering, construction, and social and
historical contexts of the Hoover Dam
"A wonderfully readable, well-organized book filled
with fascinating detail." SLJ

629.13   Aeronautics

Carson, Mary Kay, 1964-
The Wright Brothers for kids; how they
invented the airplane: 21 activities exploring the
science and history of flight; illustrations by Laura
D'Argo. Chicago Review Press 2003 146p il pa
$14.95 *
Grades: 4 5 6 7   629.13
1. Wright, Orville, 1871-1948 2. Wright, Wilbur,
1867-1912 3. Aeronautics—History 4. Science—Experiments
ISBN 1-55652-477-3   LC 2002-155449
This account of the Wright brothers' invention of the
airplane, explains the forces of flight-lift, thrust, gravity,
and drag and includes such activities as making a Chinese flying top, building a kite, bird watching, making a
paper glider and a rubber-band-powered flyer
"A treasure trove of activities awaits readers of this
wonderfully executed survey of the Wright brothers and
their invention. The narrative flows easily and is complemented by numerous photographs that give a sense of
history and this event. . . . This is a valuable resource
for student reports and projects, and for classroom units."
SLJ
Includes glossary and bibliographical references

Finkelstein, Norman H., 1941-
Three across; the great transatlantic air race of
1927; [by] Norman H. Finkelstein. Calkins Creek
2008 134p il $17.95
Grades: 5 6 7 8   629.13
1. Lindbergh, Charles, 1902-1974 2. Levine, Charles
A., 1897-1991 3. Byrd, Richard Evelyn, 1888-1957
4. Aeronautics—History
ISBN 978-1-59078-462-4; 1-59078-462-6
                              LC 2007-18345
"Framing the story in way that should enthrall any
aviation fan, Finkelstein traces the rise of aviation from
Kitty Hawk to the 1927 Orteig Prize, a $25,000 award
for the first person to fly nonstop across the Atlantic.
This book focuses on the first three flights to pull it off:
the *Spirit of St. Louis*, piloted by Charles Lindbergh; the
Columbia, led by ambitious shyster Charles A. Levine;
and the *America*, boasting Arctic explorer Richard E.
Byrd at the controls." Booklist
Includes bibliographical references

Graham, Ian, 1953-
Flight. Kingfisher (NY) 2001 63p il maps
$16.95
Grades: 5 6 7 8   629.13
1. Aeronautics 2. Airplanes
ISBN 0-7534-5326-6   LC 2001-29001
Also available in paperback with title: The world of
flight
This introduction to aeronautics devotes "one section
to military uses of flight, four to civil or research aviation, then . . . [closes] with a gallery of pioneer machines. Its art, which is mostly painted or computer generated, has a clean, uncluttered look." SLJ
Includes glossary

629.133   Aircraft types

Faber, Harold
The airplane; [by] Harold Faber. Marshall Cavendish Benchmark 2006 128p il (Great inventions) lib bdg $37.07 *
Grades: 7 8 9 10   **629.133**
1. Airplanes 2. Aeronautics—History
ISBN 0-7614-1876-8   LC 2004-22107
This is history of aviation and its influence on American history and culture.
This is presented "thoughtfully yet conversationally. . . . [It] will reward steady reading." Horn Book Guide
Includes glossary and bibliographical references

Greger, Margaret
Kites for everyone; how to make and fly them; diagrams by Del Greger. 3rd ed. Dover Publications 2006 121p il pa $9.95
Grades: 7 8 9 10 11 12 Adult   **629.133**
1. Kites
ISBN 978-0-4864-5295-1 (pa); 0-4864-5295-6 (pa)
                                      LC 2006048453
First published 1984 by Richland, WA
This is a "guide with . . . illustrated instructions for creating more than 50 . . . airborne objects—everything from simple bag kites to Vietnamese, Snake, Dutch, Dragon, Bullet, Delta, and Flowform flyers." Publisher's note
Includes bibliographical references

Nahum, Andrew
Flying machine; written by Andrew Nahum. rev ed. DK Pub. 2004 72p il (DK eyewitness books) $15.99; lib bdg $19.99
Grades: 4 5 6 7   **629.133**
1. Aeronautics—History
ISBN 0-7566-0680-2; 0-7566-0679-9 (lib bdg)
First published 1990 by Knopf
A photo essay tracing the history and development of aircraft from hot-air balloons to jetliners. Includes information on the principles of flight and the inner workings of various flying machines.

Oxlade, Chris
Airplanes; uncovering technology. Firefly Books 2006 52p il $16.95
Grades: 4 5 6 7   **629.133**
1. Airplanes
ISBN 1-55407-134-8
This "book covers civilian and military airplanes and helicopters as well as the pilots and engineers that put them in the air. . . . [The] book contains four acetate overlays, used in some cases to show changes over time, in others to show a cutaway interior." Publisher's note
This offers "appealing visuals and plenty of well-chosen facts." SLJ

629.22   Types of vehicles

Balmer, Alden J.
Doc Fizzix mousetrap racers; the complete builder's manual; [by] Alden J. Balmer; [illustrations by Mike Harnisch] Fox Chapel 2008 142p il pa $14.95
Grades: 6 7 8 9   **629.22**
1. Automobiles—Models 2. Physics
ISBN 978-1-56523-359-1; 1-56523-359-X
"Building a mousetrap-powered model racer is more complex than it first appears, and Balmer uses this project as a springboard for teaching principles of physics such as energy, forces, torque, friction, and traction. . . . The author's enthusiasm for the topic and for teaching are apparent throughout, and his focus on safety is consistent. The thorough instructions are complemented by clear, captioned, full-color photos and line drawings and diagrams that illustrate each step of the construction process." SLJ

629.222   Passenger automobiles

Collier, James Lincoln, 1928-
The automobile; by James Lincoln Collier. Marshall Cavendish Benchmark 2005 112p il (Great inventions) lib bdg $37.07 *
Grades: 7 8 9 10   **629.222**
1. Automobiles
ISBN 0-7614-1877-6   LC 2004-22109
This is a history of the automobile and its affects on American culture.
This is presented "thoughtfully yet conversationally. . . . [It] will reward steady reading." Horn Book Guide
Includes glossary and bibliographical references

Edmonston, Louis-Philippe
Car smarts; hot tips for the car crazy; [by] Phil Edmonston and Maureen Sawa; illustrated by Gordon Suavé. Tundra 2004 76p il pa $15.95 *
Grades: 7 8 9 10   **629.222**
1. Automobiles
ISBN 0-88776-646-3
This offers a "look at the history and design of automobiles. . . . [It] discusses how cars work. . . . A chapter on ownership talks about financial issues, negotiating, and maintenance. The closing section covers the automotive future, with information on ecological issues, alternative fuels, hybrids, and fuel cells." SLJ
"Written in a lively style, the book provides solid information. . . . The many illustrations include colorful paintings, drawings, and photos as well as excellent diagrams of a car's working parts." Booklist

Mueller, Mike, 1959-
Corvette; by Mike Mueller with Bob Woods. Motorbooks 2006 80p il pa $9.95
Grades: 6 7 8 9   **629.222**

Mueller, Mike, 1959-—*Continued*
1. Automobiles
ISBN 0-7603-3231-3
"Mueller and Woods chart the evolution of what enthusiasts consider America's first sports car, following the vehicle's development, inside and out, through six generations of change. . . . But history actually comes in second to the great magazine-style photo gallery. . . . This is bound to draw a crowd." Booklist

Woods, Bob
Hottest muscle cars; by Bob Woods. Enslow Publishers 2008 48p il (Wild wheels!) lib bdg $23.93; pa $7.95
Grades: 4 5 6 7   629.222
1. Automobiles
ISBN 978-0-7660-2872-2 (lib bdg); 0-7660-2872-0 (lib bdg); 978-0-7660-3611-6 (pa); 0-7660-3611-1 (pa)
LC 2007007423
This focuses on "the beginning of America's love for muscle cars, and see why they are still loved today." Publisher's note
Includes glossary and bibliographical references

Hottest sports cars; by Bob Woods. Enslow Publishers 2008 48p il (Wild wheels!) lib bdg $23.93; pa $7.95
Grades: 4 5 6 7   629.222
1. Automobiles
ISBN 978-0-7660-2873-9 (lib bdg); 0-7660-2873-9 (lib bdg); 978-0-7660-3609-3 (pa); 0-7660-3909-X (pa)
LC 2007007428
This focuses on "some of the world's most famous sports cars; how they began, and where they are going in the future." Publisher's note
Includes glossary and bibliographical references

629.227 Cycles

Haduch, Bill
Go fly a bike! the ultimate book about bicycle fun, freedom & science; illustrated by Chris Murphy. Dutton Children's Books 2004 83p il $16.99 *
Grades: 4 5 6 7   629.227
1. Bicycles 2. Cycling
ISBN 0-525-47024-7
Gives the history, science, types of cycles, safety and the basics and maintenance of bicycles
"Halftone cartoonlike illustrations are scattered throughout, and a funny fact or joke appears in an inset on most pages. . . . This is a versatile, fact-packed book that can work for both research and recreational reading." Booklist

Sidwells, Chris, 1956-
Complete bike book. DK Pub. 2003 240p il hardcover o.p. pa $17.95 *
Grades: 8 9 10 11 12 Adult   629.227
1. Bicycles 2. Cycling
ISBN 0-7894-9337-3; 0-7566-1427-9 (pa)
LC 2003-40985

"The author begins with a short history of the bicycle, charting its evolution from a simple two-wheeled machine propelled by foot power . . . to today's ultramodern, high-tech vehicle. Individual chapters discuss such matters as proper cycling attire, how to teach a child to ride, how to tailor your diet to maximize its effectiveness, and how to maintain and repair your bike. . . . The book is perfect for newbies, for someone who cycles to work, and for the off-roader, the racer, and the person who sees cycling as a healthy workout." Booklist
Includes bibliographical references

Smedman, Lisa
From boneshakers to choppers; the rip-roaring history of motorcycles. Annick Press 2007 120p il $24.95; pa $14.95
Grades: 5 6 7 8   629.227
1. Motorcycles
ISBN   978-1-55451-016-0;   1-55451-016-3;
978-1-55451-015-3 (pa); 1-55451-015-5 (pa)
"Smedman defines 'motorcycles' broadly enough to include everything from Harleys to Vespas, and even bicycles, in this lively, wide-ranging history. . . . Illustrated with a generous array of action photos, historical shots, and period advertisements." Booklist
Includes bibliographical references

Woods, Bob
Hottest motorcycles; by Bob Woods. Enslow Publishers 2008 48p il (Wild wheels!) lib bdg $23.93; pa $7.95
Grades: 4 5 6 7   629.227
1. Motorcycles
ISBN 978-0-7660-2874-6 (lib bdg); 0-7660-2874-7 (lib bdg); 978-0-7660-3608-6 (pa); 0-7660-3608-1 (pa)
LC 2007007425
This focuses on "the motorcycle's beginning, the chopper phenomenon, and motorcycle racing." Publisher's note
Includes bibliographical references

629.4 Astronautics

Carlisle, Rodney P.
Exploring space. Facts on File 2005 152p il (Discovery and exploration) $40
Grades: 7 8 9 10   629.4
1. Astronautics 2. Outer space—Exploration
ISBN 978-0-8160-5265-3; 0-8160-5265-4
This title explores "multiple aspects of the history of [space] exploration. . . . Writing is generally clear, with data and quotes smoothly woven into the narrative." SLJ
Includes bibliographical references

Chaikin, Andrew, 1956-
Space; a history of space exploration in photographs; [by] Andrew Chaikin; foreword by James A. Lovell. Firefly Books 2004 c2002 249p il pa $24.95 *
Grades: 6 7 8 9   629.4

Chaikin, Andrew, 1956-—Continued
1. Outer space—Exploration
ISBN 1-55297-987-3
First published 2002 in the United Kingdom
This is a "collection of more than 300 images that pay tribute to and trace the history of space exploration." Publisher's note
"This book is proof that scientific photos not only can educate but also can be admired for their beauty. Text explains the intriguing photos and helps introduce each chapter." Voice Youth Advocates

Cole, Michael D.
Living on Mars; mission to the Red Planet. Enslow Pubs. 1999 48p il (Countdown to space) lib bdg $23.93
Grades: 4 5 6   **629.4**
1. Space flight to Mars 2. Mars (Planet)—Exploration
ISBN 0-7660-1121-6   LC 98-13125
"Half summary account of what we know about Mars from observations and space probes, and half a speculative mission profile for the first crewed expedition that will be sent there, this book sets the stage for one of our space program's next big objectives. The text is backed by endnotes citing almost as many Web sites as print sources." SLJ
Includes bibliographical references

Crompton, Samuel
Sputnik/Explorer 1; the race to conquer space; [by] Samuel Willard Crompton. Chelsea House 2007 106p il (Milestones in American history) lib bdg $35
Grades: 7 8 9 10   **629.4**
1. Astronautics 2. Space flight
ISBN 0-7910-9357-3 (lib bdg); 978-0-7910-9357-3 (lib bdg)   LC 2006034127
"This book begins in 1957 with Russia's successful launch of the first artificial sattellite. With the Cold War as a backdrop, the text goes on to describe the space race between the United States and Russia. . . . Many photographs, quotations, and sidebars detail the roles played by key figures." Horn Book Guide
Includes bibliographical references

Jedicke, Peter
Great moments in space exploration. Chelsea House 2007 72p il (Scientific American) $30
Grades: 5 6 7 8   **629.4**
1. Astronautics 2. Outer space—Exploration
ISBN 978-0-7910-9046-6; 0-7910-9046-9
LC 2006-14774
This "introduction to the history of space exploration is well illustrated with numerous photos, many from NASA. The history is well told, with the achievements of the Soviet Union, in particular, covered quite nicely." Sci Books Films
Includes glossary and bibliographical references

Miller, Ron, 1947-
Space exploration. Twenty-First Century Books 2008 112p il (Space innovations) lib bdg $31.93
Grades: 4 5 6 7   **629.4**
1. Astronautics 2. Outer space—Exploration
ISBN 978-0-8225-7155-1; 0-8225-7155-2
LC 2007002863
"Ron Miller describes the long, hard trek from the first tentative attempts to fly rocket-powered vehicles, to the first humans to brave traveling beyond Earth's atmosphere, to the explorers who left their footprints in the soil of the Moon." Publisher's note
"Busy pages include text, photographs, sidebars, and diagrams. . . . The information . . . is accurate and focused." Horn Book Guide
Includes glossary and bibliographical references

Nagel, Rob
Space exploration, Almanac; [by] Rob Nagel; Sarah Hermsen, project editor: Almanac. U.X.L, Thomson Gale 2005 2v il (Space exploration reference library) set$115
Grades: 7 8 9 10   **629.4**
1. Astronautics 2. Outer space—Exploration
ISBN 0-7876-9209-3   LC 2004-15823
Presenting key developments, discussion ranges from ancient views of a sun-centered universe to current understanding of planetary motion and gravity
Includes bibliographical references

Saari, Peggy
Space exploration, Primary sources; [by] Peggy Saari: Primary sources. U.X.L, Thomson Gale 2005 203p il (Space exploration reference library) $63
Grades: 7 8 9 10   **629.4**
1. Astronautics
ISBN 0-7876-9213-1   LC 2004-15879
This volume contains excerpts from 17 documents and speeches, beginning with a chapter from a Jules Verne book and ending with remarks made in early 2004 by George W. Bush on a new vision for space exploration. Each selection is introduced with material on the context, key points, and information on the author
Includes glossary and bibliographical references

Stone, Tanya Lee
Almost astronauts; 13 women who dared to dream. Candlewick Press 2008 133p il $24.99; pa $17.99 *
Grades: 5 6 7 8 9   **629.4**
1. Project Mercury—History 2. Women astronauts 3. Sex discrimination
ISBN 978-0-7636-3611-1; 0-7636-3611-8; 978-0-7636-4502-1 (pa); 0-7636-4502-8 (pa)
LC 2008-17487
"In 1960, thirteen American women passed the physical exams required to become astronauts as surely as any of the men already involved in NASA's early space flight endeavors, but they were disqualified solely because of their gender. This book is their story. . . . Many historical photographs help tell the story. . . . Any

Stone, Tanya Lee—*Continued*
girl with an interest in space flight or the history of
women's rights will enjoy this account and applaud these
courageous pioneers." Voice Youth Advocates
Includes bibliographical references

Stott, Carole
Space exploration; written by Carole Stott;
photographed by Steve Gorton. rev ed. DK Pub.
2004 72p il (DK eyewitness books) $15.99; lib
bdg $19.99
Grades: 4 5 6 7   **629.4**
1. Astronautics 2. Outer space—Exploration
ISBN 0-7566-0731-0; 0-7566-0730-2 (lib bdg)
First published 1997 by Knopf
Describes rockets, exploratory vehicles, and other
technological aspects of space exploration, satellites,
space stations, and the life and work of astronauts.

629.43 Unmanned space flight

Kerrod, Robin, 1938-
Space probes; [by] Robin Kerrod. World
Almanac Library 2005 48p il (History of space
exploration) lib bdg $30; pa $11.95 *
Grades: 5 6 7 8   **629.43**
1. Space probes
ISBN 0-8368-5708-9 (lib bdg); 0-8368-5715-1 (pa)
LC 2004-48207
Discusses how technology has changed the way we
look at the celestial bodies of our Solar System, and examines how the space probes have helped discover black
holes, star clusters, and nebulae
This "is profusely illustrated with sharply reproduced
space photos and artists' conceptions. . . . [This] makes
an important addition for any collection supporting avid
young scientists or strong science curricula." SLJ
Includes bibliographical references

Miller, Ron, 1947-
Robot explorers. Twenty-First Century Books
2007 112p il (Space innovations) lib bdg $31.93
Grades: 4 5 6   **629.43**
1. Space probes 2. Robots
ISBN 978-0-8225-7152-0 (lib bdg); 0-8225-7152-8 (lib
bdg)   LC 2007002864
This describes how robots are used for space explora-
tion
Includes bibliographical references

Siy, Alexandra
Cars on Mars; roving the red planet.
Charlesbridge 2009 57p il $18.95 *
Grades: 5 6 7 8   **629.43**
1. Mars (Planet)—Exploration 2. Space vehicles
ISBN 978-1-57091-462-1; 1-57091-462-1
LC 2008-40751
Presents an introduction to the Mars Exploration Ro-
vers (MERS), 'Spirit' and 'Opportunity,' with photo-

graphs of the Mars landscape taken over a five-year period as the rovers searched for water on the red planet.
"This title will sweep readers up in an exploratory
mission that has come closer than any other so far to
finding sure signs of extraterrestrial life." SLJ
Includes glossary and bibliographic references

Wunsch, Susi Trautmann
The adventures of Sojourner; the mission to
Mars that thrilled the world. Mikaya Press 1998
60p il lib bdg $22.95; pa $9.95
Grades: 5 6 7 8   **629.43**
1. Space flight to Mars 2. Mars (Planet)—Exploration
ISBN 0-9650493-5-3 (lib bdg); 0-9650493-6-1 (pa)
LC 98-7660
Tells the story of the mission that placed the Sojourn-
er remote-control rover on Mars on July 4, 1997
"The photographs not only cover *Sojourner's move-
ments* about the surface of Mars, but also track the entire
Mars project from its inception. In addition to an index,
there is a time line of all the Mars voyages and a page
of astronomical facts." Sci Books Films

629.44 Auxiliary spacecraft

Cole, Michael D.
The Columbia space shuttle disaster; from first
liftoff to tragic final flight. Enslow Pubs. 2003 48p
il (Countdown to space) lib bdg $18.95
Grades: 4 5 6   **629.44**
1. Columbia (Space shuttle) 2. Space vehicle accidents
ISBN 0-7660-2295-1   LC 2003-4823
First published 1995 with title: Columbia
Contents: A new kind of spaceship; Columbia in orbit;
Flight and reentry; Welcome home, Columbia!; Colum-
bia's last mission
Details the first flight of the space shuttle Columbia,
as well as its tragic final flight
"The account offers a lot of information, helping to
make sense of a highly complicated subject. . . . The
color and b&w photographs complement the story." Libr
Media Connect
Includes glossary and bibliographical references

Kerrod, Robin, 1938-
Space shuttles; [by] Robin Kerrod. World
Almanac Library 2005 48p il (History of space
exploration) lib bdg $30; pa $11.95
Grades: 5 6 7 8   **629.44**
1. Space shuttles
ISBN 0-8368-5709-7 (lib bdg); 0-8368-5716-X (pa)
LC 2004-49217
Explores the successes of the shuttle program, includ-
ing the daring recovery and repair of satellites by space-
walking astronauts, and examines the human and techno-
logical costs of its tragic failures, such as the losses the
Challenger and Columbia
This "is profusely illustrated with sharply reproduced
space photos and artists' conceptions. . . . [This] makes
an important addition for any collection supporting avid
young scientists or strong science curricula." SLJ
Includes bibliographical references

Kerrod, Robin, 1938-—Continued

Space stations; [by] Robin Kerrod. World Almanac Library 2005 48p il (History of space exploration) lib bdg $30; pa $11.95
Grades: 5 6 7 8   **629.44**
1. Space stations
ISBN 0-8368-5710-0 (lib bdg); 0-8368-5717-8 (pa)
                                    LC 2004-49071

Explores the history of space homes such as the Soviet's Salyut 1, Mir, the United States's Skylab, and the International Space Station, a truly international venture between several countries and scheduled for completion in 2008
This "is profusely illustrated with sharply reproduced space photos and artists' conceptions. . . . [This] makes an important addition for any collection supporting avid young scientists or strong science curricula." SLJ
Includes bibliographical references

Miller, Ron, 1947-
Satellites; by Ron Miller. Twenty-First Century Books 2007 112p il (Space innovations) lib bdg $31.93
Grades: 7 8 9 10   **629.44**
1. Artificial satellites
ISBN 978-0-8225-7154-4   LC 2007001075
This "begins with the science of Newton, the history of rockets, and the vivid imaginations of nineteenth-century science-fiction writers. It traces the historical development of man-made satellites from *Sputnik 1* to the Earth orbiters currently transmitting everything from Earth-based communications signals to images of the universe. . . . Illustrations include many small color photos and some paintings, diagrams, satellite images, and black-and-white photos. . . . Miller synthesizes his evident research into a well-organized discussion." Booklist
Includes bibliographical references

629.45 Manned space flight

Chaikin, Andrew, 1956-
Mission control, this is Apollo; the story of the first voyages to the moon; by Andrew Chaikin, with Victoria Kohl; with paintings by Alan Bean. Penguin Group 2009 114p il $23.99 *
Grades: 5 6 7 8   **629.45**
1. Project Apollo 2. Space flight to the moon 3. Astronautics
ISBN 978-0-670-01156-8; 0-670-01156-8
                                    LC 2009000833
"Based on interviews with 28 astronauts, this history of the Apollo program masterfully describes the missions and personalizes them with astronauts' own words. Chaikin starts with a brief overview of its origins and of the Mercury and Gemini missions. He then highlights the significance of each manned Apollo mission in chronological chapters, with full-page sidebars on such topics as food, TV coverage, space sickness and going to the bathroom in space. The handsome design has many photographs, diagrams of the rockets and modules and more than 30 well-reproduced paintings by Apollo 12 astronaut Bean." Kirkus
Includes bibliographical references

Collins, Michael, 1930-
Flying to the moon; an astronaut's story. 2nd ed, with a preface & a revised final chapter. Farrar, Straus & Giroux 1994 162p il pa $6.95
Grades: 5 6 7 8   **629.45**
1. Space flight to the moon 2. Astronauts
ISBN 0-374-42356-3   LC 93-42001
"A Sunburst book"
First published 1976 with title: Flying to the moon, and other strange places
Based in part on author's Carrying the fire (1974)
The author recounts his early days as an Air Force test pilot, his NASA training and his experiences aboard Gemini 10 and the Apollo 11 mission to the moon. Collins also advocates continued exploration of the universe
"A well told tale, which includes a lot of easily explained science." BAYA Book Rev

Dyer, Alan, 1953-
Mission to the moon. Simon & Schuster Books for Young Readers 2009 80p il $19.99
Grades: 5 6 7   **629.45**
1. Project Apollo (U.S.)—Juvenile literature. 2. Space flight to the moon 3. Moon—Exploration
ISBN 978-1-4169-7935-7; 1-4169-7935-2
                                    LC 2008061118
"A Weldon Owen production"
"Sporting a highly visual encyclopedic format, this informative book features 200 photographs documenting early research into mankind's history with the moon, early space exploration and the space race, and the Apollo missions. Detailed cross-sections of modules, space suits and other equipment offer a sound technological overview, while information on the phases, structure and surface of the moon provides added insight. . . . A DVD and poster are included." Publ Wkly

Dyson, Marianne J.
Home on the moon; living on a space frontier. National Geographic Soc. 2003 64p il $18.95
Grades: 4 5 6 7   **629.45**
1. Moon
ISBN 0-7922-7193-9   LC 2002-5280
Considers the moon as a frontier that has been only partially explored, looking at its history, geography, and weather, as well as what people would require to live and work there. Includes activities
"Clear writing, vivid images, interesting details, and quotes from astronauts and scientists make this a lively, fact-filled introduction." Booklist
Includes glossary and bibliographical references

Godwin, Robert
Project Apollo; exploring the Moon. Apogee Books 2006 49p il (Pocket space guide) pa $9.95
Grades: 7 8 9 10 11 12   **629.45**
1. Project Apollo 2. Space flight to the moon 3. Moon—Exploration
ISBN 978-1-894959-37-7 (pa); 1-894959-37-X (pa)
                                    LC 2007-5457
"Facts and images for Apollo missions 12 through 17 are covered in this concise guide to the program's essen-

Godwin, Robert—*Continued*

tials—mission objectives, dates, flight plans, astronauts, space suits, and vehicles—for collectors, educators, space enthusiasts, and those just discovering the history of the space program." Publisher's note

Goodman, Susan, 1952-

Ultimate field trip 5; blasting off to Space Academy; by Susan E. Goodman; photographs by Michael J. Doolittle. Atheneum Bks. for Young Readers 2001 41p il $17 paperback o.p.

Grades: 4 5 6 7   **629.45**

1. U.S. Space Camp (Huntsville, Ala.) 2. Astronauts 3. Space flight

ISBN 0-689-83044-0; 0-689-84863-3 (pa)

             LC 00-38082

"This book follows student trainees through a weeklong session at the U.S. Space Academy in Huntsville, AL, as they are exposed to what it takes to become an astronaut and to the inner workings of the entire space program. . . . Varied-colored pages, replete with outstanding full-color, captioned photos, are artistically appealing as well as informative." SLJ

Includes glossary and bibliographical references

Kuhn, Betsy

The race for space; the United States and Soviet Union compete for the new frontier. Lerner 2006 c2007 112p il (People's history) lib bdg $31.93 *

Grades: 6 7 8 9   **629.45**

1. Astronautics

ISBN 978-0-8225-5984-9 (lib bdg); 0-8225-5984-6 (lib bdg)

This book "tells the story of the competition between the United States and the Soviet Union to become the world leader in space exploration." Sci Books Films

"Kuhn has seamlessly woven the history into a compelling story." Booklist

Includes bibliographical references

Platt, Richard, 1953-

Moon landing; a pop-up celebration of Apollo 11; by Richard Platt; paper engineering by David Hawcock. Candlewick Press 2008 unp il $29.99

Grades: 4 5 6 7   **629.45**

1. Apollo 11 (Spacecraft) 2. Space flight to the moon 3. Pop-up books

ISBN 978-0-7636-4046-0; 0-7636-4046-8

"This is a handsome, carefully engineered compendium. The text begins with the so-called space race between the United States and the Soviet Union in the 1950s and '60s and then offers brief descriptions of the 17 flights that made up the Apollo program. Here the emphasis is on the famous landing of the *Eagle* on the Moon in July 1969. The pop-ups and foldout pages on sturdy, shiny paper demonstrate the mechanical aspects of the spacecraft and offer a bold sense of both the rocketry and the trip. Small photographs and drawings surround the larger views." SLJ

Saari, Peggy

Space exploration, Biographies; [by] Peggy Saar; Lawrence W. Baker, Sarah Hermsen, and Deborah J. Baker, project editors. U.X.L, Thomson Gale 2005 219p il (Space exploration reference library) $63

Grades: 7 8 9 10   **629.45**

1. Astronauts 2. Outer space—Exploration

ISBN 0-7876-9212-3   LC 2004-15822

This volume profiles 25 astronauts, scientists, theorists, and writers involved in space exploration, including Sally Ride, Yuri A. Gagarin, Neil Armstrong, John H. Glenn, Jr., Ellen Ochoa, Hermann Oberth and others

Includes bibliographical references

Solway, Andrew

Can we travel to the stars? space flight and space exploration. Heinemann Library 2006 48p il (Stargazers guides) lib bdg $31.43; pa $8.99

Grades: 4 5 6   **629.45**

1. Interplanetary voyages 2. Astronautics 3. Outer space—Exploration 4. Space flight

ISBN 978-1-4034-7711-8 (lib bdg); 1-4034-7711-6 (lib bdg); 978-1-4034-7718-7 (pa); 1-4034-7718-3 (pa)

           LC 2005-29086

Realistically explores the possibility of mankind ever achieving the goal of traveling to the planets and to other stars

This book "is clearly written and engaging . . . with just the right level of information and explanation." Horn Book Guide

Includes glossary and bibliographical references

Thimmesh, Catherine

Team moon; how 400,000 people landed Apollo 11 on the moon. Houghton Mifflin Company 2006 80p il $19.95 *

Grades: 5 6 7 8   **629.45**

1. Apollo 11 (Spacecraft) 2. Space flight to the moon

ISBN 0-618-50757-4   LC 2005-10755

"Thimmesh retraces the course of the space mission that landed an actual man, on the actual Moon. It's an oft-told tale, but the author tells it from the point of view not of astronauts or general observers, but of some of the 17,000 behind-the-scenes workers at Kennedy Space Center, the 7500 Grumman employees who built the lunar module, the 500 designers and seamstresses who actually constructed the space suits, and other low-profile contributors who made the historic flight possible. . . . This dramatic account will mesmerize even readers already familiar with the event. . . . This stirring, authoritative tribute to the collective effort . . . belongs in every collection." SLJ

Includes glossary and bibliographical references

629.46 Engineering of unmanned spacecraft

Johnson, Rebecca L., 1956-
Satellites. Lerner Publications Co. 2006 48p il (Cool science) lib bdg $25.26
Grades: 4 5 6   **629.46**
1. Artificial satellites
ISBN 978-0-8225-2908-8; 0-8225-2908-4
LC 2004-30298
This book has "an attractive, colorful layout that will appeal to readers. Each spread includes captioned, color photographs and/or illustrations; text boxes; and, often, a 'fun fact.' . . . [This] title explains what a satellite is and discusses many aspects of satellites, including how they pertain to television broadcasts, weather forecasting, and locating black holes. Numerous amazing facts are included to pique readers' interest." SLJ
Includes bibliographical references

629.8 Automatic control engineering

Domaine, Helena
Robotics. Lerner 2005 48p il (Cool science) lib bdg $25.26
Grades: 4 5 6   **629.8**
1. Robots
ISBN 0-8225-2112-1   LC 2004-13938
This "offers a brief history of efforts to create machines that can perform functions in place of humans, then brings readers up-to-date on applications of robotic technology in exploration, industry, and medicine." Booklist
This has "an attractive, colorful layout that will appeal to readers. Each spread includes captioned, color photographs and/or illustrations; text boxes; and, often, a fun fact. . . . The content is sound and should be accessible to most students." SLJ

Henderson, Harry, 1951-
Modern robotics; building versatile machines. Chelsea House 2006 xx, 188p il (Milestones in discovery and invention) $35
Grades: 7 8 9 10 11 12   **629.8**
1. Robots
ISBN 0-8160-5745-1   LC 2005-31805
This book presents "biographies of the men and women who were and are the leaders in bringing about this change through research and new technologies." Publisher's note
Includes glossary and bibliographical references

Jones, David
Mighty robots; mechanical marvels that fascinate and frighten. Annick Press 2006 126p il $24.95; pa $14.95 *
Grades: 5 6 7 8 9 10   **629.8**

1. Robots
ISBN 1-55037-929-1; 1-55037-928-3 (pa)
"From the development of robotic technology to the history of robots in books and films, this informative offering surveys the field broadly but zeroes in with detailed accounts of many topics. . . . Many clear color photos and detailed sidebars expand the text. . . . Jones presents a great deal of information in a well-organized, accessible manner." Booklist

Lockman, Darcy
Robots. Benchmark Bks. (Tarrytown) 2001 48p il (Kaleidoscope) $25.64
Grades: 4 5 6   **629.8**
1. Robots
ISBN 0-7614-1047-3   LC 99-58311
Provides a brief history of robotics, describes tasks for which robots are useful, and suggests future development
Includes bibliographical references

Stefoff, Rebecca, 1951-
Robots. Marshall Cavendish Benchmark 2007 c2008 144p il (Great inventions) lib bdg $27.95
Grades: 6 7 8 9   **629.8**
1. Robots
ISBN 978-0-7614-2601-1
This is a history of robots in the imagination, from ancient myths to motion pictures, and in reality, including toy robots and robots in medicine, manufacturing, the military, science, and space exploration
Includes glossary and bibliographical references

VanVoorst, Jennifer, 1972-
Rise of the thinking machines; the science of robots. Compass Point Books 2009 48p il (Headline science) lib bdg $27.93; pa $7.95
Grades: 5 6 7   **629.8**
1. Robots
ISBN 978-0-7565-3377-9 (lib bdg); 0-7565-3377-5 (lib bdg); 978-0-7565-3518-6 (pa); 0-7565-3518-2 (pa)
LC 2008-05732
"Describes various types of robots and their functions, discusses technological advancements in the field of robotics, and considers the ethical issues surrounding autonomous robots." Publisher's note
Includes glossary and bibliographical references

630 Agriculture

Casper, Julie Kerr
Agriculture; the food we grow and animals we raise. Chelsea House 2007 210p il (Natural resources) $39.50
Grades: 8 9 10 11 12   **630**
1. Agriculture
ISBN 978-0-8160-6352-9; 0-8160-6352-4
LC 2006027454
This "explores why managing the land, water, and soil is a balancing act and why recycling, reducing, and reusing are concepts that affect everyone—now and in the future." Publisher's note
Includes bibliographical references

Halley, Ned

Farm. Dorling Kindersley 2000 63p il (DK eyewitness books) $15.99; lib bdg $19.99

Grades: 4 5 6 7   **630**

1. Agriculture 2. Farms

ISBN 0-7894-6040-8; 0-7894-6615-5 (lib bdg)

First published 1996 by Knopf

Text and photographs depict different aspects of farming through the ages including the equipment, domestic animals, crops, and the future of farming

Hopkins, William G.

Plant biotechnology. Chelsea House 2006 143p il (The green world) lib bdg $37.50

Grades: 7 8 9 10   **630**

1. Biotechnology 2. Plants 3. Food—Biotechnology

ISBN 0-7910-8964-9

"This is a highly accurate, very well written book about both the history of and current innovations in, plant biotechnology. The illustrative pictures are clear and attractive." Sci Books Films

Includes bibliographical references

630.9   Agriculture—Historical and geographic treatment

Rosen, Michael J., 1954-

Our farm; four seasons with five kids on one family's farm; written and photographed by Michael J. Rosen. Darby Creek Pub. 2008 144p il $18.95 *

Grades: 4 5 6 7 8   **630.9**

1. Farm life—United States 2. Ohio 3. Family life

ISBN 978-1-58196-067-9; 1-58196-067-0

A journal of one year on the Bennett farm in central Ohio. Shows how one family, with the help of relatives and friends, creates a life and livelihood on a 150-acre farm.

"This engaging book is an unsentimental, appreciative look into the world of one farm family." SLJ

633.5   Fiber crops

Meltzer, Milton, 1915-

The cotton gin. Benchmark Bks. 2003 c2004 123p il (Great inventions) lib bdg $25.95 *

Grades: 6 7 8 9   **633.5**

1. Cotton

ISBN 0-7614-1537-8   LC 2002-15308

The author describes the invention of the cotton gin and its effects on history including "the influence of mechanized cotton processing on the growth of slavery in the United States and the increase in textile mills. . . . The author expertly describes a setting that is ripe for invention. Powerful photographs . . . historical artwork, and personal narratives make the times real and relevant to readers." SLJ

Includes bibliographical references

634.9   Forestry

Colson, Mary, 1972-

Forest furnace; wildfires. Raintree 2004 48p il (Turbulent planet) lib bdg $22; pa $8.99

Grades: 6 7 8 9   **634.9**

1. Forest fires 2. Wildfires 3. Fires

ISBN 978-1-410-90588-8; 1-410-90588-8; 978-1-410-91026-4 (pa); 1-410-91026-1 (pa)

LC 2003-8295

Presents information on forest fires, giving specific examples from around the world

Includes bibliographical references

Morrison, Taylor, 1971-

Wildfire. Houghton Mifflin Co. 2006 48p il $17

Grades: 4 5 6   **634.9**

1. Wildfires 2. Forest fires

ISBN 978-0-618-50900-3; 0-618-50900-3

LC 2005-30483

"Walter Lorraine books"

This is an "overview of the people involved in fighting wildfires and the techniques and equipment they use. Detailed paintings aid in explaining how firefighters work and in describing the natural conditions that lead to initial fires and more dangerous developments. . . . The pages are packed with visual and textual information." SLJ

Includes glossary and bibliographical references

635   Garden crops (Horticulture) Vegetables

Morris, Karyn

The Kids Can Press jumbo book of gardening; written by Karyn Morris; illustrated by Jane Kurisu. Kids Can Press 2000 240p il pa $14.95 *

Grades: 4 5 6 7   **635**

1. Gardening

ISBN 1-55074-690-1

"Sections cover general information; fruit, vegetable, and flower gardens; noninvasive native plants; gardens that attract wildlife; and group projects. Projects range from a few annuals in a container and thickets designed with native wildlife in mind to community gardens. Directions are clear, with plenty of diagrams and illustrations." Booklist

Winckler, Suzanne, 1946-

Planting the seed; a guide to gardening. Lerner Publs. 2002 64p il lib bdg $25.26; pa $7.95 *

Grades: 5 6 7 8   **635**

1. Gardening

ISBN 0-8225-0081-7 (lib bdg); 0-8225-0471-5 (pa)

LC 2001-2018

"Loosely organized into the stages of planning, planting, maintaining, and harvesting a garden, the chapters offer a basic introduction to key concepts, such as growing zones, native plants, and compost. The book also ad-

Winckler, Suzanne, 1946-—*Continued*
dresses Native American gardening traditions and community gardens as well as Earth-friendly topics such as organic pest control . . . and heirloom gardens. . . . Interested young people will glean some basics and find useful resources for further exploration." Booklist
Includes glossary and bibliographical references

635.9 Flowers and ornamental plants

Rice, Barry A.
Growing carnivorous plants; [by] Barry A. Rice. Timber 2006 224p il $39.95
Grades: 7 8 9   635.9
1. Carnivorous plants
ISBN 978-0-8819-2807-5; 0-8819-2807-0
                                                LC 2007295063
A "guide to identifying and cultivating [carnivorous plants]. . . . This book will help readers select the best plants to grow on a windowsill, in a terrarium or greenhouse. Information on how to feed carnivorous plants [is included]." Publisher's note
Includes bibliographical references

636 Animal husbandry

Keenan, Sheila, 1953-
Animals in the house; a history of pets and people. Scholastic Nonfiction 2007 112p il $17.99 *
Grades: 4 5 6   636
1. Pets
ISBN 978-0-439-69286-1; 0-439-69286-5
"Kennan provides an overview of pets *and* their people. Beginning with statistics about pet ownership, the text goes on to describe how animals and humans came together . . . and discusses how this relationship has changed and deepened. . . . Eye-catchingly designed, the format uses Photoshop to best advantage, providing interesting graphics, popping borders, and plenty of pictures featuring adorable animals." Booklist
Includes bibliographical references

McAlpine, Margaret
Working with animals. Gareth Stevens Pub. 2005 64p il (My future career) lib bdg $24
Grades: 6 7 8 9   636
1. Animals 2. Vocational guidance
ISBN 0-8368-4240-5   LC 2004-45229
This describes seven occupations related to animals, such as animal groomer and zookeeper, including the responsibilities, qualifications, and best personality type for each one
"The writing is clear and interesting, and the [book is] visually well organized." SLJ
Includes bibliographical references

636.088 Animals for specific purposes

Kent, Deborah, 1948-
Animal helpers for the disabled. Watts 2003 63p il $24; pa $8.95
Grades: 4 5 6 7   636.088
1. Animals and the handicapped 2. Animals—Training 3. Guide dogs
ISBN 0-531-12017-1; 0-531-16663-5 (pa)
                                                LC 2002-8885
"Watts library"
Explores the history of guide dogs, service animals, and assistance dogs, and discusses the process of training them to help people who have physical disabilities
This is an "informative, often inspirational and thought-provoking [book]." Booklist
Includes bibliographical references

Laidlaw, Rob
Wild animals in captivity; [by] Rob Laidlaw. Fitzhenry & Whiteside 2008 48p il $19.95
Grades: 5 6 7 8   636.088
1. Animal welfare 2. Zoos
ISBN 978-1-55455-025-8; 1-55455-025-4
"A passionate, well-written, and well-researched argument against the practices of most zoos around the world. . . . Describes the damage done when animals are unnaturally confined and moved to inhospitable climates, and compares the wild and captive lives of polar bears, orcas, elephants, and great apes—the four species most harmed by captivity. . . . The issues raised in this important and powerful book will resonate with young and old." SLJ

Markle, Sandra, 1946-
Animal heroes; true rescue stories; by Sandra Markle. Millbrook Press 2009 64p il lib bdg $29.27
Grades: 4 5 6 7   636.088
1. Pets 2. Animals 3. Rescue work
ISBN 978-0-8225-7884-0 (lib bdg); 0-8225-7884-0 (lib bdg)   LC 2007-50435
"Nine stories, based on interviews with the grateful survivors, describe how brave animals rescued people in catastrophic circumstances. Each edgy retelling reveals details that only the participants could know, including sounds, smells, sights, and the knowledge that at any moment they could die, deepening the tension. Mixed in are Markle's broad and perfectly attuned insights about animal behavior." SLJ
Includes glossary and bibliographical references

636.089 Veterinary sciences. Veterinary medicine

Jackson, Donna M., 1959-
ER vets; life in an animal emergency room. Houghton Mifflin 2005 88p il $17 *
Grades: 5 6 7 8   636.089

Jackson, Donna M., 1959-—_Continued_
1. Veterinary medicine
ISBN 0-618-43663-4

"With plentiful, excellent-quality photographs, this highly visual book offers a behind-the-scenes look at an emergency animal hospital in Colorado. . . . A section on grief counseling for families with critically ill pets and a spread on how to put together a pet first-aid kit are included. Well-researched and well-written, ER Vets is an engaging book on a hot topic." SLJ

636.1   Equines. Horses

Clutton-Brock, Juliet
Horse; written by Juliet Clutton-Brock. DK Pub. 2008 72p il (DK eyewitness books) $15.99
Grades: 4 5 6 7   **636.1**
1. Horses
ISBN 978-0-7566-3775-0; 0-7566-3775-9
                           LC 2008276033
First published 2003 in the United Kingdom
Includes CD-ROM
Examines the anatomy, history, and breeds of horses, and discusses the different ways horses have been used throughout history

Ransford, Sandy
The Kingfisher illustrated horse & pony encyclopedia; written by Sandy Ransford; photographed by Bob Langrish. Kingfisher 2004 224p il $24.95 *
Grades: 4 5 6 7   **636.1**
1. Horses 2. Horsemanship
ISBN 0-7534-5781-4   LC 2003-27293
"The first part of the book covers the life cycle, domestication, and types of horses and ponies. . . . The second part deals with how to care for these animals and discusses horsemanship from taking riding lessons to training and driving a horse. . . . Filled with appealing photos of young people interacting with their four-legged friends, this title is an extremely useful addition to any collection." SLJ

Stefoff, Rebecca, 1951-
Horses. Benchmark Books 2001 112p il (Animalways) $34.21
Grades: 6 7 8 9   **636.1**
1. Horses
ISBN 978-0-7614-1139-0; 0-7614-1139-9
                           LC 99-58365
Discusses the history of horses and their domestication by humans, as well as their physical characteristics and behavior
"The information is mostly presented in clear and exhaustive detail. . . . Divided into easily navigated sections, . . . [this book is an] excellent choice[s] for students seeking report material." Booklist
Includes glossary and bibliographical references

636.2   Ruminants and Camelidae Bovidae Cattle

Freedman, Russell
In the days of the vaqueros; America's first true cowboys. Clarion Bks. 2001 70p il $18; pa $9.99 *
Grades: 4 5 6 7   **636.2**
1. Cowhands 2. Mexican Americans 3. Ranch life 4. Southwestern States
ISBN   0-395-96788-0;   978-0-395-96788-1; 978-0-547-13365-2 (pa); 0-547-13365-0 (pa)
                           LC 2001-17357
"Freedman explores the often-overlooked role of the Central American cowherders who preceded by centuries the cowboys of popular lore and legend." SLJ
The author "tells the story with depth, clarity, and a vigor that conveys the thrilling excitement of the work and the macho swagger of the culture. . . . The book's design is beautiful, with spacious type on thick paper, and the dazzling illustrations—prints, paintings, and photos on almost every page." Booklist
Includes glossary and bibliographical references

636.7   Dogs

American Kennel Club
The complete dog book; American Kennel Club. 20th ed. Ballantine Books 2006 xxi, 858p il $35
Grades: 7 8 9 10 11 12 Adult   **636.7**
1. Dogs
ISBN 0-345-47626-3; 978-0-345-47626-5
                           LC 2005-48263
"Official publication of the American Kennel Club"
First published 1935. Periodically revised
"The official guide to 124 AKC registered breeds and their history, appearance, selection, training, care and feeding, and first aid. Some color plates." N Y Public Libr. Ref Books for Child Collect. 2d edition

Bolan, Sandra
Caring for your mutt; [by] Sandra Bolan. ElDorado Ink 2008 128p (Our best friends) lib bdg $25.95
Grades: 7 8 9 10 11 12   **636.7**
1. Dogs
ISBN 978-1-932904-20-8; 1-932904-20-4
                           LC 2007051607
"Although Bolan's excellent advice on selection, training, and care applies to nearly all canines, she makes it plain that mixed breeds can be a 'challenging guessing game' when it comes to predicting size, temperment, and overall health. All the expected information is here, clearly presented and quite thorough." Booklist
Includes bibliographical references

The **Complete** dog book for kids; official publication of the American Kennel Club. Howell Book House 1996 274p il maps hardcover o.p. pa $22.95 *
Grades: 4 5 6 7   636.7
1. Dogs
ISBN 0-87605-458-0; 0-87605-460-2 (pa)
LC 96-29228
This "begins with a general section that advises readers on buying a dog, responsibilities, rewards, and how to match a dog with one's situation. . . . More than 100 dogs are profiled, with information on history, appearance, health, and 'fun facts.' Crisp color photographs accompany each article. . . . A final section gives good advice about nutrition and health issues." Booklist

Gorrell, Gena K. (Gena Kinton), 1946-
Working like a dog; the story of working dogs through history. Tundra 2003 156p il pa $16.95
Grades: 4 5 6 7   636.7
1. Working dogs
ISBN 0-88776-589-0
"Gorrell begins by tracing the evolution of 'household canids' from the wild into the civilized world. Other chapters delve into the many ways in which these animals have been viewed throughout history, what makes particular breeds right for certain jobs, dogs at war, famous pooches, etc. . . . The well-captioned, black-and-white photographs and reproductions add greatly to a narrative that's packed with intriguing details." SLJ
Includes bibliographical references

Mehus-Roe, Kristin
Dogs for kids! everything you need to know about dogs; by Kristin Mehus-Roe. BowTie Press 2007 384p il pa $14.95
Grades: 4 5 6 7   636.7
1. Dogs
ISBN 978-1-931993-83-8 (pa); 1-931993-83-1 (pa)
LC 2006035434
"If you are looking for a book about canines that is entertaining as well as immensely informative, this is it. In a lively, conversational tone, Mehus-Roe offers a vast amount of material, from the history of dogs to vacationing with a pet, and provides practical and upbeat explanations, ideas, offbeat tidbits, and pertinent details." SLJ
Includes bibliographical references

Stefoff, Rebecca, 1951-
Dogs. Benchmark Bks. 2002 110p il (Animalways) lib bdg $34.21
Grades: 6 7 8 9   636.7
1. Dogs
ISBN 0-7614-1393-6   LC 2002-1530
This describes dogs' relationship to people, their evolution, biology, behavior, life cycle, and diversity.
Includes glossary and bibliographical references

Whitehead, Sarah
How to speak dog. Scholastic Reference 2008 96p il pa $6.99
Grades: 4 5 6 7 8   636.7

1. Dogs
ISBN 978-0-545-02078-7 (pa); 0-545-02078-6 (pa)
Explains how to read a dog's body language and vocalizations and presents step-by-step instructions for training, housebreaking, teaching tricks, and playing several types of games.
This is "well-organized and interesting. . . . Whitehead discusses, and clearly shows in good-quality, full-color photographs, various canine emotions." SLJ

636.8 Cats

Bidner, Jenni
Is my cat a tiger? how your cat compares to its wild cousins. Lark Books 2006 64p il $9.95
Grades: 3 4 5 6   636.8
1. Cats 2. Wild cats
ISBN 1-57990-815-2   LC 2006023356
"This book shows how domestic cats compare with their wild cousins. Specifically, it addresses what domestic behavior reveals about wild roots. . . . The color photographs are fantastic. . . . This is a fascinating volume." SLJ

Edney, A. T. B.
ASPCA complete cat care manual; [by] Andrew Edney; foreword by Roger Caras. Dorling Kindersley 1992 192p il hardcover o.p. pa $14.95
Grades: 8 9 10 11 12 Adult   636.8
1. Cats
ISBN 1-56458-064-4; 0-7566-1742-1 (pa)
LC 92-52783
Subtitle on cover: The ultimate illustrated guide to caring for your cat
"Cat care is made easy through step-by-step photographs that illustrate grooming, handling, detecting illness, first aid, and other concerns. Difficult-to-explain procedures, such as how to administer medication or transport an injured cat, are clearly understandable." Libr J
Includes bibliographical references

Stefoff, Rebecca, 1951-
Cats. Benchmark Bks. 2004 112p il (Animalways) $34.21
Grades: 6 7 8 9   636.8
1. Cats
ISBN 0-7614-1577-7   LC 2002-155247
Contents: Cats and people; How cats developed; The biology of the cat; The life cycle; Feline behavior; Cats today
This introduction to cat biology, life cycle, behavior, and relationship to people offers "a strong combination of text and illustration." SLJ
Includes bibliographical references

Whitehead, Sarah
How to speak cat. Scholastic 2009 96p il pa $6.99
Grades: 4 5 6 7 8   636.8

Whitehead, Sarah—*Continued*
1. Cats
ISBN 978-0-545-02079-4; 0-545-02079-4
"This pet-care book focuses on developing a relationship with a pet. The author states that the communication process is a two-way street, and she describes how readers can translate a cat's body language and vocalizations. . . . the bright color photographs of children with their cats on every page will appeal greatly to readers. This is a fun book that offers a good understanding of its audience and subject." SLJ

636.9   Other mammals

McNicholas, June, 1956-
Rats. Heinemann Lib. 2003 48p il (Keeping unusual pets) $24.22
Grades: 4 5 6 7   636.9
1. Rats
ISBN 1-4034-0283-3   LC 2002-3164
Contents: What is a rat?; Ratty facts; Is a rat for you?; What do I need?; Routine care; Handling and play; Health issues; Major problems; A record of your rat
Describes how to select a pet rat, what to feed it, and when to take it to the vet, as well as how to keep a pet scrapbook
"A valuable, accessible resource." Booklist
Includes bibliographical references

Sullivant, Holly J.
Hamsters. ElDorado Ink 2009 il (Our best friends) $26.95
Grades: 7 8 9 10 11 12   636.9
1. Hamsters
ISBN 978-1-93290430-7   LC 2008040365
This is a guide to caring for a pet hamster.
"An ideal resource for those kids (or even adults) looking for a cradle-to-grave primer on responsible pet ownership. . . . Well formatted and broken up with vivid photographs and fascinating 'Fast Facts.'" Booklist

638   Insect culture

Harkins, Susan Sales
Design your own butterfly garden; by Susan Sales Harkins and William H. Harkins. Mitchell Lane Publishers 2008 48p il (Robbie reader. Gardening for kids) lib bdg $29.95
Grades: 4 5 6   638
1. Butterfly gardens
ISBN 978-1-58415-638-3; 1-58415-638-4
LC 2008-2245
Introduces the principles of butterfly gardening, discussing how to plan the garden, what flowers to plant there, and how to maintain it in all seasons.
"All the tasks delineated are well within the scope of children's abilities, and the items needed to complete them are not hard to find. . . . [The book has] excellent full-color photography and include[s] charts and diagrams to assist in the completion of the projects." SLJ
Includes bibliographical references

639.2   Commercial fishing, whaling, sealing

Foster, Mark
Whale port; a history of Tuckanucket; written by Mark Foster; illustrated by Gerald Foster. Houghton Mifflin Company 2007 64p il $18 *
Grades: 4 5 6 7   639.2
1. Whaling
ISBN 978-0-618-54722-7; 0-618-54722-3
LC 2006018772
"Walter Lorraine books"
This describes the history of whaling in New England through the fictional village of Tuckanucket and Zachariah Taber, his family and neighbors.
The village is "depicted in precisely detailed ink and crayon pictures. . . . The Fosters . . . have elegantly synthesized a tremendous amount of information into a beguiling format." Horn Book

McKissack, Patricia C., 1944-
Black hands, white sails; the story of African-American whalers; [by] Patricia C. McKissack & Fredrick L. McKissack. Scholastic Press 1999 xxiv, 152p il $17.95 *
Grades: 5 6 7 8   639.2
1. Whaling 2. African Americans
ISBN 0-590-48313-7   LC 99-11439
A Coretta Scott King honor book for text, 2000
A history of African-American whalers between 1730 and 1880, describing their contributions to the whaling industry and their role in the abolitionist movement
"A well-researched and detailed book." SLJ
Includes bibliographical references

Murphy, Jim, 1947-
Gone a-whaling; the lure of the sea and the hunt for the great whale. Clarion Bks. 1998 208p il $18; pa $8.95 *
Grades: 7 8 9 10   639.2
1. Whaling
ISBN 0-395-69847-2; 0-618-43243-4 (pa)
LC 97-13051
Diary entries form the backbone of this "look at whale hunting in America, from the nineteenth century to today." Booklist
"Murphy makes history fascinating and immediate with a lively, engrossing narrative that both informs and entertains." Voice Youth Advocates
Includes glossary and bibliographical references

Sandler, Martin W.
Trapped in ice! an amazing true whaling adventure. Scholastic Nonfiction 2006 168p il $16.99
Grades: 5 6 7 8   639.2
1. Whaling
ISBN 0-439-74363-X   LC 2005-42644

Sandler, Martin W.—*Continued*

"In 1871, people aboard 32 whaling ships discovered just how dangerous Arctic waters could be after they ignored warnings of an early winter. As conditions worsened, the ships were trapped by ice, forcing the 1,219 people to abandon the vessels or die. Sandler's account of this true story is both informative and absorbing. . . . Well-chosen illustrations and side notes on such topics as life aboard ship and women at sea extend readers' understanding." Booklist

Includes glossary and bibliographical references

639.3 Culture of cold-blooded vertebrates. Of fishes

Bartlett, Richard D., 1938-

Aquatic turtles; sliders, cooters, painted, and map turtles; [by] R.D. Bartlett, Patricia Bartlett. Barron's Educational Series 2003 46p il (Reptile keeper's guides) pa $7.99

Grades: 6 7 8 9   **639.3**

1. Turtles

ISBN 978-0-7641-2278-1 (pa); 0-7641-2278-9 (pa)

LC 2002-26264

"This guide offers . . . advice on the maintenance and care of [aquatic turtles]. . . . Readers . . . get advice on selecting a good specimen, determining sex, and providing proper housing, feeding, and health care." Publisher's note

Geckos; everything about housing, health, nutrition, and breeding; [by] R.D. Bartlett and Patricia P. Bartlett. Barron's 2006 95p il (A Complete pet owner's manual) pa $8.99

Grades: 6 7 8 9   **639.3**

1. Geckos

ISBN 978-0-7641-2855-4 (pa); 0-7641-2855-8 (pa)

LC 2005-50024

First published 1995

"Advice on purchasing geckos, as well as feeding, breeding, and health care." Publisher's note

Includes glossary and bibliograpical references

Turtles and tortoises; everything about selection, care, nutrition, housing, and behavior; [by] R.D. Bartlett and Patricia P. Bartlett; with full-color photographs; illustrations by Michele Earl-Bridges. Barron's 2006 111p il (A complete pet owner's manual) pa $8.99

Grades: 6 7 8 9   **639.3**

1. Turtles

ISBN 978-0-7641-3400-5; 0-7641-3400-0

LC 2006-40101

"Information on both land and water species, with specifics on determining sex, life expectancy, housing, feeding, and health care." Publisher's note

Includes bibliographical references

Coates, Jennifer

Lizards. ElDorado Ink 2008 il (Our best friends) $26.95

Grades: 7 8 9 10 11 12   **639.3**

1. Lizards

ISBN 978-1-93290-431-4   LC 2008033060

This is a guide to caring for lizards as pets.

"An ideal resource for those kids (or even adults) looking for a cradle-to-grave primer on responsible pet ownership. . . . Well formatted and broken up with vivid photographs and fascinating 'Fast Facts.'" Booklist

639.34 Fish culture in aquariums

Indiviglio, Frank

The everything aquarium book; all you need to build the aquarium of your dreams. Adams Media 2007 287p il (Everything series) pa $14.95

Grades: 7 8 9 10   **639.34**

1. Aquariums

ISBN 978-1-59337-715-1; 1-59337-715-0

LC 2006-28187

This book about aquariums includes information about "proper fish selection, marine plants and understanding fish behavior." Publisher's note

Includes bibliographical references

Mills, Dick

Aquarium fish. DK 2004 72p il (101 essential tips) pa $5

Grades: 7 8 9 10   **639.34**

1. Aquariums 2. Fishes

ISBN 0-7566-0611-X; 978-0-7566-0611-4

LC 2004-303366

Reprint of paperback printed by DK Pub. in 1996

This book offers advice on choosing fish for aquariums, aquarium equipment, decoration, feeding, and health care, and describes various species of tropical, coldwater, freshwater, and marine fishes.

"Accurate, clear, and concise writing is enhanced with wonderful color photographs on each page." Voice Youth Advocates [review of 1996 edition]

Wood, Kathleen

The 101 best tropical fishes; how to choose & keep hardy, brilliant, fascinating species that will thrive in your home aquarium; by Kathleen Wood; with Mary E. Sweeney and Scott W. Michael. T.F.H. Publications 2007 192p il (Adventurous aquarist guide) $18.95

Grades: 6 7 8 9   **639.34**

1. Tropical fish 2. Aquariums

ISBN 978-1-8900-8793-7; 1-8900-8793-9

LC 2008-28294

"Presents 101 full-page species accounts of fishes that not only have high survival rates in captivity but also are appealing in appearance and behave well in community tanks. Also included are 33 species to avoid—fishes that most commonly wreak havoc in home aquariums because of their size or aggressiveness, or that tend to perish in the hands of inexperienced aquarists." Publisher's note

Includes bibliographical references

641.3 Food

Dunn-Georgiou, Elisha
Everything you need to know about organic foods. Rosen Pub. Group 2002 64p il (Need to know library) lib bdg $23.95

Grades: 7 8 9 10 **641.3**
1. Natural foods 2. Organic gardening
ISBN 0-8239-3551-5   LC 2001-3789
Discusses the organic food movement and recent information about the United States Department of Agriculture's criteria for what defines an organic food.
Includes bibliographical references

Jango-Cohen, Judith
The history of food; [by] Judith Jango-Cohen. Twenty-First Century Books 2006 56p il (Major inventions through history) lib bdg $26.60

Grades: 5 6 7 8 **641.3**
1. Food—History
ISBN 0-8225-2484-8   LC 2004-23022
This history of food "discusses canning, pasteurization, refrigeration, supermarkets, and genetically modified foods. . . . The text . . . is breezy but informative; unfamiliar terms are defined. Illustrations are a mixture of period black-and-white and color photos." SLJ
Includes bibliographical references

Menzel, Peter
What the world eats; photographed by Peter Menzel; written by Faith D'Aluisio. Tricycle Press 2008 160p il map $22.99 *

Grades: 4 5 6 7 8 **641.3**
1. Food—Pictorial works 2. Diet 3. Eating customs
ISBN 978-1-58246-246-2; 1-58246-246-1
     LC 2007-41439
An adaptation of *Hungry Planet*, published 2005 by Ten Speed Press for adults
"A photographic collection exploring what the world eats featuring portraits of twenty-five families from twenty-one countries surrounded by a week's worth of food." Publisher's note
"Stunning color photographs of mealtimes and daily activities illustrate the warm, informative, anecdotal narratives. . . . This is a fascinating, sobering, and instructive look at daily life around the world." Booklist
Includes bibliographical references

Miller, Debra A.
Organic foods; by Debra A. Miller. Thomson/Gale 2008 111p il (Hot topics) lib bdg $32.45

Grades: 6 7 8 9 **641.3**
1. Natural foods 2. Natural foods industry
ISBN 978-1-59018-994-8 (lib bdg); 1-59018-994-9 (lib bdg)   LC 2007-35909
"This title about organic foods gives a concise but thorough overview of a complex issue. . . . Sidebars, study questions, ample photos, and comprehensive chapter notes complete this on-target resource." Booklist
Includes bibliographical references

Miller, Jeanne
Food science. Lerner Publications 2009 48p il (Cool science) lib bdg $27.93

Grades: 4 5 6 **641.3**
1. Food
ISBN 978-0-8225-7589-4 (lib bdg); 0-8225-7589-2 (lib bdg)
This describes how food scientists "explore how cooking changes food, create dishes that surprise the senses, and help farmers grow food in healthier ways." Publisher's note
Includes glossary and bibliographical references

Solheim, James
It's disgusting—and we ate it! true food facts from around the world—and throughout history! illustrated by Eric Brace. Simon & Schuster Bks. for Young Readers 1998 37p il hardcover o.p. pa $6.99

Grades: 4 5 6 7 **641.3**
1. Food 2. Eating customs
ISBN 0-689-80675-2; 0-689-84393-3 (pa)
     LC 96-7406
This "look at culinary culture is divided into three sections, the first discussing the global breadth of tastes, the second describing some startling dishes of history, and the third revealing some of the colorful truths behind contemporary American favorites." Bull Cent Child Books
Includes bibliographical references

641.5 Cooking

Albyn, Carole Lisa, 1955-
The multicultural cookbook for students; by Carole Lisa Albyn and Lois Sinaiko Webb. Oryx Press 1993 xxii, 287p maps pa $29.50

Grades: 7 8 9 10 **641.5**
1. Cooking
ISBN 0-89774-735-6   LC 92-41634
Presents a collection of recipes from over 120 countries and briefly discusses the culture and culinary habits of each country

Batmanglij, Najmieh, 1947-
Happy Nowruz; cooking with children to celebrate the Persian New Year; [by] Najmieh Batmanglij. Mage Publishers 2008 119p il $40

Grades: 4 5 6 7 8 **641.5**
1. Middle Eastern cooking 2. New Year 3. Eating customs 4. Iran—Social life and customs
ISBN 1-933823-16-X; 978-1-933823-16-4
     LC 2007-036047
"Combining a cookbook format with straightforward, informational text, this amply illustrated title offers a detailed introduction to the history and customs surrounding Nowruz, the Persian New Year. . . . The covered spiral binding allows pages to remain open while cooking, and the uncluttered, attractive format, featuring color photos of kids in the kitchen and whimsical illustrations, will attract interested browsers." Booklist

Bayless, Rick

Rick & Lanie's excellent kitchen adventures; chef-dad, teenage daughter, recipes and stories; [by] Rick Bayless & Lanie Bayless, with Deann Groen Bayless; photographs by Christopher Hirsheimer. Stewart, Tabori & Chang 2004 231p il $29.95

Grades: 7 8 9 10 **641.5**
1. Cooking
ISBN 1-58479-331-7 LC 2004-12627

"The volume is organized by region, with almost every continent covered. Each section begins with a few personal stories from the authors. . . . The recipes range from ultrasimple, such as 'The Simplest Fried Beans' to elaborate, such as 'Chinese Celebration Hot Pot,' which involves several exotic ingredients and numerous steps. . . . This is a volume filled with delicious recipes that are not necessarily all easy—but are always described in a way that is easy to follow." SLJ

Bloomfield, Jill

Jewish holidays cookbook; by Jill Colella Bloomfield; Janet Ozur Bass, consultant; photography by Angela Coppola. DK Pub. 2008 128p il $19.99

Grades: 4 5 6 7 **641.5**
1. Jewish cooking 2. Jewish holidays
ISBN 978-0-7566-4089-7; 0-7566-4089-X

"More than 40 recipes are included for celebrations from Shabbat to Lag B'Omer. Several introductions explain cooking tools, kitchen safety, and the general principles of keeping kosher, and brief background information is given for each holiday. Simple step-by-step instructions make the recipes easy. . . . Beautiful color photographs, both full page and spot, whet the appetite." SLJ

Canfield, Jack, 1944-

Chicken soup for the soul: kids in the kitchen; tasty recipes and fun activities for budding chefs; [by] Jack Canfield, Mark Victor Hansen, and Antonio Frontera. Health Communications 2007 248p il pa $19.95

Grades: 5 6 7 8 **641.5**
1. Cooking 2. Anecdotes
ISBN 978-0-7573-0579-5; 0-7573-0579-2
LC 2007-020559

"This title has child-friendly recipes and good tips to help kids understand and appreciate cooking." SLJ

Carle, Megan

Teens cook; how to make what you want to eat; [by] Megan and Jill Carle with Judi Carle. Ten Speed Press 2004 146p il pa $19.95

Grades: 7 8 9 10 **641.5**
1. Cooking
ISBN 1-58008-584-9

This cookbook features "recipes for a variety of dishes including chocolate chip scones, potato skins, broccoli cheese soup, steak fajitas, baked macaroni and cheese, and toffee bars. Because Megan is a vegetarian, there are several vegetarian recipes or vegetarian substitutes. . . . Attractive, engaging, and told from a teen perspective, this cookbook will make an excellent addition to any nonfiction collection." Voice Youth Advocates

Crespo, Clare

The secret life of food; photographs by Eric Staudenmaier. Hyperion 2002 108p il $19.99; pa $12.99

Grades: 4 5 6 7 **641.5**
1. Cooking
ISBN 0-7868-0846-2; 978-0-7868-3735-9 (pa); 0-7868-3735-7 (pa)

This includes "recipes for dishes that look remarkably like spiders, roses, fingers, footballs, ponds, shoes—even a chocolate moose. . . . Younger readers will need adult help to re-create Crespo's culinary delights. The stunning full-page color photos of each dish, posed in clever context, lend great 'ooh and aah' motivation, making this useful for groups as well as for kids planning parties at home." SLJ

D'Amico, Joan, 1957-

The coming to America cookbook; delicious recipes and fascinating stories from America's many cultures; [by] Joan D'Amico, Karen Eich Drummond. Wiley 2005 180p il pa $14.95 *

Grades: 5 6 7 8 **641.5**
1. Cooking 2. United States—Immigration and emigration
ISBN 0-471-48335-4 LC 2004-14947

The authors "provide information about American immigrants from 18 nations as well as recipes representing each group. . . . Accompanied by line drawings of ethnic families choosing, preparing, and eating food, . . . chapters discuss each country's climate, history, major waves of emigration, and traditional foods. Typically, three recipes follow. . . . Teachers and students looking for recipes from American immigrant cultures will make good use of this handy resource." Booklist

The healthy body cookbook; over 50 fun activities and delicious recipes for kids; [by] Joan D'Amico, Karen Eich Drummond; illustrations by Tina Cash-Walsh. Wiley 1999 184p il pa $12.95

Grades: 5 6 7 8 **641.5**
1. Cooking 2. Nutrition
ISBN 0-471-18888-3 LC 98-2776

Discusses the various parts of the human body and what to eat to keep them healthy. Includes recipes that contain nutrients important for the heart, muscles, teeth, skin, nerves, and other parts of the body

"The line drawings are helpful and the writing is informal but straightforward. The recipes are clear, thoroughly explained, and tasty." SLJ

The United States cookbook; fabulous foods and fascinating facts from all 50 states; [by] Joan D'Amico and Karen Eich Drummond; illustrations by Jeff Cline and Tina Cash-Walsh. Wiley 2000 186p il pa $12.95

Grades: 5 6 7 8 **641.5**
1. Cooking
ISBN 0-471-35839-8 LC 99-39548

D'Amico, Joan, 1957—— *Continued*

Provides information about the fifty states along with a recipe native to each of them, such as Boston baked beans from Massachusetts, crab cakes from Maryland, Key lime pie from Florida, corn dogs from Iowa, and taco soup from New Mexico

"There are helpful sections on the use of equipment; cooking skills, such as cutting, measuring, and mixing, and safety rules." SLJ

Dunnington, Rose

Big snacks, little meals; after school, dinnertime, anytime; [by] Rose Dunnington. 1st ed. Lark Books 2006 112p il $9.95 *

Grades: 6 7 8 9   **641.5**

1. Cooking

ISBN 1-57990-780-6   LC 2005030429

"This attractive cookbook aims to turn teens on to the creative and gastronomic rewards of preparing food at home. Of the 50 recipes promising 'snack magic,' those featuring meat or dairy often suggest vegetarian or vegan alternatives, and the overall lineup balances familiar dishes, such as chicken wings, with those that require specialty ingredients." Booklist

Easy menu ethnic cookbooks. rev ed. Lerner Publs. 2002-2005 37v ea $25.26

Grades: 5 6 7 8   **641.5**

1. Cooking

Replaces titles in the series published 1982-1995

Some titles also available in paperback

Series first published 1982-1995

Available volumes in the revised series are: Cooking the Australian way, by E. Germaine & A. L. Burchhardt; Cooking the Austrian way, by H. Hughes; Cooking the Brazilian way, by A. Behnke & K. L. Duro; Cooking the Caribbean way, by C. D. Kaufman; Cooking the Central American way, by A. Behnke; Cooking the Chinese way, by L. Yu; Cooking the Cuban way, by A. Behnke & V. M. Valens; Cooking the East African way, by C. Nabwire & B. V. Montgomery; Cooking the English way, by B. W. Hill; Cooking the French way, by L. M. Waldee; Cooking the German way, by H. Parnell; Cooking the Greek way, by L. W. Villios; Cooking the Hungarian way, by M. Hargittai; Cooking the Indian way, by V. Madavan; Cooking the Indonesian way, by M. Anwar & K. Cornell; Cooking the Israeli way, by J. Bacon; Cooking the Italian way, by A. Bisignano; Cooking the Japanese way, by R. Weston; Cooking the Korean way, by O. Chung and J. Monroe; Cooking the Lebanese way, by S. Amari; Cooking the Mediterranean way, by A. Behnke; Cooking the Mexican way, by R. Coronado; Cooking the Middle Eastern way, by A. Behnke; Cooking the North African way, by M. Winget & H. Cahlbi; Cooking the Norwegian way, by S. Munsen; Cooking the Polish way, by D. Zamojska-Hutchins; Cooking the Russian way, by G. & R. Plotkin; Cooking the South American way, by H. Parnell; Cooking the Southern African way, by K. Cornell & P. Thomas; Cooking the Spanish way, by R. Christian; Cooking the Thai way, by S. Harrison & J. Monroe; Cooking the Turkish way, by K. Cornell & N. Turkoglu; Cooking the Vietnamese way, by C. Nguyen & J. Monroe; Cooking the West African way, by C. Nabwire & B. V. Montgomery; Desserts around the world by L. Engfer; Holiday cooking around the world,

by R. Wolfe & D. Wolfe; Vegetarian cooking around the world, by A. Behnke

"In each volume, the front matter comprises close to half the book. Geography, history, holidays, and festivals, typical ingredients, and sample menus are all covered. . . . Each book presents about 20 recipes, mostly focusing on lunch, dinner, and holiday foods. . . . The narrative pieces are smoothly written and offer some interesting tidbits. . . . The pages are a warm buff color, and the design allows plenty of space on the pages for the text and the nicely reproduced color photos." SLJ

Gillies, Judi

The jumbo vegetarian cookbook; written by Judi Gillies and Jennifer Glossop; illustrated by Louise Phillips. Kids Can Press 2002 256p il pa $14.95 *

Grades: 4 5 6 7   **641.5**

1. Vegetarian cooking

ISBN 1-55074-977-3

"Much more than just a cookbook, this sprawling title introduces basic nutrition and how to achieve it with a vegetarian diet. Beginning sections cover safety tips and culinary basics . . . as well as types of vegetarianism, the environmental and health reasons that have led many to a meatless diet, and a list of common vegetarian ingredients. The recipe sections are extensive, with well-chosen dishes from breakfast foods through entrées and desserts." Booklist

Jacob, Jeanne

The world cookbook for students; [by] Jeanne Jacob, Michael Ashkenazi. Greenwood Press 2007 5v il map set$225

Grades: 7 8 9 10 11 12   **641.5**

1. Cooking 2. Eating customs

ISBN 0-313-33454-4; 978-0-313-33454-2

LC 2006-26184

"The volumes are organized alphabetically by country or group name. Each entry includes a brief introduction to the land and people and their cuisine and then an overview of the foodstuffs, typical dishes, and styles of eating in simple bulleted lists. Approximately 5 recipes are provided per country/ethnic group of typical dishes and holiday fare, for a total of 1,198." Publisher's note

Includes bibliographical references

Lagasse, Emeril

Emeril's there's a chef in my family! recipes to get everybody cooking; illustrated by Charles Yuen; photographs by Quentin Bacon. HarperCollins Publishers 2004 209p il $22.99 *

Grades: 5 6 7 8   **641.5**

1. Cooking

ISBN 0-06-000439-8   LC 2003-5612

Provides tips for having fun and keeping safe in the kitchen, along with dozens of world-famous chef Emeril Lagasse's favorite recipes that families can make and eat together

"The step-by-step directions are clearly laid out, and most of the dishes look delicious. The fresh and attractive design includes a mix of simple paintings (for the

Lagasse, Emeril—*Continued*
food) and photos (for the people). Emeril himself is shown throughout, conveying his enthusiasm and sense of play." SLJ

Emeril's there's a chef in my world! recipes that take you places. HarperCollins Publishers 2006 210p il $22.99 *
Grades: 5 6 7 8 **641.5**
1. Cooking
ISBN 978-0-06-073926-3; 0-06-073926-6
LC 2005-15133
"The famous chef introduces dishes from around the world, dividing the recipes into familiar food categories—sweets, snacks, sandwiches, entrees, etc. . . . The recipes, from latkes to egg-drop soup, are good choices for open-minded eaters. . . . Many children will enjoy the mix of maps, flags, cartoon drawings, and color photos . . . and the cultural facts woven into each recipe." Booklist

Locricchio, Matthew
The international cookbook for kids; by Matthew Locricchio; photographs by Jack McConnell. Marshall Cavendish 2004 175p il $18.95
Grades: 5 6 7 8 **641.5**
1. Cooking
ISBN 0-7614-5185-4 LC 2004-5894
This includes "60 classic recipes from Italy, France, China, and Mexico, . . . chef's tips discussing ingredients, nutrition, and technique, safety section discussing basic kitchen precautions, cooking terms and definitions." Publisher's note
"This is a strong collection of popular dishes attractively presented." SLJ

Super chef [series] Benchmark Books 2002-2004 c2003-2005 8v il map lib bdg group 1 set$119.71; lib bdg group 2 set$119.71
Grades: 5 6 7 8 **641.5**
1. Cooking
ISBN 0-7614-1213-1 (group 1); 0-7614-1728-1 (group 2)
Also available as single volumes $29.93 each
Contents: Group 1: The cooking of China; The cooking of France; The cooking of Italy; The cooking of Mexico; Group 2: The cooking of Brazil; The cooking of Greece; The cooking of India; The cooking of Thailand
"After a quick review of the basic principles of kitchen safety, food handling and common sense nutrition, there is a region-by-region overview of the cuisine of the country. Then it's on to a variety of authentic . . . traditional recipes!" Publisher's note
"The selection of dishes is well-rounded . . . and the directions are mostly clear and thorough. Young people will gain a solid foundation in cooking techniques as well as a cultural introduction to world cuisine with these slim volumes." Booklist

The 2nd international cookbook for kids; photographs by Jack McConnell. Marshall Cavendish 2008 176p il $18.99
Grades: 5 6 7 8 **641.5**
1. Cooking
ISBN 978-0-7614-5513-4 LC 2008003178
"Chef Matthew Locricchio brings us . . . recipes from India, Greece, Thailand, and Brazil specially designed for kids and their families" Publisher's note
The recipes are "presented in a challenging yet teen-friendly step-by-step sequence. The book is best for patient chefs with kitchen experience and adventurous appetites. Informative sidebars provide facts about the recipes and cultures." Horn Book Guide

Paul, Anthea
Girlosophy: real girls eat. Allen & Unwin 2006 199p pa $19.95 *
Grades: 8 9 10 11 12 **641.5**
1. Cooking 2. Girls—Health and hygiene
ISBN 1-74114-142-7
This "illustrated cookbook offers healthy tips for both the mind and body. Rather than pushing teens to diet, this . . . volume celebrates food and encourages girls to stop obsessing about what they should and should not eat and encourages them to indulge in what is best for them nutritionally." Publisher's note
"Paul has created a gloriously photographed and superbly art-directed text." SLJ

Smart, Denise
The cookbook for girls; written by Denise Smart; photography by Howard Shooter. DK Pub. 2009 128p il $17.99
Grades: 4 5 6 **641.5**
1. Cooking
ISBN 978-0-7566-4500-7; 0-7566-4500-X
Includes "more than fifty dishes for making with friends, serving at parties, and learning all about the kitchen, and includes craft projects designed to help young hostesses serve up their culinary achievements." Publisher's note
"The photos alone make this attractive cookbook worth the price of admission. . . . Most of these dishes will appeal to adventurous eaters and their foodie parents." SLJ

Stern, Sam, 1990-
Cooking up a storm; [by] Sam Stern, with Susan Stern. Candlewick Press 2006 128p il pa $16.99
Grades: 6 7 8 9 **641.5**
1. Cooking
ISBN 978-0-7636-2988-5; 0-7636-2988-X (pa)
LC 2006-42571
"English teen Sam Stern, with his mother's help, offers this slender, photo-packed cookbook, unusual not only because of its author but also because it focuses on guys. . . . That said, the recipes, presented in a casual but clear voice, will draw both genders. . . . The bright, energetic text and color photos of Sam and his photogenic friends and family will easily pull in aspiring foodies." Booklist

Stern, Sam, 1990——Continued
Real food, real fast; [by] Sam Stern & Susan Stern. Candlewick Press 2008 128p il $16.99
Grades: 6 7 8 9   **641.5**
1. Cooking
ISBN 978-0-7636-3533-6; 0-7636-3533-2
LC 2007025635
"This book is full of time-management advice, recipes, and tips for combining dishes. Cross-references enable novices to put together full meals, and the index encourages browsing by ingredient or type of recipe. . . . Each recipe includes serving sizes, variations to adapt the recipes to one's own taste, pictures of the author and friends, and often pictures of the finished product. The directions are easy. . . . A teen-friendly guide to healthy eating, featuring foods that are fast and easy to make." SLJ

Sam Stern's get cooking. Candlewick Press 2009 144p $17.99
Grades: 6 7 8 9   **641.5**
1. Cooking
ISBN 978-0-7636-3926-6; 0-7636-3926-5
British teenage cook Sam Stern presents over 100 new recipes based on his own favorite ingredient, chocolate, and the favorite ingredients of seven of his friends.
"Stern does an excellent job of introducing teens to the kitchen. . . . Every page boasts bright colors and pictures with large print and a user-friendly ingredients list in sidebar format. The recipes run from very easy to a bit challenging, but the step-by-step directions will help even the most challenged cook find a way around the kitchen." Voice Youth Advocates

Webb, Lois Sinaiko, 1922-
Holidays of the world cookbook for students. Oryx Press 1995 xxxiv, 297p il maps pa $36.95
Grades: 5 6 7 8 9 10   **641.5**
1. Cooking 2. Holidays
ISBN 0-89774-884-0   LC 95-26019
In this cookbook "more than 136 countries are represented, with 388 recipes. The U.S. is divided into six sections with 10 recipes for regional celebrations. History behind the holiday is included where possible, as is pertinent background information on the culture represented. . . . A discussion of different calendars used around the world is an interesting inclusion. The recipes' directions are clear and include equipment lists." SLJ
Includes glossary and bibliographical references

Zanger, Mark H.
The American ethnic cookbook for students. Oryx Press 2001 325p il $32.50
Grades: 7 8 9 10   **641.5**
1. Cooking
ISBN 1-57356-345-5   LC 00-11094
"An introduction discusses how ethnic recipes change when they are transported to new countries. Some 400 recipes from 122 ethnic groups and 21 Native American groups follow. Alphabetical entries for each ethnic group include a brief introduction about the culture followed by a few recipes." Booklist
"Using these recipes will be a great motivation for students to learn about the varied heritage of our immigrant nation." SLJ
Includes bibliographical references

641.8 Cooking specific kinds of dishes, preparing beverages

Carle, Megan
Teens cook dessert; [by] Megan and Jill Carle, with Judi Carle. Ten Speed Press 2006 158p pa $19.95
Grades: 6 7 8 9   **641.8**
1. Desserts 2. Cooking
ISBN 978-1-58008-752-0; 1-58008-752-3
LC 2005024343
The authors "start out with the all-around favorites, like classic chocolate chip cookies. There are holiday recipes for Halloween dirt pie, complete with cookie tombstones and gummy worms that seem to crawl out of the chocolate 'earth.' The final chapter has fancy foods like vanilla soufflt with chocolate sauce or fresh raspberry napoleons. . . . Not only do the recipes sound delicious, they look delicious in glossy color pictures. . . . The instructions are easy to understand." Voice Youth Advocates

Dunnington, Rose
Bake it up! desserts, breads, entire meals & more; [by] Rose Dunnington. 1st ed. Lark Books 2006 111p il $9.95
Grades: 6 7 8 9   **641.8**
1. Baking 2. Desserts 3. Bread
ISBN 1-57990-778-4   LC 2006015072
This "book describes the science involved in baking, but not before new bakers develop confidence with bread from preceding recipes. . . . Dunnington's tone will appeal to new cooks for its pithy attitude and can-do, casual approach to food, despite the sophistication of the meals presented. . . . Exceptional full-page color photos entice and provide an accurate representation of the finished products." SLJ

Super sandwiches; wrap 'em, stack 'em, stuff 'em; [by] Rose Dunnington. Lark Books 2006 112p il $9.95
Grades: 6 7 8 9   **641.8**
1. Sandwiches
ISBN 1-57990-781-4   LC 2006006330
This book "opens with a thoughtful introduction that describes best practices and suggests that teens are ready for foods more refined than peanut butter and jelly, and are capable of preparing them. The results will clearly impress the lunchroom crowd. Dunnington's tone will appeal to new cooks for its pithy attitude and can-do, casual approach to food, despite the sophistication of the meals presented. . . . Exceptional full-page color photos entice and provide an accurate representation of the finished products." SLJ

Love, Ann, 1947-
Sweet! the delicious story of candy; [by] Ann Love & Jane Drake; illustrated by Claudia Dávila. Tundra Books 2007 64p il map $19.95
Grades: 4 5 6 7   **641.8**

Love, Ann, 1947-—*Continued*

1. Candy

ISBN 978-0-88776-752-4

"This history of things sweet and sugary is a yummy feast. The prose is chatty and inviting. Color cartoon illustrations show multiethnic people in the process of making or enjoying everything from honey to ice cream to cotton candy (called candy floss here) to jelly beans and chocolate." SLJ

646.4 Clothing and accessories construction

Hantman, Clea

I wanna make my own clothes; illustrated by Azadeh Houshyar. 1st ed. Aladdin Paperbacks 2006 134p il pa $9.99

Grades: 7 8 9 10   646.4

1. Sewing 2. Clothing and dress

ISBN 0-689-87462-6   LC 2005006925

This offers instructions for sewing tee shirts, tanks, halters, and other apparel

"Varied typeface, black-and-white illustrations, and upbeat [text] written in an easy-to-read style present fun activities. . . . Teens will love the unique and fashionable designs." SLJ

Zent, Sheila

Sew teen; make your own cool clothes. Sterling 2006 160p il pa $17.95

Grades: 7 8 9 10   646.4

1. Sewing 2. Clothing and dress

ISBN 1-931543-90-9

"Zent presents 21 projects and accessory designs that will appeal to budding seamstresses and novice stitchers alike, although teens should know the basics of using a sewing machine or have assistance. . . . The step-by-step instructions include drawn renderings to assist with the construction and full-color photographs of teen models wearing each garment or accessory." SLJ

646.7 Management of personal and family life

Beker, Jeanne

The big night out; Nathalie Dion, illustrator. Tundra Books 2005 80p il pa $15.95

Grades: 7 8 9 10   646.7

1. Rites and ceremonies 2. Parties 3. Etiquette 4. Personal grooming

ISBN 0-88776-719-2

"This book is for young women who are seeking to develop and display their own sense of style as they prepare for a special event. . . . [The author] provides realistic advice on budgeting, planning ahead, and attending to all the details, from accessorizing to practicing hairstyles and makeup application in advance. . . . This book will hold an obvious appeal. Its straightforward style and playful, whimsical illustrations make it easily accessible." Voice Youth Advocates

Blatt, Jessica

The teen girl's gotta-have-it guide to embarrassing moments; how to survive life's cringe-worthy situations! illustrated by Cynthia Frenette. Watson-Guptill 2007 96p il pa $8.95

Grades: 6 7 8 9 10   646.7

1. Interpersonal relations 2. Girls—Psychology

ISBN 978-0-8230-1724-9

A guide for how teenage girls can avoid embarrassing situations, and how to deal with them when they happen anyway.

"Colorful cartoon illustrations, liberally sprinkled throughout this small guide, are relevant and amusing. The advice here is so down-to-earth and wide-ranging that even young adults in their twenties could benefit from [the author's] commonsense approach." Voice Youth Advocates

Boonyadhistarn, Thiranut

Fingernail art; dazzling fingers and terrific toes; by Thiranut Boonyadhistarn. Capstone Press 2007 32p il (Snap books) $25.26

Grades: 4 5 6 7   646.7

1. Manicuring 2. Handicraft

ISBN 978-0-7368-6474-9; 0-7368-6474-1

               LC 2006004084

This is "lively and attractive. The projects use easily obtainable materials, and the directions are simple and well numbered. . . . [This] title demonstates how to decorate nails with paper dots, acrylic paints, emoticons, stickers, and so on." SLJ

Includes bibliographical references

Esherick, Joan

Clothing, cosmetic, and self-esteem tips; making the most of the body you have. Mason Crest Publishers 2006 104p il (Obesity: modern-day epidemic) $23.95

Grades: 7 8 9 10   646.7

1. Personal grooming 2. Clothing and dress 3. Cosmetics

ISBN 978-1-59084-951-4; 1-59084-951-5

               LC 2004-26264

Shows readers how to improve self-confidence and personal appearance by taking care of their skin and body, selecting a flattering hair style, and choosing clothing to enhance their appearance.

Includes bibliographical references

Espeland, Pamela, 1951-

Life lists for teens; tips, steps, hints, and how-tos for growing up, getting along, learning, and having fun. Free Spirit 2003 264p pa $11.95

Grades: 7 8 9 10 11 12   646.7

1. Conduct of life 2. Life skills

ISBN 1-57542-125-9   LC 2002-152116

Hundreds of lists provide guidance in areas of young adult life as diverse as selecting a book or a hair color to selecting a mentor

"Espeland's well-organized book has lots of useful information and teen appeal." SLJ

Fornay, Alfred
Born beautiful; the African American teenager's complete beauty guide. John Wiley & Sons 2002 166p il pa $14.95
Grades: 8 9 10 11 12   **646.7**
1. Teenagers—Health and hygiene 2. African American women—Health and hygiene 3. Personal appearance 4. Personal grooming
ISBN 0-471-40275-3   LC 2002-18131
"An Amber book"
This book on beauty and grooming for African American teenage girls includes information on makeup, hairstyles, nail and skin care, diet, and clothing.

Irons, Diane, 1949-
Teen beauty secrets; fresh, simple & sassy tips for your perfect look. Sourcebooks 2002 263p il pa $14.95 *
Grades: 7 8 9 10   **646.7**
1. Personal appearance 2. Personal grooming 3. Girls—Health and hygiene
ISBN 1-57071-959-4   LC 2002-6705
"A book filled with dozens of practical beauty tips, diet and fitness suggestions, and fashion hints. With an emphasis on the natural, the former fashion model guides readers through bad-hair days, fashion faux pas, and the makeup techniques of the stars." SLJ

Jeffrie, Sally
The girls' book of glamour; a guide to being a goddess; written by Sally Jeffrie; illustrated by Nellie Ryan; edited by Liz Scoggins; designed by Zoe Quayle. 1st American ed. Scholastic, Inc. 2009 126p il $9.99
Grades: 6 7 8 9 10   **646.7**
1. Life skills 2. Girls 3. Etiquette
ISBN 978-0-545-08537-3; 0-545-08537-3
                                    LC 2008-17119
First published 2008 in the United Kingdom
This is "focused on lifestyle, health, and beauty. Each entry has simple instructions accompanied by entertaining illustrations. This upbeat and amusing style guide adopts a hip tone for the tween and young-teen set. . . . Jeffrie's snappy writing and Ryan's great line drawings and stylish design make [this] an easy, breezy read." SLJ

Mason, Linda
Teen makeup; looks to match your every mood. Watson-Guptill 2004 144p il pa $16.95 *
Grades: 6 7 8 9   **646.7**
1. Cosmetics 2. Personal grooming 3. Teenagers—Health and hygiene
ISBN 0-8230-2980-8
"Using a diverse group of young women as her models, Mason transforms them using seven distinctive makeup looks. . . . The colorful, well-composed photographs show each look, while additional illustrations help recreate it." SLJ

Morgenstern, Julie
Organizing from the inside out for teens; the foolproof system for organizing your room, your time, and your life; [by] Julie Morgenstern and Jessi Morgenstern-Colón; illustrations by Janet Pedersen. Holt & Co. 2002 238p il pa $15 *
Grades: 7 8 9 10   **646.7**
1. Life skills 2. Time management
ISBN 0-8050-6470-2   LC 2002-68552
The authors "offer practical advice to teenagers who want to get organized. After considering what might be holding them back and the three steps to success (analyze, strategize, attack), the discussion shifts to the two major areas of concern: managing space and managing time. . . . Useful advice in an accessible paperback format." Booklist

Rosenwald, Laurie, 1955-
All the wrong people have self esteem; an inappropriate book for young ladies (or, frankly, anybody else). Bloomsbury Children's Books 2008 unp il $16.99 *
Grades: 6 7 8 9   **646.7**
1. Life skills 2. Conduct of life
ISBN 978-1-59990-240-1; 1-59990-240-0
                                    LC 2008-14386
Rosenwald "tackles political correctness, the follies of prevailing wisdom and her favorite peeves using all the tools in her arsenal: her spread-size collages feature fonts on steriods, magazine cut-outs, photos and cartoons paired with witty diatribes confessions. . . . Funny, fresh and impossible not to read cover to cover." Publ Wkly

Warrick, Leanne
Hair trix for cool chix; the real girl's guide to great hair; [by] Leanne Warrick. Watson-Guptill 2004 96p il (Cool chix) pa $9.95 *
Grades: 6 7 8 9   **646.7**
1. Hair
ISBN 0-8230-2179-3   LC 2003-22803
Contents: Get to know your hair; Hairology 101; Salon savvy; Quiz: who do you want to be today?; Everyday styles; Hang-out styles; Special styles; Hair 911; Quiz: what's your style personality?; Make your own hair accessories
A guide to hair care and hairstyles which includes quizzes, recipes for hair products, tips on how to be "salon savvy," step-by-step instructions for casual and special hairstyles, and hair accessory projects
"Written in an upbeat, friendly style, this easy-to-follow book will have readers spending even more time in front of the bathroom mirror." SLJ

647.9 Specific kinds of public households and institutions

McAlpine, Margaret
Working in the food industry. Gareth Stevens 2006 64p il (My future career) $26
Grades: 6 7 8 9   **647.9**

McAlpine, Margaret—*Continued*
1. Food industry 2. Vocational guidance
ISBN 0-8368-4776-8
This describes seven careers in the food industry.
This is "well organized, full of beautiful photography, and [presents] honest snapshots of the featured professions. . . . Attractive, informative, and interesting." SLJ

649 Child rearing; home care of persons with disabilities and illnesses

Buckley, Annie, 1968-
Be a better babysitter; by Annie Buckley. Child's World 2007 32p il (Girls rock!) lib bdg $24.21
Grades: 5 6 7 8   649
1. Babysitting
ISBN 1-59296-740-X   LC 2006001639
This "describes what babysitting entails, examines pros and cons, discusses safety issues, offers tips for doing a good job, and suggests saving as much as half of any money earned. . . . [This] realistic [title is] well written and [provides] excellent information." SLJ
Includes bibliographical references

Crissey, Pat, 1946-
Personal hygiene? What's that got to do with me? illustrated by Noah Crissey. Jessica Kingsley 2005 94p il pa $19.95
Grades: 5 6 7   649
1. Autism 2. Asperger's syndrome 3. Hygiene
ISBN 978-1-8431-0796-5; 1-8431-0796-1
                                              LC 2004-24966
Explains the importance of personal hygiene to children with autism and asperger's syndrome.

Mehlman, Barbara
Babysitting jobs; the business of babysitting. Capstone Press 2007 32p il (Snap books. Babysitting) lib bdg $25.26
Grades: 5 6 7   649
1. Babysitting
ISBN 978-0-7368-6463-3; 0-7368-6463-6
                                              LC 2006-1733
"A guide for pre-teens and teens on how to get and keep babysitting jobs." Publisher's note
Includes bibliographical references

Raatma, Lucia
Safety for babysitters. Child's World 2005 32p il (Living well) lib bdg $25.64
Grades: 4 5 6 7   649
1. Babysitting 2. Safety education
ISBN 1-59296-239-4   LC 2003-27213
The offers advice on how to prepare for a babysitting job, what kinds of questions to ask the parents, what to do in emergencies
This has "an appealing layout with plenty of full-color photos and a triple-spaced text. . . . An excellent, easy-to-understand overview." SLJ
Includes glossary and bibliographical references

650.1 Personal success in business

Green, Donna Hayden, 1956-
Dream job profiles; the young & successful share their secrets. Graphia 2006 180p pa $7.99
Grades: 7 8 9 10   650.1
1. Occupations 2. Vocational guidance
ISBN 978-0-618-56320-3; 0-618-56320-2 (pa)
                                              LC 2006-04462
"The author interviewed nine under-thirty successful young people. Careers such as Hollywood reporter, makeup and hair artist, sports manager, Web comic strip creators, NASA astronomer, marine biologist, talent manager, outdoor educator, and mayor are unique and will be intriguing to many young people." Voice Youth Advocates

650.14 Success in obtaining jobs and promotions

Schwager, Tina, 1964-
Cool women, hot jobs . . . and how you can go for it, too! [by] Tina Schwager & Michele Schuerger. Free Spirit 2002 278p il pa $15.95
Grades: 7 8 9 10   650.14
1. Vocational guidance 2. Women—Employment 3. Occupations
ISBN 1-57542-109-7   LC 2001-40908
Profiles twenty-two women and the jobs they do, from choreographer to FBI agent, describing their education, duties, personality traits, and other factors in their career success, and gives specific ways to determine one's own future work
This "is a valuable contribution to a young adult collection. The pages burst with the inspiration and motivation." Voice Youth Advocates

652 Processes of written communication

Janeczko, Paul B., 1945-
Top secret; a handbook of codes, ciphers and secret writing; illustrated by Jenna LaReau. Candlewick Press 2004 136p il hardcover o.p. pa $7.99 *
Grades: 4 5 6 7   652
1. Cryptography 2. Ciphers
ISBN 0-7636-0971-4; 978-0-7636-2972-4 (pa); 0-7636-2972-3 (pa)
This is a "guide to secret writing. Janeczko relates how different codes came to be and why they were needed, and gives some historical examples. The book also contains information and exercises (with answers) on deciphering codes and provides children with the tools to make their own field kit. . . . Humorous black-and-white sketches . . . are found throughout the book. The author's upbeat, positive tone is refreshing and his enthusiasm about his topic is contagious." SLJ

Levy, Janey

Breaking the code with cryptography; analyzing patterns. Rosen Publishing Group's PowerKids Press 2007 32p il map (PowerMath) lib bdg $23.95

Grades: 4 5 6 7   652

1. Cryptography 2. Ciphers

ISBN 978-1-4042-3368-3 (lib bdg); 1-4042-3368-7 (lib bdg)   LC 2005-14705

A brief history of cryptography also shows how to break simple ciphers by analyzing the patterns used to create them

Pincock, Stephen

Codebreaker; the history of codes and ciphers, from the ancient pharaohs to quantum cryptography. 1st U.S. ed. Walker 2006 176p il $19.95 *

Grades: 6 7 8 9   652

1. Cryptography 2. Ciphers

ISBN 978-0-8027-1547-0; 0-8027-1547-8   LC 2007310362

"Pincock's fascinating book reveals to the reader that codes and ciphers have been used by pharaohs, queens, generals, politicians, and lovers for at least 4,000 years. . . . Beautifully written, entertaining but never shallow, and replete with fascinating insights into the arcane world of cryptography, Codebreaker is that rare work—a nonfiction title that is as appealing as a fast-paced thriller. It should be an essential purchase for libraries serving young adults." Voice Youth Advocates

Includes bibliographical references

658   General management

Bochner, Arthur Berg

The new totally awesome business book for kids (and their parents); with twenty super businesses you can start right now! [by] Arthur Bochner & Rose Bochner; foreword by Andriane G. Berg. rev and updated 3rd ed. Newmarket Press 2007 188p il pa $9.95

Grades: 4 5 6 7   658

1. Small business 2. Money-making projects for children

ISBN 978-1-55704-757-1 (pa); 1-55704-757-X (pa)   LC 2007002637

First published 1995 with title: The totally awesome business book for kids

A comprehensive look at the basic financial and management aspects of moneymaking businesses for children

"This book can certainly be thought provoking for young people with an entrepreneurial spirit. . . . The illustrations are lively and engaging, and the text non-threatening." Voice Youth Advocates

Includes bibliographical references

658.1   Organization and finance

Bielagus, Peter G.

Quick cash for teens; be your own boss and make big bucks. Sterling Pub. 2009 249p pa $12.95

Grades: 7 8 9 10 11 12   658.1

1. Entrepreneurship 2. Small business 3. Money-making projects for children

ISBN 978-1-4027-6038-9 (pa); 1-4027-6038-8 (pa)   LC 2008042793

"Young entrepreneurs wanting to own and operate their own businesses will find this practical, introductory guide an excellent source of advice. . . . Bielagus' conversational style and the frequent insertion of anecdotes from successful teen entrepreneurs make the text accessible." Booklist

659.1   Advertising

Graydon, Shari

Made you look; how advertising works and why you should know; illustrations by Warren Clark. Annick Press 2003 115p il $24.95; pa $14.95 *

Grades: 5 6 7 8   659.1

1. Advertising

ISBN 1-55037-815-5; 1-55037-814-7 (pa)

This "analysis seeks to raise preteens' awareness of themselves as targets and vectors of advertising messages. Brimming with anecdotes, facts, and quotes . . . the text covers controversial programs that bring ads into the schools, and describes traditional marketing methods as well as 'stealth' techniques. . . . Graydon . . . often ends sections with a provocative question . . . and she helpfully includes addresses of watchdog organizations, tips for writing effective complaints, and an impressive set of endnotes." Booklist

Includes bibliographical references

660.6   Biotechnology

Biotechnology: changing life through science; [by] K. Lee Lerner and Brenda Wilmoth Lerner, editors. Thomson/Gale 2007 3v il set $196

Grades: 8 9 10 11 12   660.6

1. Biotechnology 2. Reference books

ISBN 978-1-4144-0151-5

Contents: v1 Medicine; v2 Agriculture; v3 Industry

"This set introduces students to the science of biotechnology, the issues pertaining to biotechnology, and how the issues impact society. . . . The clean layout features more than 150 color photographs as well as many diagrams and boxed areas. . . . The articles contain more than enough information to meet the needs of younger students as well as general readers." Booklist

Fridell, Ron, 1943-
Genetic engineering. Lerner Pub. Group 2006
48p il (Cool science) lib bdg $25.26
Grades: 4 5 6 **660.6**
1. Genetic engineering
ISBN 978-0-8225-2633-9; 0-8225-2633-6
LC 2004-22764
This book has "an attractive, colorful layout that will
appeal to readers. Each spread includes captioned, color
photographs and/or illustrations; text boxes; and, often, a
'fun fact.' . . . Fridell offers a brief explanation of the
science and then discusses how genetics is being used to
invent plants, improve animals, and engineer people. . . .
Many intriguing examples are given. Glowing plants,
supersized mice, and shrinking watermelons are among
the topics included." SLJ

Kafka, Tina, 1950-
Cloning; by Tina Kafka. Lucent Books 2008
111p il (Hot topics) lib bdg $32.45
Grades: 7 8 9 10 **660.6**
1. Cloning
ISBN 978-1-59018-979-5; 1-59018-979-5
LC 2007-36320
"This title addresses, in an interesting and accessible
manner, a scientifically and ethically complex topic. . . .
Chapters provide background information and present
both sides of the controversy, such as whether genetically modified food should be so labeled, and whether large
seed companies, farmers, or the public benefit from the
use of cloning in agriculture. Color photos, graphs, diagrams, and highlighted information add visual impact."
SLJ
Includes bibliographical references

Moore, Pete, 1962-
The debate about genetic engineering. Rosen
Pub. Group's Rosen Central 2008 48p il (Ethical
debates) lib bdg $26.50
Grades: 5 6 7 8 **660.6**
1. Genetic engineering—Social aspects
ISBN 978-1-4042-3754-4 (lib bdg); 1-4042-3754-2 (lib
bdg) LC 2006100305
Discusses genetic engineering, including its history,
why some people are against it, and how it is used in
modern society
Includes bibliographical references

Morgan, Sally
Body doubles; cloning plants and animals.
Heinemann Lib. 2002 64p il lib bdg $32.79; pa
$9.50
Grades: 5 6 7 8 **660.6**
1. Cloning
ISBN 1-58810-698-5; 1-4034-4120-0 (pa)
LC 2001-6078
Contents: The path to Dolly; Natural cloning; Chro-
mosomes and DNA; Cloning in the lab; Cloning in ac-
tion; Spare-part surgery; Human cloning; Future develop-
ments
"Morgan presents a balanced blend of hard science
and thought-provoking topics. . . . A section on chromo-

somes and DNA is handled especially well: it is illustrated with numerous diagrams that provide great visual aid
for the well-written text." Booklist
Includes bibliographical references

Seiple, Samantha
Mutants, clones, and killer corn; unlocking the
secrets of biotechnology; [by] Samantha Seiple and
Todd Seiple. Lerner 2005 112p il (Discovery!)
$27.93 *
Grades: 7 8 9 10 **660.6**
1. Biotechnology
ISBN 0-8225-4860-7
"The Seiples present an overview of biotechnology
from its origins in selective breeding to its possible future implications. The writing is clear and a brief outline
of genetics is offered. . . . The appealing layout features
color photographs, charts, and graphs, as well as informative sidebars. . . . A solid, up-to-date addition for reports and general-interest reading." SLJ

Spangenburg, Ray, 1939-
Genetic engineering; by Ray Spangenburg and
Kit Moser. Benchmark Bks. 2003 125p il (Open
for debate) lib bdg $42.79 *
Grades: 7 8 9 10 **660.6**
1. Genetic engineering
ISBN 978-0-7614-1586-2 (lib bdg); 0-7614-1586-6 (lib
bdg) LC 2002-156286
Contents: Jack and the beanstalk; Genetically manufactured food crops; From douglas fir to bacterial sav-
iors; Is it in the wind? or not?; Cloning bossy, Mickey,
and the blue ox; Alliance or danger?; The human genome; The stem cell controversy; For and against; At the
heart of the matter
Discusses the use of genetic engineering in plants and
animals, and the hopes spurred by the mapping of human
DNA by the Human Genome Project as well as the controversy over using stem cells for disease research
"Each discussion ends with a list of 'pluses' and 'mi-
nuses' that clearly presents the arguments on each side
of these hot-button issues." Horn Book Guide
Includes bibliographical references

A **Student's** guide to biotechnology. Greenwood
Press 2002 4v il set $160
Grades: 7 8 9 10 **660.6**
1. Biotechnology 2. Reference books
ISBN 0-313-32256-2 LC 2002-72693
Contents: v1 Words and terms; v2 Important people in
biotechnology; v3 The history of biotechnology; v4 Debatable issues
This set "defines terms, profiles people who have
made significant contributions to the field, provides a
historical overview, and investigates the controversies associated with biotech research." Booklist
"This much-needed four-volume set offers readers a
wealth of well-researched and clearly written information." Libr Media Connect
Includes bibliographical references

664   Food technology

Bledsoe, Karen E., 1962-
Genetically engineered foods; written by Karen
E. Bledsoe. Blackbirch Press 2006 48p il (Science
on the edge) $23.70 *
Grades: 5 6 7 8   **664**
1. Food—Biotechnology 2. Genetic engineering
ISBN 1-4103-0602-X
This offers a brief summary of Mendel's discoveries
and the discovery of DNA, then discusses how foods are
modified by genetics and the issues associated with ge-
netic engineering of foods.
Includes glossary and bibliographical references

665   Technology of industrial oils, fats, waxes, gases

Walker, Niki, 1972-
Hydrogen; running on water; [by] Niki Walker.
Crabtree Pub. 2007 32p il (Energy revolution) lib
bdg $25.20; pa $8.95
Grades: 5 6 7 8   **665**
1. Hydrogen as fuel
ISBN 978-0-7787-2915-0 (lib bdg); 0-7787-2915-X
(lib bdg); 978-0-7787-2929-7 (pa); 0-7787-2929-X
(pa)   LC 2006014369
This describes various sources of hydrogen power, including natural gas, gasified coal, fuel from water, and
biomass gas, and how it is stored and distributed, and offers energy conservation tips.
Includes glossary

666   Ceramic and allied technologies

Kassinger, Ruth
Ceramics: from magic pots to man-made bones;
[by] Ruth G. Kassinger. Twenty-First Century Bks.
2003 80p il map (Material world) lib bdg $25.90
Grades: 7 8 9 10   **666**
1. Ceramics
ISBN 0-7613-2108-X   LC 2002-11512
Examines the discovery of pottery and ceramics and
their uses throughout history, gives a scientific explanation of the properties of clay, and looks at how ceramics
are used in modern technology
This "will catch the interest of a wide variety of readers. The color photographs are clear, interesting, and
self-explanatory." Libr Media Connect
Includes bibliographical references

667   Cleaning, color, coating, related technologies

Kassinger, Ruth
Dyes: from sea snails to synthetics; [by] Ruth
G. Kassinger. Twenty-First Century Bks. 2003 80p
il map (Material world) $25.90
Grades: 7 8 9 10   **667**
1. Dyes and dyeing 2. Color
ISBN 0-7613-2112-8   LC 2002-2102
Explains how dyes were developed, how they have
been used throughout history and discusses the history
and folklore surrounding different colors
This "will catch the interest of a wide variety of read-
ers. The color photographs are clear, interesting, and
self-explanatory." Libr Media Connect
Includes glossary and bibliographical references

669   Metallurgy

Kassinger, Ruth
Gold; from Greek myth to computer chips; [by]
Ruth G. Kassinger. Twenty-First Century Bks.
2003 80p il map (Material world) lib bdg $25.90
Grades: 7 8 9 10   **669**
1. Gold
ISBN 0-7613-2110-1   LC 2001-42729
An overview of the history, uses, and characteristics
of gold
This "will catch the interest of a wide variety of read-
ers. The color photographs are clear, interesting, and
self-explanatory." Libr Media Connect
Includes glossary and bibliographical references

670   Manufacturing

Slavin, Bill, 1959-
Transformed; how everyday things are made;
written by Bill Slavin with Jim Slavin; illustrated
by Bill Slavin. Kids Can Press 2005 160p il
$24.95
Grades: 4 5 6 7   **670**
1. Manufactures
ISBN 1-55337-179-8
This describes the manufacture of such items "as base-
balls, plastic dinosaurs, toothpaste, cereal, paper, and
bricks. Each two-page spread covers the making of one
of the 69 items in numbered paragraphs. The pictures are
the best part—clear watercolor and ink images, made all
the more engaging by folks in overalls directing the action." Booklist
Includes glossary and bibliographical references

677 Textiles

Robinson Masters, Nancy
The cotton gin. Franklin Watts 2006 80p il (Inventions that shaped the world) $30.50
Grades: 6 7 8 9   **677**
1. Whitney, Eli, 1765-1825 2. Cotton gins
ISBN 978-0-531-12406-2; 0-531-12406-1
                                    LC 2005008051
A history of the invention of Eli Whitney's cotton gin
Includes bibliographical references

681.1 Instruments for measuring time, counting and calculating machines and instruments

Collier, James Lincoln, 1928-
Clocks. Benchmark Bks. 2004 126p il (Great inventions) lib bdg $37.08 *
Grades: 6 7 8 9   **681.1**
1. Clocks and watches 2. Time
ISBN 0-7614-1538-6   LC 2002-156288
Contents: Since the beginning of time; Timekeeping marches on; The great escapement; Springs and pendulums; Setting the year straight; Navigation time; Time for everybody; Atomic time for an atomic world
This describes the history and significance of clocks and other time-keeping devices from prehistoric times to the present
Includes bibliographical references

Mara, Wil
The clock. Franklin Watts 2005 80p il (Inventions that shaped the world) lib bdg $30.50
Grades: 5 6 7 8   **681.1**
1. Clocks and watches
ISBN 978-0-531-12373-7; 0-531-12373-1
                                    LC 2004-30270
Describes the invention of the clock, the impact it has had on modern culture, and patterns of change that resulted from its use.
Includes bibliographical references

685 Leather and fur goods, and related products

Blaxland, Wendy
Sneakers. Marshall Cavendish Benchmark 2009 32p il (How are they made?) $19.95
Grades: 4 5 6   **685**
1. Sneakers
ISBN 978-0-7614-3810-6; 0-7614-3810-6
                                    LC 2008026211
This is an "introduction to athletic shoes and the global trade involved in their manufacture and marketing. . . . A typical page offers a paragraph or more of informative text as well as a color photo and, perhaps, a small sidebar." Booklist

686.2 Printing

Heinrichs, Ann
The printing press. Franklin Watts 2005 80p il (Inventions that shaped the world) lib bdg $30.50
Grades: 5 6 7 8   **686.2**
1. Printing—History
ISBN 978-0-531-12343-0; 0-531-12343-X
                                    LC 2004-1672
Describes the invention of the printing press and the impact it has had on modern culture.
Includes bibliographical references

Meltzer, Milton, 1915-
The printing press. Benchmark Bks. 2003 c2004 125p il (Great inventions) lib bdg $25.95 *
Grades: 6 7 8 9   **686.2**
1. Printing
ISBN 0-7614-1536-X   LC 2002-15307
Contents: Speaking, writing, and reading; Scribes and scrolls; Was China first?; How Gutenberg did it; Printing, printing, everywhere; The print shop: a cultural center; From apprentice to master; An aid to science; From Luther to Plymouth Rock; The printing press and democracy; Many voices; In love with the printed word; The power of print; The new place of print
"The author expertly describes a setting that is ripe for invention. . . . Historical artwork, and personal narratives make the times real and relevant to readers." SLJ
Includes bibliographical references

688.7 Recreational equipment

Fridell, Ron, 1943-
Sports technology. Lerner Publications 2009 48p il (Cool science) lib bdg $27.93
Grades: 4 5 6   **688.7**
1. Sports 2. Technology
ISBN 978-0-8225-7587-0 (lib bdg); 0-8225-7587-6 (lib bdg)   LC 2007050905
This describes "how science helps athletes stay safer, perform better, and have more fun." Publisher's notes
Includes glossary and bibliographical references

Wulffson, Don L., 1943-
Toys! amazing stories behind some great inventions; [by] Don Wulffson; with illustrations by Laurie Keller. Holt & Co. 2000 137p il $16.95
Grades: 4 5 6 7   **688.7**
1. Toys 2. Inventions
ISBN 0-8050-6196-7   LC 99-58440
Describes the creation of a variety of toys and games, from seesaws to Silly Putty and toy soldiers to Trivial Pursuit
"Each of the 25 chapters is illustrated with small, humorous drawings and discusses a particular toy or game's origin and development. The book ends with a bibliography and a list of Web sites. Good, readable fare for browsing or light research." Booklist
Includes bibliographical references

690   Building & construction

Macaulay, David, 1946-
Mill. Houghton Mifflin 1983 128p il $18; pa
$9.95 *
Grades: 4 5 6 7 8 9 10   **690**
   1. Mills 2. Textile industry—History
   ISBN 0-395-34830-7; 0-395-52019-3 (pa)
                       LC 83-10652
This is an "account of the development of four fictional 19th-Century Rhode Island cotton mills. In explaining the construction and operation of a simple water-wheel powered wooden mill, as well as the more complex stone, turbine and steam mills to follow, the author also describes the rise and decline of New England's textile industry." SLJ
"Well-researched, ambitious, and absorbing, this is another first-rate history lesson from a practiced, perfectionist hand." Booklist

Unbuilding. Houghton Mifflin 1980 78p il $18; pa $9.95 *
Grades: 4 5 6 7 8 9   **690**
   1. Empire State Building (New York, N.Y.)
   2. Building 3. Skyscrapers
   ISBN 0-395-29457-6; 0-395-45425-5 (pa)
                       LC 80-15491
This fictional account of the dismantling and removal of the Empire State Building describes the structure of a skyscraper and explains how such an edifice would be demolished
"Save for the fact that one particularly stunning double-page spread is marred by tight binding, the book is a joy: accurate, informative, handsome, and eminently readable." Bull Cent Child Books

700   ARTS

Johnson, Dolores, 1949-
The Harlem Renaissance; by Dolores Johnson with Virginia Schomp. Marshall Cavendish Benchmark 2008 80p il (Drama of African-American history) lib bdg $23.95 *
Grades: 5 6 7 8   **700**
   1. Harlem Renaissance 2. African American arts
   ISBN 978-0-7614-2641-7   LC 2007034691
This is an account of the flowering of African American art, literature, music, and political commentary of the 1920s and 1930s centered in the Harlem section of New York City.
Includes glossary and bibliographical references

Makosz, Rory
Latino arts and their influence on the United States; songs, dreams, and dances. Mason Crest Publishers 2005 112p il (Hispanic heritage) $22.95
Grades: 7 8 9 10   **700**
   1. Latin American art 2. Arts—United States
   ISBN 1-59084-938-8   LC 2004022968

This "book begins with a general discussion of the ways in which cultures express themselves through their arts. It goes on to discuss the arts of Latin American cultures and their growing prominence in the United States, with emphasis on dance and music. Writing, painting, theater arts, and holidays are also included. . . . [This is] an excellent resource both for students researching Latino arts for reports and for general readers." SLJ
Includes bibligraphical references

Nardo, Don, 1947-
Arts and literature in ancient Mesopotamia. Lucent Books 2008 104p il map (Lucent library of historical eras) $32.45
Grades: 6 7 8 9   **700**
   1. Iraq—Civilization
   ISBN 978-1-4205-0099-8; 1-4205-0099-6
                       LC 2008-22045
Introduces the cultural activities of ancient Mesopotamia, discussing art, language, metalwork, sculpture, cuneiform writing, mapmaking, epic poetry, and sacred literature.
This is "ideal for research projects. . . . [The author] provides diverse annotated suggestions (including Web sites) for further study." SLJ
Includes bibliographical references

Worth, Richard, 1945-
The Harlem Renaissance; an explosion of African-American culture; [by] Richard Worth. Enslow Publishers 2008 128p il map (America's living history) lib bdg $31.93
Grades: 5 6 7 8   **700**
   1. Harlem Renaissance
   ISBN 978-0-7660-2907-1; 0-7660-2907-7
                       LC 2007025593
"Explores the Harlem Renaissance, a reawakening of African-American culture, including literature, the arts, theater, and music, motivated by a goal to achieve equal rights." Publisher's note
This "is well sourced, includes extensive back matter, and has a full complement of supporting color photographs or other illustrations that makes it accessible and useful to report writers and general readers." SLJ
Includes glossary and bibliographical references

701   Philosophy and theory of fine and decorative arts

Dickins, Rosie
The Usborne art treasury; pictures, paintings, and projects; [by] Rosie Dickins; designed by Nicola Butler. Usborne 2007 94p il $19.99
Grades: 4 5 6 7   **701**
   1. Art appreciation 2. Painting
   ISBN 978-0-7945-1452-5
"Each project in this colorful, attractive compendium of art projects begins with a particular work of art. . . . Throughout the book, the excellent presentation of the projects makes them seem not only possible to complete but also worth doing. Illustrated step-by-step, the instructions are clearly written and practical." Booklist

Sousa, Jean

Faces, places and inner spaces; a guide to looking at art; [by] Jean Sousa. Abrams Books for Young Readers 2006 48p il $18.95 *

Grades: 5 6 7 8   **701**

1. Art appreciation

ISBN 0-8109-5966-6; 978-0-8109-5966-8

LC 2005-21053

"This introduction to art is an offshoot of an ongoing exhibit of the same name at the Art Institute of Chicago. . . . An assortment of artworks from the museum's collection is arranged into the three broad categories listed in the title, and with accessible, expert observations, Sousa pulls readers straight into the images. . . . This offers an unpretentious, dynamic approach to art education." Booklist

Includes glossary

702.8 Techniques, procedures, apparatus, equipment, materials

Luxbacher, Irene, 1970-

The jumbo book of art; written and illustrated by Irene Luxbacher. Kids Can Press 2003 208p il pa $14.95 *

Grades: 4 5 6 7   **702.8**

1. Art—Study and teaching

ISBN 1-55074-762-2

"Each of the four chapters is devoted to instructing readers in the basics of one technique—drawing, creating with color, sculpture, and mixed-media projects, respectively—and then inspires those readers to let loose and have fun making something beautiful. . . . The book features clear layouts, well-written definitions of terms, full-color illustrations, and more than 90 projects. . . . This practical, lively, and smart package is a must-have for every art and elementary school classroom, and a welcome addition to most library collections." SLJ

Includes glossary

703 Dictionaries, encyclopedias, concordances of fine and decorative arts

Greenway, Shirley

Art: an A-Z guide; selected and written by Shirley Greenway. Watts 2000 128p il lib bdg $33; pa $19.95

Grades: 7 8 9 10   **703**

1. Art—Dictionaries 2. Reference books

ISBN 0-531-11729-4 (lib bdg); 0-531-16553-1 (pa)

LC 00-24899

"Greenway highlights 59 terms that are important 'to a discussion and understanding of art.' Each term is richly illustrated with examples. While there are familiar paintings, there are also lesser-known works. . . . Sidebars highlight individual artists. . . . The text is succinct and the full-color photographs and reproductions, often several per concept, are lush and informative." SLJ

704 Special topics in fine and decorative arts

Barber, Nicola

Islamic empires; [by] Nicola Barber. Raintree 2005 48p il map (History in art) $31.43 *

Grades: 4 5 6 7   **704**

1. Islamic art 2. Islam

ISBN 1-4109-0522-5   LC 2004-7527

Contents: Art as evidence; The spread of Islam; The great empires; Life in the Islamic empires; Religion

This is an introduction to the art, culture, and history of Islamic empires.

This book has "a depth of content that is unusual in art-history books for this age group. . . . [It] is amply illustrated with full-color photographs and reproductions. . . . Well-written, informative." SLJ

Includes bibliographical references

Bolden, Tonya

Wake up our souls; a celebration of Black American artists; Published in association with Smithsonian American Art Museum. Harry N. Abrams 2004 128p il $24.95 *

Grades: 6 7 8 9   **704**

1. African American art

ISBN 0-8109-4527-4

Published in association with Smithsonian American Art Museum.

Presents a history of African American visual arts and artists from the days of slavery to the present

"Bolden's writing is rich and lyrical. She smoothly incorporates the historical context, explaining pivotal events and relevant artistic movements clearly and succinctly." SLJ

704.9 Iconography

Bingham, Jane

Emotion & relationships. Raintree 2006 56p il map (Through artists' eyes) lib bdg $32.86

Grades: 4 5 6 7   **704.9**

1. Emotions in art 2. Interpersonal relations in art

ISBN 1-4109-2238-3

"Using simple yet descriptive language and good-quality, full-color reproductions, Bingham describes works of art and links them to [emotions and relationships]. [The book] has chapters such as 'Family Feelings,' 'Happiness and Contentment,' and 'Sickness and Pain,' and includes works by Thomas Gainsborough, Frans Hals, and Frida Kahlo. . . . A variety of artwork is highlighted, including sculpture, paintings, jewelry and costume, literature, [and] opera." SLJ

Includes bibliographical references

Landscape & the environment; [by] Jane Bingham. Raintree 2006 56p il (Through artists' eyes) lib bdg $32.86

Grades: 4 5 6 7   **704.9**

1. Landscape in art

ISBN 1-4109-2240-5   LC 2005024925

Bingham, Jane—*Continued*

"Using simple yet descriptive language and good-quality, full-color reproductions, Bingham describes works of art and links them to [landscapes and environment]. . . . [The book] is broken down by location and/or time period into such topics as 'Ancient Gardens,' 'Romantic Landscapes,' and 'Landscapes of the Renaissance.' . . . A variety of artwork is highlighted, including sculpture, paintings, jewelry and costume, literature, opera, and . . . altered landscapes such as gardens and the large-scale work of Christo." SLJ

Includes bibliographical references

Science & technology; [by] Jane Bingham. Raintree 2006 56p il (Through artists' eyes) lib bdg $32.86

Grades: 4 5 6 7 **704.9**

1. Science in art 2. Technology in art

ISBN 1-4109-2241-3   LC 2005025029

"Painters such as Rembrandt and, much later, Thomas Eakins were fascinated by the advancements in medicine. Steam engines intrigued Turner and Monet. These are just a few examples of the intersecting of technology and science with art. Throughout *Science & Technology*, printing, measuring time, engineering, and communications are touched upon along with the artwork inspired by various discoveries. . . . The full-color reproductions are well chosen and of good quality. The information is brief, but it provides a well-thought-out overview of these artistic interpretations." SLJ

Includes bibliographical references

Society & class; [by] Jane Bingham. Raintree 2006 56p il map (Through artists' eyes) lib bdg $32.86

Grades: 4 5 6 7 **704.9**

1. Society in art 2. Social classes in art

ISBN 1-4109-2237-5   LC 2005025028

This "succinctly looks at how artists have depicted the lives of farmers, hunters, rulers, slaves, soldiers, and merchants throughout history. Social change such as the French and American Revolutions inspired artists, while the rise of Communism and Fascism had a chilling effect on art. . . . The full-color reproductions are well chosen and of good quality. The information is brief, but it provides a well-thought-out overview of these artistic interpretations." SLJ

Includes bibliographical references

709 Art—Historical, geographic, persons treatment of fine and decorative arts

Mason, Antony

A history of Western art; from prehistory to the 20th century; edited by John T. Spike. Abrams Books for Young Readers 2007 128p il $22.50

Grades: 7 8 9 10 **709**

1. Art—History

ISBN 978-0-8109-9421-8; 0-8109-9421-6

LC 2007-10291

This is a survey of "Western art's 50,000-year history. . . . With a few exceptions, each spread focuses on a different time period or movement, spotlighting representative work, from prehistoric cave paintings and ancient artifacts to contemporary new media. . . . A short narrative paragraph accompanies beautifully reproduced color images, extensive captions, and text boxes. . . . This overview gives students a strong visual introduction to Western art." Booklist

Raczka, Bob

Name that style; all about isms in art; by Bob Raczka. Millbrook Press 2008 32p il (Art adventures) lib bdg $25.26 *

Grades: 5 6 7 8 **709**

1. Art—History

ISBN 978-0-8225-7586-3 (lib bdg); 0-8225-7586-8 (lib bdg)   LC 2008000312

"Beginning with naturalism and ending with photorealism, with many stops along the way, this compact overview documents the shifts, both in terms of technique as well as subject matter, that differentiate each style from its predecessors. Each 'ism' gets a two-page spread, with a beautifully reproduced example. . . . This is . . . indispensible for any middle-grade classrooms introducing art history." Booklist

Sayre, Henry M., 1948-

Cave paintings to Picasso; the inside scoop on 50 art masterpieces; by Henry Sayre. Chronicle Books 2004 93p il $22.95 *

Grades: 5 6 7 8 **709**

1. Art—History

ISBN 0-8118-3767-X   LC 2002-15583

Introduces fifty celebrated works of art, including King Tut's sarcophagus and Andy Warhol's paintings of Campbell's soup cans, with historical and interpretive information for each piece.

"The author's breezy style captures interest early on. . . . Many of the world's cultures are represented and a variety of techniques are explained. . . . A dazzling and accessible introduction to art history." SLJ

Includes glossary

709.02 Art—6th-15th centuries, 500-1499

Gunderson, Jessica, 1976-

Gothic art; by Jessica Gunderson. Creative Education 2008 il (Movements in art) lib bdg $22.95

Grades: 6 7 8 9 **709.02**

1. Gothic art 2. Gothic architecture

ISBN 978-1-58341-610-5; 1-58341-610-2

LC 2007018952

"Gunderson describes how art trends, politics, and inventions informed the work that was produced during [the Gothic] movement. . . . [The] book provides an overview of the movement and its key players in continuous prose that is broken up by an occasional highlighted section of text. The color photographs, illustrations, and

Gunderson, Jessica, 1976-—*Continued*
reproductions, many of them full page, are relevant and
of high quality. . . . [The text delivers a] well-rounded
[account] that students will find accessible." SLJ
Includes glossary and bibliographical references

Spilsbury, Richard, 1963-
The Renaissance. Heinemann Library 2009 48p
il (Art on the wall) lib bdg $32.86
Grades: 5 6 7 8 9 10   **709.02**
1. Art—15th and 16th centuries 2. Renaissance
ISBN 978-1-4329-1372-4; 1-4329-1372-7
                                          LC 2008020357
This "discusses how a revival of interest in the classical world inspired a new approach to art, describes the
developments that took place in art during the Renaissance period, and examines how Renaissance artists created lifelike paintings and sculptures." Publisher's note
Includes glossary and bibliographical references

709.03   Art—Modern period, 1500-

Gunderson, Jessica, 1976-
Impressionism; by Jessica Gunderson. Creative
Education 2008 48p il (Movements in art) lib bdg
$32.80
Grades: 6 7 8 9   **709.03**
1. Impressionism (Art)
ISBN 978-1-58341-611-2 (lib bdg); 1-58341-611-0 (lib
bdg)   LC 2007008493
This "discusses the leading Impressionist artists, their
subjects, and their techniques. Quality reproductions of
many paintings and occasional sepia photos of the painters and their settings illustrate the detailed, informative
overview." Booklist
Includes glossary and bibliographical references

Realism; by Jessica Gunderson. 1st ed. Creative
Education 2009 48p il (Movements in art) lib bdg
$32.80
Grades: 6 7 8 9   **709.03**
1. Realism in art
ISBN 978-1-58341-612-9 (lib bdg); 1-58341-612-9 (lib
bdg)   LC 2007008494
"Gunderson describes how art trends, politics, and inventions informed the work that was produced during
[the Realism] movement. . . . [The] book provides an
overview of the movement and its key players in continuous prose that is broken up by an occasional highlighted
section of text. The color photographs, illustrations, and
reproductions, many of them full page, are relevant and
of high quality. . . . The [text delivers a] well-rounded
[account] that students will find accessible." SLJ
Includes glossary and bibliographical references

Romanticism; [by] Jessica Gunderson. Creative
Education 2009 48p il (Movements in art) lib bdg
$32.80
Grades: 6 7 8 9   **709.03**
1. Romanticism in art
ISBN 978-1-58341-613-6; 1-58341-613-7
                                          LC 2007008495

"Gunderson describes how art trends, politics, and inventions informed the work that was produced during
[the Romantic] movement. . . . [The] book provides an
overview of the movement and its key players in continuous prose that is broken up by an occasional highlighted
section of text. The color photographs, illustrations, and
reproductions, many of them full page, are relevant and
of high quality. . . . The [text delivers a] well-rounded
[account] that students will find accessible." SLJ
Includes glossary and bibliographical references

709.04   Art—20th century, 1900-
1999

Claybourne, Anna
Surrealism. Heinemann Library 2009 48p il (Art
on the wall) lib bdg $32.86
Grades: 5 6 7 8 9 10   **709.04**
1. Surrealism 2. Modern art
ISBN 978-1-4329-1367-0; 1-4329-1367-0
                                          LC 2008020316
This "explains the Surrealists' interest in dreams and
the subconscious, identifies the different styles and interests of many of the leading Surrealist artists, and shows
how Surrealism included writing, music, theatre, and
film, as well as art." Publisher's note
This title succeeds "in presenting a bird's-eye view of
[Surrealism] without oversimplification. Information on
individual artists is included in the broader context of the
movement. Visually exciting, with plenty of color, [the
layout is] hip and should appeal to the target audience."
SLJ
Includes glossary and bibliographical references

Demilly, Christian
Pop art; [translated from the French by Rosie
Jackson] Prestel 2007 31p il $14.95
Grades: 8 9 10 11 12   **709.04**
1. Pop art
ISBN 978-3-7913-3894-1; 3-7913-3894-3
"An excellent introduction to this artistic movement.
Demilly traces its beginnings to the work of early-20th-
century French and German artists such as Marcel Du-
champ, Kurt Schwitters, and Fernand Léger. He then
shows how Pop Art grew to comment particularly on
American society, both in its glamour and its excesses.
Each clear, one-page explanation of the various aspects
of Pop Art is set opposite a one-half or full-page, high-
quality color reproduction of a famous work." SLJ

Spilsbury, Richard, 1963-
Abstract expressionism. Heinemann Library
2009 48p il (Art on the wall) lib bdg $32.86
Grades: 5 6 7 8 9 10   **709.04**
1. Abstract expressionism 2. American art
ISBN 978-1-4329-1370-0 (lib bdg); 1-4329-1370-0 (lib
bdg)   LC 2008020361
This "explains how Abstract Expressionism developed
. . . and considers how modern artists continue to be influenced by the Abstract Expressionists." Publisher's note
This title succeeds "in presenting a bird's-eye view of

Spilsbury, Richard, 1963-—*Continued*
[Abstract expressionism] without oversimplification. Information on individual artists is included in the broader context of the movement. Visually exciting, with plenty of color, [the layout is] hip and should appeal to the target audience." SLJ
Includes glossary and bibliographical references

Pop art. Heinemann Library 2009 48p il (Art on the wall) lib bdg $23
Grades: 5 6 7 8 9 10   **709.04**
  1. Pop art
  ISBN 978-1-4329-1368-7; 1-4329-1368-9
           LC 2008020358
This describes how Pop art began, some of the movement's artists, and the influence of Pop art
This title succeeds "in presenting a bird's-eye view of [Pop art] without oversimplification. Information on individual artists is included in the broader context of the movement. Visually exciting, with plenty of color, [the layout is] hip and should appeal to the target audience." SLJ
Includes glossary and bibliographical references

709.37   Ancient Italian art. Roman art

Chrisp, Peter
Ancient Rome. Raintree 2005 48p il (History in art) lib bdg $31.43 *
Grades: 4 5 6 7   **709.37**
  1. Roman art 2. Rome—Civilization
  ISBN 1-4109-0520-9   LC 2004-7567
  Contents: The Roman empire; The story of Rome; The city of Rome; Family life; Roman religion; Timeline
While telling about her life in ancient Rome, eight-year-old Flavia includes information about the homes, families, clothing, food, gods, sports, goods traded, and things the people build
The book follows "a well-organized format that makes the history accessible for reports, but the [author takes the book] beyond a reports-only status. Captions for the two or three illustrations per spread are clear." SLJ
Includes glossary and bibliographical references

709.38   Ancient Greek art

Langley, Andrew
Ancient Greece. Raintree 2005 48p il (History in art) lib bdg $31.43; pa $8.99 *
Grades: 4 5 6 7   **709.38**
  1. Greek art 2. Greece—Civilization
  ISBN 978-1-4109-0517-8 (lib bdg); 1-4109-0517-9 (lib bdg); 978-1-4109-2035-5 (pa); 1-4109-2035-6 (pa)
           LC 2004-7523
  Contents: Art as evidence; The story of ancient Greece; Inside the city-state; Everyday life; Religion and mythology; Time line
The author shows "how art provides primary-source information about everyday and family life, beliefs and religion, and philosophy and mythology in . . . ancient

[Greece]. . . . The [book follows] a well-organized format that makes the history accessible for reports, but the [author takes the book] beyond a reports-only status. Captions for the two or three illustrations per spread are clear." SLJ
Includes glossary and bibliographical references

709.5   Asian art

Bingham, Jane
Indian art & culture. Raintree 2004 56p il map (World art & culture) lib bdg $23; pa $9.99 *
Grades: 6 7 8 9   **709.5**
  1. Indic arts
  ISBN 0-7398-6607-9 (lib bdg); 978-1-4109-2106-2 (pa); 1-4109-2106-9 (pa)   LC 2003-1956
This offers a history of the arts of India, including architecture, wall painting and decoration, stone and wood carving, painting, textiles, ceramics, music, dance, theater and film, and writing, and explains their roles in Indian culture
"Every page includes interesting and vivid color photographs of the different art forms and of artists at work. [This title is] well worth purchasing for the illustrations alone." SLJ
Includes glossary and bibliographical references

709.51   Chinese art

Anderson, Dale, 1953-
Ancient China; [by] Dale Anderson. Raintree 2005 48p il map (History in art) $22; pa $8.99 *
Grades: 4 5 6 7   **709.51**
  1. Chinese art 2. China—Civilization
  ISBN 978-1-4109-0519-2; 1-4109-0519-5; 978-1-4109-2037-9 (pa); 1-4109-2037-2 (pa)
           LC 2004-7587
  Contents: Art as evidence; The story of ancient China; Imperial government; Daily life in ancient China; Beliefs and philosophies; Timeline
The author shows "how art provides primary-source information about everyday and family life, beliefs and religion, and philosophy and mythology in . . . ancient [China]. . . . The [book follows] a well-organized format that makes the history accessible for reports, but the [author takes the book] beyond a reports-only status. Captions for the two or three illustrations per spread are clear." SLJ
Includes glossary and bibliographical references

709.52   Japanese art

Khanduri, Kamini
Japanese art & culture. Raintree 2004 56p il map (World art & culture) lib bdg $23; pa $9.99 *
Grades: 6 7 8 9   **709.52**
  1. Japanese arts 2. Japan—Civilization
  ISBN 0-7398-6609-5 (lib bdg); 978-1-4109-2107-9 (pa); 1-4109-2107-7 (pa)   LC 2003-1957

Khanduri, Kamini—*Continued*

This offers a history of the arts of Japan including painting, woodblock prints, sculpture, metalwork, pottery, lacquerware, architecture, gardens, calligraphy, and theater, and explains their places in Japanese culture

Includes glossary and bibliographical references

709.6   African art

Bingham, Jane

African art & culture. Raintree 2004 56p il map (World art & culture) lib bdg $23; pa $9.99 *

Grades: 6 7 8 9   **709.6**

1. African art

ISBN 0-7398-6606-0 (lib bdg); 978-1-4109-2105-5 (pa); 1-4109-2105-0 (pa)   LC 2003-1955

This describes a variety of art forms of the African continent and their roles in their respective cultures

This is "stunningly illustrated. . . . Every page includes interesting and vivid color photographs of the different art forms and of artists at work. [This title is] well worth purchasing for the illustrations alone." SLJ

Includes glossary and bibliographical references

709.7   North American art

January, Brendan, 1972-

Native American art & culture; [by] Brendan January. Raintree 2005 56p il map (World art & culture) lib bdg $23; pa $9.99 *

Grades: 5 6 7 8   **709.7**

1. Native American art 2. Native Americans

ISBN 978-1-4109-1108-7 (lib bdg); 1-4109-1108-X (lib bdg); 978-1-4109-2118-5 (pa); 1-4109-2118-2 (pa)
LC 2004-8072

Contents: Introduction; Beliefs and traditions; Rock art; Land art; Architecture; Body art; Carving; Masks; Images; Pottery; Weaving; Baskets; Kachina dolls; Painting; Clothing, decoration, and hair styles; Ceremonies, songs, and dance; Metals and precious stones; The powwow; Cross currents

"January investigates the many art forms of the Native American tribes. . . . Chapters are dedicated to pottery, textiles, carving, and painting as well as body art, architecture, ceremonies, songs, and dances. . . . Numerous color photographs of both ancient and modern artwork are included on each spread, and they are exceptional. . . . This fresh look at Native American culture through its artwork will be a welcome alternative for reports and classroom discussion, and the popularity of the subject matter and appealing design will attract readers outside the classroom environment." SLJ

Includes bibliographical references

Native Americans; [by] Brendan January. Raintree 2005 48p il map (History in art) lib bdg $22; pa $8.99

Grades: 4 5 6 7   **709.7**

1. Native American art 2. Native Americans

ISBN 978-1-4109-0523-9 (lib bdg); 1-4109-0523-3 (lib bdg); 978-1-4109-2041-6 (pa); 1-4109-2041-0 (pa)
LC 2004-7526

Contents: The Native Americans; A chronological history; Traditional ways; Everyday life; Beliefs and mythology

This book has "a depth of content that is unusual in art-history books for this age group. . . . [It] is amply illustrated with full-color photographs and reproductions. . . . Well-written, informative." SLJ

Includes bibliographical references

709.72   Mexican art

Lewis, Elizabeth, 1967-

Mexican art & culture. Raintree 2004 56p il map (World art & culture) lib bdg $23; pa $9.99 *

Grades: 6 7 8 9   **709.72**

1. Mexican art 2. Mexico—Social life and customs

ISBN 0-7398-6610-9 (lib bdg); 978-1-4109-2108-6 (pa); 1-4109-2108-5 (pa)   LC 2003-1958

This offers a history of the arts of Mexico including architecture, carvings and sculpture, pottery and ceramics, masks, lacquering, textiles and clothing, jewelry, painting, music and musical instruments, fiestas and festivals, death and burial customs, and toys, and explains their roles in Mexican culture

The text is "straightforward and concise, but it's the excellent selection of high-quality color photos that really stand out." Booklist

Includes glossary and bibliographical references

711   Area planning (Civic art)

Macaulay, David, 1946-

City: a story of Roman planning and construction. Houghton Mifflin 1974 112p il $18; pa $7.95 *

Grades: 4 5 6 7 8 9   **711**

1. City planning—Rome 2. Civil engineering 3. Roman architecture

ISBN 0-395-19492-X; 0-395-34922-2 (pa)
LC 74-4280

"By following the inception, construction, and development of an imaginary Roman city, the account traces the evolution of Verbonia from the selection of its site under religious auspices in 26 B.C. to its completion in 100 A.D." Horn Book

Includes glossary

720   Architecture

Bos, Samone

Super structures; [by Samone Bos; illustrated by Alessandro Rabatti] DK Pub. 2008 80p il $19.99

Grades: 5 6 7 8   **720**

1. Structural engineering 2. Architecture

ISBN 978-0-7566-4088-0; 0-7566-4088-1

"This book presents many different types of manmade structures, beginning with the wonders of the ancient world, and ranging all the way forward to Space-

Bos, Samone—*Continued*

port America, a commercial space-travel facility that is still in its planning and construction phases. . . . Readers with a developing interest in architecture or engineering or simply an appreciation for humankind's most awesome constructions will find much to pore over here." Booklist

Hosack, Karen, 1971-

Buildings; [by] Karen Hosack. Raintree 2009 32p il map (What is art?) lib bdg $27.50
Grades: 5 6 7 8   720
1. Buildings 2. Architecture
ISBN 978-1-4109-3165-8; 1-4109-3165-X
                                                        LC 2008-9700
This "features public spaces and private residences created from a variety of materials. Every page includes a paragraph about the structure with glossary terms in bold type. . . . [Title is] consistent in quality of design and content." SLJ
Includes glossary and bibliographical references

Joseph, Leonard M.

Skyscrapers: inside and out; illustrations, Leonello Calvetti [et al.] PowerKids Press 2002 47p il (Technology—blueprints of the future) lib bdg $25.25
Grades: 6 7 8 9   720
1. Skyscrapers
ISBN 0-8239-6109-5   LC 2001-1115
This "features a chronology of the world's tallest buildings, plus an intriguing look at how these amazing architectural pillars are designed, are constructed, and operate. Separate sections provide a closer look at such famous structures as the Empire State Building, the Chrysler Building, the World Trade Center, and the Sears Tower." Voice Youth Advocates
Includes bibliographical references

Laroche, Giles

What's inside; fascinating structures around the world. Houghton Mifflin Books for Children 2009 unp il $17
Grades: 4 5 6 7   720
1. Architecture
ISBN 978-0-618-86247-4; 0-618-86247-1
                                                        LC 2008-33832
"This beautiful book presents interior and exterior views of 14 extraordinary structures, from King Tut's tomb and the Temple of Kukulcan to the Sydney Opera House and the Georgia Aquarium. . . . The text is good, the organization is clever, but it's the art here that is truly masterful. The illustrations are made from layers and layers of cut and painted paper." SLJ

Macaulay, David, 1946-

Building big. Houghton Mifflin 2000 192p il $30; pa $12.95 *
Grades: 5 6 7 8 9 10   720
1. Architecture 2. Engineering
ISBN 0-395-96331-1; 0-618-46527-8 (pa)
                                                        LC 00-28116

"Walter Lorraine books"
This companion to the PBS series examines the architecture and engineering of "bridges, tunnels, dams, domes, and skyscrapers. Each section offers an implicitly chronological analysis as it focuses on several significant examples of that particular kind of structure." Bull Cent Child Books
"Macaulay combines his detailed yet vaguely whimsical illustrations with simple, straightforward prose that breaks down complex architectural and engineering accomplishments into easily digestible tidbits that don't insult the intelligence of the reader of any age." N Y Times Book Rev
Includes glossary

Oxlade, Chris

Skyscrapers; uncovering technology. Firefly Books 2006 52p il $16.95
Grades: 4 5 6 7   720
1. Skyscrapers
ISBN 1-55407-136-4
"This tour of big buildings flits around the world and through history with a kaleidoscopic mix of small, finely detailed atrists' renditions and five-sentence-or-less text muchies. . . . It also features four mylar overlays that offer an inside look at a few towering structures. . . . Blending eye-catching visuals with specific facts and comparisons, this quick survey will please both browsers and assignment-driven readers." Booklist

Roeder, Annette

13 buildings children should know; [translator, Jane Michael] Prestel 2009 46p il $14.95
Grades: 6 7 8 9   720
1. Architecture
ISBN 978-3-7913-4171-2; 3-7913-4171-5
"The famous buildings featured in this pictorial collection include Notre Dame cathedral in Paris, Neuschwanstein Castle in Germany, New York City's Guggenheim Museum and the Beijing National Stadium (built for the 2008 Olympics), each pictured in color photographs, cross-sections and/or ground plans, with time lines tracing the buildings' developments and changes over time. . . . A sound introduction to some impressive structures." Publ Wkly

Severance, John B.

Skyscrapers; how America grew up. Holiday House 2000 112p $18.95
Grades: 5 6 7 8   720
1. Skyscrapers
ISBN 0-8234-1492-2   LC 99-51842
Details some of the innovations that enabled the building of taller and taller buildings, describes the various schools of skyscraper architecture, and explores the history of several famous skyscrapers
"The many black-and-white illustrations include period prints and photos, which complement the clearly written and well-organized text." Booklist
Includes bibliographical references

720.9 Architecture—Historical, geographic, persons treatment

Clements, Gillian
A picture history of great buildings. Frances Lincoln Children's 2007 61p il map $19.95
Grades: 7 8 9 10   **720.9**
1. Buildings 2. Architecture—History
ISBN 978-1-84507-488-3; 1-84507-488-2
An illustrated history of over 9,000 years of great buildings around the world from the tombs of ancient Egypt to the modern skyscrapers of today.
This is "an excellent resource, jam-packed with information for anyone interested in a basic study of architecture throughout the ages." Libr Media Connect
Includes glossary

726 Buildings for religious and related purposes

DuTemple, Lesley A., 1952-
The Pantheon. Lerner Publs. 2003 72p il (Great building feats) lib bdg $27.93
Grades: 5 6 7 8   **726**
1. Pantheon (Rome, Italy) 2. Temples 3. Roman architecture
ISBN 0-8225-0376-X   LC 2001-05694
Describes the building of the Pantheon, discussing the role of the Roman emperor Hadrian and the significance of the Pantheon in the fields of history and architecture
This offers a "clear and straightforward text. . . . There are numerous color photographs, clear diagrams, and architectural drawings of the building and its interior." SLJ
Includes bibliographical references

The Taj Mahal. Lerner Publs. 2003 88p il (Great building feats) lib bdg $27.93
Grades: 5 6 7 8   **726**
1. Taj Mahal (Agra, India)
ISBN 0-8225-4694-9   LC 2002-151380
Contents: The Chosen One of the Palace (1519-1631); The origins of the Taj Mahal (1562-1632); Construction begins (1631-1632); Bricks and marble (1632-1637); The illumined tomb (1632-1643); The garden of paradise on earth (1640-1643); The fall of the Mughals (1643-present)
Recounts the history of the creation of the Taj Mahal, built as a tomb and memorial for the wife of the Mughal emperor Shah Jahan
The text is "enriched with interesting sidebars, diagrams that clarify the description of the building techniques, and many color photographs and reproductions." SLJ
Includes bibliographical references

Macaulay, David, 1946-
Building the book Cathedral. Houghton Mifflin 1999 112p il $29.95
Grades: 4 5 6 7 8 9   **726**
1. Cathedrals 2. Gothic architecture
ISBN 0-395-92147-3   LC 99-17975

"Walter Lorraine books"
"On its twenty-fifth anniversary, the author recounts the origins of his first book and suggests revisions he'd make in light of what he's learned. . . . Most of the original *Cathedral: the story of it's construction* is reproduced in this oversized celebratory volume, along with lots of preliminary sketches, new commentary, and revised, or newly deployed, art. . . . Touches of informal humor further enliven a book that's already mesmerizing for both its original content and its insights into this author-illustrator's incisive, ebulliently creative mind." Horn Book

Cathedral: the story of its construction. Houghton Mifflin 1973 77p il $18; pa $8.95 *
Grades: 4 5 6 7 8 9   **726**
1. Cathedrals 2. Gothic architecture
ISBN 0-395-17513-5; 0-395-31668-5 (pa)
     LC 73-6634
This is a description, illustrated with black-and-white line drawings, of the construction of an imagined representative Gothic cathedral "in southern France from its conception in 1252 to its completion in 1338. The spirit that motivated the people, the tools and materials they used, the steps and methods of constructions, all receive . . . attention." Booklist
Includes glossary

Mosque. Houghton Mifflin 2003 96p il $18 *
Grades: 4 5 6 7 8 9   **726**
1. Mosques—Design and construction
ISBN 0-618-24034-9   LC 2003-177
"Walter Lorraine books"
Using "a fictional framework to hold his nonfictional material, the author introduces readers to Admiral Suha Mehmet Pasa, a wealthy aristocrat living in Istanbul, who decides in his declining years to fund the building of a mosque and its associated buildings—religious school, soup kitchen, public baths, public fountain, and tomb. Detailing the activities of the architect and workers, Macaulay creates a from-the-ground-up look not only at the actual construction, but also at the uses of the various buildings." SLJ
"Once again Macaulay uses clear words and exemplary drawings to explore a majestic structure's design and construction. . . . In his respectful, straightforward explanation of the mosque's design, Macaulay offers an unusual, inspiring perspective into Islamic society." Booklist
Includes glossary

Pyramid. Houghton Mifflin 1975 80p il $18; pa $9.95 *
Grades: 4 5 6 7 8 9   **726**
1. Pyramids 2. Egypt—Civilization
ISBN 0-395-21407-6; 0-395-32121-2 (pa)
     LC 75-9964
The construction of a pyramid in 25th century B.C. Egypt is described. "Information about selection of the site, drawing of the plans, calculating compass directions, clearing and leveling the ground, and quarrying and hauling the tremendous blocks of granite and limestone is conveyed as much by pictures as by text." Horn Book
Includes glossary

Mann, Elizabeth, 1948-
The Parthenon; illustrations by Yuan Lee. Mikaya Press 2006 47p il (Wonders of the world) $22.95

Grades: 4 5 6 7 **726**
1. Parthenon (Athens, Greece) 2. Athens (Greece)—History 3. Greece—Civilization
ISBN 1-931414-15-7

This "volume introduces the history of ancient Athens culminating in the building of the Parthenon. . . . [The text is] well-researched and clearly written. . . . The color illustrations include an excellent map of Greece, photos of artifacts and sculptures, and many clearly deliniated, large-scale paintings." Booklist

727 Buildings for educational and research purposes

Vogel, Jennifer
A library story; by Jennifer Vogel. Millbrook Press 2006 64p il lib bdg $26.60

Grades: 4 5 6 **727**
1. Library architecture 2. Public libraries
ISBN 978-0-8225-5916-0 (lib bdg); 0-8225-5916-1 (lib bdg)   LC 2005023742

"A fact-filled look at the design and construction of the new Central Library of the Minneapolis Public Library, which opened its doors in May 2006. Vogel includes a brief overview of the library's history and plenty of details and trivia relating to this specific library system and public libraries in general. . . . A mix of color photographs and archival graphics enliven the text." SLJ

Includes bibliographical references

728.8 Large and elaborate private dwellings

Macaulay, David, 1946-
Castle. Houghton Mifflin 1977 74p il $18; pa $9.95 *

Grades: 4 5 6 7 8 9 **728.8**
1. Castles 2. Fortification
ISBN 0-395-25784-0; 0-395-32920-5 (pa)
       LC 77-7159

Macaulay depicts "the history of an imaginary thirteenth-century castle—built to subdue the Welsh hordes—from the age of construction to the age of neglect, when the town of Aberwyfern no longer needs a fortified stronghold." Economist
Includes glossary

736 Carving and carvings

Boursin, Didier
Easy origami. Firefly 2005 64p il $19.95; pa $9.95 *

Grades: 4 5 6 7 **736**

1. Origami
ISBN 1-55297-928-8; 1-55297-939-3 (pa)

This guide provides step-by-step instructions for 24 origami projects, ranked as very easy, easy, and detailed, and the book includes tips for best results.

"Paper-folding novices in particular may be drawn to this collection by its unusually clean design and bright, inviting colors." SLJ

Henry, Sally
Paper folding; [by] Sally Henry. PowerKids Press 2009 32p il (Make your own crafts) lib bdg $25.25

Grades: 3 4 5 6 **736**
1. Paper crafts 2. Origami
ISBN 978-1-4358-2507-9 (lib bdg); 1-4358-2507-1 (lib bdg)   LC 2008-4524

"After describing different kinds of paper, Henry explains the difference between a fold, a crease, and a burnished fold, and then lists all the other supplies besides paper (glue, rubber cement) that should be on hand. The rest of the book devotes two-page spreads to each project. . . . The ideas are fantastic. . . . This will keep plenty of hands and minds busy." Booklist
Includes glossary

Krier, Ann Kristen, 1962-
Totally cool origami animals. Sterling Pub. 2007 96p il $19.95

Grades: 4 5 6 **736**
1. Origami
ISBN 978-1-4027-2448-0; 1-4027-2448-9
       LC 2006029593

"Each of these twenty-eight origami animal projects is accompanied by clear step-by-step instructions and photos. Projects are conveniently labeled 'beginner,' 'intermediate,' or 'advanced.' . . . The projects . . . are typically well explained. Paper-folders of all abilities should be able to tackle these projects with success." Horn Book Guide

Nguyen, Duy
Creepy crawly animal origami; [by] Duy Nguyen. Sterling Pub. 2003 96p il hardcover o.p. pa $9.95

Grades: 5 6 7 8 **736**
1. Origami 2. Animals in art
ISBN 0-8069-9012-0; 1-4027-2229-X (pa)
       LC 2002-15507

This offers instructions for creating origami representations of animals such as alligators, turtles, tarantulas, geckos, lobsters, and grasshoppers

"Origami purists should be aware that all of the 13 creatures diagrammed here require scissors cuts, and several are assembled with glue. . . . Nguyen includes drawings and color photos of finished models, and uses standard origami notation in his easy-to-follow diagrams." SLJ

Nguyen, Duy—*Continued*
Monster origami. Sterling Pub. 2007 96p il pa $9.95
Grades: 5 6 7 8   **736**
1. Origami 2. Monsters
ISBN 978-1-4027-4014-5; 1-4027-4014-X
LC 2007003244
This "volume offers step-by-step instructions for using paper to create 'creatures of horror from books and movies.' . . . Nguyen begins with an overview of basic folds, each demonstrated in clear illustrations. . . . Nguyen shows, in easy-to-follow diagrams, how to use the folds in intricate combinations to create an array of familiar, frightening characters, ranging from Count Dracula to Godzilla's foe, King Ghidora. A final spread shows color photographs of the finished projects." Booklist

Origami birds. Sterling Pub. 2006 96p il $19.95
Grades: 5 6 7 8   **736**
1. Origami 2. Birds in art
ISBN 978-1-4027-1932-5; 1-4027-1932-9
LC 2005037669
This offers instructions for creating origami representations of 19 species of birds including cardinals, cockatoos, falcons, flying ducks, parakeets, and penguins
"The instructions are direct and thorough. . . . Spare line drawings show each step of construction, and color photos spotlight the finished project against a background photo of the bird's natural habitat." Booklist

Under the sea origami; [by] Duy Nguyen. Sterling Pub. 2004 96p il hardcover o.p. pa $9.95
Grades: 5 6 7 8   **736**
1. Origami 2. Marine animals in art
ISBN 1-4027-1541-2; 1-4027-2790-9 (pa)
LC 2004-3341
This "set of origami challenges includes step diagrams, with standard notation, for an elegant seahorse, two menacing-looking sharks, and 16 other marine models – all constructed from one or two sheets of origami paper, and many requiring scissors and/or glue." SLJ

Stern, Joel, 1953-
Jewish holiday origami; photographs by David Greenfield. Dover Publications 2006 64p il pa $5.95
Grades: 8 9 10 11 12 Adult   **736**
1. Origami 2. Jewish holidays
ISBN 0-486-45076-7; 978-0-486-45076-6
LC 2005-56934
This book contains a "year's worth of holiday projects—from Chanukah dreidels and a menorah with candles, to Passover pyramids and an image of the Red Sea parting." Publisher's note

Temko, Florence
Origami holiday decorations for Christmas, Hanukkah, and Kwanzaa. Tuttle Pub. 2003 63p il pa $8.95
Grades: 5 6 7 8   **736**
1. Origami 2. Holiday decorations
ISBN 0-8048-3477-6 (pa); 978-0-8048-3477-3 (pa)
LC 2002075060

"Among the 25 original projects are a Holiday Calendar, Jewish Star, Kwanzaa Bowl, and Santa Claus Table Decoration." Publisher's note

738.5   Mosaics

Harris, Nathaniel, 1937-
Mosaics; [by] Nathaniel Harris. 1st ed. PowerKids Press 2009 30p il (Stories in art) lib bdg $25.25
Grades: 4 5 6 7   **738.5**
1. Mosaics
ISBN 978-1-4042-4438-2; 1-4042-4438-7
LC 2007052714
"After introducing the ancient roots of mosaic art in many cultures, this colorfully illustrated book discusses the methods used in making mosaics. Each of the next six double-page spreads presents a single, narrative mosaic. . . . Four mosaic craft ideas follow, with detailed instructions and photos of key construction steps as well as finished products. . . . [Illustrated with] fine color photos. . . . This book nicely combines art appreciation with hands-on learning." Booklist

739.27   Jewelry

Macfarlane, Katherine
The jeweler's art; by Katherine Nell Macfarlane. Lucent Books 2007 112p il (Eye on art) lib bdg $32.45
Grades: 7 8 9 10 11 12   **739.27**
1. Jewelry
ISBN 978-1-59018-984-9   LC 2007-7804
A look at jewelry through the ages.
This "title is thoroughly researched and fully referenced, and contains quotations from artists and art historians. The writing is generally clear and fluid. . . . Many of the pages have good-quality photos of artwork and artists." SLJ
Includes bibliographical references

741.2   Drawing and drawings—Techniques, procedures, apparatus, equipment, materials

Ames, Lee J., 1921-
Drawing with Lee Ames; from the bestselling, award-winning creator of the Draw 50 series, a proven step-by-step guide to the fundamentals of drawing for all ages. Doubleday 1990 262p il pa $21
Grades: 6 7 8 9   **741.2**
1. Drawing
ISBN 0-385-23701-4   LC 90-31436
The author "offers a compendium of samples for beginning artists. Ames explains his approach to beginning art instruction as a form of mimicry, where students copy samples in order to get a feel for the process of drawing.

Ames, Lee J., 1921-—*Continued*

. . . This is definitely for the beginning student who possesses very little to no drawing experience. . . . Ames's approach offers a good base from which students can then move on to more in-depth instruction." Voice Youth Advocates

Includes bibliographical references

Scott, Damion

How to draw hip-hop; [by] Damion Scott and Kris Ex. Watson-Guptill 2006 144p il pa $19.95 *

Grades: 7 8 9 10   **741.2**

1. Drawing 2. Hip-hop

ISBN 0-8230-1446-0   LC 2005-29156

"This book combines the bold and energetic lines of graffiti art with the bright colors of cel-shaded video games and an obvious Japanese manga influence. . . . [It discusses] genre-specific concepts like wild style lettering [and] hip-hop clothing. The teaching . . . is unique and totally accessible. . . . There is no other book of this kind on the market, making it a necessary and relevant purchase." SLJ

Temple, Kathryn

Drawing; the only drawing book you'll ever need to be the artist you've always wanted to be; [by] Kathryn Temple. 1st ed. Lark Books 2005 112p il (Art for kids) $17.95 *

Grades: 5 6 7 8   **741.2**

1. Drawing

ISBN 1-57990-587-0   LC 2004-17909

Contents: Drawing basics; Line drawing; Light & shadow; Scale & proportion; Perspective; Faces & bodies; Still life and drawing nature; Drawing on the imagination; Composition

This "introduction to essential drawing techniques builds from the starting points of lines and simple shapes. . . . Eight concise chapters explore seeing with artist's eyes, line drawing, light and shadow, proportion and scale, perspective, drawing faces, drawing bodies, and using imagination. The succinct text reads smoothly and is written in a clear, understandable style. Sample sketches and crisp, color photographs extend the text." SLJ

741.5 Cartoons, caricatures, comics

Abadzis, Nick

Laika. First Second Books 2007 205p il $17.95 *

Grades: 5 6 7 8 9 10 11 12 Adult   **741.5**

1. Graphic novels 2. Space flight—Graphic novels

ISBN 978-1-59643-101-0; 1-59643-101-6

LC 2006-51907

Laika was the abandoned puppy destined to become Earth's first space traveler. This is her journey. Along with Laika, there is Korolev, once a political prisoner and now a driven engineer at the top of the Soviet space program, and Yelena, the lab technician responsible for Laika's health and life. The book includes a bibliography of books and websites

"Although the tightly packed and vividly inked panels of Abadzis's art tell an impressively complex tale . . . Laika's palpable spirit is what readers will remember." Publ Wkly

Akira, Shouko

Monkey High!: vol. 1; story and art by Shouko Akira; [translation and adaptation, Mai Ihara] Viz Media 2008 il pa $8.99

Grades: 7 8 9 10 11 12   **741.5**

1. Graphic novels 2. Anime 3. Romance—Graphic novels 4. High school students—Graphic novels

ISBN 978-1-4215-1518-2 (pa); 1-4215-1518-0 (pa)

"Haruna sees the students in her new school . . . as acting ike monkeys. . . . She wants to keep to herself, but because she's beautiful, the boys start vying for her attention and the girls are getting jealous. . . . The artwork is lively and bright. . . . Readers who get caught up in the couple's first fight, first hand-holding, and first kiss will wait breathlessly for the other volumes in this series." SLJ

Anderson, Eric A.

PX! Book one: a girl and her panda; written by Eric A. Anderson and Manny Trembley ; illustrated by Manny Trembley. Image Comics 2007 unp il $16.99

Grades: 6 7 8 9 10 11 12 Adult   **741.5**

1. Graphic novels 2. Humorous graphic novels 3. Adventure graphic novels 4. Science fiction graphic novels

ISBN 978-1-58240-820-0; 1-58240-820-3

A young girl named Dahlia and her trusty (robot) panda sidekick set off on a journey around the world to save her missing scientist father, who has been kidnapped by Pollo, an evil goat mastermind who wants to take over the world (and yes, people keep telling him his name means chicken" in Spanish). Along the way, Dahlia meets Weatherby Ian Poppington III, a Victorian English secret agent also known as Double Aught Seven," and Wikkity Jones, a rollerskating swordsman who talks like a hillbilly and stands ready to fight ninja any time. The absurd humor is punctuated by moments of intense violent action, especially in the side story about fighting zombies. This book collects the webcomic.

Followed by: PX! v.2: in the service of the Queen (2009)

Arai, Kiyoko

Beauty Pop, Vol. 1; story and art by Kiyoko Arai. Viz Media/Shojo Beat 2006 194p il pa $8.99

Grades: 7 8 9 10 11 12   **741.5**

1. Graphic novels 2. Manga 3. Shojo manga 4. Hair—Graphic novels

ISBN 978-1-4215-0575-6

At Kiri Koshiba's high school, three popular upper classmen do occasional "Scissors Projects," working makeovers on specially selected girls. Narumi Shogo, who cuts hair, wants to become the best beautician in Japan and has won every youth competition - except one, years ago, that a younger girl won. When girls who aren't already pretty ask Narumi for a makeover, he tells

Arai, Kiyoko—*Continued*
them they're too ugly. Kiri helps two of the girls, working a stylist's magic that makes the girls glow; she's not interested in competition, even though her family owns a salon. Narumi wants to know who dares to be the upstart and challenge him, and he sets up the school's cultural festival to be a haircutting duel. Will Kiri even bother to compete?

Other titles in this series are:
Beauty pop, Vol. 2 (2006) (978-1-4215-0576-6)
Beauty pop. Vol. 3 (2007) (978-1-4215-1009-5)
Beauty pop. Vol. 4 (2007) (978-1-4215-1010-1)
Beauty pop. Vol. 5 (2007) (978-1-4215-1011-8)
Beauty pop. Vol. 6 (2007) (978-1-4215-1323-2)
Beauty pop. Vol. 7 (2008) (978-1-4215-1784-1)
Beauty pop. Vol. 8 (2008) (978-1-4215-2310-1)
Beauty pop. Vol. 9 (2008) (978-1-4215-2310-1)
Beauty pop. Vol. 10 (2009) (978-1-4215-2594-5)

Ariyoshi, Kyoko
Swan, Vol. 1. CMX/DC Comics 2004 200p il pa $9.95
Grades: 6 7 8 9 10 **741.5**
1. Graphic novels 2. Ballet—Graphic novels 3. Manga 4. Shojo manga
ISBN 1-4012-0535-6
This is the first in an ongoing series
"Masumi, a young girl from a rural Japanese town, dreams of becoming a prima ballerina. She is picked to take part in a national ballet competition but realizes that her training lags behind that of her peers. During the competition and the subsequent professional lessons, she fights to improve her abilities and achieve her dreams. Swan is one of the most famous shoujo (girl's manga) ever published. Although it first appeared in Japan in the mid-seventies, the art and story hold up beautifully." Booklist

Atangan, Patrick
The yellow jar; two tales from Japanese tradition. NBM 2003 48p il (Songs of our ancestors) $12.92
Grades: 5 6 7 8 9 10 11 12 **741.5**
1. Graphic novels 2. Folklore—Japan—Graphic novels
ISBN 1-56163-331-3 LC 2002-32132
"To render two magical Japanese legends, one about a fisherman who discovers a fair maiden in a big pot, the other about a monk whose fastidiously kept garden is invaded by two chrysanthemums, Atangan charmingly adopts the sharp outlines, boldly juxtaposed color fields, and striking compositions of eighteenth-century Japanese woodblock prints." Booklist
Other titles in this series are:
Silk tapestry and other Chinese folktales (2004)
Tree of love (2005)

Avery, Ben
The hedge knight; [by] George R. R. Martin; Ben Avery, adapter; Mike S. Miller, artist. Marvel Enterprises 2006 160p il bookstore ed $19.95; $19.95
Grades: 9 10 11 12 Adult **741.5**
1. Graphic novels 2. Fantasy graphic novels 3. Knights and knighthood—Graphic novels
ISBN 978-0-7851-2578-5; 978-0-7851-2577-8
"Hulking young Dunk is the squire of an elderly warrior. When Dunk's master dies, he rides on to the next tournament in hopes of winning recognition for his knightly prowess. He acquires a squire of his own, a bald little boy who calls himself Egg, and gives himself the more elegant title of Duncan the Tall. . . . This heroic fantasy tale reinvigorates the tired category of sword and sorcery fiction by emphasizing the human angle." Publ Wkly

Baker, Kyle
How to draw stupid and other essentials of cartooning. Watson-Guptill 2008 110p il pa $16.95
Grades: 8 9 10 11 12 Adult **741.5**
1. Cartooning—Technique 2. Graphic novels—Drawing
ISBN 978-0-8230-0143-9 LC 2008-922161
"Baker, an award-winning cartoonist and graphic-novel illustrator, gives aspiring cartoonists irreverent advice about how to succeed in their chosen field. He offers instruction in basic drawing techniques such as choosing the right tools and discusses the importance of learning to draw shapes, exaggerating, and using references. But the author's most inspiring advice focuses on how to succeed as a cartoonist." SLJ

Through the looking-glass; by Lewis Carroll; adapted by Kyle Baker. Papercutz 2008 unp il (Classics illustrated) $9.95
Grades: 3 4 5 6 7 8 9 **741.5**
1. Carroll, Lewis, 1832-1898—Adaptations 2. Graphic novels 3. Fantasy graphic novels
ISBN 978-1-59707-115-4; 1-59707-115-3
This is Carroll's sequel to Alice's Adventures in Wonderland. This time, Alice climbs through the looking-glass in her house and finds herself in a land with talking flowers and insects, Tweedledee and Tweedledum (who recite "The Walrus and the Carpenter"), the White Queen who needs help pinning her shawl straight, Humpty Dumpty, the Red Queen, and more. The Eisner Award-winning Baker uses a different style from his usual cartoony look here, more reminiscent of Tenniel's classic illustrations of Carroll's books.

Bannister (Person)
The shadow door; art by Bannister; story by Nykko; [colors by Jaffre; translation by Carol Klio Burrell] 1st American ed. Graphic Universe 2009 46p il (The Elsewhere chronicles) lib bdg $27.93; pa $6.95
Grades: 4 5 6 7 **741.5**
1. Graphic novels 2. Horror graphic novels
ISBN 978-0-7613-4459-9 (lib bdg); 0-7613-4459-4 (lib bdg); 978-0-76133-963-2 (pa); 0-7613-3963-9 (pa)
LC 2008-39442
Four friends discover a movie projector that opens a passageway into a world threatened by creatures of shadow, where their only weapon is light
"This is an undeniably attractive offering, as the artwork, with deep darks and effervescent lights splayed

Bannister (Person)—*Continued*

across large, glossy pages, is strikingly rendered. . . .
[This] should have no problem gaining an appreciative
readership." Booklist

Other titles in this series are:

Shadow spies (2009)
Master of shadows (2009)

Beatty, Scott

Superman; the ultimate guide to the Man of
Steel; written by Scott Beatty. rev ed. DK 2006
144p il $24.99

Grades: 7 8 9 10   741.5

1. Superman (Comic strip) 2. Comic books, strips, etc.
ISBN 978-0-7566-2067-7; 0-7566-2067-8
LC 2005035040

First published 2002

Surveys the nature and history of the hero Superman,
discussing his birth, career, secrets, equipment, and enemies

Beechen, Adam, 1968-

Justice League Unlimited: the ties that bind;
written by Adam Beechen and Paul Storrie;
illustrated by Carlo Barberi, Rick Burchett and
others. DC Comics 2008 unp il (Justice league
unlimited) $12.99

Grades: 3 4 5 6 7 8 9   741.5

1. Graphic novels 2. Superhero graphic novels
3. Justice League (Fictional characters)
ISBN 978-1-4012-1691-7; 1-4012-1691-9

This version of the Justice League was created for the
Cartoon Network animated series and features such
superheroes as Superman, Batman, Wonder Woman,
Green Lantern, the Flash, Hawkgirl, J'onn Jonnz the
Martian Manhunter, Power Girl, Green Arrow, and others. The stories collected in this volume include a clash
of misunderstanding with Uncle Sam and the Freedom
Fighters, a jaunt backwards in time, getting involved in
a lovers' spat between super villains whose fight could
destroy a city, and more. The book includes superhero vs
supervillain fighting action with no bloodshed.

Another title in this series is:

Justice league unlimited. Heroes (2009)

Benjamin, P, 1970-

Hulk: misunderstood monster; Writer, Paul
Benjamin; illustrated by David Nakayama and
Juan Santacruz. Marvel 2007 v1 il (Marvel
adventures Hulk) $6.99

Grades: 5 6 7 8 9   741.5

1. The Hulk (Fictional character) 2. Graphic novels
3. Superhero graphic novels
ISBN 978-0-7851-2642-3; 0-7851-2642-2

Contains material originally published in magazine
form as Marvel Adventures Hulk #1-4.

Caught in the explosion of a gamma bomb, brilliant
scientist Bruce Banner was transformed into a hulking
beast. With no control over the transformations, Banner
lives on the run, helping those less fortunate than he,
hoping to one day find a cure to rid himself of the ram-
paging Hulk.

Other titles in this series are:

Hulk: defenders (2007)
Hulk: strongest one there is (2008)
Hulk: tales to astonish (2008)

Black, Holly, 1971-

The Good Neighbors; book one: Kin; [illustrated
by] Ted Naifeh. Graphix 2008 117p il $16.99

Grades: 7 8 9 10 11 12   741.5

1. Graphic novels 2. Fantasy graphic novels
ISBN 978-0-439-85562-4; 0-439-85562-4
LC 2007-49008

Sixteen-year-old Rue has grown up in a world much
like ours, except that the human world and the world of
faerie have co-existed, as good neighbors, for a long
time. When Rue's mother disappears and her professor
father becomes the main suspect in the murder of a
young woman, Rue's life turns strange. As she digs for
information to figure out what is happening in her life,
Rue discovers that her mother is a faerie and has returned to that realm because of a broken promise.

"This sophisticated tale is well served by Naifeh's
stylish, angular illustrations." SLJ

Blackman, Haden

Star Wars: Clone wars adventures, Vol. 1. Dark
Horse Books 2004 96p il pa $6.95

Grades: 5 6 7 8 9 10   741.5

1. Graphic novels 2. Science fiction graphic novels
ISBN 1-59307-243-0

This volume includes several adventures featuring Star
Wars characters. Obi-Wan Kenobi and Anakin Skywalker
take on the Shadowmen on the night world of Nivek;
Jedi Master Mace Windu and Saesee Tiin face a new
droid threat; and Jedi Master Kit Fisto leads an underwater hunt for the Separatists' secret base. This series is
based on the Clone Wars Adventures cartoon series
which has aired on Cartoon Network, and fits in
chronologically between Episodes Two and Three of the
motion picture series. This is the first volume, there were
four volumes as of September 2005.

Bohl, Al

Guide to cartooning. Pelican 176p il hardcover
o.p. pa $14.95

Grades: 8 9 10 11 1 2   741.5

1. Cartooning
ISBN 1-56554-367-X; 1-56554-177-4 (pa)
LC 96-44340

Provides instructions for drawing different styles of
cartooning, including political, strips, books, and illustration, and gives advice on how to get a job in the field.

This "is so chockablock with information that any teen
interested in cartooning will come away with a multitude
of tips and tricks." Booklist

Includes bibliographical references

Brooks, Terry, 1944-

Dark wraith of Shannara; [by] Terry Brooks; illustrated by Edwin David; adapted by Robert Place Napton. Ballantine Books 2008 199p il pa $13.95

Grades: 6 7 8 9   **741.5**

1. Graphic novels 2. Fantasy graphic novels

ISBN 978-0-345-49462-7 (pa); 0-345-49462-8 (pa)

     LC 2008000466

"The first graphic novel based on Brooks' popular, long-running Shannara series features an original story plotted by Brooks himself. . . . The Elven Jair embarks on a journey to keep the location of a powerful magic castle secret from a murderous cult, the Mwellrets. . . . It is . . . a solid, straightforward, highly accessible, action-heavy adventure with black-and-white art that hovers between classic comic and manga style." Booklist

Caldwell, Ben

Fantasy! cartooning; [by] Ben Caldwell. Sterling Pub. Co. 2005 95p il pa $9.95

Grades: 5 6 7 8   **741.5**

1. Cartooning—Technique 2. Fantasy in art

ISBN 1-4027-1612-5   LC 2005041676

Caldwell's "drawing style is . . . a blend of modern Disney (Hercules, Mulan), Don Bluth (Dragon's Lair), and the Cartoon Network (Powderpuff Girls, Samurai Jack, Star Wars: Clone Wars). . . . Caldwell shows original thinking, and his technique is exciting, modern, and unique." SLJ

Carey, Mike, 1959-

Confessions of a Blabbermouth; written by Mike Carey & Louise Carey; illustrated by Aaron Alexovich. DC Comics/Minx 2007 176p il pa $9.99 *

Grades: 7 8 9 10 11 12   **741.5**

1. Graphic novels 2. Family life—Graphic novels 3. Weblogs—Graphic novels 4. Humorous graphic novels

ISBN 978-1-4012-1148-6

If blabbing were an Olympic event, Tasha Flanagan would blab for her country. When Tasha's mom brings home a creepy boyfriend and his deadpan daughter, this dysfunctional family is headed for a complete mental meltdown. It becomes not only a battle of the blogs, but a battle to the bitter end to get the school yearbook finished in one piece—and keep a modern family out of prison—compliments of Tasha's blabbermouth blog. This book is co-written by comics veteran Mike Carey and his teenage daughter Louise.

"Every graphic-novel collection should have at least one copy." SLJ

Re-Gifters; written by Mike Carey; art by Sonny Liew and Marc Hempel. DC Comics/Minx 2007 148p il pa $9.99 *

Grades: 7 8 9 10 11 12   **741.5**

1. Graphic novels 2. High school students—Graphic novels 3. School stories—Graphic novels 4. Martial arts—Graphic novels 5. Romance graphic novels

ISBN 978-1-4012-0371-9 (pa); 1-4109-0371-X (pa)

"Jen Dik Seong, or Dixie, is having trouble getting her ki focused. Normally an outstanding hapkido student, she finds that her crush on classmate Adam is affecting her ability to fight. This is not good, as the national competition is fast approaching, and her parents expect her to do well. . . . Dixie makes a series of poor choices. She decides to spend the entry fee . . . on an elaborate birthday present for Adam. . . . This is a terrific read that features complex characters dealing with internal and external conflicts that make them believable and endearing. Lively black-and-white illustrations bring action and emotion to the story." SLJ

Castellucci, Cecil, 1969-

The Plain Janes; [illustrated by] Jim Rugg. DC Comics/Minx 2007 unp il pa $9.99 *

Grades: 7 8 9 10 11 12   **741.5**

1. Graphic novels 2. Friendship—Graphic novels 3. Art—Graphic novels 4. High school students—Graphic novels 5. School stories—Graphic novels

ISBN 978-1-4012-1115-8

After a bomb attack in Metro City, Jane's parents move to suburban Kent Waters, where Jane feels lost. Then she meets three other Janes at the "reject" table in the high school lunch room, and she convinces them to help her form their own secret club: P.L.A.I.N.—People Loving Art in Neighborhoods. However, their "art attacks" cause the authorities to think that P.L.A.I.N. is a terrorist group.

"The art, inspired by Dan Clowes' work, is absolutely engaging. Packaged like manga this is a fresh, exciting use of the graphic-novel format." Booklist

Another title about the Janes is:

Janes in love (2008)

Clugston, Chynna

Queen Bee. Scholastic Graphix 2005 112p il $8.99

Grades: 5 6 7 8 9   **741.5**

1. Graphic novels 2. Psychokinesis—Graphic novels

ISBN 0-439-70987-3

Haley has just started at a new middle school, where she decides to hide her nerdly psychokinetic power. She actually joins the Hive, the popular girls, which she discovers is boring. Then another new student arrives, and Haley knows instantly that Alexa also possesses psychokinetic powers. However, Alexa doesn't want to become Haley's friend—instead, it's war; can their school survive?

"With the clique theme and the cool art, this graphic novel . . . will appeal to the middle school girl readers for whom it was written." (VOYA)

Colfer, Eoin, 1965-

Artemis Fowl: the graphic novel; adapted by Eoin Colfer and Andrew Donkin; art by Giovanni Rigano; color by Paolo Lammana. Hyperion Books for Children 2007 unp il $18.99; pa $9.99

Grades: 4 5 6 7 8 9   **741.5**

1. Graphic novels 2. Fantasy graphic novels 3. Adventure graphic novels

ISBN 978-0-7868-4881-2; 0-7868-4881-2; 978-0-7868-4882-9 (pa); 0-7868-4882-0 (pa)

Twelve-year-old genius and criminal mastermind Artemis Fowl runs his missing father's crime empire and gets

Colfer, Eoin, 1965-—*Continued*

his hands on a book that will give him access to the underground fairy world. This graphic novel adaptation gives the book a European look and color palette.

"Excellent use of color and shading gives the panels a tremendous sense of light with enchanting effect. Characters are expressively brought to life with fun, exaggerated style." SLJ

Crilley, Mark, 1966-

Miki Falls, Book One: Spring. HarperCollins/HarperTeen 2007 176p il pa $7.99

Grades: 7 8 9 10 11 12   **741.5**

1. Graphic novels 2. Friendship—Graphic novels 3. High school students—Graphic novels 4. School stories—Graphic novels

ISBN 978-0-06-084616-9

"This is Miki Yoshida's final year of high school, and she's determined to make this the best year yet. Miki is in control . . . until Hiro Sakurai shows up. The tall, handsome new student is hiding something, and Miki wants to know what." Publisher's note

"Crilley uses mystery to drive the narrative and creates characters that the reader will care about. The black-and-white, manga-style art is beautiful." Voice Youth Advocates

Other titles in this series are:

Miki Falls, Book Two: Summer
Miki Falls, Book Three: Autumn
Miki Falls, Book Four: Winter

Dezago, Todd

Spider-man: Spidey strikes back Vol. 1 digest. Marvel Comics 2005 96p il pa $5.99

Grades: 4 5 6 7 8 9   **741.5**

1. Graphic novels 2. Superhero graphic novels 3. Spider-Man (Fictional character)

ISBN 0-7851-1632-X

Tired of saving the day and getting no respect, Spider-Man considers taking a break from his superhero duties, which leaves the city wide open for the likes of the Sandman and the Enforcers. Will Spidey let it all go to pot, or will he step up to the plate and take one for the team? This volume collects Marvel Age Spider-Man issues 17-20. Previous volumes were published under the series title Marvel Age Spider-Man. The Marvel Age titles are being collected and published in the digest size, similar to manga, and at an affordable price. The Marvel Age series are aimed at younger audiences than the other superhero titles from Marvel.

Dixon, Chuck, 1954-

Hobbit: an illustrated edition of the fantasy classic; [by] J. R. R. Tolkien; Chuck Dixon, adapter; David Wenzel, illustrator. Del Rey Books 2001 133p il pa $15.95

Grades: 5 6 7 8   **741.5**

1. Graphic novels

ISBN 0-345-44560-0

The tale of how dwarfs came to ask the hobbit Bilbo Baggins to leave his comfortable home in the Shire to travel with them on their quest to recover their gold from the evil dragon Smaug is adapted to comic book form, with lush, colorful illustrations by David Wenzel. All the adventures recounted in Tolkien's novel are here, retold in a format for all ages to enjoy

Fajardo, Alexis E., 1976-

Kid Beowulf and the blood-bound oath. Bowler Hat 2008 il pa $14.95

Grades: 6 7 8 9   **741.5**

1. Beowulf—Graphic novels 2. Graphic novels 3. Monsters—Graphic novels

ISBN 978-0-9801419-1-7 (pa); 0-9801419-1-5 (pa)

"In the standard Beowulf story, the character appears as a full-fledged hero, with little concept of how he actually became one. Fajardo tells the backstory, using a blend of humor and soap-opera plot twists. . . . The cartoon-style illustrations are lively and contain lots of visual humor." SLJ

Farr, James

eV: vol. 1. Tokyopop 2008 il pa $9.99

Grades: 6 7 8 9   **741.5**

1. Graphic novels 2. Science fiction—Graphic novels

ISBN 978-1-4278-0714-4 (pa); 1-4278-0714-0 (pa)

"Evie's father, Dr. Richard Wymond . . . is locked in a nearly five-year struggle to devise an advanced superhuman to send as a delegate into space. . . . Dr. Wymond has created the ZETTA serum, which . . . creates nanoscopic machines that interact with the body on an atomic level. . . . With five hours to go before the emissaries return to retrieve the delegate, Dr. Wymond learns that all of the candidates have been assassinated, and he must inject himself with the serum and travel into space. . . . Evie and her mother are slammed by a diesel truck, leaving Evie on the brink of death. . . . Dr. Wymond injects his daughter with the serum, and . . . she is saved from death, but with side effects. . . . As Evie is both brainy and beautiful, both male and female readers should enjoy this highly readable graphic novel." SLJ

Fisch, Sholly

Super friends: for justice! y; Sholly Fisch writer; Dario Brizuela ... [et. al] artists. DC Comics 2009 unp il $12.99

Grades: 5 6 7 8 9   **741.5**

1. Superhero graphic novels 2. Graphic novels 3. Batman (Fictional character) 4. Wonder Woman (Fictional character) 5. Superman (Fictional character)

ISBN 978-1-4012-2156-0; 1-4012-2156-4

"This volume features the JLA facing off with some of their biggest foes including the power-stealing android Amazo and the super-ape known as Gorilla Grodd." Publisher's note

Fisher, Jane Smith

WJHC: on the air! Wilson Place Comics, Inc. 2003 95p il pa $11.95

Grades: 4 5 6 7 8 9   **741.5**

Fisher, Jane Smith—*Continued*
1. Graphic novels 2. High school students—Graphic novels 3. Humorous graphic novels 4. Radio stations—Graphic novels
ISBN 0-9744235-0-5
"The cast of toothy, mopheaded teens includes hardworking Janey, UFO obsessed Ciel, snotty Tara O'Toole, awkward Roland, and cool, cool The Skate. Together the teens put a school radio station on the air (thus the book's title), 'chaperone' an ill-fated sixth-grade field trip, and get into a truly hilarious tangle when a love note written by one to another of the cast works its way through the hands of each one." Booklist

Flight explorer; edited by Kazu Kibuiski. Villard 2008 112p il pa $10
Grades: 4 5 6 7   **741.5**
1. Graphic novels 2. Science fiction graphic novels 3. Fantasy graphic novels 4. Adventure graphic novels 5. Humorous graphic novels
ISBN 978-0-345-50313-8; 0-345-50313-9
"In this companion book to the 'Flight' series for older readers, the editor succeeds in putting together a remarkable collection that will appeal to a younger audience. Kean Shoo's 'Jellaby,' for example, shows the humorous and contemplative moments between a girl and a friendly monster as they experience their first snowfall together. More comedic is Kibuishi's story about crossing a ravine of mushrooms. . . . Every story has a layout that promotes an acute sense of pacing and showcases the crisp, defined, full-color art." SLJ

Frampton, Otis
Oddly Normal; volume 1; written & illustrated by Otis Frampton. Viper Comics 2006 unp il pa $11.95 *
Grades: 4 5 6 7 8 9   **741.5**
1. Graphic novels 2. Fantasy graphic novels 3. Humorous graphic novels
ISBN 0-9777883-0-X
"Oddly Normal, a half witch with green hair, pointed ears, and an aversion to rain, is miserable. She is an outcast at school, and her parents are clueless about how abnormal the Normal family is. When an accidental wish on her tenth birthday goes awry, causing her parents to disappear, Oddly goes to live with her great-aunt in Fignation. . . . Frampton's art is refreshingly quirky, with strong lines and bold use of color. The world he creates is full of fun and whimsy." Booklist

Friesen, Ray
Cupcakes of doom! Don't Eat Any Bugs Productions 2008 104p il pa $12.95
Grades: 3 4 5 6 7 8   **741.5**
1. Graphic novels 2. Adventure graphic novels 3. Humorous graphic novels 4. Pirates—Graphic novels
ISBN 978-0-9802314-1-0; 0-9802314-1-8
The Pirate band led by Captain Scurvybeard must do battle with the Vikings to decide the fate of the kingdom called Pellmellia. With a decidedly shifty fellow named Flambe testing them to see if they deserve to be pirates, Yoho Joseph, Peglegless Pete (he's just a kid), Lester the parrot, Pete's sister Jamie, and the rest of the crew must find the long lost recipe for the Cupcakes of Doom, or the Deliciously-Evil Viking Pie will take over as the people's favorite baked good. The book is full of silly humor, wacky characters (including identical twin sea serpents and a Viking penguin), and a lot of action without violence or bad language. The book is suitable for younger readers, but adults will enjoy the silliness and catch more of the jokes.

Geary, Rick, 1946-
Great expectations; adapted by Rick Geary. rev ed. Papercutz 2008 56p il (Classics illustrated) $9.95
Grades: 4 5 6 7 8 9   **741.5**
1. Dickens, Charles, 1812-1870—Adaptations 2. Graphic novels 3. Great Britain—History—19th century—Graphic novels 4. Orphans—Graphic novels
ISBN 978-1-59707-097-3; 1-59707-097-1
After harsh early years, Pip, an orphan growing up in Victorian England, is given the means to become a gentleman by an unknown benefactor and learns that outward appearances can be deceiving. Presented in comic book format.
"This pleasant graphic interpretation can serve as an introduction to Dickens for younger readers and perhaps eventually steer them to the wider world of the source material and beyond." Publ Wkly

The invisible man; by H.G. Wells; adapted by Rick Geary. NBM/Papercutz 2008 unp il (Classics illustrated) $9.95
Grades: 5 6 7 8 9 10 11 12   **741.5**
1. Wells, H. G. (Herbert George), 1866-1946—Adaptations 2. Graphic novels 3. Mystery graphic novels 4. Science fiction graphic novels
ISBN 978-1-59707-106-2; 1-59707-106-4
A stranger comes to the small town of Iping, his face covered in bandages and dark lensed spectacles. After a few months, the townspeople learn that this mysterious man is invisible and responsible for recent crimes. After he escapes from Iping, he ends up in the house of Kemp, who had studied at University College with him. The man's name is Griffin, he was a scientist who became obsessed with finding the secret of invisibility and who would stop at nothing, including stealing money from his own father to fund his experiments. And he will stop at nothing including murder to remain free. The book includes a couple of panels showing partial nudity.

Giarrano, Vince, 1960-
Comics crash course; [by] Vincent Giarrano. Impact Books 2004 127p il pa $19.99 *
Grades: 5 6 7 8   **741.5**
1. Cartoons and caricatures 2. Drawing
ISBN 1-58180-533-0   LC 2004-43969
This is a guide to creating comic book stories and characters.
This offers "plenty of great art advice, striking imagery, and just enough edginess to satisfy most aspiring comic-book artists. . . . An excellent introduction to comic drawing, composition, and graphic storytelling." SLJ

Glass, Bryan J. L.

The mice templar, volume one: the prophecy; created by Bryan J.L. Glass & Michael Avon Oeming. Image Comics 2008 256p il $29.99

Grades: 6 7 8 9 10 11 12 Adult   **741.5**

1. Graphic novels 2. Fantasy graphic novels 3. Adventure graphic novels 4. Mice—Graphic novels

ISBN 978-1-58240-871-2; 1-58240-871-8

The volume is a collection of the first six issues of The mice templar

In a land populated by animals, the Mice Templar used to protect the people of the mouse kingdom, but a civil war destroyed them; the king now employs rat soldiers, and they prey upon the mouse villages. Young Karic still idolizes the Mice Templar, but everything he knows and believes is shattered when his village is raided by rats, burned, and his family captured as slaves. He survives, saved by a mysterious mouse named Pilot, who says he was once a Templar and offers to train Karic. The salmon in the river say that Karic is the one prophesied to restore the Templar, but can he truly be the one? The book includes considerable battle violence.

"Equal parts Norse myth, Arthurian legend, and Mrs. Frisby and the Rats of N.I.M.H., The Mice Templar series re-imagines the warrior animal tale with just enough of its own spin to make it well worth adding to the collection." Voice Youth Advocates

Gorman, Michele

Getting graphic! using graphic novels to promote literacy with preteens and teens; with a foreword by Jeff Smith. Linworth Pub. 2003 100p il pa $36.95 *

Grades: Professional   **741.5**

1. Graphic novels—Administration

ISBN 1-58683-089-9   LC 2003-13199

"This title serves as an introduction to the world of fiction and nonfiction comics. Collection-development policies are addressed as well as cataloging, shelving, and maintaining these . . . books. Gorman provides ideas for the genre's integration into classroom curriculum and suggests promotional activities for school and public libraries." SLJ

"A must-have first resource for school and public libraries that are considering adding graphic novels to their collections but are unsure how to proceed." Booklist

Includes bibliographical references

Gownley, Jimmy

Amelia rules! the whole world's crazy! ibooks 2003 176p il $24.95; pa $14.95

Grades: 4 5 6 7 8 9 10 11 12   **741.5**

1. Graphic novels 2. Humorous graphic novels 3. Friendship—Graphic novels 4. Family life—Graphic novels

ISBN 0-9712169-3-2; 0-9712169-2-4 (pa)

"Amelia . . . is getting used to life with her newly divorced mom and her hip, young aunt Tanner; settling in at a strange new school; and finding a group of friends. Amelia is no sweet innocent, nor are her three G.A.S.P (Gathering of Awesome Superpals) buddies: Reggie, superhero in the making; Rhonda, Amelia's tough bete noire with a fourth-grade 'thing' for Reggie; and quiet,

mysterious Pajamaman. Jealousy, meanness, sadness, and confusion, as well as surprising generosity, and love crisscross the pages in energetic, freewheeling, full-color cartoon art that unwraps a kid's eye view of life honestly, poignantly, and with a hefty dollop of melodrama." Booklist

Other titles in this series are:

Amelia rules!: What makes you happy? (2004)

Amelia rules! Superheroes (2005)

Grant, Alan, 1949-

Robert Louis Stevenson's Kidnapped; adaptation by Alan Grant; illustrator, Cam Kennedy. Tundra Books 2007 unp il pa $11.95

Grades: 6 7 8 9 10   **741.5**

1. Stevenson, Robert Louis, 1850-1894—Adaptations 2. Graphic novels 3. Adventure graphic novels

ISBN 978-0-88776-843-9 (pa); 0-88776-843-1 (pa)
                              LC 2007921350

Kidnapped is set in 1751, during the time of the Jacobite rebellion — a tumultuous and tragic period in Scottish history. When David Balfour sets out to find his uncle, he never dreamed that he would be kidnapped — but saved from a life of slavery — and thrown from one escapade to another in the company of the fugitive, masterful swordsman Alan Breck Stewart.

"This is an engaging adaptation, aided by Kennedy's vibrant illustrations in a palette dominated by blues, greens, and sepia tones. The action scenes are exciting." SLJ

Robert Louis Stevenson's Strange case of Dr. Jekyll and Mr. Hyde; adapted by Alan Grant; illustrated by Cam Kennedy; colored and lettered by Jamie Grant. Tundra Books 2008 40p il pa $11.95

Grades: 6 7 8 9 10   **741.5**

1. Stevenson, Robert Louis, 1850-1894—Adaptations 2. Graphic novels 3. Horror graphic novels

ISBN 978-0-88776-882-8; 0-88776-882-2

"Stevenson's classic tale takes on a new format in a vivid graphic novel. This mysterious story of the struggle between good and evil is one that has been popular since its publication and continues to hold its appeal. Much about this adaptation honors the original version of the story—the language of the period remains true, and the drawings of 1880s London and the furnishings and fashion within it are realistic as well." Voice Youth Advocates

Hale, Shannon

Rapunzel's revenge; [by] Shannon and Dean Hale; illustrated by Nathan Hale. Bloomsbury 2008 144p il map $18.99; pa $14.99 *

Grades: 5 6 7 8   **741.5**

1. Graphic novels 2. Humorous graphic novels 3. Fantasy graphic novels 4. Fairy tales—Graphic novels

ISBN 978-1-59990-070-4; 1-59990-070-X; 978-1-59990-288-3 (pa); 1-59990-288-5 (pa)
                              LC 2007-37670

In this graphic novel Rapunzel is raised in a grand villa surrounded by towering walls. Rapunzel dreams of a

Hale, Shannon—*Continued*

different mother than Gothel, the woman she calls Mother. She climbs over the wall and finds out the truth. Her real mother, Kate, is a slave in Gothel's gold mine. In this Old West retelling, Rapunzel uses her hair as a lasso and to take on outlaws—including Gothel.

"The dialogue is witty, the story is an enticing departure from the original, and the illustrations are magically fun and expressive." SLJ

Hart, Christopher

How to draw comic book bad guys and gals. Watson-Guptill 1998 64p il pa $10.95

Grades: 6 7 8 9 10 11 12 **741.5**
1. Comic books, strips, etc. 2. Cartoons and caricatures 3. Drawing
ISBN 0-8230-2372-9 LC 98-6411

This guide to drawing comic book villains covers such topics as head tilts, facial expressions, hands and muscle groups, the body in action, using light and shadow, composition, and storytelling

"Not for beginners, but for those who already have some knowledge of drawing and ability. . . . Boldly colored illustrations combined with the line drawings add to the professional look of the book." Voice Youth Advocates

Manga for the beginner; everything you need to start drawing right away! Watson-Guptill Publications 2008 192p il $21.95

Grades: 5 6 7 8 9 10 **741.5**
1. Graphic novels—Drawing 2. Manga—Drawing
ISBN 978-0-8230-3083-5; 0-8230-3083-0
LC 2007-40490

"Hart's latest drawing book . . . contains detailed and easy-to-follow instructions for drawing types of shojo manga (aimed at girls) and shonen manga (aimed at boys). . . . He describes in concise language and through clear illustrations how to use lettering, lighting effects, and other techniques to achieve a certain mood to advance a plot. . . . Anyone even slightly interested in drawing manga will find it appealing." Voice Youth Advocates

Manga mania romance; drawing shojo girls and bishie boys; [by] Chris Hart. Chris Hart Books 2008 147p il pa $19.95

Grades: 6 7 8 9 10 **741.5**
1. Manga—Drawing 2. Drawing 3. Cartooning—Technique
ISBN 978-1-933027-43-2; 1-933027-43-6
LC 2007-907250

"This crisply illustrated work aims to give aspiring cartoonists the basics of drawing. . . . A wonderful introduction to the shojo style. A great first choice for creating a cartooning/drawing collection." SLJ

Mecha mania; how to draw the battling robots, cool spaceships, and military vehicles of Japanese comics. Watson-Guptill 2002 128p il pa $19.95

Grades: 5 6 7 8 **741.5**
1. Cartoons and caricatures 2. Drawing
ISBN 0-8230-3056-3 LC 2002-6402

"Hart offers budding cartoonists a mix of basic instructions and savvy technical advice for creating a wide variety of generic giant robots, robotlike craft, cyborgs of both sexes, and bad-guy types . . . then posing them for maximum visual effect. . . . His 'can-do!' tone and cogent instructions, as well as the gallery of chiseled, heavily armed, hypercomplicated machines, will make this volume appealing to both casual browsers and serious young artists." SLJ

Hicks, Faith Erin

The war at Ellsmere. Slave Labor Graphics 2008 156p il pa $12.95

Grades: 6 7 8 9 10 11 **741.5**
1. Graphic novels 2. Humorous graphic novels 3. School stories—Graphic novels 4. Friendship—Graphic novels
ISBN 978-1-59362-140-7; 1-59362-140-X

Juniper is the newest scholarship student at the prestigious Ellsmere Academy; she wanted to attend there in order to increase her chances of getting into a good medical school. She's on scholarship because her mom has had to raise her alone since her father died when she was young. Jun makes one friend at Ellsmere, Cassie, who calls herself the cliche of the poor little rich girl. Wealthy Emily calls Cassie "Orphan" because her parents ignore her, and chooses to call Jun "Project," as in Headmistress Ms. Bishop's latest project. Emily is also determined to get rid of Jun, especially when Jun encourages Cassie to work harder and even win the extra credit essay contest. Now it's war, or as Jun puts it, "It's like Upstairs Downstairs meets Lord of the Flies. In plaid skirts. And sweater vests." There's one incident when Jun punches Emily in the face.

"Hicks gives readers enough tension and quirky turns to satisfy and pleasantly surprise." Booklist

Higuchi, Daisuke

Whistle! Volume 1. Viz Media, LLC 2004 192p il pa $7.99

Grades: 5 6 7 8 9 10 **741.5**
1. Graphic novels 2. Soccer—Graphic novels 3. Manga 4. Shonen manga
ISBN 1-59116-685-3

This is the first volume of an ongoing series, up to Volume 6 in July 2005.

"Although he's no Pele or David Beckham, Sho is trying to take the high school soccer world by storm. Unfortunately, he's very short and not on the first team at his new school, but he's still determined to practice as much as possible to be the best. With the rest of the second string and Tatsuya, a star player who's not into lording his ability over others like the rest of the regulars, Sho challenges the Captain to a game for leadership of the team and a starting position." Publ Wkly

Hinds, Gareth, 1971-
Beowulf; adapted and illustrated by Gareth
Hinds. Candlewick Press 2007 unp il $21.99; pa
$9.99 *

Grades: 8 9 10 11 12 Adult   **741.5**
1. Beowulf—Graphic novels 2. Graphic novels
3. Adventure graphic novels 4. Monsters—Graphic
novels
ISBN   978-0-7636-3022-5;   0-7636-3022-5;
978-0-7636-3023-2 (pa); 0-7636-3023-3 (pa)
                              LC 2006-49023
Graphic novel adaptation of the Old English epic
poem, Beowulf
"For fantasy fans both young and old, this makes an
ideal introduction to a story without which the entire fantasy genre would look very different; many scenes may
be too intense for very young readers." Publ Wkly

The merchant of Venice; a play; by William
Shakespeare; adapted and illustrated by Gareth
Hinds. Candlewick Press 2008 68p il $21.99; pa
$11.99

Grades: 8 9 10 11 12 Adult   **741.5**
1. Shakespeare, William, 1564-1616—Adaptations
2. Graphic novels
ISBN 978-0-7636-3024-9; 978-0-7636-3025-6 (pa)
                              LC 2007-938349
Hinds uses a sketchy art style and blue and gray tones
to illustrate his graphic adaptation of Shakespeare's controversial play. He sets the play in modern Venice and
uses more modern language, including prose, at the beginning of the play and then gradually returns to Shakespeare's original language for the courtroom scenes. The
play tells the story of a debt owed to a Jewish merchant
of Venice, of a strong-willed young woman who is determined to choose her own husband, and of the quest to
save a young man from the fate of having a pound of
flesh cut from him.
"Fans of the play will find this an intriguing adaptation." Publ Wkly

Horowitz, Anthony, 1955-
Point blank: the graphic novel; by Anthony
Horowitz and Antony Johnston; illustrated by
Kanako Damerum and Yuzuru Takasaki. Philomel
Books 2008 unp il (Alex Rider) pa $14.99
Grades: 5 6 7 8 9 10   **741.5**
1. Spies—Graphic novels 2. Graphic novels
3. Adventure graphic novels
ISBN 978-0-399-25026-2 (pa); 0-399-25026-3 (pa)
"Rapid-fire action, appealing *manga*-style artwork, and
a heavy reliance on the James Bond formula drive this
second graphic adaptation of Horowitz's . . . Alex Rider
books. . . . Rider, a 14-year-old British spy, is sent to
a mysterious Swiss boarding school to investigate the nefarious plot of its headmaster." Booklist

Stormbreaker: the graphic novel; [by] Anthony
Horowitz; adapted Antony Johnston; illustrated by
Kanako Damerum & Yusuru Takasaki. Philomel
Books 2006 unp il (Alex Rider) pa $14.99
Grades: 5 6 7 8   **741.5**

1. Spies—Graphic novels 2. Graphic novels
ISBN 0-399-24633-9
In this graphic novel version on Horowitz's novel,
fourteen-year-old Alex Rider is coerced into continuing
his uncle's dangerous work for Britain's intelligence
agency, MI6.
"If it's possible, this is even more rapidly paced than
the novel. Alex remains an appealing hero here, and the
idea of a heroic teen up against insidious adults continues to be an extremely powerful draw for readers."
Booklist

Hosler, Jay
Clan Apis. Active Synapse 2000 158p il pa $15
Grades: 4 5 6 7 8 9 10 11 12   **741.5**
1. Graphic novels 2. Bees—Graphic novels
3. Science—Graphic novels
ISBN 0-9677255-0-X
"Opening with a creation myth . . . and working
through the biological, sociological, and ecological
changes affecting the life of Nyuki the bee, the text is a
combination of authoritative science; appealing, detailed
black-and-white drawings; and dialogue replete with humor, pubescent angst, political sloganeering, and more.
Nyuki's colony undertakes migration to a new hive, is
beset by a woodpecker, and hibernates through a winter
that yields to a revitalizing spring." Booklist

Hotta, Yumi
Hikaru No Go, Volume 1; [by] Yumi Hotta and
Takeshi Obata. Viz Media, LLC 2004 192p il pa
$7.95
Grades: 5 6 7 8 9 10 11 12   **741.5**
1. Graphic novels 2. Manga 3. Shonen manga
4. Board games—Graphic novels
ISBN 1-59116-222-X
Sixth-grader Hikaru Shindo is not interested in intellectual pursuits, but by a twist of fate, the spirit of
Fujiwara no Sai, the ghost of an ancient Go master, manages to bond with Hikaru. Now, suddenly, Hikaru can
play Go, a complex board game of strategy, better than
almost anyone under 18 and most adults, too. Akira, who
has been raised by his Go master father, needs to know
more about the upstart Hikaru, who beats him and yet
seems so casual about the game. This is the first volume
of an ongoing series.

Huddleston, Courtney
Decoy; by Courtney Huddleston, Eli Williams,
and Dan Jensen. Penny Farthing Press 2000 112p
il pa $15.95
Grades: 7 8 9 10 11 12   **741.5**
1. Graphic novels 2. Science fiction—Graphic novels
3. Adventure graphic novels 4. Friendship—Graphic
novels
ISBN 0-9673683-2-4
Rookie cop Bobby Luck has just stumbled into a bad
situation and been shot; but, instead of dying, he ends up
physically good as new, thanks to a little, green,
shapeshifting alien he calls Decoy. With their symbiotic,
telepathic bond, Luck and Decoy must now face Nabob
and prevent him from taking over the world while keeping their bond a secret from everyone, including Luck's
senior partner, Tessa. Oh, and the life of a little girl depends on them, too.

Huddleston, Courtney—*Continued*
Another title in this series is:
Decoy: Storm of the century (2003)

Hunter, Erin
The lost warrior; created by Erin Hunter; written by Dan Jolley; art by James L. Barry. Tokyopop/HarperCollins Publishers 2007 96p il (Warriors) $6.99
Grades: 4 5 6 7 8 9   **741.5**
    1. Graphic novels 2. Adventure graphic novels 3. Cats—Graphic novels
    ISBN 978-0-06-124020-1; 0-06-124020-6
                  LC 2006-30426
Thunderclan warrior Greystripe helps clan members escape when the twolegs destroy their forest home and capture many of them, but he himself gets captured. Now he's a kittypet and desperate to return home to his clan. He meets Millie, another kittypet who wants to learn how to become a warrior, but can Greystripe find his way out of the twolegs' land?
    This series adapting Hunter's Warriors prose novel series is a co-publishing venture between Tokyopop and its book market distributor, HarperCollins.
    Other titles in this series are:
Warrior's refuge (2008)
Warrior's return (2008)
The rise of the scourge (2008)

Warriors: Tiger & Sasha #1: into the woods; created by Erin Hunter; written by Dan Jolley; art by Don Hudson. HarperCollins/Tokyopop 2008 108p il $6.99
Grades: 3 4 5 6 7 8 9   **741.5**
    1. Graphic novels 2. Adventure graphic novels 3. Cats—Graphic novels
    ISBN 978-0-06-154792-8; 0-06-154792-1
Sasha was a loved, pampered kittypet, but when one of the housefolk dies and the other moves away, they leave her behind. She had always explored the woods at night, but now she has to survive on her own. Then she meets Tigerstar, leader of ShadowClan, and they spend a lot of time together as he teaches her how to improve her hunting. He even offers her membership in the clan, but he has secrets, and when Sasha discovers one of them, she has to decide if she can trust him. There are scenes of cats hunting prey such as mice and squirrels, and fighting with foxes.
    Followed by: Warriors. Tigerstar & Sasha. #2 : Escape from the forest (2009)

Irwin, Jane, 1941-
Vögelein; clockwork faerie; [by] Jane Irwin with Jeff Berndt; foreword by Jennifer M. Contino. Fiery Studios 2003 167p il pa $12.95
Grades: 6 7 8 9 10 11 12   **741.5**
    1. Fairies—Graphic novels 2. Graphic novels 3. Fantasy graphic novels
    ISBN 0-9743110-06
Most of the material contained within was originally printed in issues 15 of the magazine "Vögelein"
    This is a "graphic novel about Vogelein, a beautiful mechanical fairy created in the seventeenth century. Al-

though she is immortal, she must be wound every 36 hours. After her old friend and caretaker dies, she must find someone new to take care of her. . . . This modern fable is a rare treasure that weaves fanciful imagination into themes of individuality, diversity, and independence. The art is beautifully shaded black and white, and it carries the narrative impeccably." Booklist

Jacques, Brian
Redwall: the graphic novel; by Brian Jacques; illustrated by Bret Blevins; adapted by Stuart Moore; lettering by Richard Starkings. Philomel Books 2007 143p il pa $12.99
Grades: 4 5 6 7 8 9   **741.5**
    1. Graphic novels 2. Fantasy graphic novels 3. Adventure graphic novels 4. Mice—Graphic novels
    ISBN 978-0-399-24481-0; 0-399-24481-6
When Cluny the rat's army attacks Redwall Abbey, young Matthias the mouse follows in the footsteps of the long-ago hero Martin the Warrior to defend his home
    "The story is a page-turner, and the detailed black-and-white drawings capture both the passion and the pathos." SLJ

Jaffe, Michele, 1970-
Bad kitty volume 1: catnipped. HarperCollins/Tokyopop 2008 176p il $9.99
Grades: 7 8 9 10 11 12   **741.5**
    1. Graphic novels 2. Mystery graphic novels 3. Humorous graphic novels
    ISBN 978-0-06-135162-4; 0-06-135162-8
Teenage aspiring detective Jasmine Callihan just wants to hang out with her boyfriend, rock star Jack, but while they're at the mall, trouble strikes. First, Jas finds a schoolmate's purse, then there's a jewelry store heist and the cops arrest the store owner whom she believes is innocent, then she says exactly the wrong thing to Jack, and her cousin Alyson with her Evil Hench Twin Veronique decided to join the investigation along with Jas and her best friends Roxy, Polly, and Tom. This global manga is an original story using the same characters as Jaffe's prose teen novels Bad Kitty and Kitty Kitty.
    "Catnipped will be especially appreciated by fans of Jaffe's novels, but it is not necessary to have read them to enjoy this rollicking, fast-paced, and funny mystery." SLJ

Jolley, Dan
Guan Yu; blood brothers to the end: a Chinese legend; story by Dan Jolley; pencils and inks by Ron Randall. Graphic Universe TM 2008 48p il (Graphic myths and legends) lib bdg $26.60
Grades: 4 5 6   **741.5**
    1. Kuan, Yu, 160-220—Graphic novels 2. China—Graphic novels 3. Graphic novels
    ISBN 978-0-8225-7527-6 (lib bdg); 0-8225-7527-2 (lib bdg)   LC 2007019742
This graphic novel offers "a look at Guan Yu, a Chinese superwarrior circa 2,000 years ago. Here chronicled is his first meeting with his 'blood brothers' and his various battles both with and against them, battles that

Jolley, Dan—*Continued*

helped to shape ancient China. . . . Most effective . . . is the unfolding of Guan Yu's life, charted not by his incredible triumphs but his failures, which provide readers . . . with a worthwhile change of perspective." Booklist

Kibuishi, Kazu

Amulet book one: the stonekeeper; [by] Kazu Kibuishi. Graphix 2008 185p il $21.99; pa $9.99 *

Grades: 3 4 5 6 7 8 9   **741.5**
1. Graphic novels 2. Fantasy graphic novels 3. Mystery graphic novels 4. Adventure graphic novels
ISBN 978-0-439-84680-6; 978-0-439-84681-3 (pa); 0-439-84680-3; 0-439-84681-1 (pa)

While still mourning the death of their father in a terrible automobile accident two years before, Emily, Navin, and their mother move to their great-grandfather's home to start a new life. On the family's very first night in the mysterious house, Emily and Navin's mother is snatched by a tentacled creature, and the two children instinctively follow. They find themselves in a strange world and befriended by a mechanical rabbit named Miskit who says he was built by their great-grandfather. Now it's up to Emily and Navin to figure out how to set things right and save their mother's life, and the strange amulet Emily found in the house may hold the key

Kim, Derek Kirk, 1974-

Good as Lily; written by Derek Kirk Kim; illustrated by Jesse Hamm; lettering by Jared K. Fletcher. DC Comics/Minx 2007 unp il pa $9.99 *

Grades: 7 8 9 10 11 12   **741.5**
1. Graphic novels 2. Humorous graphic novels 3. Fantasy graphic novels
ISBN 978-1-4012-1381-7

"On her eighteenth birthday, Korean American Grace suddenly finds herself surrounded by three very corporeal essences of herself: as a small child, as a 30-year-old woman, and as 'a cranky old fart.' Each of these incarnations is at an emotional precipice, which teenage Grace helps resolve, allowing the other self to quietly disappear. . . . Kim's pacing and plotting are excellent, and Hamm's black, white, and gray artwork is lively, witty, and full of appropriate comedy and melodrama." Booklist

Konomi, Takeshi

The Prince of Tennis, Vol. 1. Viz Media, LLC 2004 192p il pa $7.95

Grades: 6 7 8 9 10   **741.5**
1. Graphic novels 2. Tennis—Graphic novels 3. Manga 4. Shonen manga
ISBN 1-59116-435-4

This is the first of an ongoing series, up to Volume 9 in September 2005

"Ryoma is a former U.S. junior tennis champion who attends a Japanese academy, where his skill and natural talent make him nearly unbeatable. The younger students are inspired by him, but he's ruffling the feathers of the older tennis team members. Then the journalists appear, trying to discover the next champion, adding to the pres-

sure. There's lots of tennis action, dramatically illustrated, and the characters, already pretty boys, are made even more attractive with their intensity." Publ Wkly

Kovac, Tommy

Wonderland; written by Tommy Kovac; illustrated by Sonny Liew. Disney Press 2008 159p il $19.99

Grades: 4 5 6 7 8   **741.5**
1. Graphic novels 2. Fantasy graphic novels
ISBN 978-1-4231-0451-3; 1-4231-0451-X

First published as single-issue comics by SLG Publishing

Based on the tale Alice in Wonderland by Lewis Carroll

"Ever wonder what happened in Wonderland after Alice left? Follow the quirky tale of Mary Ann, the meticulous and dutiful housekeeper for the White Rabbit, as she continues the tale. Her boss is now wanted for treason by the Queen of Hearts for allowing the Alice Monster to enter the kingdom–off with his head! On the run and fearing for their lives, Mary Ann and White Rabbit encounter the meddlesome Cheshire Cat, the ever-contentious troublemaker, sending the White Rabbit straight into the clutches of the queen and poor Mary Ann tumbling into the Treacle Well. . . . This is a terrific look at a great classic. The energetic, action-packed illustrations complement the story in Disney-cartoon style, making for a great read for all ages" SLJ

Krensky, Stephen, 1953-

Comic book century; the history of American comic books. Twenty-First Century Books 2007 112p il lib bdg $30.60

Grades: 5 6 7 8 9 10   **741.5**
1. Cartoons and caricatures 2. Comic books, strips, etc.
ISBN 978-0-8225-6654-0; 0-8225-6654-0

LC 2006-20795

Provides a history of comic books in America during the twentieth century, showing how it has influenced and been influenced by American culture. Includes an epilogue about comics in the early twenty-first century.

"Frequent full-color comic-book representations and black-and-white photographs, . . . flashy sidebars, and a striking blue background combine well with the accessible text, making this . . . visually appealing as well as highly entertaining." Bull Cent Child Books

Includes bibliographical references

Larson, Hope

Chiggers; [by] Hope Larson; lettered by Jason Azzopardi. Atheneum Books for Young Readers 2008 170p il $17.99; pa $9.99

Grades: 5 6 7 8 9   **741.5**
1. Camps—Fiction 2. Graphic novels 3. Friendship—Graphic novels
ISBN 978-1-4169-3584-1; 978-1-4169-3587-2 (pa)

LC 2008-09557

When Abby returns to the same summer camp she always goes to, she is dismayed to find that her old friends have changed, and the only person who wants to be her

Larson, Hope—*Continued*
friend is the strange new girl, Shasta.

"Chiggers provides a ticket to summer fun. Larson delicately handles both the usual middle-school angst and the additional pressures that come with being somewhat different. . . . The content is perfect for upper elementary and middle school students." SLJ

Lat
Kampung boy. First Second 2006 141p il pa $16.95 *
Grades: 7 8 9 10 11 12 Adult   741.5
1. Malaysia—Graphic novels 2. Family life—Graphic novels 3. Muslims—Graphic novels 4. Graphic novels
ISBN 1-59643-121-0   LC 2005-34135
First published 1979 in Malaysia with title: Lat, the kampung boy

"Malaysian cartoonist Lat uses the graphic novel format to share the story of his childhood in a small village, or kampung. From his birth and adventures as a toddler to the enlargement of his world as he attends classes in the village, makes friends, and, finally, departs for a prestigious city boarding school, this autobiography is warm, authentic, and wholly engaging." Booklist

Town Boy. First Second Books 2007 192p il $16.95 *
Grades: 7 8 9 10 11 12 Adult   741.5
1. Graphic novels 2. Bildungsromans—Graphic novels 3. Humorous graphic novels 4. Malaysia—Graphic novels
ISBN 978-1-59643-331-1
In this sequel to Kampung Boy, it's the late 1960s and Mat is now a teenager attending a boarding school in the town of Ipoh, far from his kampung. He discovers bustling streets, hip music, heady literature, budding romance, and through it all his growing passion for art.

Lyga, Barry
Wolverine: worst day ever; by Barry Lyga; artist, Todd Nauck. Marvel Publishing 2009 184p il $14.99
Grades: 5 6 7 8 9   741.5
1. Graphic novels 2. Superhero graphic novels 3. Humorous graphic novels 4. Wolverine (Fictional 'character)
ISBN 978-0-7851-3757-3; 0-7851-3757-2
Teenager Eric Mattias has just recently discovered he has mutant powers. Very sucky mutant powers: suddenly no one notices him even when he's in the same room. He's not invisible, but he might as well be, and people don't even notice him when he speaks. Eric decides to follow Wolverine around and see if he can't pick up a few pointers about living a loner-type life, as the adamantium-clawed mutant tends to do. Only when they end up in a remote forested area does Eric realize he may not have made the smartest move, because someone else has come, someone who is as strong as Wolverine, and maybe meaner: Sabretooth.

"It's a coming-of-age tale with bursts of action that's sure to appeal to its large, built-in audience." Booklist

Macdonald, Fiona
Journey to the Center of the Earth; by Jules Verne; Fiona Macdonald, adapter; illustrated by Penko Gelev. Barron's Educational Series, Inc. 2007 48p il (Graphic classics) $15.99; pa $8.99
Grades: 3 4 5 6 7 8   741.5
1. Verne, Jules, 1828-1905—Adaptations 2. Graphic novels 3. Adventure graphic novels
ISBN 978-0-7641-5982-4; 978-0-7641-3495-1 (pa)
In Hamburg, Germany in 1863, eccentric Professor Otto Lidenbrock acquires a book by the sixteenth-century alchemist, Arne Saknussemm; the book includes a parchment page written in coded runes, and Lidenbrock's nephew Axel helps him decode it. To Axel's horror, the message tells of a way to get to the Center of the Earth, and Lidenbrock drags him along on the adventure.

The "story progresses in short two-page episodes, helped along by a few sentences of narration under each frame. Detailed illustrations in muted colors work with . . . the dim underground setting. . . . Dramatic, action-filled scenes and highly expressive faces catch readers eyes and pull them into the [story]." SLJ

Kidnapped; by Robert Louis Stevenson; Fiona Macdonald, adapter; illustrated by Penko Gelev. Barron's Educational Series, Inc. 2007 48p il (Graphic classics) $15.99; pa $8.99
Grades: 3 4 5 6 7 8   741.5
1. Stevenson, Robert Louis, 1850-1894—Adaptations 2. Graphic novels 3. Adventure graphic novels
ISBN 978-0-7641-5980-0; 978-0-7641-3494-4 (pa)
Orphaned David Balfour goes to his uncle, who first tries to kill him and then tricks him into going onboard a ship that leaves Scotland with David aboard. David befriends a passenger, Alan Breck, then learns he's a Jacobite in exile. They survive a shipwreck, witness a murder, and become fugitives on the run back in Scotland.

The "story progresses in short two-page episodes, helped along by a few sentences of narration under each frame. Detailed illustrations in muted colors work with the stormy, furtive story. . . . Dramatic, action-filled scenes and highly expressive faces catch readers eyes and pull them into the [story]." SLJ

MacHale, D. J.
Pendragon book one: the merchant of death graphic novel; adapted and illustrated by Carla Speed McNeil. Aladdin Paperbacks 2008 172p il $9.99
Grades: 5 6 7 8 9 10   741.5
1. Graphic novels 2. Adventure graphic novels 3. Fantasy graphic novels
ISBN 978-1-4169-5080-6; 1-4169-5080-X
          LC 2007-937920
Fourteen-year-old Bobby Pendragon has had a good life with a loving family, friends, and sports, but it all changes the night his Uncle Press takes him into New York City, to a deserted subway station that contains a gate that leads them to another world. On Denduron, a peaceful tribe called the Milago face annihilation from the Bedowan, and Uncle Press expects Bobby to help him stop it. Press is what he calls a Traveler, and he says Bobby is one, too, and they have a job to do. Bobby is able to write journals and send them home to his

MacHale, D. J.—*Continued*

best friends Mark and Courtney. Meanwhile, he needs to learn so much, can he do it in time to help—and stay alive?

"This graphic-format adaptation streamlines the already fast-moving experience, providing satisfying interpretations of favorite characters and situations." Booklist

Medley, Linda

Castle waiting. Fantagraphics 2006 456p il $29.95 *

Grades: 5 6 7 8 9 10 11 12   **741.5**
1. Graphic novels 2. Fairy tales—Graphic novels 3. Fantasy graphic novels
ISBN 1-56097-747-7

All of Medley's previously self-published comics are collected here in one volume for the first time. The titular castle was the home of Sleeping Beauty, whose story is retold from the viewpoint of the flibbertigibbet ladies in waiting. After the flighty princess awakens with the kiss of a handsome but not too bright prince, the castle becomes a sanctuary for various misfits. Readers will find references to many fairy tales, folk tales, and nursery rhymes in Medley's book, and her clean, clear black-and-white art reflects the works of classic illustrators such as Arthur Rackham.

Momo no Tane

Shugo chara! Peach-Pit; translated by June Kato; adapted by David Walsh; lettered by North Market Street Graphics. Del Rey/Ballantine Books 2007 v1-v6 il v1 $10.95; v2 $10.95; v3 $10.95; v4 $10.95; v5 $10.95; v6 $10.95

Grades: 5 6 7 8 9   **741.5**
1. Graphic novels
ISBN 978-0-345-49745-1 (v1); 978-0-345-49927-1 (v2); 978-0-345-50146-2 (v3); 978-0-345-50522--4 (v4); 978-0-345-50804-1 (v5); 978-0-345-51032-7 (v6)
LC 2007296632

Vol. 2-3 : translated by Satsuki Yamashita ; adapted by Nunzio Defilippis and Christina Weir.

"When Amu, a shy girl who wishes that she had the courage to truly be herself, finds three strange little eggs in her bed, she discovers that Guardian Characters are in each egg and each can give her the power to be someone new." Publisher's note

"Readers should revel in the lightly romantic and comedic plot and delight in the adorably stylized characters, from brooding mysterious cat-eared boys to small, sweet doll-like girls. Fans of CLAMP's Cardcaptor Sakura (Tokyopop) will enjoy these adventures of another plucky fourth grader uncovering magical secrets and learning of her wondrous fantasy world. Sheer bubblegum fun." SLJ

Morse, Scott

The barefoot serpent. Top Shelf Productions 2003 128p il pa $14.95

Grades: 7 8 9 10 11 12   **741.5**

1. Kurosawa, Akira, 1910-1998—Graphic novels 2. Graphic novels 3. Bereavement—Graphic novels 4. Hawaii—Graphic novels
ISBN 1-891830-37-6

"A little girl journeys to Hawaii with her parents after her older brother's death. There she meets a little-boy wheeler-dealer and tags along as he hustles a mask he has carved and plays in sand and surf. Rejoining her father, she infects him with her restored spirits; the family flies home refreshed. Sandwiching that story is a child's-picture-book-like sketch of Japanese filmmaker Akira Kurosawa." Booklist

Nagatomo, Haruno

Draw your own Manga; beyond the basics; translated by Françoise White. Kodansha International 2005 111p il pa $19.95

Grades: 7 8 9 10 11 12   **741.5**
1. Graphic novels—Drawing 2. Manga—Drawing
ISBN 4-7700-2304-9; 978-4-7700-2304-9

Also available: Draw your own Manga; all the basics (2003)

"This advanced manual looks at how to enhance manga with a range of special effects as well as how to use various types of color ink, markers, and airbrushes to reach more creative levels. Supplemented by an interview with the immensely popular Japanese sports manga artist Shinji Mizushima, this book is recommended for any cartoon or animation library." Libr J

Naifeh, Ted

Courtney Crumrin and the night things. Oni Press 2005 128p il pa $11.95

Grades: 5 6 7 8 9 10 11 12   **741.5**
1. Graphic novels 2. Fantasy graphic novels 3. Supernatural graphic novels
ISBN 1-929998-60-0

Courtney's social-climber parents take her out of her comfortable city neighborhood and move into an upscale suburb to live with her creepy Great-Uncle Aloysius in her spooky old house. She has to face uppity classmates and things that go bump in the night; but she ends up making friends with the spooks! Courtney deals with magic and the supernatural, but she's no altruistic Harry Potter; in this series, magic sometimes bites hard.

Other titles in this series are:
Courtney Crumrin and the Coven of Mystics (2003)
Courtney Crumrin in the Twilight Kingdom (2004)

Nakajo, Hisaya

Sugar Princess volume 1: skating to win; story & art by Hisaya Nakajo. Viz Media/Shojo Beat 2008 184p il $8.99

Grades: 7 8 9 10 11 12   **741.5**
1. Graphic novels 2. Manga 3. Shojo manga 4. Romance graphic novels 5. Ice skating—Graphic novels
ISBN 978-1-4215-1930-2; 1-4215-1930-5

Orginal Japanese editon, 2005

Maya Kurinoko takes her little brother to the local ice-skating rink with free tickets, but he won't skate unless she does a jump just like they saw on television the

Nakajo, Hisaya—_Continued_
night before. So, she attempts a double axel, and lands it. Skating coach Eishi Todo sees her make the jump and scouts her as an ice skater. He wants famous skater Shun Kano (who attends Maya's high school she's in junior high) to coach and then partner with her, but Shun doesn't want it. However, Maya loves ice skating and realizes it may be the one thing she can be good at doing, and she's willing to persevere.

Followed by: Sugar pincess. Vol. 2 : skating to win (2008)

O'Donnell, Liam, 1970-
Wild ride: a graphic guide adventure; written by Liam O'Donnell; illustrated by Mike Deas. Orca Book Publishers 2007 unp il pa $8.95
Grades: 3 4 5 6 7 8   **741.5**
1. Graphic novels 2. Adventure graphic novels 3. Wilderness survival—Graphic novels
ISBN 978-1-55143-756-9
Devin, his sister Nadia, smart-mouthed Marcus (all children of environmentalists), and government accountant Gerald Wiley all fly into the wilderness toward Big Horn Valley in British Columbia, but they fly into a storm and crash in the middle of nowhere. The pilot is killed, and the three young people and Wiley must survive until rescue. However, the kids soon discover Wiley is not on their side; he's taking bribes from a large corporation to stop the environmental study.

"The easy-to-follow survival adventure will engage reluctant readers. . . . Deas' full-color art is packed with action." Booklist

Another title about Devin and Nadia is:
Soccer sabotage (2008)

Parker, Jeff, 1966-
The avengers: heroes assembled; artist, Manuel Garcia. Marvel 2006 v1 il (Marvel adventures: the avengers) pa $6.99
Grades: 5 6 7 8 9   **741.5**
1. Graphic novels 2. Superhero graphic novels
ISBN 978-0-7851-2306-4; 0-7851-2306-7
Presents adventures in which various superheroes, including Captain America, Storm, Wolverine, and Spider-Man battle numerous foes. Publisher's note
Other titles in the series about the Avengers are:
The avengers v2: mischief (2007)
The avengers v3: bizarre adventures (2007)
The avengers v4: dream team (2007)
The avengers v5: some assembling required (2008)
The avengers v6: mighty marvels (2008)
The avengers v7: weirder and wilder (2008)
The avengers v8: the new recruits (2009)

Petrucha, Stefan
Beowulf; story by Stefan Petrucha; artwork by Kody Chamberlain. 1st Harper Trophy ed. HarperTrophy 2007 unp il $8.99
Grades: 6 7 8 9 11 12 Adult   **741.5**
1. Beowulf—Graphic novels 2. Graphic novels 3. Adventure graphic novels 4. Monsters—Graphic novels
ISBN 978-0-06-134390-2   LC 2007003923

For a dozen years, the monster Grendel has haunted the Danish kingdom ruled over by Hrothgar. Word of the monster spreads far and wide, and from across the sea comes the warrior Beowulf to battle the monster and free the Danes from Grendel's reign of terror.

"In this stunning graphic novel, Beowulf comes to life for young readers. . . . The illustrations are detailed and energetic and convey the sinister nature of the evil Beowulf encounters." SLJ

Poe, Edgar Allan, 1809-1849
The raven and other poems; illustrated by Gahan Wilson. Papercutz 2009 56p il (Classics illustrated) $9.95
Grades: 5 6 7 8 9 10 11 12   **741.5**
1. Poe, Edgar Allan, 1809-1849—Adaptations—Graphic novels 2. Graphic novels 3. American poetry—Graphic novels
ISBN 978-1-59707-140-6; 1-59707-140-4
Cartoonist Gahan Wilson brings his moody, macabre drawing style to illustrate poems by Edgar Allan Poe. This book includes "The Raven," "Annabel Lee," "The Sleeper," "Eldorado," "Lines on Ale," "The City in the Sea," "Alone," "The Haunted Palace," and "The Conqueror Worm." This book was first published in 1990 by First Publishing in partnership with Berkley Publishing Group.

Reed, Gary
Mary Shelley's Frankenstein: the graphic novel. Puffin Graphics 2005 176p il pa $9.99
Grades: 5 6 7 8 9 10 11 12   **741.5**
1. Shelley, Mary Wollstonecraft, 1797-1851—Adaptations 2. Graphic novels 3. Horror graphic novels
ISBN 0-14-240407-1
Scientist Victor Frankenstein decided to create a man, only to create something he deemed a monster.

"Reed concentrates on the emotional anguish of the story, ably capturing the rage, the hurt, and the guilt of both monster and creator. Irving . . . creates a hazy, suitably murky black-and-white backdrop, never exploiting the violence inherent in the monster's quest for vengeance." Booklist

Robbins, Trina, 1938-
Go girl!. Vol. 1, The time team; story, Trina Robbins, art, Anne Timmons. Dark Horse Comics 95p il pa $5.95
Grades: 3 4 5 6 7 8   **741.5**
1. Graphic novels 2. Adventure graphic novels 3. Superhero graphic novels
ISBN 1-59307-230-9
"Robbins, who has made a name for herself as a feminist in the comics world, creates a story about three stereotypical high school girls—the dismissive cheerleader, the misunderstood brain, and the daughter of a 1970s-era superheroine—who become stranded in prehistory. The girls are quick-witted, the dinosaurs are cartoony, and a late appearance by Vikings offers readers a taste of what Nordic women might have been like in a confrontation. This isn't high concept, but it's definitely good, clean fun." Booklist

Roche, Art

Comic strips; create your own comic strips from start to finish. Lark 2007 112p il (Art for kids) $17.95

Grades: 4 5 6 7   **741.5**

1. Cartoons and caricatures 2. Drawing

ISBN 978-1-57990-788-4; 1-57990-788-1

Explains the process of drawing comic strips and makes suggestions for developing a style all one's own.

"The bright, dynamic layout includes full-color illustrations. The writing is clear and concise so that after completing the book, readers will feel confident to branch out on their own." SLJ

Rocks, Misako, 1977-

Biker girl; story and art by Misako Rocks. 1st Hyperion American pa ed. Hyperion Paperbacks 2006 unp il pa $7.99

Grades: 3 4 5 6 7 8 9   **741.5**

1. Graphic novels 2. Adventure graphic novels 3. Bicycles—Graphic novels

ISBN 0-7868-3676-8   LC 2005-57428

"In this manga-style adventure, a young girl becomes a reluctant superhero after she inherits a bike with magical powers. . . . This fast-paced and well-executed story is . . . bound to be popular." Booklist

Detective Jermain, volume 1; story and art by Misako Rocks. Henry Holt and Company 2008 152p il $9.95

Grades: 6 7 8 9 10   **741.5**

1. Graphic novels 2. Mystery graphic novels

ISBN 978-0-8050-8155-8; 0-8050-8155-0

LC 2007-938579

Seventeen-year-old Jermain wants to be a detective, just like her father was before he was murdered. In her senior year of high school, she finds a mystery: a student and a teacher are killed in an automobile accident, and they were both behaving very strangely in school that day. Jermain enlists the help of her two best friends, Travis and Andy, to help her find out what is going on at school that would cost the lives of their friends.

"The author/artist is adept at portraying emotions, and employs a variety of visual effects that pull readers into the story. The b&w artwork is crisp and effectively propels the action. This is an auspicious start to a series that should prove popular with its intended audience." Libr Media Connect

Rosinsky, Natalie M. (Natalie Myra)

Write your own graphic novel. Compass Point Books 2009 64p il (Write your own) lib bdg $33.26

Grades: 5 6 7 8 9 10 11 12   **741.5**

1. Graphic novels—Authorship

ISBN 978-0-7565-3856-9; 0-7565-3856-4

LC 2008-6506

Part of the Write Your Own series

This book offers tips, advice, end encouragement to readers who might want to try their hand at writing their own comics and graphic novels. Rosinsky uses many examples from Stone Arch and Capstone Press books along with many others, and the "case study" side bars provide

glimpses into the work of such graphic novelists as Marjane Satrapi, Art Spiegelman, and Craig Thompson. The back matter includes a list of suggested graphic novels that are suitable for teen readers.

"Students wishing to explore the graphic-novel format will benefit from clear explanations of how to portray heroes and villains, use dramatic dialogue, and create a story map. Excerpts from several popular graphic novels are included. " SLJ

Russell, P. Craig, 1951-

Coraline; based on the novel by Neil Gaiman; adapted and illustrated by P. Craig Russell; colorist, Lovern Kindzierski; letterer, Todd Klein. HarperCollins 2008 186p il $18.99; lib bdg $19.89 *

Grades: 4 5 6 7   **741.5**

1. Gaiman, Neil, 1960-—Adaptations 2. Graphic novels 3. Horror graphic novels

ISBN 978-0-06-082543-0; 978-0-06-082544-7 (lib bdg)   LC 2007-930658

"An adaptation of Gaiman's 2002 novel *Coraline*, . . . a tale of childhood nightmares. As in the original story, Coraline wanders around her new house and discovers a door leading into a mirror place, where she finds her button-eyed 'other mother,' who is determined to secure Coraline's love one way or another. This version is a virtuoso adaptation. . . . A master of fantastical landscapes, Russell sharpens the realism of his imagery, perserving the humanity of the characters and heightening the horror." Booklist

Sakai, Stan

Usagi Yojimbo, Vol. 18; travels with Jotaro. Dark Horse Comics 2004 208p il $15.95

Grades: 7 8 9 10 11 12   **741.5**

1. Graphic novels 2. Adventure graphic novels

ISBN 1-59307-220-1

"Usagi, the rabbit bodyguard, is traveling with his son, although Jotaro does not know that Usagi is his father. Their adventures range from the fairly straightforward defeat of two ninja assassins to fighting powerful creatures conjured by a cursed sumi (calligraphy writing) set." SLJ

"Sakai delivers plenty of martial arts action and solid storytelling . . . and his well-researched backdrop of feudal Japan makes the story seem more like a fable than a traditional comic book." Booklist

Sakura, Kenichi

Dragon drive. Vol. 1, D-break; story & art by Ken-ichi Sakura. Viz Media/Shonen Jump 2007 195p il $7.99

Grades: 6 7 8 9 10   **741.5**

1. Graphic novels 2. Manga 3. Shonen manga 4. Video games—Graphic novels

ISBN 978-1-4215-1187-0; 1-4215-1187-8

Reiji Ozora knows that he's no good at anything, people keep telling him that. Then best friend Maiko takes him to a secret center where people play a virtual reality game, Dragon Drive. Reiji signs up and finds that, despite the fact that his virtual dragon, Chibi, is small and

Sakura, Kenichi—*Continued*

weak, together they have more power than meets the eye. While they play the game, they're in a world called Rikyu, where everything feels all too real; can Reiji, Chibi, and their friends be in real danger?

Other titles in the Dragon Drive series are:

Dragon drive. Vol. 2 : another world (2007)
Dragon drive. Vol. 3: believe (2007)
Dragon drive. Vol. 4: hero (2007)
Dragon drive. Vol. 5: mission (2007)
Dragon drive. Vol. 6: hope (2008)
Dragon drive. Vol. 7: decisive battle (2008)
Dragon drive. Vol. 8: excitement (2008)
Dragon drive. Vol. 9: reshuffle (2008)
Dragon drive. Vol. 10: departure (2008)
Dragon drive. Vol. 11: trust (2008)
Dragon drive. Vol. 12: promise (2009)
Dragon drive. Vol. 13: reunion (2009)
Dragon drive. Vol. 14: wait (2009)

Sanderson, Peter

X-men: the ultimate guide; [by] Peter Sanderson. Updated ed. Dorling Kindersley Pub. 2006 192p il $24.99

Grades: 7 8 9 10   741.5

1. X-men (Comic strip) 2. Comic books, strips, etc.

ISBN 978-0-7566-2005-9; 0-7566-2005-8
LC 2005-33592

First published 2003 with title: Ultimate X-men

This is an "overview of the history of the X-Men comics, detailing the stories and characters that have appeared on their pages." Publisher's note

Schreiber, Ellen

Vampire kisses: blood relatives. Katherine Tegen Books 2007 96p il pa $7.99

Grades: 7 8 9 10   741.5

1. Vampires—Graphic novels

ISBN 978-0-06-134081-9 (pa); 0-06-134081-2 (pa)
LC 2007-03677

"Raven is a cute Goth girl who just happens to have a vampire for a boyfriend. . . . [The] over-the-top romanticism . . . will be devoured . . . by teens who like their horror more sweet than scary. . . . The stylized artwork is an excellent match for this vampire-lite romance." SLJ

Serling, Rod, 1924-1975

The twilight zone: the after hours; by Rod Serling; adaptation by Mark Kneece; illustrated by Rebekah Isaacs. Walker & Company 2008 unp il $16.99; pa $9.99

Grades: 5 6 7 8 9 10   741.5

1. Twilight zone (Television program)—Graphic novels 2. Graphic novels 3. Supernatural graphic novels

ISBN 978-0-8027-9716-2; 978-0-8027-9717-9 (pa)
LC 2008-4310

Marsha White visits a department store to buy an advertised gold thimble, is taken by elevator to a floor with empty display cases except for one, which has the thimble, and she deals with an odd saleswoman who knows her name. When Marsha is in the elevator, she discovers the thimble is defective and tries to complain, but the manager insists there is no eighteenth floor, the store has no elevator, and the store has never carried gold thimbles. As she begins to leave, Marsha faints at the sight of a mannequin that looks exactly like the strange saleswoman, and she's put into a back room to recover. When she wakes up, the store has been closed and she's locked in. This is an actual episode of the old Twilight Zone television show. Mark Kneece, who adapted the screenplay, is one of the founders of the Sequential Art Department at Savannah College of Art and Design; artist Rebekah Isaacs graduated from Savannah College of Art and Design.

"Kneece's adaptation is quick and enjoyable and introduces a classic TV series to a new generation of readers. Isaacs's illustrations are clean, distinct and cinematic in scope, employing an interesting variety of angles." Kirkus

The Twilight Zone: walking distance; adaptation from Rod Serling's original script by Mark Kneece; illustrated by Dove McHargue. Walker & Company 2008 unp il $16.99; pa $9.99

Grades: 5 6 7 8 9 10   741.5

1. Twilight zone (Television program)—Graphic novels 2. Graphic novels 3. Supernatural graphic novels

ISBN 978-0-8027-9714-8; 978-0-8027-9715-5 (pa)
LC 2008-4273

Thirty-nine-year-old businessman Martin Sloan's car blows a tire as he's driving, and he realizes he is within walking distance of his hometown. Leaving his car to be repaired, he decides to walk there. However, when he reaches town, he has also gone back in time. Can he find his boyhood self and give his younger self advice? Or will everyone think he's just crazy? This is an actual episode of the old Twilight Zone television show. Mark Kneece, who adapted the screenplay, is one of the founders of the Sequential Art Department at Savannah College of Art and Design; artist Dove McHargue graduated from Savannah College of Art and Design and is now a faculty member with Kneece.

The story is "exceptionally well told and . . . [is] . . . brilliantly adapted to a new medium." SLJ

Sfar, Joann

Dungeon Vol. 1: Duck Heart; [by] Joann Sfar & Lewis Trondheim. NBM 2003 96p il pa $14.95

Grades: 7 8 9 10 11 12   741.5

1. Graphic novels 2. Fantasy graphic novels 3. Humorous graphic novels

ISBN 1-56163-401-8

"As a result of some unfortunate accidents, Herbert, usually a lowly messenger in the great Dungeon, is called upon to defend it from all manner of beasties. In his endeavors to become a warrior, he is helped by his friend Marvin the vegetarian dragon and by the Dungeon Keeper. Although there's a solid dose of cartoon-style violence and gore, teens will appreciate Herbert's pseudo-slacker attitude, which turns him into an accidental hero time and time again." Booklist

Other titles in this series are:

Dungeon, the early years: the night shirt (2005)
Zenith: the barbarian princess (2005)

Shelley, Mary Wollstonecraft, 1797-1851

Frankenstein; illustrated by Marion Mousse. Papercutz 2009 il (Classics illustrated) $17.95; pa $13.95

Grades: 6 7 8 9   **741.5**

1. Graphic novels 2. Monsters—Graphic novels
ISBN   978-1-597071-30-7;   1-597071-30-7; 978-1-597071-31-4 (pa); 1-597071-31-5 (pa)

"In this graphic novel adaptation of the classic story, Dr. Victor Frankenstein tries to create life, but instead creates a monster, one who vows revenge on the scientist for creating and abandoning him." Publisher's note

Siddell, Thomas

Gunnerkrigg Court: orientation; by Thomas Siddell. Archaia Studios Press 2009 298p il $26.95 *

Grades: 6 7 8 9 10 11 12   **741.5**

1. Graphic novels 2. Fantasy graphic novels
ISBN 978-1-932386-34-9; 1-932386-34-3

"The first 14 chapters of Siddell's popular webcomic are collected here in an alluring hardcover. The premise, best described as science-fantasy, involves a young girl named Antimony plopped into a strange boarding-school/industrial-complex which . . . she knows nothing about. Discrete chapters . . . all feature varying levels of jaw-dropping peculiarity, devilish bursts of humor, and sublime creativity that lurk at the ends of the school's corridors. The darkly hued artwork is deceptively simplistic and displays a flair for the crucial details of setting and atmosphere." Booklist

Sizer, Paul

Little White Mouse collection 1: Dream of the ghost. Café Digital Comics 144p il pa $12.95

Grades: 7 8 9 10   **741.5**

1. Graphic novels

In a future universe, sixteen-year-old Loo is shipwrecked on a remote, automated mining satellite when the space liner on which she and her sister were traveling was destroyed. Considered an intruder by the satellite's computer, she must survive, build a robot body for her dead sister's preserved memory, and find a way home before the satellite's life support system shuts down. Creator Sizer is now self-publishing this series of four volumes and selling it at his website, www.paulsizer.com.

Smith, Jeff

Bone: out from Boneville. Scholastic Graphix 2005 144p il $18.95; pa $9.99

Grades: 4 5 6 7 8 9 10 11 12   **741.5**

1. Graphic novels 2. Adventure graphic novels 3. Fantasy graphic novels
ISBN 0-439-70623-8; 0-439-70640-8 (pa)

Also available Bone: one volume edition $39.95 from Cartoon Books (ISBN 1-8889-6314-X)

"The story follows three cousins who have been thrown out of their town for cheating the citizens. Shortly thereafter, they are separated. Each Bone stumbles into a mysterious valley full of odd creatures that reveal strange happenings. The story is well paced with smooth

transitions. It is dark, witty, mysterious, and exciting. The full-color art reflects that of classic comic books." SLJ

Other titles in this series are:
Bone: the great cow race (vol. 2)
Bone: eyes of the storm (vol. 3)
Bone: the dragonslayer (vol. 4)
Bone: Rock Jaw Master the Eastern Border (vol. 5)
Bone: old man's cave (vol. 6)
Bone: ghost circles (vol. 7)
Bone: treasure hunters (vol. 8)
Bone: crown of horns (vol. 9)
Bone: rose (vol. 10)

Shazam!: the monster society of evil; written and drawn by Jeff Smith ; colored by Steve Hamaker ; introduction by Alex Ross. DC Comics 2007 240p il $29.99

Grades: 4 5 6 7 8 9 10 11 12 Adult

                                                   741.5

1. Graphic novels 2. Superhero graphic novels 3. Captain Marvel (Fictional character)
ISBN 978-1-4012-1466-1; 1-4012-1466-5

When young, homeless orphan Billy Batson follows a mysterious stranger onto the subway, he never imagines he's entering a strange world of powerful wizards, talking tigers, kid-eating monsters, giant robots, political intrigue, and mysterious villains. He encounters all that and more when the wizard gives him a magic word (Shazam!) that transforms him into the world's mightiest mortal, Captain Marvel. However, Billy still has to get by in a grown up world full of danger as he faces the evil schemes of Dr. Sivana and the mysterious Mr. Mind and his Monster Society of Evil. He does have the help of Talky Tawny the Tiger, who also takes the form of his old homeless friend, and of his long-lost sister Mary, but will they be enough? Smith, creator of Bone, has reworked an early Captain Marvel story for new readers.

"The excellent illustrations were drawn with confident, graceful lines, in rich colors. Striking full-page illustrations punctuate dramatic scenes, and each chapter begins with a title page styled after a vintage movie poster. Smith's trademark humor, depth, and artistic talent shine through, making this a worthy companion to 'Bone.'" SLJ

Soo, Kean

Jellaby. Hyperion Books for Children 2008 160p il $18.99; pa $9.99

Grades: 4 5 6 7 8 9 10   **741.5**

1. Fantasy graphic novels 2. Friendship—Graphic novels 3. Graphic novels
ISBN 978-1-4231-0337-0; 978-1-4231-0303-5 (pa)

Ten-year-old Portia Bennett lives with her single mom in a town near Toronto, Ontario. One night, while walking in the woods, a huge purple monster tries to eat her flashlight. Well, Portia doesn't panic, instead she takes the creature home and offers him a tuna sandwich. And just like that, lonely Portia has a new (secret) best friend whom she names Jellaby. As the days go by, Portia enjoys being with Jellaby, but she figures he's lost, and she wants to help him find his home. Their only clue is a photograph of a mysterious door in a nearby city. Is it Toronto? And how can a ten-year-old girl and a purple creature of unknown origin make their way to Toronto all by themselves? This is the first of two volumes.

Stephens, Jay, 1971-
Heroes! draw your own superheroes, gadget geeks & other do-gooders; [by] Jay Stephens. Lark Books 2007 64p il $12.95
Grades: 4 5 6 7   **741.5**
  1. Superheroes 2. Drawing 3. Cartoons and caricatures
  ISBN 978-1-57990-934-5; 1-57990-934-5
                LC 2006101661
"Stephens shows just how to draw [superheroes]. . . . Stephens does a good job organizing his material, beginning with a bit of history, then moving quickly to hero heads, . . . and on to masks, disguises, physical features, power effects, and action moves. The brightly colored illustrations offer plenty of how-to info and lots of great heroes, male and female, to use as models." Booklist

Monsters! draw your own mutants, freaks & creeps; [by] Jay Stephens. 1st ed. Lark Books 2007 64p il $12.95
Grades: 4 5 6 7   **741.5**
  1. Monsters in art 2. Drawing 3. Cartoons and caricatures
  ISBN 1-57990-935-3; 978-1-57990-935-2
                LC 2006036104
This offers instruction in drawing such cartoon monsters as Dockula, the aquatic nibbler; Skeeterman, the campground creep; and Spook Ook, the attic thumper.

Robots! draw your own androids, cyborgs & fighting bots; [by] Jay Stephens. 1st ed. Lark Books 2007 64p il pa $12.95
Grades: 4 5 6 7   **741.5**
  1. Robots in art 2. Drawing 3. Cartoons and caricatures
  ISBN 978-1-57990-937-6 (pa); 1-57990-937-X (pa)
                LC 2007027637
"With simple detailed instructions, an inviting text, and entertaining cartoon scenarios, . . . Stephens explains, step by step, how to draw a variety of robots." Booklist

Stine, R. L., 1943-
Goosebumps: Creepy creatures. Graphix 2006 139p il $16.99
Grades: 5 6 7 8 9   **741.5**
  1. Graphic novels 2. Horror graphic novels
  ISBN 0-439-84124-0
  Contents: The werewolf of Fever Swamp adapted & illustrated by Gabriel Hernandez; The scarecrow walks at midnight adapted & illustrated by Greg Ruth; The abominable snowman of Pasadena adapted & illustrated by Scott Morse
"These selections from the Goosebumps series have been abridged and put in a graphic-novel format, and the fast pace and horror elements make them perfect for this format. The black-and-white illustrations for each one are very different but fit each story well." SLJ

Storrie, Paul D.
Beowulf; monster slayer: a British legend; story by Paul D. Storrie; pencils and inks by Ron Randall. Lerner Publishing Group/Graphic Universe 2008 48p il (Graphic myths and legends) lib bdg $26.60 *
Grades: 4 5 6 7   **741.5**
  1. Beowulf—Graphic novels 2. Graphic novels 3. Monsters—Graphic novels
  ISBN 978-0-8225-6757-8 (lib bdg); 0-8225-6757-1 (lib bdg)   LC 2006-39094
An adaptation of the epic poem in which the hero Beowulf slays the monster Grendel
This "reads like ancient poetry. . . . The action and character design are strong and clear, with solid, comfortable storytelling that is strongly helped by capable color artwork." SLJ

Stuck in the middle; seventeen comics from an unpleasant age; edited by Ariel Schrag. Viking 2007 210p $18.99 *
Grades: 7 8 9 10   **741.5**
  1. Graphic novels
  ISBN 978-0-670-06221-8   LC 2006-52581
This graphic novel collects seventeen short stories about the perils of middle school, each by independent comics creators, including editor Schrag, her younger sister Tania Schrag, Aaron Renier, Daniel Clowes, Gabrielle Bell, and others.
"Highly recommended for junior high graphic novel collections on up; but please keep in mind that this graphic novel does contain some strong material, including obscenities . . . and sexual material." Kliatt

Sturm, James, 1965-
Satchel Paige; striking out Jim Crow; by James Sturm & Rich Tommaso; with an introduction by Gerald Early. Jump at the Sun 2007 89p il $16.99; pa $9.99 *
Grades: 6 7 8 9 10 11 12   **741.5**
  1. Paige, Satchel, 1906-1982—Graphic novels 2. Baseball—Graphic novels 3. Graphic novels
  ISBN 0-7868-3900-7; 0-7868-3901-5 (pa)
                LC 2007-61362
This graphic novel is "about fictional Emmet Wilson, a black farmer whose moment of glory as a player in the Negro Leagues came when he scored a run off the great pitcher, Satchel Paige. . . . This visually powerful, suspenseful, even profound story makes an excellent choice for readers interested in baseball or in the history of race relations." Booklist

The **Superhero** book; the ultimate encyclopedia of comic-book icons and Hollywood heroes; edited by Gina Misiroglu with David A. Roach. Visible Ink Press 2004 xxi, 725p il $29.95
Grades: 7 8 9 10   **741.5**
  1. Superheroes 2. Cartoons and caricatures 3. Motion pictures
  ISBN 0-7808-0772-3   LC 2004-19059
This is an "encyclopedic reference work that profiles superheroes from all companies and in all media. . . . Its 300 full entries provide information on more than 1,000

The Superhero book—*Continued*
mythic overachievers, covering . . . comic book, movie, television, and novel superheroes." Publisher's note

This "is a must-buy for comic readers interested in knowing the early roots and conceptions of comic-book heroes." SLJ

Tamaki, Mariko

Emiko superstar; written by Mariko Tamaki; illustrated by Steve Rolston. DC Comics/Minx 2008 149p il pa $9.99 *

Grades: 7 8 9 10 11 12   **741.5**
1. Graphic novels 2. Performance art—Graphic novels 3. Racially mixed people—Graphic novels

ISBN 978-1-4012-1536-1

"Emiko, a half-Japanese, half-Caucasian Canadian, is a self-described geek facing a summer of babysitting and isolation. Things change when she stumbles upon an underground performing art scene inspired by Andy Warhol's Factory. She eventually takes to the stage . . . and achieves minor celebrity. Soon, though, Emiko must face the troubling complexities in the lives of her new friends and the consequences of her own questionable actions. . . . Rolston's playful, vibrant b&w illustrations bring the characters to life." Publ Wkly

Skim; words by Mariko Tamaki; drawings by Jillian Tamaki. Groundwood Books 2008 144p il $18.95

Grades: 7 8 9 10 11 12   **741.5**
1. Graphic novels 2. Humorous graphic novels 3. School stories—Graphic novels 4. Friendship—Graphic novels

ISBN 978-0-88899-753-1; 0-88899-753-1

Skim is Kimberly Keiko Cameron, a not-slim half-Japanese would-be Wiccan goth who attends a private school. When classmate Katie Matthews' ex-boyfriend commits suicide, concerned guidance counselors descend upon the school because so many of the student body goes into mourning overdrive. The popular clique starts a new club, Girls Celebrate Life, and make Katie their project, especially after she falls off her roof and breaks both arms. Kim and her best friend Lisa observe all this, but counselors target Kim for her goth tendencies and are convinced she'll become suicidal any moment. All she is, is in love with her English teacher, Ms. Archer, who seems to reciprocate and then leaves the school. As Lisa starts to get sucked into the GLC, Kim and Katie tentatively begin a new friendship. There is only one rather chaste kiss between Kim and Ms. Archer. Artist Jillian Tamaki draws Kim to look like a classical Heian period Japanese woman.

Tan, Shaun

The arrival. Arthur A. Levine Books 2007 unp il $19.99 *

Grades: 6 7 8 9 10   **741.5**
1. Graphic novels 2. Immigrants—Graphic novels 3. Stories without words

ISBN 0-439-89529-4   LC 2006-21706

Boston Globe-Horn Book Award special citation (2008)

In this wordless graphic novel, a man leaves his homeland and sets off for a new country, where he must build a new life for himself and his family.

"Young readers will be fascinated by the strange new world the artist creates. . . . They will linger over the details in the beautiful sepia pictures and will likely pick up the book to pore over it again and again." SLJ

TenNapel, Douglas R.

Flink. Image Comics 2007 122p il $13.99

Grades: 6 7 8 9 10 11 12 Adult   **741.5**
1. Graphic novels 2. Adventure graphic novels 3. Sasquatch—Graphic novels

ISBN 978-1-58240-891-0; 1-58240-891-2

Conrad is flying with his father on his first hunting trip when the plane crashes in the wilderness. When Conrad comes to after the crash, he's completely alone, with only the clothes on his back, a handheld game player, and a pocketknife his father had just given him. When he wakes up from a sleep, he finds a deerskin wrapped around him and follows a trail of berries; a Bigfoot named Flink has saved him. Now they have to deal with a rabid she-bear that injures Flink; he needs his brother's medicine to heal, but the Bigfoot community hates humans who hunt them. How can Flink convince them that Conrad is harmless? The book includes some violence and one scene where Conrad pees on a tree.

Tommysaurus Rex. Image Comics 2005 110p il pa $11.95

Grades: 5 6 7 8 9 10 11 12   **741.5**
1. Graphic novels 2. Dinosaurs—Graphic novels

ISBN 1-58240-395-3

When Ely loses his dog, Tommy, in a car accident, his parents send him to Grandpa Joe's farm for the summer. He discovers a live, 40-foot Tyrannosaurus Rex in a cave on the farm, and soon the boy and his pet dinosaur cause a big ruckus in town. Ely promises to train the dinosaur he names Tommysaurus, but not if the town's bully, Randy, has his way.

Toriyama, Akira, 1955-

Cowa! story and art by Akira Toriyama; translation & English adaptation Alexander O. Smith, et. al. Viz Media/Shonen Jump 2008 208p il $7.99

Grades: 5 6 7 8 9 10 11 12   **741.5**
1. Graphic novels 2. Manga 3. Humorous graphic novels 4. Monsters—Graphic novels

ISBN 978-1-4215-1805-3; 1-4215-1805-8

Original Japanese edition, 1997

Mischievous Paifu is half-vampire and half-werekoala, and he's usually getting into lots of trouble with his best buddy, Jose the ghost. When the Monster Flu sweeps through town, the doctor says that without medicine, everyone will die. The only person who makes the medicine is the witch who lives hundreds of miles away, and all the adults except for the doctor are ill. Paifu and Jose team up with grumpy ex-sumo wrestler Maruyama to make the journey; will they make it before they get sick? The book includes some potty humor (Jose farts a lot) and lots of fighting scenes (Toriyama created Dragon Ball Z).

Trondheim, Lewis

Tiny Tyrant; by Lewis Trondheim; translated from the French by Alexis Siegel; illustrated by Fabrice Parme. First Second Books 2007 124p il $12.95

Grades: 4 5 6 7 8 9 10 11 12 Adult

741.5

1. Graphic novels 2. Humorous graphic novels

ISBN 978-1-59643-094-5   LC 2006021479

"Tiny child-king Ethelbert is spoiled and difficult, expecting to have his every whim fulfilled-or else. . . . In the end, though, he becomes a hero. The dynamic cartoons are filled with details and riddled with humor; most pages have between six and eight small pictures. . . . This title will have wide appeal. It's young and accessible enough for elementary-grade kids, but teens will also be charmed by the rascally king." SLJ

Vansant, Wayne

The red badge of courage; [by] Stephen Crane; Wayne Vansant, adapter. Puffin Graphics 2005 176p il pa $9.99

Grades: 5 6 7 8 9 10 11 12   **741.5**

1. Crane, Stephen, 1871-1900—Adaptations 2. Graphic novels 3. United States—History—1861-1865, Civil War—Graphic novels

ISBN 0-14-240410-1

"Artist Vansant captures Fleming's uncertainty and fear quite well, sometimes through effectively understated facial expressions." Publ Wkly

Varon, Sara, 1971-

Robot dreams. First Second 2007 205p il pa $16.95 *

Grades: 3 4 5 6 7 8 9 10 11 12 Adult

741.5

1. Graphic novels 2. Dogs—Graphic novels 3. Robots—Graphic novels

ISBN 978-1-59643-108-9 (pa); 1-59643-108-3 (pa)

LC 2006-52640

"A Junior Library Guild book"

In this wordless book, a dog builds a robot from a kit and they become friends; everything is fine until one fateful day at the beach, when the robot goes into the water and later rusts into immobility.

"Varon's drawing style is uncomplicated, and her colors are clean and refeshing. Although her story seems equally simple, it is invested with true emotion." Booklist

Vollmar, Rob

The castaways; illustrated by Pablo G. Callejo. NBM/ComicsLit 2007 64p il pa $17.95 *

Grades: 6 7 8 9 10 11 12   **741.5**

1. United States—History—1919-1933—Graphic novels 2. Graphic novels

ISBN 978-1-56163-492-7

An expanded and newly illustrated edition of the title first published 2002 by Absence of Ink Comic Press

"Afraid that he's just a burden on his family, 13-year-old Tucker Freeman lets himself be driven away from home and jumps on a freight train heading west. His inexperience makes him vulnerable to all the angry, desperate people looking for any way they can survive during America's economic collapse, but fortunately he's taken under the wing of Elijah Hopkins, an elderly colored man who introduces him to the cooperative hobo subculture. . . . Vollmer's script, based on family reminiscences, rings true; his dialogue has the vocabulary and the rhythms of real people talking. . . . Callejo's art creates a solid setting in which Tucker's experience can reveal squalor or grace." Publ Wkly

Walker, Landry Q.

The super scary monster show, featuring Little Gloomy; written by Landry Walker; drawn by Eric Jones; tones by Rikki Simons. Amaze Ink/SLG Publishing 2008 unp il $9.95

Grades: 3 4 5 6 7 8 9   **741.5**

1. Graphic novels 2. Humorous graphic novels 3. Horror graphic novels

ISBN 978-1-59362-103-2; 1-59362-103-5

This book collects the three issues (so far) of The Super Scary Monster Show comics. Little Gloomy, her friends, and her enemies, live in the world called Frightsylvania. Gloomy deals with an alien who crashlands in her backyard and wants to take over the world (she has plenty of "pet" monsters in her house who take care of her problem). Carl the squid lies to his parents about taking over the world and enslaving all its creatures, then they come for a visit. . . . Gloomy buys a golden scorpion as a gift for her friend the Mummy, but it turns out to be cursed, and everyone around her suffers accidents. The witch Evey has come up with a new spell to torment Gloomy, but it hits werewolf buddy Larry instead and shrinks him. There are plenty more stories, all written with tongue-in-cheek humor and just a touch of horror for younger readers. Gloomy does not suffer fools gladly, so the invading alien gets eaten (off page), and other inimical creatures suffer similar fates, so this book shouldn't be given to younger readers who are sensitive and don't like any violence. There is little in the way of any gore or overt violence, except for poor Frank, whose body parts often come apart.

Watson, Andi, 1969-

Clubbing. DC Comics/Minx 2007 176p il pa $9.99

Grades: 7 8 9 10 11 12   **741.5**

1. Graphic novels 2. Mystery graphic novels

ISBN 978-1-4012-0370-2

Spoiled, rebellious Charlotte "Lottie" Brook lives in London, but her parents send her to Yorkshire to work at her grandparents' country club. Lottie discovers the body of another employee. Along with Howard, the only other young person at the club, Lottie uncovers bizarre evidence and begins to suspect her own grandfather of murder. The book includes a short glossary of English slang.

"British charm radiates from every panel of this graphic novel. . . . The payoff . . . is both satisfying and humorous." Publ Wkly

Princess at midnight. Image Comics 2008 unp il $5.99

Grades: 4 5 6 7 8 9 10   **741.5**

417

Watson, Andi, 1969-—Continued
1. Graphic novels 2. Fantasy graphic novels 3. War—Graphic novels 4. Princesses—Graphic novels
ISBN 978-1-58240-928-3; 1-58240-928-5

Holly Crescent and her twin brother Henry lead sheltered lives as home-schooled children by day; their parents don't want any harm to come to their children after they were born prematurely and their early lives were so worrisome. At night, however, Holly becomes Princess of Castle Waxing, where life is good until the Horrible Horde takes over one of her favorite picnic spots. All too soon, her nights are spent in warfare against the Horde, and her days in reading books on war strategy. And when she wins, she's not satisfied with winning, she must pursue more warfare against the Horde, even as her dragon Chancellor warns her of overspending and the consequences of war on her people.

Weinstein, Lauren
Girl stories; by Lauren R. Weinstein. Henry Holt 2006 237p il pa $16.95 *
Grades: 7 8 9 10 11 12 Adult   **741.5**
1. Graphic novels 2. Humorous graphic novels 3. Girls—Graphic novels 4. Friendship—Graphic novels
ISBN 978-0-8050-7863-3; 0-8050-7863-0
LC 2005-46205
"Smart, creative Lauren sheds her geeky rep in high school in Weinstein's collection of comic strips, which have to intimacy of a teen's diary. The color-washed sketches have an edgy quality." Booklist

Wood, Don, 1945-
Into the volcano; a graphic novel. Blue Sky Press 2008 174p il map $18.99 *
Grades: 2 3 4 5 6 7 8   **741.5**
1. Graphic novels 2. Brothers—Graphic novels 3. Adventure graphic novels
ISBN 978-0-439-72671-9; 0-439-72671-9
LC 2007-51084
While their parents are away doing research, brothers Duffy and Sumo Pugg go with their cousin, Mister Come-and-Go, to Kokalaha Island, where they meet Aunt Lulu and become trapped in an erupting volcano.
"The visual format combined with nonstop action will keep reluctant readers and adventure fans turning pages to the very end." Voice Youth Advocates

Yang, Gene
American born Chinese; color by Lark Pien. First Second 2006 233p il pa $16.95 *
Grades: 7 8 9 10 11 12   **741.5**
1. Graphic novels 2. Chinese Americans—Graphic novels
ISBN 978-1-59643-152-2; 1-59643-152-0 (pa)
LC 2005-58105
Michael L. Printz Award, 2007
In three interconnected stories, the reader meets the Monkey King, who wants to be more than he is, Jin Wang, a Chinese American middle school student who desperately wants to fit in at his new school, and Caucasian-looking Danny, who unaccountably has an extremely

stereotypically Chinese cousin, Chin-Kee, whose visit causes great embarrassment.
"True to its origin as a Web comic, this story's clear, concise lines and expert coloring are deceptively simple yet expressive. Even when Yang slips in an occasional Chinese ideogram or myth, the sentiments he's depicting need no translation. Yang accomplishes the remarkable feat of practicing what he preaches with this book: accept who you are and you'll already have reached out to others." Publ Wkly

Zornow, Jeff
The legend of Sleepy Hollow; adapted and illustrated by Jeff Zornow; based upon the works of Washington Irving. Magic Wagon 2007 unp il (Graphic horror) $18.95
Grades: 5 6 7 8 9 10 11 12   **741.5**
1. New York (State)—Graphic novels
ISBN 978-1-60270-060-4; 1-60270-060-5
LC 2007-9615
This "is an entertaining and faithful, if much adapted version of Irving's classic story. Zornow's illustrations are the highlight of the work, successfully bringing the characters of the story to life." Booklist

741.6   Graphic design, illustration, commercial art

Artist to artist; 23 major illustrators talk to children about their art. Philomel Books 2007 105p il $30 *
Grades: 4 5 6 7   **741.6**
1. Illustrators 2. Illustration of books 3. Picture books for children
ISBN 978-0-399-24600-5
"This anthology celebrates and elucidates contemporary picture-book art. . . . Ashley Bryan, Quentin Blake, Leo Lionni, Alice Provensen, and Gennady Spirin are among the contributors, whose comments are formatted as signed letters illustrated with childhood photographs. . . . Each artist includes glorious self-portraits and a gatefold page that reveals a marvelous array of sketches, color mixes, and studio scenes. All readers will find something that piques curiosity or provides insight." Booklist

Ellabbad, Mohieddine, 1940-
The illustrator's notebook; [translated from the Arabic by Sarah Quinn] Groundwood Books/House of Anansi Press 2006 30p il $16.95
Grades: 5 6 7 8   **741.6**
1. Illustrators 2. Illustration of books
ISBN 0-88899-700-0
"Part children's book, part autobiography, part design treatise, this hard-to-categorize Egyptian import is full of wonders from start to finish. Ellabbad uses excerpts from his notebooks to discuss ways of seeing art from an artist's perspective and as someone from an Arabic culture. Printed like the Egyptian edition—read right to left—the pages are magnificently and surprisingly illustrated, juxtaposing Arabic script (English translations appear in the margins), watercolor paintings, pasted-in photos and pictures from comic books, and all manner of characters from Eastern and Western cultures." SLJ

Marcus, Leonard S., 1950-
A Caldecott celebration; seven artists and their paths to the Caldecott medal. rev ed. Walker & Co. 2008 55p il $19.95; lib bdg $20.85
Grades: Professional   **741.6**
1. Caldecott Medal 2. Illustrators 3. Illustration of books
ISBN 978-0-8027-9703-2; 0-8027-9703-2; 978-0-8027-9704-9 (lib bdg); 0-8027-9704-0 (lib bdg)
LC 2007-23132
First published 1998
Profiles seven Caldecott award winning books and their authors, including Robert McCloskey's "Make Way for Ducklings," Marcia Brown's "Cinderella," Maurice Sendak's "Where the Wild Things Are," William Steig's "Sylvester and the Magic Pebble," Chris Van Allsburg's "Jumanji," David Wiesner's "Tuesday," and Mordicai Gerstein's "The Man Who Walked Between the Towers"
"The value of this volume is that Marcus makes these exceptional author/illustrators, and the processes by which they created their award-winning picture books, accessible to children and to adults who value children's literature." SLJ

741.9 Collections of drawings

—I never saw another butterfly—; children's drawings and poems from Terezin concentration camp, 1942-1944; edited by Hana Volavková; foreword by Chaim Potok; afterword by Vaclav Havel. expanded 2nd ed, by U.S. Holocaust Memorial Mus. Schocken Bks. 1993 xxii, 106p il pa $17.50 hardcover o.p.   **741.9**
1. Child artists 2. Children's writings 3. Terezin (Czechoslovakia: Concentration camp)
ISBN 0-8052-1015-6   LC 92-50477
Original Czech edition, 1959; first American edition published 1964 by McGraw-Hill
"Of the 15,000 children who passed through Terezin before going to Auschwitz, only 100 lived. This book is a collection of poems and drawings by some of them. . . . This touching book adds another facet to library collections on the Holocaust." SLJ

742 Perspective in drawing

DuBosque, Doug
Draw 3-D; a step-by-step guide to perspective drawing. Peel Productions 1999 63p il pa $8.99 *
Grades: 6 7 8 9 10   **742**
1. Perspective 2. Drawing
ISBN 0-939217-14-7   LC 98-42174
"Using easy-to-follow, step-by-step sketches, DuBosque introduces readers to the techniques of three-dimensional drawing. Beginning with such elementary concepts as depth, he progresses logically through shading, reflections, and multiple vanishing points. The supportive tone encourages novices to keep trying and not become discouraged." SLJ

743 Drawing and drawings by subject

Ames, Lee J., 1921-
[Draw 50 series] Doubleday 1974-2003 21v pa each $8.95
Grades: 4 5 6 7   **743**
1. Drawing
Available titles are: Draw 50 Airplanes, aircraft, and spacecraft; Draw 50 aliens; Draw 50 animal toons; Draw 50 animals; Draw 50 athletes; Draw 50 baby animals; Draw 50 beasties; Draw 50 birds; Draw 50 boats, ships, trucks, & trains; Draw 50 buildings and other structures; Draw 50 cats; Draw 50 dinosaurs and other prehistoric animals; Draw 50 dogs; Draw 50 endangered animals; Draw 50 famous faces; Draw 50 flowers, trees, and other plants; Draw 50 holiday decorations; Draw 50 horses; Draw 50 monsters; Draw 50 people; Draw 50 people from the Bible
Each volume presents step-by-step instructions for drawing a variety of animals, people, or objects

Dobrzycki, Michael
The art of drawing dragons; mythological beasts and fantasy creatures. Walter Foster 2007 143p il pa $19.95
Grades: 8 9 10 11 12   **743**
1. Drawing 2. Dragons 3. Mythical animals
ISBN 978-1-60058-012-3
This offers instructions for drawing dragons and other mythical creatures, describing supplies and techniques and 17 creatures from diverse cultures.
"This detailed and sophisticated title for serious artists will be a popular addition." SLJ

Masiello, Ralph
Ralph Masiello's ancient Egypt drawing book. Charlesbridge 2008 unp $16.95; pa $7.95
Grades: 4 5 6 7   **743**
1. Drawing 2. Egypt—Civilization
ISBN 978-1-57091-533-8; 978-1-57091-534-5 (pa)
LC 2007027023
"Masiello starts by showing readers how to draw the Great Pyramid of Khafre using simple shapes and lines. His easy-to-follow instructions gradually build in complexity, as he moves to ancient symbols, then Egyptian gods, Queen Nefertiti, and King Tutankhamen. The finished pictures are colored with mixed media. Concise paragraphs tell more about each subject, including historical context." Horn Book Guide
Includes bibliographical references

Ralph Masiello's dragon drawing book. Charlesbridge 2007 unp $16.95; pa $7.95
Grades: 4 5 6 7   **743**
1. Dragons 2. Drawing
ISBN 978-1-57091-531-4; 1-57091-531-8; 978-1-57091-532-1 (pa); 1-57091-532-6 (pa)
LC 2006021266
"Masiello introduces 11 traditional beasts and shows how to draw them. For each, he provides a series of de-

Masiello, Ralph—*Continued*
tailed drawings that build up to the finished pictures slowly, guiding young artists line by line. . . . Well designed and practical." Booklist

Miller, Steve
  Dinosaurs: how to draw thunder lizards and other prehistoric beasts; [by] Steve Miller. Watson-Guptill Publications 2008 144p il pa $19.95
Grades: 8 9 10 11 12 Adult   **743**
  1. Dinosaurs in art 2. Drawing
  ISBN 978-0-8230-9919-1 (pa); 0-8230-9919-9 (pa)
                            LC 2008531195
  First published 2005 with title: Thunder lizards; how to draw fantastic dinosaurs
  This offers instruction in drawing dinosaurs based on scientific research and includes examples of the work of such artists as Arthur Adams, Bryan Baugh, Brett Booth, Scott Harman, Gregory S. Paul, and Bernie Wrightson
  Includes bibliographical references

Peffer, Jessica, 1983-
  DragonArt; how to draw fantastic dragons and fantasy creatures. Impact Books 2005 127p il pa $19.99
Grades: 5 6 7 8   **743**
  1. Drawing 2. Dragons 3. Mythical animals
  ISBN 1-58180-657-4   LC 2005013013
  This is a guide to drawing dragons and other mythical beasts such as griffins, guardian gargoyles, and deadly basilisks.
  "This book has great writing and superb illustrations and manages to do everything right from the front cover to the index." SLJ

745   Decorative arts

Govenar, Alan B., 1952-
  Extraordinary ordinary people; five American masters of traditional arts. Candlewick Press 2006 85p il $22.99 *
Grades: 6 7 8 9   **745**
  1. Folk art 2. Handicraft
  ISBN 0-7636-2047-5   LC 2005-44864
  "The featured artists all live in the United States but come from a variety of cultural backgrounds. The art forms they practice include singing with the Bejing Opera, boat building, waxflower making, weaving, and performing at Mardi Gras. Govenar's interviews with them not only explore their art, but also their history. . . . High-quality color and black-and-white photographs appear throughout." SLJ
  Includes bibliographical references

Panchyk, Richard, 1970-
  American folk art for kids; with 21 activities. Chicago Review Press 2004 118p il $16.95
Grades: 4 5 6 7   **745**
  1. Handicraft 2. American folk art
  ISBN 1-55652-499-4   LC 2004-4879

"Panchyk begins with a general introduction to folk art, and then explicates the main categories of these traditional crafts. He covers a variety of decorative arts, including painting, fabric work, woodworking, and found objects. Each chapter contains several related projects ranging from reverse painting on glass to quilting, stenciling, and tin-can sculpture. . . . Many quality, full-color photos are included." SLJ
  Includes bibliographical references

745.2   Industrial art and design

Welsbacher, Anne, 1955-
  Earth-friendly design; by Anne Welsbacher. Lerner Publications Company 2009 72p il (Saving our living Earth) lib bdg $30.60
Grades: 5 6 7 8   **745.2**
  1. Industrial design 2. Environmental protection
  ISBN 978-0-8225-7564-1 (lib bdg); 0-8225-7564-7 (lib bdg)   LC 2007-35925
  "Provides a thorough, interesting discussion of multiple aspects of [Earth-friendly design], including historical origins, the current situation, and potential solutions. . . . Photos from around the world accompany discussions. . . . [This is a] solid choice to replace outdated books." SLJ
  Includes glossary and bibliographical references

745.5   Handicrafts

Bell-Rehwoldt, Sheri, 1962-
  The kids' guide to building cool stuff; by Sheri Bell-Rehwoldt. Capstone Press 2009 32p il (Kids' guides) lib bdg $23.99
Grades: 4 5 6 7   **745.5**
  1. Handicraft 2. Amusements 3. Science—Experiments
  ISBN 978-1-4296-2276-9 (lib bdg); 1-4296-2276-8 (lib bdg)   LC 2008-29687
  "Edge books"
  This provides instructions for building such items as a kite, a balloon rocket, a paper boat, a milk carton bird feeder, and a plastic plate hovercraft
  Includes glossary and bibliographical references

Bruder, Mikyla
  Button girl; more than 20 cute-as-a-button projects; photographs by Scott Nobles. Chronicle Books 2005 60p il spiral bdg $12.95
Grades: 5 6 7 8   **745.5**
  1. Handicraft 2. Buttons
  ISBN 0-8118-4553-2   LC 2004-8944
  This offers instructions for creating 20 accessories including Button Barrettes and Bobbies, Hip Ribbon Button Belts, Crazy Coasters, and more.

Cano-Murillo, Kathy

The crafty diva's lifestyle makeover; awesome ideas to spice up your life; by Kathy Cano Murillo; illustrated by Carrie Wheeler; photography by John Samora. Watson-Guptill Pub. 2005 144p il pa $12.95

Grades: 5 6 7 8   **745.5**

  1. Handicraft

  ISBN 0-8230-1008-2

"Chapters include Redo Your Room, Wake Up Your Workout, and Get a Passion for Fashion. Complete with media references, each chapter includes three crafts with instructions, a difficulty meter for each one, and a list of needed supplies. A picture of the finished item, more ideas, and illustrations of supplies and the more difficult steps are included. The result is [a] fun, imaginative book." SLJ

Check, Laura, 1958-

Create your own candles; 30 easy-to-make designs; illustrations by Norma Jean Martin-Jourdenais. Williamson Books 2004 62p il (Quick starts for kids!) pa $8.95

Grades: 5 6 7 8   **745.5**

  1. Candles

  ISBN 1-88559-352-X   LC 2004-40870

"Check begins this useful resource with 'Ten Hot Safety Tips.' . . . Next, she lists and describes basic equipment. . . . The projects range from simple beeswax candles to molded candles, hand-dipped candles, and gel candles." SLJ

Corwin, Judith Hoffman

Native American crafts of the Northeast and Southeast; by Judith Hoffman Corwin. Franklin Watts 2002 48p il map hardcover o.p. pa $7.95

Grades: 4 5 6 7   **745.5**

  1. Handicraft 2. Native Americans

  ISBN 0-531-12200-X (lib bdg); 0-531-15593-5 (pa)

                    LC 2002005301

Provides step-by-step instructions for craft projects based on traditional crafts of the Cherokee, Iroquois, Seminole, and other Native Americans of the Northeastern and Southeastern United States.

Crafty activities; over 50 fun and easy things to make; by Judy Balchin [et. al.] Search 2007 unp il pa $19.95

Grades: 4 5 6 7   **745.5**

  1. Handicraft

  ISBN 1-84448-250-2 (pa); 978-1-84448-250-4 (pa)

"The book is divided into six chapters—mosaics, printing, lettering, papier-mâché, handmade cards, and origami—with projects ranging from simple leaf prints to an elaborate necklace made from dried pasta. . . . The photos of smiling kids showing off their creations, the attractive, spacious page design, and, above all the ingenious projects will attract kids—as well as teachers." Booklist

Fox, Tom

Snowball launchers, giant-pumpkin growers, and other cool contraptions; [by] Tom Fox. Sterling Pub. 2006 127p il pa $9.95

Grades: 4 5 6 7   **745.5**

  1. Handicraft

  ISBN 978-0-8069-5515-5 (pa); 0-8069-5515-5 (pa)

                    LC 2005032781

"The 20 projects in this collection range from a simple 'Heartbeat Monitor' to a fairly complex 'Moth-Bot,' a wheeled vehicle that moves toward light with the flick of a switch. Most have strong kid appeal. . . . Instructions are written in an engaging, conversational tone, with background information about concepts such as gravity and electricity woven into the text." SLJ

Haab, Sherri, 1964-

Dangles and bangles; 25 funky accessories to make and wear; by Sherri Haab and Michelle Haab; with illustrations by Barbara Pollak. Watson-Guptill Pub. 2005 96p il pa $9.95

Grades: 5 6 7 8   **745.5**

  1. Jewelry 2. Handicraft

  ISBN 0-8230-0064-8

This describes "jewelry hardware, . . . tools, glues and adhesives, and . . . craft supplies, as well as ideas about where to purchase these materials. A spread on basic techniques explains how to work with cord and elastic, glue, rings/pins, etc. The projects . . . range from necklaces to key chains to hair accessories. . . . The mix of colorful photographs, full-page paintings of stylishly dressed youngsters, and varied typefaces makes for an attractive layout. Packed full of wonderful ideas, this irresistible title will be popular with young crafters as well as with adults who plan craft programs." SLJ

Hantman, Clea

I wanna re-do my room; illustrated by Azadeh Houshyar. 1st ed. Aladdin Paperbacks 2006 134p il pa $9.99

Grades: 7 8 9 10   **745.5**

  1. Handicraft 2. Interior design

  ISBN 0-689-87463-4   LC 2005006955

"Hantman gives pointers for decorating walls and making accessories. She describes stitches, pillow forms, felting, decoupage, making photo-adorned boxes, and more. There are plenty of artistic ideas for curtains, beds, pillows, furniture, and storage." SLJ

Martin, Laura C.

Nature's art box; from t-shirts to twig baskets: 65 cool projects for crafty kids to make with natural materials you can find anywhere; written by Laura C. Martin; with drawings by David Cain. Storey Bks. 2003 215p il $23.95; pa $16.95

Grades: 4 5 6 7   **745.5**

  1. Nature craft

  ISBN 1-58017-503-1; 1-58017-490-6 (pa)

                    LC 2002-154374

"Each chapter includes information about historical and ethnic uses for the natural substances. Activities are

Martin, Laura C.—*Continued*

rated by level of difficulty; all have easy-to-follow instructions. Projects range from baskets, picture frames, wreaths, necklaces, and gift wrap to body paint, amulet bags, and painted stones. . . . The projects display a respect for nature and art, and a simple, subtle beauty." SLJ

Includes bibliographical references

O'Donnell, Rosie

Rosie O'Donnell's crafty U; 100 easy projects the whole family can enjoy all year long. 1st Simon & Schuster hardcover ed. Simon & Schuster 2008 206p il $21.95

Grades: 3 4 5 6   745.5

1. Handicraft
ISBN 978-1-4165-5341-0; 1-4165-5341-X
LC 2007031249

"Projects include bunny piñatas for spring, tie-dye T-shirts for summer, creepy costumes for Halloween, very merry garlands for the holidays, Valentine's Day bouquets, and much more. Packed with practical advice, step-by-step instructions, and . . . full-color illustrations." Publisher's note
Includes bibliographical references

Ross, Kathy, 1948-

Earth-friendly crafts; clever ways to reuse everyday items; [by] Kathy Ross; illustrated by Celine Malepart. Millbrook Press 2009 48p il lib bdg $26.60

Grades: 3 4 5 6   745.5

1. Handicraft 2. Recycling
ISBN 978-0-8225-9099-6; 0-8225-9099-9
LC 2008025481

"This clear, colorful title offers a selection of environmentally focused projects that encourage kids to reduce, reuse, and recycle. Both practical and eye-catching, the projects, from pencil cups to decorative pins, rely on everyday discarded items that many kids will find around their homes. . . . [The crafts] are presented in line drawings that demonstrate the construction step by step along with color photos of the finished product." Booklist

Torres, Laura, 1967-

Best friends forever! 199 crafts to make and share. Workman Pub. 2004 148p il pa $13.95

Grades: 5 6 7 8   745.5

1. Handicraft
ISBN 0-7611-3274-0   LC 2004-45635

"These projects are organized into seven categories: 'Photo Fun,' 'Cool Notes,' 'Gifts to Make Together,' 'Home and School,' 'Fashions,' 'Fun and Games,' and 'Jewelry.' . . . Using clear language, detailed directions, and bright color photos of the finished products, Torres has pulled together a wealth of craft ideas." SLJ

Trottier, Maxine

Native crafts; inspired by North America's first peoples; illustrated by Esperanca Melo. Kids Can Press 2000 40p il (Kids can do it) pa $6.95

Grades: 4 5 6   745.5

1. Handicraft 2. Native Americans
ISBN 978-1-55074-549-8 (pa); 1-55074-549-2 (pa)

This book "has instructions for 16 projects including seed and bead jewelry, clay pinch pots, cornhusk dolls, turtle rattles, and hoop drums. Each activity begins with a brief description of how the object was utilized and by what group." SLJ

Warwick, Ellen

Everywear; written by Ellen Warwick; illustrated by Bernice Lum. Kids Can Press 2008 80p il (Planet girl) $14.95

Grades: 5 6 7 8   745.5

1. Handicraft 2. Dress accessories
ISBN 978-1-55337-799-3; 1-55337-799-0

"After several opening pages that introduce supplies, . . . very basic stitching skills, and terminology, girls turn to the . . . issue of hair: woven-ribbon bands, jazzed-up chopsticks; fabric-flower-bedecked combs; reversible ponytail wraps. Next come body adornments . . . followed by stuff to stow it in, of clutched, dangled, and toted varieties. Each project features a list of supplies, . . . clearly numbered steps with cartoon-styled illustrations . . . and full-color photograph of the finished item. . . . [This has] genuine sleepover appeal." Bull Cent Child Books

745.54   Paper handicrafts

Diehn, Gwen, 1943-

Making books that fly, fold, wrap, hide, pop up, twist, and turn; books for kids to make. Lark Bks. 1998 96p il hardcover o.p. pa $12.95 *

Grades: 4 5 6 7   745.54

1. Paper crafts 2. Handicraft
ISBN 1-57990-023-2; 978-1-57990-326-8 (pa);
1-57990-326-6 (pa)   LC 97-41037

Presents instructions for making various kinds of books including those that carry messages across space and time as well as those that save words, ideas, and pictures

"Clear directions and diagrams and attractive full-color photographs of completed projects will make it easy for readers to duplicate 18 different folded, wrapped, and pop-up books." Booklist
Includes glossary

Prins, M. D.

Paper galaxy; out-of-this-world projects to cut, fold, & paste; [by] M.D. Prins. Sterling Pub. 2005 128p il $19.95

Grades: 6 7 8 9   745.54

1. Paper crafts 2. Astronomy
ISBN 1-4027-2131-5   LC 2005049033

This "collection includes general instructions . . . and step-by-step detailed directions for 49 projects. The attractive layout combines text with excellent color photography and clear line drawings. The exciting projects include space trivia. . . . However, patience, perseverance, and skill are called for in these eye-catching paper delights—a thunderbolt, a trapezium, a sunburst, a meteorite, spiral nebula, a comet, a quasar, Sedna, Pollux, and more." SLJ

745.58 Handicrafts from beads, found and other objects

Boonyadhistarn, Thiranut
Beading; bracelets, barrettes, and beyond; by Thiranut Boonyadhistarn. Capstone Press 2007 32p il (Snap books) $25.26

Grades: 4 5 6 7 **745.58**
1. Beadwork
ISBN 978-0-7368-6472-5; 0-7368-6472-5
LC 2006004102

This describes how to create such bead crafts as safety-pin bracelets and bag charms.

"Girls will appreciate these ideas for recreating fashion trends and for achieving the artistic effects that they want. . . . Page layouts are lively and attractive. The projects use easily obtainable materials, and the directions are simple and well numbered." SLJ

Includes bibliographical references

745.592 Toys, models, miniatures, related objects

Collins, John M., 1960-
Fantastic flight; freestyle fold and fly paper airplanes. Ten Speed Press 2004 163p il $16.95

Grades: 5 6 7 8 **745.592**
1. Airplanes—Models 2. Paper crafts
ISBN 1-58008-577-6
LC 2005298895

This "explains how to craft 25 new and amazing flying machines—like the Looper, the BAT plane, and the Manta Ray—using just single sheets of paper." Publisher's note

The gliding flight; 20 excellent fold and fly paper airplanes. Ten Speed Press 2005 146p il $16.95

Grades: 5 6 7 8 **745.592**
1. Airplanes—Models 2. Paper crafts
ISBN 1-58008-726-4; 978-1-58008-726-1
LC 2005283501

Provides instructions to create a variety of paper airplanes

Cute dolls; by Aranzi Aronzo! Vertical Inc. 2007 79p il (Let's make cute stuff) pa $14.95

Grades: 6 7 8 9 10 **745.592**
1. Dolls 2. Handicraft
ISBN 978-1-932234-78-7 (pa); 1-932234-78-0 (pa)
Original Japanese edition 2002

"Familiarity with Japan's Aranzi Aronzo brand . . . won't be necessary to muster an audience for this doll-making book. The felt-trimmed, jersey-cloth, self-consciously cute 'mascots' will be an instant draw for manga-loving teens. . . . Those who attempt one of the 21 rag dolls, for which a sewing machine is recommended, will find the techniques well explained, as well as supported by and entertainingly extended by photographs and small cartoon representations of the doll characters." Booklist

Harbo, Christopher L.
The kids' guide to paper airplanes. Capstone Press 2009 32p il (Kids' guides) $23.93

Grades: 4 5 6 7 **745.592**
1. Airplanes—Models 2. Paper crafts
ISBN 978-1-4296-2274-5; 1-4296-2274-1
LC 2008029688

"Edge books"

"Provides instructions and diagrams for making a variety of traditional paper airplanes." Publisher's note

"Using colorful, vivid, and clear step-by-step illustrations, Harbo demonstrates how to construct everything from the classic Dart to the circular Space Ring to the 18-step Silent Huntress." Booklist

Includes glossary and bibliographical references

Rigsby, Mike
Amazing rubber band cars; easy-to-build wind-up racers, models, and toys; [by] Mike Rigsby. Chicago Review Press 2007 121p il lib bdg $12.95

Grades: 4 5 6 7 **745.592**
1. Automobiles—Models 2. Toys 3. Handicraft
ISBN 978-1-55652-736-4 (lib bdg); 1-55652-736-5 (lib bdg)
LC 2007013969

This offers instructions for making toy and model cars "using mostly cardboard, glue, pencils, rubber bands, and a few other easily obtainable materials. . . . Readers will learn about corrugated and flat cardboard, and how to use glue and work with templates. Excellent instructions are accompanied by black-and-white photos every step of the way. . . . These projects are fun to construct, and inquisitive minds will be fascinated by the moving cars." SLJ

745.593 Useful objects

Hennessy, Alena, 1977-
Alter this! radical ideas for transforming books into art. Lark Books 2007 96p il $14.95

Grades: 8 9 10 11 12 **745.593**
1. Handicraft 2. Books
ISBN 1-57990-948-5
LC 2006-34669

"Hennessy offers 39 ways in which books can be scribbled in, sliced up, and otherwise transformed into vehicles for creative expression. Diverse objects, contributed by numerous artists, are shown in sharp, color photos." Booklist

Includes bibliographical references

745.594 Decorative objects

Baker, Diane, 1951-
Jazzy jewelry; power beads, crystals, chokers, and illusion and tattoo styles; [by] Diane Baker; illustrations by alexander Michaels. Williamson Pub. 2000 144p il (A Williamson kids can! book) pa $12.95

Grades: 5 6 7 8 **745.594**
1. Beadwork
ISBN 1-88559-347-3
LC 00-43712

Baker, Diane, 1951——Continued

This offers "ideas for crafters with excellent hand-eye coordination and manual dexterity, illustrated with black-and-white line drawings. Projects include fringed bobby pins, a seed-bead lattice ring, a lattice choker with dangles, hair sparklers, a butterfly hair dangler, crystal and pearl headbands, and other exotic offerings. . . . It is for dedicated bead enthusiasts." SLJ

Newcomb, Rain

The Girls' World book of jewelry: 50 cool designs to make. Lark Books 2004 127p il pa $14.95

Grades: 5 6 7 8   745.594
1. Jewelry 2. Handicraft
ISBN 1-57990-473-4   LC 2004-4990

This offers instructions for jewelry making projects such as bracelets made of copper washers or from old wooden game pieces, or chokers made from small metal flower embellishments to a ribbon.

"This exciting collection contains clear directions, sharp photos, and precise illustrations." SLJ

745.6 Calligraphy, heraldic design, illumination

Winters, Eleanor

1 2 3 calligraphy! letters and projects for beginners and beyond. Sterling Pub. Co. 2006 128p il $14.95

Grades: 4 5 6 7   745.6
1. Calligraphy
ISBN 1-4027-1839-X; 978-1-4027-1839-7
LC 2005022071

"Twenty well-written, easy-to-follow explanatory chapters are filled with plenty of practical exercises. Chapters are grouped into three parts with the first reviewing calligraphy basics, vocabulary, and types of writing instruments. The second part teaches italic, swing gothic, and modern gothic alphabets. Finally, creative projects such as stationery, envelopes, signs, and 'calligrams' are described." SLJ

Calligraphy for kids. Sterling Pub. Co. 2004 128p il $14.95 *

Grades: 6 7 8 9   745.6
1. Calligraphy
ISBN 1-4027-0664-2   LC 2003-23438

This "guide to calligraphy begins with a survey of materials, a glossary, and suggestions on posture and pen and paper positions. Succinct chapters showing how to create a variety of alphabets follow. Winters . . . folds fascinating history into her expert instructions. Her clean layouts showcase beautifully rendered examples and practical exercises." Booklist

746 Textile arts

Warwick, Ellen

Injeanuity; written by Ellen Warwick; illustrated by Bernice Lum. Kids Can Press 2006 80p il (Planet girl) spiral bdg $12.95

Grades: 5 6 7 8   746
1. Sewing 2. Handicraft
ISBN 978-1-55337-681-1 (spiral bdg); 1-55337-681-1 (spiral bdg)

"Warwick combines a love of denim with some simple crafts that will have readers thinking and feeling like fashion designers. . . . [The book] includes 17 projects from re-wearable jeans to purses and wallets to bolsters and footstools to halters and skirts and more. All include clear, easy-to-follow instructions and informative illustrations." SLJ

746.41 Weaving, braiding, matting unaltered vegetable fibers

Swett, Sarah

Kids weaving; [by] Sarah Swett; photographs by Chris Hartlove; illustrations by Lena Corwin. Stewart, Tabori & Chang 2005 128p il $19.95

Grades: 4 5 6 7   746.41
1. Weaving
ISBN 1-58479-467-4   LC 2005000650

"Swett introduces this craft with a simple weaving of a checkerboard note card—a task requiring two pieces of paper and a pair of scissors. After mastering the technique with several different small projects, she explains how to weave a hideout out of sticks and vines in the yard. She demonstrates techniques on a cardboard loom and progresses to skills for weaving on a pipe loom. These projects show the whimsical and the practical, the useful and the decorative aspects of the art. Hartlove's excellent-quality, full-color photos depict children enjoying the craft in many different settings. . . . In addition, the helpful step-by-step drawings clearly depict the processes and techniques." SLJ

Includes bibliographical references

746.43 Knitting, crocheting, tatting

Bradberry, Sarah

Kids knit! simple steps to nifty projects; [by] Sarah Bradberry. Sterling Pub. Co. 2004 96p il hardcover o.p. pa $9.95 *

Grades: 5 6 7 8   746.43
1. Knitting
ISBN 0-8069-7733-7; 978-1-4027-4057-2 (pa); 1-4027-4057-3 (pa)   LC 2004-19375

Presents basic knitting techniques and instructions for making a backpack, pillow, doll, and other simple projects

This "book works equally well for beginners and experienced knitters. . . . Besides the requisite information on knitting and purling, there are invaluable tips about

Bradberry, Sarah—*Continued*
finishing garments, fixing mistakes, and adding embellishments. The projects have been chosen with an eye toward simplicity, yet they have real appeal." Booklist

Clewer, Carolyn
Kids can knit; fun and easy projects for your small knitter. Barron's 2003 128p il pa $16.95
Grades: 4 5 6 7   746.43
1. Knitting
ISBN 0-7641-2718-7
"A Quarto book"
This "book begins by discussing types of yarn, needles, and other knitting equipment. The author explains the basic techniques of finger knitting and spool knitting, casting on, knit and purl stitches, combining stitches to create patterns, increasing and decreasing, binding off, and picking up dropped stitches. Instructions on how to make pompoms, fringes, and braiding are also provided. The 16 eye-catching projects are arranged in an orderly progression of difficulty. . . . [This is a] useful and attractive resource." SLJ

Davis, Jane
Crochet; fantastic jewelry, hats, purses, pillows & more. Lark Books 2005 112p il (Kids' crafts) $19.95; pa $9.95 *
Grades: 5 6 7 8   746.43
1. Crocheting
ISBN 1-57990-477-7; 978-1-60059-138-9 (pa); 1-60059-138-8 (pa)   LC 2004-13288
This describes basic crochet techniques and includes instructions for 50 projects.
"The book is a pleasure to look at. . . . Photographs are large and crisp. . . . Davis clearly knows what kids like. . . . Both visual and text explanations are very clear. . . . This is a must for your craft shelves." Booklist

Haden, Christen
Creepy cute crochet; zombies, ninjas, robots, and more! Quirk Books 96p il $14.95
Grades: 7 8 9 10 11 12 Adult   746.43
1. Crocheting 2. Toys
ISBN 978-1-5947-4232-3; 1-5947-42324-
"Japanese-inspired *amigurumi* (literal translation: 'knitted stuffed toy') is one of the latest crafting crazes, and Haden's first book puts a unique spin on *amigurumi* by focusing on the creepy side of crocheted creatures. . . . There are . . . crocheted ninjas, a Grim Reaper, Day of the Dead figures, and vampires, all lovingly rendered. Although some beginner information is provided, a basic knowledge of crochet stitches and techniques is assumed." Libr J

Ogawa, Narumi
Mr. Funky's super crochet wonderful. North Light Books 2007 111p il pa $16.99
Grades: 7 8 9 10   746.43
1. Crocheting
ISBN 978-1-5818-0966-4; 1-5818-0966-2
LC 2006038689

This book "features 30 projects including stuffed animals (amirgurumi) and wearable accessories such as scarves, hats, crochet flowers, headbands, a water bottle carrier, fun kids stuff and more." Publisher's note

Okey, Shannon
Knitgrrl; learn to knit with 15 fun and funky projects; photography by Shannon Fagan, Christine Okey, and Tamas Jakab; illustrations by Kathleen Jacques. Watson-Guptill 2005 96p il pa $9.95 *
Grades: 7 8 9 10   746.43
1. Knitting
ISBN 0-8230-2618-3
This offers instructions for basic knitting techniques and for such projects as scarves, hats, leg warmers, mittens, and bags.
"A lively, teen-friendly book with all the basics, plenty of additional information, and appealing color photos and illustrations." SLJ

Knitgrrl 2; learn to knit with 16 all-new patterns; photography by Shannon Fagan, Christine Okey, and Tamas Jakab; Illustrations by Kathleen Jacques. Watson-Guptill 2006 96p il pa $9.95 *
Grades: 7 8 9 10   746.43
1. Knitting
ISBN 0-8230-2619-1
This offers instructions for basic knitting techniques and for projects including flipflops, book covers, a jacket collar, a headband/choker, a pencil purse, a water-bottle holder, a beauty-to-go bag, a belt, a kerchief, a cardigan, a scarf, a necklace, wrist/ankle bracelets, a poncho, a tank top, and a beach bag.
"Varied typeface and print color as well as a mix of excellent color photography and illustrations make this book fun to read and explore. Clear, step-by-step directions are extremely helpful for learning the basics." SLJ

Rimoli, Ana Paula, 1976-
Amigurumi world; seriously cute crochet. Martingale & Co. 2008 80p il $18.95
Grades: 7 8 9 10 11 12 Adult   746.43
1. Crocheting 2. Toys
ISBN 978-1-5647-7847-5; 1-5647-7847-9
LC 2007041240
This offers instructions for crocheting toy animals such as baby monkeys, bears, owls, hedgehogs, and elephants.

Ronci, Kelli
Kids crochet; projects for kids of all ages; photographs by John Gruen; illustrations by Lena Corwin. Stewart, Tabori & Chang 2005 128p il $19.95
Grades: 4 5 6 7   746.43
1. Crocheting
ISBN 1-58479-413-5   LC 2004-17477
This offers instructions for "15 projects. All aspects of crocheting are covered. . . . Handcrafted items include a neck cozy, tool pouch, friendship cuffs, patchwork poncho, triangle-square quilt and pillow, and critter cush-

Ronci, Kelli—_Continued_
ions." SLJ

This "has projects that kids will really enjoy making.
. . . What will especially entice children are the sharply
reproduced color photographs. . . . Also excellent are
the attractive drawings." Booklist

Snow, Tamie

Tiny yarn animals; amigurumi friends to make
and enjoy; [by] Tamie Snow; photography by
Nicholas Noyes. Home 2008 61p il $12.95

Grades: 8 9 10 11 12 Adult   746.43
1. Crocheting 2. Toys
ISBN 978-1-55788-530-2; 1-55788-530-3
LC 2008-013935

This is a "book of crocheted animal patterns. The 20
toys in the collection range from the expected (pig, lamb,
and mouse) to the quirky (beaver, lemur, and hedgehog)
and they are all cheery, colorful, and cute. A beginners'
tutorial provides full-color photographic illustrations of
basic crochet stitches, and the directions are clear enough
for first-time crocheters to understand." Libr J

Turner, Sharon, 1962-
Find your style and knit it too; by Sharon
Turner. Wiley 2007 165p il pa $14.99

Grades: 6 7 8 9   746.43
1. Knitting
ISBN 978-0-470-13987-5 (pa); 0-470-13987-0 (pa)
LC 2007028419

This is a "full-service knit book for teens and preteens. . . . The book works on every level. Beginning
with knitting basics, Turner explains everything from
choosing materials to fundamental how-tos . . . to fixing
mistakes. . . . [This offers] easy-to-follow patterns, each
illustrated by a crisp color photograph." Booklist

Werker, Kim P.

Get hooked; simple steps to crochet cool stuff;
by Kim Werker; photography by Angela Fama and
Pamela Bethel; illustrations by Cynthia Frenette.
Watson-Guptill Pub. 2006 96p il $11.95 *

Grades: 6 7 8 9 10   746.43
1. Crocheting
ISBN 0-8230-5092-0

This "offers 15 patterns that will appeal to those new
to crochet. Most of the projects are simple belts, scarves,
pillows, and tiny bags. . . . Crotchet basics are shown
primarily in helpful color photographs . . . and the book
touches on subjects that such books sometimes miss:
yarn weight, edging, and custom fitting. The pop-art
graphics are very cool." Booklist
Includes bibliographical references

Get hooked again; simple steps to crochet more
cool stuff; by Kim Werker; photography by
Angela Fama and Pamela Bethel; illustrations by
Cynthia Frenette. Watson-Guptill Pub. 2007 96p il
pa $11.95 *

Grades: 6 7 8 9 10   746.43

1. Crocheting
ISBN 0-8230-5110-2 (pa); 978-0-8230-5110-6 (pa)

This book about crocheting offers "lots of solid information; clear, crisp photographs; and . . . appealing
projects. . . . The book covers crochet basics in a conversational tone that will keep readers engaged. The
easy-to-follow text and the excellent photos do a great
job of helping kids handle the crochet hook." Booklist
Includes bibliographical references

746.9 Textile products and fashion design

McAlpine, Margaret
Working in the fashion industry; [by] Margaret
McAlpine. Gareth Stevens Pub. 2006 64p il (My
future career) lib bdg $26

Grades: 6 7 8 9   746.9
1. Clothing industry 2. Vocational guidance
ISBN 0-8368-4774-1   LC 2005042524

This describes seven careers in the fashion industry.

This is "well organized, full of beautiful photography,
and [presents] honest snapshots of the featured professions. . . . Attractive, informative, and interesting." SLJ
Includes bibliographical references

747 Interior decoration

Weaver, Janice
It's your room; a decorating guide for real kids;
[by] Janice Weaver and Frieda Wishinsky;
illustrated by Claudia Dávila. Tundra Books 2006
63p il pa $14.95 *

Grades: 5 6 7 8   747
1. Interior design
ISBN 0-88776-711-7

"Budding interior designers and readers who want to
personalize their rooms will appreciate this title. It is
filled with step-by-step guidelines for creating a budget,
selecting paint colors and fabrics, organizing closets and
desks, laying everything out, and adding finishing touches. The illustrations will be a hit with first-time decora-
tors just starting to develop their own color sense." SLJ

748.2 Glassware

Emert, Phyllis Raybin
Art in glass. Lucent Books 2007 112p il map
(Eye on art) $32.45

Grades: 7 8 9 10 11 12   748.2
1. Glassware
ISBN 978-1-59018-983-2; 1-59018-983-3
LC 2007-10118

This is an introduction to the history of glassmaking,
including its ancient origins, Roman glass, Middle Eastern and Venetian glass, European and American glass,
and contemporary glass.

This "title is thoroughly researched and fully refer-

Emert, Phyllis Raybin—*Continued*

enced, and contains quotations from artists and art historians. The writing is generally clear and fluid. . . . Many of the pages have good-quality photos of artwork and artists." SLJ

Includes bibliographical references

750 Painting

Raczka, Bob

Unlikely pairs; fun with famous works of art; [by] Bob Raczka. Millbrook Press 2006 31p il lib bdg $23.93; pa $9.95

Grades: 4 5 6 7   **750**

1. Art appreciation 2. Painting

ISBN 0-7613-2936-6 (lib bdg); 0-7613-2378-3 (pa)

LC 2003-14078

Invites the reader to discover fourteen funny stories produced by pairing twenty-eight paintings from different eras and styles.

"Raczka deserves an A+ for cleverness. . . . Rodin's *The Thinker* is juxtaposed with Klee's modernistic painting of a chessboard so that the statue looks as if it is contemplating the next move. Siméon-Chardin's picture of a boy blowing soap bubbles seems to be creating Kandinsky's *Several Circles*. Each selection takes up a page and is reproduced in crisp color. . . . This book is an amusing way to introduce children to famous works of art." SLJ

750.1 Painting—Philosophy and theory

Sturgis, Alexander

Optical illusions in art. Sterling 1996 32p il hardcover o.p. pa $5.95 *

Grades: 4 5 6 7   **750.1**

1. Art appreciation 2. Optical illusions

ISBN 0-8069-6135-X; 1-4027-0650-2 (pa)

LC 95-46740

This volume includes "chapters on trompe l'oeil, surrealism, perspective, anamorphosis (distortions corrected by use of mirrors or acute viewing angles), reversible images and op art." Publ Wkly

751.4 Painting—Techniques and procedures

Self, Caroline, 1919-

Chinese brush painting; [by] Caroline Self and Susan Self. 1st ed. Tuttle 2007 64p il $16.95

Grades: 7 8 9 10 11 12   **751.4**

1. Ink painting 2. Chinese painting 3. Calligraphy

ISBN 978-0-8048-3877-1; 0-8048-3877-1

LC 2006037838

This "introduces readers to the art of Chinese calligraphy and brush painting. The text is fluid and graceful . . . and the authors wrap succinct accounts of Chinese history and lore around their clear, step-by-step, illustrated instructions." Booklist

Includes bibliographical references

759 Painting—Historical, geographic, persons, treatment

D'Harcourt, Claire, 1960-

Masterpieces up close; by Claire d'Harcourt. Chronicle Books 2006 63p il $22.95 *

Grades: 4 5 6 7   **759**

1. Painting 2. Art appreciation

ISBN 0-8118-5403-5   LC 2004-16341

"Western painting from the 14th to 20th centuries. Over 100 details to find."— jacket

"From Giotto to Warhol, d'Harcourt selects some of the most famous icons of Western art for a closer look. . . . The format of this oversize volume [consists of] boldly colored spreads featuring a central, large image surrounded by smaller details from it. Interesting tidbits and questions accompany each small picture, inviting viewers to wonder, think, and question what they see. . . . The last pages include lift-the-flap copies of the paintings and biographical sketches of the artists. A visually striking volume for browsers and art education." SLJ

759.05 Painting—1800-1899

Bingham, Jane

Impressionism. Heinemann Library 2008 48p il (Art on the wall) lib bdg $32.86

Grades: 5 6 7 8 9 10   **759.05**

1. Impressionism (Art) 2. French painting

ISBN 978-1-4329-1371-7; 1-4329-1371-9

LC 2008020468

This "discusses how and why the Impressionist movement began, looks at how the Impressionists captured the changing effects of light and color in nature, and examines the different subjects Impressionist artists chose for their paintings." Publisher's note

This title succeeds "in presenting a bird's-eye view of [Impressionism] without oversimplification. Information on individual artists is included in the broader context of the movement. Visually exciting, with plenty of color, [the layout is] hip and should appeal to the target audience." SLJ

Includes glossary and bibliographical references

Post-Impressionism. Heinemann Library 2009 48p il (Art on the wall) lib bdg $32.86

Grades: 5 6 7 8 9 10   **759.05**

1. Postimpressionism (Art) 2. French painting

ISBN 978-1-4329-1369-4; 1-4329-1369-7

LC 2008020464

This "discusses how Post-Impressstonism developed, examines the distinctive styles of individual Post-Impressionist artists, and looks at how the Post-Impressionists used colour, shape, and composition." Publisher's note

This title succeeds "in presenting a bird's-eye view of [Post-Impressionism] without oversimplification. Information on individual artists is included in the broader context of the movement. Visually exciting, with plenty of color, [the layout is] hip and should appeal to the target audience." SLJ

Includes glossary and bibliographical references

Sabbeth, Carol, 1957-
Monet and the impressionists for kids; their lives and ideas, 21 activities. Chicago Review Press 2002 140p il pa $17.95 *
Grades: 5 6 7 8   759.05
1. Impressionism (Art) 2. Art appreciation
ISBN 1-55652-397-1   LC 2001-47191
Discusses the nineteenth-century French art movement known as Impressionism, focusing on the works of Monet, Renoir, Degas, Cassatt, Cezanne, Gauguin, and Seurat
"A beautifully designed introduction to Impressionism. . . . Sabbeth also includes 21 appealing extension activities such as recipes, crafts, games, and writing suggestions. Quality color reproductions on glossy pages, and varied, attractive layouts add to the book." SLJ
Includes glossary and bibliographical references

759.13 American painting

Lawrence, Jacob, 1917-2000
The great migration; an American story; paintings by Jacob Lawrence; with a poem in appreciation by Walter Dean Myers. HarperCollins Pubs. 1993 unp il hardcover o.p. pa $8.99
Grades: 4 5 6 7   759.13
1. African Americans in art
ISBN 0-06-443428-1; 0-06-023037-1 (pa)
LC 93-16788
Published by The Museum of Modern Art, The Phillips Collection, and HarperCollins Pubs.
"A noted African-American artist chronicles the 1916-1919 migration of blacks from the South through a sequence of 60 paintings and accompanying narrative captions." SLJ
"Lawrence is a storyteller with words as well as pictures: his captions and his own 1992 introduction to this book are the best commentary on his work." Booklist

759.5 Italian painting

Barter, James, 1946-
A Renaissance painter's studio; by James E. Barter. Lucent Bks. 2003 112p il (Working life) lib bdg $21.96
Grades: 6 7 8 9   759.5
1. Artists, Italian 2. Italian painting 3. Renaissance
ISBN 1-59018-178-6   LC 2002-7892
Describes the arduous training and difficult day-to-day working lives of painters in Florence during the Renaissance and discusses how their changing approach to the art they created elevated their standing and influence in Florentine society
"Barter gives readers a fascinating glimpse . . . into the lives and work of the artists of Florence." SLJ
Includes bibliographical references

761 Relief processes (Block printing)

Boonyadhistarn, Thiranut
Stamping art; imprint your designs; by Thiranut Boonyadhistarn. Capstone Press 2007 31p il $25.26
Grades: 4 5 6 7   761
1. Rubber stamp printing
ISBN 978-0-7368-6477-0; 0-7368-6477-6
LC 2006004077
This "describes how to make stamps from common household objects, create 'embossed' cards, make a 'stained glass' lampshade, and more." SLJ
Includes bibliographical references

769.56 Postage stamps and related devices

Postal Service guide to U.S. stamps. U.S. Postal Service il pa $25
Grades: 8 9 10 11 12 Adult   769.56
1. Postage stamps—Catalogs 2. Reference books
First published 1974 with title: United States stamps and stories. Revised annually
Contains reproductions and histories of U.S. postage stamps

Scott standard postage stamp catalogue. Scott Pub. Co. (Sidney) 4v il ea $57.99
Grades: 8 9 10 11 12 Adult   769.56
1. Postage stamps—Catalogs 2. Reference books
Annual. First published 1868. Title, publisher's name and number of volumes vary
"Gives minute details, such as date of issue, design, denomination, color, perforation, and watermark, on all the stamps of the world. Most of the stamps are given a valuation." Ref Sources for Small & Medium-sized Libr. 5th edition

770 Photography & computer art

Kallen, Stuart A., 1955-
Photography. Lucent Books 2007 112p il (Eye on art) $32.45
Grades: 7 8 9 10 11 12   770
1. Photography—History
ISBN 978-1-59018-986-3   LC 2007015978
"This volume surveys the history of photography, from the ancient camera obscura to the digital camera. . . . This title offers a clear overview of an art form that many teens both practice and appreciate." Booklist
Includes bibliographical references

770.9 Photography—Historical, geographic, persons, treatment

Sandler, Martin W.
America through the lens; photographers who changed the nation. Henry Holt and Co. 2005 182p il $19.95 *
Grades: 6 7 8 9   **770.9**
1. Photographers 2. Photography
ISBN 0-8050-7367-1
This is a "collective biography of influential photographers whose work made a lasting impact on American society and the world. The chapter-length profiles begin with Civil War photographer Matthew Brady and move forward through sections on Jacob Riis, Edward Curtis, and James Van der Zee, among others. The final chapter celebrates NASA's photographs of space." Booklist
"The photographs are stunning." SLJ
Includes bibliographical references

771 Photography—Techniques, procedures, apparatus, equipment, materials

Stefoff, Rebecca, 1951-
The camera; [by] Rebecca Stefoff. Marshall Cavendish Benchmark 2007 c2008 143p il (Great inventions) lib bdg $27.95
Grades: 6 7 8 9   **771**
1. Photography—History
ISBN 978-0-7614-2596-0   LC 2007002897
"An exploration of the origin, development, and societal impact of the camera." Publisher's note
Includes glossary and bibliographical references

775 Digital photography

Bidner, Jenni
The kids' guide to digital photography; how to shoot, save, play with & print your digital photos. Lark Books 2004 96p il $14.95; pa $9.95 *
Grades: 5 6 7 8   **775**
1. Digital photography
ISBN 1-57990-604-4; 1-57990-643-5 (pa)
     LC 2004-14465
"Beginning chapters address basics, including understanding camera features, using focus and flash functions, capturing motion, and so on. Bidner then delves into picture-editing software and even how to set up a Web site. . . . Final sections offer ideas for projects. . . . Bidner introduces sophisticated technical material in enthusiastic language that is kid-friendly without being condescending." Booklist
Includes glossary

776 Computer art (Digital art)

Miller, Ron, 1947-
Digital art; painting with pixels. Twenty-First Century Books 2008 120p il lib bdg $31.93
Grades: 6 7 8 9 10   **776**
1. Digital art 2. Computer art
ISBN 978-0-8225-7516-0; 0-8225-7516-7
     LC 2007-27633
"What is digital art? Where did it come from? Is it even art at all? Ron Miller answers these questions and more." Publisher's note
"Web sites to visit, a glossary and discussions of digital art software add significantly to the book's usefulness." Voice Youth Advocates
Includes glossary and bibliographical references

778.5 Cinematography, video production, related activities

Lockman, Darcy
Computer animation. Benchmark Bks. (Tarrytown) 2001 48p il (Kaleidoscope) lib bdg $25.64 *
Grades: 4 5 6 7   **778.5**
1. Animation (Cinematography)
ISBN 0-7614-1048-1   LC 99-58310
Explains how computer animation is used to make entire films, indicates how it differs from traditional animation, and includes information on the development of the technology
Includes bibliographical references

Miller, Ron, 1947-
Special effects; an introduction to movie magic; [by] Ron Miller. Twenty-first Century Books 2006 128p il lib bdg $26.60 *
Grades: 7 8 9 10   **778.5**
1. Cinematography
ISBN 978-0-7613-2918-3 (lib bdg); 0-7613-2918-8 (lib bdg)   LC 2005013123
"The history and techniques of film, from the beginning of cinema to the current digital era, are explained." SLJ
"An excellent mix of photographs, including stills of special-effects triumphs ranging from the original *King Kong* to *The Matrix* and closeups of experts at work, will easily pull browsers and researchers alike to this comprehensive title." Booklist
Includes bibliographical references

Shaner, Peter A.
Digital filmmaking for teens; [by] Pete Shaner and Gerald Everett Jones. Thomson Course Technology Professional Trade Reference 2005 237p il $24.99 *
Grades: 7 8 9 10   **778.5**
1. Cinematography 2. Video recording
ISBN 1-59200-603-5   LC 2004-114416

Shaner, Peter A.—*Continued*

"The highlight of this guide is the DVD included in the package with which one can watch some films made by teens in a workshop in New York. . . . Only 2 of the 10 chapters are specifically about shooting the film. The other sections describe equipment, storyboarding, lighting, planning, editing, adding music, and releasing the film. . . . The instructions and suggestions are meticulously documented and easy to follow. This book . . . could serve as a superb guide for filmmaking at home or as a text for a class." SLJ

Includes bibliographical references

778.59   Video production

Shulman, Mark, 1962-

Attack of the killer video book; tips and tricks for young directors; by Mark Shulman and Hazlitt Krog; art by Martha Newbigging. Annick Press 2004 64p il $24.95; pa $12.95 *

Grades: 5 6 7 8   **778.59**

1. Video recording

ISBN 1-55037-841-4; 1-55037-840-6 (pa)

This "guide explores every stage of video production, from brainstorming, to organizing a shoot, to finally piecing it all together." Publisher's note

"This lighthearted primer uses lots of humor and colorful, cartoon-style illustrations. . . . A good choice for collections in need of an updated video-production guide that won't become dated too quickly." SLJ

779   Photographs

Delannoy, Isabelle

Our living Earth; a story of people, ecology, and preservation; by Isabelle Delannoy; photographs by Yann Arthus-Bertrand. Harry N. Abrams 2008 157p il $24.95 *

Grades: 5 6 7 8   **779**

1. Aerial photography 2. Human geography

ISBN 978-0-8109-7132-5; 0-8109-7132-1

LC 2008010324

Published in association with the Field Museum

"Wrapped around Arthus-Bertrand's magnificent aerial photographs from around the world, Delannoy's text is organized thematically, covering fresh water, biodiversity, oceans, land, cities, people, food, and climate. . . . Readers will find surprising information and images to ponder. Almost every page supports the overarching theme that social justice and environmental protection are inextricably related. . . . This volume raises awareness, and the striking images, astonishing statistics, and brief explanations will stimulate readers to investigate further and possibly to take action." SLJ

780   Music

Ardley, Neil, 1937-

A young person's guide to music; with music by Poul Ruders. DK Pub. 2004 80p il $24.99 *

Grades: 5 6 7 8   **780**

1. Music 2. Orchestra

ISBN 0-7566-0549-7

A reissue of the title first published 1995

"In association with the BBC Symphony Orchestra conducted by Andrew Davis." Title page

This "interactive guide to the orchestra is a combination of book and compact disk. The CD features a new work by the Dutch composer Poul Ruder. . . . The text itself has facts on the orchestra as a whole, the conductor, composer, and each instrument. . . . A history section features a timeline, names of musicians and composers, definitions of musical forms with examples, and a glossary." SLJ

"A rich resource for young people who want to understand orchestral music." Booklist

McAlpine, Margaret

Working in music and dance; [by] Margaret McAlpine. Gareth Stevens Pub. 2006 54p il (My future career) lib bdg $26

Grades: 6 7 8 9   **780**

1. Music 2. Dance 3. Vocational guidance

ISBN 0-8368-4777-6   LC 2005042522

Contents: Dancer; Disc jockey; Instrument maker; Music teacher; Musician Promoter/Manager; Recording engineer

This is "well organized, full of beautiful photography, and [presents] honest snapshots of the featured professions. . . . Attractive, informative, and interesting." SLJ

Includes bibliographical references

Nathan, Amy

Meet the musicians; from prodigy (or not) to pro. 1st ed. Henry Holt and Co. 2006 168p il $17.95

Grades: 5 6 7 8   **780**

1. Musicians 2. Music

ISBN 978-0-8050-7743-8; 0-8050-7743-X

LC 2005026508

The author "interviewed 13 of the New York Philharmonic's members, representing 11 different instruments, and spun their articulate comments into brief, readable profiles, supplemented by various sidebars—among them, an invaluable feature outlining pros and cons of individual instruments. . . . The practical advice mixed with inspirational words strikes just the right note for children at many different stages in their musical education." Booklist

Includes bibliographical references

780.3   Music—Encyclopedias and dictionaries

Kennedy, Michael, 1926-

The concise Oxford dictionary of music; [by] Michael Kennedy and Joyce Bourne Kennedy. 5th ed. Oxford University Press 2007 839p il (Oxford paperback reference) pa $17.99

Grades: 8 9 10 11 12 Adult   **780.3**

1. Music—Dictionaries 2. Musicians—Dictionaries 3. Reference books

ISBN 978-0-19-920383-3 (pa); 0-19-920383-0 (pa)

LC 2007008461

Kennedy, Michael, 1926-—Continued

First published 1952 as a condensation of the Oxford companion to music

This music "dictionary includes over 14,000 entries on terms from 'allegro' to 'zingaro,' and on works from 'Aida' to 'Tosca,' as well as instruments and their history, composers, librettists, musicians, singers, and orchestras. It also [includes] comprehensive works lists for major composers." Publisher's note

780.9 Music—Historical, geographic, persons, treatment

Solway, Andrew

Africa; [by] Andrew Solway. Heinemann Library 2008 48p il (World of music) lib bdg $22

Grades: 5 6 7 8   **780.9**

1. African music

ISBN 978-1-4034-9891-5 (lib bdg); 1-4034-9891-1 (lib bdg)   LC 2006100578

This introduction to African music discusses "instruments, dance, and vocal styles. The photographs presented are wonderfully colorful in quality and narrative. Topics covered include history, famous players, current styles, pop-culture, politics, world-wide connections." Libr Media Connect

Includes glossary and bibliographical references

Latin America and the Caribbean; [by] Andrew Solway. Heinemann Library 2008 48p il (World of music) lib bdg $22

Grades: 5 6 7 8   **780.9**

1. Music—Latin America 2. Music—Caribbean region

ISBN 978-1-4034-9889-2 (lib bdg); 1-4034-9889-X (lib bdg)   LC 2006100579

This introduction to music of Latin America and the Caribbean discusses "instruments, dance, and vocal styles. The photographs presented are wonderfully colorful in quality and narrative. Topics covered include history, famous players, current styles, pop-culture, politics, and world-wide connections." Libr Media Connect

Includes glossary and bibliographical references

Underwood, Deborah, 1962-

Australia, Hawaii, and the Pacific; [by] Deborah Underwood. Heinemann Library 2008 48p il (World of music) lib bdg $22

Grades: 5 6 7 8   **780.9**

1. Music—Australia 2. Music—Hawaii 3. Music—Oceania

ISBN 978-1-4034-9894-6 (lib bdg); 1-4034-9894-6 (lib bdg)   LC 2006100576

This introduction to the music of Australia, Hawaii, and the Pacific discusses "instruments, dance, and vocal styles. The photographs presented are wonderfully colorful in quality and narrative. Topics covered include history, famous players, current styles, pop-culture, politics, and world-wide connections." Libr Media Connect

Includes glossary and bibliographical references

780.94 Music of Europe

Allen, Patrick

Europe; [by] Patrick Allen. Heinemann Library 2008 48p il (World of music) lib bdg $22

Grades: 5 6 7 8   **780.94**

1. Music—Europe

ISBN 978-1-4034-9890-8 (lib bdg); 1-4034-9890-3 (lib bdg)   LC 2006100580

This introduction to European music discusses "instruments, dance, and vocal styles. The photographs presented are wonderfully colorful in quality and narrative. Topics covered include history, famous players, current styles, pop-culture, politics, and world-wide connections." Libr Media Connect

Includes glossary and bibliographical references

781.6 Traditions of music

Kallen, Stuart A., 1955-

The history of classical music. Lucent Bks. 2002 112p il (Music library) $28.70

Grades: 6 7 8 9   **781.6**

1. Music—History and criticism

ISBN 978-1-59018-123-2; 1-59018-123-9   LC 2002-3815

Contents: Music of medieval times; The musical Renaissance; The Baroque era; The classical period; The romantic era; The modern era

This follows classical music "from Medieval times into the present, closing with a description of avant-garde composer John Cage's 4'33"—4 minutes and 33 seconds of silence. . . . [The volume is] greatly enhanced by fascinating excerpts from primary material, including articles, letters, and diaries, often in the words of the composer or musician. . . . Students reading for reports or for personal interest will find much useful information." Booklist

Includes bibliographical references

781.62 Folk music

Handyside, Chris, 1972-

Folk. Heinemann Library 2006 48p il (A history of American music) lib bdg $31.43 *

Grades: 5 6 7 8   **781.62**

1. Folk music

ISBN 1-4034-8150-4

This history of folk music is an "excellent, clear [introduction]. . . . [It] starts with the post-Civil War era, when folklorists gathered slave songs. It describes the music's commercial success beginning with early recordings of the Carter family and Jimmie Rodgers in the 1920s and continuing with Leadbelly, Woody Guthrie, Pete Seeger, and the many musicians who became popular during the folk revival of the late 50s and early 60s. . . . It concludes with sections on folk rock, punk rock, and the future of folk music." SLJ

Includes bibliographical references

781.642　Country music

Bertholf, Bret
Long gone lonesome history of country music;
by Bret Bertholf. 1st ed. Little, Brown 2007 unp
il $18.99 *
Grades: 4 5 6　　　　　　　　　　　　781.642
　1. Country music
　ISBN 0-316-52393-3; 978-0-316-52393-6
　　　　　　　　　　　　LC 2005016036
"This tongue-in-cheek overview features a folksy narrative of how and why country music developed in the
barns and back roads of rural America. The text . . .
covers instruments, early recordings, yodeling, . . . the
Great Depression, gospel, movie cowboys, a 'paper-doll'
spoof of singers' costumes, hillbilly jazz, World War II,
. . . and much more. While poking fun at itself . . . the
book offers a vast amount of historical fact amid a multitude of caricatures of country stars. . . . The ever-
changing backgrounds and fonts with colored-pencil and
crayon illustrations carry an amazing variation of detail."
SLJ

Handyside, Chris, 1972-
Country. Heinemann Library 2006 48p il (A
history of American music) lib bdg $31.43 *
Grades: 5 6 7 8　　　　　　　　　　　781.642
　1. Country music
　ISBN 1-4034-8151-2
This history of Country music is an "excellent clear
[introduction]. . . . [It] follows the music's history
through honky-tonk, singing cowboys, Western Swing,
bluegrass, rockabilly, country rock, outlaw, and alternative country. Featured musicians include Uncle Dave Ma-
con, the Carter family, Jimmie Rodgers, Hank Williams,
Johnny Cash, Loretta Lynn, and John Denver." SLJ
　Includes bibliographical references

Kallen, Stuart A., 1955-
The history of country music. Lucent Bks. 2002
112p il (Music library) $28.70
Grades: 6 7 8 9　　　　　　　　　　　781.642
　1. Country music
　ISBN 1-59018-124-7　　　　　　　LC 2002-664
　Contents: The early years of country; The sounds of
bluegrass; Honky-tonk music; Cowboy music and west-
ern swing; Rockabilly music; The Nashville hit makers;
New sounds, new fans
　A history of country music which discusses its roots,
influences, and various types including bluegrass, honky
tonk, cowboy music, western swing, and rockabilly
　Includes bibliographical references

781.643　Blues

Handyside, Chris, 1972-
Blues; [by] Christopher Handyside. Heinemann
Library 2006 48p il (A history of American music)
lib bdg $31.43 *
Grades: 5 6 7 8　　　　　　　　　　　781.643
　1. Blues music
　ISBN 1-4034-8148-2　　　　　　LC 2005019280

"This book charts the development of this uniquely
American Music form from the 1600s through to the
present. It also shows how social, economic, and regional
factors have all helped to shape the blues over time and,
in turn, how this music has gone on to influence other
genres." Publisher's note
　Includes glossary and bibliographical references

781.644　Soul music

Handyside, Chris, 1972-
Soul and R&B; [by] Christopher Handyside.
Heinemann Library 2006 48p il (A history of
American music) lib bdg $31.43 *
Grades: 5 6 7 8　　　　　　　　　　　781.644
　1. Soul music 2. Rhythm and blues music
　ISBN 1-4034-8153-9　　　　　　LC 2005019324
"This book charts the development of this uniquely
American music form from the 1800s through to the
present. It also shows how social, economic, and regional
factors have all helped to shape soul and R&B over time
and, in turn, how this music has gone on to influence
other genres." Publisher's note
　Includes glossary and bibliographical references

781.65　Jazz

Handyside, Chris, 1972-
Jazz; [by] Christopher Handyside. Heinemann
Library 2006 48p il (A history of American music)
lib bdg $31.43 *
Grades: 5 6 7 8　　　　　　　　　　　781.65
　1. Jazz music
　ISBN 1-4034-8149-0　　　　　　LC 2005019305
"This book charts the development of this uniquely
American Music form from the 1600s through to the
present. It also shows how social, economic, and regional
factors have all helped to shape Jazz over time and, in
turn, how this music has gone on to influence other
genres." Publisher's note
　Includes glossary and bibliographical references

Kallen, Stuart A., 1955-
The history of jazz. Lucent Bks. 2003 112p il
(Music library) lib bdg $21.96
Grades: 6 7 8 9　　　　　　　　　　　781.65
　1. Jazz music
　ISBN 1-59018-125-5　　　　　　LC 2002-2220
　Contents: The roots of jazz; The swingin' jazz age;
Dancing to swing; The birth of bebop; The cool, the
hard, and the free; Fusion and beyond
　This follows jazz music's "evolution from its African
roots through contemporary forms. [The volume is]
greatly enhanced by fascinating excerpts from primary
material, including articles, letters, and diaries, often in
the words of the composer or musician. . . . Students
reading for reports or for personal interest will find much
useful information." Booklist
　Includes bibliographical references

Marsalis, Wynton

Jazz A-B-Z; [by] Wynton Marsalis and Paul Rogers; with biographical sketches by Phil Schaap. Candlewick Press 2005 unp il $24.99 *

Grades: 5 6 7 8 9 10   **781.65**

1. Jazz music 2. Jazz musicians

ISBN 0-7636-2135-8   LC 2005-48448

This is an illustrated alphabetically arranged introduction to jazz musicians.

This is a "witty, stunningly designed alphabet catalog. . . . The biographical sketches and notes on poetic forms by Phil Schaap are concise and genuinely informative. . . . Rogers's pastiche full-page portraits, his use of expressive typography and the smaller vignettes he sprinkles throughout are bound to heighten any reader's appreciation of both the musicians and the music. . . . [Marsalis offers] clever . . . poems, wordplays, odes and limericks." N Y Times Book Rev

781.66 Rock (Rock 'n' roll)

Goodmark, Robyn

Girls rock; how to get your group together and make some noise; [by] Robyn Goodmark; illustrated by Adrienne Yan. Billboard Books 2008 178p il pa $13.95

Grades: 6 7 8 9 10   **781.66**

1. Rock music 2. Bands (Music) 3. Women musicians

ISBN 978-0-8230-9948-1; 0-8230-9948-2

LC 2008007386

This "shows the ins, outs, and good and bad things that come with starting a band and making it successful. . . . The conversational tone and quizzes throughout give the presentation the feel of a teen magazine. . . . Clever cartoon illustrations appear throughout. . . . Not only does this book provide the technical assistance newbie musicians might need, but it also provides advice on choosing a band name and more emotional topics like how to find creative inspiration. This is a wonderful guide for any girl who wants to start a band." SLJ

Handyside, Chris, 1972-

Rock. Heinemann Library 2006 48p il (A history of American music) lib bdg $31.43 *

Grades: 5 6 7 8   **781.66**

1. Rock music

ISBN 1-4034-8150-4

This history of rock music is an "excellent, clear [introduction]. . . . [It] opens with the mid-1950s advent of rock n roll and continues with surf music, girl groups, the British invasion, psychedelic rock, heavy metal, punk, and grunge. Featured musicians range from Elvis Presley to Kurt Cobain." SLJ

Includes bibliographical references

Kallen, Stuart A., 1955-

The history of rock and roll. Lucent Bks. 2003 128p il (Music library) lib bdg $21.96

Grades: 6 7 8 9   **781.66**

1. Rock music

ISBN 1-59018-126-3   LC 2002-3923

Contents: The roots of rock; The Beatles and the British invasion; Sweet sixties soul; Folk rock turns psychedelic; Rock-and-roll superstars; The rise of punk rock; Rock's next generation

Includes bibliographical references

Kenney, Karen Latchana, 1974-

Cool hip-hop music; create & appreciate what makes music great! [by] Karen Latchana Kenney. ABDO Pub. 2008 32p il (Cool music) lib bdg $24.21

Grades: 4 5 6 7   **781.66**

1. Hip-hop

ISBN 978-1-59928-971-7 (lib bdg); 1-59928-971-7 (lib bdg)   LC 2007-40585

Introduces the reader to hip-hop music and includes activities that immerse children in musical tradition.

This book "supplies a wealth of fascinating information to those who are new to the field. Reluctant readers will be attracted to these interesting reads." Libr Media Connect

Cool rock music; create & appreciate what makes music great! [by] Karen Latchana Kenney. ABDO Pub. 2008 32p il (Cool music) lib bdg $24.21

Grades: 4 5 6 7   **781.66**

1. Rock music

ISBN 978-1-59928-974-8 (lib bdg); 1-59928-974-1 (lib bdg)   LC 2007-38169

Introduces readers to rock music and includes activities that will immerse children in musical traditions.

This book "supplies a wealth of fascinating information to those who are new to the field. Reluctant readers will be attracted to [this] interesting [read]." Libr Media Connect

Nichols, Travis

Punk rock etiquette; the ultimate how-to guide for punk, underground, DIY, and indie bands. Roaring Brook Press 2008 128p il pa $10.95 *

Grades: 7 8 9 10 11 12   **781.66**

1. Punk rock music 2. Vocational guidance

ISBN 978-1-59643-415-8; 1-59643-415-5

LC 2008-11706

Contents: Forming a band; Songs and recording; Stage etiquette; Putting out your music; Merch; Touring: preheating your oven of destruction; Touring: freeeeeeeeeeeeeeedom!!!

"Lively, knowledgeable, witty, and wise, this title offers a sound foundation in the social economics of indie rock. . . . From how to put together a band that functions rather than fights, to designing and creating appealing merchandise and running a successful tour, this heavily illustrated guide covers every aspect of how to be a bona fide DIY rock star for the twenty-first century." Voice Youth Advocates

The **Rolling** Stone encyclopedia of rock & roll; edited by Holly George-Warren and Patricia Romanowski; consulting editor, Jon Pareles. rev and updated for the 21st century. Fireside 2001 1114p il $27

Grades: 7 8 9 10 11 12 Adult   **781.66**

1. Rock music—Encyclopedias 2. Reference books

ISBN 0-7432-0120-5   LC 2001-40285

"Accompanying the biographical and discographical information on the nearly 2,000 artists included in this edition are . . . essays [about] the performers' musical influences, first breaks, and critical and commercial hits and misses, as well as evaluations of their place in rock history. Filled with hundreds of historical photos." Publisher's note

"The scope is excellent: few works can compete in terms of blanket coverage of the major rock'n'roll players." Libr J

Includes discographies

Sanna, Ellyn, 1957-

Hip hop: a short history; [by] Rosa Waters. Mason Crest Publishers 2007 c2008 64p il (Hip-hop) lib bdg $22.95; pa $7.95

Grades: 4 5 6 7   **781.66**

1. Rap music 2. Hip-hop

ISBN 1-4222-0109-0 (lib bdg); 978-1-4222-0109-1 (lib bdg); 1-4222-0261-5 (pa); 978-1-4222-0261-6 (pa)

LC 2006004320

"The book begins with a visually eye-popping time line, then moves quickly through the roots of hip-hop—through slavery, the civil rights movement, and the black church. Musical influences included gospel, blues, jazz, funk, and rock. . . . A wide-awake design, full-color photos, and a winning writing style put a positive spin on this musical phenomenon." Booklist

Includes glossary and bibliographical references

Tanner, Mike, 1960-

Flat-out rock; ten great bands of the '60s. Annick Press 2006 158p $24.95; pa $12.95

Grades: 7 8 9 10   **781.66**

1. Rock music

ISBN 1-55451-036-8; 1-55451-035-X (pa)

"Ten of the great bands in the forefront of the music scene from 1964 to 1974 are highlighted here. Tanner offers a description of how each group came together and how its distinctive style developed. The discussion includes the social and political history of the period and shows how the musicians were impacted by broader events. . . . The narrative style will hold readers' attention. . . . This book would be a helpful resource." SLJ

782.25   Sacred songs

Cooper, Michael L., 1950-

Slave spirituals and the Jubilee Singers. Clarion Bks. 2001 86p il music $16 *

Grades: 7 8 9 10   **782.25**

1. Jubilee Singers (Musical group) 2. Spirituals (Songs) 3. African American music

ISBN 0-395-97829-7   LC 00-65854

"The first half of this book traces the development of spirituals from African musical traditions and discusses the place of religion in the lives of the slaves. The second half focuses on Fisk University's Jubilee Singers. . . . Illustrated with many archival prints and photographs, the book includes extensive annotated source notes and the words and music to seven of the spirituals popularized by the Jubilee Singers." SLJ

Includes bibliographical references

Giovanni, Nikki

On my journey now; looking at African-American history through the spirituals; [by] Nikki Giovanni; foreword by Arthur C. Jones. 1st ed. Candlewick Press 2007 116p $18.99 *

Grades: 7 8 9 10   **782.25**

1. Spirituals (Songs) 2. African Americans—History

ISBN 978-0-7636-2885-7; 0-7636-2885-9

LC 2006051695

"Complete lyrics for the spirituals included."

"Personal and passionate, Giovanni's short narrative talks about the sacred songs first sung by slaves, tracing how the people in bondage created the great spirituals to tell their stories, and what the songs still mean to us today." Booklist

782.42   Songs

National anthems of the world. 11th ed. Weidenfeld & Nicolson 2006 629p $90 *

Grades: 5 6 7 8 9 10 11 12 Adult

782.42

1. National songs

ISBN 0-304-36826-1

First published 1943 in the United Kingdom with title: National anthems of the United Nations and France

This volume contains national anthems of about 198 nations, including melody and accompaniment. Words are presented in the native language with transliteration provided where necessary. English translations follow. Brief historical notes on the adoption of each anthem are included.

"An essential reference resource for all libraries." Libr J

Silverman, Jerry

Songs and stories of the Civil War. 21st Cent. Bks. (Brookfield) 2002 96p il lib bdg $30.60

Grades: 5 6 7 8   **782.42**

1. United States—History—1861-1865, Civil War—Songs

ISBN 0-7613-2305-8   LC 2001-35795

Contents: The battle cry of freedom; The battle hymn of the republic; Dixie's land; Maryland, my Maryland; Lincoln and liberty; Weeping sad and lonely; Tenting on the old camp ground; When Johnny comes marching home; Roll, Alabama, roll; The battle of Shiloh; Slavery chain done broke at last; Free at last

Provides a history of the music and lyrics of a dozen Civil War songs, describing the circumstances under which they were created and performed

"Black-and-white reproductions of period photos, en-

Silverman, Jerry—*Continued*
gravings, paintings, and drawings illustrate the text. A good resource offering an interesting sidelight on the times." Booklist
Includes discography and bibliographical references

Yolen, Jane
Apple for the teacher; thirty songs for singing while you work; collected and introduced by Jane Yolen; music arranged by Adam Stemple; art edited by Eileen Michaelis Smiles. Harry N. Abrams, Inc. 2005 117p il $24.95 *
Grades: 4 5 6 7 **782.42**
1. Songs 2. Work—Songs
ISBN 0-8109-4825-7 LC 2004-24404
"Yolen has brought together a collection of 30 work songs . . . which represent a wide variety of occupations. . . . She introduces each job, explaining unusual vocabulary and references in the songs. . . . The artwork . . . is elegant. Ranging from sculpture to paintings to needlework, each selection of Americana has been carefully matched to the occupation, beautifully reproduced on high-quality paper, and meticulously identified." Booklist

784.19 Musical instruments

Baines, Anthony
The Oxford companion to musical instruments; written and edited by Anthony Baines. Oxford University Press 1992 404p il $85
Grades: 8 9 10 11 12 Adult **784.19**
1. Musical instruments—Dictionaries 2. Reference books
ISBN 0-19-311334-1 LC 92-8635
Based on The New Oxford companion to music (1983)
This volume presents alphabetically arranged entries for musical instruments. "The individual entries cover specific instruments and families thereof (e.g., Wind Instruments) as well as their representation in different countries (e.g., Africa) and time periods (e.g., Baroque). . . . Playing techniques, a brief history, and a list of the major repertory are [discussed]." Booklist

Helsby, Genevieve
Those amazing musical instruments; [by] Genevieve Helsby; with Marin Alsop as your guide. Sourcebooks Jabberwocky 2007 176p il $19.95 *
Grades: 4 5 6 7 8 9 **784.19**
1. Musical instruments
ISBN 978-1-4022-0825-6; 1-4022-0825-1
LC 2007013821
This is "a guide to instruments commonly found in an orchestra. . . . Utilizing large print; ample, colorful illustrations; and an open format, the book is logically organized into chapters about each of the musical instrument families, including keyboards, the voice, and modern electronic instruments. Throughout, readers are prompted to listen to the accompanying CD-ROM, which features

more than 100 musical samples. Information is clearly presented, and the author's enthusiasm for her subject is contagious." SLJ

Kallen, Stuart A., 1955-
The instruments of music. Lucent Bks. 2003 112p il (Music library) lib bdg $27.45
Grades: 6 7 8 9 **784.19**
1. Musical instruments
ISBN 1-59018-127-1 LC 2001-6609
Contents: Percussion; Woodwinds; Brass; Strings; Keyboards
This volume "includes history, cultural background, and the place of individual instruments in music from classical orchestra to rock and roll." Publisher's note
Includes bibliographical references

784.2 Full orchestra (Symphony orchestra)

Ganeri, Anita, 1961-
The young person's guide to the orchestra; Benjamin Britten's composition on CD narrated by Ben Kingsley; book written by Anita Ganeri. Harcourt Brace & Co. 1996 56p il $25 *
Grades: 4 5 6 7 **784.2**
1. Orchestra 2. Musical instruments 3. Music appreciation
ISBN 0-15-201304-0 LC 95-41478
"Accompanying this book on orchestral music is a CD featuring Britten's *A Young Person's Guide to the Orchestra* . . . as well as Dukas' *The Sorcerer's Apprentice*. The book begins with an overview of the orchestra and then centers around groups of instruments, explaining a bit of their history and their sound's distinctive quality. . . . The book also introduces eight famous composers, world music, Benjamin Britten, and the background of *The Young Person's Guide to the Orchestra*. . . . Handsome and useful." Booklist
Includes glossary

784.4 Light orchestra

Bolden, Tonya
Take-off! American all-girl bands during WW II. Alfred A. Knopf 2007 76p il $18.99; lib bdg $21.99
Grades: 6 7 8 9 **784.4**
1. Jazz musicians 2. Women musicians
ISBN 978-0-375-82797-6; 0-375-82797-8; 978-0-375-92797-3 (lib bdg); 0-375-92797-2 (lib bdg)
LC 2006-24523
"To appreciate this book, readers need at least a nodding acquaintance with swing music. The accompanying CD will help, and Bolden's introduction, which features opinions from Benny Goodman, Ella Fitzgerald, and others, gets things off to a good start. Then, using fascinating archival material . . . she goes on to discuss pioneering female jazz bands. . . . Bolden [uses] a fresh style of writing, as bouncy as the music." Booklist
Includes glossary and bibliographical references

785   Chamber music

Marx, Trish, 1948-
Steel drumming at the Apollo; the road to Super Top Dog; by Trish Marx; photographs by Ellen B. Senisi. 1st ed. Lee & Low Books 2007 56p il $22
Grades: 4 5 6 7   **785**
   1. Apollo Theatre (New York, N.Y.) 2. Musicians 3. Steel drum (Musical instrument) 4. Bands (Music)
ISBN 978-1-60060-124-8; 1-60060-124-3
                      LC 2007008947
"Photo-essay about a high school steel drum band from upstate New York, that participated in a series of talent competitions for a chance to win Super Top Dog on Amateur Night at the Apollo Theater in Harlem. Includes a CD of the band performing." Publisher's note
"Marx traces the band's progress through the tiers of competition in clear evocative prose depicting the visceral experience of performing as well as the hard work of practice and composition. Senisi's color photographs enliven every page." SLJ

787.8   Plectral lute family

Ellis, Rex M., 1951-
With a banjo on my knee; a musical journey from slavery to freedom. Watts 2001 160p il lib bdg $28
Grades: 7 8 9 10   **787.8**
   1. Banjos 2. African American music
ISBN 0-531-11747-2 (lib bdg); 978-0-531-11747-7 (lib bdg)   LC 00-33035
"Ellis explains the banjo's place in African American history. . . . He includes banjo talents such as James A. Bland, who wrote 'Carry Me Back to Old Virginny,' and Johnny St. Cyr, who played with Louis Armstrong." Voice Youth Advocates
This is a "well-written, attractive work, which unveils a segment of social history both powerful and far reaching." Booklist
Includes glossary, discography and bibliographical references

790.1   General kinds of recreational activities

Bell-Rehwoldt, Sheri, 1962-
The kids' guide to classic games. Capstone Press 2009 32p il (Kids' guides) lib bdg $23.99
Grades: 4 5 6 7   **790.1**
   1. Games
ISBN 978-1-4296-2273-8; 1-4296-2273-3
                      LC 2008-29686
"Edge books"
This provides instructions and rules for indoor and outdoor games such as ping-pong soccer, ringer, paper football, spiderweb, tug-of-war, and pipeline.
Includes glossary and bibliographical references

791.43   Motion pictures

Baker, Frank W.
Coming distractions; questioning movies; by Frank W. Baker. Fact Finders 2007 32p (Media literacy) lib bdg $22.60; pa $7.95
Grades: 4 5 6 7   **791.43**
   1. Motion pictures
ISBN 978-0-7368-6766-5 (lib bdg); 0-7368-6766-X (lib bdg); 978-0-7368-7862-3 (pa); 0-7368-7862-9 (pa)
                      LC 2006021441
"Describes what media is, how movies are part of media, and encourages readers to question the medium's influential messages." Publisher's note
This is a "solid title. . . . The book's punchy headlines, sound-bite-style text, and bold design will help hold readers' attention." Booklist
Includes bibliographical references

Finch, Christopher, 1939-
The art of Walt Disney; from Mickey Mouse to the Magic Kingdoms. rev and expanded ed. Harry N. Abrams 2004 504p il $60
Grades: 7 8 9 10   **791.43**
   1. Disney, Walt, 1901-1966 2. Walt Disney Company
ISBN 0-8109-4964-4   LC 2004-10016
First published 1973
Contents: Part I: A new art form. Early enterprises; Mickey Mouse and Silly Symphonies; Hyperion days; Part II: Feature animation. Snow White: the first feature; Pinocchio; Fantasia: the grand experiment; Dumbo and Bambi; Interruptions and innovations; The end of an era; New beginnings; A second flowering; The tradition continues; Digital dreams; Part III: Live-action films and Broadway. Muskets and Mouseketeers; Expanded horizons; Broadway; Part IV: The Magic Kingdoms; Beyond film; Magic Kingdoms; Themes and variations; Renewal; Roots and branches
This is the "story of Walt Disney and the company he built, from Mickey Mouse to animated feature films to theme parks. The text is illustrated with more than 800 illustrations." Publisher's note

Hart, Christopher
Christopher Hart's animation studio. Watson-Guptill 2003 48p pa $7.95
Grades: 8 9 10 11 12   **791.43**
   1. Animated films 2. Drawing 3. Cartoons and caricatures
ISBN 0-8230-0627-1
First published 1996 with title: Christopher Hart's portable animation studio
"Christopher Hart starts with a basic overview of drawing the cartoon head and body, adding expressions, creating characters, and so on. He then takes readers on a backstage tour of a classic animation studio. . . . Future animators finish by creating an easy flip book to set their own simple sequences in motion." Publisher's note

Lace, William W.

Blacks in film; by William W. Lace. Lucent Books 2008 104p il (Lucent library of Black history) $32.45

Grades: 7 8 9 10 **791.43**

1. African Americans in motion pictures

ISBN 978-1-4205-0084-4; 1-4205-0084-8

LC 2008018289

"This volume on black actors in American cinema begins with the 'Toms' found in early silent films and goes all the way up to . . . Oscar winners Jamie Foxx and Morgan Freeman. . . . [The book includes] high quality film stills and boxed sections." Booklist

Includes bibliographical references

O'Brien, Lisa, 1963-

Lights, camera, action! making movies and TV from the inside out; [by] Lisa O'Brien; illustrated by Stephen MacEachern. 2nd ed. Maple Tree Press 2007 64p il $21.95; pa $12.95

Grades: 4 5 6 7 **791.43**

1. Motion pictures—Production and direction 2. Acting

ISBN 978-1-897066-88-1; 1-897066-88-0; 978-1-897066-89-8 (pa); 1-897066-89-9 (pa)

First published 1998 by Firefly Books

This book "follows Johnny, a young aspiring actor, as he auditions for and gets a part in a new movie called The Mists of Time. Author Lisa O'Brien examines the development and production of movies from early concept through final production. Along the way, readers get a guided tour of the world of acting, from finding an agent, through to 'acting' an audition, to handling the media." Publisher's note

Reinhart, Matthew

Star Wars: a pop-up guide to the galaxy. Orchard Books 2007 unp il $32.99 *

Grades: 4 5 6 7 **791.43**

1. Star Wars films 2. Pop-up books

ISBN 978-0-439-88282-8; 0-439-88282-6

LC 2007-19587

"Lucasfilm"

"The book has . . . six two-page spreads, each presenting a gigantic iconic character, creature, spaceship or location from the original 'Star Wars' movie trilogy. . . . The four corners of each spread contain sub-pages. These small doors open to reveal even more pop-up sculptures. . . . In all, there are 36 increasingly stunning pop-up displays." NY Times Book Rev

Reynolds, David West

Star Wars: the complete visual dictionary; written by David West Reynolds (episodes I, II and IV-VI) and James Luceno (episode III); updates and new material by Ryder Windham; special fabrications by Robert E. Barnes . . . [et. al.]; new photography by Alex Ivanov. 1st American ed. DK Pub. 2006 270p il $40

Grades: 6 7 8 9 10 11 12 Adult **791.43**

1. Star Wars films

ISBN 0-7566-2238-7; 978-0-7566-2238-1

LC 2006298949

Material in this book was originally published in various DK Pub. publications, 1998-2005

"The ultimate guide to characters and creatures from the entire Star wars saga" —Cover

"Star Wars Complete Visual Dictionary brings together all four . . . titles from The Visual Dictionary series (Episode I-III and the Trilogy) in one volume. . . . This book is [a] comprehensive visual guide to every character, weapon, starship, droid, creature and alien in the Star Wars universe." Publisher's note

791.5 Puppetry and toy theaters

Kennedy, John E., 1967-

Puppet mania; the world's most incredible puppet making book ever. North Light Books 2003 79p il pa $14.99

Grades: 4 5 6 7 **791.5**

1. Puppets and puppet plays

ISBN 1-58180-372-9

LC 2003-59965

This includes instructions for making 13 puppets and for animating them with techniques such as lip synching, body movements, eye contact and movement

Puppet planet. North Light Books 2006 79p il $16.99 *

Grades: 4 5 6 7 **791.5**

1. Puppets and puppet plays

ISBN 978-1-58180-794-3; 1-58180-794-5

LC 2005033711

This book offers twelve "puppet projects, each using a variety of techniques, [and] features 'action panels' so readers can see how each puppet comes to life. [It also] Includes staging ideas to play up each project's uniqueness." Publisher's note

792 Stage presentations

Becker, Helaine

Funny business; clowning around, practical jokes, cool comedy, cartooning, and more. . .; illustrated by Claudia Dávila. Maple Tree 2005 160p il $21.95; pa $9.95

Grades: 5 6 7 8 **792**

1. Wit and humor 2. Clowns 3. Cartooning

ISBN 1-897066-40-6; 1-897066-41-4 (pa)

"Becker offers funny facts, an informative diagram showing what goes on in the body when you laugh, brief discussions of different types of humor (situation comedy, parody, farce, riddles, puns), a How Funny Are You? quiz, tips and timing for standup routines, body lingo, props, six improvisation games, clowning material, and more. For kids who want to learn how to juggle, tell jokes, or use sight-gag items, it's all here. Cartooning is explained as well." SLJ

Belli, Mary Lou

Acting for young actors; the ultimate teen guide; [by] Mary Lou Belli & Dinah Lenney. Back Stage Books 2006 205p il pa $16.96

Grades: 7 8 9 10 11 12   **792**

    1. Acting

    ISBN 978-0-8230-4947-9 (pa); 0-8230-4947-7 (pa)

                    LC 2006007265

"Belli and Lenney, an Emmy-winning director of *Girlfriends* and a Yale-educated *ER* actress offer stage-struck teens trunks-full of sound advice packaged with a conversational tone and grounded experience. . . . The authors offer a series of questions for character analysis; suggested readings and viewings abound. . . . The handbook succeeds at communicating clearly without talking down to readers; engaging prose makes it an ideal text for classes and teens who want commonsense career prep and insight." Voice Youth Advocates

    Includes bibliographical references

Friedman, Lise

Break a leg! the kids' guide to acting and stagecraft; photographs by Mary Dowdle. Workman 2002 222p il hardcover o.p. pa $14.95
*

Grades: 4 5 6 7   **792**

    1. Acting 2. Theater

    ISBN 0-7611-2590-6; 0-7611-2208-7 (pa)

                    LC 2001-26986

A comprehensive manual for acting and theater, discussing improvisation, voice projection, breathing exercises, script analysis, and technical aspects of theater production

"The information is solid and presented well, and the sidebars, in which young actors offer comments and tips, add life to the text." Booklist

Jackson, Sheila, 1956-

Costumes for the stage; a complete handbook for every kind of play; by Sheila Jackson. 2nd ed. New Amsterdam Books 2001 153p il pa $16.95

Grades: 6 7 8 9 10 11 12 Adult   **792**

    1. Costume 2. Theater—Production and direction

    ISBN 1-56131-068-9 (pa); 978-1-56131-068-5 (pa)

                    LC 2001-32563

    First published 1978 by Dutton

This "aims at simplicity in all aspects of designing and making costumes. It is designed primarily for those who need to dress plays on a small budget, whether for amateur, semiprofessional, or professional groups." Publisher's note

"Theatres with small budgets (probably every theatre) should . . . use this handbook as a training manual. . . [It] should become a basic reference." KLIATT [review of 1st edition]

    Includes bibliographical references

Rogers, Barb, 1947-

Costumes, accessories, props, and stage illusions made easy. Meriwether Pub. 2005 205p il pa $19.95

Grades: 8 9 10 11 12   **792**

    1. Costume 2. Theater—Production and direction

    ISBN 978-1-56608-103-0 (pa); 1-56608-103-3 (pa)

                    LC 2005-4359

This book details ways to make theater "costumes with simple tools such as scissors, glue guns, and paint. In addition, there are chapters on how to make hats, gloves, armor, and animal heads, as well as other props and accessories from rummage-sale finds and a little imagination. . . . This is a useful volume for schools and community theaters with little or no budgets for costumes and props." SLJ

    Includes bibliographical references

Schumacher, Thomas L.

How does the show go on? an introduction to the theater; by Thomas Schumacher with Jeff Kurtti. 2nd ed. Disney 2008 128p il $22.95

Grades: 4 5 6 7   **792**

    1. Theater

    ISBN 978-1-4231-2031-5; 1-4231-2031-0

"Filled with lavish color photos of Disney theater productions, this eye-catching volume has clever chapter titles, beginning with 'Overture,' which tells about 'styles of theaters' and 'kinds of shows.' In 'Act One' and 'Act Two,' aspects of the front and back of the house are discussed, including the marquee, the box office, props, special effects, and so on. Interspersed throughout the facts and photos are 'Stage Notes,' where bits of trivia are doled out." SLJ

792.09   Theater—Historical, geographic, persons treatment

Currie, Stephen, 1960-

An actor on the Elizabethan stage. Lucent Bks. 2003 96p il maps (Working life) $27.45

Grades: 6 7 8 9   **792.09**

    1. Theater—History 2. Great Britain—History—1485-1603, Tudors

    ISBN 1-59018-174-3   LC 2002-9460

    Contents: Sharers and apprentices; Hired men; Preparing a production; The performance; On tour

Discusses various aspects of theatrical life, including staging and performance, financing, types of acting troupes, and social and economic influences

This is "well written and the [author draws on quotes] from many primary sources." Libr Media Connect

    Includes bibliographical references

792.5 Opera

Siberell, Anne
Bravo! brava! a night at the opera; behind the scenes with composers, cast, and crew; introduction by Frederica von Stade. Oxford Univ. Press 2001 64p il $19.95 *
Grades: 4 5 6 7   **792.5**
1. Opera
ISBN 0-19-513966-6   LC 2001-21206
This "book introduces all features of the opera, including stars, stagehands, set designers, conductors, and supernumeraries. . . . Cartoon artwork illustrates the text, and a world map highlighting the settings of well-known operas is also included, as are curtain diagrams, plot summaries of favorite operas, and sample costumes."
Horn Book Guide
"An excellent resource for reports, this unusual book has an exceptional range of topics for younger students and is an essential purchase for upper elementary and middle school music programs." SLJ
Includes glossary and bibliographical references

792.6 Musical plays

Amendola, Dana
A day at the New Amsterdam Theatre; photos by Gino Domenico; written by Dana Amendola. Disney Editions 2004 125p il $24.95 *
Grades: 4 5 6 7   **792.6**
1. New Amsterdam Theatre (New York, N.Y.)
2. Theater
ISBN 0-7868-5438-3
"This title covers a day in the life of Disney's *The Lion King*, the long-running Broadway musical. . . . A clock in a corner of each spread guides readers through the day as box-office personnel, makeup designers, dancers, actors, cleaning staff, and others do their jobs. Each spread includes several full-color photos that are often gritty, sometimes glamorous. . . . This unique volume provides an honest, realistic, eye-opening look at the behind-the-scenes work that goes into the running of a Broadway show." SLJ

792.8 Ballet and modern dance

Augustyn, Frank
Footnotes; dancing the world's best-loved ballets; [by] Frank Augustyn and Shelley Tanaka. Millbrook Press 2001 94p il lib bdg $24.90; pa $17.95 *
Grades: 5 6 7 8   **792.8**
1. Ballet
ISBN 0-7613-2323-6 (lib bdg); 0-7613-1646-9 (pa)
LC 00-50075
"*Footnotes* uses seven classical ballets as a jumping-off point to talk about the evolution of this unique art form, partnering, dancer as actor, training, costumes, choreography, and some of the world's most well-known

performers." SLJ
"Fine photographs, most in color, add enormously to the book's appeal. A well-crafted, readable volume." Booklist

Balanchine, George, 1904-1983
101 stories of the great ballets; [by] George Balanchine and Francis Mason. Dolphin Bks. (NY) 1975 541p pa $17.95
Grades: 8 9 10 11 12 Adult   **792.8**
1. Ballet—Stories, plots, etc.
ISBN 0-385-03398-2
"A Doubleday Dolphin book"
This collection contains the stories of well-known 19th and 20th century ballets

Grau, Andrée
Dance; written by Andrée Grau. rev ed. DK Pub. 2005 72p il (DK eyewitness books) $15.99; lib bdg $19.99
Grades: 4 5 6 7   **792.8**
1. Dance
ISBN 0-7566-1065-6; 0-7566-1066-4 (lib bdg)
First published 1998 by Knopf
Surveys all forms of dance throughout the world, discussing its cultural and social significance, its costume, its history, and noted dancers and choreographers

Lee, Laura, 1969-
A child's introduction to ballet; the stories, music and magic of classical dance; [by] Laura Lee; illustrated by Meredith Hamilton. Black Dog & Leventhal Publishers 2007 96p il $19.95
Grades: 4 5 6 7 8   **792.8**
1. Ballet
ISBN 978-1-57912-699-5; 1-57912-699-5
LC 2006048867
"This lively and attractive volume delves into the history of ballet from its beginnings in Italy through the 20th century. . . . Detailed and well-written descriptions of 25 of the most famous and influential ballets are provided along with colorful illustrations of scenes. A CD presents excerpts from them and the author poses some questions and gives some insights to think about as one listens to the music." SLJ

Schorer, Suki
Put your best foot forward; a young dancer's guide to life; by Suki Schorer and the School of American Ballet; illustrations by Donna Ingemanson. Workman Publishing 2005 96p il pa $9.95
Grades: 4 5 6 7   **792.8**
1. Ballet
ISBN 978-0-7611-3795-5; 0-7611-3795-5
LC 2005051428
"The words of counsel proffered by the author, who was a principal dancer for the New York City Ballet and is a teacher at the School of American Ballet, are engaging, imaginative, and right on target. . . . Practical tips

Schorer, Suki—*Continued*

such as essentials that need to be in your bag and behavioral advice such as being grateful for criticism are nicely woven into the book. The photographs, mainly of female dancers, are clear and colorful. These words of wisdom will keep dancers on their toes and stretching their minds and hearts." SLJ

Solway, Andrew

Modern dance; [by] Andrew Solway. Heinemann Library 2009 48p il (Dance) lib bdg $31.43

Grades: 4 5 6 7 8   **792.8**

1. Modern dance

ISBN 978-1-4329-1376-2; 1-4329-1376-X

LC 2008-14295

This book "is enhanced by eye-catching photography that shows costumes, famous dancers, technique and people dancing. . . . [Those] thinking about dance as a career will find this . . . helpful. . . . [This] is a definite must have." Libr Media Connect

Includes glossary and bibliographical references

793.7   Games not characterized by action

Wise, Leonard, 1940-

The way cool license plate book. Firefly Bks. 2002 64p il $19.95; pa $9.95

Grades: 4 5 6 7   **793.7**

1. Games

ISBN 1-55297-686-6; 1-55297-563-0 (pa)

LC 2003-279447

"The introduction explains what vanity license plates are and how to read them. A short history discusses the origin of license plates, the various kinds of materials that have been used to manufacture them, and collecting as a hobby, followed by six pages of directions for various license-plates-related games that can be played while traveling. . . . This is one of those titles that libraries should have just because." SLJ

793.73   Puzzles and puzzle games

Moscovich, Ivan

Big book of brain games; 1000 playthinks of art, mathematics & science; by Ivan Moscovich; foreword by Ian Stewart; illustrated by Tim Robinson. Workman Pub. 2006 420p il pa $22.95

Grades: 7 8 9 10   **793.73**

1. Scientific recreations

ISBN 0-7611-3466-2 (pa); 978-0-7611-3466-4 (pa)

LC 2006299017

First published 2001 with title: 1000 playthinks: puzzles, paradoxes, illusions & games

This is a "collection of 1,000 challenges, puzzles, riddles, illusions. . . . Twelve basic categories include Geometry, Patterns, Numbers, Logic and Probability, and Perception. [A] key at the top of each game ranks its difficulty on a scale of 1 to 10, while indices in the back cross-reference the puzzles." Publisher's note

Includes bibliographical references

793.74   Mathematical games and recreations

Ball, Johnny, 1938-

Go figure! DK Pub. 2005 96p il map $15.99

Grades: 4 5 6 7   **793.74**

1. Mathematical recreations 2. Mathematics

ISBN 0-7566-1374-4

A collection of math activities that include brainteasers, magic tricks, and mind-reading games

"A dynamic book. . . . Blocks of color, diagrams, and photo collages contribute to the exciting layout. . . . A fun romp for number and puzzle lovers." SLJ

793.8   Magic and related activities

Ottaviani, Jim

Levitation: physics and psychology in the service of deception; [by] Jim Ottaviani and Janine Johnston; lettering by Tom Orzechowski. G. T. Labs 2007 71p il pa $12.95

Grades: 6 7 8 9 10 11 12 Adult   **793.8**

1. Graphic novels 2. Magic tricks—Graphic novels

ISBN 978-0-9788037-0-4

"A General Tektronics Labs book"

This book tells the story of how John Neville Maskelyne developed the stage magic trick of levitation, of the American Harry Kellar, who acquired the trick through devious means, of the old school engineer Guy Jarrett, who perfected the magicians' tricks, and of stage performer Howard Thurston, who inherited the levitation trick from Kellar and ruined it. Or did he? The book includes notes and reprints of old posters and other information on the magicians.

Includes bibliographical references

794.1   Chess

Basman, Michael

Chess for kids; written by Michael Basman. Dorling Kindersley 2001 45p il $12.99

Grades: 4 5 6 7   **794.1**

1. Chess

ISBN 0-7894-6540-X   LC 00-59018

This guide to chess explains the rudiments of the game, techniques and winning strategies

"A solid introduction for novices and good for skilled players wanting to develop their strategies and find out about chess clubs and tournaments." Booklist

King, Daniel, 1963-

Chess; from first moves to checkmate. Kingfisher (NY) 2000 64p il $16.95 *

Grades: 5 6 7 8 9 10 11 12   **794.1**

1. Chess

ISBN 0-7534-5387-8   LC 00-26353

Introduces the rules and strategies of chess, as well as its history and some of the great players and matches

King, Daniel, 1963-—*Continued*

The author "offers training exercises, strategy quizzes, and trivia, all of which add depth and texture to his explanations. The computer-generated graphics are staggering. The colorful, multi-image illustrations are not only aesthetically appealing but also crystal clear and very effectively placed to enhance the text." Booklist

794.8 Electronic games. Computer games

Gerardi, David

Careers in the computer game industry; [by] Dave Gerardi and Peter Suciu. Rosen Pub. Group 2005 144p il (Careers in the new economy) lib bdg $31.95

Grades: 6 7 8 9   **794.8**

1. Computer games 2. Vocational guidance

ISBN 1-4042-0252-8   LC 2004-11258

"This is a realistic view of getting into the industry and the nonglamorous side of the business. The history of computer games and anecdotes of those currently working in the field will entertain and inform. Some of the topics included are: The Role of Game Testers, Computer Game Designers, Programmers, Graphic Artists and Animators, and The Future of Gaming. Qualifications and career growth are discussed." SLJ

Includes bibliographical references

Parks, Peggy J., 1951-

Video games; by Peggy J. Parks. ReferencePoint Press 2008 104p il map (Compact research) $25.95

Grades: 8 9 10 11 12   **794.8**

1. Video games

ISBN 978-1-60152-053-1; 1-60152-053-0

LC 2007049886

This "book opens with descriptions of the growing popularity of video games and the regulation and legislation of content and sales; ratings; connections with violent crime; and health effects, including addiction. An overview provides further background and context to these issues, and . . . chapters follow addressing related questions and providing other related material. . . . The accessible and objective [presentation] and lists of key people and advocacy groups make [this a] useful [resource] for research." SLJ

Includes bibliographical references

Rauf, Don

Computer game designer; [by] Don Rauf and Monique Vescia. Ferguson 2007 unp il (Virtual apprentice) lib bdg $29.95; pa $9.95

Grades: 6 7 8 9   **794.8**

1. Computer games 2. Vocational guidance

ISBN 978-0-8160-6754-1 (lib bdg); 0-8160-6754-6 (lib bdg); 978-0-8160-7550-8 (pa); 0-8160-7550-6 (pa)

LC 2006036565

"This in-depth introduction to the field of computer-game design offers specific practical advice. . . . Following a basic history of computer games and information about game types and rating levels, chapters, which

are illustrated with many color photos, profile contemporary professionals and delve into current trends and the day-to-day work of game creators." Booklist

796 Athletic and outdoor sports and games

Blumenthal, Karen

Let me play; the story of Title IX, the law that changed the future of girls in America; [by] Karen Blumenthal. 1st ed. Atheneum Books for Young Readers 2005 152p il $17.95 *

Grades: 6 7 8 9   **796**

1. Women athletes 2. Sex discrimination

ISBN 0-689-85957-0   LC 2004-1450

"The author looks at American women's evolving rights by focusing on the history and future of Title IX, which bans sex discrimination in U.S. education. . . . The images are . . . gripping, and relevant political cartoons and fact boxes add further interest. Few books cover the last few decades of American women's history with such clarity and detail" Booklist

Includes bibliographical references

ESPN sports almanac. Pearson Education il pa $12.99

Grades: 8 9 10 11 12   **796**

1. Sports 2. Reference books

ISSN 1555-8304

ISBN 978-1-93306-038-5 (pa); 1-93306-038-7 (pa)

Annual. First published 2004 as a continuation of ESPN information please sports almanac

"The almanac examines in detail baseball, college football, professional football, college basketball, professional basketball, other college sports, and hockey. The editors touch upon many other less conventional sports, such as archery, dog sledding, gymnastics, auto racing, boxing, and so on. Each section looks at statistics of the game and offers an essay highlighting an important event of the past year. Related topics cover ballparks and arenas, halls of fame and awards, who's who, and business." Recomm Ref Books in Paperback. 3d edition

Sports Illustrated almanac; by the editors of Sports Illustrated. Little, Brown 2008 il pa $12.99

Grades: 7 8 9 10 11 12 Adult   **796**

1. Sports 2. Reference books

ISBN 978-1-93382-190-0 (pa); 1-93382-190-6 (pa)

Annual. First published 1991 with title: Sports illustrated . . . sports almanac

"Provides team and individual records and highlights for all major sports. . . . A brief essay opens the section on each sport, followed by page upon page of records, both current and retrospective. Interspersed throughout . . . are black-and-white and color photographs and notable quotations by sports figures." Am Ref Books Annu, 1993

Sports rules on file; [by] the Diagram Group.
Facts on File 2000 various paging (Facts on File
reference library) loose leaf $185

Grades: Professional   **796**

1. Sports

ISBN 0-8160-4117-2   LC 00-37137

Also available CD-ROM version

"The coverage of each activity includes a synopsis; a
competition overview; some historical background; playing field or arena diagrams; information on dress and
equipment; play and scoring regulations; officials' duties;
and discussion and line drawings that focus on skills,
plays, and the basic rules. All of the major sports played
at the U.S. high school and college level are covered.
. . . An effective, easy-to-use reference tool." SLJ

Sports: the complete visual reference; François
Fortin [general editor] Firefly Bks. 2000 372p il
$39.95; pa $24.95

Grades: 8 9 10 11 12 Adult   **796**

1. Sports 2. Reference books

ISBN 1-55209-540-1; 1-55297-807-9 (pa)

This is a "reference source on 120 contemporary
sports . . . pulling together the history, physical environment for competitions, roles of the players and officials,
specific terms and expressions, and dynamics of each.
All of this is done with an emphasis on visual presentation, and each entry includes copious illustrations."
Booklist

"A sure winner for any sports reference collection."
Am Libr

Strother, Scott

The adventurous book of outdoor games; classic
fun for daring boys and girls; [by] Scott Strother.
Sourcebooks 2008 293p il pa $14.99

Grades: 4 5 6 7 Professional   **796**

1. Games

ISBN 978-1-4022-1443-1; 1-4022-1443-X

This book "outlines more than 100 games, each at different activity levels set by the amount of physical exer-
tion required. . . . Each game discusses the number of
players, ages, time allotted, and type of playing field, followed by a brief description of equipment, startup, object
of the game, and how to play. . . . The easy-to-read,
easy-to-follow format will provide hours of imaginative
play for all of those who are willing to try. An excellent
resource for parents, teachers, and activity directors and
even for children themselves." SLJ

796.2   Activities and games requiring equipment

Chambers, Veronica

Double dutch; a celebration of jump rope,
rhyme, and sisterhood. Jump at the Sun/Hyperion
Bks. for Children 2002 64p il $18.99 *

Grades: 4 5 6 7   **796.2**

1. Rope skipping 2. Jump rope rhymes

ISBN 0-7868-0512-9

"Chambers introduces readers to the world of jump
roping through personal reminiscences, wonderful action

photos, and factual narratives. The book looks like a vibrant collage, a clean typeface is interspersed with pictures and inserts of the rhymes themselves. From it, readers learn not only the history of double Dutch . . . and
its current state, but also experience some of the joy of
jumping." SLJ

Thomas, Keltie

Blades, boards & scooters; illustrated by Steve
Attoe and Allan Moon. Maple Tree Press 2003
64p il (Popular mechanics for kids) hardcover o.p.
pa $12.95 *

Grades: 5 6 7 8   **796.2**

1. In-line skating 2. Skateboarding 3. Snowboarding

ISBN 1-89437-945-4; 1-89437-946-2 (pa)

This "volume introduces scooters, in-line skates,
skateboards, and snowboards. Thomas combines sound
advice for beginners with glimpses of the 'X-treme
scene,' showcasing the amazing feats performed by the
pros and other experienced riders. . . . Throughout the
book, colorful photographs show action scenes, while
very clear pictures, evidently digital, illustrate the gear
and some of the moves used in the sports." Booklist

796.22   Skateboarding

Fitzpatrick, Jim, 1948-

Skateboarding. Cherry Lake Pub. 2009 32p il
(Innovation in sports) $27.07

Grades: 4 5 6 7   **796.22**

1. Skateboarding

ISBN 978-1-6027-9259-3; 1-6027-9259-3

     LC 2008007548

This describes skateboarding history, equipment, safety, and health benefits.

This "stands out by emphasizing monumental shifts
and advances in the events themselves. . . . Concise and
occasionally revelatory." Booklist

Includes glossary and bibliographical references

Powell, Ben

Skateboarding skills; the rider's guide. Firefly
Books 2008 128p il pa $16.95

Grades: 7 8 9 10 11 12 Adult   **796.22**

1. Skateboarding

ISBN 978-1-55407-360-3; 1-55407-360-X

     LC 2008-275044

The author "offers a colorful and useful manual for
mastering numerous skateboard tricks. Intended for riders
of all ages, the book presents step-by-step breakdowns of
skills illustrated with photographs of children around age
12; each step of a trick features a picture and a written
description." Libr J

796.323 Basketball

Ingram, Scott, 1948-
A basketball all-star. Heinemann Library 2005
48p il (Making of a champion) lib bdg $31.43; pa
$8.90 *
Grades: 5 6 7 8   **796.323**
1. Basketball
ISBN 1-4034-5363-2 (lib bdg); 1-4034-5547-3 (pa)
LC 2004-3864
Contents: A worldwide sport; Basketball beginnings;
The growth of the NBA; Changes in the rules; Basketball
basics; Coaching; Nutrition for athletes; Running; Flexibility; Basketball fitness: strength; Injuries and recovery;
Skills: dribbling; Skills: passing; Skills: shooting; On offense; Transition; Getting position; Game day; Olympic
dreams; Being a champion; Records
This overview of basketball includes "basic skills and
playing strategies, rules of the game, training, and typical
injuries. . . . Fact boxes, short vignettes on past and
present professional athletes, and lists of championships
. . . are offered. . . . The clearly presented information
is accompanied by a quality color or black-and-white
photograph on every page." SLJ
Includes bibliographical references

Labrecque, Ellen
Basketball; by Ellen Labrecque. Cherry Lake
Pub. 2009 32p il (Innovation in sports) $27.07
Grades: 4 5 6 7   **796.323**
1. Basketball
ISBN 978-1-6027-9256-2; 1-6027-9256-9
LC 2008002044
This describes basketball history, rules, equipment,
training, and great players.
This "stands out by emphasizing monumental shifts
and advances in the events themselves. . . . Concise and
occasionally revelatory." Booklist
Includes glossary and bibliographical references

Stewart, Mark
Basketball; a history of hoops. Watts 1998 160p
il (Watts history of sports) lib bdg $33.50
Grades: 7 8 9 10   **796.323**
1. Basketball
ISBN 0-531-11492-9   LC 98-25040
Discusses the origins and evolution of the sport of
basketball, as well as important events and key personali-
ties in both college and professional versions of the game
Includes bibliographical references

Swish; the quest for basketball's perfect shot; by
Mark Stewart and Mike Kennedy. Millbrook Press
2009 64p il lib bdg $25.26
Grades: 5 6 7 8   **796.323**
1. Basketball
ISBN 978-0-8225-8752-1; 0-8225-8752-1
LC 2008-24958
"Stewart and Kennedy offer an engaging history of the
sport, followed by profiles of some of the most impres-
sive shots of all time and the players who made them."
SLJ

"The wide pages offer plenty of room for well-spaced
text, sidebars, and illustrations. Each page has at least
one picture, with mostly color photos, and the many action shots make the book more exciting. With information on women's and men's basketball at both collegiate
and professional levels, this is a nice addition to sports
collections." Booklist
Includes bibliographical references

Thomas, Keltie
How basketball works. Maple Tree Press 2005
64p il $16.95; pa $6.95 *
Grades: 5 6 7 8   **796.323**
1. Basketball
ISBN 1-89706-618-X; 1-89706-619-8 (pa)
This guide to basketball offers information about the
game's origins, history, and equipment as well as positions, training, skills, stats, & rules of the game. It also
offers tips and fascinating factoids.
"The writing style is razzle-dazzle energetic. . . . The
layout features numerous sidebars and brightly colored
photos and digital drawings. Even longtime fans will
learn something from this engaging, enthusiastic book."
Booklist

796.325 Volleyball

Manley, Claudia B.
Competitive volleyball for girls. Rosen Pub.
Group 2001 64p il (Sportsgirl) lib bdg $26.50
796.325
1. Volleyball
ISBN 0-8239-3404-7   LC 00-12210
"The author shows the players in a volleyball game,
and gives a detailed look at what each player does and
how she prepares. The differences between court volleyball and beach volleyball are included." Publisher's note
Includes bibliographical references

796.332 American football

The **Child's** World encyclopedia of the NFL; by
James Buckley, Jr. . . . [et. al.] Child's World
2007 4v il set $189
Grades: 3 4 5 6 7   **796.332**
1. National Football League 2. Football—Encyclopedias 3. Reference books
ISBN 978-1-59296-922-7 (v1); 978-1-59296-923-4
(v2); 978-1-59296-924-1 (v3); 978-1-59296-925-8 (v4)
LC 2007005662
This encyclopedia of the National Football League is
"full of color photos; significant names, terms, and
events; and plenty of popular football figures. The authors are all experienced sportswriters and editors."
Booklist

Gigliotti, Jim
Football. Cherry Lake Pub. 2009 32p il
(Innovation in sports) $27.07
Grades: 4 5 6 7   **796.332**
1. Football
ISBN 978-1-6027-9257-9; 1-6027-9257-7
LC 2008002305
This describes football history, rules, equipment, training, and strategy, and innovators.
This "stands out by emphasizing monumental shifts and advances in the events themselves. . . . Concise and occasionally revelatory." Booklist
Includes glossary and bibliographical references

Ingram, Scott, 1948-
A football all-pro; [by] Scott Ingram.
Heinemann Library 2005 48p il (The making of a
champion) lib bdg $31.43; pa $8.99
Grades: 5 6 7 8 9   **796.332**
1. Football
ISBN 1-4034-5364-0 (lib bdg); 1-4034-5548-1 (pa)
LC 2004-3870
Introduction: the Super Bowl; The beginnings of football; The rise of the National Football League; Equipment; Starting young; The football basics; Weight training; The dangers of steroids; Diet and training; What a coach expects; Master the pass; Heavy-duty runners; Gifted hands; Offensive linemen; Defensive line; Linebackers; Defensive backs; The kicking game; Injuries; Game day; What it takes to make a champion; Fascinating football facts
This provides an overview of football "from [its] beginnings to contemporary times. Basic skills and playing strategies, rules of the game, training, and typical injuries are discussed, and fact boxes, short vignettes on past and present professional athletes, and lists of championships . . . are offered." SLJ
Includes bibliographical references

Madden, John
John Madden's heroes of football; the story of
America's game. Dutton Childrens Book 2006 80p
il $18.99
Grades: 5 6 7 8   **796.332**
1. Football
ISBN 0-525-47698-9   LC 2005036019
"This title traces the evolution of professional football from its humble beginnings as an Ivy League-college pastime in the 19th century to one of the most popular spectator sports in the United States. . . . This clear, well-organized account is appropriate for report writers and is a solid choice for libraries needing to update their sports-history collections." SLJ
Includes glossary and bibliographical references

796.334 Soccer

Gifford, Clive
The Kingfisher soccer encyclopedia. Kingfisher
2006 144p il $19.95 *
Grades: 5 6 7 8   **796.334**
1. Soccer—Encyclopedias 2. Reference books
ISBN 978-0-7534-5928-7; 0-7534-5928-0
LC 2005023899
"Beginning with the history of the sport, Gifford covers the basic rules as well as skills such as defending the ball, goalkeeping, and attacking. He includes brief bios of the legends of the sport, both men and women, organized by their positions. Fascinating tales of great teams and memorable competitions in events . . . will entertain fans of the sport. . . . This book could be used as a reference guide for reports or to answer specific questions. A solid purchase where an all-encompassing encyclopedia is needed." SLJ
Includes glossary

Hamm, Mia, 1972-
Go for the goal; a champion's guide to winning
in soccer and life; [by] Mia Hamm with Aaron
Heifetz. HarperCollins Pubs. 1999 222p il pa
$12.95 hardcover o.p. *
Grades: 7 8 9 10   **796.334**
1. Soccer
ISBN 0-06-093159-0 (pa)   LC 99-19592
Personal anecdotes and both action and instructional photos illustrate soccer skills and techniques

Hornby, Hugh
Soccer; written by Hugh Hornby; photographed
by Andy Crawford. DK Pub. 2008 70p il (DK
eyewitness books) $15.99
Grades: 4 5 6 7   **796.334**
1. Soccer
ISBN 978-0-7566-3779-8; 0-7566-3779-1
LC 2008276290
First published 2000
Includes CD ROM
Examines all aspects of the game of soccer: its history, rules, techniques, tactics, equipment, playing fields, competitive play, and more.

Kelley, K. C., 1960-
Soccer. Cherry Lake Pub. 2008 32p il
(Innovation in sports) $27.07
Grades: 4 5 6 7   **796.334**
1. Soccer
ISBN 978-1-6027-9261-6; 1-6027-9261-5
LC 2008006749
This describes soccer history, rules, styles of play, equipment, and innovators.
This "stands out by emphasizing monumental shifts and advances in the events themselves. . . . Concise and occasionally revelatory." Booklist
Includes glossary and bibliographical references

Scott, Nina Savin
The thinking kid's guide to successful soccer; illustrations by Anne Canevari Green. Millbrook Press 1999 96p il lib bdg $21.90 *
Grades: 4 5 6 7   **796.334**
1. Soccer
ISBN 0-7613-0324-3   LC 98-17201
Presents strategies for playing soccer under pressure, dealing with various situations during a game, setting goals, playing with teammates, coping with coaches, and dealing with doubts and fears
"This well-designed book, with genuinely funny cartoon illustrations, deserves a space on the shelf right next to those books on rules and techniques." Booklist
Includes bibliographical references

Stewart, Mark
Soccer; a history of the world's most popular game. Watts 1998 128p il (Watts history of sports) lib bdg $33.50
Grades: 7 8 9 10   **796.334**
1. Soccer
ISBN 0-531-11456-2   LC 97-17201
A comprehensive history of soccer, focusing on its evolution, momentous events, and key personalities
This book is "chock-full of outstanding full-color and black-and-white photos. There is strong coverage of memorable contests and individuals and the statistical appendix [is] useful." SLJ
Includes bibliographical references

796.34   Racket games

Swissler, Becky
Winning lacrosse for girls; foreword by Anna Maria Vesco. Facts on File 2004 192p il hardcover o.p. pa $16.95
Grades: 7 8 9 10   **796.34**
1. Lacrosse
ISBN 0-8160-5183-6; 0-8160-5184-4 (pa)
LC 2003-51446
This "teaches the game's basic skills, strategies, and drills and how to master them. Chapters cover the history of the game, the basics of stick handling, the rules of play, passing and receiving, offense and defense, key strategies, skills and tactics, conditioning, and much more." Publisher's note
This is "well organized, clear, and concise. . . . Accurate . . . pictures accompany the instruction in a logical and clear fashion." SLJ
Includes bibliographical references

796.342   Tennis

Douglas, Paul
Tennis. Dorling Kindersley 1995 72p il (101 essential tips) pa $5
Grades: 7 8 9 10   **796.342**

1. Tennis
ISBN 0-7566-0225-4
Aspects covered include strokes, positions, playing surfaces, dress and equipment
"This is a good text for those just picking up the sport, as well as for those seasoned players who want to brush up on their game or improve their strategy." Voice Youth Advocates

796.352   Golf

Kelley, K. C., 1960-
Golf. Cherry Lake Pub. 2009 32p il (Innovation in sports) $27.07
Grades: 4 5 6 7   **796.352**
1. Golf
ISBN 978-1-6027-9262-3; 1-6027-9262-3
LC 2008002045
This describes golf history, rules, balls, and club technology, and innovators.
This "stands out by emphasizing monumental shifts and advances in the events themselves. . . . Concise and occasionally revelatory." Booklist
Includes bibliographical references

796.357   Baseball

January, Brendan, 1972-
A baseball all-star. Heinemann Library 2005 48p il (Making of a champion) lib bdg $31.45; pa $8.90
Grades: 6 7 8 9   **796.357**
1. Baseball
ISBN 1-4034-5362-4 (lib bdg); 1-4034-5546-5 (pa)
LC 2004-3862
Contents: Introducing baseball; Baseball: a sport's beginnings; Little league; After little league; Equipment; Batting; Throwing; Pitching; In the outfield; In the infield; Catching; Baserunning; Coaching; Fitness; Injuries; Baseball strategies and plays; Working on skills; Knowing the game; The World Series; Life of a baseball star
This overview of baseball includes "basic skills and playing strategies, rules of the game, training, and typical injuries. . . . Fact boxes, short vignettes on past and present professional athletes, and lists of championships . . . are offered. . . . The clearly presented information is accompanied by a quality color or black-and-white photograph on every page." SLJ
Includes bibliographical references

Krasner, Steven
Play ball like the hall of famers; the inside scoop from 19 baseball greats; written by Steven Krasner; illustrations by Keith Neely. Peachtree 2005 221p $14.95
Grades: 5 6 7 8   **796.357**
1. Baseball
ISBN 1-56145-339-0
"Krasner assembles an impressive group of subjects, from Johnny Bench and Gary Carter on catching, to Don

Krasner, Steven—*Continued*

Sutton, Phil Niekro, and Tom Seaver on aspects of pitching. . . . Each entry includes anecdotes, a glossary of key terms, and mention of how the advice can be put into action. Black-and-white photos and line drawings appear throughout the succinct and readable interviews, and the perspectives are both detailed and insightful." SLJ

Play ball like the pros; tips for kids from 20 big league stars; written by Steven Krasner. Peachtree Pubs. 2002 181p il pa $12.95 *

Grades: 5 6 7 8   **796.357**

1. Baseball

ISBN 1-56145-261-0   LC 2001-7342

Nearly two dozen professional baseball players, such as Pedro Martinez and Derek Jeter, provide insights into how they prepare for and play the game.

"This title is just the sort of finely tuned analysis of baseball that many young players are looking for. . . . The tips given are detailed and insightful. . . . This is a good reference for young people working to improve their skills." Booklist

Lipsyte, Robert

Heroes of baseball; the men who made it America's favorite game; [by] Robert Lipsyte. Atheneum Books for Young Readers 2006 92p il $19.95

Grades: 4 5 6 7   **796.357**

1. Baseball—Biography

ISBN 0-689-86741-7; 978-0-689-86741-5

     LC 2005010841

"Using as a focus some of baseball's greats—Big Al Spalding, Babe Ruth, Mickey Mantle, Jackie Robinson, Curt Flood . . . —Lipsyte offers a strong history of the game and its place in American culture. . . . Although much of this material, including the pictures, might be familiar to young readers already absorbed in the game, it is nicely laid out and colorfully formatted. Lipsyte has a clear, vivid style." Booklist

Includes glossary and bibliographical references

McKissack, Patricia C., 1944-

Black diamond; the story of the Negro baseball leagues; [by] Patricia C. McKissack and Fredrick McKissack, Jr. Scholastic 1994 184p il pa $5.99 hardcover o.p. *

Grades: 6 7 8 9   **796.357**

1. Baseball 2. African American athletes

ISBN 0-590-68213-X (pa)   LC 93-22691

Traces the history of baseball in the Negro Leagues and its great heroes, including Monte Irwin, Buck Leonard, and Cool Papa Bell

This is "an engaging account. . . . It includes a chronology, player profiles and wonderful photographs from the Negro Leagues." N Y Times Book Rev

Includes bibliographical references

Owens, Tom, 1960-

Collecting baseball memorabilia; [by] Thomas S. Owens. Millbrook Press 1996 96p il lib bdg $26.90

Grades: 8 9 10 11 12   **796.357**

1. Baseball—Collectibles 2. Baseball—History

ISBN 1-56294-579-3   LC 95-19827

"This introduction delves into a wide array of baseball collectibles including tickets stubs, team schedules, autographs, and other items that can be obtained at little or no cost. . . . This book has a crisp layout with full-color photos or reproductions on nearly every page. While not a price guide, this title will be of interest to young baseball enthusiasts." SLJ

Includes glossary

Stewart, Mark

World Series. Watts 2002 159p il (Watts history of sports) $33.50

Grades: 7 8 9 10   **796.357**

1. Baseball—History 2. World series (Baseball)

ISBN 0-531-11953-X   LC 2001-5727

Contents: The 19th century; The 1900s; The 1910s; The 1920s; The 1930s; The 1940s; The 1950s; The 1960s; The 1970s; The 1980s; The 1990s; 2000 and beyond

A year-by-year account of the World Series games from the 1800s through the twentieth century

This is "fast paced, brimming with photos and sidebars and sure to be a winner for browsing or reports." Libr Media Connect

Includes bibliographical references

Teitelbaum, Michael, 1953-

Baseball; by Michael Teitelbaum. Cherry Lake Pub. 2009 32p il (Innovation in sports) lib bdg $18.95

Grades: 5 6 7 8   **796.357**

1. Baseball

ISBN 978-1-60279-255-5; 1-60279-255-0

     LC 2008-2310

This title "traces the many leaps forward in the history of baseball. [It] chronicles innovations that changed the game. . . . Nice-sized color photographs and sidebars . . . accompany the concise and easy-to-follow text." Booklist

Includes glossary and bibliographical references

Wong, Stephen

Baseball treasures; by Stephen Wong; photographs by Susan Einstein. Collins 2007 58p il $16.99; lib bdg $17.89

Grades: 5 6 7 8   **796.357**

1. Baseball—Collectibles 2. Baseball—History

ISBN 978-0-06-114464-6; 0-06-114464-9; 978-0-06-114473-8 (lib bdg); 0-06-114473-8 (lib bdg)

     LC 2006036069

This describes collectibles connected with the history of baseball, including balls, gloves and bats, jerseys, baseball cards, World Series memorabilia, and trophies.

This is "a well-designed, well-illustrated book for kids. . . . The text manages to impart the essential information without becoming bogged down in too much detail." Booklist

796.4 Weight lifting, track and field, gymnastics

Brzycki, Matt, 1957-
Wrestling strength: prepare to win. Blue River Press 2002 116p il pa $12.95 *
Grades: 7 8 9 10   **796.4**
  1. Weight lifting 2. Wrestling
  ISBN 0-9718959-1-0
The author outlines "information on anatomy and kinesiology, explains how to prevent injuries, and gives detailed instructions on performing weight-lifting exercises for maximum benefit. . . . Brzycki also discusses flexibility, diet, and safety in the weight room. . . . [This] should be mandatory reading for every young athlete about to begin weight training." Voice Youth Advocates

Wrestling strength: the competitive edge. Blue River Press 2002 112p il pa $12.95 *
Grades: 7 8 9 10   **796.4**
  1. Weight lifting 2. Wrestling
  ISBN 0-9718959-0-2
"The author offers concrete assistance on designing the appropriate weight-lifting regimen to fit the individual and his or her sport, as well as related training activities such as conditioning and skill development. . . . [This] should be mandatory reading for every young athlete about to begin weight training." Voice Youth Advocates

796.42 Track and field

Housewright, Ed
Winning track and field for girls; foreword by Buzz Andrews. Facts on File 2004 188p il $35 *
Grades: 7 8 9 10   **796.42**
  1. Track athletics
  ISBN 0-8160-5231-X   LC 2003-49241
"Housewright starts with a . . . history of women's track. The chapters are then divided into topics such as sprints, hurdles, middle and long distances, relays, jumping events, throwing events, the heptathlon, cross-country, and the triathlon. Each of these chapters then goes into detail about the individual event and concludes with a section about record holders. Helpful drills and sample workouts are also provided." SLJ
  Includes bibliographical references

Manley, Claudia B.
Competitive track and field for girls. Rosen Pub. Group 2001 64p il (Sportsgirl) lib bdg $26.50
Grades: 4 5 6 7   **796.42**
  1. Track athletics
  ISBN 0-8239-3408-X   LC 2001-752
This includes information about the origin of track and field athletics "as well as basic equipment requirements, and the fundamental skills and/or training needed." Book Rep
  Includes glossary and bibliographical references

796.48 Olympic games

Hotchkiss, Ron
The matchless six; the story of Canada's first women's Olympic team. Tundra Books 2006 194p il pa $16.95
Grades: 7 8 9 10   **796.48**
  1. Olympic games 2. Track athletics 3. Women athletes
  ISBN 0-88776-738-9; 978-0-88776-738-8
"Hotchkiss provides detailed information on the six Canadian athletes who won the track-and-field event in 1928, the first Olympics that included women. The personalities and accomplishments of Jane Bell, Myrtle Cook, Bobbie Rosenfeld, Ethel Smith, Ethel Catherwood, and Jean Thompson are highlighted with biographical information. . . . Accuracy is supported by quotes from newspapers, sports writers, coaches, and managers. . . . Anyone interested in the history of the Olympics, the history of women in the Games, or of track and field will find the book worth reading." SLJ

Macy, Sue, 1954-
Swifter, higher, stronger; a photographic history of the Summer Olympics; by Sue Macy; foreword by Bob Costas. updated for the 2008 Summer Olympics. National Geographic 2008 96p il $18.95; lib bdg $27.90 *
Grades: 4 5 6 7   **796.48**
  1. Olympic games
  ISBN 978-1-4263-0290-9; 1-4263-0290-8; 978-1-4263-0302-9 (lib bdg); 1-4263-0302-5 (lib bdg)
  First published 2004
A detailed look at the history of the Olympic Games, from their origins in Ancient Greece, through their rebirth in nineteenth century France, to the present, highlighting the contributions of individuals to the Games' success and popularity.
"While other books on the topic go into more depth on specific sports, athletes, or historical events, none are as enthusiastically broad or as enjoyable to read as this one. And, it's superbly illustrated with colorful, well-chosen, and enticing photographs." SLJ [review of 2004 ed.]
  Includes bibliographical references

796.5 Outdoor life

Paulsen, Gary
Woodsong. Bradbury Press 1990 132p map $17.95; pa $5.99 *
Grades: 7 8 9 10   **796.5**
  1. Sled dog racing 2. Outdoor life 3. Minnesota
  ISBN 0-02-770221-9; 0-689-85250-9 (pa)
                LC 89-70835
For the author and his family, life in northern Minnesota is a wild experience involving wolves, deer, and the sled dogs that make their way of life possible. Includes an account of Paulsen's first Iditarod, a dogsled race across Alaska
"The book is packed with vignettes that range among various shades of terror and lyrical beauty." Voice Youth Advocates

796.51   Walking

Hart, John, 1948-
Walking softly in the wilderness; the Sierra Club guide to backpacking. 4th ed, complete rev and updated. Sierra Club Books 2005 508p il map (Sierra Club outdoor adventure guide) pa $16.95
Grades: 8 9 10 11 12 Adult   **796.51**
   1. Backpacking 2. Wilderness areas
   ISBN 1-57805-123-1   LC 2004-56554
   First published 1977
This guide for both the novice and experienced hiker reflects the environmental concerns of the Sierra Club. Among topics covered are: clothing and equipment; making and breaking camp; problem animals and plants; hiking and camping with kids. Listings of conservation and wilderness travel organizations, map and equipment sources, land management agencies, and Internet contacts are appended.
   Includes bibliographical references

796.52   Walking and exploring by kind of terrain

Pfetzer, Mark
Within reach: my Everest story; [by] Mark Pfetzer and Jack Galvin. Dutton 1998 224p il hardcover o.p. pa $7.99
Grades: 7 8 9 10   **796.52**
   1. Mountaineering 2. Mount Everest (China and Nepal)
   ISBN 0-525-46089-6; 0-14-130497-9 (pa)
                     LC 98-29215
Mark Pfetzer describes how he spent his teenage years climbing mountains in the United States, South America, Africa, and Asia, with an emphasis on his two expeditions up Mount Everest
   "Throughout the detail-rich, briskly paced account, Pfetzer is psychologically challenging, yet always emotionally within reach." Booklist
   Includes glossary

Skreslet, Laurie
To the top of Everest; [by] Laurie Skreslet with Elizabeth MacLeod. Kids Can Press 2001 56p il $16.95; pa $8.95
Grades: 4 5 6 7   **796.52**
   1. Mountaineering 2. Mount Everest (China and Nepal)
   ISBN 1-55074-721-5; 1-55074-814-9 (pa)
This is an account of Skreslet's "1982 trek up Everest when he became one of the first Canadians to make it to the top. Skreslet takes readers through every exciting, excruciating element of the climb. Beautiful color photographs abound." Booklist
   Includes glossary

Wurdinger, Scott D.
Rock climbing; [by] Scott Wurdinger and Leslie Rapparlie. Creative Education 2007 48p il (Adventure sports) $31.35
Grades: 6 7 8 9   **796.52**
   1. Mountaineering
   ISBN 978-1-58341-394-4; 1-58341-394-4
                     LC 2005051785
This outlines "the history, gear, safety equipment, and competitions for [rock climbing]. . . . Large, full-color glossy photos . . . include action shots, closeup views of equipment and techniques, and pictures of exotic landscapes." SLJ
   Includes bibliographical references

796.54   Camping

Brunelle, Lynn
Camp out! the ultimate kids' guide, from the backyard to the backwoods; [by] Lynn Brunelle; illustrations by Brian Biggs; technical illustrations by Elara Tanguy. Workman Pub. 2007 376p il pa $11.95
Grades: 5 6 7 8   **796.54**
   1. Camping
   ISBN 978-0-7611-4122-8 (pa); 0-7611-4122-7 (pa)
                     LC 2007297580
"This book is stuffed with information about gear, packing lists, where to go, what to do while you're camping, and what to do when you get back. There are 174 games, skills, projects, recipes, songs, experiments, crafts, and more to make, learn, play, and do outdoors. . . . Line drawings give a clear picture of the instructions they represent. The book is well organized. . . . Written on a kid's level from a kid's-eye view, this volume is perfect for would-be campers." SLJ

796.6   Cycling and related activities

Buckley, Annie, 1968-
Be a better biker; by Annie Buckley. Child's World 2007 32p il (Girls rock!) lib bdg $24.21
Grades: 5 6 7 8   **796.6**
   1. Cycling 2. Bicycles
   ISBN 1-59296-741-8   LC 2006001640
This "gives the history of bicycles and describes the different types available and what they are used for. A section on safety covers helmets, bike maintenance, and basic rules of the road. . . . [The book has] clear color photos. . . . [This] realistic [title is] well written and [provides] excellent information." SLJ
   Includes bibliographical references

King, Andy
Play-by-play mountain biking; text and photographs by Andy King. rev ed. Lerner Publs. 2001 63p il pa $7.95 *
Grades: 7 8 9 10   **796.6**
   1. Mountain bikes 2. Cycling
   ISBN 0-8225-9879-5   LC 00-8852

King, Andy—*Continued*
First published 1997 with title: Fundamental mountain biking

An introduction to the sport of mountain biking, including an explanation of the required equipment and necessary skills

"There's a wealth of clearly written information in a logical format enhanced by action-packed photos." Book Rep

Includes bibliographical references

796.72   Automobile racing

Blackwood, Gary L.
The Great Race; the amazing round-the-world auto race of 1908; [by] Gary Blackwood. Abrams Books for Young Readers 2008 141p il $19.95
Grades: 6 7 8 9   796.72
1. Automobile racing 2. Voyages around the world
ISBN 978-0-8109-9489-8; 0-8109-9489-5
                                          LC 2007-22414
"In 1908, several car manufacturers sponsored a global race that was routed across America, then across Siberia and Europe, ending in Paris. . . . Blackwood presents an extremely well-researched and detailed account of this large-scale publicity stunt. . . . There's enough sheer adventure here, carried out by some eccentric characters, to attract almost every reader. Helping things along are the photographs from the event. . . . A fascinating account." Booklist

Buckley, James, Jr.
NASCAR; written by James Buckley Jr. DK Pub. 2005 72p il (DK eyewitness books) $15.99; lib bdg $19.99 *
Grades: 4 5 6 7   796.72
1. National Association for Stock Car Auto Racing
2. Automobile racing
ISBN 0-7566-1194-6; 0-7566-1193-8 (lib bdg)
This offers information about NASCAR stock car racing and its stars, including such topics as history, car construction, driving gear, the meaning of flag colors, track layouts, and race-day routines.

This is a "first-rate introduction to a hugely popular sport. Guaranteed to please both the simply curious and the avid fan." Booklist

Caldwell, Dave
Speed show; how NASCAR won the heart of America. Kingfisher 2006 126p il $16.95 *
Grades: 5 6 7 8   796.72
1. National Association for Stock Car Auto Racing
2. Automobile racing
ISBN 978-0-7534-6011-5; 0-7534-6011-4
"A New York Times book"
"Caldwell, a *New York Times* sports correspondent, gives a furiously fast but impressively thorough rundown on the National Association for Stock Auto Racing, better known as NASCAR. With his firsthand account, the history feels both personal and like fact-fueled reportage." Booklist
Includes bibliographical references

Eagen, Rachel, 1979-
NASCAR; written by Rachel Eagen. Crabtree Pub. Co. 2007 32p il (Automania!) lib bdg $25.20; pa $8.95
Grades: 4 5 6   796.72
1. National Association for Stock Car Auto Racing
2. Automobile racing
ISBN 978-0-7787-3007-1 (lib bdg); 0-7787-3007-7 (lib bdg); 978-0-7787-3029-3 (pa); 0-7787-3029-8 (pa)
                                          LC 2006012406
"Eagen has done an excellent job explaining the National Association of Stock Car Automobile Racing—the history, the modification of the cars, the drivers, and the competitions—while conveying a sense of the magnitude of the sport's current fan base. Her lucid, interesting text gets a lift from plenty of high-energy photos." Booklist

Gifford, Clive
Racing; the ultimate motorsports encyclopedia. Kingfisher 2006 144p il $19.95
Grades: 5 6 7 8   796.72
1. Automobile racing
ISBN 978-0-7534-6040-5; 0-7534-6040-8
"Glossy color photos of motorsport vehicles in action complement straightforward factual description. Some highlights include the different forms of racing, information about prominent tracks, . . . important racing figures, statistics, and the art and science of motorsport racing. This comprehensive volume . . . will be gobbled up by racing fans." Horn Book Guide
Includes glossary and bibliographical references

Gigliotti, Jim
Hottest dragsters and funny cars; by Jim Gigliotti. Enslow Publishers 2008 47p il (Wild wheels!) lib bdg $23.93
Grades: 4 5 6 7   796.72
1. Automobile racing
ISBN 978-0-7660-2870-8 (lib bdg); 0-7660-2870-4 (lib bdg)   LC 2007007424
"Learn about drag racing, funny cars, and experience what it feels like to spend the day at a drag race." Publisher's note
Includes glossary and bibliographical references

Kelley, K. C., 1960-
Hottest NASCAR machines; by K.C. Kelley. Enslow Publishers 2008 48p il (Wild wheels!) lib bdg $23.93
Grades: 4 5 6 7   796.72
1. National Association for Stock Car Auto Racing
2. Automobile racing
ISBN 978-0-7660-2869-2 (lib bdg); 0-7660-2869-0 (lib bdg)   LC 2007007426
"Experience the thrill of a NASCAR race, and learn about the cars, personalities, and races associated with this sport." Publisher's note
Includes glossary and bibliographical references

Miller, Timothy, 1951-
Vroom! motoring into the wild world of racing; [by] Tim Miller. Tundra Books 2006 58p il pa $17.95
Grades: 4 5 6 7   **796.72**
1. Automobile racing
ISBN 978-0-88776-755-5; 0-88776-755-9
"Miller offers a clear introduction to auto racing in a large-format paperback with glossy pages. The first chapter looks at the sport's history, terminology, types of racing, and safety issues. The remaining three chapters feature road racing, oval-track racing, and drag racing, respectively. Throughout the book, sidebars spotlight topics such as the costs of the sport, racing flags, and drivers as athletes. . . . It is an attractive, informative introduction to subject." Booklist
Includes glossary

Morganelli, Adrianna, 1979-
Formula One. Crabtree Pub. 2007 32p il (Automania!) lib bdg $25.20; pa $8.95
Grades: 4 5 6   **796.72**
1. Automobile racing
ISBN 978-0-7787-3009-5 (lib bdg); 0-7787-3009-3 (lib bdg); 978-0-7787-3031-6 (pa); 0-7787-3031-X (pa)
LC 2006-14362
This book "traces the history of Grand Prix racing, the development of the cars and their equipment, qualifying and racing, the tracks, safety measures, racing teams, and dominant drivers, with a sidebar on women in F1 racing. . . . Morganelli's writing is . . . organized and . . . readable. . . . [This] book is an attractive introduction." SLJ
Includes glossary

796.8   Combat sports

Inman, Roy
The judo handbook; [by] Roy Inman. North American ed. Rosen Pub. 2008 256p il (Martial arts) lib bdg $39.95
Grades: 7 8 9 10 11 12   **796.8**
1. Judo
ISBN 978-1-4042-1393-7; 1-4042-1393-7
LC 2007-37742
This features "step-by-step descriptions of various moves, accompanied by detailed, full-color photographs. [This] volume offers a background on the history of the art and its use as a sport as well as a system for self-defense. [The] handbook features a concise description of the judo fundamentals, then begins describing the techniques: throwing techniques, combination and counter-techniques, ground techniques, and combination and counter-techniques against them. The book makes good use of the Japanese terms used in judo study, integrating their meanings seamlessly into the text." SLJ
Includes bibliographical references

Martin, Ashley P.
The Shotokan karate bible; beginner to black belt. Firefly Books 2007 201p p $24.95
Grades: 6 7 8 9 10   **796.8**
1. Karate 2. Martial arts
ISBN 978-1-55407-322-1; 1-55407-322-7
LC 2008-270630
An "illustrated guide . . . [for] students of Shotokan karate, from beginners to those earning a black belt. The author outlines and explains the lessons for all 10 gradings." Publisher's note
"Each chapter outlines a grading syllabus, listing the techniques and sparring that the student must master to earn a particular belt, followed by extensive step-by-step photographs illustrating the moves involved. . . . This book of fundamentals is comprehensive and worthy. " Voice Youth Advocates
Includes bibliographical references

Pawlett, Mark
The tae kwon do handbook; [by] Mark and Ray Pawlett. Rosen Pub. 2008 256p il (Martial arts) lib bdg $39.95
Grades: 7 8 9 10 11 12   **796.8**
1. Tae kwon do
ISBN 978-1-4042-1396-8; 1-4042-1396-1
LC 2007-31559
This features "step-by-step descriptions of various moves, accompanied by detailed, full-color photographs. [The] volume offers a background on the history of the art and its use as a sport as well as a system for self-defense. . . . [The book] spends about 150 pages on techniques, and also covers dietary recommendations, a history of Korea, a description of the I Ching, and other concepts. . . . It [includes] an excellent section on strength training . . . and the text devoted to basic fundamentals of the sport, such as stances and stepping, gives those building blocks appropriate importance." SLJ
Includes bibliographical references

Pawlett, Raymond
The karate handbook; [by] Ray Pawlett. Rosen Pub. Group 2008 256p il (Martial arts) $39.95
Grades: 7 8 9 10 11 12   **796.8**
1. Karate
ISBN 978-1-4042-1394-4; 1-4042-1394-5
LC 2007-32795
This "offers a thorough introduction to karate that covers both the underlying philosophy and the physical practice. A thoughtful, sophisticated history opens the book and discusses karate's roots in Zen Buddhism, the styles of karate, and dojo etiquette. Later spreads feature lucid, step-by-step instructions." Booklist
Includes bibliographical references

Rielly, Robin L.
Karate for kids; [by] Robin Rielly. 1st ed. Tuttle Pub. 2004 48p il $11.95 *
Grades: 4 5 6 7   **796.8**
1. Karate
ISBN 0-8048-3534-9   LC 2003-27610
Contents: What is karate?; The uniform; The dojo; The class; Warming up; Practicing karate; Advancing in karate; Is karate good for me?

Rielly, Robin L.—*Continued*
"Rielly begins with a history of karate before going on to information about the uniform, including the meaning of the belt colors, the rules and etiquette of the dojo, and the interaction between student and teacher. The actual stances are clearly portrayed in watercolor-and-ink artwork that features both boys and girls in a number of stances and practicing thrusts and kicks. The book ends with advice for advancing in karate." Booklist

Ritschel, John
The kickboxing handbook; [by] John Ritschel. Rosen Pub. 2008 256p il (Martial arts) lib bdg $39.95
Grades: 7 8 9 10 11 12   **796.8**
1. Martial arts
ISBN 978-1-4042-1395-1; 1-4042-1395-3
LC 2007-37746
"This volume features step-by-step descriptions of various moves and strength-building exercises, accompanied by detailed, full-color photographs. . . . [This book] does emphasize safety, showing the correct way to punch in order to avoid injuring one's hand and displaying clear photographs on striking areas of the foot in order to perform kicks properly." SLJ

796.93   Skiing and snowboarding

Masoff, Joy, 1951-
Snowboard! your guide to freeriding, pipe & park, jibbing, backcountry, alpine, boardercross, and more; illustrations by Jack Dickason. National Geographic Soc. 2002 64p il (Extreme sports) pa $8.95 *
Grades: 4 5 6 7 8 9   **796.93**
1. Snowboarding
ISBN 0-7922-6740-0   LC 2001-44392
Describes different kinds of snowboarding—freeriding, in the pipe, jibbing, backcountry—and the techniques, equipment, and terminology involved
"Sharp, action-packed photos and punchy, magazine-style prose add to the appeal. . . . Relaxed, readable, and filled with helpful information." Booklist

Pollack, Pam
Ski; your guide to cross-country, downhill, jumping, racing, freestyle and more; by Pamela Pollack; illustrations by Jack Dickason. National Geographic Soc. 2001 64p il (Extreme sports) pa $8.95 *
Grades: 7 8 9 10   **796.93**
1. Skiing
ISBN 0-7922-6738-9   LC 2001-54445
This guide to skiing styles offers "sharp, action-packed photos and punchy, magazine-style prose. . . . Chapters are brief but packed with information for beginners. . . . Relaxed, readable, and filled with helpful information." Booklist

796.962   Ice hockey

McKinley, Michael, 1961-
Ice time; the story of hockey. Tundra Books 2006 80p il $18.95
Grades: 5 6 7 8   **796.962**
1. Hockey
ISBN 978-0-88776-762-3; 0-88776-762-1
"This straightforward history of hockey emphasizes the professional game and Canadian players. . . . Hockey enthusiasts will find this a welcome arrival." Booklist

Stewart, Mark
Hockey; a history of the fastest game on ice. Watts 1998 127p il (Watts history of sports) lib bdg $33.50
Grades: 7 8 9 10   **796.962**
1. Hockey
ISBN 0-531-11494-5   LC 98-25039
Discusses the origins and evolution of the game of hockey, as well as memorable events and key personalities in this sport
Includes bibliographical references

796.98   Winter Olympic games

Macy, Sue, 1954-
Freeze frame; a photographic history of the Winter Olympics. National Geographic 2006 96p il map $18.95 *
Grades: 5 6 7 8   **796.98**
1. Olympic games 2. Winter sports
ISBN 0-7922-7887-9; 978-0-7922-7887-0
Highlights in the history of the Winter Olympics from their inception in 1924 to today, including profiles of the Olympic athletes and information on the lesser-known winter sports. Also includes an Olympic almanac with information about each Olympiad.
This "has spectacular photographs and clear, captivating prose." SLJ
Includes bibliographical references

797.1   Boating

George, Charles, 1949-
White-water rafting; by Charles and Linda George. Riverfront Bks. 1999 48p il (Sports alive!) lib bdg $21.26 hardcover o.p.   **797.1**
1. Rafting (Sports)
ISBN 0-7368-0055-7   LC 98-7188
Describes the history, equipment, and techniques of white water rafting
Includes bibliographical references

Wurdinger, Scott D.
Kayaking; by Scott Wurdinger and Leslie Rapparlie. Creative Education 2006 48p il (Adventure sports) $21.95
Grades: 5 6 7 8   **797.1**
1. Kayaks and kayaking
ISBN 978-1-58341-397-5   LC 2005051057
"Strong, full-page color photographs illustrate this overview of kayaking. . . . Tracing the use of kayaks back thousands of years, the authors touch on the history of the boats before moving on to contemporary usage for sports and recreation. . . . The exciting views . . . will instantly draw browsers and serious readers alike." Booklist
Includes bibliographical references

797.2   Swimming and diving

Timblin, Stephen
Swimming. Cherry Lake Pub. 2009 32p il (Innovation in sports) $27.07
Grades: 4 5 6 7   **797.2**
1. Swimming
ISBN 978-1-6027-9258-6; 1-6027-9258-5
LC 2008002046
This describes swimming history, rules, equipment, training, and swimming stars.
This "stands out by emphasizing monumental shifts and advances in the events themselves. . . . Concise and occasionally revelatory." Booklist
Includes glossary and bibliographical references

797.5   Air sports

Blair, Margaret Whitman, 1951-
The roaring 20; the first cross-country air race for women. National Geographic 2006 128p il map $21.95
Grades: 6 7 8 9   **797.5**
1. Women air pilots 2. Airplane racing
ISBN 0-7922-5389-2   LC 2005-05472
"This book offers a detailed look at the first 'Powder Puff Derby' run in the summer of 1929. . . . Starting in Santa Monica, California, and ending in Cleveland, Ohio, the women flew over deserts and mountains. . . . It was an all-star event with racers including Amelia Earhart, 'Pancho' Barnes, and Louise Thaden. . . . The photos of flyers, landscapes, and memorabilia bring the story to life. This book is a welcome addition." Voice Youth Advocates
Includes bibliographical references

798.2   Horsemanship

Kimball, Cheryl
Horse show handbook for kids; everything a young rider needs to know to prepare, train, and compete in English or Western events: plus getting-ready checklists and show diary pages; [by] Cheryl Kimball. Storey Pub. 2004 151p il $26.95; pa $16.95 *
Grades: 4 5 6 7   **798.2**
1. Horsemanship
ISBN 1-58017-573-2; 1-58017-501-5 (pa)
LC 2003-21732
Paperback edition has title: Horse showing for kids
Contents: Types of shows; Types of classes; Show personnel; Choosing the right horse; Conditioning and training; Trailering; Grooming; Attire and equipment (you & your horse); Planning for a show; On the big day; After the show; Moving up the competitive ladder
"For kids who have ever wondered if there is a certain color that complements their horse more than another, what last-minute checks they need to do before entering a show ring, how to dress for success, and much more, this handbook is invaluable. Presenting a wealth of information in a well-organized and enthusiastic manner, the author also addresses the more serious issues such as safety and good sportsmanship. The format is appealing, with lots of colorful photos." SLJ

798.4   Horse racing

Tate, Nikki, 1962-
Behind the scenes: the racehorse. Fitzhenry & Whiteside 2008 72p il $22.95; pa $18.95
Grades: 5 6 7 8   **798.4**
1. Horse racing
ISBN   978-1-55455-018-0;   1-55455-018-1; 978-1-55455-032-6 (pa); 1-55455-032-7 (pa)
"A short history of horse racing opens this attractive and informative book. Tate discusses the breeding, training, and care of the horses but devotes plenty of space to the people who are involved in the sport. . . . The many color photos . . . are quite clear and well matched to the text." Booklist

798.8   Dog racing

Wood, Ted, 1965-
Iditarod dream; Dusty and his sled dogs compete in Alaska's Jr. Iditarod. Walker & Co. 1996 48p il map hardcover o.p. pa $8.95
Grades: 4 5 6 7   **798.8**
1. Sled dog racing
ISBN 0-8027-8406-2; 0-8027-7535-7 (pa)
LC 95-31084
This "photo essay follows 15-year-old Dusty Whittemore of Cantwell, AK, through the 1995 Jr. Iditarod Sled Dog Race—158 miles from Lake Lucille to Yentna and back." SLJ
"Clear, close-up color photographs portray every stage

Wood, Ted, 1965-—*Continued*
of the event and offer interesting information about the difficulties and hazards of this two-day competition."
Booklist

799.1 Fishing

Arnosky, Jim
Hook, line, & seeker; a beginner's guide to fishing, boating, and watching water wildlife; with photographs and illustrations by the author. Scholastic Nonfiction 2005 192p il $12.95 *
Grades: 4 5 6 7 **799.1**
1. Fishing 2. Boats and boating 3. Marine animals
ISBN 0-439-45584-7 LC 2004-52501
"Distilling experiences garnered from a lifetime of fishing, boating and wildlife observation, naturalist Arnosky offers outdoorsy readers a handbook that is as much memoir as vademecum. . . . Illustrated with finished paintings, quick sketches from his notebooks . . . and small but very sharp color photos, this fills in the basics on diverse topics from boating safety to artificial flies to sport fish and shore birds." Booklist

Fitzgerald, Ron
Essential fishing for teens. Children's Press 2000 48p il (Outdoor life) lib bdg $22; pa $6.95
Grades: 7 8 9 10 **799.1**
1. Fishing
ISBN 0-516-23355-6 (lib bdg); 0-516-23555-9 (pa)
LC 00-23359
Presents information about fishing, including an explanation of the different types of fishing, the equipment needed, and safety tips
"The clear, full-color photographs depict adults of both genders." SLJ
Includes glossary and bibliographical references

800 LITERATURE, RHETORIC & CRITICISM

803 Literature—Encyclopedias and dictionaries

Benet's reader's encyclopedia; edited by Bruce F. Murphy. 5th ed. Collins 2008 1210p $60
Grades: 8 9 10 11 12 Adult **803**
1. Literature—Dictionaries 2. Reference books
ISBN 978-0-06-089016-2 LC 2008-31430
First published 1948 under the editorship of William Rose Benet
This encyclopedia contains over 10,000 entries and covers world literature from early times to the present. Includes entries on authors, literary movements, principal characters, plot synopses, terms, awards, myths and legends, etc.
This is "an edifying staple for any literary library." Libr J

Brewer's dictionary of phrase & fable. 17th ed., revised by John Ayto. Collins 2005 xxvii, 1523p il $55
Grades: 5 6 7 8 9 10 11 12 Adult **803**
1. Literature—Dictionaries 2. Mythology—Dictionaries 3. Allusions 4. Reference books
ISBN 0-06-112120-7; 978-0-06-112120-3
First published 1870 under the editorship of Ebenezer Cobham Brewer
"Over 15,000 brief entries give the meanings and origins of a broad range of terms, expressions, and names of real, fictitious and mythical characters from world history, science, the arts and literature." N Y Public Libr. Ref Books for Child Collect. 2d edition
"This classic for the ages is immensely browseable; one can get lost in it for hours." Libr J

808 Rhetoric

Dunn, Jessica, 1980-
A teen's guide to getting published; publishing for profit, recognition, and academic success; [by] Jessica Dunn & Danielle Dunn. 2nd ed. Prufrock Press 2006 249p pa $14.95 *
Grades: 7 8 9 10 11 12 **808**
1. Authorship 2. Publishers and publishing
ISBN 1-59363-182-0 LC 2006005109
First published 1997
Danielle Dunn's name appears first on the earlier edition
"Adding new Internet opportunities such as online journals, writer-support blogs, and e-mail editing, this volume covers the full gamut of possibilities and pitfalls for aspiring writers. . . . In addition to standard advice on publishers and agents, the authors give practical suggestions for finding a writing environment that is accessible to teens, such as school publication staffs and local newspaper internships. . . . Annotated appendixes list Web sites, books, journals, and contests. Also provided is information on mentors, writing camps, and courses catering to young authors, and a valuable list of mainstream publishers who have expressed openness to submissions from teens. This compact, sensible book discusses all kinds of writing." SLJ

Fletcher, Ralph, 1953-
How to write your life story; [by] Ralph Fletcher. 1st ed. Collins 2007 102p $15.99; pa $5.99
Grades: 5 6 7 8 **808**
1. Authorship 2. Autobiography—Authorship
ISBN 978-0-06-050770-1; 978-0-06-050769-5 (pa)
LC 2007010990
A guide to help write an autobiography.
"Fletcher gives readers and educators many practical and supportive tips. . . . Interspersed within the text are interviews with Jack Gantos, Kathi Appelt, and Jerry Spinelli, along with passages from the author's own memoir." SLJ

Fletcher, Ralph, 1953——_Continued_

How writers work; finding a process that works for you. HarperTrophy 2000 114p pa $4.99

Grades: 4 5 6 7   **808**

1. Authorship 2. Creative writing

ISBN 0-380-79702-X   LC 00-27573

Focuses on the skills and techniques necessary for good writing, with excerpts from established writers and samples of young people's work as examples

"The book makes youngsters feel good about their writing without making light of the work involved. . . . This is a useful resource." SLJ

Includes bibliographical references

Gaines, Ann

Don't steal copyrighted stuff! avoiding plagiarism and illegal internet downloading; [by] Ann Graham Gaines. Enslow Publishers 2008 192p il (Prime) $38.60 *

Grades: 7 8 9 10   **808**

1. Plagiarism 2. Bibliographical citations 3. Copyright

ISBN 978-0-7660-2861-6; 0-7660-2861-5

LC 2007-8370

"The first three chapters explain just what plagiarism is, the types of plagiarism, and what copyright and fair use are. Two chapters explain how to find sources, take notes properly, and construct a project or paper using proper citations in MLA format. . . . Every student should be required to read this. . . . Librarians and teachers who are looking for explanations of copyright and plagiarism and illustrative examples will find this book to be a good resource." Libr Media Connect

Includes bibliographical references

Gilbert, Sara

Write your own article; newspaper, magazine, online; by Sara Gilbert. Compass Point Books 2009 64p il (Write your own) lib bdg $33.26; pa $5.95

Grades: 6 7 8 9   **808**

1. Authorship 2. Journalism

ISBN 978-0-7565-3855-2 (lib bdg); 0-7565-3855-6 (lib bdg); 978-0-7565-3945-0 (pa); 0-7565-3945-5 (pa)

LC 2008-13342

"Explains how to write articles, from getting the story to capturing speech on paper, with examples from successful articles." Publisher's note

"There is much useful information provided. . . . [The book has] full-color photos, graphics, and tinted text boxes on nearly every page. [This is a solid selection] for aspiring writers." SLJ

Includes glossary and bibliographical references

Harper, Elizabeth, 1934-

Your name in print; a teen's guide to publishing for fun, profit, and academic success; [by] Elizabeth Harper and Timothy Harper. St. Martin's Griffin 2005 186p pa $13.95

Grades: 7 8 9 10   **808**

1. Authorship 2. Publishers and publishing

ISBN 0-312-33759-0   LC 2004-24675

The authors "offer chapters and features on a variety of subjects: writing outlets (such as local papers and blogs); article topics; workspaces; book publishing and agents; tips from pros; sample columns; [and] 'glances' at current teen writers. . . . This book will be a useful addition for most libraries." Voice Youth Advocates

Includes bibliographical references

Janeczko, Paul B., 1945-

Writing winning reports and essays. Scholastic Reference 2003 224p (Scholastic guides) lib bdg $16.95; pa $7.95 *

Grades: 5 6 7 8   **808**

1. Authorship 2. Report writing

ISBN 0-439-28717-0 (lib bdg); 0-439-28718-9 (pa)

LC 2002-30543

Provides strategies for writing successful research reports and essays, including social studies reports, book reports, persuasive essays, personal essays, and descriptive essays

"A solid and useful resource." SLJ

Nobleman, Marc Tyler

Extraordinary e-mails, letters, and resumes; by Marc Tyler Nobleman. Watts 2005 128p il (F. W. Prep) $30.50 *

Grades: 7 8 9 10   **808**

1. Letter writing 2. Electronic mail systems 3. Résumés (Employment)

ISBN 0-531-16759-3

This "builds a resume step-by-step, shows examples of different types of business letters, and addresses basic and not-so-basic netiquette. . . . [It is] laid out clearly and attractively, using bulleted lists, sample writings, and tables comparing examples of outstanding versus dull writing. The language is easy to follow, and the graphics and coloring enhances the books' readability." Voice Youth Advocates

Nuwer, Hank

To the young writer; nine writers talk about their craft. Watts 2002 111p il lib bdg $23

     808

1. Authorship 2. Authors, American

ISBN 0-531-11591-7   LC 2001-24895

Nine writers, including a Hollywood screenwriter, a novelist, and a sportswriter, talk about their craft

"A concise, practical, and accessible guide. . . . A range of topics is discussed including the thrill of reporting, editing, storytelling, and writing for student publications, different audiences, and from personal experience. Also included are tips for aspiring writers. . . . This inspiring book offers a number of options for those considering the field." SLJ

Includes bibliographical references

Rosinsky, Natalie M. (Natalie Myra)
Write your own biography; by Natalie M. Rosinsky. Compass Point Books 2008 64p il (Write your own) lib bdg $31.93
Grades: 5 6 7 8 **808**
1. Biography—Authorship
ISBN 978-0-7565-3366-3 (lib bdg); 0-7565-3366-X (lib bdg) LC 2007011471
"Rosinsky adroitly leads readers through the challenging process of researching and writing a biography. Chapters include helpful suggestions, excerpts from published works, and writing exercises. Full-color photos, charts, and graphics break up the text." SLJ
Includes glossary and bibliographical references

Trueit, Trudi Strain
Keeping a journal; [by] Trudi Strain Trueit. F. Watts 2004 80p (Life balance) $20.50; pa $6.95
Grades: 5 6 7 8 **808**
1. Diaries 2. Authorship
ISBN 0-531-12262-X; 0-531-15581-1 (pa)
LC 2003-25290
Contents: Navigating the journey; Why journal?; Time travel; Getting started; Write now! A 30-day journal
"Trueit features examples . . . to spark the imaginations of young people eager to express their unique views. Tips on how to begin, exercises designed to help overcome writer's block, and a 30-day calendar of creative ideas to get started are included. . . . The enthusiastic tone, inspirational examples, and writing prompts will help even those reluctant to express themselves to pick up a pen or pencil." SLJ
Includes bibliographical references

808.06 Writing children's literature

Peck, Richard, 1934-
Invitations to the world; teaching and writing for the young. Dial Bks. 2002 204p $16.99
Grades: 8 9 10 11 12 **808.06**
1. Authorship 2. Books and reading 3. Young adult literature—Technique
ISBN 0-8037-2734-8 LC 2001-53691
First published 1994 by Delacorte Press with title: Love and death at the mall
"Peck puts down his thoughts on writing for young people and reminisces about the inspiration behind his books and his motivation to become an author. . . . The earlier version of this book addressed two questions: 'How did you get your start?' and 'Where do you get your ideas?' Here Peck adds a chapter to answer the question, 'How much longer are you going to write?'. . . . Also new to this edition is a section at the end of the book called For Sharing that includes advice to encourage reading and discussion questions for novels." Voice Youth Advocates
Includes bibliographical references

808.1 Rhetoric of poetry

Fandel, Jennifer, 1973-
Puns, allusions, and other word secrets; [by] Jennifer Fandel. Creative Education 2005 48p il (Understanding poetry) $21.95
Grades: 7 8 9 10 **808.1**
1. Poetics
ISBN 1-58341-341-3 LC 2004058229
This "deals with the importance of choosing the right word, the opportunity to create new words or strange combinations, point of view, and hidden meanings. An excellent choice of poems . . . enhances the discussion of these aspects of poetry. The text asks readers questions about their impressions and reactions to the various verses." SLJ
Includes bibliographical references

Rhyme, meter, and other word music; [by] Jennifer Fandel. Creative Education 2005 48p il (Understanding poetry) $21.95
Grades: 7 8 9 10 **808.1**
1. Poetics
ISBN 1-58341-342-1 LC 2004058230
This "title offers clear explanations and examples of perfect, slant, and internal rhymes. The various forms a poem can take, including haiku, limerick, and sonnet, are also described. . . . The selections will increase young peoples understanding and appreciation of this word music." SLJ
Includes bibliographical references

Fletcher, Ralph, 1953-
Poetry matters; writing a poem from the inside out. HarperCollins Pubs. 2002 142p hardcover o.p. pa $4.99
Grades: 4 5 6 7 **808.1**
1. Poetics
ISBN 0-06-623599-5 (lib bdg); 0-380-79703-8 (pa)
LC 2001-24640
"Chapters deal with images; creating 'music,' or sounds and rhythms; how to generate ideas for poems; the construction of the words on the page; and more. Tips on fine-tuning are also given. . . . Major poetic forms are defined, including haiku, ode, and free verse, and there is a section on ways to share your work. Interspersed are Fletcher's personal insights and interviews with three poets—Kristine O'Connell George, Janet S. Wong, and J. Patrick Lewis. . . . Since this thought-provoking book covers more of the internal, less-tangible aspects of poetry, it may be more suited for readers who have some experience with the genre." SLJ
Includes bibliographical references

Poetry from A to Z; a guide for young writers; compiled by Paul B. Janeczko; illustrated by Cathy Bobak. Bradbury Press 1994 131p il $16.95 *
Grades: 5 6 7 8 9 10 **808.1**
1. Poetics 2. American poetry—Collections
ISBN 0-02-747672-3 LC 94-10528

Poetry from A to Z—*Continued*

"In his guide, Janeczko gives many examples and ideas to get young writers started writing poetry. The book is organized alphabetically with seventy-two poems on almost any topic you could imagine. In addition, fourteen exercises labeled 'Try This' explain how to write different types of poems and help a young writer get started." Voice Youth Advocates

Includes bibliographical references

Prelutsky, Jack

Pizza, pigs, and poetry; how to write a poem. Greenwillow Books 2008 191p il $16.99; pa $5.99 *

Grades: 4 5 6   **808.1**

1. Poetics

ISBN 978-0-06-143449-5; 0-06-143449-3; 978-0-06-143448-8 (pa); 0-06-143448-5 (pa)

LC 2007-36738

"Along with easy-to-follow tips for creating verse, haiku, and concrete poetry, the reigning Children's Poet Laureate offers insights into his own thought processes, . . . glimpses of his childhood, and personal anecdotes. . . . Prelutsky tucks in more than a dozen examples of his own work, plus 10 two-and-part-of-a-third line 'poem starts.'" Booklist

Seeing the blue between; advice and inspiration for young poets; compiled by Paul B. Janeczko. Candlewick Press 2002 132p $18.99; pa $7.99

Grades: 7 8 9 10   **808.1**

1. Poetics 2. American poetry—Collections

ISBN 0-7636-0881-5; 0-7636-2909-X (pa)

LC 2001-25882

"Here, thirty-two established poets share their writing secrets in short letters addressed directly to the readers. Although each poet has a distinct voice . . . a familiar mantra quickly develops: read, observe, love words, write, rewrite. . . . Accompanying poems may connect directly to a letter's content, give a representative sample of an individual's body of work, or impart advice." Horn Book Guide

"The letters are personal, friendly, and supportive. . . . A valuable addition to public and school libraries, with the potential for much classroom and personal use." SLJ

Wolf, Allan

Immersed in verse; an informative, slightly irreverent & totally tremendous guide to living the poet's life; [by] Allan Wolf; illustrated by Tuesday Mourning. 1st ed. Lark Books 2006 112p il $14.95

Grades: 5 6 7 8   **808.1**

1. Poetics

ISBN 1-57990-628-1   LC 2005024825

Contains advice, ideas, writing activities, and encouragement from a working poet for aspiring poets. Includes poems by a variety of poets from the unknown to the famous, including Langston Hughes, E.E. Cummings, Eve Merriam, and more.

"This how-to guide—chock-full of examples—is sure to inspire and nurture young poets. The information is intensive without being overwhelming, wise without being didactic. Wolf's love of language is evident throughout." SLJ

Includes glossary and bibliographical references

808.2   Rhetoric of drama

Lawrence, Colton, 1968-

Big fat paycheck; a young person's guide to writing for the movies. Bantam Bks. 2004 269p il $11.99 paperback o.p.

Grades: 7 8 9 10   **808.2**

1. Motion picture plays—Technique

ISBN 0-553-13122-2; 0-553-13122-2 (pa)

The author addresses "the major concerns that beginning screenplay writers face—finding a voice, formatting, developing a concept and characters, plotting, rewriting, polishing, and shopping a completed script." Voice Youth Advocates

"A lively, compelling, and concisely concrete guide for creative kids with big-screen dreams." SLJ

808.3   Rhetoric of fiction

Bauer, Marion Dane, 1938-

Our stories; a fiction workshop for young authors; compiled and with commentary by Marion Dane Bauer. Clarion Bks. 1996 195p hardcover o.p. pa $6.95

Grades: 5 6 7 8   **808.3**

1. Fiction—Technique 2. Authorship 3. Creative writing

ISBN 0-395-81598-3; 0-395-81599-1 (pa)

LC 95-51091

The author presents a selection of short fiction written by students in grades four through twelve and then critiques each piece

"This book would be an excellent resource for teachers looking for a new approach to the writing process. . . . Anyone who enjoys writing cannot help but be inspired by the remarkable talent of these young authors, and by Bauer's friendly, encouraging and helpful advice." Voice Youth Advocates

Bodden, Valerie

Creating the character; dialogue and characterization; [by] Valerie Bodden. Creative Education 2009 48p il (The art of creative prose) lib bdg $22.95

Grades: 6 7 8 9   **808.3**

1. Fiction—Technique 2. Authorship 3. Characters and characteristics in literature 4. Creative writing

ISBN 978-1-58341-622-8 (lib bdg); 1-58341-622-6 (lib bdg)   LC 2007-19611

"Young authors learn the importance of showing, rather than telling, when developing a character, as well as creating well-developed protagonists and antagonists, memorable minor characters, and natural-sounding dialogue. . . . Young writers who pick [this] up . . . will find valuable guidance." SLJ

Includes glossary and bibliographical references

Bodden, Valerie—*Continued*

Painting the picture; imagery and description; by Valerie Bodden. Creative Education 2009 48p il (The art of creative prose) lib bdg $22.95

Grades: 6 7 8 9 **808.3**

1. Fiction—Technique 2. Authorship 3. Creative writing

ISBN 978-1-58341-623-5 (lib bdg); 1-58341-623-4 (lib bdg) LC 2007-18964

"Highlights the use of images that appeal to the senses, word choice, and figurative language. . . . Concludes with several suggested exercises. . . . Young writers who pick [this] up . . . will find valuable guidance." SLJ

Includes glossary and bibliographical references

Setting the style; wording and tone; [by] Valerie Bodden. Creative Education 2009 48p il (The art of creative prose) lib bdg $22.95

Grades: 6 7 8 9 **808.3**

1. Fiction—Technique 2. Authorship 3. Creative writing

ISBN 978-1-58341-625-9 (lib bdg); 1-58341-625-0 (lib bdg) LC 2007-19609

"Encourages authors to find their own voice, explaining the difference between literary and direct styles and detailing the importance of rhythm, tone, and atmosphere in fiction writing. . . . Young writers who pick [this] up . . . will find valuable guidance." SLJ

Includes glossary and bibliographical references

Telling the tale; narration and point of view; [by] Valerie Bodden. Creative Education 2009 48p il (The art of creative prose) lib bdg $22.95

Grades: 6 7 8 9 **808.3**

1. Fiction—Technique 2. Authorship 3. Creative writing

ISBN 978-1-58341-624-2 (lib bdg); 1-58341-624-2 (lib bdg) LC 2007-4198

"Covers the choice of a narrator and viewpoint, including multiple and unreliable narrators. . . . Young writers who pick [this] up . . . will find valuable guidance." SLJ

·Includes glossary and bibliographical references

Farrell, Tish

Write your own fantasy story; by Tish Farrell. Compass Point Books 2006 64p il $31.93

Grades: 4 5 6 7 **808.3**

1. Fantasy fiction—Authorship 2. Creative writing

ISBN 0-7565-1639-0 LC 2005033654

Contents: Getting started; Setting the scene; Characters; Viewpoint; Synopses and plot; Wizard words; Spellbound speech; Hints and tips; The next step; Find out more

"Full-color photographs, movie stills, and fun graphics enliven the [presentation]. . . . It's hard to think of a better way to hook emerging writers up with good advice about honing their skills." SLJ

Includes bibliographical references

Write your own mystery story; by Tish Farrell. Compass Point Books 2006 64p il $31.93

Grades: 4 5 6 7 **808.3**

1. Mystery fiction—Authorship 2. Creative writing

ISBN 0-7565-1641-2 LC 2005030730

Contents: Getting started; Setting the scene; Characters; Viewpoint; Synopses and plot; Winning words; Scintillating speech; Hints and tips; The next step; Find out more

"Full-color photographs, movie stills, and fun graphics enliven the [presentation]. . . . It's hard to think of a better way to hook emerging writers up with good advice about honing their skills." SLJ

Includes bibliographical references

Write your own science fiction story; by Tish Farrell. Compass Point Books 2006 64p il $31.93

Grades: 4 5 6 7 **808.3**

1. Science fiction—Authorship 2. Creative writing

ISBN 0-7565-1643-9 LC 2005030732

Contents: Getting started; Setting the scene; Characters; Viewpoint; Synopses and plot; Winning words; Scintillating speech; Hints and tips; The next step; Find out more

"Full-color photographs, movie stills, and fun graphics enliven the [presentation]. . . . It's hard to think of a better way to hook emerging writers up with good advice about honing their skills." SLJ

Includes bibliographical references

Hanley, Victoria

Seize the story; a handbook for teens who like to write; [by] Victoria Hanley. Cottonwood Press 2008 213p il pa $15.95 *

Grades: 7 8 9 10 **808.3**

1. Fiction—Technique 2. Authorship 3. Creative writing

ISBN 978-1-877673-81-8 (pa); 1-877673-81-1 (pa)

A guide to fiction writing for teenagers with advice on approaching the young-adult market, and discusses dialogue, plot, and other related topics; and presents interviews with established authors such as T. A. Barron, Joan Bauer, and Chris Crutcher.

"Hanley uses examples from familiar novels and authors such as 'Harry Potter' and Stephenie Meyer's *Twilight* . . . to illustrate elements of writing. . . . This book is an excellent resource for creative writing classes as well as individuals." SLJ

Includes bibliographical references

Levine, Gail Carson, 1947-

Writing magic; creating stories that fly. Collins 2006 167p $16.99; pa $5.99 *

Grades: 5 6 7 8 **808.3**

1. Fiction—Technique 2. Authorship 3. Creative writing

ISBN 978-0-06-051961-2; 0-06-051969-4; 978-0-06-051960-5 (pa); 0-06-051960-6 (pa) LC 2006-00481

"Levine, best known for *Ella Enchanted* (1997), offers middle-graders ideas about making their own writing take flight. . . . Among the topics she covers are shaping character, beginnings and endings, revising, and finding

Levine, Gail Carson, 1947-—*Continued*
ideas. . . . Each chapter concludes with writing exercises. . . . A terrific item to have on hand for writing groups or for individual young writers who want to improve." Booklist

Mlynowski, Sarah, 1977-
See Jane write; a girl's guide to writing chick lit; by Sarah Mlynowski and Farrin Jacobs. Quirk Books 2006 191p il pa $14.95
Grades: 8 9 10 11 12　　　　　　　　**808.3**
　1. Fiction—Technique 2. Authorship 3. Creative writing 4. Publishers and publishing
　ISBN 1-59474-115-8
"Fun, inspiring, and organized in a clear and encouraging style, this book covers topics from what chick lit is to how to create believable characters, develop a plot, and set a tone. The authors discuss seeing a project through to the finish and getting it published. The writing style is quirky and the advice is sound." SLJ

Otfinoski, Steven, 1949-
Extraordinary short story writing; by Steven Otfinoski. Franklin Watts 2005 128p il (F.W. prep) lib bdg $30.50; pa $9.95 *
Grades: 5 6 7 8　　　　　　　　　　**808.3**
　1. Fiction—Technique 2. Short story 3. Authorship 4. Creative writing
　ISBN 0-531-16760-7 (lib bdg); 0-531-17578-2 (pa)
　　　　　　　　　　　　　　LC 2005006650
"In this excellent resource, specific ways to write different types of stories, project ideas, and resources are presented in such a way as to make short story assignments enjoyable. Readers are given many tips and practice activities in chapters that progress from gathering ideas to the final revision. Each section includes quotes from wellknown authors such as Edgar Allan Poe, Richard Peck, and Louis Sachar." SLJ
　Includes bibliographical references

Rosinsky, Natalie M. (Natalie Myra)
Write your own fairy tale; by Natalie M. Rosinsky. Compass Point Books 2008 64p il (Write your own) lib bdg $31.93
Grades: 5 6 7 8　　　　　　　　　　**808.3**
　1. Fairy tales—Authorship 2. Creative writing
　ISBN 978-0-7565-3369-4 (lib bdg); 0-7565-3369-4 (lib bdg)
　　　　　　　　　　　　　　LC 2007015720
This offers suggestions on how to write fairy tales, discussing settings, characters, viewpoint, plots, and style.
　Includes glossary and bibliographical references

Write your own myth; by Natalie M. Rosinsky. Compass Point Books 2008 64p il (Write your own) lib bdg $31.93
Grades: 5 6 7 8　　　　　　　　　　**808.3**
　1. Creative writing
　ISBN 978-0-7565-3372-4 (lib bdg); 0-7565-3372-4 (lib bdg)
　　　　　　　　　　　　　　LC 2007011472
This offers suggestions for writing myths, discussing setting, characters, viewpoint, plots and style.
　Includes bibliographical references

Write your own tall tale; by Natalie M. Rosinsky. Compass Point Books 2008 64p il (Write your own) lib bdg $31.93
Grades: 5 6 7 8　　　　　　　　　　**808.3**
　1. Tall tales—Authorship 2. Creative writing
　ISBN 978-0-7565-3375-5 (lib bdg); 0-7565-3375-9 (lib bdg)
　　　　　　　　　　　　　　LC 2007012462
This offers suggestions for writing tall tales, discussing settings, characters, viewpoint, plots, and style.
　Includes glossary and bibliographical references

808.4　Rhetoric of essays

Orr, Tamra
Extraordinary essays. Franklin Watts 2005 128p il (F. W. Prep) $31; pa $9.95 *
Grades: 7 8 9 10　　　　　　　　　　**808.4**
　1. Essay 2. Authorship
　ISBN 0-531-16761-5; 0-531-17576-6 (pa)
"This concise, appealingly designed writing guide offers practical advice to students on how to successfully complete essay assignments. Topics covered include choosing a topic, brainstorming, researching, crafting and defending a thesis statement, and revising." Booklist
　Includes bibliographical references

808.5　Rhetoric of speech

Ryan, Margaret, 1950-
Extraordinary oral presentations. Franklin Watts 2005 128p il (F. W. Prep) $31; pa $9.95 *
Grades: 7 8 9 10　　　　　　　　　　**808.5**
　1. Public speaking
　ISBN 0-531-16758-5; 0-531-17577-4 (pa)
This offers advice on preparing oral presentations
This book provides "good, practical ideas for students." SLJ
　Includes bibliographical references

808.53　Debating

Merali, Alim, 1984-
Talk the talk; speech and debate made easy. Gravitas Pub. 2006 269p $25.95 *
Grades: 7 8 9 10 11 12　　　　　　　　**808.53**
　1. Debates and debating 2. Public speaking
　ISBN 0-9738682-0-1
"This outstanding guide to all aspects of debate is a practical and easy-to-read source for students. Beginning with helpful physical preparations and mental exercises, the book goes on to discuss kinds of speeches, ingredients of style, steps to winning an argument, and special types of speech, such as cross-examination and parliamentary exchanges." Voice Youth Advocates
　Includes glossary and bibliographical references

808.8 Literature—Collections

Beware!; R.L. Stine picks his favorite scary stories. HarperCollins Pubs. 2002 214p il $11.99; lib bdg $14.89; pa $5.99

Grades: 4 5 6 7   **808.8**
1. Horror fiction 2. Literature—Collections
ISBN 0-06-623842-0; 0-06-623843-9 (lib bdg); 0-06-055547-5 (pa)   LC 2002-18938
"A Parachute Press book"

Stine "brings together 19 brief stories, folktales, poems, and cartoons from the likes of Ray Bradbury, William Sleator, Robert W. Service . . . Gahan Wilson, and Alvin Schwartz. . . . There's something in this diverse literary buffet for every taste—including enough genuine eeriness to make it a discomfiting choice for under-the-covers reading." Booklist

Classic western stories; the most beloved stories; compiled by Cooper Edens. Chronicle Books 2009 140p il $19.99

Grades: 5 6 7 8   **808.8**
1. West (U.S.) 2. American literature—Collections
ISBN 978-0-8118-6325-4   LC 2008009819

Stories, folktales, and poems with a western setting, including stories of Paul Bunyan, Pecos Bill, Indian legends, and tales of Lewis and Clark, among others.
"Colorful, often full-page, exquisitely produced illustrations by artists such as Frederic Remington, N. C. Wyeth, and Winslow Homer bring the words to life. Overall a visual delight, this stunning book is an excellent addition to art and literature collections." SLJ

The **Coyote** Road; trickster tales; edited by Ellen Datlow and Terri Windling; introduction by Terri Windling; decorations by Charles Vess. Viking Childrens Books 2007 523p il $19.99; pa $10.99

Grades: 7 8 9 10 11 12   **808.8**
1. Literature—Collections 2. Short stories
ISBN 978-0-670-06194-5; 0-670-06194-8; 978-0-14-241300-5 (pa); 0-14-241300-3 (pa)
                                 LC 2007-12414

A collection of stories and poems about tricksters in all parts of the world by a variety of authors.
"This excellent collection is bound to find an audience among experienced readers of the genre but is attractive to less-able readers, as well, for the short, punchy stories and an always-engaging trickster character." SLJ

First kiss (then tell); [edited by] Cylin Busby. Bloomsbury Children's Books 2008 212p il $15.95; pa $8.95

Grades: 7 8 9 10   **808.8**
1. Kissing 2. Literature—Collections
ISBN 978-1-59990-199-2; 978-1-59990-241-8 (pa)
                                 LC 2007-42365

Twenty-five best-selling young adult authors share stories about their first kiss. Includes quotations, facts, advice, and illustrations.
This is an "entertaining collection. . . . These authors treat their own stories with the same freshness and respect with which they approach their YA novels. . . . Some stories are poems, one is a play, and a few are in comic form. . . . This is a good collection for browsing." Booklist

The **Green** Man: tales from the mythic forest; edited by Ellen Datlow & Terri Windling; introduction by Terri Windling; decorations by Charles Vess. Viking 2002 384p $18.99; pa $8.99

Grades: 7 8 9 10   **808.8**
1. Literature—Collections 2. Fantasy fiction
ISBN 0-670-03526-2; 0-14-240029-7 (pa)
                                 LC 2001-46976

"The stories are thematically connected yet tonally varied, and each strongly plotted tale conjures a credible fantasy world. A brief biography of and remarks by the writer are included with each story. . . . This title will be eagerly devoured." Bull Cent Child Books

Hip deep; opinions, essays, and vision from American teenagers; edited by Abe Louise Young. Next Generation Press 2006 164p pa $12.95   **808.8**
1. Teenagers' writings 2. American literature—Collections
ISBN 0-9762706-2-5

"This collection of essays and poems by teens should inspire even the most reluctant writer to press on. By writing about their feelings on subjects ranging from frustration and anger to determination and renewal, these young people expose themselves from the inside out and launch themselves onto new paths." Voice Youth Advocates

Hudson, Wade

Powerful words; more than 200 years of extraordinary writing by African Americans; illustrated by Sean Qualls; foreword by Marian Wright Edelman. Scholastic Nonfiction 2004 178p il $19.95 *

Grades: 5 6 7 8   **808.8**
1. American literature—African American authors 2. African Americans—Biography 3. African Americans—History
ISBN 0-439-40969-1   LC 2003-42792

A collection of speeches and writings by African Americans, with commentary about the time period in which each person lived, information about the speaker/writer, and public response to the words.
"Short enough to hold attention, the selections . . . are also long enough to show the writers' tone and style. Many sensitive full-page portraits are included. . . . This well-designed volume will be an excellent addition to many library collections." Booklist
Includes bibliographical references

I can't keep my own secrets; six-word memoirs by teens famous & obscure: from Smith magazine; edited by Rachel Fershleiser & Larry Smith. HarperTeen 2009 pa $8.99

Grades: 7 8 9 10   **808.8**
1. Autobiographies 2. Teenagers' writings
ISBN 978-0-06-172684-2; 0-06-172684-2
                                 LC 2009014584

"This is a book with nearly 800 authors (all aged thirteen to nineteen) and 800 characters (all real, as far as we know) and 800 stories (which can be read in any or-

I can't keep my own secrets—*Continued*
der). What every story has in common is that each was
written about the author's own life, and that each is the
exact same length: six words." Publisher's note

"The ruminations span from the haunting . . . to the
funny . . . to the inspirational. . . . A razor focus is put
on issues that hit youths the hardest. . . . It has just the
right proportion of humor and heartbreak." Booklist

Leaving home: stories; selected by Hazel
Rochman and Darlene Z. McCampbell.
HarperCollins Pubs. 1997 231p pa $11.99
hardcover o.p. *

Grades: 6 7 8 9   **808.8**
1. Youth—Fiction 2. Short stories
ISBN 0-06-440706-3   LC 96-28979

Includes the following stories: The first day, by E. P.
Jones; Dancer, by V. Sears; A gift of laughter, by A.
Sherman; Rules of the game, by A. Tan; The circuit, by
F. Jiménez; Bad influence, by J. Ortiz Cofer; Dawn, by
T. Wynne-Jones; Trip in a summer dress, by A. Sanford;
On the rainy river, by T. O'Brien; The setting sun and
the rolling world, by C. Mungoshi; Zelzah: a tale from
long ago, by N. F. Mazer; "Recitatif," by T. Morrison

An international anthology that reflects the thoughts
and feelings of young people as they make their way
into the world. Authors represented include Amy Tan,
Sandra Cisneros, Tim Wynne-Jones, and Toni Morrison

"The editors have varied the tones, the music, the
voices, and the meanings of the pieces, which provide
both humorous and heartbreaking stories of the meaning
of adolescence." ALAN

Night is gone, day is still coming; stories and
poems by American Indian teens and young
adults; edited by Annette Pina Ochoa, Betsy
Franco, and Traci L. Gourdine; with an
introduction by Simon J. Ortiz. Candlewick
Press 2003 145p $16.99

Grades: 7 8 9 10   **808.8**
1. American literature—Native American authors—
Collections
ISBN 0-7636-1518-8   LC 2002-74086

"In poems and short stories, young Indian writers,
ages 11 to 22, tell about their lives on the reservations,
in small towns, and in large cities." Booklist

"These are honest voices in a well-organized anthology that gives an excellent look into an important American culture." SLJ

Read all about it! great read-aloud stories, poems,
and newspaper pieces for preteens and teens;
edited by Jim Trelease. Penguin Bks. 1993 489p
il pa $13.95

Grades: 8 9 10 11 12   **808.8**
1. Literature—Collections 2. Authors
ISBN 0-14-014655-5   LC 93-21781

This is a collection of 52 selections of fiction, poetry,
and nonfiction from newspapers, magazines, and books
by such authors as Cynthia Rylant, Jerry Spinelli, Howard Pyle, Rudyard Kipling, Robert W. Service, Maya
Angelou, Moss Hart, Pete Hamill, and Leon Garfield. Includes biographical information about the authors

808.81   Poetry—Collections

The **Body** eclectic; an anthology of poems; edited
by Patrice Vecchione. Holt & Co. 2002 192p
$16.95

Grades: 7 8 9 10   **808.81**
1. Poetry—Collections
ISBN 0-8050-6935-6   LC 2001-51900

This collection of poetry focuses on the human body
and its parts, including works by poets such as Gary
Soto, Shel Silverstein, Paul Laurence Dunbar, Pablo
Neruda, Walt Whitman and Shakespeare

"Excellent notes at the back introduce each writer and
suggest more books to read. A great collection to show
teens that literature is about their intimate selves and
their connections with people everywhere." Booklist

Includes bibliographical references

Crush: love poems. Word of Mouth Books/KA
Productions 2007 72p pa $10 *

Grades: 8 9 10 11 12   **808.81**
1. Love poetry
ISBN 978-1-88801-840-0

"Alexander offers a cosmopolitan menu of tanka, haiku, long titles that lead into short first lines, verbal formulas that lead to sung discoveries, French phrases,
prose poems, and poems written in Spanglish. The book
is divided into three sections with various speakers, and
a fourth section that includes poems by Sherman Alexie,
Pablo Neruda, Nikki Giovanni, and the title poem,
'Crush' by Naomi Shihab Nye. . . . This well-crafted
anthology will capture the interest of teens." SLJ

A **foot** in the mouth; poems to speak, sing, and
shout; [edited by Paul B. Janeczko; illustrated
by Chris Raschka] Candlewick Press 2009 64p
il $17.99 *

Grades: 4 5 6 7   **808.81**
1. Poetry—Collections
ISBN 978-0-7636-0663-3; 0-7636-0663-4
          LC 2008-935581

"The poems in Janeczko and Raschka's collection
. . . are not complacent, although plenty are funny and
some are familiar. . . . Punchy collages flutter across
airy white pages in loose visual arrangements; torn
scraps of origami paper layer with fluid lines in tart col-
or. Janeczko introduces the collection with the idea that
'Poetry is sound,' a pleasure to vocalize and memorize.
. . . Readers will be emboldened to join in the 'song.'"
Publ Wkly

I feel a little jumpy around you; a book of her
poems & his poems collected in pairs; [by]
Naomi Shihab Nye and Paul B. Janeczko.
Simon & Schuster Bks. for Young Readers 1996
256p pa $10 hardcover o.p. *

Grades: 7 8 9 10   **808.81**
1. Poetry—Collections
ISBN 0-689-81341-4   LC 95-44904

A collection of poems, by male and female authors,
presented in pairings that offer insight into how men and
women look at the world, both separately and together

"Though the gender counterpoint really plays little
part in the juxtaposition, the pairings are piquant and

I feel a little jumpy around you—*Continued*
provide a manageable way to start talking about a very
large collection of poetry. An engaging marginal dialogue, taken from Nye's and Janeczko's collaborative fax
correspondence, appears alongside the appendix and per-
mits a revealing peek behind the scences. Highly readable notes from contributors are included, as is an index
of poems and a gender-segregated index of poets." Bull
Cent Child Books

I wouldn't thank you for a valentine; poems for
young feminists; edited by Carol Ann Duffy;
illustrated by Trisha Rafferty. Holt & Co. 1993
104p il pa $6.95 hardcover o.p.   **808.81**
1. Feminism—Poetry 2. Poetry—Collections
ISBN 0-8050-5545-2   LC 93-3172
First published 1992 in the United Kingdom
A collection of poems by women from different cultures and backgrounds, portraying the varied facets of the
female experience from childhood to old age
"The anthology draws on poets from many cultures
and includes well-known poets, such as Nikki Giovani,
Sharon Olds, and Mary Oliver, as well as several new
voices. . . . These poems open up the range of love and
family." Booklist

Index to children's poetry; a title, subject, author,
and first line index to poetry in collections for
children and youth; compiled by John E. and
Sara W. Brewton. Wilson, H.W. 1942-1965 3v
$115
Grades: Professional   **808.81**
1. Poetry—Indexes 2. Reference books
ISBN 0-8242-0021-7
Basic volume published 1942; first supplement published 1954 $85 (ISBN 0-8242-0022-5); second supple-
ment published 1965 $85 (ISBN 0-8242-0023-3)
The main volume indexes 15,000 poems by 2,500 authors in 130 collections. The two supplements analyze
another 15,000 poems by 2700 authors in 151 collec-
tions.
"This tool is an invaluable reference source." Peterson.
Ref Books for Child

Index to poetry for children and young people; a
title, subject, author, and first line index to
poetry in collections for children and young
people. Wilson, H.W. 1972-1998 6v $105
Grades: Professional   **808.81**
1. Poetry—Indexes 2. Reference books
ISBN 0-8242-0435-2
A continuation of Index to children's poetry
The volume covering 1964-1969 published 1972 and
compiled by John E. and Sara W. Brewton and G. Meredith Blackburn III; 1970-1975 published 1978 compiled
by John E. Brewton, G. Meredith Blackburn III and Lorraine A. Blackburn $105 (ISBN 0-8242-0621-5); 1976-
1981 published 1984 compiled by John E. Brewton, G.
Meredith Blackburn III and Lorraine A. Blackburn $105
(ISBN 0-8242-0681-9); 1982-1987 published 1989 compiled by G. Meredith Blackburn III and Lorraine A.
Blackburn $111 (ISBN 0-8242-0773-4); 1988-1992 pub-
lished 1994 compiled by G. Meredith Blackburn III $110
(ISBN 0-8242-0861-7); 1993-1997 published 1998 compiled by G. Meredith Blackburn III $115 (ISBN 0-8242-

0939-7)
Each volume analyzes approximately 10,000 poems by
some 2,000 authors in more than 110 collections. Over
2,000 subject headings are used in each volume.

It's a woman's world; a century of women's
voices in poetry; edited by Neil Philip. Dutton
Children's Bks. 2000 93p il $17.99 *
Grades: 7 8 9 10   **808.81**
1. Poetry—Collections 2. Women poets
ISBN 0-525-46328-3   LC 99-88363
An anthology of poetry by twentieth-century women
from around the world including, Sylvia Plath, Nigar
Hanim, Sonia Sanchez, and Nellie Wong
"Beautifully reproduced black-and-white photos intro-
duce each section. Overall, this book is dense, challeng-
ing, and provocative." SLJ

Light-gathering poems; edited by Liz Rosenberg.
Holt & Co. 2000 146p $15.95
Grades: 7 8 9 10   **808.81**
1. Poetry—Collections
ISBN 0-8050-6223-8   LC 99-49231
Companion volume to Earth-shattering poems (1997)
"Poems were chosen for their ability to 'gather light,'
some representing beauty, some joy, some fascinating
imagery, and some the illusive light at the end of a dark
tunnel. . . . Notable writers such as Robert Frost, Walt
Whitman, Langston Hughes, Edna St. Vincent Millay,
Emily Dickinson, and Allen Ginsberg share the spotlight
with contemporaries such as Gary Soto, Kate Schmitt,
Mary Oliver, Steven Dauer, and Henry M. Seiden."
Voice Youth Advocates
Includes bibliographical references

The **Oxford** book of story poems; [compiled by]
Michael Harrison and Christopher Stuart-Clark.
Oxford University Press 2006 175p il pa $18.95
Grades: 5 6 7 8   **808.81**
1. Poetry—Collections
ISBN 978-0-19-276344-0; 0-19-276344-X
LC 2007282711
First published 1990
This anthology contains "narrative verse by British
and American poets, from traditional ballads such as 'Sir
Patrick Spens' to contemporary poems such as Judith
Nicholls' 'Storytime.' . . . The poets include Carroll,
Keats, de la Mare, Kennedy, Lear, Lindsay, Longfellow,
Noyes, Poe, Southey, and Tolkien. . . . A handy collec-
tion of story poems for reading aloud or alone." Booklist
[review of 1990 edition]

The **Oxford** book of war poetry; chosen and
edited by John Stallworthy. Oxford Univ. Press
1984 xxxi, 358p hardcover o.p. pa $19.95
Grades: 8 9 10 11 12 Adult   **808.81**
1. War poetry 2. Poetry—Collections
ISBN 0-19-214125-2; 0-19-955453-6 (pa)
LC 83-19303
"This comprehensive anthology focuses on poetic
treatment of warfare ranging from the battlefields of ancient history to the conflicts in Vietnam, Northern Ireland, and El Salvador." Univ Press Books for Second
Sch Libr
This collection "reminds one of the large numbers and

The Oxford book of war poetry—*Continued*
great variety of war poems from many centuries that are
very good poems. Mr. Stallworthy's selections include
most of the best, at least the best in English." N Y
Times Book Rev
Includes bibliographical references

Revenge and forgiveness; an anthology of poems;
edited by Patrice Vecchione. Henry Holt 2004
148p $16.95
Grades: 7 8 9 10   **808.81**
1. Poetry—Collections
ISBN 0-8050-7376-0   LC 2003-56631
A collection of nearly sixty poems dealing with revenge and forgiveness, plus suggested readings about
each contributing poet
"For students who are of a philosophical bent and for
teachers of poetry, this book of poems about love, hate,
and war will be a useful resource." Libr Media Connect
Includes bibliographical references

River of words; young poets and artists on the
nature of things; edited by Pamela Michael;
introduced by Robert Hass. Milkweed Editions
2008 298p il $29 *
Grades: 4 5 6 7 8 9   **808.81**
1. Poetry—Collections 2. Nature poetry 3. Children's
writings 4. Teenagers' writings 5. Children's art
ISBN 978-1-57131-685-1; 1-57131-685-X
"In 1995 Michael and Hass . . . cofounded the River
of Words project, designed to connect students' art and
poetry education to the natural world immediately around
them. . . . The poems and pictures in this handsomely
designed volume have been culled from yearly contests.
. . . The works are startling, many of them dislocating
and highly complex." Publ Wkly

Side by side; new poetry inspired by art from
around our world; collected by Jan Greenberg.
Abrams Books for Young Readers 2008 il
$19.95 *
Grades: 8 9 10 11 12   **808.81**
1. Poetry—Collections 2. Art—Poetry
ISBN 978-0-8109-9471-3; 0-8109-9471-2
      LC 2007-11973
This is an "anthology of accomplished poems inspired
by artworks. . . . [Greenberg brings] together the work
of poets and artists from around the globe. . . . The poems are grouped loosely into categories, defined in
Greenberg's inspirational introduction. . . . Each spread
features a poem in its original language, the English
translation, and an artwork, usually from the same country or culture as the poem. With a few exceptions, the
reproductions of the art, which ranges from ancient to
contemporary work, are sharp and clear, and the moving,
often startling poems invite readers to savor the words
and then look closely at each image." Booklist

The **Space** between our footsteps; poems and
paintings from the Middle East; selected by
Naomi Shihab Nye. Simon & Schuster Bks. for
Young Readers 1998 144p il maps $19.95
Grades: 7 8 9 10   **808.81**
1. Poetry—Collections 2. Middle East—Poetry
ISBN 0-689-81233-7   LC 97-18622

"Lyrical verse about family, friendship, nature, and
daily life makes up this collection of poems from 19
countries in the Middle East, with gloriously colored
paintings in a wide range of styles." Booklist

Step lightly; poems for the journey; collected by
Nancy Willard. Harcourt Brace & Co. 1998 99p
pa $12 hardcover o.p.
Grades: 7 8 9 10   **808.81**
1. Poetry—Collections
ISBN 0-15-202052-7   LC 98-5228
A collection of poems celebrating the ordinary in an
unordinary way, by such authors as Emily Dickinson,
Theodore Roethke, and D. H. Lawrence
"Willard weaves an anthology in which readers can
find happiness, insight, inspiration, and wisdom." SLJ

War and the pity of war; edited by Neil Philip;
illustrated by Michael McCurdy. Clarion Bks.
1998 96p il $20 *
Grades: 5 6 7 8 9 10   **808.81**
1. War poetry 2. Poetry—Collections
ISBN 0-395-84982-9   LC 97-32897
"The selections, covering conflicts from ancient Persia
to modern-day Bosnia, are by a wide variety of poets,
from the well known (Tennyson, Whitman, Sandburg,
Auden), to the obscure (Anakreon from ancient Greece
and 11th-century Chinese poet Bunno). . . . The stark
and simple scratchboard drawings are reminiscent of the
Ernie Pyle illustrations from World War II and are as
memorable as the best propaganda." SLJ

What have you lost? poems; selected by Naomi
Shihab Nye; photographs by Michael Nye.
Greenwillow Bks. 1999 pa $9.99 hardcover o.p.
*
Grades: 7 8 9 10   **808.81**
1. Poetry—Collections 2. Loss (Psychology)
ISBN 0-380-73307-2   LC 98-26674
In her "introduction, the anthologist-poet considers
loss—its certainty, scope, and effect, and its ability to
give rise to art. The topic is thoroughly explored by the
one hundred and forty poets whose work is collected
here in twenty-two unlabeled, thematically arranged sections. . . . The poets are all contemporary, with a dozen
or so hailing from outside the United States." Horn Book

808.82   Drama—Collections

Actor's choice; monologues for teens; edited by
Erin Detrick. Playscripts 2008 131p pa $14.95
Grades: 6 7 8 9 10   **808.82**
1. Monologues 2. Acting 3. Drama—Collections
ISBN 978-0-9709046-6-9; 0-9709046-6-5
      LC 2007-50166
"This volume of highly entertaining monologues is
gleaned from one-act and full-length plays published by
Playscripts, Inc. . . . This is an excellent volume to help
students prepare for competitions as well as to use in
drama, speech, or English classes." SLJ

The **Book** of monologues for aspiring actors; [edited by] Marsh Cassady. NTC Pub. Group 1995 212p il pa $23.96

Grades: 7 8 9 10 **808.82**

1. Monologues 2. Acting 3. Drama—Collections

ISBN 0-8442-5771-0   LC 94-66239

"The selections range from the classical Greeks to Sam Shepard and Oscar Wilde; they give YA's the opportunity to develop characters of like ages in many different settings. Several questions to probe the actors' imaginations appear at the end of each monologue." SLJ

Great monologues for young actors; Craig Slaight, Jack Sharrar, editors. Smith & Kraus 1992-1999 3v v1 pa $11.95; v2-v3 pa ea $14.95

Grades: 8 9 10 11 12 **808.82**

1. Monologues 2. Acting 3. Drama—Collections

ISBN 1-880399-03-2 (v1); 0-57525-106-X (v2); 1-57525-408-1 (v3)

"The Young Actors series."

These volumes provide an introduction and acting notes for monologues for men and women drawn from contemporary and classic works

Great scenes for young actors from the stage; Craig Slaight, Jack Sharrar, editors. Smith & Kraus 1991 2v 256p v1 pa $11.95; v2 pa $14.95 *

Grades: 7 8 9 10 **808.82**

1. Drama—Collections 2. Acting

ISBN 0-9622722-6-4 (v1); 1-57525-107-8 (v2)

v2 has title: Great scenes for young actors

Contains scenes from classic and contemporary plays. The selections, graded according to ability level, include a range of roles for men, women, and groups. Includes a brief synopsis of each play along with special notes

New audition scenes and monologs from contemporary playwrights; the best new cuttings from around the world; edited by Roger Ellis. Meriwether Pub. 2005 177p pa $15.95

Grades: 6 7 8 9 **808.82**

1. Monologues 2. Acting 3. Drama—Collections

ISBN 1-56608-105-X

"This work presents a wide variety of scenes selected especially for performers aged 12 to 24. . . . Introductions to each scene are informative and were reviewed and approved with some reshaping by the authors. . . . A good choice for students who seek new ideas for drama, forensic, and writing classes." SLJ

Surface, Mary Hall, 1958-

More short scenes and monologues for middle school students; inspired by literature, social studies, and real life; by Mary Hall Surface. 1st ed. Smith and Kraus 2007 207p (Young actors series) pa $11.95 *

Grades: 6 7 8 9 **808.82**

1. Monologues 2. Acting 3. Drama—Collections

ISBN 978-1-57525-560-6 (pa); 1-57525-560-X (pa)

    LC 2007281299

A collection of original scenes and monologues written especially for middle-school actors

"This volume stands out for its distinct voices, multicultural characters, and engaging scenes. The book is well organized. . . . This excellent book would be useful in a variety of classrooms including speech/communication, drama, English, and social studies." SLJ

Includes bibliographical references

Short scenes and monologues for middle school actors. Smith & Kraus 1999 183p (Young actors series) pa $11.95 *

Grades: 6 7 8 9 **808.82**

1. Monologues 2. Acting 3. Drama—Collections

ISBN 1-57525-179-5   LC 99-52457

A collection of original scenes and monologues written especially for middle-school actors

"A welcome find for young actors in search of material for auditions." SLJ

Includes bibliographical references

808.85   Speeches—Collections

Lend me your ears; great speeches in history; selected and introduced by William Safire. Updated and expanded. W.W. Norton 2004 1157p $39.95

Grades: 8 9 10 11 12 Adult **808.85**

1. Speeches

ISBN 978-0-393-05931-1; 0-393-05931-6

    LC 2004-13625

First published 1992

"A compendium of more than two hundred classic and modern speeches includes Orson Welles eulogizing Darryl F. Zanuck, George Patton exhorting his D-Day troops, King Edward VIII abdicating his throne, and the never-delivered speech John F. Kennedy was scheduled to give in Dallas." Publisher's note

This "is a good addition for those . . . in need of modern speeches. With an excellent index." Libr J

808.88   Collections of miscellaneous writings

Bartlett, John, 1820-1905

Bartlett's familiar quotations; a collection of passages, phrases, and proverbs traced to their sources in ancient and modern literature. Little, Brown 2002 1431p $50

Grades: 8 9 10 11 12 Adult **808.88**

1. Quotations 2. Reference books

ISBN 0-316-08460-3   LC 2003-269668

First published 1855. Periodically revised. Editors vary

"Arranged chronologically by author, with exact references. Includes many interesting footnotes, tracing history or usage of analogous thoughts, the circumstances under which a particular remark was made, etc. Author and keyword indexes. One of the best books of quotations with a long history." Guide to Ref Books. 11th edition

Includes bibliographical references

809 Literary history and criticism

Masterpieces of world literature; edited by Frank N. Magill. Harper & Row 1989 957p $55

Grades: 8 9 10 11 12 Adult **809**

1. Literature—History and criticism

ISBN 0-06-270050-2 LC 89-45052

"The work, arranged alphabetically by title, contains plot summaries, character portrayals, and critical evaluations of 270 classics of world literature (novels, plays, stories, poems, and essays), all reprints from other Magill guides." Nichols. Guide to Ref Books for Sch Media Cent. 4th edition

809.3 Fiction—History and criticism

Campbell, Kimberly

Less is more; teaching literature with short texts, grades 6-12; [by] Kimberly Hill Campbell. Stenhouse Publishers 2007 222p il pa $18.50

Grades: Professional **809.3**

1. Literature—Study and teaching

ISBN 978-1-57110-710-7; 1-57110-710-X

LC 2007019310

"Campbell's book makes a very good case for teaching with short texts. Through chapters on short stories, essays, memoirs, poetry, picture books, and graphic novels, she shows how all aspects of literature can be taught using a variety of short pieces. She suggests structures for the classroom and strategies for eliciting both written and oral responses to these texts. She ties reading short texts to ways of looking at student writing in similar genres. . . . This book will be valuable for beginning and veteran teachers because of the lists of short texts." Voice Youth Advocates

Includes bibliographical references

810.8 American literature— Collections

33 things every girl should know; stories, songs, poems, and smart talk by 33 extraordinary women; edited by Tonya Bolden. Crown 1998 159p il pa $13 hardcover o.p.

Grades: 7 8 9 10 **810.8**

1. Girls 2. American literature—Collections

ISBN 0-517-70936-8 LC 97-29431

A mix of short stories, essays, a comic strip, a speech, an interview, poems, and more which offer insights and advice for girls

"Astute, compassionate, sometimes witty, sometimes painfully honest, the pieces are highly readable, entertaining, and educational." Booklist

911: the book of help; edited by Michael Cart; with Marianne Carus and Marc Aronson. Cricket Bks. 2002 178p $17.95; pa $9.95

Grades: 8 9 10 11 12 **810.8**

1. September 11 terrorist attacks, 2001 2. Terrorism 3. American literature—Collections

ISBN 0-8126-2659-1; 0-8126-2676-1 (pa)

LC 2002-4707

"A Marcato book"

A collection of essays, poems, and short fiction, created in response to the terrorist attacks of September 11, 2001. Contributors include Katherine Paterson, Joan Bauer, Walter Dean Myers, Nikki Giovanni, Arnold Adoff, and Russell Freedman

This "stands out for its rich prose, its unusual reporting, its search for context, its reminder of wonders." NY Times Book Rev

American dragons: twenty-five Asian American voices; edited by Laurence Yep. HarperCollins Pubs. 1993 237p pa $6.99 hardcover o.p. *

Grades: 7 8 9 10 **810.8**

1. American literature—Asian American authors—Collections

ISBN 0-06-440603-2 LC 92-28489

These "short stories, poems, and other selections are written by a cross section of Asian Americans, with roots in China, Vietnam, Japan, Korea, Tibet, and Thailand. The book is organized by theme, covering such issues of interest to adolescents as identity, family relationships, generational and cultural conflicts, and love." Horn Book

"A kaleidoscopic, occasionally brilliant, illumination of the Asian-American experience." SLJ

Includes bibliographical references

City of one; young writers speak to the world; from WritersCorps; foreword by Isabel Allende; edited by Collete DeDonato. Aunt Lute Books 2004 239p pa $10.95

Grades: 7 8 9 10 **810.8**

1. Teenagers' writings

ISBN 1-87996-069-9 LC 2004-45089

"This anthology celebrates the 10th anniversary of WritersCorps workshops, which bring creative-writing instruction to low-income kids from public schools, youth detention centers, halfway houses, and afterschool programs. More than 150 young people ranging in age from 9 to 23 write about their lives and the state of the world. . . . Poems about family, freedom, inner peace, self-identity, and the writing process round out this remarkable anthology." SLJ

Dude!; stories and stuff for boys; edited by Sandy Asher and David Harrison. Dutton Childrens Books 2006 258p il $17.99

Grades: 4 5 6 7 **810.8**

1. Boys 2. American literature—Collections

ISBN 0-525-47684-9 LC 2005025060

"These 18 original stories, plays, and poems by prize-winning writers range from entertaining to challenging and offer an array of characters and experiences. In Bill C. Davis' intimate, thought-provoking 'Family Meeting,' a boy whose stepbrother committed suicide discovers the value of life. Jamie Adoff's 'Twelve' is a rap poem about experiencing violence but still retaining hope. Jose Cruz Gonzalez's play *Watermelon Kisses* is an amusing, credible portrayal of brotherly love and squabbles. The selections, which include many well-written gems, will resonate with and also amuse middle-grade boys." Booklist

Girls got game; sports stories and poems; edited by Sue Macy. Holt & Co. 2001 152p $17.95 *
Grades: 6 7 8 9   810.8
1. Sports 2. Women athletes 3. American literature—Collections
ISBN 0-8050-6568-7   LC 00-47297
A collection of short stories and poems written by and about young women in sports
"The lineup of authors includes heavy hitters such as Virginia Euwer Wolff and Jacqueline Woodson as well as some lesser-known talents. . . . This earnest and high-minded anthology can be dipped into or devoured in one sitting; however it is read, it should empower girls and guide them along their paths toward becoming strong, independent women." SLJ

The **Great** North American prairie; edited by Sara St. Antoine; maps by Paul Mirocha; illustrations by Trudy Nicholson. Milkweed Eds. 2001 262p il (Stories from where we live) $19.95; pa $12.95   810.8
1. American literature—Collections 2. Prairies
ISBN 1-57131-630-2; 1-57131-645-0 (pa)
                                      LC 00-67886
This is a collection of stories, poems, and literary excerpts about the American prairie
"The varied selections include a song of a Sioux chief, a letter from Georgia O'Keeffe, and the recollections of a 92-year-old woman (Iron Teeth). Some contributors are authors who write books for children; others are scientists and lecturers. . . . Their voices ring with pride and poignancy." Book Rep
Includes bibliographical references

Growing up Latino; memoirs and stories; edited with an introduction by Harold Augenbraum and Ilan Stavans; foreword by Ilan Stavans. Houghton Mifflin 1993 xxix, 344p pa $15 hardcover o.p. *
Grades: 6 7 8 9   810.8
1. American literature—Hispanic American authors—Collections
ISBN 0-395-66124-2   LC 92-32624
"A Marc Jaffe book"
A collection of short stories and excerpts from novels and memoirs written by twenty-five Latino authors. Among the contributors are Julia Alvarez, Oscar Hijuelos, Denise Chávez, Rolando Hinojosa, and Sandra Cisneros.
Includes bibliographical references

Guys write for Guys Read; edited by Jon Scieszka. Viking 2005 272p il $16.99; pa $10.99 *
Grades: 6 7 8 9   810.8
1. American literature—Collections
ISBN 0-670-06007-0; 0-670-06027-5 (pa)
                                      LC 2004-28984
This is a collection of short stories, essays, columns, cartoons, anecdotes, and artwork by such writers and illustrators as Brian Jacques, Jerry Spinelli, Chris Crutcher, Mo Willems, Chris Van Allsburg, Matt Groening, and Neil Gaiman, selected by voters at the Guys Read web site.

This is "a diverse and fast-paced anthology . . . that deserves a permanent place in any collection . . . . There's something undeniably grand about this collective celebration of the intellectual life of the common boy." SLJ

Sidman, Joyce, 1956-
The world according to dog; poems and teen voices; with photographs by Doug Mindell. Houghton Mifflin 2003 71p il hardcover o.p. pa $7.95
Grades: 8 9 10 11 12   810.8
1. Dogs 2. Teenagers' writings 3. American literature—Collections
ISBN 0-618-17497-4; 0-618-28381-1 (pa)
                                      LC 2002-476
A collection of poems about dogs is accompanied by essays by young people about the dogs in their lives
"The teen essays are heartfelt and honest. . . . Sidman's poetic form is succinct, evoking images, memories, and even smells. . . . Readers of all ages who appreciate their canine companions will thoroughly enjoy this slim book." Voice Youth Advocates

Things I have to tell you; poems and writing by teenage girls; edited by Betsy Franco; photographs by Nina Nickles. Candlewick Press 2001 63p il hardcover o.p. pa $8.99
Grades: 7 8 9 10   810.8
1. Teenagers' writings 2. Girls 3. American literature—Collections
ISBN 0-7636-0905-6; 0-7636-1035-6 (pa)
                                      LC 99-46884
A collection of poems, stories, and essays written by girls twelve to eighteen years of age and revealing the secrets which enabled them to overcome the challenges they faced

Wáchale! poetry and prose on growing up Latino in America; edited by Ilan Stavans. Cricket Publs. 2001 146p $16.95
Grades: 5 6 7 8   810.8
1. Hispanic Americans 2. American literature—Hispanic American authors—Collections 3. Bilingual books—English-Spanish
ISBN 0-8126-4750-5   LC 2001-47189
A bilingual collection of poems, stories, and other writings which celebrates diversity among Latinos.
"This collection would make a fine classroom text, great for reading aloud and for stimulating students from everywhere to write about their roots and celebrate their shifting places across borders." Booklist
Includes glossary and bibliographical references

Where we are, what we see; the best young artists and writers in America: a Push anthology; edited by David Levithan. PUSH/Scholastic 2005 220p il pa $7.99
Grades: 7 8 9 10   810.8
1. Teenagers' writings 2. American literature—Collections
ISBN 0-439-73646-3   LC 2005-296492
The "young writers and artists in this anthology have been selected from the winners of the Scholastic Art &

Where we are, what we see—*Continued*
Writing Awards program. The offerings range from an intense recollection, 'What Cancer Meant,' to a whimsical dictionary of words that don't exist but should. . . . This collection is a real boon for budding writers and artists, who will feel the encouragement and see the possibility of publication." Booklist

You hear me? poems and writing by teenage boys; edited by Betsy Franco. Candlewick Press 2000 107p hardcover o.p. pa $6.99
Grades: 7 8 9 10   **810.8**
1. Teenagers' writings 2. Boys 3. American literature—Collections
ISBN 0-7636-1158-1; 0-7636-1159-X (pa)
                              LC 99-57129
This is an "anthology of poems, essays, and stories written by young men aged twelve through twenty." Harv Educ Rev
"The voices range from painfully honest to playfully ironic, but all are controlled and powerful as they speak to subjects that teen readers will be familiar with." Voice Youth Advocates

810.9 American literature—History and criticism

Aronson, Marc
Beyond the pale; new essays for a new era. Scarecrow Press 2003 145p (Scarecrow studies in young adult literature) $37.50
Grades: Professional   **810.9**
1. Young adult literature—History and criticism 2. Books and reading
ISBN 0-8108-4638-1; 978-0-8108-4638-8
                              LC 2002-151299
"A collection of essays written in the aftermath of September 11th in which Aronson weighed out how art, history, and books for younger readers could respond to the altered world." Publisher's note
"Teachers, librarians, and students of children's and young adult literature will appreciate the breadth and clarity of this book, as well as the impressive bibliographies of fantasy and of professional reading on it." SLJ
Includes bibliographical references

Crowe, Chris
More than a game; sports literature for young adults; [by] Chris Crowe. Scarecrow Press 2004 171p (Scarecrow studies in young adult literature) $45
Grades: Professional   **810.9**
1. Young adult literature—History and criticism 2. Sports in literature
ISBN 0-8108-4900-3; 978-0-8108-4900-6
                              LC 2003-13561
Contents: Is there a place for sports literature?; From the school room to the playing field: a history of young adult sports literature; Young adult sports fiction: more than just game stories; Young adult sports nonfiction and poetry; Sports literature for young women; Coaches in young adult sports fiction

This "is a comprehensive overview of adolescent sports literature, its history, and contemporary trends in the field." Publisher's note
"Readable and fascinating. . . . Categorizing and listing every sports-related book with teen appeal is an impossible feat, but the appendixes earn a medal for their impressive range. If only all professional reading could be so brainy and muscular." Voice Youth Advocates
Includes bibliographical references

Hill, Laban Carrick
Harlem stomp! a cultural history of the Harlem Renaissance. Little, Brown 2004 151p il $18.95 *
Grades: 7 8 9 10   **810.9**
1. Harlem Renaissance 2. African Americans—Intellectual life 3. African American arts
ISBN 0-316-81411-3   LC 2002-73067
"This is an account of cultural and intellectual life in Harlem during the first half of the 20th century." Bull Cent Child Books
"The vibrancy, energy, and color of the Harlem Renaissance come to life in this gem of a book packed with poetry, prose, song lyrics, art, and photography created by some of the period's most influential figures. . . . Informative and highly entertaining, it deserves to be shelved in any library." Voice Youth Advocates
Includes bibliographical references

Hillstrom, Kevin
The Harlem Renaissance. Omnigraphics 2008 228p il map (Defining moments) $49
Grades: 7 8 9 10   **810.9**
1. Harlem Renaissance 2. African American arts
ISBN 978-0-7808-1027-3; 0-7808-1027-9
                              LC 2007-51132
"Provides a detailed, factual account of the emergence and development of the Harlem Renaissance and its ongoing effect on American society. Features include a narrative overview, biographical profiles, primary source documents, detailed chronology, glossary, and annotated sources for further study." Publisher's note
"This an insightful, highly accessible subject primer for general collections." Libr J
Includes glossary and bibliographical references

811 American poetry

Adoff, Jaime
The song shoots out of my mouth; illustrated by Martin French. Dutton Children's Bks. 2002 48p il $17.99
Grades: 7 8 9   **811**
1. Music—Poetry 2. Poetry—By individual authors
ISBN 0-525-46949-4   LC 2002-284232
This is a "collection of 24 poems. Though free in form and diverse in mood and tone, all are about music, from Hip Hop to classical and from reggae to gospel. Another common element is the energy underscoring Adoff's language, which invites readers to move to the rhythm of the words. . . . All shine with the poet's obvious love of music and musicians." Booklist
Includes glossary and discography

Alexander, Elizabeth, 1962-

Miss Crandall's School for Young Ladies and Little Misses of Color; poems; by Elizabeth Alexander and Marilyn Nelson; pictures by Floyd Cooper. Wordsong 2007 47p il $17.95

Grades: 7 8 9 10 **811**
1. Crandall, Prudence, 1803-1890—Poetry 2. African Americans—Poetry 3. Schools—Poetry 4. Poetry—By individual authors
ISBN 978-1-59078-456-3; 1-59078-456-1
LC 2006-38985

"Twenty-four sonnets tell the story of Prudence Crandall and her efforts to educate young African-American women in Canterbury, CT, 1833-1834. . . . The sonnet format is challenging but compelling. . . . There are empty spaces in the pictures just as the language of the poetry leaves openness for readers' interpretation. A heartfelt, unusual presentation." SLJ

Angelou, Maya

Maya Angelou; [compiled] by Patricia Kirkpatrick. Creative Education 2003 47p il (Voices in poetry) $19.95 *

Grades: 6 7 8 9 **811**
1. Poets, American 2. African American women 3. African Americans—Poetry 4. Poetry—By individual authors
ISBN 1-58341-281-6

This is "a stunning treat for the eye. . . . Artist John Thompson creates evocative illustrations for the excerpts of Angelou's writing that capture the heart of each piece. Also included are photographs both of Angelou and of the dramatic time in which she has lived." Voice Youth Advocates
Includes bibliographical references

Maya Angelou; edited by Edwin Graves Wilson; illustrated by Jerome Lagarrigue. Sterling Pub. 2007 48p il (Poetry for young people) $14.95 *

Grades: 4 5 6 7 **811**
1. Poets, American 2. African American women 3. African Americans—Poetry 4. Poetry—By individual authors
ISBN 978-1-4027-2023-9; 1-4027-2023-8
LC 2006013803

"Wilson's introduction . . . addresses how Angelou's life has informed her imagination. . . . Twenty-five poems show her concern with the African-American experience. . . . Dignity, pride, and resiliancy are at this collection's core. . . . Footnotes offer definitions of colloquialisms and difficult words. Lagarrigue's painterly artwork uses golds, greens, and violets to capture the luminescent quality of the poems. . . . This [is a] distinguished work." SLJ

Appelt, Kathi, 1954-

Poems from homeroom; a writer's place to start. Holt & Co. 2002 114p $16.95

Grades: 7 8 9 10 **811**
1. Poetics 2. Poetry—By individual authors
ISBN 0-8050-6978-X LC 2002-67886

A collection of poems about the experiences of young people and a section with information about how each poem was written to enable readers to create their own original poems

Appelt's "poems are at times sensual, dramatic, or violent, and always rhythmic. They are fascinating, smooth, and 'with it.'" SLJ
Includes bibliographical references

Bernier-Grand, Carmen T.

Diego; bigger than life; illustrated by David Diaz. Marshall Cavendish Children 2009 64p il $18.99 *

Grades: 8 9 10 11 12 **811**
1. Rivera, Diego, 1886-1957—Poetry 2. Poetry—By individual authors
ISBN 978-0-7614-5383-3; 0-7614-5383-0
LC 2007-13761

"The life and work of the artist Diego Rivera is told through chronological poems that capture salient points in his life" Publisher's note

This is a "well written and beautifully illustrated volume. . . . Almost all written in first-person from the artist's point of view, the poems convey information succinctly within a context of colorful narrative and clearly expressed emotion. . . . Apart from four reproductions of Rivera's paintings and one photo of the artist, the illustrations are mixed-media pictures by Diaz. Depicting Rivera and his world, these iconic images glow with warmth, light, and color." Booklist
Includes bibliographical references

Frida; viva la vida! long live life! Marshall Cavendish Children 2007 64p il $18.99 *

Grades: 8 9 10 11 12 **811**
1. Kahlo, Frida, 1907-1954—Poetry 2. Poetry—By individual authors
ISBN 978-0-7614-5336-9 LC 2006014479

"Bernier-Grand introduces a famous life with lyrical free-verse poems. Nearly every double-page spread pairs a well-reproduced painting by Frida Kahlo with an original poem that defines turning points in the artist's life. Bernier-Grand's words expertly extend the autobiographical imagery so evident in the art." Booklist
Includes glossary and bibliographical references

Burleigh, Robert, 1936-

Hoops; illustrated by Stephen T. Johnson. Harcourt Brace & Co. 1997 unp il $16; pa $6 *

Grades: 6 7 8 9 **811**
1. Basketball—Poetry 2. Poetry—By individual authors
ISBN 0-15-201450-0; 0-15-216380-8 (pa)
LC 96-18440

"Silver Whistle"

Illustrations and poetic text describe the movement and feel of the game of basketball

"Burleigh's staccato text is well matched by Johnson's dynamic pastels. Muted colors and a strong sense of motion as bodies leap and lift, pounce and poke, aptly complement the words." SLJ

Crisler, Curtis L., 1965-
Tough boy sonatas; illustrations by Floyd
Cooper. Wordsong 2007 86p il $19.95 *
Grades: 8 9 10 11 12   **811**
   1. African Americans—Poetry 2. City and town life—
Poetry 3. Indiana—Poetry 4. Poetry—By individual
authors
   ISBN 978-1-932425-77-2; 1-932425-77-2
            LC 2006-11836
"Crisler presents a collection of potent, hard-hitting
poems about growing up in Gary, Indiana. Written mostly in voices of young African American males, the poems evoke the grit and ash of crumbling, burned-out
streets as well as the realities of hardscrabble life. . . .
Written with skillful manipulation of sound, rhythm, and
form, the poems are filled with sophisticated imagery
and graphic words . . . and Cooper's illustrations extend
. . . the poems' impact. Created in sooty black and gray,
the powerful drawings are mostly portraits of anguished
young men." Booklist

Dickinson, Emily, 1830-1886
My letter to the world and other poems; with
illustrations by Isabelle Arsenault. KCP Poetry
2008 unp il (Visions in poetry) $17.95; pa $9.95
Grades: 7 8 9 10 11 12   **811**
   1. Poetry—By individual authors
   ISBN   978-1-55453-103-5;   1-55453-103-9;
978-1-55453-339-8 (pa); 1-55453-339-2 (pa)
"As spare, intense, and mysterious as the words, the
surreal illustrations for seven poems in this small volume
. . . show Dickinson alone and indoors in a white dress.
. . . The long final biographical note about the introvert
and recluse . . . will take readers back to the poetry . . .
as will the clear analysis of the mixed-media illustrations." Booklist

Fields, Terri, 1948-
After the death of Anna Gonzales. Holt & Co.
2002 100p $16.95
Grades: 7 8 9 10   **811**
   1. Suicide—Poetry 2. Poetry—By individual authors
   ISBN 0-8050-7127-X   LC 2002-24074
Poems written in the voices of forty-seven people, including students, teachers, and other school staff, record
the aftermath of a high school student's suicide and the
preoccupations of teen life
"A short book, easily read, which should generate serious thought and discussion." BAYA Book Rev

Fleischman, Paul
Big talk; poems for four voices; illustrated by
Beppe Giacobbe. Candlewick Press 2000 44p il
$17.99; pa $7.99 *
Grades: 4 5 6 7   **811**
   1. Poetry—By individual authors
   ISBN 0-7636-0636-7; 0-7636-3805-6 (pa)
            LC 99-46882
A collection of poems to be read aloud by four peo-
ple, with color-coded text to indicate which lines are
read by which readers
"Each poem is more demanding, and more rewarding,

than the last. Giacobbe highlights the humor in strips of
vignettes that run along the bottom of the page. This is
'toe-tapping, tongue-flapping fun.'" Horn Book Guide

I am phoenix: poems for two voices; illustrated
by Ken Nutt. Harper & Row 1985 51p il pa $5.99
hardcover o.p. *
Grades: 4 5 6 7   **811**
   1. Birds—Poetry 2. Poetry—By individual authors
   ISBN 0-06-446092-4 (pa)   LC 85-42615
   "A Charlotte Zolotow book"
A collection of poems about birds to be read aloud by
two voices
"Devotés of the almost lost art of choral reading
should be among the first to appreciate this collection.
. . . Printed in script form, the selections . . . have a ca-
denced pace and dignified flow; their combination of
imaginative imagery and realistic detail is echoed by the
combination of stylized fantasy and representational
drawings in the black and white pictures, all soft line and
strong nuance." Bull Cent Child Books

Joyful noise: poems for two voices; illustrated
by Eric Beddows. Harper & Row 1988 44p il
$15.99; lib bdg $16.89; pa $5.99 *
Grades: 4 5 6 7   **811**
   1. Insects—Poetry 2. Poetry—By individual authors
   ISBN 0-06-021852-5; 0-06-021853-3 (lib bdg);
0-06-446093-2 (pa)   LC 87-45280
   Awarded the Newbery Medal, 1989
   "A Charlotte Zolotow book"
"This collection of poems for two voices explores the
lives of insects. Designed to be read aloud, the phrases
of the poems are spaced vertically on the page in two
columns, one for each reader. The voices sometimes alternate, sometimes speak in chorus, and sometimes echo
each other." Booklist
"There are fourteen poems in the handsomely designed volume, with stylish endpapers and wonderfully
interpretive black-and-white illustrations. Each selection
is a gem, polished perfection." Horn Book

Frost, Robert, 1874-1963
Robert Frost; edited by Gary D. Schmidt;
illustrated by Henri Sorensen. Sterling 1994 48p il
(Poetry for young people) $14.95 *
Grades: 4 5 6 7   **811**
   1. Poetry—By individual authors
   ISBN 0-8069-0633-2   LC 94-11161
   "A Magnolia Editions book"
This volume "contains a three-page overview of the
poet's life, 29 poems selected and arranged around the
seasons of the year, brief and apt commentaries on each,
and a useful index of titles and subject matter. The realistic watercolor illustrations capture the delicate beauty
of a New England spring and the glory of fall while still
suggesting the around-the-corner chill of winter, a disqui-
et echoing throughout much of Frost's poetry." SLJ

George, Kristine O'Connell

Swimming upstream; middle school poems; illustrated by Debbie Tilley. Clarion Bks. 2002 79p il $14 *

Grades: 5 6 7 8   **811**
1. Schools—Poetry 2. Poetry—By individual authors
ISBN 0-618-15250-4   LC 2002-2746
A collection of poems capture the feelings and experiences of a girl in middle school
"Students will relate to this voice 'navigating upstream,' while they try to find their own place in the middle-school wilderness." SLJ

Giovanni, Nikki

Ego-tripping and other poems for young people; illustrations by George Ford; foreword by Virginia Hamilton. 2nd ed. Hill Bks. 1993 52p il hardcover o.p. pa $10.95

Grades: 5 6 7 8   **811**
1. African Americans—Poetry 2. Poetry—By individual authors
ISBN 1-55652-189-8; 1-55652-188-X (pa)
LC 93-29578
First published 1974
Giovanni has added 10 new poems to her earlier "collection of 23 poems for young people. Ford's illustrations in sepia shades are bold and full of character and dreaming. As Virginia Hamilton says in her foreword, Giovanni's voice is personal and warm, she 'celebrates ordinary folks' and writes of struggle and liberation. She's upbeat and celebratory without minimizing hard times." Booklist

Grandits, John, 1949-

Blue lipstick; concrete poems. Clarion Books 2007 unp il $15; pa $5.95 *

Grades: 5 6 7 8 9 10   **811**
1. Poetry—By individual authors
ISBN   978-0-618-56860-4;   0-618-56860-3;
978-0-618-85132-4 (pa); 0-618-85132-1 (pa)
LC 2006-23332
"This selection introduces readers to Jessie, who impulsively purchases blue lipstick, but later, regretfully decides to give it 'the kiss-off.' Jessie is big sister to Robert, who was featured in Grandits's *Technically, It's Not My Fault* (Clarion, 2004). As he did in that terrific collection, the author uses artful arrangements of text on the page, along with 54 different typefaces, to bring his images and ideas to life. . . . This irreverent, witty collection should resonate with a wide audience." SLJ

Technically, it's not my fault; concrete poems; by John Grandits. Clarion Books 2004 unp il $15; pa $5.95 *

Grades: 5 6 7 8   **811**
1. Poetry—By individual authors
ISBN 0-618-42833-X; 0-618-50361-7 (pa)
LC 2004-231
A collection of concrete poems on such topics as roller coasters, linguini, basketball, and sisters
"Grandits combines technical brilliance and goofy good humor to provide an accessible, fun-filled collection of poems, dramatically brought to life through a brilliant book design." SLJ

Grimes, Nikki

At Jerusalem's gate; poems of Easter; with woodcuts by David Frampton. Eerdmans Books for Young Readers 2005 unp il $20

Grades: 5 6 7 8   **811**
1. Jesus Christ—Poetry 2. Easter—Poetry 3. Poetry—By individual authors
ISBN 0-8028-5183-5   LC 2003-1089
A collection of poems which tells the story of the first Easter.
"Each poem is preceded by a brief synopsis of the event, often accompanied by the author's own musings and queries, which prompt readers to think and ask questions of their own. . . . Bold, handsome woodcuts reinforce the powerful drama depicted in poetry. An outstanding effort." SLJ

A dime a dozen; pictures by Angelo. Dial Bks. for Young Readers 1998 54p il $17.99

Grades: 5 6 7 8   **811**
1. African Americans—Poetry 2. Poetry—By individual authors
ISBN 0-8037-2227-3   LC 97-5798
A collection of poems about an African-American girl growing up in New York
"Free-flowing and very accessible, the poetry may inspire readers to distill their own life experiences into precise, imaginative words and phrases." Booklist

Hopscotch love; a family treasury of love poems; illustrated by Melodye Benson Rosales. Lothrop, Lee & Shepard Bks. 1999 39p il $16.99

Grades: 4 5 6 7   **811**
1. Love poetry 2. African Americans—Poetry 3. Poetry—By individual authors
ISBN 0-688-15667-3   LC 98-21310
A collection of more than twenty poems speaking of different kinds of love
"All of the poetry is simple, written with everyday language in a straightforward style that needs no analysis or search for symbolism. . . . This small treasury will lift readers' spirits and touch their hearts." SLJ

Tai chi morning; snapshots of China; [illustrated by] Ed Young. Cricket Books 2004 51p il $15.95

Grades: 5 6 7 8   **811**
1. China—Poetry 2. Poetry—By individual authors
ISBN 0-8126-2707-5   LC 2003-16506
"In 1988, Grimes traveled to China . . . and recorded her impressions of the country. . . . She paints her personal visions of a particular area or experience in a narrative paragraph, and then knits the ideas together into a poem on the facing page. . . . Young's simple artwork complements Grimes's eloquent images. The reedy pen-and-ink drawings deftly capture the exotic and ancient culture of the country." SLJ

Grover, Lorie Ann

Loose threads. Margaret K. McElderry Bks. 2002 296p $16.95   **811**
1. Poetry—By individual authors
ISBN 0-689-84419-0   LC 2001-44724
A series of poems describes how seventh-grader Kay Garber faces her grandmother's battle with breast cancer

Grover, Lorie Ann—*Continued*
while living with her mother and great-grandmother and dealing with everyday junior high school concerns
"The poetic, spare language, written in Kay's self-possessed, first-person voice, is refreshingly frank about the disease. . . . Grover's book balances vivid emotional scenes with plenty of space between the words." Booklist
Includes bibliographical references

Harley, Avis
African acrostics; a word in edgeways; poems by Avis Harley; photographs by Deborah Noyes. Candlewick Press 2009 unp il $17.99 *
Grades: 4 5 6 7   811
1. Animals—Africa 2. Animals—Poetry 3. Acrostics 4. Poetry—By individual authors
ISBN 978-0-7636-3621-0; 0-7636-3621-5
         LC 2008017916
"Harley has written 18 poems, each one featuring a different animal. All are written as acrostics, with most of them based on the first letter of each line, but several with more unusual patterns. . . . Much of Harley's poetry consists of carefully crafted descriptive word imagery that is right on target. . . . Most of the full-page, full-color photos of the animals are perfect companions to the facing selections." SLJ

Haskins-Bookser, Laura, 1972-
The softer side of hip-hop; poetic reflections on love, family, and relationships; by Laura Haskins-Bookser; illustrated by Jami Moffett. Morning Glory Press 2008 il pa $9.95
Grades: 8 9 10 11 12   811
1. Teenage mothers—Poetry 2. Poetry—By individual authors
ISBN 978-1-932538-83-0 (pa); 1-932538-83-6 (pa)
"Haskins-Bookser brings her hip-hop sensibility to a genre—poetry—that is really at the heart and soul of both hip-hop and rap. She voices the hopes, fears, and joys of a single teen mother. . . . Her poems are at once cautionary, but are tales of hope and transcendence as well. Each poem is heartfelt and well crafted. This is a lovely treasure, enhanced by Moffett's beautifully executed drawings and quotes from teen mothers." SLJ

Hemphill, Stephanie
Your own, Sylvia; a verse portrait of Sylvia Plath. Alfred A. Knopf 2007 261p $15.99; lib bdg $18.99
Grades: 8 9 10 11 12   811
1. Plath, Sylvia—Poetry 2. Poetry—By individual authors
ISBN 978-0-375-83799-9; 978-0-375-93799-6 (lib bdg)   LC 2006-07253
Michael L. Printz Award honor book, 2008
The author interprets the people, events, influences and art that made up the brief life of Sylvia Plath.
"Hemphill's verse, like Plath's, is completely compelling: every word, every line, worth reading." Horn Book
Includes bibliographical references

Herrera, Juan Felipe, 1948-
Laughing out loud, I fly; poems in English and Spanish; drawings by Karen Barbour. HarperCollins Pubs. 1998 unp il $15.99 *
Grades: 6 7 8 9   811
1. Bilingual books—English-Spanish 2. Poetry—By individual authors 3. Mexican Americans—Poetry
ISBN 0-06-027604-5   LC 96-45476
"Joanna Cotler books"
A collection of poems in Spanish and English about childhood, place, and identity
"Barbour's black-and-white drawings accompany each poem, delicately underlining its images but allowing the strong sensuality of the words to seep into readers' minds." SLJ

Holbrook, Sara
More than friends; poems from him and her; [by] Sara Holbrook and Allan Wolf. Wordsong 2008 64p il $16.95
Grades: 6 7 8 9 10   811
1. Love poetry 2. Poetry—By individual authors
ISBN 978-1-59078-587-4; 1-59078-587-8
         LC 2007-50282
"In these parallel poems, a boy and a girl describe their progression from friendship to romance. . . . The simple language expresses strong feelings in a variety of poetic forms. . . . Small black-and-white photos never get in the way of the words, which tell the edgy truth of romance in all its joy and confusion." Booklist

Hopkins, Lee Bennett, 1938-
Been to yesterdays: poems of a life; illustrations by Charlene Rendeiro. Wordsong 1995 64p il $15.95; pa $9.95
Grades: 4 5 6 7   811
1. Poetry—By individual authors
ISBN 1-56397-467-3; 1-56397-808-3 (pa)
         LC 94-73320
"Hopkins distills the experience of his middle-grade years into 28 poems of poignant clarity. . . . Good reading and an excellent, unconventional choice for teachers doing units on poetry and autobiography." Booklist

Hovey, Kate
Ancient voices; written by Kate Hovey; with illustrations by Murray Kimber. Margaret McElderry Books 2004 unp il $18.95 *
Grades: 6 7 8 9   811
1. Classical mythology—Poetry 2. Poetry—By individual authors
ISBN 0-689-83342-3   LC 00-28359
Twenty-three poems give voice to a variety of goddesses, gods, and mortals from Greek and Roman mythology
"These lyrical poems and dramatic picture-book-size illustrations humanize the Greek myths with flashes of contemporary realism. . . . The poetry here is both intense and accessible, with unobtrusive rhyme that adds to the music of the lines." Booklist

Hughes, Langston, 1902-1967
The dream keeper and other poems; including seven additional poems; [by] Langston Hughes; illustrated by Brian Pinkney. 75th anniv. ed. Alfred A. Knopf 2007 83p il $16.99 *
Grades: 4 5 6 7   811
1. African Americans—Poetry 2. Poetry—By individual authors
ISBN 978-0-679-84421-1
First published 1932; this is a reissue of the 1994 edition
A collection of sixty-six poems, selected by the author for young readers, including lyrical poems, songs, and blues, many exploring the black experience.
"Black-and-white scratchboard illustrations in Pinkney's signature style express the emotion and beat of the poetry. . . . The poems are . . . colloquial and direct yet mysterious and complex." Booklist

Langston Hughes; edited by Arnold Rampersad & David Roessel; illustrations by Benny Andrews. Sterling Pub. 2006 48p il (Poetry for young people) $14.95 *
Grades: 5 6 7 8   811
1. African Americans—Poetry 2. Poetry—By individual authors
ISBN 1-4027-1845-4; 978-1-4027-1845-8
LC 2005025369
A brief profile of African American poet Langston Hughes accompanies some of his better known poems for children.
"This charming collection of 26 poems is vibrantly illustrated with depictions of African Americans in varied settings. . . . This will be a welcome introduction to Hughes's poetry for elementary students, and it includes sufficient detail to make it useful and enjoyable for older students." SLJ

Janeczko, Paul B., 1945-
Worlds afire. Candlewick Press 2004 92p hardcover o.p. pa $6.99   811
1. Fire—Poetry 2. Poetry
ISBN 0-7636-2235-4; 0-7636-3400-x (pa)
LC 2003-55337
"In a collection of narrative poems, Janeczko describes a circus fire that took place on July 6, 1944 in Hartford, CT, from the viewpoints of those who were there." SLJ
"Janeczko never sensationalizes the horror, but the combination of a thrilling circus and true catastrophe will grab middle-schoolers, especially for readers' theater." Booklist

Johnson, Angela, 1961-
The other side; Shorter poems. Orchard Bks. 1998 44p il hardcover o.p. pa $6.95 *
Grades: 5 6 7 8   811
1. African Americans—Poetry 2. Poetry—By individual authors
ISBN 0-531-07167-7; 0-531-30114-1 (pa)
LC 98-13736
A Coretta Scott King honor book for text, 1999
A collection of poems reminiscent of growing up as an African-American girl in Shorter, Alabama
"Photographs of the author as a child emphasize the personal nature of this captivating narrative." Horn Book

Johnston, Tony, 1942-
Voice from afar; poems of peace; by Tony Johnston; paintings by Susan Guevara. 1st ed. Holiday House 2008 32p il $16.95
Grades: 5 6 7 8   811
1. War poetry 2. Poetry—By individual authors
ISBN 978-0-8234-2012-4; 0-8234-2012-4
LC 2007031434
"Johnston offers thoughtful responses to war's senseless violence. Her free-verse word pictures call to mind scenes of terrible devastation. . . . Yet Johnston finds cause for hope amid the grimness. . . . Johnston adds her own voice, the sympathetic observer from afar, sending prayers for peace. Guevara's paintings, crafted with acrylic and oil paint with collage on textured canvas, feature subdued, neutral colors and haunting images." SLJ

Katz, Bobbi
Trailblazers; poems of exploration; by Bobbi Katz; illustrations by Carin Berger. 1st American ed. Greenwillow Books 2007 208p il $18.99; lib bdg $19.89
Grades: 5 6 7 8   811
1. Explorers—Poetry 2. Poetry—By individual authors
ISBN 978-0-688-16533-8; 0-688-16533-8; 978-0-688-16534-5 (lib bdg); 0-688-16534-6 (lib bdg)
LC 2006016696
This is a collection of poems about "the lives of more than 120 explorers, from ancient times to the present. . . . Katz challenges readers to consider not only the courage of these individuals, but also to broaden their horizons in terms of the definition of exploration and the motivations behind it. . . . All the selections encourage reading aloud, especially the poems for two voices. The few black-and-white illustrations scattered throughout are small and iconic." SLJ
Includes bibliographical references

Lawson, JonArno, 1968-
Black stars in a white night sky; [by] JonArno Lawson; illustrated by Sherwin Tjia. 1st U.S. ed. Wordsong 2008 c2006 118p il $16.95
Grades: 4 5 6 7   811
1. Humorous poetry 2. Poetry—By individual authors
ISBN 978-1-59078-521-8   LC 2007018927
First published 2006 in Canada
"This uproarious collection blends slapstick, puns, parodies, and sheer absurdity with lots of wry ideas. . . . Tjia's surreal art, in black-and-white silhouettes, is as rhythmic and absurd as the verse, which is perfect for reading aloud." Booklist

Lewis, J. Patrick
Black cat bone; [by] J. Patrick Lewis; illustrations by Gary Kelley. Creative Editions 2006 48p il $19.95 *
Grades: 6 7 8 9 10   811
1. Johnson, Robert, 1911-1938—Poetry 2. African American musicians—Poetry 3. Blues music—Poetry 4. Mississippi—Poetry 5. Poetry—By individual authors
ISBN 978-1-56846-194-6   LC 2005052298

Lewis, J. Patrick—*Continued*

"Robert Johnson, the celebrated blues musician, is said to have sold his soul to the devil for his skills on the guitar. . . . Lewis's verse echoes Johnson's music. . . . A single line of text parades ghostlike across the bottom of each page, explaining the aspect of the man's life that the poem sings of, and becoming a cumulative mini-bio in itself. A couple of Johnson's own lyrics appear with the sequence of Lewis's poems where they add to the narrative tension. Kelley's mixed-media illustrations in blues and browns add to the mood and enliven the layout." SLJ

The brothers' war; Civil War voices in verse; including photographs by Civil War photographers. National Geographic 2007 31p il $17.95; lib bdg $20.90 *

Grades: 5 6 7 8 9 10   **811**
1. United States—History—1861-1865, Civil War—Poetry 2. Poetry—By individual authors
ISBN 978-1-4263-0036-3; 978-1-4263-0037-0 (lib bdg)   LC 2006-103275
"This heartrending collection of original poems paired with photographs by Civil War photographers makes real what statistics about war cannot—that the casualties of any war have human faces. Lewis . . . writes poignantly and lyrically. . . . An elegant design of gold, silver and black handsomely frames the text and photographs." Publ Wkly

Countdown to summer; 180 poems for every day of the school year; illustrations by Ethan Long. Little, Brown and Co. 2009 180p il $15.99
Grades: 4 5 6   **811**
1. Schools—Poetry 2. Poetry—By individual authors
ISBN 978-0-316-02089-3; 0-316-02089-3
LC 2008016772
"180 poems are here gathered to be enjoyed on a vitamin-like one-a-day basis. . . . Some verses are long, some short, some thought-provoking, some laugh-provoking. Long's penciled spot art provides an agreeable visual accompaniment." Kirkus

Freedom like sunlight; praisesongs for Black Americans; [illustrated by] John Thompson. Creative Eds. 2000 40p il $17.95; pa $7.95
Grades: 5 6 7 8   **811**
1. African Americans—Poetry 2. Poetry—By individual authors
ISBN 1-56846-163-1; 0-89812-382-8 (pa)
LC 98-50909
Presents poems and brief biographical notes about such well-known African Americans as: Arthur Ashe, Harriet Tubman, Sojourner Truth, Louis Armstrong, Martin Luther King, Jr., "Satchel" Paige, Rosa Parks, Langston Hughes, Jesse Owens, Marian Anderson, Malcolm X, Wilma Rudolph, and Billie Holiday
"Stunning illustrations by John Thompson take center stage in this attractively designed poetry collection. . . . Using a range of styles and meter, the mostly rhyming poems are dramatic and reverential." Booklist

Monumental verses. National Geographic 2005 31p il $16.95; lib bdg $25.90 *
Grades: 5 6 7 8   **811**

1. Monuments—Poetry 2. Poetry—By individual authors
ISBN 0-7922-7135-1; 0-7922-7139-4 (lib bdg)
"Lewis offers 14 poems celebrating monumental structures. From the remnants of civilizations at Stonehenge, Easter Island, and Machu Picchu to the more modern achievements of the Taj Mahal, the Eiffel Tower, and the Statue of Liberty, the subjects are varied and the accompanying photos are striking." Booklist

Longfellow, Henry Wadsworth, 1807-1882

Henry Wadsworth Longfellow; edited by Frances Schoonmaker; illustrated by Chad Wallace. Sterling 1998 48p il (Poetry for young people) $14.95 *

Grades: 4 5 6 7   **811**
1. Poetry—By individual authors
ISBN 0-8069-9417-7   LC 98-14833
A collection of 27 poems, "among them, 'The Village Blacksmith,' 'The Wreck of the Hesperus.' 'The Children's Hour,' 'Paul Revere's Ride,' and 'Hiawatha's Childhood' from 'The Song of Hiawatha.' A several-page introduction to Longfellow's life also includes some of the stories behind the poems." Booklist

Hiawatha and Megissogwon; illustrated by Jeffrey Thompson; afterword by Joseph Bruchac. National Geographic Soc. 2001 unp il $16.95
Grades: 5 6 7 8   **811**
1. Native Americans—Poetry 2. Poetry—By individual authors
ISBN 0-7922-6676-5   LC 00-12719
"In this excerpt from *The Song of Hiawatha*, Hiawatha engages in battle with the evil magician Megissogwon and returns, victorious, to his people." Horn Book Guide
"Readers who persevere through the no-longer-familiar poem will be rewarded for their efforts by Hiawatha's exciting adventures, ferocious battles, and victorious homecoming. The text has been capably illustrated in a complex process utilizing original drawings, black-and-white scratchboard, and a computer program for color." SLJ

Maddox, Marjorie, 1959-
Rules of the game; baseball poems; illustrated by John Sandford. Wordsong 2009 32p il $16.95
Grades: 5 6 7 8   **811**
1. Baseball—Poetry
ISBN 978-1-59078-603-1; 1-59078-603-3
LC 2008-19018
"Sports fans will find themselves nodding in recognition of Maddox's sophisticated grasp of the game's intricacies, while language mavens will appreciate her joyous wordplay and dead-on command of poetic devices. . . . Sandford's charcoal pencil drawings, backed by sepia-toned pages . . . impart a classy timelessness to the book that's a nice match to its subject." Booklist

Mora, Pat

The desert is my mother. El desierto es mi madre; art by Daniel Lechon. Piñata Bks. 1994 unp il $14.95

Grades: 4 5 6 **811**
1. Deserts—Poetry 2. Bilingual books—English-Spanish 3. Poetry—By individual authors
ISBN 1-55885-121-6 LC 94-20047

A poetic depiction of the desert as the provider of comfort, food, spirit, and life

"Presented in both English and Spanish, the text's short verses provide opportunities for children to use their senses to explore and learn about their environment." Kaleidoscope. 2nd edition

Myers, Walter Dean, 1937-

Harlem; a poem; pictures by Christopher Myers. Scholastic 1997 unp il $16.95 *

Grades: 5 6 7 8 9 10 **811**
1. African Americans—Poetry 2. Harlem (New York, N.Y.)—Poetry 3. Poetry—By individual authors
ISBN 0-590-54340-7 LC 96-8108

A poem celebrating the people, sights, and sounds of Harlem

"Myers's paean to Harlem sings, dances, and swaggers across the pages, conveying the myriad sounds on the streets. . . . Christopher Myers's collages add an edge to his father's words, vividly bringing to life the sights and scenes of Lenox Avenue." Horn Book Guide

Here in Harlem; poems in many voices; written by Walter Dean Myers. Holiday House 2004 88p il $16.95

Grades: 7 8 9 10 **811**
1. African Americans—Poetry 2. Harlem (New York, N.Y.)—Poetry 3. Poetry—By individual authors
ISBN 0-8234-1853-7 LC 2003-67605

"In each poem here, a resident of Harlem speaks in a distinctive voice, offering a story, a thought, a reflection, or a memory. The poetic forms are varied and well chosen. . . . Expressive period photos from Myers' collection accompany the text of this handsome book." Booklist

Nelson, Marilyn, 1946-

Carver, a life in poems. Front St. 2001 103p il $16.95

Grades: 7 8 9 10 **811**
1. Carver, George Washington, 1864?-1943 2. Poetry—By individual authors
ISBN 1-88691-053-7 LC 00-63624

A Newbery Medal honor book, 2002

"A series of fifty-nine poems portrays George Washington Carver as a private, scholarly man of great personal faith and social purpose. Nelson fills in the trajectory of Carver's life with details of the cultural and political contexts that shaped him even as he shaped history. As individual works, each poem stands as a finely wrought whole of . . . high caliber." Horn Book Guide

Fortune's bones; the manumission requiem. Front Street 2004 32p il $16.95 *

Grades: 7 8 9 10 **811**
1. Slavery—Poetry 2. African Americans—Poetry 3. Poetry—By individual authors
ISBN 1-932425-12-8 LC 2004-46917

"This requiem honors a slave who died in Connecticut in 1798. His owner, a doctor, dissected his body, boiling down his bones to preserve them for anatomy studies. The skeleton . . . hung in a local museum until 1970. . . . The museum . . . uncovered the skeleton's provenance, created a new exhibit, and led to the commissioning of these six poems. The selections . . . arc from grief to triumph. . . . The facts inform the verse and open up a full appreciation of its rich imagery and rhythmic, lyrical language." SLJ

Includes bibliographical references

A wreath for Emmett Till; illustrated by Philippe Lardy. Houghton Mifflin 2005 unp il $17 *

Grades: 8 9 10 11 12 **811**
1. Till, Emmett—Poetry 2. Lynching—Poetry 3. Mississippi—Poetry 4. African Americans—Poetry 5. Poetry—By individual authors
ISBN 0-618-39752-3 LC 2004-9205

Michael L. Printz Award honor book, 2006

This is a "poetry collection about Till's brutal, racially motivated murder. The poems form a heroic crown of sonnets—a sequence in which the last line of one poem becomes the first line of the next. . . . The rigid form distills the words' overwhelming emotion into potent, heart-stopping lines that speak from changing perspectives. . . . When matched with Lardy's gripping, spare, symbolic paintings of tree trunks, blood-red roots, and wreaths of thorns, these poems are a powerful achievement that teens and adults will want to discuss together." Booklist

Nye, Naomi Shihab, 1952-

19 varieties of gazelle; poems of the Middle East. Greenwillow Bks. 2002 142p $16.95; lib bdg $16.89; pa $6.99 *

Grades: 7 8 9 10 **811**
1. Middle East—Poetry 2. Poetry—By individual authors
ISBN 0-06-009765-5; 0-06-009766-3 (lib bdg); 0-06-050404-8 (pa) LC 2002-771

In this "volume, Nye collects her poems about growing up as an Arab American (her ancestry is Palestinian), including previously published poems and newly written pieces. This rich and varied volume offers insights into the experience of childhood in two very different worlds. . . . This volume will fill a need for classroom use, for young people seeking a more personal understanding of the Middle East, and for readers seeking a connection with their own Middle Eastern background." Bull Cent Child Books

Nye, Naomi Shihab, 1952-—*Continued*

A maze me; poems for girls; pictures by Terre Maher. 1st ed. Greenwillow Books 2005 118p il $16.99; lib bdg $17.89

Grades: 7 8 9 10   **811**

1. Girls—Poetry 2. Poetry—By individual authors

ISBN 0-06-058189-1; 0-06-058190-5 (lib bdg)

LC 2004-3283

These "poems draw from Nye's observations about nature, home, school, and neighborhood to make connections to a girl's inner world. . . . Most poems . . . speak with a powerful immediacy. . . . A wide age range will respond to these deeply felt poems about everyday experiences." Booklist

Honeybee; poems & short prose. Greenwillow Books 2008 164p $16.99; lib bdg $17.89 *

Grades: 8 9 10 11 12   **811**

1. Poetry—By individual authors

ISBN   978-0-06-085390-7;   0-06-085390-5; 978-0-06-085391-4 (lib bdg); 0-06-085391-3 (lib bdg)

LC 2007-36742

This poetry "anthology is a rallying cry, a call for us to rediscover such beelike traits as interconnectedness, strong community, and honest communication. . . . Teens at the very start of their questioning years will recognize their own angst in Nye's sense of irony, their idealistic optimism in her simple wonder." SLJ

Poe, Edgar Allan, 1809-1849

The raven; with illustrations by Ryan Price. KCP Poetry 2006 unp il (Visions in poetry)

Grades: 7 8 9 10   **811**

1. Poetry—By individual authors

ISBN 978-1-55337-473-2; 1-55337-473-8

"Originally published in 1845, the poem is narrated by a melancholy scholar brooding over Lenore, a woman he loved who is now lost to him. One bleak December at midnight, a raven with fiery eyes visits the scholar and perches above his chamber door. Struggling to understand the meaning of the word his winged visitant repeats 'Nevermore!' the narrator descends by stages into madness." Publisher's note

"In this small, handsome volume, Price's grim, sepia-tone stylized pictures, decorated with feathery, black cross-hatching, do a great job of evoking the brooding guilt, terror, grief, and love in Poe's famous poem." Booklist

Rylant, Cynthia

Something permanent; photographs by Walker Evans; poetry by Cynthia Rylant. Harcourt Brace & Co. 1994 61p il $18

Grades: 7 8 9 10   **811**

1. Poetry—By individual authors

ISBN 0-15-277090-9   LC 93-3861

"Nearly 60 years ago, Walker Evans and James Agee documented the lives of poor Southern sharecroppers. Their efforts resulted in a devastating, legendary account of the Depression, *Let Us Now Praise Famous Men*. Here, Rylant pairs Evans's photographs with 29 short, lyrical poems." SLJ

"For students in junior high and high school, the jux-taposition of Evans' photos and Rylant's poems will demonstrate how emotions can be rooted in objects and how, to dig them out, you need to use strong, sturdy words." Booklist

Service, Robert W., 1874-1958

The cremation of Sam McGee; by Robert W. Service; paintings by Ted Harrison; introduction by Pierre Berton. 20th anniversary ed. Kids Can Press 2006 unp il $17.95 *

Grades: 4 5 6 7   **811**

1. Yukon Territory—Poetry 2. Poetry—By individual authors

ISBN 978-1-55453-092-2; 1-55453-092-X

Text first published 1907. This is a reissue of the edition first published 1986 in Canada and 1987 in the United States by Greenwillow Bks.

"Pledged to cremate his friend Sam, the narrator tells how, after carting the frozen body for miles, he stuffs it into a ship's roaring furnace. To his surprise, when he later opens the door he discovers Sam alive . . . and warm for the first time 'since he left Tennessee.'" Publ Wkly

This poem "has gripped readers and listeners for decades. . . . [The illustrator] obviously appreciates the humor inherent in the text. . . . As Pierre Berton observes in his introduction, [Harrison's] 'style is unique: part Oriental, part native American, part Ted Harrison.'" Horn Book

Shields, Carol Diggory

English,   fresh   squeezed!   40 thirst-for-knowledge-quenching poems; by Carol Diggory Shields; illustrations by Tony Ross. 1st ed. Handprint Books 2004 80p il $14.95

Grades: 4 5 6 7   **811**

1. English language—Poetry 2. Poetry—By individual authors

ISBN 1-59354-053-1   LC 2004-53905

"Shields presents humorous poems both celebrating and bemoaning parts of speech, grammatical rules, and other annoyances of English class. Her rhyming verse is generally snappy and pointed. . . . Ross's spot illustrations in black and white with a blue tone add visual amusement without overwhelming." SLJ

Silverstein, Shel

Falling up; poems and drawings by Shel Silverstein. HarperCollins Pubs. 1996 171p il $17.99; lib bdg $18.89

Grades: 3 4 5 6   **811**

1. Humorous poetry 2. Nonsense verses 3. Poetry—By individual authors

ISBN 0-06-024802-5; 0-06-024803-3 (lib bdg)

LC 96-75736

This "collection includes more than 150 poems. . . . As always, Silverstein has a direct line to what kids like, and he gives them poems celebrating the gross, the scary, the absurd, and the comical. The drawings are much more than decoration. They often extend a poem's meaning and, in many cases, add some great comedy." Booklist

Silverstein, Shel—*Continued*

A light in the attic. Harper & Row 1981 167p
il lib bdg $18.89

Grades: 3 4 5 6 **811**

1. Humorous poetry 2. Nonsense verses 3. Poetry—By
individual authors

ISBN 0-06-025674-5 LC 80-8453

Also available book with audio CD $22.99 (ISBN 0-06-623617-7)

This collection of more than one hundred poems "will
delight lovers of Silverstein's raucous, rollicking verse
and his often tender, whimsical, philosophical advice.
. . . The poems are tuned in to kids' most hidden feelings, dark wishes and enjoyment of the silly. . . . The
witty line drawings are a full half of the treat of this
wholly satisfying anthology by the modern successor to
Edward Lear and Hilaire Belloc." SLJ

Where the sidewalk ends; the poems &
drawings of Shel Silverstein. 30th anniversary
special ed. HarperCollins 2004 183p il $17.99; lib
bdg $18.89 *

Grades: 3 4 5 6 7 8 9 10 **811**

1. Humorous poetry 2. Nonsense verses 3. Poetry—By
individual authors

ISBN 0-06-057234-5; 0-06-058653-2 (lib bdg)
LC 2004-269335

First published 1974

This edition contains 12 new poems

"There are skillful, sometimes grotesque line drawings
with each of the 127 poems, which run in length from
a few lines to a couple of pages. The poems are tender,
funny, sentimental, philosophical, and ridiculous in turn,
and they're for all ages." Sat Rev

Singer, Marilyn, 1948-

Central heating; poems about fire and warmth;
illustrated by Meilo So. 1st ed. Alfred A. Knopf
2005 41p il $15.95; lib bdg $17.99 *

Grades: 4 5 6 7 **811**

1. Fire—Poetry 2. Heat—Poetry 3. Poetry—By individual authors

ISBN 0-375-82912-1; 0-375-92912-6 (lib bdg)
LC 2004-4274

"The complicated nature of fire is explored in Singer's
energetic short poems and So's deceptively simple sin-
gle-color illustrations. . . . This title . . . belongs on library shelves everywhere." SLJ

Footprints on the roof; poems about the earth;
illustrated by Meilo So. Knopf 2002 41p il $14.95;
lib bdg $16.99

Grades: 3 4 5 6 **811**

1. Earth—Poetry 2. Nature poetry 3. Poetry—By individual authors

ISBN 0-375-81094-3; 0-375-91094-8 (lib bdg)
LC 2001-29407

A collection of 19 poems on such topics as caves,
mud, ice, deserts, and dunes

"This elegantly presented collection of free-verse poems focuses primarily on the young narrator's emotional
response to nature—its bounties, mysteries, and delights.
Like the poems themselves, the black-and-white ink
drawings are spare and finely crafted." Horn Book Guide

Smith, Charles R.

Hoop queens; poems. Candlewick Press 2003
35p il $14.99; pa $5.99 *

Grades: 4 5 6 7 **811**

1. Basketball—Poetry 2. Women athletes—Poetry
3. Poetry—By individual authors

ISBN 0-7636-1422-X; 0-7636-3561-8 (pa)
LC 2002-41111

A collection of twelve poems that celebrate contemporary women basketball stars, including Yolanda Griffith,
Chamique Holdsclaw, and Natalie Williams

"Action photos of the athletes are pasted large on colorful, dynamic backgrounds that barely hold the motion-
filled poems to the page. Notes about each player and
poem communicate the joy Smith finds both in watching
the game and writing poetry. Pure pleasure for basketball
fans and inspiration for kids who doubted poetry was
alive." SLJ

Smith, Hope Anita

Mother poems; words and pictures by Hope
Anita Smith. Henry Holt and Co. 2009 72p il
$16.95

Grades: 4 5 6 7 **811**

1. Mothers—Poetry 2. Bereavement—Poetry
3. Death—Poetry 4. African Americans—Poetry
5. Poetry—By individual authors

ISBN 978-0-8050-8231-9; 0-8050-8231-X
LC 2008-18342

"Christy Ottaviano books"

"Smith writes about an African American child's grief
at the sudden death of her mother. . . . Like the poetry,
Smith's simple, torn-paper collages in a folk-art style
show the close embraces and vignettes without overwhelming the words." Booklist

Soto, Gary

Canto familiar; [illustrated by Annika Nelson]
Harcourt Brace & Co. 1995 79p il $18; pa $5.95

Grades: 4 5 6 **811**

1. Mexican Americans—Poetry 2. Poetry—By individual authors

ISBN 0-15-200067-4; 978-0-15-205885-2 (pa)
LC 94-24218

"This collection of simple free verse captures common
childhood moments at home, at school, and in the street.
Many of the experiences are Mexican American . . . and
occasional Spanish words are part of the easy, colloquial,
short lines. . . . The occasional full-page, richly colored
woodcuts by Annika Nelson capture the child's imaginative take on ordinary things." Booklist

A fire in my hands; poems by Gary Soto. rev
and expanded ed. Harcourt 2006 74p $16 *

Grades: 6 7 8 9 **811**

1. Mexican Americans—Poetry 2. Poetry—By individual authors

ISBN 0-15-205564-9 LC 2005024610

First published 1991 by Scholastic

"Half the poems are new to this expanded edition of
a collection first published 15 years ago, including some
great ones from Soto's adult books that speak about feeling stuck at home and growing up poor, Catholic, and

Soto, Gary—*Continued*

Mexican American. Soto's chatty introduction about writing poetry that celebrates small, common things will appeal to both readers and writers, as will the informal questions and answers at the back of the book and the brief autobiographical notes Soto includes with each poem." Booklist

A natural man. Chronicle Bks. 2000 71p pa $13.95

Grades: 7 8 9 10　　　　　　　　　　　**811**

1. Mexican Americans—Poetry 2. Poetry—By individual authors

ISBN 0-8118-2518-3　　　　　LC 99-18353

"This poetry anthology offers a photographic glimpse into the lives of California's Chicanos. But although the titles and use of Spanish words create a very particular setting, the characters, stories, and truths of these selections have a universal resonance." SLJ

Neighborhood odes; illustrated by David Diaz. Harcourt Brace Jovanovich 1992 68p il $17; pa $5.95 *

Grades: 4 5 6　　　　　　　　　　　　**811**

1. Hispanic Americans—Poetry 2. Poetry—By individual authors

ISBN 0-15-256879-4; 0-15-205364-6 (pa)
　　　　　　　　　　　　　LC 91-20710

Also available in paperback from Scholastic

"Twenty-one poems, all odes, celebrate life in a Hispanic neighborhood. Other than the small details of daily life—peoples' names or the foods they eat—these poems could be about any neighborhood. With humor, sensitivity, and insight, Soto explores the lives of children. . . . David Diaz's contemporary black-and-white illustrations, which often resemble cut paper, effortlessly capture the varied moods—happiness, fear, longing, shame, and greed—of this remarkable collection. With a glossary of thirty Spanish words and phrases." Horn Book

Partly cloudy; poems of love and longing. Harcourt 2009 100p $16

Grades: 7 8 9 10　　　　　　　　　　　**811**

1. Love poetry 2. Poetry—By individual authors

ISBN 978-0-15-206301-6; 0-15-206301-3
　　　　　　　　　　　　　LC 2008-22267

Poet Gary Soto captures the voices of young people as they venture toward their first kiss, brood over bruised hearts, and feel the thrill of first love.

"Soto's new book of verse about adolescent love is remarkable. . . . The language of the poems is spare but evocative, with not one word wasted. . . . Teens will find these poems very engaging and will relate to how the emotion of love is expressed in everyday moments." Voice Youth Advocates

Spires, Elizabeth

I heard God talking to me; William Edmondson and his stone carvings. Farrar, Straus and Giroux 2009 56p il $17.95 *

Grades: 8 9 10 11 12 Adult　　　　　**811**

1. Edmondson, William, ca. 1870-1951—Poetry 2. Artists—Poetry 3. African Americans—Poetry 4. Religious poetry 5. Sculpture—Poetry 6. Poetry—By individual authors

ISBN 978-0-374-33528-1; 0-374-33528-1
　　　　　　　　　　　　　LC 2008-02343

"Frances Foster books"

"Moved by a religious vision at age 57, Nashville janitor William Edmondson began carving tombstones and whimsical figures out of stone in 1931 and went on to attract the attention of international collectors, eventually becoming the first African American artist to have a solo show at the Museum of Modern Art in New York. This handsome picture-book-sized poetry collection pairs full-page, black-and-white photos of Edmondson and his works with poems inspired by the images. . . . Supported by an appended prose biography, these playful, thought-provoking poems introduce a fascinating artist." Booklist

Testa, Maria

Becoming Joe DiMaggio; with illustrations by Scott Hunt. Candlewick Press 2002 51p il $14.99; pa $5.99

Grades: 4 5 6 7　　　　　　　　　　　**811**

1. Italian Americans—Poetry 2. Grandfathers—Poetry 3. Poetry—By individual authors

ISBN 0-7636-1537-4; 0-7636-2444-6 (pa)
　　　　　　　　　　　　　LC 2001-25886

"Growing up in New York City during the 1940s and 1950s, Joseph Paul, an Italian boy, finds solace from a difficult life by listening to baseball games with his beloved grandfather. This powerful story, told in 24 poems, describes their relationship and their love of listening to another Italian, Joe DiMaggio, achieve success. . . . The beauty and the charm of the poetry—its concise language, its flow and descriptive power—add to the intensity of the experiences described. Hunt's charcoal-and-pastel spot illustrations are scattered throughout." SLJ

Something about America. Candlewick Press 2005 84p $14.99

Grades: 6 7 8 9　　　　　　　　　　　**811**

1. Serbian Americans—Poetry 2. Immigrants—Poetry 3. Burns and scalds—Poetry 4. Poetry—By individual authors

ISBN 0-7636-2528-0　　　　　LC 2005-47064

"In poetic free verse, a 13-year-old narrator describes her life in America after having been horribly burned during the war in Kosova." SLJ

"Testa's distilled poetry never seems forced, and her stirring words enhance a sense of the characters' experiences and emotions. . . . Based on an actual incident, this is an excellent choice for readers' theater and classroom discussion." Booklist

Thayer, Ernest Lawrence, 1863-1940

Casey at the bat; written by Ernest L. Thayer; with illustrations by Joe Morse. Kids Can Press 2006 unp il (Visions in poetry) $16.95

Grades: 5 6 7 8 **811**

1. Baseball—Poetry 2. Poetry—By individual authors

ISBN 1-55337-827-X; 978-1-55337-827-3

"Morse updates Thayer's baseball classic to a modern, urban setting with a multiracial cast filling the familiar roles. As tall buildings loom above them, metallic fences confine the players who seem pensive and watchful. The figures are strikingly rendered in oils and acrylics, their features sharply limned in thick black lines and smudges of neutral color." SLJ

Weatherford, Carole Boston, 1956-

Remember the bridge; poems of a people; designed by Semador Megged. Philomel Bks. 2002 53p il $17.99

Grades: 5 6 7 8 **811**

1. African Americans—Poetry 2. Poetry—By individual authors

ISBN 0-399-23726-7 LC 2001-36161

"Twenty-nine poems trace African-American history and include observations about Harriet Tubman, Marian Anderson, and Martin Luther King, Jr." Horn Book Guide

"The author evokes imagined and actual individual experiences of the people . . . in the historical black-and-white photos, drawings, and etchings. . . . This celebratory, visually striking book will be appreciated in most collections." SLJ

Whipple, Laura

If the shoe fits; voices from Cinderella; illustrations by Laura Beingessner. Margaret K. McElderry Bks. 2002 67p il $17.95

Grades: 5 6 7 8 **811**

1. Cinderella—Poetry 2. Fairy tales—Poetry 3. Poetry—By individual authors

ISBN 0-689-84070-5 LC 2001-30778

In this version of the fairy tale "the characters tell the story in blank verses. . . . The story unfolds just as it always does, but the multiple points of view—from Cinderella's to the prince's to the rat's to the queen's—enlarge and enrich the familiar tale to win a more sophisticated audience. . . . Paintings by Beingessner achieve just the right mixture of sorrow, beauty, and humor." Booklist

Whitman, Walt, 1819-1892

Walt Whitman; edited by Jonathan Levin; illustrated by Jim Burke. Sterling 1997 48p il (Poetry for young people) $14.95 *

Grades: 5 6 7 8 9 **811**

1. Poetry—By individual authors

ISBN 0-8069-9530-0 LC 97-433

An illustrated collection of twenty-six poems and excerpts from longer poems by the renowned nineteenth-century poet

"An outstanding introduction to Whitman's life and work. . . . This superb volume can be used to teach literature or to show a variety of poetic devices and style." SLJ

Williams, William Carlos, 1883-1963

William Carlos Williams; edited by Christopher MacGowan; illustrated by Robert Crockett. Sterling Pub. Co. 2004 48p il (Poetry for young people) $14.95

Grades: 7 8 9 10 **811**

1. Poetry—By individual authors

ISBN 1-4027-0006-7 LC 2003-6885

A collection of thirty poems with illustrations and brief introductory remarks

"The introduction and commentary that MacGowan . . . provides not only fills in biographical details but expertly illuminates the craft and sensibility behind these 31 deceptively simple imagist poems . . . Despite its simple language and clear imagery, Williams' poetry is not widely available to young readers. This gathering should help to remedy that." Booklist

Wong, Janet S., 1962-

Behind the wheel; poems about driving. Margaret K. McElderry Bks. 1999 44p $15.95

Grades: 7 8 9 10 **811**

1. Automobile drivers—Poetry 2. Poetry—By individual authors

ISBN 0-689-82531-5 LC 99-19079

Thirty-six poems look at various aspects of driving, including passing the written driver's test, being pulled over by a cop, and having an accident, and treat them as metaphors for life

"Wong's brief, clear lines will be accessible even to the most reluctant poetry readers, and readers of all ages will be moved by the intersection of poignancy and humor as she desribes the thrilling freedom of the car and an emerging adult's awareness that, although she's traveled, her road still leads to home." Booklist

Yolen, Jane

Sacred places; illustrated by David Shannon. Harcourt Brace & Co. 1996 38p il $16 *

Grades: 4 5 6 7 **811**

1. Religious poetry 2. Poetry—By individual authors

ISBN 0-15-269953-8 LC 92-30323

"The hazy moodiness of Shannon's paintings capture the mystery Yolen explores in her text, while his dense figures and literal interpretations of a passage from each poem draw Yolen's mystical flights back down to solid ground. Appended notes offer historical information on each sacred place." Bull Cent Child Books

Young, Ed

Beyond the great mountains; a visual poem about China. Chronicle Books 2005 32p il $17.95

Grades: 4 5 6 7 **811**

1. China—Poetry 2. Poetry—By individual authors

ISBN 0-8118-4343-2

"The book is comprised of 14 lines, each of which is accompanied by its own double-page illustration, done in cut and torn-paper collage. Young also provides the ancient characters for the images he presents. . . . Designed to be read vertically, each page is flipped up to reveal the accompanying illustration. In this way, the entire book becomes a piece of art, a visual treat of sublime colors and textures that joins with text and characters to describe the vastness and beauty of China." SLJ

811.008   American poetry— Collections

America at war; poems; selected by Lee Bennett Hopkins; illlustrated by Stephen Alcorn. Margaret K. McElderry Books 2008 84p il $21.99 *

Grades: 5 6 7 8   **811.008**
1. War poetry 2. United States—History—Poetry 3. American poetry—Collections
ISBN 978-1-4169-1832-5; 1-4169-1832-9
      LC 2006-08723

"This handsome anthology, expressing Americans' varied experience during wartime, is a fine selection of poems accessible to children. . . . The poems will touch readers with their sharp poignancy and undeniable power. Throughout the well-designed book, the expressive watercolor artwork enhances the poetry." Booklist

Cool salsa; bilingual poems on growing up Latino in the United States; edited by Lori M. Carlson; introduction by Oscar Hijuelos. Holt & Co. 1994 xx, 123p il hardcover o.p. Fawcett pa $6.99 *

Grades: 5 6 7 8 9 10   **811.008**
1. American poetry—Hispanic American authors—Collections 2. Bilingual books—English-Spanish
ISBN 0-8050-3135-9; 978-0-449-70436-3 (Fawcett pa); 0-449-70436-X (Fawcett pa)   LC 93-45798

"This collection presents poems by 29 Mexican-American, Cuban-American, Puerto Rican, and other Central and South American poets, including Sandra Cisneros, Luis J. Rodriguez, Pat Mora, Gary Soto, Ana Castillo, Oscar Hijuelos, Ed J. Vega, Judith Ortiz-Cofer, and other Latino writers both contemporary and historical. Brief biographical notes on the authors are provided. All the poems deal with experiences of teenagers." Book Rep

Heart to heart; new poems inspired by twentieth-century American art; edited by Jan Greenberg. Abrams 2001 80p il map $19.95 *

Grades: 5 6 7 8 9 10   **811.008**
1. American poetry—Collections 2. American art 3. Art—20th century
ISBN 0-8109-4386-7   LC 99-462335
Michael L. Printz Award honor book, 2002
A compilation of poems by Americans writing about American art in the twentieth century, including such writers as Nancy Willard, Jane Yolen, and X. J. Kennedy.

"From a tight diamante and pantoum to lyrical free verse, the range of poetic styles will speak to a wide age group. . . . Concluding with biographical notes on each poet and artist, this rich resource is an obvious choice for teachers, and the exciting interplay between art and the written word will encourage many readers to return again and again to the book." Booklist

I am the darker brother; an anthology of modern poems by African Americans; edited and with an afterword by Arnold Adoff; drawings by Benny Andrews; introduction by Rudine Sims Bishop; foreword by Nikki Giovanni. rev ed. Simon & Schuster Bks. for Young Readers 1997 208p il hardcover o.p. pa $5.99 *

Grades: 6 7 8 9   **811.008**
1. American poetry—African American authors—Collections
ISBN 0-689-81241-8; 0-689-80869-0 (pa)
      LC 97-144181
First published 1968
This anthology presents "the African-American experience through poetry that speaks for itself. . . . Because of the historical context of many of the poems, the book will be much in demand during Black History Month, but it should be used and treasured as part of the larger canon of literature to be enjoyed by all Americans at all times of the year. An indispensable addition to library collections." SLJ

I, too, sing America; three centuries of African American poetry; [selected and annotated by] Catherine Clinton; illustrated by Stephen Alcorn. Houghton Mifflin 1998 128p il $21 *

Grades: 6 7 8 9   **811.008**
1. African Americans—Poetry 2. American poetry—African American authors—Collections
ISBN 0-395-89599-5   LC 97-46137
"For each poet, Clinton provides a biography and a brief, insightful commentary on the poem(s) she has chosen, including a discussion of political as well as literary connections. Alcorn's dramatic, full-page, full-color illustrations opposite each poem evoke the quiltlike patterns and rhythmic figures of folk art." Booklist

The Invisible ladder; an anthology of contemporary American poems for young readers with the poets' own photos and commentary; edited by Liz Rosenberg. Holt & Co. 1996 210p il $21.95

Grades: 7 8 9 10   **811.008**
1. American poetry—Collections 2. Poets, American
ISBN 0-8050-3836-1   LC 96-12361
Features such poets as Robert Bly, Allen Ginsberg, Nikki Giovanni, and Galway Kinnell by including photos, selections of their work, and comments on their poetry

Rosenberg "introduces many exciting new adult voices to young people. Some of the poets' commentaries are sophisticated, some are pretentious; but most are immediate and extraordinarily moving, nearly as powerful as the poetry they lead into." Booklist

Is this forever, or what? poems and paintings from Texas; selected by Naomi Shihab Nye. Greenwillow Books 2004 164p il $19.99

Grades: 7 8 9 10   **811.008**
1. Texas—Poetry 2. Texas in art 3. American poetry—Collections
ISBN 0-06-051178-8   LC 2003-4441
"The poems include moving family tributes, furious self-revelations, and quiet, atmospheric vignettes that find

Is this forever, or what?—*Continued*

grace and beauty in sunbaked neighborhoods, basic work, and everyday faces. . . . The accompanying artworks are arresting without overpowering the words, and they echo the poems' wide range of styles." Booklist

A **Jar** of tiny stars: poems by NCTE award-winning poets; Bernice E. Cullinan, editor; illustrations by Andi MacLeod; portraits by Marc Nadel. Wordsong 1996 94p il $17.95
Grades: 4 5 6 7 **811.008**
1. American poetry—Collections
ISBN 1-56397-087-2 LC 93-60466
"Each poet who has won the NCTE Poetry Award—David McCord, Aileen Fisher, Karla Kuskin, Myra Cohn Livingston, Eve Merriam, John Ciardi, Lilian Moore, Arnold Adoff, Valerie Worth, and Barbara Esbensen—is pictured at the beginning of a section that includes several representative poems and a significant quote. The portraits are watercolor renditions from photographs, with cheerful pen-and-ink sketches accompanying the verse; all are in black and white." Bull Cent Child Books

A **kick** in the head; selected by Paul B. Janeczko; illustrated by Chris Raschka. Candlewick Press 2005 61p il $17.99; pa $9.99 *
Grades: 4 5 6 7 **811.008**
1. American poetry—Collections
ISBN 978-0-7636-0662-6; 0-7636-0662-6; 978-0-7636-4132-0 (pa); 0-7636-4132-4 (pa)
LC 2004-48508
This collection offers examples of poetic forms "building from a couplet, tercet, and quatrain to the less familiar and more complex persona poem, ballad, and pantoum." SLJ
"Raschka's high-spirited, spare torn-paper-and-paint collages ingeniously broaden the poems' wide-ranging emotional tones. . . . Clear, very brief explanations of poetic forms . . . accompany each entry; a fine introduction and appended notes offer further information. . . . This is the introduction that will ignite enthusiasm." Booklist

Lives: poems about famous Americans; selected by Lee Bennett Hopkins; illustrated by Leslie Staub. HarperCollins Pubs. 1999 31p il $15.99; lib bdg $16.89 *
Grades: 4 5 6 7 **811.008**
1. United States—Biography—Poetry 2. American poetry—Collections
ISBN 0-06-027767-X; 0-06-027768-8 (lib bdg)
LC 98-29851
A collection of poetic portraits of sixteen famous Americans from Paul Revere to Neil Armstrong, by such authors as Jane Yolen, Nikki Grimes, and X. J. Kennedy
"Hopkins's eloquent introduction praises the power of poetry. Concluding 'Notes on the Lives' give readers useful biographical information. Full-page portraits feature Staub's distinctive, flat, primitive style, and their backgrounds have details particular to the subject. . . . A winning combination of poems and illustrations." SLJ

My America; a poetry atlas of the United States; selected by Lee Bennett Hopkins; illustrated by Stephen Alcorn. Simon & Schuster Bks. for Young Readers 2000 83p il $21.95 *
Grades: 4 5 6 7 **811.008**
1. United States—Poetry 2. American poetry—Collections
ISBN 0-689-81247-7 LC 98-47402
A collection of poems evocative of seven geographical regions of the United States, including the Northeast, Southeast, Great Lakes, Plains, Mountain, Southwest, and Pacific Coast States.
"Some poems are purposive, but the best . . . capture places and people in all their diversity. Stephen Alcorn's handsome, multi-textured pictures . . . avoid literal interpretation and capture the sweep of the land and the rhythm of the words." Booklist

My black me; a beginning book of black poetry; edited by Arnold Adoff. [rev ed.] Dutton Children's Bks. 1994 83p hardcover o.p. pa $6.99
Grades: 5 6 7 8 **811.008**
1. American poetry—African American authors—Collections
ISBN 0-525-45216-8; 0-14-037443-4 (pa)
First published 1974
A compilation of poems reflecting thoughts on being black by such authors as Langston Hughes, Lucille Clifton, Nikki Giovanni, and Imamu Amiri Baraka

The **Oxford** book of American poetry; chosen and edited by David Lehman; associate editor, John Brehm. Oxford University Press 2006 lvii, 1132p $35
Grades: 8 9 10 11 12 Adult **811.008**
1. American poetry—Collections
ISBN 0-19-516251-X; 978-0-19-516251-6
LC 2005-36590
First published 1950 with title: The Oxford book of American verse
This is an anthology of "American poetry from its origins in the 17th century right up to the present." Publisher's note
"The book is not only a sound historical survey, but also gives the reader a powerful taste of poetry's impact upon the wider world." Economist
Includes bibliographical references

The **Oxford** book of children's verse in America; edited by Donald Hall. Oxford University Press 1985 xxxviii, 319p $39.95; pa $19.95
Grades: 8 9 10 11 12 Adult **811.008**
1. American poetry—Collections
ISBN 0-19-503539-9; 0-19-506761-4 (pa)
LC 84-20755
"Hall's intention, expressed in the introduction, is to create an anthology of American poetry actually written for or adopted by children during a particular historical period. The emphasis is on authenticity rather than personal taste." SLJ
"A fine and carefully winnowed collection of American poetry is gathered in a book that will interest students of children's literature and young people who simply enjoy browsing." Horn Book

The **Pain** tree, and other teenage angst-ridden poetry; collected and illustrated by Esther Pearl Watson and Mark Todd. Houghton Mifflin 2000 62p il hardcover o.p. pa $6.95

Grades: 7 8 9 10 **811.008**

1. Teenagers' writings 2. American poetry—Collections

ISBN 0-618-01588-2; 0-618-04758-1 (pa)

LC 99-48905

This is a "collection of poetry culled from teen Web sites and magazines. Throughout the 25 selections, the young people address a wide range of emotions while coping with the trials of growing up, sometimes under less than ideal circumstances." SLJ

"Readers will be struck by the brutal honesty of this collection. . . . Watson and Todd have managed to compile a collection that will strike a chord with teen readers." Voice Youth Advocates

Paint me like I am; teen poems from WritersCorps. HarperTempest 2003 128p hardcover o.p. pa $6.99

Grades: 7 8 9 10 **811.008**

1. Teenagers' writings 2. American poetry—Collections

ISBN 0-06-029288-1; 0-06-447264-7 (pa)

LC 2002-5942

"The teen voices in these poems, collected from the WritersCorps youth program, are LOUD—raging, defiant, giddy, lusty, and hopeful. Grouped into arbitrary categories, the poems explore identity, creative expressions, family, neighborhood, drugs, and relationships. . . . A foreword from Nikki Giovanni rounds out this moving collection, which also includes a few thoughtful writing exercises." Booklist

The **Place** my words are looking for; what poets say about and through their work; selected by Paul B. Janeczko. Bradbury Press 1990 150p il $17.95 *

Grades: 4 5 6 7 **811.008**

1. American poetry—Collections 2. Poetics

ISBN 0-02-747671-5 LC 89-39331

"More than forty contemporary poets are included: Eve Merriam, X. J. Kennedy, Felice Holman, Gary Soto, Mark Vinz, Karla Kuskin, and John Updike, among others. Their contributions vary widely in theme and mood and style, though the preponderance of the pieces are written in modern idiom and unrhymed meter. The accompanying comments frequently are as insightful and eloquent as the poems themselves." Horn Book

A **Poem** of her own; voices of American women yesterday and today; edited by Catherine Clinton; illustrated by Stephen Alcorn. Abrams 2003 79p il $17.95 *

Grades: 6 7 8 9 **811.008**

1. American poetry—Women authors—Collections

ISBN 0-8109-4240-2 LC 2002-12851

Presents a collection of more than twenty poems by American women published between 1678 and 2001. Includes poems by Phillis Wheatley, Gertrude Stein, Lucille Clifton, Sandra Cisneros, and Naomi Shihab Nye

"The intelligent selection is matched by the fresh, open design, highlighted by Alcorn's exciting paintings, executed in light-fast casein paint." Booklist

Poetry from the masters: the pioneers; edited by Wade Hudson; illustrated by Stephan J. Hudson. Just Us Books 2003 88p il pa $9.95

Grades: 7 8 9 10 **811.008**

1. American poetry—African American authors—Collections 2. African American authors

ISBN 0-940975-96-3

This book "focuses on a particular group of black poets, 'trailblazers' who forged a path by overcoming 'almost impossible obstacles.' Hudson puts these writers in perspective and provides a social and literary context. Eleven poets are profiled, starting with Phillis Wheatley and ending with Gwendolyn Brooks. . . . Each writer is introduced with a brief biographical sketch that highlights his or her literary significance and contributions, followed by the full text of two or more poems. . . . This is an excellent resource for students seeking research materials or just looking for wonderful examples of poetry to read." SLJ

Includes bibliographical references

A **Poke** in the I; [selected by] Paul Janeczko; illustrated by Chris Raschka. Candlewick Press 2001 35p il $16.99; pa $7.99 *

Grades: 4 5 6 7 8 9 **811.008**

1. American poetry—Collections

ISBN 0-7636-0661-8; 0-7636-2376-8 (pa)

LC 00-33675

"Thirty concrete poems of all shapes and sizes are carefully laid on large white spreads, extended by Raschka's quirky watercolor and paper-collage illustrations. . . . Beautiful and playful, this title should find use in storytimes, in the classroom, and just for pleasure anywhere." SLJ

The **Random** House book of poetry for children; selected and introduced by Jack Prelutsky; illustrated by Arnold Lobel. Random House 1983 248p il $19.95; lib bdg $21.99 *

Grades: 3 4 5 6 **811.008**

1. American poetry—Collections 2. English poetry—Collections

ISBN 0-394-85010-6; 0-394-95010-0 (lib bdg)

LC 83-2990

Opening poems for each section especially written for this anthology by Jack Prelutsky

In this anthology emphasis "is placed on humor and light verse; but serious and thoughtful poems are also included. . . . Approximately two thirds of the selections were written within the past forty years—the splendid contributions of such writers as John Ciardi, Aileen Fisher, Dennis Lee, Myra Cohn Livingston, David McCord, Eve Merriam, and Lilian Moore. [There are] . . . samplings of earlier poets from Shakespeare and Blake to Emily Dickinson and Walter de la Mare." Horn Book

Red hot salsa; bilingual poems on being young and Latino in the United States; edited by Lori Marie Carlson; introduction by Oscar Hijuelos. Henry Holt 2005 140p $14.95 *

Grades: 7 8 9 10 **811.008**

1. American poetry—Hispanic American authors—Collections 2. Hispanic Americans—Poetry 3. Bilingual books—English-Spanish

ISBN 0-8050-7616-6 LC 2004-54005

Red hot salsa—*Continued*

This is a "bilingual collection of poems that appear in both Spanish and English. Included are many well-known writers, such as Gary Soto and Luis J. Rodriguez . . . as well as emerging poets. . . . The poems often speak about the complex challenges of being bicultural. . . . Most poems are translated by the poets themselves, and many are written in an inventive blend of languages, which English speakers will easily follow with help from the appended glossary. Powerful and immediate." Booklist

Reflections on a gift of watermelon pickle—and other modern verse; [compiled by] Stephen Dunning, Edward Lueders, Hugh Smith. Lothrop, Lee & Shepard Bks. 1967 c1966 139p il $19.99 *

Grades: 6 7 8 9 10 **811.008**
1. American poetry—Collections
ISBN 0-688-41231-9

First published 1966 by Scott, Foresman in a text edition

"Although some of the [114] selections are by recognized modern writers, many are by minor or unknown poets, and few will be familiar to the reader. Nearly all are fresh in approach and contemporary in expression. . . . Striking photographs complementing or illuminating many of the poems enhance the attractiveness of the volume." Booklist

Salting the ocean; 100 poems by young poets; selected by Naomi Shihab Nye; pictures by Ashley Bryan. Greenwillow Bks. 2000 111p il $16.99

Grades: 4 5 6 7 **811.008**
1. Children's writings 2. American poetry—Collections
ISBN 0-688-16193-6 LC 99-30590

"These poems are divided into four topics: The Self and the Inner World, Where We Live, Anybody's Family, and the Wide Imagination." Horn Book Guide

"Nye presents the exceptional work of students in grades 1 through 12. . . . Illustrated with Ashley Bryan's signature bright-hued, bold-lined paintings and multicultural imagery, the poems are varied in both sophistication and subject." Booklist

Includes bibliographical references

Shimmy shimmy shimmy like my sister Kate; looking at the Harlem Renaissance through poems; [edited by] Nikki Giovanni. Holt & Co. 1995 186p $17.95 *

Grades: 8 9 10 11 12 **811.008**
1. American poetry—African American authors—Collections 2. Harlem Renaissance
ISBN 0-8050-3494-3 LC 95-38617

This anthology includes poems by such authors as Paul Laurence Dunbar, Langston Hughes, Countee Cullen, Gwendolyn Brooks, and Amiri Baraka. Commentary and a discussion of the development of African American arts known as the Harlem Renaissance is provided by editor Giovanni

Includes bibliographical references

Soul looks back in wonder; [illustrated by] Tom Feelings. Dial Bks. 1993 unp il hardcover o.p. pa $7.99 *

Grades: 4 5 6 7 **811.008**
1. American poetry—African American authors—Collections
ISBN 0-8037-1001-1; 0-14-056501-9 (pa) LC 93-824

Coretta Scott King Award for illustration

Artwork and poems by such writers as Maya Angelou, Langston Hughes, and Askia Toure portray the creativity, strength, and beauty of their African American heritage

"This thoughtful collection of poetry is unique. . . . Feelings selected sketches done while he was in West Africa, South America, and at home in America. The original drawings were enhanced with colored pencils, colored papers, stencil cut-outs, and other techniques to give a collage effect. Marbled textures bring vibrancy to the work." Horn Book

Tell the world; teen poems from WritersCorps. HarperTeen 2008 116p $16.99; pa $8.99

Grades: 7 8 9 10 11 12 **811.008**
1. Teenagers' writings 2. American poetry—Collections
ISBN 978-0-06-134505-0; 0-06-134505-9; 978-0-06-134504-3 (pa); 0-06-134504-0 (pa) LC 2007-49577

"This worthy collection of brief poems offers an array of teen voices. . . . An essay by WritersCorps teacher Michelle Matz adds a vivid picture of her students and their lives. This fine collection should inspire creativity and resonate with teens who find their own hopes, fears, and dreams eloquently voiced in the works of these young poets." SLJ

Whisper and shout; poems to memorize; edited by Patrice Vecchione. Cricket Bks. 2002 120p $16.95

Grades: 4 5 6 7 **811.008**
1. American poetry—Collections
ISBN 0-8126-2656-7 LC 2002-591

A collection of poems on different subjects and in different styles, that lend themselves to memorization. Among the poets represented are Jack Prelutsky, Edward Lear, Ogden Nash, T. S. Eliot, Edna St. Vincent Millay, Christina Rossetti, and Lewis Carroll

"With a lengthy, enthusiastic introduction and a generous final section of resources and biographies, this anthology will get as much use in the classroom as with individual readers." Booklist

Includes bibliographical references

Wicked poems; edited by Roger McGough; illustrated by Neal Layton. Bloomsbury Children's Books 2004 208p il $15

Grades: 4 5 6 7 **811.008**
1. Good and evil—Poetry 2. American poetry—Collections
ISBN 1-58234-854-5 LC 2002-38551

"The 134 poems in this . . . collection focus on people exhibiting various degrees of wickedness. The book includes works from well-known poets . . . and children's authors such as Shel Silverstein, Eve Merriam, Myra Cohn Livingston, and Jack Prelutsky. . . . Child-

Wicked poems—Continued

like, black-and-white cartoons are laugh-out-loud funny.
. . . A perfect choice for reading aloud as well as independent browsing." SLJ

Words with wings; a treasury of
African-American poetry and art; selected by
Belinda Rochelle. HarperCollins Pubs. 2001 unp
il lib bdg $16.99

Grades: 4 5 6 7 **811.008**

1. American poetry—African American authors—Collections 2. African Americans in art 3. African Americans—Poetry

ISBN 0-688-16415-3 LC 00-26864

"Amistad"

Pairs twenty works of art by African-American artists
such as Horace Pippin and Jacob Lawrence with twenty
poems by African-American poets such as Langston
Hughes, Countee Cullen, and Lucille Clifton

"Most of the combinations are stunning. . . . Short
biographical paragraphs on each poet and artist round out
this moving presentation." SLJ

811.009 American poetry—History and criticism

Borus, Audrey

A student's guide to Emily Dickinson. Enslow
Publishers 2005 152p il (Understanding literature)
$27.93

Grades: 7 8 9 10 **811.009**

1. Dickinson, Emily, 1830-1886 2. Poetry—By individual authors 3. American poetry—History and criticism

ISBN 0-7660-2285-4 LC 2004-18098

"A short discussion of Dickinson's life and times is
followed by a chapter on how to read and analyze her
poems, which would be particularly useful for students
reading her work for the first time. Subsequent chapters
focus on particular themes in the poems such as death
and eternity, truth, faith and reality, the natural world,
and the influence of the Civil War." SLJ

Includes bibliographical references

Kirk, Connie Ann, 1951-

A student's guide to Robert Frost. Enslow Pubs.
2006 160p il (Understanding literature) $27.93

Grades: 7 8 9 10 **811.009**

1. Frost, Robert, 1874-1963 2. Poetry—By individual
authors 3. American poetry—History and criticism

ISBN 0-7660-2434-2 LC 2005-13392

In this book, "the career of this literary giant is examined. . . . Poems are put into historical and biographical
context, with special emphasis placed on curriculum-
related works, including 'Stopping by Woods on a
Snowy Evening,' 'The Road Not Taken,' 'The Gift Outright,' and 'Fire and Ice.'" Publisher's note

812 American drama

Black, Ann N.

Readers theatre for middle school boys;
investigating the strange and mysterious; illustrated
by Cody Rust. Teachers Idea Press 2008 190p il
(Readers theatre) pa $30

Grades: Professional **812**

1. Drama—Collections 2. Readers' theater

ISBN 978-1-59158-535-0 (pa); 1-59158-535-X (pa)

LC 2007034923

"This book provides solid offerings of Readers Theater scripts for educators working with middle school
boys. Selections include adaptations of such creepy classics as 'The Legend of Sleepy Hollow,' 'The Masque of
the Red Death,' . . . and 'The Monkey's Paw.' The
scripts have a new, fresh feel, and contain plenty of elements to capture and maintain adolescent males' attention." Libr Media Connect

Includes bibliographical references

Levine, Karen

Hana's suitcase on stage; original story by
Karen Levine; play by Emil Sher. Second Story
2007 171p il (Holocaust remembrance book for
young readers) pa $18.95 *

Grades: 5 6 7 8 **812**

1. Brady, Hana 2. Holocaust, 1933-1945—Drama

ISBN 978-1-89718-705-0 (pa); 1-89718-705-X (pa)

"Set in the Tokyo Holocaust Center, the two-act play
opens with the woman and two of her student helpers
questioning and searching for answers to the suitcase's
history. . . . Act II blends characters of Ishioka and her
students with Hana and her family, each group individu-
ally recounting their stories in alternating voices. As with
the original book, this title succeeds in recreating a striking representation of one child's tragic and beautiful life
in a terrifying world of hate and prejudice. This volume
will serve as one of the most effective teaching models
for Holocaust curriculums available. Photographs and
facsimiles of Nazi documents are included." SLJ

Soto, Gary

Novio boy; a play. Harcourt Brace & Co. 1997
78p pa $8 *

Grades: 7 8 9 10 **812**

1. Dating (Social customs)—Drama 2. Mexican Americans—Drama

ISBN 0-15-201531-0 LC 96-32605

Rudy anxiously prepares for and then goes out on a
first date with an attractive girl who is older than he is

"A hip, funny play. . . . Since the Mexican-American
cast spouts frequent Spanish words, several lines of dialogue could be lost on an audience unfamiliar with the
language. The visual clues of a live performance might
serve to clarify some unfamiliar words. . . . Young actors should be able to perform this entertaining play with
or without adult assistance." SLJ

812.008 American drama— Collections

Acting out; six one-act plays!: six Newbery stars! edited by Justin Chanda; featuring the playwrights, Avi . . . [et. al.] Atheneum Books for Young Readers 2008 175p il $16.99
Grades: 5 6 7 8 9   812.008
1. One act plays 2. American drama—Collections
ISBN 978-1-4169-3848-4; 1-4169-3848-6
Contents: The bad room by Patricia MacLachlan; The Raven by Sharon Creech; The billionaire and the bird by Katherine Paterson; The dollop by Susan Cooper; Effigy in the outhouse by Richard Peck; Not seeing is believing by Avi
Contains six original one-act plays by Newbery Award-winning children's authors, including Sharon Creech, Susan Cooper, Avi, Patricia Maclachlan, Katherine Paterson, and Richard Peck
"Each play was inspired by a theater-improv game in which the authors started with the selection of a single word. The pieces all include the following words: 'dollop,' 'hoodwink,' 'Justin,' 'knuckleball,' 'panhandle,' and 'raven.'. . . An engaging choice for literature and acting classes as well as general reading." SLJ
Includes bibliographical references

Millennium monologs; 95 contemporary characterizations for young actors; edited by Gerald Lee Ratliff. Meriwether 2002 261p pa $15.95
Grades: 8 9 10 11 12   812.008
1. Monologues 2. Acting 3. American drama—Collections
ISBN 1-56608-082-7   LC 2002-13009
An anthology of monologues by contemporary writers, divided into four categories: "Hope and Longing," "Spirit and Soul," "Fun and Fantasy," and "Doubt and Despair." Includes audition techniques
"This fine collection of American monologues is notable for its diversity as well as for the high quality of the material." Booklist

Theatre for young audiences; 20 great plays for children; edited by Coleman A. Jennings; foreword by Maurice Sendak. St. Martin's Press 1998 604p il $35; pa $19.95   812.008
1. Drama—Collections
ISBN 0-312-18194-9; 0-312-33714-0 (pa)
LC 97-36542
Contents: Charlotte's web by J. Robinette; The Arkansaw bear by A. Harris; Really Rosie by M. Sendak; The secret garden by P. Sterling; Wiley and the Hairy Man by S. Zeder; According to Coyote by J. Kauffman; The mischief makers by L. Swortzell; The wise men of Chelm by S. F. Asher; Crow & Weasel by J. Leonard; The ice wolf by J. H. Kraus; Home on the mornin' train by K. Hines; The falcon by G. Palmer; The man-child by A. Rabin; Hush: an interview with America by J. Still; Bocón! by L. Loomer; The crane wife by B. Carlisle; Jungalbook by E. Mast; A thousand cranes by K. S. Miller; The yellow boat by D. Saar; Selkie by L. B. Gollobin

A collection of plays, many of which are based on favorite children's tales, including such titles as: "Charlotte's Web," "Really Rosie," "Wiley and the Hairy Man," "Wise Men of Chelm," and "The Crane Wife"
"Highly recommended for school and public libraries and anyone interested in a substantial collection of plays for children." Booklist

With their eyes; September 11th: the view from a high school at ground zero; edited by Annie Thoms; created by Taresh Batra [et. al.]; photos by Ethan Moses. HarperTempest 2002 228p il hardcover o.p. pa $6.99
Grades: 7 8 9 10   812.008
1. Stuyvesant High School (New York, N.Y.) 2. September 11 terrorist attacks, 2001—Drama 3. American drama—Collections 4. Teenagers' writings
ISBN 0-06-051806-5; 0-06-051718-2 (pa)
LC 2002-4552
"The students of Stuyvesant High School watched through their classroom windows as the World Trade Center was attacked on September 11. This book contains the play that they created based on what students, teachers, janitors, and others within their school community experienced." Voice Youth Advocates
"The speakers reveal their emotions with painful honesty. . . . The book is an obvious choice for reader's theater and for use across the curriculum; its deeply affecting contents will also make compelling personal-interest reading." Booklist

812.009 American drama—History and criticism

Dunkleberger, Amy
A student's guide to Arthur Miller. Enslow Publs. 2005 160p il (Understanding literature) lib bdg $27.93
Grades: 7 8 9 10   812.009
1. Miller, Arthur, 1915-2005
ISBN 0-7660-2432-6
This discusses the life of Arthur Miller and his works *All My Sons*, *Death of a Salesman*, *The Crucible*, *A View From the Bridge*, *After the Fall*, *Incident at Vichy*, and *The Price*
"Engaging and informative. . . . The very accessible format and the solid information make [this book] useful to students, and the engaging style should interest casual readers." SLJ
Includes glossary and bibliographical references

Loos, Pamela
A reader's guide to Lorraine Hansberry's A raisin in the sun. Enslow Publishers 2008 128p il (Multicultural literature) lib bdg $31.93
Grades: 7 8 9 10   812.009
1. Hansberry, Lorraine, 1930-1965. Raisin in the Sun 2. African Americans in literature 3. American drama—History and criticism
ISBN 978-0-7660-2830-2 (lib bdg); 0-7660-2830-5 (lib bdg)   LC 2006-17900

Loos, Pamela—*Continued*

"A Raisin in the Sun has become part of the literary canon and is required reading for many students. This guide is intended to help them better appreciate the social milieu out of which this play emerged . . . making this volume a fine resource." SLJ

Includes bibliographical references

813.009 American fiction—History and criticism

Bernard, Catherine

Understanding To kill a mockingbird. Lucent Books 2003 112p il map (Understanding great literature) $27.45

Grades: 7 8 9 10   **813.009**
1. Lee, Harper, 1926-
ISBN 1-56006-860-4   LC 2002-156251

An introduction to Harper Lee's famous novel, "To Kill a Mockingbird," discussing the author's life, the historical context of the novel, its plot, themes, characters, literary criticism, and pertinence for today's audiences

Includes bibliographical references

Blasingame, James B., Jr.

Gary Paulsen. Greenwood Press 2007 164p bibl (Teen reads) $45

Grades: 7 8 9 10 11 12   **813.009**
1. Paulsen, Gary 2. Authors, American
ISBN 978-0-313-33532-7; 0-313-33532-X
                                                    LC 2007-21446

"This volume examines a sample of . . . books by Paulsen. A biographical chapter demonstrates how Paulsen's life experiences, notably the Iditarod, have influenced his writing. Each book is analyzed for plot, characterization, setting, and themes." Publisher's note

Includes bibliographical references

Brave new words; the Oxford dictionary of science fiction; edited by Jeffrey Prucher; introduction by Gene Wolfe. Oxford University Press 2007 xxxi, 342p $29.95 *

Grades: 7 8 9 10 11 12 Adult   **813.009**
1. Science fiction—Dictionaries 2. Reference books
ISBN 978-0-19-530567-8; 0-19-530567-1
                                                    LC 2006-37280

This is a "dictionary of the language of science fiction based on historical principles. . . . Entries include part of speech, etymology, definition with cross references to related terms, usage status (e.g., historical, jocular, derogatory, obsolete), variant forms, and . . . dated citations and quotations illustrating the usage of the word over time." Libr J

"This new science fiction lexicon . . . is an important and entertaining reference source for any science fiction writer, magazine editor, fan, neophyte reader, or librarian." Choice

Includes bibliographical references

Carroll, Pamela S.

Sharon Creech; [by] Pamela Sissi Carroll. Greenwood Press 2007 195p (Teen reads: student companions to young adult literature) lib bdg $45

Grades: 7 8 9 10 11 12   **813.009**
1. Creech, Sharon 2. Authors, American 3. Young adult literature—History and criticism
ISBN 978-0-313-33598-3 (lib bdg); 0-313-33598-2 (lib bdg)   LC 2007-21470

This focuses on Sharon Creech's "work as a teacher and shows how she uses the practice of journal-keeping to create an emotional experience for both character and reader. Of special interest are the chapters on Creech's life and those that discuss *Absolutely Normal Chaos*, *Bloomability*, and *The Wanderer*." Voice Youth Advocates

Includes bibliographical references

Cart, Michael

The heart has its reasons; young adult literature with gay/lesbian/queer content, 1969-2004; [by] Michael Cart [and] Christine A. Jenkins. Scarecrow Press 2006 207p (Scarecrow studies in young adult literature) $42

Grades: Professional   **813.009**
1. Homosexuality in literature 2. Young adult literature—History and criticism 3. Teenagers—Books and reading
ISBN 0-8108-5071-0   LC 2005-31320

"Both a comprehensive overview and a lively, detailed discussion of individual landmark books, this highly readable title . . . discusses 35 years of YA books with gay, lesbian, bisexual, transgender, and queer/questioning (GLBTQ) content. . . . With fully annotated bibliographies, including a chronological list, this is a valuable YA and adult resource, sure to be in great demand for personal reference and group discussion." Booklist

Includes bibliographical references

Crayton, Lisa A.

A student's guide to Toni Morrison. Enslow Publs. 2006 160p il (Understanding literature) lib bdg $27.93

Grades: 7 8 9 10   **813.009**
1. Morrison, Toni, 1931-
ISBN 0-7660-2436-9   LC 2005-19069

"Each work is placed in historical and biographical context, with special emphasis placed on curriculum-related material, including The Bluest Eye, Song of Solomon, and Beloved, along with several other noteworthy works." Publisher's note

Includes glossary and bibliographical references

Diorio, Mary Ann L.

A student's guide to Herman Melville. Enslow Publs. 2006 160p il (Understanding literature) lib bdg $27.93

Grades: 7 8 9 10   **813.009**
1. Melville, Herman, 1819-1891
ISBN 0-7660-2435-0   LC 2005-10159

"Each work is placed in historical and biographical context, with special emphasis placed on curriculum-

Diorio, Mary Ann L.—*Continued*
related works, including his masterpiece, Moby Dick,
along with Billy Budd, several of his short stories, including 'Bartleby the Scrivener,' and several of his poetic works." Publisher's note
Includes glossary and bibliographical references

A student's guide to Mark Twain; [by] Mary
Ann L. Diorio. Enslow Publishers 2007 160p il
(Understanding literature) $27.93
Grades: 7 8 9 10   **813.009**
1. Twain, Mark, 1835-1910
ISBN 978-0-7660-2438-0; 0-7660-2438-5
LC 2006005888
"After a brief account of the writer's life, Diorio discusses 11 of his major works in chronological order,
starting with 'The Jumping Frog' and ending with The
Tragedy of Pudd'nhead Wilson. For each highlighted selection, she gives a bare-bones plot summary and a brief
discussion of major themes, characters, and literary devices. . . . The book is nicely formatted, with readable
font on uncluttered pages. There are a few black-and-
white photographs of Twain and some relevant reproductions." SLJ
Includes bibliographical references

Gallo, Donald R.
Richard Peck; the past is paramount; [by]
Donald R. Gallo, Wendy J. Glenn. Scarecrow
Press 2009 208p (Scarecrow studies in young adult
literature) $35
Grades: 7 8 9 10 Professional   **813.009**
1. Peck, Richard, 1934-
ISBN 978-0-8108-5848-0; 0-8108-5848-7
LC 2008036524
"Gallo and Wendy J. Glenn recount the highlights of
Peck's life, focusing on his world travels, his accom-
plishments as a teacher and his renowned writing career.
Gallo and Glenn examine Peck's 30 novels, as well as
his short stories and children's books, poems, essays and
other nonfiction." Publisher's note
Includes bibliographical references

Glenn, Wendy J., 1970-
Sarah Dessen; from burritos to box office; [by]
Wendy J. Glenn. Scarecrow Press 2005 147p
(Scarecrow studies in young adult literature) $45
Grades: 7 8 9 10 Professional   **813.009**
1. Dessen, Sarah, 1970-
ISBN 0-8108-5325-6; 978-0-8108-5325-6
LC 2004016058
This offers literary criticism of the works of Sarah
Dessen, author of such young adult novels as *The Truth
About Forever*, and *Lock and Key*
"Glenn's book is an excellent example of the kind of
meaning-making exploration that students can examine in
a work of literature written for adolescents. . . . Infor-
mative and lively." Voice Youth Advocates
Includes bibliographical references

Hinds, Maurene J.
A reader's guide to Richard Wright's Black boy.
Enslow Publishers 2010 128p il (Multicultural
literature) lib bdg $31.93
Grades: 6 7 8 9   **813.009**
1. Wright, Richard, 1908-1960 2. American literature—African American authors
ISBN 978-0-7660-3165-4; 0-7660-3165-9
LC 2008-36473
"An introduction to Richard Wright's novel Black Boy
. . . students, which includes relevant biographical background on the author, explanations of various literary devices and techniques, and literary criticism for the novice
reader." Publisher's note
Includes glossary and bibliographical references

Hinton, KaaVonia, 1973-
Angela Johnson; poetic prose; [by] KaaVonia
Hinton. Scarecrow Press 2006 107p (Scarecrow
studies in young adult literature) $35
Grades: 7 8 9 10 Professional   **813.009**
1. Johnson, Angela, 1961-
ISBN 978-0-8108-5092-7; 0-8108-5092-3
LC 2006001893
The examines the life and works of Angela Johnson,
author of such novels as *Toning the Sweep* and *A Cool
Moonlight*
"This book is a well-researched biography suitable for
reports or even thoughtful fans. Certainly teachers seek-
ing to use Johnson's books in their classes should find
the literary criticism very useful." Voice Youth Advo-
cates
Includes bibliographical references

Sharon M. Draper; embracing literacy; [by]
KaaVonia Hinton. Scarecrow Press 2009 131p
(Scarecrow studies in young adult literature) $35
Grades: 7 8 9 10 Professional   **813.009**
1. Draper, Sharon M., 1948-
ISBN 978-0-8108-5985-2; 0-8108-5985-8
LC 2008036695
"Author KaaVonia Hinton reveals how Draper became
an exceptional teacher and writer, and how she uses her
writing to urge young people to embrace literacy. Hinton
also explores how Draper has made a lasting contribution
to the field of young adult literature. This book-length
study examines both her life and work." Publisher's note
Includes bibliographical references

Hogan, Walter
Humor in young adult literature; a time to
laugh. Scarecrow Press 2005 223p (Scarecrow
studies in young adult literature) $40 *
Grades: Professional   **813.009**
1. Wit and humor—History and criticism
2. Teenagers—Books and reading
ISBN 0-8108-5072-9   LC 2004-18903
The author's "study is organized into eight chapters
that generally reflect the stages of YA development,
looking at books on family, friends, bullies, and authorities; then books dealing with self-image, love, and ironic
perception; and, finally, books that are 'coming-of-age'
novels." Booklist

Hogan, Walter—*Continued*
"As a reader's advisory tool, this book is invaluable, paving the way for many laughter-filled hours to come." Voice Youth Advocates
Includes bibliographical references

Kunzel, Bonnie Lendermon
Tamora Pierce; [by] Bonnie Kunzel and Susan Fichtelberg. Greenwood Press 2007 279p (Teen reads: student companions to young adult literature) $45
Grades: 8 9 10 11 12   **813.009**
 1. Pierce, Tamora, 1954-
 ISBN 978-0-313-33660-7; 0-313-33660-1
                               LC 2007023729
"The first section provides a biographical chapter and literary heritage. The second and third sections analyze the *Tales of Tortall* and the *Magic Circle Sagas* as a whole, providing details into the characters and settings of each. The final section of the book, Perspectives, includes both a section on literary techniques along with an interview of Tamora Pierce herself." Publisher's note
Includes bibliographical references

Loos, Pamela
A reader's guide to Amy Tan's The joy luck club. Enslow Publishers 2008 112p il (Multicultural literature) $31.93
Grades: 6 7 8 9   **813.009**
 1. Tan, Amy 2. American literature—Asian American authors 3. Mother-daughter relationships in literature 4. Literature—Women authors
 ISBN 978-0-7660-2832-6; 0-7660-2832-1
                               LC 2006102440
"An introduction to Amy Tan's The Joy Luck Club for . . . students, which includes relevant biographical background on the author, explanations of various literary devices and techniques, and literary criticism for the novice reader." Publisher's note
The book is "an excellent resource for the student wanting to do more in depth research. . . . [The] photos . . . chosen are of good quality. . . . The [volume is] well organized, clearly written, and simple to understand." Voice Youth Advocates
Includes bibliographical references

Marler, Myrna Dee
Walter Dean Myers. Greenwood Press 2008 198p (Teen reads: student companions to young adult literature) $45
Grades: 8 9 10 11 12 Professional
                                    813.009
 1. Myers, Walter Dean, 1937-
 ISBN 978-0-313-33628-7; 0-313-33628-8
                               LC 2008010070
"Marler analyzes the life and works of the accomplished author. The first two chapters are devoted to a brief biography and the historical and cultural influences on Myers's writing. The remainder of the volume looks at his books, including comparisons of plots and characters as well as thematic development within each novel." SLJ
Includes bibliographical references

McArthur, Debra
A student's guide to Edgar Allan Poe. Enslow Publishers 2006 160p il por (Understanding literature) lib bdg $27.93
Grades: 7 8 9 10   **813.009**
 1. Poe, Edgar Allan, 1809-1849
 ISBN 0-7660-2437-7   LC 2005024273
This examines the life and career of Edgar Allan Poe, discussing such works as *The Raven*, *The Fall of the House of Usher*, and *The Tell-Tale Heart*.
Includes glossary and bibliographical references

McClellan, Marilyn
Madeleine L'Engle; banned, challenged, and censored. Enslow Publishers 2008 160p il (Authors of banned books) $25.95
Grades: 8 9 10 11 12   **813.009**
 1. L'Engle, Madeleine, 1918-2007 2. Books—Censorship
 ISBN 978-0-7660-2708-4; 0-7660-2708-2
                               LC 2007015134
This "uses the attacks on one classic yet frequently challenged book, L'Engle's 1963 Newbery Medal winner, *A Wrinkle in Time*, to draw teens into a dynamic discussion of general censorship history and issues. McClellan describes the objections, frequently Christian fundamentalists citing the book's 'satanic content,' and counters them with comments from the other side. . . . Readers will also find a succinct biography of L'Engle. . . . occasional photos, a chapter of literary analysis, and summaries of both *Wrinkle* and L'Engle's *Many Waters* (1986)." Booklist
Includes bibliographical references

Nilsen, Alleen Pace
Names and naming in young adult literature; [by] Alleen Pace Nilsen, Don L. F. Nilsen. Scarecrow Press 2007 173p (Scarecrow studies in young adult literature) $45
Grades: Professional   **813.009**
 1. Young adult literature—History and criticism 2. Characters and characteristics in literature 3. Personal names in literature
 ISBN 978-0-8108-5808-4; 0-8108-5808-8
                               LC 2007-11281
This "book consists of an introduction about the role of names in young adult literature, eight essay chapters, a bibliography, and an index. . . . The authors do a good job in writing engaging content. . . . School, public, and academic libraries will find this title an asset." Booklist
Includes bibliographical references

Pingelton, Timothy J.
A student's guide to Ernest Hemingway. Enslow Publishers 2005 160p il map (Understanding literature) lib bdg $27.93
Grades: 7 8 9 10   **813.009**
 1. Hemingway, Ernest, 1899-1961
 ISBN 0-7660-2431-8
This discusses Hemingway's life and his novels *In Our Time*, *The Sun Also Rises*, *A Farewell to Arms*, and *The Old Man and the Sea*

Pingelton, Timothy J.—*Continued*
"Engaging and informative. . . . The very accessible format and the solid information make [this book] useful to students, and the engaging style should interest casual readers." SLJ
Includes glossary and bibliographical references

Reid, Suzanne Elizabeth
Virginia Euwer Wolff; capturing the music of young voices; [by] Suzanne Elizabeth Reid. Scarecrow Press 2003 137p il (Scarecrow studies in young adult literature) $49
Grades: 8 9 10 11 12 Professional
813.009
1. Wolff, Virginia Euwer
ISBN 978-0-8108-4858-0; 0-8108-4858-9
LC 2003-10897
"In five short chapters, Reid provides an intriguing exploration of this popular author's personal life along with an in-depth summary and analysis of five of her young adult novels." Voice Youth Advocates
Includes bibliographical references

Ross-Stroud, Catherine
Janet McDonald; the original project girl; [by] Catherine Ross-Stroud. Scarecrow Press 2009 137p il (Scarecrow studies in young adult literature) $35
Grades: 7 8 9 10 Professional
813.009
1. McDonald, Janet, 1953-2007
ISBN 978-0-8108-5802-2; 0-8108-5802-9
LC 2008030712
This "is a bio-critical study of McDonald and her work as it relates to the contributions she has made to the genre of teen fiction." Publisher's note
Includes bibliographical references

Stover, Lois T.
Jacqueline Woodson; the real thing; [by] Lois Thomas Stover. Scarecrow Press 2003 189p (Scarecrow studies in young adult literature) $49
Grades: 8 9 10 11 12 Professional
813.009
1. Woodson, Jacqueline
ISBN 978-0-8108-4857-3; 0-8108-4857-0
LC 2003-9881
"This volume includes a critical analysis of how Woodson's life and work intertwine and of the themes and her own goals as a writer and artist." Publisher's note
"Students who are interested in learning more about this particular author will find plenty of information that will illuminate second and deeper readings of her works. Teachers searching for ways to help make connections among the books will find Stover's work of great value." Voice Youth Advocates
Includes bibliographical references

Tighe, Mary Ann
Sharon Creech; the words we choose to say. Scarecrow Press 2006 123p (Scarecrow studies in young adult literature) $35
Grades: 7 8 9 10
813.009
1. Creech, Sharon
ISBN 978-0-8108-5086-6; 0-8108-5086-9
LC 2005037615
"Tighe bills her resource as a 'biocritical volume' on Sharon Creech, beginning with a chronology of her life before continuing with a more complete look, as well as the influence of her life experiences on her writing. . . . Tighe does an admirable and complete job of examining Creech's body of work." Voice Youth Advocates
Includes bibliographical references

Tyson, Edith S.
Orson Scott Card; writer of the terrible choice. Scarecrow Press 2003 xxv, 187p (Scarecrow studies in young adult literature) $40
Grades: 8 9 10 11 12 Professional
813.009
1. Card, Orson Scott
ISBN 0-8108-4790-6
LC 2003-5730
"Tyson begins her book with a . . . preface gleaned from Card's own explanation of the purpose of his writing, followed by a light biographical skimming of his life and development as a writer. The best features of the book are Tyson's excellent analyses of Card's books. Each book is summarized . . . and then enriched with different perspectives on the meaning, or some relevant background information, or something that Card himself wrote about that particular book. The sequence and interrelatedness of his books are also well documented. This book is a must-have for both professional and circulating collections." Voice Youth Advocates
Includes bibliographical references

The **wand** in the word; conversations with writers of fantasy; compiled and edited by Leonard S. Marcus. 1st ed. Candlewick Press 2006 202p il $19.99 *
Grades: 6 7 8 9
813.009
1. Fantasy fiction—History and criticism 2. Authors, American 3. Authors, English
ISBN 0-7636-2625-2
LC 2005-46913
"Marcus presents interviews with 13 fantasy luminaries, including Lloyd Alexander, Susan Cooper, Nancy Farmer, Brian Jacques, Garth Nix, Tamora Pierce, and Philip Pullman. The writers' distinct personalities and career paths emerge, as do intriguing similarities. . . . Each profile includes a black-and-white author's photo, a reading list, and a bit of ephemera, often a handwritten manuscript page. . . . [This is] a rich resource that will be consulted as frequently by children's literature professionals as by genre fans themselves." Booklist

814   American essays

Red; the next generation of American writers—teenage girls—on what fires up their lives today; edited by Amy Goldwasser. Hudson Street Press 2007 267p $21.95

Grades: 8 9 10 11 12 Adult   **814**
1. Teenagers' writings 2. Essays 3. Girls
ISBN 978-1-59463-040-8; 1-59463-040-2
      LC 2007027247

"Nearly sixty teenage girls from across the country speak out, writing about everything from post-Katrina New Orleans to Johnny Depp; from learning to rock climb to starting a rock band; from the loneliness of losing a best friend to the loathing or pride they feel about their bodies." Publisher's note

"The authors are complicated and real, with interests and concerns of immense scope. . . . It will be a surefire hit for girls." Voice Youth Advocates

815.008   American speeches— Collections

American Heritage book of great American speeches for young people; edited by Suzanne McIntire. Wiley 2001 292p il pa $14.95 *

Grades: 7 8 9 10   **815.008**
1. American speeches
ISBN 0-471-38942-0   LC 00-43749

This is a "compendium of more than 100 speeches that span nearly 400 years of American history, from Powhatan (1609) to Senator Charles Robb (2000). Prominent orators include Patrick Henry, Thomas Jefferson, John Kennedy, Richard Nixon, Martin Luther King, Jr., and Malcolm X. . . . The speeches inform readers and provide examples of how the spoken word has affected Americans throughout our past." SLJ

Historic speeches of African Americans; introduced and selected by Warren J. Halliburton. Watts 1993 192p il (African-American experience) lib bdg $23 *

Grades: 7 8 9 10 11 12   **815.008**
1. African Americans—History 2. American speeches
ISBN 0-531-11034-6 (lib bdg)   LC 92-39318

Presents speeches by various African American religious and political leaders from the days of slavery to the present, along with biographical information and historical background.

"Kids will dip into this for personal reading, and for curriculum research; they'll also find stirring pieces to read aloud and think about. The detailed sources at the end of the book make it easy to find out more about the individuals and their ideas." Booklist

U.X.L Asian American voices; edited by Deborah Gillan Straub. 2nd ed. U.X.L 2004 xxv, 315p il $58 *

Grades: 7 8 9 10 11 12   **815.008**
1. Asian Americans 2. American speeches
ISBN 0-7876-7600-4   LC 2003-110048

First published 1997 with title: Asian American voices

This "reference presents full or excerpted speeches, sermons, orations, poems, testimony and other notable spoken words of Asian Americans. Each entry is accompanied by an introduction and boxes explaining terms and events to which the speech refers. The volume is illustrated with photographs and drawings." Publisher's note

817   American humor and satire

Cleary, Brian P., 1959-
The laugh stand; adventures in humor; by Brian P. Cleary; illustrated by J.P. Sandy. Millbrook Press 2008 48p il lib bdg $16.95

Grades: 4 5 6   **817**
1. Wit and humor 2. Word games
ISBN 978-0-8225-7849-9   LC 2007021889

Cleary "promotes fun with words in 13 small sections that toy with puns, anagrams, daffynitions, Tom Swifties, and more. . . . Sandy's ideally matched cartoons are a google-eyed cast that includes humans, animals, food items with faces, and societal icons. This team marries humor with sublime learning." SLJ

Includes bibliographical references

818   American miscellany

Porcellino, John
Thoreau at Walden; by John Porcellino, from the writings of Henry David Thoreau; introduction by D.B. Johnson. Hyperion 2008 99p il (Center for Cartoon Studies presents) $16.99; pa $9.99

Grades: 8 9 10 11 12   **818**
1. Thoreau, Henry David, 1817-1862—Graphic novels 2. Graphic novels
ISBN   978-1-4231-0038-6;   1-4231-0038-7; 978-1-4231-0039-3 (pa); 1-4231-0039-5 (pa)
      LC 2007-61358

"Presents in graphic novel format an account of the two years that Thoreau spent at Walden Pond, excerpted from Thoreau's writings." Publisher's note

"This book is true in spirit to Thoreau's writings and to underground comics. It is fairly linear, using short quotes and simple line drawings to tell of the time the philosopher spent at Walden Pond. Porcellino chose many well-known sayings and events and placed them within a spare visual context." SLJ

Includes bibliographical references

821   English poetry

Agard, John, 1949-
Half-caste and other poems. Hodder & Stoughton 2004 80p il $16.99 *

Grades: 7 8 9 10 11 12   **821**
1. Poetry—By individual authors
ISBN 0-340-89382-6

"This collection of poems . . . deftly covers race, identity, and other topics. . . . Agard uses rhyme, repeti-

Agard, John, 1949— ***Continued*
tion, and refrains to make his work sing. His skillful use
of humor to get his serious points across is in evidence
here, and several concrete poems display both visual and
verbal wit." Horn Book Guide

Includes bibliographical references

Blake, William, 1757-1827
William Blake; edited by John Maynard;
illustrated by Alessandra Cimatoribus. Sterling
Pub. 2006 48p il (Poetry for young people) $14.95
Grades: 5 6 7 8   821
  1. Poetry—By individual authors
  ISBN 978-0-8069-3647-5; 0-8069-3647-9
                                      LC 2006013858
"The book begins with a heroic attempt to explain
some of [Blake's] themes and philosophy in a four-page
introduction. Maynard speaks of the poet with insight, eloquence, and obvious admiration. . . . He prefaces each
poem with explanatory comments that are also thought-
provoking and illuminating. . . . The artwork is well
matched to the tone of the poems. Cimatoribus's illustrations are at the same time childlike and surreal." SLJ

Carroll, Lewis, 1832-1898
Jabberwocky; the classic poem from Lewis
Carroll's Through the looking glass, and what
Alice found there; reimagined and illustrated by
Christopher Myers. Jump at the Sun/Hyperion
Books for Children 2007 unp il $15.99 *
Grades: 4 5 6 7   821
  1. Nonsense verses 2. Poetry—By individual authors
  ISBN 978-1-4231-0372-1; 1-4231-0372-6
                                      LC 2007-18337
"Myers cleverly translates Carroll's nonsense poem
into a contemporary tale through sports imagery. . . .
The spectacular paintings have silhouetted figures on vi-
brant backgrounds. . . . The jaunty text is in capital letters in an extra-large black font, with some words highlighted in color." SLJ

Cohen, Barbara, 1932-1992
Canterbury tales; [by] Geoffrey Chaucer;
selected, translated, and adapted by Barbara
Cohen; illustrated by Trina Schart Hyman.
Lothrop, Lee & Shepard Bks. 1988 87p il $24.99
*
Grades: 4 5 6 7   821
  1. Chaucer, Geoffrey, d. 1400—Adaptations
  2. Poetry—By individual authors 3. Middle Ages
  ISBN 0-688-06201-6   LC 86-21045
  Contents: The nun's priest's tale; The pardoner's tale;
The wife of Bath's tale; The franklin's tale
"Cohen's evident love and respect for Chaucer's writing keep her close to the text. Her writing retains the flavor of the times and the spirit of Chaucer's words while
her prose retelling, enriched by Hyman's lively full-color
paintings, enhances the book's appeal to young people.
. . . An excellent introduction to *The Canterbury Tales*
for young readers." Booklist

Coleridge, Samuel Taylor, 1772-1834
Samuel Taylor Coleridge; edited by James
Engell; illustrated by Harvey Chan. Sterling 2003
48p il (Poetry for young people) $14.95
Grades: 7 8 9 10   821
  1. Poetry—By individual authors
  ISBN 0-8069-6951-2   LC 2003-6549
Introduces the life of author Samuel Taylor Coleridge
and presents a sample of his poetry, including complete
works and excerpts, with a brief, explanatory introduction to each
"Chan's enchanting paintings embellish the text and
do a nice job of capturing the mood of the poetry without dominating it. . . . A useful purchase for any collection." SLJ

Kipling, Rudyard, 1865-1936
If; a father's advice to his son; [by] Rudyard
Kipling; photographs by Charles R. Smith. 1st ed.
Atheneum Books for Young Readers 2007 unp il
$14.99
Grades: 4 5 6   821
  ISBN 978-0-689-87799-5; 0-689-87799-4
                                      LC 2006005312
"Kipling's powerful poem comes to life for a contemporary audience in atmospheric photographs that use the
metaphor of sports. A lovely shot of a boy heading a
soccer ball accompanies the opening couplet: 'If you can
keep your head/when all about you/are losing theirs/and
blaming it on you.' The mood and actions in most of the
illustrations clearly invoke the verse." SLJ

Lear, Edward, 1812-1888
The owl and the pussycat; illustrations by
Stephane Jorisch. KCP Poetry 2007 unp il (Visions
in poetry) $16.95; pa $9.95
Grades: 5 6 7 8   821
  1. Nonsense verses 2. Owls—Poetry 3. Cats—Poetry
  4. Poetry—By individual authors
  ISBN   978-1-55337-828-0;   1-55337-828-8;
  978-1-55453-232-2 (pa); 1-55453-232-9 (pa)
"This striking entry in an aptly named series envisions
a darker subtext to Lear's well-known poem. Jorisch
consulted Lear's own drawings when preparing his winsome watercolor and ink illustrations, noting the melancholy quality of the title characters. The light verse is
transformed by the artist's vision into a mismatched couple seeking a place of acceptance. . . . For older readers,
this book shows true artistic vision and a great example
of the power of personal interpretation and inspiration."
SLJ

Noyes, Alfred, 1880-1958
The highwayman; [by] Alfred Noyes; with
illustrations by Murray Kimber. Kids Can Press
2005 unp il (Visions in poetry) $17.95
Grades: 7 8 9 10   821
  1. Thieves—Poetry 2. Poetry—By individual authors
  ISBN 978-1-55337-425-1; 1-55337-425-8
"Painting in an art deco style and film noir palette,
Kimber casts a motorcycle-riding rebel as the highway-
man; a curvaceous glamour girl as Bess; and tommy-gun

Noyes, Alfred, 1880-1958—*Continued*
toting cops as the soldiers who intrude upon the lovers'
tryst. . . . The dramatic artwork plays up the elements
teens will find most rewarding—particularly the protagonists' defiance of authority and the unblushingly melodramatic conclusion." Booklist

Tennyson, Alfred Tennyson, Baron, 1809-1892
The Lady of Shalott; illustrated by Geneviève
Côtè. Kids Can Press 2005 unp il (Visions in
poetry) $16.95
Grades: 7 8 9 10   **821**
1. Arthurian romances 2. Poetry—By individual authors
ISBN 978-1-55337-874-7; 1-55337-874-1
"The pictures in this small book bring an early-
twentieth-century urban setting to Tennyson's classic Arthurian poem, written in 1842, about a young woman imprisoned in a tower, endlessly weaving what she sees in
the mirror, until she dares to break free and look outside.
. . . Cote's quiet line-and-watercolor and pastel artwork
opens up the story, preserving the romance and mystery
without filling in too much." Booklist

Williams, Marcia, 1945-
Chaucer's Canterbury Tales; retold and
illustrated by Marcia Williams. Candlewick Press
2007 45p il $16.99 *
Grades: 4 5 6 7   **821**
1. Chaucer, Geoffrey, d. 1400—Adaptations
2. Middle Ages 3. Poetry—By individual authors
ISBN 978-0-7636-3197-0; 0-7636-3197-3
A retelling in comic strip form of Geoffrey Chaucer's
famous work in which a group of pilgrims in fourteenth-
century England tell each other stories as they travel on
a pilgrimage to the cathedral at Canterbury
"Chaucer's pilgrims come to life in the energetic retelling of nine tales. . . . The watercolor-and-ink car-
toon-art displayed in a comic-book format is a perfect
match for the raucous and sometimes-raw humor." SLJ

Wordsworth, William, 1770-1850
William Wordsworth; edited by Alan Liu;
illustrated by James Muir. Sterling 2003 48p il
(Poetry for young people) $14.95
Grades: 7 8 9 10   **821**
1. Poetry—By individual authors
ISBN 0-8069-8277-2   LC 2003-6163
An illustrated collection of nineteen popular poems by
William Wordsworth, who was the poet laureate of England in the mid-nineteenth century. Includes an introduction to the poet's life and work
The editor has "chosen well, bringing together about
20 of [the] great poet's most accessible, compelling poems. . . . The full color paintings on each page are
beautiful." Booklist

821.008   English poetry—Collections

Classic poetry; an illustrated collection; selected
by Michael Rosen; pictures by Paul Howard.
Candlewick Press 1998 160p il 21.99; pa $12.99
Grades: 7 8 9 10   **821.008**
1. Poetry—Collections
ISBN   978-1-5640-2890-7;   1-5640-2890-9;
978-0-7636-4210-5 (pa); 0-7636-4210-X (pa)
LC 98-18282
A collection of favorite poems by such writers as William Shakespeare, Emily Dickinson, Edward Lear, Walt
Whitman, and Langston Hughes, with portraits of the poets, brief biographical background, and illustrations.
"This handsome edition introduces major poets
through works accessible to young people. Each section
begins with a portrait of the author and a short summary
of his or her life, followed by one or two poems or parts
of poems. Each spread includes at least one illustration
evocative of the tone of the poetry as well as the times
of the poet. . . . Illustrator Paul Howard's gifts are not
diminished by the smaller size of some pictures, for
some of his best work here is in miniature. . . . Few anthologies for this age group include such a fine selection
of works from beyond the childhood classics, introduce
the poets so vividly, or provide such a rich collection of
haunting illustrations." Booklist

Committed to memory; 100 best poems to
memorize; edited, with an introduction, by John
Hollander; advisory committee, Eavan Boland
. . . [et. al.] Riverhead Books 1997 196p pa
$14
Grades: 8 9 10 11 12 Adult   **821.008**
1. English poetry—Collections 2. American poetry—
Collections
ISBN 1-57322-646-7 (pa); 978-1-57322-646-2 (pa)
Also available in hardcover from Turtle Point Press
$24.95 (ISBN 978-1885983-15-2)
First published 1996 by Academy of American Poets
Hollander "has selected 100 poems by poets—includ-
ing lyrics and narratives, meditations and counsels—
ranging from Blake and Hughes, Bishop and Thomas, to
Yeats and Hayden. These are classics that lend them-
selves to memory, being short; often in form, or at least
metrical; always rhythmic; and delightful." Libr J

The **Kingfisher** book of funny poems; selected by
Roger McGough; illustrated by Caroline Holden.
Kingfisher (NY) 2002 256p il $18.95
Grades: 4 5 6 7   **821.008**
1. Humorous poetry 2. English poetry—Collections
3. American poetry—Collections
ISBN 0-7534-5480-7   LC 2001-38942
A collection of over 200 poems, limericks, and verses
from such authors as Emily Dickinson, Lewis Carroll,
and Shel Silverstein
"This collection is chock-full of wacky, witty, and
whimsical poems that will hook readers from the first
stanza to the last. . . . What really brings out the humor
are the equally zany black-and-white drawings that appear on almost every page." SLJ

The **Oxford** book of twentieth-century English verse; chosen by Philip Larkin. Oxford University Press 1993 c1973 651p $35

Grades: 8 9 10 11 12 Adult   **821.008**

1. English poetry—Collections

ISBN 0-19-812137-7

This anthology of more than 600 poems by more than 200 twentieth-century British writers includes works by John Masefield, T. S. Eliot, W. B. Yeats, W. H. Auden, Dylan Thomas and Alan Sillitoe

"A strong vein of neo-Georgianism runs throughout the book, resulting in a clear partiality for work that is explicitly, even documentarily, English in locale, for poems that are narrative or anecdotal, for neat, well-populated fables and for moralistic ruminations." New Statesman

822 English drama

Christie, Agatha, 1890-1976

The mousetrap and other plays. New American Library 2000 742p hardcover o.p. pa $7.99

Grades: 7 8 9 10 11 12 Adult   **822**

1. English drama—Collections

ISBN 0-451-20118-3; 0-451-20114-0 (pa)

                  LC 00-64727

First published 1978 by Dodd, Mead

Contents: Ten little Indians; Appointment with death; The hollow; The mousetrap; Witness for the prosecution; Towards zero; Verdict; Go back for murder

"The noted mystery writer composed adaptations of seven novels and stories into arresting plays as well as creating one original theater piece ('Verdict'). . . . All are as delightful to read for pleasure as Christie's mystery novels, especially since some that earlier appeared in the latter form have been intriguingly altered." Booklist

822.3 William Shakespeare

Aliki

William Shakespeare & the Globe; written & illustrated by Aliki. HarperCollins Pubs. 1999 48p il hardcover o.p. lib bdg $15.89; pa $6.99 *

Grades: 4 5 6 7 8 9   **822.3**

1. Shakespeare, William, 1564-1616 2. Globe Theatre (London, England) 3. Shakespeare's Globe (London, England)

ISBN 0-06-027820-X; 0-06-027821-8 (lib bdg); 0-06-443722-1 (pa)   LC 98-7903

The "text describes Shakespeare's life, the Elizabethan world and entertainments, and the ups and downs of the theatrical industry . . . including tidbits such as the Burbage brothers' piece-by-piece theft of the original Globe Theatre. A fast-forward to the twentieth century then treats Sam Wanamaker's dream of making the Globe rise again." Bull Cent Child Books

"A logically organized and engaging text, plenty of detailed illustrations with informative captions, and a clean design provide a fine introduction to both bard and theater." Horn Book Guide

Appignanesi, Richard

As you like it; by William Shakespeare; illustrated by Chie Kutsuwada; adapted by Richard Appignanesi. Amulet Books 2009 207p (Manga Shakespeare) pa $10.95

Grades: 7 8 9 10   **822.3**

1. Shakespeare, William, 1564-1616—Adaptations

2. Graphic novels

ISBN 978-0-8109-8351-9; 0-8109-8351-6

                  LC 2008-45920

Banished to the Forest of Arden, Rosalind, disguised as a boy, reunites with true love Orlando.

"While maintaining considerable Shakespearian language, the plot is staged in a thoroughly manga manner, with Japanese settings, hairstyles, and posturing readily recognizable to the contemporary teen manga fan. . . . This is an excellent choice not only as curriculum support but also for manga readers." Booklist

Hamlet; [Richard Appignanesi, text adaptor]; illustrated by Emma Vieceli. Harry N. Abrams/Amulet Books 2007 195p (Manga Shakespeare) pa $9.95

Grades: 8 9 10 11 12 Adult   **822.3**

1. Shakespeare, William, 1564-1616—Adaptations

2. Graphic novels

ISBN 978-0-8109-9324-2; 0-8109-9324-4

First published in the United Kingdom

Shakespeare's classic play of murder and revenge is here adapted into a manga-style graphic novel. It's now set in 2107, after global climate change has devastated the Earth. Appignanesi uses the text of the play and abridges it to fit the pages, while Vieceli's art vigorously carries the story along. The book includes a summary of the plot and a brief biography of Shakespeare.

Julius Caesar; by William Shakespeare; adapted by Richard Appignanesi; illustrated by Mustashrik. Amulet Books 2008 207p (Manga Shakespeare) pa $9.95 *

Grades: 8 9 10 11 12   **822.3**

1. Shakespeare, William, 1564-1616—Adaptations

2. Graphic novels

ISBN 978-0-8109-7072-4 (pa); 0-8109-7072-4 (pa)

                  LC 2008-18764

Retells, in comic book format, Shakespeare's play about political intrigue, personal betrayal, and the aftermath of a brutal assassination

"Abridged text is spread out to render it less intimidating. . . . What truly shines in this work, though, is the superlative visualization by newcomer Mustashrik. Working in stark white and inky black, he has created a spare but intense landscape that mirrors the emotions of the characters. . . . Especially for the more artistically minded, this is a raw, striking, and powerful introduction to Shakespeare." Booklist

Manga Shakespeare: The tempest. Abrams 2008 207p pa $9.95

Grades: 7 8 9 10   **822.3**

1. Shakespeare, William, 1564-1616—Adaptations

2. Graphic novels

ISBN 978-0-8109-9476-8

Prospero and his daughter Miranda have loved on an isolated island for twelve years, after he had been de-

Appignanesi, Richard—*Continued*
posed from his rule as Duke of Naples and cast out to
sea to die. A powerful magician, Prospero has caused the
survivors of a shipwreck to land on his island, in order
to get his revenge, for these survivors are his enemies.
Problems arise when Miranda falls in love with Ferdinand; the monster Caliban tries to use the survivors to
kill Prospero, and Ariel the sprite is trying to set things
right while still obeying Prospero. The book includes a
plot summary and a brief biography of Shakespeare

"This adaptation would be useful both as an introduction to the play and as a companion piece for classroom
study of it, using images to illuminate the Bard's eloquent poetry." SLJ

A midsummer night's dream; illustrated by Kate
Brown. Abrams 2008 207p (Manga Shakespeare)
pa $9.95
Grades: 7 8 9 10   **822.3**
1. Shakespeare, William, 1564-1616—Adaptations
2. Graphic novels
ISBN 978-0-8109-9475-1; 0-8109-9475-5
Shakespeare's comedy of romance, Faerie, and she-
nanigans in the forest is adapted into a manga-style
graphic novel. Hermia is in love with Lysander, while
Demetrius is in love with Hermia, and Helen loves Demetrius. When mischievous fairy Puck decides to have
some fun with the powerful love potion he has fetched
for Fairy King Oberon, chaos reigns. While the human
foursome needs to sort itself out, Oberon seeks revenge
against his wife, Queen Titania, by having Puck use the
love potion on her so she falls in love with the first creature she sees—who happens to be a yokel to whom Puck
gave a donkey's head. The text takes dialog from the
original play. The book includes a plot summary and a
brief biography of Shakespeare.

Romeo and Juliet; by William Shakespeare;
adapted by Richard Appignanesi; illustrated by
Sonia Leong. Amulet Books 2007 195p (Manga
Shakespeare) pa $9.95
Grades: 8 9 10 11 12   **822.3**
1. Shakespeare, William, 1564-1616—Adaptations
2. Graphic novels
ISBN 978-0-8109-9325-9; 0-8109-9325-2
LC 2006-100362
First published in the United Kingdom
Shakespeare's classic play of star-crossed young lovers gets the manga treatment. Set in modern Tokyo with
rival yakuza gangs, and using somewhat abridged text
from the play for the dialogue, the story becomes an accessible, action-packed read most teens will like.
"Although the richness of the language may be lost,
the script keeps the spirit of the story intact, hitting all
the major speeches." Booklist

Cover, Arthur Byron
Macbeth; [by] William Shakespeare; Arthur
Byron Cover, adapter; Tony Leonard Tamai,
illustrator. Puffin Graphics 2005 176p il pa $9.99
Grades: 6 7 8 9 10 11 12   **822.3**

1. Shakespeare, William, 1564-1616—Adaptations
2. Graphic novels
ISBN 0-14-240409-8
Ambitious lord Macbeth murders his king to take the
throne because of the predictions of some witches, but
his position is never secure, and he takes ever more violent measures to stay in power. Shakespeare's classic
play is reinvented here with Japanese manga style art and
a futuristic setting on a vast ringworld around a sun.

Coville, Bruce
William Shakespeare's A midsummer night's
dream. Dial Bks. 1996 unp $17.95; pa $7.99
Grades: 5 6 7 8 9   **822.3**
1. Shakespeare, William, 1564-1616—Adaptations
ISBN 0-8037-1784-9; 0-14-250168-9 (pa)
LC 94-12600
A simplified prose retelling of Shakespeare's play
about the strange events that take place in a forest inhabited by fairies who magically transform the romantic fate
of two young couples.
"Coville introduces the story and also conveys something of the poetry and drama. Nolan's framed graphite
and watercolor paintings express the dreaminess and absurdity of the play, and the pictures have a theatrical
flair." Booklist

William Shakespeare's Hamlet. Dial Bks. 2004
unp $16.99
Grades: 5 6 7 8   **822.3**
1. Shakespeare, William, 1564-1616—Adaptations
ISBN 0-8037-2708-9   LC 2002-13743
Retells, in simplified prose, William Shakespeare's
play about a prince of Denmark who seeks revenge for
his father's murder
"Not only is the text incredibly faithful to the original,
but the language that surrounds the quoted dialogue is
also amazingly rich. . . . Done predominately in shades
of blue and orange, Gore's acrylic-and-pastel artwork underscores the sharp contrast between the protagonist's periods of brooding and his angry outbursts." SLJ

William Shakespeare's Romeo and Juliet. Dial
Bks. 1999 unp $16.99
Grades: 5 6 7 8 9   **822.3**
1. Shakespeare, William, 1564-1616—Adaptations
ISBN 0-8037-2462-4   LC 98-36178
A simplified prose retelling of Shakespeare's play
about two young people who defy their warring families'
prejudices and dare to fall in love.
"Coville's treatment is generally faithful to the original and is nicely enhanced by Dennis Nolan's lushly romantic illustrations. . . . This is an accessible and enticing introduction to one of Shakespeare's most popular
works." Booklist

William Shakespeare's The winter's tale. Dial
Books for Young Readers 2007 unp $16.99
Grades: 5 6 7 8   **822.3**
1. Shakespeare, William, 1564-1616—Adaptations
ISBN 978-0-8037-2709-0   LC 2006038485
When King Leontes unfairly accuses his wife of infi-
delity, he sets off a terrible chain of events.
"Coville does a good job of retelling the story for

Coville, Bruce—*Continued*

young people. Some of the watercolor-and-gouache paintings seem overly theatrical or romantic in style, but others show more restraint and depth." Booklist

Dunton-Downer, Leslie

Essential Shakespeare handbook; [by] Leslie Dunton-Downer, Alan Riding. DK Pub. 2004 480p il pa $25

Grades: 8 9 10 11 12 Adult   **822.3**

   1. Shakespeare, William, 1564-1616—Criticism

   ISBN 0-7894-9333-0   LC 2004-274586

This is an "illustrated guide to every play in the Shakespeare canon, as well as a portrait of the Bard's life and the world of Elizabethan and Jacobean theater." Publisher's note

"This is an excellent basic tool for gaining insight into the Bard's poetic genius. . . . It is an informative, visually enticing introduction to the world's most famous dramatist." SLJ

Garfield, Leon, 1921-1996

Shakespeare stories [I]-II; illustrated by Michael Foreman. Houghton Mifflin 1991-1995 c1985-c1994 2v il v1 $26; pa $17; v2 $26

Grades: 7 8 9 10 11 12   **822.3**

   1. Shakespeare, William, 1564-1616—Adaptations

   ISBN 0-395-56397-6 (v1); 0-395-86140-3 (v1 pa); 0-395-70893-1 (v2)

Original volume first published 1985 by Schocken Bks.

In these volumes Garfield has rewritten twenty-one of Shakespeare's plays in narrative form, retaining much of the original language

Hilliam, David

William Shakespeare; England's greatest playwright and poet; [by] David Hilliam. 1st ed. Rosen Central 2005 112p il (Rulers, scholars, and artists of the Renaissance) lib bdg $31.95

Grades: 6 7 8 9   **822.3**

   1. Shakespeare, William, 1564-1616

   ISBN 1-4042-0318-4   LC 2004-9274

Contents: Shakespeare's boyhood and sixteenth century England; The invention of the first modern theater; Shakespeare and the London theater scene; Shakespeare's plays and poems; Shakespeare's final years; Shakespeare in the twenty-first century

In this biography of William Shakespeare the author "carefully separates supposition and fact, piecing together an accessible, lively account of his extraordinary subject's life and times. . . . Throughout the smoothly written text are beautiful, well-integrated quotes from Shakespeare's works." Booklist

Includes bibliographical references

Hinds, Gareth, 1971-

King Lear. Thecomic.com 2007 122p il $30; pa $15.95 *

Grades: 7 8 9 10   **822.3**

   1. Shakespeare, William, 1564-1616—Adaptations

   2. Graphic novels

   ISBN 978-1-893131-07-1; 978-1-893131-06-4 (pa)

This graphic novel adaptation of Shakespeare's King Lear is "an excellent rendition of one the bard's great tragedies. Using splash pages that open up the settings, washes of otherworldly colors, grotesquely expressive faces . . . and figural work . . . Hinds occasionally attains a visual poetry." Booklist

McKeown, Adam

Julius Caesar; a retelling by Adam McKeown; illustrated by Janet Hamlin. Sterling Pub. Co. 2008 80p il (Young reader's Shakespeare) $14.95

Grades: 6 7 8 9   **822.3**

   1. Caesar, Julius, 100-44 B.C.—Fiction 2. Brutus, Marcus Junius—Fiction 3. Shakespeare, William, 1564-1616—Adaptations 4. Rome—History—Fiction

   ISBN 978-1-4027-3579-0; 1-4027-3579-0

                   LC 2007030733

"This handsomely illustrated retelling . . . stays true both to the rousing action of [Shakespeare's] play and to the characters' inner conflicts. McKeown's clear, stimulating introduction raises the complex moral issues. . . . Hamlin's dramatic, full-color art . . . ably captures the personal torment as well as the dynamics of the battlefield." Booklist

Nettleton, Pamela Hill, 1955-

William Shakespeare; playwright and poet; by Pamela Hill Nettleton. Compass Point Books 2005 112p il map (Signature lives) $30.60

Grades: 5 6 7 8   **822.3**

   1. Shakespeare, William, 1564-1616

   ISBN 0-7565-0816-9   LC 2004-23081

Contents: All the world's a stage; Shakespeare's time; Shakespeare as a boy; At school and beyond; Shakespeare in love; Shakespeare in London; Shakespeare's poems; Success as a playwrite; At the peak of his powers; The final years

Profiles the life and work of William Shakespeare

"This biography is one of the best available for younger students. Nettleton supplements what little is actually known about the bard's life with detailed and accurate information about everyday life in England during the period, the theater, and publishing practices of the time. The text is enhanced by full-color illustrations and black-and-white reproductions." SLJ

Includes bibliographical references

Packer, Tina, 1938-

Tales from Shakespeare; retold by Tina Packer; illustrated by Gail de Marcken . . . [et. al.] Scholastic Press 2004 192p il $24.95 *

Grades: 5 6 7 8   **822.3**

   1. Shakespeare, William, 1564-1616—Adaptations

   ISBN 0-439-32107-7   LC 2003-42710

Tina Packer retells ten of Shakespeare's plays. The stories are illustrated by various artists: Macbeth by Barry Moser, The Tempest by Mark Teague, Othello by Kadir Nelson, Twelfth Night by Chesley McLaren, Romeo and Juliet by David Shannon, Much Ado About

Packer, Tina, 1938——*Continued*

Nothing by Mary GrandPre, King Lear by Leo and Diane Dillon, As You Like It by Barbara McClintock, A Midsummer Night's Dream by Gail De Marcken, and Hamlet by P.J. Lynch

This is "a treasure trove of well-told tales. In these adaptations, Packer captures the essence of the playwright's words and ideas, placing them in concise and clearly told stories. . . . Each illustrator sets the appropriate tone for and conveys the mood of the tale, and the breadth of artistic interpretations gives the book appeal to a wide audience." SLJ

Rosen, Michael, 1946-

Shakespeare; his work and his world; illustrated by Robert Ingpen. Candlewick Press 2001 96p il hardcover o.p. pa $9.99

Grades: 5 6 7 8 9   **822.3**

1. Shakespeare, William, 1564-1616

ISBN 0-7636-1568-4; 0-7636-3201-5 (pa)

LC 00-66689

"The volume begins with plot teasers from the plays and progresses through an explanation of Shakespeare's time and the locations important to his life and works. . . . There is a plethora of historical information, as well as an explanation of the types of theaters and plays common at the time." Book Rep

"In exceptionally fresh and vivid terms, the author plies readers with abundant, accurate information. . . . The copious and engaging pencil-and-watercolor illustrations have the burnished look of old pictures and are as glorious as the text." SLJ

Includes bibliographical references

Shakespeare, William, 1564-1616

One hundred and eleven Shakespeare monologues; the ultimate audition book for teens; edited by Lisa Bansavage and L. E. McCullough; introduction by Jill K. Swanson. Smith & Kraus 2003 176p (Young actors series) pa $11.95

Grades: 7 8 9 10 11 12   **822.3**

1. Monologues 2. Acting

ISBN 1-57525-356-9

"These monologues are divided into three sections: those for female actors, male actors, or either. They are further subdivided into comedies, histories, and tragedies. . . . The genius of this book is in the introduction, which offers a wealth of information for teens who have never encountered Shakespeare." SLJ

Stanley, Diane, 1943-

Bard of Avon: the story of William Shakespeare; by Diane Stanley and Peter Vennema; illustrated by Diane Stanley. Morrow Junior Bks. 1992 unp il hardcover o.p. pa $6.99 *

Grades: 4 5 6 7   **822.3**

1. Shakespeare, William, 1564-1616

ISBN 0-688-09108-3; 0-688-09109-1 (lib bdg); 0-688-16294-0 (pa)   LC 90-46564

A brief biography of the world's most famous playwright, using only historically correct information

"A remarkably rounded picture of Shakespeare's life

and the period in which he lived is presented . . . together with a thoughtful attempt to relate circumstances in his personal life to the content of his plays. . . . The text is splendidly supported by the illustrations, which are stylized, yet recognizable, and present a clear view of life in the late sixteenth century. A discerning, knowledgeable biography, rising far above the ordinary." Horn Book

Includes bibliographical references

823.009   English fiction—History and criticism

Beahm, George W.

Discovering The golden compass; a guide to Philip Pullman's Dark Materials; [by] George Beahm; art by Tim Kirk. Hampton Roads Pub. Co. 2007 xxiv, 206p il $16.95

Grades: 7 8 9 10 11 12   **823.009**

1. Pullman, Philip, 1946-

ISBN 978-1-57174-506-4   LC 2007020694

"This accessible guide to the author and *His Dark Materials* trilogy is the perfect passport to Pullman's imaginative universe. Fans will appreciate the information provided about the author and his world in all formats: books, . . . plays, audiobooks, and the upcoming movie. . . . Fascinating and well-written." Voice Youth Advocates

Includes bibliographical references

Cooling, Wendy

D is for Dahl; a gloriumptious A-Z guide to the world of Roald Dahl; illustrations by Quentin Blake; compiled by Wendy Cooling. Viking 2005 149p il hardcover o.p. pa $5.99

Grades: 4 5 6 7   **823.009**

1. Dahl, Roald

ISBN 0-670-06023-2; 0-14-240934-0 (pa)

This is an alphabetically arranged collection of facts about the life and work of the popular author of children's books

"This dictionary-of-sorts is entertaining, insightful, and of particular interest to Dahl's fans. . . . The writing is clear, wicked, and fun. An occasional black-and-white photograph complements Blake's illustrations." SLJ

Gribbin, Mary

The science of Philip Pullman's His Dark Materials; [by] Mary and John Gribbon; with an introduction by Philip Pullman. Knopf 2005 203p il $15.95; lib bdg $17.99; pa $5.99

Grades: 6 7 8 9   **823.009**

1. Pullman, Philip, 1946-. His dark materials 2. Science

ISBN 0-375-83144-4; 0-375-93144-9 (lib bdg); 0-375-83146-0 (pa)   LC 2004-57731

"The Gribbins show how concepts are the real magic of Pullman's trilogy. Each chapter begins with a quote drawn from the books, which leads to an elegantly written explanation of the science. . . . The authors do an amazing job teasing an introduction to string theory from

Gribbin, Mary—*Continued*

Will's 'subtle knife.' . . . Naturally, fans of the series will be the best audience, but the book offers much to readers simply interested in the advanced sciences, who then may be led back to His Dark Materials." Booklist

Latham, Don, 1959-

David Almond; memory and magic. Scarecrow Press 2006 151p (Scarecrow studies in young adult literature) $40

Grades: 7 8 9 10 11 12 Professional

823.009

1. Almond, David, 1951-
ISBN 978-0-8108-5500-7; 0-8108-5500-3
LC 2006002300

This "explores the writings of the critically acclaimed YA author best known for *Skellig* . . . and *Kit's Wilderness*. . . . After a brief biography and thematic overview, Latham addresses Almond's published works one by one. . . . Weaving his explorations almost as seamlessly as Almond wove the original stories, Latham clearly illustrates the novels' inherent depth and teachability." Voice Youth Advocates

Includes bibliographical references

Nardo, Don, 1947-

Understanding Frankenstein. Lucent Bks. 2003 128p il (Understanding great literature) lib bdg $27.45

Grades: 7 8 9 10

823.009

1. Shelley, Mary Wollstonecraft, 1797-1851
ISBN 1-59018-147-6
LC 2002-12560

Discusses Mary Shelley's sources of ideas for the compelling plot, well-developed characters, and universal themes of "Frankenstein" which have led to its enduring popularity.

"The text is easy to understand. A solid introduction for middle school students." SLJ

Includes bibliographical references

Shea, George, 1940-

A reader's guide to Chinua Achebe's Things fall apart; [by] George Shea. Enslow Publishers 2008 128p il (Multicultural literature) lib bdg $31.93

Grades: 7 8 9 10

823.009

1. Achebe, Chinua, 1930-. Things fall apart
ISBN 978-0-7660-2831-9 (lib bdg); 0-7660-2831-3 (lib bdg)
LC 2006038486

"Shea explores why many consider the book to be the greatest African novel ever written. . . . Extensive back matter includes a chronology, glossary, chapter notes, and a bibliography of books and Web sites." Booklist

Includes glossary and bibliographical references

Squires, Claire, 1972-

Philip Pullman, master storyteller; a guide to the worlds of His Dark Materials. Continuum 2006 214p $60; pa $14.95

Grades: 8 9 10 11 12

823.009

1. Pullman, Philip, 1946-
ISBN 978-0-8264-2764-9; 0-8264-2764-2;
978-0-8264-1716-9 (pa); 0-8264-1716-7 (pa)
LC 2006019766

A comprehensive study of Philip Pullman, with focus on the contexts, sources, influences and controversies of the his Dark Materials trilogy.

"Squires does not shy away from the controversy that Pullman's themes have stirred up. . . . [This is an] accessible study." SLJ

Includes bibliographical references

828 English miscellaneous writings

Jones, Diana Wynne

The tough guide to Fantasyland. rev and updated ed. Firebird 2006 234p pa $9.99 *

Grades: 8 9 10 11 12

828

1. Fantasy fiction
ISBN 0-14-240722-4
LC 2006041153

First published 1996

This "book contains alphabetic entries for people, places, and events in a fantasy world and information on how travelers can best find their way to the epic final battle. Icons conveniently identify lodging, food, and other necessary elements that travelers will need in their journey. . . . This brilliantly written satire perfectly celebrates and skewers the clichés of the fantasy genre." Voice Youth Advocates

Means, A. L.

A student's guide to George Orwell. Enslow Pubs. 2005 176p il (Understanding literature) lib bdg $27.93

Grades: 7 8 9 10

828

1. Orwell, George, 1903-1950
ISBN 0-7660-2433-4

An introduction to the life and work of the author of *1984, Animal Farm* and other works

Includes glossary and bibliographical references

860.8 Spanish literature— Collections

The **Tree** is older than you are; a bilingual gathering of poems & stories from Mexico with paintings by Mexican artists; selected by Naomi Shihab Nye. Simon & Schuster Bks. for Young Readers 1995 111p il hardcover o.p. pa $13.95 *

Grades: 7 8 9 10

860.8

1. Mexican literature—Collections 2. Bilingual books—English-Spanish
ISBN 0-689-82097-8; 0-689-82087-9 (pa)
LC 95-1565

"This bilingual anthology of poems, stories, and paintings by Mexican writers and artists brims over with a sense of wonder and playful exuberance, its themes as varied and inventive as a child's imagination." Voice Youth Advocates

883 Classical Greek epic poetry and fiction

Homer

The Iliad; translated by Robert Fagles; introduction and notes by Bernard Knox. Viking 1990 683p $40; pa $15.95

Grades: 8 9 10 11 12 Adult 883

1. Poetry—By individual authors

ISBN 978-0-670-83510-2; 978-0-14-027536-0 (pa)

LC 89-70695

Homer's epic of the Trojan War.

"Fagles gives us a stark and terrible poem, an Iliad about, as its first word announces, rage. He conveys, far better than either Lattimore or Fitzgerald, the psychological experience of combat and war." Classical World

The Odyssey; translated by Robert Fagles; introduction and notes by Bernard Knox. Viking 1996 541p $35; pa $16

Grades: 8 9 10 11 12 Adult 883

1. Poetry—By individual authors

ISBN 978-0-670-82162-4; 978-0-14-026886-7 (pa)

LC 96-17280

This is a verse translation of Homer's epic poem

"Fagles' *Odyssey* is the one to put into the hands of younger, first-time readers, not least because of its paucity of notes, which, though sometimes frustrating, is a sign that translation has been used to do the work of explanation. Altogether, an outstanding piece of work." Booklist

Includes bibliographical references

Lister, Robin

The odyssey; retold by Robin Lister; illustrated by Alan Baker. reformatted ed. Kingfisher 2004 175p il (Kingfisher epics) pa $7.95

Grades: 5 6 7 8 883

1. Homer—Adaptations 2. Odysseus (Greek mythology)

ISBN 0-7534-5723-7

First published 1988

A retelling of Homer's epic poem that describes the wanderings of Odysseus after the fall of Troy.

McCarty, Nick

The Iliad; retold by Nick McCarty; illustrated by Victor Ambrus. Kingfisher (NY) 2000 95p il hardcover o.p. pa $15.95

Grades: 5 6 7 8 9 10 883

1. Homer—Adaptations 2. Trojan War

ISBN 0-7534-5330-4; 0-7534-5321-5 (pa)

LC 00-30442

A retelling of Homer's story of the Trojan War

"An exciting text in large print and action-packed illustrations create an accessible version of a classic tale." SLJ

Osborne, Mary Pope, 1949-

The gray-eyed goddess; with artwork by Troy Howell. Hyperion Bks. for Children 2003 120p il (Mary Pope Osborne's Tales from the Odyssey) $9.99; pa $4.99

Grades: 4 5 6 7 883

1. Homer—Adaptations 2. Odysseus (Greek mythology)

ISBN 0-7868-0773-3; 0-7868-0931-0 (pa)

Retells a part of the Odyssey in which Odysseus' wife, Penelope, and their son, Telemachus, are desperately warding off the men who want to marry her. Then a visit from a mysterious stranger gives Telemachus the courage to confront the suitors, and to search for his long-lost father

The land of the dead; illustrated by Troy Howell. Hyperion Bks. for Children 2002 105p il (Mary Pope Osborne's Tales from the Odyssey) $9.99; pa $4.99

Grades: 4 5 6 7 883

1. Homer—Adaptations 2. Odysseus (Greek mythology)

ISBN 0-7868-0771-7; 0-7868-0929-9 (pa)

LC 2002-69078

A retelling of part of the Odyssey in which Odysseus and his fleet continue their journey and encounter giant cannibals, a beautiful witch, and the Land of the Dead

"Osborne's simple, engaging narrative will surely capture interest as it presents a great hero in bold, yet human, dimensions." Booklist

The one-eyed giant; with artwork by Troy Howell. Hyperion Bks. for Children 2002 105p il (Mary Pope Osborne's Tales from the Odyssey) $9.99

Grades: 4 5 6 7 883

1. Homer—Adaptations 2. Odysseus (Greek mythology)

ISBN 0-7868-0770-9 LC 2002-68539

Retells a part of the Odyssey in which King Odysseus fights the cyclops

"In brief chapters and concise sentences, Osborne pares down . . . [this adventure] into easily absorbed, swiftly paced episodes." Publ Wkly

Return to Ithaca; with artwork by Troy Howell. Hyperion Books for Children 2004 105p (Mary Pope Osborne's Tales from the Odyssey) $9.99

Grades: 4 5 6 7 883

1. Homer—Adaptations 2. Odysseus (Greek mythology)

ISBN 0-7868-0774-1 LC 2003-60355

Retells part of Homer's Odyssey in which Odysseus, with the help of the goddess Athena, plans to get revenge on those who have plagued his wife and son during his absence

895.1 Chinese literature

Liu Siyu, 1964-
A thousand peaks; poems from China; [by] Siyu Liu and Orel Protopopescu; illustrated by Siyu Liu. Pacific View Press 2002 52p il $19.95 *
Grades: 5 6 7 8 9   **895.1**
1. Chinese poetry 2. Bilingual books—English-Chinese
ISBN 1-88189-624-2   LC 2001-34008
A collection of thirty-five poems spanning nineteen centuries, representing both famous and lesser-known poets, including both the Chinese text and a literal translation.
This "is an anthology of considerable fascination and broad utility. . . . The layout is neat, tidily fitting each poem's material on a single page and adding a line drawing featuring a relevant Chinese character. The wealth of material here provides a more stimulating entree to Chinese history than any dry textbook." Bull Cent Child Books
Includes bibliographical references

896 African literatures

Talking drums; a selection of poems from Africa south of the Sahara; edited and illustrated by Véronique Tadjo. Bloomsbury Children's Books 2003 96p il map $15.95 *
Grades: 5 6 7 8   **896**
1. African poetry—Collections
ISBN 1-58234-813-8   LC 2003-52173
Contents: Our universe; The animal kingdom; Love and celebrations; People; Death; Pride and defiance; The changing times
A collection of traditional and twentieth-century poems from sub-Saharan Africa, written in or translated into English, that expresses the spirit and history of this region
"The contemporary and the traditional are both well represented in this lively anthology. . . . Illustrated with small, black-and-white folk-art drawings, the collection ranges widely, including poems of love, sorrow, and pride. . . . This [is a] fine resource for social studies and literature classes, which will also be great for reading aloud." Booklist
Includes glossary

897 Literatures of North American native languages

Dancing teepees: poems of American Indian youth; selected by Virginia Driving Hawk Sneve, with art by Stephen Gammell. Holiday House 1989 32p il $17.95; pa $8.95 *
Grades: 4 5 6   **897**
1. Native Americans—Poetry
ISBN 0-8234-0724-1; 0-8234-0879-5 (pa)
                                      LC 88-11075
An illustrated collection of poems from the oral tradition of Native Americans
This is an "eclectic collection, drawn from a variety of tribal traditions. Printed on heavy paper, the book is illustrated with a catalogue of marvelously rendered designs and motifs, ranging from those of the Northwest Coast to the intricate beadwork patterns of the Great Lakes and the zigzag geometric borders of Southwestern pottery." N Y Times Book Rev

900 HISTORY

901 Philosophy and theory of history

Beller, Susan Provost, 1949-
The history puzzle; how we know what we know about the past; [by] Susan Provost Beller. Twenty-First Century Books 2006 128p il lib bdg $26.60 *
Grades: 7 8 9 10   **901**
1. History—Philosophy
ISBN 978-0-7613-2877-3; 0-7613-2877-7
                                      LC 2005017745
"Beller looks at more than 20 historical sites or archaeological excavations . . . in order to present the varying interpretations of history and how they have been colored by tradition, socioeconomic factors, and religious beliefs. . . . Frequent, well-placed sepia-toned photographs and period reproductions serve to enhance the text, and the source notes, further reading, and list of Web sites give students an ample list of resources for further study." SLJ
Includes bibliographical references

902 Miscellany of history

Timelines of history. Grolier 2005 10v il map set$339
Grades: 6 7 8 9   **902**
1. Historical chronology 2. Reference books
ISBN 0-7172-6002-X   LC 2005040222
Contents: v1 The early empires, prehistory-500 B.C.; v2 The Classical Age, 500 B.C.-500 A.D.; v3 Raiders and conquerors, 500-1000 A.D.; v4 The fuedal era, 1000-1250; v5 The end of the Middle Ages. 1250-1500; v6 A wider world, 1500-1600; v7 Royalty and revolt, 1600-1700; v8 The Age of Reason, 1700-1800; v9 Industry and empire, 1800-1900; v10 The modern world, 1900-2000
"This set of 10 brief volumes presents an overview of world history from prehistory (6.8 million years ago) up until 2005. . . . The content consists of alternating types of two-page spreads: time-line pages and feature pages. . . . The feature pages highlight topics such as individuals, events, or a civilization presented in the time lines. . . . The narratives in the features are clear and simply written. . . . The design is clean and colorful and features hundreds of illustrations, including maps, on every page." Booklist

Tomaselli-Moschovitis, Valerie

Junior timelines on file. updated ed. Facts on File 2002 various paging il $185

Grades: Professional   **902**

1. Historical chronology 2. World history

ISBN 0-8160-5122-4   LC 2002-27167

Also available CD-ROM version

First published 1997

This looseleaf binder provides more than 250 reproducible timelines covering "the history of the world on a country-by-country basis; different periods of time, such as the Reorganization of Empires (300 A.D. to 1500 A.D.) and Nationalism, Imperialism, and Revolution (1700 to 1914); human thought and achievement within various fields." Publisher's note

Includes bibliographical references

904   Collected accounts of events

Beyer, Rick

The greatest stories never told; 100 tales from history to astonish, bewilder, & stupefy. HarperResource 2003 214p il $17.95

Grades: 7 8 9 10   **904**

1. History—Miscellanea

ISBN 0-06-001401-6   LC 2004-296419

Based on the television program: Timelab 2000

"Beginning with the year 46 B.C. and ending in 1990, Beyer presents a chronological account of one hundred unknown, partially known, and familar tales about an array of people and events that have shaped the world. . . . They range from the mundane to the fantastic. . . . Extensive research went into the production of this charming work. Primary documents in the form of letters, laws, illustrations, and photographs bring to life these unique and incredible anecdotes." Voice Youth Advocates

Includes bibliographical references

Blackwood, Gary L.

Enigmatic events; [by] Gary L. Blackwood. Marshall Cavendish Benchmark 2005 72p il (Unsolved history) lib bdg $29.93

Grades: 4 5 6 7   **904**

1. History—Miscellanea 2. Disasters 3. Curiosities and wonders

ISBN 0-7614-1889-X   LC 2004-23755

Contents: The death of the dinosaurs; The lost colony; The Salem witch trials; *The Mary Celeste*; *The Maine*; The Tunguska event; *The Hindenburg*

Explores several events that have baffled scientists and historians for years, such as the demise of the dinosaurs, the "lost colony" of Roanoke, the sinking of the Main, and the Hindenburg disaster

This collection of "tidbits about lingering mysteries of the past . . . [offers] more substance than most. . . . [This offers] a full-page illustration opening each chapter; reproductions, many in color; and a generously spaced format." SLJ

Includes glossary and bibliographical references

909   World history

Altman, Linda Jacobs, 1943-

Forever outsiders; Jews and history from ancient times to August 1935. Blackbirch Press 1998 80p il maps (Holocaust) lib bdg $26.20 *

Grades: 6 7 8 9   **909**

1. Jews—History

ISBN 1-56711-200-5   LC 96-48179

This volume "provides a social and economic history of the Jews, shaped and punctuated by repeated acts of persecution, actions that in modern times lead to the growth of Zionism and the Holocaust." SLJ

"Authoritative, readable." Booklist

Includes glossary and bibliographical references

Burrell, R. E. C. (Roy Eric Charles), 1923-

Oxford first ancient history; [by] Roy Burrell; with many illustrations by Peter Connolly. Oxford University Press 1994 c1991 320p il maps (Rebuilding the past) hardcover o.p. pa $25

Grades: 6 7 8 9   **909**

1. Ancient history

ISBN 0-19-521058-1; 0-19-521373-4 (pa)

First published 1991 in the United Kingdom

"Beginning with prehistory, this book surveys ancient civilizations, primarily in the Mediterranean region. . . . Every page includes at least one full-color illustration, a map, a cutaway drawing, a painting re-creating the times, or a photograph of a wall painting, sculpture, artifact, site, or explorer. Not only is the format inviting, but the text is also quite readable. . . . A lively, helpful resource." Booklist

Eamer, Claire

Traitors' Gate and other doorways to the past. Annick Press 2008 154p il $24.95; pa $12.95

Grades: 6 7 8 9   **909**

1. Doorways 2. World history

ISBN 978-1-55451-145-7; 1-55451-145-3; 978-1-55451-144-0 (pa); 1-55451-144-5 (pa)

"Eamer uses the concrete image of doorways to introduce famous (and not-so-famous) structures. She begins with perhaps the most amazing one, located in Petra, Jordan. Al-Khazner is hidden in a sandstone cliff. . . . Among the other structures discussed are Cape Coast Castle in Ghana, through whose doorway Africans were led to slave ships; the six doors of the Kremlin's Holy Antechamber; . . . and Spruce Tree House, an ancient cliff house in Colorado. . . . The many photographs are nicely reproduced, and Eamer's text is always solid and sometimes soars." Booklist

Includes bibliographical references

George, Charles, 1949-

Pyramids; by Charles George. ReferencePoint Press 2007 104p il (The mysterious & unknown) lib bdg $24.95

Grades: 6 7 8 9   **909**

1. Pyramids

ISBN 978-1-60152-027-2 (lib bdg); 1-60152-027-1 (lib bdg)   LC 2007010342

George, Charles, 1949-—*Continued*

"*Pyramids* addresses why, by whom, and how these massive structures were created. While the majority of the book is devoted to the well-known Egyptian and Central American creations, George also introduces the lesser-known structures of South America, Asia, and Eastern Europe. . . . The color photographs in [this] attractive [book] are excellent, and the readable [text is] interesting." SLJ

Includes bibliographical references

The **Kingfisher** history encyclopedia. rev ed. Kingfisher 2004 491p il map $24.95

Grades: 5 6 7 8   **909**
1. World history 2. Reference books
ISBN 0-7534-5784-9
First published 1999
A reference guide to world history, featuring a timeline, key date boxes, and biographies of historical figures
"Students will find this tool useful and engaging." Booklist

Mann, Kenny, 1946-

The ancient Hebrews. Benchmark Bks. (Tarrytown) 1999 80p il (Cultures of the past) $28.50

Grades: 6 7 8 9   **909**
1. Bible. O.T. —History of Biblical events 2. Jews—History
ISBN 0-7614-0302-7   LC 97-6551
This illustrated work "discusses the social and religious history of the Jewish people and its influence on modern Judaism, and touches on the relationship between present-day Israel and Arab countries." SLJ

Includes bibliographical references

Ochoa, George

The Wilson chronology of ideas; [by] George Ochoa and Melinda Corey. Wilson, H.W. 1998 431p $115

Grades: 8 9 10 11 12 Adult   **909**
1. Civilization—History 2. Philosophy 3. Reference books
ISBN 0-8242-0935-4   LC 97-17591
A chronological presentation of influential philosophical, political, theological and social thought from ancient times to the late 20th century. Sidebars feature profiles of celebrated thinkers
Includes bibliographical references

Reformation, exploration, and empire. Grolier 2005 10v il map set $389

Grades: 6 7 8 9   **909**
1. World history—16th century 2. World history—17th century 3. Renaissance 4. Modern civilization 5. Reference books
ISBN 0-7172-6071-2
"This set describes a key period of Western history from approximately 1500 to 1700. The more than 240 entries provide a sense of the development of international trade, great cultural achievements, and the spirit of learning. . . . The layout is bright and colorful and features hundreds of illustraions, including maps, charts, tables, and more. Sidebars are plentiful and are used to highlight suplemental stories, information, and primary source materials." Booklist

Roberts, J. M. (John Morris), 1928-2003

The illustrated history of the world. rev and expanded ed. Oxford University Press 1999 11v il map set $275

Grades: 7 8 9 10   **909**
1. World history 2. Civilization—History 3. Reference books
ISBN 0-19-521529-X   LC 00-27437
Revised and expanded edition of the author's one-volume History of the world (1993)
Contents: v1 Prehistory and the first civilizations; v2 Eastern Asia and classical Greece; v3 Rome and the classical West; v4 The age of diverging traditions; v5 The Far East and a new Europe; v6 The making of the European age; v7 The age of revolution; v8 The European empires; v9 Emerging powers; v10 The new global era; v11 Series index
"The clear design features bold headings, explanatory captions (sometimes lengthy), easy-to-read maps, explanatory boxes on essential figures or movements, and a great use of white space. Though packed with information, the pages look clean and uncluttered, and it's easy to find a quick bit of information on a certain period or person." SLJ

Spilsbury, Louise, 1963-

The Islamic Empires; [by] Louise and Richard Spilsbury. Raintree 2007 64p il map (Time travel guide) lib bdg $34.29; pa $9.99

Grades: 6 7 8 9   **909**
1. Islamic civilization
ISBN 978-1-4109-2911-2 (lib bdg); 978-1-4109-2917-4 (pa)   LC 2007006035
"Raintree FreeStyle"
This describes life in the ancient Islamic world in the form of a travel guide.
Includes glossary and bibliographical references

Technology in world history; W. Bernard Carlson, editor. Oxford University Press 2005 7v il maps set $299

Grades: 7 8 9 10   **909**
1. Technology and civilization 2. Reference books
ISBN 0-19-521820-5; 978-0-19-521820-6   LC 2003-55300
"Seeking to explore how people have used technology to shape societies, Carlson and 10 other scholars examine the distinctive development and effects of technology in 18 cultures—defined either geographically (Pacific Peoples, Sub-Saharan Africa) or by historical period (Stone Age, The World Since 1970)." SLJ
Includes bibliographical references

World history on file. 2nd ed. Facts on File 2006 4v il loose-leaf set $560

Grades: 6 7 8 9 Professional   **909**
1. World history
ISBN 978-0-8160-6372-7; 0-8160-6372-9
Also available CD-ROM version

World history on file—*Continued*

First published 1999

Contents: v1 Early civilizations: prehistory to 300 CE; v2 The expanding world (300-1750); v3 The age of revolution, 1750 to 1914; v4 The 20th century

Each volume includes approximately 500 maps, charts, timelines, and line drawings with explanatory text regarding a period of world history

909.07   World history—ca. 500- 1450/1500

Adams, Simon

The Kingfisher atlas of the medieval world. Kingfisher 2007 44p il map $15.95

Grades: 4 5 6 7   **909.07**

1. Medieval civilization 2. Historical geography 3. Reference books

ISBN 978-0-7534-5946-1; 0-7534-5946-9

LC 2006005554

"Sixteen colorful maps depict the world from A.D. 500 to 1500. A chronology appears in the right margin of the first map. Specific time lines for India, China, Japan and Korea, Southeast Asia, the Pacific Islands, the Vikings, Europe, African kingdoms, and North and Central America help students integrate the major historical events of the period. Topics include cathedrals and monasteries, Islamic culture, knights and castles, and the Aztec capital of Tenochtitlán." SLJ

Exploring the Middle Ages. Marshall Cavendish 2006 11v set$514.21 *

Grades: 6 7 8 9   **909.07**

1. Middle Ages—Encyclopedias 2. Medieval civilization 3. Reference books

ISBN 0-7614-7613-X   LC 2005042161

This set " presents a truly international survey of global events that occurred between 500 and 1500 C.E. . . . The alphabetically arranged articles range from two to six pages. . . . Abundant color photographs as well as charts, sidebars, time lines, and maps complement the text. . . . Ideal for reports, and equally satisfying for browsers, . . . [this is] lavishly illustrated." Booklist

George, Linda S., 1949-

800. Benchmark Bks. 2003 96p il maps (Around the world in—) lib bdg $28.50   **909.07**

1. Middle Ages 2. World history

ISBN 0-7614-1085-6   LC 00-50758

This "book divides its subject geographically into four parts—Europe, Asia, Africa, and the Americas. . . . 800 presents chapters on the Vikings; the Abbasid Empire, centered in Baghdad; the Golden Empire of Ghana; and the Maya." Booklist

This work is "well written, informative, attractively designed and illustrated, and logically organized." Libr Media Connect

Includes glossary and bibliographical references

Hatt, Christine

The Crusades. Watts 2001 62p il (Documenting history) $22

Grades: 7 8 9 10   **909.07**

1. Crusades

ISBN 0-531-14610-3   LC 00-51351

First published 1999 in the United Kingdom

This focuses on the Crusades through primary source documents including "letters, biographies, autobiographies, speeches, newspapers, and excerpts from government documents and political commentaries. . . . This attractive [book] may encourage browsing and will be especially useful to students looking for information in a brief, inviting format, as well as for those who want a topic review or introduction." Book Rep

Hinds, Kathryn, 1962-

The city; [by] Kathryn Hinds. Marshall Cavendish Benchmark 2008 c2009 96p il map (Life in the Medieval Muslim world) lib bdg $23.93 *

Grades: 6 7 8 9   **909.07**

1. Islamic countries 2. Middle Ages 3. Medieval civilization 4. City and town life

ISBN 978-0-7614-3089-6 (lib bdg); 0-7614-3089-X (lib bdg)   LC 2008019432

"A social history of the Islamic world from the eighth through the mid-thirteenth century, with a focus on life in the cities" Publisher's note

Includes glossary and bibliographical references

The countryside; [by] Kathryn Hinds. Marshall Cavendish Benchmark 2008 c2009 95p il map (Life in the Medieval Muslim world) lib bdg $23.95 *

Grades: 6 7 8 9   **909.07**

1. Islamic countries 2. Deserts 3. Middle Ages 4. Medieval civilization 5. Country life

ISBN 978-0-7614-3091-9 (lib bdg); 0-7614-3091-1 (lib bdg)   LC 2008019266

"Presents a social history of the Islamic world from the eighth through the mid-thirteenth century, with a focus on life in the desert and countryside." Publisher's note

"This . . . fills its niche beautifully." SLJ

Includes glossary and bibliographical references

The palace; [by] Kathryn Hinds. Marshall Cavendish Benchmark 2008 c2009 96p il map (Life in the Medieval Muslim world) lib bdg $23.95 *

Grades: 6 7 8 9   **909.07**

1. Islamic countries 2. Elite (Social sciences) 3. Middle Ages 4. Medieval civilization

ISBN 978-0-7614-3088-9 (lib bdg); 0-7614-3088-1 (lib bdg)   LC 2008010734

"A social history of the Islamic world from the eighth through the mid-thirteenth century, with a focus on life in the upper echelons of society." Publisher's note

Includes glossary and bibliographical references

Knight, Judson
Middle ages: almanac; edited by Judy Galens.
U.X.L 2001 lxv, 226p il map $60
Grades: 8 9 10 11 12   **909.07**
1. Middle Ages 2. World history 3. Medieval civilization 4. Reference books
ISBN 0-7876-4856-6   LC 00-59442
This reference's 19 chapters review world history from the fall of the Roman Empire in 500 A.D. to the beginning of the Renaissance in 1500 A.D.
"The volume's strength is its broad coverage; it includes material on India, Southeast Asia, China, Japan, the Americas, and Africa as well as Europe and the Middle East, making it unique among other books for this age group." SLJ
Includes bibliographical references

Medieval world. Grolier Educ. 2001 10v il maps set$345
Grades: 7 8 9 10   **909.07**
1. Middle Ages 2. Medieval civilization 3. Reference books
ISBN 0-7172-5520-4   LC 00-46649
Contents: v1 Abelard-Burgundy; v2 The Byzantine Empire-Constantinople; v3 Copts-Feudalism; v4 Florence-Hospitals; v5 House and home-Joan of Arc; v6 Justinian-The Mediterranean; v7 Mehmet II-Painting and sculpture; v8 The papacy-Roman Empire; v9 Rome-Thomas Aquinas; v10 Tools and technology-Writing
"The 226 alphabetical entries in this set cover all aspects of the time period between 476 A.D. and 1453 A.D. . . . The set focuses on Europe, but it also shows how other civilizations were developing during this time period." Book Rep
This "is an attractive and helpful reference source that will provide information on a variety of subjects related to this complex historical period." Booklist
Includes bibliographical references

Middle ages: primary sources; [compiled by] Judson Knight; Judy Galens, editor. U.X.L 2000 xxxiv, 161p il $60
Grades: 8 9 10 11 12   **909.07**
1. Middle Ages
ISBN 0-7876-4860-4   LC 00-59441
This volume contains "19 full or excerpted documents written during this period, including the work of celebrated writers such as St. Augustine, Marco Polo, and Dante as well as less familiar individuals such as Anna Comnena and Lo Kuan-chung. Each selection is placed in its historical context and followed by a section entitled 'What happened next'. . . . Unfamiliar words or terms are defined in sidebars. Each entry has a box profiling the author of the documents and at least two illustrations." Booklist
Includes bibliographical references

Service, Alexandra
1200; by Alexandra F. Service and Pamela F. Service. Benchmark Bks. 2003 96p il maps (Around the world in—) lib bdg $28.50
Grades: 6 7 8 9   **909.07**
1. World history—13th century 2. Medieval civilization
ISBN 0-7614-1081-3   LC 00-46848

This overview of the thirteenth century "covers events happening around the world—important historical developments in Africa, Asia, Australia, Europe, and North and South America. . . . Illustrated throughout with captioned color maps and pictures. . . . [This title is] well written, informative, attractively designed and illustrated, and logically organized." Libr Media Connect
Includes glossary and bibliographical references

909.08   Modern history, 1450/1500-

Huff, Toby E., 1942-
An age of science and revolutions, 1600-1800; [by] Toby Huff. Oxford University Press 2005 173p il map (Medieval & early modern world) lib bdg $32.95 *
Grades: 7 8 9 10   **909.08**
1. World history—17th century 2. World history—18th century 3. Europe—Civilization
ISBN 0-19-517724-X   LC 2004-21612
This volume "looks at 200 years of world history. . . . [It includes] overview chapters on China, India, and the Middle East . . . [and] discusses the Enlightenment in Europe in some depth. . . . [This is a] useful book, which may spark discussion about current controversies about connections between science and religion." Booklist
Includes bibliographical references

Schomp, Virginia, 1953-
1500. Benchmark Bks. 2003 96p il maps (Around the world in—) lib bdg $28.50
Grades: 6 7 8 9   **909.08**
1. World history—16th century
ISBN 0-7614-1082-1   LC 00-41449
This overview of the 16th century "covers events happening around the world—important historical developments in Africa, Asia, Australia, Europe, and North and South America. . . . The section on Asia in 1500 covers developments in China, Japan, and the Ottoman Middle East. . . . [This volume is] well written, informative, attractively designed and illustrated, and logically organized." Libr Media Connect
Includes glossary and bibliographical references

Wiesner, Merry E., 1952-
An age of voyages, 1350-1600; [by] Merry E. Wiesner-Hanks. Oxford University Press 2005 189p il map (Medieval & early modern world) $32.95 *
Grades: 7 8 9 10   **909.08**
1. World history—16th century 2. Middle Ages
ISBN 0-19-517672-3; 978-0-19-517672-8
                                 LC 2004021178
"This book provides coverage of the political, cultural, and social history of the world from 1350 to 1600. . . . With a strong focus on the Renaissance, Reformation, and Ming China, the text comes from ordinary people, travelers, bureaucrats, children, housewives, poets, and religious thinkers." Publisher's note
"In accessible language supported by prolific illustra-

Wiesner, Merry E., 1952—_Continued_
tions and primary sources, [this volume describes an era]
that transformed the world." SLJ
Includes bibliographical references

909.7   World history—18th century, 1700-1799

Reynoldson, Fiona
Conflict and change. Facts on File 1993 79p il
maps (Illustrated history of the world) lib bdg $25
Grades: 6 7 8 9   **909.7**
1. Modern history
ISBN 0-8160-2790-0   LC 92-20460
First published 1991 in the United Kingdom
Explores the history of the world from 1650 to 1800
with emphasis on the agricultural revolution, the Enlight-
enment, the Industrial Revolution, the American and
French Revolutions, Manchu China, and Shogunate Japan
Includes glossary and bibliographical references

909.8   World history—1800-

Adams, Simon
The Kingfisher atlas of the modern world; [by]
Simon Adams; illustrated by Kevin Maddison
2007 45p il map $15.95
Grades: 4 5 6 7   **909.8**
1. World history—19th century 2. World history—
20th century 3. Historical geography
ISBN 978-0-7534-6034-4
This atlas examines world history and geography
"from 1800 to the present. . . . Each map focuses on a
major region, exploring the conflicts, changes, and social
movements that took place during a specific period of
time. The subjects are arranged chronologically." Publisher's note

Ashby, Ruth
1800. Benchmark Bks. 2003 96p il maps
(Around the world in—) lib bdg $28.50
Grades: 6 7 8 9   **909.8**
1. World history—19th century
ISBN 0-7614-1084-8   LC 00-65136
This overview of the 19th century "covers events happening around the world—important historical developments in Africa, Asia, Australia, Europe, and North and
South America. . . . The section on Africa is broken
down into three segments on North, West, and South Africa. . . . [This title is] well written, informative, attrac-
tively designed and illustrated, and logically organized."
Libr Media Connect
Includes glossary and bibliographical references

909.81   World history—19th century, 1800-1899

1800-1820: the nineteenth century; Jodie L. Zdrok,
book editor. Greenhaven Press 2005 173p map
(Events that changed the world) lib bdg $34.95
Grades: 7 8 9 10 11 12   **909.81**
1. World history—19th century
ISBN 0-7377-2029-8   LC 2004-52322
Events covered in this book include "the end of the
Holy Roman Empire, the Louisiana Purchase, the War of
1812, and the Battle of Waterloo." Publisher's note
Includes bibliographical references

1820-1840: the nineteenth century; Jennifer
Bussey, book editor. Greenhaven Press 2005
143p il map (Events that changed the world) lib
bdg $34.95
Grades: 7 8 9 10 11 12   **909.81**
1. World history—19th century
ISBN 0-7377-2031-X   LC 2004-52393
"This anthology highlights the most influential events
between 1820 and 1840, with special attention to the far-
reaching effects those events had in world history." Publisher's note
Includes bibliographical references

1840-1860: the nineteenth century; Jodie L. Zdrok,
book editor. Greenhaven Press 2005 175p il
map (Events that changed the world) lib bdg
$34.95
Grades: 7 8 9 10 11 12   **909.81**
1. World history—19th century
ISBN 0-7377-2033-6   LC 2004-42513
"This title encompasses the political actions, military
conflicts, social movements, and scientific and cultural
innovations of this period." Publisher's note
Includes bibliographical references

1860-1880: the nineteenth century; Kelly Doyle,
book editor. Greenhaven Press 2005 224p il
(Events that changed the world) lib bdg $34.95
Grades: 7 8 9 10 11 12   **909.81**
1. World history—19th century
ISBN 0-7377-2035-2   LC 2004-42443
Events described in this book include the abolition of
slavery, the birth of new secular governments in Europe,
and the beginnings of the labor movement.
Includes bibliographical references

1880-1900: the nineteenth century; Jodie L. Zdrok,
book editor. Greenhaven 2004 187p il (Events
that changed the world) lib bdg $34.95
Grades: 7 8 9 10 11 12   **909.81**
1. World history—19th century
ISBN 0-7377-2037-9   LC 2003-67762
Events described in this book include the birth of
Adolf Hitler, the Boxer rebellion, and the discovery of
radium. Both primary and secondary sources are used.
Includes bibliographical references

909.82 World history—20th century, 1900-1999

1900-1920: the twentieth century; Gary Zacharias, book editor. Greenhaven Press 2004 224p il map (Events that changed the world) lib bdg $34.95
Grades: 7 8 9 10 11 12   **909.82**
1. World history—20th century
ISBN 0-7377-1752-1   LC 2003-48332
"The period from 1900-1920 marked not only the beginning of a new century but also the seed of many trends and movements that would bear fruit throughout the rest of the 20th century. This book covers major events of this time period, including wars, theories, inventions, disasters, and revolutions." Publisher's note
"There's plenty to intrigue history students, who will relish seeing disparate pieces of history slide smoothly together." Booklist
Includes bibliographical references

1920-1940: the twentieth century; Sharon M. Himsl, book editor. Greenhaven Press 2004 204p il (Events that changed the world) lib bdg $34.95
Grades: 7 8 9 10 11 12   **909.82**
1. World history—20th century
ISBN 0-7377-1754-8   LC 2003-44864
"Ratification of Nineteenth Amendment, first assembly of League of Nations, . . . Mussolini's March on Rome, Lindbergh's transatlantic flight, Jazz Singer debut, Gandhi's 'Salt March,' Hitler's rise, stock market crash, and 'Operation Dynamo' (rescue at Dunkirk) are among the events discussed, describing a . . . period that begins with the aftermath of World War I and ends with the outbreak of World War II." Publisher's note
Includes bibliographical references

1940-1960: the twentieth century; Jennifer Bussey, book editor. Greenhaven Press 2004 188p il (Events that changed the world) lib bdg $34.95
Grades: 7 8 9 10 11 12   **909.82**
1. World history—20th century
ISBN 0-7377-1756-4   LC 2002-192798
"The world in 1960 was a very different place than it had been in 1940. . . . How did so much change unfold in twenty years' time? This anthology retraces those fateful footsteps, presenting articles about events spanning from the attack on Pearl Harbor to the launch of Sputnik." Publisher's note
"Several articles (e.g., an excerpt describing the killing of unarmed German guards by concentration camp liberators) are vivid enough to disturb some readers. . . . There's plenty to intrigue history students, who will relish seeing disparate pieces of history slide smoothly together." Booklist
Includes bibliographical references

1960-1980: the twentieth century; Jennifer A. Bussey, book editor. Greenhaven Press 2004 176p il (Events that changed the world) lib bdg $34.95
Grades: 7 8 9 10 11 12   **909.82**
1. World history—20th century
ISBN 0-7377-1758-0   LC 2003-53929
"This anthology covers the major events that shaped the world during the pivotal decades of the 1960s and 1970s. Topics covered include the Bay of Pigs invasion, the building of the Berlin Wall, U.S. president Kennedy's assassination, the first moon landing, the U.S. legalization of abortion, the Vietnam War, and the Ayatollah Khomeini's deposition of the shah of Iran." Publisher's note
Includes bibliographical references

1980-2000: the twentieth century; Bryan Grapes, book editor. Greenhaven Press 2004 187p il map (Events that changed the world) lib bdg $34.95
Grades: 7 8 9 10 11 12   **909.82**
1. World history—20th century
ISBN 0-7377-1760-2   LC 2003-53928
"This anthology follows the 1980s and 1990s as the world moved through the rise of the AIDS epidemic, the fall of the Berlin Wall and the demise of communism in Eastern Europe, the death of the Soviet Union, and the rise of the computer age. Also covered in this volume: The birth of MTV, the nuclear disaster at Chernobyl, the Chinese government's bloody crackdown in Tiananmen Square, the death of apartheid, the dissolution of Yugoslavia, and the cloning of Dolly." Publisher's note
Includes bibliographical references

Bodden, Valerie
The Cold War; by Valerie Bodden. Creative Education 2007 c2008 48p il (Days of change) lib bdg $31.35
Grades: 6 7 8 9   **909.82**
1. Cold war 2. World politics—1945-1991
ISBN 978-1-58341-546-7 (lib bdg); 1-58341-546-7 (lib bdg)   LC 2006019825
This is a "cogent [overview] of [The Cold War]. . . . Carefully selected photographs help to explicate the text, and quotes from those involved in and affected by events—from world leaders to ordinary citizens—add compelling detail and immediacy." Horn Book Guide
Includes bibliographical references

The **Cold** War; Louise I. Gerdes, book editor. Greenhaven Press 2003 255p (Great speeches in history series) lib bdg $32.45; pa $21.20
Grades: 7 8 9 10 11 12   **909.82**
1. Cold war 2. Speeches 3. United States—Foreign relations—Soviet Union 4. Soviet Union—Foreign relations—United States
ISBN 0-7377-0869-7 (lib bdg); 0-7377-0868-9 (pa)   LC 2002-34718
"This collection brings together speeches by some of the most distinguished political leaders of the twentieth century together with political analysis that traces the West's volatile relationship with Communist forces. . . . The chronologically arranged selections are organized into five chapters that focus on mounting fears about Communism, the international crisis and coercion, the menace of nuclear war, the struggle for peace, and the Berlin Wall. . . . The combination of the original speeches and the present-day analysis provides a fine starting point for reports and class discussion." Booklist
Includes bibliographical references

Feinstein, Stephen

Decades of the 20th Century [series] rev ed. Enslow Pubs. 2006 10v il ea $27.93

Grades: 5 6 7 8   **909.82**

1. World history—20th century

First published 2001

Contents: The 1900s, from Teddy Roosevelt to flying machines; The 1910s, from World War I to ragtime music; The 1920s, from Prohibition to Charles Lindbergh; The 1930s, from the Great Depression to the Wizard of Oz; The 1940s, from World War II to Jackie Robinson; The 1950s, from the Korean War to Elvis; The 1960s, from the Vietnam War to Flower Power; The 1970s, from Watergate to disco; The 1980s, from Ronald Reagan to MTV; The 1990s, from the Persian Gulf War to Y2K

"Taking a popular-culture approach, each book begins with a look at 'Lifestyles, Fashion, and Fads,' followed by arts and entertainment, sports, and then politics, with science, technology, and medicine coming last. . . . The books are visually exciting, and the texts are clear and vigorous." SLJ

Includes bibliographical references

Kallen, Stuart A., 1955-

Primary sources. Lucent Bks. 2003 112p il map (American war library, Cold War) $27.45

Grades: 8 9 10 11 12   **909.82**

1. Cold war 2. United States—Foreign relations—Soviet Union 3. Soviet Union—Foreign relations—United States

ISBN 1-59018-243-X   LC 2002-7896

This "contains documents and essays relating to the Cold War written by some of its key players including diplomats, ambassadors, presidents, and premiers." Publisher's note

Includes bibliographical references

Kaufman, Michael T.

1968. Roaring Brook Press 2009 148p il $22.95
*

Grades: 7 8 9 10 11 12   **909.82**

1. World history—20th century

ISBN 978-1-59643-428-8; 1-59643-428-7

LC 2008-15471

Kaufman "expertly draws young readers into the worldwide events of a single, watershed year: 1968. . . . Each chapter focuses on a different hot spot around the globe, beginning with the Tet Offensive and the Vietnam War and moving through uprisings in New York, Paris, Prague, Chicago, and Mexico City, as well as the assassinations of Martin Luther King Jr. and Robert F. Kennedy. . . . The images, drawn from the *[New York] Times* archives, are riveting and will easily draw young people into the fascinating, often horrifying events." Booklist

Sherman, Josepha

The Cold War; by Josepha Sherman. Lerner Pub. Co. 2004 96p il map (Chronicle of America's wars) lib bdg $27.93

Grades: 6 7 8 9   **909.82**

1. Cold war 2. Soviet Union—Foreign relations—United States 3. United States—Foreign relations—Soviet Union

ISBN 0-8225-0150-3   LC 2002-156559

Contents: Beginning of the Cold War, 1920-1945; The Cold War grows hotter, 1946-1948; Continuing Cold War trouble, 1949-1950s; The Cold War at home, 1950s; Thaws and freezes, 1950s; "Brinkmanship," 1960s; Hot war and a hot racehot war, Cold War, 1960s-1970s; The Cold War ends, 1980s-present

Chronicles the Cold War, from its origins in the Soviet Revolution as the twentieth century began to the collapse of the Soviet Union as the century closed

This offers a "concise, well-written [overview]. . . . Abundantly illustrated with color and black-and-white photographs as well as maps." Booklist

Includes bibliographical references

Winkler, Allan M., 1945-

The Cold War; a history in documents. Oxford Univ. Press 2000 159p il map (Pages from history) $39.95; pa $22.95

Grades: 8 9 10 11 12   **909.82**

1. Cold war 2. United States—Foreign relations—Soviet Union 3. Soviet Union—Foreign relations—United States

ISBN 0-19-512356-5; 0-19-516637-X (pa)

LC 00-27270

Uses contemporary documents to explore the Cold War struggle of the 1950s and 1960s and the lasting effects on American social and cultural patterns

Includes bibliographical references

909.83   World history—21st century, 2000-2099

Lace, William W.

The Indian Ocean tsunami of 2004. Chelsea House 2008 127p il map (Great historic disasters) $35

Grades: 7 8 9 10   **909.83**

1. Indian Ocean earthquake and tsunami, 2004

ISBN 978-0-7910-9642-0; 0-7910-9642-4

LC 2007-36950

"The author explains in detail the seismic activities that caused the 2004 Indian Ocean tsunami, as well as the lack of systems in place to quickly notify those in danger. Also included are many well-captioned photos . . . and short but interesting personal stories of both survivors and victims." Horn Book Guide

Includes glossary and bibliographical references

Stewart, Gail, 1949-

Catastrophe in southern Asia; the Tsunami of 2004; by Gail B. Stewart. Lucent Books 2005 112p il map (Lucent overview series) $28.70

Grades: 7 8 9 10 **909.83**

1. Indian Ocean earthquake and tsunami, 2004

ISBN 1-59018-831-4 LC 2005006036

The focuses on "the December 2004 Indian disaster. . . . Stewart includes accounts of the event itself and images of destruction, following up with the causes of tsunamis, inadequate warning systems, dealing with the casualties, continuing risks for survivors, response efforts, and rebuilding of the stricken areas. The book's real strength comes in its level of detail, as the author goes well beyond the obvious in exploring issues. . . . Compelling writing is enhanced with clear, informative, and often dramatic black-and-white photos." SLJ

Includes bibliographical references

Torres, John Albert, 1965-

Disaster in the Indian Ocean, Tsunami 2004; [by] John A. Torres. Mitchell Lane 2005 48p il map (Monumental milestones) lib bdg $19.95

Grades: 5 6 7 8 **909.83**

1. Indian Ocean earthquake and tsunami, 2004

ISBN 1-58415-344-X

This "emerges from the author's personal trip to Indonesia after the December 26, 2004, catastrophe. . . . Primary-source accounts, many taken from Torres' own interviews, chillingly recreate the tsunami's initial strike, its chaotic aftermath, and the challenges of recovery." Booklist

Includes bibliographical references

910 Geography & travel

Arnold, Caroline, 1944-

The geography book; activities for exploring, mapping, and enjoying your world. Wiley 2002 108p il pa $12.95

Grades: 4 5 6 7 **910**

1. Geography

ISBN 0-471-41236-8 LC 2001-26802

"Divided into five thematic sections, the book leads children to explore topics related to maps, land formations, water, and weather. . . . Illustrated with simple line drawings, the suggested activities include making a relief map, creating a solar water heater, and building a model of a dam. . . . Clearly written and illustrated." Booklist

Includes glossary and bibliographical references

Belmont, Helen

Looking at aerial photographs; [by] Helen Belmont. Smart Apple Media 2008 46p il map (Geography skills) $22.95 *

Grades: 6 7 8 9 **910**

1. Aerial photography 2. Geography

ISBN 978-1-59920-048-4; 1-59920-048-1

LC 2006036139

Contents: What is aerial photography?; Settlements; Towns and cities; Village and city living; A journey down a river; The floodplain; Waterfalls and river deltas; Erosion at the coast; Depositional features; Mountains; Volcanoes; Living in valleys; Living on mountains; Desert environments; Shopping; Tourist attractions; New houses; Limestone quarries; Energy needs

"The text is easy to follow. . . . The examples given in the text that involve places are almost always accompanied by excellent photographs. . . . Maps, block diagrams, tables, and graphs are clearly presented and easy to interpret." Sci Books Films

Includes glossary and bibliographical references

Cunha, Stephen F.

National Geographic Bee; official study guide; by Stephen F. Cunha; [foreword by Caitlin Snaring] 3rd ed. National Geographic 2008 127p il map $9.95

Grades: 4 5 6 7 8 **910**

1. Geography

ISBN 978-1-4263-0198-8; 1-4263-0198-7

LC 2009293527

First published 2002

This is a guide to prepare for the National Geographic "annual geography competition. Featuring maps, photos, graphs, and a variety of questions actually used in past Bees, plus an extensive resource section, this guide not only reviews geographic facts but also helps readers recognize themes, identify clues that lead to correct answers, and understand how geographers think." Publisher's note

The **DK** geography of the world. DK 2003 304p il map $29.99; pa $19.99 *

Grades: 5 6 7 8 9 10 **910**

1. Geography 2. Reference books

ISBN 0-7894-8594-X; 0-7566-1952-1 (pa)

LC 2003-269290

First published 1996

Maps and text describe countries around the world and the ways of life of the inhabitants

"This surprisingly comprehensive and affordable reference source is a joy to browse." Voice Youth Advocates

Dumont-Le Cornec, Elisabeth

Wonders of the world; natural and man-made majesties; by Elisabeth Dumont-Le Cornec; illustrated by Laureen Topalian and Kristel Riethmuller. Abrams Books for Young Readers 2007 151p il $24.95

Grades: 6 7 8 9 **910**

1. Curiosities and wonders 2. Historic sites 3. Antiquities 4. Natural monuments 5. Civilization

ISBN 978-0-8109-9417-1; 0-8109-9417-8

LC 2007016198

This "volume features 71 natural and man-made wonders selected from sites on the UNESCO World Heritage list. . . . This visually stunning book presents each selected site on a double-page spread. Most of the spread is devoted to an excellent color photo reproduced on heavy, glossy paper and accompanied by several paragraphs of explanatory text, good captions, and a small washed drawing. . . . A rich visual experience." Booklist

Gritzner, Charles F.
The tropics. Chelsea House 2007 128p il map (Geography of extreme environments) $30
Grades: 6 7 8 9   **910**
     1. Tropics
     ISBN 0-7910-9233-X   LC 2006019747
     This geography of tropical lands describes their populations, weather and climate, and their plants and animals.
     Includes bibliographical references

910.3   Geography—Dictionaries, encyclopedias, concordnces, gazetteers

Countries of the world and their leaders yearbook. Gale Res. 2v il maps set$205   **910.3**
     1. Geography 2. Politicians 3. Political science 4. Reference books
     ISSN 0196-2809
     First published 1974 with title: Countries of the world; issued annually since 1980 with slight variations in title. Supplementary volume published at mid-year available at $90
     A compilation of U.S. Department of State Background Notes and other government reports, this two-volume yearbook offers geographical, social, political, and economic data on about 170 nations. In addition, it provides information on: overseas business services from the Departments of State and Commerce, U.S. embassies and consulates, travel warnings, world health, and climate

Gifford, Clive
The Kingfisher geography encyclopedia. Kingfisher 2003 488p il map $39.95
Grades: 4 5 6 7   **910.3**
     1. Geography—Encyclopedias 2. Reference books
     ISBN 0-7534-5591-9   LC 2003-47420
     Contents: The physical earth; The Arctic; North America; Central America; The Caribbean; South America; Europe; Russian Federation; Asia; Indian subcontinent; Eastern Asia; Southeast Asia; Africa; Australasia; Oceania; Antarctica
     Statistics, text, and color maps reveal the physical geography, peoples, politics, governments, languages, religions, and currencies of each nation of the world
     "The arrangement is logical and the format accessible. . . . Striking color photographs and informative captions highlight the uniqueness of each locale." SLJ

Junior Worldmark encyclopedia of the nations; [edited by] Timothy L. Gall and Susan Bevan Gall. 5th ed. Thomson Gale 2007 10v il map set $546 *
Grades: 5 6 7 8   **910.3**
     1. Geography—Encyclopedias 2. World history—Encyclopedias 3. Reference books
     ISBN 978-1-4144-1095-1   LC 2007002388
     First published 1996
     This reference "profiles 194 countries worldwide. . . . Each country chapter includes 35 core headings that describe climate, population, labor, religion, housing, education, and other key data. Also included are brief biographical profiles of the countries' leaders, and charts, graphs, and tables that highlight the current economic conditions. . . . The encyclopedia also showcases color images of flags and coats of arms. . . . New to the 5th edition is information on each country's carbon dioxide emissions. . . . This resource incorporates a wealth of information into its chapters." Am Ref Books Annu, 2008
     Includes bibliographical references

910.4   Accounts of travel and facilities for travelers

Aronson, Marc
The world made new; why the Age of Exploration happened & how it changed the world; [by] Marc Aronson & John W. Glenn. National Geographic 2007 64p il map $17.95; lib bdg $27.90 *
Grades: 4 5 6 7   **910.4**
     1. Exploration 2. Explorers
     ISBN 978-0-7922-6454-5; 978-0-7922-6978-6 (lib bdg)   LC 2006022091
     This provides an "account of the charting of the New World and the long-term effects of America's march into history." Publisher's note
     "This highly pictorial, readable overview provides significant depth of coverage. . . . The illustrations, most in full color, make ample and appropriate use of period prints as well as contemporary illustrations and photographs. The result is a visual feast that fleshes out the . . . remarkably evenhanded narrative." SLJ
     Includes glossary and bibliographical references

Baker, Julie, 1967-
The great whaleship disaster of 1871; [by] Julie Baker. Morgan Reynolds Pub. 2007 144p $27.95
Grades: 6 7 8 9   **910.4**
     1. Whaling 2. Survival after airplane accidents, shipwrecks, etc.
     ISBN 978-1-59935-043-1; 1-59935-043-2
                      LC 2007002807
     "A compelling tale of survival. In 1871, at the peak of whale hunting, a fleet of 32 ships was trapped in Arctic ice, and the 1200 men, women, and children onboard faced a long winter with limited supplies. . . . Readers are given a picture of the hazards of whaling and the endurance required in the best of conditions. In the final chapters, the events leading up to the disaster are described. . . . The account is presented in an easy-to-follow, attractive format with concise chapters and ample diagrams, full-color reproductions, illustrations, and maps." SLJ
     Includes bibliographical references

Brewster, Hugh
882 ½ amazing answers to your questions about the Titanic; by Hugh Brewster and Laurie Coulter; text research by Greg Curtis; historical consultation by Don Lynch; paintings by Ken Marschall. Scholastic 1998 96p il pa $9.99 hardcover o.p. **910.4**
  1. Titanic (Steamship) 2. Shipwrecks
  ISBN 0-439-04296-8   LC 98-27558
  "A Scholastic/Madison Press book"
  Questions and answers present information about the building, passengers, launching, sailing, sinking, and rediscovery of the Titanic. Includes illustrations, archival images, and step-by-step diagrams

Butterfield, Moira
Pirates & smugglers; foreword by Captain Stephen Bligh. Kingfisher 2005 63p il map (Kingfisher knowledge) $12.95
Grades: 5 6 7 8   **910.4**
  1. Pirates 2. Smuggling
  ISBN 0-7534-5864-0
  This is an "introduction to the highwaymen and women of the seas from the cruel Cilician pirates who terrorized the Mediterranean more than 2,000 years ago to the . . . modern-day buccaneers who target supertankers on the South China Sea and the loot they plunder and smuggle." Publisher's note
  This offers "stunning illustrations and engaging text. . . . This book is fascinating. Photographs from the movies mix with drawings and reproductions to clarify the text." SLJ
  Includes glossary

Fritz, Jean
Around the world in a hundred years; from Henry the Navigator to Magellan; illustrated by Anthony Bacon Venti. Putnam 1994 128p il map hardcover o.p. pa $6.99
Grades: 4 5 6 7   **910.4**
  1. Explorers
  ISBN 0-399-22527-7; 0-698-11638-0 (pa)
                        LC 92-27042
  "Fritz examines the voyages of ten explorers, acknowledging that their contributions, though deserving of recognition, were dearly bought. Opening and closing chapters summarize the fourteenth-century world view and indicate later expansion of geographic understanding. As always, Fritz tempers scholarship with humor in this brief volume—illustrated with drawings in pencil—which reads like an adventure story." Horn Book Guide
  Includes bibliographical references

Hanel, Rachael
Pirates; [by] Rachael Hanel. 1st ed. Creative Education 2008 48p il map (Fearsome fighters) $31.35
Grades: 4 5 6   **910.4**
  1. Pirates
  ISBN 978-1-58341-537-5; 1-58341-537-8
                        LC 2006021844

"This book explores 'the golden age of piracy' from the sixteenth through the nineteenth centuries. Hanel discusses battles, types of ships and weapons, and attire and behavior. Vignettes of well-known male and female pirates are included. Archival reproductions and sidebars provide additional information." Horn Book Guide
  Includes glossary and bibliographical references

Lawlor, Laurie
Magnificent voyage; an American adventurer on Captain James Cook's final expedition. Holiday House 2002 236p il maps $22.95
Grades: 7 8 9 10   **910.4**
  1. Ledyard, John, 1751-1789 2. Cook, James, 1728-1779 3. Resolution (Ship) 4. Oceania
  ISBN 0-8234-1575-9   LC 2002-17148
  Based on the writings of John Ledyard, an American cook on the ship Resolution, tells of explorer James Cook's final voyage in search of the Northwest Passage, discovery of the Hawaiian Islands, and murder
  "The author's detailed picture of the voyage, and of Ledyard's relatively brief career, makes engrossing, if gloomy, reading." Booklist
  Includes glossary and bibliographical references

Marschall, Ken
Inside the Titanic; illustrated by Ken Marschall; text by Hugh Brewster. Little, Brown 1997 32p il $19.95
Grades: 4 5 6 7   **910.4**
  1. Titanic (Steamship) 2. Shipwrecks
  ISBN 0-316-55716-1   LC 97-382
  "A Madison Press book"
  "Color cutaway paintings of the *Titanic* in this over-size book allow readers to view every deck as they follow two 12-year-old boys exploring the vessel, and to see how the liner struck the iceberg and sank." Booklist
  Includes glossary and bibliographical references

Matsen, Bradford
The incredible search for the treasure ship Atocha; [by] Brad Matsen. Enslow Pubs. 2003 48p il map (Incredible deep-sea adventures) lib bdg $18.95
Grades: 4 5 6 7   **910.4**
  1. Fisher, Mel 2. Nuestra Señora de Atocha (Ship) 3. Buried treasure 4. Shipwrecks
  ISBN 0-7660-2193-9   LC 2002-14311
  Contents: Today's the day; The sinking of the Atocha, 1622; Mel Fisher's quest for the ghost galleons; The search goes on and on and on; Atocha's treasure is worth more than money
  Presents background information about the sinking of the Spanish galleon, Atocha, in 1622 and describes efforts to locate the wreck and successfully salvage its treasure more than 300 years later
  "A credible title about an amazing adventure. . . . The colorful illustrations include numerous underwater photos, period reproductions, and a map." SLJ
  Includes glossary and bibliographical references

Matthews, Rupert

Explorer; written by Rupert Matthews. rev ed. DK Pub. 2005 72p il map (DK eyewitness books) $15.99; lib bdg $19.99

Grades: 4 5 6 7   **910.4**

1. Exploration 2. Explorers
ISBN 0-7566-1072-9; 0-7566-1071-0 (lib bdg)
First published 1991 by Knopf
Photographs and text examine the history of explorers and exploration, and highlight many of their discoveries.

Open your eyes; extraordinary experiences in faraway places; edited by Jill Davis. Viking 2003 201p il $16.99

Grades: 7 8 9 10   **910.4**

1. Voyages and travels 2. Authors, American
ISBN 0-670-03616-1
A collection of memories and stories about a variety of travel experiences that changed the lives of such well-known writers as Lois Lowry, Suzie Morgenstern, and Harry Mazer
"This unusual anthology spotlights 10 people whose lives were changed by living or traveling abroad during their youth. . . . Though not every piece is excellent, the voices, vivid and distinctive." Booklist

Philbrick, Nathaniel

Revenge of the whale; the true story of the whaleship Essex. Putnam 2002 164p il maps $16.99; pa $7.99 *

Grades: 7 8 9 10   **910.4**

1. Essex (Whale-ship) 2. Shipwrecks 3. Whaling
ISBN 0-399-23795-X; 0-14-240068-8 (pa)
                     LC 2002-667
Recounts the 1820 sinking of the whaleship "Essex" by an enraged sperm whale and how the crew of young men survived against impossible odds. Based on the author's adult book "In the heart of the sea"
"The story of the *Essex* crew is a compelling saga of desperation and survival that will appeal to young people. The grisly details of cannibalism necessary to the telling of the story may provoke shivers but should not give anyone nightmares." SLJ
Includes bibliographical references

Platt, Richard, 1953-

Shipwreck; written by Richard Platt; photographed by Alex Wilson and Tina Chambers. rev ed. DK Pub. 2005 72p il (DK eyewitness books) $15.99; lib bdg $19.99

Grades: 4 5 6 7   **910.4**

1. Shipwrecks
ISBN 0-7566-1089-3; 0-7566-1090-7 (lib bdg)
First published 1997 by Knopf
Describes the history of shipwrecks, famous wrecks, causes, navigation and rescue techniques, and underwater archeology and the exploration of wrecks.

Warrick, Karen Clemens

The perilous search for the fabled Northwest Passage in American history; [by] Karen Clemens Warrick. Enslow Publishers 2004 128p il map (In American history) lib bdg $26.60

Grades: 6 7 8 9   **910.4**

1. Northwest Passage 2. Explorers 3. Arctic regions—Exploration
ISBN 0-7660-2148-3   LC 2003-26603
Contents: Franklin's final voyage; Search for a new trade route; Brave explorers in small ships; Sir John Barrow's push for Arctic exploration; Overland search for the Northwest Passage; Four winters in the Arctic; Along the coast of North America; Search and discovery; Navigating the passage; The Northwest Passage on the map
"Warrick traces the search for the Northwest Passage from the 15th to the 20th century. Describing John Cabot's and Jacques Cartier's efforts and, finally, Roald Amundsen's success in 1906, the book details the many explorers and their crews who lost their lives. . . . A worthwhile addition to history collections." SLJ
Includes bibliographical references

Weatherly, Myra, 1926-

Women of the sea; ten pirate stories. Morgan Reynolds 2006 160p il map lib bdg $26.95

Grades: 7 8 9 10   **910.4**

1. Women pirates
ISBN 1-931798-80-X
A revised edition of Women pirates: eight stories of adventure (1998)
This is a collective biography of such women pirates as Lady Killigrew, Lai Choi San, and Maria Cobham
Includes glossary and bibliographical references

White, Pamela

Exploration in the world of the Middle Ages, 500-1500. Facts on File 2005 176p il map (Discovery and exploration) $40

Grades: 7 8 9 10   **910.4**

1. Exploration 2. Middle Ages
ISBN 0-8160-5264-6   LC 2004-14564
This "looks at exploration and discovery in the medieval world. Well-known adventurers like Marco Polo are discussed as well as lesser-known stories such as a fifteenth-century Chinese emperor's exploration of Africa, Muslim travelers, Vikings, the exploratory contributions of pilgrims and missionaries, and the prevalence and long-ranging impact of untrustworthy travel accounts of the day. This . . . is an intriguing and informative resource." Voice Youth Advocates
Includes bibliographical references

911   Historical geography

Adams, Simon

The Kingfisher atlas of exploration & empires; illustrated by Mark Bergin. Kingfisher 2007 44p il $15.95

Grades: 4 5 6 7   **911**

Adams, Simon—*Continued*

1. Historical geography 2. Exploration 3. Reference books

ISBN 978-0-7534-6033-7

This atlas is "pictorial guide to the world in A.D. 1450–1800, the great age of conquest. Seventeen . . . maps present the story of human civilization from continent to continent, featuring . . . tales of trade, war, innovation, and exploration." Publisher's note

Leacock, Elspeth, 1946-

Places in time; a new atlas of American history; [by] Elspeth Leacock and Susan Buckley; illustrations by Randy Jones. Houghton Mifflin 2001 48p il $15; pa $6.95

Grades: 4 5 6 7   911

1. United States—Historical geography

ISBN 0-395-97958-7; 0-618-3113-0 (pa)

LC 00-59741

This book presents "20 sites in American history at the moment of their historical significance, beginning in 1200 (Cahokia) and ending in 1953. Places and times include New Plymouth—1627, Charlestown—1739, Saratoga—1777, Philadelphia—1787, Abilene—1871, and Chicago—1893. The detailed cutaway views of homes, forts, and mills are impressive enough to keep readers looking again and again. These fascinating slices of life stir the imagination and lead to questions and further research." SLJ

Includes bibliographical references

912   Atlases. Maps

Atlas of North America; H.J. de Blij, editor; [cartography by Philip's] Oxford University Press 2004 320p il map $125

Grades: 5 6 7 8 9 10   912

1. Atlases 2. Reference books

ISBN 0-19-516993-X   LC 2004-45005

This "atlas of the three largest countries of North America . . . [features a] thematic section covering physical, historic, economic, urban, social, and cultural topics ranging from environmental change to religious practice and from indigenous peoples to migration patterns." Publisher's note

"This exhaustive, authoritative resource presents a dynamic view of Canada, the U.S., and Mexico." SLJ

Baber, Maxwell

Map basics; [by] Maxwell Baber. Heinemann Library 2007 32p il map (Map readers) $27.07; pa $7.99 *

Grades: 4 5 6   912

1. Maps

ISBN 1-4034-6794-3; 1-4034-6801-X (pa)

LC 2006003351

"The book begins with a history of mapping, then goes on to discuss globes, with an explanation of hemispheres and meridians, and the international date line. Among the other topics covered are map projections, scale, keys, various types of maps and how to use them, and the future of mapping. The book concludes with map

projects. . . . The illustrations are crisp and easy to use. A fine choice." Booklist

Includes bibliographical references

Geography on file. 2007 ed. Facts on File 2007 various paging il map loose-leaf $195

Grades: Professional   912

1. Atlases 2. Geography 3. Reference books

ISBN 978-0-8160-7079-4

Annual updates available for $55; CD-ROM version also available

First published 1991. Periodically revised

A collection of more than 250 maps, graphs, and statistical charts on both human and physical geography. Topics covered include demographic shifts, economic growth, language distribution, and political institutions

Hammond world atlas. 5th ed. Hammond World Atlas Corporation 2008 346p il map $59.95 *

Grades: 8 9 10 11 12 Adult   912

1. Atlases 2. Geography

ISBN 978-0-8437-0967-4; 0-8437-0967-7

First published 1992 with title: Hammond atlas of the world

This atlas includes an "illustrated 64-page 'Thematic Section,' a 48-page 'Satellite Section' with more than 40 color photos and a commentary, and 228 pages of . . . full-color physical and political maps representing the world, continents, and regions with detailed . . . computer-generated terrain modeling." Libr J

Maps on file. Facts on File 2v maps loose-leaf set $250

Grades: Professional   912

1. Atlases 2. Reference books

ISSN 0275-8083

Annual updates available for $75; CD-ROM version also available

First published 1981. Frequently revised

Maps copyrighted by Martin Greenwald Associates

A collection of approximately 500 black-and-white maps covering countries, every U.S. state, Canadian provinces, oceans, and continents

National Geographic student atlas of the world. third edition. National Geographic 2009 143p il map pa $12.95

Grades: 6 7 8 9   912

1. Atlases 2. Reference books

ISBN 978-1-4263-0446-0 (pa); 1-4263-0446-3 (pa)

First published 2001

This offers information "about maps and how to read them. Then [it describes] the world's physical and human systems, including Earth's geologic history, natural vegetation, and world cultures. A . . . view from space introduces each continent, and full-page, full-color maps represent its physical and political makeup, its climate and precipitation, and its population and predominant economies. A . . . photo essay highlights an issue relevant to each continent, such as the European Union, or deforestation in the Amazon." Publisher's note

National Geographic United States atlas for young explorers. 3rd ed. National Geographic 2008 175p il map $24.95 *

Grades: 4 5 6 7   912

National Geographic United States atlas for young explorers—*Continued*

1. Atlases 2. United States—Maps 3. Reference books
ISBN 978-1-4263-0255-8; 1-4263-0255-X

First published 1999

This atlas offers maps of each of the states in the United States, divided into five geographical regions, plus U.S. territories. Each state map indicates physical features such as mountains and rivers, national forests, cities, major interstate roads, and industries, and is accompanied by color photos and facts about the state. An introductory section describes how to use the companion web site for more information, maps of the United States biomes, climates, natural hazards, political states, population, ethnic diversity, and energy use.

Oxford atlas of the world. 15th ed. Oxford University Press 2008 448p il map $80 *
Grades: 7 8 9 10 11 12 Adult   912

1. Atlases 2. Reference books
ISBN 978-0-19-537451-3; 0-19-537451-7

This atlas "contains 179 pages of full-color, computer-generated political and topographical maps by reflecting the most recent geopolitical changes, including the separation of Montenegro and Kosovo from Serbia, Venezuela's new half-hour time zone shift, as well as the demarcation of the de-facto states of Abkhazia, Nagorno-Karabakh, and Somaliland. The terrain modeling is detailed and dramatic. . . . More than 70 updated world and regional thematic maps with illustrations and text explore topics ranging from demographics and economics to the environment. . . . A 32-page gazetteer section provides ready-reference information arranged alphabetically for both independent states and dependencies with data boxes, country summaries, and official flags." Libr J

Oxford new concise world atlas. 2nd ed. Oxford University Press 2006 224p il map $35
Grades: 6 7 8 9   912

1. Atlases 2. Reference books
ISBN 978-0-19-532015-2; 0-19-532015-8

First published 2003

This atlas opens "with six pages of compiled statistics on world population, climate and geography. . . . The highly illustrated 'Earth in Space' thematic section that follows provides a wide-angle overview of the planet. . . . Then, in twenty-two compact . . . essays, the Earth's human and natural processes are explained using . . . text, instructive charts and graphs, and . . . photography and cartography. . . . With 128 pages of . . . maps . . . every region from the Arctic Ocean to The Volga Basin is rendered in layer-colored contours, revealing detailed political and topographical information about each of the 192 countries recognized by the United Nations." Publisher's note

Ross, Val

The road to there; mapmakers and their stories. Tundra Books 2003 146p il map $22.95
Grades: 6 7 8 9   912

1. Maps
ISBN 0-88776-621-8

"Ross presents an intriguing look at several mapmakers and the way that their work reflected not only physical boundaries, but also important aspects of their lives and the times in which they lived. . . . The tone of the text is chatty, sometimes humorous, and never dry. . . . Filled with details and insights and written with a storyteller's touch, this book will simultaneously inform and fascinate readers." SLJ

Rubel, David

Scholastic atlas of the United States. new and updated. Scholastic Reference 2003 144p il map hardcover o.p. pa $10.95 *
Grades: 4 5 6 7   912

1. United States—Maps 2. Atlases 3. Reference books
ISBN 0-439-55494-2; 0-439-47436-1 (pa)

"An Agincourt Press book"

First published 2000

This atlas "offers students a detailed map of each of the 50 states plus the District of Columbia and Puerto Rico. [It] also features an information page about each state that uses photos, graphics, . . . facts, and a brief essay to explain what makes each state unique." Publisher's note

Student Atlas. 5th ed., rev. DK Pub. 2008 176p il map $19.95 *
Grades: 5 6 7 8   912

1. Atlases 2. Reference books
ISBN 978-0-7566-3818-4; 0-7566-3818-6

First published 1998

Maps, illustrations, and text describe various aspects of countries of the world including physical features, population, standards of living, natural resources, industries, environmental issues, and climate.

Taylor, Barbara, 1954-

Looking at maps; [by] Barbara Taylor. Smart Apple Media 2008 46p il map (Geography skills) $22.95 *
Grades: 6 7 8 9   912

1. Maps
ISBN 1-59920-050-3; 978-1-59920-050-7

LC 2006100224

Contents: What is a map?; How are maps used?; Scale; Distance; Grids; Height; Symbols; Making landscape maps; Finding the way; Mapping data; Weather maps; Pictorial maps; What is GIS?; How is GIS used?; Mapping change; Latitude and longitude; Explaining a round world; Round earth, flat maps; Where in the world?

"The text is easy to follow. . . . The examples given in the text that involve places are almost always accompanied by excellent photographs. . . . Maps, block diagrams, tables, and graphs are clearly presented and easy to interpret." Sci Books Films

Includes glossary and bibliographical references

917.3 Geography of and travel in the United States

The **Cambridge** gazetteer of the United States and Canada; a dictionary of places; edited by Archie Hobson. Cambridge Univ. Press 1995 743p maps $80
Grades: 8 9 10 11 12 Adult   **917.3**
1. United States—Gazetteers 2. Canada—Gazetteers 3. Reference books
ISBN 0-521-41579-9   LC 95-8898
The over 12,000 listings for places in the U.S. and Canada include entries for municipalities, states, countries, geographical features, notable neighborhoods, regional names, and a few legendary places. Includes definitions of about 170 geographical terms
"The inclusion of such a wide variety of places, from streets and ballparks to battlefields and forests, makes this a valuable work that will be welcome in all reference departments." Booklist

920 Biography & genealogy

Books of biography are arranged as follows: 1. Biographical collections (920) 2. Biographies of individuals alphabetically by name of biographee (92)

Aaseng, Nathan, 1953-
Business builders in real estate. Oliver Press 2002 160p il map (Business builders) $22.95
Grades: 5 6 7 8   **920**
1. Real estate business 2. Businesspeople
ISBN 1-88150-879-X   LC 2001-36369
Profiles seven real estate developers, including John Nicholson, John Jacob Astor, William Levitt, Del Webb, Walt Disney, Paul Reichmann, and the Ghermezian brothers
"Each biography is complete, with enough information for a research report. The sum total paints an excellent picture of the real estate trade in America" Libr Media Connect
Includes bibliographical references

Business builders in sweets and treats; [by] Nathan Aaseng. Oliver Press 2005 160p il (Business builders) $24.95
Grades: 5 6 7 8   **920**
1. Food industry 2. Businesspeople
ISBN 1-881508-84-6   LC 2003-64984
Contents: Milton Hershey: dreams made of chocolate; William Wrigley Jr.: Chicago's chewing-gum empire; Frand and Forrest Mars: first family of candy; Vernon Rudolph: Krispy Kreme Donuts: hottest brand going; Ellen Gordon: Tootsie Roll: making millions on penny candy; Wally Amos: the cookie manager; Ben Cohen and Jerry Greenfield: good will, good times, good ice cream
This is a "study of Hershey and chocolate, Wrigley and chewing gum, Ben and Jerry and ice cream, and others who make things we love to eat. . . . A few well-chosen sidebars document sweets that don't get a whole chapter. Excellent sources and citations, boxed facts, a lively style, and sometimes mouthwatering pictures finish the package." Booklist
Includes bibliographical references

Alegre, Cesar, 1967-
Extraordinary Hispanic Americans; by Cesar Alegre. Children's Press 2007 288p il (Extraordinary people) lib bdg $40
Grades: 5 6 7 8   **920**
1. Hispanic Americans—Biography
ISBN 0-516-25343-3 (lib bdg); 978-0-516-25343-5 (lib bdg)   LC 2005031579
"This volume has short (two to three pages) biographies of more than 200 people, from historical figures to those in present-day politics, entertainment, and sports. The writing is energetic, interesting, and without bias. . . . Black-and-white photographs appear throughout. A good general reference source for reports." SLJ
Includes bibliographical references

Altman, Susan
Extraordinary African-Americans. Children's Press 2001 288p il (Extraordinary people) $39; pa $16.95 *
Grades: 5 6 7 8   **920**
1. African Americans—Biography
ISBN 0-516-22549-9; 0-516-25962-8 (pa)   LC 00-52373
First published 1988 with title: Extraordinary Black Americans: from colonial to contemporary times
This "profiles more than 100 African-American achievers, including writers, artists, musicians, athletes, activists, politicians, and others who have made headlines. It also includes descriptions of important periods in African-American history, including the Harlem Renaissance, Reconstruction, the Great Northern Migration, and the civil rights movement." SLJ
"Perfect for quick reference, in an attractive layout that will appeal to even the most reluctant researchers." Voice Youth Advocates
Includes bibliographical references

Archer, Jules
They had a dream; the civil rights struggle from Frederick Douglass to Marcus Garvey to Martin Luther King and Malcolm X. Viking 1993 258p il (Epoch biographies) pa $7.99 hardcover o.p. *
Grades: 6 7 8 9   **920**
1. African Americans—Biography 2. African Americans—Civil rights
ISBN 0-14-034954-5 (pa)   LC 92-40071
Traces the progression of the civil rights movement and its effect on history through biographical sketches of four prominent and influential African Americans: Frederick Douglass, Marcus Garvey, Martin Luther King, Jr., and Malcolm X
"This discussion of the contributions of four pivotal civil rights activists is balanced and substantive." Publ Wkly
Includes bibliographical references

Armstrong, Mabel

Women astronomers; reaching for the stars. Stone Pine Press 2008 179p il (Discovering women in science series) pa $16.95

Grades: 7 8 9 10   **920**

1. Women astronomers

ISBN 978-0-972892-95-7 (pa); 0-972892-95-8 (pa)

LC 2007-22318

This introduces 21 women astronomers, from ancient times to the present.

"A worthy addition to science collections, this well-documented collective biography not only fills gaps in existing books on astronomers, but also offers engaging accounts of the women's careers as well as unusually clear explanations of what they achieved and why each discovery was important." Booklist

Includes bibliographical references

Atkins, Jeannine, 1953-

How high can we climb? the story of women explorers; pictures by Dušan Petričic. Farrar, Straus and Giroux 2005 209p il $17

Grades: 5 6 7 8   **920**

1. Explorers 2. Women—Biography

ISBN 0-374-33503-6   LC 2003-56378

Profiles twelve women explorers of the land, sea, and air: Jeanne Baret, Florence Baker, Annie Smith Peck, Josephine Peary, Arnarulunguaq, Elisabeth Casteret, Nicole Maxwell, Sylvia Earle, Junko Tabei, Kay Cottee, Sue Hendrickson, and Ann Bancroft.

"The stories, illustrated with Petričic's winsome pen-and-ink drawings, are greatly fictionalized. . . . The strongest justifications for purchase are the thrilling adventures and the introductions to daring, accomplished, and, in some cases, nearly forgotten women who changed history." Booklist

Axelrod-Contrada, Joan

Women who led nations. Oliver Press 1999 160p il (Profiles) lib bdg $21.25

Grades: 7 8 9 10   **920**

1. Women politicians 2. Women in politics

ISBN 1-881508-48-X   LC 98-10958

Profiles the careers of seven women elected to head their respective countries, including Golda Meir, Indira Gandhi, Margaret Thatcher, Corazón Aquino, Benazir Bhutto, Violeta Barrios de Chamorro, and Gro Harlem Brundtland

"Black-and-white photographs adequately portray each head of state and represent highlights of the events that took place during her term of office. Fourteen other women who have ruled countries receive brief mention in the final chapter. A useful resource for reports." SLJ

Includes bibliographical references

Bausum, Ann

Our country's first ladies; [by] Ann Bausum; with a foreword by First Lady Laura Bush. National Geographic 2007 127p il $19.95; lib bdg $28.90 *

Grades: 5 6 7 8   **920**

1. Presidents' spouses—United States

ISBN 978-1-4263-0006-6; 978-1-4263-0007-3 (lib bdg)   LC 2006021284

"A well-researched, thoughtfully written, attractive account. Fact boxes provide basic information such as birth and death dates, marriage dates, and children's names; a 'Did You Know' section shares interesting personal tidbits. Periodic time lines help to place the women's lives within the broader events of history. There is enough information here for simple reports. Interesting facts and anecdotes will hold readers' attention. . . . An excellent layout and clear, colorful photographs and reproductions will further entice readers." SLJ

Includes bibliographical references

Our country's presidents; all you need to know about the presidents, from George Washington to Barack Obama; [by] Ann Bausum; with a foreword by President Barack Obama. 3rd ed. National Geographic 2009 215p il map $24.95 *

Grades: 5 6 7 8   **920**

1. Presidents—United States

ISBN 978-1-4263-0375-3; 1-4263-0375-0

LC 2009290293

First published 2001

This profiles the United States Presidents from George Washington to Barack Obama, and discusses such topics as The White House, the Electoral College, past presidents as elder statesmen, presidential security, the First Ladies, the Vice Presidents, children in the White House, pollsters and polling, and the expanding global role of the president.

"This exceedingly attractive offering is . . . chock-full of information, presented . . . in such an inviting manner that children will enjoy paging through, even if there's no school report looming. . . . Full of interesting tidbits as well as solid information." Booklist

Includes bibliographical references

Beccia, Carlyn

The raucous royals; test your royal wits: crack codes, solve mysteries, and deduce which royal rumors are true. Houghton Mifflin 2008 64p il $17

Grades: 4 5 6 7   **920**

1. Kings and rulers 2. Nobility 3. Historiography

ISBN 978-0-618-89130-6; 0-618-89130-7

LC 2008-298419

"Thirteen beliefs about rulers receive an acerbic and irreverent interrogation in this blend of royal-watching and skeptical investigation. The royal rumors, arranged chronologically, start with the real story behind Prince Dracula and Richard III's murderous ways, stopping en route at Napoleon's short stature and Marie Antoinette's 'let them eat cake' utterance, and finish up with Catherine the Great's death and King George's madness. . . . The energy and gleefully gossipy nature makes this a fine companion for Krull's Lives of . . . series, while its verve particularly recommends it as an entreé into historiography and critical thinking." Bull Cent Child Books

Includes bibliographical references

Benson, Sonia

Korean War: biographies; [by] Sonia G. Benson; Gerda-Ann Raffaelle, editor. U.X.L 2002 xxx, 268p il pa $60

Grades: 7 8 9 10   **920**

1. Korean War, 1950-1953—Biography

ISBN 0-7876-5692-5   LC 2001-44241

Benson, Sonia—*Continued*

Presents biographies of twenty-six men and women who participated in or were affected by the Korean War, including politicians, military leaders, journalists, and nurses

"An excellent starting point for researching the . . . people of the Korean War." Booklist

Includes bibliographical references

Blackwood, Gary L.

Debatable deaths; [by] Gary L. Blackwood. 1st ed. Marshall Cavendish Benchmark 2005 72p il (Unsolved history) lib bdg $29.93

Grades: 4 5 6 7   920

1. Death

ISBN 0-7614-1888-1   LC 2004-22237

Explores the mystery surrounding the deaths of various historical figures: Tutkankhamen, the English Princes in the Tower, Christopher Marlowe, Mozart, Meriwether Lewis, and Amelia Earhart

This collection of "tidbits about lingering mysteries of the past . . . [offers] more substance than most. . . . [It offers] a full-page illustration opening each chapter; reproductions, many in color; and a generously spaced format." SLJ

Includes glossary and bibliographical references

Perplexing people; [by] Gary L. Blackwood. Marshall Cavendish Benchmark 2006 72p il (Unsolved history) lib bdg $29.93

Grades: 4 5 6 7   920

1. Impostors and imposture

ISBN 0-7614-1890-3   LC 2004-22238

Describes various famous pretenders in history, including those individuals who claimed to be Joan of Arc, Anastasia, the French Dauphin who would have been King Louis XVII, and the outlaw Billy the Kid

This collection "of tidbits about lingering mysteries of the past . . . [offers] more substance than most. . . . [It offers] a full-page illustration opening each chapter; reproductions, many in color; and a generously spaced format." SLJ

Includes glossary and bibliographical references

Bolden, Tonya

Portraits of African-American heroes; paintings by Ansel Pitcairn. Dutton Children's Books 2003 88p il $18.99; pa $11.99

Grades: 4 5 6 7   920

1. African Americans—Biography

ISBN 0-525-47043-3; 0-14-240473-X (pa)

LC 2002-75911

Contents: Frederick Douglass; Matthew Henson; W.E.B. Du Bois; Mary McLeod Bethune; Bessie Coleman; Paul Robeson; Satchel Paige; Thurgood Marshal; Pauli Murray; Joe Louis; Gwendolyn Brooks; Jacob Lawrence; Dizzy Gillespie; Shirley Chisholm; Malcolm X; Martin Luther King, Jr.; Charlayne Hunter-Gault; Judith Jamison; Ruth Simmons; Ben Carson

"Bolden profiles 20 people, ranging from Matthew Henson, Thurgood Marshall, and Martin Luther King, Jr., to Paul Robeson, Ruth Simmons, Judith Jamison, and Charlayne Hunter-Gault." SLJ

"Each profile lists expected biographical information, but offers even more by way of keen insights into a subject's personality based on interviews and information drawn from personal memoirs. . . . Pitcairn's beautifully rendered sepia-toned portraits make each subject jump from the page, beckoning children to come ever closer and learn." Booklist

Bostrom, Kathleen Long, 1954-

Winning authors; profiles of the Newbery medalists; [by] Kathleen Long Bostrom. Libraries Unlimited 2003 338p il (Popular authors series) $52

Grades: Professional   920

1. Authors, American 2. Newbery Medal

ISBN 1-56308-877-0   LC 2003-53878

This "resource opens with a brief history of the Newbery Medal. . . . Entries featuring each winner from 1922 to 2002 follow with basic information about the authors, including useful listings of all awards and honors they have won, a full listing of their books, and sources for further information. A two to three-page narrative linking life experiences to themes of their books is also included." SLJ

Includes bibliographical references

Bruno, Leonard C.

Math and mathematicians; the history of math discoveries around the world; Lawrence W. Baker, editor. U.X.L 1999-2002 4v il set$235 *

Grades: 7 8 9 10   920

1. Mathematicians 2. Mathematics

ISBN 1-4144-0494-8   LC 99-32424

v1 and v2 available as a 2 volume set$120; v3 and v4 also available separately pa $67

Compilation of biographies, 50 to 60 per volume, of mathematicians from throughout history and articles describing math concepts and principles

"This effective resource is marked by its attention to detail and variety of information. Readers can readily cross-reference concepts, people, and discoveries. Easy to use, this wonderful reference will be appropriate for middle, high school, and public libraries." Voice Youth Advocates [review of vols 1 & 2]

Includes glossary and bibliographical references

Bussing-Burks, Marie, 1958-

Influential economists. Oliver Press 2003 160p il (Profiles) $19.95

Grades: 7 8 9 10   920

1. Economists

ISBN 1-881508-72-2   LC 2001-59310

Presents information on the lives and work of the economists Thomas Gresham, Adam Smith, Thomas Robert Malthus, Karl Marx, John Maynard Keynes, Milton Friedman, and Alan Greenspan

"The author discusses sometimes complex theories in a straightforward, jargon-free text accessible to most sophisticated teen readers. . . . Informative, well-written, and fairly interesting." Booklist

Includes glossary and bibliographical references

Butts, Edward, 1951-
She dared; true stories of heroines, scoundrels, and renegades; [by] Ed Butts; illustrated by Heather Collins. Tundra Bks. 2005 121p il pa $8.95
Grades: 6 7 8 9   **920**
   1. Women—Biography 2. Canada—Biography
   ISBN 0-88776-718-4
This "details the lives of some of Canada's most famous and infamous women. The stories showcase explorers, spies, criminals, and pioneers in a variety of career fields. Organized chronologically from the 16th to the mid-20th century, this 12-chapter offering is historically sound and well researched." SLJ

Byrnes, Patricia, 1942-
Environmental pioneers. Oliver Press (Minneapolis) 1998 160p il (Profiles) lib bdg $19.95
Grades: 7 8 9 10   **920**
   1. Environmentalists
   ISBN 1-881508-45-5   LC 97-30233
Profiles people who have been influential in the environmental movement: John Muir, Jay Norwood "Ding" Darling, Rosalie Edge, Aldo Leopold, Olaus and Margaret Murie, Rachel Carson, David Brower, and Gaylord Nelson
"Unlike most authors of books on this topic for a young audience, Byrnes is an experienced environmental writer, and takes an affectionate tone in describing her subjects." SLJ
Includes bibliographical references

Castro, Iván A.
100 hispanics you should know. Libraries Unlimited 2007 303p bibl il $55 *
Grades: 6 7 8 9   **920**
   1. Hispanic Americans—Biography
   ISBN 1-59158-327-6
"This eye-opening and valuable reference is one of the few biographical compilations for young people that address the achievements of Spanish-speaking individuals across the world and throughout history, especially in the sciences, arts, politics, and military. The alphabetically arranged entries begin with key information about the individuals, such as birthplaces, birth and death dates, career highlights, and b&w portraits; then continue with important contributions; and end with bibliographies." Libr Media Connect

Chin-Lee, Cynthia, 1958-
Amelia to Zora; twenty-six women who changed the world; illustrated by Megan Halsey and Sean Addy. Charlesbridge 2005 32p il $15.95 *
Grades: 4 5 6 7   **920**
   1. Women—Biography
   ISBN 1-57091-522-9
"An introduction to 26 diverse, 20th-century women who have made a difference in such varied fields as the arts, sports, journalism, science, and entertainment. The entries include Dolores Huerta, Frida Kahlo, Lena Horne, Maya Lin, and Patricia Schroeder." SLJ

"The illustrations are done in a remarkable mix of media. . . . The text portions are short . . . but they are enticing. By choosing her subjects from every culture, the author introduces children to the scope of the struggles and achievements of women from many times and many places." Booklist

Colman, Penny
Adventurous women; eight true stories about women who made a difference; [by] Penny Colman. 1st ed. Henry Holt and Co. 2006 186p il map $18.95 *
Grades: 5 6 7 8   **920**
   1. Women—Biography
   ISBN 978-0-8050-7744-5; 0-8050-7744-8
                 LC 2005050311
"The eight individuals profiled are Louise Boyd, arctic explorer; Mary Gibson Henry, plant hunter and botanist; Juana Briones, a Hispanic landowner in early San Francisco; Alice Hamilton, a pioneer in industrial medicine; Mary McLeod Bethune, educator; Katharine Wormeley, nursing superintendent during the Civil War; Biddy Mason, humanitarian; and Peggy Hull, reporter. The chapters include black-and-white photos, and some have excerpts from diaries. . . . Libraries wanting readable, browsing nonfiction will want this book." SLJ
Includes bibliographical references

Cotter, Charis
Kids who rule; the remarkable lives of five child monarchs. Annick Press 2007 120p il map $24.95; pa $14.95
Grades: 5 6 7 8   **920**
   1. Kings and rulers
   ISBN 978-1-55451-062-7; 978-1-55451-061-0 (pa); 1-55451-062-7; 1-55451-061-9 (pa)
This "book discusses five people who became monarchs as children: Tutankhamen of Egypt, Mary Queen of Scots, Queen Christina of Sweden, China's Emperor Puyi, and the fourteenth Dalai Lama. . . . The illustrations, many in color, include portrait paintings, engravings, and maps as well as photos of people, places, and artifacts. . . . This appealing collective biography presents five unusual children whose stories are well worth reading." Booklist

Delano, Marfe Ferguson
American heroes. National Geographic 2005 191p il $24.95; lib bdg $45.90
Grades: 5 6 7 8   **920**
   1. United States—Biography
   ISBN 0-7922-7208-0; 0-7922-7215-3 (lib bdg)
This profiles 50 Americans each "chosen for his or her vision, strength, and commitment to exploration or change. . . . Organized chronologically from pre-Colonial times through today, the . . . entries range from Pocahontas to Senator Daniel K. Inouye. . . . The clearly written, beautifully laid out profiles include an information box with basic chronology, milestones, landmarks, honors, and a bulleted list of facts." SLJ
Includes bibliographical references

Distinguished African American scientists of the 20th century; [by] James H. Kessler [et .al.]; with Sigrid Berge, portrait artist, and Alyce Neukirk, computer graphics artist. Oryx Press 1996 382p il $73.95 *

Grades: 7 8 9 10   **920**

1. Scientists 2. African Americans—Biography

ISBN 0-89774-955-3   LC 95-43880

"One hundred famous and not-so-famous African American scientists (both living and dead) are covered in this biographical reference. . . . Men and women accomplished in anthropology, biology, chemistry, engineering, geology, mathematics, medicine, and physics are included. Those profiled include lesser-known scientists such as Christine Darden (an engineer with NASA) as well as the better known, e.g., George Washington Carver." Libr J

Includes bibliographical references

Doherty, Kieran

Ranchers, homesteaders, and traders; frontiersmen of the South-Central states. Oliver Press (Minneapolis) 2001 176p il maps (Shaping America) lib bdg $22.95

Grades: 5 6 7 8   **920**

1. Frontier and pioneer life—West (U.S.)

ISBN 1-88150-853-6   LC 00-52864

"Doherty traces the history of the settlement of various frontier lands through a study of the lives and achievements of seven men: Henry de Tonty (Arkansas), Auguste Chouteau (Missouri), Daniel Boone (Kentucky), John Sevier (Tennessee), Stephen Austin and Sam Houston (Texas), and Eli Thayer (Kansas)." SLJ

"There's enough personal history (and plenty of illustrations) to give readers a clear overview of the frontier heroes. . . . This is an excellent resource." Booklist

Includes bibliographical references

Drucker, Malka, 1945-

Portraits of Jewish American heroes; by Malka Drucker; illustrated by Elizabeth Rosen. Dutton Children's Books 2008 96p il $22.99

Grades: 4 5 6   **920**

1. Jews—United States—Biography

ISBN 978-0-525-47771-6; 0-525-47771-3

LC 2007-028481

"From Albert Einstein and Bella Abzug to Ruth Bader Ginsburg, Hank Greenberg, and Steven Spielberg, this invitingly illustrated collective biography celebrates 20 Jewish American heroes in all their diversity. . . . The nicely designed volume includes full-page portraits of the subjects in various media. . . . Drucker's eloquent, chatty style opens up big issues about Judaism as a source of idealism and for a just, compassionate society." Booklist

Includes bibliographical references

Earls, Irene

Young musicians in world history. Greenwood Press 2002 139p il $44.95

Grades: 8 9 10 11 12   **920**

1. Musicians

ISBN 0-313-31442-X   LC 2001-40559

Contents: Louis Armstrong; Johann Sebastian Bach; Ludwig van Beethoven; Pablo Casals; Sarah Chang; Ray Charles; Charlotte Church; Bob Dylan; John Lennon; Midori; Wolfgang Mozart; Niccolo Paganini; Isaac Stern

Profiles thirteen musicians who achieved high honors and fame before the age of twenty-five, representing many different time periods and musical styles

"A useful introduction to some of the musical giants of the last four centuries." SLJ

Includes glossary and bibliographical references

Engelbert, Phillis

American civil rights: biographies; Betz Des Chenes, editor. U.X.L 1999 xl, 203p il $60

Grades: 8 9 10 11 12   **920**

1. Civil rights 2. United States—Race relations 3. United States—Biography

ISBN 0-7876-3173-6   LC 99-20497

This collection of biographies of major civil rights figures, includes sidebars covering related events and issues

Includes bibliographical references

Facts about the presidents; a compilation of biographical and historical information; Joseph Nathan Kane, Janet Podell [editors] 8th ed. Wilson, H.W. 2009 720p $125

Grades: 8 9 10 11 12 Adult   **920**

1. Presidents—United States 2. Reference books

ISBN 978-0-8242-1087-8; 0-8242-1087-8

LC 2008056016

First published 1959

The main part of this work provides an individual chapter on each President, from Washington through Barack Obama, presenting such information as family, education, election, Vice President, main events and accomplishments of his administration, and First Lady. Part two contains tables and lists presenting comparative data on all the Presidents

Fortey, Jacqueline

Great scientists; written by Jacqueline Fortey. DK Pub. 2007 72p il map (DK eyewitness books) $15.99

Grades: 5 6 7 8   **920**

1. Scientists

ISBN 978-0-7566-2974-8; 0-7566-2974-8

LC 2007-298205

This introduces readers to the great scientists and their discoveries from ancient history to modern times.

"An accompanying CD provides clip art taken from the book; this art can prove invaluable to both teachers and students. . . . A very fine book for elementary and middle school students and those who teach them." Sci Books and Films

Fradin, Dennis B.

The founders; the 39 stories behind the U.S. Constitution; [by] Dennis Brindell Fradin; illustrated by Michael McCurdy. Walker & Co. 2005 162p il map $22.95; lib bdg $23.95 *

Grades: 4 5 6 7   **920**

Fradin, Dennis B.—*Continued*
1. United States. Constitution 2. Statesmen—United States 3. United States—Politics and government—1783-1809
ISBN 0-8027-8972-2; 0-8027-8973-0 (lib bdg)
"The makers of the U.S. Constitution are profiled in two or three pages each, in sections introduced by a brief note about their home states. McCurdy's black-and-white scratchboard illustrations are properly stately and engaging. Readers will find great nuggets of fact." Booklist
Includes bibliographical references

The signers; the fifty-six stories behind the Declaration of Independence; [by] Dennis Brindell Fradin; illustrations by Michael McCurdy. Walker & Co. 2002 164p il map $22.95; lib bdg $23.85
*
Grades: 4 5 6 7   **920**
1. United States. Declaration of Independence 2. Statesmen—United States 3. United States—Politics and government—1775-1783, Revolution
ISBN 0-8027-8849-1; 0-8027-8850-5 (lib bdg)
      LC 2002-66364
Profiles each of the fifty-six men who signed the Declaration of Independence, giving historical information about the colonies they represented. Includes the text of the Declaration and its history
"Fradin gives brief, fascinating glimpses into the people who have been overlooked as well as those with whom readers might be familiar. . . . An excellent resource for report writing." SLJ
Includes bibliographical references

Freedman, Russell
Indian chiefs. Holiday House 1987 151p il lib bdg $22.95; pa $12.95 *
Grades: 6 7 8 9   **920**
1. Native Americans—Biography
ISBN 0-8234-0625-3 (lib bdg); 0-8234-0971-6 (pa)
      LC 86-46198
This "book chronicles the lives of six renowned Indian chiefs, each of whom served as a leader during a critical period in his tribe's history. . . . The text relates information about the lives of each chief and aspects of Indian/white relationships that illuminate his actions. Interesting vignettes and quotations are well integrated into the narrative as are dramatic accounts of battles. While the tone of the text is nonjudgmental, an underlying sympathy for the Indians' situation is apparent." Horn Book
Includes bibliographical references

George-Warren, Holly
Shake, rattle, & roll; the founders of rock & roll; words by Holly George-Warren; pictures by Laura Levine. Houghton Mifflin 2001 unp il hardcover o.p. pa $5.95
Grades: 4 5 6 7   **920**
1. Musicians 2. Rock music
ISBN 0-618-05540-1; 0-618-43229-9 (pa)
      LC 00-33480
"Brief profiles of 15 men and women whose music 'created a sound that changed our culture forever,' including Bill Haley, Fats Domino, Little Richard, Elvis

Presley, Carl Perkins, Wanda Jackson and Ritchie Valens." N Y Times Book Rev
"A wonderfully entertaining browsing book that will also fill a gap in most music collections." SLJ

Gifford, Clive
10 kings & queens who changed the world; written by Clive Gifford; illustrated by David Cousens. Kingfisher 2009 63p il map $14.99
Grades: 4 5 6 7 8   **920**
1. Kings and rulers
ISBN 978-0-7534-6252-2; 0-7534-6252-4
"In this look at ten royals, beginning with Queen Hatshepsut of Egypt and ending with Catherine the Great, each leader's biography is linked with another based on influences, events, and geography." Publisher's note
"Cousens' bright graphic novel-style artwork is the grabber here; he uses theatrical angles to portray each historical figure as a chiseled or beautiful adventurer. . . . The writing is clear, packed with information, and presented in agile paragraphs that twist around the scenes of war, plotting, and murder." Booklist

Goldman, David J.
Presidential losers; by David J. Goldman. Lerner Publications Co. 2004 72p il lib bdg $25.26
Grades: 6 7 8 9   **920**
1. Presidents—United States—Election
ISBN 0-8225-0100-7   LC 2003-11222
Contents: Aaron Burr (1756-1836) the election of 1800; Henry Clay (1777-1852) the elections of 1824, 1832 and 1844; George McClellan (1826-1885) the election of 1864; Samuel Tilden (1814-1886) the election of 1876; William Jennings Bryan (1860-1925) the elections of 1896, 1900 and 1908; Alfred M. Landon (1887-1987) the election of 1936; Thomas E. Dewey (1902-1971) the elections of 1944 and 1948; Adlai Stevenson (1900-1965) the elections of 1952 and 1956; Richard Nixon (1913-1994) and Hubert Humphrey (1911-1978) the elections of 1960 and 1968; Albert Gore (1948-) and George Bush (1946-) the election of 2000
"Covering the period from Aaron Burr's lost election in 1800 to Al Gore's in 2000, this book discusses 10 men who ran for U.S. president and lost. . . . Occasional anecdotes and vivid details enliven the smoothly written text. . . . The black-and-white illustrations include reproductions of period paintings, posters, and political cartoons as well as many photos." Booklist
Includes bibliographical references

Gourse, Leslie
Sophisticated ladies; the great women of jazz; illustrated by Martin French. Dutton Children's Books/Penguin Young Readers Group 2007 64p il $19.99
Grades: 7 8 9 10 11 12   **920**
1. Jazz music 2. Singers 3. Women—Biography
ISBN 978-0-525-47198-1; 0-525-47198-7
      LC 2006-14852
"This lively collective biography of 14 singers begins in the 1920s with Bessie Smith and Ethel Waters and

Gourse, Leslie—*Continued*

moves on through current performers Cassandra Wilson and Diana Krall. A vibrant, full-page portrait opens each chapter, depicting the performer with bold vitality, in a style suggestive of a theater poster." SLJ

Includes discography and bibliographical references

Great Hispanic-Americans; consultant, Nicolas Kanellos; contributing writers, Robert Rodriguez, Tamra Orr. Publications International 2005 128p il $38 *

Grades: 6 7 8 9   920

1. Hispanic Americans—Biography

ISBN 1-4127-1148-7

This "alphabetically arranged compilation showcases 55 diverse Hispanic Americans from a variety of fields who have made an impact on American society. Each person's two-page story is brief and factual, yet the information is presented in a clear and interesting manner. What makes this book even more of a standout is that the individuals highlighted are not the usual people covered in other collective biographies. The excellent-quality photographs and reproductions are abundant and help in capturing the spirit of each person. A great resource." SLJ

Growing up black; from slave days to the present: 25 African-Americans reveal the trials and triumphs of their childhoods; edited by Jay David. [rev ed] Avon Bks. 1992 276p pa $12.50 *

Grades: 6 7 8 9   920

1. African Americans—Biography

ISBN 0-380-76632-9   LC 92-135054

First published 1968 by Morrow

"This compelling collection of autobiographical accounts of 25 African Americans will introduce readers to some of the best black writers—from Frederick Douglass to Audre Lorde, Claude Brown, John Wideman, and Lorene Cary—and will help students write with candor and control about their own memories." Rochman. Against borders

Hacker, Carlotta

Nobel Prize winners. Crabtree 1998 48p il maps (Women in profile) $21.28; pa $8.95

Grades: 3 4 5 6   920

1. Nobel Prizes 2. Women—Biography

ISBN 0-7787-0007-0; 0-7787-0029-1 (pa)

LC 97-53222

Chronicles the lives and achievements of women who have received Nobel Prizes in a variety of fields, including Aung San Suu Kyi, Barbara McClintock, and Nadine Gordimer

Includes glossary and bibliographical references

Hansen, Joyce

Women of hope; African Americans who made a difference; foreword by Moe Foner. Scholastic 1998 31p il hardcover o.p. pa $6.99

Grades: 4 5 6 7   920

1. African American women—Biography

ISBN 0-590-93973-4; 978-0-590-93974-4 (pa); 0-590-93974-2 (pa)   LC 96-32117

"The book developed from a series of posters issued by the Bread and Roses Cultural Project of the National Health and Human Service Employees Union. . . . Hansen has added a clear, readable, and informative single-page commentary for each of the striking black-and-white portraits." SLJ

Includes bibliographical references

Hardy, Sheila Jackson

Extraordinary people of the civil rights movement; by Sheila Jackson Hardy & P. Stephen Hardy. Children's Press 2007 288p il (Extraordinary people) lib bdg $40 *

Grades: 5 6 7 8 9 10   920

1. African Americans—Civil rights 2. African Americans—Biography 3. United States—Race relations

ISBN 0-516-25461-8   LC 2005037533

This "book looks at the achievements of seldom-mentioned leaders of the Civil Rights Movement. . . . In addition to biographical sketches of 61 key individuals and organizations of the era, most of which are accompanied by a black-and-white photograph, the text provides an overview of the events leading up to the movement." SLJ

Includes bibliographical references

Hasday, Judy L., 1957-

Extraordinary women athletes. Children's Press 2000 288p il (Extraordinary people) hardcover o.p. pa $16.95 *

Grades: 5 6 7 8   920

1. Women athletes

ISBN 0-516-21608-2 (lib bdg); 0-516-27039-7 (pa)

LC 99-49335

Presents brief biographies of nearly fifty women athletes from the twentieth century, including Ora Washington, Althea Gibson, Tenley Albright, Wilma Rudolph, Chris Evert, Nancy Lopez Knight, Jackie Joyner-Kersee, and Janet Evans

"Students will find this volume interesting and inspiring because such care is taken to show each athlete's character and drive. . . . List of women's athletic organizations and Web sites; bibliography; index." Book Rep

Haskins, James, 1941-2005

African American entrepreneurs; [by] Jim Haskins. Wiley 1998 184p il (Black stars) *

Grades: 6 7 8 9   920

1. African American businesspeople 2. African Americans—Biography

ISBN 0-471-14576-9   LC 97-37389

The author "has chosen his subjects well. . . . Haskins has done a good job of individualizing his subjects and catching a sense of the enormous obstacles they had to overcome to succeed." Booklist

Includes bibliographical references

African American military heroes; [by] Jim Haskins. Wiley 1998 182p il (Black stars) $24.95

Grades: 6 7 8 9   920

1. African American soldiers 2. United States—Armed forces 3. United States—Military history

ISBN 0-471-14577-7   LC 98-14312

Haskins, James, 1941-2005—Continued

This "volume highlights the lives and contributions of 30 individuals who served in the military from the Revolutionary War to the present day. Well-known figures such as Private Peter Salem, Scout Harriet Tubman, Lieutenant Henry O. Flipper, and General Colin Powell are here as well as others who deserve recognition." SLJ

"The broad coverage makes this an unusual resource for teachers and researchers; there's enough information for middle-graders, and older students can use it as a jumping-off point for deeper studies." Booklist

Includes bibliographical references

African American religious leaders; [by] Jim Haskins and Kathleen Benson. Wiley 2008 162p il (Black stars) lib bdg $24.95

Grades: 6 7 8 9 10 11 12 Adult   **920**
1. African Americans—Biography 2. African Americans—Religion
ISBN 978-0-471-73632-5 (lib bdg); 0-471-73632-5 (lib bdg)   LC 2007-27347

This is a collective biography of "black religious leaders who helped shape the African American experience—from colonial to modern times." Publisher's note

"It's great to have all these figures between two covers, and even a sampling of the entries captures the importance of religion, and its leaders, in African American life." Booklist

Includes bibliographical references

Hatch, Robert

The hero project; 2 teens, 1 notebook, 13 extraordinary interviews; by Robert Hatch and William Hatch. McGraw-Hill 2006 204p pa $14.95

Grades: 6 7 8 9   **920**
1. Heroes and heroines
ISBN 0-07-144904-3   LC 2005017518

Contents: Introduction; Sample letter; Pete Seeger; Madeleine L'Engle; Florence Griffith-Joyner; Jimmy Carter; Orson Scott Card; Yo Yo Ma; Elouise Cobell; Carroll Spinney; Desmond Tutu; Lance Armstrong and Linda Kelly Armstrong; Steven Wozniak; Dolores Huerta; Jackie Chan

This is a collection of interviews by two teenaged brothers with some of their heroes.

"The selections are candid and thoughtful, with the boys asking questions about political and spiritual beliefs as well as queries about childhood heroes and family pets." SLJ

Haven, Kendall F.

100 most popular scientists for young adults; biographical sketches and professional paths; by Kendall Haven and Donna Clark. Libraries Unlimited 1999 526p il (Profiles and pathways series) $59

Grades: 7 8 9 10   **920**
1. Scientists
ISBN 1-56308-674-3   LC 99-13755

"Well-known individuals such as Jacques Cousteau, Sally Ride, and Carl Sagan are assembled here along with unheralded newcomers to the field. One third of the entries are about women and many ethnic groups are represented. . . . A bibliography concludes each entry. Valuable appendixes include an extensive list of Web sites and lists of scientists by their field of specialization. The clear type and attractive layout combined with lively writing, good organization, and curriculum-related content will make the book a useful reference source." SLJ

Includes bibliographical references

Hillstrom, Kevin

American Civil War: biographies; [by] Kevin Hillstrom and Laurie Collier Hillstrom; Lawrence W. Baker, editor. U.X.L 2000 2v il set$110

Grades: 8 9 10 11 12   **920**
1. United States—History—1861-1865, Civil War—Biography
ISBN 0-7876-3820-X   LC 99-46920

This set "chronicles the lives of 60 famous and lesser-known men and women, including abolitionists, spies, commanders, and writers." SLJ

Includes bibliographical references

Vietnam War: biographies; [by] Kevin Hillstrom and Laurie Collier Hillstrom; Diane Sawinski, editor. U.X.L 2001 2v il set$110

Grades: 8 9 10 11 12   **920**
1. Vietnam War, 1961-1975—Biography 2. United States—Biography
ISBN 0-7876-4884-1   LC 00-56378

This "focuses on 60 important figures, including military and political leaders (Spiro Agnew, Ngo Dinh Diem, Pol Pot), activists (Daniel Berrigan, Jane Fonda), writers (Le Ly Hayslip, Tim O'Brien), and prominent veterans (Ron Kovic, John McCain) on both sides of the conflict. . . . A picture of each personality accompanies the informative text." Booklist

Includes bibliographical references

Howes, Kelly King

The roaring twenties biographies; [by] Kelly King Howes. U.X.L 2006 xlvi, 249p (The roaring twenties reference library) $60

Grades: 8 9 10 11 12   **920**
1. United States—Biography 2. United States—History—1919-1933
ISBN 1-4144-0211-2   LC 2005010815

This volume profiles key figures of the 1920s, including people such as Zora Neale Hurston, Rudolph Valentino, Al Capone, Bessie Smith, Babe Ruth, Duke Ellington, Henry Ford and Langston Hughes

Includes bibliographical references

World War II: biographies; [by] Kelly K. Howes; edited by Christine Slovey. U.X.L 1999 xxxiii, 288p il $60

Grades: 8 9 10 11 12   **920**
1. World War, 1939-1945—Biography
ISBN 0-7876-3895-1   LC 99-27166

"In addition to political and military leaders, the 31 alphabetical entries in Biographies include conscientious objector Franz Jaggerstatter, journalists Dorothy Thompson and Ernie Pyle, physicist J. Robert Oppenheimer, and Holocaust victim Edith Stein. The profiles range in length from 6 to 13 pages and most contain at least one

Howes, Kelly King—*Continued*
black-and-white photo. Sidebars cover myriad topics such
as Shintoism and examples of the Navajo code." SLJ
Includes bibliographical references

Jones, Charlotte Foltz, 1945-
Westward ho! eleven explorers of the West; [by]
Charlotte Foltz Jones. Holiday House 2005 233p
bibl il map $22.95
Grades: 5 6 7 8   **920**
1. West (U.S.)—History 2. Explorers
ISBN 0-8234-1586-4   LC 2003-57004
Contents: Robert Gray (1755-1806); George Vancou-
ver (1757-1798); Alexander Mackenzie (1764-1820);
John Colter (1774 or 1775-1813); Zebulon Montgomery
Pike (1779-1813); Stephen Harriman Long (1784-1864);
James Bridger (1804-1881); Jedediah Smith (1799-1831);
Joseph Reddeford Walker (1798-1876); John C. Fremont
(1813-1890); John Wesley Powell (1834-1902)
A collective biography of eleven men who explored
the American West in the 18th and 19th centuries, including ship's officers, fur traders, and Army officers
"Jones makes history a lively endeavor by writing vivid accounts of lives that were sometimes stranger, and
nearly always more exciting, than fiction. . . . Black-
and-white reproductions of period drawings, paintings,
prints, and photos illustrate the text." Booklist
Includes bibliographical references

Kaminsky, Marty
Uncommon champions; fifteen athletes who
battled back. Boyds Mills Press 2000 147p
hardcover o.p. pa $15.95
Grades: 6 7 8 9   **920**
1. Athletes
ISBN 1-56397-787-7; 1-59078-005-1 (pa)
"Kaminsky profiles 15 athletes who have dealt with
adversity (either physical or mental) and fought back.
The subjects, a mix of male and female athletes, represent a variety of sports. . . . A full-page, black-and-
white photo is included for most subjects, a few of
whom are still well known today (Michelle Akers, Chris
Zorich, Zina Garrison)." Booklist

Katz, William Loren
Black pioneers; an untold story. Atheneum Bks.
for Young Readers 1999 193p il maps $19.95
Grades: 8 9 10 11 12   **920**
1. African Americans—History 2. Frontier and pioneer
life 3. Abolitionists 4. Underground railroad
ISBN 0-689-81410-0   LC 98-19104
The author "describes the settlement of the Ohio and
Mississippi Valleys (covering Ohio, Indiana, Illinois,
Michigan, Wisconsin, Minnesota, Iowa, Kansas, and Missouri) by African Americans seeking freedom, including
biographical sketches of men and women who formed
churches, started schools, or were politically active in
their region." SLJ
"The narration is clear, fluid, and enlivened with
quotes from the pioneers themselves." Horn Book Guide
Includes bibliographical references

Kennedy, John F. (John Fitzgerald), 1917-1963
Profiles in courage. HarperCollins Pubs. 2003
xxii, 245p $19.95; pa $13.95
Grades: 7 8 9 10 11 12 Adult   **920**
1. Politicians—United States 2. Courage
ISBN 0-06-053062-6; 0-06-085493-6 (pa)
LC 2003-40676
A reissue of the title first published 1956
This series of profiles of Americans who took coura-
geous stands at crucial moments in public life includes
John Quincy Adams, Daniel Webster, Thomas Hart Ben-
ton, Sam Houston, Edmund G. Ross, Lucius Q. C. La-
mar, George Norris, Robert A. Taft and others.
Includes bibliographical references

Kennedy, Kerry
Speak truth to power; human rights defenders
who are changing our world; photographs by
Eddie Adams; edited by Nan Richardson. Crown
2000 256p il $50
Grades: 7 8 9 10   **920**
1. Human rights
ISBN 0-8129-3062-2   LC 00-34557
"An Umbrage editions book"
This book "is composed of fifty three-page interviews
with people who have made strides in the global fight to
ensure basic human rights for everyone. . . . The Dalai
Lama, Desmond Tutu, and Elie Wiesel are included, but
most subjects are everyday people who have survived
imprisonment, death threats, and torture to bring about
change. . . . Their reports are sad but inspiring. . . . The
haunting photographs and stories are gripping." Voice
Youth Advocates

Kent, Jacqueline, 1947-
Business builders in fashion. Oliver Press
(Minneapolis) 2003 160p il (Business builders) lib
bdg $22.95
Grades: 5 6 7 8   **920**
1. Fashion design 2. Businesspeople
ISBN 1-88150-880-3   LC 2001-59313
"Drawing from a multitude of sources on Charles
Worth, Levi Strauss, Coco Chanel, Christian Dior, Mary
Quant, Ralph Lauren, and Vera Wang, Kent describes
the lives and businesses of these high-profile names in
the industry." SLJ
"This provides a well-focused consideration of a top-
ic." Booklist
Includes glossary and bibliographical references

Kenyon, Karen, 1938-
The Brontë family; passionate literary geniuses;
[by] Karen Smith Kenyon. Lerner Publs. 2003
128p il (Lerner biography) lib bdg $25.26
Grades: 7 8 9 10   **920**
1. Brontë family 2. Authors, English
ISBN 0-8225-0071-X   LC 2001-4957
Contents: Setting the record straight; Storyteller;
Cowan bridge; The twelve soldiers; Roe head; Seeking
and searching; Brussels and after; Never was better stuff
penned; Gone like dreams; Charlotte alone; Charlotte and
Mr. Nicholls

Kenyon, Karen, 1938-—*Continued*

A joint biography of Charlotte, Emily, Branwell, and Anne Bronte, exploring how the siblings sparked creativity in each other and how their lives were woven into their novels

This title is "well-written and solidly researched. . . . A boon for report writers and fascinating pleasure reading as well." SLJ

Includes bibliographical references

Kimmel, Elizabeth Cody

Ladies first; 40 daring American women who were second to none; [by] Elizabeth Cody Kimmel; foreword by Stacy Allison. National Geographic 2006 192p il $18.95

Grades: 5 6 7 8   **920**

1. Women—Biography 2. United States—Biography

ISBN 0-7922-5393-0   LC 2005005113

This offers "introductions to forty of America's most brilliant and courageous women. Each essay is three pages in length and includes a fourth full-page portrait of the woman being introduced. . . . The women chosen achieved greatness in a wide range of endeavors, from athletics to the arts to politics. . . . Students will find these excellent essays useful as an introduction to the women portrayed and as a good jumping off point for further research." Voice Youth Advocates

Includes bibliographical references

The look-it-up book of explorers. Random House 2004 128p il map $17.99; pa $10.99

Grades: 5 6 7 8   **920**

1. Explorers 2. Exploration

ISBN 0-375-92478-7; 0-375-82478-2 (pa)

"Beginning with Leif Ericksson and his trip to Greenland and the Americas to Robert Ballard's 1985 expedition to search for the *Titanic*, the chronlogically arranged spreads give readers a better understanding of how the world was explored. . . . Informative black-and-white photos and reproductions appear throughout. . . . This is an excellent quick resource that will appeal to researchers and general readers alike." SLJ

Knight, Judson

Ancient civilizations: biographies; Stacy McConnell and Lawrence W. Baker, editors. U.X.L 2000 xlvii, 207p il map $60

Grades: 7 8 9 10   **920**

1. Ancient civilization

ISBN 0-7876-3985-0   LC 99-45751

Profiles sixty men and women who shaped the ancient civilizations in Egypt, Mesopotamia, Israel, China, Asia Minor, and other places

"The accessible, alphabetically arranged profiles include black-and-white photos and reproductions. Following each entry is a list of further reading and, sometimes, Web sites." SLJ

Middle ages: biographies; edited by Judy Galens. U.X.L 2000 2v set$110

Grades: 8 9 10 11 12   **920**

1. Middle ages—Biography 2. Medieval civilization

ISBN 0-7876-4857-4   LC 00-64864

Among the 50 people profiled are Eleanor of Aquitaine, Henry the Navigator, Kublai Khan, Montezuma I, and St. Patrick

Each "entry contains illustrations, date spans and pronunciations of names for individuals, sidebars, and a bibliography of books, periodicals, and Web sites." Booklist

Koopmans, Andy

Filmmakers. Lucent Books 2005 112p il (History makers) $28.70

Grades: 7 8 9 10   **920**

1. Motion picture producers and directors

ISBN 1-59018-598-6   LC 2004-12774

Contents: Alfred Hitchcock; Stanley Kubrick; Francis Ford Coppola; Spike Lee; Peter Jackson

"This collective biography . . . focuses on the struggles, successes, and setbacks of five film directors: Alfred Hitchcock, Stanley Kubrick, Francis Ford Coppola, Spike Lee, and Peter Jackson. The subjects are well chosen. . . . These biographies inform about cinema history and have the potential to inspire readers interested in pursuing a career in film." Booklist

Includes bibliographical references

Krull, Kathleen, 1952-

Lives of extraordinary women; rulers, rebels (and what the neighbors thought); written by Kathleen Krull; illustrated by Kathryn Hewitt. Harcourt 2000 95p il $20 *

Grades: 4 5 6 7   **920**

1. Women in politics

ISBN 0-15-200807-1   LC 99-6840

"The subjects range from Cleopatra in ancient Egypt to contemporary activists Wilma Mankiller, Aung San Suu Kyi, and Rigoberta Menchu." Voice Youth Advocates

"Each entry offers a tightly written biography, often filled with delicious anecdote. . . . Each biographical essay is accompanied by one of Hewitt's full-page, full-color caricatures. Both artful and witty, the illustrations provide perfect accompaniments to the often breezy and accessible text." N Y Times Book Rev

Includes bibliographical references

Lives of the presidents; fame, shame (and what the neighbors thought); illustrated by Kathryn Hewitt. Harcourt Brace & Co. 1998 96p il $20 *

Grades: 4 5 6 7   **920**

1. Presidents—United States

ISBN 0-15-200808-X   LC 97-33069

Focuses on the lives of presidents as parents, husbands, pet-owners, and neighbors while also including humorous anecdotes about hairstyles, attitudes, diets, fears, and sleep patterns

"Packed with enough detail for brief reports, these articles are also just plain entertaining. . . . Hewitt's spirited watercolor cartoons add to the presentation immensely." SLJ

Includes bibliographical references

Langley, Wanda, 1939-
Women of the wind; early women aviators; [by] Wanda Langley. Morgan Reynolds Pub. 2006 160p il map lib bdg $26.95
Grades: 6 7 8 9   **920**
  1. Women air pilots
  ISBN 978-1-931798-81-5; 1-931798-81-8
               LC 2005022951
"This collective biography celebrates the accomplishments of nine American women who pioneered in the field of aviation: Harriet Quimby, Katherine Stinson, Ruth Law, Bessie Coleman, Amelia Earhart, Ruth Nichols, Louise Thaden, Anne Morrow Lindbergh, and Jacqueline Cochran. . . . Well reproduced and often in color, the illustrations include a great many photos, as well as maps and period advertisements. . . . Langley . . . offers information, anecdotes, and inspiring stories." Booklist
Includes bibliographical references

Lyman, Darryl, 1944-
Holocaust rescuers; ten stories of courage. Enslow Pubs. 1999 128p il (Collective biographies) lib bdg $26.60
Grades: 6 7 8 9   **920**
  1. World War, 1939-1945—Jews 2. Holocaust, 1933-1945
  ISBN 0-7660-1114-3   LC 98-21584
Discusses the efforts of ten individuals who did what they could to save Jews from the Nazis, including Anna Borkowska, Varian Fry, Irene Gut Opdyke, Mustafa Hardaga, Jorgen Kieler, Oskar Schindler, Andrew Sheptitsky, Sempo Sugihara, Marion van Binsbergen Pritchard, and Raoul Wallenberg
Includes bibliographical references

Major, John S., 1942-
Caravan to America; living arts of the Silk Road; [by] John S. Major and Betty J. Belanus. Cricket Bks. 2002 130p il map $24.95; pa $15.95 *
Grades: 4 5 6 7   **920**
  1. Arts
  ISBN 0-8126-2666-4; 0-8126-2677-X (pa)
               LC 2002-5477
"A Marcato book"
Contents: Qi Shu Fang: Peking opera performer; Doug Kim: Korean American martial artist; Yeshi Dorjee: Tibetan artist-monk; Abdul Khaliq Muradi: Turkmen rug restorer; Tamara Katayev: Bukharan singer; Najmieh Batmanglij: Iranian American cook; La Verne J. Magarian: Armenian American calligrapher and paper artist; Peter Kyvelos, Greek American oud maker
Profiles eight artists and artisans now living in America who are originally from the "Silk Road," an ancient network of caravan trails through which trade goods, ideas, and arts pass between Asia and the Mediterranean
"Full of colorful and informative archival and contemporary photographs and drawings. . . . Each person's story is told in an interesting manner, and information about their specialty and its history is woven throughout the text. . . . Not only is the work informative, but it is handsome as well." SLJ
Includes glossary and bibliographical references

Maydell, Natalie
Extraordinary women from the Muslim world; [by] Natalie Maydell and Sep Riah; paintings by Heba Amin. Global Content Publishing 2008 117p il map $16.95 *
Grades: 5 6 7 8   **920**
  1. Muslim women 2. Women—Biography
  ISBN 978-0-97999-010-6; 0-97999-010-6
This "is an illustrative introduction to 13 Muslim women in history who have lived extraordinary lives and influenced their communities in a positive way, often overcoming extreme hardship and inaccurate stereotypes that have been placed on the role of women in Islam." Publisher's note

Meltzer, Milton, 1915-
Ten kings; and the worlds they ruled; illustrated by Bethanne Andersen. Orchard Bks. 2002 132p il map $21.95 *
Grades: 5 6 7 8   **920**
  1. Kings and rulers
  ISBN 0-439-31293-0   LC 2001-33202
This "volume comprises biographies of ten legendary leaders, including Hammurabi, Alexander the Great, Attila, Kublai Khan, and Peter the Great. Meltzer's sources for discussing these lives and their cultural contexts are impeccable, and he writes knowledgeably and thoughtfully." Horn Book Guide
Includes bibliographical references

Ten queens; portraits of women of power; illustrated by Bethanne Andersen. Dutton Children's Bks. 1998 134p il map pa $14.99 *
Grades: 5 6 7 8   **920**
  1. Queens
  ISBN 0-525-47158-8 (pa); 0-525-45643-0 (hc)
               LC 97-36428
"The 10 women Meltzer showcases are Esther, Cleopatra, Boudicca, Zenobia, Eleanor of Aquitaine, Isabella of Spain, Elizabeth I, Christine of Sweden, Maria Theresa, and Catherine the Great." Booklist
Meltzer "has a storyteller's flair and an eye for the small details and anecdotes that bring these queens to life. . . . Colorful expressionistic paintings, boldly stroked onto unframed panels, enrich the pages." SLJ
Includes bibliographical references

Mendoza, Patrick M.
Extraordinary people in extraordinary times; heroes, sheroes, and villains. Libraries Unlimited 1999 142p il pa $21
Grades: 7 8 9 10   **920**
  1. United States—Biography
  ISBN 1-56308-611-5   LC 99-14238
Stories of little-known historical characters from American history. Subjects range from that of the first woman to receive the Congressional Medal of Honor to the first woman to be hanged in the United States. Jeanette Rankin, Jose Marti and two survivors of the Sand Creek Massacre are among those profiled
Includes bibliographical references

Mour, Stanley I.

American jazz musicians. Enslow Pubs. 1998 128p il (Collective biographies) lib bdg $26.60

Grades: 6 7 8 9   **920**

1. Jazz musicians 2. Jazz music

ISBN 0-7660-1027-9   LC 97-27173

Profiles ten notable jazz musicians, including Louis Armstrong, John Coltrane, Miles Davis, Duke Ellington and Wynton Marsalis

Includes discography and bibliographical references

Nardo, Don, 1947-

Great Elizabethan playwrights. Lucent Bks. 2003 112p il (Lucent library of historical eras, Elizabethan England) lib bdg $27.45

Grades: 6 7 8 9   **920**

1. English drama—History and criticism 2. Dramatists 3. Theater—History 4. Great Britain—History—1485-1603, Tudors

ISBN 1-59018-017-8   LC 2001-6602

Contents: Introduction: Birth of the English-speaking theater; "On Your Imaginary Forces Work": the Elizabethan theater; The courtly dreamer: John Lyly; Father of the revenge tragedy: Thomas Kyd; Poet of pageant and drama: George Peele; A man at war within himself: Robert Greene; Risk-taker and mystery-maker: Christopher Marlowe; A playwright for all time: William Shakespeare; Shrewd critic of human follies: Ben Jonson

Discusses the origins of English-speaking theater and includes facts about seven early Elizabethan playwrights, including William Shakespeare

Includes bibliographical references

Nathan, Amy

Meet the dancers; from ballet, broadway, and beyond. Henry Holt 2008 231p il $18.95

Grades: 5 6 7 8   **920**

1. Dancers 2. Dance

ISBN 978-0-8050-8071-1; 0-8050-8071-6

                LC 2007-27589

"This collective biography reveals the paths that 16 diverse dancers followed to become professionals and to join prestigious companies. . . . The tone of the text is conversational. . . . The pictures dramatically capture how talented these performers are. Anyone, whether considering a career in dance or not, will be inspired and educated by these up-close-and-personal accounts." SLJ

Open the unusual door; true life stories of challenge, adventure, and success by black Americans; edited and with an introduction by Barbara Summers. Graphia 2005 206p pa $7.99

Grades: 7 8 9 10   **920**

1. African Americans—Biography

ISBN 0-618-58531-1

"A wonderful cross section of excerpts from published autobiographies. The 16 stories tell of challenges met and opportunities recognized and realized. Colin Powell's recollection of his introduction to the military life at City College in New York City stands alongside Russell Simmons's retelling of the turning point in his life when, at 16 years of age, he shot at and missed a fellow drug dealer. . . . This little gem of a book should be a first purchase for public and school libraries." SLJ

Orgill, Roxane

Shout, sister, shout! the girl singers who shaped a century. Margaret K. McElderry Bks. 2001 148p il hardcover o.p. pa $12.95 *

Grades: 6 7 8 9   **920**

1. Popular music 2. Singers

ISBN 0-689-81991-9; 978-1-4169-6391-2 (pa); 1-4169-6391-X (pa)   LC 99-54374

"The lives of ten 'girl singers,' representing different genres of popular music, from vaudeville to blues to jazz to country, are arranged by decade. Profiles of Sophie Tucker, Ma Rainey, Bessie Smith, Ethel Merman, Judy Garland, Anita O'Day, Joan Baez, Bette Midler, Madonna, and Lucinda Williams are included." Voice Youth Advocates

Includes discography and bibliographical references

Ottaviani, Jim

Dignifying science: stories about women scientists; written by Jim Ottaviani and illustrated by Donna Barr [et. al.] 2nd ed. G. T. Labs 2003 142p il pa $16.95 *

Grades: 6 7 8 9 10 11 12   **920**

1. Graphic novels 2. Women scientists—Graphic novels 3. Biographical graphic novels

ISBN 0-9660106-4-7   LC 2003-91534

Ottaviani provides biographical sketches of women scientists such as Lise Meitner, Rosalind Franklin, Barbara McClintock, and Hedy Lamarr (yes, the actress was also an inventor); all the stories are illustrated by women comics artists, including Lea Hernandez, Linda Medley, Anne Timmons, and others

Outman, James L., 1946-

Industrial Revolution: biographies; [by] James L. Outman, Elisabeth M. Outman. U.X.L 2003 218p il (Industrial revolution reference library) $55

Grades: 8 9 10 11 12   **920**

1. Industrial revolution

ISBN 0-7876-6514-2   LC 2002-155421

Contents: Henry Bessemer; Andrew Carnegie; Henry Ford; Robert Fulton; Samuel Gompers; Jay Gould; James J. Hill; Mother Jones; Karl Marx; Rockefeller; Theodore Roosevelt; Adam Smith; George Stephenson; Ida Tarbell; James Watt; George Westinghouse; Eli Whitney

"The 25 essays in {this volume} provide biographical information with an emphasis on each person's contribution or impact on the Industrial Revolution. . . . More than 50 black-and-white photographs complement the text. . . . This is an excellent adjunct to American and world history units and classes on economics and labor movements." Booklist

Includes bibliographical references

Pendergast, Tom, 1964-

Westward expansion: biographies. U.X.L 2001 xxv, 251p il maps $60

Grades: 8 9 10 11 12   **920**

1. Frontier and pioneer life 2. West (U.S.)—Biography

ISBN 0-7876-4863-9   LC 00-109475

This collective biography profiles a number of legendary figures of the Wild West, including Buffalo Bill, George Custer, Wyatt Earp, Kit Carson, Annie Oakley, Andrew Jackson, Sarah Winnemucca, and Belle Starr

Pendergast, Tom, 1964- — *Continued*

World War I: biographies; [by] Tom Pendergast and Sara Pendergast; Christine Slovey, editor. U.X.L 2002 183p il $58

Grades: 8 9 10 11 12   920
1. World War, 1914-1918—Biography
ISBN 0-7876-5477-9   LC 2001-53162

A collection of thirty biographies of world figures who played important roles in World War I, including Mata Hari, T.E. Lawrence, and Alvin C. York

Includes bibliographical references

Pinkney, Andrea Davis

Let it shine; stories of Black women freedom fighters; illustrated by Stephen Alcorn. Harcourt 2000 107p il $20 *

Grades: 4 5 6 7   920
1. African American women—Biography 2. African Americans—Civil rights 3. United States—Race relations
ISBN 0-15-201005-X   LC 99-42806
"Gulliver books"

This "collective biography tells of 10 extraordinary black women. From Sojourner Truth to Shirley Chisholm, this is also a view of African American history through individual lives. . . . Stephen Alcorn's allegorical oil portraits are dramatic and beautiful. . . . The immediacy of the text and the spacious design of the large volume make this a natural for reading aloud." Booklist

Includes bibliographical references

Pioneers of human rights; Cheryl Fisher Phibbs, book editor. Greenhaven Press 2005 240p il (Profiles in history) lib bdg $34.95

Grades: 7 8 9 10   920
1. Political activists 2. Human rights
ISBN 0-7377-2146-4   LC 2003-68585

"This collective biography focuses on human rights activists, with lengthy sections on Mohandas Gandhi and Nelson Mandela and chapters on Iqbal Masih, Eleanor Roosevelt, Frederick Douglass, Natasia Kandic (fighter against abuse in Serbia and Kosovo), and others. . . . The personal stories about courageous resistance that changed the world will draw activist teens as well as students researching the history." Booklist

Includes bibliographical references

Pouy, Jean-Bernard, 1946-

The big book of dummies, rebels and other geniuses; [by] Jean-Bernard Pouy & Serge Bloch; Anne Blanchard. 1st American ed. Enchanted Lion Books 2008 123p il $19.95

Grades: 6 7 8 9   920
1. Reference books 2. Celebrities 3. Biography—Dictionaries
ISBN 978-1-59270-103-2; 1-59270-103-5
                                      LC 2008-12278

Original French edition, 2006

"Pouy offers a wide variety of biographical sketches of famous names . . . from Charlie Chaplin to Louis Armstrong and Albert Einstein. The author nicely makes sure to include little-known details. . . . [This book] will sell itself." Voice Youth Advocates

Includes bibliographical references

Price-Groff, Claire

Extraordinary women journalists. Childrens Press 1997 272p il (Extraordinary people) lib bdg $39 *

Grades: 5 6 7 8   920
1. Women journalists
ISBN 0-516-20474-2   LC 96-50341

Profiles the life and work of notable women journalists, including Sarah Hale, Margaret Fuller, and Nellie Bly

"Chapters are short but full of useful information and are accompanied by large black-and-white photos. Because these women's chosen field intersects with so many other subjects, students learn about American and world history, politics, and culture as they read these short biographies. . . . Good for reports or leisure reading." SLJ

Includes glossary and bibliographical references

Twentieth-century women political leaders. Facts on File 1998 142p il (Global profiles) $25

Grades: 7 8 9 10   920
1. Women politicians 2. Women in politics
ISBN 0-8160-3672-1   LC 97-32373

Presents biographies of twelve women who have held positions of political leadership around the world, including Golda Meir, Margaret Thatcher, Winnie Mandela, Corazon Aquino, Wilma Mankiller, and Benazir Bhutto

"The detailed index provides easy points of access for students doing research, and the variety of women included make this title a useful reference resource." SLJ

Includes bibliographical references

Reed, Jennifer

The Saudi royal family; [by] Jennifer Bond Reed. Chelsea House Publishers 2007 120p il (Modern world leaders) lib bdg $30

Grades: 6 7 8 9 10   920
1. Saudi Arabia—Kings and rulers
ISBN 978-0-7910-9218-7; 0-7910-9218-6
                                      LC 2006-10613

First published 2003 by Chelsea House in the series: Major world leaders

"Reed profiles each of the five Saudi kings, beginning with King Abdul Aziz and ending with the current leader, King Fahd." SLJ

This book "deciphers the nuances of Islamic law, an integral part of the Arabian peninsula's history. Tumultuous and violent times are recorded, and democratic-like changes are chronicled as well. The result is as neutral and evenhanded an approach as a Westerner can use to describe this succession of Arab leaders." Libr Media Connect

Includes bibliographical references

Renaissance & Reformation: biographies; Peggy Saari & Aaron Saari, editors. U.X.L 2002 2v il set$105

Grades: 8 9 10 11 12   920
1. Renaissance
ISBN 0-7876-5470-1   LC 2001-8609

Renaissance & Reformation: biographies—*Continued*

Profiles fifty people who played a significant role during the Renaissance and Reformation periods in Europe, including John Calvin, Peter Paul Rubens, Catherine de Medici, and Johannes Kepler

Includes bibliographical references

Reynolds, Moira Davison

American women scientists; 23 inspiring biographies, 1900-2000. McFarland & Co. 1999 149p il hardcover o.p. pa $24.95

Grades: 7 8 9 10   **920**
  1. Women scientists
  ISBN 0-7864-0649-6; 0-7864-2161-4 (pa)
                                    LC 99-14603
"Four-to-six page profiles of 23 of the century's premier women scientists, representing a wide variety of disciplines. The entries are arranged chronologically beginning with Cornelia Clapp (1849-1934) and ending with Mary Good (1931-). . . . Each entry includes a black-and-white portrait." SLJ

Includes bibliographical references

Richie, Jason, 1966-

Space flight; crossing the last frontier. Oliver Press (Minneapolis) 2002 144p il (Innovators) lib bdg $21.95

Grades: 5 6 7 8   **920**
  1. Scientists 2. Space flight
  ISBN 1-881508-77-3   LC 2001-36507
Profiles seven engineers and scientists who made space flight possible, including Robert Goddard, Sergei Korolev, and Wernher von Braun

"The biographies are readable, entertaining, and informative." SLJ

Includes glossary and bibliographical references

Roberts, Russell, 1953-

Leaders and generals. Lucent Bks. 2001 112p il (American war library, Vietnam War) lib bdg $27.45

Grades: 7 8 9 10   **920**
  1. Vietnam War, 1961-1975—Biography
  ISBN 1-56006-717-9   LC 00-12859
"Roberts covers the principal civilian and military leaders who were involved in the Vietnam War: Ho Chi Minh, Ngo Dinh Diem, Lyndon B. Johnson, William Westmoreland, Richard Nixon, and Henry Kissinger. Personal and political details combine to give insight into the personality, successes, and failures of each man." SLJ

Includes bibliographical references

Robinson Masters, Nancy

Extraordinary patriots of the United States of America; Colonial times to pre-Civil War; [by] Nancy Robinson Masters. Children's Press 2005 288p il (Extraordinary people) $40 *

Grades: 5 6 7 8   **920**
  1. United States—Biography
  ISBN 0-516-24404-3   LC 2004030940

"This book provides biographical sketches of dozens of individuals and groups of people. The three to five-page sketches are arranged chronologically by the patriot's birth year, beginning with Benjamin Franklin and ending with Sam Houston. . . . Although these sketches are very brief, they are interesting and readable." SLJ

Includes bibliographical references

Ross, Stewart

Leaders of World War II. Raintree Steck-Vaughn Pubs. 2000 64p il (World Wars) lib bdg $32.79

Grades: 5 6 7 8   **920**
  1. World War, 1939-1945—Biography
  ISBN 0-7398-2756-1   LC 00-59216
This profiles Winston Churchill, Franklin Roosevelt, Joseph Stalin, Adolph Hitler, Dwight D. Eisenhower, George S. Patton, Bernard L. Montgomery, Georgii Zhukov, Erwin Rommel, Hideki Tojo, and Benito Mussolini

"Captioned black-and-white photographs, original documents, maps, and sidebars border the clear and engaging text." Horn Book Guide

Includes glossary and bibliographical references

Rubel, David

Scholastic encyclopedia of the presidents and their times; with a foreword by James M. McPherson. updated. Scholastic Reference 2009 246p il map $21.99 *

Grades: 5 6 7 8   **920**
  1. Presidents—United States
  ISBN 978-0-545-10149-3; 0-545-10149-2
First published 1994
This reference "documents the tenure of each of the American presidents. It also includes information about the headlines, people, and fads that were defining America during each presidency. . . . Each profile includes a fact box that lists the president's birthday, birthplace, vice president, wife, children, and nickname." Publisher's note

"This is an attractive, inexpensive resource . . . providing concise information in an easy-to-read format." Booklist [review of 1997 edition]

Scandiffio, Laura

Evil masters; the frightening world of tyrants. Annick Press 2005 230p il map $24.95; pa $12.95

Grades: 7 8 9 10   **920**
  1. Dictators
  ISBN 1-55037-895-3; 1-55037-894-5 (pa)
This "title examines the lives and reigns of seven rulers. The profiles range from the frightening ancient world of the first emperor of China and Nero, emperor of Rome during the first century, to Ivan the Terrible and Robespierre. More recent rulers include Hitler, Stalin, and Saddam Hussein. . . . Maps, photos, reproductions, and half-page fact boxes make the events easier to understand. . . . This is an excellent and thought-provoking resource." SLJ

Includes bibliographical references

Schmittroth, Linda

American Revolution: biographies; [by] Linda Schmittroth and Mary Kay Rosteck; Stacy A. McConnell, editor. U.X.L 2000 2v il set$110

Grades: 7 8 9 10 11 12   **920**

1. United States—History—1775-1783, Revolution 2. United States—Biography

ISBN 0-7876-3792-0   LC 99-46941

Profiles sixty men and women who were key players on the British or American side of the American Revolution, from John Adams, who became the second president, to Eliza Wilkinson, who wrote of the day British soldiers looted her South Carolina home

Includes bibliographical references

Shipton, Alyn

Jazz makers; vanguards of sound. Oxford Univ. Press 2002 263p il (Oxford profiles) $39.95

Grades: 7 8 9 10   **920**

1. Jazz musicians 2. Jazz music

ISBN 0-19-512689-0   LC 2001-53148

"The book is divided into six sections that represent particular jazz styles or eras. Each section contains biographies of musicians who played a significant role in the development of jazz during that period. . . . The introductions and biographies are written in a lively style, which includes personal glimpses, quotations, and anecdotes." Libr Media Connect

Includes discography and bibliographical references

Sills, Leslie

In real life: six women photographers. Holiday House 2000 80p il $19.95; pa $9.95 *

Grades: 7 8 9 10   **920**

1. Women photographers

ISBN 0-8234-1498-1; 0-8234-1752-5 (pa)

     LC 99-51832

"The book explores the lives of Imogen Cunningham, Dorothea Lange, Lola Alvarez Bravo, Carrie Mae Weems, Elsa Dorfman, and Cindy Sherman. . . . Each artist is featured in a clearly written, easy-to-understand chapter, and the chapters include numerous and excellent examples of each artist's work, in both color and b&w." Book Rep

Includes bibliographical references

Sinnott, Susan

Extraordinary Asian Americans and Pacific Islanders. rev ed. Children's Press 2003 288p il (Extraordinary people) lib bdg $39; pa $16.95 *

Grades: 5 6 7 8   **920**

1. Asian Americans—Biography

ISBN 0-516-22655-X (lib bdg); 0-516-29355-9 (pa)

     LC 2002-11220

First published 1993 with title: Extraordinary Asian-Pacific Americans

Biographical sketches of notable Asian Americans and Pacific Islander Americans, from the nineteenth century up to the present

"This well-written resource is accompanied by black-and-white photographs, and will be useful for both browsers and report writers." SLJ

Includes bibliographical references

Spitz, Bob

Yeah! yeah! yeah! the Beatles, Beatlemania, and the music that changed the world. Little, Brown 2007 234p il $18.99

Grades: 7 8 9 10   **920**

1. Beatles 2. Rock musicians

ISBN 978-0-316-11555-1; 0-316-11555-X

     LC 2006-39575

Based on the author's title for adults: The Beatles (2005)

This is "packed with all the fun and fabulousness that were the Beatles. The book begins at the church festival where John and Paul met as teens, and ends with Paul's formal declaration to leave the group. . . . [This is] comprehensive, sensitive to its subjects, and told with a flow that carries readers along. Many smartly chosen black-and-white photographs help re-create the times." Booklist

Staeger, Rob

Ancient mathematicians. Morgan Reynolds Pub. 2006 112p il map (Profiles in mathematics) $28.95

Grades: 7 8 9 10   **920**

1. Mathematicians 2. Greece—Biography 3. Mathematics—History

ISBN 978-1-59935-065-3; 1-59935-065-3

     LC 2008-7533

"After a brief overview of the role of mathematics in ancient Greece, the book profiles Pythagoras, Euclid, Archimedes, and Hypatia. The presentation is greatly enhanced by full-color maps, reproductions, and artifacts, as well as numerous sidebars, diagrams, and time lines." SLJ

Includes bibliographical references

Stille, Darlene R., 1942-

Extraordinary women of medicine. Childrens Press 1997 288p il (Extraordinary people) lib bdg $39; pa $16.95 *

Grades: 5 6 7 8   **920**

1. Women physicians 2. Women in medicine

ISBN 0-516-20307-X (lib bdg); 0-516-26145-2 (pa)

     LC 96-43196

Presents biographical sketches highlighting the contributions of women, mostly American, to the field of medicine in the nineteenth and twentieth centuries

"The thick volume, which spans two centuries of history, is made user-friendly by large type, occasional black-and-white photographs, and short biographical chapters." Booklist

Includes glossary and bibliographical references

Streissguth, Thomas

Legendary labor leaders. Oliver Press (Minneapolis) 1998 160p il (Profiles) $19.95

Grades: 7 8 9 10   **920**

1. Labor movement

ISBN 1-881508-44-7   LC 97-29017

Traces the history of the labor movement in the United States through brief biographies of labor leaders: Samuel Gompers, Eugene Debs, William Haywood, "Mother" Jones, John Lewis, A. Philip Randolph, Jimmy Hoffa, and Cesar Chavez

Includes bibliographical references

Sullivan, Otha Richard, 1941-

African American inventors; Jim Haskins, general editor. Wiley 1998 164p il (Black stars) $24.95 *

Grades: 5 6 7 8   920

1. African American inventors

ISBN 0-471-14804-0   LC 97-46932

Profiles the lives of twenty-five African American inventors who made significant scientific contributions from the eighteenth century to modern times

This is "a particularly engaging book to read; Sullivan highlights those aspects of the subjects' lives that will interest readers the most and writes about them with insight. The book is attractive, too, with lots of historical engravings and photographs." Booklist

Includes bibliographical references

African American millionaires. John Wiley & Sons 2004 c2005 158p il (Black stars) $24.95

Grades: 6 7 8 9   920

1. African Americans—Biography

ISBN 0-471-46928-9   LC 2004-14694

This profiles 25 African American millionaires

"Sullivan offers an exemplary compilation of a relatively unexplored subject area. . . . The book is well organized, highly readable, and inspiring." SLJ

Includes bibliographical references

African American women scientists and inventors; Jim Haskins, general editor. Wiley 2002 150p il (Black stars) $24.95 *

Grades: 6 7 8 9   920

1. African American inventors 2. Women scientists 3. African American women—Biography

ISBN 0-471-38707-X   LC 2001-17924

This profiles 25 African American women "such as Ellen Elgin, who invented the clothes-wringer in the 1880s; Madame C.J. Walker, who produced her secret haircare formula; and Dr. Jane Wright, who worked in the field of cancer tissue studies and was the first woman elected president of the New York Cancer Society. These historical biographies . . . provide a unique glimpse into the struggle of the African-American woman." Book Rep

Includes bibliographical references

Tate, Eleanora E., 1948-

African American musicians; Jim Haskins, general editor. Wiley 2000 70p il (Black stars) $24.95 *

Grades: 6 7 8 9   920

1. African American musicians

ISBN 0-471-25356-1   LC 99-51360

"Many genres and skills are represented from spirituals, gospel, ragtime, blues, jazz, and soul. Scott Joplin, Marian Anderson, Duke Ellington, and Aretha Franklin are here as well as Michael Jackson and a few lesser-known individuals. Each entry includes a black-and-white photo or reproduction and sidebars on pertinent topics." SLJ

Includes bibliographical references

Tessitore, John

Extraordinary American writers; [by] John Tessitore. Children's Press 2004 288p il (Extraordinary people) $40

Grades: 5 6 7 8   920

1. Authors, American 2. American literature—History and criticism

ISBN 0-516-22656-8   LC 2003-4445

Profiles over sixty United States authors representing different eras, cultures, and genres who have made their mark in history, including Benjamin Franklin, Emily Dickinson, and W.E.B. DuBois

"This book is a solid addition to any collective-biography collection as well as a good starting point for research on these authors." SLJ

Thimmesh, Catherine

Girls think of everything; illustrated by Melissa Sweet. Houghton Mifflin 2000 57p $16; pa $6.95 *

Grades: 5 6 7 8   920

1. Women inventors 2. Inventions

ISBN 0-395-93744-2; 0-618-19563-7 (pa)

LC 99-36270

"Ten women and two girls are given a few pages each. Included are Mary Anderson, who invented the windshield wiper (after she was told it wouldn't work); Ruth Wakefield, who, by throwing chunks of chocolate in her cookie batter, gave Toll House cookies to the world; and young Becky Schroeder, who invented Glo-paper because she wanted to write in the dark. The text is written in a fresh, breezy manner, but it is the artwork that is really outstanding." Booklist

Uschan, Michael V., 1948-

Political leaders. Lucent Bks. 2003 112p il map (American war library, Cold War) $27.45

Grades: 7 8 9 10   920

1. Cold war

ISBN 1-59018-211-1   LC 2002-1837

This profiles Cold War political leaders, Joseph Stalin, Harry Truman, Mao Tse-tung, John F. Kennedy, Ho Chi Minh, Ronald Reagan, and Fidel Castro

Includes bibliographical references

Yolen, Jane

Sea queens; women pirates around the world; illustrated by Christine Joy Pratt. Charlesbridge 2008 103p il $18.95

Grades: 4 5 6 7   920

1. Women pirates

ISBN 978-1-58089-131-8; 1-58089-131-4

LC 2007026983

This offers "12 portraits of sword-swinging, seafaring women throughout history, from Artemisia, in 500 B.C.E. Persia, to Madame Ching, an early nineteenth-century Chinese woman and named here as 'the most successful pirate in the world.' . . . The scratchboard illustrations work well as portraits. . . . The book is filled with fascinating, dramatically told stories and sidebars." Booklist

Includes bibliographical references

Zarin, Cynthia
Saints among the animals; illustrated by Leonid Gore. Atheneum Books for Young Readers 2006 88p il $17.95
Grades: 4 5 6 7 **920**
1. Christian saints
ISBN 978-0-689-85031-8; 0-689-85031-X
LC 2004-7259
"A Richard Jackson book"
This tells the "stories of 10 saints, most living in the Dark Ages, and their often miraculous relationship with animals. The most famous is Saint Francis and the oft-told tale of how he dealt with the wolf of Gubbio. There are also stories of Saint Werburge, an English abbess who takes on troublesome geese; Saint Kenneth, a mis-shapen young man saved by birds; and Saint Hilda, who tames an infestation of snakes. . . . The tales are neatly told, and the book's effective format-tall, with handsome charcoal artwork-is a pleasure to hold in hand." Booklist

920.003 Dictionaries, encyclopedias, concordances of biography as a discipline

African American biography. U.X.L 1994-2001 7v (African American reference library) v1-4 set$215; v5, 6, 7 ea $60
Grades: 7 8 9 10 11 12 **920.003**
1. African Americans—Biography—Dictionaries 2. Reference books
ISBN 0-8103-9234-8 (v1-4); 0-7876-3562-6 (v5); 0-7876-3563-4 (v6); 0-7876-3564-2 (v7)
LC 93-45651
"Individuals were selected from sports, entertainment, politics, literature, religion, and science areas as well as from history. For each person there is a picture, a quote, a summary significance, a life history which emphasizes their career. Controversy is not ignored. . . . A classified index to all volumes is in each volume. This is an attractive and useful set." Safford. Guide to Ref Materials for Sch Libr Media Cent. 5th edition

Almanac of famous people; a comprehensive reference guide to more than 39,000 famous and infamous newsmakers from biblical times to the present; project editor, Jennifer Mossman. 9th ed. Thomson Gale 2007 2v set $232
Grades: 7 8 9 10 11 12 Adult **920.003**
1. Biography—Dictionaries 2. Reference books
ISBN 978-1-41441-241-2; 1-41441-241-X
First published 1981 with title: Biography almanac
This is a reference "source for biographical information on more than 30,000 famous individuals and groups. Entries provide: subject's best-known name, complete name, nickname, name of group; dates and places of birth and death (when appropriate); nationality and occupation. Most entries include citations to sources that provide additional biographical information. Four indexes [are included]: geographic, occupation, chronological index by date and chronological index by year." Publisher's note

American authors, 1600-1900; a biographical dictionary of American literature; edited by Stanley J. Kunitz and Howard Haycraft. Wilson, H.W. 1938 846p il (Authors series) $120
Grades: 8 9 10 11 12 Adult **920.003**
1. Authors, American—Dictionaries 2. American literature—Bio-bibliography 3. Reference books
ISBN 0-8242-0001-2
"Complete in one volume with 1300 biographies and 400 portraits." Title page
"This volume contains biographies of 1,300 authors who contributed to the development of American literature, from the founding of Jamestown (1607) to the end of the nineteenth century. Each essay describes the author's life, discusses past and present significance, and evaluates principal works." Safford. Guide to Ref Materials for Sch Media Cent. 5th edition

American Indian biographies; edited by Carole Barrett, Harvey Markowitz, project editor, R. Kent Rasmussen. rev ed. Salem Press 2005 623p il map (Magill's choice) $62
Grades: 8 9 10 11 12 Adult **920.003**
1. Native Americans—Biography 2. Reference books
ISBN 1-58765-233-1; 978-1-58765-233-2
LC 2004-28872
First published 1999; some essays originally appeared in Dictionary of world biography, Great lives from history: the Renaissance & early modern era, 1454-1600 (2005), and American ethnic writers (2000)
"The book contains essays on religious, social, and political leaders; warriors; and reformers from the past as well as modern activists, writers, artists, entertainers, scientists, and athletes. . . . A great bargain and an asset in any library that supports an American history curriculum." Booklist
Includes bibliographical references

American men & women of science; a biographical directory of today's leaders in physical, biological and related sciences. 25th ed. Gale Group 2008 8v set$1530.75
Grades: 8 9 10 11 12 Adult **920.003**
1. Scientists—Dictionaries 2. Reference books
ISSN 0192-8570
ISBN 1-4144-3291-7; 978-1-4144-3291-5
Also available eBook version
Irregular. First published 1906 by Science Press with title: American men of science. Some editions were divided into two sections: Physical and biological sciences and Social sciences
"Brief biographical sketches of . . . scientists and engineers active in the United States and Canada. Arranged alphabetically, with discipline index." Ref Sources for Small & Medium-sized Libr. 6th edition

American presidents in world history; [by] Creative Media Applications. Greenwood Press 2003 5v il (Middle school reference) set$200
Grades: 6 7 8 9 **920.003**
1. Presidents—United States 2. United States—Politics and government 3. United States—Foreign relations 4. Reference books
ISBN 0-313-32564-2
LC 2002-35205

American presidents in world history—*Continued*

Contents: v1 George Washington to Martin Van Buren; v2 William Henry Harrison to Abraham Lincoln; v3 Andrew Johnson to William H. Taft; v4 Woodrow Wilson to John F. Kennedy; v5 Lyndon B. Johnson to George W. Bush

This set "examines each president's actions and policies from a global perspective. . . . With its unique emphasis on foreign relations, *American Presidents in World History* is a wonderful supplement to reference sources." Booklist

Includes bibliographical references

Biography today; profiles of people of interest to young readers. Omnigraphics apply to publisher for subscription options   **920.003**
1. Biography—Periodicals
ISSN 1058-2347

Three issues a year with bound annual cumulations. First published 1992

"This periodical provides short, biographical profiles of people of current interest. Four-to-six page entries are arranged alphabetically. . . . There is at least one photograph of the subject, a contact address, and a bibliography of accessible books and articles. . . . Useful name, subject, and place of birth indexes will cumulate with each new issue. Written in a friendly, almost chatty tone, the profiles offer quick and objective information." SLJ

Current biography yearbook, 2008; editor, Clifford Thompson; senior editors, Miriam Helbok, Mari Rich. 69th annual cumulation. Wilson, H.W. 2008 il $175
Grades: 8 9 10 11 12 Adult   **920.003**
1. Biography—Periodicals
ISSN 0084-9499
ISBN 978-0-8242-1095-3

Also available online; Current biography: cumulated index, 1940-2005 available $90 (ISBN 0-8242-1054-9)

Annual. First published 1940 with title: Current biography

Also issued monthly except December at a subscription price of $175 per year (ISSN 0011-3344). Yearbooks 1940-2003 available ea $160; yearbooks 2004-2006 available ea $175

"Biographies of prominent people written in lively, popular prose. Emphasis is on entertainers, star athletes, politicians, and other celebrities. Series is cumulative, with biographies revised and updated occasionally. Each volume has seven-year index." N Y Public Libr Book of How & Where to Look It Up

Eighth book of junior authors and illustrators; edited by Connie C. Rockman. Wilson, H.W. 2000 592p il $110 *
Grades: Professional   **920.003**
1. Authors—Dictionaries 2. Illustrators—Dictionaries 3. Children's literature—Bio-bibliography 4. Reference books
ISBN 0-8242-0968-0   LC 99-86615

This volume contains "information about 202 current authors and illustrators of books for children and young adults. In addition to the many fresh voices, the book contains revised entries on 15 artists and writers, such as

Tom Feelings, Beverly Cleary, and Charlotte Zolotow, whose works continue to have an impact." SLJ

Includes bibliographical references

Ergas, G. Aimée

Artists: from Michelangelo to Maya Lin. U.X.L 1995-2001 4v il 4v set$215; 2v sets [vols 1 & 2 or vol 3 & 4] ea $110 *
Grades: 6 7 8 9   **920.003**
1. Artists—Biography 2. Reference books
ISBN 0-8103-9862-1 (v1&2); 0-7876-5363-2 (v3 & 4)
LC 95-186053

"Biographies of 62 artists, arranged alphabetically. . . . The scope of the work concentrates on North America and Europe from the Renaissance to the present. Each 5-10 page entry contains a portrait of the artist, birth and death dates, and a quote by or about the subject. There are nearly 140 black-and-white illustrations throughout. Each volume begins with an index of artists by field and media (architecture, cartoons, ceramics, etc.); a timeline; and a glossary of key art terms. As an introductory text, this title is useful for students since the focus is on the individual rather than an artistic movement or period." SLJ [review of vol 1 & 2]

Explorers; from ancient times to the space age; consulting editors, John Logan Allen, E. Julius Dasch, Barry M. Gough. Macmillan Ref. USA 1999 3v il maps set$370
Grades: 5 6 7 8   **920.003**
1. Explorers—Dictionaries 2. Reference books
ISBN 0-02-864893-5   LC 98-8809

"This set profiles 333 world explorers, including cartographers, merchants, navigators, botanists, archaeologists, treasure hunters, and astronauts. . . . Well-selected, high-quality black-and-white portraits and maps abound. . . . This is a solid resource with considerable browsing appeal." SLJ

Explorers & discoverers; from Alexander the Great to Sally Ride; [edited by] Peggy Saari, Daniel B. Baker. U.X.L 1995-1999 7v il maps v1-7 set$350; v1-4 set$215; v5, v6, & v7 ea $60   **920.003**
1. Explorers—Dictionaries 2. Adventure and adventurers 3. Reference books
ISBN 0-8103-9787-8 (v1-4 set); 0-7876-1990-6 (v5); 0-7876-2946-4 (v6); 0-7876-3681-9 (v7)
LC 95-166826

V5-7 edited by Nancy Pear and Daniel B. Baker

Profiles men and women explorers from ancient Greek scholars and travelers to contemporary astronauts and oceanographers

Hispanic American biographies. Grolier 2006 8v il set$429 *
Grades: 6 7 8 9 10 11 12   **920.003**
1. Hispanic Americans—Dictionaries 2. Reference books
ISBN 0-7172-6124-7   LC 2006-12294

"This comprehensive set features more than 750 clearly written biographical entries of one or two pages each, covering figures who were born in, or immigrated to, the

Hispanic American biographies—*Continued*
United States. . . . There is enough information to provide a strong sense of the person's place in history, without giving an overwhelming parade of facts." SLJ

Includes bibliographical references

Lincoln Library of shapers of society; 101 men and women who shaped our world; edited by Timothy Gall and Susan Gall. Lincoln Library Press 2008 7v il map set$273
Grades: 7 8 9 10 11 12   920.003
1. Biography—Dictionaries 2. Reference books
ISBN 978-0-91216-823-4
"This set offers multipage biographies of 101 individuals who, in the opinion of the editors, have exerted profound influence on contemporary society. . . . Each entry begins with a brief summary covering basic biographical facts and outlining personal accomplishments. Black-and-white full-page portraits, illustrated time lines, reproductions of primary sources, maps, archival photographs, and cartoonlike drawings complement the text. . . . Each entry entails a satisfying amount of information delivered in a variety of visual formats." Booklist

MacNee, Marie J.
Outlaws, mobsters & crooks; from the Old West to the Internet; edited by Jane Hoehner. U.X.L 1998-2002 5v il 3v set$165; ea $60
Grades: 8 9 10 11 12   920.003
1. Reference books 2. Criminals—Dictionaries
ISBN 0-7876-2803-4 (v1-3); 0-7876-6482-0 (v4); 0-7876-6483-9 (v5)   LC 98-14861
Contents: v1 Mobsters, racketeers & gamblers, robbers; v2 Computer criminals, spies, swindlers, terrorists; v3 Bandits & gunslingers, bootleggers, pirates; v4 From the Old West to the Internet [1]; v5 From the Old West to the Internet [2]
Presents the lives of seventy-five North American criminals including the nature of their crimes, their motivations, and information relating to the law officers who challenged them
"Browsers and researchers alike will make good use of this enjoyable reference set due to its fact-filled content and peek into the lives of such a wide variety of outlaws." Voice Youth Advocates

Ninth book of junior authors and illustrators; edited by Connie C. Rockman. Wilson, H.W. 2004 [i.e. 2005] 583p il $115 *
Grades: Professional   920.003
1. Authors—Dictionaries 2. Illustrators—Dictionaries 3. Children's literature—Bio-bibliography 4. Reference books
ISBN 0-8242-1043-3   LC 2004-61627
This volume covers some 200 authors and illustrators of books for children and young adults including Kate DiCamillo, Pura Belpré, Julia Alvarez and Kadir Nelson. For 20 authors and artists whose careers include significant new works and honors since their profile in earlier editions of the series, newly written entries are featured
This "offers solid and appealing information for students, librarians, and educators. . . . School and public libraries would be well served by this informative and easy-to-read text." Booklist

Notable mathematicians; from ancient times to the present; Robyn V. Young, editor; Zoran Minderovic, associate editor. Gale Res. 1998 xxi, 612p il $120
Grades: 7 8 9 10   920.003
1. Mathematicians—Dictionaries 2. Reference books
ISBN 0-7876-3071-3   LC 97-33662
This work profiles "300 mathematicians chosen for their historical importance, discoveries, familiarity to the public, awards and prizes, and involvement in mathematics education. . . . Female and minority mathematicians have been expressly represented." Libr J

Includes bibliographical references

Notable women scientists; Pamela Proffitt, editor. Gale Group 1999 xxvi, 668p il $120
Grades: 7 8 9 10   920.003
1. Women scientists 2. Reference books
ISBN 0-7876-3900-1   LC 99-35741
Biographical profiles of 500 women around the world who have made significant contributions to the field of science, from antiquity to the present
"Each alphabetically arranged entry includes basic biographical information (dates, nationality, and specialty), an essay of 400-to-2000 words, a list of selected writings by the subject, and a list of further reading. The informative, clearly written essays present excellent material for reports." SLJ

Includes bibliographical references

People of the Holocaust; [edited by] Linda Schmittroth and Mary Kay Rosteck. U.X.L 1998 2v il set$110
Grades: 7 8 9 10 11 12   920.003
1. Holocaust, 1933-1945 2. Jews—Biography 3. Reference books
ISBN 0-7876-1743-1   LC 98-4988
Profiles sixty women and men who were caught up in the Holocaust, including Nazi perpetrators and their victims, world leaders and policy makers, and those who showed their humanity and courage by resisting Hitler's reign of genocidal terror
"This unique resource will be in constant demand." SLJ

Podell, Janet
Old worlds to new; the age of exploration and discovery; [by] Janet Podell and Steven Anzovin. Wilson, H.W. 1993 286p il maps (They changed the world) $75
Grades: 7 8 9 10 11 12 Adult   920.003
1. Explorers—Dictionaries 2. Scientists—Dictionaries 3. Reference books
ISBN 0-8242-0838-2   LC 92-19264
This "compilation of important discoveries begins with approximately 1000 and continues through 1800. The book is divided into logical areas of discovery with individual explorers covered in chronological order within the division. Section topics include the empires of Spain and Portugal, mariners and pirates, the exploration of Africa, and the age of scientific discovery. Individuals are treated in articles of two to four pages. Portraits, maps and period art are included." Book Rep

Popular contemporary writers; editor, Michael D. Sharp. Marshall Cavendish Reference 2005 11v il set$657.07

    Grades: 8 9 10 11 12 Adult   **920.003**
    1. Authors—Dictionaries 2. Literature—Bibliography 3. Reference books
    ISBN 0-7614-7601-6   LC 2005-42005

"This alphabetically arranged encyclopedia offers information on 96 contemporary writers, primarily British and North American, whose works tend to mine populist as well as artistic veins—usually with bestselling results. Each extensive, readable entry opens with stage-setting biographical and critical comments, then goes on in successive sections to describe the writers life and career to date, examine his or her dominant themes in a critical light, summarize and evaluate major works, and close with leads to Web-based resources of interest." SLJ

Includes bibliographical references

Riley, Sam G.
    African Americans in the media today; an encyclopedia; [by] Sam G. Riley. Greenwood Press 2007 2v 581p set$175

    Grades: 7 8 9 10 11 12   **920.003**
    1. African Americans in television broadcasting 2. African Americans—Biography—Dictionaries 3. Mass media 4. Reference books
    ISBN 978-0-313-33679-9; 0-313-33679-2 (set); 978-0-313-33680-5 (v1); 0-313-33680-6 (v1); 978-0-313-33681-2 (v2); 0-313-33681-4 (v2)
        LC 2007008192

"This concise, alphabetically arranged work describes hundreds of people . . . in various fields of communications. It includes, for example, reporters, anchormen and women, talk-show hosts, and television producers. . . . Each of the mostly one to two-page entries includes biographical information, . . . work experience, awards, and, in some cases, includes anecdotes or articles by or about the individual. . . . A worthwhile resource for biography or communications projects." SLJ

Includes bibliographical references

Scientists: their lives and works; Peggy Saari and Stephen Allison, editors. U.X.L 1996-2002 7v il v1-7 set$350; v1-3 set $165; v4, 5, 6, & 7 ea $60

    Grades: 8 9 10 11 12   **920.003**
    1. Scientists—Dictionaries 2. Reference books
    ISBN 1-4144-0487-5 (v1-7); 0-7876-0959-5 (v1-3); 0-7876-1874-8 (v4); 0-7876-2797-6 (v5); 0-7876-3682-7 (v6); 0-7876-6383-2 (v7)
        LC 96-25579

Volume 4-6 edited by Marie C. Ellavich; volume 7 edited by Tanya Lee Stone; original 3 volume set has subtitle: the lives and works of 150 scientists

"The alphabetically arranged volumes profile figures . . . ranging from the Industrial Revolution to the present. Each entry lists birth and death dates and birthplace, followed by an accessible, fact-filled text that accurately chronicles the subject's early life, educational background, career milestones, discoveries, and awards." SLJ [review of original 3 volume set]

Something about the author; facts and pictures about authors and illustrators of books for young people. Gale Res. il ea $140

    Grades: Professional   **920.003**
    1. Authors—Dictionaries 2. Illustrators—Dictionaries 3. Children's literature—Bio-bibliography 4. Reference books
    ISSN 0276-816X

Also available Major authors and illustrators for children and young adults: a selection of sketches from Something about the author, 8 volume set$605 (ISBN 0-7876-1234-0)

First published 1971. Frequency varies

Editors vary

"This important series gives comprehensive coverage of the individuals who write and illustrate books for children. Each new volume adds about 100 profiles. Entries include career and personal data, a bibliography of the author's works, information on works in progress and references to further information." Safford. Guide to Ref Materials for Sch Libr Media Cent. 5th edition

Something about the author: autobiography series. Gale Res. il ea $149

    Grades: Professional   **920.003**
    1. Authors—Dictionaries 2. Illustrators—Dictionaries 3. Children's literature—Bio-bibliography 4. Reference books
    ISSN 0885-6842

First published 1986

Editors vary

An "ongoing series in which juvenile authors discuss their lives, careers, and published works. Each volume contains essays by 20 established writers or illustrators (e.g., Evaline Ness, Nonny Hogrogian, Betsy Byars, Jean Fritz) who represent all types of literature, preschool to young adult. . . . Some articles focus on biographical information, while others emphasize the writing career. Most, however, address young readers and provide family background, discuss the writing experience, and cite some factors that influenced it. Illustrations include portraits of the authors as children and more recent action pictures and portraits. There are cumulative indexes by authors, important published works, and geographical locations mentioned in the essays." Safford. Guide to Ref Books for Sch Libr Media Cent. 5th edition

Sonneborn, Liz
    A to Z of American Indian women. rev ed. Facts on File 2007 320p il map (Facts on File library of American history) $60 *

    Grades: 8 9 10 11 12   **920.003**
    1. Native American women—Dictionaries 2. Reference books
    ISBN 978-0-8160-6694-0   LC 2007-8162

First published 1998 with title: A to Z of Native American women

This book "profiles 152 American Indian women who have had an impact on American Indian society and the world at large." Publisher's note

"This resource is of exceptionally high quality." SLJ

Includes bibliographical references

Tenth book of junior authors and illustrators; edited by Connie C. Rockman. Wilson, H.W. 2008 803p il $120 *
Grades: Professional **920.003**
1. Children's literature—Bio-bibliography 2. Authors—Dictionaries 3. Illustrators—Dictionaries 4. Reference books
ISBN 978-0-8242-1066-3; 0-8242-1066-2
LC 2008043312

This volume covers some 200 authors and illustrators of books for children and young adults including David Almond, Blue Balliett, Terry Pratchett, and Laura Vaccaro Seeger. For 17 authors and artists whose careers include significant new works and honors since their profile in earlier editions of the series, newly written entries are featured

"Standard resource for libraries serving young readers and students studying children's and young adult literature." Booklist

Includes bibliographical references

World authors, 1995-2000; editors, Clifford Thompson, Mari Rich [et. al.] Wilson, H.W. 2003 872p il (Authors series) $160
Grades: 8 9 10 11 12 Adult **920.003**
1. Authors—Dictionaries 2. Literature—Bio-bibliography 3. Reference books
ISBN 0-8242-1032-8 LC 2003-45062

This reference includes 320 novelists, poets, dramatists, essayists, social scientists, and biographers who have published significant works from 1995 through 2000. Each profile details the author's life and career, the circumstances under which their works were produced, and their literary significance.

Includes bibliographical references

Yount, Lisa
A to Z of women in science and math. rev ed. Facts on File 2007 368p il (Facts on File library of world history) $60
Grades: 8 9 10 11 12 **920.003**
1. Women scientists—Dictionaries 2. Women mathematicians—Dictionaries 3. Reference books
ISBN 978-0-8160-6695-7; 0-8160-6695-7
LC 2007-23966

First published 1999

"More than 195 alphabetically arranged articles detail the lives of women from antiquity through modern day, including well-known scientists and mathematicians and less well-documented individuals. . . . The usefulness of this resource lies not only in the balanced group of profiles that have been assembled, providing a valuable tool for teachers and curriculum developers, but also in the readable and engaging entries themselves." Booklist

Includes bibliographical references

92 Individual biography

Lives of individuals are arranged alphabetically under the name of the person written about. Some subject headings have been added to aid in curriculum work.

Aaron, Hank, 1934-
Stanton, Tom. Hank Aaron and the home run that changed America. William Morrow 2004 249p il hardcover o.p. pa $13.95
Grades: 7 8 9 10 **92**
1. Baseball—Biography 2. African American athletes 3. United States—Race relations
ISBN 0-06-057976-5; 0-06-072290-8 (pa)
LC 2004-46092

The author "covers the time from the funeral of Jackie Robinson in 1972 to the spring of 1974, when Hank Aaron hit his 715th home run and passed Babe Ruth's record." Booklist

"Stanton deftly balances the story of Aaron's professional career, his personal life, and the changes in baseball between the years of Jackie Robinson and today's megastars, such as Ken Griffey, Jr. and Barry Bonds. . . . This book is a must for young adult collections." Voice Youth Advocates

Includes bibliographical references

Abbott, Berenice, 1898-1991
Sullivan, George. Berenice Abbott, photographer; an independent vision. Clarion Books 2006 170p il $20 *
Grades: 7 8 9 10 **92**
1. Women photographers
ISBN 978-0-618-44026-9; 0-618-44026-7
LC 2005-30736

A biography of Berenice Abbott, who was a pioneer in the field of professional photography and is particularly acclaimed for her photographs of the streets and buildings of New York City before they were replaced by skyscrapers during a building boom in the 1920s and early 1930s.

"Sullivan brings together an enormous amount of information about Abbott and presents it in a clear, thoughtful manner. . . . Large, clear reproductions of Abbott's photos appear throughout the book." Booklist

Includes bibliographical references

Abū al-Qāsim Khalaf ibn Abbās al-Zahrāwī, d. 1013?
Ramen, Fred. Albucasis (Abu al-Qasim al-Zahrawi); renowned Muslim surgeon of the Tenth Century; [by] Fred Ramen. Rosen Pub. Group 2006 112p il map (Great Muslim philosophers and scientists of the Middle Ages) lib bdg $33.25
Grades: 5 6 7 8 **92**
1. Physicians 2. Arabs 3. Medieval civilization 4. Spain—History
ISBN 1-4042-0510-1 LC 2005015786

"Acknowledging the skimpy historical record on his subject, Ramen fleshes out this profile of an influential Spanish physician with sweeping histories of ancient

Abū al-Qāsim Khalaf ibn Abbās al-Zahrāwī, d. 1013?—*Continued*

Mediterranean civilizations, early medicine, the rise of Islam, and the rise and fall of Muslim culture in Spain. Readers will come away impressed by the surgeon's contributions to medicine, which ranged from an encyclopedic surgical text to the invention of the forceps to the pioneering use of sutures. The information is buttressed by color photos of architectural remains and manuscript pages." Booklist

Includes glossary and bibliographical references

Adams, Abigail, 1744-1818

Bober, Natalie. Abigail Adams; witness to a revolution; [by] Natalie S. Bober. Atheneum Bks. for Young Readers 1995 248p il maps hardcover o.p. pa $9.99

Grades: 7 8 9 10   92

1. Presidents' spouses—United States
ISBN 0-689-31760-3; 0-689-81916-1 (pa)
LC 94-19259

"By interweaving excerpts from Adams's correspondence into a coherent biography, Bober creates a vibrant, three-dimensional portrait of a fascinating person whose comments on women's place have reverberated throughout history. This scholarly, thoroughly documented study will appeal to more mature readers, but it is more formidable in appearance than in presentation. Black-and-white reproductions are included." Horn Book Guide

Includes bibliographical references

Adams, Ansel, 1902-1984

Gherman, Beverly. Ansel Adams; America's photographer; a biography for young people. Little, Brown and Company 2002 110p il $19.95 *

Grades: 7 8 9 10   92

1. Photographers
ISBN 0-316-82445-3; 978-0-316-82445-3
LC 2002-103229

This is a "look into Adams' life, beginning with his childhood in San Francisco, following him as he becomes enamored with both photography and the piano, and detailing the long-range effects that growing up amid natural beauty had on him. . . . Readers being introduced to Adams' work for the first time will be awed by the photographs, and Adams' fans will appreciate both the numerous offerings and the book's handsome design." Booklist

Includes bibliographical references

Adams, John, 1735-1826

Adams, John. John Adams the writer; a treasury of letters, diaries, and public documents; compiled and edited by Carolyn P. Yoder. 1st ed. Calkins Creek 2007 144p il $16.95

Grades: 8 9 10 11 12   92

1. Presidents—United States
ISBN 978-1-59078-247-7; 1-59078-247-X
LC 2006101748

In the "collection, illustrated with photographs, prints, paintings, and artifacts, Carolyn Yoder has selected writings that chart the life and ideas of John Adams." Publisher's note

"Yoder's succinct introductions provide ample context for each selection, and the diverse writings give a sense of the man's intelligence, resolve, and dedication to the ideals that created America. . . . Numerous black-and-white illustrations and a list of historic sites round out the title. . . . Those who seek an easily digestible overview of the second president's life and times will find this book both informative and appealing." SLJ

Includes bibliographical references

Mara, Wil. John Adams. Marshall Cavendish Benchmark 2009 112p il (Presidents and their times) lib bdg $23.95

Grades: 5 6 7 8   92

1. Presidents—United States
ISBN 978-0-7614-2840-4; 0-7614-2840-2
LC 2007023410

"Provides comprehensive information on President John Adams and places him within his historical and cultural context. Also explored are the formative events of his times and how he responded." Publisher's note

Includes glossary and bibliographical references

Adams, Samuel, 1722-1803

Fradin, Dennis B. Samuel Adams; the father of American Independence; [by] Dennis Brindell Fradin. Clarion Bks. 1998 182p il $18 *

Grades: 6 7 8 9   92

1. United States—History—1775-1783, Revolution
ISBN 0-395-82510-5   LC 97-20027

"Archival reproductions effectively complement a descriptive and accurate narrative that imaginatively integrates details of Adams's life with the social and political milieu of the time." Horn Book Guide

Includes bibliographical references

Irvin, Benjamin. Samuel Adams; son of liberty, father of revolution; [by] Benjamin H. Irvin. Oxford University Press 2002 176p il (Oxford portraits) $28

Grades: 7 8 9 10   92

1. United States—History—1775-1783, Revolution
ISBN 0-19-513225-4   LC 2002-4283

Contents: The elusive Samuel Adams; Samuel Adams's Boston; Raised for rebellion; Tis not in mortals to command success; Sam the publican and the Stamp Act Riots; Mobs and massacre; To save the country; The Coercive Acts and the Continental Congress; Is not America already independent; The storm is now over

Examines the life of Samuel Adams, a hero of the American Revolution who is credited by some with having fired the first shot at Lexington Green, the "shot heard 'round the world"

"Irvin's account of events is exciting and written in a compelling narrative style. He presents an unbiased assessment of Adams's actions and character." SLJ

Includes bibliographical references

Addams, Jane, 1860-1935

Caravantes, Peggy. Waging peace; the story of Jane Addams; [by] Peggy Caravantes. rev ed. Morgan Reynolds Publishing 2004 144p il lib bdg $23.95 *

Grades: 5 6 7 8   92
ISBN 1-93179-840-0   LC 2004-8357
Contents: Young Jane; Search for life's work; Turning point; Social justice; Praise to insult; The progressives; Work for peace; Most-admired woman
This is a "biography of the social reformer, humanitarian, and winner of the 1931 Nobel Peace Prize. . . . Archival black-and-white photos . . . grace the book. This is a solid addition to women's history collections." SLJ
Includes bibliographical references

Fradin, Judith Bloom. Jane Addams; champion of democracy; by Judith Bloom Fradin and Dennis Brindell Fradin. Clarion Books 2006 216p il $21
Grades: 7 8 9 10   92
1. Hull House (Chicago, Ill.) 2. Chicago (Ill.)—Social conditions
ISBN 0-618-50436-1
A biography of the social activist, pacifist, author, founder of Hull House in Chicago, and winner of the Nobel Peace Prize.
"A fascinating and rich life is related in strong, unfussy prose." Booklist
Includes bibliographical references

Aguirre, Hank, 1932-1994

Copley, Bob. The tall Mexican: the life of Hank Aguirre, all-star pitcher, businessman, humanitarian; with a foreword by Jose F. Niño. Piñata Bks. 1998 159p il pa $9.95 hardcover o.p.
Grades: 7 8 9 10   92
1. Baseball—Biography 2. Businesspeople
ISBN 1-55885-294-8   LC 98-3185
A biography of the All-Star major-league pitcher whose commitment to his Hispanic heritage led him to found Mexican Industries to help provide economic opportunities to the inner-city Detroit community
"Myriad reminiscences from friends, family, employees, colleagues, and fellow athletes provide readers with the sense of true admiration felt for the subject." SLJ

Ailey, Alvin

Cruz, Bárbara. Alvin Ailey; celebrating African-American culture in dance; [by] Bárbara C. Cruz. Enslow Pub. 2004 112p il lib bdg $26.60
                                                     92
1. African American dancers 2. Choreographers
ISBN 0-7660-2293-5
Profiles the life of one of the most popular and acclaimed dancers and choreographers in the world.
"A solid addition to any biography collection." SLJ

Albright, Madeleine Korbel, 1937-

Hasday, Judy L. Madeleine Albright. Chelsea House 1999 134p il (Women of achievement) lib bdg $23.95; pa $9.95   92
1. Women politicians 2. Cabinet officers
ISBN 0-7910-4708-3 (lib bdg); 0-7910-4709-1 (pa)
                                        LC 98-14110
Focuses on the accomplishments of the former United States ambassador to the United Nations who became the first woman to serve as Secretary of State
"Good for assignments year-round, and especially valuable for women's history month." SLJ
Includes bibliographical references

Alexander, the Great, 356-323 B.C.

Adams, Simon. Alexander; the boy soldier who conquered the world. National Geographic 2005 64p il map (World history biographies) $17.95; lib bdg $27.90 *
Grades: 4 5 6 7   92
1. Ancient civilization
ISBN 0-7922-3660-2; 0-7922-3661-0 (lib bdg)
This describes the life and times of Alexander the Great.
This is a "handsomely designed [book]. . . . illustrated with maps and many color photographs of art and sculpture that give substance to [the era]. . . . Adams does not downplay Alexander's brutality or all-consuming ambition and includes examples of both." SLJ
Includes bibliographical references

Behnke, Alison. The conquests of Alexander the Great; by Alison Behnke. Twenty-First Century Books 2008 159p il map (Pivotal moments in history) lib bdg $38.60
Grades: 6 7 8 9   92
1. Greece—History—323-1453 2. Kings and rulers
ISBN 978-0-8225-5920-7 (lib bdg); 0-8225-5920-X (lib bdg)   LC 2006-11824
Presents a profile of the young military leader and king of ancient Macedonia, who conquered most of the known world of his era, before his untimely death at the age of thirty-three.
This is a "very thorough account. . . . Behnke gives enough background information about Greece and the world in which Alexander was raised to bring him to life for readers. . . . Helpful maps of the route through the Middle East and Asia and interesting sidebars and illustrations of Alexander and his contemporaries appear throughout." SLJ
Includes bibliographical references

Alhazen, 965-1039

Steffens, Bradley. Ibn al-Haytham; first scientist. Morgan Reynolds Pub. 2007 128p il (Profiles in science) lib bdg $27.95
Grades: 7 8 9 10   92
1. Scientists 2. Mathematicians
ISBN 978-1-59935-024-0 (lib bdg); 1-59935-024-6 (lib bdg)   LC 2006-23970
The author "has organized what is known of his subject's life and work into a coherent narrative. . . . Like the history of mathematics, the history of science is in-

Alhazen, 965-1039—*Continued*
complete without an acknowledgment of early scholars in the Middle East. This clearly written introduction to al-Haytham, his society, and his contributions does that." Booklist
Includes bibliographical references

Ali, Muhammad, 1942-
Myers, Walter Dean. The greatest: Muhammad Ali. Scholastic 2001 172p il hardcover o.p. pa $4.99
Grades: 7 8 9 10   92
1. Boxing—Biography 2. African American athletes
ISBN 0-590-54342-3; 0-590-54343-1 (pa)
In this biography Myers combines "reportage of Ali's major fights (especially against Sonny Liston, Joe Frazier, and George Foreman) with his own reflections about the sport's destructiveness and about Ali's unpopular views." Horn Book
"Readers will enjoy the fast-paced action, crisp writing, photographs of significant events and personalities, and the vivid fight scenes." Voice Youth Advocates

Smith, Charles R. Twelve rounds to glory: the story of Muhammad Ali; illustrated by Bryan Collier. Candlewick Press 2007 80p il $19.99 *
Grades: 5 6 7 8   92
1. Boxing—Biography 2. African American athletes
ISBN 978-0-7636-1692-2; 0-7636-1692-3
LC 2007-25998
"Rap-style cadences perfectly capture the drama that has always surrounded the boxer's life. . . . Collier's compelling watercolor collages with their brown overtones beautifully portray Ali's determination and strength." SLJ

Allende, Isabel
Main, Mary. Isabel Allende; award-winning Latin American author. Enslow Pubs. 2005 128p il map (Latino biography library) lib bdg $31.93
Grades: 6 7 8 9   92
1. Authors, Chilean 2. Women authors
ISBN 0-7660-2488-1
A biography of the Chilean author
"An interesting, well-written biography. Many black-and-white and color photographs, maps, and sidebars enhance the enticing glimpse into her Chilean world. The author does a superior job in presenting the facts of Allende's personal and professional life within the framework of an engaging narrative." SLJ
Includes bibliographical references

McNeese, Tim. Isabel Allende. Chelsea House 2006 112p bibl il por (Great Hispanic heritage) lib bdg $30
Grades: 6 7 8 9   92
1. Authors, Chilean 2. Women authors
ISBN 0-7910-8836-7   LC 2006008379
A biography of the Chilean-American novelist
Includes bibliographical references

Alvarez, Julia, 1950-
Aykroyd, Clarissa. Julia Alvarez; novelist and poet; by Clarissa Aykroyd. Lucent Books 2008 104p il (The twentieth century's most influential Hispanics) $32.45
Grades: 7 8 9 10   92
1. Poets, American 2. Hispanic American women 3. Women authors
ISBN 978-1-4205-0022-6; 1-4205-0022-8
LC 2007025974
"This introduction to author Alvarez gives a comprehensive look at the Dominican American writer's life and literary career. The lively writing . . . is supported by numerous quotes from Alvarez and details . . . that will pique kids' interest." Booklist
Includes bibliographical references

Andersen, Hans Christian, 1805-1875
Varmer, Hjørdis. Hans Christian Andersen; his fairy tale life; illustrated by Lilian Brogger; translated by Tiina Nunnally. Groundwood Books 2005 111p il $19.95 *
Grades: 5 6 7 8   92
1. Authors, Danish
ISBN 0-88899-690-X
"Most of this book describes Andersen's childhood and belated schooling, showing his poverty and the grief he experienced over the death of his beloved father, as well as several horrifying events such as being forced by a teacher to witness the beheading of three young people. . . . The biography is divided into 11 chapters, set up as if they were stories. . . . The writing flows smoothly, with many details provided to help students picture the places and events. Brøgger's haunting, mixed-media illustrations add to the somber and at times surreal feeling of the text." SLJ

Anderson, Marian, 1897-1993
Freedman, Russell. The voice that challenged a nation; Marian Anderson and the struggle for equal rights. Clarion Books 2004 114p il $18 *
Grades: 5 6 7 8   92
1. African American singers 2. African American women—Biography 3. African Americans—Civil rights
ISBN 0-618-15976-2   LC 2003-19558
A Newbery Medal honor book, 2005
Contents: Easter Sunday, April 9, 1939; Twenty-five cents a song; A voice in a thousand four: Marian fever; Banned by the DAR; Singing to the nation; Breaking barriers; "What I had was singing."
In the mid-1930s, Marian Anderson was a famed vocalist who had been applauded by European royalty and welcomed at the White House. But, because of her race, she was denied the right to sing at Constitution Hall in Washington, D.C. This is the story of her resulting involvement in the civil rights movement of the time.
"In his signature prose, plain yet eloquent, Freedman tells Anderson's triumphant story, with numerous black-and-white photos and prints that convey her personal struggle, professional artistry, and landmark civil rights role." Booklist
Includes bibliographical references

Anderson, Marian, 1897-1993—*Continued*

Jones, Victoria Garrett. Marian Anderson; a voice uplifted; [by] Victoria Garrett Jones. Sterling Pub. 2007 124p il (Sterling biographies) $12.95

Grades: 6 7 8 9   **92**
1. African American singers 2. African American women—Biography
ISBN 978-1-4027-4239-2; 1-4027-4239-8
                                    LC 2007019268
"Filled with archival photographs and quotes, this stirring biography of Anderson gives a concise, yet thorough introduction to the famous contralto's life." Booklist
Includes bibligraphical references

Andreessen, Marc

Ehrenhaft, Daniel. Marc Andreessen; Web warrior. 21st Cent. Bks. (Brookfield) 2001 77p il (Techies) lib bdg $23.90

Grades: 6 7 8 9   **92**
1. Netscape Communications Corporation 2. Internet 3. Businesspeople
ISBN 0-7613-1964-6   LC 00-57710
The author "introduces the man who coauthored the early Web-browsing software Mosaic, co-founded the firm Netscape, and was a multimillionaire at the age of 24." Booklist
This offers "a breezy style, short length, large font, numerous photographs, and attractive page design." Voice Youth Advocates
Includes bibliographical references

Andrews, Roy Chapman, 1884-1960

Bausum, Ann. Dragon bones and dinosaur eggs: a photobiography of Roy Chapman Andrews. National Geographic Soc. 2000 64p il map $17.95 *

Grades: 5 6 7 8   **92**
1. Fossils 2. Dinosaurs 3. Naturalists
ISBN 0-7922-7123-8   LC 99-38363
A biography of the great explorer-adventurer, who discovered huge finds of dinosaur bones in Mongolia, pioneered modern paleontology field research, and became the director of the American Museum of Natural History
"Bausum's account reads smoothly, and a layout dense with captioned sepia photographs and quotes from Andrews provides plenty of oases for readers as they follow him through the desert." Bull Cent Child Books
Includes bibliographical references

Anning, Mary, 1799-1847

Goodhue, Thomas W. Curious bones: Mary Anning and the birth of paleontology. Morgan Reynolds 2002 112p il lib bdg $21.95 *

Grades: 7 8 9 10   **92**
1. Fossils
ISBN 1-88384-693-5   LC 2002-8540
Contents: The girl on the cliff; A new vocation; The fish lizard; The monster on the beach; The old fossil depot; The flying dragon and the winged fish; The lioness of Lyme Regis; Praise; Through the storm

Recounts the life and work of Mary Anning, who collected fossils throughout her life and made major discoveries in paleontology when that branch of science was first emerging

This "accessible biography gives readers not only insight into Anning's life but also the time in which she lived. The documentation is excellent." Booklist
Includes glossary and bibliographical references

Archimedes, ca. 287-212 B.C.

Gow, Mary. Archimedes; mathematical genius of the ancient world. Enslow Pub. 2005 128p il (Great minds of science) lib bdg $26.60

Grades: 5 6 7 8   **92**
1. Mathematicians
ISBN 0-7660-2502-0   LC 2004-28480
"Because more information has survived about Archimedes's contributions than about his life, most of this book wisely focuses on his mathematical observations 22 centuries ago. Descriptions of Syracuse and Alexandria . . . introduce readers to ancient Greek society and give them a fuller understanding of the importance of Archimedes's discoveries. The next chapters describe the significance of his work regarding levers, buoyancy, geometry, and pi; and of such inventions as the pulley and Archimedes's screw. . . . Good-quality, black-and-white illustrations add information to the clear text." SLJ
Includes glossary and bibliographical references

Aristotle, 384-322 B.C.

Anderson, Margaret Jean. Aristotle; philosopher and scientist; [by] Margaret J. Anderson and Karen F. Stephenson. Enslow Publishers 2004 112p il map (Great minds of science) lib bdg $26.60

Grades: 5 6 7 8   **92**
1. Philosophers 2. Scientists
ISBN 0-7660-2096-7   LC 2003-2270
Contents: Living in interesting times; Aristotle's childhood; Athens, the City of Wonder; The Academy; A new direction; The Father of Zoology; Alexander; The Lyceum; "A Desire for Knowledge;" The end of the road; His writings live on; Aristotle's influence
"After opening with an overview of the time during which Aristotle lived, the authors discuss his childhood, his student days at the Academy in Athens, his tutoring of Alexander, and his founding of the Lyceum. The bulk of the text focuses on Aristotle's contributions to philosophy and science. . . . The text is clear and concise. . . . This easy-to-understand offering will prove useful for reports." SLJ
Includes bibliographical references

Katz Cooper, Sharon. Aristotle; philosopher, teacher, and scientist. Compass Point Books 2006 112p il (Signature lives) $31.93

Grades: 6 7 8 9   **92**
ISBN 978-0-7565-1873-8; 0-7565-1873-3
                                    LC 2006005403
A biography of the Greek philosopher
Includes glossary and bibliographical references

Armstrong, John Barclay, 1850-1913
Alter, Judy. John Barclay Armstrong; Texas Ranger; by Judy Alter. Bright Sky Press 2007 59p il $14.95
Grades: 4 5 6 7   92
   1. Texas Rangers 2. West (U.S.)—History
   ISBN 978-1-931721-86-8
"Born in 1850 and raised in Tennessee, Armstrong went west to seek his fortune. At 25, he joined the Texas Rangers and soon came to embody the legendary qualities of these remarkable lawmen. He is an interesting character, and the author aptly tells his tale. The archival black-and-white photos add authenticity and help bring the man to life." SLJ

Armstrong, Lance
Stewart, Mark. Sweet victory: Lance Armstrong's incredible journey; the amazing story of the greatest comeback in sports. Millbrook Press 2000 64p il lib bdg $24.90; pa $8.95
Grades: 5 6 7 8   92
   1. Bicycle racing
   ISBN 0-7613-1861-5 (lib bdg); 0-7613-1387-7 (pa)
                                    LC 99-53173
The story of the bicyclist who, having won the battle against cancer, went on to win the world's most grueling bicycle race, the Tour de France
"This easy-to-read title is as inspirational as it is informational." SLJ

Arnold, Benedict, 1741-1801
Fritz, Jean. Traitor: the case of Benedict Arnold. Putnam 1981 191p il hardcover o.p. pa $5.99
Grades: 5 6 7 8   92
   1. Generals 2. United States—History—1775-1783, Revolution
   ISBN 0-399-20834-8; 0-698-11553-8 (pa)
                                    LC 81-10584
"The writing is smooth, the material carefully organized and used in the best of biographical style—that is, Arnold is presented accurately and the reader is left to judge the strength and weaknesses of his character rather than being told by the author." Bull Cent Child Books
   Includes bibliographical references

Murphy, Jim. The real Benedict Arnold. Clarion Books 2007 264p il map $20 *
Grades: 7 8 9 10   92
   1. United States—History—1775-1783, Revolution
   2. Generals
   ISBN 978-0-395-77609-4; 0-395-77609-0
                                    LC 2007-5700
"Using Arnold's surviving military journals and political documents, Murphy carefully contrasts popular myth with historical fact. . . . As far as possible, he meticulously traces Arnold's life, revealing a complex man who was actually as much admired as he was loathed." Booklist
   Includes bibliographical references

Ashe, Arthur, 1943-1993
Cunningham, Kevin. Arthur Ashe; athlete and activist; by Kevin Cunningham. Child's World 2005 40p il (Journey to freedom) lib bdg $28.50
Grades: 5 6 7 8   92
   1. Tennis—Biography 2. African American athletes
   ISBN 1-59296-228-9   LC 2003-27076
"With an open design, clear text, and lots of action photographs, this biography . . . tells the compelling story of the tennis champion and his politics. The facts of prejudice are here as Ashe learns tennis on segregated courts. But words and pictures show him in glorious action on the court, where he makes sports history." Booklist
   Includes glossary and bibliographical references

Asimov, Isaac, 1920-1992
Hoppa, Jocelyn. Isaac Asimov; science fiction trailblazer; [by] Jocelyn Hoppa. Enslow Publishers 2009 104p il (Authors teens love) lib bdg $31.93
Grades: 6 7 8 9   92
   1. Authors, American
   ISBN 978-0-7660-2961-3; 0-7660-2961-1
                                    LC 2008-12299
"A biography of Russian-American science-fiction author Isaac Asimov." Publisher's note
   Includes bibliographical references

Attila, King of the Huns, d. 453
Price, Sean. Attila the Hun; leader of the barbarian hordes; [by] Sean Stewart Price. Franklin Watts 2009 128p il (A wicked history) $30; pa $5.95 *
Grades: 6 7 8 9   92
   1. Huns 2. Kings and rulers
   ISBN   978-0-531-21801-3;   0-531-21801-5;
   978-0-531-20737-6 (pa); 0-531-20737-4 (pa)
                                    LC 2008040520
"In fascinating detail, the book not only introduces Attila, but gives the backstory on what made the rise of the Huns possible. The exciting yet concise writing brings readers close to the battlefield, but the fighting and intrigue are neatly set against the sweep of history." Booklist
   Includes bibliographical references

Augustus, Emperor of Rome, 63 B.C.-14 A.D.
Forsyth, Fiona. Augustus: the first emperor. Rosen Pub. Group 2003 110p il maps (Leaders of ancient Rome) $23.95
Grades: 6 7 8 9   92
   1. Emperors—Rome
   ISBN 0-8239-3588-4   LC 2001-6261
A biography of the emperor of Rome who lived from 63 B.C. to 14 A.D.
"Written in a conversational tone, with large type and plentiful illustrations, [this] user-friendly [title] will draw readers into the history and intrigues of ancient Rome." Libr Media Connect
   Includes glossary and bibliographical references

Austen, Jane, 1775-1817

Locke, Juliane Poirier. England's Jane; the story of Jane Austen; [by] Juliane Locke. Morgan Reynolds Pub. 2006 144p il lib bdg $26.95
Grades: 7 8 9 10   92
1. Women authors 2. Authors, English
ISBN 978-1-931798-82-2 (lib bdg); 1-931798-82-6 (lib. bdg.)   LC 2005026279
"Drawing on letters, biographical works, archival pictures, and Austens novels, Locke offers a readable biography for students who cant manage a larger work. The language is uncomplicated and the topics are aimed at helping readers better understand *Pride and Prejudice*, *Emma*, and Austen's other writings." SLJ
Includes bibliographical references

Wagner, Heather Lehr. Jane Austen. Chelsea House 2003 c2004 112p (Who wrote that?) $23.95
Grades: 6 7 8 9   92
1. Authors, English 2. Women authors
ISBN 0-7910-7623-7   LC 2003-14409
Describes the life and novels of the nineteenth century British author, Jane Austen
"This clearly written, short biography contains descriptions of Austen's family life, her early education, writing career, and influences. Illustrations and photographs of movie adaptations, the family home, engravings from original publications, and places familiar to the writer help to familiarize students with aspects of her writing and her life." SLJ
Includes bibliographical references

Avi, 1937-

Sommers, Michael A. Avi; [by] Michael A. Sommers. 1st ed. Rosen Pub. Group 2004 112p il (Library of author biographies) lib bdg $26.50
Grades: 5 6 7 8   92
1. Authors, American
ISBN 0-8239-4522-7   LC 2003-9180
Discusses the life and work of this popular author, including his writing process and methods, inspirations, a critical discussion of his books, biographical timeline, and awards.

Babbage, Charles, 1791-1871

Collier, Bruce. Charles Babbage and the engines of perfection; [by] Bruce Collier and James MacLachlan. Oxford Univ. Press 1998 123p il (Oxford portraits in science) $28
Grades: 7 8 9 10   92
1. Mathematicians 2. Computers—History
ISBN 0-19-508997-9   LC 98-17054
Traces the life and work of the man whose nineteenth century inventions led to the development of the computer
"This is a fascinating portrait of Charles Babbage. . . . Generous b&w illustrations enliven the work." Book Rep
Includes bibliographical references

Baker, Ella, 1903-1986

Bohannon, Lisa Frederiksen. Freedom cannot rest; Ella Baker and the civil rights movement; [by] Lisa Frederiksen Bohannon. 1st ed. Morgan Reynolds Pub. 2005 176p il map (Portraits of Black Americans) lib bdg $26.95
Grades: 7 8 9 10   92
1. African Americans—Civil rights
ISBN 978-1-931798-71-6; 1-931798-71-0
LC 2005007156
"Baker was a major player in the Civil Rights movement of the 1960s. She was the principal organizer of SNCC, the Student Nonviolent Coordinating Committee. . . . Bohannon . . . makes good use of vintage photographs, artwork, and text boxes that further explain historical events. . . . Her biography might be a good place to start to get a good overview of Baker's life and the times in which she lived." SLJ
Includes bibliographical references

Balboa, Vasco Núñez de, 1475-1519

Otfinoski, Steven. Vasco Nuñez de Balboa; explorer of the Pacific; by Steven Otfinoski. Benchmark Books 2005 79p il map (Great explorations) lib bdg $29.93 *
Grades: 5 6 7 8   92
1. Explorers 2. America—Exploration
ISBN 0-7614-1609-9   LC 2003-14927
Contents: A daring youth; To the New World; From stowaway to governor; The first conquistador; To the South Sea; Discoverer of the Pacific; A new rival; Last adventure; The final treachery
Describes the life of Vasco Nuñez de Balboa, the Spanish explorer who was the first European to see the Pacific Ocean and who conceived the idea of a canal connecting the Atlantic and Pacific.
Includes bibliographical references

Banneker, Benjamin, 1731-1806

Litwin, Laura Baskes. Benjamin Banneker; astronomer and mathematician. Enslow Pubs. 1999 112p il (African-American biographies) lib bdg $26.60
Grades: 8 9 10 11 12   92
1. Astronomers 2. African Americans—Biography
ISBN 0-7660-1208-5   LC 98-34913
A biography of the eighteenth-century African-American who taught himself mathematics and astronomy and helped survey what would become Washington, D.C.
Includes bibliographical references

Barakat, Ibtisam

Barakat, Ibtisam. Tasting the sky; a Palestinian childhood. Farrar, Straus & Giroux 2007 176p $16 *
Grades: 6 7 8 9 10   92
1. Israel-Arab conflicts 2. Palestinian Arabs
ISBN 0-374-35733-1; 978-0-374-35733-7
LC 2006-41265
"Melanie Kroupa books."

Barakat, Ibtisam—*Continued*

"In 1981 the author, then in high school, boarded a bus bound for Ramallah. The bus was detained by Israeli soldiers at a checkpoint on the West Bank, and she was taken to a detention center before being released. The episode triggers sometimes heart-wrenching memories of herself as a young child, at the start of the 1967 Six Days' War, as Israeli soldiers conducted raids, their planes bombed her home, and she fled with her family across the border to Jordan. . . . What makes the memoir so compelling is the immediacy of the child's viewpoint, which depicts both conflict and daily life without exploitation or sentimentality." Booklist

Barnum, P. T. (Phineas Taylor), 1810-1891

Fleming, Candace. The great and only Barnum; the tremendous, stupendous life of showman P.T. Barnum. Schwartz & Wade Books 2009 160p il $18.99; lib bdg $21.99 *

Grades: 5 6 7 8   92

1. Circus

ISBN   978-0-375-84197-2;   0-375-84197-0; 978-0-375-94597-7 (lib bdg); 0-375-94597-0 (lib bdg)

LC 2008045847

"In this sweeping yet cohesive biography, Fleming so finely tunes Barnum's legendary ballyhoo that you can practically hear the hucksterism and smell the sawdust. . . . The material is inherently juicy, but credit Fleming's vivacious prose, bountiful period illustrations, and copious source notes for fashioning a full picture on one of the forebearers of modern celebrity." Booklist

Includes bibliographical references

Barton, Clara, 1821-1912

Somervill, Barbara A. Clara Barton; founder of the American Red Cross. Compass Point Books 2007 112p bibl il por lib bdg $23.95

Grades: 5 6 7 8   92

1. American Red Cross 2. Nurses

ISBN 978-0-7565-1888-2 (lib bdg); 0-7565-1888-1 (lib bdg)   LC 2006027071

"With an open design, clear type, and period prints and photos on every double-page spread, this highly readable biography . . . does a great job of setting Barton's personal story within the history of her time." Booklist

Includes bibliographical references

Whitelaw, Nancy. Clara Barton; Civil War nurse. Enslow Pubs. 1997 128p il maps (Historical American biographies) lib bdg $26.60

Grades: 6 7 8 9   92

1. Nurses

ISBN 0-89490-778-6   LC 97-7270

Traces the life of the Civil War nurse who cared for wounded soldiers and earned the title, "Angel of the Battlefield"

"Whitelaw makes use of her subject's original diaries from the Library of Congress, along with her published work. The chapters consist of easy, short sentences, lots of footnotes, and some direct quotes. Occasionally a box offers interesting incidental information." SLJ

Includes glossary and bibliographical references

Bates, Daisy

Fradin, Judith Bloom. The power of one; Daisy Bates and the Little Rock Nine; by Judith Bloom Fradin & Dennis Brindell Fradin. Clarion Books 2004 178p il $19

Grades: 7 8 9 10   92

1. Central High School (Little Rock, Ark.) 2. School integration 3. Arkansas—Race relations

ISBN 0-618-31556-X   LC 2004-4618

This is a biography of Daisy Bates. Born in a small town in rural Arkansas, Bates was a journalist and activist. In 1957 she mentored the nine black students who were integrated into Central High School in Little Rock, Arkansas

"This compelling biography clearly demonstrates that one person can indeed make a difference." SLJ

Includes bibliographical references

Bauer, Marion Dane, 1938-

Bauer, Marion Dane. A writer's story; from life to fiction. Clarion Bks. 1995 134p $14.95; pa $6.95

Grades: 7 8 9 10   92

1. Authors, American 2. Women authors

ISBN 0-395-72094-X; 0-395-75053-9 (pa)

LC 94-48800

"Drawing on her own experiences, the novelist examines the origins of inspiration and the subconscious drives that compel authors to write. She points out that many components of fiction—characters, settings, plot details—need not be autobiographical, yet the text does suggest that a story's meaning is directly linked to the unique experiences of its creator. . . . Bauer provides invaluable information for both writers and readers of fiction." Publ Wkly

Beethoven, Ludwig van, 1770-1827

Martin, Russell. The mysteries of Beethoven's hair; [by Russell Martin and Lydia Nibley] Charlesbridge 2009 120p il lib bdg $15.95

Grades: 5 6 7 8   92

1. Composers

ISBN 978-1-57091-714-1; 1-57091-714-0

LC 2008-07257

"Based on Martin's adult book Beethoven's Hair: An Extraordinary Historical Odyssey and Scientific Mystery Solved (Broadway, 2000), this reworking for a young audience presents an intriguing interdisciplinary story. Martin and Nibley trace the labyrinthine journey of a lock of Beethoven's hair encased in a glass and wooden locket from the 18th century to the present. . . . This is a most unusual, thoroughly researched detective story written in a clearly accessible and lively tone. Black-and-white photos and reproductions appear throughout. . . . It is . . . an incredibly readable and absorbing selection that demonstrates the multidimensional nature of true scholarship." SLJ

Viegas, Jennifer. Beethoven's world; [by] Jennifer Viegas. Rosen Pub. Group 2008 64p il (Music throughout history) lib bdg $29.25

Grades: 5 6 7 8   92

1. Composers

ISBN 1-4042-0724-4 (lib bdg); 978-1-4042-0724-0 (lib bdg)   LC 2005028917

Beethoven, Ludwig van, 1770-1827—_Continued_

This "book begins with an introduction briefly addressing social issues of the day, historical background, or other significant information. . . . Successive chapters discuss the [man's] early [life], family background, social status, personality characteristics, musical training and education, obstacles or challenges, and influences. A chapter . . . focuses on the musician's well-known compositions, describing through lively and colorful language some of the musical elements employed . . . The format and layout are appealing and uncluttered." SLJ

Includes glossary and bibliographical references

Bell, Alexander Graham, 1847-1922

Carson, Mary Kay. Alexander Graham Bell; giving voice to the world; [by] Mary Kay Carson. Sterling 2007 124p il (Sterling biographies) lib bdg $12.95; pa $5.95

Grades: 6 7 8 9   92
1. Inventors
ISBN 978-1-4027-4951-3 (lib bdg); 1-4027-4951-1 (lib bdg); 1-4027-3230-9 (pa); 978-1-4027-3230-0 (pa)
LC 2007003502

"Carson introduces Bell's life, giving readers an excellent picture of why this man became so famous. . . . [The book provides] clear, concise information in an easy-to-follow format with captioned photographs and illustrations on most pages." SLJ

Includes glossary and bibliographical references

Matthews, Tom L. Always inventing: a photobiography of Alexander Graham Bell. National Geographic Soc. 1999 64p il $17.95; pa $7.95 *

Grades: 4 5 6 7   92
1. Inventors
ISBN 0-7922-7391-5; 0-7922-5932-7 (pa)
LC 98-27209

A biography, with photographs and quotes from Bell himself, which follows this well known inventor from his childhood in Scotland through his life-long efforts to come up with ideas that would improve people's lives

"Succinct, lively, and readable, the text is illustrated with many well-captioned period photographs of Bell, his family, his associate, and his inventions as well as a host of diagrams." Booklist

Includes bibliographical references

Bell, Cool Papa, 1903-1991

McCormack, Shaun. Cool Papa Bell. Rosen Pub. Group 2002 112p il (Baseball Hall of Famers of the Negro leagues) lib bdg $29.25

Grades: 5 6 7 8   92
1. Baseball—Biography 2. African American athletes
ISBN 0-8239-3474-8   LC 2001-3121

This is a biography of the African American who played in the Negro Leagues and was elected to the Baseball Hall of Fame in 1974

This "title presents an unvarnished picture of the racism in this country and how it impacted amateur and professional baseball from 1868 onward. . . . The layout . . . is attractive, the style . . . is engaging, and the b&w photographs enhance the narrative." Book Rep

Includes glossary and bibliographical references

Berlin, Irving, 1888-1989

Furstinger, Nancy. Say it with music; the story of Irving Berlin. Morgan Reynolds 2003 128p il (Masters of music) lib bdg $21.95

Grades: 6 7 8 9   92
1. Composers—United States
ISBN 1-931798-12-5   LC 2003-6039

Contents: On the bum; Making the country hum; The hit maker; New music for new action; A crack of insecurity; God bless America; Show business; Counting his blessings; Out of tune; The melody lingers

A biography of the Russian immigrant who came to America as a boy and became one of the most successful composers of popular songs, including "White Christmas" and "God Bless America"

"Written in a lively style, the text is clearly documented with source notes, and well-placed, black-and-white photographs appear throughout." SLJ

Includes bibliographical references

Bernstein, Leonard, 1918-1990

Blashfield, Jean F. Leonard Bernstein; conductor and composer. Ferguson, J.G. 2000 127p il (Ferguson's career biographies) lib bdg $21.95

Grades: 7 8 9 10   92
1. Conductors (Music) 2. Composers
ISBN 0-89434-337-8   LC 00-37580

This illustrated biography looks at the life, career, and influence of the prominent composer/conductor

"A comprehensive time line of Bernstein's life and information about becoming a conductor or a composer are appended. There are three lists of further reading that give books, Web sites, and related places to contact or visit." SLJ

Bezos, Jeffrey, 1964-

Garty, Judy. Jeff Bezos; business genius of Amazon.com. Enslow Pubs. 2003 48p il (Internet biographies) lib bdg $18.95

Grades: 6 7 8 9   92
1. Amazon.com Inc. 2. Entrepreneurs
ISBN 0-7660-1972-1   LC 2002-153174

Contents: The visionary; The explorer; The mastermind; The pioneer; The hurricane's eye

Explores the life and career of the creator of the online bookstore Amazon.com, discussing his early interest in computers, business philosophy, and plans for the future

"Brief but thorough. . . . _Jeff Bezos_ is written in approachable, descriptive language. . . . The accompanying photographs are not to be missed." Booklist

Includes bibliographical references

Bitton-Jackson, Livia

Bitton-Jackson, Livia. My bridges of hope; searching for life and love after Auschwitz. Simon & Schuster Bks. for Young Readers 1999 258p pa $4.99 hardcover o.p.

Grades: 7 8 9 10   92
1. Holocaust survivors
ISBN 0-689-84898-6 (pa)   LC 98-8046

Sequel to: I have lived a thousand years

Bitton-Jackson, Livia—_Continued_

In 1945, after surviving a harrowing year in Auschwitz, fourteen-year-old Elli returns, along with her mother and brother, to the family home, now part of Slovakia, where they try to find a way to rebuild their shattered lives

The author's "story is utterly involving, and adds an important chapter to the ongoing attempt to understand the Holocaust and its consequences." Publ Wkly

Includes glossary

Blake, William, 1757-1827

Bedard, Michael. William Blake; the gates of paradise. Tundra Books 2006 192p il $28.99

Grades: 8 9 10 11 12   92

1. Poets, English

ISBN 978-0-88776-763-0; 0-88776-763-X

"Bedard provides a satisfying biography of English artist, poet, and visionary William Blake. . . . Illustrated with drawings, paintings, engravings, and photos of sites and artifacts, the book is handsomely produced. . . . Bedard writes with precision, simplicity, and grace." Booklist

Includes bibliographical references

Blume, Judy

Ludwig, Elisa. Judy Blume; [by] Elisa Ludwig; revised by Dennis Abrams. 2nd ed. Chelsea House 2009 120p bibl il por (Who wrote that?) $30

Grades: 6 7 8 9   92

1. Authors, American 2. Women authors

ISBN 978-1-60413-334-9; 1-60413-334-1

      LC 2008035047

First published 2004

A biography of the popular author for children and young adults.

Includes bibliographical references

Bonetta, Sarah Forbes, b. 1843?

Myers, Walter Dean. At her majesty's request; an African princess in Victorian England. Scholastic Press 1999 146p il map $17.95 *

Grades: 5 6 7 8   92

1. Africans

ISBN 0-590-48669-1   LC 98-7217

Biography of the African princess saved from execution and taken to England where Queen Victoria oversaw her upbringing and where she lived for a time before marrying an African missionary

"Myers tells an extraordinary tale which will intrigue young readers. . . . A fascinating narrative of a little-known facet of Victorian history, this book is rich with illustrations, including photographs, sketches, portraits, and maps." ALAN

Includes bibliographical references

Boone, Daniel, 1734-1820

Calvert, Patricia. Daniel Boone; beyond the mountains. Benchmark Bks. 2002 79p il (Great explorations) lib bdg $23.90

Grades: 5 6 7 8   92

1. West (U.S.)—Biography 2. Frontier and pioneer life—West (U.S.)

ISBN 0-7614-1243-3   LC 00-51902

A biography of the Western pioneer

This "well-researched [book] . . . will be useful to students writing reports." Horn Book Guide

Includes bibliographical references

Booth, Edwin, 1833-1893

Giblin, James. Good brother, bad brother. See entry under Booth, John Wilkes, 1838-1865

Booth, John Wilkes, 1838-1865

Giblin, James. Good brother, bad brother; the story of Edwin Booth and John Wilkes Booth. Clarion Books 2005 244p il $22 *

Grades: 5 6 7 8   92

1. Booth, Edwin, 1833-1893 2. Lincoln, Abraham, 1809-1865—Assassination 3. Actors 4. United States—History—1861-1865, Civil War 5. Brothers

ISBN 0-618-09642-6   LC 2004-21260

Giblin "frames the intertwined tale of two brothers with accounts of their families, friends, the Civil War, and nineteenth-century theater. . . . Alcoholism and depression afflicted the family, but Giblin is brilliant at showing that darkness was only one part of a life. . . . Giblin's book will engross readers until the very last footnote." Booklist

Includes bibliographical references

Swanson, James L. Chasing Lincoln's killer; the search for John Wilkes Booth. Scholastic Press 2009 194p il map $16.99 *

Grades: 7 8 9 10   92

1. Lincoln, Abraham, 1809-1865—Assassination 2. Actors 3. United States—History—1861-1865, Civil War

ISBN 978-0-439-90354-7; 0-439-90354-8

      LC 2008-17994

"This volume is an adaptation of Swanson's _Manhunt: The 12-Day Chase for Lincoln's Killer_ (HarperCollins, 2006). Divided into 14 chapters and an epilogue, the sentences are shorter and chapters are condensed from the original but the rich details and suspense are ever present. . . . Excellent black-and-white illustrations complement the text. . . . Readers will be engrossed by the almost hour-by-hour search and by the many people who encountered the killer as he tried to escape. It is a tale of intrigue and an engrossing mystery." SLJ

Borges, Jorge Luis, 1899-1986

McNeese, Tim. Jorge Luis Borges; [by] Tim McNeese. Chelsea House 2008 119p il (The great Hispanic heritage) $30

Grades: 6 7 8 9   92

1. Authors, Argentine

ISBN 978-0-7910-9665-9; 0-7910-9665-3

      LC 2007032008

Borges, Jorge Luis, 1899-1986—*Continued*

This biography provides a "substantive [portrait], including background information and historical context, of . . . beloved writer Borges. . . . The well-documented [text] effectively [combines] anecdotes, quotations, and historical details. Many photographs and sidebars are also included." Horn Book Guide

Includes bibliographical references

Bourgeois, Louise

Greenberg, Jan. Runaway girl: the artist Louise Bourgeois; [by] Jan Greenberg and Sandra Jordan. Abrams 2003 80p il $19.95 *

Grades: 7 8 9 10   **92**
1. Artists—United States
ISBN 0-8109-4237-2   LC 2002-11922
Contents: Family tapestry; Family secrets; A young artist in Paris; Runaway girl; The New York art scene; The great decade; Spider, spider burning bright

Introduces the life of renowned modern artist Louise Bourgeois, who is known primarily for her sculptures

"In clear, elegant prose, bolstered with numerous quotes from the artist, the authors seamlessly juxtapose stories of Bourgeois' life with relevant artworks. . . . Beautifully reproduced photographs, printed on well-designed pages, offer an excellent mix of the artist's personal life and her art." Booklist

Includes bibliographical references

Bowie, Jim, 1796-1836

Edmondson, J. R. Jim Bowie; frontier legend, Alamo hero. PowerPlus Bks. 2003 112p il map (Library of American lives and times) lib bdg $31.95

Grades: 4 5 6 7   **92**
1. West (U.S.)—Biography 2. Frontier and pioneer life—West (U.S.)
ISBN 0-8239-5734-9   LC 2001-4954
Describes the tumultuous times in early Texas history that formed the character of Jim Bowie, who is known both for inventing the Bowie knife and for fighting and dying at the Alamo

"This is a captivating, exciting biography. . . . Students will use this attractive book for reports and general reading." SLJ

Includes glossary and bibliographical references

Boyle, Robert, 1627-1691

Baxter, Roberta. Skeptical chemist; the story of Robert Boyle. Morgan Reynolds Pub. 2006 128p il (Profiles in science) lib bdg $27.95

Grades: 7 8 9 10   **92**
1. Scientists
ISBN 978-1-59935-025-7; 1-59935-025-4
                            LC 2006-23969
The author makes a "case for Boyle's significance as a key figure in the field of scientific experimentation as well as his contributions to modern chemistry and physics. Well organized and clearly written, her book offers a good view of changes in science and society at this pivotal time and presents a well-rounded view of Boyle, whose interests extended beyond scientific inquiry and discussion." Booklist

Includes bibliographical references

Gow, Mary. Robert Boyle; pioneer of experimental chemistry; [by] Mary Gow. Enslow Publishers 2005 128p il (Great minds of science) $26.60

Grades: 5 6 7 8   **92**
1. Scientists
ISBN 0-7660-2501-2   LC 2004-9194
Contents: "Which seems to prove--"; One who loves virtue; "Transported and bewitched;" The spring of the air; Boyle's law; The sceptical chymist; The Royal Society and the gospel in New England; London; "Whose writings they most desired"

This is an introduction to the seventeenth-century chemist who contributed to science not only through his discoveries, such as Boyle's Law (relating air pressure to volume), but also in developing the method of experimentation that enabled him to make those discoveries.

This is "well-organized [and] accessible. . . . The page layout contributes to the book's readability. Among the black-and-white illustrations are many reproductions of period paintings and engravings as well as photos of historical sites." Booklist

Bradford, William, 1590-1657

Doherty, Kieran. William Bradford; rock of Plymouth. 21st Cent. Bks. (Brookfield) 1999 192p il lib bdg $24.90

Grades: 6 7 8 9   **92**
1. Pilgrims (New England colonists)
2. Massachusetts—History—1600-1775, Colonial period
ISBN 0-7613-1304-4   LC 99-10631
A biography of one of the founders of the Plymouth Colony in Massachusetts and a history of the Pilgrims' difficult times during their early years in the New World

Includes bibliographical references

Brady, Mathew B., ca. 1823-1896

Pflueger, Lynda. Mathew Brady; photographer of the Civil War. Enslow Pubs. 2001 128p il (Historical American biographies) lib bdg $26.60

Grades: 6 7 8 9   **92**
1. Photographers 2. United States—History—1861-1865, Civil War
ISBN 0-7660-1444-4   LC 00-10732
A biography of "the preeminent photographer in the 1850s who zealously recorded the Civil War in photographs yet died a poor man." Voice Youth Advocates

This "book is interesting to read, well researched, and well documented." SLJ

Includes glossary and bibliographical references

Brahe, Tycho, 1546-1601

Boerst, William J. Tycho Brahe; mapping the heavens. Morgan Reynolds 2003 144p il maps (Renaissance scientists) lib bdg $23.95

Grades: 7 8 9 10   **92**
1. Astronomers
ISBN 1-88384-697-8   LC 2002-153640
Contents: Noble genius; Student days; Stargazer gets an offer; His Lordship of Uraniborg; Life at Hven; The star with a tail; Calamity; Starting over; Enter Kepler; Rebirth

Brahe, Tycho, 1546-1601—*Continued*
Presents the life and work of the famous sixteenth-century Danish astronomer
"Boerst provides a clearly written account of Brahe's education, background, personality, and career. Full-color illustrations, including many reproductions of period portraits and other artwork, appear throughout the book." Booklist
Includes bibliographical references

Nardo, Don. Tycho Brahe; pioneer of astronomy; by Don Nardo. Compass Point Books 2008 112p il (Signature lives) lib bdg $23.95
Grades: 6 7 8 9   92
1. Astronomers
ISBN 978-0-7565-3309-0 (lib bdg); 0-7565-3309-0 (lib bdg)   LC 2007004608
A biography of the sixteenth-century Danish astronomer Tycho Brahe.
"Nardo brings his lively, informative approach to this stanout biography." Booklist
Includes bibliographical references

Braille, Louis, 1809-1852
Freedman, Russell. Out of darkness: the story of Louis Braille; illustrated by Kate Kiesler. Clarion Bks. 1997 81p il $16.95; pa $7.95 *
Grades: 4 5 6 7   92
1. Blind—Books and reading
ISBN 0-395-77516-7; 0-395-96888-7 (pa)
                                                   LC 95-52353
This biography "tells about Braille's life and the development of his alphabet system for the blind." SLJ
"Without melodrama, Freedman tells the momentous story in quiet chapters in his best plain style, making the facts immediate and personal. . . . A diagram explains how the Braille alphabet works, and Kate Kessler's full-page shaded pencil illustrations are part of the understated poignant drama." Booklist

Brave Bird, Mary
Brave Bird, Mary. Lakota woman; by Mary Crow Dog and Richard Erdoes. 1st HarperPerennial ed. HarperPerennial 1991 263p il pa $13.95
Grades: 8 9 10 11 12 Adult   92
1. American Indian Movement 2. Political activists 3. Dakota Indians
ISBN 0-06-097389-7   LC 90-55980
First published 1990 by Grove Weidenfeld
"Born in 1955 and raised in poverty on the Rosebud Reservation, Mary Crow Dog escaped an oppressive Catholic boarding school but fell into a marginal life of urban shoplifting and barhopping. A 1971 encounter with AIM (the American Indian Movement), participation in the 1972 Trail of Broken Treaties march on Washington, and giving birth to her first child while under fire at the 1973 siege of Wounded Knee radicalized her." Libr J
"The story of Mary Crow Dog's coming of age in the Indian civil rights movement is simply told—and, at times, simply horrifying." N Y Times Book Rev

Breazeal, Cynthia
Brown, Jordan. Robo world; the story of robot designer Cynthia Breazeal; by Jordan D. Brown. Franklin Watts 2005 108p il (Women's adventures in science) $31
Grades: 7 8 9 10   92
1. Robots 2. Women scientists
ISBN 0-531-16782-8   LC 2005000826
Also available in paperback from Joseph Henry Press
A biography of Cynthia Breazeal who designs, builds, and experiments with robots at the MIT Media Lab.
Includes bibliographical references

Breckinridge, Mary, 1881-1965
Wells, Rosemary. Mary on horseback; three mountain stories; pictures by Peter McCarty. Dial Bks. for Young Readers 1998 53p il $16.99; pa $4.99 *
Grades: 4 5 6 7   92
1. Nurses
ISBN 0-670-88923-7; 0-14-130815-x (pa)
                                                   LC 97-43409
Tells the stories of three families who were helped by the work of Mary Breckinridge, the first nurse to go into the Appalachian Mountains and give medical care to the isolated inhabitants. Includes an afterword with facts about Breckinridge and the Frontier Nursing Service she founded
"These beautifully written stories will remain with the reader long after the book is closed." Booklist

Bridgman, Laura Dewey, 1829-1889
Alexander, Sally Hobart. She touched the world: Laura Bridgman, deaf-blind pioneer; by Sally Hobart Alexander and Robert Alexander. Clarion Books 2008 100p il $18
Grades: 5 6 7 8   92
1. Howe, Samuel Gridley, 1801-1876 2. Blind 3. Deaf
ISBN 978-0-618-85299-4; 0-618-85299-9
"At the age of three, in 1832, Laura Bridgman contracted scarlet fever and lost her sight, her hearing, her sense of smell, and much of her sense of taste. Her family sent her to Dr. Samuel [Gridley] Howe at the New England Institute for the Education of the Blind, and by the age of 10, Laura was world-famous for her accomplishments. . . . Alexander . . . presents a well-written and thoroughly researched biography of this remarkable woman, with numerous black-and-white photos." Booklist
Includes bibliographical references

Brin, Sergey
White, Casey. Sergey Brin and Larry Page; the founders of Google; [by] Casey White. Rosen Pub. Group 2007 112p il (Internet career biographies) lib bdg 31.95
Grades: 6 7 8 9   92
1. Page, Larry 2. Google, Inc. 3. Internet
ISBN 1-4042-0716-3 (lib bdg); 978-1-4042-0716-5
                                                   LC 2005031027

Brin, Sergey—*Continued*

In this dual "biography, a wealth of information is presented on the development of Silicon Valley. When [Sergey] Brin and [Larry] Page first met at Stanford in 1995, little did they know that the project they worked on together, a graduate thesis, would develop into the now-famous search engine known as Google. . . . There is enough information for reports, and it's fairly easy to access." SLJ

Includes bibliographical references

Brontë, Charlotte, 1816-1855

Reiff, Raychel Haugrud. Charlotte Brontë; by Raychel Haugrud Reiff. Marshall Cavendish Benchmark 2005 159p il (Writers and their works) lib bdg $37.07

Grades: 7 8 9 10   92

1. Authors, English 2. Women authors

ISBN 0-7614-1948-9   LC 2004-23809

Contents: How Charlotte Brontë became a writer; Brontë and her times; *Jane Eyre*; *Villette*; Brontë's place in literature

This discusses Charlotte Brontë's life, times, and works.

Includes bibliographical references

Brooks, Gwendolyn

Hill, Christine M. Gwendolyn Brooks; "poetry is life distilled". Enslow Publishers 2005 128p il (African-American biography library) lib bdg $31.93

Grades: 7 8 9 10   92

1. Poets, American 2. African American authors 3. Women poets

ISBN 0-7660-2292-7   LC 2004-16801

"The first African American to win the Pulitzer Prize, in 1950, Brooks wrote poetry about the people she knew in her segregated South Side Chicago neighborhood. Later, feminists would credit her for being one of the first writers to treat the lives of everyday women in serious poetry. . . . This lively, readable title . . . provides plenty about Brooks' personal life and her politics." Booklist

Includes bibliographical references

Rhynes, Martha E. Gwendolyn Brooks; poet from Chicago. Morgan Reynolds 2003 112p il (World writers) lib bdg $21.95

Grades: 7 8 9 10   92

1. Poets, American 2. African American authors 3. Women poets

ISBN 1-931798-05-2   LC 2002-151122

Presents a biography of the African American poet who has received the National Book Award and the Pulitzer Prize

"The writing is clear, lively, and detailed." SLJ

Includes bibliographical references

Brown, Molly, 1867-1932

Landau, Elaine. Heroine of the Titanic: the real unsinkable Molly Brown. Clarion Bks. 2001 132p il $18

Grades: 5 6 7 8   92

ISBN 0-395-93912-7   LC 00-57015

This is a biography of the survivor of the Titanic who supported such causes as worker's rights and feminism

"A realistic biography of an independent and strong-willed woman. . . . Black-and-white archival illustrations and photos highlight her life as well as greater relevant aspects of the period in which she lived." SLJ

Includes bibliographical references

Bruchac, Joseph, 1942-

Bruchac, Joseph. Bowman's store; a journey to myself. 1st Lee & Low ed. Lee & Low Books 2001 315p il pa $9.95 *

Grades: 7 8 9 10   92

1. Abnaki Indians 2. Authors, American

ISBN 1-58430-027-2 (pa); 978-1-58430-027-4 (pa)

LC 2001-16435

A reissue of the title first published 1997 by Dial Books

"Combining Native American stories with personal memories and dreams, Bruchac crafts a memoir of his childhood growing up with his grandparents in upstate New York." Horn Book Guide

"Each episode is constructed with a true storyteller's attention to language and plot development. Students of modern Native American cultures will find plenty of food for thought." Booklist

Buffett, Warren E.

Johnson, Anne Janette. Warren Buffett; [by] Anne Janette Johnson. Morgan Reynolds Pub. 2008 c2009 128p il (Business leaders) $28.95

Grades: 7 8 9 10   92

1. Capitalists and financiers

ISBN 978-1-59935-080-6; 1-59935-080-7

LC 2007045963

"This book answers many questions about the unassuming billionaire from Omaha. Buffett's life . . . is detailed on both personal and professional levels. . . . Anecdotes make the book accessible and demystify the sometimes-confusing world of stocks and investments. . . . A fair number of color photos is included." SLJ

Includes bibliographical references

Burns, Anthony, 1834-1862

Hamilton, Virginia. Anthony Burns: the defeat and triumph of a fugitive slave. Knopf 1988 193p pa $5.50 hardcover o.p. *

Grades: 5 6 7 8   92

1. Slavery—United States 2. African Americans—Biography

ISBN 0-679-83997-6 (pa)   LC 87-38063

A biography of the slave who escaped to Boston in 1854, was arrested at the instigation of his owner, and whose trial caused a furor between abolitionists and those determined to enforce the Fugitive Slave Act

"This book does exactly what good biography for children ought to do: takes readers directly into the life of the subject and makes them feel what it was like to be that person in those times." Horn Book

Includes bibliographical references

Burr, Aaron, 1756-1836

St. George, Judith. The duel: the parallel lives of Alexander Hamilton and Aaron Burr. Viking 2009 97p il $16.99 *

Grades: 6 7 8 9   92

1. Hamilton, Alexander, 1757-1804

ISBN 978-0-670-01124-7; 0-670-01124-X

LC 2009005660

"After a prologue following the steps of Alexander Hamilton and Aaron Burr on the morning of their famous duel, St. George backtracks to trace the 'parallel lives' mentioned in the subtitle. . . . Well researched and organized, the book offers insights into the personalities, lives, and times of Burr and Hamilton." Booklist

Burroughs, John, 1837-1921

Wadsworth, Ginger. John Burroughs; the sage of Slabsides. Clarion Bks. 1997 95p il $16.95

Grades: 5 6 7 8   92

1. Naturalists

ISBN 0-395-77830-1   LC 95-48400

A photobiography of the naturalist, ornithologist, author, poet, teacher, and pioneer of the conservation movement who lived and worked in his rustic cabin in the Catskill Mountains

"The pictures are mostly informal and candid, taken from personal collections, with a few studio portraits interspersed. Written with a familiar, almost intimate tone, the text is liberally sprinkled with quotes from Burroughs's publications." SLJ

Includes bibliographical references

Burton, Sir Richard Francis, 1821-1890

Young, Serinity. Richard Francis Burton; explorer, scholar, spy; [by] Serinity Young. Marshall Cavendish Benchmark 2006 80p il map (Great explorations) lib bdg $32.79

Grades: 5 6 7 8   92

1. Explorers

ISBN 978-0-7614-2222-8; 0-7614-2222-6

LC 2005027932

A biography of the 19th century English explorer of Asia and Africa

Includes bibliographical references

Busby, Cylin, 1970-

Busby, Cylin. The year we disappeared; a father-daughter memoir; [by] Cylin Busby & John Busby. Bloomsbury 2008 329p $16.99 *

Grades: 8 9 10 11 12   92

1. Busby, John, 1942- 2. Police 3. Father-daughter relationship 4. Violence

ISBN 978-1-59990-141-1; 1-59990-141-2

LC 2008017215

"No one with even a marginal interest in true crime writing should miss this page-turner, by turns shocking and almost unbearably sad. In 1979, in an underworld-style hit, a gunman shot John Busby, a policeman in Cape Cod; a fluke saved John's life, but he was permanently disfigured and disabled, and the family placed under 24-hour protection. Eventually the family went into hiding in Tennessee, but arguably their 'disappearance'

takes place long before they move—as John and his daughter, Cylin, alternately narrate, readers can see how the shooting erased the family's sense of themselves. . . . Where John's chapters provide the grim facts, it is Cylin's authentically childlike perspective that, in revealing the cost to her innocence, renders the tragic experience most searingly." Publ Wkly

Includes bibliographical references

Busby, John, 1942-

Busby, Cylin. The year we disappeared. See entry under Busby, Cylin, 1970-

Byars, Betsy Cromer, 1928-

Byars, Betsy Cromer. The moon and I. Beech Tree Bks. 1996 96p il pa $5.99

Grades: 4 5 6 7   92

1. Authors, American 2. Women authors

ISBN 0-688-13704-0   LC 95-53100

First published 1991 by Messner

A "personal narrative that gives readers some info about snakes, a fair amount of insight into how writers do what they do, and the unmistakable impression that autobiographies are great entertainment. Byars's genuine, humorous outlook on life shines through on every page." SLJ

Cammarano, Rita. Betsy Byars. Chelsea House 2002 106p il (Who wrote that?) $22.95

Grades: 4 5 6 7   92

1. Authors, American 2. Women authors

ISBN 0-7910-6720-3   LC 2001-8337

Contents: Planes, people and pets; Miss Harriet, Bubba, and the zoo; Books, a river, and a fox; Swan time; Wings and things; From swimming to soaring; Golly blossom bingo; Reaching for the moon; A well that never goes dry

Describes the personal life and successful writing career of the Newbery Award-winning author, whose memorable characters include Bingo Brown, Herculeah Jones, and the Golly sisters

"An excellent resource for author studies and creative writing classes." Book Rep

Includes bibliographical references

Caesar, Julius, 100-44 B.C.

Galford, Ellen. Julius Caesar; the boy who conquered an empire; [by] Ellen Galford. National Geographic 2007 64p il map (World history biographies) $17.95; lib bdg $27.90

Grades: 5 6 7 8   92

1. Rome—History 2. Emperors—Rome

ISBN 978-1-4263-0064-6; 978-1-4263-0065-3 (lib bdg)   LC 2006020777

A biography of the Roman emperor

This "visually appealing [title is] packed with excellent photographs and reproductions, interesting sidebars, and [has] a time line running along the bottom of every page. . . . [This book is] useful, well-written." SLJ

Includes glossary and bibliographical references

Caesar, Julius, 100-44 B.C.—*Continued*

Julius Caesar; Don Nardo, book editor. Greenhaven Press 2002 186p il (People who made history) lib bdg $34.95; pa $23.70

Grades: 7 8 9 10 11 12   **92**
    1. Emperors—Rome 2. Rome—History
    ISBN 0-7377-0665-1 (lib bdg); 0-7377-0664-3 (pa)
           LC 2001-23902

This profiles the life of the Roman emperor and includes essays and primary source documents

Includes bibliographical references

Kent, Zachary. Julius Caesar; ruler of the Roman world; [by] Zachary Kent. Enslow Publishers 2006 160p il map (Rulers of the ancient world) $27.93

Grades: 6 7 8 9   **92**
    1. Emperors—Rome 2. Rome—History
    ISBN 0-7660-2563-2   LC 2005022485

A biography of the Roman emperor

"With balance and lucidity, Kent presents the life and times of one of Western civilization's most significant political leaders." SLJ

Includes glossary and bibliographical references

Nardo, Don. Julius Caesar; Roman general and statesman. Compass Point Books 2009 112p il (Signature lives) lib bdg $34.60

Grades: 6 7 8 9   **92**
    1. Rome—History 2. Emperors—Rome
    ISBN 978-0-7565-3834-7; 0-7565-3834-3
           LC 2008005725

Presents the life and accomplishments of the Roman general and statesman whose brilliant military leadership helped make Rome the center of a vast empire.

Includes glossary and bibliographical references

Calcines, Eduardo F., 1955-

Calcines, Eduardo F. Leaving Glorytown; one boy's struggle under Castro. Farrar, Straus & Giroux 2009 221p il $17.95 *

Grades: 7 8 9 10   **92**
    1. Cuban refugees 2. Cuba—History—1959-
    ISBN 978-0-374-34394-1; 0-374-34394-2
           LC 2008-07506

"Calcines's spirited memoir captures the political tension, economic hardship, family stress, and personal anxiety of growing up during the early years of the Castro regime in Cuba. . . . The author shares startling, clear memories about his life in the Glorytown barrio of Cienfuegos. . . . Calcines writes about Cuba with immediacy, nostalgia, and passion. This personal account will acquaint readers with the oppressive and ironic effects of communism." SLJ

Callwood, June, 1924-2007

Dublin, Anne. June Callwood; a life of action. Second Story Press 2007 140p il pa $14.95

Grades: 7 8 9 10 11 12   **92**
    1. Women journalists 2. Social action 3. Canadians
    ISBN 978-1-89718-714-2

"This biography of the Canadian journalist and social activist chronicles Callwood's long life with loving care and places her activism within the cultural and historical context of pre and postwar Canada. . . . This is a well-told life story, with many black-and-white photographs that infuse the subject with personality." SLJ

Canaletto, 1697-1768

Rice, Earle. Canaletto; by Earle Rice Jr. Mitchell Lane Publishers 2007 48p il (Art profiles for kids) lib bdg $29.95

Grades: 7 8 9 10   **92**
    1. Artists, Italian
    ISBN 978-1-58415-561-4 (lib bdg); 1-58415-561-2 (lib bdg)   LC 2007023412

This offers "well-documented information for teens doing reports. [The] volume covers the painter's childhood, training, travels, influences, and historical context. The chronological chapters build a survey of the [artist's] oeuvres, including the style and subject matter of [his] works and past and present critical reaction." SLJ

Includes glossary and bibliographical references

Card, Orson Scott

Willett, Edward. Orson Scott Card; architect of alternate worlds. Enslow Publishers 2006 128p bibl por (Authors teens love) $31.93

Grades: 6 7 8 9   **92**
    1. Authors, American
    ISBN 0-7660-2354-0   LC 2005020832

"This solid and well-researched biography does an able job of balancing information on the subject's numerous publications with the events in his personal life. . . . Card's *Ender's Game* is popular with teens, and this book will help them to understand how he came to create the 'Enderverse.'" SLJ

Includes bibliographical references

Carnegie, Andrew, 1835-1919

Edge, Laura Bufano. Andrew Carnegie; industrial philanthropist; [by] Laura B. Edge. Lerner Publications Co. 2004 128p il (Lerner biography) lib bdg $27.93

Grades: 6 7 8 9   **92**
    1. Capitalists and financiers 2. Philanthropists 3. Steel industry
    ISBN 0-8225-4965-4   LC 2002-152936

Contents: Triumphant return; Simple beginnings; Climbing the ladder; The goose that laid the golden egg; Railroads and war; A little of this, a little of that; A moral tug of war; Choosing a specialty; Building an empire; The star-spangled Scotchman; War at homestead; The richest man in the world; Scientific philanthropy; Ambassador for peace; Timeline

Chronicles the rags-to-riches tale of a Scottish immigrant who used most of the millions he earned as a steel tycoon to set up a fund for the advancement of science, education, and peace.

"Children will come away with a good sense of a man driven by contradictory impulses." Booklist

Includes bibliographical references

Carnegie, Andrew, 1835-1919—*Continued*
Kent, Zachary. Andrew Carnegie; steel king and friend to libraries. Enslow Pubs. 1999 128p il maps (Historical American biographies) lib bdg $26.60
Grades: 6 7 8 9   92
1. Capitalists and financiers 2. Philanthropists 3. Steel industry
ISBN 0-7660-1212-3   LC 98-3160
A biography of the Scottish immigrant who made a fortune in the steel industry and used much of it for philanthropic causes
Includes glossary and bibliographical references

Carr, Emily, 1871-1945
Debon, Nicolas. Four pictures by Emily Carr. Douglas & McIntyre 2003 unp il $15.95 *
Grades: 4 5 6 7   92
1. Artists, Canadian 2. Women artists
ISBN 0-88899-532-6
"Debon has distilled four periods in the Canadian artist's life (1871-1945) into enticing vignettes that illuminate her passions, determination, health problems, relationships with fellow Group of Seven artists, and, most of all, her dramatic progression as a painter. . . . Engaging artwork and brisk storytelling make this a consideration for most libraries." SLJ

Carroll, Lewis, 1832-1898
Carpenter, Angelica Shirley. Lewis Carroll; through the looking glass. Lerner Publs. 2003 128p il map (Lerner biography) lib bdg $27.93
Grades: 7 8 9 10   92
1. Authors, English
ISBN 0-8225-0073-6   LC 2002-3266
A biography of the mathematician, teacher, photographer, and author who wrote "Alice in Wonderland"
"An accessible, well-documented portrait." SLJ
Includes bibliographical references

Carson, Kit, 1809-1868
Calvert, Patricia. Kit Carson; he led the way; [by] Patricia Calvert. Marshall Cavendish Benchmark 2006 c2007 96p il (Great explorations) lib bdg $32.79
Grades: 5 6 7 8   92
1. Frontier and pioneer life—West (U.S.)
ISBN 978-0-7614-2223-5; 0-7614-2223-4
                                           LC 2005037375
"An examination of the life and frontier explorations of legendary trapper and Indian agent Christopher 'Kit' Carson." Publisher's note
Includes bibliographical references

Carson, Rachel, 1907-1964
Levine, Ellen. Rachel Carson; a twentieth-century life. Viking 2007 224p il (Up close) $15.99 *
Grades: 6 7 8 9 10   92

1. Women scientists
ISBN 0-670-06220-1
A biography of the environmental scientist.
"Direct, eloquent, and precise. . . . A balanced, thoroughly researched introduction to an original scientist whose work remains of urgent importance today." Booklist
Includes bibliographical references

Carvalho, Solomon Nunes, 1815-1897
Hirschfelder, Arlene B. Photo odyssey: Solomon Carvalho's remarkable Western adventure, 1853-54. Clarion Bks. 2000 118p il $18
Grades: 6 7 8 9   92
1. Photographers 2. West (U.S.)—Exploration
ISBN 0-395-89123-X   LC 99-42201
Describes the life of Carvalho, a Jewish photographer who accompanied John Charles Fremont on his last expedition to the West
"Through the author's historically accurate, vivid descriptions of the various stages of this journey, the reader gains incredible insight into the rigors endured by those who explored the vastness of our country during the 19th century." Book Rep
Includes bibliographical references

Carver, George Washington, 1864?-1943
Abrams, Dennis. George Washington Carver; scientist and educator; [by] Dennis Abrams. Chelsea House 2008 119p il (Black Americans of achievement) $30
Grades: 6 7 8 9   92
1. African Americans—Biography 2. Scientists
ISBN 978-0-7910-9717-5; 0-7910-9717-X
                                           LC 2007035677
This biography details the African American scientist's "rise from adversity to . . . recognition. The [book goes] beyond the typical personal information to provide some social history relevant to the subject's time. Captioned photographs and boxed inserts enhance the conversational [text]." Horn Book Guide
Includes bibliographical references

Harness, Cheryl. The groundbreaking, chance-taking life of George Washington Carver and science & invention in America; by Cheryl Harness. National Geographic 2008 143p il map (Cherly Harness histories) $16.95; lib bdg $25.90
Grades: 4 5 6 7   92
1. African Americans—Biography 2. Scientists
ISBN   978-1-4263-0196-4;   1-4263-0196-0;
978-1-4263-0197-1 (lib bdg); 1-4263-0197-9 (lib bdg)
                                           LC 2007029316
"Harness presents Carver as a man who, regardless of constant hardship and racial prejudice, persevered to become a beloved teacher and devoted scientist. . . . The author raises challenging questions throughout. . . . The lively prose style conveys his sense of passion and adventure about the man and his intellectual pursuits, and the simple black-and-white drawings add a further sense of drama." SLJ
Includes bibliographical references

Carver, George Washington, 1864?-1943—Continued

MacLeod, Elizabeth. George Washington Carver; an innovative life; written by Elizabeth MacLeod. Kids Can Press 2007 32p il $14.95 *
Grades: 4 5 6 7   **92**
1. Scientists 2. African Americans—Biography
ISBN 978-1-55337-906-5; 1-55337-906-3

"MacLeod chronicles Carver's life from childhood to the end of his career, and the recognition he received posthumously. Each spread has a page of text with a quote from Carver in the margin and a page filled with many graphics in black and white and color, including photographs, illustrations, and reproductions of artifacts, all with captions. . . . With the richness of detail presented, even reluctant readers will find something of interest about this exceptional individual." SLJ

Cash, Johnny

Neimark, Anne E. Johnny Cash; a twentieth-century life. Viking Childrens Books 2007 207p il (Up close) $15.99
Grades: 8 9 10 11 12   **92**
1. Country musicians
ISBN 978-0-670-06215-7   LC 2006-10198

"The life of the deeply troubled and powerfully influential music legend is brought vividly to life in this richly detailed biography. . . . Cash's genius as a songwriter and musician as well as his incalculable influence upon music are skillfully explored, and Neimark frequently uses excerpts from Cash's own songs to enrich his compelling life story." Booklist
Includes bibliographical references

Castro, Fidel, 1926-

Woog, Adam. Fidel Castro. Lucent Bks. 2003 112p il map (Importance of) lib bdg $27.45
Grades: 7 8 9 10   **92**
1. Cuba—Politics and government
ISBN 1-59018-231-6   LC 2002-14363

A biography of the Cuban leader
This is a "well-researched account. . . . Black-and-white photos enhance the text. . . . A good choice for research where needed." SLJ
Includes bibliographical references

Cather, Willa, 1873-1947

Meltzer, Milton. Willa Cather; a biography. Twenty-First Century Books 2008 160p il (Literary greats) $33.26
Grades: 7 8 9 10 11 12   **92**
1. Authors, American 2. Women authors
ISBN 978-0-8225-7604-4; 0-8225-7604-X
                                     LC 2007-25629
A biography of the author of such novels as *O Pioneers!* and *My Antonia.*
"With signature clarity, Meltzer's . . . biography . . . sets his detailed discussion of Cather's life and work against the larger backdrop of her times. . . . The book's handsome, inviting design includes photos on almost every spread." Booklist
Includes bibliographical references

Catherine II, the Great, Empress of Russia, 1729-1796

Vincent, Zu. Catherine the Great; Empress of Russia. Franklin Watts 2009 128p il map (A wicked history) $30; pa $5.95 *
Grades: 6 7 8 9   **92**
1. Empresses 2. Russia—History 3. Russia—Kings and rulers
ISBN 978-0-531-21802-0 (lib bdg); 0-531-21802-3 (lib bdg); 978-0-531-20738-3 (pa); 0-531-20738-2 (pa)
                                     LC 2008041543
"Catherine the Great might be . . . known as a cruel dictator with lots of lovers, but author Vincent shows how the Empress of Russia actually took on her position (well, after she had her husband murdered) with some good intentions. . . . Young readers will find the manipulation of Catherine's early days particularly interesting." Booklist
Includes bibliographical references

Catlin, George, 1796-1872

Reich, Susanna. Painting the wild frontier: the art and adventures of George Catlin. Clarion Books 2008 160p il map $21 *
Grades: 7 8 9 10 11 12   **92**
1. Artists—United States 2. Native Americans in art 3. West (U.S.) in art
ISBN 978-0-618-71470-4; 0-618-71470-7
                                     LC 2007-38847
This is a "biography of nineteenth-century painter George Catlin, famous for his portraits of Native American life. . . . A great introduction to Catlin's work as well as an excellent title to use in social studies, history, and art classes." Booklist
Includes bibliographical references

Cavell, Edith, 1865-1915

Batten, Jack. Silent in an evil time: the brave war of Edith Cavell. Tundra Books 2007 135p il pa $16.95
Grades: 7 8 9 10   **92**
1. Nurses 2. World War, 1914-1918
ISBN 978-0-88776-737-1
A biography of the British nurse who was executed by the Germans for sheltering British and French soldiers in Brussels during World War I
"This exceptional biography reads like an adventure novel. . . . The historical facts are well explained and Cavell is placed clearly in context." SLJ

Cézanne, Paul, 1839-1906

Burleigh, Robert. Paul Cezanne; a painter's journey. H.N. Abrams 2006 31p il $17.95
Grades: 4 5 6 7   **92**
1. Artists, French
ISBN 0-8109-5784-1   LC 2005011779
Published in association with the National Gallery of Art
"Burleigh offers brief insights into Cézanne's personal life, such as his relationship with his father, who did not support his sons interest in art. However, the emphasis is on interpreting some individual paintings and under-

Cézanne, Paul, 1839-1906—*Continued*
standing the artist's various styles, including the impact
of the Impressionists and his evolution to a freer and
simpler manner of expression in his later years. . . . The
high-quality reproductions demonstrate Burleigh's points.
. . . A solid, lively introduction." SLJ

Champlain, Samuel de, 1567-1635
Faber, Harold. Samuel de Champlain; explorer
of Canada; Harold Faber. Benchmark Books 2005
80p il map (Great explorations) lib bdg $29.93 *
Grades: 5 6 7 8   92
1. Explorers 2. America—Exploration
ISBN 0-7614-1608-0   LC 2003-974
Contents: Growing up; First voyage to Canada; The
fur trade; Founding of Quebec; The battle of Lake
Champlain; More voyages to Canada; Disappointments;
Governor of New France
"Faber draws on Champlain's own accounts to trace
his exploration of and dogged determination to colonize
Canada. . . . Illustrated with beautiful reproductions of
period illustrations, paintings, and maps. . . . Well-
written." SLJ
Includes bibliographical references

Charles, Ray
Duggleby, John. Uh huh!: the story of Ray
Charles. Morgan Reynolds Pub. 2005 160p il
$26.95
Grades: 7 8 9 10   92
1. African American singers
ISBN 1-931798-65-6   LC 2005-1287
The author "traces Charles' long career and displays
a sensitivity to the events surrounding his life (including
his bitter battles with heroin and alcohol addiction), as
well as a genuine understanding of his music and the
breadth of his musical influence. Sidebars on 'race' music, Braille, the Grammys, soul, and rock and roll enrich
the narrative." Booklist
Includes bibliographical references

Woog, Adam. Ray Charles and the birth of soul;
[by] Adam Woog. Lucent Books 2006 112p il
(Lucent library of Black history) lib bdg $28.70 *
Grades: 7 8 9 10   92
1. African American singers 2. Soul music
ISBN 1-59018-844-6   LC 2005022586
"Woog does an excellent job of describing Charles's
rare talent and the trajectory of his long and legendary
career. . . . The text is clearly written and well organized. Black-and-white photographs illustrate and inform." SLJ
Includes bibliographical references

Chavez, Cesar, 1927-1993
Cesar Chavez; Michelle Houle, book editor.
Greenhaven Press 2003 186p (People who made
history) hardcover o.p. pa $22.45
Grades: 7 8 9 10   92
1. Migrant labor 2. Mexican Americans—Biography
ISBN 0-7377-1298-8 (lib bdg); 0-7377-1299-6 (pa)
LC 2002-27152

"Chavez is the subject of 17 essays excerpted from
various biographies, social histories, and magazine articles. . . . A conflation of opinions and personal observations about the nonviolent reformer, the book is also a
piecemeal history of a social movement and its imperfect
leader. Excellent for reports." SLJ
Includes bibliographical references

Cruz, Bárbara. César Chávez; a voice for
farmworkers; [by] Bárbara C. Cruz. Enslow
Publishers, Inc. 2005 128p il (Latino biography
library) lib bdg $31.93 *
Grades: 7 8 9 10   92
1. Migrant labor 2. Mexican Americans
ISBN 0-7660-2489-X   LC 2004-27538
"Cruz takes readers from Chavez's first job as a migrant worker in California at age 10 through his decision
to help his fellow workers: his fasts, his activism, the
founding and continued involvement in the United Farm
Workers Union until his death in 1993. Black-and-white
and full-color photos appear throughout." SLJ

Young, Jeff C. Cesar Chavez; by Jeff C. Young.
Morgan Reynolds Pub. 2007 160p lib bdg $27.95
Grades: 6 7 8 9   92
1. Migrant labor 2. Mexican Americans—Biography
ISBN 978-1-59935-036-3 (lib bdg); 1-59935-036-X
(lib bdg)   LC 2006025973
Describes the life of the famous fighter for migrants
rights in the United States.
"The design makes the text easy to read, and there are
plenty of quotes that clarify Chavez's ideals and tactics.
. . . There are also lots of news photographs, some in
color. . . . This clear, sympathetic account provides good
readers with a look at both the man and the issues."
Booklist
Includes bibliographical references

Chávez Frías, Hugo
Levin, Judith. Hugo Chávez. Chelsea House
Publishers 2007 128p il (Modern world leaders)
$30
Grades: 7 8 9 10   92
1. Venezuela 2. Presidents—Venezuela
ISBN 0-7910-9258-5; 978-0-7910-9258-3
LC 2006-10611
This is a biography of the Venezuelan president.
Includes bibliographical references

Young, Jeff C. Hugo Chavez; leader of
Venezuela. Morgan Reynolds Pub. 2007 128p il
(World leaders) $27.95
Grades: 7 8 9 10 11 12   92
1. Venezuela 2. Presidents—Venezuela
ISBN 978-1-59935-068-4; 1-59935-068-8
LC 2007016946
"Young briefly covers the history of Venezuela, Cha-
vez's early years, and his service in the military before
getting to the book's focus: Chavez's time as Venezue-
la's very controversial president. The text is supported by
well-documented quotes from a variety of sources and
some photographs." Horn Book Guide
Includes bibliographical references

Child, Lydia Maria Francis, 1802-1880
Kenschaft, Lori. Lydia Maria Child; the quest for racial justice. Oxford Univ. Press 2002 126p il (Oxford portraits) lib bdg $24
Grades: 7 8 9 10   92
1. Women authors 2. Abolitionists 3. Authors, American
ISBN 0-19-513257-2   LC 2001-52339
A biography of the popular writer who, in the mid-nineteenth century, gave up her literary success to fight for the abolition of slavery, for women's rights, and for the fair treatment of American Indians
"This well-done book will give young people an opportunity to learn more about one woman and the ideals for which she stood." SLJ
Includes bibliographical references

Cho, Margaret, 1968-
Tiger, Caroline. Margaret Cho. Chelsea House 2007 111p bibl il por (Asian Americans of achievement) lib bdg $30
Grades: 7 8 9 10   92
1. Comedians 2. Korean Americans—Biography
ISBN 0-7910-9275-5; 978-0-7910-9275-0
                                   LC 2006028385
This is "a lively introduction to the comedian, from her rebellious childhood and teen years to her current successes. . . . The frequent quotes from Cho's funny insightful material will guide readers to seek out her performances." Booklist
Includes glossary and bibliographical references

Chopin, Frédéric, 1810-1849
Malaspina, Ann. Chopin's world; [by] Ann Malaspina. 1st ed. Rosen Pub. Group 2008 64p il (Music throughout history) lib bdg $29.25
Grades: 5 6 7 8   92
1. Composers
ISBN 1-4042-0723-6 (lib bdg); 978-1-4042-0723-3 (lib bdg)   LC 2005031281
This "book begins with an introduction briefly addressing social issues of the day, historical background, or other significant information. . . . Successive chapters discuss the [man's] early [life], family background, social status, personality characteristics, musical training and education, obstacles or challenges, and influences. A chapter . . . focuses on the musician's well-known compositions, describing through lively and colorful language some of the musical elements employed. . . . The format and layout are appealing and uncluttered." SLJ
Includes glossary and bibliographical references

Christo, 1935-
Greenberg, Jan. Christo & Jeanne-Claude; through the Gates and beyond; [by] Jan Greenberg and Sandra Jordan. Roaring Brook Press 2008 50p il $19.95 *
Grades: 6 7 8 9   92
1. Christo, Jeanne-Claude, 1935- 2. Gates: Project for Central Park, New York 3. Artists—Biography
ISBN 978-1-59643-071-6; 1-59643-071-0
                                   LC 2007-19951
"A Neal Porter book"

"In 2005, the dull gray of a New York City winter was interrupted when two indomitable artists, Christo and his partner, Jeanne-Claude, brought Central Park brilliantly to life with their outdoor work The Gates. . . . This book, chronicling both The Gates as well as the artists' other projects, is as thoughtful, eye-opening, and meticulous as the work it celebrates." Booklist
Includes bibliographical references

Christo, Jeanne-Claude, 1935-
Greenberg, Jan. Christo & Jeanne-Claude. See entry under Christo, 1935-

Churchill, Sir Winston, 1874-1965
Binns, T. B. Winston Churchill; soldier and politician; [by] Tristan Boyer Binns. Franklin Watts 2004 127p il (Great life stories) $30.50
Grades: 5 6 7 8   92
1. Prime ministers—Great Britain 2. Great Britain—Politics and government—20th century
ISBN 0-531-12361-8   LC 2004-2946
Contents: The early years; Enter the army; The young statesman; World War One; Roaring through the twenties; The wilderness years; Back in power; The tide turns; Victory in Europe; After the war; A great life ends
This is an introduction to the life of Winston Churchill, British Prime Minister during World War II
"Binns does an excellent job of looking at the statesman's major successes, struggles, downfalls, and rises to political prominence. . . . Archival photographs and reproductions and boxes of information are attractive." SLJ
Includes bibliographical references

Macdonald, Fiona. Winston Churchill. World Almanac 2003 48p il (Trailblazers of the modern world) lib bdg $26.60
Grades: 5 6 7 8   92
1. Great Britain—Politics and government—20th century 2. Prime ministers—Great Britain
ISBN 0-8368-5082-3   LC 2002-38044
Examines the childhood, war years, political career, and personal life of the twentieth-century British statesman, soldier, and historian
"A fascinating peek into British society, the army, and Parliament. . . . Suitable as a first purchase." SLJ
Includes bibliographical references

Severance, John B. Winston Churchill; soldier, statesman, artist. Clarion Bks. 1996 144p il map $17.95 *
Grades: 5 6 7 8   92
1. Great Britain—Politics and government—20th century 2. Prime ministers—Great Britain
ISBN 0-395-69853-7   LC 94-25129
This "biography presents an affectionate portrait of Britain's renowned Prime Minister. Although Severance focuses on Churchill's contributions during World War II, he also describes the statesman's boyhood, Boer War adventures, and political ascendancy." SLJ
"This fair, balanced, and duly appreciative biography is handsomely produced and illustrated with a fine collection of photographs." Horn Book Guide
Includes bibliographical references

Churchill, Sir Winston, 1874-1965—*Continued*

Wrigley, Chris. Winston Churchill: a biographical companion. ABC-CLIO 2002 xxvi, 367p il (ABC-CLIO biographical companion) $55

Grades: 7 8 9 10   92

1. Great Britain—Politics and government—20th century 2. Prime ministers—Great Britain

ISBN 0-87436-990-8   LC 2002-2178

"This book is an A-Z compilation of events, people, issues, laws, places, and groups having some historical association with Churchill. Easy to use, it presents material in readable topics with B&W photos, related entries, and suggestions for further reading. . . . This book is a valuable resource for browsing or for research on specific people, places, or events connected to Churchill." Libr Media Connect

Includes bibliographical references

Cleary, Beverly

Cleary, Beverly. A girl from Yamhill: a memoir. Morrow 1988 279p il hardcover o.p. pa $12.99

Grades: 6 7 8 9   92

1. Authors, American 2. Women authors

ISBN 0-688-07800-1; 0-380-72740-4 (pa)
                                                LC 87-31554

Follows the popular children's author from her childhood years in Oregon through high school and into young adulthood, highlighting her family life and her growing interest in writing

"The author sees her child self with the same clarity and objectivity as she has seen her fictional characters, and her reminiscences have a resultant integrity and candor." Bull Cent Child Books

Clemente, Roberto, 1934-1972

Ford, Carin T. Roberto Clemente; baseball legend. Enslow Pubs. 2005 128p il (Latino biography library) lib bdg $31.93

Grades: 5 6 7 8   92

1. Baseball—Biography 2. Puerto Ricans—Biography

ISBN 0-7660-2485-7

This "account of the major leagues' first Puerto Rican superstar highlights the player's extraordinary talent and humanitarian drive as well as his less-admirable hot temper and often cocky demeanor. . . . The basic arc of Clemente's biography, particularly his tragic death, ensures an exciting read, with special appeal for sports fans." Booklist

Includes bibliographical references

Márquez, Herón. Roberto Clemente; baseball's humanitarian hero; by Herón Márquez. Carolrhoda Books 2005 112p il (Trailblazer biography) lib bdg $27.93

Grades: 4 5 6 7   92

1. Baseball—Biography 2. Puerto Ricans—Biography

ISBN 1-57505-767-0   LC 2004-2319

Contents: Introduction; Field of dreams; Turning heads, turning pro; Don't cry for me, Puerto Rico; The man of steel; Good night, Clemente; An immortal moment; Death of a hero

This "biography of the baseball great begins with Clemente's early life in Puerto Rico and ends with his death delivering supplies to earthquake victims in Nicaragua in 1972." Booklist

"This excellent biography is well organized and enlivened with interesting details and anecdotes. . . . Balancing facts with insightful perspective, this is a readable, well-rounded portrait." SLJ

Includes bibliographical references

Cleopatra, Queen of Egypt, d. 30 B.C.

Morgan, Julian. Cleopatra; ruling in the shadow of Rome. Rosen Pub. Group 2003 112p il (Leaders of ancient Egypt) lib bdg $31.95

Grades: 5 6 7 8   92

1. Queens 2. Egypt—History

ISBN 0-8239-3591-4   LC 2002-1214

"This title focuses on Cleopatra VII and her volatile relationship with Rome. A brief history of the Ptolemies and their rule in Egypt provides readers with essential background information. Vivid descriptions of Cleopatra's relationships with Julius Caesar and Mark Antony include possible motives for the alliances she formed. Clear discussions of the intricate politics, fragile unions, and the possibility of foreign invasions and internal rebellion are also provided. . . . Full-color photographs of the art, architecture, and artifacts of this time period enhance understanding." SLJ

Includes bibliographical references

Sapet, Kerrily. Cleopatra; ruler of Egypt; [by] Kerrily Sapet. Morgan Reynolds Pub. 2007 176p il map (World leaders) lib bdg $27.95

Grades: 8 9 10 11 12   92

1. Queens 2. Egypt—History

ISBN 978-1-59935-035-6 (lib bdg); 1-59935-035-1 (lib bdg)   LC 2006033381

"This biography of the legendary but somewhat mysterious Cleopatra provides a balanced account of her life and legacy. . . . The text is strongest in its descriptions of Egyptian culture and religion, the role of women, and life in the Nile Valley. . . . Numerous color reproductions and illustrations brighten the text." SLJ

Includes bibliographical references

Stanley, Diane. Cleopatra; [by] Diane Stanley, Peter Vennema; illustrated by Diane Stanley. Morrow Junior Bks. 1994 unp il map hardcover o.p. pa $7.99 *

Grades: 4 5 6 7   92

1. Queens 2. Egypt—History

ISBN 0-688-10413-4; 0-688-10414-2 (lib bdg); 0-688-15480-8 (pa)   LC 93-27032

This is a biography of the ancient Egyptian queen

"Lucid writing combines with carefully selected anecdotes, often attributed to the Greek historian Plutarch to create an engaging narrative. . . . Stanley's stunning, full-color gouache artwork is arresting in its large, well-composed images executed in flat Greek style." SLJ

Includes bibliographical references

Clinton, Hillary Rodham, 1947-
Burgan, Michael. Hillary Rodham Clinton; First Lady and Senator; by Michael Burgan. Compass Point Books 2008 112p il (Signature lives) lib bdg $34.60
Grades: 6 7 8 9   **92**
1. Women politicians 2. Presidents' spouses—United States
ISBN 0-7565-1588-2 (lib bdg); 978-0-7565-1588-1 (lib bdg)   LC 2005025209
"This biography of one of the most powerful women in U.S. politics is sure to be a hot book right now and in the future. . . . This title . . . is jacketed and boasts a clean, attractive design and lots of photos." Booklist
Includes glossary and bibliographical references

Guernsey, JoAnn Bren. Hillary Rodham Clinton; by JoAnn Bren Guernsey. Lerner Pub. Co. 2005 112p il (A & E biography) lib bdg $27.93; pa $7.95
Grades: 6 7 8 9   **92**
1. Women politicians 2. Presidents' spouses—United States
ISBN 0-8225-2372-8 (lib bdg); 0-8225-9613-X (pa)   LC 2004-21746
Contents: A young activist; An explosion of ideas; From Yale to Arkansas; First lady of Arkansas; "The race is on;" Woman in the West Wing; Vast right-wing conspiracy; Senator Clinton
This biography "covers Clinton's many achievements. . . . Guernsey does not shy away from the controversial aspects of her subject's story. . . . [This is a] solid biography." SLJ
Includes bibliographical references

Tracy, Kathleen. The Clinton view; the historic fight for the 2008 Democratic presidential nomination. Mitchell Lane Publishers 2009 il (Monumental milestones) lib bdg $29.95
Grades: 6 7 8 9   **92**
1. Women politicians 2. Presidents—United States—Election—2008 3. Presidents' spouses—United States
ISBN 978-1-58415-731-1; 1-58415-731-3   LC 2008053545
This looks at the 2008 presidential campaign from the point of view of candidate Hillary Clinton
This "begins with the Iowa caucus, the effect the loss had on front-runner Clinton, and how her win in New Hampshire made her the second Clinton 'comeback kid.' Then, the book goes back to Clinton's early years, her academic successes, and her tenures as First Lady and senator. Tracy captures some of the excitement of the campaign. . . . The design is lively and colorful, and the photos will draw readers." Booklist
Includes bibliographical references

Wells, Catherine. Hillary Clinton; by Catherine Wells. Morgan Reynolds Pub. 2007 112p il (Political profiles) lib bdg $27.95
Grades: 6 7 8 9   **92**
1. Women politicians 2. Presidents' spouses—United States
ISBN 978-1-59935-047-9 (lib bdg); 1-59935-047-5 (lib bdg)   LC 2007028950

This "hits the major points in Clinton's life. . . . Readers gain glimpses of Clinton's girlhood in suburban Chicago, most of the book's emphasis falls on the former First Lady's impressive career. . . . Broken up with numerous color photos, the text concludes with a time line, source list, bibliography, and suggestions for Web research." Booklist
Includes bibliographical references

Cobain, Kurt, 1967-1994
Burlingame, Jeff. Kurt Cobain; "oh well, whatever, nevermind". Enslow Publishers 2006 160p il (American rebels) lib bdg $27.93
Grades: 6 7 8 9   **92**
1. Rock musicians
ISBN 0-7660-2426-1   LC 2006001742
A biography of the Rock musician belonging to the group Nirvana
This "is an unusually intimate account of the rock legend. A resident of Cobain's hometown, Burlingame supports his well-researched portrait with personal interviews with Cobain's family, friends, and other local acquaintances." Booklist
Includes glossary and bibliographical references

Coleman, Bessie, 1896?-1926
Hart, Philip S. Up in the air: the story of Bessie Coleman. Carolrhoda Bks. 1996 80p il (Trailblazers) pa $8.95 hardcover o.p.
Grades: 5 6 7 8   **92**
1. Women air pilots 2. African American pilots
ISBN 0-87614-978-6 (pa)   LC 95-32906
Presents the story of Bessie Coleman, an American, who in 1920 traveled to France to become the first black woman to earn a pilot's license
This "will be useful for research and recreational reading." SLJ
Includes bibliographical references

Collins, Michael, 1930-
Schyffert, Bea Uusma. The man who went to the far side of the moon: the story of Apollo 11 astronaut Michael Collins. Chronicle 2003 77p il $14.95
Grades: 5 6 7 8   **92**
1. Astronauts 2. Space flight
ISBN 0-8118-4007-7
A biography of the astronaut, Michael Collins, who circled the moon in the Apollo 12 space capsule while his colleagues Neil Armstrong and Buzz Aldrin landed the lunar module and walked on the moon.
"This excellent book—illustrated scrapbook-style with a cleverly presented mix of photographs, illustrations, and charts—communicates the excitement of space travel." Booklist

Columbus, Christopher
Collier, James Lincoln. Christopher Columbus; to the New World; [by] James Lincoln Collier. Marshall Cavendish Benchmark 2006 80p il map (Great explorations) lib bdg $32.79 *
Grades: 5 6 7 8   **92**

Columbus, Christopher—*Continued*
1. Explorers 2. America—Exploration
ISBN 978-0-7614-2221-1; 0-7614-2221-8
An account of the life and times of the explorer credited with the European discovery of America
Includes bibliographical references

Colvin, Claudette
Hoose, Phillip M. Claudette Colvin; twice toward justice; by Phillip Hoose. Melanie Kroupa Books 2009 133p il $19.95 *
Grades: 6 7 8 9 10   92
1. African American women—Biography 2. African Americans—Civil rights
ISBN 978-0-374-31322-7; 0-374-31322-9
              LC 2008-05435
"Teenager Claudette Colvin's significant contribution to the struggle for equal accommodation is presented in this biography that smoothly weaves excerpts from Hoose's extensive interviews with Colvin and his own supplementary commentary. . . . Readers learn . . . why her arrest for refusing to give up her bus seat to a white passenger never became the crucial incident to spark the Montgomery Bus Boycott. . . . Plenty of black-and-white photographs and well-deployed sidebars enhance the text." Bull Cent Child Books
Includes bibliographical references

Confucius
Freedman, Russell. Confucius; the golden rule; illustrated by Frédéric Clément. Levine Bks. 2002 48p il $15.95 *
Grades: 4 5 6 7   92
1. Philosophers
ISBN 0-439-13957-0   LC 2001-29372
This is a "biography of the 5th-century B.C. philosopher Confucius, whose teachings have influenced the development of modern government and education in both China and the West." Publ Wkly
"The fascinating narrative seamlessly intersperses stories from the *Analects* with Chinese history and biographical information about Confucius. . . . Clement's muted, elegant paintings of towns, temples, and the bucktoothed Confucius himself have a suitably ancient feel with jagged borders and fading colors." Booklist

Copernicus, Nicolaus, 1473-1543
Andronik, Catherine M. Copernicus; founder of modern astronomy. Rev ed. Enslow Publishers 2009 128p bibl il (Great minds of science) lib bdg $31.93
Grades: 5 6 7 8   92
1. Astronomers
ISBN 978-0-7660-3013-8 (lib bdg); 0-7660-3013-X (lib bdg)   LC 2008-23940
Fisrt published 2002
"A highly readable book that presents a good balance between the biographical information needed to understand Copernicus as a man and the scientific explanations necessary to understand his work. . . . Good-quality, black-and-white reproductions, illustrations, and photographs add interest to the clearly written text." SLJ [review of 2002 edition]
Includes glossary and bibliographical references

Goble, Todd. Nicholas Copernicus and the founding of modern astronomy. Morgan Reynolds 2004 144p il (Renaissance scientists) lib bdg $23.95
Grades: 7 8 9 10   92
1. Astronomers
ISBN 1-88384-699-4   LC 2003-4659
Contents: Born at the right time; From Koppernigk to Copernicus; The perks of the office; The return to Italy; The wages of nepotism; The duties of the canon; The astronomer emerges; On revolutions; An elder canon; Publication; The retreat of the stars
Presents the life and work of the famous sixteenth-century Polish astronomer
"This methodical biography places the astronomer within the turbulent political and religious events of his times and the concurrent intellectual riptides that marked the shift from medieval to modern science." SLJ

Sakolsky, Josh. Copernicus and modern astronomy. Rosen Pub. Group 2005 64p il (Primary sources of revolutionary scientific discoveries and theories) $29.25
Grades: 6 7 8 9   92
1. Astronomers 2. Astronomy
ISBN 1-4042-0305-2; 978-1-4042-0305-1
              LC 2004011296
An introduction to the life and work of the pioneering astronomer who proved that the earth revolved around the sun
Includes bibliographical references

Cormier, Robert
Beckman, Wendy Hart. Robert Cormier; banned, challenged, and censored. Enslow Publishers 2008 160p bibl il por (Authors of banned books) lib bdg $34.60
Grades: 6 7 8 9 10   92
1. Authors, American 2. Censorship
ISBN 978-0-7660-2691-9; 0-7660-2691-4
              LC 2007-28003
"Cormier is generally cited as one of the finest and most challenged writers for teens. This combination of biography and literary criticism explains his appeal to readers as well as the most common objections to his works from parents and school districts. A history of other censorship, including several recent court cases involving the First Amendment, and a biographical sketch of Cormier precede the discussion of *The Chocolate War* (1974), *I Am the Cheese* (1977), and *After the First Death* (1979, all Knopf). . . . A helpful overview of the works of a major YA author." SLJ
Includes glossary and bibliographical references

Cousteau, Jacques Yves, 1910-1997
Olmstead, Kathleen A. Jacques Cousteau; a life under the sea; [by] Kathleen Olmstead. Sterling Pub. Co. 2008 124p il (Sterling biographies) pa $5.99
Grades: 7 8 9 10   92
1. Ocean 2. Oceanography 3. Scientists
ISBN 978-1-4027-4440-2; 1-4027-4440-4
              LC 2007048195

Cousteau, Jacques Yves, 1910-1997—*Continued*

"Most of the text . . . is concerned with Cousteau's evolving inventions for breathing and exploring underwater. Olmstead describes how his films and television specials opened a new world to viewers, and how he became a leading advocate for the oceans. She also makes mention of Cousteau's secret second family and his dispute with his son Jean-Michel over using the family name for an ecotourist resort. . . . [This] attractively formatted [title has] black-and-white and full-color photographs or reproductions as well as sidebars. [A] solid [addition] to biography shelves." SLJ

Includes glossary and bibliographical references

Coville, Bruce

Marcovitz, Hal. Bruce Coville. Chelsea House 2006 124p bibl il por (Who wrote that?) $30

Grades: 6 7 8 9   **92**

1. Authors, American

ISBN 0-7910-8656-9   LC 2005008182

A biography of the popular author of children's and young adult fantasy and science fiction books.

Includes bibliographical references

Crandall, Prudence, 1803-1890

Jurmain, Suzanne. The forbidden schoolhouse; the true and dramatic story of Prudence Crandall and her students. Houghton Mifflin 2005 150p il $18 *

Grades: 5 6 7 8   **92**

1. African Americans—Education 2. Educators 3. Abolitionists

ISBN 0-618-47302-5

This is the story of Prudence Crandall, who, in 1831, opened a school for African American girls in Canterbury, Connecticut.

"A compelling, highly readable book. . . . Writing with a sense of drama that propels readers forward . . . Jurmain makes painfully clear what Crandall and her students faced. . . . Including a number of sepia-toned and color photographs as well as historical engravings, the book's look will draw in readers." Booklist

Includes bibliographical references

Crazy Horse, Sioux Chief, ca. 1842-1877

Freedman, Russell. The life and death of Crazy Horse; drawings by Amos Bad Heart Bull. Holiday House 1996 166p il maps $22.95 *

Grades: 5 6 7 8 9 10   **92**

1. Oglala Indians

ISBN 0-8234-1219-9   LC 95-33303

A biography of the Oglala Indian leader who relentlessly resisted the white man's attempt to take over Indian lands

This is "a compelling biography that is based on primary source documents and illustrated with pictographs by a Sioux band historian." Voice Youth Advocates

Includes bibliographical references

Cromwell, Oliver, 1599-1658

Aronson, Marc. John Winthrop, Oliver Cromwell, and the Land of Promise. See entry under Winthrop, John, 1588-1649

Crutcher, Chris, 1946-

Crutcher, Chris. King of the mild frontier: an ill-advised autobiography. Greenwillow Bks. 2003 260p il $16.99; pa $6.99 *

Grades: 8 9 10 11 12   **92**

1. Authors, American

ISBN 0-06-050249-5; 0-06-050251-7 (pa)

LC 2002-11224

Chris Crutcher, author of young adult novels such as "Ironman" and "Whale Talk," as well as short stories, tells of growing up in Cascade, Idaho, and becoming a writer

"Like his novels, Crutcher's autobiography is full of heartbreak, poignancy, and hilarity. . . . This honest, insightful, revealing autobiography is a joy to read." Booklist

Sommers, Michael A. Chris Crutcher; Michael A. Sommers. 1st ed. Rosen Pub. Group 2005 112p il (Library of author biographies) lib bdg $26.50

Grades: 5 6 7 8   **92**

1. Authors, American

ISBN 1-4042-0325-7   LC 2004-13100

"Sommers describes Crutcher as an author who writes from his experience as a teacher, therapist, and writer. . . . Selections of book reviews of [his] work are included. . . . [This is] well-written." SLJ

Includes bibliographical references

Cummings, E. E. (Edward Estlin), 1894-1962

Reef, Catherine. E. E. Cummings. Clarion Books 2006 149p il $21

Grades: 7 8 9 10 11 12   **92**

1. Poets, American

ISBN 978-0-618-56849-9; 0-618-56849-2

LC 2006-10453

Subtitle on cover: A poet's life

This "is an engaging look behind the typography at one of the twentieth century's most familiar poets." Bull Cent Child Books

Includes bibliographical references

Curie, Marie, 1867-1934

Borzendowski, Janice. Marie Curie; mother of modern physics. Sterling Pub 2009 124p il map (Sterling biographies) $12.95; pa $5.95

Grades: 7 8 9 10   **92**

1. Physicists 2. Chemists 3. Women scientists

ISBN 978-1-4027-6543-8; 1-4027-6543-6; 978-1-4027-5318-3 (pa); 1-4027-5318-7 (pa)

LC 2008-30701

"This interesting, informative biography of the scientist and Nobel Prize winner explores both Curie's personal and professional life. It includes numerous archival and modern photos and reproductions. . . . The book is far more thorough and satisfying than most biographies of Curie for teens." SLJ

Includes bibliographical references

Cregan, Elizabeth R. Marie Curie; pioneering physicist. Compass Point Books 2009 40p il map (Mission: Science) lib bdg $26.60

Grades: 4 5 6   **92**

Curie, Marie, 1867-1934—*Continued*
1. Chemists 2. Women scientists
ISBN 978-0-7565-3960-3
This biography of the discoverer of radium "does a good job of connecting the scientist?s work to our lives today. . . . [The] book has a variety of graphics including diagrams, photos, and reproductions of paintings and sketches. [This volume is] a definite plus for a school library or the juvenile collection in a public library." Libr Media Connect

Krull, Kathleen. Marie Curie; [illustrations by] Boris Kulikov. Viking 2007 128p il (Giants of science) $15.99 *
Grades: 5 6 7 8   92
1. Chemists 2. Women scientists
ISBN 978-0-670-05894-5; 0-670-05894-7
LC 2007-24251
A biography of "Marie Curie, the woman who coined the term radioactivity, [and who] won not just one Nobel prize but two—in physics and in chemistry." Publisher's note
"The compelling and conversational narrative (ably assisted by Kulikov's black-and-white drawings) portrays a brilliant . . . woman with plenty of idiosyncrasies, and the story of her discovery of radium . . . is as engaging as any of her personal dramas and challenges." Horn Book

MacLeod, Elizabeth. Marie Curie; a brilliant life; written by Elizabeth MacLeod. Kids Can Press 2004 32p il $14.95; pa $6.95
Grades: 5 6 7 8   92
1. Chemists 2. Women scientists
ISBN 1-55337-570-X; 1-55337-571-8 (pa)
"The drive and self-sacrifice that enabled Marie Curie to win two Nobel Prizes and become the most acclaimed female scientist to date are explored in this accessible biography, which covers Curie's personal and professional lives. Illustrated with well-chosen archival photos." Horn Book Guide

McClafferty, Carla Killough. Something out of nothing; Marie Curie and radium. Farrar, Straus & Giroux 2006 134p il $18 *
Grades: 5 6 7 8 9 10   92
1. Chemists 2. Women scientists
ISBN 0-374-38036-8   LC 2004-56414
This "biography examines Curie's life and work as a groundbreaking scientist and as an independent woman. . . . The groundbreaking science is as thrilling as the personal story. . . . The spacious design makes the text easy to read, and occasional photos . . . bring the story closer." Booklist

Poynter, Margaret. Marie Curie; discoverer of radium. rev ed. Enslow Publishers 2007 112p il map (Great minds of science) lib bdg $31.93
Grades: 5 6 7 8   92
1. Chemists 2. Women scientists
ISBN 978-0-7660-2795-4 (lib bdg); 0-7660-2795-3 (lib bdg)   LC 2006-20080
A biography of the chemist who, with her husband, Pierre Curie, won the Nobel Prize in physics in 1903 for the discovery of radioactivity.
Includes glossary and bibliographical references

Steele, Philip. Marie Curie; the woman who changed the course of science. National Geographic 2006 64p il map (World history biographies) $17.95
Grades: 4 5 6 7   92
1. Chemists 2. Women scientists
ISBN 0-7922-5387-6
A biography of the French chemist famous for the discovery of radium
This "book is written in a clear, readable style. . . . It will be an excellent and accessible resource for libraries." Voice Youth Advocates
Includes glossary and bibliographical references

Yannuzzi, Della A. New elements; the story of Marie Curie; [by] Della Yannuzzi. Morgan Reynolds Pub. 2006 144p il (Profiles in science) lib bdg $27.95
Grades: 7 8 9 10   92
1. Chemists 2. Women scientists
ISBN 978-1-59935-023-3; 1-59935-023-8
LC 2006-18887
This is a biography "of the first woman to win a Nobel Prize in science. . . . Readers will come away with a strong portrait of the heralded scientist's life and times (the historical context is nicely integrated), and serious researchers will turn to the bibliography's sturdy selection of titles." Booklist
Includes bibliographical references

Dahl, Roald
Dahl, Roald. Boy: tales of childhood. Farrar, Straus & Giroux 1984 160p il Penguin pa $6.99 hardcover o.p. *
Grades: 6 7 8 9   92
1. Authors, English
ISBN 978-0-14-130305-5 (Penguin pa); 0-14-130305-0 (Penguin pa)   LC 84-48462
"In these memoirs, Dahl reminisces about growing up in a large Norwegian family living in Wales during the 1920s and 1930s. The text is illustrated with sketches, old photographs and excerpts of letters he wrote as a boy." SLJ
"This should be of particular interest to Dahl's fans, but it should also appeal to anyone who likes writing that is direct, candid, and free-flowing." Bull Cent Child Books

Dalai Lama XIV, 1935-
Demi. The Dalai Lama; a biography of the Tibetan spiritual and political leader. Holt & Co. 1998 unp il $18.95 *
Grades: 4 5 6 7   92
1. Buddhism 2. Tibet (China)
ISBN 0-8050-5443-X   LC 97-30654
In this biography of the Buddhist spiritual leader, Demi "uses straightforward prose and fluid, eastern-influenced art—small pen-and-ink and watercolor images with fine, intricate detail. . . . Told with respect and devotion, this is an inspirational picture-book biography." Horn Book

Dalai Lama XIV, 1935-—_Continued_

Kimmel, Elizabeth Cody. Boy on the lion throne; the childhood of the 14th Dalai Lama; with a foreword by His Holiness the Dalai Lama. Roaring Brook Press 2009 146p il map $18.95

Grades: 4 5 6 7   **92**
1. Tibet (China)
ISBN 978-1-59643-394-6; 1-59643-394-9

Follows the childhood of Lhamo Thondup, who was identified at the age of two as the fourteenth reincarnation of the Dalai Lama, describing the humble life he was born into and how his life changed after he was recognized.

"Kimmel is reverent without being adulatory, and her explanation of the Dalai Lama's relationship with Maoist China is presented in simple, clear language. This is a strange and fascinating story told in an egaging style, and young readers will find lots to keep them turning the pages." Bull Cent Child Books

Includes bibliographical references

Dalí, Salvador, 1904-1989

McNeese, Tim. Salvador Dali; [by] Tim McNeese. Chelsea House Publishers 2006 122p il (Great Hispanic heritage) lib bdg $30

Grades: 7 8 9 10   **92**
1. Artists, Spanish
ISBN 0-7910-8837-5   LC 2005025998

A biography of the 20th century surrealist painter.

"McNeese does a wonderful job of describing [this man's life] and, more importantly, the times in which [he] lived. . . . [The book is] expertly researched." SLJ

Includes bibliographical references

D'Angelo, Pascal, 1894-1932

Murphy, Jim. Pick & shovel poet: the journeys of Pascal D'Angelo. Clarion Bks. 2000 162p il $20

Grades: 6 7 8 9   **92**
1. Italian Americans 2. Poets 3. Immigrants
ISBN 0-395-77610-4   LC 00-22573

"Murphy has written an inspiring biography of a truly remarkable man. Through words and moving archival photographs, he has given readers a glimpse of the difficult life that many immigrants led in the early twentieth century." Book Rep

Includes bibliographical references

Dante Alighieri, 1265-1321

Davenport, John. Dante; poet, author, and proud Florentine; [by] John Davenport. Chelsea House 2006 140p il (Makers of the Middle Ages and Renaissance) lib bdg $30

Grades: 6 7 8 9   **92**
1. Authors, Italian
ISBN 0-7910-8634-8   LC 2005007492

This biography of the Italian Renaissance author of _The Divine Comedy_ describes his "childhood and background as well as his influences, career, and writing. The colorful illustrations, many from illuminated manuscripts, short chapters, simple vocabulary, and large print present an attractive format. Sidebars and captions contain additional information." SLJ

Includes bibliographical references

Danziger, Paula, 1944-2004

Reed, Jennifer. Paula Danziger; voice of teen troubles; [by] Jennifer Bond Reed. Enslow Publishers 2006 104p bibl il por (Authors teens love) lib bdg $31.93

Grades: 5 6 7 8   **92**
1. Women authors 2. Authors, American
ISBN 0-7660-2444-X   LC 2005030332

A biography of the author of _The Cat Ate My Gymsuit_ and other books for young people.

Danziger's "many fans will be fascinated to learn how much of her lively, funny fiction draws on her own troubled childhood in a dysfunctional home." Booklist

Includes bibliographical references

Darwin, Charles, 1809-1882

Anderson, Margaret Jean. Charles Darwin; naturalist; [by] Margaret J. Anderson. rev ed. Enslow Publishers 2007 128p bibl il por (Great minds of science) lib bdg $31.93

Grades: 5 6 7 8   **92**
1. Naturalists 2. Evolution
ISBN 978-0-7660-2794-7 (lib bdg); 0-7660-2794-5 (lib bdg)   LC 2007003430
First published 1994

A biography of the 19th century English naturalist who formulated the theory of evolution

Includes glossary and bibliographical references

Ashby, Ruth. Young Charles Darwin and the voyage of the Beagle; written by Ruth Ashby. Peachtree 2009 116p il map $12.95

Grades: 4 5 6   **92**
1. Beagle Expedition (1831-1836) 2. Naturalists 3. Evolution
ISBN 978-1-56145-478-5; 1-56145-478-8
                                    LC 2008-36747

"Beginning with the letter inviting him to sail aboard the Beagle, this traditional biography relates Darwin's life with an emphasis on the trip that led him to forge his theory about natural selection. Ashby makes good use of Darwin's own writing, sprinkling quotes throughout the text, which allow his adventures and opinions to come to life. . . . This biography will work well for book reports . . . providing accurate and readable information about the scientist and his journey." Booklist

Includes bibliographical references

Gibbons, Alan. Charles Darwin; illustrated by Leo Brown. Kingfisher 2008 63p il $16.95

Grades: 3 4 5 6   **92**
1. Beagle Expedition (1831-1836) 2. Naturalists 3. Evolution
ISBN 978-0-7534-6251-5; 0-7534-6251-6
                                    LC 2007-48365

"From the perspective of a young boy, this historical story tells of Charles Darwin and his attempt to further study plants and animals aboard the HMS Beagle from 1832 to 1836." Libr Media Connect

"Large, brightly colored line-and-wash pictures appear throughout the diary section, along with smaller photos of period artifacts. Illustrated mainly with drawings and photos, the last third of the book offers straightforward discussions of topics such as the ship, the route of the

Darwin, Charles, 1809-1882—_Continued_
voyage, life at sea, Darwin's later life and work, and other notable nineteenth-century scientists." Booklist

Includes glossary

Heiligman, Deborah. Charles and Emma; the Darwins' leap of faith. Henry Holt and Company 2009 268p il $18.95 *
Grades: 7 8 9 10 11 12   92
1. Darwin, Emma Wedgwood, 1808-1896
2. Naturalists 3. Evolution
ISBN 978-0-8050-8721-5; 0-8050-8721-4
LC 2008-26091
"This rewarding biography of Charles Darwin investigates his marriage to his cousin Emma Wedgwood. . . . Embracing the paradoxes in her subjects' personalities, the author unfolds a sympathetic and illuminating account, bolstered by quotations from their personal writings as well as significant research into the historical context." Publ Wkly

Includes bibliographical references

Leone, Bruno. Origin: the story of Charles Darwin; by Bruno Leone. Morgan Reynolds Pub. 2009 il (Profiles in science) $28.95
Grades: 6 7 8 9   92
1. Naturalists 2. Evolution
ISBN 978-1-59935-110-0; 1-59935-110-2
LC 2008047204
This "focuses primarily on Darwin's scientific achievements. . . . Leone offers a vivid portrait of Darwin as an avid naturalist, keen and patient observer, cautious scientist, and master of synthesizing and articulating his theories and observations. . . . The book is illustrated throughout with photographs, diagrams, and drawings." Booklist

Includes bibliographical references

Schanzer, Rosalyn. What Darwin saw; the journey that changed the world. National Geographic 2009 47p il map $17.95; lib bdg $26.90
Grades: 3 4 5 6   92
1. Beagle Expedition (1831-1836) 2. Naturalists 3. Evolution
ISBN 978-1-4263-0396-8; 1-4263-0396-3; 978-1-4263-0397-5 (lib bdg); 1-4263-0397-1 (lib bdg)
LC 2008-39809
"Schanzer uses Darwin's own words, taken from his journals, books, and letters, in the speech balloons of her graphic depiction of the voyage of the Beagle. This is not a full biography, but begins with Darwin's acceptance of the offer to sail on the expedition and ends with the presentation of his theory of evolution in 1860. Bright, watercolor cartoons accurately portray landscapes and specimens while also creating a vivid sense of adventure." SLJ

Includes bibliographical references

Stefoff, Rebecca. Charles Darwin and the evolution revolution. Oxford Univ. Press 1996 126p il (Oxford portraits in science) $28; pa $11.95
Grades: 7 8 9 10   92
1. Naturalists 2. Evolution
ISBN 0-19-508996-0; 0-19-512028-0 (pa)
LC 95-35802
"Extensive photos of Darwin and his family, friends, and colleagues, as well as reproductions of public notices and cartoons, are handsome additions to the nicely laid-out text. . . . It offers generally thorough, clear explanations of Darwin's scientific theories and sheds light on his personality." Booklist

Includes glossary and bibliographical references

Darwin, Emma Wedgwood, 1808-1896
Heiligman, Deborah. Charles and Emma. See entry under Darwin, Charles, 1809-1882

Davis, Miles
Dell, Pamela. Miles Davis; jazz master. Child's World 2005 40p il (Journey to freedom) $28.50
Grades: 5 6 7 8   92
1. Jazz musicians 2. African American musicians
ISBN 1-59296-232-7
In this biography of the jazz musician "Dell discusses Davis's battle with heroin addiction and his difficult personality, as well as his development as a performer and his fame. . . . Excellent historical and current photos enhance the easy-to-read [text] on every spread." SLJ

Includes bibliographical references

De Paola, Tomie, 1934-
De Paola, Tomie. Christmas remembered; [by] Tomie dePaola. G. P. Putnam Sons 2006 86p il $19.99
Grades: 5 6 7 8   92
1. Christmas 2. Authors, American 3. Illustrators
ISBN 0-399-24622-3   LC 2005032658
The children's author and artist shares his love of Christmas in 15 memories, which span six decades.
"Brightening the pages are illustrations in varied styles and media, from an intriguing portrait of dePaola's Italian grandmother to decorative paper collages to iconic paintings of great stillness and beauty. . . . Written with dialogue and humor as well as reflection." Booklist

Délano, Poli, 1936-
Délano, Poli. When I was a boy Neruda called me Policarpo; illustrated by Manuel Monroy. Groundwood Books/House of Anansi Press 2006 84p il $15.95 *
Grades: 5 6 7 8   92
1. Neruda, Pablo, 1904-1973 2. Poets, Chilean 3. Mexico
ISBN 0-88899-726-4
"Based on the author's childhood remembrances of when he and his diplomat parents lived with Tío Pablo [Neruda] in Mexico, these seven chapters reveal both the

Délano, Poli, 1936-—*Continued*
genius and the eccentricities of the Nobel Prize-winning Chilean poet. . . . The chapters are short, well written, and filled with interesting details that will open up a new and exotic world. . . . Monroy's pen-and-sepia-toned drawings are . . . at times humorous, at times dramatic, but always enticing." SLJ

Dickens, Charles, 1812-1870
Caravantes, Peggy. Best of times: the story of Charles Dickens. Morgan Reynolds Pub. 2005 160p il (World writers) $26.95
Grades: 7 8 9 10   **92**
1. Authors, English
ISBN 1-931798-68-0   LC 2005-8405
"Beginning with Dickens' childhood trauma (his father was put in debtors' prison, and Charles, 12, had to work in a blacking factory), this highly readable [book] . . . relates the extraordinary writer's stories to his life and times. . . . [It includes] many interesting quotes, color prints, and photos." Booklist
Includes bibliographical references

Rosen, Michael. Dickens; his work and his world; illustrated by Robert Ingpen. Candlewick Press 2005 95p il $19.99 *
Grades: 5 6 7 8   **92**
1. Authors, English
ISBN 0-7636-2752-6   LC 2004-61847
"Opening with Dickens's touring life and final London performance, Rosen then turns to the writer's humble beginnings and nomadic childhood, paying particular attention to the people he met, the sights he saw, and the situations he endured—all of which were to find their way into his writings. The author looks at 1800s London, pointing out the societal changes that were to influence Dickens's progressive thinking." SLJ
"The art adds to the richness of a volume designed and written with care." Booklist

Dickinson, Emily, 1830-1886
Dommermuth-Costa, Carol. Emily Dickinson; singular poet. Lerner Publs. 1998 112p il $27.93
Grades: 8 9 10 11 12   **92**
1. Poets, American 2. Women poets
ISBN 0-8225-4958-1   LC 97-40081
Examines the life, work, and significance of the visionary poet from Amherst, Massachusetts
"Extensive quotations from poems and letters help bring the major figures to life and offer a period flavor as well. A solid addition to biography collections." Booklist
Includes bibliographical references

Meltzer, Milton. Emily Dickinson; a biography. Twenty-first Century Books 2006 128p il (American literary greats) lib bdg $31.93 *
Grades: 7 8 9 10   **92**
1. Poets, American 2. Women poets
ISBN 0-7613-2949-8; 978-0-7613-2949-7
                                                LC 2003-22978
Examines the life of the reclusive nineteenth-century Massachusetts poet whose posthumously published poetry

brought her the public attention she had carefully avoided during her lifetime.
"This introduction to an important American literary figure is notable for its clear and succinct writing. . . . Excerpts from her letters and poems appear throughout. A worthwhile book for students who might have difficulty with more scholarly works." SLJ
Includes bibliographical references

Douglass, Frederick, 1817?-1895
Schuman, Michael. Frederick Douglass; "truth is of no color"; [by] Michael A. Schuman. Enslow Publishers 2009 128p il map (Americans: the spirit of a nation) lib bdg $31.93
Grades: 6 7 8 9   **92**
1. Abolitionists 2. African Americans—Biography
ISBN 978-0-7660-3025-1 (lib bdg); 0-7660-3025-3 (lib bdg)   LC 2008-29634
This "is an engaging introduction to famous abolitionist. Well-sourced excerpts, including many passages from Douglass' own writings, and vivid description enliven the text. . . . The visuals ably support the writing, with a strong mix of engravings, maps, and photos." Booklist
Includes glossary and bibliographical references

Doyle, Sir Arthur Conan, 1859-1930
Pascal, Janet B. Arthur Conan Doyle; beyond Baker Street. Oxford Univ. Press 1999 158p il (Oxford portraits) $28
Grades: 7 8 9 10   **92**
1. Authors, Scottish
ISBN 0-19-512262-3   LC 99-36643
In this biography of the creator of Sherlock Holmes the author examines the "events and people in his life that later showed up in his books, . . . paints him as a decent, likable fellow with a talent for forceful, vivid writing and unwavering enthusiasm for new ideas and enterprises." Booklist
"Pascal does a fine job of conveying the era in which her object lived." SLJ
Includes bibliographical references

Drew, Charles
Schraff, Anne E. Dr. Charles Drew; blood bank innovator; [by] Anne Schraff. Enslow Publishers 2003 112p il (African-American biographies) lib bdg $26.60   **92**
1. Surgeons 2. African Americans—Biography
ISBN 0-7660-2117-3   LC 2002-10402
Contents: Blood for Britain; Foggy Bottom beginnings; The calling; North to Canada; Howard and Freedmen's, a new era; Meeting Minnie Lenore Robbins; Blood for life; "My greatest contribution"
A biography of the pioneering African American doctor famous for his work with blood plasma
Includes bibliographical references

Du Bois, W. E. B. (William Edward Burghardt), 1868-1963

Bolden, Tonya. W.E.B. Du Bois; a twentieth-century life. Viking Children's Books 2008 224p il (Up close) $16.99

Grades: 7 8 9 10   **92**

1. African Americans—Biography 2. African Americans—Civil rights

ISBN 978-0-670-06302-4; 0-670-06302-9

LC 2007-52380

"The author covers her subject's life, which spanned 95 years, from Reconstruction to the modern Civil Rights Movement. . . . This balanced, lively account records his many contributions as a teacher, speaker, Civil Rights activist, sociologist, writer, and cofounder of several organizations, including the NAACP, as well as his failings." SLJ

Includes bibliographical references

Hinman, Bonnie. A stranger in my own house; the story of W.E.B. Du Bois. Morgan Reynolds Pub. 2005 176p il map $26.95

Grades: 7 8 9 10   **92**

1. African Americans—Biography 2. African Americans—Civil rights

ISBN 1-931798-45-1   LC 2004-26460

"The long, complex life of this scholar and controversial civil rights leader is examined in this . . . biography. Hinman offers insights into the background, beliefs, and conflicts that shaped and defined Du Bois. . . . The engaging, informative, balanced text is enhanced with documentary photographs and illustrations." SLJ

Includes bibliographical references

Dunbar, Paul Laurence, 1872-1906

Reef, Catherine. Paul Laurence Dunbar; portrait of a poet. Enslow Pubs. 2000 128p il (African-American biographies) lib bdg $26.60 *

Grades: 6 7 8 9   **92**

1. Poets, American 2. African American authors

ISBN 0-7660-1350-2   LC 99-16456

A biography of the poet who faced racism and devoted himself to depicting the black experience in America

"Excerpts from select poems and numerous quotes by and about the subject, cited in the lengthy source notes, enliven the text. Black-and-white photographs and reproductions appear throughout." SLJ

Includes bibliographical references

Duncan, Lois, 1934-

Campbell, Kimberly Edwina. Lois Duncan; author of I know what you did last summer; [by] Kimberly Campbell. Enslow Publishers 2009 104p bibl il por (Authors teens love) lib bdg $31.93

Grades: 6 7 8 9   **92**

1. Authors, American 2. Women authors

ISBN 978-0-7660-2963-7 (lib bdg); 0-7660-2963-8 (lib bdg)   LC 2008013874

This discusses the life and work of author Lois Duncan

Includes glossary and bibliographical references

Earhart, Amelia, 1898-1937

Micklos, John. Unsolved: what really happened to Amelia Earhart? [by] John Micklos, Jr. Enslow Publishers 2006 144p bibl il map por lib bdg $31.93 *

Grades: 5 6 7 8   **92**

1. Women air pilots

ISBN 0-7660-2365-6   LC 2005020875

"Micklos discusses the pilot's childhood, including what made her tick and what made her fly. However, the book's real focus is on the events of her fateful round-the-world adventure. . . . There are several theories about what happened to her and her copilot, Fred Noonan, on July 2, 1937. . . . As the plane and remains have never been found and identified, no one really knows. Fully half of this book is devoted to the famous flight and the possible explanations for what occurred. Chock-full of photos . . . *Unsolved* captures the imagination." SLJ

Includes glossary and bibliographical references

Edison, Thomas A. (Thomas Alva), 1847-1931

Baxter, Roberta. Illuminated progress; the story of Thomas Edison; [by] Roberta Baxter. Morgan Reynolds Pub. 2009 144p il (Profiles in science) lib bdg $27.95

Grades: 6 7 8 9   **92**

1. Inventors

ISBN 978-1-59935-085-1 (lib bdg); 1-59935-085-8 (lib bdg)   LC 2008007411

This title "offers a concise, informative overview of the inventor who ushered in the world the Age of Electricity. . . . This well-documented biography is illustrated throughout with photographs." Booklist

Includes bibliographical references

Carlson, Laurie M. Thomas Edison for kids; his life and ideas: 21 activities; [by] Laurie Carlson. Chicago Review Press 2006 147p il $14.95 *

Grades: 5 6 7 8   **92**

1. Inventors 2. Science—Experiments

ISBN 1-55652-584-2   LC 2005025659

"Part biography, part science activity book, this resource will appeal to casual researchers and novice inventors. It contains a wealth of full-page primary source archival photographs, sidebars, and short biographical profiles of Edison's contemporaries, in addition to short and straightforward experiments." Voice Youth Advocates

Includes bibliographical references

Delano, Marfe Ferguson. Inventing the future: a photobiography of Thomas Alva Edison. National Geographic Soc. 2002 64p il $18.95; pa $7.95 *

Grades: 5 6 7 8   **92**

1. Inventors

ISBN 0-7922-6721-4; 0-7922-5934-3 (pa)   LC 2001-7357

Presents a biography of the tireless Thomas Edison, illustrated with many photos of his life and inventions

"Well-written and -illustrated. . . . This biography would inspire young people who are interested in experimenting with new ideas and methods." Libr Media Connect

Includes bibliographical references

Edison, Thomas A. (Thomas Alva), 1847-1931—
Continued

Tagliaferro, Linda. Thomas Edison; inventor of the age of electricity. Lerner Publs. 2003 128p il (Lerner biography) lib bdg $25.26
Grades: 7 8 9 10   **92**
1. Inventors
ISBN 0-8225-4689-2   LC 2002-7603
A biography of Thomas Alva Edison, the inventor of the electric lighting system and the phonograph.
"The life of this remarkable inventor and scientific genius is explored in lively and accessible detail. . . . In this clearly written and thoroughly researched volume, the information flows smoothly and logically." SLJ
Includes bibliographical references

Woodside, Martin. Thomas A. Edison; the man who lit up the world; [by] Martin Woodside. Sterling 2007 124p (Sterling biographies) lib bdg $12.95; pa $5.95
Grades: 5 6 7 8   **92**
1. Inventors
ISBN 978-1-4027-4955-1 (lib bdg); 1-4027-4955-4 (lib bdg); 978-1-4027-3229-4 (pa); 1-4027-3229-5 (pa)
LC 2007003509
"Woodside presents the life, struggles, failures, and successes of a man whose motto was 'the most important way to succeed is always to try one more time.' [The book provides] clear, concise information in an easy-to-read format with captioned photographs and illustrations on most pages." SLJ
Includes glossary and bibliographical references

Einstein, Albert, 1879-1955
Bernstein, Jeremy. Albert Einstein and the frontiers of physics. Oxford Univ. Press 1996 189p il (Oxford portraits in science) lib bdg $24; pa $12.95
Grades: 7 8 9 10   **92**
1. Physicists
ISBN 0-19-509275-9 (lib bdg); 0-19-512029-9 (pa)
LC 95-37500
"Bernstein devotes considerable space in this . . . biography to explanations of relativity, quantum mechanics, gravitation, and the relevant mathematical formulas, and to the various scientists whose theories influenced Einstein in some way." SLJ
"Einstein's personal life, his political and religious beliefs, and his work for control of nuclear arms are well covered. . . . Recommended for those who want to know as much about Einstein's science as about his life." Voice Youth Advocates
Includes bibliographical references

Delano, Marfe Ferguson. Genius; a photobiography of Albert Einstein. National Geographic 2005 64p il $17.95; lib bdg $27.90; pa $7.95 *
Grades: 5 6 7 8   **92**
1. Physicists
ISBN 0-7922-9544-7; 0-7922-9545-5 (lib bdg); 1-4263-0294-0 (pa)   LC 2004-15001

A biography of the German American physicist.
This "combines a solid text with a particularly attractive format. . . . Delano offers just enough information about Einstein's theories to give a sense of his work. . . . Oversize and filled with well-selected photographs, the book is very handsome." Booklist

Lassieur, Allison. Albert Einstein; genius of the twentieth century. Franklin Watts 2005 128p il (Great life stories) lib bdg $30.50
Grades: 5 6 7 8   **92**
1. Physicists
ISBN 0-531-12401-0   LC 2004-14313
"A clear, chronological look at Einstein's life and contributions with respect to gravity, energy, matter, light, and time. . . . Photo captions and sidebars provide further insights into this Noble Prize winner." SLJ
Includes bibliographical references

MacLeod, Elizabeth. Albert Einstein; a life of genius; written by Elizabeth MacLeod. Kids Can Press 2003 32p il $14.95; pa $6.95 *
Grades: 4 5 6 7   **92**
1. Physicists
ISBN 1-55337-396-0; 1-55337-397-9 (pa)
A brief introduction to the life and work of the physicist
"It looks like a scrapbook, with information offered in small bites accompanied by lots of small photos and illustrations, but this introduction to the life of Einstein is as informative as it is appealing. . . . This is concise, but there's still plenty here for students and browsers alike." Booklist

Sullivan, Anne Marie. Albert Einstein. Mason Crest Publs. 2003 unp il $19.95
Grades: 4 5 6 7   **92**
1. Physicists
ISBN 1-59084-140-9   LC 2003-6034
This is a brief introduction to the life and work of the physicist
"Einstein comes alive in this delightful, entertaining, well-written, and beautifully illustrated biography." Libr Media Connect

Eisenhower, Dwight D. (Dwight David), 1890-1969
Young, Jeff C. Dwight D. Eisenhower; soldier and president. Morgan Reynolds 2002 128p il (Notable Americans) lib bdg $21.95
Grades: 7 8 9 10   **92**
1. Presidents—United States 2. Generals
ISBN 1-88384-676-5   LC 2001-30822
A biography of the World War II commander general who became the thirty-fourth President of the United States
"Young reveals Ike's story with a flair that makes both the man's questionable and admirable traits interesting. . . . There is enough drama here to make the story of the thirty-fourth president a surprisingly dynamic tale." Booklist
Includes bibliographical references

Eisner, Will, 1917-2005

Greenberger, Robert. Will Eisner; [by] Robert Greenberger. Rosen Pub. Group 2005 112p il (Library of graphic novelists) lib bdg $31.95

Grades: 6 7 8 9   **92**

1. Cartoons and caricatures

ISBN 1-4042-0286-2   LC 2004-16656

Contents: Early days; The Eisner-Iger Studio; The spirit; Mr. Eisner goes to war; Eisner the graphic novelist; Breaking new ground

This "book focuses on the artist's work rather than on his life. It sketches in major events, . . . but dwells heavily on the characters he created and his influence on the graphic-novel format. This is a well-organized and easy-to-read volume." SLJ

Includes bibliographical references

Eleanor, of Aquitaine, Queen, consort of Henry II, King of England, 1122?-1204

Kramer, Ann. Eleanor of Aquitaine; the queen who rode off to battle. National Geographic 2006 64p il map (World history biographies) $17.95; lib bdg $27.90 *

Grades: 5 6 7 8   **92**

1. Queens 2. France—History—0-1328 3. Great Britain—History—1154-1399, Plantagenets

ISBN 0-7922-5895-9; 0-7922-5896-7 (lib bdg)

An illustrated biography of the medieval queen who traveled to the Crusades with her first husband King Louis VII of France and later married King Henry II of England.

Includes glossary and bibliographical references

Elizabeth I, Queen of England, 1533-1603

Adams, Simon. Elizabeth I; the outcast who became England's queen; [by] Simon Adams. National Geographic 2005 64p il map (World history biographies) $17.95; lib bdg $27.90 *

Grades: 4 5 6 7   **92**

1. Queens 2. Great Britain—Kings and rulers 3. Great Britain—History—1485-1603, Tudors

ISBN 0-7922-3649-1; 0-7922-3654-8 (lib bdg)

     LC 2005001359

An illustrated introduction to the life and times of the 16th century queen of England

"Accomplishments and hardships are clearly explained with supporting quotes and facts. . . . Beautifully illustrated and visually appealing." SLJ

Includes glossary and bibliographical references

Stanley, Diane. Good Queen Bess: the story of Elizabeth I of England; by Diane Stanley and Peter Vennema; illustrated by Diane Stanley. HarperCollins Pubs. 2001 c1990 unp il $16.99 *

Grades: 4 5 6 7   **92**

1. Queens 2. Great Britain—Kings and rulers 3. Great Britain—History—1485-1603, Tudors

ISBN 0-688-17961-4   LC 00-47267

A reissue of the title first published 1990 by Four Winds Press

Follows the life of the strong-willed queen who ruled England in the time of Shakespeare and the defeat of the

Spanish Armada

"The handsome illustrations . . . are worthy of their subject. Although the format suggests a picture-book audience, this biography needs to be introduced to older readers who have the background to appreciate and understand this woman who dominated and named an age." SLJ

Includes bibliographical references

Thomas, Jane Resh. Behind the mask: the life of Queen Elizabeth I. Clarion Bks. 1998 196p il maps $20

Grades: 7 8 9 10   **92**

1. Queens 2. Great Britain—Kings and rulers 3. Great Britain—History—1485-1603, Tudors

ISBN 0-395-69120-6   LC 94-31975

This biography "begins with Elizabeth's father, King Henry VIII. . . . Thomas then covers the Tudor queen's life from her negotiation of pre-accession pitfalls to the major aspects of her tenure, both political and personal." Bull Cent Child Books

This is a "vital and intelligent biography. Throughout, Thomas has a good story to tell—one full of intrigue, passion, and larger-than-life characters—and her documentation backs it up. This handsome book, filled with black-and-white photographs, contains a stunning eight-page color insert of the queen's life in portraits." Horn Book Guide

Includes bibiographical references

Weatherly, Myra. Elizabeth I; Queen of Tudor England; by Myra Weatherly. Compass Point Books 2006 112p il (Signature lives) $30

Grades: 6 7 8 9   **92**

1. Queens 2. Great Britain—Kings and rulers 3. Great Britain—History—1485-1603, Tudors

ISBN 0-7565-0988-2   LC 2005002790

This "describes the political wrangling behind the English Crown set against the backdrop of the power struggle between the Church of England and the Roman Catholic Church." Voice Youth Advocates

"This engaging biography brings the monarch's complicated and fascinating life to light. . . . The text is clearly written and highly readable." SLJ

Includes bibliographical references

Ellington, Duke, 1899-1974

Brown, Gene. Duke Ellington: jazz master. Blackbirch Press 2001 128p il (Giants of art and culture) lib bdg $27.45

Grades: 7 8 9 10   **92**

1. Jazz musicians 2. African American musicians

ISBN 1-56711-505-5   LC 00-52993

First published 1990 by Silver Burdett

A biography of the jazz musician and composer

This is "solidly grounded in the times. . . . Numerous historical photographs add interest." Booklist

Includes glossary and bibliographical references

Stein, Stephanie. Duke Ellington; his life in jazz with 21 activities; [by] Stephanie Stein Crease. 1st ed. Chicago Review Press 2009 148p il $16.95

Grades: 4 5 6 7 8   **92**

1. Jazz musicians 2. African American musicians

ISBN 978-1-5565-2724-1; 1-5565-2724-1

     LC 2008023742

Ellington, Duke, 1899-1974—*Continued*

"This biography begins with a brief discussion of the lives of Ellington's parents and his childhood introduction to music and instruments. As each chapter introduces separate highlights of the man's life and musical growth, sidebar articles emphasize historical milestones in music . . . and the impact of individuals or events on his life. The book also features 21 interactive activities, each of which is positioned to provide a greater understanding of an instrument, performance, or music theory in jazz style. . . . Illustrations include performance photographs and portraits of notable names from the Big Band era." SLJ

Includes bibliographical references, discography, and filmography

Ellison, Lawrence J., 1944-

Ehrenhaft, Daniel. Larry Ellison; sheer nerve. 21st Cent. Bks. (Brookfield) 2001 80p il (Techies) lib bdg $23.93   **92**
1. Oracle Corp. 2. Computer software industry 3. Businesspeople
ISBN 0-7613-1962-X   LC 2001-27167
This is a profile of the computer software executive who founded the Oracle Corporation
This "will appeal not only to report writers, but also to recreational readers." SLJ
Includes bibliographical references

Estefan, Gloria

Lee, Sally. Gloria Estefan; superstar of song. Enslow Pubs. 2005 128p il (Latino biography library) lib bdg $31.93
Grades: 7 8 9 10   **92**
1. Singers 2. Cuban Americans
ISBN 0-7660-2490-3
A biography of the Cuban American singing star

Evans, Walker, 1903-1975

Nau, Thomas. Walker Evans; photographer of America. Roaring Brook Press 2007 63p il $19.95
Grades: 6 7 8 9   **92**
1. Photographers
ISBN 978-1-59643-225-3; 1-59643-225-X
                    LC 2006012900
"Walker Evans traversed the country taking photographs throughout much of the twentieth century. He sought to document everyday life as it was, especially as seen through the lives of the poor. . . . Nau divides his biography of Evans into varying groups of years. . . . Evans's excellent photographs fill the book. . . . [A] good and interestingly written introduction to an important American photographer." Voice Youth Advocates
Includes bibliographical references

Evers, Medgar Wiley, 1925-1963

Ribeiro, Myra. The assassination of Medgar Evers. Rosen Pub. Group 2002 64p il (Library of political assassinations) $26.50
Grades: 5 6 7 8   **92**
1. African Americans—Civil rights
ISBN 0-8239-3544-2   LC 2001-2389

This is the story of the life and untimely death of a leader "on the forefront in the important fight for civil rights in the South." Book Rep
The author "does a good job of introducing the inspiring leader and the cause he fought for." Booklist
Includes glossary and bibliographical references

Fermi, Enrico, 1901-1954

Cooper, Dan. Enrico Fermi and the revolutions in modern physics. Oxford Univ. Press 1999 117p il (Oxford portraits in science) lib bdg $28
Grades: 7 8 9 10   **92**
1. Physicists
ISBN 0-19-511762-X   LC 98-34471
A biography of the Nobel Prize-winning physicist whose work led to the discovery of nuclear fission, the basis of nuclear power and the atom bomb
"This book will be useful for reports. . . . The extensive list for further reading includes biographies of Fermi, books on both scientific and political aspects of the atomic-bomb project, and information on tours of laboratories involved in nuclear research today." SLJ

Filipovic, Zlata

Filipovic, Zlata. Zlata's diary; a child's life in Sarajevo; with an introduction by Janine Di Giovanni; translated with notes by Christina Pribichevich-Zoric. Penguin Books 2006 195p il pa $13
Grades: 6 7 8 9   **92**
1. Sarajevo (Bosnia and Hercegovina)
ISBN 0-14-303687-4
A reissue with a new preface of the title first published 1994 by Viking
"In September 1991, at the beginning of a new school year and while war was already as close as Croatia, Filipovic, a ten-year-old girl in Sarajevo began keeping a diary about her school friends, her classes, and her after-school activities. The following spring that childhood world disappeared when the war moved to Sarajevo." Libr J
"Filipovic's diary personalizes the tragedy in war-torn Sarajevo." Booklist

Fillmore, Millard, 1800-1874

Gottfried, Ted. Millard Fillmore; by Ted Gottfried. Marshall Cavendish Benchmark 2007 96p il (Presidents and their times) lib bdg $22.95
Grades: 5 6 7 8   **92**
1. Presidents—United States
ISBN 978-0-7614-2431-4   LC 2006019707
This "explores the presidency of a man from humble beginnings who, throughout his presidency, battled the question of slavery and maintaining the unity of the nation." Publisher's note
"Primary-source materials and quotes, helpful insets, and carefully selected . . . reproductions bring history to life and help make [this] clearly written [biography] highly readable." SLJ
Includes glossary and bibliographical references

Filo, David
Sherman, Josepha. Jerry Yang and David Filo.
See entry under Yang, Jerry, 1968-

Fitzgerald, Ella
Stone, Tanya Lee. Ella Fitzgerald. Viking 2008
203p il (Up close) $16.99 *
Grades: 7 8 9 10   92
1. African American singers 2. African American
women—Biography
ISBN 978-0-670-06149-5; 0-670-06149-2
                                        LC 2007-23117
This is a "strong biography [of the African American
singer]. . . . Stone's smooth, straightforward narrative
draws from authoritative sources. . . . The abundant
quotes from Fitzgerald and her musician peers greatly
develop the narrative." Booklist
Includes bibliographical references

Fitzgerald, F. Scott (Francis Scott), 1896-1940
Boon, Kevin A. F. Scott Fitzgerald; [by] Kevin
Alexander Boon. Marshall Cavendish Benchmark
2005 c2006 142p (Writers and their works) lib bdg
$25.95
Grades: 7 8 9 10   92
1. Authors, American
ISBN 0-7614-1947-0
"A biography of writer F. Scott Fitzgerald, that describes his era, his major works, his life, and the legacy
of his writing." Publisher's note
This "attractive, well-organized [book fills] a gap in
literary criticism for intermediate readers. Heavily illustrated with color and black-and-white photographs, [it]
will appeal to students who might be intimidated by longer or more scholarly titles." SLJ
Includes bibliographical references

Fleischman, Sid, 1920-
Fleischman, Sid. The abracadabra kid; a writer's
life. Greenwillow Bks. 1996 198p il $16.99; pa
$4.95 *
Grades: 5 6 7 8   92
1. Authors, American
ISBN 0-688-14859-X; 0-688-15855-2 (pa)
                                        LC 95-47382
This autobiography, "turns real life into a story com-
plete with cliffhangers. And it's a classic *boy's* story,
from card tricks and traveling magic shows to World
War II naval experiences and screen-writing gigs for
John Wayne movies. En route, we learn how Fleischman
learned the craft of writing." Bull Cent Child Books
Includes bibliographical references

Freedman, Jeri. Sid Fleischman; [by] Jeri
Freedman. 1st ed. Rosen Pub. Group 2004 112p
(Library of author biographies) $26.50
Grades: 5 6 7 8   92
1. Authors, American 2. Authorship
ISBN 0-8239-4019-5   LC 2003-5203
Discusses the life and work of this popular author, in-
cluding his writing process and methods, inspirations, a

critical discussion of his books, biographical timeline,
and awards
"Libraries looking to expand their biography section
will be well served by [this] informative [title]." SLJ
Includes bibliographical references

Fleming, Alexander, 1881-1955
Birch, Beverley. Alexander Fleming; pioneer
with antibiotics. Blackbirch Press 2002 64p il
(Giants of science) lib bdg $21.96
Grades: 5 6 7 8   92
1. Bacteriologists 2. Penicillin
ISBN 1-56711-656-6   LC 2002-3242
Recounts the life story of Alexander Fleming, his
study of medicine and bacteriology, and his discovery of
penicillin
"Short and richly illustrated with drawings and full-
color and black-and-white photographs. The writing will
appeal to middle-school science fans." SLJ
Includes glossary and bibliographical references

Fletcher, Ralph, 1953-
Fletcher, Ralph. Marshfield dreams; when I was
a kid. Holt & Co. 2005 183p il $16.95
Grades: 4 5 6 7   92
1. Authors, American
ISBN 0-8050-7242-X   LC 2004-60746
"Fletcher reminisces about growing up in Marshfield,
VT, recalling boyhood friendships, sibling attachments,
and romps through the woods. . . . Written with saga-
cious eloquence and gentle humor, this work stands
strong in the ranks of authors' memoirs and autobiographies." SLJ

Ford, Henry, 1863-1947
Tilton, Rafael. Henry Ford. Lucent Bks. 2002
112p il (Importance of) $21.96
Grades: 7 8 9 10   92
1. Automobile industry
ISBN 1-56006-846-9   LC 2001-6212
Discusses the early life of Henry Ford, including his
moving to the big city and his success as an inventor,
engineer, and pioneer of the automobile
Includes bibliographical references

Fortune, Amos, 1709 or 10-1801
Yates, Elizabeth. Amos Fortune, free man;
illustrations by Nora S. Unwin. Dutton 1950 181p
il $16.99; pa $5.99
Grades: 4 5 6 7   92
1. African Americans—Biography 2. Slavery—United
States
ISBN 0-525-25570-2; 0-14-034158-7 (pa)
Awarded the Newbery Medal, 1951
"Born free in Africa, Amos Fortune was sold into
slavery in America in 1725. After more than 40 years of
servitude Amos was able to purchase his freedom and, in
time, that of several others. He died a tanner of enviable
reputation, a landowner, and a respected citizen of his
community. Based on fact, this is a . . . story of a life
dedicated to the fight for freedom and service to others."
Booklist

Fossey, Dian

Nicholson, Lois. Dian Fossey; primatologist; [by] Lois P. Nicholson. Chelsea House 2002 120p il map (Women in science) lib bdg $22.95

Grades: 7 8 9 10 **92**

1. Gorillas 2. Women scientists

ISBN 0-7910-6907-9   LC 2002-15592

Profiles the life of the scientist who studied mountain gorillas in central Africa and worked to ensure their survival

"The writing is clear and engaging, enhanced by well-captioned, color photographs." SLJ

Includes bibliographical references

Fox, Paula

Daniel, Susanna. Paula Fox; [by] Susanna Daniel. 1st ed. Rosen Central 2004 112p il (Library of author biographies) lib bdg $26.50

Grades: 7 8 9 10 **92**

1. Authors, American 2. Women authors

ISBN 0-8239-4525-1   LC 2003-9176

Discusses the life and work of this award-winning author, including her writing process and methods, inspirations, a critical discussion of her books, biographical timeline, and awards.

Includes bibliographical references

France, Diane L.

Hopping, Lorraine Jean. Bone detective; the story of forensic anthropologist Diane France. Franklin Watts 2005 118p il (Women's adventures in science) lib bdg $31.50 *

Grades: 7 8 9 10 **92**

1. Forensic anthropology 2. Women scientists

ISBN 0-531-16776-3   LC 2005-0784

Also available in paperback from Joseph Henry Press

This "introduces the life and work of a contemporary forensic anthropologist, from her rural childhood to her work identifying the victims of the 9/11 tragedies. . . . The extensive detail gives readers a vivid sense of the daily work of a 'bone detective,' and clear explanations of the science will intrigue and inspire readers." Booklist

Includes glossary and bibliographical references

Frank, Anne, 1929-1945

Frank, Anne. The diary of a young girl: the definitive edition; edited by Otto H. Frank and Mirjam Pressler; translated by Susan Massotty. Doubleday 1995 340p $27.50; pa $6.99

Grades: 6 7 8 9 **92**

1. World War, 1939-1945—Jews 2. Netherlands—History—1940-1945, German occupation 3. Jews—Netherlands 4. Holocaust, 1933-1945

ISBN 0-385-47378-8; 0-553-57712-3 (pa)

     LC 94-41379

"This new translation of Frank's famous diary includes material about her emerging sexuality and her relationship with her mother that was originally excised by Frank's father, the only family member to survive the Holocaust." Libr J

Rol, Ruud van der. Anne Frank, beyond the diary; a photographic remembrance; by Ruud van der Rol and Rian Verhoeven; in association with the Anne Frank House; translated by Tony Langham and Plym Peters; with an introduction by Anna Quindlen. Viking 1993 113p il map hardcover o.p. pa $10.99 *

Grades: 5 6 7 8 **92**

1. World War, 1939-1945—Jews 2. Netherlands—History—1940-1945, German occupation 3. Jews—Netherlands 4. Holocaust, 1933-1945

ISBN 0-670-84932-4; 0-14-036926-0 (pa)

     LC 92-41528

Original Dutch edition, 1992

Photographs, illustrations, and maps accompany historical essays, diary excerpts, and interviews, providing an insight to Anne Frank and the massive upheaval which tore apart her world

"Readers will become absorbed in the richness of the detail and careful explanation which revisit and expand the familiar, well-loved story." Horn Book

Wukovits, John F. Anne Frank. Lucent Bks. 1999 96p il maps (Importance of) $28.70

Grades: 7 8 9 10 **92**

1. World War, 1939-1945—Jews 2. Netherlands—History—1940-1945, German occupation 3. Jews—Netherlands 4. Holocaust, 1933-1945

ISBN 1-56006-353-X   LC 98-4327

Discusses the life of Anne Frank, focusing on the years she and her family spent in hiding and the impact of her story upon the world

"Do we need yet another book about Anne Frank? The answer is yes, if junior-high and high-school readers want a context for the diary. . . . This combines biography, history, and commentary, in a highly readable format, with photos and boxed quotes from the diary and from other sources." Booklist

Includes bibliographical references

Franklin, Benjamin, 1706-1790

Adler, David A. B. Franklin, printer. Holiday House 2001 126p il lib bdg $19.95 *

Grades: 4 5 6 7 **92**

1. Statesmen—United States

ISBN 0-8234-1675-5   LC 2001-24535

This "surveys Benjamin Franklin's life as a printer, a scientist, an inventor, a writer, and a statesman. . . . Throughout the book, details, anecdotes, and quotations bring the man's portrait into clearer focus, while period illustrations . . . help readers envision the background of his times." Booklist

Includes bibliographical references

Benjamin Franklin; Tanja Lee, book editor. Greenhaven Press 2002 252p il (People who made history) lib bdg $34.95; pa $23.70

Grades: 7 8 9 10 **92**

1. Statesmen—United States

ISBN 0-7377-0899-9 (lib bdg); 0-7377-0898-0 (pa)

     LC 2001-33795

This profiles the American statesman and scientist and includes essays and primary source documents

Includes bibliographical references

Franklin, Benjamin, 1706-1790—*Continued*

Dash, Joan. A dangerous engine; Benjamin Franklin, from scientist to diplomat; pictures by Dusan Petricic. Frances Foster Books 2006 246p il $17 *

Grades: 7 8 9 10   92
  1. Statesmen—United States
  ISBN 0-374-30669-9   LC 2004-63204
"Franklin's long, productive, and interesting life is vividly recounted in a lively manner. Familiar aspects are covered, from his days as a printer in Philadelphia to his diplomatic service and his role in the development of the fledgling United States democracy. What may be new to some readers is Franklin's dedication to, and life-long love of, science and invention. . . . Witty pen-and-ink illustrations appear throughout." SLJ

Fleming, Candace. Ben Franklin's almanac; being a true account of the good gentleman's life. Atheneum Bks. for Young Readers 2003 120p il $19.95 *

Grades: 5 6 7 8   92
  1. Statesmen—United States
  ISBN 0-689-83549-3   LC 2002-6136
"An Anne Schwartz book"
Brings together eighteenth century etchings, artifacts, and quotations to create the effect of a scrapbook of the life of Benjamin Franklin
"An authoritative work of depth, humor, and interest, presenting Franklin in all his complexity, ranging from the heroic to the vulgar, the saintly to the callous." SLJ

Franklin, Rosalind, 1920-1958

Polcovar, Jane. Rosalind Franklin and the structure of life. Morgan Reynolds 2006 144p il lib bdg $26.95

Grades: 7 8 9 10   92
  1. Women scientists 2. DNA
  ISBN 978-1-59935-022-6 (lib bdg); 1-59935-022-X (lib bdg)   LC 2006-16864
A biography of the scientist whose unpublished research led to the discovery of the structure of DNA
"Polcovar writes a rattling good story on two fronts: a woman becoming a scientist in an age when that was still unusual and the complex dynamics of personalities in a field sometimes thought of as impersonal." Booklist
Includes bibliographical references

Senker, Cath. Rosalind Franklin. Raintree Steck-Vaughn Pubs. 2003 48p il (Scientists who made history) lib bdg $27.12

Grades: 5 6 7 8   92
  1. Women scientists 2. DNA
  ISBN 0-7398-5226-4   LC 2001-48961
Describes the life and career of Rosalind Franklin, a British molecular biologist who played a vital role in the discovery of the structure of DNA
This book has "ample full-color and black-and-white photos, reproductions, and maps to supplement the accessible [text]." SLJ
Includes glossary and bibliographical references

Freud, Sigmund, 1856-1939

Krull, Kathleen. Sigmund Freud; illustrated by Boris Kulikov. Viking 2006 144p il (Giants of science) $15.99 *

Grades: 5 6 7 8   92
  1. Psychiatrists
  ISBN 0-670-05892-0
"Krull unravels just how much the inventor of psychoanalysis and student of the human mind has shaped the way we think . . . while at the same time noting his personal and professional short-comings. . . . Illustrator Kulikov provides knowing and witty illustrations." Booklist
Includes bibliographical references

Muckenhoupt, Margaret. Sigmund Freud; explorer of the unconscious. Oxford Univ. Press 1997 157p il (Oxford portraits in science) lib bdg $28

Grades: 7 8 9 10   92
  1. Psychiatrists
  ISBN 0-19-509933-8   LC 95-42340
The author discusses "Freud's groundbreaking work in psychoanalysis and includes examples of some of his actual cases to illustrate his theories. His personal life, from his struggle with his Jewish identity to family relationships is explored and related to developments in his work. . . . The writing is clear and concise; terms of psychoanalysis are defined and explained." SLJ
Includes bibliographical references

Reef, Catherine. Sigmund Freud: pioneer of the mind. Clarion Bks. 2001 152p il $19 *

Grades: 7 8 9 10   92
  1. Psychiatrists
  ISBN 0-618-01762-3   LC 00-43008
"Reef weaves the developing theories of the first psychoanalyst into a chronological report of his eventful life, setting both in the political and social currents of his era." Horn Book
"Effective use of personal details that reveal Freud's intellect, emotions, and personality, plus photos of his family, friends, and professional life, make this book rich and visually appealing." Voice Youth Advocates
Includes bibliographical references

Fritz, Jean

Fritz, Jean. Homesick: my own story; illustrated with drawings by Margot Tomes and photographs. Putnam 1982 163p il $16.99; pa $5.99 *

Grades: 5 6 7 8   92
  1. China 2. Women authors
  ISBN 0-399-20933-6; 0-698-11782-4 (pa)
                                                   LC 82-7646
A Newbery Medal honor book, 1983
Companion volume to China homecoming
This is a somewhat fictionalized memoir of the author's childhood in China. "Born in Hankow, where her father was director of the YMCA, Jean loved the city. . . . But she knew she 'belonged on the other side of the world'—in Pennsylvania with her grandmother and her other relations." Horn Book
"The descriptions of places and the times are vivid in

Fritz, Jean—*Continued*
a book that brings to the reader, with sharp clarity and candor, the yearnings and fears and ambivalent loyalties of a young girl." Bull Cent Child Books

Frost, Robert, 1874-1963

Caravantes, Peggy. Deep woods; the story of Robert Frost. Morgan Reynolds 2006 176p il (World writers) lib bdg $27.95 *
Grades: 7 8 9 10   92
1. Poets, American
ISBN 978-1-931798-92-1 (lib bdg); 1-931798-92-3 (lib bdg)   LC 2005037514
This "introduces poet Robert Frost. . . . Though focused on the man, Caravantes' presentation includes a few short selections from Frost's verse and, in sidebars, a bit of information about poetic forms. . . . Well organized and clearly written, the book offers a very readable account of Frost's often troubled life as an individual, a family man, a poet, and a public figure." Booklist
Includes bibliographical references

Wooten, Sara McIntosh. Robert Frost; the life of America's poet. Enslow Publishers 2006 128p (People to know today) lib bdg $31.93
Grades: 6 7 8 9   92
1. Poets, American
ISBN 0-7660-2627-2 (lib bdg); 978-0-7660-2627-8 (lib bdg)   LC 2005034882
"In this insightful biography, Wooten recounts Frost's difficult life from his childhood with an abusive, alcoholic father, through his many financial challenges as he tried to establish a career, to his constant struggle with shyness and depression. . . . Her book is thoroughly researched." SLJ
Includes bibliographical references

Fry, Varian, 1907-1967

McClafferty, Carla Killough. In defiance of Hitler; the secret mission of Varian Fry. Farrar, Straus & Giroux 2008 196p il $19.95 *
Grades: 7 8 9 10 11 12   92
1. World War, 1939-1945—Jews—Rescue 2. Holocaust, 1933-1945 3. World War, 1939-1945—France 4. Journalists
ISBN 978-0-374-38204-9; 0-374-38204-2
                                     LC 2007-33271
"This stirring account of a young New York City journalist who secretly helped more than 2,000 refugees escape Nazi-occupied France blends exciting adventure with the grim history. . . . The author begins with a brief overview of Hitler's rise and the threat to the Jews, and then draws heavily on Fry's autobiography and his letters home." Booklist

Fulton, Robert, 1765-1815

Herweck, Don. Robert Fulton; engineer of the steamboat. Compass Point Books 2009 40p il (Mission: Science) lib bdg $26.60
Grades: 4 5 6 7   92
1. Inventors 2. Steamboats
ISBN 978-0-7565-3961-0; 0-7565-3961-7
                                     LC 2008007728

Covers the life and accomplishments of American inventor and mechanic, Robert Fulton, who is best known for building the first successful steamboat.

Kroll, Steven. Robert Fulton; from submarine to steamboat; illustrated by Bill Farnsworth. Holiday House 1999 unp il $16.95 *
Grades: 4 5 6 7   92
1. Inventors 2. Steamboats
ISBN 0-8234-1433-7   LC 98-29944
Describes the life and work of the inventor who developed the steamboat and made it a commercial success
"Report writers will find most of what they need to know about Fulton's early career as a painter of miniatures and panoramas, his later business ventures into marine engineering, and his eventual perfection of the commercially viable steamship which plied the Hudson River." Bull Cent Child Books

Pierce, Morris A. Robert Fulton and the development of the steamboat. PowerPlus Books 2003 112p il map (Library of American lives and times) lib bdg $31.95
Grades: 4 5 6 7   92
1. Inventors 2. Steamboats
ISBN 0-8239-5737-3   LC 2001-5541
Contents: Childhood, 1765-1780; Apprentice, 1780-1787; Artist, 1787-1793; Canal engineer, 1793-1797; Submarines, 1797-1802; Steamboats, 1802-1804; Torpedoes, 1804-1806; Pioneer, 1806-1807; Entrepreneur, 1807-1815
"The life and times of this complex and creative man are captured in this attractive presentation replete with maps and full-color reproductions of building sketches and period paintings." SLJ
Includes glossary and bibliographical references

Fung, Inez, 1949-

Skelton, Renee. Forecast Earth; the story of climate scientist Inez Fung. Franklin Watts 2005 116p il (Women's adventures in science) lib bdg $31.50
Grades: 7 8 9 10   92
1. Climate 2. Women scientists
ISBN 0-531-16777-1   LC 2005-05618
Also available in paperback from Joseph Henry Press
This is a biography of Inez Fung, "a climate scientist, someone who studies the causes of weather patterns and how they change over time." Publisher's note
This "volume is filled with full-color photographs of the subject and her work. Students will be comfortable with the style [of this book] and the easy reading level makes [it] accessible for even nonscience-oriented students." SLJ
Includes bibliographical references

Galen, ca. 129-ca. 200

Yount, Lisa. The father of anatomy; Galen and his dissections. Enslow Publishers 2010 128p il (Great minds of ancient science and math) lib bdg $31.93

Grades: 6 7 8 9   92

1. Human anatomy

ISBN 978-0-7660-3380-1; 0-7660-3380-5

                 LC 2008-29633

"A biography of ancient Greek physician Galen, whose dissections of animals led to discoveries about human anatomy. He was the authority on medical knowledge in the Western world for more than fifteen hundred years." Publisher's note

Includes glossary and bibliographical references

Galilei, Galileo, 1564-1642

Hightower, Paul. Galileo; astronomer and physicist. rev ed. Enslow Publishers 2008 128p il (Great minds of science) lib bdg $31.93

Grades: 5 6 7 8   92

1. Astronomers

ISBN 978-0-7660-3008-4 (lib bdg); 0-7660-3008-3 (lib bdg)   LC 2007020302

First published 1997

"A biography of the seventeenth-century Italian astronomer and physicist Galileo and includes related activities for readers." Publisher's note

Includes glossary and bibliographical references

Panchyk, Richard. Galileo for kids; his life and ideas: 25 activities; foreword by Buzz Aldrin. Chicago Review Press 2005 166p il map pa $16.95 *

Grades: 5 6 7 8   92

1. Astronomers

ISBN 1-55652-566-4   LC 2004-22936

A biography of the Renaissance scientist and his times with related activities

"Clear . . . writing places Galileo squarely within the historical context of the turbulent Italian Renaissance. . . . Panchyk's title is a good choice for those interested in integrating history and science curriculums." SLJ

Includes bibliographical references

Steele, Philip. Galileo; the genius who faced the Inquisition. National Geographic 2005 64p il (World history biographies) $17.95; lib bdg $27.90 *

Grades: 4 5 6 7   92

1. Astronomers

ISBN 0-7922-3656-4; 0-7922-3657-2 (lib bdg)

                 LC 2005-01357

An illustrated introduction to the 16th century astronomer and his times

"Accomplments and hardships are clearly explained wiwth supporting quotes and facts. . . . Beautifully illustrated and visually appealing." SLJ

Gama, Vasco da, 1469-1524

Calvert, Patricia. Vasco da Gama; so strong a spirit; [by] Patricia Calvert. Benchmark Books 2005 96p il map (Great explorations) lib bdg $29.93 *

Grades: 5 6 7 8   92

1. Explorers

ISBN 0-7614-1611-0   LC 2003-22946

Recounts the voyages undertaken by fifteenth-century Portuguese explorer Vasco da Gama to strengthen his nation's power by establishing a sea trade route to India.

Includes bibliographical references

Goodman, Joan E. A long and uncertain journey: the 27,000 mile voyage of Vasco da Gama; by Joan Elizabeth Goodman; illustrated by Tom McNeely. Mikaya Press 2001 47p il map (Great explorers book) $22.95

Grades: 4 5 6 7   92

1. Explorers

ISBN 0-9650493-7-X   LC 00-63795

"Goodman reviews the accomplishments of 15th century Portuguese explorer Vasco da Gama and his role in the rise of the Portuguese Empire." Book Rep

"McNeely's full-page illustrations, which vibrate with life and action, lighten the format, and quotations from the diary of an anonymous sailor on the voyage add fascinating detail and vivid description. . . . A good resource for reports, but the book is also intelligently written and exciting." Booklist

Gandhi, Mahatma, 1869-1948

Adams, Simon. Mahatma Gandhi. Raintree Steck-Vaughn Pubs. 2003 112p il map (20th-century history makers) lib bdg $32.82

Grades: 7 8 9 10   92

1. India—Politics and government 2. Passive resistance

ISBN 0-7398-5255-8   LC 2002-15706

A biography of Mahatma Gandhi, the Indian political and spiritual leader who led his country to freedom from British rule through his policy of nonviolent resistance

This biography is "insightful . . . detailed and well researched." SLJ

Includes glossary and bibliographical references

Severance, John B. Gandhi, great soul. Clarion Bks. 1997 143p il map $18

Grades: 5 6 7 8   92

1. India—Politics and government 2. Passive resistance

ISBN 0-395-77179-X   LC 95-20887

Severance "begins with an introduction to Gandhi's message and gives a brief overview of the mahatma's personal evolution as well as India's external and internal struggles. He then chronicles Gandhi's life. . . . Severance details Gandhi's philosophy of *satyagraha*, or peaceful resistance." Booklist

"It is not only Gandhi who comes alive in this considered, well-documented biography but the multifarious personalities and politics of his world." Horn Book Guide

Includes bibliographical references

Gandhi, Mahatma, 1869-1948—*Continued*

Wilkinson, Philip. Gandhi; the young protester who founded a nation. National Geographic 2005 64p il (World history biographies) $17.95; lib bdg $27.90 *

Grades: 4 5 6 7   92

1. India—Politics and government 2. Passive resistance

ISBN 0-7922-3647-5; 0-7922-3648-3 (lib bdg)

"Double-page spreads describe phases in Gandhi's life, from childhood to his tragic death, detailed in Wilkinson's straightforward, succinct language and in anecdotes, which will capture young people's attention and also humanize the great leader." Booklist

Includes glossary and bibliographical references

Gantos, Jack

Gantos, Jack. Hole in my life. Farrar, Straus & Giroux 2002 199p il $16; pa $8 *

Grades: 7 8 9 10   92

1. Authors, American

ISBN 0-374-39988-3; 0-374-43089-6 (pa)

LC 2001-40957

Michael L. Printz Award honor book, 2003

The author relates how, as a young adult, he became a drug user and smuggler, was arrested, did time in prison, and eventually got out and went to college, all the while hoping to become a writer

"Gantos' spare narrative style and straightforward revelation of the truth have, together, a cumulative power that will capture not only a reader's attention but also empathy and imagination." Booklist

García Márquez, Gabriel, 1928-

Darraj, Susan Muaddi. Gabriel García Márquez. Chelsea House 2006 112p bibl il por (Great Hispanic heritage) lib bdg $30

Grades: 6 7 8 9   92

1. Authors, Colombian

ISBN 0-7910-8839-1   LC 2006010615

A biography of the Colombian novelist who won the Nobel Prize for Literature in 1982

"A great deal of biographical information and some historical context is imparted in [this volume]. . . . Scattered throughout are many photographs and helpful boxed historical asides." Horn Book Guide

Includes bibliographical references

Garvey, Marcus, 1887-1940

Kallen, Stuart A. Marcus Garvey and the Back to Africa Movement. Lucent Books 2006 112p il map (Lucent library of Black history) $32.45

Grades: 7 8 9 10   92

1. African Americans—Civil rights

ISBN 1-59018-838-1   LC 2005027286

"Kallen seeks . . . to discuss and expand on [Garvey's] contributions to Black Nationalism, and to place his particular movement within the context of his times. Here, Garvey emerges as a man who anticipated those later movements that centered on black pride and black power. In an exceptionally evenhanded manner, the au-

thor also shows Garvey to have been naive, unrealistic, and lacking in management skills. A superb speechmaker, a charismatic leader, and an excellent propagandist, he seemed ill prepared to deal with the powerful enemies he made. . . . Kallen describes this all in clear, well-written prose. Archival photographs are placed throughout to good advantage." SLJ

Includes bibliographical references

Lawler, Mary. Marcus Garvey; Black nationalist leader; with additional text by John Davenport. Chelsea House 2004 94p il (Black Americans of achievement) lib bdg $30

Grades: 6 7 8 9   92

1. Universal Negro Improvement Association 2. African Americans—Civil rights

ISBN 978-0-7910-8159-4; 0-7910-8159-1

LC 2004-12658

Revised edition of the title first published 1988

"Marcus Garvey, a champion of black rights, started the Back to Africa movement, which sought to establish a central homeland for blacks in Africa." Publisher's note

Includes bibliographical references

Gates, Bill, 1955-

Aronson, Marc. Bill Gates. Penguin Group 2008 192p il (Up close) $16.99 *

Grades: 7 8 9 10   92

1. Microsoft Corporation 2. Businesspeople 3. Computer software industry

ISBN 978-0-670-06348-2; 0-670-06348-7

LC 2008-15552

This is a biography of the businessman who co-founded Microsoft.

"Well researched, thought-provoking, and up-to-date, this biography . . . offers insights into Gates' character as well as an engaging account of his life." Booklist

Lesinski, Jeanne M. Bill Gates; entrepreneur and philanthropist. rev ed. Twenty-First Century Books 2009 112p il (Lifeline biographies) lib bdg $33.26

Grades: 6 7 8 9   92

1. Microsoft Corporation 2. Businesspeople 3. Computer software industry

ISBN 978-1-58013-570-2; 1-58013-570-6

LC 2008008565

A revised edition of the title first published 2000

This biography "boasts lively, credible writing and a compelling layout. Particularly interesting are the reprints of USA Today articles found throughout, which flesh out the [narrative] in a unique and appealing manner. . . . Full-color and black-and-white photos appear on almost every spread." SLJ

Includes bibliographical references

Gehry, Frank

Bodden, Valerie. Frank Gehry. Creative Education 2009 48p il (Xtraordinary artists) lib bdg $32.80

Grades: 4 5 6 7   92

1. Architects

ISBN 978-1-58341-662-4 (lib bdg); 1-58341-662-5 (lib bdg)   LC 2007004201

Gehry, Frank—*Continued*
This is a biography of architect Frank Gehry

This offers an "interesting [layout]; big, high-quality reproductions and photographs on heavy paper; insightful quotes from diverse sources; and . . . an excerpt from an essay about [Gehry] at the end of the book. Readers get a strong sense of [the] artist's personality along with an excellent survey of his work." SLJ

Includes bibliographical references

Lazo, Caroline Evensen. Frank Gehry. Twenty-First Century Books 2006 112p il (A & E biography) lib bdg $27.93 *
Grades: 7 8 9 10   92
1. Architects
ISBN 0-8225-2649-2   LC 2005002903
"Known as a sculptor and as the architect of many famous structures, Gehry has created unique buildings from materials as varied as chain-link fencing and titanium. This biography links the creative artists professional and personal lives, pointing out great influences and shaping experiences. . . . The book is well organized and includes full-color photos and reproductions of relevant and important sites." SLJ

Includes bibliographical references

Genghis Khan, 1162-1227
Demi. Genghis Khan. Marshall Cavendish Children 2009 c1991 unp il $19.99 *
Grades: 4 5 6 7   92
1. Mongols 2. Kings and rulers
ISBN 978-0-7614-5547-9; 0-7614-5547-7
                                        LC 2008006001
A reissue of Chingis Khan, published 1991 by Henry Holt & Co.

A biography of the Mongol leader and military-strategist who, at the height of his power, was supreme master of the largest empire ever created in the lifetime of one man.

"Demi has managed to portray a fierce conqueror as a sympathetic character who follows a strict code that places loyalty, obedience, and discipline above all else. . . . The artist achieves a clever grandeur with the liberal use of iridescent gold and detailed scenes that spill out of their gilded borders and nearly off the pages. . . . This handsome biography is a feast for the eyes from cover to cover." Booklist

Lange, Brenda. Genghis Khan. Chelsea House 2003 100p il map (Ancient world leaders) lib bdg $23.95; pa $9.95
Grades: 7 8 9 10   92
1. Mongols
ISBN 0-7910-7222-3 (lib bdg); 0-7910-7496-X (pa)
                                        LC 2002-152057
Traces the life of the chief of a small Mongol tribe who established a vast empire from Peking to the Black Sea in the twelfth century.

Includes bibliographical references

George, Jean Craighead, 1919-
George, Jean Craighead. A tarantula in my purse; and 172 other wild pets; written and illustrated by Jean Craighead George. HarperCollins Pubs. 1996 134p il hardcover o.p. pa $4.99
Grades: 4 5 6   92
1. Women authors 2. Authors, American 3. Naturalists 4. Pets
ISBN 0-06-023626-4; 0-06-446201-3 (pa)
                                        LC 95-54151
"George tells of the many wild pets that lived with her family, particularly while her children were growing up. Each chapter describes a different animal or incident." Booklist

"Told in a casual and thoroughly engaging manner, the stories will enchant all animal lovers and even those who aren't." SLJ

Gibson, Josh, 1911-1947
Twemlow, Nick. Josh Gibson. Rosen Pub. Group 2002 112p il (Baseball Hall of Famers of the Negro leagues) lib bdg $29.25
Grades: 5 6 7 8   92
1. Baseball—Biography 2. African American athletes
ISBN 0-8239-3475-6   LC 2001-4143
Presents a biography of the powerful home run hitter and chronicles the history of African American participation in organized baseball, the formation of the Negro leagues, and racial politics in America

Includes glossary and bibliographical references

Giff, Patricia Reilly
Giff, Patricia Reilly. Don't tell the girls; a family memoir; by Patricia Reilly Giff. 1st ed. Holiday House 2005 131p il $16.95
Grades: 4 5 6 7   92
1. Women authors 2. Authors, American
ISBN 0-8234-1813-8   LC 2004-47452
"Giff reflects on her childhood and her family, going back through several generations. Spotlighting her two grandmothers, she lovingly relates remembered conversations and incidents involving the one she knew well before turning to the other grandmother, whom she never met. . . . This little book has much to offer thoughtful children. . . . With . . . sharply reproduced family photos and documents, this handsome book's small format reflects its intimate, conversational style." Booklist

Giuliani, Rudolph W.
Sharp, Anna Layton. Rudy Giuliani; [by] Anna Layton Sharp. Morgan Reynolds Pub. 2007 128p il (Political profiles) lib bdg $27.95
Grades: 6 7 8 9   92
1. Politicians—United States 2. New York (N.Y.)—Politics and government
ISBN 978-1-59935-048-6 (lib bdg); 1-59935-048-3 (lib bdg)   LC 2007023570
A biography of the former Mayor of New York City and presidential candidate.

Includes bibliographical references

Glenn, John, 1921-
  Mitchell, Don. Liftoff; a photobiography of John Glenn. National Geographic Society 2006 64p il $17.95; lib bdg $27.90
  Grades: 5 6 7 8   92
    1. Astronauts 2. Statesmen—United States
    ISBN 0-7922-5899-1; 0-7922-5900-9 (lib bdg)
                                       LC 2005-30916
  This is a biography of the American astronaut, pilot, and U.S. Senator from Ohio.
  This is "well-written and well-illustrated." Sci Books Films
  Includes bibliographical references

Goeppert-Mayer, Maria, 1906-1972
  Ferry, Joseph. Maria Goeppert Mayer; [by] Joseph P. Ferry. Chelsea House 2003 110p il (Women in science) lib bdg $22.95
  Grades: 7 8 9 10   92
    1. Physicists 2. Women scientists
    ISBN 0-7910-7247-9   LC 2002-15580
  A biography of Maria Goeppert-Mayer, a physicist who contributed to the development of the atomic bomb and who, in 1963, was cowinner of the Nobel Prize in Physics for her work on the nuclear shell model theory
  This is "well written and well organized." SLJ
  Includes bibliographical references

Gogh, Vincent van, 1853-1890
  Bassil, Andrea. Vincent van Gogh; by Andrea Bassil. New ed. World Almanac Library 2004 48p il (Lives of the artists) lib bdg $30; pa $11
  Grades: 4 5 6 7   92
    1. Artists, Dutch
    ISBN 0-8368-5602-3 (lib bdg); 0-8368-5607-4 (pa)
                                       LC 2003-67236
  Original Italian edition 2003
  This is a biography of the Dutch painter.
  This is "concise and straightforward, and there's no sensationalizing: Van Gogh's famous ear injury is only mentioned in a brief, matter-of-fact note. The interesting mix of photos and art is the biggest attraction." Booklist

  Bodden, Valerie. Vincent van Gogh. Creative Education 2009 48p il (Xtraordinary artists) lib bdg $32.80
  Grades: 4 5 6 7   92
    1. Artists, Dutch
    ISBN 978-1-58341-663-1; 1-58341-663-3
                                       LC 2007002118
  This biography of the artist offers an "interesting [layout]; big, high-quality reproductions and photographs on heavy paper; insightful quotes from diverse sources; and meaty selections of the artist's own writing . . . at the end of the book. Readers get a strong sense of [the] artist's personality along with an excellent survey of his work." SLJ
  Includes bibliographical references

  Crispino, Enrica. Van Gogh; illustrated by Simone Boni . . . [et. al.]; [English translation, Susan Ashley] Oliver Press 2008 64p il (Art masters) $27.95
  Grades: 6 7 8 9 10   92

    1. Artists, Dutch
    ISBN 978-1-934545-05-8; 1-934545-05-8
  "Using generous, colorful, and cleanly designed two-page spreads, Crispino situates Van Gogh among other artists within certain time periods and locations, portraying his work and life as a counterpoint to various traditions and trends. Most topics are centered by an original drawing that is surrounded by photographs, paintings, artifacts, and descriptions. . . . Consider this volume the equivalent of an unusually insightful museum tour guide." Booklist

  Greenberg, Jan. Vincent Van Gogh; portrait of an artist; [by] Jan Greenberg and Sandra Jordan. Delacorte Press 2001 132p il hardcover o.p. pa $6.99 *
  Grades: 8 9 10 11 12   92
    1. Artists, Dutch
    ISBN 0-385-32803-6; 0-440-41917-4 (pa)
                                       LC 00-31850
  This "book begins with van Gogh's boyhood and traces the various career paths (art dealer, missionary) he pursued before dedicating himself to painting. The authors draw on the artist's voluminous correspondence with his brother Theo to elicit his thoughts and feelings. . . . This outstanding, well-researched biography is fascinating reading." SLJ
  Includes glossary and bibliographical references

  Whiting, Jim. Vincent Van Gogh; by Jim Whiting. Mitchell Lane 2007 48p il (Art profiles for kids) lib bdg $29.95
  Grades: 7 8 9 10   92
    1. Artists, Dutch
    ISBN 978-1-58415-564-5 (lib bdg); 1-58415-564-7 (lib bdg)   LC 2007000662
  This offers "well-documented information for teens doing reports. [The] volume covers the painter's childhood, training, travels, influences, and historical context. The chronological chapters build a survey of the [artist's] oeuvres, including the style and subject matter of [his] works and past and present critical reaction." SLJ
  Includes glossary and bibliographical references

Goh, Chan Hon, 1969-
  Goh, Chan Hon. Beyond the dance; a ballerina's life; [by] Chan Hon Goh with Cary Fagan. Tundra Bks. 2002 151p lib bdg $15.95
  Grades: 6 7 8 9   92
    1. Ballet
    ISBN 0-88776-596-3   LC 2002-101724
  This "autobiography introduces a prima ballerina with the National Ballet of Canada. Goh was born in Beijing but raised in Vancouver by her dancer parents. She discusses the events in her homeland that led her family to emigrate, their adjustment to life in Vancouver, and her parents' struggles to build the Goh Ballet Company. . . . The book is lavishly illustrated with black-and-white photographs, and balletomanes will enjoy poring over every detail." SLJ

Goodall, Jane, 1934-

Bardhan-Quallen, Sudipta. Jane Goodall; a twentieth-century life. Penguin Group 2008 218p (Up close) $16.99

Grades: 7 8 9 10   92

1. Women scientists

ISBN 978-0-670-06263-8; 0-670-06263-4

LC 2007-38206

"This profile of the renowned primatologist highlights her independent spirit and deep love of animals as well as the significant roles Goodall's long-lived mother, Vanne, and the scientist Louis B. Leakey . . . played in shaping her character and career. . . . Readers will be inspired by this account." Booklist

Kozleski, Lisa. Jane Goodall. Chelsea House 2003 116p il (Women in science) lib bdg $22.95

Grades: 7 8 9 10   92

1. Chimpanzees 2. Women scientists

ISBN 0-7910-6905-2   LC 2002-15591

A biography of the zoologist, discussing her personal life as well as her work with chimpanzees at the Gombe Stream Reserve in Tanzania

"The writing is clear and engaging, enhanced by well-captioned, color photographs." SLJ

Includes bibliographical references

Gore, Al, 1948-

Sapet, Kerrily. Al Gore; [by] Kerrily Sapet. Morgan Reynolds Pub. 2008 112p il map (Political profiles) lib bdg $27.95

Grades: 6 7 8 9   92

1.   Vice-presidents—United   States 2. Environmentalists

ISBN 978-1-59935-070-7 (lib bdg); 1-59935-070-X (lib bdg)   LC 2007031247

A biography of the U.S. Vice President, presidential candidate, and environmentalist who won the Nobel Peace Prize and the Academy Award for his work educating the public about global warming.

Includes bibliographical references

Graham, Martha

Freedman, Russell. Martha Graham, a dancer's life. Clarion Bks. 1998 175p il $18 *

Grades: 7 8 9 10   92

1. Dancers 2. Choreographers 3. Modern dance

ISBN 0-395-74655-8   LC 97-15832

A photo-biography of the American dancer, teacher, and choreographer who was born in Pittsburgh in 1895 and who became a leading figure in the world of modern dance

"A showstopping biography that captures its dynamic subject's personality, vision, and artistry." SLJ

Includes bibliographical references

Grant, Ulysses S. (Ulysses Simpson), 1822-1885

Aronson, Billy. Ulysses S. Grant; [by] Billy Aronson. Marshall Cavendish Benchmark 2008 96p il (Presidents and their times) lib bdg $22.95

Grades: 5 6 7 8   92

1. Presidents—United States 2. Generals 3. United States—History—1861-1865, Civil War

ISBN 978-0-7614-2430-7 (lib bdg); 0-7614-2430-X (lib bdg)   LC 2006011087

A biography of the president and Civil War general

Includes bibliographical references

Sapp, Richard. Ulysses S. Grant and the road to Appomattox; [by] Richard Sapp. World Almanac Library 2006 64p il map (In the footsteps of American heroes) lib bdg $33.27; pa $11.95 *

Grades: 5 6 7 8   92

1. Presidents—United States 2. Generals 3. United States—History—1861-1865, Civil War

ISBN 0-8368-6431-X (lib bdg); 0-8368-6436-0 (pa)

LC 2005054471

"This smoothly written, informative book spotlights the life and accomplishments of Ulysses S. Grant. After conveying a vivid sense of Grant's personality in the opening sections, the focus shifts toward a more standard account of the strategy and the events of the Civil War. The closing chapter concerns Grant's troubled presidency and his lasting reputation." Booklist

Includes bibliographical references

Greene, Charles Sumner, 1868-1957

Thorne-Thomsen, Kathleen. Greene & Greene for kids; art, architecture, activities. Gibbs Smith 2004 112p il $17.95

Grades: 5 6 7 8   92

1. Greene, Henry Mather, 1870-1954 2. Architecture 3. Handicraft

ISBN 1-58685-440-2

"Charlie and Henry Greene were born in Cincinnati, OH, during the late 19th century, a time period the author elucidates through full-color photographs and illustrations to make it more accessible to her audience. . . . The book [introduces] readers to their architecture after detailing a history of their ideas, concepts, and life experiences. . . . Thorne-Thomsen presents the history, culture, and art of Greene and Greene through clear descriptions, fun activities, and lots of pictures." SLJ

Greene, Henry Mather, 1870-1954

Thorne-Thomsen, Kathleen. Greene & Greene for kids. See entry under Greene, Charles Sumner, 1868-1957

Greene, Nathanael, 1742-1786

Mierka, Gregg A. Nathanael Greene; the general who saved the Revolution; [by] Gregg A. Mierka. OTTN Pub. 2007 88p il map (Forgotten heroes of the American Revolution) $23.95; pa $12.95

Grades: 5 6 7 8   **92**

1. Generals 2. Society of Friends 3. United States— History—1775-1783, Revolution

ISBN   978-1-59556-012-4;   1-59556-012-2; 978-1-59556-017-9 (pa); 1-59556-017-3 (pa)

LC 2006021044

"A biography of the general whose successful campaign in the South, in what seemed an impossible situation, turned the tide of the American Revolution and led to a Patriot victory." Publisher's note

"This lively profile combines an engrossing account of the Revolutionary War with healthy measures of images and passages drawn from primary—and sometimes previously unpublished—sources." Booklist

Includes bibliographical references

Grimberg, Tina

Grimberg, Tina. Out of line; growing up Soviet. Tundra Books 2007 117p il $22.95

Grades: 7 8 9 10   **92**

1. Soviet Union 2. Jews—Russia 3. Jews—Biography

ISBN 978-0-88776-803-3; 0-88776-803-2

"In this warm memoir, Grimberg recalls her childhood in Kiev during the '60s and '70s. She shares the difficulties of Soviet life and explains how members of her family coped with challenges such as shortages. . . . Interwoven with her own experience of growing up in a Jewish family are the stories of her maternal and paternal grandparents. . . . The book is an exemplar of clear, graceful writing and fine storytelling skills." SLJ

Gross, Elly Berkovits, 1929-

Gross, Elly Berkovits. Elly; my true story of the Holocaust; [by] Elly Berkovits Gross. Scholastic Press 2009 125p il $14.99

Grades: 4 5 6 7   **92**

1. Holocaust survivors 2. Holocaust, 1933-1945—Personal narratives 3. Jews—Romania

ISBN 978-0-545-07494-0; 0-545-07494-0

Relates how the author was torn from her happy home and sent to Birkenau by the Nazis, describing how she worked long hours and fought for survival before being set free at the end of the war and beginning a new life in America.

"As a powerful reminder of man's capacity for inhumanity, this memoir is essential reading." Booklist

Guevara, Ernesto, 1928-1967

Havelin, Kate. Che Guevara; by Kate Havelin. Twenty-First Century Books 2007 112p il map (A & E biography) lib bdg $30.60

Grades: 7 8 9 10   **92**

1. Cuba—History—1959- 2. Guerrillas

ISBN 978-0-8225-5951-1 (lib bdg); 0-8225-5951-X (lib bdg)   LC 2005034948

The author "briefly recounts Che's childhood, then, with increasing detail, his early adulthood and revolutionary years. His famous motorcycle journey and his meeting with Fidel Castro in Mexico are discussed, as are his success as a revolutionary and failure as a bureaucrat. . . . Black-and-white archival photographs and grayscale maps add to the text, as do insets explaining everything from leprosy to the Cold War to the underlying social conditions in Cuba in the 1950s." SLJ

Includes bibliographical references

Miller, Calvin Craig. Che Guevara; in search of revolution. Morgan Reynolds Pub. 2006 192p il map (World leaders) lib bdg $27.95 *

Grades: 7 8 9 10   **92**

1. Cuba—History—1959- 2. Guerrillas

ISBN 978-1-931798-93-8 (lib bdg); 1-931798-93-1 (lib bdg)   LC 2006-5975

This biography of the guerilla leader is "woven into . . . [an] account of the global politics of his day, including his role in the Cuban revolution and the showdown with the U.S. The design is appealing, with clear type, occasional photos, and maps, and teens will be drawn to the account of the young leader who made a difference in spite of an inglorious defeat." Booklist

Includes bibliographical references

Uschan, Michael V. Che Guevara, revolutionary. Lucent Books 2007 104p il map (The twentieth century's most influential Hispanics) lib bdg $32.45

Grades: 7 8 9 10   **92**

1. Cuba—History—1959- 2. Guerrillas

ISBN 978- 1-590189-70-2 (lib bdg); 1-590189-70-1 (lib bdg)   LC 2006016801

"This title surveys the brief but remarkable life of a legendary guerilla fighter and revolutionary. Following an exploration of Guevara's privileged childhood and the origins of his socialist views, Uschan offers clear accounts of his subject's associations with Cuban revolutionary Fidel Castro, Congolese rebels in Africa, and peasants in Bolivia, where, at 39, he was executed with the help of U.S. operatives." Booklist

Includes bibliographical references

Gunther, John, 1929-1947

Gunther, John. Death be not proud; a memoir. Harper & Row 1949 261p il pa $13.95 hardcover o.p.

Grades: 7 8 9 10   **92**

1. Brain—Tumors 2. Cancer

ISBN 0-06-123097-9

A memoir of John Gunther's seventeen-year-old son, who died after a series of operations for a brain tumor. Not only a tribute to a remarkable boy but an account of a brave fight against disease

Guthrie, Woody, 1912-1967

Partridge, Elizabeth. This land was made for you and me: the life and songs of Woody Guthrie. Viking 2002 217p il $21.99 *

Grades: 7 8 9 10   **92**

1. Singers

ISBN 0-670-03535-1   LC 2001-46770

Guthrie, Woody, 1912-1967—*Continued*

A biography of Woody Guthrie, a singer who wrote over 3,000 folk songs and ballads as he traveled around the United States, including "This Land is Your Land" and "So Long It's Been Good to Know Yuh"

This "presents an unflinchingly accurate portrait of a rambling and unpredictable man. . . . In addition to a panoply of archival photographs, which add realism to this engrossing story of a life, the book includes carefully selected quotes from songs, acquaintances, and documents to punctuate the story with authenticating detail without detracting from the momentum of the narrative." Bull Cent Child Books

Includes bibliographical references

Halley, Edmond, 1656-1742

Fox, Mary Virginia. Scheduling the heavens; the story of Edmond Halley; [by] Mary Virginia Fox. Morgan Reynolds Pub. 2007 128p il map por (Profiles in science) lib bdg $27.95

Grades: 6 7 8 9   92

1. Astronomers

ISBN 978-1-59935-021-9 (lib bdg); 1-59935-021-1 (lib bdg)   LC 2006031269

"Though best known for calculating the orbit and predicting the return on a regular schedule of the eponymous comet, the brilliant scientist Halley excelled in many other fields besides astronomy. . . . Fox conveys Halley's life and times, and his lasting contributions to science, in vivid detail. The informative text is supported with maps and portraits."

Includes bibliographical references

Hamilton, Alexander, 1757-1804

St. George, Judith. The duel: the parallel lives of Alexander Hamilton and Aaron Burr. See entry under Burr, Aaron, 1756-1836

Hammel, Heidi B.

Bortz, Alfred B. Beyond Jupiter; the story of planetary astronomer Heidi Hammel; [by] Fred Bortz. Franklin Watts 2005 110p il (Women's adventures in science) lib bdg $31.50 *

Grades: 7 8 9 10   92

1. Women astronomers

ISBN 0-531-16775-5   LC 2005-0778

Also available in paperback from Joseph Henry Press

This is a biography of the American astronomer Heidi Hammel

The author "has captured some of the engaging qualities of Heidi Hammel's personality through extensive work with her and with the cooperation of her friends and family." Sci Books Films

Includes glossary and bibliographical references

Handel, George Frideric, 1685-1759

Getzinger, Donna. George Frideric Handel and music for voices; [by] Donna Getzinger and Daniel Felsenfeld. Morgan Reynolds Pub. 2004 144p il (Classical composers) lib bdg $28.95

Grades: 7 8 9 10   92

1. Composers

ISBN 1-931798-23-0   LC 2003-26729

Contents: A precocious child; Hamburg and Italy; Her Majesty's Theater; The Music Academy; Handel's Academy; Oratorios; Competing troupes; The Messiah; Respect; The last great masterpieces timeline

"Handel's importance in the field of music is described in this carefully researched and highly detailed biography. The authors explain how the composer's focus on music began at an early age and how he managed to pursue his interests despite his father's belief that music was not an acceptable profession. A social history of the time underscores the details of Handel's career. Black-and-white and full-color reproductions appear throughout." SLJ

Includes bibliographical references

Lee, Lavina. Handel's world; [by] Lavina Lee. Rosen Pub. Group 2008 64p il (Music throughout history) lib bdg $29.25

Grades: 5 6 7 8   92

1. Composers

ISBN 978-1-4042-0726-4 (lib bdg); 1-4042-0726-0 (lib bdg)   LC 2005030127

This "book begins with an introduction briefly addressing social issues of the day, historical background, or other significant information. . . . Successive chapters discuss the [man's] early [life], family background, social status, personality characteristics, musical training and education, obstacles or challenges, and influences. A chapter . . . focuses on the musician's well-known compositions, describing through lively and colorful language some of the musical elements employed." SLJ

Includes glossary and bibliographical references

Hannibal, 247-183 B.C.

Mills, Cliff. Hannibal; [by] Cliff Mills. Chelsea House 2008 120p bibl il map (Ancient world leaders) lib bdg $30

Grades: 6 7 8 9   92

1. Generals 2. Rome—History

ISBN 978-0-7910-9580-5 (lib bdg); 0-7910-9580-0 (lib bdg)   LC 2007-50493

"Mills's informative biography starts with Hannibal preparing to attack the Romans and then goes back in time to explain the founding of Carthage and the history of its conflict with Rome, mainly focusing on the Second Punic War and the subject's journey and battles during that time. . . . Frequent inserts add extra information . . . without distracting readers from the narrative. Colorful reproductions are also interspersed throughout. . . . [This offers] clear, descriptive writing." SLJ

Includes bibliographical references

Warrick, Karen Clemens. Hannibal; great general of the ancient world. Enslow Pubs. 2006 160p il map (Rulers of the ancient world) lib bdg $27.93

Grades: 6 7 8 9   92

1. Generals 2. Rome—History

ISBN 0-7660-2564-0

"Warrick first describes Hannibal crossing the Alps with his elephants and then chronicles the steps leading to the attack on Rome. [The book describes] battles and strategies in great detail. Insets, a few small black-and-white illustrations, and maps provide additional informa-

Hannibal, 247-183 B.C.—*Continued*

tion. [This book is] useful for reports and for pleasure reading." SLJ

Includes glossary and bibliographical references

Harrison, John, 1693-1776

Dash, Joan. The longitude prize; pictures by Dusan Petricic. Farrar, Straus and Giroux 1999 200p il $16

Grades: 5 6 7 8 **92**

1. Longitude

ISBN 0-374-34636-4 LC 97-44257

"Frances Foster books"

The story of John Harrison, inventor of watches and clocks, who spent forty years working on a time-machine which could be used to accurately determine longitude at sea

"Students looking for new subjects for reports will discover . . . an excellent resource on a topic seldom addressed in a book for youth. Charming ink drawings by Dusan Petricic illustrate. A glossary, an afterword, a time line, and a bibliography conclude." Booklist

Harvey, William, 1578-1657

Yount, Lisa. William Harvey; discoverer of how blood circulates; [by] Lisa Yount. rev ed. Enslow Publishers 2008 128p il map (Great minds of science) lib bdg $31.93

Grades: 5 6 7 8 **92**

1. Blood—Circulation 2. Physicians

ISBN 978-0-7660-3010-7 (lib bdg); 0-7660-3010-5 (lib bdg) LC 2007020301

First published 1994

"A biography of the seventeenth-century English physician William Harvey and includes related activities for readers." Publisher's note

Includes glossary and bibliographical references

Haskell, Katharine Wright, 1874-1929

Maurer, Richard. The Wright sister; Katharine Wright and her famous brothers. Millbrook Press 2003 127p il $18.95; lib bdg $25.90

Grades: 5 6 7 8 **92**

1. Wright, Wilbur, 1867-1912 2. Wright, Orville, 1871-1948 3. Air pilots

ISBN 0-7613-1546-2; 0-7613-2564-6 (lib bdg) LC 2002-151080

"Maurer chronicles the events surrounding Wilbur and Orville, while all along filling in the details of their younger sister's life and the relationship among the three." SLJ

"Quotations from diaries and letters bring the close-knit Wright family to life. . . . The layout is spacious, and the many well chosen, black-and-white photos help visualize the Wrights and their times." Booklist

Hatshepsut, Queen of Egypt

Dell, Pamela. Hatshepsut; Egypt's first female pharaoh. Compass Point Books 2009 112p il map (Signature lives) lib bdg $34.60

Grades: 6 7 8 9 **92**

1. Egypt—History 2. Egypt—Civilization 3. Kings and rulers

ISBN 978-0-7565-3835-4 (lib bdg); 0-7565-3835-1 (lib bdg) LC 2008005721

This biography of the Egypt's first female pharaoh offers "details about the history and daily life of Egypt's New Kingdom era. . . . It also discusses . . . topics concerning women, such as giving birth and the role of female royalty. The book expects some sophistication from its readers. . . . [The text is] accompanied by high-quality photographs of artifacts, maps, and floor plans. [The] book's detailed time line, comparing events in Egypt to those throughout the world, is helpful for placing the lives of the pharaohs in context." SLJ

Includes glossary and bibliographical references

Galford, Ellen. Hatshepsut; the princess who became king. National Geographic 2005 64p il map (World history biographies) $17.95; lib bdg $27.90 *

Grades: 4 5 6 7 **92**

1. Egypt—History 2. Egypt—Civilization 3. Kings and rulers

ISBN 0-7922-3645-9; 0-7922-3646-7 (lib bdg)

This "presents the life of Queen Hatshepsut, who ruled Egypt as pharaoh during the New Kingdom, around 3500 years ago. Illustrated with clear, color photos of artifacts and sites as well as colorful maps, the text discusses aspects of Egyptian life such as education and religion in Hatshepsut's life. . . . With a clearly written text and many handsome photos, this provides an accessible introduction to Hatshepsut and her times." Booklist

Hawk, Tony, 1968-

Hawk, Tony. Hawk; occupation, skateboarder; [by] Tony Hawk with Sean Mortimer. ReganBooks 2000 289p il hardcover o.p. pa $15

Grades: 8 9 10 11 12 **92**

1. Skateboarding

ISBN 0-06-019860-5; 0-06-095831-6 (pa) LC 00-40279

In this memoir, the author recalls how he diverted the rebellious nature of his childhood into his love for and determination to excel in skateboarding. He also discusses his experiences with such skateboarding figures as Stacy Peralta, Mark Gonzalez, and Bob Burnquist

Hawking, Stephen W., 1942-

Bankston, John. Stephen Hawking; breaking the boundaries of time and space; [by] John Bankston. Enslow Publishers 2005 128p il (Great minds of science) $26.60 *

Grades: 5 6 7 8 **92**

1. Physicists 2. Physically handicapped

ISBN 0-7660-2281-1 LC 2004-9193

Contents: A lucky man; Controversy; A lazy student?; Cosmic eggs and big bangs; The beginning of time; The big and the small of it; Black holes and white dwarfs; A new beginning; The brief history

Hawking, Stephen W., 1942-—*Continued*

This biography of the English physicist, who suffers from amyotrophic lateral sclerosis, includes explanations of his theories and experiments

"This excellent book features large font size and double spacing that makes it easy for any one to read. . . . The activities part of the book is outstanding." Sci Books Films

Includes glossary and bibliographical references

Hawthorne, Nathaniel, 1804-1864

Meltzer, Milton. Nathaniel Hawthorne; a biography. Twenty-First Century Books 2007 160p il (American literary greats) lib bdg $31.93

Grades: 7 8 9 10   92

1. Authors, American

ISBN 978-0-7613-3459-0 (lib bdg); 0-7613-3459-9 (lib bdg)   LC 2005000018

"The legendary novelist's life is portrayed as being as dramatic as the plotlines of his novels, and readers will be captivated by the detailed accounts of the family tragedies that made up his childhood and the financial and literary vicissitudes of his adult life. Meltzer provides sufficient background about New England at the time as well as accounts of the historical events that were shaping the country." SLJ

Includes bibliographical references

Haydn, Joseph, 1732-1809

Norton, James R. Haydn's world; [by] James R. Norton. Rosen Pub. Group 2008 64p il (Music throughout history) lib bdg $29.25

Grades: 5 6 7 8   92

1. Composers

ISBN 978-1-4042-0727-1 (lib bdg); 1-4042-0727-9 (lib bdg)   LC 2007000907

This "book begins with an introduction briefly addressing social issues of the day, historical background, or other significant information. . . . Successive chapters discuss the [man's] early [life], family background, social status, personality characteristics, musical training and education, obstacles or challenges, and influences. A chapter . . . focuses on the musician's well-known compositions, describing through lively and colorful language some of the musical elements employed. . . . The format and layout are appealing and uncluttered." SLJ

Includes glossary and bibliographical references

Hemingway, Ernest, 1899-1961

Reef, Catherine. Ernest Hemingway; a writer's life. Clarion Books 2009 183p il $20 *

Grades: 8 9 10 11 12   92

1. Authors, American

ISBN 978-0-618-98705-4; 0-618-98705-3

LC 2008032885

"Reef creates a memorable portrait of the writer and his times, and even readers too young for most of Hemingway's oeuvre will enjoy armchair traveling to the bullfights in Spain, fishing expeditions to the Dry Tortugas and the Marquesas Keys, big-game hunting on the Serengeti and covering the Spanish Civil War. Along the way, they will gain a sense of the writer and his times and will even pick up some writing tips." Kirkus

Includes bibliographical references

Whiting, Jim. Ernest Hemingway. Mitchell Lane 2005 48p il (Classic storytellers) lib bdg $19.95

Grades: 7 8 9 10   92

1. Authors, American

ISBN 1-58415-376-8

A biography of the American author.

"A brief, accessible introduction to this classic writer. Whiting balances the extremes in Hemingway's life, from his literary successes to his risky stunts, drinking, and bullying. . . . The book's design is attractive, with good use of color and photos." SLJ

Hendrix, Jimi

Gelfand, Dale Evva. Jimi Hendrix; musician; [by] Dale Evva Gelfand. Legacy ed. Chelsea House 2006 120p bibl il por (Black Americans of achievement) lib bdg $30

Grades: 6 7 8 9   92

1. Rock musicians 2. African American musicians

ISBN 0-7910-9214-3   LC 2006004574

A biography of the rock musician

This book goes "beyond the typical personal information to provide some social history relevant to the subject's time. Captioned photographs and boxed inserts enhance the conversational [text]." Horn Book Guide

Includes bibliographical references

Willett, Edward. Jimi Hendrix; "kiss the sky.". Enslow Publishers 2006 160p bibl por (American rebels) lib bdg $27.93

Grades: 7 8 9 10   92

1. Rock musicians 2. African American musicians

ISBN 0-7660-2449-0   LC 2005033751

"This biography introduces electric-guitar virtuouso Jimi Hendrix. . . . [This is a] good, basic introduction to Hendrix's life and the reasons for his enduring fame." Booklist

Includes bibliographical references

Henry, John William, 1847?-ca. 1875

Nelson, Scott Reynolds. Ain't nothing but a man; my quest to find the real John Henry; [by] Scott Reynolds Nelson with Marc Aronson. National Geographic 2008 64p il $18.95; lib bdg $27.90 *

Grades: 4 5 6 7 8   92

1. African Americans—Biography 2. John Henry (Legendary character) 3. Railroads—History

ISBN 978-1-4263-0000-4; 1-4263-0000-X; 978-1-4263-0001-1 (lib bdg); 1-4263-0001-8 (lib bdg)

LC 2007-12446

This describes the author's research to find the real man who inspired the songs and legends about the African American steel-driving hero.

"The layout is attractive, with a sepia and beige background for the text and sepia-toned photographs. . . . This is an excellent example of how much detective work is needed for original research." SLJ

Includes bibliographical references

Henry, O., 1862-1910

Caravantes, Peggy. Writing is my business; the story of O. Henry. Morgan Reynolds Pub. 2006 160p il map (World writers) lib bdg $27.95
Grades: 7 8 9 10   92
1. Authors, American
ISBN 978-1-59935-031-8 (lib bdg); 1-59935-031-9 (lib bdg)   LC 2006-16126
This is a biography of the short story writer
"This title grabs readers' attention and never lets go." SLJ
Includes bibliographical references

Henson, Matthew Alexander, 1866-1955

Johnson, Dolores. Onward; a photobiography of African-American polar explorer Matthew Henson. National Geographic 2006 64p il $17.95 *
Grades: 5 6 7 8   92
1. Explorers 2. North Pole 3. African Americans—Biography
ISBN 0-7922-7914-X   LC 2005-05837
"The quest to be the first to reach the North Pole is an exciting adventure story, and Henson got there first, as part of the ninth expedition led by Robert Peary in 1909. But Henson was African American, labeled as Peary's 'Negro manservant,' and he did not get full recognition until 2001. This . . . focuses on the physical details of the dangerous Arctic journeys . . . the repeated failures and the teamwork, as well as Henson's skills, stamina, and essential role in forging relationships with the Inuit. . . . The book design is beautiful: thick paper, spacious type, and stirring photos that capture the icy storms as well as the people involved in the history." Booklist

Olmstead, Kathleen A. Matthew Henson; the quest for the North Pole; [by] Kathleen Olmstead. Sterling Pub. Co. 2008 124p il (Sterling biographies) pa $5.95
Grades: 7 8 9 10   92
1. Explorers 2. North Pole 3. African Americans—Biography
ISBN 978-1-4027-4441-9 (pa); 1-4027-4441-2 (pa)   LC 2007048106
"Henson's own contradictory and partially fabricated writing about his effort to reach the North Pole with Robert Peary presented some challenges to the biographer, but she gamely sorts out the most likely version of the story, letting readers know what is unsubstantiated and what is corroborated fact. . . . [This] attractively formatted [title has] black-and-white and full-color photographs or reproductions as well as sidebars. [A] solid [addition] to biography shelves." SLJ
Includes glossary and bibliographical references

Hickam, Homer H., 1943-

Hickam, Homer H. The Coalwood way; by Homer H. Hickam, Jr. Delacorte Press 2000 318p pa $6.99 hardcover o.p.
Grades: 7 8 9 10 11 12 Adult   92
1. Authors, American 2. Aerospace engineers 3. West Virginia
ISBN 0-440-23716-5   LC 00-35884

This sequel to Rocket boys "continues the author's life story with his senior year in high school, 1959, in the declining West Virginia mining town of Coalwood. The rocket club, featured in the last book, is pushed to the periphery, and the focus shifts to Hickam's teenage problems, which include his parents, girls, and a sadness whose cause he cannot divine." Booklist

Hickam, Homer H. Rocket boys; a memoir; [by] Homer H. Hickam, Jr. Delacorte Press 1998 368p $25.95; pa $14 *
Grades: 7 8 9 10 11 12 Adult   92
1. Authors, American 2. West Virginia 3. Aerospace engineers
ISBN 0-385-33320-X; 0-385-33321-8 (pa)   LC 98-19304
"Raised in Appalachian coal country, Homer H. Hickam, Jr., might well have followed his father and grandfather into the mine. But when he was 14, his life was changed by a space launch on the other side of the world. Hickam's story of how a teenage boy's handmade rockets lifted the hopes of a hardscrabble town is told in his [memoir]." Smithsonian
"Even if Hickam stretched the strict truth to metamorphose his memories into Stand By Me-like material for Hollywood . . . the embellishing only converts what is a good story into an absorbing, rapidly readable one that is unsentimental but artful about adolescence, high school, and family life." Booklist

Hillary, Sir Edmund

Brennan, Kristine. Sir Edmund Hillary, modern day explorer. Chelsea House 2001 63p il (Explorers of new worlds) lib bdg $21.85; pa $11.95
Grades: 4 5 6 7   92
1. Mount Everest (China and Nepal) 2. Mountaineering
ISBN 0-7910-5953-7 (lib bdg); 0-7910-6163-9 (pa)   LC 00-43077
A biography of the New Zealander who, with his Sherpa climbing partner Tenzing Norgay, first reached the Summit of Mount Everest in 1953
"Accessible and well organized. . . . Fresh, appealing, and well written." SLJ
Includes glossary and bibliographical references

Elish, Dan. Edmund Hillary; first to the top; [by] Dan Elish. Marshall Cavendish Benchmark 2007 80p il map (Great explorations) lib bdg $32.79 *
Grades: 5 6 7 8   92
1. Mount Everest (China and Nepal) 2. Mountaineering
ISBN 978-0-7614-2224-2 (lib bdg); 0-7614-2224-2 (lib bdg)   LC 2005027929
"An examination of the life and accomplishments of the famed explorer from New Zealand who was one of the first to scale Mount Everest." Publisher's note
This "appealing [title features] readable [text], solid research, and variety of color illustrations." SLJ
Includes bibliographical references

Hines, Gregory

Abrams, Dennis. Gregory Hines; entertainer; [by] Dennis Abrams. Legacy ed. Chelsea House 2008 98p il (Black Americans of achievement) lib bdg $30

Grades: 6 7 8 9   92

1. African American actors

ISBN 978-0-7910-9718-2 (lib bdg); 0-7910-9718-8 (lib bdg)   LC 2007045506

This biography details the African American actor's "rise from adversity to . . . recognition. The [book goes] beyond the typical personal information to provide some social history relevant to the subject's time. Captioned photographs and boxed inserts enhance the conversational [text]." Horn Book Guide

Includes bibliographical references

Hinton, S. E.

Kjelle, Marylou Morano. S.E. Hinton; author of The outsiders. Enslow Publishers 2007 112p bibl il por (Authors teens love) lib bdg $31.93 *

Grades: 6 7 8 9   92

1. Authors, American 2. Women authors

ISBN 978-0-7660-2720-6 (lib bdg); 0-7660-2720-1 (lib bdg)   LC 2006036820

"This well-written and informative biography weaves facts about Hinton's life with analyses of and reflections on her novels." SLJ

Includes glossary and bibliographical references

Wilson, Antoine. S.E. Hinton. Rosen Central 2003 112p il (Library of author biographies) lib bdg $26.50

Grades: 6 7 8 9   92

1. Authors, American 2. Women authors

ISBN 0-8239-3778-X   LC 2002-7905

Discusses the life, novels, and writing habits of S.E. Hinton, author of such popular books as "The Outsiders" and "That Was Then, This Is Now"

"This is an informative and interesting resource." SLJ

Includes bibliographical references

Hitler, Adolf, 1889-1945

Rice, Earle. Adolf Hitler and Nazi Germany. Morgan Reynolds 2005 176p il map lib bdg $28.95

Grades: 7 8 9 10   92

1. Dictators 2. National socialism 3. Germany—Politics and government—1933-1945

ISBN 978-1-931798-78-5 (lib bdg); 1-931798-78-8 (lib bdg)   LC 2005-17825

"Rice begins with details about Hitler's childhood, his early years as an artist, and his time as a soldier in World War I. He then focuses on Hitler's rise to power as dictator and leader of the Nazi Party, the causes and course of World War II, and the Fuhrer's obsessive determination to exterminate the Jews and other 'undesirables.'" Booklist

"Clear, concise writing coupled with impressive illustrations that include black-and-white and color photos of cityscapes and individuals make this book a useful resource." SLJ

Hooke, Robert, 1635-1703

Gow, Mary. Robert Hooke; creative genius, scientist, inventor. Enslow Publishers 2006 128p il (Great minds of science) lib bdg $31.93

Grades: 5 6 7 8   92

1. Scientists

ISBN 0-7660-2547-0   LC 2005-31651

This is a biography of the 17th century English scientist "famous for the law of elasticity which bears his name. . . . In addition to Hooke's law, he also built the first Gregorian telescope, discovered plant cells by using an early microscope, and stated the law of inverse squares." Publisher's note

"The accessible [text has] an inviting, open format and [offers] many anecdotes. . . . Good-quality photos and illustrations complement the [narrative]." SLJ

Includes glossary and bibliographical references

Hoover, Herbert, 1874-1964

Holford, David M. Herbert Hoover. Enslow Pubs. 1999 128p il (United States presidents) lib bdg $26.60

Grades: 5 6 7 8   92

1. Presidents—United States

ISBN 0-7660-1035-X   LC 98-11688

A biography of Herbert Hoover, thirty-first president of the United States, describing his career as mining engineer, businessman, and president during the Great Depression

"This biography is insightful. . . . The writing is lucid, and the information is not overwhelming." SLJ

Includes bibliographical references

Hopper, Edward, 1882-1967

Rubin, Susan Goldman. Edward Hopper; painter of light and shadow. Abrams Books for Young Readers 2007 47p il $18.95 *

Grades: 5 6 7 8   92

1. Artists—United States

ISBN 978-0-8109-9347-1; 0-8109-9347-3   LC 2006-31978

"On every page of this beautifully designed biography, readers will find a reproduction of Hopper's work, matched to clear, eloquent commentary. . . . Readers . . . will come back to read about the man and look at his art again and again." Booklist

Includes bibliographical references

Horowitz, Anthony, 1955-

Abrams, Dennis. Anthony Horowitz; [by] Dennis Abrams; foreword by Kyle Zimmer. Chelsea House Publishers 2006 123p il map (Who wrote that?) lib bdg $30

Grades: 6 7 8 9   92

1. Authors, English

ISBN 0-7910-8968-1   LC 2005030090

A biography of the author of the popular Alex Rider series

"Even teens who don't know Horowitz's books will enjoy reading this frank account that describes how his unhappy childhood . . . influenced his books. . . . Just as compelling are Horowitz's perspectives on what makes good horror and spy fiction." Booklist

Includes bibliographical references

Houdini, Harry, 1874-1926

Carlson, Laurie M. Harry Houdini for kids; his life and adventures with 21 magic tricks and illusions. Chicago Review Press 2009 136p il pa $16.95

Grades: 4 5 6 7   **92**

1. Magicians 2. Magic tricks
ISBN 978-1-55652-782-1 (pa); 1-55652-782-9 (pa)
LC 2008021404

"Reluctant readers (as well as budding troublemakers) will flock to this biography/handbook hybrid about one of the most famous magicians who ever lived. Even for those familiar with Houdini's fascinating story, Carlson's snappy writing gives it new life. . . . Nearly every page is enlivened with period photographs, boxed sections containing biographies and definitions, and, most important, 21 magic tricks that will have readers breaking out their deck of cards and practicing their sleight of hand." Booklist

Fleischman, Sid. Escape! the story of the great Houdini. Greenwillow Books 2006 210p il $18.99; lib bdg $19.89 *

Grades: 5 6 7 8   **92**

1. Magicians
ISBN 978-0-06-085094-4; 0-06-085094-9; 978-0-06-085095-1 (lib bdg); 0-06-0850957-1 (lib bdg)
LC 2005052631

"Fleischman looks at Houdini's life through his own eyes, as a fellow magician. . . . Fleischman's tone is lively and he develops a relationship with readers by revealing just enough truth behind Houdini's razzle-dazzle to keep the legend alive. . . . Engaging and fascinating." SLJ

Includes bibliographical references

Lutes, Jason. Houdini: the handcuff king. Hyperion Books for Children/Jump at the Sun 2007 90p il (Center for Cartoon Studies presents) $16.99; pa $9.99 *

Grades: 4 5 6 7 8 9 10   **92**

1. Graphic novels 2. Magicians—Graphic novels 3. Biographical graphic novels
ISBN 978-0-7868-3902-5; 978-0-7868-3903-2 (pa)

On May 1, 1908, magician Harry Houdini performed one of his famous handcuff escapes, this time in handcuffs and leg irons, while jumping off the Cambridge Bridge in Massachusetts into the frigid Boston River. This graphic novel takes the reader through Houdini's day, from 5:00 a.m. as he makes his preparations, makes a practice jump, coaches his wife Bess on how she's to help him, and then makes the jump.

This is a "fascinating graphic novel. . . . The format will instantly draw a lot of attention from readers and then hold on to it. Lutes and Bertozzi use grayscale comic panels to share their story about the life of Harry Houdini in a unique way. . . . The book resembles a hybrid between fiction and nonfiction, and the ingenious choice of format will appeal to a broad age range of readers." Voice Youth Advocates

Hubble, Edwin Powell, 1889-1953

Datnow, Claire L. Edwin Hubble; discoverer of galaxies. rev ed. Enslow Publishers 2007 128p il (Great minds of science) lib bdg $31.93

Grades: 5 6 7 8   **92**

1. Astronomers
ISBN 978-0-7660-2791-6 (lib bdg); 0-7660-2791-0 (lib bdg)
LC 2006-20111
First published 1997

Traces the life and work of the man whose study of galaxies led to a new understanding of the universe
Includes glossary and bibliographical references

Hudson, Henry, d. 1611

Edwards, Judith. Henry Hudson and his voyages of exploration in world history. Enslow Pubs. 2002 128p il maps (In world history) lib bdg $26.60

Grades: 7 8 9 10   **92**

1. Explorers 2. America—Exploration
ISBN 0-7660-1885-7   LC 2001-4119

Examines the life and career of Henry Hudson, tracing his voyages in the Arctic and North America and his discovery of the Hudson River and other bodies of water during his unsuccessful search for a Northwest Passage to Asia
Includes bibliographical references

Otfinoski, Steven. Henry Hudson; in search of the Northwest Passage; [by] Steven Otfinoski. Marshall Cavendish Benchmark 2006 80p il map (Great explorations) lib bdg $32.79 *

Grades: 5 6 7 8   **92**

1. Explorers 2. America—Exploration
ISBN 978-0-7614-2225-9; 0-7614-2225-0

"An examination of the life and accomplishments of the famed explorer who lent his name to several geographic locations in North America" Publisher's note
Includes bibliographical references

Hughes, Langston, 1902-1967

Wallace, Maurice O. Langston Hughes; the Harlem Renaissance; [by] Maurice Wallace. Marshall Cavendish Benchmark 2007 144p il (Writers and their works) lib bdg $42.79

Grades: 8 9 10 11 12   **92**

1. Poets, American
ISBN 978-0-7614-2591-5 (lib bdg); 0-7614-2591-8 (lib bdg)
LC 2006-38162

"A biography of writer Langston Hughes that describes his era, his major works—especially his most famous and influential prose and poetry, his life, and and the legacy of his writing." Publisher's note

"The language, pictures, and other references are user-friendly for younger researchers. The [book is] illustrated with photos and reproductions. Useful . . . for circulation or for reference collections." SLJ

Includes filmography and bibliographical references

Hunter, Clementine, 1886?-1988

Whitehead, Kathy. Art from her heart: folk artist Clementine Hunter; [illustrated by] Shane Evans. G.P. Putnam's Sons 2008 unp il $16.99

Grades: 4 5 6 7   **92**

1. African American artists 2. Women artists 3. Folk art

ISBN 978-0-399-24219-9; 0-399-24219-8

LC 2006-34458

A biography of "folk artist Clementine Hunter. Her paintings went from hanging on her clothesline to hanging in museums, yet because of the color of her skin, a friend had to sneak her in when the gallery was closed." Publisher's note

"Whitehead's lyrical text speaks of Hunter's perseverance and talent as well as of the simplicity, love of nature, and caring of friends and family that informed her work. Evans bolsters Whitehead's words with bold mixed-media illustrations that portray Hunter in hard times and in good." SLJ

Hurston, Zora Neale, 1891-1960

Litwin, Laura Baskes. Zora Neale Hurston; "I have been in sorrow's kitchen.". Enslow Publishers 2007 c2008 128p bibl il por (African-American biography library) lib bdg $23.95 *

Grades: 7 8 9 10   **92**

1. African American authors 2. Women authors

ISBN 978-0-7660-2536-5 (lib bdg); 0-7660-2536-5 (lib bdg)   LC 2005034881

Litwin "offers an engaging portrait of legendary author and folklorist Zora Neale Hurston. . . . Well-paced . . . chapters follow Hurston through her remarkable career. . . . Generously sprinkled with excerpts from Hurston's own works and illustrated with numerous black-and-white portraits of Hurston and her prominent friends and collaborators." Booklist

Includes bibliographical references

Lyons, Mary E. Sorrow's kitchen; the life and folklore of Zora Neale Hurston. 1st Collier Books ed. Collier Books 1993 144p il (Great achievers) pa $7.99 *

Grades: 7 8 9 10   **92**

1. African American authors 2. Women authors

ISBN 0-02-044445-1   LC 92-30600

First published 1990 by Scribner

This biography details "Hurston's migration from Florida to Baltimore, Washington, D.C., and finally Harlem as well as her travels through the West Indies to collect folklore. The text contains eleven excerpts from Hurston's books. . . . Lyons has created a prime example of biography—fascinating, enlightening, stimulating, and satisfying." Horn Book

Includes bibliographical references

Sapet, Kerrily. Rhythm and folklore; the story of Zora Neale Hurston. Morgan Reynolds Pub. 2008 160p il lib bdg $27.95

Grades: 7 8 9 10 11 12   **92**

1. African American authors 2. Women authors

ISBN 978-1-59935-067-7 (lib bdg); 1-59935-067-X (lib bdg)   LC 2008-844

A biography of the African American author and folklorist

"With lots of personal quotes, this lively biography stays true to Hurston's defiant, independent spirit. . . . Sapet give a strong sense of the times, including the Harlem Renaissance. . . . With lots of full-page photos, this biography will encourage teens to read and discuss Hurston's work." Booklist

Includes bibliographical references

Hutchinson, Anne Marbury, 1591-1643

Stille, Darlene R. Anne Hutchinson; Puritan protester; by Darlene R. Stille. Compass Point Books 2006 112p il map (Signature lives) lib bdg $31.93

Grades: 6 7 8 9   **92**

1. Puritans 2. Massachusetts—History—1600-1775, Colonial period

ISBN 978-07565-1577-5 (lib bdg); 0-7565-1577-7 (lib bdg)   LC 2005025093

A biography of Anne Hutchinson, who was put on trial in colonial Massachusetts for challenging Puritan beliefs

This is an "excellent biography. . . . Stille neither glorifies nor condemns her but rather reveals her strength of character in the context of her historical era, enhancing the interesting, accessible narrative with numerous full-color illustrations." Booklist

Includes bibliographical references

Inouye, Daniel K.

Slavicek, Louise Chipley. Daniel Inouye. Chelsea House 2007 128p bibl il por (Asian Americans of achievement) lib bdg $30

Grades: 6 7 8 9   **92**

1. Statesmen—United States 2. Asian Americans—Biography

ISBN 978-0-7910-9271-2 (lib bdg); 0-7910-9271-2 (lib bdg)   LC 2006026062

A biography of the Senator from Hawaii

This is "well-researched . . . attractive . . . solid." SLJ

Includes glossary and bibliographical references

Jackson, Andrew, 1767-1845

Marrin, Albert. Old Hickory; Andrew Jackson and the American people. Dutton Children's Books 2004 262p il $35 *

Grades: 7 8 9 10   **92**

1. Presidents—United States

ISBN 0-525-47293-2   LC 2003-28299

"More than a biography, this fine study of our seventh president is also a history and analysis of the times in which he lived. . . . Marrin discusses the changes to society brought about by the Industrial Revolution, the railroads, and the rise of the market economy. Written in an engaging style and with a wealth of detail, the book is enhanced by numerous black-and-white illustrations." SLJ

Includes bibliographical references

Jackson, Robert Houghwout, 1892-1954

Jarrow, Gail. Robert H. Jackson; New Deal lawyer, Supreme Court Justice, Nuremberg prosecutor. Calkins Creek 2008 128p il $18.95

Grades: 7 8 9 10   92

1. Judges 2. Nuremberg Trial of Major German War Criminals, 1945-1946

ISBN 978-1-59078-511-9   LC 2007-18858

"Framed by Jackson's famous speech as chief American prosecutor at the 1945 international Nuremberg trial of Nazi war criminals, this detailed biography sets his law career within the history and politics of his time and raises essential issues of human rights." Booklist

Includes bibliographical references

Jackson, Shirley Ann, 1946-

O'Connell, Diane. Strong force; the story of physicist Shirley Ann Jackson. Franklin Watts 2005 110p il (Women's adventures in science) lib bdg $31

Grades: 7 8 9 10   92

1. Physicists 2. Women scientists 3. African American women—Biography

ISBN 0-5311-6784-4   LC 2005-827

A biography of African American physicist Shirley Ann Jackson.

This is "interesting, substantive, and eminently readable." SLJ

Includes bibliographical references

Jackson, Stonewall, 1824-1863

Pflueger, Lynda. Stonewall Jackson; Confederate general. Enslow Pubs. 1997 128p il (Historical American biographies) lib bdg $26.60   92

1. Confederate States of America. Army—Biography—Juvenile literature 2. Generals 3. United States—History—1861-1865, Civil War

ISBN 0-89490-781-6   LC 96-8827

A biography of the Confederate general who gained the nickname Stonewall for his stand at the first battle of Bull Run during the Civil War

"The content is thorough and includes valuable historical background." Horn Book Guide

Includes glossary and bibliographical references

Jalāl al-Dīn Rūmī, Maulana, 1207-1273

Demi. Rumi; whirling dervish; written and illustrated by Demi. Marshall Cavendish Children 2009 31p il $19.99 *

Grades: 4 5 6 7   92

1. Persian poetry 2. Poets

ISBN 978-0-7614-5527-1; 0-7614-5527-2

LC 2008012920

"Demi presents this picture-book introduction to the thirteenth-century mystical poet. . . . Demi condenses her famous subject's life into a brief but substantive text. . . . She adds frequent excerpts from Rumi's poems and writings. . . . In an introductory note, Demi cites Turkish miniatures as her inspiration for the small-scale, elaborately patterned pictures, rendered in Turkish and Chinese inks with gold overlay. . . . The gilded, celebratory pictures create shimmering beauty from the smallest details. " Booklist

James, LeBron

Rappoport, Ken. Lebron James; king on and off the court. Enslow Publishers 2006 128p bibl il por (Sports stars with heart) $31.93

Grades: 6 7 8 9   92

1. Basketball—Biography 2. African American athletes

ISBN 0-7660-2420-2; 978-0-7660-2420-5

LC 2006012538

In this biography of the basketball star "Lebron James's good deeds are well documented. . . . There is plenty of action and game details in [this title]. . . . This . . . has an attractive format with color photos that will impress reluctant readers. . . . Excellent." Voice Youth Advocates

Includes bibliographical references

Jefferson, Thomas, 1743-1826

Severance, John B. Thomas Jefferson; architect of democracy. Clarion Bks. 1998 192p il map $18

Grades: 7 8 9 10   92

1. Presidents—United States

ISBN 0-395-84513-0   LC 97-31010

Explores the life of the third president, from his childhood in Virginia, through his involvement in the Revolutionary War, to his years in office

"In this respectful, literate, and handsomely illustrated biography, Severance focuses equally on Jefferson's remarkable accomplishments and the beliefs behind them." Booklist

Includes bibliographical references

Whitelaw, Nancy. Thomas Jefferson; philosopher and president. Morgan Reynolds 2002 144p il $21.95 *

Grades: 7 8 9 10   92

1. Presidents—United States

ISBN 1-88384-681-1   LC 2001-44960

An account of Jefferson's life highlighting his many accomplishments as governor, architect, gardener, inventor, and president

"A clear, crisp biography. . . . A solid and practical book for reports." SLJ

Includes bibliographical references

Jemison, Mae C.

Jemison, Mae C. Find where the wind goes; moments from my life; [by] Mae Jemison. Scholastic Press 2001 196p il $16.95; pa $4.99

Grades: 5 6 7 8   92

1. Astronauts 2. African American women—Biography

ISBN 0-439-13195-2; 0-439-13196-0 (pa)

LC 00-41008

"Dr. Jemison, the first woman of color to travel in space, shares her life story in this autobiographical selection." Book Rep

"Jemison's vitality, intelligence, and humor shine through the book, and she has a fascinating and inspiring life story to tell." Booklist

Jenner, Edward, 1749-1823

Rodriguez, Ana Maria. Edward Jenner; conqueror of smallpox. Enslow Pubs. 2006 128p il map (Great minds of science) lib bdg $31.93

Grades: 5 6 7 8   92

1. Physicians 2. Smallpox

ISBN 0-7660-2504-7   LC 2005-19088

A biography of the discoverer of the smallpox vaccine

"Rodriguez's excellent biography reveals the whole man." Sci Books Films

Includes bibliographical references

Jeter, Derek, 1974-

Mills, Cliff. Derek Jeter; [by] Clifford W. Mills. Chelsea House 2007 122p il (Baseball superstars) lib bdg $30

Grades: 6 7 8 9   92

1. Baseball—Biography

ISBN 978-0-7910-9422-8 (lib bdg); 0-7910-9422-7 (lib bdg)   LC 2007005913

Profiles the shortstop for the New York Yankees, who is the only player in history to be named MVP of the All-Star Game and the World Series in the same season

Includes bibliographical references

Robinson, Tom. Derek Jeter; captain on and off the field; [by] Tom Robinson. Enslow Publishers 2006 128p bibl il por (Sports stars with heart) lib bdg $31.93

Grades: 6 7 8 9   92

1. Baseball—Biography

ISBN 0-7660-2819-4 (lib bdg); 978-0-7660-2819-7 (lib bdg)   LC 2006012542

A look at the life of the baseball star and his philanthropy.

"There is plenty of action and game details in [this title]. . . . This . . . has an attractive format with color photos that will impress reluctant readers. . . . Excellent." Voice Youth Advocates

Includes bibliographical references

Joan, of Arc, Saint, 1412-1431

Stanley, Diane. Joan of Arc. Morrow Junior Bks. 1998 unp il hardcover o.p. pa $7.99 *

Grades: 4 5 6 7   92

1. Christian saints 2. France—History—1328-1589, House of Valois

ISBN 0-688-14329-6; 0-06-443748-5 (pa); 978-0-06-443748-6 (pa)   LC 97-45652

A biography of the fifteenth-century peasant girl who led a French army to victory against the English and was burned at the stake for witchcraft

Stanley "orchestrates the complexities of history into a gripping, unusually challenging story in this exemplary biography. . . . Judiciously chosen details build atmosphere in both the text and the artwork—painstakingly wrought, gilded paintings modeled after the illuminated manuscripts of Joan's day." Publ Wkly

Includes bibliographical references

Wilkinson, Philip. Joan of Arc; the teenager who saved her nation; [by] Philip Wilkinson. National Geographic Society 2007 64p il map (World history biographies) $17.95; lib bdg $27.90

Grades: 4 5 6 7   92

1. Christian saints 2. France—History—1328-1589, House of Valois

ISBN 978-1-4263-0116-2; 1-4263-0116-2; 978-1-4263-0117-9 (lib bdg); 1-4263-0117-0 (lib bdg)   LC 2006026106

A look at the life, death, and continuing influence of Joan of Arc.

This book is "attractively illustrated and pleasingly presented. . . . Dates, highlighted across the bottom of pages in a colorful band, note biographical points of reference and historical events. The writing is competent . . . and covers all the essentials." SLJ

Includes glossary and bibliographical references

Jobs, Steven, 1955-

Corrigan, Jim. Steve Jobs; [by] Jim Corrigan. Morgan Reynolds Pub. 2007 128p il (Business leaders) lib bdg $27.95

Grades: 7 8 9 10   92

1. Apple Computer Inc. 2. Computer industry 3. Businesspeople

ISBN 978-1-59935-076-9 (lib bdg); 1-59935-076-9 (lib bdg)   LC 2007-39052

This biography addresses "Jobs's California childhood, early collaborations with Steve Wozniak (especially their 1976 founding of Apple Computer), 1985 resignation from Apple and return a decade later, and 1986 purchase of Pixar. Personal details include his tyrannical management style, his search for his biological parents, and his remarkable recovery from pancreatic cancer. The text concludes with the successful debut of the iPhone in 2007. [This volume contains] full-color photos that add visual appeal. . . . [This is] serious and balanced." SLJ

Includes glossary and bibliographical references

Imbimbo, Anthony. Steve Jobs; the brilliant mind behind Apple. Gareth Stevens Pub. 2008 112p il map (Life portraits) lib bdg $34

Grades: 7 8 9 10   92

1. Apple Computer Inc. 2. Computer industry 3. Businesspeople

ISBN 978-1-4339-0060-0 (lib bdg); 1-4339-0060-2 (lib bdg)   LC 2008041004

"Imbimbo offers an absorbing portrait of his charismatic subject, beginning with Jobs' introduction of the iPhone and then tracing back to Jobs' first early teen encounters with computers. . . . Numerous quotes from coworkers and from Jobs himself add to the balanced profile. . . . [Illustrated with] clear color photos of Jobs throughout his life. . . . [This is] well-researched . . . high interest." Booklist

Includes bibliographical references

John Paul II, Pope, 1920-2005

Behnke, Alison. Pope John Paul II. Lerner Publs. 2005 112p (A & E biography) $27.93; pa $8.95

Grades: 7 8 9 10   92

John Paul II, Pope, 1920-2005—*Continued*
1. Popes
ISBN 0-8225-2798-7; 0-8225-3387-1 (pa)
This "presents the dramatic story of Karol Wojtyla. The account follows him from his youth in a small Polish village during the dark days of the Holocaust and his training as a priest in an underground Krakow seminary, to his work as teacher, priest, and bishop under Communist rule and his 25 years as head of the Roman Catholic Church. Behnke's writing style is clear and direct, and the inviting design includes lots of black-and-white photos and occasional sidebars." Booklist
Includes bibliographical references

Renehan, Edward J. Pope John Paul II; [by] Edward J. Renehan, Jr. Chelsea House 2007 109p il (Modern world leaders) lib bdg $30
Grades: 7 8 9 10 11 12   **92**
1. Popes
ISBN 978-0-7910-9227-9 (lib bdg); 0-7910-9227-5 (lib bdg)   LC 2006-10612
This "biography follows the arch of the pontiff's life in the context of world politics." Publisher's note
Includes bibliographical references

Johnson, Lyndon B. (Lyndon Baines), 1908-1973
Gold, Susan Dudley. Lyndon B. Johnson. Marshall Cavendish Benchmark 2009 112p il (Presidents and their times) lib bdg $34.21
Grades: 5 6 7 8   **92**
1. Presidents—United States
ISBN 978-0-7614-2837-4 (lib bdg); 0-7614-2837-2 (lib bdg)   LC 2007038518
A biography of the thirty-sixth president of the United States discusses his personal life, education, and political career and covers the formative events of his time
Includes glossary and bibliographical references

Johnson, Mamie, 1935-
Green, Michelle Y. A strong right arm: the story of Mamie "Peanut" Johnson; introduction by Mamie Johnson. Dial Bks. for Young Readers 2002 111p il $15.99; pa $5.99 *
Grades: 4 5 6 7   **92**
1. Baseball—Biography 2. Women athletes 3. African American athletes
ISBN 0-8037-2661-9; 0-14-240072-6 (pa)   LC 2001-28616
"Johnson was a pitcher with the Negro Leagues' Indianapolis Clowns from 1953 to 1955. In the introduction, Johnson speaks directly and movingly to the reader about her meeting with author Green, who then lets the famous ballplayer tell her own story in a lively first-person narrative. Johnson's ebullient personality and determination fairly leap off the page." Booklist
Includes bibliographical references

Jones, John Paul, 1747-1792
Brager, Bruce L. John Paul Jones; America's sailor. Morgan Reynolds Pub. 2006 160p il map lib bdg $26.95
Grades: 7 8 9 10   **92**
1. Admirals
ISBN 978-1-931798-84-6 (lib bdg); 1-931798-84-2 (lib bdg)   LC 2005-30443
The author "begins with Jones's Scottish childhood, where he developed a bitter resentment of the British class system. He then traces the man's career as a commercial seaman, privateer, naval commander, and soldier of fortune. . . . This often-unflattering portrait of Jones will require readers who can place his good and bad traits in perspective and judge his place in history, making it a good choice for mature students." SLJ
Includes bibliographical references

Cooper, Michael L. Hero of the high seas; John Paul Jones and the American Revolution. National Geographic 2006 128p il map $21.95; lib bdg $32.90
Grades: 5 6 7 8   **92**
1. Admirals 2. United States—History—1775-1783, Revolution
ISBN 0-7922-5547-X; 0-7922-5548-8 (lib bdg)   LC 2005-36256
"Cooper charts his subject's life from a scandal-ridden Scottish captain on a trading ship to a man of self-invention who came to the American colonies to start a new life and became a naval hero. Jones is presented as a loyal captain, an arrogant leader, a determined sailor, and a flagrant social climber. The narrative style will appeal to reluctant readers, for it reads like a chronicle of thrilling naval adventures. . . . The text is clear and understandable." SLJ
Includes bibliographical references

Joseph, Nez Percé Chief, 1840-1904
Scott, Robert Alan. Chief Joseph and the Nez Percés; [by] Robert A. Scott. Facts on File 1993 134p il maps (Makers of America) lib bdg $25
Grades: 8 9 10 11 12   **92**
1. Nez Percé Indians
ISBN 0-8160-2475-8   LC 92-15885
A biography of the nineteenth-century Nez Percé chief, concentrating on his unending struggle to win peace and equality for his people
Includes bibliographical references

Juárez, Benito, 1806-1872
Stein, R. Conrad. Benito Juarez and the French intervention; [by] R. Conrad Stein. Morgan Reynolds Pub. 2008 160p il map (The story of Mexico) lib bdg $27.95
Grades: 6 7 8 9   **92**
1. Mexico—History
ISBN 978-1-59935-052-3 (lib bdg); 1-59935-052-1 (lib bdg)   LC 2007016005
The book provides "detailed information in a readable format, and [a] lively writing style. . . . Colorful reproductions and photographs help to maintain interest. [This] title tells the story of Juárez, a Zapotec Indian, and his

Juárez, Benito, 1806-1872—_Continued_
rise to political leadership. Born into poverty in 1806, he
became Mexico's first Indian president, presiding over a
country in turmoil." SLJ
Includes glossary and bibliographical references

Kahlo, Frida, 1907-1954
Hillstrom, Laurie. Frida Kahlo; painter; by
Laurie Collier Hillstrom. Lucent Books 2008 104p
il (The twentieth century's most influential
Hispanics) lib bdg $32.45
Grades: 6 7 8 9 10   **92**
1. Artists, Mexican 2. Women artists
ISBN 978-1-4205-0019-6 (lib bdg); 1-4205-0019-8 (lib
bdg)   LC 2007-32106
"Kahlo's life . . . is chronicled as are the influences
of her marriage to Rivera and her physical pain on on
her art. . . . The layout draws the eye with colorful
chapter headings and highlighted quotes." Lib Media
Connect
Includes bibliographical references

Laidlaw, Jill A. Frida Kahlo. Watts 2003 46p il
(Artists in their time) lib bdg $22.50; pa $6.95
Grades: 5 6 7 8   **92**
1. Artists, Mexican 2. Women artists
ISBN 0-531-12236-0 (lib bdg); 0-531-16642-2 (pa)
                             LC 2003-535333
A biography of the Mexican artist and Communist ac-
tivist
"The text is clear, concise, and written with vigor.
. . . The large, full-color reproductions of [Kahlo's]
paintings are excellent, and numerous archival photo-
graphs and quotes add a personal and immediate connec-
tion to the artist's life." SLJ

Sabbeth, Carol. Frida Kahlo and Diego Rivera:
their lives and ideas; 24 activities; [by] Carol
Sabbeth. 1st ed. Chicago Review Press 2005 147p
il map pa $17.95 *
Grades: 5 6 7 8   **92**
1. Rivera, Diego, 1886-1957 2. Artists, Mexican
3. Women artists
ISBN 1-55652-569-9   LC 2004-24525
"An overview of two complicated and controversial
figures whose personal affairs, political ideas and affiliations, and artworks were out of the mainstream, even
radical. . . . The pages are colorfully designed with
bright borders at the tops of the pages, colored sidebars,
and appropriately placed photos and reproductions, including works by both artists. The 24 related activities
range from artwork to cultural projects." SLJ
Includes bibliographical references

Wooten, Sara McIntosh. Frida Kahlo; her life in
paintings. Enslow Publishers, Inc. 2005 128p bibl
il por (Latino biography library) lib bdg $31.93
Grades: 7 8 9 10   **92**
1. Artists, Mexican 2. Women artists
ISBN 0-7660-2487-3   LC 2004-27539
This "book captures the dynamic life of the intriguing
painter. Politically active, artistically cutting-edge, physically tortured from an accident in her late teens, Kahlo
was born and lived most of her life in Mexico. Wooten

discusses her subject's physical and mental struggles, including her volatile marriage to Diego Rivera. This title
includes numerous full-color reproductions of Kahlo's
work in addition to black-and-white photographs of her
family and friends." SLJ

Karzai, Hamid
Abrams, Dennis. Hamid Karzai. Chelsea House
2007 128p bibl il por (Modern world leaders) lib
bdg $30
Grades: 7 8 9 10 11 12   **92**
1. Afghanistan—Politics and government
ISBN 0-7910-9267-4 (lib bdg); 978-0-7910-9267-5 (lib
bdg)   LC 2006032695
"Abrams opens with a chapter describing Karzai's
2004 inauguration as the president of Afghanistan and
then continues with five chapters of historical background. . . . The final chapter focuses on the current attempts to rebuild Afghanistan and the challenges Karzai
is facing. . . . [The book has] archival news photographs
throughout. [It] would be [a] good [choice] for updating
a collection, as [it is] current and [contains] solid information." SLJ
Includes bibliographical references

Keckley, Elizabeth, ca. 1818-1907
Jones, Lynda. Mrs. Lincoln's dressmaker: the
unlikely friendship of Elizabeth Keckley and Mary
Todd Lincoln; by Lynda D. Jones. National
Geographic 2009 80p il $18.95; lib bdg $27.90
Grades: 5 6 7 8   **92**
1. Lincoln, Mary Todd, 1818-1882 2. African Ameri-
can women—Biography 3. Slavery—United States
4. Presidents' spouses—United States 5. Washington
(D.C.)—Social life and customs 6. United States—
Race relations
ISBN   978-1-4263-0377-7;   1-4263-0377-7;
978-1-4263-0378-4 (lib bdg); 1-4263-0378-5 (lib bdg)
                             LC 2008-29314
"In 1868, a controversial tell-all called _Behind the
Scenes_ introduced readers to Elizabeth Hobbs Keckley.
Mrs. Keckley was a former slave who had been Mary
Todd Lincoln's dressmaker and friend during the White
House years, and in the aftermath of President Lincoln's
assassination." Publisher's note
"Readers may be familiar with the ups and downs of
Lincoln's life, but details of Keckley's story . . . will
give them new insights into the life of a slave, in this
case, one who was educated and had a profession."
Booklist
Includes bibliographical references

Keller, Helen, 1880-1968
Delano, Marfe Ferguson. Helen's eyes: a
photobiography of Annie Sullivan, Helen Keller's
teacher. See entry under Sullivan, Anne,
1866-1936

Keller, Helen, 1880-1968—*Continued*

Garrett, Leslie. Helen Keller. DK Publishing 2004 127p il (DK biography) hardcover o.p. pa $4.99

Grades: 5 6 7 8   92
    1. Blind 2. Deaf
    ISBN 0-7566-0488-5; 0-7566-0339-0 (pa)
                                    LC 2004-8451
This is a "first look at the . . . woman, blind and deaf since childhood, who . . . learned to read and speak and traveled the world as an inspiring public speaker and political activist. The . . . illustration-rich page design works well . . . and the smooth [narrative is] broken up on every page with boxed facts and quotes as well as well-chosen, small color photos." Booklist

Includes bibliographical references

Keller, Helen. The story of my life; edited and with a preface by James Berger. The restored ed. Modern Library 2003 xlvi, 343p il hardcover o.p. pa $9.95 *

Grades: 8 9 10 11 12 Adult   92
    1. Blind 2. Deaf
    ISBN 0-679-64287-0; 0-8129-6886-7 (pa)
                                    LC 2002-40971
First published 1903
This biography of the inspirational Keller contains accounts of her home life and her relationship with her devoted teacher Anne Sullivan.

Includes bibliographical references

Lawlor, Laurie. Helen Keller: rebellious spirit. Holiday House 2001 168p il $22.95

Grades: 5 6 7 8   92
    1. Blind 2. Deaf
    ISBN 0-8234-1588-0   LC 00-36950
A "biography of the most famous deaf and blind person in history. Drawing on social and scientific studies of deafness and blindness as well as on American history texts, Lawlor puts Keller's experiences in context. . . . At the same time, readers get a strong feel for Keller's personality and for the personalities of Annie Sullivan, Alexander Graham Bell, and other major figures in her life. Aided by numerous well-chosen photographs and excerpts from Keller's writings." Horn Book

Includes bibliographical references

MacLeod, Elizabeth. Helen Keller; a determined life; written by Elizabeth MacLeod. Kids Can Press 2004 32p il (Snapshots: Images of People and Places in History) $14.95; pa $6.95

Grades: 4 5 6   92
    1. Blind 2. Deaf
    ISBN 1-55337-508-4; 1-55337-509-2 (pa)
An illustrated biography of the woman renowned for overcoming her handicaps of being blind and deaf
"This biography tells Keller's story in a readable, sometimes fictionalized narrative and busy, colorful page layouts. On each spread, the main text appears on the left, while the opposite page consists of a visually appealing collage of black-and-white, full-color, and tinted photos and interesting tidbits set against a pastel background." SLJ

Sullivan, George. Helen Keller; her life in pictures; foreword by Keller Johnson Thompson. Scholastic Nonfiction 2007 80p il $17.99

Grades: 4 5 6 7   92
    1. Blind 2. Deaf
    ISBN 0-439-91815-4; 978-0-439-91815-2
                                    LC 2006-51401
"Accompanied by brief, simply phrased commentary from Sullivan, this suite of photos portrays Keller from early childhood into her 80s. . . . This profile will serve equally well as an introduction, or as supplementary reading for confirmed admirers." Booklist

Includes bibliographical references

Kennedy, Edward Moore, 1932-

Sapet, Kerrily. Ted Kennedy. Morgan Reynolds Pub. 2009 144p il (Political profiles) lib bdg $28.95

Grades: 6 7 8 9   92
    1. Statesmen
    ISBN 978-1-59935-089-9 (lib bdg); 1-59935-089-0 (lib bdg)   LC 2008034943
This offers "a detailed examination of the senator's life and career. . . . This is a meaty offering that is especially good at setting Kennedy's story against the events of his time. . . . Black-and-white and color photos are well chosen." Booklist

Includes bibliographical references

Kennedy, John F. (John Fitzgerald), 1917-1963

Burgan, Michael. John F. Kennedy. World Almanac 2001 48p il (Trailblazers of the modern world) lib bdg $30

Grades: 5 6 7 8   92
    1. Presidents—United States
    ISBN 0-8368-5065-3   LC 2001-34178
A biography of the thirty-fifth president of the United States, who served from 1961 until his assassination in 1963
"Students will enjoy reading . . . [this book] for both pleasure and research." Book Rep

Includes glossary and bibliographical references

Cooper, Ilene. Jack: the early years of John F. Kennedy. Dutton Children's Bks. 2003 168p il $22.99

Grades: 8 9 10 11 12   92
    1. Presidents—United States
    ISBN 0-525-46923-0   LC 2002-75912
A description of the childhood and youth of John Fitzgerald Kennedy, the thirty-fifth president of the United States
"Intelligent design and numerous fabulous, well-placed, and well-captioned black-and-white photographs enrich Cooper's clear prose. . . . This sensitive, well-researched biography will enhance any collection." Voice of Youth Advocates

Includes bibliographical references

Kennedy, John F. (John Fitzgerald), 1917-1963—*Continued*

Heiligman, Deborah. High hopes; a photobiography of John F. Kennedy. National Geographic 2003 63p il map $17.95 *

Grades: 4 5 6 7   92

1. Presidents—United States

ISBN 0-7922-6141-0   LC 2003-7819

Photographs and text trace the life of President John F. Kennedy.

The text "successfully captures the spirit that makes Kennedy an enduring figure in our history. . . . This well-designed book features large, well-chosen, black-and-white photographs." SLJ

Includes bibliographical references

Sommer, Shelley. John F. Kennedy; his life and legacy; introduction by Caroline Kennedy. HarperCollins Publishers 2005 152p il $16.99; lib bdg $17.89

Grades: 5 6 7 8   92

1. Presidents—United States

ISBN 0-06-054135-0; 0-06-054136-9 (lib bdg)

A "portrait of our 35th president. In discussing his curious mind, his love of reading, and his sense of humor, Sommer creates an empathetic connection with readers early in the book. . . . In an easy-to-read style, Sommer does a fine job of painting an interesting and sympathetic picture of a leader who left his mark." SLJ

Includes bibliographical references

Kennedy, Robert F., 1925-1968

Aronson, Marc. Robert F. Kennedy; a twentieth-century life. Viking 2007 204p il (Up close) $15.99

Grades: 8 9 10 11 12   92

1. Politicians

ISBN 978-0-670-06066-5; 0-670-06066-6

LC 2006-102150

Explores Robert F. Kennedy's life from his childhood to his adult years as Attorney General, New York state senator, and candidate for the presidency of the United States.

"Aronson draws on a wide variety of sources and is very honest in examining his subject as a complete human being, warts and all. . . . This text stands as an unbiased and illuminating resource." SLJ

Includes bibliographical references

Kepler, Johannes, 1571-1630

Boerst, William J. Johannes Kepler; discovering the laws of celestial motion. Morgan Reynolds 2003 144p il maps (Renaissance scientists) lib bdg $23.95

Grades: 7 8 9 10   92

1. Astronomers

ISBN 1-88384-698-6   LC 2003-708

A biography of Johannes Kepler, the seventeenth-century German astronomer and mathematician who formulated the three laws of planetary motion

"Boerst not only offers a good portrait of the astronomer and his work but also shows the effects of the contentious political and religious forces that created upheaval in his society and made scholarship anything but a safe haven. The well-designed pages feature excellent color illustrations." Booklist

Includes bibliographical references

Gow, Mary. Johannes Kepler; discovering the laws of planetary motion; [by] Mary Gow. Enslow Publishers 2003 128p il map (Great minds of science) $26

Grades: 5 6 7 8   92

1. Astronomers

ISBN 0-7660-2098-3   LC 2002-14588

Contents: The plan of the universe; Childhood; Discovering Copernicus; Solids and spheres; Turmoil and Tycho; Two laws of planetary motion; Snowflakes, Galileo and Prague; Brides, barrels and witches; Harmony and the third law; Final years

"Gow traces the life and work of the 16th-century mathematician and astronomer and sets him in the context of the German reformation and the politics of the Holy Roman Empire." SLJ

"With its balance of biographical information and scientific fact, this . . . is both informative and entertaining." Voice Youth Advocates

Includes bibliographical references

Hasan, Heather. Kepler and the laws of planetary motion. Rosen Pub. Group 2005 64p il (Primary sources of revolutionary scientific discoveries and theories) lib bdg $29.25

Grades: 6 7 8 9   92

1. Astronomers

ISBN 1-40420-308-7   LC 2004007794

"Using primary sources, this book illustrates the timeline of Kepler's discovery of planetary motion. . . . Also included are Kepler's notes and manuscripts as well as reproductions of some of the tools he used." Publisher's note

Includes bibliographical references

Kim, Jong Il

Behnke, Alison. Kim Jong Il's North Korea; [by] Alison Behnke. Twenty-First Century Books 2008 160p il lib bdg $38.60

Grades: 7 8 9 10   92

1. Korea (North)

ISBN 978-0-8225-7282-4   LC 2006100763

A biography of the North Korean dictator

This gives "students a glimpse into the repression and daily struggle for survival under [this] brutal [government]. . . . Good . . . for research." SLJ

Includes glossary and bibliographical references

King, Martin Luther, Jr., 1929-1968

Bolden, Tonya. M.L.K.; journey of a King; photography editor, Bob Adelman. Abrams Books for Young Readers 2006 128p il $19.95 *

Grades: 7 8 9 10   92

1. African Americans—Biography 2. African Americans—Civil rights

ISBN 978-0-8109-5476-2; 0-8109-5476-1

LC 2006-13332

King, Martin Luther, Jr., 1929-1968—*Continued*
"Do libraries need another biography of King? Yes, if it's as good as this one, which will reach a wide audience. . . . Stirring, beautifully reproduced, well-captioned photos . . . accompany the text." Booklist

King, Stephen, 1947-
Baughan, Michael Gray. Stephen King. Chelsea House 2009 136p il (Who wrote that?) lib bdg $30
Grades: 6 7 8 9   92
  1. Authors, American
  ISBN 978-0-7910-9852-3 (lib bdg); 0-7910-9852-4 (lib bdg)   LC 2008-35031
This biography of Stephen King "explores his path from a childhood of poverty to success as a screenwriter, film producer, director, and author of classics of the horror genre like *The Shining* and *Cujo*." Publisher's note
  Includes bibliographical references

Whitelaw, Nancy. Dark dreams; the story of Stephen King. Morgan Reynolds 2005 128p il map (World writers) $26.95
Grades: 7 8 9 10   92
  1. Authors, American 2. Horror fiction
  ISBN 1-931798-77-X   LC 2005-20112
"This well-documented look at King's life introduces the man who has become a legend for reinventing and legitimizing horror. Whitelaw has put together a seamless synthesis of interviews, biographies, and King's own writing, pared down for younger readers and illustrated with plenty of full-color photographs." Booklist

Koehl, Mimi, 1948-
Parks, Deborah. Nature's machines; the story of biomechanist Mimi Koehl; by Deborah Amel Parks. Joseph Henry Press 2005 118p il (Women's adventures in science) lib bdg $31; pa $9.95
Grades: 7 8 9 10   92
  1. Biologists 2. Human engineering 3. Women scientists
  ISBN 0-531-16780-1 (lib bdg); 0-309-09559-X (pa)
                                                 LC 2005-10201
Mimi Koehl "wanted to know more about sea anemones, particularly how they survive the turbulent surf on rocky beaches. Her inquiries and experiments led to discoveries in a new field, biomechanics, in which scientists examine how form determines movement and function in the animal kingdom. . . . This [book] should spark the curiosity of any reader." Voice Youth Advocates
  Includes bibliographical references

Kwan, Michelle
Koestler-Grack, Rachel A. Michelle Kwan. Chelsea House 2007 127p bibl por (Asian Americans of achievement) lib bdg $30
Grades: 7 8 9 10   92
  1. Ice skating—Biography 2. Asian Americans—Biography
  ISBN 0-7910-9273-9 (lib bdg); 978-0-7910-9273-6 (lib bdg)   LC 2006026069
Profiles the life and career of figure skating champion Michelle Kwan.

"With clear, full-color photos and lots of detail about training and competition, this lively biography . . . will grab fans." Booklist
  Includes bibliographical references

La Salle, Robert Cavelier, sieur de, 1643-1687
Faber, Harold. La Salle; down the Mississippi. Benchmark Bks. 2002 80p il map (Great explorations) lib bdg $29.93 *
Grades: 5 6 7 8   92
  1. Explorers 2. Mississippi River valley
  ISBN 0-7614-1239-5   LC 00-51901
A biography of the 17th century French explorer of North America
This "well-researched [book] . . . will be useful to students writing reports. Maps and archival reproductions in both black and white and color extend the text." Horn Book Guide
  Includes bibliographical references

Goodman, Joan E. Despite all obstacles: La Salle and the conquest of the Mississippi; by Joan Elizabeth Goodman; illustrated by Tom McNeely. Mikaya Press 2001 47p il map (Great explorers book) $19.95
Grades: 4 5 6 7   92
  1. Explorers 2. Mississippi River valley
  ISBN 1-931414-01-7   LC 2001-31732
A biography of the man who explored the St. Lawrence, Ohio, Illinois, and Mississippi rivers, and who claimed America's heartland for King Louis XIV and France
"Vivid color illustrations and Goodman's exciting writing style will attract both researchers and pleasure readers." Voice Youth Advocates

Lang, Lang, 1982-
Lang, Lang. Lang Lang; playing with flying keys; by Lang Lang with Michael French; introduction by Daniel Barenboim. Delacorte Press 2008 215p il $16.99; lib bdg $19.99 *
Grades: 7 8 9 10   92
  1. Pianists 2. China
  ISBN   978-0-385-73578-0;   0-385-73578-2;
  978-0-385-90564-0 (lib bdg); 0-385-90564-5 (lib bdg)
                                                 LC 2007-51597
"Although he is only 26, Chinese-born Lang is recognized as one of the world's most accomplished classical pianists. This smoothly paced, often rivetingly candid autobiography . . . follows the musician through his first encounters with the keyboard and grueling training to his triumphant debut concerts with the Chicago Symphony." Booklist

Lange, Dorothea, 1895-1965
Partridge, Elizabeth. Restless spirit: the life and work of Dorothea Lange. Viking 1998 122p il hardcover o.p. pa $10.99 *
Grades: 6 7 8 9   92
  1. Women photographers
  ISBN 0-670-87888-X; 0-14-230024-1 (pa)
                                                 LC 98-9807

Lange, Dorothea, 1895-1965—*Continued*

A biography of Dorothea Lange, whose photographs of migrant workers, Japanese American internees, and rural poverty helped bring about important social reforms

"Generously placed throughout this accessibly written biography are the photographic images that make Lange a pre-eminent artist of the century. The book is elegantly designed and the photographic reproductions are excellent." Bull Cent Child Books

Includes bibliographical references

Lavoisier, Antoine Laurent, 1743-1794

Van Gorp, Lynn. Antoine Lavoisier; and his impact on modern chemistry. Compass Point Books 2009 40p il (Mission: Science) lib bdg $26.60

Grades: 4 5 6 7   92
1. Chemists 2. Scientists
ISBN 978-0-7565-3959-7; 0-7565-3959-5
LC 2008007283
Profiles the life and career of the Frenchman who is considered the founder of chemistry.

"Color photographs, reproductions, diagrams, and maps are liberally sprinkled throughout [this] attractive [book]. Numerous sidebars offer tangential information." SLJ

Yount, Lisa. Antoine Lavoisier; founder of modern chemistry; [by] Lisa Yount. rev ed. Enslow Publishers 2008 128p il (Great minds of science) lib bdg $31.93

Grades: 5 6 7 8   92
1. Chemistry 2. Scientists
ISBN 978-0-7660-3011-4 (lib bdg); 0-7660-3011-3 (lib bdg)
LC 2007020299
"Antoine Lavoisier used experiments and careful measurements to create a system to help chemists understand how matter behaved. His experiments on combustion showed that oxygen played a key part in the burning process. . . . In this biography, you will learn why Antoine Lavoisier is remembered as the founder of modern chemistry." Publisher's note

Includes glossary and bibliographical references

Lawrence, Jacob, 1917-2000

Duggleby, John. Story painter: the life of Jacob Lawrence. Chronicle Bks. 1998 55p il $16.95 *
Grades: 4 5 6 7   92
1. African American artists
ISBN 0-8118-2082-3   LC 98-4513
A biography of the African American artist who grew up in the midst of the Harlem Renaissance and became one of the most renowned painters of the life of his people

"Lawrence's expressionistic, stark paintings, in excellent full-page color reproduction . . . nicely complement Duggleby's measured account of a materially poor but culturally rich childhood and Lawrence's subsequent struggles and successes." Publ Wkly

Includes bibliographical references

Layson, Annelex Hofstra

Layson, Annelex Hofstra. Lost childhood; my life in a Japanese prison camp during World War II; [by] Annelex Hofstra Layson; with Herman Viola. National Geographic 2008 111p $15.95; lib bdg $23.90

Grades: 5 6 7 8 9   92
1. World War, 1939-1945—Prisoners and prisons
2. World War, 1939-1945—Personal narratives
ISBN   978-1-4263-0321-0;   1-4263-0321-1;
978-1-4263-0322-7 (lib bdg); 1-4263-0322-X (lib bdg)
LC 2008-11671
In a shockingly honest narrative, a former prisoner-of-war tells how her family, along with ten thousand other Dutch residents living in the Dutch East Indies were shipped off to interment camps where food rationing, terrible sanitary conditions, and an uncertain future were the norms for more than three years

The author's narrative is warm and enthralling. . . . Layson's voice captivates and engages. Libr Media Connect

Includes bibliographical references

Lee, Harper, 1926-

Madden, Kerry. Harper Lee; a twentieth-century life. Viking Children's Books 2009 223p il map (Up close) $16.99 *
Grades: 7 8 9 10   92
1. Authors, American 2. Women authors
ISBN 978-0-670-01095-0; 0-670-01095-2
LC 2008-53911
"In a straightforward, easy-to-read biography, Madden limns familiar incidents from the life of Nelle Harper Lee." Horn Book

"A narrative both well paced and richly detailed . . . this biography will appeal to fans of the novel and to newcomers. . . . Extensive source notes and an excellent bibliography round out this superb biography." Kirkus

Includes bibliographical references

Shields, Charles J. I am Scout: the biography of Harper Lee. Henry Holt & Co. 2008 245p il $18.95
Grades: 7 8 9 10   92
1. Authors, American 2. Women authors
ISBN 978-0-8050-8334-7; 0-8050-8334-0
LC 2007-27572
A biography of the author of *To Kill a Mockingbird* Shields "offers a fascinating look at the unconventional Lee, which captures his elusive subject and her lifelong friend, Truman Capote. . . . Shields' formidable research . . . will impress any student who has ever written a term paper." Booklist

Includes bibliographical references

Lee, Robert E. (Robert Edward), 1807-1870

Robertson, James I., Jr. Robert E. Lee; Virginian soldier, American citizen; [by] James I. Robertson, Jr. Atheneum Books for Young Readers 2005 159p il maps $21.95
Grades: 7 8 9 10   92
1. Generals 2. United States—History—1861-1865, Civil War
ISBN 0-689-85731-4   LC 2003-22108

Lee, Robert E. (Robert Edward), 1807-1870—
Continued

Contents: The making of a soldier; Nation vs. country; Rocky path to army command; Brilliance in the field; The bloodiest day; Loss of an arm; Gettysburg; Forced on the defensive; From siege to defeat; National symbol

This portrait of the Confederate general "puts particular emphasis on his life during the Civil War years but provides plenty of information on his youth, his early military career, and his postwar years. . . . Useful for reports and interesting in its own right, this well-researched biography will be a solid addition to library collections." Booklist

Includes bibliographical references

Lee, Stan

Miller, Raymond H. Stan Lee; creator of Spider-man; [by] Raymond H. Miller. KidHaven Press 2006 48p il (Inventors and creators) lib bdg $23.70

Grades: 4 5 6 7   92

1. Comic books, strips, etc.

ISBN 0-7377-3447-7   LC 2005026845

The author "tells how Lee came up with the idea of Spider-Man, and how the Depression, World War II, and immigration shaped his life. . . . The book also highlights The Hulk, Fantastic Four, and other major works. The photos are fun and engaging, and will make superhero fans want to read more." SLJ

Includes glossary and bibliographical references

Leeuwenhoek, Antoni van, 1632-1723

Yount, Lisa. Antoni van Leeuwenhoek; first to see microscopic life; [by] Lisa Yount. rev ed. Enslow Publishers 2008 128p il map (Great minds of science) lib bdg $31.93

Grades: 5 6 7 8   92

1. Biologists 2. Microscopes

ISBN 978-0-7660-3012-1 (lib bdg); 0-7660-3012-1 (lib bdg)   LC 2007020300

First published 1996

This biography of seventeenth-century Dutch scientist Antoni van Leeuwenhoek includes related activities

Includes glossary and bibliographical references

Lennon, John, 1940-1980

Partridge, Elizabeth. John Lennon; all I want is the truth; a photographic biography by Elizabeth Partridge. Viking 2005 232p il $24.99 *

Grades: 8 9 10 11 12   92

1. Beatles 2. Rock musicians

ISBN 0-670-05954-4   LC 2005-11850

Michael L. Printz Award honor book, 2006

The author presents a "portrait of a legendary musician, tracing Lennon's life from his birth in 1940 during a German air raid on Liverpool to his murder in Manhattan 40 years later." Publ Wkly

"This handsome book will be eagerly received by both Beatles fans, who are legion, and their elders, who will enjoy reliving the glory days of the Fab Four and exploring the inner workings of a creative talent." SLJ

Includes bibliographical references

Rappaport, Doreen. John's secret dreams; the life of John Lennon; written by Doreen Rappaport; illustrated by Bryan Collier. Hyperion Books for Children 2004 unp il $16.99 *

Grades: 4 5 6 7   92

1. Beatles 2. Rock musicians

ISBN 0-7868-0817-9   LC 2003-57116

"Using a combination of simple prose, song lyrics, and illustration, this heartfelt picture-book biography traces Lennon's life from his childhood to his death. Striking in both its simplicity and complexity, it captures this enigmatic singer, artist, songwriter, and folk hero in a way that will move and fascinate those too young to remember the man but are surrounded by his music and myth." SLJ

Leonard, Buck, 1907-1997

Payment, Simone. Buck Leonard. Rosen Pub. Group 2002 112p il (Baseball Hall of Famers of the Negro leagues) lib bdg $29.25

Grades: 5 6 7 8   92

1. Baseball—Biography 2. African American athletes

ISBN 0-8239-3473-X   LC 2001-3151

A biography of first-baseman who played in the Negro Leagues and was inducted into the Baseball Hall of Fame in 1972

This "title presents an unvarnished picture of the racism in this country and how it impacted amateur and professional baseball from 1868 onward. . . . The layout . . . is attractive, the style . . . is engaging." Book Rep

Includes glossary and bibliographical references

Leonardo, da Vinci, 1452-1519

Anderson, Maxine. Amazing Leonardo da Vinci inventions you can build yourself. Nomad Press 2006 122p il map (Learn some hands-on history) pa $14.95

Grades: 5 6 7 8   92

1. Inventions 2. Handicraft 3. Artists, Italian 4. Scientists 5. Renaissance

ISBN 0-9749344-2-9

"Anderson has combined biography with doable activities that mirror ideas found in Leonardo's notebooks. Using common household objects (duct tape, foil, cereal boxes, paper-towel tubes, etc.), readers can make a parachute, hydrometer, invisible ink, walk-on-water shoes, etc. Anderson introduces each project with an explanation of why Leonardo came up with the idea and whether he created just the sketch or the sketch and the object. Detailed steps and illustrations provide clarity." SLJ

Krull, Kathleen. Leonardo da Vinci; illustrated by Boris Kulikov. Viking 2005 128p il (Giants of science) $15.99 *

Grades: 5 6 7 8   92

1. Artists, Italian 2. Scientists 3. Renaissance

ISBN 0-670-05920-X

This is a "biography of Leonardo da Vinci that highlights his scientific approach to understanding the physical world. The first half of the book describes Leonardo's apprenticeship and his work as an artist in Milan. The second half relates events in his later life,

Leonardo, da Vinci, 1452-1519—*Continued*
emphasizing his observation and investigation of the human body and nature. . . . Six excellent ink drawings illustrate this attractive volume. A very readable, vivid portrait set against the backdrop of remarkable times." Booklist

Includes bibliographical references

O'Connor, Barbara. Leonardo da Vinci; Renaissance genius. Carolrhoda Bks. 2003 112p il (Trailblazer biography) lib bdg $27.93
Grades: 5 6 7 8   **92**
   1. Artists, Italian 2. Scientists 3. Renaissance
ISBN 0-87614-467-9   LC 2001-6470
A biography of the notable Italian Renaissance artist, scientist, and inventor
"Outstanding writing and design result in a compelling and accessible portrait of this master artist." SLJ
Includes bibliographical references

Phillips, John. Leonardo da Vinci; the genius who defined the Renaissance. National Geographic 2006 64p bibl il (World history biographies) $27.90
Grades: 5 6 7 8   **92**
   1. Artists, Italian 2. Scientists 3. Renaissance
ISBN 978-0-7922-5386-0; 0-7922-5386-8
Examines the life of Renaissance genius Leonardo da Vinci, discussing his inquiries and accomplishments in art and various fields of science
Includes bibligraphical references

Levine, Gail Carson, 1947-
Abrams, Dennis. Gail Carson Levine; [by] Dennis Abrams; foreword by Kyle Zimmer. Chelsea House 2007 120p bibl il por (Who wrote that?) $30
Grades: 6 7 8 9   **92**
   1. Authors, American 2. Women authors
ISBN 978-0-7910-8970-5; 0-7910-8970-3
                LC 2007019449
This biography examines the "writer's life, including the inspiration behind some of [her] works. [The] volume includes photographs and quotations from interviews, as well as descriptions of main characters and annotated lists of books and awards. Useful for aspiring authors as well as book report writers." Horn Book Guide
Includes bibliographical references

Li, Moying, 1954-
Li, Moying. Snow falling in spring; coming of age in China during the cultural revolution. Farrar, Straus and Giroux 2008 176p $16 *
Grades: 7 8 9 10 11 12   **92**
   1. China—History—1949-1976—Personal narratives
ISBN 978-0-374-39922-1; 0-374-39922-0
                LC 2006-38356
"This memoir . . . offers a highly personal look at China's Cultural Revolution. The author is four years old when Mao initiates the Great Leap Forward in 1958. . . . Li effectively builds the climate of fear that accompanies the rise of the Red Guard, while accounts of her

headmaster's suicide and the pulping of her father's book collection give a harrowing, closeup view of the persecution. Sketches about her grandparents root the narrative within a broader context of Chinese traditions as well as her own family's values." Publ Wkly

Li Cunxin
Li Cunxin. Mao's last dancer; [by] Li Cunxin. Young readers' ed. Walker & Co. 2008 290p il map $16.99
Grades: 6 7 8 9   **92**
   1. Ballet dancers 2. China—History—1949-1976 3. Defectors
ISBN 978-0-8027-9779-7; 0-8027-9779-2
                LC 2008-6104
An adaptation of the title published 2003 by Putnam for adults
Chosen from millions of children to serve in Mao's cultural revolution by studying at the Beijing Dance Academy, Li knew ballet would be his family's best opportunity to escape the bitter poverty in his rural China home. From one hardship to another, Li persevered, never forgetting the family he left behind.
"Cunxin's tale is a wonderfully crafted coming-of-age story. . . . He paints a clear picture of harsh realities of life in communist China but does so without being overly negative. . . . Photographs provide readers with a glimpse of varying aspects of Cunxin's life, a short note on the history of China, and a time line of China in the twentieth century." Voice Youth Advocates

Lichtenstein, Roy, 1923-1997
Rubin, Susan Goldman. Whaam!: the art & life of Roy Lichtenstein. Abrams 2008 47p il $18.95
*
Grades: 4 5 6 7   **92**
   1. Artists—United States 2. Pop art
ISBN 978-0-8109-9492-8; 0-8109-9492-5
                LC 2007-42048
"Rubin presents an overview of a modern master with clear writing and an abundance of his eye-popping works, all framed on pages that mirror the artist's signature use of primary colors and Benday dots." Booklist

Lin, Maya Ying
Lashnits, Tom. Maya Lin; [by] Tom Lashnits. Chelsea House 2007 128p il (Asian Americans of achievement) lib bdg $30
Grades: 7 8 9 10   **92**
   1. Women architects 2. Asian Americans—Biography 3. Vietnam Veterans Memorial (Washington, D.C.)
ISBN 978-0-7910-9268-2 (lib bdg); 0-7910-9268-2 (lib bdg)   LC 2006026064
A biography of the architect who designed the Vietnam Veterans' Memorial in Washington D.C.
This is "well-researched . . . attractive . . . solid." SLJ
Includes glossary and bibliographical references

Lincoln, Abraham, 1809-1865

Aronson, Billy. Abraham Lincoln. Marshall Cavendish Benchmark 2009 112p il (Presidents and their times) lib bdg $23.95

Grades: 5 6 7 8   **92**
1. Presidents—United States 2. United States—History—1861-1865, Civil War
ISBN 978-0-7614-2839-8 (lib bdg); 0-7614-2839-9 (lib bdg)   LC 2007019190

This provides "information on President Abraham Lincoln and places him within his historical and cultural context. Also explored are the formative events of his times and how he responded." Publisher's note

Includes glossary and bibliographical references

Denenberg, Barry. Lincoln shot! a president's life remembered; chief writer, Barry Denenberg; artist, Christopher Bing. Feiwel and Friends 2008 40p il $24.95 *

Grades: 5 6 7 8   **92**
1. Presidents—United States 2. United States—History—1861-1865, Civil War
ISBN 978-0-312-37013-8; 0-312-37013-X   LC 2007-48851

"The concept is that this is a commemorative edition of 'The National News' published one year after Lincoln's death . . . Also included is an engaging, readable yet detailed account of Lincoln's life. . . . [This book] is an example of how high-quality bookmaking can turn a history lesson into an authentic experience." Booklist

Fleming, Candace. The Lincolns; a scrapbook look at Abraham and Mary. Schwartz & Wade Books 2008 177p il map $24.99; lib bdg $28.99 *

Grades: 7 8 9 10 11 12   **92**
1. Lincoln, Mary Todd, 1818-1882 2. Presidents—United States 3. Presidents' spouses—United States 4. United States—History—1861-1865, Civil War
ISBN 978-0-375-83618-3; 0-375-83618-7; 978-0-375-93618-0 (lib bdg); 0-375-93618-1 (lib bdg)   LC 2007-44113

Fleming twines "accounts of two lives—Abraham and Mary Todd Lincoln—into one fascinating whole. On spreads that combine well-chosen visuals with blocks of headlined text, Fleming gives a full, birth-to-death view of the 'inextricably bound' Lincolns." Booklist

Freedman, Russell. Lincoln: a photobiography. Clarion Bks. 1987 149p il $18; pa $7.95 *

Grades: 5 6 7 8 9 10   **92**
1. Presidents—United States 2. United States—History—1861-1865, Civil War
ISBN 0-89919-380-3; 0-395-51848-2 (pa)   LC 86-33379

Awarded the Newbery Medal, 1988

The author "begins by contrasting the Lincoln of legend to the Lincoln of fact. His childhood, self-education, early business ventures, and entry into politics comprise the first half of the book, with the rest of the text covering his presidency and assassination." SLJ

This is "a balanced work, elegantly designed and enhanced by dozens of period photographs and drawings, some familiar, some refreshingly unfamiliar." Publ Wkly

Includes bibliographical references

Lincoln, Abraham. Abraham Lincoln the writer; a treasury of his greatest speeches and letters; compiled and edited by Harold Holzer. Boyds Mills Press 2000 106p il lib bdg $15.95

Grades: 7 8 9 10   **92**
1. Presidents—United States 2. United States—History—1861-1865, Civil War
ISBN 1-56397-772-9   LC 99-66551

"Lincoln's writings include personal letters, notes on the law, excerpts from speeches, debates, and inaugural addresses, letters to parents of fallen soldiers, and telegrams to his family. Reproductions of period photos, portraits, and documents illustrate the text effectively. . . . Highly interesting and a fine resource for students seeking quotations or for those wanting to meet Lincoln through his own words." Booklist

Sandler, Martin W. Lincoln through the lens; how photography revealed and shaped an extraordinary life. Walker Pub. Co. 2008 97p il $19.99; lib bdg $20.89 *

Grades: 6 7 8 9 10   **92**
1. Presidents—United States 2. United States—History—1861-1865, Civil War—Pictorial works 3. Photography—History
ISBN 978-0-8027-9666-0; 0-8027-9666-4; 978-0-8027-9667-7 (lib bdg); 0-8027-9667-2 (lib bdg)   LC 2008-0219

"When Lincoln became president, photography was new and he joined the 'very first generation of human beings ever to be photographed.' . . . This extraordinary book is a tribute to the way contemporary and future generations came to view Lincoln. . . . Part biography, part history of of the Civil War, the book touches on many interesting topics. . . . Every step of the way there are fascinating photographs. . . . Although it's the pictures that provide the 'wow factor,' Sandler's perceptive words have their own elegance." Booklist

Sullivan, George. Picturing Lincoln; famous photographs that popularized the president. Clarion Bks. 2000 88p il $16

Grades: 8 9 10 11 12   **92**
1. Presidents—United States 2. United States—History—1861-1865, Civil War 3. Photography—History
ISBN 0-395-91682-8   LC 00-27576

Examines some of the famous photographs taken of President Abraham Lincoln, discussing the circumstances under which they were taken and how these images were used

"This unique and sharply focused volume offers an introductory exploration of photographic processes and photographers while tracing the political fortunes of our 16th president." SLJ

Includes bibliographical references

Waldman, Neil. Voyages; reminiscences of young Abe Lincoln. 1st ed. Calkins Creek 2009 32p $16.95

Grades: 4 5 6 7   **92**
1. Presidents—United States 2. Slavery—United States 3. Mississippi River
ISBN 978-1-59078-471-6   LC 2008024022

This "volume integrates some of Lincoln's own words with an imagined narrative based on documented ac-

Lincoln, Abraham, 1809-1865—*Continued*
counts of river voyages he took between the ages of 18
and 22. . . . The two narratives blend fairly smoothly,
and the book offers both a quick read and extensive opportunities for study and discussion. . . . The nostalgic
design, featuring a distressed sepia-toned appearance and
the author's own illustrations, further adds to the book's
appeal." Booklist
Includes bibliographical references

Lincoln, Mary Todd, 1818-1882
Fleming, Candace. The Lincolns. See entry
under Lincoln, Abraham, 1809-1865

Jones, Lynda. Mrs. Lincoln's dressmaker: the
unlikely friendship of Elizabeth Keckley and Mary
Todd Lincoln. See entry under Keckley, Elizabeth,
ca. 1818-1907

Lindbergh, Anne Morrow, 1906-2001
Gherman, Beverly. Anne Morrow Lindbergh;
between the sea and the stars; [by] Beverly
Gherman. Twenty-first Century Books 2008 160p
(Lerner biography) lib bdg $27.93
Grades: 6 7 8 9   92
1. Lindbergh, Charles, 1902-1974 2. Women air pilots
ISBN 978-0-8225-5970-2 (lib bdg); 0-8225-5970-6 (lib
bdg)   LC 2005022498
Explores the life and career of Anne Morrow Lindbergh, including her marriage to Charles Lindbergh, flying experiences, and success as an author.
"Clearly written and illustrated with frequent, clear
black-and-white photos, the book is strongest in demonstrating Gherman's thorough understanding of Anne's
emotional core. . . . A solid resource for reports as well
as a fascinating portrait for biography fans." Booklist
Includes bibliographical references

Lindbergh, Charles, 1902-1974
Giblin, James. Charles A. Lindbergh; a human
hero; [by] James Cross Giblin. Clarion Bks. 1997
212p il $22 *
Grades: 6 7 8 9   92
1. Air pilots
ISBN 0-395-63389-3   LC 96-9501
A biography of the pilot whose life was full of controversy and tragedy, but also fulfilling achievements
"This sympathetic and informed account (beautifully
illustrated with contemporary photographs) is an excellent introduction to Lindbergh and also to the early years
of the celebrity society in which we live now." N Y
Times Book Rev
Includes bibliographical references

Koopmans, Andy. Charles Lindbergh. Lucent
Bks. 2003 112p il maps (Importance of) lib bdg
$27.45
Grades: 5 6 7 8   92
1. Air pilots
ISBN 1-59018-245-6   LC 2002-9882
Profiles the childhood, education, interest in aviation,
fame, tragedy, and controversy surrounding the first man

to fly solo across the Atlantic Ocean
"This well-written book gives insight into a shy but
purposeful man. . . . Framed inserts from primary
sources and many high-quality, black-and-white photographs are well placed within the text." SLJ
Includes bibliographical references

Linné, Carl von, 1707-1778
Anderson, Margaret Jean. Carl Linnaeus; father
of classification; [by] Margaret J. Anderson. rev
ed. Enslow Publishers 2009 128p il (Great minds
of science) lib bdg $31.93
Grades: 5 6 7 8 9   92
1. Naturalists
ISBN 978-0-7660-3009-1 (lib bdg); 0-7660-3009-1 (lib
bdg)   LC 2008-23941
First published 1997
"A biography of eighteenth-century Swedish botanist
Carl Linneaeus, who established the modern system of
classifying plants and animals." Publisher's note
"Budding scientists will surely draw inspiration from
this biography of Linnaeus. . . . Anderson creates a dramatic narrative fully capable of keeping readers enthralled." Kirkus
Includes glossary and bibliographical references

Livingstone, David, 1813-1873
Otfinoski, Steven. David Livingstone; deep in
the heart of Africa. Marshall Cavendish
Benchmark 2006 79p il map (Great explorations)
lib bdg $32.79 *
Grades: 5 6 7 8   92
1. Explorers 2. Africa—Exploration
ISBN 978-0-7614-2226-6 (lib bdg); 0-7614-2226-9 (lib
bdg)   LC 2005027930
"An examination of the life and accomplishments of
the explorer and missionary who traveled southern Africa
and was the first European to reach Victoria Falls." Publisher's note
This "appealing [title features] readable [text], solid
research, and a variety of color illustrations." SLJ
Includes bibliographical references

Lobel, Anita, 1934-
Lobel, Anita. No pretty pictures; a child of war.
Greenwillow Bks. 1998 193p il hardcover o.p. pa
$7.99 *
Grades: 7 8 9 10   92
1. Jews—Poland 2. Holocaust, 1933-1945—Personal
narratives 3. Holocaust survivors
ISBN 0-688-15935-4; 0-06-156589-X (pa)
                                            LC 97-48392
The author, known as an illustrator of children's
books, describes her experiences as a Polish Jew during
World War II and for years in Sweden afterwards
"Lobel brings to these dramatic experiences an artist's
sensibility for the telling detail, a seemingly unvarnished
memory and heartstopping candor." Publ Wkly

Lockwood, Belva Ann, 1830-1917

Norgren, Jill. Belva Lockwood; equal rights pioneer; by Jill Norgren. Twenty-First Century Books 2009 112p il (Trailblazer biography) lib bdg $31.93

Grades: 6 7 8 9   **92**
1. Women lawyers 2. Women's rights
ISBN 978-0-8225-9068-2 (lib bdg); 0-8225-9068-9 (lib bdg)   LC 2007-50265
First published 2007 by New York University Press with title: Belva Lockwood: the woman who would be president
"Through a clear and engaging text, this biography shows how Lockwood, a relatively unknown historical figure, was an inspiring pioneer of the equal-rights movement." SLJ
Includes bibliographical references

London, Jack, 1876-1916

Stefoff, Rebecca. Jack London; an American original. Oxford Univ. Press 2002 127p il maps (Oxford portraits) lib bdg $28

Grades: 7 8 9 10   **92**
1. Authors, American
ISBN 0-19-512223-2   LC 2001-53087
"This volume does an excellent job of illuminating London's extraordinary life and career. The narrative is exciting and accessible. . . . The text is supplemented by interesting and informative illustrations, and includes excerpts from primary-source material." SLJ
Includes bibliographical references

Lopez, Jennifer

Woog, Adam. Jennifer Lopez; [by] Adam Woog. Chelsea House 2008 117p il (The great Hispanic heritage) lib bdg $30

Grades: 6 7 8 9   **92**
1. Hispanic American women 2. Actors 3. Singers
ISBN 978-0-7910-9724-3 (lib bdg); 0-7910-9724-2 (lib bdg)   LC 2007031663
This biography provides a "substantive [portrait], including background information and historical context, of . . . world-wide celebrity Lopez. The well-documented [text] effectively [combines] anecdotes, quotations, and historical details. Many photographs and sidebars are also included." Horn Book Guide
Includes bibliographical references

Louis, Joe, 1914-1981

Sullivan, George. Knockout!: a photobiography of boxer Joe Louis. National Geographic 2008 64p il $17.95; lib bdg $27.90

Grades: 6 7 8 9   **92**
1. Boxing—Biography 2. African American athletes
ISBN   978-1-4263-0328-9;   1-4263-0328-9;
978-1-4263-0329-6 (lib bdg); 1-4263-0329-7 (lib bdg)   LC 2008-25036
"This oversize biography of Joe Louis is just the thing for getting the blood of reluctant readers and sports fans pumping. Using copious period photographs . . . and full-color reproductions of fight posters and memoriblia, Sullivan relays in straightforward language the rags-to-

riches saga of the 'Brown Bomber,' and sets the story against the rampant racism of 1920s America. . . . Sullivan's fight recaps are clear and vivid." Booklist
Includes bibliographical references

Lowry, Lois

Albert, Lisa Rondinelli. Lois Lowry; the giver of stories and memories. Enslow Publishers 2008 128p il (Authors teens love) lib bdg $31.93

Grades: 5 6 7 8   **92**
1. Authors, American 2. Women authors
ISBN 978-0-7660-2722-0 (lib bdg); 0-7660-2722-8 (lib bdg)   LC 2006034045
A biography of the author of the Anastasia Krupnik series, as well as the Newbery Medal winning novels *The giver* and *Number the Stars*
Includes bibliographical references

Bankston, John. Lois Lowry; [by] John Bankston. Chelsea House 2009 127p bibl il (Who wrote that?) lib bdg $30

Grades: 6 7 8 9   **92**
1. Authors, American 2. Women authors
ISBN 978-1-6041-3335-6 (lib bdg); 1-6041-3335-X (lib bdg)   LC 2008035039
This examines the life and work of the popular author for children and young adults
Includes bibliographical references

Lowry, Lois. Looking back; a book of memories. Houghton Mifflin 1998 181p il $17 *

Grades: 5 6 7 8   **92**
1. Authors, American 2. Women authors
ISBN 0-395-89543-X   LC 98-11376
Also available in paperback from Delacorte Press
"A Walter Lorraine book"
Using family photographs and quotes from her books, the author provides glimpses into her life
"A compelling and inspirational portrait of the author emerges from these vivid snapshots of life's joyful, sad and surprising moments." Publ Wkly

Lugovskaia, Nina, 1918-1993

Lugovskaia, Nina. I want to live; the diary of a young girl in Stalin's Russia; translated by Andrew Bromfield. Houghton Mifflin 2006 280p il $17.99

Grades: 7 8 9 10 11 12   **92**
1. Persecution 2. Soviet Union—Politics and government
ISBN 978-0-618-60575-0; 0-618-60575-4
Original Russian edition, 2003
Reveals the life of a teenage girl in Stalin's Russia, where fear of arrest was a fact of daily life.
"Lugovskaya's diary, which was found in the NKVD archives, stands as a compelling historical artifact and Nina's story gives a moving—if relentlessly melancholy—personal account of life in Communist Russia." Publ Wkly
Includes bibliographical references

Lyons, Maritcha Rémond, 1848-1929

Bolden, Tonya. Maritcha; a nineteenth-century American girl. Abrams 2005 47p il $17.95 *

Grades: 4 5 6 7 8 9 10   **92**

1. African American women—Biography 2. New York (N.Y.)—Race relations 3. African Americans—New York (N.Y.)

ISBN 0-8109-5045-6   LC 2004-05849

This is a "life history of Maritcha Rémond Lyons, born a free black in 1848 in lower Manhattan. The author draws her biographical sketch primarily from Lyons's unpublished memoir, dated one year before her death in 1929. . . . One of the . . . sections of the book documents the Draft Riots . . . of July 1868, and the impact of them on Maritcha and other citizens." Publ Wkly

"The high quality of writing and the excellent documentation make this a first choice for all collections." SLJ

Ma, Yo-Yo, 1955-

Chippendale, Lisa A. Yo-Yo Ma; a cello superstar brings music to the world. 1st ed. Enslow Publishers 2004 112p il (People to know) lib bdg $26.60

Grades: 5 6 7 8   **92**

1. Violoncellists 2. Chinese Americans

ISBN 0-7660-2286-2   LC 2003-14972

Contents: Inspired by Bach; Choosing a "big instrument;" From high school to Harvard; An emerging star; Yo-yo Ma branches out; Seeking new musical forms; Traveling the Silk Road (1997-1999); When strangers meet

Tracks the life and career of violoncellist Yo-Yo Ma, a child prodigy who grew to become world famous for his playing ability, as well as for experimenting with different kinds of music and performance

"The author does a commendable job of presenting Ma in a professional light as well as a personal one." SLJ

Includes bibliographical references

Worth, Richard. Yo-Yo Ma. Chelsea House 2006 c2007 119p bibl il por (Asian Americans of achievement) lib bdg $30

Grades: 7 8 9 10   **92**

1. Violoncellists 2. Chinese Americans

ISBN 978-0-7910-9270-5 (lib bdg); 0-7910-9270-4 (lib bdg)   LC 2006026335

A biography of the cellist

This is "well-researched . . . attractive . . . solid." SLJ

Includes glossary and bibliographical references

Madison, James, 1751-1836

Elish, Dan. James Madison; [by] Dan Elish. Marshall Cavendish Benchmark 2007 96p il (Presidents and their times) lib bdg $22.95

Grades: 5 6 7 8   **92**

1. Presidents—United States

ISBN 978-0-7614-2432-1   LC 2006036856

A biography of the fourth president of the United States.

"Primary-source materials and quotes, helpful insets,

and carefully selected . . . . reproductions bring history to life and help make [this] clearly written [biography] highly readable." SLJ

Includes glossary and bibliographical references

Malone, Mary. James Madison. Enslow Pubs. 1997 128p il (United States presidents) lib bdg $26.60

Grades: 5 6 7 8   **92**

1. Presidents—United States

ISBN 0-89490-834-0   LC 96-39133

Chronicles the life and career of the fourth President with emphasis on his many contributions to the government of the United States including his role in writing the Constitution and the Bill of Rights

This "is a well-researched, smoothly written biography." Booklist

Includes bibliographical references

Magellan, Ferdinand, 1480?-1521

Levinson, Nancy Smiler. Magellan and the first voyage around the world. Clarion Bks. 2001 132p il map $19

Grades: 5 6 7 8   **92**

1. Explorers 2. Voyages around the world

ISBN 0-395-98773-3   LC 00-52350

This "biography of the great explorer, navigator, and adventurer presents him as a man of action who overcame political, social, and financial obstacles to sail around the globe." Horn Book Guide

"This clearly written book shows through involving narrative and vivid detail what a monumental achievement the journey was. . . . A well-designed volume, useful for research and interesting as biography." Booklist

Includes bibliographical references

Mah, Adeline Yen, 1937-

Mah, Adeline Yen. Chinese Cinderella. Delacorte Press 1999 205p hardcover o.p. pa $5.99

Grades: 7 8 9 10   **92**

1. China—Social life and customs

ISBN 0-385-32707-2; 0-440-22865-4 (pa)   LC 99-11007

An adaptation for young readers of the author's Falling leaves (1998)

The author, blamed for her mother's death shortly after childbirth, recalls "her sad and lonely childhood in China during the 1940s and 1950s. Wu Mei, whose English name is Adeline, faces the anger and cruelty of her family; only an aunt and frail grandfather are supportive. Shunted off to boarding schools, left out of family activities, Adeline nevertheless thrives academically and hopes desperately (and futilely) to please her father." Booklist

Malcolm X, 1925-1965

Draper, Allison Stark. The assassination of Malcolm X. Rosen Pub. Group 2002 64p il (Library of political assassinations) lib bdg $26.50

Grades: 5 6 7 8   **92**

1. African Americans—Biography 2. Black Muslims

ISBN 0-8239-3542-6   LC 2001-3323

Malcolm X, 1925-1965—*Continued*

Contents: The assassination; The making of Malcolm X; Minister Malcolm X; The death of Malcolm X; The assassination revisited

This "book begins with an introduction, followed by a . . . description of the assassination, and account of the subject's earlier life, and a concluding chapter on his impact on America." Book Rep

"Draper confronts the important issues with exceptional candor and clarity, including the ongoing controversy of who ordered the murder." Booklist

Includes glossary and bibliographical references

Mandela, Nelson

Keller, Bill. Tree shaker; the story of Nelson Mandela. Kingfisher 2008 128p il $17.95

Grades: 8 9 10 11 12 **92**

1. South Africa—Race relations 2. South Africa—Politics and government
ISBN 978-0-7534-5992-8; 0-7534-5992-2
LC 2007-03559

"A New York Times book"

The author "offers a balanced, thoughtful account of Mandela's political activism and accomplishments and his pivotal role in South Africa's modern history. . . . [The book is] packed with dramatic photos, swathes of paint, handprints and images of the African continent." Publ Wkly

Includes bibliographical references

Kramer, Ann. Mandela; the rebel who led his nation to freedom. National Geographic 2005 63p il (World history biographies) $17.95; lib bdg $27.90 *

Grades: 4 5 6 7 **92**

1. South Africa—Race relations 2. South Africa—Politics and government
ISBN 0-7922-3658-0; 0-7922-3659-9 (lib bdg)

"This biography introduces readers not only to Mandela, but also to the political turmoil that affected South Africa for over a century. It begins with his birth, and covers his school years, his political ventures, imprisonment, release, presidency, Nobel Peace Prize, and retirement. Full-color photographs appear throughout and a time line runs along the bottom of each spread. . . . the book is well worth purchasing." SLJ

Includes glossary and bibliographical references

Kramer, Ann. Nelson Mandela. Raintree Pubs. 2003 112p il (Twentieth-century history makers) lib bdg $32.85

Grades: 7 8 9 10 **92**

1. South Africa—Race relations 2. South Africa—Politics and government
ISBN 0-7398-5258-2
LC 2002-15933

Contents: Early years; Johannesburg; European dominance; From union to apartheid; Defiance; Treason; Underground; Rivonia trial; Robben Island struggle continues; Mandela freed; Mr. President

This biography of the South African leader is "accurate and eloquent about the man and the political struggle, and it has dramatic, well-chosen news photos of both." Booklist

Includes glossary and bibliographical references

Manzano, Juan Francisco, 1797-1854

Engle, Margarita. The poet slave of Cuba; a biography of Juan Francisco Manzano; art by Sean Qualls. Henry Holt 2006 183p il $16.95

Grades: 7 8 9 10 **92**

1. Poets
ISBN 0-8050-7706-5; 978-0-8050-7706-3
LC 2005-46200

In "free verse, Engle dramatizes the boyhood of the nineteenth-century Cuban slave Juan Francisco Manzano, who secretly learned to read and wrote poetry about beauty and courage in his world of unspeakable brutality." Booklist

"This is a book that should be read by young and old, black and white, Anglo and Latino." SLJ

Mao Zedong, 1893-1976

Naden, Corinne J. Mao Zedong and the Chinese Revolution. Morgan Reynolds Pub. 2009 144p il map (World leaders) lib bdg $28.95

Grades: 7 8 9 10 11 12 **92**

1. Heads of state 2. China—History—1949-1976
ISBN 978-1-59935-100-1 (lib bdg); 1-59935-100-5 (lib bdg)
LC 2008-27829

This "discusses Chariman Mao Zedong's rise to power and his crucial role in national and international history. . . . Naden's analysis of the significant role of young people will draw YA readers for reports and for personal interest. The readable design, with clear type and lots of historic color photos as well as screens and detailed maps, includes spacious back matter." Booklist

Includes bibliographical references

Slavicek, Louise Chipley. Mao Zedong. Chelsea House 2004 116p il (Great military leaders of the 20th century) lib bdg $23.95

Grades: 6 7 8 9 **92**

1. Heads of state 2. China—History—1949-1976
ISBN 0-7910-7407-2
LC 2003-6929

Contents: From the barrel of a gun: October 1, 1949; Finding a road: the early years: 1893-1921; Mao and the young Chinese communist movement: 1921-1930; The encirclement campaigns and the long march: 1930-1935; Fighting the Japanese and the Nationalists: 1936-1949; Confronting challenges at home and abroad: 1949-1959; An era of turmoil: 1960-1976

A biography of Chinese leader Mao Zedong, discussing the battles that helped shape him and reasons behind his popularity among his countrymen

"Slavicek blends personal, philosophical, and historical information to trace Mao's journey to power. Clear accounts of the communist movement, the Long March, and the eventual battle with the Nationalists and Japanese are included." SLJ

Includes bibliographical references

Marconi, Guglielmo, 1874-1937

Zannos, Susan. Guglielmo Marconi and the story of radio waves. Mitchell Lane Publishers 2004 48p il (Uncharted, unexplored and unexplained) lib bdg $29.95

Grades: 6 7 8 9   92

1. Telegraph 2. Radio—History 3. Inventors
ISBN 978-1-58415-265-1 (lib bdg); 1-58415-265-6 (lib bdg)
LC 2003-24133

Tells the story of Guglielmo Marconi and his invention of the wireless telegraph
Includes bibliographical references

Marley, Bob

Medina, Tony. I and I; Bob Marley; by Tony Medina; illustrated by Jesse Joshua Watson. Lee & Low Books 2009 unp il $19.95

Grades: 4 5 6   92

1. Singers 2. Jamaica
ISBN 978-1-60060-257-3; 1-60060-257-6
LC 2008-33485

"A biography in verse about the Jamaican reggae musician Bob Marley, offering an overview of key events and themes in his life, including his biracial heritage, Rastafarian beliefs, and love of music. End notes on poems provide further biographical information." Publisher's note

"In the words and rhythms of Jamaican patois, Medina's lyrical, direct lines make the most sense when read in tandem with the extensive appended notes. . . . Like the words, Watson's beautifully expressive acrylic paintings evoke a strong sense of Marley's remarkable life and his Caribean homeland." Booklist
Includes bibliographical references

Miller, Calvin Craig. Reggae poet: the story of Bob Marley. Morgan Reynolds Pub. 2007 128p il $27.95

Grades: 7 8 9 10   92

1. Reggae music 2. Musicians
ISBN 978-1-59935-071-4; 1-59935-071-8
LC 2007-27476

In this biography of the Jamaican musician "Miller does a fine job showing the effect the music and the politics had on each other. He also skillfully weaves in the complicated topic of the Rastaferian religion and the part ganja (marijuana) plays in it, and he doesn't hesitate when explaining Marley's complicated romantic life. The . . . photos are well chosen." Booklist
Includes bibliographical references

Paprocki, Sherry Beck. Bob Marley; musician; [by] Sherry Beck Paprocki. legacy ed. Chelsea House 2006 111p bibl il por (Black Americans of achievement) lib bdg $30

Grades: 6 7 8 9   92

1. Reggae music 2. Musicians
ISBN 0-7910-9213-5   LC 2006004578

A biography of the Jamaican reggae musician.
The book goes "beyond the typical personal information to provide some social history revelant to the subject's time. Captioned photographs and boxed inserts enhance the conversational [text]." Horn Book Guide
Includes bibliographical references

Marquette, Jacques, 1637-1675

Harkins, Susan Sales. The life and times of Father Jacques Marquette; by Susan Sales Harkins and William H. Harkins. Mitchell Lane Publishers 2008 48p il (Profiles in American history) lib bdg $29.95

Grades: 6 7 8 9   92

1. Explorers 2. Canada—History 3. Mississippi River valley—History
ISBN 978-1-58415-528-7; 1-58415-528-0
LC 2007000793

This is a biography of Father Jacques Marquette who, with his companion explorer Louis Jolliet, hoped to discover the Northwest Passage across North America in 1673.

This biography offers "a wealth of concise and well-organized information. . . . [The] book is fair and balanced and includes viewpoints from those who opposed or disagreed with [the subject's] accomplishments. The design is crisp and colorful without overwhelming the words on the page." SLJ
Includes bibliographical references

Marshall, Thurgood, 1908-1993

Crowe, Chris. Thurgood Marshall; a twentieth-century life; by Chris Crowe. Viking 2008 248p il (Up close) $16.99

Grades: 7 8 9 10   92

1. United States. Supreme Court 2. Judges
ISBN 978-0-670-06228-7; 0-670-06228-6
LC 2007-42794

"Marshall served 24 years as the first African American judge on the U.S. Supreme Court, but this biography . . . focuses on his pioneer work as a lawyer and civil rights activist and on the landmark cases in which he fought segregation in public education and elsewhere. . . . The chatty, immediate discussion relates Marshall's personal experience to the political history. . . . The eloquent quotes from his speeches are the core of this biography. The back matter is extensive, with Crowe including personal discussion of sources." Booklist
Includes bibliographical references

Martinez, Pedro, 1971-

Lashnits, Tom. Pedro Martinez. Chelsea House 2006 131p il (Great Hispanic heritage) lib bdg $30

Grades: 6 7 8 9   92

1. Baseball—Biography
ISBN 0-7910-8840-5

This "is packed with statistics and play-by-play baseball action from the beginning of the athlete's American career through the 2004 and 2005 Red Sox seasons. The conversational text and sidebars are accurate and engaging." SLJ
Includes bibliographical references

Matisse, Henri

Welton, Jude. Henri Matisse. Watts 2002 46p il (Artists in their time) $22; pa $6.95

Grades: 5 6 7 8   92

1. Artists, French
ISBN 0-531-12228-X; 0-531-16621-X (pa)
LC 2002-69106

Matisse, Henri—*Continued*

Discusses the life and career of this French artist, describing and giving examples of his work

This offers a "clear and lively [text]. . . . Captioned, full-color and black-and-white photographs and art reproductions are liberally scattered throughout." SLJ

Mawson, Sir Douglas, 1882-1958

Bredeson, Carmen. After the last dog died; the true-life, hair-raising adventure of Douglas Mawson and his 1912 Antarctic Expedition. National Geographic 2003 63p il map $18.95

Grades: 5 6 7 8   92

1. Antarctica—Exploration

ISBN 0-7922-6140-2   LC 2003-0756

Describes the life and career of the Australian explorer, Sir Douglas Mawson, focusing on his 1912 scientific expedition to Antarctica

"Bredson's compelling story of courage and survival draws heavily on quotes from Mawson and other primary source documents; there are also charts, maps, and many photographs." Booklist

McAuliffe, Christa

Jeffrey, Laura S. Christa McAuliffe; a space biography. Enslow Pubs. 1998 48p il (Countdown to space) lib bdg $23.93

Grades: 4 5 6 7   92

1. Challenger (Space shuttle) 2. Women astronauts

ISBN 0-89490-976-2   LC 97-22114

A biography of the school teacher turned astronaut whose life was tragically ended when the space shuttle Challenger exploded just after liftoff

"An accurate, well-researched . . . biography." SLJ

Includes glossary and bibliographical references

McCain, John S., 1936-

Wells, Catherine. John McCain. 1st ed. Morgan Reynolds Pub. 2007 112p il map (Political profiles) lib bdg $27.95

Grades: 5 6 7 8   92

1. Statesmen—United States

ISBN 978-1-59935-046-2 (lib bdg); 1-59935-046-7 (lib bdg)   LC 2007027133

A biography of the U.S. senator and canidate for president.

"The key exciting portion of the book for most students will be the narrative of McCain's experiences as a fighter pilot and a prisoner of war in Vietnam. . . . [This book] should be painless, even enjoyable reading for reluctant readers." Voice Youth Advocates

Includes bibliographical references

McClintock, Barbara

Cullen, J. Heather. Barbara McClintock, geneticist. Chelsea House 2003 122p il (Women in science) lib bdg $22.95

Grades: 7 8 9 10   92

1. Genetics 2. Women scientists

ISBN 0-7910-7248-7   LC 2002-15549

Presents the life and career of the geneticist who in 1983 was awarded the Nobel Prize for her study of maize cells

This is "well written and well organized." SLJ

Includes bibliographical references

Pasachoff, Naomi E. Barbara McClintock; genius of genetics; by Naomi Pasachoff. Enslow Publishers 2006 128p il (Great minds of science) lib bdg $31.93

Grades: 5 6 7 8   92

1. Genetics 2. Women scientists

ISBN 0-7660-2505-5   LC 2005014915

A biography of "a pioneering scientist in the field of genetics at a time when nearly all scientists were men. Her experiments with corn led to the . . . discovery that genes can move over generations from one place on the genome to another and even from one type of organism to another." Publisher's note

Includes glossary and bibliographical references

Spangenburg, Ray. Barbara McClintock; pioneering geneticist; by Ray Spangenburg and Diane Kit Moser. Chelsea House 2008 xxi, 136p il (Makers of modern science) $29.95

Grades: 8 9 10 11 12   92

1. Genetics 2. Women scientists

ISBN 978-0-8160-6172-3; 0-8160-6172-6

LC 2006032356

A biography of the Nobel Prize winning geneticist.

Includes glossary and bibliographical references

Mead, Margaret, 1901-1978

Mark, Joan T. Margaret Mead; coming of age in America; [by] Joan Mark. Oxford Univ. Press 1998 110p il (Oxford portraits in science) $28

Grades: 7 8 9 10   92

1. Anthropologists

ISBN 0-19-511679-8   LC 98-18604

An "account of the life and works of the influential, pioneering anthropologist. . . . Mark does a fine job of abstracting Mead's research and published works and showing why they were both critically acclaimed and criticized. The reader-friendly prose is peppered with fascinating anecdotes and photos. Mead herself is presented as a complex, intriguing figure, with fascinating, often contradictory, public and private lives." Booklist

Includes bibliographical references

Meitner, Lise, 1878-1968

Hamilton, Janet. Lise Meitner; pioneer of nuclear fission. Enslow Pubs. 2002 128p il map (Great minds of science) lib bdg $26.60

Grades: 5 6 7 8   92

1. Physicists 2. Women scientists 3. Nuclear physics

ISBN 0-7660-1756-7   LC 2001-2119

A biography of the German physicist who discovered nuclear fission in 1938

"Hamilton does a fine job of outlining the political climate of the time, which helps place the events of Meitner's life in historical context." SLJ

Includes glossary and bibliographical references

Meltzer, Milton, 1915-

Meltzer, Milton. Milton Meltzer; writing matters. Franklin Watts 2004 160p il lib bdg $29 *

Grades: 7 8 9 10   92

1. Authors, American

ISBN 0-531-12257-3   LC 2004-2947

Meltzer "writes about his own life through the prism of his craft. He tells about his growing up in Worcester, Massachusetts, the child of immigrants from the Austro-Hungarian empire, and his coming-of-age during the Depression." Booklist

"The author includes clear, interesting explanations about the American historical and economic events that influenced his life. While this book is a pleasure to read for general interest, it would also supplement units on American history." SLJ

Includes bibliographical references

Menchú, Rigoberta

Kallen, Stuart A. Rigoberta Menchu, Indian rights activist; by Stuart A. Kallen. Lucent Books 2007 104p il (The 20th century's most influential Hispanics) $31.20

Grades: 6 7 8 9   92

1. Mayas 2. Guatemala 3. Native Americans—Civil rights

ISBN 1-59018-975-2   LC 2006025690

Presents the life and accomplishments of the human rights activist who won the Noble Peace Prize in 1992 for her work to stop the oppression of her people, the Mayas of Guatemala.

This is a "stirring biography. . . . The selection of photos and captions enhance the text." SLJ

Includes bibliographical references

Mendel, Gregor, 1822-1884

Edelson, Edward. Gregor Mendel, and the roots of genetics. Oxford Univ. Press 1999 105p il (Oxford portraits in science) lib bdg $28; pa $11.95

Grades: 7 8 9 10   92

1. Genetics

ISBN 0-19-512226-7 (lib bdg); 0-19-515020-1 (pa)

LC 98-37541

"This biography provides details of the scientist's life and his experiments as well as the political and social context of his times. . . . A two-page chronology tracks important events in his life and the vital contributions he made to the study of genetics. Black-and-white photographs, reproductions of artwork, and pages from the scientist's notebooks and manuscripts accompany the text." SLJ

Includes bibliographical references

Klare, Roger. Gregor Mendel; father of genetics. Enslow Pubs. 1997 128p il (Great minds of science) lib bdg $26.60

Grades: 5 6 7 8   92

1. Genetics

ISBN 0-89490-789-1   LC 96-35791

Examines the life and work of the nineteenth-century Austrian monk who discovered the laws of genetics

"Easy-to-understand explanations of groundbreaking discoveries. . . . An activity section encourages readers to try their hands at the techniques and principles under discussion. Black-and-white photos, reproductions, and diagrams enhance the [presentation]. Useful . . . especially for reports." SLJ

Includes bibliographical references

Mercator, Gerardus, 1512-1594

Heinrichs, Ann. Gerardus Mercator; father of modern mapmaking; by Ann Heinrichs. Compass Point Books 2008 112p il map (Signature lives) lib bdg $31.93

Grades: 6 7 8 9   92

1. Maps

ISBN 978-0-7565-3312-0 (lib bdg); 0-7565-3312-0 (lib bdg)   LC 2007004902

A biography of the sixteenth-century geographer who created a world map in 1569 which introduced a new way of showing the spherical earth on a flat sheet of paper.

"Clear explanations of scientific thought and fact are presented in conversational tones and illuminated by easily grasped examples. . . . [The book includes] sidebars, maps, and well-captioned illustrations." SLJ

Includes glossary and bibliographical references

Mexia, Ynes, 1870-1938

Anema, Durlynn. Ynes Mexia, botanist and adventurer; [by] Durlynn Anema. 1st ed. Morgan Reynolds Pub. 2005 144p il (Women adventurers) lib bdg $26.95

Grades: 6 7 8 9   92

1. Botanists 2. Women scientists 3. Mexican Americans—Biography

ISBN 1-931798-67-2; 978-1-931798-67-9

LC 2005010694

A biography of the botanist who traveled on expeditions throughout South America and Mexico during the 1920s and collected over 500 new plant species.

"An interesting and colorful look at a Mexican-American scientist. The easy-to-read narrative draws on the woman's correspondences." SLJ

Includes bibliographical references

Michelangelo Buonarroti, 1475-1564

Stanley, Diane. Michelangelo. HarperCollins Pubs. 2000 unp il $16.99; lib bdg $17.89; pa $7.99 *

Grades: 4 5 6 7   92

1. Artists, Italian 2. Renaissance

ISBN 0-688-15085-3; 0-688-15086-1 (lib bdg); 0-06-052113-9 (pa)

A biography of the Renaissance sculptor, painter, architect, and poet, well known for his work on the Sistine Chapel in Rome's St. Peter's Cathedral

This is "as readable as it is useful. . . . Integrating Michelangelo's art with Stanley's watercolor, gouache, and colored-pencil figures and settings has the desired effect: readers will be dazzled with the master's ability, while at the same time pulled into his daily life and struggles." SLJ

Includes bibliographical references

Michelangelo Buonarroti, 1475-1564—*Continued*

Wilkinson, Philip. Michelangelo; the young artist who dreamed of perfection. National Geographic 2006 64p il map (World history biographies) $17.95; lib bdg $27.09 *
Grades: 5 6 7 8   92
1. Artists, Italian 2. Renaissance
ISBN 0-7922-5533-X; 0-7922-5534-8 (lib bdg)
An illustrated biography of Michelangelo, the Italian Renaissance painter and sculptor
Includes glossary and bibliographical references

Miller, Arthur, 1915-2005

Andersen, Richard. Arthur Miller. Marshall Cavendish Benchmark 2005 c2006 144p il (Writers and their works) lib bdg $25.95
Grades: 7 8 9 10   92
1. Authors, American
ISBN 0-7614-1946-2
"A biography of writer Arthur Miller that describes his era, his major works, his life, and the legacy of his writing." Publisher's note
This "attractive, well-organized [book fills] a gap in literary criticism for intermediate readers. Heavily illustrated with color and black-and-white photographs, [it] will appeal to students who might be intimidated by longer or more scholarly titles." SLJ

Mitchell, Maria, 1818-1889

Anderson, Dale. Maria Mitchell, astronomer. Chelsea House 2003 110p il (Women in science) $22.95
Grades: 7 8 9 10   92
1. Women astronomers
ISBN 0-7910-7249-5   LC 2002-13738
Contents: Watching the sun disappear; A child of Nantucket: 1818-1835; Teaching and learning: 1835-1847; Earning a medal: 1847-1855; Expanding the horizon: 1855-1861; Mitchell as professor: 1862-1869; Carrying the torch for women: 1869-1876; The force of personal character
Profiles a Vassar professor who was one of the most famous astronomers in the United States at the end of the nineteenth century and whose central message to her students was never cease to wonder
"Color prints or photographs with brief descriptions are interspersed throughout and add considerably to the [text]." Libr Media Connect
Includes bibliographical references

Gormley, Beatrice. Maria Mitchell; the soul of an astronomer; [by] Beatrice Gormley. Eerdmans Books for Young Readers 2004 c1995 137p il pa $12
Grades: 7 8 9 10   92
1. Women astronomers
ISBN 978-0-8028-5264-9 (pa); 0-8028-5264-5 (pa)
First published 1995
A biography of the first female science professor at Vassar College and the first American woman astronomer

"With a smoothly flowing and lively style, this biography introduces readers to the 19th-century astronomer. Well-chosen, primary-source quotations and quality black-and-white photos add authenticity to the text, and contribute greatly to the author's objective and comprehensive description of Mitchell's accomplishments." SLJ [review of 1995 edition]
Includes bibliographical references

Mohapatra, Jyotirmayee, 1978-

Woog, Adam. Jyotirmayee Mohapatra; by Adam Woog. KidHaven Press 2006 48p il $24.95
Grades: 4 5 6 7   92
1. Women—India 2. Social action
ISBN 0-7377-3611-9   LC 2006009121
"Mohapatra grew up in a rural village in India and became a leader in the fight for the rights of girls and women. . . . The power of one individual to inspire others to action is clearly expressed in this well-written profile. Full-color photos and a map enhance the presentation." SLJ
Includes bibliographical references

Monet, Claude, 1840-1926

Kallen, Stuart A. Claude Monet. Lucent Books 2009 112p il (Eye on art) lib bdg $32.45
Grades: 7 8 9 10   92
1. Artists, French 2. Impressionism (Art)
ISBN 978-1-4205-0074-5; 1-4205-0074-0
                                      LC 2008-20640
An introduction to the life and career of the artist Claude Monet, and how he painted his way into history.
"This biography paints a clear picture of the artist's life, work, and legacy. . . . The accompanying color reproductions of the artworks and black-and-white photographs of Monet contribute to the book's clean and attractive design. . . . This work stands out as a balanced description of the man's legacy and an enjoyable read." SLJ
Includes glossary and bibliographical references

Monroe, James, 1758-1831

Naden, Corinne J. James Monroe; [by] Corinne J. Naden and Rose Blue. Marshall Cavendish Benchmark 2009 96p il map (Presidents and their times) lib bdg $34.21
Grades: 5 6 7 8   92
1. Presidents—United States
ISBN 978-0-7614-2838-1 (lib bdg); 0-7614-2838-0 (lib bdg)   LC 2007-29480
"Provides comprehensive information on President James Monroe and places him within his historical and cultural context. Also explored are the formative events of his times and how he responded." Publisher's note
Includes glossary and bibliographical references

Mora, Pat

Marcovitz, Hal. Pat Mora; [by] Hal Marcovitz; forward by Kyle Zimmer. Chelsea House 2008 134p il (Who wrote that?) $30

Grades: 6 7 8 9   **92**

1. Poets, American 2. Mexican American authors 3. Women authors 4. Mexican Americans—Biography
ISBN 978-0-7910-9528-7; 0-7910-9528-2

LC 2007019452

This biography examines the "writer's life, including the inspiration behind some of [her] works. [The] volume includes photographs and quotations from interviews, as well as descriptions of main characters and annotated lists of books and awards. Useful for aspiring authors as well as book report writers." Horn Book Guide

Includes bibliographical references

Morrison, Toni, 1931-

Andersen, Richard. Toni Morrison. Marshall Cavendish Benchmark 2005 c2006 144p il (Writers and their works) lib bdg $25.95

Grades: 7 8 9 10   **92**

1. Authors, American 2. African American authors 3. Women authors
ISBN 0-7614-1945-4

A biography of writer Toni Morrison that describes her era, her major works, her life, and the legacy of her writing.

This "attractive, well-organized [book fills] a gap in literary criticism for intermediate readers. Heavily illustrated with color and black-and-white photographs, [it] will appeal to students who might be intimidated by longer or more scholarly titles." SLJ

Includes bibliographical references

Haskins, James. Toni Morrison; the magic of words; [by] Jim Haskins. Millbrook Press 2001 48p il (Gateway biography) lib bdg $23.90 *

Grades: 4 5 6 7   **92**

1. Authors, American 2. African American authors 3. Women authors
ISBN 0-7613-1806-2   LC 00-32868

Haskins discusses Morrison's "childhood, her career as an editor . . . and he gives a very brief outline of each of her books and its critical reception, from *The Bluest Eye* to *Beloved*." Booklist

"This introductory biography is well organized, attractive, and inspiring." SLJ

Includes bibliographical references

Mowat, Farley

Mowat, Farley. Born naked. Houghton Mifflin 1994 c1993 256p il maps pa $13 hardcover o.p.

Grades: 7 8 9 10   **92**

1. Naturalists 2. Authors, Canadian
ISBN 0-395-73528-9   LC 93-23702

"A Peter Davison book"

First published 1993 in Canada

The "renowned naturalist and writer gives us a glimpse of his parents, his growing up in Canada, and the roots of his love for animals." Booklist

"There are no dull pages here; every man, woman, child, and animal mentioned even casually makes an impression. . . . Highly recommended to all those who like good writing." Libr J

Mozart, Wolfgang Amadeus, 1756-1791

Riggs, Kate. Wolfgang Amadeus Mozart. Creative Education 2009 48p il (Xtraordinary artists) lib bdg $32.80

Grades: 4 5 6 7   **92**

1. Composers
ISBN 978-1-58341-664-8; 1-58341-664-1

LC 2007008963

This biography of the composer offers an "interesting [layout]; big, high-quality reproductions and photographs on heavy paper; insightful quotes from diverse sources; and meaty selections of the artist's own writing . . . at the end of the book. Readers get a strong sense of [Mozart's] personality along with an excellent survey of his work." SLJ

Includes bibliographical references

Weeks, Marcus. Mozart; the boy who changed the world with his music; [by] Marcus Weeks. National Geographic 2007 64p il map (World history biographies) $17.95; lib bdg $27.90

Grades: 5 6 7 8   **92**

1. Composers
ISBN   978-1-4263-0002-8;   1-4263-0002-6; 978-1-4263-0003-5 (lib bdg); 1-4263-0003-4 (lib bdg)

LC 2006020783

An introduction to the life and music of the composer and musician Mozart.

This "visually appealing [title is] packed with excellent photographs and reproductions, interesting sidebars, and have a time line running along the bottom of every page. . . . [The book is] useful, well-written." SLJ

Includes bibliographical references

Mubarak, Hosni

Darraj, Susan Muaddi. Hosni Mubarak. Chelsea House 2007 104p bibl il por (Modern world leaders) lib bdg $30

Grades: 7 8 9 10 11 12   **92**

1. Egypt—Politics and government 2. Heads of state
ISBN 0-7910-9280-1 (lib bdg); 978-0-7910-9280-4 (lib bdg)   LC 2006-32696

A biography of the man who became president of Egypt after the assassination of Anwar Sadat in 1981

The book has "archival photographs throughout. [It] would be [a] good [choice] for updating a collection, as [it is] current and [contains] solid information." SLJ

Includes bibliographical references

Mugabe, Robert Gabriel, 1924-

Arnold, James R. Robert Mugabe's Zimbabwe; by James R. Arnold and Roberta Wiener. Twenty-First Century Books 2008 160p (Dictatorships) lib bdg $38.60

Grades: 7 8 9 10   **92**

1. Zimbabwe 2. Heads of state
ISBN 978-0-8225-7283-1   LC 2006-100765

A biography of the dictator of Zimbabwe

This gives "students a glimpse into the repression and daily struggle for survival under [this] brutal [government]." SLJ

Includes glossary and bibliographical references

Muir, John, 1838-1914

Naden, Corinne J. John Muir; saving the wilderness; [by] Corinne J. Naden and Rose Blue. Millbrook Press 1992 48p il (Gateway biography) pa $9.95 hardcover o.p.
Grades: 4 5 6 7   **92**
1. Naturalists 2. Nature conservation
ISBN 1-56294-797-4 (pa)   LC 91-18106
This book profiles the life and times of naturalist John Muir
"Attractively designed with clear framed text and lots of photographs. . . . Kids will be intrigued by Muir's work for conservation, especially his role in founding the national parks." Booklist
Includes bibliographical references

Warrick, Karen Clemens. John Muir: crusader for the wilderness. Enslow Pubs. 2002 128p il map (Historical American biographies) lib bdg $26.60
Grades: 6 7 8 9   **92**
1. Naturalists 2. Nature conservation
ISBN 0-7660-1622-6   LC 2001-3000
Describes the life of the naturalist who became a founder of the Sierra Club and a proponent of the establishment of national parks in America
"Thorough and interesting, this is a good choice for most collections." SLJ
Includes glossary and bibliographical references

Munch, Edvard, 1863-1944

Whiting, Jim. Edvard Munch; by Jim Whiting. Mitchell Lane 2009 48p il (Art profiles for kids) lib bdg $20.95
Grades: 7 8 9 10   **92**
1. Artists, Norwegian
ISBN 978-1-58415-712-0; 1-58415-712-7
     LC 2008-2250
"The profile of Munch explains how the artist attempted to convey his deep feelings of anxiety in his paintings. . . . [Goes] beyond basic facts, providing historical context and significance of the art and the artist. . . . Provide[s] plenty of information for reports in a reader-friendly format." SLJ
Includes glossary and bibliographical references

Myers, Walter Dean, 1937-

Myers, Walter Dean. Bad boy; a memoir. HarperCollins Pubs. 2001 214p $15.95; lib bdg $16.89; pa $6.99 *
Grades: 7 8 9 10   **92**
1. Authors, American 2. African American authors
ISBN 0-06-029523-6; 0-06-029524-4 (lib bdg); 0-06-447288-4 (pa)   LC 00-52978
In this memoir "young adult author Walter Dean Myers recalls the life path that lead him to a career in writing. . . . His personal account allows the reader to get a glimpse of Myers, the man, touching on the issues of racism, adoption, self-identity, alcoholism, gang violence, and a speech impediment that almost altered Myers's path to the written word." Voice Youth Advocates
This "is a story full of funny anecdotes, lofty ideals, and tender moments." SLJ

Sickels, Amy. Walter Dean Myers; [by] Amy Sickels. Chelsea House 2008 128p il (Who wrote that?) $30
Grades: 6 7 8 9   **92**
1. Authors, American 2. African American authors
ISBN 978-0-7910-9524-9; 0-7910-9524-X
     LC 2007045507
This biography examines the "writer's life, including the inspiration behind some if [his] works. [The] volume includes photographs and quotations from interviews, as well as descriptions of main characters and annotated lists of books and awards. Useful for aspiring authors as well as book report writers." Horn Book Guide
Includes bibliographical references

Nakahama, Manjirō, 1827-1898

Blumberg, Rhoda. Shipwrecked!: the true adventures of a Japanese boy. HarperCollins Pubs. 2000 80p il map $16.95; pa $7.99 *
Grades: 5 6 7 8   **92**
1. Japan—History
ISBN 0-688-17484-1; 0-688-17485-X (pa)
     LC 99-86664
In 1841, rescued by an American whaler after a terrible shipwreck leaves him and his four companions castaways on a remote island, fourteen-year-old Manjiro learns new laws and customs as he becomes the first Japanese person to set foot in the United States
"Exemplary in both her research and writing, Blumberg hooks readers with anecdotes that astonish without sensationalizing, and she uses language that's elegant and challenging, yet always clear. Particularly notable is the well-chosen reproductions of original artwork." Booklist
Includes bibliographical references

Napoleon I, Emperor of the French, 1769-1821

Burleigh, Robert. Napoleon; the story of the little corporal. Abrams Books for Young Readers 2007 43p il map $18.95
Grades: 4 5 6 7   **92**
1. France—History—1799-1815 2. France—Kings and rulers
ISBN 978-0-8109-1378-3; 0-8109-1378-X
     LC 2006-23610
"Published in association with the American Federation of Arts."
"Burleigh's straightforward style and clear focus make accessible this account of the rapid rise and fall of the skilled military leader and emperor of France. The period artwork, accompanied by helpful captions, enhances the cleanly designed presentation." Horn Book Guide

Nefertiti, Queen, consort of Akhenaton, King of Egypt, 14th cent. B.C.

Lange, Brenda. Nefertiti. Chelsea House Publishers 2009 108p bibl il (Ancient world leaders) lib bdg $30
Grades: 6 7 8 9   **92**
1. Queens 2. Egypt—History
ISBN 978-0-7910-9581-2 (lib bdg); 0-7910-9581-9 (lib bdg)   LC 2008004869

Nefertiti, Queen, consort of Akhenaton, King of Egypt, 14th cent. B.C.—*Continued*
This biography of Nefertiti "deals less with the specifics of the [ancient Egyptian queen] and more with [her world] and times, including religious and political issues. The [author uses] speculation, derived from both tradition and scholarship, as to who [this] ancient [leader] may have been and how [she] might have governed." SLJ
Includes bibliographical references

Neruda, Pablo, 1904-1973
Délano, Poli. When I was a boy Neruda called me Policarpo. See entry under Délano, Poli, 1936-

Newton, Sir Isaac, 1642-1727
Anderson, Margaret Jean. Isaac Newton; the greatest scientist of all time; [by] Margaret J. Anderson. rev ed. Enslow Publishers 2008 128p il (Great minds of science) lib bdg $31.93 *
Grades: 5 6 7 8   92
1. Scientists
ISBN 978-0-7660-2793-0 (lib bdg); 0-7660-2793-7 (lib bdg)   LC 2007-29382
First published 1996
This is a biography of the eighteenth-century English scientist
"The book is well illustrated. . . . A unique aspect of the volume is that it lists a series of experiments that students can perform to sharpen their understanding of a number of Newton's scientific theories." Sci Books Films
Includes glossary and bibliographical references

Boerst, William J. Isaac Newton; organizing the universe. Morgan Reynolds Pub. 2004 144p il (Renaissance scientists) lib bdg $23.95
Grades: 7 8 9 10   92
1. Scientists
ISBN 1-931798-01-X   LC 2003-14571
"Boerst describes Newton's life from his premature birth through an isolated adulthood dominated by study and experimentation to his death at the age of 84. The author deftly explores his subject's accomplishments in relation to the scientific community and notable historical events of the time and includes information concerning his religious views. . . . This well-written book makes an excellent choice for teens exploring scientists or just looking for a good biography." SLJ
Includes bibliographical references

Christianson, Gale E. Isaac Newton and the scientific revolution. Oxford Univ. Press 1996 155p il (Oxford portraits in science) lib bdg $28
Grades: 7 8 9 10   92
1. Scientists
ISBN 0-19-509224-4   LC 96-13179
Explores the life and scientific contributions of the famed English mathematician and natural philosopher
This book "reads easily and with a pleasant and comfortable flow. Structured around pivotal moments in Newton's life, the book is an excellent reference for biographical data on the great English scientist; in addition, it affords a fine historical perspective of the scientific revolution." Sci Books Films
Includes bibliographical references

Hollihan, Kerrie Logan. Isaac Newton and physics for kids; his life and ideas with 21 activities. Chicago Review Press 2009 131p il map pa $16.95
Grades: 4 5 6 7   92
1. Scientists
ISBN 978-1-55652-778-4 (pa); 1-55652-778-0 (pa)   LC 2008048635
"Hollihan introduces readers to the scientific brilliance, as well as the social isolation, of this giant figure, blending a readable narrative with an attractive format that incorporates maps, diagrams, historical photographs, and physics activities." Booklist
Includes bibliographical references

Krull, Kathleen. Isaac Newton; illustrated by Boris Kulikov. Viking 2006 126p il (Giants of science) $15.99 *
Grades: 5 6 7 8   92
1. Scientists
ISBN 0-670-05921-8   LC 2005017741
This "profiles Sir Isaac Newton, the secretive, obsessive, and brilliant English scientist who invented calculus, built the first reflecting telescope, developed the modern scientific method, and discerned many of our laws of physics and optics. . . . The lively, conversational style will appeal to readers. . . . Kulikov's humorous pen-and-ink drawings complement the lighthearted text of this fascinating introduction." Booklist

Steele, Philip. Isaac Newton; the scientist who changed everything; [by] Philip Steele. National Geographic Society 2007 64p il map (World history biographies) $17.95; lib bdg $27.90
Grades: 4 5 6 7   92
1. Scientists
ISBN 978-1-4263-0114-8; 978-1-4263-0115-5 (lib bdg)   LC 2006020772
"The cradle-to-grave text includes vivid descriptions of Newton's youth. . . . The dynamic format is a draw; numerous mostly archival images . . . and a time-line border add interest and cultural context on each spacious page." Booklist
Includes bibliographical references

Nezahualcóyotl, King of Texcoco, 1402-1472
Serrano, Francisco. The poet king of Tezcoco; a great leader of Ancient Mexico; illustrated by Pablo Serrano; biography translated and adapted by Trudy Balch; poetry translated by Jo Anne Engelbert. Groundwood Books/House of Anansi Press 2007 35p il $18.95 *
Grades: 4 5 6 7   92
1. Aztecs 2. Mexico—History
ISBN 978-0-88899-787-6; 0-88899-787-6
"In the fifteenth century, the land where Mexico City now sprawls was a vast, green kingdom called Tezcoco. This . . . introduces one of Tezcoco's greatest rulers, a Toltec royal named Nezahualcoyotl. . . . The folk-art inspired illustrations echo the area's artistic traditions with beautiful patterning and symbolic imagery and flat, simplified characters reminiscent of hieroglyphics. Groundbreaking in its coverage of exciting history, this book offers details that are rarely presented to young people." Booklist

Nixon, Richard M. (Richard Milhous), 1913-1994

Aronson, Billy. Richard M. Nixon; [by] Billy Aronson. Marshall Cavendish Benchmark 2007 c2008 96p il (Presidents and their times) lib bdg $22.95 *

Grades: 5 6 7 8 **92**

1. Presidents—United States

ISBN 978-0-7614-2428-4   LC 2006013839

Aronson "is able to paint a picture so full that readers will come away feeling that they know the man and understand at least some of the forces that shaped him. . . . The narrative moves chronologically, marching through the war years, Nixon's tenure in Congress and as vice-president, his presidential loss to JFK, his successful efforts to remake himself as a politician, and his years as president. . . . The typeface is clear, the photographs are well chosen." Booklist

Includes glossary and bibliographical references

Barron, Rachel. Richard Nixon; American politician. rev ed. Morgan Reynolds 2004 128p il (Notable Americans) lib bdg $24.95

Grades: 7 8 9 10 **92**

1. Presidents—United States

ISBN 1-93179-830-3 (lib bdg); 978-1-93179-830-3 (lib bdg)   LC 2003-27425

First published 1998

"A comprehensive portrait of the statesman's political career and personal life. . . . Barron is objective about her subject, giving him credit for his considerable successes and holding him responsible for his failures." SLJ [review of 1998 edition]

Includes bibliographical references

Noguchi, Isamu, 1904-1988

Tiger, Caroline. Isamu Noguchi. Chelsea House 2007 112p bibl il por (Asian Americans of achievement) lib bdg $30

Grades: 6 7 8 9 **92**

1. Sculptors 2. Japanese Americans—Biography

ISBN 0-7910-9276-3 (lib bdg); 978-0-7910-9276-7 (lib bdg)   LC 2006026230

A biography of the artist, born in 1904 to an American mother and a Japanese poet father, who created sculpture, furniture, stage sets, and public gardens.

"This engaging account of the prolific and diverse artist will add depth to any biography collection." SLJ

Includes bibliographical references

Nuñez Cabeza de Vaca, Alvar, 16th cent.

Childress, Diana. Barefoot conquistador; Cabeza de Vaca and the struggle for Native American rights. Twenty-First Century Books 2008 160p il map lib bdg $30.60

Grades: 7 8 9 10 **92**

1. Explorers 2. America—Exploration

ISBN 978-0-8225-7517-7 (lib bdg); 0-8225-7517-5 (lib bdg)   LC 2007-22059

"This clearly written biography introduces a 16th-century Spanish explorer who made two expeditions to North and South America and eventually became a champion for Native Americans. . . . Childress's well-researched, lively text will fascinate readers. . . . The pages are sprinkled with period illustrations and maps." SLJ

Includes bibliographical references

Nye, Naomi Shihab, 1952-

Nye, Naomi Shihab. I'll ask you three times, are you ok? tales of driving and being driven. Greenwillow Books 2007 242p $15.99; lib bdg $16.89

Grades: 7 8 9 10 11 12 **92**

1. Voyages and travels

ISBN 978-0-06-085392-1; 978-0-06-085393-8 (lib bdg)   LC 2006-36548

The author "writes about sudden intimate connections with strangers, especially taxi drivers, who often yield glimpses of family and exile that can sometimes change us. . . . The prose is chatty, fast, and unpretentious, and teens will enjoy the driving stuff and the idea of her kissing in the backseat, and they'll feel her sense of control when she is behind the wheel herself." Booklist

Oakley, Annie, 1860-1926

Macy, Sue. Bulls-eye: a photobiography of Annie Oakley. National Geographic Soc. 2001 64p il $17.95; pa $7.95 *

Grades: 4 5 6 7 **92**

1. Entertainers

ISBN 0-7922-7008-8; 978-0-7922-7008-9; 978-0-7922-5933-6 (pa); 0-7922-5933-5 (pa)   LC 2001-125

A biography of the woman born Phoebe Ann Moses, who, under the name Annie Oakley, became a famous sharpshooter touring with Buffalo Bill's Wild West Show

"This book is exemplary nonfiction: well documented, lots of period photos with credits, a resource list, and a chronology. Equally important is its engaging and well crafted account of this famous woman of the West." SLJ

Includes bibliographical references

Wills, Charles A. Annie Oakley: a photographic story of a life; [by] Chuck Wills. DK Pub. 2007 128p il (DK biography) $14.99

Grades: 4 5 6 7 **92**

1. Entertainers

ISBN 978-0-7566-2986-1

A biography of the sharp-shooter in Buffalo Bill's Wild West Show, from her humble Quaker heritage, her childhood filled with poverty and abuse, to her rise to international fame.

"This highly readable book has a rich layout of photographs and illustrations on every spread." SLJ

Obama, Barack, 1961-

Abramson, Jill. Obama; the historic journey. Young reader's ed. Callaway 2009 94p il map $24.95

Grades: 5 6 7 8 **92**

1. Presidents—United States 2. African Americans—Biography 3. Racially mixed people

ISBN 978-0-670-01208-4; 0-670-01208-4   LC 2009-5051

Obama, Barack, 1961——_Continued_

"This scaled down, teen-friendly version of The New York Times's adult biography is geared for middle school students. Containing many of the same photos, it provides a brief overview of the President's life, information that has been revealed over the election year and during his administration. . . . Its allure is in the many photographs with captions, sidebars, speech quotes, and charts. The book is nicely organized. The writing is direct and simple, explaining things such as convention delegates. . . . The book should entice young readers to explore his life further." Voice Youth Advocates

Brill, Marlene Targ. Barack Obama; working to make a difference; [by] Marlene Targ Brill. Millbrook Press 2006 48p il (Gateway biography) lib bdg $23.93

Grades: 5 6 7 8   **92**
1. Presidents—United States 2. African Americans—Biography 3. Racially mixed people
ISBN 978-0-8225-3417-4 (lib bdg); 0-8225-3417-7 (lib bdg)   LC 2005016298

"Brill offers a warm, personal portrait of the politician, beginning with his parents' disparate backgrounds and his multinational upbringing and moving through his political awakenings, higher education, and public life. . . . Brill offers an intimate portrait that is bolstered by her own interviews with Obama's colleagues, schoolmates, and friends." Booklist

Includes bibliographical references

Davis, William. Barack Obama; the politics of hope. OTTN Pub. 2008 168p il (Shapers of America) $25.95; pa $16.99 *

Grades: 6 7 8 9 10   **92**
1. Presidents—United States 2. African Americans—Biography 3. Racially mixed people
ISBN   1-59556-024-6;   978-1-59556-024-7; 1-59556-032-7 (pa); 978-1-59556-032-2 (pa)

This biography of the president "will give readers a real feel for the man and the forces that shaped him. . . . It thoroughly and sensitively dissects Obama's complicated ethnic background and what it meant to him. . . . Davis also does a good job of explaining the realities associated with Obama's losses and wins in the political arena." Booklist

Includes bibliographical references

Gibson, Karen Bush. The Obama view; the historic fight for the 2008 Democratic presidential nomination. Mitchell Lane Publishers 2009 il (Monumental milestones) lib bdg $20.95

Grades: 6 7 8 9   **92**
1. Presidents—United   States—Election—2008 2. African Americans—Biography 3. Racially mixed people
ISBN 978-1-5841-5732-8; 1-5841-5732-1
                     LC 2008053464

This book is "clearly and crisply written. Starting with Obama's career in Illinois politics, the book then details his unlikely journey to the presidency, starting with his childhood in Hawaii and Indonesia. The final chapter deals with the presidential election and doesn't shy away from such issues as the way race was an election subtext. . . . The design is lively and colorful, and the photos

will draw readers." Booklist

Includes bibliographical references

Obama, Barack. Dreams from my father; a story of race and inheritance. Crown Publishers 2007 c2004 442p $25.95

Grades: 7 8 9 10 11 12 Adult   **92**
1. Presidents—United States 2. African Americans—Biography 3. Racially mixed people
ISBN 978-0-307-38341-9   LC 2007-271892

Also available in paperback from Three Rivers Press

First published 1995 by Times Books

This is the autobiography of the Illinois senator who would later become the 44th president of the United States.

The author "offers an account of his life's journey that reflects brilliantly on the power of race consciousness in America. . . . Obama writes well; his account is sensitive, probing, and compelling." Choice [review of 1995 edition]

Sapet, Kerrily. Barack Obama; by Kerrily Sapet. Morgan Reynolds Pub. 2007 128p il map (Political profiles) lib bdg $27.95

Grades: 6 7 8 9   **92**
1. Presidents—United States 2. African Americans—Biography 3. Racially mixed people
ISBN 978-1-59935-045-5 (lib bdg); 1-59935-045-9 (lib bdg)   LC 2007018657

A biography of the African American U.S. president.

"Photos and descriptions of [Obama's] trips to his father's native Kenya will intrigue students. . . . The political threads in [this] biography focus particularly on urban issues. . . . [This book] should be painless, even enjoyable reading for reluctant readers." Voice Youth Advocates

Includes bibliographical references

Schuman, Michael. Barack Obama; "we are one people"; [by] Michael A. Schuman. rev & exp. Enslow Publishers 2009 160p il (African-American biography library) lib bdg $34.60

Grades: 5 6 7 8   **92**
1. Presidents—United States 2. African Americans—Biography 3. Racially mixed people
ISBN 978-0-7660-3649-9 (lib bdg); 0-7660-3649-9 (lib bdg)   LC 2008-53678

First published 2008

"A biography of Barack Obama, the 44th president of the United States and the first African American to hold office." Publisher's note

"The text is straightforward and concise. . . . [The book is illustrated with] many color photos. . . . [This is a] timely, sturdy title." Booklist [review of 2008 edition]

Includes bibliographical references

Obama, Barack, 1961-—*Continued*

Thomson, Sarah L. Obama; a promise of change; [by] David Mendell; adaptation by Sarah L. Thomson. HarperCollins 2009 182p $16.99; pa $6.99

Grades: 6 7 8 9 10   **92**

  1. Presidents—United States 2. African Americans—Biography 3. Racially mixed people

  ISBN   978-0-06-169701-2;   0-06-169701-X; 978-0-06-169700-5 (pa); 0-06-169700-1 (pa)

                           LC 2008-14071

  Adapted from Obama: from promise to power by David Mendell

  "This adaptation of Mendell's adult book Obama: From Promise to Power (HarperCollins, 2007) summarizes the life of Obama through March 2008, describing his upbringing, changing family, education, and political work. The text is accurate and well researched, with endnotes providing citations for each chapter." SLJ

  Includes bibliographical references

Wagner, Heather Lehr. Barack Obama; [by] Heather Lehr Wagner. Chelsea House Publishers 2008 98p il (Black Americans of achievement) lib bdg $30

Grades: 6 7 8 9   **92**

  1. Presidents—United States 2. African Americans—Biography 3. Racially mixed people

  ISBN 978-0-7910-9716-8 (lib bdg); 0-7910-9716-1 (lib bdg)   LC 2007045642

  This biography details Obama's "rise from adversity to . . . international recognition. The [book goes] beyond the typical personal information to provide some social history relevant to the subject's time. Captioned photographs and boxed inserts enhance the conversational [text]." Horn Book Guide

  Includes bibliographical references

Obama, Michelle

Brophy, David. Michelle Obama; meet the First Lady; by David Bergen Brophy. Harper Collins 2009 114p il $16.99; pa $6.99

Grades: 5 6 7 8   **92**

  1. Presidents' spouses—United States 2. African American women—Biography

  ISBN   978-0-06-177991-6;   0-06-177991-1; 978-0-06-177990-9 (pa); 0-06-177990-3 (pa)

  A brief biography of Michelle Obama, wife of President Barack Obama.

  "The author . . . mixes personal data with information about the political process that brought the Obamas to the White House. . . . This biography is a must-have for all school libraries." Voice Youth Advocates

  Includes glossary

Colbert, David. Michelle Obama; an American story. Houghton Mifflin Harcourt 2009 151p il $16

Grades: 5 6 7 8   **92**

  1. Presidents' spouses—United States 2. African American women—Biography

  ISBN 978-0-547-24941-4; 0-547-24941-1

  This biography delves into "the subject of The First Lady's family roots. . . . It offers a strong sense of who

Obama was as a child, her solid upbringing, and her adult choices, all bolstered with numerous quotes from Obama and those who know her best. . . . Two sections of color photos and appended source notes for direct quotes complete this timely, highly readable biography." Booklist

Ocampo, Adriana C., 1955-

Hopping, Lorraine Jean. Space rocks; the story of planetary geologist Adriana Ocampo. Franklin Watts 2005 118p il (Women's adventures in science) $9.95

Grades: 7 8 9 10   **92**

  1. Geologists 2. Women scientists

  ISBN 0-531-16783-6   LC 2005006644

  "Adriana Ocampo grew up in Argentina. . . . When her father moved the family to the United States. . . . her enthusiasm for satellite design and interest in geology eventually led to a job [with NASA]. First helping to design a Mars rover, she then got involved in the search for a crater created by a massive asteroid collision that evidently caused mass extinctions in the age of dinosaurs. She now examines photos of distant planets taken by 'flyby' space probes and [plans] new geological expeditions." Voice Youth Advocates

  Includes bibliographical references

Ochoa, Ellen, 1958-

Paige, Joy. Ellen Ochoa; the first Hispanic woman in space; Joy Paige. 1st ed. Rosen Pub. Group 2004 112p il (Library of astronaut biographies) lib bdg $29.25

Grades: 6 7 8 9   **92**

  1. Women astronauts

  ISBN 0-8239-4457-3   LC 2003-10700

  Contents: A dream of success; Getting a good education; Laying the groundwork; Joining NASA; Up in space; Conclusion: A new beginning

  A biography of the woman who became an astronaut in 1991 and served on space shuttle and space station missions from 1993 until 2002

  Includes bibliographical references

O'Dell, Scott, 1898-1989

Marcovitz, Hal. Scott O'Dell; [by] Hal Marcovitz; foreword by Kyle Zimmer. Chelsea House 2008 128p il (Who wrote that?) lib bdg $30

Grades: 6 7 8 9   **92**

  1. Authors, American

  ISBN 978-0-7910-9526-3 (lib bdg); 0-7910-9526-6 (lib bdg)   LC 2007019577

  This biography examines the "writer's life, including the inspiration behind some of [his] works. [The] volume includes photographs and quotations from interviews, as well as descriptions of main characters and annotated lists of books and awards. Useful for aspiring authors as well as book report writers." Horn Book Guide

  Includes bibliographical references

Omidyar, Pierre

Viegas, Jennifer. Pierre Omidyar; the founder of eBay; [by] Jennifer Viegas. Rosen Pub. Group 2007 112p (Internet career biographies) lib bdg $31.95

Grades: 6 7 8 9   92

1. eBay Inc. 2. Internet

ISBN 1-4042-0715-5   LC 2005028804

"In Viegas's fascinating, accessible biography, readers learn about the early days of AuctionWeb and how it evolved into the eBay site." SLJ

Includes bibliographical references

Oppenheimer, J. Robert, 1904-1967

Allman, Toney. J. Robert Oppenheimer; theoretical physicist, atomic pioneer; [by] Toney Allman. Blackbirch Press 2005 64p il map (Giants of science) $24.95

Grades: 5 6 7 8   92

1. Physicists 2. Atomic bomb

ISBN 1-56711-889-5   LC 2004-11199

Subtitle on cover: Father of the atomic bomb

This is a biography of the nuclear physicist who was instrumental in the development of the atomic bomb in the United States

This is a "readable, inviting overview. . . . Full-color and black-and-white photographs and diagrams energize the text and clarify the complex ideas discussed." SLJ

Includes bibliographical references

Scherer, Glenn. J. Robert Oppenheimer; the brain behind the bomb; [by] Glenn Scherer and Marty Fletcher. MyReportLinks.com Books 2007 128p il (Inventors who changed the world) $33.27

Grades: 7 8 9 10   92

1. Physicists 2. Atomic bomb

ISBN 978-1-59845-050-7; 1-59845-050-6

LC 2006-20820

"This biography shows both the complexity of the man and the importance of his work as the leader of a team of scientists who created the atom bomb. . . . The featured Internet sources provide balance in the form of additional perspectives, including many primary documents. They offer reports, photos, and films featuring Oppenheimer and information concerning the atom bomb. Four activities explore the atom and the impact of a bomb on a city and an individual." SLJ

Includes bibliographical references

Osama bin Laden

Landau, Elaine. Osama bin Laden; a war against the West. 21st Cent. Bks. (Brookfield) 2002 144p il lib bdg $23.90

Grades: 7 8 9 10   92

1. Terrorism

ISBN 0-7613-1709-0   LC 2001-41465

Presents biographical information about militant Islamic leader Osama bin Laden, including his role in international terrorism and the beliefs that fuel his actions

"Landau's book is a comprehensive, well-researched, and in-depth look at arguably the most hated man in the country." Voice Youth Advocates

Includes bibliographical references

Page, Larry

White, Casey. Sergey Brin and Larry Page. See entry under Brin, Sergey

Parks, Rosa, 1913-2005

Parks, Rosa. Rosa Parks: my story; by Rosa Parks with Jim Haskins. Dial Bks. 1992 192p il $17.99; pa $6.99 *

Grades: 5 6 7 8   92

1. African American women—Biography 2. African Americans—Civil rights 3. Montgomery (Ala.)—Race relations

ISBN 0-8037-0673-1; 0-14-130120-7 (pa)

LC 89-1124

Rosa Parks describes her early life and experiences with race discrimination, and her participation in the Montgomery bus boycott and the civil rights movement

"A remarkable story, a record of quiet bravery and modesty, a document of social significance, a taut drama told with candor." Bull Cent Child Books

Tracy, Kathleen. The life and times of Rosa Parks. Mitchell Lane Publishers 2009 48p il (Profiles in American history) lib bdg $29.95

Grades: 6 7 8 9   92

1. African American women—Biography 2. African Americans—Civil rights 3. Montgomery (Ala.)—Race relations

ISBN 978-1-58415-666-6 (lib bdg); 1-58415-666-X (lib bdg)   LC 2008020927

This a biography of the American American seamstress who refused to give up her seat on a Montgomery, Albama, city bus to a white passenger, which led to challenging the constitutionality of Montgomery's bus segregation laws

This offers "a wealth of concise and well-organized information. . . . [The] book is fair and balanced and includes viewpoints from those who opposed or disagreed with [Parks'] accomplishments. The design is crisp and colorful without overwhelming the words on the page." SLJ

Includes glossary and bibliographical references

Pasteur, Louis, 1822-1895

Ackerman, Jane. Louis Pasteur and the founding of microbiology. Morgan Reynolds Pub. 2003 144p il (Renaissance scientists) lib bdg $23.95

Grades: 7 8 9 10   92

1. Scientists

ISBN 1-931798-13-3   LC 2003-17655

Follows the life and career of the French scientist who proved the existence of germs and their connection with diseases

"Students interested in science, biography, or medicine will find this an interesting account." SLJ

Includes bibliographical references

Robbins, Louise E. Louis Pasteur; and the hidden world of microbes. Oxford Univ. Press 2001 140p il (Oxford portraits in science) lib bdg $28

Grades: 7 8 9 10   92

1. Scientists

ISBN 0-19-512227-5   LC 2001-31405

Pasteur, Louis, 1822-1895—*Continued*

This provides a "view of one of microbiology's best-known scientists, from his childhood in France as a tanner's son to his death 73 years later. The inviting format is easy to read and includes many well-captioned, black and white photographs. . . . The chronology will be especially helpful for reports. This is a valuable research tool for any library." SLJ

Includes glossary and bibliographical references

Smith, Linda Wasmer. Louis Pasteur; disease fighter. rev ed. Enslow Publishers 2007 c2008 128p bibl il por (Great minds of science) lib bdg $31.93

Grades: 5 6 7 8 **92**

1. Scientists

ISBN 978-0-7660-2792-3 (lib bdg); 0-7660-2792-9 (lib bdg)   LC 2006036434

First published 1997

A biography of the noted French scientist whose discoveries, including a rabies vaccine and the process of pasteurization, had important practical applications in both medicine and industry

Includes glossary and bibliographical references

Zamosky, Lisa. Louis Pasteur; founder of microbiology. Compass Point Books 2009 40p il map (Mission: Science) lib bdg $26.60

Grades: 4 5 6 **92**

1. Scientists

ISBN 978-0-7565-3962-7   LC 2008007726

This biography of the father of microbiology "does a good job of connecting the scientist's work to our lives today. . . . [The] book has a variety of graphics including diagrams, photos, and reproductions of paintings and sketches. [This volume is] a definite plus for a school library or the juvenile collection in a public library." Libr Media Connect

Includes glossary and bibliographical references

Paterson, Katherine

McGinty, Alice B. Katherine Paterson; [by] Alice B. McGinty. 1st ed. Rosen Publishing Group 2005 112p il (Library of author biographies) lib bdg $26.50

Grades: 5 6 7 8 **92**

1. Women authors

ISBN 1-4042-0328-1   LC 2004-11420

This biography of the Newbery award-winning author "explains that Paterson's experiences growing up as the daughter of missionaries shaped her commitment to reflect the realistic feelings of children in her literature. . . . [This is] well-written." SLJ

Includes bibliographical references

Patrick, Danica, 1982-

Hinman, Bonnie. Danica Patrick; by Bonnie Hinman. Morgan Reynolds Pub. 2007 112p il (Xtreme athletes) lib bdg $27.95

Grades: 6 7 8 9 **92**

1. Automobile racing 2. Women athletes

ISBN 978-1-59935-079-0 (lib bdg); 1-59935-079-3 (lib bdg)   LC 2007-42944

This is a biography of "the first woman driver to lead laps in the history of the Indy 500. . . . Fans will be thrilled with the detailed accounts of action on the track, illustrated with numerous sharp color photos of cars and their drivers." Booklist

Includes bibliographical references

Pauling, Linus C., 1901-1994

Hager, Thomas. Linus Pauling and the chemistry of life. Oxford University Press 1998 142p il (Oxford portraits in science) $28

Grades: 7 8 9 10 **92**

1. Chemists

ISBN 0-19-510853-1   LC 97-43403

Profiles the Nobel Prize-winning chemist who described the nature of chemical bonds, made important discoveries in the fields of quantum mechanics, immunology, and evolution, and used his scientific fame to help advance political causes

"Students with a strong science background will get the most out of this biography, but even young people who don't like science will be able to identify with a man whose scientific curiosity and political principles led him to try to change the world. Chronology and recommended readings." Booklist

Includes bibliographical references

Paulsen, Gary

Paulsen, Gary. Caught by the sea; my life on boats. Delacorte Press 2001 103p maps $15.95; pa $5.50 *

Grades: 5 6 7 8 **92**

1. Authors, American 2. Boats and boating 3. Ocean travel

ISBN 0-385-32645-9; 0-440-40716-8 (pa)   LC 2001-17336

"Paulsen traces his life at sea, from buying his first sailboat to getting lost in the Pacific to encountering sharks. . . . His sometimes comic, sometimes near-fatal sea-going errors make for absorbing, captivating reading." Booklist

Paulsen, Gary. Guts; the true stories behind Hatchet and the Brian books. Delacorte Press 2001 148p hardcover o.p. pa $5.50 *

Grades: 6 7 8 9 **92**

1. Authors, American 2. Hunting 3. Wilderness survival

ISBN 0-385-32650-5; 0-440-40712-5 (pa)   LC 00-34061

Paulsen offers an autobiographical "collection of wilderness survival/hunting essays that concentrates on drawing parallels between his own life and the fictional adventures and misadventures of Brian Robeson in *Hatchet* . . . and its sequels." SLJ

"Readers squeamish about hunting or the death of animals will find many of the stories disturbing . . . but those who embrace the sport or have enjoyed the novels will see in Paulsen a responsible role model—a man who respects life and death as equal partners." Booklist

Paulsen, Gary—*Continued*

Paulsen, Gary. How Angel Peterson got his name; and other outrageous tales about extreme sports. Wendy Lamb Bks. 2003 111p hardcover o.p. pa $5.99 *

Grades: 5 6 7 8   92

1. Authors, American
  ISBN 0-385-72949-9; 0-385-90090-2 (lib bdg); 978-0-440-22935-3 (pa); 0-440-22935-9 (pa)

LC 2002-7668

Author Gary Paulsen relates tales from his youth in a small town in northwestern Minnesota in the late 1940s and early 1950s, such as skiing behind a souped-up car and imitating daredevil Evel Knievel

"Writing with humor and sensitivity, Paulsen shows boys moving into adolescence believing they can do anything. . . . None of them dies (amazingly), and even if Paulsen exaggerates the teensiest bit, his tales are side-splittingly funny and more than a little frightening." Booklist

Paulsen, Gary. My life in dog years; with drawings by Ruth Wright Paulsen. Delacorte Press 1998 137p il $15.95; pa $5.99 *

Grades: 4 5 6 7   92

1. Authors, American 2. Dogs
  ISBN 0-385-32570-3; 0-440-41471-7 (pa)

LC 97-40254

The author describes some of the dogs that have had special places in his life, including his first dog, Snowball, in the Philippines; Dirk, who protected him from bullies; and Cookie, who saved his life

"Paulsen differentiates his canine friends beautifully, as only a keen observer and lover of dogs can. At the same time, he presents an intimate glimpse of himself, a lonely child of alcoholic parents, who drew strength and solace from his four-legged companions and a love of the great outdoors. Poignant but never saccharine, honest, and open." Booklist

Pavlov, Ivan Petrovich, 1849-1936

Saunders, Barbara R. Ivan Pavlov; exploring the mysteries of behavior. Enslow Publishers 2006 112p il por (Great minds of science) lib bdg $31.93

Grades: 5 6 7 8   92

1. Scientists 2. Behaviorism
  ISBN 0-7660-2506-3   LC 2005031648

This is a biography of Russian scientist Ivan Pavlov, best known for his experiments with dogs, which were key to the development of behaviorism, and who won the 1904 Nobel Prize for his research on digestion

"The accessible [text has] an inviting, open format and [offers] many anecdotes. . . . Good-quality photos and illustrations complement the [narrative]." SLJ

Includes glossary and bibliographical references

Peary, Marie Ahnighito, 1893-1978

Kirkpatrick, Katherine A. Snow baby; the Arctic childhood of Admiral Robert E. Peary's daring daughter; [by] Katherine Kirkpatrick. Holiday House 2007 50p il map $16.95

Grades: 5 6 7 8   92

1. Peary, Robert Edwin, 1856-1920 2. Arctic regions 3. Explorers
  ISBN 978-0-8234-1973-9; 0-8234-1973-8

LC 2006-02016

"Born north of the Arctic Circle in 1893, Marie Ahnighito Peary published her own version of her youth in 1934 (*The Snowbaby's Own Story*), on which this book is based. Kirkpatrick's engaging text captures the girl's adventurous spirit and the opportunities that her father's life as an explorer presented, as well as her love of the North and her Inuit friends." SLJ

Peary, Robert Edwin, 1856-1920

Calvert, Patricia. Robert E. Peary; to the top of the world. Benchmark Bks. 2002 80p il map (Great explorations) lib bdg $29.93 *

Grades: 5 6 7 8   92

1. Explorers 2. North Pole
  ISBN 0-7614-1242-5   LC 00-51900

A biography of Admiral Robert Peary whose expedition reached the North Pole in 1909

"The well-researched [book] . . . will be useful to students writing reports. Maps and archival reproductions in both black and white and color extend the text." Horn Book Guide

Includes bibliographical references

Peck, Richard, 1934-

Campbell, Kimberly. Richard Peck; a spellbinding storyteller. Enslow Publishers 2008 112p bibl por (Authors teens love) lib bdg $31.93

Grades: 6 7 8 9   92

1. Authors, American
  ISBN 978-0-7660-2723-7 (lib bdg); 0-7660-2723-6 (lib bdg)   LC 2006034069

A biography of the 2001 Newbery-winning book, *A Year Down Yonder*

Includes bibliographical references

Peet, Bill

Peet, Bill. Bill Peet: an autobiography. Houghton Mifflin 1989 190p il $22; pa $15 *

Grades: 4 5 6 7   92

1. Walt Disney Productions 2. Authors, American 3. Illustrators
  ISBN 0-395-50392-7; 0-395-68982-1 (pa)

LC 88-37067

A Caldecott Medal honor book, 1990

This memoir "describes the life of the well-known children's book author who worked as an illustrator for Walt Disney from the making of 'Dumbo' until 'Mary Poppins.'" N Y Times Book Rev

"Every page of this oversized book is illustrated with Peet's unmistakable black-and-white drawings of himself and the people, places, and events described in the text. Familiar characters from his books and movies appear often." SLJ

Pelé, 1940-
Buckley, James, Jr. Pelé. DK Pub. 2007 128p il (DK biography) $14.99; pa $4.99
Grades: 6 7 8 9   92
1. Soccer—Biography
ISBN 978-0-7566-2996-0; 978-0-7566-2987-8 (pa)
This "introduces Edson Arantes do Nascimento, know to the world as soccer legend Pelé. The chapters stretch from Pelé's Brazilian youth . . . through is astonishing career and his current retirement. . . . Buckley grounds his enthusiasm with well-integrated facts and quotes. . . . Crisply reproduced photographs appear on every page." Booklist
Includes bibliographical references

Pelosi, Nancy, 1940-
Marcovitz, Hal. Nancy Pelosi; politician. Chelsea House Publishers 2009 144p il (Women of achievement) lib bdg $30
Grades: 7 8 9 10   92
1. Women politicians
ISBN 978-1-60413-075-1 (lib bdg); 1-60413-075-X (lib bdg)   LC 2008-34674
This is a biography of the first woman to serve as speaker of the U.S. House of Representatives
Includes bibliographical references

Shichtman, Sandra H. Nancy Pelosi. Morgan Reynolds Pub. 2007 112p il (Political profiles) lib bdg $28.95
Grades: 6 7 8 9   92
1. Women politicians
ISBN 978-1-59935-049-3 (lib bdg); 1-59935-049-1 (lib bdg)   LC 2007023576
A biography of the U.S. Speaker of the House of Representatives
Includes bibliographical references

Perkins, Frances, 1882-1965
Keller, Emily. Frances Perkins; first woman cabinet member. Morgan Reynolds Pub. 2006 160p il lib bdg $27.95
Grades: 8 9 10 11 12   92
1. Cabinet officers 2. Women politicians
ISBN 978-1-931798-91-4 (lib bdg); 1-931798-91-5 (lib bdg)   LC 2006023971
"This clearly written title highlights the groundbreaking accomplishments of the woman who served under Franklin D. Roosevelt as the U.S. Secretary of Labor. . . . The narrative is well researched and includes numerous quotes that are cited in a source notes section. Good-quality photographs depict many of the individuals mentioned in the text and illustrate the historical period." SLJ
Includes bibliographical references

Picasso, Pablo, 1881-1973
Hodge, Susie. Pablo Picasso; by Susie Hodge. new ed. World Almanac Library 2004 48p il (Lives of the artists) lib bdg $30; pa $11
Grades: 4 5 6 7   92
1. Artists, French
ISBN 0-8368-5601-5 (lib bdg); 0-8368-5606-6 (pa)   LC 2003-67238

Original Italian edition 2003
This discusses the life and work of the twentieth century artist
This is "concise and straightforward. . . . [It] includes remarkably accomplished sketches and paintings from the artist's childhood and adolescence." Booklist
Includes bibliographical references

McNeese, Tim. Pablo Picasso. Chelsea House Publishers 2006 122p il (Great Hispanic heritage) lib bdg $30
Grades: 7 8 9 10   92
1. Artists, French
ISBN 0-7910-8843-X   LC 2005025999
A biography of the 20th century artist.
"McNeese does a wonderful job of describing [this man's life] and, more importantly, the times in which [he] lived. . . . [The book] includes representative pictures from each phase of the artist's career." SLJ
Includes bibliographical references

Scarborough, Kate. Pablo Picasso. Watts 2002 46p il map (Artists in their time) lib bdg $22; pa $6.95
Grades: 5 6 7 8   92
1. Artists, French
ISBN 0-531-12229-8 (lib bdg); 0-531-16622-8 (pa)   LC 2002-27017
Discusses the life, art, and legacy of the artist Pablo Picasso. Includes a timeline linking the events in his life with world events
This offers a "clear and lively [text]. . . . Captioned, full-color and black-and-white photographs and art reproductions are liberally scattered throughout." SLJ
Includes glossary

Pierce, Tamora, 1954-
Dailey, Donna. Tamora Pierce; foreword by Kyle Zimmer. Chelsea House Publishers 2006 146p bibl il por (Who wrote that?) lib bdg $30
Grades: 6 7 8 9   92
1. Authors, American 2. Women authors
ISBN 978-0-7910-8795-4 (lib bdg); 0-7910-8795-6 (lib bdg)   LC 2005025041
This biography, which examines the "writer's personal life and writing career, [is] ideal for fans. . . . The synopses of most popular books, and lists of works, well-known characters, and major awards may help report writers." Horn Book Guide
Includes bibliographical references

Pike, Zebulon Montgomery, 1779-1813
Calvert, Patricia. Zebulon Pike; lost in the Rockies; by Patricia Calvert. Benchmark Books 2005 96p il map (Great explorations) lib bdg $29.93 *
Grades: 5 6 7 8   92
1. Explorers 2. West (U.S.)—Exploration
ISBN 0-7614-1612-9   LC 2003-17583
This "discusses the explorer's military service, relationship with the corrupt general James Wilkinson, the historical speculation about his motives for his meander-

Pike, Zebulon Montgomery, 1779-1813—*Continued*

ing expedition to the Spanish west, and his failure to climb the mountain named for him. . . . Illustrated with beautiful reproductions of period illustrations, paintings, and maps. . . . Well-written." SLJ

Includes bibliographical references

Pizarro, Francisco, ca. 1475-1541

Meltzer, Milton. Francisco Pizarro; the conquest of Peru; by Milton Meltzer. Benchmark Books 2005 80p il map (Great explorations) lib bdg $29.93 *

Grades: 5 6 7 8   92

1. Explorers 2. America—Exploration

ISBN 0-7614-1607-2   LC 2002-156000

Contents: Where Pizarro came from; The Spanish conquistadores; The business of conquest; A glimpse of gold; The Inca empire; Epidemics and civil wars; The decisive day; Turning an empire into a colony

Introduces the life of the explorer who was sent to Peru in the sixteenth century by the king of Spain to conquer the Incas and claim their land and wealth for the Spanish crown.

Includes bibliographical references

Poe, Edgar Allan, 1809-1849

Binns, Tristan Boyer. Edgar Allan Poe; master of suspense; [by] Tristan Boyer Binns. F. Watts 2005 127p il (Great life stories) lib bdg $30.50

Grades: 5 6 7 8   92

1. Authors, American

ISBN 0-531-16751-8   LC 2005011163

"Although not much detail is known about Poe's life, Binns explains that the writer lost his parents at a young age, had a rocky relationship with his foster parents, and was described by a fellow student as being excitable & restless, at times wayward, melancholic & morose as a young man. . . . [This book makes] excellent use of archival photos and reproductions, and extensive time lines provide historical connections and insights." SLJ

Includes bibliographical references

Lange, Karen E. Nevermore; a photobiography of Edgar Allan Poe. National Geographic 2009 64p il $19.95; lib bdg $28.90

Grades: 6 7 8 9   92

1. Authors, American

ISBN   978-1-4263-0398-2;   1-4263-0398-X; 978-1-4263-0399-9 (lib bdg); 1-4263-0399-8 (lib bdg)

LC 2008-39833

"The drama of Poe's tortured life unfolds in accessible prose. Textual information is interspersed with photos, artistic interpretations, and revealing quotations presented in script. . . . This volume offers a fairly complete and thoroughly readable description of Poe's life and his importance to literature." SLJ

Includes bibliographical references

Meltzer, Milton. Edgar Allan Poe; a biography. Twenty-First Century Books 2003 144p $31.90 *

Grades: 7 8 9 10   92

1. Authors, American

ISBN 0-7613-2910-2   LC 2002-155802

Contents: Theater in the blood; A quick and clever boy; The teenager; Soldier and poet; In West Point, and out; Satire and science fiction; Editor, novelist, husband; Hoaxes and horrors; The first ever detective story; A popular lecturer; New York: the rich and the poor; "The raven" and fame; Death of the beloved; The last years; Chronology of Poe's life

"More than most other biographers for young people, Meltzer places his subject within the framework of his society. Readers will come away not only with greater knowledge of Poe's life and accomplishments but also a clearer picture of American life in the first half of the nineteenth century." Booklist

Includes bibliographical references

Polo, Marco, 1254-1323?

Demi. Marco Polo; written and illustrated by Demi. Marshall Cavendish 2008 unp il map $19.99 *

Grades: 4 5 6 7   92

1. Voyages and travels 2. Explorers

ISBN 978-0-7614-5433-5; 0-7614-5433-0

"This elegant, scholarly picture-book biography brings the explorer's fantastic journey to life. . . . Demi weaves her subject's own accounts into a seamless tale of wonder. . . . The delicately rendered illustrations, painted with Chinese inks and gold overlays . . . capture the exotic beauty of 13th-century China." SLJ

Freedman, Russell. The adventures of Marco Polo; with illustrations by Bagram Ibatoulline; accompanied by archival, period artwork. Arthur A. Levine Books 2006 63p il map $17.99 *

Grades: 5 6 7 8   92

1. Voyages and travels 2. Explorers

ISBN 0-439-52394-X   LC 2005-22791

"Using Polo's own descriptions (as told to a writer he met in prison) Freedman shepherds readers across deserts, down the Silk Road, and over mountains until the adventurer reaches the magnificent kingdom of Kublai Khan. Supporting Freedman's informative yet evocative prose are enchanting illustrations. Ibatoulline follows the follows the historic journey with are inspired by different periods. . . . This is a glorious piece of bookmaking." Booklist

McCarty, Nick. Marco Polo; the boy who traveled the medieval world. National Geographic 2006 64p il map (World history biographies) $17.95; lib bdg $27.90

Grades: 5 6 7 8   92

1. Voyages and travels 2. Explorers

ISBN 0-7922-5893-2; 0-7922-5894-0 (lib bdg)

A biography of the Italian explorer who became famous for his travels in Asia

Includes glossary and bibliographical references

Otfinoski, Steven. Marco Polo; to China and back. Benchmark Bks. 2003 77p il map (Great explorations) lib bdg $19.95 *

Grades: 5 6 7 8   92

1. Voyages and travels 2. Explorers

ISBN 0-7614-1480-0   LC 2002-68

Polo, Marco, 1254-1323?—*Continued*

Contents: A distant world; A father's journey; Marco joins the adventure; Mountain and desert; In the court of Kublai Khan; A most trusted aide; Escort for a princess; Strange homecoming; A prisoner of war; Marco millions

This describes the life of the medieval explorer and his travels through Asia

"Maps, contemporary drawings and paintings, and diary excerpts reveal not only the complexities of Polo's groundbreaking adventures but also the awe and exhilaration they brought him." SLJ

Includes bibliographical references

Ponce de Leon, Juan, 1460?-1521

Otfinoski, Steven. Juan Ponce de Leon; discoverer of Florida; by Steven Otfinoski. Benchmark Books 2005 77p il map (Great explorations) lib bdg $29.93 *

Grades: 5 6 7 8   92

1. Explorers 2. America—Exploration

ISBN 0-7614-1610-2   LC 2003-17582

Contents: The soldier's way; Westward with Columbus; The Governor of Higuey; Father of Puerto Rico; The Fountain of Youth; An island called Florida; The King's favorite; At war with the Carib; To die in Florida

A biography of the Spanish explorer who was called the Father of Puerto Rico and who discovered Florida in his search for the Fountain of Youth.

Includes bibbliographical references

Powell, Colin L., 1937-

Finlayson, Reggie. Colin Powell; by Reggie Finlayson. Lerner Publications Co. 2004 112p il map (A & E biography) lib bdg $27.93; pa $7.95   92

1. Generals 2. Statesmen—United States 3. African Americans—Biography

ISBN 0-8225-4966-2 (lib bdg); 0-8225-9698-9 (pa)   LC 2002-156556

Contents: Ordinary or extraordinary?; The streets of New York; Soldiering on; Over where?; The home front; Lessons in leadership; Stepping stones to power; Center of the storm; Powell, peace, and war

A biography covering the childhood and military and political careers of General Colin Powell.

Includes bibliographical references

Shichtman, Sandra H. Colin Powell; "Have a vision. Be demanding"; [by] Sandra H. Shichtman. Enslow 2005 128p il (African-American biography library) lib bdg $31.93

Grades: 5 6 7 8   92

1. Generals 2. Statesmen—United States 3. African Americans—Biography

ISBN 0-7660-2464-4   LC 2004-16799

Contents: Introduction: the long wait ends; A childhood of love, learning, and discipline (1937-1954); A college student's commitment (1954-1958); "You're in the Army now" (1958-1962); Tours of duty [in Vietnam] (1962-1969); The "yo-yo" years (1969-1983); Back in Washington (1983-1989); Becomes Chairman of the Joint Chiefs of Staff (1989-1993); Private citizen; Another return to public service

A biography of the former Secretary of State and Chairman of the Joint Chiefs of Staff of the Armed Forces

This is "clearly written. . . . The captioned color photos add to the visual appeal." SLJ

Includes bibliographical references

Presley, Elvis, 1935-1977

Hampton, Wilborn. Elvis Presley; a twentieth century life. Viking 2007 197p il (Up close) $15.99

Grades: 7 8 9 10   92

1. Rock musicians 2. Singers

ISBN 978-0-670-06166-2   LC 2006029074

A biography of the legendary "King of rock and roll." The author's "enthusiasm and passion for his subject are evident throughout this appealing biography, yet he remains objective about the performer's virtues as well as his tragic flaws. The striking cover photograph complements the lively and accessible text that delves not only into Elvis's life but also his impact on music and American culture." SLJ

Priestley, Joseph, 1733-1804

Conley, Kate A. Joseph Priestley and the discovery of oxygen. Mitchell Lane 2006 48p il (Uncharted, unexplored, and unexplained) $19.95

Grades: 6 7 8 9   92

1. Chemists 2. Oxygen

ISBN 1-58415-367-9

"This introductory title follows the scientist from his childhood in Fieldhead, England, to his death in Northumberland, PA. . . . Color photographs and illustrations are featured throughout. The attractive, open layout makes this title especially appealing to reluctant readers." SLJ

Puente, Tito, 1923-2000

McNeese, Tim. Tito Puente; [by] Tim McNeese. Chelsea House 2008 118p il (The great Hispanic heritage) lib bdg $30

Grades: 6 7 8 9   92

1. Musicians 2. Puerto Ricans—Biography

ISBN 978-0-7910-9666-6 (lib bdg); 0-7910-9666-1 (lib bdg)   LC 2007031984

This biography provides a "substantive [portrait], including background information and historical context of . . . charismatic band leader Puente. . . . The well-documented [text] effectively [combines] anecdotes, quotations, and historical details. Many photographs and sidebars are also included." Horn Book Guide

Includes bibliographical references

Pujols, Albert, 1980-

Needham, Tom. Albert Pujols; MVP on and off the field. Enslow Publishers 2007 128p bibl por (Sports stars with heart) lib bdg $23.95

Grades: 4 5 6 7   92

1. Baseball—Biography

ISBN 978-0-7660-2866-1 (lib bdg); 0-7660-2866-6 (lib bdg)   LC 2006031843

Pujols, Albert, 1980-—Continued

"Baseball fans know Pujols from his outstanding record: Rookie of the Year, a National League MVP, a team leader helping the St. Louis Cardinals win the World Series in 2006. However, with its combination of sharp writing, eye-catching design, and well-chosen photos, this . . . is so pleasing that even those who don't follow baseball will enjoy learning about Pujols." Booklist

Includes bibliographical references

Pullman, Philip, 1946-

Speaker-Yuan, Margaret. Philip Pullman. Chelsea House 2006 118p il (Who wrote that?) lib bdg $30

Grades: 6 7 8 9   92

1. Authors, English

ISBN 0-7910-8658-5   LC 2005-8184

This "draws upon an impressive array of sources—particularly Pullman's own writings—to present the groundbreaking author's life and work. . . . What may thrill readers most . . . are the insights into the writing process." Booklist

Includes bibliographical references

Putin, Vladimir

Shields, Charles J. Vladimir Putin. 2nd ed. Chelsea House 2007 120p il (Modern world leaders) lib bdg $30

Grades: 7 8 9 10   92

1. Russia (Federation)—Politics and government

ISBN 0-7910-9215-1   LC 2006013657

First published 2003

A biography of the Russian president.

Includes bibliographical references

Streissguth, Thomas. Vladimir Putin; by Tom Streissguth. Lerner 2005 112p il (A & E biography) lib bdg $27.93; pa $7.95

Grades: 7 8 9 10   92

1. Russia (Federation)—Politics and government

ISBN 0-8225-2374-4 (lib bdg); 0-8225-9630-X (pa)

LC 2004-17725

Contents: A boyhood dream; The young agent; Walls crumble; End of a superpower; Reaching the Kremlin; Into the deep end; Law and disorder; Facing down terrorism

This biography of the Russian president "begins with teenage Putin going straight to the offices of the KGB and inquiring about how to become an employee. Advised to study law, Putin found his path to a political career that would take several detours over the decades as the former Soviet Union changed ideologically and socially. Frequent color photos and sidebars on specific topics—from World War II to Chechnya—add vitality to the otherwise straightforward narrative." Booklist

Includes bibliographical references

Raleigh, Sir Walter, 1552?-1618

Aronson, Marc. Sir Walter Ralegh and the quest for El Dorado. Clarion Bks. 2000 222p il map $20
*

Grades: 7 8 9 10   92

1. Explorers

ISBN 0-395-84827-X   LC 99-43096

In this biographical portrait "Ralegh—warrior, champion of North American colonialism, court favorite of Queen Elizabeth I, adventurer and writer—is placed in the center of a broad canvas depicting life in sixteenth-century England and beyond." Horn Book

"Incorporating critical examinations of period art and poetry as well as standard historical documentary evidence and pausing frequently to review and explicitly support its thesis, this title is at once lively, accessible, and challenging. Period illustrations, an index, and fastidiously annotated endnotes and bibliography are included." Bull Cent Child Books

Includes bibliographical references

Ramses II, King of Egypt

Fitzgerald, Stephanie J. Ramses II; Egyptian pharaoh, warrior, and builder. Compass Point Books 2009 112p il map (Signature lives) lib bdg $34.60

Grades: 6 7 8 9   92

1. Egypt—History 2. Egypt—Civilization 3. Kings and rulers

ISBN 978-0-7565-3836-1 (lib bdg); 0-7565-3836-X (lib bdg)   LC 2008005726

This biography of the pharaoh Ramses II offers "details about the history and daily life of Egypt's New Kingdom era. . . . [The texts is] accompanied by high-quality photographs of artifacts, maps, and floor plans. [The] book's detailed time line, comparing events in Egypt to those throughout the world, is helpful for placing the lives of the pharaohs in context." SLJ

Includes glossary and bibliographical references

Randolph, Asa Philip, 1889-1979

Miller, Calvin Craig. A. Philip Randolph and the African American labor movement. Morgan Reynolds 2005 160p il (Portraits of Black Americans) $24.95

Grades: 8 9 10 11 12   92

1. African Americans—Biography 2. African Americans—Civil rights 3. Labor unions

ISBN 1-931798-50-8   LC 2004-23706

A biography of the African American leader

"Miller lucidly traces Randolph's spectacular career while presenting a case study in the effective use of hard-nosed rhetoric and nonviolent tactics to achieve breakthroughs in the fight against segregation. Profusely illustrated with photographs, sometimes in color, and capped by resource lists." Booklist

Includes bibliographical references

Rankin, Jeannette, 1880-1973

Woelfle, Gretchen. Jeannette Rankin; political pioneer. Calkins Creek Books 2007 104p il $18.95
*

Grades: 6 7 8 9   92

Rankin, Jeannette, 1880-1973—*Continued*
1. Women politicians 2. Feminism
ISBN 978-1-59078-437-2
Jeannette Rankin "was Montana's representative in Congress before women in other states even had the right to vote. Woelfle does a terrific job introducing Rankin. . . . The high standard of writing is matched by the book's format. Informative sidebars are well integrated, and from the intense portrait on the cover to the well-chosen photos and historical material, the volume offers interesting things to look at on every page." Booklist

Rasputin, Grigoriĭ Efimovich, 1871-1916
Goldberg, Enid A. Grigory Rasputin; holy man or mad monk? [by] Enid A. Goldberg & Norman Itzkowitz. Scholastic 2008 128p il map (Wicked history) lib bdg $30
Grades: 6 7 8 9   92
1. Russia—History
ISBN 978-0-531-12594-6 (lib bdg); 0-531-12594-7 (lib bdg)   LC 2007001692
"This engaging, thought-provoking book provides a chronological account of Rasputin's life as well as the historical background necessary to understand it in context. Was Rasputin a holy man, or was he simply a philandering charlatan who rose to power because of his unique relationship with Tsar Nicholas and Tsarina Alexandra? . . . Captioned, black-and-white period photographs enhance the text. Recommended for both curricular pursuits and pleasure reading." SLJ
Includes glossary and bibliographical references

Rawlings, Marjorie Kinnan, 1896-1953
Cook, Judy. Natural writer: a story about Marjorie Kinnan Rawlings; by Judy Cook and Laura Lee Smith; illustrated by Laurie Harden. Carolrhoda Bks. 2001 64p il (Creative minds biography) lib bdg $21.27
Grades: 4 5 6   92
1. Authors, American 2. Women authors 3. Frontier and pioneer life
ISBN 1-57505-468-X   LC 00-9657
"This biography begins with Rawling's childhood in the early 1900s and shows her development as a writer through her death. . . . This easy-to-read biography has an attractive cover and a full-page charcoal illustration in each chapter." SLJ
Includes bibliographical references

Ray, Rachael
Abrams, Dennis. Rachael Ray; food entrepreneur. Chelsea House Publishers 2009 128p bibl il por (Women of achievement) lib bdg $30
*
Grades: 6 7 8 9   92
1. Cooks
ISBN 978-1-60413-078-2 (lib bdg); 1-60413-078-4 (lib bdg)   LC 2008034642
"Rachael Ray will be familiar to kids for her talk show and other television appearances, and that will draw them in. But once there, they'll respond to the story of Ray. . . . As a cook who never went to culinary

school, Ray knows that her career is an unlikely one. Abrams does a particularly good job of capturing that unpredictability as well as Ray's uniquely exuberant personality. . . . Enjoyable and useful." Booklist
Includes bibliographical references

Reagan, Ronald, 1911-2004
Sutherland, James. Ronald Reagan; a twentieth century life. Penguin Group 2008 252p il (Up close) $16.99
Grades: 6 7 8 9 10   92
1. Presidents—United States
ISBN 978-0-670-06345-1; 0-670-06345-2
                                            LC 2008-021328
"Both a character portrait and an account of Ronald Reagan's life and career(s), this profile sheds as much light on his goals and outlook as it does on his accomplishments. . . . This entry in the valuable Up Close series is a thought-provoking alternative to the plethora of routine assignment titles." Booklist

Reiss, Johanna
Reiss, Johanna. The journey back. Crowell 1976 212p hardcover o.p. pa $17.95
Grades: 5 6 7 8 9 10   92
1. Jews—Netherlands
ISBN 978-0-690-01252-1; 978-0-59543-050-5 (pa)
Sequel to The upstairs room
"The journey is the return home in the spring of 1945 for thirteen-year-old Annie and her older sister Sini. . . . The background of the early years is recapitulated. . . . The book offers an intensely provocative story, recalling many personal crises and tests of human nature cruelly beset by the dangers and deprivations of war." Horn Book

Reiss, Johanna. The upstairs room. Crowell 1972 273p $19.99; pa $5.99 *
Grades: 5 6 7 8 9 10   92
1. World War, 1939-1945—Jews 2. Netherlands—History—1940-1945, German occupation 3. Jews—Netherlands 4. Holocaust, 1933-1945—Personal narratives
ISBN 0-690-85127-8; 0-06-440370-X (pa)
A Newbery Medal honor book, 1973
"In a vital, moving account the author recalls her experiences as a Jewish child hiding from the Germans occupying her native Holland during World War II. . . . Ten-year-old Annie and her twenty-year-old sister Sini, . . . are taken in by a Dutch farmer, his wife, and mother who hide the girls in an upstairs room of the farm house. Written from the perspective of a child the story affords a child's-eye-view of the war." Booklist
Followed by The journey back

Rembert, Winfred
Rembert, Winfred. Don't hold me back; my life and art; with Charles and Rosalie Baker. Cricket Books 2003 40p il $19.95
Grades: 4 5 6 7   92
1. African Americans—Biography 2. African American artists
ISBN 0-8126-2703-2   LC 2003-9980
"A Marcato book"

Rembert, Winfred—*Continued*

Through words and paintings, an artist tells about growing up on a cotton plantation in Cuthbert, Georgia, serving time in prison for his actions during a civil rights demonstration, and finding a purpose and direction in life.

"Rembert's unusual pictures are classified as 'outsider art.' . . . Each one is a piece of leather that has been carved, tooled, and dyed with rich colors. . . . This beautifully designed, very accessible book offers a vivid impression of an African American man's experiences in the mid-twentieth-century South." Booklist

Includes bibliographical references

Rembrandt Harmenszoon van Rijn, 1606-1669

Roberts, Russell. Rembrandt; [by] Russell Roberts. Mitchell Lane 2009 48p il (Art profiles for kids) lib bdg $20.95

Grades: 7 8 9 10   92

1. Artists, Dutch

ISBN 978-1-58415-710-6 (lib bdg); 1-58415-710-0 (lib bdg)   LC 2008-2241

"Tracks the artist's rise to fame and the bitter years and bankruptcy that followed. . . . [Goes] beyond basic facts, providing historical context and significance of the art and the artist. . . . Provide[s] plenty of information for reports in a reader-friendly format." SLJ

Includes glossary and bibliographical references

Renoir, Auguste, 1841-1919

Somervill, Barbara A. Pierre-Auguste Renoir; [by] Barbara Somervill. Mitchell Lane 2007 48p il (Art profiles for kids) lib bdg $29.95

Grades: 5 6 7 8   92

1. Artists, French

ISBN 978-1-58415-566-9 (lib bdg); 1-58415-566-3 (lib bdg)   LC 2007000661

Profiles the famous French artist best known for his portraits and his paintings such as "The Luncheon of the Boating Party" that depict people enjoying themselves

"The glossy pages allow for good reproductions of paintings as well as a few photos. . . . Back matter includes a glossary, chronology, chapter notes for quotes, lists of books and Internet sites, and a Timeline in History . . . offers a concise, readable account of the artist's life." Booklist

Includes glossary and bibliographical references

Revere, Paul, 1735-1818

Giblin, James. The many rides of Paul Revere; by James Cross Giblin. Scholastic Press 2007 85p il map $17.99 *

Grades: 4 5 6 7   92

1. United States—History—1775-1783, Revolution

ISBN 978-0-439-57290-3; 0-439-57290-8   LC 2006-38369

"This well-organized biography presents a lucid account of Revere's childhood, his limited education, his training in his father's workshop, his brief military career, and his adult life as a silversmith, family man, and Revolutionary War leader. . . . Giblin presents salient facts and intriguing details to create a well-rounded and

credible image of the man. Among the many illustrations are period portraits, narrative paintings, engravings, drawings, and maps as well as photos of significant sites and artifacts." Booklist

Includes bibliographical references

Rhodes-Courter, Ashley Marie

Rhodes-Courter, Ashley Marie. Three little words; a memoir. Atheneum Books for Young Readers 2008 304p il $17.99

Grades: 8 9 10 11 12 Adult   92

1. Adopted children 2. Foster children 3. Foster home care

ISBN 978-1-4169-4806-3; 1-4169-4806-6   LC 2007-21629

The author "chronicles her hardscrabble childhood in foster care, detailing glitches in the system and infringements of laws that led to a string of unsuitable—and sometimes nightmarish—placements for her and her younger half-brother, Luke. Using a matter-of-fact tone at times laced with bitterness, the author recounts how she was wrenched away from her teenage mother at age three and was later removed from her unstable grandfather's home to live in cramped quarters with strangers." Publ Wkly

"This memoir lends a powerful voice to thousands of 'boomerang kids' who repeatedly wind up back in foster care." SLJ

Rice, Condoleezza, 1954-

Hubbard-Brown, Janet. Condoleezza Rice; [stateswoman]; [by] Janet Hubbard-Brown. Chelsea House Publishers 2008 113p il (Black Americans of achievement) lib bdg $30

Grades: 6 7 8 9   92

1. Statesmen 2. African American women—Biography 3. Women politicians

ISBN 978-0-7910-9715-1 (lib bdg); 0-7910-9715-3 (lib bdg)   LC 2007035678

This biography details the African American stateswoman's "rise from adversity to . . . recognition. The [book goes] beyond the typical personal information to provide some social history relevant to the subject's time. Captioned photographs and boxed inserts enhance the conversational [text]." Horn Book Guide

Includes bibliographical references

Rivera, Diego, 1886-1957

Hillstrom, Kevin. Diego Rivera; muralist; by Kevin Hillstrom. Lucent Books 2008 104p il (The twentieth century's most influential Hispanics) lib bdg $32.45

Grades: 6 7 8 9 10   92

1. Artists, Mexican

ISBN 978-1-4205-0018-9 (lib bdg); 1-4205-0018-X (lib bdg)   LC 2007-32104

"Rivera's life, beginnning with his childhood, is placed in the context of the artistic, political, and economic influences on family and his career. . . . The layout draws the eye with colorful headings and highlighted quotes." Libr Media Connect

Includes bibliographical references

Rivera, Diego, 1886-1957—*Continued*

Litwin, Laura Baskes. Diego Rivera; legendary Mexican painter; [by] Laura Baskes Litwin. 1st ed. Enslow Pub. 2005 128p il (Latino biography library) lib bdg $31.93

Grades: 7 8 9 10 **92**
1. Artists, Mexican
ISBN 0-7660-2486-5   LC 2004027540

A biography of the Mexican painter known for his murals and revolutionary politics

"Accessible, well-documented. . . . Litwin's clear, straightforward language includes succinct references to the background political and cultural history. . . . Archival photos and color reproductions of Rivera's works are among the illustrations." Booklist

Includes bibliographical references

Sabbeth, Carol. Frida Kahlo and Diego Rivera: their lives and ideas. See entry under Kahlo, Frida, 1907-1954

Rizal, José, 1861-1896

Arruda, Suzanne Middendorf. Freedom's martyr; the story of Jose Rizal, national hero of the Phillipines; [by] Suzanne Middendorf Arruda. Avisson Press 2003 106p il (Avisson young adult series) pa $19.95

Grades: 7 8 9 10 **92**
1. Philippines
ISBN 1-88810-555-0   LC 2003-45320

"Born in the Philippines on June 19, 1861, Rizal was executed by the Spanish for treason on December 30, 1896. . . . Rizal wanted representation for native peoples in the Spanish government and wrote three novels and several poems detailing their plight. . . . This well-written, readable biography will prove useful for reports and background information on the history of the Philippines." SLJ

Includes bibliographical references

Robeson, Paul, 1898-1976

Wright, David K. Paul Robeson; actor, singer, political activist. Enslow Pubs. 1998 128p il (African-American biographies) $26.60

Grades: 5 6 7 8 **92**
1. African Americans—Biography
ISBN 0-89490-944-4   LC 97-34194

"This book chronicles the life of 'actor, singer, political activist' Paul Robeson, and the times and country that shaped him. While style and format are targeted at young YAs, older teens doing reports will find much of value here. In addition to the index, further reading and notes on each chapter, there is also a discography, filmography and chronology of Robeson's life." BAYA Book Rev

Includes bibliographical references

Robinson, Jackie, 1919-1972

Robinson, Sharon. Promises to keep: how Jackie Robinson changed America. Scholastic 2004 64p il $16.95 *

Grades: 4 5 6 7 **92**
1. Baseball—Biography 2. African American athletes
ISBN 0-439-42592-1   LC 2003-42709

"Robinson's daughter, Sharon, describes her father's youth, his rise to become major-league baseball's first African American player, and his involvement in the civil rights movement. . . . Her private view of her father's accomplishments, placed within the context of American sports and social history, makes for absorbing reading. An excellent selection of family and team photographs and other materials . . . illustrate this fine tribute." Booklist

Wukovits, John F. Jackie Robinson and the integration of baseball; [by] John F. Wukovits. Lucent Books 2007 104p il (Lucent library of Black history) $28.70

Grades: 7 8 9 10 **92**
1. Baseball—Biography 2. African American athletes
ISBN 1-59018-913-2; 978-1-59018-913-9
          LC 2006010831

"Wukovits does a credible job of adding historical perspective to a straightforward account of Robinson's life and accomplishments. He sets the stage by focusing on baseball's history of racial exclusion, and on the discrimination faced by the athlete and his family. He covers Robinson's military career and his brief stint in the Negro Leagues before he signed with the Brooklyn Dodgers. Robinson's triumphant career in the major leagues and his later life are detailed as well. This is a well-researched and concise account." SLJ

Includes bibliographical references

Rockefeller, John D. (John Davison), 1839-1937

Segall, Grant. John D. Rockefeller; anointed with oil. Oxford University Press 2000 125p il (Oxford portraits) $28

Grades: 7 8 9 10 **92**
1. Capitalists and financiers 2. Philanthropists
ISBN 0-19-512147-3   LC 00-44616

This biography presents a "view of the man, his business and personal interests, and his philanthropic legacy." Booklist

"Included in the biography are some primary documents, such as letters, photos, and cartoons, as well as references to some of the other giants of industry, such as Flagler, Carnegie, and Gould." Book Rep

Includes bibliographical references

Rockwell, Norman, 1894-1978

Gherman, Beverly. Norman Rockwell; storyteller with a brush. Atheneum Bks. for Young Readers 2000 57p il $19.95

Grades: 4 5 6 7 **92**
1. Artists—United States
ISBN 0-689-82001-1   LC 98-36546

Describes the life and work of the popular American artist who depicted both traditional and contemporary subjects, including children, family scenes, astronauts, and the poor

"The format of the biography is appealing and attractive. The pages are replete with color reproductions of Rockwell's paintings as well as photographs of the man and his family. The text is well researched and authentic; the writing style is free-flowing and the words capture the naturalness of Rockwell's paintings." SLJ

Includes bibliographical references

Roosevelt, Eleanor, 1884-1962

Fleming, Candace. Our Eleanor; a scrapbook look at Eleanor Roosevelt's remarkable life. Atheneum Books for Young Readers 2005 176p il $19.95 *

Grades: 5 6 7 8   **92**
1. Presidents' spouses—United States
ISBN 0-689-86544-9   LC 2004-22825
"An Anne Schwartz book"

Told in scrapbook style, this biography looks behind the politics to present First Lady Eleanor Roosevelt in her many roles: wife and mother, United Nations delegate, popular columnist, civil rights crusader, and champion of the underprivileged.

"Each of the seven chapters leads readers through the subject's busy life with short sections of text filled with well-documented first-person accounts and direct quotes. . . . Not a spread goes by without incredible archival photographs or reproductions, newspaper and magazine clippings, handwritten letters, and diary entries. . . . They all provide relevant and fascinating insight." SLJ

Freedman, Russell. Eleanor Roosevelt; a life of discovery. Clarion Bks. 1993 198p il $17.95; pa $10.95 *

Grades: 5 6 7 8 9 10   **92**
1. Presidents' spouses—United States
ISBN 0-89919-862-7; 0-395-84520-3 (pa)
     LC 92-25024

A Newbery Medal honor book, 1994

This "traces the life of the former First Lady from her early childhood through the tumultuous years in the White House to her active role in the founding of the United Nations after World War II." Publisher's note

"This impeccably researched, highly readable study of one of this country's greatest First Ladies is nonfiction at its best. . . . Approximately 140 well-chosen black-and-white photos amplify the text." Publ Wkly

Includes bibliographical references

MacLeod, Elizabeth. Eleanor Roosevelt; an inspiring life; written by Elizabeth MacLeod. Kids Can Press 2006 32p il (Snapshots) $14.95; pa $6.95

Grades: 4 5 6   **92**
1. Presidents' spouses—United States
ISBN   978-1-55337-778-8;   1-55337-778-8; 978-1-55337-811-2 (pa); 1-55337-811-3 (pa)

"Fourteen short chapters take readers from Roosevelt's privileged but sad childhood through her marriage, political and family life, and post-FDR humanitarian work. . . . The period photographs . . . [are] plentiful and engrossing. . . . This attractive title will appeal to browsers and report writers." SLJ

Roosevelt, Franklin D. (Franklin Delano), 1882-1945

Elish, Dan. Franklin Delano Roosevelt. Marshall Cavendish Benchmark 2009 96p il (Presidents and their times) $23.95

Grades: 5 6 7 8   **92**
1. Presidents—United States 2. United States—Politics and government—1933-1945
ISBN 978-0-7614-2841-1; 0-7614-2841-0
     LC 2007-25619

"Provides comprehensive information on President Franklin Delano Roosevelt and places him within his historical and cultural context. Also explored are the formative events of his times and how he responded." Publisher's note

Includes glossary and bibliographical references

Freedman, Russell. Franklin Delano Roosevelt. Clarion Bks. 1990 200p il $20; pa $9.95 *

Grades: 5 6 7 8 9 10   **92**
1. Presidents—United States 2. United States—Politics and government—1933-1945
ISBN 0-89919-379-X; 0-395-62978-0 (pa)
     LC 89-34986

The author "traces the personal and public events in a life that led to the formation of one of the most influential and magnetic leaders of the twentieth century." Horn Book

"The carefully researched, highly readable text and extremely effective coordination of black-and-white photographs chronicle Roosevelt's priviledged youth, his early influences, and his maturation. . . . Even students with little or no background in American history will find this an intriguing and inspirational human portrait." SLJ

Includes bibliographical references

Panchyk, Richard. Franklin Delano Roosevelt for kids; his life and times with 21 activities; [by] Richard Panchyk. 1st ed. Chicago Review Press 2007 147p il pa $14.95

Grades: 4 5 6 7   **92**
1. Presidents—United States 2. United States—Politics and government—1933-1945
ISBN 978-1-55652-657-2 (pa); 1-55652-657-1 (pa)
     LC 2007003484

"Franklin Delano Roosevelt's enduring legacy upon the history, culture, politics, and economics of the United States is introduced to children in this . . . activity book." Publisher's note

"There are many interesting photos . . . and they are all sufficiently captioned. . . . Information about the Roosevelts [is] presented in a lively, engaging manner." SLJ

Includes bibliographical references

Roosevelt, Theodore, 1858-1919

Cooper, Michael L. Theodore Roosevelt. Viking 2009 il (Up close) $16.99 *

Grades: 7 8 9 10   **92**
1. Presidents—United States
ISBN 978-0-670-01134-6; 0-670-01134-7

"This biography presents an evenhanded account of the life and presidency of Theodore Roosevelt. . . . This clearly written biography includes many anecdotes and well-chosen quotes that help bring Roosevelt to life. . . . Cooper offers a solid portrayal of this noteworthy American president." Booklist

Includes biblographical references

Fritz, Jean. Bully for you, Teddy Roosevelt! illustrations by Mike Wimmer. Putnam 1991 127p il hardcover o.p. pa $5.99 *

Grades: 5 6 7 8   **92**
1. Presidents—United States
ISBN 0-399-21769-X; 0-698-11609-7 (pa)
     LC 90-8142

Roosevelt, Theodore, 1858-1919—*Continued*

Follows the life of the twenty-sixth president, discussing his conservation work, hunting expeditions, family life, and political career

"Jean Fritz gives a rounded picture of her subject and deftly blends the story of a person and a picture of an era." Bull Cent Child Books

Includes bibliographical references

Harness, Cheryl. The remarkable, rough-riding life of Theodore Roosevelt and the rise of empire America; painstakingly written and illustrated by Cheryl Harness. National Geographic 2007 144p il map $16.95; lib bdg $25.90

Grades: 4 5 6 7   92

1. Presidents—United States
ISBN   978-1-4263-0008-0;   1-4263-0008-5;
978-1-4263-0009-7 (lib bdg); 1-4263-0009-3 (lib bdg)
LC 2006029039

"Animated writing and intricate black-and-white illustrations drive this biography of the ever-enthusiastic twenty-sixth president of the United States. An extensive running timeline at the bottom of the pages emphasizes the dramatic changes that occurred during Roosevelt's life. The book is jam-packed with information." Horn Book Guide

Includes bibliographical references

Kraft, Betsy Harvey. Theodore Roosevelt; champion of the American spirit. Clarion Bks. 2003 180p il $19

Grades: 5 6 7 8   92

1. Presidents—United States
ISBN 0-618-14264-9   LC 2002-152825

A biography of the energetic New Yorker who became the twenty-sixth president of the United States and who once exclaimed "No one has ever enjoyed life more than I have"

"Interwoven with the well-told story of Roosevelt's public activities is Kraft's vivid portrayal of his personal life, laced with anecdotes and quotations (mainly from letters) that help bring the famous figure to life. The spacious layout and the many black-and-white reproductions of photos, drawings, and prints add to the book's appeal." Booklist

Includes bibliographical references

Marrin, Albert. The great adventure: Theodore Roosevelt and the rise of modern America. Dutton Children's Books 2007 248p il $30 *

Grades: 8 9 10 11   92

1. Presidents—United States
ISBN 978-0-525-47659-7; 0-525-47659-8
LC 2006-35912

"Marrin offers a twin portrait of American society in a time of profound change and the life of a figure so dominant in the politics and self-image of the time that he has become an enduring symbol. . . . Marrin gives him 'a place in the front rank of our country's heroes,' particularly for his achievements in environmental conservation, but also shows him acting badly. . . . Numerous endnotes and contemporary photos and prints add to this scholarly profile, which . . . will give serious history students a solid grounding in the man's times, career, and forceful character." Booklist

Includes bibliographical references

Rowling, J. K.

Chippendale, Lisa A. Triumph of the imagination: the story of writer J.K. Rowling; introduction by James Scott Brady. Chelsea House 2002 112p il (Overcoming adversity) lib bdg $22.95

Grades: 5 6 7 8   92

1. Authors, English 2. Women authors
ISBN 0-7910-6312-7   LC 2001-47604

"This title blends biographical data, literary review, and the effects of the 'Harry Potter' books on the world, written at a reading level that is accessible to many of Rowling's fans." SLJ

Includes bibliographical references

Harmin, Karen Leigh. J. K. Rowling; author of Harry Potter; [by] Karen Leigh Harmin. Enslow Publishers 2006 128p bibl il por (People to know today) lib bdg $31.93

Grades: 4 5 6 7   92

1. Women authors 2. Authors, English
ISBN 0-7660-1850-4   LC 2005020400

This introduces the author of the Harry Potter book series.

"Well researched and clearly written. . . . Attactively designed, the book includes a number of excellent color photos as well as informative sidebars . . . Up-to-date and very readable." Booklist

Includes bibliographical references

Sickels, Amy. Mythmaker: the story of J.K. Rowling; foreword by Kyle Zimmer. 2nd ed. Chelsea House Pubs. 2008 136p bibl il por (Who wrote that?) lib bdg $30

Grades: 5 6 7 8   92

1. Authors, English 2. Women authors
ISBN 978-0-7910-9632-1 (lib bdg); 0-7910-9632-7 (lib bdg)   LC 2008001202

A revised edition of Mythmaker by Charles J. Shields published 2002

"Sickels discusses the plots of the 'Harry Potter' novels and delves into Rowling's life story. The text concludes with extensive notes and lists of works by Rowling, popular Potter characters, major awards, and so on." SLJ

"Useful for report writers and aspiring authors." Horn Book Guide

Includes bibliographical references

Runyon, Brent

Runyon, Brent. The burn journals. Alfred A. Knopf 2004 373p $17.95; lib bdg $18.99; pa $13.95

Grades: 7 8 9 10   92

1. Burns and scalds 2. Suicide
ISBN 0-375-82621-1; 0-375-92621-6 (lib bdg);
1-4000-9642-1 (pa)   LC 2004-5643

"One February day in 1991, Runyon came home from eighth grade . . . and set himself on fire. . . . The dialogue between Runyon and his nurses, parents, and especially his hapless psychotherapists is natural and believable, and his inner dialogue is flip, often funny, and sometimes raw. . . . The authentically adolescent voice of the journals will engage even those reluctant to read such a dark story." SLJ

Rustin, Bayard, 1910-1987

Brimner, Larry Dane. We are one: the story of Bayard Rustin. Calkins Creek 2007 48p il $17.95 *

Grades: 5 6 7 8   92

1. African Americans—Civil rights 2. African Americans—Biography

ISBN 1-59078-498-7

"Brimner sets Rustin's personal story against the history of segregation in his time and focuses on his leadership role . . . in the struggle for civil rights. On each page, the clearly written, informal text is accompanied by eloquently captioned archival photos." Booklist

Includes bibliographical references

Miller, Calvin Craig. No easy answers; Bayard Rustin and the civil rights movement. Morgan Reynolds Pub. 2005 160p il lib bdg $24.95 *

Grades: 7 8 9 10   92

1. African Americans—Civil rights 2. African Americans—Biography

ISBN 1-931798-43-5   LC 2004-18518

"Miller combines the life story of a great social activist with the history of the struggle for civil rights in the U.S. The politics are exciting, with details of the radical campaigns in the 1940s and 1950s, Rustin's impassioned call for nonviolent protest, and his role in organizing both the Montgomery Bus Boycott and the 1963 March on Washington." Booklist

Includes bibliographical references

Ruth, Babe, 1895-1948

Hampton, Wilborn. Babe Ruth; a twentieth-century life. Viking 2009 203p il (Up close) $16.99

Grades: 6 7 8 9 10   92

1. Baseball—Biography

ISBN 978-0-670-06305-5; 0-670-06305-3
                                     LC 2008-21550

"Hampton announces early in this biography of Babe Ruth that his emphasis is on separating fact from legend, and he is not afraid to dig up some of the more tawdry aspects of the slugger's life. . . . The focus here is on Ruth's sad early life and his career as a pitcher with the Boston Red Sox. Throughout, an attempt is made to give some sense of the grace, power, and skill of Ruth on the field. . . . This title . . . illustrated with a nice selection of photos, has the advantage of telling the complete, unvarnished story in a snappy, concise style." Booklist

Includes bibliographical references

Rutherford, Ernest, 1871-1937

Pasachoff, Naomi E. Ernest Rutherford; father of nuclear science; [by] Naomi Pasachoff. Enslow Publishers 2005 128p il (Great minds of science) lib bdg $26.60

Grades: 5 6 7 8   92

1. Physicists

ISBN 0-7660-2441-5   LC 2004-13402

"Pasachoff details how Rutherford rose from early childhood poverty in rural New Zealand to become one of the world's greatest scientists. His groundbreaking discoveries include elements' mutability and radioactivity and the nuclear structure of the atom. The experiments behind these discoveries are carefully explained. . . . Pasachoff's book not only introduces students to nuclear physics and the life of Rutherford, but may also instill in them the joys and rewards of learning." SLJ

Sacagawea, b. 1786

Crosby, Michael T. Sacagawea; shoshone explorer; [by] Michael T. Crosby. OTTN Pub. 2008 144p il map (Shapers of America) lib bdg $25.95

Grades: 6 7 8 9 10   92

1. Lewis and Clark Expedition (1804-1806) 2. Shoshoni Indians 3. West (U.S.)—Biography

ISBN 978-1-59556-026-1 (lib bdg); 1-59556-026-2 (lib bdg)   LC 2007-24698

"This attractive title introduces the young Shoshone woman who accompanied the Lewis and Clark Expedition. . . . Full of clear maps, historical paintings, reproductions of period documents (including journals), and color photographs of landmarks along the route, this is a visually attractive package. . . . Detailed endnotes show the depth of the author's research, and the suggested reading includes books for both younger and older students and Internet sources." SLJ

Includes glossary and bibliographical references

St. George, Judith. Sacagawea. Putnam 1997 115p maps $16.99

Grades: 4 5 6   92

1. Lewis and Clark Expedition (1804-1806) 2. Shoshoni Indians

ISBN 0-399-23161-7   LC 96-49311

Tells the story of the Shoshoni Indian girl who served as interpreter, peacemaker, and guide for the Lewis and Clark Expedition to the Northwest in 1805-1806

"In a well-written and well-researched account, St. George humanizes her subject. . . . Adventure lovers will find much to like in the book." Booklist

Includes bibliographical references

Sachar, Louis, 1954-

Greene, Meg. Louis Sachar. Rosen Pub. Group 2004 112p il (Library of author biographies) lib bdg $26.50

Grades: 5 6 7 8   92

1. Authors, American

ISBN 0-8239-4017-9   LC 2002-154252

Contents: Meet Louis Sachar; "Louis the yard teacher"; Success; From middle school to grade school; Holes; How does he do it?; Interview with Louis Sachar; Timeline

Discusses life and work of the popular children's author, including his writing process and methods, inspirations, a critical discussion of his books, biographical timeline, and awards

A "solid [introduction]. . . . Libraries looking to expand their biography section will be well served by [this] informative [title]." SLJ

Includes bibliographical references

Saint-Georges, Joseph Boulogne, chevalier de, 1745-1799

Brewster, Hugh. The other Mozart; the life of the famous Chevalier de Saint George; [by] Hugh Brewster; illustrated by Eric Velasquez. Abrams Books for Young Readers 2007 48p il $18.95

Grades: 4 5 6 7 **92**
1. Composers 2. Racially mixed people 3. Nobility
ISBN 0-8109-5720-5; 978-0-8109-5720-6
LC 2006-07488

"Born to a white plantation owner and a black slave in eighteenth-century Guadeloupe, Joseph Bologne grew up to become the Chevalier de Saint-George, one of France's most accomplished composers. In this picture-book biography for middle-graders, Brewster introduces his subject's fascinating life. . . . Archival images and Velasquez's arresting full-page portraits will captivate many young readers." Booklist

Saladin, Sultan of Egypt and Syria, 1137-1193

Geyer, Flora. Saladin; the Muslim Warrior who defended his people. National Geographic 2006 64p il map (World history biographies) $17.95; lib bdg $27.90 *

Grades: 4 5 6 7 **92**
1. Crusades 2. Kings and rulers
ISBN 0-7922-5535-6; 0-7922-5536-4 (lib bdg)

Presents an illustrated biography Saladin, from his birth into a prominent Kurdish family in Tikrit, Mesopotamia, in 1138, through his wars to regain holy lands in and around Jerusalem, to his death in Damascus on March 4, 1193.

Includes glossary and bibliographical references

Stanley, Diane. Saladin: noble prince of Islam. HarperCollins Pubs. 2002 unp il $16.99; lib bdg $18.89 *

Grades: 4 5 6 7 **92**
1. Crusades 2. Kings and rulers
ISBN 0-688-17135-4; 0-688-17136-2 (lib bdg)
LC 2001-24636

A biography of the Islamic leader who defended his people during the Crusades

The author demonstrates "her trademark ability to research and then distill complex topics in terms accessible to middle-graders. . . . Stanley's precise, detailed artwork pays homage to period architecture. She evokes the colors of Persian miniatures (and medieval stained glass) as her paintings incorporate the complex patterning associated with Islamic art." Publ Wkly

Includes glossary and bibliographical references

Salisbury, Graham, 1944-

Gill, David Macinnis. Graham Salisbury; island boy; David Macinnis Gill. Scarecrow Press 2005 109p (Scarecrow studies in young adult literature) $35 *

Grades: 7 8 9 10 **92**
1. Authors, American
ISBN 0-8108-5338-8 LC 2004031042

"Part literary analysis and part biography, this is a well-balanced look at an unusual talent, a writer who has

an eye for the frailties of life and the rites of adolescence. Gill discusses how growing up in Hawaii in the '50s influenced Salisbury's writing and does a fine job of showing the complexity of his work." SLJ

Includes bibliographical references

Salk, Jonas, 1914-1995

Sherrow, Victoria. Jonas Salk; beyond the microscope. 2nd rev ed. Chelsea House 2008 146p il (Makers of modern science) $35

Grades: 7 8 9 10 **92**
1. Scientists 2. Poliomyelitis vaccine
ISBN 978-0-8160-6180-8; 0-8160-6180-7
LC 2006-33429

First published 1993 by Facts on File

This biography of Jonas Salk "describes this respected immunologist's medical research and his lifelong efforts to promote scientific and human progress on a global scale." Publisher's note

Includes glossary and bibliographical references

Tocci, Salvatore. Jonas Salk; creator of the polio vaccine. Enslow Pubs. 2003 128p il (Great minds of science) lib bdg $20.95

Grades: 5 6 7 8 **92**
1. Scientists 2. Poliomyelitis vaccine
ISBN 0-7660-2097-5 LC 2002-3888

Contents: Innocent victims; Survival and success; A change of plans; Relationships; His own project; His next project; The polio vaccine; The polio pioneers; An American hero

A biography of the American doctor and medical researcher who helped to develop successful influenza and polio vaccines, then turned his attention to vaccines for cancer and AIDS prevention

This is an "effective volume. . . . Tocci does a good job of showing how the fear of polio affected the public during the 1950s." Booklist

Includes glossary and bibliographical references

Santana, Carlos, 1947-

Slavicek, Louise Chipley. Carlos Santana. Chelsea House Publishers 2006 120p il (Great Hispanic heritage) lib bdg $30

Grades: 6 7 8 9 **92**
1. Rock musicians 2. Mexican Americans—Biography
ISBN 978-0-7910-8844-9 (lib bdg); 0-7910-8844-8 (lib bdg)
LC 2005026000

This biography of rock musician Santana is filled "with excellent details—music and familial [history sheds] light on the man's roots and focus strongly on his humanitarian efforts. . . . Color photos and sidebars add interest, and quotes from magazines, newspapers, and interviews are meticulously cited in the endnotes." SLJ

Includes bibliographical references

Sarkozy, Nicolas, 1955-

Abrams, Dennis. Nicolas Sarkozy. Chelsea House 2009 136p il (Modern world leaders) lib bdg $30

Grades: 6 7 8 9 **92**
1. Presidents 2. France—Politics and government
ISBN 978-1-60413-081-2 (lib bdg); 1-60413-081-4 (lib bdg)
LC 2008-26567

Sarkozy, Nicolas, 1955-—*Continued*
"Examines the life and career of the president of France." Publisher's note
"Abrams deftly explores both the personal and public spheres of this 'most untraditional politician.' . . . Probing, evenhanded." Booklist
Includes bibliographical references

Schaller, George B.
Turner, Pamela S. A life in the wild; George Schaller's struggle to save the last great beasts. Farrar, Straus, and Giroux 2008 103p il map $21.95 *
Grades: 5 6 7 8   92
1. Zoologists 2. Wildlife conservation
ISBN 978-0-374-34578-5; 0-374-34578-3
                                            LC 2007-42844
"Melanie Kroupa books"
"The author interviewed Schaller and had access to his photos, which allowed her to capture beautifully the spirit of Schaller's work. The book is organized chronologically, and each chapter covers a geographic area and the principal animals that Schaller studied there. . . . Animal lovers and conservation-minded students will enjoy this excellent introduction to Schaller and his ideals." Voice Youth Advocates
Includes bibliographical references

Schulke, Flip
Schulke, Flip. Witness to our times; my life as a photojournalist; [by] Flip Schulke; in association with Matt Schudel. Cricket Books 2003 112p il $19.95
Grades: 8 9 10 11 12   92
1. Photographers
ISBN 0-8126-2682-6   LC 2002-151457
"A Marcato book"
Contents: Early years; The divine seed of discontent; The hardest pictures I ever took; The greatest man I ever met; Views of a troubled age; The space race and beyond; A life in pictures
An autobiography of a man whose documentary photographs in American magazines helped to shape public opinion on such issues as the civil rights movement and the space race
"Photojournalist Schulke shot some of the most important photographs of the twentieth century, and the passion, concentration, and sensitivity that characterize his photos come across as powerfully in his prose. . . . His black-and-white photos make up most of the book, and they express such strong emotion that readers will feel the depth of his passion even on pages without a word of text." Booklist
Includes bibliographical references

Schumann, Clara, 1819-1896
Reich, Susanna. Clara Schumann; piano virtuoso. Clarion Bks. 1999 118p il $18; pa $9.95 *
Grades: 5 6 7 8   92
1. Pianists 2. Women composers
ISBN 0-395-89119-1; 0-618-55160-3 (pa)
                                            LC 98-24510

Describes the life of the German pianist and composer who made her professional debut at age nine and who devoted her life to music and to her family
"This thoroughly researched book draws on primary sources, both Clara's own diaries and her voluminous correspondence with her husband. . . . Reich's lucid, quietly passionate biography is liberally illustrated with photographs and reproductions." Horn Book Guide

Schutz, Samantha, 1978-
Schutz, Samantha. I don't want to be crazy; a memoir of anxiety disorder. PUSH Books 2006 280p $16.99
Grades: 8 9 10 11 12   92
1. Anxiety 2. Panic disorders
ISBN 0-439-80518-X   LC 2005028964
"In this moving memoir, Schutz details her struggle with anxiety disorder. . . . Written in verse, this memoir successfully conveys what it is like to suffer from panic attacks." Voice Youth Advocates

Schwarzenegger, Arnold
Young, Jeff C. Arnold Schwarzenegger; by Jeff C. Young. Morgan Reynolds Pub. 2007 112p il map (Political profiles) lib bdg $27.95
Grades: 6 7 8 9   92
1. Governors 2. California—Politics and government 3. Bodybuilders 4. Actors
ISBN 978-1-59935-050-9 (lib bdg); 1-59935-050-5 (lib bdg)   LC 2007020841
A biography of the Governor of California, and former actor and body builder.
Includes bibliographical references

Scieszka, Jon, 1954-
Scieszka, Jon. Knucklehead; tall tales and mostly true stories of growing up Scieszka. Viking 2008 106p il $16.99; pa $12.99
Grades: 4 5 6 7   92
1. Authors, American
ISBN   978-0-670-01106-3;   0-670-01106-1; 978-0-670-01138-4 (pa); 0-670-01138-X (pa)
                                            LC 2008-16870
"Scieszka . . . has written an autobiography about boys, for boys and anyone else interested in baseball, fire and peeing on stuff. . . . The text is divided into two- to three- page nonsequential chapters and peppered with scrapbook snapshots and comic-book-ad reproductions. . . . By themselves, the chapters entertain with abrupt, vulgar fun. Taken together, they offer a look at the makings of one very funny author." Booklist

Selkirk, Alexander, 1676-1721
Kraske, Robert. Marooned; the strange but true adventures of Alexander Selkirk, the real Robinson Crusoe; illustrated by Robert Andrew Parker. Clarion Books 2005 120p il map $15
Grades: 5 6 7 8   92
1. Survival after airplane accidents, shipwrecks, etc.
ISBN 0-618-56843-3   LC 2004-28769

Selkirk, Alexander, 1676-1721—*Continued*
"In 1704, English sailing master Alexander Selkirk was marooned on Juan Fernandez, an isolated Pacific island. . . . In 1709, two English ships rescued him, hired him as a second mate, and later captured a Spanish treasure ship. . . . Kraske offers a well-focused look at life in several quite different settings during the early eighteenth century as well as an absorbing telling of Selkirk's story." Booklist
Includes glossary and bibliographical references

Sendak, Maurice
Marcovitz, Hal. Maurice Sendak; [by] Hal Marcovitz. Chelsea House Publishers 2006 136p bibl il por (Who wrote that?) $30
Grades: 6 7 8 9   **92**
1. Authors, American
ISBN 0-7910-8796-4   LC 2005031615
"Marcovitz takes an in-depth look at Sendak's art, storytelling, sources, themes, and lasting influence, including extensive quotes from published interviews and literary criticism. The page design is attractive, with full-color art as well as boxed insets that focus on issues such as censorship, . . . the Caldecott Medal, and Sendak's lifelong concern with the Holocaust." Booklist
Includes bibliographical references

Seuss, Dr.
Dean, Tanya. Theodor Geisel. Chelsea House 2002 112p il (Who wrote that?) $22.95
Grades: 4 5 6 7   **92**
1. Authors, American 2. Illustrators
ISBN 0-7910-6724-6   LC 2002-166
Describes the life and career of the author and illustrator known as Dr. Seuss who created such popular children's picture books as *The cat in the hat, How the Grinch stole Christmas*, and *Horton hears a Who*
"Well organized and clearly written." Booklist
Includes bibliographical references

Sewall, May Wright, 1844-1920
Boomhower, Ray E. Fighting for equality; a life of May Wright Sewall; [by] Ray E. Boomhower. Indiana Historical Society Press 2007 160p il $17.95
Grades: 4 5 6   **92**
1. Feminism 2. Reformers
ISBN 978-0-87195-253-0; 0-87195-253-X
LC 2007008517
"This accessible volume tells of the life and work of suffragist and educator [May] Wright Sewall. . . . Archival black-and-white photos enhance the text." Horn Book Guide
Includes bibliographical references

Shackleton, Sir Ernest Henry, 1874-1922
Calvert, Patricia. Sir Ernest Shackleton; by endurance we conquer. Benchmark Bks. 2003 80p il map (Great explorations) lib bdg $19.95 *
Grades: 5 6 7 8   **92**
1. Endurance (Ship) 2. Imperial Trans-Antarctic Expedition (1914-1917) 3. Antarctica—Exploration 4. Explorers
ISBN 0-7614-1485-1   LC 2002-3784
Contents: A pig-headed, obstinate boy; Afraid of nothing; Don't expect a feather bed; No eagles in the barnyard; An old dog for the hard road; The long road home; He never spares himself; A lone star above the bay
Presents the life and Arctic explorations of Sir Ernest Shackleton
"This concise and straightforward account is enhanced by archival photos, reproductions, and maps." SLJ
Includes bibliographical references

Johnson, Rebecca L. Ernest Shackleton; gripped by the Antarctic. Carolrhoda Bks. 2003 112p il map (Trailblazer biography) lib bdg $25.26
Grades: 6 7 8 9   **92**
1. Endurance (Ship) 2. Imperial Trans-Antarctic Expedition (1914-1917) 3. Antarctica—Exploration 4. Explorers
ISBN 0-87614-920-4   LC 2002-6816
A biography of Sir Ernest Shackleton, the daring, charismatic Antarctic explorer who fell short of his goal of crossing Antarctica, but accomplished a far greater feat by bringing every member of his crew back alive
"The writing is lively and clear and the story is compelling. A useful title for reports and recreational reading." SLJ
Includes bibliographical references

Sharpton, Al, 1954-
Mallin, Jay, Sr. Al Sharpton; community activist. Franklin Watts 2007 111p il (Great life stories) lib bdg $30.50; pa $16.95
Grades: 6 7 8 9   **92**
1. African Americans—Biography
ISBN 978-0-531-13872-4 (lib bdg); 0-531-13872-0 (lib bdg); 978-0-531-17845-4 (pa); 0-531-17845-5 (pa)
LC 2005024622
"In the time that Sharpton has been on the public stage, he has drawn a great deal of controversy, so it is a pleasure to read a biography of him that is both objective and dispassionate. This volume chronicles his life from his early years in Brooklyn as a boy minister, through his street activism, to his run for the presidency of the United States. . . . The plentiful, informative, color and black-and-white photographs will help students get a better sense of Sharpton's life and times." SLJ
Includes bibliographical references

Sheba, Queen of
Lucks, Naomi. Queen of Sheba. Chelsea House Publishers 2009 112p il (Ancient world leaders) lib bdg $30
Grades: 6 7 8 9   **92**
1. Queens
ISBN 978-0-7910-9579-9 (lib bdg); 0-7910-9579-9 (lib bdg)   LC 2008004872

Sheba, Queen of—*Continued*

This biography of the Queen of Sheba "references various oral traditions from Europe, the Middle East, and Ethiopia to reveal aspects of the woman's personality. Classical paintings and full-color photographs of sculptures, landscapes, and archaeological finds complement the text. . . . The [text is] easily digestible and appropriate for the intended age group." SLJ

Includes glossary and bibliographical references

Shepard, Alan B., Jr.

Orr, Tamra. Alan Shepard; the first American in space; [by] Tamra B. Orr. 1st ed. Rosen Pub. Group 2004 112p il (Library of astronaut biographies) lib bdg $29.95

Grades: 4 5 6 7   92

1. Astronauts

ISBN 0-8239-4455-7   LC 2003-10703

Contents: A decade of contrasts; The launching of a future astronaut; The Mercury 7 astronauts; Freedom 7; The terror and triumph of Apollo; Into the business world; A quiet ending

This describes Alan Shepard's childhood, education, and training as an astronaut.

"The writing is fast paced and lively. Many color photographs and occasional full-page sidebars enhance the [text]." SLJ

Includes glossary and bibliographical references

Shivack, Nadia

Shivack, Nadia. Inside out; portrait of an eating disorder; written and illustrated by Nadia Shivack. Atheneum Books for Young Readers 2007 unp il $17.99

Grades: 6 7 8 9   92

1. Bulimia—Graphic novels 2. Graphic novels

ISBN 0-689-85216-9; 978-0-689-85216-9

     LC 2004016096

"In this heartfelt, honest memoir, the author uses a graphic novel format to reveal her anguished, ongoing struggle with bulimia. . . . Though intensely personal and—perhaps of necessity—repetitious, this harrowing chronicle may well provide support and solace to teens facing a similar crisis." Publ Wkly

Siegal, Aranka

Siegal, Aranka. Memories of Babi; stories. Farrar, Straus & Giroux 2008 116p $16

Grades: 4 5 6 7   92

1. Jews—Biography 2. Grandmothers 3. Ukraine 4. Farm life

ISBN 978-0-374-39978-8; 0-374-39978-6

     LC 2007007002

Siegal's *Upon the Head of the Goat* (1981) is about her childhood in Hungary as Hitler comes to power. In this follow-up, written in nine wry sketches, she remembers the years before that—especially her close relationship with her Jewish grandmother, who lived on a small farm just across the Hungarian border in Ukraine." Booklist

Siegal, Aranka. Upon the head of the goat: a childhood in Hungary, 1939-1944. Farrar, Straus & Giroux 1981 213p hardcover o.p. pa $5.95 *

Grades: 6 7 8 9   92

1. World War, 1939-1945—Jews 2. Jews—Hungary 3. Holocaust, 1933-1945—Personal narratives

ISBN 0-374-38059-7; 0-374-48079-6 (pa)

     LC 81-12642

A Newbery Medal honor book, 1982

The author "recalls her childhood in Hungary at the time of Hitler's rise to power. As the book opens, she is nine years old and is trapped in the Ukraine at her grandmother's as the border is temporarily closed. When she returns to Hungary, she begins to feel more acutely the impact of the war on her life. . . . As the story ends the author and her family are boarded on a train for Auschwitz." Voice Youth Advocates

"The story is familiar . . . but a few pages into Aranka Siegal's fine memoir . . . you feel the power and interest of her particular experience and remember that this story cannot be told too often." Newsweek

Silverstein, Shel

Baughan, Michael Gray. Shel Silverstein; [by] Michael Gray Baughan. Chelsea House 2008 120p il (Who wrote that?) lib bdg $30

Grades: 6 7 8 9   92

1. Authors, American

ISBN 978-0-7910-9676-5 (lib bdg); 0-7910-9676-9 (lib bdg)   LC 2007045336

This biography of the popular author of *Where the Sidewalk Ends* examines the writer's "life, including the inspiration behind some of [his] works. [The] volume includes photographs and quotations from interviews, as well as descriptions of main characters and annotations lists of books and awards. Useful for aspiring authors as well as book report writers." Horn Book Guide

Includes bibliographical references

Simmons, Philip

Lyons, Mary E. Catching the fire: Philip Simmons, blacksmith; with photographs by Mannie Garcia. Houghton Mifflin 1997 47p il $17 *

Grades: 4 5 6 7   92

1. African American artists

ISBN 0-395-72033-8   LC 96-38643

Tells the story of this African American artist, the great-grandson of slaves, who has achieved fame and admiration for his ornamental wrought-iron creations

"The narrative, based on Simmons' memories and words, involves readers through its lively presentation of an intriguing subject. . . . Photographs appear on every spread, with black-and-white pictures of Simmons' early days and beautifully lit and composed color shots of the man today." Booklist

Includes bibliographical references

Simmons, Russell, 1957-

Baughan, Brian. Russell Simmons; [by] Brian Baughan. Morgan Reynolds 2009 112p il (Business leaders) lib bdg $27.95

Grades: 6 7 8 9   **92**
1. Record producers
ISBN 978-1-59935-075-2 (lib bdg); 1-59935-075-0 (lib bdg)   LC 2007-37797

"Baughan describes Simmons's childhood in Queens, NY, his college days as a rap promoter, his teen years when he was involved with drugs, his early efforts as a music producer, business collaborations, and media empire. . . . Contain[s] full-color photos that add visual appeal, sidebars about related topics, and helpful time lines." SLJ

Includes bibliographical references

Lommel, Cookie. Russell Simmons. Chelsea House 2007 104p bibl il por (Hip-hop stars) lib bdg $30

Grades: 7 8 9 10   **92**
1. Record producers
ISBN 978-0-7910-9467-9 (lib bdg); 0-7910-9467-7 (lib bdg)   LC 2007001463

This "weaves a concise history of hip-hop music and culture into a solid biography of one of its originators, Def Jam Records founder Russell Simmons. . . . [This is an] inspiring title that's sure to find wide circulation among hip-hop fans." Booklist

Includes glossary and bibliographical references

Sís, Peter, 1949-

Sís, Peter. The wall; growing up behind the Iron Curtain. Farrar, Straus and Giroux 2007 unp il $18
*

Grades: 4 5 6 7 8 9 10   **92**
1. Cold war 2. Prague (Czech Republic)
ISBN 978-0-374-34701-7; 0-374-34701-8   LC 2006-49149

Boston Globe-Horn Book Award: Nonfiction (2008)
"Frances Foster books"
"The author pairs his remarkable artistry with journal entries, historical context and period photography to create a powerful account of his childhood in Cold War-era Prague." Publ Wkly

Smalls, Robert, 1839-1915

Kennedy, Robert F. Robert Smalls; the boat thief; illustrations by Patrick Faricy. Hyperion Books for Children 2008 40p il map (Robert F. Kennedy Jr.'s American heroes) $16.99

Grades: 5 6 7 8   **92**
1. Planter (Steamship) 2. African Americans—Biography 3. Slavery—United States 4. United States—History—1861-1865, Civil War 5. African Americans—Civil rights
ISBN 978-1-4231-0802-3; 1-4231-0802-7

"Kennedy focuses not only on the daring escape Smalls made to freedom but also on Smalls as a political hero, especially his important role in the emancipation of slaves and in improving things for blacks during Reconstruction. . . . The volume features many illustrations—black-and-white portraits, and stirring, full-color scenes of ocean battles." Booklist

Smith, John, 1580-1631

Doherty, Kieran. To conquer is to live: the life of Captain John Smith of Jamestown. 21st Cent. Bks. (Brookfield) 2001 144p il lib bdg $23.90

Grades: 6 7 8 9   **92**
1. United States—History—1600-1775, Colonial period 2. Jamestown (Va.)—History
ISBN 0-7613-1820-8   LC 00-44309

A biography of the English soldier and adventurer who helped establish the colony of Jamestown, Virginia

A "well-written, appealing biography. . . . This book reads much like a swashbuckling adventure and most likely will inspire further interest in the man." SLJ

Includes bibliographical references

Snicket, Lemony, 1970-

Haugen, Hayley Mitchell. Daniel Handler; the real Lemony Snicket. Kidhaven Press 2005 48p il (Inventors and Creators) $23.70

Grades: 4 5 6 7   **92**
1. Authors, American
ISBN 0-7377-3117-6

In this biography of the author of the A Series on Unfortunate Events series "Haugen explains Handler's reasons for writing under a pen name. . . . He also explains Snicket's many interruptions, for vocabulary lessons, throughout the titles. A brief section presents some of the criticism of the series and Snicket's creative allusions to other literature and authors within his work. The full-color photos of Handler are sure to please the fans who've been longing for a glimpse. . . . This book will be read for reports and by adoring fans." SLJ

Socrates

Dell, Pamela. Socrates; ancient Greek in search of truth; [by] Pamela Dell. Compass Point Books 2006 112p il (Signature lives) lib bdg $31.93

Grades: 6 7 8 9   **92**
ISBN 978-0-7565-1874-5 (lib bdg); 0-7565-1874-1 (lib bdg)   LC 2006005405

"Relying extensively on Plato's accounts, Dell portrays Socrates as a doggedly determined seeker of information about human nature. . . . The book offers a solid portrait of Socrates as an individual, an explanation of his profound influence upon philosophy, and insight into the cultural, political, and social climates of ancient Athens." Booklist

Includes bibliographical references

Soto, Gary

Abrams, Dennis. Gary Soto; foreword by Kyle Zimmer. Chelsea House Pubs. 2008 120p bibl il por (Who wrote that?) $30

Grades: 5 6 7 8   **92**
1. Authors, American 2. Mexican Americans—Biography 3. Mexican American authors
ISBN 978-0-7910-9529-4; 0-7910-9529-0   LC 2007045509

A biography of the popular Mexican American author for children and young adults.

Includes bibliographical references

Spinelli, Jerry, 1941-
Spinelli, Jerry. Knots in my yo-yo string; the autobiography of a kid. Knopf 1998 148p il hardcover o.p. pa $10.95 *
Grades: 4 5 6 7   92
  1. Authors, American
  ISBN 0-679-98791-6; 0-679-88791-1 (pa)
                                        LC 97-30827
This Italian-American Newbery Medalist presents a humorous account of his childhood and youth in Norristown, Pennsylvania
"There is an 'everyboy' universality to Spinelli's experiences, but his keen powers of observation and recall turn the story into a richly rewarding personal history." Horn Book Guide

Standish, Myles, 1584?-1656
Harness, Cheryl. The adventurous life of Myles Standish; and the amazing-but-true survival story of Plymouth Colony; painstakingly written and illustrated by Cheryl Harness. National Geographic 2006 144p il map (Cheryl Harness history) $16.95; lib bdg $25.90
Grades: 4 5 6 7   92
  1. Pilgrims (New England colonists)
  2. Massachusetts—History—1600-1775, Colonial period
  ISBN   978-0-7922-5918-3;   0-7922-5918-1;
  978-0-7922-5919-0 (lib bdg); 0-7922-5919-X (lib bdg)
"Harness chronicles the history of the Plymouth Pilgrims from their troubles in England to their first years in North America, with the focus on Standish. Separating documented history from speculation, the narrative explains religious movements, introduces key figures, and gives a balanced account of Pilgrim-Indian relationships. . . . The tone is casual. . . . A reader-friendly approach to history." Booklist
Includes bibliographical references

Stanton, Elizabeth Cady, 1815-1902
Sigerman, Harriet. Elizabeth Cady Stanton; the right is ours. Oxford Univ. Press 2001 143p il (Oxford portraits) $28
Grades: 7 8 9 10   92
  1. Feminism
  ISBN 0-19-511969-X   LC 2001-31404
A biography of one of the first leaders of the women's rights movement, whose work led to women's right to vote
"This inspiring biography . . . is both interestingly written and easy to follow. . . . Black-and-white photographs and original documents add greatly to the appeal of this resource." SLJ
Includes bibliographical references

Steinbeck, John, 1902-1968
Meltzer, Milton. John Steinbeck; a twentieth-century life. Viking 2008 237p il (Up close) $16.99 *
Grades: 7 8 9 10   92
  1. Authors, American
  ISBN 978-0-670-06139-6; 0-670-06139-5
                                       LC 2007-36424

"This compact biography makes excellent connections between the themes of social and economic justice found in Steinbeck's work and the changes that were occurring in America around the time of the Depression. . . . Meltzer's language is concise and easy to understand, and powerful excerpts from Steinbeck's work are integrated throughout. A dozen or so small, black-and-white photographs of Steinbeck at different stages of his life are included." SLJ
Includes bibliographical references

Reef, Catherine. John Steinbeck. Clarion Bks. 1996 163p il $17.95; pa $8.95 *
Grades: 7 8 9 10   92
  1. Authors, American
  ISBN 0-395-71278-5; 0-618-43244-2 (pa)
                                        LC 95-11500
"The book traces Steinbeck's life from his childhood in California, to his burgeoning writing career and his passion for social justice, to his worldwide recognition. Reef does an excellent job of synthesizing Steinbeck's work, his private life, and his politics and philosophy." Bull Cent Child Books
Includes bibliographical references

Steiner, Matt
Warren, Andrea. Escape from Saigon; how a Vietnam War orphan became an American boy. Farrar, Straus and Giroux 2004 110p il map $17; pa $9.95
Grades: 6 7 8 9 10   92
  1. Vietnamese Americans 2. Vietnam War, 1961-1975
  3. Racially mixed people 4. Interracial adoption
  ISBN   978-0-374-32224-3;   0-374-32224-4;
  978-0-374-40023-1 (pa); 0-374-40023-7 (pa)
                                        LC 2003-60672
"Melanie Kroupa books"
Chronicles the experiences of Matt Steiner, an orphaned Amerasian boy, from his birth and early childhood in Saigon through his departure from Vietnam in the 1975 Operation Babylift and his subsequent life as the adopted son of an American family in Ohio.
"The child-at-war story and the facts about the Operation Babylift rescue are tense and exciting. Just as gripping is the boy's personal conflict." Booklist

Steller, Georg Wilhelm, 1700-1746
Arnold, Ann. Sea cows, shamans, and scurvy: Alaska's first naturalist: Georg Wilhelm Steller. Farrar, Straus & Giroux 2008 227p il map $21
Grades: 6 7 8 9   92
  1. Explorers 2. Naturalists 3. Alaska
  ISBN 978-0-374-39947-4; 0-374-39947-6
                                       LC 2006037400
"Frances Foster books"
"This is a detailed and lavishly illustrated biography of Georg Wilhelm Steller (1707-1746), Alaska's first naturalist. . . . He is the only scientist ever to describe, dissect, and eat the flightless spectacled cormorant. Species bear his name, including Steller's albatross, eider, jay, sculpin, sea cow, sea eagle, and sea lion. Arnold's exciting, harrowing account is personalized by excerpts from Steller's journal." KLIATT
Includes bibliographical references

Stevenson, Robert Louis, 1850-1894
Murphy, Jim. Across America on an emigrant train. Clarion Bks. 1993 150p il $18; pa $9.95 *
Grades: 5 6 7 8   92
   1. Authors, Scottish 2. Railroads—History 3. United States—Description and travel
   ISBN 0-395-63390-7; 0-395-76483-1 (pa)
                    LC 92-38650
"Murphy presents a forthright and thoroughly engrossing history of the transcontinental railway, with entries from Robert Louis Stevenson's 1879 journal as he rode cross country. It's also an inviting introduction to Stevenson, with a romance in the bargain." SLJ
Includes bibliographical references

Stine, R. L., 1943-
Marcovitz, Hal. R.L. Stine; foreword by Kyle Zimmer. Chelsea House Publishers 2006 134p bibl il por (Who wrote that?) lib bdg $30
Grades: 6 7 8 9   92
   1. Authors, American
   ISBN 0-7910-8659-3   LC 2005008186
   A biography of the popular author of *Goosebumps* and other children's horror stories.
Includes bibliographical references

Stoker, Bram, 1847-1912
Otfinoski, Steven. Bram Stoker; the man who wrote Dracula; by Steven Otfinoski. Franklin Watts 2005 111p il (Great life stories) lib bdg $30.50
Grades: 5 6 7 8   92
   1. Authors, English
   ISBN 0-531-16750-X   LC 2005000374
"Otfinoski discusses Stoker's early childhood, including the stories his mother told him while he recovered from chronic illness, his days in college, and influences of other writers. An entire chapter is devoted to the many presentations of Dracula both on stage and screen. [This book makes] excellent use of archival photos and reproductions, and extensive time lines [provides] historical connections and insights." SLJ
Includes bibliographical references

Stone, Miriam
Stone, Miriam. At the end of words; a daughter's memoirs. Candlewick Press 2003 55p $14
Grades: 7 8 9 10   92
   1. Stone, Martha Kaufman, 1949-1999 2. Cancer 3. Death 4. Mother-daughter relationship
   ISBN 0-7636-1854-3   LC 2002-73703
   The author records her feelings and experiences as she realizes that her mother is dying of cancer
"What moves the book beyond message is the raw, simple, personal imagery. . . . The prose is as rhythmic and poetic as the verse. . . . Anyone who mourns a loved one will relate to this." Booklist

Stowe, Harriet Beecher, 1811-1896
Fritz, Jean. Harriet Beecher Stowe and the Beecher preachers. Putnam 1994 144p il $15.99; pa $5.99 *
Grades: 5 6 7 8   92
   1. Beecher family 2. Women authors 3. Authors, American 4. Abolitionists
   ISBN 0-399-22666-4; 0-698-11660-7 (pa)
                  LC 93-6408
This is a biography of the abolitionist author of "Uncle Tom's Cabin" with an emphasis on the influence of her preacher father and her family on her life and work.
"Written with vivacity and insight, this readable and engrossing biography is an important contribution to women's history as well as to the history of American letters." Horn Book
Includes bibliographical references

Sullivan, Anne, 1866-1936
Delano, Marfe Ferguson. Helen's eyes: a photobiography of Annie Sullivan, Helen Keller's teacher; [foreword by Keller Johnson Thompson] National Geographic 2008 63p il map $17.95; lib bdg $27.90
Grades: 4 5 6 7   92
   1. Keller, Helen, 1880-1968 2. Blind 3. Teachers
   ISBN   978-1-4263-02-9-1;   1-4263-0209-6; 978-1-4263-0210-7 (lib bdg); 1-4263-0210-X (lib bdg)
"There are many biographies of Helen Keller and Annie Sullivan, but this one is very nicely done. . . . The book is honest in its portrayals, expecially of Sullivan. . . . What makes this oversize book so appealing is the clean design, with large typeface. The many fascinating photographs are sometimes placed over historical documents." Booklist
Includes bibliographical references

Tan, Amy
Angel, Ann. Amy Tan; weaver of Asian-American tales. Enslow Publishers 2009 128p bibl il por (Authors teens love) lib bdg $31.93
Grades: 6 7 8 9   92
   1. Chinese Americans—Biography 2. Authors, American 3. Women authors
   ISBN 978-0-7660-2962-0 (lib bdg); 0-7660-2962-X (lib bdg)   LC 2008012440
   This examines the life and work of the Chinese American author
Includes bibliographical references

Taylor, Major, 1878-1932
Brill, Marlene Targ. Marshall "Major" Taylor; world champion bicyclist, 1899-1901; by Marlene Targ Brill. Twenty-First Century Books 2008 112p il (Trailblazer biography) lib bdg $31.93
Grades: 5 6 7 8   92
   1. Bicycle racing 2. African American athletes
   ISBN 978-0-8225-6610-6 (lib bdg); 0-8225-6610-9 (lib bdg)   LC 2006003883

Taylor, Major, 1878-1932—*Continued*
"Marshall Taylor, an African American bicyclist who, despite facing prejudice in racing and in life, achieved world renown at the turn of the last century. . . . Brill's accessible, personable prose vividly relates Taylor's experiences." Booklist
Includes bibliographical references

Taylor, Mildred D.
Houghton, Gillian. Mildred Taylor. Rosen Pub. Group 2005 112p il (Library of author biographies) lib bdg $26.50
Grades: 5 6 7 8   92
1. Women authors 2. African American authors
ISBN 1-4042-0330-3
"Houghton presents readers with an understanding of Taylor's work as based on family stories and the history of African Americans in the United States. The result is a blend of history with the author's life and literature. . . . [This is] well-written." SLJ

Tecumseh, Shawnee Chief, 1768-1813
Collier, James Lincoln. The Tecumseh you never knew; [by] James Lincoln Collier; [illustrations by Greg Copeland] Children's Press 2004 80p il map lib bdg $25.95 *
Grades: 4 5 6 7   92
1. Shawnee Indians
ISBN 0-516-24426-4   LC 2003-28205
Contents: An Indian boy grows up; The war heats up; Rebuilding the confederacy; Tippecanoe; Triumph and tragedy
A biography of the Shawnee Indian chief who struggled to build a confederacy of Indians in order to thwart American expansionism after the Revolutionary war.
"A mix of realistic paintings and reproductions depict Tecumseh's life. Easy-to-read type on spacious white pages may tempt children into reading biographies." SLJ
Includes bibliographical references

Teresa, Mother, 1910-1997
Slavicek, Louise Chipley. Mother Teresa; caring for the world's poor. Chelsea House 2007 113p bibl il por (Modern peacemakers) lib bdg $30
Grades: 7 8 9 10   92
1. Nuns
ISBN 0-7910-9433-2 (lib bdg); 978-0-7910-9433-4 (lib bdg)   LC 2006028383
A biography of the nun who won the Nobel Peace Prize for her work with the poor of India
"This book is well organized and well written, and reads like a story. It is balanced in that it points out the critics of Mother Teresa's selection for the Nobel Peace Prize . . . as well as her admirers." SLJ
Includes bibliographical references

Terrell, Mary Church, 1863-1954
Fradin, Dennis B. Fight on!: Mary Church Terrell's battle for integration; [by] Dennis Brindell Fradin & Judith Bloom Fradin. Clarion Bks. 2003 181p il $17 *
Grades: 6 7 8 9   92
1. African American women—Biography 2. African Americans—Civil rights
ISBN 0-618-13349-6   LC 2002-151356
Profiles the first black Washington D.C. Board of Education member, who helped to found the NAACP and organized pickets and boycotts that led to the 1953 Supreme Court decision to integrate D.C. area restaurants
"In this carefully researched, fascinating biography, the life of the feisty, courageous, and determined woman . . . vividly unfolds." SLJ
Includes bibliographical references

Thiebaud, Wayne, 1920-
Rubin, Susan Goldman. Delicious: the life & art of Wayne Thiebaud. Chronicle Books 2007 108p $15.95
Grades: 5 6 7 8   92
1. Artists—United States
ISBN 978-0-8118-5168-8; 0-8118-5168-0   LC 2006-31168
"Wayne Thiebaud's droll paintings, many of cakes and other sweets, make him a natural subject for a children's biography. This profile . . . stands out for its grounding in interviews with Thiebaud and for its alluring design, featuring thick paper, amply sized and spaced text, and pages drenched in colors inspired by the artist's pastel palette." Booklist
Includes bibliographical references

Thoreau, Henry David, 1817-1862
Meltzer, Milton. Henry David Thoreau; a biography. Twenty-First Century Books 2007 160p il lib bdg $31.93 *
Grades: 7 8 9 10 11 12   92
1. Authors, American 2. Naturalists
ISBN 978-0-8225-5893-4 (lib bdg); 0-8225-5893-9 (lib bdg)   LC 2006013747
In this biography "readers see Thoreau through a variety of lenses—brother, friend, pencil maker, abolitionist, naturalist, and transcendentalist—to name only a few. Meltzer's clear and succinct writing style is punctuated with well-chosen and good-quality photographs and reproductions. . . . A first-rate choice for any student seeking a well-organized introduction to the life of the author and philosopher." SLJ
Includes bibliographical references

Thorpe, Jim, 1888-1953
Bruchac, Joseph. Jim Thorpe; original All-American. Dial Books/Walden Media 2006 277p il $16.99
Grades: 6 7 8 9   92
1. Native Americans—Biography 2. Athletes
ISBN 0-8037-3118-3   LC 2005-32173

Thorpe, Jim, 1888-1953—Continued
A biography of Native American athlete Jim Thorpe, focusing on his early athletic career.
"Bruchac relates the story in first person as if the reader is listening to Thorpe tell about his early life. . . . This conceit is extremely effective, and combined with Bruchac's excellently written first-person reminiscences of key football plays and Olympic competition, will make the book appeal to reluctant readers who might otherwise not read biographies." Voice Youth Advocates
Includes bibliographical references

Tienda, Marta
O'Connell, Diane. People person; the story of sociologist Marta Tienda. Franklin Watts 2005 108p il map (Women's adventures in science) lib bdg $31
Grades: 7 8 9 10   92
1. Sociology 2. Mexican Americans—Biography
ISBN 0-531-16781-X   LC 2005000825
Also available in paperback from Joseph Henry Press
A biography of Mexican American sociologist Marta Tienda.
This is "interesting, substantive, and eminently readable." SLJ
Includes bibliographical references

Tillage, Leon, 1936-
Tillage, Leon. Leon's story; [by] Leon Walter Tillage; collage art by Susan L. Roth. Farrar, Straus & Giroux 1997 107p il $15; pa $4.95 *
Grades: 4 5 6 7 8 9 10   92
1. African Americans—Biography 2. North Carolina—Race relations
ISBN 0-374-34379-9; 0-374-44330-0 (pa)
                                LC 96-43544
The son of a North Carolina sharecropper recalls the hard times faced by his family and other African Americans in the first half of the twentieth century and the changes that the civil rights movement helped bring about
The author's "voice is direct, the words are simple. There is no rhetoric, no commentary, no bitterness. . . . This quiet drama will move readers of all ages . . . and may encourage them to record their own family stories." Booklist

Tolkien, J. R. R. (John Ronald Reuel), 1892-1973
Lynch, Doris. J.R.R. Tolkien; creator of languages and legends. Franklin Watts 2003 127p il (Great life stories) $29.50
Grades: 6 7 8 9   92
1. Authors, English
ISBN 0-531-12253-0   LC 2003-958
Contents: An ocean voyage; A home in Hobbitland; Animalic, Nevbosh, and Naffarin; Tea clubs and poetry; From Quenya to secret codes; In the shadow of war; From hospital elves to forest muses; Walrus to Leeds; Oxford again; On hobbits and fairy stories; Hobbits and beyond; Birth of a trilogy; The Shire lives on

"Lynch explains how the beloved hobbit came to be created by a man whose fascination with dead languages led him to write fantasy stories, as well as to create and study language throughout his lifetime. Tolkien's fans will meet the man behind the tales. . . . Readers will be touched and inspired by this carefully crafted portrait." SLJ
Includes bibliographical references

Willett, Edward. J.R.R. Tolkien; master of imaginary worlds. Enslow Publishers 2004 128p il (Authors teens love) lib bdg $26.60
Grades: 6 7 8 9   92
1. Authors, English
ISBN 0-7660-2246-3   LC 2003-15657
Examines the personal life and literary career of the author of the Lord of the Rings trilogy
This "clearly goes a step beyond the typical series book, offering a more perceptive and more detailed, satisfying portrayal of its subject. . . . [The] volume includes a great deal of back matter: a time line, a list of selected works, a glossary, detailed chapter notes, and lists of recommended books and Internet sites." Booklist
Includes bibliographical references

Toussaint Louverture, 1743?-1803
Rockwell, Anne F. Open the door to liberty!: a biography of Toussaint L'Ouverture; illustrated by R. Gregory Christie. Houghton Mifflin Books for Children 2009 64p il $18 *
Grades: 5 6 7 8   92
1. Haiti—History 2. Slavery—West Indies 3. Blacks—Biography 4. Generals
ISBN 978-0-618-60570-5; 0-618-60570-3
                                LC 2007-25746
"In this eye-opening biography, Rockwell makes a strong case that Toussaint L'Ouverture is one of the most overlooked heroes of the eighteenth century. A freed slave of the French colony of St. Domingue (what we now know as Haiti), L'Ouverture was 48 when he was so inspired by his people's uprising against the French that he joined them and, through his oratory and strategical skills, became their leader. In 1793, he led history's first triumphant slave rebellion, but the resulting freedom would not last long. . . . Evocative paintings in primary colors help tell the story." Booklist
Includes bibliographical references

Truth, Sojourner, d. 1883
Brezina, Corona. Sojourner Truth's "Ain't I a woman?" speech; a primary source investigation; [by] Corona Brezina. RosenCentral Primary Source 2005 64p il (Great historic debates and speeches) $29.25 *
Grades: 6 7 8 9   92
1. African American women—Biography 2. Feminism 3. Abolitionists
ISBN 1-4042-0154-8   LC 2004-1443
"Brezina faces an unusual challenge in this volume. . . . Because Sojourner Truth could neither read nor write, there is no authoritative version of the speech under discussion. The book does a good job with the topic, though, by providing clearly written biographical infor-

Truth, Sojourner, d. 1883—*Continued*
mation about Truth, offering a straightforward account of the versions of the speech that were reported, discussing their relative merits, and including two texts in an appendix." Booklist

Butler, Mary G. Sojourner Truth; from slave to activist for freedom. PowerPlus Bks. 2003 112p il map (Library of American lives and times) lib bdg $31.95

Grades: 5 6 7 8   92
  1. African American women—Biography
  2. Abolitionists 3. Feminism
  ISBN 0-8239-5736-5   LC 2001-6169
Contents: Slavery in America; The slave Isabella; Living free; The sojourn begins; The Northampton Association; On the lecture circuit; The Battle Creek years; The legend grows; The nation divided; The last crusade
A biography of the former slave who became an abolitionist and advocate for women's rights
"The text is well documented, and the numerous illustrations, photos, and reproductions, both in color and in black and white, are authoritative and informative." SLJ
Includes glossary and bibliographical references

Tubman, Harriet, 1820?-1913
Allen, Thomas B. Harriet Tubman, secret agent; how daring slaves and free Blacks spied for the Union during the Civil War; featuring illustrations by Carla Bauer. National Geographic Society 2006 191p il map $16.95; lib bdg $25.90 *

Grades: 6 7 8 9   92
  1. African American women—Biography
  2. Underground railroad 3. Slavery—United States
  4. Abolitionists
  ISBN 0-7922-7889-5; 0-7922-7890-9 (lib bdg)
                                                LC 2005030927
"Allen brings readers much more than the usual biography of the brave rescuer on the Underground Railroad. This small, packed volume tells of Harriet Tubman's astonishing roles as spy, secret agent, and military leader, and it combines her personal story with a history of the abolitionist movement and the Civil War, focusing on how ex-slaves and free blacks served the Union cause. . . . The dense history is illustrated with numerous archival images, maps, and woodcuts, and the documentation is meticulous." Booklist
Includes bibliographical references

Turing, Alan Mathison, 1912-1954
Corrigan, Jim. Alan Turing. Morgan Reynolds Pub. 2008 112p il (Profiles in mathematics) lib bdg $27.95

Grades: 7 8 9 10   92
  1. Mathematicians
  ISBN 978-1-59935-064-6; 1-59935-064-5
                                                LC 2007-11704
"Corrigan's descriptions of English mathematician Turing as sporting 'ragged, wrinkled clothes' and few social graces will fit many readers' mental image of a numbers genius. But other aspects of this portrait push against stereotypes. . . . Throughout, candid mentions of Turing's homosexuality help readers contextualize the

scandal he endured after running afoul of the era's discriminatory legislation. Equal sensitivity distinguishes Corrigan's handling of Turing's death, officially (but not decisively) a suicide." Booklist
Includes bibliographical references

Twain, Mark, 1835-1910
Caravantes, Peggy. A great and sublime fool; the story of Mark Twain. Morgan Reynolds Pub. 2009 176p il map (World writers) lib bdg $28.95

Grades: 7 8 9 10   92
  1. Authors, American
  ISBN 978-1-599-35088-2; 1-599-35088-2
                                                LC 2008034139
This "offers a workmanlike but readable account of one of America's first great writers. . . . A nice selection of photographs and artwork complement the narrative. . . . Detailed source notes and an in-depth time line round out this even and reliable . . . biography." Booklist
Includes bibliographical references

Fleischman, Sid. The trouble begins at 8: a life of Mark Twain in the wild, wild West. Greenwillow Books 2008 224p il $18.99; lib bdg $19.89 *

Grades: 5 6 7 8   92
  1. Authors, American
  ISBN 978-0-06-134431-2; 0-06-134431-1;
  978-0-06-134432-9 (lib bdg); 0-06-134432-X (lib bdg)
                                                LC 2007-37891
"Fleischman writes a charming biography of Samuel Clemens before he became Mark Twain, the great American novelist. . . . Written with a sense of humor and wit that honors Twain, this book is sprinkled with famous Twain quotes, excerpts of his writing, and pictures of Twain and other primary documents from the era Clemens spent both on the Mississippi River and in the West." Voice Youth Advocates
Includes bibliographical references

Houle, Michelle M. Mark Twain; banned, challenged, and censored. Enslow Publishers 2008 160p il (Authors of banned books) lib bdg $34.60

Grades: 8 9 10 11 12   92
  1. Authors, American 2. Censorship
  ISBN 978-0-7660-2689-6 (lib bdg); 0-7660-2689-2 (lib bdg)
                                                LC 2007-22362
"This book combines biography, criticism, and an exploration of the role of censorship in literature and education. . . . Houle offers a brief history of censorship in literature in order to place Twain's case in context, and a history of the challenges and defenses of the author's work from his contemporaries and modern critics. Illustrations include color photographs of related modern scenes (such as one that shows book burning), reproductions of artwork from early editions of Twain's works, and period cartoons and photographs." SLJ
Includes glossary and bibliographical references

Twain, Mark, 1835-1910—*Continued*

Lasky, Kathryn. A brilliant streak: the making of Mark Twain; illustrated by Barry Moser. Harcourt Brace & Co. 1998 41p il $18 *

Grades: 4 5 6 7   **92**

1. Authors, American

ISBN 0-15-252110-0   LC 95-18479

An illustrated biography of young Samuel Clemens

"An obvious delight in her subject makes Lasky's biography an appealing choice, and a similar enthusiasm invests Moser's illustrations." Horn Book Guide

Includes bibliographical references

McArthur, Debra. Mark Twain. Marshall Cavendish Benchmark 2005 c2006 158p il (Writers and their works) lib bdg $42.79

Grades: 7 8 9 10   **92**

1. Authors, American

ISBN 978-0-7614-1950-1 (lib bdg); 0-7614-1950-0 (lib bdg)

"A biography of writer Mark Twain, describing his life, his major works, and the legacy of his writing." Publisher's note

Includes bibliographical references

Vázquez de Coronado, Francisco, 1510-1554

Otfinoski, Steven. Francisco Coronado; in search of the seven cities of gold. Benchmark Bks. 2003 76p il map (Great explorations) lib bdg $19.95 *

Grades: 5 6 7 8   **92**

1. Explorers

ISBN 0-7614-1484-3   LC 2002-3935

Contents: A gentleman of Spain; A new life in the New World; The grandest expedition; The battle of Cibola; Lands of wonders; Trouble at Tiguex; The sea of grass; End of the rainbow; A conquistador's fall

This describes Coronado's life and his explorations in the Southwestern United States in the 1540s

Includes bibliographical references

Vedder, Amy

Ebersole, Rene. Gorilla mountain; the story of wildlife biologist, Amy Vedder; [by] Rene Ebersole. F. Watts 2005 118p il (Women's adventures in science) lib bdg $31

Grades: 7 8 9 10   **92**

1. Gorillas 2. Women scientists

ISBN 0-531-16779-8   LC 2005-00823

A biography of wildlife biologist Amy Vedder

This is "interesting, substantive, and eminently readable." SLJ

Includes bibliographical references

Verne, Jules, 1828-1905

Schoell, William. Remarkable journeys: the story of Jules Verne. Morgan Reynolds 2002 112p il (World writers) lib bdg $21.95   **92**

1. Authors, French

ISBN 1-88384-692-7   LC 2002-2016

A biography of the nineteenth-century Frenchman whose childhood love of literature, science, and adven-

ture, along with his vivid imagination, led him to become a highly successful science fiction author

"Thanks to Schoell's smooth, crisp writing, this fascinating, approachable biography, which lends insight into Verne's eccentric characters and relatives, proves nearly as exciting as the writer's best stories." Booklist

Includes bibliographical references

Vincent, Erin

Vincent, Erin. Grief girl; my true story. Delacorte Press 2007 306p $15.99; lib bdg $18.99

Grades: 8 9 10 11 12   **92**

1. Bereavement

ISBN   978-0-385-73353-3;   0-385-73353-4; 978-0-385-90368-4 (lib bdg); 0-385-90368-5 (lib bdg)

LC 2006-11650

"In 1983, Vincent, then 14, lost both her parents in a road accident. In this poignant memoir, she chronicles her rocky journey through adolescence as she, her 17-year-old sister, Tracy, and their brother, Trent, learn to cope on their own." Booklist

Waldman, Neil, 1947-

Waldman, Neil. Out of the shadows; an artist's journey. Boyds Mills Press 2006 144p il $21.95 *

Grades: 5 6 7 8   **92**

1. Illustrators 2. Artists—United States 3. Jews—Biography

ISBN 1-59078-411-1

Neil Waldman reveals how his passion for art emerged in the kitchen of his family's apartment, where he discovered the work of Vincent Van Gogh and the ability to use illustration as a means to escape the sadness that plagued his home.

"Young artists, as well as readers who wonder about the person behind the pictures they have seen, will appreciate every element of this book: well-constructed story, visual richness, and uncompromising honesty." Booklist

Wallenberg, Raoul

McArthur, Debra. Raoul Wallenberg; rescuing thousands from the Nazis' grasp. Enslow Publishers 2005 160p il (Holocaust heroes and Nazi criminals) lib bdg $27.93

Grades: 6 7 8 9   **92**

1. Holocaust, 1933-1945 2. Jews—Hungary

ISBN 0-7660-2530-6   LC 2004-16153

This book "brings to light the . . . efforts of the Swedish diplomat who created a huge network of resistance workers and shrewdly played both sides of the political arena to successfully save the largest community of Jews in a Nazi-occupied country. McArthur explores the myriad theories behind the mysterious fate of Wallenberg, who disappeared shortly after the end of the war. This updated version of his life is much needed in any Holocaust collection." SLJ

Includes glossary and bibliographical references

Wang, Vera

Krohn, Katherine E. Vera Wang; enduring style; by Katherine Krohn. Twenty-First Century Books 2009 112p il (Lifeline biographies) lib bdg $33.26

Grades: 6 7 8 9   **92**
1. Fashion designers
ISBN 978-1-58013-572-6 (lib bdg); 1-58013-572-2 (lib bdg)   LC 2008009198
This biography "boasts lively, credible writing and a compelling layout. Particularly interesting are the reprints of USA Today articles found throughout, which flesh out the [narrative] in a unique and appealing manner. . . . Full-color and black-and-white photos appear on almost every spread." SLJ
Includes bibliographical references

Todd, Anne M. Vera Wang; [by] Anne M. Todd. Chelsea House 2007 120p bibl il por (Asian Americans of achievement) lib bdg $30

Grades: 7 8 9 10   **92**
1. Fashion designers
ISBN 978-0-7910-9272-9 (lib bdg); 0-7910-9272-0 (lib bdg)   LC 2006028386
A biography of the fashion designer
This is "well-researched . . . attractive . . . solid." SLJ

Warhol, Andy, 1928?-1987

Greenberg, Jan. Andy Warhol; prince of pop; [by] Jan Greenberg & Sandra Jordan. Delacorte Press 2004 193p il $16.95 *

Grades: 7 8 9 10   **92**
1. Artists—United States 2. Pop art
ISBN 0-385-73056-X   LC 2003-24102
A biography of the 20th century American artist famous for his Pop art images of Campbell's soup cans and Marilyn Monroe.
"Greenberg and Jordan offer a riveting biography that humanizes their controversial subject without making judgments or sensationalizing." Booklist
Includes glossary and bibliographical references

Rubin, Susan Goldman. Andy Warhol; pop art painter. H.N. Abrams 2006 48p il $18.95 *

Grades: 4 5 6 7   **92**
1. Artists—United States 2. Pop art
ISBN 0-8109-5477-X   LC 2005-13238
"Andy Warhol was a colorful figure who revolutionized how the world looks at art. Rubin's coherent and interesting narrative is filled with quotes by the artist and people who knew him. . . . Excellent-quality black-and-white and full-color photographs of Warhol and his family and reproductions of his paintings and those of others who influenced him appear throughout." SLJ

Washington, Booker T., 1856-1915

Washington, Booker T. Up from slavery; with a new introduction by Ishmael Reed. New American Library 2000 xxii, 228p (Edwards Black Heritage Collection) pa $4.95 *

Grades: 7 8 9 10 11 12 Adult   **92**
1. Tuskegee Institute 2. African Americans—Biography
ISBN 0-451-52754-2   LC 99-34954

First published 1901
"The classic autobiography of the man who, though born in slavery, educated himself and went on to found Tuskegee Institute." N Y Public Libr
Includes bibliographical references

Washington, George, 1732-1799

Adler, David A. George Washington; an illustrated biography; by David A. Adler. 1st ed. Holiday House 2004 274p il map $24.95 *

Grades: 5 6 7 8   **92**
1. Presidents—United States
ISBN 0-8234-1838-3   LC 2003-67606
This "look at America's premier founding father literally spans his lifetime and attempts to focus . . . on how Washington's early character formation impacted his decisions as a military officer and later as president. . . . The illustrations are largely engravings from the late 19th century. . . . The writing style is accessible without ever falling prey to oversimplification." SLJ

Allen, Thomas B. George Washington, spymaster; how America outspied the British and won the Revolutionary War; featuring illustrations by Cheryl Harness. National Geographic 2004 184p il $16.95

Grades: 6 7 8 9   **92**
1. United States—History—1775-1783, Revolution 2. Spies 3. Presidents—United States
ISBN 0-7922-5126-1   LC 2003-6019
Contents: Birth of a spymaster; Spy against spy; A spy must die; George Washington, Agent 711; Tools of the spymaster; Franklin's French friends; Spymaster at work; The General is a spy; Victory in the spy war
A biography of Revolutionary War general and first President of the United States, George Washington, focusing on his use of spies to gather intelligence that helped the colonies win the war.
"Allen presents the facts with a gleeful edge, clearly enjoying his subject and writing with vigor. . . . Set in an antique typeface, [the book] is well illustrated with black-and-white reproductions of archival art and Harness's charming pen-and-ink sketches." SLJ
Includes glossary and bibliographical references

Dolan, Edward F. George Washington; [by] Edward F. Dolan. Marshall Cavendish Benchmark 2008 96p il (Presidents and their times) lib bdg $32.79

Grades: 5 6 7 8   **92**
1. Presidents—United States
ISBN 978-0-7614-2427-7 (lib bdg); 0-7614-2427-X (lib bdg)   LC 2006037802
This biography of the first president of the United States "is illustrated with color photos and contains boxed descriptions of key historical events, artwork, and political concepts experienced during the time period. . . . This . . . will be of great use both for biographical research and for enriching the curriculum." Libr Media Connect
Includes glossary and bibliographical references

Washington, George, 1732-1799—*Continued*
Miller, Brandon Marie. George Washington for kids; his life and times with 21 activities; [by] Brandon Marie Miller. Chicago Review Press 2007 130p il pa $14.95
Grades: 4 5 6 7   **92**
1. Presidents—United States
ISBN 1-55652-655-5 (pa); 978-1-55652-655-8 (pa)
This book covers Washington's life and includes 21 hands-on projects based on his experiences and the times in which he lived.
This is "accessible and absorbing . . . clearly written and informative. . . . Primary quotes are interposed throughout, and illustrations, photographs, and visual aids are plentiful and well placed." SLJ

Weber, EdNah New Rider
Weber, EdNah New Rider. Rattlesnake Mesa; stories from a native American childhood; by EdNah New Rider Weber; photographs by Richela Renkun. 1st ed. Lee & Low Books 2004 132p il $18.95
Grades: 4 5 6 7   **92**
1. Native Americans
ISBN 1-58430-231-3   LC 2004-2385
"Weber grew up in the early twentieth century on the Crown Point Navajo Reservation . . . and she attended a government boarding school for Native American children. She recounts childhood experiences in both places." Booklist
"Weber describes her experiences with warmth and affection in this unusually compelling memoir. Striking black-and-white photos . . . add to the book's appeal." Horn Book Guide

Wells-Barnett, Ida B., 1862-1931
Fradin, Dennis B. Ida B. Wells; mother of the civil rights movement; [by] Dennis Brindell Fradin and Judith Bloom Fradin. Clarion Bks. 2000 178p il $19 *
Grades: 5 6 7 8   **92**
1. African American women—Biography 2. African Americans—Civil rights
ISBN 0-395-89898-6   LC 99-37038
This "biography chronicles the life of teacher, writer, publisher and civil rights champion, Ida B. Wells." ALAN
"This stellar biography of one of history's most inspiring women offers an excellent overview of Wells's life and contributions. . . . Black-and-white photographs and reproductions enhance the clear, well-written text." SLJ
Includes bibliographical references

Schraff, Anne E. Ida B. Wells-Barnett; "strike a blow against a glaring evil;"; [by] Anne Schraff. Enslow Publishers 2008 128p il map (African-American biography library) lib bdg $23.95
Grades: 6 7 8 9 10   **92**
1. African Americans—Civil rights 2. United States—Race relations 3. African American women—Biography
ISBN 978-0-7660-2704-6 (lib bdg); 0-7660-2704-X (lib bdg)   LC 2007016051

"Discusses Ida B. Wells-Barnett's life, her work as a teacher, writer, civil rights activist, and her strong stand against lynching in the late 19th and early 20th centuries." Publisher's note
"Short chapters, succinct text, frequent sidebars, and numerous period photographs keep the narrative from becoming overwhelming. . . . This will . . . aid report writers." Booklist
Includes bibliographical references

Wexler, Nancy S.
Glimm, Adele. Gene hunter; the story of neuropsychologist Nancy Wexler. Franklin Watts 2005 118p il (Women's adventures in science) lib bdg $31.50
Grades: 7 8 9 10   **92**
1. Huntington's chorea 2. Women scientists
ISBN 978-0-531-16778-6 (lib bdg); 0-531-16778-X (lib bdg)   LC 2005-06645
Also available in paperback from Joseph Henry Press
Contents: The dancing disease; Family secrets; Taking on the world; We won't give up; Risk and death; We are all one family; Testing the future; We found it!; In quest of cure
This is a biography of neuropsychologist Nancy Wexler who is searching for the gene responsible for a fatal, inherited sickness called Huntington's disease
This "volume is filled with full-color photographs of the subject and her work. Students will be comfortable with the style of [this book], and the easy reading level makes [it] accessible for even nonscience-oriented students." SLJ
Includes bibliographical references

Whitman, Narcissa Prentiss, 1808-1847
Harness, Cheryl. The tragic tale of Narcissa Whitman and a faithful history of the Oregon Trail; written and illustrated by Cheryl Harness. National Geographic Society 2006 144p il map (Cheryl Harness history) $16.95; lib bdg $25.90
Grades: 4 5 6 7   **92**
1. Frontier and pioneer life 2. Overland journeys to the Pacific
ISBN 0-7922-5920-3; 0-7922-7890-9 (lib bdg)
                                          LC 2005-30930
This "introduces a nineteenth-century pioneer and missionary. . . . [She and her husband Marcus Whitman] journeyed along the Oregon Trail to the Waiilatpu Mission, where they ministered to the Cayuse. . . . Harness' chatty, conversational style makes the pair accessible to modern readers, and frequent quotes from Narcissa's diaries and letters and a time line help to frame the story in light of world and national events. Harness' black-line illustrations . . . help to break up the text for younger readers." Booklist
Includes bibliographical references

Whitman, Walt, 1819-1892
Kerley, Barbara. Walt Whitman; words for America; illustrated by Brian Selznick. Scholastic Press 2004 unp il $16.95
Grades: 4 5 6 7   **92**
1. Poets, American
ISBN 0-439-35791-8   LC 2003-20085

Whitman, Walt, 1819-1892—*Continued*

A biography of the American poet whose compassion led him to nurse soldiers during the Civil War, to give voice to the nation's grief at Lincoln's assassination, and to capture the true American spirit in verse

"Delightfully old-fashioned in design, [the book's] oversized pages are replete with graceful illustrations and snippets of poetry. The brilliantly inventive paintings add vibrant testimonial to the nuanced text." SLJ

Meltzer, Milton. Walt Whitman; a biography. 21st Cent. Bks. (Brookfield) 2002 160p il lib bdg $31.90 *

Grades: 7 8 9 10   92

1. Poets, American

ISBN 0-7613-2272-8   LC 2001-27798

"The book honestly explores Whitman's character and actions, including his racial prejudice and his tendency to write anonymous (and effective) praises of his own writing. Ultimately, this has a definite edge and relevance that gives it more resonance than blander overviews of the poet. . . . Photographs of Whitman and his family, images of his work, and reproductions of period illustrations . . . liven up the formatting." Bull Cent Child Books

Includes bibliographical references

Reef, Catherine. Walt Whitman. Clarion Bks. 1995 148p il $16.95; pa $7.95

Grades: 7 8 9 10   92

1. Poets, American

ISBN 0-395-68705-5; 0-618-24616-9 (pa)

LC 94-7405

"Here is a biography of Whitman that presents the life of the subject, the world in which he lived, and representative passages from his writings." Voice Youth Advocates

"This is not a biography for pleasure reading, but it could be a source for those interested in historical events of 19th century America. It also would be a good resource for students doing a critique of Whitman's work for an American literature course." Book Rep

Includes bibliographical references

Wickenheiser, Hayley, 1978-

Etue, Elizabeth. Hayley Wickenheiser; born to play. Kids Can Press 2005 40p il pa $6.95

Grades: 4 5 6 7   92

1. Hockey 2. Women athletes

ISBN 1-55337-791-5

"The first woman to play professional hockey, Hayley Wickenheiser took up the sport in her family's backyard rink in a small Saskatchewan town at the age of three. . . . In 2003, Wickenheiser played professional hockey in a men's league in Finland. Fully illustrated with clear, colorful photos of Wickenheiser in action as well as posed shots off the ice, this appealing, large-format paperback offers a look at one woman's career in a 'man's' sport and shows the drive that propelled her to the top." Booklist

Wiesenthal, Simon

Rubin, Susan Goldman. The Anne Frank Case: Simon Wiesenthal's search for the truth; illustrated by Bill Farnsworth. Holiday House 2009 40p il $18.95 *

Grades: 4 5 6 7   92

1. Jews—Biography 2. Holocaust survivors 3. Holocaust, 1933-1945

ISBN 978-0-8234-2109-1; 0-8234-2109-0

LC 2007-28396

"In 1958, Holocaust deniers disrupted a theater performance of *The Diary of Anne Frank*. In response, the well-known Nazi hunter Simon Wiesenthal vowed to prove Anne's story true. . . . This 'hook' is the framing story for a picture-book biography chronicling Wiesenthal's experiences during World War II and illustrating the development of his unusual career." SLJ

"Even those who have heard of Wiesenthal will be thrilled by this account. . . . Farnsworth's stirring full-page oil paintings are filled with emotion." Booklist

Includes glossary and bibliographical references

Wilder, Laura Ingalls, 1867-1957

Anderson, William T. Laura Ingalls Wilder; a biography; by William Anderson. HarperCollins Pubs. 1992 240p il hardcover o.p. pa $6.99

Grades: 4 5 6 7   92

1. Authors, American 2. Frontier and pioneer life 3. Women authors

ISBN 0-06-020113-4; 0-06-088552-1 (pa)

LC 91-33805

A biography of the writer whose pioneer life on the American prairie became the basis for her "Little House" books

"A readable biography that is easily accessible to middle grade children who are likely to read the Little House books. Particularly interesting are the sections that fill in the gaps in Wilder's stories." Booklist

Berne, Emma Carlson. Laura Ingalls Wilder; by Emma Carlson Berne. ABDO Pub. 2008 112p il map $22.95

Grades: 4 5 6 7   92

1. Authors, American 2. Frontier and pioneer life 3. Women authors

ISBN 978-1-59928-843-7; 1-59928-843-5

LC 2007012513

"Beginning in 1929 with the events that led up to the publication of Little House in the Big Woods, this readable biography further amplifies Wilder's life and correlates it with her books. . . . This volume is packed with relevant material, a time line, archival photographs, quotes from primary sources, and an official Web site." SLJ

Includes glossary and bibliographical references

Sickels, Amy. Laura Ingalls Wilder; [by] Amy Sickels. Chelsea House 2007 125p il (Who wrote that?) lib bdg $30

Grades: 6 7 8 9   92

1. Authors, American 2. Women authors 3. Frontier and pioneer life

ISBN 978-0-7910-9525-6 (lib bdg); 0-7910-9525-8 (lib bdg)   LC 2007019615

Wilder, Laura Ingalls, 1867-1957—*Continued*
This biography examines the "writer's life, including the inspiration behind some of [her] works. [The] volume includes photographs and quotations from interviews, as well as descriptions of main characters and annotated lists of books and awards. Useful for aspiring writers as well as book report writers." Horn Book Guide
Includes bibliographical references

Wilder, Laura Ingalls. A Little House traveler; writings from Laura Ingalls Wilder's journeys across America; by Laura Ingalls Wilder. HarperCollins 2006 344p il $16.99
Grades: 5 6 7 8   **92**
    1. Women authors 2. Authors, American 3. United States—Description and travel
    ISBN 978-0-06-072491-7   LC 2005014975
"This volume combines three Wilder travel diaries: *On the Way Home*, recounting the 1894 trip from South Dakota to Missouri, with husband Almanzo and daughter Rose; *West from Home*, featuring letters written by Laura to Almanzo during her 1915 solo visit to Rose in San Francisco; and *The Road Back*, highlighting Laura's previously unpublished record of a 1931 trip with Almanzo to De Smet, South Dakota, and the Black Hills. . . . This offers an amazing look at a beloved author, as well as a fascinating account of travel before interstate highways and air-conditioning." Booklist

Williams, Lindsey, 1987-
Houle, Michelle E. Lindsey Williams; gardening for impoverished families; [by] Michelle Houle. KidHaven Press 2008 48p il (Young heroes) lib bdg $27.45
Grades: 4 5 6 7   **92**
    1. Food relief 2. Social action 3. Gardening
    ISBN 978-0-7377-3867-4 (lib bdg); 0-7377-3867-7 (lib bdg)   LC 2007022923
This "introduces 20-year-old Lindsey Williams, who has won numerous awards, including the International Eco-Hero Award, for her groundbreaking work with agriculture and hunger issues. . . . Williams has developed growing techniques that produce more food using fewer natural resources. . . . The straightforward text, with many quotes from Williams, will draw children into the science and environmental issues." Booklist
Includes glossary and bibliographical references

Williams, Serena, 1981-
Williams, Venus. Venus & Serena. See entry under Williams, Venus, 1980-

Williams, Venus, 1980-
Williams, Venus. Venus & Serena; serving from the hip, ten rules for living, loving, and winning; [by] Venus and Serena Williams with Hilary Beard. Houghton Mifflin 2005 133p il pa $14
Grades: 7 8 9 10   **92**
    1. Williams, Serena, 1981- 2. Tennis—Biography 3. African American athletes 4. Women athletes
    ISBN 0-618-44913-2   LC 2004-13204

"The sisters and tennis players . . . give teens advice on everyday living, showing them how to aim high and reach their goals. The 10 rules for success include building a 'dream team' (people who support your goals), doing well in school, learning self-respect, valuing friendships, taking care of yourself emotionally and physically, obtaining financial security, and overcoming setbacks. The final chapter discusses the virtues of volunteerism and charity. . . . Never preachy and always practical, this is a welcome addition to most collections." SLJ

Wilson, Woodrow, 1856-1924
Lukes, Bonnie L. Woodrow Wilson and the Progressive Era. Morgan Reynolds 2005 192p il lib bdg $26.95
Grades: 7 8 9 10   **92**
    1. Presidents—United States 2. United States—Politics and government—1898-1919
    ISBN 978-1-93179-879-2; 1-93179-879-6
                                        LC 2005-15999
"This well-documented, chronological account begins with Wilson's birth in 1856, describes his varied careers, and continues through his death in 1924. . . . The author describes the intense political conflicts of the time, mostly concerning Americas involvement in World War I and then in the League of Nations. Lukes's approach is balanced. . . . Good-quality, full-color and black-and-white photos and reproductions appear throughout." SLJ
Includes bibliographical references

Winfrey, Oprah
Cooper, Ilene. Oprah Winfrey. Viking 2007 204p il (Up close) $15.99 *
Grades: 7 8 9 10   **92**
    1. African American women—Biography 2. African American actors
    ISBN 978-0-670-06162-4   LC 2006-9805
"Cooper discusses her subject's early traumatic and dramatic experiences. She shows how a poor, abused, bright child from Mississippi overcame her past, becoming perhaps the most influential woman in America. Much of the book focuses on Winfrey's work and philanthropy. . . . This well-documented, easy-to-read biography is a good resource for reports." SLJ

Krohn, Katherine E. Oprah Winfrey; global media leader; by Katherine Krohn. rev ed. Twenty-First Century Books 2009 112p il (Lifeline biographies) lib bdg $33.26
Grades: 6 7 8 9   **92**
    1. African American women—Biography 2. African American actors
    ISBN 978-1-58013-571-9 (lib bdg); 1-58013-571-4 (lib bdg)   LC 2008016951
First published 2002 by Lerner Publications
This biography "boasts lively, credible writing and a compelling layout. Particularly interesting are the reprints of USA Today articles found throughout, which flesh out the [narrative] in a unique and appealing manner. . . . Full-color and black-and-white photos appear on almost every spread." SLJ
Includes bibliographical references

Winfrey, Oprah—*Continued*

Westen, Robin. Oprah Winfrey; "I don't believe in failure". Enslow Pubs. 2005 128p il (African-American biography library) lib bdg $31.93

Grades: 5 6 7 8   92

1. African American women—Biography 2. African American actors

ISBN 978-0-7660-2462-5 (lib bdg); 0-7660-2462-8 (lib bdg)   LC 2004016800

A biography of the actress and TV personality

"Background information is included without being sensationalistic, yet it does not avoid controversy. . . . Students writing reports on modern-day African Americans will appreciate the presentation and content of this [book]." Voice Youth Advocates

Includes bibliographical references

Winthrop, John, 1588-1649

Aronson, Marc. John Winthrop, Oliver Cromwell, and the Land of Promise. Clarion Books 2004 205p il map $20

Grades: 7 8 9 10   92

1. Cromwell, Oliver, 1599-1658 2. Puritans 3. Massachusetts—History—1600-1775, Colonial period 4. Great Britain—History—1603-1714, Stuarts

ISBN 0-618-18177-6   LC 2003-16418

"The accessible text is accompanied by excerpts from primary source documents and vivid illustrations. The author's passion for the period comes across in his writing. Aronson provides an excellent source for historical and biographical data." Voice Youth Advocates

Includes bibliographical references

Woodhull, Victoria C., 1838-1927

Havelin, Kate. Victoria Woodhull. Twenty-First Century Books 2007 112p (Trailblazer biography) lib bdg $30.60

Grades: 7 8 9 10   92

1. Feminism

ISBN 978-0-8225-5986-3 (lib bdg); 0-8225-5986-2 (lib bdg)   LC 2005022824

A biography of the nineteenth century feminist who became the first woman to run for president of the U.S.

"A well-researched, well-organized biography. . . . [Woodhull's] fascinating and full life is expertly detailed in this narrative." SLJ

Includes bibliographical references

Woods, Tiger, 1975-

Roberts, Jeremy. Tiger Woods; golf's master; by Jeremy Roberts. Twenty-First Century Books 2009 112p il (Lifeline biographies) lib bdg $33.26

Grades: 6 7 8 9   92

1. Golf

ISBN 978-1-58013-569-6 (lib bdg); 1-58013-569-2 (lib bdg)   LC 2008-3098

"There are a number of biographies about the world's best golfer, but this one is particularly good. Not only does it chronicle the life of Woods but it offers a solid look at family influences, various tournaments, and personal relationships. . . . Color photographs are well chosen." Booklist

Includes bibliographical references

Woodson, Jacqueline

Hinton, KaaVonia. Jacqueline Woodson; by KaaVonia Hinton. Mitchell Lane Publishers 2008 48p il (Classic storytellers) lib bdg $29.95

Grades: 5 6 7 8   92

1. Women authors 2. African American authors

ISBN 978-1-58415-533-1 (lib bdg); 1-58415-533-7 (lib bdg)   LC 2007-669

"This biography details the life of a popular African-American author. It covers her childhood, the challenges she faced growing up during the height of the Civil Rights Movement, what inspired her to begin to write, and her many literary successes. The book is filled with photos of the writer at various stages of her life and the covers of some of her books. Young people should find inspiration in Woodson's story." SLJ

Includes glossary and bibliographical references

Wright, Frank Lloyd, 1867-1959

Adkins, Jan. Frank Lloyd Wright; a twentieth-century life; by Jan Adkins. Viking 2007 301p il (Up close) $16.99

Grades: 7 8 9 10 11 12   92

1. Architects

ISBN 978-0-670-06138-9; 0-670-06138-7

The story of the man who changed architecture from "dark, Victorian clutter" to space open to air and movement.

"Adkins skillfully illuminates the man's complex, brilliant career and the major turning points in his work and life, while seamlessly inserting an informed introduction to architectural concepts and movements." Booklist

Includes bibliographical references

Wright, Orville, 1871-1948

Collins, Mary. Airborne: a photobiography of Wilbur and Orville Wright. National Geographic Soc. 2003 63p il maps $18.95 *

Grades: 4 5 6 7   92

1. Wright, Wilbur, 1867-1912 2. Aeronautics—History

ISBN 0-7922-6957-8   LC 2002-5279

Examines the lives of the Wright brothers and discusses their experiments and triumphs in the field of flight

"The well-chosen photos give readers a feel for Kitty Hawk—windy, sandy, solitary. This is an exceptionally well-informed picture of the Wright brothers and what their 100-year-old achievement really meant." SLJ

Crompton, Samuel. The Wright brothers; first in flight; [by] Samuel Willard Crompton. Chelsea House 2007 110p il (Milestones in American history) lib bdg $35

Grades: 7 8 9 10   92

1. Wright, Wilbur, 1867-1912 2. Aeronautics—History

ISBN 978-0-7910-9356-6 (lib bdg); 0-7910-9356-5
                                        LC 2006034131

Describes the careers and achievements of the Wright Brothers, who are credited with the invention of the airplane in 1903.

An "interesting and factual account of the Wright brothers. . . . [This book has] well-reproduced archival photos and drawings with explanatory captions . . . [and an] open layout and lively [text]." SLJ

Includes bibliographical references

Wright, Orville, 1871-1948—*Continued*

Dixon-Engel, Tara. The Wright brothers; first in flight; [by] Tara Dixon-Engel and Mike Jackson. Sterling 2007 128p il (Sterling biographies) $12.95; pa $5.95
Grades: 5 6 7 8   **92**
1. Wright, Wilbur, 1867-1912 2. Aeronautics—History
ISBN 978-1-4027-4954-4; 1-4027-4954-6; 978-1-4027-3231-7 (pa); 1-4027-3231-7 (pa)
     LC 2007003631
This "follows the Wright brothers from their early lives through first diagrams to their historic flight. . . . [The book provides] clear, concise information in an easy-to-follow format with captioned photographs and illustrations on most pages." SLJ
Includes glossary and bibliographical references

Freedman, Russell. The Wright brothers: how they invented the airplane; with original photographs by Wilbur and Orville Wright. Holiday House 1991 129p il hardcover o.p. pa $14.95 *
Grades: 5 6 7 8 9 10   **92**
1. Wright, Wilbur, 1867-1912 2. Aeronautics—History
ISBN 0-8234-0875-2; 0-8234-1082-X (pa)
     LC 90-48440
In this "combination of photography and text, Freedman reveals the frustrating, exciting, and ultimately successful journey of these two brothers from their bicycle shop in Dayton, Ohio, to their Kitty Hawk flights and beyond. . . . An essential purchase for younger YAs." Voice Youth Advocates
Includes bibliographical references

Wright, Richard, 1908-1960
Levy, Debbie. Richard Wright. Twenty-First Century Books 2008 160p (Literary greats) $33.26
Grades: 7 8 9 10 11 12   **92**
1. African American authors
ISBN 978-0-8225-6793-6   LC 2006-101189
A biography of the African American author of *Native Son* and *Black Boy*
This "absorbing biography . . . does a fine job of placing Wright's personal life in the context of black history. . . . Cleanly designed and featuring a small photo on every double-page spread." Booklist
Includes bibliographical references

Wright, Wilbur, 1867-1912
Collins, Mary. Airborne: a photobiography of Wilbur and Orville Wright. See entry under Wright, Orville, 1871-1948

Crompton, Samuel. The Wright brothers. See entry under Wright, Orville, 1871-1948

Dixon-Engel, Tara. The Wright brothers. See entry under Wright, Orville, 1871-1948

Freedman, Russell. The Wright brothers: how they invented the airplane. See entry under Wright, Orville, 1871-1948

Yang, Jerry, 1968-
Sherman, Josepha. Jerry Yang and David Filo; chief yahoos of Yahoo! 21st Cent. Bks. (Brookfield) 2001 80p il (Techies) lib bdg $23.90
Grades: 6 7 8 9   **92**
1. Filo, David 2. Yahoo! Inc. 3. Computer software industry 4. Businesspeople
ISBN 0-7613-1961-1   LC 00-66790
This is a dual biography of the executives who founded the Yahoo! internet search engine
"Fairly short and definitely accessible, the [book] will appeal not only to report writers, but also to recreational readers." SLJ
Includes bibliographical references

Yep, Laurence
Marcovitz, Hal. Laurence Yep; [by] Hal Marcovitz. Chelsea House 2008 136p il (Who wrote that?) $30
Grades: 6 7 8 9   **92**
1. Authors, American 2. Chinese Americans—Biography
ISBN 978-0-7910-9527-0; 0-7910-9527-4
     LC 2007045508
This biography of the Chinese American author examines the "writer's life, including the inspiration behind some of [his] works. [The] volume includes photographs and quotations from interviews, as well as descriptions of main characters and annotated lists of books and awards. Useful for aspiring authors as well as book report writers." Horn Book Guide
Includes bibliographical references

Yep, Laurence. The lost garden. Messner 1991 117p il (In my own words) pa $4.95 o.p. *
Grades: 5 6 7 8   **92**
1. Authors, American 2. Chinese Americans—Biography
ISBN 0-688-13701-6 (HarperCollins pa)
     LC 90-40647
The author describes how he grew up as a Chinese American in San Francisco and how he came to use his writing to celebrate his family and his ethnic heritage
"The writing is warm, wry, and humorous. . . . *The Lost Garden* will be welcomed as a literary autobiography for children and, more, a thoughtful probing into what it means to be an American." SLJ

Yolen, Jane
Carpan, Carolyn. Jane Yolen; [by] Carolyn Carpan. Chelsea House 2006 128p bibl il (Who wrote that?) lib bdg $30
Grades: 6 7 8 9   **92**
1. Authors, American 2. Women authors
ISBN 978-0-7910-8660-5 (lib bdg); 0-7910-8660-7 (lib bdg)
     LC 2005007828
This describes the life and work of author Jane Yolen
"The photographs that illustrate the text show places from the author's life or period photos. . . . The extensive quotes from Yolen share her feelings as she wrote full time and published more than 250 books while raising a family. . . . [The book includes] extensive notes, a chronology, works by the author listed by publication

Yolen, Jane—*Continued*
date, major awards, and most wellknown characters."
Voice Youth Advocates
Includes bibliographical references

Zaharias, Babe Didrikson, 1911-1956
Freedman, Russell. Babe Didrikson Zaharias; the making of a champion. Clarion Bks. 1999 192p il $18
Grades: 5 6 7 8 9 10   **92**
  1. Women athletes
  ISBN 0-395-63367-2   LC 98-50208
A biography of Babe Didrikson, who broke records in golf, track and field, and other sports, at a time when there were few opportunities for female athletes
"Freedman's measured yet lively style captures the spirit of the great athlete. . . . Plenty of black-and-white photos capture Babe's spirit and dashing good looks; the documentation . . . is impeccable." Horn Book
Includes bibliographical references

Zenatti, Valérie, 1970-
Zenatti, Valérie. When I was a soldier; a memoir; translated by Adriana Hunter. Bloomsbury Children's Books 2005 235p $16.95
Grades: 7 8 9 10   **92**
  1. Women soldiers 2. Israel
  ISBN 1-58234-978-9
In this "memoir, Zenatti, first among her group of friends to be called for compulsory military service, chronicles two years of growing up in the Israeli army between 1988 and 1990." SLJ
A "fast, wry, present-tense memoir. . . . Readers on all sides of the war-peace continuum, here and there, will find much to talk about." Booklist

Zindel, Paul
Daniel, Susanna. Paul Zindel. Rosen Publishing Group 2004 112p il (Library of author biographies) lib bdg $26.50
Grades: 5 6 7 8   **92**
  1. Authors, American
  ISBN 0-8239-4524-3
Discusses the life and work of this popular author, including his writing process and methods, inspirations, a critical discussion of his books, biographical timeline, and awards.
Includes bibliographical references

929   Genealogy, names, insignia

Perl, Lila
The great ancestor hunt; the fun of finding out who you are; drawings by Erika Weihs; illustrated with photographs. Clarion Bks. 1989 104p il hardcover o.p. pa $8.95
Grades: 5 6 7 8   **929**
  1. Genealogy
  ISBN 0-89919-745-0; 0-395-54790-3 (pa)
                         LC 88-36211

The author "weaves the how-to of genealogy with a historical perspective on immigration. All the basics are covered: drawing an ancestry chart, conducting interviews with relatives, finding family memorabilia, and, for those who wish to continue their quest, writing away for documentation. The format is also a plus. Interesting black-and-white photos alternate with charts, diagrams, and a few (softly executed) drawings by Erika Weihs." Booklist
Includes bibliographical references

Taylor, Maureen, 1955-
Through the eyes of your ancestors. Houghton Mifflin 1999 86p il hardcover o.p. pa $8.95
Grades: 4 5 6 7   **929**
  1. Genealogy
  ISBN 0-395-86980-3; 0-395-86982-X (pa)
                          LC 98-8776
Discusses genealogy, the study of one's family, examining how such an interest develops, how to get started, how to use family stories and keepsakes, where to get help, and the positive effects of such study
"Motivated young researchers with adult help will find the book a good starting place." SLJ
Includes bibliographical references

Wolfman, Ira
Climbing your family tree; online and offline genealogy for kids: the official Ellis Island handbook; foreword by Alex Haley; illustrations by Michael Klein. Workman 2002 228p il pa $13.95
Grades: 5 6 7 8   **929**
  1. Genealogy
  ISBN 0-7611-2539-6   LC 2002-16797
A revised edition of Do people grow on family trees? published 1990
A guide to finding out one's own family history using web sites, libraries, archives and other public records
This "is so fascinating that one becomes motivated to start a genealogical search. . . . Throughout the book, photographs and special boxed portions add to the text to make it interesting. Bibliographies and Web sites are included throughout the chapters." Libr Media Connect
Includes bibliographical references

929.9   Flags. Forms of insignia and identification

Bateman, Teresa
Red, white, blue, and Uncle who? the stories behind some of America's patriotic symbols; illustrated by John O'Brien. Holiday House 2001 64p il $16.95; pa $6.95
Grades: 4 5 6 7   **929.9**
  1. National emblems 2. National monuments
  ISBN 0-8234-1285-7; 0-8234-1784-0 (pa)
                          LC 00-57258
This "volume presents 17 'patriotic symbols,' an umbrella term that encompasses everything from the flag to Uncle Sam, from Mount Rushmore to the Korean War

Bateman, Teresa—*Continued*
Memorial. Bateman finds plenty of interesting information to share about each symbol or site, and browsers will be entertained by the many stories of origination, construction, and history." Booklist
Includes bibliographical references

Shearer, Benjamin F.
State names, seals, flags, and symbols; a historical guide; [by] Benjamin F. Shearer and Barbara S. Shearer. 3rd ed, rev and expanded. Greenwood Press 2001 495p il $73.95
Grades: 8 9 10 11 12 Adult   **929.9**
  1. Geographic names—United States 2. Seals (Numismatics) 3. Flags—United States 4. Reference books
  ISBN 0-313-31534-5   LC 2001-23525
  First published 1987
  "Chapters on mottoes, flowers, trees, birds, songs, holidays, and license plates are just a sampling of what is covered, and the format is such that the concisely written material can be found as expeditiously as possible. Even though the book is touted predominantly as a reference tool, the information provided makes fascinating and enlightening reading." Libr J [review of 1994 edition]
  Includes bibliographical references

World Book's encyclopedia of flags. World Book 2007 12v il map set$347
Grades: 4 5 6 7   **929.9**
  1. Flags 2. Reference books
  ISBN 978-0-7166-7901-1; 0-7166-7901-9
  First published 2005
  "This set includes articles on flags of every nation in the world as well as on historical flags and flags of organizations and political groups. . . . With more than 380 flags, this set would be a valuable resource for students in elementary and middle school." Booklist [review of 2005 edition]
  Includes bibliographical references

930   History of ancient world (to ca.499)

Adams, Simon
The Kingfisher atlas of the ancient world; illustrated by Katherine Baxter. Kingfisher 2006 44p il $15.95
Grades: 4 5 6 7   **930**
  1. Ancient civilization 2. Historical geography 3. Reference books
  ISBN 978-0-7534-5914-0; 0-7534-5914-0
  "Featuring seventeen . . . hand-illustrated maps and . . . with . . . information about ancient civilizations and peoples, this is [a] . . . pictorial guide to what the world was like between 10,000 B.C. and A.D. 1000. Each . . . map shows the major sites from a particular civilization or group of civilizations. . . . Feature spreads use photographs of cultural and architectural artifacts, as well as additional information, to focus in greater depth on the key cultures of Egypt, Greece, and Rome." Publisher's note

Knight, Judson
Ancient civilizations: almanac; Stacy A. McConnell and Lawrence W. Baker, editors. U.X.L 1999 2v set$110
Grades: 7 8 9 10   **930**
  1. Ancient civilization 2. Reference books
  ISBN 0-7876-3982-6   LC 99-46791
  Provides historical information and interpretation on ancient civilizations in Egypt, Mesopotamia, Asia Minor, China, Africa, Israel, and elsewhere
  Includes bibliographical references

Merrill, Yvonne Young
Hands-on ancient people. Kits Pub. 2003-2004 2v il map pa ea $20
Grades: 5 6 7 8   **930**
  1. Ancient civilization 2. Handicraft
  ISBN 0-9643177-8-8 (v1); 0-9643177-9-6 (v2)
  Contents: v1 Art activities about Mesopotamia, Egypt, and Islam; v2 Art activities about Minoans, Trojans, Ancient Greeks, Etruscans and Romans
  Each volume offers instructions for creating 60 objects based on ancient artifacts such as a cardboard model of the Parthenon, masks, Greek vases, war shields, mosaics, toys, banners, tomb paintings, a wheel, board games, and the ziggurat.
  "These exciting art projects are illustrated with dramatic full-page, full-color photographs. Each activity occupies an inviting spread with a list of materials, clear instructions, and background information on the artifacts and the culture they represent." SLJ [review of v2]
  Includes bibliographical references

Service, Pamela F.
300 B.C. Benchmark Bks. 2003 96p il maps (Around the world in—) lib bdg $28.50
Grades: 6 7 8 9   **930**
  1. Ancient history
  ISBN 0-7614-1080-5   LC 00-36026
  Surveys important occurrences in Europe, Africa, Asia, and the Americas 2300 years ago
  "Well written, informative, attractively designed and illustrated, and logically organized." Libr Media Connect
  Includes glossary and bibliographical references

The **world** in ancient times; primary sources and reference volume; Ronald Mellor & Amanda Podany, general editors. Oxford University Press 2005 188p il map (World in ancient times) $32.95
Grades: 7 8 9 10   **930**
  1. Ancient history 2. Ancient civilization 3. Reference books
  ISBN 978-0-19-522220-3; 0-19-522220-2
             LC 2004026578
  "An excellent introduction to the use of primary resources in historical research. The 76 selections include poems, letters, inscriptions, and other contemporary accounts from antiquity as well as more modern descriptions and excerpts. Materials from Asia, Europe, and the Americas are highlighted." SLJ
  Includes bibliograghical references

930.1   Archaeology

Barnes, Trevor, 1951-
Archaeology; foreword by Tony Robinson.
Kingfisher 2004 63p il map (Kingfisher
knowledge) $11.95
Grades: 5 6 7 8   930.1
1. Archeology
ISBN 0-7534-5768-7
Explores the science of excavating and examining the
debris of centuries of human life, from the Iron Age to
recent history
Includes glossary and bibliographical references

Deem, James M.
Bodies from the bog. Houghton Mifflin 1998
42p il hardcover o.p. pa $5.95 *
Grades: 4 5 6 7   930.1
1. Mummies 2. Prehistoric peoples 3. Archeology
ISBN 0-395-85784-8; 0-618-35402-6 (pa)
LC 97-12010
Describes the discovery of bog bodies in northern Eu-
rope and the evidence which their remains reveal about
themselves and the civilizations in which they lived
"The text is engaging and accessible, and the starkly
dramatic photos are given dignity by the spacious and
understated page design." Horn Book Guide
Includes bibliographical references

Getz, David, 1957-
Frozen man; illustrated by Peter McCarty. Holt
& Co. 1994 68p il maps hardcover o.p. pa $8.95
Grades: 5 6 7 8   930.1
1. Mummies 2. Prehistoric peoples 3. Archeology
ISBN 0-8050-3261-4; 0-8050-4645-3 (pa)
LC 94-9109
"A Redfeather book"
"This is an account of the mummified stone-age
corpse who was found in Austria in 1991. . . . Getz's
generally well-organized information and smooth exposi-
tion makes the effort to understand the Iceman, as this
book calls him, into an intriguing detective story. This
could well stimulate the interest of kids who didn't think
they liked science or archeology. Black-and-white drawings include useful maps and diagrams." Bull Cent Child
Books
Includes glossary and bibliographical references

McIntosh, Jane
Archeology; written by Jane McIntosh. Dorling
Kindersley 2000 63p il (DK eyewitness books)
$15.99; lib bdg $19.99
Grades: 4 5 6 7   930.1
1. Archeology
ISBN 0-7894-5864-0; 0-7894-6605-8 (lib bdg)
First published 1994 by Knopf
This book contains "photographs, illustrations, and
terms covering the specialized field of archeology. Inside
are a contents page, an index, and 26 sections of two to
three pages each, covering . . . the various techniques
used by archeologists and historians to learn about past
civilizations." Sci Books Films [review of 1994 edition]

Smith, KC
Exploring for shipwrecks. Watts 2000 63p
$24.50; pa $8.95
Grades: 4 5 6   930.2
1. Underwater exploration 2. Shipwrecks
3. Excavations (Archeology)
ISBN 0-531-20377-8; 0-531-16471-3 (pa)
LC 99-40537
"Watts library"
Introduces the discipline of underwater archaeology
and the techniques used to find and study submerged
ships. Ancient ships such as the Cheops vessel from
Egypt and the Ulubrurn wreck of the Bronze Age are
highlighted
Includes bibliographical references

931   China to 420 A.D.

Ball, Jacqueline A.
Ancient China; archaeology unlocks the secrets
of China's past; by Jacqueline Ball and Richard
Levey, Robert Murowchick, consultant. National
Geographic 2006 c2007 64p il (National
Geographic investigates) $17.95; lib bdg $27.90 *
Grades: 5 6 7 8   931
1. China—Antiquities 2. China—Civilization
ISBN   978-0-7922-7783-5;   0-7922-7783-X;
978-0-7922-7858-6 (lib bdg); 0-7922-7856-9 (lib bdg)
"This volume spotlights archaeological finds from An-
cient China. . . . While the discussions of archaeology
will hold readers' interest, the accompanying illustrations
steal the show." Booklist

Cotterell, Arthur
Ancient China; written by Arthur Cotterell. rev
ed. Dorling Kindersley 2005 63p il map (DK
eyewitness books) $15.99
Grades: 4 5 6 7   931
1. China—Civilization 2. China—History
ISBN 0-7566-1391-4
First published 1994 by Knopf
"This volume touches upon such topics as Chinese
history, the first emperor, inventions, health and medicine, waterways, food and drink, clothing, the Silk Road,
and arts and crafts. Material from as recent as the last
dynasty, which ended in 1911, is included." SLJ [review
of 1994 edition]

Dean, Arlan
Terra-cotta soldiers; army of stone; [by] Arlan
Dean. Children's Press 2005 48p il map (Digging
up the past) lib bdg $23; pa $6.95
Grades: 4 5 6 7   931
1. Ch'in Shih-huang, Emperor of China, 259-210
B.C.—Tomb 2. China—Antiquities
ISBN 0-516-25124-4 (lib bdg); 0-516-25093-0 (pa)
LC 2005002699
"Hi-lo interest books"
This "discusses ancient Chinese history, including the
first emperor and his tomb, which was found to contain
8000 clay soldiers, made to protect him in his afterlife.

Dean, Arlan—*Continued*

Beliefs about life after death are explained. The author also discusses Qin Shi Huangdis role in creating the Great Wall." SLJ

This consists of "short chapters, with text sharing space with mostly snapshot-size photos. . . . Reluctant readers at ease with the High Interest series format may want to start with this." Booklist

Includes glossary and bibliographical references

DuTemple, Lesley A., 1952-

The Great Wall of China. Lerner Publs. 2003 80p il maps (Great building feats) lib bdg $27.93

Grades: 5 6 7 8   **931**

1. Great Wall of China 2. China—History

ISBN 0-8225-0377-8   LC 2001-3271

A history of the building of the various pieces of the Great Wall of China, with details of how the walls were built through the ages

"A well-researched and engaging account of one of humankind's most fascinating engineering feats. . . . Full-color photos, diagrams, as well as reproductions of ancient illustrations are plentiful and enliven the presentation." SLJ

Includes bibliographical references

Greenblatt, Miriam

Han Wu Di and ancient China; by Miriam Greenblatt. Marshall Cavendish Benchmark 2006 80p il map (Rulers and their times) lib bdg $29.93

                                                                            931

1. Han Wu-ti, Emperor of China, 156-87 B.C. 2. China—Civilization

ISBN 0-7614-1835-0   LC 2004-22

Partial contents: Part One: The martial emperor; Part Two: Everyday life in ancient China; Part Three: The Chinese in their own words

This describes the life and times of Hu Wu Di, the emperor of China from 156-87 B.C., with information on ancient Chinese civilization.

Includes glosssary and bibliographical references

Kleeman, Terry F., 1955-

The ancient Chinese world; [by] Terry Kleeman & Tracy Barrett. Oxford University Press 2005 174p il map (World in ancient times) $32.95

Grades: 7 8 9 10   **931**

1. China—History

ISBN 0-19-517102-0   LC 2004-14408

This book "uses primary sources to describe the history of ancient China and how it still influences the lives of billions of people today." Publisher's note

"Readers seriously interested in history, in archaeology—or in China—will be well served by this engrossing book." SLJ

Includes bibliographical references

O'Connor, Jane, 1947-

The emperor's silent army; terracotta warriors of Ancient China. Viking 2002 48p il $17.99 *

Grades: 4 5 6 7   **931**

1. Ch'in Shih-huang, Emperor of China, 259-210 B.C.—Tomb 2. China—Antiquities

ISBN 0-670-03512-2   LC 2001-46900

Describes the archaeological discovery of thousands of life-sized terracotta warrior statues in northern China in 1974, and discusses the emperor who had them created and placed near his tomb

"This intriguing book is enhanced by beautiful illustrations—pictures of stone engravings, colorful paintings, drawings, and maps—while numerous photographs show the clay soldiers from different perspectives. . . . The author's writing style is entertaining, yet informative." Book Rep

Includes bibliographical references

Schomp, Virginia, 1953-

The ancient Chinese; written by Virginia Schomp. Franklin Watts 2004 112p il map (People of the ancient world) $29.50; pa $9.95 *

Grades: 5 6 7 8   **931**

1. China—Civilization

ISBN 0-531-11817-7; 0-531-16737-2 (pa)

                                                                  LC 2004-2174

Contents: At the center of the world; Kings and emperors; Civil servants and nobles; Philosophers and holy men; Peasant farmers and soldiers; Artisans and silk makers; Merchants and traders; Inventors, scientists, and healers; Writers and artists; The legacy of ancient China

"Focusing mainly on the Shang, Zhou, Qin, and Han dynasties, this book explores ancient China through its social structure. It takes a look at its people and details the duties of an emperor, the activities of a merchant, and . . . more. It also describes some of the discoveries and writings that have led to our present-day understanding of this . . . civilization." Publisher's note

"Crisp reproductions of visuals, along with impressive ancilliary content. . . . help make [this title] among the best available on ancient [China]." Booklist

Includes bibliographical references

Shuter, Jane, 1955-

Ancient China; [by] Jane Shuter. Raintree 2007 64p il map (Time travel guide) lib bdg $34.29; pa $9.99

Grades: 6 7 8 9   **931**

1. China—Civilization

ISBN 978-1-4109-2729-3 (lib bdg); 1-4109-2729-6 (lib bdg); 978-1-4109-2736-1 (pa); 1-4109-2736-9 (pa)

                                                                LC 2006033868

"Raintree FreeStyle"

This describes life in Ancient China in the form of a travel guide.

Includes glossary and bibliographical references

932 Egypt to 640 A.D.

Baker, Rosalie F.

Ancient Egyptians; people of the pyramids; [by] Rosalie F. and Charles F. Baker. Oxford Univ. Press 2001 189p il maps (Oxford profiles) $50

Grades: 7 8 9 10   **932**

1. Egypt—Civilization 2. Egypt—Biography

ISBN 0-19-512221-6   LC 2001-21209

"Divided into five periods from the Old Kingdom, about 2686 B.C., to the declining New Kingdom, about 245 B.C., this book profiles some 30 Egyptian leaders, devoting a three- to seven-page chapter to each one. . . . The entries are well written and researched. . . . A useful addition for report writers and subject enthusiasts." SLJ

Includes glossary and bibliographical references

Berger, Melvin, 1927-

Mummies of the pharaohs; exploring the Valley of the Kings; [by] Melvin Berger & Gilda Berger. National Geographic Soc. 2001 64p il $17.95 *

Grades: 4 5 6 7   **932**

1. Egypt—Antiquities 2. Mummies

ISBN 0-7922-7223-4   LC 00-55411

"Beginning with the . . . discovery of King Tut's tomb, . . . the book continues through other . . . finds, introducing a few of the major rulers and their relationships, as well as speculation on the political scandals that surrounded some burials." SLJ

This offers "stunning photographs and clear, compelling text. . . . A fascinating historical resource that kids will read straight through for pleasure and also find useful for report writing." Booklist

Biesty, Stephen

Egypt in spectacular cross-section; text by Stewart Ross. Scholastic Nonfiction 2005 28p il $18.99

Grades: 4 5 6 7   **932**

1. Egypt—Antiquities 2. Egypt—Civilization

ISBN 0-439-74537-3   LC 2004-59185

"Employing his large, trademark cross-section or cutaway style illustrations that are full of detail and bustling small figures, Biesty, supported by Ross, uses the fictional construct of family members traveling to a wedding as a way of exploring various aspects of daily life in Egypt around the year 1230 B.C.E." SLJ

Includes glossary

Cline, Eric H.

The ancient Egyptian world; [by] Eric Cline & Jill Rubalcaba. Oxford University Press 2005 190p il (World in ancient times) $32.95 *

Grades: 7 8 9 10   **932**

1. Egypt—Civilization

ISBN 0-19-517391-0   LC 2004-17720

"This book offers chronologically arranged chapters, each of which addresses an important topic in ancient Egyptian culture or history. Geography, religion, the intersection of medicine and magic, fashion and clothing, the arts, and other subjects are explored. . . . The volume is distinguished by its profuse quotations from ancient monuments and ancient authors. Another plus is its broad scope, reaching from the earliest pre-pyramid dynasties through to the conquest of Egypt by Rome. The mostly color photographs are plentiful." SLJ

Includes bibliographical references

Filer, Joyce

Pyramids; [by] Joyce Filer. 2nd ed. Oxford University Press 2005 48p il map $16.95; lib bdg $18.95

Grades: 4 5 6 7   **932**

1. Pyramids 2. Egypt—Civilization

ISBN 978-0-19-530521-0; 0-19-530521-3; 978-0-19-530525-8 (lib bdg); 0-19-530525-6 (lib bdg)

        LC 2005017117

Previously published as: Pyramids and people of ancient Egypt

"Brief chapters explain what a pyramid is and how Egyptians lived before the Old Kingdom; more detailed chapters examine, in chronological order, Djoser and the Step Pyramid, the major pyramids of the 4th Dynasty, and the almost entirely collapsed pyramid of Ahmose of the 18th Dynasty. . . . This is a solid, well-organized introduction." SLJ

Giblin, James, 1933-

Secrets of the Sphinx; by James Cross Giblin; illustrated by Bagram Ibatoulline. Scholastic Press 2004 47p il map $17.95

Grades: 4 5 6 7   **932**

1. Egypt—Antiquities 2. Egypt—Civilization

ISBN 0-590-09847-0   LC 2003-19666

Discusses some of Egypt's most famous artifacts and monuments, including the pyramids, the Rosetta Stone, and, especially, the Great Sphinx, presenting research and speculation about their origins and their future

"In his signature plain style the . . . author presents a wealth of scholarship. . . . He vividly conveys the drama of recent discoveries. . . . The photorealistic gouache and watercolor illustrations are beautiful." Booklist

Includes bibliographical references

Harris, Geraldine, 1951-

Ancient Egypt. 3rd ed. Chelsea House 2007 96p il map (Cultural atlas for young people) $35

Grades: 5 6 7 8   **932**

1. Egypt—Civilization 2. Egypt—Antiquities

ISBN 978-0-8160-6823-4; 0-8160-6823-2

First published 1990

Maps, charts, illustrations, and text explore the history and culture of ancient Egypt.

"Filled with excellent captioned, color maps, photographs, and illustrations of primary source materials. There are sidebars, gazetteers, and timelines of events in politics, war, art, technology, etc." Libr Media Connect

Includes glossary and bibliographical references

Hart, George, 1945-
Ancient Egypt; written by George Hart. rev ed. DK Pub. 2004 72p il map (DK eyewitness books) $15.99; lib bdg $19.99
Grades: 4 5 6 7   **932**
   1. Egypt—Civilization 2. Egypt—Antiquities
   ISBN 0-7566-0646-2; 0-7566-0652-7 (lib bdg)
               LC 2004-302392
   First published 1990 by Knopf
   A photo essay on ancient Egypt and the people who lived there, documented through the mummies, pottery, weapons, and other objects they left behind. Describes their society, religion, obsession with the afterlife, and methods of mummification

Hawass, Zahi A.
Curse of the pharaohs; my adventures with mummies. National Geographic Society 2004 144p il $19.95; lib bdg $29.90 *
Grades: 5 6 7 8   **932**
   1. Egypt—Antiquities 2. Archeology
   ISBN 0-7922-6963-2; 0-7922-6665-X (lib bdg)
               LC 2003-18813
   "Hawass delineates and attempts to debunk the alleged curses attached to the entering of the pharaohs' tombs." Publ Wkly
   "Hawass' writing is passionate, informative, and kid friendly. . . . Even so, what will probably most attract aspiring archeologists are the National Geographic-quality photographs, which lend tantalizing immediacy to real-life tales from the crypt." Booklist
   Includes glossary and bibliographical references

Hinds, Kathryn, 1962-
The city. Marshall Cavendish Benchmark 2006 c2007 72p il map (Life in Ancient Egypt) lib bdg $32.79 *
Grades: 6 7 8 9   **932**
   1. Egypt—Civilization 2. City and town life
   ISBN 978-0-7614-2184-9; 0-7614-2184-X
   "Describes daily life in the cities of ancient Egypt during the New Kingdom period, from about 1550 BCE to about 1070 BCE, including the roles of women and men and what it was like to be a child in that era." Publisher's note
   This is "distinguished by elegant design and high-quality reproductions. . . . Hinds's writing is solid . . . and quotations are meticulously documented." SLJ
   Includes glossary and bibliographical references

The countryside. Marshall Cavendish Benchmark 2006 c2007 70p il map (Life in Ancient Egypt) lib bdg $32.79 *
Grades: 6 7 8 9   **932**
   1. Egypt—Civilization 2. Country life
   ISBN 978-0-7614-2185-6; 0-7614-2185-8
   "Describes the social and economic structure of country life during the New Kingdom period (c. 1550 BCE 1070 BCE) of ancient Egypt, including the distinctive roles of men and women and what it was like to be a child in a peasant community." Publisher's note
   This is "distinguished by elegant design and high-quality reproductions. . . . Hinds's writing is solid . . . and quotations are meticulously documented." SLJ

The Pharaoh's court. Marshall Cavendish Benchmark 2006 c2007 72p il map (Life in Ancient Egypt) lib bdg $32.79 *
Grades: 6 7 8 9   **932**
   1. Egypt—Civilization 2. Courts and courtiers
   ISBN 978-0-7614-2183-2; 0-7614-2183-1
   "Describes the daily life of the upper classes during the New Kingdom period of ancient Egypt, from about 1550 BCE to about 1070 BCE, including the structure of society, the differing roles of men and women, and what it was like to be a child in that era." Publisher's note
   This is "distinguished by elegant design and high-quality reproductions. . . . Hinds's writing is solid . . . and quotations are meticulously documented." SLJ
   Includes glossary and bibliographical references

Lace, William W.
The curse of King Tut; by William W. Lace. ReferencePoint Press 2007 104p il (The mysterious & unknown) lib bdg $24.95
Grades: 6 7 8 9   **932**
   1. Tutankhamen, King of Egypt 2. Egypt—Civilization 3. Egypt—Antiquities
   ISBN 978-1-60152-024-1 (lib bdg); 1-60152-024-7 (lib bdg)   LC 2007010987
   This "explores Egyptian history, mummy making, the discovery and opening of the tomb of Tutankhamen in 1922, and the events that happened after that. Much of the book is based on archaeologist Howard Carter's diaries and letters, and on period newspaper articles. The color photographs in [this attractive [book] are excellent, and the readable [text is] interesting." SLJ
   Includes bibliographical references

Langley, Andrew
Ancient Egypt; [by] Andrew Langley. Raintree 2005 48p il map (History in art) $31.43
Grades: 4 5 6 7   **932**
   1. Egyptian art 2. Egypt—Civilization
   ISBN 1-4109-0518-7   LC 2004-7524
   Contents: Art of ancient Egypt; Art as evidence; Beginnings; The old kingdom; The middle kingdom; The new kingdom; Land of the pharaohs; Building the pyramids; Trade and empire; The Valley of the Kings; Greeks and Romans; Homes and families; Eating and drinking; At work; Entertainment; Scribes and hieroglyphs; Gods and the afterlife; Mummification; Burial; Priests and rituals
   This book has "a depth of content that is unusual in art-history books for this age group. . . . [It] is amply illustrated with full-color photographs and reproductions. . . . Well-written, informative." SLJ
   Includes bibliographical references

Malam, John, 1957-
Ancient Egyptian jobs. Heinemann Lib. 2003 48p il map (People in the past) $29.93; pa $8.50
Grades: 5 6 7 8   **932**
   1. Egypt—Civilization
   ISBN 1-4034-0311-2; 1-4034-0515-8 (pa)
               LC 2002-12595

Malam, John, 1957-—*Continued*
Contents: Egypt: gift of the Nile; Who worked in ancient Egypt?; Organizing the workforce; Professions of ancient Egypt; Priest; Doctor; Merchant; Dancer; Farmer; Fisher; Hunter; Baker; Carpenter; Spinner and weaver; Jeweler; Who built the tombs of ancient Egypt?; Pyramid builder; Artist; Embalmer; How do we know?
This "volume begins with a brief introduction that offers geographical and historical background. [It] covers an assortment of workers including scribe, priest, dancer, baker, hunter, pyramid builder, and embalmer. Training, daily routines, and other pertinent information is included. . . . Color photographs of sites and artifacts and maps enhance the [presentation]. Insets provide additional tidbits of information." SLJ
Includes bibliographical references

Nardo, Don, 1947-
Ancient Alexandria. Lucent Bks. 2003 112p il maps (Travel guide to) $21.96
Grades: 7 8 9 10   **932**
1. Alexandria (Egypt) 2. Egypt—Civilization
ISBN 1-59018-142-5   LC 2002-6599
A historical look at ancient Alexandria and its people, education, weather, transportation, hotels, shopping, festivals, sporting events, banks, government, and sightseeing
"This well-written, easy-to-understand text will be a useful addition." SLJ
Includes bibliographical references

Artistry in stone; great structures of ancient Egypt. Lucent Books 2005 112p il map (Lucent library of historical eras, Ancient Egypt) $28.70
Grades: 7 8 9 10   **932**
1. Egypt—Antiquities 2. Pyramids 3. Egypt—Civilization
ISBN 1-59018-661-3
This describes ancient Egyptian pyramids, colossal statues, tombs, and temples, and the lives of the workers who built them.
"Quoting extensively from 19th- and 20th-century Egyptologists, as well as from available ancient sources, Nardo presents a great deal of information in a smooth narrative, accompanied by archival photographs and reproductions of artifacts, illustrations from the past century or so, and even scenes taken from films and documentaries." SLJ

Arts, leisure, and sport in ancient Egypt. Lucent Books 2005 112p il map (Lucent library of historical eras, Ancient Egypt) $28.70
Grades: 7 8 9 10   **932**
1. Egypt—Civilization 2. Egyptian art
ISBN 1-59018-706-7   LC 2004030542
Contents: Artistry in stone; Production of pottery and glass; Clothmaking and leatherworking; Working with metal and wood; Jewelry-making and painting; Writing and literature; Leisure games and sports; Hunting and fishing; Music, singing, and dancing
"Quoting extensively from 19th- and 20th-century Egyptologists, as well as from available ancient sources, Nardo presents a great deal of information in a smooth narrative, accompanied by archival photographs and reproductions of artifacts, illustrations from the past centu-

ry or so, and even scenes taken from films and documentaries." SLJ
Includes bibliographical references

Netzley, Patricia D.
The Greenhaven encyclopedia of ancient Egypt. Greenhaven Press 2003 336p (Greenhaven encyclopedia of) $74.95
Grades: 8 9 10 11 12   **932**
1. Egypt—Antiquities—Encyclopedias 2. Reference books
ISBN 0-7377-1150-7   LC 2002-6965
"Alphabetical entries range from prehistory to the time of Greco-Roman domination and are generally between a paragraph and a page in length. Coverage includes individual pharaohs, places, practices, trades, beliefs, artwork, and aspects of daily and family life with entries such as 'furniture,' 'children,' and 'entertaining guests.' Important individuals such as archaeologist Howard Carter are also included." SLJ
Includes bibliographical references

Perl, Lila
The ancient Egyptians; written by Lila Perl. Franklin Watts 2004 112p il map (People of the ancient world) $29.50; pa $9.95 *
Grades: 5 6 7 8   **932**
1. Egypt—Civilization
ISBN 0-531-12345-6; 0-531-16738-0 (pa)
                                     LC 2004-1940
Contents: How we know about ancient Egypt; Farmers, bakers, and brewers; Priests and scribes; Kings, queens, and pharaohs; Builders in stone; Quarrymen and craft workers; Warriors and captives; Mummy makers; The legacy of ancient Egypt
"Crisp reproductions of visuals, along with impressive ancillary content. . . . help make [this title] among the best available on ancient [Egypt]." Booklist
Includes bibliographical references

Rubalcaba, Jill
Ancient Egypt; archaeology unlocks the secrets of Egypt's past; by Jill Rubalcaba. National Geographic 2007 64p il map (National Geographic investigates) $17.95; lib bdg $27.90 *
Grades: 5 6 7 8   **932**
1. Egypt—Civilization 2. Egypt—Antiquities 3. Excavations (Archeology)—Egypt
ISBN 0-7922-7784-8; 978-0-7922-7784-2; 0-7922-7857-7 (lib bdg); 978-0-7922-7857-3 (lib bdg)
                                     LC 2006032111
This describes how archeologists have learned about Ancient Egypt.
This offers "the beautiful photography and illustrations characteristic of the National Geographic Society, [a] well-written [text] and sidebars, and information on recent archaeological finds." SLJ
Includes bibliographical references

Sharp, Anne Wallace
Women of Ancient Egypt. Lucent Books 2005 112p il map (Women in history) $28.70
Grades: 7 8 9 10   **932**

Sharp, Anne Wallace—*Continued*
1. Egypt—Civilization 2. Women—Egypt
ISBN 1-59018-361-4
This discusses the roles of women in ancient Egyptian society, as peasants and nobility, in religion and in medicine, as royalty, scribes, dancers, artisans and politicians.

Smith, Stuart Tyson
Valley of the Kings; [by] Stuart Tyson Smith and Nancy Stone Bernard. Oxford Univ. Press 2002 47p il map (Digging for the past) $19.95
Grades: 4 5 6 7   **932**
1. Egypt—Antiquities
ISBN 0-19-514770-7   LC 2002-4288
Contents: Tourists and plunderers; Explorers, observers, and patrons; Sensation of the century; The last lost tomb?; Where did all the mummies go?; Interview with Stuart Tyson Smith
Explores Egypt's Valley of the Kings, a vast burial ground containing more than seventy tombs, and discusses archaeologists' findings and challenges during nearly two hundred years of excavation
"The easy-to-read text is enhanced by good-quality, color photographs of artifacts, period photographs, reproductions of artwork, and maps." SLJ
Includes glossary and bibliographical references

Taylor, John H.
Mummy; the inside story. Abrams 2004 48p il map pa $14.95 *
Grades: 5 6 7 8   **932**
1. Mummies 2. Egypt—Antiquities
ISBN 0-8109-9181-0
Using non-invasive cutting-edge technology, this exhibit by the British Museum reveals the secrets of one mummy, the priest Nesperennub, while leaving him undisturbed.
"There are many excellent mummy books available, but this one explores the impact and potential of cutting-edge technology especially well." SLJ

Weitzman, David L., 1936-
Pharaoh's boat; written and illustrated by David Weitzman. Houghton Mifflin Harcourt 2009 unp il map $17 *
Grades: 4 5 6 7   **932**
1. Cheops, King of Egypt, fl. 2900-2877 B.C.
2. Ships 3. Egypt—Civilization
ISBN 978-0-547-05341-7; 0-547-05341-X
LC 2008036081
"Weitzman recounts the construction of a boat made for the Pharaoh Cheops and discusses its rediscovery and restoration in the 20th century. He weaves the history, texts, mythology, and customs of ancient Egypt into an effective narrative. . . . The volume's stylized illustrations are inspired by the two-dimensional depictions from ancient Egyptian art. The paintings' earth tones, accentuated by bright greens and blues, are both appropriate for the subject matter and pleasing to the eye." SLJ

933 Palestine to 70 A.D.

Sherman, Josepha
Your travel guide to ancient Israel. Lerner Publications 2004 80p il map (Passport to history) lib bdg $26.60
Grades: 6 7 8 9   **933**
1. Palestine—Civilization
ISBN 0-8225-3072-4   LC 2003-5622
Takes readers on a journey back in time in order to experience life in Israel at the time of King Solomon, describing clothing, accommodations, foods, local customs, transportation, a few notable personalities, and more
"Written in a lively conversational style, [this] book contains boxed trivia and informative photos, reproductions, drawings, and maps. Useful for reports or just browsing." SLJ

934 India to 647 A.D.

Schomp, Virginia, 1953-
Ancient India; written by Virginia Schomp. Franklin Watts 2005 112p il map (People of the ancient world) lib bdg $30.50; pa $9.95 *
Grades: 5 6 7 8   **934**
1. India—Civilization
ISBN 0-531-12379-0 (lib bdg); 0-531-16846-8 (pa)
LC 2004-25156
Contents: Brahman priests; Kings, queens, and princes; Government leaders and warriors; Farmers and merchants; Servants, laborers, and craftspeople; Outcastes and slaves; Poets and playwrights
This examines the society of ancient India through its "literature, artifacts, and documents. Religion, farming, levels of society, art, government, and fine arts are covered in [this] well-written and attractive [book]. . . . Quality full-color photos and reproductions on glossy pages will give readers insight into the daily lives, arts, and contributions of [this culture]." SLJ
Includes bibliographical references

935 Mesopotamia and Iranian Plateau to 637 A.D.

Barter, James, 1946-
The ancient Persians; [by] James Barter. Lucent Books 2006 112p il map $28.70
Grades: 5 6 7 8   **935**
1. Iran—Civilization
ISBN 1-59018-621-4   LC 2005013197
Examines the ancient civilization of the Persians, who first made and used coins, established gardens, and designed a system of roads in the modern country of Iran.
"This brief, well-organized book will provide students with material for reports and projects." SLJ
Includes bibliographical references

Gruber, Beth

Ancient Iraq; archaeology unlocks the secrets of Iraq's past; by Beth Gruber; Tony Wilkinson, consultant. National Geographic 2007 64p il map (National Geographic investigates) $17.95; lib bdg $27.90 *

Grades: 5 6 7 8   **935**

1. Iraq—Antiquities 2. Excavations (Archeology)—Iraq 3. Iraq—Civilization

ISBN 978-0-7922-5382-2; 978-0-7922-5383-9 (lib bdg)   LC 2006032109

This explores the "world of ancient Iraq, in the region once known as Mesopotamia, the cradle of civilization. Join scientists as they study the Citadel in northern Iraq; explore the ancient city of Nineveh; and see how ancient treasures help scientists reassemble the mosaic-like puzzle of Iraq's past." Publisher's note

Includes bibliographical references

Schomp, Virginia, 1953-

Ancient Mesopotamia; the Sumerians, Babylonians, and Assyrians; written by Virginia Schomp. Franklin Watts 2004 112p il map (People of the ancient world) $29.50; pa $9.95 *

Grades: 5 6 7 8   **935**

1. Iraq—Civilization

ISBN 0-531-11818-5; 0-531-16741-0 (pa)   LC 2004-1947

Contents: Cradle of civilization; The warrior-kings; Nobles, government officials, and priests; Merchants and traders; Artisans and artists; Peasant farmers; Soldiers and slaves; Doctors and scientists; Scribes and poets; The legacy of ancient Mesopotamia

"This book explores the cultures of ancient Mesopotamia through their social structure. It takes a look at the people and details the duties of a king, the activities of a peasant farmer, and . . . more. It also describes some of the discoveries and writings that have led to our present-day understanding of this . . . civilization." Publisher's note

"Crisp reproductions of visuals, along with impressive ancillary content . . . help make [this title] among the best available on ancient [Mesopotamia]." Booklist

Includes bibliographical references

The ancient Mesopotamians; [by] Virginia Schomp. Marshall Cavendish Benchmark 2008 94p il map (Myths of the world) lib bdg $23.95

Grades: 6 7 8 9   **935**

1. Iraq—Civilization

ISBN 978-0-7614-3095-7 (lib bdg); 0-7614-3095-4 (lib bdg)   LC 2008007052

"A retelling of several major ancient Mesopotamian myths, with background information describing the history, geography, belief systems, and customs of Mesopotamia" Publisher's note

Includes glossary and bibliographical references

936   Europe north and west of Italian peninsula to ca. 499 A.D.

Calvert, Patricia, 1931-

The ancient Celts; written by Patricia Calvert. Watts 2005 112p il map (People of the ancient world) $29.50; pa $9.95 *

Grades: 5 6 7 8   **936**

1. Celts

ISBN 0-531-12359-6; 0-531-16845-X (pa)

This book portrays the lives of the ancient Celts "by examining their arts, culture, economy, government, religious beliefs, and societal [structure]. . . . Attractively designed and illustrated, the [book features] excellent color representations of architecture, artwork, and other cultural and historical artifacts." SLJ

Includes bibliographical references

Green, Jen

Ancient Celts; archaeology unlocks the secrets of the Celts' past; by Jen Green; Bettina Arnold, consultant. National Geographic 2008 64p il map (National Geographic investigates) $17.95; lib bdg $27.90 *

Grades: 4 5 6 7   **936**

1. Celts 2. Celtic civilization 3. Great Britain—Antiquities 4. Ireland—Antiquities 5. Excavations (Archeology)—Europe

ISBN 978-1-4263-0225-1; 1-4263-0225-8; 978-1-4263-0226-8 (lib bdg); 1-4263-0226-6 (lib bdg)   LC 2007047836

This describes ancient Celtic civilization and how archeologists have found out about it.

"With excellent-quality photographs and a well-written text, this is a thorough presentation of the most up-to-date knowledge about this ancient European culture." SLJ

Includes glossary and bibliographical references

Millard, Anne

A street through time; written by Anne Millard; illustrated by Steve Noon. DK Pub. 1998 32p col il $17.99

Grades: 4 5 6 7   **936**

1. Cities and towns

ISBN 0-7894-3426-1   LC 98-3226

Traces the development of one street from the Stone Age to the present day, from dirt track to the rebuilding of inns as wine bars, showing how people lived and what they did all day

"The time-line construct is a useful demonstration for children, and the busy vistas would make a fine springboard for encouraging students to create scenes of local history." Horn Book Guide

Includes glossary

937 Roman Empire

Beller, Susan Provost, 1949-

Roman legions on the march; soldiering in the ancient Roman Army; by Susan Provost Beller. Twenty-First Century Books 2008 112p il map (Soldiers on the battlefront) lib bdg $33.26

Grades: 5 6 7 8   **937**

1. Soldiers—Rome 2. Rome—Civilization
ISBN 978-0-8225-6781-3   LC 2006037829

"In about 100 B.C., Gaius Marius took command of the Roman citizen army and created a professional fighting force—the Roman legions. . . . Author Susan Provost Beller describes how legionaries brought Roman ways to the local populations, influenced the creation of roads and buildings, and much more." Publisher's note

"The format is inviting with a variety of fonts at the beginning of each chapter, quotations, and a multitude of illustrations. . . . The text is clear and to the point, and chapters are divided into short topics." SLJ

Includes bibliographical references

Biesty, Stephen

Rome: in spectacular cross section; text by Andrew Solway. Scholastic Nonfiction 2003 29p il $18.95

Grades: 4 5 6 7   **937**

1. Rome—Civilization 2. Rome—Social life and customs
ISBN 0-439-45546-4   LC 2002-70694

Detailed illustrations with explanatory captions and narrative text survey some sites in ancient Rome, including the house of a wealthy family, the Colosseum, the Baths of Trajan, and the Temple of Jupiter

This "is a visually intriguing, reader-friendly introduction to ancient Rome." Booklist

Includes glossary

Blacklock, Dyan, 1951-

The Roman Army; the legendary soldiers who created an empire; illustrations by David Kennett. Walker & Company 2004 48p il map $17.95; lib bdg $18.85

Grades: 4 5 6 7   **937**

1. Rome—Military history
ISBN 0-8027-8896-3; 0-8027-8897-1 (lib bdg)
                                          LC 2003-57574

An illustrated history of the Roman Army, including information about its composition, organization, training, methods, weapons, and campaigns.

"Blacklock's writing is clear and lively and the book, packed with dramatic cartoon illustrations, will captivate readers." SLJ

Includes bibliographical references

Connolly, Peter, 1935-

The ancient city; life in classical Athens & Rome; [by] Peter Connolly, Hazel Dodge. Oxford University Press 1998 256p il maps hardcover o.p. pa $21.95

Grades: 8 9 10 11 12 Adult   **937**

1. Classical civilization 2. Rome—Civilization
3. Athens (Greece) 4. Greece—Civilization
ISBN 0-19-917242-0; 0-19-521582-6 (pa)
                                          LC 98-201131

The authors "focus specifically on city life in two 'golden ages' of ancient times: Athens in fifth-century B.C. and Rome in second-century A.D. [They] place each city in its historical and geographical perspective, and then highlight how people really lived in those times and places. Detailed color drawings, cutaways, photographs, and maps make this an extremely useful as well as an outstandingly attractive book." Voice Youth Advocates

Includes bibliographical references

Pompeii; written and illustrated by Peter Connolly. Oxford University Press 1990 77p il maps pa $12.95 hardcover o.p.

Grades: 4 5 6 7   **937**

1. Pompeii (Extinct city) 2. Excavations (Archeology)—Italy
ISBN 0-19-917158-0 (pa)

Presents archeological information about Pompeii through text, photographs, and reconstructive drawings

"This is as complete and thorough a documentation of the story of Pompeii as any that can currently be found in children's collections." SLJ

Includes glossary

Deckker, Zilah

Ancient Rome; archaeology unlocks the secrets of Rome's past; by Zilah Deckker; Robert Lindley Vann, Consultant. National Geographic 2007 64p il map (National Geographic investigates) $17.95; lib bdg $27.90 *

Grades: 4 5 6 7   **937**

1. Rome—Civilization 2. Rome—Antiquities
3. Archeology
ISBN 978-1-4263-0128-5; 978-1-4263-0129-2 (lib bdg)   LC 2007024795

This describes what archeologists have learned about Ancient Rome

Includes glossary and bibliographical references

Deem, James M.

Bodies from the ash. Houghton Mifflin 2005 50p il $16 *

Grades: 4 5 6 7   **937**

1. Pompeii (Extinct city)
ISBN 0-618-47308-4   LC 2004-26553

"On August 24, 79 C.E., the long-silent Mt. Vesuvius erupted, and volcanic ash rained down on the 20,000 residents of Pompeii. This photo-essay explains what happened when the volcano exploded—and how the results of this disaster were discovered hundreds of years later. . . . [This offers an] enormous amount of information.

Deem, James M.—*Continued*
. . . But the jewels here are the numerous . . . photographs, especially those featuring the plaster casts and skeletons of people in their death throes. . . . Excellent for browsers as well as researchers." Booklist

Greenblatt, Miriam
Julius Caesar and the Roman Republic; by Miriam Greenblatt. Marshall Cavendish Benchmark 2006 96p il map (Rulers and their times) lib bdg $29.93 *
Grades: 7 8 9 10   **937**
1. Caesar, Julius, 100-44 B.C. 2. Rome—Civilization 3. Rome—History
ISBN 0-7614-1836-9   LC 2004-16678
This covers the life of Roman emperor Julius Caesar, Roman history, and everyday life in the Roman Republic.
"Interesting facts . . . are highlighted. Achival art, paired with clear text on plentiful white space, illustrates [the book]." Horn Book Guide
Includes glossary and bibliographical references

Hanel, Rachael
Gladiators. Creative Education 2008 48p il (Fearsome fighters) lib bdg $31.35
Grades: 4 5 6   **937**
1. Gladiators 2. Rome—Civilization
ISBN 978-1-58341-535-1 (lib bdg); 1-58341-535-1 (lib bdg)   LC 2006021842
This "recounts the brutality and cruelty of fighting for sport celebrated during Roman times. . . . [The book does] an adequate job of covering fighting techniques, weapons, and history. Photographs and archival reproductions enhance the [presentation]; sidebars provide additional information." Horn Book Guide
Includes glossary and bibliographical references

Hinds, Kathryn, 1962-
The city. Benchmark Books 2004 c2005 87p il (Life in the Roman Empire) lib bdg $20.95 *
Grades: 6 7 8 9   **937**
1. Rome—Civilization 2. City and town life
ISBN 0-7614-1655-2   LC 2004-8255
Contents: An empire of cities; Public places and private spaces; Working for a living; Roman men : from high to low; City women; An urban childhood; Rest and recreation; Surviving in the city
This considers city life in the Roman empire, describing public and private spaces, work, roles of men and women, childhood, and recreation.
Includes glossary and bibliographical references

The countryside. Benchmark Books 2004 c2005 72p il (Life in the Roman Empire) lib bdg $32.79 *
Grades: 6 7 8 9   **937**
1. Rome—Civilization 2. Country life
ISBN 0-7614-1656-0   LC 2004-9496
Contents: The empire's support system; Country communities Country homes; Working the land; Men of the soil; Rural women; Growing up in the countryside; Hard times and holidays

This examines country life during the Roman Empire, describing the economy, homes, labor, roles of men and women, childhood, and holidays.
Includes glossary and bibliographical references

The Patricians. Benchmark Books 2004 c2005 72p il (Life in the Roman Empire) $20.95 *
Grades: 6 7 8 9   **937**
1. Rome—Civilization 2. Social classes
ISBN 0-7614-1654-4   LC 2004-3080
Contents: The man at the top; Monuments to power; The imperial court; A man's world; Imperial women; Children of the empire; Privileges and peril
This considers life of the ruling class during the Roman empire, describing the Senate, the emperors, the imperial court, the roles of men and women, children, and the perils of privilege.
Includes glossary and bibliographical references

James, Simon, 1957-
Ancient Rome; written by Simon James. rev. ed. DK Pub. 2008 72p il map (DK eyewitness books) $15.99
Grades: 4 5 6 7   **937**
1. Rome—Civilization 2. Rome—Antiquities
ISBN 978-0-7566-3766-8; 0-7566-3766-X   LC 2008-276034
First published 1990 by Knopf
A photo essay documenting ancient Rome and the people who lived there as revealed through the many artifacts they left behind, including shields, swords, tools, toys, cosmetics, and jewelry.
Includes glossary

Lassieur, Allison
The ancient Romans; written by Allison Lassieur. Franklin Watts 2004 112p il map (People of the ancient world) lib bdg $29.50; pa $9.95 *
Grades: 5 6 7 8   **937**
1. Rome—Civilization
ISBN 0-531-12338-3 (lib bdg); 0-531-16742-9 (pa)   LC 2004-1955
Contents: The rulers of Rome; Power and influence of the Roman senate; People of the Roman government; Scholars and writers; Soldiers and the Roman army; The lives of Roman women; Priests and the Roman religion; Architects and engineers; Working-class Romans; Slaves and slavery; Legacy of the Roman empire
"This attractive, thorough, and comprehensible book . . . offers a stellar introduction to life in ancient Rome." Booklist
Includes bibliographical references

Mann, Elizabeth, 1948-
The Roman Colosseum; with illustrations by Michael Racz. Mikaya Press 1998 45p il (Wonders of the world) $19.95
Grades: 4 5 6   **937**
1. Colosseum (Rome, Italy) 2. Rome—Antiquities
ISBN 0-9650493-3-7   LC 98-20060

Mann, Elizabeth, 1948-—*Continued*
Describes the building of the Colosseum in ancient Rome, and tells how it was used
This offers "a clear, well-written text and full-color drawings and paintings." SLJ
Includes glossary

Markel, Rita J.
The fall of the Roman Empire; by Rita J. Markel. Twenty-First Century Books 2008 160p il map (Pivotal moments in history) lib bdg $38.60
Grades: 7 8 9 10 11 12 **937**
  1. Rome—History 2. Rome—Civilization
  ISBN 978-0-8225-5919-1 (lib bdg); 0-8225-5919-6 (lib bdg)   LC 2006100918
This offers a brief history of the rise of the Roman Empire and explores the factors that contributed to its decline.
"Sure to satisfy history buffs. . . . Numerous sidebars, illustrations, maps, and art reproductions provide additional information." Horn Book Guide
Includes glossary and bibliographical references

Mellor, Ronald
The ancient Roman world; [by] Ronald J. Mellor & Marni McGee. Oxford University Press 2004 190p il map (World in ancient times) $32.95
Grades: 7 8 9 10 **937**
  1. Rome—History 2. Rome—Civilization
  ISBN 0-19-515380-4   LC 2003-17799
Introduces the history, culture, and people of ancient Rome and examines its many contributions to the development of Western society.
This volume is "somewhat more inclusive than many other works for this audience. What makes this book accessible is the lively writing. . . . The numerous illustrations include full-color photographs and reproductions of sites, artifacts, period artwork, and an occasional movie still." SLJ
Includes bibliographical references

Moser, Barry
Ashen sky; the letters of Pliny the Younger on the eruption of Vesuvius; illustrated by Barry Moser; written and translated by Benedicte Gilman. The J. Paul Getty Museum 2007 39p il map $19.95
Grades: 7 8 9 10 11 12 Adult **937**
  1. Pompeii (Extinct city)
  ISBN 978-0-89236-900-3; 0-89236-900-0
    LC 2007-2781
Barry Moser's "relief engravings decorate this translation of Pliny the Younger's two famous letters to Tacitus about the eruption of Mount Vesuvius in A.D. 79 and the death of his uncle, Pliny the Elder." Publisher's note
This is a "handsome volume. Using an advanced vocabulary and sophisticated sentence structure, the text sets the event in historical context and gives brief biographical information about the elder and younger Pliny and Tacitus. . . . Moser's engravings reflect the darkness described in the text as day was turned to night by clouds of ash." SLJ
Includes bibliographical references

Nardo, Don, 1947-
Ancient Rome. Lucent Bks. 2003 128p il maps (History of weapons and warfare) $27.45
Grades: 7 8 9 10 **937**
  1. Military art and science 2. Rome—Civilization
  ISBN 1-59018-067-4   LC 2002-6601
Contents: The early Roman army; The development of manipular tactics; The professional Imperial military forces; Fortifications and siege warfare; Naval weapons and tactics
Discusses the weapons used by the ancient Romans and their different means of warfare
Includes glossary and bibliographical references

Arts, leisure, and entertainment; life of the ancient Romans. Lucent Books 2004 128p il (The Lucent library of historical eras, Ancient Rome) $27.45
Grades: 6 7 8 9 **937**
  1. Rome—Civilization
  ISBN 1-59018-317-7   LC 2003-7625
An overview of Rome's leisure pursuits, dinners, the theater, literature, games and sports, and chariot races and battles
This is "an excellent overview of the history and culture of the civilization and {includes} numerous quotations from ancient sources." SLJ
Includes bibliographical references

From founding to fall: a history of Rome. Lucent Books 2003 128p il map (Lucent library of historical eras: Ancient Rome) $27.45
Grades: 6 7 8 9 **937**
  1. Rome—History
  ISBN 1-59018-254-5
Explores the Roman Empire from its mythical founding by Romulus, through development and expansion to decline after the barbarian invasions of the fourth and fifth centuries
This offers "an excellent overview of the history and culture of the civilization and {includes} numerous quotations from ancient sources." SLJ

Words of the ancient Romans; primary sources; Don Nardo, editor. Lucent Books 2003 128p il (The Lucent library of historical eras, Ancient Rome) $27.45
Grades: 6 7 8 9 **937**
  1. Rome—History
  ISBN 1-59018-318-5   LC 2003-1645
Contents: Rome's founding and early expansion; Julius Caesar's exploits and conquests; Reign of Augustus, the first emperor; The home and family life; Entertainment and leisure activities; Gods and religious worship; Chronology of ancient Rome
"Excerpts from historians such as Plutarch, Livy, and Suetonius, as well as the satires of Juvenal and poetry of Ovid, are included in this history of ancient Rome as told through the words of those who lived at the time. Various chapters cover the founding of the city, Julius Caesar's life, the reign of Augustus, home and family life, entertainment, leisure, and religion. . . . Each chapter . . . [begins] with an introduction that helps to put the subject in perspective for modern readers." SLJ

Sonneborn, Liz
Pompeii; by Liz Sonneborn. Twenty-First Century Books 2008 80p il map (Unearthing ancient worlds) lib bdg $30.60
Grades: 5 6 7 8   937
   1. Pompeii (Extinct city) 2. Excavations (Archeology)—Italy 3. Rome (Italy)—Antiquities
   ISBN 978-0-8225-7505-4 (lib bdg); 0-8225-7505-1 (lib bdg)   LC 2007022058
This describes the excavation of the Roman city buried in lava and ash when the volcano Mount Vesuvius erupted in A.D. 79.
This "clearly written [title is] illustrated with large photographs and period artwork, and the pages are broken up with text boxes featuring quotes and interesting anecdotes." SLJ
Includes glossary and bibliographical references

938   Greece to 323 A.D.

Baker, Rosalie F.
Ancient Greeks; creating the classical tradition; [by] Rosalie F. Baker and Charles F. Baker. Oxford Univ. Press 1997 254p il maps (Oxford profiles) $50
Grades: 7 8 9 10   938
   1. Greece—Biography 2. Greece—Civilization
   ISBN 0-19-509940-0   LC 95-26637
"The influence of ancient Greek civilization is chronicled in concise biographies of over 37 Greek statesmen, playwrights, artists, mathematicians, philosophers, and military leaders." Book Rep
"Students looking for biographical or historical information on ancient Greece will find it valuable, as will teachers seeking to integrate the classics into other disciplines." Booklist
Includes glossary and bibliographical references

Hart, Avery
Ancient Greece! 40 hands-on activities to experience this wondrous age; [by] Avery Hart & Paul Mantell; illustrations by Michael Kline. Williamson 1999 104p il pa $12.95
Grades: 4 5 6 7   938
   1. Greece—Civilization 2. Handicraft
   ISBN 1-885593-25-2   LC 98-35762
"A Kaleidoscope Kids book"
Introduces the places, people, historical events, myths, culture, and philosophy of ancient Greece. Includes forty hands-on activities, such as making an early Greek theater, building an Ionic temple, and pressing olives for oil
This is "a clever title that encourages learning and creativity." SLJ
Includes bibliographical references

Lassieur, Allison
The ancient Greeks; written by Allison Lassieur. Franklin Watts 2004 112p il map (People of the ancient world) $29.50 *
Grades: 5 6 7 8   938
   1. Greece—Civilization
   ISBN 0-531-12339-1   LC 2004-1942

Contents: The people of the government; Scientists of Greece; Greek athletes and sport; Philosophers and thinkers; Priests, priestesses, and the Greek religion; Poets and playwrights; Artists and architects; Warriors; Slaves and workers; Legacy of the ancient Greeks
This title offers "useful information that would help report writers and would also engage interested readers." SLJ
Includes bibliographical references

Malam, John, 1957-
Ancient Greece. Enchanted Lion 2004 32p il map (Picturing the past) $15.95
Grades: 5 6 7 8   938
   1. Greece—Civilization 2. Greece—Antiquities
   ISBN 1-59270-022-5
This "touches on such topics as ancient Greek religion, sport, theater, and government, each one introduced with an accompanying image of painted pottery, a statue, or photos of the present-day ruins of ancient structures. . . . Brief but substantive, [this] attractive [title] will spark students' curiosity about the specifics of ancient life and the importance of archaeology." Booklist
Includes bibliographical references

McGee, Marni
Ancient Greece; archaeology unlocks the secrets of Greece's past; by Marni McGee; Michael Shanks, consultant. National Geographic 2007 64p il map (National Geographic investigates) $17.95; lib bdg $27.90 *
Grades: 5 6 7 8   938
   1. Greece—Civilization 2. Greece—Antiquities 3. Excavations (Archeology)—Greece
   ISBN 978-0-7922-7826-9; 978-0-7922-7872-6 (lib bdg); 0-7922-7826-7 (lib bdg); 0-7922-7872-0
                LC 2006032108
This describes how archeologists have found out about Ancient Greek civilization.
This offers "the beautiful photography and illustrations characteristic of the National Geographic Society, [a] well-written [text] and sidebars, and information on recent archaeological finds." SLJ
Includes bibliographical references

Powell, Anton
Ancient Greece. 3rd ed. Chelsea House 2007 96p il map (Cultural atlas for young people) $35
Grades: 5 6 7 8   938
   1. Greece—History—0-323 2. Greece—Civilization
   ISBN 978-0-8160-6821-0; 0-8160-6821-6
First published 1989
Maps, charts, illustrations, and text trace the history and culture of ancient Greece.
"Filled with excellent captioned, color maps, photographs, and illustrations of primary source materials. There are sidebars, gazetteers, and timelines of events in politics, war, art, technology, etc." Libr Media Connect
Includes glossary and bibliographical references

Stefoff, Rebecca, 1951-
The ancient Mediterranean. Benchmark Books
2004 c2005 48p il map (World historical atlases)
lib bdg $18.95
Grades: 5 6 7 8   **938**
   1. Mediterranean region—History 2. Greece—History—0-323 3. Rome—Civilization 4. Greece—Civilization
   ISBN 0-7614-1641-2   LC 2003-12027
   Contents: Greece: Bronze Age ancestors; The Dark
Age; Greek civilization is born; The Persian wars; Athens against Sparta; Alexander's empire: Macedonian
might; To rule the world; The Hellenistic age; Conquest
by Rome; Rome: The Kingdom; The Republic; Conquest
and war; The birth of an empire; East and West; An empire falls
   Text plus historical and contemporary maps provide a
look at the history of cultures that flourished along the
Mediterranean Sea
   The text is "clearly written and well organized. The
[book includes] large, full-color photographs and illustrations reproduced from original pieces of art found in diverse national museums. Maps placed throughout clearly
show the boundaries and areas of the empires. [This volume makes an] excellent [supplement] to history lessons
and [a] good starting [point] for research." SLJ

939   Other parts of ancient world to ca. 640

Marston, Elsa
The Phoenicians. Benchmark Bks. 2001 80p il
(Cultures of the past) lib bdg $29.93 *
Grades: 6 7 8 9   **939**
   1. Phoenicians
   ISBN 0-7614-0309-4   LC 00-41452
   This describes the civilization of the ancient Phoenicians, including history, culture, beliefs, and their modern
legacy
   This offers "balanced, thoughtfully interpreted material. . . . Reinforcing the text are a number of extensions,
including illustrations, color photos of artifacts, a map,
time line, and brief samples of literature." Horn Book
Guide
   Includes glossary and bibliographical references

Podany, Amanda H.
The ancient Near Eastern world; [by] Amanda
H. Podany & Marni McGee. Oxford University
Press 2005 174p il map (World in ancient times)
$32.95
Grades: 7 8 9 10   **939**
   1. Middle East—Civilization 2. Middle East—Antiquities
   ISBN 0-19-516159-9   LC 2004-13622
   This "traces the history of the Fertile Crescent until
Alexander the Great's conquest in 330 B.C.E. . . . The
text is matched with a great deal of supporting matter including time lines, maps, dramatis personae, high-quality
photos, and artists' renderings. [This] fine [volume is a]
worthy [addition] to most libraries." SLJ
   Includes bibliographical references

Sherrow, Victoria
Ancient Africa; archaeology unlocks the secrets
of Africa's past; by Victoria Sherrow; James
Denbow, consultant. National Geographic Society
2007 64p il map (National Geographic
investigates) $17.95
Grades: 4 5 6 7   **939**
   1. Africa—Civilization 2. Africa—Antiquities
   ISBN 978-0-7922-5384-6; 0-7922-5384-1
                                LC 2007277594
   This describes archeological discoveries about ancient
peoples of Africa including the Dogon people of Mali,
the ancient city of Jenne-jeno, and the Kushite temples
at Jebel Barkal.
   Includes bibliographical references

Sonneborn, Liz
The ancient Kushites. Franklin Watts 2005 112p
il map (People of the ancient world) lib bdg
$30.50; pa $9.95 *
Grades: 5 6 7 8   **939**
   1. Cushites
   ISBN 0-531-12380-4 (lib bdg); 0-531-16847-6 (pa)
                                LC 2004-13908
   This book portrays the lives of the ancient Kushites
"by examining their arts, culture, economy, government,
religious beliefs, and societal [structure]. . . . Attractively designed and illustrated, the [book features] excellent
color representations of architecture, artwork, and other
cultural and historical artifacts." SLJ
   Includes bibliographical references

Stefoff, Rebecca, 1951-
The ancient Near East; [by] Rebecca Stefoff.
Benchmark Books 2004 c2005 48p il map (World
historical atlases) lib bdg $27.07
Grades: 5 6 7 8   **939**
   1. Middle East—History 2. Middle East—Civilization
   ISBN 0-7614-1639-0   LC 2003-12030
   Contents: Mesopotamia – Empires and invasions: Beginnings; The rise of city-states; Sumer and Akkad; Babylonia and Assyria; The Persian conquest; Anatolia –
Cultures of the crossroads: Where three worlds meet;
Early Anatolian states; Trade and war; The Hittite empire; Phrygia and Lydia; Egypt – Land of the river: Before the pharaohs; The old kingdom; The middle kingdom; The new kingdom; Foreign rulers
   Text plus historical and contemporary maps provide a
look at the history of the Ancient Near East
   This is "clearly written and well organized. The [book
includes] large, full-color photographs and illustrations
reproduced from original pieces of art found in diverse
national museums. . . . [This volume makes an] excellent [supplement] to history lessons and [a] good starting
[point] for research." SLJ
   Includes bibliographical references

940   History of Europe

Pavlovic, Zoran
Europe. Chelsea House 2006 118p il map
(Modern world cultures) lib bdg $30
Grades: 7 8 9 10   **940**

Pavlovic, Zoran—*Continued*
1. Europe
ISBN 0-7910-8143-5
This describes the geography, history, population, culture, politics, economy, and possible future of Europe.
Includes bibliographical references

Stafford, James, 1963-
The European Union: facts and figures; by James Stafford. Mason Crest Publishers 2006 88p il map (European Union) $18 *
Grades: 8 9 10 11 12   **940**
1. European Union 2. Europe
ISBN 1-4222-0045-0   LC 2005018272
"In-depth and up-to-date, this introductory title in the European Union series combines the big picture of how the EU was formed with details about how it works and the social, political, and economic advantages it provides for contemporary Europeans." Booklist
Includes bibliographical references

940.1   Europe—Early history to 1453

Barter, James, 1946-
A medieval knight. Lucent Books 2005 112p il map (Working life) $28.70
Grades: 6 7 8 9   **940.1**
1. Knights and knighthood 2. Medieval civilization
ISBN 1-59018-580-3   LC 2004-19389
Contents: Introduction: Who were the knights?; The apprenticeship of a knight; Equipping a knight; The knight at war; Crusading knights; Tournaments; Knights of fortune; Village administration
This defines knighthood and describes "apprenticeship and equipment, fighting wars, the Crusades, tournaments, and village administration. [It details] the difficult training endured and the numerous and important roles knights played in society and in upholding the law of the land. . . . [This] well-written, carefully researched [book provides] insight into the struggles and difficulties of the lives of [medieval knights] complemented by numerous black-and-white drawings, maps, and reproductions." SLJ
Includes bibliographical references

Chrisp, Peter
Town and country life; by Peter Chrisp. Lucent Books 2004 48p il (Medieval realms) $28.70
Grades: 5 6 7 8   **940.1**
1. Medieval civilization
ISBN 1-59018-536-6   LC 2003-24516
This briefly describes life in Europe in the Middle Ages for landholders, peasants, monks and nuns, on manors and in churches and villages.
Includes glossary and bibliographical references

Corbishley, Mike
The Middle Ages. 3rd ed. Chelsea House 2007 96p il map (Cultural atlas for young people) $35
Grades: 5 6 7 8   **940.1**

1. Medieval civilization 2. Middle Ages
ISBN 978-0-8160-6825-8; 0-8160-6825-9
First published 1989
Maps, charts, illustrations, and text explore the history and culture of the Middle Ages.
"The maps are excellent, precise, clear, and easy to read and understand, and the illustrations, particularly those of works of art, are wonderful. . . . This attractive volume provides an intriguing cross-cultural look at the medieval world. An excellent addition." SLJ
Includes glossary and bibliographical references

Currie, Stephen, 1960-
Miracles, saints, and superstition; the medieval mind; [by] Stephen Currie. Lucent Books 2007 104p il map (Lucent library of historical eras, Middle Ages) lib bdg $32.45 *
Grades: 6 7 8 9   **940.1**
1. Church history—600-1500, Middle Ages 2. Religion 3. Middle Ages
ISBN 978-1-59018-861-3 (lib bdg); 1-59018-861-6 (lib bdg)   LC 2006012436
This "title goes a long way in explaining the whys of the Crusades as Currie deftly examines the mindset and worldview of the medieval era. The perceptions of time and space, the order of the universe, and religion and superstition are given thorough treatment. . . . [This book has] numerous color reproductions. Clear, concise writing makes [it] highly readable, while the scholarship makes [it a] valuable [resource]." SLJ
Includes bibliographical references

Davenport, John, 1960-
The age of feudalism; [by] John Davenport. Lucent Books 2007 104p il map (World history series) lib bdg $32.45
Grades: 8 9 10 11 12   **940.1**
1. Feudalism 2. Middle Ages
ISBN 978-1-59018-649-7 (lib bdg); 1-59018-649-4 (lib bdg)   LC 2007015981
Introduces European history from the fall of Rome to the rise of nation-states.
This is "well-organized. . . . The chapters showing the gradual weakening of feudalism are particularly strong. . . . The often-colorful illustrations include reproductions of paintings, prints, and maps. . . . This book provides a useful and readable introduction." Booklist
Includes bibliographical references

Gravett, Christopher
Knight; written by Christopher Gravett; photographed by Geoff Dann. rev ed. DK Pub. 2004 72p il (DK eyewitness books) $15.99; lib bdg $19.99
Grades: 4 5 6 7   **940.1**
1. Knights and knighthood 2. Medieval civilization
ISBN 0-7566-0696-9; 0-7566-0695-0 (lib bdg)
First published 1993 by Knopf
Discusses the age of knighthood, covering such aspects as arms, armor, training, ceremonies, tournaments, the code of chivalry, and the Crusades

Hanel, Rachael
Knights. Creative Education 2008 48p il
(Fearsome fighters) lib bdg $31.35
Grades: 4 5 6   **940.1**
1. Knights and knighthood 2. Medieval civilization
ISBN 978-1-58341-536-8 (lib bdg); 1-58341-536-X
(lib bdg)   LC 2006021843
This "deals with the chivalry and battlefield encoun-
ters in medieval Europe. [The books does] an adequate
job of covering fighting techniques, weapons, and histo-
ry. Photographs and archival reproductions enhance the
[presentation]; sidebars provide additional information."
Horn Book Guide
Includes glossary and bibliographical references

Hart, Avery
Knights & castles; 50 hands-on activities to
experience the Middle Ages; [by] Avery Hart &
Paul Mantell. Williamson 1998 96p il pa $10.95
Grades: 4 5 6 7   **940.1**
1. Medieval civilization 2. Middle Ages 3. Knights
and knighthood 4. Handicraft
ISBN 1-885593-17-1   LC 97-32863
"A Kaleidoscope Kids book"
Introduces the Middle Ages, including activities and
crafts that are representative of medieval life, for example creating an hour glass, a catapult, a coat of arms, and
a code of honor
"The text is written in a breezy tone and illustrated
with a combination of line drawings and blue-or-purple-
ink reproductions of medieval art and woodcuts." SLJ
Includes bibliographical references

Haywood, John, 1956-
Medieval Europe; [by] John Haywood. Raintree
2007 64p il (Time travel guide) lib bdg $34.29; pa
$9.99
Grades: 6 7 8 9   **940.1**
1. Medieval civilization 2. Middle Ages
ISBN   978-1-4109-2909-9   (lib   bdg);
978-1-4109-2915-0 (pa)   LC 2007005625
"Raintree FreeStyle"
This describes life in Europe in the 12th and 13th cen-
turies in the form of a travel guide.
The book "is chock-full of color photographs and re-
productions, maps, sidebars, and age-appropriate humor.
. . . The [author has] done a commendable job of writ-
ing [text] that [measures] up to the rich visual layout."
SLJ
Includes glosssary and bibliographical references

Hinds, Kathryn, 1962-
The castle. Benchmark Books 2001 80p il (Life
in the Middle Ages) lib bdg $34.21; pa $6.99
Grades: 6 7 8 9   **940.1**
1. Castles 2. Medieval civilization
ISBN 978-0-7614-1007-2 (lib bdg); 0-7614-1007-4;
978-0-7614-3604-1 (pa); 0-7614-3604-9 (pa)
                             LC 99-86102
Describes daily life in the castles of Europe from the
years 500 to 1500
"Informative and beautifully illustrated. . . . Quality

period reproductions of paintings and clear, color photos
appear throughout." SLJ
Includes glossary and bibliographical references

The city. Benchmark Books 2001 80p il (Life in
the Middle Ages) lib bdg $34.21
Grades: 6 7 8 9   **940.1**
1. Medieval civilization 2. City and town life
ISBN 978-0-7614-1005-8 (lib bdg); 0-7614-1005-7-
(lib bdg)   LC 99-86689
Describes the development of cities during the late
Middle Ages, 1100 through 1400, discussing how they
varied in government, commerce, population, and culture
and how they influenced the shaping of European civilization
Readers of this title "will be struck first by the beauty
of its design, then by the intriguing information. . . .
The many period illustrations include medieval paintings
reproduced in rich, heraldic colors." Booklist
Includes glossary and bibliographical references

The countryside. Benchmark Books 2001 80p il
(Life in the Middle Ages) lib bdg $34.21
Grades: 6 7 8 9   **940.1**
1. Medieval civilization 2. Country life
ISBN 978-0-7614-1006-5 (lib bdg); 0-7614-1006-6 (lib
bdg)   LC 99-86687
Describes the social and economic structure of country
life during the late Middle Ages, 1100 through 1400, and
the role of the peasants, villagers, and landowners in the
shaping of European civilization
"The layout of a medieval village as well as its residents, their work, recreation, and customs are vividly described. The many period illustrations include medieval
paintings reproduced in rich, heraldic colors." Booklist
Includes glossary and bibliographical references

Everyday life in medieval Europe; by Kathryn
Hinds. Marshall Cavendish Benchmark 2009 285p
il lib bdg $42.79
Grades: 6 7 8 9   **940.1**
1. Medieval civilization 2. Middle Ages 3. Europe—
History—476-1492 4. Europe—Social life and customs 5. Europe—Social conditions 6. Europe—Economic conditions
ISBN 978-0-7614-3927-1 (lib bdg); 0-7614-3927-7 (lib
bdg)   LC 2008012748
"Describes the social and economic structure of life in
the High Middle Ages (1100-1400), including the ruling
classes, the peasantry, the urban dwellers, and members
of the Church and the role each group played in shaping
European civilization." Publisher's note
Includes glossary and bibliographical references

Kallen, Stuart A., 1955-
A medieval merchant. Lucent Books 2005 112p
il map (Working life) $28.70
Grades: 6 7 8 9   **940.1**
1. Merchants 2. Commerce 3. Medieval civilization
ISBN 1-59018-581-1   LC 2004-17471
Contents: Introduction: the rise of the merchant class;
Traveling the trade routes; Merchants at markets and
fairs; Merchant guilds; Education and training the merchant class; Buying respect; Merchant bankers: brokers
of power

Kallen, Stuart A., 1955-—*Continued*

This describes "the development of trade, trade routes, markets and fairs, guilds, education and training, and the power of medieval bankers. [This] well-written, carefully researched [book provides] insight into the struggles and difficulties of the lives of [medieval merchants] complemented by numerous black-and-white drawings, maps, and reproductions." SLJ

Includes bibliographical references

Langley, Andrew

Medieval life; written by Andrew Langley; photographed by Geoff Brightling. rev ed. DK Pub. 2004 72p il (DK eyewitness books) $15.99; lib bdg $19.99

Grades: 4 5 6 7   **940.1**
1. Medieval civilization
ISBN 0-7566-0705-1; 0-7566-0704-3 (lib bdg)
First published 1996 by Knopf

An illustrated look at various aspects of life in medieval Europe, covering everyday life, religion, royalty, and more.

Martin, Alex, 1953-

Knights & castles; exploring history through art; [by] Alex Martin. Two-Can Pub 2005 64p il (Picture that!) $19.95 *

Grades: 5 6 7 8   **940.1**
1. Knights and knighthood 2. Castles 3. Medieval civilization 4. Medieval art
ISBN 1-58728-441-3   LC 2004-14902

This "introduces readers to the . . . world of the medieval knight and his entourage. Including works by Paolo Uccello, Lucas Cranach, Pietr Brueghel the Younger, and Hieronymous Bosch, the book [also examines] . . . a section of the Bayeux tapestry and . . . [the] illuminated manuscript, *Les Tres Riches Heures du Duc de Berry*." Publisher's note

"Art and history meld with entertaining and successful results. . . . [This] unique, well-thought-out [title is] good for reports, and browsers would enjoy [it] too." SLJ

Includes glossary and bibliographical references

Nardo, Don, 1947-

Lords, ladies, peasants, and knights; class in the Middle Ages; [by] Don Nardo. Lucent Books 2007 104p il (Lucent library of historical eras, Middle Ages) lib bdg $32.45 *

Grades: 6 7 8 9   **940.1**
1. Social classes 2. Medieval civilization 3. Middle Ages
ISBN 978-1-59018-928-3 (lib bdg); 1-59018-928-0 (lib bdg)   LC 2006007162

"Nardo does a good job of defining the social hierarchy that represented the European medieval world. . . . The writing is compelling and full-color, contemporary pictures complement the text. This comprehensive, well-organized, and worthy effort is especially useful for reports." SLJ

Includes bibliographical references

Ross, Stewart

Monarchs; [by] Stewart Ross. Lucent 2004 48p il map (Medieval realms) lib bdg $28.70 *

Grades: 5 6 7 8   **940.1**
1. Kings and rulers 2. Medieval civilization
ISBN 978-1-59018-535-3 (lib bdg); 1-59018-534-8 (lib bdg)   LC 2003-60387

This describes medieval kings and queens of Europe and their governments, courts, succession, relationships to the church, wars, the Crusades, and the beginnings of nations

This is "attractive, informative. . . . Well reproduced and mostly colorful, the illustrations include a great many reproductions of period paintings and prints, along with maps and a few photos." Booklist

Includes glossary and bibliographical references

Schlitz, Laura Amy

Good masters! Sweet ladies! voices from a medieval village; [by] Laura Amy Schlitz; illustrated by Robert Byrd. Candlewick Press 2007 85p il $19.99; pa $9.99 *

Grades: 5 6 7 8   **940.1**
1. Middle Ages—Drama 2. Monologues
ISBN   978-0-7636-1578-9;   0-7636-1578-1; 978-0-7636-4332-4 (pa); 0-7636-4332-7 (pa)

Awarded the Newbery Medal, 2008

A collection of short one-person plays featuring characters, between ten and fifteen years old, who live in or near a thirteenth-century English manor.

"Designed for performance and excellent for use in interdisciplinary history classrooms, the book offers students an incredibly approachable format for learning about the Middle Ages that makes the period both realistic and relevant. . . . Byrd's illustrations evoke the era and give dramatists ideas for appropriate costuming and props." SLJ

Woolf, Alex

Education; by Alex Woolf. Lucent Books 2004 48p il map (Medieval realms) $28.70 *

Grades: 5 6 7 8   **940.1**
1. Medieval civilization 2. Education—History
ISBN 1-59018-532-3   LC 2003-18309

Discusses the development of formal education during the Middle Ages, describing various methods of education, types of schools, curricula, who went to school, the rise of higher education, and more

"Clear, well-organized [text] along with full-color reproductions of art and artifacts and photos of period structures immerse readers in . . . medieval life and offer sufficient information for reports." SLJ

Includes glossary and bibliographical references

940.2   Europe—1453-

Claybourne, Anna
The Renaissance; [by] Anna Claybourne. Raintree 2008 64p il map (Time travel guide) lib bdg $34.29; pa $9.99
Grades: 6 7 8 9 **940.2**
1. Renaissance
ISBN 978-1-4109-2910-5 (lib bdg); 978-1-4109-2916-7 (pa) LC 2007006027
"Raintree FreeStyle"
This describes life in 15th and 16th century Europe in the form of travel guide.
The book "is chock-full of color photographs and reproductions, maps, sidebars, and age-appropriate humor. . . . The [author has] done a commendable job of writing [text] that [measures] up to the rich visual layout." SLJ
Includes bibliographical references

Encyclopedia of women in the Renaissance; Italy, France, and England; Diana Robin, Anne R. Larsen, Carole Levin, editors. ABC-CLIO 2007 xx, 459p il $95
Grades: 7 8 9 10 11 12 **940.2**
1. Renaissance 2. Women—History 3. Women—Europe
ISBN 1-85109-772-4; 978-1-85109-772-2
LC 2006038854
"This work covers how women of the [Renaissance] lived; how they were treated and viewed; and literary, artistic musical, social, political, scientific, and religious contributions they made. Most of the roughly 150 entries are biographies. . . . Each of the alphabetically arranged essays is about one-half to two pages long, and is signed, concise, and well written. . . . An excellent addition." SLJ
Includes bibliographical references

Hinds, Kathryn, 1962-
The city. Benchmark Bks. 2003 c2004 95p il (Life in the Renaissance) lib bdg $20.95 *
Grades: 6 7 8 9 **940.2**
1. Renaissance 2. City and town life 3. Europe—Civilization
ISBN 0-7614-1678-1 LC 2003-1477
Describes the social and economic structure of city life during the Renaissance, from about 1400 to 1600, explaining how cities varied in government, commerce, population, and culture, and how they influenced the shaping of European civilization
"Report writers will be richly rewarded. . . . Interesting sidebars feature recipes, games, and stories. Black-and-white and full-color reproductions of artwork taken from libraries and museums appear throughout." SLJ
Includes glossary and bibliographical references

The countryside. Benchmark Bks. 2004 93p il (Life in the Renaissance) lib bdg $20.95 *
Grades: 6 7 8 9 **940.2**
1. Renaissance 2. Country life 3. Europe—Civilization
ISBN 0-7614-1677-3 LC 2003-1449

Describes the social and economic structure of country life during the Renaissance, from about 1400-1600, and the role of the peasants, villagers, and landowners in the shaping of European civilization
"Report writers will be richly rewarded. . . . Interesting sidebars feature recipes, games, and stories. Black-and-white and full-color reproductions of artwork taken from libraries and museums appear throughout." SLJ
Includes glossary and bibliographical references

The court. Benchmark Bks. 2004 80p il (Life in the Renaissance) lib bdg $32.79 *
Grades: 6 7 8 9 **940.2**
1. Renaissance 2. Courts and courtiers 3. Kings and rulers 4. Europe—Civilization
ISBN 0-7614-1676-5 LC 2003-1126
Describes court life during the Renaissance, from about 1400 to 1600, explaining how various rulers governed and help shape European civilization
This features "well-written [text] and excellent color illustrations in a format that is unusually attractive. . . . Most impressive are the beautiful reproductions of period paintings and prints." Booklist
Includes glossary and bibliographical references

The **Renaissance**; Jeff Hay, book editor. Greenhaven Press 2002 255p il maps (World history by era) lib bdg $44.95; pa $28.70
Grades: 8 9 10 11 12 **940.2**
1. Renaissance
ISBN 0-7377-0765-8 (lib bdg); 0-7377-0764-X (pa)
LC 2001-23842
This collection of primary and secondary source articles examines the Renaissance in Europe, Africa and the Americas, the Ottoman Turkish Empire and the Mughal Empire in India
Includes bibliographical references

Renaissance & Reformation: almanac; [by] Peggy Saari & Aaron Saari, editors; Julie Carnagie, project editor. U.X.L 2002 2v il set$105
Grades: 8 9 10 11 12 **940.2**
1. Renaissance 2. Reformation
ISBN 0-7876-5467-1 LC 2002-6152
This "is organized into topical chapters that include sidebars with additional information and more than 100 black-and-white illustrations. Volume 1 begins with a time line of important events. Following the time line are a 17-page vocabulary list and a research and activity guide. Chapters . . . deal with topics such as the rise of European monarchies, the Protestant and Catholic Reformations, the scientific revolution, the status of women, and daily life. A concluding bibliography lists books, Web sites, and video recordings and DVDs." Booklist
Includes bibliographical references

Renaissance & Reformation: primary sources; [by] Peggy Saari & Aaron Saari, editors; Julie Carnagie, project editor. U.X.L 2002 201p il $58
Grades: 8 9 10 11 12 **940.2**
1. Renaissance 2. Reformation
ISBN 0-7876-5473-6 LC 2002-3928
Contents: On the equal or unequal sin of Eve and Adam, by I. Nogarola; The Prince, by N. Machiavelli;

Renaissance & Reformation: primary sources—
Continued
The Muqaddimah, by I. Khaldûn; Notebooks, by L. da
Vinci; The Starry messenger, "A grand revolution" (box)
by G. Galilie; Merchant of Venice, William Shakespeare
(box) by W. Shakespeare; Heptaméron, by Margaret of
Navarre; Don Quixote, by M. Cervantes; "Of cannibals,"
by M. de Montaigne; The description of the new world
called the blazing world, by M. Cavendish; "The ninety-
five theses or disputation on the power and efficacy of
indulgences," by M. Luther; "The sixty-seven articles of
Ulrich Zwingli," by H. Zwingli; Ecclesiastical ordi-
nances, Institutes of the Christian religion, by J. Calvin;
"Elizabeth, a dutch anabaptist martyr: a letter," by Elizabeth; Spiritual exercises, by Ignatius of Loyola; Centuries, by Nostradamus; The life of Teresa of Jesus, by Teresa de Avila; "Profession of the Tridentine faith," by
The Roman Catholic Church; Malleus maleficarum, by
H. Kramer and J. Sprenger

This "provides selected specific writings of the time.
Introductory information about the original author begins
each section, and sidebars list definitions of obscure or
antiquated words. Following each document piece is a
discussion of the historical effects of the piece along
with additional readings." Booklist

Includes bibliographical references

Thomson, Melissa
Women of the Renaissance; [by] Melissa
Thomson and Ruth Dean. Lucent Books 2004
128p il map (Women in history) $32.45
Grades: 8 9 10 11 12   **940.2**
   1. Renaissance 2. Women—History
   ISBN 1-59018-473-4   LC 2004-10849
Contents: Introduction: worlds of the Renaissance;
Wives, mothers, and caregivers; Women at work; Wom-
en in religious life; Women who filled the role of queen;
Political leaders, rebels, and pirates; Women scholars and
scientists; Women writers; Women artists

This discusses the roles of women in the Renaissance,
as wives, mothers, workers, religious figures, queens,
politicians, pirates, scholars and scientists, writers, and
artists

"A concise, accessible account of life during this period and the issues specific to women. . . . The index is
comprehensive, the endnotes are extensive, and the full-
color reproductions and a few maps are well placed. This
attractive title will serve report writers and general readers." SLJ

Includes bibliographical references

940.3   World War I, 1914-1918

Adams, Simon
World War I; written by Simon Adams;
photographed by Andy Crawford. rev ed. DK Pub.
2004 72p il (DK eyewitness books) $15.99; lib
bdg $19.99
Grades: 4 5 6 7   **940.3**
   1. World War, 1914-1918
   ISBN 0-7566-0740-X; 0-7566-0741-8 (lib bdg)
   First published 2001

This study covers how and why the First World War
started, equipment used, and what it was like in trenches
and at home

Bosco, Peter I.
World War I; revised by Antoinette Bosco.
updated ed. Facts on File 2003 162p il map
(America at war) $35 *
Grades: 7 8 9 10   **940.3**
   1. World War, 1914-1918—United States
   ISBN 0-8160-4940-8   LC 2002-5106
   First published 1991
In words and pictures this "illustrates the military
strategies and tactics of combatants involved as well as
the national mindsets of the nations and soldiers who
fought in World War I. . . . [It is] a must-read volume
for both adults and younger readers. . . . Highly recommended for both public and school libraries." Am Ref
Books Annu, 2004

Includes bibliographical references

Carlisle, Rodney P.
World War I. Facts on File 2006 454p il map
(Eyewitness history) $75
Grades: 8 9 10 11 12   **940.3**
   1. World War, 1914-1918—Personal narratives
   ISBN 0-8160-6061-4; 978-0-8160-6061-0
                     LC 2005-27236
   First published 1992 under the authorship of Joe H.
Kirchberger with title: The First World War
This book "provides hundreds of firsthand accounts—
from diary entries, letters, speeches, and newspaper accounts—that focus on different warfare issues and on the
social and cultural impacts of the war on Europe and the
United States. . . . This volume also includes critical
documents related to this topic, as well as capsule biographies of key figures, narrative sections, eyewitness testimonies, 102 black-and-white photographs, maps and
graphs, a bibliography, notes, a glossary, chronologies,
appendixes, and an index." Publisher's note

Includes bibliographical references

Coetzee, Frans, 1955-
World War I: a history in documents; [by] Frans
Coetzee and Marilyn Shevin-Coetzee. Oxford
Univ. Press 2002 174p il maps (Pages from
history) lib bdg $36.95 *
Grades: 7 8 9 10   **940.3**
   1. World War, 1914-1918—Sources
   ISBN 0-19-513746-9   LC 2001-36605
"Introductory essays define 'document' and then point
out strategies for analyzing and evaluating one so that it
can be of value to students. Personal letters, posters,
song lyrics, and poems are among the documents included. The book has extensive citations and sidebar quotes
with dates, speaker, position held, and the context." SLJ

Includes bibliographical references

Feldman, Ruth Tenzer

World War I; [by] Ruth Tenzer Feldman. Lerner 2004 88p il map (Chronicle of America's wars) lib bdg $27.93

Grades: 5 6 7 8   **940.3**
1. World War, 1914-1918
ISBN 0-8225-0148-1   LC 2003-18806

Contents: Entanglements; Widening war; Turning points; Over there; Over the top; Pershing's Army; Uneasy peace; Epilogue

"Feldman provides a thorough background of the complicated alliances and disagreements of countries prior to World War I. Discussions of propaganda, the draft, and fear as a result of the Sedition Act help readers understand how ordinary Americans were affected by the conflict." SLJ

Includes bibliographical references

Hatt, Christine

World War I, 1914-18. Watts 2001 62p il maps (Documenting history) lib bdg $23.50

Grades: 7 8 9 10   **940.3**
1. World War, 1914-1918
ISBN 0-531-14611-1   LC 00-51354

First published 2000 in the United Kingdom

This "discusses the causes of the conflict and offers a chronological recounting of major campaigns. . . . Sources, which range from diaries, interviews, and advertisements to government documents and works of literature, are identified and put into context." Booklist

Includes glossary

Pendergast, Tom, 1964-

World War I almanac; [by] Tom Pendergast, Sara Pendergast; edited by Christine Slovey. U.X.L 2001 xl, 210p $60

Grades: 8 9 10 11 12   **940.3**
1. World War, 1914-1918
ISBN 0-7876-5476-0   LC 2001-53012

This "contains 12 chapters covering major topics related to the period, including the roots of the war; causes of U.S. involvement; the Espionage Act and Sedition Act; weapons of mass destruction; and more. Other features include maps, a detailed chronology of events, sidebars featuring related information, a glossary of 'Words to Know,' research and activity ideas, and a list of further reading sources." Publisher's note

Includes bibliographical references

World War I primary sources; [by] Tom Pendergast, Sara Pendergast; Christine Slovey, editor. U.X.L 2001 xxxlx, 215p $60

Grades: 8 9 10 11 12   **940.3**
1. World War, 1914-1918
ISBN 0-7876-5478-7   LC 2001-53163

Provides approximately thirty full or excerpted speeches, diary entries, novels, poems, correspondence, and artwork related to World War I, with information placing each in context

Includes bibliographical references

Ross, Stewart

The technology of World War I. Raintree Steck-Vaughn 2003 64p il map (World Wars) $32.79

Grades: 5 6 7 8   **940.3**
1. World War, 1914-1918 2. Technology—History
ISBN 0-7398-5482-8   LC 2002-69812

Contents: A new kind of war; Stalemate: defensive technology on land; Breakthrough: offensive technology on land; War at sea: ships of steel; War in the air: the third dimension; Behind the lines; Conclusion: total war

Describes the new military technology used during World War I on land, sea, and in the air

"The vintage photos are of good quality and not heavily duplicated in other sources." SLJ

Includes bibliographical references

Ruggiero, Adriane

American voices from World War I. Benchmark Bks. 2002 c2003 117p il map (American voices from--) lib bdg $32.79 *

Grades: 6 7 8 9   **940.3**
1. World War, 1914-1918
ISBN 0-7614-1203-4   LC 2001-8747

Presents the history of the United States's involvement in World War I through excerpts taken from letters, newspaper articles, speeches and songs dating from the period

"Period photos and posters (many in full color) with informative captions give readers a better understanding of the [conflict]." SLJ

Includes glossary and bibliographical references

World War I; Donald J. Murphy, book editor. Greenhaven Press 2002 289p il (Turning points in world history) lib bdg $34.95; pa $23.70

Grades: 7 8 9 10   **940.3**
1. World War, 1914-1918
ISBN 0-7377-0933-2 (lib bdg); 0-7377-0932-4 (pa)
                            LC 2001-33513

This is a collection of essays about World War I, with an introduction placing the essays in context and summaries of each one

Includes bibliographical references

940.4 Military history of World War I

Beller, Susan Provost, 1949-

The doughboys over there; soldiering in World War I; by Susan Provost Beller. Twenty-First Century Books 2008 112p il map (Soldiers on the battlefront) lib bdg $33.26

Grades: 5 6 7 8   **940.4**
1. World War, 1914-1918 2. Soldiers—United States
ISBN 978-0-8225-6295-5 (lib bdg); 0-8225-6295-2 (lib bdg)   LC 2006026249

The is an account of the U.S. soldiers who fought in Europe in the First World War.

"The format is inviting with a variety of fonts at the beginning of each chapter, quotations, and a multitude of

Beller, Susan Provost, 1949-—Continued
illustrations. . . . The text is clear and to the point, and
chapters are divided into short topics." SLJ
Includes bibliographical references

Myers, Walter Dean, 1937-
The Harlem Hellfighters; when pride met
courage; [by] Walter Dean Myers and Bill Miles.
HarperCollins 2006 150p il map hardcover o.p. lib
bdg $18.89 *
Grades: 5 6 7 8   **940.4**
1. World War, 1914-1918 2. African American soldiers
ISBN 0-06-001136-X; 0-06-001137-8 (lib bdg)
LC 2005-08951
This is a "tribute to the 369th Infantry Regiment,
comprised entirely of African American soldiers (many
from Harlem), who fought in World War I. . . . The
clear prose; effective use of white space; and numerous,
often full-page black-and-white photographs will attract
reluctant readers while enticing more dedicated history
buffs." Booklist
Includes bibliographical references

940.53   World War II, 1939-1945

Adams, Simon
World War II; written by Simon Adams;
photographed by Andy Crawford. rev ed. DK Pub.
2004 il (DK eyewitness books) $15.99; lib bdg
$19.99
Grades: 4 5 6 7   **940.53**
1. World War, 1939-1945
ISBN 0-7566-0742-6; 0-7566-0743-4 (lib bdg)
First published 2000
In photographs and text this introduces the events of
World War II, briefly covering such topics as bombing
raids, the role of women, the atomic bomb, the American
home front, the Holocaust, the D-Day invasion and propaganda.

Adler, David A., 1947-
We remember the Holocaust. Holt & Co. 1989
147p il pa $16.95 hardcover o.p.
Grades: 8 9 10 11 12   **940.53**
1. Holocaust, 1933-1945—Personal narratives
2. World War, 1939-1945—Jews
ISBN 0-8050-3715-2   LC 87-21139
"Survivors of the Holocaust share their unique stories
in an informative, moving account that serves to remind
readers of the terrible effects of hatred." Soc Educ
Includes glossary and bibliographical references

Alma, Ann
Brave deeds; how one family saved many from
the Nazis. Groundwood Books 2008 95p il map
$17.95
Grades: 4 5 6 7   **940.53**

1. Holocaust, 1933-1945 2. World War, 1939-1945—
Netherlands 3. World War, 1939-1945—Jews—Rescue
ISBN 978-0-88899-791-3; 0-88899-791-4
This recounts "how the Braal family, living in Holland
near the end of World War II, set up a hideout on the
island of Voorne and rescued many from the Nazis. . . .
What will excite kids are the facts, full explained in a
long historical note, accompanied by a map, and the
many archival black-and-white photos." Booklist
Includes glossary

Altman, Linda Jacobs, 1943-
Crimes and criminals of the Holocaust. Enslow
Publishers 2004 104p il map (Holocaust in history)
lib bdg $26.60
Grades: 6 7 8 9   **940.53**
1. Holocaust, 1933-1945 2. Nuremberg Trial of Major
German War Criminals, 1945-1946
ISBN 0-7660-1995-0   LC 2003-19759
Describes the atrocities committed against Jews, Gyp-
sies, the handicapped, and other minorities in the German
concentration camps, and the many trials which brought
to justice some of those who were responsible
This covers the "facts without sensationalism and
[raises] important issues about evil and human rights for
class discussion. . . . The documentation is excellent."
Booklist
Includes bibliographical references

The forgotten victims of the Holocaust. Enslow
Pubs. 2003 104p il map (Holocaust in history) lib
bdg $20.95
Grades: 6 7 8 9   **940.53**
1. Holocaust, 1933-1945
ISBN 0-7660-1993-4   LC 2002-151085
Contents: Building the "Master Race"; The Polish vic-
tims; The Russian Campaign; The Gypsies of Europe;
The race criminals
This focuses on the non-Jewish victims of the Holo-
caust, including Poles, Russians, Slavs, gypsies, homo-
sexuals, and the disabled
This "will fill a gap even in large Holocaust collec-
tions, with statistics and searing eyewitness accounts."
Booklist
Includes glossary and bibliographical references

Impact of the Holocaust. Enslow Publishers
2004 104p il map (Holocaust in history) lib bdg
$20.95
Grades: 6 7 8 9   **940.53**
1. Holocaust, 1933-1945
ISBN 0-7660-1996-9   LC 2003-21118
Contents: Introduction: World War II and the Holocaust; "Never again!;" Interrupted lives; Childhood lost;
The taint of evil; History and memory; Legacy of the
Holocaust
Discusses the effects and legacy of the Holocaust, in-
cluding the experiences of survivors, the urgency to es-
tablish a Jewish homeland in Palestine, the need for a
worldwide human rights policy, and the need to examine
the terrible cost of racism and hatred
This covers "the facts without sensationalism and
[raises] important issues about evil and human rights.
. . . The documentation is excellent." Booklist
Includes bibliographical references

Altman, Linda Jacobs, 1943—*Continued*

The Jewish victims of the Holocaust. Enslow Pubs. 2003 104p il maps (Holocaust in history) lib bdg $20.95

Grades: 6 7 8 9   **940.53**

1. Holocaust, 1933-1945 2. Jews—Europe
ISBN 0-7660-1992-6   LC 2002-151084
Contents: A people dispossessed; The ghettos of Eastern Europe; Organizing murder; Living and dying in the camps; Marching to nowhere

This is an introduction to the Holocaust and its Jewish victims in the ghettos of Eastern Europe, in the concentration camps and their liberation at the end of World War II

This is "well organized and accurate, and the writing is sound." SLJ

Includes glossary and bibliographical references

Ambrose, Stephen E.

The good fight; how World War II was won. Atheneum Bks. for Young Readers 2001 96p il maps $19.95 *

Grades: 5 6 7 8   **940.53**

1. World War, 1939-1945
ISBN 0-689-84361-5   LC 00-49600
"A Byron Preiss Visual Publications Inc. book"

"Beginning with an explanation of the origin of the war in Europe and Asia, the text moves on to Pearl Harbor through the major battles to the war-crimes trials and the Marshall Program." SLJ

"An excellent balance between the big picture and the humanizing details, well supported by fact boxes, tinted photographs, and battlefield maps that are both simple and clear. . . . Ambrose's style is authoritative and warm." Booklist

Includes glossary and bibliographical references

Ayer, Eleanor H.

In the ghettos; teens who survived the ghettos of the Holocaust. Rosen Pub. Group 1998 64p il map (Teen witnesses to the Holocaust) $26.50

Grades: 7 8 9 10   **940.53**

1. Holocaust, 1933-1945—Personal narratives
ISBN 0-8239-2845-4   LC 98-43859
Chronicles the deportation of Jews into ghettos during Hitler's Third Reich and presents the narratives of three individuals who, as teenagers, lived in the ghettos of Lodz, Theresienstadt, and Warsaw and survived physical deprivations, abuse, and deportation to the death camps

Includes bibliographical references

Barr, Gary, 1951-

World War II home front; [by] Gary E. Barr. Heinemann Library 2004 56p il (Witness to history) lib bdg $31.36; pa $8.95

Grades: 6 7 8 9   **940.53**

1. World War, 1939-1945—United States
ISBN 1-4034-4571-0 (lib bdg); 1-4034-4579-6 (pa)
                                    LC 2003-18146

This "covers America's efforts to mobilize for war by inviting readers to think about what it is like to be involved in civil defense, volunteer for military service, buy war bonds, and use ration coupons; photos and first-person accounts are included. The segregation of and discrimination against African Americans, Japanese Americans, and women are discussed along with the change in the roles of women and families as a result of the war." SLJ

Includes bibliographical references

Bitton-Jackson, Livia

I have lived a thousand years; growing up in the Holocaust; by Livia E. Bitton-Jackson. Simon & Schuster Bks. for Young Readers 1997 224p hardcover o.p. pa $5.99 *

Grades: 7 8 9 10   **940.53**

1. Holocaust, 1933-1945—Personal narratives
2. Jews—Hungary
ISBN 0-689-81022-9; 0-689-82395-9 (pa)
                                    LC 96-19971
Based on the author's book for adults, Elli: coming of age in the Holocaust (1980)

"This memoir covers the last fourteen months of World War II, during which thirteen-year-old Elli Friedmann (as the author was then named) and members of her family are deported from their home . . . to two ghettos and several camps, including Auschwitz." Bull Cent Child Books

"This is a memorable addition to the searing accounts of Holocaust survivors." Horn Book

Includes glossary

Bodden, Valerie

The Holocaust; by Valerie Bodden. Creative Education 2007 48p il (Days of change) lib bdg $32.80

Grades: 6 7 8 9   **940.53**

1. Holocaust, 1933-1945
ISBN 978-1-58341-547-4 (lib bdg); 1-58341-547-5 (lib bdg)   LC 2006019826
"Bodden details the grim economic conditions in Germany and throughout the world in the wake of the 1930s Depression. . . . A succinct overview of anti-Semitism throughout Europe and a description how Hitler's own hatred of Jews and persuasive leadership help to explain what made the Holocaust possible. Life in the concentration camps and Jewish ghettos, the eventual liberation of the death camps, and the Nuremberg war-crimes trials are vividly described with captioned photos and supported by survivors' first-person quotes. . . . [This is] written in simple language and filled with maps, photographs, and sidebars." Voice Youth Advocates

Cooper, Michael L., 1950-

Fighting for honor; Japanese Americans and World War II. Clarion Bks. 2000 118p il map $16 *

Grades: 6 7 8 9   **940.53**

1. Japanese Americans—Evacuation and relocation, 1942-1945 2. World War, 1939-1945—United States
ISBN 0-395-91375-6   LC 00-26855

Cooper, Michael L., 1950——Continued

Examines the history of Japanese in the United States, focusing on their treatment during World War II, including the mass relocation to internment camps and the distinguished service of Japanese Americans in the American military

The author's "description of life in the camps is vivid, and the battlefield accounts are graphic and dramatic. Both are enlivened with first-person testimony." Booklist

Includes bibliographical references

Remembering Manzanar; life in a Japanese relocation camp; by Michael Cooper. Clarion Bks. 2002 68p il $15

Grades: 6 7 8 9   **940.53**

1. Manzanar War Relocation Center 2. Japanese Americans—Evacuation and relocation, 1942-1945 3. World War, 1939-1945—United States

ISBN 0-618-06778-7   LC 2002-2745

Uses firsthand accounts, oral histories, and essays from school newspapers and yearbooks to tell the story of the Japanese Americans who were sent to live in government-run internment camps during World War II

"On nearly every double-page spread are haunting photos from the time by Dorothea Lange, Ansel Adams, and others that document what happened. . . . Cooper tells it quietly, drawing on the records of Manzanar's daily newspaper, and, most movingly, on primary archival sources." Booklist

Includes bibliographical references

DeSaix, Debbi Durland

Hidden on the mountain; stories of children sheltered from the Nazis in Le Chambon; [by] Deborah Durland DeSaix [and] Karen Gray Ruelle. Holiday House 2007 275p il map $24.95

Grades: 7 8 9 10   **940.53**

1. Holocaust, 1933-1945 2. World War, 1939-1945—France 3. World War, 1939-1945—Jews—Rescue

ISBN 978-0-8234-1928-9; 0-8234-1928-2

LC 2006-02033

This is the "story of the thousands of children who were sheltered in the tiny mountainous French village of Le Chambon-sur-Lignon during the Holocaust. The first chapters provide readers with an introduction to World War II, the Vichy government, and the region in southern France of La Montange Protestante. Subsequent chapters contain first-person accounts by individuals who, as children, were hidden on the mountain, along with black-and-white photographs and an epilogue detailing their lives after the war. . . . The book is an invaluable resource for Holocaust educators, and many of the children's narratives would read beautifully out loud." SLJ

Includes glossary and bibliographical references

Downing, David, 1946-

The origins of the Holocaust; [by] David Downing. World Almanac Library 2006 48p il map (World Almanac Library of the Holocaust) lib bdg $30 *

Grades: 7 8 9 10   **940.53**

1. Holocaust, 1933-1945 2. Antisemitism

ISBN 0-8368-5943-X   LC 2005042114

This "adds essential background history to the many accounts of the Nazi genocide. Downing goes back nearly 2,000 years to show the roots of antiSemitism and the long persecution of the Jews. . . . The clear overview connects that history with the rise of the Nazi Party and Hitler's vision of the Aryan master race. . . . The book design is spacious, with many photos, clear maps, and boxed insets." Booklist

Includes glossary and bibliographical references

Feldman, George

Understanding the Holocaust. U.X.L 1998 2v il maps set$110

Grades: 8 9 10 11 12   **940.53**

1. Holocaust, 1933-1945 2. Germany—Politics and government—1933-1945 3. Germany—History—1933-1945

ISBN 0-7876-1740-7   LC 97-26864

"This overview describes the Holocaust, the events that led up to it, and how the Nazis attempted to eradicate an entire people while fighting a war on two fronts. Sidebars provide information on related individuals, events, and policies. Black-and-white photographs help clarify the text." SLJ

Includes bibliographical references

Finkelstein, Norman H., 1941-

Remember not to forget; a memory of the Holocaust; [by] Norman H. Finkelstein; illustrated by Lois and Lars Hokanson. 1st Jewish Publication Society ed. Jewish Publication Society 2004 31p il pa $9.95

Grades: 4 5 6 7   **940.53**

1. Holocaust, 1933-1945 2. Jews—History

ISBN 0-82760-770-9   LC 2004556462

A reissue of the title first published 1985 by Watts

"This spare, starkly illustrated book explains what the Holocaust was and how it is remembered on Yom Hashoa, Holocaust Remembrance Day. The explanation reaches back to the explusion of the Jews from Jerusalem in A.D. 70 and describes how Jews . . . became targets of anti-Semitism, which culminated in the systematic murder of six million by the Nazis in World War II. The tone is straightforward and matter-of-fact. Black-and-white woodcuts accompany the text with somber scenes reflective of the narrative." Booklist [review of 1985 edition]

Fitzgerald, Stephanie J.

Kristallnacht, the night of broken glass; igniting the Nazi War against Jews; by Stephanie Fitzgerald. Compass Point Books 2008 96p il map (Snapshots in history) lib bdg $33.26

Grades: 6 7 8 9   **940.53**

1. Kristallnacht, 1938 2. Holocaust, 1933-1945 3. Jews—Germany

ISBN 978-0-7565-3489-9; 0-7565-3489-5

LC 2007-32701

"Opening with an overview of November 9, 1938, Kristallnacht goes on to provide background on anti-Semitism, the rise of the Nazis, . . . the impact of Herschel Grynszpan's shooting of Ernst vom Rath . . . and

Fitzgerald, Stephanie J.—*Continued*

its aftermath. . . . Abundant archival photographs (some full color), quotes from eyewitnesses, and accessible maps enhance chapter content. An excellent time line and information on related historic sites further enrich the [work]." SLJ

Includes bibliographical references

Fox, Anne L., 1926-

Ten thousand children; true stories told by children who escaped the Holocaust on the Kindertransport; by Anne L. Fox and Eva Abraham-Podietz. Behrman House 1998 128p il pa $11.75

Grades: 5 6 7 8   **940.53**
   1. Holocaust, 1933-1945—Personal narratives 2. Jewish refugees
   ISBN 0-87441-648-5   LC 98-33600
Accompanied by Teaching guide for Ten thousand children

Tells the true stories of children who escaped Nazi Germany on the Kindertransport, a rescue mission led by concerned British to save Jewish children from the Holocaust

"The design is like an open scrapbook, with different size typefaces, snapshots, news photos, and marginal notes; and the combination of the general overview with personal memories will bring readers, from middle grades through adult, close to the experience." Booklist

Friedman, Ina R.

The other victims; first-person stories of non-Jews persecuted by the Nazis. Houghton Mifflin 1990 214p pa $6.95 hardcover o.p. *

Grades: 6 7 8 9   **940.53**
   1. Holocaust, 1933-1945—Personal narratives 2. Holocaust survivors
   ISBN 0-395-74515-2 (pa)   LC 89-27036
Personal narratives of Christians, Gypsies, deaf people, homosexuals, and blacks who suffered at the hands of the Nazis before and during World War II.

"Well organized and edited, the tales are harrowing, though they all end happily, often with escape or immigration to America and highly successful careers. Friedman points out that these were the lucky ones, and her book serves as a much-needed reminder that the Nazi nightmare extended far beyond Europe's Jewish population." Bull Cent Child Books

Includes bibliographical references

Goldstein, Margaret J.

World War II, Europe; by Margaret J. Goldstein. Lerner Publications Co. 2004 96p il map (Chronicle of America's wars) lib bdg $27.93

Grades: 5 6 7 8   **940.53**
   1. World War, 1939-1945
   ISBN 0-8225-0139-2   LC 2003-12846
A chronicle of the United States and Allied forces' involvement in World War II Europe, including the political and social motivations for entering the war as well as major air, land, and sea campaigns

Includes glossary and bibliographical references

Gottfried, Ted, 1928-

Children of the slaughter; young people of the Holocaust; illustrations by Stephen Alcorn. 21st Cent. Bks. (Brookfield) 2001 112p il (Holocaust) lib bdg $29.90

Grades: 7 8 9 10   **940.53**
   1. Hitler-Jugend 2. Holocaust, 1933-1945 3. World War, 1939-1945—Children
   ISBN 0-7613-1716-3   LC 00-30222
This discusses "the effect of the Holocaust not only on the Jewish children but also on the German youngsters who were forced to join the Hitler youth and on the offspring of Holocaust survivors." Voice Youth Advocates

"With clear, direct prose and a very spacious, readable design [this volume presents] the history without rhetoric or exploitation. There is much here for classroom discussion. . . . Stephen Alcorn's illustrations at the start of each chapter are jagged and dramatic; even more moving are the occasional black-and-white archival photos." Booklist

Includes glossary and bibliographical references

Displaced persons; the liberation and abuse of Holocaust survivors. 21st Cent. Bks. (Brookfield) 2001 127p il maps (Holocaust) lib bdg $29.90

Grades: 7 8 9 10   **940.53**
   1. Jewish refugees 2. Holocaust survivors
   ISBN 0-7613-1924-7   LC 00-51225
This book "looks at the suffering of survivors immediately following [World War II] when many people returned 'home' to face racism, displacement, even massacre, and when countries, including the U.S., denied shelter to most refugees. . . . [This volume is] rich with topics for discussion, and the documentation is meticulous." Booklist

Includes glossary and bibliographical references

The Great Fatherland War; the Soviet Union in World War II; illustrated by Melanie Reim. Twenty-first Century Books 2003 128p il map (Rise and fall of the Soviet Union) lib bdg $28.90

Grades: 7 8 9 10   **940.53**
   1. World War, 1939-1945—Soviet Union 2. Soviet Union—History
   ISBN 0-7613-2559-X   LC 2002-5328
Contents: The Wehrmacht invasion; Stalin as warlord; The Siege of Leningrad; Operation Typhoon: the Battle of Moscow; Behind enemy lines; Stalingrad!; Tactics, tanks, and librarians; The scorched-earth policy; Vengeance and victory; The iron curtain descends

Discusses the Soviet Union's involvement in World War II, from their nonaggression pact with Germany to their subsequent invasion and eventual defeat, highlighting the hardships endured by the Soviet people during the war years.

"Highly readable prose, and an attractive layout work together to draw students into this absorbing study." Booklist

Includes glossary and bibliographical references

Gottfried, Ted, 1928—*Continued*
Heroes of the Holocaust; illustrations by
Stephen Alcorn. 21st Cent. Bks. (Brookfield) 2001
112p il (Holocaust) lib bdg $29.90
Grades: 7 8 9 10   **940.53**
1. Holocaust, 1933-1945 2. World War, 1939-1945—
Jews—Rescue 3. World War, 1939-1945—Under-
ground movements
ISBN 0-7613-1717-1   LC 00-32571
This book "focuses on the Jews and Gentiles who
risked their lives to save others." Horn Book Guide
This offers "clear, direct prose and a very spacious,
readable design. . . . There is much here for classroom
discussion." Booklist
Includes bibliographical references

Grant, R. G. (Reg G.)
World War II; the events and their impact on
real people; written by Reg Grant. DK Pub. 2008
192p il map $24.99
Grades: 5 6 7 8 9 10   **940.53**
1. World War, 1939-1945
ISBN 978-0-7566-3830-6; 0-7566-3830-5
                                           LC 2008-299455
Includes DVD
Discusses the factors that led to World War II; describes the events of the war, from the invasion of Poland that began it to its end with the dropping of atomic
bombs on Hiroshima and Nagasaki; and explores its aftermath
"The volume is visually stunning—50 to 80 percent of
each page is art. A potentially drab layout of black-and-
white photographs is avoided by sepia tones, color
blocks, maps, and color photos from museums. . . .
Readers young and old will gain understanding of their
world today by perusing this engrossing history." Voice
Youth Advocates
Includes glossary

Hillman, Laura, 1923-
I will plant you a lilac tree; a memoir of a
Schindler's list survivor. Atheneum Books for
Young Readers 2005 243p il map $16.95
Grades: 7 8 9 10   **940.53**
1. Jews—Germany 2. Holocaust, 1933-1945—Personal
narratives
ISBN 0-689-86980-0   LC 2004-10534
"In 1942 Berlin, Hannelore, 16, bravely volunteers to
be deported with her mother and two younger brothers
to Poland. . . . They are soon separated, and during the
next three years Hannelore is moved through eight concentration camps. In clipped, first-person narrative, she
remembers the worst. . . . She tells it as she endured it,
quietly relaying the facts without sensationalism or sentimentality." Booklist

The **Holocaust**; edited by Jeff Hill; foreword by
Stephen C. Feinstein. Omnigraphics 2006 387p
il (Primary sourcebook series) lib bdg $65 *
Grades: 7 8 9 10 11 12   **940.53**
1. Holocaust, 1933-1945
ISBN 0-7808-0935-1
"Provides coverage of all aspects of the Holocaust,
from roots of anti-Semitism to Nazi 'Final Solution' ac-

tions and policies. Features include narrative overviews
of key events and trends, 100+ primary source documents, chronology, glossary, bibliography, and subject
index." Publisher's note
"Hill has done an outstanding job of putting together
this unique resource. . . . This must-have sourcebook
provides libraries with the needed documenta-
tion/evidence for students to better understand the topic."
SLJ
Includes bibliographical references

Houston, Jeanne Wakatsuki, 1934-
Farewell to Manzanar; a true story of Japanese
American experience during and after the World
War II internment; [by] Jeanne Wakatsuki Houston
and James D. Houston. Houghton Mifflin 2002
c1973 188p $15 *
Grades: 7 8 9 10   **940.53**
1. Manzanar War Relocation Center 2. Japanese
Americans—Evacuation and relocation, 1942-1945
3. World War, 1939-1945—United States
ISBN 0-618-21620-0   LC 2002-727748
Also available in paperback from Bantam Bks.
A reissue with a new afterword of the title first pub-
lished 1973
"The author tells of the three years she and her family
spent at Manzanar, a Japanese internment camp. . . .
The last part of the book deals with her postwar adoles-
cence and reentry into American life." Libr J
"A spare, powerful memoir." Rochman. Against bor-
ders

Isserman, Maurice
World War II. Updated ed. Facts on File 2003
226p il map (America at war) $35 *
Grades: 7 8 9 10   **940.53**
1. World War, 1939-1945—United States 2. United
States—History—1933-1945
ISBN 0-8160-4938-6   LC 2002-5504
First published 1991
This describes and interprets the role of the United
States in World War II
The "emphasis on personalities enhances the narration
of the actual events and issues, thus keeping the text
both lively and absorbing. . . . [This] will prove to be
a valuable tool for students doing research." Am Ref
Books Annu, 2004
Includes glossary and bibliographical references

Kacer, Kathy, 1954-
Hiding Edith; a true story. Second Story 2006
120p (Holocaust remembrance book for young
readers) pa $10.95
Grades: 4 5 6 7   **940.53**
1. Schwalb, Edith 2. Holocaust, 1933-1945 3. Jews—
France
ISBN 1-897187-06-8
"Kacer recounts some extraordinary history: in
Moissac, France, under Nazi occupation, a French Jewish
couple hid 100 Jewish refugee children—with the support of the townspeople. Kacer, who based her account
on interviews, tells the story of one child, Edith Schwalb.

Kacer, Kathy, 1954-—*Continued*

Captioned black-and-white photos on almost every page show Edith at home in Vienna before the war, then in Belgium, and then, separated from her parents, living with the rescuers." Booklist

The underground reporters. Second Story Press 2005 155p il map (Holocaust remembrance series for young readers) pa $11.95

Grades: 6 7 8 9   **940.53**
1. Holocaust, 1933-1945 2. Newspapers 3. Reporters and reporting 4. Jews—Czechoslovakia
ISBN 1-896764-85-1

"The young people of Budejovice, Czechoslovakia, put out a newspaper during the years of Nazi occupation. . . . The newspaper, *Klepy* (Gossip), is a featured part of the book, and its photographed pages are a fascinating centerpiece of the art, but the real story here is the erosion of life in one small town and how a group of Jewish young people . . . fare during terrible times. . . . The writing . . . is captivating, and the book makes the terror very personal." Booklist

Kent, Deborah, 1948-

The tragic history of the Japanese-American internment camps; [by] Deborah Kent. Enslow Pub. 2007 c2008 128p il (From many cultures, one history) lib bdg $31.93

Grades: 6 7 8 9   **940.53**
1. Japanese Americans—Evacuation and relocation, 1942-1945 2. World War, 1939-1945—United States
ISBN 978-0-7660-2797-8 (lib bdg); 0-7660-2797-X (lib bdg)   LC 2007015125

"Examines the sad history of the Japanese-American internment camps, including adapting to the American lifestyle before Pearl Harbor, life and the conditions inside the camps, and creating a new life after leaving the camps." Publisher's note

This "will provide clear, easy-to-understand facts with critical analysis and will be useful for reports." Libr Media Connect

Includes glossary and bibliographical references

Krinitz, Esther Nisenthal

Memories of survival; [by] Esther Nisenthal Krinitz & Bernice Steinhardt. Hyperion Books for Children 2005 63p il $15.99 *

Grades: 6 7 8 9   **940.53**
1. Holocaust, 1933-1945—Personal narratives 2. Jews—Poland
ISBN 0-7868-5126-0

"Krinitz set down the story of her Holocaust survival in a series of 36 exquisite, hand-embroidered fabric collages and hand-stitched narrative captions. For this picture-book presentation, Steinhardt, Krinitz's daughter, reproduced those panels, adding eloquent commentary to fill in the facts and the history. . . . The telling is quiet, and the hand-stitched pictures are incredibly detailed, with depth and color that will make readers look closely." Booklist

Laskier, Rutka, 1929-1943

Rutka's notebook; a voice from the Holocaust. Time Books 2008 90p il map $19.95

Grades: 7 8 9 10 11 12   **940.53**
1. Holocaust, 1933-1945—Personal narratives 2. Jews—Poland
ISBN 978-1-60320-019-6; 1-60320-019-3

"Rutka Laskier was a Jewish teenager in Poland during World War II. For a few short months, before being deported to a concentration camp, she kept a diary describing her experiences. It was kept safe by a non-Jewish friend for 60 years following the war, and was finally published in Poland and Israel. This is the first U.S. edition. The diary itself is a combination of wartime horrors, social gossip, and teen angst. Photos and editorial notes clarify the situations that Laskier describes. . . . A must-have for Holocaust collections, and a solid purchase for general YA collections." SLJ

Lee, Carol Ann

Anne Frank and the children of the Holocaust. Viking 2006 242p il map $16.99

Grades: 6 7 8 9 10   **940.53**
1. Frank, Anne, 1929-1945 2. Holocaust, 1933-1945
ISBN 0-670-06107-7

"Lee provides an overview that broadens the story that Anne Frank started in her diary. She details the girl's life before her family went into hiding and places Anne in context with other persecuted children and their attempts to survive." SLJ

"This book will still serve as an excellent overview in the classroom and for personal reading." Booklist

Includes bibliographical references

A friend called Anne; one girl's story of war, peace, and a unique friendship with Anne Frank; by Jacqueline van Maarsen; retold for children by Carol Ann Lee. Viking Children's Books 2005 163p il $15.99 *

Grades: 4 5 6 7   **940.53**
1. Frank, Anne, 1929-1945 2. Jews—Netherlands 3. Holocaust, 1933-1945
ISBN 0-670-05958-7   LC 2004-21418

Contents: The Road to war; Anne; Getting to know each other; Separation; Removing the yellow star; Last goodbyes; The hunger winter; Liberation; The Diary of Anne Frank; Fame

"Jacqueline van Maarsen met Anne Frank in 1941, and the two girls quickly became best friends. A Friend Called Anne details their relationship. . . . The book also shares Jacqueline's own chilling experience of narrowly escaping Nazi deportation thanks to her Catholic mother." Publisher's note

"This is a clearly written, demonstrative memoir. . . . Black-and-white photos of family and school settings, letters, poems, and a time line of events in wartime Netherlands are included." SLJ

Levine, Ellen, 1939-
Darkness over Denmark; the Danish resistance and the rescue of the Jews. Holiday House 2000 164p $22.95; pa $14.95   **940.53**
1. Holocaust, 1933-1945 2. Jews—Denmark 3. World War, 1939-1945—Jews—Rescue 4. Denmark—History
ISBN 0-8234-1447-7; 0-8234-1755-7 (pa)
         LC 99-25607
This "narrative history, which weaves together events of the Nazi occupation of Denmark with eyewitness testimonies, is based on personal interviews with more than 20 Danish survivors, rescuers, and Resistance fighters, many of whom helped Jews hide and escape." Booklist
Includes bibliographical references

Levine, Karen
Hana's suitcase; a true story. Whitman, A. 2003 111p il lib bdg $15.95
Grades: 4 5 6 7   **940.53**
1. Brady, Hana 2. Holocaust, 1933-1945
ISBN 0-8075-3148-0   LC 2002-27439
Also available in paperback with CD-ROM from Second Story Press
First published 2002 in Canada
A biography of a Czech girl who died in the Holocaust, told in alternating chapters with an account of how the curator of a Japanese Holocaust center learned about her life after Hana's suitcase was sent to her
"The account, based on a radio documentary Levine did in Canada . . . is part history, part suspenseful mystery, and always anguished family drama, with an incredible climactic revelation." Booklist

Levy, Patricia, 1951-
The home front in World War II. Raintree 2004 64p il (World wars) lib bdg $32.79
Grades: 5 6 7 8   **940.53**
1. World War, 1939-1945
ISBN 0-7398-6065-8   LC 2003-993
Contents: Home fronts across the world; Bombing civilians; Occupation and resistance; The war effort at home; Hardships; Foreigners; Changed lives
Explores life in various countries during World War II for the ordinary citizens who contributed to war efforts in factories and other venues and who, in some cases, experienced the horrors of war firsthand
This is "brief but effective. . . . [It includes] high-quality photos and illustrations." SLJ
Includes glossary and bibliographical references

Meltzer, Milton, 1915-
Never to forget: the Jews of the Holocaust. Harper & Row 1976 217p maps pa $9.99 hardcover o.p. *
Grades: 6 7 8 9   **940.53**
1. Holocaust, 1933-1945
ISBN 0-06-446118-1 (pa)
"The mass murder of six million Jews by the Nazis during World War II is the subject of this compelling history. Interweaving background information, chilling statistics, individual accounts and newspaper reports, it provides an excellent introduction to its subject." Interracial Books Child Bull
Includes bibliographical references

Rescue: the story of how Gentiles saved Jews in the Holocaust. Harper & Row 1988 168p maps hardcover o.p. pa $9.99 *
Grades: 6 7 8 9   **940.53**
1. Holocaust, 1933-1945 2. World War, 1939-1945—Jews—Rescue
ISBN 0-06-024210-8; 0-06-446117-3 (pa)
         LC 87-47816
A recounting drawn from historic source material of the many individual acts of heroism performed by righteous gentiles who sought to thwart the extermination of the Jews during the holocaust
"This is an excellent portrayal of a difficult topic. Meltzer manages to both explain without accusing, and to laud without glorifying. . . . The discussion of the complicated relations between countries are clear, but not simplistic. An impressive aspect of this book is its lack of didacticism." Voice Youth Advocates
Includes bibliographical references

Millman, Isaac, 1933-
Hidden child. Farrar, Straus and Giroux 2005 73p il $18 *
Grades: 4 5 6 7   **940.53**
1. Holocaust, 1933-1945—Personal narratives 2. Jews—France
ISBN 0-374-33071-9   LC 2003-60688
"Frances Foster books"
The author details his difficult experiences as a young Jewish child living in Nazi-occupied France during the 1940s.
"Millman tells his story in a straightforward, yet compelling voice. . . . Dense text pages—with occasional black-and-white photos—alternate with double-page montage paintings in which Millman presents images that emphasize his fears, emotions, and reactions to the events he describes. . . . An inspiring and powerful view of this tragic period in human history." SLJ

Ng, Wendy L.
Japanese American internment during World War II; a history and reference guide; [by] Wendy Ng. Greenwood Press 2002 xxvi, 204p $45
Grades: 8 9 10 11 12 Adult   **940.53**
1. Japanese Americans—Evacuation and relocation, 1942-1945
ISBN 0-313-31375-X   LC 00-69128
Contents: Chronology of events in Japanese American history: The Japanese in America before World War II; Evacuation; Life within barbed wire; The question of loyalty: Japanese Americans in the military and draft resisters; Legal challenges to the evacuation and internment; After the war: Resettlement and redress; Photographic essay
"The combination of historical facts as presented in the essays and the ideas and sentiments expressed in the primary documents gives readers a vivid sense of this period in history. This readable book would be a solid addition to high school, public, and academic libraries." Voice Youth Advocates
Includes bibliographical references

Nicholson, Dorinda Makanaõnalani

Remember World War II; kids who survived tell their stories. National Geographic 2005 61p il map $17.95; lib bdg $27.90 *

Grades: 5 6 7 8   **940.53**

1. World War, 1939-1945—Personal narratives

ISBN 0-7922-7179-3; 0-7922-7191-2 (lib bdg)

This book offers "views of the Second World War through the eyes of those who experienced it as children. . . . Providing enough background information to give a framework for the progression of the war as a whole and the particular conditions and events surrounding the interviewees' memories, Nicholson lets the first-person accounts bring the experiences to life. Photographs of these individuals as children, other period photos, excellent maps, and pictures of artifacts illustrate the text." Booklist

Includes bibliographical references

Opdyke, Irene Gut, 1921-2003

In my hands; memories of a Holocaust rescuer; [by] Irene Gut Opdyke with Jennifer Armstrong. Knopf 1999 276p il hardcover o.p. pa $12

Grades: 7 8 9 10   **940.53**

1. World War, 1939-1945—Jews—Rescue 2. World War, 1939-1945—Personal narratives 3. Holocaust, 1933-1945—Personal narratives 4. World War, 1939-1945—Poland

ISBN 0-679-89181-1; 0-385-72032-7 (pa)

LC 98-54095

Recounts the experiences of the author who, as a young Polish girl, hid and saved Jews during the Holocaust

"No matter how many Holocaust stories one has read, this one is a must, for its impact is so powerful. . . . Opdyke's remarkable story is simply told, with clarity and feeling." SLJ

Oppenheim, Joanne

Dear Miss Breed; true stories of the Japanese American incarceration during World War II and a librarian who made a difference; foreword by Elizabeth Kikuchi Yamada; afterword by Snowden Becker. Scholastic 2006 287p il $22.99 *

Grades: 7 8 9 10   **940.53**

1. Breed, Clara E., 1906-1994 2. Japanese Americans—Evacuation and relocation, 1942-1945 3. World War, 1939-1945—United States 4. Librarians

ISBN 0-439-56992-3; 978-0-439-56992-7

LC 2004-59009

This "account focuses on Clara Breed, a children's librarian at the San Diego Public Library, and the Japanese-American children she served prior to World War II and whom she continued to serve after their families were sent to an Arizona internment camp. . . . Illustrated with numerous photographs . . . and incorporating copious letters and documents, the book is . . . compelling." Horn Book

Includes bibliographical references

Perl, Lila

Four perfect pebbles; a Holocaust story; by Lila Perl and Marion Blumenthal Lazan. Greenwillow Bks. 1996 130p il $16.99; pa $5.99

Grades: 6 7 8 9   **940.53**

1. Holocaust, 1933-1945—Personal narratives 2. Jews—Germany

ISBN 0-688-14294-X; 0-380-73188-6 (pa)

LC 95-9752

"Starting with a description of one of the days that Marion Blumenthal Lazan survived in Bergen-Belsen, this chronicle of her experiences during the Holocaust then goes further back for a look at her family's secure prewar life in Germany." Bull Cent Child Books

"This book warrants attention both for the uncommon experiences it records and for the fullness of that record. . . . Quotes from Lazan's 87-year-old mother are invaluable—her memories of the family's experiences afford Marion's story a precision and wholeness rarely available to child survivors." Publ Wkly

Includes bibliographical references

Rogasky, Barbara, 1933-

Smoke and ashes; the story of the Holocaust. rev and expanded ed. Holiday House 2002 256p il maps $27.50; pa $14.95 *

Grades: 6 7 8 9   **940.53**

1. Holocaust, 1933-1945

ISBN 0-8234-1612-7; 0-8234-1677-1 (pa)

LC 2001-16797

First published 1988

The author "details the dark horror of Nazism—from the beginning pogroms the Nazis organized against German Jews to the setting up of concentration camps and death factories. . . . In clear and simple prose, she relates how the Jews lived and died in the camps . . . and how a small number of non-Jews helped them in their struggle. She concludes with an account of the Nuremburg Trials and the many instances of contemporary anti-Semitism that have outlived Hitler." SLJ [review of 1988 edition]

Includes bibliographical references

Rosenberg, Maxine B., 1939-

Hiding to survive; stories of Jewish children rescued from the Holocaust. Clarion Bks. 1994 166p il hardcover o.p. pa $8.95

Grades: 5 6 7 8   **940.53**

1. Holocaust, 1933-1945—Personal narratives 2. Jews—Europe

ISBN 0-395-65014-3; 0-395-90020-4 (pa)

LC 93-28328

First person accounts of fourteen Holocaust survivors who as children were hidden from the Nazis by non-Jews

"Told in the plain, unvarnished language of childhood memories, these harrowing first-person accounts are particularly moving in their straightforward simplicity, and all are accompanied by photos of the survivors as children and as they are today." Voice Youth Advocates

Includes glossary and bibliographical references

Ruggiero, Adriane

American voices from World War II. Benchmark Bks. 2002 c2003 117p (American voices from--) lib bdg $22.95 *

Grades: 6 7 8 9   **940.53**
    1. World War, 1939-1945
    ISBN 0-7614-1206-9   LC 2002-3247

Presents the history of the United States participation in World War II, including the role of women and African Americans and the internment of Japanese Americans

"News articles, first-person accounts, diary and journal entries, and more offer insights from combatants, civilians, writers, and poets, and provide a wide variety of viewpoints. . . . Period photos and posters (many in full color) with informative captions give readers a better understanding of the [conflict]." SLJ

Includes glossary and bibliographical references

Schroeder, Peter W., 1942-

Six million paper clips; the making of a children's Holocaust memorial; [by] Peter W. Schroeder & Dagmar Schroeder-Hildebrand. Kar-Ben Publishing 2004 64p il lib bdg $17.95; pa $7.95

Grades: 5 6 7 8   **940.53**
    1. Holocaust, 1933-1945—Study and teaching
    ISBN 1-58013-169-7 (lib bdg); 1-58013-176-X (pa)
          LC 2004-19598

"In rural Whitwell, Tennessee, all 1,600 residents are alike, 'white, Anglo-Saxon, and Protestant.' When the community middle school decided to teach diversity by focusing on the Holocaust, the students did not believe that the Nazis had killed six million Jews and five million others. To help them grasp the numbers, they collected 11 million paper clips, which they placed in a memorial made from a German World War II railcar." Booklist

"With clear and concise language, color photographs, and an attractive layout, this book tells [an] inspiring and touching story." SLJ

Sender, Ruth Minsky, 1926-

The cage. Macmillan 1986 245p hardcover o.p. pa $5.99

Grades: 7 8 9 10   **940.53**
    1. Holocaust, 1933-1945—Personal narratives
    2. Jews—Poland
    ISBN 0-02-781830-6; 0-689-81321-X (pa)
          LC 86-8562

This "Holocaust memoir presents a series of brief scenes from 1939, when the author was 12 and Hitler invaded Poland, through the Russian liberation of the Mitelsteine labor camp in 1945. . . . Older students with previous knowledge of the subject will find Sender's narrative moving and thought provoking." SLJ

Shuter, Jane, 1955-

The camp system. Heinemann Lib. 2003 56p il map (Holocaust) lib bdg $28.50

Grades: 7 8 9 10   **940.53**
    1. Holocaust, 1933-1945 2. Concentration camps
    ISBN 1-4034-0809-2   LC 002-6754

Contents: Camps and the Holocaust; Types of camps; Prisoners; How camps were used; Running the camps; Camp discipline; Efficient camps; Processing arrivals at Auschwitz; The main camps

This is an "account of the carefully planned concentration camp network where millions suffered and died. . . . [The book combines] a good historical overview with moving personal accounts." Booklist

Includes glossary and bibliographical references

Soumerai, Eve Nussbaum

A voice from the Holocaust; [by] Eve Nussbaum Soumerai and Carol D. Schulz. Greenwood Press 2003 xxvii, 128p il (Voices of twentieth century conflict) $35   **940.53**
    1. Holocaust, 1933-1945—Personal narratives
    2. Germany—History—1933-1945
    ISBN 0-313-32358-5   LC 2003-45528

"Eve Soumerai recounts her childhood as a Jewish girl growing up in Nazi Berlin, as a teenaged refugee in the United Kingdom, and later as a young adult searching for answers in postwar Germany." Publisher's note

"Readers will get to know Soumerai's family through photos and vivid personal anecdotes. . . . Personal postscripts and extensive discussion questions and endnotes round out this memorable title." SLJ

Includes bibliographical references

Spiegelman, Art

Maus; a survivor's tale. Pantheon Bks. 1996 2v in 1 il $35 *

Grades: 7 8 9 10 11 12 Adult   **940.53**
    1. Spiegelman, Vladek—Graphic novels 2. Holocaust, 1933-1945—Graphic novels 3. Graphic novels 4. Biographical graphic novels
    ISBN 0-679-40641-7   LC 96-32796

Also available CD-ROM version, The complete Maus; available paperback boxed set edition $28 (ISBN 0-679-74840-7)

A combined edition of Maus (1986) and Maus II (1991)

Contents: My father bleeds history; And here my troubles began

In this work "Spiegelman takes the comic book to a new level of seriousness, portraying Jews as mice and Nazis as cats. Depicting himself being told about the Holocaust by his Polish survivor father, Spiegelman not only explores the concentration-camp experience, but also the guilt, love, and anger between father and son." Rochman. Against borders

Talbott, Hudson

Forging freedom; a true story of heroism during the Holocaust. Putnam 2000 64p il $15.99

Grades: 4 5 6 7   **940.53**
    1. Penraat, Jaap 2. World War, 1939-1945—Jews—Rescue 3. Holocaust, 1933-1945
    ISBN 0-399-23434-9   LC 99-52551

"Talbott tells the story of his friend Jaap Penraat, who, as a young architectural student in Amsterdam under the Nazi occupation, saved hundreds of Jews from arrest, first by forging their ID cards, and then by devising an elaborate escape plan to smuggle them over the border to freedom." Booklist

Taylor, Peter Lane

The secret of Priest's Grotto; a Holocaust survival story; [by] Peter Lane Taylor with Christos Nicola. Kar-Ben Pub. 2007 64p il map lib bdg $10.95; pa $8.95 *

Grades: 5 6 7 8 9 10 11 12   **940.53**
   1. Holocaust, 1933-1945 2. Jews—Ukraine 3. Caves
   ISBN 978-1-58013-260-2 (lib bdg); 1-58013-260-X
   (lib bdg); 978-1-58013-261-9 (pa); 1-58013-261-8 (pa)
                 LC 2006-21709

"This volume relays the tale of 38 Ukrainian Jews who sought refuge in a local cave to escape the invading Nazis in fall of 1942 and remained there for 344 days. . . . At once sobering and uplifting, this is an astounding story of survival, powerfully told." Publ Wkly

Tunnell, Michael O.

The children of Topaz; the story of a Japanese-American internment camp; based on a classroom diary; by Michael O. Tunnell and George W. Chilcoat. Holiday House 1996 74p il $19.95 *

Grades: 5 6 7 8   **940.53**
   1. Central Utah Relocation Center 2. Japanese Americans—Evacuation and relocation, 1942-1945 3. World War, 1939-1945—Children
   ISBN 0-8234-1239-3   LC 95-49360

"Interned behind barbed wire in a desert relocation camp in Topaz, Utah, Japanese American teacher Lillian 'Anne' Yamauchi Hori kept a classroom diary with her third-grade class from May to August 1943. . . . Twenty of the small diary entries appear in this book, together with several black-and-white archival photos of the camps. Tunnell and Chilcoat provide a long historical introduction and then detailed commentary that puts each diary entry in the context of what was happening in the camp and in the country at war. . . . The primary sources have a stark authority; it's the very ordinariness of the children's concerns that grabs you." Booklist

Includes bibliographical references

Warren, Andrea

Surviving Hitler; a boy in the Nazi death camps. HarperCollins Pubs. 2001 146p il $16.99; lib bdg $17.89; pa $6.99

Grades: 5 6 7 8   **940.53**
   1. Mandelbaum, Jack 2. Holocaust, 1933-1945
   ISBN 0-688-17497-3; 0-06-029218-0 (lib bdg);
   0-06-000767-2 (pa)   LC 00-38899

"Jack Mandelbaum, a Polish Jew, had a happy family life until 1939, when Germany invaded Poland, beginning World War II. Fifteen-year-old Jack is sent to Nazi concentration camps. Despite fear, starvation, and other horrors, he survives." Voice Youth Advocates

"Simply told, Warren's powerful story blends the personal testimony of Holocaust survivor Jack Mandelbaum with the history of his time, documented by stirring photos from the archives of the U.S. Holocaust Memorial Museum. . . . An excellent introduction for readers who don't know much about the history." Booklist

Includes bibliographical references

Whiteman, Dorit Bader

Lonek's journey; the true story of a boy's escape to freedom. Star Bright Books 2005 142p il map $15.95

Grades: 5 6 7 8   **940.53**
   1. Holocaust, 1933-1945 2. Jews—Poland 3. Jewish refugees
   ISBN 1-59572-021-9   LC 2005010898

"Lonek is 11 when the Nazis invade his Polish hometown in 1939. First he hides in a hole under the stable of friendly neighbors; then his family makes the dangerous escape to Russian-occupied Poland, from where the family members are deported in a horrific three-week crossing to the harsh Siberian slave-labor camps. But following a deal with the British, Stalin lets them go, and for two years Lonek travels on foot, by train, and by ship, until, with 1,000 other orphans, he reaches safety in Palestine. . . . The story . . . is told in short, stark chapters, each ending on a note of mounting suspense. . . . With occasional black-and-white photos, clear maps, and extensive historical notes, this is an important addition to history collections." Booklist

Wood, Angela

Holocaust; the events and their impact on real people; written by Angela Gluck Wood; [forward by Steven Spielberg] DK 2007 191p il map $29.99 *

Grades: 7 8 9 10   **940.53**
   1. Holocaust, 1933-1945
   ISBN 978-0-7566-2535-1; 0-7566-2535-1
                 LC 2007-298461

"In association with USC Shoah Foundation, Institute for Visual History and Education"

Includes DVD

"DK's signature editorial aesthetic, combined with the searing testimony of Holocaust survivors collected by the USC Shoah Foundation Institute of Visual History and Education, makes for a sobering and visually compelling work of history. An extraordinary array of materials—Nazi propaganda, documentary photos, artwork, artifacts—are employed in the service of a broadly sweeping chronicle. . . . Each chapter includes a two-page spread entitled Voices, devoted largely to excerpts from 23 interviews in the Foundation's video archives (an accompanying 40-minute DVD contains the actual interviews)." Publ Wkly

World War II: primary sources; [compiled by] Barbara C. Bigelow; Christine Slovey, editor. U.X.L 1999 xxxix, 222p il $60

Grades: 8 9 10 11 12   **940.53**
   1. World War, 1939-1945—Sources
   ISBN 0-7876-3896-X   LC 99-27170

Presents fifteen excerpts from primary sources related to World War II, including speeches, diary entries, newspaper accounts, novels, poems, and memoirs

The "documents are accompanied by clearly written introductory and background material. Notes in the side margins explain terms and expressions." SLJ

Includes bibliographical references

World War II; Myra Immell, book editor. Greenhaven Press 2001 283p il maps (Turning points in world history) lib bdg $34.95; pa $23.70

Grades: 7 8 9 10   **940.53**
1. World War, 1939-1945
ISBN 0-7377-0699-6 (lib bdg); 0-7377-0698-8 (pa)
LC 2001-16033

This is a collection of essays about World War II, with an introduction placing the essays in context and summaries of each one
Includes bibliographical references

940.54 Military history of World War II

Aaseng, Nathan, 1953-
Navajo code talkers. Walker & Co. 1992 114p il map hardcover o.p. pa $9.99 *

Grades: 6 7 8 9   **940.54**
1. World War, 1939-1945 2. Navajo Indians
3. Cryptography
ISBN 0-8027-8182-9; 0-8027-7627-2 (pa)
LC 92-11408

Describes how the American military in World War II used a group of Navajo Indians to create an indecipherable code based on their native language.
"A good choice for an offbeat 'war book,' this would also make an unusual complement for both history and language arts classes. Historical photos of the code-talkers in action are included." Bull Cent Child Books
Includes bibliographical references

Allen, Thomas B., 1929-
Remember Pearl Harbor; American and Japanese survivors tell their stories; foreword by Robert D. Ballard. National Geographic Soc. 2001 57p il maps $17.95 *

Grades: 5 6 7 8   **940.54**
1. Pearl Harbor (Oahu, Hawaii), Attack on, 1941
2. World War, 1939-1945—Personal narratives
ISBN 0-7922-6690-0   LC 2001-796

Personal accounts of the Japanese attack on Pearl Harbor, with background information.
"Eyewitness testimony of Japanese and American men and women from various backgrounds enriches this balanced treatment of World War II. . . . The first-person voices along with dozens of black-and-white photos and several full-color maps make this a draw for both browsers and World War II buffs." Booklist
Includes bibliographical references

Beller, Susan Provost, 1949-
Battling in the Pacific; soldiering in World War II; by Susan Provost Beller. Twenty-First Century Books 2007 112p il map (Soldiers on the battlefront) lib bdg $33.26

Grades: 5 6 7 8   **940.54**
1. World War, 1939-1945—Pacific Ocean
2. Soldiers—United States
ISBN 978-0-8225-6381-5 (lib bdg); 0-8225-6381-9 (lib bdg)   LC 2006028168

This is an account of the U.S. troops who fought in the Pacific during World War II.
"The format is inviting with a variety of fonts at the beginning of each chapter, quotations, and a multitude of illustrations. . . . The text is clear and to the point, and chapters are divided into short topics." SLJ
Includes bibliographical references

Bodden, Valerie
The bombing of Hiroshima and Nagasaki; by Valerie Bodden. Creative Education 2007 48p il (Days of change) $21.95

Grades: 6 7 8 9   **940.54**
1. Hiroshima (Japan)—Bombardment, 1945
2. Nagasaki (Japan)—Bombardment, 1945 3. World War, 1939-1945
ISBN 978-1-58341-545-0   LC 2006019824

"This book unflinchingly reveals the horrific experience of people who were right there when the atomic bomb was dropped. General World War II history is discussed in some detail. . . . But most memorable are the personal testimonies of the survivors of the bombings. . . . The strikingly designed book features clear type on thick paper and includes many full-page photos with lengthy captions." Booklist
Includes bibliographical references

Bradley, James
Flags of our fathers; heroes of Iwo Jima; [by] James Bradley with Ron Powers; adapted for young people by Michael French. Delacorte Press 2001 211p il $15.95; pa $8.95

Grades: 7 8 9 10   **940.54**
1. Rosenthal, Joe, 1911-2006 2. United States. Marine Corps 3. Iwo Jima, Battle of, 1945
ISBN 0-385-72932-4; 0-385-73064-0 (pa)
LC 00-50914

"A journalistic, accessible adaptation of the earlier book for adult readers, this account by a survivor's son centers on [Rosenthal's] famous photo of six Marines raising a U.S. flag on Iwo Jima. The accurate, engaging text provides the men's pre-war backgrounds, their war service to that time, what they actually did on the island and afterward, and the consequences of the famous photo." Horn Book Guide
Includes bibliographical references

Cartlidge, Cherese
Life of a Nazi soldier; by Cherese Cartlidge and Charles Clark. Lucent Bks. 2001 96p il (Way people live) lib bdg $27.45

Grades: 7 8 9 10   **940.54**
1. National socialism 2. Germany—History—1933-1945
ISBN 1-56006-484-6   LC 00-9559

"This examination of a German soldier's experience begins by describing the rise of the country's militarized culture under Hitler and his requirements of universal military service. The authors then describe the army's rigorous training and devote chapters to Germany's major campaigns in Poland, France, Russia, and Africa, as well as its final defense of its homeland at the end of the

Cartlidge, Cherese—*Continued*

war. . . . [This helps] readers see beyond the leaders and the larger strategic picture to the human face of the young men who carried out orders. A strong choice for history collections." SLJ

Includes bibliographical references

DeMallie, H. R.

Behind enemy lines; a young pilot's story; [by] Howard R. DeMallie. Updated ed. Sterling Pub. 2007 178p il map $12.95; pa $6.95

Grades: 6 7 8 9　　　　　　　　　　**940.54**

1. World War, 1939-1945—Personal narratives
ISBN　978-1-4027-4517-1;　1-4027-4517-6;
978-1-4027-4137-1 (pa); 1-4027-4137-5 (pa)
　　　　　　　　　　　　　　LC 2006032134

First published 2000 by Dry Bones Press with title: Beyond the dikes

"The story follows the 22-year-old American Air Force officer who was forced to bail out of his B-17 in 1944, highlighting his hiding out in the Netherlands, imprisonment in a German POW camp, and liberation by Russian soldiers. There are vivid recollections of hunger, loneliness, and uncertainty. . . . This a a good choice for nonfiction enthusiasts." SLJ

Drez, Ronald J.

Remember D-day; the plan, the invasion, survivor stories. National Geographic Books 2004 61p il map $17.95 *

Grades: 5 6 7 8　　　　　　　　　　**940.54**

1. World War, 1939-1945—Campaigns—France
ISBN 0-7922-6666-8　　　　LC 2003-17733

Discusses the events and personalities involved in the momentous Allied invasion of France on June 6, 1944.

"This well-organized, clearly written account provides a solid overview for readers unfamiliar with the subject. A first-rate purchase." SLJ

Includes bibliographical references

Fleischman, John

Black and white airmen; their true history. Houghton Mifflin 2007 160p il map $20

Grades: 6 7 8 9　　　　　　　　　　**940.54**

1. World War, 1939-1945 2. Air pilots 3. African American pilots 4. African Americans—Social conditions
ISBN 978-0-618-56297-8; 0-618-56297-4
　　　　　　　　　　　　　　LC 2006-17059

"Fleischman fleshes out an article originally published in *Air & Space Smithsonian* about a late-blooming friendship between white bomber pilot Herb Heilbrun and Tuskegee Airman John Leahr with compellingly written war reminiscences, a stinging indictment of the U.S. Army Air Force's discrimination against blacks, and a sometimes-surprising picture of segregation's local realities before and during World War II." Booklist

Includes bibliographical references

Gorman, Jacqueline Laks, 1955-

Pearl Harbor; a primary source history; by Jacqueline Laks Gorman. Gareth Stevens Pub. 2008 48p il (In their own words) lib bdg $27 *

Grades: 5 6 7 8　　　　　　　　　　**940.54**

1. Pearl Harbor (Oahu, Hawaii), Attack on, 1941
2. World War, 1939-1945
ISBN 978-1-4339-0047-1; 1-4339-0047-5
　　　　　　　　　　　　　　LC 2008044081

This book "begins with the events of December 7, 1941, but succeeding chapters go further back, to the opening of Japan, and Hitler's war in Europe. . . . Readers get a sense of not just how the war developed but, thanks to primary sources, what was happening behind the scenes. Decoded Japanese documents are fascinating, and especially moving are the reminiscences of those present on the fateful day." Booklist

Includes bibliographical references

Hama, Larry

The battle of Iwo Jima; guerilla warfare in the Pacific; by Larry Hama; illustrated by Anthony Williams. 1st ed. Rosen Pub. 2007 48p il map (Graphic battles of World War II) lib bdg $29.25 *

Grades: 5 6 7 8 9　　　　　　　　　　**940.54**

1. Iwo Jima, Battle of, 1945—Graphic novels
2. Graphic novels 3. War—Graphic novels
ISBN 978-1-4042-0781-3 (lib bdg); 1-4042-0781-3 (lib bdg)　　　　　　　　LC 2006007645

"Using a graphic novel to introduce the battle for Iwo Jima makes it very accessible. Before the graphic-novel section of the book begins, Hama provides a short, informative background piece describing the run-up to World War II, the significance of the Japanese war machine, and the importance of the tiny island of Iwo Jima. Then the graphic novel, illustrated by Williams in camouflage colors, does a terrific job of examining the ups and downs of the battle as well as the horror of so many losses—on both sides." Booklist

Includes bibliographical references

Holm, Tom, 1946-

Code talkers and warriors; Native Americans and World War II. Chelsea House 2007 168p il map (Landmark events in Native American history) $35

Grades: 7 8 9 10　　　　　　　　　　**940.54**

1. World War, 1939-1945—Native Americans
ISBN 978-0-7910-9340-5; 0-7910-9340-9
　　　　　　　　　　　　　　LC 2006102263

"In this title about Native Americans in World War II, Holm . . . expands considerably on his specific topic to highlight significant miliary roles played by Native Americans in conflicts dating back to the sixteenth century. . . . [This is] outstanding. . . . [A] valuable resource." Booklist

Includes bibliographical references

Kuhn, Betsy

Angels of mercy; the Army nurses of World War II. Atheneum Bks. for Young Readers 1999 114p il map $18

Grades: 5 6 7 8   **940.54**

1. United States. Army Nurse Corps 2. World War, 1939-1945—Women 3. Women in the armed forces

ISBN 0-689-82044-5   LC 98-36610

Relates the experiences of World War II Army nurses, who brought medical skills, courage, and cheer to hospitals throughout Europe, North Africa, and the Pacific

"Excellent reproductions, maps and a time line accompany the clear, well-written text." SLJ

Includes bibliographical references

Lawton, Clive, 1951-

Hiroshima; the story of the first atom bomb; [by] Clive A. Lawton. 1st U.S. ed. Candlewick Press 2004 48p il map $18.99 *

Grades: 5 6 7 8   **940.54**

1. Hiroshima (Japan)—Bombardment, 1945 2. Atomic bomb 3. World War, 1939-1945—Japan

ISBN 0-7636-2271-0   LC 2004-45166

The author "explores the politics and the science behind the military decision that began the nuclear arms race. . . . He investigates the events that led up to the disaster at Hiroshima in 1945 and discusses the consequences that we are still living with today." Publisher's note

"Engaging text and powerful photographs are intricately woven together to make a long-lasting impact on readers." Libr Media Connect

Maruki, Toshi, 1912-

Hiroshima no pika; words and pictures by Toshi Maruki. Lothrop, Lee & Shepard Bks. 1982 c1980 unp il $17.99

Grades: 5 6 7 8   **940.54**

1. Hiroshima (Japan)—Bombardment, 1945 2. Atomic bomb 3. World War, 1939-1945—Japan

ISBN 0-688-01297-3   LC 82-15365

First published 1980 in Japan

Focusing on the experiences of a real family "the horrifying story of the atomic bombing or 'flash' of Hiroshima is told here with a remarkable eloquence, including many poignant details. The story is terribly disturbing and painful to read, but the narrative is at the same time so spare and compelling one must go on. . . . Young people twelve and over, as well as adults, should know this terrible story. This superb book can begin to tell it to them." Appraisal

McGowen, Tom

Air raid; bombing campaigns of World War II. 21st Cent. Bks. (Brookfield) 2001 64p il (Military might) lib bdg $26.90

Grades: 5 6 7 8   **940.54**

1. World War, 1939-1945—Aerial operations 2. Military airplanes

ISBN 0-7613-1810-0   LC 00-41806

This describes the history of military aircraft and how they became formidable weapons in World War II, with a discussion of bombing campaigns

Assault from the sky; airborne infantry of World War II. 21st Cent. Bks. (Brookfield) 2002 64p il (Military might) lib bdg $26.90

Grades: 5 6 7 8   **940.54**

1. World War, 1939-1945—Aerial operations 2. Parachute troops

ISBN 0-7613-1809-7   LC 00-47934

A history of parachute troops operations during World War II

Includes bibliographical references

Carrier war; aircraft carriers in World War II. 21st Cent. Bks. (Brookfield) 2001 64p il (Military might) lib bdg $26.90

Grades: 5 6 7 8   **940.54**

1. Aircraft carriers 2. World War, 1939-1945—Naval operations 3. World War, 1939-1945—Aerial operations

ISBN 0-7613-1808-9   LC 00-42303

This begins with a "history of the evolution of aircraft carriers, followed by a discussion of the world situation in 1941 and the importance of the U.S. military bases at Pearl Harbor. Another chapter tells briefly of the Japanese attack on Pearl Harbor. The remainder of the text describes the major battles in the Pacific and the shift in the role of battleships as carriers became more important. . . . A good introduction for readers who are becoming familiar with this period of history." SLJ

Nathan, Amy

Yankee doodle gals; women pilots of World War II; foreword by Eileen Collins. National Geographic Soc. 2001 86p il maps $21

Grades: 6 7 8 9   **940.54**

1. Women air pilots 2. World War, 1939-1945—Aerial operations

ISBN 0-7922-8216-7   LC 2001-560

This describes the Women's Air Force Service Pilots of World War II

"There's plenty of action to involve readers, and the women's perseverance in the face of obstacles is inspiring. Wonderful black-and-white photos extend the text." Booklist

Includes bibliographical references

Nelson, Pete

Left for dead; a young man's search for justice for the USS Indianapolis; [by] Peter Nelson; with a preface by Hunter Scott. Delacorte Press 2002 xx, 201p il hardcover o.p. pa $8.95

Grades: 7 8 9 10   **940.54**

1. McVay, Charles Butler, III 2. Scott, Hunter 3. Indianapolis (Cruiser) 4. World War, 1939-1945—Naval operations

ISBN 0-385-72959-6; 0-385-73091-8 (pa)

      LC 2001-53774

Recalls the sinking of the U.S.S. Indianapolis at the end of World War II, the navy cover-up and unfair court martial of the ship's captain, and how a young boy helped the survivors set the record straight fifty-five years later.

"Written in simple chronological order, it tells a powerful story." Book Rep

Includes bibliographical references

Shapiro, Stephen, 1983-

Hoodwinked; deception and resistance; by Stephen Shapiro and Tina Forrester; art by David Craig. Annick Press 2004 96p il lib bdg $29.95; pa $14.95 *

Grades: 7 8 9 10   **940.54**

1. World War, 1939-1945
ISBN 1-55037-833-3 (lib bdg); 1-55037-832-5 (pa)

This "focuses on specific stories of deception that the Allied forces used to outwit the Axis powers and win the war. The stories . . . share blow-by-blow details of ingenious tricks that turned the tide of war. Some include constructing fake towns in England to confuse air raiders and broadcasting false radio news to befuddle the Germans. A mix of original paintings that imagine the action mix with archival images. The narration of each story reads like a clever mystery." Booklist

Sheehan, Sean, 1951-

The technology of World War II. Raintree Steck-Vaughn Pubs. 2003 64p il map (World wars) $32.79

Grades: 5 6 7 8   **940.54**

1. World War, 1939-1945 2. Technology—History
ISBN 0-7398-6064-X   LC 2002-151935

Contents: Victories and defeats; Technology and people; Improving the tools of war; The secret war; Inventions and discoveries; Did technology win the war?

Describes the new military technology used during World War II on land, at sea, and in the air

"The vintage photos are of good quality and not heavily duplicated in other sources." SLJ

Includes bibliographical references

Tanaka, Shelley

Attack on Pearl Harbor; the true story of the day America entered World War II; text by Shelley Tanaka; paintings by David Craig; maps by Jack McMaster; historical consultation by John Lundstrom. Hyperion Bks. for Children 2001 64p il $19.99 *

Grades: 4 5 6 7   **940.54**

1. Pearl Harbor (Oahu, Hawaii), Attack on, 1941
2. World War, 1939-1945
ISBN 0-7868-0736-9   LC 2001-16634

"An I was there book; A Hyperion/Madison Press book"

"Tanaka reconstructs key events of the attack on Pearl Harbor, based on the harrowing, real-life experiences of four young men. . . . The account is riveting. She includes plenty of sensory details and writes in a clipped, concise manner that clearly conveys the danger and frenzied pace of the events. . . . Dramatic, full-color paintings, black-and-white photos, maps, and diagrams contribute much to the readers' understanding of the events." Booklist

Includes glossary and bibliographical references

Uschan, Michael V., 1948-

The bombing of Pearl Harbor. World Almanac Library 2003 48p il map (Landmark events in American history) lib bdg $29.27; pa $14.60

Grades: 5 6 7 8   **940.54**

1. Pearl Harbor (Oahu, Hawaii), Attack on, 1941
ISBN 0-8368-5373-3 (lib bdg); 0-8368-5401-2 (pa)
                                                           LC 2002-36022

Contents: World War II; The United States in the Pacific; The attack on Pearl Harbor; After the attack; The United States in World War II

This describes the 1941 attack on Pearl Harbor and its effects

The book is "heavily illustrated with well-chosen and carefully placed archival photographs. . . . [It] will be useful for reports." SLJ

Includes glossary and bibliographical references

Whiting, Jim

The story of the attack on Pearl Harbor; [by] Jim Whiting. Mitchell Lane Publishers 2006 48p il map (Monumental milestones) lib bdg $19.95 *

Grades: 5 6 7 8   **940.54**

1. Pearl Harbor (Oahu, Hawaii), Attack on, 1941
2. World War, 1939-1945—Pacific Ocean
ISBN 1-58415-397-0   LC 2004030309

Contents: A morning of missed warnings; The long road to war; "This is no drill;" "A date which will live in infamy;" Months of misfortune, a day of reckoning

The author decribes the attack on Pearl Harbor and highlights a series of turning points in relations between the United States and Japan.

This is "first-rate. . . . Supported by frequent, relevant photographs and maps, as well as generous lists of recent and classic multimedia resources, [this book combines an] absorbing [narrative] with sharp cause-and-effect analyses." SLJ

Includes bibliographical references

Williams, Barbara

World War II, Pacific; by Barbara Williams. Lerner Publications 2005 96p il map (Chronicle of America's wars) lib bdg $27.93

Grades: 5 6 7 8   **940.54**

1. World War, 1939-1945
ISBN 0-8225-0138-4   LC 2004-3371

This chronicles World War II in the Pacific focusing on the war's impact on America and its people

"A precise, well-documented chronology of the major battles in the Pacific theater. Though the narration is brief, it is informative and avoids misconceptions." SLJ

Includes glossary and bibliographical references

940.55   Europe—1945-

Blohm, Craig E., 1948-

An uneasy peace, 1945-1980. Lucent Bks. 2003 128p il map (American war library, Cold War) $27.45

Grades: 7 8 9 10   **940.55**

1. Cold war
ISBN 1-59018-201-4   LC 2002-434

Blohm, Craig E., 1948-—*Continued*
Discusses the Cold War, its origins and the resulting conflicts, including the arms race, The Korean War, the Cuban missile crisis, and the Vietnam War
Includes bibliographical references

941 British Isles

Fuller, Barbara, 1961-
Britain. 2nd ed. Benchmark Books 2005 144p il map (Cultures of the world) lib bdg $37.07 *
Grades: 5 6 7 8   **941**
1. Great Britain
ISBN 0-7614-1845-8
First published 1994
Cover title: Great Britain
"Explores the geography, history, government, people, and culture of Britain" Publisher's note
Includes glossary and bibliographical references

941.1 Scotland

Levy, Patricia, 1951-
Scotland. Benchmark Bks. 2001 128p il map (Cultures of the world) lib bdg $37.07
Grades: 5 6 7 8   **941.1**
1. Scotland
ISBN 0-7614-1159-3   LC 00-39831
An illustrated look at the geography, history, government, politics, people, religion, language, food and culture of Scotland
Includes glossary and bibliographical references

941.5 Ireland

Bartoletti, Susan Campbell, 1958-
Black potatoes; the story of the great Irish famine, 1845-1850. Houghton Mifflin 2001 184p il $18; pa $9.95 *
Grades: 7 8 9 10   **941.5**
1. Famines 2. Ireland—History
ISBN 0-618-00271-5; 0-618-54883-1 (pa)
                                           LC 2001-24156
The author "examines the causes of the famine, considering the roles of both the potato blight and of social conditions in mid-nineteenth century Ireland." Voice Youth Advocates
"The bibliography (also narrative) provides some of the most fascinating historical reading in the book. Overall, a useful addition to collections, for both personal and research uses." SLJ
Includes bibliographical references

Dolan, Edward F., 1924-
The Irish potato famine; the story of Irish-American immigration. Benchmark Bks. 2003 109p il map (Great journeys) lib bdg $32.79
Grades: 5 6 7 8   **941.5**
1. Ireland—History 2. Famines 3. Irish Americans 4. United States—Immigration and emigration
ISBN 0-7614-1323-5   LC 2001-6237
Discusses the potato famine that devastated Ireland in the nineteenth century and led to a widespread immigration to the United States
Includes bibliographical references

Feed the children first; Irish memories of the Great Hunger; edited by Mary E. Lyons. Atheneum Bks. for Young Readers 2002 43p il $17
Grades: 5 6 7 8   **941.5**
1. Ireland—History 2. Famines
ISBN 0-689-84226-0   LC 00-49606
Lyons "compiles quotations from Irish citizens on the devastating effects of the potato famine that ravaged Ireland between 1845 and 1852." Publ Wkly
"This brief book is a powerful introduction to Ireland's history and to the human devastation of a country in extreme poverty." Horn Book
Includes bibliographical references

Levy, Patricia, 1951-
Ireland. 2nd ed. Benchmark Books 2004 144p il map (Cultures of the world) lib bdg $29.95 *
Grades: 5 6 7 8   **941.5**
1. Ireland
ISBN 0-7614-1784-2   LC 2004-12902
First published 1994
This describes the geography, history, government, economy, environment, lifestyle, religion, and culture of Ireland.
Includes glossary and bibliographical references

McQuinn, Colm
Ireland; [by] Anna and Colm McQuinn; Elizabeth Malcolm and John McDonagh, consultants. National Geographic 2008 64p il map (Countries of the world) lib bdg $27.90 *
Grades: 4 5 6 7   **941.5**
1. Ireland
ISBN 978-1-4263-0299-2 (lib bdg); 1-4263-0299-1 (lib bdg)
This describes the geography, nature, history, people and culture, government, and economy of Ireland.
Includes glossary and bibliographical references

942 England and Wales

Lister, Maree
England; [written by Maree Lister and Marti Sevier] Stevens, G. 1998 96p il (Countries of the world) lib bdg $30
Grades: 5 6 7 8   **942**
1. England
ISBN 0-8368-2125-4   LC 98-13067

Lister, Maree—*Continued*
Introduces the geography, history, economy, government, culture, food, and people of England
This book "will provide students with a solid introduction." SLJ
Includes glossary and bibliographical references

942.01 England—Early history to 1066

Crossley-Holland, Kevin
The world of King Arthur and his court; people, places, legend, and lore; illustrated by Peter Malone. Dutton Children's Bks. 1999 c1998 125p il hardcover o.p. pa $14.99
Grades: 5 6 7 8   **942.01**
   1. Arthur, King 2. Great Britain—History—0-1066
   3. Middle Ages
   ISBN 0-525-46167-1; 0-525-47321-1 (pa)
                                                   LC 98-37698
First published 1998 in the United Kingdom
Surveys the known history of King Arthur, the legends and lore surrounding him, his treatment in literature, and the possible historical background of his associates and stories
An "eminently browsable, stylishly written trove of Arthuriana. . . . Lavishly detailed, both the full-spread paintings and spot illustrations are ripe with mystery and romance." Publ Wkly

Nardo, Don, 1947-
King Arthur. Lucent Bks. 2003 96p il (Heroes and villains) lib bdg $24.45
Grades: 5 6 7 8   **942.01**
   1. Arthur, King 2. Great Britain—History—0-1066
   ISBN 1-56006-948-1   LC 2001-8668
   Contents: Arthur in history, legend, and literature; The coming of Arthur; The order of the Round Table; The coming of Lancelot; The treachery of Mordred; The passing of Arthur
Surveys the known history of King Arthur, the legends and lore surrounding him, his treatment in literature, and the possible historical background of his associates and stories
"Nardo does a nice job of mixing the exciting stories with historical background of first-millennium England." Booklist
Includes bibliographical references

942.02 England—Norman period, 1066-1154

Hamilton, Janice
The Norman conquest of England; by Janice Hamilton. Twenty-First Century Books 2008 unp il map (Pivotal moments in history) lib bdg $38.60
Grades: 7 8 9 10   **942.02**
   1. William I, the Conqueror, King of England, 1027 or 8-1087 2. Great Britain—History—1066-1154, Norman period 3. Normans
   ISBN 978-0-8225-5902-3   LC 2006102629

This is an account of the invasion and conquest of England by the Normans in 1066 and its consequences.
This is "clearly written and interesting enough for browsers as well as report writers. Maps, full-color and black-and-white photos, and reproductions of manuscripts contribute to the attractive format and make the subject matter come alive." SLJ
Includes glossary and bibliographical references

942.03 England—Period of House of Plantagenet, 1154-1399

Hinds, Kathryn, 1962-
Medieval England. Benchmark Bks. 2002 79p il maps (Cultures of the past) lib bdg $29.93 *
Grades: 6 7 8 9   **942.03**
   1. Great Britain—Social life and customs 2. Medieval civilization
   ISBN 0-7614-0308-6   LC 00-46769
This introduction to medieval England is divided into five sections: history, cultural history, belief system; beliefs and society, the legacy of the medieval England
This offers "balanced, thoughtfully interpreted material. . . . Reinforcing the text are a number of extensions, including illustrations, color photos of artifacts, a map, time line, and brief samples of literature." Horn Book Guide
Includes glossary and bibliographical references

Levy, Debbie
The signing of the Magna Carta. Twenty-First Century Books 2008 160p il map (Pivotal moments in history) lib bdg $38.60
Grades: 7 8 9 10 11 12   **942.03**
   1. Magna Carta 2. Great Britain—History—1154-1399, Plantagenets
   ISBN 978-0-8225-5917-7 (lib bdg); 0-8225-5917-X (lib bdg)   LC 2005-20971
This "research source explains the intent of the treaty of 1215 that became the Magna Carta, the factors that produced it, as well as its evolution, historical significance, and relevance today. . . . The clear explanation of the 'Great Charter's' historical context accompanied by informative inserts and beautiful, relevant illustrations make this a book to dip into as well as to read through." Voice Youth Advocates
Includes glossary and bibliographical references

Plain, Nancy
Eleanor of Aquitaine and the High Middle Ages; by Nancy Plain. Marshall Cavendish Benchmark 2006 95p il map (Rulers and their times) lib bdg $29.93 *
Grades: 7 8 9 10   **942.03**
   1. Eleanor, of Aquitaine, Queen, consort of Henry II, King of England, 1122?-1204 2. Middle Ages 3. Queens 4. Great Britain—History—1154-1399, Plantagenets 5. France—History—0-1328
   ISBN 0-7614-1834-2   LC 2004-33
   Contents: Eleanor, the Queen; Everyday life in Eleanor's realm; The French and the English in their own words

Plain, Nancy—*Continued*
This covers the life of Queen Eleanor of Aquitaine, married to King Louis VII of France and later to King Henry II of England, the history her times, and everyday life in the Middle Ages in England and France.

"Interesting facts . . . are highlighted. Archival art, paired with clear text on plentiful white space, illustrates [the book]." Horn Book Guide

Includes glossary and bibliographical references

942.05   England—Tudor period, 1485-1603

Ashby, Ruth
Elizabethan England. Benchmark Bks. (Tarrytown) 1999 80p il (Cultures of the past) lib bdg $29.93 *
Grades: 6 7 8 9   **942.05**
1. Great Britain—History—1485-1603, Tudors
2. World history—16th century 3. England—Social life and customs
ISBN 0-7614-0269-1   LC 96-43868
This is "an effective presentation, enhanced by colorful illustrations and graphics." SLJ
Includes glossary and bibliographical references

Elizabethan world reference library. Gale 2007 4v set$181
Grades: 8 9 10 11 12   **942.05**
1. Elizabeth I, Queen of England, 1533-1603 2. Great Britain—History—1485-1603, Tudors
ISBN 978-1-4144-0188-1
Also available as separate volumes; contact publisher for more information
Contents: Almanac; Biographies; Primary Sources; Cumulative Index
"This accessible set consists of three volumes: *Almanac*, which offers chapter-length essays on political, social, and cultural events and movements that shaped each era; *Biographies*, in-depth treatments of luminaries who represent various levels of society and diverse experiences and viewpoints; and *Primary Sources*, collections of facsimiles and excerpted documents that attempt to provide insights into the past for the series' intended audience. The new topic will support both social studies and literature research assignments and will be welcomed by secondary library media collections." Booklist

Hinds, Kathryn, 1962-
The city; [by] Kathryn Hinds. Marshall Cavendish Benchmark 2007 80p il (Life in Elizabethan England) lib bdg $34.21 *
Grades: 6 7 8 9   **942.05**
1. Great Britain—History—1485-1603, Tudors
2. City and town life
ISBN 978-0-7614-2544-1 (lib bdg); 0-7614-2544-6 (lib bdg)   LC 2007-6385
This describes city life in Elizabethan England, describing the roles of men and women, childhood, recreation and hardships
This offers "good-quality, full-color reproductions. . . . The attractive, open format and the engaging pre-

sentation of the subject matter, combined with documented primary-source quotations and sidebars . . . will appeal to both researchers and those who are just interested in learning more about this period." SLJ
Includes glossary and bibliographical references

The countryside. Marshall Cavendish Benchmark 2007 80p il (Life in Elizabethan England) lib bdg $34.21 *
Grades: 6 7 8 9   **942.05**
1. Great Britain—History—1485-1603, Tudors
2. Country life
ISBN 978-0-7614-2543-4 (lib bdg); 0-7614-2543-8 (lib bdg)   LC 2007-13185
This describes country life in Elizabeth England, discussing country communities, homes, the roles of men and women, families and children, amusements and hardships.
This offers "good-quality, full-color reproductions. . . . The attractive, open format and the engaging presentation of the subject matter, combined with documented primary-source quotations and sidebars . . . will appeal to both researchers and those who are just interested in learning more about this period." SLJ
Includes glossary and bibliographical references

Elizabeth and her court; [by] Kathryn Hinds. Marshall Cavendish Benchmark 2007 80p il (Life in Elizabethan England) lib bdg $34.21 *
Grades: 6 7 8 9   **942.05**
1. Elizabeth I, Queen of England, 1533-1603 2. Great Britain—History—1485-1603, Tudors 3. Courts and courtiers
ISBN 978-0-7614-2542-7 (lib bdg); 0-7614-2542-X (lib bdg)   LC 2006029587
This describes the court of Queen Elizabeth I of England including the homes of the nobility, the queen's advisors, the ladies of the court, noble children, celebrations and spectacles, and palace problems
This offers "good-quality, full-color reproductions. . . . The attractive, open format and the engaging presentation of the subject matter, combined with documented primary-source quotations and sidebars . . . will appeal to both researchers and those who are just interested in learning more about this period." SLJ
Includes glossary and bibliographical references

942.06   England—Stuart and Commonwealth periods, 1603-1714

Barter, James, 1946-
Shakespeare's London. Lucent Bks. 2003 112p il maps (Travel guide to) lib bdg $27.45
Grades: 7 8 9 10   **942.06**
1. London (England)—History 2. Great Britain—History—1603-1714, Stuarts
ISBN 1-59018-146-8   LC 2002-3286
A visitors' guide to London in 1604, including what to see, where to stay, and where to eat, with sidebars on such topics as proper etiquette, famous residents, and student life at Oxford
"This is a very enjoyable approach to history and definitely succeeds in transporting students to another place and time." SLJ
Includes bibliographical references

942.1 London

Stacey, Gill
London; by Gill Stacey. World Almanac Library 2004 48p il map (Great cities of the world) lib bdg $30; pa $11.95
Grades: 4 5 6 7   942.1
1. London (England)
ISBN 0-8368-5022-X (lib bdg); 0-8368-5182-X (pa)
LC 2003-49693
Contents: Introduction; History of London; People of London; Living in London; London at work; London at play; Looking forward
This "up-to-date, attractively formatted [title contains an] interesting, informative [text] set in an easy-to-read font. Well-chosen, excellent-quality color photos, quotations, and sidebars appear throughout." SLJ
Includes bibliographical references

942.9 Wales

Hestler, Anna
Wales. Marshall Cavendish 2001 128p il maps (Cultures of the world) lib bdg $37.07
Grades: 5 6 7 8   942.9
1. Wales
ISBN 0-7614-1195-X   LC 00-47426
This title provides "information on the geography, history, government, lifestyles, religion, festivals, arts, and contemporary life in [Wales]. . . . The concise writing offers enough material for report writers without overwhelming them." SLJ
Includes glossary and bibliographical references

943 Central Europe. Germany

Burgan, Michael
The Berlin airlift; by Michael Burgan. Compass Point Books 2007 48p il map (We the people) lib bdg $25.26; pa $8.95
Grades: 4 5 6 7   943
1. Berlin (Germany)—History—Blockade, 1948-1949
ISBN 978-0-7565-2024-3 (lib bdg); 0-7565-2024-X (lib bdg); 978-0-7565-2036-6 (pa); 0-7565-2036-3 (pa)
LC 2006006766
Examines the joint effort of the United States and Great Britain who flew in around the clock to deliver supplies to Berlin during the Soviet blockade of 1948-49.
"The writing is clear and concise and the vocabulary is age-appropriate. [This] title contains excellent contemporary photographs." SLJ
Includes glossary and bibliographical references

Fuller, Barbara, 1961-
Germany; [by] Barbara Fuller, Gabriele Vossmeyer. 2nd ed. Benchmark Bks. 2003 c2004 144p il map (Cultures of the world) lib bdg $37.07 *
Grades: 5 6 7 8   943
1. Germany
ISBN 0-7614-1667-6   LC 2003-8186

First published 1993
Explores the geography, history, government, economy, people, and culture of Germany
Includes glossary and bibliographical references

Kort, Michael
The handbook of the new Eastern Europe; [by] Michael G. Kort. 21st Cent. Bks. (Brookfield) 2001 256p il maps lib bdg $39.90
Grades: 7 8 9 10   943
1. Eastern Europe 2. Central Europe
ISBN 0-7613-1362-1   LC 00-57708
This handbook begins with a "overview of the region. Economic and historical profiles are given for seven nations plus those in the former Yugoslavia, with an emphasis on post-1989 events after the fall of Communism. . . . Other reference material includes flags of each nation, a chronology of events since 1989, and an encyclopedia. The latter emphasizes names and places, with a few general topics such as environmental pollution." Voice Youth Advocates
"The book will be useful for serious students needing research materials." Horn Book Guide
Includes bibliographical references

Russell, Henry, 1954-
Germany; [by] Henry Russell; Benedict Kork and Antje Schlottmann, consultants. National Geographic 2007 64p il map (Countries of the world) lib bdg $27.90 *
Grades: 4 5 6 7   943
1. Germany
ISBN 978-1-4263-0059-2   LC 2007024677
Describes the geography, nature, history, people and culture, government and economy of Germany.
This "appealing [title has] wonderful photographs and maps. . . . The [book offers] reliable sources for country research, and the interesting and current material holds browsing potential as well." SLJ
Includes glossary and bibliographical references

Schmemann, Serge
When the wall came down; the Berlin Wall and the fall of Soviet Communism. Kingfisher 2006 127p il map $15.95 *
Grades: 7 8 9 10   943
1. Berlin Wall (1961-1989) 2. Germany (East)—Politics and government 3. Germany—History—1945-1990 4. Cold war
ISBN 0-7534-5994-9; 978-0-7534-5994-2
LC 2005-23892
"A New York Times book"
The author "describes the rise and defeat of the Nazis and the events that made Berlin and Germany a focal point for the Cold War. He then describes life in divided Germany and the events that led to the fall of the Berlin Wall and the reunification of Germany. A writer with a unique perspective, Schmemann creates an informative and quite readable account. The volume is well illustrated with black-and-white photos." Voice Youth Advocates
Includes bibliographical references

943.086　Germany—Period of Third Reich, 1933-1945

Altman, Linda Jacobs, 1943-
Hitler's rise to power and the Holocaust. Enslow Pubs. 2003 104p il map (Holocaust in history) lib bdg $20.95
Grades: 6 7 8 9　　　　　　　　**943.086**
1. Hitler, Adolf, 1889-1945 2. National socialism 3. Germany—History—1933-1945 4. Holocaust, 1933-1945
ISBN 0-7660-1991-8　　　　　LC 2002-151083
Explores events in Germany that led up to World War II including Hitler's rise to power and the creation of the Third Reich
Includes glossary and bibliographical references

Bartoletti, Susan Campbell, 1958-
Hitler Youth; growing up in Hitler's shadow. Scholastic Nonfiction 2005 176p il map $19.95 *
Grades: 7 8 9 10　　　　　　　**943.086**
1. National socialism 2. Germany—History—1933-1945 3. Holocaust, 1933-1945
ISBN 0-439-35379-3　　　　　LC 2004-51040
A Newbery Medal honor book, 2006
The author "explores how Hitler gained the loyalty, trust, and passion of so many of Germany's young people." Publisher's note
"Bartoletti draws on oral histories, diaries, letters, and her own extensive interviews with Holocaust survivors, Hitler Youth, resisters, and bystanders to tell the history from the viewpoints of people who were there. . . . The stirring photos tell more of the story. . . . The extensive back matter is a part of the gripping narrative." Booklist
Includes bibliographical references

Living in Nazi Germany; Elaine Halleck, book editor. Greenhaven Press 2004 158p il map (Exploring cultural history) $29.95; pa $21.20
Grades: 7 8 9 10　　　　　　　**943.086**
1. Germany—Politics and government—1933-1945 2. National socialism
ISBN 0-7377-1731-9; 0-7377-1732-7 (pa)
　　　　　　　　　　　　　　LC 2003-57961
This includes "eyewitness accounts from victims of Hitler's brutality as well as from those who found places in the Nazi machine. . . . Most of the accounts are from less well known sources, and many are compelling. Excerpts from a few familiar volumes, such as Albert Speer's memoirs and the wartime diaries of Joseph Goebbels, also appear. . . . An effective, insightful look at aspects of the Nazi system." Booklist
Includes bibliographical references

Shuter, Jane, 1955-
Resistance to the Nazis. Heinemann Lib. 2003 56p il map (Holocaust) lib bdg $28.50; pa $8.95
Grades: 7 8 9 10　　　　　　　**943.086**
1. Holocaust, 1933-1945 2. World War, 1939-1945—Underground movements 3. Germany—History—1933-1945
ISBN 1-4034-0814-9 (lib bdg); 1-4034-3206-6 (pa)
　　　　　　　　　　　　　　LC 2002-6853

This is "an excellent blend of overview and personal stories." SLJ
Includes glossary and bibliographical references

943.6　Austria and Liechtenstein

Sheehan, Sean, 1951-
Austria. 2nd ed. Benchmark Bks. 2003 144p il map (Cultures of the world) lib bdg $25.95 *
Grades: 5 6 7 8　　　　　　　　**943.6**
1. Austria
ISBN 0-7614-1497-5　　　　　LC 2002-11623
First published 1993
Presents the geography, history, economy, and social life and customs of Austria, the birthplace of such people as Kurt Waldheim, Wolfgang Amadeus Mozart, Sigmund Freud, and Arnold Schwarzenegger
Includes glossary and bibliographical references

943.7　Czech Republic and Slovakia

Bultje, Jan Willem
The Czech Republic. Oliver Press 2006 48p il map (Looking at Europe) lib bdg $22.95
Grades: 5 6 7 8　　　　　　　　**943.7**
1. Czech Republic
ISBN 1-881508-29-3
This describes the history, topography, culture, cuisine, transportation, economy, and nature of the Czech Republic.
This is "attractively designed. . . . The content is solid enough for a basic report. The format is pleasing, with good-quality, full-color photos on every spread." SLJ
Includes bibliographical references

Sioras, Efstathia
Czech Republic. Benchmark Bks. 1999 128p il maps (Cultures of the world) lib bdg $37.07
Grades: 5 6 7 8　　　　　　　　**943.7**
1. Czech Republic
ISBN 0-7614-0870-3　　　　　　LC 98-30290
Describes the geography, history, government, economy, people, lifestyle, religion, language, arts, leisure, festivals, and food of the Czech Republic
Includes glossary and bibliographical references

943.8　Poland

Deckker, Zilah
Poland; [by] Zilah Deckker; Richard Butterwick and Iwona Sagan, consultants. National Geographic 2008 64p il map (Countries of the world) lib bdg $27.90 *
Grades: 4 5 6 7　　　　　　　　**943.8**
1. Poland
ISBN 978-1-4263-0201-5　　　LC 2007047823
This describes the geography, nature, history, people and culture, government, and economy of Poland.
Includes glossary and bibliographical references

Heale, Jay
Poland; [by] Jay Heale & Pawel Grajnert. 2nd ed. Benchmark Books 2005 144p il map (Cultures of the world) lib bdg $37.07 *
Grades: 5 6 7 8   **943.8**
1. Poland
ISBN 0-7614-1847-4
First published 1994
Describes the geography, history, government, economy, environment, people, and culture of Poland
"Richly detailed and illustrated with numerous striking, full-color photographs. . . . [This is] well-organized, carefully researched, readable." SLJ
Includes glossary and bibliographical references

943.9 Hungary

Ake, Anne, 1943-
Hungary. Lucent Books 2003 112p il map (Modern nations of the world) $27.45
Grades: 7 8 9 10   **943.9**
1. Hungary
ISBN 1-56006-970-8   LC 2001-5699
Discusses the diversity of Hungary and the struggle between the East and West for control of it
Includes bibliographical references

Esbenshade, Richard S.
Hungary. 2nd ed. Benchmark Books 2005 144p il map (Cultures of the world) lib bdg $37.07 *
Grades: 5 6 7 8   **943.9**
1. Hungary
ISBN 0-7614-1846-6
First published 1994
Describes the geography, history, government, economy, environment, and culture of Hungary
Includes glossary and bibliographical references

944 France and Monaco

Gofen, Ethel, 1937-
France; [by] Ethel Caro Gofen, Blandine Pengili Reymann. 2nd ed. Benchmark Bks. 2002 144p il maps (Cultures of the world) lib bdg $37.07
Grades: 5 6 7 8   **944**
1. France
ISBN 0-7614-1498-3   LC 2002-11624
First published 1992 under the authorship of Ethel Caro Gofen
Introduces the geography, history, economy, cultures, and people of France
Includes glossary and bibliographical references

King, David C., 1933-
Monaco; [by] David C. King. Marshall Cavendish Benchmark 2008 144p il map (Cultures of the world) lib bdg $27.95 *
Grades: 5 6 7 8   **944**
1. Monaco
ISBN 978-0-7614-2567-0   LC 2006030238

This describes the geography, history, government, economy, environment, people, and culture of Monaco.
Includes glossary and bibliographical references

NgCheong-Lum, Roseline, 1962-
France. Stevens, G. 1999 96p il (Countries of the world) lib bdg $30.60
Grades: 4 5 6 7   **944**
1. France
ISBN 978-0-8368-2260-1 (lib bdg); 0-8368-2260-9 (lib bdg)   LC 98-33770
An overview of France, discussing its history, geography, government, economy, culture, and relations with North America
"The full-color photos on every page are outstanding and the style of writing is graceful." SLJ
Includes glossary and bibliographical references

Plain, Nancy
Louis XVI, Marie Antoinette, and the French Revolution. Benchmark Bks. 2002 88p il maps (Rulers and their times) lib bdg $29.93 *
Grades: 6 7 8 9   **944**
1. Louis XVI, King of France, 1754-1793 2. Marie Antoinette, Queen, consort of Louis XVI, King of France, 1755-1793 3. France—History—1789-1799, Revolution
ISBN 0-7614-1029-5   LC 00-57152
This covers the lives of King Louis XVI of France and his queen Marie Antoinette "as well as everyday life and the literature of the times. Interesting facts about society, clothing, housing, food, cosmetics, sports, and other daily activities are brought to life. . . . Illustrated with plentiful archival art." Horn Book Guide
Includes glossary and bibliographical references

944.05 France—Period of First Empire, 1804-1815

Greenblatt, Miriam
Napoleon Bonaparte and Imperial France; by Miriam Greenblatt. Marshall Cavendish Benchmark 2005 96p il map (Rulers and their times) lib bdg $29.93 *
Grades: 7 8 9 10   **944.05**
1. Napoleon I, Emperor of the French, 1769-1821 2. France—History—1799-1815 3. France—Kings and rulers
ISBN 0-7614-1837-7   LC 2004-22239
"This book covers the life of Napoleon, as well as everyday life in the home and the literature of eighteenth-century France. Interesting facts about society, clothing, housing, food sports, and other daily activities are highlighted. Archival art, paired with clear text on plentiful white space, illustrates each page." Horn Book Guide
Includes glossary and bibliographical references

945   Italian Peninsula and adjacent islands. Italy

Behnke, Alison

Italy in pictures. Lerner Publs. 2003 80p il maps (Visual geography series) lib bdg $27.93

Grades: 5 6 7 8   **945**

1. Italy

ISBN 0-8225-0368-9   LC 2001-5483

A historical and current look at Italy, discussing the land, the government, the people, and the economy

Includes glossary and bibliographical references

Cohen, Elizabeth Storr, 1946-

Daily life in Renaissance Italy; [by] Elizabeth S. Cohen and Thomas V. Cohen. Greenwood Press 2001 316p il maps (Greenwood Press "Daily life through history" series) $57.95; pa $25

Grades: 7 8 9 10   **945**

1. Renaissance 2. Italy—Civilization

ISBN   978-0-313-30426-2;   0-313-30426-2; 978-0-313-6114-2 (pa); 0-313-6114-2 (pa)

LC 00-69150

Also available online

"A brief historical background precedes chapters covering society, families, morality, schooling, marriage, disease, and death, as well as many aspects of rural and city life. . . . The documented information is ideal for student reports and reference questions." Voice Youth Advocates

Includes bibliographical references

Foster, Leila Merrell

Italy. Lucent Bks. 1999 112p il (Modern nations of the world) lib bdg $28.70

Grades: 7 8 9 10   **945**

1. Italy

ISBN 1-56006-481-1   LC 98-36878

Examines the land, people, and history of Italy and discusses its state of affairs and place in the world today

"Collapsing several millennia into a survey that is both succinct and readable is a daunting task, but Foster succeeds admirably." SLJ

Includes bibliographical references

Hinds, Kathryn, 1962-

Venice and its merchant empire. Benchmark Bks. 2002 80p il maps (Cultures of the past) lib bdg $29.93

Grades: 6 7 8 9   **945**

ISBN 0-7614-0305-1   LC 97-50353

Examines the history, culture, religion, society, and achievements of the Italian city of Venice, from its founding to its surrender to Napoleon at the end of the eighteenth century

This offers a "good, balanced [overview]. . . . Clearly written, the discussion wisely does not presume prior knowledge of subjects, such as the beliefs of Catholics. . . . Greatly enhanced by many richly colored and beautifully reproduced works of art and by photographs of artifacts and historical sites." Booklist

Includes glossary and bibliographical references

Schomp, Virginia, 1953-

The Italian Renaissance. Benchmark Bks. 2002 c2003 80p il map (Cultures of the past) lib bdg $29.93 *

Grades: 6 7 8 9   **945**

1. Renaissance 2. Italy—Civilization

ISBN 0-7614-1492-4   LC 2002-1971

Contents: Birthplace of the Renaissance; A new age; The power of the church; The impact of Humanism; Our Renaissance world

Discusses how and why the Renaissance began in Italy, the cultural and intellectual achievements of the Italian Renaissance, and the lasting effects of these achievements on Western civilization

This is "sure to draw report writers and history buffs alike. . . . Copiously illustrated with period reproductions and modern-day photos." Horn Book Guide

Includes glossary and bibliographical references

Sheehan, Sean, 1951-

Malta. Benchmark Bks. 2000 128p il map (Cultures of the world) lib bdg $37.07

Grades: 5 6 7 8   **945**

1. Malta

ISBN 0-7614-0993-9   LC 99-53436

The text covers Malta's "government, economy, people, lifestyles, religion, language, arts and leisure, festivals, and food. . . . Copious colorful photographs and reproductions complement and reinforce the facts presented." SLJ

Includes glossary and bibliographical references

Winter, Jane Kohen, 1959-

Italy; [by] Jane Kohen Winter, Leslie Jermyn. 2nd ed. Benchmark Bks. 2003 144p il maps (Cultures of the world) lib bdg $37.07 *

Grades: 5 6 7 8   **945**

1. Italy

ISBN 0-7614-1500-9   LC 2002-11628

First published 1995

Describes the geography, history, government, economy, and culture of Italy

"Colorful photographs with informative captions decorate almost every page of [this book]." SLJ

Includes glossary and bibliographical references

946   Iberian Peninsula and adjacent islands. Spain

Augustin, Byron

Andorra; by Byron D. Augustin. Marshall Cavendish Benchmark 2009 144p il map (Cultures of the world) lib bdg $29.95

Grades: 5 6 7 8   **946**

1. Andorra

ISBN 978-0-7614-3122-0; 0-7614-3122-5

LC 2007040356

"Provides comprehensive information on the geography, history, governmental structure, economy, cultural diversity, peoples, religion, and culture of Andorra." Publisher's note

Includes glossary and bibliographical references

Mann, Kenny, 1946-
Isabel, Ferdinand and fifteenth-century Spain. Benchmark Bks. 2002 80p il maps (Rulers and their times) lib bdg $29.93 *
Grades: 6 7 8 9   946
1. Ferdinand V, King of Spain, 1452-1516 2. Isabella I, Queen of Spain, 1451-1504 3. Spain—History
ISBN 0-7614-1030-9   LC 00-41450
This covers the lives of King Ferdinand and Queen Isabella of Spain "as well as everyday life and the literature of the times. Interesting facts about society, clothing, housing, food, cosmetics, sports, and other daily activities are brought to life. . . . Illustrated with plentiful archival art." Horn Book Guide
Includes glossary and bibliographical references

Pavlovic, Zoran
Spain; [by] Zoran Pavlovic and Reuel Hanks. Chelsea House Pubs. 2006 104p il map (Modern world nations) lib bdg $30 *
Grades: 7 8 9 10   946
1. Spain
ISBN 978-0-7910-6697-3 (lib bdg); 0-7910-6697-5 (lib bdg)
This describes the geography, history, people, and culture of Spain

946.9   Portugal

Deckker, Zilah
Portugal. National Geographic 2009 64p il map (Countries of the world) lib bdg $27.90 *
Grades: 4 5 6 7   946.9
1. Portugal
ISBN 978-1-4263-0390-6; 1-4263-0390-4
                                              LC 2009275584
This describes the geography, nature, history, people and culture, government and economy of Portugal.
Includes glossary and bibliographical references

Heale, Jay
Portugal; [by] Jay Heale & Angeline Koh. 2nd ed. Marshall Cavendish Benchmark 2006 144p il map (Cultures of the world) lib bdg $37.07 *
Grades: 5 6 7 8   946.9
1. Portugal
ISBN 0-7614-2053-3   LC 2005022922
First published 1995
Describes the geography, history, government, economy, culture, peoples, and religion of Portugal
Includes glossary and bibliographical references

947   Eastern Europe. Russia

Gottfried, Ted, 1928-
The road to Communism; illustrated by Melanie Reim. 21st Cent. Bks. (Brookfield) 2002 144p il lib bdg $28.90
Grades: 8 9 10 11 12   947
1. Soviet Union—History—1917-1921, Revolution
ISBN 0-7613-2557-3   LC 2001-52252
Chronicles the Czarist Russian Empire in the 1800s, the birth of Bolshevism, events leading to the Russian Revolution of 1917, and the development of new political structures in its aftermath
"Gottfried writes with clarity and distance even as he narrates the dramatic details of the political conflict and the emotion of the 'dream that failed.'" Booklist
Includes glossary and bibliographical references

Kort, Michael
Russia. 3rd ed. Facts on File 2004 228p il map (Nations in transition) $40
Grades: 7 8 9 10   947
1. Russia (Federation)
ISBN 0-8160-5075-9
First published 1995
Examines the people, religion, environmental problems, politics, culture, history, and geography of Russia, emphasizing its transition, since 1991, from a communist to a free nation
Includes bibliographical references

McCray, Thomas R.
Russia and the former Soviet republics. Chelsea House Publishers 2006 127p il map (Modern world cultures) lib bdg $30 *
Grades: 7 8 9 10   947
1. Russia 2. Former Soviet republics
ISBN 0-7910-8144-3   LC 2005015057
This describes the geography, history, population, culture, economy, politics, and possible future of Russia and the former Soviet republics.
Includes bibliographical references

Russell, Henry, 1954-
Russia; [by] Henry Russell; Laurie Bernstein and Ilya Utekhin, consultants. National Geographic 2008 64p il map (Countries of the world) lib bdg $27.90 *
Grades: 4 5 6 7   947
1. Russia
ISBN 978-1-4263-0259-6 (lib bdg); 1-4263-0259-2 (lib bdg)
This describes the geography, nature, history, people and culture, government, and economy of Russia.
Includes glossary and bibliographical references

Torchinskiĭ, Oleg, 1937-
Russia; [by] Oleg Torchinsky, Angela Black. 2nd ed. Benchmark Books 2005 144p il map (Cultures of the world) lib bdg $37.07 *
Grades: 5 6 7 8   947

Torchinskiĭ, Oleg, 1937-—*Continued*
1. Russia
ISBN 0-7614-1849-0
First published 1994
Describes the history, geography, government, economy, environment, and culture of Russia
"This title provides a well-written look at Russian history and culture up to the present day. . . . The high-quality, full-color photographs and reproductions are crisply printed, well composed, and perfectly placed." SLJ
Includes glossary and bibliographical references

947.084   Russia (Soviet Union)— 1917-1991

Gay, Kathlyn, 1930-
The aftermath of the Russian Revolution. Twenty-First Century Books 2009 160p il (Aftermath of history) lib bdg $38.60
Grades: 8 9 10 11 12   **947.084**
1. Soviet Union—History
ISBN 978-0-8225-9092-7; 0-8225-9092-1
LC 2008-25276
This book "begins with an overview of the Czar's Russia and the political machinations that brought about revolution. The disputes between different revolutionary groups led to the eventual triumph of the Bolsheviks and the reigns of Lenin and Stalin. Stalin's brutality in particular receives a lot of attention. The final chapters cover the transition to a more open society, the fall of the Soviet Union, and the age of Putin." SLJ
Includes glossary and bibliographical references

Gottfried, Ted, 1928-
The Stalinist empire; illustrated by Melanie Reim. 21st Cent. Bks. (Brookfield) 2002 127p il lib bdg $28.90
Grades: 8 9 10 11 12   **947.084**
1. Stalin, Joseph, 1879-1953 2. Soviet Union—History
ISBN 0-7613-2558-1   LC 2001-52251
Chronicles the years of Joseph Stalin's iron-fisted reign in the Soviet Union, from the time of Lenin's death to the dawn of World War II
"The book treats the subject matter frankly, in a straightforward and readable fashion." Voice Youth Advocates
Includes glossary and bibliographical references

The **Rise** of the Soviet Union; Tom Streissguth, book editor. Greenhaven Press 2002 256p (Turning points in world history) hardcover o.p. pa $23.70
Grades: 7 8 9 10   **947.084**
1. Soviet Union—History
ISBN 0-7377-0929-4; 0-7377-0928-6 (pa)
LC 2001-40866
A collection of essays concerning the social, economic and political issues in the history of the Soviet Union
Includes bibliographical references

947.085   Russia (Soviet Union)— 1953-1991

Langley, Andrew
The collapse of the Soviet Union; the end of an empire. Compass Point Books 2006 96p il map (Snapshots in history) lib bdg $31.93
Grades: 7 8 9 10   **947.085**
1. Soviet Union—History
ISBN 978-0-7565-2009-0 (lib bdg); 0-7565-2009-6 (lib bdg)   LC 2006003003
This "describes leaders, their plans, and their ultimate downfalls, from the removal of Tsar Nicholas II to the problems of present-day Russia. [This book is] great for research . . . brief but comprehensive." SLJ
Includes glossary and bibliographical references

947.5   Caucasus

Beliaev, Edward
Dagestan; [by] Edward Beliaev & Oksana Buranbaeva. 1st ed. Marshall Cavendish Benchmark 2006 144p il map (Cultures of the world) lib bdg $37.07 *
Grades: 5 6 7 8   **947.5**
1. Dagestan (Russia)
ISBN 0-7614-2015-0   LC 2005013698
An exploration of the geography, history, government, economy, people, and culture of the former Soviet republic of Dagestan
Includes glossary and bibliographical references

Dhilawala, Sakina, 1964-
Armenia; [by] Sakina Dhilawala. 2nd ed. Marshall Cavendish Benchmark 2008 144p il map (Cultures of the world) lib bdg $39.93 *
Grades: 5 6 7 8   **947.5**
1. Armenia
ISBN 978-0-7614-2029-3   LC 2007014890
First published 1997
"Provides comprehensive information on the geography, history, wildlife, governmental structure, economy, cultural diversity, peoples, religion, and culture of Armenia." Publisher's note
Includes glossary and bibliographical references

King, David C., 1933-
Azerbaijan; [by] David C. King. 1st ed. Marshall Cavendish Benchmark 2006 144p il map (Cultures of the world) lib bdg $37.07 *
Grades: 5 6 7 8   **947.5**
1. Azerbaijan
ISBN 0-7614-2011-8   LC 2004028443
An overview of the history, culture, peoples, religion, government, and geography of Azerbaijan
Includes glossary and bibliographical references

Robbins, Gerald
Azerbaijan. Mason Crest 2005 128p il map
(Growth and influence of Islam in the nations of
Asia and Central Asia) lib bdg $25.95
Grades: 7 8 9 10   **947.5**
1. Azerbaijan
ISBN 1-59084-878-0   LC 2004-19825
Contents: Place in the world; The land; History; Poli-
tics, the economy, and religion; The people; Communi-
ties; Foreign relations
This describes the geography, history, economy, poli-
tics, and people of Azerbaijan
Includes bibliographical references

Spilling, Michael
Georgia; [by] Michael Spilling & Winnie Wong.
2nd ed. Marshall Cavendish Benchmark 2008
c2009 144p il map (Cultures of the world) lib bdg
$29.95 *
Grades: 5 6 7 8   **947.5**
1. Georgia (Republic)
ISBN 978-0-7614-3033-9 (lib bdg); 0-7614-3033-4 (lib
bdg)   LC 2007050796
First published 1998
This describes the geography, nature, history, people
and culture, government and economy of Georgia
Includes glossary and bibliographical references

947.6   Moldova

Sheehan, Patricia, 1954-
Moldova. Benchmark Bks. 2000 128p il map
(Cultures of the world) lib bdg $37.07
Grades: 5 6 7 8   **947.6**
1. Moldova
ISBN 0-7614-0997-1   LC 99-53433
An illustrated look at the history and culture of the
small landlocked country between Russia and the
Ukraine that proclaimed its independence in August,
1991
Includes glossary and bibliographical references

947.7   Ukraine

Bassis, Volodymyr
Ukraine; [by] Volodymyr Bassis & Sakina
Dhilawala. 2nd ed. Marshall Cavendish Benchmark
2008 144p il map (Cultures of the world) lib bdg
$39.93 *
Grades: 5 6 7 8   **947.7**
1. Ukraine
ISBN 978-0-7614-2090-3   LC 2007019179
First published 1997
"Provides comprehensive information on the geogra-
phy, history, wildlife, governmental structure, economy,
cultural diversity, peoples, religion, and culture of
Ukraine." Publisher's note
Includes glossary and bibliographical references

Cooper, Catherine W.
Ukraine; [by] Catherine W. Cooper; with
additional text by Zoran Pavlovic. 2nd ed. Chelsea
House 2006 120p il map (Modern world nations)
lib bdg $30
Grades: 7 8 9 10   **947.7**
1. Ukraine
ISBN 0-7910-9207-0   LC 2006015643
First published 2003
This describes the geography, history, people, and cul-
ture of Ukraine.
Includes bibliographical references

Kummer, Patricia K.
Ukraine. Children's Press 2001 144p il
(Enchantment of the world, Second series) lib bdg
$35
Grades: 5 6 7 8   **947.7**
1. Ukraine
ISBN 0-516-21101-3   LC 00-57040
Describes the geography, history, culture, and people
of Ukraine
The chapters "are clearly written and have the details
needed for reports, but many of the sidebars set off with-
in the chapters are more engaging. . . . Excellent-quality,
full-color photos and reproductions enhance the presentation." SLJ
Includes bibliographical references

Otfinoski, Steven, 1949-
Ukraine. Second ed. Facts on File 2004 139p il
map (Nations in transition) $40
Grades: 7 8 9 10   **947.7**
1. Ukraine
ISBN 0-8160-5115-1   LC 2004-43241
First published 1999
Gives a historical and cultural overview of the country
of Ukraine with particular emphasis on changes that have
occurred since the collapse of the Soviet Union
Includes bibliographical references

947.9   Lithuania, Latvia, Estonia

Barlas, Robert
Latvia. Benchmark Bks. 2000 128p il map
(Cultures of the world) lib bdg $37.07
Grades: 5 6 7 8   **947.9**
1. Latvia
ISBN 0-7614-0977-7   LC 99-30168
Describes the geography, history, government, econo-
my, people, religion, language, arts, leisure, festivals, and
food of Latvia
Includes glossary and bibliographical references

947.93 Lithuania

Kagda, Sakina, 1939-
Lithuania; [by] Sakina Kagda & Zawiah Abdul
Latif. 2nd ed. Marshall Cavendish Benchmark
2008 144p il map (Cultures of the world) lib bdg
$39.93 *
Grades: 5 6 7 8   **947.93**
  1. Lithuania
  ISBN 978-0-7614-2087-3   LC 2007016290
  First published 1997
"Provides comprehensive information on the geogra-
phy, history, wildlife, governmental structure, economy,
cultural diversity, peoples, religion, and culture of Lithu-
ania." Publisher's note
Includes glossary and bibliographical references

948 Scandinavia

Margeson, Susan M.
Viking; written by Susan M. Margeson;
photographed by Peter Anderson. rev ed. DK Pub.
2005 72p il map (DK eyewitness books) $15.99;
lib bdg $19.99
Grades: 4 5 6 7   **948**
  1. Vikings
  ISBN 0-7566-1095-8; 0-7566-1096-6 (lib bdg)
  First published 1994 by Knopf
Presents an illustrated look at the Vikings—their ships
and weapons, heroes and myths, and great adventures in
war and exploration

Robinson, Deborah B.
The Sami of Northern Europe. Lerner Publs.
2002 48p il map (First peoples) lib bdg $23.93
Grades: 4 5 6   **948**
  1. Sami (European people)
  ISBN 0-8225-4175-0   LC 2001-4237
Describes the history, modern and traditional cultural
practices and economies, geographic background, and ongoing oppression and struggles of the Sami
"Each topic is discussed on a spread that features colorful, engaging, and well-selected photographs. The text
is primarily written in simple, declarative sentences." SLJ
Includes glossary and bibliographical references

Schomp, Virginia, 1953-
The Vikings. Franklin Watts 2005 112p il map
(People of the ancient world) lib bdg $30.50; pa
$9.95 *
Grades: 5 6 7 8   **948**
  1. Vikings
  ISBN 0-531-12382-0 (lib bdg); 0-531-16849-2 (pa)
                  LC 2004-24311
Contents: Legends and history; Warrior kings; Upper-
class men and women; Farmers and settlers; Artisans and
artists; Merchants and traders; Warriors; Poets and rune
masters; Slaves; The legacy of the Vikings

This examines the culture of the Vikings "through
their literature, artifacts, and documents. Religion, farming, levels of society, art, government, and fine arts are
covered in [this] well-written and attractive [book]."
Booklist
Includes bibliographical references

948.1 Norway

Kagda, Sakina, 1939-
Norway; [by] Sakina Kagda & Barbara Cooke.
2nd ed. Marshall Cavendish Benchmark 2006 144p
il map (Cultures of the world) lib bdg $37.07 *
Grades: 5 6 7 8   **948.1**
  1. Norway
  ISBN 978-0-7614-2067-5 (lib bdg); 0-7614-2067-3 (lib
  bdg)
  First published 1995
This provides "information on the geography, history,
governmental structure, economy, cultural diversity, peoples, religion, and culture of Norway." Publisher's note
"Organization is clear and user friendly. Fine-quality,
full-color photographs and reproductions draw readers in
and help to hold their interest." SLJ [review of 1995 edi-
tion]
Includes glossary and bibliographical references

948.5 Sweden

Gan, Delice, 1954-
Sweden; [by] Delice Gan, Leslie Jermyn. 2nd
ed. Benchmark Bks. 2003 144p il maps (Cultures
of the world) lib bdg $37.07 *
Grades: 5 6 7 8   **948.5**
  1. Sweden
  ISBN 0-7614-1502-5   LC 2002-152559
  First published 1993 under the authorship of Delice
  Gan
Introduces the geography, history, economy, culture,
and people of the fourth largest country in Europe
Includes glossary and bibliographical references

Phillips, Charles
Sweden. National Geographic 2009 64p il map
(Countries of the world) lib bdg $27.90 *
Grades: 4 5 6 7   **948.5**
  1. Sweden
  ISBN 978-1-4263-0389-0 (lib bdg); 1-4263-0389-0 (lib
  bdg)   LC 2009275585
This describes the geography, nature, history, people
& culture, and government & economy of Sweden
Includes glossary and bibliographical references

948.9   Denmark and Finland

Pateman, Robert, 1954-
Denmark; [by] Robert Pateman. 2nd ed.
Marshall Cavendish Benchmark 2006 144p il map
(Cultures of the world) lib bdg $37.07 *
Grades: 5 6 7 8   **948.9**
1. Denmark
ISBN 0-7614-2024-X   LC 2005021610
First published 1995
Introduces the geography, history, economics, culture,
and people of Denmark
Includes glossary and bibliographical references

948.97   Finland

Skog, Jason
Teens in Finland. Compass Point Books 2008
96p il map (Global connections) lib bdg $31.93
Grades: 7 8 9 10   **948.97**
1. Teenagers 2. Finland
ISBN 978-0-7565-3405-9 (lib bdg); 0-7565-3405-4 (lib
bdg)   LC 2007032691
Uncovers the challenges, pastimes, customs and culture of teens in Finland
"Informaion is solid, giving readers an informed and
realistic view of life in that country. A historical timeline
is included, and suggestions for other nonfiction and fiction titles for further reading." Youth Voice Advocate
Includes glossary and bibliographical references

Tan, Chung Lee, 1949-
Finland; [by] Tan Chung Lee. 2nd ed. Marshall
Cavendish Benchmark 2007 144p il map (Cultures
of the world) lib bdg $39.93 *
Grades: 5 6 7 8   **948.97**
1. Finland
ISBN 978-0-7614-2073-6 (lib bdg); 0-7614-2073-8 (lib
bdg)   LC 2006015897
First published 1996
This provides "information on the geography, history,
governmental structure, economy, cultural diversity, peo-
ples, religion, and culture of Finland." Publisher's note
Includes glossary and bibliographical references

949.12   Iceland

Wilcox, Jonathan, 1960-
Iceland; [by] Jonathan Wilcox & Zawiah Abdul
Latif. 2nd ed. Marshall Cavendish Benchmark
2007 144p il map (Cultures of the world) lib bdg
$39.93 *
Grades: 5 6 7 8   **949.12**
1. Iceland
ISBN 978-0-7614-2074-3 (lib bdg); 0-7614-2074-6 (lib
bdg)   LC 2006047548
First published 1996

This provides "information on the geography, history,
wildlife, governmental structure, economy, diversity, peoples, religion, and culture of Iceland." Publisher's note
Includes glossary and bibliographical references

949.2   Netherlands

Seward, Pat, 1939-
Netherlands; [by] Pat Seward & Sunandini
Arora Lal. 2nd ed. Marshall Cavendish Benchmark
2006 144p il map (Cultures of the world) lib bdg
$37.07 *
Grades: 5 6 7 8   **949.2**
1. Netherlands
ISBN 0-7614-2052-5   LC 2005019823
First published 1995
Describes the geography, history, government, econo-
my, culture, peoples, and religion of the Netherlands.
Includes glossary and bibliographical references

949.3   Southern Low Countries. Belgium

Pateman, Robert, 1954-
Belgium; [by] Robert Pateman & Mark Elliott.
2nd ed. Marshall Cavendish Benchmark 2006 144p
il map (Cultures of the world) lib bdg $37.07 *
Grades: 5 6 7 8   **949.3**
1. Belgium
ISBN 978-0-7614-2059-0 (lib bdg); 0-7614-2059-2 (lib
bdg)
First published 1995
This provides "information on the geography, history,
governmental structure, economy, cultural diversity, peoples, religion, and culture of Belgium." Publisher's note
"Organization is clear and user friendly. Fine-quality,
full-color photographs and reproductions draw readers in
and help to hold their interest." SLJ [review of 1995 edi-
tion]
Includes glossary and bibliographical references

949.35   Luxembourg

Sheehan, Patricia, 1954-
Luxembourg; [by Patricia Sheehan & Sakina
Dhilawala. 2nd ed. Marshall Cavendish Benchmark
2008 144p il map (Cultures of the world) lib bdg
$39.93 *
Grades: 5 6 7 8   **949.35**
1. Luxembourg
ISBN 978-0-7614-2088-0   LC 2007014891
First published 1997
Discusses the geography, history, government, econo-
my, and customs of the smallest of the Benelux coun-
tries.
Includes glossary and bibliographical references

949.4   Switzerland

Levy, Patricia, 1951-
Switzerland; [by] Patricia Levy & Richard Lord.
2nd ed. Benchmark Books 2005 144p il map
(Cultures of the world) lib bdg $37.70 *
Grades: 5 6 7 8   **949.4**
  1. Switzerland
  ISBN 0-7614-1850-4
  First published 1994
  Describes the geography, history, government, econo-
my, people, and culture of Switzerland.
  Includes glossary and bibliographical references

949.5   Greece

DuBois, Jill, 1952-
Greece; [by] Jill Dubois, Xenia Skoura, Olga
Gratsaniti. 2nd ed. Benchmark Bks. 2003 143p il
maps (Cultures of the world) lib bdg $37.07
Grades: 5 6 7 8   **949.5**
  1. Greece
  ISBN 0-7614-1499-1   LC 2002-11625
  First published 1992 under the authorship of Jill Du-
Bois
  Introduces the geography, history, economics, culture,
and people of the Mediterranean country of Greece
  "An attractive, lively, and perceptive look at Greece."
SLJ
  Includes glossary and bibliographical references

Feldman, Ruth Tenzer
The fall of Constantinople. Twenty-First Century
Books 2008 160p il map (Pivotal moments in
history) lib bdg $38.60
Grades: 7 8 9 10   **949.5**
  1. Byzantine Empire 2. Istanbul (Turkey)—History—
Siege, 1453
  ISBN 978-0-8225-5918-4 (lib bdg); 0-8225-5918-8 (lib
bdg)   LC 2006037501
  "This volume examines the fall of Constantinople,
marking the end of the Middle Ages. Sure to satisfy history buffs, the book not only relates military facts but
also delves into the events leading up to Constantinople's
defeat as well as exploring its effects throughout history.
Numerous sidebars, illustrations, maps, and art reproductions provide additional information." Horn Book Guide
  Includes glossary and bibliographical references

Marston, Elsa
The Byzantine Empire. Benchmark Books 2003
80p il map (Cultures of the past) lib bdg $28.50
Grades: 6 7 8 9   **949.5**
  1. Byzantine Empire
  ISBN 0-7614-1495-9   LC 2002-3222
  Traces the history, society, culture, and lasting influences of the Byzantine Empire, which grew from the decaying Roman empire and ruled from Constantinople
from the fourth to the end of the fifteenth century

"Copiously illustrated with period reproductions as
well as modern-day photos, this book provides a well-
rounded history of the Byzantines." Horn Book Guide
  Includes glossary and bibliographical references

949.65   Albania

Knowlton, MaryLee, 1946-
Albania; by MaryLee Knowlton. Marshall
Cavendish Benchmark 2005 144p il map (Cultures
of the world) lib bdg $37.07 *
Grades: 5 6 7 8   **949.65**
  1. Albania
  ISBN 0-7614-1852-0   LC 2004-22236
  Contents: Geography; History; Government; Economy;
Environment; Albanians; Lifestyle; Religion; Language;
Arts; Leisure; Festivals; Food
  An overview of the history, culture, peoples, religion,
government, and geography of Albania
  Includes glossary and bibliographical references

949.7   Serbia and Montenegro, Croatia, Slovenia, Bosnia and Hercegovina, Macedonia

Cooper, Robert, 1945-
Croatia. Benchmark Bks. 2001 128p il map
(Cultures of the world) lib bdg $37.07
Grades: 5 6 7 8   **949.7**
  1. Croatia
  ISBN 0-7614-1156-9   LC 00-29510
  "The initial chapters go over basic geography, history,
and government, while the bulk of the book examines
Croatia's culture and contemporary life. The short chap-
ters are divided into highlighted segments of a page or
two. This format allows easy access to information." SLJ
  Includes glossary and bibliographical references

Halilbegovich, Nadja, 1979-
My childhood under fire; a Sarajevo diary. Kids
Can Press 2006 120p il $14.95
Grades: 5 6 7 8   **949.7**
  1. Yugoslav War, 1991-1995 2. Sarajevo (Bosnia and
Hercegovina)
  ISBN 1-55337-797-4
  "In 1992, when the bombing started in Sarajevo,
Halilbegovich, 12, kept a diary of her terrifying daily life
under siege. Her terse vignettes replay the horror of her
comfortable home torn apart." Booklist

King, David C., 1933-
Serbia and Montenegro; by David C. King.
Benchmark Bks. 2005 144p il map (Cultures of
the world) lib bdg $37.07 *
Grades: 5 6 7 8   **949.7**
  1. Serbia 2. Montenegro
  ISBN 0-7614-1855-5   LC 2004-22248
  Contents: Geography; History; Government; Economy;
Environment; Serbs and Montenegrins; Lifestyle; Reli-
gion; Language; Arts; Leisure; Festivals; Food

King, David C., 1933--- *Continued*

This offers "historical, geographical, and cultural information as well as observations about contemporary lifestyles and issues. In general the writing is clear; at times it is lively. . . . The photographs are excellent." SLJ

Includes glossary and bibliographical references

Knowlton, MaryLee, 1946-

Macedonia; by MaryLee Knowlton. Benchmark Books 2005 144p il map (Cultures of the world) lib bdg $25.95 *

Grades: 5 6 7 8   **949.7**

1. Macedonia (Republic)

ISBN 0-7614-1854-7   LC 2004-22735

Contents: Geography; History; Government; Economy; Environment; Macedonians; Lifestyle; Religion; Language; Arts; Leisure; Festivals; Food

Describes the geography, history, government, economy, people, and culture of Macedonia

Includes glossary and bibliographical references

Milivojevic, JoAnn

Bosnia and Herzegovina. Children's Press 2004 144p il map (Enchantment of the world, Second series) lib bdg $35

Grades: 5 6 7 8   **949.7**

1. Bosnia and Hercegovina

ISBN 0-516-24247-4   LC 2002-15581

Contents: Wrapped; Land of forests and mountains; What lives high and low; Bosnia through the centuries; Forming a new country; Economy past, present, future; One country, three ethnic groups; Three faiths; Artistic expressions; Enjoying life

Describes the history, geography, economy, and culture of Bosnia and Herzegovina

This offers "lucid commentary, digestible quantities of facts and statistics, eye-catching color photos, and eminently useful back matter." Booklist

Includes bibliographical references

Serbia. rev ed. Children's Press 2003 144p il map (Enchantment of the world, Second series) lib bdg $35

Grades: 5 6 7 8   **949.7**

1. Serbia

ISBN 0-516-22695-9   LC 2002-8262

First published 1999

Contents: Crossroads; From the mountains to the Valleys; Where the wild things grow; When Serbia began; Citizens revolt, a new president leads; Money, money, money; Who lives in Serbia?; Traditions, faith, and folklore; Pictures, words, and music; At home, school, and play

An introduction to the geography, history, economy, government, and culture of Serbia

Includes bibliographical references

O'Grady, Scott F.

Basher five-two; the true story of F-16 fighter pilot Captain Scott O'Grady; [by] Scott O'Grady with Michael French. Doubleday 1997 133p il map hardcover o.p. pa $4.99

Grades: 5 6 7 8   **949.7**

1. Yugoslav War, 1991-1995

ISBN 0-385-32300-X; 0-440-41313-3 (pa)

LC 96-51181

"O'Grady writes about being shot down, escaping capture, and surviving in enemy territory in Bosnia in 1995." Book Rep

This account "is smartly paced, with care taken over the particulars young readers will want to know. An insert of photos is included." Horn Book Guide

Orr, Tamra

Slovenia; by Tamra Orr. Children's Press 2004 144p il map (Enchantment of the world, Second series) lib bdg $35

Grades: 5 6 7 8   **949.7**

1. Slovenia

ISBN 0-516-24249-0   LC 2003-15253

Contents: A small but mighty country; Frigid Alps to underground caverns; Animal and plant life; From instability to independence; A new independence; Economic stability and strength; Proud Slovenes; Faith and tradition; The arts and sports; Daily life

Discusses the geography and climate, history, wildlife, economy, government, people, religion, and culture of Slovenia.

This "basically well-written [book] should engage a wide range of readers with varied interests. . . . The excellent quality of the photos contributes to the attractiveness of [this volume]." SLJ

Includes bibliographical references

War-torn Bosnia; Helen Cothran, book editor. Greenhaven Press 2002 192p il maps (History firsthand) lib bdg $34.95; pa $23.70

Grades: 7 8 9 10   **949.7**

1. Yugoslav War, 1991-1995 2. Bosnia and Hercegovina

ISBN 0-7377-0889-1 (lib bdg); 0-7377-0888-3 (pa)

LC 2001-40608

This is a compilation of eyewitness accounts of war in Bosnia from a variety of perspectives

Includes bibliographical references

949.9   Bulgaria

Otfinoski, Steven, 1949-

Bulgaria. 2nd ed. Facts on File 2004 144p il map (Nations in transition) $35

Grades: 7 8 9 10   **949.9**

1. Bulgaria

ISBN 0-8160-5116-X   LC 2004-43274

First published 1998

Examines the people, religion, daily life, politics, culture, history, and geography of Bulgaria, including the return of former king Simeon II, who became prime minister in June 2001 as head of the newly formed National Movement party

Includes bibliographical references

950 History of Asia

Des Forges, Roger V.

The Asian world, 600-1500; [by] Roger Des Forges & John S. Major. Oxford University Press 2005 173p il map (The medieval & early modern world) $32.95 *

Grades: 7 8 9 10   **950**
1. Asia—History
ISBN 0-19-517843-2; 978-0-19-517843-2
LC 2004021415

"Through the framework of an imaginary dinner party, the authors skillfully introduce the blend and diversity of cultures that comprised the ancient Asian world. Chapters highlight the contributions, culture, empires, and conflicts of China, Japan, India, and Korea over nine centuries. . . . Students will appreciate the wealth of material in this volume." SLJ

Includes bibliographical references

Greenblatt, Miriam

Genghis Khan and the Mongol Empire. Benchmark Bks. 2002 80p il maps (Rulers and their times) lib bdg $29.93 *

Grades: 6 7 8 9   **950**
1. Genghis Khan, 1162-1227 2. Mongols
ISBN 0-7614-1027-9   LC 99-86634

"This book covers the life of the infamous Genghis Khan, as well as everyday life and literature of the twelveth- and thirteenth-century Mongolian Empire. Illustrated with plentiful archival art, the facts about society, sports, housing, food, clothing, cosmetics, and other topics are brought to life." Horn Book Guide

Includes glossary and bibliographical references

Major, John S., 1942-

The Silk Route; 7,000 miles of history; illustrated by Stephen Fieser. HarperCollins Pubs. 1995 32p il maps pa $6.99 hardcover o.p.

Grades: 4 5 6 7   **950**
1. Trade routes 2. China—History
ISBN 0-06-443468-0   LC 92-38169

"Major traces the journey of a caravan as it leaves Chang'an, China, in A.D.700, travels along the established silk traders' route, and finally arrives at its destination in Byzantium several months later. The 7,000-mile trek crosses cities, deserts, mountains, and the Mediterranean Sea." SLJ

"The pictures and short segments make the book a teaching tool as well as a resource when learning about China and its silk industry." Child Book Rev Serv

Pascoe, Elaine

The Pacific rim; East Asia at the dawn of a new century. 21st Cent. Bks. (Brookfield) 1999 128p il lib bdg $25.90

Grades: 7 8 9 10   **950**
1. Pacific rim
ISBN 0-7613-3015-1   LC 98-28556

Examines the history and current economic and political importance of Japan, China, Taiwan, the Koreas, Southeast Asia, Indonesia, and Malaysia

"Teenagers investigating the current economic crisis in the Pacific Rim will benefit from the encapsulated histories and the relative currency of the text." Booklist

Includes bibliographical references

Peoples of Western Asia. Marshall Cavendish 2007 11v il map set$359.80

Grades: 5 6 7 8   **950**
1. Asia 2. Reference books
ISBN 978-0-7614-7677-1; 0-7614-7677-6

Contents: v1 Afghanistan-Armenia; v2 Azerbaijan-Georgia; v3 Iran-Iraq; v4 Israel-Kazakhstan; v5 Kuwait-Lebanon; v6 Maldives-Pakistan; v7 Qatar-Russian Federation; v8 Saudi Arabia-Tajikistan; v9 Turkey-Turkmenistan; v10 United Arab Emirates-Yemen; v11 Index

This describes the cultures and histories of countries as far west as Turkey, Israel, and Saudi Arabia, and as far east as Kazakhstan, Kyrgyzstan, and the Siberian region of the Russian Federation

"All of the entries are clearly written. . . . The hundreds of photographs . . . are of high quality and invaluable as illustrations for the text." Booklist

Phillips, Douglas A.

East Asia; series consulting editor Charles F. Gritzner. Chelsea House Pubs. 2006 128p il map (Modern world cultures) lib bdg $30

Grades: 7 8 9 10   **950**
1. East Asia
ISBN 0-7910-8148-6

This describes the natural environment, history, people, governments, economics, and possible future of East Asia.

Includes bibliographical references

Stefoff, Rebecca, 1951-

The Asian empires; by Rebecca Stefoff. Benchmark Books 2004 c2005 48p il map (World historical atlases) lib bdg $27.07

Grades: 5 6 7 8   **950**
1. China—History 2. China—Civilization 3. India 4. Turkey
ISBN 0-7614-1643-9   LC 2004-8703

This introduces the empires of Imperial China, early India, and Ottoman Turkey

This is "clearly written and well organized. The [book includes] large, full-color photographs and illustrations reproduced from original pieces of art found in diverse national museums. . . . [This volume makes an] excellent [supplement] to history lessons and [a] good starting [point] for research." SLJ

Includes bibliographical references

The **Wilson** chronology of Asia and the Pacific; edited by David M. Brownstone and Irene M. Franck. Wilson, H.W. 1999 442p $105

Grades: 8 9 10 11 12 Adult   **950**
1. Asia—History 2. Pacific region—History 3. Reference books
ISBN 0-8242-0950-8   LC 99-29402

The Wilson chronology of Asia and the Pacific—*Continued*

"This volume features events in politics, government, and law; war; religion; education; economic life; arts and entertainment; science and technology; and medicine. A subject index is included." Publisher's note

Includes bibliographical references

Woods, Michael, 1946-

Seven wonders of Ancient Asia; by Michael Woods and Mary B. Woods. Twenty-First Century Books 2008 80p il map (Seven wonders) lib bdg $33.26

Grades: 6 7 8 9   950

1. Asian architecture 2. Asia—History

ISBN 978-0-8225-7569-6 (lib bdg); 0-8225-7569-8 (lib bdg)   LC 2007-40824

"This handsome volume presents seven notable 'wonders' of ancient Asia: the Great Wall of China, Mahabodhi Temple in India, Angkor Wat in Cambodia, Todaiji Temple in Japan, Pha That Luang in Laos, Borobudur Temple on Java in Indonesia, and the Banaue Rice Terraces of the Philippines. . . . With good writing and a nice design, this book offers a fine introduction to some historically significant places." Booklist

Includes glossary and bibliographical references

951   China and adjacent areas

Behnke, Alison

China in pictures. rev and expanded. Lerner Publs. 2003 80p il maps (Visual geography series) lib bdg $27.93

Grades: 5 6 7 8   951

1. China

ISBN 0-8225-0370-0   LC 2001-7217

First published 1989

Text and illustrations present detailed information on the geography, history and government, economy, people, cultural life and society of traditional and modern China, home to over one-fifth of the earth's population

This "entices readers with its handsome open format, clear maps, informative sidebars, and well-chosen illustrations." SLJ

Includes glossary and bibliographical references

Ferroa, Peggy Grace, 1959-

China; [by] Peggy Ferroa, Elaine Chan. 2nd ed. Benchmark Bks. 2002 144p il map (Cultures of the world) lib bdg $37.07

Grades: 5 6 7 8   951

1. China

ISBN 0-7614-1474-6   LC 2002-19209

First published 1991

Describes the geography, history, government, economy, environment, people, and culture of China

Includes glossary and bibliographical references

Kummer, Patricia K.

Tibet; [by] Patricia K. Kummer. Children's Press 2003 144p il map (Enchantment of the world, second series) lib bdg $35

Grades: 5 6 7 8   951

1. Tibet (China)

ISBN 0-516-22693-2   LC 2002-156704

Introduces Tibet, including its geography and climate, history, government, economy, people, culture, religion, language, and activities of daily life

Includes bibliographical references

Langley, Andrew

Cultural Revolution; years of chaos in China; by Andrew Langley. Compass Point Books 2008 96p il map (Snapshots in history) lib bdg $33.26

Grades: 6 7 8 9   951

1. China—History—1949-1976

ISBN 978-0-7565-3483-7 (lib bdg); 0-7565-3483-6 (lib bdg)   LC 2007032699

This book "provides more than just a 'snapshot' of China's violent Cultural Revolution . . . The inviting layout has a photo and boxed data on almost every double-page spread, and the main account is buoyed by extensive back matter, including chapter notes for quotations." Booklist

Includes bibliographical references

Levy, Patricia, 1951-

Tibet; [by] Patricia Levy & Don Bosco. 2nd ed. Marshall Cavendish Benchmark 2007 144p il map (Cultures of the world) lib bdg $39.93 *

Grades: 5 6 7 8   951

1. Tibet (China)

ISBN 978-0-7614-2076-7 (lib bdg); 0-7614-2076-2 (lib bdg)   LC 2006015826

First published 1996

This provides "information on the geography, history, wildlife, governmental structure, economy, diversity, peoples, religion, and culture of Tibet." Publisher's note

Includes glossary and bibliographical references

Mah, Adeline Yen, 1937-

China; land of dragons and emperors. Delacorte Press 2009 240p $17.99; lib bdg $29.99

Grades: 8 9 10 11 12 Adult   951

1. China—History

ISBN   978-0-385-73748-7;   0-385-73748-3; 978-0-385-90669-2 (lib bdg); 0-385-90669-2 (lib bdg)   LC 2008035331

Mah "brings East to West in this concise, reader-friendly history of China that contains more than 80 photographs of famous figures and artifacts. Spanning 2,000 years of strife and victories, the book mainly focuses on China's six dynasties, which are introduced in chronological order and are followed by brief portraits of post-dynasty leaders. . . . This accessible work will be an invaluable resource for students and young history buffs." Publ Wkly

Includes bibliographical references

Marx, Trish, 1948-

Elephants and golden thrones; inside China's Forbidden City; written by Trish Marx; photographs and photograph selection by Ellen B. Senisi; foreword by Li Ji. Abrams Books for Young Readers 2008 48p il $18.95

Grades: 4 5 6 7   **951**

1. Forbidden City (Beijing, China) 2. China

ISBN 978-0-8109-9485-0; 0-8109-9485-2

LC 2007-022413

Introduces Beijing's Forbidden City, recounting some of the most famous incidents from its past, and describing its rooms, their function, and some of the daily rituals of palace life.

The author "brings the Forbidden City to life by telling stories about six different royal inhabitants from Zhengde, 'one of the worst emperors in Chinese history,' to Puyi, who became a pawn of the invading Japanese. . . . Beautiful drawings and photographs, some provided by the Palace Museum and some taken for this book, lend color and provide additional information. Of particular note are the photos of the interiors of buildings, a number of which are not regularly open to the public." Booklist

Includes bibliographical references

Sís, Peter, 1949-

Tibet; through the red box. Farrar, Straus & Giroux 1998 unp il maps $25 *

Grades: 4 5 6 7   **951**

1. Tibet (China)

ISBN 0-374-37552-6   LC 97-50175

"Frances Foster books"

"When Sis opens the red lacquered box that has sat on his father's table for decades, he finds the diary his father kept when he was lost in Tibet in the mid-1950s. The text replicates the diary's spidery handwriting, while the illustrations depict elaborate mazes and mandalas, along with dreamlike spreads that are filled with fragmented details of the father's and son's lives. . . . Impeccably designed and beautifully made, the book has a dreamlike quality that will keep readers of many ages coming back to find more in its pages." Booklist

951.04   China—Period of Republic, 1912-1949

Gay, Kathlyn, 1930-

The aftermath of the Chinese nationalist revolution. Twenty-First Century Books 2008 c2009 160p il (Aftermath of history) lib bdg $38.60

Grades: 7 8 9 10   **951.04**

1. China—History—1912-1949

ISBN 978-0-8225-7601-3 (lib bdg); 0-8225-7601-5 (lib bdg)   LC 2007-15082

This book "offers a lucid account of the civil turmoil that began in China with the successful revolution led by Dr. Sun Yat-sen in 1911, and culminated in the establishment of the People's Republic in 1949." Booklist

Includes bibliographical references

951.05   China—Period of People's Republic, 1949-

Jiang, Ji-li

Red scarf girl; a memoir of the Cultural Revolution; foreword by David Henry Hwang. HarperCollins Pubs. 1997 285p $16.99; pa $6.99 *

Grades: 6 7 8 9   **951.05**

1. China—History—1949-1976—Personal narratives

ISBN 0-06-027585-5; 0-06-446208-0 (pa)

LC 97-5089

"This is an autobiographical account of growing up during Mao's Cultural Revolution in China in 1966. . . . Jiang describes in terrifying detail the ordeals of her family and those like them, including unauthorized search and seizure, persecution, arrest and torture, hunger, and public humiliation. . . . Her voice is that of an intelligent, confused adolescent, and her focus on the effects of the revolution on herself, her family, and her friends provides an emotional focal point for the book, and will allow even those with limited knowledge of Chinese history to access the text." Bull Cent Child Books

Ma Yan, 1987-

The diary of Ma Yan; the struggles and hopes of a Chinese schoolgirl; edited and introduced by Pierre Haski; translated from the French by Lisa Appignanesi. 1st American ed. HarperCollins 2005 166p $15.99; lib bdg $16.89

Grades: 5 6 7 8   **951.05**

1. China

ISBN 0-06-076496-1; 0-06-076497-X (lib bdg)

LC 2004-16136

Original French edition, 2002

"The diaries were originally translated from the Mandarin by He Yanping."

"In 2001, while a French journalist was visiting remote Ningxia province in northwest China, a Muslim woman wearing the white headscarf of the Hui people thrust the diaries of her daughter into his hands. The three small notebooks described the girl's struggle to get an education despite extreme poverty. . . . The girl's feelings for her mother were powerful and complex, and she alternated between overwhelming love and rage at the injustices she suffered." SLJ

Yu Chun, 1966-

Little Green; growing up during the Chinese Cultural Revolution; [by] Chun Yu. Simon & Schuster Books for Young Readers 2005 112p il $15.95

Grades: 6 7 8 9   **951.05**

1. China—History—1949-1976

ISBN 0-689-86943-6   LC 2003-27433

"A Paula Wiseman book"

"Chun Yu was born in China in 1966, the year the Great Cultural Revolution began, and in spare poetry she remembers the first 10 years of her life. True to a child's bewildered viewpoint and augmented by occasional, small black-and-white family photos, Yu gets across the grief at home and the school indoctrination." Booklist

Zhang, Ange
Red land, yellow river; a story from the Cultural
Revolution. Douglas & McIntyre 2004 55p il
$16.95
Grades: 5 6 7 8   **951.05**
1. China—History—1949-1976—Personal narratives
ISBN 0-88899-489-3
"A Groundwood book"
"Zhang was a teen living in Beijing when Mao
Zedong began the Cultural Revolution. In a youthful
voice he records his experiences in the early years of
that turbulent decade that began in 1966. . . . This mov-
ing account of a youngster swept up in the revolutionary
fervor and then beginning to question its goals is accompanied by attractive, digitally rendered illustrations." SLJ

951.2 Taiwan, Hong Kong, Macau

Moiz, Azra, 1963-
Taiwan; [by] Azra Moiz & Janice Wu. 2nd ed.
Marshall Cavendish Benchmark 2006 144p il map
(Cultures of the world) lib bdg $39.93 *
Grades: 5 6 7 8   **951.2**
1. Taiwan
ISBN 978-0-7614-2069-9 (lib bdg); 0-7614-2069-X
(lib bdg)
First published 1995
This describes "the geography, history, government,
economy, people, religion, food, and other facets of [Tai-
wan]. . . . Organization is clear and user friendly. Fine-
quality, full-color photographs and reproductions draw
readers in and help to hold their interest." SLJ [review
of 1995 edition]
Includes glossary and bibliographical references

Waterlow, Julia
The Yangtze. World Almanac Lib. 2003 48p il
map (Great rivers of the world) lib bdg $26.60; pa
$14.60
Grades: 4 5 6 7   **951.2**
1. Yangtze River valley (China)
ISBN 0-8368-5447-0 (lib bdg); 0-8368-5454-3 (pa)
                                LC 2002-33134
Contents: The course of the Yangtze; The Yangtze in
history; Cities and settlements; Farming, transportation
and industry; Animals and plants; Environmental issues;
Recreation and leisure; The future
This covers the Yangtze River's "geography, wildlife,
and history . . . and its impact on nearby peoples. The
presentation is exceptionally clear and lively. . . . Exquisite, full-color photos and maps." SLJ
Includes glossary and bibliographical references

951.25 Hong Kong

Kagda, Falaq
Hong Kong; [by] Falaq Kagda & Magdalene
Koh. 2nd ed. Marshall Cavendish Benchmark 2008
c2009 144p il map (Cultures of the world) lib bdg
$29.95 *
Grades: 5 6 7 8   **951.25**
1. Hong Kong (China)
ISBN 978-0-7614-3034-6 (lib bdg); 0-7614-3034-2 (lib
bdg)   LC 2007048285
First published 1998
Surveys the geography, history, government, economy,
and culture of Hong Kong.
Includes glossary and bibliographical references

951.7 Mongolia

Pang, Guek-Cheng, 1950-
Mongolia. Benchmark Bks. 1999 128p il maps
(Cultures of the world) lib bdg $37.07
Grades: 5 6 7 8   **951.7**
1. Mongolia
ISBN 0-7614-0954-8   LC 98-31897
Describes the geography, history, government, econo-
my, people, lifestyle, religion, language, arts, leisure, fes-
tivals, and food of Mongolia
"High-quality, full-color photography combines with
clearly written text and meaningful sidebars." SLJ
Includes glossary and bibliographical references

951.9 Korea

Benson, Sonia
Korean War: almanac and primary sources; [by]
Sonia G. Benson; Gerda-Ann Raffaelle, editor.
U.X.L 2002 xxxiv, 318p il maps $60
Grades: 8 9 10 11 12   **951.9**
1. Korean War, 1950-1953
ISBN 0-7876-5691-7   LC 2001-44242
An overview of the Korean War, including biogra-
phies and full or excerpted memoirs, speeches, and other
source documents
"An excellent starting point for researching the events
. . . of the Korean War." Booklist
Includes glossary and bibliographical references

DuBois, Jill, 1952-
Korea. 2nd ed. Benchmark Books 2004 144p il
map (Cultures of the world) lib bdg $25.95 *
Grades: 5 6 7 8   **951.9**
1. Korea
ISBN 0-7614-1786-9   LC 2004-7678
First published 1994
Describes the geography, history, government, econo-
my, environment, people, and culture of Korea
Includes glossary and bibliographical references

Feldman, Ruth Tenzer

The Korean War; by Ruth Tenzer Feldman. Lerner Publications Co. 2004 88p il map (Chronicle of America's wars) lib bdg $27.93

Grades: 5 6 7 8   **951.9**

1. Korean War, 1950-1953

ISBN 0-8225-4716-3   LC 2002-156557

Contents: Korea sometime in January 1951; Drawing the line; Storm!; Saving the South; North to the Yalu almost; "An entirely new war;" Setting limits; The talking war; Epilogue; Timeline

This "begins briefly with the events that led to Korea's division before focusing in greater detail on North Korea's invasion of South Korea. The author offers good overviews of the roles of the major players, and she outlines the significant battles and campaigns, and the lengthy negotiations that resulted in armistice. . . . [This is] abundantly illustrated with color and black-and-white photographs as well as maps." Booklist

Includes glossary and bibliographical references

Granfield, Linda

I remember Korea; veterans tell their stories of the Korean War, 1950-53. Clarion Books 2003 136p il $16

Grades: 8 9 10 11 12   **951.9**

1. Korean War, 1950-1953—Personal narratives

ISBN 0-618-17740-X   LC 2003-5397

Personal accounts of more than thirty men and women who served with the American and Canadian forces in Korea during the years 1950-1953

This title "has much to recommend it. . . . The text is timely, given both the renewed U.S.-North Korean tension and the increasing age of the veterans of the conflict. . . . The stories range from short anecdotes to more developed reminiscences; none are more than a few pages. Many are moving, some are surprisingly funny, and all offer insight into life at war from an insider's perspective." Quill & Quire

Includes bibliographical references

Grant, Reg, 1954-

The Korean War; by Reg Grant. World Almanac Library 2005 64p il map (Atlas of conflicts) lib bdg $32.66; pa $11.95

Grades: 6 7 8 9   **951.9**

1. Korean War, 1950-1953

ISBN 0-8368-5666-X (lib bdg); 0-8368-5673-2 (pa)
                                LC 2004-45526

Contents: Front one war to the next; The Korean War erupts; The tables turned; The Chinese enter the War; Fighting to a halt; Stalemate and negotiation; Consequences of the War; Profiles of military and political leaders; Significant dates; Statistics concerning cambatant nations

The author recounts "the background to the [Korean War], and then [provides an] objective [overview] of [its] military, diplomatic, and political aspects. Grant concludes with an analysis of the consequences of the Korean War. . . . Black-and-white and color photos and reproductions add interest." SLJ

Includes bibliographical references

Isserman, Maurice

Korean war. updated ed. Facts on File 2003 146p il map (America at war) lib bdg $35

Grades: 7 8 9 10   **951.9**

1. Korean War, 1950-1953

ISBN 0-8160-4939-4   LC 2002-7916

First published 1992

Contents: Task force Smith; Background to war; Defeat and retreat; Pusan and Inchon; Disaster in the north; Ridgway takes command; Long road to peace; Lessons from a forgotten war

Examines the political climate and military situation that led to the Korean War and discusses the key people and events involved in the conflict itself.

This volume provides "a great deal of information." Libr J

Includes bibliographical references

Santella, Andrew

The Korean War; by Andrew Santella. Compass Point Books 2007 48p il map (We the people) lib bdg $25.26; pa $8.95

Grades: 4 5 6 7   **951.9**

1. Korean War, 1950-1953

ISBN 978-0-7565-2027-4 (lib bdg); 0-7565-2027-4 (lib bdg); 978-0-7565-2039-7 (pa); 0-7565-2039-8 (pa)
                                LC 2006006767

This "begins by explaining how North and South Korea became divided; the involvement of the United Nations and the United States; conflict between President Harry Truman and General Douglas MacArthur; eventual peace talks; and the division still occurring today. Accessible and straightforward, this book is an excellent one for the intended audience." SLJ

Includes bibliographical references

951.93 North Korea (People's Democratic Republic of Korea)

Kummer, Patricia K.

North Korea; by Patricia K. Kummer. Children's Press 2008 144p il map (Enchantment of the world, second series) lib bdg $38

Grades: 5 6 7 8 9   **951.93**

1. Korea (North)

ISBN 978-0-531-18485-1 (lib bdg); 0-531-18485-4 (lib bdg)   LC 2007025693

In this introduction to North Korea "geography is the focus, but Kummer also discusses ancient and recent history, . . . the economy, religion, sports, education, and more. Without discounting the rich culture, the book doesn't shy away from more sensitive issues. . . . The open design will draw readers, with clear type on thick, high-quality paper; numerous maps and color photos and spacious back matter are also included." Booklist

Includes bibliographical references

951.95 South Korea (Republic of Korea)

Jackson, Tom, 1972-
South Korea; [by] Tom Jackson. National Geographic 2007 64p il map (Countries of the world) lib bdg $27.90 *
Grades: 4 5 6 7   **951.95**
1. Korea (South)
ISBN 978-1-4263-0125-4   LC 2007024663
This describes the geography, nature, history, people and culture, government, and economy of South Korea
Includes glossary and bibliographical references

952 Japan

Behnke, Alison
Japan in pictures. Lerner Publs. 2003 79p il map (Visual geography series) lib bdg $27.93
Grades: 5 6 7 8   **952**
1. Japan
ISBN 0-8225-1956-9   LC 2001-2955
First published 1989, catalogued under title
This describes Japan's "land, history and government, people, cultural life, and economy. Other information includes a timeline, fast facts, currency, flag, national anthem, famous people, sights to see . . . and Web sites. The [book is] visually appealing with photos and sidebars that complement the text." Libr Media Connect
Includes glossary and bibliographical references

Blumberg, Rhoda, 1917-
Commodore Perry in the land of the Shogun. Lothrop, Lee & Shepard Bks. 1985 144p il map $21.99; pa $8.99 *
Grades: 5 6 7 8   **952**
1. Perry, Matthew Calbraith, 1794-1858 2. United States Naval Expedition to Japan (1852-1854) 3. United States—Foreign relations—Japan 4. Japan—Foreign relations—United States 5. Japan—History
ISBN 0-688-03723-2; 0-06-008625-4 (pa)
LC 84-21800
A Newbery Medal honor book, 1986
This "is a well-written story of Matthew Perry's expedition to open Japan to American trade and whaling ports. The account is sensitive to the extreme cultural differences that both the Japanese and Americans had to overcome. Especially good are the chapters and paragraphs explaining Japanese feudal society and culture. The text is marvelously complemented by the illustrations, almost all reproductions of contemporary Japanese art." SLJ
Includes bibliographical references

Hanel, Rachael
Samurai. Creative Education 2008 48p il (Fearsome fighters) lib bdg $31.35
Grades: 4 5 6   **952**
1. Samurai 2. Japan—Civilization
ISBN 978-1-58341-538-2 (lib bdg); 1-58341-538-6 (lib bdg)   LC 2006023575

This "title explains the social conditions that led to the rise of [the Samurai] and describes the types of people who joined their ranks. Chapters detail the weapons, armor, and fighting techniques used. . . . The [book concludes] with a description of the social changes that led to a decline in the need for these warriors, but also [shows] how their legends have lived on in film and literature. . . . The [book is] well organized and clearly . . . written." SLJ
Includes glossary and bibliographical references

Heinrichs, Ann
Japan; by Ann Heinrichs. rev ed. Children's Press 2006 144p il map (Enchantment of the world, second series) lib bdg $37
Grades: 5 6 7 8   **952**
1. Japan
ISBN 0-516-24851-0 (lib bdg); 978-0-516-24851-6 (lib bdg)   LC 2005003270
First published 1998
"This book will explore the history, geography, wildlife, government, economy, religion, culture, and people of Japan. Also, students will have at their fingertips the most current facts and statistics that relate to Japan." Publisher's note
Includes bibliographical references

Schomp, Virginia, 1953-
Japan in the days of the samurai. Benchmark Bks. 2002 80p il maps (Cultures of the past) lib bdg $19.95
Grades: 6 7 8 9   **952**
1. Japan—Civilization
ISBN 0-7614-0304-3   LC 98-12228
Describes the Japanese way of life during the samurai eras through information about the politics, military, culture, and the belief system; also indicates the legacy of the period
"Offering balanced, thoughtfully interpreted material, this book effectively introduces Japan's early culture." Horn Book Guide
Includes glossary and bibliographical references

Shelley, Rex, 1930-
Japan; by Rex Shelley, Teo Chuu Yong, and Russell Mok. 2nd ed. Benchmark Bks. 2002 144p il maps (Cultures of the world) lib bdg $37.07
Grades: 5 6 7 8   **952**
1. Japan
ISBN 0-7614-1356-1   LC 2001-28609
First published 1990
This discusses the geography, history, government, economy, and culture of Japan
This book "will be helpful to report-writing. . . . The color photographs are well reproduced." Horn Book Guide
Includes glossary and bibliographical references

Turnbull, Stephen R.
Real samurai; over 20 true stories about the knights of old Japan! by Stephen Turnbull; illustrated by James Field. Enchanted Lion 2007 48p il $15.95
Grades: 4 5 6   952
  1. Samurai 2. Japan—History—0-1868
  ISBN 1-59270-060-8
"A comprehensive, highly engaging introduction to the world of the samurai for young readers. Each spread focuses on a different subject, such as training practices, codes of honor, battle accounts, castles, weapons, and profiles of famous warriors." Booklist

953   Arabian Peninsula and adjacent areas

Augustin, Byron
United Arab Emirates. Children's Press 2002 144p il map (Enchantment of the world, Second series) lib bdg $35
Grades: 5 6 7 8   953
  1. United Arab Emirates
  ISBN 0-516-20473-4   LC 00-65958
Describes the geography, history, culture, economy, and people of the United Arab Emirates
"This attractive title enhanced with full-color photographs provides everything that most students need for a basic understanding of the country." SLJ
  Includes bibliographical references

King, David C., 1933-
The United Arab Emirates; [by] David C. King. Marshall Cavendish Benchmark 2008 144p il map (Cultures of the world) lib bdg $27.95 *
Grades: 5 6 7 8   953
  1. United Arab Emirates
  ISBN 978-0-7614-2565-6   LC 2006030237
This describes the geography, history, government, economy, environment, people, and culture of the United Arab Emirates.
  Includes glossary and bibliographical references

953.3   Yemen

Hestler, Anna
Yemen. Benchmark Bks. 1999 128p il maps (Cultures of the world) lib bdg $37.07
Grades: 5 6 7 8   953.3
  1. Yemen
  ISBN 0-7614-0956-4   LC 98-53993
Presents information about the geography, history, government, and economy of this country located on the southwestern tip of the Arabian Peninsula and describes many aspects of the lifestyle of its people
  Includes glossary and bibliographical references

953.6   Persian Gulf States

Cooper, Robert, 1945-
Bahrain. Marshall Cavendish 2000 128p il map (Cultures of the world) lib bdg $37.07
Grades: 5 6 7 8   953.6
  1. Bahrain
  ISBN 0-7614-1161-5   LC 00-43116
"Cooper covers aspects of Bahraini society and daily life from the history, religion, government, and economy to the people, the arts, dress, and food. A particularly interesting chapter addresses the ancient findings of the prehistoric era. Good-quality, full-color photographs are well-matched to the text." SLJ
  Includes glossary and bibliographical references

Orr, Tamra
Qatar; [by] Tamra Orr. 1st ed. Marshall Cavendish Benchmark 2008 144p il map (Cultures of the world) lib bdg $27.95 *
Grades: 5 6 7 8   953.6
  1. Qatar
  ISBN 978-0-7614-256-3   LC 2006033626
This describes the geography, history, government, economy, environment, people, and culture of Qatar.
  Includes glossary and bibliographical references

953.67   Kuwait

Marcovitz, Hal
Kuwait. Mason Crest Publs. 2003 112p il maps (Modern Middle East nations and their strategic place in the world) lib bdg $24.95
Grades: 7 8 9 10   953.67
  1. Kuwait
  ISBN 1-59084-510-2   LC 2002-13002
Discusses the geography, history, economy, government, religion, people, foreign relations, and major cities of Kuwait
This volume is "clearly written and accurate." SLJ
  Includes glossary and bibliographical references

O'Shea, Maria
Kuwait. Benchmark Bks. 1999 128p il maps (Cultures of the world) lib bdg $37.07
Grades: 5 6 7 8   953.67
  1. Kuwait
  ISBN 0-7614-0871-1   LC 98-25833
Introduces the geography, history, religious beliefs, government, and people of Kuwait, a small country on the Persian Gulf
  Includes glossary and bibliographical references

953.8 Saudi Arabia

Broberg, Catherine
Saudi Arabia in pictures. rev & expanded. Lerner Publs. 2003 80p il maps (Visual geography series) lib bdg $27.93
Grades: 5 6 7 8   953.8
  1. Saudi Arabia
  ISBN 0-8225-1958-5   LC 2001-2967
First published 1979 by Sterling under the authorship of Eugene Gordon
This describes the geography, people, culture, and economy of Saudi Arabia
This "is an exemplary starting point for student researchers. . . . A page of specifically chosen Web sites will link kids to other information about the Arabic language, interpretation of political events, Islamic prayer, and much more." Booklist
Includes bibliographical references

Janin, Hunt, 1940-
Saudi Arabia; [by] Hunt Janin, Margaret Besheer. 2nd ed. Benchmark Bks. 2003 144p il map (Cultures of the world) lib bdg $37.07 *
Grades: 5 6 7 8   953.8
  1. Saudi Arabia
  ISBN 0-7614-1666-8   LC 2003-6931
First published 1993
  Contents: Geography; History; Government; Economy; Environment; Saudi Arabians; Lifestyle; Religion; Language; Arts; Leisure; Festivals; Food; Map of Saudi Arabia; About the economy; About the culture; Time line
  Includes glossary and bibliographical references

954 South Asia. India

Arnold, Caroline, 1944-
Taj Mahal; by Caroline Arnold and Madeleine Comora; illustrated by Rahul Bhushan. Carolrhoda Books 2007 unp il lib bdg $17.95
Grades: 4 5 6 7   954
  1. Taj Mahal (Agra, India) 2. Mogul Empire
  ISBN 978-0-7613-2609-0 (lib bdg); 0-7613-2609-X (lib bdg)   LC 2001006685
Recounts the love story behind the building of the Taj Mahal in India, discussing how it was constructed and providing information on Indian culture.
"The small, detailed paintings are . . . set on beautifully constructed pages resembling those of illuminated manuscripts. . . . The book is sumptuous in appearance and presents a bit of history not often told for children." SLJ

Benhart, John E.
South Asia; series consulting editor Charles F. Gritzner. Chelsea House Pubs. 2006 120p (Modern world cultures) lib bdg $30
Grades: 7 8 9 10   954

  1. South Asia
  ISBN 0-7910-8147-8
This describes the natural landscapes, history, peoples, economy, regional contrasts, and possible future of countries of South Asia, including India, Pakistan, Nepal, Bangladesh, and Bhutan.

Engfer, Lee, 1963-
India in pictures. Lerner Publs. 2003 80p il map (Visual geography series) lib bdg $27.93
Grades: 5 6 7 8   954
  1. India
  ISBN 0-8225-0371-9   LC 2002-950
  Contents: The land; History and government; The people; Cultural life; The economy
Text and illustrations present detailed information on the geography, history and government, economy, people, cultural life and society of traditional and modern India
The book is "visually appealing with photos and sidebars that complement the text." Libr Media Connect
Includes bibliographical references

Srinivasan, Radhika
India; [by] Radhika Srinivasan, Leslie Jermyn. 2nd ed. Benchmark Bks. 2002 144p il maps (Cultures of the world) $37.07
Grades: 5 6 7 8   954
  1. India
  ISBN 0-7614-1354-5   LC 2001-28608
First published 1990
This describes the geography, history, government, economy, environment, people, and culture of India
Includes glossary and bibliographical references

954.02 India—647-1785

Mann, Elizabeth, 1948-
Taj Mahal; a story of love and empire; by Elizabeth Mann; with illustrations by Alan Witschonke. Mikaya 2008 47p il (Wonders of the world) $22.95 *
Grades: 4 5 6 7   954.02
  1. Taj Mahal (Agra, India) 2. Mogul Empire
  ISBN 1-931414-20-3; 978-1-931414-20-3
                              LC 2008060054
This is a "dramatic retelling of the construction of the Taj Mahal. Mann begins with two pages of prose that relay the commonly told legend, but then proceeds to explode that legend with descriptive writing, colorful illustrations, ancient paintings, maps, and photographs." Booklist
Includes bibliographical references

954.9   Jurisdictions of South Asia other than India

Cooper, Robert, 1945-
Bhutan. Benchmark Bks. 2001 128p il maps (Cultures of the world) lib bdg $37.07
Grades: 5 6 7 8   **954.9**
   1. Bhutan
   ISBN 0-7614-1191-7   LC 00-47435
Describes the geography, history, government, economy, and culture of Bhutan
Includes glossary and bibliographical references

954.91   Pakistan

Kovarik, Chiara Angela
Interviews with Muslim women of Pakistan. Syren Book Comp. 2005 c2004 131p $14.95 *
Grades: 7 8 9 10   **954.91**
   1. Muslim women 2. Women in Islam 3. Pakistan
   ISBN 0-929636-49-X
"In 10 lively interviews, American teenager Kovarik, 17, talks to Pakistani Muslim women, some she met while visiting their country in 2001, some who are now living in the U.S and Canada. She asks them about their spiritual beliefs, about American misconceptions of Muslim women, how things have changed over time, how they view Western religion and culture, how 9/11 affected them, and more. . . . Prefaced with introductory material on Islam, Pakistan, and the role of women, this combination of religion, contemporary voices, and a message of tolerance is sure to engage teens." Booklist
Includes bibliographical references

Morgan, Sally
Focus on Pakistan; [by] Sally Morgan. World Almanac Library 2007 64p il map (World in focus) lib bdg $33.27; pa $11.95
Grades: 6 7 8 9   **954.91**
   1. Pakistan
   ISBN 978-0-8368-6752-7   (lib   bdg);
   978-0-8368-6759-6 (pa)   LC 2007022011
This describes the history, landscape and climate, population and settlements, government and politics, energy and resources, economy and income, global connections, transportation and communications, education and health, culture and religion, leisure and tourism, environment and conservation, and future challenges of Pakistan.
"Attractive color photographs, graphs, and charts illustrate [this] volume. . . . [This book presents] current, accurate information in a way that is not too dry or overwhelming for the intended age group." SLJ
Includes glossary and bibliographical references

Mortenson, Greg, 1957-
Three cups of tea; one man's mission to promote peace—one school at a time; [by] Greg Mortenson and David Oliver Relin; adapted for young readers by Sarah Thomson. Dial Books for Young Readers 2009 209p il $16.99; pa $8.99
Grades: 4 5 6 7   **954.91**

   1. Pakistan 2. Schools—Pakistan
   ISBN   978-0-8037-3392-3;   0-8037-3392-5;
   978-0-14-241412-5 (pa); 0-14-241412-3 (pa)
Based on Three cups of tea: one man's mission to fight terrorism and build nations one school at a time, published 2006 by Viking for adults
"In 1993, while climbing one of the world's most difficult peaks, Mortenson became lost and ill, and eventually found aid in the tiny Pakistani village of Korphe. He vowed to repay his generous hosts by building a school; his efforts have grown into the Central Asia Institute. . . . Retold for middle readers, the story remains inspirational and compelling. . . . Illustrated throughout with b&w photos, it also contains two eight-page insets of color photos." Publ Wkly

Sheehan, Sean, 1951-
Pakistan; by Sean Sheehan. 2nd ed. Benchmark Books 2004 144p il map (Cultures of the world) lib bdg $37.07 *
Grades: 5 6 7 8   **954.91**
   ISBN 0-7614-1787-7   LC 2004-7677
   First published 1994
   Contents: Geography; History; Government; Economy; Environment; Pakistanis; Lifestyle; Religion; Language; Arts; Leisure; Festivals; Food
An introduction to the geography, history, government, and culture of Pakistan
"Excellent-quality, full-color photographs and sidebars highlight special information and make this book accessible and appealing. . . . A gold mine of information for reports." SLJ
Includes glossary and bibliographical references

954.92   Bangladesh

Orr, Tamra
Bangladesh; by Tamra B. Orr. Children's Press 2007 144p il map (Enchantment of the world, second series) lib bdg $36
Grades: 5 6 7 8   **954.92**
   1. Bangladesh
   ISBN 978-0-516-25012-0 (lib bdg); 0-516-25012-4 (lib bdg)   LC 2006024160
Describes the geography, people, government, culture, history, religion, economy, and wildlife of Bagladesh.
"The strong design features highly readable type and beautiful, color photos on almost every page. . . . Includes clear maps and useful end matter." Booklist
Includes bibliographical references

Phillips, Douglas A.
Bangladesh; [by] Douglas A. Phillips and Charles F. Gritzner. Chelsea House 2007 107p il map (Modern world nations) lib bdg $30
Grades: 7 8 9 10   **954.92**
   1. Bangladesh
   ISBN 0-7910-9251-8 (lib bdg); 978-0-7910-9251-4 (lib bdg)   LC 2006032006
Describes the geography, history, people, culture, economy, and government of Bangladesh
Includes bibliographical references

Valliant, Doris
Bangladesh. Mason Crest 2005 120p il map (Growth and influence of Islam in the nations of Asia and Central Asia) lib bdg $25.95
Grades: 8 9 10 11 12   **954.92**
1. Bangladesh
ISBN 1-59084-879-9
This is an "examination of the many ways Islam has influenced the culture and politics [of Bangladesh]. Throughout the chapters on history, people, economy, and foreign relations, the importance of the religion is emphasized in every aspect of life. Valliant presents a good discussion of the significance of Islam in the establishment of Bangladesh as an independent nation." SLJ

954.93   Sri Lanka

Wanasundera, Nanda P., 1932-
Sri Lanka; [by] Nanda Pethiyagoda Wanasundera. 2nd ed. Benchmark Bks. 2002 144p il maps (Cultures of the world) lib bdg $37.07
Grades: 5 6 7 8   **954.93**
1. Sri Lanka
ISBN 0-7614-1477-0   LC 2002-25980
First published 1990
Describes the geography, history, government, economy, social life and customs, religion, culture, and more of this island country in the Indian Ocean
Includes glossary and bibliographical references

954.96   Nepal

Burbank, Jon, 1951-
Nepal. 2nd ed. Benchmark Bks. 2002 144p il map (Cultures of the world) lib bdg $37.07 *
Grades: 5 6 7 8   **954.96**
1. Nepal
ISBN 0-7614-1476-2   LC 2002-25994
First published 1991
Describes the geography, history, government, economy, people, religion, language, and culture of Nepal, a predominantly Hindu country located north of India. Includes several recipes
Includes glossary and bibliographical references

Yackley-Franken, Nicki
Teens in Nepal; by Nicki Yackley-Franken. Compass Point Books 2008 96p map (Global connections) lib bdg $31.93
Grades: 7 8 9 10   **954.96**
1. Teenagers 2. Nepal
ISBN 978-0-7565-3411-0 (lib bdg); 0-7565-3411-9 (lib bdg)   LC 2007-32693
Uncovers the challenges, pastimes, customs and cultures of teens in Nepal.
"Information is solid, giving readers an informed and realistic view of life in that country. A historical time line is included, and suggestions for other nonfiction and fiction titles for further reading." Voice Youth Advocates
Includes glossary and bibliographical references

955   Iran

Gray, Leon, 1974-
Iran; [by] Leon Gray; Edmund Herzig and Dorreh Mirheydar, consultants. National Geographic 2008 64p il map (Countries of the world) lib bdg $27.90 *
Grades: 4 5 6 7   **955**
1. Iran
ISBN 978-1-4263-0200-8   LC 2007047834
This describes the geography, nature, history, people and culture, government and economy of Iran
"With high-quality color photographs, archival art, and several excellent, full-page maps, this [is a] highly readable, detailed overview." Booklist
Includes glossary and bibliographical references

January, Brendan, 1972-
The Iranian Revolution. Twenty-First Century Books 2008 160p il map (Pivotal moments in history) lib bdg $38.60
Grades: 7 8 9 10   **955**
1. Iran—History—1979-
ISBN 978-0-8225-7521-4   LC 2007-30260
"Sure to satisfy history buffs, the book not only relates facts about the 1979 Iranian Revolution but also delves into events leading up to it, beginning with its roots in medieval Persia, as well as exploring the lasting effects. Numerous sidebars, illustrations, maps, and art reproductions provide additional information." Horn Book Guide
Includes glossary and bibliographical references

Rajendra, Vijeya, 1936-
Iran; [by] Vijeya Rajendra, Gisela Kaplan, Rudi Rajendra. 2nd ed. Benchmark Bks. 2003 c2004 144p il map (Cultures of the world) lib bdg $37.07 *
Grades: 5 6 7 8   **955**
1. Iran
ISBN 0-7614-1665-X   LC 2003-8257
First published 1993
Contents: Geography; History; Government; Economy; Environment; Iranians; Lifestyle; Religion; Language; Arts; Leisure; Festivals; Food
Explores the geography, history, government, economy, people, and culture of Iran
Includes glossary and bibliographical references

Ramen, Fred
A historical atlas of Iran. Rosen Pub. Group 2003 64p il map (Historical atlases of South Asia, Central Asia, and the Middle East) lib bdg $30.60
Grades: 8 9 10 11 12   **955**
1. Iran
ISBN 0-8239-3864-6   LC 2002-31031
This focuses on the political history of Iran "as determined by geography and religion. . . . Brief descriptions of the art and architecture of [the] country testify to the richness of [this culture]. . . . [This] well-organized and ambitious [book provides] needed information." SLJ

Seidman, David, 1958-

Teens in Iran; by David Seidman. Compass Point Books 2008 96p il map (Global connections) lib bdg $31.93

Grades: 7 8 9 10 **955**

1. Youth—Iran

ISBN 978-0-7565-3300-7 (lib bdg); 0-7565-3300-7 (lib bdg) LC 2007-5411

Explores the daily lives and customs of Iranian teenagers, discussing holidays, education, religion, employment, and culture.

"The information is solid, giving readers an informed and realistic view of life in that country. A historical time line is included, and suggestions for other nonfiction and fiction titles for further reading. Readers are directed to a Web site, where Internet links and a list of additional nonfiction titles are provided." Voice Youth Advocates

956 Middle East

Crompton, Samuel

The Third Crusade; Richard the Lionhearted vs. Saladin; [by] Samuel Willard Crompton. Chelsea House 2003 114p il map (Great battles through the ages) $22.95

Grades: 7 8 9 10 **956**

1. Richard I, King of England, 1157-1199 2. Saladin, Sultan of Egypt and Syria, 1137-1193 3. Crusades

ISBN 0-7910-7437-4 LC 2003-4593

"In 1187 King Richard I sought control of the Holy Land. This text details the Third Crusade in which the king of England lead an army of Christians to sieze the Holy Land from the Muslims." Publisher's note

"The value of this book is not so much its depictions of battles, but rather of the men who came to symbolize the reasons for the struggle. . . . Some excellent color and black-and-white illustrations are included." SLJ

Includes bibliographical references

Gritzner, Jeffrey A.

North Africa and the Middle East; [by] Jeffrey A. Gritzner and Charles F. Gritzner. Chelsea House 2006 120p il map (Modern world cultures) lib bdg $30

Grades: 7 8 9 10 **956**

1. Middle East 2. North Africa

ISBN 0-7910-8145-1 LC 2006011649

Contents: Introduction; A diverse environment; The natural landscape; Climate and ecosystems; The cradle of civilization; Western influence; Population and settlement; Cultural geography; A troubled region looks ahead; History at a glance

Includes bibliographical references

January, Brendan, 1972-

The Arab Conquests of the Middle East. Twenty First Century Books 2009 160p il (Pivotal moments in history) $38.60

Grades: 8 9 10 11 12 **956**

1. Islam—History 2. Middle East—History

ISBN 978-0-8225-8744-6; 0-8225-8744-0

"One hundred years after the death of Muhammad, Muslim armies had conquered most of North Africa, the Middle East, and parts of Spain and were fighting as far north as modern France. This attractively illustrated history begins with Muhammad's life and revelations and covers the early period of the Muslim community first as it struggled to survive and then as it gradually assumed dominance over the Arabian peninsula. . . . A section on primary-source research will intrigue historically minded readers, and a who's who and lists of further reading make this volume highly useful for reports." SLJ

Includes bibliographical references

Kort, Michael

The handbook of the Middle East; by Michael G. Kort. rev ed. Twenty-First Century Books 2008 320p il map lib bdg $39.95

Grades: 8 9 10 11 12 **956**

1. Middle East

ISBN 978-0-8225-7143-8 (lib bdg); 0-8225-7143-9 (lib bdg) LC 2006-34917

First published 2002

Examines the past, present, and future of all the countries in the Middle East, discussing their history and culture

Includes bibliographical references

The **Middle** East. Greenwood Press 2004 5v il map (Discovering world cultures) set$200

Grades: 8 9 10 11 12 **956**

1. Middle East

ISBN 0-313-32922-2

"A Creative Media Applications, Inc. production"

Contents: v1 Bahrain, Cyprus, Egypt; v2 Iran, Iraq, Israel; v3 Jordan, Kuwait, Lebanon, Oman; v4 Qatar, Saudi-Arabia, Syria; v5 Turkey, United Arab Emirates, Yemen

This "set profiles the 16 countries that lie in the geographic region between the Mediterranean Sea and India. . . . Each country . . . is covered in a multipage chapter providing detailed information on ethnic groups, land and resources, history, economy, religion, everyday life, holidays, and the arts. . . . Readers in need of a source of solid, unbiased information will be well served by this resource." Booklist

The **Middle** East: opposing viewpoints; William Dudley, book editor. Greenhaven Press 2004 203p il lib bdg $34.95; pa $23.70

Grades: 8 9 10 11 12 **956**

1. Middle East—Politics and government 2. Religion and politics

ISBN 0-7377-1805-6 (lib bdg); 0-7377-1806-4 (pa) LC 2003-49020

Replaces the edition published 2000 under the editorship of Mary E. Williams

"Opposing viewpoints series"

"This anthology features voices within and outside the region debating the Israeli/Palestinian conflict, the role of religion, and American foreign policy in the region, and other key issues." Publisher's note

Includes bibliographical references

Steele, Philip
Middle East; foreword by Paul Adams. Kingfisher 2006 63p il map (Kingfisher knowledge) $12.95
Grades: 5 6 7 8   **956**
 1. Middle East
 ISBN 978-0-7534-5984-3; 0-7534-5984-1
"A concise overview of the history and culture of the region, defined as the countries of Turkey, Syria, Lebanon, Israel, the Palestinian territories, Egypt, Jordan, Saudi Arabia, Yemen, Oman, the Gulf states, Iraq, Iran, and Afghanistan. The text is brief but informative, and current political controversies are touched on in an age-appropriate and evenhanded manner. . . . The real strength of this book is the appealing graphic design and the excellent-quality color photographs throughout." SLJ
Includes glossary and bibliographical references

956.04   Middle East—1945-1980

The **Arab-Israeli** conflict; Mark Rackers, book editor. Greenhaven Press 2004 234p (Great speeches in history series) $34.95
Grades: 8 9 10 11 12   **956.04**
 1. Israel-Arab conflicts 2. Speeches
 ISBN 0-7377-1649-5
"This book offers 20 speeches by major players in the history of this turmoil, beginning with David Ben-Gurion's 1946 address to the Anglo-American Committee that would decide the fate of the future state of Israel and ending with Ariel Sharon's 2002 plea for peace. An excellent introductory essay sets the stage for the modern conflict. . . . This volume is a core resource for Middle East collections." SLJ

Hampton, Wilborn
War in the Middle East; a reporter's story. Candlewick Press 2007 112p il map $19.99 *
Grades: 6 7 8 9 10 11 12   **956.04**
 1. Middle East—History 2. Israel-Arab War, 1973
 ISBN 978-0-7636-2493-4; 0-7636-2493-4
                                  LC 2006-51694
"Recalling experiences as a reporter assigned to cover the 1970 Jordanian civil conflict dubbed Black September, and the Yom Kippur War that began in October 1973, Hampton not only presents a clear summary of the issues that provoked each outbreak of violence but also provides both personal slant and a sense of immediacy to his account of events." Booklist
Includes bibliographical references

The **Palestinians** and the disputed territories; Neil Alger, book editor. Greenhaven Press 2004 144p il map (World's hot spots) lib bdg $28.70 *
Grades: 8 9 10 11 12   **956.04**
 1. Israel-Arab conflicts
 ISBN 0-7377-1489-1   LC 2003-48327
This "collection of essays, articles, and analyses traces the history of strife in the region and looks at the current situation from a variety of perspectives. The writers discuss the complex issues with attention toward readers who may be unfamiliar with the circumstances of the Middle Eastern conflict. The selections expound on the importance of Jerusalem and the groups, both the religious and political, that wish to control the city. International influences and involvement by the U.S., Britain, and Russia are also addressed." SLJ
Includes bibliographical references

Senker, Cath
The Arab-Israeli conflict; [by] Cath Senker. new ed. Arcturus Pub. 2008 48p il map (Timelines) lib bdg $32.80
Grades: 5 6 7 8   **956.04**
 1. Israel-Arab conflicts
 ISBN 978-1-84193-725-0 (lib bdg); 1-84193-725-8 (lib bdg)   LC 2007-7547
 First published 2005 by Smart Apple Media
This describes current conditions in Israel and the occupied territories and includes a history of major events and political developments.
"A complex situation is clearly explained. . . . [This is] well-illustrated. . . . Throughout, the tone is nonjudgmental." SLJ [review of 2005 edition]
Includes bibliographical references

956.1   Turkey

Eboch, Chris
Turkey. Lucent Bks. 2003 112p il maps (Modern nations of the world) lib bdg $27.45
Grades: 7 8 9 10   **956.1**
 1. Turkey
 ISBN 1-59018-122-0   LC 2002-11052
 Contents: Where continents collide; The passing of empires; The republic; Daily life; Art and entertainment; Today's challenges
This is an "overview of Turkey's history and geography as well as the challenges the nation faces in today's world. . . . The book is well written." SLJ
Includes bibliographical references

Ganeri, Anita, 1961-
Focus on Turkey; [by] Anita Ganeri. World Almanac Library 2007 64p il map (World in focus) lib bdg $33.27; pa $11.95
Grades: 6 7 8 9   **956.1**
 1. Turkey
 ISBN   978-0-8368-6753-4   (lib   bdg);
 978-0-8368-6760-2 (pa)   LC 2007022145
This describes the history, landscape and climate, population and settlements, government and politics, energy and resources, economy and income, global connections, transportation and communications, education and health; culture and religion, leisure and tourism, environment and conservation, and future challenges of Turkey.
"Attractive color photographs, graphs, and charts illustrate [this] volume. . . . [This book presents] current, accurate information in a way that is not too dry or overwhelming for the intended age group." SLJ
Includes glossary and bibliographical references

Greenblatt, Miriam

Süleyman the Magnificent and the Ottoman Empire. Benchmark Bks. 2002 80p il (Rulers and their times) lib bdg $28.50 *

Grades: 6 7 8 9　　　　　　　　　956.1
  1. Süleyman I, Sultan of the Turks, 1495-1566
  2. Turkey—History
  ISBN 0-7614-1489-4　　　　　　LC 2002-1974
Provides an overview of the lives of Suleyman I and his subjects in the Ottoman Empire of the late sixteenth century, and includes excerpts from poems, letters, and stories of the time

This "uses primary documents to illustrate sixteenth-century Ottoman thought. Color reproductions of art and manuscripts illustrate the text, which is spaciously designed with plenty of white space." Horn Book Guide
  Includes glossary and bibliographical references

Lace, William W.

The unholy crusade; the ransacking of medieval Constantinople; [by] William W. Lace. Lucent Books 2007 104p il map (Lucent library of historical eras, Middle Ages) lib bdg $32.45 *

Grades: 6 7 8 9　　　　　　　　　956.1
  1. Crusades 2. Istanbul (Turkey) 3. Middle Ages
  ISBN 978-1-59018-846-0 (lib bdg); 1-59018-846-2 (lib bdg)　　　　　　　　LC 2006002572
"Lace gives equal attention to the events leading up to the destruction of Constantinople and traces the planning and plotting of the Crusades. . . . [The book has] numerous color reproductions. Clear, concise writing makes [it] highly readable, while the scholarship makes [it a] valuable [resource]." SLJ
  Includes bibliographical references

Lilly, Alexandra

Teens in Turkey. Compass Point Books 2008 96p il map (Global connections) lib bdg $31.93

Grades: 7 8 9 10　　　　　　　　　956.1
  1. Teenagers 2. Turkey
  ISBN 978-0-7565-3414-1 (lib bdg); 0-7565-3414-3 (lib bdg)　　　　　　　LC 2007033090
Uncovers the challenges, pastimes, customs and culture of teens in Turkey

"Information is solid, giving readers an informed and realistic view of life in that country. A historical time line is included, and suggestions for other nonfiction and fiction titles for further reading." Youth Voice Advocates
  Includes glossary and bibliographical references

Orr, Tamra

Turkey. Children's Press 2003 144p il map (Enchantment of the world, second series) lib bdg $34

Grades: 5 6 7 8　　　　　　　　　956.1
  1. Turkey
  ISBN 0-516-22679-7　　　　　　LC 2002-1590
Contents: Traveling through time; A unique meeting point; The flora and the fauna; A 3,000 year history; The new face of the government; Shifting the economy; The richness of the people; The ways of a spiritual life; The expanding world of Turkish culture; Daily life in Turkey; Timeline; Fast facts

This describes the history, culture, flora and fauna, government, and economy of Turkey

"Good-quality graphics and lively . . . [text makes this title] readable and visually enticing." SLJ
  Includes bibliographical references

Ruggiero, Adriane

The Ottoman Empire. Benchmark Bks. 2003 80p il maps (Cultures of the past) lib bdg $28.50 *

Grades: 6 7 8 9　　　　　　　　　956.1
  1. Turkey—History
  ISBN 0-7614-1494-0　　　　　　LC 2002-2264
Contents: History: From nomads to sultans; Cultural history: The age of Suleyman the Magnificent; Belief system: The Turks and Islam; Beliefs and society: Shaping the empire; The legacy of the Ottomans: The Ottoman influence lives on

This "volume covers the history, belief system, cultural history and legacy of [the Ottoman Empire]. . . . Students of world history will find this . . . useful for basic information and research." Libr Media Connect
  Includes glossary and bibliographical references

Shields, Sarah D., 1955-

Turkey; [by] Sarah Shields. National Geographic 2009 64p il map (Countries of the world) lib bdg $27.90 *

Grades: 4 5 6 7　　　　　　　　　956.1
  1. Turkey
  ISBN 978-1-4263-0387-6 (lib bdg); 1-4263-0387-4 (lib bdg)　　　　　　　LC 2009275583
This describes the geography, nature, history, people and culture, government and economy of Turkey
  Includes glossary and bibliographical references

956.7　Iraq

Augustin, Byron

Iraq; by Byron Augustin and Jake Kubena. rev ed. Children's Press 2006 144p il map (Enchantment of the world, second series) lib bdg $36

Grades: 5 6 7 8　　　　　　　　　956.7
  1. Iraq
  ISBN 0-516-24852-9　　　　　　LC 2005032181
First published 1998
This describes the geography, history, culture, people, and government of Iraq

This edition "focuses far less on Saddam Hussein and includes more details about the nation's different ethnic groups, environmental issues and wildlife, and information about the current political situation. . . . [The book contains] more full-color photographs than the previous [edition]. . . . Libraries will definitely want [this volume]." SLJ
  Includes bibliographical references

Campbell, Geoffrey A.

Life of an American soldier. Lucent Bks. 2001 128p il (American war library, Persian Gulf War) lib bdg $27.45

Grades: 7 8 9 10 **956.7**

1. Persian Gulf War, 1991

ISBN 1-56006-713-6 LC 00-10677

"A foreword explains why it is important to look at America as a country defined by the wars it chose to wage while an introduction seeks to explain why the United States chose to wage this particular war. Campbell has clearly done his research as evidenced by the numerous interviews (both personal and culled from sources) with veterans of the Persian Gulf War that enrich this history. . . . Clear, concise, and user-friendly, it is tailor-made for reports but will still attract browsers." SLJ

Includes glossary and bibliographical references

Ellis, Deborah, 1960-

Children of war; voices of Iraqi refugees. Groundwood Books 2009 128p il $15.95 *

Grades: 7 8 9 10 11 12 **956.7**

1. Children and war 2. Iraq War, 2003- 3. Refugees

ISBN 978-0-88899-907-8; 0-88899-907-0

Ellis "interviews child refugees from Iraq, now living in Jordan, and a few who have made it to Canada. . . . Accompanying each of the . . . interviews with young people is a brief introduction and a photo. . . . What is haunting are their graphic recent memories of what they witnessed. . . . An important, current title that will have lasting significance." Booklist

Includes glossary

Hassig, Susan M., 1969-

Iraq; [by] Susan M. Hassig, Laith Muhmood Al Adely. 2nd ed. Benchmark Bks. 2003 144p il maps (Cultures of the world) lib bdg $37.07

Grades: 5 6 7 8 **956.7**

1. Iraq

ISBN 0-7614-1668-4 LC 2003-10082

First published 1993

Explores the geography, history, government, economy, people, and culture of Iraq

Lightfoot, Dale

Iraq; [by] Dale Lightfoot. Chelsea House 2007 117p il map (Modern world nations) lib bdg $30

Grades: 7 8 9 10 **956.7**

1. Iraq

ISBN 0-7910-9247-X LC 2006012725

Describes the geography, history, people and culture, politics, and economy of Iraq

Includes bibliographical references

Samuels, Charlie, 1961-

Iraq; [by] Charlie Samuels; Sarah Shields and Shakir Mustafa, consultants. National Geographic 2007 64p il map (Countries of the world) lib bdg $27.90 *

Grades: 4 5 6 7 **956.7**

1. Iraq

ISBN 978-1-4263-0061-5 LC 2007024675

This describes the geography, nature, history, people and culture, government and economy of Iraq.

Includes glossary and bibliographical references

Smithson, Ryan

Ghosts of war; my tour of duty. HarperTeen 2009 321p il $16.99; lib bdg $17.89

Grades: 8 9 10 11 12 **956.7**

1. Iraq War, 2003——Personal narratives 2. Soldiers—United States

ISBN 978-0-06-166468-7; 0-06-166468-5; 978-0-06-166470-0 (lib bdg); 0-06-166470-7 (lib bdg)

LC 2008-35420

"Ryan Smithson was a typical 16-year-old high-school student until 9/11. . . . Smithson enlisted in the Army Reserve the following year and, a year into the Iraq war, was deployed to an Army engineer unit as a heavy-equipment operator. His poignant, often harrowing account, especially vivid in sensory details, chronicles his experiences in basic training and in Iraq. . . . This memoir is a remarkable, deeply penetrating read that will compel teens to reflect on their own thoughts about duty, patriotism and sacrifice." Kirkus

Includes glossary and bibliographical references

Zeinert, Karen, 1942-2002

The brave women of the Gulf Wars; Operation Desert Storm and Operation Iraqi Freedom; [by] Karen Zeinert & Mary Miller. 21st Century Bks. 2006 112p il $30.60

Grades: 7 8 9 10 **956.7**

1. Women in the armed forces 2. Iraq War, 2003 3. Persian Gulf War, 1991—Women

ISBN 0-7613-2705-3

"Zeinert and Miller reinforce the argument that women do, indeed, belong in the U.S. military by highlighting their contributions in Operations Desert Storm (Kuwait) and Iraqi Freedom. . . . The narrative paints a picture of consistent courage under fire and, one terse mention of the abuses at Abu Ghraib Prison aside, of professional conduct. The authors extend their purview with a chapter on women journalists in the campaigns, and while thoroughly villainizing Saddam Hussein, they also indicate that the official justifications for the war in Iraq turned out to be weak at best. A utilitarian but cogent assessment of the topic, well supported by notes and sources." Booklist

Includes bibliographical references

956.91 Syria

South, Coleman, 1948-

Syria; by Coleman South & Leslie Jermyn. 2nd ed. Marshall Cavendish Benchmark 2006 144p il map (Cultures of the world) lib bdg $37.07

Grades: 5 6 7 8 **956.91**

1. Syria

ISBN 0-7614-2054-1 LC 2005023848

First published 1995

This describes the geography, history, government, economy, culture, peoples, and religion of Syria

South, Coleman, 1948-—*Continued*
"Straightforward, up-to-date. . . , well-written. . . . The attractive layout features a high-quality full-color photo on each page." SLJ
Includes glossary and bibliographical references

956.92   Lebanon

Sheehan, Sean, 1951-
Lebanon; [by] Sean Sheehan & Zawiah Abdul Latif. 2nd ed. Marshall Cavendish Benchmark 2008 144p il map (Cultures of the world) lib bdg $39.93
Grades: 5 6 7 8   **956.92**
  1. Lebanon
  ISBN 978-0-7614-2081-1 (lib bdg); 0-7614-2081-9 (lib bdg)   LC 2006101735
First published 1997
"Provides comprehensive information on the geography, history, wildlife, governmental structure, economy, cultural diversity, peoples, religion, and culture of Lebanon." Publisher's note
Includes bibliographical references

956.93   Cyprus

Spilling, Michael
Cyprus. Benchmark Bks. 2000 128p il map (Cultures of the world) lib bdg $37.07
Grades: 5 6 7 8   **956.93**
  1. Cyprus
  ISBN 0-7614-0978-5   LC 99-31942
Discusses the geography, history, government, economy, people, and culture of Cyprus
  Includes glossary and bibliographical references

956.94   Palestine. Israel

Blumberg, Arnold, 1925-
The history of Israel. Greenwood Press 1998 218p (Greenwood histories of the modern nations) $45 *
Grades: 8 9 10 11 12   **956.94**
  1. Israel—History 2. Zionism
  ISBN 0-313-30224-3   LC 97-45659
"Starting with a description of life in modern Israel, Blumberg . . . quickly covers Israel's early history, from 3,500 years ago to World War I. . . . The battles leading to independence, the isolation of Israel, conflicts within Israel, the Suez Crisis and subsequent wars, the Intifada, the development of the PLO, and the Peace Process are described in a manner that enables readers to have a much better understanding of the events happening in Israel now." Voice Youth Advocates
Includes bibliographical references

Corona, Laurel, 1949-
Israel. Lucent Bks. 2003 112p il maps (Modern nations of the world) lib bdg $27.45
Grades: 7 8 9 10   **956.94**
  1. Israel
  ISBN 1-59018-115-8   LC 2002-10428
Discusses the vision of a Jewish homeland, the founding of Israel, and the struggles and dangers of daily life in Israel
"This title is well researched and solidly written." SLJ
Includes glossary and bibliographical references

DuBois, Jill, 1952-
Israel; by Jill DuBois, Mair Rosh. 2nd ed. Benchmark Bks. 2003 c2004 144p il map (Cultures of the world) lib bdg $37.07
Grades: 5 6 7 8   **956.94**
  1. Israel
  ISBN 0-7614-1669-2   LC 2003-10083
First published 1993
Explores the geography, history, government, economy, people, and culture of Israel
Includes glossary and bibliographical references

Ellis, Deborah, 1960-
Three wishes; Palestinian and Israeli children speak. Groundwood Bks. 2004 110p il map hardcover o.p. pa $9.99 *
Grades: 5 6 7 8   **956.94**
  1. Israel-Arab conflicts 2. Palestinian Arabs
  ISBN 0-88899-608-X; 0-88899-645-4 (pa)
"Growing up separate and apart in a world of bombs, bullets, removals, checkpoints, and curfews, 20 Israeli and Palestinian young people talk about how the war has affected them." Booklist
"An excellent presentation of a confusing historic struggle, told within a palpable, perceptive and empathetic format." SLJ
Includes bibliographical references

Frank, Mitch
Understanding the Holy Land; answering questions about the Israeli-Palestinian Conflict. Viking 2005 152p il map $17.99; pa $8.99
Grades: 6 7 8 9 10   **956.94**
  1. Israel-Arab conflicts
  ISBN 0-670-06032-1; 0-670-06043-7 (pa)
                                                LC 2004-14973
The author "tackles the complex subject of the Israeli-Palestinian conflict, making it comprehensible, if not any less horrific. . . . He uses a simple yet wonderfully effective technique to present the information: questions and answers. . . . Evenhanded and honest." Booklist
Includes bibliographical references

Israel: opposing viewpoints; John Woodward, book editor. Greenhaven Press 2005 203p il lib bdg $34.95; pa $23.70
Grades: 8 9 10 11 12   **956.94**
  1. Israel 2. Zionism 3. Palestinian Arabs
  ISBN 0-7377-2589-3 (lib bdg); 0-7377-2590-7 (pa)
                                                LC 2004-60586

Israel: opposing viewpoints—*Continued*
Replaces the 1994 edition under the editorship of Charles P. Cozic
"Opposing viewpoints series"
"The authors in this book explore the founding of Israel, potential solutions to the Arab-Israeli dispute, America's relationship with the Jewish state, and the question of its right to exist." Publisher's note
Includes bibliographical references

Rosaler, Maxine
Hamas: Palestinian terrorists. Rosen Pub. Group 2003 64p il map (Inside the world's most infamous terrorist organizations) lib bdg $26.50
Grades: 8 9 10 11 12   **956.94**
1. Hamas 2. Terrorism 3. Israel-Arab conflicts 4. Palestinian Arabs
ISBN 0-8239-3820-4   LC 2002-7769
Contents: A land divided; Inside Hamas; The suicide bombers; The cycle of violence
Discusses the origins, philosophy, and most notorious attacks of the Hamas terrorist group, including their present activities, possible plans, and counter-terrorism efforts directed against them
"With color photos that aren't too shocking and long reading lists updated by links gathered on a dedicated Web site [this] will be useful for school reports." Booklist
Includes bibliographical references

Worth, Richard, 1945-
The Arab-Israeli conflict; [by] Richard Worth. Marshall Cavendish Benchmark 2006 127p il map (Open for debate) lib bdg $39.93
Grades: 7 8 9 10   **956.94**
1. Israel-Arab conflicts
ISBN 978-0-7614-2295-2 (lib bdg); 0-7614-2295-1 (lib bdg)   LC 2005029049
"The first chapter presents a brief summary of the issues involved, with subsequent sections providing more detail about historical events in the region from ancient times through the present day. Topics discussed include the Zionist movement, the Palestinians' right of return, Yasir Arafat and the PLO, and the history of the settlements. Worth is careful to present arguments from all sides of the conflict, supporting them with quotations from primary sources. The writing is clear and factual, and the information is up-to-date." SLJ
Includes bibliographical references

Young, Emma, 1973-
Israel; [by] Emma Young; Zvi Ben-Dor Benite, George Kanazi, and Aviva Halamish, consultants. National Geographic 2008 64p il map (Countries of the world) lib bdg $27.90 *
Grades: 4 5 6 7   **956.94**
1. Israel
ISBN 978-1-4263-0258-9 (lib bdg); 1-4263-0258-4 (lib bdg)
This describes the geography, nature, history, people and culture, government, and economy of Israel.
Includes glossary and bibliographical references

Zeigler, Donald J., 1951-
Israel; [by] Donald J. Zeigler. 2nd ed. Chelsea House 2007 120p il map (Modern world nations) lib bdg $30
Grades: 7 8 9 10   **956.94**
1. Israel
ISBN 0-7910-9210-0   LC 2006014242
First published 2002
Describes the geography, history, people and culture, politics, and economy of Israel
Includes bibliographical references

956.95 Jordan and West Bank

Wingate, Katherine
The Intifadas; by Katherine Wingate. Rosen Pub. Group 2004 64p il map (War and conflict in the Middle East) lib bdg $26.50
Grades: 5 6 7 8   **956.95**
1. Palestine 2. Israel-Arab conflicts
ISBN 0-8239-4546-4   LC 2003-12562
Contents: The uprising begins; Who's in control here; Are you with us or against us?; On the road to statehood; The end, or just the beginning?; The Intifada, part two
"Wingate focuses on how the Palestinians lost their land and how the Palestinians in occupied territories retaliated. . . . Wingate sees hope in the peace organizations that work with young people. The series design is spacious, with clear type, lots of well-captioned news photos, up-to-date statistics, maps, and occasional boxed profiles of important leaders. . . . There's a lot to spark discussion." Booklist
Includes glossary and bibliographical references

958.1 Afghanistan

Ali, Sharifah Enayat, 1943-
Afghanistan; by Sharifah Enayat Ali. 2nd ed. Marshall Cavendish Benchmark 2006 144p il map (Cultures of the world) lib bdg $39.93 *
Grades: 5 6 7 8   **958.1**
1. Afghanistan
ISBN 978-0-7614-2064-4 (lib bdg); 0-7614-2064-9 (lib bdg)   LC 2005034789
First published 1995
"Provides . . . information on the geography, history, governmental structure, economy, cultural diversity, peoples, religion, and culture of Afghanistan." Publisher's note
This is "well organized, informative, and entertaining. . . . Excellent-quality full-color photographs and reproductions show the people, landforms, buildings, and everyday activities of [Afghanistan]." SLJ [review of 1995 edtion]
Includes glossary and bibliographical references

Behnke, Alison

Afghanistan in pictures. rev and expanded. Lerner Publs. 2003 80p il map (Visual geography series) lib bdg $27.93

Grades: 5 6 7 8   **958.1**

1. Afghanistan

ISBN 0-8225-4683-3   LC 2002-13613

First published 1989

An introduction to the geography, history, government, people, and economy of this landlocked country with a long history of warfare and conquest

Includes glossary and bibliographical references

Corona, Laurel, 1949-

Afghanistan. Lucent Bks. 2002 112p il (Modern nations of the world) lib bdg $27.45

Grades: 6 7 8 9   **958.1**

1. Afghanistan

ISBN 1-59018-217-0   LC 2002-3615

Contents: Introduction: Afghanistan at the crossroads; The shape of a nation: land and people; Cradle to colony: Afghanistan from prehistory to the nineteenth century; In the crossfire of world history: the nineteenth and twentieth centuries; The rise and fall of the Taliban ; Life in today's Afghanistan; The crossroads of art and culture; Facing the future: contemporary challenges

Discusses the people, land, culture, history, and future of the nation of Afghanistan

The author provides "well-selected details and [a] generally balanced treatment." Booklist

Includes bibliographical references

Gaag, Nikki van der

Focus on Afghanistan; [by] Nikki van der Gaag. World Almanac Library 2008 64p il map (World in focus) lib bdg $33.27; pa $11.95

Grades: 6 7 8 9   **958.1**

1. Afghanistan

ISBN 978-0-8368-6748-0   (lib   bdg); 978-0-8368-6755-8 (pa)   LC 2007022009

This describes the history, landscape and climate, population and settlements, government and politics, energy and resources, economy and income, global connections, transportation and communications, education and health, culture and religion, leisure and tourism, environment and conservation, and future challenges of Afghanistan.

"Attractive color photographs, graphs, and charts illustrate [this] volume. . . . [This book presents] current, accurate information in a way that is not too dry or overwhelming for the intended age group." SLJ

Includes glossary and bibliographical references

Gritzner, Jeffrey A.

Afghanistan; [by] Jeffrey A. Gritzner; with additional text by John F. Shroder. 2nd ed. Chelsea House 2006 120p il map (Modern world nations) lib bdg $30

Grades: 7 8 9 10   **958.1**

1. Afghanistan

ISBN 0-7910-9209-7   LC 2006012724

First published 2002

This describes the geography, history, people, and culture of Afghanistan.

Includes bibliographical references

Kazem, Halima

Afghanistan. Stevens, G. 2003 96p il map (Countries of the world) lib bdg $29.26

Grades: 4 5 6 7   **958.1**

1. Afghanistan

ISBN 0-8368-2357-5   LC 2002-75787

Discusses the geography, history, government, economy, people, politics, and culture of Afghanistan

"A well-organized title that fills the need for an up-to-date book on this country. Clearly written information . . . is illustrated with vibrant color photographs on almost every page." SLJ

Includes glossary and bibliographical references

Otfinoski, Steven, 1949-

Afghanistan. Facts on File 2004 130p il map (Nations in transition) $35

Grades: 8 9 10 11 12   **958.1**

1. Afghanistan

ISBN 0-8160-5056-2   LC 2003-49030

This volume provides an "examination of Afghanistan's long history and the traditions, religions, and cultural heritage of its many ethnic groups. It examines the different factions vying for power in Afghanistan today, as well as the difficulties Afghan people encounter in their daily life, and it outlines the staggering problems that the country faces in the future." Publisher's note

This is "informative, thought-provoking, and well-organized . . . well-researched . . . include[s] interesting and pertinent sidebars . . . the in-depth presentations provide solid and balanced overviews." SLJ

Includes bibliographical references

Romano, Amy, 1978-

A historical atlas of Afghanistan. Rosen Pub. Group 2003 64p il map (Historical atlases of South Asia, Central Asia, and the Middle East) lib bdg $30.60

Grades: 8 9 10 11 12   **958.1**

1. Afghanistan

ISBN 0-8239-3863-8   LC 2002-31034

Maps and text chronicle the history of Afghanistan, from the Aryan invasion in 1500 B.C. to the rise of the Taliban

This "well-organized and ambitious [book provides] needed information." SLJ

Includes glossary and bibliographical references

Stewart, Gail, 1949-

Life under the Taliban; by Gail B. Stewart. Lucent Books 2005 112p il map (Way people live) lib bdg $27.45

Grades: 8 9 10 11 12   **958.1**

1. Afghanistan

ISBN 1-59018-291-X   LC 2004-10378

Contents: The land of The Great Game; The coming of the Taliban; Life under the Sharia; Women under the Taliban; A life of grinding poverty; A training ground for terrorism; Resistance to the Taliban

Discusses the history of Afghanistan, the rise and fall of the Taliban, and daily life under the regime

"Quotes from residents, journalists, aid workers, and

Stewart, Gail, 1949——*Continued*
U.N. officials enliven the clearly presented, accurate material. . . . An excellent resource for reports." SLJ
Includes bibliographical references

Whitehead, Kim
Afghanistan. Mason Crest 2005 136p il map (Growth and influence of Islam in the nations of Asia and Central Asia) lib bdg $25.95
Grades: 7 8 9 10   **958.1**
1. Afghanistan
ISBN 1-59084-833-0
This examines the ways Islam has influenced the culture and politics of Afghanistan, including how the Taliban came to power.
This "presents a cogent overview of [Afghanistan]. Excellent-quality photos and reproductions appear throughout." SLJ
Includes bibliographical references

Whitfield, Susan
Afghanistan; [by] Susan Whitfield; Thomas Barfield and Maliha Zulfacar, consultants. National Geographic 2008 64p il map (Countries of the world) lib bdg $27.90 *
Grades: 4 5 6 7   **958.1**
1. Afghanistan
ISBN 978-1-4263-0256-5 (lib bdg); 1-4263-0256-8 (lib bdg)
This describes the geography, nature, history, people and culture, government, and economy of Aghanistan.
Includes glossary and bibliographical references

958.4   Turkestan

Corrigan, Jim
Kazakhstan. Mason Crest 2005 128p il map (Growth and influence of Islam in the nations of Asia and Central Asia) lib bdg $25.95
Grades: 7 8 9 10   **958.4**
1. Kazakhstan
ISBN 1-59084-882-9   LC 2004-22664
Contents: Place in the world; The land; History; Politics, the economy, and religion; The people; Communities; Foreign relations
"This book examines the economic and political issues facing Kazakhstan today. It provides . . . information about the country's geography and climate, history, society, important cities and communities, and relations with other countries." Publisher's note
"The writing is lucid and lively; the photographs, relevant and representative of a variety of lifestyles." SLJ
Includes bibliographical references

Harmon, Dan
Kyrgyzstan; [by] Daniel E. Harmon. Mason Crest 2005 120p il map (Growth and influence of Islam in the nations of Asia and Central Asia) lib bdg $25.95
Grades: 7 8 9 10   **958.4**
1. Kyrgyzstan
ISBN 1-59084-883-7   LC 2004-19827

Contents: Place in the world; The land; History; Politics, the economy, and religion; The people; Communities; Foreign relations
"This book examines the economic and political issues facing Kyrgyzstan today. It provides . . . information about the country's geography and climate, history, society, important cities and communities, and relations with other countries." Publisher's note
This book is a "solid [source] for reports, geography lessons, and current events." SLJ
Includes bibliographical references

Khan, Aisha Karen, 1967-
A historical atlas of Kyrgyzstan; [by] Aisha Khan. Rosen 2004 64p il map lib bdg $30.60
Grades: 7 8 9 10   **958.4**
1. Kyrgyzstan
ISBN 0-8239-4499-9
Maps and illustrations present conquests and movements of populations in Kyrgyzstan from prehistory to the present.
This is "gracefully written. . . . [It includes] excellent maps and handsome illustrations." SLJ

King, David C., 1933-
Kyrgyzstan; [by] David C. King. 1st ed. Marshall Cavendish Benchmark 2005 144p il map (Cultures of the world) lib bdg $37.07
Grades: 5 6 7 8   **958.4**
1. Kyrgyzstan
ISBN 0-7614-2013-4   LC 2005001314
Describes the geography, history, government, economy, people, and culture of Kyrgyzstan
Includes glossary and bibliographical references

958.5   Turkmenistan

Knowlton, MaryLee, 1946-
Turkmenistan; [by] MaryLee Knowlton. 1st ed. Marshall Cavendish Benchmark 2006 144p il map (Cultures of the world) lib bdg $37.07
Grades: 5 6 7 8   **958.5**
1. Turkmenistan
ISBN 0-7614-2014-2   LC 2005006455
Describes the geography, history, government, economy, people, and culture of Turkmenistan
Includes glossary and bibliographical references

958.6   Tajikistan

Abazov, Rafis, 1966-
Tajikistan; [by] Rafis Abazov. 1st ed. Marshall Cavendish Benchmark 2006 144p il map (Cultures of the world) lib bdg $37.07
Grades: 5 6 7 8   **958.6**
1. Tajikistan
ISBN 0-7614-2012-6   LC 2005001166
Describes the geography, history, government, economy, people, and culture of the former Soviet republic of Tajikistan
Includes glossary and bibliographical references

958.7 Uzbekistan

Knowlton, MaryLee, 1946-
Uzbekistan; [by] MaryLee Knowlton. Marshall
Cavendish Benchmark 2005 144p il map (Cultures
of the world) lib bdg $37.07
Grades: 5 6 7 8   **958.7**
  1. Uzbekistan
  ISBN 0-7614-2016-9   LC 2005016875
  An examination of the geography, history, govern-
ment, economy, culture, and peoples of Uzbekistan
  Includes glossary and bibliographical references

959 Southeast Asia

Phillips, Douglas A.
Southeast Asia; series consulting editor Charles
F. Gritzner. Chelsea House Publishers 2006 129p
(Modern world cultures) lib bdg $30
Grades: 7 8 9 10   **959**
  1. Southeast Asia
  ISBN 0-7910-8149-4
  This describes the geography, history, people and cultures, politics, economics, and possible future of Southeast Asia.
  This "accessible [title is] generously illustrated with
colorful photos, maps, and clear charts, graphs, and other
statistical data. . . . Phillips does an excellent job of organizing each topic by providing clear and outlined information. The research is well done, and information
and statistics are up to date." SLJ

959.3 Thailand

Goodman, Jim, 1947-
Thailand. 2nd ed. Benchmark Bks. 2003 144p il
map (Cultures of the world) lib bdg $37.07
Grades: 5 6 7 8   **959.3**
  1. Thailand
  ISBN 0-7614-1478-9   LC 2002-25979
  First published 1990
  Describes the geography, history, government, econo-
my, people, religion, language, and culture of Thailand,
a predominantly Buddhist country located in Southeast
Asia. Includes several recipes
  Includes glossary and bibliographical references

Phillips, Douglas A.
Thailand. Chelsea House 2007 108p il map
(Modern world nations) lib bdg $30
Grades: 7 8 9 10   **959.3**
  1. Thailand
  ISBN 978-0-7910-9250-7 (lib bdg); 0-7910-9250-X
(lib bdg)   LC 2006032009
  Describes the geography, history, people, culture,
economy, and government of Thailand
  Includes bibliographical references

959.4 Laos

Dalal, A. Kamala
Laos; [by] A. Kamala Dalal. National
Geographic 2009 64p il (Countries of the world)
lib bdg $27.90 *
Grades: 4 5 6 7   **959.4**
  1. Laos
  ISBN 978-1-4263-0388-3 (lib bdg); 1-4263-0388-2 (lib
bdg)
  This describes the geography, nature, history, people
and culture, and govenment and economy of Laos
  Includes glossary and bibliographical references

Mansfield, Stephen
Laos; [by] Stephen Mansfield & Magdalene
Koh. 2nd ed. Marshall Cavendish Benchmark 2008
c2009 144p il map (Cultures of the world) lib bdg
$29.95 *
Grades: 5 6 7 8   **959.4**
  1. Laos
  ISBN 978-0-7614-3035-3 (lib bdg); 0-7614-3035-0 (lib
bdg)   LC 2007048292
  First published 1998
  "Provides comprehensive information on the geogra-
phy, history, wildlife, governmental structure, economy,
cultural diversity, peoples, religion, and culture of Laos."
Publisher's note
  Includes glossary and bibliographical references

959.5 Commonwealth of Nations territories. Malaysia

Munan, Heidi
Malaysia; [by] Heidi Munan, Foo Yuk Yee. 2nd
ed. Benchmark Bks. 2002 144p il map (Cultures
of the world) lib bdg $37.07
Grades: 5 6 7 8   **959.5**
  1. Malaysia
  ISBN 0-7614-1351-0   LC 2001-25302
  First published 1990
  This describes the geography, history, government,
economy, environment, people and culture of Malaysia
  Includes glossary and bibliographical references

959.57 Singapore

Layton, Lesley, 1954-
Singapore; [by] Lesley Layton, Pang Guek
Cheng. 2nd ed. Benchmark Bks. 2002 144p il map
(Cultures of the world) lib bdg $37.07
Grades: 5 6 7 8   **959.57**
  1. Singapore
  ISBN 0-7614-1352-9   LC 2001-25413
  First published 1990
  This describes the geography, history, government,
economy, environment, people, and culture of Singapore
  Includes glossary and bibliographical references

959.6 Cambodia

Green, Robert, 1969-
Cambodia. Lucent Bks. 2003 112p il maps (Modern nations of the world) lib bdg $27.45
Grades: 7 8 9 10   **959.6**
1. Cambodia
ISBN 1-59018-109-3   LC 2002-11294
This describes the geography, history, culture, religions, people and government of Cambodia
"A well-written and well-organized overview. . . . A useful resource for reports." SLJ
Includes bibliographical references

Sheehan, Sean, 1951-
Cambodia; [by] Sean Sheehan & Barbara Cooke. 2nd ed. Marshall Cavendish Benchmark 2007 144p il map (Cultures of the world) lib bdg $39.93
Grades: 5 6 7 8   **959.6**
1. Cambodia
ISBN 978-0-7614-2071-2 (lib bdg); 0-7614-2071-1 (lib bdg)   LC 2006020818
First published 1996
This provides "information on the geography, history, governmental structure, economy, cultural diversity, peoples, religion, and culture of Cambodia." Publisher's note
Includes glossary and bibliographical references

959.7 Vietnam

Dramer, Kim
The Mekong River. Watts 2001 63p il maps lib bdg $24.50; pa $8.95
Grades: 5 6 7 8   **959.7**
1. Mekong River
ISBN 0-531-11854-1 (lib bdg); 0-531-13985-9 (pa)
LC 00-31918
"Watts library"
This presents "a multifaceted look at one particular river's impact on the area's landforms, industry, and history. The [text is] sprightly and packed with facts. The focused chapters seem especially well reasoned, which enhances their readability and usefulness for research. Fine full-color photos, maps, and historical photos appear throughout." SLJ
Includes glossary and bibliographical references

Green, Jen
Vietnam; [by] Jen Green. National Geographic 2008 64p il map (Countries of the world) lib bdg $27.90 *
Grades: 4 5 6 7   **959.7**
1. Vietnam
ISBN 978-1-4263-0202-2   LC 2007047832
This describes the geography, nature, history, people and culture, government, and economy of Vietnam.
Includes glossary and bibliographical references

959.704 Vietnam—1949-

Canwell, Diane
African Americans in the Vietnam War; [by] Diane Canwell and Jon Sutherland. World Almanac Library 2005 48p il map (American experience in Vietnam) lib bdg $30; pa $11.95
Grades: 5 6 7 8   **959.704**
1. Vietnam War, 1961-1975 2. African American soldiers
ISBN 0-8368-5772-0 (lib bdg); 0-8368-5779-8 (pa)
LC 2004-58096
This is an illustrated history of the role of American Americans in the Vietnam War.
"Browsers will gravitate to this . . . given the personal stories as well as the quality . . . and subject matter of the full-color photos. . . . Readers will pick up some sense of the history here." Booklist
Includes bibliographical references

Caputo, Philip
10,000 days of thunder; a history of the Vietnam War; [by] Philip Caputo. 1st ed. Atheneum Books for Young Readers 2005 128p il $22.95 *
Grades: 6 7 8 9   **959.704**
1. Vietnam War, 1961-1975
ISBN 0-689-86231-8   LC 2004-15468
In this history of the Vietnam War "Caputo has produced what is at once an overview and a sensitive, resonant picture of the war as seen and experienced by American soldiers, the Viet Cong, North Vietnamese guerrillas, and the citizens of both South Vietnam and the United States. . . . Caputo's prose is clear and direct, and the award-winning photos . . . add an immediacy that sets this title apart from more conventional treatments." SLJ
Includes glossary and bibliographical references

Hillstrom, Kevin
Vietnam War: almanac; [by] Kevin Hillstrom and Laurie Collier Hillstrom; Diane Sawinski, editor. U.X.L 2001 293p il $60
Grades: 7 8 9 10   **959.704**
1. Vietnam War, 1961-1975
ISBN 0-7876-4883-3   LC 00-56379
This "combines early history from the colonial period, U.S. involvement, and the war years and continues through the reestablishment of diplomacy and trade in recent years. Arranged chronologically, each of the 17 chapters includes 'Words to Know' and 'People to Know.' . . . Highly recommended for the junior- and senior-high-school libraries and public libraries." Booklist
Includes bibliographical references

Vietnam War: primary sources; [by] Kevin Hillstrom and Laurie Collier Hillstrom; Diane Sawinski, editor. U.X.L 2001 various paging $60
Grades: 7 8 9 10   **959.704**
1. Vietnam War, 1961-1975
ISBN 0-7876-4887-6   LC 00-56377

Hillstrom, Kevin—*Continued*

This "presents 13 full or excerpted speeches and writings 'that reflect the painfully diversified points of view on the war.' . . . Each excerpt includes background material to provide context. Unfamiliar terms and their definitions fill sidebars, along with other relevant information and photographs. The numerous sidebars, photographs, and maps enhance the text." Booklist

Includes bibliographical references

Levy, Debbie

The Vietnam War; by Debbie Levy. Lerner Publications 2004 88p il map (Chronicle of America's wars) lib bdg $27.93

Grades: 5 6 7 8   **959.704**

1. Vietnam War, 1961-1975

ISBN 0-8225-0421-9   LC 2002-156558

Contents: A history of struggle; Deadly dominoes; From Cold War to hot war; Americans at war; Turning point; The end begins; America lets go

This describes the events of the Vietnam War, focusing on the impact the war had on America and its people.

Includes glossary and bibliographical references

Seah, Audrey, 1958-

Vietnam; [by] Audrey Seah, Charissa M. Nair. 2nd ed. Benchmark Books 2004 144p il map (Cultures of the world) lib bdg $37.07 *

Grades: 5 6 7 8   **959.704**

1. Vietnam

ISBN 0-7614-1789-3   LC 2004-12903

First published 1994

Contents: Geography; History; Government; Economy; Environment; Vietnamese; Lifestyle; Religion; Language; Arts; Leisure; Festivals; Food

This describes the geography, history, government, economy environment, and culture of Vietnam

Includes glossary and bibliographical references

The **Vietnam** War; Ryn Shane-Armstrong and Lynn Armstrong, book editors. Greenhaven Press 2003 237p il map (Great speeches in history series) lib bdg $25.96; pa $16.96

Grades: 8 9 10 11 12   **959.704**

1. Vietnam War, 1961-1975 2. Speeches

ISBN 0-7377-1433-6 (lib bdg); 0-7377-1434-4 (pa)

LC 2002-27890

This collection of speeches relating to the Vietnam War includes the words of such speakers as Ho Chi Minh, Barry Goldwater, Martin Luther King, and Bill Clinton

This "provides insight into the lengthy conflict." SLJ

Includes bibliographical references

Yancey, Diane

Life of an American soldier. Lucent Bks. 2001 128p il (American war library, Vietnam War) lib bdg $27.45

Grades: 8 9 10 11 12   **959.704**

1. Vietnam War, 1961-1975

ISBN 1-56006-676-8   LC 00-8386

Describes the men and women who fought in the Vietnam War, the kind of war they fought, and the distress and difficulty they suffered on their return to the United States

This is "liberally illustrated with good-quality, black-and-white captioned photos. Vocabulary is appropriate while at the same time describing the situation without softening the impact or tempering the language in the soldiers' statements." SLJ

Includes glossary and bibliographical references

Young, Marilyn Blatt

The Vietnam War: a history in documents; [by] Marilyn B. Young, John J. Fitzgerald, A. Tom Grunfeld. Oxford Univ. Press 2002 175p il maps (Pages from history) lib bdg $32.95; pa $19.95

Grades: 7 8 9 10   **959.704**

1. Vietnam War, 1961-1975

ISBN 0-19-512278-X (lib bdg); 0-19-516635-3 (pa)

LC 2001-52338

This is a "collection of original documents and photographs that detail the war in Vietnam. The text includes speeches, cartoons, news articles, and parallel events occurring in the United States and in Asia." Soc Educ

"The documents are skillfully tied together by brief text that gives good background information. . . . The book is well balanced in showing both sides. . . . Good-quality, black-and-white photos and illustrations are plentiful and informative." SLJ

Includes glossary and bibliographical references

959.8   Indonesia and East Timor

Mirpuri, Gouri, 1960-

Indonesia; by Gouri Mirpuri, Robert Cooper. 2nd ed. Benchmark Bks. 2002 144p il maps (Cultures of the world) lib bdg $37.07

Grades: 5 6 7 8   **959.8**

1. Indonesia

ISBN 0-7614-1355-3   LC 2001-28607

First published 1990

This describes the geography, history, government, economy, environment and culture of Indonesia

"The pictures are lush, with captions in tiny print offering much additional information. The text is written smoothly and readably, and it contains a substantial amount of information." Booklist

Includes glossary and bibliographical references

959.9   Philippines

Skog, Jason

Teens in the Philippines; by Jason Skog. Compass Point Books 2009 96p il map (Global connections) lib bdg $33.26

Grades: 6 7 8 9   **959.9**

1. Teenagers 2. Philippines

ISBN 978-0-7565-3853-8 (lib bdg); 0-7565-3853-X (lib bdg)   LC 2008-6504

Skog, Jason—*Continued*

Uncovers the challenges, pastimes, customs and culture of teens in the Philippines

This book is "concise and highly readable. . . . Clear, colorful photos and sidebars on a range of topics provide further context. . . . [This title] will enrich young adult collections." SLJ

Includes glossary and bibliographical references

Tope, Lily Rose R., 1955-

Philippines; [by] Lily R. Tope, Detch P. Nonan-Mercado. 2nd ed. Benchmark Bks. 2002 144p il maps (Cultures of the world) lib bdg $37.07

Grades: 5 6 7 8   **959.9**

1. Philippines

ISBN 0-7614-1475-4   LC 2002-19725

First published 1990

Discusses the geography, history, government, economy, people, and culture of the Philippines, an archipelago of many islands in the Western Pacific

Includes glossary and bibliographical references

960   History of Africa

Africa: an encyclopedia for students; John Middleton, editor. Scribner 2002 4v il maps set $395

Grades: 7 8 9 10   **960**

1. Africa—Encyclopedias 2. Reference books

ISBN 0-684-80650-9   LC 2001-49348

A comprehensive look at the continent of Africa and the countries that comprise it, including peoples and cultures, the land and its history, art and architecture, and daily life

Africa: opposing viewpoints; Laura K. Egendorf, book editor. Greenhaven Press 2005 208p il $34.95; pa $23.70

Grades: 8 9 10 11 12   **960**

1. Africa

ISBN 0-7377-2218-5; 0-7377-2219-3 (pa)

LC 2004-42432

Replaces the 2000 edition under the editorship of William Dudley

"Opposing viewpoints series"

"The authors in this book debate the issues facing modern Africa in the following chapters: What Problems Does Africa Face? How Can the Spread of AIDS in Africa Be Reduced? What Policies Will Best Help Africa? How Can Africa's Wild Lands Be Preserved?." Publisher's note

Includes bibliographical references

African history on file. rev ed. Facts on File 2003 various paging il maps loose-leaf $185

Grades: Professional   **960**

1. Africa—History

ISBN 0-8160-5139-9   LC 2002-192848

Also available CD-ROM version

First published 1994

More than 500 "reproducible maps, charts, timelines, and drawings visually detail the broad range of human experience in Africa, from prehistory to the present." Publisher's note

Includes bibliographical references

Habeeb, William Mark, 1955-

Africa; facts and figures; [by] William Mark Habeeb. Mason Crest Publishers 2005 87p il map (Africa: continent in the balance) lib bdg $21.95

Grades: 7 8 9 10   **960**

1. Africa

ISBN 1-59084-817-9   LC 2004-10186

Contents: Introduction by Robert I. Rotberg; Geography; History; Government; Economy; Culture and people; Cities and communities; Calendar of festivals; Recipes; Glossary; Project and report ideas; Chronology

This is an overview of the land, history, economy, people, cities and communities, maps and flags, festivals, and foods of the African continent.

This is an "excellent, detailed overview. . . . The attractive, open design, with clear type, beautiful photos, maps, and lots of extras in lists and insets, manages to pack in an extraordinary amount of information." Booklist

Includes glossary and bibliographical references

Peoples and cultures of Africa; edited by Peter Mitchell. Chelsea House 2006 6v il map set $234

Grades: 5 6 7 8   **960**

1. Africa—Civilization 2. Ethnology—Africa 3. Reference books

ISBN 0-8160-6260-9 (set); 978-0-8160-6261-4 (v1); 978-0-8160-6262-1 (v2); 978-0-8160-6263-8 (v3); 978-0-8160-6264-5 (v4); 978-0-8160-6265-2 (v5); 978-0-8160-6266-9 (v6)   LC 2006040011

Volumes also available separately $39 each

Contents: v1 North Africa; v2 West Africa; v3 East Africa; v4 Central Africa; v5 Southern Africa; v6 Nations and personalities

"This attractive and informative set provides well-written, well-researched introductory information about African geography and culture. Each of the first five volumes covers a region within the continent . . . and opens with introductory information on that area's physical features, biomes, religions, languages, and cultures, and includes an extensive time line. It is followed by color-coded, alphabetically arranged entries examining the region's tribal and ethnic groups; art, sculpture, and textiles; performing arts and literature; and religion and individual cultures in further detail. . . . The final volume is devoted to single-page geographic and economic profiles of Africa's nations. . . . This quality set will give report writers a solid introduction to the diversity of Africa." SLJ

Includes bibliographical references

961.1 Tunisia

Brown, Roslind Varghese

Tunisia; [by] Roslind Varghese Brown & Michael Spilling. 2nd ed. Marshall Cavendish Benchmark 2008 c2009 144p il map (Cultures of the world) lib bdg $29.95

Grades: 5 6 7 8   **961.1**
   1. Tunisia
   ISBN 978-0-7614-3037-7 (lib bdg); 0-7614-3037-7 (lib bdg)   LC 2007050798
   First published 1998
   "Provides comprehensive information on the geography, history, wildlife, governmental structure, economy, cultural diversity, peoples, religion, and culture of Tunisia." Publisher note
   Includes glossary and bibliographical references

961.2 Libya

Malcolm, Peter, 1937-

Libya; [by] Peter Malcolm, Elie Losleben. 2nd ed. Benchmark Bks. 2004 144p il map (Cultures of the world) lib bdg $37.07 *

Grades: 5 6 7 8   **961.2**
   1. Libya
   ISBN 0-7614-1702-8   LC 2003-20887
   First published 1993
   Contents: Geography; History; Government; Economy; Environment; Libyans minority; Lifestyle; Religion; Language; Arts; Leisure; Festivals; Food
   Examines the geography, history, government, economy, people, and culture of Libya
   Includes glossary and bibliographical references

962 Egypt and Sudan

Bowden, Rob

The Nile; [by] Rob Bowden. Raintree Steck-Vaughn Publishers 2004 48p il map (River journey) lib bdg $29.93

Grades: 5 6 7 8   **962**
   1. Nile River 2. Nile River valley
   ISBN 0-7398-6072-0   LC 2002-155378
   Contents: The source of the Nile; Calming the Nile; The rivers meet; The Nile cataracts; The Nile Valley; The Nile Delta
   The author presents information about the Nile River "as though readers are taking a trip from the river's source to where it meets the sea. This approach works surprisingly well at drawing youngsters in. . . . The author presents an integrated view of the geological, economic, and cultural aspects of [The Nile], and does not shy away from realities, such as how thousands of people lose their homes when dams are built, or the pollution that threatens wildlife. Full-color photographs appear throughout." SLJ

Heinrichs, Ann

The Nile. Marshall Cavendish Benchmark 2008 96p il map (Nature's wonders) lib bdg $24.95

Grades: 5 6 7 8   **962**
   1. Nile River valley 2. Nile River
   ISBN 978-0-7614-2854-1   LC 2007019187
   "Provides comprehensive information on the geography, history, wildlife, peoples, and environmental issues of the Nile River Basin." Publisher's note
   "It's tough to make a river interesting, but this . . . does an admirable job of it. . . . Crisp, full-color photos and original artwork decorate nearly every page. . . . [This is a] well-thought-out natural history." Booklist
   Includes glossary and bibliographical references

Kallen, Stuart A., 1955-

Egypt. Lucent Bks. 1999 111p il maps (Modern nations of the world) lib bdg $28.70

Grades: 7 8 9 10   **962**
   1. Egypt
   ISBN 1-56006-535-4   LC 98-43851
   Discusses the history, geography, people, and culture of Egypt and its significance in the world today
   "The strength of this volume is its carefully developed history of Egypt from ancient times to the present." SLJ
   Includes bibliographical references

Pateman, Robert, 1954-

Egypt; [by] Robert Pateman, Salwa El-Hamamsy. 2nd ed. Benchmark Bks. 2003 144p il map (Cultures of the world) lib bdg $37.07 *

Grades: 5 6 7 8   **962**
   1. Egypt
   ISBN 0-7614-1670-6   LC 2003-9859
   First published 1993
   Contents: Geography; History; Government; Economy; Environment; Egyptians; Lifestyle; Religion; Language; Arts; Leisure; Festivals; Food; Map of Egypt; About the economy; About the culture
   Explores the geography, history, government, economy, people, and culture of Egypt
   Includes glossary and bibliographical references

Zuehlke, Jeffrey, 1968-

Egypt in pictures. Lerner Publs. 2003 80p il map (Visual geography series) lib bdg $27.93

Grades: 5 6 7 8   **962**
   1. Egypt
   ISBN 0-8225-0367-0   LC 2001-6613
   Discusses the physical features, history, government, people, culture, and economy of Egypt
   Includes bibliographical references

962.4 Sudan

Levy, Patricia, 1951-
Sudan. 2nd ed. Marshall Cavendish Benchmark 2008 144p il map (Cultures of the world) lib bdg $39.93
Grades: 5 6 7 8   **962.4**
1. Sudan
ISBN 978-0-7614-2083-5 (lib bdg); 0-7614-2083-5 (lib bdg)   LC 2006101725
Describes the geography, history, government, economy, people, lifestyle, religion, language, arts, leisure, festivals, and food of Sudan.
Includes bibliographical references

Xavier, John
Darfur; African genocide; [by] John Xavier. 1st ed. Rosen Pub. Group 2008 64p il map (In the news) $29.95 *
Grades: 6 7 8 9   **962.4**
1. Sudan—History—Darfur conflict, 2003-
2. Genocide
ISBN 978-1-4042-1912-0; 1-4042-1912-9
                                       LC 2007002909
An overview of the crisis in Darfur, its history and why it matters.
"Informative reflection of today's headlines. . . . In-depth exploration of the crisis in Darfur, the history of the conflict, and why it matters to the rest of the world. . . . The glossaries and Web sites at the end of each are most helpful." Voice Youth Advocates
Includes glossary and bibliographical references

963 Ethiopia and Eritrea

Gish, Steven, 1963-
Ethiopia; [by] Steven Gish & Winnie Thay & Zawiah Abdul Latif. 2nd ed. Marshall Cavendish Benchmark 2007 144p il map (Cultures of the world) lib bdg $39.93 *
Grades: 5 6 7 8   **963**
1. Ethiopia
ISBN 978-0-7614-2025-5 (lib bdg); 0-7614-2025-8 (lib bdg)   LC 2006020819
First published 1996
This provides "information on the geography, history, governmental structure, economy, cultural diversity, peoples, religion, and culture of Ethiopia." Publisher's note
Includes glossary and bibliographical references

964 Northwest African coast and offshore islands. Morocco

Blauer, Ettagale
Morocco; by Ettagale Blauer and Jason Lauré. Children's Press 1999 144p il maps (Enchantment of the world, second series) lib bdg $35
Grades: 5 6 7 8   **964**
1. Morocco
ISBN 0-516-20961-2   LC 98-17644

Describes the geography, plants and animals, history, economy, language, religions, culture, and people of Morocco, a unique northern African nation surrounded by both water and desert
Includes bibliographical references

Donovan, Sandra, 1967-
Teens in Morocco; by Sandy Donovan. Compass Point Books 2008 96p il map (Global connections) lib bdg $31.93
Grades: 7 8 9 10   **964**
1. Teenagers 2. Morocco
ISBN 978-0-7565-3402-8 (lib bdg); 0-7565-3402-X (lib bdg)   LC 2007032692
Uncovers the challenges, pastimes, customs and culture of teens in Morocco
"Information is solid, giving readers an informed and realistic view of life in that country. A historical timeline is included, and suggestions for other nonfiction and fiction titles for further reading." Voice Youth Advocates
Includes glossary and bibliographical references

Seward, Pat, 1939-
Morocco; [by] Pat Seward & Orin Hargraves. 2nd ed. Marshall Cavendish Benchmark 2006 144p il map (Cultures of the world) lib bdg $37.07
Grades: 5 6 7 8   **964**
1. Morocco
ISBN 0-7614-2051-7   LC 2005020782
First published 1995
Describes the geography, history, government, economy, people, and culture of Morocco
Includes glossary and bibliographical references

965 Algeria

Hintz, Martin, 1945-
Algeria; by Martin Hintz. rev ed. Children's Press 2006 144p il map (Enchantment of the world, second series) lib bdg $30
Grades: 5 6 7 8   **965**
1. Algeria
ISBN 0-516-24855-3   LC 2005007825
First published 1993
Describes the history, geography, people, culture, and government of Algeria
This edition "has less discussion of the French colonial experience and includes more about the current government, a section on rai music, and a new chapter depicting a day in the life of a typical Algerian boy. [The book contains] more full-color photographs than the previous [edition], and the statistics, time lines, and Web sites have been . . . added. . . . Libraries will definitely want [this volume]." SLJ
Includes bibliographical references

Kagda, Falaq
Algeria; [by] Falaq Kagda & Zawiah Abdul Latif. 2nd ed. Marshall Cavendish Benchmark 2008 144p il map (Cultures of the world) lib bdg $39.93
Grades: 5 6 7 8   **965**
  1. Algeria
  ISBN 978-0-7614-2085-9 (lib bdg); 0-7614-2085-1 (lib bdg)   LC 2007014888
First published 1997
"Provides comprehensive information on the geography, history, wildlife, governmental structure, economy, cultural diversity, peoples, religion, and culture of Algeria." Publisher's note
Includes glossary and bibliographical references

966   West Africa and offshore islands

Haywood, John, 1956-
West African kingdoms; [by] John Haywood. Raintree 2008 64p il map (Time travel guide) lib bdg $34.29; pa $9.99
Grades: 6 7 8 9   **966**
  1. West Africa
  ISBN   978-1-4109-2912-9   (lib   bdg); 978-1-4109-2918-1 (pa)   LC 2007006053
"Raintree FreeStyle"
This describes life in West Africa between 1200 and 1600 AD, including the kingdoms of Mali, Songhai, and Benin, in the form of a travel guide.
Includes glossary and bibliographical references

Heinrichs, Ann
The Sahara; [by] Ann Heinrichs. Marshall Cavendish Benchmark 2009 96p il map (Nature's wonders) lib bdg $24.95
Grades: 5 6 7 8   **966**
  1. Sahara Desert
  ISBN 978-0-7614-2855-8 (lib bdg); 0-7614-2855-0 (lib bdg)   LC 2007-20326
"Provides comprehensive information on the geography, history, wildlife, peoples, and environmental issues of the Sahara Desert." Publisher's note
This book is "full of interesting information and feature[s] a format that enables students to quickly find specific information." Voice Youth Advocates
Includes glossary and bibliographical references

966.1   Mauritania

Blauer, Ettagale
Mauritania; [by] Ettagale Blauer & Jason Lauré. Marshall Cavendish Benchmark 2009 144p il map (Cultures of the world) lib bdg $29.95
Grades: 5 6 7 8   **966.1**
  1. Mauritania
  ISBN 978-0-7614-3116-9
This describes the geography, history, government, economy, environment, people, and culture of Mauritania.

966.2   Mali, Burkina Faso, Niger

Blauer, Ettagale
Mali; [by] Ettagale Blauer & Jason Lauré. 2nd ed. Marshall Cavendish Benchmark 2008 144p il map (Cultures of the world) lib bdg $27.95
Grades: 5 6 7 8   **966.2**
  1. Mali
  ISBN 978-0-7614-2568-7
First published 1997
This describes the geography, history, government, economy, environment, people, and culture of Mali
Includes glossary and bibliographical references

McKissack, Patricia C., 1944-
The royal kingdoms of Ghana, Mali, and Songhay; life in medieval Africa; [by] Patricia and Fredrick McKissack. Holt & Co. 1993 142p il maps pa $9.95 hardcover o.p.
Grades: 5 6 7 8   **966.2**
  1. Ghana Empire 2. Songhai Empire 3. Mali—History
  ISBN 0-8050-4259-8   LC 93-4838
Examines the civilizations of the Western Sudan which flourished from 700 to 1700 A.D., acquiring such vast wealth that they became centers of trade and culture for a continent
"The McKissacks are careful to distinguish what is known from what is surmised; they draw on the oral tradition, eyewitness accounts, and contemporary scholarship; and chapter source notes discuss various conflicting views of events." Booklist
Includes bibliographical references

966.3   Senegal

Berg, Elizabeth, 1953-
Senegal; [by] Elizabeth L. Berg. Benchmark Bks. 1999 128p il maps (Cultures of the world) lib bdg $37.07
Grades: 5 6 7 8   **966.3**
  1. Senegal
  ISBN 0-7614-0872-X   LC 98-7790
Describes the geography, history, economy, lifestyle, and religion of Senegal, as well as its people, languages, and festivals
Includes glossary and bibliographical references

Mulroy, Tanya
Senegal; [by] Tanya Mulroy. Mason Crest Publishers 2008 79p il map (Africa: continent in the balance) lib bdg $21.95
Grades: 5 6 7 8   **966.3**
  1. Senegal
  ISBN 978-1-4222-0091-9 (lib bdg); 1-4222-0091-4 (lib bdg)   LC 2006-17341
This book is "clear and concise, and the authors' easy-to-read texts impart a good deal of up-to-date information. . . . Chapters . . . cover the . . . country's history; politics and government; economy; and people, including

Mulroy, Tanya—*Continued*
discussions of family life, education, ethnic groups, health care, sports, and the arts, with the focus being on the largest cities." SLJ

Includes glossary and bibliographical references

966.4 Sierra Leone

Hasday, Judy L., 1957-
Sierra Leone; [by] Judy Hasday. Mason Crest Publishers 2008 79p il map (Africa: continent in the balance) lib bdg $21.95
Grades: 5 6 7 8   966.4
  1. Sierra Leone
  ISBN 978-1-4222-0092-6; 1-4222-0092-2
                LC 2006-17342
This book features the country's "history; politics and government; economy; and people, including discussions of family life, education, ethnic groups, health care, sports, and the arts, with the focus being on the largest cities. . . . Interspersed throughout are numerous color and some black-and-white photographs, with descriptive captions, as well as 'Quick Facts' regarding geography, the economy, and the people. . . . The information is presented in an engaging manner." SLJ

Includes glossary and bibliographical references

LeVert, Suzanne
Sierra Leone; [by] Suzanne LeVert. 1st ed. Marshall Cavendish Benchmark 2007 144p il map (Cultures of the world) lib bdg $39.93 *
Grades: 5 6 7 8   966.4
  1. Sierra Leone
  ISBN 978-0-7614-2334-8 (lib bdg); 0-7614-2334-6 (lib bdg)   LC 2005035964
This provides "information on the geography, history, governmental structure, economy, cultural diversity, peoples, religion, and culture of Sierra Leone." Publisher's note

Includes glossary and bibliographical references

966.62 Liberia

Reef, Catherine
This our dark country; the American settlers of Liberia. Clarion Bks. 2002 136p il maps $17 *
Grades: 7 8 9 10   966.62
  1. American Colonization Society 2. African Americans—History 3. Slavery—United States
  ISBN 0-618-14785-3   LC 2002-3966
Contents: "These Free, Sunny Shores;" "Beyond the Reach of Mixture;" Divine providence; Americans; Life upriver; Progress; "Some Fertile Country;" "The Beclouded Sun;" Epilogue: Liberia, troubled land
Explores the history of the colony, later the independent nation of Liberia, which was established on the west coast of Africa in 1822 as a haven for free African Americans
"This photo-essay is a grim, disturbing history of Liberia. . . . Reef tells it in clear, plain style, always

showing the connections between the two homelands. The handsome, very spacious design . . . makes the hard facts accessible. . . . A must for history collections." Booklist

Includes bibliographical references

966.7 Ghana

Weatherly, Myra, 1926-
Teens in Ghana. Compass Point Books 2008 96p il map (Global connections) lib bdg $33.26
Grades: 7 8 9 10   966.7
  1. Teenagers 2. Ghana
  ISBN 978-0-7565-3417-2; 0-7565-3417-8
                LC 2007-33086
Uncovers the challenges, pastimes, customs and culture of teens in Ghana
"Color photographs of native teens enliven the text and help reinforce the connection between reader and subject matter. . . . Religion is discussed, as well as technology, government, and social roles and expectations. . . . [This] would be a wonderful addition to any library." Voice Youth Advocates

Includes bibliographical references

966.83 Benin

Kneib, Martha
Benin; [by] Martha Kneib. 1st ed. Marshall Cavendish Benchmark 2006 144p il map (Cultures of the world) lib bdg $39.93
Grades: 5 6 7 8   966.83
  1. Benin
  ISBN 978-0-7614-2328-7 (lib bdg); 0-7614-2328-1 (lib bdg)   LC 2005029052
This provides "information on the geography, history, wildlife, governmental structure, economy, diversity, peoples, religion, and culture of Benin." Publisher's note

Includes glossary and bibliographical references

966.9 Nigeria

Giles, Bridget
Nigeria; [by] Bridget Giles. National Geographic 2007 64p il map (Countries of the world) lib bdg $27.90 *
Grades: 4 5 6 7   966.9
  1. Nigeria
  ISBN 978-1-4263-0124-7   LC 2007024729
This describes the geography, nature, history, people and culture, government, and economy of Nigeria
"What helps [this book] stand out from the pack is [its] high-quality, rich photography. . . . The photos provide as much information as the [text]. . . . The writing is straightforward and solid." SLJ

Includes glossary and bibliographical references

Levy, Patricia, 1951-
Nigeria. 2nd ed. Benchmark Bks. 2004 144p il map (Cultures of the world) lib bdg $25.95
Grades: 5 6 7 8   **966.9**
1. Nigeria
ISBN 0-7614-1703-6   LC 2003-20886
First published 1993
Contents: Geography; History; Government; Economy; Environment; Nigerians; Lifestyle; Religion; Language; Arts; Leisure; Festivals; Food
Examines the geography, history, government, economy, people, and culture of Nigeria
Includes glossary and bibliographical references

Walker, Ida
Nigeria. Mason Crest Publishers 2005 79p il map (Africa: continent in the balance) lib bdg $21.95
Grades: 7 8 9 10   **966.9**
1. Nigeria
ISBN 1-59084-811-X   LC 2004-7100
Contents: Geography; History; Government; Economy; Culture and people; Cities and communities; Calendar of festivals; Recipes; Glossary; Project and report ideas; Chronology
An introduction to the geography, history, government, economy, people, and customs of Nigeria
The information in this book is "is well organized and presented in a clear, logical manner. . . . The bright, attractive photographs are well matched to the [text]." SLJ
Includes glossary and bibliographical references

967   Central Africa and offshore islands

Haskins, James, 1941-2005
Africa; a look back; by James Haskins and Kathleen Benson. Marshall Cavendish Benchmark 2007 68p il map (Drama of African-American history) lib bdg $34.21 *
Grades: 5 6 7 8   **967**
1. Africa 2. Slavery 3. African Americans—History
ISBN 978-0-7614-2148-1 (lib bdg); 0-7614-2148-3 (lib bdg)   LC 2005030477
"Provides a history of the roots of African-American culture, going back to the period of the transatlantic slave trade and earlier. Much of the history is told through reminiscences of slaves or former slaves in their narratives." Publisher's note
Includes glossary and bibliographical references

Oppong, Joseph R.
Africa South of the Sahara; series consulting editor Charles F. Gritzner. Chelsea House Publishers 2006 124p il map (Modern world cultures) lib bdg $30
Grades: 6 7 8 9   **967**
1. Sub-Saharan Africa
ISBN 0-7910-8146-X
This describes the physical and historical geography, population and settlement, cultures, politics, and economy of sub-Saharan Africa.
This "accessible [title is] generously illustrated with colorful photos, maps, and clear charts, graphs, and other statistical data." SLJ

967.43   Chad

Kneib, Martha
Chad; [by] Martha Kneib. 1st ed. Marshall Cavendish Benchmark 2007 144p il map (Cultures of the world) lib bdg $39.93
Grades: 5 6 7 8   **967.43**
1. Chad
ISBN 978-0-7614-2327-0 (lib bdg); 0-7614-2327-3 (lib bdg)   LC 2005027079
This provides "information on the geography, history, governmental structure, economy, cultural diverstiy, peoples, religion, and culture of Chad." Publisher's note
Includes glossary and bibliographical references

967.51   Democratic Republic of the Congo

Heale, Jay
Democratic Republic of the Congo. Benchmark Bks. 1999 128p il maps (Cultures of the world) lib bdg $37.07
Grades: 5 6 7 8   **967.51**
1. Congo (Republic)
ISBN 0-7614-0874-6   LC 98-28538
Describes the geography, history, government, economy, people, lifestyle, religion, languages, arts, leisure, festivals, and food of the third largest country in Africa, a former colony of Belgium
Includes glossary and bibliographical references

Willis, Terri
Democratic Republic of the Congo. Children's Press 2004 143p il map (Enchantment of the world, Second series) lib bdg $34.50
Grades: 5 6 7 8   **967.51**
1. Congo (Republic)
ISBN 0-516-24250-4   LC 2003-504
Contents: Collapsing under its weight; The country and the river; Congo's bountiful diversity; Kingdoms, colonies, and corruption; Moving toward freedom; Poverty amidst plenty; People of the Congo; Overlapping faiths; Expression through the arts; Life in Congo; Timeline; Fast facts
Discusses the geography and climate, history, wildlife, economy, government, people, religion, and culture of the Congo.
This offers "lucid commentary, digestible quantities of facts and statistics, eye-catching color photos, and eminently useful back matter." Booklist
Includes bibliographical references

967.571   Rwanda

King, David C., 1933-
Rwanda; [by] David C. King. Marshall Cavendish Benchmark 2007 144p il map (Cultures of the world) lib bdg $39.93
Grades: 5 6 7 8   **967.571**
1. Rwanda
ISBN 978-0-7614-2333-1 (lib bdg); 0-7614-2333-8 (lib bdg)   LC 2005031817
This provides "information on the geography, history, governmental structure, economy, cultural diversity, peoples, religion, and culture of Rwanda." Publisher's note
Includes glossary and bibliographical references

Koopmans, Andy
Rwanda. Mason Crest Publishers 2005 87p il map (Africa: continent in the balance) lib bdg $21.95
Grades: 7 8 9 10   **967.571**
1. Rwanda
ISBN 1-59084-812-8   LC 2004-4826
This is an introduction to the geography, history, government, economy, people, and customs of Rwanda
The information in this book is "is well organized and presented in a clear, logical manner. . . . The bright, attractive photographs are well matched to the [text]." SLJ
Includes glossary and bibliographical references

967.6   Uganda and Kenya

Barlas, Robert
Uganda. Benchmark Bks. 2000 128p il map (Cultures of the world) lib bdg $37.07
Grades: 5 6 7 8   **967.6**
1. Uganda
ISBN 0-7614-0981-5   LC 99-27577
Discusses the geography, history, government, economy, people, and culture of the African nation of Uganda
Includes glossary and bibliographical references

967.62   Kenya

Bowden, Rob
Kenya. Facts on File 2003 61p il map (Countries of the world) $30
Grades: 7 8 9 10   **967.62**
1. Kenya
ISBN 0-8160-5384-7
This covers Kenya's "physical geography, resources, ethnic populations, tourism, and commerce. . . . It includes a detailed overview of the tensions between commercial development in an impoverished nation and the need to protect natural resources and wildlife. . . . [This title offers] a wealth of nearly up-to-date information and a realistic introduction to [its subject]. . . . [It also features] good-quality color photos of urban and rural homes and buildings and traditional and western lifestyles." Booklist
Includes bibliographical references

Broberg, Catherine
Kenya in pictures. rev and expanded. Lerner Publs. 2003 80p il map (Visual geography series) lib bdg $27.93
Grades: 5 6 7 8   **967.62**
1. Kenya
ISBN 0-8225-1957-7   LC 2001-3829
First published 1988 under the authorship of Joel Reuben
A brief overview of Kenya's land, history, government, people, and culture
The book is "visually appealing with photos and sidebars that complement the text." Libr Media Connect
Includes bibliographical references

Lekuton, Joseph
Facing the lion; growing up Maasai on the African savanna; by Joseph Lekuton with Herman Viola. National Geographic Soc. 2003 127p il map $15.95 *
Grades: 7 8 9 10 11 12   **967.62**
1. Masai (African people) 2. Kenya
ISBN 0-7922-5125-3   LC 2003-750
Contents: A lion hunt; The proud one; Cows; The pinching man; School; Herdsman; Initiation; Kabarak; Soccer; America; A warrior in two worlds
A member of the Masai people describes his life as he grew up in a northern Kenya village, travelled to America to attend college, and became an elementary school teacher in Virginia
"Lekuton's story touches a universal chord, and shows readers the beauty of another culture from the inside. Simple and direct enough for reluctant readers, and written in a conversational and occasionally wryly humorous style, this book will be enjoyed by a wide range of readers." SLJ

Pateman, Robert, 1954-
Kenya; by Robert Pateman. 2nd ed. Benchmark Bks. 2004 144p il map (Cultures of the world) lib bdg $37.07
Grades: 5 6 7 8   **967.62**
1. Kenya
ISBN 0-7614-1701-X   LC 2003-20921
First published 1993
Contents: Geography; History; Government; Economy; Environment; Kenyans; Lifestyle; Religion; Language; Arts; Leisure; Festivals; Foods
Examines the geography, history, government, economy, people, and culture of Kenya
Includes glossary and bibliographical references

967.73   Somalia

Hassig, Susan M., 1969-
Somalia; by Susan M. Hassig & Zawiah Abdul Latif. 2nd ed. Marshall Cavendish Benchmark 2008 144p il map (Cultures of the world) lib bdg $42.79
Grades: 5 6 7 8   **967.73**
1. Somalia
ISBN 978-0-7614-2082-8 (lib bdg); 0-7614-2082-7 (lib bdg)   LC 2006102270

Hassig, Susan M., 1969-—_Continued_
First published 1997
"Provides comprehensive information on the geography, history, wildlife, governmental structure, economy, cultural diversity, peoples, religion, and culture of Somalia." Publisher's note
Includes glossary and bibliographical references

967.8 Tanzania

Heale, Jay
Tanzania; by Jay Heale & Winnie Wong. 2nd ed. Marshall Cavendish Benchmark 2009 144p il map (Cultures of the world) lib bdg $29.95
Grades: 5 6 7 8   **967.8**
1. Tanzania
ISBN 978-0-7614-3417-7; 0-7614-3417-8
             LC 2008028802
First published 1998
"Provides comprehensive information on the geography, history, wildlife, governmental structure, economy, cultural diversity, peoples, religion, and culture of Tanzania." Publisher's note
Includes glossary and bibliographical references

MacDonald, Joan Vos
Tanzania; [by] Joan Vos MacDonald. Mason Crest Publishers 2005 85p il map (Africa: continent in the balance) $21.95
Grades: 7 8 9 10   **967.8**
1. Tanzania
ISBN 1-59084-813-6   LC 2004-7103
Contents: Geography; History; Government; Economy; Culture and people; Cities and communities; Calendar of festivals; Recipes; Glossary; Project and report ideas; Chronology
Describes the history, geography, and culture of Tanzania
"The information in [this book] is well organized and presented in a clear, logical manner. . . . [It is illustrated with] bright, attractive photographs." SLJ
Includes glossary and bibliographical references

967.9 Mozambique

King, David C., 1933-
Mozambique; [by] David C. King. 1st ed. Marshall Cavendish Benchmark 2007 144p il map (Cultures of the world) lib bdg $39.93
Grades: 5 6 7 8   **967.9**
1. Mozambique
ISBN 978-0-7614-2331-7 (lib bdg); 0-7614-2331-1 (lib bdg)   LC 2006002302
This provides "information on the geography, history, wildlife, governmental structure, economy, cultural diversity, peoples, religion, and culture of Mozambique." Publisher's note
Includes glossary and bibliographical references

Mulroy, Tanya
Mozambique; [by] Tanya Mulroy. Mason Crest Publishers 2008 87p il map (Africa: continent in the balance) lib bdg $21.95
Grades: 5 6 7 8   **967.9**
1. Mozambique
ISBN 978-1-4222-0090-2 (lib bdg); 1-4222-0090-6 (lib bdg)   LC 2006-17340
This book is "clear and concise, and the . . . easy-to-read texts impart a good deal of up-to-date information. . . . Chapters . . . cover the . . . country's history; politics and government; economy; and people, including discussions of family life, education, ethnic groups, health care, sports, and the arts, with the focus being on the largest cities." SLJ
Includes glossary and bibliographical references

968   Southern Africa. Republic of South Africa

Blauer, Ettagale
South Africa; [by] Ettagale Blauer and Jason Lauré. rev ed. Children's Press 2006 144p il map (Enchantment of the world, second series) lib bdg $25.20
Grades: 5 6 7 8   **968**
1. South Africa
ISBN 0-516-24853-7
First published 1998
This survey of South Africa "covers geography, history, constitutional development, the economy, language, religion, and current challenges. . . . Color photos are clear and thoughtfully placed. . . . Not only is the text accurate, but it also captures some of the cultural, economic, and social complexities and contradictions in a succinct and even elegant way." SLJ

Downing, David, 1946-
Apartheid in South Africa; [by] David Downing. Heinemann Library 2004 56p il (Witness to history) $31.36 *
Grades: 7 8 9 10   **968**
1. Apartheid 2. South Africa—Race relations
ISBN 1-4034-4870-1   LC 2003-18235
Contents: How do we know?; South Africa in 1910; Discrimination; Early opposition to white rule; South Africa adopts apartheid; How apartheid worked; For Europeans only; Resistance grows; Sharpeville; A change of tactics; South Africa isolated; Life for whites; Life for nonwhites; The Bantustans; Soweto; The terrorist state; Pressure from inside; Pressure from outside; First cracks; The end of apartheid; Reconciliation; Today and the future; What have we learned from apartheid?
Examines the historical forces that led to the development of the system of apartheid, what life was like under the system for both blacks and whites, and the efforts that caused the end of this system
"This dense volume is an excellent narrative overview of the apartheid struggle, drawing extensively on primary sources that provide depth, detail, drama, and authenticity." Booklist

Mace, Virginia

South Africa; [by] Virginia Mace; Kate Rowntree and Vukile Khumalo, consultants. National Geographic 2008 64p il map (Countries of the world) lib bdg $27.90 *

Grades: 4 5 6 7 **968**

1. South Africa

ISBN 978-1-4263-0203-9   LC 2007047835

This describes the geography, nature, history, people and culture, government, and economy of South Africa.

"Through its numerous maps and standout photographs, this book provides a general overview of South Africa that will satisfy the basic needs of upper-elementary research paper writers." Horn Book Guide

Includes glossary and bibliographical references

Rosmarin, Ike, 1915-

South Africa; [by] Ike Rosmarin, Dee Rissik. 2nd ed. Benchmark Bks. 2004 144p il map (Cultures of the world) lib bdg $37.07

Grades: 5 6 7 8 **968**

1. South Africa

ISBN 0-7614-1704-4   LC 2003-20923

First published 1993

Contents: Geography; History; Government; Economy; Environment; South Africans; Lifestyle; Religion; Language; Arts; Leisure; Festivals; Food

Examines the geography, history, government, economy, people, and culture of South Africa

Includes glossary and bibliographical references

Seidman, David, 1958-

Teens in South Africa; by David Seidman. Compass Point Books 2009 96p il map (Global connections) lib bdg $33.26

Grades: 6 7 8 9 **968**

1. Teenagers 2. South Africa

ISBN 978-0-7565-3854-5 (lib bdg); 0-7565-3854-8 (lib bdg)   LC 2008-9480

Uncovers the challenges, pastimes, customs and culture of teens in South Africa

This book is "concise and highly readable. . . . Clear, colorful photos and sidebars on a range of topics provide further context. . . . [This title] will enrich young adult collections." SLJ

Inlcudes glossary and bibliographical references

Weltig, Matthew Scott

The aftermath of the Anglo-Zulu war; by Matthew S. Weltig. Twenty-First Century Books 2008 c2009 160p il (Aftermath of history) lib bdg $38.60

Grades: 6 7 8 9 **968**

1. Zulu (African people) 2. South Africa—History 3. Zulu War, 1879

ISBN 978-0-8225-7599-3 (lib bdg); 0-8225-7599-X (lib bdg)   LC 2007-50826

"The well–written text provides a detailed account of the devastation and ruin brought to Zululand by the British government and by Boer settlers, replete with text boxes that provide clarification and further explanation of what are often complex and confusing issues and events. Illustrations consist of both period photographs and paintings of the fierce fighting. Reckless bravery, treachery, cruelty, betrayal, and greed are all here, resulting in an absorbing, but tragic story." SLJ

Includes glossary and bibliographical references

968.06   Period as Republic, 1961-

Beecroft, Simon

The release of Nelson Mandela; by Simon Beecroft. World Almanac Library 2004 48p il (Days that changed the world) lib bdg $30; pa $11.95

Grades: 5 6 7 8 **968.06**

1. Mandela, Nelson 2. South Africa—Politics and government 3. Apartheid

ISBN 0-8368-5571-X (lib bdg); 0-8368-5578-7 (pa)   LC 2003-65807

First published 2003 in the United Kingdom with title: The freeing of Nelson Mandela

A biography of the black South African leader who became a civil rights activist, political prisoner, and president of South Africa, told in the context of the history of his country

This does "a fine job of combining a closeup view of an earth-shattering event with what led up to the drama and a sense of the event's impact on the future. . . . The . . . design is ideal for browsing." Booklist

Includes bibliographical references

968.83   Botswana

LeVert, Suzanne

Botswana; [by] Suzanne LeVert. 1st ed. Marshall Cavendish Benchmark 2007 144p il map (Cultures of the world) lib bdg $39.93

Grades: 5 6 7 8 **968.83**

1. Botswana

ISBN 978-0-7614-2330-0 (lib bdg); 0-7614-2330-3 (lib bdg)   LC 2005032575

This offers "information on the geography, history, governmental structure, economy, cultural diversity, peoples, religion, and culture of Botswana." Publisher's note

Includes glossary and bibliographical references

Wittmann, Kelly

Botswana; [by] Kelly Wittmann. Mason Crest Publishers 2008 79p il map (Africa: continent in the balance) lib bdg $21.95

Grades: 5 6 7 8 **968.83**

1. Botswana

ISBN 978-1-4222-0087-2 (lib bdg); 1-4222-0087-6 (lib bdg)   LC 2006-17333

This book features the country's "history; politics and government; economy; and people, including discussions of family life, education, ethnic groups, health care, sports, and the arts, with the focus being on the largest cities. . . . Interspersed throughout are numerous color and some black-and-white photographs, with descriptive

Wittmann, Kelly—*Continued*

captions, as well as 'Quick Facts' regarding geography, the economy, and the people. . . . The information is presented in an engaging manner." SLJ

Includes glossary and bibliographical references

968.91 Zimbabwe

Hall, Martin, 1952-

Great Zimbabwe; [by] Martin Hall and Rebecca Stefoff. 1st ed. Oxford University Press 2006 47p il map (Digging for the past) $23

Grades: 7 8 9 10   **968.91**
  1. Zimbabwe 2. Shona (African people) 3. Archeology
  ISBN 978-0-19-515773-4; 0-19-515773-7
                                          LC 2005014607

This "explores a ruined fourteenth-century stone city in Zimbabwe and covers controversies over its origin, its artifacts, and theories about its former inhabitants. The well-written text will spur readers' curiosity, while archival and modern photos, ancient maps, and European explorers' notes add a fascinating variety to the book's visual presentation." Horn Book Guide

Includes glossary and bibliographical references

Sheehan, Sean, 1951-

Zimbabwe. 2nd ed. Benchmark Bks. 2004 144p il map (Cultures of the world) lib bdg $37.07

Grades: 5 6 7 8   **968.91**
  1. Zimbabwe
  ISBN 0-7614-1706-0   LC 2003-20883

Contents: Geography; History; Government; Economy; Environment; Zimbabweans; Lifestyle; Religion; Language; Arts; Leisure; Festivals; Foods

Examines the geography, history, govenment, economy, people, and culture of Zimbabwe

Includes glossary and bibliographical references

968.94 Zambia

Holmes, Timothy

Zambia; by Timothy Holmes & Winnie Wong. rev ed. Marshall Cavendish Benchmark 2008 c2009 144p il map (Cultures of the world) lib bdg $29.95

Grades: 5 6 7 8   **968.94**
  1. Zambia
  ISBN 978-0-7614-3039-1 (lib bdg); 0-7614-3039-3 (lib bdg)   LC 2007050794
  First published 1998

Describes the geography, history, government, economy, people, lifestyle, religion, language, arts, leisure, festivals, and food of Zambia

Includes glossary and bibliographical references

969.1 Madagascar

Heale, Jay

Madagascar; [by] Jay Heale & Zawiah Abdul Latif. 2nd ed. Marshall Cavendish Benchmark 2008 c2009 144p il map (Cultures of the world) lib bdg $29.95

Grades: 5 6 7 8   **969.1**
  1. Madagascar
  ISBN 978-0-7614-3036-0 (lib bdg); 0-7614-3036-9 (lib bdg)   LC 2007048288
  First published 1998

"Provides comprehensive information on the geography, history, wildlife, governmental structure, economy, cultural diversity, peoples, religion, and culture of Madagascar." Publisher's note

Includes glossary and bibliographical references

970 History of North America

Desaulniers, Kristi L.

Northern America; [by] Kristi L. Desaulniers and Charles F. Gritzner. Chelsea House 2006 128p il map (Modern world cultures) lib bdg $30

Grades: 7 8 9 10   **970**
  1. North America
  ISBN 0-7910-8141-9   LC 2005031766

This describes the geography, history, culture, population, politics, economy, regions, and possible future of The United States and Canada.

Includes bibliographical references

970.004 North American native peoples

Bial, Raymond

Lifeways [series] Benchmark Books 1999-2005 28v il map Each group set of four volumes $136.86

Grades: 5 6 7 8   **970.004**
  1. Native Americans
  ISBN 0-614-0800-2 (Group 1); 0-7614-0860-6 (Group 2); 0-7614-0936-X (Group 3); 0-7614-1208-5 (Group 4); 0-7614-1412-6 (Group 5); 0-7614-1680-3 (Group 6); 0-7614-1900-4 (Group 7)

Also available as separate volumes each $34.21

Contents: Group 1: The Cherokee; The Iroquois; The Navajo; The Sioux; Group 2: The Comanche; The Ojibwe; The Pueblo; The Seminole; Group 3: The Apache; The Cheyenne; The Haida; The Huron; Group 4: The Inuit; The Nez Perce; The Powhatan; The Shoshone; Group 5: The Blackfeet; The Choctaw; The Mandan; The Tlingit; Group 6: The Arapaho; The Chumash; The Shawnee; The Wampanoag; Group 7: The Cree; The Crow; The Delaware; The Menominee

"Prefaced by the creation story, each book looks at the original lifeways of a tribe. Daily life, religious beliefs and sacred rituals are . . . explored, as well as a tribe's social systems, rules of warfare and their sense of them-

Bial, Raymond—*Continued*

selves within the natural universe. In addition, the cycle of life—from birth to marriage to death—is [described]." Publisher's note

"It's the comprehensive content, the attractive presentation, and the varied and well-chosen illustrations that make these books worthy of consideration." SLJ

The Long Walk; the story of Navajo captivity. Benchmark Bks. 2003 94p il map (Great journeys) lib bdg $31.36

Grades: 5 6 7 8 **970.004**

1. Carson, Kit, 1809-1868 2. Barboncito, Navajo Chief, 1820?-1871 3. Navajo Indians

ISBN 0-7614-1322-7   LC 2001-43969

"The book is illustrated with informative black-and-white photographs and reproductions." SLJ

Includes bibliographical references

Brown, Dee Alexander

Bury my heart at Wounded Knee; an Indian history of the American West; [by] Dee Brown. Thirtieth anniversary ed. Holt & Co. 2001 487p il $35; pa $16 *

Grades: 8 9 10 11 12 Adult   **970.004**

1. Native Americans—West (U.S.) 2. Native Americans—Wars 3. West (U.S.)—History

ISBN 0-8050-6634-9; 0-8050-6669-1 (pa)

     LC 00-40958

First published 1970

This is an account of the experience of the American Indian during the white man's expansion westward

Includes bibliographical references

Collier, Christopher, 1930-

Clash of cultures, prehistory-1638; [by] Christopher Collier, James Lincoln Collier. Benchmark Bks. (Tarrytown) 1998 95p il maps (Drama of American history) lib bdg $31.36

Grades: 6 7 8 9   **970.004**

1. Native Americans 2. United States—History—1600-1775, Colonial period 3. Culture conflict

ISBN 0-7614-0436-8   LC 96-31859

This volume "examines the civilizations on both sides of the Atlantic in the years before and during European settlement in North America. . . . While consistently presenting the big picture, the Colliers paint their American portrait 'warts and all,' caring less about idealizing our history than increasing understanding of it." Booklist

Includes bibliographical references

Denetdale, Jennifer

The Long Walk; the forced Navajo exile; [by] Jennifer Denetdale. Chelsea House 2007 143p il map (Landmark events in Native American history) lib bdg $30

Grades: 7 8 9 10   **970.004**

1. Navajo Indians

ISBN 978-0-7910-9344-3 (lib bdg); 0-7910-9344-1 (lib bdg)   LC 2007021723

"In 1863, the Diné (Navajo) faced transformations to their way of life with the Americans' determination to first subjugate and then remove them to a reservation. . . . This book exposes the series of events that facilitated the Navajo's removal from their homeland, their experiences during the Long Walk, their time at the Bosque Redondo reservation, their return home, and the ways in which they remember the Long Walk and the Bosque Redondo." Publisher's note

Includes bibliographical references

Do all Indians live in tipis? questions and answers; from the National Museum of the American Indian; foreword by Rick West; introduction by Wilma Mankiller. Collins, in association with the National Museum of the American Indian, Smithsonian Institution 2007 239p il pa $14.95

Grades: 8 9 10 11 12   **970.004**

1. Native Americans

ISBN 978-0-06-115301-3 (pa); 0-06-115301-X (pa)

     LC 2007-60874

"This highly accessible and informative book aims to dispel some of the major myths and stereotypes still surrounding Native people in the United States and Canada. . . . The straightforward questions were compiled from actual phone calls, emails, letters, and in-person visits to the George Gustav Heye Center in New York, a major branch of the National Museum of the American Indian. The Native American writers who answered them did so concisely with hints of humor and an abundance of research and experience. . . . This is a topnotch resource for both people just learning about Native American cultures and those who think they know the facts." SLJ

Dolan, Edward F., 1924-

The American Indian wars; [by] Edward F. Dolan. Millbrook Press 2003 112p il map lib bdg $29.90

Grades: 5 6 7 8   **970.004**

1. Native Americans—Wars

ISBN 0-7613-1968-9   LC 2002-153012

Contents: Warpaths; The first battles; Deep into the West; Two Apache warriors; The Battle of the Little Bighorn; The magnificent march; Death at Wounded Knee

Examines the battles and treaties between native peoples and early European settlers of what was to become the United States, as conflicts arose primarily over land, but also over food and other issues

"Period drawings, paintings, and photographs effectively illustrate a text packed with history." Booklist

Includes bibliographical references

Edwards, Judith, 1940-

The history of the American Indians and the reservation; [by] Judith Edwards. Enslow Publishers 2008 128p il map (From many cultures, one history) lib bdg $31.93

Grades: 6 7 8 9   **970.004**

1. Native Americans—History

ISBN 978-0-7660-2798-5 (lib bdg); 0-7660-2798-8 (lib bdg)   LC 2007028275

Edwards, Judith, 1940-—*Continued*

"Explores the difficult changes American Indians were forced to make, including moving off their land, adapting to like on reservations, and how those reservations have changed since their creation." Publisher's note

Includes glossary and bibliographical references

Ehrlich, Amy, 1942-

Wounded Knee: an Indian history of the American West; adapted for young readers by Amy Ehrlich from Dee Brown's Bury my heart at Wounded Knee. Holt & Co. 1974 202p il maps pa $13.95 hardcover o.p. *

Grades: 6 7 8 9   **970.004**

1. Native Americans—West (U.S.) 2. Native Americans—Wars 3. West (U.S.)—History

ISBN 0-8050-2700-9

This book traces the plight of the Navaho, Apache, Cheyenne and Sioux Indians in their struggles against the white man in the West between 1860 and 1890. It recounts battles and their causes, participants, and consequences during this era

"Some chapters [of the original] have been deleted, others condensed, and in some instances sentence structure and language have been simplified. The editing is good, and this version is interesting, readable, and smooth." SLJ

Includes bibliographical references

Elish, Dan, 1960-

The Trail of Tears; the story of the Cherokee removal. Benchmark Bks. 2002 96p il maps (Great journeys) lib bdg $32.79 *

Grades: 5 6 7 8   **970.004**

1. Cherokee Indians

ISBN 0-7614-1228-X   LC 00-52902

This "begins with the Cherokees' encounter with European explorers, discusses their experiences with the American government, and gives information on their forced removal from Georgia to locations West." SLJ

This "is particularly moving. Elish does a fine job introducing the Cherokee nation. . . . Filled with crisp, well-selected photographs and historical illustrations." Booklist

Includes bibliographical references

Encyclopedia of Native American wars and warfare; general editors, William B. Kessel, Robert Wooster. Facts on File 2005 398p il map $75; pa $21.95

Grades: 7 8 9 10   **970.004**

1. Native Americans—Wars—Encyclopedias 2. Reference books

ISBN 0-8160-3337-4; 0-8160-6430-X (pa)

LC 00-56200

"More than 600 entries provide access to information about the persons, tribes, treaties, battles, places, weaponry, and concepts related to armed conflicts between Native Americans and those of European descent, for the years between 1599 and 1890 and primarily the geographic locations now within the borders of the U.S." Booklist

"This encyclopedia offers readers a wide range of information about Native American history in North America after 1492." Choice

Includes bibliographical references

Goble, Paul

All our relatives; traditional Native American thoughts about nature; compiled and illustrated by Paul Goble. World Wisdom 2005 unp il $15.95 *

Grades: 5 6 7 8   **970.004**

1. Native Americans 2. Philosophy of nature

ISBN 0-941532-77-1; 978-0-941532-77-8

LC 2005004285

"The pages of this book are chock-full of quotations, songs, and brief stories that exemplify Native American attitudes toward nature. . . . Black Elk, Standing Bear, Brave Buffalo, and others observe the importance of various animals and the sacred qualities of all living things. . . . The spaces between text blocks are filled with Goble's familiar illustrations based on traditional Native American designs and colors." SLJ

Includes bibliographical references

Jastrzembski, Joseph C.

The Apache wars; the final resistance. Chelsea House Publishers 2007 133p il map (Landmark events in Native American history) lib bdg $35

Grades: 7 8 9 10   **970.004**

1. Apache Indians

ISBN 978-0-7910-9343-6 (lib bdg); 0-7910-9343-3 (lib bdg)   LC 2007-990

"For a quarter century—1861 to 1886—the U.S. military attempted to subjugate one of the largest Indian tribes of what is today the American Southwest. . . . [This is the] tale of how . . . the Apache Indians held out longer than any other major U.S. tribe." Publisher's note

This account features "lively writing and direct quotes, and [is] enhanced by many color and black-and-white photos, drawings, and illustrations." SLJ

Includes bibliographical references

Keoke, Emory Dean

American Indian contributions to the world; [by] Emory Dean Keoke and Kay Marie Porterfield. Facts on File 2005 5v il map set $175 *

Grades: 7 8 9 10   **970.004**

1. Native Americans

ISBN 0-8160-5392-8

Also available as separate volumes $35 each

Contents: [v1] Buildings, clothing and art; [v2] Food, farming, and hunting; [v3] Medicine and health; [v4] Science and technology; [v5] Trade, transportation, and warfare

This set "focuses on the many significant contributions that members of North, Central, and South American tribes have made to both United States and world culture. . . . The appendixes are well organized. . . . This set would be an excellent addition to any school media center's collection." Voice Youth Advocates

Includes glossary and bibliographical references

King, David C., 1933-
First people; an illustrated history of American Indians. DK Pub. 2008 192p il map $19.99
Grades: 5 6 7 8   **970.004**
1. Native Americans
ISBN 978-0-7566-4092-7; 0-7566-4092-X

"This rich pictorial work serves as an entertaining, informative, and visually appealing introduction to American Indian culture and history. Each of the seven chapters covers a different time period in chronological order. . . . The glossy photographs, colorful drawings, and easily accessible paragraphs . . . make for an easy-to-use overall package." SLJ

Murdoch, David Hamilton, 1937-
North American Indian; written by David Murdoch; chief consultant, Stanley A. Freed; photographed by Lynton Gardiner. rev ed. DK Pubs. 2005 72p il (DK eyewitness books) $15.99; lib bdg $19.99
Grades: 4 5 6 7   **970.004**
1. Native Americans
ISBN 0-7566-1082-6; 0-7566-1082-6 (lib bdg)
First published 1995 by Knopf
Published in association with the American Museum of Natural History

This is a guide to the civilizations of North American Indians including full-color photographs of artifacts and descriptions ceremonies and customs.

Philip, Neil
The great circle; a history of the First Nations; foreword by Dennis Hastings. Clarion Books 2006 153p il map $25 *
Grades: 7 8 9 10 11 12 Adult   **970.004**
1. Native Americans
ISBN 978-0-618-15941-3; 0-618-15941-X
                                          LC 2005032743
"Philip takes on a huge challenge here: to present a unified narrative that explains the complex and confrontational relationships between Native Americans and white settlers. . . . He pulls it off, however, thanks to solid research, an engaging writing style, and a talent for making individual stories serve the whole. . . . Top marks, too, for the volume's photographs and historical renderings, which so intensely illustrate the pages." Booklist
Includes bibliographical references

Schomp, Virginia, 1953-
The Native Americans; [by] Virginia Schomp. Marshall Cavendish Benchmark 2007 c2008 96p il map (Myths of the world) lib bdg $34.21
Grades: 6 7 8 9   **970.004**
1. Native Americans
ISBN 978-0-7614-2550-2 (lib bdg); 0-7614-2550-0 (lib bdg)   LC 2007013511
"A retelling of various Native American myths, with background information describing the history, geography, belief systems, and customs of the indigenous peoples of North America." Publisher's note
"With [its] beautiful illustrations, high-quality produc-

tion, and focus on source material, the [book] should whet the interest of readers." SLJ
Includes glossary and bibliographical references

Student almanac of Native American history; Media Projects, Inc. Greenwood Press 2003 2v il map (Middle school reference) set$80
Grades: 6 7 8 9   **970.004**
1. Native Americans—History 2. Reference books
ISBN 0-313-32599-5   LC 2002-35215
Contents: v1 From prehistoric times to the Trail of Tears, 35,000 BCE-1838; v2 From the Trail of Tears to the present, 1839-today
Presents an overview of the history of Native Americans from before European contact up to the present day, including historical documents, legislation, statistics, court cases, and timelines
"This attractive almanac provides information on topics of interest to users in middle school and up. . . . [This] will be a welcome addition to school and public libraries where there is a need for additional information about Native Americans." Booklist
Includes bibliographical references

Terry, Michael Bad Hand
Daily life in a Plains Indian village, 1868. Clarion Bks. 1999 48p il map hardcover o.p. pa $9.95
Grades: 4 5 6 7   **970.004**
1. Native Americans—Great Plains
ISBN 0-395-94542-9; 0-395-97499-2 (pa)
                                          LC 98-32382
Depicts the historical background, social organization, and daily life of a Plains Indian village in 1868, presenting interiors, landscapes, clothing, and everyday objects
"The author presents short paragraphs of fascinating information accompanied by visuals that explain even more than the text." SLJ
Includes glossary

Waldman, Carl
Encyclopedia of Native American tribes. 3rd rev ed. Facts on File 2006 xxiv, 360p il map (Facts on File library of American history) $75; pa $21.95
Grades: 6 7 8 9 10 11 12 Adult   **970.004**
1. Native Americans—Encyclopedias 2. Reference books
ISBN   978-0-8160-6273-7;   0-8160-6273-0; 978-0-8160-6274-4 (pa); 0-8160-6274-9 (pa)
                                          LC 2006-12529
First published 1988
This book discusses "more than 200 American Indian tribes of North America, as well as prehistoric peoples and civilizations. . . . [The] text summarizes the historical record—locations, migrations, contacts with non-Indians, wars, and more—and includes present-day tribal affairs and issues. The book also covers traditional Indian lifeways, including diet, housing, transportation, tools, clothing, art, and rituals, as well as language families." Publisher's note
"This well-written and easily accessible encyclopedia of a good starting point for research on Native American tribes." Libr Media Connect
Includes bibliographical references

Yue, Charlotte
The wigwam and the longhouse; [by] Charlotte and David Yue. Houghton Mifflin 2000 118p il $15 *
Grades: 4 5 6 7　　　　　　　　　**970.004**
1. Woodland Indians
ISBN 0-395-84169-0　　　　　LC 98-28971
Describes the history, customs, religion, government, homes, and present-day status of the various native peoples that inhabited the eastern woodlands since before the coming of the Europeans
Includes bibliographical references

970.01 North America—Early history to 1599

Freedman, Russell
Who was first? discovering the Americas. Clarion Books 2007 88p il map $19 *
Grades: 6 7 8 9　　　　　　　　　**970.01**
1. America—Exploration 2. Explorers
ISBN 978-0-618-66391-0　　　　LC 2006-102485
This "looks at various ideas about the discovery of the Americas. . . . Beyond the very readable presentation of facts and theories, the book's main accomplishment is in showing that history is . . . an evolving process of logically interpreted evidence continually questioned, disputed, and revised. . . . The illustrations, many in color, include many excellent maps as well as reproductions of period drawings, paintings, engravings, and photos. . . . A well-researched, intelligent account." Booklist
Includes bibliographical references

Wulffson, Don L., 1943-
Before Columbus; early voyages to the Americas; by Don Wulffson. Twenty-First Century Books 2008 128p il map lib bdg $30.60
Grades: 6 7 8 9　　　　　　　　　**970.01**
1. America—Exploration 2. Explorers 3. America—Antiquities
ISBN 978-0-8225-5978-8 (lib bdg); 0-8225-5978-1 (lib bdg)　　　　　　　　　　　LC 2005-24487
"This engaging presentation of early exploration of the Americas offers both fact and speculation on who, when, and why voyagers came; how they traveled; and what evidence they left behind. . . . Citing legends and sagas, oral and written histories, and archaeological discoveries, Wulffson presents an intriguing array of possibilities. . . . The stories and unanswered questions about pre-Columbian voyagers will capture the imaginations of many readers, offer fascinating glimpses of different cultural groups, [and] stimulate further research." SLJ
Includes bibliographical references

971 Canada

Braun, Eric
Canada in pictures. Lerner Publs. 2003 80p il map (Visual geography series) lib bdg $27.93
Grades: 5 6 7 8　　　　　　　　　**971**
1. Canada
ISBN 0-8225-4679-5　　　　　LC 2002-8107

First published 1989, catalogued under title
A historical and current look at Canada, discussing the land, the government, the culture, the people, and the economy
"An excellent introduction. . . . [This offers] easy-to-read and informative text, maps, charts, and full-color photographs." SLJ
Includes glossary and bibliographical references

Exploring Canada. Lucent Bks. 2003 10v il maps lib bdg ea $29.45
Grades: 6 7 8 9　　　　　　　　　**971**
1. Canada 2. Reference books
Contents: Alberta, by G. D. Laws & L. M. Laws; British Columbia, by B. J. Palana; Manitoba, by G. D. Laws & L. M. Laws; Maritime Provinces, by G. D. Laws & L. M. Laws; Newfoundland, by M. Mayell; Northwest Territory, by G. D. Laws & L. M. Laws; Ontario, by S. Ferry; Quebec, by S. Ferry; Saskatchewan, by M. Mayell; Yukon Territory, by S. Ferry, B. Harris, & L. Szynkowski
"These volumes provide overviews of the geography, history, and culture of each province or territory, along with an idea of how it fits into Canada as a whole. The maps are clear and well labeled. 'Facts About' sections provide ready-reference information. Interesting and well-produced black-and-white photographs appear throughout. . . . The strength of these titles is in their organization and the amount of information they provide." SLJ

Garrington, Sally, 1953-
Canada. Facts on File 2005 61p il map (Countries of the world) lib bdg $30
Grades: 7 8 9 10　　　　　　　　**971**
1. Canada
ISBN 0-8160-6009-6　　　　　LC 2005040676
This describes Canada's "culture, history, geography, government, and economy. [It is] competently written and [contains] current information." SLJ

Harris, Tim
The Mackenzie River; by Tim Harris. Gareth Stevens Pub. 2003 32p il map (Rivers of North America) lib bdg $24.67
Grades: 5 6 7 8　　　　　　　　　**971**
1. Mackenzie River (N.W.T.)
ISBN 0-8368-3756-8　　　　　LC 2003-42741
Contents: River of the North; From source to mouth; The life of the river; Northern people; Land of black gold; Places to visit
This describes the longest river in Canada, which runs from its source east of the Rocky Mountains in the Northwest Territories to its mouth at the Arctic Ocean
This "clearly describes [the Mackenzie River's], colorful history, and strong impact on the development of towns found along its banks. In well-organized fashion, the [author delves] into wild life, environmental issues facing [this region], and the people who live there. The color photographs enhance the [text] nicely to enrich readers' understanding." SLJ
Includes bibliographical references

Hughes, Susan, 1960-
Coming to Canada; building a life in a new land. Maple Tree Press 2005 104p il $28.95; pa $18.95 *
Grades: 6 7 8 9   **971**
1. Canada—Immigration and emigration
ISBN 1-897066-45-7; 1-897066-46-5 (pa)
"A Wow Canada! book"
This is a history of Canada's immigrants from all over the world
A "fabulous offering. . . . The lively text is well supported by an abundance of color and black-and-white photographs." SLJ

Junior Worldmark encyclopedia of the Canadian provinces; [Timothy L. Gall and Susan Bevan Gall, editors] 5th ed. U.X.L 2007 294p il map $70 *
Grades: 5 6 7 8 9 10   **971**
1. Canada 2. Reference books
ISBN 978-1-4144-1060-9; 1-4144-1060-3
LC 2007003908
First published 1997
"Arranged by 40 . . . subheadings . . . this . . . resource provides . . . information on all of Canada's provinces and territories. [It includes] details on Canada's arts, climate, government, health, languages, notable persons, ethnic groups and . . . more." Publisher's note
Includes bibliographical references

Pang, Guek-Cheng, 1950-
Canada. 2nd ed. Benchmark Books 2004 144p il map (Cultures of the world) lib bdg $37.07
Grades: 5 6 7 8   **971**
1. Canada
ISBN 0-7614-1788-5   LC 2004-8584
First published 1994
This describes the geography, history, government, economy, environment, and culture of Canada
"There is excellent coverage of Canadian arts. . . . Full-color photos appear throughout, and the maps are current and easy to read." SLJ
Includes glossary and bibliographical references

Shea, Kitty
Teens in Canada. Compass Point Books 2008 96p il map (Global connections) lib bdg $31.93
Grades: 7 8 9 10   **971**
1. Teenagers 2. Canada
ISBN 978-0-7565-3303-8 (lib bdg); 0-7565-3303-1 (lib bdg)   LC 2007-4899
Explores the culture and customs of Canadian teenagers
"Information is solid, giving readers an informed and realistic view of life in that country." Voice Youth Advocates
Includes glossary and bibliographical references

Weaver, Janice
Mirror with a memory; a nation's story in photographs. Tundra Books 2007 159p il $29.95
Grades: 6 7 8 9   **971**

1. Canada—History
ISBN 0-88776-747-8; 978-0-88776-747-0
"Defining moments in Canadian history are thematically presented in this photography collection. . . . In the conversational commentary that accompanies each image, Weaver provides historical context. Thought-provoking media literacy issues are also raised. . . . A great visual retrospective of a nation's people, places, and events." SLJ

Williams, Brian, 1943-
Canada; [by] Brian Williams; Tom Carter and Ben Cecil, consultants. National Geographic 2007 64p il map (Countries of the world) lib bdg $27.90 *
Grades: 4 5 6 7   **971**
1. Canada
ISBN 978-1-4263-0025-7   LC 2007296572
A basic overview of the history, geography, climate and culture of Canada
This "clear, succinct [overview] will support assignments without overwhelming casual readers. . . . A good selection of recent, high-quality color photographs gives the [book] visual appeal." SLJ
Includes glossary and bibliographical references

972   Middle America. Mexico

Bingham, Jane
The Aztec empire; [by] Jane Bingham. Raintree 2007 64p il map (Time travel guide) lib bdg $34.29; pa $9.99
Grades: 6 7 8 9   **972**
1. Aztecs 2. Mexico—Civilization
ISBN 978-1-4109-2730-9 (lib bdg); 1-4109-2730-X (lib bdg); 978-1-4109-2737-8 (pa); 1-4109-2737-7 (pa)   LC 2006033875
"Raintree FreeStyle"
A description of life in the Aztec empire written in the form of a travel guide.
Includes glossary and bibliographical references

Gruber, Beth
Mexico; [by] Beth Gruber; Gary S. Elbow and Jorge Zamora, consultants. National Geographic 2007 64p il map (Countries of the world) $19.90; lib bdg $27.90 *
Grades: 4 5 6 7   **972**
1. Mexico
ISBN 0-7922-7629-9; 0-7922-7669-8 (lib bdg)   LC 2004026452
"This volume introduces Mexico's geography, history, wildlife, culture, and government. The many excellent color photos and maps are a striking feature of the series. . . . This will be a useful addition to many libraries." Booklist
Includes glossary and bibliographical references

Hamilton, Janice

Mexico in pictures. Lerner Publs. 2003 80p il map (Visual geography series) lib bdg $27.93

Grades: 5 6 7 8   **972**

1. Mexico

ISBN 0-8225-1960-7   LC 2001-4238

First published 1987, catalogued under title

A historical and current look at Mexico, discussing the land, the government, the people, and the economy

The book is "visually appealing with photos and sidebars that complement the text." Libr Media Connect

Includes glossary and bibliographical references

Harris, Nathaniel, 1937-

Ancient Maya; archaeology unlocks the secrets to the Maya's past; by Nathaniel Harris; Elizabeth Graham, consultant. National Geographic 2008 64p il map (National Geographic investigates) $17.95; lib bdg $27.90 *

Grades: 4 5 6 7   **972**

1. Mayas 2. Excavations (Archeology)—Mexico 3. Mexico—Antiquities

ISBN 978-1-4263-0227-5; 1-4263-0227-4; 978-1-4263-0228-2 (lib bdg); 1-4263-0228-2 (lib bdg)   LC 2007047837

This describes ancient Mayan civilization and how archeologists found out about it.

Includes glossary and bibliographical references

Junior Worldmark encyclopedia of the Mexican states; [Timothy L. Gall and Susan Bevan Gall, editors] 2nd ed. U.X.L,Thomson/Gale 2007 423p il map $70 *

Grades: 5 6 7 8 9 10   **972**

1. Mexico 2. Reference books

ISBN 978-1-4144-1112-5   LC 2007003906

First published 2004

"Arranged by 28 . . . subheadings . . . Junior Worldmark Encyclopedia of the Mexican States provides . . . information on each of Mexico's 31 states. Topics covered include climate, plants and animals, population and ethnic groups, religions, transportation, history, state and local governments, political parties, judicial system, economy, education, arts, media, tourism, sports, famous people and . . . more." Publisher's note

Includes bibliographical references

Kops, Deborah

Palenque; by Deborah Kops. Twenty-First Century Books 2008 80p il (Unearthing ancient worlds) lib bdg $30.60

Grades: 5 6 7 8   **972**

1. Palenque site (Mexico) 2. Mayas 3. Excavations (Archeology)—Mexico 4. Mexico—Antiquities

ISBN 978-0-8225-7504-7 (lib bdg); 0-8225-7504-3 (lib bdg)   LC 2007021323

This describes the discovery of the ancient Mayan site of Palenque in 1840 by John Stephens and Frederick Catherwood, and the mid-20th century excavations of the site by Alberto Ruz Lhuillier, who discovered the tomb of the Mayan king Pakal, who died in 683 A.D., inside a pyramid

This "clearly written [title is] illustrated with large photographs and period artwork, and the pages are broken up with text boxes featuring quotes and interesting anecdotes." SLJ

Includes glossary and bibliographical references

Lourie, Peter

Hidden world of the Aztec. Boyds Mills Press 2006 48p il map $17.95 *

Grades: 4 5 6 7   **972**

1. Aztecs 2. Excavations (Archeology)—Mexico

ISBN 978-1-59078-069-5; 1-59078-069-8

The author takes a "look at the Aztecs from the perspective of archaeological digs at the Great Temple in modern-day Mexico City and at the Pyramid of the Moon in Teotihuacan. . . . The writing style is clear, informative, and interesting." SLJ

Includes glossary and bibliographical references

Perl, Lila

The ancient Maya. Franklin Watts 2005 112p il map (People of the ancient world) $29.50; pa $9.95 *

Grades: 5 6 7 8   **972**

1. Mayas

ISBN 0-531-12381-2; 0-531-16848-4 (pa)

This book portrays the lives of the ancient Maya "by examining their arts, culture, economy, government, religious beliefs, and societal structures. . . . Attractively designed and illustrated, the [book features] excellent color representations of architecture, artwork, and other cultural and historical artifacts." SLJ

Includes bibliographical references

Reilly, Mary-Jo, 1964-

Mexico; by Mary-Jo Reilly, Leslie Jermyn. 2nd ed. Benchmark Bks. 2002 144p il map (Cultures of the world) lib bdg $37.07

Grades: 5 6 7 8   **972**

1. Mexico

ISBN 0-7614-1363-4   LC 2001-47760

First published 1991

Presents the history, geography, economy, people, and social life and customs of Mexico

Includes glossary and bibliographical references

Schomp, Virginia, 1953-

The Aztecs; [by] Virginia Schomp. Marshall Cavendish Benchmark 2009 96p il map (Myths of the world) lib bdg $23.95

Grades: 6 7 8 9   **972**

1. Aztecs

ISBN 978-0-7614-3096-4 (lib bdg); 0-7614-3096-2 (lib bdg)   LC 2008007082

"A retelling of several key Aztec myths, with background information describing the history, geography, belief systems, and customs of the Aztecs." Publisher's note

Includes glossary and bibliographical references

Sonneborn, Liz
The ancient Aztecs; written by Liz Sonneborn. Franklin Watts 2005 112p il map (People of the ancient world) lib bdg $30.50; pa $9.95 *
Grades: 5 6 7 8   **972**
  1. Aztecs
  ISBN 0-531-12362-6 (lib bdg); 0-531-16844-1 (pa)
                LC 2004-13909
  Contents: Introduction; Commoners, nobles, and rulers; Warriors; Priests and scholars; Merchants and craftspeople; Farmers; Conquest and survival
  This examines ancient Aztec society "through their literature, artifacts, and documents. Religion, farming, levels of society, art, government, and fine arts are covered in [this] well-written and attractive [book]." SLJ
  Includes bibliographical references

Stein, R. Conrad, 1937-
Cortes and the Spanish Conquest; [by] R. Conrad Stein. 1st ed. Morgan Reynolds Pub. 2008 160p il map (The story of Mexico) lib bdg $27.95
Grades: 6 7 8 9 10   **972**
  1. Cortés, Hernán, 1485-1547 2. Mexico—History 3. Aztecs
  ISBN 978-1-59935-053-0 (lib bdg); 1-59935-053-X (lib bdg)   LC 2007016004
  This "identifies the 'encounter' between the Spanish and Aztecs as one that 'would put the human character itself on trial.' The author provides a look at both societies, tracing the Aztecs' rise to power and the Spaniards' interest in exploration. The Spanish conquest of the Aztecs, led by Hernando Cortés, is related in great depth, and the book ends with a discussion of its legacy. [An] excellent [introduction] to Mexican history." SLJ
  Includes bibliographical references

The Mexican Revolution. Morgan Reynolds Pub. 2008 160p il map (The story of Mexico) lib bdg $27.95
Grades: 6 7 8 9 10   **972**
  1. Mexico—History
  ISBN 978-1-59935-051-6 (lib bdg); 1-59935-051-3 (lib bdg)   LC 2007-22136
  "Opening with Porfirio Díaz's presidency (beginning in 1876), [this book] explains how Indian land was expropriated and allotted to rich hacienda owners, describes resistance movements led by Emiliano Zapata and Pancho Villa, and details 10 years of political upheaval and violent uprisings (1910-1920), ending with Alvaro Obregó's election as president of Mexico. . . . [The book has] a lively narrative style. . . . Pertinent illustrations, including photographs, historical paintings, and maps are sprinkled throughout. . . . Well-written and well-researched." SLJ
  Includes bibliographical references

The Mexican War of Independence; [by] R. Conrad Stein. Morgan Reynolds Pub. 2008 144p il map (The story of Mexico) lib bdg $27.95
Grades: 6 7 8 9 10   **972**
  1. Mexico—History
  ISBN 978-1-59935-054-7 (lib bdg); 1-59935-054-8 (lib bdg)   LC 2007022137

This "covers the years between 1521, when Hernando Cortés completed his conquest of the Aztec empire, and 1855, when Antonio Lopez Santa Anna was overthrown. The book provides excellent background information about three centuries of Spain's rule over Mexico. . . . [The book has] a lively narrative style. . . . Pertinent illustrations, including photographs, historical paintings, and maps are sprinkled throughout. . . . Well-written and well-researched." SLJ
  Includes bibliographical references

Mexico; by R. Conrad Stein. rev ed. Children's Press 2007 144p il map (Enchantment of the world, second series) lib bdg $37
Grades: 5 6 7 8   **972**
  1. Mexico
  ISBN 0-516-24868-5 (lib bdg); 978-0-516-24868-4 (lib bdg)   LC 2005024556
  First published 1998
  This describes the geography, history, culture, people, and government of Mexico
  Includes bibliographical references

972.81   Guatemala

Mann, Elizabeth, 1948-
Tikal; the center of the Maya world; with illustrations by Tom McNeely. Mikaya Press 2002 47p il map (Wonders of the world) $19.95
Grades: 4 5 6 7   **972.81**
  1. Mayas—Antiquities
  ISBN 1-931414-05-X   LC 2002-29599
  A history of the Maya Indians in the city of Tikal, founded in 800 B.C.
  "Mann's narrative flows smoothly, and frequent, full-color illustrations . . . help to clarify the details mentioned in the text." Booklist
  Includes glossary

972.82   Belize

Shields, Charles J., 1951-
Belize. Mason Crest Pubs. 2003 63p il map (Discovering Central America) lib bdg $19.95
Grades: 4 5 6 7   **972.82**
  1. Belize
  ISBN 1-59084-092-5   LC 2002-8937
  Contents: A warm, sultry land cooled by sea breezes; A history different from the rest of Central America; Careful land use strengthens the economy; A mosaic of backgrounds and languages; Communities and cultures clustered by districts; A calendar of Belizean festivals; Recipes
  This describes the history, geography, and culture of Belize
  "Tailored for the quick research needs of students, the . . . [title presents its] information smoothly and in well-organized fashion." Booklist
  Includes glossary and bibliographical references

972.83   Honduras

Kras, Sara Louise
Honduras; by Sara Louise Kras. Children's
Press 2006 144p il map (Enchantment of the
world, second series) lib bdg $37
Grades: 5 6 7 8   **972.83**
1. Honduras
ISBN 978-0-516-24871-4 (lib bdg); 0-516-24871-5 (lib
bdg)   LC 2005024240
Describes the geography, history, culture, religion, and
people of Honduras
Includes bibliographical references

Shields, Charles J., 1951-
Honduras. Mason Crest Pubs. 2003 63p il map
(Discovering Central America) lib bdg $19.95
Grades: 4 5 6 7   **972.83**
1. Honduras
ISBN 1-59084-096-8   LC 2002-9089
Contents: Honduras, the knee of Central America;
Honduras becomes the "Banana Republic;" A fragile
economy; The people of Honduras; Language, religion,
and home life; A calendar of Honduran festivals; Recipes
This describes the history, geography, and culture of
Honduras
This is "jam-packed with useful information. . . . [It
contains] straightforward writing, clearly titled chapters,
high quality color, and well-captioned photographs and
graphics." Libr Media Connect
Includes glossary and bibliographical references

972.84   El Salvador

Foley, Erin, 1967-
El Salvador; [by] Erin Foley, Rafiz Hapipi. 2nd
ed. Benchmark Bks. 2005 144p il map (Cultures
of the world) lib bdg $37.07
Grades: 5 6 7 8   **972.84**
1. El Salvador
ISBN 0-7614-1967-5   LC 2005009360
First published 1994
This describes the geography, history, government,
economy, environment, people, lifestyle, religion, lan-
guage, arts, leisure, festivals, and food of El Salvador
Includes glossary and bibliographical references

972.85   Nicaragua

Kallen, Stuart A., 1955-
The aftermath of the Sandinista Revolution.
Twenty-First Century Books 2009 160p il
(Aftermath of history) lib bdg $38.60
Grades: 8 9 10 11 12   **972.85**
1. Nicaragua—Politics and government
ISBN 978-0-8225-9091-0; 0-8225-9091-3
LC 2008025356

"The 1979 overthrow of the corrupt Nicaraguan government by the Marxist Sandinistas brought change to
one of the poorest countries in the Americas and instilled
in the U.S. new fears about the spread of Communism.
. . . Kallen offers a good overview of one of the Latin
American theaters of the Cold War." SLJ
Includes glossary and bibliographical references

Kott, Jennifer, 1971-
Nicaragua; [by] Jennifer Kott, Kristi Streiffert.
2nd ed. Benchmark Bks. 2005 144p il map
(Cultures of the world) lib bdg $37.07
Grades: 5 6 7 8   **972.85**
1. Nicaragua
ISBN 0-7614-1969-1   LC 2005009240
First published 1994
An illustrated overview of the geography, economy,
history, government, politics, and culture of Nicaragua
Includes glossary and bibliographical references

972.86   Costa Rica

Foley, Erin, 1967-
Costa Rica; [by] Erin Foley and Barbara Cooke.
2nd ed. Marshall Cavendish Benchmark 2008 144p
il map (Cultures of the world) lib bdg $42.79
Grades: 5 6 7 8   **972.86**
1. Costa Rica
ISBN 978-0-7614-2079-8 (lib bdg); 0-7614-2079-7 (lib
bdg)   LC 2006101736
First published 1997
This offers "information on the geography, history,
wildlife, governmental structure, economy, cultural diversity, peoples, religion, and culture of Costa Rica." Publisher's note
Includes glossary and bibliographical references

Morrison, Marion
Costa Rica; by Marion Morrison. rev ed.
Children's Press 2007 144p il (Enchantment of the
world, second series) lib bdg $37
Grades: 5 6 7 8   **972.86**
1. Costa Rica
ISBN 0-516-24884-7 (lib bdg); 978-0-516-24884-4 (lib
bdg)   LC 2006010384
First published 1998
Describes the geography, history, culture, religion, and
people of the small Central American nation of Costa
Rica
Includes bibliographical references

972.87   Panama

DuTemple, Lesley A., 1952-
The Panama Canal. Lerner Publs. 2003 96p il
maps (Great building feats) lib bdg $27.93
Grades: 6 7 8 9   **972.87**
1. Panama Canal
ISBN 0-8225-0079-5   LC 2001-4656

DuTemple, Lesley A., 1952-—*Continued*

Contents: The path between two oceans; The United States and Panama; One canal, three engineers; Culebra cut; Taming the Chagres; Sculpting bays and building locks; The Panama Canal

A history of the building of the Panama Canal, with emphasis on the difficulties of digging a canal where some engineers said it could not be done

"The text is peppered with quotes from letters, speeches, and diaries of those involved in the project. . . . Sidebars present interesting asides. . . . A fascinating and well-documented blend of history and engineering." SLJ

Includes bibliographical references

Hassig, Susan M., 1969-

Panama; [by] Susan Hassig & Lynette Quek. 2nd ed. Marshall Cavendish Benchmark 2007 144p il map (Cultures of the world) lib bdg $42.79 *
Grades: 5 6 7 8   **972.87**
1. Panama
ISBN 978-0-7614-2028-6 (lib bdg); 0-7614-2028-2 (lib bdg)   LC 2006020824
First published 1996

This provides "information on the geography, history, wildlife, governmental structure, economy, cultural diversity, peoples, religion, and culture of Panama." Publisher's note

Includes glossary and bibliographical references

972.91 Cuba

Castro's Cuba; Charles W. Carey Jr., book editor. Greenhaven Press 2004 205p il (History firsthand) $37.95; pa $23.70 *
Grades: 8 9 10 11 12   **972.91**
1. Castro, Fidel, 1926- 2. Cuba—Politics and government
ISBN 0-7377-1654-1; 0-7377-1655-X (pa)
LC 2003-47286

"Through the use of interviews, articles, and first-person narratives, this book focuses on the significance of the 1959 revolution and its aftermath. An extensive introduction explaining events precipitating the rise of Fidel Castro, the revolution, and the current situation in Cuba provides readers with a necessary overview to understand the succeeding chapters." SLJ

Includes bibliographical references

Donovan, Sandra, 1967-

Teens in Cuba; by Sandy Donovan. Compass Point Books 2009 96p il (Global connections) lib bdg $33.26
Grades: 6 7 8 9   **972.91**
1. Teenagers 2. Cuba
ISBN 978-0-7565-3851-4 (lib bdg); 0-7565-3851-3 (lib bdg)   LC 2008-6284

Uncovers the challenges, pastimes, customs and culture of teens in Cuba

This book is "concise and highly readable. . . . Clear, colorful photos and sidebars on a range of topics provide further context. . . . [This title] will enrich young adult collections." SLJ

Includes glossary and bibliographic references

Sheehan, Sean, 1951-

Cuba; [by] Sean Sheehan, Leslie Jermyn. 2nd ed. Benchmark Bks. 2005 144p il map (Cultures of the world) lib bdg $37.07
Grades: 5 6 7 8   **972.91**
1. Cuba
ISBN 0-7614-1965-9   LC 2005009362
First published 1994

This describes the geography, history, government, economy, population, lifestyle, religion, language, arts, leisure, festivals, and food of Cuba

Includes glossary and bibliographical references

Wright, David K., 1943-

Cuba; by David K. Wright. Children's Press 2009 144p il map (Enchantment of the world, second series) lib bdg $38
Grades: 5 6 7 8   **972.91**
1. Cuba
ISBN 978-0-531-12096-5 (lib bdg); 0-531-12096-1 (lib bdg)   LC 2008008423

This describes the geography, history, culture, people, and government of Cuba

Includes bibliographical references

972.92 Jamaica and Cayman Islands

Green, Jen

Jamaica; [by] Jen Green; David J. Howard and Joel Frater, consultants. National Geographic 2008 64p il map (Countries of the world) lib bdg $27.90 *
Grades: 4 5 6 7   **972.92**
1. Jamaica
ISBN 978-1-4263-0300-5 (lib bdg); 1-4263-0300-9 (lib bdg)

This describes the geography, nature, history, people and culture, government, and economy of Jamaica.

Includes glossary and bibligraphical references

Sheehan, Sean, 1951-

Jamaica; [by] Sean Sheehan & Angela Black. 2nd ed. Benchmark Books 2004 144p il map (Cultures of the world) lib bdg $37.07
Grades: 5 6 7 8   **972.92**
1. Jamaica
ISBN 0-7614-1785-0   LC 2004-7676
First published 1996

Introduces the geography, history, religion, government, economy, and culture of Jamaica

"An informative book with captivating pictures, a visually attractive layout, and flowing text. . . . A well-balanced and interesting look at one country's culture." SLJ

Includes glossary and bibliographical references

972.93   Dominican Republic

Foley, Erin, 1967-
Dominican Republic; [by] Erin Foley & Leslie Jermyn. 2nd ed. Marshall Cavendish Benchmark 2005 144p (Cultures of the world) lib bdg $25.95 *

Grades: 5 6 7 8   **972.93**
  1. Dominican Republic
  ISBN 0-7614-1966-7
  First published 1995
"Explores the geography, history, government, economy, people, and culture of the Dominican Republic." Publisher's note
"The material is well organized in easily readable sections, accurately illustrated with well-placed, full-color photographs on every page." SLJ

Rogers Seavey, Lura, 1977-
Dominican Republic; by Lura Rogers and Barbara Radcliffe Rogers. Children's Press 2009 144p il map (Enchantment of the world, second series) lib bdg $37
Grades: 5 6 7 8   **972.93**
  1. Dominican Republic
  ISBN 0-531-12097-X; 978-0-531-12097-2
                        LC 2008000087
Describes the geography, history, culture, religion, and people of the Caribbean island nation of the Dominican Republic.
Includes bibliographical references

972.94   Haiti

Blashfield, Jean F.
Haiti; by Jean F. Blashfield. Children's Press/Scholastic 2008 144p il map (Enchantment of the world, second series) lib bdg $37
Grades: 5 6 7 8   **972.94**
  1. Haiti
  ISBN 978-0-516-25949-9 (lib bdg); 0-516-25949-0 (lib bdg)   LC 2006036853
This describes the geography, history, culture, people, and government of Haiti
Includes bibliographical references

Cheong-Lum, Roseline Ng, 1962-
Haiti; [by] Roseline Ng Cheong-Lum & Leslie Jermyn. 2nd ed. Marshall Cavendish Benchmark 2005 144p il map (Cultures of the world) lib bdg $37.07 *
Grades: 5 6 7 8   **972.94**
  1. Haiti
  ISBN 0-7614-1968-3
  First published 1995
Describes the geography, history, government, economy, culture, peoples, and religion of Haiti
Includes glossary and bibliographical references

972.95   Puerto Rico

Levy, Patricia, 1951-
Puerto Rico; [by] Patricia Levy & Nazry Bahrawi. 2nd ed. Marshall Cavendish Benchmark 2005 144p il map (Cultures of the world) lib bdg $37.07

Grades: 5 6 7 8   **972.95**
  1. Puerto Rico
  ISBN 0-7614-1970-5
  First published 1995
This introduction to Puerto Rico "covers geography, history, government, economy, population, lifestyle, religion, language, arts, leisure, festivals, and food. . . . The material is well organized in easily readable sections, accurately illustrated with well-placed, full-color photographs on every page." SLJ
Includes glossary and bibliographical references

López, José Javier, 1969-
Puerto Rico; [by] José Javier López. Chelsea House Pub. 2006 108p il map (Modern world nations) lib bdg $30
Grades: 7 8 9 10   **972.95**
  1. Puerto Rico
  ISBN 0-7910-8798-0   LC 2005028216
Describes the geography, history, people and culture, politics, and economy of Puerto Rico
Includes bibliographical references

Worth, Richard, 1945-
Puerto Rico in American history. Enslow Publishers 2008 128p il map (From many cultures, one history) lib bdg $23.95
Grades: 6 7 8 9 10   **972.95**
  1. Puerto Rico
  ISBN 978-0-7660-2836-4 (lib bdg); 0-7660-2836-4 (lib bdg)   LC 2006-37087
This is a "book about the ties between Puerto Rico and the U.S. . . . Worth's overview will help to acclimate readers new to the island's history. . . . Writing in short, plain sentences, the author touches upon the commonwealth's ongoing struggle with poverty, migration, and language and the current conflicts about statehood and independence. The book's clean design is inviting, with lots of color-screened boxes, full-color photos, archival artwork, and maps." Booklist
Includes glossary and bibliographical references

972.96   Bahama Islands

Barlas, Robert
Bahamas. Benchmark Bks. 2000 128p il map (Cultures of the world) lib bdg $37.07
Grades: 5 6 7 8   **972.96**
  1. Bahamas
  ISBN 0-7614-0992-0   LC 99-88028
Introduces the geography, history, government, economy, religion, language, arts, leisure activities, festivals, food, and people of this archipelago lying in the Atlantic Ocean off the coast of Florida
Includes bibliographical references

972.97 Leeward Islands

Kras, Sara Louise
Antigua and Barbuda; [by] Sara Louise Kras. Marshall Cavendish Benchmark 2008 144p il map (Cultures of the world) lib bdg $27.95
Grades: 5 6 7 8   **972.97**
1. Antigua and Barbuda
ISBN 978-0-7614-2570-0   LC 2006031537
This describes the geography, history, government, economy, environment, people, and culture of Antigua and Barbuda
Includes glossary and bibliographical references

972.98 Windward and other southern islands

Orr, Tamra
Saint Lucia; [by] Tamra Orr. 2nd ed. Marshall Cavendish Benchmark 2008 144p il map (Cultures of the world) lib bdg $27.95
Grades: 5 6 7 8   **972.98**
1. Saint Lucia
ISBN 978-0-7614-2569-4
First published 1997
This describes the geography, history, government, economy, environment, people, and culture of Saint Lucia
Includes glossary and bibliographical references

Pang, Guek-Cheng, 1950-
Grenada. Benchmark Bks. 2001 128p il map (Cultures of the world) lib bdg $37.07
Grades: 5 6 7 8   **972.98**
1. Grenada
ISBN 0-7614-1160-7   LC 00-47583
Discusses the geography, history, government, economy, and culture of this Caribbean island country
Includes glossary and bibliographical references

972.983 Trinidad and Tobago

Sheehan, Sean, 1951-
Trinidad & Tobago. Benchmark Bks. 2001 128p il maps (Cultures of the world) lib bdg $37.07
Grades: 5 6 7 8   **972.983**
1. Trinidad and Tobago
ISBN 0-7614-1194-1   LC 00-47457
"The exuberance of the many different ethnic groups shines out of the photographs." Horn Book Guide
Includes glossary and bibliographical references

973 United States

America the Beautiful, third series. Children's Press 2008 22v il map lib bdg set$266
Grades: 4 5 6 7   **973**

1. United States
ISBN 0-531-20407-3 (lib bdg); 978-0-531-20407-8 (lib bdg)
Volumes also available separately, $38 each
Replaces America the Beautiful, second series, published 1998-2001; Original series published 1987-1992
Contents: Alabama by Barbara A. Somervill; Alaska by Tamra B. Orr; Arizona by Barbara A. Somervill; California by Tamra B. Orr; Colorado by Barbara A. Somervill; Connecticut by Zachary Kent; Florida by Tamra B. Orr; Georgia by G. S. Prentzas; Hawai'i by Deborah Kent; Illinois by Michael Burgan; Kentucky by Andrew Santella; Louisiana by Allison Lassieur; Maine by Ann Heinrichs; Maryland by Jean F. Blashfield; Massachusetts by Trudi Strain Trueit; Michigan by Lucia Raatma; Nebraska by Ann Heinrichs; Nevada by Ann Heinrichs; New Jersey by Deborah Kent; New York by Barbara A. Somervill; Oklahoma by Tamra B. Orr; Wisconsin by Jean F. Blashfield
This series describes the geography, history, people, economy, and government of each state
"Most students should be able to satisfy their information needs with these polished new editions, and the copious extras and lively presentation will help keep them interested too." Booklist

American history on file; [by] George Ochoa and Melinda Corey, editors. Facts on File 2002 2v unp il set$297
Grades: Professional   **973**
1. United States—History
ISBN 0-8160-4661-1   LC 2002-1673
Also available CD-ROM version
This includes maps, timelines, illustrations and text divided into ten eras of United States history, which may be reproduced for classroom use
Includes bibliographical references

Armstrong, Jennifer, 1961-
The American story; 100 true tales from American history; illustrated by Roger Roth. Alfred A. Knopf 2006 358p il map $34.95; lib bdg $39.99 *
Grades: 4 5 6 7   **973**
1. United States—History
ISBN 0-375-81256-3; 0-375-91256-8 (lib bdg)
                                          LC 2005-34822
"This large, fully illustrated compendium features 100 stories, familiar and lesser known, drawn from America's past and arranged in chronological order. . . . Thanks to writing that is consistently good and sometimes excellent, the tales will certainly hold readers' attention, and brightening nearly every page are lively drawings enhanced by watercolor washes." Booklist
Includes bibliographical references

Bockenhauer, Mark H.

Our fifty states; by Mark H. Bockenhauer and Stephen F. Cunha; foreword by former president Jimmy Carter. National Geographic Society 2004 239p il map $25.95; lib bdg $45.90

Grades: 4 5 6 7　　　　　　　　　**973**

1. United States 2. Reference books

ISBN 0-7922-6402-9; 0-7922-6992-6 (lib bdg)

LC 2004-1190

This "book is organized by regions: the Northeast, Southeast, Midwest, Southwest, and West, with a map of each region and a short history. Four pages are devoted to each state and include basic facts and a map. The full-color photographs are outstanding. Reproductions of archival illustrations depict four important events from each state's history. The final sections offer a paragraph about each of the territories and a page of facts and figures about the United States." SLJ

Includes bibliographical references

Brownstone, David M.

The young nation: America 1787-1861; [by] David M. Brownstone, Irene M. Franck. Grolier Educ. 2002 10v il maps set$339　　**973**

1. United States—History—1783-1865

ISBN 0-7172-5645-6　　　　LC 2002-20047

Contents: v1 A new nation; v2 The early years; v3 The way West; v4 Beyond the Mississippi; v5 Slavery and the coming storm; v6 The new Americans; v7 Women's lives, women's rights; v8 Science, technology, and everyday life; v9 The arts, literature, religion, and education; v10 A growing nation

This "set covers American history during the period beginning with the Constitution and ending with the Civil War. . . . A handsome layout and many excellent pictures, most in full color, give the books an inviting look. The illustrations include many period paintings and engravings as well as maps, documents, and photos of historic sites and reenactments of events." Booklist

Includes bibliographical references

Buckley, Susan

Journeys for freedom; a new look at America's story; [by] Susan Buckley and Elspeth Leacock; illustrations by Rodica Prato. Houghton Mifflin Co. 2006 48p il map $17 *

Grades: 4 5 6 7　　　　　　　　　**973**

1. United States—History

ISBN 978-0-618-22323-7; 0-618-22323-1

LC 2004000974

This "history focuses on 20 individuals' quest for freedom across U.S. history. Some . . . will be familiar, but most will not. The stories, both varied and fascinating, often go beyond the personal. . . . Running along the bottom of each double-page spread is a pictorial map keyed to the text. . . . The authors make excellent use of primary sources. . . . As powerful as it is useful." Booklist

Kids make history; a new look at America's story; [by] Susan Buckley and Elspeth Leacock; Illustrations by Randy Jones. Houghton Mifflin 2006 48p il $17

Grades: 4 5 6 7　　　　　　　　　**973**

1. United States—History

ISBN 978-0-618-22329-9; 0-618-22329-0

LC 2005036309

"This book introduces 20 children in extraordinary times, starting in 1607 with Pocahontas and ending in 2001 with 9/11 as experienced by high school senior Jukay Hsu. Laura Ingalls Wilder; John Rankin, Jr.; and Susie Baker, a young slave celebrating her independence in 1863, are among those included. The text and the highly detailed watercolor illustrations are married with numbers in small red boxes keyed to both elements for clarification. . . . A good browsing choice for children interested in American history." SLJ

Celebrate the states. 2nd ed. Marshall Cavendish Benchmark 2005-2008 40v il map Each group 5v set$213.93 *

Grades: 4 5 6 7　　　　　　　　　**973**

1. United States

ISBN 978-0-7614-1733-0 (group 1); 978-0-7614-2017-0 (group 2); 978-0-7614-2150-4 (group 3); 978-0-7614-2347-8 (group 4); 978-0-7614-2557-1 (group 5); 978-0-7614-2714-8 (group 6); 978-0-7614-0668-6 (group 7); 978-0-7614-3395-8 (group 8)

Also available separate volumes $39.93 each

Replaces the set published 1996-2001

Contents: Group 1: California by Linda Jacobs Altman; Illinois by Marlene Targ Brill; New York by Virginia Schomp; Texas by Carmen Bredeson and Mary Dodson Wade; Virginia by Tracy Barrett; Group 2: Colorado by Eleanor Ayer and Dan Elish; Indiana by Marlene Targ Brill; Louisiana by Suzanne LeVert; Oregon by Rebecca Stefoff; Vermont by Dan Elish; Group 3: Alaska by Rebecca Stefoff; Connecticut by Victoria Sherrow; South Dakota by Melissa McDaniel; Tennessee by Tracy Barrett; Wisconsin by Karen Zeinert and Joyce Hart; Group 4: Florida by Perry Chang and Joyce Hart; Hawaii by Jake Goldberg and Joyce Hart; Iowa by Polly Morrice and Joyce Hart; Michigan by Marlene Targ Brill; Washington, D.C. by Dan Elish; Group 5: Minnesota by Martin Schwabacher and Patricia K Kummer; Ohio by Victoria Sherrow; Rhode Island by Ted Klein; Washington by Rebecca Stefoff; West Virginia by Nancy Hoffman and Joyce Hart; Group 6: Kentucky by Tracy Barrett; Mississippi by David Shirley & Patricia K. Kummer; New Hampshire by Steve Otfinoski; New Mexico by Melissa McDaniel, Ettagale Blauer & Jason Lauré; Wyoming by Guy Baldwin & Joyce Hart; Group 7: Arkansas by Linda Jacobs Altman, Ettagale Blauer, and Jason Lauré; Idaho by Rebecca Stefoff; Maryland by Leslie Pietrzyk and Martha Kneib; Massachusetts by Suzanne LeVert and Tamra B. Orr; New Jersey by Wendy Moragne and Tamra B. Orr; Group 8: Alabama by David Shirely and Joyce Hart; Arizona by Melissa McDaniel and Wendy Mead; Delaware by Michael Schuman and Marlee Richards; Kansas by Ruth Bjorklund and Trudi Strain Trueit; Pennsylvania by Stephen Peters and Joyce Hart

"These titles cover standard facts: geography, history, government, economy, landmarks, and regions. They are attractively illustrated with clear maps, charts, and pie

Celebrate the states—*Continued*
graphs. Photos and reproductions of original documents add to overall effectiveness. . . . Excellent additions for reports or general interest." SLJ

Cole, Sheila
To be young in America; growing up with the country, 1776-1940; [by] Sheila Cole. 1st ed. Little, Brown 2005 146p il $19.99

Grades: 5 6 7 8   **973**
1. Children—United States 2. United States—Social life and customs
ISBN 0-316-15196-3   LC 2004-15109
"Using topics such as home, life in an orphanage, sickness and health, work, school, crime, and war, [the author] shows how each one affected young people over the course of American history. For each of these subject areas, she highlights the experiences of one real child, drawing on historical diaries and other documents that give readers an opportunity to learn about life through that individual's own voice. This is a fascinating book, and also a beautiful one." SLJ
Includes bibliographical references

Hoose, Phillip M., 1947-
We were there, too! young people in U.S. history; [by] Phillip Hoose. Farrar, Straus & Giroux 2001 264p il $28 *

Grades: 5 6 7 8   **973**
1. United States—History 2. Children 3. Youth
ISBN 0-374-38252-2   LC 99-89052
"Melanie Kroupa books"
Biographies of dozens of young people who made a mark in American history, including explorers, planters, spies, cowpunchers, sweatshop workers, and civil rights workers
"A treasure chest of history come to life, this is an inspired collection. . . . Because the book is packed with historical documents, evocatively illustrated . . . and full of eyewitness quotations, it should prove valuable to young historians and researchers." SLJ
Includes bibliographical references

Johnston, Robert D. (Robert Dougall)
The making of America; the history of the United States from 1492 to the present; with a foreword by Laura Bush. National Geographic Soc. 2002 240p il maps $29.95 *

Grades: 5 6 7 8   **973**
1. United States—History
ISBN 0-7922-6944-6   LC 2002-4825
Contents: A new world from many old worlds: beginnings to 1763; A revolutionary age: 1763-1789; The new republic: 1789-1848; A new birth of freedom: Civil War and Reconstruction, 1848-1877; Industry and empire: 1876-1900; Progressivism and the New Deal, 1900-1941; War, prosperity, and social change: 1941-1968; The age of conservatism: 1969-present
This is a "narrative of American history from Columbus through the terrorist attacks on Sept. 11, 2001." Libr Media Connect
"Johnston takes on an enormous, complex topic and

presents an excellent overview for young people. . . . This well-written book does a particularly good job of balancing political and social history." Booklist
Includes bibliographical references

Junior state maps on file. Facts on File 2002 unp il loose-leaf $185
Grades: Professional   **973**
1. United States—Maps
ISBN 0-8160-4752-9
Also available CD-ROM version
"This title offers more than 400 reproducible state maps and fact sheets in a looseleaf, three-ring binder format. . . . After a general section on the United States and its regions, the maps are arranged by geographic region. . . . Five maps and a fact sheet are provided for each state: major cities, outline map, physical features, industry, agriculture and state facts and flag. . . . This is an excellent U.S. geography resource for school and public libraries that do not subscribe to the online version." Am Ref Books Annu, 2003

Leacock, Elspeth, 1946-
Journeys in time; a new atlas of American history; [by] Elspeth Leacock and Susan Buckley; illustrations by Rodica Prato. Houghton Mifflin 2001 48p il maps $15; pa $6.95
Grades: 4 5 6 7   **973**
1. United States—History 2. United States—Historical geography
ISBN 0-395-97956-0; 0-618-31114-9 (pa)
       LC 00-40803
Each double-page spread of this book "takes an individual who was part of a historic movement (such as the Underground Railroad or immigration) and gives a brief narrative outlining his or her circumstances. Added to the text are sequential numbers that indicate major events in each of the twenty journeys. A double-page location map traces the routes each took, using illustrative vignettes marked with corresponding numbers that reference the text." Horn Book

Our country's founders; a book of advice for young people; edited with commentary by William J. Bennett. Simon & Schuster 1998 314p il hardcover o.p. pa $16.95
Grades: 7 8 9 10   **973**
1. United States—History—Sources 2. Social ethics
ISBN 0-689-82106-9; 0-689-84469-7 (pa)
       LC 98-6592
Based on: Our sacred honor (1997)
A book of advice from our nation's founders on how to be a good citizen and a worthy member of civil society
Bennett "draws on a wide variety of primary, secondary, and tertiary sources, ranging from the love letters of John and Abigail Adams to Mason Weems' apocryphal tale of George Washington and the cherry tree. Few young adults are likely to pick this up on their own, but teachers will find it a valuable resource." Booklist
Includes bibliographical references

Panchyk, Richard, 1970-
The keys to American history; understanding
our most important historic documents. Chicago
Review Press 2009 c2008 241p il map $24.95; pa
$19.95 *
Grades: 7 8 9 10 11 12   **973**
   1. United States—History—Sources
   ISBN   978-1-55652-716-6;   1-55652-716-0;
978-1-55652-804-0 (pa); 1-55652-804-3 (pa)
"From the 1606 Great Patent of James I to the 2002
Joint Resolution to Authorize the Use of United States
Armed Forces in Iraq, each document is presented in
context with a concise introductory comment, appearing
both as facsimile reproduction and typescript, and followed by 'What They Were Saying' (excerpts from primary sources that provide perspectives on those documents from major players and other contemporaries)."
Kirkus
"This impressive collection is a valuable resource for
gaining a greater appreciation for and understanding of
our nation's dynamic history." SLJ
   Includes bibliographical references

Yorinks, Adrienne
Quilt of states; quilts by Adrienne Yorinks;
written by Adrienne Yorinks and 50 librarians
from across the nation; librarian contributions
compiled and edited by Jeanette Larson. National
Geographic 2005 122p il $19.95
Grades: 5 6 7 8   **973**
   1. United States—History
   ISBN 0-7922-7285-4   LC 2004-17796
"The United States is stitched together chronologically
in this stunning book that features a quilted spread for
each state. Yorinks enlisted a librarian from each state to
contribute a short entry to point up a few significant
facts that add to the tapestry of the emerging nation. . . .
The quilted representations are not only artistically intricate and beautiful, but also informative. A handsome
book to linger over and learn from." SLJ

973.03   United States—History—
Encyclopedias and dictionaries

Benson, Sonia
UXL encyclopedia of U.S. history; [by] Sonia
Benson, Daniel E. Brannen Jr., and Rebecca
Valentine; Lawrence W. Baker and Sarah
Hermsen, project editors. U.X.L 2008 8v il map
set$485
Grades: 6 7 8 9 10 11 12   **973.03**
   1.   United   States—History—Encyclopedias
2. Reference books
   ISBN 978-1-4144-3043-0   LC 2008022347
"This set offers more than 700 entries addressing various cultural, political, economic, and social events,
trends, movements, and developments that shaped American history. . . . Black-and-white illustrations, reproductions, archival photographs, maps, sidebars, and inserts
accompany the text. . . . Most school and public library
collections that serve students in grades 6 through 12
will want to have this recommended resource." Booklist
   Includes bibliographical references

Exploring American history: from colonial times
to 1877; editors, Tom Lansford, Thomas E.
Woods, Jr. Marshall Cavendish Reference 2008
11v il map set$359.95 *
Grades: 6 7 8 9   **973.03**
   1. United States—History—1600-1775, Colonial period—Encyclopedias 2. United States—History—1775-
1783, Revolution—Encyclopedias 3. Reference books
   ISBN 978-0-7614-7746-4; 0-7614-7746-2
                         LC 2007060896
"This set contains 219 signed articles on the nearly
250 years of American life. . . . The articles have a uniform format and are color coded to indicate broad subject areas—culture, government, laws, people, or places.
. . . The articles present a solid overview of current research as well as a rich array of information. . . . The
set is thoughtfully arranged, easy to use, and accessible
for a wide range of students." Booklist
   Includes bibliographical references

Junior Worldmark encyclopedia of the states;
[Timothy L. Gall and Susan Bevan Gall,
editors] 5th ed. Thomson Gale 2007 4v il map
set $235 *
Grades: 5 6 7 8 9 10   **973.03**
   1. United States—Encyclopedias 2. Reference books
   ISBN 978-1-4144-1106-4 (set); 1-4144-1106-5 (set)
                         LC 2007003910
First published 1996
   Contents: v1 Alabama to Illinois; v2 Indiana to Nebraska; v3 Nevada to South Dakota; v4 Tennessee to
Wyoming, Washington, D.C., Puerto Rico, U.S. Pacific
and Caribbean dependencies and U.S. overview
This reference "includes facts and details on every
state in the U.S., including the District of Columbia and
U.S. dependencies. Entries cover the geography, history,
politics, economy and other facts about each state. Alphabetically arranged entries feature . . . subheadings for
each state. . . . An index of people, places and subjects
[is included]." Publisher's note
   Includes bibliographical references

King, David C., 1933-
Children's encyclopedia of American history.
DK Pub. 2003 304p il map $29.99 *
Grades: 5 6 7 8   **973.03**
   1.   United   States—History—Encyclopedias
2. Reference books
   ISBN 0-7894-8330-0   LC 2002-73388
Full-color maps, photographs, and paintings illustrate
a comprehensive reference guide to American history
"A visually enticing and textually fascinating survey."
SLJ

973.1 United States—Early history to 1607

Stefoff, Rebecca, 1951-
Exploration and settlement. M.E. Sharpe 2008
95p il map (Colonial life) $37.95
Grades: 6 7 8 9 10 11 12   **973.1**
1. America—Exploration 2. Explorers 3. United
States—History—1600-1775, Colonial period
4. Frontier and pioneer life
ISBN 978-0-7656-8108-9   LC 2007-3960
This "presents a solid and highly readable overview of
the theories regarding the peopling of America. Stefoff
skillfully interweaves world events that led up to the European exploration race of the 15th and 16th centuries
and shares illuminating biographies of the key explorers
of the period. . . . The author's conversational tone and
generous use of full-color reproductions, maps, and
sidebars will engage readers." SLJ
Includes glossary and bibliographical references

973.2 United States—Colonial period, 1607-1775

Cooper, Michael L., 1950-
Jamestown, 1607. Holiday House 2007 98p il
$18.95
Grades: 6 7 8 9   **973.2**
1. Jamestown (Va.)—History 2. United States—Histo-
ry—1600-1775, Colonial period
ISBN 978-0-8234-1948-7; 0-8234-1948-7
     LC 2006-02018
This " book presents a history of Jamestown from late
1606, when the *Discovery*, the *Susan Constant*, and the
Godspeed set sail from London to Virginia, to 1609,
when John Smith's injuries forced his return to England.
Based largely on the writings of those present, notably
Smith, the book offers a very readable, detailed account
of the settlers' exploration, deprivation, starvation, illness, and political infighting as well as their relations
with Native Americans. . . . Large black-and-white reproductions of period paintings, engravings, drawings,
maps, and documents illustrate the book." Booklist
Includes bibliographical references

Doherty, Craig A.
The thirteen colonies [series]; by Craig A.
Doherty and Katherine M. Doherty. Facts on File
2005 13v il map set$455
Grades: 4 5 6   **973.2**
1. United States—History—1600-1775, Colonial peri-
od
ISBN 0-8160-5406-1
Also available as separate volumes $35 each
Contents: Connecticut; Delaware; Georgia; Maryland;
Massachusetts; New Hampshire; New Jersey; New York;
North Carolina; Pennsylvania; Rhode Island; South Caro-
lina; Virginia
"Beginning with a brief introduction that discusses
some of the broad reasons why Europeans came to the

New World, both as explorers and settlers, each book's
. . . narrative highlights the people, places, and events
that were important to the development of each colony."
Publisher's note
"The clear narrative style is interesting and accessible.
. . . Clear explanations of events often explored in classrooms make this a valuable resource for school libraries." Voice Youth Advocates
Includes bibliographical references

Gray, Edward G., 1964-
Colonial America: a history in documents.
Oxford Univ. Press 2003 191p il maps (Pages
from history) lib bdg $36.95
Grades: 7 8 9 10   **973.2**
1. United States—History—1600-1775, Colonial period
ISBN 0-19-513747-7   LC 2002-4285
Contents: England expands; New lands, new lives;
Colonists confront first nations; Who built the colonies?;
Ties that bind; A spiritual people; Gentle women and
gentle men; A world of things
This title "presents excerpts from printed and pictorial
primary sources that together form a compact portrait of
the Colonial era in America from the late 15th century
through 1763. . . . Each chapter begins with concise introductory remarks that create a clear context for the
lists, letters, drawings, maps, portraits, ads, diagrams,
news stories, diary entries, poems, and other documentation that follow. . . . A fine source for reports about this
period." SLJ
Includes bibliographical references

Mandell, Daniel R., 1956-
King Philip's war; the conflict over New
England. Chelsea House 2007 144p il map
(Landmark events in Native American history) lib
bdg $35
Grades: 7 8 9 10   **973.2**
1. King Philip's War, 1675-1676 2. Wampanoag Indians 3. New England—History—1600-1775, Colonial
period
ISBN 978-0-7910-9346-7 (lib bdg); 0-7910-9346-8 (lib
bdg)   LC 2006-102258
"Between 1675 and 1676, King Philip's War shattered
native tribes and devastated the new English colonies.
. . . [The] Pequot and Narragansett tribes were subjugat-
ed, and Wampanoag leader King Philip (Metacom) saw
his lands taken and his counselors executed. In July
1675, his warriors started an uprising that gained the
support of other tribes and sent refugees streaming into
Boston. King Philip's War is [an] account of this . . .
confrontation." Publisher's note
This account features "lively writing and direct quotes,
and [is] enhanced by many color and black-and-white
photos, drawings, and illustrations." SLJ
Includes bibliographical references

Philbrick, Nathaniel
The Mayflower and the Pilgrims' New World.
G.P. Putnam's Sons 2008 338p il map $19.99 *
Grades: 7 8 9 10 11 12   **973.2**
1. Bradford, William, 1590-1657 2. Church, Benjamin,
1639-1718 3. Pilgrims (New England colonists)
4. Massachusetts—History—1600-1775, Colonial period 5. Native Americans
ISBN 978-0-399-24795-8; 0-399-24795-5
                                    LC 2007-30669
An adaptation of Mayflower: a story of community,
courage, and war, published 2006 by Viking for adults
"This volume highlights both the Pilgrims' determination to find and settle a home where they could worship
freely and the perilous journey that it took to make that
happen. In accessible prose, the author shatters the
American myth of the landing at Plymouth Rock and the
first Thanksgiving. . . . The various maps, reproductions
of historical documents, photographs of significant locations, and illustrations all come together with the text to
help separate fact from legend and create a realistic,
readable portrayal of the Pilgrims and their first 50 years
in America." SLJ
Includes bibliographical references

Saari, Peggy
Colonial America: almanac. U.X.L 2000 2v
set$110
Grades: 8 9 10 11 12   **973.2**
1. Almanacs 2. United States—History—1600-1775,
Colonial period 3. Reference books
ISBN 0-7876-3763-7   LC 99-39081
Examines the colonial period in America, discussing
both the Native American culture before the arrival of
Europeans and the exploration and settlement of different
parts of the New World
Includes bibliographical references and index

Colonial America: primary sources; Julie
Carnagie, editor. U.X.L 1999 297p il $67
Grades: 8 9 10 11 12   **973.2**
1. United States—History—1600-1775, Colonial period
ISBN 0-7876-3766-1   LC 99-34460
Presents the historical events and social issues of colonial America through twenty-four primary documents, including diary entries, poems, and personal narratives
"Each chapter adds helpful material before and after
the excerpt to explain its importance. Illustrations and
sidebars are used in this volume also, and difficult words
are defined." Booklist

Stanley, George Edward, 1942-
The European settlement of North America
(1492-1763); by George E. Stanley. World
Almanac Library 2005 48p il (Primary source
history of the United States) $30 *
Grades: 5 6 7 8   **973.2**
1. America—Exploration 2. Frontier and pioneer life
3. United States—History—1600-1775, Colonial period
ISBN 0-8368-5824-7
"Stanley includes the efforts of Columbus to gain the
support of the Spanish royals, a lithograph of Columbus

and Queen Isabella, and primary-source material containing the permission for exploration. The motivation of
other early explorers and their financial supporters is
treated in a similar manner. Coverage of Native Americans includes text from the Constitution of the Iroquois
Confederation, c. 1500, used by Benjamin Franklin during the creation of the United States Constitution. . . .
Well-organized, highly attractive." SLJ
Includes bibliographical references

The New Republic (1763-1815); by George E.
Stanley. World Almanac Library 2005 48p il
(Primary source history of the United States) lib
bdg $30 *
Grades: 5 6 7 8   **973.2**
1. United States—History—1600-1775, Colonial period 2. United States—History—1775-1783, Revolution
3. United States—History—1783-1865
ISBN 0-8368-5825-5
"The series of events that lead to the American Revolution is explained, helping readers to understand the
connections of events inherent in historical study. Stanley's analysis of the constitutional debates of the Federal-
ists and Anti-Federalists is exceptionally clear. Well-
organized, highly attractive." SLJ
Includes bibliographical references

Stefoff, Rebecca, 1951-
American voices from Colonial life. Benchmark
Bks. 2003 119p (American voices from--) lib bdg
$32.79 *
Grades: 6 7 8 9   **973.2**
1. United States—History—1600-1775, Colonial peri-
od
ISBN 0-7614-1205-0   LC 2002-3223
Presents the history of the British colonies in North
America, beginning with the Jamestown settlement,
through excerpts from letters, pamphlets, journal entries,
and other documents of the time
Includes glossary and bibliographical references

Cities and towns. M.E. Sharpe 2008 95p il map
(Colonial life) $37.95
Grades: 5 6 7 8 9 10 11 12   **973.2**
1. Cities and towns 2. United States—History—1600-
1775, Colonial period
ISBN 978-0-7656-8109-6   LC 2007-7843
This provides "an informative look into how the forts
and fishing camps of the early Colonial period became
the cities and towns of the 17th and 18th centuries, and
what life was like in these developing communities. The
author's conversational tone and generous use of full-
color reproductions, maps, and sidebars will engage readers." SLJ
Includes glossary and bibliographical references

Voices from colonial America [series] National
Geographic 2005-2007 18v il map ea $21.95
Grades: 5 6 7 8   **973.2**
1. United States—History—1600-1775, Colonial peri-
od
Contents: California 1542-1850 by Robin Doak with
Andrés Reséndez; Connecticut by Michael Burgan; Dela-
ware 1638-1776 by Karen Hossel with Karin Wulf; Flor-

Voices from colonial America [series]—*Continued*

ida 1513-1821 by Matthew C. Cannavale; Georgia 1521-1776 by Robin Doak; Louisiana 1682-1803 by Richard Worth; Maryland 1634-1776 by Robin S. Doak; Massachusetts 1620-1776 by Michael Burgan; New France 1534-1763 by Richard Worth; New Hampshire 1603-1776 by Scott Auden; New Jersey 1609-1776 by Robin Doak with Brendan McConville; New York 1609-1776 by Michael Burgan; North Carolina 1524-1776 by Matthew C. Cannavale; Pennsylvania 1643-1776 by Lisa Trumbauer; Rhode Island 1636-1776 by Jesse McDermott; South Carolina by Robin Doak; Texas 1527-1836 by Michael Teitelbaum; Virginia 1607-1776 by Sandy Pobst

Each volume in this series describes the colonial history of a state illustrated with historical maps and reprints of period artwork, and includes excerpts from first-person accounts.

"Presented in clear, succinct text. . . . this resource, containing a great deal of information, will be a welcome addition to history classes and a great source for report writers." Booklist [review of New Jersey volume]

Includes bibliographical references

973.3 United States—Periods of Revolution and Confederation, 1775-1789

Allen, Thomas B., 1929-

Remember Valley Forge; patriots, Tories, and Redcoats tell their stories; [by] Thomas B. Allen. National Geographic 2007 61p il map $17.95; lib bdg $27.90 *

Grades: 5 6 7 8   973.3

1. Washington, George, 1732-1799 2. Valley Forge (Pa.)—History 3. United States—History—1775-1783, Revolution

ISBN 978-1-4263-0149-0; 978-1-4263-0150-6 (lib bdg)   LC 2007024821

The author "recounts here the activities of Washington and his soldiers during the winter of 1777-8, spent regrouping at Valley Forge, Pennsylvania. . . . Allen's strength is his attention to military details and strategies, but his account is clearly presented and succinctly written as well. . . . Illustrated with reproductions of period artwork, drawings, maps, and a few contemporary photographs." Booklist

American Revolution: primary sources; [compiled by] Linda Schmittroth; Lawrence W. Baker and Stacy A. McConnell, editors. U.X.L 2000 xxxiii, 264p il lib bdg $60

Grades: 8 9 10 11 12   973.3

1. United States—History—1775-1783, Revolution

ISBN 0-7876-3790-4   LC 99-46940

This volume "presents 32 excerpted documents, beginning with the 1765 Stamp Act and ending with Washington's farewell address to the Continental Army in 1783. Each entry has helpful material to give the context for the document. The adjoining margins contain definitions of terms that may be unfamiliar. . . . [This volume] is attractive and easy to use." Booklist

Includes bibliographical references

The **American** revolutionaries: a history in their own words, 1750-1800; edited by Milton Meltzer. Crowell 1987 210p il pa $8.99 hardcover o.p.

Grades: 6 7 8 9   973.3

1. United States—History—1775-1783, Revolution 2. United States—History—1755-1763, French and Indian War

ISBN 0-06-446145-9   LC 86-47846

"Meltzer has assembled a collage of eyewitness accounts, speech and diary excerpts, letters, and other documents for a chronological account of the half century that included the American Revolution. . . . The voices of women who accompanied the troops and of blacks who fought with the army are both represented." Bull Cent Child Books

Aronson, Marc

The real revolution; the global story of American independence. Clarion Books 2005 238p il map lib bdg $21 *

Grades: 7 8 9 10   973.3

1. United States—History—1775-1783, Revolution

ISBN 0-618-18179-2   LC 2005-1088

In this "volume, Aronson investigates the origins of the American Revolution and discovers some startling global connections. The colonies' quest for independence is tied to such seemingly unrelated incidents as Robert Clive's triumph over the French in India in 1750 and John Wilkes's accusations against the king in his newspaper, The North Briton, in the 1760s. . . . This outstanding work is highly compelling reading and belongs in every library." SLJ

Includes bibliographical references

Bigelow, Barbara Carlisle

American Revolution: almanac; [by] Barbara Bigelow and Linda Schmittroth; Stacy A. McConnell, editor. U.X.L 2000 xxxiii, 188, xxxv-xlip il map lib bdg $60

Grades: 5 6 7 8   973.3

1. Almanacs 2. United States—History—1775-1783, Revolution 3. Reference books

ISBN 0-7876-3795-5   LC 99-46939

Provides in-depth background and interpretation of the American Revolution, with short biographies of people relevant to the topics discussed in each chapter

"Illustrations, sidebars, a time line, glossary, and activity ideas enhance the value of the volume." Booklist

Includes bibliographical references

Bobrick, Benson, 1947-

Fight for freedom; the American Revolutionary War. Atheneum Books for Young Readers 2004 96p il map $22.95

Grades: 5 6 7 8   973.3

1. United States—History—1775-1783, Revolution

ISBN 0-689-86422-1   LC 2003-25548

"This large-format volume profiles significant individuals and discusses the progress of the Revolutionary War. . . . Printed in color, most of the illustrations are

Bobrick, Benson, 1947-—*Continued*
period paintings and prints. . . . Students will find the book a well-organized and clearly written introduction to the war." Booklist
Includes glossary and bibliographical references

Fleming, Thomas J., 1927-
Everybody's revolution; a new look at the people who won America's freedom; [by] Thomas Fleming. Scholastic Nonfiction 2006 96p il $19.99 *
Grades: 4 5 6 7   973.3
1. United States—History—1775-1783, Revolution
ISBN 0-439-63404-0   LC 2005051814
A history of the American Revolution, focusing on the roles played by women, young people, and various ethnic groups.
"With an open layout and clean typeface, this clearly written title is attractive and inviting. . . . Fleming's sound offering is an excellent starting point for discussions of the implications of the Revolutionary War in terms of freedom for all people." SLJ
Includes glossary and bibliographical references

The **Founding** of America; Leora Maltz, book editor. Greenhaven Press 2002 236p il (Great speeches in history series) lib bdg $34.95; pa $23.70
Grades: 8 9 10 11 12 Adult   973.3
1. American speeches 2. United States—Politics and government
ISBN 0-7377-0871-9 (lib bdg); 0-7377-0870-0 (pa)
LC 2001-40736
This collection of American speeches from the late 18th and early 19th centuries includes an introductory essay, introductions to each speech and an appendix of biographical sketches
Includes bibliographical references

Freedman, Russell
Give me liberty! the story of the Declaration of Independence. Holiday House 2000 90p il $24.95; pa $12.95 *
Grades: 5 6 7 8 9   973.3
1. United States. Declaration of Independence 2. United States—Politics and government—1775-1783, Revolution
ISBN 0-8234-1448-5; 0-8234-1753-0 (pa)
LC 99-57513
Describes the events leading up to the Declaration of Independence as well as the personalities and politics behind its framing
"Handsomely designed with a generous and thoughtful selection of period art, the book is dramatic and inspiring." Horn Book
Includes bibliographical references

Washington at Valley Forge. Holiday House 2008 100p il map $24.95 *
Grades: 5 6 7 8 9   973.3
1. Washington, George, 1732-1799 2. Valley Forge (Pa.)—History 3. Pennsylvania—History 4. United States—History—1775-1783, Revolution
ISBN 978-0-8234-2069-8; 0-8234-2069-8
LC 2007-52467
This is an "account of the survival of American soldiers while camped at Valley Forge during a crucial period in the American Revolution." Publisher's note
"With his usual clarity of focus and keen eye for telling quotations, Freedman documents how Washington struggled to maintain morale despite hunger, near-nakedness, and freezing conditions. . . . Throughout, high-quality reproductions depict Washington among the men, and with the numerous other influential people who played crucial roles." Booklist

Hughes, Christopher, 1968-
The Constitutional Convention; by Chris Hughes. Blackbirch Press 2005 48p il map (People at the center of) $23.70 *
Grades: 5 6 7 8   973.3
1. United States. Constitutional Convention (1787) 2. United States—Politics and government—1775-1783, Revolution
ISBN 1-56711-918-2   LC 2004-17601
This profiles men who participated in the United States Constitutional Convention such as George Washington, Benjamin Franklin, James Madison, and Alexander Hamilton
"Maps, photos, drawings, and a two-page artistic rendition of the event add to the appeal of [this title]. Great for reports and as supplemental teaching [material]." SLJ
Includes bibliographical references

Hull, Mary
The Boston Tea Party in American history; [by] Mary E. Hull. Enslow Pubs. 1999 128p il map (In American history) lib bdg $26.60
Grades: 6 7 8 9   973.3
1. Boston Tea Party, 1773 2. United States—History—1775-1783, Revolution
ISBN 0-7660-1139-9   LC 98-5798
Presents the people and events connected with the dynamic episode called the Boston Tea Party, which helped to spawn the American Revolution
Includes bibliographical references

Lefkowitz, Arthur S.
Bushnell's submarine; the best kept secret of the American Revolution. Scholastic Nonfiction 2006 136p il map $16.99
Grades: 7 8 9 10   973.3
1. Bushnell, David, 1742-1824 2. United States—History—1775-1783, Revolution 3. Submarines
ISBN 0-439-74352-4   LC 2005-42645
This "book relates the story of America's first submarine, the *Turtle*. Constructed by David Bushnell in time to see action during the American Revolution, the barrel-shaped submersible housed a single man, who sat blindly

Lefkowitz, Arthur S.—*Continued*
in the dark, wet contraption with no power source and dwindling fresh air while operating a variety of levers, pumps, and other devices. The climax of the account is a dramatic attempt to attach a mine to a British warship anchored near New York. Lefkowitz vividly conveys the ingenuity of the inventor, the courage of the Turtle's operator, and the pleasure of discovering lost bits of history." Booklist

Miller, Brandon Marie
Growing up in revolution and the new nation, 1775 to 1800. Lerner Publs. 2003 59p il map (Our America) $26.60
Grades: 5 6 7 8   **973.3**
   1. United States—History—1775-1783, Revolution 2. United States—Social life and customs 3. Children—United States
   ISBN 0-8225-0078-7   LC 2001-4654
Presents details of daily life of American children during the period from 1775 to 1800
The author "does a good job presenting this information by using quotes from primary sources, historical photographs, and artwork from this time period." Libr Media Connect
Includes bibliographical references

Murphy, Jim, 1947-
A young patriot; the American Revolution as experienced by one boy. Clarion Bks. 1996 101p il maps $16; pa $7.95
Grades: 5 6 7 8   **973.3**
   1. Martin, Joseph Plumb, 1760-1850 2. United States—History—1775-1783, Revolution
   ISBN 0-395-60523-7; 0-395-90019-0 (pa)
                    LC 93-38789
"Using Joseph Plumb Martin's first person account of his participation in the Revolutionary War as primary source material, Murphy intertwines this story of one teenager's life as a soldier with broader information about the Revolution, to put Martin's story in context. The handsome, informative, and fascinating look at American history is illustrated with many period reproductions." Horn Book Guide
Includes bibliographical references

Nash, Gary B.
Landmarks of the American Revolution. Oxford University Press 2003 158p il map (American landmarks) lib bdg $30
Grades: 6 7 8 9   **973.3**
   1. Historic sites 2. United States—History—1775-1783, Revolution
   ISBN 0-19-512849-4   LC 2002-14152
"Published in association with the National Register of Historic Places, National Park Service, and the National Parks Foundation"
   Contents: Lexington Green; Independence Hall, Independence National; Valley Forge National Historic Park; Marblehead Historic District; Faneuil Hall; Peyton Randolph House; John and Abigail Adams House, Adams; Johnson Hall; Old Saint Mary's Episcopal Church; Old South Meeting House; Francis Hopkinson House; Yorktown Battlefield, Colonial National Historic Park

"Written with the idea that historic sites can be considered primary sources, this book skillfully demonstrates the 'power of places.' Traditional documents, such as excerpts from letters, broadsides, and maps, as well as well-placed quotes, are incorporated into the text. The places include churches, halls, homes, and battlefields, covering the many facets of the Revolution: political, religious, and actual battles. . . . This well-organized book includes clear, full-color photographs or reproductions and a small inset map for each site." SLJ
Includes bibliographical references

Renehan, Edward J., 1956-
The Treaty of Paris; the precursor to a new nation; [by] Edward J. Renehan, Jr. Chelsea House 2007 121p il map (Milestones in American history) lib bdg $35
Grades: 7 8 9 10   **973.3**
   1. Treaty of Paris (1783) 2. United States—History—1775-1783, Revolution
   ISBN 0-7910-9352-2 (lib bdg); 978-0-7910-9352-8 (lib bdg)   LC 2006034129
This describes the treaty signed in Paris in 1782 in which Benjamin Franklin, John Adams, and John Jay worked to bring about British recognition of American independence and a cessation to hostilities.
The book has "well-reproduced archival photos and drawings with explanatory captions. . . . [and an] open layout and lively [text]." SLJ
Includes bibliographical references

The **Revolutionary** War. Grolier Educ. 2002 10v il maps set$309   **973.3**
   1. United States—History—1775-1783, Revolution 2. Reference books
   ISBN 0-7172-5553-0   LC 2001-18998
   Contents: v1 The road to rebellion; v2 The shot heard around the world; v3 Taking up arms; v4 The spirit of 1776; v5 1777, year of decision; v6 The road to Valley Forge; v7 War of attrition; v8 The American cause in peril; v9 The turn of the tide; v10 An independent nation
This "set provides broad coverage of the American Revolution. Each volume chronicles a specific period, beginning with the causes; moving through the political and military events of the conflict; and ending with the adoption of the Constitution, Washington's presidency, and Westward expansion after the war. The books offer considerable background material and objectively discuss how civilian, governmental, diplomatic, and military actions influenced the course of events. . . . These books provide enough detail to serve researchers, but they are also interesting enough to appeal to general readers." SLJ
Includes bibliographical references

Stewart, Gail, 1949-
Life of a soldier in Washington's army; by Gail B. Stewart. Lucent Bks. 2003 112p il map (American war library, American Revolution) lib bdg $21.96
Grades: 7 8 9 10   **973.3**
   1. Soldiers—United States 2. United States—History—1775-1783, Revolution
   ISBN 1-59018-215-4   LC 2002-6602

Stewart, Gail, 1949— *Continued*

Discusses the training, organization, diversity, fighting and survival skills, daily routine, diseases, fears, and morale of the first army of the United States

This volume is "thorough, but not overwhelming." SLJ

Includes bibliographical references

973.4　United States—Constitutional period, 1789-1809

Collier, Christopher, 1930-

Building a new nation; the Federalist era, 1789-1801; [by] Christopher Collier, James Lincoln Collier. Benchmark Bks. 1999 95p il (Drama of American history) lib bdg $35.64 *

Grades: 6 7 8 9　　　　　　　　　**973.4**

1. United States—Politics and government—1783-1809 2. United States—History—1783-1809

ISBN 978-0-7614-0777-5 (lib bdg); 0-7614-07774 (lib bdg)　　　　　　　　LC 97-26491

Examines the events and personalities involved in the political development of the United States in the period following the creation of the Constitution

Includes bibliographical references

Corrick, James A.

The Louisiana Purchase. Lucent Bks. 2001 108p il maps (World history series) lib bdg $27.45

Grades: 7 8 9 10　　　　　　　　　**973.4**

1. Louisiana Purchase

ISBN 1-56006-637-7　　　　　　LC 00-9156

Examines the Louisiana Purchase, discussing the negotiation of the treaty with France, the formation of Louisiana, taking possession of the land, and the exploration, growth, and settlement of the territory

This overview is "well-written . . . [and] thought-provoking." SLJ

Includes bibliographical references

Lanier, Shannon

Jefferson's children; the story of one American family; by Shannon Lanier and Jane Feldman; with photographs by Jane Feldman; and an introduction by Lucian K. Truscott IV. Random House 2000 144p il hardcover o.p. pa $16.95

Grades: 7 8 9 10　　　　　　　　　**973.4**

1. African Americans—Biography 2. Racially mixed people 3. United States—Race relations

ISBN 0-375-80597-4; 0-375-82168-6 (pa)

LC 00-44551

This is an "anthology of personal meditations by a variety of Jefferson's living descendants. Edited by Shannon Lanier, a descendant through Sally's son Madison Hemings's line, the portraits that emerge are as generous and jumbled as America itself. The statements range from hostile to conciliatory to indifferent to eloquent." NY Times Book Rev

Includes bibliographical references

Schlaepfer, Gloria G.

The Louisiana Purchase; [by] Gloria G. Schlaepfer. Franklin Watts 2005 63p il map lib bdg $25.50

Grades: 5 6 7 8　　　　　　　　　**973.4**

1. Louisiana Purchase

ISBN 0-531-12300-6　　　　　LC 2005001465

"Watts library"

"Schlaepfer tells the story of 'the greatest land deal in American history.'. . . Black-and-white and color illustrations, maps, sidebars, and time lines enhance the well-organized [text]." SLJ

Includes bibliographical references

Stefoff, Rebecca, 1951-

American voices from the new republic, 1783-1830. Benchmark Books 2004 c2005 xxiii, 116p (American voices from--) lib bdg $34.21 *

Grades: 6 7 8 9　　　　　　　　　**973.4**

1. United States—History—1783-1865

ISBN 0-7614-1695-1　　　　　　LC 2004-11391

Contents: Birth of a nation; Forming a new government; Presidents and parties; International affairs; American affairs; African Americans and slavery; Arts and sciences; The age of new possibilities

Describes, through excerpts from diaries, speeches, newspaper articles, and other documents of the time, United States history from 1783 to 1830. Includes review questions.

973.5　United States—1809-1845

Bowes, John P., 1973-

Black Hawk and the War of 1832; removal in the north; [by] John P. Bowes. Chelsea House 2007 131p bibl il map (Landmark events in Native American history) lib bdg $35

Grades: 6 7 8 9　　　　　　　　　**973.5**

1. Black Hawk, Sauk chief, 1767-1838 2. Sauk Indians 3. Black Hawk War, 1832

ISBN 978-0-7910-9342-9 (lib bdg); 0-7910-9342-5 (lib bdg)　　　　　　　　LC 2007004927

This "provides a clear overview of early American expansion in the Northwest Territory, from the 1780s through the 1930s, detailing government actions and policies of Indian Removal and how they specifically affected the Sauks and Mesquakies, now known as the Sac and Fox tribes. . . . The battles that ensued (both intertribal and against the U.S. forces) are described, as are the policies created during this period. . . . Attractive color paintings, maps, and photographs appear throughout." SLJ

Includes bibliographical references

Childress, Diana

The War of 1812; [by] Diana Childress. Lerner Publications Co. 2004 80p il map (Chronicle of America's wars) lib bdg $27.93

Grades: 5 6 7 8　　　　　　　　　**973.5**

1. War of 1812

ISBN 0-8225-0800-1　　　　　　LC 2003-18805

Childress, Diana—*Continued*
Contents: The road to war; Losses on land, victories at sea; The pattern changes; A new front and a victory in the Northwest; The Creek vanquished, the last invasion; The British counterattack; A dramatic end
This describes the events of the War of 1812 and focusing on the impact the war had on America and its people.
Includes glossary and bibliographical references

Edelman, Rob
The War of 1812; by Rob Edelman and Audrey Kupferberg. Blackbirch Press 2005 48p il map (People at the center of) $23.70
Grades: 5 6 7 8   **973.5**
  1. War of 1812
  ISBN 1-56711-926-3   LC 2004-16944
This profiles 15 people connected with the War of 1812 such as Thomas Jefferson, Tecumseh, Jean Laffite, Francis Scott Key, William Henry Harrison, and Oliver Hazard Perry.
Includes bibliographical references

Greenblatt, Miriam
War of 1812; John S. Bowman, general editor. updated ed. Facts on File 2003 166p il maps (America at war) lib bdg $35
Grades: 7 8 9 10   **973.5**
  1. War of 1812
  ISBN 0-8160-4933-5   LC 2002-9555
  First published 1994
Contents: "The darkest day;" "Free trade and sailors' rights;" Warriors and war hawks; The United States on the eve of war; "Go march to Canada;" The naval war; "O'er the land of the free"; The war in the South; Ghent, Hartford, and peace
An account of the events surrounding the War of 1812 between the newly established United States and Great Britain
This offers "high-quality writing . . . [a] wealth of information and good organization." SLJ
Includes glossary and bibliographical references

Marker, Sherry, 1941-
Plains Indian wars; John S. Bowman, general editor. Updated ed. Facts on File 2003 164p il maps (America at war) lib bdg $35 *
Grades: 7 8 9 10   **973.5**
  1. Native Americans—Wars 2. Native Americans—Great Plains
  ISBN 0-8160-4931-9   LC 2002-9556
  First published 1996
This is an account of the wars between Plains Indians and white settlers in the American West in the 19th century.
"Marker does an excellent job of detailing the cultural and social complexity of the many tribes of the Great Plains while offering both a political and social picture of the U.S. Army at this time. The work concludes with an excellent chapter on the history of the stereotypes of the Plains Indians." SLJ
Includes glossary and bibliographical references

Stewart, Mark
The Indian Removal Act; forced relocation; by Mark Stewart. Compass Point Books 2007 96p il map (Snapshots in history) $23.95
Grades: 6 7 8 9   **973.5**
  1. Cherokee Indians 2. Native Americans—Government relations
  ISBN 978-0-7565-2452-4; 0-7565-2452-0
              LC 2006027084
Profiles the "Trail of Tears," the forced removal of five Southeastern Native American tribes to land west of the Mississippi River during the winter of 1838 and 1839.
"The book organizes a good deal of historical information into a cogent presentation. . . . Illustrations, many in color, include photos and maps as well as period engravings, portraits, and documents." Booklist
Includes glossary and bibliographical references

Warrick, Karen Clemens
The War of 1812; "We have met the enemy and they are ours". Enslow Pubs. 2002 128p il maps (American war series) lib bdg $26.60
Grades: 6 7 8 9   **973.5**
  1. War of 1812
  ISBN 0-7660-1854-7   LC 2001-4120
Traces the history of the War of 1812, examining the maritime and boundary issues that caused it and highlighting the roles of famous personalities, including Oliver Hazard Perry, Andrew Jackson, and Dolley Madison
"With a text that is less dry than many history books, this title will earn its keep as a circulating resource for assignments. . . . [This book has] numerous black-and-white illustrations, a time line, solid footnotes, and chapters that begin with relevant quotes." SLJ
Includes bibliographical references

973.6   United States—1845-1861

Bardhan-Quallen, Sudipta
The Mexican-American War; by Sudipta Bardhan-Quallen. Blackbirch Press 2005 48p il map (People at the center of) $23.70
Grades: 5 6 7 8   **973.6**
  1. Mexican War, 1846-1848
  ISBN 1-56711-927-1   LC 2004-13973
This offers biographical profiles of 15 people prominent in the Mexican War of 1846-1848.
This is a "unique and easily accessible [presentation] of biographical and historical information. . . . Maps, photos, drawings, . . . add to the appeal. . . . Great for reports." SLJ
Includes bibliographical references

Carey, Charles W.
The Mexican War; "Mr. Polk's war"; [by] Charles W. Carey, Jr. Enslow Pubs. 2002 128p il (American war series) lib bdg $26.60
Grades: 6 7 8 9   **973.6**
  1. Mexican War, 1846-1848
  ISBN 0-7660-1853-9   LC 2001-817

Carey, Charles W.—*Continued*

This "account of the 1846-1848 war addresses the origins, strategies, battles, and people involved in the conflict. The ramifications of the war for each country are discussed in separate chapters. . . . [This volume has] numerous black-and-white illustrations, a time line, solid footnotes, and chapters that begin with relevant quotes." SLJ

Includes bibliographical references

Collier, Christopher, 1930-

Hispanic America, Texas, and the Mexican War, 1835-1850; [by] Christopher Collier, James Lincoln Collier. Benchmark Bks. (Tarrytown) 1999 94p il map (Drama of American history) $31.36 *

Grades: 6 7 8 9   **973.6**

1. Mexican War, 1846-1848 2. Southwestern States—History

ISBN 0-7614-0780-4   LC 97-34962

Examines the settlement of the area that became the southwestern portion of the United States, detailing how it evolved from land settled by Native Americans, to Spanish territory, to states that were pawns between the North and South prior to the Civil War

Includes bibliographical references

Slavery and the coming of the Civil War, 1831-1861; [by] Christopher Collier, James Lincoln Collier. Benchmark Bks. (Tarrytown) 2000 93p il map (Drama of American history) lib bdg $31.36 *

Grades: 6 7 8 9   **973.6**

1. Slavery—United States 2. United States—History—1815-1861 3. United States—History—1861-1865, Civil War

ISBN 0-7614-0817-7   LC 98-2620

Discusses attitudes and events that led up to the Civil War, particularly the institution of slavery

This title is "clearly written. . . . Includes many maps and full color as well as black-and-white photos and reproductions." SLJ

Includes bibliographical references

Feldman, Ruth Tenzer

The Mexican-American War; [by] Ruth Tenzer Feldman. Lerner Publications Co. 2004 88p il map (Chronicle of America's wars) lib bdg $27.93

Grades: 5 6 7 8   **973.6**

1. Mexican War, 1846-1848

ISBN 0-8225-0831-1   LC 2003-23395

Contents: Bordering on war; Manifest destiny; Rough and ready; Continuing conflict; Conquering peace; March to Mexico City; The struggle for peace; Two nations, one border

This chronicles the events of the Mexican War of 1846-1848 focusing the impact the war had on America and its people.

Includes glossary and bibliographical references

973.7   United States— Administration of Abraham Lincoln, 1861-1865. Civil War

Allen, Thomas B., 1929-

Mr. Lincoln's high-tech war; how the North used the telegraph, railroads, surveillance balloons, ironclads, high-powered weapons, and more to win the Civil War; [by] Thomas B. Allen and Roger MacBride Allen. National Geographic 2009 144p il $18.95; lib bdg $25.90 *

Grades: 5 6 7 8 9 10   **973.7**

1. Lincoln, Abraham, 1809-1865 2. United States—History—1861-1865, Civil War 3. Technology—History

ISBN   978-1-4263-0379-1;   1-4263-0379-3; 978-1-4263-0380-7 (lib bdg); 1-4263-0380-7 (lib bdg)
LC 2008024546

"Well researched and clearly written, the book discusses the course of the Civil War in terms of new technology, from the ironclad and the submarine to the rapid-fire, repeating rifle and the use of railroads to carry troops and supplies. . . . The many illustrations include captioned black-and-white reproductions of period prints, paintings, and photos as well as clearly labeled drawings. . . . [Readers] will gain a fascinating perspective on why the war progressed as it did and how it was ultimately won." Booklist

Includes bibliographical references

Anderson, Maxine

Great Civil War projects you can build yourself. Nomad Press 2005 140p il $14.95

Grades: 7 8 9 10   **973.7**

1. United States—History—1861-1865, Civil War 2. Handicraft

ISBN 0-9749344-1-0

From uniforms and submarines to potato cannons and regimental flags, this interactive book explores the history and inventions of the Civil War by providing building projects and activities.

"Besides the drawings that accompany these projects, other illustrations include many period photographs and engravings. . . . Useful for Civil War reenactments as well as school projects." Booklist

Includes glossary and bibliographical references

Armstrong, Jennifer, 1961-

Photo by Brady; a picture of the Civil War. Atheneum Books For Young Readers 2005 160p il $18.95

Grades: 6 7 8 9 10   **973.7**

1. Brady, Mathew B., ca. 1823-1896 2. United States—History—1861-1865,   Civil   War 3. Photography—History

ISBN 0-689-85785-3   LC 2004-8967

"Armstrong chronicles the Civil War from Lincoln's election to his death with both a storylike narrative of events and a photo-essay. . . . This book is also a look at early photographic techniques and offers a description of [Mathew] Brady's rare collection. . . . When readers

Armstrong, Jennifer, 1961-—*Continued*

remember that the pictures are more than 100 years old, they should recognize their exquisiteness, grandeur, and genius." SLJ

Includes bibliographical references

Barney, William L.

The Civil War and Reconstruction; a student companion. Oxford Univ. Press 2001 368p il maps (Oxford student companions to American history) $60

Grades: 7 8 9 10   **973.7**

1. Reconstruction (1865-1876) 2. United States—History—1861-1865, Civil War

ISBN 0-19-511559-7   LC 00-57444

This reference guide includes "articles on the military, political, social, economic, and cultural aspects of the war and its aftermath, as well as biographical sketches of major figures." SLJ

"The book is encyclopedic in format, with many useful access points, and bibliographic information is located both at the ends of the articles and in several appendixes that suggest books, historic sites and addresses, and Web sites." Voice Youth Advocates

Includes bibliographical references

Beller, Susan Provost, 1949-

Billy Yank and Johnny Reb; soldiering in the Civil War. Twenty-First Century Books 2008 112p il map (Soldiers on the battlefront) lib bdg $33.26

Grades: 5 6 7 8   **973.7**

1. Soldiers—United States 2. United States—History—1861-1865, Civil War

ISBN 978-0-8225-6803-2; 0-8225-6803-9

       LC 2006010240

First published 2000

Describes military life for the average soldier in the Civil War, including camp life, diseases, and conditions for the wounded and prisoners of war. Includes excerpts from first-person accounts, letters, and diaries

The author "presents a good deal of solid information in an interesting manner. . . . Good black-and-white reproductions, mainly of photographs from the 1860s, appear throughout the book." Booklist [review of 2000 ed]

Includes bibliographical references

Bolden, Tonya

Cause: Reconstruction America, 1863-1877. Knopf 2005 138p il $19.95; lib bdg $21.99 *

Grades: 7 8 9 10   **973.7**

1. Reconstruction (1865-1876) 2. United States—History—1865-1898

ISBN 0-375-82795-1; 0-375-92795-6 (lib bdg)

"This examination of America during Reconstruction covers Lincoln's Proclamation of Amnesty and Reconstruction, the Civil Rights Act of 1866, the troubles of freed slaves, the expansion of the nation and the plight of Native Americans, the 15th Amendment, and the women's suffrage movement. While this is well-documented nonfiction, Bolden writes in the voice of a storyteller. The excellent graphics include archival photos, political cartoons, and primary resources." SLJ

Bolotin, Norm, 1951-

Civil War A to Z; a young readers' guide to over 100 people, places, and points of importance; [by] Norman Bolotin. Dutton Children's Bks. 2002 148p il map $19.99

Grades: 4 5 6 7   **973.7**

1. United States—History—1861-1865, Civil War

ISBN 0-525-46268-6   LC 2001-33370

Alphabetically arranged articles present over 100 people, places, and points of importance of the Civil War

"Bolotin has a good eye for what students need to understand about the war and provides a great deal of information, skillfully whittled down to its most salient points. . . . The format is attractive, with numerous photographs." Booklist

Includes glossary and bibliographical references

Carlisle, Rodney P.

Civil War and Reconstruction. Facts on File 2008 452p il map (Eyewitness history) $75

Grades: 7 8 9 10   **973.7**

1. United States—History—1861-1865, Civil War—Sources 2. Reconstruction (1865-1876)

ISBN 978-0-8160-6347-5   LC 2006-35425

First published 1991 under the authorship of Joe H. Kirchberger

"This illustrated chronology of the Civil War contains over 100 black-and-white photographs (mostly from the Library of Congress Prints and Photographs Division), 16 maps, and biographies of 50 key figures in the era. Each period-based chapter offers a narrative that delves into deeper issues of the causation of war; a chronicle of events, detailed to the week; and eyewitness testimony, including diaries, journals, correspondence, editorials, and news accounts." Choice

Includes bibliographical references

The **Civil** War. Grolier 2004 10v il map set$309

Grades: 5 6 7 8   **973.7**

1. United States—History—1861-1865, Civil War 2. Reference books

ISBN 0-7172-5883-1   LC 2003-49315

Contents: v1 Abolition-Camp followers; v2 Camp life-Custer, George A.; v3 Daily life-Flags; v4 Florida-Hill, Ambrose P.; v5 Home Front, Confederacy-Legacy of the Civil War; v6 Lincoln, Abraham-Mobile Bay, Battle of; v7 Money and banking-Politics, Confederate; v8 Politics, Union-Shenandoah Valley; v9 Sheridan, Philip H.-Trade; v10 Training-Zouaves

This set "features detailed multipage articles that address significant individuals, battles, events, and conditions of the American Civil War." Booklist

"The variety of topics addressed in this set will give students a wide perspective on the conflict. . . . The clearly written, objective entries, ranging in length from one to six pages, all offer basic analysis." SLJ

The **Civil** War; James Tackach, book editor. Greenhaven Press 2004 186p il (Turning points in world history) lib bdg $34.95

Grades: 7 8 9 10   **973.7**

1. United States—History—1861-1865, Civil War

ISBN 0-7377-1114-0   LC 2003-64297

The Civil War—*Continued*

"Comprised of 17 essays, this book is divided into four chapters: 'A Nation Divides: The Causes of the Civil War,' 'Early Battlefield Victories and the Prospect of European Intervention Fuel the South's Hope for Independence,' 'The North Gains the Advantage,' and 'A Changed Nation.' Many of the most respected Civil War historians . . . are excerpted. . . . Outstanding features of the book are discussion questions and the appendix of documents that are sure to inspire additional research and assist classroom teachers." SLJ

Includes bibliographical references

Cloud Tapper, Suzanne

The abolition of slavery; fighting for a free America; [by] Suzanne Cloud Tapper. Enslow Publishers 2006 128p il (The American saga) lib bdg $31.93

Grades: 7 8 9 10   **973.7**

1. Slavery—United States 2. Abolitionists
ISBN 0-7660-2605-1   LC 2006001739

"The book begins with descriptions of two murders. . . . The killings point to the indiscriminate hatred of both slave and anti-slaver. Following the account of the murders, the author describes the dilemma of slavery that faced the Founding Fathers, then moves through the decades to discuss the growing political, ethical, and religious opposition to the institution, and ends with the Civil War. . . . The author makes great use of direct quotes from those who lived the events, newspaper accounts, and excerpts from court proceedings. Black-and-white and color archival photographs and illustrations depict slave life. Clearly written and well researched, this logically organized book is an excellent purchase for most libraries." SLJ

Includes glossary and bibliographical references

Collier, Christopher, 1930-

The Civil War, 1860-1865; [by] Christopher Collier, James Lincoln Collier. Benchmark Bks. (Tarrytown) 1998 95p il map (Drama of American history) lib bdg $31.36 *

Grades: 6 7 8 9   **973.7**

1. United States—History—1861-1865, Civil War
ISBN 0-7614-0818-5   LC 97-49178

Examines the people and events involved in the bloody war that pitted the Northern states against those that seceded to form the Confederacy

Includes bibliographical references

DeFord, Deborah H.

African Americans during the Civil War; [by] Deborah H. DeFord. Chelsea House 2006 112p il map (Slavery in the Americas) $35

Grades: 6 7 8 9   **973.7**

1. African American soldiers 2. United States—History—1861-1865, Civil War 3. African Americans—History
ISBN 0-8160-6138-6   LC 2005021497

This "covers not only African Americans but also the forces that created the 'U.S. Colored Troops' and the spread of rights during and after the war. . . . Clearly

written, accessible, and well organized, [this] volume is illustrated with black-and-white drawings, period photographs, and explanatory text boxes." SLJ

Includes bibliographical references

Golay, Michael, 1951-

Civil War. updated ed. Facts on File 2003 xxi, 234p il map (America at war) $35

Grades: 7 8 9 10   **973.7**

1. United States—History—1861-1865, Civil War
ISBN 0-8160-4934-3   LC 2002-6371
First published 1992

Contents: Irrepressible conflict; Purged with blood; On to Richmond; The river war; The uses of sea power; America's bloodiest day; The war at home; Jubilee; Battles lost and won; Long remember: Gettysburg; Siege at Vicksburg; In the charnel house; The battle for Chattanooga; Tecumseh the Great; Grant and Lee; Epilogue: touched with fire

This includes "not only the military history of the American Civil War, but also the politics on both sides, the homefronts, the prologue, and the aftermath. . . . The battle maps are unusually clear. . . . The text throughout the book is precise and yet interesting and even colorful. The author has used many contemporary accounts and quotations." Am Ref Books Annu, 2004

Includes glossary and bibliographical references

Hansen, Joyce

Freedom roads: searching for the Underground Railroad; [by] Joyce Hansen and Gary McGowan. Cricket Bks. 2003 164p il maps $18.95 *

Grades: 5 6 7 8   **973.7**

1. Underground railroad 2. Slavery—United States
ISBN 0-8126-2673-7   LC 2002-13711

Contents: Running South: artifacts from Fort Mose; Land of the free: History on a ship's log; A more perfect Union: learning from the law; Running: The WPA slave narratives; Steal away: the enslaved speak through spirituals; I will be heard: archaeology meets an oral tradition; Midnight seekers after liberty: anecdotes and memories uncover the past; The last stop: outrunning the fugitive slave laws; A mystery: when history keeps a secret; The search continues

The authors "explore the ways historians have traced the path of the enslaved as they traveled northward to freedom. . . . The authors demonstrate how the study of artifacts, laws, slave narratives and more contribute to an understanding of how this crucial chapter of American history evolved. Reproductions of period photographs and documents extend the value of this well-researched volume." Publ Wkly

Includes bibliographical references

Hillstrom, Kevin

American Civil War: almanac; [by] Kevin Hillstrom and Laurie Collier Hillstrom; Lawrence W. Baker, editor. U.X.L 2000 xlvi, 251, xlvii-lxip il $60

Grades: 8 9 10 11 12   **973.7**

1. Almanacs 2. United States—History—1861-1865, Civil War 3. Reference books
ISBN 0-7876-3823-4   LC 99-46918

Hillstrom, Kevin—_Continued_
Describes and interprets the era of the Civil War, its events, and topics with viewpoints, definitions, report topics, chronologies, sidebars, and statistics

"Added features such as 'Words to Know' and 'People to Know' sidebars in each chapter and research and activity ideas help make the volume a good jumping-off point for research on Civil War-era events." Booklist
Includes bibliographical references

American Civil War: primary sources; [by] Kevin Hillstrom and Laurie Collier Hillstrom; Lawrence W. Baker, editor. U.X.L 2000 xxxi, 176, xxxiii-xliiip il $60
Grades: 8 9 10 11 12   **973.7**
   1. United States—History—1861-1865, Civil War—Sources
   ISBN 0-7876-3824-2   LC 99-46919
   This volume "offers 14 full or excerpted speeches and written works. Each entry provides context, telling students what to keep in mind while reading the sources, as well as 'what happened next.' The speeches and writings come from Frederick Douglass, Abraham Lincoln, William Tecumseh Sherman, and Harriet Beecher Stowe, among others." Booklist

Experiencing the American Civil War; [by] Kevin Hillstrom and Laurie Collier Hillstrom; Lawrence W. Baker, editor. U.X.L 2002 2v il maps lib bdg set$105
Grades: 8 9 10 11 12   **973.7**
   1. United States—History—1861-1865, Civil War
   2. Reference books
   ISBN 0-7876-5585-6
   Contents: v1 Novels; nonfiction books; v2 Short stories; poems; plays; films; songs
   "Discussing 25 original works . . . this set serves as an introduction for young adults to the wide range of creative treatments of the Civil War." Booklist
   "Although most useful as a supplementary source for classroom study, this reference tool has sufficient visual and textual appeal to arouse browers' curiosity about the materials discussed." SLJ
   Includes bibliographical references

Holzer, Harold
The president is shot! the assassination of Abraham Lincoln. Boyds Mills Press 2004 181p il $17.95
Grades: 5 6 7 8   **973.7**
   1. Lincoln, Abraham, 1809-1865—Assassination
   ISBN 1-56397-985-3
   This is a "description of the violent end to Lincoln's life. Holzer provides the Civil War context of the event and then details April 14 and 15, 1865." SLJ
   "A page-turner of a text, a fascinating array of photos and archival illustrations, and an event that changed the course of history: all these elements combine in this strong, highly readable book." Booklist
   Includes bibliographical references

Hughes, Chris
The Battle of Antietam. Blackbirch Press 2001 32p il maps (Civil War) $22.45
Grades: 6 7 8 9   **973.7**
   1. Antietam (Md.), Battle of, 1862
   ISBN 1-56711-551-9   LC 01-1572
   "Triangle histories"
   Describes the 1862 battle in Maryland
   This offers "a readable text that makes judicious use of quotes from participants. . . . Supplemental information about notable figures, locations, and incidents is included in sidebars, while historical reproductions and occasional photographs add further accessibility." Horn Book Guide
   Includes glossary and bibliographical references

Jordan, Anne Devereaux, 1943-
The Civil War; by Anne Devereaux Jordan; with Virginia Schomp. Marshall Cavendish Benchmark 2007 72p il (Drama of African-American history) lib bdg $34.21 *
Grades: 5 6 7 8   **973.7**
   1. United States—History—1861-1865, Civil War
   2. African Americans—History
   ISBN 978-0-7614-2179-5 (lib bdg); 0-7614-2179-3 (lib bdg)   LC 2006012472
   Describes the role of African Americans during the Civil War (1861-1865)
   Includes glossary and bibliographical references

King, David C., 1933-
The Battle of Gettysburg. Blackbirch Press 2001 32p il maps (Civil War) $22.45
Grades: 6 7 8 9   **973.7**
   1. Gettysburg (Pa.), Battle of, 1863
   ISBN 1-56711-550-0   LC 2001-2569
   "Triangle histories"
   Discusses the strategy, tactics, actual fighting, aftermath, and key figures involved in one of the Civil War's pivotal battles at Gettysburg, Pennsylvania
   This offers "a readable text that makes judicious use of quotes from participants. . . . Supplemental information about notable figures, locations, and incidents is included in sidebars, while historical reproductions and occasional photographs add further accessibility." Horn Book Guide
   Includes glossary and bibliographical references

Landau, Elaine
Fleeing to freedom on the Underground Railroad; the courageous slaves, agents, and conductors. Twenty-First Century Books 2006 88p il map (People's history) lib bdg $26.60 *
Grades: 5 6 7 8   **973.7**
   1. Underground railroad 2. Slavery—United States
   3. Abolitionists
   ISBN 978-0-8225-3490-7 (lib bdg); 0-8225-3490-8 (lib bdg)   LC 2005020358
   "Landau discusses the history of slavery in the United States, slave life, the Underground Railroad, and the leaders, both black and white, of antislavery organizations. Three chapters outline specifics of slaves' escapes.

Landau, Elaine—*Continued*

. . . An outstanding feature of this book is the use of primary sources and quotes from former slaves, contemporary newspaper accounts, and reminiscences of escaped slaves. . . . Excellent historical photographs and illustrations enhance the text." SLJ

Includes bibliographical references

Matthews, Tom L., 1949-

Grierson's raid; a daring cavalry strike through the heart of the Confederacy; [by] Tom Lalicki; original maps by David Cain. Farrar, Straus and Giroux 2004 200p il map $18

Grades: 7 8 9 10   **973.7**

1. United States—History—1861-1865, Civil War—Campaigns

ISBN 0-374-32787-4   LC 2003-49253

Describes Colonel Benjamin H. Grierson's sixteen-day raid through central Mississippi in the spring of 1863, which distracted Confederate attention while Union troops moved on Vicksburg

"The use of firsthand accounts brings the events vividly to life in a way that makes the book read more like an adventure story than a history text. . . . Accessibly written and scrupulously researched." Booklist

Includes glossary and bibliographical references

McKissack, Patricia C., 1944-

Days of Jubilee; the end of slavery in the United States; [by] Patricia C. & Fredrick L. McKissack. Scholastic Press 2003 134p il $18.95 *

Grades: 5 6 7 8   **973.7**

1. Slavery—United States 2. African Americans—History 3. United States—History—1861-1865, Civil War

ISBN 0-590-10764-X   LC 2001-57568

Uses slave narratives, letters, diaries, military orders, and other documents to chronicle the various stages leading to the emancipation of slaves in the United States

"The balanced perspective, vivid telling, and well-chosen details give this book an immediacy that many history books lack." Booklist

McNeese, Tim

The abolitionist movement; ending slavery. Chelsea House 2007 142p il (Reform movements in American history) lib bdg $30

Grades: 8 9 10 11 12   **973.7**

1. Abolitionists 2. Slavery—United States

ISBN 978-0-7910-9502-7 (lib bdg); 0-7910-9502-9 (lib bdg)   LC 2007-14766

"Complex, detailed, and yet very readable, this title . . . discusses the struggles and differences within the antislavery movement as well as the fight for emancipation and its crucial role in the Civil War. . . . The book offers a sound exploration of the topic." Booklist

Includes bibliographical references

McPherson, James M.

Fields of fury; the American Civil War. Atheneum Bks. for Young Readers 2002 96p il map $22.95

Grades: 5 6 7 8   **973.7**

1. United States—History—1861-1865, Civil War

ISBN 0-689-84833-1   LC 2001-46048

"A Byron Preiss Visual Publications, Inc. book"

Examines the events and effects of the American Civil War

"McPherson writes with authority, offering a broad overview as well as many details and anecdotes that give his account a human dimension. . . . The many fine illustrations include period photographs, paintings, prints, some excellent maps." Booklist

Includes glossary and bibliographical references

Murphy, Jim, 1947-

The boys' war; Confederate and Union soldiers talk about the Civil War. Clarion Bks. 1990 110p il hardcover o.p. pa $8.95 *

Grades: 5 6 7 8 9 10   **973.7**

1. United States—History—1861-1865, Civil War

ISBN 0-89919-893-7; 0-395-66412-8 (pa)   LC 89-23959

This book includes diary entries, personal letters, and archival photographs to describe the experiences of boys, sixteen years old or younger, who fought in the Civil War.

"An excellent selection of more than 45 sepia-toned contemporary photographs augment the text of this informative, moving work." SLJ

Includes bibliographical references

The long road to Gettysburg. Clarion Bks. 1992 116p il maps $17; pa $7.95 *

Grades: 5 6 7 8 9 10   **973.7**

1. Gettysburg (Pa.), Battle of, 1863

ISBN 0-395-55965-0; 0-618-05157-0 (pa)   LC 90-21881

Describes the events of the Battle of Gettysburg in 1863 as seen through the eyes of two actual participants, nineteen-year-old Confederate lieutenant John Dooley and seventeen-year-old Union soldier Thomas Galway. Also discusses Lincoln's famous speech delivered at the dedication of the National Cemetery at Gettysburg

The author "uses all of his fine skills as an information writer—clarity of detail, conciseness, understanding of his age group, and ability to find the drama appealing to readers—to frame a well-crafted account of a single battle in the war." Horn Book

Includes bibliographical references

Nardo, Don, 1947-

The Civil War. Lucent Bks. 2003 109p il maps (History of weapons and warfare) $27.45

Grades: 7 8 9 10   **973.7**

1. Military art and science 2. United States—History—1861-1865, Civil War

ISBN 1-59018-068-2   LC 2002-11032

Contents: Muskets and rifles; Artillery guns and batteries; Infantry units and tactics; Cavalry units and tactics; Ships and naval warfare; Espionage and experimental weapons

Nardo, Don, 1947-—*Continued*
Discusses the weapons of American Civil War soldiers and different means of warfare used during that conflict.
Includes glossary and bibliographical references

Netzley, Patricia D.
Civil War. Greenhaven Press 2004 336p il (Greenhaven encyclopedia of) lib bdg $74.95
Grades: 8 9 10 11 12   973.7
1. United States—History—1861-1865, Civil War—Encyclopedias 2. Reference books
ISBN 0-7377-0438-1   LC 2003-11808
An alphabetical presentation of definitions and descriptions of terms, people, and events of the Civil War
"Basic, accurate information about many aspects of the war. . . . The well-written, objective entries are cross-referenced. . . . Netzley's solid volume will be helpful to students needing introductory research material." SLJ
Includes bibliographical references

Osborne, Linda Barrett, 1949-
Traveling the freedom road; from slavery and the Civil War through Reconstruction; by Linda Barrett Osborne; in association with the Library of Congress. Abrams Books for Young Readers 2009 128p il map $24.95 *
Grades: 6 7 8 9 10   973.7
1. African Americans—History 2. Slavery—United States 3. United States—History—1861-1865, Civil War 4. Reconstruction (1865-1876) 5. United States—Politics and government—1783-1865 6. United States—Politics and government—1865-1898
ISBN 978-0-8109-8338-0; 0-8109-8338-9
                                LC 2008-22298
"This fascinating, well-designed volume offers an essential introduction to the experiences of African Americans between 1800 and 1877. . . . Osborne moves from . . . personal stories to broader historical milestones, and in highly accessible language, she provides basic background even as she challenges readers with philosophical questions. . . . This fluid exchange between political events and intimate, human stories creates a highly absorbing whole." Booklist

Porterfield, Jason
The Lincoln-Douglas senatorial debates of 1858; a primary source investigation; [by] Jason Porterfield. 1st ed. Rosen Central Primary Sources 2005 64p il map (Great historic debates and speeches) lib bdg $29.25
Grades: 5 6 7 8   973.7
1. Lincoln, Abraham, 1809-1865 2. Douglas, Stephen Arnold, 1813-1861
ISBN 1-4042-0153-X   LC 2003-25408
Discusses the debates between Lincoln and Douglas and how they influenced political campaigns throughout history.
This "readable [text provides a] balanced [overview]. Primary-source materials include archival maps, photos, reproductions, letters, and speeches that are examined in context." SLJ
Includes bibliographical references

Rappaport, Doreen, 1939-
United no more! stories of the Civil War; by Doreen Rappaport and Joan Verniero; illustrated by Rick Reeves. 1st ed. HarperCollinsPublishers 2006 132p il map $15.99; lib bdg $16.89 *
Grades: 4 5 6 7   973.7
1. United States—History—1861-1865, Civil War
ISBN 0-06-050599-0; 0-06-050600-8 (lib bdg)
                                LC 2005005724
"An interesting and readable introduction to the Civil War. Drawn from primary sources, the seven short narratives reflect the experiences of people on both sides of the conflict. . . . Maps and occasional black-and-white, pen-and-ink drawings add detail and drama to the narratives." SLJ
Includes bibliographical references

Seidman, Rachel Filene
The Civil war: a history in documents. Oxford University Press 2001 206p il map (Pages from history) lib bdg $39.95
Grades: 8 9 10 11 12   973.7
1. United States—History—1861-1865, Civil War—Sources
ISBN 978-0-19-511558-1 (lib bdg); 0-19-511558-9 (lib bdg)   LC 00-37523
"Seidman's documents bookend the Civil War with the territorial expansion that preceded the conflict and with the Reconstruction that followed it. In this structure the documents, under the guidance of Seidman's linking narrative, all make a powerful impression of immediacy about ordinary people's experience of, and condemnation or defense of, slavery." Booklist
Includes bibliographical references

Silvey, Anita
I'll pass for your comrade; women soldiers in the Civil War. Clarion Books 2008 115p il map $17 *
Grades: 6 7 8 9   973.7
1. United States—History—1861-1865, Civil War 2. Women soldiers
ISBN 978-0-618-57491-9; 0-618-57491-3
                                LC 2008018053
This "spotlights Union and Confederate women who fought on the battlefields. . . . Period photos, prints, drawings, and documents are among the many illustrations. . . . Well researched and clearly written, this attractive book illuminates an aspect of the Civil War that is often overlooked." Booklist
Includes bibliographical references

Stein, R. Conrad, 1937-
Escaping slavery on the Underground Railroad; [by] R. Conrad Stein. Enslow Publishers 2008 128p il (From many cultures, one history) lib bdg $31.93
Grades: 6 7 8 9   973.7
1. Underground railroad 2. Abolitionists 3. Slavery—United States
ISBN 978-0-7660-2799-2 (lib bdg); 0-7660-2799-6 (lib bdg)   LC 2007015124

Stein, R. Conrad, 1937——_Continued_

This is an account of American slavery, the Abolitionist movement, and escapes from slavery on the The Underground Railroad.

This "will provide clear, easy-to-understand facts with critical analysis and will be useful for reports." Libr Media Connect

Includes glossary and bibliographical references

Sullivan, George

The Civil War at sea. 21st Cent. Bks. (Brookfield) 2001 80p il lib bdg $27.90

Grades: 8 9 10 11 12 **973.7**

1. United States—History—1861-1865, Civil War—Naval operations

ISBN 0-7613-1553-5 LC 00-41805

"Sullivan tells of the struggle between the Union and Confederate forces at sea and in America's bays, rivers, and harbors. He describes the two rival navies and their most famous ships, most significant battles, and most memorable commanders. He also looks at the lives of ordinary sailors." Booklist

"The illustrations and reproductions included here and the lively text will appeal to every Civil War buff, and will be an excellent source of information for reports." SLJ

Includes bibliographical references

Trudeau, Noah Andre, 1949-

Like men of war; black troops in the Civil War, 1862-1865. Little, Brown 1998 xxii, 548p il maps hardcover o.p. pa $18

Grades: 7 8 9 10 **973.7**

1. African American soldiers 2. United States—History—1861-1865, Civil War

ISBN 0-316-85325-9; 0-316-85344-5 (pa)

LC 97-15380

A "study of the battlefield experiences of black Union regiments. Some 60 maps help the reader make sense of famous engagements (Fort Wagner and the Crater) and notorious incidents (Fort Pillow) in which black soldiers fought, as well as scores of lesser-known clashes. Rich archival research is integrated into a lively narrative that places the raising and deployment of black regiments in broader contexts. This book will become a basic source of information on the subject." Libr J

Includes bibliographical references

Uschan, Michael V., 1948-

The cavalry during the Civil War. Lucent Bks. 2003 112p il maps (Working life) $27.45

Grades: 6 7 8 9 **973.7**

1. United States—History—1861-1865, Civil War 2. Soldiers—United States

ISBN 1-59018-175-1 LC 2002-11840

Contents: Recruiting and training the cavalry; Life in the saddle: the varied duties of the cavalry trooper; Cavalry raiders and guerillas; Cavalry soldiers in combat; Noncombat life of the cavalry

This examines the life of cavalry soldiers during the civil war

This is "well written and the authors draw on and quote from many primary sources." Libr Media Connect

Includes bibliographical references

Walker, Sally M.

Secrets of a Civil War submarine; solving the mysteries of the H.L. Hunley. Carolrhoda Books 2005 112p il lib bdg $17.95

Grades: 7 8 9 10 **973.7**

1. Hunley (Submarine) 2. United States—History—1861-1865, Civil War—Naval operations 3. Shipwrecks 4. Underwater exploration 5. Submarines

ISBN 1-57505-830-8 LC 2004-19646

Contents: Prologue: a lost treasure; A seafaring stealth weapon; Climb aboard; Disaster; Lieutenant Dixon's mission; A stunning discovery; The Hunley talks; Buried treasures; In touch with the past; Forensic tales

This discusses "the Confederate submarine H. L. Hunley. . . . Walker begins with the history of the Hunley's design and construction as well as its place in Civil War and naval history. She really hits her stride, though, in explaining the complex techniques and loving care used in raising the craft, recovering its contents, and even reconstructing models of the crewmembers' bodies. . . . Thoroughly researched, nicely designed, and well illustrated with clear, color photos." Booklist

Includes glossary and bibliographical references

Warren, Andrea

Under siege! three children at the Civil War battle for Vicksburg; by Andrea Warren. Melanie Kroupa Books 2009 166p il map $21.95 *

Grades: 7 8 9 10 **973.7**

1. Vicksburg (Miss.)—Siege, 1863 2. United States—History—1861-1865, Civil War

ISBN 978-0-374-31255-8; 0-374-31255-9

LC 2008-1136

"Warren creates a compelling account of the 1863 siege at Vicksburg that follows three young people from December 1862 through the aftermath of the surrender on July 4, 1863. . . . The author uses primary sources throughout, including scores of quotes, many attributed to the children themselves, period photographs, maps, and paintings. . . . The back matter is extensive, including an annotated list of recommended Civil War books, a longer bibliography of sources, and extensive endnotes and illustration credits." Voice Youth Advocates

Includes bibliographical references

Watkins, Samuel R., 1839-1901

The diary of Sam Watkins, a confederate soldier; edited by Ruth Ashby; illustrations by Laszlo Kubinyi. Benchmark Bks. 2004 95p il (In my own words) lib bdg $18.95

Grades: 5 6 7 8 **973.7**

1. Watkins, Samuel R., 1839-1901 2. United States—History—1861-1865, Civil War

ISBN 0-7614-1646-3 LC 2003-1478

Excerpts from the diary of a Confederate soldier from Tennessee, describing the battles he fought in during the Civil War

This offers "an engaging history lesson." Horn Book Guide

Includes bibliographical references

Zeinert, Karen, 1942-2002
Those courageous women of the Civil War.
Millbrook Press 1998 96p il map lib bdg $30.60
Grades: 7 8 9 10   **973.7**
1. Women—United States—History 2. United States—
History—1861-1865, Civil War
ISBN 0-7613-0212-3   LC 97-21485
Examines the important contributions of various wom-
en, Northern, Southern, and slave, to the American Civil
War, on the battlefield, in print, on the home front, and
in other areas where they challenged traditional female
roles
"A solid work that is sure to open the eyes of many
readers and add a different dimension to studies about
this era." SLJ
Includes bibliographical references

973.8   United States—Reconstruction period, 1865-1901

Collier, Christopher, 1930-
The United States enters the world stage: from
the Alaska Purchase through World War I,
1867-1919; [by] Christopher Collier, James
Lincoln Collier. Benchmark Bks. (Tarrytown) 2001
94p il map (Drama of American history) lib bdg
$31.36 *
Grades: 6 7 8 9   **973.8**
1. United States—History—1865-1898 2. United
States—History—1898-1919 3. United States—Foreign
relations   4.   World   War,   1914-1918
5. Spanish-American War, 1898
ISBN 0-7614-1053-8   LC 00-29483
This discusses topics in United States history and poli-
tics including Westward expansion, imperialism, the
Spanish-American War, the Panama Canal, and World
War I
Includes bibliographical references

Custer, Elizabeth Bacon, 1842-1933
The diary of Elizabeth Bacon Custer; on the
plains with General Custer; edited by Nancy Plain;
illustrations and map by Laszlo Kubinyi.
Benchmark Bks. 2004 95p il map (In my own
words) lib bdg $18.95
Grades: 5 6 7 8   **973.8**
1. Custer, George Armstrong, 1839-1876 2. Native
Americans—Wars
ISBN 0-7614-1647-1   LC 2003-1432
Presents the diary of the wife of General George Arm-
strong Custer, focusing on their life on the Great Plains
from 1873 to 1876, when Custer and his Seventh Caval-
ry were clearing the way for the Northern Pacific Rail-
road and battling Native Americans
This offers "an engaging history lesson." Horn Book
Guide
Includes glossary and bibliographical references

Custer's last stand; Thomas Streissguth, book
editor. Greenhaven Press 2003 142p il maps (At
issue in history) lib bdg $21.96; pa $14.96
Grades: 7 8 9 10   **973.8**
1. Custer, George Armstrong, 1839-1876 2. Little Bighorn, Battle of the, 1876
ISBN 0-7377-1358-5 (lib bdg); 0-7377-1359-3 (pa)
                                          LC 2002-27875
"Using primary and secondary sources, this volume
examines the controversial history of the Battle at the
Little Bighorn in June, 1876. . . . Each of the 11 entries
is preceded by a summary of the author's main points
and conclusions. This excellent volume helps students
understand the 'what' and 'why' of history." SLJ
Includes bibliographical references

Ferrell, Nancy Warren
The Battle of the Little Bighorn in American
history. Enslow Pubs. 1996 128p il maps lib bdg
$18.95
Grades: 6 7 8 9   **973.8**
1. Little Bighorn, Battle of the, 1876
ISBN 0-89490-768-9   LC 96-11592
Describes the Battle of Little Bighorn and the events
that led up to it
Includes bibliographical references

The **Gilded** Age: a history in documents;
[compiled by] Janette Thomas Greenwood.
Oxford Univ. Press 2000 191p il map (Pages
from history) $39.95; pa $24.95
Grades: 7 8 9 10   **973.8**
1. United States—History—1865-1898
ISBN   978-0-19-510523-0;   0-19-510523-0;
978-0-19-516638-5 (pa); 0-19-516638-8 (pa)
                                          LC 99-98194
Uses a wide variety of documents to show how Americans dealt with an age of extremes from 1887 to 1900,
including rapid industrialization, unemployment, unprece-
dented wealth, and immigration
"There's plenty to absorb and much to capture the
imagination. . . . Greenwood presents the history as a
seamless tapestry sewn by the people who lived it."
Booklist
Includes bibliographical references

Hansen, Joyce
Bury me not in a land of slaves;
African-Americans in the time of Reconstruction.
Watts 2000 160p il lib bdg $23 *
Grades: 7 8 9 10   **973.8**
1. African Americans—History 2. Reconstruction
(1865-1876) 3. United States—Race relations
ISBN 0-531-11539-9   LC 99-30040
An account of African-American life in the period of
Reconstruction following the Civil War, based on first-
person narratives, contemporary documents, and other
historical sources
"Readers of this balanced, well-written account will
come away with a solid understanding of the period's
events and how they contributed to the twentieth century's segregation and prejudice." Booklist
Includes bibliographical references

January, Brendan, 1972-

Little Bighorn, June 25, 1876. Enchanted Lion Books 2004 32p il map (American battlefields) $14.95

Grades: 5 6 7 8   **973.8**

1. Little Bighorn, Battle of the, 1876 2. Native Americans—Great Plains

ISBN 1-59270-028-4   LC 2003-64300

This "describes the Native American and U.S. Cavalry clashes at Little Bighorn: the history, the leaders and their actions on that day, and the aftermath of the battle. . . . The [text is] well written . . . The books' many illustrations . . . include excellent reproductions of period photos, drawings, engravings, and paintings, along with clearly drawn maps and a few photos of sites." Booklist

Includes glossary and bibliographical references

Kupferberg, Audrey E.

The Spanish-American War; by Audrey Kupferberg. Blackbirch Press 2005 48p il (People at the center of) $23.70

Grades: 5 6 7 8   **973.8**

1. Spanish-American War, 1898

ISBN 1-56711-924-7

This profiles 15 people connected with the Spanish-American War, such as Grover Cleveland, Clara Barton, Mark Twain, Theodore Roosevelt, and William McKinley.

Ruggiero, Adriane

American voices from Reconstruction. Marshall Cavendish Benchmark 2006 103p il (American voices from--) lib bdg $37.07 *

Grades: 6 7 8 9 10 11 12   **973.8**

1. Reconstruction (1865-1876)

ISBN 978-0-7614-2168-9 (lib bdg); 0-7614-2168-8 (lib bdg)   LC 2005-24949

"Presents the history of the era of Reconstruction, 1865-1877, through a variety of primary source documents, such as diary entries, newspaper accounts, political speeches, laws, popular songs, and personal letters." Publisher's note

This "does an excellent job of bringing history close. . . . The spacious design . . . is very approachable, and the combination of voices and commentary will readers think critically." Booklist

Includes glossary and bibliographical references

Stroud, Bettye, 1939-

The Reconstruction era; by Bettye M. Stroud with Virginia Schomp. Marshall Cavendish Benchmark 2007 70p il (Drama of African-American history) lib bdg $34.21 *

Grades: 5 6 7 8   **973.8**

1. Reconstruction (1865-1876) 2. African Americans—History

ISBN 978-0-7614-2181-8 (lib bdg); 0-7614-2181-5 (lib bdg)   LC 2006012149

"Traces the history of Reconstruction, from the end of the Civil War in 1865 to 1877, when federal troops were removed from the South." Publisher's note

Includes glossary and bibliographical references

Uschan, Michael V., 1948-

The Battle of the Little Bighorn. World Almanac 2002 48p il map (Landmark events in American history) lib bdg $26.60

Grades: 5 6 7 8   **973.8**

1. Custer, George Armstrong, 1839-1876 2. Little Bighorn, Battle of the, 1876

ISBN 0-8368-5338-5   LC 2002-24632

Describes the causes, events, and aftermath of the fateful encounter at the Little Bighorn River on June 25, 1876, between the Seventh Cavalry troops commanded by Lieutenant Colonel Custer and the Cheyenne and Lakota Sioux led by Chiefs Sitting Bull and Crazy Horse

The "design is attractive, with drawings, maps, paintings, and photos; primary sources, such as excerpts from diaries, letters, and newspapers, support and enhance the [text]." Booklist

Includes glossary and bibliographical references

Walker, Paul Robert

Remember Little Bighorn; Indians, soldiers, and scouts tell their stories; [by] Paul Robert Walker; [foreword by John A. Doerner] National Geographic Society 2006 61p il map $17.95; lib bdg $27.90 *

Grades: 5 6 7 8   **973.8**

1. Little Bighorn, Battle of the, 1876

ISBN 0-7922-5521-6; 0-7922-5522-4 (lib bdg)   LC 2005030929

This "volume gives an almost blow-by-blow account of the famous battle that came to be known as Custer's Last Stand. Walker concentrates on the battle itself, fought on the Great Plains in 1876, and the book includes diagrams of each side's tactics. . . . Walker's exhaustive research . . . [brings] together the conflicting viewpoints of the whites and the Lakota Sioux, Cheyenne, and Arapaho fighters, documenting everything in source notes. The handsome book design, with thick paper, clear type, maps, stirring photos, and archival images, will attract readers to the battle story and then start them thinking about lasting historical issues." Booklist

Includes bibliographical references

Worth, Richard, 1945-

African Americans during Reconstruction; [by] Richard Worth. Chelsea House 2006 112p il map (Slavery in the Americas) $35

Grades: 6 7 8 9   **973.8**

1. Reconstruction (1865-1876) 2. African Americans—Civil rights

ISBN 0-81606-139-4   LC 2005015720

Tells the history of African Americans from the end of the Civil War through the nation's reconstruction.

Includes bibliographical references

973.91 United States—1901-1953

Burg, David F.
The Great Depression. updated ed. Facts on File 2005 xx, 444p il (Eyewitness history) $75
Grades: 8 9 10 11 12   973.91
 1. Great Depression, 1929-1939 2. United States—Economic conditions—1919-1933 3. United States—Economic conditions—1933-1945
 ISBN 0-8160-5709-5; 978-0-8160-5709-2
                         LC 2004-29126
First published 1996
"The book is divided into seven chapters, each covering a specific timeframe beginning with causative events preceding the crisis (1919-1928) and ending with the emerging Second World War (1939-1941.) Each chapter opens with a narrative summary and analysis of the period, followed by a chronological listing of significant events and then by primary-source contemporary quotations from private citizens, politicians, radio broadcasts, and more." Voice Youth Advocates
Includes bibliographical references

Collier, Christopher, 1930-
Progressivism, the Great Depression, and the New Deal, 1901 to 1941; by Christopher Collier, James Lincoln Collier. Benchmark Bks. (Tarrytown) 2001 95p il map (Drama of American history) lib bdg $31.36 *
Grades: 6 7 8 9   973.91
 1. United States—History—20th century 2. Great Depression, 1929-1939 3. United States—Economic conditions—1933-1945
 ISBN 0-7614-1054-6   LC 00-29481
This "follows events and movements during the first four decades of the twentieth century, including the growing involvement of government in reforming business practices, the impact of the Great Depression, and the social policies of Franklin D. Roosevelt's New Deal. . . . Illustrations, many in color, include period photographs and engravings as well as maps and charts. . . . Highly readable and informative." Booklist
Includes bibliographical references

Davis, Barbara J., 1952-
The Teapot Dome Scandal; corruption rocks 1920s America; by Barbara J. Davis. Compass Point Books 2008 96p il map (Snapshots in history) lib bdg $31.93
Grades: 6 7 8 9   973.91
 1. Teapot Dome Scandal, 1921-1924
 ISBN 978-0-7565-3336-6 (lib bdg); 0-7565-3336-8 (lib bdg)   LC 2007004920
"Describes the signature scandal of the 1920s, through which political appointees and personal friends of President Warren G. Harding used their positions to solicit bribes from powerful oil companies in return for rich Western oil leases. . . . [This] volume includes a minimal glossary, a helpful time line, and suggestions for further reading." Voice Youth Advocates
Includes glossary

Howes, Kelly King
The roaring twenties almanac and primary sources; [by] Kelly King Howes; Julie L. Carnagie, project editor. U.X.L 2006 liv, 286p il (The roaring twenties reference library) $60
Grades: 7 8 9 10   973.91
 1. United States—History—1919-1933
 ISBN 1-4144-0212-0   LC 2005007800
This volume begins with a timeline placing the 1920s in historical context. Illustrated entries highlight such topics as politics, economics, technological advances, women's changing roles, creationism vs. evolution, anti-immigrationism, Prohibition, and writers such as Sinclair Lewis, and Langston Hughes
Includes bibliographical references

Living through the Great Depression; Tracy Brown Collins, book editor. Greenhaven Press 2004 160p il (Exploring cultural history) $29.95
Grades: 7 8 9 10   973.91
 1. Great Depression, 1929-1939 2. United States—Social conditions
 ISBN 0-7377-2096-4   LC 2003-56833
"Beginning with the stock market crash of 1929 and continuing throughout the 1930s, the Great Depression was a time of economic crisis and social and political change in America. This book explores everyday life for those who lived through this difficult period." Publisher's note
Includes bibliographical references

McElvaine, Robert S., 1947-
The Depression and New Deal; a history in documents. Oxford Univ. Press 2000 192p il (Pages from history) hardcover o.p. pa $19.95 *
Grades: 7 8 9 10   973.91
 1. Great Depression, 1929-1939 2. United States—Economic conditions—1933-1945
 ISBN 0-19-510493-5; 0-19-516636-1 (pa)
                         LC 99-36644
"A vast assortment of diary entries, newspaper articles, campaign memos and speeches, political cartoons, songs, poetry, art, advertisements, photographs, and personal letters provide students with a political, economic, and social picture of this nation during the Depression. . . . [This] provides a balanced, inclusive picture of the period through the senses of the people who lived it." SLJ
Includes bibliographical references

The Roaring twenties; Phillip Margulies, book editor. Greenhaven Press 2004 267p (Turning points in world history) $34.95
Grades: 7 8 9 10   973.91
 1. United States—Politics and government—1919-1933 2. United States—Social conditions 3. United States—Social life and customs
 ISBN 0-7377-1809-9   LC 2003-49370
"The twenties are seen today as a watershed, a time that saw the birth of mass consumer society as it exists today. This anthology examines the ingredients of that new society as well as individual turning points in the decade that brought us modern sales promotion, chain stores, radio, tabloid newspapers, jazz, mixed drinks, or-

The Roaring twenties—*Continued*
ganized crime and the 1929 stock market crash." Publisher's note

Includes bibliographical references

Stanley, George Edward, 1942-
An emerging world power (1900-1929); [by] George E. Stanley. World Almanac Library 2005 48p il (Primary source history of the United States) lib bdg $30

Grades: 5 6 7 8   **973.91**
1. United States—Politics and government—1919-1933 2. United States—History—1919-1933 3. United States—Foreign relations

ISBN 0-8368-5828-X   LC 2004-61501
The author describes United States politics and foreign relations in the 1920s.

"Stanley explains and connects events utilizing clear language and a blending of text, images, and primary accounts. . . . Well-organized, highly attractive." SLJ

Includes bibliographical references

973.917 United States— Administration of Franklin D. Roosevelt, 1933-1945

Cooper, Michael L., 1950-
Dust to eat; drought and depression in the 1930's. Clarion Books 2004 81p il map $15 *

Grades: 4 5 6 7   **973.917**
1. Great Depression, 1929-1939 2. Migrant labor 3. Droughts

ISBN 0-618-15449-3   LC 2003-17807
Contents: The "Okie" problem; The dirty thirties; "Dust to eat, dust to breathe, dust to drink"; California-bound; Harvest gypsies; Crisis in the valley; World War II ends the Depression

This is a history of the Great Depression and the Dust Bowl drought of the 1930s that drove desperate families to California in search of work.

This includes "lots of stunning black-and-white archival photos and a clear, spacious text that draws on eloquent eyewitness reports—including comments from John Steinbeck and Woody Guthrie. . . . This is an excellent historical account." Booklist

Includes bibliographical references

Ruggiero, Adriane
American voices from The Great Depression. Benchmark Books 2004 xxi, 116p il (American voices from--) lib bdg $32.21 *

Grades: 6 7 8 9   **973.917**
1. Great Depression, 1929-1939 2. United States—Economic conditions—1919-1933 3. United States—Economic conditions—1933-1945

ISBN 0-7614-1696-X   LC 2004-865
Presents the history of the Great Depression through excerpts from letters, newspaper articles, speeches, and songs dating from the period. Includes review questions.

This "excellent [resource stands] out . . . because [it

deals] strictly with primary sources, [contains] topnotch illustrations, and [enables] students to grasp the concepts without being overwhelmed." SLJ

Includes glossary and bibliographical references

973.92 United States—1953-2001

Anderson, Dale, 1953-
The Cold War years. Raintree Steck-Vaughn Pubs. 2001 96p il (Making of America) lib bdg $35.64

Grades: 5 6 7 8   **973.92**
1. Cold war 2. United States—History—1945- 3. United States—Social conditions

ISBN 0-8172-5711-X   LC 00-62827
This discusses factors that led to the Cold War and the formation of alliances in reaction to it, as well as domestic issues such as the demand for equality for women and African Americans

"Written in a clear and concise fashion [this book provides] . . . enough details to give a taste for the era without overwhelming students." SLJ

Includes bibliographical references

Campbell, Geoffrey A.
The home front. Lucent Bks. 2003 112p il map (American war library, Cold War) $27.45

Grades: 7 8 9 10   **973.92**
1. Cold war 2. United States—Social conditions 3. United States—History—1945-

ISBN 1-59018-213-8   LC 2002-663
Examines how the Cold War period in America, lasting roughly fifty years following World War II, was a contradictory time of prosperity and optimism coupled with concerns over Soviet espionage infiltrating American institutions and fear of nuclear apocalypse

Includes bibliographical references

Collier, Christopher, 1930-
The changing face of American society: 1945-2000; [by] Christopher Collier, James Lincoln Collier. Benchmark Bks. 2002 94p il (Drama of American history) lib bdg $31.36 *

Grades: 6 7 8 9   **973.92**
1. United States—History—1945- 2. United States—Social conditions 3. United States—Social life and customs

ISBN 0-7614-1319-7   LC 2001-25963
This outlines American social conditions from 1945 to 2000, including greater prosperity, the movements for African American civil rights and women's rights, the 1960s counterculture, the Vietnam War, scientific advancements and social changes

"Illustrations are plentiful, uniformly well chosen, and include photographs, paintings, posters, and in some titles, maps. . . . [This title is] easy to read and informative." Book Rep

Includes bibliographical references

Collier, Christopher, 1930-—*Continued*

The middle road: American politics, 1945-2000; [by] Christopher Collier, James Lincoln Collier. Benchmark Bks. 2002 95p il maps (Drama of American history) lib bdg $31.36 *

Grades: 6 7 8 9   **973.92**

1. United States—Politics and government—1945-

ISBN 0-7614-1318-9   LC 2001-25615

This outlines the course of American politics from the end of World War II, through McCarthyism, the 1960s, President Nixon and the Watergate scandal, and Presidents Carter, Reagan, Bush, and Clinton

"Illustrations are plentiful, uniformly well chosen, and include photographs, paintings, posters, and in some titles, maps. . . . [This title is] easy to read and informative." Book Rep

Includes bibliographical references

Stanley, George Edward, 1942-

America in today's world (1969-2004); by George E. Stanley. World Almanac Library 2005 48p il (Primary source history of the United States) lib bdg $30

Grades: 5 6 7 8   **973.92**

1. United States—Politics and government—1945- 2. United States—History—1945- 3. Presidents—United States

ISBN 0-8368-5831-X

This "covers the end of the Vietnam War through the 2004 presidential election. The terms of Presidents Nixon through George W. Bush are highlighted through brief but evenhanded descriptions of the major events of each administration. . . . Well-organized, highly attractive." SLJ

Includes bibliographical references

973.921 United States— Administration of Dwight D. Eisenhower, 1953-1961

Fitzgerald, Brian, 1972-

McCarthyism; the red scare. Compass Point Books 2007 96p il map (Snapshots in history) lib bdg $31.93

Grades: 7 8 9 10   **973.921**

1. McCarthy, Joseph, 1908-1957 2. Communism—United States 3. Cold war 4. United States—History—1945-1953

ISBN 978-0-7565-2007-6 (lib bdg); 0-7565-2007-X (lib bdg)   LC 2006003005

This "vividly portrays the fear of Communism in the U.S., beginning after the Russian Revolution. This book shows, in clear language, how McCarthy spread paranoia throughout the country and ruined many lives and careers." SLJ

Includes glossary and bibliographical references

Lindop, Edmund

America in the 1950s. 21st Cent. Bks. (Brookfield) 2002 128p il lib bdg $25.90

Grades: 7 8 9 10   **973.921**

1. United States—Civilization 2. United States—History—1945-1953 3. United States—History—1953-1961

ISBN 0-7613-2551-4   LC 2001-52254

Contents: The Korean War; A Red scare haunts Americans; "I Like Ike" and "I'm Madly for Adlai"; African Americans seek racial justice; The Cold War escalates; Big changes come to the United States; Television takes center stage; More entertainment; A golden age of sports

Outlines life in the United States in the 1950s, including the development of suburbia, advances in technology and entertainment, politics, the space race, and the Cold War

"Lindop's book offers a solid, serious discussion in a relatively appealing package." SLJ

Includes bibliographical references

The **McCarthy** hearings; Jesse G. Cunningham, book editor; Laura K. Egendorf, assistant book editor. Greenhaven Press 2003 144p (At issue in history) lib bdg $21.96; pa $14.96

Grades: 7 8 9 10   **973.921**

1. McCarthy, Joseph, 1908-1957 2. United States—Politics and government—1945-1953 3. United States—Politics and government—1953-1961

ISBN 0-7377-1346-1 (lib bdg); 0-7377-1347-X (pa)   LC 2002-69323

"This anthology focuses on the hearings that resulted from McCarthy's famous efforts to expose communists in government positions and his use of dubious tactics such as smearing and guilt by association." Publisher's note

"Because of the evenhanded presentation, the title makes a strong and lasting impression. The writings are well chosen." SLJ

Includes bibliographical references

973.922 United States— Administration of John F. Kennedy, 1961-1963

Hampton, Wilborn

Kennedy assassinated! the world mourns: a reporter's story. Candlewick Press 1997 96p il $17.99 paperback o.p. *

Grades: 5 6 7 8 9   **973.922**

1. Kennedy, John F. (John Fitzgerald), 1917-1963—Assassination 2. Journalism

ISBN 1-56402-811-9; 0-7636-1564-1 (pa)   LC 96-25801

This is the author's "account of November 22, 1963, when, as a cub reporter for UPI in Dallas, he was drafted to cover JFK's assassination. His personal response to the tragedy is fluidly juxtaposed with the nuts and bolts of scooping the story in this insider's view of one of the most pivotal events of our nation's recent history." Publ Wkly

Includes bibliographical references

973.923 United States— Administration of Lyndon B. Johnson, 1963-1969

Schomp, Virginia, 1953-
American voices from the Vietnam era.
Benchmark Books 2004 c2005 xxiii, 134p
(American voices from--) lib bdg $34.21 *
Grades: 6 7 8 9   **973.923**
1. Vietnam War, 1961-1975 2. United States—History—1961-1974
ISBN 0-7614-1693-5   LC 2003-1475
Contents: A television war; The unseen enemy; The
war at home: "doves" for peace; The war at home:
"hawks" for war; American youth and the counterculture;
The battle for civil rights; The women's liberation movement; The credibility gap; Coming home
Describes, through excerpts from diaries, speeches,
newspaper articles, and other documents of the time, the
Vietnam War and related events that occurred in the
United States during the 1960's, including the women's
movement, the struggle for civil rights, and the generation gap. Includes review questions.
Includes glossary and bibliographical references

973.929 United States— Administration of Bill Clinton, 1993-2001

Cohen, Daniel, 1936-
The impeachment of William Jefferson Clinton.
21st Cent. Bks. (Brookfield) 2000 112p il lib bdg
$23.90
Grades: 7 8 9 10   **973.929**
1. Clinton, Bill, 1946-—Impeachment 2. United
States—Politics and government—1989-
ISBN 0-7613-1711-2   LC 99-56179
Examines the events leading to the impeachment of
President Bill Clinton, including the Whitewater investigation, the media coverage, the grand jury proceedings,
impeachment by the Senate, and the legacy of this scandal
"The chronology of events is smoothly presented, and
issues of national importance which became part of the
public debate . . . are clearly explained." Bull Cent
Child Books
Includes bibliographical references

973.931 United States— Administration of George W. Bush, 2001-

America under attack: primary sources; Tamara
Roleff, book editor. Lucent Bks. 2002 96p il
map (Lucent terrorism library) $27.45
Grades: 7 8 9 10   **973.931**
1. September 11 terrorist attacks, 2001 2. Terrorism
ISBN 1-59018-216-2   LC 2002-1816
Contents: On the scene; America's response; Response
from abroad; Who is to blame?; War on terrorism

Looks at the September 11, 2001 terrorist attack on
the World Trade Center and Pentagon, U.S. response,
world reaction, and the war on terrorism
"Roleff's useful compendium offers thematically arranged perspectives from witnesses in New York and
Washington, DC, U.S. and world leaders, the blamed and
the accusers, and war proponents and opponents. . . .
This will be a sought-after research tool." SLJ
Includes bibliographical references

Frank, Mitch
Understanding September 11th; answering
questions about the attacks on America. Viking
2002 136p il maps $16.99; pa $8.99
Grades: 7 8 9 10   **973.931**
1. September 11 terrorist attacks, 2001 2. Terrorism
ISBN 0-670-03582-3; 0-670-03587-4 (pa)
                                    LC 2002-1725
Explains the historical and religious issues that
sparked terrorists to attack America on September 11,
2001, including information on Islam, Osama bin Laden,
and the Middle East
This is written "in remarkably simple, accessible language. . . . Direct, unflinching, intelligent, and humane,
this is an invaluable resource." Booklist
Includes glossary and bibliographical references

Hampton, Wilborn
September 11, 2001; attack on New York City.
Candlewick Press 2003 145p il $17.99 *
Grades: 6 7 8 9   **973.931**
1. September 11 terrorist attacks, 2001 2. Terrorism
ISBN 0-7636-1949-3   LC 2002-41204
Describes the September 11 attacks in the United
States and presents several personal stories of tragedy
told by New Yorkers who lived through the collapse of
the World Trade Center.
"Hampton re-creates the terrible events of that day
clearly. . . . There are many . . . books about 9/11 written for young people, but this is one of the best."
Booklist
Includes bibliographical references

Lalley, Pat
9.11.01: terrorists attack the U.S.; by Patrick
Lalley. Raintree Steck-Vaughn Pubs. 2002 48p il
$29.93; pa $8.50
Grades: 4 5 6 7   **973.931**
1. September 11 terrorist attacks, 2001 2. Terrorism
ISBN 0-7398-6021-6; 0-7398-6356-8 (pa)
                                    LC 2002-277397
"Lalley covers the events of September 11th and provides brief background on the World Trade Center, Islamic extremism, and Osama bin Laden. He also comments on the impact the terrorists' attacks have had both
here and abroad." SLJ
"This compact book does an excellent job of explaining the terrorist attacks on September 11, but equally important is its presentation of the background that led to
the events." Booklist

Margulies, Phillip

Al Qaeda: Osama bin Laden's army of terrorists. Rosen Pub. Group 2003 64p il (Inside the world's most infamous terrorist organizations) lib bdg $26.50

Grades: 6 7 8 9   **973.931**
  1. Al Qaeda (Organization) 2. Terrorism
  3. September 11 terrorist attacks, 2001
  ISBN 0-8239-3817-4   LC 2002-7526
  Contents: Mujahedeen; Inside al-Qaeda; September 11; The investigation; Conclusion

Discusses the Islamic organization known as Al-Qaeda, focusing on its presumed role in the September 11 terrorist attacks in the United States

"With color photos that aren't too shocking and long reading lists updated by links gathered on a dedicated Web site. [This] will be useful for school reports." Booklist

Includes bibliographical references

Marquette, Scott

America under attack. Rourke Pub. 2003 48p il (America at war) lib bdg $29.93; pa $6.95

Grades: 4 5 6 7   **973.931**
  1. September 11 terrorist attacks, 2001 2. Terrorism
  3. United States—Foreign relations—Middle East
  ISBN 1-58952-386-5 (lib bdg); 1-58952-471-3 (pa)
                                              LC 2002-1215
  Contents: Introduction: "A War to Save Civilization"; Map of Middle East/Central Asia, 2001; Timeline; Roots of terror; "An Act of War"; A war of many fronts; "The New Normal"; America changed forever

The author "begins with 9/11 and then presents a chronology of prior events of terrorism against the U.S. He goes on to describe the war in Afghanistan and changes in American life. Even within the limits of 48 pages, he is able to point out some of the dissent in American policy concerning the Patriot Act." Booklist

Includes glossary and bibliographical references

A **Nation** challenged; a visual history of 9/11 and its aftermath; [by] The New York Times; introduction by Howell Raines; photographs edited by Nancy Lee and Lonnie Schlein; text edited by Mitchel Levitas. Young reader's ed. Scholastic 2002 96p il map $18.95 *

Grades: 4 5 6 7   **973.931**
  1. September 11 terrorist attacks, 2001—Pictorial works 2. Terrorism
  ISBN 0-439-48803-6   LC 2002-26879
  Contents: September 11, 2001; The days after; Meeting the challenge abroad; Meeting the challenge at home

In this Young Reader's edition of the title published for adults by the New York Times and Calloway, text, photographs, and illustrations from the New York Times section, "A Nation Challenged," record how the world was changed due to the September 11, 2001, terrorist attacks on the United States and their aftermath

This "is beautifully designed with unforgettable images on every page. . . . The book is an excellent resource for every library desiring a sweeping visual account of this momentous time in America's history." Libr Media Connect

Includes glossary and bibliographical references

Stewart, Gail, 1949-

America under attack; September 11, 2001; [by] Gail B. Stewart. Lucent Bks. 2002 96p il (Terrorism library) lib bdg $27.45

Grades: 7 8 9 10   **973.931**
  1. September 11 terrorist attacks, 2001 2. Terrorism
  ISBN 1-59018-208-1   LC 2001-7506
  Contents: "The mouth of hell"; Two new targets; A nation reacts; Looking for answers; Taking stock

Discusses the events surrounding the attacks on the World Trade Center and the Pentagon on September 11, 2001, and describes the experiences of those involved and the impact of these attacks

"An excellent resource that demonstrates thorough research and opens up issues for discussion." Booklist

Includes bibliographical references

Wachtel, Alan

September 11; a primary source history. Gareth Stevens Pub. 2009 48p il (In their own words) lib bdg $27 *

Grades: 5 6 7 8   **973.931**
  1. September 11 terrorist attacks, 2001 2. Terrorism
  ISBN 978-1-4339-0048-8; 1-4339-0048-3
                                            LC 2008045132
  "The horror of *September 11* feels very immediate, and uses both quotes from those who lived through it and stills from the attacks. The book does a fine job of chronicling the events, up to and including the controversies surrounding the New York memorial. The use of transcripts of phone conversations that took place aboard the doomed planes gives the book's beginning an almost 'you are there' effect. Later chapters feature such diverse sources as text from the Patriot Act and lyrics from Neil Young's song 'Let's Roll' to amplify the mood of the country." Booklist

Includes bibliographical references

Wheeler, Jill C., 1964-

September 11, 2001: the day that changed America. Abdo & Daughters 2002 64p il (War on terrorism) lib bdg $25.65

Grades: 3 4 5 6   **973.931**
  1. September 11 terrorist attacks, 2001 2. Terrorism
  ISBN 1-57765-656-3   LC 2001-53930
  Describes the events and immediate aftermath of the September 11, 2001 terrorist attacks on the United States, in which planes were crashed into the Twin Towers buildings in New York City as well as into the Pentagon building near Washington, D.C.

"The tone of the writing is matter-of-fact, and the color photos illustrate the text effectively." Booklist

Includes glossary

974 Northeastern United States

Johnson, Claudia D.
Daily life in colonial New England; [by] Claudia Durst Johnson. Greenwood Press 2002 xxvii, 215p (Daily life through history) $49.95
Grades: 7 8 9 10   **974**
1. New England—History 2. United States—Social life and customs—1600-1775, Colonial period
ISBN 0-313-31458-6   LC 00-61721
This description of colonial life in New England covers such topics as the clergy and the church, crime and punishment, government and law, labor, shelter and attire, food and health, marriage and sex, arts and amusements, and Native Americans and Africans in New England
"In this excellent volume, Johnson draws a remarkably clear and complete picture of the day-to-day existence of the first European settlers in New England." Voice Youth Advocates
Includes bibliographical references

Rylant, Cynthia
Appalachia; the voices of sleeping birds; illustrated by Barry Moser. Harcourt Brace Jovanovich 1991 21p il $17; pa $6 *
Grades: 4 5 6 7   **974**
1. Appalachian region
ISBN 0-15-201605-8; 0-15-201893-X (pa)
                    LC 90-36798
"This is a running narrative description of the dogs, people, houses, seasons, and lifestyles of Appalachia." Bull Cent Child Books
"Taking her subtitle from a passage by James Agee, the author conveys with a marvelous economy of words the essence of the very special part of America where she was raised. A poetic text projects emotion as well as information. . . . Moser's watercolors capture the scene perfectly. . . . The book is a treasure—simply a beautiful combination of text and art." Horn Book

974.4 Massachusetts

Armentrout, David, 1962-
The Mayflower Compact; [by] David & Patricia Armentrout. Rourke Pub. 2005 48p il map (Documents that shaped the nation) $29.93; pa $8.45
Grades: 4 5 6 7   **974.4**
1. Mayflower (Ship) 2. Pilgrims (New England colonists) 3. Massachusetts—History—1600-1775, Colonial period
ISBN 1-59515-229-6; 1-59515-334-9 (pa)
                    LC 2004-14413
Contents: The Pilgrims; Before the Pilgrims; The Church of England; The Scrooby separatists; William Bradford; Escape; Life in Holland; Choosing America; Merchant adventurers; Saints and strangers; A leaky mess; The Mayflower; Life at sea; Land!; The Mayflower Compact; A new settlement

The book introduces "the cultural and political factors that lead to the creation of [The Mayflower Compact], admirably distilling pertinent events into simple language that still manages to explain the complex issues and connections. . . . A wide mix of archival etchings, portraits, maps, and other images illustrate the [text]." Booklist
Includes glossary and bibliographical references

Collier, Christopher, 1930-
Pilgrims and Puritans, 1620-1676; [by] Christopher Collier, James Lincoln Collier. Benchmark Bks. (Tarrytown) 1998 94p il maps (Drama of American history) lib bdg $31.36 *
Grades: 6 7 8 9   **974.4**
1. Pilgrims (New England colonists) 2. Puritans 3. Massachusetts—History—1600-1775, Colonial period
ISBN 0-7614-0438-4   LC 96-49382
Recounts the religious, political, and social history of the Massachusetts Bay Colony, and its influence on our lives today
Includes bibliographical references

Edwards, Judith
The Plymouth Colony and the Pilgrim adventure in American history. Enslow Pubs. 2003 128p il map (In American history) lib bdg $26.60
Grades: 7 8 9 10   **974.4**
1. Pilgrims (New England colonists) 2. Massachusetts—History—1600-1775, Colonial period
ISBN 0-7660-1989-6   LC 2002-12809
Contents: Landahoy!; In search of religious freedom; The first emigration; Setting out for America; The Mayflower Compact; The howling of wolves; Betrayal and the threat of war; Hunger, treachery and pirates; Daily life at Plymouth; Expansion and legacy
Traces the dangers and adventures surrounding the history of the Pilgrim settlement at Plymouth, Massachusetts, highlighting the roles played by William Brewster, Miles Standish, and other individuals
Includes bibliographical references

Erickson, Paul, 1976-
Daily life in the Pilgrim colony, 1636. Clarion Bks. 2001 48p il map $20; pa $9.95
Grades: 4 5 6 7   **974.4**
1. Pilgrims (New England colonists) 2. Massachusetts—History—1600-1775, Colonial period
ISBN 0-618-05846-X; 0-395-98841-1 (pa)
                    LC 2001-17203
This "describes the day-to-day activities of the Prentiss family, owners of a small farm just outside the colony of Plymouth. Full-color photographs, maps, line drawings, and detailed illustrations accompany engaging present-tense text to provide insight into Pilgrim society as a whole, and into the lives of specific family members as well." Book Rep

974.7   New York

Bial, Raymond
Tenement; immigrant life on the Lower East Side. Houghton Mifflin 2002 48p il $16 *
Grades: 4 5 6 7   **974.7**
1. Poor 2. Immigrants—United States 3. Lower East Side (New York, N.Y.)
ISBN 0-618-13849-8   LC 2002-00407
Presents a view of New York City's tenements during the peak years of foreign immigration, discussing living conditions, laws pertaining to tenements, and the occupations of their residents
"The writing is particularly clear and sharp. Calling upon and quoting the writing of reformer Jacob Riis (and featuring his compelling photographs), Bial explains simply, yet engagingly, what tenement life was like. . . . Along with Riis' photographs, Bial provides some of his own, taken at the Lower East Side Tenement Museum in New York City." Booklist
Includes bibliographical references

Getzinger, Donna, 1968-
The Triangle Shirtwaist Factory fire. Morgan Reynolds Pub. 2008 128p il map (American workers) $27.95 *
Grades: 7 8 9 10   **974.7**
1. Triangle Shirtwaist Company, Inc. 2. New York (N.Y.)—History 3. Labor—Law and legislation
ISBN 978-1-59935-099-8; 1-59935-099-8
                                        LC 2008-4077
"Beginning with a brief account of the disaster, a description of the popular shirtwaist and the fabric used to make the blouse, the women who lost their lives, and the impact of the lack of communication among the workers, the first chapter is sure to hook readers. Successive chapters look more closely at New York City's growth, the varied immigrant population at that time, overcrowded factory conditions, the failure to enforce building regulations, and the many sweatshops developed from the desire of contractors to make money. . . . Archival photos and diagrams with captions add to the meaning of this devastating and important event in the history of labor." SLJ
Includes bibliographical references

Hansen, Joyce
Breaking ground, breaking silence; the story of New York's African burial ground; by Joyce Hansen and Gary McGowan. Holt & Co. 1998 130p il maps $19.95 *
Grades: 8 9 10 11 12 Adult   **974.7**
1. African Americans—History 2. Cemeteries 3. Excavations (Archeology) 4. New York (N.Y.)—Antiquities
ISBN 0-8050-5012-4   LC 97-19105
Describes the discovery and study of the African burial site found in Manhattan in 1991, while excavating for a new building, and what it reveals about the lives of black people in Colonial times
"This book is well written and attractively designed, and readers should have access to it in social studies

classrooms as well as in libraries. It will generate lots of class discussion and writing projects." Voice Youth Advocates

Hopkinson, Deborah
Shutting out the sky; life in the tenements of New York, 1880-1924. Orchard Bks. 2003 134p il $17.95
Grades: 5 6 7 8 9 10   **974.7**
1. Poor 2. Immigrants—United States 3. Lower East Side (New York, N.Y.)
ISBN 0-439-37590-8   LC 2002-44781
Contents: Coming to the golden land; Tenements: shutting out the sky; Settling in: greenhorns and boarders; Everyone worked on; On the streets: pushcarts, pickles and play; A new language, a new life; Looking to the future: will it ever be different?
Photographs and text document the experiences of five individuals who came to live in the Lower East Side of New York City as children or young adults from Belarus, Italy, Lithuania, and Romania at the turn of the twentieth century.
"The text is supported by numerous tinted archival photos of living and working conditions. Although this book will appeal to students looking for material for projects, the writing lends immediacy and vivid images make it simply a fascinating read." SLJ
Includes bibliographical references

Houle, Michelle M.
Triangle Shirtwaist Factory fire; flames of labor reform. Enslow Pubs. 2002 48p il (American disasters) lib bdg $23.93
Grades: 4 5 6 7   **974.7**
1. Triangle Shirtwaist Company, Inc. 2. Factories 3. Clothing industry
ISBN 0-7660-1785-0   LC 2001-7667
Discusses the 1911 fire that killed 146 New York garment factory workers, the conditions that led up to it, and some of the legislation that came about to prevent the occurrence of similar disasters
"The short chapters are enlivened with period photographs, including a horrific view of the bodies of women who had leaped to their deaths to escape the flames. Although the text is easy to read, the horror is not sugarcoated." SLJ
Includes bibliographical references

Matsen, Bradford
Go wild in New York City; [by] Brad Matsen; illustrations by Paul Corio; scientific illustration by Kate Lake. National Geographic 2005 79p il map $16.95
Grades: 4 5 6 7   **974.7**
1. Natural history 2. New York (N.Y.)
ISBN 0-7922-7982-4
This is a "picture-book tour through New York City's 'true wildness,' with chapters that cover the area's water, rocks, air, plants, and animals as well as a closing section about food production and waste removal. . . . Packed with color photographs, cartoons, diagrams, and numerous sidebars. . . . There's an impressive array of

Matsen, Bradford—*Continued*

basic science here, described mostly in accessible, enthusiastic text. Students will find enough to support reports, and the open format will attract browsers." Booklist

Pellowski, Michael, 1949-

The terrorist trial of the 1993 bombing of the World Trade Center; a headline court case. Enslow Pubs. 2003 112p il (Headline court cases) lib bdg $26.60

Grades: 6 7 8 9　　　　　　　　　　　　**974.7**

1. Trials 2. World Trade Center Bombing, New York, N.Y., 1993 3. Terrorism

ISBN 0-7660-2045-2　　　　　LC 2002-156033

Contents: Smoke, terror, and death; A plot unravels; Islam and Terrorism: a history; Tracking the terrorists; Terror on trial; A worldwide manhunt; Justice revisited; The terrorism continues

Examines the trials of Mahmoud Abouhalima, Ramzi Yousef, Mohammad Salameh, Sheik Omar Abdel-Rahman, and others for their roles in the 1993 bombing of the World Trade Center

"A well-balanced look at the events leading up to, during, and after the 1993 bombing. . . . The text is clear and succinct." SLJ

Includes glossary and bibliographical references

Talbott, Hudson

River of dreams; the story of the Hudson River. G. P. Putnam's Sons 2009 unp il map $17.99 *

Grades: 4 5 6 7　　　　　　　　　　　　**974.7**

1. Hudson River (N.Y. and N.J.)

ISBN 978-0-399-24521-3; 0-399-24521-9

Talbott offers a "compelling blend of political and natural history in this beautifully illustrated celebration of the Hudson River. Combining delicate watercolor-and-pencil illustrations with accessible text, the spreads move briskly through the Hudson's River's history." Booklist

Whitcraft, Melissa

The Hudson River. Watts 1999 63p il lib bdg $24.50; pa $8.95

Grades: 5 6 7 8　　　　　　　　　　　　**974.7**

1. Hudson River (N.Y. and N.J.)

ISBN 0-531-11739-1 (lib bdg); 0-531-16425-X (pa)
　　　　　　　　　　　　　　　　　　LC 99-28585

Examines the history, uses, changing nature, and ecological aspects of the Hudson River

The text is "well researched and thoughtful, making sure both the geographic concepts and the history are understandable. The spacious layout includes large color photographs on every spread, with sidebars adding further information. . . . Lists of further readings, organizations, Internet sites, and a glossary are appended." Booklist

Includes bibliographical references

975.3　District of Columbia (Washington)

Ashabranner, Brent K., 1921-

No better hope; what the Lincoln Memorial means to America; [by] Brent Ashabranner; photographs by Jennifer Ashabranner. 21st Cent. Bks. (Brookfield) 2001 64p il (Great American memorials) lib bdg $25.90

Grades: 4 5 6 7　　　　　　　　　　　　**975.3**

1. Lincoln, Abraham, 1809-1865 2. Lincoln Memorial (Washington, D.C.)

ISBN 0-7613-1523-3　　　　　　LC 00-61546

"Seven brief chapters review Lincoln's presidency, discuss preliminary plans for a permanent memorial, describe the processes by which architect Henry Bacon and sculptor Daniel French developed and executed their creation, and suggest how the site has 'become a symbol of the "patient confidence" that Lincoln had in the wisdom and courage of the common people.'" Bull Cent Child Books

A "well-designed volume. . . . Excellent color photographs by Jennifer Ashabranner appear throughout the book." Booklist

Includes bibliographical references

Our White House; looking in, looking out; created by The National Children's Book and Literacy Alliance; introduction by David McCullough. Candlewick Press 2008 241p il $29.99 *

Grades: 5 6 7 8　　　　　　　　　　　　**975.3**

1. White House (Washington, D.C.)

ISBN 978-0-7636-2067-7; 0-7636-2067-X

"The White House is the focus of this handsome, large-format compendium of writings, both factual and fictional, and illustrations. . . . Poems and essays, stories and memoirs—all combine to create a mosaic of impressions of the house's residents and visitors and of the important events that occurred there. . . . The often-spectacular, beautifully reproduced on glossy paper, is particularly striking." Booklist

975.6　North Carolina

Miller, Lee

Roanoke; the mystery of the Lost Colony. Scholastic Nonfiction 2007 112p il map $18.99

Grades: 4 5 6 7　　　　　　　　　　　　**975.6**

1. Roanoke Island (N.C.)—History 2. United States—History—1600-1775, Colonial period

ISBN 0-439-71266-1; 978-0-439-71266-8
　　　　　　　　　　　　　　　　　　LC 2005-51820

"Miller, author of *Roanoke: solving the mystery of the Lost Colony* (2001), here reprises for a young audience her historical theory that a certain man sabotaged the expedition eventually known as the Lost Colony. . . . Miller does an exceptional job of presenting the Native American culture and viewpoint. . . . This handsomely designed book features one or two illustrations on each spread, many in color, including reproductions or period drawings, paintings, and maps, as well as modern photos of sites and wildlife." Booklist

Includes bibliographical references

Reed, Jennifer
Cape Hatteras National Seashore; adventure, explore, discover; [by] Jennifer Reed. MyReportLinks.com Books 2008 128p il map (America's national parks) lib bdg $33.27
Grades: 5 6 7 8   **975.6**
  1. National parks and reserves—United States 2. Cape Hatteras National Seashore (N.C.)
  ISBN 978-1-59845-086-6 (lib bdg); 1-59845-086-7 (lib bdg)   LC 2006102321
  This "informative, well-written book contains a physical description of the park; a summary of its history including the Native peoples of the area; activities such as hiking trails, campsites, and visitor centers; information about the park's plants, animals, and weather; full-color photographs; and numerous approved links available through the publisher's Web page. . . . Thorough, useful, and appealing, this . . . is a great update for collections." SLJ
  Includes glossary and bibliographical references

975.9 Florida

Jankowski, Susan
Everglades National Park; adventure, explore, discover; [by] Susan Jankowski. MyReportLinks.com Books 2009 128p il map (America's national parks) lib bdg $33.27
Grades: 5 6 7 8   **975.9**
  1. National parks and reserves—United States 2. Everglades National Park (Fla.)
  ISBN 978-1-59845-091-0 (lib bdg); 1-59845-091-3 (lib bdg)   LC 2007-38262
  This "informative, well-written book contains a physical description of the park; a summary of its history including the Native peoples of the area; activities such as hiking trails, campsites, and visitor centers; information about the park's plants, animals, and weather; full-color photographs; and numerous approved links available through the publisher's Web page. . . . Thorough, useful, and appealing, this . . . is a great update for collections." SLJ
  Includes glossary and bibliographical references

976.4 Texas

Levy, Janey
The Alamo; a primary source history of the legendary Texas mission. Rosen Central Primary Source 2003 64p il maps (Primary sources in American history) lib bdg $29.25
Grades: 7 8 9 10   **976.4**
  1. Alamo (San Antonio, Tex.) 2. Texas—History
  ISBN 0-8239-3681-3   LC 2002-2368
  Contents: The first settlers and explorers; Timeline; Life on Mexico's northern frontier; The gathering clouds of war; The Alamo's defenders; The siege and battle of the Alamo; After the Alamo; The legend of the Alamo
  A collection of primary source materials highlights the story behind the Alamo and its place in the history of San Antonio, Texas

This "will be extremely effective when introducing students to primary source material." Libr Media Connect
  Includes bibliographical references

McNeese, Tim
The Alamo. Chelsea House 2003 136p il map (Sieges that changed the world) lib bdg $22.95
Grades: 5 6 7 8   **976.4**
  1. Alamo (San Antonio, Tex.) 2. Texas—History
  ISBN 0-7910-7101-4   LC 2002-12914
  Contents: The lands of Tejas; Gone to Texas; A land of revolution; The Texans defend themselves; The siege begins; Victory or death; The Mexicans are coming; Will you come to the bower?
  Describes the historical background, events, and aftermath of the 1836 attack on the Alamo, in which Jim Bowie and Davy Crockett were among the many Texans killed or captured by Santa Ana's troops
  The author presents "an excellent overview of Texas history in the first half of the book and details the two-week siege in the second. . . . A well-written, well-researched chronicle." SLJ
  Includes bibliographical references

Walker, Paul Robert
Remember the Alamo; Texians, Tejanos, and Mexicans tell their stories; by Paul Robert Walker. National Geographic 2007 61p il map $17.95; lib bdg $27.90
Grades: 5 6 7 8   **976.4**
  1. Alamo (San Antonio, Tex.) 2. Texas—History
  ISBN 978-1-4263-0010-3; 978-1-4263-0011-0 (lib bdg)   LC 2006034497
  "Opening with clear context about why tensions between Texas residents and the Mexican government were brought to a head, the book then chronicles events directly leading to the siege of the Alamo and its immediate aftermath, following up with an epilogue on the decisive battle of San Jacinto 10 months later. Bringing the history to life is a healthy selection of dramatic, modern paintings along with plenty of archival drawings, maps, and old photos." Booklist
  Includes bibliographical references

Worth, Richard, 1945-
The Texas war of independence: the 1800s; by Richard Worth. Marshall Cavendish Benchmark 2009 79p il map (Hispanic America) lib bdg $23.95
Grades: 6 7 8 9   **976.4**
  1. Texas—History 2. Mexican War, 1846-1848 3. Mexican Americans
  ISBN 978-0-7614-2934-0   LC 2007029478
  "Provides comprehensive information on the history of Spanish exploration in the United States, focusing on the Texas Revolt and the Mexican War." Publisher's note
  This "provides a solid overview of these pivotal events in Hispanic American history. Illustrated throughout with maps and archival images." Booklist
  Includes glossary and bibliographical references

976.8   Tennessee

Graham, Amy
Great Smoky Mountains National Park;
adventure, explore, discover; [by] Amy Graham.
MyReportLinks.com Books 2009 128p il map
(America's national parks) lib bdg $33.27
Grades: 5 6 7 8   **976.8**
1. National parks and reserves—United States
2. Great Smoky Mountains National Park (N.C. and
Tenn.)
ISBN 978-1-59845-093-4 (lib bdg); 1-59845-093-X
(lib bdg)   LC 2007-13456
This "informative, well-written book contains a physical description of the park; a summary of its history including the Native peoples of the area; activities such as
hiking trails, campsites, and visitor centers; information
about the park's plants, animals, and weather; full-color
photographs; and numerous approved links available
through the publisher's Web page. . . . Thorough, useful, and appealing, this . . . is a great update for collections." SLJ
Includes glossary and bibliographical references

977   North Central United States. Lake states

Kummer, Patricia K.
The Great Lakes; [by] Patricia K. Kummer.
Marshall Cavendish Benchmark 2008 c2009 96p il
map (Nature's wonders) lib bdg $24.95
Grades: 5 6 7 8   **977**
1. Great Lakes
ISBN 978-0-7614-2853-4 (lib bdg); 0-7614-2853-4 (lib
bdg)   LC 2007019728
"Provides comprehensive information on the geogra-
phy, history, wildlife, peoples, and environmental issues
of the Great Lakes." Publisher's note
Includes glossary and bibliographical references

977.3   Illinois

Hurd, Owen
Chicago history for kids; triumphs and tragedies
of the Windy city, includes 21 activities; [by]
Owen Hurd. 1st ed. Chicago Review Press 2007
182p il map $14.95
Grades: 5 6 7 8   **977.3**
1. Chicago (Ill.)—History
ISBN 978-1-55652-654-1; 1-55652-654-7
LC 2006031807
"This attractive overview begins with geography and
moves to the colorful stories that characterize the city.
Hurd tapped local experts and collections, using primary
and secondary sources and the responses of young readers to craft this engaging resource. . . . Excellent-quality
photos, maps, illustrations, or boxed facts appear on every page." SLJ
Includes bibliographical references

Murphy, Jim, 1947-
The great fire. Scholastic 1995 144p il maps
$16.95 *
Grades: 5 6 7 8 9 10   **977.3**
1. Fires—Chicago (Ill.)
ISBN 0-590-47267-4   LC 94-9963
Newbery honor book, 1996
"Firsthand descriptions by persons who lived through
the 1871 Chicago fire are woven into a gripping account
of this famous disaster. Murphy also examines the origins of the fire, the errors of judgment that delayed the
effective response, the organizational problems of the
city's firefighters, and the postfire efforts to rebuild the
city. Newspaper lithographs and a few historical photographs convey the magnitude of human suffering and
confusion." Horn Book Guide
Includes bibliographical references

978   Western United States

The **American** frontier; James D. Torr, book
editor. Greenhaven Press 2002 240p il (Turning
points in world history) lib bdg $34.95; pa
$23.70
Grades: 7 8 9 10   **978**
1. Frontier and pioneer life—West (U.S.) 2. United
States—Territorial expansion 3. West (U.S.)—History
ISBN 0-7377-0786-0 (lib bdg); 0-7377-0785-2 (pa)
LC 2001-33514
This is a collection of essays about the American
frontier, with an introduction and summaries
Includes bibliographical references

Blumberg, Rhoda, 1917-
The incredible journey of Lewis and Clark.
Lothrop, Lee & Shepard Bks. 1987 143p il maps
pa $12.99 *
Grades: 5 6 7 8   **978**
1. Lewis, Meriwether, 1774-1809 2. Clark, William,
1770-1838 3. Lewis and Clark Expedition (1804-1806)
4. West (U.S.)—Exploration
ISBN 0-688-14421-7   LC 87-4235
Also available in hardcover from Smith, P.
Describes the expedition led by Lewis and Clark to
explore the unknown western regions of America at the
beginning of the nineteenth century
"Blumberg's writing is dignified but never dry, and
her sense of narrative makes familiar history an exciting
story." Bull Cent Child Books
Includes bibliographical references

York's adventures with Lewis and Clark; an
African-American's part in the great expedition.
HarperCollins 2004 88p il map $17.99; lib bdg
$18.89 *
Grades: 5 6 7 8   **978**
1. York, ca. 1775-ca. 1815 2. Lewis and Clark Expe-
dition (1804-1806) 3. West (U.S.)—Exploration
4. African Americans—Biography
ISBN 0-06-009111-8; 0-06-009112-6 (lib bdg)
LC 2003-9425

Blumberg, Rhoda, 1917-—_Continued_

Relates the adventures of York, a slave and "body servant" to William Clark, who journeyed west with the Lewis and Clark Expedition of 1804-1806

"This well-researched selection helps to round out the study of an amazing event in our country's history. . . . Meticulously documented and illustrated with black-and-white photos and reproductions, this is a solid purchase for all collections." SLJ

Includes bibliographical references

Calabro, Marian

The perilous journey of the Donner Party. Clarion Bks. 1999 192p il maps $20 *

Grades: 5 6 7 8 **978**

1. Donner party 2. Frontier and pioneer life—West (U.S.) 3. Overland journeys to the Pacific

ISBN 0-395-86610-3 LC 98-29610

Uses materials from letters and diaries written by survivors of the Donner Party to relate the experiences of that ill-fated group as they endured horrific circumstances on their way to California in 1846-47

"Calabro's offering is a fine addition to the Donner Party canon and particularly well suited to its young audience, for whom the story of hardship and survival will be nothing short of riveting. . . . From the haunting cover with its lonely campfire to the recounting of a survivors' reunion, this is a page-turner." Booklist

Includes bibliographical references

Clark, William, 1770-1838

Off the map; the journals of Lewis and Clark; edited by Peter and Connie Roop; illustrations by Tim Tanner. Walker & Co. 1993 40p il pa $8.95 hardcover o.p.

Grades: 5 6 7 8 **978**

1. Lewis and Clark Expedition (1804-1806) 2. West (U.S.)—Exploration

ISBN 0-8027-7546-2 LC 92-18340

A compilation of entries and excerpts from the journals of William Clark and Meriwether Lewis, describing their historic expedition

"The full-color illustrations, mainly in warm earth tones, give the pages an attractive look, but the most vivid pictures come from the journals themselves. . . . This vivid source material would be a welcome part of any classroom study of the subject." Booklist

Collier, Christopher, 1930-

Indians, cowboys, and farmers and the battle for the Great Plains, 1865-1910; [by] Christopher Collier, James Lincoln Collier. Benchmark Bks. (Tarrytown) 2001 95p il map (Drama of American history) lib bdg $31.36 *

Grades: 6 7 8 9 **978**

1. Great Plains—History 2. Native Americans—Great Plains

ISBN 0-7614-1052-X LC 00-21103

Discusses the settling of the area between the Missouri River and the Rocky Mountains and the conflicting interests of the different groups involved—the Indians, cowboys, farmers, sheepherders, and railroad barons

Includes bibliographical references

Croy, Anita

Ancient Pueblo; archaeology unlocks the secrets of America's past; by Anita Croy; J. Jefferson Reid, consultant. National Geographic 2007 64p il map (National Geographic investigates) $17.95; lib bdg $27.90 *

Grades: 4 5 6 7 **978**

1. Pueblo Indians 2. Archeology 3. Southwestern States—Antiquities

ISBN 978-1-4263-0130-8; 978-1-4263-0131-5 (lib bdg) LC 2007024800

This describes the prehistoric sites of the American Southwest, and what archeologists have learned from them about the lives of ancient Pueblo peoples.

Includes glossary and bibliographical references

Faber, Harold

Lewis and Clark; from ocean to ocean. Benchmark Bks. 2002 80p il map (Great explorations) lib bdg $29.93 *

Grades: 5 6 7 8 **978**

1. Lewis, Meriwether, 1774-1809 2. Clark, William, 1770-1838 3. Lewis and Clark Expedition (1804-1806) 4. West (U.S.)—Exploration

ISBN 0-7614-1241-7 LC 00-51898

This "discusses the 1804 expedition that set out to explore the American continent. . . . Supplementing Faber's account are journal quotations that offer firsthand reportage of events, conditions, and reflections about the journey. The last chapter tells what happened to significant members of the expedition and includes information on the Lewis and Clark Trail. . . . The colorful and sometimes quite beautiful illustrations include paintings, drawings, and prints, as well as a few photographs of sites and artifacts." Booklist

Includes bibliographical references

Galford, Ellen

The trail West; exploring history through art; [by] Ellen Galford. Two-Can Pub. 2005 64p il (Picture that!) $19.95 *

Grades: 5 6 7 8 **978**

1. West (U.S.)—History 2. West (U.S.) in art

ISBN 1-58728-442-1 LC 2004-8334

This examines pioneer life in the American West through the works of such artists as Wislow Homer, Eastman Johnson, George Catlin, and George Caleb Bingham

"Art and history meld with entertaining and successful results. . . . [This] unique, well-thought-out [title is] good for reports, and browsers would enjoy [it], too." SLJ

Josephson, Judith Pinkerton

Growing up in pioneer America, 1800 to 1890. Lerner Publs. 2003 64p il map (Our America) lib bdg $26.60

Grades: 5 6 7 8 **978**

1. Frontier and pioneer life—West (U.S.) 2. West (U.S.)—History

ISBN 0-8225-0659-9 LC 2001-6825

Josephson, Judith Pinkerton—*Continued*
Describes what life was like for young people moving to and living on the western frontier

"Primary-source materials including selections from letters and diaries join numerous reproductions and archival photos to deliver a clear picture of the varied experiences of children living in the U.S. during the 1800s. Accessible, attractive, and useful." SLJ
Includes bibliographical references

Katz, William Loren
Black women of the Old West. Atheneum Bks. for Young Readers 1995 84p il $19.95
Grades: 5 6 7 8 9   **978**
    1. African American women 2. Frontier and pioneer life—West (U.S.) 3. West (U.S.)—History
    ISBN 0-689-31944-4   LC 95-9969
This work contains "vignettes and photographs of dozens of women, some famous, others unknown outside their own family circles, who lived across the West in the 19th and early 20th centuries." N Y Times Book Rev

"Katz succeeds in establishing that women of color were an important, if unsung, presence on the westward-shifting frontier." Bull Cent Child Books

Lawlor, Laurie
Window on the West; the frontier photography of William Henry Jackson. Holiday House 1999 132p il $18.95
Grades: 7 8 9 10   **978**
    1. Jackson, William Henry, 1843-1942 2. West (U.S.)—History 3. Photography—History
    ISBN 0-8234-1380-2   LC 98-56083
Presents the photographs taken by William Henry Jackson from 1869 to 1893, discussing his life and how his work captured and introduced the American West to the public

"Jackson's images are balanced by Lawlor's eloquent text, which folds in details about everything from the wonder of Yellowstone's geysers to the debasement of the Native Americans. . . . A memorable, bittersweet valentine to the Old West." Booklist
Includes glossary and bibliographical references

Murdoch, David Hamilton, 1937-
Cowboy; written by David H. Murdoch; photographed by Geoff Brightling. Dorling Kindersley 2000 63p il map (DK eyewitness books) $19.99
Grades: 4 5 6 7   **978**
    1. Cowhands
    ISBN 0-7894-6594-9
    First published 1993
Text and photographs trace the history and lore of cowboys around the globe.

Olson, Tod, 1962-
How to get rich on the Oregon Trail; my adventures among cows, crooks & heroes on the road to fame and fortune; [illustrations by Scott Allred & Gregory Proch; afterword by Marc Anonson] National Geographic 2009 47p il (How to get rich) $18.95; lib bdg $27.90 *
Grades: 4 5 6 7   **978**
    1. Frontier and pioneer life 2. Oregon Trail 3. Overland journeys to the Pacific 4. West (U.S.)—History
    ISBN 978-1-4263-0412-5; 1-4263-0412-9; 978-1-4263-0413-2 (lib bdg); 1-4263-0413-7 (lib bdg)
"The action follows young Will Reed and his family as they set off from Illinois to find their fortune along the 2,000-mile Oregon Trail. . . . Informing Will's impish sketches and wry journal entries is a wealth of information about life along the trail. . . . An ongoing ledger calculates the family's balance as it fluctuates from $10.70 to $3,021.70, but it's clear that this journey is more about survival than riches. The illustrations, historical anecdotes, and run-ins with everyone from the Mormons to escaped slaves to Abraham Lincoln form a perfect blend of history and humbuggery." Booklist

Patent, Dorothy Hinshaw
Animals on the trail with Lewis and Clark; photographs by William Muñoz. Clarion Bks. 2002 118p il map $18
Grades: 4 5 6 7   **978**
    1. Lewis and Clark Expedition (1804-1806) 2. Animals—United States 3. West (U.S.)—Exploration
    ISBN 0-395-91415-9   LC 2001-42200
Retraces the Lewis and Clark journey and blends their observations of previously unknown animals with modern information about those same animals

"The spacious page layouts, beautiful illustrations, and well-written text help ensure that this historically significant story will be read and enjoyed." Booklist
Includes bibliographical references

The buffalo and the Indians; a shared destiny; photographs by William Muñoz. Clarion Books 2006 85p il $18
Grades: 5 6 7   **978**
    1. Native Americans—Great Plains 2. Bison 3. West (U.S.)—History
    ISBN 0-618-48570-8; 978-0-618-48570-3
Provides a review of the bond between Native Americans and buffalos throughout history and examines how European settlers disrupted nature's balance and nearly caused the extinction of an animal so highly respected by the native tribes

"Patent's narrative is clear and her writing is almost lyrical. Muñoz's breathtaking color photos of bison, landscapes, and artifacts are mixed with reproductions of period art and illustrations." SLJ
Includes bibliographical references

Patent, Dorothy Hinshaw—*Continued*

Plants on the trail with Lewis and Clark; photographs by William Muñoz. Clarion Bks. 2003 104p il map $18

Grades: 4 5 6 7 **978**
1. Lewis and Clark Expedition (1804-1806) 2. Plants—United States 3. West (U.S.)—Exploration
ISBN 0-618-06776-0 LC 2002-10383

Contents: Jefferson, Lewis, and plants; The importance of trees; Plants as food; Wildflowers and their uses; The fate of Lewis's specimens

Describes the journey of Lewis and Clark through the western United States, focusing on the plants they cataloged, their uses for food and medicine, and the plant lore of Native American people

"Good-quality, full-color photos and reproductions clearly extend the text. . . . The author's knowledge of and keen interest in her subject matter is very evident in this fascinating account." SLJ

Includes bibliographical references

Pendergast, Tom, 1964-

Westward expansion: almanac; [by] Tom Pendergast and Sara Pendergast; Christine Slovey, editor. U.X.L 2000 xlvi, 254p il $60

Grades: 8 9 10 11 12 **978**
1. Frontier and pioneer life—West (U.S.) 2. West (U.S.)—History 3. Reference books
ISBN 0-7876-4862-0 LC 00-36375

This almanac "documents the chronological events that created a romantic national mythology around the pioneers who blazed trails through the wilderness." Publisher's note

Includes bibliographical references

Westward expansion: primary sources; [by] Tom Pendergast and Sara Pendergast; Christine Slovey, editor. U.X.L 2001 xxix, 260p $60

Grades: 7 8 9 10 **978**
1. United States—Territorial expansion 2. West (U.S.)—History
ISBN 0-7876-4864-7 LC 00-107861

This volume provides "full text or excerpts from diaries, books, letters and many other documents." Publisher's note

Includes bibliographical references

Reis, Ronald A.

The Dust Bowl. Chelsea House Publishers 2008 128p il (Great historic disasters) lib bdg $35

Grades: 6 7 8 9 **978**
1. Great Plains—History 2. Dust storms 3. Droughts
ISBN 978-0-7910-9737-3 (lib bdg); 0-7910-9737-4 (lib bdg) LC 2008004952

This describes the conditions that led up to the disastrous dust storms of the 1930s in the American Great Plains, and their consequences

The book covers its topic "thoroughly and [includes] high-quality photographs and occasional sidebars. . . . Reis includes solid research and numerous points of view." SLJ

Includes glossary and bibliographical references

Schlissel, Lillian

Black frontiers; a history of African American heroes in the Old West. Simon & Schuster Bks. for Young Readers 1995 80p il hardcover o.p. pa $7.99

Grades: 5 6 7 8 **978**
1. African Americans—History 2. Frontier and pioneer life—West (U.S.) 3. West (U.S.)—History
ISBN 0-689-80285-4; 0-689-83315-6 (pa)
LC 92-120

Focuses on the experiences of blacks as mountain men, soldiers, homesteaders, and scouts on the frontiers of the American West

"Good-quality period photos and black-and-white reproductions appear on nearly every page, adding human interest and realism to the text. An excellent addition to black history or westward movement units." Booklist

Includes bibliographical references

Sonneborn, Liz

The Mormon Trail; [by] Liz Sonneborn. Franklin Watts 2005 63p il $25.50

Grades: 5 6 7 8 **978**
1. Mormons 2. Frontier and pioneer life—West (U.S.)
ISBN 0-531-12317-0 LC 2005001466

"Watts library"

This "title tells how in the 19th century Mormons traveled west to establish a community where they could practice their religion without fear of persecution. Black-and-white and color illustrations, maps, sidebars, and time lines enhance the well-organized [text]." SLJ

Includes bibliographical references

Steele, Christy

Cattle ranching in the American West; by Christy Steele. World Almanac Library 2005 48p il map (America's westward expansion) lib bdg $30; pa $11.95

Grades: 5 6 7 8 **978**
1. Ranch life 2. Cattle 3. West (U.S.)—History
ISBN 0-8368-5787-9 (lib bdg); 0-8368-5794-1 (pa)
LC 2004-56769

This volume describing Western cattle ranching is "richly illustrated with historical photographs, illustrations, maps, and quotes from primary sources presented in sidebars." SLJ

Includes bibliographical references

Pioneer life in the American West; by Christy Steele. World Almanac Library 2005 48p il map (America's westward expansion) lib bdg $30; pa $11.95

Grades: 5 6 7 8 **978**
1. Frontier and pioneer life 2. West (U.S.)—History
ISBN 0-8368-5790-9 (lib bdg); 0-8368-5797-6 (pa)
LC 2004-56772

This description of pioneer life in the American West is "richly illustrated with historical photographs, illustrations, maps, and quotes from primary sources presented in sidebars." SLJ

Includes bibliographical references

Stefoff, Rebecca, 1951-

American voices from the opening of the West.
Benchmark Bks. 2002 c2003 105p (American
voices from--) lib bdg $32.79 *
Grades: 6 7 8 9   **978**
1. Frontier and pioneer life—West (U.S.) 2. West
(U.S.)—History
ISBN 0-7614-1201-8   LC 2001-8681
Contents: The frontier; The explorers; Mountain men
and miners; The Overland Trails; Women and children in
the West; Living and working on the land; Building the
new West; The fate of the Native Americans
Presents the history of the westward expansion of the
United States in the eighteenth and nineteenth centuries
through excerpts from letters, newspaper articles, journal
entries, and laws of the time
Includes glossary and bibliographical references

American voices from the Wild West. Marshall
Cavendish Benchmark 2007 111p (American
voices from--) lib bdg $37.07 *
Grades: 6 7 8 9   **978**
1. West (U.S.)—History
ISBN 978-0-7614-2170-2 (lib bdg); 0-7614-2170-X
(lib bdg)   LC 2005028192
"Presents the history of the Wild West through a variety of primary source images and documents, such as diary entries, newspaper accounts, public speeches, popular
literature, and personal letters." Publisher's note
Includes glossary and bibliographical references

Tunis, Edwin, 1897-1973

Frontier living; written and illustrated by Edwin
Tunis. Lyons Press 2000 165p il map pa $18.95 *
Grades: 5 6 7 8 9 10   **978**
1. Frontier and pioneer life—West (U.S.) 2. West
(U.S.)—History
ISBN 1-58574-137-X   LC 00-710694
Companion volume to Colonial living (1976)
First published 1961 by World Publishing Company
On cover: An illustrated guide to pioneer life in
America, including log cabins, furniture, tools, clothing,
and more
This volume "portrays the manners and customs of the
frontiersman and his family from the beginning of the
westward movement through the 19th century in . . .
text and more than 200 drawings." Wis Libr Bull

Vivian, R. Gwinn

Chaco Canyon; [by] R. Gwinn Vivian and
Margaret Anderson. Oxford University Press 2002
47p il maps (Digging for the past) $19.95
Grades: 5 6 7 8   **978**
1. Pueblo Indians 2. Cliff dwellers and cliff dwellings
3. Chaco Culture National Historical Park (N.M.)
4. Archeology
ISBN 0-19-514280-2   LC 2001-54855
Relates the nineteenth-century discovery of cliff dwellings in the Chaco Canyon of northwest New Mexico, the
excavations of the ancient ruins, and what the artifacts
reveal about the civilization of the ancient Pueblo Indians
This "brings young readers up close to the field of archaeology. . . . Sharp color photos show the sites, arti-

facts, and the scientists at work." Booklist
Includes glossary and bibliographical references

Westward expansion; James D. Torr, book editor.
Greenhaven Press 2003 208p map (Interpreting
primary documents) $33.70; pa $22.45
Grades: 7 8 9 10   **978**
1. Frontier and pioneer life—West (U.S.) 2. West
(U.S.)—History
ISBN 0-7377-1134-5; 0-7377-1133-7 (pa)
    LC 2002-499
Contents: The lure of the west; Conquest of native
America; Manifest Destiny; The Western railroads
Uses primary source materials, including letters and
magazine articles of the time, to examine the exploration
and conquest of the American West by explorers and settlers of European descent.
"Students will welcome the summary provided at the
beginning of each document and the questions for consideration. A good choice for those who are eager to understand arguments and attitudes that shaped the history
of the West." SLJ
Includes bibliographical references

978.03   Western United States— Encyclopedias and dictionaries

The **Old** West: history and heritage; editor,
Edward Countryman. Marshall Cavendish
Reference 2009 11v il map set $359.95 *
Grades: 6 7 8 9   **978.03**
1. West (U.S.)—History—Encyclopedias 2. Reference
books
ISBN 978-0-7614-7829-4; 0-7614-7829-9
    LC 2008062302
In this set "each volume contains about 100 pages
with 18 to 21 signed articles that vary in length from 3
to 10 pages and are arranged in an easy-to-use alphabetical sequence. The overall style is lively and enticing. The
scope of the 193 articles includes the Canadian West and
the Mexican territory and deals with the time period
from 1787 to 1912. . . . The set is thoughtfully arranged
and can be used by a wide range of students. The articles
are interesting and enlightening." Booklist
Includes glossary and bibliographical references

978.1   Kansas

McArthur, Debra

The Kansas-Nebraska Act and "Bleeding
Kansas" in American history. Enslow Pubs. 2003
128p il map (In American history) lib bdg $26.60
Grades: 6 7 8 9   **978.1**
1. Abolitionists 2. Slavery—United States 3. Kansas—
History
ISBN 0-7660-1988-8   LC 2002-152064
Describes the violent period of Kansas Territory histo-
ry, prior to statehood and the Civil War, when abolition-
ists and pro-slavery factions openly murdered in defense
of their cause
Includes bibliographical references

979.1   Arizona

Rawlins, Carol
The Colorado River; [by] Carol B. Rawlins. Watts 1999 63p il (Watts library) lib bdg $24.50; pa $8.95

Grades: 5 6 7 8   **979.1**
1. Colorado River (Colo.-Mexico)
ISBN 0-531-11738-3 (lib bdg); 0-531-16421-7 (pa)
LC 98-52125

This title discusses "the course of the river and its related landforms, including the Grand Canyon. There is also an extensive section on dams and their ability to produce hydroelectric power, as well as on the many irrigation canals and ditches built along the river. The ancient peoples of the area are described, as are Spanish and American explorers." SLJ

Includes glossary and bibliographical references

979.4   California

Murphy, Claire Rudolf
Children of Alcatraz; growing up on the rock. Walker & Co. 2006 64p il map $17.95; lib bdg $18.85

Grades: 5 6 7 8   **979.4**
1. Alcatraz Island (Calif.)
ISBN   0-8027-9577-3;   978-0-8027-9577-9;
0-8027-9578-1 (lib bdg); 978-0-8027-9578-1 (lib bdg)
LC 2006-10588

"Murphy's clearly written history starts with the island's use by Native Americans in the pre-Colonial era and continues through its various incarnations as a lighthouse, military post, and then prison. She follows the federal penitentiary years, the island's rearming during World War II, the Native American occupation of 1969-71, and the island's current incarnation as a National Historical Park. . . . Liberally illustrated with black-and-white archival photographs, the book also includes print, AV, and Internet resources. While useful for reports, this title will appeal to general readers." SLJ

Includes bibliographical references

O'Donnell, Kerri, 1972-
The gold rush; a primary source history of the search for gold in California. Rosen Central Primary Source 2003 64p il maps (Primary sources in American history) lib bdg $29.25

Grades: 4 5 6 7   **979.4**
1. California—Gold discoveries 2. Frontier and pioneer life—California
ISBN 0-8239-3682-1   LC 2002-1367

Contents: El Dorado; Timeline; The great discovery; Gold fever; To California by sea; The Overlanders; Life in the mines; The lawless West

Uses primary source documents, narrative, and illustrations to recount how the mid-nineteenth century California gold rush affected Americans and immigrants and how it shaped history

This "will be extremely effective when introducing students to primary source material." Libr Media Connect

Includes glossary and bibliographical references

Olson, Tod, 1962-
How to get rich in the California Gold Rush; an adventurer's guide to the fabulous riches discovered in 1848 . . .; illustrations by Scott Allred; afterword by Marc Aronson. National Geographic 2008 47p il map (How to get rich) $16.95; lib bdg $25.90 *

Grades: 4 5 6 7   **979.4**
1. California—Gold discoveries 2. Frontier and pioneer life—California 3. Gold mines and mining 4. California—History
ISBN   978-1-4263-0315-9;   1-4263-0315-7;
978-1-4263-0316-6 (lib bdg); 1-4263-0316-5 (lib bdg)
LC 2008-19601

The fictional Thomas Hartley gives readers a historical portrait of life in the California gold fields

This "deftly blends story with history to not only give readers an understanding of a gold rush but also to provide a lighthearted and engaging entry point into frontier life. . . . Period lithographs are reproduced alongside original illustrations. . . . A ledger on each page tracks the young men's finances in a genuinely exciting way, adding a sly element of math to this well-conceived and compulsively appealing book." Booklist

Includes bibliographical references

979.7   Washington

Jankowski, Susan
Olympic National Park; adventure, explore, discover;   [by]   Susan   Jankowski. MyReportLinks.com Books 2009 128p il map (America's national parks) lib bdg $33.27

Grades: 5 6 7 8   **979.7**
1. National parks and reserves—United States 2. Olympic National Park (Wash.)
ISBN 978-1-59845-092-7 (lib bdg); 1-59845-092-1 (lib bdg)   LC 2007-17341

This "informative, well-written book contains a physical description of the park; a summary of its history including the Native peoples of the area; activities such as hiking trails, campsites, and visitor centers; information about the park's plants, animals, and weather; full-color photographs; and numerous approved links available through the publisher's Web page. . . . Thorough, useful, and appealing, this . . . is a great update for collections." SLJ

Includes glossary and bibliographical references

980   History of South America

Gorrell, Gena K. (Gena Kinton), 1946-
In the land of the jaguar; South America and its people; illustrated by Andrej Krystoforski. Tundra Books 2007 149p il $22.95 *

Grades: 5 6 7 8 9   **980**
1. South America
ISBN 978-0-88776-756-2

"This beautifully designed volume, with an engaging narrative, combines a highly informative overview of the continent with country-by-country detail. . . . The spa-

Gorrell, Gena K. (Gena Kinton), 1946-—_Continued_

cious design includes big maps, clear type on thick paper, and small, beautiful, fully captioned illustrations." Booklist

981   Brazil

Berkenkamp, Lauri

Discover the Amazon; the world's largest rainforest; illustrated by Blair Shedd. Nomad Press 2008 90p il map pa $16.95

Grades: 4 5 6 7   **981**

1. Amazon River valley

ISBN 978-1-9346702-7-9; 1-9346702-7-8

"Berkenkamp's introduction to the [Amazon] river basin incorporates maps, drawings, and photos in various shades of green and brown on recycled paper. . . . The conversational style provides a 'you are there' feeling, conveying information and anecdotes while stressing outdoor survival skills. . . . Even readers who never travel to Amazonia will appreciate the region's complexity and significance after perusing this book." SLJ

Deckker, Zilah

Brazil; [by] Zilah Deckker; David Robinson and Joao Cezar de Castro Rocha, consultants. National Geographic 2008 64p il (Countries of the world) lib bdg $27.90 *

Grades: 4 5 6 7   **981**

1. Brazil

ISBN 978-1-4263-0298-5 (lib bdg); 1-4263-0298-3 (lib bdg)

This describes the geography, nature, history, people and culture, government, and economy of Brazil.

Includes glossary and bibliographical references

Streissguth, Thomas

Brazil in pictures; by Tom Streissguth. rev and expanded. Lerner Publs. 2003 80p il map (Visual geography series) lib bdg $21.27

Grades: 5 6 7 8   **981**

1. Brazil

ISBN 0-8225-1959-3   LC 2001-3275

Replaces the edition published 1987 prepared by Nathan A. Haverstock

An introduction to Brazil, discussing its history, government, economy, people, and culture

Includes bibliographical references

982   Argentina

Fearns, Les, 1951-

Argentina; [by] Les and Daisy Fearns. Facts on File 2005 61p il map (Countries of the world) $30

Grades: 7 8 9 10   **982**

1. Argentina

ISBN 0-8160-6008-8   LC 2005040675

This is an introduction to Argentina's "culture, history, geography, government, and economy. [It is] competently written and [contains] current information. [The text is] clear but the level of vocabulary is quite high, which might prove challenging for less competent readers. Visually, the [book is] quite impressive, with full-color photographs, maps, tables, and graphs distributed throughout." SLJ

Includes bibliographical references

Gofen, Ethel, 1937-

Argentina; by Ethel Caro Gofen, Leslie Jermyn. 2nd ed. Benchmark Bks. 2002 144p il map (Cultures of the world) lib bdg $37.07

Grades: 5 6 7 8   **982**

1. Argentina

ISBN 0-7614-1358-8   LC 2001-47759

First published 1991

Presents the history, geography, government, economy, people, and social life and customs of Argentina

Includes glossary and bibliographical references

983   Chile

Winter, Jane Kohen, 1959-

Chile; by Jane Kohen Winter, Susan Roraff. 2nd ed. Benchmark Bks. 2002 144p il map (Cultures of the world) lib bdg $37.07

Grades: 5 6 7 8   **983**

1. Chile

ISBN 0-7614-1360-X   LC 2001-47827

First published 1991

Introduces the history, geography, culture, and lifestyles of Chile

Includes glossary and bibliographical references

984   Bolivia

Pateman, Robert, 1954-

Bolivia; [by] Robert Pateman & Marcus Cramer. 2nd ed. Marshall Cavendish Benchmark 2006 144p il map (Cultures of the world) lib bdg $39.93

Grades: 5 6 7 8   **984**

1. Bolivia

ISBN 978-0-7614-2066-8 (lib bdg); 0-7614-2066-5 (lib bdg)   LC 2006002425

First published 1995

This provides "information on the geography, history, governmental structure, economy, cultural diversity, peoples, religion, and culture of Bolivia." Publisher's note

This is "well organized, informative, and entertaining. . . . Excellent-quality full-color photographs and reproductions show the people, landforms, buildings, and everyday activities." SLJ

Includes bibliographical references

985 Peru

Bingham, Jane
The Inca empire; [by] Jane Bingham. Raintree 2007 64p il map (Time travel guide) lib bdg $34.29; pa $9.99
Grades: 6 7 8 9   **985**
1. Incas 2. Peru
ISBN 978-1-4109-2731-6 (lib bdg); 1-4109-2731-8 (lib bdg); 978-1-4109-2738-5 (pa); 1-4109-2738-5 (pa)
LC 2006033877
"Raintree FreeStyle"
This describes life in the ancient Inca empire in the form of a travel guide.
Includes glossary and bibliographical references

Calvert, Patricia, 1931-
The ancient Inca; written by Patricia Calvert. Franklin Watts 2004 128p il (People of the ancient world) lib bdg $29.50; pa $9.95 *
Grades: 5 6 7 8   **985**
1. Incas
ISBN 0-531-12358-8 (lib bdg); 0-531-16740-2 (pa)
LC 2004-1956
Contents: The science of the past: why it matters; Before the Inca; Children of the sun; Life in a highland family; Growing up among the Inca; Medicine, magic, and death; The top of the Inca pyramid; Warriors, war, and keeping the peace; Buildings, bridges, and roads; The war of two brothers; Suncasapa, the bearded one; The aftermath of conquest
This "well-written, attractive [title has] extensive collections of quality color photographs of ruins and artifacts." SLJ
Includes bibliographical references

Donovan, Sandra, 1967-
Teens in Peru; by Sandy Donovan. Compass Point Books 2009 95p il (Global connections) lib bdg $33.26
Grades: 6 7 8 9   **985**
1. Peru 2. Teenagers
ISBN 978-0-7565-3852-1 (lib bdg); 0-7565-3852-1 (lib bdg)
LC 2008-6503
Uncovers the challenges, pastimes, customs and culture of teens in Peru
This book is "concise and highly readable. . . . Clear, colorful photos and sidebars on a range of topics provide further context. . . . [This title] will enrich young adult collections." SLJ
Includes glossary and bibliographic references

Falconer, Kieran, 1970-
Peru; [by] Kieran Falconer & Lynette Quek. 2nd ed. Marshall Cavendish Benchmark 2006 144p il map (Cultures of the world) lib bdg $37.07 *
Grades: 5 6 7 8   **985**
1. Peru
ISBN 978-0-7614-2068-2 (lib bdg); 0-7614-2068-1 (lib bdg)
First published 1995

This provides "information on the geography, history, governmental structure, economy, cultural diversity, peoples, religion, and culture of Peru." Publisher's note
Includes glossary and bibliographical references

Gruber, Beth
Ancient Inca; archaeology unlocks the secrets of the Inca's past; by Beth Gruber; Johan Reinhard, consultant. National Geographic 2007 64p il map (National Geographic investigates) $17.95; lib bdg $27.90 *
Grades: 5 6 7 8   **985**
1. Incas 2. Excavations (Archeology)—Peru 3. Peru—Antiquities
ISBN 978-0-7922-7827-6; 978-0-7922-7873-3 (lib bdg)
LC 2006032104
This describes how archeologists have found out about ancient Incan civilization.
This offers "the beautiful photography and illustrations characteristic of the National Geographic Society, [a] well-written [text] and sidebars, and information on recent archaeological finds." SLJ
Includes bibliographical references

986.1 Colombia

Croy, Anita
Colombia; [by] Anita Croy; Ulrich Oslender and Mauricio Pardo, consultants. National Geographic 2008 64p il map (Countries of the world) $27.90 *
Grades: 4 5 6 7   **986.1**
1. Colombia
ISBN 978-1-4263-0257-2; 1-4263-0257-6
This describes the geography, nature, history, people and culture, government, and economy of Colombia
Includes glossary and bibliographical references

DuBois, Jill, 1952-
Colombia; by Jill DuBois, Leslie Jermyn. 2nd ed. Benchmark Bks. 2002 144p il map (Cultures of the world) lib bdg $37.07
Grades: 5 6 7 8   **986.1**
1. Colombia
ISBN 0-7614-1361-8   LC 2001-47264
First published 1991
Presents the geography, history, government, economy, and social life and customs of the country of Colombia
Includes glossary and bibliographical references

986.6 Ecuador

Foley, Erin, 1967-
Ecuador; [by] Erin L. Foley & Leslie Jermyn. 2nd ed. Marshall Cavendish Benchmark 2006 144p il map (Cultures of the world) lib bdg $37.07 *
Grades: 5 6 7 8   **986.6**
1. Ecuador
ISBN 0-7614-2050-9   LC 2005022671

Foley, Erin, 1967——*Continued*
First published 1995
This briefly describes Ecuador's "history, government, economy, and geography. . . . Particularly useful is the information on religion, the arts, food, leisure activities, and social roles. The [book has] great visual appeal with excellent full-color photographs on every page. [It] is especially successful in explaining social and economic hierarchies within the country." SLJ
Includes glossary and bibliographical references

Kras, Sara Louise
The Galapagos Islands; [by] Sara Louise Kras. 1st ed. Marshall Cavendish Benchmark 2008 c2009 96p il map (Nature's wonders) lib bdg $24.95
Grades: 5 6 7 8   **986.6**
1. Galapagos Islands
ISBN 978-0-7614-2856-5 (lib bdg); 0-7614-2856-9 (lib bdg)   LC 2007020416
"Provides comprehensive information on the geography, history, wildlife, peoples, and environmental issues of the Galapagos Islands." Publisher's note
Includes glossary and bibliographical references

987   Venezuela

Winter, Jane Kohen, 1959-
Venezuela; [by] Jane Kohen Winter, Kitt Baguley. 2nd ed. Benchmark Bks. 2002 144p il map (Cultures of the world) lib bdg $37.07
Grades: 5 6 7 8   **987**
1. Venezuela
ISBN 0-7614-1362-6   LC 2001-53877
First published 1990
Presents the geography, history, economy, and social life and customs of Venezuela
Includes glossary and bibliographical references

988.1   Guyana

Jermyn, Leslie
Guyana. Benchmark Bks. 2000 128p il map (Cultures of the world) lib bdg $37.07
Grades: 5 6 7 8   **988.1**
1. Guyana
ISBN 0-7614-0994-7   LC 99-55063
Examines the geography, history, government, economy, people, and culture of Guyana
Includes glossary and bibliographical references

Morrison, Marion
Guyana. Children's Press 2003 144p il map (Enchantment of the world, Second series) lib bdg $38
Grades: 5 6 7 8   **988.1**
1. Guyana
ISBN 978-0-516-22377-3 (lib bdg); 0-516-22377-1 (lib bdg)   LC 2001-6915

Describes the geography, history, culture, religion, and people of Guyana
Includes bibliographical references

989.2   Paraguay

Jermyn, Leslie
Paraguay. Benchmark Bks. 2000 128p il map (Cultures of the world) lib bdg $37.07
Grades: 5 6 7 8   **989.2**
1. Paraguay
ISBN 0-7614-0979-3   LC 99-27257
Describes the geography, history, government, economy, people, lifestyle, religion, language, arts, leisure, festivals, and food of Paraguay
Includes glossary and bibliographical references

989.5   Uruguay

Jermyn, Leslie
Uruguay. Benchmark Bks. (Tarrytown) 1999 128p il maps (Cultures of the world) lib bdg $37.07
Grades: 5 6 7 8   **989.5**
1. Uruguay
ISBN 0-7614-0873-8   LC 98-27375
Describes the geography, history, government, economy, people, lifestyle, religion, language, arts, leisure, festivals, and food of the smallest country in South America
Includes glossary and bibliographical references

993   New Zealand

Gillespie, Carol Ann
New Zealand; [by] Carol Ann Gillespie. updated ed. Chelsea House Publishers 2005 100p il map (Modern world nations) lib bdg $30
Grades: 7 8 9 10   **993**
1. New Zealand
ISBN 0-7910-8708-5   LC 2005045445
First published 1992
This describes the natural landscapes, unique plant and animal life, history, culture, people, government and politics, and future outlook of New Zealand
Includes bibliographical references

Jackson, Barbara
New Zealand; [by] Barbara Jackson; Vaughan Wood and Simon Milne, consultants. National Geographic 2008 64p il map (Countries of the world) lib bdg $27.90 *
Grades: 4 5 6 7   **993**
1. New Zealand
ISBN 978-1-4263-0301-2 (lib bdg); 1-4263-0301-7 (lib bdg)
This describes the geography, nature, history, people and culture, government, and economy of New Zealand.

Smelt, Roselynn

New Zealand; by Roselynn Smelt. 2nd ed. Marshall Cavendish Benchmark 2009 128p il map (Cultures of the world) lib bdg $42.79

Grades: 5 6 7 8 **993**

1. New Zealand

ISBN 978-0-7614-3415-3 (lib bdg); 0-7614-3415-1 (lib bdg) LC 2008028792

First published 1998

"Provides comprehensive information on the geography, history, wildlife, governmental structure, economy, cultural diversity, peoples, religion, and culture of New Zealand." Publisher's note

Includes glossary and bibliographical references

994 Australia

Arnold, Caroline, 1944-

Uluru, Australia's Aboriginal heart; photographs by Arthur Arnold. Clarion Books 2003 64p il $16 *

Grades: 5 6 7 8 **994**

1. Aboriginal Australians 2. Australia 3. Uluru-Kata Tjuta National Park (Australia)

ISBN 0-618-18181-4 LC 2002-15542

Describes Uluru, formerly known as Ayers Rock, in Australia's Uluru-Kata Tjuta National Park, its plant and animal life, and the country's Aboriginal people for whom the site is sacred

"The book's greatest accomplishment . . . is to give readers a sense of the ongoing spiritual importance of Uluru to the Anangu, who have lived around it for 10,000 years. Clear, colorful photos of Uluru and its surroundings appear on nearly every page, illustrating the text with beauty and finesse." Booklist

Einfeld, Jann

Life in the Australian Outback. Lucent Bks. 2003 112p il map (Way people live) lib bdg $21.96

Grades: 6 7 8 9 **994**

1. Australia

ISBN 1-59018-014-3 LC 2001-7504

Contents: An ancient people; Cattle mustering and sheep shearing; At home on the station; School by air; Opal fever; Outback town life

"An in-depth look at a unique culture that exists in Australia's remote interior. Well detailed and meticulously documented, this book does an excellent job of illustrating the diversity of the outback population as well as the challenges faced by its inhabitants." SLJ

Includes glossary and bibliographical references

Grabowski, John F.

Australia. Lucent Bks. 2002 112p il (Modern nations of the world) $29.95

Grades: 7 8 9 10 **994**

1. Australia

ISBN 1-56006-566-4 LC 2001-6626

Discusses Australia's history, geography, government, people, and culture

"The strength of the work is . . . its readability. The author . . . uses his writing skills to present basic facts about Australian history and culture in an entertaining manner." Am Ref Books Annu, 2003

Includes bibliographical references

Heinrichs, Ann

Australia; by Ann Heinrichs. rev ed. Children's Press 2007 144p il map (Enchantment of the world, second series) lib bdg $38

Grades: 5 6 7 8 **994**

1. Australia

ISBN 978-0-516-24873-8 (lib bdg); 0-516-24873-1 (lib bdg) LC 2006017586

First published 1998

Describes the geography, people, government, culture, history, religion, economy, and wildlife of Australia

Includes bibliographical references

Leppman, Elizabeth J.

Australia and the Pacific; series consulting editor Charles F. Gritzner. Chelsea House Pubs. 2006 118p il map (Modern world cultures) lib bdg $30

Grades: 7 8 9 10 **994**

1. Australia 2. Oceania

ISBN 0-7910-8150-8

This describes the natural landscapes, history, people, culture, geopolitics, economy, regional contrasts, and future outlook of Australia and the Pacific.

Includes bibliographical references

Rajendra, Vijeya, 1936-

Australia; [by] Vijeya & Sundran Rajendra. 2nd ed. Benchmark Bks. 2002 143p il map (Cultures of the world) lib bdg $37.07

Grades: 5 6 7 8 **994**

1. Australia

ISBN 0-7614-1473-8 LC 2002-19206

First published 1990

Presents the history, geography, government, economy, environment, religion, people, and social life and customs of the island continent of Australia

Includes glossary and bibliographical references

Turner, Kate

Australia; [by] Kate Turner; Elaine Stratford and Joseph Powell, consultants. National Geographic 2007 64p il map (Countries of the world) lib bdg $27.90 *

Grades: 4 5 6 7 **994**

1. Australia

ISBN 978-1-4263-0055-4

Describes the geography, nature, history, people and culture, government and economy of Australia

This "appealing [title has] wonderful photographs and maps. . . . [This book is a] reliable [source] for country research, and the interesting current material hold browsing potential as well." SLJ

Includes glossary and bibliographical references

995.3 Papua New Guinea. New Guinea region

Gascoigne, Ingrid
Papua New Guinea; [by] Ingrid Gascoigne. 2nd
ed. Marshall Cavendish Benchmark 2009 144p il
map (Cultures of the world) lib bdg $29.95
Grades: 5 6 7 8   995.3
1. Papua New Guinea
ISBN 978-0-7614-3416-0   LC 2008028794
First published 1998
"Provides comprehensive information on the geogra-
phy, history, wildlife, governmental structure, economy,
cultural diversity, peoples, religion, and culture of Papua
New Guinea" Publisher's note
Includes glossary and bibliographical references

996 Other parts of Pacific. Polynesia

NgCheong-Lum, Roseline, 1962-
Tahiti; [by] Roseline NgCheong-Lum. 2nd ed.
Marshall Cavendish Benchmark 2008 144p il map
(Cultures of the world) lib bdg $39.93
Grades: 5 6 7 8   996
1. Tahiti (French Polynesia)
ISBN 978-0-7614-2089-7   LC 2007014901
"Provides comprehensive information on the geogra-
phy, history, wildlife, governmental structure, economy,
cultural diversity, peoples, religion, and culture of Tahi-
ti." Publisher's note
Includes glossary and bibliographical references

Pelta, Kathy
Rediscovering Easter Island. Lerner Publs. 2000
112p il maps (How history is invented) lib bdg
$23.93
Grades: 5 6 7 8   996
1. Easter Island
ISBN 0-8225-4890-9   LC 00-9163
Discusses the many visits made by explorers,
missionaries, businessmen, scientists, and others to Easter
Island since the late 1600s and what they revealed about
life on this remote Pacific island
"Coverage is serious, generally evenhanded, and
smoothly presented, making this a fine foundation for
readers who enjoy digging up the past." Bull Cent Child
Books
Includes bibliographical references

998 Arctic islands and Antarctica

Beattie, Owen
Buried in ice; by Owen Beattie and John Geiger
with Shelley Tanaka. Scholastic 1992 64p il maps
(Time quest book) pa $6.95 hardcover o.p.
Grades: 4 5 6 7   998
1. Franklin, Sir John, 1786-1847 2. Arctic regions
ISBN 0-590-43849-2 (pa)   LC 91-23897

"A Scholastic/Madison Press book"
Probes the tragic and mysterious fate of Sir John
Franklin's failed expedition to the Arctic to find the
Northwest Passage in 1845
"The narrative is interspersed with an imaginative section that relates the story of the expedition from the
point of view of 19-year-old Luke, a member of the
crew. While the text is exciting, the book's greatest
strength is its superb illustrations: drawings, paintings,
and historic and present day photographs are used to enrich each page." SLJ
Includes glossary and bibliographical references

Bledsoe, Lucy Jane
How to survive in Antarctica; written and
photographed by Lucy Jane Bledsoe. Holiday
House 2006 101p il map $16.95 *
Grades: 5 6 7 8   998
1. Antarctica
ISBN 0-8234-1890-1   LC 2004-60639
"Bledsoe, who made three trips to study Antarctica,
bases her informal, chatty narrative on her thrilling adventure, bringing close the amazing science and geography as well as the gritty facts of human survival in the
frigid environment. . . . Bledsoe's own black-and-white
photos . . . will grab students across the curriculum."
Booklist
Includes glossary

Kimmel, Elizabeth Cody
Ice story; Shackleton's lost expedition. Clarion
Bks. 1999 120p il maps $18 *
Grades: 4 5 6 7   998
1. Shackleton, Sir Ernest Henry, 1874-1922
2. Endurance (Ship) 3. Imperial Trans-Antarctic Expe-
dition (1914-1917) 4. Antarctica—Exploration
ISBN 0-395-91524-4   LC 98-29956
Describes the events of the 1914 Shackleton Antarctic
expedition, when the ship the Endurance was crushed in
a frozen sea and the men made the perilous journey
across ice and stormy seas to reach inhabited land
"The amazing story is well served in this account,
which includes photos by expedition photographer Frank
Hurley." Horn Book Guide
Includes bibliographical references

Lourie, Peter
Arctic thaw; the people of the whale in a
changing climate. Boyds Mills Press 2007 47p il
map $17.95
Grades: 5 6 7 8   998
1. Inupiat 2. Human ecology 3. Whaling 4. Alaska
5. Greenhouse effect
ISBN 978-1-59078-436-5; 1-59078-436-7
                                  LC 2006-20045
"A somewhat sobering, yet upbeat examination of the
probable effects of global warming on the culture of the
Iñupiaq whale hunters of Alaska's North Slope. . . .
[Lourie's] lively, straightforward text describes the mixture of traditional and modern ways of the present-day
Iñupiaq, as well as the work of [Paul] Shepson and his
team to record weather and climate changes and to pre-
dict what effect they will have locally and globally." SLJ
Includes bibliographical references

Lynch, Wayne

Arctic; text and photographs by Wayne Lynch; assisted by Aubrey Lang. NorthWord Books for Young Readers 2007 64p il map (Our wild world: ecosystems) $16.95; pa $8.95

Grades: 4 5 6 7   **998**
   1. Arctic regions 2. Animals—Arctic regions
   ISBN 978-1-55971-960-5; 978-1-55971-961-2 (pa)
                                        LC 2006021920

"With accessible first-person writing, Lynch describes the Arctic ecosystem, discussing both the high and low Arctic. . . . Stunning photographs include close-ups and more expansive views." Horn Book Guide
   Includes bibliographical references

Myers, Walter Dean, 1937-

Antarctica; journeys to the South Pole. Scholastic Press 2004 134p il maps $18.95 *

Grades: 6 7 8 9   **998**
   1. Antarctica
   ISBN 0-439-22001-7   LC 2004-2501

This is an "overview of the discovery and exploration of Antarctica. . . . What drives the narrative is the personal adventures of those who raced to reach the South Pole first, especially the fierce rivalry between Norwegian explorer Roald Amundsen . . . and Britain's Robert Scott."
   This is "a lucid, well-written text." SLJ
   Includes bibliographical references

Revkin, Andrew

The North Pole was here; puzzles and perils at the top of the world; [by] Andrew C. Revkin. 1st ed. Kingfisher 2006 128p il map $15.95 *

Grades: 7 8 9 10   **998**
   1. North Pole 2. Arctic regions 3. Greenhouse effect
   ISBN 0-7534-5993-0; 978-0-7534-5993-5
                                        LC 2005-24307

"A New York Times book"
   The author "relates his journey to the top of the world in the company of scientists studying climate changes. The informative chapters weave together accounts of his experiences and observations with details about the environment, its exploration, and scientific concepts. . . . The illustrations include full-color photographs of the author's trek, archival reproductions and photos of previous excursions, original diagrams that clarify concepts, and maps. . . . The wonderfully written narrative will pull youngsters into the book and hold them there willingly until the last page." SLJ
   Includes bibliographical references

Scott, Elaine, 1940-

Poles apart; why penguins and polar bears will never be neighbors. Viking 2004 63p il maps $17.99

Grades: 5 6 7 8   **998**
   1. Arctic regions 2. Antarctica
   ISBN 0-670-05925-0   LC 2004-4270
   Contents: Drifting apart: Gondwanaland and Eurasia; Poles apart: summer and winter; Mutual attraction: the magnetic poles; The people: Inuit and None; Never

neighbors: penguins in the south; Never neighbors: polar bears in the north; Great races: first to see them; Great races: first to claim them; The poles today: lessons from the ice
   This "book introduces the North and South Poles: their origins, seasons, composition, magnetism, people, animals, exploration, and recent changes. . . . The many excellent color illustrations include clear photographs of wildlife and mysterious, beautiful shots of the northern lights as well as maps and period photos. Scott writes well, never talking down to her audience but making scientific and historical information understandable." Booklist

Tulloch, Coral

Antarctica; the heart of the world. 1st American ed. Enchanted Lion Books 2006 48p il map $17.95

Grades: 6 7 8 9   **998**
   1. Antarctica
   ISBN 1-59270-054-3   LC 2005-40162
   Originally published: Singapore : ABC Books for the Australian Broadcasting Co., 2003.
   "Tulloch writes out of her experiences as a voyager on an Antarctic resupply ship to illuminate the continent's geologic history, its flora and fauna, and its importance to the global ecosystem. She also addresses the early and continuing human explorations and their impact on the region as well as the area's rich potential and possible future problems. The writing is clear, and the science is comprehensible without the slightest sense of talking down to youthful readers." Voice Youth Advocates
   Includes bibliographical references

Fic   FICTION

A number of subject headings have been added to the books in this section to aid in curriculum work. It is not necessarily recommended that these subjects be used in the library catalog.

Abbott, Ellen Jensen

Watersmeet. Marshall Cavendish 2009 341p il $16.99

Grades: 6 7 8 9   **Fic**
   1. Fantasy fiction
   ISBN 978-0-7614-5536-3; 0-7614-5536-1
                                        LC 2008-00315

Fourteen-year-old Absina escapes the escalating violence, prejudice, and religious fervor of her home town, Vranille, and sets out with a dwarf, Haret, to seek the father she has never met in a place called Watersmeet.
   "The relationship between Abisina and Haret is warm and engaging, and the dialogue between them cleverly captures the slow development of their camaraderie. . . . Fans of Ursula Le Guin's character-driven fantsies will enjoy this story of Abisina's quest to unify both her divided country and her dividied self." Bull Cent Child Books

Abbott, Tony

The postcard. Little, Brown 2008 358p il $15.99
*

Grades: 5 6 7 8   **Fic**
1. Mystery fiction 2. Grandmothers—Fiction
3. Florida—Fiction 4. Books and reading—Fiction
ISBN 978-0-316-01172-3; 0-316-01172-X
LC 2007-31074

While in St. Petersburg, Florida, to help clean out his
recently-deceased grandmother's house, thirteen-year-old
Jason finds an old postcard which leads him on an adventure that blends figures from an old, unfinished detective story with his family's past.

"Mystery fans will appreciate the depth and intrigue of
the dual level mysteries, and will also enjoy the wit and
banter of the main characters." Libr Media Connect

Abdel-Fattah, Randa

Does my head look big in this? Orchard Books
2007 360p $16.99 *

Grades: 7 8 9 10 11 12   **Fic**
1. Muslims—Fiction 2. Clothing and dress—Fiction
3. School stories 4. Australia—Fiction
ISBN 978-0-439-91947-0; 0-439-91947-9
LC 2006-29117

Year Eleven at an exclusive prep school in the suburbs of Melbourne, Australia, would be tough enough,
but it is further complicated for Amal when she decides
to wear the hijab, the Muslim head scarf, full-time as a
badge of her faith—without losing her identity or sense
of style.

"While the novel deals with a number of serious issues, it is extremely funny and entertaining." SLJ

Ten things I hate about me. Orchard Books
2009 297p $16.99

Grades: 7 8 9 10 11 12   **Fic**
1. Muslims—Fiction 2. Prejudices—Fiction 3. School
stories 4. Lebanese—Fiction 5. Australia—Fiction
ISBN 978-0-5450-5055-5; 0-5450-5055-3
LC 2008-13667

Lebanese-Australian Jamilah, known in school as
Jamie, hides her heritage from her classmates and tries
to pass by dyeing her hair blonde and wearing blue-
tinted contact lenses, until her conflicted feelings become
too much for her to bear.

"The teen's present-tense narrative is . . . hilarious
. . . and . . . honest about the shocking prejudice
against Muslims. Teens will love the free-flowing, funny
dialogue." Booklist

Abrahams, Peter, 1947-

Down the rabbit hole; an Echo Falls mystery.
Laura Geringer Books 2005 375p $15.99; lib bdg
$16.89; pa $6.99

Grades: 7 8 9 10   **Fic**
1. Mystery fiction
ISBN 0-06-073701-8; 0-06-073702-6 (lib bdg);
0-06-073703-4 (pa)   LC 2004-14778

"Ingrid Levin-Hill . . . has just been cast as the lead
in Alice in Wonderland when she finds herself in a different role—murder detective. The corpse is that of
'Cracked-Up Katie,' whom Ingrid encountered when she

attempted to get from her orthodontist to soccer practice." Publ Wkly

Ingrid "and the other main characters are all solidly
drawn. . . . Deft use of literary allusions and ironic humor add further touches of class to a topnotch mystery."
SLJ

Other titles about Ingrid Levin-Hill are:
Behind the curtain (2006)
Into the dark (2008)

Reality check. HarperTeen 2009 330p $16.99;
lib bdg $17.89

Grades: 7 8 9 10   **Fic**
1. Missing persons—Fiction 2. Social classes—Fiction
3. School stories 4. Gambling—Fiction
ISBN 978-0-06-122766-0;   0-06-122766-8;
978-0-06-122767-7 (lib bdg); 0-06-122767-6 (lib bdg)
LC 2008-22593

"Laura Geringer books"

After a knee injury destroys sixteen-year-old Cody's
college hopes, he drops out of high school and gets a job
in his small Montana town, but when his ex-girlfriend
disappears from her Vermont boarding school, Cody
travels cross-country to join the search.

"Abrahams writes a fine thriller that is pitched to attract everyone from reluctant readers to sports fans to romantic idealists." Voice Youth Advocates

Ackermann, Joan

In the space left behind. HarperTeen 2007 394p
$17.99; lib bdg $18.89

Grades: 7 8 9 10   **Fic**
1. Father-son relationship—Fiction 2. Travel—Fiction
ISBN 978-0-06-072255-5;   0-06-072255-X;
978-0-06-072256-2 (lib bdg); 0-06-072256-8 (lib bdg)
LC 2006-22172

Fifteen-year-old Colm embarks on a cross-country
journey with the father who abandoned him as a child.

"Packed with surprising turns of events, this skillfully
crafted novel offers a new twist on father/son rituals."
Publ Wkly

Adams, Douglas, 1952-2001

The hitchhiker's guide to the galaxy. 25th
anniversary illustrated collector's ed. Harmony
Books 2004 271p il $35 *

Grades: 7 8 9 10 11 12 Adult   **Fic**
1. Science fiction

ISBN 1-4000-5293-9   LC 2004-558987
Also available in paperback from Ballantine Bks.
First published 1980

"Based on a BBC radio series, . . . this is the episodic story of Arthur Dent, a contemporary Englishman who
discovers first that his unpretentious house is about to be
demolished to make way for a bypass, and second that
a good friend is actually an alien galactic hitchhiker who
announces that Earth itself will soon be demolished to
make way for an intergalactic speedway. A suitably bewildered Dent soon finds himself hitching . . . rides
throughout space, aided by a . . . reference book, The
Hitchhiker's Guide to the Galaxy, a compendium of
'facts,' philosophies, and wild advice." Libr J

Other titles featuring Arthur Dent are:

Adams, Douglas, 1952-2001—*Continued*
Life, the universe and everything (1982)
Mostly harmless (1992)
The restaurant at the end of the universe (1981)
So long, and thanks for all the fish (1984)

Adams, Richard, 1920-
Watership Down. Scribner classics ed. Scribner 1996 c1972 429p $30; pa $15
Grades: 6 7 8 9   **Fic**
1. Rabbits—Fiction 2. Allegories
ISBN 0-684-83605-X; 0-7432-7770-8 (pa)
First published 1972 in the United Kingdom; first United States edition 1974 by Macmillan
"Faced with the annihilation of its warren, a small group of male rabbits sets out across the English downs in search of a new home. Internal struggles for power surface in this intricately woven, realistically told adult adventure when the protagonists must coordinate tactics in order to defeat an enemy rabbit fortress. It is clear that the author has done research on rabbit behavior, for this tale is truly authentic." Shapiro Fic for Youth. 3d edition

Adler, C. S. (Carole S.), 1932-
One unhappy horse. Clarion Bks. 2000 156p $15
Grades: 5 6 7 8   **Fic**
1. Horses—Fiction 2. Friendship—Fiction
ISBN 0-618-04912-6   LC 00-25907
Things are difficult for twelve-year-old Jan and her mother after her father's death, and when it turns out that her beloved horse needs an operation, Jan reluctantly gets money from an elderly woman whom she has befriended
"A well-paced story with interesting and mostly sympathetic characters." SLJ

Adler, David A., 1947-
Don't talk to me about the war. Viking 2008 216p $15.99
Grades: 4 5 6 7   **Fic**
1. Bronx (New York, N.Y.)—Fiction 2. Family life—Fiction 3. Friendship—Fiction 4. World War, 1939-1945—Fiction
ISBN 978-0-670-06307-9; 0-670-06307-X
       LC 2007017889
In 1940, thirteen-year-old Tommy's routine of school, playing stickball in his Bronx, New York, neighborhood, talking with his friend Beth, and listening to Dodgers games on the radio changes as his mother's illness and his increasing awareness of the war in Europe transform his world.
"An engaging and very accessible historical novel." Booklist

Adlington, L. J., 1970-
Cherry Heaven. Greenwillow Books 2008 458p $16.99; lib bdg $17.89
Grades: 7 8 9 10   **Fic**
1. Orphans—Fiction 2. Science fiction
ISBN   978-0-06-143180-7;   0-06-143180-X; 978-0-06-143181-4 (lib bdg); 0-06-143181-8 (lib bdg)
       LC 2007-24679

Companion volume to The Diary of Pelly D (2005)
Kat and Tanka J leave the wartorn city, move with their adoptive parents to the New Frontier, and are soon settled into a home called Cherry Heaven, but Luka, an escaped factory worker, confirms their suspicion that New Frontier is not the utopia it seems to be.
"In this complex, absorbing, and sometimes disquieting novel, Adlington creates a world that is distinctly different from our own, yet chillingly familiar." Booklist

The diary of Pelly D. Greenwillow Books 2005 282p $15; lib bdg $16.89
Grades: 7 8 9 10   **Fic**
1. Science fiction
ISBN 0-06-076615-8; 0-06-076616-6 (lib bdg)
       LC 2004-52258
When Toni V, a construction worker on a futuristic colony, finds the diary of a teenage girl whose life has been turned upside-down by holocaust-like events, he begins to question his own beliefs.
"Adlington has crafted an original and disturbing dystopian fantasy told in a smart and sympathetic teen voice." Booklist

Agell, Charlotte, 1959-
Shift. Henry Holt and Co. 2008 230p $16.95
Grades: 7 8 9 10   **Fic**
1. Despotism—Fiction 2. Religion—Fiction 3. Environmental degradation—Fiction 4. Resistance to government—Fiction 5. Family life—Fiction 6. Science fiction
ISBN 978-0-8050-7810-7; 0-8050-7810-X
       LC 2007-46942
In fifteen-year-old Adrian Havoc's world, HomeState rules every aspect of society and religious education is enforced but Adrian, refusing to believe that the Apocalypse is at hand, goes north through the Deadlands and joins a group of insurgents.
"The story is made particularly compelling by the economy and lyricism of the writing style. . . . Readers seeking contemplative and philosophical science fiction will find this a haunting exploration of government gone awry and one boy's steadfast pursuit of justice." Bull Cent Child Books

Aguiar, Nadia
The lost island of Tamarind; [by] Nadia Aguiar. Feiwel and Friends 2008 437p il map (The Book of Tamarind) $17.95
Grades: 5 6 7 8   **Fic**
1. Adventure fiction 2. Islands—Fiction 3. Magic—Fiction 4. Siblings—Fiction 5. Pirates—Fiction 6. Giants—Fiction 7. War stories
ISBN 978-0-312-38029-8; 0-312-38029-1
       LC 2008-5623
Thirteen-year-old Maya, who has spent her life at sea with her marine biologist parents, yearns for a normal life, but when a storm washes her parents overboard, life becomes anything but normal for Maya, her younger brother and baby sister, as they land at a mysterious, uncharted island filled with danger.
"Each detail of this fantasy is crafted with care; readers will be drawn into this dangerous, magical world where anything is possible and nothing can be fully explained." SLJ

Aiken, Joan, 1924-2004

The wolves of Willoughby Chase; illustrated by
Pat Marriott. Delacorte Press 2000 c1962 181p
hardcover o.p. pa $6.50 *

Grades: 5 6 7 8 **Fic**

1. Great Britain—Fiction
ISBN 0-385-32790-0; 0-440-49603-9 (pa)

First published 1962 in the United Kingdom; first
United States edition 1963 by Doubleday

"In this burlesque of a Victorian melodrama, two London children are sent to a country estate while their parents are away. Here they outwit a wicked governess, escape from packs of hungry wolves, and restore the estate
to its rightful owner." Hodges. Books for Elem Sch Libr

"Plot, characterization, and background blend perfectly
into an amazing whole. . . . Highly recommended." SLJ
Other titles in this series are:
Black hearts in Battersea (1964)
Cold Shoulder Road (1996)
The cuckoo tree (1971)
Dangerous games (1999)
Is underground (1993)
Midwinter nightingale (2003)
The stolen lake (1981)
The witch of Clatteringshaws (2005)

Ain, Beth Levine

The revolution of Sabine; [by] Beth Levine Ain.
1st ed. Candlewick Press 2008 214p $16.99

Grades: 6 7 8 9 **Fic**

1. Franklin, Benjamin, 1706-1790—Fiction
2. Fragonard, Jean-Honoré, 1732-1806—Fiction
3. Social classes—Fiction 4. Mother-daughter relationship—Fiction 5. France—History—1589-1789, Bourbons—Fiction
ISBN 978-0-76363-396-7; 0-76363-396-8

LC 2007022121

During Benjamin Franklin's visit to Paris in 1776, sixteen-year-old Sabine Durand rails against the strict rules
of society and her social-climbing mother by rejecting
her arranged marriage and spending more time with servants and others who accept Franklin's political ideals
and those she read in Voltaire's Candide while having
her portrait painted by the renowned artist, Fragonard.

"Written in a first-person narrative, this historical novel is also a coming-of-age story with a hint of romance.
Sabine is likable from the beginning and her transition
from silly aristocrat to thoughtful young woman is gradual and realistic." SLJ

Alcott, Louisa May, 1832-1888

Little women; [by] Louisa May Alcott;
illustrated in color by Jessie Willcox Smith and in
black and white by Frank T. Merrill. Gramercy
books 2002 388p il (Illustrated children's library)
$12.99 *

Grades: 5 6 7 8 **Fic**

1. Family life—Fiction 2. Sisters—Fiction 3. New England—Fiction
ISBN 978-0-517-22116-7; 0-517-22116-0

First published 1868

Chronicles the joys and sorrows of the four March sisters as they grow into young ladies in nineteenth-century
New England.

Other titles about members of the March family are:
Eight cousins (1875)
Jo's boys (1886)
Little men (1871)
Rose in bloom (1876)

Alegría, Malín

Estrella's quinceanera. Simon & Schuster Books
for Young Readers 2006 272p $14.95

Grades: 7 8 9 10 **Fic**

1. Mexican Americans—Fiction 2. Quinceañera (Social custom)—Fiction
ISBN 0-689-87809-5

Estrella's mother and aunt are planning a gaudy, traditional quinceañera for her, even though it is the last thing
she wants.

"Alegria writes about Mexican American culture, first
love, family, and of moving between worlds with poignant, sharp-sighted humor and authentic dialogue."
Booklist

Alender, Katie

Bad girls don't die. Hyperion Books 2009 352p
$15.99

Grades: 7 8 9 10 **Fic**

1. Demoniac possession—Fiction 2. Sisters—Fiction
3. School stories 4. Horror fiction
ISBN 978-1-4231-0876-4; 1-4231-0876-0

LC 2008-46179

When fifteen-year-old Lexi's younger sister Kasey begins behaving strangely and their old Victorian house
seems to take on a life of its own, Lexi investigates and
discovers some frightening facts about previous occu-
pants of the house, leading her to believe that many lives
are in danger.

This "novel is both a mystery and a trip into the paranormal. . . . With just enough violence, suspense, and
romance to keep readers turning pages, this . . . will be
a popular additon to any YA collection." Booklist

Alexander, Alma

Gift of the Unmage. Eos 2007 389p
(Worldweavers) $16.99; lib bdg $17.89

Grades: 6 7 8 9 10 **Fic**

1. Magic—Fiction
ISBN 978-0-06-083955-0; 0-06-083955-4;
978-0-06-083956-7 (lib bdg); 0-06-083956-2 (lib bdg)

LC 2006-20123

As the seventh child born of the union of two seventh
children, fourteen-year-old Thea has not fulfilled her parents' hope of having special magical powers, and they
try a last, desperate measure before sending her to a
school for those with no magical ability.

"This novel combines elements of magic, culture, and
spirituality with a firm grounding in the very real world."
Voice Youth Advocates
Other titles in this series are:
Spellspam (2008)
Worldweavers (2009)

Alexander, Lloyd, 1924-2007

The book of three. rev ed. Holt & Co. 1999 190p (Chronicles of Prydain) $19.95 *
Grades: 5 6 7 8   **Fic**
1. Fantasy fiction
ISBN 0-8050-6132-0   LC 98-40901
Also available in paperback from Yearling Bks
First published 1964
"The first of five books about the mythical land of Prydain finds Taran, an assistant pig keeper, fighting with Prince Gwydion against the evil which theatens the kingdom." Hodges. Books for Elem Sch Libr
"Related in a simple, direct style, this fast-paced tale of high adventure has a well-balanced blend of fantasy, realism, and humor." SLJ
Other titles about the mythical land of Prydain are:
The black cauldron (1965)
The castle of Llyr (1966)
The foundling and other tales of Prydain (1999)
The high king (1968)
Taran Wanderer (1967)

The golden dream of Carlo Chuchio. H. Holt 2007 306p il $16.95 *
Grades: 5 6 7 8 9   **Fic**
1. Fantasy fiction 2. Buried treasure—Fiction 3. Middle East—Fiction 4. Voyages and travels—Fiction
ISBN 978-0-8050-8333-0; 0-8050-8333-2
LC 2006-49710
Naive and bumbling Carlo, his shady camel-puller Baksheesh, and Shira, a girl determined to return home, follow a treasure map through the deserts and cities of the infamous Golden Road, as mysterious strangers try in vain to point them toward real treasures.
This "is an exuberant and compassionate tale of adventure." Publ Wkly

The Illyrian adventure. Dutton 1986 132p pa $5.99 hardcover o.p. *
Grades: 5 6 7 8   **Fic**
1. Adventure fiction
ISBN 0-14-130313-1 (pa)   LC 85-30762
"Sixteen-year-old Vesper Holly drags her long-suffering guardian, Brinnie, off to Illyria to vindicate her late father's reputation as a scholar. With humor, beguiling charm, and intelligence she manages to find a treasure, thwart a conspiracy to murder Illyria's King Osman, and guide two rival factions to the peace table." Wilson Libr Bull
"Alexander's archeological mystery has intricate plotting and witty wording." Bull Cent Child Books
Other adventure titles featuring Vesper Holly are:
The Drackenberg adventure (1988)
The El Dorado adventure (1987)
The Jedera adventure (1989)
The Philadelphia adventure (1990)
The Xanadu adventure (2005)

The iron ring. Dutton Children's Bks. 1997 283p pa $5.99 hardcover o.p. *
Grades: 5 6 7 8   **Fic**
1. Adventure fiction 2. India—Fiction
ISBN 0-14-130348-4   LC 96-29730

"Young Tamar, ruler of a small Indian kingdom, wagers with a visiting king and loses his kingdom and his freedom. Traveling to the king's land to make good on his debt, he collects quite an entourage and eventually overcomes his enemies with his friends' help. This tale offers delightful characters, a philosophical interest in the meaning of life, a thoughtful look at the caste system, and a clever use of Indian animal folktales." Horn Book Guide

The remarkable journey of Prince Jen. Dutton Children's Bks. 1991 273p pa $6.99 hardcover o.p. *
Grades: 5 6 7 8   **Fic**
1. Adventure fiction 2. China—Fiction
ISBN 0-14-240225-7 (pa)   LC 91-13720
Bearing six unusual gifts, young Prince Jen in Tang Dynasty China embarks on a perilous quest and emerges triumphantly into manhood
"Alexander satisfies the taste for excitement, but his vivid characters and the food for thought he offers will nourish long after the last page is turned." SLJ

Westmark. Dutton 1981 184p pa $5.99 hardcover o.p. *
Grades: 5 6 7 8   **Fic**
1. Adventure fiction
ISBN 0-14-131068-5 (pa)
A boy fleeing from criminal charges falls in with a charlatan, his dwarf attendant, and an urchin girl, travels with them about the kingdom of Westmark, and ultimately arrives at the palace where the king is grieving over the loss of his daughter
The author "peoples his tale with a marvelous cast of individuals, and weaves an intricate story of high adventure that climaxes in a superbly conceived conclusion, which, though predictable, is reached through carefully built tension and subtly added comic relief." Booklist
Other titles in this series are:
The Beggar Queen (1984)
The Kestrel (1982)

Alexie, Sherman, 1966-

The absolutely true diary of a part-time Indian; art by Ellen Forney. Little, Brown 2007 229p il $16.99 *
Grades: 7 8 9 10   **Fic**
1. Native Americans—Fiction 2. Family life—Fiction 3. School stories 4. Friendship—Fiction
ISBN 0-316-01368-4; 978-0-316-01368-0
LC 2007-22799
Boston Globe-Horn Book Award: Fiction and Poetry (2008)
Budding cartoonist Junior leaves his troubled school on the Spokane Indian Reservation to attend an all-white farm town school where the only other Indian is the school mascot.
"The many characters, on and off the rez, with whom he has dealings are portrayed with compassion and verve. . . . Forney's simple pencil cartoons fit perfectly within the story and reflect the burgeoning artist within Junior." Booklist

Allison, Jennifer

Gilda Joyce, psychic investigator. Sleuth/Dutton 2005 321p $10.99 *

Grades: 5 6 7 8   Fic

1. Mystery fiction 2. Cousins—Fiction

ISBN 0-525-47375-0   LC 2004-10834

During the summer before ninth grade, intrepid Gilda Joyce invites herself to the San Francisco mansion of distant cousin Lester Splinter and his thirteen-year-old daughter, where she uses her purported psychic abilities and detective skills to solve the mystery of the mansion's boarded-up tower.

"Allison pulls off something special here. She not only offers a credible mystery . . . but also . . . provides particularly strong characterizations." Booklist

Other titles about Gilda Joyce are:

Gilda Joyce: the Ladies of the Lake (2006)

Gilda Joyce: the ghost sonata (2007)

Gilda Joyce: the dead drop (2009)

Almond, David, 1951-

Clay. Delacorte Press 2006 247p $15.95; lib bdg $17.99

Grades: 7 8 9 10   Fic

1. Supernatural—Fiction 2. Horror fiction

ISBN 0-385-73171-X; 0-385-90208-5 (lib bdg)

LC 2005-22681

The developing relationship between teenager Davie and a mysterious new boy in town morphs into something darker and more sinister when Davie learns firsthand of the boy's supernatural powers.

"Rooted in the ordinariness of a community and in one boy's chance to play God, this story will grab readers with its gripping action and its important ideas." Booklist

The fire-eaters. Delacorte Press 2004 c2003 218p $15.95 *

Grades: 7 8 9 10   Fic

1. Great Britain—Fiction

ISBN 0-385-73170-1   LC 2003-55709

First published 2003 in the United Kingdom

In 1962 England, despite observing his father's illness and the suffering of the fire-eating Mr. McNulty, as well as enduring abuse at school and the stress of the Cuban Missile Crisis, Bobby Burns and his family and friends still find reasons to rejoice in their lives and to have hope for the future.

"The author's trademark themes . . . are here in full, and resonate long after the last page is turned." SLJ

Kit's wilderness. Delacorte Press 1999 229p hardcover o.p. pa $5.99 *

Grades: 5 6 7 8 9   Fic

1. Coal mines and mining—Fiction 2. Ghost stories 3. Great Britain—Fiction

ISBN 0-385-32665-3; 0-440-41605-1 (pa)

LC 99-34332

Michael L. Printz Award, 2001

Thirteen-year-old Kit goes to live with his grandfather in the decaying coal mining town of Stoneygate, England, and finds both the old man and the town haunted by ghosts of the past

The author "explores the power of friendship and fam-

ily, the importance of memory, and the role of magic in our lives. This is a highly satisfying literary experience." SLJ

The savage; illustrated by Dave McKean. Candlewick Press 2008 79p il $17.99 *

Grades: 5 6 7 8   Fic

1. Death—Fiction 2. Fathers—Fiction

ISBN 978-0-7636-3932-7; 0-7636-3932-X

LC 2008-928388

A boy tells about a story he wrote when dealing with his father's death about a savage kid living in a ruined chapel in the woods-and the tale about the savage kid coming to life in the real world.

"This illustrated novella, a graphic novel within a novel, will satisfy Almond's fans and newcomers alike. McKean's illustrations-ink and watercolor in black, blues, and greens-add an appropriately eerie touch." Horn Book Guide

Skellig. 10th anniversary ed. Delacorte Press 2009 c1998 182p $16.99; pa $6.99 *

Grades: 5 6 7 8 9 10   Fic

1. Fantasy fiction

ISBN 978-0-385-32653-7; 0-385-32653-X; 978-0-440-41602-9 (pa); 0-440-41602-7 (pa)

Michael L. Printz Award honor book

First published 1998 in the United Kingdom; first United States edition 1999

Unhappy about his baby sister's illness and the chaos of moving into a dilapidated old house, Michael retreats to the garage and finds a mysterious stranger who is something like a bird and something like an angel.

"The plot is beautifully paced and the characters are drawn with a graceful, careful hand. . . . A lovingly done, thought-provoking novel." SLJ

Alvarez, Julia, 1950-

Before we were free. Knopf 2002 167p $15.95; lib bdg $17.99; pa $5.99 *

Grades: 7 8 9 10   Fic

1. Trujillo Molina, Rafael Leónidas, 1891-1961—Fiction 2. Dominican Republic—Fiction 3. Family life—Fiction

ISBN 0-375-81544-9; 0-375-91544-3 (lib bdg); 0-440-23784-X (pa)   LC 2001-50520

In the early 1960s in the Dominican Republic, twelve-year-old Anita learns that her family is involved in the underground movement to end the bloody rule of the dictator, General Trujillo

This "is a realistic and compelling account of a girl growing up too quickly while coming to terms with the cost of freedom." Horn Book

How Tía Lola came to visit/stay. Knopf 2001 147p $15.95; lib bdg $17.99; pa $5.50 *

Grades: 4 5 6 7   Fic

1. Aunts—Fiction 2. Dominican Americans—Fiction 3. Divorce—Fiction 4. Vermont—Fiction

ISBN 0-375-80215-0; 0-375-90215-5 (lib bdg); 0-440-41870-4 (pa)   LC 00-62932

On title page "visit" is crossed out

Although ten-year-old Miguel is at first embarrassed by his colorful aunt, Tia Lola, when she comes to Ver-

Alvarez, Julia, 1950——*Continued*

mont from the Dominican Republic to stay with his mother, his sister, and him after his parents' divorce, he learns to love her

"Readers will enjoy the funny situations, identify with the developing relationships and conflicting feelings of the characters, and will get a spicy taste of Caribbean culture in the bargain." SLJ

Return to sender. Alfred A. Knopf 2009 325p $16.99; lib bdg $19.99

Grades: 4 5 6 7   **Fic**

1. Farm life—Fiction 2. Friendship—Fiction 3. Migrant labor—Fiction 4. Illegal aliens—Fiction 5. Vermont—Fiction

ISBN   978-0-375-85838-3;   0-375-85838-5; 978-0-375-95838-0 (lib bdg); 0-375-95838-X (lib bdg)

LC 2008-23520

After his family hires migrant Mexican workers to help save their Vermont farm from foreclosure, eleven-year-old Tyler befriends the oldest daughter, but when he discovers they may not be in the country legally, he realizes that real friendship knows no borders.

"Readers will be moved by small moments. . . . A tender, well-constructed book." Publ Wkly

Amateau, Gigi, 1964-

A certain strain of peculiar. Candlewick Press 2009 261p $16.99

Grades: 6 7 8 9   **Fic**

1. Ranch life—Fiction 2. Grandmothers—Fiction

ISBN 978-0-7636-3009-6; 0-7636-3009-8

Tired of the miserable life she lives, Mary Harold leaves her mother behind and moves back to Alabama and her grandmother, where she receives support and love and starts to gain confidence in herself and her abilities.

"Mary Harold is a wonderfully complex and honest character. . . . [Her] narrative is heartfelt and poignant, and the message that being 'different' is nothing to be ashamed of will resonate with readers." Voice Youth Advocates

Anderson, John David, 1975-

Standard hero behavior; [by] John David Anderson. Clarion Books 2007 273p $16 *

Grades: 6 7 8 9   **Fic**

1. Heroes and heroines—Fiction 2. Adventure fiction 3. Fantasy fiction

ISBN 0-618-75920-4; 978-0-618-75920-0

LC 2007013059

When fifteen-year-old Mason Quayle finds out that their town of Darlington is about to be attacked by orcs, goblins, ogres, and trolls, he goes in search of some heroes to save the day.

"Mason is thoroughly believable. . . . Using imaginative details, witty language with a scattering of modern idiom, and lots of allusions, Anderson manages the difficult task of constructing a satisfying story while poking large fun at all genre traditions. Fantasy fans are ensured a good laugh." Booklist

Anderson, Laurie Halse, 1961-

Chains; seeds of America. Simon & Schuster Books for Young Readers 2008 316p $16.99

Grades: 6 7 8 9 10   **Fic**

1. New York (N.Y.)—Fiction 2. United States—History—1775-1783, Revolution—Fiction 3. Slavery—Fiction 4. African Americans—Fiction 5. Spies—Fiction

ISBN 978-1-4169-0585-1; 1-4169-0585-5

LC 2007-52139

After being sold to a cruel couple in New York City, a slave named Isabel spies for the rebels during the Revolutionary War.

"This gripping novel offers readers a startlingly provocative view of the Revolutionary War. . . . [Anderson's] solidly researched exploration of British and Patriot treatment of slaves during a war for freedom is nuanced and evenhanded, presented in service of a fast-moving, emotionally involving plot." Publ Wkly

Fever, 1793. Simon & Schuster Bks. for Young Readers 2000 251p $17.99; pa $6.99 *

Grades: 5 6 7 8   **Fic**

1. Yellow fever—Fiction 2. Epidemics—Fiction 3. Philadelphia (Pa.)—Fiction

ISBN   978-0-689-83858-3;   0-689-83858-1; 978-0-689-84891-9 (pa); 0-689-84891-9 (pa)

LC 00-32238

ALA YALSA Margaret A. Edwards Award (2009)

In 1793 Philadelphia, sixteen-year-old Matilda Cook, separated from her sick mother, learns about perseverance and self-reliance when she is forced to cope with the horrors of a yellow fever epidemic.

"A vivid work, rich with well-drawn and believable characters. Unexpected events pepper the top-flight novel that combines accurate historical detail with a spellbinding story line." Voice Youth Advocates

Speak. Farrar, Straus & Giroux 1999 197p $16

Grades: 7 8 9 10   **Fic**

1. Rape—Fiction 2. School stories

ISBN 0-374-37152-0   LC 98-31933

Also available in paperback from Puffin Bks.

Michael L. Printz Award honor book, 2000

"Having broken up an end-of-summer party by calling the police, high school freshman Melinda Sordino begins the school year as a social outcast. She's the only person who knows the real reason behind her call: she was raped at the party by Andy Evans, a popular senior at her school." Booklist

The novel is "keenly aware of the corrosive details of outsiderhood and the gap between home and daily life at high school; kids whose exclusion may have less concrete cause than Melinda's will nonetheless find the picture recognizable. This is a gripping account of personal wounding and recovery." Bull Cent Child Books

Wintergirls. Viking 2009 288p $17.99 *

Grades: 8 9 10 11 12   **Fic**

1. Anorexia nervosa—Fiction 2. Self-mutilation—Fiction 3. Friendship—Fiction 4. Death—Fiction

ISBN 978-0-670-01110-0; 0-670-01110-X

LC 2008-37452

Eighteen-year-old Lia comes to terms with her best friend's death from anorexia as she struggles with the same disorder.

Anderson, Laurie Halse, 1961-—*Continued*

"As events play out, Lia's guilt, her need to be thin, and her fight for acceptance unravel in an almost poetic stream of consciousness in this startlingly crisp and pitch-perfect first-person narrative." SLJ

Anderson, M. T., 1968-

Feed. Candlewick Press 2002 237p $16.99; pa $7.99

Grades: 8 9 10 11 12   **Fic**

1. Science fiction 2. Satire

ISBN 0-7636-1726-1; 0-7636-2259-1 (pa)

     LC 2002-23738

In a future where most people have computer implants in their heads to control their environment, a boy meets an unusual girl who is in serious trouble

"An ingenious satire of corporate America and our present-day value system." Horn Book Guide

The Game of Sunken Places; [by] M. T. Anderson. Scholastic Press 2004 260p $16.95; pa $5.99

Grades: 5 6 7 8   **Fic**

1. Games—Fiction 2. Vermont—Fiction

ISBN 0-439-41660-4; 0-439-41661-2 (pa)

     LC 2003-20055

When two boys stay with an eccentric relative at his mansion in rural Vermont, they discover an old-fashioned board game that draws them into a mysterious adventure.

"Deliciously scary, often funny, and crowned by a pair of deeply satisfying surprises, this tour de force leaves one marveling at Anderson's ability to slip between genres as fluidly as his middle-grade heroes straddle worlds." Booklist

Whales on stilts; illustrations by Kurt Cyrus. Harcourt 2005 188p il $15; pa $5.95

Grades: 4 5 6 7   **Fic**

1. Science fiction

ISBN 0-15-205340-9; 0-15-205394-8 (pa)

     LC 2004-17754

Racing against the clock, shy middle-school student Lily and her best friends, Katie and Jasper, must foil the plot of her father's conniving boss to conquer the world using an army of whales.

"A story written with the author's tongue shoved firmly into his cheek. . . . It's full of witty pokes at other series novels and Jasper's nutty inventions." SLJ

Other titles about Lily, Kate, and Jasper are:

The clue of the linoleum lederhosen (2006)

Jasper Dash and the Flame-pits of Delaware (2009)

Anderson, R. J.

Spell Hunter. HarperCollinsPublishers 2009 329p (Faery rebels) $16.99

Grades: 7 8 9 10 11 12   **Fic**

1. Fairies—Fiction 2. Magic—Fiction 3. Fantasy fiction

ISBN 978-0-06-155474-2; 0-06-155474-X

In a dying faery realm, only the brave and rebellious faery Knife persists in trying to discover how her people's magic was lost and what is needed to restore their powers and ensure their survival, but her quest is endangered by her secret friendship with a human named Paul.

"Filled with delicate, fantastical creatures; evil and dangerous crows; and a human who believes in love, this is a highly readable, sophisticated tale of romance and self-sacrifice." Booklist

Angle, Kimberly Greene

Hummingbird; [by] Kimberly Greene Angle. Farrar Straus Giroux 2008 243p $16.95

Grades: 5 6 7 8   **Fic**

1. Bereavement—Fiction 2. Death—Fiction 3. Family life—Fiction 4. Farm life—Fiction 5. Georgia—Fiction 6. Grandmothers—Fiction

ISBN 978-0-374-33376-8; 0-374-33376-9

     LC 2007-9156

In spite of a busy life on the family pumpkin and watermelon farm in Jubilee, Georgia, twelve-year-old March Anne Tanner feels that something is missing, and when Grenna, the grandmother who has helped raise her since her mother died when she was three, also passes on, March Anne finds that she must act on her feelings of loss.

"The novel is a call to notice nature's bounty as well as the story of a search for identity; and it reveals much about the hard work and simple life on a farm in rural Georgia. Charmingly told, the pace is slow but as compelling as the return of spring." KLIATT

Antieau, Kim

Ruby's imagine; written by Kim Antieau. Houghton Mifflin Co. 2008 201p $16

Grades: 6 7 8 9   **Fic**

1. Hurricane Katrina, 2005—Fiction 2. African Americans—Fiction 3. New Orleans (La.)—Fiction

ISBN 978-0-618-99767-1; 0-618-99767-9

     LC 2007047736

Tells the story of Hurricane Katrina from the point of view of Ruby, an unusually intuitive girl who lives with her grandmother in New Orleans but has powerful memories of an earlier life in the swamps.

"Antieau offers a complex, personal account of Katrina and its aftermath. . . . Ruby's atmospheric narrative is as dense and pungent as the bayou." Booklist

Appelbaum, Susannah

The Hollow Bettle. Alfred A. Knopf 2009 (The Poisons of Caux) $16.99; lib bdg $19.99

Grades: 4 5 6 7   **Fic**

1. Poisons and poisoning—Fiction 2. Uncles—Fiction 3. Fantasy fiction

ISBN 978-0-375-85173-5; 0-375-85173-9; 978-0-375-95173-2 (lib bdg); 0-375-95173-3 (lib bdg)

     LC 2008022626

Eleven-year-old Ivy Manx sets out with her new friend, a young "taster," to find her missing uncle, an outlawed healer, in the dangerous kingdom of Caux where magic, herbs, and poisons rule.

This "is a deeply satisfying, humor-laced quest with elements of wizardry and herbology, deeds of a dastardly nature, and, ultimately, redemption." Booklist

Applegate, Katherine

Home of the brave. Feiwel & Friends 2007
249p $16.95 *

Grades: 5 6 7 8   **Fic**
1. Immigrants—Fiction 2. Refugees—Fiction
3. Africans—Fiction 4. Cattle—Fiction 5. Minnesota—
Fiction 6. Novels in verse
ISBN 0-312-36765-1; 978-0-312-36765-7
LC 2006-32053

Kek, an African refugee, is confronted by many
strange things at the Minneapolis home of his aunt and
cousin, as well as in his fifth grade classroom, and longs
for his missing mother, but finds comfort in the company
of a cow and her owner.

"This beautiful story of hope and resilience is written
in free verse." Voice Youth Advocates

Armstrong, Kelley

The summoning. HarperCollinsPublishers 2008
390p (Darkest powers) $17.99; lib bdg $18.89

Grades: 7 8 9 10   **Fic**
1. Supernatural—Fiction 2. Ghost stories
ISBN   978-0-06-166269-0;   0-06-166269-0;
978-0-06-166272-0 (lib bdg); 0-06-166272-0 (lib bdg)
LC 2008-14221

After fifteen-year-old Chloe starts seeing ghosts and is
sent to Lyle House, a mysterious group home for mentally disturbed teenagers, she soon discovers that neither
Lyle House nor its inhabitants are exactly what they
seem, and that she and her new friends are in danger.

"Suspenseful, well-written, and engaging, this page-
turning . . . [novel] will be a hit." Voice Youth Advocates

Followed by: The awakening (2009)

Armstrong, William Howard, 1914-1999

Sounder; [by] William H. Armstrong;
illustrations by James Barkley. Harper & Row
1969 116p il $15.99; pa $5.99 *

Grades: 5 6 7 8   **Fic**
1. Dogs—Fiction 2. African Americans—Fiction
3. Family life—Fiction
ISBN 0-06-020143-6; 0-06-440020-4 (pa)
Awarded the Newbery Medal, 1970

"Set in the South in the era of sharecropping and segregation, this succinctly told tale poignantly describes the
courage of a father who steals a ham in order to feed his
undernourished family; the determination of the eldest
son, who searches for his father despite the apathy of
prison authorities; and the devotion of a coon dog named
Sounder." Shapiro. Fic for Youth. 3d edition

Asher, Jay

Thirteen reasons why; a novel. Razorbill 2007
288p $16.99

Grades: 8 9 10 11 12   **Fic**
1. Suicide—Fiction 2. School stories
ISBN 978-1-59514-171-2   LC 2007-03097

When high school student Clay Jenkins receives a box
in the mail containing thirteen cassette tapes recorded by
his classmate Hannah, who committed suicide, he spends
a bewildering and heartbreaking night crisscrossing their

town, listening to Hannah's voice recounting the events
leading up to her death.

"Clay's pain is palpable and exquisitely drawn in gripping casually poetic prose. The complex and soulful
characters expose astoundingly rich and singularly
teenage inner lives." SLJ

Atinsky, Steve

Tyler on prime time. Delacorte Press 2002 168p
hardcover o.p. pa $5.50

Grades: 5 6 7 8   **Fic**
1. Television—Fiction
ISBN 0-385-72917-0; 0-440-41803-8 (pa)
LC 2001-32468

While visiting his uncle, a writer on the most popular
show on television, twelve-year-old Tyler auditions for a
part on the show

"Written with a light touch, the novel features likable
characters and a well-detailed setting. . . . The vagaries
of show business . . . are convincingly portrayed." Horn
Book Guide

Atkins, Catherine

Alt ed. Putnam 2003 198p $17.99; pa $6.99

Grades: 7 8 9 10   **Fic**
1. School stories
ISBN 0-399-23854-9; 0-14-240235-4 (pa)
LC 2002-16942

Participating in a special after-school counseling class
with other troubled students, including a sensitive gay
classmate, helps Susan, an overweight tenth grader, develop a better sense of herself

"Most of the characters . . . come to life in new and
interesting ways, and Susan's story is strong, because she
is reinventing family relationships as well as trying to
communicate with her peers." Booklist

Atwater-Rhodes, Amelia, 1984-

Persistence of memory. Delacorte Press 2008
212p $15.99; lib bdg $18.99

Grades: 8 9 10 11 12   **Fic**
1. Supernatural—Fiction 2. Schizophrenia—Fiction
3. Vampires—Fiction 4. Witches—Fiction
ISBN   978-0-385-73437-0;   0-385-73437-9;
978-0-385-90443-8 (lib bdg); 0-385-90443-6 (lib bdg)
LC 2008-16062

Diagnosed with schizophrenia as a child, sixteen-year-
old Erin has spent half of her life in therapy and on
drugs, but now must face the possibility of weird things
in the real world, including shapeshifting friends and her
"alter," a centuries-old vampire.

"What sets this novel apart . . . are the two narrators—Erin, grown used to, and even comfortable with,
the idea that she is mentally ill; and Shevaun, willing to
do anything to protect the family she's cobbled together.
Secondary characters are equally compelling, and the
world that Atwater-Rhodes has created is believable and
intriguing." SLJ

Auch, Mary Jane

Ashes of roses. Holt & Co. 2002 250p $16.95;
pa $6.50

Grades: 7 8 9 10 11 12 Adult   **Fic**
1. Triangle Shirtwaist Company, Inc. —Fiction
2. Immigrants—Fiction 3. Irish Americans—Fiction
4. New York (N.Y.)—Fiction

ISBN 0-8050-6686-1; 0-440-23851-X (pa)
         LC 2001-51896

Sixteen-year-old Margaret Rose Nolan, newly arrived
from Ireland, finds work at New York City's Triangle
Shirtwaist Factory shortly before the 1911 fire in which
146 employees died

"Fast-paced, populated by distinctive characters, and
anchored in Auch's convincing sense of time and place,
this title is a good choice for readers who like historical
fiction." SLJ

Wing nut; [by] MJ Auch. 1st ed. Henry Holt
2005 231p $16.95

Grades: 5 6 7 8   **Fic**
1. Moving—Fiction 2. Birds—Fiction 3. Old age—
Fiction

ISBN 0-8050-7531-3   LC 2004-54046

When twelve-year-old Grady and his mother relocate
yet again, they find work taking care of an elderly man,
who teaches Grady about cars, birds, and what it means
to have a home

"Auch's story . . . is engaging. . . . What will attract
readers . . . is the author's careful integration of bird
lore and the unusual challenges of creating and maintaining a purple martin colony." Booklist

Avi, 1937-

The Book Without Words; a fable of medieval
magic. Hyperion Books for Children 2005 203p
$15.99

Grades: 5 6 7 8   **Fic**
1. Supernatural—Fiction 2. Magic—Fiction 3. Middle
Ages—Fiction 4. Great Britain—History—0-1066—
Fiction

ISBN 0-7868-0829-2

"At the dawning of the Middle Ages, Thorston, an old
alchemist, works feverishly to create gold and to dose
himself with a concoction that will enable him to live
forever. The key to his success lies in a mysterious book
with blank pages that can only be read by desperate,
green-eyed people. . . . Avi's compelling language
creates a dreary foreboding. . . . Clearly this is a story
with a message, a true fable. Thoughtful readers will devour its absorbing plot and humorous elements, and learn
a 'useful truth' along the way." SLJ

Crispin: the cross of lead. Hyperion Bks. for
Children 2002 262p $15.99; lib bdg $16.49; pa
$6.99 *

Grades: 5 6 7 8   **Fic**
1. Orphans—Fiction 2. Middle Ages—Fiction
3. Great Britain—History—1154-1399, Plantagenets—
Fiction

ISBN 0-7868-0828-4; 0-7868-2647-9 (lib bdg);
0-7868-1658-9 (pa)   LC 2001-51829

Awarded the Newbery Medal

Falsely accused of theft and murder, an orphaned
peasant boy in fourteenth-century England flees his village and meets a larger-than-life juggler who holds a
dangerous secret

This "book is a page-turner from beginning to end.
. . . A meticulously crafted story, full of adventure,
mystery, and action." SLJ

Followed by: Crispin at the edge of the world (2006)

Don't you know there's a war on?
HarperCollins Pubs. 2001 200p $14.95; pa $5.99
*

Grades: 4 5 6 7   **Fic**
1. World War, 1939-1945—Fiction 2. Teachers—Fiction 3. Brooklyn (New York, N.Y.)—Fiction

ISBN 0-380-97863-6; 0-380-81544-3 (pa)
         LC 00-46102

In wartime Brooklyn in 1943, eleven-year-old Howie
Crispers mounts a campaign to save his favorite teacher
from being fired

"The 1943 Brooklyn setting is well evoked in Howie's
lively, slang-spangled narration. The novel's uncomplicated, compact structure invites reading aloud." Horn
Book Guide

Hard gold; The Colorado gold rush of 1859.
Hyperion 2008 224p map (I witness) $15.99

Grades: 5 6 7 8   **Fic**
1. Colorado—Gold discoveries—Fiction 2. Uncles—
Fiction

ISBN 978-1-4231-0519-0; 1-4231-0519-2

Early Whitcomb, whose family's farm in Iowa is failing due to drought, is enticed by his uncle Jesse to go
west and dig for gold to help prevent foreclosure, but
during their adventure, Jesse gets into trouble, and Early
makes hard decisions while trying to find his relative and
the riches that lay hidden in the mountains.

"The chapters are short and broken up into diary format so as to mimic travel journals of the early wagon
train adventurers. A rewarding addition." SLJ

Includes glossary and bibliographical references

Iron thunder; the battle between the Monitor and
the Merrimac, a civil war novel. Hyperion 2007
205p il $15.99 *

Grades: 4 5 6   **Fic**
1. United States—History—1861-1865, Civil War—
Fiction 2. Ships—Fiction 3. Brooklyn (New York,
N.Y.)—Fiction

ISBN 978-1-423-10446-9

"This fascinating adventure taken from U.S. history
begins in Brooklyn in 1862, when Tom Carroll, 13, is
hired at the Iron Works in Greenpoint for a secret project, derisively known around the borough as Ericsson's
Folly. John Ericsson, a Swedish inventor, is trying to
build an ironclad ship that can battle the *Merrimac*, a
Confederate ship being outfitted with metal plates in Virginia. . . . Illustrated with period engravings, this is
gripping historical fiction from a keenly imagined perspective." Publ Wkly

Avi, 1937——*Continued*

The man who was Poe; a novel. Orchard Bks. 1989 208p hardcover o.p. pa $5.99

Grades: 4 5 6 7   **Fic**
1. Poe, Edgar Allan, 1809-1849—Fiction 2. Mystery fiction

ISBN 0-531-08433-7; 0-380-73022-7 (pa)
LC 89-42537

"A Richard Jackson book"

In Providence, R.I., in 1848, Edgar Allan Poe reluctantly investigates the problems of eleven-year-old Edmund, whose family has mysteriously disappeared and whose story suggests a new Poe tale with a ghastly final twist

Avi blends "drama, history, and mystery without a hint of pastiche or calculation. And, as in the best mystery stories, readers will be left in the end with both the comfort of puzzles solved and the unease of mysteries remaining." Bull Cent Child Books

Nothing but the truth; a documentary novel. Orchard Bks. 1991 177p hardcover o.p. pa $6.99 *

Grades: 6 7 8 9   **Fic**
1. School stories

ISBN 0-531-05959-6; 0-380-71907-X (pa)
LC 91-9200

A Newbery Medal honor book, 1992

"A Richard Jackson book"

A ninth-grader's suspension for singing "The Star-Spangled Banner" during homeroom becomes a national news story.

"The book is effectively set entirely in monologue or dialogue; conversations, memos, letters, diary entries, talk-radio transcripts, and newspaper articles are all interwoven to present an uninterrupted plot. The construction is nearly flawless; the characters seem painfully human and typically ordinary. . . . A powerful, explosive novel that involves the reader from start to finish." Horn Book

The seer of shadows. HarperCollinsPublishers 2008 202p $16.99; lib bdg $17.89 *

Grades: 4 5 6 7   **Fic**
1. Photography—Fiction 2. Ghost stories 3. Swindlers and swindling—Fiction 4. New York (N.Y.)—Fiction

ISBN   978-0-06-000015-8;   0-06-000015-8; 978-0-06-000016-5 (lib bdg); 0-06-000016-3 (lib bdg)
LC 2007-10891

In New York City in 1872, fourteen-year-old Horace, a photographer's apprentice, becomes entangled in a plot to create fraudulent spirit photographs, but when Horace accidentally frees the real ghost of a dead girl bent on revenge, his life takes a frightening turn.

"Fast-paced yet haunting. . . . This engaging novel has great immediacy and strong narrative drive." Booklist

Traitor's gate. Atheneum Books for Young Readers 2007 351p $17.99 *

Grades: 5 6 7 8   **Fic**
1. London (England)—Fiction 2. Spies—Fiction 3. Family life—Fiction 4. Poverty—Fiction

ISBN 0-689-85335-7

When his father is arrested as a debtor in 1849 London, fourteen-year-old John Huffman must take on unexpected responsibilities, from asking a distant relative for

help to determining why people are spying on him and his family.

"With plenty of period detail, this action-packed narrative of twists, turns, and treachery is another winner from a master craftsman." SLJ

Ayres, Katherine

Macaroni boy. Delacorte Press 2003 182p hardcover o.p. pa $5.99

Grades: 5 6 7 8   **Fic**
1. School stories 2. Great Depression, 1929-1939—Fiction

ISBN 0-385-73016-0; 0-440-41884-4 (pa)
LC 2002-6768

In Pittsburgh in 1933, sixth-grader Mike Costa notices a connection between several strange occurrences, but the only way he can find out the truth about what's happening is to be nice to the class bully. Includes historical facts

"Actual places and events are interwoven with a heartwarming story of a close-knit family facing difficult times." Voice Youth Advocates

North by night; a story of the Underground Railroad. Delacorte Press 1998 176p hardcover o.p. pa $4.99

Grades: 6 7 8 9   **Fic**
1. Underground railroad—Fiction 2. Slavery—Fiction

ISBN 0-385-32564-9; 0-440-22747-x (pa)
LC 98-10039

Companion volume to: Stealing south

Presents the journal of Lucinda, a sixteen-year-old girl whose family operates a stop on the Underground Railroad

This "is an absorbing tale. Ayres slips in a lot of evocative detail about the hard work of running a farm and a household before the Civil War, as well as some rather charming musing about kissing and its myriad effects on the psyche." Booklist

Baggott, Julianna

The   Prince   of   Fenway   Park. HarperCollinsPublishers 2009 322p $16.99; lib bdg $17.89

Grades: 4 5 6 7   **Fic**
1. Boston Red Sox (Baseball team)—Fiction
2. Fenway Park (Boston, Mass.)—Fiction
3. Baseball—Fiction 4. Orphans—Fiction
5. Father-son relationship—Fiction 6. Supernatural—Fiction

ISBN   978-0-06-087242-7;   0-06-087242-X; 978-0-06-087243-4 (lib bdg); 0-06-087243-8 (lib bdg)
LC 2008-19666

In the fall of 2004, twelve-year-old Oscar Egg is sent to live with his father in a strange netherworld under Boston's Fenway Park, where he joins the fairies, pooka, banshee, and other beings that are trapped there, waiting for someone to break the eighty-six-year-old curse that has prevented the Boston Red Sox from winning a World Series.

"Both whimsical and provocative (the 'N' word crops up in some historical references), this story will engage readers who like clever tales, and also those who enjoy chewing over controversial themes." SLJ

Baker, Julie
Up Molasses Mountain. Wendy Lamb Bks. 2002
209p lib bdg $17.99
Grades: 6 7 8 9   **Fic**
   1. Coal mines and mining—Fiction
   ISBN 0-385-90048-1   LC 2001-50692
When union members arrive to organize their West
Virginia coal mining town, fourteen-year-old Clarence
Henderson, shunned for his cleft lip, and his neighbor
Elizabeth Braxton narrate the changes in their own lives
and in the lives of everyone in their community
   "Baker does an excellent job of presenting both sides
of the issues. . . . Baker also offers a deeply moving
psychological portrait of a tormented boy who finds a
way outside himself." Booklist

Baldwin, James, 1924-1987
Go tell it on the mountain. Knopf 1953 303p
$15.95; pa $6.99
Grades: 7 8 9 10   **Fic**
   1. African Americans—Fiction 2. Harlem (New York,
N.Y.)—Fiction
   ISBN 0-679-60154-6; 0-440-33007-6 (pa)
Also available in paperback from Laurel-Leaf Bks.
   This novel is an "autobiographical story of a Harlem
child's relationship with his father against the back-
ground of his being saved in the pentecostal church." Be-
net's Reader's Ency of Am Lit

Balliett, Blue, 1955-
Chasing Vermeer; illustrated by Brett Helquist.
Scholastic Press 2004 254p il $16.95 *
Grades: 5 6 7 8   **Fic**
   1. Vermeer, Johannes, 1632-1675—Fiction
2. Mystery fiction 3. Art—Fiction
   ISBN 0-439-37294-1   LC 2002-152106
When seemingly unrelated and strange events start to
happen and a precious Vermeer painting disappears, elev-
en-year-olds Petra and Calder combine their talents to
solve an international art scandal.
   Balliett's purpose "seems to be to get children to
think—about relationships, connections, coincidences,
and the subtle language of artwork. . . . [This is] a book
that offers children something new upon each reading.
. . . Helquist . . . outdoes himself here, providing an interactive mystery in his pictures." Booklist
   Other titles about Petra and Calder are:
The Wright 3 (2006)
The Calder game (2008)

Banghart, Tracy
What the sea wants; illustrated by Julia C.
Blum. Lizstar Books 2006 71p il $16 *
Grades: 6 7 8 9   **Fic**
   1. Ocean—Fiction 2. Seashore—Fiction 3. Maine—
Fiction
   ISBN 978-0-9779753-0-3; 0-9779753-0-4
"Victoria has always been drawn to the sea. Living on
the windswept Maine coast with her mother and Grannie
Foster, she spends most of her days and nights walking
the shore. . . . On the last day of summer, Victoria near-
ly drowns and is saved by Sam, but the sea always ex-

acts a price from those who would deny it what it wants.
Banghart's first novel . . . is striking and exquisite. . . .
In quiet yet purposeful prose, she paints a tale full of
rich atmosphere and vivid setting." Voice Youth Advocates

Banks, Kate, 1960-
Walk softly, Rachel. Farrar, Straus & Giroux
2003 149p $16
Grades: 7 8 9 10   **Fic**
   1. Family life—Fiction 2. Death—Fiction
   ISBN 0-374-38230-1   LC 2002-26503
"Frances Foster books"
   When fourteen-year-old Rachel reads the journal of
her brother, who died when she was seven, she learns se-
crets that help her understand her parents and herself
   "While Banks's poetic prose may consist of simple
words, its effect on the ear and heart is remarkable." SLJ

Barber, Tiki, 1975-
Go long! [by] Tiki and Ronde Barber with Paul
Mantell. 1st ed. Simon & Schuster Books for
Young Readers 2008 153p $15.99
Grades: 4 5 6 7   **Fic**
   1. Football—Fiction 2. Twins—Fiction 3. Brothers—
Fiction
   ISBN 978-1-416-93619-0; 1-416-93619-X
      LC 2007045843
"A Paula Wiseman book"
   When Coach Spangler leaves at the start of their sec-
ond year of junior high school, thirteen-year-old twins
Tiki and Ronde wonder if his replacement, history teach-
er Mr. Wheeler, can coach the Eagles to another winning
football season.
   "Football fans will find the on-field action scenes and
even the coaching sessions very readable." Booklist
   Another title about Tiki and Ronde is:
Kickoff (2007)

Barker, M. P., 1960-
A difficult boy. Holiday House 2008 298p
$16.95
Grades: 5 6 7 8   **Fic**
   1. Contract labor—Fiction 2. Irish Americans—Fiction
3. Massachusetts—Fiction 4. Swindlers and swindling—Fiction
   ISBN 978-0-8234-2086-5; 0-8234-2086-8
      LC 2007-37059
In Farmington, Massachusetts, in 1839, nine-year-old
Ethan experiences hardships as an indentured servant of
the wealthy Lyman family alongside Daniel, a boy
scorned simply for being Irish, and the boys bond as
they try to right a terrible wrong.
   "A memorable tale of friendship and a fascinating
glimpse into mid-19th-century Massachusetts." SLJ

Barkley, Brad
Dream factory; [by] Brad Barkley + Heather
Hepler. Dutton Books 2007 250p $16.99; pa $8.99
Grades: 8 9 10 11 12   **Fic**

Barkley, Brad—_Continued_
1. Walt Disney World (Fla.)—Fiction 2. Love stories
3. Summer employment—Fiction
ISBN   978-0-525-47802-7;   0-525-47802-7;
978-0-14-241298-5 (pa); 0-14-241298-8 (pa)
Alternating chapters present the view points of two
teenagers who find summer employment as costumed
cartoon characters at Disney World and try to resist falling in love.
"Able writing moves the story along while strong
characterization makes even secondary players come
alive." SLJ

Jars of glass; [by] Brad Barkley & Heather
Hepler. Dutton Childrens Books 2008 246p $16.99
Grades: 7 8 9 10 11 12   Fic
1. Family life—Fiction 2. Mental illness—Fiction
3. Siblings—Fiction 4. Adoption—Fiction
ISBN 978-0-525-47911-6; 0-525-47911-2
                                        LC 2007-52657
Two sisters, aged fourteen and fifteen, offer their
views of events that occur during the year after their
mother is diagnosed with schizophrenia and their family,
including a recently adopted Russian orphan, begins to
disintegrate.
"Barkley and Hepler are the masters of alternating
narration, with Chloe's and Shana's voices both believable, clearly different, and usefully complementary. . . .
This is an affecting story about families struggling to re-
adjust in the face of one member's affliction." Bull Cent
Child Books

Scrambled eggs at midnight; by Brad Barkley,
Heather Hepler. Dutton Books 2006 262p $16.99
Grades: 7 8 9 10   Fic
1. Love stories 2. Fairs—Fiction 3. North Carolina—
Fiction
ISBN 0-525-47760-8   LC 2005029187
Calliope and Eliot, two fifteen-year-olds in Asheville,
North Carolina, begin to acknowledge some unpleasant
truths about their parents and form their own ideas about
love.
"This coauthored love story unfolds in alternating
chapters narrated in Cal and Eliot's hilarious, heart-
tugging voices. . . . The authors raise a potentially routine summer romance into a refreshing, poetic, memorable story." Booklist

Barnes, Jennifer Lynn
The Squad: perfect cover. Delacorte Press 2008
275p pa $6.99
Grades: 7 8 9 10   Fic
1. Spies—Fiction 2. Cheerleading—Fiction 3. School
stories 4. Computers—Fiction
ISBN 978-0-385-73454-7 (pa); 0-385-73454-9 (pa)
                                        LC 2007-09352
High school sophomore Toby Klein enjoys computer
hacking and wearing combat boots, so she thinks it is a
joke when she is invited to join the cheerleading squad
but soon learns cheering is just a cover for an elite group
of government operatives known as the Squad.
"In addition to offering crafty plotting and time-
honored, typical teen conflicts and rivalries, Barnes
maintains a sharp sense of humor in this action-adventure
series." Bull Cent Child Books
Another title in this series is:

The Squad: killer spirit (2008)

Barrett, Tracy, 1955-
The 100-year-old secret; by Tracy Barrett.
Henry Holt 2008 157p (The Sherlock files) $15.95
Grades: 4 5 6 7   Fic
1. Brothers and sisters—Fiction. 2. Great Britain—Fiction 3. Mystery fiction
ISBN 978-0-8050-8340-8; 0-8050-8340-5
                                        LC 2007034004
Xena and Xander Holmes, an American brother and
sister living in London for a year, discover that Sherlock
Holmes was their great-great-great grandfather when they
are inducted into the Society for the Preservation of Famous Detectives and given his unsolved casebook, from
which they attempt to solve the case of a famous missing
painting.
"The main characters are observant, bright, and gifted
with powers of deduction." SLJ
Another title in this series is:
The beast of Blackslope (2009)

Barron, T. A.
The lost years of Merlin. Philomel Bks. 1996
326p $19.99; $10.99; pa $6.99; pa $2.99 *
Grades: 5 6 7 8   Fic
1. Merlin (Legendary character)—Fiction 2. Fantasy
fiction
ISBN   0-399-23018-1;   0-399-25020-4;
978-0-4410-06687- (pa); 978-0-4410-1028-8 (pa)
                                        LC 96-33920
"A boy, hurled on the rocks by the sea, regains consciousness unable to remember anything—not his parents, not his own name. He is sure that the secretive
Branwen is not his mother, despite her claims, and that
Emrys is not his real name. The two soon find them-
selves feared because of Branwen's healing abilities and
Emrys' growing powers. . . . Barron has created not
only a magical land populated by remarkable beings but
also a completely magical tale, filled with ancient Celtic
and Druidic lore, that will enchant readers." Booklist
Other titles in this series are:
The fires of Merlin (1998)
The mirror of Merlin (1999)
The seven songs of Merlin (1997)
The wings of Merlin (2000)

The Merlin effect. Philomel Bks. 1994 254p
$19.99; pa $6.99
Grades: 5 6 7 8   Fic
1. Merlin (Legendary character)—Fiction 2. Buried
treasure—Fiction 3. Fantasy fiction
ISBN 0-399-22689-3; 0-441-01222-1 (pa)
                                        LC 93-36234
Also available in paperback from TOR Bks.
When she joins her father and several others investigating a strange whirlpool and possible sunken treasure
ship off the coast of Baja California, thirteen-year-old
Kate, featured in Heartlight (1990) and The Ancient One
(1992), is drawn into a centuries-old conflict between
Merlin and the evil Vagar
The author "blends a wealth of sea lore with ancient
myth and fast-paced adventure." Libr J

Barron, T. A.—*Continued*
Merlin's dragon; by T.A. Barron. Philomel
Books 2008 305p $19.99
Grades: 6 7 8 9   **Fic**
1. Dragons—Fiction 2. Magic—Fiction 3. Fantasy fiction
ISBN 978-0-399-24750-7; 0-399-24750-5
LC 2008-2469
Basil, a small, flying lizard who is searching for others like himself, discovers that there is more to him than he knows, as he becomes engaged in Avalon's great war between the evil Rhita Gawr and the forces of good.
"Basil is an appealing, complex character. . . . This first book in a new series will captivate readers already familiar with the fantasist's Merlin chronicles." Booklist

Bartoletti, Susan Campbell, 1958-
The boy who dared. Scholastic Press 2008 202p
$16.99 *
Grades: 5 6 7 8   **Fic**
1. Hübener, Helmuth, 1925-1942—Fiction
2. Courage—Fiction 3. National socialism—Fiction
4. Germany—History—1933-1945—Fiction
ISBN 978-0-439-68013-4; 0-439-68013-1
LC 2007014166
In October, 1942, seventeen-year-old Helmuth Hübener, imprisoned for distributing anti-Nazi leaflets, recalls his past life and how he came to dedicate himself to bringing the truth about Hitler and the war to the German people.
Bartoletti "does and excellent job of conveying the political climate surrounding Hitler's ascent to power, seamlessly integrating a complex range of socioeconomic conditions into her absorbing drama." Publ Wkly

Baskin, Nora Raleigh, 1961-
All we know of love. Candlewick Press 2008
201p $16.99
Grades: 6 7 8 9 10   **Fic**
1. Mothers—Fiction 2. Loss (Psychology)—Fiction
3. Voyages and travels—Fiction
ISBN 978-0-7636-3623-4; 0-7636-3623-1
LC 2007-22396
Natalie, almost sixteen, sneaks away from her Connecticut home and takes the bus to Florida, looking for the mother who abandoned her father and her when she was ten years old.
"Baskin takes a familiar story line and examines it in a new and interesting way that will engage readers." Voice Youth Advocates

Anything but typical. Simon & Schuster Books for Young Readers 2009 195p il $15.99 *
Grades: 4 5 6 7   **Fic**
1. Autism—Fiction 2. School stories 3. Family life—Fiction 4. Authorship—Fiction
ISBN 978-1-416-96378-3; 1-416-96378-2
LC 2008-20994
Jason, a twelve-year-old autistic boy who wants to become a writer, relates what his life is like as he tries to make sense of his world.
"This is an enormously difficult subject, but Baskin, without dramatics or sentimentality, makes it universal." Booklist

The truth about my Bat Mitzvah. Simon & Schuster Books for Young Readers 2008 138p
$15.99
Grades: 5 6 7 8   **Fic**
1. Jews—Fiction 2. Bat mitzvah—Fiction
3. Grandmothers—Fiction
ISBN 978-1-4169-3558-2; 1-4169-3558-4
LC 2007-01248
After her beloved grandmother, Nana, dies, non-religious twelve-year-old Caroline becomes curious about her mother's Jewish ancestry.
"Readers will identify with Caroline and her preoccupations. . . . This quick read will be a hit with preteens contemplating their own identities." Booklist

Bastedo, Jamie, 1955-
On thin ice. Red Deer Press 2006 348p pa
$10.95
Grades: 8 9 10 11 12   **Fic**
1. Polar bear—Fiction 2. Arctic regions—Fiction
3. Greenhouse effect—Fiction 4. Inuit—Fiction
ISBN 978-0-88995-337-6
"Set in the remote Arctic village of Nanurtalik, this novel follows Ashley as she journeys on the shaman path chosen for her through the Inuit line of her father. Disturbed by haunting—sometimes frightening—dreams of a gigantic polar bear that seems bent on destroying her, Ashley furiously draws her dreams onto paper, capturing the very essence of the bear within. . . . This novel is told with richness of language, culture, and emotion, but its sense of place sparkles brightest." Voice Youth Advocates

Basye, Dale E.
Heck; where the bad kids go; by Dale E. Basye; illustrated by Bob Dob. Random House 2008 304p
il $16.99; lib bdg $19.99
Grades: 5 6 7 8   **Fic**
1. Siblings—Fiction 2. Future life—Fiction 3. School stories
ISBN   978-0-375-84075-3;   0-375-84075-3;
978-0-375-94075-0 (lib bdg); 0-375-94075-8 (lib bdg)
LC 2007-8379
When timid Milton and his older, scofflaw sister Marlo die in a marshmallow bear explosion at Grizzly Mall, they are sent to Heck, an otherworldly reform school from which they are determined to escape.
"The author's umpteen clever allusions—characters' eternal fates are decided by standardized 'Soul Aptitude Tests'; Mr. R. Nixon teaches ethics to evildoers in room 1972—make this book truly sparkle." Publ Wkly
Followed by: Rapacia : the second circle of Heck (2009)

Bateson, Catherine, 1960-
Being Bee. Holiday House 2007 126p il $16.95
*
Grades: 4 5 6   **Fic**
1. Family life—Fiction 2. Father-daughter relationship—Fiction 3. Guinea pigs—Fiction 4. Australia—Fiction
ISBN 978-0-8234-2104-6; 0-8234-2104-X
LC 2006-101561

Bateson, Catherine, 1960-—*Continued*

Bee faces friction at home and at school when her widowed father begins seriously dating Jazzi, who seems to take over the house and their lives, but as shared secrets and common interests finally begin to draw them together, Jazzi accidentally makes a terrible mistake.

"Bee's emotions are perspectives are honest and clearly presented. . . . She is a likable, believable character." SLJ

Bauer, A. C. E.

No castles here. 1st ed. Random House 2007 270p $15.99; lib bdg $18.99

Grades: 4 5 6 7   **Fic**

1. New Jersey—Fiction 2. City and town life—Fiction 3. Books and reading—Fiction 4. Choirs (Music)—Fiction 5. Magic—Fiction

ISBN 978-0-375-83921-4; 978-0-375-93921-1 (lib bdg)   LC 2006023601

Eleven-year-old Augie Boretski dreams of escaping his rundown Camden, New Jersey, neighborhood, but things start to turn around with help from a Big Brother, a music teacher, and a mysterious bookstore owner, so when his school is in trouble, he pulls the community together to save it.

This is a "heartwarming novel." Booklist

Bauer, Joan

Peeled. G.P. Putnam's Sons 2008 256p $16.99 *

Grades: 6 7 8 9 10   **Fic**

1. Journalism—Fiction 2. Farm life—Fiction 3. Ghost stories 4. School stories 5. New York (State)—Fiction

ISBN 978-0-399-23475-0; 0-399-23475-6   LC 2007-42835

In an upstate New York farming community, high school reporter Hildy Biddle investigates a series of strange occurrences at a house rumored to be haunted.

This is "a warm and funny story full of likable, off-beat characters led by a strongly voiced, independently minded female protagonist on her way to genuine, well-earned maturity." SLJ

Squashed; [by] Joan Bauer. 1st G.P. Putnam's Sons ed. Puffin Books 2001 c1992 194p hardcover o.p. pa $7.99 *

Grades: 6 7 8 9   **Fic**

1. Country life—Fiction 2. Iowa—Fiction

ISBN 0-399-23750-X; 0-14-240426-8 (pa)   LC 2001-18595

A reissue of the title first published 1992 by Delacorte Press

As sixteen-year-old Ellie pursues her two goals—growing the biggest pumpkin in Iowa and losing twenty pounds herself—she strengthens her relationship with her father and meets a young man with interests similar to her own.

"Skillful plot development and strong characterization are real stengths here. Ellie's perspetive, intelligent, and funny narrative keeps the story lively right up to its satisfying conclusion." SLJ

Stand tall. Putnam 2002 182p $16.99; pa $6.99

Grades: 5 6 7 8   **Fic**

1. Divorce—Fiction 2. Grandfathers—Fiction

ISBN 0-399-23473-X; 0-14-240148-X (pa)   LC 2002-23876

Tree, a six-foot-three-inch twelve-year-old, copes with his parents' recent divorce and his failure as an athlete by helping his grandfather, a Vietnam vet and recent amputee, and Sophie, a new girl at school

The "swiftly paced story artfully blends poignant and outright funny moments, resulting in a triumphant tale that will resonate with many young readers." Publ Wkly

Bauer, Marion Dane, 1938-

On my honor. Clarion Bks. 1986 90p $15 *

Grades: 4 5 6 7   **Fic**

1. Accidents—Fiction

ISBN 0-89919-439-7   LC 86-2679

Also available in paperback from Dell

A Newbery Medal honor book, 1987

When his best friend drowns while they are both swimming in a treacherous river that they had promised never to go near, Joel is devastated and terrified at having to tell both sets of parents the terrible consequences of their disobedience

"Bauer's association of Joel's guilt with the smell of the polluted river on his skin is particularly noteworthy. Its miasma almost rises off the pages. Descriptions are vivid, characterization and dialogue natural, and the style taut but unforced. A powerful, moving book." SLJ

Beaty, Andrea

Cicada summer. Amulet Books 2008 167p $15.95

Grades: 4 5 6 7   **Fic**

1. Siblings—Fiction 2. Bereavement—Fiction 3. Illinois—Fiction

ISBN 978-0-8109-9472-0; 0-8109-9472-0   LC 2007-22266

Twelve-year-old Lily mourns her brother, and has not spoken since the accident she feels she could of prevented but the summer Tinny comes to town she is the only one who realizes Lily's secret.

"This is compelling fiction that will be a hit with young readers. . . . Rich and thought-provoking and yet . . . accessible." Horn Book

Beaufrand, Mary Jane

Primavera; by Mary Jane Beaufrand. 1st ed. Little, Brown 2007 260p $16.99

Grades: 6 7 8 9   **Fic**

1. Botticelli, Sandro, 1444 or 5-1510—Fiction 2. Italy—History—0-1559—Fiction 3. Renaissance—Fiction 4. Artists—Fiction

ISBN 978-0-316-01644-5; 0-316-01644-6   LC 2006025288

Growing up in Renaissance Italy, Flora sees her family's fortunes ebb, but encounters with the artist Botticelli and the guidance of her nurse teach her to look past the material world to the beauty already in her life.

"Political, historical, and art historical details provide a canvas on which this tale of murder, intrigue, and young romance is played out, but are painted with a broad stroke." SLJ

Beck, Ian

The secret history of Tom Trueheart. Greenwillow Books 2007 341p il $16.99; lib bdg $17.89

Grades: 4 5 6 7   **Fic**

1. Storytelling—Fiction 2. Fairy tales 3. Brothers—Fiction

ISBN   978-0-06-115210-8;   0-06-115210-2; 978-0-06-115211-5 (lib bdg); 0-06-115211-0 (lib bdg)

LC 2006043362

When young Tom Trueheart's seven older brothers all go missing during their adventures in the Land of Stories, he embarks on a perilous mission to save them and to capture the rogue story-writer who wants to do away with the heroes.

This "is a charming twist on fairy tales. . . . Silhouette drawings interspersed throughout add a wonderfully nostalgic touch." SLJ

Another title about Tom Trueheart is:

Tom Trueheart and the Land of Dark Stories (2008)

Becker, Tom, 1981-

Darkside; [by] Tom Becker. Orchard Books 2008 294p (Darkside) $16.99

Grades: 7 8 9 10   **Fic**

1. Supernatural—Fiction 2. London (England)—Fiction 3. Horror fiction

ISBN 978-0-545-03739-6; 0-545-03739-5

LC 2007-23634

Jonathan Starling's father is in an asylum and his home has been attacked when, while running away from kidnappers, he stumbles upon Darkside, a terrifying and hidden part of London ruled by the descendents of Jack the Ripper, where Jonathan is in mortal danger if he cannot find the way out.

"This fast-paced, unrelentingly entertaining story has plenty of suspense and lots of scares." Booklist

Followed by: Lifeblood (2008)

Beil, Michael D.

The Red Blazer Girls: the ring of Rocamadour. Alfred A. Knopf 2009 299p $15.99; lib bdg $18.99 *

Grades: 5 6 7 8   **Fic**

1. Puzzles—Fiction 2. Friendship—Fiction 3. School stories 4. Mystery fiction

ISBN   978-0-375-84814-8;   0-375-84814-2; 978-0-375-94814-5 (lib bdg); 0-375-94814-7 (lib bdg)

LC 2008-25254

Catholic-schooled seventh-graders Sophie, Margaret, Rebecca, and Leigh Ann help an elderly neighbor solve a puzzle her father left for her estranged daughter twenty years ago.

"The dialogue is fast and funny, the clues are often solvable." Booklist

Bell, Cathleen Davitt, 1971-

Slipping. Bloomsbury 2008 215p $16.95

Grades: 6 7 8 9   **Fic**

1. Grandfathers—Fiction 2. Death—Fiction 3. Ghost stories

ISBN 978-1-59990-258-6; 1-59990-258-3

LC 2008-04420

Thirteen-year-old Michael and an unlikely group of allies journey to the river of the dead to help Michael's grandfather release his hold on a ghostly life and, in the process, heal wounds that have kept Michael's father distant.

"The balance between the supernatural and genuine human feelings creates a compelling mix." Booklist

Bell, Hilari, 1958-

Flame; The book of Sorahb, volume one. Simon & Schuster Bks. for Young Readers 2003 344p (Farsala trilogy) hardcover o.p. pa $6.99

Grades: 7 8 9 10   **Fic**

1. Fantasy fiction

ISBN 0-689-85413-7; 0-689-8541-5 (pa)

LC 2003-114815

Paperback has title: Fall of a Kingdom

"The story is set in Farsala, a peaceful land now targeted for invasion by the Hrum, who have already conquered 28 other countries. As the enemy advances, routing the overconfident Farsalan army, three young people caught up in the fray move inexorably toward new futures in which they will play leading roles in the outcome and aftermath of the war. They are Soraya, the spoiled daughter of the Farsalan army's high commander; Jiaan, the high commander's peasant-born bastard son; and Kavi, an itinerant peddler and sometime con artist." Booklist

"The crisp dialogue, finely tuned characterizations, and vivid descriptions make the people and landscape seem as real as those in any grand historical epic." SLJ

Other titles in this series are:

Forging the sword (2006)

Rise of a hero (2005)

The Goblin Wood. Eos/HarperCollins Pubs. 2003 294p hardcover o.p. pa $7.99

Grades: 5 6 7 8   **Fic**

1. Fantasy fiction

ISBN 0-06-051371-3; 0-06-51373-3 (pa)

LC 2002-15281

A young Hedgewitch, an idealistic knight, and an army of clever goblins fight against the ruling hierarchy that is trying to rid the land of all magical creatures.

"Leavened by humor and a dollop of romance, this well-crafted fantasy adventure demonstrates Bell's talent for creating enduring characters and worlds." Booklist

The last knight. Eos 2007 357p (Knight and rogue) $16.99; lib bdg $17.89

Grades: 7 8 9 10   **Fic**

1. Knights and knighthood—Fiction 2. Fantasy fiction

ISBN   978-0-06-082503-4;   0-06-082503-0; 978-0-06-082504-1 (lib bdg); 0-06-082504-9 (lib bdg)

LC 2006-36427

In alternate chapters, eighteen-year-old Sir Michael Sevenson, an anachronistic knight errant, and seventeen-year-old Fisk, his streetwise squire, tell of their noble quest to bring Lady Ceciel to justice while trying to solve her husband's murder.

"The novel is brimming with saved-by-a-hair escapades and fast-paced realistic action. . . . This well-created fantasy is a great read with worthwhile moral issues pertinent to its intended audience." SLJ

Followed by: Rogue's home (2008)

Bell, Hilari, 1958-—*Continued*
Shield of stars. Simon & Schuster Books For Young Readers 2007 267p (The shield, the sword and the crown) $16.99
Grades: 6 7 8 9   **Fic**
1. Fantasy fiction
ISBN 978-1-4169-0594-3; 1-4169-0594-4
LC 2005-35571

When the Justice he works for is condemned for treason, fourteen-year-old and semi-reformed pickpocket Weasel sets out to find a notorious bandit who may be able to help save his master's life.

"Bell's trademark shades of gray help shift readers' perceptions of the characters and their motivations, adding an unusual layer of depth that moves this story beyond simple adventure. Weasel's choices are complex and believable." SLJ

Followed by: Sword of waters (2008)

Bell, Ted
Nick of time; [by] Ted Bell. St. Martin's Griffin 2008 434p il $17.95 *
Grades: 6 7 8 9   **Fic**
1. Nelson, Horatio Nelson, Viscount, 1758-1805—Fiction 2. Churchill, Sir Winston, 1874-1965—Fiction 3. Adventure fiction 4. World War, 1939-1945—Fiction 5. Pirates—Fiction 6. France—History—1799-1815—Fiction 7. Fantasy fiction
ISBN 978-0-312-38068-7; 0-312-38068-2
LC 2008-13634

First published 2000 by Xlibris

With the help of Lord Hawke, whose children have been taken by the evil pirate Captain Billy Blood, young Nick McIver uses a time machine to rescue the two children as well as change the course of events in two time periods, the Napoleonic Wars and World War II.

"This is an immensely appealing book. . . . [The book is filled] with great battle scenes; lots of nautical jargon; and themes of courage, integrity, and honor." SLJ

Bellairs, John
The curse of the blue figurine. Dial Bks. for Young Readers 1983 200p hardcover o.p. pa $5.99 *
Grades: 5 6 7 8   **Fic**
1. Mystery fiction
ISBN 0-8446-7138-4; 0-14-240258-3 (pa)
LC 82-73217

Also available Brad Strickland's titles based on John Bellairs characters; Hardcover available from P. Smith

"The terror for young Johnny Dixon begins when cranky eccentric Professor Childermass tells him that St. Michael's Church is haunted by Father Baart, an evil sorcerer who mysteriously disappeared years ago. When Johnny finds a blue Egyptian figurine hidden in the church basement, he takes it home in spite of the warning note from Father Baart threatening harm to anyone who removes it from the church." SLJ

The author "intertwines real concerns with sorcery in a seamless fashion, bringing dimension to his characters and events with expert timing and sharply honed atmosphere." Booklist

Other titles about Johnny Dixon and Professor Childermass are:

The chessmen of doom (1989)
The eyes of the killer robot (1986)
The mummy, the will and the crypt (1983)
The revenge of the wizard's ghost (1985)
The secret of the underground room (1990)
The spell of the sorcerer's skull (1984)
The trolley to yesterday (1989)

Bemis, John Claude
The nine pound hammer. Random House 2009 368p (Clockwork dark) $16.99; lib bdg $19.99
Grades: 6 7 8 9   **Fic**
1. Orphans—Fiction 2. Siblings—Fiction 3. Fantasy fiction 4. John Henry (Legendary character)
ISBN   978-0-375-85564-1;   0-375-85564-5; 978-0-375-95564-8 (lib bdg); 0-375-95564-X (lib bdg)
LC 2008-22503

Drawn by the lodestone his father gave him years before, twelve-year-old orphan Ray travels south, meeting along the way various characters from folklore who are battling against an evil industry baron known as the Gog.

"If readers still possess a twinkle of wonder for the step-right-up days of side-show hucksterism, Bemis' debut will shock and amaze them." Booklist

Bennett, Jay, 1912-
Coverup; a novel. Watts 1991 144p hardcover o.p. pa $4.50
Grades: 7 8 9 10   **Fic**
1. Mystery fiction
ISBN 0-531-15224-3; 0-449-70409-2 (pa)
LC 91-18506

Teenage Brad is tormented by confused memories of a drunken ride with his best friend Alden, during which they may have hit and killed a man

"Bennett has created another suspenseful mystery that is sure to please his confirmed fans and attract new ones." Booklist

Berlin, Eric
The puzzling world of Winston Breen; the secret in the box. Putnam 2007 215p il $16.99 *
Grades: 4 5 6 7   **Fic**
1. Siblings—Fiction 2. Puzzles—Fiction 3. Mystery fiction
ISBN 978-0-399-24693-7; 0-399-24693-2
LC 2006-20531

Puzzle-crazy, twelve-year-old Winston and his ten-year-old sister Katie find themselves involved in a dangerous mystery involving a hidden ring. Puzzles for the reader to solve are included throughout the text.

"A delightfully clever mystery. . . . There is plenty of suspense to engage readers." SLJ

Berry, Julie
The Amaranth enchantment. Bloomsbury U.S.A. Children's Books 2009 308p $16.99
Grades: 6 7 8   **Fic**
1. Fantasy fiction 2. Orphans—Fiction 3. Extraterrestrial beings—Fiction
ISBN 978-1-59990-334-7; 1-59990-334-2
LC 2008-22354

Berry, Julie—*Continued*

Orphaned at age five, Lucinda, now fifteen, stands with courage against the man who took everything from her, aided by a thief, a clever goat, and a mysterious woman called the Witch of Amaranth, while the prince she knew as a child prepares to marry, unaware that he, too, is in danger.

"A lively, quick, stylish, engaging first novel with some lovely, familiar fairy-tale elements." Publ Wkly

Berryhill, Shane

Chance Fortune and the Outlaws; [by] Shane Berryhill. Starscape 2006 269p (The adventures of Chance Fortune) $17.95

Grades: 4 5 6 7   **Fic**

1. Science fiction 2. Adventure fiction

ISBN 0-7653-1468-1   LC 2005036400

"A Tom Doherty Associates book"

"Josh Blevins, resident of a planet almost but not quite like earth, has only one dream. He longs to attend the Burlington Academy for the Superhuman. . . . His application is rejected because he has no superpowers, but he reapplies and gets admitted as Chance Fortune, claiming the power of unnaturally good luck. . . . Berryhill blends elements of space opera, comic book adventure, [and] classic horror literature . . . into a lively and engrossing tale that neither takes itself too seriously nor underestimates its readers." Voice Youth Advocates

Another title about Chance Fortune is:

Chance Fortune in the shadow zone (2008)

Bertagna, Julie, 1962-

Exodus; [by] Julie Bertagna. Walker 2008 345p $16.95 *

Grades: 6 7 8 9 10   **Fic**

1. Voyages and travels—Fiction 2. Greenhouse effect—Fiction 3. Floods—Fiction 4. Science fiction

ISBN 978-0-8027-9745-2; 0-8027-9745-8

LC 2007-23116

In the year 2100, as the island of Wing is about to be covered by water, fifteen-year-old Mara discovers the existence of New World sky cities that are safe from the storms and rising waters, and convinces her people to travel to one of these cities in order to save themselves.

"Astonishing in its scope and exhilarating in both its action and its philosophical inquiry." Booklist

Followed by: Zenith (2009)

Binder, Mark

The brothers Schlemiel; [by] Mark Binder; illustrated by Zevi Blum. 1st ed. Jewish Publication Society 2008 247p $19.95

Grades: 6 7 8 9   **Fic**

1. Brothers—Fiction 2. Twins—Fiction 3. Poland—Fiction 4. Jews—Fiction

ISBN 978-0-8276-0865-8   LC 2007036044

"The Brothers Schlemiel was originally serialized in the Houston Jewish Herald-Voice. The first episode was run in February of 2000. One-hundred installments later, the novel was concluded on January 16, 2002."

Born in Chelm, a small Jewish settlement known for being full of fools, identical twin brothers Abraham and Adam are alike in so many ways that they, themselves, are not always sure who is who, as they grow to adulthood encountering gypsies, thieves, kings, and love along the way.

"Binder's droll characters . . . will delight readers, particularly those who have previously heard stories about the residents of Chelm. Blum's fanciful illustrations have an Old World feel." Booklist

Binding, Tim

Sylvie and the songman. Random House 2009 il $15.99 *

Grades: 5 6 7 8   **Fic**

1. Fantasy fiction

ISBN 978-0-385-75159-9; 0-385-75159-1

"Sylvie's composer father . . . goes missing and that's the first odd thing that interrupts her happy routine. Next, the animals seem to have lost their voices. The third is the arrival of the eerie, malevolent Woodpecker Man. . . . The dense narrative is packed with surreal imagery. . . . It's a testament to Binding's assured writing that the abstractions become visceral thrills, like a dream you just can't shake. . . . An unforgettable tale." Booklist

Bingham, Kelly, 1967-

Shark girl. Candlewick Press 2007 276p $16.99 *

Grades: 7 8 9 10   **Fic**

1. Amputees—Fiction 2. Artists—Fiction 3. Novels in verse

ISBN 978-0-7636-3207-6; 0-7636-3207-4

LC 2006049120

After a shark attack causes the amputation of her right arm, fifteen-year-old Jane, an aspiring artist, struggles to come to terms with her loss and the changes it imposes on her day-to-day life and her plans for the future.

"In carefully constructed, sparsely crafted free verse, Bingham's debut novel offers a strong view of a teenager struggling to survive and learn to live again." Booklist

Birney, Betty G., 1947-

The princess and the Peabodys. HarperCollinsPublishers 2007 249p $15.99; lib bdg $16.89

Grades: 5 6 7 8   **Fic**

1. Princesses—Fiction 2. School stories 3. Family life—Fiction

ISBN 0-06-084720-4; 978-0-06-084720-3; 978-0-06-084721-0 (lib bdg); 0-06-084721-2 (lib bdg)

LC 2006-100447

When a medieval princess named Eglantine (Egg for short) appears out of a rusty box bought at a yard sale, fourteen-year-old tomboy Casey Peabody and her family are stuck with her royal snobbiness until the young wizard who had trapped her there figures out the spell to send her home.

"Eglantine and Casey . . . make terrific narrative foils for eachother. . . . Their eventual warm and lasting friendship is all the more satisfying because it is so realistically hard-won." Bull Cent Child Books

Blacker, Terence, 1948-

Boy2girl. Farrar, Straus and Giroux 2005 296p
$16

Grades: 7 8 9 10   **Fic**
  1. Cousins—Fiction 2. Sex role—Fiction
  ISBN 0-374-30926-4   LC 2004-53268

After the death of his mother, thirteen-year-old Sam
comes to live with his cousin and as a prank, he dresses
up as a girl for school, but it soon gets out of hand.

"Sam's tale is told in very short chapters, each narrated by one of the many lively supporting characters who
Sam meets. This unconventional technique works exceptionally well, telling the fast-paced story from different
perspectives while delving into the ever-complicated
world of sex roles." Booklist

Blackwood, Gary L.

The Shakespeare stealer; [by] Gary Blackwood.
Dutton Children's Bks. 1998 216p $15.99; pa
$5.99 *

Grades: 5 6 7 8   **Fic**
  1. Shakespeare, William, 1564-1616—Fiction
  2. Theater—Fiction 3. Orphans—Fiction 4. Great Britain—History—1485-1603, Tudors—Fiction
  ISBN 0-525-45863-8; 0-14-130595-9 (pa)
                                         LC 97-42987

A young orphan boy is ordered by his master to infiltrate Shakespeare's acting troupe in order to steal the
script of "Hamlet," but he discovers instead the meaning
of friendship and loyalty

"Wry humor, cliffhanger chapter endings, and a
plucky protagonist make this a fitting introduction to
Shakespeare's world." Horn Book
  Other titles in this series are:
Shakespeare's scribe (2000)
Shakespeare's spy (2003)

The year of the hangman; [by] Gary Blackwood.
Dutton Children's Bks. 2002 261p $16.99; pa
$5.99

Grades: 8 9 10 11 12   **Fic**
  1. United States—History—1775-1783, Revolution—
  Fiction
  ISBN 0-525-46921-4; 0-14-240078-5 (pa)
                                        LC 2002-67498

In 1777, having been kidnapped and taken forcibly
from England to the American colonies, fifteen-year-old
Creighton becomes part of developments in the political
unrest there that may spell defeat for the patriots and
change the course of history

"Packed with action, convincing historical speculation,
and compelling portrayals of real-life and fictional characters, this page-turner will appeal to fans of both history
and fantasy." SLJ

Bloor, Edward, 1950-

London calling. 1st ed. Alfred A. Knopf 2006
289p $16.96; lib bdg $18.99

Grades: 6 7 8 9   **Fic**
  1. London (England)—Fiction 2. World War, 1939-
  1945—Fiction 3. Science fiction 4. School stories
  ISBN 0-375-83635-7; 0-375-93635-1 (lib bdg)
                                        LC 2005-33330

Seventh-grader Martin Conway believes that his life is
monotonous and dull until the night the antique radio he
uses as a night-light transports him to the bombing of
London in 1940.

"Evocative descriptions and elegant phrasings make
the writing most enjoyable, and because the author uses
a first-person voice, the story seems very personal." SLJ

Taken. Alfred A. Knopf 2007 247p $17; lib bdg
$19.99 *

Grades: 6 7 8 9 10   **Fic**
  1. Science fiction 2. Kidnapping—Fiction 3. Social
  classes—Fiction
  ISBN   978-0-375-83636-7;   0-375-83636-5;
  978-0-375-93636-4 (lib bdg); 0-375-93636-X (lib bdg)
                                        LC 2006-35561

In 2036 kidnapping rich children has become an industry, but when thirteen-year-old Charity Meyers is tak-
en and held for ransom, she soon discovers that this particular kidnapping is not what it seems.

"Deftly constructed, this is as riveting as it is thought-
provoking." Publ Wkly

Tangerine. Harcourt Brace & Co. 1997 294p
$17

Grades: 7 8 9 10   **Fic**
  1. Soccer—Fiction 2. Brothers—Fiction 3. Florida—
  Fiction
  ISBN 0-15-201246-X   LC 96-34182
  Also available in paperback from Scholastic

Twelve-year-old Paul, who lives in the shadow of his
football hero brother Erik, fights for the right to play
soccer despite his near blindness and slowly begins to remember the incident that damaged his eyesight

"Readers will cheer for this bright, funny, decent kid."
Horn Book Guide

Blos, Joan W., 1928-

Letters from the corrugated castle; a novel of
gold rush California, 1850-1852. Atheneum Books
for Young Readers 2007 310p $17.99 *

Grades: 5 6 7 8   **Fic**
  1.   Frontier   and   pioneer   life—Fiction
  2. Mother-daughter relationship—Fiction 3. Gold
  mines and mining—Fiction 4. Mexican Americans—
  Fiction 5. California—Fiction
  ISBN 978-0-689-87077-4; 0-689-87077-9
                                        LC 2007-02673

"Ginee Seo books."

A series of letters and newspaper articles reveals life
in California in the 1850s, especially for thirteen-year-old
Eldora, who was raised in Massachusetts as an orphan
only to meet her influential mother in San Francisco, and
Luke, who hopes to find a fortune in gold.

"It is Blos' sturdy characters, whose experiences reveal the complexity of human relationships and wisdom
about 'the salt and the sweet of life,' who will make this
last." Booklist

Blubaugh, Penny
Serendipity Market. HarperTeen 2009 268p
$16.99
Grades: 7 8 9 10   **Fic**
1. Fairy tales 2. Magic—Fiction 3. Storytelling—Fiction
ISBN   978-0-06-146875-9;   0-06-146875-4;
978-0-06-146876-6 (lib bdg); 0-06-146876-2 (lib bdg)
      LC 2008-10187
"Laura Geringer books"
When the world begins to seem unbalanced, Mama
Inez calls ten storytellers to the Serendipity Market and,
through the power of their magical tales, the balance of
the world is corrected once again.
"In this debut storytelling tour de force, Blubaugh re-
packages familiar folk and fairy-tale themes with contemporary verve and wit." Kirkus

Blume, Judy
Are you there God?, it's me, Margaret. rev
format ed. Atheneum 2001 c1970 149p $17.95 *
Grades: 5 6 7 8   **Fic**
1. Religion—Fiction
ISBN 0-689-84158-2
Also available in paperback from Dell
A reissue of the title first published 1970 by Bradbury
Press
A "story about the emotional, physical, and spiritual
ups and downs experienced by 12-year-old Margaret,
child of a Jewish-Protestant union." Natl Counc of Teach
of Engl. Adventuring with Books. 2d edition
"The writing style is lively, the concerns natural, and
the problems are treated with both humor and sympathy,
but the story is intense in its emphasis on the four girls'
absorption in, and discussions of, menstruation and bras-
sieres." Bull Cent Child Books

Here's to you, Rachel Robinson. Orchard Bks.
1993 196p hardcover o.p. pa $5.99
Grades: 5 6 7 8   **Fic**
1. Siblings—Fiction 2. Gifted children—Fiction
3. Friendship—Fiction
ISBN 0-531-06801-3; 0-440-21974-4 (pa)
      LC 93-9631
"A Richard Jackson book"
Expelled from boarding school, Charles' presence at
home proves disruptive, especially for sister Rachel, a
gifted seventh grader juggling friendships and school activities
"Blume once again demonstrates her ability to shape
multidimensional characters and to explore—often
through very convincing dialogue—the tangled interactions of believable, complex people." Publ Wkly

Tiger eyes; a novel. Bradbury Press 1981 206p
$16.95; pa $6.99
Grades: 7 8 9 10   **Fic**
1. Death—Fiction
ISBN 0-689-85872-8; 0-440-98469-6 (pa)
      LC 81-6152
Resettled in the "Bomb City" with her mother and
brother, Davey Wexler recovers from the shock of her
father's death during a holdup of his 7-Eleven store in
Atlantic City

"The plot is strong, interesting and believable. . . .
The story though intense and complicated flows smoothly and easily." Voice Youth Advocates

Blume, Lesley M. M.
The rising star of Rusty Nail; [by] Lesley M.M.
Blume. 1st ed. Alfred A. Knopf 2007 270p
$15.99; lib bdg $18.99 *
Grades: 4 5 6   **Fic**
1. Pianists—Fiction 2. Musicians—Fiction 3. Russian
Americans—Fiction 4. Minnesota—Fiction
ISBN 978-0-375-83524-7; 978-0-375-93524-4 (lib
bdg)   LC 2006024252
In the small town of Rusty Nail, Minnesota, in the
early 1950s, musically talented ten-year-old Franny wants
to take advanced piano lessons from newcomer Olga Ma-
lenkov, a famous Russian musician suspected of being a
communist spy by gossipy members of the community.
"Blume has skillfully combined humor, history, and
music to create an enjoyable novel that builds to a surprising crescendo." SLJ

Tennyson. Alfred A. Knopf 2008 288p $15.99;
lib bdg $18.99
Grades: 6 7 8 9 10 11 12   **Fic**
1. Great Depression, 1929-1939—Fiction 2. Family
life—Fiction 3. New Orleans (La.)—Fiction
ISBN 978-0-375-84703-5; 978-0-375-94703-2 (lib
bdg)   LC 2007-25983
After their mother abandons them during the Great
Depression, eleven-year-old Tennyson Fontaine and her
little sister Hattie are sent to live with their eccentric
Aunt Henrietta in a decaying plantation house
"Many readers will respond to this novel's Southern
gothic sensibility, especially Blume's beautiful, poetic
writing about how the past resonates through the generations." Booklist

Blundell, Judy
What I saw and how I lied. Scholastic Press
2008 284p $16.99 *
Grades: 8 9 10 11 12   **Fic**
1. Florida—Fiction 2. Mystery fiction
ISBN 978-0-439-90346-2; 0-439-90346-7
      LC 2008-08503
In 1947, with her jovial stepfather Joe back from the
war and family life returning to normal, teenage Evie,
smitten by the handsome young ex-GI who seems to
have a secret hold on Joe, finds herself caught in a complicated web of lies whose devastating outcome change
her life and that of her family forever.
"Using pitch-perfect dialogue and short sentences
filled with meaning, Blundell has crafted a suspenseful,
historical mystery." Booklist

Bodeen, S. A., 1965-
The Compound. Feiwel and Friends 2008 248p
$16.95
Grades: 7 8 9 10   **Fic**
1. Survival after airplane accidents, shipwrecks, etc.—
Fiction 2. Twins—Fiction 3. Fathers—Fiction
ISBN 978-0-312-37015-2; 0-312-37015-6
      LC 2007-36148

Bodeen, S. A., 1965-—*Continued*

After his parents, two sisters, and he have spent six years in a vast underground compound built by his wealthy father to protect them from a nuclear holocaust, fifteen-year-old Eli, whose twin brother and grandmother were left behind, discovers that his father has perpetrated a monstrous hoax on them all.

"The audience will feel the pressure closing in on them as they, like the characters, race through hairpin turns in the plot toward a breathless climax." Publ Wkly

Boie, Kirsten, 1950-

The princess plot; translated by David Henry Wilson. 1st American ed. Chicken House/Scholastic 2009 378p $17.99

Grades: 5 6 7 8   Fic

1. Princesses—Fiction 2. Conspiracies—Fiction

ISBN 978-0-545-03220-9; 0-545-03220-2

LC 2008-24403

Orginal German edition, 2005

Believing that she is on a film set after auditioning and winning the role of a princess, fourteen-year-old Jenna becomes the unsuspecting pawn in a royal conspiracy.

"This novel takes simple, straightforward writing and layers it with kidnappings, political intrigue, and an abundance of secret plots. Readers will enjoy leisurely uncovering the mystery of Jenna's heritage, right along with Jenna herself." Booklist

Boles, Philana Marie

Little divas. Amistad 2006 164p $16.89

Grades: 5 6 7 8   Fic

1. African Americans—Fiction 2. Father-daughter relationship—Fiction 3. Divorce—Fiction 4. Cousins—Fiction

ISBN 0-06-073300-4

"Amistad"

The summer before seventh grade, Cassidy Carter must come to terms with living with her father, practically a stranger, as well as her relationships with her cousins, all amidst the overall confusion of adolescence.

"Boles portrays this variable age well, and readers will feel for Cassidy's trials." SLJ

Boniface, William

The hero revealed; [by] William Boniface; illustrations by Stephen Gilpin. 1st ed. HarperCollins Pub. 2006 294p il (The extraordinary adventures of Ordinary Boy) $15.99; lib bdg $16.89

Grades: 4 5 6 7   Fic

1. Superheroes—Fiction

ISBN 978-0-06-077464-6; 0-06-077464-9; 978-0-06-077465-3 (lib bdg); 0-06-077465-7 (lib bdg)

LC 2005018676

Ordinary Boy, the only resident of Superopolis without a superpower, uncovers and foils a sinister plot to destroy the town.

"This first book in a new series is great fun. . . . Boniface wields a cynical, but definitely kid-friendly, sense of humor, and Gilpin's illustrations are sharp and witty." SLJ

Other titles in this series are:
The return of Meteor Boy? (2007)
The great powers outage (2008)

Bonk, John J.

Dustin Grubbs; one-man show; [by] John J. Bonk. 1st ed. Little, Brown and Co. 2005 243p $15.99

Grades: 5 6 7 8   Fic

1. School stories 2. Theater—Fiction

ISBN 0-316-15636-1   LC 2004021268

A sixth-grader, who longs to see his name in lights, recounts life at Buttermilk Falls Elementary in preparation for the school drama production.

"There are plenty of hilarious scenes, occasionally interrupted by thoughtful, bittersweet moments; and everything is wrapped up with a very satisfying ending." Booklist

Another title about Dustin Grubbs is:
Dustin Grubbs: take two (2006)

Booraem, Ellen

The unnameables. Harcourt 2008 317p $16

Grades: 6 7 8 9   Fic

1. Utopias—Fiction 2. Friendship—Fiction 3. Fantasy fiction

ISBN 978-0-1520-6368-9; 0-1520-6368-4

LC 2007-48844

On an island in whose strict society only useful objects are named and the unnamed are ignored or forbidden, thirteen-year-old Medford encounters an unusual and powerful creature, half-man, half-goat, and together they attempt to bring some changes to the community.

"Island, a creepy and restrictive world masquerading as a utopia, is as memorable as the intricately developed inhabitants." Bull Cent Child Books

Bowers, Laura, 1969-

Beauty shop for rent; --fully equipped, inquire within; [by] Laura Bowers. 1st ed. Harcourt 2007 328p $17; pa $6.95

Grades: 6 7 8 9   Fic

1. Mother-daughter relationship—Fiction 2. Beauty shops—Fiction

ISBN 0-15-205764-1; 978-0-15-205764-0; 978-0-15-206385-6 (pa); 0-15-206385-4 (pa)

LC 2006016761

Raised by a great-grandmother and a bunch of beauty shop buddies, fourteen-year-old Abbey resolves to overcome her unhappy childhood and disillusionment with the mother who deserted her.

"This deceptively simple book reveals Abbey as a wonderful character who will appeal to a broad spectrum of readers." SLJ

Bowler, Tim, 1953-

Blade; playing dead. Philomel Books 2009 231p $16.99

Grades: 7 8 9 10   Fic

1. Violence—Fiction 2. Gangs—Fiction 3. Homeless persons—Fiction 4. Great Britain—Fiction

ISBN 978-0-399-25186-3; 0-399-25186-3

LC 2008-37813

Bowler, Tim, 1953-—*Continued*

Originally published in the United Kingdom in 2008.

A fourteen-year-old British street person with extraordinary powers of observation and self-control must face murderous thugs connected with a past he has tried to forget, when his skills with a knife earned him the nickname, Blade.

"Bowler delivers an intense, gripping novel. . . . Readers who like their thrillers brutally realistic will find much to enjoy." Publ Wkly

Frozen fire; [by] Tim Bowler. Philomel Books 2008 328p $17.99

Grades: 7 8 9 10   **Fic**

1. Supernatural—Fiction 2. Missing children—Fiction 3. Brothers—Fiction

ISBN 978-0-399-25053-8; 0-399-25053-0

LC 2007-43880

First published 2006 in the United Kingdom

Fifteen-year-old Dusty gets a mysterious call from a boy who says he is going to kill himself, and while he claims to have called her randomly, he seems to know her intimately.

"Bowler plunges readers into a mystery of psychological, supernatural, and sociological dimensions. . . . The book's wintry setting is brittle and otherworldly, and the story never lacks for tension." Horn Book Guide

Bradbury, Jennifer

Shift. Atheneum Books for Young Readers 2008 245p $16.99 *

Grades: 7 8 9 10 11 12   **Fic**

1. Cycling—Fiction 2. Travel—Fiction 3. Missing persons—Fiction 4. Friendship—Fiction

ISBN 978-1-4169-4732-5; 1-4169-4732-9

LC 2007-23558

When best friends Chris and Win go on a cross country bicycle trek the summer after graduating and only one returns, the FBI wants to know what happened.

"Bradbury's keen details . . . add wonderful texture to this exciting [novel.] . . . Best of all is the friendship story." Booklist

Bradbury, Ray, 1920-

The Halloween tree; [by] Ray Bradbury; illustrated by Joseph Mugnaini. Alfred A. Knopf 2007 c1972 145p il $15.99

Grades: 6 7 8 9   **Fic**

1. Halloween—Fiction 2. Fantasy fiction

ISBN 978-0-394-82409-3; 0-394-82409-1

A reissue of the title first published 1972

A group of boys meet a spirit-being and are carried back in time to the origins of Halloween celebrations.

This is "fast-moving, genuinely eerie." Booklist

Something wicked this way comes. Avon Bks. 1999 293p $15.95; pa $7.99

Grades: 7 8 9 10   **Fic**

1. Horror fiction 2. Fantasy fiction

ISBN 0-380-97727-3; 0-380-72940-7 (pa)

A reissue of the title first published 1962 by Simon and Schuster

"We read here of the loss of innocence, the recognition of evil, the bond between generations, and the purely fantastic. These forces enter Green Town, Illinois, on the wheels of Cooger and Dark's Pandemonium Shadow Show. Will Halloway and Jim Nightshade, two 13-year-olds, explore the sinister carnival for excitement, which becomes desperation as the forces of the dark threaten to engulf them. Bradbury's gentle humanism and lyric style serve this fantasy well." Shapiro. Fic for Youth. 3d edition

Bradford, Chris

Young samurai; the way of the warrior. Hyperion Books for Children 2009 359p $16.99 *

Grades: 4 5 6 7   **Fic**

1. Samurai—Fiction 2. Martial arts—Fiction 3. Adventure fiction 4. Japan—Fiction

ISBN 978-1-4231-1871-8; 1-4231-1871-5

LC 2008-46180

First published 2008 in the United Kingdom

Orphaned by a ninja pirate attack off the coast of Japan in 1611, twelve-year-old English lad Jack Fletcher is determined to prove himself, despite the bullying of fellow students, when the legendary sword master who rescued him begins training him as a samurai warrior.

"Jack's story alone makes for a page-turner, but coupling it with intriguing bits of Japanese history and culture, Bradford produces an adventure novel to rank among the genre's best." Publ Wkly

Includes bibliographical references

Bradley, Alex

24 girls in 7 days. Dutton 2005 265p $15.99

Grades: 7 8 9 10   **Fic**

1. Dating (Social customs)—Fiction

ISBN 0-525-47369-6

"When the love of his life rejects his invitation to the senior prom, Jack Grammar's so-called best friends pose as Jack and run a personal ad in the online school newspaper soliciting a date. . . . The result is a hilarious adventure as Jack tries to speed-date 24 girls in 7 days. . . . This entertaining guy's eye view on dating, friendship, and understanding one's self is one that most libraries will want to own." SLJ

Bradley, Kimberly Brubaker

The lacemaker and the princess. Margaret K. McElderry Books 2007 199p $16.99

Grades: 4 5 6 7 8   **Fic**

1. Marie Antoinette, Queen, consort of Louis XVI, King of France, 1755-1793—Fiction 2. France—History—1789-1799, Revolution—Fiction 3. Friendship—Fiction 4. Lace and lace making—Fiction

ISBN 978-1-4169-1920-9; 1-4169-1920-1

In 1788, eleven-year-old Isabelle, living with her lacemaker grandmother and mother near the palace of Versailles, becomes close friends with Marie Antoinette's daughter, Princess Therese, and finds their relationship complicated not only by their different social class but by the growing political unrest and resentment of the French people.

"Skillfully integrated historical facts frame this engrossing, believable story." Booklist

Bradley, Kimberly Brubaker—*Continued*

Leap of faith. Dial Books for Young Readers 2007 185p $16.99 *

Grades: 6 7 8 9   **Fic**

1. School stories 2. Religion—Fiction

ISBN 978-0-8037-3127-1; 0-8037-3127-2

LC 2006-21322

Forced to attend a Catholic middle school because of her conduct, Abigail discovers a talent for theater and develops a true religious faith.

"Bradley does not pull back from the questions and confusion that adolescents face when it comes to religion, and packs alot of power into this slim volume." SLJ

Brande, Robin

Evolution, me, & other freaks of nature. Alfred A. Knopf 2007 268p $15.99; lib bdg $18.99

Grades: 7 8 9 10   **Fic**

1. Evolution—Fiction 2. Christian life—Fiction 3. School stories

ISBN   978-0-375-84349-5;   0-375-84349-3; 978-0-375-94349-2 (lib bdg); 0-375-94349-8 (lib bdg)

LC 2006-34158

Following her conscience leads high school freshman Mena to clash with her parents and former friends from their conservative Christian church, but might result in better things when she stands up for a teacher who refuses to include "Intelligent Design" in lessons on evolution.

"Readers will appreciate this vulnerable but ultimately resilient protagonist who sees no conflict between science and her own deeply rooted faith." Booklist

Brashares, Ann, 1967-

3 willows; the sisterhood grows. Delacorte Press 2009 318p $18.99; lib bdg $21.99

Grades: 6 7 8 9 10   **Fic**

1. Friendship—Fiction 2. Maryland—Fiction

ISBN   978-0-385-73676-3;   0-385-73676-2; 978-0-385-90628-9 (lib bdg); 0-385-90628-5 (lib bdg)

LC 2008-34873

Ama, Jo, and Polly, three close friends from Bethesda, Maryland, spend the summer before ninth grade learning about themselves, their families, and the changing nature of their friendship.

"Brashares gets her characters' emotions and interactions just right." Publ Wkly

Breen, M. E.

Darkwood. Bloomsbury 2009 273p il $16.99

Grades: 5 6 7 8   **Fic**

1. Adventure fiction 2. Orphans—Fiction 3. Sisters—Fiction 4. Wolves—Fiction 5. Fantasy fiction

ISBN 978-1-59990-259-3; 1-59990-259-1

LC 2008-44413

A clever and fearless orphan endures increasing danger while trying to escape from greedy, lawless men and elude the terrifying "kinderstalks"—animals who steal children—before discovering her true destiny.

"Breen's finely tuned storytelling—pithy description, quick and keen emotion, broad trust of readers' intelligence—offers equal gratification whether readers spot clues and connections early or late. Both grounded and wondrous." Kirkus

Brewer, Heather

The chronicles of Vladimir Tod: eighth grade bites. Dutton Children's Books 2007 182p (The chronicles of Vladimir Tod) $16.99

Grades: 6 7 8 9   **Fic**

1. Vampires—Fiction 2. Orphans—Fiction 3. School stories

ISBN 978-0-525-47811-9; 0-525-47811-6

LC 2006030455

For thirteen years, Vlad, aided by his aunt and best friend, has kept secret that he is half-vampire, but when his missing teacher is replaced by a sinister substitute, he learns that there is more to being a vampire, and to his parents' deaths, than he could have guessed.

This "is an exceptional current-day vampire story. The mix of typical teen angst and dealing with growing vampiric urges make for a fast-moving, engaging story." Voice Youth Advocates

Other titles about Vladimir Tod are:

Ninth grade slays (2008)

Tenth grade bleeds (2009)

Brittain, Bill

The wish giver; three tales of Coven Tree; drawings by Andrew Glass. Harper & Row 1983 181p il $16.89; pa $5.99

Grades: 5 6 7 8   **Fic**

1. Wishes—Fiction 2. Magic—Fiction

ISBN 0-06-020687-X; 0-06-440168-5 (pa)

LC 82-48264

A Newbery Medal honor book, 1984

"Witchy and devilish things happen in Coven Tree, New England, and their chronicler is Stew Meat, proprietor of the Coven Tree store. . . . Stew relates the King Midas luck that came to three young people, each of whom had a wish fulfilled, and each of whom rued that fulfillment." SLJ

"Captivating, fresh, and infused with homespun humor." Horn Book

Other titles about Coven Tree are:

Dr. Dredd's wagon of wonders (1987)

Professor Popkin's prodigious polish (1990)

Brittney, L.

Dangerous times; the first Nathan Fox mission; [by] L. Brittney. Feiwel & Friends 2008 283p (Nathan Fox) $16.95

Grades: 5 6 7 8   **Fic**

1. Walsingham, Sir Francis, 1530?-1590—Fiction 2. Shakespeare, William, 1564-1616—Fiction 3. Spies—Fiction 4. Adventure fiction 5. Actors—Fiction 6. Great Britain—History—1485-1603, Tudors—Fiction

ISBN 978-0-312-36962-0; 0-312-36962-X

"The setting is Elizabethan England, and young Nathan Fox is an actor who works with the likes of Will Shakespeare. Because of his many talents, he is recruited by the Queen's spymaster, the all-powerful Sir Francis

Brittney, L.—*Continued*

Walsingham. . . . Nathan is in the thick of much action in the Eastern Mediterranean, accompanying the Venetian general Othello on the way to gaining back Cyprus for the Venetians. . . . There is no question that it is cleverly written by Brittney, and we look forward to more tales about Nathan." KLIATT

Broach, Elise, 1963-

Masterpiece; illustrated by Kelly Murphy. Henry Holt & Co. 2008 292p il $16.95 *

Grades: 4 5 6 7   **Fic**
1. Artists—Fiction 2. Mystery fiction 3. Beetles—Fiction 4. New York (N.Y.)—Fiction
ISBN 978-0-8050-8270-8; 0-8050-8270-0
"Christy Ottaviano books"

After Marvin, a beetle, makes a miniature drawing as an eleventh birthday gift for James, a human with whom he shares a house, the two new friends work together to help recover a Durer drawing stolen from the Metropolitan Museum of Art.

Broach "packs this fast-moving story with perennially seductive themes: hidden lives and secret friendships, miniature worlds lost to disbelievers. . . . Loosely implying rather than imitating the Old Masters they reference, the finely hatched drawings depict the settings realistically and the characters, especially the beetles, with joyful comic license." Publ Wkly

Shakespeare's secret; [by] Elise Broach. Henry Holt 2005 250p il $16.95 *

Grades: 5 6 7 8   **Fic**
1. Mystery fiction
ISBN 0-8050-7387-6   LC 2004-54020

Named after a character in a Shakespeare play, misfit sixth-grader Hero becomes interested in exploring this unusual connection because of a valuable diamond supposedly hidden in her new house, an intriguing neighbor, and the unexpected attention of the most popular boy in school.

"The mystery alone will engage readers. . . . The main characters are all well developed, and the dialogue is both realistic and well planned." SLJ

Brooks, Bruce, 1950-

All that remains. Atheneum Bks. for Young Readers 2001 168p $16; pa $6.99

Grades: 7 8 9 10   **Fic**
1. Death—Fiction
ISBN 0-689-83351-2; 0-689-83442-X (pa)
         LC 00-56912

Three novellas explore the effects of death on young lives. "In the title story, two cousins become caught in a scheme to cremate their Aunt Judith's remains. State law forbids her cremation because Judith died of AIDS. . . . The second story, *Playing the Creeps,* is about another set of cousins, Hank and Bobby. . . . When Bobby tries out for the hockey team, Hank is torn between a deathbed promise to Bobby's father to 'help' Bobby, and his embarrassment over Bobby's effeminate nature. . . . The final story, *Teeing Up,* takes place on a golf course. Three guys form a reluctant foursome with a girl who never removes her backpack. The backpack, the boys

eventually discover, contains her father's cremated remains." Voice Youth Advocates

"All three offerings feature believable dialogue and attitudes true to the emotions of their young characters as well as intriguingly offbeat events." Horn Book Guide

The moves make the man; a novel. HarperCollins Pubs. 1984 280p hardcover o.p. pa $6.99

Grades: 7 8 9 10 11 12   **Fic**
1. African Americans—Fiction 2. Friendship—Fiction
ISBN 0-06-020679-9; 0-06-440564-8 (pa)

A Newbery Medal honor book, 1985

"Jerome Foxworthy's consuming passion is 'hoops,' and he gets excited when he sees a shortstop who has the same kind of love for baseball. 'Jayfox', 13, is the first and only black kid to integrate the junior high in Wilmington, N.C. His mother has a terrible accident, and in order to cook for his older brothers, he takes home economics, and finds that the only other male is that shortstop, Bix. Bix's mother is in a mental institution, and his stepfather will not allow Bix to visit her. Bix's problem becomes Jerome's with all sorts of consequences." BAYA Book Rev

This is an "excellent novel about values and the way people relate to one another." N Y Times Book Rev

Brooks, Laurie

Selkie girl; a novel. Alfred A. Knopf 2008 262p $15.99; lib bdg $18.99

Grades: 7 8 9 10   **Fic**
1. Seals (Animals)—Fiction 2. Scotland—Fiction 3. Fantasy fiction
ISBN 978-0-375-85170-4; 0-375-85170-4; 978-0-375-95170-1 (lib bdg); 0-375-95170-9 (lib bdg)
         LC 2008-03547

When sixteen-year-old Elin Jean finds a seal pelt hidden at home and realizes that her mother is actually a selkie, she returns the pelt to her mother, only to find her life taking many unexpected turns.

"An extraordinary, beautifully written tale about belonging, love, and the laws of nature. . . . Brooks's rich prose reverberates with vivid, cinematic images." SLJ

Brooks, Martha, 1944-

Mistik Lake. Farrar, Straus and Giroux 2007 207p $16 *

Grades: 7 8 9 10   **Fic**
1. Mothers—Fiction 2. Manitoba—Fiction 3. Family life—Fiction
ISBN 978-0-374-34985-1; 0-374-34985-1
         LC 2006-37391

After Odella's mother leaves her, her sisters, and their father in Manitoba and moves to Iceland with another man, she then dies there, and the family finally learns some of the many secrets that have haunted them for two generations.

"All of the characters seem distinct and real, thanks to the author's exceptional skill with details." Publ Wkly

True confessions of a heartless girl. Farrar, Straus & Giroux 2003 181p $16

Grades: 7 8 9 10   **Fic**
1. Canada—Fiction 2. City and town life—Fiction
ISBN 0-374-37806-1   LC 2002-72461

Brooks, Martha, 1944-—*Continued*

"Melanie Kroupa books"

A confused seventeen-year-old girl, a single mother and her young son, two elderly women, and a sad and lonely man, with their own individual tragedies to bear, come together in a small Manitoba town and find a way to a better future

"The writing is plain, with a flatness about it that mirrors the Canadian prairie where the story is set. The style also suits the novel's bleak mood; even the most horrific events seem somehow expected. The characterizations are bare-to-the-bones as well, but the people are so expertly revealed that their pain is palpable." Booklist

Brothers, Meagan

Debbie Harry sings in French. Henry Holt 2008 232p $16.95 *

Grades: 8 9 10 11 12   **Fic**

1. Rock music—Fiction 2. Sex role—Fiction 3. Transvestites—Fiction

ISBN 978-0-8050-8080-3; 0-8050-8080-5

LC 2007-27322

When Johnny completes an alcohol rehabilitation program and his mother sends him to live with his uncle in North Carolina, he meets Maria, who seems to understand his fascination with the new wave band Blondie, and he learns about his deceased father's youthful forays into "glam rock," which gives him perspective on himself, his past, and his current life.

"The brisk pace and the strong-willed, empathetic narrator will keep readers fully engaged." Publ Wkly

Brown, Don, 1949-

The train jumper. Roaring Brook Press 2007 122p $16.95

Grades: 6 7 8 9   **Fic**

1. Great Depression, 1929-1939—Fiction 2. Poverty—Fiction 3. Tramps—Fiction

ISBN 978-1-59643-218-5; 1-59643-218-7

LC 2007-03440

"A Deborah Brodie book."

Jumping freight trains during the Great Depression leads fourteen-year-old Collie to a friendship with men and boys on their way to "somewhere else."

"The matter-of-fact dialogue is easy to follow and draws readers into an accurate picture of life on the rails during the Depression." SLJ

Brown, Jason Robert

13; [by] Jason Robert Brown & Dan Elish. Laura Geringer Books 2008 201p il $15.99; lib bdg $16.89

Grades: 5 6 7 8   **Fic**

1. Jews—Fiction   2. Bar   mitzvah—Fiction 3. Divorce—Fiction 4. School stories 5. Indiana—Fiction

ISBN   978-0-06-078749-3;   0-06-078749-X; 978-0-06-078750-9 (lib bdg); 0-06-078750-3 (lib bdg)

LC 2008000777

Almost thirteen-year-old Evan Goldman learns what it means to be a man when his parents separate and he and his mother move from New York City to Appleton, Indi-

ana, right before his bar mitzvah.

"This quick read, accented with humor, takes up a vast array of themes while hewing rather closely to the strand of finding oneself. . . . A fine school story with characters that are limned with enough thoroughness to make them real." Booklist

Bruchac, Joseph, 1942-

Bearwalker; [by] Joseph Bruchac; illustrations by Sally Wern Comport. HarperCollinsPublishers 2007 208p il $15.99; lib bdg $16.89

Grades: 5 6 7 8   **Fic**

1. Camping—Fiction 2. Bears—Fiction 3. Mohawk Indians—Fiction 4. Adirondack Mountains (N.Y.)—Fiction

ISBN   978-0-06-112309-2;   0-06-112309-9; 978-0-06-112311-5 (lib bdg); 0-06-112311-0 (lib bdg)

LC 2006-30420

Although the littlest student in his class, thirteen-year-old Baron Braun calls upon the strength and wisdom of his Mohawk ancestors to face both man and beast when he tries to get help for his classmates, who are being terrorized during a school field trip in the Adirondacks.

"This exciting horror story, illustrated with b/w drawings, is based on Native American folklore." Kliatt

Code talker; a novel about the Navajo Marines of World War Two. Dial 2005 240p $16.99 *

Grades: 6 7 8 9   **Fic**

1. Navajo Indians—Fiction 2. World War, 1939-1945—Fiction

ISBN 0-8037-2921-9

After being taught in a boarding school run by whites that Navajo is a useless language, Ned Begay and other Navajo men are recruited by the Marines to become Code Talkers, sending messages during World War II in their native tongue.

"Bruchac's gentle prose presents a clear historical picture of young men in wartime. . . . Nonsensational and accurate, Bruchac's tale is quietly inspiring." SLJ

Includes bibliographical references

Geronimo. Scholastic Press 2006 360p $16.99

Grades: 7 8 9 10   **Fic**

1. Geronimo, Apache Chief, 1829-1909—Fiction 2. Apache Indians—Fiction

ISBN 0-439-35360-2   LC 2005-50007

"Starting in 1886 with Geronimo's final surrender, this novel is told from the perspective of his adopted grandson Little Foot, and follows the Chiricahua Apaches from their home in Arizona to Florida. . . . The fictional Little Foot affords Bruchac the perfect point of view to observe and interpret Geronimo's life, explaining where the history books got it wrong, and offering insights that won't be found there." SLJ

Hidden roots; by Joseph Bruchac. 1st ed. Scholastic 2004 136p hardcover o.p. pa $5.99

Grades: 5 6 7 8   **Fic**

1. Family life—Fiction 2. Native Americans—Fiction 3. Prejudices—Fiction 4. New York (State)—Fiction

ISBN 0-439-35358-0; 0-439-35359-9 (pa)

LC 2003-50396

Bruchac, Joseph, 1942-—Continued

Although he is uncertain why his father is so angry and what secret his mother is keeping from him, eleven-year-old Sonny knows that he is different from his classmates in their small New York town.

"Bruchac's story takes its roots in the 1930s Native American sterilization program known as the Vermont Eugenics Program. . . . This purposeful but discerning book will prompt discussion and further research into the plight of the Native people from the Green Mountain State." SLJ

Whisper in the dark; illustrations by Sally Wern Comport. 1st ed. HarperCollins Pub. 2005 174p il $15.99; lib bdg $16.89

Grades: 5 6 7 8　　　　　　　　　　　　Fic

1. Narragansett Indians—Fiction 2. Traffic accidents—Fiction 3. Horror fiction 4. Rhode Island—Fiction

ISBN 0-06-058087-9; 0-06-058088-7 (lib bdg)

LC 2004-22561

An ancient and terrifying Narragansett native-American legend begins to come true for a teenage long-distance runner, whose recovery from the accident that killed her parents has stunned everyone, including her guardian aunt in Providence, Rhode Island.

"This fast-paced, macabre novel is perfect for reluctant readers." SLJ

The winter people. Dial Bks. 2002 168p $16.99; pa $5.99 *

Grades: 5 6 7 8　　　　　　　　　　　　Fic

1. Abnaki Indians—Fiction 2. United States—History—1755-1763, French and Indian War—Fiction

ISBN 0-8037-2694-5; 0-14-240229-X (pa)

LC 2002-338

As the French and Indian War rages in October of 1759, Saxso, a fourteen-year-old Abenaki boy, pursues the English rangers who have attacked his village and taken his mother and sisters hostage

"The narrative itself is thrilling, its spiritual aspects enlightening." Booklist

Bryant, Jennifer

Kaleidoscope eyes; [by] Jen Bryant. Alfred A. Knopf 2009 264p $15.99; lib bdg $18.99

Grades: 5 6 7 8　　　　　　　　　　　　Fic

1. Novels in verse 2. Buried treasure—Fiction 3. Vietnam War, 1961-1975—Fiction 4. New Jersey—Fiction 5. Mystery fiction

ISBN 978-0-375-84048-7; 0-375-84048-6; 978-0-375-94048-4 (lib bdg); 0-375-94048-0 (lib bdg)

LC 2008027345

In 1968, with the Vietnam War raging, thirteen-year-old Lyza inherits a project from her deceased grandfather, who had been using his knowledge of maps and the geography of Lyza's New Jersey hometown to locate the lost treasure of Captain Kidd.

"Bryant weaves an emotional novel in poems based on a true story of buried treasure. Tensions among families are drawn with heart-wrenching prose, and her depiction of segregation is flawless. . . . The characters are witty and well developed." Voice Youth Advocates

Pieces of Georgia; a novel; [by] Jen Bryant. Knopf 2006 166p $15.95; lib bdg $17.99

Grades: 6 7 8 9　　　　　　　　　　　　Fic

1. Bereavement—Fiction 2. Artists—Fiction

ISBN 0-375-83259-9; 0-375-93259-3 (lib bdg)

LC 2005-43593

In journal entries to her mother, a gifted artist who died suddenly, thirteen-year-old Georgia McCoy reveals how her life changes after she receives an anonymous gift membership to a nearby art museum.

"This is a remarkable book. . . . [The] story is a universal one of love, friendship, and loss and will be appreciated by a wide audience." SLJ

Ringside, 1925; views from the Scopes trial, a novel; [by] Jen Bryant. Alfred A. Knopf 2008 228p $15.99; lib bdg $18.99 *

Grades: 8 9 10 11 12　　　　　　　　　　Fic

1. Scopes, John Thomas—Fiction 2. Evolution—Study and teaching—Fiction 3. Tennessee—Fiction 4. Novels in verse

ISBN 978-0-375-84047-0; 0-375-84047-8; 978-0-375-94047-7 (lib bdg); 0-375-94047-2 (lib bdg)

LC 2007-7177

Visitors, spectators, and residents of Dayton, Tennessee, in 1925 describe, in a series of free-verse poems, the Scopes 'monkey trial' and its effects on that small town and its citizens.

"Bryant offers readers a ringside seat in this compelling and well-researched novel. It is fast-paced, interesting, and relevant to many current first-amendment challenges." SLJ

Buckingham, Royce

Demonkeeper. G. P. Putnam's Sons 2007 216p $15.99

Grades: 4 5 6 7　　　　　　　　　　　　Fic

1. Horror fiction 2. Supernatural—Fiction

ISBN 978-0-399-24649-4; 0-399-24649-5

LC 2006-26541

When Nat, the weirdest boy in Seattle, leaves for a date with the plainest girl in town, chaos breaks out in the houseful of demons of which he is the sole guardian.

"This is horror on the mild side. . . . The easygoing, breezy humor adds appeal to an already engaging premise." Bull Cent Child Books

Buckley-Archer, Linda

Gideon the cutpurse; being the first part of the Gideon trilogy. Simon & Schuster Books for Young Readers 2006 404p (Gideon trilogy) $17.95

Grades: 5 6 7 8　　　　　　　　　　　　Fic

1. Science fiction 2. Thieves—Fiction 3. Great Britain—History—1714-1837—Fiction

ISBN 978-1-4169-1525-6; 1-4169-1525-7

LC 2006-42204

Ignored by his father and sent to Derbyshire for the weekend, twelve-year-old Peter and his new friend, Kate, are accidentally transported back in time to 1763 England where they are befriended by a reformed cutpurse

"This wonderfully rich and complex novel, written in lyrical and vivid language, is destined to be a classic." SLJ

Followed by The time thief (2008)

Budhos, Marina Tamar

Ask me no questions; [by] Marina Budhos. Atheneum Books for Young Readers 2006 162p $16.95

Grades: 7 8 9 10   **Fic**

1. School stories 2. Asian Americans—Fiction 3. Family life—Fiction 4. New York (N.Y.)—Fiction

ISBN 1-4169-0351-8   LC 2005-1831

"Ginee Seo Books"

Fourteen-year-old Nadira, her sister, and their parents leave Bangladesh for New York City, but the expiration of their visas and the events of September 11, 2001, bring frustration, sorrow, and terror for the whole family.

"Nadira and Aisha's strategies for surviving and succeeding in high school offer sharp insight into the narrow margins between belonging and not belonging." Horn Book Guide

Buffie, Margaret, 1945-

Out of focus. Kids Can Press 2006 239p $16.95; pa $6.95

Grades: 7 8 9 10   **Fic**

1. Alcoholism—Fiction 2. Mother-daughter relationship—Fiction

ISBN   978-1-55337-955-3;   1-55337-955-1; 978-1-55337-956-0 (pa); 1-55337-956-X (pa)

"Amateur photographer Bernie, 16, tries desperately to keep life together for her two younger siblings despite their alcoholic single mother's string of broken promises, lost jobs, and lack of stable housing. . . . Buffie excels at creating credible characters and placing them in situations that allow them to grow and develop." SLJ

Bunce, Elizabeth C.

A curse dark as gold; [by] Elizabeth C. Bunce. Arthur A. Levine Books 2008 395p $17.99 *

Grades: 7 8 9 10   **Fic**

1. Factories—Fiction 2. Uncles—Fiction 3. Orphans—Fiction 4. Sisters—Fiction 5. Magic—Fiction

ISBN 978-0-439-89576-7; 0-439-89576-6

LC 2007019759

ALA YALSA Morris Award, 2009

Upon the death of her father, seventeen-year-old Charlotte struggles to keep the family's woolen mill running in the face of an overwhelming mortgage and what the local villagers believe is a curse, but when a man capable of spinning straw into gold appears on the scene she must decide if his help is worth the price.

"This is a rich, compelling story that fleshes out the fairy tale, setting it in the nonspecific past of the Industrial Revolution. Readers unfamiliar with 'Rumplestilskin' will not be at a disadvantage here." KLIATT

Bunting, Eve, 1928-

Blackwater. HarperCollins Pubs. 1999 146p hardcover o.p. pa $5.99

Grades: 5 6 7 8   **Fic**

1. Death—Fiction 2. Guilt—Fiction

ISBN 0-06-027843-9 (lib bdg); 0-06-440890-6 (pa)

LC 99-24895

"Joanna Cotler books"

When a boy and girl are drowned in the Blackwater River, thirteen-year-old Brodie must decide whether to confess that he may have caused the accident

"Bunting's thought-provoking theme, solid characterization and skillful juggling of suspense and pathos make this a top-notch choice." Publ Wkly

The man with the red bag. HarperCollins 2007 230p $15.99; lib bdg $16.89

Grades: 5 6 7 8   **Fic**

1. Terrorism—Fiction 2. Travel—Fiction 3. Mystery fiction

ISBN 978-0-06-081828-9; 978-0-06-081835-7 (lib bdg); 0-06-081828-X; 0-06-081835-2 (lib bdg)

LC 2006-103558

In the months following the September 11, 2001 terrorist attacks, twelve-year-old Kevin, an aspiring mystery writer traveling cross-country with his grandmother on a sightseeing trip to various national parks and monuments, suspects a sinister-looking man in his tour group of carrying a bomb.

"Bunting writes an effective psychological thriller." Voice Youth Advocates

SOS Titanic. Harcourt Brace & Co. 1996 240p hardcover o.p. pa $6

Grades: 7 8 9 10   **Fic**

1. Titanic (Steamship)—Fiction 2. Shipwrecks—Fiction

ISBN 0-15-200271-5; 0-15-201305-9 (pa)

LC 95-10712

Fifteen-year-old Barry O'Neill, traveling from Ireland to America on the maiden voyage of the Titanic, finds his life endangered when the ship hits an iceberg and begins to sink

"Bunting accurately and dramatically describes the ship's sinking and, at the same time, immerses readers in the many human tragedies. . . . This fast-paced story will satisfy readers looking for the human element in the *Titanic's* history." Booklist

Spying on Miss Müller. Clarion Bks. 1995 179p $15; pa $6.99 *

Grades: 5 6 7 8   **Fic**

1. World War, 1939-1945—Fiction 2. School stories 3. Ireland—Fiction

ISBN 0-395-69172-9; 0-4497-0455-6 (pa)

LC 94-15003

At Alveara boarding school in Belfast at the start of World War II, thirteen-year-old Jessie must deal with her suspicions about a teacher whose father was German and with her worries about her own father's drinking problem

"A thoughtful, moving coming-of-age novel. Jessie and her world . . . are portrayed with page-turning immediacy." Horn Book

The summer of Riley. HarperCollins Pubs. 2001 170p $15.95; lib bdg $16.89; pa $5.99

Grades: 4 5 6   **Fic**

1. Dogs—Fiction 2. Divorce—Fiction

ISBN 0-06-029141-9; 0-06-029142-7 (lib bdg); 0-06-440927-9 (pa)   LC 00-63203

"Joanna Cotler books"

"William is still adjusting to his parents' separation and his father's engagement when his beloved grandfa-

Bunting, Eve, 1928-—*Continued*
ther dies. He knows his mother is letting him adopt a dog so he'll start feeling better, and Riley appears to be a perfect pet. . . . But when Riley violates a state law by chasing a neighbor's horse, William has to convince the county commissioners not to destroy his friend. . . . Bunting's story will have strong appeal for middle-graders who will relish the bittersweet but satisfying resolution." Booklist

Burg, Ann E., 1954-
All the broken pieces; a novel in verse. Scholastic Press 2009 218p $16.99 *
Grades: 7 8 9 10   **Fic**
1. Vietnam War, 1961-1975—Fiction 2. Novels in verse 3. Vietnamese Americans—Fiction 4. Adoption—Fiction
ISBN 978-0-545-08092-7; 0-545-08092-4
      LC 2008-12381
Two years after being airlifted out of Vietnam in 1975, Matt Pin is haunted by the terrible secret he left behind and, now, in a loving adoptive home in the United States, a series of profound events forces him to confront his past.
This is written "in rapid, simple free verse. . . . The intensity of the simple words . . . will make readers want to rush to the end and then return to the beginning again to make connections between past and present, friends and enemies." Booklist

Burg, Shana, 1968-
A thousand never evers. Delacorte Press 2008 301p $15.99; lib bdg $18.99
Grades: 6 7 8 9   **Fic**
1. African Americans—Fiction 2. Race relations—Fiction
ISBN 978-0-385-73470-7; 978-0-385-90468-1 (lib bdg)
As the civil rights movement in the South gains momentum in 1963—and violence against African Americans intensifies—the black residents, including seventh-grader Addie Ann Pickett, in the small town of Kuckachoo, Mississippi, begin their own courageous struggle for racial justice.
This is "gripping. . . . References to significant historical events . . . add authenticity and depth, while Addie's frank, expertly modulated voice delivers an emotional wallop." Publ Wkly

Burnett, Frances Hodgson, 1849-1924
The secret garden; illustrated by Inga Moore. Candlewick Press 2008 278p il $21.99 *
Grades: 3 4 5 6   **Fic**
1. Orphans—Fiction 2. Gardens—Fiction 3. Great Britain—Fiction
ISBN 0-7636-3161-2; 978-0-7636-3161-1
      LC 2006051838
First published 1911
A ten-year-old orphan comes to live in a lonely house on the Yorkshire moors where she discovers an invalid cousin and the mysteries of a locked garden.
"Burnett's tale . . . is presented in an elegant, over-

size volume and handsomely illustrated with Moore's detailed ink and watercolor paintings. Cleanly laid-out text pages are balanced by artwork ranging from delicate spot images to full-page renderings." SLJ

Burton, Rebecca, 1970-
Leaving Jetty Road; [by] Rebecca Burton. 1st ed. Knopf 2006 248p $15.95; lib bdg $17.99
Grades: 8 9 10 11 12   **Fic**
1. Friendship—Fiction 2. School stories 3. Anorexia nervosa—Fiction 4. Australia—Fiction
ISBN 0-375-83488-5; 0-375-93488-X (lib bdg)
      LC 2005018140
"In their final year of high school, best friends Lise, Nat, and Sofia make a New Year's resolution to become vegetarians. . . . As they prepare for the next steps in their lives, the girls become so wrapped up in themselves that they fail to see how their friends are growing, changing, and . . . hurting. Burton does an effective job of weaving the symptoms and personality characteristics of anorexia into an absorbing story about the tug and pull of old friendships as a teen's world expands." Booklist

Butler, Dori Hillestad
The truth about Truman School; by Dori Hillestad Butler. Albert Whitman 2008 170p $15.95
Grades: 5 6 7 8   **Fic**
1. School stories 2. Bullies—Fiction 3. Newspapers—Fiction 4. Journalism—Fiction
ISBN 978-0-8075-8095-0; 0-8075-8095-3
      LC 2007-29977
Tired of being told what to write by the school newspaper's advisor, Zibby and her friend Amr start an underground newspaper online where everyone is free to post anything, but things spiral out of control when a cyberbully starts using the site to harrass one popular girl.
"The story moves at a good pace and the timely subject of cyberbullying will be relevant to readers. The language is accessible and the students' voices ring true." SLJ

Byars, Betsy Cromer, 1928-
The burning questions of Bingo Brown; [by] Betsy Byars. Viking 1988 166p pa $5.99 hardcover o.p. *
Grades: 4 5 6 7   **Fic**
1. School stories
ISBN 0-14-032479-8 (pa)   LC 87-21022
A boy is puzzled by the comic and confusing questions of youth and worried by disturbing insights into adult conflicts
"A fully worked out novel. . . . Readers will recognize the pitfalls, agonies, and joys of elementary school life in this book. . . . The short chapters and comic style are designed to appeal to young readers and to move them right into other books." Christ Sci Monit
Other titles about Bingo Brown are:
Bingo Brown and the language of love (1989)
Bingo Brown, gypsy lover (1990)
Bingo Brown's guide to romance (1992)

Byars, Betsy Cromer, 1928-—*Continued*

Cracker Jackson; [by] Betsy Byars. Viking Kestrel 1985 147p pa $5.99 hardcover o.p.

Grades: 5 6 7 8   **Fic**

1. Wife abuse—Fiction 2. Child abuse—Fiction

ISBN 0-670-80546-7 (pa)   LC 84-24684

"Young Jackson discovers that his ex-baby sitter has been beaten by her husband; and, spurred by affection for her, the boy enlists his friend Goat to help drive her to a home for battered women. The pathetic story of Alma, with her adored baby, tidy home, and treasured collection of Barbie dolls, is relieved by flashbacks to the two boys' antics at school and by their hilarious, if potentially lethal, attempt to drive her to safety." Horn Book

"Suspense, danger, near-tragedy, heartbreak and tension-relieving, unwittingly comic efforts at seriously heroic action mark this as the best of middle-grade fiction to highlight the problems of wife-battering and child abuse." SLJ

The dark stairs; a Herculeah Jones mystery; by Betsy Byars. Viking 1994 130p hardcover o.p. pa $5.99 *

Grades: 4 5 6   **Fic**

1. Mystery fiction

ISBN 0-670-85487-5; 0-14-240592-2 (pa)

LC 94-14012

The intrepid Herculeah Jones helps her mother, a private investigator, solve a puzzling and frightening case

"There is plenty to laugh at in this book, including classic chapter headings guaranteed to cause shivers for the uninitiated; practiced mystery readers may feel that they are in on a bit of a joke and appreciate the hint of parody. This is a page-turner that is sure to entice the most reluctant readers." SLJ

Other titles about Herculeah Jones are:

The black tower (2006)
Dead letter (1996)
Death's door (1997)
Disappearing acts (1998)
King of murder (2006)
Tarot says beware (1995)

The keeper of the doves; by Betsy Byars. Viking 2002 121p $14.99; pa $5.99

Grades: 4 5 6 7   **Fic**

1. Sisters—Fiction 2. Family life—Fiction 3. Kentucky—Fiction

ISBN 0-670-03576-9; 0-14-240063-7 (pa)

LC 2002-9283

In the late 1800s in Kentucky, Amie McBee and her four sisters both fear and torment the reclusive and seemingly sinister Mr. Tominski, but their father continues to provide for his needs

"This is Byars at her best—witty, appealing, thought-provoking." Horn Book

The summer of the swans; [by] Betsy Byars; illustrated by Ted CoConis. Viking 1970 142p il $15.99; pa $5.99 *

Grades: 5 6 7 8   **Fic**

1. Mentally handicapped children—Fiction 2. Siblings—Fiction

ISBN 0-670-68190-3; 0-14-031420-2 (pa)

Awarded the Newbery Medal, 1971

"The thoughts and feelings of a young girl troubled by a sense of inner discontent which she cannot explain are tellingly portrayed in the story of two summer days in the life of fourteen-year-old Sara Godfrey. Sara is jolted out of her self-pitying absorption with her own inadequacies by the disappearance of her ten-year-old retarded brother who gets lost while trying to find the swans he had previously seen on a nearby lake. Her agonizing, albeit ultimately successful, search for Charlie and the reactions of others to this traumatic event help Sara gain a new perspective on herself and life." Booklist

Cabot, Meg, 1967-

Airhead. Scholastic/Point 2008 340p $16.99 *

Grades: 7 8 9 10   **Fic**

1. Fashion models—Fiction 2. New York (N.Y.)—Fiction 3. Transplantation of organs, tissues, etc.—Fiction

ISBN 978-0-545-04052-5; 0-545-04052-3

LC 2007-38269

Sixteen-year-old Emerson Watts, an advanced placement student with a disdain for fashion, is the recipient of a "whole body transplant"; and finds herself transformed into one of the world's most famous teen supermodels.

"Cabot's portrayal of Emerson is brilliant. . . . Pure fun, this first series installment will leave readers clamoring for the next." Publ Wkly

Another title in this series is:
Being Nikki (2009)

All-American girl. HarperCollins Pubs. 2002 247p hardcover o.p. pa $7.99

Grades: 7 8 9 10   **Fic**

1. Presidents—Fiction

ISBN 0-06-029469-8; 0-06-029470-1 (lib bdg); 0-06-147989-6 (pa)   LC 2002-19049

Samantha stops a presidential assassination attempt, is appointed Teen Ambassador to the United Nations, and catches the eye of the very cute First Son

There's "surprising depth in the characters and plenty of authenticity in the cultural details and the teenage voices—particularly in Sam's poignant, laugh-out-loud narration." Booklist

Another title about Samantha is:
Ready or not (2005)

How to be popular. HarperTempest 2006 288p $16.99; lib bdg $17.89

Grades: 7 8 9 10   **Fic**

1. School stories

ISBN 978-0-06-088012-5; 0-06-088012-0; 978-0-06-088013-2 (lib bdg); 0-06-088013-9 (lib bdg)

LC 2006-00367

"Preparing for eleventh grade, Steph studies an old book entitled *How to Be Popular* and plots her path into the A-Crowd. . . . Soon, though, Steph discovers that the love of her life is *not* sitting at the popular kids' table in the school cafeteria. . . . [This is an] appealing, first-person story of teen yearning, befuddlement, and love." Booklist

Cabot, Meg, 1967-—*Continued*

The princess diaries. Avon Bks. 2000 238p
$15.95; lib bdg $15.89; pa $6.99 *
Grades: 6 7 8 9   **Fic**
  1. Princesses—Fiction 2. New York (N.Y.)—Fiction
  ISBN 0-380-97848-2; 0-06-029210-5 (lib bdg);
  0-380-81402-1 (pa)   LC 99-46479
Fourteen-year-old Mia, who is trying to lead a normal
life as a teenage girl in New York City, is shocked to
learn that her father is the Prince of Genovia, a small
European principality, and that she is a princess and the
heir to the throne
  "Readers will relate to Mia's bubbly, chatty voice and
enjoy the humor of this unlikely fairy tale." SLJ
  Other titles about Princess Mia are:
Forever princess (2008)
Party princess (2006)
Princess in pink (2004)
Princess in the spotlight (2001)
Princess in training (2005)
Princess in waiting (2003)
The princess present (2004)
Sweet sixteen princess (2006)
Valentine princess (2006)

Cadnum, Michael
The book of the Lion. Viking 2000 204p
hardcover o.p. pa $5.99
Grades: 7 8 9 10   **Fic**
  1. Knights and knighthood—Fiction 2. Crusades—Fiction 3. Middle Ages—Fiction
  ISBN 0-670-88386-7; 0-14-230034-9 (pa)
                                           LC 99-39370
In twelfth-century England, after his master, a maker
of coins for the king, is brutally punished for alleged
cheating, seventeen-year-old Edmund finds himself traveling to the Holy Land as squire to a knight crusader on
his way to join the forces of Richard Lionheart
  "Cadnum brilliantly captures both the grisly horror
and the taut, sinewy excitement of hard travel and battle
readiness. . . . There's bawdy and violent talk, but religion as part of the heart and bone of life is present, too."
Booklist
  Followed by: The leopard sword (2002)

Daughter of the wind; a novel. Orchard Books
2003 266p $17.95
Grades: 7 8 9 10   **Fic**
  1. Vikings—Fiction
  ISBN 0-439-35224-X   LC 2002-72286
In medieval times as various groups of Vikings fight
for supremacy of the northern lands and waters,
Hallgerd, Gauk, and Hego, three young people from the
quiet coastal village of Spjothof, find their fates intertwined as a series of events take them into danger far
from home.
  "The story is . . . gripping, and full of graphic scenes
of violence, which may be unpleasant reading for some.
Yet it is Cadnum's glimpses of everyday life and the
stirring sagas that bring the inner world of these Northern people to life." SLJ

Forbidden forest; the story of Little John and
Robin Hood. Orchard Bks. 2002 218p $17.95
Grades: 7 8 9 10   **Fic**
  1. Robin Hood (Legendary character)—Fiction
  2. Great Britain—History—1154-1399, Plantagenets—
Fiction 3. Middle Ages—Fiction
  ISBN 0-439-31774-6   LC 2001-32932
Companion volume to In a dark wood
Profiles Little John, from his quiet life before joining
Robin Hood through his adventures protecting a beautiful
lady when she is wrongfully accused of murdering her
husband
  "The book is fast paced and exciting yet does not sug-
arcoat the grim realities of medieval life. Cadnum gives
the familiar tale of Robin Hood a fresh look by making
minor characters the focus of the story." Voice Youth
Advocates

The king's arrow. Viking Childrens Books 2008
224p $16.99
Grades: 7 8 9 10   **Fic**
  1. William II, King of England, 1056?-1100—Fiction
  2. Middle Ages—Fiction 3. Great Britain—History—
1066-1154, Norman period—Fiction
  ISBN 978-0-670-06331-4   LC 2007-25313
In England's New Forest on the second day of August, 1100, eighteen-year-old Simon Foldre, delighted to
be allowed to participate in a royal hunt as squire to the
Anglo-Norman nobleman Walter Tirel, finds his future
irrevocably altered when, during the hunt, he witnesses
the possible murder of King William II.
  "This story is rich in details that lend credibility to the
period setting and help bring even historical figures to
life as strongly realized and believable characters."
Booklist

Nightsong; the legend of Orpheus and Eurydice;
[by] Michael Cadnum. 1st ed. Orchard Books
2006 133p $16.99
Grades: 7 8 9 10   **Fic**
  1. Classical mythology—Fiction
  ISBN 0-439-54535-8   LC 2006000711
Expands on the myth of Orpheus, a young poet and
musician who undertakes a terrifying journey to ask the
rulers of the Underworld to return the princess Euridice,
his beloved bride, after she is killed by a venomous serpent.
  "Skillfully creating a complex, multidimensional portrait of Orpheus . . . Cadnum brings new meaning to an
ancient romance." Publ Wkly

Peril on the sea. Farrar, Straus and Giroux 2009
245p $16.95
Grades: 7 8 9 10   **Fic**
  1. Pirates—Fiction 2. Adventure fiction 3. Great Britain—History—1485-1603, Tudors—Fiction
  ISBN 978-0-374-35823-5; 0-374-35823-0
                                          LC 2008-5421
In the tense summer of 1588, eighteen-year-old Sherwin Morris, after nearly perishing in a shipwreck, finds
himself aboard the privateer Vixen, captained by the notorious and enigmatic Brandon Fletcher who offers him
adventure and riches if Sherwin would write and dissem-
inate a flattering account of the captain's exploits.
  "Cadnum's prose is vivid and evocative, brilliantly

Cadnum, Michael—*Continued*
recreating life at sea in the Elizabethan era. . . . The tale is expertly paced, the varied threads of the tale elegantly woven. There's plenty here to appeal to a wide audience." Kirkus

Calame, Don
Swim the fly. Candlewick Press 2009 345p $16.99
Grades: 8 9 10 11 12   **Fic**
1. Swimming—Fiction 2. Summer—Fiction
ISBN 978-0-7636-4157-3; 0-7636-4157-X
                                            LC 2009-920818
"Fifteen-year-old Matt has two summer goals: attract his crush Kelly's attention by learning to 'swim the fly' and see a real girl naked. Matt and pals Cooper and Sean cook up several plots to catch a betty in the buff, but all attempts fail. . . . Fully realized secondary characters, realistically raunchy dialogue and the scatological subject matter assure that this boisterous and unexpectedly sweet read will be a word-of-mouth hit." Kirkus

Caletti, Deb
The fortunes of Indigo Skye. Simon & Schuster Books for Young Readers 2008 304p $15.99; pa $9.99 *
Grades: 8 9 10 11 12   **Fic**
1. Waiters and waitresses—Fiction 2. Restaurants—Fiction 3. Wealth—Fiction 4. Family life—Fiction 5. Single parent family—Fiction 6. Washington (State)—Fiction
ISBN   978-1-4169-1007-7;   1-4169-1007-7; 978-1-4169-1008-4 (pa); 1-4169-1008-4 (pa)
                                            LC 2007-08744
Eighteen-year-old Indigo is looking forward to becoming a full-time waitress after high school graduation, but her life is turned upside down by a $2.5 million tip given to her by a customer.
The author "builds characters with so much depth that readers will be invested in her story. . . . Caletti spins a network of relationships that feels real and enriching." Publ Wkly

Calvert, Patricia, 1931-
Bigger. Scribner 1994 137p hardcover o.p. pa $4.99 *
Grades: 5 6 7 8   **Fic**
1. Frontier and pioneer life—Fiction 2. Father-son relationship—Fiction 3. Dogs—Fiction
ISBN 0-684-19685-9; 0-689-86003-X (pa)
                                            LC 93-14415
When his father disappears near the Mexican border at the end of the Civil War, twelve-year-old Tyler decides to go after him and bring him home, acquiring on the journey a strange dog which he names Bigger
"Calvert's story has many tantalizing elements: Tyler is likable and realistically portrayed, the book raises some provocative issues, and the ending is sad but satisfying. . . . This is an entertaining story even reluctant readers will relish." Booklist
Other titles in this series are:
Betrayed! (2002)
Sooner (1998)

Canales, Viola, 1957-
The tequila worm. Wendy Lamb Books 2005 199p $15.95; lib bdg $17.99 *
Grades: 6 7 8 9   **Fic**
1. Mexican Americans—Fiction 2. Texas—Fiction
ISBN 0-385-74674-1; 0-385-90905-5 (lib bdg)
                                            LC 2004-24533
Sofia grows up in the close-knit community of the barrio in McAllen, Texas, then finds that her experiences as a scholarship student at an Episcopal boarding school in Austin only strengthen her ties to family and her "comadres."
"The explanations of cultural traditions . . . are always rooted in immediate, authentic family emotions, and in Canales' exuberant storytelling, which . . . finds both humor and absurdity in sharply observed, painful situations." Booklist

Cantor, Jillian
The September sisters. HarperTeen 2009 361p $16.99
Grades: 7 8 9 10 11 12   **Fic**
1. Missing persons—Fiction 2. Sisters—Fiction 3. Family life—Fiction
ISBN 978-0-06-168648-1; 0-06-168648-4
                                            LC 2008-07120
"Laura Geringer books"
A teenaged girl tries to keep her family and herself together after the disappearance of her younger sister.
"Cantor treats the shape of Abby's agony with poignant credibility. . . . This is a sensitive and perceptive account of the way tragedy unfolds both quickly and slowly and life reassembles itself around it." Bull Cent Child Books

Carbone, Elisa Lynn, 1954-
Blood on the river; James Town 1607; [by] Elisa Carbone. Viking 2006 237p $16.99
Grades: 5 6 7 8   **Fic**
1. Jamestown (Va.)—History—Fiction 2. Powhatan Indians—Fiction 3. United States—History—1600-1775, Colonial period—Fiction
ISBN 0-670-06060-7   LC 2005023646

Carbone, Elisa Lynn, 1954-—*Continued*

Traveling to the New World in 1606 as the page to Captain John Smith, twelve-year-old orphan Samuel Collier settles in the new colony of James Town, where he must quickly learn to distinguish between friend and foe.

"A strong, visceral story of the hardship and peril settlers faced, as well as the brutal realities of colonial conquest." Booklist

Stealing freedom; [by] Elisa Carbone. Knopf 1998 258p hardcover o.p. pa $5.50

Grades: 6 7 8 9   **Fic**
　　1. Weems, Anne-Marie—Fiction 2. Slavery—Fiction 3. Underground railroad—Fiction 4. African Americans—Fiction
　　ISBN 0-679-89307-5; 0-440-41707-4 (pa)
　　　　　　　　　　　　　　　　　　LC 98-36929

A novel based on the events in the life of Anne-Marie Weems, a young slave girl from Maryland who endures all kinds of mistreatment and cruelty, including being separated from her family, but who eventually escapes to freedom in Canada

"This is a fine piece of historical fiction with a strong, appealing heroine." SLJ

Card, Orson Scott

Ender's game. TOR Bks. 1991 c1985 xxi, 226p $24.95; pa $6.99 *

Grades: 7 8 9 10 11 12 Adult   **Fic**
　　1. Science fiction 2. Interplanetary voyages—Fiction 3. Science fiction
　　ISBN 0-312-93208-1; 0-8125-5070-6 (pa)

"A Tom Doherty Associates book"

A reissue of the title first published 1985

"Chosen as a six-year-old for his potential military genius, Ender Wiggin spends his childhood in outer space at the Battle School of the Belt. Severed from his family, isolated from his peers, and rigorously tested and trained, Ender pours all his talent into the war games that will one day repel the coming alien invasion." Libr J

"The key, of course, is Ender Wiggin himself. Mr. Card never makes the mistake of patronizing or sentimentalizing his hero. Alternately likable and insufferable, he is a convincing little Napoleon in short pants." N Y Times Book Rev

Other titles in the author's distant future series about Ender Wiggin are:
Speaker for the dead (1986)
Xenocide (1991)
Children of the mind (1996)
Ender's shadow (1999)
Shadow of the Hegemon (2001)
Shadow puppets (2002)
Shadow of the giant (2005)
A war of gifts (2007)

Cárdenas, Teresa, 1970-

Letters to my mother; translated by David Unger. Groundwood Books/House of Anansi Press 2006 103p $15.95; pa $7.95

Grades: 7 8 9 10   **Fic**

　　1. Blacks—Fiction 2. Race relations—Fiction 3. Cuba—Fiction
　　ISBN 0-88899-720-5; 0-88899-721-3 (pa)

A young African-Cuban girl is sent to live with her aunt and cousins after the death of her mother and begins to write letters to her deceased mother telling of the misery, racial prejudice, and mistreatment at the hands of those around her.

"The main character's voice is authentic, and the other characters, sketched with spare lines, are believable and sympathetic. . . . Short chapters and lucid writing will appeal to reluctant readers." SLJ

Old dog; translated by David Unger. Groundwood Books/House of Anansi Press 2007 144p $16.95

Grades: 7 8 9 10 11 12   **Fic**
　　1. Slavery—Fiction 2. Cuba—Fiction
　　ISBN 978-0-88899-757-9; 0-88899-757-4

Perro Viejo, an elderly slave on a Cuban sugar plantation, "recalls his life and the endless acts of atrocity and inhumanity he has witnessed. . . . [This is a] slender but powerful story that will invite classroom discussion." Booklist

Carey, Janet Lee

The beast of Noor. 1st ed. Atheneum Books for Young Readers 2006 497p $16.95

Grades: 6 7 8 9   **Fic**
　　1. Fantasy fiction
　　ISBN 978-0-689-87644-8; 0-689-87644-0
　　　　　　　　　　　　　　　　　　LC 2005-17731

Fifteen-year-old Miles Ferrell uses the rare and special gift he is given to break the curse of the Shriker, a murderous creature reportedly brought to Shalem Wood by his family's clan centuries

"Carey delivers an eerie, atmospheric tale, full of terror and courage, set in a convincingly realized magical realm." Booklist

Dragon's Keep. Harcourt 2007 302p $17 *

Grades: 7 8 9 10   **Fic**
　　1. Princesses—Fiction 2. Dragons—Fiction 3. Mother-daughter relationship—Fiction 4. Great Britain—History—1066-1154, Norman period—Fiction 5. Fantasy fiction
　　ISBN 978-0-15-205926-2; 0-15-205926-1
　　　　　　　　　　　　　　　　　　LC 2006-24669

In 1145 A.D., as foretold by Merlin, fourteen-year-old Rosalind, who will be the twenty-first Pendragon Queen of Wilde Island, has much to accomplish to fulfill her destiny, while hiding from her people the dragon's claw she was born with that reflects only one of her mother's dark secrets.

This is told "in stunning, lyrical prose. . . . Carey smoothly blends many traditional fantasy tropes here, but her telling is fresh as well as thoroughly compelling." Booklist

Carlson, Drew

Attack of the Turtle; a novel; by Drew Carlson; illustrations by David A. Johnson. Eerdmans Books for Young Readers 2007 149p il $16

Grades: 4 5 6 7   **Fic**

1. Bushnell, David, 1742-1824—Fiction 2. United States—History—1775-1783, Revolution—Fiction 3. Submarines—Fiction 4. Inventors—Fiction

ISBN 978-0-8028-5308-0; 0-8028-5308-0

LC 2005032068

During the Revolutionary War, fourteen-year-old Nathan joins forces with his older cousin, the inventor David Bushnell, to secretly build the first submarine used in naval warfare.

"Though Nate makes for a sympathetic character and the plot is well constructed, the actual tale of the *Turtle* is quite involving, too." Booklist

Carman, Patrick

The Dark Hills divide; [by] Patrick Carman. 1st Orchard Books ed. Orchard Books 2005 253p (The land of Elyon) $11.95

Grades: 4 5 6 7   **Fic**

1. Fantasy fiction

ISBN 0-439-70093-0   LC 2004-16312

When she finds the key to a secret passageway leading out of the walled city of Bridewell, twelve-year-old Alexa realizes her lifelong wish to explore the mysterious forests and mountains that lie beyond the wall.

"Narrator Aasne Vigesaa clearly portrays Alexa's thoughtful, inquisitive nature and unsettled feelings. . . . Vigesaa's excellent use of pace, pitch, and tone help differentiate each character." SLJ

Other titles in this series are:

Beyond the Valley of Thorns (2005)
The tenth city (2006)
Into the mist (2007)
Stargazer (2008)

Carmichael, Clay

Wild things; [written and illustrated by Clay Carmichael] Front Street 2009 248p il $18.95

Grades: 5 6 7 8   **Fic**

1. Family life—Fiction 2. Orphans—Fiction 3. Uncles—Fiction 4. Artists—Fiction 5. Cats—Fiction

ISBN 978-159078-627-7; 1-59078-627-0

LC 2007-49911

Stubborn, self-reliant, eleven-year-old Zoe, recently orphaned, moves to the country to live with her prickly half-uncle, a famous doctor and sculptor, and together they learn about trust and the strength of family.

"Carmichael gives a familiar plot a fresh new life in this touching story with a finely crafted sense of place." Booklist

Carmody, Isobelle

Alyzon Whitestarr. 1st American ed. Random House 2009 c2005 501p $17.99; lib bdg 20.99

Grades: 8 9 10 11 12   **Fic**

1. Extrasensory perception—Fiction 2. Family life—Fiction 3. Supernatural—Fiction 4. Australia—Fiction

ISBN   978-0-375-83938-2;   0-375-83938-0; 978-0-375-93938-9 (lib bdg); 0-375-93938-5 (lib bdg); 978-0-375-83939-9 (pa); 978-0-375-83940-5 (pa)

LC 2008033796

First published 2005 in Australia

When Alyzon, the ordinary member of an extraordinary family, develops enhanced senses, she becomes aware of an evil virus that preys on people's spirits, and realizes that the sickness and its disseminators are aware of her and are a menace to her family.

"Alyzon is fully believable. . . . This will keep teen readers turning the pages." Booklist

Carney, Jeff

The adventures of Michael MacInnes. Farrar, Straus and Giroux 2006 244p $17

Grades: 6 7 8 9   **Fic**

1. School stories 2. Orphans—Fiction 3. Poetry—Fiction

ISBN 978-0-374-30146-0; 0-374-30146-8

LC 2004-57669

In 1924, high school junior Michael MacInnes, a freethinking poet and orphaned scholarship student, stirs up trouble when he challenges the rules and traditions of his prep school.

"There is plenty of action, mystery, and suspense to appeal to both genders in this riveting debut novel." Voice Youth Advocates

Carter, Anne, 1953-

The shepherd's granddaughter; [by] Anne Laurel Carter. Groundwood Books 2008 224p $17.95; pa $12.95

Grades: 5 6 7 8   **Fic**

1. Palestine—Fiction 2. Shepherds—Fiction

ISBN   978-0-88899-902-3;   0-88899-902-X; 978-0-88899-903-0 (pa); 0-88899-903-8 (pa)

Amani longs to be a shepherd like her grandfather, Seedo. Like many Palestinians, her family has grazed sheep above the olive groves of the family homestead for generations, and she has been steeped in Seedo's stories, especially one about a secret meadow called the Firdoos and the wolf that once showed him the path there.

"Carter strikes a splendid balance in character development, portraying both parties' flaws while demonstrating Palestinian sympathies. Background and cultural information are seamlessly woven into the narrative, which is written simply and clearly in a skillful depiction of sensitive situation." SLJ

Carvell, Marlene

Sweetgrass basket. Dutton Childrens Books 2005 243p $16.99

Grades: 7 8 9 10   **Fic**

1. Sisters—Fiction 2. Mohawk Indians—Fiction 3. School stories

ISBN 0-525-47547-8   LC 2004-24374

Carvell, Marlene—*Continued*

In alternating passages, two Mohawk sisters describe their lives at the Carlisle Indian Industrial School, established in 1879 to educate Native Americans, as they try to assimilate into white culture and one of them is falsely accused of stealing.

"Carvell has put together a compelling, authentic, and sensitive portrayal of a part of our history that is still not made accurately available to young readers." SLJ

Who will tell my brother? Hyperion Bks. for Children 2002 150p hardcover o.p. pa $5.99

Grades: 7 8 9 10   **Fic**

1. Mohawk Indians—Fiction 2. School stories
ISBN 0-7868-0827-6; 0-7868-1657-0 (pa)
LC 2001-51759

During his lonely crusade to remove offensive mascots from his high school, Evan, part-Mohawk Indian, learns more about his heritage, his ancestors, and his place in the world

"The blank verse format will be appealing, especially to reluctant readers. . . . [A] lovely, heart-wrenching and profound little book." Voice Youth Advocates

Cary, Kate

Bloodline; a novel. Razor Bill 2005 324p $16.99

Grades: 7 8 9 10   **Fic**

1. Vampires—Fiction 2. World War, 1914-1918—Fiction 3. Horror fiction
ISBN 1-59514-012-3

In this story told primarily through journal entries, a British soldier in World War I makes the horrifying discovery that his regiment commander is descended from Count Dracula.

"This story is an interesting blend of mystery, horror, and romance, and readers who love vampire novels will find it a refreshing twist to the classic story." SLJ

Followed by Bloodline: reckoning (2007)

Casanova, Mary

The klipfish code; by Mary Casanova. Houghton Mifflin Company 2007 227p map $16

Grades: 4 5 6 7   **Fic**

1. Norway—Fiction 2. World War, 1939-1945—Norway—Fiction 3. World War, 1939-1945—Underground movements—Fiction 4. Family life—Fiction
ISBN 978-0-618-88393-6; 0-618-88393-2
LC 2007012752

Sent with her younger brother to Godøy Island to live with her aunt and grandfather after Germans bomb Norway in 1940, ten-year-old Merit longs to join her parents in the Resistance and when her aunt, a teacher, is taken away two years later, she resents even more the Nazis' presence and her grandfather's refusal to oppose them.

"Casanova spins an adventure-filled and harrowing story." SLJ

Includes glossary and bibliographical references

Cashore, Kristin

Graceling. Harcourt 2008 471p map $17

Grades: 8 9 10 11 12   **Fic**

1. Fantasy fiction
ISBN 978-0-15-206396-2; 0-15-206396-X
LC 2007-45436

ALA YALSA Morris Award Finalist, 2009

In a world where some people are born with extreme and often-feared skills called Graces, Katsa struggles for redemption from her own horrifying Grace, the Grace of killing, and teams up with another young fighter to save their land from a corrupt king.

"This is gorgeous storytelling: exciting, stirring, and accessible. Fantasy and romance readers will be thrilled." SLJ

Cassidy, Cathy, 1962-

Scarlett; [by] Cathy Cassidy. Viking 2006 261p $16.99

Grades: 5 6 7 8   **Fic**

1. Stepfamilies—Fiction 2. Country life—Fiction 3. Ireland—Fiction
ISBN 0-670-06068-2   LC 2006001029

After being expelled from yet another school in London, twelve-year-old Scarlett is sent by her exasperated mother to live with her father, stepmother, and stepsister in Ireland, where, with the help of a mysterious boy, she eventually overcomes her anger and resentment and feels part of a family again.

"Infused with a bit of fairy-tale magic, this is a fast-paced yet thoughtful story. The heroine is feisty and troublesome, yet quirky and lovable." SLJ

Castellucci, Cecil, 1969-

Boy proof. Candlewick Press 2005 203p $15.99; pa $7.99

Grades: 7 8 9 10   **Fic**

1. Motion pictures—Fiction 2. Los Angeles (Calif.)—Fiction
ISBN 0-7636-2333-4; 0-7636-2796-6 (pa)
LC 2004-50256

Feeling alienated from everyone around her, Los Angeles high school senior and cinephile Victoria Denton hides behind the identity of a favorite movie character until an interesting new boy arrives at school and helps her realize that there is more to life than just the movies.

This "novel's clipped, funny, first-person, present-tense narrative will grab teens . . . with its romance and the screwball special effects, and with the story of an outsider's struggle both to belong and to be true to herself." Booklist

Catanese, P. W., 1961-

Happenstance found. Aladdin 2009 342p il (The books of Umber) $16.99

Grades: 4 5 6   **Fic**

1. Adventure fiction 2. Magic—Fiction 3. Fantasy fiction
ISBN 978-1-4169-7519-9; 1-4169-7519-5
LC 2008-45966

A boy awakens, blindfolded, with no memory of even his name, but soon meets Lord Umber, an adventurer and

Catanese, P. W., 1961-—_Continued_
inventor, who calls him Happenstance and tells him that
he has a very important destiny—and a powerful enemy.

"Catanese packs a lot into the book: rich characterizations, . . . well-choreographed action sequences and genuinely surprising twists at the end." Publ Wkly

Caveney, Philip
Sebastian Darke: Prince of Fools. Delacorte
Press 2008 338p $15.99; lib bdg $18.99
Grades: 7 8 9 10   Fic
1. Fantasy fiction 2. Fools and jesters—Fiction
3. Princesses—Fiction
ISBN 978-0-385-73467-7; 978-0-385-90465-0 (lib
bdg)   LC 2006-25262
First published 2007 in the United Kingdom
Accompanied by his sardonic buffalope Max, seventeen-year-old Sebastian Darke meets a spoiled princess
and a diminutive soldier who aid in his quest to become
court jester to the evil King Septimus.

"In a very plot-driven book, the central characters are
nonetheless well developed. Max is a particularly cre-
ative invention. . . . There are enough sword fights,
treachery, and wicked creatures for any adventure reader.
The sense of humor . . . makes it a fun read." Voice
Youth Advocates
Another title about Sebastian Darke is:
Sebastian Darke: Prince of Pirates (2009)

Chabon, Michael
Summerland. Hyperion Bks. for Children 2002
500p hardcover o.p. pa $8.95
Grades: 5 6 7 8   Fic
1. Fantasy fiction 2. Baseball—Fiction 3. Magic—Fiction
ISBN 0-7868-0877-2; 0-7868-1615-5 (pa)
                                        LC 2002-27497
Ethan Feld, the worst baseball player in the history of
the game, finds himself recruited by a 100-year-old scout
to help a band of fairies triumph over an ancient enemy.

"Much of the prose is beautifully descriptive as
Chabon navigates vividly imagined other worlds and offers up some timeless themes." Horn Book

Chaltas, Thalia
Because I am furniture. Viking Children's
Books 2009 352p $16.99
Grades: 8 9 10 11   Fic
1. Novels in verse 2. Child abuse—Fiction 3. Child
sexual abuse—Fiction 4. Guilt—Fiction 5. School stories
ISBN 978-0-670-06298-0; 0-670-06298-7
                                        LC 2008-23235
The youngest of three siblings, fourteen-year-old Anke
feels both relieved and neglected that her father abuses
her brother and sister but ignores her, but when she
catches him with one of her friends, she finally becomes
angry enough to take action.

"Incendiary, devastating, yet—in total—offering em-
powerment and hope, Chaltas's poems leave an indelible
mark." Publ Wkly

Chan, Gillian
A foreign field. Kids Can Press 2002 184p
$16.95; pa $5.95
Grades: 7 8 9 10   Fic
1. World War, 1939-1945—Fiction 2. Love stories
ISBN 1-55337-349-9; 1-55337-350-2 (pa)
"Fourteen-year-old Ellen, who lives near a Canadian
air base that the Royal Air Force is using for training
during WWII, has what she considers a tedious job as
her war work: looking after her disobedient, airplane-mad
younger brother, Colin. Colin introduces her to Stephen,
a very young RAF trainee. . . . They find common
ground and their friendship grows and deepens into love.
. . . Chan beautifully captures the particular tensions and
intensity of wartime relationships in this quiet, absorbing
novel." Booklist

Chappell, Crissa-Jean
Total constant order. Katherine Tegen Books
2007 278p $16.99; lib bdg $17.89
Grades: 8 9 10 11 12   Fic
1.   Obsessive-compulsive   disorder—Fiction
2. Florida—Fiction
ISBN   978-0-06-088605-9;   0-06-088605-6;
978-0-06-088606-6 (lib bdg); 0-06-088606-4 (lib bdg)
                                      LC 2006-102964
Resentful and upset when her family moves from Vermont to Miami, Florida, and her parents' fighting escalates, high-schooler Fin develops OCD (Obsessive-
Compulsive Disorder) and becomes consumed with numbers, counting, irrational worrying, and avoiding germs.

"Likable characters and an intense pace make this a
good purchase for most collections." SLJ

Charlton-Trujillo, e. E.
Feels like home. Delacorte Press 2007 213p
$15.99; lib bdg $18.99
Grades: 7 8 9 10   Fic
1. Siblings—Fiction 2. Bereavement—Fiction
3. Texas—Fiction
ISBN   978-0-385-73332-8;   0-385-73332-1;
978-0-385-90349-3 (lib bdg); 0-385-90349-9 (lib bdg)
                                       LC 2006-00275
Following the death of their father, seventeen-year-old
Michelle's older brother—who had disappeared six years
earlier—returns to their small Texas town where, with
the help of S.E. Hinton's "The Outsiders," the two siblings try to find a way to move beyond a past tragedy.

"Charlton-Trujillo has created a roster of multidimensional characters. . . . Teens . . . will surely be taken by
the story's winning mix of tragedy, romance and chemistry." Publ Wkly

Cheaney, J. B.
The middle of somewhere. Alfred A. Knopf
2007 218p $15.99; lib bdg $18.99
Grades: 5 6 7 8   Fic
1. Automobile travel—Fiction 2. Siblings—Fiction
3.   Attention   deficit   disorder—Fiction
4. Grandfathers—Fiction 5. Kansas—Fiction
ISBN 978-0-375-83790-6; 978-0-375-93790-3 (lib
bdg)   LC 2006-29202

Cheaney, J. B.—*Continued*

Twelve-year-old Ronnie loves organization, especially because her brother has attention-deficit hyperactivity disorder, but traveling with their grandfather who is investigating wind power in Kansas brings some pleasant, if chaotic, surprises.

"The main characters are particularly well drawn and believable, and readers will root for both children as they attempt to overcome the obstacles placed in front of them." Booklist

Chen, Da, 1962-

Sword. Laura Geringer Books 2008 232p (Forbidden tales) $16.99; lib bdg $17.89

Grades: 6 7 8 9 10   **Fic**

1. Martial arts—Fiction 2. China—Fiction
ISBN   978-0-06-144758-7;   0-06-144758-7; 978-0-06-144759-4 (lib bdg); 0-06-144759-5 (lib bdg)
LC 2008-10774

When Miu Miu turns fifteen, she learns the truth about her father's violent death and discovers that she must avenge his murder before she can marry the man to whom she is betrothed. Based on a story told to the author by a former prisoner during China's Cultural Revolution.

"Exciting, exotic, and thoughtful, this book will appeal to fans of high-class maritial arts films." Booklist

Cheng, Andrea, 1957-

The bear makers. 1st ed. Front Street 2008 170p $16.95

Grades: 5 6 7 8   **Fic**

1. Hungary—Fiction 2. Family life—Fiction
ISBN 978-1-59078-518-8; 1-59078-518-5
LC 2007049005

In post-World War II Budapest, a young girl and her family struggle against the oppressive Hungarian Worker's Party policies and try to find a way to a better life.

"Cheng has crafted a cast of characters and palpable setting that are vivid and compelling, and she offers a glimpse into history that many children will find easy to relate to and powerfully affecting." Booklist

Eclipse. Front Street 2006 129p $16.95

Grades: 4 5 6 7   **Fic**

1. Immigrants—Fiction 2. Hungarian Americans—Fiction 3. Ohio—Fiction
ISBN 978-1-932425-21-5; 1-932425-21-7
LC 2006-00785

In Cincinnati, Ohio, in the summer of 1952, eight-year-old Peti gives up his room to his Hungarian relatives, including a twelve-year-old cousin who bullies him, and worries about his grandfather who cannot escape from behind the Iron Curtain.

"The pain of the immigrant experience . . . is compellingly captured in this spare, unsentimental novel." Booklist

Cheva, Cherry

She's so money. HarperTeen 2008 290p $16.99; lib bdg $17.99

Grades: 7 8 9 10 11 12   **Fic**

1. Cheating (Education)—Fiction 2. School stories 3. Thai Americans—Fiction 4. Restaurants—Fiction
ISBN   978-0-06-128855-5;   0-06-128855-1; 978-0-06-128852-4 (lib bdg); 0-06-128852-7 (lib bdg)
LC 2007-37432

Maya, a high school senior bound for Stanford University, goes against her better judgement when she and a popular but somewhat disreputable boy start a profitable school-wide cheating ring in order to save her family's Thai restaurant, which she fears will be shut down due to her irresponsible actions.

"Cheva's writing, full of sarcastic wit and snappy comebacks, raises the bar, and the flirty banter between Maya and Camden makes this romantic comedy more than bearable." SLJ

Chima, Cinda Williams

The warrior heir. Hyperion Books for Children 2006 426p $16.99; pa $8.99 *

Grades: 7 8 9 10 11 12   **Fic**

1. Magic—Fiction 2. Fantasy fiction
ISBN   0-7868-3916-3;   978-0-7868-3916-2; 0-7868-3917-1 (pa); 978-0-7868-3917-9 (pa)
LC 2005-52720

After learning about his magical ancestry and his own warrior powers, sixteen-year-old Jack embarks on a training program to fight enemy wizards.

"Twists and turns abound in this remarkable, nearly flawless debut novel that mixes a young man's coming-of-age with fantasy and adventure. Fast paced and brilliantly plotted." Voice Youth Advocates

Other titles in this series are:
The wizard heir (2007)
The dragon heir (2008)

Choi, Sook Nyul

Year of impossible goodbyes. Houghton Mifflin 1991 171p $16 *

Grades: 5 6 7 8   **Fic**

1. Korea—Fiction
ISBN 0-395-57419-6; 0-440-40759-1 (Yearling pa)
LC 91-10502

Also available in paperback from Yearling

Sookan, a young Korean girl survives the oppressive Japanese and Russian occupation of North Korea during the 1940s, to later escape to freedom in South Korea

"Tragedies are not masked here, but neither are they overdramatized. . . . The observations are honest, the details authentic, the characterizations vividly developed." Bull Cent Child Books

Other titles about Sookan are:
Echoes of the white giraffe (1993)
Gathering of pearls (1994)

Choldenko, Gennifer, 1957-
Al Capone does my shirts. G.P. Putnam's Sons
2004 225p il $15.99 *
Grades: 5 6 7 8   **Fic**
1. Alcatraz Island (Calif.)—Fiction 2. Autism—Fiction
3. Siblings—Fiction
ISBN 0-399-23861-1   LC 2002-31766
A Newbery Medal honor book, 2005
A twelve-year-old boy named Moose moves to Alcatraz Island in 1935 when guards' families were housed
there, and has to contend with his extraordinary new environment in addition to life with his autistic sister.
"With its unique setting and well-developed characters, this warm, engaging coming-of-age story has plenty
of appeal, and Choldenko offers some fascinating historical background on Alcatraz Island in an afterword."
Booklist

Notes from a liar and her dog. Putnam 2001
216p hardcover o.p. pa $5.99
Grades: 5 6 7 8   **Fic**
1. Family life—Fiction 2. Truthfulness and falsehood—Fiction
ISBN 0-399-23591-4; 0-14-250068-2 (pa)
                                 LC 00-55354
Eleven-year-old Ant, stuck in a family that she does
not like, copes by pretending that her "real" parents are
coming to rescue her, by loving her dog Pistachio, by
volunteering at the zoo, and by bending the truth and
telling lies
"Choldenko's writing is snappy and tender, depicting
both Ant's bravado and her isolation with sympathy."
Bull Cent Child Books

Chotjewitz, David, 1964-
Daniel half human; and the good Nazi;
translated by Doris Orgel. Atheneum Books for
Young Readers 2004 298p $17.95
Grades: 7 8 9 10   **Fic**
1. Jews—Fiction 2. Germany—Fiction 3. National socialism—Fiction
ISBN 0-689-85747-0   LC 2003-25554
"A Richard Jackson Book"
In 1933, best friends Daniel and Armin admire Hitler,
but as anti-Semitism buoys Hitler to power, Daniel learns
he is half Jewish, threatening the friendship even as life
in their beloved Hamburg, Germany, is becoming nightmarish. Also details Daniel and Armin's reunion in 1945
in interspersed chapters.
"Orgel's translation reads smoothly and movingly. An
outstanding addition to the large body of World War
II/Holocaust fiction." SLJ

Choyce, Lesley, 1951-
Deconstructing   Dylan.   Boardwalk
Books/Dundurn Press 2006 174p pa $12.99
Grades: 7 8 9 10 11 12   **Fic**
1. Cloning—Fiction 2. Science fiction
ISBN 1-55002-603-8
"The year is 2014. . . . The only child of well-known
genetics researchers, Dylan has always felt that he is dif-
ferent from his peers in some fundamental way that he
cannot define. . . . [His parents] confess that Dylan is a

clone of his dead brother. . . . Choyce uses a tantalizing
story line to ask some difficult questions about the consequences of scientific progress. Dylan is an unforgettable character." Voice Youth Advocates

Christopher, John, 1922-
The White Mountains. 35th anniversary ed.
Simon & Schuster Bks. for Young Readers 2003
c1967 164p hardcover o.p. pa $5.99 *
Grades: 5 6 7 8   **Fic**
1. Science fiction
ISBN 0-689-85504-4; 0-689-85672-5 (pa)
                                 LC 2002-70808
A reissue of the title first published 1967 by Macmil-
lan
Young Will Parker and his companions make a peril-
ous journey toward an outpost of freedom where they
hope to escape from the ruling Tripods, who capture ma-
ture human beings and make them docile, obedient ser-
vants
This "remarkable story . . . belongs to the school of
science-fiction which puts philosophy before technology
and is not afraid of telling an exciting story." Times Lit
Suppl
Other titles about the Tripods are:
The city of gold and lead (2003 c1967)
The pool of fire (2003 c1968)
When the Tripods came (2003 c1988)

Cirrone, Dorian
Prom kings and drama queens; [by] Dorian
Cirrone. HarperTeen 2008 200p $16.99; lib bdg
$17.89
Grades: 8 9 10 11 12   **Fic**
1. School stories 2. Florida—Fiction
ISBN   978-0-06-114372-4;   0-06-114372-3;
978-0-06-114373-1 (lib bdg); 0-06-114373-1 (lib bdg)
                                 LC 2007-20883
When high school junior Emily Bennet is caught between a new relationship with the boy of her dreams and
planning an alternative prom with her longtime rival on
the student newspaper, it forces her to think about her
values and make a difficult decision.
"Narration and commentary skewering and usually hilarious." Voice Youth Advocates

Cisneros, Sandra
The house on Mango Street. Knopf 1994 134p
$24 *
Grades: 7 8 9 10   **Fic**
1. Chicago (Ill.)—Fiction 2. Mexican Americans—Fiction
ISBN 0-679-43335-X   LC 93-43564
"Originally published by Arte Público Press in 1984."
Verso of title page
Composed of a series of interconnected vignettes, this
"is the story of Esperanza Cordero, a young girl growing
up in the Hispanic quarter of Chicago. For Esperanza,
Mango Street is a desolate landscape of concrete and
run-down tenements, where she discovers the hard realities of life—the fetters of class and gender, the specter
of racial enmity, the mysteries of sexuality, and more."

Cisneros, Sandra—*Continued*
Publisher's note

This is "a composite of evocative snapshots that manages to passionately recreate the milieu of the poor quarters of Chicago." Commonweal

Clark, Clara Gillow, 1951-
Hill Hawk Hattie. Candlewick Press 2003 159p hardcover o.p. pa $6.99
Grades: 4 5 6 7   **Fic**
1. Father-daughter relationship—Fiction 2. Death—Fiction 3. Sex role—Fiction
ISBN 0-7636-1963-9; 0-7636-2559-0 (pa)
            LC 2002-73740

Angry and lonely after her mother dies, eleven-year-old Hattie pretends to be a boy and joins her father on an adventure-filled rafting trip down the Delaware River in the late 1800s to transport logs from New York to Philadelphia.

"With beautiful rhythmic sentences, the simple first-person narrative captures [Hattie's] rustic innocence, the thrilling rafting adventure, and the heartfelt struggle of a tough girl who feels useful to her father only in the role of a boy." Booklist

Other titles about Hattie are:
Hattie on her way (2005)
Secrets of Greymoor (2009)

Clarke, Arthur C., 1917-2008
2001: a space odyssey. New Am. Lib. 1968 221p pa $7.99 hardcover o.p. *
Grades: 7 8 9 10 11 12 Adult   **Fic**
1. Science fiction
ISBN 0-451-45799-4 (pa)

"Based on a screenplay by Stanley Kubrick and Arthur C. Clarke." Title page

Astronauts of the spaceship Discovery, aided by their computer, HAL, blast off in search of proof that extraterrestrial beings had a part in the development of intelligent life forms on Earth millions of years ago.

"By standing the universe on its head, the author makes us see the ordinary universe in a different light. . . . [This novel becomes] a complex allegory about the history of the world." New Yorker

Clarke, Judith, 1943-
One whole and perfect day. Front Street 2007 250p $16.95
Grades: 7 8 9 10   **Fic**
1. Grandfathers—Fiction 2. Family life—Fiction 3. Australia—Fiction
ISBN 978-1-932425-95-6; 1-932425-95-0
            LC 2006-20126
Michael L. Printz Award honor book, 2008

As her irritating family prepares to celebrate her grandfather's eightieth birthday, sixteen-year-old Lily yearns for just one whole perfect day together.

The author's "sharp, poetic prose evokes each character's inner life with rich and often amusing vibrancy." Horn Book

Starry nights. Front St. 2003 148p $15.95
Grades: 6 7 8 9   **Fic**
1. Ghost stories 2. Death—Fiction
ISBN 1-88691-082-0   LC 2002-192884

Guilty over their older brother's drowning and their mother's subsequent breakdown, fourteen-year-old Vida ventures into the occult but it is ten-year-old Jess who meets the ghost who is trying to help them

"This tantalizing ghost story . . . will keep readers on the edge of their seats. . . . A spine-tingler with staying power." Publ Wkly

Clayton, Emma, 1968-
The roar. Chicken House/Scholastic Inc. 2009 481p $17.99
Grades: 5 6 7 8   **Fic**
1. Twins—Fiction 2. Science fiction
ISBN 978-0-439-92593-8; 0-439-92593-2
            LC 2008-8311

In an overpopulated world where all signs of nature have been obliterated and a wall has been erected to keep out plague-ridden animals, twelve-year-old Mika refuses to believe that his twin sister was killed after being abducted, and continues to search for her in spite of the dangers he faces in doing so.

"This is an unusually gripping adventure that targets a younger audience than most young adult sci-fi." Bull Cent Child Books

Cle, Troy
The marvelous effect; a.k.a., the marvelous world of the supposedly soon to be phenomenal young Mr. Louis Proof, book 1; [by] Troy Cle. 1st ed. Simon & Schuster Books for Young Readers 2007 369p (Marvelous world) $14.99
Grades: 6 7 8 9   **Fic**
1. Fantasy fiction 2. African Americans—Fiction
ISBN 978-1-4169-3958-0; 1-4169-3958-X
            LC 2006039685

Strange things are happening on Earth, and twelve-year-old Louis Proof discovers that he is one of the few people able to see—and combat—those responsible.

"The narration has the free-flowing, engrossing rhythm of oral storytelling, punctuated by poetic interludes that comment . . . on the action." SLJ

Cleary, Beverly
Dear Mr. Henshaw; illustrated by Paul O. Zelinsky. Morrow 1983 133p il $15.99; lib bdg $16.89; pa $5.99 *
Grades: 4 5 6 7   **Fic**
1. Divorce—Fiction 2. Parent-child relationship—Fiction 3. School stories
ISBN 0-688-02405-X; 0-688-02406-8 (lib bdg); 0-380-70958-9 (pa)   LC 83-5372
Awarded the Newbery Medal

"Leigh Botts started writing letters to his favorite author, Boyd Henshaw, in the second grade. Now, Leigh is in the sixth grade, in a new school, and his parents are recently divorced. This year he writes many letters to Mr. Henshaw, and also keeps a journal. Through these the reader learns how Leigh adjusts to new situations,

Cleary, Beverly—*Continued*

and of his triumphs." Child Book Rev Serv

"The story is by no means one of unrelieved gloom, for there are deft touches of humor in the sentient, subtly wrought account of the small triumphs and tragedies in the life of an ordinary boy." Horn Book

Followed by: Strider (1991)

Cleaver, Vera

Where the lillies bloom; [by] Vera & Bill Cleaver; illustrated by Jim Spanfeller. Lippincott 1969 174p il $15.95; pa $5.99 *

Grades: 5 6 7 8   **Fic**

1. Orphans—Fiction   2. Siblings—Fiction
3. Appalachian region—Fiction

ISBN 0-397-31111-7; 0-06-447005-9 (pa)

Mary Call Luther is "fourteen years old and made of granite. When her sharecropper father dies, Mary Call becomes head of the household, responsible for a boy of ten and a retarded, gentle older sister. Mary and her brother secretly bury their father so they can retain their home [in the Appalachian hills]; tenaciously she fights to keep the family afloat by selling medicinal plants and to keep them together by fending off [Kiser Pease, their landlord], who wants to marry her sister." Saturday Rev

"The setting is fascinating, the characterization good, and the style of the first-person story distinctive." Bull Cent Child Books

Followed by Trial Valley (1977)

Clements, Andrew, 1949-

The school story; illustrated by Brian Selznick. Simon & Schuster Bks. for Young Readers 2001 196p il $16; pa $5.99

Grades: 4 5 6 7   **Fic**

1. Authorship—Fiction 2. Publishers and publishing—Fiction

ISBN 0-689-82594-3; 0-689-85186-3 (pa)

LC 00-49683

After twelve-year-old Natalie writes a wonderful novel, her friend Zoe helps her devise a scheme to get it accepted at the publishing house where Natalie's mother works as an editor

"The girls are believable characters. . . . Selznick's black-and-white illustrations add humorous details. A comic novel that's a sure winner." SLJ

Things not seen. Philomel Bks. 2002 251p $15.99; pa $5.99

Grades: 7 8 9 10   **Fic**

1. Blind—Fiction 2. Science fiction

ISBN 0-399-23626-0; 0-14-240076-9 (pa)

LC 00-69900

When fifteen-year-old Bobby wakes up and finds himself invisible, he and his parents and his new blind friend Alicia try to find out what caused his condition and how to reverse it.

"The author spins a convincing and affecting story." Publ Wkly

Other titles in this series are:

Things hoped for (2006)

Things that are (2008)

Click; [by] Linda Sue Park [et al.] Arthur A. Levine Books 2007 217p $16.99

Grades: 7 8 9 10   **Fic**

1. Photojournalism—Fiction 2. Adventure fiction

ISBN 0-439-41138-6; 978-0-439-41138-7

LC 2006-100069

Contents: Maggie by Linda Sue Park; Annie by David Almond; Jason by Eoin Colfer; Lev by Deborah Ellis; Maggie by Nick Hornby; Vincent by Roddy Doyle; Min by Timy Wynne-Jones; Jiro by Ruth Ozeki; Afela by Margo Lanagan; Margaret by Gregory Maguire

"Ten distinguished authors each write a chapter of this intriguing novel of mystery and family, which examines the lives touched by a photojournalist George Keane, aka Gee. . . . The authors' distinctive styles remain evident; although readers expecting a more straightforward or linear story may find the leaps through time and place challenging, the thematic currents help the chapters gel into a cohesive whole." Publ Wkly

Clinton, Cathryn

A stone in my hand. Candlewick Press 2002 191p $15.99; pa $5.99

Grades: 8 9 10 11   **Fic**

1. Family life—Fiction

ISBN 0-7636-1388-6; 0-7636-2561-2 (pa)

LC 2001-58423

Eleven-year-old Malaak and her family are touched by the violence in Gaza between Jews and Palestinians when first her father disappears and then her older brother is drawn to the Islamic Jihad

"With a sharp eye for nuances of culture and the political situation in the Middle East, Clinton has created a rich, colorful cast of characters and created an emotionally charged novel." SLJ

Clippinger, Carol

Open court. Alfred A. Knopf 2007 262p $15.99; lib bdg $18.99

Grades: 6 7 8 9   **Fic**

1. Tennis—Fiction

ISBN   978-0-375-84049-4;   0-375-84049-4; 978-0-375-94049-1 (lib bdg); 0-375-94049-9 (lib bdg)

LC 2006-24250

Hall Braxton, a thirteen-year-old tennis prodigy, grapples with her seemingly incompatible desires to be an exceptional athlete and a normal teenager.

"The first-person narrative intersperses Hall's thoughts and activities with the ever-present and relentless demands of the game, creating a tension and rhythm that will capture readers' attention to the finish." SLJ

Cochran, Thomas, 1955-

Roughnecks. Harcourt Brace & Co. 1997 248p hardcover o.p. pa $6

Grades: 7 8 9 10   **Fic**

1. Football—Fiction

ISBN 0-15-201433-0; 0-15-202200-7 (pa)

LC 96-43939

"Gulliver books"

Travis Cody prepares for the final game of his high school football career, a rematch with his school's chief

Cochran, Thomas, 1955-—_Continued_
rival

"Travis is an appealing, positive character. . . . Football descriptions are authentic, intense, even lyrical at times." Booklist

Running the dogs. Farrar Straus & Giroux 2007 153p $16

Grades: 4 5 6 7   **Fic**
1. Dogs—Fiction 2. Louisiana—Fiction
ISBN 0-374-36360-9; 978-0-374-36360-4
       LC 2006-46515

When an unexpected snowstorm hits his part of Louisiana, ten-year-old Tal demonstrates his determination and responsibility after his hunting dogs become lost in the woods.

"Cochran's greatest strength lies in evoking hushed yet intense moods; his light-handed conjuration of rural Louisiana is also admirable." Horn Book Guide

Cochrane, Mick
The girl who threw butterflies. Alfred A. Knopf 2009 177p $15.99; $18.99

Grades: 6 7 8 9   **Fic**
1. Baseball—Fiction 2. Sex role—Fiction
3. Bereavement—Fiction 4. Mother-daughter relationship—Fiction
ISBN 978-0-375-85682-2; 0-375-85682-X; 978-0-375-95682-9 (lib bdg); 0-375-95682-4 (lib bdg)
       LC 2008-15986

Eighth-grader Molly's ability to throw a knuckleball earns her a spot on the baseball team, which not only helps her feel connected to her recently deceased father, who loved baseball, it helps in other aspects of her life, as well.

"Cochrane crafts an awkward yet engaging heroine whose perceptions and interactions with family, friends, and supporting characters ring true. Crisply written sports action balances the internal drama." SLJ

Cockcroft, Jason
Counter clockwise. HarperCollins Publishers 2009 202p il $15.99; lib bdg $16.89

Grades: 5 6 7 8   **Fic**
1. Fantasy fiction 2. Time travel—Fiction
3. Father-son relationship—Fiction 4. London (England)—Fiction
ISBN 978-0-06-125554-0; 0-06-125554-8; 978-0-06-125555-7 (lib bdg); 0-06-125555-6 (lib bdg)

With the aid of Bartleby, an enormous Tower of London guard known as a Beefeater, Nathan travels through time to stop his father from changing the past.

"Cockcroft employs a cleverness that keeps the story fresh. . . . [This book] should appeal to fantasy fans." Voice Youth Advocates

Cohen, Tish, 1963-
The invisible rules of the Zoë Lama. Dutton 2007 247p $15.99

Grades: 4 5 6 7   **Fic**

1. School stories 2. Grandmothers—Fiction
3. Mother-daughter relationship—Fiction
4. Alzheimer's disease—Fiction
ISBN 978-0-525-47810-2

Twelve-year-old Zoë, famous for advising other people using her unwritten rules, has her hands full with chairing a school dance committee, training a new student to fit in, keeping her grandmother out of a nursing home, and trying to find a husband for her mother.

"Periodic cartoon drawings and scanned cookie images add whimsy and visual interest. An entertaining read." Booklist

Followed by: The one and only Zoe Lama (2008)

Cohn, Rachel
The Steps. Simon & Schuster Bks. for Young Readers 2003 137p $15.95; pa $4.99

Grades: 5 6 7 8   **Fic**
1. Stepfamilies—Fiction 2. Family life—Fiction
3. Australia—Fiction
ISBN 978-0-689-84549-9; 0-689-84549-9; 978-0-689-87414-7 (pa); 0-689-87414-6 (pa)
       LC 2001-57566

Over Christmas vacation, Annabel goes from her home in Manhattan to visit her father, his new wife, and her half- and step-siblings in Sydney, Australia

"Packed with humorous incident, life lessons learned, Australian travel tidbits, and a litany of preteen-girl touchstones." Horn Book

Another title about this family is:
Two steps forward (2006)

You know where to find me. Simon & Schuster Books for Young Readers 2008 208p $15.99; pa $8.99 *

Grades: 8 9 10 11 12   **Fic**
1. Suicide—Fiction 2. Obesity—Fiction 3. Drug abuse—Fiction 4. Cousins—Fiction 5. Washington (D.C.)—Fiction
ISBN 978-0-689-87859-6; 0-689-87859-1; 978-0-689-87860-2 (pa); 0-689-87860-5 (pa)
       LC 20070-0851

In the wake of her cousin's suicide, overweight and introverted seventeen-year-old Miles experiences significant changes in her relationships with her mother and father, her best friend Jamal and his family, and her cousin's father, while gaining insights about herself, both positive and negative.

"Cohn once again excels at crafting a multidimensional, in-the-moment teenage world. . . . Her work is heartbreaking . . . but it rings with authenticity." Publ Wkly

Cole, Brock, 1938-
The goats; written and illustrated by Brock Cole. Farrar, Straus & Giroux 1987 184p il hardcover o.p. pa $5.99

Grades: 7 8 9 10   **Fic**
1. Camps—Fiction 2. Friendship—Fiction
ISBN 0-374-32678-9; 0-374-42575-2 (pa)
       LC 87-45362

"A boy and the girl have been chosen as 'the goats' at summer camp. Stripped naked, they are marooned on Goat Island, as part of an annual prank played on camp-

Cole, Brock, 1938-—*Continued*

ers who don't fit in. But the goats have much more spirit than their fellow campers expect, and they decide to disappear completely." Publ Wkly

"This is an unflinching book, and there is a quality of raw emotion that may score some discomfort among adults. Such a first novel restores faith in the cultivation of children's literature." Bull Cent Child Books

Cole, Stephen, 1971-

Thieves like us. Bloomsbury 2006 349p $16.95

Grades: 8 9 10 11 12   **Fic**
1. Adventure fiction
ISBN 978-1-58234-653-3; 1-58234-653-4

LC 2005030616

A mysterious benefactor hand-picks a group of teen geniuses to follow a set of clues leading to the secrets of everlasting life, secrets which they must steal and for which they risk being killed.

"This novel relies on fast action, cool gadgets, and clever problem solving." Booklist

Followed by Thieves till we die (2007)

Colfer, Eoin, 1965-

Airman; [by] Eoin Colfer. Hyperion Books for Children 2008 412p $17.99 *

Grades: 4 5 6 7 8 9 10   **Fic**
1. Airplanes—Fiction   2. Prisoners—Fiction
3. Adventure fiction 4. Inventors—Fiction 5. Ireland—Fiction
ISBN 978-1-4231-0750-7; 1-4231-0750-0

LC 2007-38415

In the late nineteenth century, when Conor Broekhart discovers a conspiracy to overthrow the king, he is branded a traitor, imprisoned, and forced to mine for diamonds under brutal conditions while he plans a daring escape from Little Saltee prison by way of a flying machine that he must design, build, and, hardest of all, trust to carry him to safety.

This is "polished, sophisticated storytelling. . . . A tour de force." Publ Wkly

Artemis Fowl. Hyperion Bks. for Children 2001 277p $16.95; pa $7.99 *

Grades: 5 6 7 8   **Fic**
1. Fairies—Fiction 2. Fantasy fiction
ISBN 0-7868-0801-2; 0-7868-1707-0 (pa)

LC 2001-16632

When a twelve-year-old evil genius tries to restore his family fortune by capturing a fairy and demanding a ransom in gold, the fairies fight back with magic, technology, and a particularly nasty troll

"Colfer's antihero, techno fantasy is cleverly written and filled to the brim with action, suspense, and humor." SLJ

Other titles in this series are:
Artemis Fowl: the Arctic incident (2002)
Artemis Fowl: the Eternity code (2003)
Artemis Fowl: the lost colony (2006)
Artemis Fowl: the Opal deception (2005)
Artemis Fowl: the time paradox (2008)

Benny and Omar. Miramax Books/Hyperion Books for Children 2007 280p $18.95

Grades: 5 6 7 8   **Fic**
1. Friendship—Fiction 2. Hurling (Game)—Fiction
3. Tunisia—Fiction
ISBN 978-1-4231-0281-6; 1-4231-0281-9

LC 2006-100644

First published 1998 in Ireland

Twelve-year-old Benny, a hurling fanatic, moves to Tunisia, North Africa, when his father is transferred and has a hard time adjusting to the new land until he meets Omar.

"Colfer does such a masterful job of mixing humor and tragedy with Benny's smart-alecky remarks that youngsters will like him in spite of themselves. This is a funny, fast-paced read." SLJ

Another title about Benny is:
Benny and Babe (2007)

Half-Moon investigations. Miramax Books/Hyperion Books for Children 2006 290p $16.95

Grades: 4 5 6 7   **Fic**
1. Mystery fiction
ISBN 0-7868-4957-6

"Diminutive Fletcher Moon may not be the most popular 12-year-old in his Irish town but he's proud . . . of the badge that he constantly flashes to let everyone know that he's an online graduate of a private detective academy in Washington, DC. . . . But when . . . April Devereux hires him to find a lock of a pop star's hair that she claims was stolen . . . everything starts going wrong for Fletcher." SLJ

"The private-eye lingo has a great, comical grade-school snap, and . . . the kid's goofy charm and stubborn dedication to crime solving will win him a hefty, enthusiastic following." Booklist

Collier, James Lincoln, 1928-

The dreadful revenge of Ernest Gallen; [by] James Lincoln Collier. 1st U.S. ed. Bloomsbury Children's Books 2008 232p $16.95 *

Grades: 5 6 7 8   **Fic**
1. Supernatural—Fiction 2. Great Depression, 1929-1939—Fiction 3. Horror fiction
ISBN 978-1-59990-220-3; 1-59990-220-6

LC 2007044453

When Eugene starts hearing a voice inside his head telling him to do awful things, it leads him to look into his small town's past before the Depression, and to discover long-hidden secrets about his neighbors and his town.

"Collier has written an eerily weird and strangely believable historical mystery. . . . A complex, spooky page-turner." Booklist

The empty mirror. Bloomsbury 2004 192p $16.95

Grades: 5 6 7 8   **Fic**
1. Ghost stories 2. Influenza—Fiction 3. Orphans—Fiction
ISBN 1-58234-949-5

"Nick's an admitted troublemaker, but when his mysterious doppleganger starts committing increasingly sinis-

Collier, James Lincoln, 1928-—*Continued*
ter crimes, his small New England town is ready to
string Nick up. The secret of this ghostly presence might
lie in the recent influenza epidemic of 1918. . . . Collier's challenging novel effectively combines historical
fiction with a genuinely spooky supernatural tale." Horn
Book Guide

Jump ship to freedom; [by] James Lincoln
Collier, Christopher Collier. Delacorte Press 1981
198p pa $5.99 hardcover o.p. *
Grades: 6 7 8 9 **Fic**
 1. United States—History—1783-1809—Fiction
 2. Slavery—Fiction 3. African Americans—Fiction
 ISBN 0-440-44323-7 (pa) LC 81-65492
Companion volume to War comes to Willie Freeman
and Who is Carrie?
In 1787 Dan Arabus, a fourteen-year-old slave, anx-
ious to buy freedom for himself and his mother, escapes
from his dishonest master and tries to find help in cash-
ing the soldier's notes received by his father, Jack
Arabus, for fighting in the Revolution
"The period seems well researched, and the speech
has an authentic ring without trying to imitate a dialect."
SLJ

My brother Sam is dead; by James Lincoln
Collier and Christopher Collier. Four Winds Press
1985 c1974 216p $17.95 *
Grades: 6 7 8 9 **Fic**
 1. United States—History—1775-1783, Revolution—
 Fiction
 ISBN 0-02-722980-7 LC 84-28787
Also available in paperback from Scholastic
A Newbery Medal honor book, 1975
A reissue of the title first published 1974
"In 1775 the Meeker family lived in Redding, Con-
necticut, a Tory community. Sam, the eldest son, allied
himself with the Patriots. The youngest son, Tim,
watched a rift in the family grow because of his broth-
er's decision. Before the war was over the Meeker fami-
ly had suffered at the hands of both the British and the
Patriots." Shapiro. Fic for Youth. 3d edition

War comes to Willy Freeman; [by] James
Lincoln Collier, Christopher Collier. Delacorte
Press 1983 178p pa $5.99 hardcover o.p. *
Grades: 6 7 8 9 **Fic**
 1. United States—History—1775-1783, Revolution—
 Fiction 2. African Americans—Fiction 3. Slavery—
 Fiction
 ISBN 0-440-49504-0 (pa) LC 82-70317
This deals with events prior to those in Jump ship to
freedom, and involves members of the same family.
"Willy is thirteen when she begins her story, which takes
place during the last two years of the Revolutionary War;
her father, a free man, has been killed fighting against
the British, her mother has disappeared. Willy makes her
danger-fraught way to Fraunces Tavern in New York,
her uncle, Jack Arabus, having told her that Mr.
Fraunces may be able to help her. She works at the tavern until the war is over, goes to the Arabus home to
find her mother dying, and participates in the trial (historically accurate save for the fictional addition of Willy)
in which her uncle sues for his freedom and wins." Bull
Cent Child Books

With every drop of blood; [by] James Lincoln
Collier, Christopher Collier. Delacorte Press 1994
235p maps hardcover o.p. pa $6.99
Grades: 5 6 7 8 **Fic**
 1. United States—History—1861-1865, Civil War—
 Fiction 2. Race relations—Fiction 3. African Americans—Fiction
 ISBN 0-385-32028-0; 0-440-21983-3 (pa)
    LC 93-37655
This is a "docu-novel of the Civil War. Johnny, 14, a
young, white rebel soldier, is captured by a black Union
soldier, Cush, a runaway slave. As they get to know each
other in the mess and slaughter of battle and retreat, the
two boys gradually lose their mutual distrust, and each
risks his life to save the other." Booklist
"The relationship of Cush and Johnny and the convincingly conversational tone of Johnny's voice make
this book an effectively immediate evocation of a distant
and sometimes difficult-to-understand time." Horn Book

Collins, Pat Lowery, 1932-
Hidden voices; the orphan musicians of Venice.
Candlewick 2009 345p $17.99
Grades: 8 9 10 11 12 **Fic**
 1. Vivaldi, Antonio, 1678-1741—Fiction
 2. Musicians—Fiction 3. Orphans—Fiction 4. Venice
 (Italy)—Fiction
 ISBN 978-0-7636-3917-4; 0-7636-3917-6
Anetta, Rosalba, and Luisa, find their lives taking unexpected paths while growing up in eighteenth century
Venice at the orphanage Ospedale della Pieta, where
concerts are given to support the orphanage as well as
expose the girls to potential suitors.
"Collins's descriptive prose makes Venice and a
unique slice of history come alive as the three connecting
narrative strains create a rich story of friendship and self-
realization." SLJ

Collins, Suzanne
Gregor the Overlander. Scholastic Press 2003
311p (Underland chronicles) $16.95; pa $5.99
Grades: 4 5 6 7 **Fic**
 1. Fantasy fiction
 ISBN 0-439-43536-6; 0-439-67813-7 (pa)
    LC 2002-155865
When eleven-year-old Gregor and his two-year-old
sister are pulled into a strange underground world, they
trigger an epic battle involving men, bats, rats, cock-
roaches, and spiders while on a quest foretold by ancient
prophecy
"Collins creates a fascinating, vivid, highly original
world and a superb story to go along with it." Booklist
 Other titles in this series are:
Gregor and the prophecy of Bane (2004)
Gregor and the curse of the warmbloods (2005)
Gregor and the marks of secret (2006)
Gregor and the code of claw (2007)

The Hunger Games. Scholastic Press 2008 374p
$17.99 *
Grades: 7 8 9 10 **Fic**
 1. Science fiction
 ISBN 978-0-439-02348-1; 0-439-02348-3
    LC 2007-39987

Collins, Suzanne—_Continued_

In a future North America, where the rulers of Panem maintain control through an annual televised survival competition pitting young people from each of the twelve districts against one another, sixteen-year-old Katniss's skills are put to the test when she voluntarily takes her younger sister's place.

"Collins's characters are completely realistic and sympathetic. . . . The plot is tense, dramatic, and engrossing." SLJ

Followed by: Catching fire (2009)

Collins, Yvonne

The Black Sheep; [by] Yvonne Collins and Sandy Rideout. Hyperion Books for Children 2007 348p $15.99

Grades: 8 9 10 11 12   **Fic**

1. Television programs—Fiction 2. Family life—Fiction 3. Otters—Fiction 4. Wildlife conservation—Fiction 5. California—Fiction

ISBN 978-1-4231-0156-7; 1-4231-0156-1

LC 2006035591

Fifteen-year-old Kendra Bishop quickly regrets her rash decision to write to a new reality television show when she finds herself in Monterey, California, living with a large family of activists rather than in a Manhattan apartment with her uptight, money-oriented parents.

"This fun book should enthrall most girls. . . . The television twist makes it fresh and new." Voice Youth Advocates

Comerford, Lynda B.

Rissa Bartholomew's declaration of independence. Scholastic Press 2009 250p $16.99

Grades: 4 5 6 7   **Fic**

1. Friendship—Fiction 2. Illinois—Fiction 3. School stories

ISBN 978-0-545-05058-6; 0-545-05058-8

LC 2008-26618

Having told off all of her old friends at her eleventh birthday party, Rissa starts middle school determined to make new friends while being herself, not simply being part of a herd.

"Rissa's troubles are ones that many middle-schoolers will identify with: new schools, shifting allegiances, new feelings, and changing bodies. First-time novelist Comerford gives her readers an appealing heroine who, despite her flaws and quirks, finds herself along the way." Booklist

Compestine, Ying Chang

Revolution is not a dinner party; a novel. Henry Holt and Company 2007 256p map $16.95

Grades: 5 6 7 8   **Fic**

1. China—History—1949-1976—Fiction 2. Communism—Fiction 3. Persecution—Fiction

ISBN 978-0-8050-8207-4; 0-8050-8207-7

LC 2006035465

Starting in 1972 when she is nine years old, Ling, the daughter of two doctors, struggles to make sense of the communists' Cultural Revolution, which empties stores of food, homes of appliances deemed "bourgeois," and

people of laughter.

"Readers should remain rapt by Compestine's storytelling throughout this gripping account of life during China's Cultural Revolution." Publ Wkly

Conly, Jane Leslie

Racso and the rats of NIMH; illustrations by Leonard Lubin. Harper & Row 1986 278p il lib bdg $17.89; pa $5.99 *

Grades: 4 5 6 7   **Fic**

1. Mice—Fiction 2. Rats—Fiction

ISBN 0-06-021362-0 (lib bdg); 0-06-440245-2 (pa)

LC 85-42634

Sequel to Mrs. Frisby and the rats of NIMH by Robert C. O'Brien

This book "continues the NIMH saga with a focus on the second rodent generation: Timothy, Mrs. Frisby's son, and Racso, son of the rebel rat Jenner. On his way to classes at Thorn Valley, Timothy saves Racso's life but is himself severely injured. Both reach the Utopian colony only to discover that the valley and surrounding farms are to be turned into a tourist lake and campgrounds." SLJ

"The book is cleverly and gracefully built upon both the philosophy of self-sufficiency and the details of the plot of its predecessor. Given the difficulty of writing good sequels, _Racso and the Rats of NIMH_ is an outstanding success." Horn Book

Another title about the rats of NIMH by this author is: RT, Margaret, and the rats of NIMH (1990)

Connor, Leslie

Dead on town line; illustrations by Gina Triplett. Dial Books 2005 131p il $15.99

Grades: 7 8 9 10   **Fic**

1. Ghost stories 2. Homicide—Fiction

ISBN 0-8037-3021-7   LC 2004-15312

"Cassie's body lies hidden in a crevice, where she tries to figure out what happens next. She meets the ghost of Birdie, another murdered girl who was hidden in the same crevice years earlier. . . . Each verse/chapter adds a piece to the puzzle of Cassie's death until her body is found and the crime is solved. . . . This is an absorbing and moving story." SLJ

Waiting for normal. Katherine Tegen Books 2008 290p $16.99; lib bdg $17.89 *

Grades: 5 6 7 8   **Fic**

1. Family life—Fiction 2. Mothers—Fiction 3. New York (State)—Fiction

ISBN 978-0-06-089088-9; 0-06-089088-6; 978-0-06-089089-6 (lib bdg); 0-06-089089-4 (lib bdg)

LC 2007-06881

Twelve-year-old Addie tries to cope with her mother's erratic behavior and being separated from her beloved stepfather and half-sisters when she and her mother go to live in a small trailer by the railroad tracks on the outskirts of Schenectady, New York.

"Connor . . . treats the subject of child neglect with honesty and grace in this poignant story. . . . Characters as persuasively optimistic as Addie are rare, and readers will gravitate to her." Publ Wkly

Conrad, Pam, 1947-1996

My Daniel. Harper & Row 1989 137p lib bdg
$16.89; pa $5.99 *

Grades: 5 6 7 8   **Fic**

1. Nebraska—Fiction
ISBN 0-06-021314-0 (lib bdg); 0-06-440309-2 (pa)
                                         LC 88-19850

"When she's 80 years old, Julia Summerwaithe decides to visit her grandchildren, Ellie and Stevie, in New
York City, for the first time. She has something important to show them; in the Natural History Museum is the
dinosaur she and her brother discovered on their farm in
Nebraska when they were young. But even more important to Julia than seeing the dinosaur is sharing her memories of the discovery and excavation with her
grandchildren." SLJ

"Rendering scenes from both the past and the present
with equal skill, Conrad is at the peak of her storytelling
powers." Publ Wkly

Constable, Kate

The singer of all songs. Arthur A. Levine Books
2004 c2002 297p $16.95; pa $6.99

Grades: 7 8 9 10   **Fic**

1. Fantasy fiction 2. Magic—Fiction
ISBN 0-439-55478-0; 0-439-55479-4 (pa)
                                         LC 2003-9034

First published 2002 in Australia

Calwyn, a young priestess of ice magic, or chantment,
joins with other chanters who have different magical
skills to fight a sorcerer who wants to claim all powers
for his own

"An impressive debut by an author who clearly has
much to contribute to the fantasy genre." Booklist

Other available titles in this series are:
The waterless sea (2005)
The tenth power (2006)

Conway, Celeste

The goodbye time. Delacorte Press 2008 98p
$14.99; lib bdg $17.99 *

Grades: 4 5 6   **Fic**

1. Friendship—Fiction 2. New York (N.Y.)—Fiction
ISBN   978-0-385-73555-1;   0-385-73555-3;
978-0-385-90540-4 (lib bdg); 0-385-90540-8 (lib bdg)
                                         LC 2008-35675

The close friendship of two eleven-year-old girls, who
live in New York City, begins to unravel as each struggles to deal with a brother who is leaving home.

"The writing is simple and clear, and gently delivers
the message that growing up is inextricably linked with
change." Publ Wkly

Coombs, Kate

The runaway princess. Farrar, Straus and Giroux
2006 279p $17 *

Grades: 5 6 7 8   **Fic**

1. Fairy tales
ISBN 0-374-35546-0   LC 2005-51225

Fifteen-year-old Princess Meg uses magic and her wits
to rescue a baby dragon and escape the unwanted atten-
tions of princes hoping to gain her hand in marriage

through a contest arranged by her father, the king.

"This witty, humorous tale will be popular with fantasy buffs who enjoy takeoffs on fairy tales." Booklist

Cooney, Caroline B., 1947-

Code orange. Delacorte 2005 200p $15.95

Grades: 7 8 9 10   **Fic**

1. Smallpox—Fiction 2. School stories 3. New York
(N.Y.)—Fiction
ISBN 0-385-90277-8   LC 2004-26422

While conducting research for a school paper on
smallpox, Mitty finds an envelope containing 100-year-
old smallpox scabs and fears that he has infected himself
and all of New York City.

"Readers won't soon forget either the profoundly disturbing premise of this page-turner or its likable, ultimately heroic slacker protagonist." Booklist

Diamonds in the shadow. Delacorte Press 2007
228p $15.99; lib bdg $18.99

Grades: 7 8 9 10 11 12   **Fic**

1. Refugees—Fiction 2. Africans—United States—Fiction 3. Family life—Fiction 4. Connecticut—Fiction
ISBN 978-0-385-73261-1; 978-0-385-90278-6 (lib
bdg)   LC 2006-27811

The Finches, a Connecticut family, sponsor an African
refugee family of four, all of whom have been scarred by
the horrors of civil war, and who inadvertently put their
benefactors in harm's way.

"Tension mounts in a novel that combines thrilling
suspense and a story about innocence lost." Booklist

The face on the milk carton. Delacorte Press
2006 184p $15.95; pa $6.99 *

Grades: 7 8 9 10   **Fic**

1. Kidnapping—Fiction
ISBN   978-0-385-32328-4;   0-385-32328-X;
978-0-440-22065-7 (pa); 0-440-22065-3 (pa)

A reissue of the title first published 1990 by Bantam
Books

A photograph of a missing girl on a milk carton leads
Janie on a search for her real identity.

Cooney "demonstrates an excellent ear for dialogue
and a gift for portraying responsible middle-class
teenagers trying to come to terms with very real concerns." SLJ

Other titles in this series are:
Whatever happened to Janie? (1993)
The voice on the radio (1996)
What Janie found (2000)

Hit the road. Delacorte Press 2006 183p $15.95;
lib bdg $17.99

Grades: 6 7 8 9   **Fic**

1. Grandmothers—Fiction 2. Automobile travel—Fiction 3. Kidnapping—Fiction 4. Old age—Fiction
ISBN 0-385-72944-8; 0-385-90174-7 (lib bdg)
                                         LC 2004-10106

Sixteen-year-old Brittany acts as chauffeur for her
grandmother and three other eighty-plus-year-old women
going to what is supposedly their college reunion, on a
long drive that involves lies, theft, and kidnappings.

"Cooney masterfully combines nonstop, cleverly plotted action with heartfelt emotion." Booklist

Cooney, Caroline B., 1947-—*Continued*
If the witness lied. Delacorte Press 2009 213p
$16.99; lib bdg $19.99
Grades: 6 7 8 9   **Fic**
  1. Siblings—Fiction 2. Bereavement—Fiction
3. Orphans—Fiction 4. Connecticut—Fiction
  ISBN   978-0-385-73448-6;   0-385-73448-4;
978-0-385-90451-3 (lib bdg); 0-385-90451-7 (lib bdg)
                    LC 2008-23959
Torn apart by tragedies and the publicity they brought,
siblings Smithy, Jack, and Madison, aged fourteen to sixteen, tap into their parent's courage to pull together and
protect their brother Tris, nearly three, from further media exploitation and a much more sinister threat.
"The pacing here is pure gold. Rotating through various perspectives to follow several plot strands . . .
Cooney draws out the action, investing it with the slow-
motion feel of an impending collision. . . . This family-
drama-turned-thriller will have readers racing, heart in
throat, to reach the conclusion." Horn Book

Cooper, Susan, 1935-
The Boggart. Margaret K. McElderry Bks. 1993
196p $15.95; pa $5.99
Grades: 4 5 6 7   **Fic**
  1. Supernatural—Fiction 2. Scotland—Fiction
3. Canada—Fiction
  ISBN 0-689-50576-0; 0-689-86930-4 (pa)
                    LC 92-15527
After visiting the castle in Scotland which her family
has inherited and returning home to Canada, twelve-year-
old Emily finds that she has accidentally brought back
with her a boggart, an invisible and mischievous spirit
with a fondness for practical jokes
"Using both electronics and theater as metaphors for
magic, Cooper has extended the world of high fantasy
into contemporary children's lives through scenes super-
imposing the ordinary and the extraordinary." Bull Cent
Child Books
Another title about the Boggart is:
The Boggart and the monster (1997)

Over sea, under stone; illustrated by Margery
Gill. Harcourt Brace Jovanovich 1966 c1965 252p
il $18; pa $4.99 *
Grades: 5 6 7 8   **Fic**
  1. Fantasy fiction 2. Good and evil—Fiction 3. Great
Britain—Fiction
  ISBN 0-15-259034-X; 0-689-84035-7 (pa)
Also available in paperback from Simon & Schuster
First published 1965 in the United Kingdom
Three children on a holiday in Cornwall find an an-
cient manuscript which sends them on a dangerous quest
for a grail that would reveal the true story of King Ar-
thur and that entraps them in the eternal battle between
the forces of the Light and the forces of the Dark.
"The air of mysticism and the allegorical quality of
the continual contest between good and evil add much
value to a fine plot, setting, and characterization." Horn
Book
Other titles in this series are:
The dark is rising (1973)
Greenwitch (1974)
The grey king (1975)
Silver on the tree (1977)

Corbett, Sue
Free baseball; [by] Sue Corbett. 1st ed. Dutton
Children's Books 2006 152p $15.99
Grades: 5 6 7 8   **Fic**
  1. Baseball—Fiction 2. Cuban Americans—Fiction
3. Florida—Fiction
  ISBN 0-525-47120-0   LC 2005004792
Angry with his mother for having too little time for
him, eleven-year-old Felix takes advantage of an opportunity to become bat boy for a minor league baseball
team, hoping to someday be like his father, a famous
Cuban outfielder. Includes glossaries of baseball terms
and Spanish words and phrases.
"An engaging, well-written story with a satisfying
ending." SLJ

Cormier, Robert
After the first death. Dell Publishing 1991
c1979 233p pa $6.50 *
Grades: 7 8 9 10   **Fic**
  1. Terrorism—Fiction
  ISBN 0-440-20835-1
  ALA YALSA Margaret A. Edwards Award (1991)
First published 1979 by Pantheon Bks.
"A busload of children is hijacked by a band of terrorists whose demands include the exposure of a military
brainwashing project. The narrative line moves from the
teenage terrorist Milo to Kate the bus driver and the involvement of Ben, whose father is the head of the military operation, in this confrontation. The conclusion has
a shocking twist." Shapiro. Fic for Youth. 2d edition

I am the cheese; a novel. Pantheon Bks. 1977
233p hardcover o.p. pa $6.50 *
Grades: 7 8 9 10 11 12 Adult   **Fic**
  1. Intelligence service—Fiction
  ISBN 0-394-83462-3; 0-440-94060-5 (pa)
                    LC 76-55948
  ALA YALSA Margaret A. Edwards Award (1991)
"Adam Farmer's mind has blanked out; his past is revealed in bits and pieces—partly by Adam himself, partly through a transcription of Adam's interviews with a
government psychiatrist. Adam's father, a newspaper reporter, gave evidence at the trial of a criminal organization which had infiltrated the government itself. He and
his family, marked for death, came under the protection
of the super-secret Department of Re-Identification,
which changed the family's name and kept them under
constant surveillance. Now an adolescent, Adam is finally let in on his parents' terrible secret." SLJ
"The suspense builds relentlessly to an ending that, although shocking, is entirely plausible." Booklist

The rag and bone shop; a novel. Delacorte Press
2001 154p $15.95; lib bdg $17.99; pa $5.99
Grades: 7 8 9 10   **Fic**
  1. Homicide—Fiction 2. Police—Fiction
  ISBN 0-385-72962-6; 0-385-90027-9 (lib bdg);
0-440-22971-5 (pa)   LC 2001-28540
Trent, an ace interrogator from Vermont, works to
procure a confession from an introverted twelve-year-old
accused of murdering his seven-year-old friend in Monu-
ment, Massachusetts
"Terse and terrifying, this final book from Cormier

Cormier, Robert—*Continued*

will leave a lasting impression. . . . The book's horrifying, surprising conclusion will engender discussion."
Booklist

Cornwell, Autumn

Carpe diem. Feiwel & Friends 2007 360p
$16.95 *

Grades: 7 8 9 10   **Fic**
 1. Grandmothers—Fiction 2. Artists—Fiction
3. Authorship—Fiction 4. Southeast Asia—Fiction
 ISBN 0-312-36792-9; 978-0-312-36792-3
         LC 2006-32054

Sixteen-year-old Vassar Spore's detailed plans for the next twenty years of her life are derailed when her bohemian grandmother insists that she join her in Southeast Asia for the summer, but as she writes a novel about her experiences, Vassar discovers new possibilities.

"Suspenseful and wonderfully detailed, the well-crafted story maintains its page-turning pace while adding small doses of insight and humor." SLJ

Cotten, Cynthia

Fair has nothing to do with it. Farrar, Straus and Giroux 2007 153p $16

Grades: 4 5 6 7   **Fic**
 1. Bereavement—Fiction 2. Grandfathers—Fiction
3. Drawing—Fiction
 ISBN 0-374-39935-2; 978-0-374-39935-1
         LC 2006-45170

When Michael's beloved grandfather dies, he has a hard time admitting how much it hurts and allowing himself to trust anyone again.

"The dramatic portrayal of Michael's grief, true to the child's viewpoint, is far from sentimental. . . . A excellent book for discussion." Booklist

Cottrell Boyce, Frank

Framed. HarperCollins 2006 306p $16.99; lib bdg $17.89

Grades: 5 6 7 8   **Fic**
 1. Automobiles—Fiction 2. Art—Fiction 3. Business enterprises—Fiction 4. Family life—Fiction 5. Wales—Fiction
 ISBN 0-06-073402-7; 0-06-073403-5 (lib bdg)
         LC 2006-00557

Dylan and his sisters have some ideas about how to make Snowdonia Oasis Auto Marvel into a more profitable business, but it is not until some strange men arrive in their small town of Manod, Wales with valuable paintings, and their father disappears, that they consider turning to crime.

"The colorful characters steal the show—even the secondary players are cleverly drawn. But it is Dylan's narrative voice . . . that is truly a masterpiece." SLJ

Couloumbis, Audrey

Love me tender. Random House 2008 209p $16.99; lib bdg $19.99 *

Grades: 5 6 7 8   **Fic**
 1. Family life—Fiction 2. Pregnancy—Fiction
3. Grandmothers—Fiction 4. Memphis (Tenn.)—Fiction
 ISBN 978-0-375-83839-2; 0-375-83839-2; 978-0-375-93839-9 (lib bdg); 0-375-93839-7 (lib bdg)
         LC 2006033162

Thirteen-year-old Elvira worries about her future when, after a fight, her father heads to Las Vegas for an Elvis impersonator competition and her pregnant mother takes her and her younger sister to Memphis to visit a grandmother the girls have never met.

"Tart characterizations, lively dialogue and Elvira's frank narration keep this perceptive novel both credible and buoyant." Publ Wkly

The misadventures of Maude March; or, Trouble rides a fast horse; [by] Audrey Couloumbis. Random House 2005 295p $15.95; lib bdg $17.99 *

Grades: 5 6 7 8   **Fic**
 1. Frontier and pioneer life—Fiction 2. Orphans—Fiction 3. Adventure fiction
 ISBN 0-375-83245-9; 0-375-93245-3 (lib bdg)
         LC 2004-16464

After the death of the stern aunt who raised them since they were orphaned, eleven-year-old Sallie and her fifteen-year-old sister escape their self-serving guardians and begin an adventure resembling those in the dime novels Sallie loves to read.

"Sallie's narration is delightful, with understatements that are laugh-out-loud hilarious. . . . Hard to put down, and a fun read-aloud." SLJ

Another title about Maude March is:
Maude March on the run! (2007)

Couvillon, Jacques

The chicken dance; [by] Jacques Couvillon. 1st U.S. ed. Bloomsbury Children's Books 2007 326p $16.95

Grades: 6 7 8 9   **Fic**
 1. Chickens—Fiction 2. Family life—Fiction
3. Country life—Fiction 4. Louisiana—Fiction
 ISBN 978-1-59990-043-8; 1-59990-043-2
         LC 2006102093

When eleven-year-old Don Schmidt wins a chicken-judging contest in his small town of Horse Island, Louisiana and goes from outcast to instant celebrity, even his neglectful mother occasionally takes notice of him and eventually he discovers some shocking family secrets.

"A funny, sometimes poignant novel. . . . [This offers] strong characters, interesting concepts, and a deft comedic touch." SLJ

Coville, Bruce

Aliens ate my homework; illustrated by Katherine Coville. Pocket Bks. 1993 179p il pa $4.99 hardcover o.p. *

Grades: 4 5 6   **Fic**
 1. Science fiction 2. Extraterrestrial beings—Fiction
 ISBN 0-671-72712-5 (pa)   LC 93-3945

Coville, Bruce—*Continued*
"A Minstrel book"
Rod is surprised when a miniature spaceship lands in his school science project and reveals five tiny aliens, who ask his help in apprehending an interstellar criminal
"A funny and suspenseful romp, with appealing illustrations throughout." Horn Book Guide
Other titles in this series are:
Aliens stole my body (1998)
I left my sneakers in dimension X (1994)
The search for Snout (1995)

Juliet Dove, Queen of Love; a magic shop book. Harcourt 2003 190p $17 *
Grades: 4 5 6 **Fic**
1. Magic—Fiction 2. Classical mythology—Fiction
ISBN 0-15-204561-9   LC 2003-11846
A shy twelve-year-old girl must solve a puzzle involving characters from Greek mythology to free herself from a spell which makes her irresistible to boys
"Although humorous, the story has surprising depth. . . . Coville capably interweaves mythological characters with realistic modern ones, keeping readers truly absorbed." SLJ

The monsters of Morley Manor. Harcourt 2001 224p $16; pa $5.95
Grades: 4 5 6 **Fic**
1. Monsters—Fiction 2. Extraterrestrial beings—Fiction
ISBN 0-15-216382-4; 0-15-204705-0 (pa)
                              LC 00-12912
Anthony and his younger sister discover that the monster figures he got in an unusual box at an estate sale are alive, but they have no way of knowing that the "monsters" will lead them on fantastical adventures to other worlds in an effort to try to save Earth
"Coville's rollicking tale has an unbelievable plot and exaggerated characters, but this is exactly what makes it so entertaining." Horn Book Guide

The skull of truth; a magic shop book; illustrated by Gary A. Lippincott. Harcourt Brace & Co. 1997 195p il $17 *
Grades: 4 5 6 7 **Fic**
1. Truthfulness and falsehood—Fiction 2. Fantasy fiction
ISBN 0-15-275457-1   LC 97-9264
Also available in paperback from Pocket Bks.
Charlie, a sixth-grader with a compulsion to tell lies, acquires a mysterious skull that forces its owner to tell only the truth, causing some awkward moments before he understands its power
"Coville has structured the story very carefully, with a great deal of sensitivity to children's thought processes and emotions. The mood shifts from scary to funny to serious are fused with understandable language and sentence structures." SLJ

Coy, John, 1958-
Box out. Scholastic Press 2008 276p $16.99 *
Grades: 6 7 8 9 10 **Fic**
1. Basketball—Fiction 2. Prayer—Fiction 3. School stories
ISBN 978-0-439-87032-0; 0-439-87032-1
                              LC 2007-45354

High school sophomore Liam jeopardizes his new position on the varsity basketball team when he decides to take a stand against his coach who is leading prayers before games and enforcing teamwide participation.
"Plainly acquainted with teenagers and well as b-ball play and lingo, Coy adds subplots and supporting characters to give Liam's life dimension, but he weaves plenty of breathlessly compelling game action too." Booklist

Crackback. Scholastic 2005 201p $16.99
Grades: 7 8 9 10 **Fic**
1. School stories 2. Football—Fiction 3. Drug abuse—Fiction 4. Father-son relationship—Fiction
ISBN 0-439-69733-6   LC 2004-30972
Miles barely recalls when football was fun after being sidelined by a new coach, constantly criticized by his father, and pressured by his best friend to take performance-enhancing drugs.
The author "writes a moving, nuanced portrait of a teen struggling with adults who demand, but don't always deserve, respect." Booklist

Crabtree, Julie
Discovering pig magic. Milkweed Editions 2008 184p $16.95; pa $6.95
Grades: 5 6 7 8 **Fic**
1. Friendship—Fiction 2. Magic—Fiction 3. School stories
ISBN   978-1-57131-683-7;   1-57131-683-3;
978-1-57131-684-4 (pa); 1-57131-684-1 (pa)
                              LC 2008-00625
After three sixth-grade best friends perform a "magic" ritual, they experience what they think are unintended consequences of their wishes and they must all find ways to deal with their lives—with or without magic.
"Crabtree's portrayals both of the charm and power of friendship and of the internal emotional life of a young teen are deft and complex, and her confident pacing never drags." Kirkus

Craig, Colleen
Afrika. Tundra Books 2008 233p pa $9.95 *
Grades: 7 8 9 10 **Fic**
1. South Africa. Commission for Truth and Reconciliation—Fiction 2. Fathers—Fiction 3. Mothers—Fiction 4. South Africa—Fiction
ISBN 978-0-88776-807-1; 0-88776-807-5
"Growing up in Canada with her white South African mother, Kim van der Merwe does not know who her father is. Now, at 13, she goes to Cape Town for the first time, shortly after independence in the mid-1990s, because her mother, a journalist, is going to report on the Truth and Reconciliation Commission. . . . Visiting and meeting her family for the first time, she decides that her mission will be to discover her father's identity. . . . . The realities of the society are carefully and skillfully portrayed, so that Kim's story is truly the emotional heart of the book, and not a vehicle for ideas." SLJ

Crane, E. M.
Skin deep; [by] E. M. Crane. Delacorte Press 2008 273p $16.99; lib bdg $19.99
Grades: 7 8 9 10 11 12 **Fic**

Crane, E. M.—*Continued*

1. Death—Fiction 2. Friendship—Fiction 3. Dogs—Fiction

ISBN 978-0-385-73479-0; 0-385-73479-4; 978-0-385-90477-3 (lib bdg); 0-385-90477-0 (lib bdg)

When sixteen-year-old Andrea Anderson begins caring for a sick neighbor's dog, she learns a lot about life, death, pottery, friendship, hope, and love.

"Teenage girls who can empathize with Andrea's journey of self-discovery and its triumphs and losses will find a well-written story, with lyrical explorations of nature, and memorable characters." Voice Youth Advocates

Crawford, Brent

Carter finally gets it. Disney Hyperion Books 2009 300p $15.99 *

Grades: 7 8 9 10   Fic

1. School stories

ISBN 978-1-4231-1246-4; 1-4231-1246-6

LC 2008-46541

Awkward freshman Will Carter endures many painful moments during his first year of high school before realizing that nothing good comes easily, focus is everything, and the payoff is usually incredible.

"Crawford expertly channels his inner 14-year-old for this pitch-perfect comedy. . . . His stream-consciousness, first-person narrative flails around in an excellent imitation of a freshman." Booklist

Creech, Sharon

Absolutely normal chaos. HarperCollins Pubs. 1995 c1990 230p $16.99; lib bdg $16.89; pa $5.99

Grades: 5 6 7 8   Fic

1. Family life—Fiction

ISBN 0-06-026989-8; 0-06-026992-8 (lib bdg); 0-06-440632-6 (pa)   LC 95-22448

First published 1990 in the United Kingdom

"Mary Lou Finney's summer journal describes family life in a high-spirited household in Ohio that includes five children." N Y Times Book Rev

"Those in search of a light, humorous read will find it; those in search of something a little deeper will also be rewarded." SLJ

Bloomability. HarperCollins Pubs. 1998 273p $16.99; pa $5.99

Grades: 5 6 7 8   Fic

1. School stories 2. Switzerland—Fiction

ISBN 0-06-026993-6; 0-06-440823-X (pa)

LC 98-14601

"Joanna Cotler books"

When her aunt and uncle take her from New Mexico to Lugano, Switzerland, to attend an international school, thirteen-year-old Dinnie discovers her world expanding

"As if fresh, smart characters in a picturesque setting weren't engaging enough, Creech also poses an array of knotty questions, both personal and philosophical. . . . A story to stimulate both head and heart." Booklist

The Castle Corona; illuminated by David Diaz. Joanna Cotler Books 2007 320p il $18.99; lib bdg $19.89

Grades: 4 5 6 7   Fic

1. Orphans—Fiction 2. Siblings—Fiction 3. Italy—Fiction 4. Kings and rulers—Fiction

ISBN 978-0-06-084621-3; 0-06-084621-6; 978-0-06-084622-0 (lib bdg); 0-06-084622-4 (lib bdg)

LC 2006-32004

Two orphaned peasant children discover a mysterious pouch, the contents of which lead them to the majestic Castle Corona, where their lives may be transformed forever.

"The engaging, puzzle-like plot will attract readers, as the novel's heady themes, from wisdom to empathy to the fate-changing power of story, prompt them to deeper thought. Diaz's full-color chapter-heading artwork and ornamental flourishes lend the novel substantial aesthetic appeal." Booklist

Love that dog. HarperCollins Pubs. 2001 86p $15.99; lib bdg $14.89; pa $5.99

Grades: 4 5 6 7   Fic

1. Poetry—Fiction 2. School stories

ISBN 0-06-029287-3; 0-06-029289-X (lib bdg); 0-06-440959-7 (pa)   LC 00-54233

"Joanna Cotler books"

"Jack's free-verse journal charts his evolution from doubt to delight in poetry. His teacher, Miss Stretchberry, introduces him to poetry, serves as an advocate for his writing, and flatters him into believing he's a poet." Horn Book

"Creech has created a poignant, funny picture of a child's encounter with the power of poetry. . . . This book is a tiny treasure." SLJ

Another title about Jack is:

Hate that cat (2008)

Replay; a new book. Joanna Cotler Books 2005 180; 31p $15.99; lib bdg $16.89

Grades: 5 6 7 8   Fic

1. Family life—Fiction 2. Theater—Fiction 3. Italian Americans—Fiction

ISBN 0-06-054019-2; 0-06-054020-6 (lib bdg)

While preparing for a role in the school play, twelve-year-old Leo finds an autobiography that his father wrote as a teenager and ponders the ways people change as they grow up. Includes the text for the play, "Rumpopo's Porch."

"Both uproarious and tender, this story . . . captures [Leo's] big, noisy, extended Italian family with pitch-perfect dialogue that will sweep readers right to the end of the story." Booklist

Walk two moons. HarperCollins Pubs. 1994 280p $16.99; lib bdg $17.89; pa $6.99 *

Grades: 6 7 8 9   Fic

1. Death—Fiction 2. Grandparents—Fiction 3. Family life—Fiction 4. Friendship—Fiction

ISBN 0-06-023334-6; 0-06-023337-0 (lib bdg); 0-06-440517-6 (pa)   LC 93-31277

Awarded the Newbery Medal, 1995

After her mother leaves home suddenly, thirteen-year-old Sal and her grandparents take a car trip retracing her mother's route. Along the way, Sal recounts the story of

Creech, Sharon—*Continued*
her friend Phoebe, whose mother also left
"An engaging story of love and loss, told with humor
and suspense. . . . A richly layered novel about real and
metaphorical journeys." SLJ

The Wanderer; drawings by David Diaz.
HarperCollins Pubs. 2000 305p il $16.99; lib bdg
$17.89; pa $6.99
Grades: 5 6 7 8   **Fic**
1. Sailing—Fiction 2. Family life—Fiction 3. Sea sto-
ries
ISBN 0-06-027730-0; 0-06-027731-9 (lib bdg);
0-06-076673-5 (pa)   LC 99-42699
A Newbery Medal honor book, 2001
"Joanna Cotler books"
Thirteen-year-old Sophie and her cousin Cody record
their transatlantic crossing aboard the Wanderer, a forty-
five foot sailboat, which, along with uncles and another
cousin, is en route to visit their grandfather in England
"The story is exciting, funny, and brimming with life.
. . . This is a beautifully written and imaginatively con-
structed novel." SLJ

Crichton, Michael, 1942-2008
Jurassic Park; a novel. Knopf 1990 399p
$28.95; pa $7.99
Grades: 7 8 9 10 11 12 Adult   **Fic**
1. Science fiction 2. Dinosaurs—Fiction 3. Genetic en-
gineering—Fiction
ISBN 0-394-58816-9; 0-345-37077-5 (pa)
                                            LC 90-52960
This novel "tells of a modern-day scientist bringing to
life a horde of prehistoric animals." N Y Times Book
Rev
"Crichton is a master at blending technology with fic-
tion. . . . Suspense, excitement, and good adventure per-
vade this book." SLJ
Followed by The lost world (1995)

Crist-Evans, Craig
Amaryllis. Candlewick Press 2003 184p $15.99;
pa $7.99
Grades: 7 8 9 10   **Fic**
1. Brothers—Fiction 2. Father-son relationship—Fiction 3. Vietnamese Conflict, 1961-1975—Fiction
4. Florida—Fiction
ISBN 0-7636-1863-2; 0-7636-2990-1 (pa)
                                         LC 2002-34997
Jimmy and his older brother Frank share a love of
surfing and their problems with a drunken father, until
Frank turns eighteen and goes to Vietnam
"Crist-Evans has written an interesting, although somber, account of a troubled family in emotional turmoil.
Both teens are believable and likable characters with
whom many young adults will identify. . . . This is a
crisply written and a worthwhile addition to fiction collections." SLJ

Crocker, Nancy
Billie Standish was here. Simon & Schuster
Books for Young Readers 2007 281p $16.99 *
Grades: 6 7 8 9   **Fic**
1. Friendship—Fiction 2. Rape—Fiction 3. Child
abuse—Fiction 4. Missouri—Fiction
ISBN 978-1-4169-2423-4; 1-4169-2423-X
                                         LC 2006-32688
When the river jeopardizes the levee and most of the
town leaves, Miss Lydia, an elderly neighbor, and Billie
form a friendship that withstands tragedy and time.
"This story is beautiful, painful, and complex, and the
descriptions of people, events, and emotions are graphic
and tangible. The rape scene is described but not
sensationalized." SLJ

Cross, Gillian, 1945-
The dark ground. Dutton Children's Books 2004
264p (The dark ground trilogy) $15.99
Grades: 6 7 8 9   **Fic**
1. Science fiction
ISBN 0-525-47350-5
"Robert wakes up naked and alone in a thick jungle.
The last thing he remembers is being in a plane with his
family, but there is no sign of a crash or survivors. . . .
He is in the park near his house, but his familiar world
has been transformed into an alien landscape. When he
finds others in the same position, he enlists their help in
getting back home." Publisher's note
"This is a fast-moving, suspenseful science-fiction ad-
venture. The ending is surprising and satisfying." SLJ
Other titles in this series are:
The black room (2006)
The nightmare game (2007)

Crossley-Holland, Kevin
Crossing to Paradise. Arthur A. Levine Books
2008 c2006 339p $17.99
Grades: 7 8 9 10   **Fic**
1. Arthur, King—Fiction 2. Pilgrims and pilgrim-
ages—Fiction 3. Christian life—Fiction 4. Literacy—
Fiction 5. Singing—Fiction 6. Middle Ages—Fiction
7. Great Britain—History—1154-1399, Plantagenets—
Fiction
ISBN   978-0-545-05866-7;   0-545-05866-X;
978-0-545-05868-1 (pa); 0-545-05868-6 (pa)
                                         LC 2007-51853
First published 2006 in the United Kingdom with title:
Gatty's tale
When fifteen-year-old Gatty, an illiterate field-girl
who sings beautifully, is selected for a pilgrimage, she
travels from her home on an English estate to London,
Venice, and eventually Jerusalem, and experiences great
changes in her circumstances and in herself.
"Gatty, the irrepressible peasant girl first introduced in
Crossley-Holland's 'Arthur' trilogy . . . comes into her
own in this sweeping, vibrant story." SLJ

Crossley-Holland, Kevin—*Continued*

The seeing stone; Arthur trilogy book one.
Levine Bks. 2001 c2000 342p $17.95; pa $6.99

Grades: 7 8 9 10   **Fic**
1. Arthur, King—Fiction 2. Magic—Fiction
3. Middle Ages—Fiction 4. Great Britain—History—
1154-1399, Plantagenets—Fiction
ISBN 0-439-26326-3; 0-439-43524-2 (pa)

LC 00-61883

First published 2000 in the United Kingdom

In late twelfth-century England, a thirteen-year-old
boy named Arthur recounts how Merlin gives him a
magical seeing stone which shows him images of the
legendary King Arthur, the events of whose life seem to
have many parallels to his own

"The novel unfolds in short, lucid chapters, vividly describing events, personalities, and life on a medieval
manor." Booklist

Other titles in the Arthur trilogy are:
At the crossing-places [book two] (2002)
King of the Middle March [book three] (2004)

Crowe, Chris

Mississippi trial, 1955. Penguin Putnam 2002
231p $17.99; pa $5.99

Grades: 7 8 9 10   **Fic**
1. Till, Emmett—Fiction 2. Grandfathers—Fiction
ISBN 0-8037-2745-3; 0-14-250192-1 (pa)

LC 2001-40221

"Phyllis Fogelman books"

In Mississippi in 1955, a sixteen-year-old finds himself at odds with his grandfather over issues surrounding
the kidnapping and murder of a fourteen-year-old African
American from Chicago named Emmett Till

"By combining real events with their impact upon a
single fictional character, Crowe makes the issues in this
novel hard-hitting and personal. The characters are complex." Voice Youth Advocates

Crowley, Suzanne, 1963-

The very ordered existence of Merilee
Marvelous. Greenwillow 2007 380p $16.99; lib
bdg $17.89

Grades: 5 6 7 8   **Fic**
1. Asperger's syndrome—Fiction 2. Family life—Fiction 3. Texas—Fiction
ISBN 0-06-123197-5; 0-06-123198-3 (lib bdg)

LC 2006-50983

In the small town of Jumbo, Texas, thirteen-year-old
Merilee, who has Asperger's Syndrome, tries to live a
"Very Ordered Existence," but disruptions begin when a
boy and his father arrive in town and the youngster
makes himself a part of the family.

This is "a beautifully crafted story that will give children much to talk about." Booklist

Crutcher, Chris, 1946-

Deadline. Greenwillow Books 2007 316p
$16.99; lib bdg $17.89 *

Grades: 8 9 10 11 12   **Fic**
1. Terminally ill—Fiction 2. Death—Fiction
3. School stories
ISBN 978-0-06-085089-0; 0-06-085089-2;
978-0-06-085090-6 (lib bdg); 0-06-085090-6 (lib bdg)

LC 2006-31526

Given the medical diagnosis of one year to live, high
school senior Ben Wolf decides to fulfill his greatest fantasies, ponders his life's purpose and legacy, and con-
verses through dreams with a spiritual guide known as
"Hey-Soos."

"Ben's sensitive voice uses self-deprecating humor,
philosophical pondering, and effective dramatic irony."
Voice Youth Advocates

Ironman; a novel. Greenwillow Bks. 1995 181p
$16.99; pa $6.99

Grades: 8 9 10 11 12   **Fic**
1. Father-son relationship—Fiction 2. School stories
3. Triathlon—Fiction
ISBN 0-688-13503-X; 0-06-059840-9 (pa)

LC 94-1657

While training for a triathlon, seventeen-year-old Bo
attends Mr. Nak's anger management group at school
which leads him to examine his relationship with his father.

"Through Crutcher's masterful character development,
readers will believe in Bo, empathize with the other
members of the anger-management group, absorb the
wisdom of Mr. Nak and despise, yet at times pity, the
boy's father. This is not a light read, as many serious issues surface, though the author's trademark dark humor
(and colorful use of street language) is abundant." SLJ

Staying fat for Sarah Byrnes. Greenwillow Bks.
1993 216p $17.99; pa $6.99

Grades: 7 8 9 10   **Fic**
1. Obesity—Fiction 2. Child abuse—Fiction
3. Friendship—Fiction 4. Swimming—Fiction
ISBN 0-688-11552-7; 0-06-009489-3 (pa)

LC 91-40097

"An obese boy and a disfigured girl suffer the emotional scars of years of mockery at the hands of their
peers. They share a hard-boiled view of the world until
events in their senior year hurl them in very different directions. A story about a friendship with staying power,
written with pathos and pointed humor." SLJ

Stotan! HarperTempest 2003 c1986 261p pa
$6.99

Grades: 7 8 9 10   **Fic**
1. Swimming—Fiction
ISBN 0-06-009492-3   LC 85-12712

"A Greenwillow book"

First published 1986

A high school coach invites members of his swimming team to a memorable week of rigorous training that
tests their moral fiber as well as their physical stamina.

"A subplot involving the boys' fight against local
Neo-Nazi activists provides some immediate action,
while the various characters' conflicts tighten the middle
and ending. The pace lags through the story's introduc-

Crutcher, Chris, 1946-—*Continued*
tion; nevertheless, this is a searching sports novel, with a tone varying from macho-tough to sensitive." Bull Cent Child Books

Whale talk. Greenwillow Bks. 2001 220p $15.99; lib bdg $16.89; pa $5.99
Grades: 7 8 9 10   **Fic**
1. Swimming—Fiction 2. School stories 3. Racially mixed people—Fiction
ISBN 0-688-18019-1; 0-06-029369-1 (lib bdg); 0-440-22938-3 (pa)   LC 00-59292
Intellectually and athletically gifted, TJ, a multiracial, adopted teenager, shuns organized sports and the gung-ho athletes at his high school until he agrees to form a swimming team and recruits some of the school's less popular students
"This remarkable novel is vintage Crutcher: heart-pounding athletic competitions, raw emotion, an insufferable high school atmosphere that allows bullying and reveres athletes, and a larger-than-life teen hero who champions the underdog while skewering both racists and abusers with his rapier-sharp wit." Book Rep

Cullen, Lynn
I am Rembrandt's daughter. Bloomsbury Children's Books 2007 307p $16.95 *
Grades: 7 8 9 10   **Fic**
1. Rembrandt Harmenszoon van Rijn, 1606-1669—Fiction 2. Father-daughter relationship—Fiction 3. Artists—Fiction 4. Plague—Fiction 5. Poverty—Fiction 6. Netherlands—Fiction
ISBN 978-1-59990-046-9; 1-59990-046-7
                                    LC 2006-28197
In Amsterdam in the mid-1600s, Cornelia's life as the illegitimate child of renowned painter Rembrandt is marked by plague, poverty, and despair at ever earning her father's love, until she sees hope for a better future in the eyes of a weathy suitor.
"Historical fiction, mystery, and romance are masterfully woven. . . . Cullen's novel is a reader's delight." Voice Youth Advocates

Cumbie, Patricia
Where people like us live. Laura Geringer Books/HarperTeen 2008 210p $16.99; lib bdg $17.89
Grades: 7 8 9 10 11 12   **Fic**
1. Friendship—Fiction 2. Stepfamilies—Fiction 3. Moving—Fiction 4. Child sexual abuse—Fiction 5. Wisconsin—Fiction
ISBN   978-0-06-137597-2;   0-06-137597-7; 978-0-06-137598-9 (lib bdg); 0-06-137598-5 (lib bdg)
                                    LC 2007-18675
In 1978, when her restless father moves the family to Racine, Wisconsin, fourteen-year-old Libby quickly becomes friends with neighbor Angie, but there is something strange about Angie's stepfather and when Libby learns the truth, she must make a very difficult choice.
Cumbie's "characters have a dignity and innate courage that readers will not soon forget." Booklist

Cummings, John Michael, 1963-
The night I freed John Brown; [by] John Michael Cummings. Philomel Books 2008 251p $17.99
Grades: 6 7 8 9   **Fic**
1. Father-son relationship—Fiction 2. West Virginia—Fiction
ISBN 978-0-399-25054-5; 0-399-25054-9
                                    LC 2007-23648
In Harpers Ferry, West Virginia, twelve-year-old Josh uncovers family secrets involving his overly strict father, whose anger threatens to tear the family apart.
"This is a compelling and intriguing tale that is timeless." Libr Media Connect

Cummings, Priscilla, 1951-
Red kayak; Priscilla Cummings. 1st ed. Dutton Children's Books 2004 209p $15.99; pa $6.99
Grades: 7 8 9 10   **Fic**
1.   Friendship—Fiction   2.   Death—Fiction 3. Maryland—Fiction
ISBN 0-525-47317-3; 0-14-240573-4 (pa)
                                    LC 2003-63532
Living near the water on Maryland's Eastern Shore, thirteen-year-old Brady and his best friends J.T. and Digger become entangled in a tragedy which tests their friendship and their ideas about right and wrong.
"This well-crafted story will have broad appeal." SLJ

Currier, Katrina Saltonstall, 1969-
Kai's journey to Gold Mountain; an Angel Island story; illustrated by Gabhor Utomo. Angel Island Association 2005 39p il $16.95
Grades: 4 5 6 7   **Fic**
1. Chinese Americans—Fiction 2. Immigrants—Fiction 3. Los Angeles (Calif.)—Fiction
ISBN 0-9667352-4-2   LC 2004-14821
In 1934, twelve-year-old Kai leaves China to join his father in America, but first he must take a long sea voyage, then endure weeks of crowded conditions and harsh examinations on Angel Island, fearing that he or his new friend will be sent home.
"The character Kai is based on a real person, whose photos, then and now, are part of the historical notes at the back of the book. Opposite each page of the intensely moving, detailed text are beautiful full-page watercol-or-and-pencil illustrations that capture the crowded holding place, and, in unforgettable closeups, the characters' heartbreak and strength." Booklist

Curry, Jane Louise, 1932-
The Black Canary. Margaret K. McElderry Books 2005 279p $16.95
Grades: 5 6 7 8   **Fic**
1. Essex, Robert Devereux, 2nd Earl of, 1566-1601—Fiction 2. Racially mixed people—Fiction 3. Singers—Fiction 4. London (England)—Fiction 5. Great Britain—History—1485-1603, Tudors—Fiction
ISBN 0-689-86478-7   LC 2003-26150
As the child of two musicians, twelve-year-old James has no interest in music until he discovers a portal to

Curry, Jane Louise, 1932-—*Continued*

seventeenth-century London in his uncle's basement, and finds himself in a situation where his beautiful voice and the fact that he is biracial might serve him well.

"A genuinely good story that conveys a sense of darkness and mystery in the textured backdrop of a storied time and place." Booklist

Curtis, Christopher Paul

Bud, not Buddy. Delacorte Press 1999 245p $16.95; pa $6.50 *

Grades: 4 5 6 7   Fic

1. Orphans—Fiction 2. African Americans—Fiction 3. Great Depression, 1929-1939—Fiction

ISBN 0-385-32306-9; 0-440-41328-1 (pa)

LC 99-10614

Newbery Medal

Ten-year-old Bud, a motherless boy living in Flint, Michigan, during the Great Depression, escapes a bad foster home and sets out in search of the man he believes to be his father—the renowned bandleader, H. E. Calloway of Grand Rapids

"Curtis says in a afterword that some of the characters are based on real people, including his own grandfathers, so it's not surprising that the rich blend of tall tale, slapstick, sorrow, and sweetness has the wry, teasing warmth of family folklore." Booklist

Elijah of Buxton. Scholastic 2007 341p $16.99 *

Grades: 5 6 7 8   Fic

1. Slavery—Fiction 2. Canada—Fiction

ISBN 0-439-02344-0; 978-0-439-02344-3

LC 2007-05181

A Newbery Medal honor book, 2008

In 1859, eleven-year-old Elijah Freeman, the first freeborn child in Buxton, Canada, which is a haven for slaves fleeing the American south, uses his wits and skills to try to bring to justice the lying preacher who has stolen money that was to be used to buy a family's freedom.

"Many readers drawn to the book by humor will find themselves at times on the edges of their seats in suspense and, at other moments, moved to tears." Booklist

The Watsons go to Birmingham—1963; a novel. Delacorte Press 1995 210p $16.95; pa $6.50 *

Grades: 4 5 6 7   Fic

1. African Americans—Fiction 2. Family life—Fiction 3. Prejudices—Fiction

ISBN 0-385-32175-9; 0-440-41412-1 (pa)

LC 95-7091

A Newbery Medal honor book, 1996

The ordinary interactions and everyday routines of the Watsons, an African American family living in Flint, Michigan, are drastically changed after they go to visit Grandma in Alabama in the summer of 1963

"Curtis's ability to switch from fun and funky to pinpoint-accurate psychological imagery works unusually well. . . . Ribald humor, sly sibling digs, and a totally believable child's view of the world will make this book an instant hit." SLJ

Cushman, Karen, 1941-

Catherine, called Birdy. Clarion Bks. 1994 169p $16 *

Grades: 6 7 8 9   Fic

1. Middle Ages—Fiction 2. Great Britain—Fiction

ISBN 0-395-68186-3   LC 93-23333

Also available in paperback from HarperCollins

A Newbery Medal honor book, 1995

The fourteen-year-old daughter of an English country knight keeps a journal in which she records the events of her life, particularly her longing for adventures beyond the usual role of women and her efforts to avoid being married off

"In the process of telling the routines of her young life, Birdy lays before readers a feast of details about medieval England. . . . Superb historical fiction." SLJ

The loud silence of Francine Green. Clarion Books 2006 225p $16

Grades: 6 7 8 9   Fic

1. School stories 2. Family life—Fiction 3. United States—Politics and government—1945-1953—Fiction 4. Los Angeles (Calif.)—Fiction

ISBN 978-0-618-50455-8; 0-618-50455-9

LC 2005-29774

In 1949, thirteen-year-old Francine goes to Catholic school in Los Angeles where she becomes best friends with a girl who questions authority and is frequently punished by the nuns, causing Francine to question her own values.

Readers will "savor the story of friends and family tensions, the sly humor, and the questions about patriotism, activism, and freedom." Booklist

The midwife's apprentice. Clarion Bks. 1995 122p $12; pa $5.99 *

Grades: 6 7 8 9   Fic

1. Middle Ages—Fiction 2. Midwives—Fiction 3. Great Britain—Fiction

ISBN 0-395-69229-6; 0-06-440630-X (pa)

LC 94-13792

Awarded the Newbery Medal, 1996

In medieval England, a nameless, homeless girl is taken in by a sharp-tempered midwife, and in spite of obstacles and hardship, eventually gains the three things she most wants: a full belly, a contented heart, and a place in this world

"Earthy humor, the foibles of humans both high and low, and a fascinating mix of superstition and genuinely helpful herbal remedies attached to childbirth make this a truly delightful introduction to a world seldom seen in children's literature." SLJ

Rodzina. Clarion Bks. 2003 215p $16 *

Grades: 5 6 7 8   Fic

1. Polish Americans—Fiction 2. Orphans—Fiction

ISBN 0-618-13351-8   LC 2002-15976

A twelve-year-old Polish American girl is boarded onto an orphan train in Chicago with fears about traveling to the West and a life of unpaid slavery

"The story features engaging characters, a vivid setting, and a prickly but endearing heroine. . . . Rodzina's musings and observations provide poignancy, humor, and a keen sense of the human and topographical landscape." SLJ

Includes bibliographical references

Cusick, Richie Tankersley, 1952-

Walk of the spirits. Speak 2008 328p pa $8.99

Grades: 7 8 9 10   **Fic**

1. Ghost stories 2. Space and time—Fiction
3. Louisiana—Fiction 4. Mystery fiction

ISBN 978-0-14-241050-9; 0-14-241050-0

LC 2007-36073

"The parallels with Hurricane Katrina are obvious, even though here the setting is an urban Florida community that is ravished, and the escape route is to a sleepy, small town in Louisiana. Add cries in the night, old historic homes with secrets to hide, and a supernatural love story, and you have a surefire reader favorite." Booklist

D'Adamo, Francesco

Iqbal; a novel; written by Francesco D'Adamo; translated by Ann Leonori. Atheneum Bks. for Young Readers 2003 120p $15.95; pa $4.99

Grades: 5 6 7 8   **Fic**

1. Masih, Iqbal, d. 1995—Fiction 2. Child labor—Fiction 3. Pakistan—Fiction

ISBN 0-689-85445-5; 1-4169-0329-1 (pa)

LC 2002-153498

Original Italian edition, 2001

A fictionalized account of the Pakistani child who escaped from bondage in a carpet factory and went on to help liberate other children like him before being gunned down at the age of thirteen

"The situation and setting are made clear in this novel. Readers cannot help but be moved by the plight of these youngsters. . . . This readable book will certainly add breadth to most collections." SLJ

Danziger, Paula, 1944-2004

The cat ate my gymsuit; [by] Paula Danziger. 30th anniversary edition. G.P. Putnam's Sons 2004 c1974 151p $15.99; pa $5.99

Grades: 4 5 6 7   **Fic**

1. School stories 2. Teachers—Fiction

ISBN 0-399-24307-0; 0-14-240654-6 (pa)

LC 2004001892

A reissue of the title first published 1974 by Delacorte Press

When the unconventional English teacher who helped her conquer many of her feelings of insecurity is fired, thirteen-year-old Marcy Lewis uses her new found courage to campaign for the teacher's reinstatement.

"Paula Danziger's compassionate and accurate portrayal of a young girl struggling to find her own voice rings as true today as it did 30 years ago. A full cast brings this modern American classic of teenage angst to life with humor and pathos." SLJ

The Divorce Express. Delacorte Press 1982 148p il pa $5.99 hardcover o.p.

Grades: 6 7 8 9   **Fic**

1. Divorce—Fiction 2. Parent-child relationship—Fiction

ISBN 0-14-240712-7 (pa)   LC 82-70318

The protagonist, fourteen year old Phoebe, shuttles "back and forth between her father's home in Woodstock and her mother's apartment in Manhattan via the bus she calls 'The Divorce Express' because there are so many children like her who ride it. She has not become adjusted to the man her mother is planning to marry, and feels more and more at home in Woodstock, especially when she makes a new friend, Rosie, whose parents . . . are also divorced." Bull Cent Child Books

This is "a warm, tender book for adolescents who must deal with the complexities of growing up." Child Book Rev Serv

P.S. Longer letter later; [by] Paula Danziger & Ann M. Martin. Scholastic 1998 234p $16.95; pa $4.99

Grades: 5 6 7 8   **Fic**

1. Friendship—Fiction 2. Letters—Fiction

ISBN 0-590-21310-5; 0-590-21311-3 (pa)

LC 97-19120

Companion volume to Snail mail no more

Twelve-year-old best friends Elizabeth and Tara-Starr continue their friendship through letter-writing after Tara-Starr's family moves to another state

"The authenticity of the well-drawn characters gives life and vitality to the story. . . . Readers will thoroughly enjoy this fast-paced read." SLJ

Snail mail no more; [by] Paula Danziger & Ann M. Martin. Scholastic Press 2000 307p $16.95; pa $5.99 *

Grades: 5 6 7 8   **Fic**

1. Friendship—Fiction 2. Letters—Fiction

ISBN 0-439-06335-3; 0-439-06336-1 (pa)

LC 99-33593

Companion volume to P.S. Longer letter later

Now that they live in different cities, thirteen-year-old Tara and Elizabeth use e-mail to "talk" about everything that is occurring in their lives and to try to maintain their closeness as they face big changes

"A funny, thought-provoking page-turner that will delight readers and leave them ready for more messages." Booklist

Daswani, Kavita, 1964-

Indie girl. Simon Pulse 2007 232p pa $8.99

Grades: 7 8 9 10   **Fic**

1. East Indian Americans—Fiction 2. Fashion—Fiction 3. Journalists—Fiction

ISBN 1-4169-4892-9

"Fifteen-year-old Indie Konkipuddi has always dreamed of becoming a fashion reporter. She'd do anything to land an internship with glamorous Celebrity Style magazine, even babysit publisher Aaralyn Taylor's two-year-old son." Publisher's note

"What sets this novel apart is Daswani's nuanced take on her character's Indian-American subculture, the pressure she feels to be like her more conventional cousins, her desire for independence, American-style, and her pride in her heritage. Indie is a heroine worth meeting." Publ Wkly

Davies, Jacqueline

Where the ground meets the sky. Marshall Cavendish 2002 224p hardcover o.p. pa $5.95

Grades: 5 6 7 8 **Fic**

1. Manhattan Project—Fiction 2. World War, 1939-1945—Fiction 3. New Mexico—Fiction

ISBN 0-7614-5105-6; 0-7614-5187-0 (pa)

LC 2001-32519

During World War II, a twelve-year-old girl is uprooted from her quiet, East coast life and moved to a secluded army post in the New Mexico desert where her father and other scientists are working on a top secret project

"The story is told in Hazel's lively, if self-conscious voice. . . . Davies skillfully describes the secrecy and intensity of the work and how it affected every aspect of the researchers' and their families' lives." Booklist

Davies, Jacqueline, 1962-

Lost. Marshall Cavendish 2009 242p $16.99

Grades: 7 8 9 10 **Fic**

1. Triangle Shirtwaist Company, Inc. —Fiction 2. Bereavement—Fiction 3. Factories—Fiction 4. New York (N.Y.)—Fiction 5. Sisters—Fiction

ISBN 978-0-7614-5535-6; 0-7614-5535-3

LC 2008-40560

In 1911 New York, sixteen-year-old Essie Rosenfeld must stop taking care of her irrepressible six-year-old sister when she goes to work at the Triangle Waist Company, where she befriends a missing heiress who is in hiding from her family and who seems to understand the feelings of heartache and grief that Essie is trying desperately to escape.

The "unusual pacing adds depth and intrigue as the plot unfolds. There are many layers to this story, which will appeal to a variety of interests and age levels." SLJ

Davis, Deborah

Not like you. Clarion Books 2007 268p $16

Grades: 8 9 10 11 12 **Fic**

1. Mother-daughter relationship—Fiction 2. Alcoholism—Fiction 3. Single parent family—Fiction

ISBN 978-0-618-72093-4; 0-618-72093-6

LC 2006-21867

When she and her mother move once again in order to make a new start, fifteen-year-old Kayla is hopeful that her mother will be able to stop drinking and begin a better life, as she has been promising for years.

"Written in Kayla's believable voice, Davis' moving, gritty novel builds to a hopeful, realistic close." Booklist

Davis, Katie

The curse of Addy McMahon. 1st ed. Greenwillow Books 2008 271p $16.99; lib bdg $17.89

Grades: 4 5 6 **Fic**

1. Authorship—Fiction 2. Cartoons and caricatures—Fiction 3. Bereavement—Fiction 4. Family life—Fiction 5. Friendship—Fiction

ISBN 978-0-06-128711-4; 0-06-128711-3; 978-0-06-128712-1 (lib bdg); 0-06-128712-1 (lib bdg)

LC 2007041154

After her father's death, aspiring sixth-grade writer Addy McMahon feels like she is cursed with bad luck, and when she temporarily loses her best friend, and is forced to admit that her mother is dating again, she vows she will never write another word.

"Peppered with authentic preteen conversations, the novel combines traditional narrative with graphic-novel stories, emails, and IMs. . . . The book is a fast-paced and interesting read." SLJ

Davis, Tanita S.

A la carte. Alfred A. Knopf Books for Young Readers 2008 288p $15.99; lib bdg $18.99

Grades: 7 8 9 10 **Fic**

1. Cooking—Fiction 2. African Americans—Fiction

ISBN 978-0-375-84815-5; 0-375-84815-0; 978-0-375-94815-2 (lib bdg); 0-375-94815-5 (lib bdg)

LC 2007-49656

Lainey, a high school senior and aspiring celebrity chef, is forced to question her priorities after her best friend (and secret crush) runs away from home.

"The relationships and characters in this book are authentic. The actions and dialogue seem true to those represented. Even though it is a quick read, the story is a meaningful one." Voice Youth Advocate

Mare's war. Alfred A. Knopf 2009 341p $16.99; lib bdg $19.99

Grades: 7 8 9 10 **Fic**

1. United States. Army. Women's Army Corps—Fiction. 2. Automobile travel—Fiction 3. Grandmothers—Fiction 4. African Americans—Fiction 5. World War, 1939-1945—Fiction 6. Sisters—Fiction 7. Alabama—Fiction

ISBN 978-0-375-85714-0; 0-375-85714-1; 978-0-375-95714-7 (lib bdg); 0-375-95714-6 (lib bdg)

LC 2008-33744

Teens Octavia and Tali learn about strength, independence, and courage when they are forced to take a car trip with their grandmother, who tells about growing up Black in 1940s Alabama and serving in Europe during World War II as a member of the Women's Army Corps.

"The parallel travel narratives are masterfully managed, with postcards from Octavia and Tali to the folks back home in San Francisco signaling the shift between 'then' and 'now.' Absolutely essential reading." Kirkus

Day, Karen

No cream puffs. 1st ed. Wendy Lamb Books 2008 209p $15.99; lib bdg $18.99

Grades: 6 7 8 9 **Fic**

1. Baseball—Fiction 2. Sex role—Fiction 3. Friendship—Fiction 4. Michigan—Fiction

ISBN 978-0-375-83775-3; 0-375-83775-2; 978-0-375-93775-0 (lib bdg); 0-375-93775-7 (lib bdg)

LC 2007030018

In 1980, when twelve-year-old Madison, who loves to play baseball, decides to play in her town's baseball league, she never envisions the uproar it causes when she becomes the first girl to join.

This is a "perceptive, enjoyable title, packed with exciting baseball." Booklist

De Guzman, Michael
The bamboozlers; [by] Michael de Guzman. 1st ed. Farrar, Straus & Giroux 2005 167p $16
Grades: 5 6 7 8 **Fic**
1. Grandfathers—Fiction 2. Swindlers and swindling—Fiction
ISBN 0-374-30512-9 LC 2004-57670
Nothing exciting ever happens to twelve-year-old Albert Rosegarden until he meets his grandfather for the first time, and the pair travel to Seattle, Washington, where Albert becomes a partner in his grandfather's elaborate scheme to "con a con man."
"Plot progression is steady, well paced, and broken up into short chapters of clear, concise detail. Language and writing style are visual and uncomplicated, with engaging characters that lend an authentic feel to the story." SLJ

Beekman's big deal; [by] Michael de Guzman. 1st ed. Farrar Straus Giroux 2004 213p $16 *
Grades: 5 6 7 8 **Fic**
1. New York (N.Y.)—Fiction 2. Moving—Fiction
ISBN 0-374-30672-9 LC 2003-60773
Tired of the frequent moves that he and his father must make, twelve-year-old Beekman begins to make connections with neighbors and classmates after settling in a small, unusual New York City neighborhood
"Featuring interesting, well-developed characters and sprinkled with gentle humor, this novel strikes a pleasing balance between heart-wrenching and heartwarming moments." SLJ

Finding Stinko. Farrar, Straus and Giroux 2007 136p $16 *
Grades: 5 6 7 8 **Fic**
1. Foster home care—Fiction 2. Ventriloquism—Fiction 3. Dolls—Fiction 4. Runaway children—Fiction
ISBN 0-374-32305-4; 978-0-374-32305-9
LC 2006-40859
Having spent his life trying to escape the foster care system, eventually becoming mute to keep out of trouble, twelve-year-old Newboy finally hits the streets, where a discarded ventriloquist's dummy gives him back his voice and his hope.
This is a "gritty, engagingly offbeat page-turner. . . . Readers will be riveted." Booklist

De la Cruz, Melissa, 1971-
Fresh off the boat. HarperCollins Publishers 2005 243p hardcover o.p. lib bdg $16.89; pa $7.99
Grades: 7 8 9 10 **Fic**
1. Filipino Americans—Fiction 2. Immigrants—Fiction 3. School stories
ISBN 0-06-054540-2; 0-06-054541-0 (lib bdg); 0-06-054542-9 (pa) LC 2004-15513
When her family emigrates from the Philippines to San Francisco, California, fourteen-year-old Vicenza Arambullo struggles to fit in at her exclusive, all-girl private school.
"This well-written, heartfelt novel is a worthy addition to most YA collections, but especially where there are strong immigrant populations." SLJ

De la Peña, Matt
Mexican whiteboy. Delacorte Press 2008 249p $15.99; lib bdg $18.99
Grades: 8 9 10 11 12 **Fic**
1. Mexican Americans—Fiction 2. Racially mixed people—Fiction 3. Cousins—Fiction 4. California—Fiction
ISBN 978-0-385-73310-6; 0-385-73310-0; 978-0-385-90329-5 (lib bdg); 0-385-90329-4 (lib bdg) LC 2007-32302
Sixteen-year-old Danny searches for his identity amidst the confusion of being half-Mexican and half-white while spending a summer with his cousin and new friends on the baseball fields and back alleys of San Diego County, California.
"The author juggles his many plotlines well, and the portrayal of Danny's friends and neighborhood is rich and lively." Booklist

De Lint, Charles, 1951-
The blue girl; Charles de Lint. Viking 2004 368p $17.99; pa $7.99
Grades: 7 8 9 10 **Fic**
1. Fairies—Fiction 2. Ghost stories 3. School stories
ISBN 0-670-05924-2; 0-14-240545-0 (pa)
LC 2004-19051
New at her high school, Imogene enlists the help of her introverted friend Maxine and the ghost of a boy who haunts the school after receiving warnings through her dreams that soul-eaters are threatening her life
"The book combines the turmoil of high school intertwined with rich, detailed imagery drawn from traditional folklore and complex characters with realistic relationships. . . . This book is not just another ghost story, but a novel infused with the true sense of wonder and magic that is De Lint at his best. It is strongly recommended." Voice Youth Advocates

De Mari, Silvana, 1953-
The last dragon; translated from the Italian by Shaun Whiteside. Miramax Books/Hyperion Books for Children 2006 361p $16.95
Grades: 5 6 7 8 **Fic**
1. Dragons—Fiction 2. Fantasy fiction
ISBN 0-7868-3636-9
"In a post-apocalyptic world . . . a young elf named Yorsh struggles to survive. When his village is destroyed by the torrential waters, Yorsh finds himself suddenly orphaned and alone-the earth's last elf. But soon Yorsh discovers he is part of a powerful prophecy: when the last dragon and the last elf break the circle, the past and the future will meet, and the sun of a new summer will shine in the sky." Publisher's note
"With its combination of humor and deeply felt emotion, *The Last Dragon* . . . will leave readers enthralled." Horn Book

Dee, Barbara
Just another day in my insanely real life; a novel. Margaret K. McElderry Books 2006 252p $15.95
Grades: 5 6 7 8 **Fic**

Dee, Barbara—_Continued_

1. Single parent family—Fiction 2. Authorship—Fiction
ISBN 978-1-4169-0861-6; 1-4169-0861-7

With her father "out of the picture" and her mother working long hours, twelve-year-old Cassie unconsciously describes her anger and confusion in a fantasy novel she is writing for school.

"It's the drama and seething anger in Cassie's first-person narrative that's so compelling." Booklist

Solving Zoe. Margaret K. McElderry Books 2009 230p $15.99

Grades: 4 5 6 7   **Fic**

1. School stories 2. Cryptography—Fiction 3. Family life—Fiction 4. Gifted children—Fiction 5. Brooklyn (New York, N.Y.)—Fiction
ISBN 978-1-4169-6128-4; 1-4169-6128-3
LC 2008-06217

Zoe's sixth-grade year at a Brooklyn school for gifted students is marked by changing relationships with her fellow students and teachers, recognition of her talent for cryptography, and a greater awareness of her passion.

"The novel realistically portrays Zoe's general unhappiness and her pain at losing a close friend while it shows her finding a way out of the emotional tangle. . . . This vivid middle-school novel offers readers plenty to think about." Booklist

Defoe, Daniel, 1661?-1731

Robinson Crusoe; edited with an introduction by Thomas Keymer and notes by Thomas Keymer and James Kelly. Oxford University Press 2007 368p (Oxford world's classics) pa $7.95

Grades: 8 9 10 11 12 Adult   **Fic**

1. Survival after airplane accidents, shipwrecks, etc.—Fiction
ISBN 0-19-283342-1; 978-0-19-283342-6
LC 2006-26022

Also available from other publishers
First published 1719

"A minutely circumstantial account of the hero's shipwreck and escape to an uninhabited island, and the methodical industry whereby he makes himself a comfortable home. The story is founded on the actual experiences of Alexander Selkirk, who spent four years on the island of Juan Fernandez in the early 18th century." Lenrow. Reader's Guide to Prose Fic

DeKeyser, Stacy, 1959-

Jump the cracks. Flux 2008 216p pa $9.95

Grades: 6 7 8 9 10   **Fic**

1. Abandoned children—Fiction
ISBN 978-0-7387-1274-1 (pa); 0-7387-1274-4 (pa)
LC 2007-42333

On the way to visit her father in New York City, fifteen-year-old Victoria finds an apparently abused child in the train's bathroom and soon finds herself branded a kidnapper and on the run while trying to fulfill her promise to protect the boy at all costs.

"With a combination of lively adventure and humane treatment of its characters, this is an absorbing and emotionally effective read." Bull Cent Child Books

Dekker, James C.

Scum. Orca 2008 95p $16.95; pa $9.95

Grades: 7 8 9 10   **Fic**

1. Siblings—Fiction 2. Drug abuse—Fiction 3. Violence—Fiction
ISBN 978-1-55143-926-6; 978-1-55143-924-2 (pa)
LC 2008-928741

After her brother Danny is killed in a bar in an apparent robbery and the police are not motivated to solve the case, Megan's attempts to discover the truth are complicated by people who will kill to keep it hidden.

"The book's willingness to forego hackneyed messages is refreshing and there's considerable realism. . . . The fast pace, big pring, and compact . . . size make the title accessible to reluctant readers and a quick but satisfying drama." Bull Cent Child Books

Delaney, Joseph, 1904-1991

Revenge of the witch; illustrations by Patrick Arrasmith. Greenwillow Bks. 2005 344p il (The last apprentice) $14.99; lib bdg $15.89 *

Grades: 5 6 7 8   **Fic**

1. Supernatural—Fiction 2. Witches—Fiction
ISBN 0-06-076618-2; 0-06-076619-0 (lib bdg)
LC 2004-54003

Young Tom, the seventh son of a seventh son, starts work as an apprentice for the village spook, whose job is to protect ordinary folk from "ghouls, boggarts, and all manner of wicked beasties."

"Delaney grabs readers by the throat and gives them a good shake in a smartly crafted story. . . . This is a gristly thriller. . . . Yet the twisted horror is amply buffered by an exquisitely normal young hero, matter-of-fact prose, and a workaday normalcy." Booklist

Other titles in this series are:
Curse of the bane (2006)
Night of the soul-stealer (2007)
Attack of the fiend (2008)

Deming, Sarah

Iris, messenger. Harcourt 2007 209p $16

Grades: 5 6 7 8   **Fic**

1. Classical mythology—Fiction 2. Pennsylvania—Fiction
ISBN 978-0-15-205823-4; 0-15-205823-0
LC 2006-22943

After discovering that the immortals of Greek mythology reside in her hometown of Middleville, Pennsylvania, twelve-year-old Iris listens to their life stories, gaining wisdom, beauty, and startling revelations about her past.

"This engaging story of an unhappy girl whose dreaming pays off in wonderful ways will be a hit with adolescents dealing with those difficult middle school years." SLJ

Denman, K. L., 1957-

Rebel's tag; [by] K. L. Denman. Orca Book Pub. 2007 104p pa $8.95

Grades: 6 7 8 9   **Fic**

Denman, K. L., 1957-—*Continued*
1. Grandfathers—Fiction 2. Family life—Fiction
ISBN 978-1-55143-740-8 (pa); 1-55143-740-6 (pa)
"When fourteen-year-old Sam hears from the grandfather who abandoned the family after Sam's father died, Sam wants nothing to do with him. All he cares about is illicitly climbing roofs at night; he has always felt free on rooftops. After meeting some of his grandfather's friends, though, and then being forgiven by an elderly couple whose roof he tagged, Sam begins to change. . . . The book addresses weighty concepts succinctly, comprehensibly, and without pretense, and those looking for a hi-lo story with more depth will find it here." Voice Youth Advocates

Deriso, Christine Hurley, 1961-
Talia Talk. Delacorte Press 2009 184p $15.99; lib bdg $18.99
Grades: 4 5 6 7   **Fic**
1. Mother-daughter relationship—Fiction 2. Friendship—Fiction 3. School stories 4. Television programs—Fiction
ISBN 978-0-385-73620-6; 0-385-73620-7; 978-0-385-90592-3 (lib bdg); 0-385-90592-0 (lib bdg)
LC 2007-50556
Trying to fit in despite having a loud, embarrassing best friend, eleven-year-old Talia becomes a commentator on her middle school's closed-circuit television program and turns the tables on her mother, a talk show host who has been revealing Talia's most humiliating experiences for years.
This is "breezy, readable, and full of gentle insight." Bull Cent Child Books

Dessen, Sarah, 1970-
Along for the ride; a novel. Viking 2009 383p $19.99 *
Grades: 7 8 9 10   **Fic**
1. Stepfamilies—Fiction 2. Infants—Fiction 3. Dating (Social customs)—Fiction 4. Divorce—Fiction
ISBN 978-0-670-01194-0; 0-670-01194-0
LC 2009-5661
When Auden impulsively goes to stay with her father, stepmother, and new baby sister the summer before she starts college, all the trauma of her parents' divorce is revived, even as she is making new friends and having new experiences such as learning to ride a bike and dating.
"Dessen explores the dynamics of an extended family headed by two opposing, flawed personalities, revealing their parental failures with wicked precision yet still managing to create real, even sympathetic characters. . . . [This book] provides the interpersonal intricacies fans expect from a Dessen plot." Horn Book

That summer. Orchard Books 1996 198p hardcover o.p. pa $8.99
Grades: 7 8 9 10   **Fic**
1. Sisters—Fiction 2. Weddings—Fiction
ISBN 0-531-09538-X; 0-531-08888-X (lib bdg); 978-0-14-240172-9 (pa); 0-14-240172-2 (pa)
LC 96-7643
During the summer of her divorced father's remarriage and her sister's wedding, fifteen-year-old Haven comes

into her own by letting go of the myths of the past
"Dessen adds a fresh twist to a traditional sister-of-the-bride story with her keenly observant narrative full of witty ironies. Her combination of unforgettable characters and unexpected events generates hilarity as well as warmth." Publ Wkly

The truth about forever. Viking 2004 382p $16.99; pa $6.50
Grades: 7 8 9 10   **Fic**
1. Death—Fiction 2. Catering—Fiction
ISBN 0-670-03639-0; 0-440-21928-0 (pa)
LC 2003-28298
The summer following her father's death, Macy plans to work at the library and wait for her brainy boyfriend to return from camp, but instead she goes to work at a catering business where she makes new friends and finally faces her grief.
"All of Dessen's characters . . . are fully and beautifully drawn. Their dialogue is natural and believable, and their care for one another is palpable. . . . Dessen charts Macy's navigation of grief in such an honest way it will touch every reader who meets her. " SLJ

Deuker, Carl, 1950-
Gym candy. Houghton Mifflin Company 2007 313p $16 *
Grades: 7 8 9 10 11 12   **Fic**
1. Football—Fiction 2. Father-son relationship—Fiction 3. School stories 4. Steroids—Fiction 5. Washington (State)—Fiction
ISBN 978-0-618-77713-6; 0-618-77713-X
LC 2007-12749
Groomed by his father to be a star player, football is the only thing that has ever really mattered to Mick Johnson, who works hard for a spot on the varsity team his freshman year, then tries to hold onto his edge by using steroids, despite the consequences to his health and social life.
"Deuker skillfully complements a sobering message with plenty of exciting on-field action and locker-room drama, while depicting Mick's emotional struggles with loneliness and insecurity as sensitively and realistically as his physical ones." Booklist

High heat. Houghton Mifflin 2003 277p $16; pa $6.99
Grades: 7 8 9 10   **Fic**
1. Fathers—Fiction 2. School stories
ISBN 0-618-31117-3; 0-06-057248-5 (pa)
LC 2002-15324
When high school sophomore Shane Hunter's father is arrested for money laundering at his Lexus dealership, the star pitcher's life of affluence and private school begins to fall apart
This is "a story that delivers baseball action along with a rich psychological portrait, told through a compelling first-person narration." SLJ

Night hoops. Houghton Mifflin 2000 212p $15; pa $6.99
Grades: 7 8 9 10   **Fic**
1. Basketball—Fiction 2. Friendship—Fiction
ISBN 0-395-97936-6; 0-06-447275-2 (pa)
LC 99-47882

Deuker, Carl, 1950-—*Continued*

Also available in paperback from HarperCollins Pubs.

While trying to prove that he is good enough to be on his high school's varsity basketball team, Nick must also deal with his parents' divorce and erratic behavior of a troubled classmate who lives across the street

"The descriptions of the games are well written and accurate. Best of all, the complexities of basketball are contrasted with the complexities of life." SLJ

Painting the black. Avon Books 1999 248p pa $5.99

Grades: 8 9 10 11 12   **Fic**

1. Baseball—Fiction 2. School stories

ISBN 0-380-73104-5

"An Avon Flare book"

First published 1997 by Houghton Mifflin

"After a disastrous fall from a tree, senior Ryan Ward wrote off baseball. But he is swept back into the game when cocky, charismatic Josh Daniels—a star quarterback with the perfect spiral pass as well as a pitcher with a mean slider—moves into the neighborhood. . . . The well-written sports scenes—baseball and football—will draw reluctant readers, but it is Ryan's moral courage that will linger when the reading is done." Booklist

DiCamillo, Kate, 1964-

Because of Winn-Dixie. Candlewick Press 2000 182p $15.99; pa $6.99 *

Grades: 4 5 6 7   **Fic**

1. Dogs—Fiction 2. Florida—Fiction

ISBN   978-0-7636-0776-0;   0-7636-0776-2; 978-0-7636-4432-1 (pa); 0-7636-4432-3 (pa)

                LC 99-34260

A Newbery honor book, 2001

Ten-year-old India Opal Buloni describes her first summer in the town of Naomi, Florida, and all the good things that happen to her because of her big ugly dog Winn-Dixie

"This well-crafted, realistic, and heartwarming story will be read and reread as a new favorite deserving a long-term place on library shelves." SLJ

The magician's elephant; illustrated by Yoko Tanaka. Candlewick Press 2009 il $16.99 *

Grades: 4 5 6 7   **Fic**

1. Orphans—Fiction 2. Missing children—Fiction 3. Elephants—Fiction 4. Adventure fiction 5. Siblings—Fiction

ISBN 978-0-7636-4410-9; 0-7636-4410-2

              LC 2009007359

When ten-year-old orphan Peter Augustus Duchene encounters a fortune teller in the marketplace one day and she tells him that his sister, who is presumed dead, is in fact alive, he embarks on a remarkable series of adventures as he desperately tries to find her.

"The profound and deeply affecting emotions at work in the story are buoyed up by the tale's succinct, lyrical text; gentle touches of humor; and uplifting message." Booklist

Dickens, Charles, 1812-1870

A Christmas carol; [by] Charles Dickens; illustrated by P.J. Lynch. 1st U.S. ed. Candlewick Press 2006 156p il $19.99

Grades: 5 6 7 8   **Fic**

1. Christmas—Fiction 2. Ghost stories 3. Great Britain—Fiction

ISBN 978-0-7636-3120-8; 0-7636-3120-5

              LC 2005058122

A miser learns the true meaning of Christmas when three ghostly visitors review his past and foretell his future.

Lynch's "watercolor-and-gouache illustrations lavishly enhance this handsome edition." SLJ

Dickinson, Peter, 1927-

Angel Isle; illustrations by Ian Andrew. Wendy Lamb Books 2007 500p il $17.99; lib bdg $20.99 *

Grades: 7 8 9 10   **Fic**

1. Magic—Fiction 2. Fantasy fiction

ISBN 978-0-385-74690-8; 978-0-385-90928-0 (lib bdg)   LC 2007-7053

Sequel to The Ropemaker (2001)

While seeking the Ropemaker to restore the ancient magic that will protect their valley, Saranja, Maja, and Ribek must outwit twenty-four of the empire's most powerful and evil magicians.

"The characters are as well developed as those in the first book, and the complex, multilayered story includes more heady explorations of time and magic, joined here by thoughts on the meaning of true love." Booklist

The ropemaker. Delacorte Press 2001 375p $15.95; pa $7.95 *

Grades: 7 8 9 10   **Fic**

1. Magic—Fiction 2. Fantasy fiction

ISBN 0-385-72921-9; 0-385-73063-2 (pa)

              LC 2001-17422

Michael L. Printz Award honor book, 2002

When the magic that protects their Valley starts to fail, Tilja and her companions journey into the evil Empire to find the ancient magician Faheel, who originally cast those spells

"The suspense does not let up until the very last pages. While on one level this tale is a fantasy, it is also a wonderful coming-of-age story." SLJ

Followed by: Angel Isle

Tears of the salamander. Wendy Lamb Bks. 2003 197p hardcover o.p. pa $7.95

Grades: 7 8 9 10   **Fic**

1. Magic—Fiction 2. Volcanoes—Fiction 3. Italy—Fiction

ISBN 0-385-73098-5; 0-385-90125-9 (lib bdg); 0-440-23823-4 (pa); 978-0-440-23823-2 (pa)

              LC 2003-584

When Alfredo, a twelve-year-old choir boy in eighteenth-century Italy, loses his family in a fire, he goes to live with Uncle Giorgio, who he discovers is a sorcerer in control of the fires of Mt. Etna with sinister plans for his nephew

"Pitch-perfect, unobtrusive storytelling gracefully cedes center stage to the story's near-mythic elements.

Dickinson, Peter, 1927—_Continued_
Thoughtful readers will find much to ponder." Publ
Wkly

Dionne, Erin, 1975-
Models don't eat chocolate cookies. Dial Books
for Young Readers 2009 243p pa $7.99
Grades: 6 7 8 9   **Fic**
1. Obesity—Fiction 2. Fashion models—Fiction
ISBN 978-0-8037-3296-4; 0-8037-3296-1
                                        LC 2008020612
Overweight thirteen-year-old Celeste begins a campaign to lose weight in order to make sure she does not
win the Miss HuskeyPeach modeling challenge, in which
her mother and aunt have entered her--against her wishes.
"Wry first-person narrative also provides convincing
views of middle-school friendships, family dynamics, and
incremental personal growth. . . . A light, well-paced
first novel." Booklist

Divakaruni, Chitra Banerjee, 1956-
The conch bearer. Roaring Brook Press 2003
265p (Brotherhood of the conch) hardcover o.p. pa
$5.99
Grades: 5 6 7 8   **Fic**
1. Magic—Fiction 2. India—Fiction
ISBN 0-7613-1935-2; 0-6898-7242-9 (pa)
                                        LC 2003-8578
"A Neal Porter book"
In India, a healer invites twelve-year-old Anand to
join him on a quest to return a magical conch to its safe
and rightful home, high in the Himalayan mountains
"Divakaruni keeps her tale fresh and riveting." Publ
Wkly
Other titles in this series are:
The mirror of fire and dreaming (2005)
Shadowland (2009)

D'Lacey, Chris
The fire within; [by] Chris D'Lacey. 1st
Scholastic ed. Orchard Books 2005 340p $15.99
Grades: 6 7 8 9   **Fic**
1. Dragons—Fiction 2. Supernatural—Fiction
3. Authorship—Fiction
ISBN 0-439-67244-9   LC 2004-58327
When college student David Rain rents a room in an
unusual boardinghouse full of clay dragons, he has no
idea that they, along with some lively squirrels, will help
jumpstart his writing career.
This "has a satisfying domestic reality, spiced with
some very unusual dragons." SLJ
Other titles in this series are:
Icefire (2006)
Fire star (2007)
The fire eternal (2008)

Dobkin, Bonnie
Neptune's children; [by] Bonnie Dobkin. Walker
& Co. 2008 262p map $16.99
Grades: 7 8 9 10   **Fic**
1. Amusement parks—Fiction 2. Resistance to government—Fiction 3. Terrorism—Fiction
ISBN 978-0-8027-9734-6; 0-8027-9734-2
                                        LC 2008-2680
When a biological terrorist attack kills all adults on
Earth, children stranded at an amusement park work together to survive, led by Milo whose father was an engineer there, but when new threats arise and suspicions
grow, rebellion erupts.
"This thriller has gripping writing that makes it hard
to put down. The characterizations of the older children
are well done. . . . Even with the large number of survival stories on the market, this is one worth adding to
your collection." SLJ

Docherty, James, 1976-
The ice cream con; [by] Jimmy Docherty.
Scholastic 2008 250p $16.99
Grades: 5 6 7 8 9   **Fic**
1. Bullies—Fiction 2. Thieves—Fiction 3. Scotland—
Fiction
ISBN 978-0-545-02885-1; 0-545-02885-X
                                        LC 2007-35321
In Glasgow, Scotland, after getting mugged twice in
ten minutes, thirteen-year-old Jake comes up with a plan
to con the criminals on his estate with the help of his
closest friends, until events start to snowball out of control.
"Docherty keeps the action coming fast and furious
from beginning to end. . . . It is bound to be a huge hit
with tween boys and especially reluctant readers." Voice
Youth Advocates

Doctorow, Cory
Little brother. Tor Teen 2008 380p $17.95 *
Grades: 8 9 10 11 12   **Fic**
1. United States. Dept. of Homeland Security—Fiction
2. Terrorism—Fiction 3. Computers—Fiction 4. Civil
rights—Fiction 5. San Francisco (Calif.)—Fiction
ISBN 978-0-76531-985-2; 0-76531-985-3
                                        LC 2008-1827
"A Tom Doherty Associates book"
After being interrogated for days by the Department of
Homeland Security in the aftermath of a major terrorist
attack on San Francisco, California, seventeen-year-old
Marcus, released into what is now a police state, decides
to use his expertise in computer hacking to set things
right.
"The author manages to explain naturally the necessary technical tools and scientific concepts in this fast-
paced and well-written story. . . . The reader is privy to
Marcus's gut-wrenching angst, frustration, and terror,
thankfully offset by his self-awareness and humorous observations." Voice Youth Advocates

Doherty, Berlie

The girl who saw lions. Roaring Brook Press 2008 249p $16.95

Grades: 6 7 8 9 **Fic**

1. Adoption—Fiction 2. AIDS (Disease)—Fiction 3. Great Britain—Fiction 4. Tanzania—Fiction

ISBN 978-1-59643-377-9; 1-59643-377-9

LC 2007-44054

In alternating voices, thirteen-year-old Rosa and her mother are trying to adopt a Tanzanian child in England, while in Tanzania, nine-year-old Abela watches her family die and her uncle illegally sends her to England, in the hopes of selling her.

"Packs in a great deal of information about the AIDS crisis in Africa, female genital mutilation, international adoptions, the foster care system, and the many challenges facing parentless children and the social workers who try to place them. Girls will love this emotionally powerful novel." Voice Youth Advocates

Donofrio, Beverly

Thank you, Lucky Stars; [by] Beverly Donofrio. Schwartz & Wade 2008 234p $16.99; lib bdg $19.99

Grades: 4 5 6 **Fic**

1. Friendship—Fiction 2. Bullies—Fiction 3. School stories

ISBN 978-0-375-83964-1; 0-375-83964-X; 978-0-375-93964-8 (lib bdg); 0-375-93964-4 (lib bdg)

LC 2007-00853

Ally has looked forward to a new school year, especially since she and her best friend, Betsy, have planned since kindergarten to sing in the fifth grade talent show, but Betsy has a new best friend and Ally, shy and prone to cry, is targeted by bullies and a strange new student who is looking for a friend.

"Young readers with friendship issues of their own may find it easy to identify with shy Ally and rejoice at her final performance, while the bittersweet ending may come as a surprise." Booklist

Dorris, Michael

Morning Girl. Hyperion Bks. for Children 1992 74p pa $4.99 hardcover o.p.

Grades: 4 5 6 7 **Fic**

1. Taino Indians—Fiction 2. America—Exploration—Fiction

ISBN 0-78681-358-X (pa) LC 92-52989

Twelve year old Morning Girl, a Taino Indian who loves the day, and her younger brother Star Boy, who loves the night, take turns describing their life on a Bahamian island in 1492; in Morning Girl's last narrative, she witnesses the arrival of the first Europeans to her world

"The author uses a lyrical, yet easy-to-follow, style to place these compelling characters in historical context. . . . Dorris does a superb job of showing that family dynamics are complicated, regardless of time and place. . . . A touching glimpse into the humanity that connects us all." Horn Book

Sees Behind Trees. Hyperion Bks. for Children 1996 104p pa $4.99 hardcover o.p.

Grades: 4 5 6 7 **Fic**

1. Native Americans—Fiction 2. Vision disorders—Fiction

ISBN 0-7868-1357-1 (pa) LC 96-15859

"For the partially sighted Walnut, it is impossible to prove his right to a grown-up name by hitting a target with his bow and arrow. With his highly developed senses, however, he demonstrates that he can do something even better: he can see 'what cannot be seen' which earns him the name Sees Behind Trees. . . . Set in sixteenth-century America, this richly imagined and gorgeously written rite-of-passage story has the gravity of legend. Moreover, it has buoyant humor and the immediacy of a compelling story that is peopled with multidimensional characters." Booklist

Dowd, Siobhan

Bog child. David Fickling Books 2008 321p $16.99; lib bdg $19.99 *

Grades: 8 9 10 11 12 **Fic**

1. Northern Ireland—Fiction 2. Mummies—Fiction 3. Prisoners—Fiction 4. Family life—Fiction 5. Violence—Fiction 6. Terrorism—Fiction

ISBN 978-0-385-75169-8; 0-385-75169-9; 978-0-385-75170-4 (lib bdg); 0-385-75170-2 (lib bdg)

LC 2008-2998

In 1981, the height of Ireland's 'Troubles,' eighteen-year-old Fergus is distracted from his upcoming A-level exams by his imprisoned brother's hunger strike, the stress of being a courier for Sinn Fein, and dreams of a murdered girl whose body he discovered in a bog.

"Dowd raises questions about moral choices within a compelling plot that is full of surprises, powerfully bringing home the impact of political conflict on innocent bystanders." Publ Wkly

The London Eye mystery. David Fickling Books 2008 c2007 322p $15.99; lib bdg $18.99 *

Grades: 5 6 7 8 **Fic**

1. Asperger's syndrome—Fiction 2. Missing children—Fiction 3. Siblings—Fiction 4. Cousins—Fiction 5. Mystery fiction 6. London (England)—Fiction

ISBN 978-0-375-84976-3; 978-0-375-94976-0 (lib bdg); 0-375-84976-3; 0-375-94976-3 (lib bdg)

LC 2007-15119

First published 2007 in the United Kingdom

When Ted and Kat's cousin Salim disappears from the London Eye ferris wheel, the two siblings must work together—Ted with his brain that is "wired differently" and impatient Kat—to try to solve the mystery of what happened to Salim.

"Everything rings true here, the family relationships, the quirky connections of Ted's mental circuitry, and . . . the mystery. . . . A page turner with heft." Booklist

Dowell, Frances O'Roark

Chicken boy. Atheneum Books for Young Readers 2005 201p $15.95; pa $5.99

Grades: 4 5 6 7 **Fic**

1. Chickens—Fiction 2. Friendship—Fiction 3. Family life—Fiction

ISBN 0-689-85816-7; 1-4169-3482-0 (pa)

LC 2004-10928

Dowell, Frances O'Roark—*Continued*

Since the death of his mother, Tobin's family life and school life have been in disarray, but after he starts raising chickens with his seventh-grade classmate, Henry, everything starts to fall into place.

"There is no glib resolution, here. But the strong narration and the child's struggle with forgiveness make for poignant, aching drama." Booklist

Dovey Coe. Atheneum Bks. for Young Readers 2000 181p $16; pa $5.99 *

Grades: 5 6 7 8   **Fic**
1. Mountain life—Fiction 2. North Carolina—Fiction
ISBN 0-689-83174-9; 0-689-84667-3 (pa)
LC 99-46870

When accused of murder in her North Carolina mountain town in 1928, Dovey Coe, a stronged-willed twelve-year-old girl, comes to a new understanding of others, including her deaf brother

"Dowell has created a memorable character in Dovey, quick-witted and honest to a fault. . . . This is a delightful book, thoughtful and full of substance." Booklist

The kind of friends we used to be. Atheneum Books for Young Readers 2009 234p $16.99

Grades: 5 6 7 8   **Fic**
1. Friendship—Fiction 2. School stories
ISBN 978-1-416-95031-8; 1-416-95031-1
LC 2008-22245

Sequel to: The secret language of girls (2004)

Twelve-year-olds Kate and Marylin, friends since pre-school, draw further apart as Marylin becomes involved in student government and cheerleading, while Kate wants to play guitar and write songs, and both develop unlikely friendships with other girls and boys.

"Dowell gets middle-school dynamics exactly right, and while her empathetic portraits of Kate and Marylin are genuine and heartfelt, even secondary characters are memorable. A realistic and humorous look at the trials and tribulations of growing up and growing independent." SLJ

Shooting the moon. Atheneum Books for Young Readers 2008 163p $16.99 *

Grades: 4 5 6 7   **Fic**
1. Vietnam War, 1961-1975—Fiction 2. Soldiers—Fiction 3. Family life—Fiction
ISBN 978-1-4169-2690-0; 1-4169-2690-9
LC 2006-100347

When her brother is sent to fight in Vietnam, twelve-year-old Jamie begins to reconsider the army world that she has grown up in.

"The clear, well-paced first-person prose is perfectly matched to this novel's spare setting and restrained plot. . . . This [is a] thoughtful and satisfying story. . . . Readers will find beauty in its resolution, and will leave this eloquent heroine reluctantly." SLJ

Where I'd like to be. Atheneum Bks. for Young Readers 2003 232p hardcover o.p. pa $5.99

Grades: 4 5 6 7   **Fic**
1. Foster home care—Fiction 2. Tennessee—Fiction 3. Friendship—Fiction
ISBN 0-689-84420-4; 0-689-87067-1 (pa)
LC 2002-2183

"When a new girl moves into the East Tennessee Children's Home, her charisma has an immediate effect on Maddie, the story's narrator. Maddie's scrapbooks filled with pictures of the houses she dreams of living in serve as a catalyst for Murphy, as she gathers a fledgling group of unlikely friends around her. . . . The foster children's backgrounds are believable, diverse, and engaging, and readers familiar with eastern Tennessee will appreciate the references to real towns and cities that are sprinkled throughout the text." SLJ

Downer, Ann, 1960-

Hatching magic. Atheneum Bks. for Young Readers 2003 242p $16.95 *

Grades: 4 5 6 7   **Fic**
1. Dragons—Fiction 2. Magic—Fiction
ISBN 0-689-83400-4   LC 00-56570

When a thirteenth-century wizard confronts twenty-first century Boston while seeking his pet dragon, he is followed by a rival wizard and a very unhappy demon, but eleven-year-old Theodora Oglethorpe may hold the secret to setting everything right

"With likable characters, and laced with plenty of humor and adventure, Downer's fantasy will have solid appeal for young genre fans." Booklist

Another title about Theodora is:
The dragon of never-was (2006)

Downham, Jenny

Before I die. David Fickling Books 2007 326p $15.99; lib bdg $18.99 *

Grades: 8 9 10 11 12   **Fic**
1. Terminally ill—Fiction 2. Death—Fiction
ISBN 978-0-385-75155-1; 978-0-385-75158-2 (lib bdg)   LC 2007-20284

A terminally ill teenaged girl makes and carries out a list of things to do before she dies.

"Downham holds nothing back in her wrenchingly and exceptionally vibrant story." Publ Wkly

Dowswell, Paul

Powder monkey; adventures of Sam Witchall; [by] Paul Dowswell. 1st U.S. ed. Bloomsbury Pub. 2005 275p $16.95

Grades: 6 7 8 9   **Fic**
1. France—History—1799-1815—Fiction 2. Sea stories 3. Great Britain—History—1714-1837—Fiction 4. Adventure fiction
ISBN 978-1-58234-675-5; 1-58234-675-5
LC 2005013049

Thirteen-year-old Sam endures harsh conditions, battles, and a shipwreck after being pressed into service aboard the HMS Miranda during the Napoleonic Wars.

"Readers will be absorbed in the day-to-day life of young Sam, and his vivid tale will keep them on edge." SLJ

Other titles in this series are:
Prison ship (2006)
Battle fleet (2008)

Doyle, Brian, 1935-

Boy O'Boy. Douglas & McIntyre 2003 161p hardcover o.p. pa $12.95

Grades: 6 7 8 9 **Fic**

1. Child sexual abuse—Fiction 2. Canada—Fiction

ISBN 0-88899-588-1; 0-88899-590-3 (pa)

"A Groundwood book"

Living in Ottawa in 1945, Martin O'Boy must deal with a drunken father, an overburdened mother, a disabled twin brother, and a sexual predator at his church.

"Martin O'Boy is an expert observer and narrator. . . . Martin's world is believably real. Even the description of the sexual encounter seems like what a confused 11 or 12-year-old might say. " SLJ

Followed by: Pure Spring

Pure Spring. Groundwood Books 2007 158p $16.95; pa $8.95

Grades: 6 7 8 9 **Fic**

1. Canada—Fiction

ISBN 978-0-88899-774-6; 978-0-88899-775-3 (pa)

Sequel to: Boy O'Boy

It's spring in post-World War II Ottawa and Martin has found a true home. He's also working even though he had to lie about his age to get the job. Martin is also in love, but his boss is robbing the family of the one he loves.

"Doyle lovingly shapes his characters. . . . Doyle rounds out the grimness with comedic scenes." Horn Book

Doyle, Marissa

Bewitching season; [by] Marissa Doyle. Henry Holt 2008 346p $16.95 *

Grades: 7 8 9 10 **Fic**

1. Twins—Fiction 2. Sisters—Fiction 3. Magic—Fiction 4. Missing persons—Fiction 5. London (England)—Fiction 6. Great Britain—History—19th century—Fiction

ISBN 978-0-8050-8251-7; 0-8050-8251-4

In 1837, as seventeen-year-old twins, Persephone and Penelope, are starting their first London Season they find that their beloved governess, who has taught them everything they know about magic, has disappeared.

"Doyle takes as much care with characters . . . as with story details. This [is a] delightful mélange of genres." Booklist

Doyle, Roddy, 1958-

Wilderness. Arthur A. Levine Books 2007 211p $16.99

Grades: 6 7 8 9 **Fic**

1. Mothers—Fiction 2. Wilderness survival—Fiction 3. Sledding—Fiction 4. Finland—Fiction

ISBN 978-0-439-02356-6; 0-439-02356-4

LC 2007-11688

As Irish teenager Gráinne anxiously prepares for a reunion with her mother, who abandoned the family years before, Gráinne's half-brothers and their mother take a dogsledding vacation in Finland.

"The drama and adventure are leavened by generous helpings of Doyle's characteristic charm, laugh-out-loud humor, and wonderful way with words." SLJ

Draanen, Wendelin van

Confessions of a serial kisser. Alfred A. Knopf 2008 294p $15.99; lib bdg $18.99

Grades: 7 8 9 10 **Fic**

1. Kissing—Fiction 2. Friendship—Fiction 3. School stories

ISBN 978-0-375-84248-1; 0-375-84248-9; 978-0-375-94248-8 (lib bdg); 0-375-94248-3 (lib bdg)

LC 2007-49027

After reading her mother's secret collection of romance novels during her parent's difficult separation, seventeen-year-old Evangeline Logan begins a quest for the perfect kiss.

"The playful title and premise are matched by tender and convincing storytelling." Publ Wkly

Flipped. Knopf 2001 212p $14.95; lib bdg $16.99; pa $8.95

Grades: 6 7 8 9 **Fic**

ISBN 0-375-81174-5; 0-375-91174-X (lib bdg); 0-375-82544-4 (pa)

LC 2001-29238

In alternating chapters, eighth-graders Juli and Bryce, describe how their feelings about themselves, each other, and their families have changed over the years

"There's lots of laugh-out-loud egg puns and humor in this novel. There's also, however, a substantial amount of serious social commentary woven in, as well as an exploration of the importance of perspective in relationships." SLJ

Runaway. Knopf 2006 250p $15.95; lib bdg $17.99

Grades: 6 7 8 9 **Fic**

1. Runaway children—Fiction 2. Orphans—Fiction 3. Homeless persons—Fiction

ISBN 0-375-83522-9; 0-375-93522-3 (lib bdg)

LC 2005-33276

After running away from her fifth foster home, Holly, a twelve-year-old orphan, travels across the country, keeping a journal of her experiences and struggle to survive.

"The ending of this taut, powerful story seems possible and deeply hopeful." Booklist

Sammy Keyes and the hotel thief. Knopf 1998 163p il hardcover o.p. pa $6.50 *

Grades: 4 5 6 7 **Fic**

1. Mystery fiction

ISBN 978-0-679-88839-0; 0-679-89264-8 (pa)

LC 97-40776

Thirteen-year-old Sammy's penchant for speaking her mind gets her in trouble when she involves herself in the investigation of a robbery at the "seedy" hotel across the street from the seniors' building where she is living with her grandmother

"This is a breezy novel with vivid characters." Bull Cent Child Books

Other titles about Sammy Keyes are:

Sammy Keyes and the art of deception (2003)

Sammy Keyes and the cold hard cash (2008)

Sammy Keyes and the curse of Moustache Mary (2000)

Sammy Keyes and the dead giveaway (2005)

Sammy Keyes and the Hollywood mummy (2001)

Sammy Keyes and the psycho Kitty Queen (2004)

Sammy Keyes and the runaway elf (1999)

Draanen, Wendelin van—*Continued*
Sammy Keyes and the search for snake eyes (2002)
Sammy Keyes and the Sisters of Mercy (1999)
Sammy Keyes and the skeleton man (1998)
Sammy Keyes and the wild things (2007)

Draper, Sharon M., 1948-
The Battle of Jericho. Atheneum Books for
Young Readers 2003 297p $16.95; pa $6.99
Grades: 7 8 9 10   Fic
1. Clubs—Fiction 2. School stories 3. Cousins—Fiction 4. Death—Fiction
ISBN 0-689-84232-5; 0-689-84233-3 (pa)
LC 2002-8612
"The Warriors of Distinction has been the school's
most exclusive club for 50 years, so when 16-year-old
Jericho is asked to pledge, he's excited—and intimidated.
. . . When the ceremony turns cruel—with the one girl
pledge being singled out for abuse—Jericho begins to
have second thoughts. Then the affair turns deadly."
Booklist
"This title is a compelling read that drives home important lessons about making choices." SLJ
Other titles in this series are:
November blues (2007)
Just another hero (2009)

Double Dutch. Atheneum Bks. for Young
Readers 2002 183p $16; pa $4.99
Grades: 6 7 8 9   Fic
1. Rope skipping—Fiction 2. Friendship—Fiction
3. African Americans—Fiction
ISBN 0-689-84230-9; 0-689-84231-7 (pa)
LC 00-50247
Three eighth-grade friends, preparing for the International Double Dutch Championship jump rope competition in their home town of Cincinnati, Ohio, cope with
Randy's missing father, Delia's inability to read, and Yo
Yo's encounter with the class bullies
"Teens will like the high-spirited, authentic dialogue
. . . the honest look at tough issues, and the team workout scenes that show how sports can transform young
lives." Booklist

Fire from the rock. Dutton Children's Books
2007 229p $16.99 *
Grades: 6 7 8 9   Fic
1. Central High School (Little Rock, Ark.)—Fiction
2. African Americans—Fiction 3. Race relations—Fiction 4. School stories 5. Arkansas—Fiction
ISBN 978-0-525-47720-4; 0-525-47720-9
LC 2006-102952
In 1957, Sylvia Patterson's life is disrupted by the impending integration of Little Rock's Central High when
she is selected to be one of the first black students to attend the previously all white school.
"This historical fiction novel is a must have. It keeps
the reader engaged with vivid depictions of a time that
most young people can only imagine." Voice Youth Advocates

Forged by fire. Atheneum Bks. for Young
Readers 1997 151p $16.95; pa $4.99
Grades: 7 8 9 10   Fic
1. Child abuse—Fiction 2. Siblings—Fiction
3. African Americans—Fiction
ISBN 0-689-80699-X; 0-689-81851-3 (pa)
LC 96-2763
Companion volume to Tears of a tiger
Teenage Gerald, who has spent years protecting his
fragile half-sister from their abusive father, faces the
prospect of one final confrontation before the problem
can be solved
"What started out as an award-winning short story in
Ebony magazine was expanded into this sad but inspirational story. . . . With non-stop excitement, this is well-written, easy to read, and possibly an inspiration for anyone trapped in family situations involving child abuse or
domestic violence." Voice Youth Advocates

Duble, Kathleen Benner
Hearts of iron. Margaret K. McElderry Books
2006 248p $15.95
Grades: 6 7 8 9   Fic
1. Iron industry—Fiction 2. Connecticut—Fiction
ISBN 1-4169-0850-1   LC 2005-29258
In early 1800s Connecticut, fifteen-year-old Lucy tries
to decide whether to marry her childhood friend who unhappily toils at the Mt. Riga iron furnace or the young
man from Boston who has come to work in her father's
store.
"Well-written historical fiction with a unique setting
and a touch of mystery, Lucy's story will both inform
and entertain readers." SLJ

Quest. 1st ed. Margaret K. McElderry Books
2008 240p $16.99
Grades: 7 8 9 10   Fic
1. Hudson, Henry, d. 1611—Fiction 2. Explorers—Fiction 3. Spies—Fiction 4. Seafaring life—Fiction
5. America—Exploration—Fiction 6. Netherlands—Fiction
ISBN 978-1-4169-3386-1; 1-4169-3386-7
LC 2006102712
Relates events of explorer Henry Hudson's final voyage in 1602 from four points of view, those of his seventeen-year-old son aboard ship, a younger son left in London, a crewmember, and a young English woman acting
as a spy in Holland in hopes of restoring honor to her
family's name.
"The author's skillful juxtaposition of these four narratives creates an absorbing work of historical fiction that
manages to incorporate the viewpoints of explorers, investors, sailors, governments, family members, and
neighbors of those who played a part in this fascinating
era." SLJ

The sacrifice. Margaret K. McElderry Books
2005 211p $15.95
Grades: 6 7 8 9   Fic
1. Witchcraft—Fiction 2. Puritans—Fiction
3. Massachusetts—History—1600-1775, Colonial period—Fiction
ISBN 0-689-87650-5   LC 2004-18355

Duble, Kathleen Benner—*Continued*

Two sisters, aged ten and twelve, are accused of witchcraft in Andover, Massachusetts, in 1692 and await trial in a miserable prison while their mother desperately searches for some way to obtain their freedom.

"Well written with accessible language, this book will appeal to a wide range of readers." SLJ

Includes bibliographical references

Duey, Kathleen

Skin hunger. Atheneum Books for Young Readers 2007 357p (Resurrection of magic) $17.99

Grades: 7 8 9 10   **Fic**

1. Fantasy fiction 2. Magic—Fiction

ISBN 978-0-689-84093-7; 0-689-84093-4

LC 2006-34819

In alternate chapters, Sadima travels from her farm home to the city and becomes assistant to a heartless man who is trying to restore knowledge of magic to the world, and a group of boys fights to survive in the academy that has resulted from his efforts.

This is a "compelling new fantasy. . . . Duey sweeps readers up in the page-turning excitement." Horn Book

Dumas, Alexandre, 1802-1870

The three musketeers; translated by Jacques Le Clercq. Modern Library 1999 xxi, 598p $24.95

Grades: 7 8 9 10 11 12 Adult   **Fic**

1. France—History—1589-1789, Bourbons—Fiction

ISBN 0-679-60332-8

Also available from other publishers

Original French edition, 1844

"D'Artagnan arrives in Paris one day in 1625 and manages to be involved in three duels with three musketeers . . . Athos, Porthos and Aramis. They become d'Artagnan's best friends. The account of their adventures from 1625 on develops against the rich historical background of the reign of Louis XIII and the early part of that of Louis XIV, the main plot being furnished by the antagonism between Cardinal de Richelieu and Queen Anne d'Autriche." Haydn. Thesaurus of Book Dig

Duncan, Lois, 1934-

I know what you did last summer. Little, Brown 1973 199p pa $6.50 hardcover o.p.

Grades: 7 8 9 10 11 12   **Fic**

1. Mystery fiction

ISBN 0-440-22844-1 (pa)

"Julie, Barry, Helen, and Ray have almost made themselves forget the terrible night when their joyriding had ended in tragedy. Barry hit and killed a young cyclist on the road and kept on going; they all swear to keep the accident a secret. A year passes and they all believe they are safe, but one day Julie gets a note in the mail which says, 'I know what you did last summer.' Barry is shot and lying paralyzed in the hospital when Helen is attacked and their silent menace goes about completing his scheme to exact revenge." Publ Wkly

This book "has vivid characterization, good balance, and the boding sense of impending danger that adds excitement to the best mystery stories." Bull Cent Child Books

Killing Mr. Griffin. Dell 1990 223p pa $6.50 hardcover o.p. *

Grades: 7 8 9 10   **Fic**

1. School stories 2. Kidnapping—Fiction

ISBN 0-440-94515-1 (pa)

First published 1978 by Little, Brown

"Mr. Griffin, the stern highschool English teacher, is loathed by those who should appreciate his determination to educate them. Mark, a student, uses his cool glamour and cleverness to mesmerize classmates Jeff, David, Betsy and Sue, persuading them to kidnap Mr. Griffin, with the idea of scaring the teacher into handing out high grades for inferior work. They leave the man trussed and gagged in a remote spot, where he dies. Sue wants to go to the police with a confession, but Mark masterminds a frantic coverup." Publ Wkly

The author's "skillful plotting builds layers of tension that draws readers into the eye of the conflict. The ending is nicely handled in a manner which provides relief without removing any of the chilling implications." SLJ

Locked in time. Little, Brown 1985 210p hardcover o.p. pa $6.50

Grades: 7 8 9 10   **Fic**

1. Mystery fiction 2. Louisiana—Fiction

ISBN 0-316-19555-3; 0-440-94942-4 (pa)

LC 85-23

"Shortly after arriving at her strangely youthful stepmother's isolated Louisiana mansion, Nore realizes that Lisette and her two children—handsome, 17-year-old Gabe and moody 13-year-old Josie—hide a sinister, century-old secret, a secret that threatens the lives of Nore and her infatuated father." Booklist

"The writing style is smooth, the characters strongly developed, and the plot, which has excellent pace and momentum, is an adroit blending of fantasy and realism." Bull Cent Child Books

Stranger with my face. Little, Brown 1981 250p pa $8.95 hardcover o.p.

Grades: 7 8 9 10   **Fic**

1. Supernatural—Fiction 2. Twins—Fiction

ISBN 0-440-98356-8   LC 81-8299

"There are small things, at first—a face in the mirror, a presence in an empty room, a beckoning figure on treacherous rocks—that portend 17-year-old Laurie's confrontation with the astral projection of her previously unknown, malevolent identical twin. . . . The jealous twin, Lia, pursues her, prodding her to explore astral projection so that Lia may enter Laurie's body." SLJ

"The ghostly Lia is deliciously evil; the idea of astral projection—Lia's method of travel—is novel; the island setting is vivid; and the relationships among the young people are realistic in the smoothly written supernatural tale." Horn Book

Dunkle, Clare B.

The sky inside. Atheneum Books for Young Readers 2008 229p $16.99 *

Grades: 6 7 8 9   **Fic**

1. Science fiction

ISBN 978-1-41692-422-7; 1-41692-422-1

"Ginee Seo books"

Dunkle, Clare B.—*Continued*

After the disappearance of his sister, Cassie, and other children who ask questions about their carefully choreographed life in a domed suburb cut off from the outside world, Martin and his intelligent dog investigate.

"Dunkle surrounds her protagonists with an enthralling range of settings, a memorable cast of characters. . . . Fans of the author will . . . recognize her evocative storytelling and intricate plotting." Bull Cent Child Books

Followed by: The walls have eyes (2009)

Dunlap, Susanne Emily

The musician's daughter; [by] Susanne Dunlap. Bloomsbury 2009 322p $16.99

Grades: 8 9 10 11 12   **Fic**

1. Haydn, Joseph, 1732-1809—Fiction 2. Musicians—Fiction 3. Homicide—Fiction 4. Gypsies—Fiction 5. Vienna (Austria)—Fiction 6. Mystery fiction

ISBN 978-1-59990-332-3; 1-59990-332-6

LC 2008-30307

In eighteenth-century Vienna, Austria, fifteen-year-old Theresa seeks a way to help her mother and brother financially while investigating the murder of her father, a renowned violinist in Haydn's orchestra at the court of Prince Esterhazy, after his body is found near a gypsy camp.

"Dunlap skillfully builds suspense until the final page. . . . Readers will root for courageous Theresa through the exciting intrigue even as they absorb deeper messages about music and art's power to lift souls and inspire change." Booklist

Dunmore, Helen, 1952-

Ingo. HarperCollins Pubs. 2005 328p $16.99; lib bdg $17.89

Grades: 6 7 8 9   **Fic**

1. Mermaids and mermen—Fiction 2. Great Britain—Fiction

ISBN 978-0-06-081852-4; 0-06-081852-2; 978-0-06-081853-1 (lib bdg); 0-06-081853-0 (lib bdg)

LC 2005-19079

As they search for their missing father near their Cornwall home, Sapphy and her brother Conor learn about their family's connection to the domains of air and of water.

"Strong character development combines with an engaging plot and magical elements to make this a fine choice for fantasy readers, who will look forward to the next installments in this planned trilogy." SLJ

Other titles about Sapphire are:

The tide knot (2008)
The deep (2009)

DuPrau, Jeanne, 1944-

The city of Ember. Random House 2003 270p (Books of Ember) $15.95; lib bdg $17.99 *

Grades: 5 6 7 8   **Fic**

1. Science fiction

ISBN 0-375-82273-9; 0-375-92274-1 (lib bdg)

LC 2002-10239

"More than 200 years after an unspecified holocaust, the residents of Ember have lost all knowledge of any-

thing beyond the area illuminated by the floodlamps on their buildings. . . . Food and other supplies are running low, and the power failures that plunge the town into impenetrable darkness are becoming longer and more frequent. Then Lina, a young foot messenger, discovers a damaged document from the mysterious Builders that hints at a way out." SLJ

"The writing and storytelling are agreeably spare and remarkably suspenseful." Horn Book

Other titles in this series are:

The people of Sparks (2004)
The prophet of Yonwood (2006)
The diamond of Darkhold (2008)

Durango, Julia, 1967-

The walls of Cartagena; by Julia Durango; illustrated by Tom Pohrt. 1st ed. Simon & Schuster Books for Young Readers 2008 152p il $15.99

Grades: 5 6 7 8   **Fic**

1. Slavery—Fiction 2. Leprosy—Fiction 3. Catholic Church—Fiction 4. Colombia—Fiction

ISBN 978-1-416-94102-6; 1-416-94102-9

LC 2007041861

Thirteen-year-old Calepino, an African slave in the seventeenth-century Caribbean city of Cartagena, works as a translator for a Jesuit priest who tends to newly-arrived slaves and, after working for a Jewish doctor in a leper colony and helping an Angolan boy and his mother escape, he realizes his true calling.

"Illustrated with occasional small ink sketches, the ultimate rescue adventure is gripping, but more compelling is the authentic history of people desperate and brave." Booklist

Durbin, William, 1951-

Blackwater Ben. Wendy Lamb Bks. 2003 199p $15.95; lib bdg $17.99

Grades: 5 6 7 8   **Fic**

1. Lumber and lumbering—Fiction 2. Father-son relationship—Fiction 3. Frontier and pioneer life—Fiction 4. Minnesota—Fiction

ISBN 0-385-72928-6; 0-385-90149-6 (lib bdg)

LC 2002-155586

In the winter of 1898, a seventh-grade boy drops out of school to work with his father, the cook at Blackwater Logging Camp in Minnesota

"Lively details about logging add depth to this warm, colorful historical novel." Booklist

The broken blade. Delacorte Press 1997 163p hardcover o.p. pa $5.50

Grades: 5 6 7 8   **Fic**

1. Fur trade—Fiction 2. Canada—Fiction

ISBN 0-385-32224-0; 0-440-41184-X

LC 96-22114

When an injury prevents his father from going into northern Canada with fur traders, thirteen-year-old Pierre decides to take his father's place as a voyageur

"This look at the early nineteenth-century Canadian fur trade should appeal to reluctant readers as well as adventure buffs, and it may be a welcome suggestion for middle-school historical fiction reports." Bull Cent Child Books

Durbin, William, 1951——*Continued*
The darkest evening. Orchard Books 2004 232p
$15.95
Grades: 6 7 8 9   **Fic**
1. Finnish Americans—Fiction 2. Communism—Fiction 3. Russia—Fiction
ISBN 0-439-37307-7   LC 2003-20255
In the 1930s, a young Finnish-American boy reluctantly moves with his family to Karelia, a communist-Finnish state founded in Russia, where his idealistic father soon realizes that his conception of a communist utopia is flawed.
"Many readers who enjoy tales of courage under fire . . . will find this exciting stuff." Booklist

The Winter War; [by] William Durbin. 1st ed.
Wendy Lamb Books 2008 231p $15.99; lib bdg
$18.99
Grades: 6 7 8 9   **Fic**
1. Russo-Finnish War, 1939-1940—Fiction
2. Soldiers—Fiction 3. Poliomyelitis—Fiction
4. Finland—Fiction
ISBN 978-0-385-74652-6; 0-385-74652-0;
978-0-385-90889-4 (lib bdg); 0-385-90889-X (lib bdg)
LC 2007007048
When Russian troops invade Finland during the winter of 1939–40, Marko, a young polio victim determined to keep his homeland free, joins the Finnish Army as a messenger boy.
"Durbin's graphic depictions of the realities of war are not for the faint of heart. . . . More than a war story, though, this is a tale of resilience and self-discovery. . . . An engaging novel for adventure lovers and fans of historical fiction alike." SLJ
Includes bibliographical references

Durrant, Lynda, 1956-
Imperfections. Clarion Books 2008 172p $16
Grades: 6 7 8 9   **Fic**
1. Shakers—Fiction 2. Siblings—Fiction
3. Kentucky—Fiction 4. Abandoned children—Fiction
5. United States—History—1861-1865, Civil War—Fiction
ISBN 978-0-5470-0357-3; 0-5470-0357-9
LC 2008-23533
In 1862 Pleasant Hill, Kentucky, fourteen-year-old Rosemary Elizabeth strives to fit in with the Shaker sisters of this "Heaven on Earth," but yearns to be reunited with her mother and siblings from whom she was separated when they sought refuge from her abusive father.
Includes facts about Shakers and Morgan's Raiders.
"This fine coming-of-age novel rewards readers with an unusual glimpse into a rarely portrayed religion as well as a different perspective on the Civil War." Booklist
Includes bibliographical references

My last skirt; the story of Jennie Hodgers, Union soldier; by Lynda Durrant. Clarion Books 2006 199p $16
Grades: 6 7 8 9   **Fic**
1. Hodgers, Jennie, 1844-1915—Fiction 2. Irish Americans—Fiction 3. United States—History—1861-1865, Civil War—Fiction 4. Sex role—Fiction
ISBN 978-0-618-57490-2; 0-618-57490-5
LC 2005027746

Enjoying the freedom afforded her while dressing as a boy in order to earn higher pay after emigrating from Ireland, Jennie Hodgers serves in the 95th Illinois Infantry as Private Albert Cashier, a Union soldier in the American Civil War.
"Based on a true story, Jennie's tale is gripping. . . . Her loneliness, longing, and missed opportunities will resonate deeply with readers." SLJ
Includes bibliographical references

Durst, Sarah Beth
Into the Wild. Razorbill 2007 260p $15.99
Grades: 6 7 8 9   **Fic**
1. Fairy tales 2. Magic—Fiction
ISBN 978-1-59514-156-9; 1-59514-156-1
LC 2007-01942
Having escaped from the Wild and the preordained fairy tale plots it imposes, Rapunzel, along with her daughter Julie Marchen, tries to live a fairly normal life, but when the Wild breaks free and takes over their town, it is Julie who has to prevent everyone from being trapped in the events of a story.
"The novel is a creative romp through the fairy tale genre, highlighting the strength of the female characters whose stories we all know so well." Kliatt
Another title about Julie is:
Out of the wild (2008)

Dygard, Thomas J., 1931-1996
Second stringer. Morrow Junior Bks. 1998 174p
$15.99
Grades: 7 8 9 10   **Fic**
1. Football—Fiction
ISBN 0-688-15981-8   LC 98-11361
When Kevin replaces the quarterback and football hero who suffers a knee injury, the second stringer needs to prove that he can do the job and is not just a substitute
"Dygard offers just enough conflict and character development to add texture to the fast-paced plot." Booklist

Easton, Kelly, 1960-
White magic; spells to hold you: a novel.
Wendy Lamb Books 2007 193p $15.99; lib bdg
$18.99
Grades: 8 9 10 11 12   **Fic**
1. Witchcraft—Fiction 2. Friendship—Fiction
3. School stories 4. California—Fiction
ISBN 978-0-375-83769-2; 978-0-375-93769-9 (lib bdg)
LC 2006-39735
Three high school girls in Santa Monica form a coven to try to get what they feel is missing from their lives.
This offers "Easton's elegant, fluid writing, . . . believable teenage emotions and situations, and strong characterizations." Horn Book

Efaw, Amy

Battle dress. HarperCollins Pubs. 2000 291p lib bdg $16.89 paperback o.p.

Grades: 7 8 9 10   **Fic**

1. United States Military Academy—Fiction
2. Military education—Fiction

ISBN 0-06-028411-0 (lib bdg); 0-06-053520-2

LC 99-34516

As a newly arrived freshman at West Point, seventeen-year-old Andi finds herself gaining both confidence and self esteem as she struggles to get through the grueling six weeks of new cadet training known as the Beast

"This book by a West Point graduate is a gripping, hard-to-put-down look at a young woman's struggle to succeed in a traditionally all-male environment." Voice Youth Advocates

Ehrenberg, Pamela, 1972-

Ethan, suspended; written by Pamela Ehrenberg. Eerdmans Books for Young Readers 2007 266p $16 *

Grades: 7 8 9 10   **Fic**

1. Grandparents—Fiction 2. Race relations—Fiction
3. Jews—Fiction 4. Washington (D.C.)—Fiction

ISBN 978-0-8028-5324-0   LC 2006032697

After a school suspension and his parents' separation, Ethan is sent to live with his grandparents in Washington, D.C., which is worlds apart from his home in a Philadelphia suburb.

"Ehrenberg focuses on themes of race and class without sounding preachy. . . . Best of all are the portraits of [Ethan's] scrappy Jewish grandparents." Booklist

Elkeles, Simone

How to ruin my teenage life; [by] Simone Elkeles. 1st ed. Flux 2007 281p pa $8.95

Grades: 7 8 9 10 11 12   **Fic**

1. Jews—Fiction   2. Israelis—Fiction
3. Father-daughter relationship—Fiction 4. Chicago (Ill.)—Fiction

ISBN 978-0-7387-0961-1 (pa); 0-7387-1019-9 (pa)

LC 2007005535

Living with her Israeli father in Chicago, seventeen-year-old Amy Nelson-Barak feels like a walking disaster, worried about her "non-boyfriend" in the Israeli army, her mother, new stepfather, and the baby they are expecting, a new boy named Nathan who has moved into her apartment building and goes to her school, and whether or not she really is the selfish snob that Nathan says she is.

"This book has laugh-out-loud moments. . . . Amy's thoughtfulness and depth raise this book above most of the chick-lit genre." Voice Youth Advocates

Elliott, Laura

Give me liberty; [by] L. M. Elliott. Katherine Tegen Books 2006 376p $16.99; lib bdg $17.89

Grades: 5 6 7 8   **Fic**

1. United States—History—1775-1783, Revolution—Fiction 2. Virginia—Fiction

ISBN 0-06-074421-9; 0-06-074422-7 (lib bdg)

Follows the life of thirteen-year-old Nathaniel Dunn, from May 1774 to December 1775, as he serves his indentureship with a music teacher in Williamsburg, Virginia, and witnesses the growing rift between patriots and loyalists, culminating in the American Revolution.

"Elliott packs a great deal of historical detail into a novel already filled with action, well-drawn characters, and a sympathetic understanding of many points of view." Booklist

Under a war-torn sky; [by] L.M. Elliott. Hyperion Bks. for Children 2001 284p hardcover o.p. pa $5.99

Grades: 7 8 9 10   **Fic**

1. World War, 1939-1945—Fiction 2. France—Fiction

ISBN 0-7868-0755-5; 0-7868-1753-4 (pa)

LC 2001-16633

After his plane is shot down by Hitler's Luftwaffe, nineteen-year-old Henry Forester of Richmond, Virginia, strives to walk across occupied France, with the help of the French Resistance, in hopes of rejoining his unit

"It's packed with action, intrigue, and suspense, but this novel celebrates acts of kindness and heroism without glorifying war." Booklist

Ellis, Ann Dee

Everything is fine. Little, Brown and Co. Books for Young Readers 2009 154p il $16.99

Grades: 6 7 8 9 10   **Fic**

1. Depression (Psychology)—Fiction 2. Family life—Fiction 3. Mothers—Fiction 4. Bereavement—Fiction

ISBN 978-0-316-01364-2; 0-316-01364-1

LC 2008-05847

When her father leaves for a job out of town, Mazzy is left at home to try to cope with her mother, who has been severely depressed since the death of Mazzy's baby sister.

"What makes [this book] so extraordinary is the narrative device that Ellis employs to searing effect. . . . [This] is a story so painful you want to read it with your eyes closed. It is a stunning novel." Voice Youth Advocates

This is what I did. Little, Brown 2007 157p $16.99 *

Grades: 6 7 8 9   **Fic**

1. Bullies—Fiction 2. School stories

ISBN 978-0-316-01363-5; 0-316-01363-3

LC 2006-01388

Bullied because of an incident in his past, eighth-grader Logan is unhappy at his new school and has difficulty relating to others until he meets a quirky girl and a counselor who believe in him.

"Part staccato prose, part transcript, this haunting first novel will grip readers right from the start. . . . A particularly attractive book design incorporates small drawings between each segment of text." Publ Wkly

Ellis, Deborah, 1960-

Bifocal; [by] Deborah Ellis and Eric Walters. Fitzhenry & Whiteside 2007 280p $18.95; pa $12.95

Grades: 7 8 9 10   **Fic**

Ellis, Deborah, 1960-—*Continued*
1. Muslims—Fiction 2. Prejudices—Fiction 3. School stories
ISBN   978-1-55455-036-4;   1-55455-036-X;
978-1-55455-062-3 (pa); 1-55455-062-9 (pa)
When a Muslim boy is arrested at a high school on suspicion of terrorist affiliations, growing racial tensions divide the student population.
"The story is told in the alternating voices of two students. . . . Their individual struggles to understand the flaring prejudice and their journeys toward self-discovery are subtle and authentic. . . . This is a story that will leave readers looking at their schools and themselves with new eyes." Booklist

Ellis, Sarah, 1952-
Odd man out. Groundwood Books/House of Anansi Press 2006 162p $18.95; pa $9.95
Grades: 5 6 7 8   Fic
1. Cousins—Fiction 2. Grandmothers—Fiction 3. Fathers—Fiction
ISBN 0-88899-702-7; 978-0-88899-703-6 (pa); 0-88899-703-5 (pa)
"While his mother and new stepfather are on their honeymoon, 12-year-old Kip is sent to his grandmother's island home for a holiday that he will share with his five . . . female cousins. . . . No sooner has he settled into his new surroundings than he discovers a mysterious binder in his attic bedroom and gradually begins to uncover the disturbing truth about the father he has never known." Booklist
"This is a thoughtful and often funny book of a boy on the verge of adolescence challenged to think—of his father, mother, cousins, life—in a different way." SLJ

Emerson, Kevin
Carlos is gonna get it; [by] Kevin Emerson. Arthur A. Levine Books 2008 291p $16.99 *
Grades: 4 5 6 7   Fic
1. School stories 2. African Americans—Fiction 3. Boston (Mass.)—Fiction 4. New Hampshire—Fiction
ISBN   978-0-439-93525-8;   0-439-93525-3;
978-0-439-93526-5 (pa); 0-439-93526-1 (pa)
LC 2007037088
Recounts the events that occur at the end of seventh grade, when a group of friends plan to trick Carlos, an annoying "problem" student who says he is visited by aliens, while they are on a field trip in the mountains of New Hampshire.
This is a "gripping story. . . . The dialogue is right on, as is the hurt of betrayal and the guilt that cannot be resolved." Booklist

Enderle, Dotti, 1954-
Man in the moon. Delacorte Press 2008 152p $14.99; lib bdg $17.99
Grades: 4 5 6   Fic
1. Siblings—Fiction 2. Moon—Fiction
ISBN   978-0-385-73566-7;   0-385-73566-9;
978-0-385-90554-1 (lib bdg); 0-385-90554-8 (lib bdg)
LC 2008-000476

"Janine is prepared for a sticky, boring summer on her family's land in the middle of nowhere. Far from town and with only her ailing brother Ricky for company, Janine spends half her time stuck inside with him, wishing that their mother would let them out to play. But when Mr. Lunas—a mysterious man who saved Janine's father's life in the war—arrives through the cornfields, strange things begin happening." Publisher's note
"This well-constructed novel satisfies on many levels, with wonderful dialogue, a vividness of place, and memorable characters that allow even the magical elements to ring true." SLJ

Engdahl, Sylvia Louise, 1933-
Enchantress from the stars; foreword by Lois Lowry. Firebird 2003 288p pa $6.99
Grades: 7 8 9 10 11 12   Fic
1. Science fiction
ISBN 0-14-250037-2
A Newbery Medal honor book, 1971
A reissue of the title first published 1970 by Atheneum Pubs.
When young Elana unexpectedly joins the team leaving the spaceship to study the planet Andrecia, she becomes an integral part of an adventure involving three very different civilizations, each one centered on the third planet from the star in its own solar system
"Emphasis is on the intricate pattern of events rather than on characterization, and readers will find fascinating symbolism-and philosophical parallels to what they may have observed or thought. The book is completely absorbing and should have a wider appeal than much science fiction." Horn Book
Another title about Elana is:
The far side of evil (2003)

Engle, Margarita
The surrender tree; poems of Cuba's struggle for freedom. Henry Holt and Co. 2008 169p $17.95
Grades: 7 8 9 10 11 12   Fic
1. Cuba—Fiction 2. Novels in verse
ISBN 978-0-8050-8674-4; 0-8050-8674-9
LC 2007-27591
A Newbery Medal honor book, 2009
This "book is written in clear, short lines of stirring free verse. . . . [The author] draws on her own Cuban American roots . . . to describe those who fought in the nineteenth-century Cuban struggle for independence. At the center is Rosa, a traditional healer, who nurses runaway slaves and deserters in caves and other secret hideaways. . . . Many readers will be caught by the compelling narrative voices and want to pursue the historical accounts in Engle's bibliography." Booklist

Tropical secrets; Holocaust refugees in Cuba. Henry Holt 2009 199p $16.95 *
Grades: 7 8 9 10 11   Fic
1. Jews—Fiction 2. Holocaust, 1933-1945—Fiction 3. Cuba—Fiction 4. Refugees—Fiction 5. Novels in verse
ISBN 978-0-8050-8936-3; 0-8050-8936-5
LC 2008-36782

Engle, Margarita—*Continued*

Escaping from Nazi Germany to Cuba in 1939, a young Jewish refugee dreams of finding his parents again, befriends a local girl with painful secrets of her own, and discovers that the Nazi darkness is never far away.

"Readers who think they might not like a novel in verse will be pleasantly surprised at how quickly and smoothly the story flows. . . . The book will provide great fodder for discussion of the Holocaust, self-reliance, ethnic and religious bias, and more." Voice Youth Advocates

English, Karen

Francie. Farrar, Straus & Giroux 1999 199p $17; pa $5.95 *

Grades: 5 6 7 8   Fic
    1. African Americans—Fiction 2. Race relations—Fiction 3. Alabama—Fiction
    ISBN 0-374-32456-5; 0-374-42459-4 (pa)
                                        LC 98-53047
Coretta Scott King honor book for text, 2000
"The best student in her small, all-black school in preintegration Alabama, 12-year-old Francie hopes for a better life. . . . When Jessie, an older school friend who is without family, is forced on the run by a racist employer, Francie leaves her mother's labeled canned food for him in the woods. Only when the sheriff begins searching their woods . . . does she realize the depth of the danger she may have brought to her family. Francie's smooth-flowing, well-paced narration is gently assisted by just the right touch of the vernacular. Characterization is evenhanded and believable, while place and time envelop readers." SLJ

Enthoven, Sam

Tim, defender of the Earth! by Sam Enthoven. Razorbill 2008 288p $19.99

Grades: 6 7 8 9   Fic
    1. Dinosaurs—Fiction 2. Genetic engineering—Fiction 3. Science fiction
    ISBN 978-1-59514-184-2; 1-59514-184-7
                                        LC 2007-23903
When two gargantuan, human-made monsters clash over the future of the human race and the planet, fourteen-year-old Anna Mallahide has a hard time convincing her classmate, Chris Pitman, that he must play any role in the outcome of their epic battle.

"Action-packed absurdity saves the day in this strongly plotted tale of epic proportions." Horn Book Guide

Ephron, Delia

Frannie in pieces; drawings by Chad W. Beckerman. HarperTeen 2007 374p il $16.99; lib bdg $17.89

Grades: 7 8 9 10   Fic
    1. Father-daughter relationship—Fiction 2. Bereavement—Fiction 3. Puzzles—Fiction
    ISBN 978-0-06-074716-9; 0-06-074716-1; 978-0-06-074717-6 (lib bdg); 0-06-074717-X (lib bdg)
                                        LC 2007-10909

When fifteen-year-old Frannie's father dies, only a mysterious jigsaw puzzle that he leaves behind can help her come to terms with his death.

"This is a tender, moving story dealing with grief and growing up and the power of art to heal." SLJ

Erdrich, Louise

The birchbark house. Hyperion Bks. for Children 1999 244p il hardcover o.p. pa $6.99 *

Grades: 5 6 7 8   Fic
    1. Ojibwa Indians—Fiction
    ISBN 0-7868-0300-2; 0-7868-1454-3 (pa)
                                        LC 98-46366
Omakayas, a seven-year-old Native American girl of the Ojibwa tribe, lives through the joys of summer and the perils of winter on an island in Lake Superior in 1847.

"Erdrich crafts images of tender beauty while weaving Ojibwa words seamlessly into the text. Her gentle spot art throughout complements this first of several projected stories that will 'attempt to retrace [her] own family's history.'" Horn Book Guide

Followed by: The game of silence (2004)

The game of silence; [by] Louise Erdrich. 1st ed. HarperCollins 2004 256p $15.99; lib bdg $16.89; pa $5.99 *

Grades: 5 6 7 8   Fic
    1. Ojibwa Indians—Fiction
    ISBN 0-06-029789-1; 0-06-029790-5 (lib bdg); 0-06-441029-3 (pa)   LC 2004-6018
Sequel to: The birchbark house (1999)
Nine-year-old Omakayas, of the Ojibwa tribe, moves west with her family in 1849.

"Erdrich's captivating tale of four seasons portrays a deep appreciation of our environment, our history, and our Native American sisters and brothers." SLJ

Followed by: The porcupine year (2008)

The porcupine year. HarperCollinsPublishers 2008 193p $15.99; lib bdg $16.89 *

Grades: 5 6 7 8   Fic
    1. Ojibwa Indians—Fiction 2. Family life—Fiction 3. Voyages and travels—Fiction
    ISBN 978-0-06-029787-9; 0-06-029787-5; 978-0-06-029788-6 (lib bdg); 0-06-029788-3 (lib bdg)
                                        LC 2008000757

Sequel to: The game of silence (2004)
In 1852, forced by the United States government to leave their beloved Island of the Golden Breasted Woodpecker, fourteen-year-old Omokayas and her Ojibwe family travel in search of a new home.

"Based on Erdrich's own family history, this celebration of life will move readers with its mischief, its anger, and its sadness. What is left unspoken is as powerful as the story told." Booklist

Ernst, Kathleen, 1959-

Hearts of stone; [by] Kathleen Ernst. 1st ed. Dutton Children's Books 2006 248p $16.99

Grades: 6 7 8 9   Fic
    1. United States—History—1861-1865, Civil War—Fiction 2. Tennessee—Fiction 3. Orphans—Fiction
    ISBN 0-525-47686-5   LC 2005032756

Ernst, Kathleen, 1959-—*Continued*

Orphaned when her father dies fighting for the Union and her mother expires from exhaustion, and also estranged from their Confederate neighbors, fifteen-year-old Hannah struggles to find a way for her family to survive during the Civil War in Tennessee.

"Ernst movingly shows that the calamity and upheaval of war extends far beyond the battlefields." Booklist

Erskine, Kathryn

Quaking. Philomel Books 2007 236p $16.99

Grades: 7 8 9 10   Fic
1. Patriotism—Fiction 2. Toleration—Fiction
3. School stories 4. Society of Friends—Fiction
5. Family life—Fiction 6. Pennsylvania—Fiction
ISBN 978-0-399-24774-3; 0-399-24774-2
                                      LC 2006-34563

In a Pennsylvania town where antiwar sentiments are treated with contempt and violence, Matt, a fourteen-year-old girl living with a Quaker family, deals with the demons of her past as she battles bullies of the present, eventually learning to trust in others as well as herself.

"This is a compelling story, which enfolds the political issues into a deeper focus on the characters' personal stories." Booklist

Esckilsen, Erik E.

The last mall rat. Houghton Mifflin 2003 182p $15; pa $5.95

Grades: 7 8 9 10   Fic
1. Shopping centers and malls—Fiction
ISBN 0-618-23417-9; 0-618-60896-6 (pa)
                                      LC 2002-14436

"Walter Lorraine books"

Too young to get a job at the Onion River Mall, fifteen-year-old Mitch earns money from salesclerks to harrass rude shoppers

"Realistic dialogue and a keen sense of what matters to teens will draw them to this quick read." Booklist

Offsides; a novel; by Erik E. Esckilsen. Houghton Mifflin 2004 172p $15

Grades: 7 8 9 10   Fic
1. Mohawk Indians—Fiction 2. Soccer—Fiction
ISBN 0-618-46284-8   LC 2004-735

Tom Gray, a Mohawk Indian and star soccer player, moves to a new high school and refuses to play for the Warriors with their insulting mascot.

"Fast-paced game scenes alternating with thoughtful passages focusing on Tom's developing maturity make for a balanced, enjoyable read." Booklist

Estevis, Anne

Chicken Foot Farm; by Anne Estevis. Pinata Books 2008 154p pa $10.95

Grades: 5 6 7 8   Fic
1. Mexican Americans—Fiction 2. Ranch life—Fiction
3. Family life—Fiction 4. Texas—Fiction
ISBN 978-1-55885-505-2 (pa); 1-55885-505-X (pa)
                                      LC 2007048338

Alejandro grows from ten years old to the age of seventeen, learning about life from his extended Mexican American family on a small ranch in 1940s South Texas.

"The vignettes are filled with nostalgia and range in tone from funny and tender to tragic and wistful. . . . The emotional intimacy and deep love between its characters is *Chicken Foot Farm's* greatest charm." SLJ

Evangelista, Beth

Gifted. Walker & Co. 2005 180p $16.95

Grades: 5 6 7 8   Fic
1. Gifted children—Fiction 2. Camping—Fiction
3. Bullies—Fiction
ISBN 0-8027-8994-3

Arrogant, mentally gifted George Clark has dreaded the eighth-grade class camping trip and its inevitable bullying, but a hurricane and a friend's loyalty make him realize what is important in life.

"It's hard to write a successful book with an unlikable protagonist . . . but that's what first-time author Evangelista has done. . . . Fresh and funny." Booklist

Fahy, Thomas Richard

The unspoken; [by] Tom Fahy. Simon & Schuster Books for Young Readers 2008 166p $15.99

Grades: 8 9 10 11 12   Fic
1. Horror fiction 2. Cults—Fiction
ISBN 978-1-4169-4007-4; 1-4169-4007-3
                                      LC 2007-00850

Six teens are drawn back to the small, North Carolina town where they once lived and, one by one, begin to die of their worst fears, as prophesied by the cult leader they killed five years earlier, and who they believe poisoned their parents.

"Teeth-clenching suspenseful at times and deliciously creepy at others, Fahy . . . delivers a classic horror story." Publ Wkly

Falcone, L. M., 1951-

Walking with the dead. Kids Can Press 2005 196p $16.95; pa $6.95

Grades: 6 7 8 9   Fic
1. Classical mythology—Fiction 2. Mummies—Fiction
ISBN 1-55337-708-7; 1-55337-709-5 (pa)

"Twelve-year-old Alex's dad is about to open a museum of oddities. Among the items on display is a corpse from ancient Greece. When a surge of electricity awakes the corpse and it starts running around the town, Alex realizes that he needs to step in and help the cadaver out. His efforts take him on the classic hero's journey to the underworld, where Alex and his friend Freddie must outwit a host of monsters from Greek mythology. . . . An amusing adventure, this offers an inventive and lighthearted introduction to the Greek myths." Booklist

Fantaskey, Beth

Jessica's guide to dating on the dark side. Harcourt 2009 354p $17

Grades: 8 9 10 11 12   Fic
1. Horror fiction 2. Vampires—Fiction
ISBN 978-0-15-206384-9; 0-15-206384-6
                                      LC 2007-49002

Fantaskey, Beth—*Continued*

Seventeen-year-old Jessica, adopted and raised in Pennsylvania, learns that she is descended from a royal line of Romanian vampires and that she is betrothed to a vampire prince, who poses as a foreign exchange student while courting her.

"Fantaskey makes this premise work by playing up its absurdities without laughing at them. . . . The romance sizzles, the plot develops ingeniously and suspensefully, and the satire sings." Publ Wkly

Fardell, John, 1967-

The 7 professors of the Far North. G. P. Putnam's Sons 2005 217p il $14.99

Grades: 4 5 6 7   **Fic**

1. Adventure fiction 2. Arctic regions—Fiction 3. Science fiction

ISBN 0-399-24381-X

Eleven-year-old Sam finds himself involved in a dangerous adventure when he and his new friends, brother and sister Ben and Zara, set off for the Arctic to try and rescue the siblings' great-uncle and five other professors from the mad scientist holding them prisoner.

"Action is nonstop and very exciting. This inventive, funny, suspenseful, and exciting book will appeal to most readers." SLJ

Followed by: The flight of the Silver Turtle (2006)

The flight of the Silver Turtle. G. P. Putnam's Sons 2006 233p $15.99

Grades: 4 5 6 7   **Fic**

1. Adventure fiction 2. Airplanes—Fiction 3. Science fiction

ISBN 0-399-24382-8   LC 2006-08241

Sequel to: The 7 professors of the Far North (2005)

Ben, Zara, Sam, and Marcia begin their summer vacation by helping Professor Ampersand and a new friend build the Silver Turtle, a futuristic airplane, but on the day the first test flight is planned, a strange woman steals the airplane with the children inside.

"The writing is consistently upbeat and energetic. . . . Fans of Fardell's previous book will enjoy following the characters and their wacky high-speed adventures." SLJ

Farmer, Nancy, 1941-

The Ear, the Eye, and the Arm; a novel. Orchard Bks. 1994 311p $18.95; lib bdg $19.99 *

Grades: 6 7 8 9   **Fic**

1. Science fiction 2. Zimbabwe—Fiction

ISBN 0-531-06829-3; 0-531-08679-8 (lib bdg)

LC 93-11814

Also available in paperback from Puffin Bks. and Thorndike Press large print edition

A Newbery Medal honor book, 1995

"A Richard Jackson book"

In 2194 in Zimbabwe, General Matsika's three children Tendai, Rita, and Kuda, are kidnapped and put to work in a plastic mine, while three mutant detectives named The Ear, the Eye and the Arm use their special powers to search for them

"Throughout the story, it's the thrilling adventure that will grab readers, who will also like the comic, tender characterizations." Booklist

A girl named Disaster. Orchard Bks. 1996 309p $19.95; pa $7.99

Grades: 6 7 8 9   **Fic**

1. Supernatural—Fiction 2. Adventure fiction 3. Mozambique—Fiction 4. Zimbabwe—Fiction

ISBN 0-531-09539-8; 0-14-038635-1 (pa)

LC 96-15141

A Newbery Medal honor book, 1997

"A Richard Jackson book"

While journeying from Mozambique to Zimbabwe to escape an arranged marriage, eleven-year-old Nhamo struggles to escape drowning and starvation and in so doing comes close to the luminous world of the African spirits

"This story is humorous and heartwrenching, complex and multilayered." SLJ

The house of the scorpion. Atheneum Bks. for Young Readers 2002 380p $17.95; pa $7.99 *

Grades: 7 8 9 10   **Fic**

1. Cloning—Fiction 2. Science fiction

ISBN 0-689-85222-3; 0-689-85223-1 (pa)

LC 2001-56594

A Newbery Medal honor book, 2003

In a future where humans despise clones, Matt enjoys special status as the young clone of El Patrón, the 140-year-old leader of a corrupt drug empire nestled between Mexico and the United States.

"This is a powerful, ultimately hopeful, story that builds on today's sociopolitical, ethical, and scientific issues and prognosticates a compelling picture of what the future could bring." Booklist

The Land of the Silver Apples. Atheneum Books for Young Readers 2007 496p il $18.99; pa $9.99 *

Grades: 5 6 7 8 9   **Fic**

1. Norse mythology—Fiction 2. Vikings—Fiction 3. Druids and Druidism—Fiction 4. Fantasy fiction

ISBN   978-1-4169-0735-0;   1-4169-0735-1; 978-1-4169-0736-7 (pa); 1-4169-0736-x (pa)

LC 2006-31433

Sequel to The Sea of Trolls

"A Richard Jackson book."

After escaping from the Sea of Trolls, the apprentice bard Jack plunges into a new series of adventures, traveling underground to Elfland and uncovering the truth about his little sister Lucy.

"Farmer beautifully balances pell-mell action and quieter thematic points. . . . This hearty adventure, as personal as it is epic, will cradle readers in the 'hollow it its hand.'" Booklist

The Sea of Trolls. Atheneum Books for Young Readers 2004 459p $17.95; pa $9.99 *

Grades: 5 6 7 8 9   **Fic**

1. Norse mythology—Fiction 2. Druids and Druidism—Fiction 3. Vikings—Fiction 4. Fantasy fiction

ISBN 0-689-86744-1; 0-689-86746-8 (pa)

LC 2003-19091

"A Richard Jackson book"

After Jack becomes apprenticed to a Druid bard, he and his little sister Lucy are captured by Viking Berserkers and taken to the home of King Ivar the Boneless and

Farmer, Nancy, 1941-—*Continued*
his half-troll queen, leading Jack to undertake a vital
quest to Jotunheim, home of the trolls.

"This exciting and original fantasy will capture the
hearts and imaginations of readers." SLJ

Includes bibliographical references

Followed by The Land of the Silver Apples (2007)

Farr, Richard, 1960-
Emperors of the ice; a true story of disaster and
survival in the Antarctic, 1910-13. Farrar, Straus &
Giroux 2008 215p il map $19.95
Grades: 6 7 8 9   **Fic**
1. Cherry-Garrard, Apsley, 1886-1959—Fiction
2. Wilson, Edward Adrian, 1872-1912—Fiction
3. Scott, Robert Falcon, 1868-1912—Fiction
4. British Antarctic ("Terra Nova") Expedition (1910-
1913). : (1910-1913)—Fiction 5. Explorers—Fiction
6. Penguins—Fiction 7. Antarctica—Fiction
ISBN 978-0-374-31975-5; 0-374-31975-8
LC 2007-52347
Apsley 'Cherry' Cherry-Garrard shares his adventures
as the youngest member of Robert Scott's expedition to
Antarctica in the early twentieth century, during which
he and Edward Wilson try to learn the evolutionary history of emperor penguins. Includes historical notes.

"Heavily illustrated with paintings, photos, and documents from the actual expedition, the book brings vividly
to life the explorers and scientists of nearly a century
ago." Voice Youth Advocates

Includes bibliographical references

Fehler, Gene, 1940-
Beanball; by Gene Fehler. Clarion Books 2008
119p $16
Grades: 7 8 9 10   **Fic**
1. Baseball—Fiction 2. School stories 3. Novels in
verse
ISBN 0-618-84348-5; 978-0-618-84348-0
LC 2007013058
Relates, from diverse points of view, events surrounding the critical injury of popular and talented high school
athlete, Luke "Wizard" Wallace, when he is hit in the
face by a fastball.

This is a "moving baseball novel in free verse. . . .
This swift read will appeal to both reluctant readers and
baseball players." KLIATT

Feinstein, John
Last shot; a Final Four mystery. Knopf 2005
251p $16.95; lib bdg $18.99
Grades: 6 7 8 9   **Fic**
1. Journalists—Fiction 2. Basketball—Fiction
3. Mystery fiction
ISBN 0-375-83168-1; 0-375-93168-6 (lib bdg)
LC 2004-26535
After winning a basketball reporting contest, eighth
graders Stevie and Susan Carol are sent to cover the Final Four tournament, where they discover that a talented
player is being blackmailed into throwing the final game.

"The action on the court is vividly described. . . .
Mystery fans will find enough suspense in this fast-paced
narrative to keep them hooked." SLJ

Other titles in this series are:
Vanishing act (2006)
Cover-up (2007)
Change-up (2009)

Fensham, Elizabeth
Helicopter man. Bloomsbury 2005 159p il
$15.95
Grades: 6 7 8 9   **Fic**
1. Father-son relationship—Fiction 2. Mentally ill—
Fiction 3. Homeless persons—Fiction 4. Australia—
Fiction
ISBN 1-58234-981-9
Peter Sinclair cares for his father, who is mentally ill,
and tries to make the most of their homeless life togeth-
er.

"Fensham uses the diary format to excellent advantage. . . . This compact, intense read, set in Australia,
will speak directly to teens growing up with a schizo-
phrenic parent, as well as to a wide range of readers who
will finish the affecting story with more questions about
and compassion for the mentally ill." Booklist

Ferraiolo, Jack D.
The big splash; by Jack D. Ferraiolo. Amulet
Books 2008 277p $15.95
Grades: 4 5 6 7   **Fic**
1. School stories 2. Mystery fiction
ISBN 978-0-8109-7067-0; 0-8109-7067-8
LC 2007-49978
Matt Stevens, an average middle schooler with a glib
tongue and a knack for solving crimes, uncovers a mys-
tery while working with "the organization," a mafia-like
syndicate run by seventh-grader Vincent "Mr. Biggs"
Biggio, specializing in forged hall passes, test-copying
rings, black market candy selling, and taking out hits
with water guns.

This "novel delivers plenty of laughs, especially in the
opening chapters, and fans of private-eye spoofs will enjoy this entertaining read." Booklist

Ferris, Jean, 1939-
Much ado about Grubstake. Harcourt, Inc. 2006
265p $17
Grades: 5 6 7 8   **Fic**
1. Gold mines and mining—Fiction 2. Orphans—Fiction 3. City and town life—Fiction 4. Colorado—Fiction
ISBN 0-15-205706-6
When two city folks arrive in the depressed mining
town of Grubstake, Colorado in 1888, sixteen-year-old
orphaned Arley tries to discover why they want to buy
the supposedly worthless mines in the area.

"Ferris combines adventure, love, and off-the-wall
characters in a page-turning story full of good laughs and
common sense messages." Voice Youth Advocates

Underground. Farrar, Straus and Giroux 2007
167p $16
Grades: 7 8 9 10   **Fic**
1. Slavery—Fiction 2. Underground railroad—Fiction
3. Caves—Fiction 4. Kentucky—Fiction
ISBN 978-0-374-37243-9; 0-374-37243-8
LC 2006-37385

Ferris, Jean, 1939——*Continued*

In 1839, Charlotte Brown is sold north to Kentucky, where she becomes a maid at Mammoth Cave Hotel, falls in love with one of the tour guides there, and gets involved in the Underground Railroad.

"Ferris manages to strike a good balance between history and her imagination. Her prose is vivid, the characters strong, the narrative well constructed." NY Times Book Rev

Fienberg, Anna, 1956-

Number 8. Walker 2007 288p $16.95

Grades: 7 8 9 10   Fic

1. Organized crime—Fiction 2. Family life—Fiction 3. Singers—Fiction 4. Mathematics—Fiction 5. Australia—Fiction

ISBN 978-0-8027-9660-8; 0-8027-9660-5

LC 2007-14706

While hiding out from the mob in the suburbs with his mother, a singer, Jackson uses his fascination with math and numbers to make friends, but strange phone calls and even greater threats endanger not only Jackson and his mother, but his new girlfriend, as well.

"The fact that each character has an idiosyncratic passion that somehow helps them understand the others adds dimension to an already effective suspense plot." Bull Cent Child Books

Finn, Mary

Anila's journey. Candlewick Press 2008 309p $16.99

Grades: 7 8 9 10   Fic

1. Racially mixed people—Fiction 2. Missing persons—Fiction 3. India—History—1765-1947, British occupation—Fiction

ISBN 978-0-7636-3916-7; 0-7636-3916-8

LC 2008-17917

In late eighteenth-century Calcutta, half-Indian half-Irish Anila Tandy finds herself alone with nothing but her artistic talent to rely on, searching for her father who is presumed dead.

This is "an engrossing trek with a truly admirable young woman who refuses to compromise either her independence or family loyalty." Bull Cent Child Books

Fisher, Catherine, 1957-

The oracle betrayed; book one of The Oracle Prophecies; by Catherine Fisher. 1st American ed. Greenwillow Books 2004 341p (Oracle prophecies) $16.99; lib bdg $17.89; pa $6.99

Grades: 7 8 9 10   Fic

1. Fantasy fiction

ISBN 0-06-057157-8; 0-06-057158-6 (lib bdg); 0-06-057159-4 (pa)   LC 2003-48498

After she is chosen to be "Bearer-of-the-god," Mirany questions the established order and sets out, along with a musician and a scribe, to find the legitimate heir of the religious leader known as the Archon.

"This [is] a well-developed world with its own culture, some sharply realized settings, and several strong, distinctive characters." Booklist

Other titles in this series :

Day of the scarab: book three of The Oracle Prophecies (2006)

The Sphere of Secrets: book two of The Oracle Prophecies (2005)

Fitzgerald, Dawn

Soccer chick rules. Roaring Brook Press 2006 150p $16.95

Grades: 5 6 7 8   Fic

1. School stories 2. Soccer—Fiction 3. Politics—Fiction

ISBN 1-59643-137-7

"A Deborah Brodie book"

While trying to focus on a winning soccer season, thirteen-year-old Tess becomes involved in local politics when she learns that all sports programs at her school will be stopped unless a tax levy is passed.

This is "a fast-moving, true-to-life, amusing take on school life. The dialogue is especially spot-on." Booklist

Flake, Sharon G.

Bang! Jump at the Sun/Hyperion Books for Children 2005 298p $16.99

Grades: 8 9 10 11 12   Fic

1. Violence—Fiction 2. Family life—Fiction 3. African Americans—Fiction

ISBN 0-7868-1844-1   LC 2005-47434

A teenage boy must face the harsh realities of inner city life, a disintegrating family, and destructive temptations as he struggles to find his identity as a young man.

"This disturbing, thought-provoking novel will leave readers with plenty of food for thought and should fuel lively discussions." SLJ

The broken bike boy and the Queen of 33rd Street. Jump at the Sun/Hyperion Books for Children 2007 132p il $15.99 *

Grades: 4 5 6 7   Fic

1. Friendship—Fiction 2. School stories 3. African Americans—Fiction

ISBN 978-1-4231-0032-4; 1-4231-0032-8

LC 2006-35590

Ten-year-old Queen, a spoiled and conceited African American girl who is disliked by most of her classmates, learns a lesson about friendship from an unlikely "knight in shining armor."

"Complex intergenerational characters and a rich urban setting defy stereotyping. . . . Infrequent detailed pencil illustrations . . . add a welcome dimension." Horn Book

The skin I'm in. Jump at the Sun 1998 171p $14.95; pa $5.99

Grades: 6 7 8 9   Fic

1. African Americans—Fiction 2. Teachers—Fiction 3. School stories

ISBN 0-7868-0444-0; 0-7868-1307-5 (pa)

LC 98-19615

Thirteen-year-old Maleeka, uncomfortable because her skin is extremely dark, meets a new teacher with a birthmark on her face and makes some discoveries about how to love who she is and what she looks like

This "novel is fast-paced and realistic." Horn Book Guide

Flanagan, John

The ruins of Gorlan. Philomel Bks. 2005 249p (Ranger's apprentice) $15.99 *

Grades: 5 6 7 8   **Fic**

1. Fantasy fiction

ISBN 0-399-24454-9

When fifteen-year-old Will is rejected by battleschool, he becomes the reluctant apprentice to the mysterious Ranger Halt, and winds up protecting the kingdom from danger.

"Flanagan concentrates on character, offering readers a young protagonist they will care about and relationships that develop believably over time." Booklist

Other titles in this series are:

The burning bridge (2006)

The icebound land (2007)

The battle for Skandia (2008)

The socerer of the north (2008)

Fleischman, Paul

Bull Run; woodcuts by David Frampton. HarperCollins Pubs. 1993 104p il lib bdg $16.89; pa $4.99 *

Grades: 6 7 8 9   **Fic**

1. Bull Run, 1st Battle of, 1861—Fiction 2. United States—History—1861-1865, Civil War—Fiction

ISBN 0-06-021447-3 (lib bdg); 0-06-440588-5 (pa)

LC 92-14745

"A Laura Geringer book"

"In a sequence of sixty one- to two-page narratives, fifteen fictional characters (and one real general) recount their experiences during the Civil War. A few encounter each other, most meet unawares or not at all, but they have in common a battle, Bull Run, that affects—and sometimes ends—their lives." Bull Cent Child Books

"Abandoning the conventions of narrative fiction, Fleischman tells a vivid, many-sided story in this original and moving book. An excellent choice for readers' theater in the classroom or on stage." Booklist

A fate totally worse than death. Candlewick Press 1995 124p hardcover o.p. pa $5.99

Grades: 7 8 9 10   **Fic**

1. School stories

ISBN 1-56402-627-2; 0-7636-2189-7

LC 94-48433

In this horror novel parody, three self-centered members of Cliffside High School's ruling clique, who are beginning to age rapidly, become convinced that the beautiful new exchange student is the ghost of the girl whose death they caused the year before

"The fun is in the vapid thinking of the girls, the trendy teen scenes, and the parody of YA actions and dialogue. This hilarious farce should have teen-horror fans screaming with laughter." SLJ

Seedfolks; illustrations by Judy Pedersen. HarperCollins Pubs. 1997 69p $14.99; lib bdg $15.89; pa $4.99 *

Grades: 4 5 6 7   **Fic**

1. Gardens—Fiction 2. City and town life—Fiction

ISBN 0-06-027471-9; 0-06-027472-7 (lib bdg); 0-06-447207-8 (pa)   LC 96-26696

"Joanna Cotler books"

This "novel tells about an urban garden started by a child and nurtured by people of all ages and ethnic and economic backgrounds. Each of the thirteen chapters is narrated by a different character, allowing the reader to watch as a community develops out of disconnected lives and prior suspicions." Horn Book Guide

"The characters' vitality and the sharply delineated details of the neighborship make this not merely an exercise in craftsmanship or morality but an engaging, entertaining novel as well." Booklist

Seek. Front St./Cricket Bks. 2001 167p $16.95

Grades: 7 8 9 10   **Fic**

1. Fathers—Fiction 2. Radio—Fiction

ISBN 0-8126-4900-1   LC 2001-28869

"A Marcato book"

"Using a script format, Rob relates his experiences growing up listening to local and distant radio stations, searching for the disk jockey father who abandoned him before birth." Horn Book Guide

"Fleischman has orchestrated a symphony that is both joyful and poignant with this book designed for reader's theatre." Voice Youth Advocates

Fleischman, Sid, 1920-

The entertainer and the dybbuk. Greenwillow Books 2007 180p $16.99; lib bdg $17.89 *

Grades: 6 7 8 9   **Fic**

1. Holocaust, 1933-1945—Fiction 2. Jews—Fiction 3. Supernatural—Fiction 4. Ghost stories 5. Ventriloquism—Fiction

ISBN 978-0-06-134445-9; 0-06-13444-1; 978-0-06-134446-6 (lib bdg); 0-06-134446-X (lib bdg)

LC 2007-17267

A struggling American ventriloquist in post-World War II Europe is possessed by the mischievous spirit of a young Jewish boy killed in the Holocaust.

"This exciting and thought-provoking book belongs in every collection." SLJ

The whipping boy; illustrations by Peter Sis. Greenwillow Bks. 1986 90p il $16.99; pa $5.99

Grades: 5 6 7 8   **Fic**

1. Thieves—Fiction 2. Adventure fiction

ISBN 0-688-06216-4; 0-06-052122-8 (pa)

LC 85-17555

Awarded the Newbery Medal, 1987

"A round tale of adventure and humor, this follows the fortunes of Prince Roland (better known as Prince Brat) and his whipping boy, Jemmy, who has received all the hard knocks for the prince's mischief. . . . There's not a moment's lag in pace, and the stock characters, from Hold-Your-Nose Billy to Betsy's dancing bear Petunia, have enough inventive twists to project a lively air to it all." Bull Cent Child Books

Fletcher, Charlie

Stoneheart. Hyperion Books for Children 2007 450p (Stoneheart trilogy) $16.99

Grades: 5 6 7 8   **Fic**

1. Fantasy fiction

ISBN 978-1-4231-0175-8; 1-4231-0175-8

LC 2007-01138

Fletcher, Charlie—*Continued*

When twelve-year-old George accidentally decapitates a stone statue in London, England, he falls into a parallel dimension where he must battle ancient "live" statues and solve a dangerous riddle.

This "is an action-packed fantasy filled with battles, chases, and an intriguing variety of characters." SLJ

Other titles in this series are:

Ironhand (2008)

Silvertongue (2009)

Fletcher, Ralph, 1953-

The one o'clock chop; [by] Ralph Fletcher. 1st ed. Henry Holt 2007 183p $16.95

Grades: 7 8 9 10 **Fic**

1. Cousins—Fiction 2. Boats and boating—Fiction 3. New York (State)—Fiction

ISBN 978-0-8050-8143-5; 0-8050-8143-7

LC 2006035470

In New York, fourteen-year-old Matt spends the summer of 1973 digging clams to earn money for his own boat and falling for Jazzy, a beautiful and talented girl from Hawaii who happens to be his first cousin.

"Plenty of universal teen fascinations and concerns exist for those readers willing to enter Matt's world and give themselves over to this smoothly paced and competently written novel." SLJ

Fletcher, Susan, 1951-

Alphabet of dreams. Atheneum Books for Young Readers 2006 294p map $16.95

Grades: 6 7 8 9 **Fic**

1. Jesus Christ—Nativity—Fiction 2. Iran—Fiction 3. Dreams—Fiction 4. Zoroastrianism—Fiction

ISBN 0-689-85042-5

"Ginee Seo Books"

Fourteen-year-old Mitra, of royal Persian lineage, and her five-year-old brother Babak, whose dreams foretell the future, flee for their lives in the company of the magus Melchoir and two other Zoroastrian priests, traveling through Persia as they follow star signs leading to a newly-born king in Bethlehem. Includes historical notes

"The characters are vivid and whole, the plot compelling, and the setting vast." Voice Youth Advocates

Dragon's milk. Atheneum Pubs. 1989 242p hardcover o.p. pa $5.99

Grades: 7 8 9 10 **Fic**

1. Dragons—Fiction 2. Fantasy fiction

ISBN 0-689-31579-1; 0-689-71623-0 (pa)

LC 88-35059

"A Jean Karl book"

Kaeldra, an outsider adopted by an Elythian family as a baby, possesses the power to understand dragons and uses this power to try to save her younger sister who needs dragon's milk to recover from an illness

"High-fantasy fans will delight in the clash of swords, the flash of magic, the many escape-and-rescue scenes." Booklist

Other titles in this series are:

Flight of the Dragon Kyn (1993)

Sign of the dove (1996)

Walk across the sea. Atheneum Bks. for Young Readers 2001 214p hardcover o.p. pa $4.99

Grades: 5 6 7 8 **Fic**

1. Chinese Americans—Fiction 2. Prejudices—Fiction

ISBN 0-689-84133-7; 0-689-85707-1 (pa)

LC 00-50246

In late nineteenth-century California, when Chinese immigrants are being driven out or even killed for fear they will take jobs from whites, fifteen-year-old Eliza Jane McCully defies the townspeople and her lighthouse-keeper father to help a Chinese boy who has been kind to her

"This is a gripping and complex story, and Fletcher's lyrical depiction of 19th-century life, her exceptionally well-drawn protagonist, and her deft analysis of racial discrimination make the book even more powerful." SLJ

Flinn, Alex

Beastly. HarperTeen 2007 304p $16.99; lib bdg $17.89

Grades: 6 7 8 9 10 **Fic**

1. Fantasy fiction 2. New York (N.Y.)—Fiction

ISBN 978-0-06-087416-2; 0-06-087416-3; 978-0-06-087417-9 (lib bdg); 0-06-087417-1 (lib bdg)

LC 2006-36241

A modern retelling of "Beauty and the Beast" from the point of view of the Beast, a vain Manhattan private school student who is turned into a monster and must find true love before he can return to his human form.

This "is creative enough to make it an engaging read. . . . [This is an] engrossing tale that will have appeal for fans of fantasy and realistic fiction." Voice Youth Advocates

Breaking point; [by] Alex Flinn. HarperTempest 2002 241p hardcover o.p. pa $6.99

Grades: 7 8 9 10 **Fic**

1. Friendship—Fiction 2. School stories

ISBN 0-06-623847-1; 0-06-623848-X; 0-06-447371-6 (pa)

LC 2001-39504

"Gate-Brickell Christian is a toney private school attended by the rich and privileged—and a few despised offspring of the staff, like Paul Richmond. . . . Charlie, the magnetic class ringleader, becomes the center of Paul's world. . . . Paul's loyalty to Charlie takes him from vandalism (battering mailboxes) to cheating . . . to, finally, leaving a Charlie-made bomb in a classroom." Bull Cent Child Books

"In this intense story of peer pressure and the need to be accepted, the characters are realistically drawn and reflect the nature of high school relationships." SLJ

Fogelin, Adrian, 1951-

The big nothing. 1st ed. Peachtree 2004 235p $14.95

Grades: 7 8 9 10 **Fic**

1. Family life—Fiction 2. Pianists—Fiction

ISBN 1-56145-326-9 LC 2004-6327

Thirteen-year-old Justin Riggs struggles to cope with major family problems, including a brother who might be heading for the Persian Gulf, but finds an escape in piano lessons and the dream of a romance with a popular girl.

Fogelin, Adrian, 1951-—_Continued_

"Serious and humorous by turns, this seemingly simple story is actually quite complex but not weighty and will be enthusiastically embraced." SLJ

The real question. Peachtree 2006 234p $15.95
Grades: 7 8 9 10   **Fic**
    1. Father-son relationship—Fiction 2. Florida—Fiction
ISBN 1-56145-383-8   LC 2006013996

Fisher Brown, a sixteen-year-old over-achiever, is on the verge of academic burnout when he impulsively decides to stop cramming for the SATs for one weekend and accompany his ne'erdowell neighbor to an out-of-town job repairing a roof.

"Fisher's first-person narration is dead-on. . . . This amazing title . . . should be required reading for every teen . . . who feels the weight of a parent's expectations but cannot quite figure out what to do about it." Voice Youth Advocates

Fombelle, Timothée de, 1973-

Toby alone; translated by Sarah Ardizzone; illustrated by François Place. Candlewick Press 2009 384p il $17.99
Grades: 5 6 7 8   **Fic**
    1. Trees—Fiction 2. Fantasy fiction
ISBN 978-0-7636-4181-8; 0-7636-4181-2
Original French edition 2006

Toby is just one and a half millimeters tall, and he's the most wanted person in his world of the great oak Tree. When Toby's father discovers that the Tree is alive, he realizes that exploiting it could do damage to their world. Refusing to reveal the secret to an enraged community, Toby's parents have been imprisoned. Only Toby has managed to escape, but for how long?

"The impressive debut novel from French playwright de Fombelle deftly weaves mature political commentary, broad humor and some subtle satire into a thoroughly enjoyable adventure." Publ Wkly

Ford, Christine, 1953-

Scout; [by] Christine Ford. Delacorte Press 2006 213p $14.95; lib bdg $16.99
Grades: 5 6 7 8   **Fic**
    1. Friendship—Fiction 2. Family life—Fiction
3. Texas—Fiction 4. Novels in verse
ISBN 0-385-73234-1; 0-385-90260-3 (lib bdg)
       LC 2005005696

After her mother dies, eleven-year-old Cecelia befriends a new boy at school, but soon realizes that the scruffy youth's home life is the reason for his introspective personality, which is so much like her own.

"With short lines and an immediate first-person narrative, the free verse in this first novel is that rare combination—an easy read and beautiful poetry." Booklist

Ford, John C., 1971-

The morgue and me. Viking 2009 313p $17.99
Grades: 8 9 10 11 12   **Fic**
    1. Criminal investigation—Fiction 2. Homicide—Fiction 3. Journalists—Fiction 4. Michigan—Fiction
5. Mystery fiction
ISBN 978-0-670-01096-7; 0-670-01096-0
       LC 2009-01956

Eighteen-year-old Christopher, who plans to be a spy, learns of a murder cover-up through his summer job as a morgue assistant and teams up with Tina, a gorgeous newspaper reporter, to investigate, despite great danger.

"Ford spins a tale that's complex but not confusing, never whitewashing some of the harsher crimes people commit. The result is a story that holds its own as a mainstream mystery as well as a teen novel." Publ Wkly

Ford, Michael, 1980-

The Fire of Ares; [by] Michael Ford. Walker & Co. 2008 244p (Spartan quest) $16.95
Grades: 4 5 6 7   **Fic**
    1. Lysander, d. 395 B.C.—Fiction 2. Slavery—Fiction
3. Social classes—Fiction 4. Sparta (Extinct city)—Fiction 5. Greece—History—Fiction
ISBN 978-0-8027-9744-5; 0-8027-9744-X
       LC 2007024237

When slaves rebel in ancient Sparta, twelve-year-old Lysander, guarded by an heirloom amulet, the Fire of Ares, is caught between the Spartan ruling class, with whom he has been training as a warrior since his noble heritage was revealed, and those among whom he was recently laboring as a slave.

"Middle-grade boys who love action and vividly depicted battles will seize upon Ford's children's book debut . . . and they'll encounter a large number of interesting facts about ancient Greece along the way." Booklist

Another title in this series is:
Birth of a warrior (2008)

Ford, Michael Thomas

Suicide notes; a novel. HarperTeen 2008 295p $16.99; lib bdg $17.89 *
Grades: 8 9 10 11 12   **Fic**
    1. Suicide—Fiction 2. Psychiatric hospitals—Fiction
3. Homosexuality—Fiction
ISBN   978-0-06-073755-9;   0-06-073755-7; 978-0-06-073756-6 (lib bdg); 0-06-073756-5 (lib bdg)
       LC 2008-19199

Brimming with sarcasm, fifteen-year-old Jeff describes his stay in a psychiatric ward after attempting to commit suicide.

Ford's "characterizations run deep, and without too much contrivance the teens' interactions slowly dislodge clues about what triggered Jeff's suicide attempt." Publ Wkly

Forester, Victoria

The girl who could fly. Feiwel and Friends 2008 329p $16.95 *
Grades: 4 5 6 7   **Fic**
    1. Science fiction 2. Flight—Fiction 3. School stories
ISBN 978-0-312-37462-4; 0-312-37462-3
       LC 2008-06882

When homeschooled farm girl Piper McCloud reveals her ability to fly, she is quickly taken to a secret government facility to be trained with other exceptional children, but she soon realizes that something is very wrong and begins working with brilliant and wealthy Conrad to escape.

"The story soars, just like Piper, with enough loop-de-

Forester, Victoria—*Continued*

loops to keep kids uncertain about what will come next. . . . Best of all are the book's strong, lightly wrapped messages about friendship and authenticity and the difference between doing well and doing good." Booklist

Forman, Gayle

If I stay; a novel. Dutton Children's Books 2009 201p $16.99 *

Grades: 7 8 9 10   Fic

1. Coma—Fiction 2. Death—Fiction 3. Medical care—Fiction 4. Oregon—Fiction

ISBN 978-0-525-42103-0; 0-525-42103-3

LC 2008-23938

While in a coma following an automobile accident that killed her parents and younger brother, seventeen-year-old Mia, a gifted cellist, weights whether to live with her grief or join her family in death.

"Intensely moving, the novel will force readers to take stock of their lives and the people and things that make them worth living." Publ Wkly

Foxlee, Karen, 1971-

The anatomy of wings. Alfred A. Knopf 2009 361p $16.99; lib bdg $19.99 *

Grades: 8 9 10 11 12   Fic

1. Suicide—Fiction 2. Bereavement—Fiction 3. Sisters—Fiction 4. Family life—Fiction 5. Australia—Fiction

ISBN 978-0-375-85643-3; 0-375-85643-9; 978-0-375-95643-0 (lib bdg); 0-375-95643-3 (lib bdg)

LC 2008-19373

First published 2007 in Australia

After the suicide of her troubled teenage sister, eleven-year-old Jenny struggles to understand what actually happened.

Jenny's "observations are . . . poetic and washed with magic realism. . . . With heart-stopping accuracy and sly symbolism, Foxlee captures the small ways that humans reveal themselves, the mysterious intensity of female adolescence, and the surreal quiet of a grieving house, which slowly and with astonishing resilience fills again with sound and music." Booklist

Foyt, Victoria

The virtual life of Lexie Diamond. HarperTempest 2007 310p $16.99; lib bdg $17.89

Grades: 6 7 8 9 10   Fic

1. Supernatural—Fiction 2. Homicide—Fiction 3. California—Fiction

ISBN 978-0-06-082563-8; 0-06-082563-4; 978-0-06-082564-5 (lib bdg); 0-06-082564-2 (lib bdg)

LC 2006-29873

Fourteen-year-old Lexie is only at peace while using her computer, so when her mother dies suddenly, Lexie tries to connect with her online. Lexie not only discovers that her mother was murdered, she learns that her father's new girlfriend is big trouble.

"Lexie's internal dialogue and unique spiritual perspective make her a fascinating central character." SLJ

Frank, E. R.

Life is funny; a novel. DK Ink 2000 263p $19.99

Grades: 7 8 9 10   Fic

1. Brooklyn (New York, N.Y.)—Fiction

ISBN 0-7894-2634-X   LC 99-23452

Also available in paperback from Puffin Bks.

"A Richard Jackson book"

The lives of eleven young people of different races, economic backgrounds, and family situations living in Brooklyn, New York, become intertwined over a seven year period

"The voices ring true, and the talk is painful, vulgar, rough, sexy, funny, fearful, furious, gentle." Booklist

Wrecked. Atheneum Books for Young Readers 2005 247p $15.95

Grades: 8 9 10 11 12   Fic

1. Traffic accidents—Fiction 2. Bereavement—Fiction

ISBN 0-689-87383-2   LC 2004-18448

"A Richard Jackson Book"

After a car accident seriously injures her best friend and kills her brother's girlfriend, sixteen-year-old Anna tries to cope with her guilt and grief, while learning some truths about her family and herself.

"This story is compulsively readable both because Anna is likable and imperfect and because Frank's writing is so fluid." SLJ

Franklin, Emily

The other half of me. Delacorte Press 2007 247p $15.99; lib bdg $18.99

Grades: 8 9 10 11 12   Fic

1. Identity (Psychology)—Fiction 2. Sisters—Fiction 3. Artists—Fiction

ISBN 978-0-385-73445-5; 0-385-73445-X; 978-0-385-90449-0 (lib bdg); 0-385-90449-5 (lib bdg)

LC 2006-36825

Feeling out of place in her athletic family, artistic sixteen-year-old Jenny Fitzgerald, whose biological father was a sperm donor, finds her half sister through the Sibling Donor Registry and contacts her, hoping that this will finally make her feel complete.

"Franklin offers readers an engaging protagonist whose humor and unusual situation highlight the lonely and displaced feelings common to many teens." SLJ

Frazer, Megan, 1977-

Secrets of truth and beauty. Hyperion 2009 $15.99

Grades: 7 8 9 10   Fic

1. Sisters—Fiction 2. Obesity—Fiction 3. Farm life—Fiction 4. Massachusetts—Fiction

ISBN 978-1-4231-1711-7; 1-4231-1711-5

"At age seven, Dara Cohen tap-danced and sang her way to stardom, winning the title of Little Miss Maine. Now, at 17, Dara carries a lot of baggage, both around her hips and in her heart. . . . When her autobiographical English presentation about society's obsession with thinness is horribly misunderstood, Dara decides to seek out her estranged older sister, now living on a Massachusetts goat farm. . . . Readers will quickly become intrigued with the unraveling of family secrets and the cast

Frazer, Megan, 1977——*Continued*
of memorable characters. . . . Dara emerges as a likable, complex heroine, whose growing self-confidence is touching and inspiring." Publ Wkly

Frederick, Heather Vogel
The voyage of Patience Goodspeed. Simon & Schuster Bks. for Young Readers 2002 219p hardcover o.p. pa $4.99
Grades: 5 6 7 8   **Fic**
1. Seafaring life—Fiction 2. Whaling—Fiction 3. Navigation—Fiction
ISBN 0-689-84851-X; 0-689-84869-2 (pa)
LC 2001-49039
Following their mother's death in Nantucket, Captain Goodspeed brings twelve-year-old Patience and six-year-old Tad aboard his whaling ship, where a new crew member incites a mutiny and Patience puts her mathematical ability to good use
"This is an exciting voyage of peril and self-discovery." N Y Times Book Rev
Another title about Patience is:
The education of Patience Goodspeed (2004)

Fredericks, Mariah
Crunch time. Atheneum Bks. for Young Readers 2006 317p $15.95
Grades: 8 9 10 11 12   **Fic**
1. Friendship—Fiction 2. School stories
ISBN 0-689-86938-X   LC 2004-20008
"A Richard Jackson book"
Four students, who have formed a study group to prepare for the SAT exam, sustain each other through the emotional highs and lows of their junior year in high school.
"Fredericks writes about high school academics and social rules with sharp insight and spot-on humor." Booklist

Head games. Atheneum Books for Young Readers 2004 260p $15.95
Grades: 7 8 9 10   **Fic**
1. Dating (Social customs)—Fiction 2. School stories
ISBN 0-689-85532-X   LC 2003-17012
"A Richard Jackson book"
Two teenagers connect online in a roleplaying game which leads them into their own face-to-face, half-acknowledged courtship.
"This novel realistically portrays young adults trying to find themselves, fit in, and resist the labels put on them." SLJ

Love; illustrated by Liselotte Watkins. Atheneum Books for Young Readers 2007 270p il (In the cards) $15.99
Grades: 5 6 7 8   **Fic**
1. Tarot—Fiction 2. Fortune telling—Fiction 3. School stories 4. Friendship—Fiction
ISBN 978-0-689-87654-7; 0-689-87654-8
LC 2005-31956
"A Richard Jackson book"
Thirteen-year-old Anna hopes that her newly inherited tarot cards will predict an exciting future, including be-

coming the girlfriend of eighth-grade hottie, Declan Kelso.
"Fredericks displays a keen ear for dialogue and a knack for expressing some complex, real middle school emotions." SLJ
Other titles in this series are:
Fame (2008)
Life (2008)

Freitas, Donna, 1972-
The possibilities of sainthood. Farrar, Straus & Giroux 2008 272p $16.95 *
Grades: 7 8 9 10 11 12   **Fic**
1. Saints—Fiction 2. Catholics—Fiction 3. Italian Americans—Fiction 4. Family life—Fiction 5. School stories 6. Rhode Island—Fiction
ISBN 978-0-374-36087-0; 0-374-36087-1
LC 2007-33298
"Frances Foster books"
While regularly petitioning the Vatican to make her the first living saint, fifteen-year-old Antonia Labella prays to assorted patron saints for everything from help with preparing the family's fig trees for a Rhode Island winter to getting her first kiss from the right boy.
"With a satisfying ending, this novel about the realistic struggles of a chaste teen is a great addition to all collections." SLJ

French, Jackie, 1950-
Rover. HarperCollins Publishers 2007 283p $16.99; lib bdg $17.89 *
Grades: 5 6 7 8   **Fic**
1. Freydis Eriksdottir, ca. 971-ca. 1010—Fiction 2. Vikings—Fiction 3. Slavery—Fiction 4. Dogs—Fiction 5. Sex role—Fiction
ISBN   978-0-06-085078-4;   0-06-085078-7; 978-0-06-085079-1 (lib bdg); 0-06-085079-5 (lib bdg)
LC 2006-19545
Captured by Vikings, young Hekja is taken as a slave to Greenland by the daughter of Erik the Red, and accompanied by no one from her homeland but her loyal dog, shares adventures with her new mistress.
"In French's accessible, historically accurate telling, Hekja both suffers and profits from her experiences. . . . French has created compelling, fully realized characters." Booklist

French, Vivian
The robe of skulls; [illustrated by] Ross Collins. Candlewick Press 2008 208p il (Tales from the five kingdoms series) $14.99; pa $5.99
Grades: 4 5 6   **Fic**
1. Fairy tales 2. Bats—Fiction 3. Trolls—Fiction 4. Magic—Fiction
ISBN   978-0-7636-3531-2;   0-7636-3531-6; 978-0-7636-4364-5 (pa); 0-7636-4364-5 (pa)
LC 2007-38290
The sorceress Lady Lamorna has her heart set on a very expensive new robe, and she will stop at nothing—including kidnapping and black magic—to get the money to pay for it.
"Collins' black-and-white line drawings, dropped hap-

French, Vivian—*Continued*

hazardly into the text, perfectly complement the story, offering visual metaphors for the heady narrative mix of melodrama and humor." Bull Cent Child Books

Followed by: The Bag of bones (2009)

Freymann-Weyr, Garret, 1965-

My heartbeat. Houghton Mifflin 2002 154p $15

Grades: 7 8 9 10 **Fic**

1. Siblings—Fiction 2. Homosexuality—Fiction

ISBN 0-618-14181-2 LC 2001-47059

Also available in paperback from Puffin Bks.

Michael L. Printz Award honor book, 2003

As she tries to understand the closeness between her older brother and his best friend, fourteen-year-old Ellen finds her relationship with each of them changing

"This beautiful novel tells a frank, upbeat story of teen bisexual love in all its uncertainty, pain, and joy. . . . The fast, clipped dialogue will sweep teens into the story, as will Ellen's immediate first-person, present-tense narrative." Booklist

Friðrik Erlingsson

Benjamin Dove. North-South 2007 206p $15.95; pa $7.95

Grades: 6 7 8 9 **Fic**

1. Friendship—Fiction

ISBN 978-0-7358-2150-7; 0-7358-2150-X; 978-0-7358-2149-1 (pa); 0-7358-2149-6 (pa)

"Benjamin tells the story of the summer her was 12, when free-spirited Roland moved into the neighborhood and changed the lives of Benjamin and his friends Jeff and Manny forever. . . . This is a well-written, attention-grabbing tale of desire for acceptance, conflict between good and evil, and coming-of-age." SLJ

Friedman, Aimee, 1979-

The year my sister got lucky. Scholastic 2008 370p $16.99

Grades: 7 8 9 10 **Fic**

1. Sisters—Fiction 2. Moving—Fiction 3. Country life—Fiction 4. City and town life—Fiction 5. New York (State)—Fiction

ISBN 978-0-439-92227-2; 0-439-92227-5

LC 2007-16416

When fourteen-year-old Katie and her older sister, Michaela, move from New York City to upstate New York, Katie is horrified by the country lifestyle but is even more shocked when her sister adapts effortlessly, enjoying their new life, unlike Katie.

"Friedman gets the push and pull of the sister bond just right in this delightful, funny, insightful journey." Booklist

Friedman, D. Dina

Escaping into the night. Simon & Schuster for Young Readers 2006 199p $15.95

Grades: 6 7 8 9 **Fic**

1. Holocaust, 1933-1945—Fiction 2. Jewish refugees—Fiction 3. Poland—Fiction 4. World War, 1939-1945—Fiction

ISBN 1-4169-0258-9

"Halina, a Jewish teen, is expelled from her Polish ghetto just before residents are being exterminated or sent to concentration camps. She joins a group of refugees who have banded together in an underground encampment in the Belorussian forests during World War II. . . . This compelling story offers an unusual insight into a different war experience." Voice Youth Advocates

Friedman, Robin, 1968-

The importance of wings. Charlesbridge 2009 170p $15.95

Grades: 6 7 8 9 **Fic**

1. Friendship—Fiction 2. Israelis—Fiction 3. New York (N.Y.)—Fiction

ISBN 978-1-58089-330-5; 1-58089-330-9

LC 2008025326

Although she longs to be an all-American girl, Roxanne, a timid, Israeli-born thirteen-year-old who idolizes Wonder Woman, begins to see things differently when the supremely confident Liat, also from Israel, moves into the "cursed house" next door and they become friends.

"Friedman does an exquisite job in bringing the two older girls to life and showing how each has responded to her family's upheavals and current circumstances. Minor characters are also compelling and, for the most part, endearing." Booklist

Friend, Natasha, 1972-

Bounce; [by] Natasha Friend. Scholastic Press 2007 188p $16.99 *

Grades: 6 7 8 9 **Fic**

1. Remarriage—Fiction 2. Stepfamilies—Fiction 3. Moving—Fiction 4. Massachusetts—Fiction

ISBN 978-0-439-85350-7; 0-439-85350-8

LC 2006038126

Thirteen-year-old Evyn's world is turned upside-down when her father, widowed since she was a toddler, suddenly decides to remarry a woman with six children, move with Ev and her brother from Maine to Boston, and enroll her in private school.

The author "presents, through hip conversations and humor, believable characters and a feel-good story with a satisfying amount of pathos." SLJ

Lush. Scholastic Press 2006 178p $16.99

Grades: 7 8 9 10 **Fic**

1. Alcoholism—Fiction 2. Fathers—Fiction

ISBN 0-439-85346-X LC 2005-031333

Unable to cope with her father's alcoholism, thirteen-year-old Sam corresponds with an older student, sharing her family problems and asking for advice.

"Friend adeptly takes a teen problem and turns it into a believable, sensitive, character-driven story, with realistic dialogue." Booklist

Friend, Natasha, 1972-—*Continued*

Perfect. Milkweed Editions 2004 172p $16.95;
pa $6.95

Grades: 6 7 8 9 **Fic**

1. Bereavement—Fiction 2. Bulimia—Fiction

ISBN 1-57131-652-3; 1-57131-651-5 (pa)

LC 2004-6371

Following the death of her father, thirteen-year-old Isabelle uses bulimia as a way to avoid her mother's and
ten-year-old sister's grief, as well as her own.

"Isabelle's grief and anger are movingly and honestly
portrayed, and her eventual empathy for her mother is
believable and touching." Booklist

Friesen, Gayle, 1960-

The Isabel factor. KCP Fiction 2005 252p
$16.95; pa $6.95

Grades: 7 8 9 10 **Fic**

1. Friendship—Fiction 2. Camps—Fiction

ISBN 1-55337-737-0; 1-55337-738-9 (pa)

"Anna and Zoe are inseparable—at least until Zoe
breaks her arm and Anna finds herself on her way to
summer camp without her best friend. . . . By the time
Zoe arrives at camp (with her arm still in a sling), Anna
is already embroiled in keeping peace between the indi-
vidualistic Isabel and everyone else in Cabin 7. . . .
Girls addicted to friendship stories will welcome this particularly well-crafted novel." Booklist

Friesner, Esther M.

Nobody's princess; [by] Esther Friesner.
Random House 2007 305p $16.99; lib bdg $19.99

Grades: 6 7 8 9 10 **Fic**

1. Helen of Troy (Legendary character)—Fiction
2. Sex role—Fiction 3. Classical mythology—Fiction
4. Adventure fiction

ISBN   978-0-375-87528-1;   0-375-87528-X;
978-0-375-97528-8 (lib bdg); 0-375-97528-4 (lib bdg)

LC 2006-06515

Determined to fend for herself in a world where only
men have real freedom, headstrong Helen, who will be
called queen of Sparta and Helen of Troy one day, learns
to fight, hunt, and ride horses while disguised as a boy,
and goes on an adventure throughout the Mediterranean
world.

This "is a fascinating portrait. . . . Along the way,
Friesner skillfully exposes larger issues of women's
rights, human bondage, and individual destiny. It's a rollicking good story." Booklist

Followed by: Nobody's prize (2008)

Temping fate. Dutton Books 2006 279p $16.99

Grades: 6 7 8 9 **Fic**

1. Classical mythology—Fiction

ISBN 0-525-47730-6   LC 2005-56039

Ilana gets a summer job at "The Divine Relief Temp
Agency, where she is given her extraordinary assignment: temping for the Greek mythological goddesses, the
Fates. . . . The lightning pace, over-the-top characters,
and witty dialogue are all as essential to the novel's success as her personal growth." Bull Cent Child Books

Frost, Gregory

Shadowbridge; [by] Gregory Frost. Ballantine
Books 2008 255p pa $14

Grades: 7 8 9 10 **Fic**

1. Orphans—Fiction 2. Fantasy fiction

ISBN 978-0-345-49758-1 (pa); 0-345-49758-9 (pa)

LC 2007033139

"Orphaned 16-year-old Leodora, a talented puppeteer
and storyteller, is forced to hide her identity and gender
as she travels the spans and tunnels of the ocean-crossing
Shadowbridge in Frost's exciting first of a diptych. . . .
Frost (Fitcher's Brides) draws richly detailed human
characters and embellishes his multilayered stories with
intriguing creatures—benevolent sea dragons, trickster
foxes, death-eating snakes and capricious gods—that
make this fantasy a sparkling gem of mythic invention
and wonder." SLJ

Frost, Helen, 1949-

The braid. Farrar, Straus and Giroux 2006 95p
$16

Grades: 7 8 9 10 **Fic**

1. Scotland—Fiction 2. Canada—Fiction 3. Sisters—
Fiction 4. Immigrants—Fiction 5. Novels in verse

ISBN 0-374-30962-0   LC 2005-40148

"Frances Foster books"

Two Scottish sisters, living on the western island of
Barra in the 1850s, relate, in alternate voices and linked
narrative poems, their experiences after their family is
forcible evicted and separated with one sister accompanying their parents and younger siblings to Cape Breton,
Canada, and the other staying behind with other family
on the small island of Mingulay.

"The book will inspire both students and teachers to
go back and study how the taut poetic lines manage to
contain the powerful feelings." Booklist

Diamond Willow. Farrar, Straus and Giroux
2008 111p $16

Grades: 6 7 8 9 **Fic**

1. Alaska—Fiction 2. Dogs—Fiction 3. Athapascan Indians—Fiction 4. Novels in verse

ISBN 978-0-374-31776-8; 0-374-31776-3

LC 2006-37438

"Frances Foster books"

In a remote area of Alaska, twelve-year-old Willow
helps her father with their sled dogs when she is not at
school, wishing she were more popular, all the while unaware that the animals surrounding her carry the spirits
of dead ancestors and friends who care for her.

"Willow relates her story in one-page poems, each of
which contains a hidden message printed in darker type.
. . . Her poems offer pensive imagery and glimpses of
character, and strong emotion. This complex and elegant
novel will resonate with readers who savor powerful drama and multifaceted characters." SLJ

Keesha's house. Frances Foster Bks./Farrar,
Straus & Giroux 2003 116p $16; pa $8

Grades: 7 8 9 10 **Fic**

1. Home—Fiction

ISBN 0-374-34064-1; 0-374-40012-1 (pa)

LC 2002-22698

Frost, Helen, 1949-—*Continued*

Seven teens facing such problems as pregnancy, closeted homosexuality, and abuse each describe in poetic forms what caused them to leave home and where they found home again

"Spare, eloquent, and elegantly concise. . . . Public, private, or correctional educators and librarians should put this must-read on their shelves." Voice Youth Advocates

Fullerton, Alma, 1969-

Walking on glass. HarperTempest 2007 131p $15.99; lib bdg $16.89

Grades: 8 9 10 11 12   Fic

1. Mother-son relationship—Fiction 2. Suicide—Fiction 3. Novels in verse

ISBN   978-0-06-077851-4;   0-06-077851-2;
978-0-06-077852-1 (lib bdg); 0-06-077852-0 (lib bdg)
LC 2006-20037

A teenage boy recounts, in a free verse journal, his attempts to come to terms with the realities of his mother's near-death coma.

"This is a quick yet powerful read with an authentic teen voice." SLJ

Funke, Cornelia Caroline

Inkheart; [by] Cornelia Funke; translated from the German by Anthea Bell. Scholastic 2003 534p $19.95; pa $9.99 *

Grades: 5 6 7 8   Fic

1. Books and reading—Fiction 2. Fantasy fiction

ISBN 0-439-53164-0; 0-439-70910-5 (pa)
LC 2003-45844

"The Chicken House"

Twelve-year-old Meggie learns that her father, who repairs and binds books for a living, can "read" fictional characters to life when one of those characters abducts them and tries to force him into service.

The author "proves the power of her imagination; readers will be captivated by the chilling and thrilling world she has created here." Publ Wkly

Other titles in this series are:
Inkspell (2005)
Inkdeath (2008)

Fuqua, Jonathon Scott

The Willoughby Spit wonder. Candlewick 2004 145p $15.99

Grades: 5 6 7 8   Fic

1. Sick—Fiction 2. Father-son relationship—Fiction 3. Virginia—Fiction

ISBN 0-7636-1776-8   LC 2002-41141

In 1950s Norfolk, Virginia, as Carter and his sister watch their dying father struggle to remain cheerful, Carter decides to emulate Prince Namor, comic superhero, in order to inspire his father to stay alive.

"Carter . . . is a compelling character, and his growing understanding and acceptance of the world is shown quietly through an array of accurately observed details. A subtle, engaging novel." Booklist

Gaiman, Neil, 1960-

Coraline; [by] Neil Gaiman; with illustrations by Dave McKean. HarperCollins Pubs. 2002 162p il $15.99; lib bdg $17.89; pa $5.99 *

Grades: 5 6 7 8   Fic

1. Supernatural—Fiction 2. Horror fiction

ISBN 0-380-97778-8; 0-06-623744-0 (lib bdg);
0-380-80734-3 (pa)   LC 2002-18937

Looking for excitement, Coraline ventures through a mysterious door into a world that is similar, yet disturbingly different from her own, where she must challenge a gruesome entity in order to save herself, her parents, and the souls of three others

"Gaiman twines his taut tale with a menacing tone and crisp prose fraught with memorable imagery . . . yet keeps the narrative just this side of terrifying." Publ Wkly

The graveyard book; with illustrations by Dave McKean. HarperCollins 2008 312p il $17.99; lib bdg $18.89 *

Grades: 5 6 7 8 9 10   Fic

1.   Death—Fiction   2.   Supernatural—Fiction 3. Cemeteries—Fiction

ISBN   978-0-06-053092-1;   0-06-053092-8;
978-0-06-053093-8 (lib bdg); 0-06-053093-6 (lib bdg)
LC 2008-13860

Nobody Owens is a normal boy, except that he has been raised by ghosts and other denizens of the graveyard.

"Gaiman writes with charm and humor, and again he has a real winner." Voice Youth Advocates

Interworld; [by] Neil Gaiman [and] Michael Reaves. Eos 2007 239p $16.99; lib bdg $17.89

Grades: 6 7 8 9 10   Fic

1. Space and time—Fiction 2. Science fiction

ISBN 978-0-06-123896-3; 978-0-06-123897-0 (lib bdg)   LC 2007-08617

At nearly fifteen years of age, Joey Harker learns that he is able to travel between dimensions. Soon, he joins a team of different versions of himself, each from another dimension, to fight the evil forces striving to conquer all the worlds.

This offers "vivid, well-imagined settings and characters. . . . [A] rousing sf/fantasy hybrid." Booklist

Galante, Cecilia, 1971-

Hershey herself; [by] Cecilia Galante. Aladdin Mix 2008 330p pa $5.99

Grades: 5 6 7 8   Fic

1. Music—Fiction 2. Friendship—Fiction 3. Abused women—Fiction

ISBN 978-1-4169-5463-7; 1-4169-5463-5

"When twelve-year-old Hershey must run away with her mother to a women's shelter, she wonders how, among other things, she'll compete in the town talent show with her best friend, Phoebe." Publisher's note

"Subplots with multiple themes of self-respect, abuse, poverty, friendship, music, depression and dreams are all skillfully blended into an engaging novel for middle school readers." Libr Media Connect

Galante, Cecilia, 1971-—*Continued*

The patron saint of butterflies. Bloomsbury 2008
292p $16.95

Grades: 6 7 8 9 10   **Fic**

1. Cults—Fiction 2. Christian life—Fiction

ISBN 978-1-59990-249-4; 1-59990-249-4

LC 2007-51368

When her grandmother takes fourteen-year-old Agnes,
her younger brother, and best friend Honey and escapes
Mount Blessing, a Connecticut religious commune, Agnes clings to the faith she loves while Honey looks toward a future free of control, cruelty, and preferential
treatment.

"If both girls occasionally seem wise beyond their
years, readers will nevertheless cheer them on as they
ponder the limits of faith and duty." SLJ

Gantos, Jack

Jack on the tracks; four seasons of fifth grade.
Farrar, Straus & Giroux 1999 182p il $16; pa
$5.95 *

Grades: 5 6 7 8   **Fic**

1. School stories 2. Family life—Fiction 3. Miami
(Fla.)—Fiction

ISBN 0-374-33665-2; 0-374-43717-3 (pa)

LC 99-27897

Moving with his unbearable sister to Miami, Florida,
Jack tries to break some of his bad habits but finds himself irresistibly drawn to things disgusting, gross, and
weird

"Jack is a likable and appealing fifth grader. His first-
person preadolescent musings and worries are poignant,
funny, and real." SLJ

Other titles in this series are:

Heads or tails (1994)

Jack's black book (1997)

Jack's new power (1995)

Joey Pigza swallowed the key. Farrar, Straus &
Giroux 1998 153p $16 *

Grades: 5 6 7 8   **Fic**

1. Attention deficit disorder—Fiction 2. School stories

ISBN 0-374-33664-4   LC 98-24264

Also available in paperback from HarperCollins

To the constant disappointment of his mother and his
teachers, Joey has trouble paying attention or controlling
his mood swings when his prescription meds wear off
and he starts getting worked up and acting wired

This "frenetic narrative pulls at heartstrings and tickles
funny bones." SLJ

Other titles about Joey Pigza are:

Joey Pigza loses control (2000)

What would Joey do? (2002)

I am not Joey Pigza (2007)

García, Cristina, 1958-

I wanna be your shoebox. Simon & Schuster
Books for Children 2008 198p $16.99 *

Grades: 4 5 6 7   **Fic**

1. Racially mixed people—Fiction 2. Grandfathers—
Fiction 3. Jews—Fiction 4. Cuban Americans—Fiction
5. Family life—Fiction 6. California—Fiction

ISBN 978-1-4169-3928-3; 1-4169-3928-8

Thirteen-year-old, clarinet-playing, Southern California
surfer, Yumi Ruiz-Hirsch, comes from a complex family—her father is Jewish-Japanese, her mother is Cuban,
and her parents are divorced—and when her grandfather
Saul is diagnosed with terminal cancer, Yumi asks him
to tell her his life story, which helps her to understand
her own history and identity.

"García's . . . exceptional ability to channel a range
of voices lights up her first children's novel. . . . The
large personalities propel the story and bring tenderness
and credibility to a classic message about change." Publ
Wkly

Garden, Nancy, 1938-

Endgame. Harcourt 2006 287p $17

Grades: 8 9 10 11 12   **Fic**

1. School stories 2. Bullies—Fiction 3. Family life—
Fiction 4. Violence—Fiction

ISBN 0-15-205416-2; 978-0-15-205416-8

LC 2005-19486

Fifteen-year-old Gray Wilton, bullied at school and
ridiculed by an unfeeling father for preferring drums to
hunting, goes on a shooting rampage at his high school.

"This is a hard-hitting and eloquent look at the impact
of bullying, and the resulting destruction of lives touched
by the violence." SLJ

Gardner, Lyn

Into the woods; pictures by Mini Grey. David
Fickling Books 2007 427p il $16.99; lib bdg
$19.99 *

Grades: 5 6 7 8   **Fic**

1. Sisters—Fiction 2. Fantasy fiction

ISBN 978-0-385-5115-5; 0-385-75115-X;
978-0-385-75116-2 (lib bdg); 0-385-75116-8 (lib bdg)

LC 2006-24350

Pursued by the sinister Dr. DeWilde and his ravenous
wolves, three sisters—Storm, the inheritor of a special
musical pipe, the elder Aurora, and the baby Any—flee
into the woods and begin a treacherous journey filled
with many dangers as they try to find a way to defeat
their pursuer and keep him from taking the pipe and control of the entire land.

"Gardner's fast-paced fantasy-adventure cleverly bor-
rows from well-known fairy tales, and astute readers will
enjoy identifying the many folkloric references. . . .
Grey's appealing black-and-white illustrations add humor
and detail to the story." Booklist

Gardner, Sally

I, Coriander; [illustrations by Lydia Corry] Dial
Bks. 2005 280p il $16.99

Grades: 6 7 8 9   **Fic**

1. Magic—Fiction 2. Fairies—Fiction

ISBN 0-8037-3099-3   LC 2005--06050

In 17th century London, Coriander, a girl who has inherited magic from her mother, must find a way to use
this magic in order to save both herself and an inhabitant
of the fairy world where her mother was born

Gardner, Sally—_Continued_

"Seamlessly meshing fact and fantasy, the author composes a suspenseful masterpiece that will have audience members gladly suspending their disbelief." Publ Wkly

The red necklace; a story of the French Revolution. Dial Books 2008 378p $16.99 *

Grades: 8 9 10 11 12   **Fic**

1. France—History—1789-1799, Revolution—Fiction 2. Social classes—Fiction 3. Gypsies—Fiction 4. Orphans—Fiction 5. Adventure fiction

ISBN 978-0-8037-3100-4; 0-8037-3100-0

LC 2007-39813

In the late eighteenth-century, Sido, the twelve-year-old daughter of a self-indulgent marquis, and Yann, a fourteen-year-old Gypsy orphan raised to perform in a magic show, face a common enemy at the start of the French Revolution.

"Scores are waiting to be settled on every page; this is a heart-stopper." Booklist

Garland, Sherry, 1948-

The silent storm. Harcourt Brace Jovanovich 1993 240p hardcover o.p. pa $7

Grades: 4 5 6 7   **Fic**

1. Orphans—Fiction 2. Grandfathers—Fiction 3. Hurricanes—Fiction

ISBN 0-15-274170-4; 0-15-200016-X (pa)

LC 92-33690

Thirteen-year-old Alyssa has not spoken since seeing her parents die in a hurricane, and now, three years later, another storm threatens the home she shares with her grandfather on Galveston Island

"Garland writes evocatively of her coastal setting, developing a solid sense of place. . . . The characterizations of family members made fearful by previous losses are well developed. . . . This book will have appeal for lovers of the outdoors as well as anyone who appreciates an exciting, atmospheric story." SLJ

Gates, Susan, 1950-

Beyond the billboard. Harcourt 2007 210p $16

Grades: 6 7 8 9   **Fic**

1. Wetlands—Fiction 2. Family life—Fiction 3. Siblings—Fiction 4. Twins—Fiction

ISBN 978-0-15-205983-5; 0-15-205983-0

LC 2006-31527

First published 2005 in the United Kingdom with title: Firebird

Firebird and her twin brother Ford have always accepted their father's isolated way of life and secluded home in the middle of a desolate swamp until the discovery of old family secrets changes everything.

"The pace and action are rapid-fire, and readers willing to puzzle through the ambiguities about place and time will be rewarded with an unusual tale of teens trying to make their way in an altered world." Booklist

Gavin, Jamila, 1941-

The blood stone. Farrar, Straus & Giroux 2005 340p il $18

Grades: 6 7 8 9   **Fic**

1. Taj Mahal (Agra, India)—Fiction 2. Diamonds—Fiction 3. Voyages and travels—Fiction

ISBN 0-374-30846-2   LC 2004-53257

In the early seventeenth century, young Venetian Filippo Veroneo travels from Venice to Afghanistan to rescue his imprisoned father, Geronimo, and stops in India to raise the ransom by selling his father's beautiful diamond to the ruler Shah Jehan, who later uses the stone as the model for the Taj Mahal.

"Gavin has created fascinating, multidimensional characters whose actions and motives remain suspicious through much of the story." SLJ

Coram boy. Farrar, Straus & Giroux 2001 c2000 327p hardcover o.p. pa $7.95

Grades: 7 8 9 10   **Fic**

1. Adventure fiction 2. Great Britain—Fiction

ISBN 0-374-31544-2; 0-374-41374-6 (pa)

LC 00-67200

First published 2000 in the United Kingdom

In the mid-eighteenth century, an unsavory character and his simpleton son become involved in the lives of a wealthy English family when that family's eldest son is disinherited because of his love of music

"Gavin provides a chilling, terrifying, and painful portrayal of life in this era. . . . Gavin's rich prose will entice any devotee of historical fiction as well as any reader intrigued by graceful language or a solid adventure." Voice Youth Advocates

Genesse, Paul, 1973-

The golden cord. Five Star 2008 398p (Iron dragon) $25.95

Grades: 7 8 9 10   **Fic**

1. Dragons—Fiction 2. Magic—Fiction 3. Fantasy fiction

ISBN 978-1-5941-4659-6; 1-5941-4659-4

LC 2007044408

"The plateau world of Ae'leron lives in fear of the griffins and dragons that threaten them from the air and the dwarven Drobin Empire that rules the humans with an iron fist. When Drake Bloodstone, a young guardian of the hidden human enclave of Cliffton, is forced to lead a party of Drobin to the lair of the Dragon King, he knows that the fate of his loved ones hangs in the balance. This debut novel promises to unlock a realm of magic and warfare in a unique world of cloud-bound lands and a mysterious Underworld." Libr J

George, Jean Craighead, 1919-

Charlie's raven; written and illustrated by Jean Craighead George. Dutton Children's Books 2004 190p il $15.99

Grades: 5 6 7 8   **Fic**

1. Ravens—Fiction 2. Grandfathers—Fiction 3. Naturalists—Fiction

ISBN 0-525-47219-3

Charlie's friend, Singing Bird, a Teton Sioux, tells him that ravens have curing powers, so Charlie steals a

George, Jean Craighead, 1919-—*Continued*
baby bird from its nest, hoping to heal his ailing
Granddad, a retired naturalist.

"The story is technically accurate and offers a vivid
sense of place and a window into Native American beliefs through storytelling." SLJ

Julie; illustrated by Wendell Minor.
HarperCollins Pubs. 1994 226p il pa $5.99
hardcover o.p. *
Grades: 6 7 8 9 **Fic**
1. Inuit—Fiction 2. Arctic regions—Fiction
3. Wolves—Fiction
ISBN 0-06-440573-7 (pa); 0-06-023528-4 (hc)
LC 93-27738

This sequel to Julie of the wolves "details Julie's adjustment to family and modernization after returning
home. Her father's musk oxen enterprise depicts the
problems inherent to environment-versus-economics issues as Julie struggles to save her wolf friends." Sci
Child

Followed by Julie's wolf pack

Julie of the wolves; pictures by John
Schoenherr. Harper & Row 1972 170p il $15.99;
lib bdg $16.89; pa $5.99 *
Grades: 6 7 8 9 **Fic**
1. Inuit—Fiction 2. Arctic regions—Fiction
3. Wilderness survival—Fiction 4. Wolves—Fiction
ISBN 0-06-021943-2; 0-06-021944-0 (lib bdg);
0-06-440058-1 (pa)
Awarded the Newbery Medal, 1973

"Lost in the Alaskan wilderness, thirteen-year old
Miyax [Julie in English], an Eskimo girl, is gradually accepted by a pack of Arctic wolves that she comes to
love." Booklist

"The superb narration includes authentic descriptions
and details of the Eskimo way-of-life and of Eskimo rituals. . . . The whole book has a rare, intense reality
which the artist enhances beautifully with animated
drawings." Horn Book

Followed by Julie

George, Jessica Day, 1976-
Dragon slippers. Bloomsbury Children's Books
2007 324p $16.95
Grades: 5 6 7 8 **Fic**
1. Dragons—Fiction 2. Orphans—Fiction 3. Fantasy
fiction
ISBN 978-1-59990-057-5; 1-59990-057-2
LC 2006-21142

Orphaned after a fever epidemic, Creel befriends a
dragon and unknowingly inherits an object that can either
save or destroy her kingdom.

"The plot is fast paced with all the right touches of
romance and adventure. . . . The characters are wonderfully drawn." Voice Youth Advocates

Followed by: Dragon flight (2008)

Princess of the midnight ball. Bloomsbury
Children's Books 2009 280p $16.99
Grades: 6 7 8 9 10 **Fic**
1. Fairy tales
ISBN 978-1-59990-322-4; 1-59990-322-9
LC 2008-30310

A retelling of the tale of twelve princesses who wear
out their shoes dancing every night, and of Galen, a former soldier now working in the king's gardens, who follows them in hopes of breaking the curse.

"Fans of fairy-tale retellings . . . will enjoy this story
for its magic, humor, and touch of romance." SLJ

Sun and moon, ice and snow. Bloomsbury 2008
336p $16.95
Grades: 7 8 9 10 11 12 **Fic**
1. Fantasy fiction
ISBN 978-1-59990-109-1; 1-59990-109-9
LC 2007-30848

A girl travels east of the sun and west of the moon
to free her beloved prince from a magic spell.

"George has adapted Norse myths and fairy tales to
create this eerily beautiful, often terrifying world. . . .
Mystery, adventure, and the supernatural, and a touch of
love are woven together to create a vivid, well-crafted,
poetic fantasy." Booklist

George, Madeleine
Looks. Viking 2008 240p $16.99 *
Grades: 8 9 10 11 12 **Fic**
1. Anorexia nervosa—Fiction 2. Obesity—Fiction
3. Friendship—Fiction 4. School stories
ISBN 978-0-670-06167-9; 0-670-06167-0
LC 2007-38218

"Meghan and Aimee are on opposite ends of the outcast spectrum. Meghan is extremely overweight. . . .
Aimee, on the other hand, is classic anorexic. Both girls
have been hurt by one of the popular girls at school.
They join forces to bring Cara down in a stunning bit of
public humiliation. . . . The story will make readers
think about the various issues touched upon, and it is difficult to put down." SLJ

Gephart, Donna
As if being 12 3/4 isn't bad enough, my mother
is running for president! by Donna Gephart.
Delacorte Press 2008 227p $15.99; lib bdg $18.99
Grades: 4 5 6 **Fic**
1. Politics—Fiction 2. Mother-daughter relationship—
Fiction 3. School stories 4. Florida—Fiction
ISBN 978-0-385-73481-3; 978-0-385-90479-7 (lib
bdg) LC 2007027601

Preparing for spelling bees, having a secret admirer,
and waiting for her chest size to catch up with her enormous feet are pressure enough, but twelve-year-old Vanessa must also deal with loneliness and very real fears
as her mother, Florida's Governor, runs for President of
the United States.

"Gephart creates a likable protagonist. . . . Vanessa's
emotional and social life . . . will keep readers engaged,
and also the kid's-eye view of a candidate's campaigning." Booklist

Geras, Adèle
Ithaka. Harcourt 2006 360p $17; pa $6.95 *
Grades: 7 8 9 10 **Fic**
1. Classical mythology—Fiction 2. Trojan War—Fic-
tion 3. Odysseus (Greek mythology)—Fiction
ISBN 0-15-205603-3; 0-15-206104-5 (pa)
LC 2005-7569

Geras, Adèle—*Continued*

Companion volume to: Troy

The island of Ithaka is overrun with uncouth suitors demanding that Penelope choose a new husband, as she patiently awaits the return of Odysseus from the Trojan War.

This book "can introduce young people to the power of story in Homer's epics as well as being a beautifully written story in its own right." Voice Youth Advocates

Troy. Harcourt 2001 340p pa $6.95 *

Grades: 7 8 9 10 Fic

1. Trojan War—Fiction

ISBN 0-15-216492-8; 0-15-204570-8 (pa)

LC 00-57262

Homer's "tales of Paris and Helen, Achilles and Hector, and Odysseus and the Trojan horse are recast in the form of a modern novel, using the heroes' fates as background and focus for the real subjects: the women of Troy." Horn Book Guide

"Mythology buffs will savor the author's ability to embellish stories of old without diminishing their original flavor, while the uninitiated will find this a captivating introduction to a pivotal event in classic Greek literature." Publ Wkly

Geus, Mireille, 1964-

Piggy; translated by Nancy Forest-Flier. Front Street 2008 110p $14.95

Grades: 6 7 8 9 10 Fic

1. Autism—Fiction 2. Friendship—Fiction 3. Criminal investigation—Fiction 4. Bullies—Fiction

ISBN 978-1-59078-636-9; 1-59078-636-X

LC 2007-48847

Original Dutch edition 2005

Lizzie struggles to overcome the closed, internal world of autism when a new girl moves into her neighborhood, befriends her, then insists that Lizzie join her in seeking revenge on the boys who tease them.

"The title's compactness adds accessibility for readers who prefer sprint reads to distance, and this would be a natural discussion-starter for readers ranging from reluctant to adventurous." Bull Cent Child Books

Giff, Patricia Reilly

Eleven. Wendy Lamb Books 2008 164p $15.99; lib bdg $18.99

Grades: 4 5 6 7 Fic

1. Kidnapping—Fiction 2. Friendship—Fiction 3. Learning disabilities—Fiction 4. Woodwork—Fiction

ISBN 978-0-385-73069-3; 978-0-385-90098-0 (lib bdg) LC 2007-12638

When Sam, who can barely read, discovers an old newspaper clipping just before his eleventh birthday, it brings forth memories just from his past, and, with the help of a new friend at school and the castle they are building for a school project, his questions are eventually answered.

This is an "exquisitely rendered story of self-discovery." Publ Wkly

A house of tailors. Wendy Lamb Books 2004 148p $15.95; lib bdg $17.99

Grades: 5 6 7 8 Fic

1. Immigrants—Fiction 2. German Americans—Fiction 3. Brooklyn (New York, N.Y.)—Fiction

ISBN 0-385-73066-7; 0-385-90879-2 (lib bdg)

LC 2003-26103

When thirteen-year-old Dina emigrates from Germany to America in 1871, her only wish is to return home as soon as she can, but as the months pass and she survives a multitude of hardships living with her uncle and his young wife and baby, she finds herself thinking of Brooklyn as her home.

"This novel is rich with believable, endearing characters as well as excitement and emotion." SLJ

Nory Ryan's song. Delacorte Press 2000 148p hardcover o.p. pa $5.99 *

Grades: 5 6 7 8 Fic

1. Ireland—Fiction 2. Famines—Fiction

ISBN 0-385-32141-4; 0-440-41829-1 (pa)

LC 00-27690

When a terrible blight attacks Ireland's potato crop in 1845, twelve-year-old Nory Ryan's courage and ingenuity help her family and neighbors survive

"Giff brings the landscape and the cultural particulars of the era vividly to life and creates in Nory a heroine to cheer for. A beautiful, heart-wrenching novel that makes a devastating event understandable." Booklist

Another title about Nory is:

Maggie's door (2003)

Pictures of Hollis Woods. Wendy Lamb Bks. 2002 166p $15.95; lib bdg $17.99; pa $6.50

Grades: 5 6 7 8 Fic

1. Artists—Fiction 2. Foster home care—Fiction 3. Old age—Fiction

ISBN 0-385-32655-6; 0-385-90070-8 (lib bdg); 0-439-69239-3 (pa) LC 2002-426

A Newbery Medal honor book, 2003

"She was named for the place where she was found as an abandoned baby. Twelve-year-old Hollis Woods has been through many foster homes—and she runs away, every time. In her latest placement, with an artist named Josie, the tightly wound Hollis begins to relax ever so slightly. . . . But Josie is slowly slipping into dementia, and Hollis knows that she'll be taken away from her if Josie is found out. . . . Giff has a sure hand with language, and the narrative is taut and absorbing." Booklist

Water Street. Wendy Lamb Books 2006 164p $15.95

Grades: 5 6 7 8 Fic

1. Irish Americans—Fiction 2. Brooklyn (New York, N.Y.)—Fiction 3. Family life—Fiction

ISBN 978-0-385-90097-3; 0-385-73068-3

LC 2006-02024

In the shadow of the construction of the Brooklyn Bridge, eighth-graders and new neighbors Bird Mallon and Thomas Neary make some decisions about what they want to do with their lives.

"Continuing the Irish American immigration story begun in *Nory Ryan's Song* (2000) and *Maggie's Door* (2003), [this] novel, set in 1875, is about the next gener-

Giff, Patricia Reilly—*Continued*
ation. . . . A poignant immigration story of friendship, work, and the meaning of home." Booklist

Willow run. Wendy Lamb Bks. 2005 149p $15.95
Grades: 4 5 6 7   **Fic**
  1. World War, 1939-1945—Fiction
  ISBN 0-385-73067-5   LC 2004-24541
During World War II, after moving with her parents to Willow Run, Michigan, when her father gets a job in the B24 bomber-building factory, eleven-year-old Meggie learns about different kinds of bravery from all of the people around her.
"Giff artfully carves the sentiments so prevalent in times of war—anxiety, inspiration, boredom—into sharp relief while creating a cast of finely drawn characters." Booklist

Giles, Gail
Right behind you. Little, Brown 2007 292p $15.99
Grades: 8 9 10 11 12   **Fic**
  1. Psychotherapy—Fiction 2. Family life—Fiction 3. Homicide—Fiction
  ISBN 978-0-316-16636-2; 0-316-16636-7
      LC 2007-12336
After spending over four years in a mental institution for murdering a friend in Alaska, fourteen-year-old Kip begins a completely new life in Indiana with his father and stepmother under a different name, but not only has trouble fitting in, he finds there are still problems to deal with from his childhood.
"The story-behind-the-headlines flavor gives this a voyeuristic appeal, while the capable writing and sympathetic yet troubled protagonist will suck readers right into the action." Bull Cent Child Books

Gilman, David
The devil's breath. Delacorte Press 2008 391p (Danger zone) $15.99; lib bdg $18.99
Grades: 7 8 9 10 11 12   **Fic**
  1. Adventure fiction 2. Environmental protection—Fiction 3. Namibia—Fiction
  ISBN 978-0-385-73560-5; 978-0-385-90546-6 (lib bdg)   LC 2007-46744
When fifteen-year-old Max Gordon's environmentalist-adventurer father goes missing while working in Namibia and Max becomes the target of a would-be assassin at his school in England, he decides he must follow his father to Africa and find him before they both are killed.
"The action is relentless. . . . Gilman has a flair for making the preposterous seem possible." Booklist

Gilman, Laura Anne
Grail quest: the Camelot spell; book one. HarperCollins 2006 291p $10.99; lib bdg $14.89
Grades: 5 6 7 8   **Fic**
  1. Arthur, King—Fiction 2. Knights and knighthood—Fiction 3. Middle Ages—Fiction 4. Magic—Fiction
  ISBN 0-06-077279-4; 0-06-077280-8 (lib bdg)
Three teenagers living in Camelot are forced to undertake a dangerous mission when King Arthur's court falls under a mysterious enchantment on the eve of the quest for the Holy Grail.
"The believable dialogue, succint plot, and uncomplicated references to court life will appeal to middle graders who are beginning to explore Aurthurian legend." Voice Youth Advocates
  Other titles in this series are:
Grail quest: Morgain's revenge (2006)
Grail quest: The shadow companion (2006)

Gilmore, Kate, 1931-
The exchange student. Houghton Mifflin 1999 216p $15; pa $6.95
Grades: 7 8 9 10   **Fic**
  1. Science fiction 2. Extraterrestrial beings—Fiction
  ISBN 0-395-57511-7; 0-618-68948-6 (pa)
      LC 97-47162
When her mother arranges to host one of the young people coming to Earth from Chela, Daria is both pleased and intrigued by the keen interest shown by the Chelan in her work breeding endangered species
"Gilmore makes a farfetched premise seem more reasonable with everyday details of life in the twenty-first century, sympathetic characters, and logical consequences. . . . A story that will appeal to readers on many levels." Booklist

Gipson, Frederick Benjamin, 1903-1973
Old Yeller; [by] Fred Gipson; drawings by Carl Burger. Harper & Row 1956 158p il $23; pa $5.99
Grades: 6 7 8 9   **Fic**
  1. Dogs—Fiction 2. Texas—Fiction 3. Frontier and pioneer life—Fiction
  ISBN 0-06-011545-9; 0-06-440382-3 (pa)
      LC 56-8780
A Newbery Medal honor book, 1957
"Travis at fourteen was the man of the family during the hard summer of 1860 when his father drove his herd of cattle from Texas to the Kansas market. It was the summer when an old yellow dog attached himself to the family and won Travis' reluctant friendship. Before the summer was over, Old Yeller proved more than a match for thieving raccoons, fighting bulls, grizzly bears, and mad wolves. This is a skillful tale of a boy's love for a dog as well as a description of a pioneer boyhood and it can't miss with any dog lover." Horn Book

Glatstein, Jacob, 1896-1971
Emil and Karl; by Yankev Glatshteyn; translated by Jeffrey Shandler. Roaring Brook Press 2006 194p $17.95
Grades: 5 6 7 8   **Fic**
  1. Holocaust, 1933-1945—Fiction 2. Jews—Fiction 3. Vienna (Austria)—Fiction 4. Friendship—Fiction
  ISBN 1-59643-119-9   LC 2005-26800
Original Yiddish edition 1940
A story about the dilemma faced by two young boys—one Jewish, the other not—when they suddenly find themselves without homes or families in Vienna on the eve of World War II.
"The fast-moving prose is stark and immediate. Glatshteyn was, of course, writing about what was happening to children in his time. . . . The translation, 65 years after the novel's original publication, is nothing short of haunting." Booklist

Gliori, Debi

Pure dead frozen. Alfred A. Knopf 2007 311p $15.99

Grades: 4 5 6 7 **Fic**
1. Magic—Fiction 2. Witches—Fiction 3. Scotland—Fiction
ISBN 978-0-375-83317-5; 0-375-83317-X

First published 2006 in the United Kingdom with title: Deep fear

The Strega-Borgias make one last stand to defend their home against invaders who seek the Chronostone—and one little baby who may not be what he appears.

"Gliori clearly delights in word play and elicits laughter with her descriptions of characters, both good and evil. Playful language and inept evildoers make this book a fun but not scary read." Voice Youth Advocates

Other titles in this series are:
Pure dead magic (2001)
Pure dead wicked (2002)
Pure dead brilliant (2004)
Pure dead trouble (2005)
Pure dead batty (2006)

Godbersen, Anna

The luxe. HarperCollins Pub. 2007 433p $17.99; lib bdg $18.89

Grades: 8 9 10 11 12 **Fic**
1. Social classes—Fiction 2. Wealth—Fiction 3. New York (N.Y.)—Fiction
ISBN 978-0-06-134566-1; 0-06-134566-0; 978-0-06-134567-8 (lib bdg); 0-06-134567-9 (lib bdg)
LC 2007-20876

In Manhattan in 1899, five teens of different social classes lead dangerously scandalous lives, despite the strict rules of society and the best-laid plans of their parents and others.

"It's all scandalous, steamy—though never graphic—fun, with just enough period detail to make the Gilded Age come alive." SLJ

Other titles in the author's series are:
Rumors (2008)
Envy (2009)

Godwin, Jane, 1964-

Falling from Grace; [by] Jane Godwin. Holiday House 2007 187p $16.95

Grades: 5 6 7 8 **Fic**
1. Missing children—Fiction 2. Sisters—Fiction 3. Australia—Fiction
ISBN 978-0-8234-2105-3; 0-8234-2105-8
LC 2006101432

Relates, from varying points of view, events surrounding the search for a twelve-year-old girl lost during a storm off the coast of Australia.

"Readers of all abilities will appreciate the short, descriptive chapters; teachers and librarians will value the possibilities for discussion in this unusual mystery that's sure to prompt readers to examine the consequences of their choices." SLJ

Going, K. L.

Fat kid rules the world. Putnam 2003 187p $17.99; pa $6.99 *

Grades: 7 8 9 10 **Fic**
1. Obesity—Fiction 2. Musicians—Fiction 3. Friendship—Fiction
ISBN 0-399-23990-1; 0-14-240208-7 (pa)
LC 2002-67956

Michael L. Printz Award honor book, 2004

Seventeen-year-old Troy, depressed, suicidal, and weighing nearly 300 pounds, gets a new perspective on life when a homeless teenager who is a genius on guitar wants Troy to be the drummer in his rock band

"Going has put together an amazing assortment of characters. . . . This is an impressive debut that offers hope for all kids." Booklist

The garden of Eve. Harcourt 2007 234p $17

Grades: 4 5 6 7 **Fic**
1. Magic—Fiction 2. Death—Fiction 3. Bereavement—Fiction 4. New York (State)—Fiction
ISBN 978-0-15-205986-6; 0-15-205986-5
LC 2007-05074

Eve gave up her belief in stories and magic after her mother's death, but a mysterious seed given to her as an eleventh-birthday gift by someone she has never met takes her and a boy who claims to be a ghost on a strange journey, to where their supposedly cursed town of Beaumont, New York, flourishes.

"Believably and with delicacy, Going paints a suspenseful story suffused with the poignant questions of what it means to be alive, and what might await on the other side." Horn Book

Goldblatt, Stacey

Stray; a novel. Delacorte Press 2007 276p $15.99; lib bdg $18.99

Grades: 7 8 9 10 11 12 **Fic**
1. Mother-daughter relationship—Fiction 2. Dogs—Fiction 3. Dating (Social customs)—Fiction
ISBN 978-0-385-73443-1; 0-385-73443-3; 978-0-385-90448-3 (lib bdg); 0-385-90448-7 (lib bdg)
LC 2006-31828

Natalie's mother, a veterinarian with a dogs-only practice, has the sixteen-year-old on such a short leash that, when the teenaged son of her old school friend comes to stay with them for the summer, Natalie is tempted to break her mother's rules and follow her own instincts for a change.

"This fresh treatment of a familiar teen feeling will attract readers who love dogs as well as a good first-love story." Booklist

Golding, Julia

The diamond of Drury Lane. Roaring Brook Press 2008 424p (Cat Royal Quartet) $12.50 *

Grades: 6 7 8 9 **Fic**
1. Drury Lane Theatre (London, England)—Fiction 2. Orphans—Fiction 3. Theater—Fiction 4. London (England)—Fiction 5. Great Britain—History—1714-1837—Fiction
ISBN 978-1-59643-351-9; 1-59643-351-5
LC 2007-23604

Golding, Julia—*Continued*

Orphan Catherine "Cat" Royal, living at the Drury Lane Theater in 1790s London, tries to find the "diamond" supposedly hidden in the theater, which unmasks a treasonous political cartoonist, and involves her in the street gangs of Covent Garden and the world of nobility.

This is "a story with as many cliff-hangers as there are chapters. But the real thrills also come from the varied, sharply drawn cast. . . . [Golding] offers a view of London readers can grasp with all their senses." Booklist

Other titles in this series are:

Cat among the pigeons (2008)

Den of thieves (2009)

Secret of the sirens; [by] Julia Golding. 1st Marshall Cavendish ed. Marshall Cavendish 2007 c2006 357p (The companions quartet) $16.99

Grades: 7 8 9 10   **Fic**

1. Mythical animals—Fiction 2. Environmental protection—Fiction 3. Supernatural—Fiction

ISBN 978-0-7614-5371-0; 0-7614-5371-7

LC 2006052799

First published 2006 in the United Kingdom

Upon moving to her aunt's seaside home in the British Isles, Connie becomes part of a secret society that shelters mythical creatures, and must use her ability to communicate with these beings to protect them from evil and the incursions of humans.

This "packs a serious environmental message, yet never feels heavyhanded. . . . The contemporary setting and its modern villains . . . make for an entertaining read." Publ Wkly

Other titles in this series are:

The gorgon's gaze (2007)

Mines of the minotaur (2008)

The chimera's curse (2008)

Golding, William, 1911-1993

Lord of the Flies; introduction by E. M. Forster. Coward, McCann & Geoghegan 1962 243p il $22.95; pa $13

Grades: 8 9 10 11 12 Adult   **Fic**

1. Boys—Fiction 2. Survival after airplane accidents, shipwrecks, etc.—Fiction

ISBN 0-399-52920-9; 1-57322-612-2 (pa)

First published 1954 in the United Kingdom; first United States edition, 1955

"Stranded on an island, a group of English schoolboys leave innocence behind in a struggle for survival. A political structure modeled after English government is set up and a hierarchy develops, but forces of anarchy and aggression surface. The boys' existence begins to degenerate into a savage one. They are rescued from their microcosmic society to return to an adult, stylized milieu filled with the same psychological tensions and moral voids. Adventure and allegory are brilliantly combined in this novel." Shapiro. Fic for Youth. 3d edition

Goldschmidt, Judy

The secret blog of Raisin Rodriguez; by Judy Goldschmidt. Razorbill 2005 202p $12.99

Grades: 6 7 8 9   **Fic**

1. School stories

ISBN 1-59514-018-2   LC 2004-18361

In a weblog she sends to her best friends back in Berkeley, seventh-grader Raisin Rodriguez chronicles her successes and her more frequent humiliating failures as she attempts to make friends at her new Philadelphia school.

"This readable novel features solid writing and an engaging main character." Horn Book Guide

Other titles about Raisin Rodriguez are:

Raisin Rodriguez and the big-time smooch (2005)

Will the real Raisin Rodriguez please stand up? (2007)

Gonzalez, Julie, 1958-

Imaginary enemy. Delacorte Press 2008 241p $15.99; lib bdg $18.99

Grades: 6 7 8 9 10   **Fic**

1. Imaginary playmates—Fiction

ISBN 978-0-385-73552-0; 0-385-73552-9; 978-0-385-90530-5 (lib bdg); 0-385-90530-0 (lib bdg)

LC 2007-45752

Although her impetuous behavior, smart-mouthed comments, and slacker ways have landed her in trouble over the years, sixteen-year-old Jane has always put the blame on her "imaginary enemy," until a new development forces her to decide whether or not to assume responsibility for her actions.

"Gonzalez has written a witty, realistic novel . . . peppered with funny, authentic dialogue." Booklist

Wings. Delacorte Press 2005 197p $15.95; lib bdg $17.99

Grades: 7 8 9 10   **Fic**

1. Flight—Fiction 2. Brothers—Fiction

ISBN 0-385-73227-9; 0-385-73097-7 (lib bdg)

LC 2004-7158

Ever since he was a little boy, Ben, who wanted to be called Icarus, persisted in believing that he would grow wings and would fly, a belief that perplexed and worried his family and friends.

"Short chapters take readers from event to event, moving the action along while gradually revealing more about each character. Ben's fight against gravity and his study of natural history add a nice subtext, and the evolving relationship between the brothers is as absorbing as the wait for wings." Booklist

Goobie, Beth, 1959-

Before wings; a novel. Orca Bk. Pubs. 2001 203p hardcover o.p. pa $8.95

Grades: 7 8 9 10   **Fic**

1. Death—Fiction 2. Camps—Fiction

ISBN 1-55143-161-0; 1-55143-163-7 (pa)

LC 00-105582

"Since surviving a brain aneurysm, fifteen-year-old Adrian has been seeing spirits. Working at her aunt's summer camp, Adrian meets a boy who is also clouded by visions of his own death, then discovers that the spirits she sees are connected to the dark mystery surround-

Goobie, Beth, 1959-—*Continued*

ing her aunt." Horn Book Guide

"Full of magic realism and beautifully written, this is a story of good triumphing over evil, life triumphing over death, the power of love, friendship, and the hope for an afterlife." Booklist

Goodman, Alison, 1966-

Eon: Dragoneye reborn. Viking 2009 531p $19.99 *

Grades: 7 8 9 10   **Fic**

1. Fantasy fiction 2. Dragons—Fiction 3. Sex role—Fiction 4. Apprentices—Fiction 5. Magic—Fiction

ISBN 978-0-670-06227-0; 0-670-06227-8

LC 2008-33223

Sixteen-year-old Eon hopes to become an apprentice to one of the twelve energy dragons of good fortune and learn to be its main interpreter, but to do so will require much, including keeping secret that she is a girl.

"Entangled politics and fierce battle scenes provide a pulse-quickening pace, while the intriguing characters add interest and depth." Booklist

Singing the Dogstar blues. Viking 2003 c1998 261p $16.99

Grades: 7 8 9 10   **Fic**

1. Australia—Fiction 2. Science fiction

ISBN 0-670-03610-2   LC 2002-12161

First published 1998 in Australia

In a future Australia, the saucy eighteen-year-old daughter of a famous newscaster and a sperm donor teams up with a hermaphrodite from the planet Choria in a time travel adventure that may significantly change both of their lives

"This wildly entertaining novel successfully mixes adventure, humor, mystery, and sf into a fast-paced, thrilling story that will apeal to a wide audience." Booklist

Goodman, Allegra

The other side of the island. Razorbill 2008 280p $16.99

Grades: 6 7 8 9   **Fic**

1. Science fiction

ISBN 978-1-59514-195-8; 1-59514-195-2

LC 2007-50915

Born in the eighth year of Enclosure, ten-year-old Honor lives in a highly regulated colony with her defiant parents, but when they have an illegal second child and are taken away, it is up to Honor and her friend Helix, another 'Unpredictable,' to uncover a terrible secret about their Island and the Corporation that runs everything.

"A satisfying and compelling read." Bull Cent Child Books

Gordon, Roderick

Tunnels; [by] Roderick Gordon [and] Brian Williams. Chicken House/Scholastic 2008 480p il $17.99

Grades: 6 7 8 9   **Fic**

1. Adventure fiction 2. London (England)—Fiction

ISBN 978-0-439-87177-8; 0-439-87177-8

LC 2007-09169

When Will Burrows and his friend Chester embark on a quest to find Will's archaeologist father, who has inexplicably disappeared, they are led to a labyrinthine world underneath London, full of sinister inhabitants with evil intentions toward 'Topsoilers' like Will and his father.

This is "compelling. . . . The authors add distinctive, vivid touches to the . . . premise . . . and the murderous, refreshingly competant Styx makes an uncommonly challenging adversary." Booklist

Followed by: Deeper (2009)

Gorman, Carol

Games. HarperCollinsPublishers 2007 279p $16.99; lib bdg $17.89

Grades: 6 7 8 9   **Fic**

1. Games—Fiction 2. School stories

ISBN   978-0-06-057027-9;   0-06-057027-X; 978-0-06-057028-6 (lib bdg); 0-06-057028-8 (lib bdg)

LC 2006-31759

When fourteen-year-old rivals Boot Quinn and Mick Sullivan fight once too often, the new principal devises the punishment of having to play games together at his office, where they learn which battles are worth fighting.

"This novel is a great book for middle school students, well scripted, realistic, and entertaining. The characters are true and understandable." Voice Youth Advocates

Gould, Peter L.

Write naked; [by] Peter Gould. Farrar, Straus and Giroux 2008 247p $16.95

Grades: 7 8 9 10 11 12   **Fic**

1. Authorship—Fiction 2. Greenhouse effect—Fiction 3. Vermont—Fiction

ISBN 978-0-374-38483-8; 0-374-38483-5

LC 2007-16023

"Melanie Kroupa Books"

When Victor finds an old Royal typewriter at a yard sale and takes it to his uncle's isolated cabin in the Vermont woods to attempt to write, he meets up with an unusual girl, and together they explore their concerns about the world, themselves, and each other.

"The converging personal journeys of two thoughtful young people unfold beautifully in Victor's quirky but honest voice and in Rose Anna's self-revealing fable. . . . Young adult readers will not want to put down this exceptional debut novel." Voice Youth Advocates

Grabenstein, Chris

The crossroads. 1st ed. Random House 2008 325p $16.99; lib bdg $19.99

Grades: 5 6 7 8   **Fic**

1. Ghost stories 2. Stepmothers—Fiction 3. Connecticut—Fiction

ISBN   978-0-375-84697-7;   0-375-84697-2; 978-0-375-94697-4 (lib bdg); 0-375-94697-7 (lib bdg)

LC 2007024803

When eleven-year-old Zack Jennings moves to Connecticut with his father and new stepmother, they must deal with the ghosts left behind by a terrible accident, as well as another kind of ghost from Zack's past.

"An absorbing psychological thriller . . . as well as a rip-roaring ghost story, this switches points of view among humans, trees, and ghosts with astonishing élan." Booklist

Graff, Lisa, 1981-

The life and crimes of Bernetta Wallflower; a novel. Laura Geringer Books 2008 250p $15.99; lib bdg $17.89

Grades: 4 5 6 **Fic**

1. Swindlers and swindling—Fiction 2. Magic tricks—Fiction 3. Money-making projects for children—Fiction 4. School stories

ISBN 978-0-06-087592-3; 0-06-087592-5; 978-0-06-087593-0 (lib bdg); 0-06-087593-3 (lib bdg)
LC 2006-103470

After her supposed best friend implicates her in a cheating and blackmail scam, twelve-year-old Bernie loses her private school scholarship but, with the help of a new friend, spends the summer using her knowledge of magic and sleight-of-hand both to earn the $9,000 in tuition money and to get revenge.

"The characters are well drawn, and Bernetta's growing qualms of conscience are believable. Readers will appreciate the well-constructed plot and intriguing snippets of magic slipped in here and there." SLJ

Grant, K. M.

Blood red horse. Walker & Co. 2005 c2004 277p $16.95; pa $8.99

Grades: 6 7 8 9 **Fic**

1. Crusades—Fiction 2. Horses—Fiction 3. Middle Ages—Fiction

ISBN 0-8027-8960-9; 0-8027-7734-8 (pa)
LC 2005-42280

First published 2004 in the United Kingdom

A special horse named Hosanna changes the lives of two English brothers and those around them as they fight with King Richard I against Saladin's armies during the Third Crusades.

This "story . . . transcends boundaries of gender and genre, with something to offer fans of equestrian fare, historical fiction, and battlefield drama alike." Booklist

Other titles in this series are:
Green jasper (2006)
Blaze of silver (2007)

Blue flame; book one of the Perfect Fire trilogy. Walker & Co. 2008 246p (Perfect fire trilogy) $16.99 *

Grades: 7 8 9 10 **Fic**

1. Knights and knighthood—Fiction 2. France—History—0-1328—Fiction 3. Middle Ages—Fiction

ISBN 978-0-8027-9694-3; 0-8027-9694-X
LC 2007-51384

In 1242 in the restive Languedoc region of France, Parsifal, having been charged as a child to guard an important religious relic, has lived in hiding for much of his life until he befriends a young couple on opposite sides of the escalating conflict between the Catholics and the Cathars.

"Characters are as complex as the moral issues they face, and Grant's nuanced, thought-provoking look at the religious conflicts they face will resonate today." Booklist

How the hangman lost his heart. Walker & Co. 2007 244p $16.95 *

Grades: 7 8 9 10 **Fic**

1. Great Britain—History—1714-1837—Fiction 2. Adventure fiction

ISBN 978-0-8027-9672-1; 0-8027-9672-9
LC 2006-53182

When her Uncle Frank is executed for treason against England's King George in 1746, and his severed head is mounted on a pike for public viewing, daring Alice tries to reclaim the head for a proper burial, finding an unlikely ally in the softhearted executioner, while incurring the wrath of the royal guard.

"The story is filled with action and interesting characters. . . . This is a rousing read." SLJ

Grant, Michael, 1954-

Gone. HarperTeen 2008 576p $17.99; lib bdg $18.89 *

Grades: 7 8 9 10 **Fic**

1. Supernatural—Fiction 2. Good and evil—Fiction

ISBN 978-0-0614-4876-8; 978-0-0614-4877-5 (lib bdg)
LC 2007-36734

In a small town on the coast of California, everyone over the age of fourteen suddenly disappears, setting up a battle between the remaining town residents and the students from a local private school, as well as those who have "The Power" and are able to perform supernatural feats and those who do not.

"A tour de force that will leave readers dazed, disturbed, and utterly breathless." Booklist

Followed by: Hunger (2009)

Grant, Vicki

Pigboy. Orca Book Pub. 2006 101p (Orca currents series) $14.95; pa $8.95

Grades: 6 7 8 9 **Fic**

1. School stories 2. Pigs—Fiction

ISBN 1-55143-666-3; 1-55143-643-4 (pa)

"When one's last name is Hogg and the class field trip involves a trip to a pig farm, there is a good chance there will be some tough times ahead. But Dan Hogg does not bargain for the fact that the pig farmer has been tied up by a would-be burglar who now is planning a tragic accident to do away with all the witnesses, including Dan." Voice Youth Advocates

"Dan's wry sense of humor catches readers' attention and has them rooting for him practically from the first page." SLJ

Quid pro quo. Orca 2005 160p $16.95; pa $7.95

Grades: 7 8 9 10 **Fic**

1. Lawyers—Fiction 2. Mother-son relationship—Fiction 3. Missing persons—Fiction 4. Mystery fiction

ISBN 1-55143-394-X; 1-55143-370-2 (pa)

"Cyril Floyd MacIntyre, 13, is perplexed over the disappearance of his mother, a 28-year-old law-school graduate. . . . Cyril becomes involved in a web of intrigue and deceit searching for her. His discovery of resurfacing shady characters who played a role in Andy's disappearance makes for a suspense-filled, well-plotted legal thriller." SLJ

Followed by: Res judicata (2008)

Gratz, Alan, 1972-

The Brooklyn nine; a novel in nine innings. Dial Books 2009 299p $16.99 *

Grades: 5 6 7 8   **Fic**
1. Baseball—Fiction 2. Brooklyn (New York, N.Y.)—Fiction 3. Family life—Fiction 4. United States—History—Fiction 5. German Americans—Fiction
ISBN 978-0-8037-3224-7; 0-8037-3224-4
LC 2008-21263

Follows the fortunes of a German immigrant family through nine generations, beginning in 1845, as they experience American life and play baseball.

Gratz "builds this novel upon a clever . . . conceit . . . and executes it with polish and precision." Booklist

Samurai shortstop. Dial Books 2006 280p $17.99

Grades: 7 8 9 10   **Fic**
1. Father-son relationship—Fiction 2. Baseball—Fiction 3. School stories 4. Tokyo (Japan)—Fiction
ISBN 0-8037-3075-6; 978-0-8037-3075-5
LC 2005-22081

While obtaining a Western education at a prestigious Japanese boarding school in 1890, sixteen-year-old Toyo also receives traditional samurai training which has profound effects on both his baseball game and his relationship with his father. This book features some scenes of graphic violence.

"This is an intense read about a fascinating time and place in world history." Publ Wkly

Gray, Claudia

Evernight. HarperTeen 2008 327p $16.99; lib bdg $17.89

Grades: 8 9 10 11 12   **Fic**
1. Horror fiction 2. School stories 3. Vampires—Fiction
ISBN 978-0-06-128439-7; 0-06-128439-4; 978-0-06-128443-4 (lib bdg); 0-06-128443-2 (lib bdg)
LC 2007-36733

Sixteen-year-old Bianca, a new girl at the sinister Evernight boarding school, finds herself drawn to another outsider, Jared, but dark forces threaten to tear them apart and destroy Bianca's entire world.

"Gray's writing hooks readers from the first page and reels them in with surprising plot twists and turns. . . . A must-have for fans of vampire stories." SLJ

Followed by: Stargazer (2009)

Gray, Dianne E.

Together apart. Houghton Mifflin 2002 193p $16

Grades: 7 8 9 10   **Fic**
1. Sex role—Fiction 2. Blizzards—Fiction
ISBN 0-618-18721-9   LC 2002-408

In 1888 in Prairie Hill, Nebraska, a few months after barely surviving a deadly blizzard that has killed two of her brothers, fourteen-year-old Hannah goes to work at the home of a wealthy widow with progressive social ideas, where she finds Isaac, who is also trying to make a new life for himself. Told from alternating points of view of Hannah and Isaac

"The blossoming love story will keep readers in-

volved, and Gray's memorable characters reveal the late 19th-century society's attitudes toward women's rights and class consciousness." Publ Wkly

Tomorrow, the river; [illustrations by Stephanie Cooper] Houghton Mifflin Company 2006 233p il $16

Grades: 6 7 8 9   **Fic**
1. Sisters—Fiction 2. Steamboats—Fiction 3. Mississippi River—Fiction 4. Photography—Fiction
ISBN 978-0-618-56329-6; 0-618-56329-6
LC 2005038068

In 1896, fourteen-year-old Megan joins her sister and family on their steamboat for the summer riding up the Mississippi River towards St. Paul, Minnesota, and through all of their adventures, Megan realizes what is her "true calling."

"History and river life are skillfully woven into the fast-moving plot, and the characters are fully realized." SLJ

Green, Tim

Baseball great. 1st ed. HarperCollinsPublishers 2009 250p $16.99; lib bdg $17.89

Grades: 5 6 7 8   **Fic**
1. Baseball—Fiction 2. Father-son relationship—Fiction 3. School stories
ISBN 978-0-06-162686-9; 0-06-162686-4; 978-0-06-162687-6 (lib bdg); 0-06-162687-2 (lib bdg)
LC 2008051778

All twelve-year-old Josh wants to do is play baseball but when his father, a minor league pitcher, signs him up for a youth championship team, Josh finds himself embroiled in a situation with potentially illegal consequences.

"Issues of peer and family pressure are well handled, and the short, punchy chapters and crisp dialogue are likely to hold the attention of young baseball fans." SLJ

Football genius. HarperCollinsPublishers 2007 244p $16.99; lib bdg $17.89

Grades: 5 6 7 8   **Fic**
1. Football—Fiction 2. Atlanta (Ga.)—Fiction
ISBN 978-0-06-112270-5; 0-06-112270-X; 978-0-06-112272-9 (lib bdg); 0-06-112272-6 (lib bdg)
LC 2006-29470

Troy, a sixth-grader with an unusual gift for predicting football plays before they occur, attempts to use his ability to help his favorite team, the Atlanta Falcons, but he must first prove himself to the coach and players.

The author "imparts many insider details that football fans will love. Green makes Troy a winning hero, and he ties everything together with a fast-moving plot." Booklist

Followed by: Football champ (2009)

Football hero. HarperCollinsPublishers 2008 297p $16.99; lib bdg $17.89

Grades: 5 6 7 8   **Fic**
1. Football—Fiction 2. Mafia—Fiction 3. New Jersey—Fiction
ISBN 978-0-06-112274-3; 0-06-112274-2; 978-0-06-112275-0 (lib bdg); 0-06-112275-0 (lib bdg)
LC 2007-24184

Green, Tim—*Continued*

When twelve-year-old Ty's brother Thane is recruited out of college to play for the New York Jets, their Uncle Gus uses Ty to get insider information for his gambling ring, landing Ty and Thane in trouble with the Mafia.

"The novel is briskly paced and undemanding, and might be a good bet for sports-minded reluctant readers." SLJ

Greene, Bette, 1934-

Summer of my German soldier. Dial Bks. for Young Readers 1973 230p pa $6.99 hardcover o.p.

Grades: 6 7 8 9   **Fic**

1. World War, 1939-1945—Fiction 2. German prisoners of war—Fiction 3. Arkansas—Fiction

ISBN 0-14-130636-X (pa)

"Patty knows the pain of loneliness, rejection, and beatings in a family where she is the ugly duckling, unable to gain her parents' love. This is in contrast to the affection shown to her beautiful and submissive sister. Anton Reiker is a German prisoner-of-war in a camp outside of Jenkinsville, Arkansas, and when he escapes, Patty helps him. Because her family is Jewish, she pays dearly for this intervention." Shapiro. Fic for Youth. 3d edition

Followed by Morning is a long time coming (1978)

Greene, Michele

Chasing the jaguar; [by] Michele Domínguez Greene. HarperCollins Pubs. 2006 227p $15.99; lib bdg $16.89

Grades: 7 8 9 10   **Fic**

1. Mayas—Fiction 2. Mexican Americans—Fiction 3. Los Angeles (Calif.)—Fiction 4. Mystery fiction 5. Kidnapping—Fiction

ISBN 0-06-076353-1; 0-09-076354-X (lib bdg)

After having unsettling dreams about the kidnapped daughter of her mother's employer, fifteen-year-old Martika learns that she is a descendant of a long line of curanderas—Mayan medicine women with special powers. Includes glossary of Spanish words.

"Los Angeles is vibrantly described. . . . This unusual mystery is sure to attract teens, and should encourage them to find out more about Mayan culture." SLJ

Greenwald, Lisa

My life in pink and green. Amulet Books 2009 267p $16.95

Grades: 4 5 6 7   **Fic**

1.   Mother-daughter   relationship—Fiction 2. Cosmetics—Fiction 3. Environmental protection—Fiction

ISBN 978-0-8109-8352-6; 0-8109-8352-4

LC 2008025577

When the family's drugstore is failing, seventh-grader Lucy uses her problem solving talents to come up with solution that might resuscitate the business, along with helping the environment.

"Greenwald deftly blends eco-facts and makeup tips, friendship dynamics, and spot-on middle-school politics into a warm, uplifting story." Booklist

Gregory, Kristiana

Eleanor: crown jewel of Aquitaine. Scholastic 2002 187p il (Royal diaries) $10.95

Grades: 6 7 8 9   **Fic**

1. Eleanor, of Aquitaine, Queen, consort of Henry II, King of England, 1122?-1204—Fiction 2. France—History—0-1328—Fiction

ISBN 0-439-16484-2   LC 2001-57628

The diary of Eleanor, first daughter of the duke of Aquitaine, from 1136 until 1137, when at age fifteen she becomes queen of France. Includes historical notes on her later life

"With attention focused on the small details of life and her youthful dreams, Eleanor comes to life. . . . An epilogue, historical note, family tree, photographs, and glossary of characters round out the book." SLJ

My darlin' Clementine. 1st ed. Holiday House 2009 206p $16.95

Grades: 5 6 7 8   **Fic**

1. Frontier and pioneer life—Fiction 2. Family life—Fiction 3. Sisters—Fiction 4. Sex role—Fiction 5. Miners—Fiction 6. Idaho—Fiction

ISBN 978-0-8234-2198-5; 0-8234-2198-8

LC 2008039203

Expands on the folk song to tell of seventeen-year-old Clementine, whose dream of being a doctor is complicated by her drunken, gambling father, the lawlessness of 1866 Idaho Territory, and the affections of handsome Boone Reno.

"Clem is an inspiring character, and Gregory provides plenty of cliff-hangers and historical background to keep avid fans of the author, or the genre, reading." SLJ

Seeds of hope; the gold rush diary of Susanna Fairchild. Scholastic 2001 182p il map (Dear America) $10.95

Grades: 5 6 7 8   **Fic**

1. California—Gold discoveries—Fiction 2. Frontier and pioneer life—Fiction

ISBN 0-590-51157-2; 0-439-55509-4

LC 00-63725

A diary account of fourteen-year-old Susanna Fairchild's life in 1849, when her father succumbs to gold fever on the way to establish his medical practice in Oregon after losing his wife and money on their steamship journey from New York. Includes a historical note

"A gripping, realistic fictional glimpse of history." Booklist

Gregory, Nan, 1944-

I'll sing you one-o. Clarion Books 2006 220p $16

Grades: 5 6 7 8   **Fic**

1. Foster home care—Fiction 2. Siblings—Fiction 3. Twins—Fiction 4. Family life—Fiction

ISBN 978-0-618-60708-2; 0-618-60708-0

LC 2005-32709

Reunited with her long-lost twin brother, twelve-year-old Gemma constantly tests the boundaries of acceptable behavior while relying on angels to help her connect with her new family.

"Fine characterization provides a broad cast. . . . The child's enormous need to verify her birth mother's love for her is achingly real." SLJ

Grey, Christopher

Leonardo's shadow; or, my astonishing life as Leonardo da Vinci's servant. Atheneum Books for Young Readers 2006 394p $16.95 *

Grades: 6 7 8 9   Fic

1. Leonardo, da Vinci, 1452-1519—Fiction
2. Household employees—Fiction 3. Artists—Fiction
ISBN 1-4169-0543-X

Fifteen-year-old Giacomo—servant to Leonardo da Vinci—helps his procrastinating master finish painting "The Last Supper" while also trying to find clues to his parentage and pursue his own career as an artist in late fifteenth-century Milan.

"Grey seamlessly blends fact and research about the inventor/artist with imagination. . . . Easily readable, this novel incorporates adventure and mystery with history." SLJ

Griffin, Adele

My almost epic summer. G. P. Putnam's Sons 2006 170p $15.99; pa $6.99

Grades: 7 8 9 10   Fic

1. Babysitters—Fiction 2. Summer—Fiction
ISBN 0-399-23784-4; 0-14-240860-3 (pa)
                                              LC 2005013491

Stuck babysitting during the summer while her friends take glamorous vacations, fourteen-year-old Irene learns some lessons about life after meeting a beautiful, yet troubled, girl.

"Griffin has created vivid scenes, believable dilemmas, and satisfyingly human characters in this novel of self-discovery." SLJ

Where I want to be. G.P. Putnam's Sons 2005 150p pa $6.99

Grades: 7 8 9 10   Fic

1. Sisters—Fiction 2. Mental illness—Fiction
3. Death—Fiction 4. Rhode Island—Fiction
ISBN 0-399-23783-6; 0-14-240948-0 (pa)
                                               LC 2004-1887

Two teenaged sisters, separated by death but still connected, work through their feelings of loss over the closeness they shared as children that was later destroyed by one's mental illness, and finally make peace with each other

"Thoughtful, unique, and ultimately life-affirming, this is a fascinating take on the literary device of a main character speaking after death." SLJ

Griffin, Paul, 1966-

Ten Mile River. Dial Books 2008 188p $16.99

Grades: 8 9 10 11 12   Fic

1. Juvenile delinquency—Fiction 2. Homeless persons—Fiction 3. Runaway teenagers—Fiction 4. New York (N.Y.)—Fiction
ISBN 978-0-8037-3284-1; 0-8037-3284-8
                                              LC 2007-047870

Having escaped from juvenile detention centers and foster care, two teenaged boys live on their own in an abandoned shack in a New York City park, making their way by stealing, occasionally working, and trying to keep from being arrested.

"The language is tough but convincing, the setting authentic, the characters memorable and their struggles played out with a complexity that respects the audience's intelligence." Publ Wkly

Griffin, Peni R.

The ghost sitter. Dutton Children's Bks. 2001 131p $14.99; pa $5.99

Grades: 4 5 6 7   Fic

1. Ghost stories
ISBN 0-525-46676-2; 0-14-230216-3 (pa)
                                                  LC 00-65859

When she realizes that her new house is haunted by the ghost of a ten-year-old girl who used to live there, Charlotte tries to help her find peace

"Griffin's book has several strong appeals: new best friends solving a mystery together, a just-scary-enough ghost girl, and a deathless bond between sisters that provides the book with its resoundingly satisfying conclusion and bang-up last sentence." Horn Book

Grimes, Nikki

Bronx masquerade. Dial Bks. 2002 167p $16.99; pa $5.99 *

Grades: 7 8 9 10   Fic

1. School stories 2. African Americans—Fiction
3. Bronx (New York, N.Y.)—Fiction
ISBN 0-8037-2569-8; 0-14-250189-1 (pa)
                                                  LC 00-31701

While studying the Harlem Renaissance, students at a Bronx high school read aloud poems they've written, revealing their innermost thoughts and fears to their formerly clueless classmates

"Funny and painful, awkward and abstract, the poems talk about race, abuse, parental love, neglect, death, and body image. . . . Readers will enjoy the lively, smart voices that talk bravely about real issues and secret fears. A fantastic choice for readers' theater." Booklist

Dark sons. Jump at the Sun 2005 216p $15.99

Grades: 6 7 8 9   Fic

1. Father-son relationship—Fiction 2. Stepfamilies—Fiction 3. Novels in verse
ISBN 0-7868-1888-3   LC 2004-54208

Alternating poems compare and contrast the conflicted feelings of Ishmael, son of the Biblical patriarch Abraham, and Sam, a teenager in New York City, as they try to come to terms with being abandoned by their fathers and with the love they feel for their younger stepbrothers.

"The simple words eloquently reveal what it's like to miss someone. . . . but even more moving is the struggle to forgive and the affection each boy feels for the baby that displaces him. The elemental connections and the hope. . . will speak to a wide audience." Booklist

Jazmin's notebook. Dial Bks. 1998 102p $15.99 *

Grades: 6 7 8 9   Fic

1. African Americans—Fiction 2. Authorship—Fiction
3. Harlem (New York, N.Y.)—Fiction
ISBN 0-8037-2224-9   LC 97-5850

Also available in paperback from Puffin Bks.

A Coretta Scott King honor book for text, 1999

Grimes, Nikki—*Continued*

Jazmin, an Afro-American fourteen-year-old who lives with her older sister in a small Harlem apartment in the 1960s, finds strength in writing poetry and keeping a record of the events in her sometimes difficult life

"An articulate, admirable heroine, Jazmin leaps over life's hurdles with agility and integrity." Publ Wkly

The road to Paris. G. P. Putnam's Sons 2006 153p $15.99

Grades: 4 5 6 7   Fic

1. Foster home care—Fiction 2. Racially mixed people—Fiction 3. Siblings—Fiction

ISBN 0-399-24537-5; 978-0-399-24537-4

LC 2005-28920

Inconsolable at being separated from her older brother, eight-year-old Paris is apprehensive about her new foster family but just as she learns to trust them, she faces a life-changing decision.

"In clear, short chapters, Grimes tells a beautiful story of family, friendship, and faith from the viewpoint of a child in search of home in a harsh world." Booklist

Gruber, Michael

The witch's boy. HarperTempest 2005 377p $16.99; lib bdg $17.89; pa $7.99

Grades: 7 8 9 10   Fic

1. Witches—Fiction 2. Fairy tales

ISBN 0-06-076164-4; 0-06-076165-2 (lib bdg); 0-06-076167-9 (pa)   LC 2004-20845

A grotesque foundling turns against the witch who sacrificed almost everything to raise him when he becomes consumed by the desire for money and revenge against those who have hurt him, but he eventually finds his true heart's desire.

"Gruber cleverly weaves elements from familiar fairy tales into a saga that moves across forest, earth, and sea." Booklist

Gutman, Dan

The million dollar putt; [by] Dan Gutman. 1st ed. Hyperion Books for Children 2006 169p $15.99

Grades: 6 7 8 9   Fic

1. Golf—Fiction 2. Contests—Fiction 3. Blind—Fiction 4. Hawaii—Fiction

ISBN 0-7868-3641-5   LC 2005052519

Assisted by his neighbor, Birdie, blind thirteen-year-old Ed "Bogie" Bogard will win one million dollars if he can sink a ten-foot putt in Hawaii's fifth annual Angus Killick Memorial Tournament.

"This novel's appeal is enhanced by humorous, lively dialogue; the innocence of the main characters; and the positive portrayal of their relationship and disabilities. An interesting read." SLJ

The million dollar shot. Hyperion Bks. for Children 1997 114p hardcover o.p. pa $5.99

Grades: 4 5 6 7   Fic

1. Basketball—Fiction 2. Contests—Fiction

ISBN 0-7868-2275-9; 1-4231-0084-0 (pa)

LC 97-6461

Eleven-year-old Eddie gets a chance to win a million dollars by sinking a foul shot at the National Basketball Association finals

This "will appeal to both sports readers and general audiences. Gutman's subtle humor, exciting sports action, and excruciating suspense make this title an outstanding choice for reluctant readers." SLJ

Shoeless Joe & me; a baseball card adventure. HarperCollins Pubs. 2002 163p hardcover o.p. pa $5.99

Grades: 4 5 6 7   Fic

1. Jackson, Joe, 1888-1951—Fiction 2. Baseball—Fiction

ISBN 0-06-029253-9; 0-06-447259-0 (pa)

LC 2001-24638

Joe Stoshack travels back to 1919, where he meets Shoeless Joe Jackson and tries to prevent the fixing of the World Series in which Jackson was wrongly implicated

"Shoeless Joe is compelling, and Joe's adventures are exciting." Voice Youth Advocates

Other titles in the Baseball card adventures series are:

Abner & me (2005)

Babe & me (2000)

Honus & me (1997)

Jackie & me (1999)

Jim & me (2008)

Mickey & me (2003)

Ray & me (2009)

Satch & me (2006)

Gwaltney, Doris

Homefront. Simon & Schuster Books for Young Readers 2006 310p $16.99

Grades: 5 6 7 8   Fic

1. Family life—Fiction 2. World War, 1939-1945—Fiction 3. Virginia—Fiction

ISBN 0-689-86842-1   LC 2006-283492

"As Margaret Ann Motley looks forward to seventh grade, the only changes she sees on the horizon are her sister's leaving for college and, immediately afterwards, moving . . . into her sister's old room. With the U.S. on the brink of World War II, though, greater changes are in store. . . . Gwaltney provides vivid character portrayals. . . . Well grounded in the Tidewater area of Virginia, the novel's social context is made real." Booklist

Haas, Jessie

Chase. Greenwillow Books 2007 250p $16.99; lib bdg $17.89

Grades: 5 6 7 8   Fic

1. Coal mines and mining—Fiction 2. Irish Americans—Fiction 3. Pennsylvania—Fiction

ISBN 978-0-06-112850-9; 0-06-112850-3; 978-0-06-112851-6 (lib bdg); 0-06-112851-1 (lib bdg)

LC 2006-41240

In the coal mining region of mid-nineteenth century eastern Pennsylvania, Phin witnesses a murder and runs for his life, pursued by a mysterious man and a horse with the instincts of a bloodhound.

"This exciting story is soaked in historical detail and psychological credibility." Booklist

Haddix, Margaret Peterson, 1964-

Among the hidden. Simon & Schuster Bks. for Young Readers 1998 153p $16.95; pa $5.99 *

Grades: 5 6 7 8   **Fic**

  1. Science fiction

  ISBN 0-689-81700-2; 0-689-82475-0 (pa)

                       LC 97-33052

In a future where the Population Police enforce the law limiting a family to only two children, Luke has lived all his twelve years in isolation and fear on his family's farm, until another 'third' convinces him that the government is wrong

"The fully realized setting, honest characters, and fast paced plot combine for a suspenseful tale." ALAN

  Other titles in this series are:

Among the Barons (2003)

Among the betrayed (2002)

Among the brave (2004)

Among the enemy (2005)

Among the free (2006)

Among the impostors (2001)

Double identity. Simon & Schuster Books for Young Readers 2005 218p $15.95 *

Grades: 5 6 7 8   **Fic**

  1. Cloning—Fiction 2. Science fiction

  ISBN 0-689-87374-3   LC 2004-13448

Thirteen-year-old Bethany's parents have always been overprotective, but when they suddenly drop out of sight with no explanation, leaving her with an aunt she never knew existed, Bethany uncovers shocking secrets that make her question everything she thought she knew about herself and her family.

This is a "suspenseful sf novel guaranteed to keep readers riveted." Booklist

Found. Simon & Schuster Books for Young Readers 2008 314p (The missing) $15.99 *

Grades: 5 6 7 8   **Fic**

  1. Adoption—Fiction 2. Science fiction

  ISBN 978-1-4169-5417-0; 1-4169-5417-1

                       LC 2007-23614

When thirteen-year-olds Jonah and Chip, who are both adopted, learn they were discovered on a plane that appeared out of nowhere, full of babies with no adults on board, they realize that they have uncovered a mystery involving time travel and two opposing forces, each trying to repair the fabric of time.

This is "a tantalizing opener to a new series. . . . Readers will be hard-pressed to wait for the next installment." Publ Wkly

Just Ella. Simon & Schuster Bks. for Young Readers 1999 185p hardcover o.p. pa $5.99

Grades: 7 8 9 10   **Fic**

  1. Princesses—Fiction 2. Sex role—Fiction

  ISBN 0-689-82186-7; 0-689-83128-5 (pa)

                       LC 98-8384

Companion volume to: Palace of Mirrors (2008)

In this continuation of the Cinderella story, fifteen-year-old Ella finds that accepting Prince Charming's proposal ensnares her in a suffocating tangle of palace rules and royal etiquette, so she plots to escape

"In lively prose, with well-developed characters, creative plot twists, wit, and drama, Haddix transforms the Cinderella tale into an insightful coming-of-age story." Booklist

Leaving Fishers. Simon & Schuster Bks. for Young Readers 1997 211p hardcover o.p. pa $5.99

Grades: 7 8 9 10   **Fic**

  1. Cults—Fiction

  ISBN 0-689-81125-X; 0-689-86793-X (pa)

                       LC 96-47857

After joining her new friends in the religious group called Fishers of Men, Dorry finds herself immersed in a cult from which she must struggle to extricate herself

"The novel does a credible job of showing the effect of a cult on a vulnerable person, without disavowing strong religious beliefs." Child Book Rev Serv

Uprising. Simon & Schuster Books for Young Readers 2007 346p $16.99 *

Grades: 6 7 8 9 10   **Fic**

  1. Triangle Shirtwaist Company, Inc. —Fiction

  2. Strikes—Fiction 3. Fires—Fiction

  ISBN 978-1-4169-1171-5; 1-4169-1171-5

                       LC 2006-34870

In 1927, at the urging of twenty-one-year-old Harriet, Mrs. Livingston reluctantly recalls her experiences at the Triangle Shirtwaist factory, including miserable working conditions that led to a strike, then the fire that took the lives of her two best friends, when Harriet, the boss's daughter, was only five years old. Includes historical notes.

"This deftly crafted historical novel unfolds dramatically with an absorbing story and well-drawn characters who readily evoke empathy and compassion." SLJ

Hahn, Mary Downing, 1937-

Hear the wind blow. Clarion Bks. 2003 212p $15 *

Grades: 5 6 7 8   **Fic**

  1. United States—History—1861-1865, Civil War—Fiction 2. Siblings—Fiction

  ISBN 0-618-18190-3   LC 2002-15977

With their mother dead and their home burned, a thirteen-year-old boy and his little sister set out across Virginia in search of relatives during the final days of the Civil War

The author "gives readers an entertaining and thought-provoking combination: a strong adventure inextricably bound to a specific time and place, but one that resonates with universal themes." Horn Book

Stepping on the cracks. Clarion Bks. 1991 216p $16; pa $5.99 *

Grades: 5 6 7 8   **Fic**

  1. World War, 1939-1945—Fiction

  ISBN 0-395-58507-4; 0-547-07660-6 (pa)

                       LC 91-7706

Also available in paperback from Avon Bks.

In 1944, while her brother is overseas fighting in World War II, eleven-year-old Margaret gets a new view of the school bully Gordy when she finds him hiding his own brother, an army deserter, and decides to help him

"Well-drawn characters and a satisfying plot. . . . There is plenty of action and page-turning suspense to please those who want a quick read, but there is much to ponder and reflect on as well." SLJ

Haig, Matt, 1975-
Samuel Blink and the forbidden forest; [by]
Matt Haig. Putnam 2007 316p il $16.99
Grades: 4 5 6 7   **Fic**
   1. Siblings—Fiction 2. Magic—Fiction 3. Dogs—Fiction 4. Orphans—Fiction 5. Norway—Fiction
   ISBN 978-0-399-24739-2   LC 2006024827
Accompanied by his aunt's Norwegian elkhound, Ib-
sen, twelve-year-old Samuel ventures into a weird forest
filled with strange and dangerous creatures to rescue his
younger sister, Martha, who has been mute since their
parents' recent death.
   "Crisp dialogue, fast-paced action, short chapters, and
a wry narrative voice bring this tale to life." SLJ
   Followed by: Samuel Blink and the runaway troll
(2008)

Halam, Ann
Siberia; a novel. Wendy Lamb Books 2005
262p hardcover o.p. pa $5.99
Grades: 7 8 9 10   **Fic**
   1. Endangered species—Fiction 2. Wilderness survival—Fiction 3. Science fiction
   ISBN 0-385-74659-4; 0-553-49414-7 (pa)
After spending two years at a prison school, thirteen-
year-old Sloe sets off on a trek across frozen wastelands,
tending to the secret "seeds" of wild animals her mother
left in her care, trying to reach a new life for all of
them.
   "Halam intertwines issues of ecology, climate change,
and nature conservancy with more personal themes of
loneliness, identity, and trust. . . . The bitterly cold setting, the hunger, and fear are almost palpable." SLJ

Snakehead. Wendy Lamb Books 2008 289p il
map $16.99; lib bdg $19.99
Grades: 6 7 8 9 10   **Fic**
   1. Classical mythology—Fiction 2. Perseus (Greek
mythology)—Fiction 3. Medusa (Greek mythology)—
Fiction 4. Gods and goddesses—Fiction
   ISBN 978-0-375-84108-8; 978-0-375-94108-5 (lib
bdg)   LC 2007-28318
Compelled by his father Zeus to accept the evil king
Polydectes's challenge to bring the head of the monstrous Medusa to the Aegean island of Serifos, Perseus,
although questioning the gods' interference in human
lives, sets out, accompanied by his beloved Andromeda,
a princess with her own harsh destiny to fulfill.
   "Mythology buffs will appreciate the plethora of classical figures, while periodic references to contemporary
culture (e.g., a band of rich, rowdy teens are dubbed the
Yacht Club kids) and occasional slang drive the story
home for the target audience without sacrificing its heroic dimensions." Publ Wkly

Hale, Marian
Dark water rising. Henry Holt 2006 233p il
$16.95 *
Grades: 6 7 8 9   **Fic**
   1. Hurricanes—Fiction   2.   Floods—Fiction
3. Galveston (Tex.)—Fiction 4. Father-son relationship—Fiction
   ISBN 0-8050-7585-2   LC 2005-36678

While salvaging and rebuilding in the aftermath of the
Galveston flood of 1900, sixteen-year-old Seth proves
himself in a way that his previous efforts never could,
but he still must face his father man-to-man.
   "Character development is as vital here as the historical facts, and because the pack is quick and descriptions
are sharp and focused, the book will draw even reluctant
readers." Booklist

The truth about sparrows; [by] Marian Hale. 1st
ed. H. Holt 2004 260p $16.95
Grades: 5 6 7 8   **Fic**
   1. Friendship—Fiction 2. Moving—Fiction 3. Great
Depression, 1929-1939—Fiction
   ISBN 0-8050-7584-4   LC 2003-56981
Twelve-year-old Sadie promises that she will always
be Wilma's best friend when their families leave
drought-stricken Missouri in 1933, but once in Texas,
Sadie learns that she must try to make a new home—and
new friends, too
   "Rich with social history, this first novel is informative, enjoyable, and evocative." SLJ

Hale, Shannon
Book of a thousand days; illustrations by James
Noel Smith. Bloomsbury Children's Books 2007
305p il $17.95 *
Grades: 7 8 9 10   **Fic**
   1. Fantasy fiction 2. Love stories
   ISBN 978-1-59990-051-3; 1-59990-051-3
                            LC 2006-36999
Fifteen-year-old Dashti, sworn to obey her sixteen-
year-old mistress, the Lady Saren, shares Saren's years
of punishment locked in a tower, then brings her safely
to the lands of her true love, where both must hide who
they are as they work as kitchen maids.
   This is a "captivating fantasy filled with romance,
magic, and strong female characters." Booklist

Princess Academy. Bloomsbury Children's Bks.
2005 314p $16.95; pa $7.95
Grades: 6 7 8 9   **Fic**
   1. Princesses—Fiction
   ISBN 1-58234-993-2; 1-59990-073-4 (pa)
                            LC 2004065958
   A Newbery Medal honor book, 2006
   While attending a strict academy for potential princesses with the other girls from her mountain village,
fourteen-year-old Miri discovers unexpected talents and
connections to her homeland.
   "Hale weaves an intricate, multilayered story about
families, relationships, education, and the place we call
home." SLJ

Hall, Barbara, 1960-
The Noah confessions. Delacorte Press 2007
215p $15.99
Grades: 8 9 10 11 12   **Fic**
   1. Family life—Fiction 2. Father-daughter relationship—Fiction 3. Mothers—Fiction
   ISBN 978-0-385-73328-1; 0-385-73328-3
                            LC 2006-15640

Hall, Barbara, 1960- —*Continued*

Instead of a car for her sixteenth birthday, Lynnie receives a manuscript from her father in which her deceased mother writes about family secrets, helping Lynnie to understand more about her parents and the complexity of growing up.

"This novel will grab readers' attention. . . . A solid story . . . that teaches about self-examination and the ability to move away from the past." SLJ

Tempo change. Delacorte Press 2009 247p $16.99; lib bdg $19.99

Grades: 8 9 10 11 12   **Fic**
1. Coachella Valley Music & Arts Festival—Fiction 2. Bands (Music)—Fiction 3. Father-daughter relationship—Fiction 4. Single parent family—Fiction 5. Fame—Fiction 6. California—Fiction
ISBN   978-0-385-73607-7;   0-385-73607-X; 978-0-385-90585-5 (lib bdg); 0-385-90585-8 (lib bdg)
LC 2008-30968

Sixteen-year-old Blanche forms a band that wins a spot at Coachella, a southern California music festival, where she hopes to reconnect with her father, a famous but reclusive musician who left when she was six years old.

"Hall's cast of characters is quirky . . . [and] Blanche's witty, sensitive narration will have readers rooting for her throughout." Booklist

Halpern, Julie, 1975-

Get well soon. Feiwel & Friends 2007 193p $16.95

Grades: 7 8 9 10   **Fic**
1. Mental illness—Fiction 2. Psychiatric hospitals—Fiction
ISBN 0-312-36795-3; 978-0-312-36795-4
LC 2006-32358

When her parents confine her to a mental hospital, Anna, an overweight teenage girl who suffers from panic attacks, describes her experiences in a series of letters to a friend.

"Halpern creates a narrative that reflects the changes in Anna with each passing day that includes self-reflection and a good dose of humor." Voice Youth Advocates

Halpin, Brendan

Forever changes. Farrar, Straus & Giroux 2008 181p $16.95

Grades: 7 8 9 10 11 12   **Fic**
1. Death—Fiction 2. Mathematics—Fiction 3. School stories 4. Massachusetts—Fiction
ISBN 978-0-374-32436-0; 0-374-32436-0
LC 2007-26494

Although encouraged to apply to colleges, Brianna Pelletier, a mathematically-gifted high school senior with cystic fibrosis, dwells on her mortality and the unfairness of life.

"Teens looking for a novel with a sad ending and a touch of bibliotherapy will not be disappointed by Brianna's story." Voice Youth Advocates

How ya like me now. Farrar, Straus & Giroux 2007 201p $16 *

Grades: 7 8 9 10 11 12   **Fic**
1. School stories 2. Boston (Mass.)—Fiction 3. Cousins—Fiction 4. Race relations—Fiction
ISBN 0-374-33495-1; 978-0-374-33495-6
LC 2006-40989

After his father dies and his mother goes into rehab, Eddie moves from the suburbs into his cousin's Boston loft, where he gradually adjusts to being one of the few white kids in a progressive private school, and learns how to feel like a normal teenager.

"An engaging YA slice-of-life story, capped by an upbeat resolution and endowed with both laughter and healing." Booklist

Hamilton, Virginia, 1936-2002

The house of Dies Drear; illustrated by Eros Keith. Macmillan 1968 246p il $18.95; pa $5.99 *

Grades: 5 6 7 8   **Fic**
1. African Americans—Fiction 2. Mystery fiction 3. Ohio—Fiction
ISBN 0-02-742500-2; 0-02-043520-7 (pa)

"A hundred years ago, Dies Drear and two slaves he was hiding in his house, an Underground Railroad station in Ohio, had been murdered. The house, huge and isolated, was fascinating, Thomas thought, but he wasn't sure he was glad Papa had bought it—funny things kept happening, frightening things." Bull Cent Child Books

"The answer to the mystery comes in a startling dramatic dénouement that is pure theater. This is gifted writing; the characterization is unforgettable, the plot imbued with mounting tension." Saturday Rev

Followed by The mystery of Drear House (1987)

The planet of Junior Brown. Macmillan 1971 210p hardcover o.p. pa $5.99 *

Grades: 6 7 8 9   **Fic**
1. Friendship—Fiction 2. African Americans—Fiction
ISBN 0-689-71721-0; 1-4169-1410-2 (pa)

A Newbery Medal honor book, 1972

"This is the story of a crucial week in the lives of two black, eighth-grade dropouts who have been spending their time with the school janitor. Each boy is presented as a distinct individual. Jr. is a three-hundred pound musical prodigy as neurotic as his overprotective mother. Buddy has learned to live by his wits in a world of homeless children. Buddy becomes Jr. Brown's protector and says to the other boys, 'We are together because we have to learn to live for each other.'" Read Ladders for Hum Relat. 6th edition

Hamley, Dennis, 1935-

Without warning; Ellen's story 1914-1918; [by] Dennis Hamley. 1st U.S. ed. Candlewick Press 2007 326p $17.99

Grades: 6 7 8 9   **Fic**
1. World War, 1914-1918—Fiction 2. Great Britain—Fiction
ISBN 978-0-7636-3338-7; 0-7636-3338-0
LC 2007025248

First published 2006 in the United Kingdom with title: Ellen's people

Hamley, Dennis, 1935——*Continued*

During World War I, an English teenager leaves the safety of home and begins a journey of self-discovery that takes her close to the front lines to pursue her calling as a nurse.

"This intense narrative dramatically offers insight into the effects of World War I on the English home front. . . . This is a highly readable selection with many well-drawn characters." SLJ

Han, Jenny

Shug; [by] Jenny Han. 1st ed. Simon & Schuster Books for Young Readers 2006 248p $14.95

Grades: 5 6 7 8   Fic

1. School stories 2. Family life—Fiction

ISBN 978-1-4169-0942-2; 1-4169-0942-7

LC 2005009367

"Tall, freckled, gawky seventh-grader Annemarie Wilcox (whose family calls her Shug) has a beautiful, popular older sister; a gorgeous, alcoholic mother who doesn't fit in their small Georgia town; and a father who's always away on business. She also has a huge crush on Mark, the neighborhood boy who has always been her best friend. . . . Shug's direct, honest narration reveals a wholly believable, endearing, hot-tempered young woman who faces painful truths and survives." Booklist

The summer I turned pretty. Simon & Schuster Books for Young Readers 2009 276p $16.99 *

Grades: 7 8 9 10   Fic

1. Beaches—Fiction   2. Summer—Fiction
3. Vacations—Fiction 4. Friendship—Fiction

ISBN 978-1-4169-6823-8; 1-4169-6823-7

LC 2008-27070

Belly spends the summer she turns sixteen at the beach just like every other summer of her life, but this time things are very different.

"Romantic and heartbreakingly real. . . . The novel perfectly blends romance, family drama, and a coming-of-age tale, one that is substantially deeper than most." SLJ

Hansen, Joyce

One true friend. Clarion Bks. 2001 154p $14; pa $6.95

Grades: 6 7 8 9   Fic

1. Friendship—Fiction 2. African Americans—Fiction

ISBN 0-395-84983-7; 0-618-60991-1 (pa)

LC 2001-28483

Fourteen-year-old orphan Amir, living in Syracuse, exchanges letters with his friend Doris, still living in their old Bronx neighborhood, in which they share their lives and give each other advice on friendship, family, foster care, and making decisions

"Both sad and hopeful, this story dramatizes the struggle for survival, the primal pull of family, and the gift of 'one true friend.'" Booklist

Other titles about Amir and Doris are:

The gift-giver (1980)

Yellow Bird and me (1985)

Harazin, S. A.

Blood brothers. Delacorte Press 2007 224p $15.99; lib bdg $18.99 *

Grades: 8 9 10 11 12   Fic

1. Drug abuse—Fiction 2. Friendship—Fiction
3. Georgia—Fiction

ISBN 978-0-385-73364-9; 978-0-385-90379-0 (lib bdg)   LC 2006-19637

With his best friend on life-support after taking drugs at a party, seventeen-year-old Clay, a medical technician, recalls their long friendship, future plans, and recent disagreement, and tries to figure out who is responsible for the accidental overdose.

"Settings and characters are extremely well drawn. The compelling serious story line is punctuated by smatters of Clay's self-deprecating humor." Voice Youth Advocates

Hardinge, Frances

Fly by night. HarperCollinsPublishers 2006 487p $16.99; lib bdg $17.89 *

Grades: 5 6 7 8   Fic

1. Fantasy fiction

ISBN 978-0-06-087627-2; 0-06-087627-1; 978-0-06-087629-6 (lib bdg); 0-06-087629-8 (lib bdg)   LC 2005-20598

First published 2005 in the United Kingdom

Mosca Mye and her homicidal goose, Saracen, travel to the city of Mandelion on the heels of smooth-talking con-man, Eponymous Clent.

"Through rich, colorful language and a sure sense of plot and pacing, Hardinge has created a distinctly imaginative world full of engaging characters, robust humor, and true suspense." SLJ

The lost conspiracy. Bowen Press 2009 576p $16.99; lib bdg $17.89 *

Grades: 6 7 8 9   Fic

1. Sisters—Fiction 2. Fantasy

ISBN 978-0-06-088041-5; 0-06-088041-4; 978-0-06-088042-2 (lib bdg); 0-06-088042-2 (lib bdg)   LC 2008-45380

When a lie is exposed and their tribe turns against them, Hathin must find a way to save her sister Arilou--once considered the tribe's oracle--and herself.

"A deeply imaginative story, with nuanced characters, intricate plotting, and an amazingly original setting. . . . A perfectly pitched, hopeful ending caps off this standout adventure." Booklist

Well witched; [by] Frances Hardinge. HarperCollins Publishers 2008 390p $16.99; lib bdg $17.89 *

Grades: 5 6 7 8   Fic

1. Witches—Fiction   2. Magic—Fiction
3. Friendship—Fiction 4. Great Britain—Fiction

ISBN 978-0-06-088038-5; 0-06-088038-4; 978-0-06-088039-2 (lib bdg); 0-06-088039-2 (lib bdg)   LC 2007020877

Three friends fall prey to the demands of the Well Witch when they trespass in her wishing well and steal some coins.

"This novel is alive with quirky, idiosyncratic characters. . . . There is no doubt that the book's hypnotic cover and inventive plot will attract many readers." Voice Youth Advocates

Harlow, Joan Hiatt

Joshua's song. Margaret K. McElderry Bks. 2001 176p $16; pa $4.99

Grades: 4 5 6 7   **Fic**

1. Newspaper carriers—Fiction 2. Disasters—Fiction 3. Boston (Mass.)—Fiction

ISBN 0-689-84119-1; 0-689-85542-7 (pa)

       LC 00-52537

Needing to earn money after his father's death during the influenza epidemic of 1918, thirteen-year-old Joshua works as a newspaper boy in Boston, one day finding himself in the vicinity of an explosion that sends tons of molasses coursing through the streets.

"Even readers who don't usually like historical fiction will enjoy Harlow's vivid depiction of early-twentieth-century working-class life and conditions. They will also like the fast-paced story, which revolves around an actual incident." Booklist

Harmel, Kristin

When you wish; [by] Kristin Harmel. 1st ed. Delacorte Press 2008 273p $15.99; lib bdg $18.99

Grades: 7 8 9 10   **Fic**

1. Fame—Fiction 2. Singers—Fiction 3. Mother-daughter relationship—Fiction 4. Father-daughter relationship—Fiction 5. Florida—Fiction

ISBN 978-0-385-73475-2; 0-385-73475-1; 978-0-385-90474-2 (lib bdg); 0-385-90474-6 (lib bdg)

       LC 2007020472

When sixteen-year-old pop singing sensation Star Beck learns that her father, who left when she was three, has been writing to her for six years, she disguises herself, leaves her controlling mother and adoring fans behind, and goes to find him—and, perhaps, a normal life—in St. Petersburg, Florida.

"Harmel has created a character and a story that will have wide appeal. There is enough complexity to hold the interest of a more demanding reader, even while remaining basically an entertaining reading experience." KLIATT

Harmon, Michael, 1941-

Skate. Alfred A. Knopf 2006 242p $15.95

Grades: 8 9 10 11   **Fic**

1. Runaway teenagers—Fiction 2. Brothers—Fiction

ISBN 0-375-87516-6   LC 2005-28270

Facing a disintegrating home life and trouble at school, teenager Ian McDermott runs away with his younger brother to Washington State in search of safety, justice and their long-absent father.

"This well-written, fast-paced novel offers a believable narrator for whom readers will root." Voice Youth Advocates

Harness, Cheryl

Just for you to know. HarperCollins 2006 308p $16.99; lib bdg $17.89

Grades: 5 6 7 8   **Fic**

1. Family life—Fiction 2. Death—Fiction 3. Missouri—Fiction

ISBN 0-06-078313-3; 0-06-078314-1 (lib bdg)

       LC 2006-281855

In Independence, Missouri, in 1963, twelve-year-old Carmen already has her hands full dealing with a dreamy mother, a sometimes reckless father, and five noisy little brothers, but must find a way to hold onto her own dreams when tragedy strikes.

"Carmen's pain and loneliness are brought to life through her narrative. The writing flows nicely." SLJ

Harper, Suzanne

The Juliet club. Greenwillow Books 2008 402p $17.99; lib bdg $18.89

Grades: 8 9 10 11 12   **Fic**

1. Shakespeare, William, 1564-1616—Fiction 2. Italy—Fiction 3. Letters—Fiction

ISBN 978-0-06-136691-8; 0-06-136691-9; 978-0-06-136692-5 (lib bdg); 0-06-136692-7 (lib bdg)

       LC 2007-41315

When high school junior Kate wins an essay contest that sends her to Verona, Italy, to study Shakespeare's 'Romeo and Juliet' over the summer, she meets both American and Italian students and learns not just about Shakespeare, but also about star-crossed lovers—and herself.

"An amalgam of familiar Shakespearean plot elements, character names, and devices make up this delightful, light, and romantic read. . . . The chapter titles are each given act and scene designations to keep the structure of a play. Following the formula of a Shakespearean comedy, the novel ends with a grand ball where misunderstandings are resolved and couples are revealed in a magical evening." Voice Youth Advocates

The secret life of Sparrow Delaney. Greenwillow Books 2007 364p $16.99; lib bdg $17.89

Grades: 7 8 9 10   **Fic**

1. Spiritualism—Fiction 2. Family life—Fiction 3. New York (State)—Fiction

ISBN 978-0-06-113158-5; 0-06-113158-X; 978-0-06-113159-2 (lib bdg); 0-06-113159-8 (lib bdg)

       LC 2006-41339

In Lily Dale, New York, a community dedicated to the religion of Spiritualism, tenth-grader Sparrow Delaney, the youngest daughter in an eccentric family of psychics, agonizes over whether or not to reveal her special abilities in order to help a friend.

"For all of the imagination the author displays in inventing a spirit world, she shows equal skill in probing the nuances of tender emotions, too." Publ Wkly

Harrington, Jane

Four things my geeky-jock-of-a-best-friend must do in Europe. Darby Creek Pub. 2006 160p lib bdg $15.95

Grades: 6 7 8 9   **Fic**

1. Vacations—Fiction 2. Friendship—Fiction 3. Mother-daughter relationship—Fiction

ISBN 1-58196-041-7

Written in the form of letters to her best friend, Delia, back home, Brady tells of her adventures while on a Mediterranean cruise with her mother, and her progress on Delia's list of things she must do, including the search for a "code-red Euro-hottie."

"The author cleverly entwines the embarrassments of

Harrington, Jane—*Continued*

adolescence with travel episodes. The cover illustration provides a tantalizing invitation to this laugh-out-loud summer read." SLJ

Another title about these characters is:

My best friend, the Atlantic Ocean, and other great bodies standing between me and my life with Giulio (2008)

Harris, Joanne

Runemarks. Alfred A. Knopf 2008 526p map $18.99; lib bdg $21.99

Grades: 7 8 9 10 11 12   **Fic**

1. Norse mythology—Fiction 2. Magic—Fiction 3. Fantasy fiction

ISBN 978-0-375-84444-7; 978-0-375-94444-4 (lib bdg); 0-375-84444-9; 0-375-94444-3 (lib bdg)

LC 2007-28928

Maddy Smith, who bears the mysterious mark of a rune on her hand, learns that she is destined to join the gods of Norse mythology and play a role in the fate of the world.

"Harris demonstrates a knack for moving seamlessly between the serious and comic. . . . She creates a glorious and complex world replete with rune-based magic spells, bickering gods, exciting adventures, and difficult moral issues." Publ Wkly

Harrison, Mette Ivie, 1970-

The princess and the hound. 1st ed. Eos 2007 410p $17.99; lib bdg $18.89

Grades: 7 8 9 10 11 12   **Fic**

1. Fairy tales 2. Princesses—Fiction 3. Magic—Fiction

ISBN   978-0-06-113187-5;   0-06-113187-3; 978-0-06-113188-2 (lib bdg); 0-06-113188-1 (lib bdg)

LC 2007-09306

George has always felt burdened by his princely duties, and even more by the need to hide the magic through which he speaks with animals, but when he is betrothed to the strange princess of a neighboring kingdom, his secret, and the persecution of people like himself, must come to an end.

"This is polished storytelling, satisfyingly old-fashioned in tone, with a dreamy, naive quality that will draw young romantics." Bull Cent Child Books

Followed by: The princess and the bear (2009)

Hart, Alison, 1950-

Gabriel's horses; by Alison Hart. 1st ed. Peachtree 2007 161p (Racing to freedom) $14.95

Grades: 6 7 8 9   **Fic**

1. Horse racing—Fiction 2. United States—History—1861-1865, Civil War—Fiction 3. Slavery—Fiction 4. African Americans—Fiction 5. Kentucky—Fiction

ISBN 978-1-56145-398-6; 1-56145-398-6

LC 2006027697

In Kentucky, during the Civil War, the twelve-year-old slave Gabriel, contends with a cruel new horse trainer and skirmishes with Confederate soldiers as he pursues his dream of becoming a jockey.

"The author grounds this fast-paced tale in historical fact by providing a nonfiction epilogue. Readers will find this wonderful blend of history and horses appealing." SLJ

Another title in this series is:

Gabriel's triumph (2007)

Hartnett, Sonya, 1968-

What the birds see. Candlewick Press 2003 196p $15.99

Grades: 7 8 9 10   **Fic**

1. Missing children—Fiction

ISBN 0-7636-2092-0   LC 2002-73717

While the residents of his town concern themselves with the disappearance of three children, a lonely, rejected nine-year-old boy worries that he may inherit his mother's insanity

"Tightly composed and ripe with symbolism, this complex book will offer opportunities for rich discussion." SLJ

Hartry, Nancy

Watching Jimmy. Tundra Books 2009 152p $16.95

Grades: 5 6 7 8   **Fic**

1. Brain—Wounds and injuries—Fiction 2. Child abuse—Fiction

ISBN 978-0-88776-871-2; 0-88776-871-7

In Canada, in 1958, 11-year-old Carolyn secretly witnessed the abuse of her friend, Jimmy, at the hands of his drunken Uncle Ted, which caused Jimmy's severe brain damage. Now Jimmy's mother can't afford health insurance and is struggling to survive, and Carolyn is trying to protect Jimmy.

"Like a steady beat that pulses louder and louder, the story unfolds against a backdrop of postwar social and political concerns and Remembrance Day. Carolyn is a passionate and feisty character, delineated with love and precision, and readers will be drawn to her. A compelling and satisfying novel." SLJ

Hausman, Gerald

A mind with wings; the story of Henry David Thoreau; [by] Gerald & Loretta Hausman. 1st ed. Trumpeter Books for Young Readers; distributed by Random House 2006 148p $15.95

Grades: 6 7 8 9   **Fic**

1. Thoreau, Henry David, 1817-1862—Fiction 2. Naturalists—Fiction 3. Massachusetts—Fiction

ISBN 1-59030-228-1   LC 2005018094

"This well-researched novel expertly captures Thoreau's character and life in mid-19th-century Massachusetts. . . . Careful readers will have much to mull over, and they will savor the adventures of this great American thinker." SLJ

Includes bibliographical references

Hautman, Pete, 1952-

All-in. Simon & Schuster Books for Young Readers 2007 181p $15.99 *

Grades: 7 8 9 10   **Fic**

1. Poker—Fiction 2. Gambling—Fiction 3. Las Vegas (Nev.)—Fiction

ISBN 978-1-4169-1325-2; 1-4169-1325-4

LC 2006-23871

Sequel to No limit (2005)

Hautman, Pete, 1952-—*Continued*

Having won thousands of dollars playing high-stakes poker in Las Vegas, seventeen-year-old Denn Doyle hits a losing streak after falling in love with a young casino card dealer named Cattie Hart.

"Skillfully using the multiple-voice approach, Hautman brings to life the intricacies of poker, crafting a thrilling story of loss, good versus evil, and redemption." Voice Youth Advocates

Godless. Simon & Schuster Books for Young Readers 2004 208p $15.95; pa $8.99 *
Grades: 7 8 9 10   **Fic**
1. Religion—Fiction
ISBN 0-689-86278-4; 1-4169-0816-1 (pa)
                                            LC 2003-10468
When sixteen-year-old Jason Bock and his friends create their own religion to worship the town's water tower, what started out as a joke begins to take on a power of its own

"The witty text and provocative subject will make this a supremely enjoyable discussion-starter as well as pleasurable read." Bull Cent Child Books

Hole in the sky. Simon & Schuster Bks. for Young Readers 2001 179p $16; pa $11.95
Grades: 7 8 9 10   **Fic**
1. Science fiction 2. Grand Canyon (Ariz.)—Fiction
ISBN 0-689-83118-8; 1-4169-6822-9 (pa)
                                            LC 00-58324
In a future world ravaged by a mutant virus, sixteen-year-old Ceej and three other teenagers seek to save the Grand Canyon from being flooded, while trying to avoid capture by a band of renegade Survivors

"Readers will appreciate the novel's intense action and fascinating premise." Horn Book Guide

Snatched; [by] Pete Hautman and Mary Logue. Putnam 2006 200p (Bloodwater mysteries) $15.99
Grades: 7 8 9 10   **Fic**
1. Mystery fiction 2. Kidnapping—Fiction
ISBN 0-399-24377-1   LC 2005-28558
Too curious for her own good, Roni, crime reporter for her high school newspaper, teams up with Brian, freshman science geek, to investigate the beating and kidnapping of a classmate.

"Give this solid marks for plotting and characterization, as well as for suspense." Booklist

Other titles in this series are:
Skullduggery (2007)
Doppelganger (2008)

Sweetblood. Simon & Schuster Bks. for Young Readers 2003 180p $16.95; pa $6.99 *
Grades: 7 8 9 10   **Fic**
1. Diabetes—Fiction
ISBN 0-689-85048-4; 0-689-87324-7 (pa)
                                            LC 2002-11179
"Lucy Szabo has been an insulin-dependent diabetic since she was 6, and now, at age 16, she has developed an interesting theory that links vampirism with diabetic ketoacidosis." SLJ

"Hautman does an outstanding job of making Lucy's theory and her struggle to accept herself credible. . . . Lucy's clever, self-deprecating voice is endlessly original." Booklist

Haven, Paul

Two hot dogs with everything; illustrated by Tim Jessell. Random House 2006 307p il $15.95; lib bdg $17.89; pa $6.50
Grades: 4 5 6 7   **Fic**
1. Baseball—Fiction 2. Superstition—Fiction
ISBN 0-375-83348-X; 0-375-93348-4 (lib bdg);
0-375-83349-8 (pa)   LC 2005-08344
Although everyone credits him and his superstitions for the Slugger's first winning streak in 108 baseball seasons, eleven-year-old Danny Gurkin believes that his discovery of a secret from the team's past may be the real reason behind the ball club's success.

"Haven's first novel will delight readers with its whimsically exaggerated detail. . . . The intricate plot . . . will keep readers on the edge of their seats." SLJ

Havill, Juanita

Eyes like Willy's. HarperCollins 2004 135p $15.99; lib bdg $16.89
Grades: 5 6 7 8   **Fic**
1. World War, 1914-1918—Fiction
ISBN 0-688-13672-9; 0-688-13673-7 (lib bdg)
                                            LC 2003-14954
While vacationing over the course of several summers in Austria, French siblings Guy and Sarah Masson become best friends with a German boy, until the outbreak of World War I puts them on opposing sides.

"This spare, thoughtful story does a superb job of personalizing the pain of this brutal, futile war." Booklist

Haydon, Elizabeth

The Floating Island; the lost journals of Ven Polypheme; text compiled by Elizabeth Haydon; illustrations restored by Brett Helquist. 1st ed. Starscape 2006 368p il $17.95
Grades: 5 6 7 8   **Fic**
1. Fantasy fiction
ISBN 0-7653-0867-3   LC 2006005768
"A Tom Doherty Associates book"
Ven, the youngest son of a long line of famous shipwrights, dreams of sailing to far-off lands where magic thrives. He gets his chance when he is chosen to direct the Inspection of his family's latest ship and sets sail on the journey of a lifetime.

The author's "world building is as successful as her characters, with Helquist's occasional loose sketches providing some visual distraction and additional atmosphere. A delightful epic fantasy." Booklist
Followed by The Thief Queen's daughter (2007)

The Thief Queen's daughter; text compiled by Elizabeth Haydon; illustrations restored by Jason Chan. 1st hardcover ed. Tom Doherty Associates 2007 319p (Lost journals of Ven Polypheme) $17.95
Grades: 5 6 7 8   **Fic**
1. Fantasy fiction
ISBN 978-0-7653-0868-9; 0-7653-0868-1
                                            LC 2007007933
Sequel to The Floating Island (2006)
"Starscape book"

Haydon, Elizabeth—*Continued*

Young Ven Polypheme is sent on a secret mission within the walls of the Gated City, a former penal colony in the land of Serendair, where he and his friends face kidnapping and even worse dangers from the ruthless Thief Queen, who is trying to reclaim her runaway daughter.

"Haydon uses snippets of Ven's diary entries, fast-paced action, and plenty of humorous touches to keep readers engaged." SLJ

Headley, Justina Chen, 1968-

North of beautiful. Little, Brown 2009 373p $16.99 *

Grades: 7 8 9 10 11 12   **Fic**

1. Aesthetics—Fiction

ISBN 978-0-316-02505-8; 0-316-02505-4

LC 2008-09260

Headley's "finely crafted novel traces a teen's uncharted quest to find beauty. Two things block Terra's happiness: a port-wine stain on her face and her verbally abusive father. . . . A car accident brings her together with Jacob, an Asian-born adoptee with unconventional ideas. . . . The author confidently addresses very large, slippery questions about the meaning of art, travel, love and of course, beauty." Publ Wkly

Hearn, Julie, 1958-

Ivy; a novel. Atheneum Books for Young Readers 2008 355p $17.99 *

Grades: 8 9 10 11 12   **Fic**

1. Artists—Fiction 2. Drug abuse—Fiction 3. Criminals—Fiction 4. London (England)—Fiction 5. Great Britain—History—19th century—Fiction

ISBN 978-1-4169-2506-4; 1-4169-2506-6

LC 2007-045463

"ginee seo books"

In mid-nineteenth-century London, young, mistreated, and destitute Ivy, whose main asset is her beautiful red hair, comes to the attention of an aspiring painter of the pre-Raphaelite school of artists who, with the connivance of Ivy's unsavory family, is determined to make her his model and muse.

"Quirky characters, darkly humorous situations, and quick action make this enjoyable historical fiction." SLJ

The minister's daughter. Atheneum Books for Young Readers 2005 263p $16.95; pa $7.99

Grades: 7 8 9 10   **Fic**

1. Witchcraft—Fiction 2. Supernatural—Fiction 3. Great Britain—History—1642-1660, Civil War and Commonwealth—Fiction 4. Salem (Mass.)—Fiction

ISBN 0-689-87690-4; 0-689-87691-2 (pa)

LC 2004-18324

Published in United Kingdom with title: The Merrybegot

In 1645 in England, the daughters of the town minister successfully accuse a local healer and her granddaughter of witchcraft to conceal an out-of-wedlock pregnancy, but years later during the 1692 Salem trials their lie has unexpected repercussions.

"With its thought-provoking perceptions about human nature, magic and persecution, this tale will surely cast a spell over readers." Publ Wkly

Heath, Jack, 1986-

The Lab. Scholastic Press 2008 311p $17.99

Grades: 7 8 9 10   **Fic**

1. Spies—Fiction 2. Adventure fiction 3. Genetic engineering—Fiction 4. Science fiction

ISBN 978-0-545-06860-4; 0-545-06860-6

"A gritty dystopic world exists under the iron rule of the mega-corporation Chao-Sonic, with only a few vigilante groups around to act as resistance. Six of Hearts is easily the best agent on one such group, the Deck, and he is fiercely dedicated to justice, using his extensive genetic modifications to his advantage. . . . The compelling and memorable protagonist stands out even against the intricately described and disturbing city whose vividness makes the place's questionable fate a suspenseful issue in its own right." Bull Cent Child Books

Hegamin, Tonya

M+O 4evr; [by] Tonya Cherie Hegamin. Houghton Mifflin Co. 2008 165p $16

Grades: 8 9 10 11   **Fic**

1. Friendship—Fiction 2. Death—Fiction 3. Family life—Fiction 4. Lesbians—Fiction 5. Slavery—Fiction 6. Pennsylvania—Fiction

ISBN 978-0-618-49570-2; 0-618-49570-3

LC 2007-34293

In parallel stories, Hannah, a slave, finds love while fleeing a Maryland plantation in 1842, and in the present, Opal watches her life-long best friend, Marianne, pull away and eventually lose her life in the same Pennsylvania ravine where Hannah died.

"Hegamin's first novel is richly imaginative as it deals with difficult subjects. . . . [The] parallel stories of love and loss blend seamlessly in this small book that packs a big wallop." SLJ

Pemba's song; a ghost story; [by] Tonya Hegamin & Marilyn Nelson. Scholastic Press 2008 109p $16.99

Grades: 7 8 9 10   **Fic**

1. Parapsychology—Fiction 2. African Americans—Fiction 3. Moving—Fiction 4. Slavery—Fiction 5. Connecticut—Fiction

ISBN 978-0-545-02076-3; 0-545-02076-X

LC 2007051044

As fifteen-year-old Pemba adjusts to leaving her Brooklyn, New York, home for small-town Connecticut, a Black history researcher helps her understand the paranormal experiences drawing her into the life of a mulatto girl who was once a slave in her house.

"Written in shifting voices and styles, this vivid, collaborative novella tells a supernatural story of a young girl's connection with history." Booklist

Hegedus, Bethany

Between us Baxters. WestSide Books 2009 306p $17.95

Grades: 7 8 9 10   **Fic**

1. Friendship—Fiction 2. Race relations—Fiction

ISBN 978-1-934813-02-7; 1-934813-02-8

"In 1959, in Holcolm County, GA, there is a palpable tension. Times are slowly changing, causing resentment among some folks and optimism among others. The vol-

Hegedus, Bethany—_Continued_

atile mix sets the tone for this story of family, friendship, and racial discrimination. . . .When suspicious fires, vandalism, and threats to successful black business owners cause fear and distrust among the townspeople, the strength of Polly and Timbre Ann's bond is tested. . . . The connection between the two girls and their families is beautifully described and believable, and the richness of the characters is apparent. The pacing of the story is deliberate and suspenseful with twists and turns that add to the bittersweet conclusion." SLJ

Helgerson, Joseph

Crows & cards; a novel; written with diligence by Mr. Joseph Helgerson; to which are added fine illustrations by Mr. Peter Desève; also included is Dictionarium Americannicum; being the words herein most arcane and alien and their definitions. Houghton Mifflin Harcourt 2009 344p il $16

Grades: 4 5 6 7   **Fic**
  1. Apprentices—Fiction 2. Gambling—Fiction 3. Slavery—Fiction 4. Native Americans—Fiction 5. Saint Louis (Mo.)—Fiction
ISBN 978-0-618-88395-0; 0-618-88395-9
                         LC 2008013308
In 1849, Zeb's parents ship him off to St. Louis to become an apprentice tanner, but the naive twelve-year-old rebels, casting his lot with a cheating riverboat gambler, while a slave and an Indian medicine man try to get Zeb back on the right path. Includes historical notes, glossary, and bibliographical references.
"Helgerson surrounds Zeb with a lively cast. . . . A solid choice for fans fo high-spun yarns and not-too-tall tales." Booklist
Bibliography: p. [290]-294

Horns & wrinkles; [by] Joseph Helgerson; [illustrations by Nicoletta Ceccoli] Houghton Mifflin 2006 357p il $16 *

Grades: 4 5 6 7   **Fic**
  1. Magic—Fiction 2. Trolls—Fiction 3. Bullies—Fiction 4. Mississippi River—Fiction
ISBN 0-618-61679-9   LC 2005025448
Along a magic-saturated stretch of the Mississippi River near Blue Wing, Minnesota, twelve-year-old Claire and her bullying cousin Duke are drawn into an adventure involving Bodacious Deepthink the Great Rock Troll, a helpful fairy, and a group of trolls searching for their fathers.
"Tongue-in-cheek humor brings a delightful zing to the playfully inventive storytelling and fast-paced plot. Enchanting sketches foreshadow each chapter, adding to the wonder." SLJ

Hemphill, Helen, 1955-

The adventurous deeds of Deadwood Jones. Front Street 2008 228p $16.95

Grades: 5 6 7 8   **Fic**
  1. Cowhands—Fiction 2. African Americans—Fiction 3. Race relations—Fiction 4. Cousins—Fiction 5. West (U.S.)—Fiction
ISBN 978-1-59078-637-6; 1-59078-637-8
                         LC 2008005422

Thirteen-year-old Prometheus Jones and his eleven-year-old cousin Omer flee Tennessee and join a cattle drive that will eventually take them to Texas, where Prometheus hopes his father lives, and they find adventure and face challenges as African Americans in a land still recovering from the Civil War.
"Prometheus is an always sympathetic and engaging character, and the dangers and misadventures he encounters . . . make for compelling reading." Booklist

Long gone daddy. Front Street 2006 176p $16.95

Grades: 8 9 10 11 12   **Fic**
  1. Father-son relationship—Fiction 2. Grandfathers—Fiction 3. Christian life—Fiction 4. Las Vegas (Nev.)—Fiction
ISBN 1-932425-38-1   LC 2005-25105
Young Harlan Q. Stank gets a taste of life in the fast lane when he accompanies his preacher father on a road trip to Las Vegas to bury his grandfather and to fulfill the terms of the old man's will.
"Many teens will see their own questions about faith, worship, and independence in Harlan's heart-twisting feelings." Booklist

Hemphill, Stephanie

Things left unsaid; a novel in poems. Hyperion Books for Children 2005 261p $16.99

Grades: 7 8 9 10   **Fic**
  1. Friendship—Fiction 2. Suicide—Fiction 3. Novels in verse
ISBN 0-7868-1850-6   LC 2003-56968
After a lifetime of conforming to the image of what her parents and high school friends want her to be, Sarah must come to terms with her own identity when her destructive best friend tries to commit suicide. Told in the form of free-verse poems.
"A thought-provoking read." SLJ

Henderson, Jan-Andrew, 1962-

Bunker 10. Harcourt 2007 253p $17

Grades: 7 8 9 10   **Fic**
  1. Virtual reality—Fiction 2. Genetic engineering—Fiction
ISBN 978-0-15-206240-8; 0-15-206240-8
                         LC 2006-38694
Something is going terribly wrong at the top secret Pinewood Military Installation as the teenage geniuses who study and work there are about to discover a horrible truth.
"Henderson ably balances intriguing plot twists and hauntingly well-developed characters with gripping pace and dramatic showdowns." Bull Cent Child Books

Heneghan, James, 1930-

Bank job; written by James Heneghan and Norma Charles. Orca Book Publishers 2009 pa $9.95

Grades: 5 6 7 8   **Fic**
  1. Foster home care—Fiction 2. Theft—Fiction
ISBN 978-1-55143-855-9; 1-55143-855-0
"Nell, Billy and Tom call themselves the Three Musketeers. . . . Hearing their foster parents need $10,000 to

Heneghan, James, 1930-—*Continued*
make necessary home improvements, the teens start robbing banks. . . . Short sentences, clear and direct writing
and tense situations make this an excellent choice for reluctant readers." Booklist

Payback. Groundwood/House of Anansi Press
2007 184p $16.95; pa $8.95
Grades: 6 7 8 9   **Fic**
1. Suicide—Fiction 2. Irish—Canada—Fiction
3. Bullies—Fiction 4. Immigrants—Fiction 5. Guilt—
Fiction
ISBN   0-88899-701-9;   978-0-88899-701-2;
978-0-88899-704-3 (pa); 0-88899-704-3 (pa)
"After his eighth-grade classmate Benny commits suicide, Charley blames himself. . . . Why did he do nothing when he saw the bullies torment Benny and call him
'fag'? Was it because, as a new Irish immigrant in Vancouver, Charley himself was threatened and bullied? . . .
The drama of guilt, sorrow, and redemption is honest and
heartfelt, told in Charley's spare, fast, first-person narrative." Booklist

Safe house. Orca Book Publishers 2006 151p pa
$7.95
Grades: 6 7 8 9   **Fic**
1. Belfast (Northern Ireland)—Fiction
ISBN 1-55143-640-X (pa); 978-1-55143-640-1 (pa)
"In 1999, in Belfast, Liam Fogarty's parents are murdered by intruders. Because he gets a good look at one
of the gunmen, the 12-year-old is also a target." SLJ
"Readers will be drawn by the fast action and the
breathless escape adventure, but they'll also respond to
the politics of war in Belfast." Booklist

Heneghan, Judith, 1965-
The magician's apprentice. Holiday House 2008
c2005 168p $16.95
Grades: 4 5 6 7   **Fic**
1. Swindlers and swindling—Fiction 2. Adventure fiction 3. Magicians—Fiction 4. Orphans—Fiction
5. Great Britain—History—19th century—Fiction
ISBN 978-0-8234-2150-3; 0-8234-2150-3
LC 2007-35186
First published 2005 in the United Kingdom with title:
Stonecipher
In 1874 Winchester, England, Jago Stonecipher, magician's assistant to his unscrupulous uncle, becomes involved in a series of plots and deceits revolving around
a lady's maid and her employer's family, and finally escapes to sea, where the trouble follows him, even aboard
ship.
"The complex plot is full of unexpected twists and
hairbreadth escapes, and the dialogue rings true to the
period. An exciting choice for historical fiction fans."
SLJ

Henkes, Kevin, 1960-
Bird Lake moon. Greenwillow Books 2008 179p
$15.99; lib bdg $16.89 *
Grades: 4 5 6 7   **Fic**
1. Divorce—Fiction 2. Bereavement—Fiction
3. Lakes—Fiction 4. Friendship—Fiction 5. Family
life—Fiction 6. Wisconsin—Fiction
ISBN 978-0-06147-076-9; 978-0-06147-078-3 (lib
bdg); 0-06147-076-7; 0-06147-078-3 (lib bdg)
LC 2007-36564
Twelve-year-old Mitch and his mother are spending
the summer with his grandparents at Bird Lake after his
parents separate, and ten-year-old Spencer and his family
have returned to the lake where Spencer's little brother
drowned long ago, and as the boys become friends and
spend time together, each of them begins to heal.
"Characters are gently and believably developed as the
story weaves in and around the beautiful Wisconsin setting. The superbly crafted plot moves smoothly and
unhurriedly, mirroring a slow summer pace." SLJ

Olive's ocean. Greenwillow Bks. 2003 217p
$15.99; lib bdg $16.89; pa $6.99 *
Grades: 5 6 7 8   **Fic**
1. Grandmothers—Fiction 2. Family life—Fiction
ISBN 0-06-053543-1; 0-06-053544-X (lib bdg);
0-06-053545-8 (pa)   LC 2002-29782
A Newbery Medal honor book, 2004
On a summer visit to her grandmother's cottage by
the ocean, twelve-year-old Martha gains perspective on
the death of a classmate, on her relationship with her
grandmother, on her feelings for an older boy, and on
her plans to be a writer.
"Rich characterizations move this compelling novel to
its satisfying and emotionally authentic conclusion." SLJ

Protecting Marie. Greenwillow Bks. 1995 195p
$18.99; pa $5.99
Grades: 5 6 7 8   **Fic**
1. Father-daughter relationship—Fiction 2. Dogs—Fic-
tion
ISBN 0-688-13958-2; 0-06-053545-8 (pa)
LC 94-16387
Also available in paperback from Puffin Bks.
Relates twelve-year-old Fanny's love-hate relationship
with her father, a temperamental artist, who has given
Fanny a new dog
"The characters ring heartbreakingly true in this quiet,
wise story; they are complex and difficult—like all of
us—and worthy of our attention." Horn Book

Hennesy, Carolyn, 1962-
Pandora gets jealous. Bloomsbury Children's
Books 2008 264p $14.95
Grades: 4 5 6 7   **Fic**
1. Pandora (Legendary character)—Fiction
2. Classical mythology—Fiction
ISBN 978-1-59990-196-1; 1-59990-196-X
LC 2007-23975
Thirteen-year-old Pandy is hauled before Zeus and
given six months to gather all of the evils that were re-
leased when the box she brought to school as her annual
project was accidentally opened.
"Hennesy's Hollywood comedian background shows

Hennesy, Carolyn, 1962—*Continued*
in her witty juxtapositions of modern popular culture and classical Greek legend. . . . Accurate where it counts, this loosely interpreted myth rarely misses a comic twist." Publ Wkly
 Another title in this series is:
Pandora gets vain (2008)

Henry, April
   Torched. G.P. Putnam's Sons 2009 224p $16.99
Grades: 8 9 10 11   **Fic**
  1. Environmental movement—Fiction 2. Terrorism—Fiction
  ISBN 978-0-399-24645-6; 0-399-24645-2
                       LC 2008-01145
  In order to save her parents from going to jail for possession of marijuana, sixteen-year-old Ellie must help the FBI uncover the intentions of a radical environmental group by going undercover.
  "The mix of politics and thrilling action will grab teens. . . . This suspenseful story will spark discussion about what it means to fight for right 'by any means necessary.'" Booklist

Henson, Heather
   Here's how I see it, here's how it is. 1st ed. Atheneum Books for Young Readers 2009 270p $16.99
Grades: 5 6 7   **Fic**
  1. Theater—Fiction 2. Actors—Fiction 3. Asperger's syndrome—Fiction
  ISBN 978-1-4169-4901-5; 1-4169-4901-1
                       LC 2008-22213
  At almost-thirteen, Junebug has never felt right except as stagehand at her father's summer theater, but after her parents separate and an irritating intern takes over her responsibilities, she discovers how hard life can be without a script to follow.
  "Henson . . . creates a funny, bittersweet story filled with colorful personalities and plenty of backstage detail and drama." Publ Wkly

Herlong, Madaline
   The great wide sea; [by] M. H. Herlong. Viking Children's Books 2008 283p $16.99
Grades: 7 8 9 10   **Fic**
  1. Sailing—Fiction 2. Brothers—Fiction 3. Father-son relationship—Fiction 4. Bereavement—Fiction 5. Survival after airplane accidents, shipwrecks, etc.—Fiction
  ISBN 978-0-670-06330-7; 0-670-06330-4
                       LC 2008-8384
  Still mourning the death of their mother, fifteen-year-old Ben and his two younger brothers go with their father on an extended sailing trip off the Florida Keys and have a harrowing adventure at sea.
  "Herlong makes the most of the three boys' characters, each exceptionally well developed here, to make this as much a novel of brotherhood as a sea story." Bull Cent Child Books

Hernandez, David, 1964-
   No more us for you. HarperTeen 2009 281p $16.99
Grades: 8 9 10 11 12   **Fic**
  1. Friendship—Fiction 2. Death—Fiction 3. Bereavement—Fiction 4. School stories 5. California—Fiction
  ISBN 978-0-06-117333-2; 0-06-117333-9
                       LC 2008-19203
  Isabel and Carlos, both seventeen, find themselves growing closer after an unexpected accident forces them to confront both the harshness and the beauty of life.
  "Hernandez builds Isabel and Carlos into characters that readers come to root for and love." Voice Youth Advocates

   Suckerpunch. HarperTeen 2008 217p $17.89
Grades: 8 9 10 11 12   **Fic**
  1. Child abuse—Fiction 2. Brothers—Fiction 3. Father-son relationship—Fiction 4. Drug abuse—Fiction 5. Hispanic Americans—Fiction
  ISBN 978-0-06-117330-1; 0-06-117331-2
  Accompanied by two friends, teenage brothers Marcus and Enrique head on a road trip to confront the abusive father who walked out on them a year earlier.
  "The author's imagery, sometimes subtle, sometimes searing, invariably hits its mark." Publ Wkly

Herrera, Juan Felipe, 1948-
   Cinnamon girl; letters found inside a cereal box. Joanna Cotler Books 2005 164p $15.99; lib bdg $16.89
Grades: 7 8 9 10   **Fic**
  1. September 11 terrorist attacks, 2001—Fiction 2. Puerto Ricans—Fiction 3. Uncles—Fiction 4. New York (N.Y.)—Fiction
  ISBN 0-06-057984-6; 0-06-057985-4 (lib bdg)
                       LC 2004-26185
  Yolanda, a Puerto Rican girl, tries to come to terms with her painful past as she waits to see if her uncle recovers from injuries he suffered when the towers collapsed on September 11, 2001
  "Herrera depicts the immigration experience with intensity and drama, and even readers who aren't Latino will understand Yolanda's feelings." Booklist

Herrick, Steven, 1958-
   By the river. Front Street 2006 238p $16.95
Grades: 8 9 10 11 12   **Fic**
  1. Brothers—Fiction 2. Death—Fiction 3. Single parent family—Fiction 4. Australia—Fiction
  ISBN 1-932425-72-1   LC 2005-23967
  First published 2004 in the United Kingdom
  A fourteen-year-old describes, through prose poems, his life in a small Australian town in 1962, where, since their mother's death, he and his brother have been mainly on their own to learn about life, death, and love.
  "The poems are simple but potent in their simplicity, blending together in a compelling, evocative story of a gentle, intelligent boy growing up and learning to deal with a sometimes-ugly little world that he . . . will eventually escape." Voice Youth Advocates

Hershey, Mary

10 lucky things that have happened to me since I nearly got hit by lightning; [by] Mary Hershey. Wendy Lamb Books 2008 230p $15.99

Grades: 4 5 6 7   **Fic**

1. Friendship—Fiction 2. Priests—Fiction 3. School stories

ISBN 978-0-385-73541-4; 0-385-73541-3

LC 2007-030939

Sequel to: My big sister is so bossy she says you can't read this book (2005)

Even though her father is in prison for embezzlement, ten-year-old Effie considers herself pretty lucky until her mother's old friend, Father Frank, comes to stay with them, Effie's friend Aurora decides to quit their Catholic school to attend public school, and her contrary sister begins to transform herself into "Saint Maxey."

"Humor, warmth, and Effie's Catholic values shine through in this entertaining story." Booklist

Hesse, Karen

Brooklyn Bridge; a novel. Feiwel and Friends 2008 229p il map $17.95 *

Grades: 5 6 7 8 9 10   **Fic**

1. Family life—Fiction 2. Social classes—Fiction 3. Homeless persons—Fiction 4. Immigrants—Fiction 5. Russian Americans—Fiction 6. Brooklyn (New York, N.Y.)—Fiction

ISBN 978-0-312-37886-8; 0-312-37886-6

LC 2008-05624

In 1903 Brooklyn, fourteen-year-old Joseph Michtom's life changes for the worse when his parents, Russian immigrants, invent the teddy bear and turn their apartment into a factory, while nearby the glitter of Coney Island contrasts with the dismal lives of children dwelling under the Brooklyn Bridge.

Hesse "applies her gift for narrative voice to this memorable story. . . . The novel explodes with dark drama before its eerie but moving resolution." Publ Wkly

Letters from Rifka. Holt & Co. 1992 148p $16.95 *

Grades: 5 6 7 8   **Fic**

1. Immigrants—Fiction 2. Jews—Fiction 3. Letters—Fiction

ISBN 0-8050-1964-2   LC 91-48007

Also available in paperback from Puffin Bks.

In letters to her cousin, Rifka, a young Jewish girl, chronicles her family's flight from Russia in 1919 and her own experiences when she must be left in Belgium for a while when the others emigrate to America

"Based on the true story of the author's great-aunt, the moving account of a brave young girl's story brings to life the day-to-day trials and horrors experienced by many immigrants as well as the resourcefulness and strength they found within themselves." Horn Book

Out of the dust. Scholastic 1997 227p $16.95; pa $6.99 *

Grades: 5 6 7 8   **Fic**

1. Dust storms—Fiction 2. Farm life—Fiction 3. Great Depression, 1929-1939—Fiction 4. Oklahoma—Fiction 5. Novels in verse

ISBN 0-590-36080-9; 0-590-37125-8 (pa)

LC 96-40344

Awarded the Newbery Medal, 1998

"After facing loss after loss during the Oklahoma Dust Bowl, Billie Jo begins to reconstruct her life." SLJ

"Hesse's writing transcends the gloom and transforms it into a powerfully compelling tale of a girl with enormous strength, courage, and love. The entire novel is written in very readable blank verse." Booklist

Witness. Scholastic Press 2001 161p $16.95; pa $5.99

Grades: 6 7 8 9   **Fic**

1. Ku Klux Klan—Fiction 2. Prejudices—Fiction 3. Vermont—Fiction 4. Novels in verse

ISBN 0-439-27199-1; 0-439-27200-9 (pa)

LC 00-54139

A series of poems express the views of eleven people in a small Vermont town, including a young black girl and a young Jewish girl, during the early 1920s when the Ku Klux Klan is trying to infiltrate the town

"The story is divided into five acts, and would lend itself beautifully to performance. The plot unfolds smoothly, and the author creates multidimensional characters." SLJ

Hesser, Terry Spencer

Kissing doorknobs. Delacorte Press 1998 149p hardcover o.p. pa $6.50

Grades: 7 8 9 10   **Fic**

1. Obsessive-compulsive disorder—Fiction

ISBN 0-385-32329-8; 0-440-41314-1 (pa)

LC 97-26937

Fourteen-year-old Tara describes how her increasingly strange compulsions begin to take over her life and affect her relationships with her family and friends

"An honest, fresh, and multilayered story to which readers will instantly relate. . . . The prose is forthright, economical, and peppered with wry humor." SLJ

Heuston, Kimberley Burton, 1960-

The Book of Jude; [by] Kimberley Heuston. Front Street 2008 217p $17.95

Grades: 8 9 10 11 12   **Fic**

1. Family life—Fiction 2. Personality disorders—Fiction 3. Mormons—Fiction 4. Christian life—Fiction 5. Communism—Fiction 6. Moving—Fiction 7. Twins—Fiction 8. Prague (Czech Republic)—Fiction 9. Czech Republic—Fiction

ISBN 978-1-932425-26-0; 1-932425-26-8

LC 2007-17971

In 1989, when fifteen-year-old Jude's mother wins a Fulbright fellowship to study art in Czechoslovakia, the family postpones a planned move to Utah to join her, but the political situation and the move itself are too much for Jude, who is overwhelmed by a previously undiagnosed psychological disorder.

"Heuston constructs a solid cast and setting, against which her protagonist's breakdown proceeds in a convincing way. Jude's Mormon faith is a strong subsidiary element here, as well." Booklist

Heuston, Kimberley Burton, 1960-—*Continued*

The Shakeress; [by] Kimberley Heuston. Front St. 2002 207p $16.95; pa $11.95
Grades: 7 8 9 10   **Fic**
1. Shakers—Fiction 2. Orphans—Fiction
ISBN 1-88691-056-1; 1-59078-575-4 (pa)
                                        LC 2001-40298
While searching for her true self and for the way to meet the needs of her personal sense of spirituality, an orphaned teenaged girl joins a Shaker community in mid-nineteenth century New England and learns about a new religion called Mormonism
"This is an introspective story that will attract readers seeking their own spiritual path." Booklist

Hiaasen, Carl, 1953-

Flush. Knopf 2005 263p $16.95; pa $8.99 *
Grades: 5 6 7 8   **Fic**
1. Environmental protection—Fiction 2. Florida—Fiction 3. Boats and boating—Fiction
ISBN 0-375-82182-1; 0-375-84185-7 (pa)
                                        LC 2005-05259
With their father jailed for sinking a river boat, Noah Underwood and his younger sister, Abbey, must gather evidence that the owner of this floating casino is emptying his bilge tanks into the protected waters around their Florida Keys home.
"This quick-reading, fun, family adventure harkens back to the Hardy Boys in its simplicity and quirky characters." SLJ

Hoot. Knopf 2002 292p $15.95; lib bdg $17.99; pa $8.95 *
Grades: 5 6 7 8   **Fic**
1. Owls—Fiction 2. Environmental protection—Fiction 3. Florida—Fiction
ISBN 0-375-82181-3; 0-375-92181-8 (lib bdg); 0-375-82916-4 (pa)   LC 2002-25478
A Newbery Medal honor book, 2003
Roy, who is new to his small Florida community, becomes involved in another boy's attempt to save a colony of burrowing owls from a proposed construction site
"The story is full of offbeat humor, buffoonish yet charming supporting characters, and genuinely touching scenes of children enjoying the wildness of nature." Booklist

Scat. Knopf 2009 371p $16.99; lib bdg $19.99
Grades: 5 6 7 8   **Fic**
1. Teachers—Fiction 2. Missing persons—Fiction 3. Wildlife conservation—Fiction 4. Florida—Fiction
ISBN   978-0-375-83486-8;   0-375-83486-9; 978-0-375-93486-5 (lib bdg); 0-375-93486-3 (lib bdg)
                                        LC 2008-28266
Nick and his friend Marta decide to investigate when a mysterious fire starts near a Florida wildlife preserve and an unpopular teacher goes missing.
"Once again, Hiaasen has written an edge-of-the-seat eco-thriller. . . . From the first sentence, readers will be hooked. . . . This well-written and smoothly plotted story, with fully realized characters, will certainly appeal to mystery lovers." SLJ

Hicks, Betty

Busted! Roaring Brook Press 2004 168p hardcover o.p. pa $6.99
Grades: 5 6 7 8   **Fic**
1. Mothers—Fiction 2. Single parent family—Fiction
ISBN 1-59643-004-4; 0-312-38053-4 (pa)
                                        LC 2003-17830
"A Deborah Brodie book"
"Twelve-year-old Stuart Ellis finds that his relationship with his single-parent mom is becoming increasingly prickly. When he is forced to quit the soccer team after he breaks a household rule, he asks his best friend, Mack, for help." Booklist
"A winning combination of sports and humor with a subtle message about personal responsibility." SLJ

Get real. Roaring Brook Press 2006 184p $16.95
Grades: 5 6 7 8   **Fic**
1. Adoption—Fiction   2. Friendship—Fiction 3. Family life—Fiction 4. North Carolina—Fiction
ISBN 1-59643-089-3   LC 2005-28749
"A Deborah Brodie book"
Destiny, a thirteen-year-old control freak who feels alienated in her messy, haphazard family, helps her adopted best friend when she finds her birth mother and decides to have a relationship with her.
"Hicks offers a solid YA novel featuring strong characters, deep friendships, supportive families, and the joy and pain of growing up." Booklist

Higgins, F. E.

The Black Book of Secrets. Feiwel and Friends 2007 273p $14.95 *
Grades: 4 5 6 7   **Fic**
1. Pawnbrokers—Fiction 2. Apprentices—Fiction
ISBN 978-0-312-36844-9; 0-312-36844-5
                                        LC 2007-32559
Companion volume to: The bone magician (2008)
When Ludlow Fitch runs away from his thieving parents in the City, he meets up with the mysterious Joe Zabbidou, who calls himself a secret pawnbroker, and who takes Ludlow as an apprentice to record the confessions of the townspeople of Pagus Parvus, where resentments are many and trust is scarce.
This is "an intriguing blend of adventure and historical fiction spiced with a light touch of the fantastic." Voice Youth Advocates

Higgins, Jack, 1929-

Sure fire; [by] Jack Higgins with Justin Richards. 1st American ed. G.P. Putnam's Sons 2007 c2006 237p $16.99 *
Grades: 6 7 8 9   **Fic**
1. Spies—Fiction 2. Adventure fiction 3. Twins—Fiction 4. Fathers—Fiction
ISBN 978-0-399-24784-2   LC 2007008144
First published 2006 in the United Kingdom
Resentful of having to go and live with their estranged father after the death of their mother, fifteen-year-old twins, Rich and Jade, soon find they have more complicated problems when their father is kidnapped and their attempts to rescue him involve them in a dangerous in-

Higgins, Jack, 1929——*Continued*

ternational plot to control the world's oil.

This is a "standout YA spy novel. . . . Each chapter ends with a cliff-hanger, maintaining the high level of suspense." Publ Wkly

Followed by: Death run (2008)

Hightman, Jason

Spirit; [by] J. P. Hightman. HarperTeen 2008 224p $16.99; lib bdg $17.89

Grades: 6 7 8 9 10 11 12   Fic

1. Witchcraft—Fiction 2. Ghost stories 3. Supernatural—Fiction 4. Salem (Mass.)—Fiction

ISBN   978-0-06-085063-0;   0-06-085063-9; 978-0-06-085064-7 (lib bdg); 0-06-085064-7 (lib bdg)

LC 2007-41934

In 1892, a wealthy, seventeen-year-old married couple, Tess and Tobias Goodraven, lay ghosts to rest for the thrill of it but, separated by the terrible witch who was responsible for the Salem witchcraft horrors, they may not have strength to survive, much less help the dead.

"Fans of horror and spirit-world stories will be entranced by this vivid, spooky offering." Booklist

Hill, Kirkpatrick, 1938-

Do not pass go. Margaret K. McElderry Books 2007 229p $15.99

Grades: 6 7 8 9   Fic

1. Prisoners—Fiction 2. Fathers—Fiction 3. Alaska—Fiction

ISBN 978-1-4169-1400-6; 1-4169-1400-5

LC 2006-03254

When Deet's father is jailed for using drugs, Deet learns that prison is not what he expected, nor are other people necessarily the way he thought they were.

"Hill does not sugar-coat the hardships that plague Deet's family. . . . Deet emerges as a sensitive, courageous protagonist who is smart enough and open-minded enough to look past people's mistakes." Publ Wkly

Hill, Stuart, 1958-

The cry of the Icemark. Scholastic 2005 472p (The Icemark chronicles) $18.95

Grades: 7 8 9 10   Fic

1. Fantasy fiction

ISBN 978-0-439-68626-6; 0-439-68626-1

A young princess warrior, Thirrin Freer Strong-in-the-Arm Lindenshield, befriends a warlock and forges a coalition of snow leopards, ancient vampires, and wolf-folk to protect her tiny kingdom against a cunning general and his conquering army.

"This novel is filled with captivating characters, exciting battles, and a plot line that grows progessively tighter with every page." Horn Book Guide

Other titles in the author's series about Icemark are:

Blade of fire (2007)

Last battle of the Icemark (2009)

Himelblau, Linda

The trouble begins. Delacorte Press 2005 200p $14.95

Grades: 4 5 6 7   Fic

1. Vietnamese Americans—Fiction 2. Immigrants—Fiction

ISBN 0-385-73273-2   LC 2004-28253

"After years in a refugee camp in the Philippines, Du Nguyen and his grandmother are finally joining the rest of the family, who escaped Vietnam long ago. American life is nothing like he imagined. . . . Du's narration nimbly conveys not just his own cultural confusion but also how he is misunderstood by others. . . . The book is often funny and bitter-sweet simultaneously." Horn Book

Hinton, Nigel

Time bomb; [by] Nigel Hinton. Tricycle Press 2006 284p map $15.95

Grades: 5 6 7 8   Fic

1. Friendship—Fiction 2. Great Britain—History—1945-1952—Fiction

ISBN 978-1-58246-186-1; 1-58246-186-4

LC 2006007451

Now grown, Andy tells the story of the summer of 1949 when, embittered after enduring injustice at their English school and disappointed by the adults in their lives, he and his friends wrestle with thoughts of revenge and deal with several life-changing secrets.

"Hinton has created a compelling story about the impact of secrets and the complexities of friendship." SLJ

Hinton, S. E.

The outsiders. Viking 1967 188p $16.99; pa $6.99 *

Grades: 7 8 9 10   Fic

1. Juvenile delinquency—Fiction

ISBN 0-670-53257-6; 0-14-038572-X (pa)

Also available in paperback from Puffin Books

ALA YALSA Margaret A. Edwards Award (1988)

"From the perspective of Ponyboy Curtis, the author relates the story of the Greasers, who are from the lower class, and their conflict with the Socs, who are their middle-class opposite number. For the Greasers, the gang comprises their street family, all the family that some of them have. In the collision between the two social factions, two buddies die, one as a hood, the other, a hero." Shapiro. Fic for Youth. 3d edition

"This remarkable novel by a seventeen-year-old girl gives a moving, credible view of the outsiders from the inside—their loyalty to each other, their sensitivity under tough crusts, their understanding of self and society." Horn Book

Rumble fish. Delacorte Press 1975 132p hardcover o.p. pa $5.99

Grades: 7 8 9 10   Fic

1. Brothers—Fiction 2. Juvenile delinquency—Fiction

ISBN 0-385-28675-9; 0-440-97534-4 (pa)

"Young Rusty-James rapidly loses everything meaningful to him—his girl, his 'rep' as number one tough guy, and, most important, his idolized older brother—a James Dean look- and act-alike known only as the Motorcycle Boy. And, although it is the Motorcycle Boy

Hinton, S. E.—*Continued*

who is gunned down at the end after breaking into a pet store, it is Rusty-James, emotionally burnt out at 14, who is the ultimate victim." SLJ

"Believable, written convincingly in first person, the story line is less a plot than a picture of personality disintegration. Memorable, but with no relief from depression, no note of hope." Bull Cent Child Books

That was then, this is now. Viking 1971 159p $15.99; pa $6.99

Grades: 7 8 9 10　　　　　　　　　　　　**Fic**

1. Drug abuse—Fiction 2. Juvenile delinquency—Fiction

ISBN 0-670-69798-2; 0-14-038966-0 (pa)

"Mark had lived with Byron's family since he was nine (his parents had shot each other) and the two boys were like brothers. Now they are adolescent, skirmishing on the edge of delinquency. Bryon, who tells the story, is in love with a girl whose younger brother is a gentle, candid thirteen-year-old; when he and Cathy find that the boy has taken drugs and is on a bad trip, Bryon is deeply upset. Then he finds a cache of pills in Mark's room and realizes that Mark is a pusher. . . . The book has a bitter realism . . . it is distinguished by percipience in characterization, natural dialogue, and a sensitivity toward the complexity of human relationships." Sutherland. The Best in Child Books

Hirahara, Naomi, 1962-

1001 cranes. Delacorte Press 2008 230p $15.99

Grades: 5 6 7 8　　　　　　　　　　　　**Fic**

1. Japanese Americans—Fiction 2. Family life—Fiction 3. Grandparents—Fiction

ISBN 978-0-385-73556-8; 0-385-73556-1

LC 2007-27655

With her parents on the verge of separating, Angela, a twelve-year-old Japanese American girl, spends the summer in Los Angeles with her grandparents, where she folds paper cranes into wedding displays, becomes involved with a young skateboarder, and learns how complicated relationships can be.

Angela's "colorful, bold voice captures the excitement of her first love as well as the anxiety of not understanding the many secrets of the adults around her. By experiencing her family's support, by learning about her Japanese heritage, and by acknowledging the various ways that love is expressed, Angela emerges into a strong, caring person." SLJ

Hite, Sid, 1954-

A hole in the world. Scholastic Press 2001 204p $16.95; pa $5.99

Grades: 7 8 9 10　　　　　　　　　　　　**Fic**

1. Farm life—Fiction

ISBN 0-439-09830-0; 0-439-09831-9 (pa)

LC 00-53149

Fifteen-year-old Paul Shackleford experiences an eye-opening and transformative summer living and working on the central Virginia farm belonging to a distant relative, where everyone seems to be haunted by the death of a much-loved and admired farmhand the year before

"Leavened with a healthy dose of humor, a dash of tender and respectful romance, and tantalizing bits of supernatural intrigue." Bull Cent Child Books

I'm exploding now; [by] Sid Hite. 1st ed. Hyperion Books for Children 2007 185p $16.99

Grades: 8 9 10 11 12　　　　　　　　　　**Fic**

1. New York (State)—Fiction 2. Aunts—Fiction

ISBN 0-7868-3757-8; 978-0-7868-3757-1

LC 2007002163

The summer he turns seventeen, Max Whooten is feeling off his game with no job and nothing to do, but after spending a lot of time hanging out in Manhattan, thinking about life, writing down his thoughts, and visiting his aunt in Woodstock, he develops a personal philosophy called "coolism" which seems to help turn things around.

"The fast-paced coming-of-age story has wide appeal." SLJ

Hobbs, Will

Bearstone. Atheneum Pubs. 1989 154p pa $4.99 hardcover o.p. *

Grades: 7 8 9 10　　　　　　　　　　　　**Fic**

1. Ute Indians—Fiction

ISBN 0-689-87071-X (pa)　　　　　　LC 89-6641

"Rebellious at being forced to abandon his family and his Ute Indian heritage to attend high school, Cloyd is sent to spend a summer with a lonely old rancher in Colorado. Upon arriving, Cloyd accidentally finds a turquoise bear totem in an Anasazi grave site, which serves as a touchstone between his cultural roots and his feelings. As time goes by, he also develops a mutual respect and friendship for the old man." ALAN

"The growth and maturity that Cloyd acquires as the summer progresses is juxtaposed poetically against the majestic Colorado landscape. Hobbs has creatively blended myth and reality as Cloyd forges a new identity for himself." Voice Youth Advocates

Followed by Beardance (1993)

Crossing the wire. HarperCollins 2006 216p $15.99; lib bdg $16.89

Grades: 5 6 7 8　　　　　　　　　　　　**Fic**

1. Illegal aliens—Fiction 2. Mexicans—Fiction

ISBN　978-0-06-074138-9;　0-06-074138-4; 978-0-06-074139-6 (lib bdg); 0-06-074139-2 (lib bdg)

LC 2005-19697

Fifteen-year-old Victor Flores journeys north in a desperate attempt to cross the Arizona border and find work in the United States to support his family in central Mexico.

This is "an exciting story in a vital contemporary setting." Voice Youth Advocates

Downriver. Atheneum Pubs. 1991 204p hardcover o.p. pa $6.99

Grades: 7 8 9 10　　　　　　　　　　　　**Fic**

ISBN 0-689-31690-9; 0-440-22673-2 (pa)

LC 90-1044

Fifteen-year-old Jessie and the other rebellious teenage members of a wilderness survival school team abandon their adult leader, hijack his boats, and try to run the dangerous white water at the bottom of the Grand Canyon

"The book is exquisitely plotted, with nail-biting suspense and excitement." SLJ

Hobbs, Will—*Continued*

Ghost canoe. Morrow Junior Bks. 1997 195p $16.99

Grades: 5 6 7 8   **Fic**
1. Buried treasure—Fiction 2. Adventure fiction 3. Pacific Northwest—Fiction
ISBN 0-688-14193-5   LC 96-34417
Also available in paperback from HarperTrophy

Fourteen-year-old Nathan, fishing with the Makah in the Pacific Northwest, finds himself holding a vital clue when a mysterious stranger comes to town looking for Spanish treasure

"Hobbs blends together a number of elements to create an exciting adventure set in 1874. . . . A winning tale that artfully combines history, nature, and suspense." SLJ

Jason's gold. Morrow Junior Bks. 1999 221p $16.99; pa $5.99 *

Grades: 5 6 7 8   **Fic**
1. Klondike River Valley (Yukon)—Gold discoveries—Fiction 2. Voyages and travels—Fiction 3. Orphans—Fiction
ISBN 0-688-15093-4; 0-380-72914-8 (pa)
                       LC 99-17973

When news of the discovery of gold in Canada's Yukon Territory in 1897 reaches fifteen-year-old Jason, he embarks on a 10,000-mile journey to strike it rich

"The successful presentation of a fascinating era, coupled with plenty of action, makes this a good historical fiction choice." SLJ

Followed by Down the Yukon (2001)

Leaving Protection. HarperCollins 2004 178p il map $15.99; pa $5.99

Grades: 7 8 9 10   **Fic**
1. Fishing—Fiction 2. Buried treasure—Fiction 3. Alaska—Fiction
ISBN 0-688-17475-2; 0-380-73312-9 (pa)
                       LC 2003-15545

Sixteen-year-old Robbie Daniels, happy to get a job aboard a troller fishing for king salmon off southeastern Alaska, finds himself in danger when he discovers that his mysterious captain is searching for long-buried Russian plaques that lay claim to Alaska and the Northwest

This "nautical thriller brims with detail about the fishing life and weaves in historical facts as well. . . . Robbie's doubts build to a climactic finale involving a dramatic and fateful storm at sea, grippingly rendered. Fans of maritime tales will relish the atmosphere and the bursts of action." Publ Wkly

Wild Man Island. HarperCollins Pubs. 2002 184p $15.99; lib bdg $16.89; pa $5.99

Grades: 6 7 8 9   **Fic**
1. Wilderness survival—Fiction 2. Alaska—Fiction
ISBN 0-688-17473-6; 0-06-029810-3 (lib bdg); 0-380-73310-2 (pa)   LC 2001-39818

After fourteen-year-old Andy slips away from his kayaking group to visit the wilderness site of his archaeologist father's death, a storm strands him on Admiralty Island, Alaska, where he manages to survive, encounters unexpected animal and human inhabitants, and looks for traces of the earliest prehistoric immigrants to America

"A well-paced adventure, this novel combines survival saga, mystery, and archaeological expedition." Voice Youth Advocates

Hoeye, Michael, 1947-

Time stops for no mouse; a Hermux Tantamoq adventure. Putnam 2002 250p $14.99; pa $7.99 *

Grades: 5 6 7 8   **Fic**
1. Mice—Fiction 2. Animals—Fiction 3. Mystery fiction
ISBN 0-399-23878-6; 0-698-11991-6 (pa)
                       LC 2001-48486
First published 2000 by Terfle Bks.

When Linka Perflinger, a jaunty mouse, brings a watch into his shop to be repaired and then disappears, Hermux Tantamoq is caught up in a world of dangerous search for eternal youth as he tries to find out what happened to her

"The snappy, sophisticated writing makes this adventure a delight from start to finish. The city of Pinchester comes alive brilliantly with its multispecies population of rats, mice, gophers, and other small furry folk. . . . A delightful romp for imaginative readers and fantasy fans." Voice Youth Advocates

Other titles in this series are:
No time like show time (2004)
The sands of time (2002)
Time to smell the roses (2007)

Hoffman, Mary, 1945-

The falconer's knot; a story of friars, flirtation and foul play. Bloomsbury Children's Books 2007 297p $16.95 *

Grades: 7 8 9 10   **Fic**
1. Religious life—Fiction 2. Renaissance—Fiction 3. Italy—History—0-1559—Fiction
ISBN 978-1-59990-056-8; 1-59990-056-4
                       LC 2006-16365

Silvano and Chiara, teens sent to live in a friary and a nunnery in Renaissance Italy, are drawn to one another and dream of a future together, but when murders are committed in the friary, they must discover who is behind the crimes before they can realize their love.

"Hoffman creates utterly engaging characters and vivid settings, and she skillfully turns up the suspense, wrapping her varied plot threads into a satisfying whole." Booklist

Stravaganza: city of masks. Bloomsbury Children's Bks. 2002 344p hardcover o.p. pa $7.95

Grades: 7 8 9 10   **Fic**
1. Space and time—Fiction 2. Adventure fiction
ISBN 1-58234-791-3; 1-58234-917-7 (pa)
                       LC 2001-56464

While sick in bed with cancer, Lucien begins making journeys to a place in a parallel world that resembles Venice, Italy, and he becomes caught up in the political intrigues surrounding the Duchessa who rules the city.

"Utterly fascinating, this rich, rip-roaring adventure—the first in a series—will no doubt whet readers' appetites for Italian history and culture as well as the next installment." Booklist

Other available titles in this series are:
Stravaganza: city of flowers (2005)
Stravaganza: city of secrets (2008)
Stravaganza: city of stars (2003)

Hoffman, Nina Kiriki
A stir of bones. Viking 2003 211p $15.99
Grades: 7 8 9 10   Fic
1. Ghost stories 2. Wife abuse—Fiction
ISBN 0-670-03551-3   LC 2003-5029
Prequel to the author's adult novels, A red heart of
memories (1999) and Past the size of dreaming (2000)
Fourteen-year-old Susan Blackstrom "begins the painful process of breaking away from her abusive father,
with help from allies both human and supernatural. A
chance encounter with three classmates leads Susan to an
abandoned house that . . . harbors an uncommonly substantial ghost named Nathan. . . . Richly endowed with
complex relationships, a strange and subtle brand of
magic, evocative language, and suspenseful storytelling,
this will draw readers into a world less safe and simple
than it seems at first glance." Booklist

Hogan, Mary, 1957-
Pretty face. HarperTeen 2008 213p $16.99; lib
bdg $17.89
Grades: 7 8 9 10   Fic
1. Self-acceptance—Fiction 2. Obesity—Fiction
3. Dating (Social customs)—Fiction 4. Italy—Fiction
5. Santa Monica (Calif.)—Fiction
ISBN   978-0-06-084111-9;   0-06-084111-7;
978-0-06-084112-6 (lib bdg); 0-06-084112-5 (lib bdg)
LC 2007-11869
When an overweight high school student from Santa
Monica spends the summer in Italy, she learns to relish
life and understand the true meaning of beauty.
"A bolstering blend of empowering and wish-
fulfilling, this will be a splendid escape for those who
can't quite swing the real Italian thing." Bull Cent Child
Books

Hokenson, Terry, 1948-
The winter road. 1st ed. Front Street 2006 175p
$16.95
Grades: 7 8 9 10   Fic
1. Survival after airplane accidents, shipwrecks, etc.—
Fiction 2. Canada—Fiction
ISBN 1-932425-45-4   LC 2005027030
Seventeen-year-old Willa, still grieving over the death
of her older brother and the neglect of her father, decides
to fly a small plane to fetch her mother from Northern
Ontario, but when the plane crashes she is all alone in
the snowy wilderness.
"The mortal challenges Willa faces make for a grip-
ping narrative, one sharpened by visceral details."
Booklist

Hollyer, Belinda
River song; by Belinda Hollyer. 1st American
ed. Holiday House 2008 170p $16.95
Grades: 4 5 6 7   Fic
1.   Mother-daughter   relationship—Fiction
2. Grandmothers—Fiction 3. Maori (New Zealand)—
Fiction
ISBN 978-0-8234-2149-7; 0-8234-2149-X
LC 2007035995
First published 2007 in the United Kingdom

Jessye loves living with her grandmother in a traditional Maori village, but when her free-wheeling mother
comes back into her life, Jessye must decide whether to
stay or move to the city.
"The natural-sounding first-person narrative draws
readers into a story of a girl learning to make sense of
all the strands that make up her life and heritage." SLJ

Secrets, lies and my sister Kate. Holiday House
2009 c2007 135p $16.95
Grades: 6 7 8 9   Fic
1. Sisters—Fiction 2. Missing persons—Fiction
3. Family life—Fiction
ISBN 978-0-8234-2179-4; 0-8234-2179-1
LC 2008-16601
First published 2007 in the United Kingdom
When her beloved older sister begins to act strangely
and then disappears, twelve-year-old Mini tries to find
her, uncovering family secrets along the way.
"Hollyer has written a story of a likable, seemingly
average family ensnarled in good intensions gone awry."
Booklist

Holm, Jennifer L.
Boston Jane: an adventure. HarperCollins Pubs.
2001 273p hardcover o.p. pa $6.99 *
Grades: 6 7 8 9   Fic
1. Chinook Indians—Fiction 2. Frontier and pioneer
life—Fiction 3. Washington (State)—Fiction
ISBN 0-06-028738-1; 0-06-028739-X; 0-06-440849-3
(pa)   LC 2001-16753
Schooled in the lessons of etiquette for young ladies
of 1854, Miss Jane Peck of Philadelphia finds little use
for manners during her long sea voyage to the Pacific
Northwest and while living among the American traders
and Chinook Indians of Washington Territory
"Strong characterizations, meticulous attention to his-
torical details . . . and a perceptive understanding of hu-
man nature make this a first-rate story not to be missed."
Booklist
Other available titles about Boston Jane are:
Boston Jane: the claim (2004)
Boston Jane: wilderness days (2002)

Middle school is worse than meatloaf; a year
told through stuff; by Jennifer L. Holm; pictures
by Elicia Castaldi. Atheneum Books for Young
Readers 2007 unp il $12.99 *
Grades: 5 6 7 8   Fic
1. School stories 2. Family life—Fiction
ISBN 0-689-85281-9
"Ginny Davis begins seventh grade with a list of
items to accomplish. This list, along with lots of other
'stuff'—including diary entries, refrigerator notes, cards
from Grandpa, and IM screen messages—convey a year
full of ups and downs. Digitally rendered collage illustrations realistically depict the various means of communication, and the story flows easily from one colorful page
to the next. . . . The story combines honesty and humor
to create a believable and appealing voice." SLJ

Holm, Jennifer L.—*Continued*
Our only May Amelia. HarperCollins Pubs.
1999 253p il hardcover o.p. pa $5.99 *
Grades: 5 6 7 8   **Fic**
1. Frontier and pioneer life—Fiction 2. Family life—
Fiction 3. Finnish Americans—Fiction 4. Washington
(State)—Fiction
ISBN 0-06-027822-6; 0-06-440856-6 (pa)
                                         LC 98-47504
A Newbery Medal honor book, 2000
As the only girl in a Finnish American family of sev-
en brothers, May Amelia Jackson resents being expected
to act like a lady while growing up in Washington State
in 1899
"The voice of the colloquial first-person narrative
rings true and provides a vivid picture of frontier and pioneer life. . . . An afterword discusses Holm's research
into her own family's history and that of other Finnish
immigrants." Horn Book Guide

Penny from heaven. Random House 2006 274p
il $15.95; lib bdg $17.99 *
Grades: 5 6 7 8   **Fic**
1. Family life—Fiction 2. New Jersey—Fiction
3. Italian Americans—Fiction
ISBN 0-375-83687-X; 0-375-93687-4 (lib bdg)
                                         LC 2005-13896
A Newbery Medal honor book, 2007
As she turns twelve during the summer of 1953, Penny gains new insights into herself and her family while
also learning a secret about her father's death.
"Holm impressively wraps pathos with comedy in this
coming-of-age story, populated by a cast of vivid characters." Booklist

Holmes, Elizabeth Ann, 1957-
Tracktown summer; [by] Elizabeth Holmes.
Dutton Children's Books 2009 248p $16.99
Grades: 5 6 7 8   **Fic**
1. Father-son relationship—Fiction 2. Lakes—Fiction
3. Mental illness—Fiction
ISBN 978-0-525-47946-8; 0-525-47946-5
                                         LC 2008-34223
Spending the summer with his father at a run-down
house between a railroad track and a polluted section of
a lake, twelve-year-old Jake gets involved with a fourteen-year-old neighbor who is hiding a secret within his
home.
"Holmes' ever-graceful style captures the shifting
moods of summer. Without melodrama, she subtly presents Jake's complex emotions, as he tries to resolve
problems of friendship, separated parents, and a distant
father. Readers will welcome this quiet, realistic story."
Booklist

Holt, K. A.
Mike Stellar: nerves of steel. Random House
2009 262p $15.99; lib bdg $18.99
Grades: 4 5 6 7   **Fic**
1. Space flight to Mars—Fiction 2. Space colonies—
Fiction 3. Family life—Fiction 4. Science fiction
ISBN   978-0-375-84556-7;   0-375-84556-9;
978-0-375-94556-4 (lib bdg); 0-375-94556-3 (lib bdg)
                                         LC 2008027272

Mike is suspicious when his family joins an expedition to Mars at the last minute, and his fears are confirmed when all of the adults on the colonizing mission,
including his parents, begin to act strangely.
This "whizzes by at warp speed—the suspenseful plot
and the precocious yet complex hero combine for a fun
ride with a satisfying resolution." Publ Wkly

Holt, Kimberly Willis
When Zachary Beaver came to town. Holt &
Co. 1999 227p $16.95 *
Grades: 5 6 7 8   **Fic**
1. Obesity—Fiction 2. Friendship—Fiction 3. Texas—
Fiction
ISBN 0-8050-6116-9   LC 99-27998
Also available in paperback from Dell
During the summer of 1971 in a small Texas town,
thirteen-year-old Toby and his best friend Cal meet the
star of a sideshow act, 600-pound Zachary, the fattest
boy in the world
"Holt writes with a subtle sense of humor and sensi-
tivity, and reading her work is a delightful experience."
Voice Youth Advocates

Holt, Simon
The Devouring. Little, Brown 2008 231p (The
devouring) $16.99
Grades: 7 8 9 10   **Fic**
1.   Siblings—Fiction   2.   Fear—Fiction
3. Supernatural—Fiction 4. Horror fiction
ISBN 978-0-316-03573-6; 0-316-03573-4
                                         LC 2008-09258
The existence of Vours, supernatural creatures who
feast on fear and attack on the eve of the winter solstice,
becomes a terrifying reality for fifteen-year-old Reggie
when she begins to suspect that her timid younger brother might be one of their victims.
"Comparable to books by R. L. Stine and Stephen
King, *The Devouring* will keep readers on the edge of
their seats. . . . The book has some graphic content,
blood, and gore, which only add to the chills. A must-
have for horror fans." SLJ

Holub, Josef, 1926-
An innocent soldier; translated by Michael
Hofmann. Arthur A. Levine Books 2005 231p
$16.99; pa $6.99
Grades: 8 9 10 11 12   **Fic**
1. France—History—1799-1815—Fiction 2. Russia—
Fiction 3. War stories
ISBN 0-439-62771-0; 0-439-62772-9 (pa)
A sixteen-year-old farmhand is tricked into fighting in
the Napoleonic Wars by the farmer for whom he works,
who secretly substitutes him for the farmer's own son.
"This is a well-wrought psychological tale. . . . [It]
has a lot to offer to those seeking to build a deep historical fiction collection." SLJ

Hoobler, Dorothy

The ghost in the Tokaido Inn; [by] Dorothy and Thomas Hoobler. Philomel Bks. 1999 214p $17.99; pa $6.99 *

Grades: 6 7 8 9   Fic
  1. Japan—Fiction 2. Mystery fiction
  ISBN 0-399-23330-X; 0-698-11879-0 (pa)
                            LC 98-14089

While attempting to solve the mystery of a stolen jewel, Seikei, a merchant's son who longs to be a samurai, joins a group of kabuki actors in eighteenth-century Japan

"Precise characterization, suspenseful plot twists, and a pace defined by swift and sometimes violent action make this a lively period thriller." Bull Cent Child Books

Other titles about Seikei are:

The demon in the teahouse (2001)

In darkess, death (2004)

The sword that cut the burning grass (2005)

A samurai never fears death (2007)

Seven paths to death (2008)

Hood, Ann, 1956-

How I saved my father's life (and ruined everything else). Scholastic Press 2008 218p $16.99

Grades: 6 7 8 9   Fic
  1. Family life—Fiction 2. Divorce—Fiction 3. Remarriage—Fiction 4. Catholics—Fiction
  ISBN 978-0-439-92819-9; 0-439-92819-2
                            LC 2007-10868

After her father leaves and marries the glamorous Ava Pomme, Madeline blames her mother for their difficult new life, but in spite of the twelve-year-old's efforts to achieve sainthood, it takes a summer trip to Italy to put her family into perspective.

"Hood is a witty and poignant writer; Madeline's fascination with faith . . . is explored with both humor and sympathy, and her near-allergic recoiling from her mother is painfully vivid." Bull Cent Child Books

Hooper, Mary

At the sign of the Sugared Plum. Bloomsbury Children's Bks. 2003 169p $16.95; pa $8.77

Grades: 6 7 8 9   Fic
  1. Sisters—Fiction 2. Plague—Fiction 3. London (England)—Fiction
  ISBN 1-58234-849-9; 0-7475-6124-8 (pa)
                            LC 2003-51863

In June 1665, excited at the prospect of coming to London to work at her sister Sarah's candy shop, teenaged Hannah is unconcerned about rumors of Plague until, as the hot summer advances and increasing numbers of people succumb to the disease, she and Sarah find themselves trapped in the city with no means of escape

"The story moves quickly and the tension builds at a rapid pace and will hold readers' interest. . . . A captivating entry in the historical fiction genre." SLJ

Includes bibliographical references

Followed by: Petals in the ashes (2004)

Newes from the dead; being a true story of Anne Green, hanged for infanticide at Oxford Assizes in 1650, restored to the world and died again 1665. Roaring Brook Press 2008 263p $15.95

Grades: 8 9 10 11 12   Fic
  1. Death—Fiction 2. Household employees—Fiction 3. Great Britain—History—1603-1714, Stuarts—Fiction 4. Pregnancy—Fiction
  ISBN 978-1-59643-355-7; 1-59643-355-8
                            LC 2007-16591

In 1650, while Robert, a young medical student, steels himself to assist with her dissection, twenty-two-year-old housemaid Anne Green recalls her life as she lies in her coffin, presumed dead after being hanged for murdering her child that was, in fact, stillborn.

"Loosely based on a true story-hence the title, taken from broadsides published at the time-with a decidedly unromantic view of the era, this is a must-read for teens learning about Cromwell and the Puritan revolution, or for young feminists who appreciate narratives about the treatment of women in history." SLJ

Includes bibliographical references.

Hopkinson, Deborah

Into the firestorm; a novel of San Francisco, 1906. Alfred A. Knopf 2006 200p $15.95; lib bdg $17.99

Grades: 5 6 7 8   Fic
  1. San Francisco (Calif.)—Fiction 2. Earthquakes—Fiction 3. Orphans—Fiction
  ISBN 0-375-83652-7; 0-375-93652-1 (lib bdg)
                            LC 2005-37189

Days after arriving in San Francisco from Texas, eleven-year-old orphan Nicholas Dray tries to help his new neighbors survive the 1906 San Francisco earthquake and the subsequent fires.

"The terror of the 1906 disaster is brought powerfully alive in this fast-paced tale. . . . Nick is a thoroughly developed protagonist, as are the supporting characters." SLJ

Includes bibliographical references

Horowitz, Anthony, 1955-

Public enemy number two; a Diamond brothers mystery. Philomel Books 2004 c1997 190p $16.99; pa $5.99 *

Grades: 5 6 7 8   Fic
  1. Mystery fiction
  ISBN 0-399-24154-X; 0-14-240218-4 (pa)
                            LC 2004-10418

When thirteen-year-old Nick is framed for a jewel robbery, he and his brother, the bumbling detective Tim Diamond, attempt to clear his name by capturing the master criminal known as the Fence.

"Horowitz has a knack for puns and humor, and he successfully combines it with a nonstop action mystery that has everything from hydraulically controlled buses to secret caverns. A readable and exciting adventure." SLJ

Other titles in the Diamond Brothers Mystery series are:

The falcon's Maltester (2004)

South by southeast (2005)

Three of Diamonds (2005)

The Greek who stole Christmas (2008)

Horowitz, Anthony, 1955——*Continued*

Raven's gate; book one of the Gatekeepers; [by] Anthony Horowitz. 1st ed. Scholastic Press 2005 254p (Gatekeepers) $17.95; pa $7.99

Grades: 6 7 8 9 **Fic**
1. Witchcraft—Fiction 2. Supernatural—Fiction 3. Great Britain—Fiction

ISBN 0-439-67995-8; 0-439-68009-7 (pa)

LC 2004-21512

Sent to live in a foster home in a remote Yorkshire village, Matt, a troubled fourteen-year-old English boy, uncovers an evil plot involving witchcraft and the site of an ancient stone circle.

"The creepy activities and the overall atmosphere of fear are well defined, and once the action starts, it doesn't let up. . . . This powerful struggle between good and evil is a real page-turner." SLJ

Other titles in the Gatekeepers series are:

Evil star (2006)

Nightrise (2007)

Necropolis (2009)

Stormbreaker. Philomel Bks. 2001 c2000 192p (An Alex Rider adventure) $17.99; pa $5.99 *

Grades: 5 6 7 8 **Fic**
1. Spies—Fiction 2. Terrorism—Fiction 3. Orphans—Fiction 4. Great Britain—Fiction

ISBN 0-399-23620-1; 0-14-240165-X (pa)

LC 00-63683

First published 2000 in the United Kingdom

After the death of the uncle who had been his guardian, fourteen-year-old Alex Rider is coerced to continue his uncle's dangerous work for Britain's intelligence agency, MI6

"Horowitz thoughtfully balances Alex's super-spy finesse with typical teen insecurities to create a likable hero living a fantasy come true. An entertaining, nicely layered novel." Booklist

Other titles about Alex Rider are:

Alex Rider, the gadgets (2006)

Ark angel (2006)

Eagle strike (2004)

Point blank (2002)

Scorpia (2005)

Skeleton key (2003)

Snakehead (2007)

Horvath, Polly

The canning season. Farrar, Straus & Giroux 2003 195p $16; pa $6.95

Grades: 6 7 8 9 **Fic**
1. Aunts—Fiction

ISBN 0-374-39956-5; 0-374-41042-9 (pa)

LC 2002-66296

Thirteen-year-old Ratchet spends a summer in Maine with her eccentric great-aunts Tilly and Penpen, hearing strange stories from the past and encountering a variety of unusual and colorful characters

"Offbeat, slapstick humor is mitigated by poignancy in Horvath's distinctive rollicking style. There is occasional use of strong language, and the family stories are woven with death, often gruesomely described. . . . Readers are in for a wise and wacky ride when they open this novel." SLJ

The Corps of the Bare-Boned Plane. Farrar, Straus and Giroux 2007 261p $17

Grades: 7 8 9 10 11 12 **Fic**
1. Death—Fiction 2. Bereavement—Fiction 3. Cousins—Fiction 4. Airplanes—Fiction 5. Uncles—Fiction 6. Islands—Fiction 7. British Columbia—Fiction

ISBN 978-0-374-31553-5; 0-374-31553-1

LC 2006-41281

When their parents are killed in a train accident, cousins Meline and Jocelyn, who have little in common, are sent to live with their wealthy, eccentric, and isolated Uncle Marten on his island off the coast of British Columbia, where they are soon joined by other oddly disconnected and troubled people.

"The savagely dark humor allows Horvath to place her characters in increasingly bizarre psychic positions, building to an almost painful crescendo in a remarkable examination of the extremes of emotional distress." Horn Book

Everything on a waffle. Farrar, Straus & Giroux 2001 149p $16; pa $5.95

Grades: 4 5 6 7 **Fic**
1. Uncles—Fiction 2. British Columbia—Fiction

ISBN 0-374-32236-8; 0-374-42208-7 (pa)

LC 00-35399

A Newbery Medal honor book, 2002

Eleven-year-old Primrose living in a small fishing village in British Columbia recounts her experiences and all that she learns about human nature and the unpredictability of life in the months after her parents are lost at sea

"The story is full of subtle humor and wisdom, presented through the eyes of a uniquely appealing young protagonist." SLJ

My one hundred adventures. Schwartz & Wade Books 2008 260p $16.99; lib bdg $19.99 *

Grades: 4 5 6 **Fic**
1. Siblings—Fiction 2. Single parent family—Fiction 3. Summer—Fiction 4. Beaches—Fiction 5. Babysitters—Fiction

ISBN 978-0-375-84582-6; 0-375-84582-8; 978-0-375-95582-2 (lib bdg); 0-375-95582-8 (lib bdg)

LC 2008-02243

Twelve-year-old Jane, who lives at the beach in a rundown old house with her mother, two brothers, and sister, has an eventful summer accompanying her pastor on bible deliveries, meeting former boyfriends of her mother's, and being coerced into babysitting for a family of ill-mannered children.

"With writing as foamy as waves, as gritty as sand, or as deep as the sea, this book may startle readers with the freedom given the heroine. . . . Unconventionality is Horvath's stock and trade, but here the high quirkiness quotient rests easily against Jane's inner story with its honest, childlike core." Booklist

The vacation; [by] Polly Horvath. 1st ed. Farrar, Straus & Giroux 2005 197p $16

Grades: 6 7 8 9 **Fic**
1. Vacations—Fiction 2. Family life—Fiction 3. Automobile travel—Fiction 4. Aunts—Fiction

ISBN 0-374-38070-8 LC 2004-57667

Horvath, Polly—*Continued*

When his parents go to Africa to work as missionaries, twelve-year-old Henry's eccentric aunts, Pigg and Mag, take him on a cross-country car trip, allowing him to gain insight into his family and himself.

"Horvath spins another delightfully offbeat yarn, complete with her signature cast of eccentric characters, wacky situations, poignant moments, and snappy dialogue." SLJ

Hostetter, Joyce

Blue; [by] Joyce Moyer Hostetter. 1st ed. Boyds Mills Press 2005 197p $16.95

Grades: 5 6 7 8   **Fic**
    1. Poliomyelitis—Fiction 2. North Carolina—Fiction
    ISBN 1-59078-389-1   LC 2005033570

"Calkins Creek books"

"Thirteen-year-old Ann Fay contracts polio after her brother dies from it. Set in North Carolina during the polio epidemic of 1944, Hostetter's novel examines the complexities of the disease and its effect on the nation. The characters' authentic reactions result in a compelling story." Horn Book Guide
    Followed by: Comfort (2009)

Comfort; [by] Joyce Moyer Hostetter. Calkins Creek 2009 306p $17.95

Grades: 5 6 7 8   **Fic**
    1. Poliomyelitis—Fiction 2. North Carolina—Fiction
    ISBN 978-1-59078-606-2; 1-59078-606-8
                           LC 2008-43664

Sequel to: Blue (2006)

In 1945 Hickory, North Carolina, Ann Fay's father is back from the war but she must still rely on her own strength and determination as she faces the problems of her polio-induced disability and her father's failure to get a job. Includes facts about the disability rights movement.

"This continuation of Ann Fay's story contains vivid descriptions of postwar rural America, polio treatment, small-town life, the ravages of war and the importance of family, all related in her homespun voice. Helpful appendices provide further information." Kirkus

Healing water; a Hawaiian story; [by] Joyce Moyer Hostetter. Calkins Creek 2008 217p $17.95

Grades: 6 7 8 9 10   **Fic**
    1. Leprosy—Fiction 2. Hawaii—Fiction
    ISBN 978-1-59078-514-0   LC 2007-18349

This novel tells the story of Pia, who is sent to Hawaii's leprosy settlement on Molokai Island in the 1860s.

"Readers will find their compassion stirred and their interest piqued through this truly fine historical novel." Bull Cent Child Books

Houston, Julian, 1944-

New boy. Houghton Mifflin Co. 2005 282p $16

Grades: 8 9 10 11 12   **Fic**
    1. Prejudices—Fiction 2. African Americans—Fiction
    3. School stories
    ISBN 0-618-43253-1   LC 2004-27207

"As the first black student in an elite Connecticut boarding school in the late 1950s, Rob Garrett, 16,

knows he is making history. . . . When his friends in the South plan a sit-in against segregation, he knows he must be part of it. . . . The honest first-person narrative makes stirring drama. . . . This brings up much for discussion about then and now." Booklist

Houts, Michelle

The Beef Princess of Practical County. Delacorte Press 2009 226p $16.99; lib bdg $19.99

Grades: 6 7 8 9   **Fic**
    1. Cattle—Fiction 2. Farm life—Fiction 3. Indiana—Fiction
    ISBN 978-0-385-73584-1; 978-0-385-90568-8 (lib bdg)   LC 2008-34712

Twelve-year-old Libby, the daughter of an Indiana cattle farmer, raises two calves in hopes of winning the annual steer competition at the county fair, but fails to follow her father's warning about developing a bond with animals that are destined to be sold at auction.

"Houts paints an idyllic yet authentic picture of farm life as she takes Libby and her family through the ups and downs of cattle raising and fair showing with sly humor and a flair for description and characterization." Booklist

Hoving, Isabel

The dream merchant; translated by Hester Velmans. Candlewick Press 2005 630p $17.99

Grades: 8 9 10 11 12   **Fic**
    1. Dreams—Fiction 2. Fantasy fiction
    ISBN 0-7636-2880-8

Having been hired by a mysterious corporation called Gippart, twelve-year-old Josh-along with two friends and the ghost of his dead twin sister-finds himself trapped in "umaya," a place between dreams, time, and reality.

"The intricate plot is deep and gratifying. Despite the sprawling, fast-paced action, it's a personal story." SLJ

Howe, James, 1946-

The misfits. Atheneum Bks. for Young Readers 2001 274p $16; pa $5.99

Grades: 5 6 7 8   **Fic**
    1. School stories 2. Elections—Fiction 3. Friendship—Fiction
    ISBN 0-689-83955-3; 0-689-83956-1 (pa)
                           LC 00-66390

Four students who do not fit in at their small-town middle school decide to create a third party for the student council elections to represent all students who have ever been called names

This is a "timely, sensitive, laugh-out-loud must-read for all middle school students and teachers." Voice Youth Advocates

Totally Joe. Atheneum Books for Young Readers 2005 189p $15.95

Grades: 6 7 8 9   **Fic**
    1. Homosexuality—Fiction
    ISBN 0-689-83957-X   LC 2004-22242

"Ginee Seo books"

As a school assignment, a thirteen-year-old boy writes an alphabiography—life from A to Z—and explores is-

Howe, James, 1946-—*Continued*
sues of friendship, family, school, and the challenges of
being a gay teenager.

"Howe deals with weighty issues, but uses Joe's affa-
ble personality to interject ample humor." Publ Wkly

Howe, Peter, 1942-
Waggit's tale; by Peter Howe; [illustrations by
Omar Rayyan] 1st ed. HarperCollinsPublishers
2008 288p $16.99; lib bdg $17.89
Grades: 5 6 7 8   Fic
1. Dogs—Fiction
ISBN   978-0-06-124261-8;   0-06-124261-6;
978-0-06-124262-5 (lib bdg); 0-06-124262-4 (lib bdg)
       LC 2007020878
Followed by: Waggit again (2009)
When Waggit is abandoned by his owner as a puppy,
he meets a pack of wild dogs who become his friends
and teach him to survive in the city park, but when he
has a chance to go home with a kind woman who wants
to adopt him, he takes it.

"The novel celebrates the wild freedom of the feral
dog pack, while also emphasizing the many hazards of
urban life for homeless companion animals." Voice
Youth Advocates

Hughes, Carol, 1961-
Dirty magic. Random House 2006 416p map
$17.95; lib bdg $19.99; pa $5.99
Grades: 6 7 8 9   Fic
1. Fantasy fiction 2. Siblings—Fiction 3. Death—Fiction
ISBN   978-0-375-83187-4;   0-375-83187-8;
978-0-375-93187-1 (lib bdg); 0-375-93187-2 (lib bdg);
978-0-375-83188-1 (pa); 0-375-83188-6 (pa)
       LC 2004-10087
After his little sister Hannah becomes mortally ill, ten-
year-old Joe follows a shadowy figure to the wartorn
land of Asphodel, a mysterious and dangerous world of
dying children, where he entrusts himself to a devious
blind guide, faces ruthless killing machines, and discovers a shocking truth about himself.

"This dense but quick-paced fantasy offers suspense;
inventive and plentiful though sometimes graphic details
(Joe is tortured); and a dizzying array of plot turns."
Booklist

Hughes, Dean, 1943-
Search and destroy. Atheneum Books for Young
Readers 2006 216p $16.95
Grades: 7 8 9 10   Fic
1. Vietnam War, 1961-1975—Fiction
ISBN 0-689-87023-X   LC 2005-11255
"Ginee Seo Books"
Recent high school graduate Rick Ward, undecided
about his future and eager to escape his unhappy home
life, joins the army and experiences the horrors of the
war in Vietnam.

"This is a compelling, insightful story about the emotional, physical, and psychological scars that wars leave
upon soldiers." Booklist

Soldier boys. Atheneum Bks. for Young Readers
2001 162p $16.95; pa $5.99
Grades: 7 8 9 10   Fic
1. World War, 1939-1945—Fiction 2. Ardennes, Battle of the, 1944-1945—Fiction 3. Soldiers—Fiction
ISBN 0-689-81748-7; 0-689-86021-8 (pa)
       LC 00-46920
"This World War II novel tells the parallel stories of
two young soldiers fighting on opposite sides of the conflict—a paratrooper from Utah and a Hitler Youth who
joins the German army. Spence and Dieter's paths cross
briefly on a snow-covered Belgian hill in a scene both
compassionate and tragic. Hughes tells their tales in assured prose that's harrowing without being exploitive."
Horn Book Guide

Hughes, Mark Peter
I am the wallpaper. Delacorte Press 2005 228p
$15.95; lib bdg $17.99
Grades: 5 6 7 8   Fic
ISBN 0-385-73241-4; 0-385-90265-4 (lib bdg)
       LC 2004-10163
Thirteen-year-old Floey Packer, jealous of her attractive and popular older sister, shares her home with two
younger cousins and experiences a summer vacation
filled with embarrassing events, with herself as the star.

"Humorous incidents abound, character growth is convincing, and the plot moves irresistibly forward." SLJ

Hughes, Pat, 1933-
Open ice. Wendy Lamb Books 2005 271p
$15.95; lib bdg $17.89
Grades: 8 9 10 11 12   Fic
1. Hockey—Fiction 2. Brain—Wounds and injuries—
Fiction 3. School stories
ISBN 0-385-74675-X; 0-385-90906-3 (lib bdg)
       LC 2004-23113
Hockey has been Nick Taglio's life since he was five
years old, so when a massive concussion benches him—
possibly for good—everything seems to fall apart, including his schoolwork, his family relationships, his friendships, and his love life.

"Hughes's attention to detail in terms of both head injuries and the sport adds lots of pith and interest to this
story, and her accurate portrayal of middle-class teen life
(which includes sex, obscenities, and pot smoking)
should keep reluctant readers turning pages." Booklist

Hull, Nancy L., 1952-
On rough seas; [by] Nancy L. Hull. Clarion
Books 2008 261p $16
Grades: 6 7 8 9   Fic
1. World War, 1939-1945—Fiction 2. Great Britain—
Fiction 3. Dunkerque (France), Battle of, 1940—Fic-
tion
ISBN 978-0-618-89743-8; 0-618-89743-8
       LC 2007-37933
In Dover, England in 1940, fourteen-year-old Alec
Curtis wants nothing more than to go to sea, to absolve
himself of the guilt he feels over the earlier drowning of
his cousin and to help the war effort, but when he sneaks
aboard a small boat going across the English Channel to

Hull, Nancy L., 1952-—_Continued_
Dunkirk, his experience changes him forever.

"Hull offers a sensitive portrayal of Alec's seesawing emotions and gradual recognition of what matters to him, culminating in subtle changes that show his newfound maturity in sometimes unexpected yet wholly convincing ways. A well-researched historical novel." Booklist

Hulme, John, 1970-
The glitch in sleep; by John Hulme and Michael Wexler; illustrations by Gideon Kendall. Bloomsbury Children's Books 2007 277p il (The Seems) $16.95 *
Grades: 4 5 6 7   **Fic**
   1. Sleep—Fiction 2. Science fiction
   ISBN 978-1-59990-129-9; 1-59990-129-3
                         LC 2007-2598
When twelve-year-old Becker Drane is recruited by The Seems, a parallel universe that runs everything in The World, he must fix a disastrous glitch in the Department of Sleep that threatens everyone's ability to ever fall asleep again.

"The story is upbeat and full of humor. . . . Dynamic full-page illustrations appear throughout." SLJ
   Another title in this series is:
The split second (2008)

Humphreys, Chris
The fetch; [by] Chris Humphreys. Knopf 2006 357p (The Runestone saga) $15.95; lib bdg $17.99
Grades: 7 8 9 10   **Fic**
   1. Supernatural—Fiction 2. Adventure fiction 3. Cousins—Fiction
   ISBN   0-375-83292-0;   978-0-375-83292-5; 0-375-93292-5 (lib bdg); 978-0-375-93292-5 (lib bdg)
                         LC 2005033349
After he and his cousin Kristin discover a sea chest full of runes and a journal belonging to their deceased Norwegian grandfather, fifteen-year-old Sky summons the old man's ghost, who teaches him how to use the power of the runestones to travel through time and space.

"Both Sky and Kristin are well-developed, interesting characters. . . . The use of runestone divination and old Norse history and culture is effective, and may draw teens to seek further information on those subjects." SLJ
   Other titles in this series are:
Vendetta (2007)
Possession (2008)

Hunter, Erin
Into the wild. HarperCollins Pubs. 2003 272p il map (Warriors) $15.99; lib bdg $16.89; pa $5.99 *
Grades: 6 7 8 9   **Fic**
   1. Cats—Fiction 2. Fantasy fiction
   ISBN 0-06-000002-3; 0-06-052548-7 (lib bdg); 0-06-052550-9 (pa)
For generations, four clans of wild cats have shared the forest. When their warrior code is threatened by mysterious deaths, a house cat named Rusty may turn out to be the bravest warrior of all.

"The author has created an intriguing world with an intricate structure and mythology, and an engaging young hero." SLJ

Other titles in the Warriors series are:
Code of the clans (2009)
A dangerous path (2004)
The darkest hour (2004)
Fire and ice (2003)
Forest of secrets (2003)
Rising storm (2004)

Midnight. HarperCollins 2005 303p (Warriors: the new prophecy) $15.99; lib bdg $16.89; pa $6.99
Grades: 6 7 8 9   **Fic**
   1. Cats—Fiction 2. Fantasy fiction
   ISBN 0-06-074449-9; 0-06-074450-2 (lib bdg); 0-06-07445-0 (pa)
Called by StarClan to fulfill a new prophecy, a group of young cats sets out on a long and dangerous journey, knowing only that trouble threatens the forest, as the adventures of the warrior clans continue.
   Other titles in this series are:
Moonrise (2005)
Dawn (2005)
Starlight (2006)
Twilight (2006)
Sunset (2007)

The sight; [by] Erin Hunter. HarperCollins Pub. 2007 363p (Warriors: power of three) $16.99; lib bdg $17.89
Grades: 6 7 8 9   **Fic**
   1. Cats—Fiction 2. Fantasy fiction
   ISBN   978-0-06-089201-2;   0-06-089201-3; 978-0-06-089203-6 (lib bdg); 0-06-089203-X (lib bdg)
                         LC 2007-11860
In a troubled time for the Clans, three young cats, grandchildren of the legendary Firestar, begin their training as warriors and, in the course of many adventures, discover their true destiny.

"Plenty of action and solid characterizations make this an enticing choice for fans of the long-running enterprise." Booklist
   Other titles in this series are:
Dark river (2008)
Outcast (2008)
Eclipse (2008)
Long shadows (2009)
Sunrise (2009)

Hurley, Tonya
Ghostgirl. Little, Brown and Co. 2008 328p $17.99 *
Grades: 7 8 9 10   **Fic**
   1. Popularity—Fiction 2. School stories 3. Death—Fiction 4. Ghost stories
   ISBN 978-0-316-11357-1; 0-316-11357-3
                         LC 2007-31541
After dying, high school senior Charlotte Usher is as invisible to nearly everyone as she always felt, but despite what she learns in a sort of alternative high school for dead teens, she clings to life while seeking a way to go to the Fall Ball with the boy of her dreams.

"Hurley combines afterlife antics, gothic gore, and high school hell to produce an original, hilarious satire. . . . Tim Burton and Edgar Allan Poe devotees will die for this fantastic, phantasmal read." SLJ

Hurley, Tonya—*Continued*

Another title about Charlotte Usher is:

Ghostgirl: Homecoming (2009)

Hurst, Carol Otis

Through the lock. Houghton Mifflin 2001 160p $15

Grades: 5 6 7 8   **Fic**

1. Orphans—Fiction   2.   Canals—Fiction
3. Connecticut—Fiction

ISBN 0-618-03036-0   LC 99-28510

"Walter Lorraine books"

Etta, a twelve-year-old orphan in nineteenth-century Connecticut, meets Walter, a boy living in an abandoned cabin on the New Haven and Northampton Canal and has adventures with him while trying to be reunited with her siblings

"Etta and Walter's terse conversations, anguished and funny, are the best part of the book, and the history is fascinating." Booklist

Huxley, Aldous, 1894-1963

Brave new world. Harper & Row 1946 xx, 311p pa $13.95 hardcover o.p.

Grades: 7 8 9 10   **Fic**

1. Utopias—Fiction 2. Technology and civilization—Fiction

ISBN 0-06-085052-3 (pa)

Also available in hardcover from Buccaneer Bks.

First published 1932 by Doubleday, Doran & Company

"The ironic title, which Huxley has taken from Shakespeare's 'The Tempest,' describes a world in which science has taken control over morality and humaneness. In this utopia humans emerge from test tubes, families are obsolete, and even pleasure is regulated. When a so-called savage who believes in spirituality is found and is imported to the community, he cannot accomodate himself to this world and ends his life." Shapiro. Fic for Youth. 3d edition

Hyde, Catherine Ryan

The year of my miraculous reappearance. Alfred A. Knopf 2007 228p $15.99; lib bdg $18.99

Grades: 7 8 9 10   **Fic**

1. Alcoholism—Fiction 2. Down syndrome—Fiction
3. Siblings—Fiction

ISBN 978-0-375-83257-4; 978-0-375-93257-1 (lib bdg); 0-375-83257-2; 0-375-93257-7 (lib bdg)

LC 2006-29194

Thirteen-year-old Cynnie has had to deal with her mother's alcoholism and stream of boyfriends all her life, but when her grandparents take custody of her brother, Bill, who has Down Syndrome, Cynnie becomes self-destructive and winds up in court-mandated Alcoholics Anonymous meetings.

"Cynnie's love for and devotion to Bill are wholly believable, as are her attempts to snare a stable adult presence in her life. Secondary characters are multidimensional and well drawn." Booklist

Ibbotson, Eva

The beasts of Clawstone Castle; illustrated by Kevin Hawkes. Dutton Children's Books 2006 243p il hardcover o.p. pa $6.99

Grades: 4 5 6   **Fic**

1. Ghost stories 2. Castles—Fiction 3. Cattle—Fiction
4. Great Britain—Fiction

ISBN 0-525-47719-5; 0-14-240931-6 (pa)

LC 2005-29188

While spending the summer with elderly relatives at Clawstone Castle in northern England, Madlyn and her brother Rollo, with the help of several ghosts, attempt to save the rare cattle that live on the castle grounds.

"Ibbotson's charismatic ghosts are great. . .—as human as they are horrific—and there's plenty of quirky humor in this energetic, diverting read, loaded with charm." Booklist

The dragonfly pool; illustrated by Kevin Hawkes. Dutton Children's Books 2008 377p il $17.99 *

Grades: 5 6 7 8   **Fic**

1. World War, 1939-1945—Fiction 2. School stories

ISBN 978-0-525-42064-4; 0-525-42064-9

"At first Tally doesn't want to go to the boarding school called Delderton. But she soon discovers that it is a wonderful place. . . . Tally organizes a ragtag dance troupe so the school can participate in an international folk dancing festival in Bergania in the summer of 1939. There she befriends Karil, the crown prince. . . . When Karil's father is assassinated, it is up to Tally and her friends to help Karil escape the Nazis and the bleak future he has inherited." Publisher's note

"Ibbotson's trademark eccentric characters and strongly contrasted principles of right and wrong brighten and broaden this uplifting tale." Booklist

The star of Kazan; illustrated by Kevin Hawkes. Dutton 2004 405p il $16.99 *

Grades: 5 6 7 8   **Fic**

1. Vienna (Austria)—Fiction 2. Germany—Fiction
3. Mystery fiction

ISBN 0-525-47347-5   LC 2004-45455

After twelve-year-old Annika, a foundling living in late nineteenth-century Vienna, inherits a trunk of costume jewelry, a woman claiming to be her aristocratic mother arrives and takes her to live in a strangely decrepit mansion in Germany

"This is a rich saga . . . full of stalwart friends, sly villains, a brave heroine, and good triumphing over evil. . . . An intensely satisfying read." SLJ

Ingold, Jeanette

The Big Burn. Harcourt 2002 295p $17; pa $6.95

Grades: 7 8 9 10   **Fic**

1. Forest fires—Fiction

ISBN 0-15-216470-7; 0-15-204924-X (pa)

LC 2001-5667

Three teenagers battle the flames of the Big Burn of 1910, one of the century's biggest wildfires

"A solid adventure story with a well-realized setting." Booklist

Ingold, Jeanette—*Continued*

Hitch. Harcourt, Inc 2005 272p $17; pa $6.95
Grades: 7 8 9 10   **Fic**
1. Civilian Conservation Corps (U.S.)—Fiction
2. Great Depression, 1929-1939—Fiction
3. Montana—Fiction
ISBN 0-15-204747-6; 0-15-20561-9 (pa)
      LC 2004-19447

To help his family during the Depression and avoid becoming a drunk like his father, Moss Trawnley joins the Civilian Conservation Corps, helps build a new camp near Monroe, Montana, and leads the other men in making the camp a success.

This is "a credible, involving story. . . . Both [the author's] writing style and her 1930s setting feels totally true to the time." Booklist

Mountain solo. Harcourt 2003 309p $17; pa $6.95
Grades: 7 8 9 10   **Fic**
1. Violinists—Fiction 2. Family life—Fiction
ISBN 0-15-202670-3; 0-15-205358-1 (pa)
      ·LC 2003-42326

Back at her childhood home in Missoula, Montana, after a disastrous concert in Germany, a teenage violin prodigy contemplates giving up life with her mother in New York City and her music as she, her father, stepmother, and stepsister hike to a pioneer homesite where another violinist once faced difficult decisions of his own

"Mountain Solo is a good read for anyone fascinated by the power of music and its effects on individuals' lives." SLJ

Includes bibliographical references (p. {307}-309)

Irving, Washington, 1783-1859

The Legend of Sleepy Hollow; illustrated by Gris Grimly. Atheneum Books for Young Readers 2007 unp il $16.99
Grades: 4 5 6   **Fic**
1. New York (State)—Fiction 2. Ghost stories
ISBN 1-4169-0625-8; 978-1-4169-0625-4
      LC 2005-27502

A superstitious schoolmaster, in love with a wealthy farmer's daughter, has a terrifying encounter with a headless horseman.

"The tale, . . . slightly condensed but with language and ambiguities intact, is reimagined here with humor, vigor, [and] clarity. . . . Irving's language is challenging . . . but Grimly's numerous Halloween-hued panel and spot illustrations . . . parse it into comprehensible tidbits. The comically amplified emotions and warm yellow and orange tones balance the horror aspects of the text." Horn Book

Isaacs, Anne, 1949-

Torn thread. Scholastic 2000 188p hardcover o.p. pa $4.99
Grades: 7 8 9 10   **Fic**
1. World War, 1939-1945—Fiction 2. Holocaust, 1933-1945—Fiction 3. Jews—Fiction
ISBN 0-590-60363-9; 0-590-60364-7 (pa)
      LC 95-31655

In an attempt to save his daughter's life, Eva's father sends her from Poland to a labor camp in Czechoslovakia where she and her sister survive the war

"Given its precise detail and sensitivity to unimaginable suffering, this gripping novel reads like the strongest of Holocaust memoirs." Publ Wkly

Ives, David

Scrib; some characters, adventures, letters and conversations from the year 1863, including a deadly chase in the wilderness of the Fearsome Canyon, all as told by Billy Christmas, who was there; a novel. HarperCollins 2005 188p $15.99; lib bdg $16.89
Grades: 5 6 7 8   **Fic**
1. West (U.S.)—Fiction 2. United States—History—1861-1865, Civil War—Fiction 3. Adventure fiction
ISBN 0-06-059841-7; 0-06-059842-5 (lib bdg)
      LC 2004-12483

In 1863, a sixteen-year-old boy nicknamed Scrib travels around the West making his living writing and delivering letters, an occupation that leads to him nearly getting killed, being jailed as a criminal, joining up with the notorious Crazy James Kincaid, and delivering a letter from President Abraham Lincoln to a Paiute Indian.

"Ives's witty wordplay is lively and the plot is fast and funny in this great read-aloud." Horn Book Guide

Voss; how I came to America and am hero, mostly. G.P. Putnam's Sons 2008 200p $17.99
Grades: 7 8 9 10   **Fic**
1. Illegal aliens—Fiction 2. Immigrants—Fiction
3. Donation of organs, tissues, etc.—Fiction
ISBN 978-0-399-24722-4; 0-399-24722-X
      LC 2007-46207

Through a series of letters home, fifteen-year-old Vospop "Voss" Vsklzwczdztwczky shares his experiences as he is smuggled out of Slobovia in a crate of black-market cheese puffs, tries to find a job in an American city, and foils a sinister plot.

"The language, the nutty plotting . . . and even nuttier sendups of classical stereotypes . . . are enough to make readers roar with laughter. Yet Ives . . . delivers a pointed social commentary that not only steers clear of cynicism but preserves its narrator's sturdy idealism." Publ Wkly

Jackson, Alison, 1953-

Rainmaker. Boyds Mills Press 2005 192p $16.95
Grades: 5 6 7 8   **Fic**
1. Droughts—Fiction 2. Great Depression, 1929-1939—Fiction 3. Florida—Fiction
ISBN 1-59078-309-3

"For 13-year-old Pidge Martin, the summer of 1939 brings changes and challenges. Her town, Frostfree, Florida, faces its longest drought in 40 years, and if it doesn't rain soon, area families . . . may lose their farms. A miracle is in order, and Pidge's father hopes a rainmaker can provide one. . . . Pidge is a well-characterized, sympathetic protagonist that readers will connect with." Booklist

Jacques, Brian

Castaways of the Flying Dutchman; illustrated by Ian Schoenherr. Philomel Bks. 2001 327p il $22.95; pa $7.99

Grades: 6 7 8 9   **Fic**

1. Orphans—Fiction 2. Dogs—Fiction 3. Angels—Fiction 4. Adventure fiction

ISBN 0-399-23601-5; 0-14-250118-2 (pa)

LC 00-59822

In 1620, a boy and his dog are rescued from the doomed ship, Flying Dutchman, by an angel who guides them in travelling the world, eternally helping those in great need

"The swashbuckling language brims with color and melodrama; the villains are dastardly and stupid; and buried treasure, mysterious clues, and luscious culinary descriptions . . . keep the pages turning." Booklist

Other titles in this series are:
The angel's command (2003)
Voyage of slaves (2006)

Redwall; illustrated by Gary Chalk. 20th anniv. ed. Philomel 2007 351p il $23.99; pa $7.99 *

Grades: 5 6 7 8 9   **Fic**

1. Mice—Fiction 2. Animals—Fiction 3. Fantasy fiction

ISBN 978-0-399-24794-1; 0-399-24794-7; 978-0-4410-0548-2 (pa); 0-4410-0548-9 (pa)

First published 1986

"Only the lost sword of Martin the Warrior can save Redwall Abbey from the evil rat Cluny and his greedy horde. The young mouse Matthias (formerly Redwall's most awkward novice) vows to recover the legendary weapon." Publ Wkly

"Thoroughly engrossing, this novel captivates despite its length. . . . The theme will linger long after the story is finished." Booklist

Other titles in this series are:
The Bellmaker (1995)
Doomwyte (2008)
Eulalia! (2007)
High Rhulain (2005)
The legend of Luke (2000)
Loamhedge (2003)
The long patrol (1998)
Lord Brocktree (2000)
Mariel of Redwall (1992)
Marlfox (1998)
Martin the Warrior (1994)
Mattimeo (1990)
Mossflower (1998)
The outcast of Redwall (1996)
Pearls of Lutra (1997)
Rakkety Tam (2004)
Salamandastron (1993)
Taggerung (2001)
Triss (2002)

James, Brian, 1976-

Zombie blondes. Feiwel and Friends 2008 232p $16.95

Grades: 7 8 9 10   **Fic**

1. Moving—Fiction 2. Father-daughter relationship—Fiction 3. School stories 4. Cheerleading—Fiction 5. Horror fiction 6. Zombies—Fiction 7. Vermont—Fiction

ISBN 978-0-312-37298-9; 0-312-37298-1

LC 2007-50869

Each time fifteen-year-old Hannah and her out-of-work father move she has some fears about making friends, but a classmate warns her that in Maplecrest, Vermont, the cheerleaders really are monsters.

"James has created a believable novel about starting over, making friends, bullying, and ostracism, while adding a dash of the supernatural." SLJ

Jansen, Hanna

Over a thousand hills I walk with you; translated from the German by Elizabeth D. Crawford. Carolrhoda Books 2006 342p $16.95

Grades: 7 8 9 10   **Fic**

1. Rwanda—Fiction

ISBN 1-57505-927-4 (lib bdg); 978-1-57505-927-3

LC 2005-21123

Original German edition, 2002

"Eight-year-old Jeanne was the only one of her family to survive the 1994 Rwanda genocide. Then a German family adopted her, and her adoptive mother now tells Jeanne's story in a compelling fictionalized biography that stays true to the traumatized child's bewildered viewpoint." Booklist

Jaramillo, Ann, 1949-

La linea. Roaring Brook Press 2006 131p $16.95

Grades: 5 6 7 8   **Fic**

1. Siblings—Fiction 2. Immigrants—Fiction 3. Mexicans—Fiction

ISBN 1-59643-154-7   LC 2005-20133

"A Deborah Brodie book"

When fifteen-year-old Miguel's time finally comes to leave his poor Mexican village, cross the border illegally, and join his parents in California, his younger sister's determination to join him soon imperils them both.

"A gripping contemporary survival adventure, this spare first novel is also a heart-wrenching family story of courage, betrayal, and love." Booklist

Jarvis, Robin

The alchemist's cat; book one of the Deptford histories. Seastar Books 2004 304p $17.95 *

Grades: 5 6 7 8   **Fic**

1. Witchcraft—Fiction 2. Horror fiction 3. London (England)—Fiction

ISBN 1-58717-257-7

Prequel to the Deptford mice trilogy that includes The dark portal, The crystal prison, and The final reckoning

First published 1989 in the United Kingdom

When Will Godwin, assistant to a wicked alchemist in 1664 London, takes in a mother cat and her kittens, a

Jarvis, Robin—*Continued*
story of villainy unfolds which reveals how Jupiter, Lord of Darkness, became so evil and powerful.

"Jarvis delivers a vivid tale of treachery, cruelty, and sorcery, leavened only by Will's innate goodness. It's also a real page-turner." Booklist

Followed by The oaken throne

The Whitby witches; book one of the Whitby witches trilogy; [by] Robin Jarvis; illustrated by Jeff Petersen. Chronicle Books 2006 295p il $17.95 *

Grades: 5 6 7 8 **Fic**
1. Orphans—Fiction 2. Witches—Fiction 3. Supernatural—Fiction 4. Great Britain—Fiction
ISBN 978-0-8118-5413-9; 0-8118-5413-2
LC 2005026778

First published 1991 in the United Kingdom

Ben and Jennet, an orphaned brother and sister, are taken in by an old woman in the quaint fishing village of Whitby, where they soon learn of the town's ancient lore and become involved in an epic struggle between good and evil.

This "is a dark but delightful read. . . . There is just the right amount of suspense to make the book creepy, but not enough to make it truly scary for younger readers." SLJ

Jean, Mark, 1952-
Puddlejumpers; [by] Mark Jean, Christopher C. Carlson. 1st ed. Hyperion Books for Children 2008 328p lib bdg $16.99

Grades: 6 7 8 **Fic**
1. Kidnapping—Fiction 2. Courage—Fiction 3. Fantasy fiction
ISBN 978-1-4231-0759-0 (lib bdg); 1-4231-0759-4 (lib bdg)
LC 2008004511

Kidnapped as a baby by Puddlejumpers, little people who live in a world below puddles, twelve-year-old Ernie must find courage to save the Puddlejumpers by leading them into battle against their mortal enemies, the Troggs.

"Fast-paced, adventurous fantasy with interesting characters and an explicitly green environmental theme." SLJ

Jenkins, A. M. (Amanda McRaney)
Night road. HarperTeen 2008 362p $16.99; lib bdg $17.89

Grades: 8 9 10 11 12 **Fic**
1. Vampires—Fiction 2. Horror fiction 3. Automobile travel—Fiction
ISBN 978-0-06-054604-5; 0-06-054604-2; 978-0-06-054605-2 (lib bdg); 0-06-054605-0 (lib bdg)
LC 2007-31703

Battling his own memories and fears, Cole, an extraordinarily conscientious vampire, and Sandor, a more impulsive acquaintance, spend a few months on the road, trying to train a young man who recently joined their ranks.

"The real strength of the novel lies in the noirish atmosphere, accessible prose, and crisp, sharp dialogue." Horn Book

Repossessed. HarperTeen 2007 218p $15.99; lib bdg $16.89

Grades: 7 8 9 10 **Fic**
1. Demoniac possession—Fiction 2. Devil—Fiction 3. School stories
ISBN 978-0-06-083568-2; 0-06-083568-0; 978-0-06-083569-9 (lib bdg); 0-06-083569-9 (lib bdg)
LC 2007-09142

Michael L. Printz Award honor book, 2008

A fallen angel, tired of being unappreciated while doing his pointless, demeaning job, leaves Hell, enters the body of a seventeen-year-old boy, and tries to experience the full range of human feelings before being caught and punished, while the boy's family and friends puzzle over his changed behavior.

"Funny and clever. . . . It's a quick, quirky and entertaining read, with some meaty ideas in it, too." Kliatt

Jenkins, Martin, 1959-
Don Quixote; [by] Miguel de Cervantes; retold by Martin Jenkins; illustrated by Chris Riddell. 1st U.S. ed. Candlewick Press 2009 347p il $27.99

Grades: 5 6 7 8 **Fic**
1. Knights and knighthood—Fiction 2. Spain—Fiction
ISBN 978-0-7636-4081-1; 0-7636-4081-6
LC 2008026500

An illustrated retelling of the exploits of an idealistic Spanish country gentleman and his shrewd squire who set out, as knights of old, to search for adventure, right wrongs, and punish evil.

"Jenkins' rendition is faithful almost to a fault. . . . The book does a fine job of capturing the sly satire and the duo's slapstick schtick. The chapter headings are especially mirthful. . . . Jenkins' always impressive and expressive artwork—characters are both gnarled and caricaturish—is an ideal medium in which to mix the tale's deadpan silliness with Quixote's unhinged fantasies." Booklist

Jennings, Patrick, 1962-
Barb and Dingbat's crybaby hotline; [by] Patrick Jennings. Holiday House 2007 161p $16.95

Grades: 8 9 10 11 **Fic**
1. Friendship—Fiction 2. Vietnam War, 1961-1975—Fiction
ISBN 0-8234-2055-8; 978-0-8234-2055-1
LC 2006049300

In the middle 1970s, a high school ladies' man and a brainy, no-nonsense girl engage in verbal combat and soul-baring revelations through their telephone calls.

"This laugh-out-loud novel is ideal for reluctant readers and those looking for a 'short book'." SLJ

Jennings, Richard W., 1945-
Orwell's luck; [by] Richard Jennings. Houghton Mifflin 2000 146p $15; pa $6.95 *

Grades: 5 6 7 8 **Fic**
1. Rabbits—Fiction 2. Magic—Fiction
ISBN 0-618-03628-8; 0-618-69335-1 (pa)
LC 99-33501

"Walter Lorraine books"

Jennings, Richard W., 1945-—*Continued*

While caring for an injured rabbit which becomes her confidant, horoscope writer, and source of good luck, a thoughtful seventh grade girl learns to see things in more than one way

"This absolutely captivating tale is about everyday magic . . . filled with quiet humor and seamless invention. The characters . . . are the sort that readers fall in love with." Booklist

Stink City. Houghton Mifflin Company 2006 186p $16

Grades: 5 6 7 8   **Fic**
1. Fishing—Fiction 2. Animal rights movement—Fiction
ISBN 978-0-618-55248-1; 0-618-55248-0
                                        LC 2006-05863
"Walter Lorraine books"

As fifteen-year-old Cade gets involved in animal rights activism in his struggle to atone for the suffering of fish used in his family's smelly catfish bait business, his neighbor Leigh Ann tries to keep him out of trouble.

"Many kids will enjoy the fishing lore, eccentric diversions, and exaggerated humor in this whopper of a yarn." Booklist

Jiménez, Francisco, 1943-

Breaking through. Houghton Mifflin 2001 195p il $15; pa $6.95 *

Grades: 7 8 9 10 11 12   **Fic**
1. Mexican Americans—Fiction 2. Migrant labor—Fiction 3. California—Fiction
ISBN 0-618-01173-0; 0-618-34248-6 (pa)
                                        LC 2001-16941
Sequel to: The circuit (1997)

Having come from Mexico to California ten years ago, fourteen-year-old Francisco is still working in the fields but fighting to improve his life and complete his education

"For all its recounting of deprivation, this is a hopeful book, told with rectitude and dignity." Horn Book

The circuit: stories from the life of a migrant child. Houghton Mifflin 1999 c1997 $16 *

Grades: 7 8 9 10 11 12   **Fic**
1. Mexican Americans—Fiction 2. Migrant labor—Fiction 3. California—Fiction 4. Family life—Fiction
ISBN 0-395-7902-1; 978-0-395-97902-0

First published 1997 by University of New Mexico Press

The story "begins in Mexico when the author is very young and his parents inform him that they are going on a very long trip to 'El Norte.' What follows is a series of stories of the family's unending migration from one farm to another as they search for the next harvesting job. Each story is told from the point of view of the author as a young child. The simple and direct narrative stays true to this perspective. . . . Lifting the story up from the mundane, Jiménez deftly portrays the strong bonds of love that hold this family together." Publ Wkly

Followed by: Breaking through (2001)

Reaching out. Houghton Mifflin 2008 196p $16 *

Grades: 7 8 9 10 11 12   **Fic**

1. Mexican Americans—Fiction 2. California—Fiction 3. Father-son relationship—Fiction
ISBN 978-0-618-03851-0; 0-618-03851-5

Sequel to: Breaking through (2001)

"Papa's raging depression intensifies young Jiménez's personal guilt and conflict in the 1960s. . . . He is the first in his Mexican American migrant family to attend college in California. . . . Like his other fictionalized autobiographies, *The Circuit* (1997) and *Breaking Through* (2001), this sequel tells Jiménez's personal story in self-contained chapters that join together in a stirring narrative. . . . The spare episodes will draw readers with the quiet daily detail of work, anger, sorrow, and hope." Booklist

Jinks, Catherine, 1963-

Babylonne; [by] Catherine Jinks. Candlewick Press 2008 384p map $18.99

Grades: 7 8 9 10 11 12   **Fic**
1. War stories 2. Orphans—Fiction 3. Middle Ages—Fiction 4. France—History—0-1328—Fiction
ISBN 978-0-7636-3650-0; 0-7636-3650-9
                                        LC 2007-21958

In the violent and predatory world of thirteenth-century Languedoc, Pagan's sixteen-year-old daughter disguises herself as a boy and runs away with a priest who claims to be a friend of her dead father and mother, not knowing whether or not she can trust him, or anyone.

"Complete with snappy dialogue, humorous asides, and colorful descriptions . . . this novel stands on its own as a very fine historical fiction book about a period in history that is not commonly written about for teens." Voice Youth Advocates

Evil genius. Harcourt 2007 486p $17 *

Grades: 7 8 9 10   **Fic**
1. Genius—Fiction 2. Crime—Fiction 3. Good and evil—Fiction 4. School stories 5. Australia—Fiction
ISBN 978-0-15-205988-0; 0-15-205988-1
                                        LC 2006-14476
First published 2005 in Australia

Child prodigy Cadel Piggot, an antisocial computer hacker, discovers his true identity when he enrolls as a first-year student at an advanced crime academy.

"Cadel's turnabout is convincingly hampered by his difficulty recognizing appropriate outlets for rage, and Jinks' whiplash-inducing suspense writing will gratify fans of Anthony Horowitz's high-tech spy scenarios." Booklist

Another title about Cadel Piggot is:
Genius squad (2008)

The reformed vampire support group. Houghton Mifflin Harcourt 2009 362p $17

Grades: 8 9 10 11 12   **Fic**
1. Vampires—Fiction 2. Mystery fiction
ISBN 978-0-15-206609-3; 0-15-206609-8
                                        LC 2008-25115

Fifteen-year-old vampire Nina has been stuck for fifty-one years in a boring support group for vampires, and nothing exciting has ever happened to them—until one of them is murdered and the others must try to solve the crime.

Jinks, Catherine, 1963-—*Continued*

"Jinks's signature facility with plot and character development is intact. . . . The plot twists . . . ramp up the giddiness." Publ Wkly

Jocelyn, Marthe, 1956-

How it happened in Peach Hill. Wendy Lamb Books 2007 232p $15.99; lib bdg $18.99 *

Grades: 6 7 8 9   Fic

1. Mother-daughter relationship—Fiction 2. Swindlers and swindling—Fiction 3. Clairvoyance—Fiction 4. New York (State)—Fiction

ISBN   978-0-375-83701-2;   0-375-93701-9; 978-0-375-93701-9 (lib bdg); 0-375-93701-3 (lib bdg)

LC 2006-26688

When fifteen-year-old Annie Grey and her "clairvoyant" mother arrive in Peach Hill, New York, in 1924, each finds a reason for wanting to finally settle down, but to reach their goals they will have to do some serious lying and Annie will have to stand up for herself.

"The blend of coming-of-age, adventure, and intrigue, framed by details of small-town life and a classic con, will appeal to fans of spunky female characters and readers of historical fiction alike." Booklist

Mable Riley; a reliable record of humdrum, peril, and romance. Candlewick Press 2004 279p $15.99

Grades: 5 6 7 8   Fic

1. Teachers—Fiction 2. Women's rights—Fiction 3. Canada—Fiction

ISBN 0-7636-2120-X   LC 2003-55322

In 1901, fourteen-year-old Mable Riley dreams of being a writer and having adventures while stuck in Perth County, Ontario, assisting her sister in teaching school and secretly becoming friends with a neighbor who holds scandalous opinions on women's rights.

"This book is a funny and inspiring tale of a young girl finding her voice and the courage to make it heard." Voice Youth Advocates

Would you. Wendy Lamb Books 2008 165p $15.99; lib bdg $18.99 *

Grades: 8 9 10 11 12   Fic

1. Sisters—Fiction 2. Medical care—Fiction 3. Coma—Fiction 4. Traffic accidents—Fiction 5. Family life—Fiction

ISBN   978-0-375-83703-6;   0-375-83703-5; 978-0-375-93703-3 (lib bdg); 0-375-93703-X (lib bdg)

LC 2007-18913

When her beloved sister, Claire, steps in front of a car and winds up in a coma, Nat's anticipated summer of working, hanging around with friends, and seeing Claire off to college is transformed into a nightmare of doctors, hospitals, and well-meaning neighbors.

"Jocelyn captures a teen's thoughts and reactions in a time of incredible anguish without making her overly dramatic. Readers will fly through the pages of this book, crying, laughing, and crying some more." SLJ

Johansen, K. V. (Krista V.), 1968-

The Cassandra Virus. Orca Book Publishers 2006 153p pa $7.95

Grades: 6 7 8 9   Fic

1. Computers—Fiction 2. Science fiction

ISBN 1-55143-497-0

When Jordan creates a computer program that communicates with him via e-mail, he has no idea the havoc the program will create for him and his friend Helen.

"Endearing characters . . . add depth to this fast-paced, futuristic, middle school thriller." Voice Youth Advocates

Followed by: The Drone War (2008)

Johnson, Angela, 1961-

A cool moonlight. Dial Bks. 2003 133p $14.99 *

Grades: 4 5 6   Fic

1. Skin—Diseases—Fiction

ISBN 0-8037-2846-8   LC 2002-31521

Nine-year-old Lila, born with xeroderma pigmentosum, a skin disease that make her sensitive to sunlight, makes secret plans to feel the sun's rays on her tenth birthday

"The book's real magic resides in the spell cast by Johnson's spare, lucid, lyrical prose. Using simple words and vivid sensory images, she creates Lila's inner world as a place of quiet intensity." Booklist

The first part last. Simon & Schuster Bks. for Young Readers 2003 131p $15.95; pa $5.99 *

Grades: 7 8 9 10   Fic

1. Teenage fathers—Fiction 2. Infants—Fiction 3. African Americans—Fiction

ISBN 0-689-84922-2; 0-689-84923-0 (pa)

LC 2002-36512

Michael L. Printz Award, 2004

Prequel to Heaven (1998)

Bobby's carefree teenage life changes forever when he becomes a father and must care for his adored baby daughter.

"Brief, poetic, and absolutely riveting." SLJ

Heaven. Simon & Schuster Bks. for Young Readers 1998 138p $16.95; pa $5.99

Grades: 6 7 8 9   Fic

1. Adoption—Fiction 2. African Americans—Fiction

ISBN 0-689-82229-4; 0-689-82290-1 (pa)

LC 98-3291

Fourteen-year-old Marley's seemingly perfect life in the small town of Heaven is disrupted when she discovers that her father and mother are not her real parents

"In spare, often poetic prose . . . Johnson relates Marley's insightful quest into what makes a family." SLJ

Toning the sweep. Orchard Bks. 1993 103p hardcover o.p. pa $5.99 *

Grades: 6 7 8 9   Fic

1. Grandmothers—Fiction 2. Family life—Fiction 3. Death—Fiction 4. African Americans—Fiction

ISBN 0-531-05476-4; 0-531-08626-7 (lib bdg); 978-0-590-48142-7 (pa); 0-590-48142-8 (pa)

LC 92-34062

Coretta Scott King Award for text

"A Richard Jackson book"

On a visit to her grandmother Ola, who is dying of cancer in her house in the desert, fourteen-year-old Emmie hears many stories about the past and her family

Johnson, Angela, 1961-—*Continued*

history and comes to a better understanding of relatives
both dead and living

"Full of subtle nuance, the novel is overlaid with
meaning about the connections of family and the power
of friendship." SLJ

Johnson, Jane, 1951-

The secret country; chapter illustrations by
Adam Stower. Simon & Schuster Books for
Young Readers 2006 c2005 323p il (Eidolon
chronicles) $14.95

Grades: 4 5 6 7   **Fic**
1. Fantasy fiction
ISBN 1-4169-0712-2   LC 2005-04449

First published 2005 in the United Kingdom

Having learned from a talking cat that he and his sisters are the half-elfin royalty of a parallel world called
Eidolon, twelve-year old Ben Arnold attempts to stop his
evil uncle from smuggling magical creatures between the
two worlds to sell on the black market.

"The writing is smooth and clear, and the action flows
quickly, enlivened by touches of humor." SLJ

Another title in this series is:
The shadow world (2007)

Johnson, Lindsay Lee

Worlds apart. Front Street 2005 166p il $16.95

Grades: 7 8 9 10   **Fic**
1. Moving—Fiction 2. Psychiatric hospitals—Fiction
ISBN 1-932425-28-4   LC 2005-12052

A thirteen-year-old daughter of a surgeon finds herself
wrenched away from a comfortable lifestyle to a home
on the grounds of a mental hospital, where her father has
accepted a five year contract.

"This story brings bias and prejudice to the forefront
in a discussable and readable narrative." SLJ

Johnson, Maureen, 1973-

13 little blue envelopes. HarperCollins
Publishers 2005 317p $15.99; lib bdg $16.89; pa
$8.99

Grades: 8 9 10 11 12   **Fic**
1. Voyages and travels—Fiction 2. Aunts—Fiction
3. Europe—Fiction
ISBN 0-06-054141-5; 0-06-054142-3 (lib bdg);
0-06-054143-1 (pa)   LC 2005-02658

When seventeen-year-old Ginny receives a packet of
mysterious envelopes from her favorite aunt, she leaves
New Jersey to criss-cross Europe on a sort of scavenger
hunt that transforms her life.

"Equal parts poignant, funny and inspiring, this tale is
sure to spark wanderlust." Publ Wkly

The Bermudez Triangle; a novel. Razorbill 2004
370p $16.99; pa $7.99

Grades: 8 9 10 11 1 2   **Fic**
1. Lesbians—Fiction 2. Friendship—Fiction 3. School
stories
ISBN 1-59514-019-0; 1-59514-033-6 (pa)
      LC 2004-5093

The friendship of three high school girls and their relationships with their friends and families are tested
when two of them fall in love with each other.

"Johnson accurately and effectively interweaves characters of various classes, backgrounds, values, and
dreams, credibly mixing them with empathy and care."
Voice Youth Advocates

Devilish. Razorbill/Penguin Putnam 2006 263p
$16.99

Grades: 8 9 10 11 12   **Fic**
1. Devil—Fiction 2. Supernatural—Fiction
3. Friendship—Fiction 4. School stories
ISBN 1-59514-060-3   LC 2006-10230

Jane Jarvis, a senior at a Catholic girl's school in
Providence, Rhode Island, tries to save her best friend by
making a pact with a demon—in the form of a cupcake-
eating, very friendly teenage girl.

"Decorated in fine detail and well served by a terrific
supporting cast, this page-turner will have high appeal
and get great word-of-mouth." Booklist

Suite Scarlett. Scholastic Point 2008 353p
$16.99 *

Grades: 6 7 8 9   **Fic**
1. Hotels and motels—Fiction 2. Family life—Fiction
3. Authorship—Fiction 4. New York (N.Y.)—Fiction
ISBN 978-0-439-89927-7; 0-439-89927-3
      LC 2007-041903

Fifteen-year-old Scarlett Marvin is stuck in New York
City for the summer working at her quirky family's historic hotel, but her brother's attractive new friend and a
seasonal guest who offers her an intriguing and challenging writing project improve her outlook.

"Utterly winning, madcap Manhattan farce, crafted
with a winking, urbane narrative and tight, wry dialogue." Booklist

Johnson, Peter, 1951-

What happened. Front Street 2007 133p $16.95
*

Grades: 8 9 10 11 12   **Fic**
1. Father-son relationship—Fiction 2. Traffic accidents—Fiction
ISBN 978-1-932425-67-3; 1-932425-67-5
      LC 2006-12028

When Duane is involved in a hit-and-run accident during a snowstorm, passengers Kyle and his younger brother must face Duane's powerful father, a man whose hatred of their own absent father may lead him to harm the
boys.

"The voice that Johnson has given this boy . . . is
breathtakingly good, each word conspiring with every
other word to create an irresistibly seductive tone that is
a haunting combination of sadness and fragile hope."
Booklist

Johnston, Julie

In spite of killer bees. Tundra Bks. 2001 253p
hardcover o.p. pa $9.95

Grades: 7 8 9 10   **Fic**

Johnston, Julie—*Continued*
1. Sisters—Fiction
ISBN 0-88776-537-8; 0-88776-601-3 (pa)

"Fourteen-year-old Agatha and her two older sisters, Jeannie and Helen, have been eking out their existence since the death of their father and the departure of their mother, but all that's going to change now that their wealthy grandfather has died, leaving them his heirs. Or so they think." Bull Cent Child Books

"Johnston's descriptive, present-tense narrative is compelling, fluctuating between distance, edginess, and heartfelt intimacy." Booklist

A very fine line. Tundra Books 2006 198p $18.95
Grades: 5 6 7 8   Fic
1. Clairvoyance—Fiction 2. Canada—Fiction
ISBN 978-0-88776-746-3; 0-88776-746-X

Then thirteen-year-old Rosalind's "aunt informs her that as the seventh daughter of a seventh daughter, she can . . . see glimpses of the future, she balks. . . . The story begins in Kepston, Ontario, in 1941. . . . Readers who come to the book intrigued by the idea of clairvoyance will fine much more: several vivid characters, a well-realized setting, and a sensitively nuanced resolution." Booklist

Johnston, Tony
Any small goodness; a novel of the barrio; illustrations by Raúl Colón. Blue Sky Press (NY) 2001 128p il $16.95; pa $4.99
Grades: 4 5 6 7   Fic
1. Mexican Americans—Fiction 2. Los Angeles (Calif.)—Fiction
ISBN 0-439-18936-5; 0-439-23384-4 (pa)
LC 99-59877

Arturo and his family and friends share all kinds of experiences living in the barrio of East Los Angeles—reclaiming their names, playing basketball, championing the school librarian, and even starting their own gang

"The characters are likable and warm. . . . The message is positive and the episodes, while occasionally serious, are more often humorous and gratifying." SLJ

Bone by bone by bone. 1st ed. Roaring Brook Press 2007 184p $16.95 *
Grades: 6 7 8 9   Fic
1. Race relations—Fiction 2. Friendship—Fiction 3. African Americans—Fiction 4. Father-son relationship—Fiction 5. Tennessee—Fiction
ISBN 978-1-59643-113-3; 1-59643-113-X
LC 2006-32923

"A Deborah Brodie book."

In 1950s Tennessee, ten-year-old David's racist father refuses to let him associate with his best friend Malcolm, an African American boy.

"Like most of her characters, Johnston's novel is layered with disturbing contradictions that add depth and a vivid sense of the time and place." Booklist

Jolin, Paula
In the name of God. Roaring Brook Press 2007 208p $16.95
Grades: 8 9 10 11 12   Fic
1. Muslims—Fiction 2. Family life—Fiction 3. Islamic fundamentalism—Fiction 4. Syria—Fiction
ISBN 978-1-59643-211-6; 1-59643-211-X
LC 2006-23834

Determined to follow the laws set down in the Qur'an, seventeen-year-old Nadia becomes involved in a violent revolutionary movement aimed at supporting Muslim rule in Syria and opposing the Western politics and materialism that increasingly affect her family.

"The well-written prose and short chapters give stories in the news a face and a character. Readers of this book will not be able to read or watch the news in the same way." Voice Youth Advocates

Jonell, Lynne, 1956-
Emmy and the incredible shrinking rat; art by Jonathan Bean. Henry Holt 2007 346p il $16.95 *
Grades: 4 5 6   Fic
1. Rats—Fiction
ISBN 978-0-8050-8150-3; 0-8050-8150-X
LC 2006-35461

Followed by: Emmy and the Home for Troubled Girls (2008)

When Emmy discovers that she and her formerly loving parents are being drugged by their evil nanny with rodent potions that can change people in frightening ways, she and some new friends must try everything possible to return things to normal.

"This tale turns smoothly on its fanciful premise and fabulous characters." Booklist

Jones, Allan Frewin, 1954-
The faerie path. Eos 2007 312p $16.99; lib bdg $17.89
Grades: 6 7 8 9   Fic
1. Fairies—Fiction 2. Fantasy fiction
ISBN 978-0-06-087102-4; 0-06-087102-4; 978-0-06-087103-1 (lib bdg); 0-06-087102-4 (lib bdg)
LC 2006-18955

Anita, an ordinary sixteen-year-old girl, is transported from modern-day London to the realm of Faerie where she discovers that she is Princess Tania, the long-lost daughter of King Oberon and Queen Titania.

"The book is appealing. The images are vivid, the characters are charming." Voice Youth Advocates

Other titles in this series are:
The lost queen (2007)
The Sorcerer King (2008)

Warrior princess. 1st ed. Eos 2009 346p $16.99
Grades: 8 9 10 11 12   Fic
1. Princesses—Fiction 2. War stories 3. Magic—Fiction 4. Wales—Fiction 5. Great Britain—History—0-1066—Fiction
ISBN 978-0-06-087143-7; 0-06-087143-1
LC 2008023936

After a deadly attack on her home, fifteen-year-old Princess Branwen meets a mystical woman in white who prophesies that Branwen will save her homeland from

Jones, Allan Frewin, 1954-—_Continued_
falling to the Saxons.

"Filled with battle scenes, fully realized characters, and a conclusion that will keep readers guessing, this story has surefire appeal." SLJ

Jones, Diana Wynne
Charmed life. Greenwillow Bks. 2000 272p $15.95; pa $5.99 *
Grades: 6 7 8 9   **Fic**
1. Witches—Fiction 2. Magic—Fiction
ISBN 0-06-029876-6; 0-688-15546-4 (pa)
The first four titles in this series also available in 2 volume compilation, The chronicles of Chrestomanci
A reissue of the title first published 1977
Gwendolen Chant and her brother Cat find the Chrestomanci Castle family's magic powers difficult to counter with the inferior powers of the Coven Street witches.

"The concept is ingenious." Horn Book
Other titles in this series are:
Conrad's fate (2005)
The lives of Christoper Chant (1988)
The magicians of Caprona (1980)
The Pinhoe egg (2006)
Witch week (1982)

The game. Firebird 2007 179p $11.99
Grades: 6 7 8 9   **Fic**
1. Classical mythology—Fiction 2. Cousins—Fiction 3. Fantasy fiction
ISBN 0-14-240718-6   LC 2006-41330
Sent to a boisterous family gathering in Ireland by her overly strict grandmother, orphaned Hayley feels out of place until her unruly cousins include her in a special game involving travel through the mythosphere, the place where all the world's stories can be found, and where some secrets of her past are revealed.

"The strength of this story is the finesse with which it draws readers into a realistic story that gradually becomes more and more fantastic." Booklist

House of many ways. Greenwillow Books 2008 404p $17.99; lib bdg $18.89
Grades: 5 6 7 8   **Fic**
1. Houses—Fiction 2. Magic—Fiction 3. Uncles—Fiction 4. Fantasy fiction
ISBN 978-0-06-147795-9; 0-06-147795-8; 978-0-06-147796-6 (lib bdg); 0-06-147796-6 (lib bdg)
LC 2007036147
Sequel to: Howl's moving castle (1986)
When Charmain is asked to housesit for Great Uncle William, the Royal Wizard of Norland, she is ecstatic to get away from her parents, but finds that his house is much more than it seems.

This is "a buoyantly entertaining read. . . . [Jones'] comic pacing and wit are amply evident." Horn Book

Howl's moving castle. Greenwillow Books 1986 212p pa $6.99 hardcover o.p. *
Grades: 5 6 7 8   **Fic**
1. Fantasy fiction
ISBN 978-0-06-147878-9 (pa); 0-06-147878-4 (pa); 0-688-06233-4 (hc)   LC 85-21981

"When the wicked Witch of the Waste turns Sophie Hatter into an ugly crone, the girl seeks refuge in Wizard Howl's moving castle. To her surprise and dismay, she finds herself embroiled in a contest between the witch and the wizard, in the tangled love affairs of the wizard, and in a perplexing mystery." Child Book Rev Serv

"Satisfyingly, Sophie meets a fate far exceeding her dreary expectations. This novel is an exciting, multifaceted puzzle, peopled with vibrant, captivating characters. A generous sprinkling of humor adds potency to this skillful author's spell." Voice Youth Advocates
Followed by: House of many ways (2008)

Jones, Kimberly K., 1957-
Sand dollar summer; [by] Kimberly K. Jones. Margaret K. McElderry Books 2006 206p $15.95
Grades: 5 6 7 8   **Fic**
1. Islands—Fiction 2. Maine—Fiction 3. Family life—Fiction
ISBN 978-1-4169-0362-8; 1-4169-0362-3
LC 2005012740
When twelve-year-old Lise spends the summer on an island in Maine with her self-reliant mother and bright—but oddly mute—younger brother, her formerly safe world is complicated by an aged Indian neighbor, her mother's childhood friend, and a hurricane.

"The drama in [the] smart, tough, first-person narrative is understated; the spaces between the words are as eloquent as what is said. . . . The family story . . . is exquisitely told." Booklist

Jones, Traci L.
Standing against the wind. 1st ed. Farrar, Straus and Giroux 2006 184p $16
Grades: 6 7 8 9   **Fic**
1. African Americans—Fiction 2. School stories 3. City and town life—Fiction
ISBN 978-0-374-37174-6; 0-374-37174-1
LC 2005-51226
As she tries to escape her poor Chicago neighborhood by winning a scholarship to a prestigious boarding school, shy and studious eighth-grader Patrice discovers that she has more options in life than she previously realized.

"Handled without obscenity, the lively street talk will draw readers to the gripping story of a contemporary kid who works to make her dreams come true." Booklist

Jones, V. M., 1958-
Out of reach. Marshall Cavendish 2008 c2003 264p $16.99
Grades: 7 8 9 10   **Fic**
1. Father-son relationship—Fiction 2. Mountaineering—Fiction 3. Soccer—Fiction
ISBN 978-0-7614-5514-1; 0-7614-5514-0
LC 2007-49515
First published 2003 in New Zealand with title: Juggling with mandarins
Pressured by his agressively competitive father to play soccer, teenaged Pip McLeod secretly pursues a sport that he truly enjoys—indoor rock climbing.

"Pip is a likable character and both his conflict with his father and his journey of self-discovery are believable. A heartwarming story about finding one's strengths and confronting problems." SLJ

Jongman, Mariken, 1965-
Rits; translated from the Dutch by Wanda
Boeke. Front Street 2008 236p $17.95
Grades: 6 7 8 9   **Fic**
1. Uncles—Fiction 2. Friendship—Fiction
ISBN 978-1-59078-545-4; 1-59078-545-2
LC 2007021596
When his father runs off with his girlfriend and his
distraught mother is admitted to an institution, thirteen-
year-old Rits goes to live with his uncle and tries to
make the best of his unusual circumstances.
Rits' "voice transcends the awkwardness with its utter
believability, making for a quietly funny and heartfelt
story." Booklist

Jonsberg, Barry, 1951-
Dreamrider. Knopf 2008 239p $15.99; lib bdg
$18.99
Grades: 8 9 10 11 12   **Fic**
1. Bullies—Fiction 2. Dreams—Fiction 3. Obesity—
Fiction 4. Australia—Fiction 5. School stories
ISBN   978-0-375-84457-7;   0-375-84457-0;
978-0-375-94457-4 (lib bdg); 0-375-94457-5 (lib bdg)
LC 2007-28929
First published 2006 in Australia
Harangued by his father about his weight and bullied
in all the many schools he has attended, teenaged Michael finds some comfort in his ability to experience "lucid" dreaming but then starts to notice that the things
that happen in his dreams are starting to occur in the real
world as well.
"Readers will be chilled by the author's unflinching
and innovative treatment of the horrors and hopelessness
engulfing the victim of bullying. Jonsberg's prose is
spare, his pacing excellent, his plotting memorable." Publ
Wkly

Jordan, Rosa, 1939-
Lost Goat Lane. Peachtree Publisher 2004 197p
$14.95
Grades: 5 6 7 8   **Fic**
1. Goats—Fiction 2. Race relations—Fiction
3. African Americans—Fiction 4. Florida—Fiction
ISBN 1-56145-325-0   LC 2004-5343
Two families—one white, one black—living near one
another in rural Florida overcome their suspicions of
each other and find ways to work together, with the help
of their children and a few goats
"The fully realized characters and the warmth of the
story make up for the small sermons. A tender, satisfying
offering." SLJ
Other titles in this series are:
The goatnappers (2007)
The last wild place (2008)

Jordan, Sherryl, 1949-
Time of the eagle. Eos 2007 464p $17.99; lib
bdg $18.89
Grades: 7 8 9 10   **Fic**
1. Fantasy fiction
ISBN   978-0-06-059555-5;   0-06-059555-8;
978-0-06-059554-8 (lib bdg); 0-06-059554-X (lib bdg)
LC 2006-19371

Sequel to: Secret sacrament (2001)
Avala, the daughter of Gabriel Eshban Vala, dreams
of becoming a healer like her mother, but she is instead
destined to bring about the Time of the Eagle, in which
tribes hunted by the Navoran director will unite and win
their freedom.
This is a "long saga, filled with excitement, romance,
and mystery." Kliatt

Joseph, Lynn
The color of my words. HarperCollins Pubs.
2000 138p hardcover o.p. pa $5.99
Grades: 5 6 7 8   **Fic**
1. Family life—Fiction 2. Siblings—Fiction
3. Dominican Republic—Fiction
ISBN 0-06-028232-0; 0-06-447204-3 (pa)
LC 00-22440
"Joanna Cotler books"
When life gets difficult for Ana Rosa, a twelve-year-
old would-be writer living in a small village in the Dominican Republic, she can depend on her older brother
to make her feel better—until the life-changing events on
her thirteenth birthday
"A finely crafted novel, lovely and lyrical." SLJ

Joyce, Graham
The exchange. Viking 2008 241p $16.99
Grades: 7 8 9 10   **Fic**
1. Supernatural—Fiction 2. Dating (Social customs)—
Fiction 3. Tattooing—Fiction 4. Single parent family—Fiction
ISBN 978-0-670-06207-2; 0-670-06207-3
LC 2007-32160
Cursed by the elderly recluse whose home she and a
friend were creeping through late one night, fourteen-
year-old Caz soon finds her life disintegrating and realizes she must find a way of lifting the curse—or at least
understanding its power.
"Joyce has crafted a bizarre, magically realistic tale.
. . . . It's a wild ride with subtly moralistic undertones
and a surprisingly happy ending that will stay with readers." Booklist

Juby, Susan, 1969-
Alice, I think. HarperTempest 2003 290p
hardcover o.p. pa $7.99
Grades: 7 8 9 10   **Fic**
1. Family life—Fiction 2. Psychotherapy—Fiction
ISBN 0-06-051543-0; 0-06-051545-7 (pa)
LC 2002-27360
"A very different form of this book was previously
published in 2000 in Canada." Verso of title page
Fifteen-year-old Alice keeps a diary as she struggles
to cope with the embarrassments and trials of family,
dating, school, work, small town life, and a serious case
of "outcastitis"
"While Juby's novel stands out more for her narrator's
voice than for its plot, her dark wit virtually glitters on
every page." Publ Wkly
Other titles about Alice are:
Alice Macleod, realist at last (2005)
Miss Smithers (2004)

Juby, Susan, 1969-—*Continued*
Another kind of cowboy. HarperTeen 2007 344p
$16.99; lib bdg $17.89
Grades: 8 9 10 11 12 **Fic**
1. Horsemanship—Fiction 2. Horses—Fiction
3. Homosexuality—Fiction 4. Friendship—Fiction
5. British Columbia—Fiction
ISBN 0-06-076517-8; 978-0-06-076517-0;
0-06-076518-6 (lib bdg); 978-0-06-076518-7 (lib bdg)
LC 2006-36336
In Vancouver, British Columbia, two teenage dressage
riders, one a spoiled rich girl and the other a closeted
gay sixteen-year-old boy, come to terms with their identities and learn to accept themselves.
"Wry humor infuses this quiet story with a gentle
warmth, and the secondary characters are well developed." Booklist

Getting the girl; a guide to private investigation,
surveillance, and cookery; [by] S. Juby.
HarperTeen 2008 341p $16.99; lib bdg $17.89
Grades: 6 7 8 9 10 **Fic**
1. School stories 2. Popularity—Fiction 3. British Columbia—Fiction 4. Mystery fiction
ISBN 978-0-06-076525-5; 0-06-076525-9;
978-0-06-076527-9 (lib bdg); 0-06-076527-5 (lib bdg)
LC 2008-00788
Ninth-grader Sherman Mack investigates the "Defil-
ers," a secret group at his British Columbia high school
that marks certain female students as pariahs, at first because he is trying to protect the girl he has a crush on,
but later as a matter of principle.
Juby "applies her signature brand of humor to a detective novel. . . . [This offers a] strong and memorable female cast. . . . Here's hoping that Juby delivers on the
promise of sequels." Horn Book

Jukes, Mavis
Smoke. Farrar, Straus and Giroux 2009 164p
$16.95
Grades: 5 6 7 8 **Fic**
1. Single parent family—Fiction 2. Cats—Fiction
3. Lost and found possessions—Fiction 4. California—
Fiction
ISBN 978-0-374-37085-5; 0-374-37085-0
LC 2008-07157
Twelve-year-old Colton and his mother move to a
farm in California, away from his grandfather and his ro-
deo-champion father in Idaho, and after his cat Smoke
goes missing, Colt feels even more lonely for his old
life.
"Jukes's prose is straightforward and unadorned, with
strong dialogue and an abundance of exclamation points.
It's a tender, audience-appropriate story that subtly handles themes of home, family and community." Kirkus

Jung, Reinhardt
Dreaming in black and white; translated by
Anthea Bell. Phyllis Fogelman Books 2003 112p
$15.99
Grades: 5 6 7 8 **Fic**
1. Handicapped—Fiction 2. Germany—Fiction
3. Holocaust, 1933-1945—Fiction
ISBN 0-8037-2811-5 LC 2002-19918

Original German edition, 1996
A boy dreams that he is a student during the period
of the Nazi Third Reich in Germany, where he is persecuted for being physically handicapped
"This spare, deeply felt novel adds a new dimension
to Holocaust literature." Horn Book Guide

Kaaberbol, Lene
The Shamer's daughter. Henry Holt 2004 235p
$16.95; pa $7.95
Grades: 6 7 8 9 **Fic**
1. Fantasy fiction
ISBN 0-8050-7541-0; 0-8050-8111-9 (pa)
LC 2003-56580
After her mother, a Shamer, is summoned to Dunark
for a mission, ten-year-old Dina is forced to use her own
special powers as she is caught up in an adventure of po-
litical intrigue and survival
"Classic adventure fantasy, with the right combination
of personalities, power, intrigue, and dragons. . . . It will
prove to be a sure hit." Voice Youth Advocates
Other titles about Dina are:
The Shamer's signet (2005)
The Shamer's war (2006)
The serpent gift (2006)

Kadohata, Cynthia
Cracker! the best dog in Vietnam; [by] Cynthia
Kadohata. Atheneum Books for Young Readers
2007 312p $16.99
Grades: 5 6 7 8 **Fic**
1. Dogs—Fiction 2. Vietnam War, 1961-1975—Fic-
tion
ISBN 978-1-4169-0637-7; 1-4169-0637-1
LC 2006-22022
The author "tells a stirring, realistic story of Ameri-
ca's war in Vietnam, using the alternating viewpoints of
an army dog named Cracker and her 17-year-old handler,
Rick Hanski. . . . The heartfelt tale explores the close
bond of the scout-dog team." Booklist

Kira-Kira. Atheneum Bks. for Young Readers
2004 244p $15.95 *
Grades: 5 6 7 8 **Fic**
1. Sisters—Fiction 2. Japanese Americans—Fiction
3. Death—Fiction 4. Georgia—Fiction
ISBN 0-689-85639-3
Awarded the Newbery Medal, 2005
Chronicles the close friendship between two Japanese-
American sisters growing up in rural Georgia during the
late 1950s and early 1960s, and the despair when one
sister becomes terminally ill.
"This beautifully written story tells of a girl struggling
to find her own way in a family torn by illness and horrendous work conditions. . . . All of the characters are
believable and well developed." SLJ

Outside beauty. Atheneum Books for Young
Readers 2008 265p $16.99 *
Grades: 5 6 7 8 **Fic**
1. Sisters—Fiction 2. Father-daughter relationship—
Fiction 3. Mother-daughter relationship—Fiction
ISBN 978-0-689-86575-6; 0-689-86575-9
LC 2007-39711

Kadohata, Cynthia—*Continued*

Thirteen-year-old Shelby and her three sisters must go to live with their respective fathers while their mother, who has trained them to rely on their looks, recovers from a car accident that scarred her face.

Kadohata's "gifts for creating and containing drama and for careful definition of character prove as powerful as ever in this wise, tender and compelling novel." Publ Wkly

Weedflower. Atheneum Books for Young Readers 2006 260p $16.95

Grades: 5 6 7 8   **Fic**
1. Japanese Americans—Evacuation and relocation, 1942-1945—Fiction 2. World War, 1939-1945—Fiction 3. Arizona—Fiction
ISBN 0-689-86574-0   LC 2004-24912

After twelve-year-old Sumiko and her Japanese-American family are relocated from their flower farm in southern California to an internment camp on a Mojave Indian reservation in Arizona, she helps her family and neighbors, becomes friends with a local Indian boy, and tries to hold on to her dream of owning a flower shop.

Sumiko "is a sympathetic heroine, surrounded by well-crafted, fascinating people. The concise yet lyrical prose conveys her story in a compelling narrative." SLJ

Kantor, Melissa

The breakup bible; a novel. Hyperion Books for Children 2007 272p $15.99

Grades: 8 9 10 11 12   **Fic**
1. Dating (Social customs)—Fiction
ISBN 978-0-7868-0962-2

Jennifer thinks she and Max are the perfect couple, until he decides he just wants to be friends.

"Written with wit and featuring a few fine plot twists, this will have teen girls nodding sympathetically." Booklist

Confessions of a not it girl. Hyperion 2004 247p $15.99; pa $8.99

Grades: 7 8 9 10   **Fic**
1. School stories
ISBN 0-7868-1837-9; 0-7868-1808-5 (pa)

"Jan Miller is a . . . teen seeking her first romance during her senior year in high school. . . . Jan obsesses about the college applications she has not yet begun; the size of her butt; and Josh. . . . Lots of fun, lots of truth, very satisfying." SLJ

If I have a wicked stepmother, where's my prince? Hyperion 2005 283p $15.99; pa $8.99

Grades: 8 9 10 11 12   **Fic**
1. Stepfamilies—Fiction
ISBN 0-7868-0960-4; 0-7868-0961-2 (pa)

When the father of high school sophomore, Lucy Norton, remarries, Lucy finds herself tormented by two bratty stepsisters and a wicked stepmother.

"While savvy readers will anticipate Lucy's ultimate pairing and improved family relationships, most teens won't be disappointed in the pleasant confection of wit, teen angst, shopping, girl talk, and flirtation." SLJ

Karasyov, Carrie, 1972-

Bittersweet sixteen; [by] Carrie Karasyov and Jill Kargman. HarperCollins Publishers 2006 230p $15.99; lib bdg $16.89

Grades: 7 8 9 10   **Fic**
1. School stories 2. Birthdays—Fiction 3. Parties—Fiction 4. Friendship—Fiction 5. New York (N.Y.)—Fiction
ISBN 978-0-06-077844-6; 0-06-077844-X; 978-0-06-077845-3 (lib bdg); 0-06-077845-8 (lib bdg)
LC 2005017975

A student at New York's most exclusive preparatory school for girls deals with the mayhem of "Sweet Sixteen" birthday parties given by the ultrawealthy.

This is "is a fast-paced, entertaining read." Voice Youth Advocates

Summer intern; [by] Carrie Karasyov & Jill Kargman. 1st ed. HarperTeen 2007 184p $16.99; lib bdg $17.89

Grades: 7 8 9 10 11 12   **Fic**
1. Internship programs—Fiction 2. Clothing industry—Fiction 3. New York (N.Y.)—Fiction
ISBN 0-06-115375-3; 0-06-115376-1 (lib bdg)
LC 2006028651

Through the course of a summer internship at the fashion magazine Skirt, Kira experiences weird roommates, a not-so-perfect romance, an accusation of theft, and continual confrontation with a fellow intern who happens to be the owner's daughter.

"The authors do a great job of describing the ins and outs of fashion couture. This addition to the chick-lit genre is funny and lighthearted." SLJ

Karim, Sheba

Skunk girl. Farrar, Straus & Giroux 2009 231p $16.95

Grades: 8 9 10 11 12   **Fic**
1. Pakistani Americans—Fiction 2. Family life—Fiction 3. School stories 4. Muslims—Fiction 5. Dating (Social customs)—Fiction 6. New York (State)—Fiction
ISBN 978-0-374-37011-4; 0-374-37011-7
LC 2008-07482

Nina Khan is not just the only Asian or Muslim student in her small-town high school in upstate New York, she is also faces the legacy of her "Supernerd" older sister, body hair, and the pain of having a crush when her parents forbid her to date.

This novel is "rife with smart, self-deprecating humor." Kirkus

Karr, Kathleen

Born for adventure. Marshall Cavendish 2007 193p $16.99

Grades: 7 8 9 10   **Fic**
1. Stanley, Henry M. (Henry Morton), 1841-1904—Fiction 2. Adventure fiction 3. Central Africa—Fiction 4. Voyages and travels—Fiction
ISBN 978-0-7614-5348-2; 0-7614-5348-2
LC 2006-30232

In 1887, as assistant to Henry Morton Stanley, renowned explorer of the African continent, sixteen-year-

Karr, Kathleen—*Continued*

old Tom Ormsby makes a perilous trek to help rescue the kidnapped Emin Pasha, learning much about leadership, African people, and himself along the way.

"Karr suffuses this coming-of-age story with a wealth of historical detail and a steady stream of action." Publ Wkly

Fortune's fool. Alfred A. Knopf 2008 201p $15.99; lib bdg $18.99

Grades: 5 6 7 8   **Fic**

1. Middle Ages—Fiction 2. Fools and jesters—Fiction 3. Germany—History—0-1517—Fiction

ISBN 978-0-375-84816-2; 0-375-84816-2; 978-0-375-94816-9 (lib bdg); 0-375-84816-3 (lib bdg)

LC 2007-49034

In medieval Germany, fifteen-year-old Conrad, a court jester, and his beloved Christa, a servant girl, escape from a cruel master and journey through the countryside on a quest to find a kind lord who will give them sanctuary.

"Karr does an splendid job of recreating the medieval milieu, especially the life of a professional entertainer with all of its challenges and hardships." Booklist

Kass, Pnina

Real time; by Pnina Moed Kass. Clarion Books 2004 186p $15; pa $7.99

Grades: 7 8 9 10   **Fic**

1. Israel—Fiction 2. Germans—Israel—Fiction 3. Terrorism—Fiction

ISBN 0-618-44203-0; 0-618-69174-X (pa)

LC 2004-8481

Sixteen-year-old Tomas Wanninger persuades his mother to let him leave Germany to volunteer at a kibbutz in Israel, where he experiences a violent political attack and finds answers about his own past

This "volume is an exhausting but illuminating read that will provide much-needed insight into life in modern Israel. . . . The characters are deeply developed and painfully sympathetic." SLJ

Katcher, Brian

Playing with matches. Delacorte Press 2008 294p $15.99; lib bdg $18.99

Grades: 8 9 10 11 12   **Fic**

1. Burns and scalds—Fiction 2. School stories 3. Missouri—Fiction 4. Dating (Social customs)—Fiction

ISBN 978-0-385-73544-5; 0-385-73544-8; 978-0-385-90525-1 (lib bdg); 0-385-90525-4 (lib bdg)

LC 2007-27654

While trying to find a girl who will date him, Missouri high school junior Leon Sanders befriends a lonely, disfigured female classmate.

"This is a strong debut novel with a cast of quirky, multidimensional characters struggling with issues of acceptance, sexuality, identity, and self-worth." SLJ

Keaney, Brian

The hollow people; [illustrated by Nicoletta Ceccoli] Knopf 2007 224p il (The promises of Dr. Sigmundus) $16.99; lib bdg $19.99

Grades: 6 7 8 9   **Fic**

1. Science fiction

ISBN 978-0-375-84332-7; 0-375-84332-9; 978-0-375-94332-4 (lib bdg); 0-375-94332-3 (lib bdg)

LC 2006-31137

On an island that houses the asylum where lawbreakers are imprisoned, two teenagers rebel against a rigidly controlled society where dreams are considered antisocial and all citizens over the age of fourteen take a drug to control their behavior.

"Keaney's concoction of science fiction, horror, and fantasy is remarkably effective." Bull Cent Child Books

Followed by: The cracked mirror (2008)

Jacob's ladder. Candlewick Press 2007 218p $15.99

Grades: 6 7 8 9 10   **Fic**

1. Amnesia—Fiction 2. Death—Fiction

ISBN 978-0-7636-3071-3; 0-7636-3071-3

LC 2006-51795

When Jacob wakes up in the middle of a field, he realizes that the only thing he remembers is his name. When he arrives at a nearby town, he becomes aware that everyone there is also suffering from amnesia.

"This intriguing novel starts like science fiction, but ends as something entirely different. . . . An accessible, discussable read." SLJ

Keehn, Sally M., 1947-

Gnat Stokes and the Foggy Bottom Swamp Queen; [by] Sally M. Keehn. Philomel Books 2005 152p il $16.99

Grades: 5 6 7 8   **Fic**

1. Magic—Fiction 2. Tennessee—Fiction

ISBN 0-399-24287-2   LC 2003-26635

In Mary's Cove, Tennessee, in 1869, twelve-year-old Gnat Stokes decides to prove she's not just a trouble maker by rescuing a boy who was spirited away seven years earlier by the evil Swamp Queen of Foggy Bottom.

"Keehn's tale is by turns, creepy, laugh-aloud funny, touching, and utterly satisfying. Her voice is sassy and straight out of the Tennessee hills." Booklist

Magpie Gabbard and the quest for the buried moon; [by] Sally M. Keehn. Philomel Books 2007 198p $16.99

Grades: 5 6 7 8   **Fic**

1. Family life—Fiction 2. Moon—Fiction 3. Fairies—Fiction 4. Kentucky—Fiction 5. Tall tales

ISBN 978-0-399-24340-0; 0-399-24340-2

LC 2006008920

In Kentucky in 1872, when goblins capture the moon, thirteen-year-old Magpie must rise above her family's fighting legacy and put her "cussedness" to use to save the moon and her loved ones, according to "the age-old prophecy."

"Keehn captures Appalachian colloquialisms and language to perfection while maintaining an action-packed, rip-snorting, hilarious pace that never lets readers go." SLJ

Kehret, Peg, 1936-

Abduction! [by] Peg Kehret. 1st ed. Dutton Children's Books 2004 215p $16.99

Grades: 5 6 7 8   **Fic**

1. Kidnapping—Fiction

ISBN 0-525-47294-0   LC 2003-63531

Thirteen-year-old Bonnie has a feeling of foreboding on the very day that her six-year-old brother Matt and their dog Pookie are abducted, and she becomes involved in a major search effort as well as a frightening adventure

"This novel has enough suspense to keep children interested, and it will also appeal to reluctant readers." SLJ

Don't tell anyone. Dutton Children's Bks. 2000 137p $15.99; pa $5.99

Grades: 5 6 7 8   **Fic**

1. Cats—Fiction 2. Criminals—Fiction

ISBN 0-525-46388-7; 0-14-230031-4 (pa)

LC 99-89605

Twelve-year-old Megan does not realize that feeding a group of feral cats living in a field near her house will involve her as a witness to a traffic accident and in the dangerous plan of an unstable criminal

"There are subplots galore in this quick read . . . but they all hang together, and thanks to Kehret's even tone, the scary aspects won't frighten younger readers." Booklist

The ghost's grave. Dutton Children's Books 2005 210p $16.99

Grades: 5 6 7 8   **Fic**

1. Ghost stories 2. Coal miners—Fiction 3. Washington (State)—Fiction

ISBN 0-525-46162-0   LC 2004-22064

Apprehensive about spending the summer in Washington State with his Aunt Ethel when his parents get an overseas job, twelve-year-old Josh soon finds adventure when he meets the ghost of a coal miner.

"This fast-paced and engaging book should be a hit with fans of ghost stories. Josh is a rich character to whom readers can relate." SLJ

Trapped! [by] Peg Kehret and Pete the Cat. 1st ed. Dutton Children's Books 2006 177p $16.99

Grades: 4 5 6 7   **Fic**

1. Trapping—Fiction 2. Cats—Fiction 3. Mystery fiction

ISBN 0-525-47728-4; 978-0-525-47728-0

LC 2005032962

When his owner, Alex, finds an illegal animal trap in the woods, Pete the cat faces grave danger as he tries to help his human friends find the culprit who set the trap.

"Animal lovers will get a kick out of this intriguing mystery." Booklist

Keith, Harold, 1903-1998

Rifles for Watie. Crowell 1957 332p $16.89; pa $5.99 *

Grades: 6 7 8 9   **Fic**

1. Watie, Stand, 1806-1871—Fiction 2. United States—History—1861-1865, Civil War—Fiction

ISBN 0-690-04907-2; 0-06-447030-X (pa)

Awarded the Newbery Medal, 1958

"Young Jeff Bussey longs for the life of a Union soldier during the Civil War, but before long he realizes the cruelty and savagery of some men in the army situation. The war loses its glamor as he sees his very young friends die. When he is made a scout, his duties take him into the ranks of Stand Watie, leader of the rebel troops of the Cherokee Indian Nation, as a spy. He makes good friends among the enemy troops and falls in love with Lucy Washbourne, beautiful part-Cherokee girl and rebel sympathizer." Stensland. Lit By & About the Am Indian

"An exceptionally well-written story of the Civil War as it was fought in the western states." Bull Cent Child Books

Kelly, Jacqueline

The evolution of Calpurnia Tate. Henry Holt and Co. 2009 340p $16.99 *

Grades: 4 5 6 7   **Fic**

1. Nature—Fiction 2. Family life—Fiction 3. Grandfathers—Fiction 4. Naturalists—Fiction 5. Texas—Fiction

ISBN 978-0-8050-8841-0; 0-8050-8841-5

LC 2008-40595

In central Texas in 1899, eleven-year-old Callie Vee Tate is instructed to be a lady by her mother, learns about love from the older three of her six brothers, and studies the natural world with her grandfather, the latter of which leads to an important discovery.

"Callie is a charming, inquisitive protagonist; a joyous, bright, and thoughtful creation. . . . Several scenes . . . mix gentle humor and pathos to great effect." SLJ

Kelly, Tom, 1961-

Finn's going. Greenwillow Books 2007 278p $16.99; lib bdg $17.89

Grades: 6 7 8 9   **Fic**

1. Death—Fiction 2. Bereavement—Fiction 3. Runaway children—Fiction 4. Twins—Fiction 5. Brothers—Fiction 6. Great Britain—Fiction

ISBN 978-0-06-121453-0; 978-0-06-121454-7 (lib bdg); 0-06-121453-1; 0-06-121454-X (lib bdg)

LC 2006-50121

A ten-year-old English boy decides to run away after the sadness at home becomes unbearable following the death of his twin brother.

"Though sad, this is an ultimately life-affirming book, full of poignant insights." Booklist

Kennedy, James, 1973-

The Order of Odd-Fish; [by] James Kennedy. Delacorte Press 2008 403p $15.99; lib bdg $18.99

Grades: 6 7 8 9   **Fic**

1. Aunts—Fiction 2. Adventure fiction

ISBN 978-0-385-73543-8; 0-385-73543-X; 978-0-385-90524-4 (lib bdg); 0-385-90524-6 (lib bdg)

LC 2008-00711

Thirteen-year-old Jo suddenly finds her humdrum life turned upside down when Colonel Anatoly Kordakov shows up at her aunt's party and announces he has come to protect her.

"This clever, creative story will keep readers engaged and laughing." Libr Media Connect

Kent, Rose

Kimchi & calamari. HarperCollinsPublishers 2007 220p $15.99; lib bdg $16.89

Grades: 4 5 6 7   **Fic**

1. Korean Americans—Fiction 2. Italian Americans—Fiction 3. Adoption—Fiction

ISBN   978-0-06-083769-3;   0-06-083769-1; 9780060837709 (lib bdg); 0-06-083770-5 (lib bdg)

LC 2006-20041

"Fourteen-year-old Korean adoptee Joseph Calderaro is stumped when his social studies teacher assigns an ancestry essay. . . . Kent's debut novel humorously captures the feelings of a young teen who thoroughly enjoys his Italian-American family but still wonders about his birth parents." Booklist

Kephart, Beth

House of Dance. HarperTeen 2008 263p $16.99; lib bdg $17.89 *

Grades: 7 8 9 10   **Fic**

1. Cancer—Fiction 2. Death—Fiction 3. Dancers—Fiction 4. Grandfathers—Fiction 5. Mother-daughter relationship—Fiction

ISBN   978-0-06-142928-6;   0-06-142928-7; 978-0-06-142929-3 (lib bdg); 0-06-142929-5 (lib bdg)

LC 2007-26011

"Laura Geringer books"

During one of her daily visits across town to visit her dying grandfather, fifteen-year-old Rosie discovers a dance studio that helps her find a way to bring her family members together.

This is "distinguished more by its sharp, eloquent prose than by its plot. . . . Poetically expressed memories and moving dialogue both anchor and amplify the characters' emotions." Publ Wkly

Undercover. HarperTeen 2007 278p $16.99; lib bdg $17.89 *

Grades: 8 9 10 11 12   **Fic**

1. Poetry—Fiction 2. School stories 3. Family life—Fiction

ISBN   978-0-06-123893-2;   0-06-123893-7; 978-0-06-123894-9 (lib bdg); 0-06-123894-5 (lib bdg)

LC 2007-2981

"Laura Geringer books"

High school sophomore Elisa is used to observing while going unnoticed except when classmates ask her to write love notes for them, but a teacher's recognition of her talent, a "client's" desire for her friendship, a love of ice skating, and her parent's marital problems draw her out of herself.

"Kephart tells a moving story. . . . Readers will fall easily into the compelling premise and Elisa's memorable, graceful voice." Booklist

Kerley, Barbara

Greetings from planet Earth. Scholastic Press 2007 246p $16.99

Grades: 5 6 7 8   **Fic**

1. Father-son relationship—Fiction 2. Vietnam War, 1961-1975—Fiction 3. Family life—Fiction

ISBN 0-439-80203-2; 978-0-439-80203-1

LC 2006-11300

In 1977, as twelve-year-old Theo struggles with a science class project on space exploration, questions emerge about why his father never returned from Vietnam and why Theo's mother has been keeping secrets for many years.

"The novel convincingly portrays a family overshadowed by secrets." Booklist

Kerr, M. E., 1927-

Gentlehands. Harper & Row 1978 183p pa $5.99 hardcover o.p.

Grades: 7 8 9 10   **Fic**

1. Grandfathers—Fiction 2. Social classes—Fiction 3. Criminals—Fiction

ISBN 978-0-06-447067-4 (pa); 0-06-447067-9 (pa)

LC 77-11860

"Buddy Boyle falls for Skye and her affluent, breezy way of life. Finding his own parents not 'cultured' enough for this new relationship, Buddy turns to his grandfather, whose love of opera and other refinements make him more suitable to make Skye's acquaintance. A shocking surprise awaits Buddy when Mr. DeLucca, pursuer of an infamous Nazi, finally identifies his quarry." Shapiro. Fic for youth. 3rd edition

Slap your sides; a novel. HarperCollins Pubs. 2001 198p pa $5.99 hardcover o.p.

Grades: 7 8 9 10   **Fic**

1. World War, 1939-1945—Fiction 2. Brothers—Fiction 3. Conscientious objectors—Fiction 4. Society of Friends—Fiction

ISBN 0-06-447274-4 (pa)   LC 00-54037

Life in their Pennsylvania hometown changes for Jubal Shoemaker and his family when his older brother witnesses to his Quaker beliefs by becoming a conscientious objector during World War II

"The ideas are gripping, not only because Kerr is fair to all sides but also because the characters are complicated." Booklist

Snakes don't miss their mothers; a novel. HarperCollins 2003 195p hardcover o.p. pa $5.99

Grades: 4 5 6   **Fic**

1. Animal shelters—Fiction 2. Animals—Fiction

ISBN 0-06-052624-6; 0-06-052626-2 (pa)

LC 2002-153772

The animals at Critters animal shelter look forward to Christmas as well as the ever-present possiblility of adoption

"Kerr poignantly gives voice to the loneliness and needs of these abandoned animals." Voice Youth Advocates

Someone like summer. HarperTempest 2007 263p $16.99; lib bdg $17.89 *

Grades: 7 8 9 10   **Fic**

1. Immigrants—Fiction 2. Prejudices—Fiction 3. Father-daughter relationship—Fiction 4. Love stories

ISBN   978-0-06-114099-0;   0-06-114099-6; 978-0-06-114100-3 (lib bdg); 0-06-114100-3 (lib bdg)

LC 2006-21465

An upper-middle-class white girl from Long Island and an immigrant worker from Colombia fall in love de-

Kerr, M. E., 1927-—*Continued*

spite objections from both their families and their community.

This is a "stirring teen romance. . . . The main characters disturb all the stereotypes." Booklist

Kerr, Philip

One small step; [by] P.B. Kerr. Margaret K. McElderry Books 2008 309p $16.99

Grades: 6 7 8 9   **Fic**

1. Air pilots—Fiction 2. Father-son relationship—Fiction 3. Space flight—Fiction 4. Houston (Tex.)—Fiction

ISBN 978-1-4169-4213-9; 1-4169-4213-0

LC 2007-35660

In 1969 Houston, Texas, thirteen-year-old Scott learns to fly from his father, an Air Force flight instructor, but when NASA needs him for a secret space mission, Scott's elation is tempered by concern that his mother, who has moved to Florida, will find out.

"This is a gripping and well-researched piece of space-age historical fiction." SLJ

Key, Watt, 1970-

Alabama moon. 1st ed. Farrar, Straus & Giroux 2006 294p $16

Grades: 5 6 7 8   **Fic**

1. Orphans—Fiction 2. Wilderness survival—Fiction 3. Alabama—Fiction

ISBN 0-374-30184-0   LC 2005-40165

After the death of his father, ten-year-old Moon leaves their forest shelter home and is sent to an Alabama institution, becoming entangled in the outside world he has never known and making good friends, a relentless enemy, and finally a new life.

"The book is well written with a flowing style, plenty of dialogue, and lots of action. The characters are well drawn and three-dimensional." SLJ

Khan, Rukhsana, 1962-

Wanting Mor. Groundwood Books/House of Anansi Press 2009 190p $17.95

Grades: 6 7 8 9   **Fic**

1. Afghanistan—Fiction 2. Birth defects—Fiction 3. Bereavement—Fiction 4. Sex role—Fiction

ISBN 978-0-8889-9858-3; 0-8889-9858-9

Jameela and her family live in a poor, war-torn village in Afghanistan. Even with her cleft lip and lack of educational opportunities, Jameela feels relatively secure, sustained by her Muslim faith and the love of her mother, Mor. But when Mor dies, Jameela's father impulsively decides to start a new life in Kabul.

"This compelling story is based on real incidents. Jameela's matter-of-fact, first person narrative will awaken young readers to life and conditions in Afghanistan." Booklist

Kidd, Ronald, 1948-

Monkey town; the summer of the Scopes trial. Simon & Schuster Books for Young Readers 2006 259p $15.95

Grades: 6 7 8 9   **Fic**

1. Scopes, John Thomas—Fiction 2. Evolution—Study and teaching—Fiction 3. Father-daughter relationship—Fiction 4. Tennessee—Fiction

ISBN 1-4169-0572-3   LC 2005-08920

When her father hatches a plan to bring publicity to their small Tennessee town by arresting a local high school teacher for teaching about evolution, the resulting 1925 Scopes trial prompts fifteen-year-old Frances to rethink many of her beliefs about religion and truth, as well as her relationship with her father.

"A unique and heartfelt story of a likable girl maturing through an unforgettable summer in American history. An excellent read and a wonderful piece of literature." SLJ

On Beale Street. Simon & Schuster Books for Young Readers 2008 244p $16.99

Grades: 7 8 9 10 11 12   **Fic**

1. Presley, Elvis, 1935-1977—Fiction 2. Rock music—Fiction 3. Race relations—Fiction 4. Segregation—Fiction 5. Memphis (Tenn.)—Fiction

ISBN 978-1-4169-3387-8; 1-4169-3387-5

LC 2007-22583

In Memphis, in the 1950's, when fifteen-year-old Johnny is introduced to the blues, he ventures to the infamous Beale Street and finds the friendship with an up-and-coming young musician Elvis Presley.

"This novel is a fascinating glimpse into the musical world of Beale Street, the society that was the segregated South, [and] the origins of rock and roll. . . . Accurate historical details are skillfully woven into what becomes an absorbing search for personal identity." School Library Journal

Kilworth, Garry

Attica. Little, Brown 2009 334p pa $11.95

Grades: 5 6 7 8   **Fic**

1. Fantasy fiction 2. Stepfamilies—Fiction

ISBN 978-1-9042-3356-5; 1-9042-3356-2

"New stepsiblings Jordy, Chloe and Alex move into a duplex landlorded by initially crotchety Mr. Grantham. When the children venture into the attic to find Grantham's pocket watch, they find a vast world that they dub Attica." Kirkus

"The children have distinct personalities and react to Attica in realistic ways, finding their own strengths in this exhilarating, unpredictable environment. This book is a rare find." Booklist

Kimmel, Elizabeth Cody

Lily B. on the brink of cool. HarperCollins Pubs. 2003 245p $15.99; lib bdg $16.89 *

Grades: 5 6 7 8   **Fic**

1. Authorship—Fiction 2. Family life—Fiction

ISBN 0-06-000586-6; 0-06-000587-4 (lib bdg)

LC 2002-13385

"The eventually internationally recognized writer Lily Blennerhassett" spends her thirteenth summer missing her

Kimmel, Elizabeth Cody—*Continued*

best friend and keeping a journal of her boring life at home and exciting newly-discovered relatives

"The pacing of the book is fast and smooth." SLJ

Other titles about Lily B. are:

Lily B. on the brink of love (2005)

Lily B. on the brink of Paris (2006)

Spin the bottle. Dial Books for Young Readers 2008 240p $16.99

Grades: 5 6 7 8   **Fic**

1. School stories 2. Theater—Fiction 3. Friendship—Fiction

ISBN 978-0-8037-3191-2; 0-8037-3191-4

LC 2007-17127

When aspiring actress Phoebe and her best friend, the brainy Harper, enter middle school, their friendship is briefly tested by Phoebe's admiration of some of the drama club students and the intensity of her first crush, but ultimately they find that their relationship can withstand the stresses of their expanding lives.

"Brainy, self-contained Harper is a cool and tough-minded character, an intriguing contrast to Phoebe. . . . Top that with the jammy goodness of a theatrical story and the rich spinklings of sweet, rueful humor . . . and you've got a tasty concoction." Bull Cent Child Books

Kindl, Patrice, 1951-

Lost in the labyrinth; a novel. Houghton Mifflin 2002 194p $16

Grades: 6 7 8 9   **Fic**

1. Classical mythology—Fiction

ISBN 0-618-16684-X   LC 2002-406

Fourteen-year-old Princess Xenodice tries to prevent the death of her half-brother, the Minotaur, at the hands of the Athenian prince, Theseus, who is aided by Icarus, Daedalus, and her sister Ariadne

"Attentive to both archaeological detail and emotional probity, Kindl fleshes out the Minotaur myth's bare bones and brings it to life." Horn Book

Owl in love. Houghton Mifflin 1993 204p hardcover o.p. pa $6.99 *

Grades: 6 7 8 9   **Fic**

1. Supernatural—Fiction 2. Owls—Fiction 3. Teachers—Fiction

ISBN 0-395-66162-5; 0-618-43910-2 (pa)

LC 92-26952

Also available in paperback from Penguin Bks.

A fourteen-year-old girl, who can transform into an owl, has a crush on her science teacher which leads her into interesting new relationships with both humans and owls

"Kindl's prose is remarkably even in its wit, one of many virtues in this tautly plotted and touching novel." Publ Wkly

King, Ron

The quantum July; [by] Ron King. 1st ed. Delacorte Press 2007 244p $15.99; lib bdg $18.99

Grades: 6 7 8 9   **Fic**

1. Quantum theory—Fiction 2. Siblings—Fiction 3. Family life—Fiction

ISBN 978-0-385-73418-9; 978-0-385-90432-2 (lib bdg)   LC 2007002409

As problems escalate between their parents, a Harvard-educated stock boy and a would-be physicist, thirteen-year-old Danny agrees to participate in his twelve-year-old sister's experiments with quantum physics, through which he hopes he can change their lives for the better.

"The boy's longings for a better life and a better father are moving, while the complexities of the choices he must make and the mind-expanding speculative aspects of the novel will challenge and engage readers' imaginations." Booklist

Kinney, Jeff

Diary of a wimpy kid: Greg Heffley's journal. Amulet Books 2007 217p pa $14.95 *

Grades: 5 6 7 8   **Fic**

1. Friendship—Fiction 2. School stories

ISBN 978-0-8109-9313-6; 0-8109-9313-9

LC 2006-31847

Greg records his sixth grade experiences in a middle school where he and his best friend, Rowley, undersized weaklings amid boys who need to shave twice daily, hope just to survive, but when Rowley grows more popular, Greg must take drastic measures to save their friendship.

"Kinney's background as a cartoonist is apparent in this hybrid book that falls somewhere between traditional prose and graphic novel. . . . The pace moves quickly. The first of three installments, it is an excellent choice for reluctant readers, but more experienced readers will also find much to enjoy and relate to." SLJ

Other titles about Greg are:

Diary of a wimpy kid: Rodrick rules (2008)

Diary of a wimpy kid: the last straw (2009)

Kirk, Daniel

Elf realm: the low road. Amulet Books 2008 498p il $18.95 *

Grades: 5 6 7 8   **Fic**

1. Fantasy fiction 2. Fairies—Fiction 3. Magic—Fiction

ISBN 978-0-8109-7069-4; 0-8109-7069-4

LC 2007039751

When Matt and his family move to a new development, they stumble into the middle of massive upheaval in the Fairy world, and as the elves' territory disintegrates and dark factions try to seize control, an apprentice mage sees in Matt the key to saving the realms from destruction.

"The complex, suspense-filled plot pits humans against elves and elves against elves. Highly imaginative, intricately described, and filled with a wide cast of memorable characters, this is a thoroughly engaging fantasy that never lags." Booklist

Kladstrup, Kristin

The book of story beginnings. Candlewick Press 2006 360p $15.99

Grades: 4 5 6 7   **Fic**

1. Authorship—Fiction 2. Storytelling—Fiction 3. Magic—Fiction 4. Space and time—Fiction

ISBN 0-7636-2609-0   LC 2005054262

Kladstrup, Kristin—*Continued*

After moving with her parents to Iowa, twelve-year-old Lucy discovers a mysterious notebook that can bring stories to life and which has a link to the 1914 disappearance of her great uncle.

"Kladstrup's first novel offers mystery, adventure, and fantasy, as well as reflections on family dynamics, time travel, and the structure of stories." Booklist

Klages, Ellen, 1954-

The green glass sea. Viking 2006 321p $16.99
*

Grades: 5 6 7 8   Fic
1. Scientists—Fiction 2. Atomic bomb—Fiction 3. World War, 1939-1945—Fiction 4. New Mexico—Fiction
ISBN 0-670-06134-4

It is 1943, and 11-year-old Dewey Kerrigan is traveling west on a train to live with her scientist father—but no one will tell her exactly where he is. When she reaches Los Alamos, New Mexico, she learns why: he's working on a top secret government program.

"Many readers will know as little about the true nature of the project as the girls do, so the gradual revelation of facts is especially effective, while those who already know about Los Alamos's historical significance will experience the story in a different, but equally powerful, way." SLJ

Followed by: White sands, red menace (2008)

Klass, David, 1960-

Dark angel. Farrar, Straus & Giroux 2005 311p $17

Grades: 7 8 9 10   Fic
1. Brothers—Fiction 2. School stories
ISBN 0-374-39950-6   LC 2004-53340
Also available in paperback from HarperCollins
"Frances Foster books"

When his older brother is released from prison, seventeen-year-old Jeff's family secret is revealed, causing upheaval in his home, school and love life.

"The plot builds ferociously in tandem with Jeff's suffocating conflict and burgeoning courage. . . . Recommend this fast-paced, thoughtful story to older reluctant readers, especially boys." SLJ

Firestorm. 1st ed. Frances Foster Books 2006 289p (The Caretaker trilogy) $17

Grades: 8 9 10 11 12   Fic
1. Science fiction
ISBN 0-374-32307-0   LC 2005-52112

After learning that he has been sent from the future for a special purpose, eighteen-year-old Jack receives help from an unusual dog and a shape-shifting female fighter.

"The sobering events and tone are leavened with engaging humor, and the characters are multidimensional. The relentless pace, coupled with issues of ecology, time travel, self-identity, and sexual awakening, makes for a thrilling and memorable read." SLJ

Followed by Whirlwind (2008)

Home of the Braves. Farrar, Straus & Giroux 2002 312p $18

Grades: 7 8 9 10   Fic
1. Soccer—Fiction 2. School stories
ISBN 0-374-39963-8   LC 2002-19391
Also available in paperback from HarperCollins
"Frances Foster books"

Eighteen-year-old Joe, captain of the soccer team, is dismayed when a hotshot player shows up from Brazil and threatens to take over both the team and the girl whom Joe hopes to date.

"A gritty, realistic story of a robust insider with his feet planted solidly on the ground. . . . More than a sports story, [this] is a first-rate coming-of-age novel." Voice Youth Advocates

Klass, Sheila Solomon

Soldier's secret; the story of Deborah Sampson. Henry Holt 2009 215p $17.95 *

Grades: 6 7 8 9 10   Fic
1. Sampson, Deborah, 1760-1827—Fiction 2. United States—History—1775-1783, Revolution—Fiction 3. Soldiers—Fiction
ISBN 978-0-8050-8200-5; 0-8050-8200-X
     LC 2008-36783
"Christy Ottaviano books"

During the Revolutionary War, a young woman named Deborah Sampson disguises herself as a man in order to serve in the Continental Army.

In this novel, Sampson "is strong, brave, and witty. . . . Klass doesn't shy away from the horrors of battle; she also is blunt regarding details young readers will wonder about, like how Sampson dealt with bathing, urination, and menstruation. . . . Sampson's romantic yearnings for a fellow soldier . . . is given just the right notes or restraint and realism." Booklist

Klause, Annette Curtis

The silver kiss. Delacorte Press 1990 198p hardcover o.p. pa $5.99

Grades: 8 9 10 11 12   Fic
1. Vampires—Fiction 2. Death—Fiction
ISBN 0-385-30160-X; 0-440-21346-0 (pa)
     LC 89-48880

"One evening, when 17-year-old Zoë is sitting in the park contemplating her mother's imminent death due to cancer, her father's lack of support, and her best friend's move, she meets Simon. Simon is startlingly handsome and strangely compelling. As their friendship grows over time, Simon reveals to Zoë his true identity: he is a vampire, trying to kill his younger vampire brother." SLJ

"There's inherent romantic appeal in the vampire legend, and Klause weaves all the gory details into a poignant love story that becomes both sensuous and suspenseful." Booklist

Klein, Lisa M., 1958-

Two girls of Gettysburg; [by] Lisa Klein. Bloomsbury U.S.A. Children's Books 2008 393p $16.99

Grades: 7 8 9 10   **Fic**

1. Gettysburg (Pa.), Battle of, 1863—Fiction 2. United States—History—1861-1865, Civil War—Fiction 3. Cousins—Fiction

ISBN 978-1-59990-105-3; 1-59990-105-6

LC 2008-10322

When the Civil War breaks out, two cousins, Lizzie and Rosanna, find themselves on opposite sides of the conflict until the war reunites them in the town of Gettysburg.

"Terrific action and lively characterizations move the story along well." Booklist

Kline, Lisa Williams, 1954-

Write before your eyes; [by] Lisa Williams Kline. Delacorte Press 2008 178p $15.99; lib bdg $18.99

Grades: 5 6 7 8   **Fic**

1. Magic—Fiction 2. Friendship—Fiction 3. Family life—Fiction 4. School stories 5. Georgia—Fiction

ISBN   978-0-385-73568-1;   0-385-73568-5; 978-0-385-90556-5 (lib bdg); 0-385-90556-4 (lib bdg)

LC 2008-35674

An old journal seems to be eighth-grader Gracie's ticket to the worlds of magic of which she has read, but her writings not only come true, they have unexpected consequences for her family and her best friend, would-be boyfriend Dylan.

"The author provides an excellent depiction of family communications and a pre-teen hierarchy of school life. Fantasy is interwoven into the realistic setting in a very believable way." Libr Media Connect

Klinger, Shula

The Kingdom of Strange; a novel; by Shula Klinger. 1st ed. Marshall Cavendish 2008 298p $16.99

Grades: 6 7 8 9   **Fic**

1. Authorship—Fiction 2. School stories

ISBN 978-0-76145-395-6; 0-76145-395-4

LC 2007015853

An English class project to find one's audience as a writer by posting original works on a blog leads fourteen-year-old Thisbe on a journey of self-discovery and new friendship.

"Young would-be authors will identify with Thisbe's steady determination to be a writer and benefit from her exercises and not-quite lectures as well." Booklist

Klise, Kate

Deliver us from Normal; by Kate Klise. 1st ed. Scholastic Press 2005 226p $16.95 *

Grades: 6 7 8 9   **Fic**

1. Family life—Fiction 2. Illinois—Fiction

ISBN 0-439-52322-2   LC 2004-42906

With a mother who buys Christmas cards in August and a younger brother who describes the Trinity as a toasted marshmallow on a graham cracker, life for elev-

en-year-old Charles Harrisong is anything but normal in Normal, Illinois.

"Through Charles's narration, Klise offers a stunningly realistic look at the concatenations that the boy's obsessive thinking weaves. . . . A superb psychological novel." SLJ

Another title about Charles Harrisong is:

Far from Normal (2006)

Letters from camp; illustrated by M. Sarah Klise. Avon Bks. 1999 178p il hardcover o.p. pa $5.99

Grades: 4 5 6 7   **Fic**

1. Camps—Fiction 2. Siblings—Fiction 3. Letters—Fiction

ISBN 0-380-97539-4; 0-380-79348-2 (pa)

LC 98-52315

Sent to Camp Happy Harmony to learn how to get along with each other, pairs of brothers and sisters chronicle in letters home how they come to suspect the intentions of the singing family running the camp

This is a "delightfully wacky story. . . . The humor is very gentle and tongue-in-cheek. . . . An entirely satisfying camp adventure." Booklist

Regarding the sink; where, oh where, did Waters go? illustrated by M. Sarah Klise. Harcourt 2004 127p il $15

Grades: 4 5 6 7   **Fic**

1. School stories

ISBN 0-15-205019-1   LC 2003-26560

A series of letters reveals the selection of the famous fountain designer, Florence Waters, to design a new sink for the Geyser Creek Middle School cafeteria, her subsequent disappearance, and the efforts of a class of sixth-graders to find her

"Piecing the story and clues together is satisfying. Introduce this book to savvy readers who are ready for the jump to a clever, unconventional reading experience." SLJ

Other titles in this series are:

Regarding the bathrooms (2006)

Regarding the bees (2007)

Regarding the fountain (1998)

Regarding the trees (2005)

Kluger, Jeffrey

Nacky Patcher and the curse of the dry-land boats; a novel; with illustrations by David Elliot. Philomel Books 2007 374p il $18.99

Grades: 7 8 9 10   **Fic**

1. Shipbuilding—Fiction 2. Orphans—Fiction 3. Fantasy fiction

ISBN 978-0-399-24604-3; 0-399-24604-5

LC 2006-34534

When thief and swindler Nacky Patcher and orphaned eleven-year-old Teedie Flinn discover a huge wrecked boat in a small mountain lake near their town, they try to unite all the inhabitants to help rebuild the vessel – an endeavor that forever changes all of their lives.

"Eager readers with an appreciation for imaginative language and storytelling will be rewarded by this singular novel." Voice Youth Advocates

Kluger, Steve

My most excellent year; a novel of love, Mary Poppins, & Fenway Park. Dial Books 2008 403p $16.99; pa $8.99 *

Grades: 8 9 10 11 12   **Fic**
1. Boston (Mass.)—Fiction 2. Friendship—Fiction
ISBN   978-0-8037-3227-8;   0-8037-3227-9;
978-0-14-241343-2 (pa); 0-14-2413437 (pa)
LC 2007-26651

"Three bright and funny Brookline, MA, eleventh graders look back on their most excellent year—ninth grade—for a school report. Told in alternating chapters by each of them, this enchanting, life-affirming coming-of-age story unfolds through instant messages, emails, memos, diary entries, and letters. . . . This is a rich and humorous novel for older readers." SLJ

Knudsen, Michelle

The dragon of Trelian. Candlewick Press 2009 407p $16.99

Grades: 4 5 6 7   **Fic**
1. Fantasy fiction 2. Dragons—Fiction 3. Princesses—Fiction 4. Magic—Fiction
ISBN 978-0-7636-3455-1; 0-7636-3455-7
LC 2008025378

A mage's apprentice, a princess, and a dragon combine their strength and magic to bring down a traitor and restore peace to the kingdom of Trelian.

"Knudsen does a fantastic job of creating sympathetic and realistic characters that really drive the story. The tale is adventurous and exciting with many twists and turns along the way." SLJ

Koertge, Ronald

Stoner & Spaz; [by] Ron Koertge. Candlewick Press 2002 169p hardcover o.p. pa $6.99 *

Grades: 7 8 9 10   **Fic**
1. Cerebral palsy—Fiction 2. School stories
ISBN 0-7636-1608-7; 0-7636-2150-1 (pa)
LC 2001-43050

A troubled youth with cerebral palsy struggles toward self-acceptance with the help of a drug-addicted young woman

"Funny, touching, and surprising, it is a hopeful yet realistic view of things as they are and as they could be." Booklist

Strays; [by] Ron Koertge. Candlewick Press 2007 167p $16.99 *

Grades: 7 8 9 10 11 12   **Fic**
1. Foster home care—Fiction 2. Orphans—Fiction
ISBN 978-0-7636-2705-8; 0-7636-2705-4
LC 2007-24096

After his parents are killed in a car accident, high school senior Sam wonders whether he will ever feel again or if he will remain numbed by grief.

"Though Koertge never soft pedals the horrors faced by some foster children, this thoughtful novel about the lost and abandoned is a hopeful one." Booklist

Kogler, Jennifer Anne

Ruby Tuesday. HarperCollins Publishers 2005 307p $15.99; lib bdg $16.89

Grades: 7 8 9 10   **Fic**
1. Family life—Fiction 2. Gambling—Fiction 3. Las Vegas (Nev.)—Fiction
ISBN 0-06-073956-8; 0-06-073957-6 (lib bdg)
LC 2004-21507

The 1988 World Series win by the Los Angeles Dodgers sets off a chain of life-changing events for thirteen-year-old Ruby Tuesday as she travels to Las Vegas and learns some surprising truths about her family members and their careers as gamblers and musicians.

"Kogler's characters are entertaining, captivating, and in general, fun to read about. . . . The book is a page-turner." Voice Youth Advocates

Koja, Kathe

Buddha Boy. Farrar, Straus & Giroux 2003 117p $16 *

Grades: 7 8 9 10   **Fic**
1. Artists—Fiction 2. Buddhism—Fiction 3. School stories
ISBN 0-374-30998-1   LC 2002-25067
"Frances Foster books"

"When Jinsen arrives at Edward Rucher High School coatless in winter, sporting a bald head, begging for money in the school cafeteria, and talking about karma, he is immediately dubbed 'Buddha Boy' by the resident bullies. Justin, the narrator . . . is forced to work on a school project with Jinsen and discovers the newcomer's incredible artistic talent. . . . Mesmerized by Jinsen's art and philosophy, Justin befriends him and learns about Jinsen's hostile past." Voice Youth Advocates

"A compelling introduction to Buddhism and a credible portrait of how true friendship brings out the best in people." Publ Wkly

Headlong. Farrar, Straus and Giroux 2008 195p $16.95 *

Grades: 8 9 10 11 12   **Fic**
1. School stories 2. Social classes—Fiction 3. Orphans—Fiction
ISBN 978-0-374-32912-9; 0-374-32912-5
LC 2007-23612

"Frances Foster books"

High school sophomore Lily opens herself to new possibilities when, despite warnings, she becomes friends with 'ghetto girl' Hazel, a new student at the private Vaughn School which Lily, following in her elitist mother's footsteps, has attended since preschool.

"Class, identity and friendship are the intersecting subjects of this intelligent novel. . . . [The author] relays this story with her usual insight and, through her lightning-fast characterizations, an ability to project multiple perspectives simultaneously." Publ Wkly

Kissing the bee. Farrar, Straus and Giroux 2007 121p $16 *

Grades: 8 9 10 11 12   **Fic**
1. School stories 2. Bees—Fiction 3. Love stories 4. Friendship—Fiction
ISBN 978-0-374-39938-2; 0-374-39938-7
LC 2006-37378

"Frances Foster books"

Koja, Kathe—*Continued*

While working on a bee project for her advanced biology class, quiet high school senior Dana reflects on her relationship with gorgeous best friend Avra and Avra's boyfriend Emil, whom Dana secretly loves.

The "understated, tightly focused language evokes vivid scenes and heady emotions." Publ Wkly

Straydog. Farrar, Straus & Giroux 2002 105p $16

Grades: 7 8 9 10 **Fic**
1. Dogs—Fiction 2. Animal shelters—Fiction
ISBN 0-374-37278-0 LC 2001-16030
"Frances Foster books"

Rachel, a teenager with a healthy dose of both aptitude and attitude, begins to feel at home volunteering at an animal shelter until the arrival of a feral dog with whom she senses a special kinship

"The strong characters, rich detail, and well-articulated emotions . . . make a powerful story that will resonate with many teens." Booklist

Konigsburg, E. L.

The mysterious edge of the heroic world. Atheneum Books for Young Readers 2007 244p $16.99

Grades: 5 6 7 8 **Fic**
1. Friendship—Fiction 2. Art museums—Fiction
3. Florida—Fiction
ISBN 978-1-4169-4972-5; 1-4169-4972-0

"Amedeo Kaplan (son of characters met in *The Outcasts of 19 Schuyler Place*) has just moved to coastal Florida and made friends with William Wilcox, son of an estate sale manager. . . . As the boys help William's mother pack up the palatial home of Amedeo's next-door neighbor, a larger-than-life retired opera singer, Amedeo finds a signed Modigliani drawing. . . . Amedeo is primed to uncover the history behind the drawing—a dark provenance that links the retired opera singer, the Vanderwaals and the Nazi occupation of Amsterdam." Publ Wkly

"This humorous, poignant, tragic, and mysterious story has intertwining plots that peel away like the layers of an onion." SLJ

The outcasts of 19 Schuyler Place. Atheneum Bks. for Young Readers 2004 296p $16.95

Grades: 5 6 7 8 **Fic**
1. Social action—Fiction
ISBN 0-689-86636-4 LC 2003-8067

A prequel to Silent to the bone

Upon leaving an oppressive summer camp, twelve-year-old Margaret Rose Kane spearheads a campaign to preserve three unique towers her grand uncles have been building in their back yard for over forty years

"The plot is well paced and has excellent foreshadowing. Konigsburg's characters are particularly well motivated. . . . Funny and thought-provoking by turns, this is Konigsburg at her masterful best." SLJ

Silent to the bone. Atheneum Bks. for Young Readers 2000 261p hardcover o.p. pa $5.99

Grades: 7 8 9 10 **Fic**
1. Siblings—Fiction 2. Babysitters—Fiction
3. Mystery fiction
ISBN 0-689-83601-5; 0-689-83602-3 (pa)
LC 00-20043

"A Jean Karl book"

When he is wrongly accused of gravely injuring his baby half-sister, thirteen-year-old Branwell loses his power of speech and only his friend Connor is able to reach him and uncover the truth about what really happened

"A compelling mystery that is also a moving story of family, friendship, and seduction." Booklist

The view from Saturday. Atheneum Bks. for Young Readers 1996 163p $16.95; pa $5.99 *

Grades: 4 5 6 7 **Fic**
1. School stories 2. Friendship—Fiction 3. Physically handicapped—Fiction
ISBN 0-689-80993-X; 0-689-81721-5 (pa)
LC 95-52624

Awarded the Newbery Medal, 1997
"A Jean Karl book"

Four students, with their own individual stories, develop a special bond and attract the attention of their teacher, a paraplegic, who choses them to represent their sixth-grade class in the Academic Bowl competition

"Glowing with humor and dusted with magic. . . . Wrought with deep compassion and a keen sense of balance." Publ Wkly

Korman, Gordon, 1963-

Born to rock. Hyperion Books for Children 2006 261p $15.99

Grades: 7 8 9 10 **Fic**
1. Father-son relationship—Fiction 2. Punk rock music—Fiction
ISBN 0-7868-0920-5 LC 2005-52652

High school senior Leo Caraway, a conservative Republican, learns that his biological father is a punk rock legend.

"Rock fans will appreciate the short riffs at chapter breaks and the intriguing music-centric premise." Publ Wkly

Jake, reinvented. Hyperion 2003 213p $15.99; pa $5.99

Grades: 7 8 9 10 **Fic**
1. School stories
ISBN 0-7868-1957-X; 0-7868-5697-1 (pa)
LC 2003-47804

Rick becomes friends with the popular new boy, Jake Garrett, football player and host of superlative parties, and in the process discovers the true nature of his schoolmates and uncovers the mystery of Jake's past.

"Korman's reworking of The Great Gatsby places the action in a modern framework, which makes it more recognizable for today's readers and may lead them to the classic. Teens will find deeper issues to consider about popularity, being true to one's self, and taking responsibility for one's actions as they relate to the setting and characters." SLJ

Korman, Gordon, 1963-—*Continued*

The Juvie three. Hyperion 2008 249p lib bdg $15.99 *

Grades: 7 8 9 10   **Fic**

1. Juvenile delinquency—Fiction 2. Friendship—Fiction

ISBN 978-1-4231-0158-1; 1-4231-0158-8

LC 2008-19087

Gecko, Arjay, and Terence, all in trouble with the law, must find a way to keep their halfway house open in order to stay out of juvenile detention.

"Korman keeps lots of balls in the air as he handles each boy's distinct voice and character—as well as the increasingly absurd situation—with humor and flashes of sadness." Booklist

No more dead dogs. Hyperion Bks. for Children 2000 180p $15.99; pa $5.99

Grades: 5 6 7 8   **Fic**

1. Theater—Fiction 2. School stories

ISBN 0-7868-0531-5; 0-7868-1601-5 (pa)

LC 00-24313

Eighth-grade football hero Wallace Wallace is sentenced to detention attending rehearsals of the school play where, in spite of himself, he becomes wrapped up in the production and begins to suggest changes that improve not only the play but his life as well

"Humor abounds here, but underlying is the true angst of the middle school student." Voice Youth Advocates

Schooled. Hyperion Books for Children 2007 208p $15.99 *

Grades: 6 7 8 9   **Fic**

1. School stories 2. Hippies—Fiction

ISBN 0-7868-5692-0

Homeschooled by his hippie grandmother, Capricorn (Cap) Anderson has never watched television, tasted a pizza, or even heard of a wedgie. But when his grandmother lands in the hospital, Cap is forced to move in with a guidance counselor and attend the local middle school.

"This rewarding novel features an engaging main character and some memorable moments of comedy, tenderness, and reflection." Booklist

Son of the mob. Hyperion Bks. for Children 2002 262p $15.99; pa $5.99 *

Grades: 7 8 9 10   **Fic**

1. Mafia—Fiction

ISBN 0-7868-0769-5; 0-7868-1593-0 (pa)

LC 2002-68672

Seventeen-year-old Vince's life is constantly complicated by the fact that he is the son of a powerful Mafia boss, a relationship that threatens to destroy his romance with the daughter of an FBI agent

"The fast-paced, tightly focused story addresses the problems of being an honest kid in a family of outlaws—and loving them anyway. Korman doesn't ignore the seamier side of mob life, but even when the subject matter gets violent . . . he keeps things light by relating his tale in the first-person voice of a humorously sarcastic yet law-abiding wise guy." Horn Book

Another title about Vince is:

Son of the mob: Hollywood hustle (2004)

Kositsky, Lynne, 1947-

Claire by moonlight. Tundra Books 2005 271p pa $9.95

Grades: 7 8 9 10   **Fic**

1. Nova Scotia—Fiction 2. Acadians—Fiction

ISBN 0-88776-659-5

"Claire Richard has already survived the death of her parents, deportation from her beloved Acadian village, and a violent storm at sea. British and French forces are at large in 1755, but she is determined to return to Acadia with her remaining sister and brother. She also seeks her true love, Sam, a reluctant British soldier. . . . Plenty of action and the determination of the strong female heroine move the story swiftly along." Booklist

The thought of high windows. Kids Can Press 2004 175p $16.95

Grades: 7 8 9 10   **Fic**

1. Jews—Fiction 2. Holocaust, 1933-1945—Fiction

ISBN 1-55337-621-8

"Esther describes her life as one of a group of Jewish children taken from Germany to France by the Red Cross during World War II. The novel begins when she is 15 and living in a French castle; her childhood in Berlin is described through flashbacks. . . . Based on true events, this is an immediate, painfully honest story." SLJ

Koss, Amy Goldman, 1954-

The girls. Dial Bks. for Young Readers 2000 121p $16.99; pa $5.99

Grades: 5 6 7 8   **Fic**

1. Friendship—Fiction

ISBN 0-8037-2494-2; 0-14-230033-0 (pa)

LC 99-19318

"One Saturday morning a girl finds out that her group of friends, for reasons unknown, has decided to exclude her. As the short novel moves over the course of the weekend, five girls narrate in turns, each moving the story forward as well as providing sometimes unwitting commentary on her friends' versions of events." Horn Book Guide

"This provocative page-turner will be passed from one girl to the next." SLJ

Poison Ivy. Roaring Brook Press 2006 166p $16.96

Grades: 7 8 9 10   **Fic**

1. Bullies—Fiction 2. School stories

ISBN 1-59643-118-0   LC 2005-17256

"A Deborah Brodie book."

In a government class three popular girls undergo a mock trial for their ruthless bullying of a classmate.

"Realistic dialogue and fast-paced action will hold interest, and the final verdict is unsettling, but not unexpected." SLJ

Side effects. 1st ed. Roaring Brook Press 2006 143p $16.95

Grades: 6 7 8 9   **Fic**

1. Cancer—Fiction

ISBN 978-1-59643-167-6; 1-59643-167-9

LC 2005-31473

"A Deborah Brodie book."

Koss, Amy Goldman, 1954- —*Continued*
Everything changes for Isabelle, not quite fifteen, when she is diagnosed with lymphoma—but eventually she survives and even thrives.

"Koss refuses to glamorize Issy's illness or treatment. Instead, she settles for an honesty and frankness that will both challenge and enlighten readers." Booklist

Kostick, Conor
Epic. Viking 2007 364p $17.99 *
Grades: 7 8 9 10   Fic
1. Fantasy fiction 2. Video games—Fiction
ISBN 0-670-06179-4; 978-0-670-06179-2
LC 2006-19958
On New Earth, a world based on a video role-playing game, fourteen-year-old Erik pursuades his friends to aid him in some unusual gambits in order to save his father from exile and safeguard the futures of each of their families.

"There is intrigue and mystery throughout this captivating page-turner. Veins of moral and ethical social situations and decisions provide some great opportunities for discussion. Well written and engaging." SLJ
Followed by: Saga (2008)

Kostick, Conor, 1964-
Saga. Viking 2008 367p $18.99
Grades: 7 8 9 10   Fic
1. Video games—Fiction 2. Fantasy fiction
ISBN 978-0-6700-6280-5; 0-6700-6280-4
LC 2007-32175
Sequel to Epic (2007)
On Saga, a world based on a video role-playing game, fifteen-year-old Ghost lives to break rules, but the Dark Queen who controls Saga plans to enslave its people and those of New Earth, and Ghost and her airboarding friends, along with Erik and his friends from Epic, try to stop her.

"The plot and pacing are near perfect in this tale of a world cramped by fear and tradition. . . . Compulsively readable and palpable (the descriptions of airboarding are a near-physical experience), it will appeal to SF fans across the board." Voice Youth Advocates

Kress, Adrienne
Alex and the Ironic Gentleman. Weinstein Books 2007 310p $16.95
Grades: 4 5 6 7   Fic
1. Pirates—Fiction 2. Buried treasure—Fiction
3. Adventure fiction
ISBN 978-1-60286-005-6; 1-60286-005-X
Companion novel to: Timothy and the dragon's gate (2008)
"Alex, who lives with her uncle in the flat above their doorknob shop, is dreading the sixth grade . . . but on the first day she learns that a new teacher has been installed—the young Mr. Underwood. . . . He turns out to be a descendant of a famous pirate, and soon three vicious men turn up in town, looking for a map to a fabled family treasure. . . . Kress has a delightfully simple, observational prose style. . . . This inspired book should hold up to many re-readings." Publ Wkly

Krisher, Trudy
Fallout. Holiday House 2006 315p $17.95
Grades: 7 8 9 10   Fic
1. Prejudices—Fiction 2. Friendship—Fiction
3. North Carolina—Fiction
ISBN 978-0-8234-2035-3; 0-8234-2035-3
LC 2006-41193
The move of an unconventional Hollywood family to a coastal North Carolina town in the early 1950s results not only in an unlikely friendship between high school age Genevieve and newcomer Brenda but also in a challenge to traditional ways of thinking.

"This is an excellent novel for teens searching for a good story with a well-paced and action-filled plot that challenges them to think about the importance of voicing their opinions." SLJ

Uncommon Faith. Holiday House 2003 263p $17.95
Grades: 7 8 9 10   Fic
1. Women's rights—Fiction 2. Christian life—Fiction
3. Massachusetts—Fiction
ISBN 0-8234-1791-3   LC 2002-191919
In 1837-38, residents of Millbrook, Massachusetts, speak in their different voices of major issues of their day, including women's rights, slavery, religious differences, and one fiery girl named Faith

"The increasingly distinctive voices make this multilayered story richer and more compelling as it progresses." Booklist

Kropp, Paul, 1948-
The countess and me. Fitzhenry & Whiteside 2002 144p $14.95; pa $8.95
Grades: 5 6 7 8   Fic
1. Friendship—Fiction
ISBN 1-55041-680-4; 1-55041-692-8 (pa)
"Jordan befriends an elderly, eccentric neighbor, Mrs. von Loewen, a countess in her younger European days, by helping her around the house. . . . Jordan's stories of the old woman attract the attention of a clique of boys on their way to juvenile delinquenthood. Jordan is offered a chance to become part of their group—at the price of betraying Mrs. von Loewen's trust." Booklist

"Told in first person, the well-paced plot will keep kids involved, and the book is not too difficult for reluctant readers." SLJ

Kuhlman, Evan
The last invisible boy; illustrated by J.P. Coovert. Atheneum Books for Young Readers 2008 233p il $16.99 *
Grades: 4 5 6 7   Fic
1. Bereavement—Fiction 2. Father-son relationship—Fiction 3. Family life—Fiction 4. School stories 5. Ohio—Fiction
ISBN 978-1-416-95797-3; 1-416-95797-9
LC 2007-40258
"Ginee Seo books"
In the wake of his father's sudden death, twelve-year-old Finn feels he is becoming invisible as his hair and skin become whiter by the day, and so he writes and illustrates a book to try to understand what is happening

Kuhlman, Evan—*Continued*
and to hold on to himself and his father.

"Vivid details . . . add depth to the characterizations and grow in meaning as the story progresses. . . . Finn's distinct narrative voice, and the sweet precision with which the story unfolds, give this title a touching resonance." Booklist

Kwasney, Michelle D., 1960-
Itch; [by] Michelle D. Kwasney. 1st ed. Henry Holt 2008 240p $16.95
Grades: 5 6 7 8   **Fic**
1. Grandparents—Fiction 2. Mothers—Fiction 3. Child abuse—Fiction 4. Friendship—Fiction 5. School stories 6. Ohio—Fiction
ISBN 978-0-8050-8083-4; 0-8050-8083-X
                                            LC 2007027573
In 1968, after the death of her beloved Gramps, Delores "Itch" Colchester and her grandmother move from Florida to an Ohio trailer park, where she meets new people and, when she learns that a friend is being abused by her mother, tries her best to emulate her plain-spoken grandfather.

"The 1960s references provide the realistic backdrop for this moving, believable story. Sympathetic well-drawn characters draw the reader into Delores' personal struggles." Booklist

La Fevers, R. L.
Theodosia and the Serpents of Chaos; illustrated by Yoko Tanaka. Houghton Mifflin 2007 343p il $16
Grades: 4 5 6 7   **Fic**
1. Adventure fiction 2. Museums—Fiction 3. Magic—Fiction 4. Egypt—Fiction 5. London (England)—Fiction
ISBN 978-0-618-75638-4; 0-618-75638-8
                                            LC 2006-34284
Set in 1906 London and Cairo, this mystery adventure introduces an intrepid heroine—Theodosia Throckmorton, who is thrust into the heart of a mystery when she learns an ancient Egyptian amulet carries a curse that threatens to crumble the British Empire.

"It's the delicious, precise, and atmospheric details (nicely extended in Tanaka's few, stylized illustrations) that will capture and hold readers." Booklist

Another title about Theodosia is:
Theodosia and the Staff of Osiris (2008)

Lachtman, Ofelia Dumas
The truth about Las Mariposas; [by] Ofelia Dumas Lachtman. Pinata Books 2007 171p pa $9.95
Grades: 7 8 9 10   **Fic**
1. Hotels and motels—Fiction 2. Aunts—Fiction 3. Mexican Americans—Fiction 4. California—Fiction 5. Mystery fiction
ISBN 978-1-55885-494-9   LC 2007019238
When sixteen-year-old Caro Torres goes to help her Tia Matilda at her bed-and-breakfast in Two Sands, California, she ends up also helping her aunt fend off the attempts of her ex-husband to buy the property and steal

the treasures that are hidden there.

"Staying true to the young Latina's viewpoint, the story offers a lively mix of work, friendship, family, and romance that add texture to the gripping, surprising mystery." Booklist

LaFaye, A., 1970-
Stella stands alone; [by] A. LaFaye. Simon & Schuster Books for Young Readers 2008 245p map $16.99
Grades: 7 8 9 10   **Fic**
1. Reconstruction (1865-1876)—Fiction 2. Swindlers and swindling—Fiction 3. Orphans—Fiction 4. African Americans—Fiction
ISBN 978-1-4169-1164-7; 1-4169-1164-2
                                            LC 2007-38725
Fourteen-year-old Stella, orphaned just after the Civil War, fights to keep her family's plantation and fulfill her father's desire to turn land over to the people who have worked on it for generations, but first she must find her father's hidden deed and will.

"Readers will be drawn along by Stella's refusal to act helpless and sweet and her discovery of strength and kindness in unexpected places. The sadness and anger, and the wrenching legacy of slavery are present throughout." Booklist

LaFleur, Suzanne M., 1983-
Love, Aubrey; [by] Suzanne LaFleur. Wendy Lamb Books 2009 262p $15.99; lib bdg $18.99
Grades: 5 6 7 8   **Fic**
1. Abandoned children—Fiction 2. Bereavement—Fiction 3. Grandmothers—Fiction 4. Letters—Fiction 5. Friendship—Fiction 6. School stories 7. Depression (Psychology)—Fiction 8. Vermont—Fiction
ISBN   978-0-385-73774-6;   0-385-73774-2; 978-0-385-90686-9 (lib bdg); 0-385-90686-2 (lib bdg); 978-0-375-85159-9 (pa)   LC 2008031742
While living with her Gram in Vermont, eleven-year-old Aubrey writes letters as a way of dealing with losing her father and sister in a car accident, and then being abandoned by her grief-stricken mother.

Aubrey's "detailed progression from denial to acceptance makes her both brave and credible in this honest and realistic portrayal of grief." Kirkus

Laird, Elizabeth
A little piece of ground; [by] Elizabeth Laird; with Sonia Nimr. Haymarket Books 2006 216p pa $9.95
Grades: 6 7 8 9 10   **Fic**
1. Israel-Arab conflicts—Fiction 2. Palestine—Fiction
ISBN 978-1-931859-38-7; 1-931859-38-8
                                            LC 2006008707
During the Israeli occupation of Ramallah in the West Bank of Palestine, twelve-year-old Karim and his friends create a secret place for themselves where they can momentarily forget the horrors of war.

"Throughout this powerful narrative, the authors remain true to Karim's character and reactions. He is a typical self-centered adolescent. . . . [This book] deserves serious attention and discussion." SLJ

Lake, A. J.

The coming of dragons; [by] A.J. Lake. 1st U.S.
ed. Bloomsbury 2006 239p (Darkest age) $16.95
Grades: 5 6 7 8   **Fic**
1. Magic—Fiction 2. Dragons—Fiction 3. Great Britain—Fiction 4. Fantasy fiction
ISBN 978-1-58234-965-7; 1-58234-965-7
LC 2005030623
Two eleven-year-olds named Edmund and Elspeth discover that they have been given fantastic gifts to use
against the ancient and evil forces that have been awak-
ened by powerful magic during the Dark Ages in Great
Britain.
"This early medieval tale that blends adventure, suspense, friendship, and magic as well as the savage world
of wild boars, malevolent knights, dragons, and ancient
evil will appeal to boys and girls alike." Voice Youth
Advocates

Lamba, Marie

What I meant. . . Random House 2007 310p
$16.99; lib bdg $19.99 *
Grades: 7 8 9 10   **Fic**
1. East Indian Americans—Fiction 2. Family life—
Fiction 3. Aunts—Fiction 4. Pennsylvania—Fiction
ISBN   978-0-375-84091-3;   0-375-84091-5;
978-0-375-94091-0 (lib bdg); 0-375-94091-X (lib bdg)
LC 2006010898
Having to share her home with her demanding and devious aunt from India makes it all the more difficult for
fifteen-year-old Sang to deal with such things as her parents thinking she is too young to date, getting less than
perfect grades, and being shut out by her long-time best
friend.
"Lamba makes an impressive debut with this contemporary novel. . . . Readers will find much to like in
Lamba's heroine, who ultimately survives a set of trials
worthy of Job with grace and humor." Publ Wkly

Lamm, C. Drew

Bittersweet; [by] Drew Lamm. Clarion Bks.
2003 214p $15
Grades: 6 7 8 9   **Fic**
1. Grandmothers—Fiction 2. Artists—Fiction
ISBN 0-618-16443-X   LC 2003-12503
When her beloved grandmother suffers a stroke, high
school junior and talented artist Taylor finds her inspiration and creative energy disappearing until she learns to
reconnect with others and herself in unexpected ways
"Lamm has written a dramatic, poignant, realistic first
novel with a character who will find a place in readers'
hearts." SLJ

Landman, Tanya

I am Apache; [by] Tanya Landman. Candlewick
Press 2008 305p $17.99
Grades: 8 9 10 11 12   **Fic**
1. Orphans—Fiction 2. Siblings—Fiction 3. Mexico—
Fiction 4. Apache Indians—Fiction
ISBN 978-0-7636-3664-7; 0-7636-3664-9
Fourteen-year-old Siki seeks to avenge her brother's
death by becoming an Apache warrior and learns a star-

tling truth about her own identity.
"With an eloquent voice and dignified pace, Landman
creates a credible and artistic story with excellent characterization and engaging psychological and sociopolitical
questions." Booklist

Landon, Dena

Shapeshifter's quest; [by] Dena Landon. 1st ed.
Dutton Children's Books 2005 182p $16.99
Grades: 7 8 9 10   **Fic**
1. Fantasy fiction 2. Magic—Fiction
ISBN 0-525-47310-6   LC 2004-21457
To atone for the misdeed of an ancestor, teen-aged
Syanthe, a shapeshifter, journeys outside the safety of the
forest where she has always lived to learn the secret of
the evil king's magic.
"Fantasy fans will enjoy this plucky heroine and her
richly imagined world where magic abounds." Booklist

Landy, Derek

Skulduggery Pleasant. HarperCollinsPublishers
2007 392p $17.99; lib bdg $18.89 *
Grades: 4 5 6 7   **Fic**
1. Magic—Fiction 2. Fantasy fiction
ISBN   0-06-123115-0;   978-0-06-123115-5;
0-06-123116-9 (lib bdg); 978-0-06-123116-2 (lib bdg)
LC 2006-29403
When twelve-year-old Stephanie inherits her weird uncle's estate, she must join forces with Skulduggery Pleasant, a skeleton mage, to save the world from the Faceless
Ones.
This "is a rich fantasy that is as engaging in its creative protagonists and villains as it is in the lightning-
paced plot and sharp humor." Bulletin Cent Child Books
Followed by: Playing with fire (2008)

Lane, Dakota, 1959-

Gothic Lolita; a mystical thriller; words and
photographs by Dakota Lane. Atheneum Books for
Young Readers 2008 194p il $17.99
Grades: 8 9 10 11 12   **Fic**
1. Weblogs—Fiction 2. Bereavement—Fiction
3. Hollywood (Calif.)—Fiction 4. Japan—Fiction
5. Racially mixed people—Fiction
ISBN 978-1-4169-1396-2; 1-4169-1396-3
LC 2008-15390
"Ginee Seo books"
Lane "focuses on two half-Japanese, half-American
girls who forge an unusual bond over their blogs, loneliness and fascination with the gothic Lolita subculture.
Chelsea is in L.A. and Miya is in Japan. . . . Readers
will find themselves quickly engrossed." Publ Wkly

Langrish, Katherine

Troll Fell. HarperCollins 2004 264p $15.99; lib
bdg $16.89
Grades: 6 7 8 9   **Fic**
1. Vikings—Fiction 2. Trolls—Fiction 3. Adventure
fiction 4. Fantasy fiction
ISBN 0-06-058304-5; 0-06-058305-3 (lib bdg)
LC 2003-17480

Langrish, Katherine—*Continued*

Forced to live with his evil identical-twin uncles after his father's death, twelve-year-old Peer tries to find a way to stop their plan to sell the neighbor's children to the trolls.

"Langrish's tense, quick-paced story will keep readers glued to the page." Booklist

Other titles about in this series are:

Troll Mill (2006)

Troll blood (2008)

Langston, Laura

The trouble with Cupid; [by] Laura Langston. Fitzhenry & Whiteside 2009 251p pa $11.95

Grades: 5 6 7 8   **Fic**

1. School stories 2. Dogs—Fiction

ISBN 978-1-55455-059-3; 1-55455-059-9

All Erin has to do is train the school mascot to perform on cue, and she will be a hero. But none of her dog-training experience has prepared Erin for Cupid, the laziest, most unlovable dog that ever woofed.

"The story is a quick and entertaining read with believable characters. Although lighthearted, the plot introduces the themes of animal exploitation and the importance of standing up for one's principles." SLJ

Larbalestier, Justine, 1967-

How to ditch your fairy. Bloomsbury 2008 307p $16.99

Grades: 6 7 8 9   **Fic**

1. Fairies—Fiction 2. Magic—Fiction

ISBN 978-1-59990-301-9; 1-59990-301-6

LC 2008-02408

In a world in which everyone has a personal fairy who tends to one aspect of daily life, fourteen-year-old Charlie decides she does not want hers—a parking fairy—and embarks on a series of misadventures designed to rid herself of the invisible sprite and replace it with a better one, like her friend Rochelle's shopping fairy.

"Charlie is totally likable, smart, and sarcastic, a perfectly self-involved, insecure teen. At its core, this is a typical coming-of-age story, but the addition of the fairies, the slightly alternative setting, and the made-up slang make it much more." SLJ

Magic or madness. Razorbill 2005 288p $16.99; pa $7.99

Grades: 8 9 10 11 12   **Fic**

1. Magic—Fiction 2. Space and time—Fiction 3. Grandmothers—Fiction 4. New York (N.Y.)—Fiction 5. Australia—Fiction

ISBN 1-59514-022-0; 1-59514-124-3 (pa)

LC 2004-18263

From the Sydney, Australia home of a grandmother she believes is a witch, fifteen-year-old Reason Cansino is magically transported to New York City, where she discovers that friends and foes can be hard to distinguish

"Readers looking for layered, understated fantasy will follow the looping paths of Larbalestier's fine writing . . . with gratitude and awe." Booklist

Other titles about Reason Cansino are:

Magic lessons (2006)

Magic's child (2007)

LaRochelle, David, 1960-

Absolutely, positively not. Arthur A. Levine Books 2005 219p $16.95 *

Grades: 7 8 9 10   **Fic**

1. Homosexuality—Fiction 2. School stories

ISBN 0-439-59109-0   LC 2004-23558

Chronicles a teenage boy's humorous attempts to fit in at his Minnesota high school by becoming a macho, girl-loving, "Playboy" pinup-displaying heterosexual.

"The wry, first-person narrative is wonderful as it moves from personal angst to outright farce. . . . The characters are drawn with surprising depth." Booklist

Larson, Kirby, 1954-

Hattie Big Sky. Delacorte Press 2006 289p $15.95; lib bdg $17.99

Grades: 6 7 8 9 10   **Fic**

1. Frontier and pioneer life—Fiction 2. Orphans—Fiction 3. World War, 1914-1918—Fiction 4. Montana—Fiction

ISBN 0-385-73313-5; 0-385-90332-4 (lib bdg)

LC 2005-35039

A Newbery Medal honor book, 2007

After inheriting her uncle's homesteading claim in Montana, sixteen-year-old orphan Hattie Brooks travels from Iowa in 1917 to make a home for herself and encounters some unexpected problems related to the war being fought in Europe.

This is "a richly textured novel full of memorable characters." Booklist

Laser, Michael, 1954-

Cheater; a novel. Dutton Books 2008 224p $16.99

Grades: 8 9 10 11 12   **Fic**

1. Cheating (Education)—Fiction 2. School stories

ISBN 978-0-525-47826-3   LC 2007-18001

When brilliant high school student Karl Petrovsky gets talked into participating in an elaborate cheating operation at his school, he ends up involved in a bigger problem than he ever anticipated.

"The characterizations . . . are intriguingly complex, and the web of strings being pulled behind the scenes is mysteriously suggested and satisfyingly revealed." Bull Cent Child Books

Laskas, Gretchen Moran

The miner's daughter. Simon & Schuster Books for Young Readers 2007 250p $15.99

Grades: 8 9 10 11 12   **Fic**

1. Great Depression, 1929-1939—Fiction 2. Coal mines and mining—Fiction 3. Family life—Fiction 4. West Virginia—Fiction

ISBN 978-1-4169-1262-0; 1-4169-1262-2

LC 2006-00684

Sixteen-year-old Willa, living in a Depression-era West Virginia mining town, works hard to help her family, experiences love and friendship, and finds an outlet for her writing when her family becomes part of the Arthurdale, West Virginia, community supported by Eleanor Roosevelt.

"Richly drawn characters and plot make this an excellent novel that explores the struggles endured by many in America in the 1930s." SLJ

Lasky, Kathryn

Broken song; by Kathryn Lasky. Viking 2005
154p $15.99

Grades: 5 6 7 8   **Fic**

1. Jews—Fiction 2. Russia—Fiction 3. Violinists—
Fiction

ISBN 0-670-05931-5   LC 2004-17741

In 1897, fifteen-year-old Reuven Bloom, a Russian
Jew, must set aside his dreams of playing the violin in
order to save himself and his baby sister after the rest of
their family is murdered

"Through rich prose filled with imagery, distinct characterization, and historical research, Lasky breathes life
into the horrific history of anti-Semitism in Russia in the
late-19th and early-20th centuries." SLJ

Elizabeth I; red rose of the House of Tudor.
Scholastic 1999 237p il (Royal diaries) $10.95

Grades: 4 5 6 7   **Fic**

1. Elizabeth I, Queen of England, 1533-1603—Fiction
2. Great Britain—History—1485-1603, Tudors—Fiction

ISBN 0-590-68484-1   LC 99-11178

In a series of diary entries, Princess Elizabeth, the
eleven-year-old daughter of King Henry VIII, celebrates
holidays and birthdays, relives her mother's execution,
revels in her studies, and agonizes over her father's
health

"Well written and captivating." Voice Youth Advocates

Jahanara, Princess of Princesses. Scholastic 2002
186p (Royal diaries) $10.95

Grades: 4 5 6 7   **Fic**

1. Jahanara Begum—Fiction 2. Shahjahan, Emperor
of India, ca. 1592-1666—Fiction

ISBN 0-439-22350-4   LC 2001-57627

Beginning in 1627, Princess Jahanara, first daughter of
Shah Jahan of India's Mogul Dynasty, writes in her diary
about political intrigues, weddings, battles, and other experiences of her life. Includes historical notes on
Jahanara's later life and on the Mogul Empire

"The language seems true to the thoughts and sensitiv-
ities of a young teen, and Lasky's meticulous research is
evident throughout the journal." Booklist

The last girls of Pompeii; [by] Kathryn Lasky.
Viking 2007 184p $15.99

Grades: 6 7 8 9   **Fic**

1. Family life—Fiction 2. Handicapped—Fiction
3. Slavery—Fiction 4. Pompeii (Extinct city)—Fiction

ISBN 978-0-670-06196-9   LC 2006026663

Twelve-year-old Julia knows that her physical defor-
mity will keep her from a normal life, but counts on the
continuing friendship of her lifelong slave, Mitka, until
they learn that both of their futures in first-century Pompeii are about to change for the worse.

This is a "compelling novel. . . . Lasky seamlessly
weaves a great deal of history into this novel. . . . She
vividly portrays a wide swath of society." SLJ

Mary, Queen of Scots, queen without a country.
Scholastic 2002 206p (Royal diaries) $10.95

Grades: 4 5 6 7   **Fic**

1. Mary, Queen of Scots, 1542-1587—Fiction

ISBN 0-439-19404-0   LC 2001-31085

Mary, the young Scottish queen, is sent a diary from
her mother in which she records her experiences living
at the court of France's King Henry II as she awaits her
marriage to Henry's son, Francis

"Lasky creates a voice that's both accessible and believable, deftly incorporating historical detail and the intricacies of court life and behavior while showing the
teenage queen as a compelling, independent character."
Booklist

Memoirs of a bookbat. Harcourt Brace & Co.
1994 216p hardcover o.p. pa $6

Grades: 6 7 8 9   **Fic**

1. Censorship—Fiction 2. Books and reading—Fiction

ISBN 0-15-215727-1; 0-15-201259-1

LC 93-36402

Fourteen-year-old Harper, an avid reader of fantasy
who must hide her books from her fundamentalist parents, comes to realize that their public promotion of censorship threatens her freedom to make her own choices

"In this very smart (and somewhat acerbic) book . . .
Lasky . . . combines fictional characters with real-life
authors and religious groups (such as Operation Rescue)
to create a credible and entertaining story of an emerging
independent thinker." Publ Wkly

The night journey; [by] Kathryn Lasky. Viking
2005 151p $15.99; pa $5.99

Grades: 4 5 6 7   **Fic**

1. Jews—Fiction 2. Russia—Fiction

ISBN 0-670-05963-3; 0-14-240322-9 (pa)

LC 2005276376

A reissue of the title first published 1981 by Warne

Rachel ignores her parents' wishes and persuades her
great-grandmother to relate the story of her escape from
czarist Russia.

"The novel shifts back and forth from the dangerous
journey out of Russia to Rachel's own casual, secure life
at home and school. These transitions are handled with
a smoothness that doesn't break the intrinsic tension of
the story, and the contrast between the two lives demonstrates with poignant clarity the real meaning of freedom." SLJ

Lavender, William, 1921-

Aftershocks. Harcourt 2006 344p $17

Grades: 8 9 10 11 12   **Fic**

1. Sex role—Fiction 2. Father-daughter relationship—
Fiction   3.   Chinese   Americans—Fiction
4. Earthquakes—Fiction 5. San Francisco (Calif.)—
Fiction

ISBN 0-15-205882-6   LC 2005-19695

In San Francisco from 1903 to 1908, teenager Jessie
Wainwright determines to reach her goal of becoming a
doctor while also trying to care for the illegitimate child
of a liaison between her father and their Chinese maid.

This "is readable historical fiction about an engrossing
event in U.S. history." Voice Youth Advocates

Law, Ingrid, 1970-

Savvy. Dial Books for Young Readers 2008 342p $16.99 *

Grades: 4 5 6 7   **Fic**

1. Magic—Fiction 2. Family life—Fiction 3. Voyages and travels—Fiction

ISBN 978-0-8037-3306-0; 0-8037-3306-2

LC 2007-39814

A Newbery Medal honor book, 2009

Recounts the adventures of Mississippi (Mibs) Beaumont, whose thirteenth birthday has revealed her "savvy"—a magical power unique to each member of her family—just as her father is injured in a terrible accident.

"Short chapters and cliffhangers keep the pace quick, while the mix of traditional language and vernacular helps the story feel both fresh and timeless. . . . [This is] a vibrant and cinematic novel that readers are going to love." Publ Wkly

Lawlor, Laurie

Dead reckoning; a pirate voyage with Captain Drake. Simon & Schuster Books for Young Readers 2005 254p $15.95

Grades: 7 8 9 10   **Fic**

1. Drake, Sir Francis, 1540?-1596—Fiction 2. Pirates—Fiction 3. Seafaring life—Fiction 4. Orphans—Fiction

ISBN 0-689-86577-5   LC 2004-21682

Emmet, a fifteen-year-old orphan, learns hard lessons about survival when he sails from England in 1577 as a servant aboard the Golden Hind—the ship of his cousin, the explorer and pirate Francis Drake—on its three-year circumnavigation of the world.

"The tone is dark and grim, and there are scenes that might horrify younger readers. . . . But the story is authentic and harrowing, and the historical details are well done. This book would be perfect for older teens who love historical fiction, or want more on pirates." SLJ

He will go fearless; [by] Laurie Lawlor. Simon & Schuster Books for Young Readers 2006 210p $15.95

Grades: 5 6 7 8   **Fic**

1. Father-son relationship—Fiction 2. United States—History—1865-1898—Fiction 3. Overland journeys to the Pacific—Fiction

ISBN 0-689-86579-1   LC 2005-06129

With the Civil War ended and Reconstruction begun, fifteen-year-old Billy resolves to make the dangerous and challenging journey West in search of real fortune – his true father.

"Danger, adventure, and survival combine to make this a richly detailed story." SLJ

Lawrence, Caroline

The thieves of Ostia; a Roman mystery. Roaring Brook Press 2002 152p (Roman mysteries) lib bdg $22.90; pa $5.99

Grades: 4 5 6 7   **Fic**

1. Dogs—Fiction 2. Rome—History—Fiction 3. Mystery fiction

ISBN 0-7613-2602-2 (lib bdg); 0-7613-1582-9 (pa)

LC 2001-34912

First published 2001 in the United Kingdom

In Rome in the year 79 A.D., a group of children from very different backgrounds work together to discover who beheaded a pet dog—and why

"With adroit and skillful writing, the author hooks the reader into this fast-paced, sharply pieced together mystery, and doesn't let up until she reaches a convincing and satisfying solution. . . . Moreover, the book is filled with appealing and believable characters, interesting historical information, and strong narrative descriptions." ALAN

Other titles in this series are:

The assassins of Rome (2006)

The charioteer of Delphi (2007)

The Colossus of Rhodes (2006)

The dolphins of Laurentem (2003)

The enemies of Jupiter (2005)

The fugitive from Corinth (2006)

The gladiators of Capua (2005)

The pirates of Pompeii (2003)

The secrets of Vesuvius (2002)

The Sirens of Surrentum (2007)

The twelve tasks of Flavia Gemina (2004)

Lawrence, Iain, 1955-

B for Buster. Delacorte Press 2004 321p $15.95; lib bdg $17.95; pa $5.99

Grades: 7 8 9 10   **Fic**

1. World War, 1939-1945—Fiction 2. Air pilots—Fiction

ISBN 0-385-73086-1; 0-385-90108-9 (lib bdg); 0-440-23810-2 (pa)   LC 2003-17345

In the spring of 1943, sixteen-year-old Kak, desperate to escape his abusive parents, lies about his age to enlist in the Canadian Air Force and soon finds himself based in England as part of a crew flying bombing raids over Germany

"Lawrence writes a gripping, affecting story about the thrill of flying, the terrifying realities of war, and the agony of reconciling personal fears and ideals with duty and bravery." Booklist

The convicts; [by] Iain Lawrence. Delacorte Press 2005 198p $15.95; lib bdg $17.99 *

Grades: 5 6 7 8   **Fic**

1. Prisoners—Fiction 2. Adventure fiction

ISBN 0-385-73087-X; 0-385-90109-7 (lib bdg)

LC 2004-14968

His efforts to avenge his father's unjust imprisonment force thirteen-year-old Tom Tin into the streets of nineteenth-century London, but after he is convicted of murder, Tom is eventually sent to Australia where he has a surprise reunion.

"The story abounds in terrifying villains, grime, misery, and cruelty. Yet it also serves up a fair share of optimism. . . . This book is . . . action packed and . . . thoroughly researched. . . . Give it to reluctant readers who are looking for an exciting adventure." SLJ

Other titles in this series are:

The cannibals (2005)

The castaways (2007)

Lawrence, Iain, 1955-—_Continued_

The lightkeeper's daughter. Delacorte Press 2002 246p $16.95; lib bdg $18.99; pa $7.95
Grades: 7 8 9 10   **Fic**
1. Teenage mothers—Fiction 2. Islands—Fiction
ISBN 0-385-72925-1; 0-385-90062-7 (lib bdg); 0-385-73127-2 (pa)   LC 2002-578
When, after a four-year absence, seventeen-year-old Squid returns to her childhood home on a remote lighthouse island off British Columbia with her young daughter in tow, she and her parents try to come to terms with each other and the painful events of the past, especially the death of her older brother
This "is not an easy or comfortable read but for sophisticated teens, this lyrical novel is an experience not to be forgotten." SLJ

The seance. Delacorte Press 2008 262p il $15.99
Grades: 4 5 6 7   **Fic**
1. Houdini, Harry, 1874-1926—Fiction 2. Spiritualism—Fiction 3. Magicians—Fiction 4. Mystery fiction
ISBN 978-0-385-73375-5; 0-385-73375-5; 978-0-385-90392-9 (lib bdg); 0-385-90392-8 (lib bdg)   LC 2007-27994
In 1926, magician Harry Houdini arrives in the city to perform magic and to expose fradulent mediums but thirteen-year-old Scooter King, who works for his mother making her seances seem real, needs Houdini's help to solve a murder.
"Mystery lovers will get a kick out of this rollicking whodunit featuring swashbuckling soothsayers, outlandish séances, magic tricks and more." Publ Wkly

The wreckers. Delacorte Press 1998 196p hardcover o.p. pa $5.99 *
Grades: 5 6 7 8   **Fic**
1. Shipwrecks—Fiction 2. Adventure fiction 3. Great Britain—History—1714-1837—Fiction
ISBN 0-385-32535-5; 0-440-41545-4 (pa)   LC 97-31625
"In 1799 fourteen-year-old John Spencer survives a shipwreck on the coast of Cornwall. To his horror, he soon learns that the villagers are not rescuers, but pirates who lure ships ashore in order to plunder their cargoes. . . . Lawrence creates an edge-of-the-chair survival/mystery story. Fast-moving, mesmerizing." Horn Book Guide
Other titles in this series are:
The buccaneers (2001)
Ghost boy (2000)
The smugglers (1999)

Lawrence, L. S., 1951-
Escape by sea. 1st American ed. Holiday House 2009 195p $16.95
Grades: 7 8 9 10 11 12   **Fic**
1. Survival after airplane accidents, shipwrecks, etc.—Fiction 2. Sex role—Fiction 3. Rome—History—Fiction 4. Sea stories
ISBN 978-0-8234-2217-3; 0-8234-2217-8   LC 2008049495

When the city of Carthage falls to the Romans during the Punic Wars, Sara, the fifteen-year-old daughter of a Carthaginian senator, must gather her grief-stricken father and take to the seas, where, with only with a meager cargo to trade, her healing skills, her wits, and her courage, Sara must face a life wildly different from anything she thought possible.
This is "a welcome, seaworthy historical adventure in an atypical setting." Booklist

Lawrence, Michael
A crack in the line; Withern Rise, volume I; by Michael Lawrence. 1st ed. Greenwillow Books 2004 c2003 323p $15.99; lib bdg $16.89; pa $7.99
Grades: 7 8 9 10   **Fic**
1. Space and time—Fiction 2. Great Britain—Fiction
ISBN 0-06-072477-3; 0-06-072478-1 (lib bdg); 0-06-072479-X (pa)   LC 2003-56860
Sixteen-year-old Alaric discovers how to travel to an alternate reality, where his mother is alive and his place in the family is held by a girl named Naia
"The first in a trilogy, this complex story of choices, fate, and acceptance is demanding. . . . [It] is sure to spark passionate discussion." Booklist
Other titles in this series are :
Small eternities (2005)
The Underwood See (2007)

Le Guin, Ursula K., 1929-
A wizard of Earthsea; [by] Ursula K. Le Guin; illustrated by Ruth Robbins. Bantam trade pbk. ed. Bantam Books 2004 182p il pa $15 *
Grades: 6 7 8 9   **Fic**
1. Fantasy fiction 2. Science fiction 3. Magic—Fiction
ISBN 0-553-38304-3; 978-0-553-38304-1   LC 2004558962
A reissue of the title first published 1968 by Parnassus Press
"An imaginary archipelago is the setting for . . . this fantasy. . . . In a willful misuse of his limited powers, the novice wizard unleashes a shadowy, malevolent creature that endangers his life and the world of Earthsea." Booklist
A "powerful fantasy-allegory. Though set as prose, the rhythms of the langauge are truly and consistently poetical." Read Ladders for Hum Relat. 5th edition
Other titles in this series are:
The Tombs of Atuan (1971)
The farthest shore (1972)
Tehanu (1990)

Leal, Ann Haywood
Also known as Harper. Henry Holt 2009 246p $16.95
Grades: 4 5 6 7   **Fic**
1. Single parent family—Fiction 2. Poets—Fiction 3. Siblings—Fiction 4. Handicapped—Fiction
ISBN 978-0-8050-8881-6; 0-8050-8881-4   LC 2008-36940
Writing poetry helps fifth-grader Harper Lee Morgan cope with her father's absence, being evicted, and having to skip school to care for her brother while their mother

Leal, Ann Haywood—*Continued*

works, and things look even brighter after she befriends a mute girl and a kindly disabled woman.

"The characters are memorable as are the descriptive passages. . . . Most touching are Harper's pithy poems that expose the raw emotions of a bright but disadvantaged girl. This book is rich with discussion opportunity for middle school students." Voice Youth Advocates

Leavitt, Martine, 1953-

Heck, superhero. Front Street 2004 144p $16.95

Grades: 6 7 8 9 **Fic**

1. Mental illness—Fiction 2. Abandoned children—Fiction 3. Cartoons and caricatures—Fiction 4. Superheroes—Fiction

ISBN 1-88691-094-4 LC 2002-192863

Abandoned by his mentally ill mother, thirteen-year-old Heck tries to survive on his own as his mind bounces between the superhero character he imagines himself to be and the harsh reality of his life.

"Strong supporting characters . . . add depth to this engrossing, evocative novel." Booklist

Keturah and Lord Death. Front Street 2006 216p $16.95

Grades: 8 9 10 11 12 **Fic**

1. Death—Fiction

ISBN 978-1-932425-29-1; 1-932425-29-2

LC 2006-00799

When Lord Death comes to claim sixteen-year-old Keturah while she is lost in the King's Forest, she charms him with her story and is granted a twenty-four hour reprieve in which to seek her one true love

"The romance is intense, the writing is startling, and the story is spellbinding." Booklist

Lecesne, James

Absolute brightness. HarperTeen 2008 472p $17.99; lib bdg $18.89 *

Grades: 7 8 9 10 **Fic**

1. Cousins—Fiction 2. Homosexuality—Fiction 3. Good and evil—Fiction 4. New Jersey—Fiction

ISBN 978-0-06-125627-1; 0-06-125627-7; 978-0-06-125628-8 (lib bdg); 0-06-125628-5 (lib bdg)

LC 2007-02988

ALA YALSA Morris Award Finalist, 2009

"Laura Geringer books"

In the beach town of Neptune, New Jersey, Phoebe's life is changed irrevocably when her gay cousin moves into her house and soon goes missing.

"This thoughtful novel is beautifully written; its themes are haunting, and in spite of the central tragedy, it's often laugh-out-loud funny." Kliatt

Lee, Tanith

Piratica; being a daring tale of a singular girl's adventure upon the high seas; presented most handsomely by the notorious Tanith Lee. Dutton Children's Books 2004 288p $17.99

Grades: 6 7 8 9 **Fic**

1. Pirates—Fiction 2. Sex role—Fiction 3. Adventure fiction

ISBN 0-525-47324-6

First published 2003 in the United Kingdom

A bump on the head restores Art's memories of her mother and the exciting life they led, so the sixteen-year-old leaves Angels Academy for Young Maidens, seeks out the pirates who were her family before her mother's death, and leads them back to adventure on the high seas.

"Piratica is a refreshing, tongue-in-cheek, tangled tale that will entice readers who crave adventure and fantasy." SLJ

Followed by Piratica II: return to Parrot Island (2006)

Leeds, Constance

The silver cup; [by] Constance Leeds. Viking 2007 212p $16.99

Grades: 6 7 8 9 **Fic**

1. Germany—History—0-1517—Fiction 2. Middle Ages—Fiction 3. Jews—Fiction 4. Prejudices—Fiction 5. Friendship—Fiction 6. Crusades—Fiction

ISBN 978-0-670-06157-0; 0-670-06157-3

LC 2006008626

In 1096, Anna, a German Catholic girl, and Leah, a German Jewish girl, strike up a remarkable friendship and make surprising discoveries about each other.

"An intriguing and suspenseful portrayal of Europe's early medieval days." SLJ

Lekich, John

King of the Lost and Found. Raincoast Books 2007 308p pa $11.95

Grades: 6 7 8 9 10 **Fic**

1. School stories

ISBN 978-1-55192-802-9 (pa); 1-55192-802-7 (pa)

"Life for Raymond has been far from normal, coping with fainting spells, nosebleeds, allergies, being short, no social skills, and a broken family. With the intervention of popular athlete Jack and warmhearted perfectionist Janice, Raymond's life becomes a hilarious, chaotic experience. . . . Lekich effectively illustrates the culture of high school, where friends are everything and recognition is always an obsession." Voice Youth Advocates

Lemna, Don, 1936-

When the sergeant came marching home; by Don Lemna; [illustrations by Matt Collins] Holiday House 2008 215p il $16.95 *

Grades: 4 5 6 **Fic**

1. Montana—Fiction 2. Farm life—Fiction 3. Siblings—Fiction

ISBN 978-0-8234-2083-4; 0-8234-2083-3

LC 2007-22424

In 1946 when his father returns from the war, a ten year old boy and his family move from the Montana town where they had been living to an old, rundown farm in the middle of nowhere, where they work hard trying to make ends meet.

"Donald's first-person narration is filled with humor and wit. Lemna conveys a true sense of farm life and all its difficulties, with each chapter describing the brothers' various adventures. . . . The narrative is simple, with a few choice vocabulary words that can be explored through language lessons. . . . Well written and entertaining." SLJ

L'Engle, Madeleine, 1918-2007

A ring of endless light. Farrar, Straus & Giroux 1980 324p $21.99; pa $6.99 *

Grades: 6 7 8 9   Fic

1. Death—Fiction 2. Dolphins—Fiction

ISBN 0-374-36299-8; 0-312-37935-8 (pa)

LC 79-27679

A Newbery Medal honor book, 1981

During the summer her grandfather is dying of leukemia and death seems all around, 15-year-old Vicky finds comfort with the pod of dolphins with which she has been doing research

"With customary grace and firm control of an intricate plot, L'Engle has created another irresistible novel about familiar characters, the Austin family." Publ Wkly

A wrinkle in time. Farrar, Straus & Giroux 1962 211p $17 *

Grades: 5 6 7 8 9 10   Fic

1. Fantasy fiction

ISBN 0-374-38613-7

ALA YALSA Margaret A. Edwards Award (1998)

"A brother and sister, together with a friend, go in search of their scientist father who was lost while engaged in secret work for the government on the tesseract problem. A tesseract is a wrinkle in time. The father is a prisoner on a forbidding planet, and after awesome and terrifying experiences, he is rescued, and the little group returns safely to Earth and home." Child Books Too Good to Miss

"It makes unusual demands on the imagination and consequently gives great rewards." Horn Book

Followed by A wind in the door (1973)

Lennon, Joan, 1953-

Questors. Margaret K. McElderry Books 2007 358p $16.99

Grades: 5 6 7 8   Fic

1. Fantasy fiction

ISBN 978-1-4169-3658-9; 1-4169-3658-0

LC 2006-28895

Three confused children are brought together then, with little training, sent off to save three worlds that were held in perfect balance until a cataclysmic disruption in the space-time continuum threatened their existence, which is just what their enemy desires.

"Fantasy fans . . . will be enthralled by the complex plot set in this strange multilayered world." Bull Cent Child Books

Leonard, Elmore, 1925-

A coyote's in the house. HarperEntertainment 2004 149p il $15.95

Grades: 5 6 7 8   Fic

1. Dogs—Fiction 2. Coyotes—Fiction 3. Hollywood (Calif.)—Fiction

ISBN 0-06-054404-X   LC 2003-71050

"Hip coyote Antwan . . . is foraging for garbage when he makes the acquaintance of German shepherd Buddy, a retired film star. Buddy is bored and has decided he'd like the freedom of the coyote's life in the wild, while Antwan . . . is interested in getting to know Miss Betty, a prizewinning poodle who lives with Buddy's

family. . . . The story is good fun, but the real pleasure here . . . lies in listening to the characters banter with one another. . . . A poignant ending gives the tale just the right edge." Booklist

Les Becquets, Diane

Season of ice. Bloomsbury U.S.A. Children's Books 2008 281p $16.95

Grades: 8 9 10 11 12   Fic

1. Missing persons—Fiction 2. Father-daughter relationship—Fiction 3. Stepfamilies—Fiction 4. Lakes—Fiction 5. Maine—Fiction

ISBN 978-1-59990-063-6; 1-59990-063-7

LC 2007-30845

When seventeen-year-old Genesis Sommer's father disappears on Moosehead Lake near their small-town Maine home in mid-November, she must cope with the pressure of keeping her family together, even while rumors about the event plague her.

This is "a heartbreaking story from the very beginning, but Les Becquets turns it into something well beyond a mere tearjerker. . . . It's a tender story of a tough, smart, loving girl who finds that she can rise to the challenge of what she's lost because of what she's gained. Readers will understand her and admire her, and find her difficult indeed to forget." Bull Cent Child Books

Lester, Alison, 1952-

Quicksand pony. Houghton Mifflin 1998 136p $15

Grades: 5 6 7 8   Fic

1. Horses—Fiction 2. Australia—Fiction

ISBN 0-395-93749-3   LC 98-6930

"Walter Lorraine books"

First published 1997 in Australia

After her pony Bella, trapped in quicksand, is rescued by a mysterious unseen person, ten-year-old Biddy follows the trail into the Australian bush and discovers the solution to a disappearance that happened years ago

"A multilayered story of survival, love, mystery, and family relationships." SLJ

The snow pony. Houghton Mifflin 2003 194p il $15

Grades: 5 6 7 8   Fic

1. Horses—Fiction 2. Australia—Fiction

ISBN 0-618-25404-8   LC 2002-13388

"Walter Lorraine books"

Prolonged drought has strained Dusty's ranching family to the breaking point, but she finds consolation with her wild and beautiful horse

"This fast-paced 'horse and girl' adventure story has interesting, well-developed characters, and the tension among the family members is well drawn." SLJ

Lester, Julius

Day of tears; a novel in dialogue. Hyperion 2005 177p $15.99; pa $7.99

Grades: 7 8 9 10   Fic

1. Slavery—Fiction 2. African Americans—Fiction

ISBN 0-7868-0490-4; 1-42310-409-0 (pa)

Coretta Scott King Award for text

Lester, Julius—_Continued_

"Jump at the sun"

Emma has taken care of the Butler children since Sarah and Frances's mother, Fanny, left. Emma wants to raise the girls to have good hearts, as a rift over slavery has ripped the Butler household apart. Now, to pay off debts, Pierce Butler wants to cash in his slave "assets", possibly including Emma.

"The horror of the auction and its aftermath is unforgettable. . . . The racism is virulent (there's widespread use of the n-word). The personal voices make this a stirring text for group discussion." Booklist

Guardian. Amistad/HarperTeen 2008 129p $16.99; lib bdg $17.89

Grades: 7 8 9 10   **Fic**

1. Race relations—Fiction 2. African Americans—Fiction 3. Southern States—Fiction 4. Lynching—Fiction

ISBN   978-0-06-155890-0;   0-06-155890-7; 978-0-06-155891-7 (lib bdg); 0-06-155891-5 (lib bdg)
LC 2008-14251

In a rural southern town in 1946, a white man and his son witness the lynching of an innocent black man. Includes historical note on lynching.

"The author's understated, haunting prose is as compelling as it is dark; . . . the story . . . leaves a deep impression." Publ Wkly

Includes bibliographical references

Time's memory. Farrar, Straus & Giroux 2006 230p $17

Grades: 8 9 10 11 12   **Fic**

1. Slavery—Fiction 2. African Americans—Fiction

ISBN 0-374-37178-4; 978-0-374-37178-4
LC 2005-47716

Ekundayo, a Dogon spirit brought to America from Africa, inhabits the body of a young African American slave on a Virginia plantation, where he experiences loss, sorrow, and reconciliation in the months preceding the Civil War.

"More than a picture of slavery through the eyes of those enslaved or their captors, Lester's narrative evokes spiritual images of Mali's Dogon people." SLJ

Levine, Anna

Freefall. Greenwillow Books 2008 250p $16.99; lib bdg $17.89

Grades: 8 9 10 11 12   **Fic**

1. Soldiers—Fiction 2. Israelis—Fiction

ISBN   978-0-06-157654-6;   0-06-157654-9; 978-0-06-157656-0 (lib bdg); 0-06-157656-5 (lib bdg)
LC 2008003826

As war between Israel and Lebanon breaks out in 2006 and her compulsory service in the Israeli army draws near, teenaged Aggie considers joining an elite female combat unit.

Levine "writes with immediate, vivid detail. There is no talk of politics or enemies or peace in this stirring novel." Booklist

Levine, Ellen, 1939-

Catch a tiger by the toe; by Ellen Levine. Viking 2005 200p $15.99

Grades: 6 7 8   **Fic**

1. Communism—Fiction 2. Bronx (New York, N.Y.)—Fiction 3. United States—Politics and government—1945-1953—Fiction

ISBN 0-670-88461-8   LC 2004-17348

In the Bronx, New York, during the McCarthy era, twelve-year-old Jamie keeps a terrible secret about her family, but when the truth is exposed, her parents lose their jobs and she is fired from the school newspaper.

"Tension mounts to the very end. . . . The warmth, sadness, and anger humanize the issues, which are sure to spark discussion about the meaning of patriotism - then and now." Booklist

Levine, Gail Carson, 1947-

Dave at night. HarperCollins Pubs. 1999 281p hardcover o.p. pa $5.99 *

Grades: 5 6 7 8   **Fic**

1. Orphans—Fiction 2. Jews—Fiction 3. African Americans—Fiction 4. New York (N.Y.)—Fiction

ISBN 0-06-028154-5; 0-06-440747-0 (pa)
LC 98-50069

When orphaned Dave is sent to the Hebrew Home for Boys where he is treated cruelly, he sneaks out at night and is welcomed into the music- and culture-filled world of the Harlem Renaissance

"The magic comes from Levine's language and characterization. This novel will provide inspiration for all children while offering a unique view of a culturally diverse New York City." SLJ

Ella enchanted. HarperCollins Pubs. 1997 232p $16.99; lib bdg $17.89; pa $6.50 *

Grades: 5 6 7 8   **Fic**

1. Fantasy fiction

ISBN 0-06-027510-3; 0-06-027511-1 (lib bdg); 0-06-440705-5 (pa)   LC 96-30734

A Newbery Medal honor book, 1998

In this novel based on the story of Cinderella, Ella struggles against the childhood curse that forces her to obey any order given to her

"As finely designed as a tapestry, Ella's story both neatly incorporates elements of the original tale and mightily expands them." Booklist

Ever. HarperCollinsPublishers 2008 256p $16.99; lib bdg $17.89

Grades: 5 6 7 8   **Fic**

1. Fate and fatalism—Fiction 2. Gods and goddesses—Fiction 3. Winds—Fiction 4. Immortality—Fiction

ISBN   978-0-06-122962-6;   0-06-122962-8; 978-0-06-122963-3 (lib bdg); 0-06-122963-6 (lib bdg)
LC 2007-32289

Fourteen-year-old Kezi and Olus, Akkan god of the winds, fall in love and together try to change her fate—to be sacrificed to a Hyte god because of a rash promise her father made—through a series of quests that might make her immortal.

"Levine conducts a riveting journey, offering passion and profound pondering along the way." Publ Wkly

Levine, Gail Carson, 1947-—*Continued*

Fairest. HarperCollins 2006 326p $16.99; lib bdg $17.89

Grades: 6 7 8 9   **Fic**

1. Fairy tales 2. Singing—Fiction
ISBN   978-0-06-073408-4;   0-06-073408-6;
978-0-06-073409-1 (lib bdg); 0-06-073409-4 (lib bdg)
LC 2006-00337

In a land where beauty and singing are valued above all else, Aza eventually comes to reconcile her unconventional appearance and her magical voice, and learns to accept herself for who she truly is.

"The plot is fast-paced, and Aza's growth and maturity are well crafted and believable." SLJ

The wish. HarperCollins Pubs. 2000 197p hardcover o.p. lib bdg $16.89; pa $5.99

Grades: 5 6 7 8   **Fic**

1. School stories
ISBN 0-06-027900-1; 0-06-027901-X (lib bdg);
0-06-447361-9 (pa)   LC 98-19087

When granted her wish to be the most popular girl in school, Wilma, an eighth grader, forgets that she will graduate in three weeks and her popularity will vanish

"There are some laugh-out-loud moments here and plenty of scenes that are believable and fun. Kids will get a kick out of this one." Booklist

Levine, Kristin, 1974-

The best bad luck I ever had. Putnam 2009 266p $16.99 *

Grades: 5 6 7 8   **Fic**

1. Race relations—Fiction 2. Prejudices—Fiction
3. Friendship—Fiction 4. Country life—Fiction
5. Family life—Fiction 6. Alabama—Fiction
ISBN 978-0-399-25090-3; 0-399-25090-5
LC 2008-11570

In Moundville, Alabama, in 1917, twelve-year-old Dit hopes the new postmaster will have a son his age, but instead he meets Emma, who is black, and their friendship challenges accepted ways of thinking and leads them to save the life of a condemned man.

"Tension builds just below the surface of this energetic, seamlessly narrated . . . novel. . . . Levine handles the setting with grace and nuance." Publ Wkly

Levitin, Sonia, 1934-

Strange relations. Alfred A. Knopf 2007 298p $15.99; lib bdg $18.99 *

Grades: 7 8 9 10   **Fic**

1. Jews—Fiction 2. Hawaii—Fiction 3. Cousins—Fiction 4. Religion—Fiction
ISBN   978-0-375-83751-7;   0-375-83751-5;
978-0-375-93751-4 (lib bdg); 0-375-93751-X (lib bdg)
LC 2006-33275

Fifteen-year-old Marne is excited to be able to spend her summer vacation in Hawaii, not realizing the change in her lifestyle it would bring staying with her aunt, seven cousins, and uncle who is a Chasidic rabbi.

"It's rare to find such well-developed characters, empathetic and sensitive religious treatment, and carefully crafted plotlines in one novel." SLJ

Levy, Elizabeth, 1942-

Seventh grade tango. Hyperion Bks. for Children 2000 153p $15.99; pa $5.99

Grades: 5 6 7 8   **Fic**

1. Dancers—Fiction 2. Friendship—Fiction 3. School stories
ISBN 0-7868-0498-X; 0-7868-1565-5 (pa)
LC 99-53124

When Rebecca, a seventh-grader, is paired up with her friend Scott for a dance class at school, she learns a lot about who her real friends are

"Descriptive prose, snappy dialogue, and diverse characters enhance the story, which notably portrays ballroom dance as a hip, fun activity." Booklist

Lewis, C. S. (Clive Staples), 1898-1963

The lion, the witch, and the wardrobe; illustrated by Pauline Baynes. HarperCollins Pubs. 1994 189p il $16.99; lib bdg $17.89; pa $7.99 *

Grades: 4 5 6 7   **Fic**

1. Fantasy fiction
ISBN 0-06-023481-4; 0-06-023482-2 (lib bdg);
0-06-440499-4 (pa)   LC 93-8889

A reissue of the title first published 1950 by Macmillan

Four English schoolchildren find their way through the back of a wardrobe into the magic land of Narnia and assist Aslan, the golden lion, to triumph over the White Witch, who has cursed the land with eternal winter

This begins "the 'Narnia' stories, outstanding modern fairy tales with an underlying theme of good overcoming evil." Child Books Too Good to Miss

Other titles about Narnia are:
The horse and his boy (1954)
The last battle (1956)
The magician's nephew (1956)
Prince Caspian (1951)
The silver chair (1953)
The voyage of the Dawn Treader (1952)

Lewis, Richard, 1949-

The killing sea. Simon & Schuster Books for Young Readers 2006 183p $15.95

Grades: 6 7 8 9   **Fic**

1. Survival after airplane accidents, shipwrecks, etc.—Fiction 2. Indian Ocean earthquake and tsunami, 2004—Fiction 3. Indonesia—Fiction
ISBN 978-1-4169-1165-4; 1-4169-1165-0
LC 2006001050

In the aftermath of the 2004 tsunami in Sumatra, two teenagers, American Sarah and Acehnese Ruslan, meet and continue together their arduous climb inland, where Ruslan hopes to find his father and Sarah seeks a doctor for her brother.

"Drawing from his own experience as a rescue worker, Lewis creates a powerful fictional tale of survival and cooperation." Booklist

LeZotte, Ann Clare

T4; a novel in verse; written by Ann Clare LeZotte. Houghton Mifflin Co. 2008 108p $14

Grades: 6 7 8 9   **Fic**
1. Novels in verse 2. Deaf—Fiction 3. Euthanasia—Fiction 4. Germany—History—1933-1945—Fiction
ISBN 978-0-547-04684-6; 0-547-04684-7
LC 2007-47737

When the Nazi party takes control of Germany, thirteen-year-old Paula, who is deaf, finds her world-as-she-knows-it turned upside down, as she is taken into hiding to protect her from the new law nicknamed T4.

"This novel will have a lasting effect on readers, giving insight into an often-forgotten aspect of the horrors of the Third Reich." SLJ

Lieurance, Suzanne

The locket; surviving the Triangle Shirtwaist fire; [by] Suzanne Lieurance. Enslow Publishers 2008 160p il (Historical fiction adventures) lib bdg $27.93

Grades: 4 5 6 7   **Fic**
1. Triangle Shirtwaist Company, Inc. —Fiction 2. Sisters—Fiction 3. Immigrants—Fiction 4. Jews—United States—Fiction 5. Factories—Fiction
ISBN 978-0-7660-2928-6 (lib bdg); 0-7660-2928-X (lib bdg)   LC 2007-5281

After Galena, an eleven-year-old Russian immigrant, survives a terrible fire at the non-unionized Triangle Shirtwaist factory while her older sister and many others do not, she begins fighting for improved working conditions in New York City factories.

"Woven together in perfect compatibility, the historical background and fictional plot give readers a clear insight into Jewish immigrants and . . . unfair labor practices, and there is excellent foreshadowing of the fire." SLJ

Includes bibliographical references

Limb, Sue

Girl 15, charming but insane. Delacorte Press 2004 214p pa $8.95; mass market pa $5.99

Grades: 7 8 9 10   **Fic**
1. Friendship—Fiction 2. Dating (Social customs)—Fiction 3. Great Britain—Fiction
ISBN 0-385-73214-7; 0-385-90244-1 (lib bdg); 978-0-385-73215-4 (pa); 0-385-73215-5 (pa); 978-0-440-23896-6 (mass market pa); 0-440-23896-X (mass market pa)   LC 2003-21254

Fifteen-year-old Jess, living with her mum, separated from her father in Cornwall, and with a best friend who seems to do everything perfectly, finds her own assets through humor.

"Readers will relish the heady blend of rueful humor and tantalizingly uncertain romance." Bull Cent Child Books

Other titles in this series are:
Girl, (nearly) 16, absolute torture (2005)
Girl, going on 17, pants on fire (2006)
Girl, barely 15, flirting for England (2008)

Zoe and Chloe: on the prowl. Viking Childrens Books 2008 248p $16.99

Grades: 7 8 9 10   **Fic**
1. Friendship—Fiction 2. Dating (Social customs)—Fiction 3. Sisters—Fiction 4. School stories 5. Great Britain—Fiction
ISBN 978-0-670-01120-9; 0-670-01120-7
LC 2008-15551

Best friends Zoe and Chloe need suitable dates for the Earthquake Ball—the ball of the year—and time is running out, while at the university, Zoe's older sister is in serious financial trouble and needs her help.

"Limb makes the most of each comic situation with fast-paced text sprinkled with dialogue that often incorporates British slang and strong language." SLJ

Lin, Grace, 1974-

Where the mountain meets the moon. Little, Brown and Company Books for Young Readers 2009 278p il $16.99 *

Grades: 4 5 6 7   **Fic**
1. Fairy tales 2. Dragons—Fiction 3. Moon—Fiction
ISBN 978-0-316-11427-1; 0-316-11427-8
LC 2008-32818

Minli, an adventurous girl from a poor village, buys a magical goldfish, and then joins a dragon who cannot fly on a quest to find the Old Man of the Moon in hopes of bringing life to Fruitless Mountain and freshness to Jade River.

"With beautiful language, Lin creates a strong, memorable heroine and a mystical land. . . . Children will embrace this accessible, timeless story about the evil of greed and the joy of gratitude." Booklist

Lion, Melissa, 1976-

Upstream. Wendy Lamb Books 2005 149p $15.95; lib bdg $17.99

Grades: 7 8 9 10   **Fic**
1. Bereavement—Fiction 2. Alaska—Fiction
ISBN 0-385-74643-1; 0-385-90877-6 (lib bdg)
LC 2004-15145

After her boyfriend is killed in a hunting accident, Alaska high school senior Marty, with help from her mother and two younger sisters, tries to get over her grief and begin a new life.

"Lion writes with sensitivity and depth. . . . Teens will want to discuss the morally complex conclusion, which raises questions about accidents, crime, and punishment." Booklist

Lipsyte, Robert

The contender. Harper & Row 1967 182p pa $5.99 hardcover o.p. *

Grades: 7 8 9 10   **Fic**
1. Boxing—Fiction 2. Harlem (New York, N.Y.)—Fiction 3. African Americans—Fiction
ISBN 0-06-447039-3

ALA YALSA Margaret A. Edwards Award (2001)

"After a street fight in which he is the chief target, Alfred wanders into a gym in his neighborhood. He decides not only to improve his physical condition but also to become a boxer. Because of this interest Alfred's life

Lipsyte, Robert—*Continued*
is completely changed. He assumes a more positive outlook on his immediate future, even within the confines
of a black ghetto." Shapiro. Fic for Youth. 3d edition
Followed by The brave (1991) and The chief (1993)

One fat summer. Harper & Row 1977 152p
hardcover o.p. pa $5.99 *
Grades: 7 8 9 10   **Fic**
   1. Weight loss—Fiction 2. Obesity—Fiction
   ISBN 0-06-023895-X; 0-06-447073-3 (pa)
                    LC 76-49746
ALA YALSA Margaret A. Edwards Award (2001)
"Bobby Marks is 14 and fat. How fat, he doesn't
know because he jumps off the scale when it hits 200
pounds. In one action-packed summer Bobby learns that
altered physical appearance can bolster self-esteem. He's
not sure he likes his friend Joanie's new nose and new
ego, but he's certainly pleased with his own svelte new
image. The slimming is a result of his summer job; tending the grounds of the town miser." West Coast Rev
Books
"This is far superior to most of the summer-of-change
stories; any change that takes place is logical and the
protagonist learns by action and reaction to be both self-
reliant and compassionate." Bull Cent Child Books
Followed by Summer rules (1981) and The
summerboy (1982)

Lisle, Holly, 1960-
The Ruby Key. Orchard Books 2008 361p
(Moon & sun) $16.99 *
Grades: 5 6 7 8   **Fic**
   1. Fantasy fiction 2. Siblings—Fiction
   ISBN 978-0-545-00012-3; 0-545-00012-2
                    LC 2007-30217
In a world where an uneasy peace binds Humans and
Nightlings, fourteen-year-old Genna and her twelve-year-
old brother Dan learn of their uncle's plot to gain immortality in exchange for human lives, and the two strike
their own bargain with the Nightling lord, which sets
them on a dangerous journey along the Moonroads in
search of a key.
"Lisle's fertile imagination provides the nightworlds
with monsters . . . but it is her clever plotting in this
. . . fantasy, leading up to a thrilling finish . . . That
will bewitch her audience." Horn Book
Followed by: The silver door (2009)

Lisle, Janet Taylor, 1947-
The crying rocks. Atheneum Bks. for Young
Readers 2003 199p $16.95; pa $6.99
Grades: 5 6 7 8   **Fic**
   1. Orphans—Fiction 2. Native Americans—Fiction
   3. Adoption—Fiction
   ISBN 0-689-85319-X; 0-689-85320-3 (pa)
                    LC 2002-151484
"A Richard Jackson book"
Thirteen-year-old Joelle has always wondered about
her life before being adopted by the woman she calls
Aunt Louise and her husband Vernon, and she makes
some surprising discoveries while researching a 17th cen-
tury Indian tribe

"This lovely portrait of a strong girl facing her past
and present with dignity and courage will receive a wide
and enthusiastic readership." SLJ

Highway cats; illustrated by David Frankland.
Philomel Books 2008 118p il $14.99
Grades: 4 5 6 7   **Fic**
   1. Cats—Fiction
   ISBN 978-0-399-25070-5; 0-399-25070-0
                    LC 2008-17165
A hard-bitten group of mangy highway cats is
changed forever after the mysterious arrival of three kittens.
"Lisle shows that she can create and develop animal
characters that are just as convincing as the humans in
her past works. . . . Deftly written and attractively illustrated with chapter-opening silhouettes by Frankland, this
is a treat for any reader and would be a delight to read
aloud." Booklist

Littke, Lael
Lake of secrets. Holt & Co. 2002 202p $16.95
Grades: 7 8 9 10   **Fic**
   1. Reincarnation—Fiction 2. Mystery fiction
   ISBN 0-8050-6730-2   LC 2001-39933
Having arrived in her mother's home town to try to
find her long-missing brother, who disappeared three
years before she was born, fifteen-year-old Carlene finds
herself haunted by memories from a past life
"The realistic characters and plot make the idea compelling, and the story will intrigue teens." Booklist

Littman, Sarah
Confessions of a closet Catholic; [by] Sarah
Darer Littman. 1st ed. Dutton Children's Books
2005 193p $15.99
Grades: 5 6 7 8   **Fic**
   1. Jews—Fiction 2. Catholics—Fiction
   ISBN 0-525-47365-3   LC 2004-10829
To be more like her best friend, eleven-year-old Justine decides to give up Judaism to become Catholic, but
after her beloved, religious grandmother dies, she realizes
that she needs to seek her own way of being Jewish.
"The novel is injected with humor throughout and
written with the voice of a contemporary adolescent.
Readers can't help but laugh and cry with this winning
protagonist." SLJ

Llewellyn, Sam, 1948-
The well between the worlds. Orchard Books
2009 339p (Lyonesse) $17.99
Grades: 5 6 7 8   **Fic**
   1. Arthur, King—Fiction 2. Fantasy fiction
   ISBN 978-0-439-93469-5; 0-439-93469-9
                    LC 2008-20075
Eleven-year-old Idris Limpet, living with his family in
the once noble but now evil and corrupt island country
of Lyonesse, finds his life taking a dramatic turn when,
after a near-drowning incident, he is accused of being allied to the feared sea monsters and is rescued from a
death sentence by a mysterious and fearsome stranger.
"Seldom does one find a new fantasy that is so richly

Llewellyn, Sam, 1948-—*Continued*

textured, so original in concept, and with such a wonderfully interesting story. . . . Fantasy lovers will be impatient to find out where their paths take them." Voice Youth Advocates

Lockhart, E.

The disreputable history of Frankie Landau-Banks. Hyperion 2008 352p $16.99 *

Grades: 7 8 9 10 11 12 Fic

1. School stories

ISBN 0-7868-3818-3; 978-0-7868-3818-9

Michael L. Printz Award honor book, 2009

"On her return to Alabaster Prep . . . [Frankie] attracts the attention of gorgeous Matthew . . . [who] is a member of the Loyal Order of the Basset Hounds, an all-male Alabaster secret society. . . . Frankie engineers her own guerilla membership by assuming a false online identity. . . . Lockhart creates a unique, indelible character. . . . Teens will be galvanized." Booklist

Dramarama. Hyperion 2007 311p $15.99 *

Grades: 7 8 9 10 11 12 Fic

1. Actors—Fiction 2. Friendship—Fiction 3. School stories

ISBN 0-7868-3815-9; 978-0-7868-3815-8

LC 2006-49599

Spending their summer at Wildewood Academy, an elite boarding school for the performing arts, tests the bond between best friends Sadye and Demi.

"Teens will identify strongly with both the heartbreak and the humor in this authentic portrayal of friendships maturing and decaying." SLJ

Loizeaux, William

Clarence Cochran, a human boy; pictures by Anne Wilsdorf. Farrar, Straus and Giroux 2009 152p il $16 *

Grades: 4 5 6 Fic

1. Cockroaches—Fiction 2. Toleration—Fiction 3. Environmental protection—Fiction

ISBN 978-0-374-31323-4; 0-374-31323-7

LC 2007-35358

"Melanie Kroupa books"

With the threat of extermination looming, a cockroach who has been transformed into a tiny human learns to communicate with his human hosts, leading to an agreement both sides can live with, and a friendship between Clarence and ten-year-old Mimi, a human environmentalist.

"There's a serious message here about environmentalism and the power of words, and the action and suspense make this a good read-aloud or classroom-discussion choice." SLJ

London, Jack, 1876-1916

The call of the wild; pictures by Wendell Minor. Atheneum Books for Young Readers 1999 112p il $24 *

Grades: 5 6 7 8 9 10 Fic

1. Dogs—Fiction 2. Alaska—Fiction

ISBN 0-689-81836-X LC 97-45019

Also available from other publishers

First published 1903 by Macmillan

"Buck, half-St. Bernard, half-Scottish sheepdog, is stolen from his comfortable home in California and pressed into service as a sledge dog in the Klondike. At first he is abused by both man and dog, but he learns to fight ruthlessly. He becomes lead dog on a sledge team, after bettering Spitz, the vicious old leader, in a brutal fight to the death. In John Thornton, he finally finds a master whom he can respect and love. When Thornton is killed by Indians, Buck breaks away to the wilds and becomes the leader of a wolf pack, returning each year to the site of Thornton's death." Reader's Ency. 4th edition

White Fang; pictures by Ed Young. Atheneum Books for Young Readers 2000 260p il hardcover o.p. pa $5.99 *

Grades: 5 6 7 8 9 10 Fic

1. Dogs—Fiction 2. Alaska—Fiction 3. Dogs

ISBN 0-689-82431-9; 1-416-91414-5 (pa)

LC 98-19241

Also available from other publishers

First published 1906

White Fang "is about a dog, a cross-breed, sold to Beauty Smith. This owner tortures the dog to increase his ferocity and value as a fighter. A new owner Weedom Scott, brings the dog to California, and, by kind treatment, domesticates him. White Fang later sacrifices his life to save Scott." Haydn. Thesaurus of Book Dig

Lopez, Diana

Confetti girl. Little, Brown and Company 2009 198p $15.99

Grades: 4 5 6 7 Fic

1. Father-daughter relationship—Fiction 2. Mexican Americans—Fiction 3. School stories 4. Friendship—Fiction 5. Bereavement—Fiction 6. Texas—Fiction

ISBN 978-0-316-02955-1; 0-316-02955-6

LC 2008032819

After the death of her mother, Texas sixth-grader Lina's grades and mood drop as she watches her father lose himself more and more in books, while her best friend uses Lina as an excuse to secretly meet her boyfriend.

"Lopez effectively portrays the Texas setting and the characters' Latino heritage. . . . This . . . novel puts at its center a likable girl facing realistic problems on her own terms." Booklist

López, Lorraine, 1956-

Call me Henri; a novel; by Lorraine M. López. Curbstone Press 2006 237p $17.95

Grades: 6 7 8 9 Fic

1. Gangs—Fiction 2. French language—Fiction 3. School stories 4. Mexican Americans—Fiction 5. California—Fiction

ISBN 1-931896-27-5 LC 2005-35790

Faced with family problems, difficulty in school, and gangs in the barrio, Enrique dreams of some day reaching the "other America" depicted on television, while sympathetic teachers help him cope by supporting his fight to study French instead of ESL.

"Enrique is a hero who will appeal to teens of all

López, Lorraine, 1956-—*Continued*

backgrounds. . . . There is violence and some sexual allusion, but overall it is an inspirational story that will touch and inspire." Voice Youth Advocates

Lord, Cynthia

Rules; [by] Cynthia Lord. 1st ed. Scholastic Press 2006 200p $15.99 *

Grades: 4 5 6 7   **Fic**
1. Autism—Fiction   2.   Siblings—Fiction
3. Handicapped—Fiction
ISBN 0-439-44382-2   LC 2005017519

A Newbery Medal honor book, 2007

Frustrated at life with an autistic brother, twelve-year-old Catherine longs for a normal existence but her world is further complicated by a friendship with an young paraplegic.

"The details of autistic behavior are handled well, as are depictions of relationships. . . . A heartwarming first novel." Booklist

Love, D. Anne, 1949-

Defying the diva; [by] D. Anne Love. Margaret K. McElderry Books 2008 257p $16.99

Grades: 7 8 9 10   **Fic**
1. Bullies—Fiction 2. School stories
ISBN 978-1-4169-3481-3; 1-4169-3481-2
         LC 2007-10945

During Haley's freshman year of high school, a campaign of gossip and bullying causes her to be socially ostracized, but after spending the summer living with her aunt, working at a resort, making new friends, and dating a hunky lifeguard, she learns how to stand up for herself and begins to trust again.

"Concluding with a serious author's note on harassment, which includes information on getting help, this text skillfully captures the painful reality of teen bullying while also telling Haley's humorous and sincere story of growing up." Kirkus

Picture perfect; [by] D. Anne Love. 1st ed. Margaret K. McElderry Books 2007 291p $16.99

Grades: 6 7 8 9   **Fic**
1. Family life—Fiction 2. School stories 3. Texas—Fiction
ISBN 978-0-689-87390-4; 0-689-87390-5
         LC 2006003508

When her mother leaves her family suddenly to take a new job, fourteen-year-old Phoebe tries to deal with her own confused feelings and, in the process, learns some things about love and the complicated ties that bind families together.

"The family dynamics are realistic, and the protagonist's voice rings true. The uplifting ending will leave readers satisfied." SLJ

Semiprecious. 1st ed. Margaret K. McElderry Books 2006 293p $16.95

Grades: 5 6 7 8   **Fic**
1. Family life—Fiction 2. Oklahoma—Fiction
ISBN 978-0-689-85638-9; 0-689-85638-5
         LC 2005-14906

Uprooted and living with an aunt in 1960s Oklahoma, thirteen-year-old Garnet and her older sister Opal brave their mother's desertion and their father's recovery from an accident, learning that "the best home of all is the one you make inside yourself."

"An involving novel of hurt, healing, and adjustment." Booklist

Lowe, Helen, 1971-

Thornspell. Alfred A. Knopf 2008 320p $15.99; lib bdg $18.99

Grades: 6 7 8 9 10   **Fic**
1. Fairy tales 2. Princes—Fiction
ISBN 978-0-375-85581-8; 978-0-375-95581-5 (lib bdg)   LC 2008-04149

In this elaboration of "Sleeping Beauty," Prince Sigismund, having grown up in a remote castle dreaming of going on knightly quests, has had only a passing interest in the forbidden wood lying beyond the castle gates until a brief encounter with a beautiful and mysterious lady changes his life forever.

"This version fittingly has more swordplay and dangerous escapades than romance, but it still ends happily every after." Booklist

Lowell, Pamela

Returnable girl; [by] Pamela Lowell. Marshall Cavendish 2006 229p $16.99

Grades: 8 9 10 11   **Fic**
1. Foster home care—Fiction 2. Mothers—Fiction 3. Friendship—Fiction
ISBN 978-0-7614-5317-8; 0-7614-5317-2
         LC 2006006398

Friendship with an outcast classmate and memories of her mother's desertion interfere with the relationship thirteen-year-old Ronnie tries to establish with her new foster mother.

"With its clear, direct language and an appealing heroine, the book is likely to draw a wide range of teen readers." Voice Youth Advocates

Lowenstein, Sallie Claire, 1949-

Waiting for Eugene. Lion Stone Books 2005 201p il $19

Grades: 6 7 8 9   **Fic**
1. Father-daughter relationship—Fiction 2. Holocaust survivors—Fiction 3. Mentally ill—Fiction 4. Art—Fiction
ISBN 0-96584-865-5

"Sara Goldman, 12, never knows when her architect father, a Holocaust survivor, will retreat into the dark, frightening world of his childhood memories. . . . Sara nurtures a budding first romance with the boy next door, and her developing artistic skills help her father face his painful past." SLJ

"Lowenstein maintains an accessible, quietly poetic voice. Intriguing illustrations by the author are an integral part of the text. . . . Those who enjoy reading about the power of art, music, words, and memory will find treasure here." Booklist

Lowry, Brigid, 1953-

Follow the blue; Brigid Lowry. 1st American ed. Holiday House 2004 205p $16.95

Grades: 7 8 9 10   **Fic**
    1. Australia—Fiction
    ISBN 0-8234-1827-8   LC 2003-62550

Fifteen-year-old Bec, living with her family in Perth, Australia, decides to stop being sensible and follow her wilder impulses during the summer that her parents are away on a long trip to help her father recover from a breakdown.

This is an "exhilarating novel. . . . A lot goes on in this very funny romp, some of it quite profound, and Lowry manages to remain mercifully nonpreachy throughout." Booklist

Things you either hate or love; [by] Brigid Lowry. 1st ed. Holiday House 2006 179p $16.95

Grades: 8 9 10 11 12   **Fic**
    1. Obesity—Fiction 2. Summer employment—Fiction
    3. Australia—Fiction
    ISBN 978-0-8234-2004-9; 0-8234-2004-3
                                          LC 2005-52539

First published 2005 in Australia with title: With lots of love from Georgia

A cynical, overweight, and lonely Australian teenager spends her summer vacation making lists, eating comfort foods, and trying to earn enough money to attend a big rock concert.

"A compelling, enjoyable read with a complex, irresistible protagonist who will engage many readers." Booklist

Lowry, Lois

Anastasia Krupnik. Houghton Mifflin 1979 113p $16 *

Grades: 4 5 6   **Fic**
    1. Family life—Fiction
    ISBN 0-395-28629-8

Also available in paperback from Dell

Anastasia's 10th year has some good things like falling in love and really getting to know her grandmother and some bad things like finding out about an impending baby brother.

"Anastasia's father and mother—an English professor and an artist—are among the most humorous, sensible, and understanding parents to be found in . . . children's fiction, and Anastasia herself is an amusing and engaging heroine." Horn Book

Other titles about Anastasia Krupnik and her family are:
All about Sam (1988)
Anastasia, absolutely (1995)
Anastasia again! (1981)
Anastasia, ask your analyst (1984)
Anastasia at this address (1991)
Anastasia at your service (1982)
Anastasia has the answers (1986)
Anastasia on her own (1985)
Anastasia's chosen career (1987)
Attaboy Sam! (1992)
See you around Sam! (1996)
Zooman Sam (1999)

Gathering blue. Houghton Mifflin 2000 215p $16

Grades: 5 6 7 8   **Fic**
    1. Science fiction
    ISBN 0-618-05581-9   LC 00-24359

Also available in paperback from Laurel Leaf
"Walter Lorraine books"

Lame and suddenly orphaned, Kira is mysteriously removed from her squalid village to live in the palatial Council Edifice, where she is expected to use her gifts as a weaver to do the bidding of the all-powerful Guardians

"Lowry has once again created a fully realized world full of drama, suspense, and even humor." SLJ

The giver. Houghton Mifflin 1993 180p $17; pa $8.95 *

Grades: 6 7 8 9   **Fic**
    1. Science fiction
    ISBN 0-395-64566-2; 0-385-73255-4 (pa)
                                          LC 92-15034

Awarded the Newbery Medal, 1994

Given his lifetime assignment at the Ceremony of Twelve, Jonas becomes the receiver of memories shared by only one other in his community and discovers the terrible truth about the society in which he lives.

"A riveting, chilling story that inspires a new appreciation for diversity, love, and even pain. Truly memorable." SLJ

Number the stars. Houghton Mifflin 1989 137p $16 *

Grades: 4 5 6 7   **Fic**
    1. World War, 1939-1945—Fiction 2. Jews—Fiction
    3. Friendship—Fiction 4. Denmark—Fiction
    ISBN 0-395-51060-0   LC 88-37134

Also available in paperback from Dell
Awarded the Newbery Medal, 1990

In 1943, during the German occupation of Denmark, ten-year-old Annemarie learns how to be brave and courageous when she helps shelter her Jewish friend from the Nazis.

"The appended details the historical incidents upon which Lowry bases her plot. . . . The whole work is seamless, compelling, and memorable." Horn Book

The silent boy. Houghton Mifflin 2003 178p $15

Grades: 4 5 6 7   **Fic**
    1. Mentally handicapped—Fiction
    ISBN 0-618-28231-9   LC 2002-9072

"Walter Lorraine books"

Katy, the precocious eight-year-old daughter of the town doctor, befriends a retarded boy

"The author balances humor and generosity with the obstacles and injustice of Katy's world to depict a complete picture of the turn of the 20th century." Publ Wkly

Lubar, David, 1954-

Dunk. Clarion Bks. 2002 249p $15; pa $6.99
Grades: 7 8 9 10   **Fic**
    1. Amusement parks—Fiction
    ISBN 0-618-19455-X; 0-618-43909-9 (pa)
                                          LC 2001-58428

Lubar, David, 1954-—*Continued*

While hoping to work as the clown in an amusement park dunk tank on the New Jersey shore the summer before his junior year in high school, Chad faces his best friend's serious illness, hassles with police, and the girl that got away

"With painful truth, Lubar has created complex, difficult to understand characters that seem straight from real life." Booklist

Sleeping freshmen never lie. Dutton Books 2005 279p $16.99; pa $6.99 *

Grades: 7 8 9 10　　　　　　　　　　Fic
1. Authorship—Fiction 2. School stories
ISBN 0-525-47311-4; 0-14-240780-1 (pa)
LC 2004-23067

While navigating his first year of high school and awaiting the birth of his new baby brother, Scott loses old friends and gains some unlikely new ones as he hones his skills as a writer

"The plot is framed by Scott's journal of advice for the unborn baby. The novel's absurd, comical mood is evident in its entries. . . . The author brings the protagonist to three-dimensional life by combining these introspective musings with active, hilarious narration." SLJ

True talents. Tom Doherty Associates 2007 315p $17.95; pa $5.99

Grades: 6 7 8 9　　　　　　　　　　Fic
1. Extrasensory perception—Fiction 2. Kidnapping—Fiction 3. Friendship—Fiction
ISBN　978-0-7653-0977-8;　0-7653-0977-7;
978-0-7653-4856-2 (pa); 0-7653-4856-X (pa)
LC 2006-39763

Sequel to: Hidden talents
"A Starscape book"

Over a year after fourteen-year-old Eddie "Trash" Thalmeyer and his friends from Edgeview Alternative School find out about their psychic abilities, Trash is kidnapped and Torchie, Cheater, Lucky, Flinch, and Martin must join forces to rescue their friend, discovering their true talents in the process.

This is "a gripping page-turner, with a flawlessly structured plot and compelling, struggling characters who never let each other down." Voice Youth Advocates

Luddy, Karon

Spelldown. Simon & Schuster Books for Young Readers 2007 211p $15.99 *

Grades: 5 6 7 8　　　　　　　　　　Fic
1. Spelling bees—Fiction 2. School stories 3. South Carolina—Fiction
ISBN 1-4169-1610-5; 9781416916109
LC 2006-21956

In 1969, the town of Red Clover, South Carolina, led by an enthusiastic new Latin teacher, supports thirteen-year-old Karlene as she wins her school spelling bee and strives to qualify for the National Bee, despite family problems and a growing desire for romance.

"This heartrending and funny debut novel deftly evokes place, time and character." Publ Wkly

Lupica, Mike

The big field. Philomel Books 2008 243p $17.99

Grades: 5 6 7 8　　　　　　　　　　Fic
1. Baseball—Fiction 2. Father-son relationship—Fiction
ISBN 978-0-399-24625-8; 0-399-24625-8
LC 2007-23647

When fourteen-year-old baseball player Hutch feels threatened by the arrival of a new teammate named Darryl, he tries to work through his insecurities about both Darryl and his remote and silent father, who was once a great ballplayer too.

"Writing in typically fluid prose and laying in a strong supporting lineup, Lupica strikes the right balance between personal issues and game action." Booklist

Miracle on 49th Street. Philomel Books 2006 246p $17.99

Grades: 5 6 7 8　　　　　　　　　　Fic
1.　Father-daughter　relationship—Fiction
2. Basketball—Fiction 3. Boston (Mass.)—Fiction
ISBN 0-399-24488-3　　　　LC 2005-32648

After her mother's death, twelve-year-old Molly learns that her father is a basketball star for the Boston Celtics.

"Lupica creates intriguing, complex characters . . . and he paces his story well, with enough twists and cliffhangers to keep the pages turning." SLJ

Summer ball; [by] Mike Lupica. Philomel Books 2007 244p $17.99

Grades: 6 7 8 9　　　　　　　　　　Fic
1. Basketball—Fiction 2. Camps—Fiction
ISBN 978-0-399-24487-2　　　LC 2006021781

Sequel to Travel team (2004)

Thirteen-year-old Danny must prove himself all over again for a disapproving coach and against new rivals at a summer basketball camp.

"Lupica breathes life into both characters and story. Danny is . . . sympathetic and engaging. He is surrounded by a cast of supporting characters who add humor and whose interactions ring true." SLJ

Lurie, April

Brothers, boyfriends & other criminal minds; [by] April Lurie. 1st ed. Delacorte Press 2007 289p $15.99

Grades: 7 8 9 10　　　　　　　　　　Fic
1. Organized crime—Fiction 2. Friendship—Fiction 3. Siblings—Fiction
ISBN 978-0-385-73124-9　　　LC 2006035633

While living on the same block as several members of the Mafia does have the advantage of a lower crime rate, fourteen-year-old April and her brother find there are times when it is also a major disadvantage.

"A classic growing-up-in-America story with a twist, this is lighthearted yet complex." Booklist

Dancing in the streets of Brooklyn. Delacorte Press 2002 194p $15.95; lib bdg $17.99; pa $5.99

Grades: 5 6 7 8　　　　　　　　　　Fic
1. Stepfathers—Fiction 2. World War, 1939-1945—Fiction 3. Brooklyn (New York, N.Y.)—Fiction
ISBN 0-385-72942-1; 0-385-90066-X (lib bdg); 0-440-41825-9 (pa)　　　LC 2002-170

Lurie, April—*Continued*

In 1944, thirteen-year-old Judy grapples with the discovery that "Pa" isn't her biological father, experiences her first romance, and faces hardships dealt to friends in Brooklyn's Norwegian community

"Judy's crises, romantic and domestic, are thoroughly believable, and Lurie ably avoids melodrama by setting them firmly among the realistic ebb and flow of neighborhood life." Bull Cent Child Books

The latent powers of Dylan Fontaine. Delacorte Press 2008 208p $15.99; lib bdg $18.99

Grades: 8 9 10 11 12 **Fic**

1. Family life—Fiction 2. New York (N.Y.)—Fiction
ISBN 978-0-385-73125-6; 978-0-385-90153-6 (lib bdg) LC 2007-32313

Fifteen-year-old Dylan's friend Angie is making a film about him while he is busy trying to keep his older brother from getting caught with drugs, to deal with his mother having left the family, and to figure out how to get Angie to think of him as more than just a friend.

"This is a story about guys, primarily . . . brothers; fathers and sons; lonely young men who are feeling somewhat lost. Any reader will care for each one of them. Lurie does a wonderful job of making them real." Kliatt

Ly, Many

Home is east; [by] Many Ly. Delacorte Press 2005 294p $15.95; lib bdg $17.99

Grades: 5 6 7 8 **Fic**

1. Cambodian Americans—Fiction 2. Divorce—Fiction 3. Moving—Fiction 4. California—Fiction
ISBN 0-385-73222-8; 0-385-73223-6 (lib bdg) LC 2004-14969

After her mother moves out, Amy, a Cambodian American girl, and her old-fashioned father leave their home in Florida to begin a new life in San Diego, experiencing turmoil and change as they slowly adjust to their new circumstances.

"Amy's narration is convincingly plainspoken, believable in its limitations but subtle in its understandings, and she's joined by a cast of compelling supporting characters." Bull Cent Child Books

Roots and wings; [by] Many Ly. Delacorte Press 2008 262p $15.99; lib bdg $18.99

Grades: 6 7 8 9 10 **Fic**

1. Buddhism—Fiction 2. Cambodian Americans—Fiction
ISBN 978-0-385-73500-1; 978-0-385-90494-0 (lib bdg); 0-385-73500-6; 0-385-90494-0 (lib bdg) LC 2008-00474

While in St. Petersburg, Florida, to give her grandmother a Cambodian funeral, fourteen-year-old Grace, who was raised in Pennsylvania, finally gets some answers about the father she never met, her mother's and grandmother's youth, and her Asian-American heritage.

"The book is beautifully written . . . [and] the author allows family secrets to unfold carefully and explores them with sincerity." SLJ

Lyga, Barry

The astonishing adventures of Fanboy & Goth Girl. Houghton Mifflin 2006 311p $16.95 *

Grades: 7 8 9 10 11 12 **Fic**

1. Cartoons and caricatures—Fiction 2. School stories 3. Friendship—Fiction
ISBN 0-618-72392-7 LC 2005-33259

A fifteen-year-old "geek" who keeps a list of the high school jocks and others who torment him, and pours his energy into creating a great graphic novel, encounters Kyra, Goth Girl, who helps change his outlook on almost everything, including himself.

"This engaging first novel has good characterization with genuine voices. . . . The book is compulsively readable." Voice Youth Advocates

Hero-type; by Barry Lyga. Houghton Mifflin Co. 2008 295p $16

Grades: 7 8 9 10 **Fic**

1. Heroes and heroines—Fiction 2. Patriotism—Fiction 3. School stories 4. Maryland—Fiction
ISBN 978-0-547-07663-8; 0-547-07663-0 LC 2008-7276

Feeling awkward and ugly is only one reason sixteen-year-old Kevin is uncomfortable with the publicity surrounding his act of accidental heroism, but when a reporter photographs him apparently being unpatriotic, he steps into the limelight to encourage people to think about what the symbols of freedom really mean.

"Leavened by much humor . . . this neatly plotted look at what real patriotism and heroism mean will get readers thinking." KLIATT

Lynch, Chris

The Big Game of Everything. HarperTeen 2008 275p $16.99; lib bdg $17.89

Grades: 7 8 9 10 **Fic**

1. Family life—Fiction 2. Grandfathers—Fiction 3. Summer employment—Fiction 4. Golf—Fiction
ISBN 978-0-06-074034-4; 0-06-074034-5; 978-0-06-074035-1 (lib bdg); 0-06-074035-3 (lib bdg) LC 2007-49578

Jock and his eccentric family spend the summer working at Grampus's golf complex, where they end up learning the rules of "The Big Game of Everything."

"This Printz Honor-winning author offers up another touching and offbeat novel full of delightfully skewed humor." Voice Youth Advocates

Cyberia; [by] Chris Lynch. Scholastic Press 2008 158p $16.99

Grades: 5 6 7 8 **Fic**

1. Technology and civilization—Fiction 2. Animals—Fiction 3. Science fiction
ISBN 978-0-545-02793-9; 0-545-02793-4 LC 2008-05388

In a future where electronic surveillance has taken the place of love, a veterinarian is putting computer chips in animals to control them, and those creatures choose young Zane, who understands their speech, to release captives and bring them to a technology-free safety zone.

"This very funny book occasionally strikes notes of unexpected poignancy." Booklist

Lynch, Chris—*Continued*

Inexcusable. Atheneum Books for Young Readers 2005 165p $16.95; pa $6.99 *

Grades: 8 9 10 11 12 **Fic**

1. Rape—Fiction 2. Football—Fiction 3. School stories

ISBN 0-689-84789-0; 1-416-93972-5 (pa)

LC 2004-30874

"Ginee Seo books"

High school senior and football player Keir sets out to enjoy himself on graduation night, but when he attempts to comfort a friend whose date has left her stranded, things go terribly wrong

"This finely crafted and thought-provoking page-turner carefully conveys that it is simply inexcusable to whitewash wrongs, and that those responsible should (and hopefully will) pay the price." SLJ

Lyon, Annabel, 1971-

All-season Edie. Orca Book Publishers 2008 179p pa $8.95

Grades: 5 6 7 8 **Fic**

1. Family life—Fiction 2. Grandfathers—Fiction 3. Canada—Fiction

ISBN 978-1-55143-713-2 (pa); 1-55143-713-9 (pa)

"Eleven-year-old Edie Jasmine Snow has a 'perfect' thirteen-year-old sister, two loving parents, and a cat named Dusty. . . . *All-Season Edie* follows Edie through a tumultuous year in which her beloved grandfather becomes ill. In the face of family tragedy, Edie tries to practice witchcraft, learns to dance the flamenco, meets the Greek god Zeus doing his Christmas shopping at the mall, ruins the most important party of her sister's life." Publisher's note

"Wry, fast, and funny. . . . Set in a Vancouver suburb . . . [this book] gets the preteen voice perfectly." Booklist

Lyon, George Ella, 1949-

Sonny's house of spies. Atheneum Books for Young Readers 2004 298p $16.95

Grades: 5 6 7 8 **Fic**

1. Race relations—Fiction 2. Homosexuality—Fiction 3. Alabama—Fiction

ISBN 0-689-85168-5 LC 2003-7529

"A Richard Jackson book"

In a small Alabama town in 1947 - 1956, Sonny searches for answers about his father's disappearance, "Uncle Marty," who looks after the family, and Mamby, their black housekeeper.

"Lyon conveys a strong sense of Southern life through the cadence of speech, wonderful turns of phrase, and the patterns of daily life. Sonny, smart-mouthed older sister Loretta, and their mother are all well-drawn, realistic characters with whom readers will sympathize." SLJ

Lyon, Steve

The gift moves. Houghton Mifflin 2004 230p $15

Grades: 5 6 7 8 **Fic**

1. Science fiction

ISBN 0-618-39128-2 LC 2003-12293

In a futuristic United States devoid of wealth and material things, a teenage baker befriends a talented weaver's apprentice who holds a dark secret.

"Lyon mixes elements of magical realism with a coming-of-age story, incorporating issues that teens will relate to. . . . This is an unusual story that is sure to inspire much thought and contemplation." SLJ

Lyons, Mary E.

Dear Ellen Bee; a Civil War scrapbook of two Union spies; by Mary E. Lyons & Muriel M. Branch. Atheneum Bks. for Young Readers 2000 161p il $17.95

Grades: 5 6 7 8 **Fic**

1. Van Lew, Elizabeth, 1818-1900—Fiction 2. Slavery—Fiction 3. Abolitionists—Fiction 4. United States—History—1861-1865, Civil War—Fiction 5. Spies—Fiction

ISBN 0-689-82379-7 LC 99-42050

A scrapbook kept by Liza, a young black girl details her experiences and those of the older white woman, "Miss Bet," who had freed her and her family, sent her north from Richmond to get an education, and then worked to bring an end to slavery. Based on the life of Elizabeth Van Lew

"Terrific research provides a fascinating portrait of these real heroines." Voice Youth Advocates

Letters from a slave boy; the story of Joseph Jacobs. Atheneum Books for Young Readers 2007 197p il map $15.99; pa $5.99

Grades: 6 7 8 9 **Fic**

1. Jacobs, Joseph, b. 1829—Fiction 2. Slavery—Fiction 3. African Americans—Fiction 4. Letters—Fiction

ISBN 978-0-689-87867-1; 0-689-87867-2; 978-0-689-87868-8 (pa); 0-689-87868-0 (pa)

LC 2006-01277

Companion volume to *Letters from a Slave Girl* (1992)

A fictionalized look at the life of Joseph Jacobs, son of a slave, told in the form of letters that he might have written during his life in pre-Civil War North Carolina, on a whaling expedition, in New York, New England, and finally in California during the Gold Rush.

"The 'letters' are short and the pace is quick. The dialect and spelling give authenticity without making the text difficult to read and understand. . . . This title stands on its own, but children who appreciated the forthright perspective of the first book will want to read this one as well." SLJ

Letters from a slave girl; the story of Harriet Jacobs. Scribner 1992 146p il hardcover o.p. pa $5.99 *

Grades: 6 7 8 9 **Fic**

1. Jacobs, Harriet A., 1813-1897—Fiction 2. Slavery—Fiction 3. African Americans—Fiction 4. Letters—Fiction

ISBN 0-684-19446-5; 1-4169-3637-8 (pa)

LC 91-45778

A fictionalized version of the life of Harriet Jacobs, told in the form of letters that she might have written during her slavery in North Carolina and as she prepared for escape to the North in 1842

Lyons, Mary E.—_Continued_

This "is historical fiction at its best. . . . Mary Lyons has remained faithful to Jacobs's actual autobiography throughout her readable, compelling novel. . . . Her observations of the horrors of slavery are concise and lucid. The letters are written in dialect, based on Jacobs's own writing and on other slave narrations of the period." Horn Book

MacCullough, Carolyn

Drawing the ocean. Roaring Brook Press 2006 170p $16.95

Grades: 7 8 9 10　　　　　　　　　　　　　　Fic

1. Twins—Fiction 2. Siblings—Fiction 3. Death—Fiction 4. Ghost stories

ISBN 978-1-59643-092-1; 1-59643-092-3

　　　　　　　　　　　　　　　　LC 2005-31471

"A Deborah Brodie book"

A gifted artist, Sadie is determined to fit in at her new school, but her deceased twin brother Ollie keeps appearing to her.

"Characters of every age come to life with vivid descriptions and dialogue that make this spare mood piece work." SLJ

MacHale, D. J.

The pilgrims of Rayne; [by] D.J. MacHale. 1st ed. Simon & Schuster Books for Young Readers 2007 547p (Pendragon) $16.99 *

Grades: 7 8 9 10　　　　　　　　　　　　　　Fic

1. Fantasy fiction 2. Adventure fiction

ISBN 978-1-4169-1416-7; 1-4169-1416-1

　　　　　　　　　　　　　　　　LC 2006038131

With Saint Dane seemingly on the verge of toppling all of the territories, Pendragon and Courtney set out to rescue Mark and find themselves traveling—and battling—their way through different worlds as they try to save all of Halla.

This is "packed . . . with nonstop action, mindboggling plot twists, and well-imagined locales." Voice Youth Advocates

Other titles in this series are:

The merchant of death (2002)

The lost city of Faar (2003)

The never war (2003)

The reality bug (2003)

Black water (2004)

The rivers of Zadaa (2005)

Quillan games (2006)

Raven rise (2008)

Mack, Tracy, 1968-

The fall of the Amazing Zalindas; casebook no. 1; by Tracy Mack and Michael Citrin; illustrations by Greg Ruth. Orchard Books 2006 259p il (Sherlock Holmes and the Baker Street irregulars) $16.99

Grades: 4 5 6 7　　　　　　　　　　　　　　Fic

1. Mystery fiction 2. Circus—Fiction 3. Great Britain—Fiction

ISBN 0-439-82836-8　　　　　　　　LC 2005-34000

The ragamuffin boys known as the Baker Street Irregulars help Sherlock Holmes solve the mysterious deaths of a family of circus tightrope walkers.

"Colorful, well-defined characters . . . and plenty of historical detail, Cockney slang . . . and Sherlockian references bring Victorian England to life. Vintage-style design elements and evocative black-and-white illustrations further the effect." Booklist

Mackel, Kathy

Boost. Dial Books 2008 248p $16.99 *

Grades: 6 7 8 9　　　　　　　　　　　　　　Fic

1. Basketball—Fiction 2. Steroids—Fiction

ISBN 978-0-8037-3240-7; 0-8037-3240-6

　　　　　　　　　　　　　　　　LC 2007-49441

Thirteen-year-old Savvy's dreams of starting for her elite basketball team are in danger when she is accused of taking steroids.

"Mackel has turned a tough subject in the world of teen competitive sports into a highly readable blend of intense action, interfamily relationships, and intrigue." SLJ

MadCat; [by] Kathy Mackel. 1st ed. HarperCollins 2005 185p $15.99; lib bdg $16.89

Grades: 5 6 7 8　　　　　　　　　　　　　　Fic

1. Softball—Fiction 2. Friendship—Fiction 3. Women athletes—Fiction

ISBN 0-06-054869-X; 0-06-054870-3 (lib bdg)

　　　　　　　　　　　　　　　　LC 2004-6618

Fast-pitch softball catcher MadCat Campione's love for the sport—and her relationship with her best friends—is strained when her team competes on a national level.

"With a credible plot, a distinct narrative voice, and sparky dialogue, this is a winner in any league." Booklist

Mackey, Weezie Kerr

Throwing like a girl; [by] Weezie Kerr Mackey. Marshall Cavendish 2007 271p $16.99

Grades: 6 7 8 9　　　　　　　　　　　　　　Fic

1. Softball—Fiction 2. School stories 3. Family life—Fiction 4. Texas—Fiction

ISBN 978-0-7614-5342-0　　　　　　LC 2006030233

After moving from Chicago to Dallas in the spring of her sophomore year, fifteen-year-old Ella finds that joining the softball team at her private school not only helps her make friends, it also provides unexpected opportunities to learn and grow.

"Readers will be delighted with how well the athletics and the girly stuff work in tandem." Booklist

Mackler, Carolyn

The earth, my butt, and other big, round things. Candlewick Press 2003 246p $15.99; pa $8.99

Grades: 7 8 9 10　　　　　　　　　　　　　　Fic

1. Family life—Fiction 2. Obesity—Fiction 3. School stories 4. New York (N.Y.)—Fiction

ISBN 0-7636-1958-2; 0-7636-2091-2 (pa)

　　　　　　　　　　　　　　　　LC 2002-73921

Feeling like she does not fit in with the other members of her family, who are all thin, brilliant, and good-

Mackler, Carolyn—*Continued*
looking, fifteen-year-old Virginia tries to deal with her
self-image, her first physical relationship, and her disillusionment with some of the people closest to her
"The e-mails [Virginia] exchanges . . . and the lists
she makes (e.g., 'The Fat Girl Code of Conduct') add
both realism and insight to her character. The heroine's
transformation into someone who finds her own style and
speaks her own mind is believable—and worthy of ap-
plause." Publ Wkly

Love and other four-letter words. Delacorte
Press 2000 247p $14.95 hardcover o.p. paperback
available $5.99
Grades: 7 8 9 10   **Fic**
1. Divorce—Fiction 2. Mother-daughter relationship—
Fiction
ISBN 0-385-32743-9   LC 00-25189
When she and her mother move to an apartment in
New York City after her parents decide on a trial separation, sixteen-year-old Sammie learns to deal with her
mother's fragile mental state, her best friend's self-
centeredness, several new friendships, and her own budding sexuality
"Mackler gets the contemporary scene with humor and
realism." Booklist

MacLachlan, Patricia, 1938-
Two novels: Baby; Journey; [by] Patricia
MachLachlan. Delacorte Press 2007 208p $16.99;
lib bdg $19.99 *
Grades: 5 6 7 8   **Fic**
1. Infants—Fiction 2. Bereavement—Fiction
3. Islands—Fiction 4. Mother-child relationship—Fiction 5. Grandparents—Fiction 6. Family life—Fiction
ISBN   978-0-385-73423-3;   0-385-73423-9;
978-0-385-90436-0 (lib bdg); 0-385-90436-3 (lib bdg)
LC 2006050273
A compilation of two previously published novels:
Baby (1993) and Journey (1991)
"In *Baby*, MacLachlan's spare, powerful prose tells of
twelve-year-old Larkin's family, already shattered by the
loss of a baby boy when infant Sophie appears on their
doorstep. Compelling compact *Journey* is about a brother
and sister who live with their grandparents after their
mother leaves, with photography central to the family's
healing." Horn Book Guide

MacLeod, Doug, 1959-
I'm being stalked by a moonshadow. Front
Street 2007 197p $16.95
Grades: 7 8 9 10   **Fic**
1. Family life—Fiction 2. Eccentrics and eccentricities—Fiction 3. Dating (Social customs)—Fiction
ISBN 978-1-59078-501-0; 1-59078-501-0
LC 2006-101608
As his odd parents fight the regional environmental
health officer about their dung-covered house and his
melodramatic younger brother demands attention, fourteen-year-old Australian Seth Parrot simply seeks the
muscular woman of his dreams.
This is a "fast, funny contemporary novel. . . . The
conflicts of loyalty and love will attract teens as much
as the farce." Booklist

MacPhail, Catherine, 1946-
Dark waters. Bloomsbury Pub. 2003 175p
$15.95
Grades: 5 6 7 8   **Fic**
1. Brothers—Fiction 2. Ghost stories
ISBN 1-58234-846-4   LC 2002-28296
Col McCann becomes a local hero when he saves a
boy from drowning but when his older brother is suspected of a serious crime, Col must decide if he should
be loyal to his family or tell the truth about what he saw
while under the water
"This is a fast-paced, exciting tale with lively characters and realistic family friction." Booklist

Madden, Kerry
Gentle's Holler; by Kerry Madden. Viking 2005
237p $16.99
Grades: 5 6 7 8   **Fic**
1. Family life—Fiction 2. Poverty—Fiction 3. North
Carolina—Fiction
ISBN 0-670-05998-6   LC 2004-18424
In the early 1960s, twelve-year-old songwriter Livy
Two Weems dreams of seeing the world beyond the
Maggie Valley, North Carolina, holler where she lives in
poverty with her parents and eight brothers and sisters,
but understands that she must put family first.
"Livy's narration rings true and is wonderfully voiced,
and Madden's message about the importance of forgive-
ness will be well received." SLJ
Other titles in this series are:
Louisiana's song (2007)
Jessie's mountain (2008)

Maddox, Jake
Free throw; by Jake Maddox; illustrated by Sean
Tiffany; text by Anastasia Suen. Stone Arch Books
2007 65p il lib bdg $22.60; pa $5.95
Grades: 4 5 6 7   **Fic**
1. Basketball—Fiction
ISBN 978-1-59889-060-0 (lib bdg); 1-59889-060-3 (lib
bdg); 978-1-59889-238-3 (pa); 1-59889-238-X (pa)
LC 2006006076
Since Derek is now the tallest player on his basketball
team, the coach decides to have him play center but Jason, the former center, has little confidence in Derek and
will not pass him the ball.
"The clear descriptions, realistic dialogue, abundant
action, and touches of humor will appeal to younger children, as well as to middle school or older readers who
are working to bolster their skills. They will appreciate
the large font and the comic-book-style drawings that illuminate the [text]." SLJ

Madison, Bennett, 1981-
Lulu Dark and the summer of the Fox; a
mystery; by Bennett Madison. Razorbill 2006
$10.99
Grades: 7 8 9 10   **Fic**
1. Mystery fiction
ISBN 1-59514-086-7   LC 2006004960
Companion volume to Lulu Dark can see through
walls (2005)
"Sleuth"

Madison, Bennett, 1981-—*Continued*

When a mysterious person called the Fox begins to threaten young starlets, Lulu Dark investigates, even though she suspects that her own mother—an aging actress—might be behind it all.

"Teens will enjoy this smart, funny chick-lit heroine who has real problems and a satirical outlook." SLJ

Lulu Dark can see through walls; a mystery. Razorbill 2005 248p $9.99

Grades: 7 8 9 10   **Fic**

1. Mystery fiction

ISBN 1-59514-010-7   LC 2004-26073

When someone steals her purse and her identity, high school junior and reluctant girl sleuth Lulu Dark investigates.

Written "with a flip buoyancy that bops off the page. . . . Teens searching for a lighthearted mystery will adore Lulu." SLJ

Magoon, Kekla, 1980-

The rock and the river. Aladdin 2009 290p $15.99 *

Grades: 7 8 9 10   **Fic**

1. Black Panther Party—Fiction 2. African Americans—Fiction 3. Brothers—Fiction 4. Chicago (Ill.)—Fiction

ISBN 978-1-4169-7582-3; 1-4169-7582-9

LC 2008-29170

In 1968 Chicago, fourteen-year-old Sam Childs is caught in a conflict between his father's nonviolent approach to seeking civil rights for African Americans and his older brother, who has joined the Black Panther Party.

This "novel will make readers feel what it was like to be young, black, and militant 40 years ago, including the seething fury and desperation over the daily discrimination that drove the oppressed to fight back." Booklist

Maguire, Gregory

What-the-Dickens; the story of a rogue tooth fairy. Candlewick Press 2007 295p $15.99

Grades: 4 5 6 7   **Fic**

1. Fairies—Fiction   2. Orphans—Fiction
3. Storytelling—Fiction   4. Storms—Fiction
5. Cousins—Fiction

ISBN 978-0-7636-2961-8; 0-7636-2961-8

LC 2007-24186

As a terrible storm rages, ten-year-old Dinah and her brother and sister listen to their cousin Gage's tale of a newly-hatched, orphaned, skibberee, or tooth fairy, called What-the-Dickens, who hopes to find a home among the skibbereen tribe, if only he can stay out of trouble.

"The immediacy of the story and combination of fantasy and reality will grip even reluctant readers." SLJ

Mah, Adeline Yen, 1937-

Chinese Cinderella and the Secret Dragon Society; [by] Adeline Yen Mah. 1st ed. HarperCollins 2005 242p $15.99; lib bdg $16.89

Grades: 5 6 7 8   **Fic**

1. World War, 1939-1945—Fiction 2. China—Fiction 3. Martial arts—Fiction

ISBN 0-06-056734-1; 0-06-056735-X (lib bdg)

LC 2004-8852

During the Japanese occupation of parts of China, twelve-year-old Ye Xian is thrown out of her father's and stepmother's home, joins a martial arts group, and tries to help her aunt and the Americans in their struggle against the Japanese invaders.

"Full of adventure and contrivance, this somewhat old-fashioned, plot-driven novel is clear about the values that are important to the author. . . . These young people are courageous, creative, and open-minded." SLJ

Mahy, Margaret

Alchemy. Margaret K. McElderry Bks. 2003 207p $16.95; pa $7.99

Grades: 7 8 9 10   **Fic**

1. Alchemy—Fiction

ISBN 0-689-85053-0; 0-689-85054-9 (pa)

LC 2002-5973

Seventeen-year-old Roland discovers that an unpopular girl in his school is studying alchemy and finds that their destiny is linked with that of a power-hungry magician

"Mahy, whose thrillers are both complex and literary, once again provides a multilayered story that can be appreciated on several levels." Booklist

Maddigan's Fantasia. Margaret K. McElderry Books 2007 499p $15.99

Grades: 4 5 6 7   **Fic**

1. Circus—Fiction 2. Magic—Fiction 3. Fantasy fiction

ISBN 1-4169-1812-4; 978-1-4169-1817-7

LC 2006-15512

In a world made uncertain by "the Chaos," two time-traveling boys, fifteen-year-old Timon and eleven-year-old Eden, seek to protect a magic talisman, aided by twelve-year-old Garland, a member of a traveling circus known as Maddigan's Fantasia.

"A well-drawn character, Garland resembles other Mahy protagonists—cranky, assertive and filled with self-doubt—and her adventures are invariably exciting." Publ Wkly

Malley, Gemma

The Declaration. Bloomsbury; distributed by Holtzbrinck Pub. 2007 300p $16.95

Grades: 7 8 9 10   **Fic**

1. Science fiction 2. Great Britain—Fiction 3. Immortality—Fiction

ISBN 978-1-59990-119-0; 1-59990-119-6

LC 2006-102138

In 2140 England, where drugs enable people to live forever and children are illegal, teenaged Anna, an obedient "Surplus" training to become a house servant, discovers that her birth parents are trying to find her.

This is "gripping. . . . The indoctrinated teen's awakening to massive injustice makes compulsive reading." Booklist

Malley, Gemma—*Continued*
Followed by The resistance (2008)

Mankell, Henning, 1948-
A bridge to the stars. Delacorte Press 2007 164p
$15.99; lib bdg $18.99 *
Grades: 6 7 8 9   **Fic**
1. Father-son relationship—Fiction 2. Sweden—Fiction
ISBN 978-0-385-73495-0; 978-0-385-90489-6 (lib
bdg)   LC 2006-26901
In Sweden in 1956, eleven-year-old Joel and his father, a logger who was once a sailor, live alone with
their secrets, including Joel's secret society that meets at
night and his father's new romantic interest.
This is a "quiet but deeply satisfying coming-of-age
story. . . . Those who welcome character-driven fiction
will treasure this beautifully realized novel." Booklist
Followed by: Shadows in the twilight (2008)

Secrets in the fire; translated by Anne Connie
Stuksrud. Annick Press 2003 166p $17.95; pa
$7.95
Grades: 5 6 7 8   **Fic**
1. Mozambique—Fiction 2. War stories
ISBN 1-55037-801-5; 1-55037-800-7 (pa)
Originally published in Sweden
Sofia, who lost her legs from landmines in Mozam-
bique, attempts to make a new life for herself.
"A hard-hitting, eye-opening novel that brings readers
face-to-face with the horrors of war. . . . Mankell's lan-
guage and style are spare, but elicit a deeply emotional
response. " SLJ

Margolis, Leslie
Boys are dogs; [by] Leslie Margolis.
Bloomsbury Children's Books 2008 195p $15.99
Grades: 4 5 6   **Fic**
1. Moving—Fiction 2. Dogs—Fiction 3. School stories
ISBN 978-1-59990-221-0; 1-59990-221-4
                                     LC 2007052362
When her mother gets a new boyfriend, sixth-grader
Annabelle gets to cope with a new town, a new school,
and a new puppy and, while training her puppy, she decides to apply some of the same techniques to tame the
unruly boys that are making her middle-school life miserable.
Annabelle's "breakthroughs come across as genuine.
The story lines—melded household, moving, boys as
dogs—coalesce naturally, giving girl readers a thoughtful
story along with, just possibly, some substantive boy advice." Publ Wkly

Marillier, Juliet
Cybele's secret. Alfred A. Knopf 2008 432p
$17.99; lib bdg $20.99 *
Grades: 7 8 9 10   **Fic**
1. Magic—Fiction 2. Supernatural—Fiction
3. Sisters—Fiction 4. Turkey—Fiction
ISBN   978-0-375-83365-6;   0-375-83365-X;
978-0-375-93365-3 (lib bdg); 0-375-93365-4 (lib bdg)
                                     LC 2008-4758
Companion volume to: Wildwood dancing (2007)

Scholarly eighteen-year-old Paula and her merchant
father journey from Transylvania to Istanbul to buy an
ancient pagan artifact rumored to be charmed, but others,
including a handsome Portuguese pirate and an envoy
from the magical Wildwood, want to acquire the item, as
well.
This is a "honeyed draught of a [novel]. . . . Marillier
embroiders Ottoman Empire cultural details into every
fold and drape of her story." Booklist

Wildwood dancing. Knopf 2007 416p $16.99;
lib bdg $18.99
Grades: 7 8 9 10   **Fic**
1. Magic—Fiction 2. Supernatural—Fiction
3. Sisters—Fiction
ISBN 0-375-83364-1; 0-375-93364-6 (lib bdg)
                                     LC 2006-16075
Five sisters who live with their merchant father in
Transylvania use a hidden portal in their home to cross
over into a magical world, the Wildwood.
This is told "with a striking sense of place, magical
elements, beautifully portrayed characters, strong hero-
ines, and an emotional core that touches the heart."
Voice Youth Advocates
Followed by: Cybele's secret (2008)

Marley, Louise, 1952-
Singer in the snow. Viking 2005 304p $16.99;
pa $7.99
Grades: 7 8 9 10   **Fic**
1. Fantasy fiction
ISBN 0-670-05965-X; 0-14-240748-8 (pa)
                                     LC 2005-5575
"This follow-up to the Singers of Nevya trilogy (1995-
1997) features two young Singers with the psi-Gift who
journey from their beloved Conservatory to the remote
House of Tarus near the Frozen Sea. Mreen, a mute
young woman of exceptional power, is Tarus' new
Cantrix: one who uses music and magic to summon the
light and heat necessary to survive the planet's deadly
cold. Emle, whose musical talent is sublime but who for
reasons unknown cannot summon a thing, acts as
Mreen's interpreter. While Mreen adjusts to her new life,
Emle explores the flaws of her gift and connects with a
psychologically burdened stable boy. . . . This is satisfying fare for fantasy lovers and an easy entry point for
teens new to the genre." Booklist

Marr, Melissa
Ink exchange. HarperTeen 2008 325p il $16.99;
lib bdg $17.89
Grades: 8 9 10 11 12   **Fic**
1. Fairies—Fiction 2. Tattooing—Fiction 3. Kings and
rulers—Fiction 4. Fantasy fiction
ISBN   978-0-06-121468-4;   0-06-121468-X;
978-0-06-121469-1 (lib bdg); 0-06-121469-8 (lib bdg)
                                     LC 2007-40106
Seventeen-year-old Leslie wants a tattoo as a way of
reclaiming control of herself and her body, but the eerie
image she selects pulls her into the dangerous Dark
Court of the faeries, where she draws on inner strength
to make a horrible choice.
"Readers will be drawn in by Marr's darkly poetic imagery and language, her vivid portrayal of the art of tat-

Marr, Melissa—*Continued*

tooing, and her shadowy love triangle. This is indeed a delicious, smoky delight." Bull Cent Child Books

Other titles about Faerie are:

Wicked lovely (2007)

Fragile eternity (2009)

Marriott, Zoë, 1982 or 3-

The swan kingdom. Candlewick Press 2008 272p $16.99

Grades: 6 7 8 9 10 11 12   **Fic**

1. Fantasy fiction 2. Magic—Fiction

ISBN 978-0-7636-3481-0; 0-7636-3481-6

LC 2007-38291

When Alexa's mother is killed, her father marries a cunning and powerful woman and her brothers disappear, sending Alexa on a long, dangerous journey as she attempts to harness the mystical power she inherited from her mother and restore the kingdom to its proper balance.

"The mix of magic, royalty and romance will compel many teens." Publ Wkly

Marsden, Carolyn, 1950-

Sahwira; an African friendship; [by] Carolyn Marsden and Philip Matzigkeit. Candlewick Press 2009 189p $15.99

Grades: 5 6 7 8   **Fic**

1. Clergy—Fiction 2. Friendship—Fiction 3. Race relations—Fiction 4. Zimbabwe—Fiction

ISBN 978-0-7636-3575-6; 0-7636-3575-8

The strong friendship between two boys, one black and one white, who live on a mission in Rhodesia, begins to unravel as protests against white colonial rule intensify in 1964.

"The book looks beyond race to examine questions about the meaning of being Christian, fear of Communism, family loyalty, and ethical choices. Marsden and Matzigkeit . . . deftly navigate the dynamic forces at play in the two boys' lives. . . . The story crosses genres to bring in elements of historical fiction, intrigue, and mystery." Bull Cent Child Books

Marsden, John, 1950-

Tomorrow, when the war began. Houghton Mifflin 1995 286p $16 *

Grades: 7 8 9 10   **Fic**

1. War stories 2. Australia—Fiction

ISBN 0-395-70673-4   LC 94-29299

Also available in paperback from Dell

First published 1993 in Australia

"Australian teenager Ellie and six of her friends return from a winter break camping trip to find their homes burned or deserted, their families imprisoned, and their country occupied by a foreign military force in league with a band of disaffected Australians. As their shock wears off, the seven decide they must stick together if they are to survive." SLJ

"The novel is a riveting adventure through which Marsden explores the capacity for evil and the necessity of working together to oppose it." Horn Book

Other available titles in this series are:

Burning for revenge (2000)

Darkness, be my friend (1999)

The dead of night (1997)

A killing frost (1998)

The night is for hunting (2001)

The other side of dawn (2002)

While I live (2007)

Marsh, Katherine

The night tourist; [by] Katherine Marsh. 1st ed. Hyperion Books for Children 2007 232p $17.99 *

Grades: 6 7 8 9   **Fic**

1. Death—Fiction 2. Classical mythology—Fiction 3. New York (N.Y.)—Fiction

ISBN 978-1-4231-0689-0; 1-4231-0689-X

LC 2007013311

After fourteen-year-old classics prodigy Jack Perdu has a near fatal accident he meets Euri, a young ghost who introduces him to New York's Underworld, where those who died in New York reside until they are ready to move on, and Jack vows to find his dead mother there.

"Mixing numerous references to mythology and classical literature with deft touches of humor and extensive historical details . . . this intelligent and self-assured debut will compel readers from its outset and leave them satisfied." Publ Wkly

Followed by: The twilight prisoner (2009)

Martin, Ann M., 1955-

A corner of the universe. Scholastic Press 2002 189p $15.95; pa $5.99

Grades: 5 6 7 8   **Fic**

1. Uncles—Fiction 2. Mentally handicapped—Fiction 3. Friendship—Fiction

ISBN 0-439-38880-5; 0-439-38881-3 (pa)

LC 2001-57611

A Newbery Medal honor book, 2003

The summer that Hattie turns twelve, she meets the childlike uncle she never knew and becomes friends with a girl who works at the carnival that comes to Hattie's small town

"Martin delivers wonderfully real characters and an engrossing plot through the viewpoint of a girl who tries so earnestly to connect with those around her." SLJ

Here today. Scholastic 2004 308p $16.95

Grades: 5 6 7 8   **Fic**

1. Mothers—Fiction 2. Family life—Fiction

ISBN 0-439-57944-9   LC 2004-41620

In 1963, Ellie's mother was crowned a grocery store beauty queen, her classmates treated her cruelly, and President Kennedy was killed. It was also when Ellie realized that in trying to keep her life together she had to let pieces of it go

"Martin paints a well-articulated picture of the times, but it is her memorable child and adult characters that shine here." SLJ

Martin, Nora

Flight of the Fisherbird. Bloomsbury Children's
Bks. 2003 150p il $16.95

Grades: 5 6 7 8   **Fic**

1. Uncles—Fiction 2. Chinese Americans—Fiction
3. Washington (State)—Fiction

ISBN 1-58234-814-6   LC 2002-35628

In 1889 in the islands off the coast of Washington
State, thirteen-year-old Clementine pulls a nearly
drowned Chinese man out of the sea and begins to suspect that her beloved uncle may have been involved in
his attempted murder as well as other treacherous deeds.

"A fast-paced, high-stakes historical mystery." SLJ

Martin, Rafe

Birdwing; [by] Rafe Martin. 1st ed. Arthur A.
Levine Books 2005 359p $16.99

Grades: 6 7 8 9   **Fic**

1. Fairy tales

ISBN 0-439-21167-0   LC 2004-11695

Prince Ardwin, known as Birdwing, the youngest of
six brothers turned into swans by their stepmother, is unable to complete the transformation back into human
form, so he undertakes a journey to discover whether his
feathered arm will be a curse or a blessing to him.

"The many original characters and unusual adventure
scenes ensure that readers will remember this well-paced
fantasy." Booklist

Mason, Prue

Camel rider; [by] Prue Mason. 1st U.S. ed.
Charlesbridge 2007 204p $15.95

Grades: 6 7 8 9   **Fic**

1. Wilderness survival—Fiction 2. Deserts—Fiction
3. Persian Gulf region—Fiction 4. War stories

ISBN 978-1-58089-314-5; 1-58089-314-7

LC 2006034125

Two expatriates living in a Middle Eastern country,
twelve-year-old Adam from Australia and Walid from
Bangladesh, must rely on one another when war breaks
out and they find themselves in the desert, both trying to
reach the same city with no water, little food, and no
common language.

"The suspense is sustained and the wildly improbable
happy ending is very satisfying." SLJ

Mason, Timothy

The last synapsid. Delacorte Press 2009 311p il
$16.99; lib bdg $19.99

Grades: 5 6 7 8   **Fic**

1. Prehistoric animals—Fiction 2. Time travel—Fiction
3. Space and time—Fiction 4. Colorado—Fiction

ISBN   978-0-385-73581-0;   0-385-73581-2;
978-0-385-90567-1 (lib bdg); 0-385-90567-X (lib bdg)

LC 2008-35678

On a mountain near their tiny town of Faith, Colorado, best friends Rob and Phoebe discover a squat, drooly
creature from thirty million years before the dinosaurs,
that needs their help in tracking down a violent carnivore
that must be returned to its proper place in time, or humans will never evolve.

"Mason has written a highly engaging fantasy that in-

cludes something for all readers. . . . Readers will find
it difficult to put this book down until they have reached
the last page." Libr Media Connect

Mass, Wendy, 1967-

Every soul a star; a novel. Little, Brown and
Co. 2008 322p $15.99 *

Grades: 5 6 7 8   **Fic**

1. Solar eclipses—Fiction 2. Friendship—Fiction

ISBN 978-0-316-00256-1; 0-316-00256-9

LC 2008009259

Ally, Bree, and Jack meet at the one place the Great
Eclipse can be seen in totality, each carrying the burden
of different personal problems, which become dim when
compared to the task they embark upon and the friendship they find.

Mass "combines astronomy and storytelling for a well-
balanced look at friendships and the role they play in
shaping identity. . . . Information about solar eclipses
and astronomy is carefully woven into the plot to build
drama and will almost certainly intrigue readers." Publ
Wkly

Includes bibliographical references

Heaven looks a lot like the mall; a novel. Little,
Brown 2007 251p $16.99

Grades: 8 9 10 11 12   **Fic**

1. Coma—Fiction 2. School stories 3. Shopping centers and malls—Fiction

ISBN 978-0-316-05851-3; 0-316-05851-3

LC 2007-12333

When high school junior Tessa Reynolds falls into a
coma after getting hit in the head during gym class, she
experiences heaven as the mall where her parents work,
and she revisits key events from her life, causing her to
reevaluate herself and how she wants to live.

"Tessa's journey and authentic voice is one that readers will appreciate. . . . Funny, thought-provoking, and
at times heartbreaking, this story will entertain and inspire readers." SLJ

Jeremy Fink and the meaning of life. Little,
Brown 2006 289p $15.99

Grades: 5 6 7 8   **Fic**

1. Conduct of life—Fiction 2. Father-son relationship—Fiction

ISBN 978-0-316-05829-2; 0-316-05829-7

LC 2005037291

Just before his thirteenth birthday, Jeremy Fink receives a keyless locked box—set aside by his father before his death five years earlier—that purportedly contains the meaning of life.

"Mass fashions an adventure in which both journey
and destination are worth the trip." Horn Book

A mango-shaped space; a novel. Little, Brown
2003 220p $16.95

Grades: 5 6 7 8   **Fic**

1. Synesthesia—Fiction 2. School stories

ISBN 0-316-52388-7   LC 2002-72989

Afraid that she is crazy, thirteen-year-old Mia, who
sees a special color with every letter, number, and sound,
keeps this a secret until she becomes overwhelmed by
school, changing relationships, and the loss of something

Mass, Wendy, 1967——*Continued*
important to her

"Mass skillfully conveys Mia's emotions, and readers will be intrigued with this fictional depiction of an actual, and fascinating, condition." Horn Book Guide

Masson, Sophie, 1959-

Snow, fire, sword. 1st American ed. Eos 2006 359p $15.99; lib bdg $16.89

Grades: 6 7 8 9   **Fic**

1. Magic—Fiction 2. Fantasy fiction
ISBN   978-0-06-079091-2;   0-06-079091-1;
978-0-06-079092-9 (lib bdg); 0-06-079092-X (lib bdg)
LC 2005-18149

In the mythical, Indonesia-like country of Jayangan, a village girl and an apprentice swordmaker embark on a magical journey to defeat a hidden evil that threatens their land.

"The sense of a permeable membrane between spirit worlds and contemporary reality will fascinate many readers, as will the shifting images of water buffaloes and motorbikes, villages and cities, and sacred and secular ways." Booklist

Matas, Carol, 1949-

After the war. Simon & Schuster Bks. for Young Readers 1996 116p map hardcover o.p. pa $4.99

Grades: 7 8 9 10   **Fic**

1. Holocaust, 1933-1945—Fiction 2. Jews—Fiction
ISBN 0-689-80350-8; 0-689-80722-8
LC 95-43613

After being released from Buchenwald at the end of World War II, fifteen-year-old Ruth risks her life to lead a group of children across Europe to Palestine

"Rich in texture and simple in its honesty, this story resonates with feeling." Voice Youth Advocates

Followed by The garden

Sparks fly upward. Clarion Bks. 2002 180p $15
Grades: 4 5 6 7   **Fic**

1. Jews—Fiction 2. Prejudices—Fiction 3. Canada—Fiction
ISBN 0-618-15964-9   LC 2001-47188

In 1910, when a family of Russian Jews moves from Saskatchewan to Winnipeg, Canada, twelve-year-old Rebecca must live with Christians temporarily and struggles with anti-Semitism, confusion about God, and changing relationships with family and friends

"There's no sentimentality in the characterization . . . and the history is well researched. Most compelling, though, is Rebecca's personal struggle with faith, friendship, and loyalty." Booklist

The whirlwind. Orca 2007 128p pa $8.95
Grades: 6 7 8 9   **Fic**

1. Jews—Fiction 2. World War, 1939-1945—Fiction 3. Immigrants—Fiction
ISBN 978-1-55143-703-3 (pa); 1-55143-703-1 (pa)

"Benjamin Friedman, a 15-year-old Jewish boy, fears for his life in Nazi Germany. Fortunately, his family is able to escape Hitler, arriving in Seattle in the summer of 1941. Ben is relieved to be there but is upset and con-

fused by his experiences. . . . This unique and thought-provoking story shows what prejudice and indifference to suffering and wrongdoing can lead to. It imparts an understanding of the Holocaust and World War II." SLJ

Matthews, Andrew, 1948-

The way of the warrior. Dutton Children's Books 2008 152p $15.99

Grades: 7 8 9 10   **Fic**

1. Samurai—Fiction 2. Japan—Fiction
ISBN 978-0-525-42063-7; 0-525-42063-0

"In 1565, when Jimmu is 10 years old, he witnesses his father commit seppuku, a ritual suicide, to avoid bringing dishonor to his family. . . . Jimmu spends the next seven years learning the art of the samurai . . . with the sole intention of avenging his father . . . . The . . . story is an honest and engaging portrayal of a young man's struggle to do the right thing. . . . The vivid depictions of a soldier's life in 16th-century Japan will captivate samurai enthusiasts, and the amount of action that Matthews packs into this relatively short novel will appeal to reluctant readers." SLJ

Matthews, Kezi, 1928-

Flying lessons. Cricket Bks. 2002 162p $16.95
Grades: 6 7 8 9   **Fic**

1. Aunts—Fiction 2. Uncles—Fiction 3. Death—Fiction
ISBN 0-8126-2671-0   LC 2002-6047

In 1937, when LaMarr's glamorous mother is lost in a plane crash and she goes to live with her aunt and uncle, it takes the thirteen-year-old some time to reconcile herself to the idea that her mother has not gone to Hollywood to become a movie star

"Beautifully written and emotionally resonant." Horn Book

Matthews, L. S.

A dog for life; [by] L.S. Matthews. Delacorte Press 2006 144p $14.95; lib bdg $16.99

Grades: 4 5 6 7   **Fic**

1. Dogs—Fiction 2. Runaway children—Fiction 3. Great Britain—Fiction
ISBN   978-0-385-73366-3;   0-385-73366-6;
978-0-385-90381-3 (lib bdg); 0-385-90381-2 (lib bdg)
LC 2006-45664

When John, who has a special ability to communicate with animals, finds that his dog, Mouse is scheduled to go to the pound, he and Mouse decide to run away and find his uncle who may be able to help them.

"Although John and Mouse encounter some disturbing situations, the childlike tone and magical elements of the narrative keep it age appropriate. . . . Highly enjoyable." SLJ

Lexi. Delacorte Press 2008 200p $14.99; lib bdg $17.99

Grades: 4 5 6 7   **Fic**

1. Amnesia—Fiction 2. Orphans—Fiction 3. Twins—Fiction 4. Sisters—Fiction 5. Homeless persons—Fiction
ISBN   978-0-385-73574-2;   0-385-73574-X;
978-0-385-90563-3 (lib bdg); 0-385-90563-7 (lib bdg)
LC 2007-46745

Matthews, L. S.—*Continued*

When twelve-year-old Lexi wakes up in the middle of a forest with no memory of her name or anything else, she slowly reconstructs her forgotten life with the help of some shelter workers, an ex-boxer, and her long-lost grandmother.

"This is a story of improbable, sometimes frightening events told by a child narrator, in which extraordinary things seem perfectly plausible. . . . Fans of Matthews's previous work will appreciate its sense of childlike wonder and fantasy." SLJ

The outcasts. Delacorte Press 2007 259p $15.99; lib bdg $18.99

Grades: 7 8 9 10 **Fic**
1. Supernatural—Fiction 2. School stories 3. Great Britain—Fiction
ISBN 978-0-385-73367-0; 978-0-385-90382-0 (lib bdg) LC 2006-50872

First published 2005 in the United Kingdom

A much-anticipated school trip to England's West Country turns into a life-changing adventure for five high school misfits when they fall into another dimension while exploring the house in which they are staying.

"A fun, wild, and thoughtfully layered adventure." Booklist

Matthews, Tom L., 1949-

Danger in the dark; a Houdini & Nate mystery; [by] Tom Lalicki; pictures by Carlyn Cerniglia. 1st ed. Farrar, Straus and Giroux 2006 186p il $14.95

Grades: 4 5 6 7 **Fic**
1. Houdini, Harry, 1874-1926—Fiction 2. Magicians—Fiction 3. Spiritualism—Fiction 4. Mystery fiction
ISBN 0-374-31680-5 LC 2005052111

Thirteen-year-old Nathaniel, aided by the famous magician Harry Houdini, plots to unmask a phony spirit advisor attempting to relieve the boy's great-aunt of her fortune.

"The action is nonstop, and even a flurry of enormous coincidences won't spoil enthusiasm for this entertaining story." Booklist

Another title in this series is:
Shots at sea (2007)

Mayall, Beth

Mermaid Park. Razorbill 2005 248p $16.99

Grades: 7 8 9 10 **Fic**
1. Swimming—Fiction 2. Summer employment—Fiction 3. Family life—Fiction 4. New Jersey—Fiction
ISBN 1-59514-029-8

Sixteen-year-old Amy escapes family difficulties by immersing herself in her job at a mermaid-themed water show.

"This is a good read that deals with real growing-up issues." SLJ

Maynard, Joyce, 1953-

The cloud chamber. Atheneum Books for Young Readers 2005 274p $16.95; pa $7.99

Grades: 7 8 9 10 **Fic**
1. Depression (Psychology)—Fiction 2. Suicide—Fiction 3. School stories 4. Montana—Fiction
ISBN 0-689-87152-X; 1-416-92699-2 (pa) LC 2004-18607

"An Anne Schwartz book"

In 1966, when his father's attempted suicide causes the ostracism of the family in their small Montana community, fourteen-year-old Nate copes with his sadness and anger by trying to win the school science fair.

"The plot moves quickly and engagingly through Nate's trials and small triumphs." SLJ

Mazer, Harry, 1925-

A boy at war; a novel of Pearl Harbor. Simon & Schuster Bks. for Young Readers 2001 104p il hardcover o.p. pa $4.99

Grades: 7 8 9 10 **Fic**
1. Pearl Harbor (Oahu, Hawaii), Attack on, 1941—Fiction
ISBN 0-689-84161-2; 0-689-84160-4 (pa) LC 00-49687

While fishing with his friends off Honolulu on December 7, 1941, teenaged Adam is caught in the midst of the Japanese attack and through the chaos of the subsequent days tries to find his father, a naval officer who was serving on the U.S.S. Arizona when the bombs fell

"Mazer's graphic, sensory descriptions give the narrative immediacy, putting readers alongside Adam, watching with him as 'pieces of the ship and pieces of men rained down around him.' . . . This is a thought-provoking, sobering account of the human costs of war." Horn Book Guide

Other titles in this series are:
Boy no more (2004)
Heroes don't run (2005)

The last mission. Dell 1981 c1979 188p pa $5.99 *

Grades: 7 8 9 10 **Fic**
1. World War, 1939-1945—Fiction 2. Prisoners of war—Fiction 3. Jews—Fiction
ISBN 0-440-94797-9

First published 1979 by Delacorte Press

In 1944 a 15-year-old Jewish boy tells his family he will travel in the West but instead, enlists in the United States Air Corps and is subsequently taken prisoner by the Germans.

"Told in a rapid journalistic style, occasionally peppered with barrack-room vulgarities, the story is a vivid and moving account of a boy's experience during World War II as well as a skillful, convincing portrayal of his misgivings as a Jew on enemy soil and of his ability to size up—in mature human fashion—the misery around him." Horn Book

Mazer, Harry, 1925-—*Continued*

My brother Abe; Sally Lincoln's story. Simon & Schuster Books for Young Readers 2009 202p $15.99

Grades: 4 5 6 7   **Fic**

    1. Lincoln, Abraham, 1809-1865—Fiction 2. Lincoln, Sarah Bush Johnston, 1788-1869—Fiction 3. Frontier and pioneer life—Fiction

    ISBN 978-1-4169-3884-2; 1-4169-3884-2

                                    LC 2008-01106

Forced off their land in Kentucky in 1816, nine-year-old Sarah Lincoln, known as Sally, and her family, including younger brother Abe, move to the Indiana frontier.

"Drawing on a limber imagination and knack for storytelling, Mazer . . . turns a few facts from Abraham Lincoln's childhood into a vivid historical novel. . . . Abe's older sister, Sally, about whom little is known, serves as the personable narrator and protagonist." Publ Wkly

Snow bound. Delacorte Press 1973 146p pa $5.99 hardcover o.p. *

Grades: 7 8 9 10   **Fic**

    1. Wilderness survival—Fiction 2. Runaway children—Fiction

    ISBN 0-440-96134-3   LC 72-7958

"Tony Laporte is angry when his parents will not allow him to keep a stray dog, so he takes off in his mother's old car. Driving without a license in the middle of a snowstorm that soon becomes a blizzard, Tony picks up a hitchhiker, Cindy Reichert. Trying to impress the slightly older girl with his driving skill, Tony wrecks the car, leaving the two stranded in a desolate area far from a main highway, with little likelihood of rescue for days." Shapiro. Fic for Youth. 3d edition

Mazer, Norma Fox, 1931-

After the rain. Morrow 1987 291p hardcover o.p. pa $5.99

Grades: 6 7 8 9   **Fic**

    1. Grandfathers—Fiction 2. Death—Fiction

    ISBN 0-688-06867-7; 0-380-75025-2 (pa)

                                    LC 86-33270

A Newbery Medal honor book, 1988

"Adolescent Rachel has always been a little afraid of Grandpa Izzy, her mother's father; sharp-tongued and irritable, the old man seems to have no kindness or softness in his nature. After the family learns that he has terminal cancer (which Izzy isn't told), Rachel begins to visit him and walk with him daily, and by the time he is near the end and hospitalized, she has come to love him." Bull Cent Child Books

"A powerful book, dealing with death and dying and the strength of family affection." Horn Book

Girlhearts. HarperCollins Pubs. 2001 210p hardcover o.p. lib bdg $16.89; pa $6.99

Grades: 6 7 8 9   **Fic**

    1. Orphans—Fiction 2. Death—Fiction

    ISBN 0-688-13350-9; 0-688-06866-9 (lib bdg); 0-380-72290-9 (pa)   LC 00-63202

Sequel to Silver

Thirteen-year-old Sarabeth Silver's life is turned upside-down when her mother dies suddenly, leaving her orphaned, confused, and at the mercy of everyone who seems to know what is best for her

"Mazer's intimate portrait of grief is convincing and well drawn." Horn Book Guide

The missing girl. HarperTeen 2008 288p $16.99; lib bdg $17.89

Grades: 7 8 9 10   **Fic**

    1. Kidnapping—Fiction 2. Sisters—Fiction 3. Child sexual abuse—Fiction 4. New York (State)—Fiction

    ISBN 978-0-06-623776-3; 978-0-06-623777-0 (lib bdg)   LC 2007-09136

In Mallory, New York, as five sisters, aged eleven to seventeen, deal with assorted problems, conflicts, fears, and yearnings, a mysterious middle-aged man watches them, fascinated, deciding which one he likes the best.

"Fans of . . . classic tales of high-tension peril will appreciate the way this successfully plays on their deepest fears." Bull Cent Child Books

McCaffrey, Anne

Dragonflight; volume 1 of "The Dragonriders of Pern". Ballantine Bks. 1978 337p il (Dragonriders of Pern) hardcover o.p. pa $12.95

Grades: 8 9 10 11 12 Adult   **Fic**

    1. Dragons—Fiction 2. Fantasy fiction

    ISBN 0-345-27749-X; 0-345-48426-6 (pa)

                                    LC 78-16707

"A Del Rey book"

First published 1968 in paperback. Based on two award winning stories entitled: Weyr search and Dragonrider

The planet Pern, originally colonized from Earth but long out of contact with it, has been periodically threatened by the deadly silver Threads which fall from the wandering Red Star. To combat them a life form on the planet was developed into winged, fire-breathing dragons. Humans with a high degree of empathy and telepathic power are needed to train and preserve these creatures. As the story begins, Pern has fallen into decay, the threat of the Red Star has been forgotten, the Dragonriders and dragons are reduced in number and in disrepute, and the evil Lord Fax has begun conquering neighboring holds

Fantasy titles set on Pern are:

All the Weyrs of Pern (1991)

The chronicles of Pern: first fall (1993)

Dragon's fire (2006)

Dragon's kin (2003)

Dragondrums (1979)

Dragonquest (1971)

Dragonsdawn (1988)

Dragonseye (1997)

Dragonsinger (1977)

Dragonsong (1976)

The masterharper of Pern (1998)

Morets: Dragonlady of Pern (1983)

Nerilka's story (1986)

The Renegades of Pern (1989)

The skies of Pern (2001)

White dragon (1978)

McCaughrean, Geraldine, 1951-

The kite rider; a novel. HarperCollins Pubs. 2002 272p maps $15.95; lib bdg $16.89; pa $6.99
*

Grades: 5 6 7 8   Fic
1. Kublai Khan, 1216-1294—Fiction 2. China—Fiction 3. Kites—Fiction
ISBN 0-06-623874-9; 0-06-623875-7 (lib bdg); 0-06-441091-9 (pa)   LC 2001-39522

In thirteenth-century China, after trying to save his widowed mother from a horrendous second marriage, twelve-year-old Haoyou has life-changing adventures when he takes to the sky as a circus kite rider and ends up meeting the great Mongol ruler Kublai Khan

"The story is a genuine page-turner. . . . McCaughrean fully immerses her memorable characters in the culture and lore of the ancient Chinese and Mongols, which make this not only a solid adventure story but also a window to a fascinating time and place." Booklist

Not the end of the world; a novel. HarperTempest 2005 244p $16.99; lib bdg $17.89
Grades: 7 8 9 10   Fic
1. Noah's ark—Fiction
ISBN 0-06-076030-3; 0-06-076031-1 (lib bdg)
LC 2004-14786

Noah's daughter, daughters-in-law, sons, wife, and the animals describe what it was like to be aboard the ark while they watched everyone around them drown.

"This frightening retelling of the biblical Noah's Ark story is written beautifully and with brutal clarity." Voice Youth Advocates

McClintock, Norah

Dooley takes the fall. Red Deer Press 2007 314p $12.95
Grades: 7 8 9 10   Fic
1. Suicide—Fiction
ISBN 978-0-88995-403-8; 0-88995-403-8

As a troubled teen struggles to free himself from his past and the implications of the present conspiracies that surround him, Dooley tries to prove his innocence in a suicide that looks like murder.

"A fast-paced book with an involving character and a story that builds to a satisfying climax." Voice Youth Advocates

McClymer, Kelly

Must love black. Simon Pulse 2008 167p pa $8.99
Grades: 6 7 8 9   Fic
1. Sisters—Fiction 2. Twins—Fiction 3. Babysitters—Fiction
ISBN 978-1-4169-6994-5; 1-4169-4903-8

"Philippa does not consider herself a Goth but she loves the color black. When she answers a classified ad for a summer nanny position, it is the advertisement's one specification 'must love black' that attracts her to the job. . . . McClymer's novel combines understated gothic elements with traditional teen romance tropes and succeeds as a light and funny read." SLJ

McCormick, Patricia

Cut. Front St. 2000 168p $16.95
Grades: 7 8 9 10   Fic
1. Self-mutilation—Fiction 2. Psychiatric hospitals—Fiction
ISBN 1-88691-061-8   LC 00-34840
Also available in paperback from Scholastic Bks.

While confined to a mental hospital, thirteen-year-old Callie slowly comes to understand some of the reasons behind her self-mutilation, and gradually starts to get better

"Realistic, sensitive, and heartfelt." Voice Youth Advocates

My brother's keeper. Hyperion Books for Children 2004 187p $15.99
Grades: 7 8 9 10   Fic
1. Brothers—Fiction 2. Drug abuse—Fiction 3. Baseball—Fiction
ISBN 0-7868-5173-2   LC 2004-55233

Thirteen-year-old Toby, a prematurely gray-haired Pittsburgh Pirates fan and baseball card collector, tries to cope with his brother's drug use, his father's absence, and his mother dating Stanley the Food King.

"This is a clever and believable first-person narrative by a responsible, caring, and appealing kid who is doing his utmost to hold together people he loves." Booklist

McDaniel, Lurlene, 1944-

Breathless. Delacorte Press 2009 165p $13.99
Grades: 8 9 10 11 12   Fic
1. Cancer—Fiction 2. Suicide—Fiction 3. Friendship—Fiction 4. Siblings—Fiction
ISBN 978-0-385-90458-2; 0-385-90458-4
LC 2008-18427

A high school diving champion develops bone cancer in this story told from the points of view of the diver, his best friend, his sister, and his girlfriend.

"This is a heartstrings-tugging read that retains the central character's dignity and peace in the face of insurmountable odds. A sensitive book on a delicate topic." SLJ

Hit and run; [by] Lurlene McDaniel. 1st ed. Delacorte Press 2007 180p $10.99
Grades: 8 9 10 11 12   Fic
1. Traffic accidents—Fiction 2. School stories
ISBN 978-0-385-73161-4   LC 2006012738

Events surrounding the hit and run accident of a popular high school student are told from the viewpoints of those involved, including the victim.

This "demonstrates the power of love and making choices. McDaniel, known for her inspiring novels, has a simplistic style, but a weighty message—it's the way you respond to a given situation that defines who you are and who you will be." SLJ

McDonald, Janet, 1953-2007

Harlem Hustle. Frances Foster Books 2006 182p $16
Grades: 8 9 10 11   Fic
1. Rap music—Fiction 2. African Americans—Fiction 3. Harlem (New York, N.Y.)—Fiction
ISBN 978-0-374-37184-5; 0-374-37184-9
LC 2005-52108

McDonald, Janet, 1953-2007—*Continued*

Eric "Hustle" Samson, a smart and streetwise seventeen-year-old dropout from Harlem, aspires to rap stardom, a dream he naively believes is about to come true.

"The author nails the hip-hop lingo and the street slang, and her characters strike just the right attitude. . . . Young adults will love this book." SLJ

Off-color. Farrar, Straus and Giroux 2007 163p $16 *

Grades: 7 8 9 10 11 12   **Fic**
1. Racially mixed people—Fiction 2. Mother-daughter relationship—Fiction 3. Single parent family—Fiction 4. Brooklyn (New York, N.Y.)—Fiction
ISBN 0-374-37196-2   LC 2006-47334
"Frances Foster book"

Fifteen-year-old Cameron living with her single mother in Brooklyn finds her search for identity further challenged when she discovers that she is the product of a biracial relationship.

"McDonald dramatizes the big issues from the inside, showing the hard times and the joy in fast-talking dialogue that is honest, insulting, angry, tender, and very funny." Booklist

Spellbound. Frances Foster Bks. 2001 138p $16
Grades: 7 8 9 10   **Fic**
1. Teenage mothers—Fiction 2. African Americans—Fiction
ISBN 0-374-37140-7   LC 00-29381

Raven, a teenage mother and high school dropout living in a housing project, decides, with the help and sometime interference of her best friend Aisha, to study for a spelling bee which could lead to a college preparatory program and four-year scholarship

"The dialogue is lively and smart; the characters ring true." Booklist

Twists and turns. Frances Foster Bks./Farrar, Straus & Giroux 2003 135p $16; pa $6.95
Grades: 7 8 9 10   **Fic**
1. African Americans—Fiction 2. Public housing—Fiction 3. Sisters—Fiction 4. Brooklyn (New York, N.Y.)—Fiction
ISBN 0-374-39955-7; 0-374-40006-7 (pa)
                                            LC 2002-35313

With the help of a couple of successful friends, eighteen- and nineteen-year-old Teesha and Keeba try to capitalize on their talents by opening a hair salon in the rundown Brooklyn housing project where they live

"The poetry and wit are in the daily details. . . . The story is inspiring—not because of a slick resolution or a heavy message, but because McDonald shows how hard things are, even as she tells a story of teens who find the strength in themselves and in those around them to rebuild and carry on." Booklist

McDonald, Joyce

Devil on my heels. Delacorte Press 2004 263p $15.95; lib bdg $17.99
Grades: 7 8 9 10   **Fic**

1. African Americans—Fiction 2. Race relations—Fiction 3. Migrant labor—Fiction 4. Florida—Fiction
ISBN 0-385-73107-8; 0-385-90133-x (lib bdg)

In 1957 fifteen-year-old Dove, the daughter of a prosperous orange grower in Benevolence, Florida, feels increasingly uneasy after learning of acts of racism against the African American orange pickers by those close to her.

"This is certainly a page-turner and it will give readers insight into a difficult and shameful part of American history." SLJ

McDonnell, Margot

Torn to pieces. Delacorte Press 2008 258p $15.99; lib bdg $18.99
Grades: 8 9 10 11 12   **Fic**
1. Missing persons—Fiction 2. Friendship—Fiction 3. Mother-daughter relationship—Fiction 4. Grandparents—Fiction
ISBN 978-0-385-73559-9; 0-385-73559-6; 978-0-385-90542-8 (lib bdg); 0-385-90542-4 (lib bdg)
                                            LC 2007-41536

When her mother disappears during a business trip, seventeen-year-old Anne discovers that her family harbors many dark secrets.

"This teen thriller . . . builds to a gripping conclusion with a final twist that will shock and satisfy teen readers." Booklist

McDowell, Marilyn Taylor

Carolina Harmony. Delacorte 2009 288p $16.99 *

Grades: 4 5 6 7   **Fic**
1. Orphans—Fiction 2. Farm life—Fiction 3. Blue Ridge Mountains region—Fiction
ISBN 978-0-385-73590-2; 0-385-73590-1

"After Carolina's beloved Auntie Shen suffers a stroke, Carolina escapes from an unpleasant foster placement. The orphaned 10-year-old finds love at Harmony Farm, but the web of lies she spins almost leads to losing that home too. . . . This third-person narrative unwinds leisurely, with plenty of backtracking to fill in details of Carolina's life and the glories of her world in the Blue Ridge Mountains. . . . McDowell reveals her love for this part of the world, savoring the language, the environment, and the traditions of mountain culture." Booklist

McGhee, Alison, 1960-

All rivers flow to the sea. Candlewick Press 2005 168p $15.99
Grades: 8 9 10 11 12   **Fic**
1. Sisters—Fiction 2. Traffic accidents—Fiction 3. Bereavement—Fiction 4. Adirondack Mountains (N.Y.)—Fiction
ISBN 0-7636-2591-4   LC 2004-54609

After a car accident in the Adirondacks leaves her older sister Ivy brain-dead, seventeen-year-old Rose struggles with her grief and guilt as she slowly learns to let her sister go.

"This somber, philosophical look at loss and the reestablishment of identity is sensitive and perceptive, and includes passages of beautiful writing. Supporting characters are complex and lovingly rendered." Booklist

McGraw, Eloise Jarvis, 1915-2000

The moorchild; [by] Eloise McGraw. Margaret K. McElderry Bks. 1996 241p $17; pa $4.99

Grades: 4 5 6 7   **Fic**

1. Fantasy fiction 2. Fairies—Fiction

ISBN 0-689-80654-X; 0-689-82033-X (pa)

LC 95-34107

A Newbery Medal honor book, 1997

"Saaski, a half-human, half-Moorfolk child, is banished from the Mound and placed as a changeling in a human village, where she is regarded with suspicion and treated with scorn." Horn Book Guide

"Incorporating some classic fantasy motifs and icons, McGraw . . . conjures up an appreciably familiar world that, as evidence of her storytelling power, still strikes an original chord." Publ Wkly

McGuigan, Mary Ann, 1949-

Morning in a different place. Front Street 2009 195p $17.95

Grades: 7 8 9 10   **Fic**

1. Friendship—Fiction 2. Race relations—Fiction 3. African Americans—Fiction 4. Bronx (New York, N.Y.)—Fiction

ISBN 978-1-59078-551-5; 1-59078-551-7

LC 2007-17547

In 1963 in the Bronx, New York, eighth-graders Fiona and Yolanda help one another face hard decisions at home despite family and social opposition to their interracial friendship, but Fiona is on her own when popular classmates start paying attention to her and give her a glimpse of both a different way of life and a new kind of hatefulness.

This is "never didactic. McGuigan's writing is spare and low-key, and her metaphors are acute." Booklist

McKay, Hilary, 1959-

Saffy's angel. Margaret K. McElderry Bks. 2002 152p $16; pa $4.99 *

Grades: 5 6 7 8   **Fic**

1. Family life—Fiction 2. Adoption—Fiction 3. Great Britain—Fiction

ISBN 0-689-84933-8; 0-689-84934-6 (pa)

LC 2001-44110

First published 2001 in the United Kingdom

After learning that she was adopted, thirteen-year-old Saffron's relationship with her eccentric, artistic family changes, until they help her go back to Italy where she was born to find a special momento of her past

"Like the Casson household itself, the plot is a chaotic whirl that careens off in several directions simultaneously. But McKay always skillfully draws each clearly defined character back into the story with witty, well-edited details; rapid dialogue; and fine pacing." Booklist

Other titles in this series are:

Indigo's star (2004)

Permanent Rose (2005)

Caddy ever after (2006)

Forever Rose (2008)

McKenzie, Nancy

Guinevere's gift. Alfred A. Knopf 2008 327p (The Chrysalis Queen quartet) $15.99; lib bdg $18.99

Grades: 7 8 9 10   **Fic**

1. Guinevere (Legendary character)—Fiction 2. Great Britain—History—0-1066—Fiction 3. Cousins—Fiction

ISBN 978-0-375-84345-7; 0-375-84345-0; 978-0-375-94345-4 (lib bdg); 0-375-94345-5 (lib bdg)

LC 2007-28782

When the orphaned Guinevere is twelve years old, living with Queen Alyse and King Pellinore of Gwynedd, she fearlessly helps rescue her cousin from kidnappers who are plotting to seize the palace and overthrow the king, even as the queen despairs of Guinevere's rebellious nature.

"Adventure seekers can be content with this tale of a heroine and her castle while dedicated legend fans will appreciate where it fits in the overall tapestry." Bull Cent Child Books

Another title in this series is:

Guinevere's gamble (2009)

McKernan, Victoria

The devil's paintbox. Alfred A. Knopf 2009 359p $16.99; lib bdg $19.99 *

Grades: 6 7 8 9 10   **Fic**

1. Frontier and pioneer life—Fiction 2. Overland journeys to the Pacific—Fiction 3. Orphans—Fiction 4. Siblings—Fiction

ISBN 978-0-375-83750-0; 0-375-83750-7; 978-0-375-93750-7 (lib bdg); 0-375-93750-1 (lib bdg)

LC 2008-4749

In 1866, fifteen-year-old Aidan and his thirteen-year-old sister Maddy, penniless orphans, leave drought-stricken Kansas on a wagon train hoping for a better life in Seattle, but find there are still many hardships to be faced.

This is a "gripping novel. . . . Attention to detail and steady pacing keep readers fully engaged." Publ Wkly

Shackleton's stowaway. Knopf 2005 336p $15.95; lib bdg $17.99

Grades: 7 8 9 10   **Fic**

1. Shackleton, Sir Ernest Henry, 1874-1922—Fiction 2. Endurance (Ship)—Fiction 3. Adventure fiction 4. Survival after airplane accidents, shipwrecks, etc.—Fiction

ISBN 0-375-82691-2; 0-375-92691-7 (lib bdg)

LC 2004-10313

A fictionalized account of the adventures of eighteen-year-old Perce Blackborow, who stowed away for the 1914 Shackleton Antarctic expedition and, after their ship *Endurance* was crushed by ice, endured many hardships, including the loss of the toes of his left foot to frostbite, during the nearly two-year return journey across sea and ice

"This book provides historical information for history and geography classes who are interested in exploration, the Antarctic, and early history of great sea voyages." Libr Media Connect

McKinley, Robin

Beauty; a retelling of the story of Beauty & the beast. Harper & Row 1978 247p $15.99; pa $5.99
*

Grades: 7 8 9 10 **Fic**
1. Fairy tales
ISBN 0-06-024149-7; 0-06-440477-3 (pa)

LC 77-25636

"McKinley's version of this folktale is embellished with rich descriptions and settings and detailed characterizations. The author has not modernized the story but varied the traditional version to attract modern readers. The values of love, honor, and beauty are placed in a magical setting that will please the reader of fantasy." Shapiro. Fic for Youth. 3d edition

The blue sword. Greenwillow Bks. 1982 272p
$17.99; pa $6.99 *
Grades: 7 8 9 10 **Fic**
1. Fantasy fiction
ISBN 0-688-00938-7; 0-441-06880-4 (pa)

LC 82-2895

A Newbery Medal honor book, 1983

Harry, bored with her sheltered life in the remote orange-growing colony of Daria, discovers magic in herself when she is kidnapped by a native king with mysterious powers.

"This is a zesty, romantic, heroic fantasy with an appealing stalwart heroine, a finely realixed mythical kingdom, and a grounding in reality." Booklist

Chalice. G.P. Putnam's Sons 2008 263p $18.99
Grades: 7 8 9 10 11 12 **Fic**
1. Fantasy fiction 2. Bees—Fiction
ISBN 978-0-399-24676-0; 0-399-24676-2

LC 2008-704

A beekeeper by trade, Mirasol's life changes completely when she is named the new Chalice, the most important advisor to the new Master, a former priest of fire.

"The fantasy realm is evoked in thorough and telling detail. . . . A lavish and lasting treat." Publ Wkly

Dragonhaven. G.P. Putnam's Sons 2007 342p
$17.99
Grades: 7 8 9 10 11 12 **Fic**
1. Dragons—Fiction 2. Fantasy fiction
ISBN 978-0-399-24675-3; 0-399-24675-4

LC 2007-8197

When Jake Mendoza, who lives in the Smokehill National Park where his father runs the Makepeace Institute of Integrated Dragon Studies, goes on his first solo overnight in the park, he finds an infant dragon whose mother has been killed by a poacher.

Readers "will be engaged by McKinley's well-drawn characters and want to root for the Smokehill community's fight to save the ultimate endangered species." SLJ

The hero and the crown. Greenwillow Bks.
1985 246p lib bdg $16.99 *
Grades: 6 7 8 9 **Fic**
1. Fantasy fiction
ISBN 0-688-02593-5 LC 84-4074
Also available in paperback from Ace Bks.
Awarded the Newbery Medal, 1985

"A prequel rather than sequel to 'The Blue Sword' [1982], McKinley's second novel set in the . . . mythical kingdom of Damar centers on Aerin, daughter of a Damarian king and his second wife, a witchwoman from the feared, demon-ridden North. The narrative follows Aerin as she seeks her birthright, becoming first a dragon killer and eventually the savior of the kingdom." Booklist

The author "has in this suspenseful prequel . . . created an utterly engrossing fantasy, replete with a fairly mature romantic subplot as well as adventure." N Y Times Book Rev

Rose daughter. Greenwillow Bks. 1997 306p pa
$7.99
Grades: 7 8 9 10 **Fic**
1. Fairy tales
ISBN 0-688-15439-5; 0-441-00583-7 (pa)

LC 96-48783

Also available in paperback from Ace Bks.

"Nearly twenty years after the publication of *Beauty: A Retelling of the Story of Beauty and the Beast* McKinley has . . . produced another full-length novel retelling the same tale." Horn Book Guide

Compared to Beauty, this "is fuller bodied, with richer characterizations and a more mystical, darker edge. . . . There is more background on the Beast in this version . . . and Beauty's choice at the end, a departure from that in *Beauty*, is just so right. Readers will be enchanted, in the best sense of the word." Booklist

McKinnon, Hannah Roberts

Franny Parker. Farrar Straus Giroux 2009 149p
$16 *
Grades: 5 6 7 8 **Fic**
1. Family life—Fiction 2. Droughts—Fiction
3. Violence—Fiction 4. Oklahoma—Fiction
ISBN 978-0-374-32469-8; 0-374-32469-7

LC 2008001702

Through a hot, dry Oklahoma summer, twelve-year-old Franny tends wild animals brought by her neighbors, hears gossip during a weekly quilting bee, befriends a new neighbor who has some big secrets, and learns to hope.

"Franny is a relatable and consistent narrator, the homey rural setting is throughtfully rendered and the easy prose should appeal to reluctant readers." Publ Wkly

McKissack, Patricia C., 1944-

A friendship for today. Scholastic Press 2007
172p $16.99
Grades: 4 5 6 7 **Fic**
1. School integration—Fiction 2. Race relations—Fiction 3. Friendship—Fiction 4. Divorce—Fiction
5. African Americans—Fiction 6. Missouri—Fiction
ISBN 978-0-439-66098-3 LC 2006-29293
In 1954, when desegregation comes to Kirkland, Missouri, ten-year-old Rosemary faces many changes and challenges at school and at home as her parents separate.

"A real, at times raw tale about a winning and insightful young heroine during a bittersweet era." Publ Wkly

McKissack, Patricia C., 1944-—*Continued*
Let my people go; Bible stories told by a freeman of color to his daughter, Charlotte, in Charleston, South Carolina, 1806-16; by Patricia and Fredrick McKissack; illustrated by James Ransome. Atheneum Bks. for Young Readers 1998 134p il $20 *
Grades: 4 5 6 7 **Fic**
1. African Americans—Fiction 2. Bible stories 3. Slavery—Fiction
ISBN 0-689-80856-9 LC 97-19983
"An Anne Schwartz book"
Charlotte, the daughter of a free black man who worked as a blacksmith in Charleston, South Carolina, in the early 1800s recalls the stories from the Bible that her father shared with her, relating them to the experiences of African Americans
"The poignant juxtaposition of the Biblical characters and Charlotte's personal narrative is authentic and moving. . . . The occasional illustrations are powerful oil paintings in rich colors, emotional and evocative." SLJ
Includes bibliographical references

Nzinga, warrior queen of Matamba; by Patricia McKissack. Scholastic 2000 136p (Royal diaries) $10.95 *
Grades: 5 6 7 8 **Fic**
1. Nzinga, Queen of Matamba, 1582-1663—Fiction 2. Angola—Fiction 3. Princesses—Fiction 4. Slave trade—Fiction
ISBN 0-439-11210-9 LC 00-24216
Presents the diary of thirteen-year-old Nzingha, a sixteenth-century West African princess who loves to hunt and hopes to lead her kingdom one day against the invasion of the Portuguese slave traders
"The diary format will appeal to readers and the author's use of time lines, seasons, and actual place names makes the story believable and interesting." SLJ

McLaren, Clemence, 1938-
Inside the walls of Troy; a novel of the women who lived the Trojan War. Atheneum Bks. for Young Readers 1996 199p hardcover o.p. pa $5.99
Grades: 7 8 9 10 **Fic**
1. Helen of Troy (Legendary character)—Fiction
ISBN 0-689-31820-0; 0-689-87397-2 (pa)
LC 93-8127
Also available in paperback from Bantam Bks.
The events surrounding the famous battle between the Greeks and the Trojans are told from the points of view of two women, the beautiful Helen and the prophetic Cassandra
"These ancient stories are made as fresh and vivid as any modern tale by the electrifying characters and sensual details." Booklist

McMann, Lisa
Wake. Simon Pulse 2008 210p $15.99; pa $8.99
Grades: 7 8 9 10 **Fic**
1. Dreams—Fiction 2. School stories
ISBN 978-1-4169-5357-9; 1-4169-5357-4; 978-1-4169-7447-5 (pa); 1-4169-7447-4 (pa)
LC 2007036267

Ever since she was eight years old, high school student Janie Hannagan has been uncontrollably drawn into other people's dreams, but it is not until she befriends an elderly nursing home patient and becomes involved with an enigmatic fellow-student that she discovers her true power.
"A fast pace, a great mix of teen angst and supernatural experiences, and an eerie, attention-grabbing cover will make this a hit." Booklist
Followed by: Fade (2009)

McMullan, Margaret
Cashay. Houghton Mifflin Harcourt 2009 166p $15
Grades: 7 8 9 10 **Fic**
1. Bereavement—Fiction 2. Anger—Fiction 3. Mentoring—Fiction 4. Racially mixed people—Fiction
ISBN 978-0-547-07656-0; 0-547-07656-8
LC 2008-36111
When her world is turned upside down by her sister's death, a mentor is assigned to fourteen-year-old Cashay to help her through her anger and grief.
"Cashay's spirited voice and non-frothy prose will draw both confirmed and newer fans of inner-city drama." Kirkus

How I found the Strong; a Civil War story. Houghton Mifflin 2004 136p $15 *
Grades: 5 6 7 8 **Fic**
1. United States—History—1861-1865, Civil War—Fiction 2. Mississippi—Fiction 3. Slavery—Fiction
ISBN 0-618-35008-X LC 2003-12294
Frank Russell, known as Shanks, wishes he could have gone with his father and brother to fight for Mississippi and the Confederacy, but his experiences with the war and his changing relationship with the family slave, Buck, change his thinking.
"The crisply written narrative is full of regional speech and detail, creating a vivid portrait." Voice Youth Advocates

When I crossed No-Bob. Houghton Mifflin Company 2007 209p $16 *
Grades: 5 6 7 8 **Fic**
1. Farm life—Fiction 2. Mississippi—Fiction 3. Abandoned children—Fiction 4. Reconstruction (1865-1876)—Fiction 5. Race relations—Fiction
ISBN 978-0-618-71715-6; 0-618-71715-3
LC 2007-12753
Ten years after the Civil War's end, twelve-year-old Addy, abandoned by her parents, is taken from the horrid town of No-Bob by schoolteacher Frank Russell and his bride, but when her father returns to claim her she must find another way to leave her O'Donnell past behind.
"The simple prose can be pure poetry. . . . Readers will be drawn by the history close-up and by the elemental moral choice." Booklist

McNab, Andy

Traitor; [by] Andy McNab and Robert Rigby. G.P. Putnam's Sons 2005 265p $15.99

Grades: 7 8 9 10   **Fic**

1. Grandfathers—Fiction 2. Orphans—Fiction 3. Spies—Fiction 4. Great Britain—Fiction

ISBN 0-399-24464-6   LC 2005-6701

Published in the United Kingdom with title: Boy soldier

"Orphaned Londoner Danny Watts wants nothing to do with his estranged grandfather, a traitor who went MIA years ago, until the British military offers Danny a proposition: find his grandfather and he'll receive a scholarship. . . . With help from his best friend, Elena, he sets off to find his relative and the truth. . . . The well-crafted language includes a few coarse phrases. . . . With its brisk plot and unpredictable characters, this story of intrigue rises above many standard adventure stories." Booklist

Other titles in this series are:
Payback (2006)
Avenger (2007)
Meltdown (2008)

McNamee, Eoin, 1961-

The Navigator. Wendy Lamb Books 2007 c2006 342p il (Navigator trilogy) $15.99; pa $6.99

Grades: 6 7 8 9   **Fic**

1. Time—Fiction 2. Fantasy fiction

ISBN 978-0-375-83910-8; 0-375-83910-0; 978-0-385-73554-4 (pa); 0-385-73554-5 (pa)

LC 2006-26691

Owen has always been different, and not only because his father committed suicide, but he is not prepared for the knowledge that he has a mission to help the Wakeful—the custodians of time—to stop the Harsh from reversing the flow of time.

McNamee "shows a deft hand in writing for children. Excellent world-building, a thrilling and propulsive plot, internal consistency and a multitude of child heroes guarantee a following for this exciting fantasy." Kirkus

Other titles in this series are:
City of Time (2008)
The Frost Child (2009)

McNamee, Graham

Acceleration. Wendy Lamb Bks. 2003 210p hardcover o.p. lib bdg $17.99; pa $6.50

Grades: 8 9 10 11 12   **Fic**

1. Homicide—Fiction 2. Mystery fiction 3. Canada—Fiction

ISBN 0-385-73119-1; 0-385-90144-5 (lib bdg); 0-440-23836-6 (pa)   LC 2003-3708

Stuck working in the Lost and Found of the Toronto Transit Authority for the summer, seventeen-year-old Duncan finds the diary of a serial killer and sets out to stop him

"Never overexploits the sensational potential of the subject and builds suspense layer upon layer, while injecting some surprising comedy relief." Booklist

Bonechiller; [by] Graham McNamee. 1st ed. Wendy Lamb Books 2008 294p $15.99; lib bdg $18.99

Grades: 7 8 9 10 11 12   **Fic**

1. Monsters—Fiction 2. Supernatural—Fiction 3. Bereavement—Fiction 4. Canada—Fiction

ISBN 978-0-385-74658-8; 0-385-74658-X; 978-0-385-90895-5 (lib bdg); 0-385-90895-4 (lib bdg)

LC 2007039383

Four high school students face off against a soul-stealing beast that has been making young people disappear their small Ontario, Canada, town for centuries.

"This will be an easy booktalk and a spendidly enjoyable read sure to please those who respond with both hope and dread when things go bump in the night." Bull Cent Child Books

McNaughton, Janet, 1953-

An earthly knight. HarperCollins Publishers 2004 c2003 261p $15.99; lib bdg $16.89

Grades: 7 8 9 10   **Fic**

1. Fantasy fiction 2. Scotland—Fiction

ISBN 0-06-008992-X; 0-06-008993-8 (lib bdg)

LC 2003-9561

First published 2003 in Canada

In 1162 in Scotland, sixteen-year-old Jenny Avenel falls in love with the mysterious Tam Lin while being courted by the king's brother and must navigate the tides of tradition and the power of ancient magic to define her own destiny.

"The author does an excellent job of interweaving legend and history to create an exciting and engaging tale." SLJ

The secret under my skin; by Janet McNaughton. Eos 2005 264p $15.99; lib bdg $16.89

Grades: 7 8 9 10   **Fic**

1. Science fiction

ISBN 0-06-008989-X; 0-06-008990-3 (lib bdg)

LC 2004-12373

In the year 2368, humans exist under dire environmental conditions and one young woman, rescued from a workcamp and chosen for a special duty, uses her love of learning to discover the truth about the planet's future and her own dark past

"The setting and culture of the book are . . . vividly rendered, offering a depth that allows readers to believe fully in its premise. The writing is clear and crisp, evoking a magic that enchants. . . . This [is] one of the top science fiction novels in recent years." SLJ

McNeal, Laura

The decoding of Lana Morris; [by] Laura & Tom McNeal. Alfred A. Knopf 2007 289p $15.99; lib bdg $18.99

Grades: 7 8 9 10 11 12   **Fic**

1. Foster home care—Fiction 2. Handicapped—Fiction 3. Drawing—Fiction 4. Supernatural—Fiction 5. Nebraska—Fiction

ISBN 978-0-375-83106-5; 0-375-83106-1; 978-0-375-93106-2 (lib bdg); 0-375-93106-6 (lib bdg)

LC 2006-23950

McNeal, Laura—*Continued*

For sixteen-year-old Lana life is often difficult, with a flirtatious foster father, an ice queen foster mother, a houseful of special needs children to care for, and bullies harrassing her, until the day she ventures into an antique shop and buys a drawing set that may change her life.

This is "a colorful character drama with genuine spice and impact." Bull Cent Child Books

McNicoll, Sylvia, 1954-

Last chance for Paris. Fitzhenry & Whiteside 2008 204p pa $11.95

Grades: 6 7 8 9   **Fic**

1. Wolves—Fiction 2. Twins—Fiction 3. Siblings—Fiction 4. Canada—Fiction

ISBN 978-1-5545-5061-6 (pa); 1-5545-5061-0 (pa)

Fourteen-year-old Zanna goes to the Alberta ice fields with her father and twin brother, Martin, where they find a wolf pup which they name Paris. When Martin is lost, Paris helps find him.

"Written with elements of wry humor and romance, this Canadian novel features a narrator whose disarmingly candid opinions make her an appealing guide for readers who usually veer away from backwoods or survival stories." Booklist

McNish, Cliff

Angel. Carolrhoda Books 2008 312p $16.95 *

Grades: 7 8 9 10   **Fic**

1. Angels—Fiction 2. School stories 3. Popularity—Fiction 4. Bullies—Fiction 5. Mental illness—Fiction

ISBN 978-0-8225-8900-6; 0-8225-8900-1

       LC 2007-9664

An unlikely friendship develops between fourteen-year-olds Stephanie, an angel-obsessed social outcast, and Freya, a popular student whose visions of angels sent her to a mental institution and who is now seeing a dark angel at every turn.

"The author beautifuly melds a tale of the fantastic and the mundane." Voice Youth Advocates

Breathe; a ghost story; by Cliff McNish. 1st American ed. Carolrhoda Books 2006 261p lib bdg $15.95

Grades: 4 5 6 7   **Fic**

1. Ghost stories 2. Asthma—Fiction 3. Great Britain—Fiction

ISBN 978-0-8225-6443-0; 0-8225-6443-2

       LC 2006000513

When he and his mother move into an old farmhouse in the English countryside, asthmatic, twelve-year-old Jack discovers that he can communicate with the ghosts inhabiting the house and inadvertently establishes a relationship with a tormented, malevolent spirit that threatens to destroy both his mother and himself.

"The author gives his characters substance. . . . This is a well-crafted story that is weightier than the standard chiller. Filled with suspense, it will keep readers riveted to the pages." SLJ

The silver child; by Cliff McNish. 1st American ed. Carolrhoda Books 2005 192p lib bdg $15.95

Grades: 6 7 8 9   **Fic**

1. Fantasy fiction

ISBN 1-57505-825-1   LC 2004-12407

Drawn to a wasteland of garbage dumps called Coldharbour, six children undergo mysterious transformations and band together to face an unknown enemy.

The author "writes a darkly compelling fantasy, using alternating narratives to add to the suspense. His vivid, often lyrical prose will engage readers." Booklist

Other titles in this series are:

Silver City (2006)

Silver world (2007)

McPhee, Peter, 1948-

New blood. James Lorimer 2008 167p pa $8.95

Grades: 6 7 8 9 10   **Fic**

1. Bullies—Fiction 2. School stories 3. Canada—Fiction

ISBN 978-1-55028-996-1; 1-55028-996-9

When his family moves from the tough streets of Glasgow to Winnipeg, Canada, Callum finds that his high school days of dealing with bullies are far from over.

"The Scottish culture, which becomes a colorful character, adds to the fullness of the story. The writing, rich in dialogue, does not waste words and keeps the reader involved and cheering for this gutsy hero who fights his fear to stand against abuse aimed at himself and others." Voice Youth Advocates

McWilliams, Kelly

Doormat; a novel. Delacorte Press 2004 131p $15.95; lib bdg $17.99

Grades: 6 7 8 9   **Fic**

1. Pregnancy—Fiction 2. Theater—Fiction 3. Friendship—Fiction

ISBN 0-385-73168-X; 0-385-90204-2 (lib bdg)

       LC 2003-19675

Fourteen-year-old Jaime has always been a doormat, but her diary reveals how getting the lead in a school play, finding her first boyfriend, discovering her dream, and helping her best friend cope with being pregnant transform her life.

"McWilliams' first-person, present-tense vignettes are taut, funny, and touching, the dialogue is authentic, and both the teen and adult characters ring true." Booklist

Mead, Alice, 1952-

Dawn and dusk. Farrar, Straus and Giroux 2007 151p $16

Grades: 6 7 8 9   **Fic**

1. Iran-Iraq War, 1980-1988—Fiction 2. Iran—Fiction 3. Refugees—Fiction

ISBN 0-374-31708-9; 978-0-374-31708-9

       LC 2006-40850

As thirteen-year-old Azad tries desperately to cling to the life he has known, the political situation in Iran during the war with Iraq finally forces his family to flee their home and seek safety elsewhere.

"Azad is an appealing protagonist, and it is his simple and direct story that will draw readers through the complexities of a multinational ethnic longing for self-determination that remains at the heart of an international tinderbox." SLJ

Mead, Alice, 1952-—*Continued*

Swimming to America; Alice Mead. 1st ed. Farrar, Straus and Giroux 2005 153p $16 *

Grades: 6 7 8 9   Fic

1. Immigrants—Fiction 2. Brooklyn (New York, N.Y.)—Fiction

ISBN 0-374-38047-3   LC 2004-53249

Eighth grader Linda Berati struggles to understand who she is within the context of her mother's secrecy about the family background, her discomfort with her old girlfriends, her involvement with the family problems of her Cuban-American friend Ramon, and an opportunity to attend a school for "free spirits" like herself.

Written with "sensitivity and optimism. . . . [This is] an informative, empathetic, contemporary portrait of the immigrant experience." SLJ

Mebus, Scott, 1974-

Gods of Manhattan. Dutton Children's Books 2008 352p $17.99

Grades: 6 7 8 9   Fic

1. Fantasy fiction 2. Space and time—Fiction 3. Gods and goddesses—Fiction 4. Adventure fiction 5. New York (N.Y.)—Fiction

ISBN 978-0-525-47955-0; 0-525-47955-4

      LC 2007-18113

"Rory, 13, and his sister Bridget, 9, live in present-day New York City unaware of the spirits from Manhattan's or 'Mannahatta's' past that coexist alongside them. Rory has a gift for seeing this other world but has repressed this ability until the day he notices a cockroach riding a rat, an ancient Indian warrior, a papier-mâché boy, and other oddities. . . . The use of real historical figures and events lends authenticity to this compulsively readable and fast-paced fantasy." SLJ

Medina, Meg, 1963-

Milagros; girl from Away. Henry Holt and Co. 2008 279p $17.89 *

Grades: 6 7 8 9   Fic

1. Mother-daughter relationship—Fiction 2. Magic—Fiction 3. Rays (Fishes)—Fiction 4. Islands—Fiction 5. West Indies—Fiction 6. Maine—Fiction

ISBN 978-0-8050-8230-2; 0-8050-8230-1

      LC 2007-46939

Twelve-year-old Milagros barely survives an invasion of her tiny, Caribbean island home, escapes with the help of mysterious sea creatures, reunites briefly with her pirate-father, and learns about a mother's love when cast ashore on another island.

"Medina's use of magical realism keeps readers tantalizingly off-balance as she navigates among settings. . . . [This] haunting tale . . . will remain with readers." Horn Book

Meehan, Kierin

Hannah's winter. Kane/Miller Book Publishers 2009 212p $15.95

Grades: 5 6 7 8   Fic

1. Japan—Fiction 2. Adventure fiction

ISBN 978-1-933605-98-2; 1-933605-98-7

First published 2001 in Australia

Hannah would much rather be back in Australia, starting high school with her friends. But Japan turns out to be nothing like she'd imagined. When Hannah and her new friend Miki find an ancient message in the stationery shop, they are drawn into involving a mysterious riddle.

"Meehan utilizes beautifully crafted similes and metaphors as she creates a loving and detailed portrayal of Japan and its people. . . . The tale remains so grounded in reality that it never defies belief. A fine fantasy." Kirkus

Meehl, Brian

Out of Patience. Delacorte Press 2006 292p $15.95; lib bdg $17.99

Grades: 5 6 7 8   Fic

1. Family life—Fiction 2. Kansas—Fiction

ISBN 0-385-73299-6; 0-385-90320-0 (lib bdg)

      LC 2005-13873

Twelve-year-old Jake Waters cannot wait to escape the small town of Patience, Kansas, until the arrival of a cursed toilet plunger causes him to reevaluate his feelings toward his family and its history.

This includes "well-drawn characters, page-turning action, and lively prose peppered with dry humor." Bull Cent Child Books

Suck it up. Delacorte Press 2008 323p $15.99; lib bdg $18.99 *

Grades: 8 9 10 11   Fic

1. Vampires—Fiction

ISBN   978-0-385-73300-7;   0-385-73300-3; 978-0-385-90321-9 (lib bdg); 0-385-90321-9 (lib bdg)

      LC 2007-27995

After graduating from the International Vampire League, a scrawny, teenaged vampire named Morning is given the chance to fulfill his childhood dream of becoming a superhero when he embarks on a League mission to become the first vampire to reveal his identity to humans and to demonstrate how peacefully-evolved, blood-substitute-drinking vampires can use their powers to help humanity.

This "an original and light variation on the current trend in brooding teen vampire protagonists. . . . Puns abound in this lengthy, complicated romp. . . . Teens will find it delightful." Booklist

Melling, O. R.

The Hunter's Moon. Amulet Books 2005 284p (Chronicles of Faerie) $16.95; pa $7.95

Grades: 7 8 9 10   Fic

1. Magic—Fiction 2. Ireland—Fiction

ISBN 0-8109-5857-0; 0-8109-9214-0 (pa)

      LC 2004-22216

First published 1992 in Ireland

Two teenage cousins, one Irish, the other from the United States, set out to find a magic doorway to the Faraway Country, where humans must bow to the little people.

"This novel is a compelling blend of Irish mythology and geography. Characters that breathe and connect with readers, and a picturesque landscape that shifts between the present and the past, bring readers into the experience." SLJ

Other available titles in this series are:

Melling, O. R.—*Continued*
The Summer King (2006)
The Light-Bearer's daughter (2007)
The book of dreams (2009)

Meltzer, Milton, 1915-
Tough times; by Milton Meltzer. Clarion Books 2007 168p $16

Grades: 5 6 7 8   **Fic**
1. Great Depression, 1929-1939—Fiction 2. Jews—Fiction 3. Family life—Fiction 4. Massachusetts—Fiction
ISBN 978-0-618-87445-3; 0-618-87445-3
     LC 2006102765
In 1931 Worcester, Massachusetts, Joey Singer, the teenaged son of Jewish immigrants, suffers with his family through the early part of the Great Depression, trying to finish high school, working a milk delivery route, marching on Washington, and eventually even becoming a hobo, all the while trying to figure out how to go to college and realize his dream of becoming a writer.
"Joey's strong voice makes this a valuable addition to the historical-fiction shelves." Booklist

Meminger, Neesha
Shine, coconut moon. Margaret K. McElderry Books 2009 256p $16.99

Grades: 7 8 9 10   **Fic**
1. Prejudices—Fiction 2. East Indian Americans—Fiction 3. School stories 4. September 11 terrorist attacks, 2001—Fiction
ISBN 978-1-4169-5495-8; 1-4169-5495-3
     LC 2008-9836
In the days and weeks following the terrorist attacks on September 11, 2001, Samar, who is of Punjabi heritage but has been raised with no knowledge of her past by her single mother, wants to learn about her family's history and to get in touch with the grandparents her mother shuns.
"Meminger's debut book is a beautiful and sensitive portrait of a young woman's journey from self-absorbed navet to selfless, unified awareness." SLJ

Merrill, Jean, 1923-
The pushcart war; by Jean Merrill; with illustrations by Ronni Solbert. Bantam Doubleday Dell Books for Young Readers 1987 222p il pa $6.50 *

Grades: 5 6 7 8   **Fic**
1. Trucks—Fiction 2. New York (N.Y.)—Fiction
ISBN 0-440-47147-8
A reissue of the title first published 1964 by W. R. Scott
The outbreak of a war between truck drivers and pushcart peddlers brings the mounting problems of traffic to the attention of both the city of New York and the world.
"A book that is both humorous and downright funny. . . . Such a lively book will need little introducing." Horn Book

Meyer, Carolyn
Beware, Princess Elizabeth. Harcourt 2001 214p (Young royals) hardcover o.p. pa $5.95

Grades: 7 8 9 10   **Fic**
1. Elizabeth I, Queen of England, 1533-1603—Fiction 2. Great Britain—History—1485-1603, Tudors—Fiction
ISBN 0-15-202659-2; 0-15-204556-2 (pa)
     LC 00-11700
"Gulliver Books"
After the death of her father, King Henry VIII, in 1547, thirteen-year-old Elizabeth must endure the political intrigues and dangers of the reigns of her half-brother Edward and her half-sister Mary before finally becoming Queen of England eleven years later
"The story moves along swiftly with hints of romance, life-and-death plots, and snippets of everyday life." Book Rep

Duchessina; a novel of Catherine de' Medici. Harcourt 2007 261p (Young royals) $17

Grades: 7 8 9 10   **Fic**
1. Catherine de Médicis, Queen, consort of Henry II, King of France, 1519-1589—Fiction 2. Italy—Fiction 3. Queens—Fiction 4. Orphans—Fiction
ISBN 978-0-15-205588-2; 0-15-205588-6
     LC 2006028876
While her tyrannical family is out of favor in Italy, young Catherine de Medici is raised in convents, then in 1533, when she is fourteen, her uncle, Pope Clement VII, arranges for her marriage to prince Henri of France, who is destined to become king.
"With meticulous historical detail, sensitive characterizations, and Catherine's strong narration, Meyer's memorable story of a fascinating young woman who relies on her intelligence, rather than her beauty, will hit home with many teens." Booklist

The true adventures of Charley Darwin. 1st ed. Harcourt 2009 321p il $17

Grades: 7 8 9 10   **Fic**
1. Darwin, Charles, 1809-1882—Fiction 2. Beagle Expedition (1831-1836)—Fiction 3. Voyages around the world—Fiction 4. Natural history—Fiction
ISBN 978-0-15-206194-4; 0-15-206194-0
     LC 2008-17451
In nineteenth-century England, young Charles Darwin rejects the more traditional careers of physician and clergyman, choosing instead to embark on a dangerous five-year journey by ship to explore the natural world.
"Meyer's writing has a light touch that capitalizes on the humorous, romantic, and exciting events in the man's life while introducing his scientific pursuits and the beliefs of his time. . . . This novel paints a readable and detailed portrait of the young Charles Darwin." SLJ
Includes bibliographical references

Meyer, Kai, 1969-
The water mirror; translated by Elizabeth D. Crawford. Margaret K. McElderry Books 2005 250p (Dark reflections) $15.95

Grades: 5 6 7 8   **Fic**
1. Orphans—Fiction 2. Mermaids and mermen—Fiction 3. Fantasy fiction
ISBN 0-689-87787-0   LC 2005-11943

Meyer, Kai, 1969-—*Continued*

Original German edition 2001

In Venice two teenaged orphans, apprenticed to a maker of magic mirrors, begin to realize that their fates are tied to the magical protector of the city known as the Flowing Queen and to the ruler of Hell, respectively.

An "inventive and original fantasy . . . A powerful mix of political intrigue, adventure, and magic." SLJ

Other titles in this series are:

The stone light (2007)

The glass word (2008)

Meyer, L. A., 1942-

Bloody Jack; being an account of the curious adventures of Mary "Jacky" Faber, ship's boy. Harcourt 2002 278p $17; pa $6.95 *

Grades: 7 8 9 10   Fic

1. Orphans—Fiction 2. Seafaring life—Fiction 3. Pirates—Fiction 4. Sex role—Fiction 5. Adventure fiction

ISBN 0-15-216731-5; 0-15-205085-X (pa)

LC 2002-759

Reduced to begging and thievery in the streets of 18th-century London, a thirteen-year-old orphan disguises herself as a boy and connives her way onto a British warship set for high sea adventure in search of pirates

"From shooting a pirate in battle to foiling a shipmate's sexual attack to surviving when stranded alone on a Caribbean island, the action in Jacky's tale will entertain readers with a taste for adventure." Booklist

Other titles in this series are:

Curse of the blue tatoo (2004)

Under the Jolly Roger (2005)

In the belly of The Bloodhound (2006)

Mississippi Jack (2007)

My bonny light horseman (2008)

Meyer, Stephenie, 1973-

Twilight. Little, Brown and Co. 2005 498p $17.99; pa $8.99 *

Grades: 8 9 10 11 12   Fic

1. Vampires—Fiction 2. School stories 3. Washington (State)—Fiction

ISBN 0-316-16017-2; 0-316-01584-9 (pa)

LC 2004-24730

"Megan Tingley books"

When seventeen-year-old Bella leaves Phoenix to live with her father in Forks, Washington, she meets an exquisitely handsome boy at school for whom she feels an overwhelming attraction and who she comes to realize is not wholly human.

"Realistic, subtle, succinct, and easy to follow, . . . [this book] will have readers dying to sink their teeth into it." SLJ

Other titles in this series are:

New moon (2006)

Eclipse (2007)

Breaking dawn (2008)

Michael, Jan, 1947-

City boy. 1st American ed. Clarion Books 2009 188p $16

Grades: 5 6 7 8   Fic

1. Orphans—Fiction 2. Country life—Fiction 3. Malawi—Fiction

ISBN 978-0-547-22310-0; 0-547-22310-2

LC 2008-37418

First published in the United Kingdom with title: Leaving home

In the southern African country of Malawi, after the AIDS-related deaths of both of his parents, a boy leaves his affluent life in the city to live in a rural village, sharing a one-roomed hut with his aunt, his cousins, and other orphans.

"This is a powerful portrait of poverty and hardship, evenly balanced with shades of hope. Michael's simple prose subtly layers detail, building full-bodied descriptions of landscapes and characters, leaving no room for shortcuts. . . . A stoic tale of surviving life's uncertainties." Kirkus

Michael, Livi, 1960-

City of dogs. G. P. Putnam's Sons 2007 250p $16.99

Grades: 5 6 7 8   Fic

1. Dogs—Fiction 2. Fantasy fiction 3. Norse mythology—Fiction

ISBN 978-0-399-24356-1; 0-399-24356-9

LC 2006-26539

Jenny, a mysterious dog, shows up on Sam's birthday and pulls many of the other dogs in the neighborhood into her quest to prevent the destruction of the world.

"Fantasy readers seeking a thoughtful novel into which to sink their teeth will especially appreciate the unhurried pace, the frequently shifting perspectives . . . and the offbeat but quite effective dogcentric narration." Bull Cent Child Books

Michaelis, Antonia, 1979-

Tiger moon; translated from the German by Anthea Bell. Amulet Books 2008 453p $18.95 *

Grades: 8 9 10 11 12   Fic

1. Storytelling—Fiction 2. Thieves—Fiction 3. Tigers—Fiction 4. Princesses—Fiction 5. India—Fiction

ISBN 978-0-8109-9481-2; 0-8109-9481-X

LC 2007-22823

Sold to be the eighth wife of a rich and cruel merchant, Safia, also called Raka, tries to escape her fate by telling stories of Farhad the thief, his companion Nitish the white tiger, and their travels across India to retrieve a famous jewel that will save a kidnapped princess from becoming the bride of a demon king.

"The plot is fast paced and exciting, and the story gives an excellent overview of the conflicts of India at the time of British occupation, and of Hindu religious beliefs." SLJ

Michaels, Rune

Genesis Alpha; [by] Rune Michaels. 1st ed.
Atheneum Books for Young Readers 2007 193p
$15.99 *

Grades: 7 8 9 10   **Fic**
1. Brothers—Fiction 2. Homicide—Fiction 3. Genetic
engineering—Fiction 4. Video games—Fiction
ISBN 978-1-4169-1886-8; 1-4169-1886-8
                               LC 2007001446

"Ginee Seo Books"

When thirteen-year-old Josh's beloved older brother,
Max, is arrested for murder, the victim's sister leads Josh
to evidence of Max's guilt—and her own—hidden in
their favorite online role-playing game. Josh, who was
conceived to save Max's life years earlier, must consider
whether he shares that guilt.

"Skillfully interweaving science fiction and cyberspace
into a murder mystery, Michaels gives readers a story
that is not only difficult to put down but also poses questions that will linger long after the last page is turned."
Voice Youth Advocates

The reminder. Atheneum Books for Young
Readers 2008 182p $16.99

Grades: 6 7 8 9 10   **Fic**
1. Mothers—Fiction 2. Bereavement—Fiction
3. Robots—Fiction
ISBN 978-1-4169-4131-6; 1-4169-4131-2
                               LC 2008-15391

"Ginee Seo books"

A teenaged girl who hears her dead mother's voice
makes a startling discovery after breaking into her father's industrial robotics lab and finding his latest secret
project: a lifelike replica of her mother's head that looks,
talks, moves, and even smiles just like her mother.

"An intriguing story about loss and survival, with elements of science fiction." Booklist

Miéville, China, 1972-

Un Lun Dun. Ballantine Books 2007 432p il
$17.95 *

Grades: 5 6 7 8 9   **Fic**
1. Fantasy fiction
ISBN   978-0-345-49516-7;   0-345-49516-0;
978-0-345-45844-5 (pa); 0-345-45844-3 (pa)
                               LC 2007-296921

"Del Rey"

When 12-year-old Zanna and her friend Deeba find a
secret entrance leading out of London and into the
strange city of Un Lun Dun, it appears that an ancient
prophesy is coming true at last.

"Miéville's fantastical city is vivid and splendidly
crafted. . . . The story is exceptional and the action
moves along at a quick pace." SLJ

Mikaelsen, Ben, 1952-

Ghost of Spirit Bear; [by] Ben Mikaelsen. 1st
ed. HarperCollins Publishers 2008 154p $16.99; lib
bdg $17.89

Grades: 6 7 8 9   **Fic**
1. School stories 2. Bullies—Fiction
ISBN   978-0-06-009007-4;   0-06-009007-3;
978-0-06-009008-1 (lib bdg); 0-06-009008-1 (lib bdg)
                               LC 2007036732

Sequel to: Touching Spirit Bear (2001)

After a year in exile on an Alaskan island as punishment for severely beating a fellow student, Cole Matthews returns to school in Minneapolis having made
peace with himself and his victim--but he finds that surviving the violence and hatred of high school is even
harder than surviving in the wilderness.

This is "gripping and fast moving. . . [this novel] will
appeal to boys especially and to reluctant readers."
KLIATT

Touching Spirit Bear. HarperCollins Pubs. 2001
241p $15.99; lib bdg $16.89; pa $5.99

Grades: 6 7 8 9   **Fic**
1. Alaska—Fiction 2. Wilderness survival—Fiction
3. Bears—Fiction
ISBN 0-380-97744-3; 0-06-029149-4 (lib bdg);
0-380-80560-X (pa)   LC 00-40702

After his anger erupts into violence, Cole, in order to
avoid going to prison, agrees to participate in a sentencing alternative based on the native American Circle Justice, and he is sent to a remote Alaskan Island where an
encounter with a huge Spirit Bear changes his life

"Mikaelsen's portrayal of this angry, manipulative,
damaged teen is dead on. . . . Gross details about Cole
eating raw worms, a mouse, and worse will appeal to
fans of the outdoor adventure/survival genre." SLJ

Followed by: Ghost of Spirit Bear (2008)

Miklowitz, Gloria D., 1927-

The enemy has a face. Eerdmans Bks. for
Young Readers 2003 139p $16; pa $8

Grades: 7 8 9 10   **Fic**
1. Missing persons—Fiction
ISBN 0-8028-5243-2; 0-8028-5261-0 (pa)
                               LC 2002-9233

Netta and her family have relocated temporarily from
Israel to Los Angeles, and when her seventeen-year-old
brother mysteriously disappears, she becomes convinced
that he has been abducted by Palestinian terrorists

"Almost unbearably suspenseful, the plot will keep
readers turning pages as fast as they can. Nicely interspersed with the events is a thoughtful examination of
some of the reasons behind the age-old strife between
Palestinians and Israelis. Readers come away with a
greater understanding of the conflict, and Netta is given
the opportunity to modify her attitude about her former
enemies." SLJ

Miller, Kirsten, 1963-

Kiki Strike: inside the shadow city; [by] Kirsten
Miller. 1st U.S. ed. Bloomsbury Children's Books
2006 387p $16.95 *

Grades: 5 6 7 8   **Fic**
1. Mystery fiction 2. New York (N.Y.)—Fiction
ISBN 978-1-58234-960-2; 1-58234-960-6
                               LC 2005030945

Life becomes more interesting for Ananka Fishbein
when, at the age of twelve, she discovers an underground
room in the park across from her New York City apartment and meets a mysterious girl called Kiki Strike who
claims that she, too, wants to explore the subterranean
world.

Miller, Kirsten, 1963——*Continued*

"If a 12-year-old can be a hardboiled detective, Ananka Fishbein is one. Her narration is fresh and funny, and the author's unadorned, economical, yet descriptive style carries her character through with verve." SLJ

Another title about Kiki Strike is:

Kiki Strike: The empress's tomb (2007)

Miller, Mary Beth

Aimee; a novel. Dutton Bks. 2002 276p hardcover o.p. pa $6.99

Grades: 7 8 9 10   **Fic**

1. Suicide—Fiction 2. Friendship—Fiction

ISBN 0-525-46894-3; 0-14-240025-4 (pa)

                  LC 2002-283987

It seems that everyone believes that Zoe helped her best friend, Aimee, commit suicide. Zoe is paralyzed by loneliness, guilt, and anger at everyone's suppression of the truth

"Despite the topic, there's no gratuitous violence, and the realistic yet not overly graphic suicide scene doesn't romanticize Aimee's action. The portrayal of therapy is especially good, and Miller's wholly believable, often irritating characters will alienate some readers but feel like a mirror for others." Booklist

Miller, Sarah, 1979-

Miss Spitfire; reaching Helen Keller. Atheneum Books for Young Readers 2007 208p $16.99 *

Grades: 7 8 9 10 11   **Fic**

1. Sullivan, Anne, 1866-1936—Fiction 2. Keller, Helen, 1880-1968—Fiction 3. Teachers—Fiction 4. Blind—Fiction 5. Deaf—Fiction

ISBN 978-1-4169-2542-2; 1-4169-2542-2

                  LC 2006014738

At age twenty-one, partially-blind, lonely but spirited Annie Sullivan travels from Massachusetts to Alabama to try and teach six-year-old Helen Keller, deaf and blind since age two, self-discipline and communication skills. Includes historical notes and timeline.

"This excellent novel is compelling reading even for those familiar with the Keller/Sullivan experience." SLJ

Includes bibliographical references

Mills, Claudia, 1954-

Alex Ryan, stop that! Farrar, Straus & Giroux 2003 151p $16 *

Grades: 5 6 7 8   **Fic**

1. School stories 2. Fathers—Fiction

ISBN 0-374-34655-0   LC 2002-25009

Seventh-grader Alex Ryan enjoys attracting attention, though he never seems to impress his father, but when his antics cause problems with his would-be girlfriend on a school outing, he has second thoughts about his actions

"Mills has a great ear for middle-school dialogue, and her characters ring true." Booklist

Other titles in the West Creek Middle School series are:

Lizzie at last (2000)

You're a brave man, Julius Zimmerman (2000)

Loser, Inc. (1997)

Makeovers by Marcia (2005)

Mills, Sam, 1975-

The viper within; [by] Sam Mills. 1st American ed. Alfred A. Knopf 2008 296p $16.99; lib bdg $19.99

Grades: 7 8 9 10   **Fic**

1. Cults—Fiction 2. Kidnapping—Fiction 3. Religion—Fiction 4. Divorce—Fiction

ISBN 978-0-375-84465-2; 0-375-84465-1; 978-0-375-94465-9 (lib bdg); 0-375-94465-6 (lib bdg)

                  LC 2007031952

Bitter and angry after his parents' divorce, Jon joins a cult, The Religion of Hebetheus, at his high school and soon becomes embroiled in a plot to kidnap a fellow student and suspected terrorist, but their plans go terribly wrong.

"Thought provoking, tension packed, and suspenseful, Mill's novel forces readers to grapple with multiple perspectives on terrorism, cults, religion, victimization, fidelity, embedded misogyny and conscience." Voice Youth Advocates

Milway, Alex, 1978-

The mousehunter; written and illustrated by Alex Milway. Little, Brown 2009 422p il map $15.99

Grades: 4 5 6 7   **Fic**

1. Mice—Fiction 2. Pirates—Fiction 3. Adventure fiction

ISBN 978-0-316-02454-9; 0-316-02454-6

Captain Mousebeard is a feared mousehunting pirate. He seeks out the rarest and most precious breeds of mice to collect and trade. Emeline, a mousekeeper, wants the bounty her master puts on Mousebeard's head. So she heads off to adventure to capture the pirate.

"Milway has created an atmospheric and engaging world filled with hundreds of varieties of mice with different coloring, temperaments, and abilities. New creatures are introduced both within the text and in pages with information and illustrations from The Mousehunter's Almanac interspersed between chapters. Readers will enjoy the action, chases, and plot twists." SLJ

Mitchard, Jacquelyn

All we know of heaven; a novel. HarperTeen 2008 312p $16.99; lib bdg $17.89

Grades: 7 8 9 10 11 12   **Fic**

1. Traffic accidents—Fiction 2. Death—Fiction 3. Bereavement—Fiction

ISBN 978-0-06-134578-4; 0-06-134578-4; 978-0-06-134579-1 (lib bdg); 0-06-134579-2 (lib bdg)

When Maureen and Bridget, two sixteen-year-old best friends who look like sisters, are in a terrible car accident and one of them dies, they are at first incorrectly identified at the hospital, and then, as Maureen achieves a remarkable recovery, she must deal with the repercussions of the accident, the mixup, and some choices she made while she was getting better.

"Riveting, compassionate and psychologically nuanced. . . . Utterly gripping." Publ Wkly

Mitchard, Jacquelyn—*Continued*

The midnight twins. Razorbill 2008 235p
$16.99; pa $8.99

Grades: 6 7 8 9   **Fic**
1. Twins—Fiction 2. Clairvoyance—Fiction
3. Telepathy—Fiction
ISBN   978-1-59514-160-6;   1-59514-160-X;
978-1-59514-226-9 (pa); 1-59514-226-6 (pa)
LC 2007-31139

Identical twins Meredith and Mallory Brynn have always shared one another's thoughts, even as they dream,
but their connection diminishes as they approach their
thirteenth birthday, and one begins to see the future, the
other the past, leading them to discover that a high
school student they know is doing horrible things that
place the twins, and others, in grave danger.

"The plot moves quickly, propelled by the mysteries
of the sisters' relationship. . . . The girls' supernatural
knowledge is a delicious bonus." Publ Wkly

Another title about Meredith and Mallory is:
Look both ways (2009)

Now you see her. HarperTempest 2007 208p
$15.99; lib bdg $16.89

Grades: 7 8 9 10   **Fic**
1. Actors—Fiction 2. Impostors and imposture—Fiction 3. Mentally ill—Fiction
ISBN   978-0-06-111683-4;   0-06-111683-1;
978-0-06-111684-1 (lib bdg); 0-06-111684-X (lib bdg)
LC 2006-29875

Fifteen-year-old Hope describes events leading her to
agree to her boyfriend's plan to stage her abduction, and
the consequences for their relationship, her family life,
and her budding career as an actress.

"Peeling the layers of her story away reveals the truth
in bits and pieces, and the ambiguous conclusion feels
absolutely realistic. This is a riveting page-turner." SLJ

Mitchell, Todd, 1974-

The Traitor King. Scholastic Press 2007 358p
$16.99 *

Grades: 5 6 7 8   **Fic**
1. Fantasy fiction
ISBN 0-439-82788-4   LC 2006-12815

When ten-year-old Darren and his family show up at
their family reunion and find their Uncle Will missing,
Darren and his sister go in search of clues to discover
what happened.

"Humor, menace, and mystery suffuse this fast-paced
tale, which is peopled (or creatured?) with brownies,
nixies, bogels, and other fay, as well as a handful of eccentric humans. . . . This well-written tale is a must for
most fantasy readers." SLJ

Mochizuki, Ken

Beacon Hill boys. Scholastic Press 2002 201p
$16.95; pa $5.99

Grades: 7 8 9 10   **Fic**
1. Japanese Americans—Fiction 2. Washington
(State)—Fiction
ISBN 0-439-26749-8; 0-439-24906-6 (pa)
LC 2002-2343

In 1972 in Seattle, a teenager in a Japanese American
family struggles for his own identity, along with a group
of three friends who share his anger and confusion

"The author nicely balances universal experiences of
male adolescence . . . with scenes that bring readers
right into the complicated era, and his important,
thought-provoking story asks tough questions about racial
and cultural identity, prejudice, and family." Booklist

Molloy, Michael

Peter Raven under fire. Scholastic 2005 502p il
maps $17.95

Grades: 6 7 8 9   **Fic**
1. France—History—1799-1815—Fiction 2. Sea stories 3. Adventure fiction
ISBN 0-439-72454-6
"The Chicken House"

"In 1800, continuous war has depleted France's treasury, but Napoleon still wants to expand his empire. To
this end, he needs money to defeat the superior British
Navy and to exploit Louisiana for the greatest gain. In
England, midshipman Peter Raven, 13, is assigned to
HMS Torren. When powerful, sadistic pirates murder everyone on the ship except Peter and jack-of-all-trades
Matthew Book, the protagonist finds himself apprenticed
to a British spy. . . . Fast paced with multiple plot
twists. . . . Molloy's writing is intelligent and engaging."
SLJ

Moloney, James, 1954-

The Book of Lies. HarperCollinsPublishers 2007
360p $16.99; lib bdg $17.89

Grades: 5 6 7 8   **Fic**
1. Magic—Fiction 2. Orphans—Fiction 3. Fantasy fiction
ISBN   978-0-06-057842-8;   0-06-057842-4;
978-0-06-057843-5 (lib bdg); 0-06-057843-2 (lib bdg)
LC 2006-29874

On the night he was brought to an orphanage, Marcel's memories were taken by a sorceror and replaced
with new ones by his Book of Lies, but Bea, a girl with
the ability to make herself invisible, was watching and is
determined to help him discover his true identity.

"Readers who enjoy the mixture of mystery, riddles,
action, and camaraderie will be pleased that the open-
ended conclusion leads to a planned sequel." Booklist

Monninger, Joseph

Baby. Front Street 2007 173p $16.95

Grades: 8 9 10 11   **Fic**
1. Foster home care—Fiction 2. Sled dog racing—Fiction 3. Dogs—Fiction 4. New Hampshire—Fiction
ISBN 978-1-59078-502-7   LC 2006-101749

Fifteen-year-old Baby's last chance at foster care is
with the Potters, and while she likes them and enjoys
learning to race their sled dogs, she feels she should go
back on the streets with her boyfriend if she cannot find
the mother who has deserted her again.

"The girl's first-person voice, the backdrop, and the
details . . . work together well to set this story apart
from the many in which troubled teens find solace in animals." Booklist

Monninger, Joseph—*Continued*
Hippie chick. Front Street 2008 156p $16.95
Grades: 8 9 10 11 12   **Fic**
1. Survival after airplane accidents, shipwrecks, etc.—
Fiction 2. Manatees—Fiction 3. Shipwrecks—Fiction
4. Everglades (Fla.)—Fiction
ISBN 978-1-59078-598-0; 1-59078-598-3
           LC 2007-51976
After her sailboat capsizes, fifteen-year-old Lolly
Emmerson is rescued by manatees and taken to a man-
grove key in the Everglades, where she forms a bond
with her aquatic companions while struggling to survive.
"It's an affecting account, beautifully told." SLJ

Montes, Marisa, 1951-
A circle of time. Harcourt 2002 261p $17
Grades: 6 7 8 9   **Fic**
1. Space and time—Fiction
ISBN 0-15-202626-6   LC 2001-2614
"A Time travel mystery"
In 1996, Allison, a fourteen-year-old girl in a coma,
is forced back in time by Becky, a girl who died in
1906, and who needs help in righting a series of terrible
wrongs
"Fans of both mysteries and time-slip stories will like
the novel, which is liberally spiced with romance and
melodrama, and clarifies a bit of intriguing and tragic
California history." Booklist

Moore, Perry
Hero. Hyperion 2007 428p $16.99
Grades: 7 8 9 10 11 12   **Fic**
1. Superheroes—Fiction 2. Homosexuality—Fiction
3. Father-son relationship—Fiction 4. Science fiction
ISBN 978-1-4231-0195-6; 1-4231-0195-2
Thom Creed, the gay son of a disowned superhero,
finds that he, too, has special powers and is asked to join
the very League that rejected his father, and it is there
that Thom finds other misfits whom he can finally trust.
"The combination of mystery, fantasy, thriller, and romance create a delightful and compelling read." Voice
Youth Advocates

Moore, Peter
Caught in the act. Viking 2005 260p $16.99
Grades: 7 8 9 10   **Fic**
1. Theater—Fiction 2. Mental illness—Fiction
ISBN 0-670-05990-0   LC 2004-14906
Everyone believes that sophomore honors student
Ethan Lederer is a topnotch scholar and a great guy, but
a new student helps Ethan to discover and disclose that
he is just acting a role, even as she reveals her own
mental instability.
"The smart, straightforward writing with its fast-paced
action and realistic dialogue makes this novel a page-
turner." SLJ

Moore, Yvette
Freedom songs. Orchard Bks. 1991 168p
hardcover o.p. pa $5.99
Grades: 7 8 9 10   **Fic**
1. African Americans—Fiction 2. Uncles—Fiction
ISBN 0-531-05812-3; 0-14-036017-4 (pa)
           LC 88-43073

"Sheryl is a black fourteen-year-old who launches her
narrative with an account of her family's trip to North
Carolina on Easter of 1963. There she sees Jim Crow
laws in action. . . . Back in Brooklyn, she organizes a
concert to raise money for the freedom riders, one of
whom, her Uncle Pete, is killed by a bomb at the school
where he teaches black southerners registering to vote."
Bull Cent Child Books
"Humorous details of typical adolescent concerns and
escapades lighten the serious nature of a well-crafted story." Horn Book

Moran, Katy
Bloodline. Candlewick Press 2009 297p il map
$16.99
Grades: 7 8 9 10   **Fic**
1. Adventure fiction 2. War stories 3. Middle Ages—
Fiction 4. Great Britain—History—0-1066—Fiction
ISBN 978-07636-4083-5; 0-7636-4083-2
           LC 2008-21413
While traveling through early seventh-century Britain
trying to stop an impending war, Essa, who bears the
blood of native British tribes and of the invading
Anglish, makes discoveries that divide his loyalties.
"Essa is a complex, sympathetic protagonist: prickly
and quick of temper, but also clever, determined and of
unflinching integrity. If his struggle is authentically gory
and ultimately tragic, it is not without glimpses of love
and hope." Kirkus

Moranville, Sharelle Byars
Over the river. Holt & Co. 2002 228p $16.95
Grades: 5 6 7 8   **Fic**
1. Family life—Fiction 2. Illinois—Fiction
ISBN 0-8050-7049-4   LC 2002-24308
Also available in paperback from Dell
In 1947, after the war, Willa Mae's father returns to
the Illinois town where she has lived with her maternal
grandparents for the last five of her eleven years, and
Willa Mae finds herself struggling to understand old
family tensions and secrets
"Suspense builds and the troubling secrets are revealed, but there's no tidy resolution. . . . This is the
best kind of historical fiction, where details of time and
place are not a picturesque backdrop but an integral part
of the story." Booklist

The Snows. Henry Holt 2007 225p $16.95
Grades: 7 8 9 10 11 12   **Fic**
1. Family life—Fiction 2. Iowa—Fiction
ISBN 978-0-8050-7469-7; 0-8050-7469-4
           LC 2006-35468
With the thread of family that connects them through
the generations, Jim in 1931, Cathy in 1942, Jill in 1969,
and Mona in 2006 each find "sixteen" to be the pivotal
age in their lives.
"Both major and supporting characters are well drawn
and interesting. Beautifully rendered prose with precise
descriptions." SLJ

Mordecai, Martin

Blue Mountain trouble. Arthur A. Levine Books 2009 341p $16.99

Grades: 5 6 7 8 **Fic**

1. Twins—Fiction 2. Siblings—Fiction 3. Family life—Fiction 4. Mountain life—Fiction 5. Jamaica—Fiction

ISBN 978-0-545-04156-0; 0-545-04156-2

LC 2008042648

After being saved from a disastrous landslide by an extraordinary goat that blocks their usual way to school, twins Pollyread and Jackson, living with their parents high in the mountains of Jamaica, find the strange goat reappearing at crucial intervals as their day-to-day life is changed by series of mysterious events involving the return of a local troublemaker and secrets from their family's past.

"Mordecai has written a nostalgic valentine to his native island that is . . . always rich in characterization with a beautifully realized setting. The elements of magic and mystery intriguing, too." Booklist

Morden, Simon

The lost art. David Fickling Books 2008 521p $16.99; lib bdg $19.99

Grades: 8 9 10 11 12 **Fic**

1. Religion and science—Fiction 2. Science fiction

ISBN 978-0-385-75147-6; 0-385-75147-8; 978-0-385-75148-3 (lib bdg); 0-385-75148-6 (lib bdg)

LC 2007-35591

A millennium after a devastating war changed the direction of Earth's rotation, when the Church keeps science and technology suppressed, magician-like Benzamir and Va, a killer-for-hire turned monk, seek Solomon, who is surreptitiously spreading technology for nefarious purposes.

"This original and engaging science fiction adventure features adult protagonists, though they deal with classic coming-of-age questions about their place in the world." Horn Book Guide

Morgan, Clay

The boy who spoke dog. Dutton Children's Bks. 2003 166p $15.99

Grades: 5 6 7 8 **Fic**

1. Survival after airplane accidents, shipwrecks, etc.—Fiction 2. Dogs—Fiction 3. Orphans—Fiction 4. New Zealand—Fiction 5. Adventure fiction

ISBN 0-525-47159-6 LC 2003-45223

After being marooned on an island near New Zealand, Jack, an orphaned cabin boy from San Francisco, becomes allied with a group of dogs who protect the local sheep from wild dogs

"Morgan delivers an unusual, engrossing novel, using vivid language to project the reader into the sounds and smells of the animal world as he examines the ancient bonds between humans and dogs." Booklist

Followed by: The boy who returned from the sea (2007)

Morgan, Nicola, 1961-

Chicken friend; [by] Nicola Morgan. 1st U.S. ed. Candlewick Press 2005 148p $15.99

Grades: 5 6 7 8 **Fic**

1. Diabetes—Fiction 2. Country life—Fiction 3. Friendship—Fiction 4. Great Britain—Fiction

ISBN 0-7636-2735-6 LC 2004-54608

When her parents decide to move their family to the English countryside, homeschool their children, and raise chickens, Becca tries to make friends with her new neighbors by hiding her diabetes and throwing a twelfth birthday party for herself.

"The girl is believable and likable as both character and narrator, which turns an apparently simple story into one that is funny, insightful, and moving." SLJ

Fleshmarket. Delacorte Press 2004 208p hardcover o.p. lib bdg $17.99

Grades: 7 8 9 10 **Fic**

1. Knox, Robert, 1791-1862—Fiction 2. Medicine—Fiction 3. Physicians—Fiction 4. Poverty—Fiction 5. Scotland—Fiction

ISBN 0-385-73154-X; 0-385-90192-5 (lib bdg)

LC 2003-11441

In nineteenth-century Scotland, following the death of his mother during surgery, Robbie decides to take revenge on the surgeon who performed the operation, Dr. Robert Knox, and in the process, makes a gruesome discovery about the lengths the medical profession will go to advance its knowledge of anatomy.

"The protagonist's need for revenge is palpable, and Morgan's story is fast paced and absorbing. Readers who are fascinated by forensics and anatomy will find this a gripping story." SLJ

The highwayman's footsteps. Candlewick Press 2007 354p $16.99

Grades: 6 7 8 9 **Fic**

1. Great Britain—History—1714-1837—Fiction 2. Adventure fiction

ISBN 978-0-7636-3472-8; 0-7636-3472-7

LC 2007-25997

In eighteenth-century England, William runs away from his father, only to be captured by an armed highwayman who turns out to be a girl. Together, they seek vengeance against William's cruel father and the soldiers who killed the girl's parents.

"Alfred Noyes' romantic epic . . . provides the jumping off point for this beautifully written historical novel. . . . Excellent for both recreational reading and curriculum support in the humanities." Booklist

Morgenroth, Kate

Jude. Simon & Schuster Books for Young Readers 2004 277p $16.95; pa $5.99

Grades: 7 8 9 10 **Fic**

1. Crime—Fiction 2. Mother-son relationship—Fiction

ISBN 0-689-86479-5; 1-416-91267-3 (pa)

LC 2003-20475

Still reeling from his drug-dealing father's murder, moving in with the wealthy mother he never knew, and transferring to a private school, fifteen-year-old Jude is tricked into pleading guilty to a crime he did not commit

"The plot is tight, deliberately paced, and full of deli-

Morgenroth, Kate—*Continued*

cious twists. . . . The story is quick and action packed enough to engage reluctant readers, especially older boys." SLJ

Morgenstern, Susie Hoch

Secret letters from 0 to 10; translated by Gill Rosner. Viking 1998 137p $16.99; pa $4.99

Grades: 4 5 6 **Fic**

1. Friendship—Fiction 2. School stories 3. Paris (France)—Fiction

ISBN 0-670-88007-8; 0-14-130819-2 (pa)

LC 98-5559

Ten-year-old Ernest lives a boring existence in Paris with his grandmother until a lively girl named Victory enters his class at school

"Morgenstern has created extremely well-drawn, distinct, and sometimes quirky characters with eloquent dialogue." SLJ

Moriarty, Jaclyn

The murder of Bindy Mackenzie. Arthur A. Levine Books 2006 494p $16.99

Grades: 8 9 10 11 12 **Fic**

1. School stories 2. Australia—Fiction

ISBN 0-439-74051-7; 0-439-74052-5 (pa)

LC 2006-07562

Class brain Bindy Mackenzie has alienated her entire high school but when she realizes someone is trying to kill her, she has to make friends in order to get help.

"The truths about family, school, and social pressures and Bindy's unforgettable, earnest, hilariously high-strung voice . . . will capture and hold readers." Booklist

The year of secret assignments. Arthur A. Levine Books 2004 340p $16.95; pa $7.99

Grades: 7 8 9 10 **Fic**

1. Friendship—Fiction 2. School stories 3. Australia—Fiction

ISBN 0-439-49881-3; 0-439-49882-1 (pa)

LC 2003-14278

Three female students from Ashbury High write to three male students from rival Brookfield High as part of a pen pal program, leading to romance, humiliation, revenge plots, and war between the schools

"There are a few coarse moments—a reference to a blow job and some caustic outbursts. . . . This is an unusual novel with an exhilarating pace, irrepressible characters, and a screwball humor that will easily attract teens." Booklist

Morpurgo, Michael

The amazing story of Adolphus Tips; [by] Michael Morpurgo. 1st American ed. Scholastic Press 2006 140p $15.99

Grades: 4 5 6 7 **Fic**

1. World War, 1939-1945—Fiction 2. Cats—Fiction 3. Grandmothers—Fiction

ISBN 0-439-79661-X LC 2005049038

When Boowie reads the diary that his grandmother sends him, he learns of her childhood in World War II England when American and British soldiers practiced for D-Day's invasion in the area of her home, and about her beloved cat, Adolphus Tips, and the cat's namesake.

"The personal story of anger and love is as gripping as the war drama, and Morpurgo includes a fascinating note about the invasion rehearsal and why its history is seldom told." Booklist

Kensuke's kingdom. Scholastic Press 2003 c1999 164p $16.95 *

Grades: 4 5 6 7 **Fic**

1. Survival after airplane accidents, shipwrecks, etc.—Fiction

ISBN 0-439-38202-5 LC 2002-9078

First published 1999 in the United Kingdom

When Michael is swept off his family's yacht, he washes up on a desert island, where he struggles to survive—until he finds he is not alone

This is "highly readable. . . . The end is bittersweet but believable, and the epilogue is a sad commentary on the long-lasting effects of war." Booklist

The Mozart question; [by] Michael Morpurgo; illustrated by Michael Foreman. Candlewick Press 2008 66p il $15.99

Grades: 4 5 6 7 **Fic**

1. Holocaust, 1933-1945—Fiction 2. Venice (Italy)—Fiction 3. Violinists—Fiction

ISBN 978-0-7636-3552-7; 0-7636-3552-9

A young journalist goes to Venice, Italy, to interview a famous violinist, who tells the story of his parents' incarceration by the Nazis, and explains why they can no longer listen to the music of Mozart.

"Morpurgo breathes life into this touching tale, which is conveyed with compassion and honesty. Foreman's watercolors enrich the narrative." SLJ

Private Peaceful. Scholastic Press 2004 c2003 202p $16.95; pa $5.99

Grades: 7 8 9 10 **Fic**

1. World War, 1914-1918—Fiction 2. Great Britain—Fiction

ISBN 0-439-63648-5; 0-439-63653-1 (pa)

LC 2003-65347

First published 2003 in the United Kingdom

When Thomas Peaceful's older brother is forced to join the British Army, Thomas decides to sign up as well, although he is only fourteen years old, to prove himself to his country, his family, his childhood love, Molly, and himself

"In this World War I story, the terse and beautiful narrative of a young English soldier is as compelling about the world left behind as about the horrific daily details of trench warfare. . . . Suspense builds right to the end, which is shocking, honest, and unforgettable." Booklist

War horse; by Michael Morpurgo. 1st ed. Scholastic 2007 165p $16.99

Grades: 5 6 7 8 **Fic**

1. Horses—Fiction 2. World War, 1914-1918—Fiction

ISBN 978-0-439-79663-7; 0-439-79663-6

LC 2006044368

First published 1982 in the United Kingdom

Morpurgo, Michael—*Continued*

Joey the horse recalls his experiences growing up on an English farm, his struggle for survival as a cavalry horse during World War I, and his reunion with his beloved master.

"At times deeply affecting, the story balances the horror with moments of respite and care." Horn Book Guide

Morris, Gerald, 1963-

The squire's tale. Houghton Mifflin 1998 212p (Squire's tales) $15; pa $5.50 *

Grades: 6 7 8 9   **Fic**

1. Gawain (Legendary character)—Fiction 2. Knights and knighthood—Fiction 3. Great Britain—History—0-1066—Fiction

ISBN 0-395-86959-5; 0-440-22823-9 (pa)

LC 97-12447

In medieval England, fourteen-year-old Terence finds his tranquil existence suddenly changed when he becomes the squire of the young Gawain of Orkney and accompanies him on a long quest, proving Gawain's worth as a knight and revealing an important secret about his own true identity

"Well-drawn characters, excellent, snappy dialogue, detailed descriptions of medieval life, and a dry wit put a new spin on this engaging tale of the characters and events of King Arthur's time." Booklist

Other titles in this series are:
The ballad of Sir Dinadan (2003)
The lionness & her knight (2005)
Parsifal's page (2001)
The princess, the crone, and the dung-cart knight (2004)
The quest of the Fair Unknown (2006)
The savage damsel and the dwarf (2000)
The squire, his knight, & his lady (1999)

Morton-Shaw, Christine

The hunt for the seventh. HarperCollins 2008 273p il map $16.99; lib bdg $17.89

Grades: 6 7 8 9   **Fic**

1. Father-son relationship—Fiction 2. Ghost stories 3. Mystery fiction

ISBN 978-0-06-072822-9; 0-06-072822-1; 978-0-06-072823-6 (lib bdg); 0-06-072823-X (lib bdg)

LC 2007-38885

"Katherine Tegen Books"

When his father starts a new job at Minerva Hall as gardener, twelve-year-old Jim discovers an ancient curse that needs to be unraveled before disaster happens.

"Morton-Shaw skillfully weaves ancient lore into a gripping mystery. The fine plotting keeps readers turning the pages as suspense builds to the surprising end." SLJ

The riddles of Epsilon. Katherine Tegen Books 2005 375p $16.99; lib bdg $17.89

Grades: 7 8 9 10   **Fic**

1. Great Britain—Fiction 2. Supernatural—Fiction

ISBN 0-06-072819-1; 0-06-072820-5 (lib bdg)

LC 2004-14641

After moving with her parents to a remote English island, fourteen-year-old Jess attempts to dispel an ancient curse by solving a series of riddles, aided by Epsilon, a supernatural being.

Moses, Shelia P.

The baptism. Margaret K. McElderry Books 2007 130p $15.99

Grades: 5 6 7 8   **Fic**

1. Twins—Fiction 2. Baptism—Fiction 3. Family life—Fiction 4. African Americans—Fiction 5. Slavery—Fiction 6. North Carolina—Fiction

ISBN 978-1-4169-0671-1; 1-4169-0671-1

LC 2005-28408

In twentieth-century Occoneechee Neck, North Carolina—an area still affected by its history of slavery—twelve-year-old Leon Curry reflects about whether he wants to give up sinning to be baptized alongside his twin brother.

"Set in the same . . . community in the 1940s as . . . *The Legend of [Buddy] Bush* . . . this story is told by Buddy's 12-year-old cousin. . . . Sharp and immediate, the boy's narrative . . . brings close the cruel secrets of slavery's legacy as well as the powerful ties of family during hard times." Booklist

Joseph. Margaret K. McElderry Books 2008 174p $16.99

Grades: 7 8 9 10   **Fic**

1. Mother-son relationship—Fiction 2. Drug abuse—Fiction 3. African Americans—Fiction

ISBN 978-1-4169-1752-6; 1-4169-1752-7

Fourteen-year-old Joseph tries to avoid trouble and keep in touch with his father, who is serving in Iraq, as he and his alcoholic, drug-addicted mother move from one homeless shelter to another.

"Moses creates a compelling character in Joseph. His struggle to survive his current situation intact is fascinating to read. . . . Negative influences such as drug dealers and users are described in a clear, cold light. Education and hard work are praised for their positive influences. Middle school and junior high teens will enjoy this story." Voice Youth Advocates

The legend of Buddy Bush. Margaret K. McElderry Books 2004 216p $15.95

Grades: 6 7 8 9   **Fic**

1. Race relations—Fiction 2. African Americans—Fiction 3. North Carolina—Fiction

ISBN 0-689-85839-6   LC 2003-8024

In 1947, twelve-year-old Pattie Mae is sustained by her dreams of escaping Rich Square, North Carolina, and moving to Harlem when her Uncle Buddy is arrested for attempted rape of a white woman and her grandfather is diagnosed with a terminal brain tumor.

"Patti Mae's first-person voice, steeped in the inflections of the South, rings true, and her observations richly evoke a time, place, and a resilient African American community." Booklist

Another title about Buddy Bush is:
The return of Buddy Bush (2005)

Mosher, Richard, 1949-

Zazoo. Clarion Bks. 2001 248p $16; pa $6.99

Grades: 6 7 8 9   **Fic**

1. Vietnamese—Fiction 2. Grandfathers—Fiction 3. Orphans—Fiction 4. France—Fiction

ISBN 0-618-13534-0; 0-618-43904-8 (pa)

LC 2001-28291

Mosher, Richard, 1949-—*Continued*
Amid old secrets revealed and rifts healed, a thirteen-year-old Vietnamese orphan raised in rural France by her aging "Grand-Pierre" learns about life, death, and love
This "is a beautiful and lyrical novel, with poetry woven throughout." SLJ

Mosier, Elizabeth
My life as a girl. Random House 1999 193p hardcover o.p. pa $12
Grades: 8 9 10 11 12   **Fic**
1. Prisoners—Fiction 2. Waiters and waitresses—Fiction 3. Arizona—Fiction
ISBN 0-679-89035-1; 0-375-89522-1 (pa)
LC 98-8688
During her last summer in Phoenix, Arizona, before going to an eastern college, eighteen-year-old Jaime works two waitress jobs and plans her escape from a life forever changed by her father's prison sentence
"Featuring lifelike dialogue, three-dimensional characters and an upbeat outcome, the novel also serves up glossy, attention-getting prose." Publ Wkly

Mosley, Walter
47. Little, Brown 2005 232p $16.99
Grades: 7 8 9 10   **Fic**
1. Slavery—Fiction 2. Magic—Fiction 3. African Americans—Fiction
ISBN 0-316-11035-3   LC 2004-12500
Number 47, a fourteen-year-old slave boy growing up under the watchful eye of a brutal master in 1832, meets the mysterious Tall John, who introduces him to a magical science and also teaches him the meaning of freedom.
"Time travel, shape-shifting, and intergalactic conflict add unusual, provocative elements to this story. And yet, well-drawn characters; lively dialogue filled with gritty, regional dialect; vivid descriptions; and poignant reflections ground it in harsh reality." SLJ

Mourlevat, Jean-Claude
The pull of the ocean; [by] Jean-Claude Mourlevat; translated from the French by Y. Maudet. Delacorte Press 2006 190p $13.95; lib bdg $17.99 *
Grades: 5 6 7   **Fic**
1. Size—Fiction 2. Brothers—Fiction 3. Twins—Fiction 4. France—Fiction
ISBN   978-0-385-73348-9;   0-385-73348-8;
978-0-385-90364-6 (lib bdg); 0-385-90364-2 (lib bdg)
LC 2006001802
Loosely based on Charles Perrault's "Tom Thumb," seven brothers in modern-day France flee their poor parents' farm, led by the youngest who, although mute and unusually small, is exceptionally wise.
This "is a memorable novel that readers will find engaging and intellectually satisfying." SLJ

Murdock, Catherine Gilbert
Dairy Queen; a novel. Houghton Mifflin 2006 275p $16 *
Grades: 7 8 9 10   **Fic**
1. Football—Fiction 2. Farm life—Fiction
ISBN 0-618-68307-0   LC 2005-19077
After spending her summer running the family farm and training the quarterback for her school's rival football team, sixteen-year-old D.J. decides to go out for the sport herself, not anticipating the reactions of those around her.
"D. J.'s voice is funny, frank, and intelligent, and her story is not easily pigeonholed." Voice Youth Advocates
Followed by The off season (2007)

Princess Ben; being a wholly truthful account of her various discoveries and misadventures, recounted to the best of her recollection, in four parts; written by Catherine Gilbert Murdock. Houghton Mifflin 2008 344p $16 *
Grades: 7 8 9 10   **Fic**
1. Fairy tales 2. Princesses—Fiction 3. Magic—Fiction 4. Courts and courtiers—Fiction
ISBN 978-0-618-95971-6; 0-618-95971-8
LC 2007-34300
A girl is transformed, through instruction in life at court, determination, and magic, from sullen, pudgy, graceless Ben into Crown Princess Benevolence, a fit ruler of the kindgom of Montagne as it faces war with neighboring Drachensbett.
This offers "sardonic, witty repartee. . . . [The story] is thoroughly entertaining." Publ Wkly

Murphy, Claire Rudolf
Free radical. Clarion Bks. 2002 198p $15
Grades: 7 8 9 10   **Fic**
1. Baseball—Fiction
ISBN 0-618-11134-4   LC 2001-42268
In Fairbanks, Alaska, in the middle of the summer Little League baseball season, fifteen-year-old Luke is stunned when his mother confesses that she is wanted by the FBI for her role in the death of a student during an anti-Vietnam War protest thirty years ago
"The fast action of the baseball scenes will lure teens to the sports story, and the thought-provoking issues of guilt and responsibility will hold their interest." Booklist

Murphy, Jim, 1947-
Desperate journey. Scholastic Press 2006 278p il map $16.99
Grades: 5 6 7 8   **Fic**
1. Erie Canal (N.Y.)—Fiction 2. Family life—Fiction
ISBN 0-439-07806-7   LC 2006-02526
In the mid-1800s, with both her father and her uncle in jail on an assault charge, Maggie, her brother, and her ailing mother rush their barge along the Erie Canal to deliver their heavy cargo or lose everything.
This is a "gripping novel." Booklist

Murphy, Pat, 1955-
The wild girls. Viking 2007 288p $16.99
Grades: 5 6 7 8 **Fic**
1. Authorship—Fiction 2. Friendship—Fiction
3. School stories
ISBN 978-0-670-06226-3 LC 2007-14830
When thirteen-year-old Joan moves to California in
1972, she becomes friends with Sarah, who is timid at
school but an imaginative leader when they play in the
woods, and after winning a writing contest together they
are recruited for an exclusive summer writing class that
gives them new insights into themselves and others.
"Supporting characters are fully formed and intriguing.
Murphy evokes her setting with skill and plays out
themes of creativity and self-expression with grace and
intensity." SLJ

Murphy, Rita
Bird. Delacorte Press 2008 151p $15.99; lib bdg
$18.99
Grades: 5 6 7 8 **Fic**
1. Houses—Fiction 2. Supernatural—Fiction
3. Flight—Fiction 4. Kites—Fiction 5. Vermont—Fiction
ISBN 978-0-385-73018-1; 0-385-73018-7;
978-0-385-90557-2 (lib bdg); 0-385-90557-2 (lib bdg)
LC 2008-04690
Miranda, a small, delicate girl easily carried off by the
wind, lands at Bourne Manor on the coast of Lake
Champlain and is raised by the dour Wysteria Barrows,
but she begins to believe rumors that the Manor is
cursed and, aided by a new friend and kites secreted in
an attic, seeks to escape.
"This enchanting novel is well written with lyrical text
and beautiful descriptions. . . . Good for middle school
students, this book will make a nice addition to school
and public libraries alike." Libr Media Connect

Looking for Lucy Buick. Delacorte Press 2005
165p $15.95; lib bdg $17.99
Grades: 7 8 9 10 **Fic**
1. Abandoned children—Fiction 2. Family life—Fiction
ISBN 0-385-72939-1; 0-385-90176-3 (lib bdg)
LC 2004-20128
Following the death of her favorite adoptive aunt,
Lucy goes searching for her biological family who abandoned her in an old Buick eighteen years before.
"What wins the day are the people in Lucy's life, living and dead . . . who pop off the pages, and Murphy's
voice . . . which tells the story with a steadfastness and
sweetness." Booklist

Murray, Jaye
Bottled up; a novel. Dial Books 2003 220p
hardcover o.p. pa $6.99
Grades: 7 8 9 10 **Fic**
1. Brothers—Fiction 2. Alcoholism—Fiction 3. Drug
abuse—Fiction
ISBN 0-8037-2897-2; 0-1424-0240-0 (pa)
LC 2002-13744
A high school boy comes to terms with his drug ad-
diction, life with an alcoholic father, and a younger

brother who looks up to him
"With its rich language and exquisite allegories, the
book is a perfect choice for any teen who needs a humorous yet touching push in the right direction." Voice
Youth Advocates

Murray, Kirsty, 1960-
The secret life of Maeve Lee Kwong; by Kirsty
Murray. Allen & Unwin 2008 252p (Children of
the wind) pa $8.95
Grades: 5 6 7 8 **Fic**
1. Racially mixed people—Fiction 2. Australia—Fic-
tion 3. Chinese—Fiction 4. Ireland—Fiction
ISBN 978-1-86508-737-5 (pa); 1-86508-737-8 (pa)
"Being half-Chinese and half-Irish never bothered
Maeve Lee Kwong much. A lot of Australians have
mixed heritages, and she considers herself fully Aussie.
Then her mother dies in a car accident, and Maeve no
longer knows who she is, or where she belongs. . . .
This book has a lot going for it, including short and
highly varied scenes that propel the story forward at a
brisk pace. With settings in Australia, Hong Kong, and
Ireland, the descriptions are lush and appealing." SLJ

Mussi, Sarah
The door of no return. Margaret K. McElderry
Books 2008 394p $17.99 *
Grades: 8 9 10 11 12 **Fic**
1. Adventure fiction 2. Buried treasure—Fiction
3. Blacks—Fiction 4. Homicide—Fiction 5. Great
Britain—Fiction 6. Ghana—Fiction
ISBN 978-1-4169-1550-8; 1-4169-1550-8
LC 2007-18670
Sixteen-year-old Zac never believed his grandfather's
tales about their enslaved ancestors being descended
from an African king, but when his grandfather is mur-
dered and the villains come after Zac, he sets out for
Ghana to find King Baktu's long-lost treasure before the
murderers do.
"This exciting narrative takes place in England and
Africa; in jungles, dark caves, and on the sea. . . . Over-
all, this is a complex, masterful story for confident readers." SLJ

Mwangi, Meja
The Mzungu boy. House of Anansi Press 2005
150p $15.95
Grades: 5 6 7 8 **Fic**
1. Kenya—Fiction 2. Friendship—Fiction 3. Race relations—Fiction
ISBN 0-88899-653-5; 0-88899-664-0 (pa)
"A Groundwood book"
First published 1990 in Canada with title: Little white
man
"A story set in Kenya during the early 1950s. . . .
Much of the land at this time was held by European set-
tlers, and native Kenyans were relegated to working as
tenant farmers under exploitative and demeaning condi-
tions. Against this backdrop, the author created this story
of a friendship between two boys, Nigel, white and
British, grandson of a brutal landowner." Booklist
"The pace is quick, and the story is exciting, action-
packed, and full of detail. . . . This is a riveting tale."
SLJ

Myers, Anna

Assassin; [by] Anna Myers. Walker & Company 2005 212p $16.95

Grades: 7 8 9 10   **Fic**
    1. Booth, John Wilkes, 1838-1865—Fiction 2. Lincoln, Abraham, 1809-1865—Fiction 3. United States—History—1861-1865, Civil War—Fiction

ISBN 0-8027-8989-7   LC 2005042275

In alternating passages, a young White House seamstress named Bella and the actor John Wilkes Booth describe the events that lead to the latter's assassination of Abraham Lincoln.

"The novel offers a good opportunity for discussion about the assassin, his motivations, and, in this case, how he drew an unsuspecting girl into his scheme." SLJ

Spy! [by] Anna Myers. Walker & Co. 2008 211p $16.99

Grades: 5 6 7 8 9   **Fic**
    1. Hale, Nathan, 1755-1776—Fiction 2. Teachers—Fiction 3. Spies—Fiction 4. Orphans—Fiction 5. United States—History—1775-1783, Revolution—Fiction

ISBN 978-0-8027-9742-1; 0-8027-9742-3
                                      LC 2008-254

In 1774, twelve-year-old Jonah becomes a pupil of Nathan Hale, who inspires him to question his beliefs about the impending revolution, and two years later, Jonah makes a decision that leads to Nathan's execution.

"Set against clearly delineated historical events, the story employs personal thoughts and feelings to show the conflicts facing the colonists. This well-written novel is a good supplement to American history studies." SLJ

Tulsa burning. Walker & Co. 2002 152p $16.95; pa $6.95

Grades: 7 8 9 10   **Fic**
    1. Race relations—Fiction 2. Riots—Fiction 3. Oklahoma—Fiction

ISBN 0-8027-8829-7; 0-8027-7696-5 (pa)
                                      LC 2002-23457

In 1921, fifteen-year-old Noble Chase hates the sheriff of Wekiwa, Oklahoma, and is more than willing to cross him to help his best friend, a black man, who is injured during race riots in nearby Tulsa

"In this emotional page-turner, Myers expertly captures an era of poisonous racism while conveying the strong, true voice of a courageous young man." Booklist

Wart; [by] Anna Myers. Walker & Co. 2007 215p $16.95

Grades: 5 6 7 8   **Fic**
    1. Remarriage—Fiction 2. Witchcraft—Fiction

ISBN 978-0-8027-8977-8; 0-8027-8977-3
                                      LC 2007006218

Regretting his part in his father's decision not to marry the town librarian, Stewart has many misgivings about the latest woman in their lives, although her spells and charms might make Stewart popular and improve his basketball game.

"The plot moves quickly and the characters are appealing and unique." SLJ

Myers, Edward, 1950-

Storyteller; by Edward Myers. Clarion Books 2008 283p $16 *

Grades: 6 7 8 9   **Fic**
    1. Storytelling—Fiction 2. Kings and rulers—Fiction 3. Fairy tales

ISBN 978-0-618-69541-6; 0-618-69541-9
                                      LC 2007031031

Jack, a seventeen-year-old storyteller, goes to the royal city seeking his fortune and soon attracts the attention of the grief-stricken king, his beautiful eldest daughter, and his cruel young son, and he attempts to help them—and the entire kingdom—through his stories.

"This old-fashioned story has the timeless appeal of adventure, humor, and light romance, all woven together by an able teller of tales." Booklist

Myers, Walter Dean, 1937-

Amiri & Odette; a love story; a poem by Walter Dean Myers; paintings by Javaka Steptoe. Scholastic Press 2009 unp il $17.99

Grades: 7 8 9 10   **Fic**
    1. Novels in verse 2. Love stories 3. African Americans—Fiction 4. Fairy tales

ISBN 978-0-590-68041-7; 0-590-68041-2
                                      LC 2008-11563

Presents a modern, urban retelling in verse of the ballet in which brave Amiri falls in love with beautiful Odette and fights evil Big Red for her on the streets of the Swan Lake Projects.

"Myers's verse is almost overwrought—as it should be to suit the story, and the intensity of teenage love. The melodrama combines with an energy and beat that—heightened by dynamic text design—makes this ideal for performance. Steptoe's collage-on-cinderblock illustrations have a roughness, darkness, and density that suit the tone." SLJ

Autobiography of my dead brother; art by Christopher Myers. HarperTempest/Amistad 2005 212p il $15.99; lib bdg $16.89; pa $6.99

Grades: 7 8 9 10   **Fic**
    1. Violence—Fiction 2. African Americans—Fiction 3. Friendship—Fiction 4. Harlem (New York, N.Y.)—Fiction

ISBN 0-06-058291-X; 0-06-058292-8 (lib bdg); 0-06-058293-6 (pa)   LC 2004-27878

Jesse pours his heart and soul into his sketchbook to make sense of life in his troubled Harlem neighborhood and the loss of a close friend.

"This novel is like photorealism; it paints a vivid and genuine portrait of life that will have a palpable effect on its readers." SLJ

The Beast. Scholastic Press 2003 170p $16.95

Grades: 7 8 9 10   **Fic**
    1. Drug abuse—Fiction 2. African Americans—Fiction

ISBN 0-439-36841-3   LC 2002-42776

A visit to his Harlem neighborhood and the discovery that the girl he loves is using drugs give sixteen-year-old Anthony Witherspoon a new perspective both on his home and on his life at a Connecticut prep school

"The emotions of the characters, their search for meaning in a harsh setting, and their conclusions will resonate with readers." Libr Media Connect

Myers, Walter Dean, 1937——*Continued*

Dope sick. HarperTeen/Amistad 2009 186p
$16.99; lib bdg $17.89
Grades: 8 9 10 11 12   Fic
1. Drug abuse—Fiction 2. African Americans—Fiction
3. Supernatural—Fiction 4. Harlem (New York,
N.Y.)—Fiction
ISBN   978-0-06-121477-6;   0-06-121477-9;
978-0-06-121478-3 (lib bdg); 0-06-121478-7 (lib bdg)
                                          LC 2008-10568
Seeing no way out of his difficult life in Harlem, seventeen-year-old Jeremy "Lil J" Dance flees into a house
after a drug deal goes awry and meets a weird man who
shows different turning points in Lil J's life when he
could have made better choices.
"Myers uses street-style lingo to cover Lil J's sorry
history of drug use, jail time, irresponsible fatherhood
and his own childhood grief. A didn't-see-that-coming
ending wraps up the story on a note of well-earned hope
and will leave readers with plenty to think about." Publ
Wkly

Fallen angels. Scholastic 1988 309p hardcover
o.p. pa $6.99 *
Grades: 8 9 10 11 12   Fic
1. Vietnam War, 1961-1975—Fiction 2. African
American soldiers—Fiction
ISBN 0-590-40942-5; 0-545-05576-8 (pa)
                                          LC 87-23236
"Black, seventeen, perceptive and sensitive, Richie
(the narrator) has enlisted and been sent to Vietnam; in
telling the story of his year of active service, Richie is
candid about the horror of killing and the fear of being
killed, the fear and bravery and confusion and tragedy of
the war." Bull Cent Child Books
"Except for occasional outbursts, the narration is remarkably direct and understated; and the dialogue, with
morbid humor sometimes adding comic relief, is steeped
in natural vulgarity, without which verisimilitude would
be unthinkable. In fact, the foul talk, which serves as the
story's linguistic setting, is not nearly as obscene as are
the events." Horn Book

Game. HarperTeen 2008 218p $16.99; lib bdg
$17.89
Grades: 8 9 10 11 12   Fic
1. Basketball—Fiction 2. African Americans—Fiction
3. Czech Americans—Fiction 4. School stories
5. Harlem (New York, N.Y.)—Fiction
ISBN 978-0-06-058294-4; 978-0-06-058295-1 (lib
bdg)   LC 2007-18370
"A Junior Library Guild selection"
If Harlem high school senior Drew Lawson is going
to realize his dream of playing college, then professional,
basketball, he will have to improve at being coached and
being a team player, especially after a new—white—student threatens to take the scouts' attention away from
him.
"Basketball fans will love the long passages of detailed court action. . . . The authentic thoughts of a
strong, likable, African American teen whose anxieties,
sharp insights, and belief in his own abilities will captivate readers of all backgrounds." Booklist

Harlem summer. Scholastic Press 2007 176p il
$16.99
Grades: 6 7 8 9   Fic
1. Harlem (New York, N.Y.)—Fiction 2. African
Americans—Fiction 3. Harlem Renaissance—Fiction
ISBN 978-0-439-36843-8; 0-439-36843-X
                                          LC 2006-46812
In 1920s Harlem, sixteen-year-old Mark Purvis, an as-
piring jazz saxophonist, gets a summer job as an errand
boy for the publishers of the groundbreaking African
American magazine, "The Crisis," but soon finds himself
on the enemy list of mobster Dutch Shultz.
"Readers will be delighted to accompany the teen on
his action-packed adventures." Booklist

Hoops; a novel. Delacorte Press 1981 183p pa
$5.99 hardcover o.p. *
Grades: 7 8 9 10   Fic
1. Basketball—Fiction 2. Harlem (New York, N.Y.)—
Fiction 3. African Americans—Fiction
ISBN 0-440-93884-8 (pa)   LC 81-65497
"Growing up in the streets of Harlem, seventeen-year-
old Lonnie Jackson dreams of making a better life. He
has a 'game,' and sees basketball as his way out of the
ghetto." ALAN
"This story offers the reader some fast, descriptive
basketball action, a love story between Lonnie and
girlfriend Mary-Ann, peer friendship problems, and gang-
ster intrigues. Most importantly, however, it portrays the
growth of a trusting and deeply caring father-son relationship between [the coach] Cal and [fatherless] Lonnie." Voice Youth Advocates
Followed by The outside shot (1988)

Monster; illustrations by Christopher Myers.
HarperCollins Pubs. 1999 281p il $14.95; lib bdg
$14.89 *
Grades: 7 8 9 10   Fic
1. Trials—Fiction 2. African Americans—Fiction
ISBN 0-06-028077-8; 0-06-028078-6 (lib bdg)
                                          LC 98-40958
Michael L. Printz Award honor book
While on trial as an accomplice to a murder, sixteen-
year-old Steve Harmon records his experiences in prison
and in the courtroom in the form of a film script as he
tries to come to terms with the course his life has taken.
"Balancing courtroom drama and a sordid jailhouse
setting with flashbacks to the crime, Myers adeptly allows each character to speak for him or herself, leaving
readers to judge for themselves the truthfulness of the
defendants, witnesses, lawyers, and, most compellingly,
Steve himself." Horn Book Guide

Scorpions. Harper & Row 1988 216p $16.99;
lib bdg $16.89; pa $5.99
Grades: 6 7 8 9   Fic
1. African Americans—Fiction 2. Juvenile delinquency—Fiction 3. Harlem (New York, N.Y.)—Fiction
ISBN 0-06-024364-3; 0-06-024365-1 (lib bdg);
0-06-447066-0 (pa)   LC 85-45815
A Newbery Medal honor book, 1989
Set in Harlem, this "story presents a brutally honest
picture of the tragic influence of gang membership and
pressures on a young black adolescent. Jamal Hicks, age
twelve, reluctantly follows the orders of his older broth-

Myers, Walter Dean, 1937-—*Continued*

er, now serving time in prison for robbery, and takes his place as leader of the Scorpions. When Jamal's leadership is challenged, disaster follows and Jamal learns some tragic lessons about friendship and owning a gun." Child Book Rev Serv

Slam! Scholastic Press 1996 266p hardcover o.p. pa $5.99 *

Grades: 7 8 9 10 **Fic**
1. Basketball—Fiction 2. African Americans—Fiction 3. School stories
ISBN 0-590-48667-5; 0-590-48668-3 (pa)
LC 95-46647

Seventeen-year-old "Slam" Harris is counting on his noteworthy basketball talents to get him out of the inner city and give him a chance to succeed in life, but his coach sees things differently

Myers "descriptions of Slam on the court . . . use crisp details, not flowery language, to achieve their muscular poetry, and Myers is equally vivid in relating the torment Slam feels as he stares at a page of indecipherable algebra formulas. . . . [This is an] admirably realistic coming-of-age novel." Booklist

Street love. Amistad/Harper Tempest 2006 134p $15.99; lib bdg $16.89

Grades: 8 9 10 11 12 **Fic**
1. African Americans—Fiction 2. Harlem (New York, N.Y.)—Fiction 3. Novels in verse
ISBN 978-0-06-028079-6; 0-06-028079-4; 978-0-06-028080-2 (lib bdg); 0-06-028080-8 (lib bdg)
LC 2006-02457

This story told in free verse is set against a background of street gangs and poverty in Harlem in which seventeen-year-old African American Damien takes a bold step to ensure that he and his new love will not be separated.

"The realistic drama on the street and at home tells a gripping story." Booklist

Sunrise over Fallujah. Scholastic Press 2008 290p $17.99 *

Grades: 8 9 10 11 12 **Fic**
1. Iraq War, 2003-—Fiction 2. African Americans—Fiction
ISBN 978-0-439-91624-0; 0-439-91624-0
LC 2007-25444

"Instead of heading to college as his father wishes, Robin leaves Harlem and joins the army to stand up for his country after 9/11. While stationed in Iraq with a war looming that he hopes will be averted, he begins writing letters home to his parents and to his Uncle Richie. . . . Myers brilliantly freeze-frames the opening months of the current Iraq War by realistically capturing its pivotal moments in 2003 and creating a vivid setting. Memorable characters share instances of wry levity that balance the story without deflecting its serious tone." SLJ

Myracle, Lauren, 1969-

Eleven. Dutton Children's Books 2004 201p $16.99

Grades: 4 5 6 7 **Fic**
1. Friendship—Fiction 2. Family life—Fiction
ISBN 0-525-47165-0 LC 2003-49076

The year between turning eleven and turning twelve bring many changes for Winnie and her friends.

"The inclusion of details about the everyday lives of these girls . . . will make this novel enjoyable, even for reluctant readers. However, it's the book's occasional revelation of harder truths that lifts it out of the ordinary." SLJ

Followed by: Twelve

Peace, love, and baby ducks. Dutton Children's Books 2009 292p $16.99

Grades: 8 9 10 11 12 **Fic**
1. Sisters—Fiction 2. Atlanta (Ga.)—Fiction
ISBN 978-0-525-47743-3; 0-525-47743-8
LC 2008-34221

Fifteen-year-old Carly's summer volunteer experience makes her feel more real than her life of privilege in Atlanta ever did, but her younger sister starts high school pretending to be what she is not, and both find their relationships suffering.

"Myracle empathetically explores issues of socioeconomic class, sibling rivalry, and parental influence in a story that is deeper and more nuanced than the title and cutesy cover." Booklist

Twelve; [by] Lauren Myracle. 1st ed. Dutton Children's Books 2007 202p $15.99

Grades: 4 5 6 7 **Fic**
1. Friendship—Fiction 2. Family life—Fiction
ISBN 978-0-525-47784-6 LC 2006014499

Sequel to: Eleven

Winnie relates the events of her twelfth year and the many changes in her relationships and in her attitude toward growing up.

This presents "well-selected junior high school crises that middle-school girls will easily relate to such as bra shopping, periods, boys, and friendship issues." SLJ

Na, An, 1972-

The fold. G.P. Putnam's Sons 2008 280p $16.99

Grades: 8 9 10 11 12 **Fic**
1. Korean Americans—Fiction 2. Plastic surgery—Fiction 3. Identity (Psychology)—Fiction
ISBN 978-0-399-24276-2 LC 2007-19420

Korean American high school student Joyce Kim feels like a nonentity compared to her beautiful older sister, and when her aunt offers to pay for plastic surgery on her eyes, she jumps at the chance, thinking it will change her life for the better.

"Na skillfully combines solemnity, humor, and romance." Voice Youth Advocates

A step from heaven. Front St. 2000 156p $15.95 *

Grades: 7 8 9 10 **Fic**
1. Korean Americans—Fiction 2. Family life—Fiction
ISBN 1-88691-058-8 LC 00-41083

Also available in paperback from Speak

Michael L. Printz Award, 2002

A young Korean girl and her family find it difficult to learn English and adjust to life in America

"This isn't a quick read, especially at the beginning when the child is trying to decipher American words and customs, but the coming-of-age drama will grab teens

Na, An, 1972——*Continued*
and make them think of their own conflicts between
home and outside. As in the best writing, the particulars
make the story universal." Booklist

Wait for me. Putnam 2006 169p $15.99
Grades: 8 9 10 11 12   **Fic**
1. Mother-daughter relationship—Fiction 2. Korean
Americans—Fiction 3. Sisters—Fiction 4. Deaf—Fiction
ISBN 0-399-24275-9   LC 2005-30931
As her senior year in high school approaches, Mina
yearns to find her own path in life but working at the
family business, taking care of her little sister, and dealing with her mother's impossible expectations are as sti-
fling as the southern California heat, until she falls in
love with a man who offers a way out.
"This is a well-crafted tale, sensitively told. . . . The
mother-daughter conflict will resonate with teens of any
culture who have wrestled parents for the right to choose
their own paths." Bull Cent Child Books

Naidoo, Beverley
Burn my heart. HarperCollins 2009 c2007 209p
$15.99; lib bdg $16.89 *
Grades: 7 8 9 10 11 12   **Fic**
1. Kenya—Fiction 2. Race relations—Fiction
3. Friendship—Fiction
ISBN   978-0-06-143297-2;   0-06-143297-0;
978-0-06-143298-9 (lib bdg); 0-06-143298-9 (lib bdg)
                                        LC 2008-928322
First published 2007 in the United Kingdom
"Mathew and Mugo, two boys—one white, one
black—share an uneasy friendship in Kenya in the
1950s. They're friends even though Mathew's dad owns
the land and everything on it. They're friends despite the
difference in their skin color. And they're friends in the
face of the growing Mau Mau rebellion." Publisher's
note
"The dramatic plot is riveting . . . and so is the setting. . . . The friendship story is haunting." Booklist

Journey to Jo'burg; a South African story;
illustrations by Eric Velasquez. Lippincott 1986
80p il pa $4.99 hardcover o.p. *
Grades: 5 6 7 8   **Fic**
1. South Africa—Race relations—Fiction
ISBN 0-06-440237-1 (pa)   LC 85-45508
"This touching novel graphically depicts the plight of
Africans living in the horror of South Africa. Thirteen-
year-old Maledi and her 9-year-old brother leave their
small village, take the perilous journey to the city, and
encounter, firsthand, the painful struggle for justice, freedom, and dignity in the 'City of Gold.' A provocative
story with a message readers will long remember." Soc
Educ
Followed by Chain of fire (1990)

The other side of truth. HarperCollins Pubs.
2001 c2000 252p $16.99; lib bdg $17.89; pa $5.99
*
Grades: 5 6 7 8   **Fic**
1. Africans—Fiction 2. London (England)—Fiction
3. Refugees—Fiction 4. Nigeria—Fiction
ISBN 0-06-029628-3; 0-06-029629-1 (lib bdg);
0-06-441002-1 (pa)   LC 00-54112

First published 2000 in the United Kingdom
Smuggled out of Nigeria after their mother's murder,
Sade and her younger brother are abandoned in London
when their uncle fails to meet them at the airport and
they are fearful of their new surroundings and of what
may have happened to their journalist father back in Nigeria
"Part survival adventure, part docudrama, the narrative
stays true to Sade's viewpoint. . . . This powerful novel
brings the news images very close." Booklist
Followed by Web of lies (2006)

Web of lies. HarperCollins Pub. 2006 256p
$15.99; lib bdg $16.89
Grades: 6 7 8 9   **Fic**
1. Africans—Fiction 2. London (England)—Fiction
3. Refugees—Fiction 4. Gangs—Fiction
ISBN 0-06-076075-3; 0-06-076077-X (lib bdg)
"In *The Other Side of Truth* (2001), Naidoo brings
politics close through the eyes of Sade, who, following
the assassination of her mother in Nigeria, flees to London with her brother, Femi. Now, two years later, the
children have been reunited with their father, as the refugee family waits for asylum. The focus this time is on
Femi, 12, who succumbs to pressure to join a violent
gang. . . . Readers will want to talk about the issues
Naidoo raises here." Booklist

Nails, Jennifer
Next to Mexico; by Jennifer Nails. Houghton
Mifflin Harcourt 2008 235p $16
Grades: 4 5 6   **Fic**
1. Friendship—Fiction 2. School stories 3. Mexican
Americans—Fiction 4. Arizona—Fiction
ISBN 978-0-618-96635-6; 0-618-96635-8
                                        LC 2008007268
Outspoken, impulsive Lylice has skipped fifth grade,
but she finds that getting along at Susan B. Anthony
Middle School is more difficult than she expected, until
she is assigned to be the English Buddy to Mexico Men-
doza, a recent immigrant.
"Lylice humorously narrates this lively, thought-
provoking story, becoming increasingly likeable and endearing." Voice Youth Advocates

Namioka, Lensey
Mismatch; a novel. Delacorte Press 2006 217p
$15.95; lib bdg $17.99
Grades: 7 8 9 10   **Fic**
1. Japanese Americans—Fiction 2. Chinese Americans—Fiction 3. Dating (Social customs)—Fiction
4. Prejudices—Fiction
ISBN 0-385-73183-3; 0-385-90220-4 (lib bdg)
Their families clash when Andy, a Japanese-American
teenaged boy, starts dating Sue, a Chinese-American
teenaged girl.
"A story that is current, relevant, and upbeat." SLJ

An ocean apart, a world away. Delacorte Press
2002 197p hardcover o.p. pa $5.50 *
Grades: 5 6 7 8   **Fic**
1. Chinese—United States—Fiction
ISBN 0-385-73002-0; 0-440-22973-1 (pa)
                                        LC 2002-73550

Namioka, Lensey—*Continued*

Companion volume to Ties that bind, ties that break (1998)

Despite the odds facing her decision to become a doctor in 1920's Nanking, China, teenaged Yanyan leaves her family to study at Cornell University where, along with hard work, she finds prejudice and loneliness as well as friendship and a new sense of accomplishment

"Without heavy messages, Namioka explores what it means to be independent." Booklist

Ties that bind, ties that break; a novel. Delacorte Press 1999 154p hardcover o.p. pa $5.50

Grades: 5 6 7 8   **Fic**
1. Sex role—Fiction 2. China—Fiction
ISBN 0-385-32666-1; 0-440-41599-3 (pa)
                                   LC 98-27877
Companion volume to: An ocean apart, a world away

"In early twentieth-century China, Ailin's liberal father allows her to avoid the tradition of foot-binding, but a broken engagement makes her family fear for her future. Ailin's intelligence and hard work—and a lot of luck— lead her to a new life in America." Horn Book Guide

"In lyrical, descriptive prose, Namioka compassionately portrays a young girl's coming-of-age in a repressive, challenging time." Booklist

Nance, Andrew

Daemon Hall; [by] Andrew Nance; with illustrations by Coleman Polhemus. Henry Holt 2007 259p $16.95

Grades: 7 8 9 10   **Fic**
1. Authorship—Fiction 2. Horror fiction
ISBN 978-0-8050-8171-8; 0-8050-8171-2
                                   LC 2006-31044
Famous horror story writer R. U. Tremblin comes to the town of Maplewood to hold a short story writing contest, offering the five finalists the chance to spend what turns out to be a terrifying—and deadly—night with him in a haunted house.

"Readers looking for creepy chills and thrills will find plenty of satisfaction in this fast-paced book." Booklist

Nanji, Shenaaz, 1954-

Child of dandelions. Front Street 2008 214p $17.95

Grades: 7 8 9 10 11 12   **Fic**
1. Amin, Idi, 1925-2003—Fiction 2. Uganda—Fiction
3. East Indians—Fiction 4. Family life—Fiction
ISBN 978-1-93242-593-2; 1-93242-593-4
                                   LC 2007-31576
In Uganda in 1972, fifteen-year-old Sabine and her family, wealthy citizens of Indian descent, try to preserve their normal life during the ninety days allowed by President Idi Amin for all foreign Indians to leave the country, while soldiers and others terrorize them and people disappear.

"This is an absorbing story rich with historical detail and human dynamics." Bull Cent Child Books

Napoli, Donna Jo, 1948-

Alligator bayou. Wendy Lamb Books 2009 280p $16.99; lib bdg $19.99

Grades: 6 7 8 9   **Fic**
1. Prejudices—Fiction 2. Italian Americans—Fiction
3. Uncles—Fiction 4. Country life—Fiction
5. Louisiana—Fiction 6. United States—History—Fiction
ISBN 978-0-385-74654-0; 0-385-74654-7; 978-0-385-90891-7 (lib bdg); 0-385-90891-1 (lib bdg)
                                   LC 2008-14504
Fourteen-year-old Calogero Scalise and his Sicilian uncles and cousin live in small-town Louisiana in 1898, when Jim Crow laws rule and anti-immigration sentiment is strong, so despite his attempts to be polite and to follow American customs, disaster dogs his family at every turn.

"Napoli's skillful pacing and fascinating detail combine in a gripping story that sheds cold, new light on Southern history and on the nature of racial prejudice." Booklist

Beast. Atheneum Bks. for Young Readers 2000 260p hardcover o.p. pa $8 *

Grades: 7 8 9 10   **Fic**
1. Fairy tales 2. Iran—Fiction
ISBN 0-689-83589-2; 0-689-87005-1 (pa)
                                   LC 99-89923
"In this take on 'Beauty and the Beast,' Napoli focuses on Beast before French beauty Belle enters his life. The first-person story begins in Persia, where proud prince Orasmyn, who loves roses, makes an unfortunate decision that sets in motion a curse: he becomes a lion who can only be restored by the love of a woman." Booklist

"The reader is immersed in the imagery and spirituality of ancient Persia. . . . Although Napoli uses Farsi (Persian) and Arabic words in the text (there is a glossary), this only adds to the texture and richness of her remarkable piece of writing." Book Rep

Bound. Atheneum Books for Young Readers 2004 186p $16.95; pa $5.99

Grades: 8 9 10 11 12   **Fic**
1. China—Fiction 2. Sex role—Fiction
ISBN 0-689-86175-3; 0-689-86178-8 (pa)
                                   LC 2004-365
In a novel based on Chinese Cinderella tales, fourteen-year-old stepchild Xing-Xing endures a life of neglect and servitude, as her stepmother cruelly mutilates her own child's feet so that she alone might marry well

The author "fleshes out and enriches the story with well-rounded characters and with accurate information about a specific time and place in Chinese history; the result is a dramatic and masterful retelling." SLJ

Fire in the hills. Dutton Children's Books 2006 215p $16.99

Grades: 5 6 7 8   **Fic**
1. World War, 1939-1945—Fiction 2. Italy—Fiction
ISBN 0-525-47751-9
Sequel to Stones in water (1997)

Upon returning to Italy, fourteen-year-old Roberto struggles to survive, first on his own, then as a member of the resistance, fighting against the Nazi occupiers

Napoli, Donna Jo, 1948----*Continued*
while yearning to reach home safely and for an end to
the war.
"This well-written book grips the reader from the beginning and on through Roberto's adventures." Voice
Youth Advocates

The great god Pan. Wendy Lamb Bks. 2003
149p $15.95; lib bdg $17.99
Grades: 7 8 9 10   **Fic**
1. Pan (Greek deity)—Fiction 2. Classical mytholo-
gy—Fiction
ISBN 0-385-32777-3; 0-385-90120-8 (lib bdg)
                                         LC 2002-13139
A retelling of the Greek myths about Pan, both goat
and god, whose reed flute frolicking leads him to a meeting with Iphigenia, a human raised as the daughter of
King Agamemnon and Queen Clytemnestra
"Filling in gaps that appear in other myths about Pan
and Iphigenia, Napoli creates a novel filled with breathtaking language about nature, music, and desire. Teen
readers will swoon." Booklist

Hush; an Irish princess' tale. Atheneum Books
for Young Readers 2007 308p $16.99 *
Grades: 8 9 10 11 12   **Fic**
1. Slavery—Fiction 2. Princesses—Fiction 3. Middle
Ages—Fiction 4. Ireland—Fiction
ISBN 978-0-689-86176-5; 0-689-86176-1
                                          LC 2007-2676
Fifteen-year-old Melkorka, an Irish princess, is kidnapped by Russian slave traders and not only learns how
to survive but to challenge some of the brutality of her
captors, who are fascinated by her apparent muteness and
the possibility that she is enchanted.
This is a "powerful survival story. . . . Napoli does
not shy from detailing practices that will make readers
wince . . . and the Russian crew repeatedly gang-rapes
an older captive. . . . The tension over Mel's hopes for
escape paces this story like a thriller." Publ Wkly

The king of Mulberry Street; [by] Donna Jo
Napoli. Wendy Lamb Books 2005 245p $15.95;
lib bdg $17.99
Grades: 5 6 7 8   **Fic**
1. Immigrants—Fiction 2. Italian Americans—Fiction
3. Jews—Fiction
ISBN 0-385-74653-9; 0-385-90890-3 (lib bdg)
                                         LC 2004-30860
In 1892, Dom, a nine-year old Jewish stowaway from
Naples, Italy, arrives in New York and must learn to sur-
vive the perils of street life in the big city.
"The characters are drawn with depth . . . and the unsentimental story is honest about the grinding poverty
and the prejudice among various immigrant groups."
Booklist

The smile. Dutton Children's Books 2008 260p
$17.99
Grades: 7 8 9 10   **Fic**
1. Leonardo, da Vinci, 1452-1519. Mona Lisa—Fic-
tion 2. Renaissance—Fiction 3. Italy—History—0-
1559—Fiction 4. Artists—Fiction
ISBN 978-0-525-47999-4; 0-525-47999-6
                                         LC 2007-48522

In Renaissance Italy, Elisabetta longs for romance, and
when Leonardo da Vinci introduces her to Guiliano de
Medici, whose family rules Florence but is about to be
deposed, she has no inkling of the romance—and sorrow—that will ensue.
"Napoli skillfully draws readers into the vibrant settings . . . with tangible, sensory details that enliven the
novel's intriguing references to history and art.
Elisabetta's strength and individuality . . . will captivate
readers." Booklist

Stones in water. Dutton Children's Bks. 1997
209p hardcover o.p. pa $5.99 *
Grades: 5 6 7 8   **Fic**
1. World War, 1939-1945—Fiction
ISBN 0-525-45842-5; 0-14-130600-9 (pa)
                                          LC 97-14253
After being taken by German soldiers from a local
movie theater along with other Italian boys including his
Jewish friend, Roberto is forced to work in Germany, escapes into the Ukrainian winter, before desperately trying
to make his way back home to Venice
This is a "gripping, meticulously researched story
(loosely based on the life of an actual survivor)." Publ
Wkly

Zel. Dutton Children's Bks. 1996 227p
hardcover o.p. pa $5.99
Grades: 7 8 9 10   **Fic**
1. Fairy tales 2. Mother-daughter relationship—Fiction
ISBN 0-525-45612-0; 0-14-130116-3 (pa)
                                          LC 96-15135
Based on the fairy tale Rapunzel, the story is told in
alternating chapters from the point of view of Zel, her
mother, and the prince, and delves into the psychological
motivations of the characters
"This version, with its Faustian overtones, will challenge readers to think about this old story on a deeper
level. It begs for discussion in literature classes." SLJ

Naylor, Phyllis Reynolds, 1933-
Cricket man. Atheneum Books for Young
Readers 2008 208p $16.99
Grades: 6 7 8 9   **Fic**
1. Heroes and heroines—Fiction 2. Family life—Fiction 3. School stories 4. Skateboarding—Fiction
5. Pregnancy—Fiction 6. Maryland—Fiction
ISBN 978-1-416-94981-7; 1-416-94981-X
                                         LC 2008-05889
"Ginee Seo books"
Thirteen-year-old Kenny secretly calls himself "Cricket Man" after a summer of rescuing creatures from his
family's Bethesda, Maryland, pool, which gives him
more self-confidence and an urge to be a hero, especially
for his depressed sixteen-year-old neighbor, Jodie.
"Naylor sketches a sensitive portrayal of life in middle
school. . . . An involving novel by a fine storyteller."
Booklist

Naylor, Phyllis Reynolds, 1933- —*Continued*

Faith, hope, and Ivy June. Delacorte Press 2009 280p $16.99; lib bdg $19.99

Grades: 5 6 7 8 **Fic**
1. School stories 2. Kentucky—Fiction 3. Appalachian region—Fiction
ISBN 978-0-385-73615-2; 0-385-73615-0; 978-0-385-90588-6 (lib bdg); 0-385-90588-2 (lib bdg)
LC 2008-19625

During a student exchange program, seventh-graders Ivy June and Catherine share their lives, homes, and communities, and find that although their lifestyles are total opposites they have a lot in common.

"This finely crafted novel . . . depicts a deep friendship growing slowly through understanding. As both girls wait out tragedies at the book's end, they cling to hope—and each other—in a thoroughly real and unaffected way. Naylor depicts Appalachia with sympathetic realism." Kirkus

The fear place. Atheneum Pubs. 1994 118p pa $4.99 hardcover o.p.

Grades: 5 6 7 8 **Fic**
1. Brothers—Fiction 2. Pumas—Fiction 3. Camping—Fiction
ISBN 0-689-80442-3 (pa) LC 93-38891

When he and his older brother Gordon are left camping alone in the Rocky Mountains, twelve-year-old Doug faces his fear of heights and his feelings about Gordon—with the help of a cougar

This is "a solid action story, tense and involving. . . . A satisfying wilderness adventure." Publ Wkly

Reluctantly Alice. Atheneum Pubs. 1991 182p $16; pa $4.99 *

Grades: 7 8 9 10 **Fic**
1. School stories 2. Family life—Fiction
ISBN 0-689-31681-X; 0-689-81688-X (pa)
LC 90-37956

"A Jean Karl book"

Alice experiences the joys and embarrassments of seventh grade while advising her father and older brother on their love lives

"Naylor combines laugh-out-loud scenes with moments of sudden gentleness. . . . The characters are complex, the dialogue is droll, the junior high world authentic." Booklist

Other titles about Alice are:
Achingly Alice (1998)
Alice alone (2001)
Alice in-between (1994)
Alice in lace (1996)
Alice in the know (2006)
Alice on her way (2005)
Alice on the outside (1999)
Alice the brave (1995)
All but Alice (1992)
Almost Alice (2008)
Intensely Alice (2009)
Dangerously Alice (2007)
The grooming of Alice (2000)
Including Alice (2004)
Outrageously Alice (1997)
Patiently Alice (2003)
Simply Alice (2002)

Shiloh. Atheneum Pubs. 1991 144p $15; pa $5.50 *

Grades: 4 5 6 **Fic**
1. Dogs—Fiction 2. West Virginia—Fiction
ISBN 0-689-31614-3; 0-689-83583-3 (pa)
LC 90-603

Also available Shiloh trilogy as a boxed set $35; pa $14.99 (ISBN 0-689-82327-4; 0-689-01525-9 pa

Awarded the Newbery Medal, 1992

When he finds a lost beagle in the hills behind his West Virginia home, Marty tries to hide it from his family and the dog's real owner, a mean-spirited man known to shoot deer out of season and to mistreat his dogs

"A credible plot and characters, a well-drawn setting, and nicely paced narration combine in a story that leaves the reader feeling good." Horn Book

Other titles about Shiloh are:
Saving Shiloh (1997)
Shiloh season (1996)

Neff, Henry H., 1973-

The hound of Rowan. Random House 2007 414p il (The tapestry) $17.99; lib bdg $20.99; pa $6.99

Grades: 6 7 8 9 **Fic**
1. Magic—Fiction 2. School stories
ISBN 978-0-375-83894-1; 0-375-83894-5; 978-0-375-93894-8 (lib bdg); 0-375-93894-4 (lib bdg); 978-0-375-83895-8 (pa); 0-375-83895-3 (pa)
LC 2006-20970

After glimpsing a hint of his destiny in a mysterious tapestry, twelve-year-old Max McDaniels becomes a student at Rowan Academy, where he trains in "mystics and combat" in preparation for war with an ancient enemy that has been kidnapping children like him.

"Max's intelligence and goodhearted nature give the story a solid emotional core even as the surprising twists and turns keep the pages turning." Voice Youth Advocates

Followed by: The second siege (2008)

Nelson, Blake, 1960-

New rules of high school. Viking 2003 225p hardcover o.p. pa $6.99

Grades: 7 8 9 10 **Fic**
1. School stories
ISBN 0-670-03644-7; 0-1424-0242-7 (pa)
LC 2002-153369

Seventeen-year-old Max Caldwell has been the perfect high school student—on the honor roll, captain of the debate team, and soon-to-be editor of the school newspaper—but during his senior year, he begins questioning his approach to life and things start to change

"The teenage voice is dead-on, and Max pulls readers by the hand, right into his world, without missing a beat." SLJ

Paranoid Park. Viking 2006 180p $15.99

Grades: 7 8 9 10 **Fic**
1. Guilt—Fiction 2. Skateboarding—Fiction 3. Homicide—Fiction
ISBN 0-670-06118-2 LC 2006-00277

Nelson, Blake, 1960-—*Continued*

A sixteen-year-old Portland, Oregon skateboarder, whose parents are going through a difficult divorce, is engulfed by guilt and confusion when he accidentally kills a security guard at a train yard.

"Readers will have a visceral reaction to this story, but on a literary level, they'll also appreciate Nelson's clever plotting and spot-on characterizations." Booklist

They came from below. Tor 2007 299p $17.95
Grades: 7 8 9 10 **Fic**
1. Beaches—Fiction 2. Marine pollution—Fiction 3. Cape Cod (Mass.)—Fiction 4. Supernatural—Fiction
ISBN 978-0-7653-1423-9; 0-7653-1423-1
LC 2007-09542
"A Tom Doherty Associates book."

While vacationing on Cape Cod, best friends Emily, age sixteen, and Reese, seventeen, meet Steve and Dave, who seem too good to be true, and whose presence turns out to be related to a dire threat of global pollution.

"Offering wittiness, suspense and ideologies borrowed from Eastern religions, Nelson reaches a new level of depth and creativity with this intriguing depiction of one very weird summer." Publ Wkly

Nelson, Nina

Bringing the boy home; by N.A. Nelson. HarperCollinsPublishers 2008 211p $15.99; lib bdg $16.89
Grades: 5 6 7 8 **Fic**
1. Senses and sensation—Fiction 2. Extrasensory perception—Fiction 3. Rain forests—Fiction 4. Amazon River valley—Fiction
ISBN   978-0-06-088698-1;   0-06-088698-6; 978-0-06-088699-8 (lib bdg); 0-06-088699-4 (lib bdg)
LC 2007-31702

As two Takunami youths approach their thirteenth birthdays, Luka reaches the culmination of his mother's training for the tribe's manhood test while Tirio, raised in Miami, Florida, by his adoptive mother, feels called to begin preparations to prove himself during his upcoming visit to the Amazon rain forest where he was born.

"The vivid setting, imagined cultural particulars . . . and magical realism will captivate readers." Booklist

Nelson, Theresa, 1948-

Ruby electric; a novel. Atheneum Bks. for Young Readers 2003 264p $16.95
Grades: 5 6 7 8 **Fic**
1.   Fathers—Fiction   2.   Siblings—Fiction 3. Authorship—Fiction 4. California—Fiction
ISBN 0-689-83852-2   LC 2002-8034
"A Richard Jackson book"

Twelve-year-old Ruby Miller, movie buff and aspiring screen writer, tries to resolve the mysteries surrounding her little brother's stuffed woolly mammoth and their father's five year absence

"Ruby's voice is electric, and she is an unforgettable character with courage, a cause, and imagination." Booklist

Nemeth, Sally

The heights, the depths, and everything in between. 1st ed. Alfred A. Knopf 2006 263p $15.95; lib bdg $17.99
Grades: 5 6 7 8 **Fic**
1. Friendship—Fiction 2. Size—Fiction 3. Dwarfism—Fiction
ISBN 0-375-83458-3; 0-375-93458-8 (lib bdg)
LC 2005-33273

In 1977, best friends Lucy Small, a seventh grader from Wilmington, Delaware, who is five feet ten inches tall, and Jake Little, a dwarf, try unsuccessfully to go unnoticed during their first year of junior high school.

"Playwright Nemeth has a real gift for capturing teen dialogue and emotions. . . . Readers will relate to this satisfying tale." Booklist

Neri, Greg

Chess rumble; by G. Neri; art by Jesse Joshua Watson. 1st ed. Lee & Low Books 2007 64p il $18.95
Grades: 5 6 7 8 **Fic**
1. Chess—Fiction 2. African Americans—Fiction
ISBN 978-1-58430-279-7   LC 2007010772

Branded a troublemaker due to his anger over everything from being bullied to his sister's death a year before, Marcus begins to control himself and cope with his problems at home and at his inner-city school when an unlikely mentor teaches him to play chess.

"Neri expertly captures Marcus's voice and delicately teases out his alternating vulnerability and rage. The cadence and emotion of the verse are masterfully echoed through Watson's expressive acrylic illustrations." SLJ

Ness, Patrick, 1971-

The knife of never letting go. Candlewick Press 2008 479p (Chaos Walking) $18.99 *
Grades: 8 9 10 11 12 **Fic**
1. Science fiction 2. Telepathy—Fiction 3. Space colonies—Fiction
ISBN 978-0-7636-3931-0; 0-7636-3931-1
LC 2007-52334

Pursued by power-hungry Prentiss and mad minister Aaron, young Todd and Viola set out across New World searching for answers about his colony's true past and seeking a way to warn the ship bringing hopeful settlers from Old World.

"This troubling, unforgettable opener to the Chaos Walking trilogy is a penetrating look at the ways in which we reveal ourselves to one another, and what it takes to be a man in a society gone horribly wrong." Booklist

Neumeier, Rachel

The City in the Lake. Alfred A. Knopf 2008 304p $15.99; lib bdg $18.99 *
Grades: 8 9 10 11 12 **Fic**
1. Magic—Fiction 2. Fantasy fiction
ISBN   978-0-375-84704-2;   0-375-84704-9; 978-0-375-94704-9 (lib bdg); 0-375-94704-3 (lib bdg)
LC 2008-08941

Neumeier, Rachel—*Continued*

Seventeen-year-old Timou, who is learning to be a mage, must save her mysterious, magical homeland, The Kingdom, from a powerful force that is trying to control it.

"Neumeier structures her story around archetypal fantasy elements. . . . It's the poetic, shimmering language and fascinating unfolding of worlds that elevates this engrossing story beyond its formula." Booklist

Newbery, Linda, 1952-

At the firefly gate. 1st American ed. David Fickling Books 2007 152p $15.99; lib bdg $18.99

Grades: 5 6 7 8   **Fic**
1. Supernatural—Fiction 2. World War, 1939-1945—Fiction 3. Great Britain—Fiction

ISBN 978-0-385-75113-1; 978-0-385-75114-8 (lib bdg)   LC 2006-01796

After moving with his parents from London to Suffolk near a former World War II airfield, Henry sees the shadowy image of a man by the orchard gate and feels an unusual affinity with an eldery woman who lives next door.

"This is a well-written book, with an old-fashioned tone, that emphasizes character and feelings over plot. It's for thoughtful readers who appreciate a book that lingers in their minds." SLJ

Lost boy. David Fickling Books 2008 194p $15.99; lib bdg $18.99

Grades: 4 5 6 7   **Fic**
1. Mystery fiction 2. Ghost stories 3. Traffic accidents—Fiction 4. Wales—Fiction

ISBN 978-0-375-84574-1; 978-0-375-93617-3 (lib bdg)   LC 2007-15041

First published 2005 in the United Kingdom

After Matt moves to Hay-on-Wye in Wales, a boy his age who bears the same initials and was killed in a car accident many years earlier, appears to Matt.

"With its imaginative melding of present-day concerns, good storytelling, lush descriptions of the landscape and even a faithful dog, this novel will ensnare readers." Publ Wkly

Newton, Robert, 1965-

Runner. Alfred A. Knopf 2007 209p $15.99; lib bdg $18.99

Grades: 6 7 8 9   **Fic**
1. Running—Fiction 2. Poverty—Fiction 3. Criminals—Fiction 4. Australia—Fiction

ISBN 978-0-375-83744-9; 978-0-375-93744-6 (lib bdg); 0-375-83744-2; 0-375-93744-7 (lib bdg)
                                        LC 2006-29275

In Richmond, Australia, in 1919, fifteen-year-old Charlie Feehan becomes an errand boy for a notorious mobster, hoping that his ability to run will help him, his widowed mother, and his baby brother to escape poverty.

"Rich dialogue in Australian dialect creates a colorful picture of the historical urban setting, suspenseful plot, and warm characterizations." SLJ

Nicholls, Sally, 1983-

Ways to live forever; [by] Sally Nicholls. Arthur A. Levine Books 2008 212p il $16.99 *

Grades: 4 5 6 7   **Fic**
1. Leukemia—Fiction 2. Authorship—Fiction 3. Family life—Fiction 4. Death—Fiction

ISBN 978-0-545-06948-9; 0-545-06948-3
                                        LC 2007047341

Eleven-year-old Sam McQueen, who has leukemia, writes a book during the last three months of his life, in which he tells about what he would like to accomplish, how he feels, and things that have happened to him.

This "skirts easy sentiment to confront the hard questions head-on, intelligently and realistically and with an enormous range of feeling." Publ Wkly

Nicholson, William

Seeker. Harcourt 2006 413p (Noble warriors) $17; pa $7.95

Grades: 7 8 9 10   **Fic**
1. Fantasy fiction

ISBN 978-0-15-205768-8; 0-15-205768-4; 978-0-15-205866-1 (pa); 0-15-205866-4 (pa)
                                        LC 2005-17171

"Seeker, Morning Star, and Wildman are three teens who hope to join the Nomana, a society of noble warriors and worshippers of the All and Only (the god who makes all things). . . . Conjuring up a plan to prove their worth, this motley trio plays a key role in foiling the murderous plans of the royalty in a nearby town." Bull Cent Child Books

"The classic coming-of-age tale is combined with a rich setting of cold villains, strange powers, and disturbing warriors." Voice Youth Advocates

Other titles in this series are:
Jango (2007)
Noman (2008)

Nielsen, Susin

Word nerd. Tundra Books 2008 248p $18.95 *

Grades: 5 6 7 8   **Fic**
1. Friendship—Fiction 2. Mother-son relationship—Fiction 3. Scrabble (Game)—Fiction

ISBN 978-0-88776-875-0; 0-88776-875-X

"Twelve-year-old Ambrose Bukowski and his widowed, overprotective mother . . . move frequently. When he almost dies after he bites into a peanut that bullies put in his sandwich, just to see if he is really allergic, Irene . . . decides to homeschool him. . . . Ambrose gets to know 25-year-old Cosmo, recently released from jail and the son of the Bukowskis' . . . landlords. . . . Ambrose . . . talks Cosmo into taking him to a Scrabble Club. . . . This is a tender, often funny story with some really interesting characters. It will appeal to word nerds, but even more to anyone who has ever longed for acceptance or had to fight unreasonable parental restrictions." SLJ

Nigg, Joe

How to raise and keep a dragon; by John Topsell; executive editor, Joseph Nigg; illustrations, Dan Malone. Barron's 2006 128p il $18.99

Grades: 5 6 7 8   **Fic**

Nigg, Joe—*Continued*

1. Dragons—Fiction

ISBN 0-7641-5920-8

"Posing as dragon-breeder John Topsell . . . Nigg instructs readers in selecting and caring for a breed of dragon suited for them. . . . While not intended as a serious book on mythology, Nigg does share many bits of real dragon lore while spinning out details of what it might be like to live in a world where people breed, register, and show these creatures. Malone's full-color illustrations on every page offer fans many cool pictures to copy or sketch. With its tongue firmly in cheek, this book is a lot of lighthearted fun." SLJ

Nimmo, Jenny, 1944-

Midnight for Charlie Bone. Orchard Bks. 2003 c2002 401p (Children of the Red King) $12.99

Grades: 5 6 7 8   **Fic**

1. Magic—Fiction 2. School stories 3. Great Britain—Fiction

ISBN 978-0-439-47429-0; 0-439-47429-9

      LC 2002-30738

First published 2002 in the United Kingdom

Charlie Bone's life with his widowed mother and two grandmothers undergoes a dramatic change when he discovers that he can hear people in photographs talking.

"This marvelous fantasy is able to stand on its own despite inevitable comparisons to the students of Hogwarts." Voice Youth Advocates

Other titles in this series are:

Charlie Bone and the time twister (2003)

Charlie Bone and the invisible boy (2004)

Charlie Bone and the castle of mirrors (2005)

Charlie Bone and the hidden king (2006)

Charlie Bone and the beast (2007)

Charlie Bone and the shadow (2008)

The snow spider; [by] Jenny Nimmo. 1st ed. Orchard Books 2006 146p (Magician trilogy) $9.99 *

Grades: 4 5 6 7   **Fic**

1. Magic—Fiction 2. Father-son relationship—Fiction 3. Wales—Fiction

ISBN 978-0-439-84675-2; 0-439-84675-7

      LC 2006009445

A reissue of the title first published 1987 by Dutton

Gifts from Gwyn's grandmother on his ninth birthday open up a whole new world to him, as he discovers he has magical powers that help him heal the breach with his father that has existed ever since his sister's mysterious disappearance four years before.

"The narration is paced well and builds in excitement along with the tale." SLJ

Other titles in this series are:

Emlyn's moon (2007)

Chestnut solider (2007)

Nix, Garth, 1963-

Mister Monday; Keys to the kingdom, book one. Scholastic 2003 361p $15.99; pa $5.99

Grades: 6 7 8 9   **Fic**

1. Fantasy fiction

ISBN 0-439-70370-0; 0-439-55123-4 (pa)

      LC 2004-540574

Arthur Penhaligon is supposed to die at a young age, but is saved by a key that is shaped like the minute hand of a clock. The key causes bizarre creatures to come from another realm, bringing with them a plague. A man named Mister Monday will stop at nothing to get the key back. Arthur goes to a mysterious house that only he can see, so that he can learn the truth about himself and the key

"The first in a seven part series for middle graders is every bit as exciting and suspenseful as the author's previous young adult novels." SLJ

Other titles in the Keys to the Kingdom series are:

Grim Tuesday (2004)

Drowned Wednesday (2005)

Sir Thursday (2006)

Lady Friday (2007)

Superior Saturday (2008)

Sabriel. HarperCollins Pubs. 1996 c1995 292p $17.99; pa $7.99 *

Grades: 7 8 9 10   **Fic**

1. Fantasy fiction

ISBN 0-06-027322-4; 0-06-447183-7 (pa)

      LC 96-1295

First published 1995 in Australia

Sabriel, daughter of the necromancer Abhorsen, must journey into the mysterious and magical Old Kingdom to rescue her father from the Land of the Dead

"The final battle is gripping, and the bloody cost of combat is forcefully presented. The story is remarkable for the level of originality of the fantastic elements . . . and for the subtle presentation, which leaves readers to explore for themselves the complex structure and significance of the magic elements." Horn Book

Other titles in this series are:

Abhorsen (2003)

Across the wall (2005)

Lirael, daughter of the Clayr (2001)

Shade's children. HarperCollins Pubs. 1997 310p $18.99; pa $6.99

Grades: 7 8 9 10   **Fic**

1. Science fiction

ISBN 0-06-027324-0; 0-06-447196-9 (pa)

      LC 97-3841

In a savage postnuclear world, four young fugitives attempt to overthrow the bloodthirsty rule of the Overlords with the help of Shade, their mysterious mentor

"Grim, unusual, and fascinating." Horn Book

Nixon, Joan Lowery, 1927-2003

The haunting. Delacorte Press 1998 184p hardcover o.p. pa $5.50

Grades: 7 8 9 10   **Fic**

1. Ghost stories 2. Louisiana—Fiction

ISBN 0-385-32247-X; 0-440-22008-4 (pa)

      LC 97-32658

When her mother inherits an old plantation house in the Louisiana countryside, fifteen-year-old Lia seeks to rid it of the evil spirit that haunts it

"This title has it all - a hint of romance, some really scary scenes, and a plucky heroine who successfully routs both outer and inner demons." Horn Book Guide

Nixon, Joan Lowery, 1927-2003—*Continued*

Laugh till you cry. Delacorte Press 2004 99p $15.95; lib bdg $17.99

Grades: 5 6 7 8   **Fic**
1. Moving—Fiction 2. Family life—Fiction 3. School stories

ISBN 0-385-73027-6; 0-385-90186-0 (lib bdg)
      LC 2004-9557

Thirteen years old and a budding comedian, Cody has little to laugh about after he and his mother move from California to Texas to help his sick grandmother and he finds himself framed by his jealous cousin for calling in bomb threats to their school.

"The pacing of the story, Cody's humorous side, and the book's length make this mystery ideal for reluctant readers." SLJ

Nightmare. Delacorte Press 2003 166p hardcover o.p. lib bdg $17.99; pa $5.99

Grades: 6 7 8 9   **Fic**
1. Camps—Fiction 2. Homicide—Fiction 3. Mystery fiction

ISBN 0-385-73026-8; 0-385-90151-8 (lib bdg); 0-4402-3773-4 (pa)   LC 2003-43434

Emily is sent to a camp for underachievers where she discovers a murderer on the staff who might provide an explanation for her recurring nightmares

"Elements of suspense and mystery are cleverly integrated with the teen's problems resulting from what she witnessed as a child. Readers will once again fall under Nixon's spell as they enjoy this page-turner." SLJ

Nolan, Han, 1956-

A face in every window. Harcourt Brace & Co. 1999 264p hardcover o.p. pa $6.95

Grades: 7 8 9 10   **Fic**
1. Mentally handicapped—Fiction

ISBN 0-15-201915-4; 0-15-206418-4 (pa)
      LC 99-14230

Also available in paperback from Puffin Bks.

After the death of his grandmother, who held the family together, teenage JP is left with a mentally challenged father and a mother who seems ineffectual and constantly sick, and he feels everything sliding out of control

"Only a writer as talented as Nolan could make this improbable story line and bizarre cast of characters not only believable but also ultimately uplifting, intriguing, and memorable." Booklist

A summer of Kings. Harcourt 2006 334p $17

Grades: 6 7 8 9   **Fic**
1. Race relations—Fiction 2. African Americans—Fiction 3. Black Muslims—Fiction

ISBN 0-15-205108-2   LC 2005-19487

Over the course of the summer of 1963, fourteen-year-old Esther Young discovers the passion within her when eighteen-year-old King-Roy Johnson, accused of murdering a white man in Alabama, comes to live with her family.

"Infused with rhetoric that is as meaningful today as it was two generations ago, this young teen's account of a life-changing summer not only opens a window to history, but also displays Nolan's brilliant gift for crafting profoundly appealing protagonists." SLJ

Nordin, Sofia

In the wild; translated by Maria Lundin. House of Anansi Press 2005 115p $15.95; pa $6.95

Grades: 4 5 6 7   **Fic**
1. Bullies—Fiction 2. Wilderness survival—Fiction

ISBN 0-88899-648-9; 0-88899-663-2 (pa)

Originally published in Swedish

"Amanda, the target of harassment by her classmates, is on an adventure trip with her sixth-grade class. When she and one of the bullies, Philip, are separated from the group and become lost in the wilderness, they are forced to work together to survive. . . . Nordin realistically depicts the psychological effects of relentless hounding. . . . The translation is smooth and the text flows naturally. . . . Well written, and a lightning-fast read." SLJ

Norville, Rod

Moonshine express; with a history of moonshine today and yesterday. Four Seasons Pub. 2003 xxix, 195p pa $13.95

Grades: 6 7 8 9   **Fic**
1. Moonshining—Fiction 2. Florida—Fiction

ISBN 1-89129-99-2

"Thirteen-year-old Rob McKinley's world is falling apart. His mother has died and his father is drinking heavily. Rob's barely coping with the support of his friend, Katie. They live on the edge of a north Florida swamp sprinkled with half-breed Seminole moon shiners. Rob and Katie are stunned when they stumble across respectable community citizens behind a local moonshine distribution ring." Publisher's note

"This is an edge-of-the-seat thriller." SLJ

Nuzum, K. A.

The leanin' dog. Joanna Cotler Books 2008 250p $15.99; lib bdg $16.89

Grades: 4 5 6 7   **Fic**
1. Dogs—Fiction 2. Bereavement—Fiction 3. Colorado—Fiction 4. Winter—Fiction

ISBN 978-0-06-113934-5; 0-06-113934-3; 978-0-06-113935-2 (lib bdg); 0-06-113935-1 (lib bdg)   LC 2008-11855

In wintry Colorado during the 1930s, eleven-year-old Dessa Dean mourns the death of her beloved mother, but the arrival of an injured dog and the friendship they form is just what they need to change their lives forever.

"Nuzum's pacing and spare, poetic narrative create something quite wonderful. . . . This is a beautiful story in which friendship and the power of being needed trump despair." SLJ

A small white scar; [by] K.A. Nuzum. 1st ed. Joanna Cotler Books 2006 180p $15.99; lib bdg $16.89

Grades: 6 7 8 9   **Fic**
1. Mentally handicapped—Fiction 2. Brothers—Fiction 3. Twins—Fiction 4. Cowhands—Fiction 5. Colorado—Fiction

ISBN 978-0-06-075639-0; 0-06-075639-X; 978-0-06-075640-6 (lib bdg); 0-06-075640-3 (lib bdg)   LC 2005017721

Fifteen-year-old Will Bennon leaves his family and begins life as a cowboy, but his mentally retarded twin

Nuzum, K. A.—*Continued*

brother follows him and joins the journey.

"The images of the stark 1940s Colorado countryside suffering from drought, and the wild animals that populate it, are clearly drawn with poetic turns of phrase. Characters, plot, and theme all combine to make a compelling story." SLJ

Nye, Naomi Shihab, 1952-

Going going. Greenwillow Books 2005 232p il $15.99; lib bdg $16.89

Grades: 7 8 9 10 **Fic**

1. Political activists—Fiction 2. Small business—Fiction 3. San Antonio (Tex.)—Fiction

ISBN 0-688-16185-5; 0-06-029366-7 (lib bdg)

LC 2004-10146

In San Antonio, Texas, sixteen-year-old Florrie leads her friends and a new boyfriend in a campaign which supports small businesses and protests the effects of chain stores.

The "novel's strong message belongs honestly to Florrie, whose vivid individualism will engage readers. Nye evokes history through small details, inviting readers to view their own cities and towns with a new perspective." Horn Book Guide

Habibi. Simon & Schuster Bks. for Young Readers 1997 259p $16; pa $5.99 *

Grades: 7 8 9 10 **Fic**

1. Jewish-Arab relations—Fiction 2. Jerusalem—Fiction

ISBN 0-689-80149-1; 0-689-82523-4 (pa)

LC 97-10943

When fourteen-year-old Liyanne Abboud, her younger brother, and her parents move from St. Louis to a new home between Jerusalem and the Palestinian village where her father was born, they face many changes and must deal with the tensions between Jews and Palestinians

"Poetically imaged and leavened with humor, the story renders layered and complex history understandable through character and incident." SLJ

Nyoka, Gail

Mella and the N'anga; an African tale. Sumach Press 2006 158p pa $9.95

Grades: 5 6 7 8 **Fic**

1. Zimbabwe—Fiction 2. Fantasy fiction

ISBN 1-894549-49-X

In ancient mythical Zimbabwe, Mella and two other girls train with the N'anga, a mysterious, spiritual advisor, to become Daughters of the Hunt and rescue their people.

"The language reinforces the sense of the ancient court setting, and many passages glimmer with mysticism linked to the beauty of the natural world. Mella's thrilling, magical, girl-powered quest will attract many readers." Booklist

Ó Guilín, Peadar

The inferior. David Fickling Books 2008 439p $16.99

Grades: 8 9 10 11 12 **Fic**

1. Hunting—Fiction 2. Cannibalism—Fiction 3. Science fiction

ISBN 978-0-385-75145-2; 0-385-75145-1

LC 2007-34496

In a brutal world where hunting and cannibalism are necessary for survival, something is going terribly wrong as even the globes on the roof of the world are fighting, but one young man, influenced by a beautiful and mysterious stranger, begins to envision new possibilities.

This is an "epic story of survival, betrayal, and community. . . . This well-paced fantasy/science fiction blend perfectly introduces community conflict at a base level. . . . Easy to follow and intriguing at every turn, *The Inferior* will hold readers from page to page, chapter to chapter, to the very end." SLJ

Oaks, J. Adams

Why I fight; a novel. Atheneum Books for Young Readers 2009 228p $16.99 *

Grades: 8 9 10 11 12 **Fic**

1. Uncles—Fiction 2. Violence—Fiction 3. Criminals—Fiction

ISBN 978-1-416-91177-7; 1-416-91177-4

LC 2007-46433

"A Richard Jackson book"

After his house burns down, twelve-year-old Wyatt Reaves takes off with his uncle, and the two of them drive from town to town for six years, earning money mostly by fighting, until Wyatt finally confronts his parents one last time.

"Oaks' first novel is a breathtaking debut with an unforgettable protagonist. . . . The voice Oaks has created for Wyatt to tell his painful and poignant story is a wonderful combination of the unlettered and the eloquent." Booklist

Oates, Joyce Carol, 1938-

Big Mouth & Ugly Girl. HarperCollins Pubs. 2002 265p $16.99; lib bdg $17.89; pa $7.99 *

Grades: 7 8 9 10 **Fic**

1. School stories 2. Friendship—Fiction

ISBN 0-06-623756-4; 0-06-623758-0 (lib bdg); 0-06-447347-3 (pa) LC 2001-24601

When sixteen-year-old Matt is falsely accused of threatening to blow up his high school and his friends turn against him, an unlikely classmate comes to his aid.

"Readers will be propelled through these pages by an intense curiosity to learn how events will play out. Oates has written a fast-moving, timely, compelling story." SLJ

Freaky green eyes. Harper Tempest 2003 341p lib bdg $17.89; pa $6.99

Grades: 7 8 9 10 **Fic**

1. Domestic violence—Fiction

ISBN 0-06-623757-2 (lib bdg); 0-06-447348-1 (pa)

LC 2002-32868

Fifteen-year-old Frankie relates the events of the year leading up to her mother's mysterious disappearance and her own struggle to discover and accept the truth about

Oates, Joyce Carol, 1938-—*Continued*
her parents' relationship.
"Oates pulls readers into a fast-paced, first-person thriller. . . . An absorbing page-turner." Booklist

O'Brien, Robert C., 1918-1973
Mrs. Frisby and the rats of NIMH; [by] Robert C. O'Brien; illustrated by Zena Bernstein. Atheneum Books for Young Readers 2006 c1971 233p il $18 *
Grades: 4 5 6 7   **Fic**
    1. Mice—Fiction 2. Rats—Fiction
    ISBN 978-0-689-20651-1; 0-689-20651-8
    Awarded the Newbery Medal, 1972
    A reissue of the title first published 1971
    Having no one to help her with her problems, a widowed mouse visits the rats whose former imprisonment in a laboratory made them wise and long lived.
    "The story is fresh and ingenious, the style witty, and the plot both hilarious and convincing." Saturday Rev

Z for Zachariah. Atheneum Pubs. 1975 c1974 246p hardcover o.p. pa $7.99 *
Grades: 7 8 9 10   **Fic**
    1. Science fiction
    ISBN 0-689-30442-0; 1-416-93921-0 (pa)
    Seemingly the only person left alive after a nuclear war, a sixteen-year-old girl is relieved to see a man arrive into her valley until she realizes that he is a tyrant and she must somehow escape.
    "The journal form is used by O'Brien very effectively, with no lack of drama and contrast, and the pace and suspense of the story are adroitly maintained until the dramatic and surprising ending." Bull Cent Child Books

O'Connell, Tyne
True love, the sphinx, and other unsolvable riddles; a comedy in four voices; [by] Tyne O'Connell. 1st U.S. ed. Bloomsbury 2007 225p $16.95
Grades: 7 8 9 10   **Fic**
    1. School stories 2. Love stories 3. Friendship—Fiction 4. Egypt—Fiction
    ISBN 978-1-59990-050-6; 1-59990-050-5
                                            LC 2007002596
    While on a class trip in Egypt, two teenaged best friends from an American private boys' school and two teenaged best friends from a British private girls' school meet each other, and must endure many misunderstandings on their path to true love.
    "This flirty, fun romcom, told from four distinctive points of view, reads like an old-time comedy of errors. O'Connell describes Egypt with such vitality and richness that it shines as a separate character." SLJ

O'Connor, Barbara
Fame and glory in Freedom, Georgia. Frances Foster Bks./Farrar, Straus & Giroux 2003 104p $16; pa $6.95
Grades: 4 5 6 7   **Fic**
    1. School stories 2. Contests—Fiction
    ISBN 0-374-32258-9; 0-374-40018-0 (pa)
                                            LC 2002-190212

Unpopular sixth-grader Burdette Bird ̈Weaver persuades the new boy at school, whom everyone thinks is mean and dumb, to be her partner for a spelling bee that might win her everything she's ever wanted.
    "An idiosyncratic group of characters play out this touching and well-paced story about friendship, family, and connection." Horn Books

Greetings from nowhere. Farrar, Straus and Giroux 2008 198p $16
Grades: 4 5 6 7   **Fic**
    1. Hotels and motels—Fiction 2. North Carolina—Fiction
    ISBN 978-0-374-39937-5; 0-374-39937-9
                                            LC 2006-37439
    "Frances Foster books"
    In North Carolina's Great Smoky Mountains, a troubled boy and his mother, a happy family seeking adventure, a man and his lonely daughter, and the widow who must sell the rundown motel that has been her home for decades, meet and are transformed by their shared experiences.
    "The plainspoken text is clean, direct, and honest in its portrayal of pain and hope." Booklist

How to steal a dog; a novel. 1st ed. Farrar, Straus & Giroux 2007 170p $16 *
Grades: 4 5 6   **Fic**
    1. Homeless persons—Fiction 2. Siblings—Fiction 3. Dogs—Fiction
    ISBN 0-374-33497-8; 978-0-374-33497-0
                                            LC 2005-40166
    "Frances Foster books"
    Living in the family car in their small North Carolina town, Georgina persuades her younger brother to help her in an elaborate scheme to get money by stealing a dog and then claiming the reward that the owners are bound to offer.
    This is told "in stripped-down, unsentimental prose. . . . The myriad effects of homelessness and the realistic picture of a moral quandary will surely generate discussion." Booklist

O'Dell, Kathleen
Agnes Parker . . . girl in progress. Dial Bks. 2003 156p $16.99
Grades: 4 5 6 7   **Fic**
    1. Friendship—Fiction 2. School stories
    ISBN 0-8037-2648-1   LC 2001-58256
    As she starts in the sixth grade, Agnes faces challenges with her old best friend, a longtime bully, a wonderful new classmate and neighbor, and herself
    "This is a thoughtful, gently humorous, and resonant cusp-of-coming-of-age novel." Horn Book Guide
    Other titles about Agnes Parker are:
    Agnes Parker . . . Happy camper? (2005)
    Agnes Parker . . . Keeping cool in middle school (2007)

O'Dell, Scott, 1898-1989
Island of the Blue Dolphins; illustrated by Ted Lewin. Houghton Mifflin 1990 181p il $22 *
Grades: 5 6 7 8   **Fic**
    1. Native Americans—Fiction 2. Wilderness survival—Fiction 3. San Nicolas Island (Calif.)—Fiction
    ISBN 0-395-53680-4   LC 90-35331

O'Dell, Scott, 1898-1989—*Continued*

Also available in paperback from Dell

A reissue with new illustrations of the title first published 1960

"Unintentionally left behind by members of her California Native American tribe who fled a tragedy-ridden island, young Karana must construct a life for herself. Without bitterness or self-pity, she is able to extract joy and challenge from her eighteen years of solitude." Shapiro. Fic for Youth. 2d edition

Followed by Zia

Sing down the moon. Houghton Mifflin 1970 137p $18

Grades: 5 6 7 8 **Fic**

1. Navajo Indians—Fiction
ISBN 0-395-10919-1

Also available in paperback from Laurel Leaf

A Newbery Medal honor book, 1971

This story is told "through the eyes of a young Navaho girl as she sees the rich harvest in the Canyon de Chelly in 1864 destroyed by Spanish slavers and the subsequent destruction by white soldiers which forces the Navahos on a march to Fort Sumner." Publ Wkly

"There is a poetic sonority of style, a sense of identification, and a note of indomitable courage and stoicism that is touching and impressive." Saturday Rev

Streams to the river, river to the sea; a novel of Sacagawea. Houghton Mifflin 1986 191p $16

Grades: 5 6 7 8 **Fic**

1. Sacagawea, b. 1786—Fiction 2. Lewis and Clark Expedition (1804-1806)—Fiction 3. Native Americans—Fiction
ISBN 0-395-40430-4 LC 86-936

Also available in paperback from Fawcett Bks.

This novel "tells the story of the Lewis and Clark expedition through the eyes of the young Shoshone woman who served as interpreter and, often, guide." Soc Educ

"An informative and involving choice for American history students and pioneer-adventure readers." Bull Cent Child Books

Thunder rolling in the mountains; [by] Scott O'Dell and Elizabeth Hall. Houghton Mifflin 1992 128p map $17

Grades: 5 6 7 8 **Fic**

1. Nez Percé Indians—Fiction
ISBN 0-395-59966-0 LC 91-15961

Also available in paperback from Yearling

"Told from the point of view of Chief Joseph's daughter, this historical novel concerns the forced removal of the Nez Perce tribe from their homeland in 1877. Fourteen-year-old Sound of Running Feet describes her people's pain at leaving their beloved Wallowa Valley, their disagreements over whether to resist the government troops that plague them, and their suffering as every act of defense or defiance brings on a more devastating reaction." Booklist

"This is a sad, dark-hued story told in Mr. O'Dell's lean, affecting prose." Child Book Rev Serv

Zia. Houghton Mifflin 1976 179p hardcover o.p. pa $6.95 *

Grades: 5 6 7 8 **Fic**

1. Native Americans—Fiction 2. Christian missions—Fiction
ISBN 0-395-24393-9; 0-440-21956-6 (pa)
LC 75-44156

In this sequel to Island of the Blue Dolphins, the author invents a niece for Karana "in the character of Zia, a young Indian who lives at the Santa Barbara Mission and who dreams of sailing to the island to rescue her aunt. After one thwarted attempt to get there, and imprisonment for helping some fellow Indians flee the Mission, Zia finds her dream realized." N Y Times Book Rev

"Zia is an excellent story in its own right, written in a clear, quiet, and reflective style which is in harmony with the plot and characterization." SLJ

Okorafor, Nnedimma

The shadow speaker; [by] Nnedi Okorafor-Mbachu. Jump at the Sun/Hyperion Books for Children 2007 336p $16.99

Grades: 7 8 9 10 **Fic**

1. Sahara Desert—Fiction 2. West Africa—Fiction 3. Fantasy fiction 4. Science fiction
ISBN 978-1-4231-0033-1; 1-4231-0033-6
LC 2007-13313

In West Africa in 2070, after fifteen-year-old "shadow speaker" Ejii witnesses her father's beheading, she embarks on a dangerous journey across the Sahara to find Jaa, her father's killer, and upon finding her, she also discovers a greater purpose to her life and to the mystical powers she possesses.

"Okorafor-Mbachu does an excellent job of combining both science fiction and fantasy elements into this novel. . . . The action moves along at a quick pace and will keep most readers on their toes and wanting more at the end of the novel." Voice Youth Advocates

Zahrah the Windseeker; by Nnedi Okorafor-Mbachu. Houghton Mifflin 2005 308p il $16

Grades: 5 6 7 8 **Fic**

1. Fantasy fiction
ISBN 0-618-34090-4 LC 2004-15783

Zahrah, a timid thirteen-year-old girl, undertakes a dangerous quest into the Forbidden Greeny Jungle to seek the antidote for her best friend after he is bitten by a snake, and finds knowledge, courage, and hidden powers along the way.

"Okorafor-Mbachu's evocative setting will draw experienced fantasy readers with its heady mix of the familiar and the strange." Booklist

Olsen, Sylvia, 1955-

The girl with a baby. Sono Nis Press 2004 203p pa $8.95

Grades: 7 8 9 10 **Fic**

1. Teenage mothers—Fiction 2. Native Americans—Fiction 3. Canada—Fiction
ISBN 1-55039-142-9

This "novel tells of teenage mother Jane, 14, who wants to stay in school and raise her baby, Destiny, to

Olsen, Sylvia, 1955-—*Continued*
be respectful of tradition and smart in the new ways.
Jane's family left the reservation because of resentment
against Dad, who is white; now in a white area, they
face prejudice for being Indian. . . . Jane's home . . . is
drawn without romanticism, and . . . Jane's first-person
narrative never denies how hard life is, and how thrilling." Booklist

White girl. Sono Nis Press 2004 235p pa $8.95
Grades: 7 8 9 10   **Fic**
1. Native Americans—Fiction 2. Prejudices—Fiction
ISBN 1-5503-9147-X
"Until she was fourteen, Josie was pretty ordinary.
Then her Mom meets Martin, 'a real ponytail Indian,'
and before long, Josie finds herself living on a reserve
outside town, with a new stepfather, a new stepbrother,
and a new name 'Blondie.'" Publisher's note
"The talk is contemporary and relaxed, and the characters will hold readers as much as the novel's extraordinary sense of place." Booklist

Olson, Gretchen
Call me Hope; a novel; by Gretchen Olson. 1st
ed. Little, Brown & Company 2007 272p $15.99
Grades: 4 5 6   **Fic**
1. Child abuse—Fiction 2. Mother-daughter relationship—Fiction 3. Oregon—Fiction
ISBN 978-0-316-01236-2; 0-316-01236-X
                                    LC 2006027896
In Oregon, eleven-year-old Hope begins coping with
her mother's verbal abuse by devising survival strategies
for herself based on a history unit about the Holocaust,
and meanwhile she works toward buying a pair of purple
hiking boots by helping at a second-hand shop.
"Hope is a winsome character whose bravery and determination will resonate with middle-grade readers."
Booklist

Oppel, Kenneth
Airborn. Eos 2004 355p $16.99; lib bdg $17.89
Grades: 7 8 9 10   **Fic**
1. Fantasy fiction 2. Airships—Fiction
ISBN 0-06-053180-0; 0-06-053181-9 (lib bdg)
                                    LC 2003-15642
Matt, a young cabin boy aboard an airship, and Kate,
a wealthy young girl traveling with her chaperone, team
up to search for the existence of mysterious winged crea-
tures reportedly living hundreds of feet above the Earth's
surface.
"This rousing adventure has something for everyone:
appealing and enterprising characters, nasty villains, and
a little romance." SLJ
Other titles in this series are:
Skybreaker (2005)
Starclimber (2009)

Silverwing. Simon & Schuster Bks. for Young
Readers 1997 217p hardcover o.p. pa $6.99 *
Grades: 5 6 7 8   **Fic**
1. Bats—Fiction
ISBN 0-689-81529-8; 1-4169-4998-4 (pa)
                                    LC 97-10977

When a newborn bat named Shade but sometimes
called "Runt" becomes separated from his colony during
migration, he grows in ways that prepare him for even
greater journeys
"Oppel's bats are fully developed characters who, if
not quite cuddly, will certainly earn readers' sympathy
and respect. In *Silverwing* the author has created an intriguing microcosm of rival species, factions, and religions." Horn Book
Other titles in this series are:
Firewing (2003)
Sunwing (2000)
Darkwing (2007)

Orenstein, Denise Gosliner, 1950-
The secret twin. Katherine Tegen Books 2007
385p $16.99; lib bdg $17.89 *
Grades: 7 8 9 10   **Fic**
1. Twins—Fiction 2. Siamese twins—Fiction
3. Orphans—Fiction
ISBN   978-0-06-078564-2;   0-06-078564-0;
978-0-06-078565-9 (lib bdg); 0-06-078565-9 (lib bdg)
                                    LC 2006-03876
Born a conjoined twin, thirteen-year-old Noah bears
the secret guilt of being the only survivor, and now finds
himself in the care of a stranger with a secret of her
own.
"This spellbinding story will entangle readers at the
first sentence. . . . Orenstein's writing is magic—every
word and phrase precisely chosen." Booklist

Unseen companion. Katherine Tegen Bks. 2003
357p lib bdg $16.89; pa $7.99
Grades: 7 8 9 10   **Fic**
1. Inuit—Fiction 2. Alaska—Fiction
ISBN 0-06-052057-4 (lib bdg); 0-06-052058-2 (pa)
                                    LC 2002-152944
"In distinctive voices, the four narrators tell their own
involving stories. . . . A sensitive observer and a compelling storyteller, Orenstein offers a novel that is both
touching and harsh." Booklist

Orlev, Uri, 1931-
Run, boy, run; a novel; translated from the
Hebrew by Hillel Halkin. Houghton Mifflin 2003
186p $15
Grades: 7 8 9 10   **Fic**
1. Holocaust, 1933-1945—Fiction
ISBN 0-618-16465-0   LC 2003-1550
"Walter Lorraine books"
Original Hebrew edition, 2001
Based on the true story of a nine-year-old boy who
escapes the Warsaw Ghetto and must survive throughout
the war in the Nazi-occupied Polish countryside
"The story is totally engrossing as it vividly describes
the hardships faced by so many youngsters during the
war. Orlev has . . . successfully used historical fiction to
illustrate the Holocaust experience." SLJ

Ortiz Cofer, Judith, 1952-

Call me Maria; a novel. Orchard Books 2004 127p $16.95

Grades: 7 8 9 10 **Fic**

1. Puerto Ricans—Fiction 2. New York (N.Y.)—Fiction

ISBN 0-439-38577-6 LC 2004-2674

Fifteen-year-old Maria leaves her mother and their Puerto Rican home to live in the barrio of New York with her father, feeling torn between the two cultures in which she has been raised.

"Through a mixture of poems, letters, and prose, María gradually reveals herself as a true student of language and life. . . . Understated but with a brilliant combination of all the right words to convey events, Cofer aptly relates the complexities of María's two homes, her parents' lives, and the difficulty of her choice between them." SLJ

Orwell, George, 1903-1950

Animal farm; a fairy story; with a foreword to the Centennial edition by Ann Patchett; with a preface by Russell Baker; introduction by C.M. Woodhouse. Centennial ed. Harcourt Brace 2003 xxix, 97p $14

Grades: 7 8 9 10 11 12 Adult **Fic**

1. Animals—Fiction 2. Totalitarianism—Fiction

ISBN 978-0-45228-424-1; 0-45228-424-4

First published 1945 in the United Kingdom; first United States edition 1946

Orwell's 1945 fable about the power struggles among animals on a farm parallels the situation in Russia at the time as Orwell saw it; the characters include the ruthless pig Stalin, his idealistic Trotsky-like adversary, and the simple, kindly horse who represents the common man.

Nineteen eighty-four; with an introduction by Julian Symonds. Knopf 1992 xlii, 325p $19

Grades: 8 9 10 11 12 Adult **Fic**

1. Totalitarianism—Fiction

ISBN 0-679-41739-7 LC 92-52906

Also available in paperback from Plume

First published 1949 by Harcourt, Brace

"A dictatorship called Big Brother rules the people in a collectivist society where Winston Smith works in the Ministry of Truth. The Thought Police persuade the people that ignorance is strength and war is peace. Winston becomes involved in a forbidden love affair and joins the underground to resist this mind control." Shapiro. Fic for Youth. 3d edition

Osa, Nancy

Cuba 15. Delacorte Press 2003 277p $15.95; lib bdg $17.99; pa $7.95

Grades: 7 8 9 10 **Fic**

1. Cuban Americans—Fiction

ISBN 0-385-73021-7; 0-385-90086-4 (lib bdg); 0-385-73233-3 (pa) LC 2002-13389

Violet Paz, who is half Cuban American, half Polish American, reluctantly prepares for her upcoming "quince," a Spanish nickname for the celebration of an Hispanic girl's fifteenth birthday

"Violet's hilarious, cool first-person narrative veers between slapstick and tenderness, denial and truth." Booklist

Osborne, Mary Pope, 1949-

Standing in the light; the captive diary of Catherine Carey Logan. Scholastic 1998 184p il (Dear America) $10.95

Grades: 4 5 6 7 **Fic**

1. United States—History—1600-1775, Colonial period—Fiction 2. Pennsylvania—Fiction 3. Delaware Indians—Fiction 4. Society of Friends—Fiction

ISBN 0-590-13462-0 LC 97-40083

A Quaker girl's diary reflects her experiences growing up in the Delaware River Valley of Pennsylvania and her capture by Lenape Indians in 1763.

"Osborne successfully sustains readers' attention with a strong story line while informing them about American history." SLJ

Osterlund, Anne

Aurelia. Speak 2008 246p pa $8.99

Grades: 8 9 10 11 **Fic**

1. Princesses—Fiction 2. Mystery fiction

ISBN 978-0-14-240579-6; 0-14-240579-5

LC 2007-36074

The king sends for Robert, whose father was a trusted spy, when someone tries to assassinate Aurelia, the stubborn and feisty crown princess of Tyralt.

"Osterlund's characters are both believable, relatable, and enviable, which makes this book enjoyable to read. Even though the book might seem to fit the mold of a quintessential princess fairy tale, Aurelia's spitfire attitude and her resulting actions lend the story a unique twist." Voice Youth Advocates

Ostow, Micol

Emily Goldberg learns to salsa. Razorbill 2006 200p $16.99

Grades: 7 8 9 10 **Fic**

1. Racially mixed people—Fiction 2. Puerto Ricans—Fiction 3. Jews—Fiction 4. Family life—Fiction

ISBN 1-59514-081-6 LC 2006-14651

Forced to stay with her mother in Puerto Rico for weeks after her grandmother's funeral, half-Jewish Emily, who has just graduated from a Westchester, New York high school, does not find it easy to connect with her Puerto Rican heritage and relatives she had never met.

This is "a moving story that has a solid plotline and plenty of family secrets." Booklist

So punk rock (and other ways to disappoint your mother); a novel; with art by David Ostow. Flux 2009 246p il pa $9.95 *

Grades: 8 9 10 11 12 **Fic**

1. Rock music—Fiction 2. Jews—United States—Fiction 3. Bands (Music)—Fiction 4. School stories 5. New Jersey—Fiction

ISBN 978-0-7387-1471-4; 0-7387-1471-2

LC 2009008216

Four suburban New Jersey students from the Leo R. Gittleman Jewish Day School form a rock band that becomes inexplicably popular, creating exhiliration, friction, confrontation, and soul-searching among its members.

The "comic-strip-style illustrations are true showstoppers. . . . A rollicking, witty, and ultra-contemporary book that drums on the funny bone and reverberates through the heart." Booklist

Oswald, Nancy, 1950-

Nothing here but stones; a Jewish pioneer story; [by] Nancy Oswald. 1st ed. H. Holt 2004 215p $16.95

Grades: 5 6 7 8   **Fic**

1. Jews—Fiction 2. Frontier and pioneer life—Fiction 3. Colorado—Fiction 4. Immigrants—Fiction

ISBN 0-8050-7465-1   LC 2003-56969

In 1882, ten-year-old Emma and her family, along with other Russian Jewish immigrants, arrive in Cotopaxi, Colorado, where they face inhospitable conditions as they attempt to start an agricultural colony, and lonely Emma is comforted by the horse whose life she saved.

"This well-paced, vivid account should capture readers' attention." SLJ

Owen, James A.

Here, there be dragons; written and illustrated by James A. Owen. Simon & Schuster Books for Young Readers 2006 326p il (The Chronicles of the Imaginarium Geographica) $17.95

Grades: 8 9 10 11 12   **Fic**

1. Fantasy fiction

ISBN 978-1-4169-1227-9; 1-4169-1227-4

LC 2005-30486

Three young men are entrusted with the Imaginarium Geographica, an atlas of fantastical places to which they travel in hopes of defeating the Winter King whose bid for power is related to the First World War raging in the Real World.

"From the arresting prologue, the reader is gripped by a finely crafted fantasy tale and compelled to continue. . . . This superb saga has interesting characters and plenty of action." Voice Youth Advocates

Other titles in this series are:
The search for the Red Dragon (2007)
The indigo king (2008)

Padian, Maria

Brett McCarthy: work in progress. Knopf 2008 276p $15.99; lib bdg $18.99

Grades: 5 6 7 8   **Fic**

1. Grandmothers—Fiction 2. Friendship—Fiction 3. Cancer—Fiction 4. School stories 5. Family life—Fiction 6. Maine—Fiction

ISBN   978-0-375-84675-5;   0-375-84675-1;
978-0-375-94675-2 (lib bdg); 0-375-94675-6 (lib bdg)

LC 2007-04415

Eighth-grader Brett McCarthy—once good student and best-friend-to-Diane, now suspended and friendless—faces school and family troubles as she grapples with her redefined life.

"It is Padian's fully developed characters and ear for teenage voices that make this a story that will resonate with anyone who has ever felt isolated in the middle of a crowd." SLJ

Paley, Sasha

Huge. Simon & Schuster Books for Young Readers 2007 259p $15.99

Grades: 7 8 9   **Fic**

1.   Obesity—Fiction   2.   Camps—Fiction
3. Friendship—Fiction

ISBN 978-1-4169-3517-9; 1-4169-3517-7

LC 2007-03510

When Wilhelmina and April find themselves roommates at a fat camp, both with very different goals, they find they have very little in common until they are both humiliated by the same person.

"The characters are sharply drawn, and the often-amusing story does a good job of showing how everyday concerns are often overshadowed by the issue of weight." Booklist

Paolini, Christopher

Eragon. Knopf 2003 509p (Inheritance) $18.95; lib bdg $20.99; pa $6.99 *

Grades: 7 8 9 10   **Fic**

1. Dragons—Fiction 2. Fantasy fiction

ISBN 0-375-82668-8; 0-375-92668-2 (lib bdg);
0-440-23848-X (pa)   LC 2003-47481

First published 2002 in different form by Paolini International

In Aagaesia, a fifteen-year-old boy of unknown lineage called Eragon finds a mysterious stone that weaves his life into an intricate tapestry of destiny, magic, and power, peopled with dragons, elves, and monsters

"This unusual, powerful tale . . . is the first book in the planned Inheritance trilogy. . . . The telling remains constantly fresh and fluid, and [the author] has done a fine job of creating an appealing and convincing relationship between the youth and the dragon." Booklist

Other titles in this series are:
Eldest (2005)
Brisningr (2008)

Papademetriou, Lisa

Drop. Alfred A. Knopf 2008 169p $15.99; lib bdg $18.99

Grades: 8 9 10 11 12   **Fic**

1. Gambling—Fiction 2. Las Vegas (Nev.)—Fiction

ISBN   978-0-375-84244-3;   0-375-84244-6;
978-0-375-94244-0 (lib bdg); 0-375-94244-0 (lib bdg)

LC 2008-02568

Sixteen-year-old math prodigy Jerrica discovers she has the ability to predict outcomes in blackjack and roulette, and joins forces with Sanjay and Kat to develop her theories while helping them get the money they desperately need.

"The characters are well drawn and the excitement of the gambling scenes is well executed. Additionally, some surprising details about the teens turn the story upside down, unraveling everything that readers thought they knew about them. A page-turner." SLJ

M or F? a novel; [by] Lisa Papademetriou and Chris Tebbetts. Razorbill 2005 296p $16.99

Grades: 8 9 10 11 12   **Fic**

1. Homosexuality—Fiction 2. Friendship—Fiction

ISBN 1-59514-034-4   LC 2005008149

Papademetriou, Lisa—*Continued*

Gay teen Marcus helps his friend Frannie chat up her crush online, but then becomes convinced that the crush is falling for him instead.

"This is a creative, funny romance, written with style and sophistication." Booklist

Park, Barbara, 1947-

The graduation of Jake Moon. Atheneum Bks. for Young Readers 2000 115p $15; pa $4.99

Grades: 4 5 6 7   **Fic**

1. Alzheimer's disease—Fiction 2. Grandfathers—Fiction

ISBN 0-689-83912-X; 0-689-83985-5 (pa)

LC 99-87475

Fourteen-year-old Jake recalls how he has spent the last four years of his life watching his grandfather descend slowly but surely into the horrors of Alzheimer's disease

"Jake is a well-rounded and believable character surrounded by colorful and equally realistic supporting characters. . . . This novel . . . is written in an accessible style that will appeal to a wide audience." SLJ

Park, Linda Sue, 1960-

Archer's quest. Clarion Books 2006 167p $16

Grades: 4 5 6 7   **Fic**

1. Science fiction 2. Korea—Fiction 3. Korean Americans—Fiction

ISBN 978-0-618-59631-7; 0-618-59631-3

LC 2005-29789

Twelve-year-old Kevin Kim helps Chu-mong, a legendary king of ancient Korea, return to his own time.

This "is a breezy, fun read." Voice Youth Advocates

Keeping score. Clarion Books 2008 202p map $16

Grades: 4 5 6 7   **Fic**

1. Baseball—Fiction 2. Brooklyn (New York, N.Y.)—Fiction 3. Family life—Fiction

ISBN 978-0-618-92799-9; 0-618-92799-9

LC 2007-46522

In Brooklyn in 1951, a die-hard Giants fan teaches nine-year-old Maggie, who is a "Bums" (Dodgers) fan, how to use a technique to keep score of a baseball game which creates a special friendship between them.

"Maggie's perspective is authentically childlike and engaging, and her relations with her family and friends ring true. . . . This finely crafted novel should resonate with a wide audience of readers." SLJ

Project Mulberry; a novel. Clarion 2005 225p $16

Grades: 5 6 7 8   **Fic**

1. Korean Americans—Fiction

ISBN 0-618-47786-1   LC 2004-18159

While working on a project for an afterschool club, Julia, a Korean American girl, and her friend Patrick learn not just about silkworms, but also about tolerance, prejudice, friendship, patience, and more. Between the chapters are short dialogues between the author and main character about the writing of the book.

"The unforgettable family and friendship story, the quiet, almost unspoken racism, and the excitement of the science make this a great cross-curriculum title." Booklist

A single shard. Clarion Bks. 2001 152p $15; pa $6.99 *

Grades: 5 6 7 8   **Fic**

1. Pottery—Fiction 2. Korea—Fiction

ISBN 0-395-97827-0; 0-440-41851-8 (pa)

LC 00-43102

Awarded the Newbery Medal, 2002

Tree-ear, a thirteen-year-old orphan in medieval Korea, lives under a bridge in a potters' village, and longs to learn how to throw the delicate celadon ceramics himself

"This quiet, but involving, story draws readers into a very different time and place. . . . A well-crafted novel with an unusual setting." Booklist

When my name was Keoko. Clarion Bks. 2002 199p $16

Grades: 5 6 7 8   **Fic**

1. Korea—Fiction 2. World War, 1939-1945—Fiction

ISBN 0-618-13335-6   LC 2001-32487

With national pride and occasional fear, a brother and sister face the increasingly oppressive occupation of Korea by Japan during World War II, which threatens to suppress Korean culture entirely

"Park is a masterful prose stylist, and her characters are developed beautifully. She excels at making traditional Korean culture accessible to Western readers." Voice Youth Advocates

Includes bibliographical references

Parker, Marjorie Hodgson

David and the Mighty Eighth; a British boy and a Texas airman in World War II; by Marjorie Hodgson Parker; illustrated by Mark Postlethwaite. Bright Sky Press 2007 176p il $17.95

Grades: 4 5 6 7   **Fic**

1. World War, 1939-1945—Fiction 2. Great Britain—Fiction

ISBN 978-1-931721-93-6; 1-931721-93-9

LC 2007025999

When, during the London Blitz, he and his older sister are evacuated to go live on their grandparents' East Anglia farm, a young English boy finds it difficult to adjust to his new life until the arrival of the pilots and crews of the U.S. Eight Air Force at nearby airfields brings excitement, friendship, and hope for the future.

This is an "exciting novel, based on a true story. . . . The story is framed by extensive historical notes. . . . Spacious type, thick paper, and an occasional black-and-white drawings make this an appealing package all around." Booklist

Parker, Robert B., 1932-

The Edenville Owls. Philomel Books 2007 194p $17.99

Grades: 6 7 8 9   **Fic**

1. Friendship—Fiction 2. Basketball—Fiction 3. Teachers—Fiction 4. Mystery fiction 5. Massachusetts—Fiction

ISBN 978-0-399-24656-2; 0-399-24656-8

LC 2006-34533

Fourteen-year-old Bobby, living in a small Massachusetts town just after World War II, finds himself facing

Parker, Robert B., 1932-—*Continued*

many new challenges as he tries to pull together his coachless basketball team, cope with new feelings for his old friend Joanie, and discover the identity of the mysterious stranger who seems to be threatening his teacher.

"The poignant, well-articulated coming-of-age moments deepen the heart-pounding suspense." Booklist

Parkinson, Curtis

Domenic's war; a story of the Battle of Monte Cassino. Tundra Books 2006 191p pa $9.95
Grades: 6 7 8 9   **Fic**
  1. World War, 1939-1945—Fiction 2. Italy—Fiction
  ISBN 0-88776-751-6

"Based on actual experiences, this World War II novel tells the stories of Italians living near Monte Cassino, caught between the German army and the Allied forces. Young Domenic Luppino and his family live north of the fighting, but fear the advancing troops. Fifteen-year-old Antonio lost his entire family when fighting moved into the town, and now he's on his own. Both boys face hardships and risk their lives for friends and family. Their stories of strength, resourcefulness, and survival are deftly placed within the context of the Monte Cassino campaign and will give readers a poignant look at the ways in which the war affected average citizens." SLJ

Parkinson, Siobhán

Blue like Friday. Roaring Brook Press 2008 160p $16.95
Grades: 4 5 6 7   **Fic**
  1. Family life—Fiction 2. Missing persons—Fiction
  3. Synesthesia—Fiction 4. Ireland—Fiction
  ISBN 978-1-59643-340-3; 1-59643-340-X

When Olivia helps her quirky friend Hal, whose synesthesia causes him to experience everything in colors, with a prank intended to get rid of Hal's potential stepfather, there are unexpected consequences, including the disappearance of Hal's mother.

"Parkinson creates a warm, moving story of real families facing real problems. . . . The economy of her prose is admirable; all the characters are well drawn." Booklist

Second fiddle; or how to tell a blackbird from a sausage. Roaring Brook Press 2007 180p $16.95
Grades: 6 7 8 9   **Fic**
  1. Father-daughter relationship—Fiction 2. Violinists—Fiction 3. Friendship—Fiction
  ISBN 978-1-59643-122-5; 1-59643-122-9
                                LC 2006-19924

Outspoken Mags decides to help her new friend Gillian, a talented violin student, reconcile with her estranged father so that he will allow her to attend a prestigious music school in England.

"This wise and winning story plants truths about the frailty of life, the dreadfulness of some parents and the often fractious nature of friendship." Publ Wkly

Parry, Rosanne

Heart of a shepherd; [by] Rosanne Parry. Random House Children's Books 2009 161p $15.99; lib bdg $18.99
Grades: 4 5 6 7   **Fic**
  1. Ranch life—Fiction 2. Family life—Fiction 3. Christian life—Fiction 4. Iraq War, 2003-—Fiction 5. Oregon—Fiction
  ISBN 978-0-375-84802-5; 0-375-84802-9; 978-0-375-94802-2 (lib bdg); 0-375-94802-3 (lib bdg)
                                  LC 2007-48094

Ignatius 'Brother' Alderman, nearly twelve, promises to help his grandparents keep the family's Oregon ranch the same while his brothers are away and his father is deployed to Iraq, but as he comes to accept the inevitability of change, he also sees the man he is meant to be.

There is "more action than introspection afoot, with sibling tensions, a wildfire, and the grandfather's death along the journey. It's refreshing . . . to find a protagonist with his eyes and heart open to positive adult examples . . . and who matches his mettle to theirs." Bull Cent Child Books

Paterson, Katherine

Bread and roses, too. Clarion Books 2006 275p $16
Grades: 5 6 7 8   **Fic**
  1. Strikes—Fiction 2. Immigrants—Fiction 3. United States—History—1898-1919—Fiction 4. Lawrence (Mass.)—Fiction
  ISBN 978-0-618-65479-6; 0-618-65479-8
                                  LC 2005-31702

Jake and Rosa, two children, form an unlikely friendship as they try to survive and understand the 1912 Bread and Roses strike of mill workers in Lawrence, Massachusetts.

"Paterson has skillfully woven true events and real historical figures into the fictional story and created vivid settings, clearly drawn characters, and a strong sense of the hardship and injustice faced by the mostly immigrant mill workers." SLJ

Bridge to Terabithia; illustrated by Donna Diamond. Crowell 1977 128p il $15.99; lib bdg $16.89; pa $5.99 *
Grades: 4 5 6 7   **Fic**
  1. Friendship—Fiction 2. Death—Fiction 3. Virginia—Fiction
  ISBN 0-690-01359-0; 0-690-04635-9 (lib bdg); 0-06-440184-7 (pa)   LC 77-2221
  Awarded the Newbery Medal, 1978

The life of Jess, a ten-year-old boy in rural Virginia expands when he becomes friends with a newcomer who subsequently meets an untimely death trying to reach their hideaway, Terabithia, during a storm

"Jess and his family are magnificently characterized; the book abounds in descriptive vignettes, humorous sidelights on the clash of cultures, and realistic depictions of rural school life." Horn Book

The great Gilly Hopkins. Crowell 1978 148p $15.99; lib bdg $16.89; pa $5.99 *
Grades: 5 6 7 8   **Fic**
  1. Foster home care—Fiction
  ISBN 0-690-03837-2; 0-690-03838-0 (lib bdg); 0-06-440201-0 (pa)   LC 77-27075

Paterson, Katherine—*Continued*

A Newbery Medal honor book, 1979

"Cool, scheming, and deliberately obstreperous, 11-year-old Gilly is ready to be her usual obnoxious self when she arrives at her new foster home. . . . But Gilly's old tricks don't work against the all-encompassing love of the huge, half-illiterate Mrs. Trotter. . . . Determined not to care she writes a letter full of wild exaggerations to her real mother that brings, in return, a surprising visit from an unknown grandmother." Booklist

"A well-structured story, [this] has vitality of writing style, natural dialogue, deep insight in characterization, and a keen sense of the fluid dynamics in human relationships." Bull Cent Child Books

Jacob have I loved. Crowell 1980 216p $15.99; lib bdg $17.89; pa $6.99 *

Grades: 5 6 7 8   **Fic**

1. Twins—Fiction 2. Sisters—Fiction 3. Chesapeake Bay (Md. and Va.)—Fiction

ISBN 0-690-04078-4; 0-690-04079-2 (lib bdg); 0-06-440368-8 (pa)   LC 80-668

Awarded the Newbery Medal, 1981

Filled with resentment over the attention showered upon her twin sister, and awaiting the day she can leave her town behind, young Louise meets a wise old sea captain and begins learning how to let go of her anger.

"Each incident and feeling in the life of her young protagonist rings true because the younger voice is so alive and direct. This is a book full of humor and compassion and sharpness." Bull Cent Child Books

Jip; his story. Lodestar Bks. 1996 181p pa $5.99 hardcover o.p.

Grades: 5 6 7 8   **Fic**

1. Slavery—Fiction 2. African Americans—Fiction 3. Vermont—Fiction 4. Racially mixed people—Fiction

ISBN 0-14-038674-2 (pa); 0-525-67543-4 (hc)   LC 96-2680

While living on a Vermont poor farm during 1855 and 1856, Jip learns that his mother was a runaway slave, and that his father, the plantation owner, plans to reclaim him as property

"This historically accurate story is full of revelations and surprises, one of which is the return appearance of the heroine of *Lyddie*. . . . The taut, extremely readable narrative and its tender depictions of friendship and loyalty provide first-rate entertainment." Publ Wkly

Lyddie. Lodestar Bks. 1991 182p $17.99; pa $6.99 *

Grades: 5 6 7 8 9   **Fic**

1. United States—History—1815-1861—Fiction 2. Massachusetts—Fiction 3. Factories—Fiction

ISBN 0-525-67338-5; 0-14-034981-2 (pa)   LC 90-42944

Impoverished Vermont farm girl Lyddie Worthen is determined to gain her independence by becoming a factory worker in Lowell, Massachusetts, in the 1840s

"Not only does the book contain a riveting plot, engaging characters, and a splendid setting, but the language—graceful, evocative, and rhythmic—incorporates the rural speech patterns of Lyddie's folk, the simple Quaker expressions of the farm neighbors, and the lilt of fellow mill girl Bridget's Irish brogue. . . . A superb story of grit, determination, and personal growth." Horn Book

Park's quest. Lodestar Bks. 1988 148p pa $5.99 hardcover o.p.

Grades: 5 6 7 8   **Fic**

1. Farm life—Fiction 2. Vietnamese Americans—Fiction

ISBN 0-14-034262-1   LC 87-32422

Eleven-year-old Park makes some startling discoveries when he travels to his grandfather's farm in Virginia to learn about his father who died in the Vietnam War and meets a Vietnamese-American girl named Thanh

The author "confronts the complexity, the ambiguity, of the war and the emotions of those it involved with an honesty that young readers are sure to recognize and appreciate." N Y Times Book Rev

Preacher's boy. Clarion Bks. 1999 168p $15; pa $4.95

Grades: 5 6 7 8   **Fic**

1. Family life—Fiction 2. Christian life—Fiction 3. Vermont—Fiction

ISBN 0-395-83897-5; 0-06-447233-7 (pa)   LC 98-50083

In 1899, ten-year-old Robbie, son of a preacher in a small Vermont town, gets himself into all kinds of trouble when he decides to give up being Christian in order to make the most of his life before the end of the world

"With warmth, humor, and her powerful yet plain style, Paterson draws empathetic and memorable characters." SLJ

The same stuff as stars. Clarion Bks. 2002 242p $15

Grades: 5 6 7 8   **Fic**

ISBN 0-618-24744-0   LC 2002-3967

When Angel's self-absorbed mother leaves her and her younger brother with their poor great-grandmother, the eleven-year-old girl worries not only about her mother and brother, her imprisoned father, the frail old woman, but also about a mysterious man who begins sharing with her the wonder of the stars

"Paterson's deft hand at characterization, her insight into the human soul, and her glorious prose make this book one to rejoice over." Voice Youth Advocates

Patneaude, David, 1944-

A piece of the sky; [by] David Patneaude; [cover illustration by Layne Johnson] Albert Whitman 2007 178p $15.95

Grades: 5 6 7 8   **Fic**

1. Meteorites—Fiction 2. Mountaineering—Fiction 3. Oregon—Fiction

ISBN 978-0-8075-6536-0   LC 2006023529

Fourteen-year-old Russell, his friend Phoebe, and her brother Isaac must find a legendary meteor in the Oregon mountains before it is exploited.

"This old-fashioned adventure story has contemporary appeal." Booklist

Patneaude, David, 1944——*Continued*

Thin wood walls. Houghton Mifflin 2004 231p
$16

Grades: 7 8 9 10 **Fic**

1. Japanese Americans—Evacuation and relocation,
1942-1945—Fiction 2. World War, 1939-1945—Fiction

ISBN 0-618-34290-7 LC 2004-1014

When the Japanese bomb Pearl Harbor, Joe Hamada
and his family face growing prejudice, eventually being
torn away from their home and sent to a relocation camp
in California, even as his older brother joins the United
States Army to fight in the war.

"Basing his story on extensive research and interviews, the author does a fine job of bringing the daily
experience up close through the story of an American kid
torn from home." Booklist

Paton, Alan

Cry, the beloved country. Scribner Classics 2003
316p $28; pa $15

Grades: 7 8 9 10 11 12 Adult **Fic**

1. Race relations—Fiction 2. South Africa—Fiction

ISBN 0-7432-6195-X; 0-7432-6217-4 (pa)

First published 1948

"Reverend Kumalo, a black South African preacher, is
called to Johannesburg to rescue his sister. There he
learns that his son Absalom has been accused of murdering a young white attorney whose interests and sympathies had been with the natives. Despite this, the attorney's father comes to the aid of the minister to help the
natives in their struggle to survive a drought." Shapiro.
Fic for Youth. 3d edition

Paton Walsh, Jill, 1937-

A parcel of patterns. Farrar, Straus & Giroux
1983 136p hardcover o.p. pa $5.95

Grades: 7 8 9 10 **Fic**

1. Plague—Fiction 2. Great Britain—Fiction

ISBN 0-374-35750-1; 0-374-45743-3

LC 83-48143

Mall Percival tells how the plague came to her Derbyshire village of Eyam in the year 1665, how the villagers
determined to isolate themselves to prevent further
spread of the disease, and how three-fourths of them died
before the end of the following year.

"Historical in broad outline, the narrative blends superb characterizations, skillful plotting, and convincing
speech for a hauntingly memorable story that offers a
richly textured picture of the period." Child Book Rev
Serv

Patterson, James

Maximum Ride: the angel experiment. Little,
Brown 2005 422p $16.99

Grades: 7 8 9 10 **Fic**

1. Science fiction 2. Genetic engineering—Fiction

ISBN 0-316-15556-X LC 2004-18623

After the mutant Erasers abduct the youngest member
of their group, the "bird kids," who are the result of genetic experimentation, take off in pursuit and find themselves struggling to understand their own origins and
purpose.

"Smart-mouthed sympathetic characters and copious
butt-kicking make this fast read pure escapist pleasure."
Horn Book Guide

Other titles in this series are:

School's out – forever (2006)

Saving the world and other extreme sports (2007)

Final warning (2008)

Pattou, Edith

East. Harcourt 2003 498p $18

Grades: 7 8 9 10 **Fic**

1. Fairy tales 2. Bears—Fiction

ISBN 0-15-204563-5 LC 2003-2338

A young woman journeys to a distant castle on the
back of a great white bear who is the victim of a cruel
enchantment

"Readers with a taste for fantasy and folklore will embrace Pattou's . . . lushly rendered retelling of 'East of
the Sun and West of the Moon'." Publ Wkly

Paulsen, Gary

Dogsong. Atheneum Books for Young Readers
2000 c1985 177p $17.99; pa $6.99 *

Grades: 6 7 8 9 **Fic**

1. Inuit—Fiction 2. Sled dog racing—Fiction
3. Arctic regions—Fiction

ISBN 0-689-83960-X; 1-416-93962-8 (pa)

A Newbery Medal honor book, 1986

"A Richard Jackson book"

A reissue of the title first published 1985 by Bradbury
Press

A fourteen-year-old Eskimo boy who feels assailed by
the modernity of his life takes a 1400-mile journey by
dog sled across ice, tunda, and mountains seeking his
own "song" of himself

The author's "mystical tone and blunt prose style are
well suited to the spare landscape of his story, and his
depictions of Russell's icebound existence add both authenticity and color to a slick rendition of the visionquest plot, which incorporates human tragedy as well as
promise." Booklist

Harris and me; a summer remembered. Harcourt
Brace & Co. 1993 157p $16 *

Grades: 5 6 7 8 **Fic**

1. Farm life—Fiction 2. Cousins—Fiction

ISBN 0-15-292877-4 LC 93-19788

Sent to live with relatives on their farm because of his
unhappy home life, an eleven-year-old city boy meets his
distant cousin Harris and is given an introduction to a
whole new world

"Readers will experience hearts as large as farmers'
appetites, humor as broad as the country landscape and
adventures as wild as boyhood imaginations. All this
adds up to a hearty helping of old-fashioned, rip-roaring
entertainment." Publ Wkly

Hatchet; [by] Gary Paulsen; illustrated by Drew
Willis. 20th anniversary ed. Simon & Schuster
Books for Young Readers 2007 188p il $19.99; pa
$6.99 *

Grades: 6 7 8 9 **Fic**

Paulsen, Gary—*Continued*
1. Survival after airplane accidents, shipwrecks, etc.—Fiction 2. Divorce—Fiction
ISBN   978-1-416-92508-8;   1-416-92508-2;
978-1-416-93647-3 (pa); 1-416-93647-5 (pa)
A Newbery Medal honor book, 1988
A reissue of the title first published 1987 by Bradbury Press

After a plane crash, thirteen-year-old Brian spends fifty-four days in the wilderness, learning to survive initially with only the aid of a hatchet given him by his mother, and learning also to survive his parents' divorce
"Paulsen's knowledge of our national wilderness is obvious and beautifully shared." Voice Youth Advocates
Other titles in this series are:
Brian's return (1999)
Brian's winter (1996)
The river (1991)

The island. Orchard Bks. 1988 202p hardcover o.p. pa $5.99
Grades: 8 9 10 11 12   **Fic**
1. Islands—Fiction
ISBN 0-531-05749-6; 0-439-78662-2 (pa)
                    LC 87-24761
"A Richard Jackson book"
"Wil Neuton moves with his parents from Madison, Wis., to a small house in the north woods, miles from the nearest village, because of his father's work with the state highway department. He then discovers a lake with a single island in the middle of it; or rather, he feels as though the island had discovered him and drawn him to it for some mysterious and important purpose." N Y Times Book Rev
"With humor and psychological genius, Paulsen develops strong adolescent characters who lend new power to youth's plea to be allowed to apply individual skills in their risk-taking." Voice Youth Advocates

Nightjohn. Delacorte Press 1993 92p $15.95; pa $5.99
Grades: 7 8 9 10   **Fic**
1. Slavery—Fiction 2. Reading—Fiction 3. African Americans—Fiction
ISBN 0-385-30838-8; 0-440-21936-1 (pa)
                    LC 92-1222
Twelve-year-old Sarny's brutal life as a slave becomes even more dangerous when a newly arrived slave offers to teach her how to read
"Paulsen is at his best here: the writing is stark and bareboned, without stylistic pretensions of any kind. The narrator's voice is strong and true, the violence real but stylized with an almost mythic tone. . . . The simplicity of the text will make the book ideal for older reluctant readers who can handle violence but can't or won't handle fancy writing in long books. Best of all, the metaphor of reading as an act of freedom speaks for itself through striking action unembroidered by didactic messages." Bull Cent Child Books

The Schernoff discoveries. Delacorte Press 1997 103p pa $4.99
Grades: 5 6 7 8   **Fic**
1. Friendship—Fiction 2. School stories
ISBN 0-440-41463-6 (pa)   LC 96-45390

Harold and his best friend, both hopeless geeks and societal misfits, try to survive unusual science experiments, the attacks of the football team, and other dangers of junior high school
"The tone is breezy, funny, and sometimes touching (but not too mushy) and bound to keep the most reluctant reader chuckling." Bull Cent Child Books

Soldier's heart; a novel of the Civil War. Delacorte Press 1998 106p $15.95; pa $5.99
Grades: 7 8 9 10   **Fic**
1. United States—History—1861-1865, Civil War—Fiction 2. Post-traumatic stress disorder—Fiction
ISBN 0-385-32498-7; 0-440-22838-7 (pa)
                    LC 98-10038
"Being the story of the enlistment and due service of the boy Charley Goddard in the First Minnesota Volunteers." Title page
"This compelling and realistic depiction of war is based on a true story. . . . Paulsen's writing is crisp and fast-paced, and this soldier's story will haunt readers long after they finish reading the novel." Book Rep

The Transall saga. Delacorte Press 1998 248p pa $6.50
Grades: 5 6 7 8   **Fic**
1. Science fiction
ISBN 0-440-21976-0 (pa)   LC 97-40773
While backpacking in the desert, thirteen-year-old Mark falls into a tube of blue light and is transported into a more primitive world, where he must use his knowledge and skills to survive
"A riveting tale of adventure and action." Voice Youth Advocates

The winter room. Orchard Bks. 1989 103p $16.95; pa $5.99
Grades: 5 6 7 8   **Fic**
1. Farm life—Fiction 2. Minnesota—Fiction
ISBN 0-531-05839-5; 0-545-08534-9 (pa)
                    LC 89-42541
A Newbery Medal honor book, 1990
"A Richard Jackson book"
A young boy growing up on a northern Minnesota farm describes the scenes around him and recounts his old Norwegian uncle's tales of an almost mythological logging past
"While this seems at first to be a collection of anecdotes organized around the progression of the farm calendar, Paulsen subtly builds a conflict that becomes apparent in the last brief chapters, forceful and well-prepared. . . . Lyrical and only occasionally sentimental, the prose is clean, clear, and deceptively simple." Bull Cent Child Books

Pausewang, Gudrun, 1928-
Dark hours; translated by John Brownjohn. Annick Press 2006 208p $21.95
Grades: 6 7 8 9   **Fic**
1. World War, 1939-1945—Fiction 2. Germany—Fiction 3. Refugees—Fiction
ISBN 1-55451-042-2
"Forced to flee her Silesian home to escape the advancing Russian army, fifteen-year-old Gisela Beck

Pausewang, Gudrun, 1928-—_Continued_
struggles to reach Dresden with her family in the waning days of World War II." Voice Youth Advocates

"Well written with suspense and powerful sentiments, this story will spark discussion." SLJ

Traitor; translated from the German by Rachel Ward. Carolrhoda Books 2006 220p $16.95
Grades: 7 8 9 10 Fic
   1. World War, 1939-1945—Fiction 2. Germany—Fiction 3. Prisoners of war—Fiction
   ISBN 0-8225-6195-6 LC 2005033379
During the closing months of World War II, a fifteen-year-old German girl must decide whether or not to help an escaped Russian prisoner of war, despite the serious consequences if she does so.

"Pausewang presents an exciting and thought-provoking novel." SLJ

Paver, Michelle
Wolf brother; by Michelle Paver. 1st American ed. HarperCollins 2005 c2004 295p (Chronicles of ancient darkness) $16.99; lib bdg $17.89
Grades: 5 6 7 8 Fic
   1. Prehistoric peoples—Fiction 2. Wolves—Fiction 3. Demoniac possession—Fiction 4. Bears—Fiction
   ISBN 0-06-072825-6; 0-06-072826-4 (lib bdg)
  LC 2004-8857
First published 2004 in the United Kingdom
6,000 years in the past, twelve-year-old Tarak and his guide, a wolf cub, set out on a dangerous journey to fulfill an oath the boy made to his dying father—to travel to the Mountain of the World Spirit seeking a way to destroy a demon-possessed bear that threatens all the clans.

"Paver's depth of research into the spiritual world of primitive peoples makes this impressive British import, slated to be the first in a six-book series, intriguing and believable." SLJ
   Other titles in this series are:
Spirit walker (2006)
Soul eater (2007)
Outcast (2008)
Oath breaker (2009)

Peacock, Shane
Eye of the crow. Tundra Books 2007 264p (The boy Sherlock Holmes) $24.99 *
Grades: 6 7 8 9 10 Fic
   1. Mystery fiction 2. Great Britain—Fiction
   ISBN 978-0-88776-850-7; 0-88776-850-4
"A young woman is brutally murdered in a dark back street of Whitechapel; a young Arab is discovered with the bloody murder weapon; and a thirteen-year-old Sherlock Holmes, who was seen speaking with the alleged killer as he was hauled into jail, is suspected to be his accomplice. . . . Although imaginative reconstruction of Holmes childhood has been the subject of literary and cinematic endeavors, Peacock's take ranks among the most successful." Bull Cent Child Books
   Another title in this series is:
Death in the air (2008)

Pearce, Jacqueline, 1962-
Manga touch; [by] Jacqueline Pearce. Orca Books 2007 105p pa $8.95
Grades: 6 7 8 Fic
   1. Japan—Fiction 2. Travel—Fiction
   ISBN 978-1-55143-746-0 (pa); 1-55143-746-5 (pa)
Dana takes a school trip to Japan to learn about Japanese culture and artwork. She surprisingly discovers she has a lot to learn about people as well as manga art.

"Readers will enjoy the skillful way Pearce weaves in facts regarding Japanese culture while still keeping things interesting." Voice Youth Advocates

Pearsall, Shelley
All of the above; a novel; illustrations by Javaka Steptoe. Little, Brown 2006 234p il $15.99
Grades: 5 6 7 8 Fic
   1. School stories 2. City and town life—Fiction
   ISBN 0-316-11524-X; 978-0-316-11524-7
  LC 2005-33109
Five urban middle school students, their teacher, and other community members relate how a school project to build the world's largest tetrahedron affects the lives of everyone involved.

"Pearsall's novel, based on a real event in 2002—is a delightful story about the power of a vision and the importance of a goal. The authentic voices of the students and the well-intentioned, supportive adults surrounding them illustrate all that is good about schools, family, friendship, and community." Booklist

All shook up; [by] Shelley Pearsall. Alfred A. Knopf 2008 261p il $15.99; lib bdg $18.99
Grades: 6 7 8 9 Fic
   1. Father-son relationship—Fiction 2. Chicago (Ill.)—Fiction
   ISBN 978-0-375-83698-5; 0-375-83698-5; 978-0-375-93698-2 (lib bdg); 0-375-93698-X (lib bdg)
  LC 2007-22931
When thirteen-year-old Josh goes to stay with his father in Chicago for a few months, he discovers—to his horror—that his dad has become an Elvis impersonator.

"This affecting story of a typical, clever middle-school boy dealing with divorce and the new families that sometimes replace the old is also a very funny tale told by a terrifically engaging young narrator." Voice Youth Advocates

Crooked river; [by] Shelley Pearsall. 1st ed. Knopf 2005 249p $15.95; lib bdg $17.99
Grades: 5 6 7 8 Fic
   1. Ojibwa Indians—Fiction 2. Frontier and pioneer life—Fiction 3. Ohio—Fiction
   ISBN 0-375-82389-1; 0-375-92389-6 (lib bdg)
  LC 2004-10310
When twelve-year old Rebecca Carter's father brings a Native American accused of murder into their 1812 Ohio settlement town, Rebecca, witnessing the town's reaction to the Indian, struggles with the idea that an innocent man may be convicted and sentenced to death.

"Pearsall quickly engages readers with her captivating tale of fear, ignorance, and bravery. . . . Packed with believable characters wrapped in a thoroughly researched plot." SLJ

Pearson, Mary

The adoration of Jenna Fox; [by] Mary E. Pearson. Henry Holt and Co. 2008 272p $16.95 *

Grades: 7 8 9 10 11 12   **Fic**

1. Science fiction 2. Bioethics—Fiction

ISBN 978-0-8050-7668-4; 0-8050-7668-9

LC 2007-27314

In the not-too-distant future, when biotechnological advances have made synthetic bodies and brains possible but illegal, a seventeen-year-old girl, recovering from a serious accident and suffering from memory lapses, learns a startling secret about her existence.

"The science . . . and the science fiction are fascinating, but what will hold readers most are the moral issues of betrayal, loyalty, sacrifice, and survival." Booklist

Peck, Dale

Drift House: the first voyage; [by] Dale Peck. Bloomsbury Children's Books 2005 437p $16.95; pa $7.95

Grades: 6 7 8 9   **Fic**

1. Time—Fiction 2. Uncles—Fiction 3. Mermaids and mermen—Fiction 4. Pirates—Fiction

ISBN 1-58234-969-X; 978-1-58234-969-5; 1-59990-005-X (pa); 978-1-59990-005-6 (pa)

LC 2005-47067

Sent to stay with their uncle in a ship-like home called Drift House, twelve-year-old Susan and her two younger stepbrothers embark on an unexpected adventure involving duplicitous mermaids, pirates, and an attempt to stop time forever.

"Readers will find themselves drawn in by the appealing characters, generous doses of humor, and the palpable presence of the narrator." SLJ

Followed by: The lost cities, a Drift House voyage (2007)

The lost cities; a Drift House voyage. Bloomsbury Children's Books 2007 392p $16.95

Grades: 6 7 8 9   **Fic**

1. Time—Fiction 2. Uncles—Fiction 3. Siblings—Fiction 4. Extinct cities—Fiction

ISBN 978-1-58234-859-9; 1-58234-859-6

LC 2006-16139

Sequel to: Drift House, the first voyage (2005)

Siblings Susan and Charles receive a mysterious book before leaving to visit their Uncle Farley at his time-traveling house, where they become separated in the Sea of Time and struggle to find their way home.

This is "challenging and thought-provoking reading." Voice Youth Advocates

Peck, Richard, 1934-

Are you in the house alone? Viking 1976 156p pa $5.99

Grades: 8 9 10 11 12   **Fic**

1. Rape—Fiction

ISBN 0-14-130693-9 (pa)   LC 76-28810

"Gail is frightened by the obscene telephone calls she receives and the notes that are left on her school locker. It is after she has been raped by a classmate while she is babysitting that she begins to understand the real meaning of fear. Although she is a victim, she is doubted by her family, friends, and the police. Most unendurable is the fact that she is forced frequently to cross the path of her attacker, the son of a prominent member of the community." Shapiro. Fic for Youth. 2d edition

Fair weather; a novel. Dial Bks. 2001 130p il $16.99; pa $5.99

Grades: 5 6 7 8   **Fic**

1. Buffalo Bill, 1846-1917—Fiction 2. Russell, Lillian, 1861-1922—Fiction 3. Family life—Fiction 4. Chicago (Ill.)—Fiction

ISBN 0-8037-2516-7; 0-14-250034-8 (pa)

LC 00-55561

In 1893, thirteen-year-old Rosie and members of her family travel from their Illinois farm to Chicago to visit Aunt Euterpe and attend the World's Columbian Exposition which, along with an encounter with Buffalo Bill and Lillian Russell, turns out to be a life-changing experience for everyone

"Peck's unforgettable characters, cunning dialogue and fast-paced action will keep readers in stitches." Publ Wkly

Here lies the librarian. Dial Books 2006 145p $16.99

Grades: 4 5 6   **Fic**

1. Automobiles—Fiction 2. Librarians—Fiction 3. Country life—Fiction 4. Indiana—Fiction

ISBN 0-8037-3080-2   LC 2005-20279

Fourteen-year-old Eleanor "Peewee" McGrath, a tomboy and automobile enthusiast, discovers new possibilities for her future after the 1914 arrival in her small Indiana town of four young librarians.

"Another gem from Peck, with his signature combination of quirky characters, poignancy, and outrageous farce." SLJ

A long way from Chicago; a novel in stories. Dial Bks. for Young Readers 1998 148p $15.99; pa $5.99 *

Grades: 5 6 7 8   **Fic**

1. Grandmothers—Fiction 2. Great Depression, 1929-1939—Fiction

ISBN 0-8037-2290-7; 0-14-240110-2 (pa)

LC 98-10953

A Newbery Medal honor book, 1999

Joe recounts his annual summer trips to rural Illinois with his sister during the Great Depression to visit their larger-than-life grandmother

"The novel reveals a strong sense of place, a depth of characterization, and a rich sense of humor." Horn Book

Followed by A year down yonder (2000)

On the wings of heroes. Dial Books 2007 148p $16.99 *

Grades: 4 5 6 7   **Fic**

1. World War, 1939-1945—Fiction 2. Illinois—Fiction

ISBN 0-8037-3081-0   LC 2006011906

A boy in Illinois remembers the homefront years of World War II, especially his two heroes, his brother in the Air Force and his father, who fought in the previous war.

"Peck's masterful, detail-rich prose describes wartime in the United States. . . . Peck's characters are memorable. . . . This book is an absolute delight." SLJ

Peck, Richard, 1934-—*Continued*

The river between us. Dial Bks. 2003 164p $16.99; pa $6.99

Grades: 7 8 9 10 **Fic**

1. United States—History—1861-1865, Civil War—Fiction 2. Racially mixed people—Fiction 3. Race relations—Fiction

ISBN 0-8037-2735-6; 0-14-240310-5 (pa)

LC 2002-34815

During the early days of the Civil War, the Pruitt family takes in two mysterious young ladies who have fled New Orleans to come north to Illinois

"The harsh realities of war are brutally related in a complex, always surprising plot that resonates on mutiple levels." Horn Book Guide

A season of gifts. Dial Books for Young Readers 2009 156p $16.99

Grades: 5 6 7 8 **Fic**

1. Moving—Fiction 2. Illinois—Fiction

ISBN 978-0-8037-3082-3; 0-8037-3082-9

LC 2008-48050

A companion novel to: A long way from Chicago (1998) and A year down yonder (2000)

Relates the surprising gifts bestowed on twelve-year-old Bob Barnhart and his family, who have recently moved to a small Illinois town in 1958, by their larger-than-life neighbor, Mrs. Dowdel.

"The type of down-home humor and vibrant characterizations Peck fans have come to adore re-emerge in full as Peck resurrects Mrs. Dowdel, the irrepressible, self-sufficient grandmother featured in *A Year Down Yonder* and *A Long Way from Chicago*." Publ Wkly

Strays like us. Dial Bks. 1998 155p hardcover o.p. pa $4.99

Grades: 6 7 8 9 **Fic**

ISBN 0-8037-2291-5; 0-14-130619-X (pa)

LC 97-18575

When her drug-addict mother can no longer care for her, twelve-year-old Molly comes to stay with her great-aunt and slowly begins to realize that others in the small town also feel as if they don't belong

This novel's "easy-flowing action readily absorbs the reader into the lives of contemporary characters and a realistic, believable plot." Voice Youth Advocates

The teacher's funeral; a comedy in three parts. Dial Books 2004 190p $16.99 *

Grades: 5 6 7 8 **Fic**

1. Teachers—Fiction 2. Indiana—Fiction 3. Country life—Fiction

ISBN 0-8037-2736-4 LC 2004-4361

In rural Indiana in 1904, fifteen-year-old Russell's dream of quitting school and joining a wheat threshing crew is disrupted when his older sister takes over the teaching at his one-room schoolhouse after mean, old Myrt Arbuckle "hauls off and dies."

"The dry wit and unpretentious tone make the story's events comical, its characters memorable, and its conclusion unexpectedly moving." Booklist

A year down yonder. Dial Bks. for Young Readers 2000 130p $16.99; pa $5.99 *

Grades: 5 6 7 8 **Fic**

1. Grandmothers—Fiction 2. Great Depression, 1929-1939—Fiction

ISBN 0-8037-2518-3; 0-14-230070-5 (pa)

LC 99-43159

Awarded the Newbery Medal, 2001

This sequel to A long way from Chicago "tells the story of Joey's younger sister, Mary Alice, 15, who spends the year of 1937 back with Grandma Dowdel in a small town in Illinois." Booklist

"Peck has created a delightful, insightful tale that resounds with a storyteller's wit, humor, and vivid description." SLJ

Peck, Robert Newton, 1928-

A day no pigs would die. Knopf 1973 c1972 150p $25; pa $5.50 *

Grades: 6 7 8 9 **Fic**

1. Shakers—Fiction 2. Farm life—Fiction 3. Vermont—Fiction 4. Pigs—Fiction 5. Family life—Fiction 6. Father-son relationship—Fiction

ISBN 0-394-48235-2; 0-679-85306-5 (pa)

"Rob lives a rigorous life on a Shaker farm in Vermont in the 1920s. Since farm life is earthy, this book is filled with Yankee humor and explicit descriptions of animals mating. A painful incident that involves the slaughter of Rob's beloved pet pig is instrumental in urging him toward adulthood. The death of his father completes the process of his accepting responsibility." Shapiro. Fic for Youth. 3d edition

Horse thief; a novel. HarperCollins Pubs. 2002 231p $16.95; lib bdg $16.89; pa $5.99

Grades: 7 8 9 10 **Fic**

1. Rodeos—Fiction

ISBN 0-06-623791-2; 0-06-623792-0 (lib bdg); 0-06-441075-7 (pa) LC 2001-39733

In 1938, with the help of a doctor and her elderly, horse-thieving father, a seventeen-year-old orphan steals thirteen horses from Chickalookee, Florida's doomed rodeo and finds a family in the process

This is "a convoluted and surprisingly funny odyssey, chock-full of engaging characters. Peck's dialect and comic timing are right on target. Even sophisticated urban teens may find themselves drawn by the rip-roaring story and gentle humor." Booklist

Peet, Mal

Keeper. Candlewick Press 2005 c2003 225p $15.99

Grades: 8 9 10 11 12 **Fic**

1. Soccer—Fiction 2. Brazil—Fiction

ISBN 0-7636-2749-6 LC 2005-50786

First published 2003 in the United Kingdom

In an interview with a young journalist, World Cup hero, El Gato, describes his youth in the Brazilian rain forest and the events, experiences, and people that helped make him a great goalkeeper and renowned soccer star.

"This is a well-written, fast-paced sports story that addresses far more than just the sport itself." SLJ

Peet, Mal—*Continued*

Tamar. Candlewick Press 2007 424p $17.99 *

Grades: 8 9 10 11 12   **Fic**
1. Grandfathers—Fiction 2. World War, 1939-1945—
Fiction 3. Netherlands—Fiction
ISBN 978-0-7636-3488-9; 0-7636-3488-3
                                   LC 2006-51837

In 1995, 15-year-old Tamar inherits a box containing
a series of coded messages from his late grandfather. The
messages show Tamar the life that his grandfather lived
during World War II the life of an Allied undercover op-
erative in Nazi-occupied Holland.

"Peet's plot is tightly constructed, and striking, descriptive language, full of metaphor, grounds the story."
Booklist

Pennington, Kate

Brief candle; [by] Kate Pennington. Hodder
Children's 2004 262p pa $12.95

Grades: 6 7 8 9   **Fic**
1. Brontë, Emily, 1818-1848—Fiction 2. Great Britain—Fiction
ISBN 0-12-92965-2

"Along with losing herself in romantic poetry, 14-
year-old Emily Bronte loves to wander the wild landscape around her father's parsonage. . . . Her two passions thrillingly collide when she encounters a distraught
young man, whose courtship of a girl outside his station
has left him jobless and desperate. . . . Pennington's
homage offers the most to teens familiar with Bronte's
Wuthering Heights. . . . But even readers without much
previous knowledge about the book's underpinnings . . .
will enjoy the universally accessible view of an ill-fated
love and the dreamy restless teen who acts on its behalf." SLJ

Pérez, L. King

Remember as you pass me by. Milkweed 2007
184p $16.95; pa $6.95

Grades: 5 6 7 8   **Fic**
1. Race relations—Fiction 2. Texas—Fiction
3. African Americans—Fiction 4. Friendship—Fiction
ISBN 978-1-57131-677-6; 978-1-57131-678-3 (pa)

In small-town Texas in the mid-1950s, twelve-year-old
Silvy tries to make sense of her parent's financial problems, a Supreme Court ruling that will integrate her
school, the prejudice of her family and friends, and her
own behavior, which always seems to be wrong.

"The story flows chronologically with enough drama
to keep readers turning the pages." SLJ

Perez, Marlene

Dead is the new black. Harcourt 2008 190p pa
$7.95

Grades: 7 8 9 10   **Fic**
1. Supernatural—Fiction 2. Cheerleading—Fiction
3. Extrasensory perception—Fiction 4. School stories
ISBN 978-0-15-206408-2; 0-15-206408-7
                                   LC 2007027677

While dealing with her first boyfriend and suddenly
being pressed into service as a substitute cheerleader,
seventeen-year-old Daisy Giordano, daughter and sister

of psychics but herself a 'normal', attempts to help her
mother discover who is behind a series of bizarre attacks
on teenage girls in their little town of Nightshade, California.

"This is the witty and humorous first installment in a
series; it provides romance, mystery, friendship, adventure, and the supernatural all rolled up in a fast-paced,
plot-twisting story." SLJ

Other titles in this series are:
Dead is a state of mind (2009)
Dead is so last year (2009)

Perkins, Lynne Rae

All alone in the universe. Greenwillow Bks.
1999 140p il $15.95; pa $5.99

Grades: 5 6 7 8   **Fic**
1. Friendship—Fiction
ISBN 0-688-16881-7; 0-380-73302-1 (pa)
                                   LC 98-50093

Debbie is dismayed when her best friend Maureen
starts spending time with ordinary, boring Glenna

"A poignant story written with sensitivity and tenderness." SLJ

Criss cross. Greenwillow Books 2005 337p
$16.99; lib bdg $17.89 *

Grades: 6 7 8 9   **Fic**
ISBN 0-06-009272-6; 0-06-009273-4 (lib bdg)
                                   LC 2004-54023

Awarded the Newbery Medal, 2006

Teenagers in a small town in the 1960s experience
new thoughts and feelings, question their identities, connect, and disconnect as they search for the meaning of
life and love.

"Debbie . . . and Hector . . . narrate most of the
novel. Both are 14 years old. Hector is a fabulous character with a wry humor and an appealing sense of self-
awareness. . . . The descriptive, measured writing includes poems, prose, haiku, and question-and-answer formats. There is a great deal of humor in this gentle story." SLJ

Perkins, Mitali, 1963-

First daughter: extreme American makeover.
Dutton Children's Books 2007 277p $16.99

Grades: 7 8 9 10   **Fic**
1. Pakistani Americans—Fiction 2. Politics—Fiction
3. Adoption—Fiction
ISBN 978-0-525-47800-3   LC 2006024467

During her father's presidential campaign, sixteen-
year-old Sameera Righton, who was adopted from Pakistan at the age of three, struggles with campaign staffers
who want to give her a more "all-American" image and
create a fake weblog in her name.

"Sameera is a savvy and appealing character, and
while teen girls will love reading about her makeover,
they will also come away with a sense of the demands
made on those who are constantly in the public eye."
SLJ

Followed by: First daughter: White House rules (2008)

Perkins, Mitali, 1963-—*Continued*

Monsoon summer. Delacorte Press 2004 257p
$15.95; pa $6.50

Grades: 7 8 9 10   **Fic**
  1. India—Fiction 2. East Indians—United States—Fiction

ISBN 0-385-73123-X; 0-440-23840-4 (pa)
                 LC 2003-15168

Secretly in love with her best friend and business partner Steve, fifteen-year-old Jazz must spend the summer away from him when her family goes to India during that country's rainy season to help set up a clinic.

This "novel, written in Jazz's smart, funny, self-deprecating voice, vividly evokes the smells, sights, and sounds of India in the monsoon season." Booklist

Secret keeper. Delacorte Press 2009 225p
$16.99; lib bdg $19.99

Grades: 7 8 9 10   **Fic**
  1. Sisters—Fiction 2. Family life—Fiction 3. India—Fiction

ISBN   978-0-385-73340-3;   0-385-73340-2;
978-0-385-90356-1 (lib bdg); 0-385-90356-1 (lib bdg)
                 LC 2008-21475

In 1974 when her father leaves New Delhi, India, to seek a job in New York, Ashi, a tomboy at the advanced age of sixteen, feels thwarted in the home of her extended family in Calcutta where she, her mother, and sister must stay, and when her father dies before he can send for them, they must remain with their relatives and observe the old-fashioned traditions that Ashi hates.

"The plot is full of surprising secrets rooted in the characters' conflicts and deep connections with each other. The two sisters and their mutual sacrifices are both heartbreaking and hopeful." Booklist

Peters, Julie Anne, 1952-

Between Mom and Jo. Little, Brown 2006 232p
$16.99

Grades: 7 8 9 10   **Fic**
  1. Mother-son relationship—Fiction 2. Lesbians—Fiction 3. Family life—Fiction 4. Prejudices—Fiction

ISBN 0-316-73906-5   LC 2005-22012

Fourteen-year-old Nick has a three-legged dog named Lucky 2, some pet fish, and two mothers, whose relationship complicates his entire life as they face prejudice, work problems, alcoholism, cancer, and finally separation.

"A powerful, moving examination of the relationships we forge within the family we are given." Horn Book Guide

Define "normal"; a novel. Little, Brown 2000
196p $14.95; pa $5.95

Grades: 7 8 9 10   **Fic**
  1. School stories 2. Friendship—Fiction

ISBN 0-316-70631-0; 0-316-73489-6 (pa)
                 LC 99-42774

When she agrees to meet with Jasmine as a peer counselor at their middle school, Antonia never dreams that this girl with the black lipstick and pierced eyebrow will end up helping her deal with the serious problems she faces at home and become a good friend

"Readers who are looking for believable characters and a good story about friendship, being different, and growing wiser will appreciate *Define 'Normal'*" Voice Youth Advocates

Peterson, Will

Triskellion; [by] Will Peterson. Candlewick
Press 2008 365p $16.99

Grades: 6 7 8 9   **Fic**
  1.   Siblings—Fiction   2.   Twins—Fiction
3. Supernatural—Fiction 4. Great Britain—Fiction

ISBN 978-0-7636-3971-6; 0-7636-3971-0

After their parents' divorce, Rachel and Adam are sent to live with their grandmother in the English village of Triskellion, where they find danger and paranormal activity as they discover hidden secrets that some will kill to keep buried.

"The plot moves along at a brisk pace, and there's plenty of adventure, dark and creepy atmosphere, and a touch of the paranormal." SLJ

Followed by: Triskellion 2: The burning (2009)

Petrucha, Stefan

The Rule of Won. Walker & Co. 2008 227p
$16.99

Grades: 8 9 10 11 12   **Fic**
  1. Supernatural—Fiction 2. Clubs—Fiction 3. School stories 4. Books and reading—Fiction

ISBN 978-0-8027-9651-6; 0-8027-9651-6
                 LC 2008-00255

Caleb Dunne, the quintessential slacker, is pressured by his girlfriend to join a high school club based on The Rule of Won, which promises to fulfill members' every "crave," but when nonbelievers start being ostracized and even hurt, Caleb must act.

"The book is fast paced and gripping enough to draw in reluctant readers. . . . Raising questions about issues such as personal responsibility, freedom of speech and the press, and standing up for unpopular beliefs, this novel would be a terrific choice for book-group and class discussions." SLJ

Teen, Inc.; [by] Stefan Petrucha. Walker 2007
244p $16.95 *

Grades: 8 9 10 11 12   **Fic**
  1. Orphans—Fiction 2. Business ethics—Fiction 3. Pollution—Fiction

ISBN 978-0-8027-9650-9; 0-8027-9650-8
                 LC 2007-2368

Fourteen-year-old Jaiden has been raised by NECorp. since his parents were killed when he was a baby, so when he discovers that the corporation has been lying about producing illegal levels of mercury emissions, he and his two friends decide to try to do something about it.

"Witty and provocative without being preachy, this novel has both daring characters and a heady plot." Booklist

Pfeffer, Susan Beth, 1948-

The dead & the gone. Harcourt 2008 321p $17

Grades: 7 8 9 10 11   **Fic**

1. Natural disasters—Fiction 2. Family life—Fiction
3. Science fiction

ISBN 978-0-15-206311-5; 0-15-206311-0

LC 2007-29606

Companion volume to: Life as we knew it (2006)

After a meteor hits the moon and sets off a series of
horrific climate changes, seventeen-year-old Alex Mora-
les must take care of his sisters alone in the chaos of
New York City.

"The writing draws in readers with palpable descriptions, allowing them to experience the fear, stench,
numbness, and grief alongside the characters. With its
accessible language, rich imagery, and gripping premise,
this book will appeal to readers who enjoy a wide range
of fiction, from survival stories to apocalyptic tales to
heart wrenching, coming-of-age novels." Voice Youth
Advocates

Life as we knew it. Harcourt 2006 337p $17

Grades: 7 8 9 10   **Fic**

1. Natural disasters—Fiction 2. Family life—Fiction
3. Science fiction

ISBN 978-0-15-205826-5; 0-15-205826-5

LC 2005-36321

Companion volume to: The dead and the gone (2008)

Through journal entries sixteen-year-old Miranda describes her family's struggle to survive after a meteor
hits the moon, causing worldwide tsunamis, earthquakes,
and volcanic eruptions.

"Each page is filled with events both wearying and
terrifying and infused with honest emotions. Pfeffer
brings cataclysmic tragedy very close." Booklist

Philbrick, W. R. (W. Rodman)

The mostly true adventures of Homer P. Figg;
[by] Rodman Philbrick. Blue Sky Press 2009 224p
$16.99 *

Grades: 5 6 7 8   **Fic**

1. Adventure fiction 2. Orphans—Fiction
3. Brothers—Fiction 4. United States—History—1861-
1865, Civil War—Fiction

ISBN 978-0-439-66818-7; 0-439-66818-2

LC 2008-16925

Twelve-year-old Homer, a poor but clever orphan, has
extraordinary adventures after running away from his evil
uncle to rescue his brother, who has been sold into service in the Civil War.

"The book wouldn't be nearly as much fun without
Homer's tall tales, but there are serious moments, too,
and the horror of war and injustice of slavery ring clearly above the din of playful exaggerations." Publ Wkly

Pierce, Tamora, 1954-

Circle of magic: Sandry's book. Scholastic Press
1997 252p hardcover o.p. pa $6.99 *

Grades: 6 7 8 9   **Fic**

1. Fantasy fiction

ISBN 0-590-55356-9; 0-590-55408-5 (pa)

LC 95-39540

Four young misfits find themselves living in a strictly
disciplined temple community where they become friends
while also learning to do crafts and to use their powers,
especially magic

"Pierce has created an excellent new world where
magic is a science and utterly believable and populated
it with a cast of well-developed characters." Booklist

Other available titles in this series are:

Circle of magic: Briar's book (1999)

Circle of magic: Daja's book (1998)

Circle of magic: Tris's book (1998)

First test. Random House 1999 216p (Protector
of the small) hardcover o.p. lib bdg $17.99; pa
$5.99 *

Grades: 6 7 8 9   **Fic**

1. Fantasy fiction

ISBN 0-679-88914-0; 0-679-98914-5 (lib bdg);
0-679-88917-5 (pa)   LC 98-30903

Set in the imaginary kingdom of Tortall, setting for
the author's Lioness quartet and the Immortals series

First title in the Protector of the small series. Ten-
year-old Keladry of Mindalen, daughter of nobles, serves
as a page but must prove herself to the males around her
if she is ever to fulfill her dream of becoming a knight

"Pierce spins a whopping good yarn, her plot balanced
on a solid base of action and characterization." Bull Cent
Child Books

Other available titles in this series are:

Lady knight (2002)

Page (2001)

Squire (2002)

Melting stones. Scholastic Press 2008 312p
$17.99 *

Grades: 8 9 10 11 12   **Fic**

1. Magic—Fiction 2. Fantasy fiction

ISBN 978-0-545-05264-1; 0-545-05264-5

LC 2007045036

Residents of the island of Starns send for help from
Winding Circle temple, and when prickly green mage
Rosethorn and young stone mage trainee Evvy respond,
Evvy finds that the problem is with a long-dormant vol-
cano and tries to use her talents to avert the looming de-
struction.

This "is a riveting story that has many inventive and
exciting plot twists and turns. . . . The story features excellent character development." SLJ

Terrier. Random House 2006 581p il map (Beka
Cooper) $18.95; lib bdg $20.99 *

Grades: 7 8 9 10   **Fic**

1. Police—Fiction 2. Fantasy fiction 3. Magic—Fiction

ISBN   978-0-375-81468-6;   0-375-81468-X;
978-0-375-91468-3 (lib bdg); 0-375-91468-4 (lib bdg)

LC 2006-14834

When sixteen-year-old Beka becomes "Puppy" to a
pair of "Dogs," as the Provost's Guards are called, she
uses her police training, natural abilities and a touch of
magic to help them solve the case of a murdered baby
in Tortall's Lower City.

"Pierce deftly handles the novel's journal structure,
and her clear homage to the police-procedural genre applies a welcome twist to the girl-legend-in-the-making
story line." Booklist

Pierce, Tamora, 1954-—*Continued*
Followed by: Bloodhound (2009)

Trickster's choice. Random House 2003 422p
$17.95; pa $8.95 *
Grades: 7 8 9 10   **Fic**
  1. Fantasy fiction
  ISBN 0-375-81466-3; 0-375-82879-6 (pa)
                        LC 2003-5202
Alianne must call forth her mother Alanna's courage
and her father's wit in order to survive on the Copper
Isles in a royal court rife with political intrigue and murderous conspiracy
  "This series opener is packed with Pierce's alluring
mix of fantasy, adventure, romance, and humor, making
the book an essential purchase for school and public libraries." Voice Youth Advocates
  Another title in this series is:
Trickster's queen (2004)

The will of the empress. Scholastic Press 2005
550p $17.99; pa $8.99 *
Grades: 8 9 10 11 12   **Fic**
  1. Fantasy fiction
  ISBN 0-439-44171-4; 0-439-44172-2 (pa)
                       LC 2005-02874
On visit to Namorn to visit her vast landholdings and
her devious cousin, Empress Berenene, eighteen-year-old
Sandry must rely on her childhood friends and fellow
mages, Daja, Tris, and Briar, despite the distance that has
grown between them
  "This novel begins two years after the Circle of Magic
and The Circle Opens series. . . . Readers will enjoy being reacquainted with these older but still very well-
developed characters." SLJ

Pignat, Caroline, 1970-
  Greener grass; the famine years. Red Deer Press
2009 276p pa $12.95
Grades: 7 8 9 10   **Fic**
  1. Ireland—Fiction 2. Famines—Fiction
  ISBN 0-88995-402-1; 0-88995-402-X
  "In 1847, 15-year-old Kit is jailed for digging up potatoes on confiscated land to feed her starving family,
and during the three weeks that she is incarcerated, she
reflects on the past year in Ireland: the blight, the famine, evictions, and deaths. . . . True to Kat's voice, the
plain, rhythmic language . . . is lyrical but never ornate.
The tension in the story and in the well-developed characters is always rooted in daily detail." Booklist

Pike, Aprilynne
  Wings. HarperTeen 2009 294p $16.99; lib bdg
$17.89
Grades: 6 7 8 9   **Fic**
  1. Fairies—Fiction 2. Plants—Fiction 3. Trolls—Fiction 4. Fantasy fiction
  ISBN   978-0-06-166803-6;   0-06-166803-6;
978-0-06-166804-3 (lib bdg); 0-06-166804-4 (lib bdg)
                      LC 2008-24653
When a plant blooms out of fifteen-year-old Laurel's
back, it leads her to discover the fact that she is a faerie
and that she has a crucial role to play in keeping the
world safe from the encroaching enemy trolls.
  "Replete with budding romance, teen heroics, a good
smattering of evil individuals, and an ending that serves
up a ready sequel, this novel nonetheless provides an unusual approach to middle level fantasy through its startlingly creative premise that faeries are of the plant world
and not the animal world. . . . Both male and female
fantasy readers will enjoy this fast-paced action fantasy."
Voice Youth Advocates

Pinkwater, Daniel Manus, 1941-
  The Neddiad; how Neddie took the train, went
to Hollywood, and saved civilization; by Daniel
Pinkwater; illustrations by Calef Brown. Houghton
Mifflin 2007 307p il $16
Grades: 5 6 7 8   **Fic**
  1. Turtles—Fiction 2. Los Angeles (Calif.)—Fiction
  ISBN 978-0-618-59444-3; 0-618-59444-2
                      LC 2006033944
Followed by: The Yggyssey (2009)
  When shoelace heir Neddie Wentworthstein and his
family take the train from Chicago to Los Angeles in the
1940s, he winds up in possession of a valuable Indian
turtle artifact whose owner is supposed to be able to prevent the impending destruction of the world, but he is
not sure exactly how.
  "A bright and breezy adventure with a smart and funny narrator. . . . [This is a] goofy and lovingly nostalgic
historical fantasy." SLJ

The Yggyssey; how Iggy wondered what
happened to all the ghosts, found out where they
went, and went there; illustrations by Calef Brown.
Houghton Mifflin Co. 2009 245p il $16
Grades: 4 5 6   **Fic**
  1. Ghost stories 2. Hotels and motels—Fiction
3. Hollywood (Calif.)—Fiction
  ISBN 978-0-618-59445-0; 0-618-59445-0
                      LC 2008-01874
Sequel to: The Neddiad
  In the mid-1950s, Yggdrasil Birnbaum and her friends,
Seamus and Neddie, journey to Old New Hackensack,
which is on another plane, to try to learn why ghosts are
disappearing from the Birnbaum's hotel and other Holly-
wood, California, locations.
  "Once again, Pinkwater combines a goofy plot, myth
and fairy tale references, and an obvious affection for
yesteryear Los Angeles in a supernaturally funny read."
Booklist

Pixley, Marcella
  Freak. Farrar, Straus and Giroux 2007 131p $16
*
Grades: 6 7 8 9 10   **Fic**
  1. Bullies—Fiction 2. School stories
  ISBN 0-374-32453-0; 978-0-374-32453-7
                      LC 2006-50683
  Twelve-year-old Miriam, poetic, smart, and quirky, is
considered a freak by the popular girls at her middle
school, and she eventually explodes in response to their
bullying, revealing an inner strength she did not know
she had.
  "The story's conflicts are exceptionally riveting and
believable." Booklist

Plum-Ucci, Carol, 1957-
The night my sister went missing. Harcourt
2006 202p $17
Grades: 8 9 10 11 12   **Fic**
1. Missing children—Fiction 2. Incest—Fiction
3. City and town life—Fiction
ISBN 978-0-15-204758-0; 0-15-204758-1
       LC 2005035081
When his sister goes missing under mysterious circumstances, seventeen-year-old Kurt spends a night at
the local police station overhearing statements from a variety of witnesses that reveal the deep prejudices and
shocking secrets of his small beach community.
"Readers will be turning pages as new information is
dispensed in each chapter, moving and changing the story in unexpected ways. They'll race to the ending and
won't guess until they get there." Booklist

Plummer, Louise
Finding Daddy; [by] Louise Plummer. 1st ed.
Delacorte Press 2007 176p $15.99; lib bdg $18.99
Grades: 6 7 8 9   **Fic**
1. Father-daughter relationship—Fiction
2. Criminals—Fiction 3. Family life—Fiction
4. Utah—Fiction
ISBN 978-0-385-73092-1; 0-385-73092-6;
978-0-385-90113-0 (lib bdg); 0-385-90113-5 (lib bdg)
       LC 2006023938
Just before her sixteenth birthday, Mira finally tracks
down the father she has never known, but a few days before meeting him—without her mother's or grandmother's knowledge—someone breaks into her home, beginning an escalating series of crimes.
"A fast-paced thriller that will keep readers turning
pages." Booklist

Polak, Monique
What world is left. Orca Book Pub. 2008 215p
pa $12.95 *
Grades: 7 8 9 10 11 12   **Fic**
1. Holocaust, 1933-1945—Fiction 2. Jews—Nether-
lands—Fiction 3. World War, 1939-1945—Netherlands—Fiction 4. Netherlands—History—1940-1945,
German occupation—Fiction
ISBN 978-1-5514-3847-4; 1-5514-3847-X
"Growing up in a secular Jewish home in Holland,
Anneke cares little about Judaism, so she has no faith to
lose when, in 1943, her family is deported to
Theresienstadt, the Nazi concentration camp. . . . Based
on the experiences of the author's mother . . . this novel
is narrated in Anneke's first-person, present-tense voice.
The details are unforgettable. . . . An important addition
to the Holocaust curriculum." Booklist

Pollet, Alison
Nobody was here; 7th grade in the life of me,
Penelope; by Alison Pollet. 1st ed. Orchard Books
2004 218p $15.95; pa $5.99
Grades: 4 5 6 7   **Fic**
1. School stories 2. New York (N.Y.)—Fiction
ISBN 0-439-58394-2; 0-439-58395-0 (pa)
       LC 2003-19380

Life in New York in the 1980s is made more difficult
for Penelope Schwartzbaum by problems at home and at
school.
"Pollet has created a believable set of characters who
experience nasty, spiteful behavior that most girls over
the age of 12 will easily recognize, and her perceptive,
often humorous story is sure to be welcomed by readers
approaching, as well as those stuck in, seventh grade."
Booklist
Another title in this series is:
The pity party: 8th grade In the life of me, Cass (2005)

Porter, Tracey
Billy Creekmore. Joanna Cotler Books 2007
305p $16.99; lib bdg $17.89 *
Grades: 5 6 7 8   **Fic**
1. Orphanages—Fiction 2. Coal mines and mining—
Fiction 3. Circus—Fiction 4. West Virginia—Fiction
ISBN 978-0-06-077570-4; 0-06-0-77570-X;
978-0-06-077571-1 (lib bdg); 0-06-077571-8 (lib bdg)
       LC 2007-00001
In 1905, ten-year-old Billy is taken from an orphanage
to live with an aunt and uncle he never knew he had,
and he enjoys his first taste of family life until his work
in a coal mine and involvement with a union brings trouble, then he joins a circus in hopes of finding his father.
"Porter's writing is strong, and the story, told in Billy's steadfast yet child-true voice, makes the shocking
history about the lives of children at the turn of the last
century come alive for today's readers." Booklist

Potter, Ellen, 1963-
Slob. Philomel Books 2009 199p $16.99 *
Grades: 5 6 7 8   **Fic**
1. Obesity—Fiction 2. Bereavement—Fiction
3. Siblings—Fiction 4. Inventions—Fiction
5. Orphans—Fiction 6. New York (N.Y.)—Fiction
ISBN 978-0-399-24705-7; 0-399-24705-X
       LC 2008040476
Picked on, overweight genius Owen tries to invent a
television that can see the past to find out what happened
the day his parents were killed.
"An intriguingly offbeat mystery, . . . at turns humorous, suspenseful and poignant." Kirkus

Pow, Tom, 1950-
The pack; [by] Tom Pow. 1st American ed.
Roaring Brook Press 2006 228p $16.95
Grades: 6 7 8 9   **Fic**
1. Science fiction
ISBN 978-1-59643-159-1; 1-59643-159-8
       LC 2005-24543
"A Neal Porter book"
A band of children must scavenge to survive in a
post-apocalyptic future where forbidden territories exist
and the line between man and beast is blurred.
"The suspense is palpable, and the characters are viv-
idly realized. . . . Truly an edge-of-the-chair read."
Booklist

Powell, Randy

Swiss mist. Farrar, Straus & Giroux 2008 210p
$16.95

Grades: 6 7 8 9 10   **Fic**
 1. Divorce—Fiction 2. Washington (State)—Fiction
 ISBN 978-0-374-37356-6; 0-374-37356-6
                                    LC 2007-27680

Follows Milo from fifth grade, when his mother and
philosopher father get divorced, through tenth grade,
when his mother has married a wealthy businessman and
Milo is still a bit of a loner, looking for the meaning of
life.

"This book is rewardingly remarkable for the characters and bits of truth that Milo never stops pursuing,
even as he learns that truth is not what matters most."
SLJ

Three clams and an oyster. Farrar, Straus &
Giroux 2002 216p $16; pa $6.95

Grades: 7 8 9 10   **Fic**
 1. Friendship—Fiction 2. Football—Fiction
 ISBN 0-374-37526-7; 0-374-40007-5 (pa)
                                    LC 2001-54833

During their humorous search to find a fourth player
for their flag football team, three high school juniors are
forced to examine their long friendship, their individual
flaws, and their inability to try new experiences

"Sometimes philosophical, sometimes comical, but always touching, Randy Powell writes an unusually moving story of adolescent male friends." Book Rep

Pratchett, Terry

The amazing Maurice and his educated rodents.
HarperCollins Pubs. 2001 241p hardcover o.p. lib
bdg $17.89; pa $6.99 *

Grades: 7 8 9 10   **Fic**
 1. Fantasy fiction 2. Rats—Fiction 3. Cats—Fiction
 ISBN 0-06-001233-1; 0-06-001234-X (lib bdg);
 0-06-001235-8 (pa)   LC 2001-42411

A talking cat, intelligent rats, and a strange boy coop-
erate in a Pied Piper scam until they try to con the
wrong town and are confronted by a deadly evil rat king

"In this laugh-out-loud fantasy, his first 'Discworld'
novel for younger readers, Pratchett rethinks a classic
story and comes up with a winner." SLJ

Nation. HarperCollins 2008 367p $16.99; lib
bdg $17.89 *

Grades: 7 8 9 10 11 12   **Fic**
 1. Survival after airplane accidents, shipwrecks, etc.—
 Fiction 2. Tsunamis—Fiction 3. Islands—Fiction
 ISBN   978-0-06-143301-6;   0-06-143301-2;
 978-0-06-143302-3 (lib bdg); 0-06-143302-0 (lib bdg)
                                    LC 2008-20211

Michael L. Printz Award honor book, 2009

After a devastating tsunami destroys all that they have
ever known, Mau, an island boy, and Daphne, an aristocratic English girl, together with a small band of refugees, set about rebuilding their community and all the
things that are important in their lives.

"Quirky wit broad vision make this a fascinating survival story on many levels." Booklist

Only you can save mankind. HarperCollins 2005
c1992 207p $15.99; lib bdg $16.89 *

Grades: 5 6 7 8   **Fic**
 1. Computer games—Fiction 2. War stories
 ISBN 0-06-054185-7; 0-06-054186-5 (lib bdg)
 First published 1992 in the United Kingdom

Twelve-year-old Johnny endures tensions between his
parents, watches television coverage of the Gulf War,
and plays a computer game called Only You Can Save
Mankind, in which he is increasingly drawn into the reality of the alien ScreeWee.

This is "a wild ride, full of Pratchett's trademark humor; digs at primitive, low-resolution games . . . ; and
some not-so-subtle philosophy about war and peace."
Booklist

Other title in this trilogy are:
Johnny and the dead (2006)
Johnny and the bomb (2006)

Preller, James, 1961-

Six innings; a game in the life. Feiwel and
Friends 2008 147p $16.95 *

Grades: 4 5 6 7   **Fic**
 1. Baseball—Fiction 2. Cancer—Fiction
 ISBN 978-0-312-36763-3; 0-312-36763-5
                                    LC 2007-32846

Earl Grubb's Pool Supplies plays Northeast Gas &
Electric in the Little League championship game, while
Sam, who has cancer and is in a wheelchair, has to call
the play-by-play instead of participating in the game.

"The outcome is predictable but the journey is
nailbitingly tense. Kids will be nodding in agreement at
the truths laid bare." Publ Wkly

Prévost, Guillaume, 1964-

The book of time; [by] Guillaume Prévost;
translated by William Rodarmor. Arthur A. Levine
Books 2007 213p $16.99

Grades: 5 6 7 8   **Fic**
 1. Science fiction 2. Missing persons—Fiction
 ISBN 978-0-439-88375-7; 0-439-88375-x
                                    LC 2006-38446

Original French edition 2006

Sam Faulkner travels back in time to medieval Ireland, ancient Egypt and Renaissance Bruges in search of
his missing father.

"The appeal of the novel . . . comes from both well-
drawn characters and a swiftly moving story." Booklist

Prineas, Sarah

The magic thief; illustrations by Antonio Javier
Caparo. HarperCollins Pub. 2008 419p il map
$16.99 *

Grades: 4 5 6 7   **Fic**
 1.   Magic—Fiction   2.   Thieves—Fiction
 3. Apprentices—Fiction 4. Fantasy fiction
 ISBN 978-0-06-137587-3; 0-06-137587-X
                                    LC 2007-31704

"Conn is a thief but, through desire and inevitability,
becomes a wizard . . . This evolution begins when Conn
picks the pocket of the wizard Nevery. . . . What works
wonderfully well here is the boy's irresistable voice."
Booklist

Prineas, Sarah—_Continued_
Another title in this series is:
Lost (2009)

Prose, Francine, 1947-
After. HarperCollins Pubs. 2003 330p $15.99;
lib bdg $16.89
Grades: 7 8 9 10   **Fic**
1. School stories 2. School violence—Fiction
3. Conspiracies—Fiction
ISBN 0-06-008081-7; 0-06-008082-5 (lib bdg)
                                        LC 2002-14386
In the aftermath of a nearby school shooting, a grief
and crisis counselor takes over Central High School and
enacts increasingly harsh measures to control students,
while those who do not comply disappear
"This drama raises all-too-relevant questions about the
fine line between safety as a means of protection versus
encroachment on individual rights and free will. Sure to
spur heated discussions." Publ Wkly

Touch. HarperTeen 2009 262p $16.99; lib bdg
$17.89
Grades: 7 8 9 10   **Fic**
1. Friendship—Fiction 2. Family life—Fiction
3. Stepmothers—Fiction 4. School stories
ISBN   978-0-06-137517-0;   0-06-137517-9;
978-0-06-137518-7 (lib bdg); 0-06-137518-7 (lib bdg)
                                        LC 2008-20208
Ninth-grader Maisie's concepts of friendship, loyalty,
self-acceptance, and truth are tested to their limit after a
schoolbus incident with the three boys who have been
her best friends since early childhood.
"Readers will be fascinated by this convincing tale
and the questions that it raises, from its gripping first
chapter to its poignant and surprising conclusion." Voice
Youth Advocates

Pullman, Philip, 1946-
The golden compass; his dark materials book I;
[appendix illustrations by Ian Beck] Deluxe 10th
anniversary ed. Alfred A. Knopf 2006 399p il
$22.95; lib bdg $24.99 *
Grades: 7 8 9 10 11 12   **Fic**
1. Fantasy fiction
ISBN   978-0-375-83830-9;   0-375-83830-9;
978-0-375-93830-6 (lib bdg); 0-375-93830-3 (lib bdg)
                                        LC 2005-32556
First published 1995 in the United Kingdom with title:
Northern lights
Includes "Some papers from the Library at Jordan
College" and other materials that complement the original text
This first title in a fantasy trilogy "introduces the
characters and sets up the basic conflict, namely, a race
to unlock the mystery of a newly discovered type of
charged particles simply called 'dust' that may be a
bridge to an alternate universe. The action follows 11-
year-old protagonist Lyra Belacqua from her home at
Oxford University to the frozen wastes of the North on
a quest to save dozens of kidnapped children from the
evil 'Gobblers,' who are using them as part of a sinister
experiment involving dust." Libr J [review of 1996 edi-
tion]

Other titles in the His dark materials series are:
The amber spyglass (2000)
The subtle knife (1997)

Once upon a time in the North; illustrated by
John Lawrence. Knopf 2008 95p il $12.99 *
Grades: 7 8 9 10 11 12   **Fic**
1. Fantasy fiction
ISBN 978-0-375-84510-9; 0-375-84510-0
                                        LC 2007-43993
Prequel to: The golden compass
"A David Fickling book"
In a time before Lyra Silvertongue was born, the
tough American balloonist Lee Scoresby and the great
armoured bear Iorek Byrnison meet when Lee and his
hare daemon Hester crash-land their trading balloon onto
a port in the far Arctic North and find themselves right
in the middle of a political powder keg.
"The precise narrative prose is spiced up with Lee's
flights of 'oratorical flamboyancy,' and the sardonic banter between Lee and his daemon Hester is as amusing as
ever. [Illustrated with] engraved spot illustrations and 'reproduced' documents." Horn Book

Purtill, C. Leigh
Love, Meg; [by] C. Leigh Purtill. Razorbill
2007 297p $16.99
Grades: 7 8 9 10   **Fic**
1. Family life—Fiction 2. Moving—Fiction 3. New
York (N.Y.)—Fiction
ISBN 978-1-59514-116-3   LC 2007001941
High school sophomore Meg longs for a "normal life"
instead of constantly moving whenever Lucie, her older
sister and guardian, finds a new boyfriend, but after Meg
discovers a family secret, she leaves Lucie and Hollywood, California, for Queens, New York, in search of
answers and loving relatives.
"Purtill's writing is a pleasure to read. She creates a
world for Meg that teen girls will recognize." Voice
Youth Advocates

Qamar, Amjed
Beneath my mother's feet. Atheneum Books for
Young Readers 2008 198p $16.99
Grades: 7 8 9 10   **Fic**
1. Household employees—Fiction 2. Pakistan—Fiction
3. Sex role—Fiction 4. Poverty—Fiction
ISBN 978-1-4169-4728-8; 1-4169-4728-0
                                        LC 2007-19001
When her father is injured, fourteen-year-old Nazia is
pulled away from school, her friends, and her preparations for an arranged marriage, to help her mother clean
houses in a wealthy part of Karachi, Pakistan, where she
finally rebels against the destiny that is planned for her.
"This first novel by a Muslim Indian-American provides a fascinating glimpse into a world remarkably distant from that of most American teens, and would be an
excellent suggestion for readers who want to know about
how other young people live." SLJ

Qualey, Marsha, 1953-
Just like that. Dial Books 2005 233p $16.99
Grades: 7 8 9 10   Fic
    1. Bereavement—Fiction 2. Accidents—Fiction
    ISBN 0-8037-2840-9   LC 2004-24177
"Eighteen-year-old Hanna believes that she may have
been able to save two teens before they died on a
subzero Minneapolis night. Consumed with guilt, she visits the tragedy's site, where she spots Will, a boy who
harbors his own shame about the deaths." Booklist
"Qualey writes with quiet fierceness, giving her characters depth and the plot complexities that transcend the
sometimes hackneyed trend toward grim realism in YA
novels." SLJ

Rabin, Staton, 1958-
Black powder. Margaret K. McElderry Books
2005 245p $16.95
Grades: 6 7 8 9   Fic
    1. Science fiction 2. African Americans—Fiction
    ISBN 0-689-86876-4
"Fourteen-year-old Langston Davis's best friend,
Neely, has been shot and killed in a gang fight. . . .
When his science teacher invents a century-hopping time
machine, Langston [wants to] go back in time to stop the
invention of gunpowder." Publisher's note
This is "a touching story of two great scientific minds
discovering the humanity behind the ideas. Langston is
particularly well-developed as an intelligent, mostly responsible African-American finding his way." SLJ

Randall, David, 1972-
Clovermead; [by] David Randall. 1st ed.
Margaret K. McElderry Books 2004 288p (In the
shadow of the bear) $15.95
Grades: 7 8 9 10   Fic
    1. Fantasy fiction
    ISBN 0-689-86639-9   LC 2003-9934
Clovermead, twelve-year-old tomboy, learns that her
father has been lying about the past and that the truth
may be the key to ending the epic battle raging between
the followers of Lord Ursus and those of Lady Moon.
    "Excellent characterization and a well-developed story
make for an intricate and action-packed adventure." SLJ
    Other titles in this series are:
Chandlefort (2006)
Sorrel (2007)

Ravel, Edeet
The saver; [by] Edeet Ravel. Groundwood
Books/House of Anansi Press 2008 214p $17.95
Grades: 7 8 9 10 11   Fic
    1. Death—Fiction 2. Orphans—Fiction 3. Uncles—
    Fiction
    ISBN 978-0-88899-882-8; 0-88899-882-1
When 17-year-old Fern's mother dies of a heart attack, she has to make her own way in the world. She
takes over her mother's housecleaning jobs, takes a job
as a janitor, and adds two other part-time jobs. Then her
Uncle Jack, whom she's never met, shows up to help
her.
    "Written as a series of letters to an imaginary friend
on another planet, this is a compelling story of determination and the will to survive." SLJ

Rawlings, Marjorie Kinnan, 1896-1953
The yearling; with pictures by N. C. Wyeth.
Scribner 1985 c1938 400p il $28; pa $5.95
Grades: 5 6 7 8   Fic
    1. Florida—Fiction 2. Deer—Fiction
    ISBN 0-684-18461-3; 0-02-044931-3 (pa)
                                       LC 85-40301
Reissue of the title first published 1938; awarded Pulitzer Prize, 1939
    "Young Jody Baxter lives a lonely life in the scrub
forest of Florida until his parents unwillingly consent to
his adopting an orphan fawn. The two become inseparable until the fawn destroys the meager crops. Then Jody
realizes that this situation offers no compromise. In the
sacrifice of what he loves best, he leaves his own yearling days behind." Read Ladders for Hum Relat. 5th edition
    "With its excellent descriptions of Florida scrub land-
scapes, its skillful use of native vernacular, its tender relation between Jody and his pet fawn, The Yearling is a
simply written, picturesque story of boyhood." Time

Rawls, Wilson, 1913-1984
Where the red fern grows; the story of two dogs
and a boy. Bantam Bks. 1996 212p $16.95; pa
$5.99
Grades: 4 5 6 7   Fic
    1. Dogs—Fiction 2. Ozark Mountains—Fiction
    ISBN 0-385-32330-1; 0-440-41267-6 (pa)
    First published 1961 by Doubleday
"Looking back more than 50 years to his boyhood in
the Ozarks, the narrator, recalls how he achieved his
heart's desire in the ownership of two redbone hounds,
how he taught them all the tricks of hunting, and how
they won the championship coon hunt before Old Dan
was killed by a mountain lion and Little Ann died of
grief. Although some readers may find this novel hackneyed and entirely too sentimental, others will enjoy the
fine coonhunting episodes and appreciate the author's
feelings for nature." Booklist

Ray, Delia
Ghost girl; a Blue Ridge Mountain story.
Clarion Bks. 2003 216p il $15
Grades: 5 6 7 8   Fic
    1. Hoover, Herbert, 1874-1964—Fiction 2. Hoover,
    Lou Henry, 1874-1944—Fiction 3. School stories
    4. Teachers—Fiction 5. Virginia—Fiction
    ISBN 0-618-33377-0   LC 2003-4115
Eleven-year-old April is delighted when President and
Mrs. Hoover build a school near her Madison County,
Virginia, home but her family's poverty, grief over the
accidental death of her brother, and other problems may
mean that April can never learn to read from the wonderful teacher, Miss Vest
    "This excellent portrayal of four important years in a
girl's life rises to the top. Based on a real school and
teacher, this novel seamlessly incorporates historical facts
into the narrative." SLJ

Singing hands. Clarion Books 2006 248p il $16
Grades: 4 5 6 7   Fic
    1. Deaf—Fiction 2. Family life—Fiction 3. Clergy—
    Fiction 4. Alabama—Fiction
    ISBN 0-618-65762-2   LC 2005-22972

Ray, Delia—*Continued*

In the late 1940s, twelve-year-old Gussie, a minister's daughter, learns the definition of integrity while helping with a celebration at the Alabama School for the Deaf—her punishment for misdeeds against her deaf parents and their boarders.

"While the portrayal of a signing household is natural and convincing, the focus is on Gussie's rebellion and growth, the real heart of the story." Horn Book Guide

Rees, Douglas C.

Vampire High. Delacorte Press 2003 226p $15.95; lib bdg $17.99

Grades: 7 8 9 10   **Fic**

1. Vampires—Fiction 2. School stories 3. Massachusetts—Fiction

ISBN 0-385-73117-5; 0-385-90143-7 (lib bdg)

LC 2003-41992

When his family moves from California to New Sodom, Massachusetts and Cody enters Vlad Dracul Magnet School, many things seem strange, from the dark-haired, pale-skinned, supernaturally strong students to Charon, the wolf who guides him around campus on the first day

"There's barely a false note in this rollicking tale of horror, humor, and light romance that will appeal to both girls and boys." Booklist

Reeve, Philip, 1966-

Here lies Arthur. Scholastic Press 2008 339p $16.99 *

Grades: 7 8 9 10   **Fic**

1. Arthur, King—Fiction 2. Magic—Fiction 3. Great Britain—History—0-1066—Fiction

ISBN 978-0-545-09334-7; 0-545-09334-1

LC 2008-05787

When her village is attacked and burned, Gwyna seeks protection from the bard Myrddin, who uses Gwyna in his plan to transform young Arthur into the heroic King Arthur.

"Powerfully inventive. . . . Events rush headlong toward the inevitable ending, but Gwyna's observations illuminate them in a new way." Booklist

Starcross; or The coming of the moobs!, or Our adventures in the fourth dimension; a stirring adventure of spies, time travel and curious hats; as narrated by Art Mumby, Esq. (& Miss Myrtle Mumby) to their amanuensis, Mr Philip Reeve & illuminated throughout by David Wyatt. Bloomsbury U.S.A. Children's Books 2007 368p il $16.95

Grades: 5 6 7 8   **Fic**

1. Science fiction

ISBN 978-1-59990-121-3; 1-59990-121-8

LC 2007-12002

Another title in the author's series about the Mumby family

Sequel to: Larklight (2006)

Young Arthur Mumby, his sister Myrtle, and their mother accept an invitation to take a holiday at an up-and-coming resort in the asteroid belt, where they become involved in a dastardly plot involving spies, time travel, and mind-altering clothing.

"It's all very tongue-in-cheek with plenty of jokes and puns in the best traditions of British humor." Booklist

Followed by: Mothstorm (2008)

Reger, Rob

Emily the Strange: the lost days; [by] Rob Reger and Jessica Gruner; illustrated by Rob Reger and Buzz Parker. Harper 2009 266p il $16.99

Grades: 7 8 9 10   **Fic**

1. Amnesia—Fiction 2. Runaway teenagers—Fiction 3. Adventure fiction

ISBN 978-0-06-145229-1; 978-0-06-145230-7 (lib bdg)

LC 2008027225

Emily the Strange has lost her memory and finds herself in the town of Blackrock with nothing more than her diary, her slingshot, and the clothes on her back.

"The action moves along with no lulls, and none of the entries or illustrations are superfluous. This is a highly enjoyable read." SLJ

Reinhardt, Dana

How to build a house; a novel. Wendy Lamb Books 2008 227p $15.99; lib bdg $18.99 *

Grades: 8 9 10 11 12   **Fic**

1. Building—Fiction 2. Divorce—Fiction 3. Stepfamilies—Fiction 4. Volunteer work—Fiction 5. Tennessee—Fiction

ISBN 978-0-375-84453-9; 0-375-84453-8; 978-0-375-94454-3 (lib bdg); 0-375-94454-0 (lib bdg)

LC 2007-33403

Seventeen-year-old Harper Evans hopes to escape the effects of her father's divorce on her family and friendships by volunteering her summer to build a house in a small Tennessee town devastated by a tornado.

"This meticulously crafted book illustrates how both homes and relationships can be resurrected through hard work, hope and teamwork." Publ Wkly

Reisman, Michael, 1972-

Simon Bloom, the gravity keeper. Dutton Children's Books 2007 298p $15.99 *

Grades: 5 6 7 8   **Fic**

1. Extraterrestrial beings—Fiction 2. Physics—Fiction 3. Science fiction

ISBN 978-0-525-47922-2   LC 2006039046

Nerdy sixth-grader Simon Bloom finds a book that enables him to control the laws of physics, but when two thugs come after him, he needs the formulas in the book to save himself.

This is a "fast-paced, cinematic . . . novel. . . . It makes scientific concepts interesting and accessible." Publ Wkly

Another title about Simon Bloom is:

Simon Bloom, the octopus effect (2009)

Resau, Laura

Red glass. Delacorte Press 2007 275p $15.99; lib bdg $18.99 *

Grades: 7 8 9 10 **Fic**

1. Automobile travel—Fiction 2. Orphans—Fiction 3. Mexico—Fiction 4. Guatemala—Fiction 5. Family life—Fiction

ISBN 978-0-385-73466-0; 0-385-73466-2; 978-0-385-90464-3 (lib bdg); 0-385-90464-9 (lib bdg)

LC 2007-02408

Sixteen-year-old Sophie has been frail and delicate since her premature birth, but discovers her true strength during a journey through Mexico, where the six-year-old orphan her family hopes to adopt was born, and to Guatemala, where her would-be boyfriend hopes to find his mother and plans to remain.

"The vivid characters, the fine imagery, and the satisfying story arc make this a rewarding novel." Booklist

What the moon saw; a novel. Delacorte Press 2006 258p $15.95; lib bdg $17.99 *

Grades: 5 6 7 8 **Fic**

1. Mexico—Fiction 2. Country life—Fiction 3. Grandparents—Fiction

ISBN 0-385-73343-7; 0-385-90360-X (lib bdg)

LC 2006-04571

Fourteen-year-old Clara Luna spends the summer with her grandparents in the tiny, remote village of Yucuyoo, Mexico, learning about her grandmother's life as a healer, her father's decision to leave home for the United States, and her own place in the world.

This is an "exquisitely crafted narrative. . . . The characters are well developed. . . . Resau does an exceptional job of portraying the agricultural society sympathetically and realistically." SLJ

Rettig, Liz

My desperate love diary. Holiday House 2007 313p $16.95

Grades: 7 8 9 10 11 12 **Fic**

1. Love stories 2. Family life—Fiction

ISBN 978-0-8234-2033-9; 0-8234-2033-7

LC 2006-43647

High-school student Kelly chronicles her year of family problems and the pursuit of the guy she has a crush on, while not realizing that she herself is the object of pursuit by Chris, her closest male friend.

"Rettig freshens a standard story through clever humor and subplots." Bull Cent Child Books

Rex, Adam

The true meaning of Smekday. Hyperion Books for Children 2007 423p il $16.99 *

Grades: 5 6 7 8 **Fic**

1. End of the world—Fiction 2. Science fiction 3. Extraterrestrial beings—Fiction

ISBN 0-7868-4900-2; 978-0-7868-4900-0

When her mother is abducted by aliens on Christmas Eve (or "Smekday" Eve since the Boov invasion), 11 year-old Tip hops in the family car and heads south to find her and meets an alien Boov mechanic who agrees to help her and save the planet from disaster.

"Incorporating dozens of his weird and wonderful illustrations and fruitfully manipulating the narrative structure, Rex skewers any number of subjects." Publ Wkly

Rich, Naomi

Alis. Viking Children's Books 2009 274p $17.99 *

Grades: 7 8 9 10 **Fic**

1. Marriage—Fiction 2. Runaway teenagers—Fiction 3. Religion—Fiction

ISBN 978-0-670-01125-4; 0-670-01125-8

LC 2008-23234

Raised within the strict religious confines of the Community of the Book, Alis flees from an arranged marriage to the much older Minister of her town and her life takes a series of unexpected twists before she returns to accept her fate.

"Rich's sympathetic portrayal of Alis and her desperate struggle to exercise free will in a theocracy will have audiences firmly gripped." Publ Wkly

Richards, Justin, 1961-

The chaos code. Bloomsbury Children's Books 2007 388p $17.95

Grades: 7 8 9 10 **Fic**

1. Ciphers—Fiction 2. Adventure fiction 3. Supernatural—Fiction 4. Atlantis—Fiction 5. Mystery fiction

ISBN 978-1-59990-124-4; 1-59990-124-2

LC 2006-102609

Fifteen-year-old Matt and his new friend Robin search the globe to retrieve an ancient code—rumored to have brought down the ancient civilization of Atlantis—from the hands of a madman who is bent on destroying the modern world.

"This novel combines intrigue, adventure, and cryptography with masterful pacing and age-old mysteries. . . . Riveting." Voice Youth Advocates

Richter, Conrad, 1890-1968

The light in the forest. Everyman's Library 2005 c1953 176p $14.95; pa $6.50

Grades: 7 8 9 10 **Fic**

1. Frontier and pioneer life—Fiction 2. Delaware Indians—Fiction

ISBN 1-4000-4426-X; 1-4000-7788-5 (pa)

First published 1953 by Knopf

"A boy stolen in early childhood and brought up by the Delawares is at fifteen suddenly returned to the family he has forgotten. He resents his loss of independence, hates the brutality of the white man's civilization, and longs only for a return to the Indians whom he remembers as peace-loving and kind. His return to the Delawares does not, however, bring him peace; rather, he must make a bitter choice between helping his indian brothers kill agroup of unsuspecting white men or helping the white men escape. This is both vivid re-creation of outdoor life and a provocative study in conflicting loyalties." Horn Book

Rinaldi, Ann, 1934-
Come Juneteenth. Harcourt 2007 246p (Great episodes) $17
Grades: 6 7 8 9   **Fic**
1. Slavery—Fiction 2. African Americans—Fiction
3. Family life—Fiction 4. Texas—Fiction
5. Juneteenth—Fiction
ISBN 978-0-15-05947-7; 0-15-205947-4
LC 2006-21458
Fourteen-year-old Luli and her family face tragedy after failing to tell their slaves that President Lincoln's Emancipation Proclamation made them free.
"Luli's authentic voice demonstrates Rinaldi's ability to evoke the human side of history." SLJ

The Ever-After Bird. Harcourt 2007 232p $17
Grades: 7 8 9 10 11 12   **Fic**
1. Slavery—Fiction 2. Abolitionists—Fiction
3. Underground railroad—Fiction 4. Birds—Fiction
5. Uncles—Fiction 6. Georgia—Fiction
ISBN 978-0-15-202620-2; 0-15-202620-7
LC 2006-101592
In 1851, thirteen-year-old Cecilia has her eyes opened to the horrors of slavery when she accompanies her ornithologist uncle on an expedition in search of the rare Scarlet Ibis, and watches as he shows slaves the way to the Underground Railroad.
"This riveting historical novel will push young teens through the black-and-white questions of childhood into the inevitable gray areas of adolescence." Booklist

The fifth of March; a story of the Boston Massacre. Harcourt Brace & Co. 1993 335p (Great episodes) pa $6.95 *
Grades: 7 8 9 10   **Fic**
1. Adams family—Fiction 2. Boston Massacre, 1770—Fiction 3. United States—History—1600-1775, Colonial period—Fiction
ISBN 0-15-205078-7 (pa)   LC 93-17821
"Gulliver books"
Fourteen-year-old Rachel Marsh, an indentured servant in the Boston household of John and Abigail Adams, is caught up in the colonists' unrest that eventually escalates into the massacre of March 5, 1770.
"The story moves along briskly, and details of life in 18th-century Boston are woven into the narrative." SLJ

Girl in blue. Scholastic Press 2001 310p hardcover o.p. pa $5.99
Grades: 6 7 8 9   **Fic**
1. Greenhow, Rose O'Neal, 1817-1864—Fiction
2. United States—History—1861-1865, Civil War—Fiction 3. Sex role—Fiction 4. Spies—Fiction
ISBN 0-439-07336-7; 0-439-67646-0 (pa)
LC 00-41945
To escape an abusive father and an arranged marriage, fourteen-year-old Sarah, dressed as a boy, leaves her Michigan home to enlist in the Union Army, and becomes a soldier on the battlefields of Virginia as well as a Union spy working in the house of Confederate sympathizer Rose O'Neal Greenhow in Washington, D.C.
"This first-person novel will engage readers through its sympathetic main character and exciting action." Booklist

The redheaded princess. HarperCollinsPublishers 2008 214p $15.99; lib bdg $16.89
Grades: 6 7 8 9   **Fic**
1. Elizabeth I, Queen of England, 1533-1603—Fiction
2. Great Britain—History—1485-1603, Tudors—Fiction
ISBN 978-0-06-073374-2; 0-06-073374-8;
978-0-06-073375-9 (lib bdg); 0-06-073375-6 (lib bdg)
LC 2007-18577
In 1542, nine-year-old Lady Elizabeth lives on an estate near London, striving to get back into the good graces of her father, King Henry VIII, and as the years pass she faces his death and those of other close relatives until she finds herself next in line to ascend the throne of England in 1558.
"The rich scene-setting and believable, appealing heroine will satisfy Rinaldi's many fans." Booklist

An unlikely friendship; a novel of Mary Todd Lincoln and Elizabeth Keckley. Harcourt 2007 241p $17
Grades: 6 7 8 9   **Fic**
1. Lincoln, Mary Todd, 1818-1882—Fiction
2. Keckley, Elizabeth, ca. 1818-1907—Fiction
3. Slavery—Fiction 4. Friendship—Fiction
ISBN 0-15-205597-5   LC 2005-30210
Relates the lives of Mary Todd Lincoln, raised in a wealthy Virginia family, and Lizzy Keckley, a dressmaker born a slave, as they grow up separately then become best friends when Mary's childhood dream of living in the White House comes true.
This "story is fascinating and filled with remarkable gems of historical memorabilia to create a very satisfying read." Voice Youth Advocates

Riordan, Rick
The lightning thief. Miramax Books/Hyperion Books for Children 2005 377p (Percy Jackson & the Olympians) $17.95 *
Grades: 6 7 8 9   **Fic**
1. Classical mythology—Fiction
ISBN 0-7868-5629-7   LC 2005-299400
Twelve-year-old Percy Jackson learns he is a demigod, the son of a mortal woman and Poseidon, god of the sea. His mother sends him to a summer camp for demigods where he and his new friends set out on a quest to prevent a war between the gods.
"Riordan's fast-paced adventure is fresh, dangerous, and funny." Booklist
Other titles in this series are:
The Sea of Monsters (2006)
The Titan's curse (2007)
The battle of the Labyrinth (2008)
The last Olympian (2009)

The maze of bones. Scholastic 2008 220p il (The 39 clues) $12.99 *
Grades: 4 5 6 7   **Fic**
1. Ciphers—Fiction 2. Family—Fiction
ISBN 978-0-545-06039-4; 0-545-06039-7
At the reading of their grandmother's will, Dan and Amy Cahill are given the choice of receiving a million dollars or uncovering the 39 clues hidden around the world that will lead to the source of the family's power,

Riordan, Rick—*Continued*
but by taking on the clues, they end up in a dangerous race against their own family members.

"Adeptly incorporating a genuine kids' perspective, the narrative unfolds like a boulder rolling downhill and keeps readers glued to the pages. . . . The book dazzles with suspense, plot twists, and snappy humor." SLJ

Other titles in this series are:
One false note by Gordon Korman (2008)
The sword thief by Peter Lerangis (2009)
Beyond the grave by Jude Watson (2009)

Ritter, John H., 1951-
The boy who saved baseball. Philomel Books 2003 216p $17.99
Grades: 5 6 7 8   **Fic**
1. Baseball—Fiction
ISBN 0-399-23622-8   LC 2002-15792
A prequel to this title is: The desperado who stole baseball (2009)

The fate of a small California town rests on the outcome of one baseball game, and Tom Gallagher hopes to lead his team to victory with the secrets of the now disgraced player, Dante Del Gato

"This tale is peppered with both optimism and dilemmas; it has plenty of play-by-play action, lots of humor, and a triumphant ending." SLJ

Choosing up sides. Philomel Bks. 1998 166p $17.99; pa $5.99
Grades: 6 7 8 9   **Fic**
1. Left- and right-handedness—Fiction 2. Father-son relationship—Fiction 3. Baseball—Fiction
ISBN 0-399-23185-4; 0-689-11840-5 (pa)
                                              LC 97-39779
"In 1921 Ohio, a minister's son is condemned by his father because of his natural inclination for using his left hand. Luke discovers he has a talent for playing baseball, although Pa disdains sports—especially a game that utilizes Luke's 'evil' hand." Horn Book Guide

"This is an entertaining and thought-provoking coming-of-age story." Book Rep

The desperado who stole baseball. Philomel Books 2009 260p il $17.99
Grades: 5 6 7 8   **Fic**
1. Billy, the Kid—Fiction 2. Baseball—Fiction 3. Orphans—Fiction 4. Frontier and pioneer life—Fiction 5. California—Fiction
ISBN 978-0-399-24664-7; 0-399-24664-9
                                              LC 2008-16901
Prequel to: The boy who saved baseball

In 1881, the scrappy, rough-and-tumble baseball team in a California mining town enlists the help of a quick-witted twelve-year-old orphan and the notorious outlaw Billy the Kid to win a big game against the National League Champion Chicago White Stockings.

"This tall-tale page-turner stands alone though it will be most appreciated by fans of Ritter's earlier works." SLJ

Under the baseball moon. Philomel Books 2006 283p $16.99
Grades: 7 8 9 10   **Fic**
1. Softball—Fiction 2. Musicians—Fiction 3. California—Fiction
ISBN 0-399-23623-6   LC 2005-27183
Andy and Glory, two fifteen-year-olds from Ocean Beach, California, pursue their respective dreams of becoming a famous musician and a professional softball player.

"Andy's poetic first-person narrative superbly catches the weird uniqueness of Ocean Beach and briskly moves the . . . story to a satisfying conclusion." SLJ

Roberts, Kristi
My 13th season; [by] Kristi Roberts. Henry Holt 2005 154p $15.95
Grades: 5 6 7 8   **Fic**
1. Baseball—Fiction 2. Sex role—Fiction 3. Bereavement—Fiction
ISBN 0-8050-7495-3   LC 2004-52368
Already downhearted due to the loss of her mother and her father's overwhelming grief, thirteen-year-old Fran decides to give up her dream of becoming the first female in professional baseball after a coach attacks her just for being a girl.

"Funny, harsh, and poignant by turns, this strong first-person narrative establishes Fran's character through the most colorful, accessible side of her story before gradually letting readers in on her rich inner life of imagination, memory, and dreams." Booklist

Roberts, Marion, 1966-
Sunny side up. Wendy Lamb Books 2009 c2008 244p il $15.99
Grades: 4 5 6 7   **Fic**
1. Family life—Fiction 2. Friendship—Fiction 3. Australia—Fiction
ISBN 978-0-385-73672-5; 0-385-73672-X
                                              LC 2008-08633
First published 2008 in Australia

As the hot Australian summer draws to an end, eleven-year-old Sunny, content to be an only child with amicably divorced parents, finds her life getting much too complicated when her mother's boyfriend moves in with his two children, her best friend begins to develop an interest in boys, and she is contacted by her long-estranged grandmother.

"Character development is strong, as the girl is quick to observe and comment on the people in her life, and the setting forms an interesting backdrop. Small black-and-white photos are liberally scattered throughout." SLJ

Roberts, Willo Davis, 1928-2004
The kidnappers. Atheneum Bks. for Young Readers 1998 137p hardcover o.p. pa $4.99
Grades: 4 5 6 7   **Fic**
1. Kidnapping—Fiction 2. Wealth—Fiction 3. New York (N.Y.)—Fiction
ISBN 0-689-81394-5; 0-689-81393-7 (pa)
                                              LC 96-53677
"A Jean Karl book"

Roberts, Willo Davis, 1928-2004—*Continued*

No one believes eleven-year-old Joey, who has a reputation for telling tall tales, when he claims to have witnessed the kidnapping of the class bully outside their expensive New York City private school

"The combination of a witty narrative and a suspenseful plot makes this a good page-turner that will leave even the most reluctant readers glued to their seats." Booklist

Robinet, Harriette Gillem, 1931-

Walking to the bus-rider blues. Atheneum Bks. for Young Readers 2000 146p hardcover o.p. pa $4.99

Grades: 5 6 7 8   **Fic**
1. African Americans—Fiction 2. Race relations—Fiction
ISBN 0-689-83191-9; 0-689-83886-7 (pa)

                       LC 99-29054

"A Jean Karl book"

Twelve-year-old Alfa Merryfield, his older sister, and their grandmother struggle for rent money, food, and their dignity as they participate in the Montgomery, Alabama bus boycott in the summer of 1956

"Ingredients of mystery, suspense, and humor enhance and personalize this well-constructed story that offers insight into a troubled era." SLJ

Robinson, Barbara

The best Christmas pageant ever; pictures by Judith Gwyn Brown. Harper & Row 1972 80p il $15.99; lib bdg $16.89; pa $5.99 *

Grades: 4 5 6   **Fic**
1. Christmas—Fiction 2. Pageants—Fiction
ISBN 0-06-025043-7; 0-06-025044-5 (lib bdg); 0-06-447044-X (pa)

In this story the six Herdmans, "absolutely the worst kids in the history of the world," discover the meaning of Christmas when they bully their way into the leading roles of the local church nativity play

The story "romps through the festive preparations with comic relish, and if the Herdmans are so gauche as to seem exaggerated, they are still enjoyable, as are the not-so-subtle pokes at pageant-planning in general." Bull Cent Child Books

Other titles about the Herdmans are:
The best Halloween ever (2004)
The best school year ever (1994)

Rodda, Emily, 1948-

The key to Rondo. Scholastic Press 2008 342p $16.99 *

Grades: 5 6 7 8   **Fic**
1. Fantasy fiction 2. Cousins—Fiction 3. Magic—Fiction
ISBN 0-545-03535-X; 978-0-545-03535-4

                       LC 2007-16873

Through an heirloom music box, Leo, a serious, responsible boy, and his badly-behaved cousin Mimi enter the magical world of Rondo to rescue Mimi's dog from a sorceress, who wishes to exchange him for the key that allows free travel between worlds.

"Rodda fills the cousins' quest with image-rich prose and compelling action." Bull Cent Child Books

Rodgers, Mary, 1931-

Freaky Friday. Harper & Row 1972 145p $15.95; lib bdg $16.89; pa $5.99 *

Grades: 4 5 6 7   **Fic**
1. Mother-daughter relationship—Fiction
ISBN 0-06-025048-8; 0-06-025049-6 (lib bdg); 0-06-057010-5 (pa)

"'When I woke up this morning, I found I'd turned into my mother.' So begins the most bizarre day in the life of 13-year-old Annabel Andrews, who discovers one Friday morning she has taken on her mother's physical characteristics while retaining her own personality. Readers will giggle in anticipation as Annabel plunges madly from one disaster to another trying to cope with various adult situations." Publ Wkly

"A fresh, imaginative, and entertaining story." Bull Cent Child Books

Rodman, Mary Ann

Jimmy's stars. Farrar, Straus & Giroux 2008 257p $16.95 *

Grades: 5 6 7 8   **Fic**
1. World War, 1939-1945—Fiction 2. Siblings—Fiction 3. Soldiers—Fiction 4. Family life—Fiction 5. Pittsburgh (Pa.)—Fiction
ISBN 978-0-374-33703-2; 0-374-33703-9

                       LC 2007-05091

In 1943, eleven-year-old Ellie is her brother Jimmy's "best girl," and when he leaves Pittsburgh just before Thanksgiving to fight in World War II, he promises he will return, asks her to leave the Christmas tree up until he does, and reminds her to "let the joy out."

Rodman "finds beauty in every emotional nuance. . . . The lively spirit of working-class Pittsburgh . . . extends Ellie's person story with a broader sense of home-front life." Booklist

Rollins, James, 1961-

Jake Ransom and the Skull King's shadow. HarperCollins 2009 399p $16.99; lib bdg $17.89

Grades: 5 6 7 8   **Fic**
1. Adventure fiction 2. Mayas—Fiction 3. Archeology—Fiction 4. Siblings—Fiction
ISBN 978-0-06-147379-1; 0-06-147379-0; 978-0-06-147380-7 (lib bdg); 0-06-147380-4 (lib bdg)

Connecticut middle-schooler Jake and his older sister Kady are transported by a Mayan artifact to a strange world inhabited by a mix of people from long-lost civilizations who are threatened by prehistoric creatures and an evil alchemist, the Skull King.

This is an "exciting time-travel adventure. . . . Rollins . . . presents a wide range of interesting historical information while telling a rollicking good story that should please a wide range of readers." Publ Wkly

Roorda, Julie

Wings of a bee; by Julie Roorda. Sumach Press 2007 220p pa $9.95

Grades: 6 7 8 9   **Fic**

Roorda, Julie—*Continued*
1. Cerebral palsy—Fiction 2. Sisters—Fiction
3. Bees—Fiction 4. Ghost stories
ISBN 978-1-894549-68-4; 1-894549-68-6
Bronwyn doesn't see things quite like the rest of the girls do. Her little sister Carey, who has celebral palsy, is the only person who truly gets Bronwyn, But as Carey gets sicker and their mother gets more and more distracted, Bronwyn tries to carry on as usual until she is shaken by a frightening experience of her own.

"In this carefully crafted debut novel, author Roorda subtly contrasts Bronwyn's growth and maturity with Carey's gradual decline, all the while focusing on Carey's vibrant, if shortened, life and Bronwyn's expanding opportunities. Both girls are vivid characters." Booklist

Rosen, Renée
Every crooked pot. St. Martin's Griffin 2007 227p pa $8.95 *
Grades: 7 8 9 10   **Fic**
1. Father-daughter relationship—Fiction 2. Birth defects—Fiction
ISBN 978-0-312-36543-1; 0-312-36543-8
LC 2007-10457
"Rosen looks back at the life of Nina Goldman, whose growing up is tied to two pillars: a port-wine stain around her eye and her inimitable father, Artie. The birthmark, she hates; her father, she loves. Both shape her in ways that merit Rosen's minute investigation. . . . There's real power in the writing." Booklist

Rosenbloom, Fiona
You are so not invited to my bat mitzvah! Hyperion 2005 190p lib bdg $15.99
Grades: 4 5 6 7   **Fic**
1. Bat mitzvah—Fiction 2. Jews—Fiction
ISBN 0-7868-5616-5   LC 2005046398
As her bat mitzvah approaches, Stacy Adelaide Friedman of White Plains, New York, has a lot on her mind—her parents have separated, her mother dresses her like an American Girl doll, her younger brother is embarrassing, and she is totally in love with Andy Goldfarb.

"Stacy is a realistic thirteen-year-old: funny, kindhearted, loving, gossipy, envious, brand-obsessed, and self-centered. . . . This book is a fun, fast must-read." Voice of Youth Advocates

Rosten, Carrie
Chloe Leiberman (sometimes Wong); a novel. Delacorte Press 2005 210p $15.95 *
Grades: 7 8 9 10   **Fic**
1. School stories 2. Jews—Fiction 3. Chinese Americans—Fiction 4. Racially mixed people—Fiction
ISBN 0-385-73247-3
Chloe, an aspiring fashion designer, dreams of going to design school in London, but first has to tell her parents that she does not plan to go to college.

"Plainly having inherited her grandfather Leo Rosten's gift for ethnic-flavored comedy, the author places her sympathetically portrayed 17-year-old misfit in a broadly brushed Jewish-Chinese-Valley Girl milieu." Booklist

Rowling, J. K.
Harry Potter and the Sorcerer's Stone; illustrations by Mary Grandpré. Arthur A. Levine Bks. 1998 c1997 309p il $22.99; pa $8.99 *
Grades: 4 5 6 7 8 9 10   **Fic**
1. Fantasy fiction 2. Witches—Fiction
ISBN 0-590-35340-3; 0-590-35342-X (pa)
LC 97-39059
First published 1997 in the United Kingdom with title: Harry Potter and the Philosopher's Stone
Rescued from the outrageous neglect of his aunt and uncle, a young boy with a great destiny proves his worth while attending Hogwarts School for Witchcraft and Wizardry.

This "is a brilliantly imagined and beautifully written fantasy." Booklist
Other titles in this series are:
Harry Potter and the Chamber of Secrets (1999)
Harry Potter and prisoner of Azkaban (1999)
Harry Potter and Goblet of Fire (2000)
Harry Potter and the Order of the Phoenix (2003)
Harry Potter and the Half-Blood Prince (2005)
Harry Potter and the Deathly Hallows (2007)

Roy, James, 1968-
Max Quigley; technically not a bully; written and illustrated by James Roy. Houghton Mifflin Harcourt 2009 202p il $12.95
Grades: 4 5 6   **Fic**
1. Bullies—Fiction 2. Friendship—Fiction
ISBN 978-0-547-15263-9; 0-547-15263-9
LC 2008-36110
First published 2007 in Australia
After playing a prank on one of his "geeky" classmates, sixth-grader Max Quigley's punishment is to be tutored by him.

"Straightforward chronology, believable dialogue, self-contained chapters, and plenty of humor make this accessible to reluctant readers and particularly appealing to boys who may see a bit of themselves in this realistic school story." Booklist

Roy, Jennifer Rozines
Yellow star; by Jennifer Roy. Marshall Cavendish 2006 227p $16.95 *
Grades: 5 6 7 8   **Fic**
1. Holocaust, 1933-1945—Fiction 2. Jews—Fiction
3. Poland—Fiction
ISBN 978-0-7614-5277-5; 0-7614-5277-X
LC 2005-50788
From 1939, when Syvia is four and a half years old, to 1945 when she has just turned ten, a Jewish girl and her family struggle to survive in Poland's Lodz ghetto during the Nazi occupation.

"In a thoughtful, vividly descriptive, almost poetic prose, Roy retells the true story of her Aunt Syvia's experiences. . . . This book is a standout in the genre of Holocaust literature." SLJ

Ruby, Laura

Lily's ghosts. HarperCollins Pubs. 2003 258p
$16.99; lib bdg $17.89

Grades: 5 6 7 8   **Fic**
1. Ghost stories
ISBN 0-06-051829-4; 0-06-051830-8 (lib bdg)
LC 2002-154315

Strange goings-on at her great-uncle's summer home
in Cape May, New Jersey, draw Lily and a new friend
into a mystery involving lost treasure, a fake medium,
and ghosts of all sizes, shapes, and dispositions

"Ruby doesn't horrify so much as she insinuates, in
gracefully nuanced language that provides chilling support for the action." Bull Cent Child Books

Play me. HarperTeen 2008 311p $16.99

Grades: 8 9 10 11 12   **Fic**
1. Video recording—Fiction 2. Dating (Social cus-
toms)—Fiction 3. Mothers—Fiction 4. Stepfamilies—
Fiction
ISBN 978-0-06-124327-1; 0-06-124327-2
LC 2008-07117

Disappointed when he does not get the MTV production deal he so wants, high school senior Eddy leaves his
girlfriend to take a road trip to find the mother who has
left him and his younger stepbrother and taken a bit part
in a television show.

"Guy lit with a brain and a heart, this has plenty to
offer both romantics and cynics about love, film, and
transformation." Bull Cent Child Books

Ruby, Lois, 1942-

The secret of Laurel Oaks. Tom Doherty
Associates 2008 282p $16.95

Grades: 6 7 8 9   **Fic**
1. Slavery—Fiction 2. Louisiana—Fiction 3. Ghost
stories
ISBN 978-0-7653-1366-9; 0-7653-1366-9
LC 2008-28395

"A Starscape book"

While staying with her family in Louisiana's Laurel
Oaks Plantation, purported to be one of the most haunted
places in America, thirteen-year-old Lila is contacted by
the ghost of a slave girl unjustly convicted of murder.
Story inspired by the author's visit to the Myrtles Plantation in Louisiana.

"Ruby succeeds in writing a captivating story about a
time long gone, portraying the horror of slavery effectively." Libr Media Connect

Shanghai shadows. Holiday House 2006 284p
$16.95

Grades: 7 8 9 10   **Fic**
1. Jews—Fiction 2. China—Fiction 3. World War,
1939-1945—Fiction
ISBN 0-8234-1960-6; 978-0-8234-1960-9
LC 2005-50342

From 1939 to 1945, a Jewish family struggles to survive in occupied China; young Ilse by remaining optimistic, her older brother by joining a resistance movement, her mother by maintaining connections to the past,
and her father by playing the violin that had been his
livelihood.

The author's "careful research, courageous characters,
low-key descriptions of fear and misery, and understated

examples of love, friendship, and courage will further
readers' understanding and personalize the often-
horrifying epoch." Booklist

Includes bibliographical references

Runholt, Susan, 1948-

The mystery of the third Lucretia. Viking
Childrens Books 2008 288p $16.99

Grades: 5 6 7 8 9 10   **Fic**
1. Art—Fiction 2. Europe—Fiction 3. Friendship—
Fiction 4. Mystery fiction
ISBN 978-0-670-06252-2; 0-670-06252-9
LC 2007-24009

While traveling in London, Paris, and Amsterdam,
fourteen-year-old best friends Kari and Lucas solve an
international art forgery mystery.

"There are enough artistic details for fans of art mysteries and enough spying and fleeing for fans of detective
adventure." Bull Cent Child Books

Runyon, Brent

Surface tension; a novel in four summers.
Alfred A. Knopf 2009 197p $16.99; lib bdg
$19.99

Grades: 8 9 10 11   **Fic**
1. Vacations—Fiction 2. Family life—Fiction 3. New
York (State)—Fiction
ISBN   978-0-375-84446-1;   0-375-84446-5;
978-0-375-94446-8 (lib bdg); 0-375-94446-X (lib bdg)
LC 2008-9193

During the summer vacations of his thirteenth through
his sixteenth year at the family's lake cottage, Luke realizes that although some things stay the same over the
years that many more change.

"With sensitivity and candor, Runyon reveals how life
changes us all and how these unavoidable changes can
be full of both turmoil and wonder." Kirkus

Rushton, Rosie

Friends, enemies. Hyperion 2004 c2003 225p
$15.99

Grades: 6 7 8 9   **Fic**
1. Friendship—Fiction
ISBN 0-786-85177-5

First published 2003 in the United Kingdom with title:
Friends, enemies, and other tiny problems

When fourteen-year-old Tory and her circle reluctantly
befriend Hannah, they uncover deceit and hidden family
crises.

"The plot snaps along at as brisk a pace as the characters' lives. . . . The relationships are strong and realistic." SLJ

Russell, Christopher, 1947-

Dogboy. Greenwillow Books 2006 259p $15.99;
lib bdg $16.89

Grades: 5 6 7 8   **Fic**
1. Knights and knighthood—Fiction 2. Orphans—Fiction 3. Dogs—Fiction 4. Hundred Years' War, 1339-
1453—Fiction 5. Middle Ages—Fiction
ISBN   0-06-084116-8;   978-0-06-084116-4;
0-06-084117-6 (lib bdg); 978-0-06-084117-1 (lib bdg)
LC 2005-08525

Russell, Christopher, 1947-—_Continued_

First published 2005 in the United Kingdom

In 1346, twelve-year-old Brind, an orphaned kennel boy raised with hunting dogs at an English manor, accompanies his master, along with half of the manor's prized mastiffs, to France, where he must fend for himself when both his master and the dogs are lost at the decisive battle of Crécy.

"The action is fast-paced with narrow escapes at every turn and elements of dry humor at the most unlikely times." SLJ

Followed by Hunted (2007)

Russo, Marisabina, 1950-

A portrait of Pia. Harcourt 2007 221p $17

Grades: 4 5 6 7   Fic

1. Father-daughter relationship—Fiction
2. Friendship—Fiction 3. Siblings—Fiction 4. Italy—Fiction 5. Mentally ill—Fiction

ISBN 978-0-15-205577-6; 0-15-205577-6

LC 2006-08758

As childhood friendships change, her brother's schizophrenia worsens, and her mother's latest boyfriend seems likely to become her stepfather, twelve-year-old artist Pia Crossley tries to gain control of her life by contacting her father, who returned home to Italy before she was born.

"Relationships are portrayed clearly, and the school scenes are believable. Middle-school girls will find it easy to relate to Pia's uncertainties as well as to her solutions." Booklist

Rutkoski, Marie

The Cabinet of Wonders; [by] Marie Rutkoski. Farrar Straus Giroux 2008 258p (The Kronos Chronicles) $16.95 *

Grades: 5 6 7 8   Fic

1. Magic—Fiction 2. Princes—Fiction 3. Gypsies—Fiction 4. Fantasy fiction

ISBN 978-0-374-31026-4; 0-374-31026-2

LC 2007037702

Twelve-year-old Petra, accompanied by her magical tin spider, goes to Prague hoping to retrieve the enchanted eyes the Prince of Bohemia took from her father, and is aided in her quest by a Roma boy and his sister.

"Add this heady mix of history and enchantment to the season's list of astonishingly accomplished first novels. . . . Infusions of folklore (and Rutkowski's embellishments of them) don't slow the fast plot but more deeply entrance readers." Publ Wkly

Ryan, Amy Kathleen

Vibes; written by Amy Kathleen Ryan. Houghton Mifflin 2008 249p $16

Grades: 7 8 9 10   Fic

1. Parapsychology—Fiction 2. School stories
3. Family life—Fiction

ISBN 978-0-618-99530-1; 0-618-99530-7

Kristi, a sophomore in an alternative high school, is aware that nearly everyone dislikes her—even those obsessed by her large breasts—but begins to doubt her psychic insights after learning long-held family secrets and

some classmates' true feelings.

This "is a sweet, undemanding, yet consistently entertaining read with a good deal of insight into the way slightly off-center teenage girls construct their manic inner worlds." Bull Cent Child Books

Ryan, Pam Muñoz

Esperanza rising. Scholastic Press 2000 262p $15.95; pa $4.99

Grades: 5 6 7 8   Fic

1. Mexican Americans—Fiction 2. Agricultural laborers—Fiction 3. California—Fiction

ISBN 0-439-12041-1; 0-439-12042-X (pa)

LC 00-24186

Esperanza and her mother are forced to leave their life of wealth and privilege in Mexico to go work in the labor camps of Southern California, where they must adapt to the harsh circumstances facing Mexican farm workers on the eve of the Great Depression

"Ryan writes movingly in clear, poetic language that children will sink into, and the [book] offers excellent opportunities for discussion and curriculum support." Booklist

Ryan, Patrick, 1965-

Saints of Augustine; [by] P.E. Ryan. HarperTeen 2007 308p $16.99; lib bdg $17.89 *

Grades: 8 9 10 11 12   Fic

1. Friendship—Fiction 2. Homosexuality—Fiction
3. Death—Fiction 4. Florida—Fiction

ISBN 978-0-06-085810-0; 0-06-085810-9; 978-0-06-085811-7 (lib bdg); 0-06-085811-7 (lib bdg)

LC 2006019519

In St. Augustine, Florida, former best friends Charlie Perrin and Sam Findley, now both sixteen, come to realize that their friendship is the only thing that will keep them afloat when each of their worlds is turned upside down through death, divorce, and the seemingly out-of-control direction of their lives.

"Teens will find both boys' storylines (and narrative voices) thoroughly compelling right through to the end." Publ Wkly

Rylant, Cynthia

A fine white dust. Simon & Schuster 2000 c1986 106p $25; pa $2.99 *

Grades: 5 6 7 8   Fic

1. Religion—Fiction 2. Friendship—Fiction 3. Family life—Fiction

ISBN 978-0-689-84087-6; 0-689-84087-X; 978-1-4169-4828-5 (pa); 1-4169-4828-7 (pa)

A Newbery Medal honor book, 1987

A reissue of the title first published 1986 by Bradbury Press

The visit of the traveling Preacher Man to his small North Carolina town gives new impetus to thirteen-year-old Peter's struggle to reconcile his own deeply felt religious belief with the beliefs and non-beliefs of his family and friends

"Blending humor and intense emotion with a poetic use of language, Cynthia Rylant has created a taut, finely drawn portrait of a boy's growth from seeking for belief, through seduction and betrayal, to a spiritual acceptance and a readiness 'for something whole.'" Horn Book

Rylant, Cynthia—_Continued_

Missing May. Orchard Bks. 1992 89p $14.95;
pa $5.99 *

Grades: 5 6 7 8   **Fic**
1. Death—Fiction 2. West Virginia—Fiction
ISBN 0-531-05996-0; 0-439-61383-3 (pa)
LC 91-23303

Awarded the Newbery Medal, 1993
"A Richard Jackson book"
After the death of the beloved aunt who has raised
her, twelve-year-old Summer and her uncle Ob leave
their West Virginia trailer in search of the strength to go
on living
"There is much to ponder here, from the meaning of
life and death to the power of love. That it all succeeds
is a tribute to a fine writer who brings to the task a natural grace of language, an earthly sense of humor, and a
well-grounded sense of the spiritual." SLJ

Sachar, Louis, 1954-
Holes; [by] Louis Sachar. 10th anniversary ed.
Farrar, Straus and Giroux 2008 c1998 265p $18 *

Grades: 5 6 7 8   **Fic**
1. Juvenile delinquency—Fiction 2. Homeless per-
sons—Fiction 3. Friendship—Fiction 4. Buried treasure—Fiction
ISBN 978-0-374-33266-2; 0-374-33266-5
LC 2007045430

Awarded the Newbery Medal, 1999
"Frances Foster books"
A reissue of the title first published 1998. Includes additional information about the author and his Newbery
acceptance speech.
As further evidence of his family's bad fortune which
they attribute to a curse on a distant relative, Stanley
Yelnats is sent to a hellish correctional camp in the Texas desert where he finds his first real friend, a treasure,
and a new sense of himself.
"This delightfully clever story is well-crafted and
thought-provoking, with a bit of a folklore thrown in for
good measure." Voice Youth Advocates

Small steps; [by] Louis Sachar. Delacorte Press
2006 257p $16.95; lib bdg $19.99

Grades: 5 6 7 8   **Fic**
1. Juvenile delinquency—Fiction 2. Cerebral palsy—
Fiction 3. African Americans—Fiction
ISBN 0-385-73314-3; 0-385-90333-2 (lib bdg)
LC 2005-09102

Sequel to Holes
Three years after being released from Camp Green
Lake, Armpit is trying hard to keep his life on track, but
when his old pal X-Ray shows up with a tempting plan
to make some easy money scalping concert tickets, Armpit reluctantly goes along.
This "is a story of redemption, of the triumph of the
human spirit, of self-sacrifice, and of doing the right
thing. Sachar is a master storyteller who creates memorable characters." SLJ

Sachs, Marilyn, 1927-
Lost in America. Roaring Brook Press 2005
150p $16.95

Grades: 5 6 7 8   **Fic**
1. Jews—Fiction 2. Immigrants—Fiction
3. Holocaust, 1933-1945—Fiction
ISBN 1-59643-040-0   LC 2004-17551
Sequel to A pocket full of seeds (1973)
"A Deborah Brodie book"
Follows the experiences of Nicole, a teenaged French
Jew, from 1943 to 1948, as she loses her parents and sis-
ter to the concentration camps and then leaves her native
France to make a new life for herself in New York City.
"This is a moving coming-of-age story of a coura-
geous girl." SLJ

Saenz, Benjamin Alire
He forgot to say good-bye. Simon & Schuster
2008 321p $16.99 *

Grades: 8 9 10 11   **Fic**
1. Drug abuse—Fiction 2. Mexican Americans—Fic-
tion
ISBN 978-1-4169-4963-3; 1-4169-4963-1
LC 2007-21959

Two teenaged boys with very different lives find that
they share a common bond—fathers they have never met
who left when they were small boys—and in spite of
their differences, they become close when they each need
someone who understands.
"The affirming and hopeful ending is well-earned for
the characters and a great payoff for the reader. . . .
Characters are well-developed and complex. . . . Overall
it is a strong novel with broad teenage appeal." Voice
Youth Advocates

Sage, Angie
Magyk; Septimus Heap, book one; illustrations
by Mark Zug. Katherine Tegen Books 2005 576p
il $16.99; lib bdg $17.89 *

Grades: 5 6 7 8   **Fic**
1. Fantasy fiction 2. Magic—Fiction
ISBN 0-06-057731-2; 0-06-057732-0 (lib bdg)
LC 2003-28185

After learning that she is the Princess, Jenna is
whisked from her home and carried toward safety by the
Extraordinary Wizard, those she always believed were
her father and brother, and a young guard known only as
Boy 412, pursued by agents of those who killed her
mother ten years earlier.
"Youngsters will lose themselves happily in Sage's
fluent, charismatic storytelling, which enfolds supportive
allies and horrific enemies, abundant quirky details, and
poignant moments of self-discovery." Booklist
Other titles in this series are:
Flyte (2006)
Physik (2007)
Queste (2008)

Saint-Exupéry, Antoine de, 1900-1944

The little prince; written and illustrated by Antoine de Saint-Exupery; translated from the French by Richard Howard. Harcourt 2000 83p il $18; pa $12

Grades: 4 5 6 7 8 9 10 11 12 Adult   **Fic**
1. Fantasy fiction 2. Air pilots—Fiction 3. Princes—Fiction 4. Extraterrestrial beings—Fiction
ISBN 0-15-202398-4; 0-15-601219-7 (pa)
           LC 99-50439
A new translation of the title first published 1943 by Reynal & Hitchcock

"This many-dimensional fable of an airplane pilot who has crashed in the desert is for readers of all ages. The pilot comes upon the little prince soon after the crash. The prince tells of his adventures on different planets and on Earth as he attempts to learn about the universe in order to live peacefully on his own small planet. A spiritual quality enhances the seemingly simple observations of the little prince." Shapiro. Fic for Youth. 3d edition

Saldaña, René

The whole sky full of stars; [by] René Saldaña, Jr. Wendy Lamb Books 2007 131p $15.99; lib bdg $18.99

Grades: 8 9 10 11 12   **Fic**
1. Boxing—Fiction   2. Gambling—Fiction 3. Friendship—Fiction 4. Mexican Americans—Fiction
ISBN   978-0-385-73053-2;   0-385-73053-5; 978-0-385-90078-2 (lib bdg); 0-385-90078-3 (lib bdg)
         LC 2006-26698
Eighteen-year-old Barry competes in a non-sanctioned boxing match in hopes of helping his recently-widowed mother, unaware that his best friend and manager, Alby, has his own desperate need for a share of the purse that may put their friendship on the line.

This "novel challenges traditional notions of what it means to be a winner. Those, like Alby, who are enticed by the glitz and glamour of high-stakes betting, may perceive the world of gambling differently after reading this book." Publ Wkly

Salisbury, Graham, 1944-

Eyes of the emperor. Wendy Lamb Books 2005 228p $15.95; lib bdg $17.99; pa $6.50 *

Grades: 7 8 9 10   **Fic**
1. World War, 1939-1945—Fiction 2. Japanese Americans—Fiction
ISBN 0-385-72971-5; 0-385-90874-1 (lib bdg); 0-440-22956-8 (pa)   LC 2004-15142
Following orders from the United States Army, several young Japanese American men train K-9 units to hunt Asians during World War II.

"Based on the experiences of 26 Hawaiian-Americans of Japanese ancestry, this novel tells an uncomfortable story. Yet it tells of belief in honor, respect, and love of country." Libr Media Connect

House of the red fish. Wendy Lamb Books 2006 291p $16.95; lib bdg $17.99 *

Grades: 6 7 8 9   **Fic**
1. World War, 1939-1945—Fiction 2. Japanese Americans—Fiction 3. Hawaii—Fiction
ISBN 0-385-73121-3; 0-385-90145-3 (lib bdg)
         LC 2006-07544
Sequel to Under the blood-red sun (1994)

Over a year after Japan's attack on Pearl Harbor and the arrest of Tomi's father and grandfather, Tomi and his friends, battling anti-Japanese-American sentiment in Hawaii, try to find a way to salvage his father's sunken fishing boat.

"Many readers, even those who don't enjoy historical fiction, will like the portrayal of the work and the male camaraderie." Booklist

Lord of the deep. Delacorte Press 2001 182p $15.95; lib bdg $17.99; pa $7.99

Grades: 5 6 7 8   **Fic**
1. Fishing—Fiction   2. Stepfathers—Fiction 3. Hawaii—Fiction
ISBN 0-385-72918-9; 0-385-90013-9 (lib bdg); 0-440-22911-1 (pa)   LC 00-60280
Working for Bill, his stepfather, on a charter fishing boat in Hawaii teaches thirteen-year-old Mikey about fishing, and about taking risks, making sacrifices, and facing some of life's difficult choices

"With its vivid Hawaiian setting, this fine novel is a natural for book-discussion groups that enjoy pondering moral ambiguity. Its action-packed scenes will also lure in reluctant readers." SLJ

Night of the howling dogs; a novel. Wendy Lamb Books 2007 191p $16.99; lib bdg $19.99 *

Grades: 5 6 7 8   **Fic**
1. Boy Scouts of America—Fiction 2. Earthquakes—Fiction 3. Tsunamis—Fiction 4. Survival after airplane accidents, shipwrecks, etc.—Fiction 5. Camping—Fiction 6. Hawaii—Fiction
ISBN 978-0-385-73122-5; 978-0-385-90146-8 (lib bdg)   LC 2007-07054
In 1975, eleven Boy Scouts, their leaders, and some new friends camping at Halape, Hawaii, find their survival skills put to the test when a massive earthquake strikes, followed by a tsunami.

This is a "vivid adventure. . . . Salisbury weaves Hawaiian legend into the modern-day narrative to create a haunting, unusual novel." Booklist

Under the blood-red sun. Delacorte Press 1994 246p pa $5.99

Grades: 5 6 7 8   **Fic**
1. Pearl Harbor (Oahu, Hawaii), Attack on, 1941—Fiction 2. World War, 1939-1945—Fiction 3. Japanese Americans—Fiction 4. Hawaii—Fiction
ISBN 0-385-32099-X; 0-440-41139-4 (pa)
         LC 94-444
Tomikazu Nakaji's biggest concerns are baseball, homework, and a local bully, until life with his Japanese family in Hawaii changes drastically after the bombing of Pearl Harbor in December 1941

"Character development of major figures is good, the setting is warmly realized, and the pace of the story moves gently though inexorably forward." SLJ

Followed by: House of the red fish (2006)

Sanchez, Alex, 1957-

So hard to say; Alex Sanchez. 1st ed. Simon &
Schuster Books for Young Readers 2004 230p
$14.95

Grades: 6 7 8 9   **Fic**

1. Homosexuality—Fiction 2. Mexican Americans—
Fiction 3. California—Fiction

ISBN 0-689-86564-3   LC 2003-21128

Thirteen-year-old Xio, a Mexican American girl, and
Frederick, who has just moved to California from Wisconsin, quickly become close friends, but when Xio
starts thinking of Frederick as her boyfriend, he must
confront his feelings of confusion and face the fear that
he might be gay.

"Adventurous, multifaceted, funny, and unpredictably
insightful, Sanchez's novel . . . gels well-rounded characterizations with the universal excitement of first love."
SLJ

Sandell, Lisa Ann, 1977-

A map of the known world. Scholastic Press
2009 273p $16.99

Grades: 7 8 9 10   **Fic**

1. Bereavement—Fiction 2. Art—Fiction 3. Family
life—Fiction 4. School stories

ISBN 978-0-545-06970-0; 0-545-06970-X

LC 2008-50745

Devastated, along with her parents, by the death of
her older brother and apprehensive about being a freshman in the same high school he attended, fourteen-year-
old Cora finds unexpected solace in art.

Sandell's "fluid phrasing and choice of metaphors give
her prose a quiet poetic ambience." Publ Wkly

Sanderson, Brandon, 1975-

Alcatraz versus the evil Librarians. Scholastic
Press 2007 308p $16.99

Grades: 4 5 6 7   **Fic**

1. Librarians—Fiction 2. Grandfathers—Fiction
3. Fantasy fiction

ISBN 0-439-92550-9; 978-0-439-92550-1

LC 2006-38378

On his thirteenth birthday, foster child Alcatraz
Smedry receives a bag of sand which is immediately
stolen by the evil Librarians who are trying to take over
the world. Soon, Alcatraz is introduced to his grandfather
and his own special talent, and told that he must use it
to save civilization.

"Readers whose sense of humor runs toward the sub-
versive will be instantly captivated. . . . This nutty novel
isn't for everyone, but it's also sure to win passionate
fans." Publ Wkly

Another title about Alcatraz is:
Alcatraz versus the scrivener's bones (2008)

Sargent, Pamela

Farseed. Tor Books 2007 287p $17.95

Grades: 7 8 9 10 11 12   **Fic**

1. Science fiction

ISBN 978-0-765-31427-7; 0-765-31427-4

LC 2006-100252

Sequel to: Earthseed (1983)

"A Tom Doherty Associates book"

"In *Earthseed* (1983), genetically created teenagers
were taught survival skills to fulfill a desperate plan to
settle other worlds. Centuries pass; settlements are started
on an earthlike planet, Home; and children are born.
Then a small group breaks away and sets up its own society, which degenerates into a primitive existence.
Meanwhile, those who stay at the original settlement are
fearful, never straying far from their homes and pastures.
In *Farseed*, Sargent explores the resurgence of the conflict between the groups that begins after 16-year-old
Nuy, the daughter of the leader of the breakaway contin-
gent, encounters strangers who are looking for her people. The interpersonal dynamics, plus the challenges of
adapting to another world, give this long-awaited second
book in the Seed Trilogy strong appeal." Booklist

Scaletta, Kurtis, 1968-

Mudville. 1st ed. Alfred A. Knopf 2009 265p
$16.99; lib bdg $19.99

Grades: 5 6 7 8   **Fic**

1. Baseball—Fiction 2. Foster home care—Fiction
3. Rain—Fiction 4. Family life—Fiction 5. Dakota Indians—Fiction 6. Minnesota—Fiction

ISBN   978-0-375-85579-5;   0-375-85579-3;
978-0-375-95579-2 (lib bdg); 0-375-95579-8 (lib bdg)

LC 2008000166

For twenty-two years, since a fateful baseball game
against their rival town, it has rained in Moundville, so
when the rain finally stops, twelve-year-old Roy, his
friends, and foster brother Sturgis dare to face the curse
and form a team.

The author "balances perceptive explorations of personal and domestic issues perfectly with fine baseball
talk and . . . absorbing play-by-play." SLJ

Schirripa, Steven R.

Nicky Deuce; welcome to the family; [by]
Steven R. Schirripa & Charles Fleming. Delacorte
Press 2005 167p $15.95 *

Grades: 4 5 6   **Fic**

1. Italian Americans—Fiction 2. Grandmothers—Fiction 3. Uncles—Fiction 4. Brooklyn (New York,
N.Y.)—Fiction

ISBN 0-385-73257-0   LC 2004-28810

While his parents are on a cruise, twelve-year-old
Nicholas spends his summer in Brooklyn with his grandmother and uncle and learns, with unintended results,
about his Italian-American heritage.

The authors "have created a warm, funny story with
memorable characters and enough shady intrigue to keep
readers turning the pages." Booklist

Another title about Nicky Deuce is:
Nicky Deuce: home for the holidays (2007)

Schlitz, Laura Amy

A drowned maiden's hair; a melodrama.
Candlewick Press 2006 389p $15.99 *

Grades: 5 6 7 8   **Fic**

1. Orphans—Fiction 2. Spiritualism—Fiction

ISBN 978-0-7636-2930-4; 0-7636-2930-8

LC 2006-49056

Schlitz, Laura Amy—*Continued*

At the Barbary Asylum for Female Orphans, eleven-year-old Maud is adopted by three spinster sisters moonlighting as mediums who take her home and reveal to her the role she will play in their seances.

"Filled with heavy atmosphere and suspense, this story recreates life in early-20th-century New England. . . . Maud is a charismatic, three-dimensional character." SLJ

Schmidt, C. A.

Useful fools. Dutton Books 2007 262p $18.99 *

Grades: 8 9 10 11 12   Fic
1. Sendero Luminoso (Guerrilla group)—Fiction
2. Peru—Fiction 3. Family life—Fiction 4. Violence—Fiction 5. War stories
ISBN 978-0-525-47814-0   LC 2006-36508

A fifteen-year-old Peruvian boy, whose mother runs a clinic for poor village children, becomes caught up in the war after Senderistas bomb the clinic, killing his mother and throwing his family into turmoil.

This "groundbreaking novel is disturbing and complex, not only because it is told from alternating viewpoints but also because the politics and savage brutality change its characters profoundly." Booklist

Schmidt, Gary

First boy. Holt & Co. 2005 197p $16.95
Grades: 7 8 9 10   Fic
1. Farm life—Fiction 2. Presidents—Fiction 3. New Hampshire—Fiction
ISBN 0-8050-7859-2   LC 2004-60747

Dragged into the political turmoil of a presidential election year, fourteen-year-old Cooper Jewett, who runs a New Hampshire dairy farm since his grandfather's death, stands up for himself and makes it clear whose first boy he really is.

"Cooper's grief, solitude, and loneliness are poignantly and realistically drawn, and secondary characters add humor to this fast-paced tale." SLJ

Schmidt, Gary D.

Lizzie Bright and the Buckminster boy. Clarion Books 2004 219p $15; pa $6.99 *
Grades: 7 8 9 10   Fic
1. Race relations—Fiction 2. Maine—Fiction
ISBN 0-618-43929-3; 0-553-49495-3 (pa)
LC 2003-20967

A Newbery Medal honor book, 2005

In 1911, Turner Buckminster hates his new home of Phippsburg, Maine, but things improve when he meets Lizzie Bright Griffin, a girl from a poor, nearby island community founded by former slaves that the town fathers—and Turner's—want to change into a tourist spot

"Although the story is hauntingly sad, there is much humor, too. Schmidt's writing is infused with feeling and rich in imagery. With fully developed, memorable characters and a fascinating, little-known piece of history, this novel will leave a powerful impression on readers." SLJ

Trouble. Clarion Books 2008 297p $16 *
Grades: 6 7 8 9 10   Fic
1. Traffic accidents—Fiction 2. Death—Fiction
3. Family life—Fiction 4. Cambodian Americans—Fiction 5. Prejudices—Fiction
ISBN 978-0-618-92766-1; 0-618-92766-2
LC 2007-40104

Fourteen-year-old Henry, wishing to honor his brother Franklin's dying wish, sets out to hike Maine's Mount Katahdin with his best friend and dog, but fate adds another companion—the Cambodian refugee accused of fatally injuring Franklin—and reveals troubles that predate the accident.

"Schmidt creates a rich and credible world peopled with fully developed characters who have a lot of complex reckoning to do. . . . Schmidt's prose . . . is flawless, and Henry's odyssey of growth and understanding is pitch-perfect and deeply satisfying." Bull Cent Child Books

The Wednesday wars. Clarion Books 2007 264p $16 *
Grades: 5 6 7 8   Fic
1. Shakespeare, William, 1564-1616—Fiction
2. School stories
ISBN 978-0-618-72483-3; 0-618-72483-4
LC 2006-23660

A Newbery Medal honor book, 2008

During the 1967 school year, on Wednesday afternoons when all his classmates go to either Catechism or Hebrew school, seventh-grader Holling Hoodhood stays in Mrs. Baker's classroom where they read the plays of William Shakespeare and Holling learns much of value about the world he lives in.

"The serious issues are leavened with ample humor, and the supporting cast . . . is fully dimensional. Best of all is the hero." Publ Wkly

Schreck, Karen Halvorsen, 1962-

Dream journal. Hyperion 2006 250p $15.99
Grades: 7 8 9 10   Fic
1. Mother-daughter relationship—Fiction 2. Death—Fiction 3. Friendship—Fiction
ISBN 1-4231-0105-7   LC 2006-22676

Sixteen-year-old Olivia, facing the impending death of her mother from cancer, records her thoughts in a journal as she grapples with the changing behavior of her best friend and her own desire to run away from all of her problems.

"Teens who have recently lost someone close to them, or know that it's about to happen, will appreciate this sincere and thoughtful novel." SLJ

Schreiber, Ellen

Vampire kisses. Katherine Tegen Bks. 2003 197p $15.99; lib bdg $16.89
Grades: 7 8 9 10   Fic
1. Vampires—Fiction
ISBN 0-06-009334-X; 0-06-009335-8 (lib bdg)
LC 2002-155506

The first three titles in this series also available in paperback compilation, Vampire Kisses: The beginning (2009)

Schreiber, Ellen—_Continued_

Sixteen-year-old Raven, an outcast who always wears black and hopes to become a vampire some day, falls in love with the mysterious new boy in town, eager to find out if he can make her dreams come true

"Schreiber uses a careful balance of humor, irony, pathos, and romance." Booklist

Other titles in this series are:

Vampire kisses 2: Kissing coffins (2005)

Vampire kisses 3: Vampireville (2006)

Vampire kisses 4: Dance with a vampire (2007)

Vampire kisses 5: The Coffin Club (2008)

Vampire kisses 6: Royal Blood (2009)

Schroeder, Lisa

I heart you, you haunt me; [by] Lisa Schroeder. Simon Pulse 2008 226p pa $7.99

Grades: 7 8 9 10   **Fic**

1. Death—Fiction 2. Ghost stories 3. Novels in verse 4. Love—Fiction

ISBN 978-1-4169-5520-7 (pa); 1-4169-5520-8 (pa)

Fifteen year old Ava learns to deal with her boyfriend's untimely death.

"Using flashbacks, precise language and verse format, Schroeder creates vivid images that define the passion of teenage love." Voice Youth Advocates

Schumacher, Julie

The book of one hundred truths. Delacorte Press 2006 182p $15.95; lib bdg $17.99

Grades: 5 6 7 8   **Fic**

1. Honesty—Fiction 2. Grandparents—Fiction 3. Cousins—Fiction 4. New Jersey—Fiction

ISBN 978-0-385-73290-1; 0-385-73290-2; 978-0-385-90311-0 (lib bdg); 0-385-90311-1 (lib bdg)

LC 2005-34958

While visiting her grandparents in Port Harbor, New Jersey, thirteen-year-old Theodora lists one hundred truths that she discovers while babysitting her younger cousins.

"This is a compelling novel, with just the right dose of quiet reflection, self-discovery, and mystery." Bull Cent Child Books

The chain letter. Delacorte Press 2005 195p $15.95; lib bdg $17.99

Grades: 5 6 7 8   **Fic**

1. Superstition—Fiction 2. Letters—Fiction

ISBN 0-385-73169-8; 0-385-90205-0 (lib bdg)

LC 2004-73

When sixth-grader Livvie decides to throw a chain letter in the trash, bad luck ensues.

"Readers . . . will appreciate the story's suspense, humor, and many examples of fine prose." SLJ

Schumacher, Julie, 1958-

Black box; a novel. Delacorte Press 2008 168p $15.99; lib bdg $18.99 *

Grades: 8 9 10 11 12   **Fic**

1. Depression (Psychology)—Fiction 2. Sisters—Fiction 3. Family life—Fiction 4. School stories

ISBN 978-0-385-73542-1; 0-385-73542-1; 978-0-385-90523-7 (lib bdg); 0-385-90523-8 (lib bdg)

LC 2007-45774

When her sixteen-year-old sister is hospitalized for depression and her parents want to keep it a secret, fourteen-year-old Elena tries to cope with her own anxiety and feelings of guilt that she is determined to conceal from outsiders.

"The writing is spare, direct, and honest. Written in the first person, this is a readable, ultimately uplifting book about a difficult subject." SLJ

Schwabach, Karen

The Hope Chest. Random House 2008 274p $16.99; lib bdg $19.99

Grades: 4 5 6 7   **Fic**

1. Women—Suffrage—Fiction 2. Sisters—Fiction 3. Tennessee—Fiction

ISBN 978-0-375-84095-1; 0-375-84095-8; 978-0-375-94095-8 (lib bdg); 0-375-94095-2 (lib bdg)

LC 2006-36692

When eleven-year-old Violet runs away from home in 1920 and takes the train to New York City to find her older sister who is a suffragist, she falls in with people her parents would call "the wrong sort," and ends up in Nashville, Tennessee, where "Suffs" and "Antis" are gathered, awaiting the crucial vote on the nineteenth amendment.

This confronts "heavy issues such as racism and sexism, but the narrative is leavened with humor. The story is packed with period details . . . but Schwabach's attention to character and plotting ensures that it never bogs down." SLJ

A pickpocket's tale. Random House 2006 225p $15.95; lib bdg $17.99

Grades: 5 6 7 8   **Fic**

1. Orphans—Fiction 2. Contract labor—Fiction 3. Jews—Fiction 4. New York (N.Y.)—Fiction

ISBN 978-0-375-83379-3; 0-375-83379-X; 978-0-375-93379-0 (lib bdg); 0-375-93379-4 (lib bdg)

When Molly, a ten-year-old orphan, is arrested for picking pockets in London in 1731, she is banished to America and serves as an indentured servant for a New York City family that expects her to follow their Jewish traditions.

"Written in vividly detailed prose, this debut novel introduces an engaging protagonist. . . . Enjoyable and sometimes thought-provoking historical fiction." Booklist

Schwartz, Ellen, 1949-

Stealing home. Tundra Books 2006 217p $8.95

Grades: 5 6 7 8   **Fic**

1. Orphans—Fiction 2. Racially mixed people—Fiction 3. Family life—Fiction 4. Jews—Fiction

ISBN 978-0-88776-765-4; 0-88776-765-6 (pa)

"Joey, an orphaned, mixed-race 10-year-old isn't the only one who has to make adjustments after he's taken in by Jewish relatives he never knew he had. Wondering why his mother never told him about her side of the family, Joey moves to Brooklyn—to find a warm welcome from Aunt Frieda, an instant ally in baseball-loving cousin Bobbie, and a decidedly cold shoulder from his grandfather. . . . Keenly felt internal conflicts, lightened by some sparky banter, put this more than a cut above the average." Booklist

Schwartz, Virginia Frances, 1950-
4 kids in 5E & 1 crazy year; by Virginia
Frances Schwartz. 1st ed. Holiday House 2006
265p $16.95
Grades: 4 5 6 **Fic**
1. Authorship—Fiction 2. School stories 3. New York
(N.Y.)—Fiction
ISBN 978-0-8234-1946-3; 0-8234-1946-0
LC 2006041194
Family, school, and life in general are seen through
the writings of four fifth graders who have been taken
out of an overcrowded New York City classroom and
placed with a teacher who shows them how to write and
how to believe in themselves.
This is "a book for sharing and talking about in children's creative-writing and teacher-education classes.
. . . The story is simply told. . . . Particularly great are
the kids' poems and journal comments." Booklist

Send one angel down. Holiday House 2000
163p $15.95 **Fic**
1. Slavery—Fiction 2. African Americans—Fiction
3. Racially mixed people—Fiction 4. Cousins—Fiction
ISBN 0-8234-1484-1 LC 99-52818
Abram, a young slave tries to hide the horrors of slavery from his younger cousin Eliza, a light-skinned slave
who is the daughter of the plantation owner
"Schwartz's well-developed characters are full of humanity and personality, and the story vividly acknowledges the sustaining power of music . . . in the lives of
the slaves. This is a profoundly moving tale that is ultimately hopeful but never glosses over the horrific treatment of slaves." Booklist

Scott, Elizabeth
Perfect you. Simon Pulse 2008 304p pa $9.99
Grades: 7 8 9 10 **Fic**
1. Family life—Fiction 2. Friendship—Fiction
3. School stories
ISBN 978-1-4169-5355-5 (pa); 1-4169-5355-8 (pa)
LC 2007-929324
"Kate's father quit his job and is now living his dream
by selling infomercial vitamins at a mall kiosk. The
teen's college-graduate brother is living on the couch,
her mother is working two jobs, and her friend Anna
isn't talking to her now that Anna has lost weight and
become popular. Making Kate's life completely miserable, her overbearing grandmother has moved in, and
Will, the boy Kate tries to pretend she doesn't like because of their contentious history, is constantly making
approaches. . . . Scott does a good job portraying a teen
who is simultaneously self-centered and sympathetic.
. . . Supporting characters are well fleshed out, and the
ending, while encouraging, isn't all sunshine and roses,
making it believable as well as hopeful." SLJ

Stealing Heaven. HarperTeen 2008 307p $16.99;
lib bdg $17.89
Grades: 7 8 9 10 **Fic**
1. Thieves—Fiction 2. Mother-daughter relationship—
Fiction
ISBN 978-0-06-112280-4; 0-06-112280-7;
978-0-06-112281-1 (lib bdg); 0-06-112281-5 (lib bdg)
Eighteen-year-old Dani grows weary of her life as a
thief when she and her mother move to a town where

Dani feels like she can put down roots.
"Witty dialogue gives a new perspective full of hope
to YAs who feel trapped between family and friends."
KLIATT

Scott, Kieran, 1974-
Geek magnet; a novel in five acts. G.P.
Putnam's Sons 2008 308p $16.99
Grades: 7 8 9 10 **Fic**
1. Dating (Social customs)—Fiction 2. School stories
3. Theater—Fiction
ISBN 978-0-399-24760-6; 0-399-24760-2
LC 2007-28707
Seventeen-year-old KJ Miller is determined to lose the
label of "geek magnet" and get the guy of her dreams,
all while stage managing the high school musical, with
the help of the most popular girl in school.
"An enjoyable, touching read about self-discovery
with a hopeful ending that avoids too-neat resolutions."
Booklist

I was a non-blonde cheerleader; [by] Kieran
Scott. G.P. Putnam's Sons 2005 246p $15.99
Grades: 7 8 9 10 **Fic**
1. Cheerleading—Fiction 2. School stories
3. Florida—Fiction
ISBN 0-399-24279-1 LC 2004-3788
As a brunette on the all-blonde cheerleading squad at
her new Florida high school, sophomore Annisa
Gobrowski tries to fit in with her popular teammates
without losing the friendship of Bethany, the only other
non-blonde at the school.
"The specifics are fun and definitely au courant."
Booklist
Other titles in this series are:
Brunettes strike back (2006)
A non-blonde cheerleader in love (2007)

The princess & the pauper; [by] Kate Brian.
Simon & Schuster Bks. for Young Readers 2003
266p $14.95
Grades: 7 8 9 10 **Fic**
1. Princesses—Fiction 2. Los Angeles (Calif.)—Fiction
ISBN 0-689-86173-7 LC 2003-7380
When sixteen-year-old Julia, of Los Angeles, and sixteen-year-old Princess Carina, of Vineland, switch places,
Julia dances at the ball with the incredible Markus and
Carina escapes rigid protocol to spend time with a rock
star
"Although the plot is pure fairy tale, the humor is incisive, the characters of the two girls are well drawn, and
the touch of sweet, G-rated romance will thrill the intended audience." Booklist

Scott, Michael, 1959-
The alchemyst. Delacorte Press 2007 375p (The secrets of the immortal Nicholas Flammel) $16.99; lib bdg $19.99 *

Grades: 7 8 9 10   **Fic**
1. Flamel, Nicolas, d. 1418—Fiction 2. Dee, John, 1527-1608—Fiction 3. Magic—Fiction 4. Alchemy—Fiction 5. Twins—Fiction 6. Siblings—Fiction 7. San Francisco (Calif.)—Fiction
ISBN   978-0-385-73357-1;   0-385-73357-7; 978-0-385-90372-1 (lib bdg); 0-385-90372-3 (lib bdg)
LC 2006-24417
While working at pleasant but mundane summer jobs in San Francisco, fifteen-year-old twins, Sophie and Josh, suddenly find themselves caught up in the deadly, centuries-old struggle between rival alchemists, Nicholas Flamel and John Dee, over the possession of an ancient and powerful book holding the secret formulas for alchemy and everlasting life.
"Scott uses a gigantic canvas for this riveting fantasy. . . . A fabulous read." SLJ
Other titles in this series are:
The magician (2008)
The sorceress (2009)

Scrimger, Richard, 1957-
From Charlie's point of view. Sleuth/Dutton 2005 278p $10.99
Grades: 7 8 9 10   **Fic**
1. Blind—Fiction 2. Mystery fiction
ISBN 0-525-47374-2
Charlie "is blind, and his dad has just been arrested for a crime he didn't commit. Now, with the help of his friends Bernadette and Lewis, Charlie is determined to find the real Stocking Bandit. . . . With a fast-paced plot, witty dialogue, and compelling characters, this mystery is riveting all the way to its exciting and surprising conclusion." SLJ

Into the ravine. Tundra Books 2007 260p pa $9.95
Grades: 6 7 8 9   **Fic**
1. Adventure fiction
ISBN 978-0-88776-822-4 (pa); 0-88776-822-9 (pa)
Jules, Chris, and Cory "head into the ravine for a daylong Huck Finn-like odyssey. . . . Adding to this adventure are talking toilets, older ganglike teenagers, brief first kisses, burning buildings, the great Elgin Avenue bike throw, illegal emeralds, and a mysterious villain named Bonesaw. . . . A funny, scary, exciting, and spot-on adventure." Booklist

Sedgwick, Marcus
The foreshadowing. Wendy Lamb Books 2006 293p $16.95; lib bdg $18.99
Grades: 8 9 10 11   **Fic**
1. World War, 1914-1918—Fiction 2. Extrasensory perception—Fiction
ISBN   0-385-74646-6;   978-0-385-74646-5; 0-385-90881-4 (lib bdg); 978-0-385-90881-8 (lib bdg)
LC 2006-5135
Having always been able to know when someone is going to die, Alexandra poses as a nurse to go to France

during World War I to locate her brother and to try to save him from the fate she has foreseen for him.
The author "skillfully connects young peoples' struggles for power and self-determination with the deepest questions about fate, free will, and the meaning of patriotism." Booklist

My swordhand is singing. Wendy Lamb Books 2007 205p $15.99; lib bdg $18.99 *
Grades: 7 8 9 10   **Fic**
1. Vampires—Fiction 2. Horror fiction 3. Supernatural—Fiction 4. Gypsies—Fiction
ISBN 978-0-375-84689-2; 978-0-375-94689-9 (lib bdg)
LC 2007-07051
In the dangerous dark of winter in an Eastern European village during the early seventeenth century, Peter learns from a gypsy girl that the Shadow Queen is behind the recent murders and reanimations, and his father's secret past may hold the key to stopping her.
"Sedgwick writes a compellingly fresh vampire story, combining elements from ancient myths and legends to create a believable and frightening tale." Voice Youth Advocates

Seidler, Tor, 1952-
Brainboy and the Deathmaster. Laura Geringer Bks. 2003 311p $16.99; lib bdg $17.89
Grades: 5 6 7 8   **Fic**
1. Orphans—Fiction 2. Video games—Fiction 3. Science fiction
ISBN 0-06-029181-8; 0-06-029182-6 (lib bdg)
LC 2002-33918
When Darryl, a twelve-year-old orphan, is adopted by a technology genius, he finds himself the star of his very own life-threatening video game
"A fast-paced, science-fiction adventure. . . . Seidler has created empathetic characters and writes at a level that is accessible even to readers not usually drawn to this genre." SLJ

Selfors, Suzanne, 1963-
Fortune's magic farm; illustrated by Catia Chien. Little, Brown 2009 264p il $14.99
Grades: 4 5 6   **Fic**
1. Orphans—Fiction 2. Magic—Fiction 3. Farms—Fiction
ISBN 978-0-316-01818-0; 0-316-01818-X
LC 2008-12493
Rescued from a rainy, boggy town where she works in a dismal factory, ten-year-old orphan Isabelle learns that she is the last surviving member of a family that tends the world's only remaining magic-producing farm.
"Readers will cozy up to the tale's quirky characters and enjoy the many twists and turns of this magical adventure." Kirkus

Saving Juliet. Walker & Co. 2008 242p $16.95 *
Grades: 7 8 9 10 11 12   **Fic**
1. Shakespeare, William, 1564-1616—Fiction 2. Actors—Fiction 3. Theater—Fiction 4. Space and time—Fiction 5. Italy—Fiction
ISBN 978-0-8027-9740-7; 0-8027-9740-7
LC 2007-18528

Selfors, Suzanne, 1963-—*Continued*

Seventeen-year-old Mimi Wallingford's stage fright and fight with her mother on the closing night of Romeo and Juliet are nothing compared to the troubles she faces when she and her leading man are transported to Shakespeare's Verona, where she decides to give the real Juliet a happy ending.

This is "hilarious and often very clever. . . . Readers will have fun with the characters. . . . Mimi . . . is an honest savvy narrator." Publ Wkly

Selzer, Adam, 1980-

How to get suspended and influence people; a novel. Delacorte Press 2007 c2006 183p $15.99; lib bdg $18.99

Grades: 6 7 8 9   Fic

1. Motion pictures—Fiction 2. School stories 3. Censorship—Fiction

ISBN 978-0-385-73369-4; 978-0-385-90384-4 (lib bdg)   LC 2006-20438

Gifted eighth-grader Leon Harris becomes an instant celebrity when the film he makes for a class project sends him to in-school suspension.

"This funny, fast-paced novel is filled with characters who epitomize the middle school experience, and it presents a lesson or two about free speech as well." SLJ

Another title about Leon is:
Pirates of the retail wasteland (2008)

I put a spell on you; from the files of Chrissie Woodward, spelling bee detective. 1st ed. Delacorte Press 2008 247p $15.99; lib bdg $18.99

Grades: 4 5 6 7   Fic

1. Spelling bees—Fiction 2. School stories 3. Mystery fiction

ISBN 978-0-385-73504-9; 0-385-73504-9; 978-0-385-90498-8 (lib bdg); 0-385-90498-3 (lib bdg)   LC 2008035673

When Gordon Liddy Community School's resident tattletale-detective, Chrissie Woodward, realizes that the adults are out to fix the big spelling bee, she transfers her loyalty to her fellow students and starts collecting evidence. Told through in-class letters, administrative memos, file notes from Chrissie's investigation, and testimony from spelling bee contestants.

"The wit in this school story is directed almost entirely against the grownups in a scathingly funny indictment of a shady principal and insanely competitive parents." Horn Book

Selznick, Brian

The invention of Hugo Cabret; a novel in words and pictures. Scholastic Press 2007 533p il $22.95
*

Grades: 4 5 6 7   Fic

1. Méliès, Georges, 1861-1938—Fiction 2. Robots—Fiction 3. Orphans—Fiction 4. Motion pictures—Fiction 5. Paris (France)—Fiction

ISBN 0-439-81378-6   LC 2006-07119

When twelve-year-old Hugo, an orphan living and repairing clocks within the walls of a Paris train station in 1931, meets a mysterious toyseller and his goddaughter, his undercover life and his biggest secret are jeopardized.

"With characteristic intelligence, exquisite images, and a breathtaking design, Selznick shatters conventions related to the art of bookmaking." SLJ

Sensel, Joni, 1962-

The Farwalker's quest. Bloomsbury U.S.A Children's Books 2009 372p $16.99

Grades: 5 6 7 8   Fic

1. Fantasy fiction

ISBN 978-1-59990-272-2; 1-59990-272-9   LC 2008-30523

When twelve-year-old Ariel and her friend Zeke find a mysterious artifact the like of which has not been seen in a long time, it proves to be the beginning of a long and arduous journey that will untimately reveal to them their true identities.

"This is a solid and well-paced fantasy in which the journey is more important than the conclusion." SLJ

Service, Pamela F.

Tomorrow's magic; [by] Pamela F. Service. 1st ed. Random House 2007 437p $15.99; lib bdg $18.99; pa $7.99

Grades: 7 8 9 10   Fic

1. Arthur, King—Fiction 2. Merlin (Legendary character)—Fiction 3. Morgan le Fay (Legendary character)—Fiction 4. Magic—Fiction 5. Fantasy fiction 6. Science fiction

ISBN 978-0-375-84087-6; 0-375-84087-7; 978-0-375-94087-3 (lib bdg); 0-375-94087-1 (lib bdg); 978-0-375-84087-6 (pa); 0-375-84088-5 (pa)   LC 2006016131

First published in two volumes by Atheneum: Winter of magic's return (1985), Tomorrow's magic (1987)

Two novels in which a young, resurrected Merlin and two friends attempt to bring King Arthur back to Britain, then struggle against the evil plots of Morgan Le Fey to build a new and better civilization in the wake of a nuclear holocaust.

"Service has done a terrific job melding futuristic science fiction with ancient Arthurian legend." Horn Book Guide

Followed by: Yesterday's magic (2008)

Shafer, Audrey

The mailbox. Delacorte Press 2006 178p $15.95; lib bdg $17.99

Grades: 5 6 7 8   Fic

1. Foster home care—Fiction 2. Uncles—Fiction

ISBN 978-0-385-73344-1; 0-385-73344-5; 978-0-385-90361-5 (lib bdg); 0-385-90361-8 (lib bdg)   LC 2006-04572

When twelve-year-old Gabe tries to hide his uncle's death from the local authorities, he is not prepared for what happens when this secret is discovered.

"Complex and believably imperfect characters emerge from the first page to the last in this debut novel. . . . Warm and moving." SLJ

Shahan, Sherry, 1949-

Death mountain; [by] Sherry Shahan. 1st ed.
Peachtree 2005 202p $15.95

Grades: 5 6 7 8 **Fic**

1. Wilderness survival—Fiction 2. Sierra Nevada
Mountains—Fiction

ISBN 1-56145-353-6   LC 2005010820

"A day trip to a mountain lake turns to disaster when
lightning strikes a pack mule, a mud slide kills a horse,
and hikers scatter, seeking shelter. Erin, 14, leaves her
new friend Levi with the injured hikers to search for his
sister, Mae, who has run off-trail in the confusion. . . .
A great addition to the adventure-survival genre." SLJ

Shan, Darren, 1972-

Lord Loss; [by] Darren Shan. 1st U.S. ed. Little,
Brown 2005 233p (Demonata) $15.99

Grades: 7 8 9 10 **Fic**

1. Horror fiction

ISBN 0-316-11499-5   LC 2005-0145

Presumably the only witness to the horrific and bloody
murder of his entire family, a teenage boy must outwit
not only the mental health professionals determined to
cure his delusion, but also the demonic forces only he
can see.

"The plot rolls along at high speed, but Shan is still
quite adept when it comes to capturing Grubbs' roller-
coaster emotions." Booklist

Other titles in this series are:
Demon thief (2006)
Slawter (2006)
Bec (2007)
Blood beast (2007)
Demon apocalypse (2008)
Death's shadow (2008)
Wolf island (2009)
Dark calling (2009)

Shanahan, Lisa

The sweet, terrible, glorious year I truly,
completely lost it. Delacorte Press 2007 297p
$15.99; lib bdg $18.99 *

Grades: 7 8 9 10 **Fic**

1. Theater—Fiction 2. School stories 3. Family life—
Fiction 4. Australia—Fiction

ISBN   978-0-385-73516-2;   0-385-73516-2;
978-0-385-90505-3 (lib bdg); 0-385-90505-X (lib bdg)
LC 2006-101158

Fourteen-year-old Gemma Stone struggles to understand her shifting emotions as her older sister plans her
wedding, she overcomes her nerves and tries out for the
school play, and she gets to know one of the most notorious boys in her class.

"Shanahan's quirky characters are a riot, but the depth
of Gemma's growth and heartbreak is profound." SLJ

Sharenow, Rob

My mother the cheerleader; a novel. Laura
Geringer Books 2007 288p $16.99; lib bdg $17.89

Grades: 7 8 9 10 **Fic**

1. Race relations—Fiction 2. School integration—Fiction 3. Mother-daughter relationship—Fiction 4. New
Orleans (La.)—Fiction

ISBN   978-0-06-114896-5;   0-06-114896-2;
978-0-06-114897-2 (lib bdg); 0-06-114897-0 (lib bdg)
LC 2006-21716

Thirteen-year-old Louise uncovers secrets about her
family and her neighborhood during the violent protests
over school desegregation in 1960 New Orleans.

"Through inquisitive Louise's perspective, readers get
a wrenching look at the era's turmoil and pervasive racism." Publ Wkly

Shaw, Susan

Safe. Dutton Books 2007 168p $16.99 *

Grades: 7 8 9 10 **Fic**

1. Rape—Fiction 2. Mothers—Fiction

ISBN 978-0-525-47829-4; 0-525-47829-9
LC 2006-36428

When thirteen-year-old Tracy, whose mother died
when she was three years old, is raped and beaten on the
last day of school, all her feelings of security disappear
and she does not know how to cope with the fear and
dread that engulf her.

This is an "extraordinarily tender novel. . . . Intimate,
first-person narrative honestly expresses Tracy's full
range of emotions." Publ Wkly

Shaw, Tucker

The hookup artist. HarperCollins Pubs. 2005
197p $15.99; lib bdg $16.89

Grades: 8 9 10 11 12 **Fic**

1.   Dating   (Social   customs)—Fiction
2. Homosexuality—Fiction

ISBN 0-06-075620-9; 0-06-075621-7 (lib bdg)
LC 2005-05950

"When his best friend, Cate, gets dumped, Cupid-
wannabe Lucas seizes the matchmaking opportunity to
pair her with Derek, the hot new guy in town. At first,
Cate is dubious of their match, and rightfully so, since
Derek can't seem to keep his eyes off Lucas. Lucas, who
has just been dumped by Marcus, finds himself curiously
intrigued by Derek. Soon, he and Cate . . . dupe themselves into crushing on him at the same time. Shaw's sly
twist on the old best-friends-fall-for-the-same-guy conun-
drum is fresh, funny, frolicsome, and not without genuine tension." SLJ

Shearer, Alex

Canned. Scholastic Press 2008 237p $16.99

Grades: 4 5 6 7 **Fic**

1. Collectors and collecting—Fiction 2. Great Britain—Fiction 3. Mystery fiction

ISBN 0-439-90309-2; 0-439-90310-6
LC 2007-09815

Fergal Banfield, an eccentric lad who collects cans, is
surprised to find some unexpected—and even alarming—
things in a few of his treasures, and when he meets

Shearer, Alex—*Continued*

Charlotte, another collector, they begin an investigation that leads them into dangerous territory.

"Quirky and original, funky and totally gross, this fast-paced novel blends several genres: crime, horror, mystery, and fantasy. Its black humor, balanced by a serious look at forced child labor, will keep readers hooked from the beginning." SLJ

The Great Blue Yonder. Clarion Bks. 2002 c2001 184p $15

Grades: 5 6 7 8   **Fic**

1. Future life—Fiction

ISBN 0-618-21257-4   LC 2001-47741

First published 2001 in the United Kingdom

This "novel tells the story of Harry, killed in a bicycle accident. Initially confused by his new existence in the Other Side, the flippant 12-year-old realizes he cannot move toward the peace of the Great Blue Yonder until he has addressed the unfinished business in his life. . . . Amusing, poignant, and deeply moving. A great main character and unusual topical matter combine to make a unique winner of a book that will leave readers laughing through their tears." SLJ

Sheinmel, Courtney, 1977-

My so-called family. Simon & Schuster Books for Young Readers 2008 194p $15.99

Grades: 5 6 7 8   **Fic**

1. Stepfamilies—Fiction 2. Siblings—Fiction 3. Family life—Fiction 4. Friendship—Fiction

ISBN 978-1-4169-5785-0; 1-4169-5785-5

     LC 2007-34465

Leah, who was conceived through a donor bank, decides that even though she loves her mother, stepfather, and stepbrother, she wants to find out if she has any other siblings, and sets out to investigate without telling anyone what she is doing.

"Leah's voice is right on key, whether describing the give-and-take of family life or revelations about what constitutes family. Smart, original and full of vitality." Publ Wkly

Sheldon, Dyan

Confessions of a teenage drama queen. Candlewick Press 1999 272p hardcover o.p. pa $7.99 *

Grades: 7 8 9 10   **Fic**

1. School stories

ISBN 0-7636-0822-X; 0-7636-2827-1 (pa)

     LC 98-53914

In her first year at a suburban New Jersey high school, Mary Elizabeth Cep, who now calls herself "Lola," sets her sights on the lead in the annual drama production, and finds herself in conflict with the most popular girl in school.

"An exuberant and hilarious celebration of the ups and downs of high school life. . . . The story is off-beat, outrageous, and utterly charming." SLJ

Other titles about Lola are:

My perfect life (2002)

Confessions of a Hollywood star (2006)

Sherlock, Patti

Letters from Wolfie. Viking 2004 232p $16.99

Grades: 5 6 7 8   **Fic**

1. Dogs—Fiction 2. Vietnam War, 1961-1975—Fiction

ISBN 0-670-03694-3   LC 2003-24316

Certain that he is doing the right thing by donating his dog, Wolfie, to the Army's scout program in Vietnam, thirteen-year-old Mark begins to have second thoughts when the Army refuses to say when and if Wolfie will ever return.

"In this topnotch novel, Sherlock weaves together numerous threads of emotion, information, and plot so seamlessly that readers will be surprised by how much they've learned by the time they finish this deceptively simple story." SLJ

Sherman, Delia

Changeling. Viking 2006 292p $16.99

Grades: 5 6 7 8   **Fic**

1. Fantasy fiction

ISBN 0-670-05967-6

"Neef is a changeling, a human baby stolen by fairies. She lives in 'New York Between,' an invisible parallel city, and she was raised under the protection of her godmother (a white rat) and the Green Lady of Central Park. . . . After breaking Fairy Law, Neef is expelled, and she must complete a heroic quest . . . in order to regain entry to her community. . . . Silly, profound, and lightning paced all at once, this novel will please adventure fans and fantasy readers alike." Bull Cent Child Books

Sheth, Kashmira

Blue jasmine; [by] Kashmira Sheth. 1st ed. Hyperion Books for Children 2004 186p $15.99; pa $5.99

Grades: 5 6 7 8   **Fic**

1. Immigrants—Fiction 2. East Indians—Fiction 3. India—Fiction

ISBN 0-7868-1855-7; 0-7868-5565-7 (pa)

     LC 2003-50818

When twelve-year-old Seema moves to Iowa City with her parents and younger sister, she leaves friends and family behind in her native India but gradually begins to feel at home in her new country.

"Seema's story, which articulates the ache for distant home and family, will resonate with fellow immigrants and enlighten their classmates." Booklist

Keeping corner. Hyperion 2007 281p $15.99 *

Grades: 7 8 9 10 11 12   **Fic**

1. Gandhi, Mahatma, 1869-1948—Fiction 2. India—Fiction 3. Widows—Fiction 4. Women's rights—Fiction

ISBN 978-0-7868-3859-2; 0-7868-3859-0

     LC 2007-15314

In India in the 1940s, twelve-year-old Leela's happy, spoiled childhood ends when her husband since age nine, whom she barely knows, dies, leaving her a widow whose only hope of happiness could come from Mahatma Ghandi's social and political reforms.

Sheth "sets up a thrilling premise in which politics become achingly personal." Booklist

Shinn, Sharon, 1957-

The dream-maker's magic. Viking 2006 261p
$16.99

Grades: 7 8 9 10   **Fic**
  1. Fantasy fiction
  ISBN 0-670-06070-4   LC 2006-297745
Kellen's mother insisted her only child was born a
male and raised her as a boy till she was forced to go
to school. Then she became friends with Gryffin who
would become the new Dream-Maker of their village.
Will their love survive when Gryffin is whisked away to
the castle?

"Shinn returns to the world of The *Safe-Keeper's Secret* (2004) and The *Truth-Teller's Tale* (2005) . . . creating a stand-alone story with a unique heroine. . . .
This is a fast-paced and captivating tale, sure to appeal
to fantasy fans looking for a touch of romance." SLJ

General Winston's daughter. Viking 2007 352p
$17.99; pa $7.99

Grades: 7 8 9 10   **Fic**
  1. War stories 2. Military occupation—Fiction
  3. Social classes—Fiction 4. Soldiers—Fiction
  ISBN   978-0-670-06248-5;   0-670-06248-0;
  978-0-14-241346-3 (pa); 0-14-241346-1 (pa)
                                      LC 2007-14703
Seventeen-year-old heiress Averie Winston travels
with her guardian to faraway Chiarrin, a country her father's army has occupied, and once she arrives and is reunited with her fiance, she discovers that her notions
about politics, propriety, the military, and even her intended have changed.

The author "skillfully shepherds her tale to a satisfying, believable conclusion. This thoughtful romance with
political overtones will prove irresistible to many readers." Booklist

The truth-teller's tale. Viking 2005 276p $16.99

Grades: 7 8 9 10   **Fic**
  1. Fantasy fiction
  ISBN 0-670-06000-3   LC 2005-5453
Sequel to The Safekeeper's secret
Twins Eleda, who can tell only the truth, and Adele,
who cannot reveal others' secrets, are sorely tested by a
newly arrived pair of handsome dance instructors who
seem to harbor a secret.

"The comforting, fairy-tale rhythms of the girls' stories exert an irresistible pull, and Shinn's numerous fans
will welcome a second helping of the refreshing tale
spinning and charmingly homespun, village-centered fantasy culture that marked *The Safe Keeper's Secret*."
Booklist

Followed by The Dream-keeper's magic

Shipton, Paul

The pig scrolls; by Gryllus the pig; [as
translated by] Paul Shipton. Candlewick Press
2005 c2004 274p $15.99

Grades: 5 6 7 8   **Fic**
  1. Pigs—Fiction 2. Classical mythology—Fiction
  ISBN 0-7636-2702-X   LC 2005-50177
A translation of an ancient Greek manuscript written
by Gryllus, a talking pig who was once a man, which
describes the many adventures that he and his compan-

ions—a junior prophetess named Sybil and a bumbling
goatherd—experience while traveling to Delphi to try to
prevent the universe from coming to an end.

"Shipton combines humor and action with bits of abstract thought about death and life. . . . More farce than
epic, this story does manage to provide a little bit to
chew on after the laughter stops." SLJ

Another title about Gryllus is:
The pig who saved the world (2007)

Shreve, Susan Richards

Under the Watson's porch; [by] Susan Shreve.
Alfred A. Knopf 2004 199p $15.95; lib bdg
$17.99

Grades: 5 6 7 8   **Fic**
  1. Friendship—Fiction
  ISBN 0-375-82630-0; 0-375-92630-5 (lib bdg)
                                      LC 2003-61383
Twelve-year-old Ellie's boring summer becomes exciting when she develops a crush on her new next-door
neighbor, an older boy with a troubled past, whom her
parents have forbidden her to see.

"Ellie's first-person narration is utterly and immediately believable. . . . Shreve imagines a troubled kid with
unusual sensitivity and depth, and this novel will be treasured by readers." Booklist

Shulman, Polly

Enthusiasm. G. P. Putnam's Sons 2006 198p
$15.99

Grades: 7 8 9 10   **Fic**
  1. School stories
  ISBN 0-399-24389-5   LC 2005-13490
Julie and Ashleigh, high school sophomores and Jane
Austen fans, seem to fall for the same Mr. Darcy-like
boy and struggle to hide their true feelings from one another while rehearsing for a school musical.

"While familiarity with Austen's world through her
books or, more likely, the movie renditions will deepen
readers' appreciation for Shulman's impressive . . . novel, it is by no means a prerequisite to enjoying this involving and often amusing narrative of friendship, courtship, and (of course) true love." Booklist

Shusterman, Neal

Antsy does time. Dutton Children's Books 2008
247p $16.99 *

Grades: 5 6 7 8   **Fic**
  1. Death—Fiction 2. School stories 3. Brooklyn (New
  York, N.Y.)—Fiction
  ISBN 978-0-525-47825-6; 0-525-47825-6
                                      LC 2008-00459
Sequel to: The Schwa was here (2004)
Fourteen-year-old Anthony "Antsy" Bonano learns
about life, death, and a lot more when he tries to help
a friend with a terminal illness feel hopeful about the future.

"Featuring a terrific supporting cast led by Antsy's
wise, acerbic mother, an expert blend of comedy and
near tragedy, and the wry observations of a narrator . . .
this will keep tween readers hooked from start to finish."
Booklist

Shusterman, Neal—*Continued*

Downsiders. Simon & Schuster Bks. for Young Readers 1999 246p hardcover o.p. pa $4.99 *
Grades: 9 10 11 12   **Fic**
1. Subways—Fiction 2. New York (N.Y.)—Fiction
ISBN 0-689-80375-3; 0-689-83969-3 (pa)
LC 98-38555
When fourteen-year-old Lindsay meets Talon and discovers the Downsiders world which had evolved from the subway built in New York in 1867 by Alfred Ely Beach, she and her new friend experience the clash of their two cultures.
"Shusterman has invented an alternate world in the Downside that is both original and humorous." Voice Youth Advocates

Full tilt; a novel. Simon & Schuster Bks. for Young Readers 2003 201p $16.95; pa $5.99
Grades: 7 8 9 10   **Fic**
1. Amusement parks—Fiction 2. Brothers—Fiction 3. Horror fiction
ISBN 0-689-80374-5; 0-689-87325-5 (pa)
LC 2002-13867
"An older, alluring, and slightly mysterious girl invites Blake to an amusement park that's only open from midnight to dawn. The rules: he must finish seven rides, all before sunrise, or the park absorbs him. Blake comes to realize that each ride takes him to his deepest fears." Horn Book Guide
"Shusterman has created a surreal, scary fantasy, packed with suspenseful psychological drama." Booklist

The Schwa was here; [by] Neal Shusterman. 1st ed. Dutton Children's Books 2004 228p $15.99
Grades: 5 6 7 8   **Fic**
1. Friendship—Fiction 2. Brooklyn (New York, N.Y.)—Fiction
ISBN 0-525-47182-0   LC 2004-45072
A Brooklyn eighth-grader nicknamed Antsy befriends the Schwa, an "invisible-ish" boy who is tired of blending into his surroundings and going unnoticed by nearly everyone.
"Antsy is one funny narrator. . . . Shusterman has created yet another very readable and refreshingly different story." Voice Youth Advocates
Followed by: Antsy does time (2008)

Unwind. Simon & Schuster Books for Young Readers 2007 335p $16.99 *
Grades: 6 7 8 9 10 11 12   **Fic**
1. Science fiction
ISBN 978-1-4169-1204-0; 1-4169-1204-5
LC 2006-32689
In a future world where those between the ages of thirteen and eighteen can have their lives "unwound" and their body parts harvested for use by others, three teens go to extreme lengths to uphold their beliefs—and, perhaps, save their own lives.
"Poignant, compelling, and ultimately terrifying." Voice Youth Advocates

Siebold, Jan
My nights at the Improv; by Jan Siebold. Albert Whitman & Co. 2005 98p $14.95
Grades: 4 5 6 7   **Fic**
1. Moving—Fiction 2. Acting—Fiction 3. School stories
ISBN 0-8075-5630-0   LC 2005004590
"Lizzie, an eighth-grader struggling with a move to a new town, feels as though her voice is on 30-second delay. . . . She learns to confront her fear of speaking out by secretly observing a community-education class on improvisational-drama techniques. . . . Improvisational theater is a fascinating topic that is not often represented in fiction for this age group; the concept is well covered in this high-interest novel." SLJ

Siegelson, Kim L., 1962-
Honey Bea; [by] Kim L. Siegelson. 1st ed. Jump at the Sun/Hyperion Books for Children 2006 276p $15.99
Grades: 7 8 9 10   **Fic**
1. Slavery—Fiction 2. Magic—Fiction 3. Plantation life—Fiction 4. Louisiana—Fiction
ISBN 0-7868-0853-5   LC 2003-61888
On a Louisiana sugar plantation, a young slave girl struggles with the magical powers that have been passed down from her grandmother and mother to her, unsure of the responsibilities and consequences that accompany this power.
"Siegelson crafts a mesmerizing tale heavy with the scent of honey and flowers and rooted in Louisiana soil." Booklist

Simmons, Michael
Vandal. Roaring Brook Press 2006 173p $16.95
Grades: 7 8 9 10   **Fic**
1. Brothers—Fiction 2. Bands (Music)—Fiction
ISBN 978-1-59643-070-9; 1-59643-070-2
LC 2005-28741
The love-hate relationship between high school musician Will and his older brother Jason is fueled by the abuse Will suffers at Jason's hands but a devastating accident changes the everything for the boys and their family.
This is "a deftly structured, refreshingly unsentimental, and witty analysis of the resilient, complicated bonds that connect siblings." Booklist

Simmons, Michael, 1970-
Alien feast; [by] Michael Simmons; illustrated by George O'Connor. Roaring Brook Press 2008 240p il (Chronicles of the first invasion) $9.95
Grades: 5 6 7 8   **Fic**
1. Extraterrestrial beings—Fiction 2. Kidnapping—Fiction 3. Orphans—Fiction 4. Science fiction
ISBN 978-1-59643-281-9; 1-59643-281-0
LC 2007-44050
In 2017, human-eating aliens have kidnapped two scientists who might cure the disease that is destroying them, and twelve-year-old William Aitkin, his elderly, ailing Uncle Maynard, and the scientists' daughter, Sophie, set out to rescue them.

Simmons, Michael, 1970-—*Continued*

"The youngsters are nicely developed, and, refreshingly, they act as you'd expect kids to behave in such a stressful situation, not like miniature adults. O'Connor's artwork adds to the humor." SLJ

Simner, Janni Lee

Bones of Faerie. Random House 2009 247p $16.99; lib bdg $19.99

Grades: 7 8 9 10   **Fic**

1. Fairies—Fiction 2. Magic—Fiction 3. Fantasy fiction

ISBN 978-0-375-84563-5; 978-0-375-94563-2 (lib bdg)   LC 2008-02022

Fifteen-year-old Liza travels through war-ravaged territory, accompanied by two companions, in a struggle to bridge the faerie and human worlds and to bring back her mother while learning of her own powers and that magic can be controlled.

This is a "compelling developed, highly vulnerable trio whose resolute defiance against the status quo will resonate with readers long after specific details of the story may be forgotten." Bull Cent Child Books

Singer, Nicky, 1956-

Gem X. Holiday House 2008 311p $16.95

Grades: 7 8 9 10   **Fic**

1. Genetic engineering—Fiction 2. Cloning—Fiction 3. Political corruption—Fiction 4. Science fiction

ISBN 978-0-8234-2108-4; 0-8234-2108-2   LC 2007-14975

Sixteen-year-old Maxo Strang, the most perfect human ever made, suddenly discovers a 'crack' in his face, which leads him to expose his community's dark underworld of secret scientific research and the city's corrupt supreme leader.

"This intelligent, fast-paced novel will appeal to those teens who . . . want speculative fiction with bite and satire." SLJ

Singleton, Linda Joy, 1957-

Dead girl walking; [by] Linda Joy Singleton. Flux 2008 308p (Dead girl) $9.95

Grades: 8 9 10 11 12   **Fic**

1. Death—Fiction 2. Future life—Fiction 3. School stories

ISBN 978-0-7387-1405-9; 0-7387-1405-4   LC 2008012991

When Amber, a smart, middle-class, high school student, is hit by a truck, she meets her deceased grandmother in a dreamlike place, then takes a wrong turn and awakens in the body of a wealthy, beautiful, popular classmate with serious problems.

"This page-turner has wit, love, courage, adventure, and remarkable insight." SLJ

Sitomer, Alan Lawrence

The Hoopster. Jump at the Sun/Hyperion Books for Children 2005 218p $16.99

Grades: 7 8 9 10   **Fic**

1. Basketball—Fiction 2. Race relations—Fiction 3. African Americans—Fiction 4. Authorship—Fiction

ISBN 0-7868-5483-9

First published 2002 by Milk Mug Pub.

Andre Anderson, called "The Hoopster" for his basketball skills, is brutally attacked by racists in response to an article he writes for a national magazine.

"The dialogue-filled sparring is fresh and accurately portrays the dynamics among urban teens and their families." SLJ

Other books in the Hoopster series include:

Hip-hop high school (2006)

Homeboyz (2007)

The secret story of Sonia Rodriguez. Jump at the Sun/Hyperion Books For Children 2008 312p lib bdg $17.99

Grades: 7 8 9 10   **Fic**

1. Mexican Americans—Fiction 2. Family life—Fiction

ISBN 978-1-4231-1072-9; 1-4231-1072-2   LC 2007-45265

Tenth-grader Sonia reveals secrets about her life and her Hispanic family as she studies hard to become the first Rodriguez to finish high school.

"Sonia's immediate voice will hold teens with its mix of anger, sorrow, tenderness, and humor." Booklist

Skelton, Matthew

Endymion Spring. Delacorte Press 2006 392p il $17.95; lib bdg $19.99 *

Grades: 5 6 7 8   **Fic**

1. Gutenberg, Johann, 1397?-1468—Fiction 2. Magic—Fiction 3. Books and reading—Fiction 4. Great Britain—Fiction

ISBN 0-385-73380-1; 0-385-90397-9 (lib bdg)   LC 2006-46259

Having reluctantly accompanied his academic mother and pesky younger sister to Oxford, twelve-year-old Blake Winters is at loose ends until he stumbles across an ancient and magical book, secretely brought to England in 1453 by Gutenberg's mute apprentice to save it from evil forces, and which now draws Blake into a dangerous and life-threatening quest.

"This book is certain to reach an audience looking for a page-turner, and it just might motivate readers to explore the . . . facts behind the fiction." SLJ

Skurzynski, Gloria, 1930-

Cliff hanger; by Gloria Skurzynski and Alane Ferguson. National Geographic Soc. 1999 147p il (Mysteries in our National Parks) $15.95; pa $5.95

Grades: 4 5 6   **Fic**

1. Foster home care—Fiction 2. Mystery fiction

ISBN 0-7922-7036-3; 0-7922-7654-X (pa)   LC 98-8716

Twelve-year-old Jack and his younger sister visit Mesa Verde National Park, where they delve into the park's history while gradually uncovering the mysterious past of their family's teenage foster child Lucky

"The authors do a fine job of integrating lots of material into an exciting story." Booklist

Other titles in the Mysteries in our National Parks series are:

Buried alive (2003)

Deadly waters (1999)

Escape from fear (2002)

Skurzynski, Gloria, 1930-—_Continued_
Ghost horses (2000)
Hunted (2000)
Out of the deep (2002)
Over the edge (2002)
Rage of fire (1998)
Running scared (2002)
Valley of death (2002)
Wolf stalker (1997)

The Virtual War. Simon & Schuster Bks. for Young Readers 1997 152p hardcover o.p. pa $10.95
Grades: 6 7 8 9   **Fic**
  1. Science fiction 2. Virtual reality—Fiction
  ISBN 0-689-81374-0; 1-4169-7577-2 (pa)
              LC 96-35346
In a future world where global contamination has necessitated limited human contact, three young people with unique genetically engineered abilities are teamed up to wage a war in virtual reality
"Skurzynski's anti-war message is clear yet never didactic; her characters are complex and fully realized, the pacing brisk, and the story compelling." Bull Cent Child Books
 Other titles in this series are:
The choice (2006)
The clones (2002)
The revolt (2005)

Slade, Arthur G., 1967-
Jolted; Newton Starker's rules for survival; [by] Arthur Slade. Wendy Lamb Books 2009 227p $15.99; lib bdg $18.99
Grades: 5 6 7 8   **Fic**
  1. Lightning—Fiction 2. School stories
  ISBN   978-0-385-74700-4;   0-385-74700-4; 978-0-385-90944-0 (lib bdg); 0-385-90944-6 (lib bdg)
              LC 2008-8632
First published 2008 in Canada
Many of Newton Starker's ancestors, including his mother, have been killed by lightning strikes, so when he enrolls at the eccentric Jerry Potts Academy of Higher Learning and Survival in Moose Jaw, Saskatchewan, he tries to be a model student so that he can avoid the same fate.
"The premise will snag readers immediately [and] . . . Slade's portrayal of Newton's sweep of emotions as he deals with his perceived fate–fear, fury, dogged determination–is especially convincing." Publ Wkly

Megiddo's shadow. Wendy Lamb Books 2006 290p $15.95
Grades: 7 8 9 10   **Fic**
  1. World War, 1914-1918—Fiction 2. Brothers—Fiction
  ISBN 0-385-74701-2; 978-0-385-90945-7
              LC 2006011494
After the death of his beloved older brother Hector in World War I, sixteen-year-old Edward leaves the family farm in Canada to enlist in Hector's batallion, where he attempts to come to terms with what has happened.
"An engrossing and thought-provoking story." SLJ

Slayton, Fran Cannon
When the whistle blows. Philomel Books 2009 162p $16.99 *
Grades: 7 8 9 10   **Fic**
  1. Railroads—Fiction 2. Family life—Fiction 3. Country life—Fiction 4. West Virginia—Fiction
  ISBN 978-0-399-25189-4; 0-399-25189-8
              LC 2008038435
Jimmy Cannon tells about his life in the 1940s as the son of a West Virginia railroad man, loving the trains and expecting one day to work on the railroad like his father and brothers.
"Telling details and gentle humor help set the scene and reveal a great deal about these characters and their lives. . . . A polished paean to a bygone time and place." SLJ

Sleator, William
The duplicate. Dutton 1988 154p pa $5.99 hardcover o.p. *
Grades: 7 8 9 10   **Fic**
  1. Science fiction
  ISBN 0-14-130431-6   LC 87-30562
Sixteen-year-old David, finding a strange machine that creates replicas of living organisms, duplicates himself and suffers the horrible consequences when the duplicate turns against him
"There are some points in the story when the roles of the clones (referred to as Duplicates A and B) become congested to the detriment of the book's pace, but fantasy fans will doubtless find the concept fresh enough and eerie enough to compensate for this, and Sleator is, as always, economical in casting and structuring his story." Bull Cent Child Books

House of stairs. Dutton 1974 166p hardcover o.p. pa $5.99 *
Grades: 7 8 9 10   **Fic**
  1. Science fiction
  ISBN 0-525-32335-X; 0-14-034580-9 (pa)
  Available in hardcover from P. Smith
"Five 15-year-old orphans with widely ranging personality characteristics are involuntarily placed in a house of endless stairs and subjected to psychological experiments on conditioned human responses." Booklist
"The setting is bleak, dramatic and convincing; the interaction and development of the five young people as characters trapped in an abrasive situation are compelling. A very effective and provocative suspense story that can be read for plot alone or doubly enjoyed for the mystery and the message." Bull Cent Child Books

Interstellar pig. Dutton 1984 197p pa $6.99 hardcover o.p. *
Grades: 5 6 7 8   **Fic**
  1. Science fiction
  ISBN 0-14-037595-3 (pa)   LC 84-4132
"Solitary and bored, Barney is quickly attracted by the exotic appearance and protean personalities of Zena, Manny, and Joe, who have rented the summer house next door. The interest of the sophisticated adults in sixteen-year-old Barney at first flatters, then intrigues, and finally terrifies him as he becomes absorbed in their compulsion to possess 'The Piggy.' When he realizes that the

Sleator, William—_Continued_
talisman has power, the game expands in significance."
Horn Book

The author "draws the reader in with intimations of danger and horror, but the climactic battle is more slapstick than horrific, and the victor's prize could scarcely be more ironic. Problematic as straight science fiction but great fun as a spoof on human-alien contact." Booklist

Another title about Barney is:
Parasite Pig (2002)

Singularity. Dutton 1985 170p pa $5.99
Grades: 7 8 9 10   **Fic**
1. Twins—Fiction 2. Science fiction
ISBN 0-525-44161-1; 0-14-037598-8 (pa)
LC 84-26075
Available in hardcover from P. Smith

Sixteen-year-old twins Harry and Barry stumble across a gateway to another universe, where a distortion in time and space causes a dramatic change in their competitive relationship

"The book has a title with a fine double entendre and is an unusual, suspenseful yarn told by a master storyteller." Horn Book

Smelcer, John E., 1963-
The trap; [by] John Smelcer. Henry Holt and Co. 2006 170p $15.95
Grades: 6 7 8 9   **Fic**
1. Survival after airplane accidents, shipwrecks, etc.—Fiction 2. Grandfathers—Fiction 3. Native Americans—Fiction 4. Alaska—Fiction
ISBN 978-0-8050-7939-5; 0-8050-7939-4
LC 2005035740
In alternating chapters, seventeen-year-old Johnny Least-Weasel worries about his missing grandfather, and the grandfather, Albert Least-Weasel, struggles to survive, caught in his own steel trap in the Alaskan winter.

"In this story, Smelcer . . . seems to straddle the line flawlessly between an ancient legend and contemporary fiction. . . . His characters act with quiet dignity. . . . The suspense is played on an everyday level, which is why it works." Voice Youth Advocates

Smith, Cynthia Leitich
Rain is not my Indian name. HarperCollins Pubs. 2001 135p $15.99; lib bdg $16.89
Grades: 6 7 8 9   **Fic**
1. Death—Fiction 2. Photography—Fiction 3. Native Americans—Fiction
ISBN 0-688-17397-7; 0-06-029504-X (lib bdg)
LC 00-59705
Tired of staying in seclusion since the death of her best friend, a fourteen-year-old Native American girl takes on a photographic assignment with her local newspaper to cover events at the Native American summer youth camp

"The engaging first-person narrative convincingly portrays Rain's grieving process and addresses the varying degrees of prejudice she encounters." Horn Book Guide

Smith, D. James
The boys of San Joaquin; a novel. Atheneum Books for Young Readers 2005 231p $15.95
Grades: 5 6 7 8   **Fic**
1. Family life—Fiction 2. Italian Americans—Fiction 3. Deaf—Fiction 4. California—Fiction
ISBN 0-689-87606-8   LC 2004-3075
"A Richard Jackson book"

In a small California town in 1951, twelve-year-old Paolo and his deaf cousin Billy get caught up in a search for money missing from the church collection, leading them to complicated discoveries about themselves, other family members, and townspeople they thought they knew.

"Narrator Paolo has an appealingly distinctive voice and a keen eye for observing people, and the supporting characters are equally memorable." Booklist

Other titles about Paolo and Billy are:
Probably the world's best story about a dog and the girl who loved me (2006)
It was September when we ran away the first time (2008)

Smith, Emily Wing, 1980-
The way he lived; [by] Emily Wing Smith. 1st ed. Flux 2008 232p pa $9.95 *
Grades: 8 9 10 11 12   **Fic**
1. Death—Fiction 2. Mormons—Fiction 3. Utah—Fiction
ISBN 978-0-7387-1404-2 (pa)   LC 2008024416
"When sixteen-year-old Joel Espen dies of thirst on a Boy Scout hiking trip, it shakes the small town of Haven, Utah to its socially conformist foundation. And the six teens who were closest to Joel start to view their community—and themselves—in a new light." Publisher's note

"The author preserves each narrator's complexity. . . . It's a testament to Smith's skills that although her central character speaks only through other people's recollections, his identity emerges distinctly by the end of the novel." Publ Wkly

Smith, Gordon R., 1951-
The forest in the hallway; by Gordon Smith. Clarion Books 2006 232p $16
Grades: 6 7 8 9   **Fic**
1. Magic—Fiction 2. Witches—Fiction
ISBN 978-0-618-68847-0; 0-618-68847-1
LC 2006-15659
Accompanied by a mysterious lost boy and a rowdy family with strange powers, fourteen-year-old Beatriz searches for her missing parents while evading a band of slave traders and a vengeful witch.

"This entertaining read has creative characters and a story line that will keep readers engaged." Booklist

Smith, Hope Anita
Keeping the night watch; with illustrations by E.B. Lewis. Henry Holt 2008 73p il $18.95 *
Grades: 4 5 6 7   **Fic**
1. Family life—Fiction 2. Fathers—Fiction 3. African Americans—Fiction 4. Novels in verse
ISBN 978-0-8050-7202-0; 0-8050-7202-0
LC 2007-12372

Smith, Hope Anita—*Continued*
Coretta Scott King honor book for text, 2009
Sequel to: The way a door closes (2003)
A thirteen-year-old African American boy chronicles what happens to his family when his father, who temporarily left, returns home and they all must deal with their feelings of anger, hope, abandonment, and fear.
"The words are simple . . . and the beautiful watercolor pictures of the African American family have the same quiet intensity as pictures in the first book. . . . Although mainly in free verse, there's also a sonnet." Booklist

The way a door closes; [by] Hope Anita Smith; with illustrations by Shane W. Evans. Holt & Co. 2003 52p il $18.95
Grades: 4 5 6 7   **Fic**
1. Fathers—Fiction 2. Family life—Fiction 3. African Americans—Fiction 4. Novels in verse
ISBN 0-8050-6477-X   LC 2002-67884
In this novel in verse "readers are drawn into the thoughts and feelings of a 13-year-old African American as he tries to understand and cope with a parent's departure from the family. . . . In carefully chosen, straightforward language, Smith conveys the boy's roller-coaster emotions with pinpoint accuracy. The results are poems that are heartbreaking, angry, and tender. Done in warm shades of mostly brown, blue, and gold, Evans's color spot and full-page paintings have a realistic, slightly sculptural appearance and are a perfect complement to the poems." SLJ
Followed by Keeping the night watch (2008)

Smith, Jennifer E.
The comeback season. Simon & Schuster Books for Young Readers 2008 246p $15.99
Grades: 6 7 8 9 10   **Fic**
1. Baseball—Fiction 2. Father-daughter relationship—Fiction 3. Bereavement—Fiction 4. Family life—Fiction 5. Chicago (Ill.)—Fiction
ISBN 978-1-4169-3847-7; 1-4169-3847-8
     LC 2007-17067
High school freshman Ryan Walsh, a Chicago Cubs fan, meets Nick when they both skip school on opening day, and their blossoming relationship becomes difficult for Ryan when she discovers that Nick is seriously ill and she again feels the pain of losing her father five years earlier.
"Smith deftly twines strands of grief, romance, baseball, family, and friendships lost and regained into this tale. . . . The present-tense narrative has an immediacy that will engage readers and the supporting cast is unusually vivid." Booklist

Smith, Kirsten, 1970-
The geography of girlhood. Little, Brown 2006 184p $16.99; pa $7.99
Grades: 8 9 10 11 12   **Fic**
1. Family life—Fiction 2. School stories 3. Novels in verse
ISBN 0-316-16021-0; 0-316-01735-3 (pa)
     LC 2005-938431

Novel in poetry about a girl navigating the unknown, the difficult limbo between youth and adulthood. A novel written in verse follows Penny Morrow in her transition from middle school to high school as her father remarries, she acquires a new stepbrother, and she experiences her first dance, first kiss, and other hazards of growing up.
"There is some matter-of-fact mention of sexual situations and underage drinking. However, it is the clarity, the keen understanding, and the apt metaphors that make Penny's voice so memorable." SLJ

Smith, Patricia Clark, 1943-
Weetamoo, heart of the Pocassets. Scholastic 2003 203p il (Royal diaries) $10.95
Grades: 6 7 8 9   **Fic**
1. Native Americans—Fiction 2. Massachusetts—Fiction
ISBN 0-439-12910-9   LC 00-49243
The 1653-1654 diary of a fourteen-year-old Pocasset Indian girl, destined to become a leader of her tribe, describes how her life changes with the seasons, after a ritual fast she undertakes, and with her tribe's interaction with the English "Coat-men" of the nearby Plymouth Colony
This is "a lively yet ultimately tragic tale that vividly evokes the time period." Booklist

Smith, Roland, 1951-
Cryptid hunters. Hyperion Books for Children 2005 348p $15.99
Grades: 5 6 7 8   **Fic**
1. Twins—Fiction 2. Congo (Republic)—Fiction 3. Adventure fiction
ISBN 0-7868-5161-9
Twins, Grace and Marty, along with a mysterious uncle, are dropped into the middle of the Congolese jungle in search of their missing photojournalist parents.
"The action is nonstop in this well-paced jungle adventure, and Smith adds a deeper layer in scenes of Marty and Grace discovering truths about their complicated family relationships." Booklist

Elephant run. Hyperion Books for Children 2007 318p $15.99
Grades: 6 7 8 9 10 11 12   **Fic**
1. World War, 1939-1945—Fiction 2. Myanmar—Fiction 3. Prisoners of war—Fiction 4. Elephants—Fiction
ISBN 978-1-4231-0402-5; 1-4231-0402-1
     LC 2007-13310
Nick endures servitude, beatings, and more after his British father's plantation in Burma is invaded by the Japanese in 1941.
"The Burmese setting and the role of elephants in the lumbering industry are exceptionally well integrated into this wartime adventure tale." Bull Cent Child Books

I, Q.: book one, Indepedence Hall. Sleeping Bear Press 2008 302p pa $8.95
Grades: 5 6 7 8   **Fic**

Smith, Roland, 1951--—*Continued*
1. Terrorism—Fiction 2. Spies—Fiction 3. Adventure fiction
ISBN 978-1-58536-325-4 (pa); 1-58536-325-1 (pa)

In Philadelphia, Angela realizes she's being followed, and Q soon learns the secret about Angela's real mother, a former Secret Service agent.

"Adventure, suspense, humor, fascinating characters, and plot twists galore will draw middle-graders to this series starter." Booklist

Peak. Harcourt 2007 246p $17 *
Grades: 7 8 9 10 Fic
1. Mountaineering—Fiction 2. Father-son relationship—Fiction 3. Mount Everest (China and Nepal)—Fiction
ISBN 978-0-15-202417-8 LC 2006024325

After fourteen-year-old Peak Marcello is arrested for scaling a New York City skyscraper, he is sent to live with his long-lost father, who wants him to be the youngest person to reach the Everest summit.

"This is a thrilling, multifaceted adventure story. Smith includes plenty of mountaineering facts told in vivid detail. . . . But he also explores other issues, such as the selfishness that nearly always accompanies the intensely single-minded." Booklist

Smith, Sherri L.
Flygirl. G.P. Putnam's Sons 2009 275p $16.99
*
Grades: 7 8 9 10 Fic
1. Women Airforce Service Pilots (U.S.)—Fiction 2. World War, 1939-1945—Fiction 3. Women air pilots—Fiction 4. Air pilots—Fiction 5. African Americans—Fiction
ISBN 978-0-399-24709-5; 0-399-24709-2
LC 2008-25407

During World War II, a light-skinned African American girl "passes" for white in order to join the Women Airforce Service Pilots.

"The details about navigation are exciting, but tougher than any flight maneuver are Ida Mae's loneliness, shame, and fear that she will be thrown out of the the military, feelings that culminate in an unforgettable climax." Booklist

Hot, sour, salty, sweet. Delacorte Press 2008 167p $15.99; lib bdg $18.99
Grades: 5 6 7 8 Fic
1. Cooking—Fiction 2. Family life—Fiction 3. Los Angeles (Calif.)—Fiction 4. Racially mixed people—Fiction
ISBN 978-0-385-73417-2; 0-385-73417-4; 978-0-385-90431-5 (lib bdg); 0-385-90431-2 (lib bdg)
LC 2007-15035

Disaster strikes when Ana Shen is about to deliver the salutatorian speech at her junior high school graduation, but an even greater crisis looms when her best friend invites a crowd to Ana's house for dinner, and Ana's multicultural grandparents must find a way to share a kitchen.

"Ana is a winning heroine, a real teenager trying to cope with frustrating situations through patience and humor, and sometimes losing both. The supporting characters are strongly drawn." SLJ

Smith, Sherwood
A posse of princesses. Norilana Books 2008 299p $22.95
Grades: 7 8 9 10 Fic
1. Fairy tales
ISBN 978-1-934648-26-1; 1-934648-26-4

"In this delightful novel, 16-year-old Princess Rhis travels from her small mountain kingdom of Nym to the large kingdom of Vesarja for a party in honor of newly named Crown Prince Lios. While there, the intelligent and independent teen takes a leading role in a quest to rescue an abducted princess and finds herself drawn, not to the handsome prince or one of his royal peers, but to the prince's clever, witty scribe. . . . Smith's humorous narrative, colorful descriptions of palace life, and fully realized characters will appeal to romance and fantasy buffs alike." SLJ

Smith, Yeardley, 1964-
I, Lorelei; by Yeardley Smith. Laura Geringer Books 2009 339p il $16.99; lib bdg $17.89
Grades: 4 5 6 Fic
1. Divorce—Fiction 2. Diaries—Fiction 3. Family life—Fiction
ISBN 978-0-06-149344-7; 0-06-149344-9; 978-0-06-149345-4 (lib bdg); 0-06-149345-7 (lib bdg)

In letters to her recently deceased cat Mud, eleven-year-old Lorelei chronicles the ups and downs of her sixth-grade year, during which her parents separate, she gets a part in the school play, and she becomes friends with the cutest boy in her grade.

"Lorelei's authentic and endearing voice provide a richly layered reading experience. This funny, poignant story of self-centered parents and appealing, resilient children is a winner." SLJ

Sniegoski, Tom
Sleeper code; by Tom Sniegoski. Razorbill 2006 278p (Sleeper conspiracy) pa $6.99
Grades: 8 9 10 11 12 Fic
1. Sleep disorders—Fiction 2. Multiple personality—Fiction 3. Conspiracies—Fiction
ISBN 1-59514-052-2 LC 2006009102

Just when he has met a beautiful girl and his outlook is improving, sixteen-year-old narcoleptic Tom Lovett begins to suspect that his dreams and hallucinations of killing people may be something more real and terrifying.

"Readers looking for fast-paced action and espionage will enjoy this first book in the two-part Sleeper Conspiracy." SLJ

Snow, Alan
Here be monsters! an adventure involving magic, trolls, and other creatures; written and illustrated by Alan Snow. Atheneum Books for Young Readers 2006 529p il (The Ratbridge chronicles) $17.95
Grades: 4 5 6 7 Fic
1. Fantasy fiction 2. Monsters—Fiction
ISBN 978-0-689-87047-7; 0-689-87047-7
LC 2005024438

Snow, Alan—*Continued*

While gathering food to bring to his grandfather, young Arthur becomes trapped in the city of Ratbridge, where he and some new friends try to stop a plot to shrink the monsters of Arthur's home, the Underworld, for a nefarious purpose.

"Helpful in creating the settings and bringing the more fantastic characters to life, the illustrations, which are often amusing, also make the book accessible to younger children who like lengthy books. Snow's inventive fantasy . . . combines stout hearts, terrible troubles, and inspired lunacy." Booklist

Snow, Carol, 1965-

Switch. HarperTeen 2008 215p $16.99

Grades: 8 9 10 11 12 **Fic**

1. Supernatural—Fiction

ISBN 978-0-06-145208-6; 0-06-145208-4

LC 2008020220

Living in a small beach community with her mother, fifteen-year-old Claire, an accomplished swimmer, discovers that, like her long-dead but, still very much present, grandmother, she has the ability to inhabit other people's bodies while asleep.

"Claire's quick-paced narration comes laced with bolts of sarcasm; the realistic problems blend successfully into a suspenseful, mystical story." Kirkus

Snow, Maya

Sisters of the sword. HarperCollins 2008 275p (Sisters of the sword) $16.99; lib bdg $17.89

Grades: 5 6 7 8 **Fic**

1. Samurai—Fiction 2. Sex role—Fiction 3. Sisters—Fiction 4. Japan—Fiction

ISBN 978-0-06-124387-5; 0-06-124387-6; 978-0-06-124388-2 (lib bdg); 0-06-124388-4 (lib bdg)

LC 2007-029610

Two aristocratic sisters in ancient Japan disguise themselves as samurai warriors to take revenge on the uncle who betrayed their family.

"This rousing new series . . . starts off with a bang, or more accurately, the silent thrust of a sword." Booklist

Other titles in this series are:

Chasing the secret (2009)

Journey through fire (2009)

Snyder, Zilpha Keatley

The magic nation thing; [by] Zilpha Keatley Snyder. Delacorte Press 2005 164p $15.95; lib bdg $17.99

Grades: 4 5 6 7 **Fic**

1. Extrasensory perception—Fiction 2. San Francisco (Calif.)—Fiction

ISBN 0-385-73085-3; 0-385-90107-0 (lib bdg)

LC 2004-10105

Although twelve-year-old Abby has always tried to deny that she has some kind of weird psychic power, she takes advantage of it to help her mother, a struggling private investigator, and, more importantly, to find her best friend's little brother when he goes missing at a ski resort.

"Readers will delight in Snyder's vivid descriptions of Abby's special powers, but what will draw them most is the warm, believable story." Booklist

The Unseen. Delacorte Press 2004 199p $15.95; lib bdg $17.99

Grades: 5 6 7 8 **Fic**

1. Supernatural—Fiction

ISBN 0-385-73084-5; 0-385-90106-2 (lib bdg)

LC 2003-46299

Feeling angry and out-of-place in her large family, twelve-year-old Xandra finds a magical key to a world of ghostly, sometimes frightening, phantoms that help her see herself and her siblings more clearly.

"This book is a wonderful ride into fantasy, with a lot of realistic touches to think about and relationships to ponder. . . . This perceptive story is not to be missed." SLJ

Somper, Justin

Vampirates: demons of the ocean. Little, Brown 2006 330p $15.99

Grades: 6 7 8 9 **Fic**

1. Pirates—Fiction 2. Vampires—Fiction 3. Twins—Fiction 4. Adventure fiction

ISBN 0-316-01373-0

When twins Connor and Grace's ship is wrecked in a storm and Connor is rescued by pirates, he believes that Grace has been taken aboard the mythical Vampirate's ship, and he is determined to find her.

"This winning fantasy features both pirates and vampires with adventure, bloodcurling action, and sinister characters." Voice Youth Advocates

Son, John

Finding my hat. Orchard Bks. 2003 185p (First person fiction) $16.95; pa $6.99

Grades: 5 6 7 8 **Fic**

1. Korean Americans—Fiction 2. Family life—Fiction

ISBN 0-439-43538-2; 0-439-43539-0 (pa)

LC 2002-44998

Jin-Han describes his life growing up with his mother and father, immigrants from Korea, and his little sister as they move to different cities with his parents' business

This is "a beautifully written and deeply personal account of growing up." SLJ

Sones, Sonya

Stop pretending; what happened when my big sister went crazy. HarperCollins Pubs. 1999 149p lib bdg $14.89; pa $6.99

Grades: 6 7 8 9 **Fic**

1. Mental illness—Fiction 2. Sisters—Fiction

ISBN 0-06-028386-6 (lib bdg); 0-06-446218-8 (pa)

LC 99-11473

"Based on the journals Sones wrote at the age of 13 when her 19-year-old sister was hospitalized due to manic depression, the simply crafted but deeply felt poems reflect her thoughts, fears, hopes, and dreams during that troubling time." SLJ

Sones, Sonya—*Continued*

What my girlfriend doesn't know. Simon & Schuster Books for Young Readers 2007 291p $16.99 *

Grades: 7 8 9 10   **Fic**

1. Dating (Social customs)—Fiction 2. School stories 3. Artists—Fiction 4. Boston (Mass.)—Fiction

ISBN 978-0-689-87602-8; 0-689-87602-5

LC 2006-14682

Sequel to What my mother doesn't know (2001)

Fourteen-year-old Robin Murphy is so unpopular at high school that his name is slang for "loser," and so when he begins dating the beautiful and popular Sophie her reputation plummets, but he finds acceptance as a student in a drawing class at Harvard.

"Robin's believable voice is distinctive, and Sones uses her spare words (and a few drawings) to expert effect." Booklist

What my mother doesn't know. Simon & Schuster Bks. for Young Readers 2001 259p $17; pa $7.99

Grades: 7 8 9 10   **Fic**

1. Dating (Social customs)—Fiction

ISBN 0-689-84114-0; 0-689-85553-2 (pa)

LC 00-52634

"Fourteen-year-old Sophia is searching for Mr. Right. In a story written in poetry form, Sophia describes her relationships with sexy Dylan, suspicious cyberboy, and, finally, with the mysterious masked 'stranger' who dances with her on Halloween and then disappears." Book Rep

This is "a fast, funny, touching book. . . . The very short, sometimes rhythmic lines make each page fly. Sophie's voice is colloquial and intimate." Booklist

Followed by What my girlfriend doesn't know (2007)

Sonnenblick, Jordan

Drums, girls, & dangerous pie. Scholastic Press 2005 c2004 273p $16.99

Grades: 5 6 7 8   **Fic**

1. Leukemia—Fiction 2. Brothers—Fiction

ISBN 0-439-75519-0   LC 2004-62563

First published 2004 by Turning Tide Press

When his younger brother is diagnosed with leukemia, thirteen-year-old Steven tries to deal with his complicated emotions, his school life, and his desire to support his family.

"A story that could have morphed into melodrama is saved by reality, rawness, and the wit Sonnenblick infuses into Steven's first-person voice." Booklist

Notes from the midnight driver. Scholastic Press 2006 265p $16.99 *

Grades: 8 9 10 11 12   **Fic**

1. Friendship—Fiction 2. Old age—Fiction 3. Musicians—Fiction

ISBN 0-439-75779-7   LC 2005-27972

After being assigned to perform community service at a nursing home, sixteen-year-old Alex befriends a cantankerous old man who has some lessons to impart about jazz guitar playing, love, and forgiveness.

The author "deftly infiltrates the teenage mind to produce a first-person narrative riddled with enough hapless

confusion, mulish equivocation, and beleaguered deadpan humor to have readers nodding with recognition, sighing with sympathy, and gasping with laughter—often on the same page." Horn Book

Zen and the art of faking it. Scholastic Press 2007 264p $16.99 *

Grades: 5 6 7 8   **Fic**

1. School stories 2. Zen Buddhism—Fiction 3. Asian Americans—Fiction 4. Pennsylvania—Fiction

ISBN 978-0-439-83707-1; 0-439-83707-3

LC 2006-28841

When thirteen-year-old San Lee moves to a new town and school for the umpteenth time, he is looking for a way to stand out when his knowledge of Zen Buddhism, gained in his previous school, provides the answer—and the need to quickly become a convincing Zen master.

The author gives readers "plenty to laugh at. . . . Mixed with more serious scenes, . . . lighter moments take a basic message about the importance of honesty and forgiveness and treat it with panache." Publ Wkly

Sorrells, Walter

Erratum. 1st ed. Dutton 2008 298p $17.99

Grades: 4 5 6 7   **Fic**

1. Science fiction 2. Space and time—Fiction 3. Books and reading—Fiction

ISBN 978-0-525-47832-4; 0-525-47832-9

LC 2007052647

When Jessica finds--and then loses--an unfinished book about her life, she learns that if she cannot keep it from falling into the wrong hands, the balance of the universe is in peril.

"Highly imaginative, fast-paced and a bit disorienting. . . . Sorrell presents a stew of hearty concepts, including string theory, alternate dimensions and mind control. Readers with a taste for science or science fiction will be especially intrigued." Publ Wkly

Fake ID; Hunted: book one. Sleuth/Dutton 2005 313p $12.99

Grades: 7 8 9 10   **Fic**

1. Mystery fiction

ISBN 0-525-47514-1   LC 2004-21578

After a lifetime of moving and assuming new identities, sixteen-year-old Chass begins to piece together the disturbing past that haunts her and her mother and which involves a mysterious tape, a deceased popular singer, and the secrets of several people in a small Alabama town.

"Sorrells masterfully sustains suspense throughout, spiking the drama with some truly frightening scenes that make this a terrific read." Booklist

Another title about Chastity is:

Club Dread, Hunted: book two (2006)

First shot. Dutton Children's Books 2007 279p $16.99 *

Grades: 7 8 9 10 11 12   **Fic**

1. Mystery fiction 2. Homicide—Fiction 3. Father-son relationship—Fiction

ISBN 978-0-525-47801-0; 0-525-47801-9

As David enters his senior year of high school, a family secret emerges that could solve the mystery of why

Sorrells, Walter—*Continued*

his mother was murdered two years ago.

"David's first person narration pulls readers into the young man's torment. . . . This is a fast-paced, intriguing read." Booklist

Soto, Gary

Accidental love; [by] Gary Soto. Harcourt 2006 179p $16

Grades: 6 7 8 9   **Fic**

1. Love stories 2. School stories 3. Hispanic Americans—Fiction

ISBN 0-15-205497-9   LC 2004-29900

After unexpectedly falling in love with a "nerdy" boy, fourteen-year-old Marisa works to change her life by transferring to another school, altering some of her behavior, and losing weight.

This is a "warmhearted, humorous novel." SLJ

The afterlife. Harcourt 2003 161p $16; pa $6.95

Grades: 7 8 9 10   **Fic**

1. Mexican Americans—Fiction 2. Ghost stories

ISBN 0-15-204774-3; 0-15-205220-8 (pa)

       LC 2003-44995

A senior at East Fresno High School lives on as a ghost after his brutal murder in the restroom of a club where he had gone to dance.

"In many ways, this is as much a story about a hardscrabble place as it is about a boy who is murdered. Both pulse with life and will stay in memory." Booklist

Buried onions. Harcourt Brace & Co. 1997 149p $17; pa $6.95 *

Grades: 8 9 10 11 12   **Fic**

1. Violence—Fiction 2. Mexican Americans—Fiction

ISBN 0-15-201333-4; 0-15-206265-3 (pa)

       LC 96-53112

When nineteen-year-old Eddie drops out of college, he struggles to find a place for himself as a Mexican American living in a violence-infested neighborhood of Fresno, California.

"Soto has created a beautiful, touching, and truthful story. . . . The lyrical language and Spanish phrases add to the immediacy of setting and to the sensitivity the author brings to his character's life." Voice Youth Advocates

Taking sides. Harcourt Brace Jovanovich 1991 138p $17; pa $5.95 *

Grades: 5 6 7 8   **Fic**

1. Hispanic Americans—Fiction 2. Basketball—Fiction

ISBN 0-15-284076-1; 0-15-204694-1 (pa)

       LC 91-11082

Fourteen-year-old Lincoln Mendoza, an aspiring basketball player, must come to terms with his divided loyalties when he moves from the Hispanic inner city to a white suburban neighborhood

This is a "light but appealing story. . . . Because of its subject matter and its clear, straightforward prose, it will be especially good for reluctant readers." SLJ

Includes glossary

Sparrow, Rebecca, 1972-

The year Nick McGowan came to stay; [by] Rebecca Sparrow. 1st American ed. Alfred A. Knopf 2008 c2006 198p $15.99; lib bdg $18.99

Grades: 8 9 10 11   **Fic**

1. Australia—Fiction 2. School stories

ISBN 978-0-375-84570-3; 0-375-84570-4; 978-0-375-94570-0 (lib bdg); 0-375-84570-9 (lib bdg)

       LC 2007020758

First published 2006 in Australia

In her final year of high school in 1989, Australian teenager Rachel has her world turned upside down when the most popular (and disturbed) boy in school comes to live with her family for a semester.

"This book is full of laugh-out-loud moments. . . . Sparrow is adept at accurately portraying her teenage characters and placing them in realistic scenarios that most readers will find pertinent." SLJ

Speare, Elizabeth George, 1908-1994

The sign of the beaver. Houghton Mifflin 1983 135p $16 *

Grades: 5 6 7 8   **Fic**

1. Frontier and pioneer life—Fiction 2. Native Americans—Fiction 3. Friendship—Fiction

ISBN 0-395-33890-5   LC 83-118

Also available in paperback from Dell

A Newbery Medal honor book, 1984

Left alone to guard the family's wilderness home in eighteenth-century Maine, Matt is hard-pressed to survive until local Indians teach him their skills

Matt "begins to understand the Indians' ingenuity and respect for nature and the devastating impact of the encroachment of the white man. In a quiet but not unsuspenseful story . . . the author articulates historical facts along with the adventures and the thoughts, emotions, and developing insights of a young adolescent." Horn Book

The witch of Blackbird Pond. Houghton Mifflin 1958 249p $16 *

Grades: 6 7 8 9   **Fic**

1. Connecticut—History—1600-1775, Colonial period—Fiction 2. Witchcraft—Fiction 3. Puritans—Fiction

ISBN 0-395-07114-3   LC 58-11063

Also available in paperback from Dell

Awarded the Newbery Medal, 1959

"Headstrong and undisciplined, Barbados-bred Kit Tyler is an embarrassment to her Puritan relatives, and her sincere attempts to aid a reputed witch soon bring her to trial as a suspect." Child Books Too Good to Miss

Spillebeen, Geert, 1956-

Kipling's choice; written by Geert Spillebeen; translated by Terese Edelstein. Houghton Mifflin Co 2005 147p $16; pa $7.99

Grades: 7 8 9 10   **Fic**

1. Kipling, John, 1897-1915—Fiction 2. World War, 1914-1918—Fiction 3. France—Fiction

ISBN 0-618-43124-1; 0-618-80035-2 (pa)

       LC 2004-20856

Spillebeen, Geert, 1956——*Continued*

In 1915, mortally wounded in Loos, France, eighteen-year-old John Kipling, son of writer Rudyard Kipling, remembers his boyhood and the events leading to what is to be his first and last World War I battle.

"This well-written novel combines facts with speculation about John Kipling's short life and gruesome death. A riveting account of World War I." SLJ

Spinelli, Jerry, 1941-

Crash. Knopf 1996 162p $16; pa $4.99 *

Grades: 5 6 7 8 **Fic**
1. Football—Fiction 2. Grandfathers—Fiction
3. Friendship—Fiction
ISBN 0-679-87957-9; 0-679-88550-1 (pa)
LC 95-30942

"Crash is a star football player. He torments Penn, a classmate who is everything Crash is not—friendly, small, and a pacifist. When his beloved grandfather comes to live with his family and suffers a debilitating stroke, Crash begins to see value in many of the things he has scorned." Horn Book Guide

"Readers will devour this humorous glimpse at what jocks are made of while learning that life does not require crashing helmet-headed through it." SLJ

Maniac Magee; a novel. Little, Brown 1990 184p $16.99; pa $6.99 *

Grades: 5 6 7 8 **Fic**
1. Orphans—Fiction 2. Homeless persons—Fiction
3. Race relations—Fiction
ISBN 0-316-80722-2; 0-316-80906-3 (pa)
LC 89-27144

Awarded the Newbery Medal, 1991

"Orphaned at three, Jeffery Lionel Magee, after eight unhappy years with relatives, one day takes off running. A year later, he ends up 200 miles away in Two Mills, a highly segregated community. Part tall tale and part contemporary realistic fiction, this unusual novel magically weaves timely issues of homelessness, racial prejudice, and illiteracy into an energetic story that bursts with creativity, enthusiasm, and hope for the future. In short, it's a celebration of life." Booklist

Smiles to go. Joanna Cotler Books 2008 248p $16.99; lib bdg $17.89

Grades: 6 7 8 9 10 **Fic**
1. Siblings—Fiction 2. Friendship—Fiction 3. Family life—Fiction 4. School stories
ISBN 978-0-06-028133-5; 0-06-028133-2; 978-0-06-028134-2 (lib bdg); 0-06-028134-0 (lib bdg)
LC 2007-29563

Will Tuppence's life has always been ruled by science and common sense but in ninth grade, shaken up by the discovery that protons decay, he begins to see the entire world differently and gains new perspective on his relationships with his little sister and two closest friends.

"What makes a Spinelli novel isn't plotting so much as character, dialogue, voice and humor. The Spinelli touch remains true in this funny and thoroughly enjoyable read." Publ Wkly

Stargirl. Knopf 2000 186p $15.95; lib bdg $17.99; pa $8.95 *

Grades: 7 8 9 10 **Fic**
1. School stories 2. Arizona—Fiction
ISBN 0-679-88637-0; 0-679-98637-5 (lib bdg); 0-375-82233-X (pa)
LC 99-87944

In this story about the perils of popularity, the courage of nonconformity, and the thrill of first love, an eccentric student named Stargirl changes Mica High School forever

"As always respectful of his audience, Spinelli poses searching questions about loyalty to one's friends and oneself and leaves readers to form their own answers." Publ Wkly

Another title about Stargirl is:
Love, Stargirl (2007)

There's a girl in my hammerlock. Simon & Schuster Bks. for Young Readers 1991 199p pa $5.99 hardcover o.p.

Grades: 5 6 7 8 **Fic**
1. Wrestling—Fiction 2. Sex role—Fiction 3. School stories
ISBN 1-4169-3937-7 (pa)
LC 91-8765

Thirteen-year-old Maisie joins her school's formerly all-male wrestling team and tries to last through the season, despite opposition from other students, her best friend, and her own teammates

The author "tackles a meaty subject—traditional gender roles—with his usual humor and finesse. The result, written in a breezy, first-person style, is a rattling good sports story that is clever, witty and tightly written." Publ Wkly

Wringer. HarperCollins Pubs. 1997 228p $16.99; lib bdg $16.89; pa $6.50 *

Grades: 4 5 6 7 **Fic**
1. Courage—Fiction 2. Violence—Fiction
3. Pigeons—Fiction
ISBN 0-06-024913-7; 0-06-024914-5 (lib bdg); 0-06-440578-8 (pa)
LC 96-37897

A Newbery Medal honor book, 1998

"Joanna Cotler books"

"During the annual pigeon shoot, it is a town tradition for 10-year-old boys to break the necks of wounded birds. In this riveting story told with verve and suspense, Palmer rebels." SLJ

Spinner, Stephanie, 1943-

Damosel; in which the Lady of the Lake renders a frank and often startling account of her wondrous life and times. Alfred A. Knopf 2008 198p $16.99; lib bdg $19.99

Grades: 7 8 9 10 **Fic**
1. Arthur, King—Fiction 2. Dwarfs—Fiction 3. Fools and jesters—Fiction 4. Magic—Fiction 5. Knights and knighthood—Fiction 6. Great Britain—History—0-1066—Fiction
ISBN 978-0-375-83634-3; 0-375-83634-9; 978-0-375-93634-0 (lib bdg); 0-375-93634-3 (lib bdg)
LC 2007-43519

Damosel, a rule-bound Lady of the Lake, and Twixt, a seventeen-year-old dwarf, relate their experiences as

Spinner, Stephanie, 1943-—*Continued*
they strive to help King Arthur face Morgause, Morgan, and Mordred, one through her magic and the other through his humble loyalty.

"The magic is exciting and palpable. . . . Spinner's elegant language, strong characterizations, energetic dialogue, and lively plot combine in a memorable, accessible novel." Booklist

Quicksilver. Knopf 2005 229p $15.95; lib bdg $17.99

Grades: 7 8 9 10   **Fic**
1. Classical mythology—Fiction
ISBN 0-375-82638-6; 0-375-92638-0 (lib bdg)
                             LC 2004-10311

Hermes, Prince of Thieves and son of Zeus, relates why the seasons change, the history of the Trojan War, his friendship with Pegasus, and many more adventures.

"Spinner seamlessly weaves necessary background information about the cast of celestial characters into a narrative filled with thrilling action and violence that is drawn straight from the original stories. Teens will connect with Hermes' immediate, often very funny voice." Booklist

Quiver. Knopf 2002 177p $15.95; lib bdg $17.99; pa $5.99

Grades: 7 8 9 10   **Fic**
ISBN 0-375-81489-2; 0-375-91489-7 (lib bdg); 0-440-23819-6 (pa)   LC 2002-5451

When her father commands that she produce an heir, the huntress Atalanta gives her suitors a seemingly impossible task in order to uphold her pledge of chastity, as the gods of ancient Greece look on

"Spinner gives this Greek myth a fresh face and makes Atalanta a strong heroine." SLJ

Spooner, Michael
Last Child. Henry Holt 2005 230p $16.95

Grades: 7 8 9 10   **Fic**
1. Mandan Indians—Fiction 2. Smallpox—Fiction 3. Racially mixed people—Fiction 4. North Dakota—Fiction
ISBN 0-8050-7739-1   LC 2005-9957

"The horror of the smallpox epidemic that killed more than 20,000 Indians from the Upper Missouri nations in the late 1830s is told from the perspective of a young girl at a fur-company outpost, who is caught between her loving Scottish dad, who calls her Rosalie, and her Mandan family that calls her Last Child." Booklist

"Action-packed prose; sharp, witty dialogue; and strong characterization make this novel an entertaining read." Voice Youth Advocates

Spradlin, Michael P.
Keeper of the Grail. G.P. Putnam's Sons 2008 248p (The youngest Templar) $17.99

Grades: 5 6 7 8   **Fic**
1. Knights and knighthood—Fiction 2. Grail—Fiction 3. Middle Ages—Fiction 4. Crusades—Fiction
ISBN 978-0-399-24763-7; 0-399-24763-7
                             LC 2007-36143

In 1191, fifteen-year-old Tristan, a youth of unknown origin raised in an English abbey, becomes a Templar Knight's squire during the Third Crusade and soon finds himself on a mission to bring the Holy Grail to safety.

"The deadly action, uncompromising in many of its descriptions, may take center stage, but Spradlin smartly doesn't neglect story. . . . The stirring story ends with a true cliff-hanger, priming fans for the next installment." Booklist

Springer, Nancy
The case of the missing marquess; an Enola Holmes mystery. Philomel Books 2006 216p $10.99 *

Grades: 5 6 7 8   **Fic**
1. Mystery fiction 2. London (England)—Fiction 3. Missing persons—Fiction
ISBN 0-399-24304-6

Enola Holmes, much younger sister of detective Sherlock Holmes, must travel to London in disguise to unravel the disappearance of her missing mother.

"Enola's loneliness, intelligence, sense of humor, and sheer pluck make her an extremely appealing heroine." SLJ

Other titles about Enola Holmes are:
The case of the left-handed lady (2007)
The case of the bizarre bouquets (2008)
The case of the peculiar pink fan (2008)

Dusssie. Walker & Co. 2007 176p $16.95

Grades: 5 6 7 8   **Fic**
1. Classical mythology—Fiction 2. Mother-daughter relationship—Fiction 3. Snakes—Fiction 4. New York (N.Y.)—Fiction 5. Artists—Fiction
ISBN 0-8027-9649-3; 978-0-8027-9649-4

At age thirteen Dusie makes the horrifying discovery that she, like her New York artist mother, is a Gorgon—a Greek mythological monster sprouting snakes from her head and capable of turning humans into stone with one angry look.

This "is an enjoyable read, fast paced and fun, with a smart, likable character." SLJ

I am Mordred; a tale from Camelot. Philomel Bks. 1998 184p hardcover o.p. pa $6.99

Grades: 7 8 9 10   **Fic**
1. Arthur, King—Fiction 2. Mordred (Legendary character)—Fiction 3. Great Britain—History—0-1066—Fiction
ISBN 0-399-23143-9; 0-698-11841-3 (pa)
                             LC 97-39740

"Mordred, the bad seed, the son of King Arthur and his sister, spends his youth learning who he is and then trying to deal with the prophecy made by Merlin that he will kill his father." SLJ

"Springer humanizes Arthurian archvillain Mordred in a thoroughly captivating and poignant tale." Booklist

I am Morgan le Fay; a tale from Camelot. Philomel Bks. 2001 227p hardcover o.p. pa $5.99

Grades: 7 8 9 10   **Fic**
1. Arthur, King—Fiction 2. Morgan le Fay (Legendary character)—Fiction 3. Great Britain—History—0-1066—Fiction
ISBN 0-399-23451-9; 0-698-11974-6 (pa)
                             LC 99-52847

Springer, Nancy—*Continued*

In a war-torn England where her half-brother Arthur will eventually become king, the young Morgan le Fay comes to realize that she has magic powers and links to the faerie world

"Introspective, yet threaded with intrigue and adventure, this compelling study of the legendary villainess explores the ways that love, hate, jealousy, and the desire for power shape one young woman's fate and affect the destiny of others." Horn Book

Rowan Hood, outlaw girl of Sherwood Forest. Philomel Bks. 2001 170p $16.99 *

Grades: 4 5 6 7   Fic

1. Robin Hood (Legendary character)—Fiction
2. Middle Ages—Fiction 3. Adventure fiction
ISBN 0-399-23368-7   LC 00-63694

In her quest to connect with Robin Hood, the father she has never met, thirteen-year-old Rosemary disguises herself as a boy, befriends a half-wolf, half-dog, a runaway princess, and an overgrown boy whose singing is hypnotic, and makes peace with her elfin heritage

"This tale is a charmer, filled with exciting action, plenty of humor, engaging characters, and a nice fantasy twist." Booklist

Other titles about Rowan Hood are:
Lionclaw (2002)
Outlaw princess of Sherwood (2003)
Rowan Hood returns (2005)
Wild boy (2004)

St. Anthony, Jane

Grace above all; [by] Jane St. Anthony. 1st ed. Farrar Straus Giroux 2007 166p $16

Grades: 5 6 7 8   Fic

1. Mothers—Fiction 2. Family life—Fiction
3. Vacations—Fiction
ISBN 0-374-39940-9; 978-0-374-39940-5
     LC 2006047630

When thirteen-year-old Grace, her mother, and four siblings go to her mother's childhood cabin by a lake over the summer, as usual Grace is in charge of all the kids while her mother does nothing, but after meeting some relatives Grace becomes a bit more understanding, and learns to stand up for herself.

"St. Anthony effectively explores the netherworld of early adolescent friendship and love. Readers will meet a variety of unusual and lovable characters." Booklist

The summer Sherman loved me; [by] Jane St. Anthony. 1st ed. Farrar, Straus & Giroux 2006 136p $16

Grades: 5 6 7 8   Fic

1. Family life—Fiction 2. Mother-daughter relationship—Fiction 3. Friendship—Fiction
ISBN 0-374-3728-6   LC 2005046361

In addition to coping with her changing relationship with her mother, twelve-year-old Margaret spends her summer trying to sort out her feelings for the boy next door who claims to love her.

"This fluidly told, well-paced novel is set in a more innocent time. . . . The emotions experienced by the well-drawn characters, however, remain universal. A fresh and refreshing coming-of-age story." SLJ

St. Crow, Lili, 1976-

Strange angels. Razorbill 2009 293p pa $9.99

Grades: 7 8 9 10   Fic

1. Supernatural—Fiction 2. Extrasensory perception—Fiction 3. Werewolves—Fiction 4. Vampires—Fiction 5. Orphans—Fiction
ISBN 978-1-59514-251-1 (pa); 1-59514-251-7 (pa)
     LC 2008-39720

Sixteen-year-old Dru's psychic abilities helped her father battle zombies and other creatures of the "Real World," but now she must rely on herself, a "werwulf"-bitten friend, and a half-human vampire hunter to learn who murdered her parents, and why.

"The book grabs readers by the throat, sets hearts beating loudly and never lets go." Kirkus

St. John, Lauren, 1966-

The white giraffe; illustrated by David Dean. Dial Books for Young Readers 2007 180p $16.99

Grades: 4 5 6 7   Fic

1. Mythical animals—Fiction 2. Giraffes—Fiction
3. Orphans—Fiction 4. South Africa—Fiction
ISBN 978-0-8037-3211-7; 0-8037-3211-2
     LC 2006-21323

After a fire kills her parents, eleven-year-old Martine must leave England to live with her grandmother on a wildlife game reserve in South Africa, where she befriends a mythical white giraffe.

"The story is captivating and well spun." SLJ

Other titles in this series are:
Dolphin song (2008)
Last leopard (2009)

Stahler, David, Jr.

Doppelganger; [by] David Stahler, Jr. HarperCollins Publishers 2006 258p $16.99; lib bdg $17.89

Grades: 8 9 10 11 12   Fic

1. Family life—Fiction 2. Child abuse—Fiction
3. Supernatural—Fiction 4. Horror fiction
ISBN   978-0-06-087232-8;   0-06-087232-2; 978-0-06-087233-5 (lib bdg); 0-06-087233-0 (lib bdg)
     LC 2005-28484

When a sixteen-year-old member of a race of shapeshifting killers called doppelgangers assumes the life of a troubled teen, he becomes unexpectedly embroiled in human life—and it is nothing like what he has seen on television.

"This brooding story of literally stepping into someone else's shoes combines romance, horror, and angst to create a distinctive story of redemption. The abusive relationships in Chris's family are portrayed with realism and sensitivity." Voice Youth Advocates

A gathering of shades. HarperTempest 2005 289p $15.99; lib bdg $16.89

Grades: 7 8 9 10   Fic

1. Ghost stories 2. Farm life—Fiction 3. Vermont—Fiction
ISBN 0-06-052294-1; 0-06-052295-X (lib bdg)
     LC 2004-21498

Having moved with his mother to a remote corner of Vermont after his father's death, sixteen-year-old Aidan

Stahler, David, Jr.—*Continued*

learns much about his family, including that ghosts inhabit an ancient orchard on the family farm, sustained by his grandmother.

"Stahler's eloquence on grief and yearning, combined with a vision of ghosts refreshingly distinct from depictions in 'cheesy horror movies,' will exert a powerful hold on many teens' imaginations." Booklist

Stanley, Diane, 1943-

Bella at midnight; illustrated by Bagram Ibatoulline. HarperCollins Pub. 2006 278p il $15.99; lib bdg $16.89 *

Grades: 5 6 7 8   **Fic**
1. Knights and knighthood—Fiction 2. Fairy tales
ISBN 0-06-077573-4; 0-06-077574-2 (lib bdg); 9780060775742 (lib bdg)   LC 2005-05906
Raised by peasants, Bella discovers that she is actually the daughter of a knight and finds herself caught up in a terrible plot that will change her life and the kingdom forever.

"What raises this above other recreated fairy tales is the quality of the writing, dotted with jeweled description and anchored by the strong values—loyalty, truth, honor." Booklist

The mysterious matter of I.M. Fine. HarperCollins Pubs. 2001 201p hardcover o.p. lib bdg $16.89; pa $5.99

Grades: 4 5 6 7   **Fic**
1. Magic—Fiction 2. Books and reading—Fiction 3. Mystery fiction
ISBN 0-688-17546-5; 0-06-029619-4 (lib bdg); 0-380-73327-7 (pa)   LC 00-54040
Noticing that a popular series of horror novels is having a bizarre effect on the behavior of its readers, Franny and Beamer set out to find the mysterious author

"The solidly constructed mystery, well-rounded characters, and playful jab at wildly successful horror writers go down a treat." Horn Book Guide

Another title about Franny and her friends is:
The mysterious case of the Allbright Academy (2008)

Staples, Suzanne Fisher

Dangerous skies. Farrar, Straus & Giroux 1996 231p hardcover o.p. pa $7.95

Grades: 7 8 9 10   **Fic**
1. African Americans—Fiction 2. Prejudices—Fiction 3. Friendship—Fiction
ISBN 0-374-31694-5; 0-374-41670-2 (pa)
                                                                LC 95-45529
"Frances Foster books"

"At twelve, white boy Buck and black girl Tunes Smith are best friends. . . . The adolescents' idyllic world of fishing and observing nature is shattered when their much older friend Jorge Rodrigues is murdered, and Tunes is accused of the crime. . . . Staples's beautifully written and chilling tale of contemporary racism should keep young adult readers turning pages until they reach the heart-breaking end." Voice Youth Advocates

Shabanu; daughter of the wind. Knopf 1989 240p hardcover o.p. pa $6.50

Grades: 8 9 10 11 12   **Fic**
1. Sex role—Fiction 2. Pakistan—Fiction
ISBN 0-394-84815-2; 0-440-23856-0 (pa)
                                                                LC 89-2714
A Newbery Medal honor book, 1990

When eleven-year-old Shabanu, the daughter of a nomad in the Cholistan Desert of present-day Pakistan, is pledged in marriage to an older man whose money will bring prestige to the family, she must either accept the decision, as is the custom, or risk the consequences of defying her father's wishes

"Interspersing native words throughout adds realism, but may trip up readers, who must be patient enough to find meaning through context. This use of language is, however, an important element in helping Staples paint an evocative picture of life in the desert that includes references to the hard facts of reality." Booklist

Other titles in this series are:
Haveli (1993)
The house of djinn (2008)

Shiva's fire. Farrar, Straus & Giroux 1999 275p $17

Grades: 7 8 9 10   **Fic**
1. Dance—Fiction 2. India—Fiction
ISBN 0-374-36824-4   LC 99-10626
Also in paperback from HarperCollins Pubs.

"A Frances Foster book"

In India, a talented dancer sacrifices friends and family for her art

"This novel draws the reader into the exotic setting and spiritual world of sacred Hindu classical dance. The glossary with pronunciation guide helps readers understand Indian terminology. . . . Readers will relate to Parvati's dislike of being different and to her relief upon finding her place as a master dancer, a place where her unique abilities are honored, not feared." Voice Youth Advocates

Under the Persimmon tree. Farrar, Straus & Giroux 2005 275p $17 *

Grades: 7 and up   **Fic**
1. Afghanistan—Fiction 2. Pakistan—Fiction
ISBN 0-374-38025-2

During the 2001 Afghan War, the lives of Najmal, a young refugee from Kunduz, Afghanistan, and Nusrat, an American-Muslim teacher who is awaiting her huband's return from Mazar-i-Sharif, intersect at a school in Peshawar, Pakistan.

"Staples weaves a lot of history and politics into her story. . . . But . . . it's the personal story . . . that compels as it takes readers beyond the modern stereotypes of Muslims as fundamentalist fanatics. There are no sweet reunions, but there's hope in heartbreaking scenes of kindness and courage." Booklist

Staub, Wendy Corsi, 1964-

Lily Dale: awakening. Walker & Co. 2007 228p
$15.95

Grades: 7 8 9 10 **Fic**

1. Extrasensory perception—Fiction
2. Grandmothers—Fiction 3. Mothers—Fiction
4. New York (State)—Fiction 5. Mystery fiction
ISBN 978-0-8027-9654-7; 0-8027-9654-0

LC 2007-2370

When seventeen-year-old Calla's mother suddenly
dies, she goes to stay with her psychic grandmother in
Lily Dale, a spiritualist community in western New
York, where she discovers some disconcerting secrets
about her practical, down-to-earth mother, and realizes
that she herself may also have some psychic abilities.

"Deft characterization couples with a compelling plot."
Voice Youth Advocates

Other titles in this series are:
Lily Dale: believing (2008)
Lily Dale: connecting (2009)

Stauffacher, Sue, 1961-

Donuthead. Knopf 2003 144p $15.95; lib bdg
$17.99 *

Grades: 4 5 6 **Fic**

1. Fear—Fiction 2. Friendship—Fiction
ISBN 0-375-82468-5; 0-375-92468-X (lib bdg)

LC 2003-40073

Franklin Delano Donuthead, a fifth-grader obsessed
with hygiene and safety, finds an unlikely friend and
protector in Sarah Kervick, the tough new student who
lives in a dirty trailer, bonds with his mother, and is as
"irregular" as he is

"It's refreshing for a novel with problem situations to
be so light and funny. An appealing story with some
memorable characters and a lot of heart." SLJ

Another title about Franklin is:
Donutheart (2006)

Harry Sue. Knopf 2005 288p $15.95; lib bdg
$17.99

Grades: 5 6 7 8 **Fic**

1. Prisoners—Fiction 2. Handicapped—Fiction
3. Mother-daughter relationship—Fiction
ISBN 0-375-83274-2; 0-375-93274-7 (lib bdg)

LC 2004-16945

Although tough-talking Harry Sue would like to start
a life of crime in order to be "sent up" and find her incarcerated mother, she must first protect the children at
her neglectful grandmother's home day care center and
befriend a paralyzed boy.

"This is a riveting story, dramatically and well told,
with characters whom readers won't soon forget." SLJ

Stead, Rebecca

First light. Wendy Lamb Books 2007 328p
$15.99; lib bdg $18.99

Grades: 5 6 7 8 **Fic**

1. Greenland—Fiction 2. Greenhouse effect—Fiction
3. Supernatural—Fiction
ISBN 978-0-375-84017-3; 0-375-84017-6;
987-0-375-094017-0 (lib bdg); 0-375-94017-0 (lib
bdg) LC 2006-39733

"The father of 12-year-old Peter is a glaciologist, his
mother, a genetic scientist. Peter is thrilled when his father decides to take the family on his latest excursion to
Greenland to study the effects of global warming. Fourteen-year-old Thea lives in a secret society called
Gracehope under the Greenland ice. After finding a map
that leads her to the surface, she becomes obsessed with
seeing the sun and bringing her people back above
ground. Peter and Thea accidentally meet on the surface
and discover, through a secret kept by Peter's mother,
that their destinies are unexpectedly joined." Booklist

This "novel is an exciting, engaging mix of science
fiction, mystery, and adventure. . . . Peter and Thea are
fully developed main characters." SLJ

When you reach me. Wendy Lamb Books 2009
199p $15.99; lib bdg $18.99 *

Grades: 5 6 7 8 **Fic**

1. Space and time—Fiction 2. New York (N.Y.)—Fiction
ISBN 978-0-385-73742-5; 0-385-73742-4;
978-0-385-90664-7 (lib bdg); 0-385-90664-1 (lib bdg)

LC 2008024998

As her mother prepares to be a contestant on the
1980s television game show, "The $20,000 Pyramid," a
twelve-year-old New York City girl tries to make sense
of a series of mysterious notes received from an anonymous source that seems to defy the laws of time and
space.

"The '70s New York setting is an honest reverberation
of the era; the mental gymnastics required of readers are
invigorating; and the characters . . . are honest bits of
humanity." Booklist

Stein, Tammar

High dive. Alfred A. Knopf 2008 201p $15.99;
lib bdg $18.99

Grades: 7 8 9 10 **Fic**

1. Vacations—Fiction 2. Single parent family—Fiction
3. Loss (Psychology)—Fiction 4. Friendship—Fiction
5. Europe—Fiction 6. Iraq War, 2003-—Fiction
ISBN 978-0-375-83024-2; 0-375-83024-3;
978-0-375-93024-9 (lib bdg); 0-375-93024-8 (lib bdg)

LC 2007049657

With her mother stationed in Iraq as an Army nurse,
Vanderbilt University student Arden Vogel, whose father
was killed in a traffic accident a few years earlier, impulsively ends up on a tour of Europe with a group of college girls she meets on her way to attend to some family
business in Sardinia.

"Ideal for the thoughtful armchair traveler, this story
is engaging enough for readers on the long flight to the
enduring wonders of Europe and emerging adulthood."
SLJ

Light years; a novel. Knopf 2005 263p $15.95;
lib bdg $17.99

Grades: 7 8 9 10 **Fic**

1. Israel-Arab conflicts—Fiction 2. Bereavement—Fiction
ISBN 0-375-83023-5; 0-375-93023-X (lib bdg)

LC 2004-7776

Maya Laor leaves her home in Israel to study astronomy at the University of Virginia after the tragic death of
her boyfriend in a suicide bombing.

Stein, Tammar—*Continued*
"This well-paced first novel, a moving study of grief and recovery, is also a love story that should appeal particularly to students interested in other ways of seeing the world." SLJ
Includes bibliographical references

Steinbeck, John, 1902-1968
The pearl. John Steinbeck centennial ed. Penguin Books 2002 87p pa $11
Grades: 7 8 9 10   **Fic**
1. Mexico—Fiction 2. Poverty—Fiction
ISBN 0-14-200069-8   LC 2001-56113
First published 1947
"Kino, a poor pearl-fisher, lives a happy albeit spartan life with his wife and their child. When he finds a magnificent pearl, the Pearl of the World, he is besieged by dishonest pearl merchants and envious neighbors. Even a greedy doctor ties his professional treatment of their baby when it is bitten by a scorpion to the possible acquisition of the pearl. After a series of disasters, Kino throws the pearl away since it has brought him only unhappiness." Shapiro. Fic for Youth. 3d edition

The red pony. Viking 1993 100p pa $9
    Fic
1. Horses—Fiction 2. Ranch life—Fiction 3. California—Fiction
ISBN 0-670-59184-X; 0-14-017736-1 (pa)
    LC 86-1610
First published 1937
"Jody Tiflin, ten years old, begins to grow up in these four vignettes describing his life on a farm in California. He takes responsibility for his red pony and suffers when it dies. An old man arouses Jody's curiosity about what is beyond the mountains, and he anxiously awaits the birth of a colt. His grandfather's tales are a source of interest and wonder for Jody." Shapiro. Fic for Youth. 3d edition

Sternberg, Libby
The case against my brother. Bancroft Press 2007 201p $19.95
Grades: 6 7 8 9   **Fic**
1. Brothers—Fiction 2. Portland (Or.)—Fiction 3. Polish Americans—Fiction 4. Prejudices—Fiction
ISBN 978-1-890862-51-0; 1-890862-51-7
"In 1922, when their widowed mother dies, Carl Matiuski and his older brother, Adam, move to Portland, OR, to live with an uncle. . . . When [Adam] is accused of a crime he didn't commit, Carl steps in . . . to try to clear his brother's name. . . . Readers are easily swept up in the adventure as the eye-opening mystery unfolds." SLJ

Stevenson, Robert Louis, 1850-1894
Kidnapped; [by] Robert Louis Stevenson; with an introduction by Sid Hite. F. Watts 2007 213p (Scholastic classics) $25.50
Grades: 7 8 9 10 11 12 Adult   **Fic**
1. Scotland—Fiction 2. Kidnapping—Fiction 3. Adventure fiction
ISBN 978-0-531-16990-2; 0-531-16990-1
    LC 2006006816

First published 1886
A sixteen-year-old orphan is kidnapped by his villainous uncle, but later escapes and becomes involved in the struggle of the Scottish highlanders against English rule.

The strange case of Dr. Jekyll and Mr. Hyde; with an introduction by Joyce Carol Oates. Vintage Books 1991 97p pa $8.95
Grades: 7 8 9 10 11 12 Adult   **Fic**
1. Horror fiction

ISBN 0-679-73476-7   LC 90-50600
Also available from other publishers
First published 1886. Variant title: Dr. Jekyll and Mr. Hyde
"The disturbing tale of the dual personality of Dr. Jekyll, a physician. A generous and philanthropic man, he is preoccupied with the problems of good and evil and with the possibility of separating them into two distinct personalities. He develops a drug that transforms him into the demonic Mr. Hyde, in whose person he exhausts all the latent evil in his nature. He also creates an antidote that will restore him to his respectable existence as Dr. Jekyll. Gradually, however, the unmitigated evil of his darker self predominates, until finally he performs an atrocious murder. . . . The novel is of great psychological perception and strongly concerned with ethical problems." Reader's Ency. 4th edition

Treasure Island; illustrated by N.C. Wyeth. Scribner 1981 273p il $29.99
Grades: 7 8 9 10 11 12 Adult   **Fic**
1. Buried treasure—Fiction 2. Pirates—Fiction
ISBN 0-684-17160-0   LC 81-8788
Also available from various publishers
First published 1882
Young Jim Hawkins discovers a treasure map in the chest of an old sailor who dies under mysterious circumstances at his mother's inn. He shows it to Dr. Livesey and Squire Trelawney who agree to outfit a ship and sail to Treasure Island. Among the crew is the pirate Long John Silver and his followers who are in pursuit of the treasure
"A masterpiece among romances. . . . Pew, Black Dog, and Long John Silver are a villainous trio, strongly individualized, shedding an atmosphere of malignancy and terror. The scenery of isle and ocean contrasts vividly with the savagery of the action." Baker. Guide to the Best Fic

Stevenson, Robin H., 1968-
Dead in the water; [by] Robin Stevenson. Orca Book Publishers 2008 169p (Orca sports) pa $9.95
Grades: 6 7 8 9   **Fic**
1. Endangered species—Fiction 2. Sailing—Fiction 3. Adventure fiction 4. British Columbia—Fiction
ISBN 978-1-5514-3962-4 (pa); 1-5514-3962-X (pa)
"Simon ('Spacey') joins three other teenagers for a weeklong sailing course in British Columbia, Canada. . . . His weird shipmate, Olivia, insists that the men on a nearby cabin cruiser are smuggling abalone, a threatened shellfish species, and she persuades Simon to help her investigate. . . . Stevenson . . . delivers plenty of realistic, gripping detail about handling a boat in screaming winds and crashing waves, as well as a solid story about a crucial environmental issue." Booklist

Stevenson, Robin H., 1968—*Continued*

Out of order; written by Robin Stevenson. Orca Book Publishers 2007 221p pa $8.95

Grades: 8 9 10 11 12 Fic

1. Friendship—Fiction 2. School stories 3. Canada—Fiction

ISBN 978-1-55143-693-7; 1-55143-693-0

When Sophie moves to Victoria, she hopes to leave the bullying she experienced in Ontario behind, but when she makes two new friends who are polar opposites, she finds that friendships can both help and harm her sense of self.

"The visceral, emotional reactions of the characters ring true. . . . Despite weighty themes, this story is about friendship and self-worth." Voice Youth Advocates

Stewart, Jennifer J., 1960-

If that breathes fire, we're toast! Holiday House 1999 118p $15.95

Grades: 4 5 6 Fic

1. Dragons—Fiction 2. Arizona—Fiction

ISBN 0-8234-1430-2 LC 98-36883

Also available in paperback from Scholastic

When twelve-year-old Rick and his mother move from San Diego to Tucson he is not too happy about the change, but when they get a fire-breathing, time-traveling dragon to replace their broken furnace, his new life starts to get more interesting

"The sharp, funny phrasing and the likable, believable characters give the book freshness and zip." Booklist

Stewart, Paul, 1955-

The curse of the night wolf; [by] Paul Stewart and Chris Riddell; illustrated by Chris Riddell. David Fickling Books 2008 204p il (Barnaby Grimes) $15.99; lib bdg $18.99

Grades: 4 5 6 7 Fic

1. Physicians—Fiction 2. Werewolves—Fiction 3. London (England)—Fiction 4. Great Britain—History—19th century—Fiction 5. Mystery fiction

ISBN 978-0-385-75125-4; 0-385-75125-7; 978-0-385-75126-1 (lib bdg); 0-385-75126-5 (lib bdg)

LC 2008-01697

Soon after Victorian messenger Barnaby Grimes is attacked by a huge beast while crossing London's rooftops, he becomes entangled in a mystery involving patent medicine, impoverished patients, and very expensive furs.

"Moody, highly detailed pen-and-ink drawings provide ornamentation throughout, lending a classic Victorian feel to help punctuate the drama. . . . Possessing an easy confidence and quick wit . . . Barnaby is an appealing character." Booklist

Another title in this series is:

Return of the emerald skull (2009)

Stewart, Trenton Lee, 1970-

The mysterious Benedict Society; illustrated by Carson Ellis. 1st ed. Little, Brown 2007 485p il $16.99 *

Grades: 5 6 7 8 Fic

1. Adventure fiction 2. Science fiction

ISBN 978-0-316-05777-6; 0-316-05777-0

LC 2006-09925

After passing a series of mind-bending tests, four children are selected for a secret mission that requires them to go undercover at the Learning Institute for the Very Enlightened, where the only rule is that there are no rules.

"Stewart's unusual characters, threatening villains, and dramatic plot twists will grab and hold readers' attention." SLJ

Another title about the Benedict Society is:

The mysterious Benedict Society and the perilous journey (2008)

Stiefvater, Maggie, 1981-

Lament; the faerie queen's deception. Flux 2008 325p pa $9.95

Grades: 8 9 10 11 12 Fic

1. Supernatural—Fiction 2. Fairies—Fiction 3. Magic—Fiction 4. Musicians—Fiction

ISBN 978-0-7387-1370-0; 0-7387-1370-8

LC 2008-17592

On the day of an important music competition, talented but painfully introverted and nervous Deirdre Monaghan is helped to perform by the compelling and enigmatic Luke Dillon and finds herself inexorably drawn into the mysteries and dangers of the faerie world.

"Stiefvater brings to her story several layers of romance, a knowledge of Irish music and a talent for plot twists. . . . Vibrant and potent." Publ Wkly

Stoffels, Karlijn, 1947-

Heartsinger; translated by Laura Watkinson. Arthur A. Levine Books 2009 134p $16.99 *

Grades: 8 9 10 11 Fic

1. Love—Fiction 2. Fantasy fiction 3. Voyages and travels—Fiction

ISBN 978-0-545-06929-8; 0-545-06929-7; 978-0-545-06968-7 (pa); 0-545-06968-8 (pa)

LC 2008-17785

In this meditation on various kinds of love, Mee travels across the country to the court of the Princess Esperanza, singing the life stories of some of the people he meets.

"Written with clarity and grace. . . . This unusual novel offers readers limpid writing, strong storytelling, and the unblinking recognition of love in many forms." Booklist

Stolarz, Laurie Faria, 1972-

Project 17. Hyperion 2007 256p $15.99

Grades: 7 8 9 10 11 12 Fic

1. Ghost stories 2. Psychiatric hospitals—Fiction 3. Motion pictures—Fiction 4. Horror fiction

ISBN 978-0-7868-3856-1

When six high school students sneak into an abandoned mental institution to make a film about their night there, they do not expect the inexplicable and terrifying events that keep occuring within the crumbling, maze-like building.

"Page-turning action, genuine scares, and a satisfying conclusion should make this a hit with teens." SLJ

Stolls, Amy

Palms to the ground; a novel. 1st ed. Farrar, Straus and Giroux 2005 243p $17

Grades: 7 8 9 10   **Fic**

1. Family life—Fiction 2. Psychotherapy—Fiction 3. Only child—Fiction

ISBN 0-374-35731-5   LC 2004-53261

The only child of an over-protective mother and a well-meaning father, and in therapy since the age of seven, eighth-grader Calman Pulowitz spends two weeks with his pen pal in Washington State, getting drunk, running away, and learning a lot about himself.

"Delightfully quirky, but thoroughly believable characters make this . . . novel enjoyable and thought-provoking." SLJ

Stolz, Joëlle

The shadows of Ghadames; translated from the French by Catherine Temerson. Delacorte Press 2004 119p $15.95; lib bdg $17.99

Grades: 5 6 7 8   **Fic**

1. Muslims—Fiction 2. Sex role—Fiction 3. Libya—Fiction

ISBN 0-385-73104-3; 0-385-90131-3 (lib bdg)

LC 2003-21656

At the end of the nineteenth century in Libya, eleven-year-old Malika simultaneously enjoys and feels constricted by the narrow world of women, but an injured stranger enters her home and disrupts the traditional order of things.

"Stolz invigorates her tale with elegant prose and a deft portrayal of a girl verging on adolescence. The vivid backdrop is intoxicating." Booklist

Stone, Phoebe, 1947-

Deep down popular; a novel; by Phoebe Stone. 1st ed. Arthur A. Levine Books 2008 280p $16.99

Grades: 4 5 6 7   **Fic**

1. Friendship—Fiction 2. School stories 3. Country life—Fiction 4. Family life—Fiction 5. Virginia—Fiction

ISBN 0-4398-0245-8; 978-0-4398-0245-1

LC 2007017198

In a small Virginia town, sixth-grader Jessie Lou Ferguson has a crush on the hugely popular Conrad Parker Smith, and when he suddenly develops a medical problem and the teacher asks Jessie Lou to help him, they become friends, to her surprise.

"Jessie Lou tells her tale with the strong, rough-edged purity of a young poet, which she is; equally strong are the story's underpinnings, longing and laughter, and a willingness to believe in something despite the facts." Booklist

Stork, Francisco X.

Marcelo in the real world. Arthur A. Levine Books 2009 312p $17.99 *

Grades: 8 9 10 11 12   **Fic**

1. Autism—Fiction 2. Asperger's syndrome—Fiction

ISBN 978-0-545-05474-4; 0-545-05474-5

LC 2008-14729

Marcelo Sandoval, a seventeen-year-old boy on the high-functioning end of the autistic spectrum, faces new challenges, including romance and injustice, when he goes to work for his father in the mailroom of a corporate law firm.

"Stork introduces ethical dilemmas, the possibility of love, and other 'real world' conflicts, all the while preserving the integrity of his characterizations and intensifying the novel's psychological and emotional stakes." Publ Wkly

Strasser, Todd, 1950-

Boot camp. Simon & Schuster Books for Young Readers 2007 238p $15.99

Grades: 8 9 10 11 12   **Fic**

1. Juvenile delinquency—Fiction 2. Torture—Fiction

ISBN 978-1-4169-0848-7; 1-4169-0848-X

LC 2006-13634

After ignoring several warnings to stop dating his former teacher, Garrett is sent to Lake Harmony, a boot camp that uses brutal methods to train students to obey their parents.

"The ending is both realistic and disturbing. . . . Writing in the teen's mature and perceptive voice, Strasser creates characters who will provoke strong reactions from readers. . . . [This is a] fast-paced and revealing story." SLJ

Can't get there from here. Simon & Schuster Books for Young Readers 2004 198p $15.95

Grades: 7 8 9 10   **Fic**

1. Runaway teenagers—Fiction 2. Homeless persons—Fiction 3. New York (N.Y.)—Fiction

ISBN 0-689-84169-8   LC 2003-170

Tired of being hungry, cold, and dirty from living on the streets of New York City with a tribe of other homeless teenagers who are dying, one by one, a girl named Maybe ponders her future and longs for someone to care about her

"While the events described in this cautionary tale are shocking, the language is not, making these all-too-real problems accessible to a wide readership." SLJ

If I grow up. Simon & Schuster Books for Young Readers 2009 222p $16.99

Grades: 7 8 9 10   **Fic**

1. Gangs—Fiction 2. Violence—Fiction 3. Poverty—Fiction 4. African Americans—Fiction

ISBN 978-1-4169-2523-1; 1-4169-2523-6

LC 2008-00655

Growing up in the inner-city projects, DeShawn is reluctantly forced into the gang world by circumstances beyond his control.

"Strasser's writing puts the reader in the midst of the projects and offers totally real characters." Voice Youth Advocates

Includes bibliographical references

Stratton, Allan

Chanda's secrets. Annick Press 2004 193p $19.95; pa $8.95

Grades: 7 8 9 10   **Fic**

1. AIDS (Disease)—Fiction 2. Africa—Fiction

ISBN 1-55037-835-X; 1-55037-834-1 (pa)

Michael L. Printz Award honor book, 2005

Stratton, Allan—*Continued*

In this story "Chanda, a 16-year-old . . . girl living in the small city of Bonang in Africa, must confront the undercurrents of shame and stigma associated with HIV/AIDS." Publisher's note

"The details of sub-Saharan African life are convincing and smoothly woven into this moving story of poverty and courage, but the real insight for readers will be the appalling treatment of the AIDS victims. Strong language and frank description are appropriate to the subject matter." SLJ

Another title about Chanda is:

Chanda's war (2007)

Strickland, Brad

The sign of the sinister sorcerer; [by] Brad Strickland. Dial Books for Young Readers 2008 168p $16.99

Grades: 4 5 6 7   Fic
1. Magic—Fiction   2. Supernatural—Fiction
3. Uncles—Fiction 4. Witches—Fiction 5. Orphans—Fiction 6. Michigan—Fiction 7. Mystery fiction
ISBN 978-0-8037-3151-6; 0-8037-3151-5
                                    LC 2008007698
Continues John Bellairs' series about Lewis Barnavelt Based on the characters of John Bellairs

In Michigan in the mid-1950s, Lewis Barnavelt is convinced that the series of accidents he and his uncle are experiencing are the result of a curse by a mysterious, hooded figure that may be part of his uncle's past.

"For readers who enjoy trying to solve the mystery as they read, there are abundant clues including an anagram. A quick, exciting read." SLJ

Other titles about Lewis Barnavelt by Brad Strickland are:

The beast under the wizard's bridge (2000)
The house where nobody lived (2006)
The spector from the magician's museum (1998)
The tower at the end of the world (2001)
The whistle, the grave, and the ghost (2003)

Stroud, Jonathan, 1970-

The Amulet of Samarkand. Hyperion Bks. for Children 2003 462p (Bartimaeus trilogy) $17.95; pa $7.99 *

Grades: 7 8 9 10   Fic
1. Fantasy fiction
ISBN 0-7868-1859-X; 0-7868-5255-0 (pa)
                                    LC 2003-49904
Nathaniel, a magician's apprentice, summons up the djinni Bartimaeus and instructs him to steal the Amulet of Samarkand from the powerful magician Simon Lovelace.

"There is plenty of action, mystery, and humor to keep readers turning the pages. This title, the first in a trilogy, is a must for fantasy fans." SLJ

Other titles in this series are:

The golem's eye (2004)
Ptolemy's gate (2006)

Heroes of the valley. Hyperion Books for Children 2009 483p $17.99 *

Grades: 7 8 9 10   Fic

1. Adventure fiction 2. Middle Ages—Fiction
ISBN 978-1-4231-0966-2; 1-4231-0966-X

"Twelve Houses control sections of a valley. Halli Sveinsson—at 15, the youngest child of the rulers of the House of Svein—goes against tradition when he sets out to avenge the death of his murdered uncle, and his actions result in warfare among Houses for the first time in generations. . . . Smart, funny dialogue and prose, revealing passages about the exploits of the hero Svein, bouts of action and a touch of romance briskly move the story along." Publ Wkly

Sturtevant, Katherine, 1950-

A true and faithful narrative. Farrar, Straus & Giroux 2006 247p $17

Grades: 6 7 8 9   Fic
1. London (England)—Fiction 2. Great Britain—History—1603-1714, Stuarts—Fiction
ISBN 0-374-37809-6   LC 2005046922
Sequel to At the sign of the star (2000)

In London in the 1680s, Meg—now sixteen years old—tries to decide whether to marry either of the two men who court her, taking into account both love and her writing ambitions.

The author "offers readers a story depicted with great clarity and many vivid details of everyday life. Written in the first-person, the narrative reveals Meg as a strong-willed yet vulnerable young woman who emerges as a well-rounded, convincing individual." Booklist

Supplee, Suzanne

Artichoke's heart. Dutton Children's Books 2008 276p $16.99

Grades: 7 8 9 10   Fic
1. Obesity—Fiction 2. Weight loss—Fiction
3. Mother-daughter relationship—Fiction 4. School stories 5. Cancer—Fiction 6. Tennessee—Fiction
ISBN 978-0-52547-902-4; 0-52547-902-3
                                    LC 2007-28486
When she is almost sixteen years old, Rosemary decides she is sick of being overweight, mocked at school and at Heavenly Hair—her mother's beauty salon—and feeling out of control, and as she slowly loses weight, she realizes that she is able to cope with her mother's cancer, having a boyfriend for the first time, and discovering that other people's lives are not as perfect as they seem from the outside.

"Supplee brings a cast of original characters to life in this convincing and consistently entertaining narrative." Booklist

Sutcliff, Rosemary, 1920-1992

Sword song. Farrar, Straus & Giroux 1998 271p hardcover o.p. pa $6.95

Grades: 7 8 9 10   Fic
1. Vikings—Fiction 2. Great Britain—History—0-1066—Fiction
ISBN 0-374-37363-9; 0-374-46984-9 (pa)
                                    LC 98-16827
At sixteen, Bjarni is cast out of the Norse settlement in the Angles' Land for an act of oath-breaking and spends five years sailing the west coast of Scotland and witnessing the feuds of the clan chiefs living there

"This is a well-crafted story that will appeal to sophisticated readers." SLJ

Swallow, Pamela Curtis
It only looks easy. Roaring Brook Press 2003
168p $15.95
Grades: 4 5 6 7   **Fic**
    1. Alzheimer's disease—Fiction 2. School stories
    ISBN 0-7613-1790-2   LC 2002-6611
    On the first day of seventh grade when Kat "borrows"
a bicycle to go see her dog who was hit the day before
by a woman with Alzheimer's disease, she learns about
the serious consequences of impetuous actions and manages to make some new friends in the process
    "Genuine kid humor and a goodhearted, all-too-human
heroine distinguish this middle-grade novel." Booklist

Swanson, Julie A., 1964-
Going for the record. Eerdmans Books for
Young Readers 2004 217p pa $8
Grades: 7 8 9 10   **Fic**
    1. Soccer—Fiction 2. Father-daughter relationship—
Fiction 3. Cancer—Fiction
    ISBN 0-8028-5273-4
    Seventeen-year-old Leah's chance to make the nation-
al soccer team does not seem so important when she
learns that her father has cancer and may only have
months to live.
    "Each character rings true. Without being sensational
or maudlin, Swanson's novel is real: it's deeply sad and
often painful to read, but ultimately hopeful and uplifting." Booklist

Sweeney, Joyce, 1955-
The guardian. Henry Holt and Co. 2009 177p
$16.95
Grades: 7 8 9 10   **Fic**
    1. Foster home care—Fiction 2. Siblings—Fiction
3. School stories 4. Bullies—Fiction 5. Father-son relationship—Fiction
    ISBN 978-0-8050-8019-3; 0-8050-8019-8
                       LC 2008040602
    When thirteen-year-old Hunter, struggling to deal with
a harsh, money-grubbing foster mother, three challenging
foster sisters, and a school bully, returns to his childhood
faith and prays to St. Gabriel, he instantly becomes
aware that he does, indeed, have a guardian.
    "Sweeney's prose is insightful and realistic, with clev-
erly delivered descriptions. The peripheral characters are
believable, and the religious undercurrent supports the
plot. Well-paced, and with a satisfying conclusion." SLJ

Swift, Jonathan, 1667-1745
Gulliver's travels; illustrated by Scott
McKowen. Sterling Pub. Co. 2007 293p il
(Sterling unabridged classics) $9.95
Grades: 7 8 9 10 11 12 Adult   **Fic**
    1. Fantasy fiction 2. Voyages and travels—Fiction
    ISBN 978-1-4027-4339-9; 1-4027-4339-4
                       LC 2007003974
    First published 1726
    "In the account of his four wonder-countries Swift sat-
irizes contemporary manners and morals, art and politics-
in fact the whole social scheme-from four different
points of view. The huge Brobdingnagians reduce man to

his natural insignificance, the little people of Lilliput parody Europe and its petty broils, in Laputa philosophers
are ridiculed, and finally all Swift's hatred and contempt
find their satisfaction in degrading humanity to a bestial
condition." Baker. Guide to the Best Fic

Tal, Eve, 1947-
Double crossing. Cinco Puntos Press 2005 261p
$16.95
Grades: 7 8 9 10   **Fic**
    1. Immigrants—Fiction 2. Jews—Fiction
    ISBN 0-938317-94-6   LC 2005-8188
    In 1905, as life becomes increasingly difficult for
Jews in Ukraine, eleven-year-old Raizel and her father
flee to America in hopes of earning money to bring the
rest of the family there, but her father's health and Orthodox faith become barriers.
    "Tal's fictionalized account of her grandfather's jour-
ney to America is fast paced, full of suspense, and highly readable." SLJ

Tarshis, Lauren
Emma-Jean Lazarus fell out of a tree. Dial
Books for Young Readers 2007 199p $16.99 *
Grades: 5 6 7   **Fic**
    1. Friendship—Fiction 2. School stories
    ISBN 978-0-8037-3164-6; 0-8037-3164-7
                       LC 2006-18428
    A quirky and utterly logical seventh-grade girl named
Emma-Jean Lazarus discovers some interesting results
when she gets involved in the messy everyday problems
of her peers.
    "Readers will be fascinated by Emma-Jean's emotion-
less observations and her adult-level vocabulary. Tarshis
pulls off a balancing act, showing the child's detachment
yet making her a sympathetic character. Exceptionally
fleshed-out secondary characters add warmth to the story." SLJ
    Followed by: Emma-Jean Lazarus fell in love (2009)

Tashjian, Janet, 1956-
The gospel according to Larry. Holt & Co. 2001
227p il $16.95; pa $5.99
Grades: 7 8 9 10   **Fic**
    1. Web sites—Fiction
    ISBN 0-8050-6378-1; 0-440-23792-0 (pa)
                       LC 2001-24568
    Seventeen-year-old Josh, a loner-philosopher who
wants to make a difference in the world, tries to maintain
his secret identity as the author of a web site that is receiving national attention
    "Tashjian fabricates a cleverly constructed scenario
and expertly carries it out to the bittersweet end." Horn
Book Guide
    Other titles about Larry are:
Vote for Larry (2004)
Larry and the meaning of life (2008)

Tate, Eleanora E., 1948-
Celeste's Harlem Renaissance. Little, Brown
2007 279p $15.99
Grades: 4 5 6 7   **Fic**

Tate, Eleanora E., 1948—_Continued_
  1. Aunts—Fiction 2. Harlem Renaissance—Fiction
3. African Americans—Fiction 4. Harlem (New York,
N.Y.)—Fiction
  ISBN 978-0-316-52394-3
In 1921, thirteen-year-old Celeste leaves North Carolina to stay with her glamorous Aunt Valentina in Harlem,
New York, where she discovers the vibrant Harlem Renaissance in full swing, even though her aunt's life is not
exactly what she was led to believe.
  "Both sobering and inspiring, Tate's novel is a moving portrait of growing up black and female in 1920s
America." Booklist

Tayleur, Karen
  Chasing boys. Walker & Co. 2009 244p $16.99
Grades: 7 8 9 10   **Fic**
  1. Fathers—Fiction 2. School stories
  ISBN 978-0-8027-9830-5; 0-8027-9830-6
                        LC 2008-23241
First published 2007 by Black Dog Books
With her father gone and her family dealing with financial problems, El transfers to a new school, where she
falls for one of the popular boys and then must decide
whether to remain true to herself or become like the girls
she scorns.
  "All the ingredients of El's life are blended seamlessly, never downplaying the audience's intelligence, as
Tayleur captures the all-consuming nature of a teenage
crush without making El ridiculous. Moody, poetic, and
intimate, this book is billed as the 'romance for girls
who don't like pink,' but is much more than that."
Booklist

Taylor, G. P.
  Tersias the oracle. G.P. Putnam's Sons 2006
c2005 262p $17.99; pa $8.99
Grades: 8 9 10 11 12   **Fic**
  1. Occultism—Fiction 2. London (England)—Fiction
3. Prophets—Fiction
  ISBN 0-399-24258-9; 0-14-240846-8 (pa)
                        LC 2005-14347
First published 2005 in the United Kingdom
Jonah, a young thief, and his friends and Tersias, a
twelve-year-old boy who channels prophesies, become
embroiled in the machinations of a magician, a politician,
and a false prophet, as well as in the magic of a strange
alabaster box.
  "The story's gritty setting, moody tone, and brisk action will appeal to many." Booklist

Taylor, Mildred D.
  The friendship; pictures by Max Ginsburg. Dial
Bks. for Young Readers 1987 53p il $15.99; pa
$4.99
Grades: 4 5 6 7   **Fic**
  1. African Americans—Fiction 2. Race relations—Fic-
tion 3. Mississippi—Fiction
  ISBN 0-8037-0417-8; 0-14-038964-4 (pa)
                        LC 86-29309
This "story about race relations in rural Mississippi
during the Depression focuses on an incident between an
old Black man, Mr. Tom Bee, and a white storekeeper,

Mr. John Wallace. Indebted to Tom for saving his life as
a young man, John had promised they would always be
friends. But now, years later, John insists that Tom call
him 'Mister' and shoots the old man for defiantly—and
publicly—calling him by his first name. Narrator Cassie
Logan and her brothers . . . are verbally abused by Wallace's villainous sons before witnessing the encounter."
Bull Cent Child Books

  The gold Cadillac; pictures by Michael Hays.
Dial Bks. for Young Readers 1987 43p il $16.99;
pa $4.99 *
Grades: 4 5 6 7   **Fic**
  1. African Americans—Fiction 2. Prejudices—Fiction
3. Race relations—Fiction
  ISBN 0-8037-0342-2; 0-14-038963-6 (pa)
                        LC 86-11526
  "The shiny gold Cadillac that Daddy brings home one
summer evening marks a stepping stone in the lives of
Wilma and 'lois, two black sisters growing up in Ohio
during the fifties. At first neighbors and relatives shower
them with attention. But when the family begins the long
journey to the South to show off the car to their Mississippi relatives, the girls, for the first time, encounter the
undisguised ugliness of racial prejudice." Horn Book
  "Full-page sepia paintings effectively portray the characters, setting, and mood of the story events as Hays
ably demonstrates his understanding of the social and
emotional environments which existed for blacks during
this period." SLJ

  The land. Phyllis Fogelman Bks. 2001 375p
$17.99; pa $6.99 *
Grades: 7 8 9 10   **Fic**
  1. Racially mixed people—Fiction 2. African Americans—Fiction 3. Race relations—Fiction
  ISBN 0-8037-1950-7; 0-14-250146-8 (pa)
                        LC 00-39329
Prequel to Roll of Thunder, Hear My Cry
After the Civil War Paul-Edward Logan, the son of a
white father and a black mother, finds himself caught between the two worlds of colored folks and white folks as
he pursues his dream of owning land of his own.
  "Taylor masterfully uses harsh historical realities to
frame a powerful coming-of-age story that stands on its
own merits." Horn Book Guide

  Let the circle be unbroken. Dial Bks. for Young
Readers 1981 394p $17.99; pa $7.99 *
Grades: 4 5 6 7   **Fic**
  1. African Americans—Fiction 2. Mississippi—Fiction
3. Great Depression, 1929-1939—Fiction
  ISBN 0-8037-4748-9; 0-14-034892-1 (pa)
                        LC 81-65854
Sequel to Roll of thunder, hear my cry
This novel featuring the Logans covers "a series of
tangential events so that it is a family record, a picture
of the depression years in rural Mississippi, and an indictment of black-white relations in the Deep South. A
young friend is convicted of a murder of which he is innocent, a pretty cousin is insulted by some white boys
and her father taunted because he married a white woman, an elderly neighbor tries to vote, the government
pays farmers to plow their crops under, etc." Bull Cent
Child Books

Taylor, Mildred D.—*Continued*

The author "provides her readers with a literal sense of witnessing important American history. . . . Moreover, [she] never neglects the details of her volatile 9-year-old heroine's interior life. The daydreams, the jealousy, the incredible ardor of that age come alive." N Y Times Book Rev

The road to Memphis; by Mildred Taylor. Dial Bks. 1989 290p $18.99; pa $6.99 *

Grades: 4 5 6 7 **Fic**
1. Race relations—Fiction 2. African Americans—Fiction 3. Mississippi—Fiction
ISBN 0-8037-0340-6; 0-14-036077-8 (pa)
LC 88-33654

Coretta Scott King Award for text
Sadistically teased by two white boys in 1940's rural Mississippi, Cassie Logan's friend, Moe, severely injures one of the boys with a tire iron and enlists Cassie's help in trying to flee the state
"Taylor's continued smooth, easy language provides readability for all ages, with a focus on universal human pride, worthy values, and individual responsibility. This action-packed drama is highly recommended." Voice Youth Advocates

Roll of thunder, hear my cry. 25th anniversary ed. Phyllis Fogelman Books 2001 276p $17.99; pa $7.99 *

Grades: 4 5 6 7 8 9 **Fic**
1. African Americans—Fiction 2. Mississippi—Fiction
ISBN 0-8037-2647-3; 0-14-240112-9 (pa)
LC 00-39378

Also available in paperback from Puffin Bks.
Awarded the Newbery Medal, 1977
First published 1976 by Dial Press
"The time is 1933. The place is Spokane, Mississippi where the Logans, the only black family who own their own land, wage a courageous struggle to remain independent, displeasing a white plantation owner bent on taking their land. But this suspenseful tale is also about the story's young narrator, Cassie, and her three brothers who decide to wage their own personal battles to maintain the self-dignity and pride with which they were raised. . . . Ms. Taylor's richly textured novel shows a strong, proud black family . . . resisting rather than succumbing to oppression." Child Book Rev Serv

The well; David's story. Dial Bks. for Young Readers 1995 92p $16.99; pa $5.99

Grades: 4 5 6 7 **Fic**
1. African Americans—Fiction 2. Race relations—Fiction 3. Mississippi—Fiction
ISBN 0-8037-1802-0; 0-14-038642-4 (pa)
LC 94-25360

"David Logan (Cassie's father) tells this story from his childhood. . . . There's a drought, and the Logans possess the only well in the area that has not gone dry. Black and white alike come for water freely given by the family, but the Simms boys can't seem to stand the necessary charity, and their resentment explodes when David's big brother Hammer beats Charlie Simms after Charlie hits David." Bull Cent Child Books
This story "delivers an emotional wallop in a concentrated span of time and action. . . . This story reverberates in the heart long after the final paragraph is read." Horn Book

Taylor, Theodore, 1921-2006

The cay. Delacorte Press 1987 c1969 137p $16.95; pa $5.50 *

Grades: 5 6 7 8 **Fic**
1. Race relations—Fiction 2. Caribbean region—Fiction 3. Survival after airplane accidents, shipwrecks, etc.—Fiction 4. Blind—Fiction
ISBN 0-385-07906-0; 0-440-22912-X (pa)

Also available in paperback from HarperCollins
A reissue of the title first published 1969
When the freighter on which they are traveling is torpedoed by a German submarine during World War II, Phillip, an adolescent white boy blinded by a blow on the head, and Timothy, an old black man, are stranded on a tiny Caribbean island where the boy acquires a new kind of vision, courage, and love from his old companion.
"Starkly dramatic, believable and compelling." Saturday Rev
Followed by Timothy of the cay

Timothy of the cay. Harcourt Brace & Co. 1993 161p hardcover o.p. pa $5.95 *

Grades: 5 6 7 8 **Fic**
1. Race relations—Fiction 2. Caribbean region—Fiction 3. Survival after airplane accidents, shipwrecks, etc.—Fiction 4. Blind—Fiction
ISBN 0-15-288358-4; 0-15-206320-X (pa)
LC 93-7898

Sequel to The cay
Having survived being blinded and shipwrecked on a tiny Caribbean island with the old black man Timothy, twelve-year-old white Phillip is rescued and hopes to regain his sight with an operation. Alternate chapters follow the life of Timothy from his days as a young cabin boy
"Somewhat more thoughtful than its well-loved antecedent, this boldly drawn novel is no less commanding." Publ Wkly

Temple, Frances, 1945-1995

The Beduins' gazelle. HarperTrophy 1998 150p pa $5.99

Grades: 7 8 9 10 **Fic**
1. Bedouins—Fiction 2. Deserts—Fiction 3. Middle East—Fiction
ISBN 0-06-440669-5

First published 1996 by Orchard Books
"In 1302, Atiyah and Halima, cousins betrothed at birth, are separated when Atiyah travels from the desert to Fez to study. . . . While in Fez, Atiyah meets and befriends Etienne, a French pilgrim who is studying Arabic, whom readers met in 'The Ramsay Scallop'. . . . When word travels to Atiyah that Halima is lost, he and Etienne return to the desert to find her. But Halima is rescued by another tribe whose sheikh wants her as his newest wife." Voice Youth Advocates
"Told in short, rapid chapters, Temple's briskly paced story is fueled by a cast of complex, emotionally resonant characters." Publ Wkly

Temple, Frances, 1945-1995—*Continued*
The Ramsay scallop; a novel. Orchard Bks.
1994 310p hardcover o.p. pa $7.99 *
Grades: 6 7 8 9   **Fic**
   1. Middle Ages—Fiction 2. Pilgrims and pilgrim-
ages—Fiction
ISBN 0-531-06836-6; 0-06-440601-6 (pa)
                                          LC 93-29697
"A Richard Jackson book"
At the turn of the fourteenth century in England, fourteen-year-old Elenor finds her betrothal to an ambitious
lord's son launching her on a memorable pilgrimage to
far-off Spain
   "With a nod to *The Canterbury Tales*, the book highlights the stories that their fellow pilgrims share with
Elenor and Thomas; the stories are sad, romantic, and instructive, and all help shape the journey into the special
thing it becomes for the duo. . . . The leisurely pace of
the pilgrimage allows the author to introduce a large cast
of characters and to decorate her story with historical details that enlighten and intrigue." Booklist

Thal, Lilli
Mimus; translated by John Brownjohn. Annick
Press 2005 394p $19.95; pa $9.95
Grades: 7 8 9 10   **Fic**
   1. Fools and jesters—Fiction 2. Fantasy fiction
ISBN 1-55037-925-9; 1-55037-924-0 (pa)
The tale of Prince Florin, forced to become a jester in
the court of his father's enemy.
   "This outstanding translation from the German brings
an author with rich, complex, and very clever storytelling
skills to American teens. . . . This is a sophisticated and
engrossing historical tale by a writer who brings exceptional attention to detail, character development, and
theme." Booklist

Tharp, Tim, 1957-
Knights of the hill country. Alfred A. Knopf
2006 233p $16.95; lib bdg $18.99
Grades: 8 9 10 11 12   **Fic**
   1. Football—Fiction 2. School stories 3. Oklahoma—
Fiction
ISBN   978-0-375-83653-4;   0-375-83653-5;
978-0-375-93653-1 (lib bdg); 0-375-93653-X (lib bdg)
                                          LC 2005-33279
In his senior year, high school star linebacker Hampton Greene finally begins to think for himself and discovers that he might be interested in more than just football.
   "Taut scenes on the football field and the dilemmas
about choosing what feels right over what's expected are
all made memorable by Hamp's unforgettable, colloquial
voice." Booklist

Thomas, Jane Resh, 1936-
Blind mountain. Clarion Books 2006 117p $15
Grades: 4 5 6   **Fic**
   1. Wilderness survival—Fiction 2. Father-son relationship—Fiction   3.   Mountaineering—Fiction
4. Montana—Fiction
ISBN 978-0-618-64872-6; 0-618-64872-0
                                          LC 2005-34512

Unsure of himself and annoyed at having to spend a
day climbing a Montana mountain with his bossy father,
twelve-year-old Sam must become the guide on their perilous journey down when his carelessness temporarily
blinds his father
   "Thomas' wilderness knowledge comes through vividly here, particularly in the survival details, and the subplot involving the cougar will have great appeal."
Booklist

Thomason, Mark
Moonrunner. Kane/Miller 2009 c2008 $15.95
Grades: 4 5 6 7   **Fic**
   1. Australia—Fiction 2. Horses—Fiction
ISBN 978-1-935279-03-7; 1-935279-03-3
First published 2008 in Australia
   "In the 1890s, Casey and his parents immigrate to
Australia, to a homestead that they inherited from his
grandfather. The 12-year-old finds the change difficult.
He is bullied at school, and he misses his baseball team
in Montana and his horse. Then he happens upon a magnificent wild stallion, and he is determined to befriend
the brumby, whom he names Moonrunner. . . . This
well-paced story effectively portrays the family's struggles. Casey is a strong, engaging protagonist whose interactions with the other characters are believable and interesting." SLJ

Thompson, Kate
Fourth World. Bloomsbury 2005 330p (Missing
link trilogy) $16.95; pa $7.95
Grades: 6 7 8 9   **Fic**
   1. Genetic engineering—Fiction 2. Scotland—Fiction
3. Science fiction
ISBN 1-58234-650-X; 1-58234-897-9 (pa)
                                          LC 2004-62367
First published 2000 in the United Kingdom
Fifteen-year-old Christie and his older stepbrother,
Danny, travel to the home and mysterious laboratory of
the elder boy's scientist mother, where they learn a
shocking truth about the nature of her experiments.
   "The story is compelling and the questions left open
at the end are intriguing enough to lead readers . . . into
the promised sequel." SLJ
   Other titles in this series are:
Only human (2006)
Origins (2007)

The new policeman. Greenwillow Books 2007
442p $16.99; lib bdg $17.89 *
Grades: 7 8 9 10   **Fic**
   1. Space and time—Fiction 2. Fairies—Fiction
3. Music—Fiction 4. Ireland—Fiction 5. Fantasy fiction
ISBN   978-0-06-117427-8;   0-06-117427-0;
978-0-06-117428-5 (lib bdg); 0-06-117428-9 (lib bdg)
                                          LC 2006-8246
First published 2005 in the United Kingdom
Irish teenager JJ Liddy discovers that time is leaking
from his world into Tir na nOg, the land of the fairies,
and when he attempts to stop the leak he finds out a lot
about his family history, the music that he loves, and a
crime his great-grandfather may or may not have committed.

Thompson, Kate—*Continued*
"Mesmerizing and captivating, this book is guaranteed to charm fantasy fans." Voice Youth Advocates
Followed by: The last of the High Kings (2008)

Thomson, Sarah L.
The secret of the Rose. 1st ed. Greenwillow Books 2006 296p $16.99; lib bdg $17.89
Grades: 6 7 8 9   **Fic**
   1. Marlowe, Christopher, 1564-1593—Fiction 2. Sex role—Fiction 3. Theater—Fiction 4. Great Britain—History—1485-1603, Tudors—Fiction 5. Catholics—Fiction
   ISBN   978-0-06-087250-2;   0-06-087250-0; 978-0-06-087251-9 (lib bdg); 0-06-087251-9 (lib bdg)
                           LC 2005-22177
When her father is imprisoned in 1592 England for being Catholic, fourteen-year-old Rosalind disguises herself as a boy and finds an ultimately dangerous job as servant to playwright Christopher Marlowe.
"Part historical mystery, part suspense, this fast-paced story is propelled by Rosalind's desire not just to survive but also to learn who she is." Voice Youth Advocates

Thurlo, Aimée
The spirit line; [by] Aimeé & David Thurlo. Viking 2004 216p $15.99
Grades: 6 7 8 9   **Fic**
   1. Navajo Indians—Fiction 2. New Mexico—Fiction
   ISBN 0-670-03645-5
When the special rug Crystal Manyfeathers is weaving for her kinaaldá, the traditional Navajo womanhood ceremony, is stolen from her loom, there are any number of suspects.
"Carefully combining humor and seriousness, this well-paced story contains accurate portrayals of Navajo customs, mostly believable teen dialogue, and a realistic depiction of the conflicts modern Native young people face." SLJ

Tiernan, Cate, 1961-
A chalice of wind. Penguin/Razorbill 2005 250p (Balefire) pa $5.99
Grades: 8 9 10 11 12   **Fic**
   1. Witchcraft—Fiction 2. Twins—Fiction 3. Sisters—Fiction 4. New Orleans (La.)—Fiction
   ISBN 1-59514-045-X
Separated since birth, seventeen-year-old twins Thais and Clio unexpectedly meet in New Orleans where they seem to be pursued by a coven of witches who want to harness the twins' magickal powers for its own ends.
"The suspenseful story moves quickly along, and a love triangle between the twins and a mysterious young man adds some depth. The action builds toward a tantalizing twist." Booklist
Other titles in the Balefire series are:
A circle of ashes (2005)
A feather of stone (2005)
A necklace of water (2006)

Tiffany, Grace, 1958-
Ariel. Laura Geringer Books 2005 232p $16.99; lib bdg $17.89
Grades: 7 8 9 10   **Fic**
   1. Shakespeare, William, 1564-1616—Fiction 2. Survival after airplane accidents, shipwrecks, etc.—Fiction 3. Magic—Fiction
   ISBN 0-06-075327-7; 0-06-075327-6 (lib bdg)
"Tiffany takes the characters from Shakespeare's The Tempest and provides background as to how they get to the point where readers find them in the play." SLJ
"This lush, lyrical, and elegantly expressive work is a strong mix of solid narrative storytelling, sensitive characterization, and fantasy." Booklist

Tigelaar, Liz
Pretty tough. Penguin 2007 246p pa $8.99
Grades: 7 8 9 10   **Fic**
   1. Sisters—Fiction 2. Soccer—Fiction 3. School stories 4. California—Fiction
   ISBN 978-1-59514-112-5 (pa)   LC 2007-01973
Two feuding sisters from Malibu, California, take their rivalry to the soccer field when both girls make the high school team.
"This is a well-paced book with solid character development and witty, authentic dialogue." SLJ

Tilly, Meg
Porcupine. Tundra Books 2007 233p $15.95
Grades: 5 6 7 8   **Fic**
   1. Newfoundland—Fiction 2. Bereavement—Fiction 3. Family life—Fiction
   ISBN 978-0-88776-810-1
"When Jacqueline Cooper's father is killed in Afghanistan, her mother goes to pieces and takes her three children to live on a farm with a strict great-grandmother they didn't know they had. After she leaves, the 12-year-old make it her job to keep her family together and safe. . . . A very satisfying read." SLJ

Tingle, Rebecca
The edge on the sword. Putnam 2001 277p hardcover o.p. pa $6.99
Grades: 7 8 9 10   **Fic**
   1. Great Britain—History—0-1066—Fiction
   ISBN 0-399-23580-9; 0-14-250058-5 (pa)
                           LC 00-55353
In ninth-century Britain, fifteen-year-old Aethelflaed, daughter of King Alfred of West Saxony, finds she must assume new responsibilities much sooner than expected when she is betrothed to Ethelred of Mercia in order to strengthen a strategic alliance against the Danes
This "story is filled with exciting action, interesting characters, and convincing historical details of the late ninth century that bring to life this distant and violent time in Britain." SLJ
Another title about Aethelflaed and her family is:
Far traveler (2005)

Tocher, Timothy

Bill Pennant, Babe Ruth, and me. Cricket Books 2009 178p $16.95

Grades: 5 6 7 8   **Fic**

1. Ruth, Babe, 1895-1948—Fiction 2. McGraw, John Joseph, 1873-1934—Fiction 3. New York Giants (Baseball team)—Fiction 4. New York Yankees (Baseball team)—Fiction. 5. Baseball—Fiction

ISBN 978-0-8126-2755-8; 0-8126-2755-5

LC 2008026829

In 1920, sixteen-year-old Hank finds his loyalties divided when he is assigned to care for the Giants' mascot, a wildcat named Bill Pennant, as well as keep an eye on Babe Ruth in Ruth's first season with the New York Yankees.

The author "seamlessly blends fact and fiction. He recreates the era with scrupulous attention to its syntax and slang, as well as details of daily life. Ruth, McGraw and the other historical figures come alive for readers, and the fictional Hank is a sympathetic, fully developed character." Kirkus

Chief Sunrise, John McGraw, and me; Timothy Tocher. 1st ed. Cricket Books 2004 154p $15.95

Fic

1. Baseball—Fiction 2. Runaway teenagers—Fiction 3. Race relations—Fiction

ISBN 0-8126-2711-3   LC 2003-23407

In 1919, fifteen-year-old Hank escapes an abusive father and goes looking for a chance to become a baseball player, accompanied by a man who calls himself Chief Sunrise and claims to be a full-blooded Seminole.

"The story is both entertaining and thought-provoking." Booklist

Todd, Pamela, 1950-

The blind faith hotel; [by] Pamela Todd. Margaret K. McElderry Books 2008 312p $16.99

Grades: 8 9 10   **Fic**

1. Family life—Fiction 2. Prairies—Fiction 3. Nature—Fiction

ISBN 978-1-4169-5494-1; 1-4169-5494-5

LC 2007-43912

When her parents separate and she and her siblings move with their mother from the northwest coast to a midwest prairie farmhouse, fourteen-year-old Zoe, miserably unhappy to be away from the ocean and her father, begins to develop a deep attachment to her new surroundings, when, after a shoplifting episode, she is assigned to work at a nature preserve.

"This touching novel tackles many difficult issues; beautiful imagery and language keep the story vibrant." Horn Book Guide

Toksvig, Sandi

Hitler's canary. Roaring Brook Press 2007 191p $16.95 *

Grades: 5 6 7 8   **Fic**

1. World War, 1939-1945—Fiction 2. Denmark—Fiction 3. Jews—Fiction

ISBN 978-1-59643-247-5; 1-59643-247-0

LC 2006-16607

"A Deborah Brodie book"

Ten-year-old Bamse and his Jewish friend Anton participate in the Danish Resistance during World War II.

"Though . . . suspenseful episodes will thrill readers, it is Bamse's growing courage and deepening understanding that drive the story." Booklist

Tolan, Stephanie S., 1942-

Surviving the Applewhites. HarperCollins Pubs. 2002 216p $15.99; lib bdg $17.89; pa $5.99 *

Grades: 5 6 7 8   **Fic**

1. Eccentrics and eccentricities—Fiction 2. Theater—Fiction 3. Family life—Fiction

ISBN 0-06-623602-9; 0-06-623603-7 (lib bdg); 0-06-441044-7 (pa)   LC 2002-1474

A Newbery Medal honor book, 2003

Jake, a budding juvenile delinquent, is sent for home schooling to the arty and eccentric Applewhite family's Creative Academy, where he discovers talents and interests he never knew he had

This is a "thoroughly enjoyable book with humor, well-drawn characters, and a super cover." Voice Youth Advocates

Tolkien, J. R. R. (John Ronald Reuel), 1892-1973

The hobbit, or, There and back again. Houghton Mifflin 2001 330p il $18; pa $10 *

Grades: 5 6 7 8 9 10 11 12 Adult   **Fic**

1. Fantasy fiction

ISBN 0-618-16221-6; 0-618-26030-7 (pa)

LC 2001276594

Also available from Houghton Mifflin in an edition with illustrations by Michael Hague for $29.95 (ISBN 0-395-36290-3)

A reissue of the title first published 1938

"Text of this edition is based on that first published in Great Britain by Collins Modern Classics in 1998 . . . corrections have been made to that setting"—T.p. verso

"This fantasy features the adventures of hobbit Bilbo Baggins, who joins a band of dwarves led by Gandalf the Wizard. Together they seek to recover the stolen treasure that is hidden in Lonely Mountain and guarded by Smaug the Dragon. This book precedes the Lord of the Rings trilogy." Shapiro. Fic for Youth. 3d edition

Followed by The lord of the rings trilogy: The fellowship of the ring; The two towers; The return of the king

The lord of the rings. 50th Anniversary ed. Houghton Mifflin 2004 xxv, 1157p il map slip case $100 *

Grades: 7 8 9 10 11 12 Adult   **Fic**

1. Fantasy fiction

ISBN 0-618-51765-0   LC 2004-275215

Also available as separate volumes in hardcover and paperback editions

First published 1954 in the United Kingdom

Contents: The fellowship of the ring; The two towers; The return of the king

"This is a tale of imaginary gnomelike creatures who battle against evil. Led by Frodo, the hobbits embark on a journey to prevent a magic ring from falling into the grasp of the powers of darkness. The forces of good succeed in their fight against the Dark Lord of evil, and Frodo and Sam bring the Ring to Mount Doom, where it is destroyed." Shapiro. Fic for Youth. 3d edition

Tomlinson, Heather

Aurelie; a faerie tale. Henry Holt 2008 184p
$16.95 *

Grades: 7 8 9 10   **Fic**
  1. Fairies—Fiction 2. Princesses—Fiction 3. Music—
Fiction 4. Fantasy fiction
  ISBN 978-0-8050-8276-0; 0-8050-8276-X
                        LC 2007-41958
Heartsick at losing her two dearest companions, Princess Aurelie finds comfort in the glorious music of the
faeries, but the duties of the court call her, as do the
needs of her friends.
  "Graceful prose leads the reader through a complex
chronological narrative and a Shakespearean tangle of
love stories." Booklist

The swan maiden. Henry Holt 2007 292p
$16.95 *

Grades: 6 7 8 9   **Fic**
  1. Magic—Fiction 2. Fairy tales
  ISBN 978-0-8050-8275-3; 0-8050-8275-1
                        LC 2006-33774
Raised as a chastelaine-in-training unlike her sisters
who are learning the arts of sorcery, Doucette discovers
when she is sixteen years old that she too has magic in
her blood, and she must brave her mother's wrath-and
the loss of the man she loves-in order to follow her
birthright.
  "Layered, elegantly written, and filled with unexpected
twists and turns, *The Swan Maiden* soars with grace and
power." Booklist

Torrey, Michele

Voyage of midnight. Alfred A. Knopf 2006
232p $15.95; lib bdg $17.99

Grades: 6 7 8 9   **Fic**
  1. Orphans—Fiction 2. Physicians—Fiction 3. Slave
trade—Fiction 4. Voyages and travels—Fiction
5. Uncles—Fiction
  ISBN 0-375-82382-4; 0-375-92382-9 (lib bdg)
                        LC 2005036269
In the early nineteenth century, when his sea-captain
uncle invites him to assist the ship's surgeon on his next
voyage, orphaned, fourteen-and-a-half-year-old Phillip,
eager to be with family, accepts only to find out that his
uncle is a slave trader.
  "Philip is a well-developed character. . . . [This is an]
engrossing, eye-opening historical novel." Booklist

Townley, Rod

Sky; a novel in three sets and an encore; by
Roderick Townley. 1st ed. Atheneum Books for
Young Readers 2004 265p $16.95

Grades: 7 8 9 10   **Fic**
  1. Jazz musicians—Fiction 2. New York (N.Y.)—Fiction
  ISBN 0-689-85712-8   LC 2003-11354
  "A Richard Jackson book"
In New York City in 1959, fifteen-year-old Alec
Schuyler, at odds with his widowed father over his love
of music, finds a mentor and friend in a blind, black jazz
musician.
  "Townley presents a compassionate portrait of a
young man who is battling for his own place in life and
sets the story in the exciting time of the beat poets and
the explosive development of jazz music." SLJ

Townsend, Wendy

Lizard love; [by] Wendy Townsend. Front Street
2008 196p $17.95 *

Grades: 6 7 8 9   **Fic**
  1. Reptiles—Fiction 2. New York (N.Y.)—Fiction
3. City and town life—Fiction 4. Country life—Fiction
  ISBN 978-1-932425-34-5; 1-932425-34-9
                        LC 2007017975
Grace, a teenager, and her mother have moved to
Manhattan where she feels alienated and out of place, far
from the ponds and farm where she grew up playing
with bullfrogs and lizards, until she finds Fang & Claw,
a reptile store, and meets the owner's son, Walter.
  "Townsend displays a remarkable narrative gift. . . .
Her sensitive herpetological descriptions are unflinching,
evocative, and positively elegant. Even minor characterizations are full and complex." Booklist

Trottier, Maxine

Sister to the wolf. Kids Can Press 2004 348p
hardcover o.p. pa $6.95

Grades: 6 7 8 9   **Fic**
  1. Pawnee Indians—Fiction 2. Frontier and pioneer
life—Fiction
  ISBN 1-55337-519-X; 1-55337-520-3 (pa)
  "Cecile, who lives in Quebec in the early 1700s, sees
a Lesharo, 'an indien slave,' being branded by his master. She buys Lesharo and frees him, and their paths become further intertwined when he accompanies Cecile
and her father to Fort Detroit." Booklist
  "In addition to providing a rich historical background
and vividly recreating the sense of wilderness, Trottier
has drawn her characters and their relationships in a fully
satisfying manner. There is plenty of action and a sweet
romance in the mix as well." SLJ

Trueman, Terry

7 days at the hot corner. HarperTempest 2007
160p $15.99; lib bdg $16.89 *

Grades: 7 8 9 10   **Fic**
  1. Baseball—Fiction 2. Homosexuality—Fiction
3. Friendship—Fiction
  ISBN   978-0-06-057494-9;   0-06-057494-1;
978-0-06-057495-6 (lib bdg); 0-06-057495-X (lib bdg)
                        LC 2006-03706
Varsity baseball player Scott Latimer struggles with
his own prejudices and those of others when his best
friend reveals that he is gay.
  This "suspenseful story is enhanced by some late-
inning surprises, the gay subplot is treated with honesty
and integrity, and Scott and Travis are believable, sympathetic characters." Booklist

Trueman, Terry—*Continued*

Cruise control. 1st ed. HarperTempest 2004
149p $15.99; lib bdg $16.89; pa $8.99 *

Grades: 7 8 9 10　　　　　　　　　　　　**Fic**
1. Brothers—Fiction 2. Cerebral palsy—Fiction
3. Basketball—Fiction 4. Father-son relationship—Fiction

ISBN 0-06-623960-5; 0-06-623961-3 (lib bdg);
0-06-447377-5 (pa)　　　　　LC 2003-19822

Companion volume to: Stuck in neutral (2000)

A talented basketball player struggles to deal with the
helplessness and anger that come with having a brother
rendered completely dysfunctional by severe cerebral palsy and a father who deserted the family.

"This powerful tale is extremely well written and will
give readers an understanding of what it's like to have
a challenged sibling." SLJ

Hurricane; a novel. HarperCollins 2008 137p
$15.99; lib bdg $16.89

Grades: 5 6 7　　　　　　　　　　　　　**Fic**
1. Hurricanes—Fiction 2. Honduras—Fiction
3. Survival after airplane accidents, shipwrecks, etc.—
Fiction

ISBN 978-0-06-000018-9; 978-0-06-000019-6 (lib
bdg); 0-06-000018-X; 0-06-000019-8 (lib bdg)
　　　　　　　　　　　　　　　LC 2007-02990

A revised edition of Swallowing the sun, published
2004 in the United Kingdom

"Thirteen-year-old Jose lives with his family in Honduras. A hurricane hits, causing the recently clear-cut
hillside adjacent to his village to become a mudslide that
smothers and kills most of its fifty inhabitants. . . . Jose
quickly takes charge and becomes a resourceful member
of his ailing community. This survival tale is concise but
engaging. Trueman's descriptions of the village buried in
mud and of the difficulties it creates for the survivors are
vivid." Voice Youth Advocates

Inside out. HarperTempest 2003 117p $15.99;
lib bdg $16.99 *

Grades: 7 8 9 10　　　　　　　　　　　　**Fic**
1. Schizophrenia—Fiction 2. Mentally ill—Fiction
3. Juvenile delinquency—Fiction 4. Hostages—Fiction
5. Suicide—Fiction

ISBN 0-06-623962-1; 0-06-623963-X (lib bdg)
　　　　　　　　　　　　　　　LC 2002-151604

A sixteen-year-old with schizophrenia is caught up in
the events surrounding an attempted robbery by two other teens who eventually hold him hostage.

"Trueman sometimes captures moments of heartbreaking truth, and his swift, suspenseful plot will have particular appeal to reluctant readers." Booklist

Stuck in neutral. HarperCollins Pubs. 2000 114p
$14.95; lib bdg $16.89; pa $6.99 *

Grades: 7 8 9 10　　　　　　　　　　　　**Fic**
1. Cerebral palsy—Fiction 2. Euthanasia—Fiction
3. Father-son relationship—Fiction

ISBN 0-06-028519-2; 0-06-028518-4 (lib bdg);
0-06-447213-2 (pa)　　　　　LC 99-37098

Companion to: Cruise control

Fourteen-year-old Shawn McDaniel, who suffers from
severe cerebral palsy and cannot function, relates his perceptions of his life, his family, and his condition, espe-

cially as he believes his father is planning to kill him.

"Trueman has created a compelling novel that poses
questions about ability and existence while fostering
sympathy for people with severe physical limitations."
Bull Cent Child Books

Tschinag, Galsan, 1943-

The blue sky; a novel; [by] Galsan Tschinag;
translated from the German by Katharina Rout.
Milkweed Editions 2006 209p $22

Grades: 7 8 9 10　　　　　　　　　　　　**Fic**
1. Mongolia—Fiction

ISBN 978-1-57131-055-2; 1-57131-055-X
　　　　　　　　　　　　　　　LC 2006022865

"A poet, shaman, and leader of his Tuvan people describes the harshness and beauty of a childhood spent
herding sheep in Mongolia's High Altai mountains. . . .
The events described happen around 1950 in a part of
the Communist world just beginning to experience political change. The author provides a fascinating window
into an indigenous world." SLJ

Tullson, Diane, 1958-

Red Sea. Orca Book Publishers 2005 169p pa
$7.95

Grades: 7 8 9 10　　　　　　　　　　　　**Fic**
1. Adventure fiction 2. Survival after airplane accidents, shipwrecks, etc.—Fiction

ISBN 1-55143-331-1

"Libby, 14, is on a yearlong sailing adventure with
her mother and stepfather, Duncan. Stuck in Djibouti
awaiting favorable seas, she makes her discontent known
to everyone, at every turn. She deliberately dilly-dallies
on the day of departure, which causes her boat to miss
traveling with the flotilla as planned. Sailing through
dangerous waters, Libby's family is alone when pirates
attack. Duncan is killed, and her mother is badly wounded. The teen is left to her own devices to survive, nurse
her mother, and find the right course to safety. An exciting and suspenseful survival tale." SLJ

Tunnell, Michael O.

Wishing moon. Dutton Children's Books 2004
272p $17.99

Grades: 6 7 8 9　　　　　　　　　　　　**Fic**
1. Magic—Fiction 2. Orphans—Fiction 3. Middle
East—Fiction

ISBN 0-525-47193-6　　　　　LC 2003-62486

After a fourteen-year-old orphan named Aminah
comes to possess a magic lamp, the wishes granted her
by the genie inside it allow her to alter her life by choosing prosperity, purpose, and romance.

"Aminah strives to do good with her magic, and yet
the tale skips preachiness and goes for rich characterizations and a strong, suspenseful plot worthy of the Arabian Nights." Booklist

Another title about Aminah is:

Moon without magic (2007)

Turnbull, Ann

Forged in the fire. Candlewick Press 2007 312p $16.99

Grades: 7 8 9 10 11 12   **Fic**
  1. Plague—Fiction 2. Society of Friends—Fiction 3. Fires—Fiction 4. Great Britain—History—1603-1714, Stuarts—Fiction
  ISBN 978-0-7636-3144-4; 0-7636-3144-2
                   LC 2006-51830
Sequel to: No shame, no fear (2004)
After spending three years apart, eighteen-year-old Susanna is eager to be reunited with her fiance, Will, who is due to arrive from London so that they can be married. But in the summer of 1665, a plague is beginning to spread throughout the city.
  "This novel is filled with fascinating details of everyday life in seventeenth-century England. . . . Throughout, the story maintains a commanding dramatic tension." Booklist

No shame, no fear. Candlewick Press 2004 c2003 293p $15.99

Grades: 7 8 9 10 11 12   **Fic**
  1. Society of Friends—Fiction 2. Great Britain—History—1485-1603, Tudors—Fiction
  ISBN 0-7636-2505-1   LC 2003-65280
First published 2003 in the United Kingdom
In England in 1662, a time of religious persecution, fifteen-year-old Susanna, a poor country girl and a Quaker, and seventeen-year-old William, a wealthy Anglican, meet and fall in love against all odds.
  "This is a well-told historical tale, engaging and informative." Booklist
Followed by Forged in the fire (2007)

Turner, Ann Warren, 1945-

Hard hit; [by] Ann Turner. Scholastic Press 2006 167p $16.99

Grades: 7 8 9 10   **Fic**
  1. Father-son relationship—Fiction 2. Baseball—Fiction 3. Cancer—Fiction 4. Death—Fiction 5. Novels in verse
  ISBN 0-439-29680-3   LC 2005-49906
A rising high school baseball star faces his most difficult challenge when his father is diagnosed with pancreatic cancer.
  This is a "novel in verse that speaks volumes long after the book is closed." Voice Youth Advocates

Turner, Megan Whalen, 1965-

The thief. Greenwillow Bks. 1996 219p $16.99; pa $6.99 *

Grades: 7 8 9 10   **Fic**
  1. Adventure fiction 2. Thieves—Fiction
  ISBN 0-688-14627-9; 0-06-082497-2 (pa)
                   LC 95-41040
A Newbery Medal honor book, 1997
  "Gen languishes in prison for boasting of his skill as a thief. The magus—the king's powerful advisor—needing a clever thief to find an ancient ring that gives the owner the right to rule a neighboring country, bails Gen out. Their journey toward the treasure is marked by danger and political intrigue, and features a motley cast,

tales of old gods, and the revelation of Gen's true identity." Publisher's note
  "A tantalizing, suspenseful, exceptionally clever novel. . . . The author's characterization of Gen is simply superb." Horn Book
  Other titles in this series are:
The King of Attolia (2006)
The Queen of Attolia (2000)

Twain, Mark, 1835-1910

The adventures of Huckleberry Finn; illustrated by Steven Kellogg; afterword by Peter Glassman. Books of Wonder 1994 348p il $24.99 *

Grades: 5 6 7 8   **Fic**
  1. Mississippi River—Fiction 2. Missouri—Fiction
  ISBN 0-688-10656-0
Other editions also available
First published 1885
The adventures of a boy and a runaway slave as they travel down the Mississippi River on a raft.

The adventures of Tom Sawyer; illustrated by Barry Moser; afterword by Peter Glassman. Books of Wonder 1989 261p il $24.99 *

Grades: 5 6 7 8   **Fic**
  1. Mississippi River—Fiction 2. Missouri—Fiction
  ISBN 0-688-07510-X
Other editions also available
First published 1876
The adventures and pranks of a mischievous boy growing up in a Mississippi River town on the early nineteenth century.

The prince and the pauper; introduction by Christopher Paul Curtis. Modern Library 2003 211p (The Modern Library classics) pa $8.95

Grades: 5 6 7 8 9 10 11 12 Adult   **Fic**
  1. Edward VI, King of England, 1537-1553—Fiction 2. Great Britain—History—1485-1603, Tudors—Fiction
  ISBN 0-375-76112-8   LC 2002-26302
Also available in hardcover from the University of California Press and in paperback from Pocket Bks.
  First published 1881
  "Edward VI of England and a little pauper change places a few days before Henry VIII's death. The prince wanders in rags, while Tom Canty suffers the horrors of princedom. At the last moment, the mistake is rectified." Reader's Ency. 4th edition

Twomey, Cathleen

Beachmont letters. Boyds Mills Press 2003 223p $16.95

Grades: 7 8 9 10   **Fic**
  1. Fires—Fiction 2. Burns and scalds—Fiction
  ISBN 1-59078-050-7   LC 2002-111301
Scarred by a fire that killed her father, a seventeen-year-old girl begins a correspondence with a young soldier in 1944
  This "has plenty of atmosphere and an appealing, courageous heroine who gradually realizes her own strength. This unusual survivor/love story is certain to be a three-hanky read." Booklist

Uchida, Yoshiko, 1921-1992

A jar of dreams. Atheneum Pubs. 1981 131p
$16.95; pa $4.99 *

Grades: 5 6 7 8   **Fic**

1. Japanese Americans—Fiction 2. Family life—Fiction 3. Prejudices—Fiction 4. California—Fiction
ISBN 0-689-50210-9; 0-689-71672-9 (pa)

LC 81-3480

"A Margaret K. McElderry book"

"A story of the Depression Era is told by eleven-year-
old Rinko, the only girl in a Japanese-American family
living in Oakland and suffering under the double burden
of financial pressure and the prejudice that had increased
with the tension of economic competition. Into the
household comes a visitor who is a catalyst for change."
Bull Cent Child Books

"Rinko in her guilelessness is genuine and refreshing,
and her worries and concerns seem wholly natural, honest, and convincing." Horn Book

Other titles about Rinko Tsujimura and her family are:
The best bad thing (1983)
The happiest ending (1985)

Journey to Topaz; a story of the
Japanese-American evacuation; illustrated by
Donald Carrick. Scribner 1971 149p il *

Grades: 5 6 7 8   **Fic**

1. Japanese Americans—Evacuation and relocation,
1942-1945—Fiction

Available Heyday Bks. paperback edition $9.95 (ISBN
1-890771-91-0)

This is the story of eleven-year-old Yuki, her eighteen-year-old brother and her mother, who were uprooted, evacuated and interned in Topaz, the War Relocation
Center in Utah during World War II

"This tragic herding of innocent people is described
with dignity and a sorrowful sense of injustice that never
becomes bitter." Saturday Rev

Followed by Journey home

Uehashi, Nahoko, 1962-

Moribito; Guardian of the Spirit; [by] Nahoko
Uehashi; translated by Cathy Hirano; illustrated by
Yuko Shimizu. Arthur A. Levine Books 2008
248p il $17.99 *

Grades: 6 7 8 9   **Fic**

1. Fantasy fiction 2. Martial arts—Fiction 3. Japan—
Fiction
ISBN 978-0-5450-0542-5; 0-5450-0542-6

The wandering warrior Balsa is hired to protect Prince
Chagum from both a mysterious monster and the prince's
father, the Mikado.

"This book is first in a series of ten that have garnered literary and popular success in Japan. . . . Balsa
and Chagum's story is brought to America with a strong
translation. . . . Readers who are fans of action manga,
especially with strong female characters, will enjoy the
ninja-like fighting scenes. . . . The exciting premise,
combined with an attractive cover, should insure that this
title will circulate well." Voice Youth Advocates

Followed by: Moribito II: Guardian of the Darkness
(2009)

Updale, Eleanor

Montmorency; thief, liar, gentleman? Orchard
Books 2004 c2003 232p $16.95 *

Grades: 6 7 8 9 10   **Fic**

1. London (England)—Fiction 2. Great Britain—History—19th century—Fiction 3. Thieves—Fiction
ISBN 0-439-58035-8   LC 2003-56345

First published 2003 in the United Kingdom

In Victorian London, after his life is saved by a young
physician, a thief utilizes the knowledge he gains in prison and from the scientific lectures he attends as the physician's case study exhibit to create a new, highly successful, double life for himself.

"Updale adroitly works the tradition of devilish
schemes and narrow escapes, and the plot moves as nimbly as the master thief himself." Bull Cent Child Books

Other titles about Montmorency are:
Montmorency and the assassins (2006)
Montmorency on the rocks: doctor, aristocrat, murderer?
(2005)
Montmorency's revenge (2007)

Ursu, Anne, 1973-

The shadow thieves. Atheneum Books for
Young Readers 2006 424p il (Cronus chronicles)
$16.95

Grades: 7 8 9 10   **Fic**

1. Mythical animals—Fiction 2. Fantasy fiction
ISBN 1-4169-0587-1   LC 2004-27867

After her cousin Zee arrives from England, thirteen-
year-old Charlotte and he must set out to save humankind from denizens of the underworld, Nightmares,
Death, Pain, and a really nasty guy named Phil.

"This story is charmingly silly, but has enough serious
moments to carry the plot forward. It unwinds with such
unabashed cheerfulness and gusto that readers will find
much to enjoy, especially if they can connect with its
mythological base." Booklist

Another title in this series is:
The siren song (2007)

Vail, Rachel

Lucky. HarperTeen 2008 233p $16.99; lib bdg
$17.89

Grades: 7 8 9 10   **Fic**

1. Friendship—Fiction 2. Wealth—Fiction 3. School
stories
ISBN 978-0-06-089043-8; 978-0-06-089044-5 (lib
bdg)

As Phoebe and her clique of privileged girlfriends get
ready to graduate from eighth grade, a financial scandal
threatens her family's security—as well as Phoebe's social status—but ultimately it teaches her the real meaning
of friendship.

"Vail's insightful characterizations of teen girls and
their shifting loyalties is right on target." Booklist

Followed by: Gorgeous (2009)

You, maybe; the profound asymmetry of love in
high school. HarperCollins Publishers 2006 199p
$15.99

Grades: 8 9 10 11 12   **Fic**

1. School stories 2. Love stories
ISBN 0-06-056917-4   LC 2006-00365

Vail, Rachel—*Continued*

Josie, a fifteen-year-old high school sophomore, is smart, funny, and very much her own person, but when popular senior Carson Gold starts wooing her, she cannot resist his attention.

"Honest about the pain of unrequited love as well as its survivability, this is a sympathetic look at the trials of unexpected and unpredictable romance." Bull Cent Child Books

Valentine, Jenny

Broken soup. HarperTeen 2009 216p $16.99

Grades: 7 8 9 10 **Fic**

1. Bereavement—Fiction 2. Family—Fiction 3. London (England)—Fiction

ISBN 978-0-06-085071-5; 0-06-085071-X

LC 2008-11719

A photographic negative and two surprising new friends become the catalyst for healing as fifteen-year-old Rowan struggles to keep her family and her life together after her brother's death.

"The mystery Valentine sets in motion is quickly paced and packed with revelations. . . . The main appeal of the book, however, is her beautifully modulated tone. . . . Insightful details abound." Booklist

Me, the missing, and the dead. HarperTeen 2008 201p $16.99; lib bdg $17.89 *

Grades: 8 9 10 11 **Fic**

1. Death—Fiction 2. Missing persons—Fiction 3. Fathers—Fiction 4. Single parent family—Fiction 5. London (England)—Fiction

ISBN 978-0-06-085068-5; 0-06-085068-X; 978-0-06-085069-2 (lib bdg); 0-06-085069-8 (lib bdg)

LC 2007-14476

ALA YALSA Morris Award finalist, 2009

First published 2007 in the United Kingdom with title: Finding Violet Park

When a series of chance events leaves him in possession of an urn with ashes, sixteen-year-old Londoner Lucas Swain becomes convinced that its occupant, Violet Park, is communicating with him, initiating a voyage of self-discovery that forces him to finally confront the events surrounding his father's sudden disappearance.

"Part mystery, part magical realism, part story of personal growth, and in large part simply about a funny teenager making light of his and his family's pain, this short novel is engaging from start to finish." SLJ

Van de Ruit, John, 1975-

Spud. Razorbill 2007 331p $16.99

Grades: 6 7 8 9 10 **Fic**

1. School stories 2. South Africa—Fiction

ISBN 978-1-59514-170-5; 0-14-302484-1

LC 2007-6065

In 1990, thirteen-year-old John "Spud" Milton, a prepubescent choirboy, keeps a diary of his first year at an elite, boys-only boarding school in South Africa.

"This raucous autobiographical novel about a scholarship boy in an elite boys' boarding school in 1990 is mainly farce but also part coming-of-age tale." Booklist

Van Diepen, Allison, 1977-

Snitch; [by] Allison Van Diepen. Simon & Schuster 2007 297p pa $6.99

Grades: 7 8 9 10 **Fic**

1. Gangs—Fiction 2. School stories

ISBN 978-1-4169-5030-1 (pa); 1-4169-5030-3 (pa)

Julia DiVino tries hard not to get mixed up with the gangs at South Bay High School, but when Eric Valienté enters into her life, everything changes.

"Van Diepen creates a gritty tale that reveals the uneasy life of a teenager in inner-city Brooklyn. . . . The book is easy to read, full of atmosphere and action, with a swift plot and a ferocity that will draw in reluctant readers." Voice Youth Advocates

Van Etten, David

Likely story. Alfred A. Knopf 2008 230p il $15.99; lib bdg $18.99

Grades: 7 8 9 10 **Fic**

1. Television—Fiction 2. Mother-daughter relationship—Fiction 3. Hollywood (Calif.)—Fiction

ISBN 978-0-375-84676-2; 0-375-84676-X; 978-0-375-94676-9 (lib bdg); 0-375-94676-4 (lib bdg)

LC 2007-22724

Sixteen-year-old Mallory, daughter of the star of a long-running but faltering soap opera, writes her own soap opera script and becomes deeply involved in the day-to-day life of a Hollywood player, while trying to hold on to some shaky personal relationships.

"Strong-willed, quick-witted Mallory is a sympathetic heroine, and Van Etten engagingly weds melodrama to the more mundane, universal dramas of teenage life." Horn Book Guide

Other titles in this series are:

All that glitters (2008)

Red carpet riot (2009)

Van Leeuwen, Jean

Cabin on Trouble Creek. Dial Books for Young Readers 2004 119p $16.99 *

Grades: 4 5 6 7 **Fic**

1. Frontier and pioneer life—Fiction 2. Brothers—Fiction 3. Ohio—Fiction

ISBN 0-8037-2548-5 LC 2003-14151

In 1803 in Ohio, two young brothers are left to finish the log cabin and guard the land while their father goes back to Pennsylvania to fetch their mother and younger siblings.

"Excellent pacing is what makes this novel work so well. . . . The suspense builds consistently. The boys' struggle is portrayed realistically, without sugarcoating nature's harshness." SLJ

Lucy was there—. Phyllis Fogelman Bks. 2002 165p $16.99 **Fic**

1. Death—Fiction 2. Friendship—Fiction 3. Dogs—Fiction

ISBN 0-8037-2738-0 LC 2001-33974

With the help of new friends and a very special dog, Morgan begins to come to terms with the loss of her mother and five-year-old brother, who boarded a plane and never came back

"Morgan's anguish is palpable but never overwrought,

Van Leeuwen, Jean—*Continued*
and the short chapters, appealing heroine, and well-told story leavened with humor give this solid . . . appeal."
Booklist

Vande Velde, Vivian, 1951-
The book of Mordred; [illustrations by Justin Gerard] Houghton Mifflin 2005 342p $18; pa $8.99
Grades: 8 9 10 11 12   **Fic**
1. Arthur, King—Fiction 2. Mordred (Legendary character)—Fiction 3. Knights and knighthood—Fiction 4. Great Britain—History—0-1066—Fiction
ISBN 0-618-50754-X; 0-618-80916-3 (pa)
LC 2004-28223
As the peaceful King Arthur reigns, the five-year-old daughter of Lady Alayna, newly widowed of the village-wizard Toland, is abducted by knights who leave their barn burning and their only servant dead.
"All of the characters are well developed and have a strong presence throughout. . . . [This] provides an intriguing counterpoint to anyone who is interested in Arthurian legend." SLJ

Heir apparent. Harcourt 2002 315p $17; pa $6.95
Grades: 6 7 8 9   **Fic**
1. Virtual reality—Fiction 2. Science fiction
ISBN 0-15-204560-0; 0-15-205125-2 (pa)
LC 2002-2441
While playing a total immersion virtual reality game of kings and intrigue, fourteen-year-old Giannine learns that demonstrators have damaged the equipment to which she is connected, and she must win the game quickly or be damaged herself
"This adventure includes a cast of intriguing characters and personalities. The feisty heroine has a funny, sarcastic sense of humor and succeeds because of her ingenuity and determination." SLJ

Never trust a dead man. Harcourt Brace & Co. 1999 194p hardcover o.p. pa $6.95
Grades: 6 7 8 9   **Fic**
1. Mystery fiction
ISBN 0-15-201899-9; 0-15-206448-6 (pa)
LC 98-39885
Wrongly convicted of murder and punished by being sealed in the tomb with the dead man, seventeen-year-old Selwyn enlists the help of a witch and the resurrected victim to find the true killer
"Filled with engaging characters, witty dialogue, and lots of action, this is an entertaining blend of fantasy, whodunit, and comedy." SLJ

Remembering Raquel. Harcourt 2007 160p $16
Grades: 8 9 10 11   **Fic**
1. Death—Fiction 2. School stories 3. Obesity—Fiction
ISBN 978-0-15-205976-7   LC 2006-35769
Various people recall aspects of the life of Raquel Falcone, an unpopular, overweight freshman at Quail Run High School, including classmates, her parents, and the driver who struck and killed her as she was walking home from an animated film festival.
"Easily booktalked and deeper than it initially seems, this will be popular with reluctant readers." Booklist

Stolen. Marshall Cavendish 2008 158p $16.99 *
Grades: 6 7 8 9 10   **Fic**
1. Amnesia—Fiction 2. Missing children—Fiction 3. Witches—Fiction 4. Magic—Fiction
ISBN 978-0-7614-5515-8; 0-7614-5515-9
LC 2008-03184
A girl finds herself running through the forest at the edge of a village with no memory of anything, even her own name, and later learns that she might be twelve-year-old Isabelle, believed to be stolen by a witch six years before.
"Vande Velde, noted for her well-crafted riffs on fairy tales, has written her darkest yet, a story of greed, jealousy, and insidious evil that will haunt the reader for some time to come." Booklist

There's a dead person following my sister around. Harcourt Brace & Co. 1999 143p hardcover o.p. pa $5.95 *
Grades: 4 5 6 7   **Fic**
1. Ghost stories 2. Slavery—Fiction 3. Underground railroad—Fiction
ISBN 0-15-202100-0; 0-15-206467-2 (pa)
LC 99-11462
Also available in paperback from Puffin Bks.
Ted becomes concerned and intrigued when his five-year-old sister Vicki begins receiving visits from the ghosts of two runaway slaves
"There is sufficient humor, action, and scariness to keep readers engaged." SLJ

Vaupel, Robin
My contract with Henry. Holiday House 2003 244p $16.95   **Fic**
1. Thoreau, Henry David, 1817-1862—Fiction 2. Friendship—Fiction 3. School stories
ISBN 0-8234-1701-8   LC 2002-27471
A mission that begins as an eighth-grade project on Henry David Thoreau's experimental living at Walden Pond becomes a life-changing experience for a group of outsider students who become budding philosophers, environmental activists, and loyal friends
"Vaupel creates a painfully accurate portrayal of middle-school social dynamics." Booklist

Rules of the universe by Austin W. Hale. Holiday House 2007 265p $16.95
Grades: 4 5 6 7   **Fic**
1. Science fiction 2. Grandfathers—Fiction 3. Death—Fiction
ISBN 0-8234-1811-1; 978-0-8234-1811-4
LC 2003-56751
Thirteen-year-old Austin Hale, an aspiring scientist and disciple of his grandfather, a Nobel Prize-winning molecular physicist, finds himself in control of a powerful energy force that can turn back time and turn his orbit upside down.
"The captivating blend of scientific research and magic is effectively balanced against the stark realism of a boy facing his first significant losses; the overall tone is one of cautious optimism." Bull Cent Child Books

Veciana-Suarez, Ana

The flight to freedom. Orchard Bks. 2002 215p (First person fiction) $16.95; pa $6.99   **Fic**

1. Cuban Americans—Fiction 2. Immigrants—Fiction

ISBN 0-439-38199-1; 0-439-38200-9 (pa)

LC 2001-58783

Writing in the diary which her father gave her, thirteen-year-old Yara describes life with her family in Havana, Cuba, in 1967 as well as her experiences in Miami, Florida, after immigrating there to be reunited with some relatives while leaving others behind

"The story and characters ring true in their portrayal of loss, longing, and the hope of starting a new life." SLJ

Vega, Denise

Click here; (to find out how I survived seventh grade). Little, Brown 2005 211p $15.99

Grades: 5 6 7 8   **Fic**

1. Friendship—Fiction 2. School stories

ISBN 0-316-98560-0

Seventh-grader Erin Swift writes about her friends and classmates in her private blog, but when it accidentally gets posted on the school Intranet site, she learns some important lessons about friendship.

"The characters and situations are believable, and readers will relate to and sympathize with Erin's dilemmas." SLJ

Velmans, Hester

Isabel of the whales; [by] Hester Velmans. Delacorte Press 2005 192p $15.95; lib bdg $17.99

Grades: 5 6 7 8   **Fic**

1. Whales—Fiction 2. Massachusetts—Fiction

ISBN 0-385-73202-3; 0-385-90233-6 (lib bdg)

LC 2004-546

On a whale watch trip with her class off the coast of Cape Cod, Isabel, who has always had an affinity for whales, falls overboard and discovers as she finds herself swimming underwater with whales all around her that she is one of the Chosen who can change shape from human to whale and back again.

"An excellent choice for readers who enjoy animal stories, domestic fantasy, or even nonfiction." SLJ

Venkatraman, Padma

Climbing the stairs. G.P. Putnam's Sons 2008 247p $16.99 *

Grades: 6 7 8 9 10   **Fic**

1. Family life—Fiction 2. Prejudices—Fiction 3. Brain—Wounds and injuries—Fiction 4. India—History—1765-1947, British occupation—Fiction

ISBN 978-0-399-24746-0; 0-399-24746-7

LC 2007-21757

In India, in 1941, when her father becomes brain-damaged in a non-violent protest march, fifteen-year-old Vidya and her family are forced to move in with her father's extended family and become accustomed to a totally different way of life.

"Venkatraman paints an intricate and convincing backdrop of a conservative Brahmin home in a time of change. . . . The striking cover art . . . will draw readers to this vividly told story." Booklist

Verne, Jules, 1828-1905

20,000 leagues under the sea; illustrated by the Dillons; translated by Anthony Bonner. HarperCollins Pubs. 2000 394p il $21.95 *

Grades: 5 6 7 8 9 10 11 12 Adult   **Fic**

1. Science fiction 2. Submarines—Fiction

ISBN 0-688-10535-1   LC 00-24336

Also available other translations from various publishers

"Books of Wonder"

Original French edition, 1870

Translation of: Vingt milles lieues sous les mers

Retells the adventures of a French professor and his two companions as they sail above and below the world's oceans as prisoners on the fabulous electric submarine of the deranged Captain Nemo

Vernon, Ursula

Nurk; the strange, surprising adventures of a (somewhat) brave shrew; [by] Ursula Vernon. Harcourt 2008 131p il $15

Grades: 4 5 6 7   **Fic**

1. Diaries—Fiction 2. Dragonflies—Fiction 3. Courage—Fiction 4. Letters—Fiction

ISBN 978-0-15-206375-7; 0-15-206375-7

LC 2007-30788

Nurk, a sort-of brave shrew, packs up a few pairs of clean socks and sails off on an accidental adventure, guided by wisdom found in the journal of his famously brave and fierce grandmother, Lady Surka the warrior shrew.

"Vernon's clever dialogue . . ., silly characters, and even sillier situations will amuse readers right to the very last page, as will the author's line drawings that appear in each chapter." Booklist

Verrillo, Erica F.

Elissa's quest; [by] Erica Verrillo. Random House 2007 336p (Phoenix rising) $16.99; lib bdg $19.99; pa $6.99

Grades: 5 6 7 8   **Fic**

1. Magic—Fiction 2. Father-daughter relationship—Fiction 3. Fantasy fiction

ISBN 978-0-375-83946-7; 0-375-83946-1; 978-0-375-93946-4 (lib bdg); 0-375-93946-6 (lib bdg); 978-0-375-83947-4 (pa); 0-375-83947-X (pa)

LC 2006-14436

Thirteen-year-old Elissa knows nothing of her origins until her father comes and takes her to the Citadel of the evil Khan, in exchange for soldiers to protect the kingdom that will one day be hers, but upon discovering her power, she chooses to follow her own destiny.

This is a "charming and elegant story. Elissa emerges as a thoroughly lovable heroine." Publ Wkly

Other titles is this series are:

Elissa's odyssey (2008)

World's end (2009)

Vincent, Zu, 1952-

The lucky place. Front Street 2008 230p $17.95
Grades: 7 8 9 10   **Fic**
1. Father-daughter relationship—Fiction
2. Stepfathers—Fiction 3. Death—Fiction 4. Cancer—
Fiction 5. Alcoholism—Fiction
ISBN 978-1-932425-70-3; 1-932425-70-5
        LC 2007-18357
"Readers meet Cassie when she is three years old and
her inebriated father leaves her behind at the racetrack.
. . . She is returned home by the police and their mother
eventually realizes that this man is not a competent father. . . . Mom brings home Ellis, New Daddy, and
Cassie can't help but feel his strength. . . . Cassie's
voice changes as she grows into a 12-year-old who
comes to know that inside herself is the real lucky place
that she can truly count on. . . . Taking place in California in the late 1950s and early '60s . . . Vincent's novel
ably creates a world that makes promises it can't keep.
. . . A stunning fiction debut." SLJ

Vivian, Siobhan

A little friendly advice; [by] Siobhan Vivian.
Scholastic/Push 2008 248p $16.99
Grades: 7 8 9 10 11 12   **Fic**
1. Divorce—Fiction 2. Father-daughter relationship—
Fiction 3. Friendship—Fiction 4. Ohio—Fiction
ISBN 978-0-545-00404-6; 0-545-00404-7
        LC 2007-9905
When Ruby's divorced father shows up unexpectedly
on her sixteenth birthday, the week that follows is full of
confusing surprises, including discovering that her best
friend has been keeping secrets from her, her mother has
not been truthful about the past, and life is often complicated.
"Readers will find themselves and their relationships
reflected in Ruby's story—for better and worse." Publ
Wkly

Same difference. PUSH 2009 287p $17.99
Grades: 6 7 8 9   **Fic**
1. Artists—Fiction 2. School stories 3. Friendship—
Fiction 4. New Jersey—Fiction 5. Philadelphia (Pa.)—
Fiction
ISBN 978-0-545-00407-7; 0-545-00407-1
        LC 2008-30165
Feeling left out since her long-time best friend started
a serious relationship, sixteen-year-old Emily looks forward to a summer program at the Philadelphia College
of Art but is not sure she is up to the challenges to be
faced there, including finding herself and learning to balance life and art.
"Vivian . . . serves up the story with vivid description
and dialogue; the author's talent for scene-setting and
evocative imagery is especially effective." Publ Wkly

Voake, Steve

The dreamwalker's child. Bloomsbury
Children's Books 2006 300p $16.95
Grades: 6 7 8 9   **Fic**
1. Science fiction 2. Insects—Fiction
ISBN 978-1-58234-661-8; 1-58234-661-5
        LC 2005-57068
First published 2005 in the United Kingdom

After being hit by a car Sam Palmer finds himself in
Aurobon, a land of giant insects where some of the inhabitants are working to keep Earth's ecology in balance
while others are trying to wipe out humankind with a lethal virus spread by mosquitoes.
"This page-turner has something for everyone." SLJ
Followed by The web of fire (2007)

The web of fire; [by] Steve Voake. Bloomsbury
2007 318p $17.95
Grades: 6 7 8 9   **Fic**
1. Insects—Fiction 2. Science fiction
ISBN 978-1-58234-737-0; 1-58234-737-9
        LC 2006042881
Sequel to The dreamwalker's child (2006)
Four years after vanquishing Odoursin and saving humankind from his evil plans, Sam and Skipper return to
a devastated Aurobon where they must once again fight
for survival against the reemerged Odoursin and his new
army of robber flies.
This is "packed with action. . . . A high-flying sci-
fi/fantasy adventure." SLJ

Voelkel, J.

Middleworld; [by] J & P Voelkel [i.e., Jon
Voelkel, Pamela Craik Voelkel] Smith and Kraus
Publishers 2007 397p il (Jaguar stones trilogy)
$17.95
Grades: 6 7 8 9   **Fic**
1. Adventure fiction 2. Central America—Fiction
3. Mayas—Fiction
ISBN 978-1-57525-561-3
"Newly arrived in 'the snake-infested dump' of San
Xavier, a fictional Central American country, 14-year-old
Max Murphy discovers that his archaeologist parents
have disappeared. Aided in his search by resourceful
Lola, a descendent of the Maya, Max learns that the
gods of her people have chosen him for a mission involving powerful artifacts." Booklist
"Suspense and intrigue, human sacrifice, smuggling,
and secret doors and escape routes through pyramids ensure that the novel, the first in a projected trilogy, is
likely to win legions of fans." SLJ

Voigt, Cynthia

Bad girls in love. Atheneum Bks. for Young
Readers 2002 233p $15.95; pa $4.99 **Fic**
1. School stories 2. Friendship—Fiction
ISBN 0-689-82471-8; 0-689-86620-8 (pa)
        LC 2001-45898
"An Anne Schwartz book"
Now in the eighth grade, best friends Mikey and
Margalo try to figure out boys, crushes, and falling in
love
It's the girls' "talk—insulting, furious, funny, needy,
and smart—on the telephone, and in the school's cafete-
ria, bathrooms, and hallways that gets the junior-high
jungle exactly right." Booklist
Other titles in this series are:
Bad, badder, baddest (1997)
Bad girls (1996)
Bad girls, bad girls, whatcha gonna do? (2006)
It's not easy being bad (2000)

Voigt, Cynthia—*Continued*

Dicey's song. Atheneum Pubs. 1982 196p
$17.95; pa $6.99 *

Grades: 5 6 7 8   **Fic**
1. Grandmothers—Fiction 2. Siblings—Fiction
ISBN 0-689-30944-9; 0-689-86362-4 (pa)
LC 82-3882
Awarded the Newbery Medal, 1983
Sequel to Homecoming
Dicey "had brought her siblings to the grandmother
they'd never seen when their mother (now in a mental
institution) had been unable to cope. This is the story of
the children's adjustment to Gram (and hers to them) and
to a new school and a new life—but with some of the
old problems." Bull Cent Child Books
"The vividness of Dicey is striking; Voigt has
plumbed and probed her character inside out to fashion
a memorable protagonist." Booklist

Homecoming. Atheneum Pubs. 1981 312p
$18.95 *

Grades: 6 7 8 9   **Fic**
1. Siblings—Fiction 2. Abandoned children—Fiction
ISBN 0-689-30833-7   LC 80-36723
Also available in paperback from Fawcett Bks.
"When their momma abandons them in a shopping
center, Dicey Tillerman and her three younger brothers
and sisters set out on foot for where momma was osten-
sibly taking them—to Great-Aunt Cilla's in Bridgeport,
Connecticut." Booklist
"The characterizations of the children are original and
intriguing, and there are a number of interesting minor
characters encountered in their travels." SLJ
Followed by Dicey's song

Izzy, willy-nilly. Rev. format ed. Atheneum
Books for Young Readers 2005 c1986 327p
$17.95; pa $6.99 *

Grades: 7 8 9 10   **Fic**
1. Friendship—Fiction 2. Amputees—Fiction
3. Drunk driving—Fiction
ISBN   978-1-4169-0340-6;   1-4169-0340-2;
978-1-4169-0339-0 (pa); 1-4169-0339-9 (pa)
LC 2005299062
ALA YALSA Margaret A. Edwards Award (1995)
A reissue of the title first published 1986
A car accident causes fifteen-year-old Izzy to lose one
leg and face the need to start building a new life as an
amputee.
"Voigt shows unusual insight into the workings of a
15-year-old girl's mind. . . . Just as Voigt's perceptive
empathy brings Izzy to life, other characterizations are
memorable, whether of Izzy's shallow former friends or
of her egocentric 10-year-old sister." Pub Wkly [review
of 1986 edition]

A solitary blue. Atheneum Pubs. 1983 189p
hardcover o.p. pa $6.99 *

Grades: 7 8 9 10   **Fic**
1. Divorce—Fiction 2. Parent-child relationship—Fic-
tion
ISBN 0-689-31008-0; 0-689-86360-8 (pa)
LC 83-6007
A Newbery honor book, 1984

Jeff Greene, a minor character from Dicey's song, "is
abandoned by his mother at age seven and suffers from
the benign neglect of his college professor father. As a
teenager, Jeff again sees and is charmed by his mother
only to become disillusioned by her." Child Book Rev
Serv
"This is the most mature and sophisticated of Voigt's
novels. . . . Beautifully knit . . . compelling and intelligent." Bull Cent Child Books

Volponi, Paul

Black and white. Viking 2005 185p $15.99; pa
$6.99

Grades: 7 8 9 10   **Fic**
1. African Americans—Fiction 2. Race relations—Fiction 3. Basketball—Fiction
ISBN 0-670-06006-2; 0-14-240692-9 (pa)
LC 2004-24543
Two star high school basketball players, one black and
one white, experience the justice system differently after
committing a crime together and getting caught.
"These complex characters share a mutual respect and
struggle with issues of loyalty, honesty, and courage. Social conflicts, basketball fervor, and tough personal
choices make this title a gripping story." SLJ

The hand you're dealt. Atheneum Books for
Young Readers 2008 176p $16.99

Grades: 8 9 10 11   **Fic**
1. Poker—Fiction 2. Teachers—Fiction 3. School stories
ISBN 978-1-4169-3989-4; 1-4169-3989-X
LC 2007-22988
When seventeen-year-old Huck's vindictive math
teacher wins the town poker tournament and takes the
winner's watch away from Huck's father while he is in
a coma, Huck vows to get even with him no matter what
it takes.
"The varied characters are unique and add to the
book's interest quotient." Voice Youth Advocates

Homestretch. Atheneum Books for Young
Readers 2009 160p $16.99

Grades: 6 7 8 9   **Fic**
1. Horse racing—Fiction 2. Horses—Fiction
3. Prejudices—Fiction 4. Mexican Americans—Fiction
5. Father-son relationship—Fiction 6. Death—Fiction
ISBN 978-1-4169-3987-0; 1-4169-3987-3
LC 2008-30024
Five months after losing his mother, seventeen-year-
old Gas runs away from an abusive father and gets a job
working at an Arkansas race track, surrounded by the illegal Mexican immigrants that he and his father blame
for her death.
"Volponi continues his streak of well-written novels in
this simply written, coming-of-age story." Voice Youth
Advocates

Hurricane song; a novel of New Orleans. Viking
Childrens Books 2008 144p $15.99 *

Grades: 7 8 9 10 11 12   **Fic**
1. Father-son relationship—Fiction 2. Hurricane
Katrina, 2005—Fiction 3. Jazz music—Fiction
4. New Orleans (La.)—Fiction
ISBN 978-0-670-06160-0; 0-670-06160-3
LC 2007-38215

Volponi, Paul—*Continued*

Twelve-year-old Miles Shaw goes to live with his father, a jazz musician, in New Orleans, and together they survive the horrors of Hurricane Katrina in the Superdome, learning about each other and growing closer through their painful experiences.

"A brilliant blend of reality and fiction, this novel hits every chord just right." Voice Youth Advocates

Rucker Park setup. Viking 2007 149p $15.99 *
Grades: 7 8 9 10 11 12   **Fic**
1. Basketball—Fiction 2. Homicide—Fiction
3. African Americans—Fiction 4. Harlem (New York, N.Y.)—Fiction 5. Mystery fiction
ISBN 978-0-670-06130-3; 0-670-06130-1
LC 2006-28463
While playing in a crucial basketball game on the very court where his best friend was murdered, Mackey tries to come to terms with his own part in that murder and decide whether to maintain his silence or tell J.R.'s father and the police what really happened.

The author's "description of playing pickup ball on one of the toughest courts in the world feels wholly authentic. The characters also feel real." Voice Youth Advocates

Vrettos, Adrienne Maria

Sight; [by] Adrienne Maria Vrettos. Margaret K. McElderry Books 2007 254p $16.99 *
Grades: 7 8 9 10   **Fic**
1. Parapsychology—Fiction 2. Missing persons—Fiction 3. School stories 4. Criminal investigation—Fiction
ISBN 978-1-4169-0657-5; 1-4169-0657-6
LC 2006-35999
Sixteen-year-old Dylan uses her psychic abilities to help police solve crimes against children, but keeps her extracurricular activities secret from her friends at school.

"Vrettos has created a creepy scenario with a taut plot and a gripping climax. . . . She has crafted a believable setting and characters." Bull Cent Books

Skin. Margaret K. McElderry Books 2006 227p $16.95
Grades: 7 8 9 10   **Fic**
1. Siblings—Fiction 2. Anorexia nervosa—Fiction
ISBN 1-4169-0655-X   LC 2005001119
When his parents decide to separate, eighth-grader Donnie watches with horror as the physical condition of his sixteen-year old sister, Karen, deteriorates due to an eating disorder.

"The overwhelming alienation Donnie endures will speak to many teens, while his honest perspective will be welcomed by boys." Booklist

Wade, Rebecca

The theft & the miracle. 1st ed. Katherine Tegen Books 2007 351p $16.99; lib bdg $17.89
Grades: 5 6 7 8   **Fic**
1. Sculpture—Fiction 2. Artists—Fiction
3. Supernatural—Fiction 4. Cathedrals—Fiction
ISBN   978-0-06-077493-6;   0-06-077493-2;
978-0-06-077495-0 (lib bdg); 0-06-077495-9 (lib bdg)
LC 2006-00822

Overweight with acne-prone skin, twelve-year-old Hannah always feels unsure of herself, but when a wooden statue of Jesus goes missing from a cathedral, she discovers a special connection with both the statue and a larger force.

"Wade skillfully blends the Black Death of the 14th century and other historical elements into a fascinating and well-paced story. Fully developed characters give the mystery an added depth." SLJ

Wait, Lea, 1946-

Finest kind. Margaret K. McElderry Books 2006 246p $16.95
Grades: 4 5 6 7   **Fic**
1. Family life—Fiction 2. Cerebral palsy—Fiction
3. Maine—Fiction
ISBN 978-1-4169-0952-1; 1-4169-0952-4
LC 2005-25422
When his father's Boston bank fails in 1838, causing his family to relocate to a small Maine town, twelve-year-old Jake Webber works to prepare the family for the harsh winter while also keeping the existence of his disabled younger brother a secret.

"Wait's prose is straightforward, the story is filled with diverse characters and period details, and Jake is an appealing, dimensional protagonist." Booklist

Wintering well. Margaret K. McElderry Books 2004 186p hardcover o.p. pa $5.99
Grades: 5 6 7 8   **Fic**
1. Siblings—Fiction 2. Handicapped—Fiction
3. Maine—Fiction
ISBN 0-689-85646-6; 0-689-85647-4 (pa)
LC 2003-19322
Fifteen-year-old Will Ames and his sister Cassie go to stay with their sister in nearby Wiscasset, Maine, after a disabling accident ruins Will's plans for a career in farming.

"Limned with just the right amount of detail about the realities of life in the early nineteenth century, this is a quiet story of seeking." Booklist

Waite, Judy

Forbidden. Atheneum Books for Young Readers 2006 c2004 249p $16.95
Grades: 8 9 10 11 12   **Fic**
1. Cults—Fiction
ISBN 0-689-87642-4   LC 2004-27898
First published 2004 in the United Kingdom
Elinor has lived in a cult her entire life, but when she meets a boy who looks strangely familiar, she begins to question what she has been taught

"The story moves quickly to a message-laden climax that readers will not soon forget." SLJ

Shopaholic. Atheneum Bks. for Young Readers 2003 211p $16.95
Grades: 6 7 8 9   **Fic**
1. Friendship—Fiction 2. Shopping—Fiction
ISBN 0-689-85138-3   LC 2002-26246
"Fourteen-year-old Taylor feels unloved at home, where her mother has slipped into a depression after the death of Taylor's younger sister. When an older friend

Waite, Judy—*Continued*

offers to take Taylor shopping, Taylor struggles to live up to Kat's glamorous lifestyle." Horn Book Guide

This is "an engaging, emotionally wrenching read." SLJ

Walden, Mark

H.I.V.E; The Higher Institute of Villainous Education. Simon & Schuster Books for Young Readers 2007 309p $15.99

Grades: 5 6 7 8   **Fic**

1. Criminals—Fiction

ISBN 1-4169-3571-1; 978-1-4169-3571-1

LC 2007-16205

"H.I.V.E. is operated on a volcanic island in a distant ocean by G.L.O.V.E., a shadowy organization of worldwide wickedness. And, as 13-year-old master of mischief Otto Malpense soon discovers, here the slickest of young tricksters, thieves, and hackers have been brought against their will to be trained as the next generation of supervillains. . . . [This] novel is a real page-turner; those who love superhero stories will eat it up." SLJ

Another title about H.I.V.E. is:

H.I.V.E.: the Overlord protocol (2008)

Waldorf, Heather

Tripping. Red Deer Press 2008 342p pa $12.95

Grades: 8 9 10 11 12   **Fic**

1. Wilderness survival—Fiction 2. Amputees—Fiction 3. Voyages and travels—Fiction 4. Canada—Fiction

ISBN 978-0-88995-426-7 (pa); 0-88995-426-7 (pa)

"Rainey and five other teens begin an eight-week school-sponsored educational/survival trek across Canada. . . . Rainey's challenge is heightened because she has an artificial leg and she learns that her mother, who abandoned her as a baby, lives near one of their stops and wants to meet her. As the trip progresses, the individuals bond and become part of a team. . . . Waldorf has written a unique story in which six very different young people are united in a common cause. Told with wit and humor, this fast-paced novel has character development that is extraordinary." SLJ

Wallace, Bill, 1947-

Skinny-dipping at Monster Lake. Simon & Schuster Bks. for Young Readers 2003 212p $16.95

Grades: 4 5 6 7   **Fic**

ISBN 0-689-85150-2   LC 2002-152820

When twelve-year-old Kent helps his father in a daring underwater rescue, he wins the respect he has always craved.

"This old-fashioned adventure has wide appeal, and the youngsters' games and camaraderie will hook even reluctant readers." SLJ

Wallace, Rich, 1957-

One good punch. Alfred A. Knopf 2007 114p $15.99; lib bdg $17.89

Grades: 7 8 9 10 11 12   **Fic**

1. Journalism—Fiction 2. Track athletics—Fiction 3. School stories 4. Pennsylvania—Fiction

ISBN 978-0-375-81352-8;   0-375-81352-7; 978-0-375-91352-5 (lib bdg); 0-375-91352-1 (lib bdg)

LC 2006-33270

Eighteen-year-old Michael Kerrigan, writer of obituaries for the Scranton Observer and captain of the track team, is ready for the most important season of his life—until the police find four joints in his school locker, and he is faced with a choice that could change everything.

"This novel's success is in creating a multidimensional male character in a format that will appeal to all readers. The moral dilemma . . . makes this novel ripe for ethical discussions." Voice Youth Advocates

Perpetual check. Alfred A. Knopf 2009 112p $15.99; lib bdg $18.99

Grades: 8 9 10 11   **Fic**

1. Chess—Fiction 2. Brothers—Fiction 3. Father-son relationship—Fiction

ISBN 978-0-375-84058-6;   0-375-84058-3; 978-0-375-94058-3 (lib bdg); 0-375-94058-8 (lib bdg)

LC 2008-04159

Brothers Zeke and Randy participate in an important chess tournament, playing against each other while also trying to deal with their father's intensely competetive tendencies.

"Wallace cleverly positions Randy and Zeke for a win-win conclusion in this satisfying, engaging, and deceptively simple story." SLJ

Wrestling Sturbridge. Knopf 1996 135p hardcover o.p. pa $4.99 *

Grades: 7 8 9 10   **Fic**

1. Wrestling—Fiction 2. Friendship—Fiction

ISBN 0-679-87803-3; 0-679-88555-2 (pa)

LC 95-20468

"Narrator Ben, a high school senior, doesn't want to be like his father and so many others in Sturbridge, Pa., who after graduating get a job at the cinder block plant. Seemingly his only alternative is to become a state wrestling champion and thus win an athletic scholarship. But his way is firmly blocked by his buddy Al, who reigns supreme in their weight class." Publ Wkly

"The wresting scenes are thrilling. . . . Like Ben, whose voice is so strong and clear here, Wallace weighs his words carefully, making every one count in this excellent, understated first novel." Booklist

Walters, Eric, 1957-

Sketches; by Eric Walters. Viking 2008 232p $15.99

Grades: 7 8 9 10   **Fic**

1. Homeless persons—Fiction 2. Runaway teenagers—Fiction 3. Artists—Fiction

ISBN 978-0-670-06294-2; 0-670-06294-4

LC 2007-23123

After running away from home, fifteen-year-old Dana finds friends on the Toronto streets, and, eventually, a way to come to terms with what has happened to her.

Walters, Eric, 1957——*Continued*

"The characters' well-portrayed camaraderie, resourcefulness, and resiliency carry the tale, which ends on a note of promise." SLJ

Splat! written by Eric Walters. Orca Book Publishers 2008 112p $16.95; pa $9.95

Grades: 7 8 9 10 **Fic**

1. Friendship—Fiction 2. Tomatoes—Fiction 3. Canada—Fiction

ISBN 978-1-55143-988-4; 1-55143-988-3; 978-1-55143-986-0 (pa); 1-55143-986-7 (pa)

"Keegan and Alex are the only kids in Leamington who haven't volunteered to help out with the town's annual tomato festival. In an attempt to teach them a sense of responsibility, their fathers put them in charge of the tomato toss. The boys decide it's their responsibility to add a little excitement to the event." Publisher's note

"The relationship between Keegan and narrator Alex, with their relentless and often quite funny smartassed exhanges, is the core of this speedy and readable novel." Bull Cent Child Books

Waltman, Kevin

Learning the game. Scholastic Press 2005 215p $16.95

Grades: 8 9 10 11 12 **Fic**

1. Brothers—Fiction 2. Basketball—Fiction 3. Theft—Fiction 4. Indiana—Fiction

ISBN 0-439-73109-7 LC 2004-23535

When he and his high school basketball teammates steal from a fraternity house in their small Indiana town, Nate contends with his guilt, his loyalty to his friends, and his desire to help his older brother who comes under suspicion for the crime.

"The layered issues, together with excellent writing sparked with many sharp phrases, make for a compelling novel that offers no easy answers." Booklist

Ward, David, 1967-

Escape the mask. Amulet Books 2008 195p (The grassland trilogy) $15.95 *

Grades: 7 8 9 10 **Fic**

1. Science fiction 2. Slavery—Fiction

ISBN 978-0-8109-9477-5; 0-8109-9477-1

LC 2007028212

Six young friends, tortured by the Spears and forced to work as slaves in the harsh fields of Grassland, vow to escape to find the freedom that was stolen from them long ago, and their opportunity arises when Outsiders come and wage war against the Spears.

"Ward's novel bursts with action and is laden with tense scenes. His excellent descriptive writing allows the reader to visualize the action. In addition, Ward's fantasy world is so believable that the text almost reads as historical fiction." Voice Youth Advocates

Followed by: Beneath the mask (2008)

Wardlaw, Lee, 1955-

101 ways to bug your teacher; Lee Wardlaw. Dial Books 2004 246p hardcover o.p. pa $6.99

Grades: 4 5 6 7 **Fic**

1. School stories

ISBN 0-8037-2658-9; 0-14-240331-1 (pa)

LC 2003-20068

Steve "Sneeze" Wyatt attempts to thwart his parents' plan to have him skip eighth grade, but he has bigger problems when his friends disapprove of his new list and Mrs. "Fierce" Pierce threatens to keep him from the Invention Convention.

"In spite of the title, the characters show respect for their teachers and parents, and for one another. A delightful read." SLJ

Warner, Sally

It's only temporary; written and illustrated by Sally Warner. Viking Childrens Books 2008 182p il $15.99

Grades: 4 5 6 7 **Fic**

1. Siblings—Fiction 2. Bullies—Fiction 3. Brain—Wounds and injuries—Fiction 4. Grandmothers—Fiction

ISBN 978-0-670-06111-2; 0-670-06111-5

LC 2007-038220

When Skye's older brother comes home after a devastating accident, she moves from Albuquerque, New Mexico, to California to live with her grandmother and attend middle school, where she somewhat reluctantly makes new friends, learns to stand up for herself and those she cares about, and begins to craft a new relationship with her changed brother.

"Warner deftly handles Skye's anger toward her brain-injured brother, also infusing her with a convincingly developed sense of compassion. Witty line art decorates some pages." Horn Book Guide

Wasserman, Robin

Awakening. Scholastic 2007 207p (Chasing yesterday) pa $5.99 *

Grades: 6 7 8 9 **Fic**

1. Amnesia—Fiction

ISBN 978-0-439-93338-4

"A teenager wakes up just yards away from a mysterious industrial accident. . . . Although she is seriously injured and has amnesia, she should be dead. . . . As Jane Doe, or J.D., she receives national news attention. Then a woman shows up, claiming to be her mother, and J.D. goes 'home' to a house she cannot remember and begins psychiatric treatment with an old family friend, who unnervingly looks exactly like the monstrous doctor of her nightmares. . . . [Wasserman's] characters are well developed and believable, her plot is suspenseful, and her backgrounds . . . are nicely detailed." Voice Youth Advocates

Another title in this series is:
Betrayal (2007)

Waters, Dan, 1969-
Generation dead. Hyperion 2008 382p $16.99 *
Grades: 7 8 9 10   **Fic**
  1. Death—Fiction 2. Zombies—Fiction 3. Prejudices—
  Fiction 4. School stories
  ISBN 978-1-4231-0921-1; 1-4231-0921-X
                                      LC 2007-36361
  When dead teenagers who have come back to life start
showing up at her high school, Phoebe, a goth girl, becomes interested in the phenomenon, and when she starts
dating a "living impaired" boy, they encounter prejudice,
fear, and hatred.
  This "is a classic desegregation story that also skewers
adult attempts to make teenagers play nice. . . . Motivational speakers, politically correct speech and encounter
groups come in for special ridicule." N Y Times Book
Rev

Waters, Zack C., 1946-
Blood moon rider; [by] Zack C. Waters. 1st ed.
Pineapple Press 2006 126p $13.95
Grades: 5 6 7 8   **Fic**
  1. Grandfathers—Fiction 2. World War, 1939-1945—
  Fiction 3. Ranch life—Fiction 4. Florida—Fiction
  ISBN 978-1-56164-350-9; 1-56164-350-5
                                      LC 2005030749
  After his father's death in World War II, fourteen-
year-old Harley Wallace tries to join the Marines but is,
instead, sent to live with his grandfather in Peru Landing,
Florida, where he soon joins a covert effort to stop Nazis
from destroying a secret airbase on Tampa Bay.
  This is "an adventure filled with unexpected kind-
nesses and the irrepressibility of family ties, as well as
a brush with espionage and a couple of suspenseful
shoot'em-up scenes. A colorful cast of characters and a
nod to teenage romance help make this a good choice for
middle school boys." SLJ

Watkins, Steve, 1954-
Down Sand Mountain. Candlewick Press 2008
327p $16.99 *
Grades: 7 8 9 10   **Fic**
  1. Family life—Fiction 2. School stories 3. Race relations—Fiction 4. Bullies—Fiction 5. Florida—Fiction
  ISBN 978-0-7636-3839-9; 0-7636-3839-0
                                      LC 2007-52159
  In a small Florida mining town in 1966, twelve-year-
old Dewey faces one worst-day-ever after another, but
comes to know that the issues he faces about bullies,
girls, race, and identity are part of the adult world, as
well.
  "The simple, beautiful prose remains totally true to the
child's bewildered viewpoint. . . . Readers will be
haunted by the disturbing drama of harsh secrets close to
home." Booklist

Watkins, Yoko Kawashima
My brother, my sister, and I. Bradbury Press
1994 275p hardcover o.p. pa $5.99 *
Grades: 6 7 8 9   **Fic**
  1. World War, 1939-1945—Fiction 2. Japan—Fiction
  3. Korea—Fiction
  ISBN 0-689-80656-6; 0-02-792526-9 (pa)
                                      LC 93-23535

"The author continues her autobiographical account
begun in *So Far from the Bamboo Grove* with the story
of how the two sisters, Ko and Yoko, now reunited with
their brother Hideyo, try to survive in postwar Japan."
Horn Book
  "Watkins's first-person narrative is beautifully direct
and emotionally honest." Publ Wkly

So far from the bamboo grove. Lothrop, Lee &
Shepard Bks. 1986 183p map pa $5.99 hardcover
o.p. *
Grades: 6 7 8 9   **Fic**
  1. World War, 1939-1945—Fiction 2. Korea—Fiction
  3. Japan—Fiction
  ISBN 0-688-13115-8 (pa)   LC 85-15939
  A fictionalized autobiography in which eight-year-old
Yoko escapes from Korea to Japan with her mother and
sister at the end of World War II
  "An admirably told and absorbing novel." Horn Book
  Followed by My brother, my sister and I

Wayland, April Halprin, 1954-
Girl coming in for a landing; a novel in poems;
illustrations by Elaine Clayton. Knopf 2002 134p
il $14.95; lib bdg $16.99; pa $5.50
Grades: 7 8 9 10   **Fic**
  1. School stories 2. Novels in verse
  ISBN 0-375-80158-8; 0-375-90158-2 (lib bdg);
  0-440-41903-4 (pa)   LC 2001-38107
  A collection of over 100 poems recounting the ups
and downs of one adolescent girl's school year
  "Wayland's spare lines and unpretentious words get
right to the heart of situations and emotions, and the familiarity and candor in the speaker's voice—warm and
authentic—will invite teens to value the small moments
in their own experiences and put them into verse."
Booklist

Weatherford, Carole Boston, 1956-
Becoming Billie Holiday; art by Floyd Cooper.
Wordsong 2008 116p il $19.95 *
Grades: 7 8 9 10   **Fic**
  1. Holiday, Billie, 1915-1959—Fiction 2. Novels in
  verse 3. African Americans—Fiction 4. Singers—Fic-
  tion 5. Jazz music—Fiction
  ISBN 978-1-59078-507-2; 1-59078-507-X
                                      LC 2007-51214
  Coretta Scott King honor book for text, 2009
  Jazz vocalist Billie Holiday looks back on her early
years in this fictional memoir written in verse.
  "This captivating title places readers solidly into Holiday's world, and is suitable for independent reading as
well as a variety of classroom uses." SLJ
  Includes bibliographical references

Weatherly, Lee
Breakfast at Sadie's. 1st American ed. David
Fickling Books 2006 199p $15.95; lib bdg $21.59
Grades: 6 7 8 9   **Fic**
  1. Hotels and motels—Fiction 2. Wales—Fiction
  ISBN 0-385-75094-3; 0-385-75095-1 (lib bdg)
                                      LC 2004-25448

Weatherly, Lee—*Continued*
"Sadie, 13, has the weight of the world on her shoulders. Bad grades and her friends accusations of cheating arent enough; now her mother, who has Guillain-Barre Syndrome, is really ill and is leaving Sadies aunt in charge of their bed-and-breakfast. . . . Despite the seriousness of her situation, the book is a fast, light read." SLJ

Kat got your tongue. David Fickling Books 2007 195p $15.99; lib bdg $18.99
Grades: 7 8 9 10   **Fic**
1. Amnesia—Fiction 2. Great Britain—Fiction
ISBN   978-0-385-75117-9;   0-385-75117-6;
978-0-385-75122-3 (lib bdg); 0-385-75122-2 (lib bdg)
LC 2006-24408
After being hit by a car, thirteen-year-old Kat wakes up in the hospital with no memory of her previous life.
"Weatherby writes with fluid grace and makes this story line compelling, sprinkling bits of humor into Kat's journey toward recovery." Booklist

Weaver, Will
Defect. Farrar, Straus and Giroux 2007 199p $16
Grades: 7 8 9 10 11 12   **Fic**
1. Birth defects—Fiction 2. Foster home care—Fiction 3. School stories 4. Minnesota—Fiction
ISBN 0-374-31725-9; 978-0-374-31725-6
LC 2006-49152
After spending most of his life in Minnesota foster homes hiding a bizarre physical abnormality, fifteen-year-old David is offered a chance at normalcy, but must decide if giving up what makes him special is the right thing to do.
The author "skillfully interweaves the improbable with twenty-first-century realities in this provocative novel of the ultimate cost of being so, so different." Voice Youth Advocates

Full service. Farrar, Straus & Giroux 2005 231p $17
Grades: 7 8 9 10   **Fic**
1. Service stations—Fiction 2. Farm life—Fiction 3. Minnesota—Fiction
ISBN 0-374-32485-9   LC 2004-57671
In the summer of 1965, teenager Paul Sutton, a northern Minnesota farm boy, takes a job at a gas station in town, where his strict religious upbringing is challenged by new people and experiences.
"Weaver is a wonderful stylist and his beautifully chosen words put such a shine on his deeply felt story that most teens will be able to find their own faces reflected in its pages." Booklist

Saturday night dirt. Farrar, Straus and Giroux 2008 163p $14.95
Grades: 8 9 10 11   **Fic**
1. Automobile racing—Fiction 2. Minnesota—Fiction
ISBN 978-0-374-35060-4; 0-374-35060-4
LC 2007-6988
In a small town in northern Minnesota, the much-anticipated Saturday night dirt-track race at the old-fashioned, barely viable, Headwaters Speedway becomes,

in many ways, an important life-changing event for all the participants on and off the track.
"Weaver presents compelling character studies. . . . Young racing fans . . . will find much that rings true here." Booklist
Another title in this series is:
Super stock rookie (2009)

Wedekind, Annie
A horse of her own; by Annie Wedekind. Feiwel and Friends 2008 275p $16.95
Grades: 5 6 7 8   **Fic**
1. Horses—Fiction 2. Horsemanship—Fiction 3. Camps—Fiction 4. Kentucky—Fiction
ISBN 978-0-312-36927-9; 0-312-36927-1
LC 2007032769
At summer camp Jane feels like an outsider among the cliquish rich girls who board their horses at Sunny Acres farm, and when the horse she has been riding is sold to another camper, she feels even worse until her teacher asks her to help train a beautiful but skittish new horse, and the experience brings out the best in her.
"Tenacious and thoughtful, Jane is an appealing protagonist who gradually recognizes that being accepted no longer matters to her. The plot . . . has enough twists, including a hint of romance, to sustain readers' interest." SLJ

Weeks, Sarah
Jumping the scratch; a novel. 1st ed. Laura Geringer Books 2006 167p il $15.99; lib bdg $16.89 *
Grades: 5 6 7 8   **Fic**
1. Child sexual abuse—Fiction 2. Memory—Fiction 3. Aunts—Fiction
ISBN   978-0-06-054109-5;   0-06-054109-1;
978-0-06-054110-1 (lib bdg); 0-06-054110-5 (lib bdg)
LC 2005-17776
After moving with his mother to a trailer park to care for an injured aunt, eleven-year-old Jamie Reardon struggles to cope with a deeply buried secret.
"Weeks alludes to sexual abuse, but with a broad brush and no graphic details. . . . Weeks perfectly captures not only the guilt, shame, and pain of the abused boy but also the tenor of a fifth-grade classroom from the point of view of a new student who is friendless, targeted, and belittled by an insensitive teacher. Touches of humor ameliorate the pain and poignancy." SLJ

Wein, Elizabeth E., 1964-
The lion hunter. Viking 2007 223p (Mark of Solomon) $16.99 *
Grades: 7 8 9 10   **Fic**
1. Arthur, King—Fiction 2. Princes—Fiction 3. Africa—Fiction
ISBN 978-0-670-06163-1; 0-670-03638-2
Still recovering from his ordeal as a government spy, twelve-year-old Telemakos, the half-Ethiopian grandson of King Artos of Britain, is sent with his sister to live with Abreha, the ruler of Himyar. His Aunt Goewin warns him that Abreha is a dangerous man, but just how dangerous remains to be seen.

Wein, Elizabeth E., 1964-—*Continued*

"The vividly evoked setting provides a lush backdrop for the story's seemingly casual permutations, and readers' sympathies toward the embattled, wounded hero will draw them on willingly while Wein weaves her web of loyalty and intrigue." Horn Book

Followed by: The empty kingdom (2008)

Weingarten, Lynn

Wherever Nina lies. Point 2009 316p $16.99

Grades: 8 9 10 11 12   Fic

1. Sisters—Fiction 2. Missing persons—Fiction

ISBN 978-0-545-06631-0; 0-545-06631-X

LC 2008-21527

"Sixteen-year-old Ellie Wrigley is desperate to find her unconventional, beloved older sister, Nina, who disappeared two years ago, seemingly without a trace. When Ellie uncovers a clue in a local secondhand shop . . . she is determined to investigate. . . . Ellie sets off on a cross-country chase with her new crush, Sean, who has also lost a sibling. . . . Weingarten's fast-paced, chatty style will keep readers tuned in." Publ Wkly

Weinheimer, Beckie

Converting Kate. Viking Children's Books 2007 312p $16.99

Grades: 7 8 9 10   Fic

1. Religion—Fiction 2. Family life—Fiction 3. Maine—Fiction

ISBN 0-670-06152-2; 978-0-670-06152-5

LC 2006-10200

After moving from Arizona to Maine, sixteen-year-old Kate tries to recover from her father's death as she resists her mother's dogmatic religious beliefs and attempts to find a new direction to her life.

"Religion and religious differences are serious issues to many young adults, and even those breaking from their parents on more secular fronts will sympathize with Kate's struggle." Bull Cent Child Books

Wells, H. G. (Herbert George), 1866-1946

The war of the worlds; illustrated by Edward Gorey. New York Review Books [2005] c1960 251p il $16.95

Grades: 7 8 9 10 11 12 Adult   Fic

1. Science fiction 2. Extraterrestrial beings—Fiction

ISBN 1-59017-158-6   LC 2005-3693

Also available from other publishers

First published 1898

"The inhabitants of Mars, a loathsome though highly organized race, invade England, and by their command of superior weapons subdue and prey on the people." Baker. Guide to the Best Fic

In this novel the author "introduced the 'Alien' being into the role which became a cliché—a monstrous invader of Earth, a competitor in a cosmic struggle for existence. Though the Martians were a ruthless and terrible enemy, HGW was careful to point out that Man had driven many animal species to extinction, and that human invaders of Tasmania had behaved no less callously in exterminating their cousins." Sci Fic Ency

Wells, Rosemary, 1943-

Red moon at Sharpsburg. Viking 2007 236p $16.99 *

Grades: 6 7 8 9 10   Fic

1. United States—History—1861-1865, Civil War—Fiction

ISBN 0-670-03638-2; 978-0-670-03638-7

As the Civil War breaks out, India, a young Southern girl, summons her sharp intelligence and the courage she didn't know she had to survive the war that threatens to destroy her family, her Virginia home and the only life she has ever known.

"This powerful novel is unflinching in its depiction of war and the devastation it causes, yet shows the resilience and hope that can follow such a tragedy. India is a memorable, thoroughly believable character." SLJ

Werlin, Nancy, 1961-

Double helix. Dial Books 2004 252p $16.99; pa $6.99

Grades: 7 8 9 10   Fic

1. Genetic engineering—Fiction 2. Bioethics—Fiction 3. Science fiction

ISBN 0-8037-2606-6; 0-14-240327-X (pa)

LC 2003-12269

Eighteen-year-old Eli discovers a shocking secret about his life and his family while working for a Nobel Prizewinning scientist whose specialty is genetic engineering.

"Werlin clearly and dramatically raises fundamental bioethical issues for teens to ponder. She also creates a riveting story with sharply etched characters and complex relationships that will stick with readers long after the book is closed." SLJ

Impossible; a novel. Dial Books 2008 376p $17.99 *

Grades: 7 8 9 10   Fic

1. Magic—Fiction 2. Pregnancy—Fiction 3. Teenage mothers—Fiction

ISBN 978-0-8037-3002-1; 0-8037-3002-0

LC 2008-06633

When seventeen-year-old Lucy discovers her family is under an ancient curse by an evil Elfin Knight, she realizes to break the curse she must perform three impossible tasks before her daughter is born in order to save them both.

"Werlin earns high marks for the tale's graceful interplay between wild magic and contemporary reality." Booklist

The killer's cousin; [by] Nancy Werlin. Dial Books 2009 c1998 227p $16.99; pa $7.99 *

Grades: 7 8 9 10   Fic

1. Cousins—Fiction 2. Homicide—Fiction

ISBN   978-0-8037-3370-1;   0-8037-3370-4; 978-0-14-241373-9 (pa); 0-14-241373-9 (pa)

LC 2008024294

A reissue of the title first published 1998 by Delacorte

After being acquitted of murder, seventeen-year-old David goes to stay with relatives in Cambridge, Massachusetts, where he finds himself forced to face his past as he learns more about his strange young cousin Lily.

"Teens will find this tautly plotted thriller, rich in complex, finely drawn characters, an absolute page-turner." Booklist

Werlin, Nancy, 1961-—_Continued_

The rules of survival. Dial Books 2006 259p
$16.99

Grades: 8 9 10 11 12   **Fic**
1. Child abuse—Fiction 2. Siblings—Fiction
ISBN 0-8037-3001-2   LC 2006-1675

Seventeen-year-old Matthew recounts his attempts,
starting at a young age, to free himself and his sisters
from the grip of their emotionally and physically abusive
mother.

The author "tackles the topic of child abuse with
grace and insight. . . . Teens will empathize with these
siblings and the secrets they keep in this psychological
horror story." SLJ

Westerfeld, Scott
So yesterday; a novel. Razorbill 2004 225p
$16.99; pa $7.99 *

Grades: 7 8 9 10   **Fic**
1. Missing persons—Fiction 2. Mystery fiction
3. New York (N.Y.)—Fiction
ISBN 1-59514-000-X; 1-59514-032-8 (pa)
     LC 2004-2302

Hunter Braque, a New York City teenager who is paid
by corporations to spot what is "cool," combines his analytical skills with girlfriend Jen's creative talents to find
a missing person and thwart a conspiracy directed at the
heart of consumer culture

"This hip, fascinating thriller aggressively questions
consumer culture. . . . Teens will inhale this wholly entertaining, thought-provoking look at a system fueled by
their purchasing power. " Booklist

Uglies. Simon Pulse 2005 425p pa $6.99 *
Grades: 7 8 9 10   **Fic**
1. Science fiction
ISBN 0-689-86538-4

"Fifteen-year-old Tally's eerily harmonious,
postapocalyptic society gives extreme makeovers to teens
on their sixteenth birthdays. . . . When a top-secret
agency threatens to leave Tally ugly forever unless she
spies on runaway teens, she agrees to infiltrate the
Smoke, a shadowy colony of refugees from the 'tyranny
of physical perfection.'" Booklist

"Ethical concerns will provide a good source of discussion. . . . Characterization . . . is strong, and . . .
the novel is highly readable with a convincing plot." SLJ

Other titles in this series are:

Pretties (2005)
Specials (2006)
Extras (2007)

Weston, Robert Paul
Zorgamazoo. Razorbill 2008 281p il $15.99 *
Grades: 4 5 6 7   **Fic**
1. Novels in verse 2. Imagination—Fiction
3. Adventure fiction
ISBN 978-1-59514-199-6; 1-59514-199-5
     LC 2007-51682

Imaginative and adventurous Katrina eludes her mani-
acal guardian to help Morty, a member of a vanishing
breed of zorgles, with his quest to uncover the fate of the
fabled zorgles of Zorgmazoo as well as of other creatures
that seem to have disappeared from the earth.

"This book is a natural descendant to the works of Dr.
Seuss and Roald Dahl." Booklist

Weyn, Suzanne
Distant waves; a novel of the Titanic. Scholastic
Press 2009 330p $17.99

Grades: 8 9 10 11   **Fic**
1. Tesla, Nikola, 1856-1943—Fiction 2. Astor, John
Jacob, 1763-1848—Fiction 3. Stead, William Thomas,
1849-1912—Fiction 4. Titanic (Steamship)—Fiction
5. Spiritualism—Fiction 6. Sisters—Fiction
7. Mother-daughter relationship—Fiction
8. Inventors—Fiction
ISBN 978-0-545-08572-4; 0-545-08572-1
     LC 2008-40708

In the early twentieth century, four sisters and their
widowed mother, a famed spiritualist, travel from New
York to London, and as the Titanic conveys them and
their acquaintances, journalist W.T. Stead, scientist
Nikola Tesla, and industrialist John Jacob Astor, home,
Tesla's inventions will either doom or save them all.

"The interplay of science, spirituality, history and romance will satisfy." Publ Wkly

Reincarnation; [by] Suzanne Weyn. Scholastic
Press 2008 293p $17.99

Grades: 7 8 9 10   **Fic**
1. Reincarnation—Fiction 2. Space and time—Fiction
3. Love stories
ISBN 978-0-545-01323-9; 0-545-01323-2
     LC 2007-08743

When a young couple dies in prehistoric times, their
love—and link to various green stones—endures through
the ages as they are reborn into new bodies and somehow find a way to connect.

"Readers with a romantic bent will be drawn to this
story, which pushes the notion of eternal love to its limits: two spirits find each other again and again, at different moments in history." Publ Wkly

Whelan, Gloria
After the train. HarperCollins 2009 152p $15.99;
lib bdg $16.89

Grades: 6 7 8 9   **Fic**
1. Antisemitism—Fiction 2. Jews—Germany—Fiction
3. Germany—History—1945-1990—Fiction
ISBN 978-0-06-029596-7; 0-06-029596-1;
978-0-06-029597-4 (lib bdg); 0-06-029597-X (lib bdg)
     LC 2008-10185

Ten years after the end of the Second World War, the
town of Rolfen, West Germany, looks just as peaceful
and beautiful as ever, until young Peter Liebig discovers
a secret about his past that leads him to question everything, including the town's calm facade and his own
sense of comfort and belonging.

"The story offers effective suspense in the mystery of
Peter's situation and a dramatic climax. . . . Fans of
Whelan's middle-school-aimed historical fiction . . . will
definitely want to get their hands on this title." Bull Cent
Child Books

Whelan, Gloria—*Continued*

Burying the sun. HarperCollins Publishers 2004
205p $15.99; lib bdg $16.89   **Fic**
   1. Saint Petersburg (Russia)—Siege, 1941-1944—Fiction 2. World War, 1939-1945—Fiction
   ISBN 0-06-054112-1; 0-06-054113-X (lib bdg)
                    LC 2003-12487
   In Leningrad in 1941, when Russia and Germany are at war, fourteen-year-old Georgi vows to help his family and his city during the terrible siege.
   "Haunting images and elegant prose make this companion to The Impossible Journey . . . and Angel on the Square . . . memorable. . . .The lilting writing style and simple dignity of the characters help construct an honest portrait of everyday life in extraordinary circumstances." SLJ
   Includes bibliographical references

Chu Ju's house. HarperCollins 2004 227p
$15.99; lib bdg $16.89   **Fic**
   1. China—Fiction 2. Sex role—Fiction 3. Runaway teenagers—Fiction
   ISBN 0-06-050724-1; 0-06-050725-X (lib bdg)
                    LC 2003-6979
   In order to save her baby sister, fourteen-year-old Chu Ju leaves her rural home in modern China and earns food and shelter by working on a sampan, tending silk worms, and planting rice seedlings, while wondering if she will ever see her family again.
   "Whelan tells a compelling adventure story, filled with rich cultural detail, about a smart, likable teenage girl who overcomes society's gender restrictions." Booklist

The Disappeared. Dial Books 2008 136p $16.99
*
Grades: 8 9 10 11 12   **Fic**
   1. Argentina—Fiction 2. Siblings—Fiction
   ISBN 978-0-8037-3275-9; 0-8037-3275-9
                    LC 2007-43750
   Teenaged Silvia tries to save her brother, Eduardo, after he is captured by the military government in 1970s Argentina.
   "The deftly handled voices of Silvia and Eduardo follow the well-intentioned, but often grievous, mistakes of youth. Their compelling tale is a chilling account of the manipulative power of corruption." SLJ
   Includes bibliographical references

Goodbye, Vietnam. Knopf 1992 135p hardcover
o.p. pa $5.50
Grades: 4 5 6 7   **Fic**
   1. Refugees—Fiction 2. Vietnamese—Fiction
   ISBN 0-679-82376-X; 0-679-92263-6 (pa)
                    LC 91-3660
   Thirteen-year-old Mai and her family embark on a dangerous sea voyage from Vietnam to Hong Kong to escape the unpredictable and often brutal Vietnamese government
   "While the book has the suspense and appeal of any good escape story, Whelan is neither melodramatic nor sentimental, and the sometimes horrific details of the scary voyage are plain but understated." Bull Cent Child Books

Homeless bird. HarperCollins Pubs. 2000 216p
$15.95; lib bdg $16.89; pa $5.99 *
Grades: 6 7 8 9   **Fic**
   1. Women—India—Fiction 2. India—Fiction
   ISBN 0-06-028454-4; 0-06-028452-8 (lib bdg); 0-06-440819-1 (pa)   LC 99-33241
   When thirteen-year-old Koly enters into an ill-fated arranged marriage, she must either suffer a destiny dictated by India's tradition or find the courage to oppose it
   "This beautifully told, inspiring story takes readers on a fascinating journey through modern India and the universal intricacies of a young woman's heart." Booklist

Listening for lions. HarperCollins 2005 194p
$15.99; lib bdg $16.89 *
Grades: 5 6 7 8   **Fic**
   1. Orphans—Fiction 2. East Africa—Fiction 3. Physicians—Fiction 4. Great Britain—Fiction
   ISBN 0-06-058174-3; 0-06-058175-1 (lib bdg)
   Left an orphan after the influenza epidemic in British East Africa in 1918, thirteen-year-old Rachel is tricked into assuming a deceased neighbor's identity to travel to England, where her only dream is to return to Africa and rebuild her parents' mission hospital.
   "In a straightforward, sympathetic voice, Rachel tells an involving, episodic story." Booklist

The locked garden. HarperCollinsPublishers
2009 168p $15.99 *
Grades: 4 5 6 7   **Fic**
   1. Psychiatric hospitals—Fiction 2. Mental illness—Fiction 3. Family life—Fiction 4. Michigan—Fiction
   ISBN 978-0-06-079094-3; 0-06-079094-6
                    LC 2008024637
   After their mother dies of typhoid, Verna and younger sister Carlie move with their father, a psychiatrist, and stern Aunt Maude to an asylum for the mentally ill in early-twentieth-century Michigan, where new ideas in the treatment of mental illness are being proposed, but old prejudices still hold sway.
   "Whelan establishes a strong sense of time, unusual setting and characters. . . . This convincing melodrama portrays an atypical attitude toward treating mental illness." Kirkus

Parade of shadows. HarperCollins 2007 295p
$15.99; lib bdg $16.89
Grades: 7 8 9 10 11 12   **Fic**
   1. Voyages and travels—Fiction 2. Father-daughter relationship—Fiction 3. Spies—Fiction 4. Turkey—Fiction 5. Middle East—Fiction
   ISBN 978-0-06-089028-5; 978-0-06-089029-2 (lib bdg)   LC 2006-103477
   In 1907, sixteen-year-old Julia Hamilton, happy to accompany her diplomat father on a tour of the Ottoman-controlled cities of Istanbul, Damascus, Palmyra, and Aleppo, soon finds the journey increasingly hazardous as she begins to uncover her father's true mission and the secret motivations of the other travelers in their group.
   "This satisfying read is a romantic adventure in the best tradition by a master of such stories." SLJ

White, Andrea

Surviving Antarctica; reality TV 2083. HarperCollins Publishers 2005 327p $15.99; lib bdg $16.89; pa $6.99

Grades: 7 8 9 10   Fic

1. Antarctica—Fiction 2. Science fiction

ISBN 0-06-055454-1; 0-06-055455-X (lib bdg); 0-06-055456-8 (pa)   LC 2004-6249

In the year 2083, five fourteen-year-olds who were deprived by chance of the opportunity to continue their educations reenact Scott's 1910-1913 expedition to the South Pole as contestants on a reality television show, secretly aided by a Department of Entertainment employee

"A real page-turner, this novel will give readers pause as they ponder the ethics of teens risking their lives in adult-contrived situations for the entertainment of the masses." Booklist

Window boy. Bright Sky Press 2008 255p $17.95

Grades: 6 7 8 9   Fic

1. Churchill, Sir Winston, 1874-1965—Fiction 2. Cerebral palsy—Fiction 3. Imaginary playmates—Fiction 4. School stories

ISBN 978-1-933979-14-4; 1-933979-14-3
             LC 2008-492

After his mother finally convinces the principal of Greenfield Junior High to admit him, twelve-year-old Sam arrives for his first day of school, along with his imaginary friend Winston Churchill, who encourages him to persevere with his cerebral palsy.

"Strong character development is combined with an accurate representation of the lack of educational opportunities for those who were physically and mentally disabled pre-IDEA." SLJ

White, Ellen Emerson

The President's daughter. Feiwel and Friends 2008 304p pa $9.99

Grades: 7 8 9 10   Fic

1. Politics—Fiction 2. Mother-daughter relationship—Fiction 3. Moving—Fiction 4. Washington (D.C.)—Fiction

ISBN 0-312-37488-7; 978-0-312-37488-4
             LC 2008-6888

First published 1984

Sixteen-year-old Meghan Powers' happy life in Massachusetts changes drastically when her mother, one of the most prestigious senators in the country, becomes the front-runner in the race for United States President.

"Besides offering a solid look at the political system, this [book] has very strong characterizations." Booklist

Other titles about Meg are:

White House autumn (2008)

Long live the queen (2008)

Long may she reign (2007)

White, Ruth

Belle Prater's boy. Farrar, Straus & Giroux 1996 196p $17 *

Grades: 5 6 7 8   Fic

1. Cousins—Fiction 2. Virginia—Fiction 3. Appalachian region—Fiction

ISBN 0-374-30668-0   LC 94-43625

Also available in paperback from Random House

A Newbery Medal honor book, 1997

"Gypsy and her cousin Woodrow become close friends after Woodrow's mother disappears. Both sixth-graders feel deserted by their parents—Gypsy discovers that her father committed suicide—and need to define themselves apart from these tragedies. White's prose evokes the coal mining region of Virginia and the emotional quality of her characters' transformations." Horn Book Guide

Another title about Belle Prater is:

The search for Belle Prater (2005)

Little Audrey. Farrar, Straus & Giroux 2008 145p $16 *

Grades: 5 6 7 8   Fic

1. Country life—Fiction 2. Virginia—Fiction 3. Coal miners—Fiction 4. Death—Fiction

ISBN 978-0-374-34580-8; 0-374-34580-5
             LC 2007-29310

In 1948, eleven-year-old Audrey lives with her father, mother, and three younger sisters in Jewell Valley, a coal mining camp in Southwest Virginia, where her mother still mourns the death of a baby, her father goes on drinking binges on paydays, and Audrey tries to recover from the scarlet fever that has left her skinny and needing to wear glasses.

"The setting is perfectly portrayed and the characterizations ring true." Voice Youth Advocates

Memories of Summer. Farrar, Straus & Giroux 2000 135p $16

Grades: 7 8 9 10   Fic

1. Mentally ill—Fiction 2. Sisters—Fiction 3. Michigan—Fiction

ISBN 0-374-34945-2   LC 99-54793

In 1955, thirteen-year-old Lyric finds her whole life changing when her family moves from the hills of Virginia to a town in Michigan and her older sister Summer begins descending into mental illness

"A marvelous recreation of time and place and a poignant story that has much to say about compassion." SLJ

Way Down Deep. Farrar, Straus and Giroux 2007 197p $16 *

Grades: 5 6 7 8   Fic

1. Orphans—Fiction 2. West Virginia—Fiction

ISBN 0-374-38251-4; 978-0-374-38251-3
             LC 2006-46324

In the West Virginia town of Way Down Deep in the 1950s, a foundling called Ruby June is happily living with Miss Arbutus at the local boarding house when suddenly, after the arrival of a family of outsiders, the mystery of Ruby's past begins to unravel.

This is "a story as tender as a breeze and as sharp as a tack. . . . At the heart of the story are profound questions that readers will enjoy puzzling out." Booklist

White, T. H. (Terence Hanbury), 1906-1964

The once and future king. Putnam 1958 677p
$25.95 *

Grades: 8 9 10 11 12 Adult   **Fic**
1. Arthur, King—Fiction 2. Arthur, King 3. Great
Britain—History—0-1066—Fiction 4. Knights and
knighthood—Fiction 5. Fantasy fiction 6. Knights and
knighthood 7. Middle Ages 8. Chivalry
ISBN 0-399-10597-2   LC 58-10760
Also available in paperback from Ace Bks.

An omnibus edition of four novels; The sword in the
stone (1939), The witch in the wood (1939, now called
The Queen of Air and Darkness) and The ill-made knight
(1940). A number of alterations have been made in the
earlier books. Previously unpublished, The candle in the
wind "deals with the plotting of Mordred and his kinsmen of the house of Orkney, and their undying enmity
to King Arthur." Times Lit Suppl

"White's contemporary retelling of Malory's Le Morte
d'Arthur is both romantic and exciting." Shapiro. Fic for
Youth. 3d edition

Whitlock, Dean

Raven; by Dean Whitlock. Clarion Books 2007
234p $16

Grades: 6 7 8 9   **Fic**
1. Birds—Fiction 2. Magic—Fiction 3. Fantasy fiction
ISBN 978-0-618-70224-4; 0-618-70224-5
                                   LC 2006027348
Sequel to: Sky carver
Raven, a shape-shifting mage, is determined to save
her baby half-sister Sarita from the evil Steward and his
son who are equally determined to get rid of the baby
and take her inheritance for themselves.

This "is a solid tale with magic and adventure. The
protagonist is well developed and her struggles are realistic and engaging." SLJ

Sky carver; by Dean Whitlock. Clarion Books
2005 248p $16

Grades: 6 7 8 9   **Fic**
1. Fantasy fiction 2. Magic—Fiction
ISBN 0-618-44393-2   LC 2004-17819
Thomas, a talented wood carver, discovers that he can
also do weather magic and undertakes a journey that
could lead him to hone that skill and save his village
from drought, or perhaps to a completely different destiny.

"Whitlock's world combines magic and familiar inventions like bicycles and engines in believable ways.
Carver's struggle to find his identity will ring true with
adolescent readers." SLJ

Followed by: Raven

Whittenberg, Allison

Life is fine. Delacorte Press 2008 181p $15.99;
lib bdg $18.99

Grades: 8 9 10 11 12   **Fic**
1. African Americans—Fiction 2. Child abuse—Fiction 3. Mother-daughter relationship—Fiction
ISBN 978-0-385-73480-6; 978-0-385-90478-0 (lib
bdg)   LC 2007-27604

With a neglectful mother who has an abusive, live-in
boyfriend, life for fifteen-year-old Samara is not fine, but
when a substitute teacher walks into class one day and
introduces her to poetry, she starts to view life from a
different perspective.

"Samara's voice is sharp and convincing." Publ Wkly

Sweet Thang. Delacorte Press 2006 149p
$15.95; lib bdg $17.99

Grades: 5 6 7 8   **Fic**
1. African Americans—Fiction 2. Family life—Fiction
3. School stories
ISBN 0-385-73292-9; 0-385-90313-8 (lib bdg)
                                   LC 2005-03809
In 1975, life is not fair for fourteen-year-old
Charmaine Upshaw, who shares a room with her brother,
tries to impress a handsome classmate, and acts as caretaker for a rambunctious six-year-old cousin who has
taken over the family.

"Whittenberg has created a refreshing cast and a good
read." SLJ

Another title about the Upshaw family is:
Hollywood & Maine (2009)

Whyman, Matt

Icecore; a Carl Hobbes thriller. Atheneum
Books for Young Readers 2007 307p $16.99

Grades: 7 8 9 10   **Fic**
1. Prisoners—Fiction 2. Computer crimes—Fiction
3. Torture—Fiction 4. Military bases—Fiction
5. Arctic regions—Fiction
ISBN 978-1-4169-4907-7; 1-4169-4907-0
                                   LC 2007-02674
Seventeen-year-old Englishman Carl Hobbes meant no
harm when he hacked into Fort Knox's security system,
but at Camp Twilight in the Arctic Circle, known as the
Guantanamo Bay of the north, he is tortured to reveal information about a conspiracy of which he was never a
part.

"Powered by a fast-paced narrative, this exploration of
numerous timely themes . . . gives the eminently readable adventure a degree of depth." Publ Wkly

Whytock, Cherry

My cup runneth over; the life of Angelica
Cookson Potts. Simon & Schuster Bks. for Young
Readers 2003 163p il $14.95

Grades: 7 8 9 10   **Fic**
1. Weight loss—Fiction 2. School stories
ISBN 0-689-86546-5   LC 2003-45769
First published 2003 in the United Kingdom with the
title: Angel: disasters, diets, and D-cups

Believing she is too big, fourteen-year-old Angel tries
dieting and kick-boxing to lose weight, but thanks to her
friends and the school fashion show, she discovers that
her size is just right

"This is very funny stuff, and Whytock freshens up a
potentially trite template with peculiarly British recipes
. . . plus amusingly annotated doodles." Booklist

Another available title about Angelica Cookson Potts is:
My scrumpious Scottish dumplings (2005)
My saucy stuffed ravioli (2006)

Wilce, Ysabeau S.

Flora Segunda; being the magickal mishaps of a girl of spirit, her glass-gazing sidekick, two ominous butlers (one blue), a house with eleven thousand rooms, and a red dog. Harcourt 2007 431p $17

Grades: 7 8 9 10 **Fic**

1. Magic—Fiction 2. Fantasy fiction

ISBN 978-0-15-205433-5; 0-15-205433-2

Fourteen-year-old Flora Fyrdraaca, whose mother is the Warlord's Commanding General and whose father is mad, kindly helps her house's magical—and long-banished—butler, unaware that he draws strength from the Fyrdraaca will.

"Wilce creates a world so complex and delightful and a character so appealing that readers are bound to be clamoring for this heroine's further adventures." Voice Youth Advocates

Another title about Flora is:

Flora's dare (2008)

Wild, K., 1954-

Fight game; [by] Kate Wild. Chicken House/Scholastic 2007 279p $16.99

Grades: 7 8 9 10 **Fic**

1. Martial arts—Fiction 2. Genetic engineering—Fiction 3. Spies—Fiction 4. Science fiction

ISBN 978-0-439-87175-4; 0-439-87175-1

LC 2006-32889

Fifteen-year-old Freedom Smith is a fighter, just like all of his relatives who have the "Hercules gene," which leads him to a choice between being jailed for attempted murder or working with a covert law enforcement agency to break up a mysterious, illegal fight ring.

"Intriguing supporting characters pepper Wild's debut novel and bolster an already strong protagonist. . . . Wild's story pulsates with raw energy." Voice Youth Advocates

Wiles, Deborah

The Aurora County All-Stars. Harcourt 2007 242p il $16 *

Grades: 4 5 6 **Fic**

1. Baseball—Fiction 2. Death—Fiction 3. Race relations—Fiction 4. Mississippi—Fiction

ISBN 978-0-15-206068-8; 0-15-206068-5

LC 2006-102551

In a small Mississippi town, after the death of the old man to whom twelve-year-old star pitcher House Jackson has been secretly reading for a year, House uncovers secrets about the man and the history of baseball in Aurora County.

"Quotations from Walt Whitman's poetry, baseball players and Aurora County news dispatches pepper the story and add color. . . . A home run for Wiles." Publ Wkly

Wilhelm, Doug

The revealers. Farrar, Straus & Giroux 2003 207p $16 **Fic**

1. School stories 2. Friendship—Fiction

ISBN 0-374-36255-6 LC 2002-35321

Tired of being bullied and picked on, three seventh-grade outcasts join forces and, using scientific methods and the power of the Internet, begin to create a new atmosphere at Parkland Middle School

"Briskly plotted, the novel shows how bringing the stories to light transforms stereotypes into real people and provides a vehicle for others to become involved. . . . The novel is effective and will fascinate even reluctant readers." SLJ

Williams, Alex, 1969-

The deep freeze of Bartholomew Tullock. Philomel Books 2008 298p $16.99

Grades: 6 7 8 9 **Fic**

1. Adventure fiction 2. Weather—Fiction 3. Inventions—Fiction 4. Dogs—Fiction

ISBN 978-0-399-25185-6; 0-399-25185-5

LC 2008-02663

Published in the United Kingdom with title: The storm maker

In a land of never-ending snow, Rufus Breeze and his mother must protect the family home from being seized by tyrant Bartholomew Tullock, while sister Madeline and her father, an inventor of fans that are now useless, join forces with a ne'er-do-well adventurer and his blue-haired terrier, hoping to make some money.

This offers "originality of setting, a full complement of truly heinous villains, insurmountable dangers cleverly surmounted, ingenious contraptions, and plucky, appealing underdogs. . . . William handles his material with fizz and verve." Bull Cent Child Books

Williams, Carol Lynch, 1959-

The chosen one. St. Martin's Griffin 2009 213p $16.95

Grades: 7 8 9 10 **Fic**

1. Family life—Fiction 2. Cults—Fiction 3. Polygamy—Fiction

ISBN 978-0-312-55511-5; 0-312-55511-3

LC 2009-04800

In a polygamous cult in the desert, Kyra, not yet fourteen, sees being chosen to be the seventh wife of her uncle as just punishment for having read books and kissed a boy, in violation of Prophet Childs' teachings, and is torn between facing her fate and running away from all that she knows and loves.

"This book is a highly emotional, terrifying read. It is not measured or objective. Physical abuse, fear, and even murder are constants. It is a girl-in-peril story, and as such, it is impossible to put down and holds tremendous teen appeal." Voice Youth Advocates

Williams, Dar

Amalee; by Dar Williams. Scholastic 2004 180p $16.95; pa $5.99

Grades: 5 6 7 8 **Fic**

1. Single parent family—Fiction 2. Friendship—Fiction 3. Sick—Fiction

ISBN 0-439-39563-1; 0-439-39564-X (pa)

Amalee is being raised by her single father and his group of eccentric friends, and when he becomes seriously ill everyone pitches in to try to cope with the ensuing fear and chaos.

Williams, Dar—*Continued*

"Readers will be charmed by Williams' eccentric, lovable characters and her sharp observations about the world of both middle-schoolers and adults." Booklist

Another title about Amalee is:

Lights, camera, Amalee (2006)

Williams, Laura E.

Slant; [by] Laura E. Williams. 1st ed. Milkweed Editions 2008 149p $16.95; pa $6.95

Grades: 4 5 6 7   **Fic**

1. Prejudices—Fiction 2. Mothers—Fiction 3. Adoption—Fiction 4. Korean Americans—Fiction 5. Friendship—Fiction 6. Plastic surgery—Fiction

ISBN   978-1-57131-681-3;   1-57131-681-7; 978-1-57131-682-0 (pa); 1-57131-682-5 (pa)

LC 2008007093

Thirteen-year-old Lauren, a Korean-American adoptee, is tired of being called "slant" and "gook," and longs to have plastic surgery on her eyes, but when her father finds out about her wish—and a long-kept secret about her mother's death is revealed—Lauren starts to question some of her own assumptions.

"The characters are exceptionally well drawn, and the friendship between Julie and Lauren is not only believable, featuring humor, conflict, and true wit, but also captures both girls' gains in maturity." SLJ

Williams, Maiya

The golden hour. Amulet Books 2004 259p $16.95

Grades: 5 6 7 8   **Fic**

1. Fantasy fiction 2. Siblings—Fiction

ISBN 0-8109-4823-0   LC 2003-16281

Thirteen-year-old Rowan and his eleven-year-old sister Nina, still bereft by the death of their mother the year before, experience an unusual adventure through time when they come to stay with their two eccentric great-aunts in a small town on the Maine coast.

"Part realistic fiction, part fantasy, part historical adventure, this entertaining novel features several well-realized settings and some quirky, original characters. The story is particularly energized by Rowan's intelligent, wry observations." Booklist

Other titles in this series are:

The hour of the cobra (2006)

The hour of the outlaw (2007)

Williams, Susan, 1946-

Wind rider. HarperCollins 2006 309p $16.99

Grades: 7 8 9 10   **Fic**

1. Horses—Fiction 2. Sex role—Fiction 3. Prehistoric peoples—Fiction

ISBN   978-0-06-087236-6;   0-06-087236-5; 978-0-06-087237-3 (lib bdg); 0-06-087237-3 (lib bdg)

LC 2005028595

"Laura Geringer books"

Fern, a teenager living in 4000 B.C., defies the expectations of her people by displaying a unique and new ability to tame horses and by also questioning many of the traditional activities of women.

"Fern aggressively strains against her mother's expectations and her society's traditional gender roles, and it

is these timeless struggles, narrated in Fern's poetic voice, that transform Williams' impressively researched details into a vividly imagined, wholly captivating world." Booklist

Williams, Suzanne, 1949-

Bull rider; [by] Suzanne Morgan Williams. Margaret K. McElderry Books 2009 241p $16.99

Grades: 7 8 9 10   **Fic**

1. Brothers—Fiction 2. Bull riding—Fiction 3. Veterans—Fiction 4. Wounds and injuries—Fiction

ISBN 978-1-4169-6130-7; 1-4169-6130-5

LC 2007-52518

When his older brother, a bull-riding champion, returns from the Iraq War partially paralyzed, fourteen-year-old Cam takes a break from skateboarding to enter a bull-riding contest, in hopes of winning the $15,000 prize and motivating his depressed brother to continue with his rehabilitation.

"The mix of wild macho action with family anguish and tenderness will grab teens. . . . [This is a] powerful contemporary story of family, community, and work." Booklist

Williams-Garcia, Rita

Jumped. HarperTeen 2009 169p $16.99; lib bdg $17.89 *

Grades: 8 9 10 11 12   **Fic**

1. Bullies—Fiction 2. School stories

ISBN   978-0-06-076091-5;   0-06-076091-5; 978-0-06-076092-2 (lib bdg); 0-06-076092-3 (lib bdg)

LC 2008-22381

"Amistad"

The lives of Leticia, Dominique, and Trina are irrevocably intertwined through the course of one day in an urban high school after Leticia overhears Dominique's plans to beat up Trina and must decide whether or not to get involved.

"In alternating chapters narrated by Leticia, Trina, and Dominique, Williams-Garcia has given her characters strong, individual voices that ring true to teenage speech, and she lets them make their choices without judgment or moralizing." SLJ

Like sisters on the homefront. Lodestar Bks. 1995 165p hardcover o.p. pa $5.99 *

Grades: 7 8 9 10   **Fic**

1. African Americans—Fiction 2. Family life—Fiction 3. Teenage mothers—Fiction

ISBN 0-525-67465-9; 0-14-038561-4 (pa)

LC 95-3690

"It's bad enough that 14-year-old Gayle has one baby, but when she becomes pregnant again by another boy, Mama's had enough. She takes Gayle for an abortion and then ships her and her baby south to stay with religious relatives. . . . With the help of her dying great-grandmother, who leaves Gayle the family's African-American oral tradition, she begins to mature and understand her place in the family and her future." Child Book Rev Serv

"Beautifully written, the text captures the cadence and rhythm of New York street talk and the dilemma of being poor, black, and uneducated. This is a gritty, realistic, well-told story." SLJ

Williams-Garcia, Rita—*Continued*

No laughter here. HarperCollins 2004 133p
$15.99; lib bdg $16.89
Grades: 7 8 9 10 **Fic**
1. Female circumcision—Fiction 2. Friendship—Fiction 3. African Americans—Fiction 4. New York
(N.Y.)—Fiction
ISBN 0-688-16247-9; 0-688-16248-7 (lib bdg)
LC 2003-9331
In Queens, New York, ten-year-old Akilah is determined to find out why her closest friend, Victoria, is silent and withdrawn after returning from a trip to her
homeland, Nigeria.
This is a "disturbing and poignant coming-of-age novel. . . . This contemporary tale about the ancient rite of
female circumcision will no doubt leave an indelible
mark on preteens." Publ Wkly

Wilson, Diane L.

Black storm comin'. Margaret K. McElderry
Books 2005 295p $17.99
Grades: 7 8 9 10 **Fic**
1. Pony express—Fiction 2. Racially mixed people—
Fiction 3. Frontier and pioneer life—Fiction
ISBN 0-689-87137-6; 0-689-87138-2
LC 2004-9438
Twelve-year-old Colton, son of a black mother and a
white father, takes a job with the Pony Express in 1860
after his father abandons the family on their California-
bound wagon train, and risks his life to deliver an important letter that may affect the growing conflict between
the North and South.
"Wilson masterfully creates a multidimensional character in Colton. . . . Readers will absorb greater lessons
as they become engrossed in the excitement, beauty, and
terror of Colton's journey to California and manhood."
Booklist

Firehorse. Margaret K. McElderry Books 2006
325p $16.95 *
Grades: 7 8 9 10 **Fic**
1. Veterinary medicine—Fiction 2. Sex role—Fiction
3. Horses—Fiction 4. Arson—Fiction 5. Family life—
Fiction 6. Boston (Mass.)—Fiction
ISBN 1-4169-1551-6; 978-1-4169-1551-5
LC 2005-30785
Spirited fifteen-year-old horse lover Rachel Selby determines to become a veterinarian, despite the opposition
of her rigid father, her proper mother, and the norms of
Boston in 1872, while that city faces a serial arsonist and
an epidemic spreading through its firehorse population.
"Wilson paces the story well, with tension building.
. . . The novel's finest achievement, though, is the convincing depiction of family dynamics in an era when
men ruled the household and and women, who had few
opportunities, folded their dreams and put them away
with the linens they embroidered." Booklist

Wilson, Jacqueline

Best friends. Roaring Brook Press 2008 229p
$15.95
Grades: 4 5 6 7 **Fic**
1. Friendship—Fiction 2. School stories 3. Scotland—
Fiction
ISBN 978-1-59643-278-9; 1-59643-278-0
LC 2006-39716
"A Deborah Brodie book."
Rambunctious and irrepressible Gemma has been best
friends with Alice ever since they were born on the same
day, so when Alice moves miles away to Scotland, Gemma is distraught over the idea that Alice might find a
new best friend.
"Believable, sympathetic characters; recognizable
home and school situations; and plenty of humor . . .
will ensure that this becomes . . . a popular read for
middle-grade girls." Booklist

Wilson, John, 1951-

The alchemist's dream; [by] John Wilson. Key
Porter Books 2007 248p pa $12.95
Grades: 7 8 9 10 **Fic**
1. Hudson, Henry, d. 1611—Fiction 2. Bylot, Robert,
fl. 1610-1616—Fiction 3. Great Britain—History—
1603-1714, Stuarts—Fiction 4. London (England)—
Fiction 5. Navigation—Fiction 6. Explorers—Fiction
ISBN 978-1-55263-934-4 (pa); 1-55263-934-7 (pa)
"In the fall of 1669, the Nonsuch returned to London
with a load of fur from Hudson Bay. It brought something else, too—the lost journal from Henry Hudson's
tragic search for a passage to Cathay in 1611. The journal finds its way to the aged Robert Bylot and triggers
disturbing memories of his life." Publisher's note
"Middle grade readers and high school readers who
like historical fiction and stories of adventure with some
mystery thrown in will be drawn to this book." Voice
Youth Advocates

And in the morning. Kids Can Press 2003 198p
$16.95
Grades: 7 8 9 10 **Fic**
1. World War, 1914-1918—Fiction
ISBN 1-55337-400-2
"Jim Hay, 16, is caught up in the patriotic fervor
sweeping across Scotland as the British troops prepare to
enter World War I. . . . His father is killed in action and
10 days later his mother dies from shock and grief.
Within weeks, Jim has signed up and is soon in the
trenches. . . . A compelling, fascinating, and ultimately
disturbing book that is not to be missed." SLJ

Wilson, Nancy Hope, 1947-

Mountain pose. Farrar, Straus & Giroux 2001
233p $17
Grades: 5 6 7 8 **Fic**
1. Grandmothers—Fiction 2. Diaries—Fiction
3. Vermont—Fiction
ISBN 0-374-35078-7 LC 00-57269
Also available in paperback from Scholastic
When twelve-year-old Ellie inherits an old Vermont
farm from her cruel and heartless grandmother Aurelia,
she reads a set of diaries written by an ancestor and dis-

Wilson, Nancy Hope, 1947-—_Continued_
covers secrets from the past

"Beautifully written and suspenseful, this novel explores the many emotions associated with the tragedy of spousal and child abuse." Voice Youth Advocates

Wilson, Nathan D.
Leepike Ridge; [by] N.D. Wilson. Random House 2007 224p $15.99; lib bdg $18.99; pa $6.99 *

Grades: 4 5 6 7   Fic
1. Missing persons—Fiction 2. Caves—Fiction 3. Adventure fiction 4. Mother-son relationship—Fiction
ISBN   978-0-375-83873-6;   0-375-83873-2;
978-0-375-93873-3 (lib bdg); 0-375-93873-7 (lib bdg);
978-0-375-83874-3 (pa); 0-375-83874-0 (pa)
LC 2006-13352
While his widowed mother continues to search for him, eleven-year-old Tom, presumed dead after drifting away down a river, finds himself trapped in a series of underground caves with another survivor and a dog, and pursued by murderous treasure-hunters.

"While _Leepike Ridge_ is primarily an adventure story involving murder, treachery, and betrayal, Wilson's rich imagination and his quirky characters are a true delight." SLJ

Winerip, Michael
Adam Canfield of the Slash. Candlewick Press 2005 326p $15.99
Grades: 5 6 7 8   Fic
1. Journalism—Fiction 2. School stories
ISBN 0-7636-2340-7
While serving as co-editors of their school newspaper, middle-schoolers Adam and Jennifer uncover fraud and corruption in their school and in the city's government.

"This is a deceptively fun read that somehow manages to present kids with some of the most subtle social and ethical questions currently shaping their futures." SLJ
Another title about Adam Canfield is:
Adam Canfield, watch you back! (2007)

Winston, Sherri
The Kayla chronicles; a novel. Little, Brown 2007 188p $16.99 *
Grades: 6 7 8 9 10   Fic
1. African Americans—Fiction 2. Dancers—Fiction 3. Journalism—Fiction 4. School stories
ISBN 978-0-316-11430-1; 0-316-11430-8
LC 2006-933219
Kayla transforms herself from mild-mannered journalist to hot-trotting dance diva in order to properly investigate her high school's dance team, and has a hard time remaining true to her real self while in the role.

"Few recent novels for younger YAs mesh levity and substance this successfully." Booklist

Winterson, Jeanette, 1959-
Tanglewreck. 1st U.S. ed. Bloomsbury Children's Books; distributed by Holtzbrinck Publishers 2006 414p $16.95
Grades: 5 6 7 8   Fic
1. Science fiction 2. Space and time—Fiction 3. Clocks and watches—Fiction
ISBN 978-1-58234-919-0; 1-58234-919-3
LC 2005-30630
Eleven-year-old Silver sets out to find the Timekeeper—a clock that controls time—and to protect it from falling into the hands of two people who want to use the device for their own nefarious ends.

"Winterson seamlessly combines rousing adventure with time warps, quantum physics, and a few wonderfully hapless flunkies." Booklist

Winthrop, Elizabeth
Counting on Grace. Wendy Lamb Books 2006 232p $15.95
Grades: 5 6 7 8   Fic
1. Hine, Lewis Wickes, 1874-1940—Fiction 2. Child labor—Fiction   3.   Factories—Fiction 4. Photographers—Fiction 5. Vermont—Fiction
ISBN 0-385-74644-X
It's 1910 in Pownal, Vermont. At 12 Grace and her best friend Arthur must go to work in the mill, helping their mothers work the looms. Together Grace and Arthur write a secret letter to the Child Labor Board about underage children working in the mill. A few weeks later, Lewis Hine, a famous reformer, arrives undercover to gather evidence. Grace meets him and appears in some of his photographs, changing her life forever.

"Much information on early photography and the workings of the textile mills is conveyed, and history and fiction are woven seamlessly together in this beautifully written novel." SLJ

Wiseman, Eva
Puppet; a novel. Tundra Books 2009 243p $17.95 *
Grades: 7 8 9 10 11 12   Fic
1. Jews—Hungary—Fiction 2. Prejudices—Fiction
ISBN 978-0-88776-828-6; 0-88776-828-8
"Times are hard in Julie Vamosi's Hungarian village in the lat nineteenth-century, and the townspeople . . . blame the Jews. After Julie's best friend, Esther, . . . disappears, the rumor spreads that the Jews cut her throat and drained her blood to drink with their Passover matzos. . . . Based on the records of a trial in 1883, this searing novel dramatizes virulent anti-Semitism from the viewpoint of a Christian child. . . . The climax is electrifying." Booklist

Wisler, G. Clifton, 1950-
Caleb's choice. Lodestar Bks. 1996 154p pa $4.99 hardcover o.p.   Fic
1. Underground railroad—Fiction 2. Slavery—Fiction
ISBN 0-14-038256-9 (pa)   LC 96-2339
While living in Texas in 1858, fourteen-year-old Caleb faces a dilemma in deciding whether or not to assist fugitive slaves in their run for freedom

Wisler, G. Clifton, 1950-—*Continued*
"This fast-paced, easy-to-read novel proves that history can be intriguing and exciting, Wisler draws readers into this masterful, and often humorous tale." ALAN

Red Cap. Lodestar Bks. 1991 160p pa $5.99 hardcover o.p.
Grades: 4 5 6 7 **Fic**
1. Powell, Ransom J., 1849-1899—Fiction
2. Andersonville Prison—Fiction 3. United States—History—1861-1865, Civil War—Fiction
ISBN 0-14-036936-8 (pa) LC 90-21944
A young Yankee drummer boy displays great courage when he's captured and sent to Andersonville Prison
The author "presents a well-researched view of the war. He effectively interweaves the known facts of Powell's life with first-person accounts of other soldiers and prisoners to create an exciting story." SLJ

Wittlinger, Ellen, 1948-
Hard love. Simon & Schuster Bks. for Young Readers 1999 224p hardcover o.p. pa $8.99
Grades: 7 8 9 10 **Fic**
1. Authorship—Fiction 2. Lesbians—Fiction
ISBN 0-689-82134-4; 0-689-84154-X (pa)
LC 98-6668
Michael L. Printz Award honor book, 2000
"John, cynical yet vulnerable, thinks he's immune to emotion until he meets bright, brittle Marisol, the author of his favorite zine. He falls in love, but Marisol, a lesbian, just wants to be friends. A love story of a different sort—funny, poignant, and thoughtful." Booklist
Followed by: Love & lies: Marisol's story (2008)

Parrotfish. Simon & Schuster Books for Young Readers 2007 294p $16.99
Grades: 7 8 9 10 **Fic**
1. Transsexualism—Fiction 2. Family life—Fiction
3. School stories
ISBN 978-1-4169-1622-2; 1-4169-1622-9
LC 2006-9689
Grady, a transgendered high school student, yearns for acceptance by his classmates and family as he struggles to adjust to his new identity as a male.
"The author demonstrates well the complexity faced by transgendered people and makes the teen's frustration with having to fit into a category fully apparent." Publ Wkly

Zigzag. Simon & Schuster Bks. for Young Readers 2003 267p $16.95
Grades: 7 8 9 10 **Fic**
1. Automobile travel—Fiction 2. Cousins—Fiction
ISBN 0-689-84996-6 LC 2002-2145
A high-school junior makes a trip with her aunt and two cousins, discovering places she did not know existed and strengths she did not know she had
"Teens will easily hear themselves in Robin's hilarious, sharp observations and feel her excitement as she travels through new country and discovers her own strength." Booklist

Wolf, Allan
New found land; Lewis and Clark's voyage of discovery: a novel. Candlewick Press 2004 500p map $18.99
Grades: 7 8 9 10 **Fic**
1. Lewis and Clark Expedition (1804-1806)—Fiction
ISBN 0-7636-2113-7 LC 2003-65254
The letters and thoughts of Thomas Jefferson, members of the Corps of Discovery, their guide Sacagawea, and Captain Lewis's Newfoundland dog, all tell of the historic exploratory expedition to seek a water route to the Pacific Ocean.
"This is an extraordinary, engrossing book that would appeal most to serious readers, but it should definitely be added to any collection." SLJ
Includes glossary and bibliographical references

Wolf, Joan M., 1966-
Someone named Eva. Clarion Books 2007 200p $16 *
Grades: 5 6 7 8 **Fic**
1. World War, 1939-1945—Fiction 2. National socialism—Fiction 3. Europe—History—1918-1945—Fiction 4. School stories
ISBN 0-618-53579-9 LC 2006-26070
From her home in Lidice, Czechoslovakia, in 1942, eleven-year-old Milada is taken with other blond, blue-eyed children to a school in Poland to be trained as "proper Germans" for adoption by German families, but all the while she remembers her true name and history.
"This amazing, eye-opening story, masterfully written, is an essential part of World War II literature and belongs on the shelves of every library." SLJ

Wolff, Virginia Euwer
Make lemonade. Holt & Co. 1993 200p hardcover o.p. pa $7.95 *
Grades: 8 9 10 11 12 **Fic**
1. Teenage mothers—Fiction 2. Babysitters—Fiction
3. Poverty—Fiction 4. Novels in verse
ISBN 0-8050-2228-7; 978-0-8050-8070-4 (pa);
0-8050-8070-8 (pa) LC 92-41182
"Fourteen-year-old LaVaughn accepts the job of babysitting Jolly's two small children but quickly realizes that the young woman, a seventeen-year-old single mother, needs as much help and nurturing as her two neglected children. The four become something akin to a temporary family, and through their relationship each makes progress toward a better life. Sixty-six brief chapters, with words arranged on the page like poetry, perfectly echo the patterns of teenage speech." Horn Book Guide
Other titles in this trilogy are:
True believer (2001)
This full house (2009)

The Mozart season. Holt & Co. 1991 249p hardcover o.p. pa $6.99
Grades: 6 7 8 9 **Fic**
1. Violinists—Fiction
ISBN 0-8050-1571-X; 0-312-36745-7 (pa)
LC 90-23635
Allegra spends her twelfth summer practicing a Mozart concerto for a violin competition and finding many

Wolff, Virginia Euwer—*Continued*

significant connections in her world

"With a clear, fresh voice that never falters, Wolff gives readers a delightful heroine, a fully realized setting, and a slowly building tension that reaches a stunning climax." SLJ

Probably still Nick Swansen. Holt & Co. 1988 144p hardcover o.p. pa $7.99 *

Grades: 7 8 9 10 **Fic**
1. Learning disabilities—Fiction
ISBN 0-8050-0701-6; 0-689-85226-6 (pa)
LC 88-13175

Sixteen-year-old learning-disabled Nick struggles to endure a life in which the other kids make fun of him, he has to take special classes, his date for the prom makes an excuse not to go with him, and he is haunted by the memory of his older sister who drowned while he was watching

"It is a poignant, gentle, utterly believable narrative." Booklist

Wolfson, Jill

Home, and other big, fat lies. Henry Holt 2006 281p $16.95

Grades: 5 6 7 8 **Fic**
1. Foster home care—Fiction 2. Nature—Fiction 3. Environmental protection—Fiction
ISBN 978-0-8050-7670-7; 0-8050-7670-0
LC 200035843

Eleven-year-old Termite, a foster child with an eye for the beauty of nature and a talent for getting into trouble, takes on the loggers in her new home town when she tries to save the biggest tree in the forest.

"Written with humor and sensitivity." Voice Youth Advocates

What I call life. Holt & Co. 2005 270p $16.95

Grades: 5 6 7 8 **Fic**
1. Foster home care—Fiction
ISBN 0-8050-7669-7

Placed in a group foster home, eleven-year-old Cal Lavender learns how to cope with life from the four other girls who live there and from their storytelling guardian, the Knitting Lady.

"Wolfson paints her characters with delightful authenticity. Her debut novel is a treasure of quiet good humor and skillful storytelling that conveys subtle messages about kindness, compassion, and the gift of family regardless of its configuration." Booklist

Wollman, Jessica

Switched. Delacorte Press 2007 249p $15.99

Grades: 6 7 8 9 **Fic**
1. Social classes—Fiction 2. Mother-daughter relationship—Fiction 3. Household employees—Fiction 4. School stories
ISBN 978-0-385-73396-0

Laura and Willa, born the same night seventeen years ago on opposite sides of Darien, Connecticut, are both unhappy with their lives and when they discover they look remarkably alike, they decide to try out one another's lives for four months.

"Wollman turns a potentially clichéd premise . . . into an entertaining and thoughtful novel. . . . Wollman creates credible characters who should endear themselves to readers." Publ Wkly

Wood, June Rae, 1946-

The man who loved clowns. Putnam 1992 224p pa $5.99 hardcover o.p.

Grades: 5 6 7 8 **Fic**
1. Down syndrome—Fiction 2. Mentally handicapped—Fiction 3. Uncles—Fiction
ISBN 0-14-240422-5 (pa) LC 91-33861

Thirteen-year-old Delrita, whose unhappy life has caused her to hide from the world, loves her uncle Punky but sometimes feels ashamed of his behavior because he has Down's syndrome

"Wood's prose is strong and flowing, with a good balance of dialogue and narrative, and with several well-developed and memorable characters." SLJ

Another title about Delrita is:
Turtle on a fence post (1997)

Wood, Maryrose

My life the musical; by Maryrose Wood. 1st ed. Delacorte Press 2008 228p $15.99; lib bdg $18.99

Grades: 7 8 9 10 **Fic**
1. Musicals—Fiction 2. Theater—Fiction 3. School stories 4. New York (N.Y.)—Fiction
ISBN 978-0-385-73278-9; 0-385-73278-3; 978-0-385-90297-7 (lib bdg); 0-385-90297-2 (lib bdg)
LC 2007015034

Sixteen-year-old Emily Pearl's obsession with Broadway shows, and one musical in particular, lands her in trouble in school and at home, but it might also allow her and her best friend, Phillip, to find a dramatic solution to the problems.

"Teens will enjoy the fast pace and humor in this uplifting novel." SLJ

Wooding, Chris, 1977-

The haunting of Alaizabel Cray. Orchard Bks. 2004 292p $16.95; pa $7.99 *

Grades: 7 8 9 10 **Fic**
1. Horror fiction 2. Supernatural—Fiction 3. London (England)—Fiction
ISBN 0-439-54656-7; 0-439-59851-6 (pa)
LC 2003-69108

First published 2001 in the United Kingdom

In a world similar to Victorian London, Thaniel, a seventeen-year-old hunter of deadly, demonic creatures called the wych-kin, takes in a lost, possessed girl, and becomes embroiled in a plot to unleash evil on the world

"Eerie and exhilarating. . . . [The author] fuses together his best storytelling skills . . . to create a fabulously horrific and ultimately timeless underworld." SLJ

Poison. Orchard Bks. 2005 c2003 273p $16.99; pa $7.99

Grades: 7 8 9 10 **Fic**
1. Fantasy fiction 2. Storytelling—Fiction 3. Fairies—Fiction
ISBN 0-439-75570-0; 0-439-75571-9 (pa)
LC 2005-02174

Wooding, Chris, 1977-—*Continued*

First published 2003 in the United Kingdom

When Poison leaves her home in the marshes of Gull to retrieve the infant sister who was snatched by the fairies, she and a group of unusual friends survive encounters with the inhabitants of various Realms, and Poison herself confronts a surprising destiny.

"Poison's story should please crowds of horror fans who like their books fast-paced, darkly atmospheric, and melodramatic." SLJ

The storm thief. Orchard Books 2006 310p $16.99

Grades: 6 7 8 9   **Fic**

1. Science fiction

ISBN 0-439-86513-1   LC 2005-35993

With the help of a golem, two teenaged thieves try to survive on the city island of Orokos, where unpredictable probability storms continually change both the landscape and the inhabitants.

The author "delivers memorable characters, such as Vago, whose plight—Who am I and where do I belong in the world?—will be understood by many teens. Wooding also creates a unique world for his characters to explore, and the setting serves as an excellent backdrop for the author to develop his theme of order versus chaos and the need for balance between the two." Voice Youth Advocates

Woodruff, Elvira

Dear Austin; letters from the Underground Railroad; illustrated by Nancy Carpenter. Knopf 1998 137p il $16; lib bdg $17.99; pa $5.50

Grades: 4 5 6   **Fic**

1. Underground railroad—Fiction 2. Slavery—Fiction 3. African Americans—Fiction 4. Pennsylvania—Fiction

ISBN 0-679-88594-3; 0-679-98594-8 (lib bdg); 0-375-80356-4 (pa)   LC 98-5314

Sequel to Dear Levi (1994)

In 1853, in letters to his older brother, eleven-year-old Levi describes his adventures in the Pennsylvania countryside with his black friend Jupiter and his experiences with the Underground Railroad

"The smoothly written text is fast paced." Horn Book Guide

Fearless. Scholastic Press 2008 224p il $16.99

Grades: 5 6 7 8   **Fic**

1. Winstanley, Henry, 1644-1703—Fiction 2. Orphans—Fiction 3. Adventure fiction 4. Lighthouses—Fiction 5. Great Britain—History—1603-1714, Stuarts—Fiction

ISBN 978-0-439-67703-5; 0-439-67703-3   LC 2006-10137

In late seventeenth-century England, eleven-year-old Digory, forced to leave his hometown after his father is lost at sea, becomes an apprentice to the architect Henry Winstanley, who built a lighthouse on the treacherous Eddystone Reef—the very rocks that sank Digory's grandfather's ship years before.

"This fascinating, well-written story is closely based on the life of the real Henry Winstanley. . . . The characters are finely drawn and the action is nonstop." SLJ

Woods, Brenda

Emako Blue. G. P. Putnam's Sons 2004 124p $15.99

Grades: 7 8 9 10   **Fic**

1. African Americans—Fiction 2. Los Angeles (Calif.)—Fiction

ISBN 0-399-24006-3   LC 2003-16647

Monterey, Savannah, Jamal, and Eddie have never had much to do with each other until Emako Blue shows up at chorus practice, but just as the lives of the five Los Angeles high school students become intertwined, tragedy tears them apart.

"This short, succinct, and poignant story of friendship, family, and overwhelming sadness will leave some readers in tears." SLJ

My name is Sally Little Song. G.P. Putnam's Sons 2006 182p $15.99

Grades: 4 5 6 7   **Fic**

1. Slavery—Fiction 2. African Americans—Fiction 3. Seminole Indians—Fiction 4. Georgia—Fiction 5. Florida—Fiction

ISBN 0-399-24312-7   LC 2005-32651

When their owner plans to sell one of them in 1802, twelve-year-old Sally and her family run away from their Georgia plantation to look for both freedom from slavery and a home in Florida with the Seminole Indians.

"Based on historical accounts, this novel provides readers with an alternative view of the realities of slavery—an escape to the South rather than North. . . . This accessible tale will prove a rich resource for study and discussion." SLJ

Woods, Ron

The hero. Knopf 2002 215p hardcover o.p. pa $4.99

Grades: 5 6 7 8   **Fic**

1. Rafting (Sports)—Fiction 2. Death—Fiction

ISBN 0-375-80612-1; 0-440-22978-2 (pa)   LC 00-54460

In the summer of 1957 in Idaho, when 14 year old Jamie and his older cousin Jerry reluctantly include outsider Dennis in their rafting adventure, Dennis drowns and Jamie lies that Dennis made a heroic sacrifice

"The author deftly handles a convincing adventure with emotional depth and tenderness toward his characters." SLJ

Woodson, Jacqueline

After Tupac and D Foster. G.P. Putnam's Sons 2008 153p $15.99 *

Grades: 7 8 9 10   **Fic**

1. Shakur, Tupac—Fiction 2. Friendship—Fiction 3. African Americans—Fiction 4. Queens (New York, N.Y.)—Fiction

ISBN 978-0-399-24654-8   LC 2007-23725

A Newbery honor book, 2009

In the New York City borough of Queens in 1996, three girls bond over their shared love of Tupac Shakur's music, as together they try to make sense of the unpredictable world in which they live.

"The subtlety and depth with which the author conveys the girls' relationships lend this novel exceptional vividness and staying power." Publ Wkly

Woodson, Jacqueline—*Continued*

Feathers. G.P. Putnam's Sons 2007 118p $15.99; pa $6.99 *

Grades: 4 5 6 7 **Fic**

1. Race relations—Fiction 2. African Americans—Fiction 3. Religion—Fiction

ISBN 978-0-399-23989-2; 0-399-23989-8; 978-0-14-241198-8 (pa); 0-14-241198-1 (pa)

LC 2006-24713

A Newbery Medal honor book, 2008

When a new, white student nicknamed "The Jesus Boy" joins her sixth grade class in the winter of 1971, Frannie's growing friendship with him makes her start to see some things in a new light.

"Woodson creates in Frannie a strong protagonist who thinks for herself and recognizes the value and meaning of family. The story ends with hope and thoughtfulness while speaking to those adolescents who struggle with race, faith, and prejudice." SLJ

From the notebooks of Melanin Sun. Blue Sky Press (NY) 1995 141p hardcover o.p. pa $5.99 *

Grades: 7 8 9 10 **Fic**

1. Mother-son relationship—Fiction 2. African Americans—Fiction 3. Lesbians—Fiction

ISBN 0-590-45880-9; 0-590-45881-7 (pa)

LC 93-34158

Fourteen-year-old Melanin Sun's comfortable, quiet life is shattered when his mother reveals she has fallen in love with a woman

"Offering no easy answers, Woodson teaches the reader that love can lead to acceptance of all manner of differences." Publ Wkly

Hush. Putnam 2002 181p $15.99; pa $5.99

Grades: 6 7 8 9 **Fic**

1. Witnesses—Fiction 2. African Americans—Fiction

ISBN 0-399-23114-5; 0-14-250049-6 (pa)

LC 2001-19710

Thirteen-year-old Toswiah finds her life changed when her family enters the witness protection program

The author's "poetic, low-key, yet vivid writing style perfectly conveys the story's atmosphere of quiet intensity." Horn Book

If you come softly. Putnam 1998 181p $15.99; pa $5.99 *

Grades: 7 8 9 10 **Fic**

1. African Americans—Fiction 2. Race relations—Fiction 3. New York (N.Y.)—Fiction

ISBN 0-399-23112-9; 0-698-11862-6 (pa)

LC 97-32212

ALA YALSA Margaret A. Edwards Award (2006)

After meeting at their private school in New York, fifteen-year-old Jeremiah, who is black and whose parents are separated, and Ellie, who is white and whose mother has twice abandoned her, fall in love and then try to cope with people's reactions

"The gentle and melancholy tone of this book makes it ideal for thoughtful readers and fans of romance." Voice Youth Advocates

Another title about Jeremiah is:
Behind you (2004)

Lena; by Jacqueline Woodson. 1st G.P. Putnam's Sons ed. G. P. Putnam's Sons 2006 c1999 135p $17.99

Grades: 6 7 8 9 **Fic**

1. Runaway teenagers—Fiction 2. Sisters—Fiction

ISBN 0-399-24469-7 LC 2005032666

Sequel to: I hadn't meant to tell you this (1994)

A reissue of the title first published 1999 by Delacorte Press

Thirteen-year-old Lena and her younger sister Dion mourn the death of their mother as they hitchhike from Ohio to Kentucky while running away from their abusive father.

"Soulful, wise and sometimes wrenching, this taut story never loses its grip on the reader." Publ Wkly

Locomotion. Putnam 2003 100p $15.99; pa $5.99 *

Grades: 4 5 6 7 **Fic**

1. African Americans—Fiction 2. Foster home care—Fiction 3. Novels in verse

ISBN 0-399-23115-3; 0-14-240149-8 (pa); 978-0-439-63615-5 (pa) LC 2002-69779

In a series of poems, eleven-year-old Lonnie writes about his life, after the death of his parents, separated from his younger sister, living in a foster home, and finding his poetic voice at school

"In a masterful use of voice, Woodson allows Lonnie's poems to tell a complex story of loss and grief and to create a gritty, urban environment. Despite the spare text, Lonnie's foster mother and the other minor characters are three-dimensional, making the boy's world a convincingly real one." SLJ

Peace, Locomotion. G.P. Putnam's Sons 2009 134p $15.99 *

Grades: 4 5 6 7 **Fic**

1. Foster home care—Fiction 2. Siblings—Fiction 3. Orphans—Fiction 4. African Americans—Fiction 5. Letters—Fiction

ISBN 978-0-399-24655-5; 0-399-24655-X

LC 2008-18583

Companion volume to: Locomotion (2003)

Through letters to his little sister, who is living in a different foster home, sixth-grader Lonnie, also known as "Locomotion," keeps a record of their lives while they are apart, describing his own foster family, including his foster brother who returns home after losing a leg in the Iraq War.

"Woodson creates a full-bodied character in kind, sensitive Lonnie. Readers will understand his quest for peace, and appreciate the hard work he does to find it." Publ Wkly

Woodworth, Chris, 1957-

Double-click for trouble. Farrar, Straus and Giroux 2008 162p $16

Grades: 6 7 8 9 **Fic**

1. Country life—Fiction 2. Indiana—Fiction 3. Uncles—Fiction

ISBN 978-0-374-30987-9; 0-374-30987-6

LC 2006-38351

After he is caught viewing inappropriate websites on the Internet, a fatherless, thirteen-year-old Chicago boy is

Woodworth, Chris, 1957——*Continued*
sent to rural Indiana to spend school break with his eccentric great-uncle.

"Woodworth perfectly captures an eighth-grade boy on the cusp of adolescence, struggling with his identity as he learns about himself, his family, and what is really important in relationships." SLJ

When Ratboy lived next door. Farrar, Straus and Giroux 2005 181p $16
Grades: 6 7 8 9 **Fic**
1. Raccoons—Fiction 2. Friendship—Fiction 3. Indiana—Fiction
ISBN 0-374-34677-1 LC 2004-50634
When his strange family moves into her quiet southern Indiana town, sixth-grader Lydia Carson initially despises her new neighbor and classmate, who seems as wild as the raccoon that is his closest companion.

"There are serious issues present, including poverty, alcoholism, abuse, learning disabilities, and bullying. The conflicts of the plot are effectively tied up, though not too neatly to lose believability. . . . An outstanding offering." SLJ

Wrede, Patricia C., 1953-
Dealing with dragons. Harcourt Brace Jovanovich 1990 212p $17; pa $5.95
Grades: 6 7 8 9 **Fic**
1. Fairy tales 2. Dragons—Fiction
ISBN 0-15-222900-0; 0-15-204566-X (pa)
LC 89-24599
Also available in paperback from Scholastic "Jane Yolen books"
Bored with traditional palace life, a princess goes off to live with a group of dragons and soon becomes involved with fighting against some disreputable wizards who want to steal away the dragons' kingdom

"A decidedly diverting novel with plenty of action and many slightly skewed fairy-tale conventions that add to the laugh-out-loud reading pleasure and give the story a wide appeal. The good news is that this is book one in the Enchanted Forest Chronicles." Booklist
Other titles in the Enchanted Forest Chronicles are:
Calling on dragons (1993)
Searching for dragons (1991)
Talking to dragons (1993)

Sorcery and Cecelia, or, The enchanted chocolate pot; being the correspondence of two young ladies of quality regarding various magical scandals in London and the country; [by] Patricia C. Wrede and Caroline Stevermer. Harcourt 2003 316p $17; pa $6.95
Grades: 7 8 9 10 **Fic**
1. Cousins—Fiction 2. Supernatural—Fiction 3. Great Britain—Fiction
ISBN 0-15-204615-1; 0-15-205300-X (pa)
LC 2002-38706
In 1817 in England, two young cousins, Cecilia living in the country and Kate in London, write letters to keep each other informed of their exploits, which take a sinister turn when they find themselves confronted by evil wizards

"This is a fun story that quickly draws in the reader." Voice Youth Advocates

Other titles about Kate and Cecilia are:
The grand tour (2004)
The mislaid magician (2006)

The thirteenth child. Scholastic Press 2009 344p (Frontier magic) $16.99
Grades: 7 8 9 10 **Fic**
1. Magic—Fiction 2. School stories 3. Frontier and pioneer life—Fiction 4. Twins—Fiction 5. Fantasy fiction
ISBN 978-0-545-03342-8; 0-545-03342-X
LC 2008-34048
Eighteen-year-old Eff must finally get over believing she is bad luck and accept that her special training in Aphrikan magic, and being the twin of the seventh son of a seventh son, give her extraordinary power to combat magical creatures that threaten settlements on the western frontier.

Wrede "creates a rich world where steam dragons seem as normal as bears, and a sympathetic character in Eff." Publ Wkly

Wright, Bil
When the black girl sings; [by] Bil Wright. Simon & Schuster Books for Young Readers 2007 266p $16.99; pa $5.99
Grades: 6 7 8 9 10 **Fic**
1. African Americans—Fiction 2. Adoption—Fiction 3. Divorce—Fiction 4. Connecticut—Fiction
ISBN 978-1-4169-3995-5; 1-4169-3995-4; 978-1-4169-4003-6 (pa); 1-4169-4003-0 (pa)
LC 2006030837
Adopted by white parents and sent to an exclusive Connecticut girls' school where she is the only black student, fourteen-year-old Lahni Schuler feels like an outcast, particularly when her parents separate, but after attending a local church where she hears gospel music for the first time, she finds her voice.

"Readers will enjoy the distinctive characters, lively dialogue, and palette of adolescent and racial insecurities in this contemporary, upbeat story." SLJ

Wulffson, Don L., 1943-
Soldier X. Viking 2001 226p $15.99; pa $6.99
Grades: 7 8 9 10 **Fic**
1. World War, 1939-1945—Fiction 2. Russia—Fiction
ISBN 0-670-88863-X; 0-14-250073-9 (pa)
LC 99-49418
"Based on a true story"
In 1943 sixteen-year-old Erik experiences the horrors of war when he is drafted into the German army and sent to fight on the Russian front

"Erik's first-person narrative records battlefield sequences with an unflinching—and occasionally numbing—brutality, in a story notable for its unusual perspective." Horn Book Guide

Wyatt, Leslie J.
Poor is just a starting place; by Leslie J. Wyatt. 1st ed. Holiday House 2005 196p $16.95
Grades: 5 6 7 8 **Fic**
1. Great Depression, 1929-1939—Fiction 2. Poverty—Fiction 3. Kentucky—Fiction
ISBN 0-8234-1884-7 LC 2004-47451

Wyatt, Leslie J.—*Continued*

During the Great Depression, twelve-year-old Artie Wilson, determined to escape plowing and planting the fields and milking the cow on her family's farm, longs to leave Buck Creek, Kentucky, and her life of poverty.

"Written with spare beauty, this first novel tells a moving story." Booklist

Wynne-Jones, Tim

The boy in the burning house. Farrar, Straus & Giroux 2001 c2000 213p hardcover o.p. pa $5.95

Grades: 6 7 8 9   **Fic**

1. Mystery fiction 2. Canada—Fiction

ISBN 0-374-30930-2; 0-374-40887-4 (pa)

          LC 99-89534

"Melanie Kroupa books"

First published 2000 in Canada

Trying to solve the mystery of his father's disappearance from their rural Canadian community, fourteen-year-old Jim gets help from the disturbed Ruth Rose, who suspects her stepfather, a local pastor

"A gripping, fast-moving plot offers the pure adrenaline rush of a thriller." Horn Book Guide

A thief in the house of memory. Farrar, Straus & Giroux 2004 210p $17

Grades: 7 8 9 10   **Fic**

1. Memory—Fiction 2. Mothers—Fiction 3. Canada—Fiction

ISBN 0-374-37478-3   LC 2004-53263

"Melanie Kroupa books"

The death of an apparent stranger in the Steeple family's old home triggers troubling questions for sixteen-year-old Declan as he tries to make sense of his fragmented dreams, random memories, and unexplained coincidences, hoping to learn the truth about the mother who suddenly left when he was ten

"This rich and rewarding novel will appeal most to thoughtful readers who appreciate a sad and bittersweet read." SLJ

Wyss, Thelma Hatch

Bear dancer; the story of a Ute girl. Margaret K. McElderry Books 2005 181p il $15.95

Grades: 5 6 7 8   **Fic**

1. Ute Indians—Fiction

ISBN 1-4169-0285-0   LC 2005-40620

In late nineteenth-century Colorado, Elk Girl, sister of Ute chief Ouray, is captured by Cheyenne and Arapaho warriors, rescued by the white "enemy," and finally returned to her home. Includes historical notes.

"This fascinating story is based on a real person. . . . An excellent addition to historical-fiction collections." SLJ

Yancey, Richard

The extraordinary adventures of Alfred Kropp; by Rick Yancey. Bloomsbury Pub. 2005 339p $16.95; pa $7.95

Grades: 7 8 9 10   **Fic**

1. Arthur, King—Fiction 2. Adventure fiction 3. Orphans—Fiction

ISBN 1-58234-693-3; 1-59990-044-0 (pa)

          LC 2005-13044

Through a series of dangerous and violent misadventures, teenage loser Alfred Kropp rescues King Arthur's legendary sword Excalibur from the forces of evil.

"True to its action-adventure genre, the story is lighthearted, entertaining, occasionally half-witted, but by and large fun." SLJ

Other titles about Alfred Kropp are:

Alfred Kropp: the seal of Solomon (2007)

Alfred Kropp: the thirteenth skull (2008)

Yee, Lisa

Absolutely Maybe. Arthur A. Levine Books 2009 274p $16.99

Grades: 8 9 10 11 12   **Fic**

1. Mother-daughter relationship—Fiction 2. Fathers—Fiction 3. Runaway teenagers—Fiction 4. Los Angeles (Calif.)—Fiction

ISBN 978-0-439-83844-3; 0-439-83844-4

          LC 2008-17787

When living with her mother, an alcoholic ex-beauty queen, becomes unbearable, almost seventeen-year-old Maybelline "Maybe" Chestnut runs away to California, where she finds work on a taco truck and tries to track down her birth father.

"The characters are complex and their friendships layered—they sweep readers up in their path." Publ Wkly

Millicent Min, girl genius. Arthur A. Levine Books 2003 248p $16.95; pa $4.99

Grades: 5 6 7   **Fic**

1. Gifted children—Fiction 2. School stories 3. Chinese Americans—Fiction

ISBN 0-439-42519-0; 0-439-42520-4 (pa)

          LC 2003-3747

"At the tender age of eleven, Millicent Min has completed her junior year of high school. Summer school is Millie's idea of fun, so she is excited that her parents are allowing her to take a college poetry course. . . . The tension between Millie's formal, overly intellectual way of expressing herself and her emotional immaturity makes her a very funny narrator. . . . Readers considerably older than Millicent's eleven years will enjoy this strong debut novel." Voice Youth Advocates

Other titles about Millicent Min and her friends are:

Stanford Wong flunks big-time (2005)

So totally Emily Ebers (2007)

Yee, Paul

Learning to fly; [by] Paul Yee. Orca Book Pub. 2008 108p (Orca soundings) $16.95

Grades: 7 8 9 10   **Fic**

1. Chinese—Fiction 2. Immigrants—Fiction 3. Native Americans—Fiction 4. Prejudices—Fiction 5. Drug abuse—Fiction 6. Canada—Fiction 7. Friendship—Fiction

ISBN 978-1-55143-955-6; 1-55143-955-7

"Jason Chen, 17, wants to leave his small town in Canada and return to China. . . . His white high-school teachers do not know how smart he is, and his classmates jeer at him. Driven to join the crowd of potheads, he bonds especially with his Native American classmate, Charles ('Chief'). Narrated in Jason's wry, first-person, present-tense narrative, Yee's slim novel packs in a lot. . . . The clipped dialogue perfectly echoes the contem-

Yee, Paul—*Continued*

porary scene, the harsh prejudice felt by the new immigrant and the Native American, and their gripping friendship story." Booklist

Yeomans, Ellen, 1962-

Rubber houses; a novel. Little, Brown and Company 2007 152p $15.99

Grades: 7 8 9 10   **Fic**

1. Bereavement—Fiction   2.   Death—Fiction
3. Siblings—Fiction 4. Novels in verse
ISBN 978-0-316-10647-4; 0-316-10647-X

LC 2005-37297

A novel in verse that relates seventeen-year-old Kit's experiences as her younger brother is diagnosed with and dies of cancer and as she withdraws into and gradually emerges from her grief.

"This slim work speaks volumes about the grieving process. Yeomans has very precisely selected her words to convey the fear and the grief that Kit feels." SLJ

Yep, Laurence

Dragon road; Golden Mountain chronicles: 1939. HarperCollins 2008 291p $16.99; lib bdg $17.89 *

Grades: 6 7 8 9   **Fic**

1. Chinese Americans—Fiction 2. Basketball—Fiction
3. Great Depression, 1929-1939—Fiction
ISBN   978-0-06-027520-4;   0-06-027520-0;
978-0-06-027521-1 (lib bdg); 0-06-027521-9 (lib bdg)

LC 2008-00784

In 1939, unable to find regular jobs because of the Great Depression, long-time friends Cal Chin and Barney Young tour the country as members of a Chinese American basketball team.

"As always, Yep's history is impeccable; now he's written an episode with appeal to basketball fans as well." Booklist

Includes bibliographical references

Dragon's gate; Golden Mountain chronicles: 1867. HarperCollins Pubs. 1993 273p $16.99; pa $6.99 *

Grades: 6 7 8 9   **Fic**

1. Chinese—United States—Fiction 2. Railroads—Fiction
ISBN 0-06-022971-3; 0-06-440489-7 (pa)

LC 92-43649

A Newbery Medal honor book, 1994

Sequel to The serpent's children (1984) and Mountain light (1985)

When he accidentally kills a Manchu, a fifteen-year-old Chinese boy is sent to America to join his father, an uncle, and other Chinese working to build a tunnel for the transcontinental railroad through the Sierra Nevada mountains in 1867

"Yep has succeeded in realizing the primary characters and the irrepressibly dramatic story. . . . The carefully researched details will move students to thought and discussion." Bull Cent Child Books

Dragonwings; Golden Mountain chronicles: 1903. Harper & Row 1975 248p lib bdg $16.89; pa $6.99 *

Grades: 6 7 8 9   **Fic**

1. Chinese Americans—Fiction 2. San Francisco (Calif.)—Fiction
ISBN 0-06-026738-0 (lib bdg); 0-06-440085-9 (pa)

A Newbery Medal honor book, 1976

"In 1903 Moon Shadow, eight years old, leaves China for the 'Land of the Golden Mountains,' San Francisco, to be with his father, Windrider, a father he has never seen. There, beset by the trials experienced by most foreigners in America, Moonrider shares his father's dream—to fly. This dream enables Windrider to endure the mockery of the other Chinese, the poverty he suffers in this hostile place—the land of the white demons—and his loneliness for his wife and his own country." Shapiro. Fic for Youth. 3d edition

Hiroshima; a novella. Scholastic 1995 56p pa $4.99

Grades: 4 5 6 7   **Fic**

1. Hiroshima (Japan)—Bombardment, 1945—Fiction
ISBN 0-590-20832-2; 0-590-20833-0 (pa)

LC 94-18195

"This moving and detailed narrative chronicles the dropping of the atomic bomb on Hiroshima and its effects on its citizens, especially on twelve-year-old Sachi. Based on true accounts, this book describes the horrors and sadness as well as the courage and hope that result from war." Soc Educ

The traitor; Golden Mountain chronicles, 1885. HarperCollins Pubs. 2003 310p $16.99; lib bdg $17.89 *

Grades: 5 6 7 8   **Fic**

1. Prejudices—Fiction   2.   Friendship—Fiction
3. Chinese Americans—Fiction
ISBN 0-06-027522-7; 0-06-027523-5 (lib bdg)

LC 2002-22534

Sequel to Dragon's gate

In 1885, a lonely illegitimate American boy and a lonely Chinese American boy develop an unlikely friendship in the midst of prejudices and racial tension in their coal mining town of Rock Springs, Wyoming

"The short chapters read quickly, and readers will become involved through the first-person voices that capture each boy's feelings of being an outsider and a traitor." Booklist

Yohalem, Eve

Escape under the forever sky; a novel. Chronicle Books 2009 220p $16.99 *

Grades: 4 5 6 7   **Fic**

1. Wilderness survival—Fiction 2. Kidnapping—Fiction 3. Mother-daughter relationship—Fiction 4. Ethiopia—Fiction
ISBN 978-0-8118-6653-8; 0-8118-6653-X

LC 2008019565

As a future conservation zoologist whose mother is the United States Ambassador to Ethiopia, thirteen-year-old Lucy uses her knowledge for survival when she is kidnapped and subsequently escapes.

"Lucy's past and present are gracefully woven togeth-

Yohalem, Eve—*Continued*
er, through well-integrated flashbacks, into a powerful picture of the life of a foreigner in Ethiopia. The story should appeal to all with a sense of adventure." Publ Wkly

Yolen, Jane
Briar Rose. Doherty Assocs. 1992 190p (Fairy tale series) hardcover o.p. pa $6.99 *
Grades: 8 9 10 11 12 Adult   Fic
1. Fantasy fiction 2. Holocaust, 1933-1945—Fiction
3. Jews—Poland—Fiction 4. Grandmothers—Fiction
ISBN 0-312-85135-9; 0-7653-4230-8 (pa)
LC 92-25456
"A TOR book"
"Yolen takes the story of Briar Rose (commonly known as Sleeping Beauty) and links it to the Holocaust. . . . Rebecca Berlin, a young woman who has grown up hearing her grandmother Gemma tell an unusual and frightening version of the Sleeping Beauty legend, realizes when Gemma dies that the fairy tale offers one of the very few clues she has to her grandmother's past. . . . By interpolating Gemma's vivid and imaginative story into the larger narrative, Yolen has created an engrossing novel." Publ Wkly

Dragon's blood. Harcourt 2004 303p (Pit dragon chronicles) pa $6.95
Grades: 6 7 8 9   Fic
1. Dragons—Fiction 2. Fantasy fiction
ISBN 0-15-205126-0   LC 2003-56661
"Magic Carpet books"
A reissue of the title first published 1982 by Delacorte Press
Jakkin, a bond boy who works as a Keeper in a dragon nursery on the planet Austar IV, secretly trains a fighting pit dragon of his own in hopes of winning his freedom
"An original and engrossing fantasy." Horn Book
Other titles in this series are:
Heart's blood (2004)
Sending of dragons (2004)
Dragon's heart (2009)

Girl in a cage; [by] Jane Yolen & Robert J. Harris. Philomel Bks. 2002 234p hardcover o.p. pa $6.99
Grades: 7 8 9 10   Fic
1. Robert I, King of Scotland, 1274-1329—Fiction
2. Scotland—Fiction
ISBN 0-399-23627-9; 0-14-240132-3 (pa)
LC 2001-55978
As English armies invade Scotland in 1306, eleven-year-old Princess Marjorie, daughter of the newly crowned Scottish king, Robert the Bruce, is captured by England's King Edward Longshanks and held in a cage on public display
"Marjorie's first-person narration of her captivity and the events leading up to it is exciting and moving, and her strategies for coping with a hideous imprisonment are models of ingenuity and staying true to oneself." SLJ

Passager. Harcourt Brace & Co. 1996 76p (Young Merlin trilogy) $16
Grades: 4 5 6 7   Fic
1. Merlin (Legendary character)—Fiction 2. Fantasy fiction
ISBN 0-15-200391-6   LC 94-27101
Also available one volume paperback compilation of the entire trilogy $6.95 (ISBN 0-15-205211-9)
A foundling rediscovers his identity through the help of the falconer who adopts him
A "stark, poignant, and absorbing tale. . . . This 'skinny' book will entice reluctant readers, but its rich language and poetic phrasing make it compelling and challenging." SLJ
Other titles in the Young Merlin trilogy are:
Hobby (1996)
Merlin (1997)

Pay the piper; [by] Jane Yolen and Adam Stemple. Tor/Starscape 2005 175p $16.95
Grades: 6 7 8 9   Fic
1. Rock music—Fiction 2. Fantasy fiction
ISBN 0-7653-1158-5
"A Tom Doherty Associates book"
When Callie interviews the band, Brass Rat, for her school newspaper, her feelings are ambivalent, but when all the children of Northampton begin to disappear on Halloween, she knows where the dangerous search must begin.
The authors "have produced a rollicking good riff on the Pied Piper. . . . The authors keep the action moving. . . . An entertaining as well as meaty read." Booklist

The queen's own fool; a novel of Mary Queen of Scots; [by] Jane Yolen and Robert J. Harris. Philomel Bks. 2000 390p pa $7.99
Grades: 7 8 9 10   Fic
1. Mary, Queen of Scots, 1542-1587—Fiction
2. Scotland—Fiction
ISBN 0-399-23380-6; 0-698-11918-5 (pa)
LC 99-55070
When twelve-year-old Nicola leaves Troupe Brufort and serves as the fool for Mary, Queen of Scots, she experiences the political and religious upheavals in both France and Scotland
"The authors have woven fiction and historical fact into a seamless tapestry." Horn Book Guide

The Rogues; [by] Jane Yolen & Robert J. Harris. Philomel Books 2007 277p $18.99 *
Grades: 7 8 9 10   Fic
1. Scotland—Fiction 2. Adventure fiction
ISBN 978-0-399-23898-7   LC 2006-26434
After his family is evicted from their Scottish farm, fifteen-year-old Roddy forms an unlikely friendship with a notorious rogue who helps him outwit a tyrant landlord in order to find a family treasure and make his way to America.
"The suspense mounts and the plot races along flawlessly in this excellent historical adventure." Booklist

Yolen, Jane—_Continued_

Troll Bridge; a rock 'n' roll fairy tale; [by] Jane Yolen and Adam Stemple. 1st ed. Starscape 2006 240p $16.95; pa $5.99

Grades: 7 8 9 10   **Fic**

1. Fairy tales 2. Musicians—Fiction

ISBN 0-7653-1426-6; 0-7653-5284-2 (pa)

LC 2005034517

"A Tom Doherty Associates book"

Sixteen-year-old harpist prodigy Moira is transported to a strange and mystical wilderness, where she finds herself in the middle of a deadly struggle between a magical fox and a monstrous troll.

"The story ends with a grand twist that is totally satisfying. The writing is filled with humor and straightforward prose, and the song lyrics are so well written that one can almost hear the music that accompanies them." SLJ

Yoo, Paula

Good enough. HarperTeen 2008 322p $16.99; lib bdg $17.89

Grades: 7 8 9 10   **Fic**

1. Korean Americans—Fiction 2. Violinists—Fiction

ISBN 978-0-06-079085-1; 978-0-06-079086-8 (lib bdg)   LC 2007-02985

A Korean American teenager tries to please her parents by getting into an Ivy League college, but a new guy in school and her love of the violin tempt her in new directions.

"The frequent lists, . . . SAT questions, and even spam recipes are, like Patti's convincing narration, filled with laugh-out-loud lines, but it's the deeper questions about growing up with immigrant parents, confronting racism, and how best to find success and happiness that will stay with readers." Booklist

Young, E. L.

STORM: The Infinity Code. Dial 2008 311p il $16.99

Grades: 6 7 8 9   **Fic**

1. Adventure fiction 2. Great Britain—Fiction 3. Spies—Fiction

ISBN 978-0-8037-3265-0

In London, the teenaged geniuses of STORM, a secret organization dedicated to eliminating the world's misery through science and technology, uncover plans for a deadly weapon and race to find and dismantle it, then confront the corrupt scientist behind the scheme.

"Young's debut novel is full of unusual scientific creations—all based on real inventions. The novel is plot-driven and packed with unlikely escapes and improbable plot twists—exactly what many middle school and junior high readers crave." Voice Youth Advocates

Other titles in this series are:

STORM: The ghost machine (2008)

STORM: The black sphere (2009)

Zarr, Sara

Sweethearts. Little, Brown and Co. 2008 217p $16.99 *

Grades: 8 9 10 11 12   **Fic**

1. Love stories 2. School stories 3. Weight loss—Fiction 4. Utah—Fiction

ISBN 978-0-316-01455-7; 0-316-01455-9

LC 2007-41099

After losing her soul mate, Cameron, when they were nine, Jennifer, now seventeen, transformed herself from the unpopular fat girl into the beautiful and popular Jenna, but Cameron's unexpected return dredges up memories that cause both social and emotional turmoil.

"Zarr's writing is remarkable. . . . She conveys great delicacy of feeling and shades of meaning, and the realistic, moving ending will inspire excellent discussion." Booklist

Zeises, Lara M.

Contents under pressure. Delacorte Press 2004 244p $15.95; lib bdg $17.99

Grades: 7 8 9 10   **Fic**

1. Family life—Fiction 2. Pregnancy—Fiction

ISBN 0-385-73047-0; 0-385-90162-3 (lib bdg)

LC 2003-5411

Lucy, a fourteen-year-old high school freshman, experiences the happiness and confusion of dating a popular older boy, changing relationships with lifelong friends, and sharing a bedroom with her older brother's pregnant girlfriend.

"Zeises paints a convincing picture of a family facing tough decisions and a fully realistic heroine who's confused and scared. Even secondary characters have depth and add sparkle to an already absorbing plot." SLJ

Zemser, Amy Bronwen

Dear Julia. Greenwillow Books 2008 327p $16.99; lib bdg $17.89 *

Grades: 7 8 9 10   **Fic**

1. Cooking—Fiction 2. Mother-daughter relationship—Fiction 3. Contests—Fiction 4. Feminism—Fiction

ISBN   978-0-06-029458-8;   0-06-029458-2; 978-0-06-029459-5 (lib bdg); 0-06-029459-0 (lib bdg)   LC 2008-3824

Shy sixteen-year-old Elaine has long dreamed of being the next Julia Child, to the dismay of her feminist mother, but when her first friend, the outrageous Lucida Sans, convinces Elaine to enter a cooking contest, anything could happen.

"Readers will laugh throughout, but Zemser never loses sight of Elaine's frailties and hopes." Publ Wkly

Zephaniah, Benjamin, 1958-

Face. Bloomsbury Pub. 2002 c1999 207p $15.95; pa $6.95

Grades: 7 8 9 10   **Fic**

1. Burns and scalds—Fiction 2. Great Britain—Fiction

ISBN 1-58234-774-3; 1-58234-921-5 (pa)

LC 2002-22758

First published 1999 in the United Kingdom

"Something terrible has happened to Martin's face. An automobile crash and fire have left the handsome, popu-

Zephaniah, Benjamin, 1958-—*Continued*
lar 15-year-old boy horribly disfigured. . . . His life is
about to change drastically." Booklist
"This book will not only be enjoyed by teen readers
for its entertaining story, but also for its statement about
prejudice." Voice Youth Advocates

Zevin, Gabrielle, 1977-
Elsewhere. Farrar, Straus & Giroux 2005 275p
$16; pa $6.95
Grades: 7 8 9 10 **Fic**
1. Future life—Fiction 2. Death—Fiction
ISBN 0-374-32091-8; 0-312-36746-5 (pa)
LC 2004-56279
After fifteen-year-old Liz Hall is hit by a taxi and
killed, she finds herself in a place that is both like and
unlike Earth, where she must adjust to her new status
and figure out how to "live."
"Zevin's third-person narrative calmly, but surely
guides readers through the bumpy landscape of strongly
delineated characters dealing with the most difficult issue
that faces all of us. A quiet book that provides much to
think about and discuss." SLJ

Memoirs of a teenage amnesiac. Farrar, Straus
and Giroux 2007 271p $17 *
Grades: 7 8 9 10 **Fic**
1. Amnesia—Fiction 2. Friendship—Fiction 3. School
stories
ISBN 978-0-374-34946-2; 0-374-34946-0
LC 2006-35287
After a nasty fall, Naomi realizes that she has no
memory of the last four years and finds herself
reassessing every aspect of her life.
This is a "sensitive, joyful novel. . . . Pulled by the
the heart-bruising love story, readers will pause to con-
template irresistible questions." Booklist

Ziegler, Jennifer
Alpha dog; a novel; by Jennifer Ziegler.
Delacorte Press 2006 321p lib bdg $9.99; pa $7.95
Grades: 8 9 10 11 **Fic**
1. Dogs—Fiction 2. Texas—Fiction
ISBN 0-385-90302-2 (lib bdg); 0-385-73285-6 (pa)
LC 2005032702
Katie "seems to have no control over her life. . . .
After her boyfriend dumps her on her birthday, she looks
forward to a fresh start at a University of Texas summer
college-prep program. To her dismay, however, a new
set of controlling personalities takes over. . . . When
Katie adopts an adorable, homeless mutt, she thinks she
has found a true friend, but Seamus turns into a holy terror. . . . In despair, Katie tries an obedience school,
where she is told to become the alpha dog. As Katie
gradually gains control of Seamus, she wonders if she
can also be the alpha dog with the people in her life.
. . . This is a charmingly humorous romp." Booklist

How not to be popular. Delacorte Press 2008
339p $15.99; lib bdg $18.99
Grades: 7 8 9 10 11 12 **Fic**
1. Popularity—Fiction 2. School stories 3. Texas—Fiction 4. Hippies—Fiction
ISBN 978-0-385-73465-3; 0-385-73465-4;
978-0-385-90463-6 (lib bdg); 0-385-90463-0 (lib bdg)
LC 2007-27603
Seventeen-year-old Sugar Magnolia Dempsey is tired
of leaving friends behind every time her hippie parents
decide to move, but her plan to be unpopular at her new
school backfires when other students join her on the path
to "supreme dorkdom."
This "balances laugh-out-loud, sardonic commentary
with earnest reflections that will directly connect with
teens." Booklist

Zimmer, Tracie Vaughn
42 miles; illustrated by Elaine Clayton. Clarion
Books 2008 73p il $16
Grades: 4 5 6 **Fic**
1. Divorce—Fiction 2. Family life—Fiction 3. Farm
life—Fiction 4. City and town life—Fiction 5. Novels
in verse
ISBN 978-0-618-61867-5; 0-618-61867-8
LC 2007-31032
As her thirteenth birthday approaches, JoEllen decides
to bring together her two separate lives—one as Joey,
who enjoys weekends with her father and other relatives
on a farm, and another as Ellen, who lives with her
mother in an apartment near her school and friends.
"Using free verse, Zimmer shows the richness in both
places, while black-and-white composit illustrations
bright the bits and pieces together." Booklist

Reaching for sun. Bloomsbury Children's Books
2007 192p $14.95
Grades: 7 8 9 10 **Fic**
1. Cerebral palsy—Fiction 2. Friendship—Fiction
3. Novels in verse
ISBN 1-59990-037-8 LC 2006-13197
Josie, who lives with her mother and grandmother and
has cerebral palsy, befriends a boy who moves into one
of the rich houses behind her old farmhouse.
"Written in verse, this quick-reading, appealing story
will capture readers' hearts with its winsome heroine and
affecting situations." Booklist

Zindel, Paul
The Pigman; a novel. Harper & Row 1968 182p
hardcover o.p. pa $6.99 *
Grades: 7 8 9 10 **Fic**
ISBN 0-06-026828-X; 0-06-0757353-3 (pa)
ALA YALSA Margaret A. Edwards Award (2002)
"John Conlan and Lorraine Jensen, high school sophomores, are both troubled young people who have problems at home. They become friendly with an elderly
widower, Mr. Pignati, who welcomes them into his home
and shares with them his simple pleasures, including his
collection of ceramic pigs, of which he is proud. When
the Pigman, as the young people call him, goes to the
hospital after a heart attack, they take advantage of his
house for a party that becomes destructive. The conse-

Zindel, Paul—*Continued*

quences are tragic and propel the two young friends into more responsible behavior." Shapiro. Fic for Youth. 3d edition

Another title about the Pigman is:
The Pigman's legacy (1980)

Zink, Michelle, 1969-

Prophecy of the sisters. Little, Brown 2009 352p $17.99

Grades: 7 8 9 10   **Fic**
1. Supernatural—Fiction 2. Good and evil—Fiction 3. Twins—Fiction 4. Sisters—Fiction
ISBN 978-0-316-02742-7; 0-316-02742-1
LC 2008-45290

In late nineteenth-century New York state, wealthy sixteen-year-old twin sisters Lia and Alice Milthorpe find that they are on opposite sides of an ancient prophecy that has destroyed their parents and seeks to do even more harm.

"This arresting story takes readers to other planes of existence." Booklist

Zuckerman, Linda

A taste for rabbit. Arthur A. Levine Books 2007 310p $16.99

Grades: 7 8 9 10   **Fic**
1. Rabbits—Fiction 2. Foxes—Fiction 3. Resistance to government—Fiction 4. Animals—Fiction
ISBN 0-439-86977-3; 978-0-439-86977-5
LC 2007-7787

Quentin, a rabbit who lives in a walled compound run by a militaristic government, must join forces with Harry, a fox, to stop the sinister disappearances of outspoken and rebellious rabbit citizens.

"The blend of adventure, mystery and morality in this heroic tale of honor and friendship will appeal to middle-school fantasy fans." Publ Wkly

Zusak, Markus, 1975-

The book thief. Knopf 2006 552p il $16.95; lib bdg $18.99 *

Grades: 8 9 10 11 12   **Fic**
1. World War, 1939-1945—Fiction 2. Holocaust, 1933-1945—Fiction 3. Books and reading—Fiction 4. Death—Fiction
ISBN 0-375-83100-2; 0-375-93100-7 (lib bdg)
LC 2005-08942

Michael L. Printz Award honor book, 2007

Trying to make sense of the horrors of World War II, Death relates the story of Liesel—a young German girl whose book-stealing and storytelling talents help sustain her family and the Jewish man they are hiding, as well as their neighbors.

"This hefty volume is an achievement—a challenging book in both length and subject, and best suited to sophisticated older readers." Publ Wkly

S C STORY COLLECTIONS

Books in this class include collections of short stories by one author and collections by more than one author. Folklore is in class 398.2

13; thirteen stories that capture the agony and ecstasy of being thirteen; edited by James Howe. Atheneum Books for Young Readers 2003 278p $16.95; pa $7.99

Grades: 4 5 6 7   **S C**
1. Short stories
ISBN 0-689-82863-2; 1-416-92684-4 (pa)

Contents: What's the worst that could happen? by Bruce Coville; Kate the great by Meg Cabot; If you kiss a boy by Alex Sanchez; Thirteen and a half by Rachel Vail; Jeremy Goldblatt is so not Moses by James Howe; Black holes and basketball sneakers by Lori Aurelia Williams; Picky eater by Stephen Roos; Such foolishness by Maureen Ryan Griffin; Noodle soup for nincompoops by Ellen Wittlinger; Squid girl by Todd Strasser; Angel & Aly by Ron Koertge; Nobody stole Jason Grayson by Carolyn Mackler; Tina the teen fairy by Ann M. Martin and Laura Godwin.

In this "collection, familiar authors for young adults contribute short fiction about 13-year-old characters who are experiencing bewildering feelings, making discoveries, or undergoing the embarrassments typical of the age." Booklist

"The stories are a mixture of humor, pathos, and poignancy, and most are based on personal experiences. . . . Howe has chosen excellent authors for this volume and they have written oh-so-true stories about that wonderful, terrible first year of being a teenager. " SLJ

666: the number of the beast. Point 2007 330p $14.99

Grades: 7 8 9 10 11 12   **S C**
1. Horror fiction 2. Short stories
ISBN 978-0-545-02117-3; 0-545-02117-0
LC 2007-20058

Contents: Channel 99 by Peter Abrahams; The legend of Anna Barton by Laurie Faria Stolarz; Saving face by Christopher Pike; The little sacrifice by Joyce Carol Oates; If you knew Suzie by Heather Graham; Slam dance by Bentley Little; A trick of the light by Chet Williamson; Erased by Jane Mason; Empire of dirt by Amelia Atwater-Rhodes; Incident report by Joshua Gee; Scapegoat by Robin Wasserman; Imagining things by T.E.D. Klein; Grandma Kelly by David Moody; Shelter Island by Melissa de la Cruz; La fleur de nuit by P.D. Cacek; Ever after by Isobel Bird; Haunted by Ellen Schreiber; Wolfsbane by Sarah Hines Stephens

Eighteen winners of the Bram Stoker award contribute tales of evil, darkness, and beasts.

"Vampires, werewolves, evil fairies—all the usual suspects line up in this horror-star-studded collection of stories created to creep readers out. . . . The cover alone, featuring a beast with blood-red fangs, will have this book flying off the shelves. . . . Horror-seekers . . . will find something here to keep them up nights." Voice Youth Advocates

Alexander, Lloyd, 1924-2007

The foundling and other tales of Prydain. rev & expanded ed. Holt & Co. 1999 98p $19.95 *

Grades: 5 6 7 8   S C

1. Fantasy fiction 2. Short stories

ISBN 0-8050-6130-4   LC 98-42807

Also available in paperback from Penguin

First published 1973; this revised and expanded edition includes two additional stories Coll and his white pig and The truthful harp, first published separately 1965 and 1967 respectively

Contents: The foundling; The stone; The true enchanter; The rascal crow; The sword; The smith, the weaver, and the harper; Coll and his white pig; The truthful harp

Eight short stories dealing with events that preceded the birth of Taran, the Assistant Pig-Keeper and key figure in the author's five works on the Kingdom of Prydain which began with The book of three

"The stories are written with vivid grace and humor." Chicago. Children's Book Center [review of 1973 edition]

American eyes; new Asian-American short stories for young adults; introduction by Cynthia Kadohata. Fawcett Juniper 1996 c1994 138p pa $6.99 *

Grades: 7 8 9 10   S C

1. Asian Americans—Fiction 2. Short stories

ISBN 0-449-70448-3

"A Fawcett Juniper book"

First published 1994 by Holt & Co.

Includes the following stories: Knuckles by Mary F. Chen; Blonde by Katherine Min; Fortune teller by Minh Doc Ngyuen; Wild meat and the bully burgers by Lois-Ann Yamanaka; Bone by Fae Myenne Ng; Housepainting by Lan Samantha Chang; A matter of faith by Peter Bacho; Home now by Ryan Oba; Summer of my Korean soldier by Marie G. Lee; Singing apples by Cynthia Kadohata;

These ten stories reflect the conflict Asian Americans face in balancing an ancient heritage and an unknown future.

This collection is distinguished by the "excellent quality of its writing, the acuteness of characterization, and the sophistication of its themes." SLJ

Appelt, Kathi, 1954-

Kissing Tennessee and other stories from the Stardust Dance. Harcourt 2000 118p hardcover o.p. pa $5.95

Grades: 6 7 8 9   S C

1. School stories 2. Short stories

ISBN 0-15-202249-X; 0-15-205127-9 (pa)

LC 99-50505

Contents: Dance with me; Rachel's sister; Just a kiss, Annie P.; Starbears; The right word; Kissing Tennessee; The notes between the notes; These shoes

Graduating eighth graders relate their stories of love and heartbreak that have brought them to Dogwood Junior High's magical Stardust Dance.

"This collection will spark conversation in contemporary literature discussions, will quietly unsettle readers, and will elevate the quality of short-story collections." SLJ

Asimov, Isaac, 1920-1992

I, robot. Bantam hardcover ed. Bantam Books 2004 224p (Robot series) $24; pa $7.99

Grades: 7 8 9 10 11 12 Adult   S C

1. Science fiction 2. Robots—Fiction 3. Short stories 4. Science fiction 5. Short stories 6. Robots

ISBN 0-553-80370-0; 0-553-29438-5 (pa)

LC 2003-69139

First published 1950 by Gnome Press

Contents: Robbie; Runaround; Reason; Catch that rabbit; Liar!; Little lost robot; Escape!; Evidence; The evitable conflict

"These loosely connected stories cover the career of Dr. Susan Calvin and United States Robots, the industry that she heads, from the time of the public's early distrust of these robots to its later dependency on them. This collection is an important introduction to a theme often found in science fiction: the encroachment of technology on our lives." Shapiro. Fic for Youth. 3d edition

Aspin, Diana, 1947-

Ordinary miracles. Red Deer Press 2003 168p (Northern Lights young novels) pa $7.95

Grades: 7 8 9 10   S C

1. Canada—Fiction 2. Short stories

ISBN 0-88995-277-9

Contents: The home boy; The art of embalming; Cold snap; Frog palace; Jasmine, Ylang-Ylang, Rose; Roadkill; Sarah Moonglow; Hero; Moose; Mom?!; Ordinary miracles; Wings; The girl from the future

A collection of 13 short stories concerning life in a small Canadian community, covering such topics as an old man's memories of abandonment by his mother and his abusive life as an orphan, a teen's struggle with his sexuality, and issues such as alcoholism, death, adultery, and poverty.

This is "a riveting collection. . . . The author has created a work that leaves readers awash with feelings of empathy for each young protagonist." SLJ

Avi, 1937-

Strange happenings; five tales of transformation. Harcourt 2006 147p $15

Grades: 5 6 7 8   S C

1. Supernatural—Fiction 2. Short stories

ISBN 0-15-205790-0   LC 2004-29579

Contents: Bored Tom; Babette the beautiful; Curious; The shoemaker and Old Scratch; Simon

"In this short story collection, Avi offers five fantastical tales, set in both contemporary and fairy-tale lands, that explore the notion of transformation. . . . The pieces are vividly imagined and shot through with a captivating, edgy spookiness, which, along with their brevity and some droll, crackling dialogue, makes them great choices for sharing aloud in class or as inspiration in creative-writing units." Booklist

What do fish have to do with anything? and other stories; illustrated by Tracy Mitchell. Candlewick Press 1997 202p il hardcover o.p. pa $6.99

Grades: 4 5 6 7   S C

1. Short stories

ISBN 0-7636-0329-5; 0-7636-2319-9 (pa)

LC 97-1354

Avi, 1937-——*Continued*

Contents: What do fish have to do with anything?; The goodness of Matt Kaizer; Talk to me; Teacher tamer; Pets; What's inside; Fortune cookie

"Willie believes a homeless man possesses a cure for unhappiness. A minister dares his devilish son to be good. Pet-obsessed Eve receives visitations from two deceased cats. . . . These are among seven . . . stories dealing with communication in troubled relationships." Publisher's note

"While Avi's endings are not tidy, they are effective: each story brings its protagonist beyond childhood self-absorption to the realization that one is an integral part of a bigger picture." Horn Book

Baseball crazy: ten short stories that cover all the bases; edited by Nancy E. Mercado. Dial Books for Young Readers 2008 191p $16.99 *

Grades: 4 5 6 7   **S C**

1. Baseball—Fiction 2. Short stories

ISBN 978-0-8037-3162-2; 0-8037-3162-0

LC 2007-26649

Contents: The great Gus Zernial and me by Jerry Spinelli; Mark Pang and the impossible square by Frank Portman; Fall ball by Sue Corbett; Great moments in baseball by Paul Acampora; Riding the pine: a play by Ron Koertge; Tomboy forgiveness by David Rice; Just like Grampy by Charles Smith, Jr.; Smile like Jeter by Maria Testa; Baseball crazy by John H. Ritter; Ball hawk by Joseph Bruchac

"There's no shortage of great writing in this collection of 10 stories. Baseball unifies the entries, but the similarities end. . . . Readers will be drawn in by the masterful storytelling." Publ Wkly

Best shorts; favorite short stories for sharing; selected by Avi; assisted by Carolyn Shute; afterword by Katherine Paterson; [illustrations by Chris Raschka] Houghton Mifflin 2006 342p $16.95 *

Grades: 5 6 7 8   **S C**

1. Short stories

ISBN 978-0-618-47603-9; 0-618-47603-2

LC 2006011535

Contents: Rogue wave by Theodore Taylor; The caller by Robert D. San Souci; Scout's honor by Avi; The dog of Pompeii by Louis Untermeyer; LAFFF by Lensey Namioka; Rip Van Winkle by Washington Irving; Nuts by Natalie Babbitt; Flight of the swan by Marian Flandrick Bray; Ho-ichi the Earless by Rafe Martin; The lady who put salt in her coffee by Lucretia P. Hale; The town cats by Lloyd Alexander; Zlateh the goat by Isaac Bashevis Singer; To starch a spook by Andrew Benedict; The night of the pomegranate by Tim Wynne-Jones; The librarian and the robbers by Margaret Mahy; The woman in the snow by Patricia McKissack; The binnacle boy by Paul Fleischman; The baby in the night deposit box by Megan Whalen Turner; The circuit by Francisco Jiménez; The Widow Carey's chickens by Gerald Hausman; The special powers of Blossom Culp by Richard Peck; A white heron by Sarah Orne Jewett; Jimmy takes vanishing lessons by Walter R. Brooks; The lady or the tiger? by Frank Stockton

"There is no integrating theme in the 24 short stories included here—just fine writing, cultural diversity, and

timeless creativity. With such strong writers as Richard Peck, Natalie Babbitt, Lloyd Alexander, and Rafe Martin, one would expect nothing less." SLJ

The **Book** of dragons; selected and illustrated by Michael Hague. Morrow 1995 146p il $21.99; pa $10.99

Grades: 5 6 7 8   **S C**

1. Dragons—Fiction 2. Fantasy fiction 3. Short stories

ISBN 0-688-10879-2; 0-06-075968-2 (pa)

LC 94-42958

Contents: The dragon and the enchanted filly retold by Italo Calvino; The adventures of Eustace by C.S. Lewis; Perseus and Andromeda by Padraic Colum; The reluctant dragon by Kenneth Grahame; The flower queen's daughter retold by Andrew Lang; Li Chi slays the serpent by Kan Pao; Bilbo Baggins and Smaug by J.R.R. Tolkien; Uncle Lubin and the dragon by W. Heath Robinson; The deliverers of their country by E. Nesbit; The devil and his grandmother by the Brothers Grimm; Sigurd and Fafnir retold by Andrew Lang; The story of Wang Li by Elizabeth Coatsworth; St. George and the dragon retold by William H.G. Kingston; Stan Bolovan retold by Andrew Lang; The good sword retold by Ruth Bryan Owen; The dragon of Wantley; The dragon tamers by E. Nesbit

"Excerpts from classic novels such as J. R. R. Tolkien's *The Hobbit*, C. S. Lewis's *Voyage of the Dawn Treader*, and short stories such as Kenneth Grahame's 'The Reluctant Dragon' are included. In addition, there are folktales from China, Italy, and Germany. Most of the heroes are men, but occasionally children are the only ones who can outsmart the dragon. . . . Hague's beautiful full-page watercolors reflect the different moods of the stories and the temperaments of the dragons depicted." SLJ

Carter, Alden R.

Love, football, and other contact sports. Holiday House 2006 261p $16.95 *

Grades: 8 9 10 11 12   **S C**

1. Football—Fiction 2. School stories 3. Short stories

ISBN 978-0-8234-1975-3; 0-8234-1975-4

LC 2005-46094

Contents: A girl's guide to football players; A football player's guide to love; Kickoff (or never trust a girl who steals your ice cream sandwich); Trashback; Pig brains; Buck's head; Satyagraha; Elvis; The Ogre of Mensa; The gully; Kicker wanted; The briefcase; Jersey Day; Big Chicago; The ghost of Mum-Mum; The Doughnut boots his reputation; A good game.

This "collection of short stories, which revolves around Argyle West High School's football team, features an ensemble cast of students during their sophomore, junior, and senior years. . . . Written with sensitivity and conviction, the realistic stories are leavened with occasional, often ironic humor." Booklist

Cleavage; breakaway fiction for real girls; edited by Deb Loughead & Jocelyn Shipley. Sumach Press 2008 186p il pa $12.95

Grades: 8 9 10 11 12   **S C**

Cleavage—*Continued*
1. Short stories 2. Mother-daughter relationship—Fiction
ISBN 978-1-894549-76-9; 1-894549-76-7

Contents: Former juice girl eats world's largest taco by Valerie Hunter; Wax world by Anna WaSrje; Faceless on the farm by Ann Sutherland; About my curves by Robin Stevenson; The puberty theory by Kellee Ngan; Presenting Miss Gorilla Legs by Lisabeth Jackson; My mother's poison by Amanda Hartley; Change room by Patricia McCowan; Fat genes by Anne Ptasznik; The giant Regina by Wendy A. Lewis; My so not ballerina boobs by Jennifer Filipowicz; Profanity by Karen Krossing; Bare by Claire Tacon; My mom is a freak by Ev Bishop; The cake princess by Mar'ce Merrell.

"Alternately edgy, charming, funny, and sweet, these 15 stories address issues confronting adolescents. Integral to each selection is the complicated relationship between the girls and their mothers. . . . The selections touch on the multiple meanings of the word 'cleavage,' and together form an aptly named collection of stories about body image and mothers and daughters coming together and growing apart. A fresh, honest, and entertaining anthology." SLJ

The **Color** of absence; 12 stories about loss and hope; edited by James Howe. Atheneum Bks. for Young Readers 2001 238p hardcover o.p. pa $6.99
Grades: 7 8 9 10   S C
1. Short stories
ISBN 0-689-82862-4; 0-689-8567-9 (pa)
LC 00-44206

Contents: Summer of love by Annette Curtis Klause; What are you good at? by Roderick Townley; Atomic blues pieces by Angela Johnson; The tin butterfly by Norma Fox Mazer; The fire pond by Michael J. Rosen; Chair: a story for voices by Virginia Euwer Wolff; Red seven by C.B. Christiansen; Shoofly pie by Naomi Shihab Nye; You're not a winner unless your picture's in the paper by Avi; Season's end by Walter Dean Myers; The Rialto by Jacqueline Woodson and Chris Lynch; Enchanted night by James Howe

A collection of stories dealing with different kinds of loss experienced by young people.
"A solid choice for all collections." SLJ

Coville, Bruce
Oddest of all; stories by Bruce Coville. Harcourt 2008 235p $16
Grades: 6 7 8 9   S C
1. Horror fiction 2. Short stories
ISBN 978-0-15-205808-1; 0-15-205808-7
LC 2007-50298

Contents: In our own hands; What's the worst that could happen?; The ghost let go; In the frog king's court; The thing in Auntie Alma's pond; The hardest, kindest gift; The mask of Eamonn Tiyado; Herbert Hutchison in the underworld; The boy with silver eyes

A collection of nine short stories featuring ghosts, half-humans, unicorns, and other unusual creatures.
"The variety of fiction subgenres, brilliant use of themes, the stories' brief lengths, strong character viewpoints, and fast-paced action and resolution of story line make this collection a must-have." Voice Youth Advocates

Cowboy stories; illustrated by Barry Moser; introduction by Peter Glassman. Chronicle Books 2007 181p il $16.95
Grades: 7 8 9 10   S C
1. Cowhands—Fiction 2. Short stories
ISBN 978-0-8118-5418-4; 0-8118-5418-3
LC 2006-31568

Contents: Introduction by Peter Glassman; From Shane by Jack Schaefer; From Lonesome dove by Larry McMurtry; Top hand by Luke Short; A buffalo hunt by Nat Love; The gift of Cochise by Louis L'Amour; The blood bay by Annie Proulx; Three-ten to Yuma by Elmore Leonard; From The secret life of cowboys by Tom Groneberg; Twelve o'clock by Stephen Crane; From Riders of the purple sage by Zane Grey; Shallow graves by E. C. Teddy Blue Abbott; I woke up wicked by Dorothy M. Johnson; The bandana by J. Frank Dobie; From The Virginian by Owen Wister; Wine on the desert by Max Brand; From Biting the dust by Dirk Johnson; Hewey and the wagon cook by Elmer Kelton; From Breaking clean by Judy Blunt; The reformation of Calliope by O. Henry; Long ride back by Ed Gorman; Home on the range by Brewster Higley

"This collection of 20 stories by well-known writers features the most American of icons, the cowboy. . . . Some of the selections are excerpts from well-known novels such as *Shane* and *The Virginian*. Others are short stories by Western authors including Annie Proulx and Louis L'Amour. Actual cowboys, Nat Love and 'Teddy Blue' Abbott, offer exciting accounts of their lives. A significant feature here is Moser's artwork. Twenty-two stunning black-and-white engravings offer up the true grit of their cowboy subjects and galvanize readers." SLJ

Crutcher, Chris, 1946-
Athletic shorts; six short stories. Greenwillow Bks. 1991 154p $17.99; pa $6.99 *
Grades: 7 8 9 10   S C
1. Sports—Fiction 2. Short stories
ISBN 0-688-10816-4; 0-06-050783-7 (pa)
LC 91-4418

Contents: A brief moment in the life of Angus Bethune; Pin; Other pin; Goin' fishin'; Telephone man; In the time I get

A collection of short stories about high school sports
"The author seamlessly blends humor with more serious elements. . . These *Athletic Shorts* will speak to YAs, touch them deeply, and introduce them to characters they'll want to know better." SLJ

Dahl, Roald
Skin and other stories. Viking 2000 212p $15.99; pa $8.99
Grades: 7 8 9 10   S C
1. Short stories
ISBN 0-670-89184-3; 0-14-131034-0 (pa)
LC 99-58600

Contents: Skin; Lamb to the slaughter; The sound machine; An African story; Galloping Foxley; The wish; The surgeon; Dip in the pool; The champion of the world; Beware of the dog; My lady love, my dove

A collection of 13 of the author's short stories written for adults. "Full of irony and unexpected twists, they

Dahl, Roald—*Continued*

smack of the master's touch—every word carefully chosen, characters fully fleshed out in only a few pages, the sense of place immediate." Booklist

De Lint, Charles, 1951-

Waifs and strays; preface by Terri Windling. Viking 2002 394p $17.99; pa $7.99

Grades: 7 8 9 10   **S C**

1. Supernatural—Fiction 2. Short stories

ISBN 0-670-03584-X; 0-14-240158-7 (pa)

LC 2002-23314

Contents: Merlin dreams in the Moondream Wood; There's no such thing; Sisters; Fairy dust; A wish named Arnold; Wooden bones; The graceless child; A tattoo on her heart; Stick; May this be your last sorrow; One chance; Alone; But for the grace go I; Ghosts of wind and shadow; Waifs and strays; Somewhere in my mind there is a painting box

"De Lint offers sixteen of his previously published short stories about coming of age, dividing the collection into locations familiar from his previous works. . . . Throughout the stories, characters confront physical, emotional, and psychological dangers. . . . The book creates emotionally believable characters and uses their fantastical settings to deal with powerful archetypal themes such as abandonment, bereavement, and redemption." Bull Cent Child Books

Del Negro, Janice

Passion and poison; tales of shape-shifters, ghosts, and spirited women. Marshall Cavendish 2007 64p il $16.99 *

Grades: 5 6 7 8   **S C**

1. Ghost stories 2. Supernatural—Fiction 3. Short stories

ISBN 978-0-76145-361-1; 0-7614-5361-1

LC 2007-07237

Contents: The bargain; Rosie Hopewell; Skulls and bones, ghosts and gold; The severed hand; Rubies; Seachild; Hide and seek

"Including both original tales and retellings, this collection of seven stories . . . features diverse female protagonists facing challenges and perils—from human bullies to ghosts. More eerie than scary, the tales of bravery, revenge, grief, and redemption share a gothic sensibility. . . . The black-and-white illustrations . . . evoke bygone times." Booklist

Delacre, Lulu, 1957-

Salsa stories; stories and linocuts by Lulu Delacre. Scholastic Press 2000 105p il $15.95; pa $4.50 *

Grades: 4 5 6   **S C**

1. Latin America—Fiction 2. Family life—Fiction 3. Short stories

ISBN 0-590-63118-7; 0-590-63121-7 (pa)

LC 99-25534

Contents: New Years Day; A carpet for Holy Week; At the beach; The night of San Juan; Teatime; Birthday piñata; The Lord of Miracles; Aguinaldo; Carmen Teresa's gift

A collection of stories within the story of a family celebration where the guests relate their memories of growing up in various Latin American countries. Also contains recipes

"Kids will respond to both the warmth and the anxiety of the family life described in the vivid writing, and in Delacre's nicely composed linocuts." Booklist

Destination unexpected: short stories; collected by Donald R. Gallo. Candlewick Press 2003 240p hardcover o.p. pa $8.99

Grades: 7 8 9 10   **S C**

1. Short stories

ISBN 0-7636-1764-4; 0-7636-3119-1 (pa)

LC 2002-71599

Contents: Something old, something new by J. Sweeney; Brutal interlude by R. Koertge; Bread on the water by D. Lubar; My people by M. P. Haddix; Bad blood by W. Weaver; Keep smiling by A. Flinn; August lights by K. W. Holt; Mosquito by G. Salisbury; The kiss in the carry-on bag by R. Peck; Tourist trapped by E. Wittlinger

This collection "features teen protagonists experiencing a transforming experience while on some kind of journey. . . . . Whether humorous or serious, the stories are consistently well written and engaging." Booklist

Does this book make me look fat? edited by Marissa Walsh. Clarion Books 2008 215p $16

Grades: 7 8 9 10 11 12   **S C**

1. Obesity—Fiction 2. Eating disorders—Fiction 3. Short stories

ISBN 978-0-547-01496-8; 0-547-01496-1

LC 2008-25070

Contents: Circumferentially challenged by Daniel Pinkwater; Mirror, mirror by Megan McCafferty; Alterations by Eireann Corrigan; Last red light before we're there by Matt de la Peña; Sweet 16 plus by Wendy McClure; Some girls are bigger than others by Sarra Manning; Tale of a half-pint by Margo Rabb; The day before Waterlily arrived by Jaclyn Moriarty; Hello ... my name is by Carolyn Mackler; The mating habits of whales by Barry Lyga, illustrated by Jeff Dillon; It is good by Sara Zarr; Pretty, hungry by Ellen Hopkins; How to tame a wild booty by Coe Booth; Confessions of a former It Girl by Wendy Shanker

"This star-studded collection tackles a popular topic—body image—with humor, sensitivity, and creativity. . . . [It includes] Megan McCafferty's story narrated by a pair of skinny jeans. Other highlights are Matt de la Peña's wrenching story of a young man coming to terms with his sister's devastating eating disorder, and Sarra Manning's feisty protagonist, who helps a co-worker find her own style and later faces her own body issues." Booklist

Don't cramp my style; stories about that time of the month; edited by Lisa Rowe Fraustino. Simon & Schuster for Young Readers 2004 295p $15.95

Grades: 7 8 9 10   **S C**

1. Menstruation—Fiction 2. Short stories

ISBN 0-689-85882-5

Contents: Introduction "snapshots in blood" by Michelle H. Martin; Taking care of things by Pat Brisson; Heroic quest of Douglas McGawain by David Lubar;

Don't cramp my style—*Continued*

Moon time child by Alice McGill; Women's house by Dianne Ochiltree; Czarevna of muscovy by Joan Elizabeth Goodman; Sleeping beauty by Lisa Rowe Fraustino; Transfusion by Joyce McDonald; Maroon by Han Nolan; Ritual purity by Deborah Heiligman; Losing it by Julie Stockler; Uterus fairy by Linda Oatman High

A collection of eleven stories concerning menstruation. "This highly recommended collection . . . encompasses an impressive variety of times, cultures, attitudes, and moods. . . . The writing . . . is consistently excellent." Voice Youth Advocates

Doyle, Sir Arthur Conan, 1859-1930

The adventures of Sherlock Holmes; illustrated by Barry Moser; afterword by Peter Glassman. Books of Wonder 1992 342p il $27.99 *

Grades: 7 8 9 10 11 12 Adult   S C

1. Mystery fiction 2. Short stories

ISBN 0-688-10782-6; 978-0-688-10782-6

LC 91-39632

A collection of Sherlock Holmes mystery adventures, including "A Scandal in Bohemia," "The Red-headed League," and "The Adventure of the Speckled Band."

Ellis, Deborah, 1960-

Lunch with Lenin and other stories. Fitzhenry & Whiteside 2008 169p $14.95

Grades: 7 8 9 10 11 12   S C

1. Drug abuse—Fiction 2. Short stories

ISBN 978-1-55455-105-7 (pa); 1-55455-105-6 (pa)

Contents: Through the woods; Pretty flowers; Lunch with Lenin; Dancing, with beads; Prodigal; Red hero at midnight; Another night in Disneyland; Cactus people

A collection of short stories that explore the lives of teenagers affected directly or indirectly by drugs.

"The relatively short stories read quickly, offering neither judgment nor solutions but rather the opportunity for compassion and understanding. . . . The collection's quality . . . is high enough to justify placing this book in every library." Voice Youth Advocates

Estevis, Anne

Down Garrapata road; by Anne Estevis. Arte Piñata Books 2003 119p pa $12.95

Grades: 7 8 9 10   S C

1. Mexican Americans—Fiction 2. Texas—Fiction 3. Short stories

ISBN 1-55885-397-9   LC 2003-49837

Contents: The Chávez family: Tia Pina and the Chupasangre; The dancing queens of Garrapata Road; The whistle; The gift of tranquilino trujillo; Chatita's night out; The Bermúdez family: Her brother's keeper; La Tamalada; The virgin and Doña Fidelfa; The Zambrano family: A reluctant scholar; The battle of the blackbirds; The Paloma family: Crazy Rita; The prisoner; A fork in the road

A collection of short stories set in a small Mexican-American community in southern Texas during the 1940s and 1950s, revealing the traditions, love, and social concerns of the families living there.

"Sly, gentle, and written in lively, simple language, these are stories that will draw readers into the particulars of a culture while capturing universal family dramas." Booklist

Every man for himself; ten short stories about being a guy; edited by Nancy E. Mercado. Dial Books 2005 154p il $16.99; pa $6.99 *

Grades: 7 8 9 10   S C

1. Short stories 2. Boys—Fiction

ISBN 0-8037-2896-4; 0-14-240813-1 (pa)

LC 2004-24069

Contents: The prom prize by Walter Dean Myers; Jump away by René Saldaña, Jr.; No more birds will die today by Paul Acampora; Shockers by David Lubar; Pig lessons by Edward Averett; Strange powers by Craig Thompson; The unbeatable by Mo Willems; Princes by David Levithan; Fear by Terry Trueman; It's complicated by Ron Koertge

"This collection provides a refreshing look at the values, decisions, and friendships that ultimately shape a boy into a man. The stories themselves are diverse, ranging from humorous to serious." SLJ

Face relations; 11 stories about seeing beyond color. Simon & Schuster Books for Young Readers 2004 224p $17.95

Grades: 7 8 9 10   S C

1. Race relations—Fiction 2. Short stories

ISBN 0-689-85637-7

Contents: Phat acceptance by Jess Mowry; Skins by Joseph Bruchac; Snow by Sherri Winston; The heartbeat of the soul of the world by René Saldaña, Jr.; Hum by Naomi Shihab Nye; Epiphany by Ellen Wittlinger; Black and white by Kyoko Mori; Hearing flower by M.E. Kerr; Gold by Marina Budhos; Mr. Ruben by Rita Williams-Garcia; Negress by Marilyn Singer

"Contributed by familiar writers for young people, including Ellen Wittlinger, M. E. Kerr, Rita Williams-Garcia, Naomi Shihab Nye, and Jess Mowry, the stories ask challenging questions about what role race plays in family life, at school, in friendships, and in love. . . . This is a provocative collection." Booklist

Firebirds; an anthology of original fantasy and science fiction; edited by Sharyn November. Firebird Press 2003 420p il $19.99

Grades: 7 8 9 10 11 12   S C

1. Fantasy fiction 2. Science fiction 3. Short stories

ISBN 0-14-250142-5

Contents: Cotillion by Delia Sherman; The baby in the night deposit box by Megan Whalen Turner; Beauty by Sherwood Smith; Mariposa by Nancy Springer; Max Mondrosch by Lloyd Alexander; The fall of Ys by Meredith Ann Pierce; Medusa by Michael Cadnum; The black fox by Emma Bull (adaptation) and Charles Vess (illustrations); Byndley by Patricia A. McKillip; The lady of the ice garden by Kara Dalkey; Hope chest by Garth Nix; Chasing the wind by Elizabeth E. Wein; Little Dot by Diana Wynne Jones; Remember me by Nancy Farmer; Flotsam by Nina Kiriki Hoffman; The flying woman by Laurel Winter

"Teens will find much to savor and celebrate in this dazzling collection of 16 short stories by some of the best fantasy writers around." SLJ

Firebirds rising; an anthology of original science
fiction and fantasy; edited by Sharyn November.
Firebird 2006 530p $19.99
Grades: 7 8 9 10 11 12   **S C**
1. Science fiction 2. Fantasy fiction 3. Short stories
ISBN 0-14-240549-3; 978-0-14-240549-9
Contents: Huntress by Tamora Pierce; Unwrapping by
Nina Kiriki Hoffman; The real thing by Alison Good-
man; Little (Grrl) lost by Charles de Lint; I'll give you
my word by Diana Wynne Jones; In the house of the
seven librarians by Ellen Klages; Wintermoon wish by
Sharon Shinn; The wizards of Perfil by Kelly Link; Jack
o'Lantern by Patricia A. McKillip; Quill by Carol
Emshwiller; Blood roses by Francesca Lia Block; Hives
by Kara Dalkey; Perception by Alan Dean Foster; The
house on the planet by Tanith Lee; Cousins by Pamela
Dean; What used to be good still is by Emma Bull
This is a collection of sixteen science fiction and fantasy stories.
"This anthology is a wonderful choice for any young
adult collection." Voice Youth Advocates

Firebirds soaring; an anthology of original
speculative fiction; [edited by Sharyn
November; illustrated by Mike Dringenberg]
Firebird 2009 574p il $19.99
Grades: 7 8 9 10 11 12   **S C**
1. Fantasy fiction 2. Science fiction 3. Short stories
ISBN 978-0-14-240552-9; 0-14-240552-3
                     LC 2008-29516
Contents: Kingmaker by Nancy Springer; A ticket to
ride by Nancy Farmer; A thousand tails by Christopher
Barzak; All under heaven by Chris Roberson; Singing on
a star by Ellen Klages; Egg magic by Louise Marley;
Flatland by Kara Dalkey; Dolly the dog-soldier by
Candas Jane Dorsey; Ferryman by Margo Lanagan; The
ghosts of strangers by Nina Kiriki Hoffman; Twilight
tales by Jo Walton; The dignity he's due by Carol
Emshwiller; Power and magic by Marly Youmans; Court
ship by Sherwood Smith; Little Red by Jane Yolen and
Adam Stemple; The myth of Fenix by Laurel Winter;
Fear and loathing in Lalanna by Nick O'Donohoe; Bone-
chewer's legacy by Clare Bell; Something worth doing
by Elizabeth E. Wein
This anthology "contains 19 short stories by some of
the top writers in this genre. . . . The selections vary in
length, with some short stories, some novellas. Each
work is introduced by an evocative illustration that beautifully sets the scene for the written work. The variety of
styles and themes and a gathering together of so many
talented writers in one work offer readers a banquet for
the imagination. For fans of the genre, this is a must
read." SLJ

Flake, Sharon G.
Who am I without him? short stories about girls
and the boys in their lives. Jump at the
Sun/Hyperion Books for Children 2004 168p
$15.99; pa $7.99 *
Grades: 7 8 9 10   **S C**
1. African Americans—Fiction 2. Short stories
ISBN 0-7868-0693-1; 1-4231-0383-1 (pa)
Contents: So I ain't no good girl; The ugly one;
Wanted: a thug; I know a stupid boy when I see one;

Mookie in love; Don't be disrespecting me; I like white
boys; Jacob's rules; Hunting for boys; A letter to my
daughter
Ten short stories about African American teenage girls
and their relationships with boys.
"Addressing issues and situations that many girls face
in today's often complex society, this book is provocative and thought-provoking." SLJ

Fleischman, Paul
Graven images; three stories; by Paul
Fleischman; illustrations by Bagram Ibatoulline.
Candlewick Press 2006 116p il $16.99; pa $5.99
Grades: 5 6 7 8   **S C**
1. Supernatural—Fiction 2. Short stories
ISBN 0-7636-2775-5; 0-7636-2984-7 (pa)
                     LC 2005054283
A Newbery Medal honor book, 1983
A newly illustrated edition with a new afterword of
the title first published 1982 by Harper & Row
Contents: The binnacle boy; Saint Crispin's follower;
The man of influence
A collection of three stories about a child who reads
the lips of those who whisper secrets into a statue's ear;
a daydreaming shoemaker's apprentice who must find
ways to make the girl he loves notice him; and a stone
carver who creates a statue of a ghost.
"Readers will be delighted with the return to print of
[this title] with haunting new acrylic gouache illustrations
. . . evoking the spinetingling aspects of this trio of
tales. . . . Via a new afterword, the author explains the
stories' inspiration and describes this book's significance
early in his career." Publ Wkly

Friends; stories about new friends, old friends,
and unexpectedly true friends; edited by Ann M.
Martin and David Levithan. Scholastic Press
2005 185p $16.95
Grades: 5 6 7 8   **S C**
1. Friendship—Fiction 2. Short stories
ISBN 0-439-72991-2   LC 2004-27758
Contents: The friend who changed my life by Pam
Muñoz Ryan; My best friend by Jennifer L. Holm; Con-
nie Hunter Williams, psychic teacher by Meg Cabot;
Squirrel by Ann M. Martin; Smoking lessons by Patricia
McCormick; Shashikala: a brief history of love and khadi
by Tanuja Desai Hidier; The Wild Prince by Brian
Selznick; Flit by Patrick Jennings; The Justice League by
David Levithan; Minka and Meanie by Rachel Cohn;
Doll by Virginia Euwer Wolff
"This collection of stories by well-known authors
spans a broad definition of the term 'friend,' and also ap-
proaches the topic from a wide variety of viewpoints.
. . . The selections by Ann M. Martin, Pam Muñoz
Ryan, Rachel Cohn, David Levithan, and Patricia Mc-
Cormick are among the more outstanding entries. . . . It
is also likely that every reader will find at least one that
hits home." SLJ

Full house; 10 stories about poker; edited by Pete
Hautman. G. P. Putnam's Sons 2007 161p
$17.99
Grades: 7 8 9 10   **S C**
1. Poker—Fiction 2. Short stories
ISBN 978-0-399-24528-2   LC 2007-14116

Full house—*Continued*

Contents: Poker for the complete idiot by K. L. Going; Positively cheat street by Francine Pascal; Dealing with the devil by Adam Stemple; The cards that are hidden by Alex Flinn; Sportin' men by Gary Phillips; The royal couple by Mary Logue; Fiddy dolla smile by Bill Fitzhugh; Suicide king by Walter Sorrells; The scholarship game by Pete Hautman; Up the river by Will Weaver

This is a "compilation of stories about teenage encounters with poker. The characters find themselves in high-stakes situations: playing with the Devil, competing in a scholarship game, fighting to defeat a deadbeat stepdad, and staying one step ahead of an Internet poker company. . . . The stories vary from the eerily realistic to amusingly farfetched. In all cases, teen poker players will recognize themselves and their opponents in this diverse collection." SLJ

Gaiman, Neil, 1960-

M is for magic; illustrations by Teddy Kristiansen. HarperCollins Pub. 2007 260p il $16.99; lib bdg $17.89; pa $6.99 *

Grades: 7 8 9 10   S C

1. Magic—Fiction 2. Short stories

ISBN   978-0-06-118642-4;   0-06-118642-2; 978-0-06-118645-5 (lib bdg); 0-06-118645-7 (lib bdg); 978-0-06-118647-9 (pa); 0-06-118647-3 (pa)

LC 2007-14472

Contents: The case of the four and twenty blackbirds; Troll bridge; Don't ask Jack; How to sell the Ponti Bridge; October in the chair; Chivalry; The price; How to talk to girls at parties; Sunbird; The witch's headstone; Instructions

Gaiman "has selected nine of his short stories and a poem and added a segment from an upcoming children's title for this volume. . . . This well-chosen collection is sure to create a new generation of Gaiman fans who will not need to understand all the allusions to enjoy the stories." Booklist

Give me shelter; stories about children who seek asylum; edited by Tony Bradman. Frances Lincoln 2007 220p $16.95

Grades: 5 6 7 8   S C

1. Refugees—Fiction 2. Short stories

ISBN 978-1-84507-522-4; 1-84507-522-6

Contents: Baa and the angels by Nicki Cornwell; Only up from here by Sulaiman Addonia; Samir Hakkim's healthy eating diary by Miriam Halahmy; A nice quiet girl by Gaye Hicyilmaz; Little fish by Kim Kitson; Give me shelter by Solomon Gebremedhin; Cherry studel by Leslie Wilson; Writing to the president by Kathleen McCreery; Beans for tea by Lucy Henning and Saeda Elmi; A place to hide by Rob Porteous; Final border by Lily Hyde

This is a "moving collection of 11 powerful narratives, quite different in their particulars but astonishingly similar in their sense of loss and loneliness. . . . While most of the stories focus on current asylum-seekers in Britain, one looks back to a Vietnamese child's trip to Australia, and another is set in an unnamed Eastern European country." SLJ

Gothic!; ten original dark tales; edited by Deborah Noyes. Candlewick Press 2004 241p $15.99; pa $7.99

Grades: 7 8 9 10   S C

1. Horror fiction 2. Short stories

ISBN 0-7636-2243-5; 0-7636-2737-2 (pa)

LC 2004-45188

Contents: Lungewater by Joan Aiken; Morgan Roehmar's boys by Vivian Vande Velde; Watch and wake by M.T. Anderson; Forbidden brides of the faceless slaves in the nameless house of the night of dread desire by Neil Gaiman; The dead and the moonstruck by Caitlin R. Kiernan; Have no fear, Crumpot is here! by Barry Yourgrau; Stone tower by Janni Lee Simner; The prank by Gregory Maguire; Writing on the wall by Celia Rees; Endings by Garth Nix

This is a "collection features short stories by noted young adult authors such as M. T. Anderson, Caitlín R. Kiernan, Garth Nix, Celia Rees, Janni Lee Simner, and Barry Yourgrau. . . . These varied tales take place in the distant past and in the high-tech present. Some are humorous while others have surprising twists or are reminiscent of classic fairy tales full of malevolent characters, but all share a love of the surreal or supernatural. . . . A sophisticated, thought-provoking, and gripping read." SLJ

Half-human; compiled & edited by Bruce Coville; photo illustrations by Marc Tauss. Scholastic Press 2001 212p il $16.95; pa $5.99 *

Grades: 7 8 9 10   S C

1. Fantasy fiction 2. Short stories

ISBN 0-590-95944-1; 0-590-95588-8 (pa)

LC 00-50524

Contents: Becoming by Nancy Springer; Princess Dragonblood by Jude Mandell; How to make a human by Lawrence Schimel; Linnea by D.J. Malcolm; Soaring by Tim Waggoner; Water's edge by Janni Lee Simner; Elder brother by Tamora Pierce; Scarecrow by Gregory Maguire; Centaur Field by Jane Yolen; The hardest, kindest gift by Bruce Coville

A collection of 9 stories and one poem about such creatures as mermaids and centaurs, who are part-human and part-animal or part-plant.

Readers "will be intrigued with this unusual collection of well-written fantasies that illustrate the adolescent challenge of discovering both our animal and human natures." Booklist

Hearne, Betsy Gould, 1942-

The canine connection: stories about dogs and people; [by] Betsy Hearne. Margaret K. McElderry Bks. 2003 113p $15.95; pa $8.95

Grades: 5 6 7 8   S C

1. Dogs—Fiction 2. Short stories

ISBN 0-689-85258-4; 1-416-96817-2 (pa)

LC 2001-58991

Contents: Lab; Restaurant; Room 313; Cargo; The drive; A grave situation; Fiona and Tim; The nose; Nameless creek; The canine connection; The boss; Bones

Twelve short stories that reflect the varied ways that dogs and humans relate

"The emotions and dialogue are pitch perfect. . . . A rewarding collection that will stay with readers." Booklist

Hearne, Betsy Gould, 1942— —*Continued*
Hauntings, and other tales of danger, love, and sometimes loss. Greenwillow Books 2007 211p $15.99; lib bdg $16.89 *
Grades: 5 6 7 8   **S C**
1. Ghost stories 2. Death—Fiction 3. Supernatural— Fiction 4. Short stories
ISBN   978-0-06-123910-6;   0-06-123910-0; 978-0-06-123911-3 (lib bdg); 0-06-123911-9 (lib bdg)
                   LC 2006033711

Contents: Rys; Fortress; Lost; Hauntings; Coins; Nurse's fee; The crossing; The letter; Fall; Loose chippings; Angel; Unnatural guests; Secret trees; Light; The devil and the dog

Ten stories of death and hauntings, set in the past, the present, and the afterlife.

"The settings of these 15 stories are painted with sure, deft, and simple strokes that use both action and mood to focus the reader's imagination." Booklist

Heyman, Alissa
The big book of horror; 21 tales to make you tremble; [adaptation and abridgement by Alissa Heyman]; illustrated by Pedro Rodriguez. Sterling 2006 108p il $12.95
Grades: 4 5 6   **S C**
1. Horror fiction 2. Short stories
ISBN 978-1-4027-3860-9

Contents: Signalman by Charles Dickens; Green eyes by Gustavo Adolfo Becquer; Vampire by John William Polidori; Murders in the rue morgue by Edgar Allen Poe; Bodysnatcher by Robert Louis Stevenson; Hand by Guy de Maupassant; Fall the of the House of Usher by Edgar Allan Poe; Torture by hope by Villiers de Isle Adam; He? by Guy de Maupassant; Pit and the pendulum by Edgar Allan Poe; Outsider by H.P. Lovecraft; Power of mind Morella by Edgar Allen Poe; House of the nightmare by Edward Lucas White; Magnetism by Guy de Maupassant; Facts in the case of M. Valdemar by Edgar Allan Poe; Sir Dominick's bargain by Sheridan Le Fanu; Green monster 88 by Gerard de Nerval; Tropical horror 92 by William Hope Hodgson; Black cat by Edgar Allan Poe; Werewolf by Eugene Field

Presents abridged and adapted versions of twenty-one horror stories, including Charles Dickens' "The Signalman" and Edgar Allan Poe's "The Black Cat."

"These simplified stories read smoothly, and children will find this collection of 21 horror tales quite engaging. . . . Unusually well designed for a collection of scary stories, this large-format volume features dramatically composed illustrations using unusual but effective color combinations and a fine sense of the macabre." Booklist

Holt, Kimberly Willis
Part of me; stories of a Louisiana family. 1st ed. H. Holt 2006 208p $16.95
Grades: 7 8 9 10   **S C**
1. Family life—Fiction 2. Louisiana—Fiction 3. Short stories
ISBN 978-0-8050-6360-8; 0-8050-6360-9
                   LC 2005-29676
Contents: Rose: Beans and cornbread; Fisherman; Books on the bayous; Merle Henry: Trapped; Playing hooky; Annabeth: Fairy tale; Squealers; Klye: Summer job; Missing Harry; Rose: Been down that road

Ten stories trace the connections between four generations of one Louisiana family from 1939 when a young girl leaves school to help support her family to 2006 when an eighty-year-old woman embarks on a book tour.

"Holt once again excels at creating character and an evocative sense of place." SLJ

Horowitz, Anthony, 1955-
Horowitz horror; [by] Anthony Horowitz. 1st American ed. Philomel Books 2006 c1999 217p $10.99 *
Grades: 7 8 9 10   **S C**
1. Horror fiction 2. Short stories
ISBN 0-399-24489-1   LC 2005058609
First published 1999 in the United Kingdom
Contents: Bath night; Killer camera; Light moves; The night bus; Harriet's horrible dream; Scared; A career in computer games; The man with the yellow face; The monkey's ear

"In this collection of nine macabre tales, Horowitz proves himself as adept at spooky psychological horror as he is at creating breakneck adventure-suspense." Booklist

More Horowitz horror; stories you'll wish you'd never read; [by] Anthony Horowitz. 1st American ed. Philomel Books 2006 210p $11.99 *
Grades: 7 8 9 10   **S C**
1. Horror fiction 2. Short stories
ISBN 978-0-399-24519-0   LC 2006045583
Contents: The hitchhiker; The sound of murder; Burned; Flight; Howard's end; The elevator; The phone goes dead; Twist cottage; The shortest horror story ever written

A collection of frightening tales.

This "cements [Horowitz's] reputation in the horror genre by once again yanking young readers out of their safe, familiar world." Booklist

Jacques, Brian
The Ribbajack & other curious yarns. Philomel Books 2004 168p $16.99
Grades: 5 6 7 8   **S C**
1. Ghost stories 2. Short stories
ISBN 0-399-24220-1   LC 2003-66448
Contents: The Ribbajack; A smile and a wave; The All Ireland Champion versus the Nye Add; The mystery of Huma D'este; Miggy Mags and the Malabar Sailor; Rosie's pet

"Jacques offers six original ghost stories." SLJ

These are "wickedly imagined yarns filled with surprises and the cheerful satisfaction of seeing some thoroughly nasty villains come to grief." Booklist

Join in; multiethnic short stories by outstanding writers for young adults; edited by Donald R. Gallo. Delacorte Press 1993 256p pa $5.99 hardcover o.p.
Grades: 7 8 9 10   **S C**
1. Short stories
ISBN 0-440-21957-4 (pa)   LC 92-43169
Contents: Expectations: Into the game by Rita Williams-Garcia; Fox hunt by Lensey Namioka; Eagle cloud

Join in—*Continued*

and fawn by Barbara Beasley Murphy; Next month...Hollywood! by Jean Davies Okimoto; Friendships: Viva New Jersey by Gloria Gonzalez; No win phuong by Alden R. Carter; A daughter of the sea by Maureen Crane Wartski; Dilemmas: Dead end by Rudolfo Anaya; Bride price by Linda Crew; My sweet sixteenth by Brenda Wilkinson; The child by Julius Lester; Connections: Rima's song by Elsa Marston; Godmother by Sharon Bell Mathis; Blues for Bob E. Brown by T. Ernesto Bethancourt; Confrontations: The alley by Danny Romero; Coming of age by Kleya Forte-Escamilla; The winter hibiscus by Minfong Ho

"The 17 stories cross the boundaries of race and culture and probe the universal themes of belonging, acceptance, family, and friendship." Booklist

"Diverse, thought-provoking, and consistently well-written." Kirkus

Kimmel, Eric A.

The jar of fools: eight Hanukkah stories from Chelm; illustrated by Mordicai Gerstein. Holiday House 2000 56p il $18.95 *

Grades: 4 5 6 7   S C

1. Hanukkah—Fiction 2. Short stories 3. Jews—Fiction

ISBN 0-8234-1463-9   LC 99-57823

Contents: The jar of fools; How they play dreidel in Chelm; Sweeter than honey, purer than oil; The Knight of the Golden Slippers; Silent Samson, the Maccabee; The magic spoon; The soul of a menorah; Wisdom for sale

Drawing on traditional Jewish folklore, these Hanukkah stories relate the antics of the people of Chelm, thought—perhaps incorrectly—to be a town of fools

"Kimmel gets the shtetl setting, the humanity, and the farce. . . . Gerstein's detailed ink-on-oil paint artwork, one full-page picture per story, captures the intricate silliness and slapstick." Booklist

Kipling, Rudyard, 1865-1936

The jungle book: the Mowgli stories; illustrated by Jerry Pinkney; afterword by Peter Glassman. Morrow 1995 258p il $22.95 *

Grades: 4 5 6 7   S C

1. Animals—Fiction 2. India—Fiction 3. Short stories

ISBN 0-688-09979-3   LC 92-1415

Contents: Mowgli's brothers; Hunting song of the Seeonee Pack; Kaa's hunting; Road song of the bandarlog; How fear came; The law of the jungle; "TigerTiger!"; Mowglie's song; Letting in the jungle; Mowglie's song gainst people; The king's ankus; The song of the little hunter; Red dog; Chil's song; The spring running; The outsong; "Rikkitikkitavi"; Darzee's chant

Selected stories from Kipling's two "Jungle Books" chronicle the adventures of Mowgli, the boy reared by a pack of wolves in an Indian jungle. Also includes "Rikki-Tikki-Tavi"

"The handsome illustrations in dappled watercolors show to admiration the lush jungle growth, the watchful animals, and Mowgli himself. A glorious pairing of text and illustration." Horn Book

Lanagan, Margo, 1960-

White time. Eos 2006 216p $15.99; lib bdg $16.89

Grades: 8 9 10 11 12   S C

1. Short stories

ISBN   978-0-06-074393-2;   0-06-074393-X; 978-0-06-074394-9 (lib bdg); 0-06-074394-8 (lib bdg)
LC 2005019755

Contents: White time; Dedication; Tell and kiss; The queen's notice; Big rage; The night lily; The boy who didn't yearn; Midsummer mission; Welcome blue; Wealth

Presents ten short stories, both dark and hopeful, that journey into the past, the future, and altered versions of the present.

"Each story underscores Lanagan's talent for inspiring curiosity, disturbing sensibilities, and provoking thought." Booklist

Lay-ups and long shots; an anthology of short stories; by Joseph Bruchac . . . [et al.] Darby Creek Pub. 2008 112p il $15.95

Grades: 4 5 6   S C

1. Sports—Fiction 2. Short stories

ISBN 978-1-58196-078-5; 1-58196-078-6

Contents: SWISH: a basketball story by Joseph Bruchac; Fat girls don't run by Lynea Bowdish; Bounceback by David Lubar; H-O-R-S-E by Terry Trueman; Amazing dirt girl rides again by C.S. Perryess; Riding the wave by Dorian Cirrone; Red shorts, white water by Jamie McEwan; Big foot by Max Elliot Anderson; Song of hope by Peggy Duffy

"These nine new short stories feature tweens or teens who, despite lack of skill or other obstacles, engage in athletic pursuits. Some . . . have autobiographical elements. . . . Consistently readable and engaging, the collection should have as much appeal for geeks as it does for jocks." Booklist

Lester, Julius

Long journey home: stories from black history. Dial Press (NY) 1972 147p pa $5.99 hardcover o.p.

Grades: 6 7 8 9   S C

1. African Americans—Fiction 2. Short stories

ISBN 0-14-038981-4 (pa)

Contents: Satan on my track; Louis; Ben; The man who was a horse; When freedom came; Long journey home

"Six original short stories based on real characters and incidents depict the drama and tragedy of the black experience." Chicago Public Libr

"In a foreword, Julius Lester explains that he has chosen minor figures because the mass of people were the 'movers of history' while the great figures are their symbols. . . . The selections are diversified in their settings and alike in their sharply-etched effectiveness." Bull Cent Child Books

Levithan, David, 1972-
How they met, and other stories. Alfred A. Knopf 2008 244p $16.99; lib bdg $19.99 *
Grades: 7 8 9 10   S C
1. Love stories 2. Short stories
ISBN 978-0-375-84886-5; 978-0-375-94886-2 (lib bdg)   LC 2007-10586
Contents: Starbucks boy; Miss Lucy had a steamboat; The alumni interview; The good witch; The escalator, a love story; The number of people who meet on airplanes; Andrew Chang; Flirting with waiters; Lost sometimes; Princes; Breaking and entering; Skipping the prom; A romantic inclination; What a song can do; Without saying; How they met; Memory dance; Intersection
A collection of eighteen stories describing the surprises, sacrifices, doubts, pain, and joy of falling in love.
"The author is a master of texture and detail. . . . Each richly imagined story will tap familiar veins of longing, memory, and anticipation." Bull Cent Child Books

Link, Kelly
Pretty monsters; stories; decorations by Shaun Tan. Viking 2008 389p il $19.99 *
Grades: 7 8 9 10   S C
1. Short stories 2. Fantasy fiction 3. Science fiction 4. Horror fiction
ISBN 978-0-670-01090-5; 0-670-01090-1   LC 2008-33251
Contents: The wrong grave; The wizards of Perfil; Magic for beginners; The faery handbag; The specialist's hat; Monster; The surfer; The constable of Abal; Pretty monsters
"Readers as yet unfamiliar with Link . . . will be excited to discover her singular voice in this collection of nine short stories, her first book for young adults. . . . Subjects . . . range from absurd to mundane, all observed with equidistant irony. . . . The author mingles the grotesque and the ethereal to make magic on the page." Publ Wkly

Love is hell; [by] Melissa Marr . . . [et al.] HarperTeen 2008 263p $16.99; pa $9.99
Grades: 7 8 9 10   S C
1. Love stories 2. Supernatural—Fiction 3. Short stories
ISBN 978-0-06-144305-3; 0-06-144305-0; 978-0-06-144304-6 (pa); 0-06-144304-2 (pa)   LC 2007-49574
Contents: Sleeping with the spirit by Laurie Stolarz; Stupid perfect world by Scott Westerfeld; Lammas day by Justine Larbalestier; Fan fictions by Gabrielle Zevin; Love struck by Melissa Marr
"Supernatural romance is the well-chosen theme of five original stories by as many authors. . . . There's enough variety to round out the central theme, and consistently supple storytelling will lure readers through all five entries." Publ Wkly

Magic in the mirrorstone; tales of fantasy; edited by Steve Berman. Wizards of the Coast 2008 295p $14.95
Grades: 8 9 10 11   S C
1. Fantasy fiction 2. Short stories
ISBN 978-0-7869-4732-4   LC 2007-31357

Contents: Princess Bufo marinus, also known as Amy by Eugie Foster; Lights, camera, action by Cecil Castellucci; Ten thousand waves by Ann Zeddies; Mauve's quilt by Craig Laurance Gidney; Have you ever seen a shoggoth? by Cassandra Clare; The Amulet of Winter by Lawrence M. Schoen; Veronica Brown by Sean Manseau; The jewel of abandon by by Nina Kiriki Hoffman; School spirit by Jim C. Hines; Blackwater baby by Tiffany Trent; Old crimes by J.D. Everyhope; The fortunate dream by Gregory Frost; Out of her element by E. Sedia; Virgin by Holly Black; Pig, crane, fox: three hearts unfolding by Beth Bernobich
An anthology of fifteen stories featuring such themes as amphibians that speak and enchanted jewelry.
"Ranging from funny to disquieting to bittersweet, the stories in this solid collection will appeal to most genre fans, including many adults." Booklist

Make me over; 11 stories of transformation; edited by Marilyn Singer. Dutton Children's Books 2005 199p $17.99
Grades: 7 8 9 10   S C
1. Short stories
ISBN 0-525-47480-3   LC 2005-02109
Contents: Some people call me Maurice by Joyce Sweeney; Not much to it by René Saldaña, Jr.; Bedhead red, peekaboo pink by Marilyn Singer; Vision quest by Peni R. Griffin; Wabi's ears by Joseph Bruchac; Honestly, truthfully by Terry Trueman; The resurrection by Jess Mowry; Bazooka Joe and the chaos kid by Norma Howe; The plan by Marina Budhos; Lucky six by Evelyn Coleman; Butterflies by Margaret Peterson Haddix.
These stories "delve into our culture's fascination with beauty and present different views about all kinds of makeovers." Publisher's note
"Sweet and spicy, tough and raw, these well-written stories will make a lasting impression on readers." Booklist

Marston, Elsa
Santa Claus in Baghdad and other stories about teens in the Arab world. Indiana University Press 2008 198p pa $15.95
Grades: 6 7 8 9 10   S C
1. Middle East—Fiction 2. Arab countries—Fiction 3. Short stories
ISBN 978-0-253-22004-2; 0-253-22004-1   LC 2007-50768
Includes notes which place the stories in context
Contents: Santa Claus in Baghdad: a story from Iraq (2000); Faces: a story from Syria; The hand of Fatima: a story from Lebanon; The olive grove: a story from Palestine; In line: a story from Egypt; Scenes in a Roman theater: a story from Tunisia; Honor: a story from Jordan; The plan: a story from a Palestinian refugee camp in Lebanon
A collection of eight stories, most previously published in other anthologies, about what it is like to grow up in the Middle East today.
"Marston, who has lived and visited the countries of which she writes, offers a realistic portrait of the Middle East that mixes possiblity and bleakness in equal measure." Voice Youth Advocates

McKinley, Robin

The door in the hedge. Greenwillow Bks. 1981 216p hardcover o.p. pa $6.99

Grades: 7 8 9 10   S C

1. Fairy tales 2. Short stories

ISBN 0-688-00312-5; 0-698-11960-6 (pa)

LC 80-21903

Contents: The stolen princess; The princess and the frog; The hunting of the hind; The twelve dancing princesses

The author "presents four romantic tales that elaborate—to a greater or lesser degree—upon the supernatural lore of fairy tale, myth, and legend. Two of the stories are original in plot and in characters. . . . The other two stories are literary recastings of Grimm tales, 'The Princess and the Frog' . . . {and} 'The Twelve Dancing Princesses.'" Horn Book

"These tales are well-written and enjoyable to read. It is too bad they lack illustrations." Child Book Rev Serv

Water: tales of elemental spirits; [by] Robin McKinley, Peter Dickinson. Putnam 2002 266p $18.99; pa $6.99

Grades: 7 8 9 10   S C

1. Fantasy fiction 2. Mermaids and mermen—Fiction 3. Short stories

ISBN 0-399-23796-8; 0-14-240244-3 (pa)

LC 2001-41642

Contents: Mermaid song by Peter Dickinson; The sea-king's son by Robin McKinley; Sea serpent by Peter Dickinson; Water horse by Robin McKinley; Kraken by Peter Dickinson; A pool in the desert by Robin McKinley

"These six stories, three by McKinley and three by her husband, Dickinson, feature the elemental spirits that inhabit Earth's waters." Voice Youth Advocates

"The masterfully written stories all feature distinct, richly detailed casts and settings . . . and focus as strongly on action as on character. There's plenty here to excite, enthrall, and move even the pickiest readers." SLJ

McKissack, Patricia C., 1944-

The dark-thirty; Southern tales of the supernatural; illustrated by Brian Pinkney. Knopf 1992 122p il $18.95; lib bdg $20.99; pa $6.50 *

Grades: 4 5 6 7   S C

1. Ghost stories 2. African Americans—Fiction 3. Short stories

ISBN 0-679-81863-4; 0-679-91853-9 (lib bdg); 0-679-89006-8 (pa)   LC 92-3021

A Newbery Medal honor book, 1993

Contents: The legend of Pin Oak; We organized; Justice; The 11:59; The sight; The woman in the snow; The conjure brother; Boo Mama; The gingi; The chicken-coop monster

A collection of ghost stories with African American themes, designed to be told during the Dark Thirty—the half hour before sunset—when ghosts seem all too believable

"Strong characterizations are superbly drawn in a few words. The atmosphere of each selection is skillfully developed and sustained to the very end. Pinkney's stark scratchboard illustrations evoke an eerie mood, which heightens the suspense of each tale." SLJ

Porch lies; tales of slicksters, tricksters, and other wily characters; [by] Patricia C. McKissack; illustrated by André Carrilho. 1st ed. Schwartz & Wade Books 2006 146p il $18.95 *

Grades: 4 5 6 7   S C

1. African Americans—Fiction 2. Short stories

ISBN 0-375-83619-5   LC 2005-22048

Contents: When Pete Bruce came to town; Change; The devil's guitar; Aunt Gran and the outlaws; By the weight of a feather; A grave situation; The best lie ever told; The earth bone and the King of the Ghosts; Cake: Norris lives on, Part one; Cake: Norris lives on, Part two

The "original tales in this uproarious collection draw on African American oral tradition and blend history and legend with sly humor, creepy horror, villainous characters, and wild farce. McKissack based the stories on those she heard as a child while sitting on her grandparents' porch. . . . Carrilho's full-page illustrations—part cartoon, part portrait in silhouette—combine realistic characters with scary monsters." Booklist

McRobbie, David, 1934-

A whole lot of Wayne; [by] David McRobbie. Allen & Unwin 2007 396p pa $12.95

Grades: 7 8 9 10   S C

1. Boys—Fiction 2. Short stories

ISBN 978-1-74175-244-1; 1-74175-244-2

"This collection has been adapted from stories in The Wayne dynasty, Waxing with Wayne and A little drop of Wayne, published by Mammoth Australia in 1989, 1991 and 1994" verso of title page

Contents: New school; U-turn; Wojjer Willmot; Fancy dressing; The minister's cat; The Wayne manifesto; Harris Weed; You can't take him anywhere; Reuben; A Wayne's gotta do what a Wayne's gotta do; Junk; Look before you leap; Now you see it, now you still see it; Pizza; The harder they fall; Show biz; Special operations; Soap; Work experience; We babysit anything; Amy; Pastrami day; Goose-pimples; Babes in the wood; Mutiny; Girls

"McRobbie thoroughly entertains readers with this charming and heartwarming collection of stories starring Wayne Wilson. Accompanied by his friend Squocka Berrington, the teen finds himself in a variety of hilarious and oftentimes precarious situations." SLJ

Moccasin thunder; American Indians stories for today; edited by Lori Marie Carlson. HarperCollins 2005 156p $15.99; lib bdg $16.89 *

Grades: 7 8 9 10   S C

1. Native Americans—Fiction 2. Short stories

ISBN 0-06-623957-5; 0-06-623959-1 (lib bdg)

LC 2004-22186

Contents: How to get to the planet Venus by Joy Harjo; Because my father always said he was the only Indian who saw Jimi Hendrix play "The Star Spangled Banner" at Woodstock by Sherman Alexie; A real-live blond Cherokee and his equally annoyed soul mate by Cynthia Leitich Smith; The last snow of the Virgin Mary by Richard Van Camp; Crow by Linda Hogan; Ice by Joseph Bruchac; Wild Geese by Louise Erdrich; The magic pony by Greg Sarris; Summer wind by Lee Francis; Drum Kiss by Susan Power

Moccasin thunder—*Continued*

Presents ten short stories about contemporary Native American teens by members of tribes of the United States and Canada, including Louise Erdrich and Joseph Bruchac

"This distinguished anthology offers powerful, beautifully written stories that are thoughtful and important for teens to hear." SLJ

My dad's a punk; 12 stories about boys and their fathers; edited by Tony Bradman. Kingfisher 2006 271p pa $7.95

Grades: 7 8 9 10   S C

1. Father-son relationship—Fiction 2. Short stories

ISBN 0-7534-5870-5

Contents: The wordwatcher by Joseph Wallace; My dad's a punk by Sean Taylor; Twenty crows by Ron Koertge; The Journey to Ompah by Tim Wynne-Jones; Superdad by Francis McCrickland; Later by Simon Cheshire; Whoosh! by Daniel Weitzman; Street Corner dad by Alan Gibbons; Handheld by Daniel Ehrenhaft; Begi-Begi and Jill-Jillie by Farrukh Dhondy; Cut me, and I bleed khaki by Terence Blacker; Glorius Fergus by Andrew Daddo

"Authors such as Ron Koertge, Tim Wynne-Jones, and Francis McCrickard explore father-son relationships in moving stories set in the past, present, and future. From bird watching to bird slaughter, divorced dads to gay dads, and close conversations to clandestine meetings on street corners, the situations and characters in each of these stories convey the depth and breadth of what it means to be a male in a family. A strong collection." Booklist

Myers, Walter Dean, 1937-

145th Street; short stories. Delacorte Press 2000 151p $15.95; lib bdg $18.99; pa $5.50

Grades: 7 8 9 10   S C

1. Harlem (New York, N.Y.)—Fiction 2. African Americans—Fiction 3. Short stories

ISBN 0-385-32137-6; 0-385-90538-6 (lib bdg); 0-440-22916-2 (pa)   LC 99-36097

Contents: Big Joe's funeral; The baddest dog in Harlem; Fighter; Angela's eyes; The streak; Monkeyman; Kitty and Mack: a love story; A Chirstmas story; A story in three parts; Block party—145th Street style

"These ten powerful stories create a vivid mosaic of life in the Harlem neighborhood of 145th Street. Memorable characters range from outgoing Big Joe, who decides to stage his own funeral party in *Big Joe's funeral*, to book-loving *Monkeyman*, who outsmarts the Tigros gang. . . . Beautifully told, Myers's stories offer an enticing collection for teens." Voice Youth Advocates

What they found; love on 145th street. Wendy Lamb Books 2007 243p $15.99; lib bdg $18.99 *

Grades: 8 9 10 11 12   S C

1. Harlem (New York, N.Y.)—Fiction 2. African Americans—Fiction 3. Family life—Fiction 4. Short stories

ISBN   978-0-385-32138-9;   0-385-32138-4; 978-0-375-93709-5 (lib bdg); 0-375-93709-9 (lib bdg)
LC 2007-7057

Companion volume to 145th street (2000)

Contents: The fashion show, grand opening, and barbque memorial service; What would Jesus do?; Mama; The life you need to have; Burn; Some men are just funny that way; Jump at the sun; Law and order; The man thing; Society for the Preservation of Sorry-Butt Negroes; Madonna; The real deal; Marisol and Skeeter; Poets and plumbers; Combat zone

Fifteen interrelated stories explore different aspects of love, such as a dying father's determination to help start a family business—a beauty salon—and the relationship of two teens who plan to remain celibate until they marry.

"Rich in both character and setting, these urban tales combine heartbreak and hope into a vivid tableau of a community. A priority purchase for all libraries, especially those in urban settings." SLJ

Naidoo, Beverley

Out of bounds: seven stories of conflict and hope. HarperCollins Pubs. 2003 c2001 175p $16.99; lib bdg $17.89

Grades: 5 6 7 8   S C

1. South Africa—Race relations—Fiction 2. Short stories

ISBN 0-06-050799-3; 0-06-050800-0 (lib bdg)
LC 2002-68901

First published 2001 in the United Kingdom

Contents: The dare; The noose; One day, Lily, one day; The typewriter; The gun; The playground; Out of bounds

Seven stories, spanning the time period from 1948 to 2000, chronicle the experiences of young people from different races and ethnic groups as they try to cope with the restrictions placed on their lives by South Africa's apartheid laws

"Naidoo's book reveals our humanity and inhumanity with starkness and precision. . . . She honors her country's past, present, and future with these brave tales." Horn Book

Necessary noise: stories about our families as they really are; edited by Michael Cart; illustrations by Charlotte Noruzi. Joanna Cotler Bks. 2003 239p $15.99; pa $8.99

Grades: 7 8 9 10   S C

1. Family life—Fiction 2. Short stories

ISBN 0-06-027499-9; 0-06-051437-X (pa)
LC 2002-151058

Contents: Hardware by J. Bauer; Siskiyou Sloan and the eye of the giraffe by N. Howe; Necessary noise by E. Donoghue; The throwaway: a suite by N. Grimes; Visit by W. D. Myers; A family illness: a mom-son conversation by J. C. Thomas; A woman's touch by R. Williams-Garcia; Sailing away by M. Cart; Dr. Jekyll and Sister Hyde by S. Sones; Snowbound by L. Lowry

"Ten original stories provide ten distinct perspectives on the quagmire that is 'family.' The result is a collection with considerable range and depth. . . . The style of the writers varies as much as their subjects: Joyce Carol Thomas offers a 'Mom-Son Conversation' about the frightening onset of schizophrenia; Sonya Sones's prose poems portray a light-and-dark relationship with an abusive sibling in 'Dr. Jekyll and Sister Hyde'. . . . Lois Lowry gives us a terrific finale with a clever and truthful story that reads like a one-act play." Horn Book Guide

Nix, Garth, 1963-

Across the wall; a tale of the Abhorsen and other stories. Eos 2005 305p $16.99; lib bdg $17.98 *

Grades: 7 8 9 10 S C
1. Fantasy fiction 2. Short stories
ISBN 0-06-074713-7; 0-06-074714-5 (lib bdg)

Contents: Nicholas Sayre and the creature in the case; Under the lake; Charlie Rabbit; From the lighthouse; The hill; Lightning Bringer; Down to the Scum Quarter; Heart's desire; Hansel's eyes; Hope chest; My new really epic fantasy series; Three roses; Endings

In *Nicholas Sayre and the creature of case*, the opening novella, "Nick encounters a bloodsucking Free Magic monster during a visit to Ancelstierre's top-secret intelligence agency. The story teasingly refers to British mysteries and spy fiction, parodic elements that will appeal most to Nix's adult fans. Even less-experienced readers, though, will enjoy getting to know Nick on his own terms. . . . The remaining 11 stories . . . include selections clearly intended for middle-graders as well as more sophisticated offerings containing frank references to sex and violence spattered with 'blood and brains and urine.' Buy this with the understanding that the packaging will attract the full spectrum of Nix's fans but that the younger ones may get more than they bargained for." Booklist

No such thing as the real world; a short story collection; [by] An Na [et al.]; introduction by Jill Santopolo; [compiled by Laura Geringer and Jill Santopolo] HarperTeen 2009 246p $16.99

Grades: 8 9 10 S C
1. Short stories
ISBN 978-0-06-147058-5; 0-06-147058-9
LC 2008-22583

"Laura Geringer books"

Contents: The projection by M.T. Anderson; Survival by K.L. Going; The longest distance by Beth Kephart; Arrangements by Chris Lynch; Complication by An Na; The company by Jacqueline Woodson

Six award-winning young adult authors present short stories featuring teens who have to face the 'real world' for the first time.

"This unique collection will challenge students' intellect and have them questioning their own decision-making skills. A fine balance is straddled between sophisticated prose and authentic teen voices, uninhibited and peppered with profanity." SLJ

Noyes, Deborah, 1965-

The ghosts of Kerfol. Candlewick Press 2008 163p $16.99 *

Grades: 8 9 10 11 12 S C
1. Short stories 2. Ghost stories 3. Supernatural—Fiction
ISBN 978-0-7636-3000-3; 0-7636-3000-4
LC 2007-51884

Over the centuries, the inhabitants of author Edith Wharton's fictional mansion, Kerfol, are haunted by the ghosts of dead dogs, fractured relationships, and the taste of bitter revenge.

This collection includes "five wonderfully chilling short stories." Publ Wkly

On the fringe; edited by Donald R. Gallo. Dial Bks. for Young Readers 2001 224p hardcover o.p. pa $6.99

Grades: 7 8 9 10 S C
1. Short stories
ISBN 0-8037-2656-2; 0-14-250026-7 (pa)
LC 00-40521

Contents: Geeks bearing gifts by Ron Koertge; Mrs. Noonan by Graham Salisbury; Shortcut by Nancy Werlin; Standing on the roof, naked by Francess Lantz; Through a window by Angela Johnson; Muzak for Prozac by Jack Gantos; Son by M.E. Kerr; WWJD by Will Weaver; Satyagraha by Alden R. Carter; A letter from the fringe by Joan Bauer; Guns for geeks by Chris Crutcher

"Kids who are geeks, unathletic, poor, emotionally fragile, loners, or unattractive by current standards form the heart of this collection of exceptional stories by well-known YA authors such as Joan Bauer, Chris Crutcher, and M. E. Kerr." SLJ

Once upon a cuento; edited by Lyn Miller-Lachman. Curbstone Press 2003 243p pa $15.95

Grades: 9 10 11 12 S C
1. Hispanic Americans—Fiction 2. Short stories
ISBN 1-88068-499-3 LC 2003-14667

Contents: Heritage, holidays, and contemporary culture: My ciguapa; A Nuyorican Christmas in el Bronx; Adventures in Mexican wrestling; Searching for Peter Z; Family life: Leaving before the snow; A special gift; Initiation; Good trouble for Lucy; The snake; Friends and other relationships: Sara and Panchito; Armpits, hair and other marks of beauty; Learning buddies; Indian summer sun; Dealing with differences: Leti's shoe escandalo; Dancing Miranda; That October; Grease

"Fourteen Latino authors have contributed to this collection of 17 short stories " SLJ

"Writing quality is consistenly high throughout. . . . This book . . . succeeds admirably in proving, through literature, that there is no single 'Latino experience.'" Voice Youth Advocates

Outside rules; short stories about nonconformist youth; edited, with an introduction by Claire Robson. Persea Books 2007 178p pa $9.95 *

Grades: 7 8 9 10 S C
1. Short stories
ISBN 0-89255-316-2; 978-0-89255-316-7
LC 2006-22548

"A Karen and Michael Braziller book"

Contents: A minstrel visits by Sandell Morse; Mr. Softee by Wally Lamb; My Tocaya by Sandra Cisneros; Surrounded by sleep by Akhil Sharma; One extra parking space by Jacqueline Sheehan; Laughing in the dark by Rand Richards Cooper; Nobody listens when I talk by Annette Sanford; Saint Chola by K. Kvashay-Boyle; The frontiers of knowledge by Claire Robson; Gypsy girl by Caitlin Jeffrey Lonning; April by Katharine Noel; The kind of light that shines on Texas by Reginald McKnight; Playing the garden by Chris Fisher; The white room by Rebecca Rule

An anthology of fourteen short stories about youth who do not quite fit in because they are too brainy, unathletic, poor, the "wrong" religion, emotionally frag-

Outside rules—*Continued*

ile, from nontraditional families, not model-thin, or simply bent on following a unique path.

"The collection is broadly multicultural, and the stories are consistently insightful, original, and discussion provoking in addition to being well written." Bull Cent Child Books

Owning it; stories about teens with disabilities; edited by Donald R. Gallo. Candlewick Press 2008 215p $17.99 *

Grades: 7 8 9 10   **S C**
1. Handicapped—Fiction 2. Diseases—Fiction
3. Short stories
ISBN 978-0-7636-3255-7; 0-7636-3255-4
                                        LC 2007-24963
Contents: Here's to good friends by David Lubar; Tic and Shout by Gail Giles; Triclops by Julie Anne Peters; Under control by Chris Crutcher; Way too cool by Brenda Woods; Good hands by Ron Koertge; See you by Kathleen Jeffrie Johnson; Fatboy and Skinnybones by Rene Saldana, Jr.; Brainiac by Alex Flinn; Let's hear it for Fire Team Bravo by Robert Lipsyte

Presents ten stories of teenagers facing all of the usual challenges of school, parents, boyfriends and girlfriends, plus the additional complications that come with having a physical or psychological disability.

"Each of the stories is strong and will resonate with teens dealing with everything from drinking problems, migraines, Tourette's Syndrome, and even cancer." Libr Media Connect

Paterson, Katherine

Angels and other strangers; family Christmas stories; [by] Katherine Paterson; including a new introduction by the author. HarperCollins Pub. 2006 c1979 170p $9.99

Grades: 5 6 7 8   **S C**
1. Christmas—Fiction 2. Short stories
ISBN 978-0-06-078376-1; 0-06-078376-1
A reissue of the title first published 1979 by Crowell
Contents: Angels and other strangers; Guests; Many happy returns; Tidings of joy; Maggie's gift; Star of night; He came down; Woodrow Kennington works practically a miracle; Broken windows

"The author weaves stories about miracles of the Christmas season—miracles that take place on a truly human level. Each story is based on the Christian message of the birth of Christ and the significance that message takes on for the characters. She writes of the poor, the desolate, and the lonely as well as of the arrogant, the complacent, and the proud." Horn Book

Peck, Richard, 1934-

Past perfect, present tense: new and collected stories. Dial Bks. 2004 177p $16.99; pa $6.99

Grades: 7 8 9 10 11 12   **S C**
1. Short stories
ISBN 0-8037-2998-7; 0-14-240537-X (pa)
                                        LC 2003-10904
Contents: Priscilla and the wimps; The electric summer; Shotgun Cheatham's last night above ground; The special powers of Blossom Culp; By far the worst pupil

at Long Point School; Girl at the window; The most important night of Melanie's life; Waiting for Sebastian; Shadows; Fluffy the gangbuster; I go along; The kiss in the carryon bag; The three-century woman; How to write a short story; Five helpful hints

A collection of short stories, including two previously unpublished ones, that deal with the way things could be.

"The stories perfectly highlight Peck's range and expertise at characterization. Almost every one is a superb read-aloud. . . . This superior collection is a must for every library." SLJ

Places I never meant to be; original stories by censored writers; edited by Judy Blume. Atheneum Bks. for Young Readers 1999 198p hardcover o.p. pa $10 *

Grades: 7 8 9 10   **S C**
1. Short stories
ISBN 0-689-82034-8; 0-689-84258-9 (pa)
                                        LC 98-30343
Contents: Introduction Censorship : a personal view by Judy Blume; A letter from Joan Bertin; Meeting the mugger by Norma Fox Mazer; Spear by Julius Lester; Going sentimental by Rachel Vail; The red dragonfly by Katherine Paterson; July Saturday by Jacqueline Woodson; You come, too, A-ron by Harry Mazer; The beast is in the labyrinth by Walter Dean Myers; Ashes by Susan Beth Pfeffer; Baseball camp by David Klass; Love and centipedes by Paul Zindel; Lie, no lie by Chris Lynch; Something which is nonexistent by Norma Kein

"This collection of 11 original short stories and a reprint of the late Norma Klein's college writing is interspersed with personal essays about the authors' views on censorship and its effect upon their work. Among the authors included are Norma Fox Mazer, Jacqueline Woodson, Harry Mazer, and Susan Beth Pfeffer." SLJ

"The contributors are a stellar list of well-known YA authors. . . . The authors' notes about censorship add a thought-provoking dimension to the collection, as does Blume's introduction, and the stories themselves are emotionally intense." Bull Cent Child Books

Poe, Edgar Allan, 1809-1849

Edgar Allan Poe; edited by Andrew Delbanco; illustrated by Gerard DuBois. Sterling 2006 80p il (Stories for young people) $14.95 *

Grades: 6 7 8 9   **S C**
1. Horror fiction 2. Short stories
ISBN 1-4027-1515-3
Contents: The fall of the House of Usher; The masque of the red death; The telltale heart; The cask of Amontillado; The oval portrait

"Introductory comments and appropriately atmospheric paintings enhance this handsomely packaged collection of five of Poe's unsettling short stories. . . . The editor . . . provides glosses for unusual words and literary references within the narratives." Booklist

Edgar Allan Poe's tales of mystery and madness; illustrated by Gris Grimley. Atheneum Books for Young Readers 2004 135p il $17.95

Grades: 8 9 10 11 12   **S C**
1. Horror fiction 2. Short stories
ISBN 0-689-84837-4   LC 2003-10565
Contents: The black cat; The masque of the Red Death; Hop Frog; The fall of the house of Usher

Poe, Edgar Allan, 1809-1849—*Continued*

"With high-production values and gothic sensibilities thoroughly reflected in both text and art, this is an essential purchase for libraries. Adults can use it to lead young people to some great literature; readers will pluck it off the shelves themselves for creepy, entertaining fun." Booklist

Tales of terror; illustrated with an introduction and notes by Michael McCurdy. Knopf 2005 89p il $15.95; lib bdg $17.99 *

Grades: 7 8 9 10   **S C**

1. Horror fiction 2. Short stories
ISBN 0-375-83305-6; 0-375-93305-0 (lib bdg)
LC 2004-23204

Contents: The masque of the Red Death; The black cat; The pit and the pendulum; The tell-tale hear; The cask of Amontillado; The fall of the House of Usher

"This collection includes six of Poe's most famous tales. . . . In the introduction, McCurdy discusses of Poe's life and remarks on the darkness of Poe's nature, reflected in his work, and the physical darkness of his world after sundown, reflected in the illustrations. The 18 full-page, black-and-white scratchboard-style pictures are suitably dramatic and often macabre. This handsome volume, . . . accompanied by a CD that features readings of four of the tales, offers a good introduction to Poe's fiction." Booklist

Priestley, Chris, 1958-

Uncle Montague's tales of terror; [by] Chris Priestley; illustrations by David Roberts. Bloomsbury Children's Books 2007 238p il $12.95

Grades: 5 6 7 8 9   **S C**

1. Horror fiction 2. Uncles—Fiction 3. Storytelling—Fiction 4. Short stories
ISBN 978-1-59990-118-3; 1-59990-118-8

"Ghosts, demons, jinns, and deadly trees populate these 10 chilly short stories set in the late 19th century, with the language and black-and-white illustrations capturing the feel of Victorian times. Young Edgar hears these tales while visiting his eccentric Uncle Montague, and each one is connected to a strange object in his uncle's study. . . . An enjoyable collection with enough creepy atmosphere (and some gruesome action) to hold readers' attention." SLJ

The **restless** dead; ten original stories of the supernatural; edited by Deborah Noyes. Candlewick Press 2007 253p $16.99

Grades: 8 9 10 11 12   **S C**

1. Supernatural—Fiction 2. Horror fiction 3. Short stories
ISBN 0-7636-2906-5; 978-0-7636-2906-9
LC 2007-22114

Contents: The wrong grave by Kelly Link; The house and the locket by Chris Wooding; Kissing dead boys by Annette Curtis Klause; The heart of another by Marcus Sedgwick; The necromancers by Herbie Brennan; No visible power by Deborah Noyes; Bad things by Libba Bray; The gray boy's work by M.T. Anderson; The poison eaters by Holly Black; Honey in the wound by Nancy Etchemendy

This is a "collection of terrifying stories from some of the most well-known authors writing for teens, including M. T. Anderson, Holly Black, Libby Bray, and Annette Curtis Klause. From vampires to vindictive ghosts, this diverse anthology has it all, and then some." Booklist

Rice, David, 1964-

Crazy loco; stories about growing up Chicano in southern Texas. Dial Books for Young Readers 2001 135p hardcover o.p. pa $6.99

Grades: 7 8 9 10 11 12   **S C**

1. Mexican Americans—Fiction 2. Texas—Fiction 3. Short stories
ISBN 0-8037-2598-1; 0-14-250056-9 (pa)
LC 00-59042

Contents: Sugarcane fire; Her other son; Valentine; Papa Lalo; Crazy loco; Proud to be an American; She flies; The California cousins; Last mass

A collection of nine stories about Mexican American kids growing up in the Rio Grande Valley of southern Texas.

"Two great strengths of these stories are the pitch-perfect sense for the speech and thought patterns of teens and the vivid depiction of the daily lives of Mexican-Americans in Texas's Rio Grande Valley." SLJ

Rowling, J. K.

The tales of Beedle the Bard; translated from the ancient runes by Hermione Granger; commentary by Albus Dumbledore; introduction, notes, and illustrations by J.K. Rowling. Children's High Level Group in association with Arthur A. Levine 2008 111p il $12.99

Grades: 5 6 7 8   **S C**

1. Fairy tales 2. Magic—Fiction 3. Short stories
ISBN 978-0-545-12828-5; 0-545-12828-5

Contents: The wizard and the hopping pot; The fountain of fair fortune; The warlock's hairy heart; Babbitty Rabbitty and her cackling stump; The tale of the three brothers

A collection of tales from the world of Harry Potter.

"The introduction is captivating . . . [and] the tales themselves are entertaining. . . . Rowling is at the top of her game as a superb storyteller, providing her legions of fans with an enchanting collection of wizard folklore." Voice Youth Advocates

San Souci, Robert, 1946-

Dare to be scared; thirteen stories to chill and thrill; illustrations by David Ouimet. Cricket Bks. 2003 159p il $15.95 *

Grades: 4 5 6 7   **S C**

1. Horror fiction 2. Short stories
ISBN 0-8126-2688-5
LC 2002-152827

Contents: Nighttown; The dark dark house; The caller; The double dare; Space is the place; Ants; The Halloween spirit; The Bald Mountain monster; Playland; Smoke; Mrs. Moonlight (Senora de Luna); Hungry ghosts; Bakotahl

"From a horrible dream a boy can't wake up from to an alien-driven bus to an eerie house with an alarming inhabitant, these stories cover the gamut of scary

San Souci, Robert, 1946-—*Continued*
themes." SLJ

"With crisp, straightforward delivery and some intriguing endings, these 13 tales are great fun for young readers who like to be spooked." Booklist

Double-dare to be scared: another thirteen chilling tales; [by] Robert D. San Souci; illustrated by David Ouimet. Cricket Books 2004 170p il $15.95 *

Grades: 4 5 6 7   S C
1. Horror fiction 2. Short stories
ISBN 0-8126-2716-4   LC 2003-26610
Companion volume to Dare to be scared (2003)

Contents: Campfire tale; Best friends; The quilt; Circus dreams; Rosalie; Mountain childers; Class cootie; Half-past midnight; Laughter; Click-clack; Daddy Boogey; Grey; "Gulp!"

This is a "collection of 13 tales. . . . Most of the main characters are menaced by a variety of scary, unexpected threats: a madman in the woods, a giant spider, unforgiving leprechauns, and exceptionally hungry Appalachian children." Booklist

"San Souci uses elements of urban legend and folklore to weave powerful and suspenseful yet age-appropriate stories that youngsters will revisit, finding new meaning with each reading." SLJ

Triple-dare to be scared; thirteen further freaky tales; [by] Robert D. San Souci; illustrations by David Ouimet. 1st ed. Cricket Books 2007 229p il $16.95

Grades: 4 5 6 7   S C
1. Horror fiction 2. Short stories
ISBN 978-0-8126-27497; 0-8126-2749-0
                                     LC 2006025899

Contents: Second childhood; They bite, too!; Plat-eye; Tour de force; Underwater; Far site; Field of nightmares; The double; John Mouldy; Green thumb; El arroyo de los fantasmas; Bookworm; Rain

"San Souci serves up 13 more spooky tales, and Ouimet's macabre black-and-white illustrations are a perfect complement to each one. The selections are short enough for read-alouds or for independent readers to complete in one sitting." SLJ

Scary stories; illustrations by Barry Moser; introduction by Peter Glassman. Chronicle Books 2006 184p il $16.95

Grades: 6 7 8 9   S C
1. Horror fiction 2. Short stories
ISBN 978-0-8118-5414-6; 0-8118-5414-0
                                     LC 2005025226

Contents: Kittens by Dean Koontz; The Magic Shop by H.G. Wells; Miriam by Truman Capote; The telltale heart by Edgar Allan Poe; Genesis and catastrophe (a true story) by Roald Dahl; The squaw by Bram Stoker; Here there be tygers by Stephen King; Man overboard! by Winston Churchill; The lottery by Shirley Jackson; The bus-conductor by E.F. Benson; Thanksgiving by Joyce Carol Oates; Excerpt from The legend of Sleepy Hollow by Washington Irving; The terrible old man by H.P. Lovecraft; John Charrington's wedding by E. Nesbit; The furnished room by O. Henry; The man upstairs by Ray Bradbury; The music on the hill by Saki;

The boarded window by Ambrose Bierce; Fingers on the back of the neck by Margaret Mahy; The cremation of Sam McGee by Robert W. Service

"A collection of 20 previously published stories, some by well-known writers of horror such as Stephen King and H. P. Lovecraft, others by authors not generally associated with the genre, like Winston Churchill. Each selection includes a chilling black-and-white engraving, often placed near the end of the story for maximum effect." SLJ

Shattered: stories of children and war; edited by Jennifer Armstrong. Knopf 2002 166p hardcover o.p. pa $6.50

Grades: 7 8 9 10   S C
1. War stories 2. Short stories
ISBN 0-375-81112-5; 0-440-23765-3 (pa)
                                     LC 2001-18609

Contents: Second day by Ibtisam Barakat; Shattered by Marilyn Singer; Bad day for baseball by Graham Salisbury; I'll see you when this war is over by M.E. Kerr; Golpe de Estado by Dian Curtis Regan; Snap, crackle, pop by Lois Metzger; Things happen by Lisa Rowe Fraustino; Faizabad harvest 1980 by Suzanne Fisher Staples; Sounds of Thunder by Joseph Bruchac; Witness by Jennifer Armstrong; War is swell by David Lubar; Hope by Gloria D. Miklowitz

"This anthology of short stories (and one memoir), mostly by well-known writers for YAs, shows how war's violence affects individual young people in countries across the world." Booklist

"These selections will make teens cry, will make them angry, but most of all they will make them think." SLJ

Shelf life: stories by the book; edited by Gary Paulsen. Simon & Schuster Bks. for Young Readers 2003 173p $16.95 *

Grades: 5 6 7 8   S C
1. Books and reading—Fiction 2. Short stories
ISBN 0-689-84180-9   LC 2002-66901

Contents: In your hat, by E. Conford; Escape, by M. P. Haddix; Follow the water, by J. L. Holm; Testing, testing 1 . . . 2 . . . 3, by A. La Faye; Tea party ends in bloody massacre, film at 11, by G. Maguire; What's a fellow to do, by K. Karr; Wet hens, by E. Wittlinger; The good deed, by M. D. Bauer; Bacarole for paper and bones, by M. T. Anderson; Clean sweep, by J. Bauer

Ten short stories in which the lives of young people in different circumstances are changed by their encounters with books

"Covering almost every genre of fiction, including mystery, SF, fantasy and realism, these well-crafted stories by familiar authors offer sharply drawn characterizations and intriguing premises." Publ Wkly

Shining on; 11 star authors' illuminating stories; foreword by Lois Lowry. Delacorte Press 2007 159p pa $8.99; lib bdg $11.99

Grades: 8 9 10 11 12   S C
1. Short stories
ISBN 978-0-385-73472-1 (pa); 978-0-385-90470-4 (lib bdg)   LC 2006050274

Contents: Resigned by Meg Rosoff; Allie Finkelstein's rules for boyfriends by Meg Cabot; Coming home by Melvin Burgess; Getting the message by Anne Fine;

Shining on—*Continued*

You're a legend by Sue Limb; The bad sister by Jacqueline Wilson; Calling the cats by Celia Rees; Humming through my fingers by Malorie Blackman; A summer to die by Lowis Lowry; Skin deep by Rosie Rushton; John Lennon said by Cathy Hopkins

"This collection of stories primarily from British authors focuses on the ability of teens not only to deal with the problems that life brings, but also to triumph over them. . . . The stories show courage, creativity, and a core of toughness that is not always attributed to young adults." SLJ

Shusterman, Neal

Darkness creeping; twenty twisted tales. Puffin Books 2007 291p pa $7.99

Grades: 5 6 7 8   S C

1. Horror fiction 2. Short stories
ISBN 0-14-240721-6 (pa)

Contents: Catching cold; Who do we appreciate?; Soul survivor; Black box; Resting deep; Security blanket; Same time next year; River tour; Flushie; Monkeys tonight; Screaming at the wall; Growing pains; Alexander's skull; Connecting flight; Ralphy Sherman's root canal; Ear for music; Riding the raptor; Trash day; Crystalloid; Shawdows of doubt

"The author takes a walk on the dark side in this collection of spooky stories, some old, some new, all delightfully creepy. He knows his audience, providing enough horrific touches to appeal to the most challenging readers—those hard-to-reach middle school boys. Each story is introduced with a brief statement describing where he got the idea." Voice Youth Advocates

Sideshow; ten original tales of freaks, illusionists, and other matters odd and magical; edited by Deborah Noyes. Candlewick Press 2009 199p il $16.99 *

Grades: 7 8 9 10   S C

1. Short stories
ISBN 978-0-7636-3752-1; 0-7636-3752-1

LC 2008037420

Contents: The bearded girl by Aimee Bender; Those psychics on TV by Vivian Vande Velde; Year of the rat by Danica Novgorodoff; The mummy's daughter by Annette Curtis Klause; When God came to Kathleen's garden by David Almond; The shadow troupe by Shawn Cheng; Cat calls by Cynthia Leitch Smith; The bread box by Cecil Castellucci; Living curiosities by Margo Lanagan; Jargo! by Matt Phelan

"This is a masterpiece of 10 short stories by world-class authors. Contributors include David Almond, Annette Curtis Klause, and Vivian Vande Velde. . . . Not all of the stories are traditional prose; several are graphic renditions, including Matt Phelan's masterfully drawn 'Jargo!' . . . Suspending disbelief, readers of this fantastic anthology may start investing in psychics and sleeping with the light on." SLJ

Sleator, William

Oddballs; stories. Dutton Children's Bks. 1993 134p hardcover o.p. pa $5.99 *

Grades: 6 7 8 9 10   S C

1. Short stories
ISBN 0-525-45057-2; 0-14-037438-8 (pa)

LC 92-27666

Contents: Games; Frank's mother; The freedom fighters of Parkview; The hypnotist; The séance; The pitiful encounter; Leah's stories; Pituh-plays; Dad's cool; Oddballs

A collection of stories based on experiences from the author's youth and peopled with an unusual assortment of family and friends.

"Fresh, funny, and slightly gross, the quasi-autobiographical glimpses will grab the reader's attention." Horn Book Guide

Smith, Charles R.

Winning words; sports stories and photographs; [by] Charles R. Smith. Candlewick Press 2008 70p il $17.99

Grades: 5 6 7 8   S C

1. Sports—Fiction 2. Short stories
ISBN 978-0-7636-1445-4; 0-7636-1445-9

Contents: Don't say it; Stuffed eagles; I'm open; Crack-crack-crunch; A mountain of wood; Makes me wanna holla

In this collection of short stories and photographs, Charles R. Smith Jr. shows young athletes overcoming their fears and challenging themselves to do their best.

"This outstanding collection consists of six readable and engaging stories. . . . Smith does a fine job of evoking the action and character of the games, in words and in closeup photos." SLJ

Somehow tenderness survives; stories of Southern Africa; selected by Hazel Rochman. Harper & Row 1988 147p hardcover o.p. pa $5.99

Grades: 7 8 9 10   S C

1. Short stories 2. South Africa—Race relations—Fiction
ISBN 0-06-025022-4; 0-06-447063-6 (pa)

LC 88-916

Contents: When the train comes by Zoe Wicomb; A farm at Raraba by Ernst Havemann; It's quiet now by Gcina Mhlophe; Kaffir boy by Mark Mathebane; The old chief Mshlanga by Doris May Lessing; A chip of glass ruby by Nadine Gordimer; Tell freedom by Peter Abrahams; Country lovers by Nadine Gordimer; The toilet by Gcina Mhlophe; A day in the country by Dan Jacobson

A collection of eight short stories and two "autobiographical accounts which vividly evoke what it means to come of age in South Africa under apartheid. The contributors, including Doris Lessing and Nadine Gordimer, as well as lesser-known writers, are of various races and their stories cover a time span of 35 years. . . . This title should be in every YA collection. A glossary and notes on contributors are included." Voice Youth Advocates

Soto, Gary

Baseball in April, and other stories. 10th anniversary ed. Harcourt Brace Jovanovich 2000 c1990 111p $16; pa $6 *

Grades: 5 6 7 8   S C

Soto, Gary—*Continued*
1. Mexican Americans—Fiction 2. California—Fiction
3. Short stories
ISBN 0-15-202573-1; 0-15-202567-7 (pa)
A reissue of the title first published 1990
Contents: Broken chain; Baseball in April; Two
dreamers; Barbie; The no-guitar blues; Seventh grade;
Mother and daughter; The Karate Kid; La Bamba; The
marble champ; Growing up
A collection of eleven short stories focusing on the
everyday adventures of Hispanic young people growing
up in Fresno, California
Each story "gets at the heart of some aspect of growing up. The insecurities, the embarrassments, the triumphs, the inequities of it all are chronicled with wit and
charm. Soto's characters ring true and his knowledge of,
and affection for, their shared Mexican-American heritage is obvious and infectious." Voice Youth Advocates

Help wanted; stories; by Gary Soto. Harcourt
2005 216p $17; pa $6.95 *
Grades: 6 7 8 9   S C
1. Mexican Americans—Fiction 2. California—Fiction
3. Short stories
ISBN 0-15-205201-1; 978-0-15-205663-6 (pa)
LC 2004-7510
Contents: Paintball in the wild; Sorry, wrong family;
Yeah, right; How Becky Garza learned golf; The cadet;
The sounds of love; Teenage chimps; The sounds of the
house; One last kiss; Raiders nation
"Ten original short stories about Mexican-American
teens in central California. The fundamental theme of
'needing help' is the common thread among the stories,
which range from the satirical to the peculiar to the humorous to the sad." SLJ
"The stories are sometimes funny, often poignant, and
occasionally provocative." Booklist

Local news. Harcourt Brace Jovanovich 1993
148p hardcover o.p. pa $5.95 *
Grades: 5 6 7 8   S C
1. Mexican Americans—Fiction 2. California—Fiction
3. Short stories
ISBN 0-15-248117-6; 0-15-204695-X (pa)
LC 92-37905
Contents: Blackmail; Trick-or-treating; First job; El radio; Pushup; The school play; The Raiders jacket; The
challenge; Nacho loco; The squirrels; The mechanical
mind; Nickel-a-pound plane ride; New Year's Eve
A collection of thirteen short stories about the everyday lives of Mexican American young people in California's Central Valley
"These stories resonate with integrity, verve, and compassion." Horn Book

Spinelli, Jerry, 1941-
The library card. Scholastic 1997 148p pa $4.99
Grades: 4 5 6 7   S C
1. Books and reading—Fiction 2. Short stories
ISBN 0-590-38633-6 (pa)   LC 96-18412
Contents: Mongoose; Brenda; Sonseray; April Mendez
"A library card is the magical object common to each
of these four stories in which a budding street thug, a
television addict, a homeless orphan, and a lonely girl

are all transformed by the power and the possibilities that
await them within the walls of the public library.
Spinelli's characters . . . are unusual and memorable; his
writing both humorous and convincing." Horn Book
Guide

Sports shorts. Darby Creek Pub. 2005 127p il
$15.99
Grades: 5 6 7 8   S C
1. Sports—Fiction 2. Short stories
ISBN 1-58196-040-9
Contents: Bombardment by Joseph Bruchac; Two left
feet, two left hands, and too left on the bench by David
Lubar; First position by Marilyn Singer; Finishing blocks
and deadly hook shots by Terry Trueman; Finding high-
jump fame by Dorian Cirrone; Line drive by Tanya
West; Riding the century by Alexandra Siy; On being
written in by Jamie McEwan.
A collection of eight semi-autobiographical stories
about the authors' experiences with sports while growing
up.
"Some of the vignettes are laugh-out-loud funny. . . .
The book's smaller-than-standard trim size and inviting
page design will help attract readers to this rewarding
collection." Booklist

The **Starry** rift; tales of new tomorrows: an
original science fiction anthology; edited by
Jonathan Strahan. Viking 2008 530p $19.99 *
Grades: 8 9 10 11 12   S C
1. Short stories 2. Science fiction
ISBN 978-0-6700-6059-7; 0-6700-6059-3
LC 2007-32152
Contents: Ass-hat magic spider by Scott Westerfeld;
Cheats by Ann Halam; Orange by Neil Gaiman; The
surfer by Kelly Link; Repair kit by Stephen Baxter; The
dismantled invention of fate by Jeffrey Ford; Anda's
game by Cory Doctorow; Sundiver Day by Kathleen Ann
Goonan; The dust assassin by Ian McDonald; The star
surgeon's apprentice by Alastair Reynolds; An honest
day's work by Margo Lanagan; Lost continent by Greg
Egan; Incomers by Paul McAuley; Post-ironic stress syndrome by Tricia Sullivan; Infestation by Garth Nix;
Pinocchio by Walter Jon Williams
The sixteen stories by a mix of acclaimed YA and
adult authors showcase settings ranging from bleak near-
futures to careening spaceships and extraterrestrial communities. Each is followed by an author's note and brief
biography.
"Each of the tales is not only entertaining to read, but
also provides a thought-provoking element to consider.
. . . Quality stories by authors at the height of their craft
make this anthology a must-have for any library." SLJ

Swan sister; fairy tales retold; edited by Ellen
Datlow and Terri Windling. Simon & Schuster
Bks. for Young Readers 2003 165p $16.95 *
Grades: 5 6 7 8   S C
1. Fairy tales 2. Short stories
ISBN 0-689-84613-4   LC 2002-30409
Contents: Greenkid by Jane Yolen; Golden fur by
Midori Snyder; Chambers of the heart by Nina Kiriki
Hoffman; Little Red and the Big Bad by Will Shetterly;
The Fish's story by Pat York; The Children of Tilford
Fortune by Christopher Rowe; The Girl in the attic by

Swan sister—*Continued*

Lois Metzger; The Harp that sang by Gregory Frost; A life in miniature by Bruce Coville; Lupe by Kathe Koja; Awake by Tanith Lee; Inventing Aladdin by Neil Gaiman; My swan sister by Katherine Vaz

"In this anthology, noted children's and adult fantasy writers play with the bones of traditional stories, songs, and characters to create 13 vibrant, imaginative short stories. . . . There's something for everyone in this anthology." SLJ

Talking leaves; contemporary native American short stories; introduced and edited by Craig Lesley; associate editor, Katheryn Stavrakis. Dell 1991 xxvi, 385p pa $16.95 *

Grades: 8 9 10 11 12 Adult   **S C**

1. Native Americans—Fiction 2. Short stories

ISBN 0-385-31272-5   LC 92-139334

"A Laurel trade paperback"

Contents: Deer woman by Paula Gunn Allen; Turtle Lake by Gloria Bird; Swimming upstream by Beth Brant; Going home by Joseph Bruchac; A visit from Reverend Tileston by Elizabeth Cook-Lynn; Queen of Diamonds by Michael Dorris; The old marriage by Debra Earling; After Celilo by Ed Edmo; The humming of stars, bees, and waves by Anita Endrezze; The bingo van by Louise Erdrich; The way it was by Tina Marie Freeman-Villalobos; Aunt Parnetta's electric blisters by Diane Glancey; High cotton by Rayna Green; The flood by Joy Harjo; Northern lights by Joy Harjo; Taking care of business by Kathleen Shaye Hill; Aunt Moon's young man by Linda Hogan; The pebble people by Roger Jack; Wet mocassins by Maurice Kenny; A seat in the garden by Thomas King; Killing the bear by Judith Minty; She is beautiful in her whole being by N. Scott Momaday; Crow's sun by Duane Niatum; Never quite a Hollywood star by Carter Revard; The Indian basket by Mickey Roberts; It's all in how you say it by Mickey Roberts; How I got to be queen by Greg Sarris; Dancer by Vickie Sears; Snatched away by Mary Tallmountain; Cheyenne revenge [excerpt] by Clifford E. Trafzer; The Baron of Petronia by Gerold Vizenor; China Browne by Gerold Vizenor; Bicenti by Anna Lee Walters; Fools crow [excerpt] by James Welch; Summer girl by Roberta Hill Whiteman; Diamond Island: Alcatraz by Darryl Babe Wilson; White-out by Phyllis Wolf; HomeCooking by Elizabeth Woody

This anthology includes contributions by such authors as Louise Erdrich, Diane Glancey, Michael Dorris, N. Scott Momaday, Paula Gunn Allen, and Mary Tallmountain

"All these stories have a strong sense of person and place and engagingly inform of the Native American condition." Libr J

Tan, Shaun

Tales from outer suburbia. Arthur A. Levine Books 2009 92p il $19.99 *

Grades: 7 8 9 10   **S C**

1. Suburban life—Fiction 2. Short stories

ISBN 978-0-545-05587-1; 0-545-05587-3

LC 2008-13784

Contents: The water buffalo; Eric; Broken toys; Undertow; Grandpa's story; No other country; Stick figures; The nameless holiday; Alert but not alarmed; Wake; Our expedition; Night of the turtle rescue

"The term 'suburbia' may conjure visions of vast and generic sameness, but in his hypnotic collection of 15 short stories and meditations, Tan does for the sprawling landscape what he did for the metropolis in *The Arrival* . . . . Ideas and imagery both beautiful and disturbing will linger." Publ Wkly

This is PUSH; an anthology of new writing; edited by David Levithan. Scholastic 2007 232p (Push anthology) pa $6.99

Grades: 6 7 8 9   **S C**

1. Short stories

ISBN 978-0-439-89028-1; 0-439-89028-4

Contents: The lost chapter by Eireann Corrigan; The first six killers by Markus Zusak; Filthadelphia by Brian James; People watching by Chris Wooding; My boyfriend refuses to speak in iambic pentameter by Billy Merrell; Katie James beats the blues by Kristen Kemp; Ginger by Christopher Krovatin; Halfway by Coe Booth; Eight minutes by Tanuja Desai Hidier; Jack and Dean by Kevin Brooks; Picking by Samantha Schutz; Smoking lessons by Patricia McCormick; The blanket by Eddie de Oliveira; The waitress by Matthue Roth; The birds of Fleming Park by Kevin Waltman

"Fifteen new stories make up this first-class anthology. . . . Readers will be left speechless by Chris Wooding's jarring, horrific tale of two godlike beings . . . and they will no doubt be haunted by Markus Zusak's captivatingly poetic story of a gravedigger and his crush. . . . As a whole, they run the literary gamut from realistic fiction to memoir to romance to mystery to horror, and each one will no doubt be devoured by teens." SLJ

Tripping over the lunch lady and other school stories; edited by Nancy E. Mercado. Dial Books 2004 177p $16.99 *

Grades: 4 5 6 7   **S C**

1. School stories 2. Short stories

ISBN 0-8037-2873-5   LC 2003-15905

Contents: Tripping over the lunch lady by Angela Johnson; How I got my English A by Avi; Experts, incorporated by Sarah Weeks; Apple blossoms by Terry Trueman; Science friction by David Lubar; The grade school zone by James Proimos, illustrated by David Fremont; The desk by Lee Wardlaw; The crush by Rachel Vail; The girls room by Susan Shreve; Tied to Zelda by David Rice

An "anthology of 10 short stories, by authors such as Avi, Angela Johnson, David Lubar, and Rachel Vail." SLJ

"In these first-person narratives, sharply defined details and keenly observed nuances of school life often set the stage for moments of wit, surprise, realization, and tenderness." Booklist

Troll's eye view; a book of villainous tales; edited by Ellen Datlow and Terri Windling. Viking 2009 200p $16.99

Grades: 5 6 7 8   **S C**

1. Fairy tales 2. Short stories

ISBN 978-0-670-06141-9; 0-670-06141-7

Contents: Wizard's apprentice by Delia Sherman; An unwelcome guest by Garth Nix; Faery tales by Wendy Froud; Rags and riches by Nina Kiriki Hoffman; Up the down beanstalk: a wife remembers by Peter S. Beagle;

Troll's eye view—*Continued*

The shoes that were danced to pieces by Ellen Kushner; Puss in boots, the sequel by Joseph Stanton; The boy who cried wolf by Holly Black; Troll by Jane Yolen; Castle Othello by Nancy Farmer; 'Skin by Michael Cadnum; Delicate architecture by Catherynne M. Valente; Molly by Midori Snyder; Observing the formalities by Neil Gaiman; The Cinderella game by Kelly Link

Everyone thinks you know the real story behind the villains in fairy tales—evil, no two ways about it. But the villains themselves beg to differ. In this anthology for younger readers, you'll hear from the Giant's wife (from Jack and the Beanstalk), Rumpelstiltskin, the oldest of the Twelve Dancing Princesses, and more.

"A mixed bag of funny, quirky, and downright creepy entries. . . . The collection is largely accessible and very enjoyable." Booklist

Twain, Mark, 1835-1910

Mark Twain; edited by Gregg Camfield; illustrated by Sally Wern Comport. Sterling 2005 80p il (Stories for young people) $14.95 *

Grades: 6 7 8 9   S C

1. Short stories

ISBN 1-4027-1178-6

Contents: An encounter with an interviewer; The invalid's story; Advice to youth; The £1,000,000 banknote; A fable

"This collection of five stories includes 'An Encounter with an Interviewer,' 'The Invalid's Story,' 'Advice to Youth,' 'The L1,000,000 Banknote,' and 'A Fable.'. . . . Handsome illustrations with detailed, revealing facial expressions and body language appear on almost every page. The book opens with a biography, explaining the meaning of mark twain," briefly outlining Clemens's life, and quickly discussing his influence on American literature." SLJ

Twice told; original stories inspired by original art; drawings by Scott Hunt. Dutton 2006 259p il $19.99

Grades: 7 8 9 10   S C

1. Short stories

ISBN 0-525-46818-8; 978-0-525-46818-9

LC 2005-18694

Contents: Sha-la-la by Sarah Dessen; Floater by Ellen Wittlinger; Alejandro by Gene Brewer; Saying no to Nick by Bruce Coville; Just a couple of girls talking haiku by Ron Koertge; Ruby by Adele Geras; What I did last summer by Jan Marino; Word of the day by Marilyn Singer; Hope springs eternal by Audrey Couloumbis; The approximate cost of loving Caroline by John Green; Angel's food by M.T. Anderson; Chocolate almond torte by William Sleator; Rebecca by Nancy Werlin; Bunny boy by Alex Flinn; Essie and Clem by Margaret Peterson Haddix; The God of St. James and Vine by Jaime Adoff; Smells like Kafka by Neal Shusterman; Habitat for humanity by David Lubar

Presents nine drawings by a single illustrator, each of which has been translated into a story by two different authors writing about what they imagine is going on in the picture.

"The collection showcases authors' distinct voices and effectively samples a variety of styles." Horn Book Guide

Ultimate sports; short stories by outstanding writers for young adults; edited by Donald R. Gallo. Delacorte Press 1995 333p hardcover o.p. pa $6.99

Grades: 7 8 9 10   S C

1. Sports—Fiction 2. Short stories

ISBN 0-440-22707-0; 0-440-22707-0 (pa)

LC 94-49610

Contents: Joyriding by Jim Naughton; Fury by T. Ernesto Bethancourt; Superboy by Chris Crutcher; If you can't be lucky by Carl Deuker; Stealing for girls by Will Weaver; Shark bait by Graham Salisbury; Cutthroat by Norma Fox Mazer; The assault on the record by Stephen Hoffius; The defender by Robert Lipsyte; Just once by Thomas J Dygard; Brownian motion by Virginia Euwer Wolff; Bones by Todd Strasser; Sea changes by Tessa Duder; The gospel according to Krenzwinkle by David Klass; Falling off the Empire State Building by Harry Mazer; The hobbyist by Chris Lynch

A collection of sixteen short stories about teenage athletes.

"There is a terrific mix of the serious and the lighthearted, female and male characters, and traditional and nontraditional games. A winning collection." SLJ

Up all night; a short story collection; [by] Peter Abrahams [et al.]; with an introduction by Laura Geringer. Laura Geringer Books/HarperTeen 2008 227p il $16.99; lib bdg $17.89

Grades: 8 9 10 11 12   S C

1. Short stories 2. Night—Fiction

ISBN   978-0-06-137076-2;   0-06-137076-2; 978-0-06-137077-9 (lib bdg); 0-06-137077-0 (lib bdg)

LC 2007-21355

Contents: Phase 2 by Peter Abrahams; Not just for breakfast anymore by Libba Bray; The vulnerable hours by David Levithan; Orange Alert by Patricia McCormick; Superman is dead by Sarah Weeks; The motherless one by Gene Luen Yang

"Six top teen authors have contributed stories to this winning collection. Abrahams has written a modern ghost story, Libba Bray tells of a wild night partying with friends that changes a girl's relationship with her estranged father, and David Levithan gives readers a magical take on life in the city. Patricia McCormick takes a hard look at freedom and power, Sarah Weeks writes of responsibility with humor, and Yang tops off the book in his own graphic-novel style. Each story shines in its own way." SLJ

Vande Velde, Vivian, 1951-

All Hallows' Eve; 13 stories. Harcourt 2006 225p $17

Grades: 7 8 9 10   S C

1. Halloween—Fiction 2. Supernatural—Fiction 3. Short stories

ISBN 978-0-15-205576-9; 0-15-205576-2

LC 2006-05439

Contents: Come in and rest a spell; MARIAN; Morgan Roehmar's boys; Only on All Hallows' Eve; Cemetery field trip; Best friends; Pretending; I want to thank you; When and how; When my parents come to visit; Edward, lost and far from home; My real mother; Holding on

Vande Velde, Vivian, 1951-—*Continued*

Presents thirteen tales of Halloween horrors, including ghosts, vampires, and pranks gone awry.

"This mistress of the macabre draws readers in with her familiar conversational tone and easily recognizable situations . . . before skillfully shifting the narratives in unsettling, sometimes terrifying, directions. . . . Vande Velde's narrative tricks are a treat." Horn Book

Being dead; stories. Harcourt 2001 203p hardcover o.p. pa $6.95 *
Grades: 7 8 9 10   S C
1. Supernatural—Fiction 2. Horror fiction 3. Short stories
ISBN 0-15-216320-4; 0-15-204912-6 (pa)
LC 00-12996

Contents: Dancing with Marjorie's ghost; Shadow brother; For love of him; October chill; Drop by drop; The ghost; Drop dead

This is a collection of seven "creepy tales featuring ghosts, cemeteries, suicides, murders, and other death-related themes." SLJ

"Often humorous and sometimes evoking sympathy, this anthology will be enjoyed by lovers of mild horror as well as by those who like clever short stories." Voice Youth Advocates

Tales from the Brothers Grimm and the Sisters Weird. Harcourt Brace & Co. 1995 128p il hardcover o.p. pa $5.95
Grades: 7 8 9 10   S C
1. Fairy tales 2. Short stories
ISBN 0-15-200220-0; 0-15-205572-X (pa)
LC 94-26341

"Jane Yolen Books"

Contents: Straw into gold; Frog; The granddaughter; Jack; The bridge; Mattresses; Twins; Beast and Beauty

This collection presents alternative versions of such familiar fairy tales as Rumpelstiltskin, Hansel and Gretel, and The Princess and the Pea

"Vande Velde challenges readers' notions of good, bad, and ugly. . . . Modern references and sensibilities . . . add to the humor (often the gallows variety). Entertaining and provocative, these selections make good read-alouds and can be used to spark discussion or creative writing exercises." SLJ

Visions: nineteen short stories by outstanding writers for young adults; edited by Donald R. Gallo. Delacorte Press 1987 228p pa $6.99 hardcover o.p.
Grades: 7 8 9 10   S C
1. Short stories
ISBN 0-440-20208-6   LC 87-6787

Contents: Shadows by Richard Peck; Saint Agnes sends the golden boy by Cin Forshay-Lunsford; Dream job by Marjorie Weinman Sharmat; The all-American slurp by Lensey Namioka; Jason Kovak, the quick and the brave by Jean Davies Okimoto; What happened in the cemetery by Norma Fox Mazer; Amanda and the wounded birds by Colby Rodowsky; Playing God by Ouida Sebestyen; The Fuller brush man by Gloria D. Miklowitz; The good girls by Fran Arrick; On the bridge by Todd Strasser; Great moves by Sandy Asher; A hundred bucks of happy by Susan Beth Pfeffer; Cousin Alice

by Joan Aiken; Words of power by Jane Yolen; The sweet perfume of goodbye by M. E. Kerr; Jeremiah's song by Walter Dean Myers; The boy with yellow eyes by Gloria Gonzalez; The beginning of something by Sue Ellen Bridgers

"Information about the authors follows each of nineteen original short stories, most of them impressive examples of the genre, all of them written by established men and women. Among the familiar names: Joan Aiken, M.E. Kerr, Walter Dean Myers, Richard Peck. The tales are grouped under such headings as 'Adjustments' or 'Kinships,' and include both realistic and fanciful writing, most of the work being of fine quality and the rest only slightly less so." Bull Cent Child Books

Voices in first person; reflections on Latino identity; [edited by Lori Marie Carlson] Atheneum Books for Young Readers 2008 96p il $16.99
Grades: 6 7 8 9 10 11 12   S C
1. American literature—Hispanic American authors—Collections 2. Short stories
ISBN 978-1-4169-0635-3; 1-4169-0635-5
LC 2006-34161

Contents: Ritual by Claudia Quiroz Cahill; Reclaim your rights as citizen of here, here by Michele Serros; Spending money by Gary Soto; I stand at the crosswalk by Esmeralda Santiago; Angel's monologue by Gwylym Cano; Jose by Caridad de la Luz; The evil eye by Raquel Valle Senties; Poultrymorphosis by Oscar Hijuelos

A collection of brief fictional pieces about the experiences of Latinos in the United States, by such writers as Sandra Cisneros, Gary Soto, Oscar Hijuelos, and others.

"Carlson has drawn from both established and new writers, focusing on finding Latino voices that speak to contemporary readers. . . . This collection sparkles more than its predecessors because of its dynamic design, featuring black-and-white photographs and line illustrations incorporated with the text in a collage-like magazine layout." SLJ

Wallace, Rich, 1957-

Losing is not an option: stories. Knopf 2003 127p $15.95; pa $5.99
Grades: 7 8 9 10   S C
1. Short stories
ISBN 0-375-81351-9; 0-440-23844-7 (pa)
LC 2002-34036

Contents: Night game; Nailed; The amazing two-headed boy; I voted for Mary Ann; In letters that would soar a thousand feet high; What it all goes back to; Dawn; Thankgiving; Losing is not an option

Nine episodes in the life of a young man, from sneaking into his tenth football game in a row with his best friend in sixth grade to running his last high school race, the Pennsylvania state championships.

"Readers will nod with recognition as they follow this jock/poet/regular guy from the cusp of adolescence to the edge of adulthood." Horn Book Guide

What a song can do; 12 riffs on the power of music; edited by Jennifer Armstrong. Knopf 2004 200p $15.95; pa $5.99

Grades: 7 8 9 10   **S C**

1. Music—Fiction 2. Short stories

ISBN 0-375-82499-5; 0-440-23816-1 (pa)

            LC 2003-24306

Contents: Variations on a theme by Ron Koertge; A warrior song by Joseph Bruchac; Riffs by Ann Manheimer; What a song can do by David Levithan; Piano obsession by Ibtisam S. Barakat; The audition by J. Alison James; Tangled notes in watermelon by Dian Curtis Regan; Ballad of a prodigy by Jude Mandell; The song of Stones River by Jennifer Armstrong; The gypsy's violin by Gail Giles; New town by Alexandra Siy; A third kind of funny by Sarah Ellis

Twelve stories describe the power of music in young people's lives, from forming a community of individuals in a high school band to helping a young man connect to his Indian heritage through ancient songs.

These stories "show the power of both words and music to express the turbulent emotions of growing up." Booklist

What are you afraid of? stories about phobias; edited by Donald R. Gallo. Candlewick Press 2006 189p $16.99

Grades: 6 7 8 9   **S C**

1. Phobias—Fiction 2. Short stories

ISBN 0-7636-2654-6   LC 2004-62874

Contents: The door by Alex Flinn; Calle de Muerte by Ron Koertge; Thin by Joan Bauer; D'arcy by Angela Johnson; Claws and effect by Dabid Lubar; Rutabaga by Nancy Springer; Bang, bang, you're dead by Jane Yolen and Heidi E.Y. Stemple; No clown zone by Gail Giles; Instructions for tight spaces by Kelly Easton; Fear-for-all by Neal Shusterman

Presents ten short stories by well-known authors featuring teenagers with phobias, inluding fear of gaining weight, fear of clowns, and fear of cats.

"This is an excellent collection on a topic that holds a strange and fascinating allure." SLJ

Who do you think you are? stories of friends and enemies; selected by Hazel Rochman and Darlene Z. McCampbell. Little, Brown 1993 170p pa $9.99 hardcover o.p.

Grades: 7 8 9 10   **S C**

1. Friendship—Fiction 2. Short stories

ISBN 0-316-75320-3   LC 93-314

"Joy Street books"

Contents: Good grief [excerpt from Dandelion wine] by Ray Bradbury; Where are you going, where have you been? by Joyce Carol Oates; American history by Judith Ortiz-Cofer; Raymond's run by Toni Cade Bambara; A boy and his dog by Martha Brooks; The alligators by John Updike; Celia behind me by Isabel Huggan; This boy's life [excerpt] by Tobias Wolff; Priscilla and the wimps by Richard Peck; What means switch by Gish Jen; My Lucy friend who smells like corn by Sandra Cisneros; Sucker by Carson McCullers; The red convertible by Louise Erdrich; The man I killed [excerpt from The things they carried] by Tim O'Brien; Ambush [excerpt from The things they carried] by Tim O'Brien; I know why the caged bird sings [excerpt] by Maya Angelou; Poesía a la amistad/Poetry of friendship by José Martí

"Louise Erdrich, John Updike, Ray Bradbury, Joyce Carol Oates, Sandra Cisneros, Tim O'Brien, Richard Peck, and Maya Angelou are among the 15 writers represented in this anthology of stories [two prose excerpts and a poem] about friendship and loss of friendship." Booklist

"Meticulously chosen and arranged, these works crystalize moments of vulnerability, sorrow and understanding; together, they serve as an excellent introduction to modern American writing." Publ Wkly

Yee, Paul

Tales from Gold Mountain; stories of the Chinese in the New World; paintings by Simon Ng. Groundwood Books 1989 64p il $18.95 *

Grades: 4 5 6 7   **S C**

1. Chinese Americans—Fiction 2. Short stories

ISBN 0-88899-098-7   LC 89-12643

Contents: Spirits of the railway; Sons and daughters; The friends of Kwan Ming; Ginger for the heart; Gambler's eyes; Forbidden fruit; Rider Chan and the night river; The revenge of the iron chink

A collection of eight stories reflecting the gritty optimism of the Chinese who overcame prejudice and adversity to build a unique place for themselves in North America

These "brief, pithy tales strikingly reflect traditional Chinese beliefs and customs in New World circumstances. . . . Romance, family loyalty, and justice are important themes, and an element of surprise is never far away." Booklist

You never did learn to knock; 14 stories about girls and their mothers; selected by Bel Mooney. Kingfisher 2006 254p pa $7.95

Grades: 7 8 9 10   **S C**

1. Mother-daughter relationship—Fiction 2. Short stories

ISBN 0-7534-5877-2

Contents: Tantie by Adèle Geras; Becoming an M.P.G. by Candice Ransom; The dolphin bracelet by Caroline Pitcher; Making it up by Julia Jarman; Snowglobe moment by Shirley Klock; Broken flower heads by Kate Petty; Barn swallows by Amy Boesky; Not just a pretty face by Jean Ure; Sing by Linda Newbery; Missing out by Betty Hicks; The ninth dragon by Jennifer Kramer; The surprise by Jenny Land; You never did learn to knock by Cathy Hopkins; Hot cool summer by Bel Mooney

In this collection of short stories about mothers and daughters "situations include adoption, girls manipulating their mothers, divorce, and terminal illness. . . . A solid, enjoyable collection due to its breezy style and content." SLJ

Young warriors; stories of strength; edited by Tamora Pierce and Josepha Sherman. Random House 2005 312p $17.95; lib bdg $19.99; pa $8.95 *

Grades: 7 8 9 10   **S C**

1. Fantasy fiction 2. Short stories

ISBN   0-375-82962-8;   978-0-375-82962-8; 0-375-92962-2 (lib bdg); 978-0-375-92962-5 (lib bdg); 0-375-82963-6 (pa); 978-0-375-82963-5 (pa)

LC 2004-16432

Contents: Gift of Rain Mountain by Bruce Holland Rogers; Magestone by S. M. and Jan Stirling; Eli and the dybbuk by Janis Ian; Heartless by Holly Black; Lioness by Pamela F. Service; Thunderbolt by Ester Friesner; Devil wind by India Edghill; Boy who cried "dragon!" by Mike Resnick; Student of ostriches by Tamora Pierce; Serpent's rock by Laura Anne Gilman; Hidden warrors by Margaret Mahy; Emerging legacy by Doranna Durgin; Axe for men by Rosemary Edghill; Acts of faith by Lesley McBain; Swords that talk by Brent Hartinger

Fifteen original short stories by various authors relate the exploits of teenage warriors who defeat their enemies with cunning and skill as they strive to fulfill their destinies.

"This timely and appealing anthology will surely help swell the ranks of teenage fantasy readers." SLJ

AUTHOR, TITLE, AND SUBJECT INDEX

This index to the books in the Classified Catalog includes author, title, and subject entries; added entries for publishers' series, for joint authors, and for editors of works entered under title; and name and subject cross references; all arranged in one alphabet. The number or symbol in bold face type at the end of each entry refers to the Dewey Decimal Classification or to the Fiction or Story Collection Section where the book will be found. Works classed in 92 will be found under the heading for the person written about. For further information about this index and for examples of entries, see Directions for Use of the Catalog.

Adolescent prostitution *See* Juvenile prostitution

Adolescent psychology

> *See also* Boys—Psychology; Girls—Psychology
>
> Muharrar, A. More than a label   **305.23**

Adolescents *See* Teenagers

Adolf Hitler and Nazi Germany. Rice, E.   **92**

Adopted children

> Rhodes-Courter, A. M. Three little words   **92**

Adoption

> Adoption   **362.7**
> Adoption: opposing viewpoints   **362.7**
> Kaminker, L. Everything you need to know about being adopted   **362.7**
> Lanchon, A. All about adoption   **362.7**
> Warren, A. Orphan train rider   **362.7**
> Weiss, A. E. Adoptions today   **362.7**
>
> #### Fiction
>
> Barkley, B. Jars of glass   **Fic**
> Burg, A. E. All the broken pieces   **Fic**
> Doherty, B. The girl who saw lions   **Fic**
> Haddix, M. P. Found   **Fic**
> Hicks, B. Get real   **Fic**
> Johnson, A. Heaven   **Fic**
> Kent, R. Kimchi & calamari   **Fic**
> Lisle, J. T. The crying rocks   **Fic**
> McKay, H. Saffy's angel   **Fic**
> Perkins, M. First daughter: extreme American makeover   **Fic**
> Williams, L. E. Slant   **Fic**
> Wright, B. When the black girl sings   **Fic**

Adoption, Interracial *See* Interracial adoption

Adoption   **362.7**

Adoption: opposing viewpoints   **362.7**

Adoptions today. Weiss, A. E.   **362.7**

The **adoration** of Jenna Fox. Pearson, M.   **Fic**

Adventure and adventurers

> Explorers & discoverers   **920.003**
>
> #### Fiction
>
> *See* Adventure fiction

Adventure fiction

> *See also* Science fiction; Sea stories
>
> Aguiar, N. The lost island of Tamarind   **Fic**
> Alexander, L. The Illyrian adventure   **Fic**
> Alexander, L. The iron ring   **Fic**
> Alexander, L. The remarkable journey of Prince Jen   **Fic**
> Alexander, L. Westmark   **Fic**
> Anderson, J. D. Standard hero behavior   **Fic**
> Bell, T. Nick of time   **Fic**
> Berryhill, S. Chance Fortune and the Outlaws   **Fic**
> Bradford, C. Young samurai   **Fic**
> Breen, M. E. Darkwood   **Fic**
> Brittney, L. Dangerous times   **Fic**
> Cadnum, M. Peril on the sea   **Fic**
> Catanese, P. W. Happenstance found   **Fic**
> Click   **Fic**
> Cole, S. Thieves like us   **Fic**
> Colfer, E. Airman   **Fic**
> Couloumbis, A. The misadventures of Maude March   **Fic**
> DiCamillo, K. The magician's elephant   **Fic**
> Dowswell, P. Powder monkey   **Fic**

Fardell, J. The 7 professors of the Far North   **Fic**

Fardell, J. The flight of the Silver Turtle   **Fic**

Farmer, N. A girl named Disaster   **Fic**

Fleischman, S. The whipping boy   **Fic**

Friesner, E. M. Nobody's princess   **Fic**

Gardner, S. The red necklace   **Fic**

Gavin, J. Coram boy   **Fic**

Gilman, D. The devil's breath   **Fic**

Gordon, R. Tunnels   **Fic**

Grant, K. M. How the hangman lost his heart   **Fic**

Heath, J. The Lab   **Fic**

Heneghan, J. The magician's apprentice   **Fic**

Higgins, J. Sure fire   **Fic**

Hobbs, W. Ghost canoe   **Fic**

Hoffman, M. Stravaganza: city of masks   **Fic**

Humphreys, C. The fetch   **Fic**

Ives, D. Scrib   **Fic**

Jacques, B. Castaways of the Flying Dutchman   **Fic**

Karr, K. Born for adventure   **Fic**

Kennedy, J. The Order of Odd-Fish   **Fic**

Kress, A. Alex and the Ironic Gentleman   **Fic**

La Fevers, R. L. Theodosia and the Serpents of Chaos   **Fic**

Langrish, K. Troll Fell   **Fic**

Lawrence, I. The convicts   **Fic**

Lawrence, I. The wreckers   **Fic**

Lee, T. Piratica   **Fic**

MacHale, D. J. The pilgrims of Rayne   **Fic**

McKernan, V. Shackleton's stowaway   **Fic**

Mebus, S. Gods of Manhattan   **Fic**

Meehan, K. Hannah's winter   **Fic**

Meyer, L. A. Bloody Jack   **Fic**

Milway, A. The mousehunter   **Fic**

Molloy, M. Peter Raven under fire   **Fic**

Moran, K. Bloodline   **Fic**

Morgan, C. The boy who spoke dog   **Fic**

Morgan, N. The highwayman's footsteps   **Fic**

Mussi, S. The door of no return   **Fic**

Philbrick, W. R. The mostly true adventures of Homer P. Figg   **Fic**

Reger, R. Emily the Strange: the lost days   **Fic**

Richards, J. The chaos code   **Fic**

Rollins, J. Jake Ransom and the Skull King's shadow   **Fic**

Scrimger, R. Into the ravine   **Fic**

Smith, R. Cryptid hunters   **Fic**

Smith, R. I, Q.: book one, Indepedence Hall   **Fic**

Somper, J. Vampirates: demons of the ocean   **Fic**

Springer, N. Rowan Hood, outlaw girl of Sherwood Forest   **Fic**

Stevenson, R. L. Kidnapped   **Fic**

Stevenson, R. H. Dead in the water   **Fic**

Stewart, T. L. The mysterious Benedict Society   **Fic**

Stroud, J. Heroes of the valley   **Fic**

Tullson, D. Red Sea   **Fic**

Turner, M. W. The thief   **Fic**

Voelkel, J. Middleworld   **Fic**

Weston, R. P. Zorgamazoo   **Fic**

Age and employment
See also Teenagers—Employment
The **age** of feudalism. Davenport, J. **940.1**
An **age** of science and revolutions, 1600-1800.
Huff, T. E. **909.08**
An **age** of voyages, 1350-1600. Wiesner, M. E.
909.08
Agell, Charlotte, 1959-
Shift **Fic**
Agenbroad, Larry D.
Mammoths **569**
Agnes Parker . . . girl in progress. O'Dell, K.
Fic
Agricultural laborers
Atkin, S. B. Voices from the fields **331.5**
Fiction
Ryan, P. M. Esperanza rising **Fic**
Agriculture
Bowden, R. Food and farming **363.8**
Casper, J. K. Agriculture **630**
Halley, N. Farm **630**
Aguiar, Nadia
The lost island of Tamarind **Fic**
Aguilar, David A.
11 planets **523.4**
Planets, stars, and galaxies **520**
Aguirre, Hank, 1932-1994
About
Copley, B. The tall Mexican: the life of Hank
Aguirre, all-star pitcher, businessman, human-
itarian **92**
AI (Artificial intelligence) *See* Artificial intelli-
gence
AIDS (Disease)
AIDS **616.97**
Ballard, C. AIDS and other epidemics **614.5**
Ellis, D. Our stories, our songs **362.7**
Silverstein, A. The AIDS update **616.97**
See/See also pages in the following book(s):
Epidemics: opposing viewpoints **614.4**
Fiction
Doherty, B. The girl who saw lions **Fic**
Stratton, A. Chanda's secrets **Fic**
Graphic novels
Winick, J. Pedro and me **362.1**
AIDS **616.97**
AIDS and other epidemics. Ballard, C. **614.5**
The **AIDS** update. Silverstein, A. **616.97**
Aiken, Joan, 1924-2004
The wolves of Willoughby Chase **Fic**
Ailey, Alvin
About
Cruz, B. Alvin Ailey **92**
AIM *See* American Indian Movement
Aimee. Miller, M. B. **Fic**
Ain, Beth Levine
The revolution of Sabine **Fic**
Ain't nothing but a man [biography of John Wil-
liam Henry] Nelson, S. R. **92**
Air
Meiani, A. Air **533**
Parker, S. The science of air **533**

See/See also pages in the following book(s):
Knapp, B. J. Materials science **620.1**
Air pilots
See also African American pilots; Women
air pilots
Fleischman, J. Black and white airmen
940.54
Giblin, J. Charles A. Lindbergh **92**
Koopmans, A. Charles Lindbergh **92**
Maurer, R. The Wright sister [biography of
Katharine Wright Haskell] **92**
Fiction
Kerr, P. One small step **Fic**
Lawrence, I. B for Buster **Fic**
Saint-Exupéry, A. d. The little prince **Fic**
Smith, S. L. Flygirl **Fic**
Air pollution
Rapp, V. Protecting Earth's air quality **363.7**
Air raid. McGowen, T. **940.54**
Airborn. Oppel, K. **Fic**
Airborne: a photobiography of Wilbur and Orville
Wright. Collins, M. **92**
Aircraft accidents
Lace, W. W. The Hindenburg disaster of 1937
363.1
Aircraft carriers
McGowen, T. Carrier war **940.54**
Airhead. Cabot, M. **Fic**
Airman. Colfer, E. **Fic**
Airplane racing
Blair, M. W. The roaring 20 **797.5**
Airplanes
Faber, H. The airplane **629.133**
Graham, I. Flight **629.13**
Oxlade, C. Airplanes **629.133**
Accidents
See Aircraft accidents
Fiction
Colfer, E. Airman **Fic**
Fardell, J. The flight of the Silver Turtle
Fic
Horvath, P. The Corps of the Bare-Boned Plane
Fic
Models
Collins, J. M. Fantastic flight **745.592**
Collins, J. M. The gliding flight **745.592**
Harbo, C. L. The kids' guide to paper airplanes
745.592
Airplanes, Military *See* Military airplanes
Airships
Fiction
Oppel, K. Airborn **Fic**
Ake, Anne, 1943-
Hungary **943.9**
Akers, Michelle, 1966-
See/See also pages in the following book(s):
Kaminsky, M. Uncommon champions **920**
Akira, Shouko
Monkey High!: vol. 1 **741.5**
Al Adely, Laith Muhmood
(jt. auth) Hassig, S. M. Iraq **956.7**
Al Capone does my shirts. Choldenko, G. **Fic**

Al-Hazza, Tami Craft
  Books about the Middle East   **016**
Al Qaeda (Organization)
  Margulies, P. Al Qaeda: Osama bin Laden's army of terrorists   **973.931**
Al-Zahrāwī, Abū al-Qāsim Khalaf ibn Abbās
  See Abū al-Qāsim Khalaf ibn Abbās al-Zahrāwī, d. 1013?
ALA readers' advisory series
  Booth, H. Serving teens through readers' advisory   **028.5**
Alabama
Fiction
  Davis, T. S. Mare's war   Fic
  English, K. Francie   Fic
  Key, W. Alabama moon   Fic
  Levine, K. The best bad luck I ever had   Fic
  Lyon, G. E. Sonny's house of spies   Fic
  Ray, D. Singing hands   Fic
Alabama moon. Key, W.   Fic
Alamo (San Antonio, Tex.)
  Levy, J. The Alamo   **976.4**
  McNeese, T. The Alamo   **976.4**
  Walker, P. R. Remember the Alamo   **976.4**
Alaska
  Arnold, A. Sea cows, shamans, and scurvy: Alaska's first naturalist: Georg Wilhelm Steller   **92**
  Lourie, P. Arctic thaw   **998**
  Webb, S. Looking for seabirds   **598**
Fiction
  Frost, H. Diamond Willow   Fic
  Hill, K. Do not pass go   Fic
  Hobbs, W. Leaving Protection   Fic
  Hobbs, W. Wild Man Island   Fic
  Lion, M. Upstream   Fic
  London, J. The call of the wild   Fic
  London, J. White Fang   Fic
  Mikaelsen, B. Touching Spirit Bear   Fic
  Orenstein, D. G. Unseen companion   Fic
  Smelcer, J. E. The trap   Fic
Albania
  Knowlton, M. Albania   **949.65**
Albert, Lisa Rondinelli
  Lois Lowry   **92**
Albert Einstein and the frontiers of physics. Bernstein, J.   **92**
Albright, Madeleine Korbel, 1937-
About
  Hasday, J. L. Madeleine Albright   **92**
Albyn, Carole Lisa, 1955-
  The multicultural cookbook for students   **641.5**
Alcatraz Island (Calif.)
  Murphy, C. R. Children of Alcatraz   **979.4**
Fiction
  Choldenko, G. Al Capone does my shirts   Fic
Alcatraz versus the evil Librarians. Sanderson, B.   Fic
The **alchemist's** cat. Jarvis, R.   Fic
The **alchemist's** dream. Wilson, J.   Fic

Alchemy
Fiction
  Mahy, M. Alchemy   Fic
  Scott, M. The alchemyst   Fic
The **alchemyst**. Scott, M.   Fic
Alcohol
Physiological effect
  Alcohol information for teens   **616.86**
  Esherick, J. Dying for acceptance   **616.86**
Alcohol and drug abuse. Powell, J.   **362.29**
Alcohol and teenagers *See* Teenagers—Alcohol use
Alcohol information for teens   **616.86**
Alcoholic beverages
  See also Drinking of alcoholic beverages
Alcoholics
  See also Children of alcoholics
Alcoholism
  See also Children of alcoholics; Drinking of alcoholic beverages
  Addiction: opposing viewpoints   **362.29**
  Alcohol information for teens   **616.86**
  Alcoholism   **362.292**
  Aretha, D. On the rocks   **362.292**
  Gottfried, T. The facts about alcohol   **362.292**
  Powell, J. Alcohol and drug abuse   **362.29**
  Teen alcoholism   **362.292**
  The Truth about alcohol   **362.292**
Fiction
  Buffie, M. Out of focus   Fic
  Davis, D. Not like you   Fic
  Friend, N. Lush   Fic
  Hyde, C. R. The year of my miraculous reappearance   Fic
  Murray, J. Bottled up   Fic
  Vincent, Z. The lucky place   Fic
Alcoholism   **362.292**
Alcorn, Louise E., 1970-
  Wireless networking   **025.04**
Alcorn, Stephen, 1958-
  (il) America at war. See America at war   **811.008**
  (il) Gottfried, T. Children of the slaughter   **940.53**
  (il) Gottfried, T. Heroes of the Holocaust   **940.53**
  (il) I, too, sing America. See I, too, sing America   **811.008**
  (il) My America. See My America   **811.008**
  (il) Pinkney, A. D. Let it shine   **920**
  (il) A Poem of her own. See A Poem of her own   **811.008**
Alcott, Louisa May, 1832-1888
  Little women   Fic
  See/See also pages in the following book(s):
  Ellis, S. From reader to writer   **372.6**
Alderton, David
  Wild cats of the world   **599.75**
Alegre, Cesar, 1967-
  Extraordinary Hispanic Americans   **920**
Alegría, Malín
  Estrella's quinceanera   Fic

Alender, Katie
Bad girls don't die   **Fic**

Aleshire, Peter
Deserts   **551.4**
Mountains   **551.4**
Ocean ridges and trenches   **551.46**

Alessio, Amy
A year of programs for teens   **027.62**

Alex and the Ironic Gentleman. Kress, A.   **Fic**

Alex Rider [series]
Horowitz, A. Point blank: the graphic novel
    741.5
Horowitz, A. Stormbreaker: the graphic novel
    741.5

An Alex Rider adventure [series]
Horowitz, A. Stormbreaker   **Fic**

Alex Ryan, stop that!. Mills, C.   **Fic**

Alexander, the Great, 356-323 B.C.
About
Adams, S. Alexander   **92**
Behnke, A. The conquests of Alexander the
Great   **92**
See/See also pages in the following book(s):
Meltzer, M. Ten kings   **920**
Stefoff, R. The ancient Mediterranean   **938**

Alexander, Alma
Gift of the Unmage   **Fic**

Alexander, Elizabeth, 1962-
Miss Crandall's School for Young Ladies and
Little Misses of Color   **811**

Alexander, Kwame
(ed) Crush: love poems. See Crush: love poems
    808.81

Alexander, Lloyd, 1924-2007
The book of three   **Fic**
The foundling and other tales of Prydain
    S C
The golden dream of Carlo Chuchio   **Fic**
The Illyrian adventure   **Fic**
The iron ring   **Fic**
The remarkable journey of Prince Jen   **Fic**
Westmark   **Fic**

Alexander, Robert Joseph, 1944-
(jt. auth) Alexander, S. H. She touched the
world: Laura Bridgman, deaf-blind pioneer
    92

Alexander, Sally Hobart
She touched the world: Laura Bridgman, deaf-
blind pioneer   **92**

Alexandria (Egypt)
Nardo, D. Ancient Alexandria   **932**

Alexandria (Egypt). Library *See* Alexandrian Library (Egypt)

Alexandrian Library (Egypt)
Trumble, K. The Library of Alexandria   **027**

Alexie, Sherman, 1966-
The absolutely true diary of a part-time Indian
    Fic

Alexovich, Aaron, 1977-
(il) Carey, M. Confessions of a Blabbermouth
    741.5

Alger, Neil
(ed) The Palestinians and the disputed territories. See The Palestinians and the disputed
territories   **956.04**

Algeria
Hintz, M. Algeria   **965**
Kagda, F. Algeria   **965**

Algonquian Indians
See also Delaware Indians

Alhazen, 965-1039
About
Steffens, B. Ibn al-Haytham   **92**

Ali, Dominic
Media madness   **302.23**

Ali, Muhammad, 1942-
About
Myers, W. D. The greatest: Muhammad Ali
    92
Smith, C. R. Twelve rounds to glory: the story
of Muhammad Ali   **92**
Streissguth, T. Clay v. United States and how
Muhammad Ali fought the draft   **343**

Ali, Sharifah Enayat, 1943-
Afghanistan   **958.1**

Alice, I think. Juby, S.   **Fic**

Alien feast. Simmons, M.   **Fic**

Aliens
See also Illegal aliens; Immigrants
United States
See also United States—Immigration and
emigration

Aliens ate my homework. Coville, B.   **Fic**

Aliens from outer space *See* Extraterrestrial beings

Alighieri, Dante *See* Dante Alighieri, 1265-1321

Aliki
William Shakespeare & the Globe   **822.3**

Alire, Camila
Serving Latino communities   **027.6**

Alis. Rich, N.   **Fic**

Alive. Ganeri, A.   **612**

Alkouatli, Claire
Islam   **297**

All aboard!. Zimmermann, K. R.   **385**

All about adoption. Lanchon, A.   **362.7**

All about sleep from A to ZZZZ. Scott, E.
    612.8

All alone in the universe. Perkins, L. R.   **Fic**

All-American girl. Cabot, M.   **Fic**

All Hallows' Eve *See* Halloween

All Hallows' Eve. Vande Velde, V.   **S C**

All-in. Hautman, P.   **Fic**

All made up. Brashich, A.   **305.23**

All of the above. Pearsall, S.   **Fic**

All our relatives. Goble, P.   **970.004**

All rivers flow to the sea. McGhee, A.   **Fic**

All-season Edie. Lyon, A.   **Fic**

All shook up. Pearsall, S.   **Fic**

Animals—*Continued*

Fiction

Hoeye, M. Time stops for no mouse	**Fic**
Jacques, B. Redwall	**Fic**
Kerr, M. E. Snakes don't miss their mothers	**Fic**
Kipling, R. The jungle book: the Mowgli stories	**S C**
Lynch, C. Cyberia	**Fic**
Orwell, G. Animal farm	**Fic**
Zuckerman, L. A taste for rabbit	**Fic**

Folklore

See also Dragons; Monsters; Mythical animals

Lester, J. Uncle Remus, the complete tales	**398.2**
Nigg, J. Wonder beasts	**398**

Hibernation

See Hibernation

Pictorial works

See also Animals in art

Poetry

Harley, A. African acrostics	**811**

Training

Kent, D. Animal helpers for the disabled	**636.088**

Africa

Harley, A. African acrostics	**811**
Saign, G. The African cats	**599.75**

Arctic regions

Lynch, W. Arctic	**998**

United States

Patent, D. H. Animals on the trail with Lewis and Clark	**978**

Animals, Fossil *See* Fossils

Animals, Habits and behavior of *See* Animal behavior

Animals, Mythical *See* Mythical animals

Animals	**590.3**

Animals and the handicapped

Kent, D. Animal helpers for the disabled	**636.088**

Animals in art

See also Marine animals in art

Nguyen, D. Creepy crawly animal origami	**736**

Animals in order [series]

Lassieur, A. Crabs, lobsters, and shrimps	**595.3**
Animals in the house. Keenan, S.	**636**
Animals like us. Mills, A.	**333.95**
Animals on the edge. Pobst, S.	**578.68**
Animals on the trail with Lewis and Clark. Patent, D. H.	**978**

Animals' rights *See* Animal rights

Animals that hibernate. Perry, P. J.	**591.56**
Animals under the ground. Perry, P. J.	**591.56**
Animals under threat. Spilsbury, L.	**333.95**

Animalways [series]

Greenberg, D. A. Dolphins	**599.5**
Greenberg, D. A. Lizards	**597.95**
Greenberg, D. A. Whales	**599.5**

Jango-Cohen, J. Crocodiles	**597.98**
Schlaepfer, G. G. Butterflies	**595.7**
Schlaepfer, G. G. Elephants	**599.67**
Schwabacher, M. Bees	**595.7**
Stefoff, R. Bears	**599.78**
Stefoff, R. Cats	**636.8**
Stefoff, R. Deer	**599.65**
Stefoff, R. Dogs	**636.7**
Stefoff, R. Horses	**636.1**
Stefoff, R. Lions	**599.75**
Stefoff, R. Penguins	**598**
Stefoff, R. Turtles	**597.92**
Warhol, T. Eagles	**598**
Warhol, T. Hawks	**598**
Warhol, T. Owls	**598**
Zabludoff, M. Beetles	**595.7**
Zabludoff, M. Monkeys	**599.8**
Zabludoff, M. Spiders	**595.4**

Animated films

See also Anime

Hart, C. Christopher Hart's animation studio	**791.43**

Animation (Cinematography)

See also Computer animation

Lockman, D. Computer animation	**778.5**

Anime

Akira, S. Monkey High!: vol. 1	**741.5**
Brenner, R. E. Understanding manga and anime	**025.2**

Anne Frank and the children of the Holocaust. Lee, C. A.   **940.53**

The **Anne** Frank Case: Simon Wiesenthal's search for the truth. Rubin, S. G.   **92**

Annenberg Foundation Trust at Sunnylands' adolescent mental health initiative [series]

Ford, E. What you must think of me	**616.85**

Anning, Mary, 1799-1847

About

Goodhue, T. W. Curious bones: Mary Anning and the birth of paleontology	**92**

See/See also pages in the following book(s):

Fradin, D. B. With a little luck	**509**
Anorexia	**616.85**
Anorexia. Lynette, R.	**616.85**

Anorexia nervosa

Anorexia	**616.85**
Lynette, R. Anorexia	**616.85**
Silverstein, A. The eating disorders update	**616.85**

Fiction

Anderson, L. H. Wintergirls	**Fic**
Burton, R. Leaving Jetty Road	**Fic**
George, M. Looks	**Fic**
Vrettos, A. M. Skin	**Fic**

Another kind of cowboy. Juby, S.   **Fic**

Antarctica

Bledsoe, L. J. How to survive in Antarctica	**998**
Myers, W. D. Antarctica	**998**
Scott, E. Poles apart	**998**
Tulloch, C. Antarctica	**998**
Webb, S. My season with penguins	**598**

Astronomy—*Continued*

Gardner, R. Astronomy projects with an observatory you can build   **522**

Hakim, J. The story of science: Newton at the center   **509**

Lippincott, K. Astronomy   **520**

Matloff, G. L. More telescope power   **522**

NightWatch: a practical guide to viewing the universe   **520**

Pasachoff, J. M. A field guide to the stars and planets   **523**

Prins, M. D. Paper galaxy   **745.54**

Reed, G. Eyes on the universe   **520**

Rhatigan, J. Out-of-this-world astronomy   **520**

Ridpath, I. Facts on File stars & planets atlas   **520**

Ridpath, I. The monthly sky guide   **523**

Sakolsky, J. Copernicus and modern astronomy   **92**

Silverstein, A. The universe   **520**

Simon, S. Destination: space   **522**

Solway, A. What's inside a black hole?   **523.1**

Spangenburg, R. The Hubble Space Telescope   **522**

VanCleave, J. P. Janice VanCleave's A+ projects in astronomy   **520**

Yount, L. Modern astronomy   **520**

Atlases
See Stars—Atlases

Dictionaries
The Facts on File dictionary of astronomy   **520.3**

Astronomy projects with an observatory you can build. Gardner, R.   **522**

At her majesty's request [biography of Sarah Forbes Bonetta] Myers, W. D.   **92**

At issue [series]

Anorexia   **616.85**

Is Islam a religion of war or peace?   **297**

Islam in America   **297**

Should drilling be permitted in the Arctic National Wildlife Refuge?   **333.95**

What is a hate crime?   **364.1**

At issue: Health [series]

Can diets be harmful?   **613.2**

At issue in history [series]

Custer's last stand   **973.8**

The McCarthy hearings   **973.921**

At issue: National security [series]

Can the War on Terrorism be won?   **363.32**

At Jerusalem's gate. Grimes, N.   **811**

At the end of words. Stone, M.   **92**

At the firefly gate. Newbery, L.   **Fic**

At the schoolhouse gate. Pipkin, G.   **373.1**

At the sign of the Sugared Plum. Hooper, M.   **Fic**

Atahualpa, d. 1533

See/See also pages in the following book(s):

Meltzer, M. Ten kings   **920**

Atangan, Patrick

The yellow jar   **741.5**

Athabascan Indians *See* Athapascan Indians

Athapascan Indians

Fiction
Frost, H. Diamond Willow   **Fic**

Athens (Greece)

Connolly, P. The ancient city   **937**

History
Mann, E. The Parthenon   **726**

Athletes

See also African American athletes; Women athletes

Bruchac, J. Jim Thorpe   **92**

Kaminsky, M. Uncommon champions   **920**

Drug use
See also Steroids

Egendorf, L. K. Performance-enhancing drugs   **362.29**

LeVert, S. The facts about steroids   **362.29**

Porterfield, J. Doping   **362.29**

Nutrition
Shryer, D. Peak performance   **617.1**

Athletes with disabilities. Kent, D.   **371.9**

Athletic medicine *See* Sports medicine

Athletic shorts. Crutcher, C.   **S C**

Athletics

See also Sports; Track athletics

Atinsky, Steve

Tyler on prime time   **Fic**

Atkin, S. Beth

Gunstories   **363.33**

Voices from the fields   **331.5**

Atkins, Catherine

Alt ed   **Fic**

Atkins, Jeannine, 1953-

How high can we climb?   **920**

Atkinson, Linda *See* Goldenberg, Linda, 1941-

Atkinson, Mary, 1938-

The Snake book. See The Snake book   **597.96**

Atlanta (Ga.)

Fiction
Green, T. Football genius   **Fic**

Myracle, L. Peace, love, and baby ducks   **Fic**

The **Atlantic** slave trade. Nardo, D.   **326**

Atlantis

Nardo, D. Atlantis   **001.9**

Fiction
Richards, J. The chaos code   **Fic**

Atlas of conflicts [series]

Grant, R. The Korean War   **951.9**

The **atlas** of endangered species. Mackay, R.   **333.95**

Atlas of Hispanic-American history. Ochoa, G.   **305.8**

Atlas of North America   **912**

Atlases

Atlas of North America   **912**

Geography on file   **912**

Hammond world atlas   **912**

Maps on file   **912**

National Geographic student atlas of the world   **912**

Atlases—*Continued*

National Geographic United States atlas for young explorers **912**

Oxford atlas of the world **912**

Oxford new concise world atlas **912**

Rubel, D. Scholastic atlas of the United States **912**

Student Atlas **912**

Atmosphere

See also Air

Casper, J. K. Water and atmosphere **553.7**

Cosgrove, B. Weather **551.5**

Gallant, R. A. Atmosphere **551.51**

Vogt, G. The atmosphere **551.5**

Atocha (Ship) *See* Nuestra Señora de Atocha (Ship)

Atomic bomb

Allman, T. J. Robert Oppenheimer **92**

Lawton, C. Hiroshima **940.54**

Making and using the atomic bomb **355.8**

Maruki, T. Hiroshima no pika **940.54**

Scherer, G. J. Robert Oppenheimer **92**

Sullivan, E. T. The ultimate weapon **355.8**

Fiction

Klages, E. The green glass sea **Fic**

Atomic energy *See* Nuclear energy

Atomic power plants *See* Nuclear power plants

Atomic theory

Cregan, E. R. The atom **539.7**

Oxlade, C. Atoms **539.7**

Atomic universe. Jerome, K. B. **539.7**

Atomic weapons *See* Nuclear weapons

Atoms

Cregan, E. R. The atom **539.7**

Manning, P. Atoms, molecules, and compounds **539.7**

Morgan, S. From Greek atoms to quarks **530**

Oxlade, C. Atoms **539.7**

Woodford, C. Atoms and molecules **540**

Atoms and molecules. Woodford, C. **540**

Atoms, molecules, and compounds. Manning, P. **539.7**

Attack of the killer video book. Shulman, M. **778.59**

Attack of the Turtle. Carlson, D. **Fic**

Attack on Pearl Harbor. Tanaka, S. **940.54**

Attention deficit disorder

Capaccio, G. ADD and ADHD **616.85**

Corman, C. A. Positively ADD **616.85**

Menhard, F. R. The facts about ritalin **615**

Pigache, P. ADHD **616.85**

Silverstein, A. The ADHD update **616.85**

Trueit, T. S. ADHD **616.85**

Fiction

Cheaney, J. B. The middle of somewhere **Fic**

Gantos, J. Joey Pigza swallowed the key **Fic**

Attica. Kilworth, G. **Fic**

Attila, King of the Huns, d. 453

About

Price, S. Attila the Hun **92**

See/See also pages in the following book(s):

Meltzer, M. Ten kings **920**

Attila the Hun. Price, S. **92**

Attoe, Steve

(il) Thomas, K. Blades, boards & scooters **796.2**

Attorneys *See* Lawyers

Atwater-Rhodes, Amelia, 1984-

Persistence of memory **Fic**

Auch, Mary Jane

Ashes of roses **Fic**

Wing nut **Fic**

Auden, Scott

Medical mysteries **610**

Auderset, Marie-Josée

Walking tall **158**

Audiobooks

Coville, B. William Shakespeare's A midsummer night's dream **822.3**

Audiovisual materials

Catalogs

Adamson, L. G. Literature connections to world history, 7-12 **016.9**

The **Audubon** Society field guide to North American butterflies. Pyle, R. M. **595.7**

The **Audubon** Society field guide to North American fishes, whales, and dolphins. See Gilbert, C. R. National Audubon Society field guide to fishes, North America **597**

The **Audubon** Society field guide to North American insects and spiders. Milne, L. J. **595.7**

The **Audubon** Society field guide to North American mushrooms. Lincoff, G. **579.6**

The **Audubon** Society field guide to North American rocks and minerals. Chesterman, C. W. **549**

The **Audubon** Society field guide to North American seashore creatures. Meinkoth, N. A. **592**

The **Audubon** Society field guide to the night sky. Chartrand, M. R. **523**

Augenbraum, Harold

(ed) Growing up Latino. See Growing up Latino **810.8**

Augustin, Byron

Andorra **946**

Iraq **956.7**

United Arab Emirates **953**

Augustus, Emperor of Rome, 63 B.C.-14 A.D.

About

Forsyth, F. Augustus: the first emperor **92**

Augustus: the first emperor. Forsyth, F. **92**

Augustyn, Frank

Footnotes **792.8**

Aung San Suu Kyi

See/See also pages in the following book(s):

Hacker, C. Nobel Prize winners **920**

Krull, K. Lives of extraordinary women **920**

Authors, English—*Continued*
Sickels, A. Mythmaker: the story of J.K. Rowling **92**
Speaker-Yuan, M. Philip Pullman **92**
Wagner, H. L. Jane Austen **92**
The wand in the word **813.009**
Willett, E. J.R.R. Tolkien **92**

Authors, French
Schoell, W. Remarkable journeys: the story of Jules Verne **92**

Authors, Italian
Davenport, J. Dante **92**

Authors, Scottish
Murphy, J. Across America on an emigrant train [biography of Robert Louis Stevenson] **92**
Pascal, J. B. Arthur Conan Doyle **92**

Authors of banned books [series]
Beckman, W. H. Robert Cormier **92**
Houle, M. M. Mark Twain **92**
McClellan, M. Madeleine L'Engle **813.009**

Authors series
American authors, 1600-1900 **920.003**
World authors, 1995-2000 **920.003**

Authors teens love [series]
Albert, L. R. Lois Lowry **92**
Angel, A. Amy Tan **92**
Campbell, K. Richard Peck **92**
Campbell, K. E. Lois Duncan **92**
Hoppa, J. Isaac Asimov **92**
Kjelle, M. M. S.E. Hinton **92**
Reed, J. Paula Danziger **92**
Willett, E. J.R.R. Tolkien **92**
Willett, E. Orson Scott Card **92**

Authorship

See also Creative writing; Journalism
Bauer, M. D. Our stories **808.3**
Benini Pietromarchi, S. The book book: a journey into bookmaking **070.5**
Bodden, V. Creating the character **808.3**
Bodden, V. Painting the picture **808.3**
Bodden, V. Setting the style **808.3**
Bodden, V. Telling the tale **808.3**
Dunn, J. A teen's guide to getting published **808**
Fletcher, R. How to write your life story **808**
Fletcher, R. How writers work **808**
Freedman, J. Sid Fleischman **92**
Gilbert, S. Write your own article **808**
Global warming **363.7**
Hanley, V. Seize the story **808.3**
Harper, E. Your name in print **808**
Janeczko, P. B. Writing winning reports and essays **808**
Levine, G. C. Writing magic **808.3**
Mlynowski, S. See Jane write **808.3**
Nuwer, H. To the young writer **808**
Orr, T. Extraordinary essays **808.4**
Otfinoski, S. Extraordinary short story writing **808.3**
Peck, R. Invitations to the world **808.06**
Racism: an opposing viewpoints guide **305.8**
Terrorism **363.32**
Trueit, T. S. Keeping a journal **808**

Fiction
Baskin, N. R. Anything but typical **Fic**
Clements, A. The school story **Fic**
Cornwell, A. Carpe diem **Fic**
Davis, K. The curse of Addy McMahon **Fic**
Dee, B. Just another day in my insanely real life **Fic**
D'Lacey, C. The fire within **Fic**
Gould, P. L. Write naked **Fic**
Grimes, N. Jazmin's notebook **Fic**
Johnson, M. Suite Scarlett **Fic**
Kimmel, E. C. Lily B. on the brink of cool **Fic**
Kladstrup, K. The book of story beginnings **Fic**
Klinger, S. The Kingdom of Strange **Fic**
Lubar, D. Sleeping freshmen never lie **Fic**
Murphy, P. The wild girls **Fic**
Nance, A. Daemon Hall **Fic**
Nelson, T. Ruby electric **Fic**
Nicholls, S. Ways to live forever **Fic**
Schwartz, V. F. 4 kids in 5E & 1 crazy year **Fic**
Sitomer, A. L. The Hoopster **Fic**
Wittlinger, E. Hard love **Fic**

Autism
Baldwin, C. Autism **616.89**
Brill, M. T. Autism **616.85**
Crissey, P. Personal hygiene? What's that got to do with me? **649**

Fiction
Baskin, N. R. Anything but typical **Fic**
Choldenko, G. Al Capone does my shirts **Fic**
Geus, M. Piggy **Fic**
Lord, C. Rules **Fic**
Stork, F. X. Marcelo in the real world **Fic**

Autobiographies
I can't keep my own secrets **808.8**

Autobiography
Authorship
Fletcher, R. How to write your life story **808**

Autobiography of my dead brother. Myers, W. D. **Fic**

Automania! [series]
Eagen, R. NASCAR **796.72**
Morganelli, A. Formula One **796.72**

Automata *See* Robots

Automated information networks *See* Information networks

An **automation** primer for school library media centers and small libraries. Schultz-Jones, B. **027.8**

Automobile accidents *See* Traffic accidents

Automobile drivers
Poetry
Wong, J. S. Behind the wheel **811**

Automobile industry
Tilton, R. Henry Ford **92**

Automobile racing
Blackwood, G. L. The Great Race **796.72**
Buckley, J., Jr. NASCAR **796.72**
Caldwell, D. Speed show **796.72**

Baking

See also Bread

Dunnington, R. Bake it up! **641.8**

Bakke, Allan Paul

About

McPherson, S. S. The Bakke case and the affirmative action debate **344**

Stefoff, R. The Bakke case **344**

The **Bakke** case. Stefoff, R. **344**

The **Bakke** case and the affirmative action debate. McPherson, S. S. **344**

Balanchine, George, 1904-1983

101 stories of the great ballets **792.8**

Balboa, Vasco Núñez de, 1475-1519

About

Otfinoski, S. Vasco Nuñez de Balboa **92**

See/See also pages in the following book(s):

Fritz, J. Around the world in a hundred years **910.4**

Bald eagle

Patent, D. H. The bald eagle returns **598**

The **bald** eagle returns. Patent, D. H. **598**

Baldwin, Carol

Autism **616.89**

Sickle cell disease **616.1**

Baldwin, James, 1924-1987

Go tell it on the mountain **Fic**

Balefire [series]

Tiernan, C. A chalice of wind **Fic**

Balkin, Karen

(ed) Anorexia. See Anorexia **616.85**

Ball, Jacqueline A.

Ancient China **931**

Ball, Johnny, 1938-

Go figure! **793.74**

Ballard, Carol

AIDS and other epidemics **614.5**

Food for feeling healthy **613.2**

From steam engines to nuclear fusion **333.79**

Ballet

Augustyn, F. Footnotes **792.8**

Goh, C. H. Beyond the dance **92**

Lee, L. A child's introduction to ballet **792.8**

Schorer, S. Put your best foot forward **792.8**

Graphic novels

Ariyoshi, K. Swan, Vol. 1 **741.5**

Stories, plots, etc.

Balanchine, G. 101 stories of the great ballets **792.8**

Ballet dancers

Li Cunxin. Mao's last dancer [biography of Li Cunxin] **92**

Balliett, Blue, 1955-

Chasing Vermeer **Fic**

Balloons, Dirigible *See* Airships

Balmer, Alden J.

Doc Fizzix mousetrap racers **629.22**

Bancroft, Ann

See/See also pages in the following book(s):

Atkins, J. How high can we climb? **920**

A **band** of bears. Hunt, J. P. **599.78**

Bands (Music)

Goodmark, R. Girls rock **781.66**

Marx, T. Steel drumming at the Apollo **785**

Fiction

Hall, B. Tempo change **Fic**

Ostow, M. So punk rock (and other ways to disappoint your mother) **Fic**

Simmons, M. Vandal **Fic**

Bang!. Flake, S. G. **Fic**

Bangalore, Lakshmi

Brain development **612.8**

Banghart, Tracy

What the sea wants **Fic**

Bangladesh

Orr, T. Bangladesh **954.92**

Phillips, D. A. Bangladesh **954.92**

Valliant, D. Bangladesh **954.92**

Banjos

Ellis, R. M. With a banjo on my knee **787.8**

Bank job. Heneghan, J. **Fic**

Banks, Deena

Amnesty International **323**

Banks, Kate, 1960-

Walk softly, Rachel **Fic**

Bankston, John

Stephen Hawking **92**

Bankston, John, 1974-

Lois Lowry **92**

Banned books *See* Books—Censorship

Banneker, Benjamin, 1731-1806

About

Litwin, L. B. Benjamin Banneker **92**

Banner, Shawn

(il) Brashich, A. All made up **305.23**

Bannister (Person)

The shadow door **741.5**

Banqueri, Eduardo, 1966-

Weather **551.5**

Bansavage, Lisa

(ed) Shakespeare, W. One hundred and eleven Shakespeare monologues **822.3**

Baptism

Fiction

Moses, S. P. The baptism **Fic**

The **baptism**. Moses, S. P. **Fic**

Bar mitzvah

Metter, B. Bar mitzvah, bat mitzvah **296.4**

Fiction

Brown, J. R. 13 **Fic**

Bar mitzvah, bat mitzvah. Metter, B. **296.4**

Barakat, Ibtisam

Tasting the sky **92**

Barancik, Sue, 1944-

Guide to collective biographies for children and young adults **016.9**

Barb and Dingbat's crybaby hotline. Jennings, P. **Fic**

Barbara McClintock, geneticist. Cullen, J. H. **92**

Barbary States *See* North Africa

Bartimaeus trilogy [series]
Stroud, J. The Amulet of Samarkand **Fic**
Bartlett, John, 1820-1905
Bartlett's familiar quotations **808.88**
Bartlett, Patricia Pope, 1949-
(jt. auth) Bartlett, R. D. Aquatic turtles
639.3
(jt. auth) Bartlett, R. D. Geckos **639.3**
(jt. auth) Bartlett, R. D. Turtles and tortoises
639.3
Bartlett, Richard D., 1938-
Aquatic turtles **639.3**
Geckos **639.3**
Turtles and tortoises **639.3**
Bartlett's familiar quotations. Bartlett, J.
808.88
Bartlett's Roget's thesaurus **423**
Bartoletti, Susan Campbell, 1958-
Black potatoes **941.5**
The boy who dared **Fic**
Growing up in coal country **331.3**
Hitler Youth **943.086**
Kids on strike! **331.8**
Barton, Clara, 1821-1912
About
Somervill, B. A. Clara Barton **92**
Whitelaw, N. Clara Barton **92**
Barton, Hazel
About
Jackson, D. M. Extreme scientists **509**
Barton, Otis
About
Matsen, B. The incredible record-setting deep-
sea dive of the bathysphere **551.46**
Bas mitzvah *See* Bat mitzvah
Baseball
See also Softball; World series (Baseball)
January, B. A baseball all-star **796.357**
Krasner, S. Play ball like the hall of famers
796.357
Krasner, S. Play ball like the pros **796.357**
McKissack, P. C. Black diamond **796.357**
Teitelbaum, M. Baseball **796.357**
Biography
Copley, B. The tall Mexican: the life of Hank
Aguirre, all-star pitcher, businessman, human-
itarian **92**
Ford, C. T. Roberto Clemente **92**
Green, M. Y. A strong right arm: the story of
Mamie "Peanut" Johnson **92**
Hampton, W. Babe Ruth **92**
Lashnits, T. Pedro Martinez **92**
Lipsyte, R. Heroes of baseball **796.357**
Márquez, H. Roberto Clemente **92**
McCormack, S. Cool Papa Bell **92**
Mills, C. Derek Jeter **92**
Needham, T. Albert Pujols **92**
Payment, S. Buck Leonard **92**
Robinson, S. Promises to keep: how Jackie Rob-
inson changed America **92**
Robinson, T. Derek Jeter **92**
Stanton, T. Hank Aaron and the home run that
changed America **92**
Twemlow, N. Josh Gibson **92**

Wukovits, J. F. Jackie Robinson and the integra-
tion of baseball **92**
Collectibles
Owens, T. Collecting baseball memorabilia
796.357
Wong, S. Baseball treasures **796.357**
Fiction
Baggott, J. The Prince of Fenway Park **Fic**
Baseball crazy: ten short stories that cover all
the bases **S C**
Chabon, M. Summerland **Fic**
Cochrane, M. The girl who threw butterflies
Fic
Corbett, S. Free baseball **Fic**
Day, K. No cream puffs **Fic**
Deuker, C. Painting the black **Fic**
Fehler, G. Beanball **Fic**
Gratz, A. The Brooklyn nine **Fic**
Gratz, A. Samurai shortstop **Fic**
Green, T. Baseball great **Fic**
Gutman, D. Shoeless Joe & me **Fic**
Haven, P. Two hot dogs with everything
Fic
Lupica, M. The big field **Fic**
McCormick, P. My brother's keeper **Fic**
Murphy, C. R. Free radical **Fic**
Park, L. S. Keeping score **Fic**
Preller, J. Six innings **Fic**
Ritter, J. H. The boy who saved baseball
Fic
Ritter, J. H. Choosing up sides **Fic**
Ritter, J. H. The desperado who stole baseball
Fic
Roberts, K. My 13th season **Fic**
Scaletta, K. Mudville **Fic**
Smith, J. E. The comeback season **Fic**
Tocher, T. Bill Pennant, Babe Ruth, and me
Fic
Tocher, T. Chief Sunrise, John McGraw, and
me **Fic**
Trueman, T. 7 days at the hot corner **Fic**
Turner, A. W. Hard hit **Fic**
Wiles, D. The Aurora County All-Stars **Fic**
Graphic novels
Sturm, J. Satchel Paige **741.5**
History
Owens, T. Collecting baseball memorabilia
796.357
Stewart, M. World Series **796.357**
Wong, S. Baseball treasures **796.357**
Poetry
Maddox, M. Rules of the game **811**
Thayer, E. L. Casey at the bat **811**
Baseball. Teitelbaum, M. **796.357**
A **baseball** all-star. January, B. **796.357**
Baseball crazy: ten short stories that cover all the
bases **S C**
Baseball great. Green, T. **Fic**
Baseball Hall of Famers of the Negro leagues
[series]
McCormack, S. Cool Papa Bell **92**
Payment, S. Buck Leonard **92**
Twemlow, N. Josh Gibson **92**
Baseball in April, and other stories. Soto, G.
S C

Baseball superstars [series]
Mills, C. Derek Jeter — 92

Baseball treasures. Wong, S. — 796.357

Baseman, Gary
(il) Harris, J. Strong stuff — 398.2

Bases (Chemistry)
Lew, K. Acids and bases — 546
Oxlade, C. Acids and bases — 546

Basher, Simon
(jt. auth) Dingle, A. The periodic table — 546
(il) Green, D. Physics — 530

Basher five-two. O'Grady, S. F. — 949.7

Basic biology [series]
Walker, D. Inheritance and evolution — 576

Basic Japanese-English dictionary — 495.6

Basic life skills See Life skills

Basic rights See Civil rights; Human rights

The **basics** of quantum physics. Willett, E. — 539

Basketball
Ingram, S. A basketball all-star — 796.323
Labrecque, E. Basketball — 796.323
Stewart, M. Basketball — 796.323
Stewart, M. Swish — 796.323
Thomas, K. How basketball works — 796.323
Biography
Rappoport, K. Lebron James — 92
Fiction
Coy, J. Box out — Fic
Deuker, C. Night hoops — Fic
Feinstein, J. Last shot — Fic
Gutman, D. The million dollar shot — Fic
Lupica, M. Miracle on 49th Street — Fic
Lupica, M. Summer ball — Fic
Mackel, K. Boost — Fic
Maddox, J. Free throw — Fic
Myers, W. D. Game — Fic
Myers, W. D. Hoops — Fic
Myers, W. D. Slam! — Fic
Parker, R. B. The Edenville Owls — Fic
Sitomer, A. L. The Hoopster — Fic
Soto, G. Taking sides — Fic
Trueman, T. Cruise control — Fic
Volponi, P. Black and white — Fic
Volponi, P. Rucker Park setup — Fic
Waltman, K. Learning the game — Fic
Yep, L. Dragon road — Fic
Poetry
Burleigh, R. Hoops — 811
Smith, C. R. Hoop queens — 811

A **basketball** all-star. Ingram, S. — 796.323

Baskin, Nora Raleigh, 1961-
All we know of love — Fic
Anything but typical — Fic
The truth about my Bat Mitzvah — Fic

Basman, Michael
Chess for kids — 794.1

Basoalto, Ricardo Elizier Neftali Reyes See Neruda, Pablo, 1904-1973

Bassil, Andrea
Vincent van Gogh — 92

Bassis, Volodymyr
Ukraine — 947.7

Bastedo, Jamie, 1955-
On thin ice — Fic

Basye, Dale E.
Heck — Fic

Bat mitzvah
Metter, B. Bar mitzvah, bat mitzvah — 296.4
Fiction
Baskin, N. R. The truth about my Bat Mitzvah — Fic
Rosenbloom, F. You are so not invited to my bat mitzvah! — Fic

Bateman, Teresa
Red, white, blue, and Uncle who? — 929.9

Bates, Daisy
About
Fradin, J. B. The power of one [biography of Daisy Bates] — 92

Bates, Martine See Leavitt, Martine, 1953-

Bateson, Catherine, 1960-
Being Bee — Fic

Batman (Fictional character)
Fisch, S. Super friends: for justice! — 741.5

Batmanglij, Najmieh
See/See also pages in the following book(s):
Major, J. S. Caravan to America — 920

Batmanglij, Najmieh, 1947-
Happy Nowruz — 641.5

Bats
Lockwood, S. Bats — 599.4
Stokes beginner's guide to bats — 599.4
Fiction
French, V. The robe of skulls — Fic
Oppel, K. Silverwing — Fic

Batten, Jack
Silent in an evil time: the brave war of Edith Cavell — 92

Batten, Mary
Anthropologist: scientist of the people — 301

Battered children See Child abuse

Battered women See Abused women

Battered women — 362.82

Battering of wives See Wife abuse

The **battle** against polio. Peters, S. T. — 614.5

Battle dress. Efaw, A. — Fic

The **Battle** of Antietam. Hughes, C. — 973.7

The **Battle** of Gettysburg. King, D. C. — 973.7

The **battle** of Iwo Jima. Hama, L. — 940.54

The **Battle** of Jericho. Draper, S. M. — Fic

Battle of the Bulge See Ardennes, Battle of the, 1944-1945

The **Battle** of the Little Bighorn. Uschan, M. V. — 973.8

The **Battle** of the Little Bighorn in American history. Ferrell, N. W. — 973.8

Battles & weapons: exploring history through art. Chapman, C. — 355

Battling in the Pacific. Beller, S. P. — 940.54

Bauchner, Elizabeth, 1970-
What do I have to lose? — 613.2

Bauer, A. C. E.
No castles here — Fic

Bauer, Carla
(il) Allen, T. B. Harriet Tubman, secret agent
92

Bauer, Joan
Peeled   Fic
Squashed   Fic
Stand tall   Fic

Bauer, Marion Dane, 1938-
On my honor   Fic
Our stories   808.3
A writer's story   92

Bauer, Alice C. E. *See* Bauer, A. C. E.

Baughan, Brian
Russell Simmons   92

Baughan, Michael Gray, 1973-
Shel Silverstein   92
Stephen King   92

Baule, Steven M., 1966-
Facilities planning for school library and technology centers   027.8

Baumbach, Donna
Less is more   025.2

Baumfree, Isabella *See* Truth, Sojourner, d. 1883

Bausum, Ann
Denied, detained, deported   325.73
Dragon bones and dinosaur eggs: a photobiography of Roy Chapman Andrews   92
Freedom Riders   323.1
Muckrakers   070.4
Our country's first ladies   920
Our country's presidents   920
With courage and cloth   305.4

Baxter, Katherine
(il) Adams, S. The Kingfisher atlas of the ancient world   930

Baxter, Kathleen A.
Gotcha!   028.5
Gotcha again!   028.5
Gotcha for guys!   028.5
Gotcha good!   028.5

Baxter, Roberta, 1952-
Illuminated progress   92
Skeptical chemist   92

Bayless, Lanie
(jt. auth) Bayless, R. Rick & Lanie's excellent kitchen adventures   641.5

Bayless, Rick
Rick & Lanie's excellent kitchen adventures   641.5

Baynes, Pauline, 1922-2008
Questionable creatures   398.2
(il) Lewis, C. S. The lion, the witch, and the wardrobe   Fic

Bazin, Maurice
Math and science across cultures   510

Be a better babysitter. Buckley, A.   649
Be a better biker. Buckley, A.   796.6
Be confident in who you are. Fox, A.   158
Be healthy! it's a girl thing. Cheung, L. W. Y.   613

Beaches
Fiction
Han, J. The summer I turned pretty   Fic
Horvath, P. My one hundred adventures   Fic
Nelson, B. They came from below   Fic

Beachmont letters. Twomey, C.   Fic
Beacon Hill boys. Mochizuki, K.   Fic
Beading. Boonyadhistarn, T.   745.58

Beadwork
Baker, D. Jazzy jewelry   745.594
Boonyadhistarn, T. Beading   745.58

Beagle Expedition (1831-1836)
Ashby, R. Young Charles Darwin and the voyage of the Beagle   92
Gibbons, A. Charles Darwin   92
Schanzer, R. What Darwin saw   92
Fiction
Meyer, C. The true adventures of Charley Darwin   Fic

Beahm, George W.
Discovering The golden compass   823.009

Bean, Alan
(il) Chaikin, A. Mission control, this is Apollo   629.45

Bean, Jonathan, 1979-
(il) Jonell, L. Emmy and the incredible shrinking rat   Fic

Beanball. Fehler, G.   Fic
The **bear** makers. Cheng, A.   Fic
Bear rescue. Thomas, K.   599.78

Beard, Hilary
(jt. auth) Williams, V. Venus & Serena   92

Bearing witness. Rosen, P.   016.94053

Bears
    See also Polar bear
Hunt, J. P. A band of bears   599.78
Montgomery, S. Search for the golden moon bear   599.78
Stefoff, R. Bears   599.78
Thomas, K. Bear rescue   599.78
Ward, P. Bears of the world   599.78
Fiction
Bruchac, J. Bearwalker   Fic
Mikaelsen, B. Touching Spirit Bear   Fic
Pattou, E. East   Fic
Paver, M. Wolf brother   Fic

Bears of the world. Ward, P.   599.78
Bearstone. Hobbs, W.   Fic
The **Beast**. Myers, W. D.   Fic
Beast. Napoli, D. J.   Fic
The **beast** of Noor. Carey, J. L.   Fic
Beastly. Flinn, A.   Fic
The **beasts** of Clawstone Castle. Ibbotson, E.   Fic

Beatles
Partridge, E. John Lennon   92
Rappaport, D. John's secret dreams [biography of John Lennon]   92
Spitz, B. Yeah! yeah! yeah!   920

Beattie, Owen
Buried in ice   998

Behnke, Alison
Afghanistan in pictures — 958.1
China in pictures — 951
The conquests of Alexander the Great — 92
Italy in pictures — 945
Japan in pictures — 952
Kim Jong Il's North Korea — 92
Pope John Paul II — 92

Beil, Michael D.
The Red Blazer Girls: the ring of Rocamadour — Fic

Being Bee. Bateson, C. — Fic

Being caribou. Heuer, K. — 599.65

Being dead. Vande Velde, V. — S C

Being human — 612

Being Muslim. Siddiqui, H. — 297

Beingessner, Laura, 1965-
(il) Whipple, L. If the shoe fits — 811

Beka Cooper [series]
Pierce, T. Terrier — Fic

Beker, Jeanne
The big night out — 646.7

Belanus, Betty J.
(jt. auth) Major, J. S. Caravan to America — 920

Belfast (Northern Ireland)
Fiction
Heneghan, J. Safe house — Fic

Belgium
Pateman, R. Belgium — 949.3

Beliaev, Edward
Dagestan — 947.5

Belize
Shields, C. J. Belize — 972.82

Bell, Alexander Graham, 1847-1922
About
Carson, M. K. Alexander Graham Bell — 92
Matthews, T. L. Always inventing: a photobiography of Alexander Graham Bell — 92

Bell, Ann, 1945-
Handheld computers in schools and media centers — 371.3

Bell, Cathleen Davitt, 1971-
Slipping — Fic

Bell, Cool Papa, 1903-1991
About
McCormack, S. Cool Papa Bell — 92

Bell, Currer See Brontë, Charlotte, 1816-1855

Bell, Ellis See Brontë, Emily, 1818-1848

Bell, Gertrude Margaret Lowthian, 1868-1926
See/See also pages in the following book(s):
Krull, K. Lives of extraordinary women — 920

Bell, Hilari, 1958-
Flame — Fic
The Goblin Wood — Fic
The last knight — Fic
Shield of stars — Fic

Bell, Ruth
Changing bodies, changing lives — 613.9

Bell, Suzanne
Encyclopedia of forensic science — 363.2

Fakes and forgeries — 363.2

Bell, Suzanne S.
Librarian's guide to online searching — 025.5

Bell, Ted
Nick of time — Fic

Bell, Trudy E.
Earth's journey through space — 525

Bell-Rehwoldt, Sheri, 1962-
The kids' guide to building cool stuff — 745.5
The kids' guide to classic games — 790.1

Bella at midnight. Stanley, D. — Fic

Bellairs, John
The curse of the blue figurine — Fic
(jt. auth) Strickland, B. The sign of the sinister sorcerer — Fic

Belle Prater's boy. White, R. — Fic

Bellenir, Karen
(ed) Allergy information for teens. See Allergy information for teens — 616.97
(ed) Asthma information for teens. See Asthma information for teens — 616.2
(ed) Diet information for teens. See Diet information for teens — 613.2
(ed) Mental health information for teens. See Mental health information for teens — 616.89
(ed) Sports injuries information for teens. See Sports injuries information for teens — 617.1
(ed) Tobacco information for teens. See Tobacco information for teens — 362.29

Beller, Susan Provost, 1949-
Battling in the Pacific — 940.54
Billy Yank and Johnny Reb — 973.7
The doughboys over there — 940.4
The history puzzle — 901
Roman legions on the march — 937

Belli, Mary Lou
Acting for young actors — 792

Bells
Folklore
Spencer, A. And round me rings — 398.2

Belmont, Helen
Looking at aerial photographs — 910
Planning for a sustainable future — 338.9

Bemis, John Claude
The nine pound hammer — Fic

Ben Franklin's almanac. Fleming, C. — 92

Benchley, Peter, 1940-2006
Shark life — 597

Bender, Lionel
Invention — 609

Beneath my mother's feet. Qamar, A. — Fic

Benet's reader's encyclopedia — 803

Benhart, John E.
South Asia — 954

Benin
Kneib, M. Benin — 966.83

Benini Pietromarchi, Sophie
The book book: a journey into bookmaking — 070.5

Benito Juarez and the French intervention. Stein, R. C. — 92

Bielagus, Peter G.
Quick cash for teens   **658.1**

Bienvenidos! = Welcome!. Byrd, S. M.   **027.6**

Biesty, Stephen
Egypt in spectacular cross-section   **932**
Rome: in spectacular cross section   **937**

Bifocal. Ellis, D.   **Fic**

The **big** bang. Fleisher, P.   **523.1**

Big bang cosmology *See* Big bang theory

Big bang theory
Fleisher, P. The big bang   **523.1**

Big book of brain games. Moscovich, I.
    793.73

The **big** book of dummies, rebels and other geniuses. Pouy, J.-B.   **920**

The **big** book of horror. Heyman, A.   **S C**

The **big** book of teen reading lists. Keane, N. J.
    028.5

The **Big** Burn. Ingold, J.   **Fic**

Big cat conservation. Thomas, P.   **333.95**

Big fat paycheck. Lawrence, C.   **808.2**

The **big** field. Lupica, M.   **Fic**

Big foot *See* Sasquatch

Big game hunting *See* Hunting

The **Big** Game of Everything. Lynch, C.   **Fic**

Big Mouth & Ugly Girl. Oates, J. C.   **Fic**

The **big** night out. Beker, J.   **646.7**

The **big** nothing. Fogelin, A.   **Fic**

Big snacks, little meals. Dunnington, R.   **641.5**

The **big** splash. Ferraiolo, J. D.   **Fic**

Big talk. Fleischman, P.   **811**

Bigelow, Barbara Carlisle
American Revolution: almanac   **973.3**
(comp) World War II: primary sources. See
    World War II: primary sources   **940.53**

Bigfoot *See* Sasquatch

Bigger. Calvert, P.   **Fic**

Biggs, Brian
(il) Brunelle, L. Camp out!   **796.54**

Bigotry *See* Toleration

Biker girl. Rocks, M.   **741.5**

Bikes, Mountain *See* Mountain bikes

Bildungsromans
Graphic novels
Lat. Town Boy   **741.5**

Bilingual books
English-Chinese
Liu Siyu. A thousand peaks   **895.1**
English-Spanish
Cool salsa   **811.008**
Hayes, J. Dance, Nana, dance   **398.2**
Herrera, J. F. Laughing out loud, I fly   **811**
Mora, P. The desert is my mother. El desierto
    es mi madre   **811**
Red hot salsa   **811.008**
The Tree is older than you are   **860.8**
Wáchale! poetry and prose on growing up
    Latino in America   **810.8**

Bill, Buffalo *See* Buffalo Bill, 1846-1917

Bill of rights (U.S.) *See* United States. Constitution. 1st-10th amendments

The **Bill** of Rights. Patrick, J. J.   **342**

Bill Pennant, Babe Ruth, and me. Tocher, T.
    Fic

Billie Standish was here. Crocker, N.   **Fic**

Billings, Charlene W., 1941-
Supercomputers   **004**

Billitteri, Thomas J.
Alternative medicine   **615.5**

Billy, the Kid
Fiction
Ritter, J. H. The desperado who stole baseball
    Fic

Billy Creekmore. Porter, T.   **Fic**

Billy Yank and Johnny Reb. Beller, S. P.
    973.7

Bily, Cynthia A.
(ed) Endangered species. See Endangered species   **333.95**
(ed) Global warming: opposing viewpoints. See
    Global warming: opposing viewpoints
    363.7
(ed) Homosexuality: opposing viewpoints. See
    Homosexuality: opposing viewpoints
    306.76

Bilz, Rachelle Lasky
Life is tough   **028.5**

Bin Laden, Osama *See* Osama bin Laden

Binder, Mark
The brothers Schlemiel   **Fic**

Binding, Tim
Sylvie and the songman   **Fic**

Bing, Christopher
(il) Denenberg, B. Lincoln shot!   **92**

Binge-purge behavior *See* Bulimia

Bingham, Jane
African art & culture   **709.6**
The Aztec empire   **972**
Eating disorders   **616.85**
Emotion & relationships   **704.9**
Impressionism   **759.05**
The Inca empire   **985**
Indian art & culture   **709.5**
Landscape & the environment   **704.9**
Post-Impressionism   **759.05**
Science & technology   **704.9**
Society & class   **704.9**
Stress and depression   **616.85**
Why do families break up?   **306.89**

Bingham, Kelly, 1967-
Shark girl   **Fic**

Binns, T. B.
Winston Churchill   **92**

Binns, Tristan Boyer, 1968-
Edgar Allan Poe   **92**

Bioengineered foods *See* Food—Biotechnology

Bioethics
Altman, L. J. Bioethics   **174.2**
Fiction
Pearson, M. The adoration of Jenna Fox   **Fic**
Werlin, N. Double helix   **Fic**

Biofeedback. West, K.   **615.8**

Biofeedback training
West, K. Biofeedback   **615.8**

Biographical graphic novels
Lutes, J. Houdini: the handcuff king   **92**
Ottaviani, J. Dignifying science: stories about women scientists   **920**
Spiegelman, A. Maus   **940.53**
Winick, J. Pedro and me   **362.1**

Biography
    See also Autobiographies
Lukenbill, W. B. Biography in the lives of youth   **028.5**
      Authorship
Rosinsky, N. M. Write your own biography   **808**
      Bibliography
Barancik, S. Guide to collective biographies for children and young adults   **016.9**
      Dictionaries
Almanac of famous people   **920.003**
Lincoln Library of shapers of society   **920.003**
Pouy, J.-B. The big book of dummies, rebels and other geniuses   **920**
      Periodicals
Biography today   **920.003**
Current biography yearbook, 2008   **920.003**
Biography almanac. See Almanac of famous people   **920.003**

Biography as a literary form
    See also Autobiography

Biography from ancient civilizations [series]
Gedney, M. The life and times of Buddha   **294.3**

Biography in the lives of youth. Lukenbill, W. B.   **028.5**

Biography today   **920.003**

Biohazards. Grady, S. M.   **614.5**

Biological diversity
Conserving the environment   **333.7**
Gallant, R. A. The wonders of biodiversity   **333.95**

Biological invasions
Collard, S. B., III. Science warriors   **578.6**
May, S. Invasive microbes   **579**

Biological warfare
Gay, K. Silent death   **358**
Judson, K. Chemical and biological warfare   **358**
See/See also pages in the following book(s):
Weapons of mass destruction: opposing viewpoints   **358**

Biologists
Parks, D. Nature's machines [biography of Mimi Koehl]   **92**
Yount, L. Antoni van Leeuwenhoek   **92**

Biology
    See also Adaptation (Biology); Freshwater biology; Marine biology; Microbiology; Space biology
Biology   **570**
Biology matters!   **570**
The Facts on File biology handbook   **570**
Kelsey, E. Strange new species   **578**

Silverstein, A. Growth and development   **571.8**
      Classification
Stefoff, R. The conifer division   **585**

Biology   **570**

Biology! best science projects [series]
Walker, P. Ecosystem science fair projects using worms, leaves, crickets, and other stuff   **577**

Biology matters!   **570**

Biology of cancer [series]
McKinnell, R. G. Prevention of cancer   **616.99**

Bioluminescence
Sitarski, A. Cold light   **572**

Biomass. Walker, N.   **333.95**

Biomass energy
Walker, N. Biomass   **333.95**

Biomechanics See Human engineering

Biomes [series]
Miller-Schroeder, P. Boreal forests   **577.3**

Biomes and habitats [series]
Fridell, R. Life in the desert   **577.5**
Tocci, S. Alpine tundra   **577.5**
Tocci, S. Arctic tundra   **577.5**
Tocci, S. The chaparral   **577.3**
Tocci, S. Coral reefs   **577.7**
Tocci, S. Life in the temperate forests   **577.3**
Tocci, S. Life in the tropical forests   **577.3**
Toupin, L. Freshwater habitats   **577.6**
Toupin, L. Life in the temperate grasslands   **577.4**
Toupin, L. Savannas   **577.4**

Biomes atlases [series]
Burnie, D. Shrublands   **577.3**
Hoare, B. Temperate grasslands   **577.4**
Jackson, T. Tropical forests   **577.3**

Bionics
Jango-Cohen, J. Bionics   **617.9**
Rosaler, M. Bionics   **617.9**

Biotechnology
    See also Food—Biotechnology
Biotechnology: changing life through science   **660.6**
Hopkins, W. G. Plant biotechnology   **630**
Seiple, S. Mutants, clones, and killer corn   **660.6**
A Student's guide to biotechnology   **660.6**
Yount, L. Biotechnology and genetic engineering   **303.4**

Biotechnology and genetic engineering. Yount, L.   **303.4**

Biotechnology: changing life through science   **660.6**

Birch, Beverley
Alexander Fleming   **92**

The **birchbark** house. Erdrich, L.   **Fic**

Bird. Murphy, R.   **Fic**

Bird alert. Thomas, P.   **333.95**

The **bird** class. Stefoff, R.   **598**

Bird Lake moon. Henkes, K.   **Fic**

Bird song See Birdsongs

Blackman, Haden
Star Wars: Clone wars adventures, Vol. 1
741.5

Blacks
Biography
See also African Americans—Biography
Rockwell, A. F. Open the door to liberty!: a biography of Toussaint L'Ouverture **92**
Fiction
Cárdenas, T. Letters to my mother **Fic**
Mussi, S. The door of no return **Fic**
United States
See African Americans

Blacks in art
See also African Americans in art

Blacks in film. Lace, W. W. **791.43**

Blacks in literature
See also African Americans in literature

Blacksmithing
See/See also pages in the following book(s):
Lyons, M. E. Catching the fire: Philip Simmons, blacksmith **92**

Blackwater. Bunting, E. **Fic**

Blackwater Ben. Durbin, W. **Fic**

Blackwood, Gary L.
Debatable deaths **920**
Enigmatic events **904**
Extraordinary events and oddball occurrences **001.9**
Gangsters **364.1**
The Great Race **796.72**
Highwaymen **364.1**
Legends or lies? **398.2**
Outlaws **364.1**
Perplexing people **920**
The Shakespeare stealer **Fic**
Swindlers **364.1**
The year of the hangman **Fic**

Blade. Bowler, T. **Fic**

Blades, boards & scooters. Thomas, K. **796.2**

Blair, Eric *See* Orwell, George, 1903-1950

Blair, Margaret Whitman, 1951-
The roaring 20 **797.5**

Blake, Quentin, 1932-
(il) Cooling, W. D is for Dahl **823.009**

Blake, William, 1757-1827
William Blake [Poetry for young people series] **821**
About
Bedard, M. William Blake **92**

Blanchard, Anne
(jt. auth) Pouy, J.-B. The big book of dummies, rebels and other geniuses **920**

Blashfield, Jean F.
Haiti **972.94**
Leonard Bernstein **92**

Blasingame, James B., Jr.
Gary Paulsen **813.009**

Blastoff! [series]
Schwabacher, M. Jupiter **523.4**
Stefoff, R. Earth and the moon **550**
Stefoff, R. Neptune **523.4**

Stone, T. L. Mars **523.4**
Stone, T. L. Saturn **523.4**

Blatner, David
Joy of [pi] **516.2**

Blatt, Jessica
The teen girl's gotta-have-it guide to embarrassing moments **646.7**
The teen girl's gotta-have-it guide to money **332.024**

Blauer, Ettagale
Mali **966.2**
Mauritania **966.1**
Morocco **964**
South Africa **968**

Blaxland, Wendy
Sneakers **685**

Bledsoe, Karen E., 1962-
Genetically engineered foods **664**

Bledsoe, Lucy Jane
How to survive in Antarctica **998**

Blevins, Bret, 1960-
(il) Jacques, B. Redwall: the graphic novel **741.5**

Blimps *See* Airships

Blind
Alexander, S. H. She touched the world: Laura Bridgman, deaf-blind pioneer **92**
Delano, M. F. Helen's eyes: a photobiography of Annie Sullivan, Helen Keller's teacher **92**
Garrett, L. Helen Keller **92**
Keller, H. The story of my life **92**
Lawlor, L. Helen Keller: rebellious spirit **92**
MacLeod, E. Helen Keller **92**
Sullivan, G. Helen Keller **92**
Books and reading
Freedman, R. Out of darkness: the story of Louis Braille **92**
Fiction
Clements, A. Things not seen **Fic**
Gutman, D. The million dollar putt **Fic**
Miller, S. Miss Spitfire **Fic**
Scrimger, R. From Charlie's point of view **Fic**
Taylor, T. The cay **Fic**
Taylor, T. Timothy of the cay **Fic**

Blind, Dogs for the *See* Guide dogs

The **blind** faith hotel. Todd, P. **Fic**

Blind mountain. Thomas, J. R. **Fic**

Blizzards
Stewart, M. Blizzards and winter storms **551.55**
Fiction
Gray, D. E. Together apart **Fic**

Blizzards and winter storms. Stewart, M. **551.55**

Bloch, Serge
(jt. auth) Pouy, J.-B. The big book of dummies, rebels and other geniuses **920**

Blogs *See* Weblogs

Blohm, Craig E., 1948-
An uneasy peace, 1945-1980 **940.55**
Weapons of peace **327.1**

Blood
Brynie, F. H. 101 questions about blood and circulation, with answers straight from the heart
    612.1

Circulation
See also Cardiovascular system
Yount, L. William Harvey   **92**

Disease
See Hemophilia

Diseases
See also Leukemia

Transfusion
Winner, C. Circulating life   **615**

Blood & DNA evidence. Rainis, K. G.   **363.2**

Blood brothers. Harazin, S. A.   **Fic**

Blood moon rider. Waters, Z. C.   **Fic**

Blood on the river. Carbone, E. L.   **Fic**

Blood red horse. Grant, K. M.   **Fic**

Bloodline. Cary, K.   **Fic**

Bloodline. Moran, K.   **Fic**

Bloodwater mysteries [series]
Hautman, P. Snatched   **Fic**

Bloody Jack. Meyer, L. A.   **Fic**

Bloom, Ona
(jt. auth) Morgan, J. Cells of the nervous system
    611

Bloomability. Creech, S.   **Fic**

Bloomfield, Jill
Jewish holidays cookbook   **641.5**

Bloor, Edward, 1950-
London calling   **Fic**
Taken   **Fic**
Tangerine   **Fic**

Blos, Joan W., 1928-
Letters from the corrugated castle   **Fic**

Blowers, Helene
Weaving a library Web   **025.04**

Blubaugh, Penny
Serendipity Market   **Fic**

Blue, Rose
(jt. auth) Naden, C. J. Dred Scott   **342**
(jt. auth) Naden, C. J. James Monroe   **92**
(jt. auth) Naden, C. J. John Muir   **92**

Blue. Hostetter, J.   **Fic**

The **blue** book on information age inquiry, instruction and literacy. Callison, D.   **028.7**

Blue collar workers *See* Working class

Blue flame. Grant, K. M.   **Fic**

The **blue** girl. De Lint, C.   **Fic**

Blue jasmine. Sheth, K.   **Fic**

The **blue** jean book. Kyi, T. L.   **391**

Blue like Friday. Parkinson, S.   **Fic**

Blue lipstick. Grandits, J.   **811**

Blue Mountain trouble. Mordecai, M.   **Fic**

Blue Ridge Mountains region
Fiction
McDowell, M. T. Carolina Harmony   **Fic**

The **blue** sky. Tschinag, G.   **Fic**

Blue Spruce, Ida Marx
(il) Bode, J. Kids still having kids   **362.7**

The **blue** sword. McKinley, R.   **Fic**

Blues. Handyside, C.   **781.643**

Blues music
See also Jazz music; Soul music
Handyside, C. Blues   **781.643**
Poetry
Lewis, J. P. Black cat bone   **811**

Bluestein, Jane
High school's not forever   **373.1**

Bluestone, Rose *See* Blue, Rose

Blum, Julia C.
(il) Banghart, T. What the sea wants   **Fic**

Blum, Zevi
(il) Binder, M. The brothers Schlemiel   **Fic**

Blumberg, Arnold, 1925-
The history of Israel   **956.94**

Blumberg, Rhoda, 1917-
Commodore Perry in the land of the Shogun
    952
The incredible journey of Lewis and Clark
    978
Shipwrecked!: the true adventures of a Japanese boy [biography of Manjiro Nakahama]   **92**
York's adventures with Lewis and Clark
    978

Blume, Judy
Are you there God?, it's me, Margaret   **Fic**
Here's to you, Rachel Robinson   **Fic**
Tiger eyes   **Fic**
About
Ludwig, E. Judy Blume   **92**
(ed) Places I never meant to be. See Places I never meant to be   **S C**

Blume, Lesley M. M.
The rising star of Rusty Nail   **Fic**
Tennyson   **Fic**

Blumenthal, Karen
Let me play   **796**
Six days in October   **330.9**

Blundell, Judy
What I saw and how I lied   **Fic**

Boadicea, Queen, d. 62
See/See also pages in the following book(s):
Meltzer, M. Ten queens   **920**

Board games
Graphic novels
Hotta, Y. Hikaru No Go, Volume 1   **741.5**

Boat. Kentley, E.   **387.2**

Boatbuilding
See also Shipbuilding

Boats, Submarine *See* Submarines

Boats and boating
See also Rafting (Sports); Sailing; Ships
Arnosky, J. Hook, line, & seeker   **799.1**
Kentley, E. Boat   **387.2**
Paulsen, G. Caught by the sea   **92**
Sandler, M. W. On the waters of the USA
    387.2
Fiction
Fletcher, R. The one o'clock chop   **Fic**
Hiaasen, C. Flush   **Fic**

Boaz, John
(ed) Free speech. See Free speech   **342**

Bortolotti, Dan
Exploring Saturn	**523.4**
Panda rescue	**599.78**
Tiger rescue	**333.95**

Bortz, Alfred B., 1944-
Astrobiology	**576.8**
Beyond Jupiter [biography of Heidi Hammel]	**92**

Bortz, Fred *See* Bortz, Alfred B., 1944-

Borus, Audrey
A student's guide to Emily Dickinson	**811.009**

Borzendowski, Janice
Marie Curie	**92**

Bos, Samone
Super structures	**720**

Bosco, Antoinette
(jt. auth) Bosco, P. I. World War I	**940.3**

Bosco, Don
(jt. auth) Levy, P. Tibet	**951**

Bosco, Peter I.
World War I	**940.3**

Boskey, Elizabeth
America debates genetic DNA testing	**174.2**

Bosnia and Hercegovina

See also Sarajevo (Bosnia and Hercegovina)
Milivojevic, J. Bosnia and Herzegovina	**949.7**
War-torn Bosnia	**949.7**

Bosnia and Herzegovina. Milivojevic, J. **949.7**

Boston (Mass.)
Fiction
Emerson, K. Carlos is gonna get it	Fic
Halpin, B. How ya like me now	Fic
Harlow, J. H. Joshua's song	Fic
Kluger, S. My most excellent year	Fic
Lupica, M. Miracle on 49th Street	Fic
Sones, S. What my girlfriend doesn't know	Fic
Wilson, D. L. Firehorse	Fic

Boston Jane: an adventure. Holm, J. L. Fic

Boston Massacre, 1770
Fiction
Rinaldi, A. The fifth of March	Fic

Boston Red Sox (Baseball team)
Fiction
Baggott, J. The Prince of Fenway Park	Fic

Boston Tea Party, 1773
Hull, M. The Boston Tea Party in American history	**973.3**

Bostrom, Kathleen Long, 1954-
Winning authors	**920**

Botanists
Anema, D. Ynes Mexia, botanist and adventurer	**92**

Botany

See also Plants
Casper, J. K. Plants	**580**
Plant sciences	**580**
VanCleave, J. P. Janice VanCleave's plants	**580.7**

United States
See Plants—United States

Botany, Medical *See* Medical botany

Botswana
LeVert, S. Botswana	**968.83**
Wittmann, K. Botswana	**968.83**

Botswana. Wittmann, K. **968.83**

Bott, C. J., 1947-
The bully in the book and in the classroom	**371.5**

Botticelli, Sandro, 1444 or 5-1510
Fiction
Beaufrand, M. J. Primavera	Fic

Bottled up. Murray, J. Fic

Botulism
Emmeluth, D. Botulism	**616.9**

Botzakis, Stergios
Pretty in print	**050**

Bouchard, Dave
The gift of reading	**372.4**

Boudicca *See* Boadicea, Queen, d. 62

Boughn, Michael
Into the world of the dead	**398.2**

Boulogne, Joseph *See* Saint-Georges, Joseph Boulogne, chevalier de, 1745-1799

Bounce. Friend, N. Fic

Bouncing back. Jones, J. B. **158**

Bound. Napoli, D. J. Fic

Bound for America. Meltzer, M. **325.73**

Bound for the North Star. Fradin, D. B. **326**

Bourgeois, Louise
About
Greenberg, J. Runaway girl: the artist Louise Bourgeois	**92**

Bourne, Joyce
(jt. auth) Kennedy, M. The concise Oxford dictionary of music	**780.3**

Bourseiller, Philippe
(il) Burleigh, R. Volcanoes	**551.2**

Boursin, Didier
Easy origami	**736**

Boveé, Jonita Ruth Bonham- *See* Bonham-Boveé, Jonita Ruth, d. 1994

Bow, Patricia
Chimpanzee rescue	**599.8**

Bowden, Rob
Energy	**333.79**
Food and farming	**363.8**
Kenya	**967.62**
The Nile	**962**
Waste	**363.7**
Water supply	**363.6**

Bowers, Elizabeth Shimer
(jt. auth) Ehrlich, P. Living with allergies	**616.97**

Bowers, Laura, 1969-
Beauty shop for rent	Fic

Bowes, John P., 1973-
Black Hawk and the War of 1832	**973.5**

Bowie, James *See* Bowie, Jim, 1796-1836

Brooks, Bruce, 1950-
All that remains   **Fic**
The moves make the man   **Fic**

Brooks, Gwendolyn
About
Hill, C. M. Gwendolyn Brooks   **92**
Rhynes, M. E. Gwendolyn Brooks   **92**

Brooks, Laurie
Selkie girl   **Fic**

Brooks, Martha, 1944-
Mistik Lake   **Fic**
True confessions of a heartless girl   **Fic**

Brooks, Philip *See* Wilkinson, Philip, 1955-

Brooks, Terry, 1944-
Dark wraith of Shannara   **741.5**

Brooks, Wanda M., 1969-
(ed) Embracing, evaluating, and examining African children's and young adult literature. See Embracing, evaluating, and examining African American children's and young adult literature   **028.5**

Brophy, David
Michelle Obama   **92**

Brostrom, Jennifer Allison *See* Allison, Jennifer

Brother Imás. Hinojosa, R.
In Growing up Latino; memoirs and stories p250-58   **810.8**

Brotherhood of the conch [series]
Divakaruni, C. B. The conch bearer   **Fic**

Brothers, Meagan
Debbie Harry sings in French   **Fic**

Brothers
Giblin, J. Good brother, bad brother [biography of John Wilkes Booth and Edwin Booth]   **92**

Fiction
Barber, T. Go long!   **Fic**
Beck, I. The secret history of Tom Trueheart   **Fic**
Binder, M. The brothers Schlemiel   **Fic**
Bloor, E. Tangerine   **Fic**
Bowler, T. Frozen fire   **Fic**
Crist-Evans, C. Amaryllis   **Fic**
Gonzalez, J. Wings   **Fic**
Harmon, M. Skate   **Fic**
Herlong, M. The great wide sea   **Fic**
Hernandez, D. Suckerpunch   **Fic**
Herrick, S. By the river   **Fic**
Hinton, S. E. Rumble fish   **Fic**
Kelly, T. Finn's going   **Fic**
Kerr, M. E. Slap your sides   **Fic**
Klass, D. Dark angel   **Fic**
MacPhail, C. Dark waters   **Fic**
Magoon, K. The rock and the river   **Fic**
McCormick, P. My brother's keeper   **Fic**
Michaels, R. Genesis Alpha   **Fic**
Mourlevat, J.-C. The pull of the ocean   **Fic**
Murray, J. Bottled up   **Fic**
Naylor, P. R. The fear place   **Fic**
Nuzum, K. A. A small white scar   **Fic**
Philbrick, W. R. The mostly true adventures of Homer P. Figg   **Fic**
Shusterman, N. Full tilt   **Fic**
Simmons, M. Vandal   **Fic**

Slade, A. G. Megiddo's shadow   **Fic**
Sonnenblick, J. Drums, girls, & dangerous pie   **Fic**
Sternberg, L. The case against my brother   **Fic**
Trueman, T. Cruise control   **Fic**
Van Leeuwen, J. Cabin on Trouble Creek   **Fic**
Wallace, R. Perpetual check   **Fic**
Waltman, K. Learning the game   **Fic**
Williams, S. Bull rider   **Fic**
Graphic novels
Wood, D. Into the volcano   **741.5**

Brothers and sisters
Fiction.
Barrett, T. The 100-year-old secret   **Fic**

Brothers and sisters *See* Siblings; Twins

Brothers, boyfriends & other criminal minds. Lurie, A.   **Fic**

The **brothers** Schlemiel. Binder, M.   **Fic**

The **brothers'** war. Lewis, J. P.   **811**

Brower, David, 1912-2000
See/See also pages in the following book(s):
Byrnes, P. Environmental pioneers   **920**

Brown, Alan
The Bible and Christianity   **220**

Brown, Calef
(il) Pinkwater, D. M. The Neddiad   **Fic**
(il) Pinkwater, D. M. The Yggyssey   **Fic**

Brown, Dee Alexander
Bury my heart at Wounded Knee   **970.004**
Bury my heart at Wounded Knee; adaptation. See Ehrlich, A. Wounded Knee: an Indian history of the American West   **970.004**
Dee Brown's folktales of the Native American   **398.2**

Brown, Don, 1949-
The train jumper   **Fic**

Brown, Gene
Duke Ellington: jazz master   **92**

Brown, Jason Robert
13   **Fic**

Brown, Jean E., 1945-
(jt. auth) Stephens, E. C. Learning about—the Civil War   **016.973**
(ed) Your reading. See Your reading   **011.6**

Brown, Jordan
Robo world [biography of Cyntia Breazeal]   **92**

Brown, Judith Gwyn
(il) Robinson, B. The best Christmas pageant ever   **Fic**

Brown, Kate
(il) Appignanesi, R. A midsummer night's dream   **822.3**

Brown, Lauren
Grasses, an identification guide   **584**

Brown, Leo, d. 1991
(il) Gibbons, A. Charles Darwin   **92**

Brown, Margaret Tobin *See* Brown, Molly, 1867-1932

Brown, Mary E.
Exhibits in libraries   **021.7**

Bulletin of the United States Bureau of Labor Statistics [series]
United States/Bureau of Labor Statistics. Occupational outlook handbook 2008-2009   **331.7**

Bullies
Beaudoin, M.-N. Responding to the culture of bullying and disrespect   **371.5**
Bott, C. J. The bully in the book and in the classroom   **371.5**
Bullying   **302.3**
Burton, B. Girls against girls   **305.23**
Kevorkian, M. 101 facts about bullying   **302.3**
Winkler, K. Bullying   **371.5**
Fiction
Butler, D. H. The truth about Truman School   **Fic**
Docherty, J. The ice cream con   **Fic**
Donofrio, B. Thank you, Lucky Stars   **Fic**
Ellis, A. D. This is what I did   **Fic**
Evangelista, B. Gifted   **Fic**
Garden, N. Endgame   **Fic**
Geus, M. Piggy   **Fic**
Helgerson, J. Horns & wrinkles   **Fic**
Heneghan, J. Payback   **Fic**
Jonsberg, B. Dreamrider   **Fic**
Koss, A. G. Poison Ivy   **Fic**
Love, D. A. Defying the diva   **Fic**
McNish, C. Angel   **Fic**
McPhee, P. New blood   **Fic**
Mikaelsen, B. Ghost of Spirit Bear   **Fic**
Nordin, S. In the wild   **Fic**
Pixley, M. Freak   **Fic**
Roy, J. Max Quigley   **Fic**
Sweeney, J. The guardian   **Fic**
Warner, S. It's only temporary   **Fic**
Watkins, S. Down Sand Mountain   **Fic**
Williams-Garcia, R. Jumped   **Fic**

Bulls-eye: a photobiography of Annie Oakley. Macy, S.   **92**

Bully for you, Teddy Roosevelt!. Fritz, J.   **92**

The **bully** in the book and in the classroom. Bott, C. J.   **371.5**

Bullying   **302.3**

Bullying. Winkler, K.   **371.5**

Bultje, Jan Willem
The Czech Republic   **943.7**

Bunce, Elizabeth C.
A curse dark as gold   **Fic**

Bunch, Bryan H.
(ed) Diseases. See Diseases   **616**

Bunker 10. Henderson, J.-A.   **Fic**

Bunting, Anne Eve *See* Bunting, Eve, 1928-

Bunting, Eve, 1928-
Blackwater   **Fic**
The man with the red bag   **Fic**
SOS Titanic   **Fic**
Spying on Miss Müller   **Fic**
The summer of Riley   **Fic**

Buonarotti, Michelangelo *See* Michelangelo Buonarroti, 1475-1564

Buonarroti, Michel Angelo *See* Michelangelo Buonarroti, 1475-1564

Buranbaeva, Oksana
(jt. auth) Beliaev, E. Dagestan   **947.5**

Burbank, Jon, 1951-
Nepal   **954.96**

Burchett, Rick
(il) Beechen, A. Justice League Unlimited: the ties that bind   **741.5**

Burek Pierce, Jennifer
Sex, brains, and video games   **027.62**

Burg, Ann E., 1954-
All the broken pieces   **Fic**

Burg, David F.
The Great Depression   **973.91**

Burg, Shana, 1968-
A thousand never evers   **Fic**

Burgan, Michael
The Berlin airlift   **943**
Hillary Rodham Clinton   **92**
John F. Kennedy   **92**

Burger, Carl, 1888-1967
(il) Gipson, F. B. Old Yeller   **Fic**

Burial
Colman, P. Corpses, coffins, and crypts   **393**
Greene, M. Rest in peace   **393**
Sloan, C. Bury the dead   **393**

Buried in ice. Beattie, O.   **998**

Buried onions. Soto, G.   **Fic**

Buried treasure
Matsen, B. The incredible search for the treasure ship Atocha   **910.4**
Fiction
Alexander, L. The golden dream of Carlo Chuchio   **Fic**
Barron, T. A. The Merlin effect   **Fic**
Bryant, J. Kaleidoscope eyes   **Fic**
Hobbs, W. Ghost canoe   **Fic**
Hobbs, W. Leaving Protection   **Fic**
Kress, A. Alex and the Ironic Gentleman   **Fic**
Mussi, S. The door of no return   **Fic**
Sachar, L. Holes   **Fic**
Stevenson, R. L. Treasure Island   **Fic**

Burke, Jim
(il) Whitman, W. Walt Whitman   **811**

Burleigh, Robert, 1936-
Hoops   **811**
Napoleon   **92**
Paul Cezanne   **92**
Volcanoes   **551.2**

Burlingame, Jeff
Kurt Cobain   **92**

Burma *See* Myanmar

The **burn** journals. Runyon, B.   **92**

Burn my heart. Naidoo, B.   **Fic**

Burnett, Frances Hodgson, 1849-1924
The secret garden   **Fic**

Burnett, Hugh, 1919-1991
About
Cooper, J. Season of rage   **323.1**

Burnfield, Alexander
Multiple sclerosis   **616.8**

Burnham, Laurie
Rivers   **551.48**

Cárdenas, Teresa, 1970-
Letters to my mother   Fic
Old dog   Fic
Cardiovascular system
    See also Blood—Circulation; Heart
Bjorklund, R. Circulatory system   612.1
Brynie, F. H. 101 questions about blood and circulation, with answers straight from the heart   612.1
Parker, S. Heart, blood, and lungs   612.1
Simon, S. The heart   612.1
Care, Medical *See* Medical care
Care of children *See* Child care
Care of the dying *See* Terminal care
Career discovery encyclopedia   331.7
Career guidance *See* Vocational guidance
Career ideas for teens [series]
Reeves, D. L. Career ideas for teens in architecture and construction   624
Reeves, D. L. Career ideas for teens in education and training   331.7
Reeves, D. L. Career ideas for teens in health science   610.69
Career ideas for teens in architecture and construction. Reeves, D. L.   624
Career ideas for teens in education and training. Reeves, D. L.   331.7
Career ideas for teens in health science. Reeves, D. L.   610.69
Careers *See* Occupations
Careers in renewable energy. McNamee, G.   333.79
Careers in the computer game industry. Gerardi, D.   794.8
Careers in the new economy [series]
Gerardi, D. Careers in the computer game industry   794.8
The Caretaker trilogy [series]
Klass, D. Firestorm   Fic
Carey, Charles W.
The Mexican War   973.6
(ed) Castro's Cuba. See Castro's Cuba   972.91
Carey, Janet Lee
The beast of Noor   Fic
Dragon's Keep   Fic
Carey, Louise
(jt. auth) Carey, M. Confessions of a Blabbermouth   741.5
Carey, Mike, 1959-
Confessions of a Blabbermouth   741.5
Re-Gifters   741.5
Caribbean region
    See also West Indies
        Antiquities
Macaulay, D. Ship   387.2
        Fiction
Taylor, T. The cay   Fic
Taylor, T. Timothy of the cay   Fic
Caribou
Heuer, K. Being caribou   599.65

Caricatures *See* Cartoons and caricatures
Caring for your mutt. Bolan, S.   636.7
Carle, Jill
(jt. auth) Carle, M. Teens cook   641.5
(jt. auth) Carle, M. Teens cook dessert   641.8
Carle, Judi
(jt. auth) Carle, M. Teens cook   641.5
(jt. auth) Carle, M. Teens cook dessert   641.8
Carle, Megan
Teens cook   641.5
Teens cook dessert   641.8
Carlisle, Rodney P.
Civil War and Reconstruction   973.7
Exploring space   629.4
World War I   940.3
Carlos is gonna get it. Emerson, K.   Fic
Carlowicz, Michael J.
The moon   523.3
Carlson, Christopher C.
(jt. auth) Jean, M. Puddlejumpers   Fic
Carlson, Drew
Attack of the Turtle   Fic
Carlson, Laurie M., 1952-
Harry Houdini for kids   92
Thomas Edison for kids   92
Carlson, Lori M.
(ed) American eyes. See American eyes   S C
(ed) Cool salsa. See Cool salsa   811.008
(ed) Moccasin thunder. See Moccasin thunder   S C
(ed) Red hot salsa. See Red hot salsa   811.008
(ed) Voices in first person. See Voices in first person   S C
Carlson, W. Bernard
(ed) Technology in world history. See Technology in world history   909
Carman, Patrick
The Dark Hills divide   Fic
Carmichael, Clay
Wild things   Fic
Carmody, Isobelle
Alyzon Whitestarr   Fic
Carnagie, Julie
Renaissance & Reformation: almanac. See Renaissance & Reformation: almanac   940.2
Renaissance & Reformation: primary sources. See Renaissance & Reformation: primary sources   940.2
(ed) Saari, P. Colonial America: primary sources   973.2
(ed) U.X.L encyclopedia of biomes. See U.X.L encyclopedia of biomes   577.8
Carnegie, Andrew, 1835-1919
        About
Edge, L. B. Andrew Carnegie   92
Kent, Z. Andrew Carnegie   92
Whitelaw, N. The Homestead Steel Strike of 1892   331.8
Carney, Jeff
The adventures of Michael MacInnes   Fic

Chiappe, Luis M.
(jt. auth) Dingus, L. Dinosaur eggs discovered! **567.9**

Chicago (Ill.)
Fiction
Cisneros, S. The house on Mango Street **Fic**
Elkeles, S. How to ruin my teenage life **Fic**
Magoon, K. The rock and the river **Fic**
Pearsall, S. All shook up **Fic**
Peck, R. Fair weather **Fic**
Smith, J. E. The comeback season **Fic**
History
Hurd, O. Chicago history for kids **977.3**
Social conditions
Fradin, J. B. Jane Addams **92**

Chicago Children's Choir
Turck, M. Freedom song **323.1**

Chicago history for kids. Hurd, O. **977.3**

Chicanos See Mexican Americans

Chicken boy. Dowell, F. O. **Fic**

The **chicken-coop** monster. McKissack, P. C.
In McKissack, P. C. The dark-thirty; Southern tales of the supernatural p111-122
S C

The **chicken** dance. Couvillon, J. **Fic**

Chicken Foot Farm. Estevis, A. **Fic**

Chicken friend. Morgan, N. **Fic**

Chicken pox. Hoffmann, G. **616.9**

Chicken soup for the soul: kids in the kitchen. Canfield, J. **641.5**

Chicken soup for the teenage soul [I-IV]. Canfield, J. **158**

Chicken soup for the teenage soul's the real deal **158**

Chickenpox
Hoffmann, G. Chicken pox **616.9**
Silverstein, A. Chickenpox and shingles
616.9

Chickenpox and shingles. Silverstein, A. **616.9**

Chickens
Fiction
Couvillon, J. The chicken dance **Fic**
Dowell, F. O. Chicken boy **Fic**

Chief Joseph See Joseph, Nez Percé Chief, 1840-1904

Chief Joseph and the Nez Percés. Scott, R. A.
92

Chief Justice of the Supreme Court See United States. Supreme Court

Chief Sunrise, John McGraw, and me. Tocher, T.
Fic

Chien, Catia
(il) Selfors, S. Fortune's magic farm **Fic**

Chiggers. Larson, H. **741.5**

Chilcoat, George W.
(jt. auth) Tunnell, M. O. The children of Topaz
940.53

Child, Lydia Maria Francis, 1802-1880
About
Kenschaft, L. Lydia Maria Child **92**

Child abuse
See also Child sexual abuse
Gordon, S. M. Beyond bruises **362.7**
Kim, H. H. Child abuse **362.7**
Medina, S. Abuse and neglect **362.7**
Fiction
Byars, B. C. Cracker Jackson **Fic**
Chaltas, T. Because I am furniture **Fic**
Crocker, N. Billie Standish was here **Fic**
Crutcher, C. Staying fat for Sarah Byrnes
Fic
Draper, S. M. Forged by fire **Fic**
Hartry, N. Watching Jimmy **Fic**
Hernandez, D. Suckerpunch **Fic**
Kwasney, M. D. Itch **Fic**
Olson, G. Call me Hope **Fic**
Stahler, D., Jr. Doppelganger **Fic**
Werlin, N. The rules of survival **Fic**
Whittenberg, A. Life is fine **Fic**

Child and mother See Mother-child relationship
Child and parent See Parent-child relationship
Child and youth security sourcebook **362.7**

Child artists
—I never saw another butterfly— **741.9**

Child care
See also Babysitting
McAlpine, M. Working with children **362.7**

Child development
McAlpine, M. Working with children **362.7**

Child labor
Bartoletti, S. C. Growing up in coal country
331.3
Bartoletti, S. C. Kids on strike! **331.8**
Chambers, C. Living as a child laborer
331.3
Freedman, R. Kids at work **331.3**
Herumin, W. Child labor today **331.3**
Springer, J. Listen to us **331.3**
Fiction
D'Adamo, F. Iqbal **Fic**
Winthrop, E. Counting on Grace **Fic**

Child labor today. Herumin, W. **331.3**

Child molesting See Child sexual abuse

Child of dandelions. Nanji, S. **Fic**

Child prostitution See Juvenile prostitution

Child psychiatry
See also Autism

Child rearing
See also Parenting; Socialization

Child sexual abuse
Medina, S. Abuse and neglect **362.7**
Strong at the heart **362.7**
See/See also pages in the following book(s):
Jukes, M. It's a girl thing **305.23**
Fiction
Chaltas, T. Because I am furniture **Fic**
Cumbie, P. Where people like us live **Fic**
Doyle, B. Boy O'Boy **Fic**
Mazer, N. F. The missing girl **Fic**
Weeks, S. Jumping the scratch **Fic**

Childbirth
Brynie, F. H. 101 questions about reproduction
612.6

Childlessness

See also Infertility

Children

See also Abandoned children; African American children; Boys; Foster children; Girls; Handicapped children; Infants; Internet and children; Only child; Runaway children

Hoose, P. M. We were there, too! **973**

Abuse

See Child abuse

Adoption

See Adoption

Books and reading

Crossing boundaries with children's books **028.5**

Embracing, evaluating, and examining African American children's and young adult literature **028.5**

Gelman, J. The kids' book club book **028.5**

Larson, J. C. Bringing mysteries alive for children and young adults **028.5**

Lukenbill, W. B. Biography in the lives of youth **028.5**

Sutherland, Z. Children & books **028.5**

Care

See Child care

Development

See Child development

Employment

See Child labor

Law and legislation

Cohen, L. The Gault case and young people's rights **345**

Socialization

See Socialization

United States

Cole, S. To be young in America **973**

Freedman, R. Children of the Great Depression **305.23**

Miller, B. M. Growing up in revolution and the new nation, 1775 to 1800 **973.3**

Children, Adopted *See* Adopted children

Children, Retarded *See* Mentally handicapped children

Children & books. Sutherland, Z. **028.5**

Children and television *See* Television and children

Children and the Internet *See* Internet and children

Children and war

Ellis, D. Children of war **956.7**

Ellis, D. Off to war **303.6**

Making it home **305.23**

Sherrow, V. Encyclopedia of youth and war **305.23**

Wilson, J. One peace **305.23**

Children in crisis [series]

Chambers, C. Living as a child laborer **331.3**

Dalton, D. Living in a refugee camp **305.23**

Howard, H. Living as a refugee in America **305.23**

Hynson, C. Living on the street **362.7**

Children of Alcatraz. Murphy, C. R. **979.4**

Children of alcoholics

Alcohol information for teens **616.86**

Children of immigrants

Roth, R. The story road to literacy **372.6**

Children of single parents *See* Single parent family

Children of the Dust Bowl. Stanley, J. **371.9**

Children of the Red King [series]

Nimmo, J. Midnight for Charlie Bone **Fic**

Children of the slaughter. Gottfried, T. **940.53**

Children of the wind [series]

Murray, K. The secret life of Maeve Lee Kwong **Fic**

The **children** of Topaz. Tunnell, M. O. **940.53**

Children of war. Ellis, D. **956.7**

Children tell stories. Hamilton, M. **372.6**

Children's and young adult literature by Latino writers. York, S. **028.5**

The **children's** and young adult literature handbook. Gillespie, J. T. **011.6**

Children's and young adult literature reference series

Barr, C. Best new media, K-12 **011**

Gillespie, J. T. The children's and young adult literature handbook **011.6**

Gillespie, J. T. Classic teenplots **011.6**

Gillespie, J. T. The Newbery/Printz companion **028.5**

Lynn, R. N. Fantasy literature for children and young adults **016.8**

McDaniel, D. Gentle reads **028.5**

Thomas, R. L. Popular series fiction for middle school and teen readers **016.8**

Walter, V. A. War & peace **016.3**

Zbaracki, M. D. Best books for boys **028.5**

Children's art

River of words **808.81**

Children's Book Council (New York, N.Y.)

Notable social studies trade books for young people. See Notable social studies trade books for young people **016.3**

Outstanding science trade books for students K-12. See Outstanding science trade books for students K-12 **016.5**

Children's books in children's hands **028.5**

Children's catalog. 19th ed. **011.6**

Children's clothing

Sills, L. From rags to riches **391**

Children's courts *See* Juvenile courts

Children's encyclopedia of American history. King, D. C. **973.03**

Children's libraries

See also Libraries and schools; Young adults' libraries

Follos, A. M. G. Reviving reading **027.62**

Lukenbill, W. B. Biography in the lives of youth **028.5**

Reid, R. Something funny happened at the library **027.62**

Simpson, M. S. Bringing classes into the public library **027.62**

Chimpanzee rescue. Bow, P.   599.8

Chimpanzees
Bow, P. Chimpanzee rescue   599.8
Feinstein, S. The chimpanzee   599.8
Goodall, J. The chimpanzees I love   599.8
Kozleski, L. Jane Goodall   92
Lockwood, S. Chimpanzees   599.8
The **chimpanzees** I love. Goodall, J.   599.8

Chin, Jason, 1978-
(il) Winchester, S. The day the world exploded   551.2

Chin-Lee, Cynthia, 1958-
Amelia to Zora   920

Ch'in Shih-huang, Emperor of China, 259-210 B.C.
Tomb
Dean, A. Terra-cotta soldiers   931
O'Connor, J. The emperor's silent army   931

China
Behnke, A. China in pictures   951
Ferroa, P. G. China   951
Fritz, J. Homesick: my own story   92
Lang, L. Lang Lang   92
Ma Yan. The diary of Ma Yan   951.05
Marx, T. Elephants and golden thrones   951
Antiquities
Ball, J. A. Ancient China   931
Dean, A. Terra-cotta soldiers   931
O'Connor, J. The emperor's silent army   931
Civilization
Anderson, D. Ancient China   709.51
Ball, J. A. Ancient China   931
Cotterell, A. Ancient China   931
Greenblatt, M. Han Wu Di and ancient China   931
Schomp, V. The ancient Chinese   931
Shuter, J. Ancient China   931
Stefoff, R. The Asian empires   950
Whitfield, S. Philosophy and writing   181
Communism
See Communism—China
Description and travel
Childress, D. Marco Polo's journey to China   92
Fiction
Alexander, L. The remarkable journey of Prince Jen   Fic
Chen, D. Sword   Fic
Mah, A. Y. Chinese Cinderella and the Secret Dragon Society   Fic
McCaughrean, G. The kite rider   Fic
Namioka, L. Ties that bind, ties that break   Fic
Napoli, D. J. Bound   Fic
Ruby, L. Shanghai shadows   Fic
Whelan, G. Chu Ju's house   Fic
Folklore
See Folklore—China
Graphic novels
Jolley, D. Guan Yu   741.5
History
Cotterell, A. Ancient China   931
DuTemple, L. A. The Great Wall of China   931

Kleeman, T. F. The ancient Chinese world   931
Mah, A. Y. China   951
Major, J. S. The Silk Route   950
Stefoff, R. The Asian empires   950
History—1912-1949
Gay, K. The aftermath of the Chinese nationalist revolution   951.04
History—1949-1976
Langley, A. Cultural Revolution   951
Li Cunxin. Mao's last dancer [biography of Li Cunxin]   92
Naden, C. J. Mao Zedong and the Chinese Revolution   92
Slavicek, L. C. Mao Zedong   92
Yu Chun. Little Green   951.05
History—1949-1976—Fiction
Compestine, Y. C. Revolution is not a dinner party   Fic
History—1949-1976—Personal narratives
Jiang, J.-l. Red scarf girl   951.05
Li, M. Snow falling in spring   92
Zhang, A. Red land, yellow river   951.05
Poetry
Grimes, N. Tai chi morning   811
Young, E. Beyond the great mountains   811
Science
See Science—China
Social life and customs
Mah, A. Y. Chinese Cinderella   92

China (Republic of China, 1949-) *See* Taiwan

China in pictures. Behnke, A.   951

Chinese
Fiction
Murray, K. The secret life of Maeve Lee Kwong   Fic
Yee, P. Learning to fly   Fic
United States
Perl, L. To the Golden Mountain   305.8
United States—Fiction
Namioka, L. An ocean apart, a world away   Fic
Yep, L. Dragon's gate   Fic
The **Chinese**   305.8
The **Chinese** American family album. Hoobler, D.   305.8

Chinese Americans
See also Chinese—United States
The Chinese   305.8
Chippendale, L. A. Yo-Yo Ma   92
Hoobler, D. The Chinese American family album   305.8
Worth, R. Yo-Yo Ma   92
Biography
Angel, A. Amy Tan   92
Marcovitz, H. Laurence Yep   92
Yep, L. The lost garden   92
Fiction
Currier, K. S. Kai's journey to Gold Mountain   Fic
Fletcher, S. Walk across the sea   Fic
Lavender, W. Aftershocks   Fic
Martin, N. Flight of the Fisherbird   Fic
Namioka, L. Mismatch   Fic

Church and education
See/See also pages in the following book(s):
Religion in America: opposing viewpoints
200.9

Church and state
Andryszewski, T. School prayer **344**
Dudley, M. E. Engel v. Vitale (1962) **344**
Gold, S. D. Engel v. Vitale **344**
Mountjoy, S. Engel v. Vitale **344**
See/See also pages in the following book(s):
Civil liberties: opposing viewpoints **323**
Religion in America: opposing viewpoints
200.9

United States
McIntosh, K. When religion & politics mix
201

Church history
600-1500, Middle Ages
Currie, S. Miracles, saints, and superstition
940.1

1517-1648, Reformation
See Reformation

Church of England
Hinds, K. The church [Life in Elizabethan England series] **274**

Church of Jesus Christ of Latter-day Saints
Bial, R. Nauvoo **289.3**
Book of Mormon. The Book of Mormon
289.3
Bushman, C. L. Mormons in America **289.3**

Churchill, Sir Winston, 1874-1965
About
Binns, T. B. Winston Churchill **92**
Macdonald, F. Winston Churchill **92**
Severance, J. B. Winston Churchill **92**
Wrigley, C. Winston Churchill: a biographical companion **92**
See/See also pages in the following book(s):
Ross, S. Leaders of World War II **920**
Fiction
Bell, T. Nick of time **Fic**
White, A. Window boy **Fic**

Ci Xi *See* Tz'u-hsi, Empress dowager of China, 1835-1908

Cicada summer. Beaty, A. **Fic**

Ciccone, Madonna *See* Madonna, 1958-

Cimatoribus, Alessandra, 1967-
(il) Blake, W. William Blake [Poetry for young people series] **821**

Cinco de Mayo
Mattern, J. Celebrate Cinco de Mayo **394.26**

Cinderella
Poetry
Whipple, L. If the shoe fits **811**

Cinematography
Miller, R. Special effects **778.5**
Shaner, P. A. Digital filmmaking for teens
778.5

Cinnamon girl. Herrera, J. F. **Fic**

Ciphers
Janeczko, P. B. Top secret **652**
Levy, J. Breaking the code with cryptography
652
Pincock, S. Codebreaker **652**

Fiction
Richards, J. The chaos code **Fic**
Riordan, R. The maze of bones **Fic**

Cipollone, Rose, d. 1984
About
Sergis, D. K. Cipollone v. Liggett Group
346.03

Cipollone v. Liggett Group. Sergis, D. K.
346.03

Circle of magic: Sandry's book. Pierce, T. **Fic**

A **circle** of time. Montes, M. **Fic**

The **circuit**: stories from the life of a migrant child. Jiménez, F. **Fic**

Circulating life. Winner, C. **615**

Circulation of library materials *See* Library circulation

Circulatory system *See* Cardiovascular system

Circulatory system. Bjorklund, R. **612.1**

Circumcision, Female *See* Female circumcision

Circumnavigation *See* Voyages around the world

Circus
Fleming, C. The great and only Barnum **92**
Fiction
Mack, T. The fall of the Amazing Zalindas
Fic
Mahy, M. Maddigan's Fantasia **Fic**
Porter, T. Billy Creekmore **Fic**

Cirrone, Dorian
Prom kings and drama queens **Fic**

Cisneros, Sandra
The house on Mango Street **Fic**
The monkey garden
In Growing up Latino; memoirs and stories p288-91 **810.8**

Citations, Bibliographical *See* Bibliographical citations

Cities. Lorinc, J. **307.7**

Cities and towns
See also Inner cities
Lorinc, J. Cities **307.7**
Millard, A. A street through time **936**
Stefoff, R. Cities and towns **973.2**
Growth
See also Urbanization
United States
Collier, C. The rise of the cities, 1820-1920
307.7

Cities and towns, ruined, extinct, etc. *See* Extinct cities

Cities and towns. Stefoff, R. **973.2**

Citrin, Michael
(jt. auth) Mack, T. The fall of the Amazing Zalindas **Fic**

The **city** [Life in Ancient Egypt series] Hinds, K.
932

The **city** [Life in Elizabethan England series] Hinds, K. **942.05**

The **city** [Life in the Medieval Muslim world series] Hinds, K. **909.07**

The **city** [Life in the Middle Ages series] Hinds, K. **940.1**

The **Civil** War   **973.7**
Civil War. Golay, M.   **973.7**
The **Civil** War. Jordan, A. D.   **973.7**
The **Civil** War. Nardo, D.   **973.7**
Civil War. Netzley, P. D.
    973.7
    [Grolier 10v set]   **973.7**
Civil War [series]
    Hughes, C. The Battle of Antietam   **973.7**
    King, D. C. The Battle of Gettysburg   **973.7**
The **Civil** War, 1860-1865. Collier, C.   **973.7**
The **Civil** war: a history in documents. Seidman, R. F.
    973.7
Civil War A to Z. Bolotin, N.   **973.7**
The **Civil** War and Reconstruction. Barney, W. L.
    973.7
The **Civil** War at sea. Sullivan, G.   **973.7**
Civilian Conservation Corps (U.S.)
    Fiction
    Ingold, J. Hitch   **Fic**
Civilization
    See also names of continents, countries, states, etc., with the subdivision *Civilization,* e.g. United States—Civilization
    Dumont-Le Cornec, E. Wonders of the world   **910**
    History
    Ochoa, G. The Wilson chronology of ideas   **909**
    Roberts, J. M. The illustrated history of the world   **909**
Civilization, Ancient *See* Ancient civilization
Civilization, Celtic *See* Celtic civilization
Civilization, Classical *See* Classical civilization
Civilization, Islamic *See* Islamic civilization
Civilization, Medieval *See* Medieval civilization
Civilization, Modern *See* Modern civilization
Civilization and science *See* Science and civilization
Civilization and technology *See* Technology and civilization
Cixi *See* Tz'u-hsi, Empress dowager of China, 1835-1908
Claflin, Victoria *See* Woodhull, Victoria C., 1838-1927
Claire by moonlight. Kositsky, L.   **Fic**
Clairvoyance
    Fiction
    Jocelyn, M. How it happened in Peach Hill   **Fic**
    Johnston, J. A very fine line   **Fic**
    Mitchard, J. The midnight twins   **Fic**
Clan Apis. Hosler, J.   **741.5**
Clarence Cochran, a human boy. Loizeaux, W.   **Fic**
Clark, Charles, 1949-
    Islam   **297**
    (jt. auth) Cartlidge, C. Life of a Nazi soldier   **940.54**
Clark, Christopher Stuart- *See* Stuart-Clark, Christopher

Clark, Clara Gillow, 1951-
    Hill Hawk Hattie   **Fic**
Clark, Donna Lynn
    (jt. auth) Haven, K. F. 100 most popular scientists for young adults   **920**
Clark, Peter H., 1829-1925
    See/See also pages in the following book(s):
    Katz, W. L. Black pioneers   **920**
Clark, Septima Poinsette, 1898-1987
    See/See also pages in the following book(s):
    Hansen, J. Women of hope   **920**
Clark, Warren
    (il) Graydon, S. Made you look   **659.1**
Clark, William, 1770-1838
    Off the map   **978**
    About
    Blumberg, R. The incredible journey of Lewis and Clark   **978**
    Faber, H. Lewis and Clark   **978**
Clarke, Arthur C., 1917-2008
    2001: a space odyssey   **Fic**
Clarke, Barry
    Amphibian   **597.8**
Clarke, Judith, 1943-
    One whole and perfect day   **Fic**
    Starry nights   **Fic**
Clash of cultures, prehistory-1638. Collier, C.   **970.004**
Classic connections. Koelling, H.   **027.62**
Classic poetry   **821.008**
Classic storytellers [series]
    Hinton, K. Jacqueline Woodson   **92**
    Whiting, J. Ernest Hemingway   **92**
Classic teenplots. Gillespie, J. T.   **011.6**
Classic western stories   **808.8**
Classical antiquities
    See also Greece—Antiquities; Rome—Antiquities; Rome (Italy)—Antiquities
Classical art *See* Roman art
Classical civilization
    See also Rome—Civilization
    Connolly, P. The ancient city   **937**
Classical composers [series]
    Getzinger, D. George Frideric Handel and music for voices   **92**
Classical music *See* Music
Classical mythology
    Hamilton, E. Mythology   **292**
    McCaughrean, G. Hercules   **292**
    McCaughrean, G. Odysseus   **292**
    McCaughrean, G. Perseus   **292**
    Nardo, D. The Greenhaven encyclopedia of Greek and Roman mythology   **292**
    Rylant, C. The beautiful stories of life   **292**
    Schomp, V. The ancient Greeks   **292**
    Schomp, V. The ancient Romans   **292**
    Smith, C. R. The mighty 12   **292**
    Fiction
    Cadnum, M. Nightsong   **Fic**
    Coville, B. Juliet Dove, Queen of Love   **Fic**
    Deming, S. Iris, messenger   **Fic**
    Falcone, L. M. Walking with the dead   **Fic**
    Friesner, E. M. Nobody's princess   **Fic**

Classical mythology—Fiction—*Continued*

Friesner, E. M. Temping fate	Fic
Geras, A. Ithaka	Fic
Halam, A. Snakehead	Fic
Hennesy, C. Pandora gets jealous	Fic
Jones, D. W. The game	Fic
Kindl, P. Lost in the labyrinth	Fic
Marsh, K. The night tourist	Fic
Napoli, D. J. The great god Pan	Fic
Riordan, R. The lightning thief	Fic
Shipton, P. The pig scrolls	Fic
Spinner, S. Quicksilver	Fic
Springer, N. Dusssie	Fic

Poetry

Hovey, K. Ancient voices	811

Classics illustrated [series]

Baker, K. Through the looking-glass	741.5
Geary, R. Great expectations	741.5
Geary, R. The invisible man	741.5
Poe, E. A. The raven and other poems	
	741.5
Shelley, M. W. Frankenstein	741.5

Classification

Books

See Library classification

Classified catalogs

Children's catalog. 19th ed.	011.6
Senior high core collection	011.6

Clay, Cassius *See* Ali, Muhammad, 1942-

Clay. Almond, D.   Fic

Clay v. United States and how Muhammad Ali fought the draft. Streissguth, T.   343

Claybourne, Anna

The nature of matter	530.4
The Renaissance	940.2
Surrealism	709.04

Clayton, Elaine, 1961-

(jt. auth) Wayland, A. H. Girl coming in for a landing	Fic
(il) Zimmer, T. V. 42 miles	Fic

Clayton, Emma, 1968-

The roar	Fic

Cle, Troy

The marvelous effect	Fic

Cleanliness

See also Hygiene

Cleary, Beverly

Dear Mr. Henshaw	Fic
A girl from Yamhill: a memoir	92

Cleary, Brian P., 1959-

The laugh stand	817

Cleavage   S C

Cleaver, Bill

(jt. auth) Cleaver, V. Where the lillies bloom	
	Fic

Cleaver, Vera

Where the lillies bloom	Fic

Clemens, Samuel Langhorne *See* Twain, Mark, 1835-1910

Clément, Frédéric

(il) Freedman, R. Confucius	92

Clement, Gary

(il) Lottridge, C. B. Stories from Adam and Eve to Ezekiel	220.9

Clemente, Roberto, 1934-1972

About

Ford, C. T. Roberto Clemente	92
Márquez, H. Roberto Clemente	92

Clements, Andrew, 1949-

The school story	Fic
Things not seen	Fic

Clements, Gillian

A picture history of great buildings	720.9

Cleopatra, Queen of Egypt, d. 30 B.C.

About

Morgan, J. Cleopatra	92
Sapet, K. Cleopatra	92
Stanley, D. Cleopatra	92

See/See also pages in the following book(s):

Krull, K. Lives of extraordinary women	920
Meltzer, M. Ten queens	920

Clergy

See also Priests

Fiction

Marsden, C. Sahwira	Fic
Ray, D. Singing hands	Fic

Clewer, Carolyn

Kids can knit	746.43

Click   Fic

Click here. Vega, D.   Fic

Cliff dwellers and cliff dwellings

Vivian, R. G. Chaco Canyon	978

Cliff hanger. Skurzynski, G.   Fic

Climate

See also Greenhouse effect; Meteorology; United States—Climate; Weather

Arnold, C. El Niño	551.6
Christie, P. The curse of Akkad	551.6
Cosgrove, B. Weather	551.5
Silverstein, A. Weather and climate	551.5
Skelton, R. Forecast Earth [biography of Inez Fung]	92

Environmental aspects

Berne, E. C. Global warming and climate change	363.7
Cherry, L. How we know what we know about our changing climate	363.7
David, L. The down-to-earth guide to global warming	363.7
Delano, M. F. Earth in the hot seat	363.7
Desonie, D. Climate	551.6
Gore, A., Jr. An inconvenient truth	363.7
Johnson, R. L. Investigating climate change	
	551.6
Johnson, R. L. Understanding global warming	
	363.7
Morris, N. Global warming	363.7
Nardo, D. Climate crisis	363.7
Parks, P. J. Global warming	363.7
Robinson, M. America debates global warming	
	363.7
Silverstein, A. Global warming	363.7
Simpson, K. Extreme weather	551.6
Stille, D. R. The greenhouse effect	363.7
Tanaka, S. Climate change	363.7

Collier, James Lincoln, 1928-—*Continued*
The Tecumseh you never knew   **92**
Vaccines   **615**
War comes to Willy Freeman   **Fic**
With every drop of blood   **Fic**
(jt. auth) Collier, C. Building a new nation   **973.4**
(jt. auth) Collier, C. The changing face of American society: 1945-2000   **973.92**
(jt. auth) Collier, C. The Civil War, 1860-1865   **973.7**
(jt. auth) Collier, C. Clash of cultures, prehistory-1638   **970.004**
(jt. auth) Collier, C. Creating the Constitution, 1787   **342**
(jt. auth) Collier, C. Hispanic America, Texas, and the Mexican War, 1835-1850   **973.6**
(jt. auth) Collier, C. Indians, cowboys, and farmers and the battle for the Great Plains, 1865-1910   **978**
(jt. auth) Collier, C. The middle road: American politics, 1945-2000   **973.92**
(jt. auth) Collier, C. Pilgrims and Puritans, 1620-1676   **974.4**
(jt. auth) Collier, C. Progressivism, the Great Depression, and the New Deal, 1901 to 1941   **973.91**
(jt. auth) Collier, C. The rise of the cities, 1820-1920   **307.7**
(jt. auth) Collier, C. Slavery and the coming of the Civil War, 1831-1861   **973.6**
(jt. auth) Collier, C. The United States enters the world stage: from the Alaska Purchase through World War I, 1867-1919   **973.8**
(jt. auth) Collier, C. The United States in the Cold War: 1945-1989   **327.73**

Collier, Michael, 1950-
Over the mountains   **557**

Colligan, L. H.
Sleep disorders   **616.8**
Tick-borne illnesses   **616.9**

Collins, Heather
(il) Butts, E. She dared   **920**

Collins, Joan, 1946-
Motivating readers in the middle grades   **028.5**

Collins, John M., 1960-
Fantastic flight   **745.592**
The gliding flight   **745.592**

Collins, Joseph T.
(jt. auth) Conant, R. A field guide to reptiles & amphibians   **597.9**

Collins, Mary, 1961-
Airborne: a photobiography of Wilbur and Orville Wright   **92**

Collins, Matt
(il) Lemna, D. When the sergeant came marching home   **Fic**

Collins, Michael, 1930-
Flying to the moon   **629.45**
About
Schyffert, B. U. The man who went to the far side of the moon: the story of Apollo 11 astronaut Michael Collins   **92**

Collins, Pat Lowery, 1932-
Hidden voices   **Fic**

Collins, Ross
(il) French, V. The robe of skulls   **Fic**

Collins, Suzanne
Gregor the Overlander   **Fic**
The Hunger Games   **Fic**

Collins, Tracy Brown
(ed) Living through the Great Depression. See Living through the Great Depression   **973.91**

Collins, Yvonne
The Black Sheep   **Fic**

Colman, Penny
Adventurous women   **920**
Corpses, coffins, and crypts   **393**
Rosie the riveter   **331.4**
Thanksgiving   **394.26**

Colombia
Croy, A. Colombia   **986.1**
DuBois, J. Colombia   **986.1**
Fiction
Durango, J. The walls of Cartagena   **Fic**

Colombian authors *See* Authors, Colombian

Colombo, Cristoforo *See* Columbus, Christopher

Colón, Jessi Morgenstern- *See* Morgenstern-Colón, Jessi

Colón, Raúl
(il) Johnston, T. Any small goodness   **Fic**
(il) Yolen, J. Mightier than the sword   **398.2**

Colon cancer
Stokes, M. Colon cancer   **616.99**

Colonial America: a history in documents. Gray, E. G.   **973.2**

Colonial America: almanac. Saari, P.   **973.2**

Colonial America: primary sources. Saari, P.   **973.2**

Colonial life [series]
Stefoff, R. Cities and towns   **973.2**
Stefoff, R. Exploration and settlement   **973.1**

Color
Gardner, R. Physics projects with a light box you can build   **530**
Kassinger, R. Dyes: from sea snails to synthetics   **667**
See/See also pages in the following book(s):
Luxbacher, I. The jumbo book of art   **702.8**

The **Color** of absence   **S C**

The **color** of my words. Joseph, L.   **Fic**

Colorado
Fiction
Ferris, J. Much ado about Grubstake   **Fic**
Mason, T. The last synapsid   **Fic**
Nuzum, K. A. The leanin' dog   **Fic**
Nuzum, K. A. A small white scar   **Fic**
Oswald, N. Nothing here but stones   **Fic**
Gold discoveries—Fiction
Avi. Hard gold   **Fic**

Colorado River (Colo.-Mexico)
Rawlins, C. The Colorado River   **979.1**

Colosseum (Rome, Italy)
Mann, E. The Roman Colosseum   **937**

The **conjure** brother. McKissack, P. C.
   In McKissack, P. C. The dark-thirty; Southern tales of the supernatural p66-77   **S C**

Conjuring *See* Magic tricks

Conklin, Barbara Gardner
   (jt. auth) Gardner, R. Chemistry science fair projects using french fries, gumdrops, soap, and other organic stuff   **547**
   (jt. auth) Gardner, R. Health science projects about psychology   **150**

Conlan, Kathy
   Under the ice   **578.7**

Conley, Kate A., 1977-
   Joseph Priestley and the discovery of oxygen   **92**

Conly, Jane Leslie
   Racso and the rats of NIMH   **Fic**

Conly, Robert L. *See* O'Brien, Robert C., 1918-1973

Connecticut
Fiction
   Cooney, C. B. Diamonds in the shadow   **Fic**
   Cooney, C. B. If the witness lied   **Fic**
   Duble, K. B. Hearts of iron   **Fic**
   Grabenstein, C. The crossroads   **Fic**
   Hegamin, T. Pemba's song   **Fic**
   Hurst, C. O. Through the lock   **Fic**
   Wright, B. When the black girl sings   **Fic**
   History—1600-1775, Colonial period—Fiction
   Speare, E. G. The witch of Blackbird Pond
   Fic

Connecting boys with books 2. Sullivan, M.
   028.5

Connecting with reluctant teen readers. Jones, P.
   028.5

Connecting young adults and libraries. Gorman, M.   **027.62**

Connolly, Peter, 1935-
   The ancient city   **937**
   Pompeii   **937**
   (il) Burrell, R. E. C. Oxford first ancient history
   909

Connolly, Sean, 1956-
   New Testament miracles   **226**
   The right to vote   **324.6**

Connolly, Sucheta
   Anxiety disorders   **616.85**

Connor, Leslie
   Dead on town line   **Fic**
   Waiting for normal   **Fic**

The **conquests** of Alexander the Great. Behnke, A.
   92

Conrad, Pam, 1947-1996
   My Daniel   **Fic**

Conscientious objectors
Fiction
   Kerr, M. E. Slap your sides   **Fic**

Consciousness expanding drugs *See* Hallucinogens

Conservation movement *See* Environmental movement

Conservation of natural resources
   See also Nature conservation; Wildlife conservation
   Anderson, T. MySpace/OurPlanet   **333.72**
   Global resources: opposing viewpoints
   333.71
   Malaspina, A. Saving the American wilderness
   333.72
   Ravilious, K. Power   **179**

Conservation of water *See* Water conservation

Conserving the environment   **333.7**

Consider the source. Broderick, J. F.   **070.5**

Conspiracies
Fiction
   Boie, K. The princess plot   **Fic**
   Prose, F. After   **Fic**
   Sniegoski, T. Sleeper code   **Fic**

Constable, Kate
   The singer of all songs   **Fic**

Constellation (Frigate)
   Myers, W. D. USS Constellation   **359.8**

The **Constitution**. Finkelman, P.   **342**

Constitution [series]
   Fireside, H. The Fifth Amendment   **347**

The Constitution of the United States [series]
   Gonzales, D. A look at the Second Amendment
   344

The **Constitutional** Convention   **342**

Constitutional history
   Finkelman, P. The Constitution   **342**
United States
   Collier, C. Creating the Constitution, 1787
   342
   The Constitutional Convention   **342**
   Feinberg, B. S. The Articles of Confederation
   342
   Haynes, C. C. First freedoms   **342**
   Ritchie, D. A. Our Constitution   **342**

Constitutional law
United States
   Brannen, D. E. Supreme Court drama   **347**
   Panchyk, R. Our Supreme Court   **347**
   Pendergast, T. Constitutional amendments: from freedom of speech to flag burning   **342**
   Vile, J. R. The United States Constitution
   342

Constitutional rights *See* Civil rights

Construction *See* Building

Construction: building the impossible. Aaseng, N.
   624

Consumer education
   Menhard, F. R. Teen consumer smarts
   332.024

Contagious diseases *See* Communicable diseases

Contaminated food *See* Food contamination

Contemporary issues companion [series]
   Battered women   **362.82**
   Depression   **616.85**
   Eating disorders   **616.85**
   Inner-city poverty   **362.5**
   Teen alcoholism   **362.292**

The **contemporary** Torah. Bible. O.T. Pentateuch
   222

Cottee, Kay, 1954-
See/See also pages in the following book(s):
Atkins, J. How high can we climb? 920

Cotten, Cynthia
Fair has nothing to do with it Fic

Cotter, Charis
Kids who rule 920

Cotterell, Arthur
Ancient China 931

Cotton
Hopkinson, D. Up before daybreak 331.7
Meltzer, M. The cotton gin 633.5
The **cotton** gin. Meltzer, M. 633.5
The **cotton** gin. Robinson Masters, N. 677

Cotton gins
Robinson Masters, N. The cotton gin 677

Cottrell Boyce, Frank
Framed Fic

Cougars *See* Pumas

Couloumbis, Audrey
Love me tender Fic
The misadventures of Maude March Fic

Coulter, Laurie
(jt. auth) Brewster, H. 882 ½ amazing answers to your questions about the Titanic 910.4

Council on Library and Information Resources
The whole digital library handbook. See The whole digital library handbook 025.1

Counseling
See also Mentoring

Count on us. Nathan, A. 355

Countdown to space [series]
Cole, M. D. The Columbia space shuttle disaster 629.44
Cole, M. D. Hubble Space Telescope 522
Cole, M. D. Living on Mars 629.4
Jeffrey, L. S. Christa McAuliffe 92

Countdown to summer. Lewis, J. P. 811

Counter clockwise. Cockcroft, J. Fic

Counter-Reformation
See also Reformation

The **countess** and me. Kropp, P. Fic

Counting
See also Numbers

Counting on Grace. Winthrop, E. Fic

Countries of the world [series]
Bowden, R. Kenya 967.62
Croy, A. Colombia 986.1
Dalal, A. K. Laos 959.4
Deckker, Z. Brazil 981
Deckker, Z. Poland 943.8
Deckker, Z. Portugal 946.9
Fearns, L. Argentina 982
Garrington, S. Canada 971
Giles, B. Nigeria 966.9
Gray, L. Iran 955
Green, J. Jamaica 972.92
Green, J. Vietnam 959.7
Gruber, B. Mexico 972
Jackson, B. New Zealand 993
Jackson, T. South Korea 951.95
Kazem, H. Afghanistan 958.1

Lister, M. England 942
Mace, V. South Africa 968
McQuinn, C. Ireland 941.5
NgCheong-Lum, R. France 944
Phillips, C. Sweden 948.5
Russell, H. Germany 943
Russell, H. Russia 947
Samuels, C. Iraq 956.7
Shields, S. D. Turkey 956.1
Turner, K. Australia 994
Whitfield, S. Afghanistan 958.1
Williams, B. Canada 971
Young, E. Israel 956.94

Countries of the world and their leaders yearbook 910.3

Country. Handyside, C. 781.642

Country and western music *See* Country music

Country life
See also Mountain life
Hinds, K. The countryside [Life in the Middle Ages series] 940.1
Hinds, K. The countryside [Life in the Renaissance series] 940.2
Hinds, K. The countryside [Life in the Roman Empire series] 937
Hinds, K. The countryside [Life in Ancient Egypt series] 932
Hinds, K. The countryside [Life in Elizabethan England series] 942.05
Hinds, K. The countryside [Life in the Medieval Muslim world series] 909.07
Fiction
Bauer, J. Squashed Fic
Cassidy, C. Scarlett Fic
Couvillon, J. The chicken dance Fic
Friedman, A. The year my sister got lucky Fic
Levine, K. The best bad luck I ever had Fic
Michael, J. City boy Fic
Morgan, N. Chicken friend Fic
Napoli, D. J. Alligator bayou Fic
Peck, R. Here lies the librarian Fic
Peck, R. The teacher's funeral Fic
Resau, L. What the moon saw Fic
Slayton, F. C. When the whistle blows Fic
Stone, P. Deep down popular Fic
Townsend, W. Lizard love Fic
White, R. Little Audrey Fic
Woodworth, C. Double-click for trouble Fic

Country music
Bertholf, B. Long gone lonesome history of country music 781.642
Handyside, C. Country 781.642
Kallen, S. A. The history of country music 781.642

Country musicians
Neimark, A. E. Johnny Cash 92

Countryman, Edward
(ed) The Old West: history and heritage. See The Old West: history and heritage 978.03

The **countryside** [Life in Ancient Egypt series] Hinds, K. 932

Cults—Fiction—*Continued*
  Waite, J. Forbidden   **Fic**
  Williams, C. L. The chosen one   **Fic**
Cultural anthropology *See* Ethnology
Cultural atlas for young people [series]
  Corbishley, M. The Middle Ages   **940.1**
  Harris, G. Ancient Egypt   **932**
  Powell, A. Ancient Greece   **938**
Cultural diversity. Gay, K.   **305.8**
Cultural pluralism *See* Multiculturalism
Cultural programs
  Jones, E. W. Start-to-finish YA programs
     027.62
Cultural Revolution. Langley, A.   **951**
Culture, Popular *See* Popular culture
Culture conflict
  Collier, C. Clash of cultures, prehistory-1638
     970.004
Culture shock *See* Culture conflict
Cultures of the past [series]
  Ashby, R. Elizabethan England   **942.05**
  Hinds, K. Medieval England   **942.03**
  Hinds, K. Venice and its merchant empire
     945
  Mann, K. The ancient Hebrews   **909**
  Marston, E. The Byzantine Empire   **949.5**
  Marston, E. The Phoenicians   **939**
  Ruggiero, A. The Ottoman Empire   **956.1**
  Schomp, V. The Italian Renaissance   **945**
  Schomp, V. Japan in the days of the samurai
     952
Cultures of the world [series]
  Abazov, R. Tajikistan   **958.6**
  Ali, S. E. Afghanistan   **958.1**
  Augustin, B. Andorra   **946**
  Barlas, R. Bahamas   **972.96**
  Barlas, R. Latvia   **947.9**
  Barlas, R. Uganda   **967.6**
  Bassis, V. Ukraine   **947.7**
  Beliaev, E. Dagestan   **947.5**
  Berg, E. Senegal   **966.3**
  Blauer, E. Mali   **966.2**
  Blauer, E. Mauritania   **966.1**
  Brown, R. V. Tunisia   **961.1**
  Burbank, J. Nepal   **954.96**
  Cheong-Lum, R. N. Haiti   **972.94**
  Cooper, R. Bahrain   **953.6**
  Cooper, R. Bhutan   **954.9**
  Cooper, R. Croatia   **949.7**
  Dhilawala, S. Armenia   **947.5**
  DuBois, J. Colombia   **986.1**
  DuBois, J. Greece   **949.5**
  DuBois, J. Israel   **956.94**
  DuBois, J. Korea   **951.9**
  Esbenshade, R. S. Hungary   **943.9**
  Falconer, K. Peru   **985**
  Ferroa, P. G. China   **951**
  Foley, E. Costa Rica   **972.86**
  Foley, E. Dominican Republic   **972.93**
  Foley, E. Ecuador   **986.6**
  Foley, E. El Salvador   **972.84**
  Fuller, B. Britain   **941**
  Fuller, B. Germany   **943**
  Gan, D. Sweden   **948.5**

Gascoigne, I. Papua New Guinea   **995.3**
Gish, S. Ethiopia   **963**
Gofen, E. Argentina   **982**
Gofen, E. France   **944**
Goodman, J. Thailand   **959.3**
Hassig, S. M. Iraq   **956.7**
Hassig, S. M. Panama   **972.87**
Hassig, S. M. Somalia   **967.73**
Heale, J. Democratic Republic of the Congo
     967.51
Heale, J. Madagascar   **969.1**
Heale, J. Poland   **943.8**
Heale, J. Portugal   **946.9**
Heale, J. Tanzania   **967.8**
Hestler, A. Wales   **942.9**
Hestler, A. Yemen   **953.3**
Holmes, T. Zambia   **968.94**
Janin, H. Saudi Arabia   **953.8**
Jermyn, L. Guyana   **988.1**
Jermyn, L. Paraguay   **989.2**
Jermyn, L. Uruguay   **989.5**
Kagda, F. Algeria   **965**
Kagda, F. Hong Kong   **951.25**
Kagda, S. Lithuania   **947.93**
Kagda, S. Norway   **948.1**
King, D. C. Azerbaijan   **947.5**
King, D. C. Kyrgyzstan   **958.4**
King, D. C. Monaco   **944**
King, D. C. Mozambique   **967.9**
King, D. C. Rwanda   **967.571**
King, D. C. Serbia and Montenegro   **949.7**
King, D. C. The United Arab Emirates   **953**
Kneib, M. Benin   **966.83**
Kneib, M. Chad   **967.43**
Knowlton, M. Albania   **949.65**
Knowlton, M. Macedonia   **949.7**
Knowlton, M. Turkmenistan   **958.5**
Knowlton, M. Uzbekistan   **958.7**
Kott, J. Nicaragua   **972.85**
Kras, S. L. Antigua and Barbuda   **972.97**
Layton, L. Singapore   **959.57**
LeVert, S. Botswana   **968.83**
LeVert, S. Sierra Leone   **966.4**
Levy, P. Ireland   **941.5**
Levy, P. Nigeria   **966.9**
Levy, P. Puerto Rico   **972.95**
Levy, P. Scotland   **941.1**
Levy, P. Sudan   **962.4**
Levy, P. Switzerland   **949.4**
Levy, P. Tibet   **951**
Malcolm, P. Libya   **961.2**
Mansfield, S. Laos   **959.4**
Mirpuri, G. Indonesia   **959.8**
Moiz, A. Taiwan   **951.2**
Munan, H. Malaysia   **959.5**
NgCheong-Lum, R. Tahiti   **996**
Orr, T. Qatar   **953.6**
Orr, T. Saint Lucia   **972.98**
O'Shea, M. Kuwait   **953.67**
Pang, G.-C. Canada   **971**
Pang, G.-C. Grenada   **972.98**
Pang, G.-C. Mongolia   **951.7**
Pateman, R. Belgium   **949.3**
Pateman, R. Bolivia   **984**
Pateman, R. Denmark   **948.9**
Pateman, R. Egypt   **962**
Pateman, R. Kenya   **967.62**

Curricula (Courses of study) *See* Education—Curricula

Curriculum connections through the library
027.8

Curriculum materials centers *See* Instructional materials centers

Curriculum partner. Kearney, C. A.   027.8

Currie, Stephen, 1960-
An actor on the Elizabethan stage   792.09
Miracles, saints, and superstition   940.1
Slavery   326
(ed) Terrorism. See Terrorism   363.32

Currie-McGhee, L. K., 1971-
Sexually transmitted diseases   614.5

Currie-McGhee, Leanne K. *See* Currie-McGhee, L. K., 1971-

Currier, Katrina Saltonstall, 1969-
Kai's journey to Gold Mountain   Fic

Curry, Jane Louise, 1932-
The Black Canary   Fic
Hold up the sky: and other Native American tales from Texas and the Southern Plains   398.2

A **curse** dark as gold. Bunce, E. C.   Fic

The **curse** of Addy McMahon. Davis, K.   Fic

The **curse** of Akkad. Christie, P.   551.6

The **curse** of King Tut. Lace, W. W.   932

The **curse** of the blue figurine. Bellairs, J.   Fic

The **curse** of the night wolf. Stewart, P.   Fic

Curse of the pharaohs. Hawass, Z. A.   932

Curtis, Christopher Paul
Bud, not Buddy   Fic
Elijah of Buxton   Fic
The Watsons go to Birmingham—1963   Fic

Curtsinger, Bill, 1946-
(il) Cerullo, M. M. Sea soup: zooplankton
592

Curzon, Susan Carol
Managing change   025.1

Cushites
Sonneborn, L. The ancient Kushites   939

Cushman, Karen, 1941-
Catherine, called Birdy   Fic
The loud silence of Francine Green   Fic
The midwife's apprentice   Fic
Rodzina   Fic

Cusick, Richie Tankersley, 1952-
Walk of the spirits   Fic

Custer, Elizabeth Bacon, 1842-1933
The diary of Elizabeth Bacon Custer   973.8

Custer, George Armstrong, 1839-1876
About
Custer, E. B. The diary of Elizabeth Bacon Custer
973.8
Custer's last stand   973.8
Uschan, M. V. The Battle of the Little Bighorn
973.8

Custer's last stand   973.8

Cut. McCormick, P.   Fic

Cut from the same cloth. San Souci, R.   398.2

Cute dolls   745.592

Cute, furry, and deadly. Brownlee, C.   614.4

The cutting edge [series]
Oxlade, C. Electronics   621.381
Rooney, A. Computers   004

Cutting-edge medicine. Goldsmith, C.   610

Cybele's secret. Marillier, J.   Fic

Cyber journals *See* Weblogs

Cyberia. Lynch, C.   Fic

Cycling
See also Bicycles; Motorcycles
Buckley, A. Be a better biker   796.6
Gardner, R. Bicycle science projects   531
Haduch, B. Go fly a bike!   629.227
King, A. Play-by-play mountain biking
796.6
Sidwells, C. Complete bike book   629.227
Fiction
Bradbury, J. Shift   Fic

Cyclones
See also Hurricanes
Ceban, B. J. Hurricanes, typhoons, and cyclones
551.55
Encyclopedias
Longshore, D. Encyclopedia of hurricanes, typhoons, and cyclones   551.55

Cyprus
Spilling, M. Cyprus   956.93

Cyrus, Kurt, 1954-
(il) Anderson, M. T. Whales on stilts   Fic

Cystic fibrosis
Bjorklund, R. Cystic fibrosis   616.3
Giddings, S. Cystic fibrosis   616.3
Monroe, J. Cystic fibrosis   616.3

Cytology *See* Cells

Czarnecki, Monike
(il) Lanchon, A. All about adoption   362.7

Czech Americans
Fiction
Myers, W. D. Game   Fic

Czech Republic
Bultje, J. W. The Czech Republic   943.7
Sioras, E. Czech Republic   943.7
Fiction
Heuston, K. B. The Book of Jude   Fic

Czechoslovakia
See also Czech Republic

D

D is for Dahl. Cooling, W.   823.009

D.N.A. *See* DNA

Da Gama, Vasco *See* Gama, Vasco da, 1469-1524

Da Vinci, Leonardo *See* Leonardo, da Vinci, 1452-1519

Dabek, Lisa
About
Montgomery, S. Quest for the tree kangaroo
599.2

D'Adamo, Francesco
Iqbal   Fic

Daemon Hall. Nance, A.   **Fic**

Dagestan (Russia)
Beliaev, E. Dagestan   **947.5**

Dahl, Roald
Boy: tales of childhood   **92**
Skin and other stories   **S C**
        About
Cooling, W. D is for Dahl   **823.009**

Dahomey *See* Benin

Dailey, Donna
Tamora Pierce   **92**

Daily life in a Plains Indian village, 1868. Terry, M. B. H.   **970.004**

Daily life in colonial New England. Johnson, C. D.   **974**

Daily life in Renaissance Italy. Cohen, E. S.   **945**

Daily life in the Pilgrim colony, 1636. Erickson, P.   **974.4**

Daily life through history [series]
Johnson, C. D. Daily life in colonial New England   **974**

Daily prison life. Rabiger, J.   **365**

Daintith, John
(ed) The Facts on File dictionary of astronomy. See The Facts on File dictionary of astronomy   **520.3**

Dairy Queen. Murdock, C. G.   **Fic**

Dakota Indians
    See also Oglala Indians
Brave Bird, M. Lakota woman   **92**
See/See also pages in the following book(s):
Ehrlich, A. Wounded Knee: an Indian history of the American West   **970.004**
Freedman, R. Indian chiefs   **920**
        Fiction
Scaletta, K. Mudville   **Fic**

Dalai Lama XIV, 1935-
        About
Demi. The Dalai Lama   **92**
Kimmel, E. C. Boy on the lion throne [biography of the Dalai Lama]   **92**
See/See also pages in the following book(s):
Cotter, C. Kids who rule   **920**

Dalal, A. Kamala
Laos   **959.4**

Dalí, Salvador, 1904-1989
        About
McNeese, T. Salvador Dali   **92**

Dalston, Teresa R., 1965-
(jt. auth) Hallam, A. Managing budgets and finances   **025.1**

Dalton, David
Living in a refugee camp   **305.23**

D'Aluisio, Faith, 1957-
(jt. auth) Menzel, P. What the world eats   **641.3**

Daly, Melissa
(jt. auth) Mezinski, P. Drugs explained   **362.29**
(jt. auth) Piquemal, M. When life stinks   **158**

Damerum, Kanako
(il) Horowitz, A. Point blank: the graphic novel   **741.5**
(il) Horowitz, A. Stormbreaker: the graphic novel   **741.5**

D'Amico, Joan, 1957-
The coming to America cookbook   **641.5**
The healthy body cookbook   **641.5**
The United States cookbook   **641.5**

Damosel. Spinner, S.   **Fic**

Dams
See/See also pages in the following book(s):
Macaulay, D. Building big   **720**

Dance
    See also Ballet; Modern dance
Grau, A. Dance   **792.8**
McAlpine, M. Working in music and dance   **780**
Nathan, A. Meet the dancers   **920**
        Fiction
Staples, S. F. Shiva's fire   **Fic**

Dance [series]
Solway, A. Modern dance   **792.8**

Dance, Nana, dance. Hayes, J.   **398.2**

Dance of the continents. Gallant, R. A.   **551.1**

Dancers
    See also African American dancers; Ballet dancers
Freedman, R. Martha Graham, a dancer's life   **92**
Nathan, A. Meet the dancers   **920**
        Fiction
Kephart, B. House of Dance   **Fic**
Levy, E. Seventh grade tango   **Fic**
Winston, S. The Kayla chronicles   **Fic**

Dancing *See* Dance

Dancing in the streets of Brooklyn. Lurie, A.   **Fic**

Dancing teepees: poems of American Indian youth   **897**

D'Angelo, Pascal, 1894-1932
        About
Murphy, J. Pick & shovel poet: the journeys of Pascal D'Angelo   **92**

Danger in the dark. Matthews, T. L.   **Fic**

Danger zone [series]
Gilman, D. The devil's breath   **Fic**

Danger zone: dieting and eating disorders [series]
Zahensky, B. A. Diet fads   **613.2**

Dangerous animals
    See also Poisonous animals
Benchley, P. Shark life   **597**
Lewin, T. Tooth and claw   **590**
Wilkes, A. Dangerous creatures   **591.6**

The **dangerous** book for boys. Iggulden, C.   **031.02**

Dangerous creatures. Wilkes, A.   **591.6**

A **dangerous** engine [biography of Benjamin Franklin] Dash, J.   **92**

Dangerous planet. Barnard, B.   **363.34**

Dangerous planet. Engelbert, P.   **363.34**

Dangerous skies. Staples, S. F. **Fic**
Dangerous times. Brittney, L. **Fic**
Dangerous weather [series]
  Allaby, M. Droughts **551.57**
  Allaby, M. Floods **551.48**
Dangles and bangles. Haab, S. **745.5**
Danica Patrick. Hinman, B. **92**
Daniel, Susanna
  Paul Zindel **92**
  Paula Fox **92**
Daniel half human. Chotjewitz, D. **Fic**
Daniel Handler [biography of Lemony Snicket]
  Haugen, H. M. **92**
Daniels, Roger
  American immigration **325.73**
Danish authors See Authors, Danish
Dann, Geoff
  (il) Gravett, C. Knight **940.1**
  (il) Greenaway, T. Jungle **577.3**
Dante Alighieri, 1265-1321
    About
  Davenport, J. Dante **92**
D'Antona, Robin, 1946-
  (jt. auth) Kevorkian, M. 101 facts about bullying
    302.3
Danube. Bryan, N. **363.7**
Danziger, Paula, 1944-2004
  The cat ate my gymsuit **Fic**
  The Divorce Express **Fic**
  P.S. Longer letter later **Fic**
  Snail mail no more **Fic**
    About
  Reed, J. Paula Danziger **92**
Dare to be scared. San Souci, R. **S C**
Darfur. Xavier, J. **962.4**
D'Argo, Laura
  (il) Carson, M. K. The Wright Brothers for kids
    629.13
Dark Ages See Middle Ages
Dark angel. Klass, D. **Fic**
Dark dreams [biography of Stephen King]
  Whitelaw, N. **92**
The **dark** ground. Cross, G. **Fic**
The dark ground trilogy [series]
  Cross, G. The dark ground **Fic**
The **Dark** Hills divide. Carman, P. **Fic**
Dark hours. Pausewang, G. **Fic**
Dark reflections [series]
  Meyer, K. The water mirror **Fic**
Dark sons. Grimes, N. **Fic**
The **dark** stairs. Byars, B. C. **Fic**
The **dark-thirty**. McKissack, P. C. **S C**
Dark water rising. Hale, M. **Fic**
Dark waters. MacPhail, C. **Fic**
Dark wraith of Shannara. Brooks, T. **741.5**
Darkest age [series]
  Lake, A. J. The coming of dragons **Fic**
The **darkest** evening. Durbin, W. **Fic**
Darkest powers [series]
  Armstrong, K. The summoning **Fic**

Darkness creeping. Shusterman, N. **S C**
Darkness over Denmark. Levine, E. **940.53**
Darkside. Becker, T. **Fic**
Darkside [series]
  Becker, T. Darkside **Fic**
Darkwood. Breen, M. E. **Fic**
Darling, Jay Norwood, 1876-1962
  See/See also pages in the following book(s):
  Byrnes, P. Environmental pioneers **920**
Darling, Kathy, 1943-
  (jt. auth) Cobb, V. We dare you! **507.8**
Darraj, Susan Muaddi
  Gabriel García Márquez **92**
  Hosni Mubarak **92**
Darwin, Charles, 1809-1882
    About
  Anderson, M. J. Charles Darwin **92**
  Ashby, R. Young Charles Darwin and the voyage of the Beagle **92**
  Gibbons, A. Charles Darwin **92**
  Heiligman, D. Charles and Emma [dual biography of Charles Darwin and Emma Wedgwood Darwin] **92**
  Leone, B. Origin: the story of Charles Darwin **92**
  Schanzer, R. What Darwin saw **92**
  Stefoff, R. Charles Darwin and the evolution revolution **92**
  See/See also pages in the following book(s):
  Gardner, R. Genetics and evolution science fair projects **576**
    Fiction
  Meyer, C. The true adventures of Charley Darwin **Fic**
Darwin, Emma Wedgwood, 1808-1896
    About
  Heiligman, D. Charles and Emma [dual biography of Charles Darwin and Emma Wedgwood Darwin] **92**
Darwinism See Evolution
Dasch, E. Julius (Ernest Julius), 1932-
  (ed) Explorers. See Explorers **920.003**
Dasch, Ernest Julius See Dasch, E. Julius (Ernest Julius), 1932-
Dasch, Pat
  (ed) Space sciences. See Space sciences
    500.5
Dash, Joan
  A dangerous engine [biography of Benjamin Franklin] **92**
  The longitude prize [biography of John Harrison] **92**
Daswani, Kavita, 1964-
  Indie girl **Fic**
Data processing
    See also Artificial intelligence; Computer science
Data storage and retrieval systems See Information systems
Data transmission systems
    See also Computer networks; Electronic mail systems

Day

See also Night

A **day** at the New Amsterdam Theatre. Amendola, D.   **792.6**

A **day** no pigs would die. Peck, R. N.   **Fic**

Day of tears. Lester, J.   **Fic**

The **day** the Cisco Kid shot John Wayne. Candelaria, N.

In Growing up Latino; memoirs and stories p115-30   **810.8**

The **day** the Rabbi disappeared: Jewish holiday tales of magic. Schwartz, H.   **398.2**

The **day** the world exploded. Winchester, S.   **551.2**

A **day** without immigrants. Ouellette, J.   **331.6**

Days of change [series]

Bodden, V. The bombing of Hiroshima and Nagasaki   **940.54**

Bodden, V. The Cold War   **909.82**

Bodden, V. The Holocaust   **940.53**

Days of Jubilee. McKissack, P. C.   **973.7**

Days that changed the world [series]

Beecroft, S. The release of Nelson Mandela   **968.06**

De Balboa, Vasco Núñez *See* Balboa, Vasco Núñez de, 1475-1519

De Blij, Harm J.

(ed) Atlas of North America. See Atlas of North America   **912**

De Chamorro, Violeta Barrios *See* Chamorro, Violeta Barrios de

De Champlain, Samuel *See* Champlain, Samuel de, 1567-1635

De Guzman, Michael

The bamboozlers   **Fic**

Beekman's big deal   **Fic**

Finding Stinko   **Fic**

De la Bédoyère, Camilla

The discovery of DNA   **572.8**

De la Bédoyère, Guy

The discovery of penicillin   **615**

The first computers   **004**

The first polio vaccine   **615**

De la Cruz, Melissa, 1971-

Fresh off the boat   **Fic**

De la Peña, Matt

Mexican whiteboy   **Fic**

De Leal, Amy

(jt. auth) Howard, H. Living as a refugee in America   **305.23**

De Lint, Charles, 1951-

The blue girl   **Fic**

Waifs and strays   **S C**

De Marcken, Gail

(il) Packer, T. Tales from Shakespeare   **822.3**

De Mari, Silvana, 1953-

The last dragon   **Fic**

De Médicis, Catherine, Queen, consort of Henry II, King of France, 1519-1589 *See* Catherine de Médicis, Queen, consort of Henry II, King of France, 1519-1589

De Paola, Thomas Anthony *See* De Paola, Tomie, 1934-

De Paola, Tomie, 1934-

Christmas remembered   **92**

De Pinna, Simon *See* Pinna, Simon de

De Sautuola, Maria *See* Sautuola, Maria de, 1870-1946

De Seguin, Gaetan *See* Seguin, Gaetan de

De Sève, Peter

(il) Helgerson, J. Crows & cards   **Fic**

De Soto, Hernando *See* Soto, Hernando de, ca. 1500-1542

De Tonti, Henri *See* Tonti, Henri de, 1650-1704

The **dead** & the gone. Pfeffer, S. B.   **Fic**

Dead girl [series]

Singleton, L. J. Dead girl walking   **Fic**

Dead girl walking. Singleton, L. J.   **Fic**

Dead in the water. Stevenson, R. H.   **Fic**

Dead is the new black. Perez, M.   **Fic**

Dead on town line. Connor, L.   **Fic**

Dead reckoning. Lawlor, L.   **Fic**

Deadline. Crutcher, C.   **Fic**

Deadly disasters [series]

Ceban, B. J. Hurricanes, typhoons, and cyclones   **551.55**

Ceban, B. J. Tornadoes   **551.55**

Miller, M. Hurricane Katrina strikes the Gulf Coast   **363.34**

Reed, J. Earthquakes   **551.2**

Worth, R. Massacre at Virginia Tech   **364.1**

Deadly diseases and epidemics [series]

Brands, D. A. Salmonella   **615.9**

Emmeluth, D. Botulism   **616.9**

Smith, T. C. Ebola   **616.9**

Zonderman, J. Legionnaires' disease   **616.2**

Deadly invaders. Grady, D.   **614.4**

Deaf

Alexander, S. H. She touched the world: Laura Bridgman, deaf-blind pioneer   **92**

Garrett, L. Helen Keller   **92**

Keller, H. The story of my life   **92**

Lawlor, L. Helen Keller: rebellious spirit   **92**

MacLeod, E. Helen Keller   **92**

Sullivan, G. Helen Keller   **92**

Fiction

LeZotte, A. C. T4   **Fic**

Miller, S. Miss Spitfire   **Fic**

Na, A. Wait for me   **Fic**

Ray, D. Singing hands   **Fic**

Smith, D. J. The boys of San Joaquin   **Fic**

Means of communication

See also Sign language

Dealing with dragons. Wrede, P. C.   **Fic**

Dean, Arlan

Terra-cotta soldiers   **931**

Dean, David, 1976-

(il) St. John, L. The white giraffe   **Fic**

Dean, Ruth, 1947-

Teen prostitution   **362.7**

(jt. auth) Thomson, M. Women of the Renaissance   **940.2**

Des Chenes, Betz—_Continued_
(ed) Engelbert, P. American civil rights: biographies **920**

Des Forges, Roger V.
The Asian world, 600-1500 **950**

Des Moines Independent Community School District
Gold, S. D. Tinker v. Des Moines **342**

DeSaix, Debbi Durland
Hidden on the mountain **940.53**

DeSalle, Rob
(jt. auth) Tattersall, I. Bones, brains and DNA **599.93**

Desaulniers, Kristi L.
Northern America **970**

Desegregation _See_ Segregation

Desegregation in education _See_ School integration

Desert ecology
Allaby, M. Deserts **577.5**
Fridell, R. Life in the desert **577.5**
Warhol, T. Desert **577.5**

The **desert** is my mother. El desierto es mi madre.
Mora, P. **811**

Desert Storm Operation _See_ Persian Gulf War, 1991

Deserts
Aleshire, P. Deserts **551.4**
Allaby, M. Deserts **577.5**
Fridell, R. Life in the desert **577.5**
Hinds, K. The countryside [Life in the Medieval Muslim world series] **909.07**
Warhol, T. Desert **577.5**
Fiction
Mason, P. Camel rider **Fic**
Temple, F. The Beduins' gazelle **Fic**
Poetry
Mora, P. The desert is my mother. El desierto es mi madre **811**

Desetta, Al
(ed) The Courage to be yourself. See The Courage to be yourself **305.23**

Design, Industrial _See_ Industrial design

Design your own butterfly garden. Harkins, S. S. **638**

Designing a school library media center for the future. Erikson, R. **027.8**

Desktop publishing
Todd, M. Whatcha mean, what's a zine? **070.5**

Desonie, Dana
Climate **551.6**
Geosphere **333.73**
Hydrosphere **551.48**
Oceans **551.46**
Polar regions **304.2**

The **desperado** who stole baseball. Ritter, J. H. **Fic**

Desperate journey. Murphy, J. **Fic**

Despite all obstacles: La Salle and the conquest of the Mississippi. Goodman, J. E. **92**

Despotism
Fiction
Agell, C. Shift **Fic**

Desrocher, Jack
(il) Doeden, M. Eat right! **613.2**
(il) Johnson, R. L. Amazing DNA **572.8**
(il) Johnson, R. L. Powerful plant cells **581.7**
(il) Johnson, R. L. Ultra-organized cell systems **612**

Dessen, Sarah, 1970-
Along for the ride **Fic**
That summer **Fic**
The truth about forever **Fic**
About
Glenn, W. J. Sarah Dessen **813.009**

Desserts
Carle, M. Teens cook dessert **641.8**
Dunnington, R. Bake it up! **641.8**

Destination: Jupiter. Simon, S. **523.4**

Destination: space. Simon, S. **522**

Destination unexpected: short stories **S C**

Detective Jermain, volume 1. Rocks, M. **741.5**

Detrick, Erin, 1981-
(ed) Actor's choice. See Actor's choice **808.82**

Deuker, Carl, 1950-
Gym candy **Fic**
High heat **Fic**
Night hoops **Fic**
Painting the black **Fic**

Developing an information literacy program, K-12 **025.5**

Developing and promoting graphic novel collections. Miller, S. **025.2**

Developing Christian fiction collections for children and adults. Walker, B. J. **025.2**

Developing countries
Economic conditions
Garlake, T. Global debt **336.3**

Devereux, Robert, 1566-1601 _See_ Essex, Robert Devereux, 2nd Earl of, 1566-1601

Devers, Gail, 1966-
See/See also pages in the following book(s):
Kaminsky, M. Uncommon champions **920**

Devil
Fiction
Jenkins, A. M. Repossessed **Fic**
Johnson, M. Devilish **Fic**

Devil on my heels. McDonald, J. **Fic**

The **devil** on trial. Margulies, P. **345**

Devilish. Johnson, M. **Fic**

DeVillers, David
Marbury v. Madison **347**

The **devil's** breath. Gilman, D. **Fic**

The **devil's** paintbox. McKernan, V. **Fic**

DeVorkin, David H., 1944-
Hubble imaging space and time **522**

Devotional exercises
See also Meditation

The **Devouring.** Holt, S. **Fic**

Doc Fizzix *See* Balmer, Alden J.
Doc Fizzix mousetrap racers. Balmer, A. J.
    629.22

Docherty, James, 1976-
  The ice cream con   **Fic**

Doctorow, Cory
  Little brother   **Fic**

Doctors *See* Physicians

Doctors Without Borders (Organization) *See*
  Médecins Sans Frontières (Organization)

Documentary photography
See/See also pages in the following book(s):
  Schulke, F. Witness to our times   **92**

Documenting history [series]
  Hatt, C. The Crusades   **909.07**
  Hatt, C. Scientists and their discoveries   **509**
  Hatt, C. World War I, 1914-18   **940.3**

Documents that shaped the nation [series]
  Armentrout, D. The Mayflower Compact
    974.4

Dodge, Hazel
  (jt. auth) Connolly, P. The ancient city   **937**

Dodgson, Charles Lutwidge *See* Carroll, Lewis,
  1832-1898

Dodson, Shireen
  100 books for girls to grow on   **028.1**

Doeden, Matt, 1974-
  Eat right!   **613.2**

Does my head look big in this? Abdel-Fattah, R.
    Fic

Does this book make me look fat?   **S C**

A **dog** for life. Matthews, L. S.   **Fic**

Dog racing
    See also Sled dog racing

Dogboy. Russell, C.   **Fic**

Dogs
    See also Working dogs
  American Kennel Club. The complete dog book
    636.7
  Bolan, S. Caring for your mutt   **636.7**
  The Complete dog book for kids   **636.7**
  London, J. White Fang   **Fic**
  Mehus-Roe, K. Dogs for kids!   **636.7**
  Paulsen, G. My life in dog years   **92**
  Sidman, J. The world according to dog
    810.8
  Stefoff, R. Dogs   **636.7**
  Whitehead, S. How to speak dog   **636.7**
      Fiction
  Armstrong, W. H. Sounder   **Fic**
  Bunting, E. The summer of Riley   **Fic**
  Calvert, P. Bigger   **Fic**
  Cochran, T. Running the dogs   **Fic**
  Crane, E. M. Skin deep   **Fic**
  DiCamillo, K. Because of Winn-Dixie   **Fic**
  French, J. Rover   **Fic**
  Frost, H. Diamond Willow   **Fic**
  Gipson, F. B. Old Yeller   **Fic**
  Goldblatt, S. Stray   **Fic**
  Haig, M. Samuel Blink and the forbidden forest
    Fic
  Hearne, B. G. The canine connection: stories
    about dogs and people   **S C**

Henkes, K. Protecting Marie   **Fic**
Howe, P. Waggit's tale   **Fic**
Jacques, B. Castaways of the Flying Dutchman
    Fic
Kadohata, C. Cracker!   **Fic**
Langston, L. The trouble with Cupid   **Fic**
Lawrence, C. The thieves of Ostia   **Fic**
Leonard, E. A coyote's in the house   **Fic**
London, J. The call of the wild   **Fic**
London, J. White Fang   **Fic**
Margolis, L. Boys are dogs   **Fic**
Matthews, L. S. A dog for life   **Fic**
Michael, L. City of dogs   **Fic**
Monninger, J. Baby   **Fic**
Morgan, C. The boy who spoke dog   **Fic**
Naylor, P. R. Shiloh   **Fic**
Nuzum, K. A. The leanin' dog   **Fic**
O'Connor, B. How to steal a dog   **Fic**
Rawls, W. Where the red fern grows   **Fic**
Russell, C. Dogboy   **Fic**
Sherlock, P. Letters from Wolfie   **Fic**
Van Leeuwen, J. Lucy was there—   **Fic**
Williams, A. The deep freeze of Bartholomew
  Tullock   **Fic**
Ziegler, J. Alpha dog   **Fic**
      Graphic novels
Varon, S. Robot dreams   **741.5**

Dogs, Wild *See* Wild dogs

Dogs for kids!. Mehus-Roe, K.   **636.7**

Dogs for the blind *See* Guide dogs

Dogsong. Paulsen, G.   **Fic**

Doherty, Berlie
  The girl who saw lions   **Fic**

Doherty, Craig A.
  The thirteen colonies [series]   **973.2**

Doherty, Katherine M.
  (jt. auth) Doherty, C. A. The thirteen colonies
  [series]   **973.2**

Doherty, Kieran
  Ranchers, homesteaders, and traders   **920**
  To conquer is to live: the life of Captain John
    Smith of Jamestown   **92**
  William Bradford   **92**

Doing it right. Pardes, B.   **613.9**

Dolan, Edward F., 1924-
  The American Indian wars   **970.004**
  George Washington   **92**
  The Irish potato famine   **941.5**

Doll, Carol Ann
  Managing and analyzing your collection
    025.2

Dolls
  Cute dolls   **745.592**
      Fiction
  De Guzman, M. Finding Stinko   **Fic**

Dolphins
  Greenberg, D. A. Dolphins   **599.5**
  Hall, H. A charm of dolphins   **599.5**
  Montgomery, S. Encantado   **599.5**
      Fiction
  L'Engle, M. A ring of endless light   **Fic**

Domaine, Helena
  Robotics   **629.8**

Douglass, Ali
(il) Holyoke, N. A smart girl's guide to money
332.024

Douglass, Frederick, 1817?-1895
About
Schuman, M. Frederick Douglass **92**
See/See also pages in the following book(s):
Archer, J. They had a dream **920**
Cloud Tapper, S. Voices from slavery's past
326

Douglass, Jackie Leatherbury
Peterson first guide to shells of North America
594

Douglass, John
(il) Douglass, J. L. Peterson first guide to shells
of North America **594**

Doves *See* Pigeons

Dovey Coe. Dowell, F. O. **Fic**

Dowd, Siobhan
Bog child **Fic**
The London Eye mystery **Fic**

Dowdle, Mary
(il) Friedman, L. Break a leg! **792**

Dowell, Frances O'Roark
Chicken boy **Fic**
Dovey Coe **Fic**
The kind of friends we used to be **Fic**
Shooting the moon **Fic**
Where I'd like to be **Fic**

Down Garrapata road. Estevis, A. **S C**

Down Sand Mountain. Watkins, S. **Fic**

Down syndrome
Brill, M. T. Down syndrome **616.85**
Evans-Martin, F. Down syndrome **616.85**
Libal, A. My name is not Slow **362.3**
Parks, P. J. Down syndrome **616.85**
Routh, K. Down syndrome **616.85**
Fiction
Hyde, C. R. The year of my miraculous reap-
pearance **Fic**
Wood, J. R. The man who loved clowns
Fic

Down the rabbit hole. Abrahams, P. **Fic**

The **down-to-earth** guide to global warming. David, L. **363.7**

Downer, Ann, 1960-
Hatching magic **Fic**

Downham, Jenny
Before I die **Fic**

Downing, David, 1946-
Apartheid in South Africa **968**
The origins of the Holocaust **940.53**

Downloading copyrighted stuff from the Internet.
Gordon, S. M. **346.04**

Downriver. Hobbs, W. **Fic**

Downsiders. Shusterman, N. **Fic**

Dowswell, Paul
Powder monkey **Fic**

Doyle, Sir Arthur Conan, 1859-1930
The adventures of Sherlock Holmes **S C**
About
Pascal, J. B. Arthur Conan Doyle **92**

Doyle, Brian, 1935-
Boy O'Boy **Fic**
Pure Spring **Fic**

Doyle, Conan *See* Doyle, Sir Arthur Conan, 1859-
1930

Doyle, Kelly
(ed) 1860-1880: the nineteenth century. See
1860-1880: the nineteenth century **909.81**

Doyle, Marissa
Bewitching season **Fic**

Doyle, Miranda, 1972-
101+ great ideas for teen library Web sites
027.62

Doyle, Roddy, 1958-
Wilderness **Fic**

Dr. Frankenstein's human body book. Walker, R.
612

Dr. Jekyll and Mr. Hyde. See Stevenson, R. L.
The strange case of Dr. Jekyll and Mr. Hyde
Fic

Dr. Jenner and the speckled monster. Marrin, A.
614.5

Dr. Seuss *See* Seuss, Dr.

Dr. Susan's girls-only weight loss guide. Bartell,
S. S. **613.2**

Draanen, Wendelin van
Confessions of a serial kisser **Fic**
Flipped **Fic**
Runaway **Fic**
Sammy Keyes and the hotel thief **Fic**

Draft
Law and legislation
Streissguth, T. Clay v. United States and how
Muhammad Ali fought the draft **343**
Draft resisters
See also Conscientious objectors

Dragon bones and dinosaur eggs: a
photobiography of Roy Chapman Andrews.
Bausum, A. **92**

Dragon drive. Vol. 1, D-break. Sakura, K.
741.5

The **dragon** of Trelian. Knudsen, M. **Fic**

Dragon road. Yep, L. **Fic**

Dragon slippers. George, J. D. **Fic**

DragonArt. Peffer, J. **743**

Dragonflies
Fiction
Vernon, U. Nurk **Fic**

Dragonflight. McCaffrey, A. **Fic**

The **dragonfly** pool. Ibbotson, E. **Fic**

Dragonhaven. McKinley, R. **Fic**

Dragons
Dobrzycki, M. The art of drawing dragons
743
Masiello, R. Ralph Masiello's dragon drawing
book **743**
Peffer, J. DragonArt **743**
See/See also pages in the following book(s):
Nigg, J. Wonder beasts **398**
Fiction
Barron, T. A. Merlin's dragon **Fic**
The Book of dragons **S C**

Dunnick, Regan
(il) Shaskan, K. How underwear got under there
391

Dunning, Stephen
(comp) Reflections on a gift of watermelon pickle—and other modern verse. See Reflections on a gift of watermelon pickle—and other modern verse **811.008**

Dunnington, Rose
Bake it up! **641.8**
Big snacks, little meals **641.5**
Super sandwiches **641.8**

Dunton-Downer, Leslie
Essential Shakespeare handbook **822.3**

The **duplicate.** Sleator, W. **Fic**

DuPont, Kathryn Cullen- See Cullen-DuPont, Kathryn

DuPrau, Jeanne, 1944-
The city of Ember **Fic**

Durango, Julia, 1967-
The walls of Cartagena **Fic**

Durbin, William, 1951-
Blackwater Ben **Fic**
The broken blade **Fic**
The darkest evening **Fic**
The Winter War **Fic**

Durham, Michael, 1952-
Painkillers and tranquilizers **615**

Durrant, Lynda, 1956-
Imperfections **Fic**
My last skirt **Fic**

Durst, Sarah Beth
Into the Wild **Fic**

Dusssie. Springer, N. **Fic**

Dust storms
Reis, R. A. The Dust Bowl **978**
Fiction
Hesse, K. Out of the dust **Fic**

Dust to eat. Cooper, M. L. **973.917**

Dustin Grubbs. Bonk, J. J. **Fic**

Dutch artists See Artists, Dutch

DuTemple, Lesley A., 1952-
The Great Wall of China **931**
The Hoover Dam **627**
The New York subways **388.4**
The Panama Canal **972.87**
The Pantheon **726**
The Taj Mahal **726**

Duwel, Lucretia I., 1948-
(jt. auth) Simpson, M. S. Bringing classes into the public library **027.62**

Dvořák, Antonín, 1841-1904
About
Horowitz, J. Dvořák in America **92**

Dwarfism
Fiction
Nemeth, S. The heights, the depths, and everything in between **Fic**

Dwarfs
Fiction
Spinner, S. Damosel **Fic**

Dyer, Alan, 1953-
Mission to the moon **629.45**

Dyes and dyeing
Kassinger, R. Dyes: from sea snails to synthetics **667**
See/See also pages in the following book(s):
Knapp, B. J. Materials science **620.1**

Dyes: from sea snails to synthetics. Kassinger, R.
667

Dygard, Thomas J., 1931-1996
Second stringer **Fic**

Dying for acceptance. Esherick, J. **616.86**

Dying patients See Terminally ill

Dynamics
Viegas, J. Kinetic and potential energy **531**

Dyslexia
Landau, E. Dyslexia **616.85**

Dyson, Marianne J.
Home on the moon **629.45**

Dzhugashvili, Iosif Vissarionovich See Stalin, Joseph, 1879-1953

E

E-mail systems See Electronic mail systems

E.S.P. See Extrasensory perception

Eagen, Rachel, 1979-
NASCAR **796.72**

Eagles
See also Bald eagle
Warhol, T. Eagles **598**

Eamer, Claire
Super crocs & monster wings **591.3**
Traitors' Gate and other doorways to the past **909**

Ear
Simon, S. Eyes and ears **612.8**

The **Ear,** the Eye, and the Arm. Farmer, N.
Fic

Earhart, Amelia, 1898-1937
About
Micklos, J. Unsolved: what really happened to Amelia Earhart? **92**

Earle, Sylvia A., 1935-
See/See also pages in the following book(s):
Atkins, J. How high can we climb? **920**

Earls, Irene
Young musicians in world history **920**

Earls, Lindsay
About
Kowalski, K. M. The Earls case and the student drug testing debate **344**

The **Earls** case and the student drug testing debate. Kowalski, K. M. **344**

The **early** human world. Robertshaw, P.
599.93

Earth
Gravity
See Gravity

Earth
Bell, T. E. Earth's journey through space **525**
Day, T. DK guide to savage Earth **550**

Easy genius science projects [series]
 Gardner, R. Easy genius science projects with chemistry **540.7**
 Gardner, R. Easy genius science projects with light **537**
 Gardner, R. Easy genius science projects with the human body **612**
Easy genius science projects with chemistry. Gardner, R. **540.7**
Easy genius science projects with light. Gardner, R. **537**
Easy genius science projects with the human body. Gardner, R. **612**
Easy menu ethnic cookbooks [series] **641.5**
Easy origami. Boursin, D. **736**
Eat right!. Doeden, M. **613.2**
Eating customs
 Batmanglij, N. Happy Nowruz **641.5**
 Ingram, S. Want fries with that? **613.2**
 Jacob, J. The world cookbook for students **641.5**
 Menzel, P. What the world eats **641.3**
 Sanna, E. America's unhealthy lifestyle **613.2**
 Solheim, J. It's disgusting—and we ate it! **641.3**
Eating disorders
 See also Anorexia nervosa; Bulimia
 Bingham, J. Eating disorders **616.85**
 Bjorklund, R. Eating disorders **616.85**
 Eating disorders **616.85**
 Eating disorders information for teens **616.85**
 Eating disorders: opposing viewpoints **616.85**
 Esherick, J. Diet and your emotions **616.85**
 Favor, L. J. Food as foe **616.85**
 Orr, T. When the mirror lies **616.85**
 Silverstein, A. The eating disorders update **616.85**
 The Truth about eating disorders **616.85**
   Fiction
 Does this book make me look fat? **S C**
Eating disorders **616.85**
Eating disorders information for teens **616.85**
Eating disorders: opposing viewpoints **616.85**
The **eating** disorders update. Silverstein, A. **616.85**
Eating habits
 Schlosser, E. Chew on this **394.1**
Eats, shoots & leaves. Truss, L. **428**
eBay Inc.
 Viegas, J. Pierre Omidyar **92**
Ebersole, Rene, 1974-
 Gorilla mountain [biography of Amy Vedder] **92**
Eblen, Ruth A.
 (ed) The Environment encyclopedia. See The Environment encyclopedia **363.7**
Eblen, William R.
 (ed) The Environment encyclopedia. See The Environment encyclopedia **363.7**

Ebner, Aviva
 (ed) Science activities for *all* students. See Science activities for *all* students **507.8**
Ebner, David, 1942-
 (jt. auth) Elliott, K. How to prepare for the SSAT/ISEE, Secondary School Admissions Test/Independent School Entrance Exam **373.1**
Eboch, Chris
 Turkey **956.1**
Ebola virus
 Smith, T. C. Ebola **616.9**
 Willett, E. Ebola virus **616.9**
Eccentrics and eccentricities
   Fiction
 MacLeod, D. I'm being stalked by a moonshadow **Fic**
 Tolan, S. S. Surviving the Applewhites **Fic**
Ecclesiastical rites and ceremonies See Rites and ceremonies
Eclipse. Cheng, A. **Fic**
Eclipses, Solar *See* Solar eclipses
Ecological movement *See* Environmental movement
Ecology
   See also Biological diversity; Environmental protection; Food chains (Ecology); Habitat (Ecology) types of ecology
 Gardner, R. Science projects about the environment and ecology **363.7**
 Pollock, S. Ecology **577**
 Rompella, N. Ecosystems **577**
 Somervill, B. A. Our living world **577**
 Stille, D. R. Nature interrupted **577**
 Tocci, S. Coral reefs **577.7**
 Walker, P. Ecosystem science fair projects using worms, leaves, crickets, and other stuff **577**
   Encyclopedias
 The Environment encyclopedia **363.7**
 U.X.L encyclopedia of biomes **577.8**
Ecology, Human *See* Human ecology
Economic botany
 Young, K. J. Ethnobotany **581.6**
Economic conditions
   See also Natural resources
Economic policy
   United States
 Fridell, R. Environmental issues **333.7**
Economists
 Bussing-Burks, M. Influential economists **920**
Ecosystem [series]
 Allaby, M. Deserts **577.5**
 Allaby, M. Temperate forests **577.3**
 Day, T. Oceans **551.46**
 Moore, P. D. Tundra **577.5**
 Moore, P. D. Wetlands **577.6**
Ecosystem science fair projects using worms, leaves, crickets, and other stuff. Walker, P. **577**
Ecosystems. Rompella, N. **577**

Ecosystems of North America [series]
Fielding, E. The Eastern forest   **577.3**

Ecstasy (Drug)
Koellhoffer, T. Ecstasy and other club drugs
362.29
LeVert, S. The facts about ecstasy   **362.29**

Ecstasy and other club drugs. Koellhoffer, T.
362.29

Ecuador
Foley, E. Ecuador   **986.6**

Edelman, Marian Wright, 1939-
See/See also pages in the following book(s):
Hansen, J. Women of hope   **920**

Edelman, Rob
The War of 1812   **973.5**

Edelson, Edward, 1932-
Gregor Mendel, and the roots of genetics   **92**

Edens, Cooper, 1945-
(comp) Classic western stories. See Classic
western stories   **808.8**

The **Edenville** Owls. Parker, R. B.   **Fic**

Edgar Allan Poe. Meltzer, M.   **92**

Edgar Allan Poe's tales of mystery and madness.
Poe, E. A.   **S C**

Edge, Laura Bufano, 1953-
Andrew Carnegie   **92**
Locked up   **365**

Edge, Rosalie
See/See also pages in the following book(s):
Byrnes, P. Environmental pioneers   **920**

The **edge** of the sea. Carson, R.   **577.7**

The **edge** on the sword. Tingle, R.   **Fic**

Edison, Thomas A. (Thomas Alva), 1847-1931
About
Baxter, R. Illuminated progress   **92**
Carlson, L. M. Thomas Edison for kids   **92**
Delano, M. F. Inventing the future: a
photobiography of Thomas Alva Edison
92
Sonneborn, L. The electric light   **621.32**
Tagliaferro, L. Thomas Edison   **92**
Woodside, M. Thomas A. Edison   **92**

Edmonds, Marie
About
Grace, C. O. Forces of nature   **551.2**

Edmondson, J. R., 1950-
Jim Bowie   **92**

Edmondson, William, ca. 1870-1951
Poetry
Spires, E. I heard God talking to me   **811**

Edmonston, Louis-Philippe
Car smarts   **629.222**

Edney, A. T. B.
ASPCA complete cat care manual   **636.8**

Edney, Andrew See Edney, A. T. B.

Education
See also Internet in education; Military education; Schools; Teaching
Reeves, D. L. Career ideas for teens in education and training   **331.7**

Curricula
Crane, B. E. Using WEB 2.0 tools in the K-12
classroom   **371.3**
Managing curriculum and assessment   **375**
Government policy
Hester, J. P. Public school safety   **371.7**
History
Woolf, A. Education   **940.1**
Social aspects
Stanley, J. Children of the Dust Bowl   **371.9**
United States—Directories
The Handbook of private schools   **370.25**

Education, Discrimination in See Discrimination
in education

Education, Segregation in See Segregation in education

Education and church See Church and education

Education and state See Education—Government
policy

Educational achievement See Academic achievement

Educational administration See Schools—Administration

Educational counseling
See also Vocational guidance

Educational media See Teaching—Aids and devices

Educational media centers See Instructional materials centers

Educational psychology
See also Psychology of learning

Educational tests and measurements
See also Psychological tests

Educators
Jurmain, S. The forbidden schoolhouse [biography of Prudence Crandall]   **92**

Edward VI, King of England, 1537-1553
Fiction
Twain, M. The prince and the pauper   **Fic**

Edwards, Judith
Abolitionists and slave resistance   **326**
Henry Hudson and his voyages of exploration in
world history   **92**
The Plymouth Colony and the Pilgrim adventure
in American history   **974.4**

Edwards, Judith, 1940-
The history of the American Indians and the
reservation   **970.004**

Edwards Black Heritage Collection [series]
Washington, B. T. Up from slavery   **92**

Efaw, Amy
Battle dress   **Fic**

Egendorf, Laura K., 1973-
Performance-enhancing drugs   **362.29**
(ed) Africa: opposing viewpoints. See Africa:
opposing viewpoints   **960**
(ed) Guns and violence. See Guns and violence
[Current controversies]   **363.33**
(ed) Human rights: opposing viewpoints. See
Human rights: opposing viewpoints   **323**
(ed) Islam in America. See Islam in America
297

Emberley, Michael, 1960-
(il) Harris, R. H. It's perfectly normal **613.9**

Emblems *See* Signs and symbols

Emblems, National *See* National emblems

Embracing, evaluating, and examining African American children's and young adult literature **028.5**

Embryology
See also Fertilization in vitro; Reproduction

Emergency relief *See* Disaster relief

An **emerging** world power (1900-1929). Stanley, G. E. **973.91**

Emeril's there's a chef in my family!. Lagasse, E. **641.5**

Emeril's there's a chef in my world!. Lagasse, E. **641.5**

Emerson, Kevin
Carlos is gonna get it **Fic**

Emert, Phyllis Raybin
Art in glass **748.2**

Emi and the rhino scientist. Carson, M. K. **599.66**

Emigrants *See* Immigrants

Emigration *See* Immigration and emigration

Emiko superstar. Tamaki, M. **741.5**

Emil and Karl. Glatstein, J. **Fic**

Emily Goldberg learns to salsa. Ostow, M. **Fic**

Emily Post's table manners for kids. Post, P. **395**

Emily Post's The guide to good manners for kids. Post, P. **395**

Emily the Strange: the lost days. Reger, R. **Fic**

Emma-Jean Lazarus fell out of a tree. Tarshis, L. **Fic**

Emmeluth, Donald
Botulism **616.9**

Emmy and the incredible shrinking rat. Jonell, L. **Fic**

Emotion & relationships. Bingham, J. **704.9**

Emotion and stress. Evans-Martin, F. **612.8**

Emotional health issues [series]
Bingham, J. Eating disorders **616.85**
Bingham, J. Stress and depression **616.85**
Medina, S. Abuse and neglect **362.7**
Powell, J. Alcohol and drug abuse **362.29**
Powell, J. Self-harm and suicide **616.85**

Emotional intelligence. Andrews, L. W. **152.4**

Emotional stress *See* Stress (Psychology)

Emotions
See also Anxiety
Andrews, L. W. Emotional intelligence **152.4**
Canfield, J. Chicken soup for the teenage soul [I-IV] **158**
Chicken soup for the teenage soul's the real deal **158**
Evans-Martin, F. Emotion and stress **612.8**
Tym, K. Coping with your emotions **152.4**

Emotions in art
Bingham, J. Emotion & relationships **704.9**

Emperors

Rome
Forsyth, F. Augustus: the first emperor **92**
Galford, E. Julius Caesar **92**
Julius Caesar [essays about] **92**
Kent, Z. Julius Caesar **92**
Nardo, D. Julius Caesar **92**

Emperors of the ice. Farr, R. **Fic**

The **emperor's** silent army. O'Connor, J. **931**

Empire State Building (New York, N.Y.)
Macaulay, D. Unbuilding **690**

Employees

Training
See also Apprentices

Employment
See also Summer employment

Employment discrimination *See* Discrimination in employment

Employment forecasting
See also Labor supply

Employment guidance *See* Vocational guidance

Employment of children *See* Child labor

Employment of teenagers *See* Teenagers—Employment

Employment of women *See* Women—Employment

Empowered girls. Karnes, F. A. **361.3**

Empresses
See also Empresses
Vincent, Z. Catherine the Great **92**

The **empty** mirror. Collier, J. L. **Fic**

Encantado. Montgomery, S. **599.5**

Enchantment of the world, second series
Augustin, B. Iraq **956.7**
Augustin, B. United Arab Emirates **953**
Blashfield, J. F. Haiti **972.94**
Blauer, E. Morocco **964**
Blauer, E. South Africa **968**
Heinrichs, A. Australia **994**
Heinrichs, A. Japan **952**
Hintz, M. Algeria **965**
Kras, S. L. Honduras **972.83**
Kummer, P. K. Tibet **951**
Kummer, P. K. Ukraine **947.7**
Milivojevic, J. Bosnia and Herzegovina **949.7**
Milivojevic, J. Serbia **949.7**
Morrison, M. Costa Rica **972.86**
Morrison, M. Guyana **988.1**
Orr, T. Bangladesh **954.92**
Orr, T. Slovenia **949.7**
Orr, T. Turkey **956.1**
Rogers Seavey, L. Dominican Republic **972.93**
Stein, R. C. Mexico **972**
Willis, T. Democratic Republic of the Congo **967.51**
Wright, D. K. Cuba **972.91**

Enchantress from the stars. Engdahl, S. L. **Fic**

Encountering enchantment. Fichtelberg, S.
016.8

Encyclopaedia Britannica almanac, 2006
031.02

Encyclopedia horrifica. Gee, J. **001.9**
Encyclopedia of American government 320.03
The **encyclopedia** of animals **590.3**
Encyclopedia of animals. McGhee, K. **590.3**
The **encyclopedia** of birds **598**
Encyclopedia of careers and vocational guidance
331.7

Encyclopedia of forensic science. Bell, S.
363.2

Encyclopedia of hurricanes, typhoons, and cyclones. Longshore, D. **551.55**
Encyclopedia of modern everyday inventions. Cole, D. J. **609**
Encyclopedia of Native American tribes. Waldman, C. **970.004**
Encyclopedia of Native American wars and warfare **970.004**
Encyclopedia of the end. Noyes, D. **306.9**
Encyclopedia of the Jewish religion. See The Oxford dictionary of the Jewish religion
296.03

Encyclopedia of women in the Renaissance
940.2

Encyclopedia of women's history in America. Cullen-DuPont, K. **305.4**
The **encyclopedia** of world religions **200.3**
Encyclopedia of youth and war. Sherrow, V.
305.23

Encyclopedia prehistorica [series]
Sabuda, R. Dinosaurs **567.9**
Sabuda, R. Mega beasts **569**
Sabuda, R. Sharks and other sea monsters
560

Encyclopedias and dictionaries
See also Picture dictionaries names of languages with the subdivision *Dictionaries* and subjects with the subdivision *Dictionaries* or *Encyclopedias*
Britannica student encyclopedia **031**
Kane, J. N. Famous first facts **031.02**
One million things **031**
Scholastic children's encyclopedia **031**
The World Book encyclopedia **031**

End of the world
Fiction
Rex, A. The true meaning of Smekday **Fic**

Endangered. McGavin, G. **578.68**

Endangered oceans: opposing viewpoints
333.95

Endangered planet. Burnie, D. **333.95**

Endangered species
See also Rare animals; Wildlife conservation
Endangered species **333.95**
Endangered species: opposing viewpoints
578.68
Feinstein, S. The chimpanzee **599.8**
Hamilton, G. Frog rescue **597.8**

Hamilton, G. Rhino rescue **599.66**
Hickman, P. M. Birds of prey rescue **598**
Hickman, P. M. Turtle rescue **597.92**
Hoose, P. M. The race to save the Lord God Bird **598**
Imbriaco, A. The red wolf **599.77**
Mackay, R. The atlas of endangered species
333.95
McGavin, G. Endangered **578.68**
Miles, V. Wild science **591.68**
Mills, A. Animals like us **333.95**
Pobst, S. Animals on the edge **578.68**
Salmansohn, P. Saving birds **333.95**
Sheehan, S. Endangered species **333.95**
Spilsbury, L. Animals under threat **333.95**
Thomas, K. Bear rescue **599.78**
Fiction
Halam, A. Siberia **Fic**
Stevenson, R. H. Dead in the water **Fic**

Endangered species **333.95**

Endangered species: opposing viewpoints
578.68

Enderle, Dotti, 1954-
Man in the moon **Fic**

Ender's game. Card, O. S. **Fic**

Endgame. Garden, N. **Fic**

The **endless** steppe: growing up in Siberia. Hautzig, E. R. **92**

Endocrine glands
Klosterman, L. Endocrine system **612.4**

Endocrine system. Klosterman, L. **612.4**

Endurance, Physical *See* Physical fitness

Endurance (Ship)
Calvert, P. Sir Ernest Shackleton **92**
Johnson, R. L. Ernest Shackleton **92**
Kimmel, E. C. Ice story **998**
Fiction
McKernan, V. Shackleton's stowaway **Fic**

Endymion Spring. Skelton, M. **Fic**

The **enemy** has a face. Miklowitz, G. D. **Fic**

Energy *See* Force and energy

Energy. Bowden, R. **333.79**
Energy. Casper, J. K. **333.79**
Energy. Farndon, J. **531**
Energy. Juettner, B. **333.79**
Energy. Silverstein, A. **621**
Energy alternatives. Nakaya, A. C. **333.79**
Energy alternatives. Povey, K. D. **333.79**
Energy development
Bowden, R. Energy **333.79**

Energy resources
See also Hydrogen as fuel
Ballard, C. From steam engines to nuclear fusion **333.79**
Casper, J. K. Energy **333.79**
Povey, K. D. Energy alternatives **333.79**
Silverstein, A. Energy **621**
VanCleave, J. P. Janice VanCleave's energy for every kid **531**
Woodford, C. Energy **333.79**

Energy revolution [series]
Walker, N. Biomass **333.95**

The **facts** about amphetamines. Menhard, F. R.
362.29

The **facts** about antidepressants. LeVert, S.
615

The **facts** about caffeine. Klosterman, L.   **613**

The **facts** about cocaine. LeVert, S.   **362.29**

The **facts** about depressants. Klosterman, L.
615

The **facts** about drug dependence to treatment.
Klosterman, L.   **362.29**

The **facts** about drugs and society. Axelrod-
Contrada, J.   **362.29**

The **facts** about drugs and the body. Klosterman,
L.   **615**

The **facts** about ecstasy. LeVert, S.   **362.29**

The **facts** about heroin. LeVert, S.   **362.29**

The **facts** about inhalants. Menhard, F. R.
362.29

The **facts** about LSD and other hallucinogens.
LeVert, S.   **362.29**

The **facts** about marijuana. Gottfried, T.
362.29

The **facts** about nicotine. LeVert, S.   **362.29**

The **facts** about over-the-counter drugs.
Klosterman, L.   **615**

The **facts** about ritalin. Menhard, F. R.   **615**

The **facts** about steroids. LeVert, S.   **362.29**

The **facts** about the A-Z of drugs. Naden, C. J.
615

Facts about the presidents   **920**

The **Facts** on File biology handbook   **570**

The **Facts** on File chemistry handbook   **540**

The **Facts** on File dictionary of astronomy
520.3

The **Facts** on File Earth science handbook   **550**

The **Facts** On File guide to research. Lenburg, J.
025.5

Facts on File library of American history [series]
Ochoa, G. Atlas of Hispanic-American history
305.8
Sonneborn, L. A to Z of American Indian wom-
en   **920.003**
Waldman, C. Encyclopedia of Native American
tribes   **970.004**

Facts on File library of religion and mythology
[series]
The encyclopedia of world religions   **200.3**

Facts on File library of world history [series]
Yount, L. A to Z of women in science and math
920.003

The **Facts** on File physics handbook   **530**

Facts on File reference library [series]
Sports rules on file   **796**

Facts on File science library [series]
Bell, S. Encyclopedia of forensic science
363.2
The Facts on File biology handbook   **570**
The Facts on File chemistry handbook   **540**
The Facts on File dictionary of astronomy
520.3

The Facts on File Earth science handbook
550

The Facts on File physics handbook   **530**
Longshore, D. Encyclopedia of hurricanes, typhoons, and cyclones   **551.55**

Facts on File stars & planets atlas. Ridpath, I.
520

The **faerie** path. Jones, A. F.   **Fic**

Faery rebels [series]
Anderson, R. J. Spell Hunter   **Fic**

Fagan, Cary
(jt. auth) Goh, C. H. Beyond the dance   **92**

Fagan, Eleanora See Holiday, Billie, 1915-1959

Faget, Maxime A., 1921-2004
See/See also pages in the following book(s):
Richie, J. Space flight   **920**

Fagles, Robert
(tr) Homer. The Iliad   **883**
(tr) Homer. The Odyssey   **883**

Faherty, Sara
Victims and victims' rights   **362.88**

Fahy, Thomas Richard
The unspoken   **Fic**

Fahy, Tom See Fahy, Thomas Richard

Fair has nothing to do with it. Cotten, C.   **Fic**

Fair use (Copyright)
Butler, R. P. Copyright for teachers and librarians   **346.04**

Fair weather. Peck, R.   **Fic**

Fairclough, Chris
(il) Oxlade, C. Chemistry   **540.7**

Fairest. Levine, G. C.   **Fic**

Fairies
Allen, J. Fantasy encyclopedia   **398**
     Fiction
Anderson, R. J. Spell Hunter   **Fic**
Colfer, E. Artemis Fowl   **Fic**
De Lint, C. The blue girl   **Fic**
Gardner, S. I, Coriander   **Fic**
Jones, A. F. The faerie path   **Fic**
Keehn, S. M. Magpie Gabbard and the quest for
the buried moon   **Fic**
Kirk, D. Elf realm: the low road   **Fic**
Larbalestier, J. How to ditch your fairy   **Fic**
Maguire, G. What-the-Dickens   **Fic**
Marr, M. Ink exchange   **Fic**
McGraw, E. J. The moorchild   **Fic**
Pike, A. Wings   **Fic**
Simner, J. L. Bones of Faerie   **Fic**
Stiefvater, M. Lament   **Fic**
Thompson, K. The new policeman   **Fic**
Tomlinson, H. Aurelie   **Fic**
Wooding, C. Poison   **Fic**
     Graphic novels
Irwin, J. Vögelein   **741.5**

Fairs
     Fiction
Barkley, B. Scrambled eggs at midnight   **Fic**

Fairy tale series
Yolen, J. Briar Rose   **Fic**

Fairy tales

See also Fantasy fiction

Beck, I. The secret history of Tom Trueheart
                  Fic
Blubaugh, P. Serendipity Market   **Fic**
Burns, B. The king with horse's ears and other
   Irish folktales   **398.2**
Coombs, K. The runaway princess   **Fic**
Durst, S. B. Into the Wild   **Fic**
French, V. The robe of skulls   **Fic**
George, J. D. Princess of the midnight ball
                   Fic
Gruber, M. The witch's boy   **Fic**
Harrison, M. I. The princess and the hound
                   Fic
Hearne, B. G. Beauties and beasts **398.2**
Index to fairy tales   **398.2**
Levine, G. C. Fairest   **Fic**
Lin, G. Where the mountain meets the moon
                   Fic
Lowe, H. Thornspell   **Fic**
Martin, R. Birdwing   **Fic**
McKinley, R. Beauty   **Fic**
McKinley, R. The door in the hedge   **S C**
McKinley, R. Rose daughter   **Fic**
Murdock, C. G. Princess Ben   **Fic**
Myers, E. Storyteller   **Fic**
Myers, W. D. Amiri & Odette   **Fic**
Napoli, D. J. Beast   **Fic**
Napoli, D. J. Zel   **Fic**
Pattou, E. East   **Fic**
Philip, N. Celtic fairy tales   **398.2**
Rapunzel and other magic fairy tales **398.2**
Rowling, J. K. The tales of Beedle the Bard
                   S C
Smith, S. A posse of princesses   **Fic**
Stanley, D. Bella at midnight   **Fic**
Swan sister   **S C**
Tomlinson, H. The swan maiden   **Fic**
Troll's eye view   **S C**
Vande Velde, V. Tales from the Brothers
   Grimm and the Sisters Weird   **S C**
Wrede, P. C. Dealing with dragons   **Fic**
Yolen, J. Troll Bridge   **Fic**
Authorship
Rosinsky, N. M. Write your own fairy tale
                808.3
Bibliography
Lynn, R. N. Fantasy literature for children and
   young adults   **016.8**
Graphic novels
Hale, S. Rapunzel's revenge   **741.5**
Medley, L. Castle waiting   **741.5**
Poetry
Whipple, L. If the shoe fits   **811**

Faith. Hinds, K.   **297**

Faith, hope, and Ivy June. Naylor, P. R.   **Fic**

Faith in America [series]

Buxbaum, S. M. Jewish faith in America
                296
Murphy, L. African-American faith in America
                200

A **faith** like mine. Buller, L.   **200**

Fajardo, Alexis E., 1976-
  Kid Beowulf and the blood-bound oath
                741.5

Fake ID. Sorrells, W.   **Fic**

Fakes and forgeries. Bell, S.   **363.2**

Falcone, L. M., 1951-
  Walking with the dead   **Fic**

Falconer, Kieran, 1970-
  Peru   **985**

The **falconer's** knot. Hoffman, M. **Fic**

Fall of a kingdom. See Bell, H. Flame **Fic**

The **fall** of Constantinople. Feldman, R. T.
               949.5

The **fall** of the Amazing Zalindas. Mack, T.
               Fic

The **fall** of the Roman Empire. Markel, R. J.
               937

Fallen angels. Myers, W. D.   **Fic**

Falling from Grace. Godwin, J.   **Fic**

Falling stars See Meteors

Falling up. Silverstein, S.   **811**

Fallout. Krisher, T.   **Fic**

Falsehood See Truthfulness and falsehood

Fama, Angela
  (il) Werker, K. P. Get hooked   **746.43**
  (il) Werker, K. P. Get hooked again **746.43**

Fame
Fiction
Hall, B. Tempo change   **Fic**
Harmel, K. When you wish   **Fic**

Fame and glory in Freedom, Georgia. O'Connor,
  B.   **Fic**

Family
   See also types of family members
Winchester, E. Sisters and brothers **306.8**
Fiction
Riordan, R. The maze of bones   **Fic**
Valentine, J. Broken soup   **Fic**

Family finance See Personal finance

The **family** Haggadah. Schecter, E. **296.4**

Family histories See Genealogy

Family life
Rosen, M. J. Our farm   **630.9**
Fiction
Adler, D. A. Don't talk to me about the war
               Fic
Agell, C. Shift   **Fic**
Alcott, L. M. Little women   **Fic**
Alexie, S. The absolutely true diary of a part-
  time Indian   **Fic**
Alvarez, J. Before we were free   **Fic**
Angle, K. G. Hummingbird   **Fic**
Armstrong, W. H. Sounder   **Fic**
Avi. Traitor's gate   **Fic**
Banks, K. Walk softly, Rachel   **Fic**
Barkley, B. Jars of glass   **Fic**
Baskin, N. R. Anything but typical **Fic**
Bateson, C. Being Bee   **Fic**
Birney, B. G. The princess and the Peabodys
               Fic
Blume, L. M. M. Tennyson   **Fic**
Brooks, M. Mistik Lake   **Fic**

Family life—Fiction—*Continued*

Bruchac, J. Hidden roots   **Fic**
Budhos, M. T. Ask me no questions   **Fic**
Byars, B. C. The keeper of the doves   **Fic**
Caletti, D. The fortunes of Indigo Skye   **Fic**
Cantor, J. The September sisters   **Fic**
Carmichael, C. Wild things   **Fic**
Carmody, I. Alyzon Whitestarr   **Fic**
Casanova, M. The klipfish code   **Fic**
Cheng, A. The bear makers   **Fic**
Choldenko, G. Notes from a liar and her dog   **Fic**
Clarke, J. One whole and perfect day   **Fic**
Clinton, C. A stone in my hand   **Fic**
Cohn, R. The Steps   **Fic**
Collins, Y. The Black Sheep   **Fic**
Connor, L. Waiting for normal   **Fic**
Cooney, C. B. Diamonds in the shadow   **Fic**
Cottrell Boyce, F. Framed   **Fic**
Couloumbis, A. Love me tender   **Fic**
Couvillon, J. The chicken dance   **Fic**
Creech, S. Absolutely normal chaos   **Fic**
Creech, S. Replay   **Fic**
Creech, S. Walk two moons   **Fic**
Creech, S. The Wanderer   **Fic**
Crowley, S. The very ordered existence of Merilee Marvelous   **Fic**
Curtis, C. P. The Watsons go to Birmingham—1963   **Fic**
Cushman, K. The loud silence of Francine Green   **Fic**
Davis, K. The curse of Addy McMahon   **Fic**
Dee, B. Solving Zoe   **Fic**
Delacre, L. Salsa stories   **S C**
Denman, K. L. Rebel's tag   **Fic**
Dowd, S. Bog child   **Fic**
Dowell, F. O. Chicken boy   **Fic**
Dowell, F. O. Shooting the moon   **Fic**
Ellis, A. D. Everything is fine   **Fic**
Erdrich, L. The porcupine year   **Fic**
Erskine, K. Quaking   **Fic**
Estevis, A. Chicken Foot Farm   **Fic**
Fienberg, A. Number 8   **Fic**
Flake, S. G. Bang!   **Fic**
Fogelin, A. The big nothing   **Fic**
Ford, C. Scout   **Fic**
Foxlee, K. The anatomy of wings   **Fic**
Freitas, D. The possibilities of sainthood   **Fic**
Gantos, J. Jack on the tracks   **Fic**
García, C. I wanna be your shoebox   **Fic**
Garden, N. Endgame   **Fic**
Gates, S. Beyond the billboard   **Fic**
Giff, P. R. Water Street   **Fic**
Giles, G. Right behind you   **Fic**
Gratz, A. The Brooklyn nine   **Fic**
Gregory, K. My darlin' Clementine   **Fic**
Gregory, N. I'll sing you one-o   **Fic**
Gwaltney, D. Homefront   **Fic**
Hall, B. The Noah confessions   **Fic**
Han, J. Shug   **Fic**
Harness, C. Just for you to know   **Fic**
Harper, S. The secret life of Sparrow Delaney   **Fic**
Hegamin, T. M+O 4evr   **Fic**
Henkes, K. Bird Lake moon   **Fic**
Henkes, K. Olive's ocean   **Fic**
Hesse, K. Brooklyn Bridge   **Fic**

Heuston, K. B. The Book of Jude   **Fic**
Hicks, B. Get real   **Fic**
Hirahara, N. 1001 cranes   **Fic**
Hollyer, B. Secrets, lies and my sister Kate   **Fic**
Holm, J. L. Middle school is worse than meatloaf   **Fic**
Holm, J. L. Our only May Amelia   **Fic**
Holm, J. L. Penny from heaven   **Fic**
Holt, K. A. Mike Stellar: nerves of steel   **Fic**
Holt, K. W. Part of me   **S C**
Hood, A. How I saved my father's life (and ruined everything else)   **Fic**
Horvath, P. The vacation   **Fic**
Ingold, J. Mountain solo   **Fic**
Jiménez, F. The circuit: stories from the life of a migrant child   **Fic**
Jocelyn, M. Would you   **Fic**
Johnson, A. Toning the sweep   **Fic**
Johnson, M. Suite Scarlett   **Fic**
Jolin, P. In the name of God   **Fic**
Jones, K. K. Sand dollar summer   **Fic**
Joseph, L. The color of my words   **Fic**
Juby, S. Alice, I think   **Fic**
Karim, S. Skunk girl   **Fic**
Keehn, S. M. Magpie Gabbard and the quest for the buried moon   **Fic**
Kelly, J. The evolution of Calpurnia Tate   **Fic**
Kephart, B. Undercover   **Fic**
Kerley, B. Greetings from planet Earth   **Fic**
Kimmel, E. C. Lily B. on the brink of cool   **Fic**
King, R. The quantum July   **Fic**
Kline, L. W. Write before your eyes   **Fic**
Klise, K. Deliver us from Normal   **Fic**
Kogler, J. A. Ruby Tuesday   **Fic**
Kuhlman, E. The last invisible boy   **Fic**
Lamba, M. What I meant. . .   **Fic**
Laskas, G. M. The miner's daughter   **Fic**
Lasky, K. The last girls of Pompeii   **Fic**
Law, I. Savvy   **Fic**
Levine, K. The best bad luck I ever had   **Fic**
Love, D. A. Picture perfect   **Fic**
Love, D. A. Semiprecious   **Fic**
Lowry, L. Anastasia Krupnik   **Fic**
Lurie, A. The latent powers of Dylan Fontaine   **Fic**
Lynch, C. The Big Game of Everything   **Fic**
Lyon, A. All-season Edie   **Fic**
Mackey, W. K. Throwing like a girl   **Fic**
Mackler, C. The earth, my butt, and other big, round things   **Fic**
MacLachlan, P. Two novels: Baby; Journey   **Fic**
MacLeod, D. I'm being stalked by a moonshadow   **Fic**
Madden, K. Gentle's Holler   **Fic**
Martin, A. M. Here today   **Fic**
Mayall, B. Mermaid Park   **Fic**
McKay, H. Saffy's angel   **Fic**
McKinnon, H. R. Franny Parker   **Fic**
Meehl, B. Out of Patience   **Fic**
Meltzer, M. Tough times   **Fic**
Moranville, S. B. Over the river   **Fic**

Family life—Fiction—*Continued*

Moranville, S. B. The Snows	**Fic**
Mordecai, M. Blue Mountain trouble	**Fic**
Moses, S. P. The baptism	**Fic**
Murphy, J. Desperate journey	**Fic**
Murphy, R. Looking for Lucy Buick	**Fic**
Myers, W. D. What they found	**S C**
Myracle, L. Eleven	**Fic**
Myracle, L. Twelve	**Fic**
Na, A. A step from heaven	**Fic**
Nanji, S. Child of dandelions	**Fic**
Naylor, P. R. Cricket man	**Fic**
Naylor, P. R. Reluctantly Alice	**Fic**

Necessary noise: stories about our families as
they really are **S C**

Nicholls, S. Ways to live forever	**Fic**
Nixon, J. L. Laugh till you cry	**Fic**

Ostow, M. Emily Goldberg learns to salsa
Fic

Padian, M. Brett McCarthy: work in progress
Fic

Park, L. S. Keeping score	**Fic**
Parkinson, S. Blue like Friday	**Fic**
Parry, R. Heart of a shepherd	**Fic**
Paterson, K. Preacher's boy	**Fic**
Peck, R. Fair weather	**Fic**
Peck, R. N. A day no pigs would die	**Fic**
Perkins, M. Secret keeper	**Fic**
Peters, J. A. Between Mom and Jo	**Fic**
Pfeffer, S. B. The dead & the gone	**Fic**
Pfeffer, S. B. Life as we knew it	**Fic**
Plummer, L. Finding Daddy	**Fic**
Prose, F. Touch	**Fic**
Purtill, C. L. Love, Meg	**Fic**
Ray, D. Singing hands	**Fic**
Resau, L. Red glass	**Fic**
Rettig, L. My desperate love diary	**Fic**
Rinaldi, A. Come Juneteenth	**Fic**
Roberts, M. Sunny side up	**Fic**
Rodman, M. A. Jimmy's stars	**Fic**
Runyon, B. Surface tension	**Fic**
Ryan, A. K. Vibes	**Fic**
Rylant, C. A fine white dust	**Fic**

Sandell, L. A. A map of the known world
Fic

Scaletta, K. Mudville	**Fic**
Schmidt, C. A. Useful fools	**Fic**
Schmidt, G. D. Trouble	**Fic**
Schumacher, J. Black box	**Fic**
Schwartz, E. Stealing home	**Fic**
Scott, E. Perfect you	**Fic**

Shanahan, L. The sweet, terrible, glorious year
I truly, completely lost it **Fic**

Sheinmel, C. My so-called family	**Fic**

Sitomer, A. L. The secret story of Sonia Rodriguez **Fic**

Slayton, F. C. When the whistle blows	**Fic**
Smith, D. J. The boys of San Joaquin	**Fic**
Smith, H. A. Keeping the night watch	**Fic**
Smith, H. A. The way a door closes	**Fic**
Smith, J. E. The comeback season	**Fic**
Smith, K. The geography of girlhood	**Fic**
Smith, S. L. Hot, sour, salty, sweet	**Fic**
Smith, Y. I, Lorelei	**Fic**
Son, J. Finding my hat	**Fic**
Spinelli, J. Smiles to go	**Fic**
St. Anthony, J. Grace above all	**Fic**

St. Anthony, J. The summer Sherman loved me
Fic

Stahler, D., Jr. Doppelganger	**Fic**
Stolls, A. Palms to the ground	**Fic**
Stone, P. Deep down popular	**Fic**
Tilly, M. Porcupine	**Fic**
Todd, P. The blind faith hotel	**Fic**
Tolan, S. S. Surviving the Applewhites	**Fic**
Uchida, Y. A jar of dreams	**Fic**
Venkatraman, P. Climbing the stairs	**Fic**
Wait, L. Finest kind	**Fic**
Watkins, S. Down Sand Mountain	**Fic**
Weinheimer, B. Converting Kate	**Fic**
Whelan, G. The locked garden	**Fic**
Whittenberg, A. Sweet Thang	**Fic**
Williams, C. L. The chosen one	**Fic**

Williams-Garcia, R. Like sisters on the
homefront **Fic**

Wilson, D. L. Firehorse	**Fic**
Wittlinger, E. Parrotfish	**Fic**
Zeises, L. M. Contents under pressure	**Fic**
Zimmer, T. V. 42 miles	**Fic**

See/See also pages in the following book(s):

Sleator, W. Oddballs	**S C**

Graphic novels

Carey, M. Confessions of a Blabbermouth
741.5

Gownley, J. Amelia rules!	**741.5**
Lat. Kampung boy	**741.5**

Family planning *See* Birth control

Family size

    See also Birth control; Only child

Family trees [series]

Stefoff, R. The amphibian class	**597.8**
Stefoff, R. The arachnid class	**595.4**
Stefoff, R. The bird class	**598**
Stefoff, R. The conifer division	**585**
Stefoff, R. The fish classes	**597**
Stefoff, R. The fungus kingdom	**579.5**
Stefoff, R. The marsupial order	**599.2**
Stefoff, R. The Moneran kingdom	**579**
Stefoff, R. The primate order	**599.8**
Stefoff, R. The rodent order	**599.35**
Stefoff, R. Sea mammals	**599.5**
Zabludoff, M. The insect class	**595.7**
Zabludoff, M. The reptile class	**597.9**

Family violence *See* Domestic violence

Family violence   **362.82**

Famines

Bartoletti, S. C. Black potatoes	**941.5**
Dolan, E. F. The Irish potato famine	**941.5**
Feed the children first	**941.5**

Fiction

Giff, P. R. Nory Ryan's song	**Fic**
Pignat, C. Greener grass	**Fic**

Famous first facts. Kane, J. N.   **031.02**

Famous people *See* Celebrities

Famous prisons. Lock, J.   **365**

Fancy dress *See* Costume

Fandel, Jennifer, 1973-

    Puns, allusions, and other word secrets
808.1

    Rhyme, meter, and other word music   **808.1**

Fantaskey, Beth
Jessica's guide to dating on the dark side
    Fic

Fantastic feats and failures   **624**

Fantastic fiction *See* Fantasy fiction

Fantastic flight. Collins, J. M.   **745.592**

Fantasy
Hardinge, F. The lost conspiracy   **Fic**

Fantasy! cartooning. Caldwell, B.   **741.5**

Fantasy encyclopedia. Allen, J.   **398**

Fantasy fiction

    See also Fairy tales; Science fiction

Abbott, E. J. Watersmeet   **Fic**
Alexander, L. The book of three   **Fic**
Alexander, L. The foundling and other tales of
    Prydain   **S C**
Alexander, L. The golden dream of Carlo
    Chuchio   **Fic**
Almond, D. Skellig   **Fic**
Anderson, J. D. Standard hero behavior   **Fic**
Anderson, R. J. Spell Hunter   **Fic**
Appelbaum, S. The Hollow Bettle   **Fic**
Barron, T. A. The lost years of Merlin   **Fic**
Barron, T. A. The Merlin effect   **Fic**
Barron, T. A. Merlin's dragon   **Fic**
Bell, H. Flame   **Fic**
Bell, H. The Goblin Wood   **Fic**
Bell, H. The last knight   **Fic**
Bell, H. Shield of stars   **Fic**
Bell, T. Nick of time   **Fic**
Bemis, J. C. The nine pound hammer   **Fic**
Berry, J. The Amaranth enchantment   **Fic**
Binding, T. Sylvie and the songman   **Fic**
The Book of dragons   **S C**
Booraem, E. The unnameables   **Fic**
Bradbury, R. The Halloween tree   **Fic**
Bradbury, R. Something wicked this way comes
    Fic
Breen, M. E. Darkwood   **Fic**
Brooks, L. Selkie girl   **Fic**
Carey, J. L. The beast of Noor   **Fic**
Carey, J. L. Dragon's Keep   **Fic**
Carman, P. The Dark Hills divide   **Fic**
Cashore, K. Graceling   **Fic**
Catanese, P. W. Happenstance found   **Fic**
Caveney, P. Sebastian Darke: Prince of Fools
    Fic
Chabon, M. Summerland   **Fic**
Chima, C. W. The warrior heir   **Fic**
Cle, T. The marvelous effect   **Fic**
Cockcroft, J. Counter clockwise   **Fic**
Colfer, E. Artemis Fowl   **Fic**
Collins, S. Gregor the Overlander   **Fic**
Constable, K. The singer of all songs   **Fic**
Cooper, S. Over sea, under stone   **Fic**
Coville, B. The skull of truth   **Fic**
De Mari, S. The last dragon   **Fic**
Dickinson, P. Angel Isle   **Fic**
Dickinson, P. The ropemaker   **Fic**
Duey, K. Skin hunger   **Fic**
Farmer, N. The Land of the Silver Apples
    Fic
Farmer, N. The Sea of Trolls   **Fic**
Firebirds   **S C**
Firebirds rising   **S C**

Firebirds soaring   **S C**
Fisher, C. The oracle betrayed   **Fic**
Flanagan, J. The ruins of Gorlan   **Fic**
Fletcher, C. Stoneheart   **Fic**
Fletcher, S. Dragon's milk   **Fic**
Flinn, A. Beastly   **Fic**
Fombelle, T. d. Toby alone   **Fic**
Frost, G. Shadowbridge   **Fic**
Funke, C. C. Inkheart   **Fic**
Gardner, L. Into the woods   **Fic**
Genesse, P. The golden cord   **Fic**
George, J. D. Dragon slippers   **Fic**
George, J. D. Sun and moon, ice and snow
    Fic
Goodman, A. Eon: Dragoneye reborn   **Fic**
Hale, S. Book of a thousand days   **Fic**
Half-human   **S C**
Hardinge, F. Fly by night   **Fic**
Harris, J. Runemarks   **Fic**
Haydon, E. The Floating Island   **Fic**
Haydon, E. The Thief Queen's daughter   **Fic**
Hill, S. The cry of the Icemark   **Fic**
Hoving, I. The dream merchant   **Fic**
Hughes, C. Dirty magic   **Fic**
Hunter, E. Into the wild   **Fic**
Hunter, E. Midnight   **Fic**
Hunter, E. The sight   **Fic**
Jacques, B. Redwall   **Fic**
Jean, M. Puddlejumpers   **Fic**
Johnson, J. The secret country   **Fic**
Jones, A. F. The faerie path   **Fic**
Jones, D. W. The game   **Fic**
Jones, D. W. House of many ways   **Fic**
Jones, D. W. Howl's moving castle   **Fic**
Jones, D. W. The tough guide to Fantasyland
    828
Jordan, S. Time of the eagle   **Fic**
Kaaberbol, L. The Shamer's daughter   **Fic**
Kilworth, G. Attica   **Fic**
Kirk, D. Elf realm: the low road   **Fic**
Kluger, J. Nacky Patcher and the curse of the
    dry-land boats   **Fic**
Knudsen, M. The dragon of Trelian   **Fic**
Kostick, C. Epic   **Fic**
Kostick, C. Saga   **Fic**
Lake, A. J. The coming of dragons   **Fic**
Landon, D. Shapeshifter's quest   **Fic**
Landy, D. Skulduggery Pleasant   **Fic**
Langrish, K. Troll Fell   **Fic**
Le Guin, U. K. A wizard of Earthsea   **Fic**
L'Engle, M. A wrinkle in time   **Fic**
Lennon, J. Questors   **Fic**
Levine, G. C. Ella enchanted   **Fic**
Lewis, C. S. The lion, the witch, and the ward-
    robe   **Fic**
Link, K. Pretty monsters   **S C**
Lisle, H. The Ruby Key   **Fic**
Llewellyn, S. The well between the worlds
    Fic
MacHale, D. J. The pilgrims of Rayne   **Fic**
Magic in the mirrorstone   **S C**
Mahy, M. Maddigan's Fantasia   **Fic**
Marley, L. Singer in the snow   **Fic**
Marr, M. Ink exchange   **Fic**
Marriott, Z. The swan kingdom   **Fic**
Masson, S. Snow, fire, sword   **Fic**
McCaffrey, A. Dragonflight   **Fic**

Fantasy fiction—*Continued*

McGraw, E. J. The moorchild — **Fic**
McKinley, R. The blue sword — **Fic**
McKinley, R. Chalice — **Fic**
McKinley, R. Dragonhaven — **Fic**
McKinley, R. The hero and the crown — **Fic**
McKinley, R. Water: tales of elemental spirits — **S C**
McNamee, E. The Navigator — **Fic**
McNaughton, J. An earthly knight — **Fic**
McNish, C. The silver child — **Fic**
Mebus, S. Gods of Manhattan — **Fic**
Meyer, K. The water mirror — **Fic**
Michael, L. City of dogs — **Fic**
Miéville, C. Un Lun Dun — **Fic**
Mitchell, T. The Traitor King — **Fic**
Moloney, J. The Book of Lies — **Fic**
Neumeier, R. The City in the Lake — **Fic**
Nicholson, W. Seeker — **Fic**
Nix, G. Across the wall — **S C**
Nix, G. Mister Monday — **Fic**
Nix, G. Sabriel — **Fic**
Nyoka, G. Mella and the N'anga — **Fic**
Okorafor, N. The shadow speaker — **Fic**
Okorafor, N. Zahrah the Windseeker — **Fic**
Oppel, K. Airborn — **Fic**
Owen, J. A. Here, there be dragons — **Fic**
Paolini, C. Eragon — **Fic**
Pierce, T. Circle of magic: Sandry's book — **Fic**
Pierce, T. First test — **Fic**
Pierce, T. Melting stones — **Fic**
Pierce, T. Terrier — **Fic**
Pierce, T. Trickster's choice — **Fic**
Pierce, T. The will of the empress — **Fic**
Pike, A. Wings — **Fic**
Pratchett, T. The amazing Maurice and his educated rodents — **Fic**
Prineas, S. The magic thief — **Fic**
Pullman, P. The golden compass — **Fic**
Pullman, P. Once upon a time in the North — **Fic**
Randall, D. Clovermead — **Fic**
Rodda, E. The key to Rondo — **Fic**
Rowling, J. K. Harry Potter and the Sorcerer's Stone — **Fic**
Rutkoski, M. The Cabinet of Wonders — **Fic**
Sage, A. Magyk — **Fic**
Saint-Exupéry, A. d. The little prince — **Fic**
Sanderson, B. Alcatraz versus the evil Librarians — **Fic**
Sensel, J. The Farwalker's quest — **Fic**
Service, P. F. Tomorrow's magic — **Fic**
Sherman, D. Changeling — **Fic**
Shinn, S. The dream-maker's magic — **Fic**
Shinn, S. The truth-teller's tale — **Fic**
Simner, J. L. Bones of Faerie — **Fic**
Snow, A. Here be monsters! — **Fic**
Stoffels, K. Heartsinger — **Fic**
Stroud, J. The Amulet of Samarkand — **Fic**
Swift, J. Gulliver's travels — **Fic**
Thal, L. Mimus — **Fic**
Thompson, K. The new policeman — **Fic**
Tolkien, J. R. R. The hobbit, or, There and back again — **Fic**
Tolkien, J. R. R. The lord of the rings — **Fic**
Tomlinson, H. Aurelie — **Fic**

Uehashi, N. Moribito — **Fic**
Ursu, A. The shadow thieves — **Fic**
Verrillo, E. F. Elissa's quest — **Fic**
White, T. H. The once and future king — **Fic**
Whitlock, D. Raven — **Fic**
Whitlock, D. Sky carver — **Fic**
Wilce, Y. S. Flora Segunda — **Fic**
Williams, M. The golden hour — **Fic**
Wooding, C. Poison — **Fic**
Wrede, P. C. The thirteenth child — **Fic**
Yolen, J. Briar Rose — **Fic**
Yolen, J. Dragon's blood — **Fic**
Yolen, J. Passager — **Fic**
Yolen, J. Pay the piper — **Fic**
Young warriors — **S C**

Authorship
Farrell, T. Write your own fantasy story — **808.3**

Bibliography
Fichtelberg, S. Encountering enchantment — **016.8**
Lynn, R. N. Fantasy literature for children and young adults — **016.8**

History and criticism
The wand in the word — **813.009**
Fantasy for children. *See* Lynn, R. N. Fantasy literature for children and young adults — **016.8**

Fantasy graphic novels
Avery, B. The hedge knight — **741.5**
Baker, K. Through the looking-glass — **741.5**
Black, H. The Good Neighbors; book one: Kin — **741.5**
Brooks, T. Dark wraith of Shannara — **741.5**
Colfer, E. Artemis Fowl: the graphic novel — **741.5**
Flight explorer — **741.5**
Frampton, O. Oddly Normal — **741.5**
Glass, B. J. L. The mice templar, volume one: the prophecy — **741.5**
Hale, S. Rapunzel's revenge — **741.5**
Irwin, J. Vögelein — **741.5**
Jacques, B. Redwall: the graphic novel — **741.5**
Kibuishi, K. Amulet book one: the stonekeeper — **741.5**
Kim, D. K. Good as Lily — **741.5**
Kovac, T. Wonderland — **741.5**
MacHale, D. J. Pendragon book one: the merchant of death graphic novel — **741.5**
Medley, L. Castle waiting — **741.5**
Naifeh, T. Courtney Crumrin and the night things — **741.5**
Sfar, J. Dungeon Vol. 1: Duck Heart — **741.5**
Siddell, T. Gunnerkrigg Court: orientation — **741.5**
Smith, J. Bone: out from Boneville — **741.5**
Soo, K. Jellaby — **741.5**
Watson, A. Princess at midnight — **741.5**

Fantasy in art
Caldwell, B. Fantasy! cartooning — **741.5**

Fantasy literature for children and young adults. Lynn, R. N. — **016.8**

Far East *See* East Asia

Fardell, John, 1967-
The 7 professors of the Far North — **Fic**

Ferri, Giuliano
  (il) Sullivan, A. M. Albert Einstein **92**
Ferri, Vincenzo
  Tortoises and turtles **597.92**
Ferris, Jean, 1939-
  Much ado about Grubstake **Fic**
  Underground **Fic**
Ferroa, Peggy Grace, 1959-
  China **951**
Ferry, Joseph, 1954-
  Maria Goeppert Mayer **92**
Fershleiser, Rachel
  (ed) I can't keep my own secrets. See I can't
    keep my own secrets **808.8**
Fertility
  See also Infertility
Fertility control *See* Birth control
Fertilization in vitro
  Fullick, A. Test tube babies **618.1**
  Orr, T. Test tube babies **618.1**
  Winkler, K. High-tech babies **618.1**
Fertilization in vitro, Human *See* Fertilization in
    vitro
Festivals
  The American book of days **394.26**
  Breuilly, E. Festivals of the world **394.26**
  Heath, A. Windows on the world **394.2**
  Holidays, festivals, and celebrations of the world
    dictionary **394.26**
  Junior Worldmark encyclopedia of world holi-
    days **394.26**
  Marks, D. F. Let's celebrate today **394.26**
  Rajtar, S. United States holidays and obser-
    vances **394.26**
                Bibliography
  Matthew, K. I. Neal-Schuman guide to celebra-
    tions & holidays around the world **394.26**
Festivals of the world. Breuilly, E. **394.26**
The **fetch**. Humphreys, C. **Fic**
Feudalism
  Davenport, J. The age of feudalism **940.1**
Fever
  Calamandrei, C. Fever **616**
Fever. Calamandrei, C. **616**
Fever, 1793. Anderson, L. H. **Fic**
Feynman, Richard Phillips, 1918-1988
  See/See also pages in the following book(s):
  Henderson, H. Nuclear physics **539.7**
Fibers
  See/See also pages in the following book(s):
  Knapp, B. J. Materials science **620.1**
Fichtelberg, Susan
  Encountering enchantment **016.8**
  (jt. auth) Kunzel, B. L. Tamora Pierce
    813.009
Fiction
      See also Adventure fiction; Christian fic-
    tion; Fairy tales; Fantasy fiction; Historical
    fiction; Horror fiction; Love stories; Mystery
    fiction; School stories; Science fiction; Sea
    stories; Short stories; War stories
                Technique
  Bauer, M. D. Our stories **808.3**

  Bodden, V. Creating the character **808.3**
  Bodden, V. Painting the picture **808.3**
  Bodden, V. Setting the style **808.3**
  Bodden, V. Telling the tale **808.3**
  Hanley, V. Seize the story **808.3**
  Levine, G. C. Writing magic **808.3**
  Mlynowski, S. See Jane write **808.3**
  Otfinoski, S. Extraordinary short story writing
    808.3
Fiction, food, and fun. Closter, K. **028.5**
Field, James, 1959-
  (il) Turnbull, S. R. Real samurai **952**
Field athletics *See* Track athletics
Field, Elizabeth *See* Bauchner, Elizabeth, 1970-
A **field** guide to freshwater fishes: North America
    north of Mexico. Page, L. M. **597**
A **field** guide to Pacific states wildflowers.
    Niehaus, T. F. **582.13**
A **field** guide to reptiles & amphibians. Conant, R.
    597.9
A **field** guide to rocks and minerals. Pough, F. H.
    549
A **field** guide to the birds. See Peterson, R. T.
    Peterson field guide to birds of North Ameri-
    ca **598**
A **field** guide to the stars and planets. Pasachoff,
    J. M. **523**
A **field** guide to trees and shrubs. Petrides, G. A.
    582.16
A **field** guide to western trees. Petrides, G. A.
    582.16
Field guide to wildflowers, eastern region. See
    Thieret, J. W. National Audubon Society field
    guide to North American wildflowers: eastern
    region **582.13**
Field guides [series]
  Banqueri, E. Weather **551.5**
Field Museum of Natural History
  Kelly, E. Evolving planet **551**
  Relf, P. A dinosaur named Sue: the story of the
    colossal fossil: the world's most complete T.
    rex **567.9**
Fielding, Eileen
  The Eastern forest **577.3**
Fields, Terri, 1948-
  After the death of Anna Gonzales **811**
Fields of fury. McPherson, J. M. **973.7**
Fienberg, Anna, 1956-
  Number 8 **Fic**
Fieser, Stephen
  (il) Major, J. S. The Silk Route **950**
Fifteen hundred. See Schomp, V. 1500 **909.08**
The **Fifth** Amendment. Fireside, H. **347**
The **fifth** of March. Rinaldi, A. **Fic**
Fight for freedom. Bobrick, B. **973.3**
The **fight** for peace. Gottfried, T. **303.6**
Fight game. Wild, K. **Fic**
Fight on!: Mary Church Terrell's battle for inte-
    gration. Fradin, D. B. **92**
Fighting for equality. Boomhower, R. E. **92**
Fighting for honor. Cooper, M. L. **940.53**

Flake, Sharon G.
  Bang!   **Fic**
  The broken bike boy and the Queen of 33rd
    Street   **Fic**
  The skin I'm in   **Fic**
  Who am I without him?   **S C**
Flame. Bell, H.   **Fic**
Flamel, Nicolas, d. 1418
          Fiction
  Scott, M. The alchemyst   **Fic**
Flanagan, John
  The ruins of Gorlan   **Fic**
Flappers and the new American woman. Gourley,
  C.   **305.4**
Flat-out rock. Tanner, M.   **781.66**
Fleeing to freedom on the Underground Railroad.
  Landau, E.   **973.7**
Fleischman, Albert Sidney See Fleischman, Sid,
  1920-
Fleischman, John
  Black and white airmen   **940.54**
  Phineas Gage: a gruesome but true story about
    brain science   **362.1**
Fleischman, Paul
  Big talk   **811**
  Bull Run   **Fic**
  Dateline: Troy   **292**
  A fate totally worse than death   **Fic**
  Graven images   **S C**
  I am phoenix: poems for two voices **811**
  Joyful noise: poems for two voices **811**
  Seedfolks   **Fic**
  Seek   **Fic**
Fleischman, Sid, 1920-
  The abracadabra kid   **92**
  The entertainer and the dybbuk   **Fic**
  Escape! [biography of Harry Houdini] **92**
  The trouble begins at 8: a life of Mark Twain
    in the wild, wild West   **92**
  The whipping boy   **Fic**
          About
  Freedman, J. Sid Fleischman   **92**
Fleisher, Paul
  The big bang   **523.1**
  Evolution   **576.8**
  Parasites   **578.6**
Fleming, Alexander, 1881-1955
         About
  Birch, B. Alexander Fleming   **92**
  See/See also pages in the following book(s):
  Fradin, D. B. With a little luck **509**
Fleming, Candace
  Ben Franklin's almanac   **92**
  The great and only Barnum   **92**
  The Lincolns   **92**
  Our Eleanor   **92**
Fleming, Charles
  (jt. auth) Schirripa, S. R. Nicky Deuce **Fic**
Fleming, Thomas, 1945-
  Socialism   **320.5**
Fleming, Thomas J., 1927-
  Everybody's revolution   **973.3**
Fleshmarket. Morgan, N.   **Fic**

Fletcher, Alphonse, Jr.
  See/See also pages in the following book(s):
  Haskins, J. African American entrepreneurs
              920
Fletcher, Buddy See Fletcher, Alphonse, Jr.
Fletcher, Charlie
  Stoneheart   **Fic**
Fletcher, Marty
  (jt. auth) Scherer, G. J. Robert Oppenheimer
              92
Fletcher, Ralph, 1953-
  How to write your life story   **808**
  How writers work   **808**
  Marshfield dreams   **92**
  The one o'clock chop   **Fic**
  Poetry matters   **808.1**
Fletcher, Susan, 1951-
  Alphabet of dreams   **Fic**
  Dragon's milk   **Fic**
  Walk across the sea   **Fic**
Flies
  Dixon, N. Focus on flies   **595.7**
  Pascoe, E. Flies   **595.7**
Flight
         Fiction
  Forester, V. The girl who could fly **Fic**
  Gonzalez, J. Wings   **Fic**
  Murphy, R. Bird   **Fic**
Flight. Graham, I.   **629.13**
Flight explorer   **741.5**
Flight of the Fisherbird. Martin, N. **Fic**
The **flight** of the Silver Turtle. Fardell, J. **Fic**
The **flight** to freedom. Veciana-Suarez, A. **Fic**
Flink. TenNapel, D. R.   **741.5**
Flinn, Alex
  Beastly   **Fic**
  Breaking point   **Fic**
Flinn, Alexandra See Flinn, Alex
Flip it!. Yucht, A. H.   **025.5**
Flipped. Draanen, W. v.   **Fic**
The **Floating** Island. Haydon, E.   **Fic**
Flodin, Mickey
  (jt. auth) Butterworth, R. R. The Perigee visual
    dictionary of signing   **419**
Floods
  Allaby, M. Floods   **551.48**
         Fiction
  Bertagna, J. Exodus   **Fic**
  Hale, M. Dark water rising   **Fic**
Flook, Helen
  (il) Erlbach, A. The middle school survival
    guide   **373.1**
Flora Segunda. Wilce, Y. S.   **Fic**
Florczak, Robert
  (il) Hausman, G. Horses of myth **398.2**
Florida
         Fiction
  Abbott, T. The postcard   **Fic**
  Bloor, E. Tangerine   **Fic**
  Blundell, J. What I saw and how I lied **Fic**
  Chappell, C.-J. Total constant order **Fic**

Florida—Fiction—*Continued*

Cirrone, D. Prom kings and drama queens
    Fic

Corbett, S. Free baseball   **Fic**

Crist-Evans, C. Amaryllis   **Fic**

DiCamillo, K. Because of Winn-Dixie   **Fic**

Fogelin, A. The real question   **Fic**

Gephart, D. As if being 12 3/4 isn't bad enough, my mother is running for president!
    Fic

Harmel, K. When you wish   **Fic**

Hiaasen, C. Flush   **Fic**

Hiaasen, C. Hoot   **Fic**

Hiaasen, C. Scat   **Fic**

Jackson, A. Rainmaker   **Fic**

Jordan, R. Lost Goat Lane   **Fic**

Konigsburg, E. L. The mysterious edge of the heroic world   **Fic**

McDonald, J. Devil on my heels   **Fic**

Norville, R. Moonshine express   **Fic**

Rawlings, M. K. The yearling   **Fic**

Ryan, P. Saints of Augustine   **Fic**

Scott, K. I was a non-blonde cheerleader
    Fic

Waters, Z. C. Blood moon rider   **Fic**

Watkins, S. Down Sand Mountain   **Fic**

Woods, B. My name is Sally Little Song
    Fic

The **flowering** plant division. Stefoff, R.   **580**

Flowers, Helen F., 1931-
Public relations for school library media programs   **021.7**

Flowers
See also Wild flowers
Souza, D. M. Freaky flowers   **582.13**

Flu *See* Influenza

The **flu**. Hoffmann, G.   **616.2**

The **flu** and pneumonia update. Silverstein, A.
    616.2

Flush. Hiaasen, C.   **Fic**

Fly by night. Hardinge, F.   **Fic**

Flygirl. Smith, S. L.   **Fic**

Flying *See* Flight

Flying lessons. Matthews, K.   **Fic**

Flying machine. Nahum, A.   **629.133**

Flying saucers *See* Unidentified flying objects

Flying solo. Perrier, P.   **158**

Flying to the moon. Collins, M.   **629.45**

Flynn, Leonie
(ed) The ultimate teen book guide. See The ultimate teen book guide   **028.1**

Flynn, Noa
See also Walker, Ida

Focus on Afghanistan. Gaag, N. v. d.   **958.1**

Focus on flies. Dixon, N.   **595.7**

Focus on Pakistan. Morgan, S.   **954.91**

Focus on Turkey. Ganeri, A.   **956.1**

Fogelin, Adrian, 1951-
The big nothing   **Fic**
The real question   **Fic**

The **fold**. Na, A.   **Fic**

Foley, Erin, 1967-
Costa Rica   **972.86**
Dominican Republic   **972.93**
Ecuador   **986.6**
El Salvador   **972.84**

Foley, Ronan
World health   **362.1**

Folk. Handyside, C.   **781.62**

Folk art
See also American folk art
Govenar, A. B. Extraordinary ordinary people
    745
Whitehead, K. Art from her heart: folk artist Clementine Hunter   **92**

Folk lore *See* Folklore

Folk music
Handyside, C. Folk   **781.62**
United States
See also Country music

Folk songs
United States
See also Spirituals (Songs)

Folk stories of the Hmong. Livo, N. J.   **398.2**

Folklore
See also Animals—Folklore; Dragons; Legends topics as themes in folklore and names of ethnic or national groups with the subdivision *Folklore*

Forest, H. Wisdom tales from around the world
    398.2

Hausman, G. Horses of myth   **398.2**

Hearne, B. G. Beauties and beasts   **398.2**

Jaffe, N. The cow of no color: riddle stories and justice tales from around the world   **398.2**

Norman, H. Between heaven and earth
    398.2

Olson, A. N. Ask the bones: scary stories from around the world   **398.2**

Olson, A. N. More bones   **398.2**

Rapunzel and other magic fairy tales   **398.2**

San Souci, R. A terrifying taste of short & shivery   **398.2**

Spencer, A. And round me rings   **398.2**

Tchana, K. H. Changing Woman and her sisters
    398.2

Yolen, J. Mightier than the sword   **398.2**
Dictionaries
The Dictionary of folklore   **398**
Myths and legends   **398**
Indexes
Index to fairy tales   **398.2**
Africa
African folktales   **398.2**
Bryan, A. Ashley Bryan's African tales, uh-huh
    398.2
Appalachian Mountains
Shelby, A. The adventures of Molly Whuppie and other Appalachian folktales   **398.2**
Australia
See also Aboriginal Australians—Folklore
China
Bedard, M. The painted wall and other strange tales   **398.2**
Krasno, R. Cloud weavers   **398.2**

Fools and jesters
Fiction
Caveney, P. Sebastian Darke: Prince of Fools

Fic

Karr, K. Fortune's fool Fic
Spinner, S. Damosel Fic
Thal, L. Mimus Fic
A **foot** in the mouth 808.81
Football

See also Soccer

Gigliotti, J. Football 796.332
Ingram, S. A football all-pro 796.332
Madden, J. John Madden's heroes of football
796.332
Encyclopedias
The Child's World encyclopedia of the NFL
796.332
Fiction
Barber, T. Go long! Fic
Carter, A. R. Love, football, and other contact
sports S C
Cochran, T. Roughnecks Fic
Coy, J. Crackback Fic
Deuker, C. Gym candy Fic
Dygard, T. J. Second stringer Fic
Green, T. Football genius Fic
Green, T. Football hero Fic
Lynch, C. Inexcusable Fic
Murdock, C. G. Dairy Queen Fic
Powell, R. Three clams and an oyster Fic
Spinelli, J. Crash Fic
Tharp, T. Knights of the hill country Fic
A **football** all-pro. Ingram, S. 796.332
Football genius. Green, T. Fic
Football hero. Green, T. Fic
Footnotes. Augustyn, F. 792.8
Footprints on the roof. Singer, M. 811
For boys only. Aronson, M. 031.02
Forbidden. Waite, J. Fic
Forbidden City (Beijing, China)
Marx, T. Elephants and golden thrones 951
Forbidden forest. Cadnum, M. Fic
The **forbidden** schoolhouse [biography of Pru-
dence Crandall] Jurmain, S. 92
Forbidden tales [series]
Chen, D. Sword Fic
Force and energy
Farndon, J. Energy 531
Gardner, R. Forces and motion science fair proj-
ects 531
Nardo, D. Force and motion 531
Pinna, S. d. Transfer of energy 531
Silverstein, A. Forces and motion 531
Snedden, R. Forces and motion 531
Solway, A. Exploring forces and motion
531
VanCleave, J. P. Janice VanCleave's energy for
every kid 531
Viegas, J. Kinetic and potential energy 531
Woodford, C. Energy 333.79
Force and motion. Nardo, D. 531
Forced labor *See* Slavery
Forces and motion. Silverstein, A. 531

Forces and motion. Snedden, R. 531
Forces and motion science fair projects. Gardner,
R. 531
Forces in nature. Sonneborn, L. 537
Forces of nature. Grace, C. O. 551.2
Ford, Carin T.
Roberto Clemente 92
Ford, Christine, 1953-
Scout Fic
Ford, Emily, 1979-
What you must think of me 616.85
Ford, George
(il) Giovanni, N. Ego-tripping and other poems
for young people 811
Ford, Henry, 1863-1947
About
Tilton, R. Henry Ford 92
Ford, Jean
Diseases and disabilities caused by weight prob-
lems 616.3
The truth about diets 613.2
Ford, John C., 1971-
The morgue and me Fic
Ford, Michael, 1980-
The Fire of Ares Fic
Ford, Michael Thomas
Suicide notes Fic
Ford, Wayne, 1944-
(il) Lorbiecki, M. Prairie dogs 599.3
The **forebrain**. Tully, E. 612.8
Forecast Earth [biography of Inez Fung] Skelton,
R. 92
Forecasting

See also Weather forecasting

A **foreign** field. Chan, G. Fic
Foreign population *See* Immigrants
Foreigners *See* Immigrants
Foreman, Michael, 1938-
(il) Garfield, L. Shakespeare stories [I]-II
822.3
(jt. auth) Morpurgo, M. Beowulf 398.2
(il) Morpurgo, M. The Mozart question Fic
(il) Morpurgo, M. Sir Gawain and the Green
Knight 398.2
Forensic anthropology
Denega, D. Skulls and skeletons 363.2
Hopping, L. J. Bone detective [biography of Di-
ane France] 92
Forensic evidence [series]
Innes, B. DNA and body evidence 363.2
Innes, B. Fingerprints and impressions 363.2
Forensic medicine *See* Medical jurisprudence
Forensic science projects [series]
Rainis, K. G. Blood & DNA evidence 363.2
Rainis, K. G. Fingerprints 363.2
Rainis, K. G. Forgery 363.2
Rainis, K. G. Hair, clothing and tire track evi-
dence 363.2
Forensic science projects with a crime lab you can
build. Gardner, R. 363.2
Forensic sciences
Allman, T. The medical examiner 363.2

Galleries, Art *See* Art museums

Gallo, Donald R.
Richard Peck   **813.009**
(ed) Destination unexpected: short stories. See Destination unexpected: short stories   **S C**
(ed) Join in. See Join in   **S C**
(ed) On the fringe. See On the fringe   **S C**
(ed) Owning it. See Owning it   **S C**
(ed) Ultimate sports. See Ultimate sports   **S C**
(ed) Visions: nineteen short stories by outstanding writers for young adults. See Visions: nineteen short stories by outstanding writers for young adults   **S C**
(ed) What are you afraid of? See What are you afraid of?   **S C**

Gallup Youth Survey [series]
Marcovitz, H. Teens & gay issues   **306.76**
Marcovitz, H. Teens & volunteerism   **361.3**

Gallup Youth Survey, major issues and trends [series]
Hernández, R. E. Teens & relationships   **158**

Galveston (Tex.)
Fiction
Hale, M. Dark water rising   **Fic**

Galvin, Jack
(jt. auth) Pfetzer, M. Within reach: my Everest story   **796.52**

Gama, Vasco da, 1469-1524
About
Calvert, P. Vasco da Gama   **92**
Goodman, J. E. A long and uncertain journey: the 27,000 mile voyage of Vasco da Gama   **92**

See/See also pages in the following book(s):
Fritz, J. Around the world in a hundred years   **910.4**

Gamble, Cyndi
Leopards   **599.75**

Gambling
Fiction
Abrahams, P. Reality check   **Fic**
Hautman, P. All-in   **Fic**
Helgerson, J. Crows & cards   **Fic**
Kogler, J. A. Ruby Tuesday   **Fic**
Papademetriou, L. Drop   **Fic**
Saldaña, R. The whole sky full of stars   **Fic**

The **game**. Jones, D. W.   **Fic**

Game. Myers, W. D.   **Fic**

The **game** of silence. Erdrich, L.   **Fic**

The **Game** of Sunken Places. Anderson, M. T.   **Fic**

Game protection
See also Birds—Protection

Games
See also Computer games; Sports; Video games; Word games and names of individual games
Bell-Rehwoldt, S. The kids' guide to classic games   **790.1**
Strother, S. The adventurous book of outdoor games   **796**
Wise, L. The way cool license plate book   **793.7**

Fiction
Anderson, M. T. The Game of Sunken Places   **Fic**
Gorman, C. Games   **Fic**

Gammell, Stephen, 1943-
(il) Dancing teepees: poems of American Indian youth. See Dancing teepees: poems of American Indian youth   **897**
(il) Schwartz, A. More scary stories to tell in the dark   **398.2**
(il) Schwartz, A. Scary stories 3   **398.2**
(il) Schwartz, A. Scary stories to tell in the dark   **398.2**

Gan, Delice, 1954-
Sweden   **948.5**

Gandhi, Indira, 1917-1984
See/See also pages in the following book(s):
Axelrod-Contrada, J. Women who led nations   **920**
Krull, K. Lives of extraordinary women   **920**
Price-Groff, C. Twentieth-century women political leaders   **920**

Gandhi, Mahatma, 1869-1948
About
Adams, S. Mahatma Gandhi   **92**
Severance, J. B. Gandhi, great soul   **92**
Wilkinson, P. Gandhi   **92**
Fiction
Sheth, K. Keeping corner   **Fic**

Gandhi, Mohandas Karamchand *See* Gandhi, Mahatma, 1869-1948

Gandhi, great soul. Severance, J. B.   **92**

Ganeri, Anita, 1961-
Alive   **612**
Buddhism   **294.3**
Focus on Turkey   **956.1**
The Ramayana and Hinduism   **294.5**
The young person's guide to the orchestra   **784.2**

Gangi, Carol Kelly- *See* Kelly-Gangi, Carol

Gangs
Gangs   **364.1**
Johnson, J. Why do people join gangs?   **364.1**
Fiction
Bowler, T. Blade   **Fic**
López, L. Call me Henri   **Fic**
Naidoo, B. Web of lies   **Fic**
Strasser, T. If I grow up   **Fic**
Van Diepen, A. Snitch   **Fic**

Gangs   **364.1**

Gangsters *See* Mafia

Gangsters. Blackwood, G. L.   **364.1**

Gannett, Deborah Sampson *See* Sampson, Deborah, 1760-1827

Gantos, Jack
Hole in my life   **92**
Jack on the tracks   **Fic**
Joey Pigza swallowed the key   **Fic**

Garbage *See* Refuse and refuse disposal

Garcha, Rajinder
The world of Islam in literature for youth   **016.3058**

García, Cristina, 1958-
I wanna be your shoebox   **Fic**
Garcia, Mannie
(il) Lyons, M. E. Catching the fire: Philip Simmons, blacksmith   **92**
Garcia, Manuel, 1949-
(il) Parker, J. The avengers: heroes assembled   **741.5**
Garcia, Rita Williams- *See* Williams-Garcia, Rita
García de Paredes, Angel
Cassell's Spanish-English, English-Spanish dictionary. See Cassell's Spanish-English, English-Spanish dictionary   **463**
García Márquez, Gabriel, 1928-
About
Darraj, S. M. Gabriel García Márquez   **92**
Garden, Nancy, 1938-
Endgame   **Fic**
The **garden** of Eve. Going, K. L.   **Fic**
Gardening
Houle, M. E. Lindsey Williams   **92**
Mackey, B. A librarian's guide to cultivating an elementary school garden   **372**
Morris, K. The Kids Can Press jumbo book of gardening   **635**
Winckler, S. Planting the seed   **635**
Gardening, Organic *See* Organic gardening
Gardens
See also Butterfly gardens
Fiction
Burnett, F. H. The secret garden   **Fic**
Fleischman, P. Seedfolks   **Fic**
Gardiner, Lynton
(il) Murdoch, D. H. North American Indian   **970.004**
Gardner, Lyn
Into the woods   **Fic**
Gardner, Robert, 1929-
Astronomy projects with an observatory you can build   **522**
Bicycle science projects   **531**
Chemistry projects with a laboratory you can build   **540**
Chemistry science fair projects using acids, bases, metals, salts, and inorganic stuff   **540**
Chemistry science fair projects using french fries, gumdrops, soap, and other organic stuff   **547**
Easy genius science projects with chemistry   **540.7**
Easy genius science projects with light   **537**
Easy genius science projects with the human body   **612**
Forces and motion science fair projects   **531**
Forensic science projects with a crime lab you can build   **363.2**
Genetics and evolution science fair projects   **576**
Health science projects about psychology   **150**
Light, sound, and waves science fair projects   **507.8**
Meteorology projects with a weather station you can build   **551.5**

Physics projects with a light box you can build   **530**
Planet Earth science fair projects using the moon, stars, beach balls, frisbees, and other far-out stuff   **507.8**
Science project ideas about kitchen chemistry   **540.7**
Science project ideas about rain   **551.57**
Science project ideas about trees   **582.16**
Science projects about physics in the home   **530**
Science projects about plants   **580.7**
Science projects about temperature and heat   **536**
Science projects about the environment and ecology   **363.7**
Sound projects with a music lab you can build   **534**
Gardner, Sally
I, Coriander   **Fic**
The red necklace   **Fic**
Gareth Stevens vital science: life science [series]
Somervill, B. A. The human body   **612**
Gareth Stevens vital science: physical science [series]
Claybourne, A. The nature of matter   **530.4**
Parker, S. Electricity and magnetism   **537**
Pinna, S. d. Transfer of energy   **531**
Snedden, R. Forces and motion   **531**
Garfield, James A., 1831-1881
See/See also pages in the following book(s):
St. George, J. In the line of fire   **364.1**
Garfield, Leon, 1921-1996
Shakespeare stories [I]-II   **822.3**
Garlake, Teresa
Global debt   **336.3**
Garland, Judy
See/See also pages in the following book(s):
Orgill, R. Shout, sister, shout!   **920**
Garland, Sherry, 1948-
The silent storm   **Fic**
Garment industry *See* Clothing industry
Garments *See* Clothing and dress
Garner, Andrew
(jt. auth) Horst, H. A. Jamaican Americans   **305.8**
Garner, Joe
We interrupt this broadcast   **070.1**
Garrard, Apsley Cherry- *See* Cherry-Garrard, Apsley, 1886-1959
Garratt, Richard
(il) Allaby, M. Deserts   **577.5**
(il) Allaby, M. Temperate forests   **577.3**
(il) Day, T. Oceans   **551.46**
(il) Moore, P. D. Tundra   **577.5**
Garrett, Leslie, 1932-
Helen Keller   **92**
Garrington, Sally, 1953-
Canada   **971**
Garrison, William Lloyd, 1805-1879
See/See also pages in the following book(s):
Cloud Tapper, S. Voices from slavery's past   **326**

George Washington, spymaster. Allen, T. B.
                                                          92

Georgia
Fiction
Angle, K. G. Hummingbird   **Fic**
Harazin, S. A. Blood brothers   **Fic**
Kadohata, C. Kira-Kira   **Fic**
Kline, L. W. Write before your eyes   **Fic**
Rinaldi, A. The Ever-After Bird   **Fic**
Woods, B. My name is Sally Little Song
                                                  Fic

Georgia (Republic)
Spilling, M. Georgia   **947.5**

Georgia (Soviet Union) *See* Georgia (Republic)

Geosphere. Desonie, D.   **333.73**

Gephart, Donna
As if being 12 3/4 isn't bad enough, my mother
is running for president!   **Fic**

Geraci, Carmen
(jt. auth) Elliott, K. How to prepare for the
SSAT/ISEE, Secondary School Admissions
Test/Independent School Entrance Exam
                                                  373.1

Gerardi, David
Careers in the computer game industry
                                                  794.8

Geras, Adèle
Ithaka   **Fic**
Troy   **Fic**

Gerdes, Louise
(ed) Addiction: opposing viewpoints. See Addiction: opposing viewpoints   **362.29**
(ed) Cloning. See Cloning [Introducing issues
with opposing viewpoints series]   **176**
(ed) The Cold War. See The Cold War [Great
speeches in history series]   **909.82**
(ed) Endangered oceans: opposing viewpoints.
See Endangered oceans: opposing viewpoints
                                         333.95
(ed) Pollution: opposing viewpoints. See Pollution: opposing viewpoints   **363.7**
(ed) War: opposing viewpoints. See War: opposing viewpoints   **355**

Germ theory. Herbst, J.   **616**

Germ theory of disease
Herbst, J. Germ theory   **616**

Germ warfare *See* Biological warfare

The **German** American family album. Hoobler, D.
                                                  305.8

German Americans
The Germans   **305.8**
Hoobler, D. The German American family al-
bum   **305.8**
Fiction
Giff, P. R. A house of tailors   **Fic**
Gratz, A. The Brooklyn nine   **Fic**

German Democratic Republic *See* Germany
(East)

German language
Dictionaries
Cassell's German-English, English-German dictionary   **433**

German prisoners of war
Fiction
Greene, B. Summer of my German soldier
                                                  Fic

Germans
Israel—Fiction
Kass, P. Real time   **Fic**

The **Germans**   **305.8**

Germany
Fuller, B. Germany   **943**
Russell, H. Germany   **943**
Fiction
Chotjewitz, D. Daniel half human   **Fic**
Ibbotson, E. The star of Kazan   **Fic**
Jung, R. Dreaming in black and white   **Fic**
Pausewang, G. Dark hours   **Fic**
Pausewang, G. Traitor   **Fic**
History—0-1517—Fiction
Karr, K. Fortune's fool   **Fic**
Leeds, C. The silver cup   **Fic**
History—1933-1945
Altman, L. J. Hitler's rise to power and the
Holocaust   **943.086**
Bartoletti, S. C. Hitler Youth   **943.086**
Cartlidge, C. Life of a Nazi soldier   **940.54**
Feldman, G. Understanding the Holocaust
                                             940.53
Shuter, J. Resistance to the Nazis   **943.086**
Soumerai, E. N. A voice from the Holocaust
                                             940.53
History—1933-1945—Fiction
Bartoletti, S. C. The boy who dared   **Fic**
LeZotte, A. C. T4   **Fic**
History—1945-1990
Schmemann, S. When the wall came down
                                             943
History—1945-1990—Fiction
Whelan, G. After the train   **Fic**
Politics and government—1933-1945
Feldman, G. Understanding the Holocaust
                                             940.53
Living in Nazi Germany   **943.086**
Rice, E. Adolf Hitler and Nazi Germany   **92**

Germany (East)
Politics and government
Schmemann, S. When the wall came down
                                             943

Germs *See* Bacteria

Geronimo, Apache Chief, 1829-1909
See/See also pages in the following book(s):
Brown, D. A. Bury my heart at Wounded Knee
                                             970.004
Ehrlich, A. Wounded Knee: an Indian history of
the American West   **970.004**
Fiction
Bruchac, J. Geronimo   **Fic**

Gerontology
See also Old age

Gerstein, Mordicai, 1935-
(il) Kimmel, E. A. The jar of fools: eight Hanukkah stories from Chelm   **S C**

Get hooked. Werker, K. P.   **746.43**

Get hooked again. Werker, K. P.   **746.43**

Giacobbe, Beppe
(il) Fleischman, P. Big talk   811
Giant panda
Bortolotti, D. Panda rescue   599.78
Giants
Fiction
Aguiar, N. The lost island of Tamarind   Fic
Giants (Baseball team) *See* New York Giants
(Baseball team)
Giants of art and culture [series]
Brown, G. Duke Ellington: jazz master   92
Giants of science [series]
Allman, T. J. Robert Oppenheimer   92
Birch, B. Alexander Fleming   92
Krull, K. Isaac Newton   92
Krull, K. Leonardo da Vinci   92
Krull, K. Marie Curie   92
Krull, K. Sigmund Freud   92
Giarrano, Vince, 1960-
Comics crash course   741.5
Gibbons, Alan, 1953-
Charles Darwin   92
Giblin, James, 1933-
Charles A. Lindbergh   92
Good brother, bad brother [biography of John
Wilkes Booth and Edwin Booth]   92
The many rides of Paul Revere   92
The mystery of the mammoth bones   569
The riddle of the Rosetta Stone   493
Secrets of the Sphinx   932
Gibson, J. Phil
Plant diversity   580
Gibson, Josh, 1911-1947
About
Twemlow, N. Josh Gibson   92
Gibson, Karen Bush
The Obama view   92
Gibson, Terri R.
(jt. auth) Gibson, J. P. Plant diversity 580
Gibson girls and suffragists. Gourley, C. 305.4
Giddens, Owen
(jt. auth) Giddens, S. Future techniques in sur-
gery   617
Giddens, Sandra
Future techniques in surgery   617
Giddings, Sharon
Cystic fibrosis   616.3
Gideon, Clarence Earl
About
Fridell, R. Gideon v. Wainwright   345
Sherrow, V. Gideon v. Wainwright   345
Gideon the cutpurse. Buckley-Archer, L.   Fic
Gideon trilogy [series]
Buckley-Archer, L. Gideon the cutpurse   Fic
Gideon v. Wainwright. Fridell, R.   345
Gideon v. Wainwright. Sherrow, V.   345
Gidgets and women warriors. Gourley, C.
                                         305.4
Giff, Patricia Reilly
Don't tell the girls   92
Eleven   Fic
A house of tailors   Fic

Nory Ryan's song   Fic
Pictures of Hollis Woods   Fic
Water Street   Fic
Willow run   Fic
Gifford, Clive
10 kings & queens who changed the world
                                         920
The arms trade   382
The Kingfisher geography encyclopedia
                                         910.3
The Kingfisher soccer encyclopedia   796.334
Pollution   363.7
Racing   796.72
Violence on the screen   303.6
The **gift** moves. Lyon, S.   Fic
The **gift** of reading. Bouchard, D.   372.4
Gift of the Unmage. Alexander, A.   Fic
Gifted. Evangelista, B.   Fic
Gifted children
Karnes, F. A. Competitions for talented kids
                                         371.95
Fiction
Blume, J. Here's to you, Rachel Robinson
                                          Fic
Dee, B. Solving Zoe   Fic
Evangelista, B. Gifted   Fic
Yee, L. Millicent Min, girl genius   Fic
Gigliotti, Jim
Football   796.332
Hottest dragsters and funny cars   796.72
Gilbert, Carter Rowell, 1930-
National Audubon Society field guide to fishes,
North America   597
Gilbert, Sara
Write your own article   808
Gilchrist, Jane E.
(ed) Cataloging correctly for kids. See Catalog-
ing correctly for kids   025.3
Gilda Joyce, psychic investigator. Allison, J.
                                          Fic
The **Gilded** Age: a history in documents
                                         973.8
Giles, Bridget
Nigeria   966.9
Giles, Gail
Right behind you   Fic
Gilgamesh
McCaughrean, G. The epic of Gilgamesh
                                         398.2
Gilgamesh the hero. See McCaughrean, G. The
epic of Gilgamesh   398.2
Gill, David Macinnis, 1963-
Graham Salisbury   92
Gill, Margery, 1925-
(il) Cooper, S. Over sea, under stone   Fic
Gillam, Scott
Civil liberties   323
Gilles de la Tourette's syndrome *See* Tourette
syndrome
Gillespie, Carol Ann
New Zealand   993

Girls rock. Goodmark, R.   **781.66**

Girls rock! [series]

  Buckley, A. Be a better babysitter   **649**

  Buckley, A. Be a better biker   **796.6**

Girls think of everything. Thimmesh, C.   **920**

The **Girls'** World book of jewelry: 50 cool designs to make. Newcomb, R.   **745.594**

Girlwonder. Hartman, H.   **305.23**

GIs See Soldiers—United States

Gish, Steven, 1963-

  Ethiopia   **963**

Gist, E. M.

  (il) Olson, A. N. More bones   **398.2**

Gist, Erik M. See Gist, E. M.

Giuliani, Rudolph W.

About

  Sharp, A. L. Rudy Giuliani   **92**

Give me liberty. Elliott, L.   **Fic**

Give me liberty!. Freedman, R.   **973.3**

Give me shelter   **S C**

The **giver**. Lowry, L.   **Fic**

Glacial epoch See Ice Age

Glaciers

  Deem, J. M. Bodies from the ice   **599.9**

Gladiators

  Hanel, R. Gladiators   **937**

Gladstone, Dale M.

  (il) Julius, E. H. Arithmetricks   **513**

Glass, Andrew, 1949-

  (il) Brittain, B. The wish giver   **Fic**

Glass, Bryan J. L.

  The mice templar, volume one: the prophecy   **741.5**

Glass

  Kassinger, R. Glass   **620.1**

  See/See also pages in the following book(s):

  Knapp, B. J. Materials science   **620.1**

Glassware

  Emert, P. R. Art in glass   **748.2**

Glatshteyn, Yankev See Glatstein, Jacob, 1896-1971

Glatstein, Jacob, 1896-1971

  Emil and Karl   **Fic**

GLBTQ (Gay, Lesbian, Bisexual, Transgender, Questioning). Huegel, K.   **306.76**

Glenn, John, 1921-

About

  Mitchell, D. Liftoff [biography of John Glenn]   **92**

Glenn, John W.

  (jt. auth) Aronson, M. The world made new   **910.4**

Glenn, Wendy J., 1970-

  Sarah Dessen   **813.009**

  (jt. auth) Gallo, D. R. Richard Peck   **813.009**

Glick, Susan

  War and peace   **201**

The **gliding** flight. Collins, J. M.   **745.592**

Glimm, Adele

  Gene hunter [biography of Nancy Wexler]   **92**

Gliori, Debi

  Pure dead frozen   **Fic**

Glisson, Susan M., 1967-

  (jt. auth) Haynes, C. C. First freedoms   **342**

The **glitch** in sleep. Hulme, J.   **Fic**

Global connections [series]

  Donovan, S. Teens in Cuba   **972.91**

  Donovan, S. Teens in Morocco   **964**

  Donovan, S. Teens in Peru   **985**

  Lilly, A. Teens in Turkey   **956.1**

  Seidman, D. Teens in Iran   **955**

  Seidman, D. Teens in South Africa   **968**

  Shea, K. Teens in Canada   **971**

  Skog, J. Teens in Finland   **948.97**

  Skog, J. Teens in the Philippines   **959.9**

  Weatherly, M. Teens in Ghana   **966.7**

  Yackley-Franken, N. Teens in Nepal   **954.96**

Global debt. Garlake, T.   **336.3**

Global profiles [series]

  Price-Groff, C. Twentieth-century women political leaders   **920**

Global resources: opposing viewpoints   **333.71**

Global warming See Greenhouse effect

Global warming   **363.7**

Global warming. Morris, N.   **363.7**

Global warming. Parks, P. J.   **363.7**

Global warming. Silverstein, A.   **363.7**

Global warming and climate change. Berne, E. C.   **363.7**

Global warming: opposing viewpoints   **363.7**

GlobaLinks: resources for world studies, grades K-8. Beck, P.   **016.9**

Globe Theatre (London, England)

  See also Shakespeare's Globe (London, England)

  Aliki. William Shakespeare & the Globe   **822.3**

Glossaries See Encyclopedias and dictionaries

Glossop, Jennifer

  (jt. auth) Gillies, J. The jumbo vegetarian cookbook   **641.5**

Gnat Stokes and the Foggy Bottom Swamp Queen. Keehn, S. M.   **Fic**

Go figure!. Ball, J.   **793.74**

Go fly a bike!. Haduch, B.   **629.227**

Go for the goal. Hamm, M.   **796.334**

Go girl!. Vol. 1, The time team. Robbins, T.   **741.5**

Go long!. Barber, T.   **Fic**

Go tell it on the mountain. Baldwin, J.   **Fic**

Go wild in New York City. Matsen, B.   **974.7**

Goats

Fiction

  Jordan, R. Lost Goat Lane   **Fic**

The **goats**. Cole, B.   **Fic**

Goble, Paul

  All our relatives   **970.004**

Goble, Todd, 1962-

  Nicholas Copernicus and the founding of modern astronomy   **92**

The **Goblin** Wood. Bell, H.   **Fic**

Gove, Philip Babcock, 1902-1972
(ed) Webster's third new international dictionary of the English language, unabridged. See Webster's third new international dictionary of the English language, unabridged **423**

Govenar, Alan B., 1952-
Extraordinary ordinary people **745**

Government See Political science

Government, Resistance to See Resistance to government

Government debts See Public debts

Government housing See Public housing

Governors
Young, J. C. Arnold Schwarzenegger **92**

Gow, Mary
Archimedes **92**
Johannes Kepler **92**
Robert Boyle **92**
Robert Hooke **92**

Gowell, Elizabeth Tayntor
Fountains of life **577.7**

Gownley, Jimmy
Amelia rules! **741.5**

Grabenstein, Chris
The crossroads **Fic**

Grabowski, John F.
Australia **994**

Grace, Catherine O'Neill, 1950-
Forces of nature **551.2**

Grace above all. St. Anthony, J. **Fic**

Graceling. Cashore, K. **Fic**

The **graduation** of Jake Moon. Park, B. **Fic**

Grady, Denise
Deadly invaders **614.4**

Grady, Sean M., 1965-
Biohazards **614.5**
(jt. auth) Billings, C. W. Supercomputers **004**
(jt. auth) Facklam, M. Modern medicines **615**

Graff, Lisa, 1981-
The life and crimes of Bernetta Wallflower **Fic**

Graff Hysell, Shannon
(ed) Recommended reference books for small and medium-sized libraries and media centers. See Recommended reference books for small and medium-sized libraries and media centers **011**

Graham, Amy
Great Smoky Mountains National Park **976.8**

Graham, Bette Nesmith, 1924-1980
See/See also pages in the following book(s):
Thimmesh, C. Girls think of everything **920**

Graham, Ian, 1953-
Flight **629.13**
Military technology **355**

Graham, Kennon See Harrison, David Lee, 1937-

Graham, Martha
About
Freedman, R. Martha Graham, a dancer's life **92**

Graham Salisbury. Gill, D. M. **92**

Grail
Fiction
Pyle, H. The story of the Grail and the passing of Arthur **398.2**
Spradlin, M. P. Keeper of the Grail **Fic**

Grail quest: the Camelot spell. Gilman, L. A. **Fic**

Grajnert, Paul
(jt. auth) Heale, J. Poland **943.8**

Grammar
See also English language—Grammar

Grand Canyon (Ariz.)
Fiction
Hautman, P. Hole in the sky **Fic**

Grandfathers
Fiction
Bauer, J. Stand tall **Fic**
Bell, C. D. Slipping **Fic**
Cheaney, J. B. The middle of somewhere **Fic**
Clarke, J. One whole and perfect day **Fic**
Cotten, C. Fair has nothing to do with it **Fic**
Crowe, C. Mississippi trial, 1955 **Fic**
De Guzman, M. The bamboozlers **Fic**
Denman, K. L. Rebel's tag **Fic**
García, C. I wanna be your shoebox **Fic**
Garland, S. The silent storm **Fic**
George, J. C. Charlie's raven **Fic**
Hemphill, H. Long gone daddy **Fic**
Kelly, J. The evolution of Calpurnia Tate **Fic**
Kephart, B. House of Dance **Fic**
Kerr, M. E. Gentlehands **Fic**
Lynch, C. The Big Game of Everything **Fic**
Lyon, A. All-season Edie **Fic**
Mazer, N. F. After the rain **Fic**
McNab, A. Traitor **Fic**
Mosher, R. Zazoo **Fic**
Park, B. The graduation of Jake Moon **Fic**
Peet, M. Tamar **Fic**
Sanderson, B. Alcatraz versus the evil Librarians **Fic**
Smelcer, J. E. The trap **Fic**
Spinelli, J. Crash **Fic**
Vaupel, R. Rules of the universe by Austin W. Hale **Fic**
Waters, Z. C. Blood moon rider **Fic**
Poetry
Testa, M. Becoming Joe DiMaggio **811**

Grandits, John, 1949-
Blue lipstick **811**
Technically, it's not my fault **811**

Grandmothers
Siegal, A. Memories of Babi **92**
Fiction
Abbott, T. The postcard **Fic**
Amateau, G. A certain strain of peculiar **Fic**
Angle, K. G. Hummingbird **Fic**
Baskin, N. R. The truth about my Bat Mitzvah **Fic**
Cohen, T. The invisible rules of the Zoë Lama **Fic**
Cooney, C. B. Hit the road **Fic**

The **great** adventure: Theodore Roosevelt and the rise of modern America. Marrin, A. **92**

Great American memorials [series]
Ashabranner, B. K. No better hope **975.3**

The **great** ancestor hunt. Perl, L. **929**

The **great** and only Barnum. Fleming, C. **92**

A **great** and sublime fool. Caravantes, P. **92**

The **great** apes. Saign, G. **599.8**

Great-aunts See Aunts

Great Barrier Reef (Australia)
Collard, S. B., III. Lizard Island **577.7**
Kummer, P. K. The Great Barrier Reef **578.7**

Great battles through the ages [series]
Crompton, S. The Third Crusade **956**

The **Great** Blue Yonder. Shearer, A. **Fic**

The **great** brain book. Newquist, H. P. **612.8**

Great Britain

See also England
Fuller, B. Britain **941**

Antiquities
Green, J. Ancient Celts **936**

Fiction
Aiken, J. The wolves of Willoughby Chase **Fic**
Almond, D. The fire-eaters **Fic**
Almond, D. Kit's wilderness **Fic**
Barrett, T. The 100-year-old secret **Fic**
Bowler, T. Blade **Fic**
Burnett, F. H. The secret garden **Fic**
Cooper, S. Over sea, under stone **Fic**
Cushman, K. Catherine, called Birdy **Fic**
Cushman, K. The midwife's apprentice **Fic**
Dickens, C. A Christmas carol [illustrated by P.J. Lynch] **Fic**
Doherty, B. The girl who saw lions **Fic**
Dunmore, H. Ingo **Fic**
Gavin, J. Coram boy **Fic**
Hamley, D. Without warning **Fic**
Hardinge, F. Well witched **Fic**
Horowitz, A. Raven's gate **Fic**
Horowitz, A. Stormbreaker **Fic**
Hull, N. L. On rough seas **Fic**
Ibbotson, E. The beasts of Clawstone Castle **Fic**
Jarvis, R. The Whitby witches **Fic**
Kelly, T. Finn's going **Fic**
Lake, A. J. The coming of dragons **Fic**
Lawrence, M. A crack in the line **Fic**
Limb, S. Girl 15, charming but insane **Fic**
Limb, S. Zoe and Chloe: on the prowl **Fic**
Mack, T. The fall of the Amazing Zalindas **Fic**
Malley, G. The Declaration **Fic**
Matthews, L. S. A dog for life **Fic**
Matthews, L. S. The outcasts **Fic**
McKay, H. Saffy's angel **Fic**
McNab, A. Traitor **Fic**
McNish, C. Breathe **Fic**
Morgan, N. Chicken friend **Fic**
Morpurgo, M. Private Peaceful **Fic**
Morton-Shaw, C. The riddles of Epsilon **Fic**
Mussi, S. The door of no return **Fic**
Newbery, L. At the firefly gate **Fic**

Nimmo, J. Midnight for Charlie Bone **Fic**
Parker, M. H. David and the Mighty Eighth **Fic**
Paton Walsh, J. A parcel of patterns **Fic**
Peacock, S. Eye of the crow **Fic**
Pennington, K. Brief candle **Fic**
Peterson, W. Triskellion **Fic**
Shearer, A. Canned **Fic**
Skelton, M. Endymion Spring **Fic**
Weatherly, L. Kat got your tongue **Fic**
Whelan, G. Listening for lions **Fic**
Wrede, P. C. Sorcery and Cecelia, or, The enchanted chocolate pot **Fic**
Young, E. L. STORM: The Infinity Code **Fic**
Zephaniah, B. Face **Fic**

Folklore
See Folklore—Great Britain

History—0-1066
Crossley-Holland, K. The world of King Arthur and his court **942.01**
Nardo, D. King Arthur **942.01**

History—0-1066—Fiction
Avi. The Book Without Words **Fic**
Jones, A. F. Warrior princess **Fic**
McKenzie, N. Guinevere's gift **Fic**
Moran, K. Bloodline **Fic**
Morris, G. The squire's tale **Fic**
Reeve, P. Here lies Arthur **Fic**
Spinner, S. Damosel **Fic**
Springer, N. I am Mordred **Fic**
Springer, N. I am Morgan le Fay **Fic**
Sutcliff, R. Sword song **Fic**
Tingle, R. The edge on the sword **Fic**
Vande Velde, V. The book of Mordred **Fic**
White, T. H. The once and future king **Fic**

History—19th century—Graphic novels
Geary, R. Great expectations **741.5**

History—1066-1154, Norman period
Hamilton, J. The Norman conquest of England **942.02**

History—1066-1154, Norman period—Fiction
Cadnum, M. The king's arrow **Fic**
Carey, J. L. Dragon's Keep **Fic**

History—1154-1399, Plantagenets
Kramer, A. Eleanor of Aquitaine **92**
Levy, D. The signing of the Magna Carta **942.03**
Plain, N. Eleanor of Aquitaine and the High Middle Ages **942.03**

History—1154-1399, Plantagenets—Fiction
Avi. Crispin: the cross of lead **Fic**
Cadnum, M. Forbidden forest **Fic**
Crossley-Holland, K. Crossing to Paradise **Fic**
Crossley-Holland, K. The seeing stone **Fic**

History—1485-1603, Tudors
Adams, S. Elizabeth I **92**
Ashby, R. Elizabethan England **942.05**
Currie, S. An actor on the Elizabethan stage **792.09**
Elizabethan world reference library **942.05**
Hinds, K. The church [Life in Elizabethan England series] **274**
Hinds, K. The city [Life in Elizabethan England series] **942.05**

Greenland
Fiction
Stead, R. First light   **Fic**

Greenspan, Alan
See/See also pages in the following book(s):
Bussing-Burks, M. Influential economists
    920

Greenwald, Lisa
My life in pink and green   **Fic**

Greenway, Shirley
Art: an A-Z guide   **703**

Greenwood, Janette Thomas
(comp) The Gilded Age: a history in documents.
See The Gilded Age: a history in documents
    973.8

Greenwood histories of the modern nations [series]
Blumberg, A. The history of Israel   **956.94**

Greenwood Press "Daily life through history" series
Cohen, E. S. Daily life in Renaissance Italy
    945

Greenwood professional guides in school librarianship [series]
Craver, K. W. Creating cyber libraries   **027.8**
Kearney, C. A. Curriculum partner   **027.8**

Greetings from nowhere. O'Connor, B.   **Fic**

Greetings from planet Earth. Kerley, B.   **Fic**

Greger, Margaret
Kites for everyone   **629.133**

Gregor Mendel, and the roots of genetics. Edelson, E.   **92**

Gregor the Overlander. Collins, S.   **Fic**

Gregory, Kristiana
Eleanor: crown jewel of Aquitaine   **Fic**
My darlin' Clementine   **Fic**
Seeds of hope   **Fic**

Gregory, Nan, 1944-
I'll sing you one-o   **Fic**

Greiner, Tony
Analyzing library collection use with Excel
    025.2

Grenada
Pang, G.-C. Grenada   **972.98**

Gresham, Sir Thomas, 1519?-1579
See/See also pages in the following book(s):
Bussing-Burks, M. Influential economists
    920

Grey, Christopher
Leonardo's shadow   **Fic**

Grey, Mini
(il) Gardner, L. Into the woods   **Fic**

Gribbin, John R.
(jt. auth) Gribbin, M. The science of Philip Pullman's His Dark Materials   **823.009**

Gribbin, Mary
The science of Philip Pullman's His Dark Materials   **823.009**

Grief girl. Vincent, E.   **92**

Grierson's raid. Matthews, T. L.   **973.7**

Griffin, Adele
My almost epic summer   **Fic**

Where I want to be   **Fic**

Griffin, Paul, 1966-
Ten Mile River   **Fic**

Griffin, Peni R.
The ghost sitter   **Fic**

Griffin, Robert, 1951-
(ed) Junior Worldmark encyclopedia of world holidays. See Junior Worldmark encyclopedia of world holidays   **394.26**

Griffiths, Rodney
(il) Gamble, C. Leopards   **599.75**

Griggs, Jack L.
All the birds of North America   **598**

Grimberg, Tina
Out of line   **92**

Grimes, Nikki
At Jerusalem's gate   **811**
Bronx masquerade   **Fic**
Dark sons   **Fic**
A dime a dozen   **811**
Hopscotch love   **811**
Jazmin's notebook   **Fic**
The road to Paris   **Fic**
Tai chi morning   **811**

Grimes, Sharon
Reading is our business   **027.8**

Grimly, Gris
(il) Irving, W. The Legend of Sleepy Hollow
    Fic
(il) Poe, E. A. Edgar Allan Poe's tales of mystery and madness   **S C**

Gritzner, Charles F.
The tropics   **910**
(jt. auth) Desaulniers, K. L. Northern America
    970
(jt. auth) Gritzner, J. A. North Africa and the Middle East   **956**
(jt. auth) Phillips, D. A. Bangladesh   **954.92**

Gritzner, Jeffrey A.
Afghanistan   **958.1**
North Africa and the Middle East   **956**

Groff, Claire Price- *See* Price-Groff, Claire

Grooming, Personal *See* Personal grooming

Gross, Elly Berkovits, 1929-
Elly   **92**

Groth-Fleming, Candace, 1962-
See also Fleming, Candace

The **groundbreaking**, chance-taking life of George Washington Carver and science & invention in America. Harness, C.   **92**

Groundwork guides [series]
Forssberg, M. Sex for guys   **306.7**
Laxer, J. Democracy   **321.8**
Lorinc, J. Cities   **307.7**
Siddiqui, H. Being Muslim   **297**
Springer, J. Genocide   **304.6**
Tanaka, S. Climate change   **363.7**

Groups, Social *See* Social groups

Grover, Lorie Ann
Loose threads   **811**

Growing carnivorous plants. Rice, B. A.   **635.9**

Guns and violence [Current controversies]
363.33

Gunsmithing *See* Firearms industry

Gunstories. Atkin, S. B.   363.33

Gunther, John, 1901-1970
Death be not proud   92

Gunther, John, 1929-1947
About
Gunther, J. Death be not proud   92

Gupta, Dipak K.
Who are the terrorists?   303.6

Gurstelle, William
The art of the catapult   623.4

Gut-eating bugs. Denega, D.   363.2

Gutenberg, Johann, 1397?-1468
Fiction
Skelton, M. Endymion Spring   Fic

Guthrie, Woody, 1912-1967
About
Partridge, E. This land was made for you and
me: the life and songs of Woody Guthrie
92

Gutman, Bill
(jt. auth) Madden, J. John Madden's heroes of
football   796.332

Gutman, Dan
The million dollar putt   Fic
The million dollar shot   Fic
Shoeless Joe & me   Fic

Guts. Simon, S.   612.3

The **guy** book. Jukes, M.   305.23

The **guy-friendly** YA library. Welch, R. J.
027.62

Guyana
Jermyn, L. Guyana   988.1
Morrison, M. Guyana   988.1

Guys write for Guys Read   810.8

Gwaltney, Doris
Homefront   Fic

Gym candy. Deuker, C.   Fic

Gynecology *See* Women—Health and hygiene

Gypsies
See/See also pages in the following book(s):
Altman, L. J. The forgotten victims of the Holo-
caust   940.53
Fiction
Dunlap, S. E. The musician's daughter   Fic
Gardner, S. The red necklace   Fic
Rutkoski, M. The Cabinet of Wonders   Fic
Sedgwick, M. My swordhand is singing   Fic

H

H.I.V.E. Walden, M.   Fic

Haab, Michelle
(jt. auth) Haab, S. Dangles and bangles
745.5

Haab, Sherri, 1964-
Dangles and bangles   745.5

Haas, Jessie
Chase   Fic

Habeeb, William Mark, 1955-
Africa   960

Habibi. Nye, N. S.   Fic

Habitat (Ecology)
See also types of ecology, e.g. Desert ecol-
ogy; Marine ecology
Habitats of the world   577

Habitats of the world   577

Hacker, Carlotta
Nobel Prize winners   920

Haddix, Margaret Peterson, 1964-
Among the hidden   Fic
Double identity   Fic
Found   Fic
Just Ella   Fic
Leaving Fishers   Fic
Uprising   Fic

Haden, Christen
Creepy cute crochet   746.43

Haduch, Bill
Go fly a bike!   629.227
Science fair success secrets   507.8

Haerens, Margaret
(ed) Illegal immigration: opposing viewpoints.
See Illegal immigration: opposing viewpoints
325.73

Haesly, Richard, 1969-
(ed) The Constitutional Convention. See The
Constitutional Convention   342

Hafiz, Dilara
The American Muslim teenager's handbook
297

Hafiz, Imran
(jt. auth) Hafiz, D. The American Muslim
teenager's handbook   297

Hafiz, Yasmine
(jt. auth) Hafiz, D. The American Muslim
teenager's handbook   297

Hager, Thomas
Linus Pauling and the chemistry of life   92

Hague, Michael, 1948-
(comp) The Book of dragons. See The Book of
dragons   S C

Hahn, Daniel
(ed) The ultimate teen book guide. See The ultimate teen book guide   028.1

Hahn, Mary Downing, 1937-
Hear the wind blow   Fic
Stepping on the cracks   Fic

Haig, Matt, 1975-
Samuel Blink and the forbidden forest   Fic

Hains, Bryan C.
Brain disorders   616.8
Pain   616

Hair
Warrick, L. Hair trix for cool chix   646.7
Graphic novels
Arai, K. Beauty Pop, Vol. 1   741.5

Hair, clothing and tire track evidence. Rainis, K.
G.   363.2

Hair trix for cool chix. Warrick, L.   646.7

Haiti
Blashfield, J. F. Haiti **972.94**
Cheong-Lum, R. N. Haiti **972.94**
History
Rockwell, A. F. Open the door to liberty!: a biography of Toussaint L'Ouverture **92**

Hakim, Joy
The story of science: Aristotle leads the way **509**
The story of science: Einstein adds a new dimension **509**
The story of science: Newton at the center **509**

Halam, Ann
Siberia **Fic**
Snakehead **Fic**

Hale, Dean, 1972-
(jt. auth) Hale, S. Rapunzel's revenge **741.5**

Hale, Marian
Dark water rising **Fic**
The truth about sparrows **Fic**

Hale, Nathan, 1755-1776
Fiction
Myers, A. Spy! **Fic**

Hale, Nathan, 1976-
(il) Hale, S. Rapunzel's revenge **741.5**

Hale, Shannon
Book of a thousand days **Fic**
Princess Academy **Fic**
Rapunzel's revenge **741.5**

Haley, James L.
Stephen F. Austin and the founding of Texas **92**

Half-caste and other poems. Agard, J. **821**

Half-human **S C**

Half-Moon investigations. Colfer, E. **Fic**

Halilbegovich, Nadja, 1979-
My childhood under fire **949.7**

Hall, Alvin
Show me the money **332.024**

Hall, Barbara, 1960-
The Noah confessions **Fic**
Tempo change **Fic**

Hall, Derek, 1930-
(ed) Being human. See Being human **612**

Hall, Donald, 1928-
(ed) The Oxford book of children's verse in America. See The Oxford book of children's verse in America **811.008**

Hall, Eleanor J.
Recycling **363.7**

Hall, Elizabeth, 1929-
(jt. auth) O'Dell, S. Thunder rolling in the mountains **Fic**

Hall, Howard
A charm of dolphins **599.5**

Hall, Loretta
Arab American voices **305.8**

Hall, Margaret, 1947-
Skin deep **612.7**

Hall, Martin, 1952-
Great Zimbabwe **968.91**

Hall, Melanie
(jt. auth) Szabo, R. Behind happy faces **616.89**

Hall, Susan, 1940-
Using picture storybooks to teach literary devices v4 **016.8**

Hall-Ellis, Sylvia Dunn, 1949-
Grants for school libraries **025.1**
Grantsmanship for small libraries and school library media centers. See Grantsmanship for small libraries and school library media centers **025.1**

Hallam, Arlita
Managing budgets and finances **025.1**

Halleck, Elaine
(ed) Living in Nazi Germany. See Living in Nazi Germany **943.086**

Hallett, Mark, 1947-
(il) Becker, J. E. Wild cats: past & present **599.75**
(il) Halls, K. M. Wild horses **599.66**

Halley, Edmond, 1656-1742
About
Fox, M. V. Scheduling the heavens [biography of Edmond Halley] **92**

Halley, Ned
Farm **630**

Halliburton, Warren J.
(comp) Historic speeches of African Americans. See Historic speeches of African Americans **815.008**

Halloween
Fiction
Bradbury, R. The Halloween tree **Fic**
Vande Velde, V. All Hallows' Eve **S C**
The **Halloween** tree. Bradbury, R. **Fic**

Hallowell, Edward M.
(jt. auth) Corman, C. A. Positively ADD **616.85**

Halls, Kelly Milner, 1957-
Dinosaur mummies **567.9**
Mysteries of the mummy kids **393**
Tales of the cryptids **001.9**
Wild dogs **599.77**
Wild horses **599.66**

Hallucinogenic drugs *See* Hallucinogens

Hallucinogenic plants *See* Hallucinogens

Hallucinogens
See also Ecstasy (Drug)
Barter, J. Hallucinogens **362.29**
LeVert, S. The facts about LSD and other hallucinogens **362.29**

Halpern, Julie, 1975-
Get well soon **Fic**

Halpern-Cordell, Julie *See* Halpern, Julie, 1975-

Halpin, Brendan
Forever changes **Fic**
How ya like me now **Fic**

Halpin, Mikki
It's your world—if you don't like it, change it **361.2**

Halsey, Megan
(il) Chin-Lee, C. Amelia to Zora **920**

Health alert—*Continued*

Bjorklund, R. Cystic fibrosis	**616.3**
Bjorklund, R. Eating disorders	**616.85**
Bjorklund, R. Epilepsy	**616.8**
Bjorklund, R. Food-borne illnesses	**615.9**
Brill, M. T. Alzheimer's disease	**616.8**
Brill, M. T. Autism	**616.85**
Brill, M. T. Down syndrome	**616.85**
Brill, M. T. Lung cancer	**616.99**
Brill, M. T. Multiple sclerosis	**616.8**
Buckmaster, M. L. Skin cancer	**616.99**
Calamandrei, C. Fever	**616**
Capaccio, G. ADD and ADHD	**616.85**
Colligan, L. H. Sleep disorders	**616.8**
Colligan, L. H. Tick-borne illnesses	**616.9**
Haney, J. Heart disease	**616.1**
Haney, J. Juvenile diabetes	**616.4**
Hicks, T. A. Allergies	**616.97**
Hicks, T. A. The common cold	**616.2**
Hicks, T. A. Obesity	**616.3**
Hoffmann, G. Chicken pox	**616.9**
Hoffmann, G. The flu	**616.2**
Hoffmann, G. Mononucleosis	**616.9**
Hoffmann, G. Osteoporosis	**616.7**
Klosterman, L. Leukemia	**616.99**
Klosterman, L. Meningitis	**616.8**
Klosterman, L. Rabies	**616.9**
Petreycik, R. Headaches	**616.8**
Roy, J. R. Depression	**616.85**

Health care *See* Medical care

Health foods *See* Natural foods

Health issues [series]

Elliot-Wright, S. Epilepsy	**616.8**

Health matters! **613**

Health matters [series]

Baldwin, C. Autism	**616.89**
Baldwin, C. Sickle cell disease	**616.1**

Health science projects about psychology. Gardner, R. **150**

Health zone [series]

Doeden, M. Eat right!	**613.2**

The **healthy** body cookbook. D'Amico, J. **641.5**

Hear me out: true stories of Teens Educating and Confronting Homophobia **306.76**

Hear that train whistle blow!. Meltzer, M. **385.09**

Hear the wind blow. Hahn, M. D. **Fic**

Hearing
Simon, S. Eyes and ears **612.8**

Hearing impaired
See also Deaf

Hearn, Julie, 1958-
Ivy **Fic**
The minister's daughter **Fic**

Hearne, Betsy Gould, 1942-
Beauties and beasts **398.2**
The canine connection: stories about dogs and people **S C**
Hauntings, and other tales of danger, love, and sometimes loss **S C**

Hearne, Elizabeth G. *See* Hearne, Betsy Gould, 1942-

Hearst, Patricia Campbell
See/See also pages in the following book(s):
Aaseng, N. You are the juror **345**

Heart
See also Blood—Circulation
Brynie, F. H. 101 questions about blood and circulation, with answers straight from the heart **612.1**
Parker, S. Heart, blood, and lungs **612.1**
Simon, S. The heart **612.1**
The **heart**. Simon, S. **612.1**

Heart attack *See* Heart diseases

Heart, blood, and lungs. Parker, S. **612.1**

Heart diseases
Haney, J. Heart disease **616.1**
Silverstein, A. Heart disease **616.1**

A **heart** divided. Bennett, C.

The **heart** has its reasons. Cart, M. **813.009**

Heart of a shepherd. Parry, R. **Fic**

Heart to heart **811.008**

Hearts of iron. Duble, K. B. **Fic**

Hearts of stone. Ernst, K. **Fic**

Heartsinger. Stoffels, K. **Fic**

Heat
Gardner, R. Science projects about temperature and heat **536**
Sullivan, N. Temperature **536**
Poetry
Singer, M. Central heating **811**

Heath, Alan
Windows on the world **394.2**

Heath, Jack, 1986-
The Lab **Fic**

Heaven. Johnson, A. **Fic**

Heaven looks a lot like the mall. Mass, W. **Fic**

Heck. Basye, D. E. **Fic**

Heck, superhero. Leavitt, M. **Fic**

The **hedge** knight. Avery, B. **741.5**

Hegamin, Tonya
M+O 4evr **Fic**
Pemba's song **Fic**

Hegedus, Bethany
Between us Baxters **Fic**

Heifetz, Aaron
(jt. auth) Hamm, M. Go for the goal **796.334**

Height, Dorothy I., 1912-
See/See also pages in the following book(s):
Pinkney, A. D. Let it shine **920**

The **heights,** the depths, and everything in between. Nemeth, S. **Fic**

Heiligman, Deborah
Charles and Emma [dual biography of Charles Darwin and Emma Wedgwood Darwin] **92**
High hopes [biography of John F. Kennedy] **92**

Heilman, Carl, 1954-
(il) Weber, S. Two in the wilderness **508**

Holocaust, 1933-1945—Personal narratives—Continued

Opdyke, I. G. In my hands	**940.53**
Perl, L. Four perfect pebbles	**940.53**
Reiss, J. The upstairs room	**92**
Rosenberg, M. B. Hiding to survive	**940.53**
Sender, R. M. The cage	**940.53**
Siegal, A. Upon the head of the goat: a childhood in Hungary, 1939-1944	**92**
Soumerai, E. N. A voice from the Holocaust	**940.53**

Study and teaching

Schroeder, P. W. Six million paper clips	**940.53**
The **Holocaust**	**940.53**

Holocaust [21st Century Bks. series]

Gottfried, T. Children of the slaughter	**940.53**
Gottfried, T. Displaced persons	**940.53**
Gottfried, T. Heroes of the Holocaust	**940.53**

Holocaust [Blackbirch Press series]

Altman, L. J. Forever outsiders	**909**

Holocaust [Heinemann Lib. series]

Shuter, J. The camp system	**940.53**
Shuter, J. Resistance to the Nazis	**943.086**

Holocaust heroes and Nazi criminals [series]

McArthur, D. Raoul Wallenberg	**92**

Holocaust in history [series]

Altman, L. J. Crimes and criminals of the Holocaust	**940.53**
Altman, L. J. The forgotten victims of the Holocaust	**940.53**
Altman, L. J. Hitler's rise to power and the Holocaust	**943.086**
Altman, L. J. Impact of the Holocaust	**940.53**
Altman, L. J. The Jewish victims of the Holocaust	**940.53**

Holocaust remembrance book for young readers [series]

Kacer, K. Hiding Edith	**940.53**
Levine, K. Hana's suitcase on stage	**812**
Kacer, K. The underground reporters	**940.53**

Holocaust rescuers. Lyman, D. | **920**

Holocaust survivors

Bitton-Jackson, L. My bridges of hope	**92**
Friedman, I. R. The other victims	**940.53**
Gottfried, T. Displaced persons	**940.53**
Gross, E. B. Elly	**92**
Lobel, A. No pretty pictures	**92**
Rubin, S. G. The Anne Frank Case: Simon Wiesenthal's search for the truth	**92**

Fiction

Lowenstein, S. C. Waiting for Eugene	**Fic**

Holt, K. A.

Mike Stellar: nerves of steel	**Fic**

Holt, Kimberly Willis

Part of me	**S C**
When Zachary Beaver came to town	**Fic**

Holt, Simon

The Devouring	**Fic**

Holtz, Thomas R., 1965-

Dinosaurs	**567.9**

Holub, Josef, 1926-

An innocent soldier	**Fic**

The **Holy** Bible [New Revised Standard Version] Bible | **220.5**

Holy days See Religious holidays

Holy Grail See Grail

Holyoke, Nancy

A smart girl's guide to money	**332.024**

Holzer, Harold

The president is shot!	**973.7**
(ed) Lincoln, A. Abraham Lincoln the writer	**92**

Home

Fiction

Frost, H. Keesha's house	**Fic**

Home, and other big, fat lies. Wolfson, J. | **Fic**

Home decoration See Interior design

A **home** for foundlings. Jocelyn, M. | **362.7**

The **home** front. Campbell, G. A. | **973.92**

The **home** front in World War II. Levy, P. | **940.53**

Home instruction See Home schooling

Home is east. Ly, M. | **Fic**

Home life See Family life

Home of the brave. Applegate, K. | **Fic**

Home of the Braves. Klass, D. | **Fic**

Home on the moon. Dyson, M. J. | **629.45**

Home schooling

Lerch, M. T. Serving homeschooled teens and their parents	**027.6**

Home video systems

See also Video recording

Homecoming. Voigt, C. | **Fic**

Homefront. Gwaltney, D. | **Fic**

Homeless bird. Whelan, G. | **Fic**

The **Homeless:** opposing viewpoints | **362.5**

Homeless persons

See also Refugees; Runaway children; Runaway teenagers; Tramps

The Homeless: opposing viewpoints	**362.5**
Hynson, C. Living on the street	**362.7**

Fiction

Bowler, T. Blade	**Fic**
Draanen, W. v. Runaway	**Fic**
Fensham, E. Helicopter man	**Fic**
Griffin, P. Ten Mile River	**Fic**
Hesse, K. Brooklyn Bridge	**Fic**
Matthews, L. S. Lexi	**Fic**
O'Connor, B. How to steal a dog	**Fic**
Sachar, L. Holes	**Fic**
Spinelli, J. Maniac Magee	**Fic**
Strasser, T. Can't get there from here	**Fic**
Walters, E. Sketches	**Fic**

Homer

The Iliad	**883**
The Odyssey	**883**

Adaptations

Lister, R. The odyssey	**883**
McCarty, N. The Iliad	**883**

Human fertility
See also Infertility

Human Genome Project
Boon, K. A. The human genome project
    599.93

Human geography
Delannoy, I. Our living Earth   **779**

Human impact. Vogel, C. G.   **333.91**

Human influence on nature
Burnie, D. Endangered planet   **333.95**
Desonie, D. Geosphere   **333.73**
Desonie, D. Polar regions   **304.2**
Vogel, C. G. Human impact   **333.91**

Human origins
See also Evolution; Fossil hominids; Pre-
    historic peoples
Anderson, D. How do we know the nature of
    human origins   **599.93**
Poynter, M. The Leakeys   **92**
Robertshaw, P. The early human world
    599.93
Sloan, C. The human story   **599.93**
Tattersall, I. Bones, brains and DNA   **599.93**
Thimmesh, C. Lucy long ago   **599.93**

Human physiology on file   **612**

Human relations *See* Interpersonal relations

Human rights
Altman, L. J. Human rights   **323**
Every human has rights   **323**
Herumin, W. Child labor today   **331.3**
Human rights: opposing viewpoints   **323**
Kennedy, K. Speak truth to power   **920**
Pioneers of human rights   **920**
Stewart, G. Human rights in the Middle East
    323

See/See also pages in the following book(s):
Africa: opposing viewpoints   **960**

Human rights in the Middle East. Stewart, G.
    323

Human rights: opposing viewpoints   **323**

Human settlements
Anderson, J. Looking at settlements   **307**

The **human** story. Sloan, C.   **599.93**

Hummingbird. Angle, K. G.   **Fic**

Hummingbirds
Aziz, L. Hummingbirds   **598**
Rauzon, M. J. Hummingbirds   **598**

Humor *See* Wit and humor

Humor in young adult literature. Hogan, W.
    813.009

Humorous graphic novels
Anderson, E. A. PX! Book one: a girl and her
    panda   **741.5**
Carey, M. Confessions of a Blabbermouth
    741.5
Fisher, J. S. WJHC: on the air!   **741.5**
Flight explorer   **741.5**
Frampton, O. Oddly Normal   **741.5**
Friesen, R. Cupcakes of doom!   **741.5**
Gownley, J. Amelia rules!   **741.5**
Hale, S. Rapunzel's revenge   **741.5**
Hicks, F. E. The war at Ellsmere   **741.5**

Jaffe, M. Bad kitty volume 1: catnipped
    741.5
Kim, D. K. Good as Lily   **741.5**
Lat. Town Boy   **741.5**
Lyga, B. Wolverine: worst day ever   **741.5**
Sfar, J. Dungeon Vol. 1: Duck Heart   **741.5**
Tamaki, M. Skim   **741.5**
Toriyama, A. Cowa!   **741.5**
Trondheim, L. Tiny Tyrant   **741.5**
Walker, L. Q. The super scary monster show,
    featuring Little Gloomy   **741.5**
Weinstein, L. Girl stories   **741.5**

Humorous poetry
The Kingfisher book of funny poems
    821.008
Lawson, J. Black stars in a white night sky
    811
Silverstein, S. Falling up   **811**
Silverstein, S. A light in the attic   **811**
Silverstein, S. Where the sidewalk ends   **811**

Humphreys, C. C. *See* Humphreys, Chris

Humphreys, Chris
The fetch   **Fic**

The **hundred-year-old** secret. See Barrett, T. The
    100-year-old secret   **Fic**

Hundred Years' War, 1339-1453
Fiction
Russell, C. Dogboy   **Fic**

Hungarian Americans
Fiction
Cheng, A. Eclipse   **Fic**

Hungary
Ake, A. Hungary   **943.9**
Esbenshade, R. S. Hungary   **943.9**
Fiction
Cheng, A. The bear makers   **Fic**

The **Hunger** Games. Collins, S.   **Fic**

Hunley (Submarine)
Walker, S. M. Secrets of a Civil War submarine
    973.7

Huns
Price, S. Attila the Hun   **92**

Hunt, Joni Phelps, 1956-
A band of bears   **599.78**

Hunt, Robert
See also Crockett, Robert

Hunt, Scott
(il) Testa, M. Becoming Joe DiMaggio   **811**
(il) Twice told. See Twice told   **S C**

The **hunt** for the seventh. Morton-Shaw, C.
    Fic

Hunter, Clementine, 1886?-1988
About
Whitehead, K. Art from her heart: folk artist
    Clementine Hunter   **92**

Hunter, David, 1947-
Born to smoke   **616.86**

Hunter, Erin
Into the wild   **Fic**
The lost warrior   **741.5**
Midnight   **Fic**
The sight   **Fic**
Warriors: Tiger & Sasha #1: into the woods
    741.5

Hunter, William, 1971-
DNA analysis   363.2

The **Hunter's** Moon. Melling, O. R.   **Fic**

Hunting
See also Tracking and trailing
Paulsen, G. Guts   92
Fiction
Ó Guilín, P. The inferior   **Fic**

Huntington's chorea
Glimm, A. Gene hunter [biography of Nancy Wexler]   92

Hurd, Owen
Chicago history for kids   **977.3**

Hurley, Jennifer A., 1973-
Teen pregnancy   362.7
(ed) The Homeless: opposing viewpoints. See The Homeless: opposing viewpoints   **362.5**
(ed) Teens at risk: opposing viewpoints. See Teens at risk: opposing viewpoints   **362.7**

Hurley, Tonya
Ghostgirl   **Fic**

Hurling (Game)
Fiction
Colfer, E. Benny and Omar   **Fic**

Hurricane. Trueman, T.   **Fic**

Hurricane force. Treaster, J. B.   **551.55**

Hurricane Katrina, 2005
Miller, D. A. Hurricane Katrina   363.34
Miller, M. Hurricane Katrina strikes the Gulf Coast   363.34
Palser, B. Hurricane Katrina   363.34
Pietras, J. Hurricane Katrina   363.34
Fiction
Antieau, K. Ruby's imagine   **Fic**
Volponi, P. Hurricane song   **Fic**

Hurricane Katrina. Palser, B.   **363.34**

Hurricane Katrina strikes the Gulf Coast. Miller, M.   **363.34**

Hurricane song. Volponi, P.   **Fic**

Hurricanes
See also Typhoons
Ceban, B. J. Hurricanes, typhoons, and cyclones   **551.55**
Fradin, J. B. Hurricanes   551.55
Miller, M. Hurricane Katrina strikes the Gulf Coast   363.34
Palser, B. Hurricane Katrina   363.34
Ryback, C. Hurricanes   551.55
Treaster, J. B. Hurricane force   551.55
Encyclopedias
Longshore, D. Encyclopedia of hurricanes, typhoons, and cyclones   **551.55**
Fiction
Garland, S. The silent storm   **Fic**
Hale, M. Dark water rising   **Fic**
Trueman, T. Hurricane   **Fic**

Hurricanes, tsunamis, and other natural disasters. Langley, A.   **363.34**

Hurricanes, typhoons, and cyclones. Ceban, B. J.   **551.55**

Hurst, Carol Otis
Through the lock   **Fic**

Hurston, Zora Neale, 1891-1960
About
Litwin, L. B. Zora Neale Hurston   92
Lyons, M. E. Sorrow's kitchen [biography of Zora Neale Hurston]   92
Sapet, K. Rhythm and folklore [biography of Zora Neale Hurston]   92
Adaptations
Thomas, J. C. The skull talks back and other haunting tales   **398.2**

Hurtado, A. Magdalena
About
Batten, M. Anthropologist: scientist of the people   **301**

Hush. Napoli, D. J.   **Fic**

Hush. Woodson, J.   **Fic**

Hutchinson, Anne Marbury, 1591-1643
About
Stille, D. R. Anne Hutchinson   92

Huxley, Aldous, 1894-1963
Brave new world   **Fic**

Hyde, Catherine Ryan
The year of my miraculous reappearance   **Fic**

Hyde, Margaret Oldroyd, 1917-
Diabetes   **616.4**
Smoking 101   **616.86**
Stress 101   **616.85**

Hydrogen. Walker, N.   **665**

Hydrogen as fuel
Walker, N. Hydrogen   **665**

Hydrosphere. Desonie, D.   **551.48**

Hydrothermal vents *See* Ocean bottom

Hygiene
See also Health
Crissey, P. Personal hygiene? What's that got to do with me?   **649**

Hyman, Bruce M.
Obsessive-compulsive disorder   **616.85**

Hyman, Trina Schart, 1939-2004
(il) Cohen, B. Canterbury tales   821
(il) Rogasky, B. The golem   398.2
(il) Tchana, K. H. Changing Woman and her sisters   398.2
(il) Tchana, K. H. The serpent slayer: and other stories of strong women   398.2

Hymns
See also Spirituals (Songs)

Hynes, Margaret, 1970-
Rocks & fossils   **552**

Hynson, Colin
Living on the street   **362.7**

Hyperactive children
See also Attention deficit disorder

I

I am Apache. Landman, T.   **Fic**

I am Mordred. Springer, N.   **Fic**

I am Morgan le Fay. Springer, N.   **Fic**

I am phoenix: poems for two voices. Fleischman, P. **811**

I am Rembrandt's daughter. Cullen, L. **Fic**

I am Scout: the biography of Harper Lee. Shields, C. J. **92**

I am the cheese. Cormier, R. **Fic**

I am the darker brother **811.008**

I am the wallpaper. Hughes, M. P. **Fic**

I and I [biography of Bob Marley] Medina, T. **92**

I can't keep my own secrets **808.8**

I don't want to be crazy. Schutz, S. **92**

I feel a little jumpy around you **808.81**

I have lived a thousand years. Bitton-Jackson, L. **940.53**

I heard God talking to me. Spires, E. **811**

I heart you, you haunt me. Schroeder, L. **Fic**

I know what you did last summer. Duncan, L. **Fic**

I, Lorelei. Smith, Y. **Fic**

—I never saw another butterfly— **741.9**

I once was a monkey. Lee, J. M. **294.3**

I put a spell on you. Selzer, A. **Fic**

I, Q.: book one, Indepedence Hall. Smith, R. **Fic**

I remember Korea. Granfield, L. **951.9**

I, robot. Asimov, I. **S C**

I-search for success. Duncan, D. **025.5**

I, too, sing America **811.008**

I wanna be your shoebox. García, C. **Fic**

I wanna make my own clothes. Hantman, C. **646.4**

I wanna re-do my room. Hantman, C. **745.5**

I want to live. Lugovskaia, N. **92**

I was a non-blonde cheerleader. Scott, K. **Fic**

I was dreaming to come to America **325.73**

I was there books [series]
Tanaka, S. Attack on Pearl Harbor **940.54**

I will plant you a lilac tree. Hillman, L. **940.53**

I witness [series]
Avi. Hard gold **Fic**

I wouldn't thank you for a valentine **808.81**

Ibatoulline, Bagram
(il) Fleischman, P. Graven images **S C**
(il) Freedman, R. The adventures of Marco Polo **92**
(il) Giblin, J. Secrets of the Sphinx **932**
(jt. auth) Stanley, D. Bella at midnight **Fic**

Ibbotson, Eva
The beasts of Clawstone Castle **Fic**
The dragonfly pool **Fic**
The star of Kazan **Fic**

Ibn al-Haytham See Alhazen, 965-1039

Ibn al-Haytham. Steffens, B. **92**

Ice Age
Harrison, D. L. Cave detectives **560**

The **ice** cream con. Docherty, J. **Fic**

Ice hockey See Hockey

Ice skating
Biography
Koestler-Grack, R. A. Michelle Kwan **92**
Graphic novels
Nakajo, H. Sugar Princess volume 1: skating to win **741.5**

Ice story. Kimmel, E. C. **998**

Ice time. McKinley, M. **796.962**

Icecore. Whyman, M. **Fic**

Iceland
Wilcox, J. Iceland **949.12**

The Icemark chronicles [series]
Hill, S. The cry of the Icemark **Fic**

Icenoggle, Jodi, 1967-
Schenck v. United States and the freedom of speech debate **342**

Iconography See Christian art; Religious art

Id al-Adha
Jeffrey, L. S. Celebrate Ramadan **297.3**

Ida B. Wells-Barnett. Schraff, A. E. **92**

Idaho
Fiction
Gregory, K. My darlin' Clementine **Fic**

Ideal states See Utopias

Ideas of the modern world [series]
Grant, R. G. Protesting Capitalism **330.1**
Stearman, K. Feminism **305.4**
Tames, R. Nationalism **320.5**

Identification
See also DNA fingerprinting; Forensic anthropology

Identifying trees. Williams, M. D. **582.16**

Identity (Psychology)
Fiction
Franklin, E. The other half of me **Fic**
Na, A. The fold **Fic**

Idioms See English language—Idioms

Iditarod dream. Wood, T. **798.8**

If. Kipling, R. **821**

If I grow up. Strasser, T. **Fic**

If I have a wicked stepmother, where's my prince? Kantor, M. **Fic**

If I stay. Forman, G. **Fic**

If that breathes fire, we're toast!. Stewart, J. J. **Fic**

If the shoe fits. Whipple, L. **811**

If the witness lied. Cooney, C. B. **Fic**

If you come softly. Woodson, J. **Fic**

Iggulden, Conn, 1971-
The dangerous book for boys **031.02**

Iggulden, Hal, 1972-
(jt. auth) Iggulden, C. The dangerous book for boys **031.02**

The **Iliad.** Homer **883**

The **Iliad.** McCarty, N. **883**

I'll ask you three times, are you ok? Nye, N. S. **92**

The **ill-made** knight. White, T. H.
In White, T. H. The once and future king **Fic**

I'll pass for your comrade. Silvey, A. **973.7**
I'll sing you one-o. Gregory, N. **Fic**
Illegal aliens
Illegal immigration: opposing viewpoints
 325.73
 Kenney, K. L. Illegal immigration **325.73**
 Miller, D. A. Illegal immigration **325.73**
 Ouellette, J. A day without immigrants
 331.6
Fiction
 Alvarez, J. Return to sender **Fic**
 Hobbs, W. Crossing the wire **Fic**
 Ives, D. Voss **Fic**
Illegal immigration. Kenney, K. L. **325.73**
Illegal immigration. Miller, D. A. **325.73**
Illegal immigration: opposing viewpoints
 325.73
Illinois
Fiction
 Beaty, A. Cicada summer **Fic**
 Comerford, L. B. Rissa Bartholomew's declaration of independence **Fic**
 Klise, K. Deliver us from Normal **Fic**
 Moranville, S. B. Over the river **Fic**
 Peck, R. On the wings of heroes **Fic**
 Peck, R. A season of gifts **Fic**
History
 Bial, R. Nauvoo **289.3**
Illiteracy *See* Literacy
Illness *See* Diseases
Illuminated progress. Baxter, R. **92**
Illusions *See* Optical illusions
Illustrated children's library [series]
 Alcott, L. M. Little women **Fic**
Illustrated dictionary of mythology. Wilkinson, P.
 201
The **illustrated** history of the world. Roberts, J. M. **909**
Illustrated history of the world [series]
 Reynoldson, F. Conflict and change **909.7**
Illustration of books
 See also Picture books for children
 Artist to artist **741.6**
 Ellabbad, M. The illustrator's notebook
 741.6
 Marcus, L. S. A Caldecott celebration **741.6**
Illustrations, Humorous *See* Cartoons and caricatures
Illustrators
 Artist to artist **741.6**
 De Paola, T. Christmas remembered **92**
 Dean, T. Theodor Geisel [Dr. Seuss] **92**
 Ellabbad, M. The illustrator's notebook
 741.6
 Marcus, L. S. A Caldecott celebration **741.6**
 Peet, B. Bill Peet: an autobiography **92**
 Waldman, N. Out of the shadows **92**
Dictionaries
 Eighth book of junior authors and illustrators
 920.003
 Ninth book of junior authors and illustrators
 920.003
 Something about the author **920.003**

Something about the author: autobiography series **920.003**
Tenth book of junior authors and illustrators
 920.003
The **illustrator's** notebook. Ellabbad, M. **741.6**
The **Illyrian** adventure. Alexander, L. **Fic**
I'm a vegetarian. Schwartz, E. **613.2**
I'm being stalked by a moonshadow. MacLeod, D.
 Fic
I'm exploding now. Hite, S. **Fic**
Images and issues of women in the twentieth century [series]
 Gourley, C. Flappers and the new American woman **305.4**
 Gourley, C. Gibson girls and suffragists
 305.4
 Gourley, C. Gidgets and women warriors
 305.4
 Gourley, C. Rosie and Mrs. America **305.4**
Imaginary enemy. Gonzalez, J. **Fic**
Imaginary playmates
Fiction
 Gonzalez, J. Imaginary enemy **Fic**
 White, A. Window boy **Fic**
Imagination
Fiction
 Weston, R. P. Zorgamazoo **Fic**
Imbimbo, Anthony
 Steve Jobs **92**
Imbriaco, Alison
 The red wolf **599.77**
Imhoff, Kathleen R.
 Library contests **021.7**
Imhotep, 27th cent. B.C.
See/See also pages in the following book(s):
 Aaseng, N. Construction: building the impossible **624**
Immell, Myra
 (ed) World War II. See World War II [Turning points in world history series] **940.53**
Immersed in verse. Wolf, A. **808.1**
Immigrants
 Murphy, J. Pick & shovel poet: the journeys of Pascal D'Angelo **92**
Fiction
 Applegate, K. Home of the brave **Fic**
 Auch, M. J. Ashes of roses **Fic**
 Cheng, A. Eclipse **Fic**
 Currier, K. S. Kai's journey to Gold Mountain
 Fic
 De la Cruz, M. Fresh off the boat **Fic**
 Frost, H. The braid **Fic**
 Giff, P. R. A house of tailors **Fic**
 Heneghan, J. Payback **Fic**
 Hesse, K. Brooklyn Bridge **Fic**
 Hesse, K. Letters from Rifka **Fic**
 Himelblau, L. The trouble begins **Fic**
 Ives, D. Voss **Fic**
 Jaramillo, A. La linea **Fic**
 Kerr, M. E. Someone like summer **Fic**
 Lieurance, S. The locket **Fic**
 Matas, C. The whirlwind **Fic**
 Mead, A. Swimming to America **Fic**

Indians (of India) *See* East Indians

Indians, cowboys, and farmers and the battle for the Great Plains, 1865-1910. Collier, C.
978

Indians of North America *See* Native Americans

Indic arts
Bingham, J. Indian art & culture **709.5**

Indie girl. Daswani, K. **Fic**

Indigenous peoples *See* Ethnology

Indiviglio, Frank
The everything aquarium book **639.34**

Indonesia
Mirpuri, G. Indonesia **959.8**
Fiction
Lewis, R. The killing sea **Fic**

Industrial arts
See also Technology

Industrial design
Welsbacher, A. Earth-friendly design **745.2**

Industrial materials *See* Materials

Industrial plants *See* Factories

Industrial revolution
Arnold, J. R. The industrial revolution **330.9**
Outman, J. L. Industrial Revolution: almanac
330.9
Outman, J. L. Industrial Revolution: biographies
920
Outman, J. L. Industrial Revolution: primary sources **330.9**

Industrial Revolution: biographies. Outman, J. L.
920

Industrial revolution reference library [series]
Outman, J. L. Industrial Revolution: almanac
330.9
Outman, J. L. Industrial Revolution: biographies
920
Outman, J. L. Industrial Revolution: primary sources **330.9**

Industries
See also Defense industry

Inexcusable. Lynch, C. **Fic**

Infantile paralysis *See* Poliomyelitis

Infants
Birth defects
See Birth defects
Care
See also Babysitting
Fiction
Dessen, S. Along for the ride **Fic**
Johnson, A. The first part last **Fic**
MacLachlan, P. Two novels: Baby; Journey
Fic

Infection and infectious diseases *See* Communicable diseases

The inferior. Ó Guilín, P. **Fic**

Infertility
Fullick, A. Test tube babies **618.1**
Orr, T. Test tube babies **618.1**
Winkler, K. High-tech babies **618.1**

Influential economists. Bussing-Burks, M. **920**

Influenza
Goldsmith, C. Influenza: the next pandemic?
614.5
Hoffmann, G. The flu **616.2**
Kupperberg, P. The influenza pandemic of 1918-1919 **614.5**
Silverstein, A. The flu and pneumonia update
616.2
Fiction
Collier, J. L. The empty mirror **Fic**
The **influenza** pandemic of 1918-1919. Kupperberg, P. **614.5**

Influenza: the next pandemic? Goldsmith, C.
614.5

Information literacy
Callison, D. The blue book on information age inquiry, instruction and literacy **028.7**
Riedling, A. M. Learning to learn **028.7**
Taylor, J. Information literacy and the school library media center **028.7**
Wan Guofang. Virtually true **025.04**

Information literacy. Riedling, A. M. **025.5**

Information literacy and the school library media center. Taylor, J. **028.7**

Information literacy series
Rankin, V. The thoughtful researcher **027.62**

Information literacy skills, grades 7-12 **027.62**

Information networks
See also Computer networks; Internet
Riedling, A. M. Information literacy **025.5**

Information Please girls' almanac. See Hartman, H. Girlwonder **305.23**

Information power. American Association of School Librarians **027.8**

The **Information-powered** school **027.8**

Information resources
See also Internet resources
Lenburg, J. The Facts On File guide to research
025.5

Information society
See also Information technology
See/See also pages in the following book(s):
Managing the Internet controversy **025.04**

Information storage and retrieval systems *See* Information systems

Information systems
See also Digital libraries
Wolinsky, A. Internet power research using the Big6 approach **025.04**

Information technology
Braun, L. W. Teens, technology, and literacy; or, Why bad grammar isn't always bad
373.1
Farmer, L. S. J. Technology-infused instruction for the educational community **025.5**
Woodford, C. Digital technology **621.381**
See/See also pages in the following book(s):
Managing the Internet controversy **025.04**

Ingemanson, Donna
(il) Schorer, S. Put your best foot forward
792.8

Ingo. Dunmore, H. **Fic**

Ingold, Jeanette

The Big Burn   **Fic**

Hitch   **Fic**

Mountain solo   **Fic**

Ingpen, Robert R.

(il) Rosen, M. Dickens   92

(il) Rosen, M. Shakespeare   822.3

Ingram, Scott, 1948-

A basketball all-star   796.323

A football all-pro   796.332

King George III   92

Marijuana   362.29

Want fries with that?   613.2

Inhalant abuse

Koellhoffer, T. Inhalants and solvents

     362.29

Inhalants and solvents. Koellhoffer, T.   362.29

Inhalation abuse of solvents See Solvent abuse

Inheritance [series]

Paolini, C. Eragon   **Fic**

Inheritance and evolution. Walker, D.   576

Initiation rites

See also Female circumcision

Injeanuity. Warwick, E.   746

Injuries See Accidents; Wounds and injuries

Ink exchange. Marr, M.   **Fic**

Ink painting

Self, C. Chinese brush painting   751.4

Inkheart. Funke, C. C.   **Fic**

Inman, Roy

The judo handbook   796.8

Inner cities

Inner-city poverty   362.5

Inner-city poverty   362.5

Innes, Brian, 1928-

DNA and body evidence   363.2

Fingerprints and impressions   363.2

Forensic science   363.2

International terrorism   303.6

An **innocent** soldier. Holub, J.   **Fic**

Innovation in sports [series]

Fitzpatrick, J. Skateboarding   796.22

Gigliotti, J. Football   796.332

Kelley, K. C. Golf   796.352

Kelley, K. C. Soccer   796.334

Labrecque, E. Basketball   796.323

Teitelbaum, M. Baseball   796.357

Timblin, S. Swimming   797.2

Innovators [series]

Aaseng, N. Construction: building the impossible   624

DeAngelis, G. Computers   004

Richie, J. Space flight   920

Inns See Hotels and motels

Innuit See Inuit

Inoculation See Vaccination

Inouye, Daniel K.

About

Slavicek, L. C. Daniel Inouye   92

Inquiry learning through librarian-teacher partnerships. Harada, V. H.   371.1

Insane See Mentally ill

Hospitals

See Psychiatric hospitals

The **insect** class. Zabludoff, M.   595.7

Insectivorous plants See Carnivorous plants

Insects

See also Ants; Butterflies; Dragonflies; Moths

Bradley, T. J. Paleo bugs   560

Denega, D. Gut-eating bugs   363.2

Evans, A. V. National Wildlife Federation field guide to insects and spiders & related species of North America   595.7

Jackson, D. M. The bug scientists   595.7

Milne, L. J. The Audubon Society field guide to North American insects and spiders   595.7

Rodriguez, A. M. Secret of the plant-killing ants . . . and more!   595.7

Wilkes, S. Insects   595.7

Zabludoff, M. The insect class   595.7

Fiction

Voake, S. The dreamwalker's child   **Fic**

Voake, S. The web of fire   **Fic**

Poetry

Fleischman, P. Joyful noise: poems for two voices   811

Inside ancient China [series]

Strapp, J. Science and technology   609

Whitfield, S. Philosophy and writing   181

Inside Delta Force. Haney, E. L.   356

Inside government [series]

Feinberg, B. S. The cabinet   352.24

Inside out. Shivack, N.   92

Inside out. Trueman, T.   **Fic**

Inside the Titanic. Marschall, K.   910.4

Inside the walls of Troy. McLaren, C.   **Fic**

Inside the world's most infamous terrorist organizations [series]

Margulies, P. Al Qaeda: Osama bin Laden's army of terrorists   973.931

Rosaler, M. Hamas: Palestinian terrorists

     956.94

Insiders [series]

Calabresi, L. Human body   612

Long, J. A. Dinosaurs   567.9

McMillan, B. Oceans   551.46

Vogt, R. C. Rain forests   577.3

Insignia

See also National emblems

Instruction See Teaching

Instructional materials See Teaching—Aids and devices

Instructional materials centers

See also School libraries

American Association of School Librarians. Information power   027.8

Bell, A. Handheld computers in schools and media centers   371.3

Church, A. P. Leverage your library program to help raise test scores   027.8

Everhart, N. Evaluating the school library media center   027.8

Farmer, L. S. J. Collaborating with administrators and educational support staff   027.8

Internet library [series]

Souter, G. Creating animation for your Web page **006.6**

Wolinsky, A. Internet power research using the Big6 approach **025.04**

The **Internet:** opposing viewpoints **303.4**

Internet power research using the Big6 approach. Wolinsky, A. **025.04**

Internet predators. Allman, T. **364.1**

Internet resources

See also subjects with the subdivision Internet resources, for materials about information available on the Internet on a subject, e.g. Job hunting—Internet resources

Braun, L. W. Hooking teens with the Net **025.04**

Craver, K. W. Creating cyber libraries **027.8**

Diaz, K. R. IssueWeb: a guide and sourcebook for researching controversial issues on the Web **025.04**

Riedling, A. M. Learning to learn **028.7**

Valenza, J. K. Power research tools **001.4**

Internet searching

Bell, S. S. Librarian's guide to online searching **025.5**

Riedling, A. M. Learning to learn **028.7**

Valenza, J. K. Power research tools **001.4**

Study and teaching

Braun, L. W. Hooking teens with the Net **025.04**

Diaz, K. R. IssueWeb: a guide and sourcebook for researching controversial issues on the Web **025.04**

Gordon, R. S. Teaching the Internet in libraries **025.04**

Internment camps See Concentration camps

Internship programs

Fiction

Karasyov, C. Summer intern **Fic**

Interpersonal relations

Amblard, O. Friends forever? **158**

Blatt, J. The teen girl's gotta-have-it guide to embarrassing moments **646.7**

Burningham, S. O. Boyology **306.7**

Canfield, J. Chicken soup for the teenage soul [I-IV] **158**

Chicken soup for the teenage soul's the real deal **158**

Hernández, R. E. Teens & relationships **158**

Kreiner, A. Everything you need to know about creating your own support system **158**

McIntyre, T. The behavior survival guide for kids **158**

Romain, T. Cliques, phonies & other baloney **158**

Interpersonal relations in art

Bingham, J. Emotion & relationships **704.9**

Interplanetary voyages

Adams, D. The hitchhiker's guide to the galaxy **Fic**

Solway, A. Can we travel to the stars? **629.45**

Fiction

Card, O. S. Ender's game **Fic**

Interpreting primary documents [series]

Westward expansion **978**

Interracial adoption

Warren, A. Escape from Saigon [biography of Matt Steiner] **92**

Interracial America: opposing viewpoints **305.8**

Interracial marriage

Law and legislation

Gold, S. D. Loving v. Virginia **346**

Interracial relations See Race relations

Interstellar pig. Sleator, W. **Fic**

Intervention (International law)

See also Monroe Doctrine

See/See also pages in the following book(s):

War: opposing viewpoints **355**

Interviews with Muslim women of Pakistan. Kovarik, C. A. **954.91**

Interworld. Gaiman, N. **Fic**

The **Intifadas.** Wingate, K. **956.95**

Intner, Sheila S., 1935-

Standard cataloging for school and public libraries **025.3**

(ed) Cataloging correctly for kids. See Cataloging correctly for kids **025.3**

Into focus **028.1**

Into the firestorm. Hopkinson, D. **Fic**

Into the ravine. Scrimger, R. **Fic**

Into the volcano. Wood, D. **741.5**

Into the Wild. Durst, S. B. **Fic**

Into the wild. Hunter, E. **Fic**

Into the woods. Gardner, L. **Fic**

Into the world of the dead. Boughn, M. **398.2**

Intolerance See Toleration

Intoxicants See Narcotics; Stimulants

Introducing issues with opposing viewpoints [series]

Bullying **302.3**

Civil liberties **342**

Cloning **176**

Death and dying **179.7**

Endangered species **333.95**

Gangs **364.1**

Smoking **362.29**

Inuit

Fiction

Bastedo, J. On thin ice **Fic**

George, J. C. Julie **Fic**

George, J. C. Julie of the wolves **Fic**

Orenstein, D. G. Unseen companion **Fic**

Paulsen, G. Dogsong **Fic**

Folklore

Houston, J. A. James Houston's Treasury of Inuit legends **398.2**

Inupiat

Lourie, P. Arctic thaw **998**

Invalids See Sick

Invasion of privacy See Right of privacy

Invasive microbes. May, S. **579**

Invasive species [series]

May, S. Invasive microbes **579**

Invective
Gordon, S. M. Beyond bruises   **362.7**

Inventing the future: a photobiography of Thomas Alva Edison. Delano, M. F.   **92**

The **invention** of Hugo Cabret. Selznick, B.   **Fic**

Inventions
Anderson, M. Amazing Leonardo da Vinci inventions you can build yourself   **92**
Bender, L. Invention   **609**
Horne, R. 101 things you wish you'd invented—and some you wish no one had   **609**
Macaulay, D. The new way things work   **600**
Thimmesh, C. Girls think of everything   **920**
Tucker, T. Brainstorm!   **609**
Woodford, C. Cool Stuff 2.0 and how it works   **600**

Fiction
Potter, E. Slob   **Fic**
Williams, A. The deep freeze of Bartholomew Tullock   **Fic**

History
Bridgman, R. F. 1,000 inventions & discoveries   **609**
Cole, D. J. Encyclopedia of modern everyday inventions   **609**
Historical inventions on file   **609**
Inventors and inventions   **609**
Jedicke, P. Great inventions of the 20th century   **609**
Landau, E. The history of everyday life   **609**
MacLeod, J. How nearly everything was invented . . . by the Brainwaves   **609**
Robinson, J. Inventions   **609**
Rossi, A. Bright ideas   **609**
Sandler, M. W. Inventors   **609**
Tomecek, S. What a great idea!   **609**

Inventions that shaped the world [series]
Heinrichs, A. The printing press   **686.2**
Kummer, P. K. The calendar   **529**
Kummer, P. K. Currency   **332.4**
Kummer, P. K. The telephone   **621.385**
Mara, W. The clock   **681.1**
Matthews, J. R. The light bulb   **621.32**
Petersen, C. The microscope   **502.8**
Robinson Masters, N. The cotton gin   **677**
Trueit, T. S. Gunpowder   **623.4**

Inventors
Baxter, R. Illuminated progress   **92**
Carlson, L. M. Thomas Edison for kids   **92**
Carson, M. K. Alexander Graham Bell   **92**
Delano, M. F. Inventing the future: a photobiography of Thomas Alva Edison   **92**
Herweck, D. Robert Fulton   **92**
Inventors and inventions   **609**
Kroll, S. Robert Fulton   **92**
Matthews, T. L. Always inventing: a photobiography of Alexander Graham Bell   **92**
Pierce, M. A. Robert Fulton and the development of the steamboat   **92**
Sandler, M. W. Inventors   **609**
Tagliaferro, L. Thomas Edison   **92**
Tucker, T. Brainstorm!   **609**

Woodside, M. Thomas A. Edison   **92**
Zannos, S. Guglielmo Marconi and the story of radio waves   **92**

Fiction
Carlson, D. Attack of the Turtle   **Fic**
Colfer, E. Airman   **Fic**
Weyn, S. Distant waves   **Fic**

Inventors, African American See African American inventors

Inventors and Creators [series]
Haugen, H. M. Daniel Handler   **92**
Miller, R. H. Stan Lee   **92**

Inventors and inventions   **609**

Inventors who changed the world [series]
Scherer, G. J. Robert Oppenheimer   **92**

Invertebrates
Meinkoth, N. A. The Audubon Society field guide to North American seashore creatures   **592**

Investigating climate change. Johnson, R. L.   **551.6**

Investments
McGowan, E. N. Stock market smart   **332.6**

Invincible Louisa [May Alcott] Meigs, C. L.   **92**

Invisible allies. Farrell, J.   **579**

Invisible enemies. Farrell, J.   **614.4**

Invisible force. Phelan, G.   **531**

Invisible invaders. Goldsmith, C.   **614.4**

The **Invisible** ladder   **811.008**

The **invisible** man. Geary, R.   **741.5**

The **invisible** rules of the Zoë Lama. Cohen, T.   **Fic**

Invitations to the world. Peck, R.   **808.06**

Iowa
Fiction
Bauer, J. Squashed   **Fic**
Moranville, S. B. The Snows   **Fic**

Iqbal. D'Adamo, F.   **Fic**

Iran
Social life and customs
Batmanglij, N. Happy Nowruz   **641.5**

Iran
Gray, L. Iran   **955**
Rajendra, V. Iran   **955**
Ramen, F. A historical atlas of Iran   **955**
Civilization
Barter, J. The ancient Persians   **935**
Fiction
Fletcher, S. Alphabet of dreams   **Fic**
Mead, A. Dawn and dusk   **Fic**
Napoli, D. J. Beast   **Fic**
History—1979-
See also Iran-Iraq War, 1980-1988
January, B. The Iranian Revolution   **955**

Iran-Iraq War, 1980-1988
Fiction
Mead, A. Dawn and dusk   **Fic**

The **Iranian** Revolution. January, B.   **955**

Iraq
Augustin, B. Iraq   **956.7**
Hassig, S. M. Iraq   **956.7**

Jemison, Mae C.—*Continued*
See/See also pages in the following book(s):
Hansen, J. Women of hope   **920**

Jenkins, A. M. (Amanda McRaney)
Night road   **Fic**
Repossessed   **Fic**

Jenkins, Amanda McRaney See Jenkins, A. M.
(Amanda McRaney)

Jenkins, Christine, 1949-
(jt. auth) Cart, M. The heart has its reasons
    813.009

Jenkins, Leonard
(il) Thomas, J. C. The skull talks back and other
haunting tales   **398.2**

Jenkins, Martin, 1959-
Don Quixote   **Fic**

Jenner, Edward, 1749-1823
About
Marrin, A. Dr. Jenner and the speckled monster
    614.5
Rodriguez, A. M. Edward Jenner   **92**

Jennings, Coleman A., 1933-
(ed) Theatre for young audiences. See Theatre
for young audiences   **812.008**

Jennings, Patrick, 1962-
Barb and Dingbat's crybaby hotline   **Fic**

Jennings, Richard W., 1945-
Orwell's luck   **Fic**
Stink City   **Fic**

Jennings, Thomas L., 1791-1859
See/See also pages in the following book(s):
Haskins, J. African American entrepreneurs
    920

Jensen, Dan
(jt. auth) Huddleston, C. Decoy   **741.5**

Jerabek, Ann
(jt. auth) Hall-Ellis, S. D. Grants for school libraries   **025.1**

Jeremy Fink and the meaning of life. Mass, W.
    Fic

Jermyn, Leslie
Guyana   **988.1**
Paraguay   **989.2**
Uruguay   **989.5**
(jt. auth) Cheong-Lum, R. N. Haiti   **972.94**
(jt. auth) DuBois, J. Colombia   **986.1**
(jt. auth) Foley, E. Dominican Republic
    972.93
(jt. auth) Foley, E. Ecuador   **986.6**
(jt. auth) Gan, D. Sweden   **948.5**
(jt. auth) Gofen, E. Argentina   **982**
(jt. auth) Reilly, M.-J. Mexico   **972**
(jt. auth) Sheehan, S. Cuba   **972.91**
(jt. auth) South, C. Syria   **956.91**
(jt. auth) Srinivasan, R. India   **954**
(jt. auth) Winter, J. K. Italy   **945**

Jerome, Kate Boehm
Atomic universe   **539.7**

Jerry Yang and David Filo. Sherman, J.   **92**

Jerusalem
Fiction
Nye, N. S. Habibi   **Fic**
The **Jerusalem** Bible. See Bible. The new Jerusa-
lem Bible   **220.5**

Jessell, Tim
(il) Haven, P. Two hot dogs with everything
    Fic

Jessica's guide to dating on the dark side.
Fantaskey, B.   **Fic**

Jesters See Fools and jesters

Jesus Christ
About
Lottridge, C. B. Stories from the life of Jesus
    232.9
Nativity
Fiction
Fletcher, S. Alphabet of dreams   **Fic**
Poetry
Grimes, N. At Jerusalem's gate   **811**

Jeter, Derek, 1974-
About
Mills, C. Derek Jeter   **92**
Robinson, T. Derek Jeter   **92**

The **jeweler's** art. Macfarlane, K.   **739.27**

Jewelry
Haab, S. Dangles and bangles   **745.5**
Macfarlane, K. The jeweler's art   **739.27**
Newcomb, R. The Girls' World book of jewel-
ry: 50 cool designs to make   **745.594**

Jewels See Precious stones

Jewish-Arab relations
See also Israel-Arab conflicts
Fiction
Nye, N. S. Habibi   **Fic**

Jewish cooking
Bloomfield, J. Jewish holidays cookbook
    641.5

Jewish faith in America. Buxbaum, S. M.   **296**

Jewish holiday origami. Stern, J.   **736**

Jewish holidays
See also Hanukkah; Passover
Berger, G. Celebrate!   **296.4**
Bloomfield, J. Jewish holidays cookbook
    641.5
Stern, J. Jewish holiday origami   **736**
Fiction
Schwartz, H. The day the Rabbi disappeared:
Jewish holiday tales of magic   **398.2**

Jewish holidays cookbook. Bloomfield, J.
    641.5

Jewish holocaust (1933-1945) *See* Holocaust,
1933-1945

Jewish legends
Chaikin, M. Angels sweep the desert floor
    296.1
Pinsker, M. In the days of sand and stars
    296.1

Jewish refugees
Fox, A. L. Ten thousand children   **940.53**
Gottfried, T. Displaced persons   **940.53**
Whiteman, D. B. Lonek's journey   **940.53**
Fiction
Friedman, D. D. Escaping into the night   **Fic**
The **Jewish** victims of the Holocaust. Altman, L.
J.   **940.53**

Jews
See also Israelis

Judaism—*Continued*
See/See also pages in the following book(s):
Osborne, M. P. One world, many religions
200

Customs and practices
See also Bar mitzvah; Bat mitzvah
Dictionaries
The Oxford dictionary of the Jewish religion
296.03

Jude. Morgenroth, K. **Fic**

Judges
Crowe, C. Thurgood Marshall **92**
Jarrow, G. Robert H. Jackson **92**

Judo
Inman, R. The judo handbook **796.8**
The **judo** handbook. Inman, R. **796.8**

Judson, Karen, 1941-
Animal testing **179**
Chemical and biological warfare **358**
Resolving conflicts **303.6**

Juettner, Bonnie, 1968-
Energy **333.79**

Juggling with mandarins. See Jones, V. M. Out of reach **Fic**

Jukes, Mavis
Growing up: it's a girl thing **612.6**
The guy book **305.23**
It's a girl thing **305.23**
Smoke **Fic**
(jt. auth) Cheung, L. W. Y. Be healthy! it's a girl thing **613**

Julie. George, J. C. **Fic**

Julie of the wolves. George, J. C. **Fic**

The **Juliet** club. Harper, S. **Fic**

Juliet Dove, Queen of Love. Coville, B. **Fic**

Julius, Edward H., 1952-
Arithmetricks **513**

Julius Caesar. Appignanesi, R.
822.3
[essays about] **92**

Julius Caesar and the Roman Republic. Greenblatt, M. **937**

The **jumbo** book of art. Luxbacher, I. **702.8**
The **jumbo** vegetarian cookbook. Gillies, J.
641.5

Jump rope See Rope skipping
Jump rope rhymes
Chambers, V. Double dutch **796.2**
Jump ship to freedom. Collier, J. L. **Fic**
Jump the cracks. DeKeyser, S. **Fic**
Jumped. Williams-Garcia, R. **Fic**
Jumping the scratch. Weeks, S. **Fic**

Juneteenth
Fiction
Rinaldi, A. Come Juneteenth **Fic**

Jung, Reinhardt
Dreaming in black and white **Fic**
Jungle. Greenaway, T. **577.3**
The **jungle** book: the Mowgli stories. Kipling, R.
S C

Junior authors & illustrators series
Eighth book of junior authors and illustrators
920.003
Ninth book of junior authors and illustrators
920.003
Tenth book of junior authors and illustrators
920.003

Junior drug awareness [series]
Breguet, A. Vicodin, OxyContin, and other pain relievers **362.29**
Ingram, S. Marijuana **362.29**
Koellhoffer, T. Ecstasy and other club drugs
362.29
Koellhoffer, T. Inhalants and solvents
362.29
Kreske, D. P. How to say no to drugs
362.29
Price, S. Nicotine **616.86**
Warburton, L. Amphetamines and other stimulants **362.29**
West, K. Cocaine and crack **362.29**

Junior high school libraries *See* High school libraries

Junior high schools
See also Middle schools
Junior state maps on file **973**
Junior timelines on file. Tomaselli-Moschovitis, V. **902**
Junior Worldmark encyclopedia of the Canadian provinces **971**
Junior Worldmark encyclopedia of the Mexican states **972**
Junior Worldmark encyclopedia of the nations
910.3
Junior Worldmark encyclopedia of the states
973.03
Junior Worldmark encyclopedia of world holidays
394.26

Jupiter (Planet)
Miller, R. Jupiter **523.4**
Schwabacher, M. Jupiter **523.4**
Simon, S. Destination: Jupiter **523.4**

Jurassic Park. Crichton, M. **Fic**
Jurassic poop. Berkowitz, J. **567.9**

Jurmain, Suzanne
The forbidden schoolhouse [biography of Prudence Crandall] **92**

Jury
Aaseng, N. You are the juror **345**
Just add water **546**
Just another day in my insanely real life. Dee, B.
Fic
Just Ella. Haddix, M. P. **Fic**
Just for you to know. Harness, C. **Fic**
Just like that. Qualey, M. **Fic**
Just the facts [series]
Burnfield, A. Multiple sclerosis **616.8**
Durham, M. Painkillers and tranquilizers
615
Gillie, O. Cancer **616.99**
Mason, P. Body piercing and tattooing **391**
Parker, S. Allergies **616.97**

Just the facts—*Continued*
Pigache, P. ADHD   **616.85**
Routh, K. Down syndrome   **616.85**
Routh, K. Epilepsy
Routh, K. Meningitis   **616.8**
Justice. McKissack, P. C.
    In McKissack, P. C. The dark-thirty; Southern tales of the supernatural p22-34   **S C**
Justice League (Fictional characters)
Beechen, A. Justice League Unlimited: the ties that bind   **741.5**
Justice league unlimited [series]
Beechen, A. Justice League Unlimited: the ties that bind   **741.5**
Justice League Unlimited: the ties that bind. Beechen, A.   **741.5**
Juvenile courts
Cohen, L. The Gault case and young people's rights   **345**
Jacobs, T. A. They broke the law, you be the judge   **345**
Juvenile delinquency
    See also Gangs
Hile, K. S. The trial of juveniles as adults   **345**
Kuklin, S. No choirboy   **364.66**
Youth violence   **364.36**
See/See also pages in the following book(s):
Teens at risk: opposing viewpoints   **362.7**
Fiction
Griffin, P. Ten Mile River   **Fic**
Hinton, S. E. The outsiders   **Fic**
Hinton, S. E. Rumble fish   **Fic**
Hinton, S. E. That was then, this is now   **Fic**
Korman, G. The Juvie three   **Fic**
Myers, W. D. Scorpions   **Fic**
Sachar, L. Holes   **Fic**
Sachar, L. Small steps   **Fic**
Strasser, T. Boot camp   **Fic**
Trueman, T. Inside out   **Fic**
Juvenile diabetes. Haney, J.   **616.4**
Juvenile prostitution
Dean, R. Teen prostitution   **362.7**
The **Juvie** three. Korman, G.   **Fic**
Jweid, Rosann, 1933-
Building character through literature   **028.5**
The library-classroom partnership   **027.8**

K

Kaaberbol, Lene
The Shamer's daughter   **Fic**
Kacer, Kathy, 1954-
Hiding Edith   **940.53**
The underground reporters   **940.53**
Kadohata, Cynthia
Cracker!   **Fic**
Kira-Kira   **Fic**
Outside beauty   **Fic**
Weedflower   **Fic**
Kafirs (African people) *See* Zulu (African people)

Kafka, Tina, 1950-
Cloning   **660.6**
Gay rights   **306.76**
Kagda, Falaq
Algeria   **965**
Hong Kong   **951.25**
Kagda, Sakina, 1939-
Lithuania   **947.93**
Norway   **948.1**
Kahlo, Frida, 1907-1954
About
Hillstrom, L. Frida Kahlo   **92**
Laidlaw, J. A. Frida Kahlo   **92**
Sabbeth, C. Frida Kahlo and Diego Rivera: their lives and ideas   **92**
Wooten, S. M. Frida Kahlo   **92**
Poetry
Bernier-Grand, C. T. Frida   **811**
Kai's journey to Gold Mountain. Currier, K. S.   **Fic**
Kajder, Sara B., 1975-
Bringing the outside in   **028.5**
Kaleidoscope [series]
Lockman, D. Computer animation   **778.5**
Lockman, D. Robots   **629.8**
Kaleidoscope eyes. Bryant, J.   **Fic**
Kallen, Stuart A., 1955-
The aftermath of the Sandinista Revolution   **972.85**
Claude Monet   **92**
Egypt   **962**
The history of classical music   **781.6**
The history of country music   **781.642**
The history of jazz   **781.65**
The history of rock and roll   **781.66**
The instruments of music   **784.19**
Marcus Garvey and the Back to Africa Movement   **92**
A medieval merchant   **940.1**
National security   **355**
Photography   **770**
Primary sources [American war library, The Cold War]   **909.82**
Rigoberta Menchu, Indian rights activist   **92**
Shamans   **201**
Shinto   **299.5**
Women of the civil rights movement   **323.1**
Kaminker, Laura
Everything you need to know about being adopted   **362.7**
Everything you need to know about dealing with sexual assault   **364.1**
Kaminsky, Marty
Uncommon champions   **920**
Kampuchea *See* Cambodia
Kampung boy. Lat   **741.5**
Kan, Katharine
Sizzling summer reading programs for young adults   **027.62**
Kane, Joseph Nathan, 1899-2002
Famous first facts   **031.02**
(ed) Facts about the presidents. See Facts about the presidents   **920**

Keates, Colin
(il) Whalley, P. E. S. Butterfly & moth
595.7

Keckley, Elizabeth, ca. 1818-1907
About
Jones, L. Mrs. Lincoln's dressmaker: the unlikely friendship of Elizabeth Keckley and Mary Todd Lincoln **92**
See/See also pages in the following book(s):
Haskins, J. African American entrepreneurs
920

Fiction
Rinaldi, A. An unlikely friendship **Fic**

Keding, Dan
(ed) English folktales. See English folktales
398.2

Keedle, Jayne
(jt. auth) Ryback, C. Hurricanes **551.55**

Keehn, Sally M., 1947-
Gnat Stokes and the Foggy Bottom Swamp Queen **Fic**
Magpie Gabbard and the quest for the buried moon **Fic**

Keeley, Jennifer, 1974-
Espionage **327.12**

Keen, Dan
(jt. auth) Bonnet, R. L. 46 science fair projects for the evil genius **507.8**

Keenan, Sheila, 1953-
Animals in the house **636**

Keene, Michael
Judaism **296**

Keeper. Peet, M. **Fic**

The **keeper** of the doves. Byars, B. C. **Fic**

Keeper of the Grail. Spradlin, M. P. **Fic**

Keeping a journal. Trueit, T. S. **808**

Keeping corner. Sheth, K. **Fic**

Keeping score. Park, L. S. **Fic**

Keeping the night watch. Smith, H. A. **Fic**

Keeping unusual pets [series]
McNicholas, J. Rats **636.9**

Keesha's house. Frost, H. **Fic**

Kehret, Peg, 1936-
Abduction! **Fic**
Don't tell anyone **Fic**
The ghost's grave **Fic**
Trapped! **Fic**

Keintpoos *See* Kintpuash, Modoc Chief, 1837?-1873

Keith, Eros, 1942-
(il) Hamilton, V. The house of Dies Drear
Fic

Keith, Harold, 1903-1998
Rifles for Watie **Fic**

Keller, Bill
Tree shaker **92**

Keller, Emily
Frances Perkins **92**

Keller, Helen, 1880-1968
The story of my life **92**

About
Delano, M. F. Helen's eyes: a photobiography of Annie Sullivan, Helen Keller's teacher
92
Garrett, L. Helen Keller **92**
Lawlor, L. Helen Keller: rebellious spirit **92**
MacLeod, E. Helen Keller **92**
Sullivan, G. Helen Keller **92**
Fiction
Miller, S. Miss Spitfire **Fic**

Keller, Laurie
(il) Wulffson, D. L. Toys! **688.7**

Kelley, Gary
(jt. auth) Lewis, J. P. Black cat bone **811**

Kelley, K. C., 1960-
Golf **796.352**
Hottest NASCAR machines **796.72**
Soccer **796.334**

Kellogg, Steven, 1941-
(il) Twain, M. The adventures of Huckleberry Finn **Fic**

Kelly, Erica
Evolving planet **551**

Kelly, Evelyn B.
Alzheimer's disease **616.8**

Kelly, Jacqueline
The evolution of Calpurnia Tate **Fic**

Kelly, Tom, 1961-
Finn's going **Fic**

Kelly-Gangi, Carol
Miranda v. Arizona and the rights of the accused **345**

Kelsey, Elin
Canadian dinosaurs **567.9**
Strange new species **578**

Kemer, Eric
(jt. auth) Gardner, R. Science projects about temperature and heat **536**

Kendall, Gideon, 1966-
(il) Hulme, J. The glitch in sleep **Fic**

Kennebec Indians *See* Abnaki Indians

Kennedy, Cam, 1944-
(il) Grant, A. Robert Louis Stevenson's Kidnapped **741.5**
(il) Grant, A. Robert Louis Stevenson's Strange case of Dr. Jekyll and Mr. Hyde **741.5**

Kennedy, Edward Moore, 1932-
About
Sapet, K. Ted Kennedy **92**

Kennedy, James, 1973-
The Order of Odd-Fish **Fic**

Kennedy, John E., 1967-
Puppet mania **791.5**
Puppet planet **791.5**

Kennedy, John F. (John Fitzgerald), 1917-1963
Profiles in courage **920**
About
Burgan, M. John F. Kennedy **92**
Cooper, I. Jack: the early years of John F. Kennedy **92**
Heiligman, D. High hopes [biography of John F. Kennedy] **92**
Sommer, S. John F. Kennedy **92**

Kennedy, John F. (John Fitzgerald), 1917-1963—About—*Continued*
See/See also pages in the following book(s):
St. George, J. In the line of fire   364.1
Uschan, M. V. Political leaders   920
Assassination
Hampton, W. Kennedy assassinated!   973.922
Kennedy, Kerry
Speak truth to power   920
Kennedy, Michael, 1926-
The concise Oxford dictionary of music   780.3
Kennedy, Mike, 1965-
(jt. auth) Stewart, M. Swish   796.323
Kennedy, Robert F.
Robert Smalls   92
Kennedy, Robert F., 1925-1968
About
Aronson, M. Robert F. Kennedy   92
Kennedy, Ted *See* Kennedy, Edward Moore, 1932-
Kennedy assassinated!. Hampton, W.   973.922
Kennedy Cuomo, Kerry *See* Kennedy, Kerry
Kennett, David, 1959-
(il) Blacklock, D. The Roman Army   937
Kenney, Karen Latchana, 1974-
Cool hip-hop music   781.66
Cool rock music   781.66
Illegal immigration   325.73
Kenny, Kevin *See* Krull, Kathleen, 1952-
Kenschaft, Lori
Lydia Maria Child   92
Kensuke's kingdom. Morpurgo, M.   Fic
Kent, Deborah, 1948-
Animal helpers for the disabled   636.088
Athletes with disabilities   371.9
Snake pits, talking cures, & magic bullets   616.89
The tragic history of the Japanese-American internment camps   940.53
Kent, Jacqueline, 1947-
Business builders in fashion   920
Kent, Rose
Kimchi & calamari   Fic
Kent, Zachary
Andrew Carnegie   92
Julius Caesar   92
Kentley, Eric
Boat   387.2
Kentucky
Fiction
Byars, B. C. The keeper of the doves   Fic
Durrant, L. Imperfections   Fic
Ferris, J. Underground   Fic
Hart, A. Gabriel's horses   Fic
Keehn, S. M. Magpie Gabbard and the quest for the buried moon   Fic
Naylor, P. R. Faith, hope, and Ivy June   Fic
Wedekind, A. A horse of her own   Fic
Wyatt, L. J. Poor is just a starting place   Fic
Kenya
Bowden, R. Kenya   967.62

Broberg, C. Kenya in pictures   967.62
Lekuton, J. Facing the lion   967.62
Pateman, R. Kenya   967.62
Fiction
Mwangi, M. The Mzungu boy   Fic
Naidoo, B. Burn my heart   Fic
Kenya in pictures. Broberg, C.   967.62
Kenyon, Karen, 1938-
The Brontë family   920
Kenyon, Linda, 1956-
Rainforest bird rescue   598
Keoke, Emory Dean
American Indian contributions to the world   970.004
Kephart, Beth
House of Dance   Fic
Undercover   Fic
Kepler, Johannes, 1571-1630
About
Boerst, W. J. Johannes Kepler   92
Gow, M. Johannes Kepler   92
Hasan, H. Kepler and the laws of planetary motion   92
Kepler and the laws of planetary motion. Hasan, H.   92
Keppler, Johannes *See* Kepler, Johannes, 1571-1630
Kerley, Barbara
Greetings from planet Earth   Fic
Walt Whitman   92
Kerr, Jim
Food   178
Kerr, M. E., 1927-
Gentlehands   Fic
Slap your sides   Fic
Snakes don't miss their mothers   Fic
Someone like summer   Fic
Kerr, Philip
One small step   Fic
Kerrigan, Michael
The history of punishment   364.6
Kerrod, Robin, 1938-
Space probes   629.43
Space shuttles   629.44
Space stations   629.44
The star guide   523.8
Kessel, William B.
(ed) Encyclopedia of Native American wars and warfare. See Encyclopedia of Native American wars and warfare   970.004
Kessler, James H.
Distinguished African American scientists of the 20th century. See Distinguished African American scientists of the 20th century   920
Kett, Joseph F.
(jt. auth) Hirsch, E. D. The new dictionary of cultural literacy   031
Keturah and Lord Death. Leavitt, M.   Fic
Kevorkian, Meline
101 facts about bullying   302.3
Key, Watt, 1970-
Alabama moon   Fic

The **key** to Rondo. Rodda, E.   **Fic**

Keynes, John Maynard, 1883-1946
See/See also pages in the following book(s):
Bussing-Burks, M. Influential economists
    920

The **keys** to American history. Panchyk, R.
    973

Keys to the kingdom [series]
Nix, G. Mister Monday   **Fic**

Khan, Aisha Karen, 1967-
A historical atlas of Kyrgyzstan   **958.4**

Khan, Rukhsana, 1962-
Wanting Mor   **Fic**

Khanduri, Kamini
Japanese art & culture   **709.52**

Khufu *See* Cheops, King of Egypt, fl. 2900-2877 B.C.

Kibuishi, Kazu
Amulet book one: the stonekeeper   **741.5**
(ed) Flight explorer. See Flight explorer
    741.5

A **kick** in the head   **811.008**

The **kickboxing** handbook. Ritschel, J.   **796.8**

Kid, Thomas *See* Kyd, Thomas, 1558-1594

Kid Antrim *See* Billy, the Kid

Kid Beowulf and the blood-bound oath. Fajardo, A. E.   **741.5**

Kidd, J. S. (Jerry S.)
New genetics   **576.5**
Nuclear power   **621.48**
Potent natural medicines   **615**

Kidd, Jerry S. *See* Kidd, J. S. (Jerry S.)

Kidd, Renee A.
(jt. auth) Kidd, J. S. New genetics   **576.5**
(jt. auth) Kidd, J. S. Nuclear power   **621.48**
(jt. auth) Kidd, J. S. Potent natural medicines
    615

Kidd, Ronald, 1948-
Monkey town   **Fic**
On Beale Street   **Fic**

Kidnapped. Macdonald, F.   **741.5**

Kidnapped. Stevenson, R. L.   **Fic**

The **kidnappers**. Roberts, W. D.   **Fic**

Kidnapping
Wiloch, T. Everything you need to know about protecting yourself and others from abduction
    613.6

Fiction
Bloor, E. Taken   **Fic**
Cooney, C. B. The face on the milk carton
    Fic
Cooney, C. B. Hit the road   **Fic**
Duncan, L. Killing Mr. Griffin   **Fic**
Giff, P. R. Eleven   **Fic**
Greene, M. Chasing the jaguar   **Fic**
Hautman, P. Snatched   **Fic**
Jean, M. Puddlejumpers   **Fic**
Kehret, P. Abduction!   **Fic**
Lubar, D. True talents   **Fic**
Mazer, N. F. The missing girl   **Fic**
Mills, S. The viper within   **Fic**
Roberts, W. D. The kidnappers   **Fic**
Simmons, M. Alien feast   **Fic**

Stevenson, R. L. Kidnapped   **Fic**
Yohalem, E. Escape under the forever sky
    Fic

Kids at work. Freedman, R.   **331.3**

The **kids'** book club book. Gelman, J.   **028.5**

Kids can do it [series]
Trottier, M. Native crafts   **745.5**

Kids can knit. Clewer, C.   **746.43**

The **Kids** Can Press jumbo book of gardening. Morris, K.   **635**

Kids' crafts [series]
Davis, J. Crochet   **746.43**

Kids crochet. Ronci, K.   **746.43**

A **kid's** guide to America's Bill of Rights. Krull, K.   **342**

The **kids'** guide to building cool stuff. Bell-Rehwoldt, S.   **745.5**

The **kids'** guide to classic games. Bell-Rehwoldt, S.   **790.1**

Kid's guide to creating Web pages for home and school. See Selfridge, B. A teen's guide to creating Web pages and blogs   **006.7**

The **kids'** guide to digital photography. Bidner, J.
    775

A **kid's** guide to giving. Zeiler, F.   **361.2**

A **kid's** guide to Latino history. Petrillo, V.
    305.8

The **kids'** guide to paper airplanes. Harbo, C. L.
    745.592

The **kids'** guide to working out conflicts. Drew, N.
    303.6

Kids' guides [series]
Bell-Rehwoldt, S. The kids' guide to building cool stuff   **745.5**
Bell-Rehwoldt, S. The kids' guide to classic games   **790.1**
Harbo, C. L. The kids' guide to paper airplanes
    745.592

Kids knit!. Bradberry, S.   **746.43**

Kids make history. Buckley, S.   **973**

Kids on strike!. Bartoletti, S. C.   **331.8**

Kids still having kids. Bode, J.   **362.7**

Kids weaving. Swett, S.   **746.41**

Kids who rule. Cotter, C.   **920**

Kieler, Jørgen, 1919-
See/See also pages in the following book(s):
Lyman, D. Holocaust rescuers   **920**

Kiesler, Kate, 1971-
(il) Freedman, R. Out of darkness: the story of Louis Braille   **92**

Kiki Strike: inside the shadow city. Miller, K.
    Fic

Kiland, Taylor Baldwin, 1966-
The U.S. Navy and military careers   **359**

Killer bees. Landau, E.   **595.7**

Killer rocks from outer space. Koppes, S. N.
    523.5

The **killer's** cousin. Werlin, N.   **Fic**

Killing germs, saving lives. Phelan, G.   **615**

Killing Mr. Griffin. Duncan, L.   **Fic**

The **killing** sea. Lewis, R.   **Fic**

Kilworth, Garry
  Attica   **Fic**

Kim, Chong Il *See* Kim, Jong Il

Kim, Derek Kirk, 1974-
  Good as Lily   **741.5**

Kim, Doug
  See/See also pages in the following book(s):
  Major, J. S. Caravan to America   **920**

Kim, Henny H., 1968-
  Child abuse   **362.7**
  (ed) Youth violence. See Youth violence
      364.36

Kim, Jong Il
      About
  Behnke, A. Kim Jong Il's North Korea   **92**

Kim Jong Il *See* Kim, Jong Il

Kim Jong Il's North Korea. Behnke, A.   **92**

Kimball, Chad T.
  (ed) Child and youth security sourcebook. See Child and youth security sourcebook
      362.7

Kimball, Cheryl
  Horse show handbook for kids   **798.2**

Kimber, Murray
  (il) Hovey, K. Ancient voices   **811**
  (il) Noyes, A. The highwayman   **821**

Kimchi & calamari. Kent, R.   **Fic**

Kimmel, Elizabeth Cody
  Boy on the lion throne [biography of the Dalai Lama]   **92**
  Dinosaur bone war   **560**
  Ice story   **998**
  Ladies first   **920**
  Lily B. on the brink of cool   **Fic**
  The look-it-up book of explorers   **920**
  Spin the bottle   **Fic**

Kimmel, Eric A.
  The jar of fools: eight Hanukkah stories from Chelm   **S C**
  Wonders and miracles   **296.4**

Kincher, Jonni, 1949-
  Psychology for kids vol. 1: 40 fun tests that help you learn about yourself   **150**
  Psychology for kids vol. 2: 40 fun experiments that help you learn about others   **150**

The **kind** of friends we used to be. Dowell, F. O.   **Fic**

Kindl, Patrice, 1951-
  Lost in the labyrinth   **Fic**
  Owl in love   **Fic**

Kinetic and potential energy. Viegas, J.   **531**

Kinetics *See* Dynamics

King, Andy
  Play-by-play mountain biking   **796.6**

King, Coretta Scott, 1927-2006
  (jt. auth) King, M. L., Jr. The words of Martin Luther King, Jr.   **323.1**

King, Daniel, 1963-
  Chess   **794.1**

King, Dave
  (il) Redmond, I. Elephant   **599.67**

  (il) The Snake book. See The Snake book
      597.96
  (il) Whalley, P. E. S. Butterfly & moth
      595.7

King, David C., 1933-
  Azerbaijan   **947.5**
  The Battle of Gettysburg   **973.7**
  Children's encyclopedia of American history
      973.03
  First people   **970.004**
  Kyrgyzstan   **958.4**
  Monaco   **944**
  Mozambique   **967.9**
  Rwanda   **967.571**
  Serbia and Montenegro   **949.7**
  The United Arab Emirates   **953**

King, Martin Luther, Jr., 1929-1968
  The words of Martin Luther King, Jr.   **323.1**
      About
  Boerst, W. J. Marching in Birmingham
      323.1
  Bolden, T. M.L.K. [biography of Martin Luther King]   **92**
  Jeffrey, L. S. Celebrate Martin Luther King, Jr., Day   **394.26**
  See/See also pages in the following book(s):
  Archer, J. They had a dream   **920**
  Freedman, R. Freedom walkers   **323.1**

King, Ron
  The quantum July   **Fic**

King, Stephen, 1947-
      About
  Baughan, M. G. Stephen King   **92**
  Whitelaw, N. Dark dreams [biography of Stephen King]   **92**
  Wukovits, J. F. Stephen King   **92**

King, Martin Luther, holiday *See* Martin Luther King Day

King Arthur. Nardo, D.   **942.01**

King Lear. Hinds, G.   **822.3**

The **king** of Mulberry Street. Napoli, D. J.
      Fic

King of the Lost and Found. Lekich, J.   **Fic**

King of the mild frontier: an ill-advised autobiography. Crutcher, C.   **92**

King Philip's War, 1675-1676
  Mandell, D. R. King Philip's war   **973.2**

The **king** with horse's ears and other Irish folktales. Burns, B.   **398.2**

The **Kingdom** of Strange. Klinger, S.   **Fic**

Kingdoms of life [series]
  Silverstein, A. Vertebrates   **596**

The **Kingfisher** atlas of exploration & empires. Adams, S.   **911**

The **Kingfisher** atlas of the medieval world. Adams, S.   **909.07**

The **Kingfisher** atlas of the modern world. Adams, S.   **909.8**

The **Kingfisher** book of funny poems   **821.008**

Kingfisher epics [series]
  Lister, R. The odyssey   **883**

The **Kingfisher** geography encyclopedia. Gifford, C.   **910.3**

Knitting—*Continued*
Turner, S. Find your style and knit it too
746.43

Knockout!: a photobiography of boxer Joe Louis.
Sullivan, G. **92**

Knop, Kathi
(jt. auth) Anderson, C. Write grants, get money
025.1

Knots in my yo-yo string. Spinelli, J. **92**

Knowles, Elizabeth, 1946-
Boys and literacy **028.5**
Reading rules! **028.5**
Talk about books! **372.4**

Knowlton, MaryLee, 1946-
Albania **949.65**
Macedonia **949.7**
Turkmenistan **958.5**
Uzbekistan **958.7**

Knox, Robert, 1791-1862
Fiction
Morgan, N. Fleshmarket **Fic**

Knucklehead [biography of Jon Scieszka]
Scieszka, J. **92**

Knudsen, Michelle
The dragon of Trelian **Fic**

Kochel, Marcia Agness
(jt. auth) Baxter, K. A. Gotcha! **028.5**
(jt. auth) Baxter, K. A. Gotcha again! **028.5**
(jt. auth) Baxter, K. A. Gotcha for guys!
028.5
(jt. auth) Baxter, K. A. Gotcha good! **028.5**

Koehl, Mimi, 1948-
About
Parks, D. Nature's machines [biography of Mimi
Koehl] **92**

Koellhoffer, Tara
Ecstasy and other club drugs **362.29**
Inhalants and solvents **362.29**
(jt. auth) Sohn, E. The environment **363.7**

Koelling, Holly
Classic connections **027.62**
(ed) Best books for young adults. See Best
books for young adults **028.1**

Koertge, Ronald
Stoner & Spaz **Fic**
Strays **Fic**

Koestler-Grack, Rachel A., 1973-
Michelle Kwan **92**

Kogler, Jennifer Anne
Ruby Tuesday **Fic**

Koh, Angeline, 1982-
(jt. auth) Heale, J. Portugal **946.9**

Koh, Magdalene
(jt. auth) Kagda, F. Hong Kong **951.25**
(jt. auth) Mansfield, S. Laos **959.4**

Kohl, Victoria
(jt. auth) Chaikin, A. Mission control, this is
Apollo **629.45**

Koja, Kathe
Buddha Boy **Fic**
Headlong **Fic**
Kissing the bee **Fic**
Straydog **Fic**

Konigsburg, E. L.
The mysterious edge of the heroic world
Fic
The outcasts of 19 Schuyler Place **Fic**
Silent to the bone **Fic**
The view from Saturday **Fic**

Konomi, Takeshi
The Prince of Tennis, Vol. 1 **741.5**

Koopmans, Andy
Charles Lindbergh **92**
Filmmakers **920**
Rwanda **967.571**

Koppes, Steven N.
Killer rocks from outer space **523.5**

Kops, Deborah
Palenque **972**
Racial profiling **363.2**

Koran
The Koran **297.1**
The meaning of the glorious Koran **297.1**

Korea
See also Korea (North); Korea (South)
DuBois, J. Korea **951.9**
Fiction
Choi, S. N. Year of impossible goodbyes
Fic
Park, L. S. Archer's quest **Fic**
Park, L. S. A single shard **Fic**
Park, L. S. When my name was Keoko **Fic**
Watkins, Y. K. My brother, my sister, and I
Fic
Watkins, Y. K. So far from the bamboo grove
Fic

Korea (Democratic People's Republic) *See* Korea (North)

Korea (North)
Behnke, A. Kim Jong Il's North Korea **92**
Kummer, P. K. North Korea **951.93**

Korea (Republic) *See* Korea (South)

Korea (South)
Jackson, T. South Korea **951.95**

Korean Americans
Choi, A. S. Korean Americans **305.8**
Biography
Tiger, C. Margaret Cho **92**
Fiction
Kent, R. Kimchi & calamari **Fic**
Na, A. The fold **Fic**
Na, A. A step from heaven **Fic**
Na, A. Wait for me **Fic**
Park, L. S. Archer's quest **Fic**
Park, L. S. Project Mulberry **Fic**
Son, J. Finding my hat **Fic**
Williams, L. E. Slant **Fic**
Yoo, P. Good enough **Fic**

Korean language
Dictionaries
Shapiro, N. The Oxford picture dictionary, English-Korean **495.7**

Korean War, 1950-1953
Benson, S. Korean War: almanac and primary
sources **951.9**
Feldman, R. T. The Korean War **951.9**
Grant, R. The Korean War **951.9**

Kwan, Michelle
About
Koestler-Grack, R. A. Michelle Kwan   92
Kwanzaa
Altman, L. J. Celebrate Kwanzaa   394.26
Kwasney, Michelle D., 1960-
Itch   Fic
Kwolek, Stephanie L., 1923-
See/See also pages in the following book(s):
Thimmesh, C. Girls think of everything   920
Kyd, Thomas, 1558-1594
See/See also pages in the following book(s):
Nardo, D. Great Elizabethan playwrights
920
Kyi, Tanya Lloyd, 1973-
The blue jean book   391
Kynaston, Suzanne, 1971-
(jt. auth) Ward, P. Bears of the world
599.78
Kyrgyzstan
Harmon, D. Kyrgyzstan   958.4
Khan, A. K. A historical atlas of Kyrgyzstan
958.4
King, D. C. Kyrgyzstan   958.4
Kyvelos, Peter
See/See also pages in the following book(s):
Major, J. S. Caravan to America   920

L

L is for lollygag   428
La Fevers, R. L.
Theodosia and the Serpents of Chaos   Fic
La Pierre, Yvette
Neandertals   599.93
La Salle, René Robert Cavelier *See* La Salle,
Robert Cavelier, sieur de, 1643-1687
La Salle, Robert Cavelier, sieur de, 1643-1687
About
Faber, H. La Salle   92
Goodman, J. E. Despite all obstacles: La Salle
and the conquest of the Mississippi   92
The **Lab**. Heath, J.   Fic
Labor
See also Agricultural laborers; Migrant la-
bor; Teenagers—Employment; Work; Work-
ing class
Law and legislation
Getzinger, D. The Triangle Shirtwaist Factory
fire   974.7
Labor and laboring classes *See* Working class
Labor disputes
See also Strikes
Labor movement
Streissguth, T. Legendary labor leaders   920
History
Laughlin, R. The Ludlow massacre of 1913-14
331.8
Laughlin, R. The Pullman strike of 1894
331.8
Whitelaw, N. The Homestead Steel Strike of
1892   331.8

Labor policy
See also Vocational education
Labor supply
See also Teenagers—Employment
Ching, J. Outsourcing U.S. jobs   331.1
Labor unions
Miller, C. C. A. A Philip Randolph and the Afri-
can American labor movement   92
Skurzynski, G. Sweat and blood   331.8
Laboratory animal experimentation *See* Animal
experimentation
Labrecque, Ellen
Basketball   796.323
Lace, William W.
Blacks in film   791.43
Christianity   230
The curse of King Tut   932
The Hindenburg disaster of 1937   363.1
The Indian Ocean tsunami of 2004   909.83
The unholy crusade   956.1
Lace and lace making
Fiction
Bradley, K. B. The lacemaker and the princess
Fic
The **lacemaker** and the princess. Bradley, K. B.
Fic
Lachmann, Lyn Miller- *See* Miller-Lachmann,
Lyn, 1956-
Lachtman, Ofelia Dumas
The truth about Las Mariposas   Fic
Lacrosse
Swissler, B. Winning lacrosse for girls
796.34
Ladies first. Kimmel, E. C.   920
The **Lady** of Shalott. Tennyson, A. T., Baron
821
LaFaye, A., 1970-
Stella stands alone   Fic
LaFleur, Suzanne M., 1983-
Love, Aubrey   Fic
Lagarrigue, Jerome
(il) Angelou, M. Maya Angelou   811
Lagasse, Emeril
Emeril's there's a chef in my family!   641.5
Emeril's there's a chef in my world!   641.5
Laidlaw, Jill A.
Frida Kahlo   92
Laidlaw, Rob
Wild animals in captivity   636.088
Laika. Abadzis, N.   741.5
Laird, Elizabeth
A little piece of ground   Fic
Lake, A. J.
The coming of dragons   Fic
Lake, Kate
(il) Matsen, B. Go wild in New York City
974.7
Lake and pond. Sayre, A. P.   577.6
Lake ecology
Josephs, D. Lakes, ponds, and temporary pools
577.6
Sayre, A. P. Lake and pond   577.6

Lasky, Kathryn—*Continued*
Mary, Queen of Scots, queen without a country
    Fic
Memoirs of a bookbat   **Fic**
Monarchs   **595.7**
The most beautiful roof in the world   **577.3**
The night journey   **Fic**

Lassieur, Allison
Albert Einstein   **92**
The ancient Greeks   **938**
The ancient Romans   **937**
Crabs, lobsters, and shrimps   **595.3**

The last apprentice [series]
Delaney, J. Revenge of the witch   **Fic**

Last chance for Paris. McNicoll, S.   **Fic**

The **last** dragon. De Mari, S.   **Fic**

The **last** girls of Pompeii. Lasky, K.   **Fic**

The **last** invisible boy. Kuhlman, E.   **Fic**

The **last** knight. Bell, H.   **Fic**

The **last** mall rat. Esckilsen, E. E.   **Fic**

Last-minute science fair projects. Bardhan-Quallen, S.   **507.8**

The **last** mission. Mazer, H.   **Fic**

Last shot. Feinstein, J.   **Fic**

The **last** synapsid. Mason, T.   **Fic**

Lat
Kampung boy   **741.5**
Town Boy   **741.5**

The **latent** powers of Dylan Fontaine. Lurie, A.
    Fic

Latham, Don, 1959-
David Almond   **823.009**

Latif, Zawiah Abdul
(jt. auth) Gish, S. Ethiopia   **963**
(jt. auth) Hassig, S. M. Somalia   **967.73**
(jt. auth) Heale, J. Madagascar   **969.1**
(jt. auth) Kagda, F. Algeria   **965**
(jt. auth) Kagda, S. Lithuania   **947.93**
(jt. auth) Levy, P. Sudan   **962.4**
(jt. auth) Sheehan, S. Lebanon   **956.92**
(jt. auth) Wilcox, J. Iceland   **949.12**

Latimer, Jonathan P.
Backyard birds   **598**
Birds of prey   **598**
Bizarre birds   **598**
Butterflies   **595.7**
Caterpillars   **595.7**
Shorebirds   **598**
Songbirds   **598**
(ed) Simon & Schuster thesaurus for children.
    See Simon & Schuster thesaurus for children
    423

Latin America
    See also South America
    Bibliography
Schon, I. The best of Latino heritage 1996-2002
    011.6
    Fiction
Delacre, L. Salsa stories   **S C**

Folklore
    See Folklore—Latin America
Latin America and the Caribbean. Solway, A.
    780.9

Latin American art
Makosz, R. Latino arts and their influence on the United States   **700**

Latin American literature
    See also Mexican literature
Latin American music *See* Music—Latin America

Latin Americans
    Social life and customs
Sanna, E. Latino folklore and culture   **398.2**

Latin language
    Dictionaries
Cassell's Latin dictionary   **473**

Latino American history [series]
Doak, R. S. Struggling to become American
    305.8

Latino arts and their influence on the United States. Makosz, R.   **700**

Latino biography library [series]
Cruz, B. César Chávez   **92**
Ford, C. T. Roberto Clemente   **92**
Lee, S. Gloria Estefan   **92**
Litwin, L. B. Diego Rivera   **92**
Main, M. Isabel Allende   **92**
Wooten, S. M. Frida Kahlo   **92**

Latino folklore and culture. Sanna, E.   **398.2**

Latinos (U.S.) *See* Hispanic Americans

Latta, Sara L.
The good, the bad, the slimy   **579**

Latter-day Saints *See* Church of Jesus Christ of Latter-day Saints

Latvia
Barlas, R. Latvia   **947.9**

Laubach, Christyna M.
Raptor! a kid's guide to birds of prey   **598**

Laubach, René
(jt. auth) Laubach, C. M. Raptor! a kid's guide to birds of prey   **598**

Laugh & learn [series]
Fox, J. S. Get organized without losing it
    371.3

The **laugh** stand. Cleary, B. P.   **817**

Laugh till you cry. Nixon, J. L.   **Fic**

Laughing out loud, I fly. Herrera, J. F.   **811**

Laughlin, Rosemary, 1941-
The Ludlow massacre of 1913-14   **331.8**
The Pullman strike of 1894   **331.8**

Lauré, Jason, 1940-
(jt. auth) Blauer, E. Mali   **966.2**
(jt. auth) Blauer, E. Mauritania   **966.1**
(jt. auth) Blauer, E. Morocco   **964**
(jt. auth) Blauer, E. South Africa   **968**

Lauren, Ralph
    See/See also pages in the following book(s):
Kent, J. Business builders in fashion   **920**

Lavender, William, 1921-
Aftershocks   **Fic**

Leap of faith. Bradley, K. B. **Fic**

Lear, Edward, 1812-1888
The owl and the pussycat **821**

Learn some hands-on history [series]
Anderson, M. Amazing Leonardo da Vinci inventions you can build yourself **92**

Learning, Art of *See* Study skills

Learning, Psychology of *See* Psychology of learning

Learning about—the Civil War. Stephens, E. C. **016.973**

Learning and memory. Hudmon, A. **153.1**

Learning and scholarship
See also Education

Learning disabilities
See also Attention deficit disorder
Brinkerhoff, S. Why can't I learn like everyone else? **371.9**
Paquette, P. H. Learning disabilities **371.9**
Fiction
Giff, P. R. Eleven **Fic**
Wolff, V. E. Probably still Nick Swansen **Fic**

Learning resource centers *See* Instructional materials centers

Learning the game. Waltman, K. **Fic**

Learning to fly. Yee, P. **Fic**

Learning to learn. Riedling, A. M. **028.7**

Leaving Cuba. Gay, K. **362.87**

Leaving Fishers. Haddix, M. P. **Fic**

Leaving Glorytown. Calcines, E. F. **92**

Leaving home. See Michael, J. City boy **Fic**

Leaving home: stories **808.8**

Leaving Jetty Road. Burton, R. **Fic**

Leaving Protection. Hobbs, W. **Fic**

Leavitt, Martine, 1953-
Heck, superhero **Fic**
Keturah and Lord Death **Fic**

Lebanese
Fiction
Abdel-Fattah, R. Ten things I hate about me **Fic**

Lebanon
Sheehan, S. Lebanon **956.92**

Lecesne, James
Absolute brightness **Fic**

Lechón, Daniel
(il) Mora, P. The desert is my mother. El desierto es mi madre **811**

LeConte, Joseph, 1823-1901
See/See also pages in the following book(s):
Cloud Tapper, S. Voices from slavery's past **326**

Ledyard, John, 1751-1789
About
Lawlor, L. Magnificent voyage **910.4**

Lee, Carol Ann
Anne Frank and the children of the Holocaust **940.53**
A friend called Anne **940.53**

Lee, Cora
The great number rumble **510**

Lee, Harper, 1926-
About
Bernard, C. Understanding To kill a mockingbird **813.009**
Madden, K. Harper Lee **92**
Shields, C. J. I am Scout: the biography of Harper Lee **92**

Lee, Jeanne M.
I once was a monkey **294.3**

Lee, Kimberly Fekany
Cells **571.6**

Lee, Laura, 1969-
A child's introduction to ballet **792.8**

Lee, Lavina
Handel's world **92**

Lee, Robert E. (Robert Edward), 1807-1870
About
Robertson, J. I., Jr. Robert E. Lee **92**

Lee, Sally, 1943-
Gloria Estefan **92**

Lee, Spike
See/See also pages in the following book(s):
Haskins, J. African American entrepreneurs **920**
Koopmans, A. Filmmakers **920**

Lee, Stan
About
Miller, R. H. Stan Lee **92**

Lee, Tanith
Piratica **Fic**

Lee, Tanja
(ed) Benjamin Franklin. See Benjamin Franklin [essays about] **92**

Lee, Yuan
(il) Mann, E. The Parthenon **726**

Leeds, Constance
The silver cup **Fic**

Leeming, David Adams, 1937-
(ed) The Dictionary of folklore. See The Dictionary of folklore **398**

Leeper, Angela
Poetry in literature for youth **016.8**

Leepike Ridge. Wilson, N. D. **Fic**

Leeuwenhoek, Antoni van, 1632-1723
About
Yount, L. Antoni van Leeuwenhoek **92**

Lefkowitz, Arthur S.
Bushnell's submarine **973.3**

Left- and right-handedness
Fiction
Ritter, J. H. Choosing up sides **Fic**

Left for dead. Nelson, P. **940.54**

Legal aid
Fridell, R. Gideon v. Wainwright **345**
Sherrow, V. Gideon v. Wainwright **345**

Legal profession *See* Lawyers

Legal rights. Johnson, T. **342**

Legalizing marijuana. Ruschmann, P. **345**

The **legend** of Buddy Bush. Moses, S. P. **Fic**

The **legend** of Lao Tzu and the Tao te ching. Demi **299.5**

The **legend** of Pin Oak. McKissack, P. C.
In McKissack, P. C. The dark-thirty; Southern tales of the supernatural p3-16 **S C**

The **Legend** of Sleepy Hollow. Irving, W. **Fic**

The **legend** of Sleepy Hollow. Zornow, J. **741.5**

Legendary labor leaders. Streissguth, T. **920**

Legends
> *See also* Folklore; Mythology
Blackwood, G. L. Legends or lies? **398.2**
Indexes
Index to fairy tales **398.2**

Legends, Jewish *See* Jewish legends

Legends or lies? Blackwood, G. L. **398.2**

Legionnaires' disease
Zonderman, J. Legionnaires' disease **616.2**

LeGuin, Ursula *See* Le Guin, Ursula K., 1929-

Lehman, David, 1948-
(ed) The Oxford book of American poetry. See The Oxford book of American poetry **811.008**

Leidesdorff, William Alexander, 1810-1848
See/See also pages in the following book(s):
Haskins, J. African American entrepreneurs **920**

Lekich, John
King of the Lost and Found **Fic**

Lekuton, Joseph
Facing the lion **967.62**

Lemna, Don, 1936-
When the sergeant came marching home **Fic**

LeMond, Greg, 1961-
See/See also pages in the following book(s):
Kaminsky, M. Uncommon champions **920**

Lena. Woodson, J. **Fic**

Lenape Indians *See* Delaware Indians

Lenburg, Jeff
The Facts On File guide to research **025.5**

Lend me your ears **808.85**

Lending of library materials *See* Library circulation

L'Engle, Madeleine, 1918-2007
A ring of endless light **Fic**
A wrinkle in time **Fic**
About
McClellan, M. Madeleine L'Engle **813.009**

Leningrad (Russia) *See* Saint Petersburg (Russia)

Lenney, Dinah
(jt. auth) Belli, M. L. Acting for young actors **792**

Lennon, Joan, 1953-
Questors **Fic**

Lennon, John, 1940-1980
About
Partridge, E. John Lennon **92**
Rappaport, D. John's secret dreams [biography of John Lennon] **92**

Lent, ReLeah Cossett
(jt. auth) Pipkin, G. At the schoolhouse gate **373.1**

Leon, Juan Ponce de *See* Ponce de Leon, Juan, 1460?-1521

León, Vicki, 1942-
A pod of killer whales **599.5**

Leonard, Buck, 1907-1997
About
Payment, S. Buck Leonard **92**

Leonard, Elmore, 1925-
A coyote's in the house **Fic**

Leonardo, da Vinci, 1452-1519
About
Anderson, M. Amazing Leonardo da Vinci inventions you can build yourself **92**
Krull, K. Leonardo da Vinci **92**
O'Connor, B. Leonardo da Vinci **92**
Phillips, J. Leonardo da Vinci **92**
Fiction
Grey, C. Leonardo's shadow **Fic**
Napoli, D. J. The smile **Fic**
Mona Lisa; criticism
> *In* Napoli, D. J. The smile **Fic**

Leonardo's shadow. Grey, C. **Fic**

Leone, Bruno, 1939-
Origin: the story of Charles Darwin **92**

Leong, Sonia
(il) Appignanesi, R. Romeo and Juliet **822.3**

Leon's story. Tillage, L. **92**

Leopards
Gamble, C. Leopards **599.75**

Leopold, Aldo, 1886-1948
See/See also pages in the following book(s):
Byrnes, P. Environmental pioneers **920**

Leppman, Elizabeth J.
Australia and the Pacific **994**

Leprosy
Lynette, R. Leprosy **616.9**
Fiction
Durango, J. The walls of Cartagena **Fic**
Hostetter, J. Healing water **Fic**

Lerch, Maureen T.
Serving homeschooled teens and their parents **027.6**

Lerner, Brenda Wilmoth, 1956-
(ed) Biotechnology: changing life through science. See Biotechnology: changing life through science **660.6**

Lerner, K. Lee, 1957-
(ed) Biotechnology: changing life through science. See Biotechnology: changing life through science **660.6**

Lerner biography [series]
Carpenter, A. S. Lewis Carroll **92**
Edge, L. B. Andrew Carnegie **92**
Gherman, B. Anne Morrow Lindbergh **92**
Kenyon, K. The Brontë family **920**
Tagliaferro, L. Thomas Edison **92**

Lerner long biographies [series]
Lazo, C. E. F. Scott Fitzgerald **92**

Les Becquets, Diane
Season of ice **Fic**

Lesbian and gay voices. Day, F. A. **016.8**

Lesbian marriage *See* Same-sex marriage

Lesbians

See also Gay couples; Gay parents

The Full spectrum   **306.76**

Martin, H. J., Jr. Serving lesbian, gay, bisexual, transgender, and questioning teens   **027.62**

Civil rights

Alsenas, L. Gay America   **306.76**

Hudson, D. L. Gay rights   **306.76**

Kafka, T. Gay rights   **306.76**

Marcovitz, H. Teens & gay issues   **306.76**

Fiction

Hegamin, T. M+O 4evr   **Fic**

Johnson, M. The Bermudez Triangle   **Fic**

Peters, J. A. Between Mom and Jo   **Fic**

Wittlinger, E. Hard love   **Fic**

Woodson, J. From the notebooks of Melanin Sun   **Fic**

Lesinski, Jeanne M., 1960-

Bill Gates   **92**

Lesley, Craig

(ed) Talking leaves. See Talking leaves   **S C**

Leslie, Roger

(jt. auth) Wilson, P. J. Center stage   **027.8**

Less developed countries *See* Developing countries

Less is more. Baumbach, D.   **025.2**

Less is more. Campbell, K.   **809.3**

Lest we forget. Thomas, V. M.   **326**

Lester, Alison, 1952-

Quicksand pony   **Fic**

The snow pony   **Fic**

Lester, Julius

Day of tears   **Fic**

From slave ship to freedom road   **326**

Guardian   **Fic**

Long journey home: stories from black history   **S C**

Time's memory   **Fic**

Uncle Remus, the complete tales   **398.2**

Let it shine. Pinkney, A. D.   **920**

Let me play. Blumenthal, K.   **796**

Let my people go. McKissack, P. C.   **Fic**

Let the circle be unbroken. Taylor, M. D.   **Fic**

Let's celebrate today. Marks, D. F.   **394.26**

Let's clear the air: 10 reasons not to start smoking   **362.29**

Let's make cute stuff [series]

Cute dolls   **745.592**

Letter writing

Nobleman, M. T. Extraordinary e-mails, letters, and resumes   **808**

Letters

Fiction

Danziger, P. P.S. Longer letter later   **Fic**

Danziger, P. Snail mail no more   **Fic**

Harper, S. The Juliet club   **Fic**

Hesse, K. Letters from Rifka   **Fic**

Klise, K. Letters from camp   **Fic**

LaFleur, S. M. Love, Aubrey   **Fic**

Lyons, M. E. Letters from a slave boy   **Fic**

Lyons, M. E. Letters from a slave girl   **Fic**

Schumacher, J. The chain letter   **Fic**

Vernon, U. Nurk   **Fic**

Woodson, J. Peace, Locomotion   **Fic**

Letters from a slave boy. Lyons, M. E.   **Fic**

Letters from a slave girl. Lyons, M. E.   **Fic**

Letters from camp. Klise, K.   **Fic**

Letters from Rifka. Hesse, K.   **Fic**

Letters from the corrugated castle. Blos, J. W.   **Fic**

Letters from Wolfie. Sherlock, P.   **Fic**

Letters to my mother. Cárdenas, T.   **Fic**

Leukemia

Klosterman, L. Leukemia   **616.99**

Fiction

Nicholls, S. Ways to live forever   **Fic**

Sonnenblick, J. Drums, girls, & dangerous pie   **Fic**

Leventhal, Alice Walker *See* Walker, Alice, 1944-

Leverage your library program to help raise test scores. Church, A. P.   **027.8**

LeVert, Suzanne

Botswana   **968.83**

The facts about antidepressants   **615**

The facts about cocaine   **362.29**

The facts about ecstasy   **362.29**

The facts about heroin   **362.29**

The facts about LSD and other hallucinogens   **362.29**

The facts about nicotine   **362.29**

The facts about steroids   **362.29**

Sierra Leone   **966.4**

Levey, Richard H.

(jt. auth) Ball, J. A. Ancient China   **931**

Levin, Carole, 1948-

(ed) Encyclopedia of women in the Renaissance. See Encyclopedia of women in the Renaissance   **940.2**

Levin, Jack, 1941-

Domestic terrorism   **303.6**

Levin, Judith, 1956-

Anxiety and panic attacks   **616.85**

Hugo Chávez   **92**

Japanese mythology   **299.5**

Levine, Anna

Freefall   **Fic**

Levine, Charles A., 1897-1991

About

Finkelstein, N. H. Three across   **629.13**

Levine, Ellen, 1939-

Catch a tiger by the toe   **Fic**

Darkness over Denmark   **940.53**

Rachel Carson   **92**

Levine, Gail Carson, 1947-

Dave at night   **Fic**

Ella enchanted   **Fic**

Ever   **Fic**

Fairest   **Fic**

The wish   **Fic**

Writing magic   **808.3**

About

Abrams, D. Gail Carson Levine   **92**

Levine, Karen

Hana's suitcase   **940.53**

Hana's suitcase on stage   **812**

Levine, Kristin, 1974-
The best bad luck I ever had   **Fic**
Levine, Laura
(il) George-Warren, H. Shake, rattle, & roll
    920
Levine, Shar, 1953-
The ultimate guide to your microscope
    502.8
Levinson, David, 1947-
(ed) The Wilson chronology of the world's religions. See The Wilson chronology of the world's religions   **200**
Levinson, Nancy Smiler, 1938-
Magellan and the first voyage around the world
    92
Levitas, Mitchel
(ed) A Nation challenged. See A Nation challenged   **973.931**
Levitation: physics and psychology in the service of deception. Ottaviani, J.   **793.8**
Levithan, David, 1972-
How they met, and other stories   **S C**
(ed) Friends. See Friends   **S C**
(ed) The Full spectrum. See The Full spectrum   **306.76**
(ed) This is PUSH. See This is PUSH   **S C**
(ed) Where we are, what we see. See Where we are, what we see   **810.8**
Levitin, Sonia, 1934-
Strange relations   **Fic**
Levitt, William, 1907-1994
See/See also pages in the following book(s):
Aaseng, N. Business builders in real estate
    920
Levy, Debbie
Richard Wright   **92**
The signing of the Magna Carta   **942.03**
The Vietnam War   **959.704**
Levy, Elizabeth, 1942-
Seventh grade tango   **Fic**
Levy, Janey
The Alamo   **976.4**
Breaking the code with cryptography   **652**
Levy, Matthys
Earthquakes, volcanoes, and tsunamis   **551.2**
Engineering the city   **624**
Levy, Patricia, 1951-
The home front in World War II   **940.53**
Ireland   **941.5**
Nigeria   **966.9**
Puerto Rico   **972.95**
Scotland   **941.1**
Sudan   **962.4**
Switzerland   **949.4**
Tibet   **951**
Lew, Kristi, 1968-
Acids and bases   **546**
Goodbye, gasoline   **621.31**
Lewandowski, Christine Laura *See* Lew, Kristi, 1968-
Lewin, Ted, 1935-
Tooth and claw   **590**
(il) O'Dell, S. Island of the Blue Dolphins
    Fic

Lewis, C. S. (Clive Staples), 1898-1963
The lion, the witch, and the wardrobe   **Fic**
See/See also pages in the following book(s):
Ellis, S. From reader to writer   **372.6**
Lewis, Clive Staples *See* Lewis, C. S. (Clive Staples), 1898-1963
Lewis, E. B. (Earl B.), 1956-
(il) Smith, H. A. Keeping the night watch
    Fic
Lewis, Earl B. *See* Lewis, E. B. (Earl B.), 1956-
Lewis, Elizabeth, 1967-
Mexican art & culture   **709.72**
Lewis, J. Patrick
Black cat bone   **811**
The brothers' war   **811**
Countdown to summer   **811**
Freedom like sunlight   **811**
Monumental verses   **811**
Lewis, John, 1940-
About
Bausum, A. Freedom Riders   **323.1**
Lewis, John L., 1880-1969
See/See also pages in the following book(s):
Streissguth, T. Legendary labor leaders   **920**
Lewis, Meriwether, 1774-1809
About
Blumberg, R. The incredible journey of Lewis and Clark   **978**
Faber, H. Lewis and Clark   **978**
(jt. auth) Clark, W. Off the map   **978**
Lewis, Reginald F., 1922-1993
See/See also pages in the following book(s):
Haskins, J. African American entrepreneurs
    920
Lewis, Richard, 1949-
The killing sea   **Fic**
Lewis and Clark. Faber, H.   **978**
Lewis and Clark Expedition (1804-1806)
Blumberg, R. The incredible journey of Lewis and Clark   **978**
Blumberg, R. York's adventures with Lewis and Clark   **978**
Clark, W. Off the map   **978**
Crosby, M. T. Sacagawea   **92**
Faber, H. Lewis and Clark   **978**
Patent, D. H. Animals on the trail with Lewis and Clark   **978**
Patent, D. H. Plants on the trail with Lewis and Clark   **978**
St. George, J. Sacagawea   **92**
Fiction
O'Dell, S. Streams to the river, river to the sea
    Fic
Wolf, A. New found land   **Fic**
Lexi. Matthews, L. S.   **Fic**
LeZotte, Ann Clare
T4   **Fic**
Li, Moying, 1954-
Snow falling in spring   **92**
Li Cunxin
Mao's last dancer [biography of Li Cunxin]
    92
Li-Marcus, Moying *See* Li, Moying, 1954-

Llanes, Peggie
(jt. auth) Coleman, T. The hipster librarian's guide to teen craft projects **027.62**

Llewellyn, Sam, 1948-
The well between the worlds **Fic**

Lloyd, J. D., 1959-
(ed) Family violence. See Family violence **362.82**

Loans
See also Public debts

Lobbying
Schuckett, S. Political advocacy for school librarians **027.8**

Lobel, Anita, 1934-
No pretty pictures **92**

Lobel, Arnold
(il) The Random House book of poetry for children. See The Random House book of poetry for children **811.008**

Lobsters
See/See also pages in the following book(s):
Lassieur, A. Crabs, lobsters, and shrimps **595.3**

Local news. Soto, G. **S C**

Lock, Joan
Famous prisons **365**

Locke, Juliane Poirier, 1959-
England's Jane **92**

The **locked** garden. Whelan, G. **Fic**

Locked in time. Duncan, L. **Fic**

Locked up. Edge, L. B. **365**

The **locket**. Lieurance, S. **Fic**

Lockhart, E.
The disreputable history of Frankie Landau-Banks **Fic**
Dramarama **Fic**

Lockhart, Laura
(jt. auth) Duncan, D. I-search for success **025.5**

Lockman, Darcy
Computer animation **778.5**
Robots **629.8**

Lockouts *See* Strikes

Lockwood, Belva Ann, 1830-1917
About
Norgren, J. Belva Lockwood **92**

Lockwood, Sophie
Baboons **599.8**
Bats **599.4**
Chimpanzees **599.8**
Elephants **599.67**
Foxes **599.77**
Giraffes **599.63**
Lions **599.75**
Polar Bears **599.78**
Sea otters **599.7**
Sea turtles **597.92**
Skunks **599.7**
Whales **599.5**
Zebras **599.66**

Locomotion. Woodson, J. **Fic**

Locomotives
Zimmermann, K. R. Steam locomotives **385**

Locricchio, Matthew
The international cookbook for kids **641.5**
Super chef [series] **641.5**
The 2nd international cookbook for kids **641.5**

Loehle, Richard
(il) Tucker, T. Brainstorm! **609**

Loertscher, David V., 1940-
(ed) The Whole school library handbook. See The Whole school library handbook **027.8**

Logging *See* Lumber and lumbering

Logue, Mary, 1952-
(jt. auth) Hautman, P. Snatched **Fic**

Loizeaux, William
Clarence Cochran, a human boy **Fic**

Lommel, Cookie
Russell Simmons **92**

London, Jack, 1876-1916
The call of the wild **Fic**
White Fang **Fic**
About
Stefoff, R. Jack London **92**

London (England)
Stacey, G. London **942.1**
Fiction
Avi. Traitor's gate **Fic**
Becker, T. Darkside **Fic**
Bloor, E. London calling **Fic**
Cockcroft, J. Counter clockwise **Fic**
Curry, J. L. The Black Canary **Fic**
Dowd, S. The London Eye mystery **Fic**
Doyle, M. Bewitching season **Fic**
Golding, J. The diamond of Drury Lane **Fic**
Gordon, R. Tunnels **Fic**
Hearn, J. Ivy **Fic**
Hooper, M. At the sign of the Sugared Plum **Fic**
Jarvis, R. The alchemist's cat **Fic**
La Fevers, R. L. Theodosia and the Serpents of Chaos **Fic**
Naidoo, B. The other side of truth **Fic**
Naidoo, B. Web of lies **Fic**
Springer, N. The case of the missing marquess **Fic**
Stewart, P. The curse of the night wolf **Fic**
Sturtevant, K. A true and faithful narrative **Fic**
Taylor, G. P. Tersias the oracle **Fic**
Updale, E. Montmorency **Fic**
Valentine, J. Broken soup **Fic**
Valentine, J. Me, the missing, and the dead **Fic**
Wilson, J. The alchemist's dream **Fic**
Wooding, C. The haunting of Alaizabel Cray **Fic**
History
Barter, J. Shakespeare's London **942.06**

London calling. Bloor, E. **Fic**

The **London** Eye mystery. Dowd, S. **Fic**

Lonek's journey. Whiteman, D. B. **940.53**

Long, Ethan
(il) Lewis, J. P. Countdown to summer **811**

Long, John A., 1957-
Dinosaurs 567.9
Feathered dinosaurs 567.9

A long and uncertain journey: the 27,000 mile voyage of Vasco da Gama. Goodman, J. E. 92

Long gone daddy. Hemphill, H. Fic

Long gone lonesome history of country music. Bertholf, B. 781.642

Long journey home: stories from black history. Lester, J. S C

The long road to Gettysburg. Murphy, J. 973.7

The Long Walk. Bial, R. 970.004

The Long Walk. Denetdale, J. 970.004

A long way from Chicago. Peck, R. Fic

Longevity
See also Old age

Longfellow, Henry Wadsworth, 1807-1882
Henry Wadsworth Longfellow 811
Hiawatha and Megissogwon 811

Longitude
Dash, J. The longitude prize [biography of John Harrison] 92

The longitude prize [biography of John Harrison] Dash, J. 92

Longshore, David
Encyclopedia of hurricanes, typhoons, and cyclones 551.55

Look again!. Serritella, J. 373.1

A look at earth. Tabak, J. 550

A look at Mercury. Spangenburg, R. 523.4

A look at Neptune. Tabak, J. 523.4

A look at the Second Amendment. Gonzales, D. 344

A look at Uranus. Tocci, S. 523.4

The look-it-up book of explorers. Kimmel, E. C. 920

Looking at aerial photographs. Belmont, H. 910

Looking at Europe [series]
Bultje, J. W. The Czech Republic 943.7

Looking at maps. Taylor, B. 912

Looking at settlements. Anderson, J. 307

Looking back. Lowry, L. 92

Looking for life in the universe. Jackson, E. B. 576.8

Looking for Lucy Buick. Murphy, R. Fic

Looking for seabirds. Webb, S. 598

Looks. George, M. Fic

Loos, Pamela
A reader's guide to Amy Tan's The joy luck club 813.009
A reader's guide to Lorraine Hansberry's A raisin in the sun 812.009

Loose threads. Grover, L. A. 811

Lopes, Tom
(il) Baker, R. F. In a word 422

Lopez, Diana
Confetti girl Fic

Lopez, Jennifer
About
Woog, A. Jennifer Lopez 92

López, José Javier, 1969-
Puerto Rico 972.95

López, Lorraine, 1956-
Call me Henri Fic

Lorbiecki, Marybeth
Prairie dogs 599.3

Lord, Cynthia
Rules Fic

Lord, Richard
(jt. auth) Levy, P. Switzerland 949.4

Lord Loss. Shan, D. Fic

Lord of the deep. Salisbury, G. Fic

Lord of the Flies. Golding, W. Fic

The lord of the rings. Tolkien, J. R. R. Fic

Lords, ladies, peasants, and knights. Nardo, D. 940.1

Lorinc, John, 1963-
Cities 307.7

Los Angeles (Calif.)
Fiction
Castellucci, C. Boy proof Fic
Currier, K. S. Kai's journey to Gold Mountain Fic
Cushman, K. The loud silence of Francine Green Fic
Greene, M. Chasing the jaguar Fic
Johnston, T. Any small goodness Fic
Pinkwater, D. M. The Neddiad Fic
Scott, K. The princess & the pauper Fic
Smith, S. L. Hot, sour, salty, sweet Fic
Woods, B. Emako Blue Fic
Yee, L. Absolutely Maybe Fic

Losing is not an option: stories. Wallace, R. S C

Losing things *See* Lost and found possessions

Losleben, Elie
(jt. auth) Malcolm, P. Libya 961.2

Loss (Psychology)
Hantman, C. 30 days to getting over the dork you used to call your boyfriend 158
Myers, E. When will I stop hurting? 155.9
What have you lost? 808.81
Fiction
Baskin, N. R. All we know of love Fic
Stein, T. High dive Fic

Lost. Davies, J. Fic

Lost and found possessions
Fiction
Jukes, M. Smoke Fic

The lost art. Morden, S. Fic

Lost boy. Newbery, L. Fic

Lost childhood [biography of Annelex Hofstra Layson] Layson, A. H. 92

Lost children *See* Missing children

The lost cities. Peck, D. Fic

The lost conspiracy. Hardinge, F. Fic

The lost garden. Yep, L. 92

Lost Goat Lane. Jordan, R. Fic

Lost in America. Sachs, M. **Fic**

Lost in the labyrinth. Kindl, P. **Fic**

The **lost** island of Tamarind. Aguiar, N. **Fic**

Lost journals of Ven Polypheme [series]
Haydon, E. The Thief Queen's daughter **Fic**

The **lost** warrior. Hunter, E. **741.5**

The **lost** years of Merlin. Barron, T. A. **Fic**

Lottridge, Celia Barker
Stories from Adam and Eve to Ezekiel
220.9
Stories from the life of Jesus **232.9**

The **loud** silence of Francine Green. Cushman, K.
Fic

Loughead, Deb, 1955-
(ed) Cleavage. See Cleavage **S C**

Louis XIV, King of France, 1638-1715
See/See also pages in the following book(s):
Meltzer, M. Ten kings **920**

Louis XVI, King of France, 1754-1793
About
Plain, N. Louis XVI, Marie Antoinette, and the
French Revolution **944**

Louis, Joe, 1914-1981
About
Sullivan, G. Knockout!: a photobiography of
boxer Joe Louis **92**

Louis Pasteur and the founding of microbiology.
Ackerman, J. **92**

Louis XVI, Marie Antoinette, and the French Revolution. Plain, N. **944**

Louisiana
Fiction
Cochran, T. Running the dogs **Fic**
Couvillon, J. The chicken dance **Fic**
Cusick, R. T. Walk of the spirits **Fic**
Duncan, L. Locked in time **Fic**
Holt, K. W. Part of me **S C**
Napoli, D. J. Alligator bayou **Fic**
Nixon, J. L. The haunting **Fic**
Ruby, L. The secret of Laurel Oaks **Fic**
Siegelson, K. L. Honey Bea **Fic**

Louisiana Purchase
Corrick, J. A. The Louisiana Purchase **973.4**
Schlaepfer, G. G. The Louisiana Purchase
973.4

Lourie, Peter
Arctic thaw **998**
Hidden world of the Aztec **972**
On the Texas trail of Cabeza de Vaca **92**

Love, Ann, 1947-
Sweet! **641.8**

Love, D. Anne, 1949-
Defying the diva **Fic**
Picture perfect **Fic**
Semiprecious **Fic**

Love
Fiction
Schroeder, L. I heart you, you haunt me
Fic
Stoffels, K. Heartsinger **Fic**
Love. Fredericks, M. **Fic**
Love and death at the mall. See Peck, R. Invita-
tions to the world **808.06**

Love and other four-letter words. Mackler, C.
Fic

Love, Aubrey. LaFleur, S. M. **Fic**

Love Canal. Bryan, N. **363.7**

**Love Canal Chemical Waste Landfill (Niagara
Falls, N.Y.)**
Bryan, N. Love Canal **363.7**

Love, football, and other contact sports. Carter, A.
R. **S C**

Love is hell **S C**

Love me tender. Couloumbis, A. **Fic**

Love, Meg. Purtill, C. L. **Fic**

Love poetry
Crush: love poems **808.81**
Grimes, N. Hopscotch love **811**
Holbrook, S. More than friends **811**
Soto, G. Partly cloudy **811**

Love stories
Barkley, B. Dream factory **Fic**
Barkley, B. Scrambled eggs at midnight **Fic**
Chan, G. A foreign field **Fic**
Hale, S. Book of a thousand days **Fic**
Kerr, M. E. Someone like summer **Fic**
Koja, K. Kissing the bee **Fic**
Levithan, D. How they met, and other stories
S C
Love is hell **S C**
Myers, W. D. Amiri & Odette **Fic**
O'Connell, T. True love, the sphinx, and other
unsolvable riddles **Fic**
Rettig, L. My desperate love diary **Fic**
Soto, G. Accidental love **Fic**
Vail, R. You, maybe **Fic**
Weyn, S. Reincarnation **Fic**
Zarr, S. Sweethearts **Fic**

Love that dog. Creech, S. **Fic**

Lovegrove, Ray
Health **174.2**

Loving, Mildred Jeter
About
Gold, S. D. Loving v. Virginia **346**

Loving, Richard
About
Gold, S. D. Loving v. Virginia **346**

Loving v. Virginia. Gold, S. D. **346**

Low income housing *See* Public housing

Lowe, Helen, 1971-
Thornspell **Fic**

Lowe, Joy L.
(jt. auth) Matthew, K. I. Neal-Schuman guide to
celebrations & holidays around the world
394.26

Lowell, Pamela
Returnable girl **Fic**

Lowenstein, Sallie Claire, 1949-
Waiting for Eugene **Fic**

Lower East Side (New York, N.Y.)
Bial, R. Tenement **974.7**
Hopkinson, D. Shutting out the sky **974.7**

Lowman, Margaret
About
Lasky, K. The most beautiful roof in the world
577.3

Lum, Roseline Ng Cheong- *See* Cheong-Lum, Roseline Ng, 1962-

Lum, Roseline NgCheong- *See* NgCheong-Lum, Roseline, 1962-

Lumber and lumbering

Fiction

Durbin, W. Blackwater Ben | Fic

Un **Lun** Dun. Miéville, C. | Fic

Lunar expeditions *See* Space flight to the moon

Lunch with Lenin and other stories. Ellis, D.
| S C

Lundgren, Orrin

(il) Harris, E. S. Save the Earth science experiments | 507.8

Lung cancer

Brill, M. T. Lung cancer | 616.99

Lungs

Diseases

See also Asthma

Lupica, Mike

The big field | Fic

Miracle on 49th Street | Fic

Summer ball | Fic

Lurie, April

Brothers, boyfriends & other criminal minds
| Fic

Dancing in the streets of Brooklyn | Fic

The latent powers of Dylan Fontaine | Fic

Lush. Friend, N. | Fic

Lutes, Jason, 1967-

Houdini: the handcuff king | 92

Lutz, Richard A.

About

Mallory, K. Diving to a deep-sea volcano
| 551.46

Luxbacher, Irene, 1970-

The jumbo book of art | 702.8

The **luxe.** Godbersen, A. | Fic

Luxembourg

Sheehan, P. Luxembourg | 949.35

Ly, Many

Home is east | Fic

Roots and wings | Fic

Lyddie. Paterson, K. | Fic

Lyga, Allyson A. W.

Graphic novels in your media center | 025.2

Lyga, Barry

The astonishing adventures of Fanboy & Goth Girl | Fic

Hero-type | Fic

Wolverine: worst day ever | 741.5

(jt. auth) Lyga, A. A. W. Graphic novels in your media center | 025.2

Lying *See* Truthfulness and falsehood

Lyly, John, 1554?-1606

See/See also pages in the following book(s):

Nardo, D. Great Elizabethan playwrights
| 920

Lyman, Darryl, 1944-

Holocaust rescuers | 920

Lyme disease

Silverstein, A. Lyme disease | 616.9

Lynch, Chris

The Big Game of Everything | Fic

Cyberia | Fic

Inexcusable | Fic

Lynch, Doris

J.R.R. Tolkien | 92

Lynch, Patricia Ann

African mythology A to Z | 299.6

Lynch, Patrick James

(il) Dickens, C. A Christmas carol [illustrated by P.J. Lynch] | Fic

Lynch, Wayne

Arctic | 998

The Everglades | 508

Rocky Mountains | 577.4

Lynching

Aretha, D. The murder of Emmett Till
| 364.1

Crowe, C. Getting away with murder: the true story of the Emmett Till case | 364.1

Uschan, M. V. Lynching and murder in the deep South | 364.1

Fiction

Lester, J. Guardian | Fic

Poetry

Nelson, M. A wreath for Emmett Till | 811

Lynching and murder in the deep South. Uschan, M. V. | 364.1

Lynette, Rachel

Anorexia | 616.85

Leprosy | 616.9

Lynn, Ruth Nadelman, 1948-

Fantasy literature for children and young adults
| 016.8

Lyon, Annabel, 1971-

All-season Edie | Fic

Lyon, George Ella, 1949-

Sonny's house of spies | Fic

Lyon, Steve

The gift moves | Fic

Lyonesse [series]

Llewellyn, S. The well between the worlds
| Fic

Lyons, Maritcha Rémond, 1848-1929

About

Bolden, T. Maritcha [biography of Maritcha Rémond Lyons] | 92

Lyons, Mary E.

Catching the fire: Philip Simmons, blacksmith
| 92

Dear Ellen Bee | Fic

Letters from a slave boy | Fic

Letters from a slave girl | Fic

Sorrow's kitchen [biography of Zora Neale Hurston] | 92

(ed) Feed the children first. See Feed the children first | 941.5

Lysander, d. 395 B.C.

Fiction

Ford, M. The Fire of Ares | Fic

Lysergic acid diethylamide *See* LSD (Drug)

Macquitty, Miranda
Shark **597**

Macy, Anne Sullivan *See* Sullivan, Anne, 1866-1936

Macy, Sue, 1954-
Bulls-eye: a photobiography of Annie Oakley
92
Freeze frame **796.98**
Swifter, higher, stronger **796.48**
(ed) Girls got game. See Girls got game
810.8

Madagascar
Heale, J. Madagascar **969.1**

Madaras, Area
(jt. auth) Madaras, L. The "what's happening to my body?" book for boys **613.9**
(jt. auth) Madaras, L. The "what's happening to my body?" book for girls **613.9**

Madaras, Lynda, 1947-
The "what's happening to my body?" book for boys **613.9**
The "what's happening to my body?" book for girls **613.9**

MadCat. Mackel, K. **Fic**

Madden, John
John Madden's heroes of football **796.332**

Madden, Kerry
Gentle's Holler **Fic**
Harper Lee **92**

Maddigan's Fantasia. Mahy, M. **Fic**

Maddison, Kevin W.
(il) Adams, S. The Kingfisher atlas of the modern world **909.8**

Maddox, Jake
Free throw **Fic**

Maddox, Marjorie, 1959-
Rules of the game **811**

Made you look. Graydon, S. **659.1**

Madikizela-Mandela, Winnie *See* Mandela, Winnie

Madison, Bennett, 1981-
Lulu Dark and the summer of the Fox **Fic**
Lulu Dark can see through walls **Fic**

Madison, James, 1751-1836
About
DeVillers, D. Marbury v. Madison **347**
Elish, D. James Madison **92**
Malone, M. James Madison **92**

Madonna, 1958-
See/See also pages in the following book(s):
Orgill, R. Shout, sister, shout! **920**

Mafia
Fiction
Green, T. Football hero **Fic**
Korman, G. Son of the mob **Fic**

Magarian, La Verne J.
See/See also pages in the following book(s):
Major, J. S. Caravan to America **920**

Magazines *See* Periodicals

Magellan, Ferdinand, 1480?-1521
About
Levinson, N. S. Magellan and the first voyage around the world **92**

See/See also pages in the following book(s):
Fritz, J. Around the world in a hundred years
910.4

Magellan and the first voyage around the world.
Levinson, N. S. **92**

Maghreb *See* North Africa

Magic
Black magic and witches **133.4**
Stefoff, R. Magic **133.4**
Fiction
Aguiar, N. The lost island of Tamarind **Fic**
Alexander, A. Gift of the Unmage **Fic**
Anderson, R. J. Spell Hunter **Fic**
Avi. The Book Without Words **Fic**
Barron, T. A. Merlin's dragon **Fic**
Bauer, A. C. E. No castles here **Fic**
Blubaugh, P. Serendipity Market **Fic**
Brittain, B. The wish giver **Fic**
Bunce, E. C. A curse dark as gold **Fic**
Catanese, P. W. Happenstance found **Fic**
Chabon, M. Summerland **Fic**
Chima, C. W. The warrior heir **Fic**
Constable, K. The singer of all songs **Fic**
Coville, B. Juliet Dove, Queen of Love **Fic**
Crabtree, J. Discovering pig magic **Fic**
Crossley-Holland, K. The seeing stone **Fic**
Dickinson, P. Angel Isle **Fic**
Dickinson, P. The ropemaker **Fic**
Dickinson, P. Tears of the salamander **Fic**
Divakaruni, C. B. The conch bearer **Fic**
Downer, A. Hatching magic **Fic**
Doyle, M. Bewitching season **Fic**
Duey, K. Skin hunger **Fic**
Durst, S. B. Into the Wild **Fic**
French, V. The robe of skulls **Fic**
Gaiman, N. M is for magic **S C**
Gardner, S. I, Coriander **Fic**
Genesse, P. The golden cord **Fic**
Gilman, L. A. Grail quest: the Camelot spell
Fic
Gliori, D. Pure dead frozen **Fic**
Going, K. L. The garden of Eve **Fic**
Goodman, A. Eon: Dragoneye reborn **Fic**
Haig, M. Samuel Blink and the forbidden forest
Fic
Hardinge, F. Well witched **Fic**
Harris, J. Runemarks **Fic**
Harrison, M. I. The princess and the hound
Fic
Helgerson, J. Horns & wrinkles **Fic**
Jennings, R. W. Orwell's luck **Fic**
Jones, A. F. Warrior princess **Fic**
Jones, D. W. Charmed life **Fic**
Jones, D. W. House of many ways **Fic**
Keehn, S. M. Gnat Stokes and the Foggy Bottom Swamp Queen **Fic**
Kirk, D. Elf realm: the low road **Fic**
Kladstrup, K. The book of story beginnings
Fic
Kline, L. W. Write before your eyes **Fic**
Knudsen, M. The dragon of Trelian **Fic**
La Fevers, R. L. Theodosia and the Serpents of Chaos **Fic**
Lake, A. J. The coming of dragons **Fic**
Landon, D. Shapeshifter's quest **Fic**
Landy, D. Skulduggery Pleasant **Fic**

The **Mambo** Kings play songs of love [excerpt]
Hijuelos, O.
In Growing up Latino; memoirs and stories
p16-21   **810.8**

Mammals

See also Fossil mammals groups of mammals; and names of mammals

Hare, T. Animal fact-file   **599**
Rodriguez, A. M. Secret of the singing mice
. . . and more!   **599**
Whitaker, J. O., Jr. National Audubon Society
field guide to North American mammals
    599

Encyclopedias

Exploring mammals   **599**
Exploring the world of mammals   **599**

Mammals, Marine *See* Marine mammals

Mammoths

Agenbroad, L. D. Mammoths   **569**
Giblin, J. The mystery of the mammoth bones
    569

Man *See* Human beings

Influence on nature

See Human influence on nature

Origin

See Human origins

Man, Fossil *See* Fossil hominids

Man, Prehistoric *See* Prehistoric peoples

The **man-eating** tigers of Sundarbans. Montgomery, S.   **599.75**

Man in the moon. Enderle, D.   **Fic**

The **man** who loved clowns. Wood, J. R.   **Fic**

The **man** who was Poe. Avi   **Fic**

The **man** who went to the far side of the moon:
the story of Apollo 11 astronaut Michael Collins. Schyffert, B. U.   **92**

The **man** with the red bag. Bunting, E.   **Fic**

Management

See also Conflict management

Management of conflict *See* Conflict management

Managing 21st century libraries. Pugh, L.
    025.1

Managing and analyzing your collection. Doll, C. A.   **025.2**

Managing budgets and finances. Hallam, A.
    025.1

Managing change. Curzon, S. C.   **025.1**

Managing curriculum and assessment   **375**

Managing the Internet controversy   **025.04**

Manatees

Swinburne, S. R. Saving manatees   **599.5**
Fiction
Monninger, J. Hippie chick   **Fic**

Mancall, Jacqueline C., 1932-
(jt. auth) Hughes-Hassell, S. Collection management for youth   **025.2**

Mandan Indians
Fiction
Spooner, M. Last Child   **Fic**

Mandela, Nelson
About
Beecroft, S. The release of Nelson Mandela
    968.06
Keller, B. Tree shaker   **92**
Kramer, A. Mandela   **92**
Kramer, A. Nelson Mandela   **92**

Mandela, Winnie
See/See also pages in the following book(s):
Price-Groff, C. Twentieth-century women political leaders   **920**

Mandelbaum, Jack
About
Warren, A. Surviving Hitler   **940.53**

Mandell, Daniel R., 1956-
King Philip's war   **973.2**

Manga

See also Shojo manga; Shonen manga
Arai, K. Beauty Pop, Vol. 1   **741.5**
Ariyoshi, K. Swan, Vol. 1   **741.5**
Higuchi, D. Whistle! Volume 1   **741.5**
Hotta, Y. Hikaru No Go, Volume 1   **741.5**
Konomi, T. The Prince of Tennis, Vol. 1
    741.5
Nakajo, H. Sugar Princess volume 1: skating to win   **741.5**
Sakura, K. Dragon drive. Vol. 1, D-break
    741.5
Toriyama, A. Cowa!   **741.5**
Drawing
Hart, C. Manga for the beginner   **741.5**
Hart, C. Manga mania romance   **741.5**
Nagatomo, H. Draw your own Manga   **741.5**
Study and teaching
Brenner, R. E. Understanding manga and anime
    025.2

Manga for the beginner. Hart, C.   **741.5**

Manga mania romance. Hart, C.   **741.5**

Manga Shakespeare [series]
Appignanesi, R. As you like it   **822.3**
Appignanesi, R. Hamlet   **822.3**
Appignanesi, R. Julius Caesar   **822.3**
Appignanesi, R. A midsummer night's dream
    822.3
Appignanesi, R. Romeo and Juliet   **822.3**

Manga Shakespeare: The tempest. Appignanesi, R.
    822.3

Manga touch. Pearce, J.   **Fic**

Mangelsen, Thomas D.
(il) Hirschi, R. Lions, tigers, and bears
    591.5

A **mango-shaped** space. Mass, W.   **Fic**

Manhattan Project
Making and using the atomic bomb   **355.8**
Sullivan, E. T. The ultimate weapon   **355.8**
Fiction
Davies, J. Where the ground meets the sky
    Fic

Manheimer, Ann S.
Martin Luther King Jr   **92**

Maniac Magee. Spinelli, J.   **Fic**

Manic-depressive illness

 See also Depression (Psychology)

 Silverstein, A. The depression and bipolar disorder update   **616.89**

Manicuring

 Boonyadhistarn, T. Fingernail art   **646.7**

Manipulating light. Stille, D. R.   **535**

Manitoba

Fiction

 Brooks, M. Mistik Lake   **Fic**

Mankell, Henning, 1948-

 A bridge to the stars   **Fic**

 Secrets in the fire   **Fic**

Mankiller, Wilma

 See/See also pages in the following book(s):

 Krull, K. Lives of extraordinary women   **920**

 Price-Groff, C. Twentieth-century women political leaders   **920**

Manley, Claudia B.

 Competitive track and field for girls   **796.42**

 Competitive volleyball for girls   **796.325**

Manmade disasters [series]

 Mayell, M. Tragedies of space exploration   **363.1**

Mann, Elizabeth, 1948-

 Hoover Dam   **627**

 The Parthenon   **726**

 The Roman Colosseum   **937**

 Taj Mahal   **954.02**

 Tikal   **972.81**

Mann, Gurinder Singh

 Buddhists, Hindus, and Sikhs in America   **294**

Mann, Jonathan H.

 (ed) The Election of 2000 and the administration of George W. Bush. See The Election of 2000 and the administration of George W. Bush   **324**

Mann, Kenny, 1946-

 The ancient Hebrews   **909**

 Isabel, Ferdinand and fifteenth-century Spain   **946**

Mann, Murray Gell- *See* Gell-Mann, Murray, 1929-

Manners *See* Etiquette

Manners and customs

 See also Country life

Manning, Phillip, 1936-

 Atoms, molecules, and compounds   **539.7**

Manning, Phillip Lars, 1967-

 Dinomummy   **567.9**

Manpower

 See also Draft

Mansa Musa *See* Musa, d. 1337

Mansfield, Stephen

 Laos   **959.4**

Manslaughter *See* Homicide

Mantell, Paul

 (jt. auth) Barber, T. Go long!   **Fic**

 (jt. auth) Hart, A. Ancient Greece!   **938**

 (jt. auth) Hart, A. Knights & castles   **940.1**

Manual workers *See* Working class

Manufactures

 Slavin, B. Transformed   **670**

Many peoples, one land. Helbig, A.   **016.8**

The **many** rides of Paul Revere. Giblin, J.   **92**

Manzanar War Relocation Center

 Cooper, M. L. Remembering Manzanar   **940.53**

 Houston, J. W. Farewell to Manzanar   **940.53**

Manzano, Juan Francisco, 1797-1854

About

 Engle, M. The poet slave of Cuba   **92**

Mao, Tse-tung *See* Mao Zedong, 1893-1976

Mao Zedong, 1893-1976

About

 Naden, C. J. Mao Zedong and the Chinese Revolution   **92**

 Slavicek, L. C. Mao Zedong   **92**

 See/See also pages in the following book(s):

 Uschan, M. V. Political leaders   **920**

Mao Zedong and the Chinese Revolution. Naden, C. J.   **92**

Maori (New Zealand)

Fiction

 Hollyer, B. River song   **Fic**

Mao's last dancer [biography of Li Cunxin] Li Cunxin   **92**

Map basics. Baber, M.   **912**

A **map** of the known world. Sandell, L. A.   **Fic**

Map readers [series]

 Baber, M. Map basics   **912**

Maps

 See also Atlases

 Baber, M. Map basics   **912**

 Heinrichs, A. Gerardus Mercator   **92**

 Morrison, T. The coast mappers   **623.89**

 Ross, V. The road to there   **912**

 Taylor, B. Looking at maps   **912**

Maps on file   **912**

Mara, W. P. *See* Mara, Wil

Mara, Wil

 The clock   **681.1**

 John Adams   **92**

Mara, William P. *See* Mara, Wil

Marburg virus

 See/See also pages in the following book(s):

 Grady, D. Deadly invaders   **614.4**

Marbury, William, 1761?-1835

About

 DeVillers, D. Marbury v. Madison   **347**

Marbury v. Madison. DeVillers, D.   **347**

Marcelo in the real world. Stork, F. X.   **Fic**

March of the penguins. Jacquet, L.   **598**

Marches (Demonstrations) *See* Demonstrations

Marching in Birmingham. Boerst, W. J.   **323.1**

Marching toward freedom. Schomp, V.   **305.8**

Marco Polo. Demi   **92**

Marco Polo's journey to China. Childress, D.   **92**

Marine sciences
Yount, L. Modern marine science   **551.46**

Marines (U.S.) *See* United States. Marine Corps

Maritcha [biography of Maritcha Rémond Lyons]
Bolden, T.   **92**

Mark, Joan T., 1937-
Margaret Mead   **92**

Mark of Solomon [series]
Wein, E. E. The lion hunter   **Fic**

Mark Twain. Twain, M.
  S C
[essays about]   **92**

Markel, Rita J.
The fall of the Roman Empire   **937**

Marker, Sherry, 1941-
Plains Indian wars   **973.5**

Markle, Sandra, 1946-
Animal heroes   **636.088**
Outside and inside mummies   **393**
Prairie dogs   **599.3**
Rescues!   **363.34**

Markowitz, Harvey
(ed) American Indian biographies. See American
Indian biographies   **920.003**

Marks, Diana F.
Let's celebrate today   **394.26**

Markuson, Carolyn A.
(jt. auth) Erikson, R. Designing a school library
media center for the future   **027.8**

Marler, Myrna Dee
Walter Dean Myers   **813.009**

Marley, Bob
About
Medina, T. I and I [biography of Bob Marley]
  92
Miller, C. C. Reggae poet: the story of Bob
Marley   **92**
Paprocki, S. B. Bob Marley   **92**

Marley, Louise, 1952-
Singer in the snow   **Fic**

Marlowe, Christopher, 1564-1593
See/See also pages in the following book(s):
Nardo, D. Great Elizabethan playwrights
  920
Fiction
Thomson, S. L. The secret of the Rose   **Fic**

Marooned [biography of Alexander Selkirk]
Kraske, R.   **92**

Marquette, Jacques, 1637-1675
About
Harkins, S. S. The life and times of Father
Jacques Marquette   **92**

Marquette, Scott
America under attack   **973.931**

Márquez, Gabriel García *See* García Márquez,
Gabriel, 1928-

Márquez, Herón
Roberto Clemente   **92**

Marr, Melissa
Ink exchange   **Fic**

Marriage
  See also Divorce; Family; Polygamy; Remarriage; Same-sex marriage; Weddings

Stefoff, R. Marriage   **306.8**
The truth about divorce   **306.89**
Fiction
Rich, N. Alis   **Fic**

Marriage, Interracial *See* Interracial marriage

Marrin, Albert, 1936-
Dr. Jenner and the speckled monster   **614.5**
The great adventure: Theodore Roosevelt and
the rise of modern America   **92**
Oh, rats!   **599.35**
Old Hickory [biography of Andrew Jackson]
  92
Saving the buffalo   **599.64**

Marriott, Pat, 1920-
(il) Aiken, J. The wolves of Willoughby Chase
  Fic

Marriott, Zoë, 1982 or 3-
The swan kingdom   **Fic**

Mars (Planet)
Miller, R. Mars   **523.4**
Scott, E. Mars and the search for life   **576.8**
Skurzynski, G. Discover Mars   **523.4**
Stone, T. L. Mars   **523.4**
Ward, D. J. Exploring Mars   **523.4**
Exploration
Cole, M. D. Living on Mars   **629.4**
Siy, A. Cars on Mars   **629.43**
Wunsch, S. T. The adventures of Sojourner
  629.43

Mars and the search for life. Scott, E.   **576.8**

Marsalis, Wynton
Jazz A-B-Z   **781.65**
See/See also pages in the following book(s):
Mour, S. I. American jazz musicians   **920**

Marschall, Ken
Inside the Titanic   **910.4**
(il) Brewster, H. 882 ½ amazing answers to your
questions about the Titanic   **910.4**

Marsden, Carolyn, 1950-
Sahwira   **Fic**

Marsden, John, 1950-
Tomorrow, when the war began   **Fic**

Marsh, Katherine
The night tourist   **Fic**

Marsh, Othniel Charles, 1831-1899
About
Kimmel, E. C. Dinosaur bone war   **560**

Marsh ecology
Wechsler, D. Marvels in the muck   **578.7**

Marshall, James Vance, 1924-
Stories from the Billabong   **398.2**

Marshall, Robina MacIntyre
The Library of Alexandria   **027**

Marshall, Samuel D.
About
Montgomery, S. The tarantula scientist   **595.4**

Marshall, Thurgood, 1908-1993
About
Crowe, C. Thurgood Marshall   **92**

Marshfield dreams. Fletcher, R.   **92**

Marston, Elsa
The Byzantine Empire   **949.5**
The Phoenicians   **939**

Marston, Elsa—*Continued*

Santa Claus in Baghdad and other stories about teens in the Arab world   **S C**

(jt. auth) Harik, R. M. Women in the Middle East   **305.4**

The **marsupial** order. Stefoff, R.   **599.2**

Marsupials

Collard, S. B., III. Pocket babies and other amazing marsupials   **599.2**

Stefoff, R. The marsupial order   **599.2**

Martha Graham, a dancer's life. Freedman, R.   **92**

Martí, José, 1853-1895

See/See also pages in the following book(s):

Mendoza, P. M. Extraordinary people in extraordinary times   **920**

Martial arts

See also Tae kwon do

Martin, A. P. The Shotokan karate bible   **796.8**

Ritschel, J. The kickboxing handbook   **796.8**

Fiction

Bradford, C. Young samurai   **Fic**

Chen, D. Sword   **Fic**

Mah, A. Y. Chinese Cinderella and the Secret Dragon Society   **Fic**

Uehashi, N. Moribito   **Fic**

Wild, K. Fight game   **Fic**

Graphic novels

Carey, M. Re-Gifters   **741.5**

Martial arts [series]

Inman, R. The judo handbook   **796.8**

Pawlett, M. The tae kwon do handbook   **796.8**

Pawlett, R. The karate handbook   **796.8**

Ritschel, J. The kickboxing handbook   **796.8**

Martians. Nardo, D.   **001.9**

Martin, Alex, 1953-

Knights & castles   **940.1**

Martin, Ann M.

7 steps to an award-winning school library program   **027.8**

Martin, Ann M., 1955-

A corner of the universe   **Fic**

Here today   **Fic**

(jt. auth) Danziger, P. P.S. Longer letter later   **Fic**

(jt. auth) Danziger, P. Snail mail no more   **Fic**

(ed) Friends. See Friends   **S C**

Martin, Ashley P.

The Shotokan karate bible   **796.8**

Martin, Fay Evans- *See* Evans-Martin, Fay

Martin, George R. R.

The hedge knight; adaptation. See Avery, B.

The hedge knight   **741.5**

Martin, Gilles

(il) Dubois, P. J. Birds   **598**

Martin, Hillias J., Jr.

Serving lesbian, gay, bisexual, transgender, and questioning teens   **027.62**

Martin, Joel

Native American religion   **299.7**

Martin, Joseph Plumb, 1760-1850

About

Murphy, J. A young patriot   **973.3**

Martin, Laura C.

Nature's art box   **745.5**

Martin, Nora

Flight of the Fisherbird   **Fic**

Martin, Patricia A. Fink, 1955-

Prairies, fields, and meadows   **577.4**

Woods and forests   **577.3**

Martin, Patricia Preciado

The ruins

In Growing up Latino; memoirs and stories p73-84   **810.8**

Martin, Rafe

Birdwing   **Fic**

Martin, Rafe, 1946-

The world before this one   **398.2**

Martin, Russell, 1952-

The mysteries of Beethoven's hair   **92**

Martin, Victoria C. Woodhull *See* Woodhull, Victoria C., 1838-1927

Martin-Jourdenais, Norma Jean

(il) Check, L. Create your own candles   **745.5**

Martin Luther King Day

Jeffrey, L. S. Celebrate Martin Luther King, Jr., Day   **394.26**

Martinez, Miriam G., 1948-

Children's books in children's hands. See Children's books in children's hands   **028.5**

Martinez, Pedro, 1971-

About

Lashnits, T. Pedro Martinez   **92**

Marty, Martin E., 1928-

(jt. auth) Breuilly, E. Religions of the world   **200**

Maruki, Toshi, 1912-

Hiroshima no pika   **940.54**

Marvel adventures Hulk [series]

Benjamin, P. Hulk: misunderstood monster   **741.5**

Marvel adventures: the avengers [series]

Parker, J. The avengers: heroes assembled   **741.5**

The **marvelous** effect. Cle, T.   **Fic**

Marvelous world [series]

Cle, T. The marvelous effect   **Fic**

Marvels in the muck. Wechsler, D.   **578.7**

Marx, Trish, 1948-

Elephants and golden thrones   **951**

Steel drumming at the Apollo   **785**

Marxism

See also Communism; Socialism

Mary, Queen of Scots, 1542-1587

See/See also pages in the following book(s):

Cotter, C. Kids who rule   **920**

Fiction

Lasky, K. Mary, Queen of Scots, queen without a country   **Fic**

Yolen, J. The queen's own fool   **Fic**

Mary on horseback [biography of Mary Breckinridge] Wells, R.   **92**

Mary Pope Osborne's Tales from the Odyssey [series]
Osborne, M. P. The gray-eyed goddess   **883**
Osborne, M. P. The land of the dead   **883**
Osborne, M. P. The one-eyed giant   **883**
Osborne, M. P. Return to Ithaca   **883**

Mary, Queen of Scots, queen without a country. Lasky, K.   **Fic**

Mary Shelley's Frankenstein: the graphic novel. Reed, G.   **741.5**

Maryland
    Fiction
Brashares, A. 3 willows   **Fic**
Cummings, P. Red kayak   **Fic**
Lyga, B. Hero-type   **Fic**
Naylor, P. R. Cricket man   **Fic**
    History
Walker, S. M. Written in bone   **614**

Marzilli, Alan, 1970-
Election reform   **324.6**
Stem cell research and cloning   **174.2**

Masai (African people)
Lekuton, J. Facing the lion   **967.62**

Masiello, Ralph
Ralph Masiello's ancient Egypt drawing book   **743**
Ralph Masiello's dragon drawing book   **743**

Masih, Iqbal, d. 1995
    Fiction
D'Adamo, F. Iqbal   **Fic**

Masks (Facial)
Finley, C. The art of African masks   **391**

Maslin, Ruthie, 1966-
(jt. auth) Imhoff, K. R. Library contests   **021.7**

Masoff, Joy, 1951-
The African American story   **305.8**
Snowboard!   **796.93**
We are all Americans   **325.73**

Mason, Antony
A history of Western art   **709**

Mason, Biddy, 1818-1891
See/See also pages in the following book(s):
Colman, P. Adventurous women   **920**
Pinkney, A. D. Let it shine   **920**

Mason, Bob
    About
Montgomery, S. The snake scientist   **597.96**

Mason, Chris, 1944-
(jt. auth) Brownlie, A. Why do people fight wars?   **355**

Mason, Francis
(jt. auth) Balanchine, G. 101 stories of the great ballets   **792.8**

Mason, Linda
Teen makeup   **646.7**

Mason, Paul, 1967-
Body piercing and tattooing   **391**
Population   **363.9**
Poverty   **362.5**

Mason, Prue
Camel rider   **Fic**

Mason, Timothy
The last synapsid   **Fic**

Mass, Wendy, 1967-
Every soul a star   **Fic**
Gods and goddesses   **201**
Heaven looks a lot like the mall   **Fic**
Jeremy Fink and the meaning of life   **Fic**
A mango-shaped space   **Fic**

Mass communication *See* Telecommunication

Mass extinction. Andryszewski, T.   **576.8**

Mass extinction of species
Andryszewski, T. Mass extinction   **576.8**
Mehling, R. Great extinctions of the past   **576.8**

Mass media
Ali, D. Media madness   **302.23**
Gelletly, L. Violence in the media   **303.6**
Gifford, C. Violence on the screen   **303.6**
Mass media: opposing viewpoints   **302.23**
Media violence: opposing viewpoints   **363.3**
Riley, S. G. African Americans in the media today   **920.003**
Streissguth, T. Media bias   **302.23**
See/See also pages in the following book(s):
Teens at risk: opposing viewpoints   **362.7**

Mass media: opposing viewpoints   **302.23**

Massachusetts
    Fiction
Barker, M. P. A difficult boy   **Fic**
Frazer, M. Secrets of truth and beauty   **Fic**
Friend, N. Bounce   **Fic**
Halpin, B. Forever changes   **Fic**
Hausman, G. A mind with wings   **Fic**
Krisher, T. Uncommon Faith   **Fic**
Meltzer, M. Tough times   **Fic**
Parker, R. B. The Edenville Owls   **Fic**
Paterson, K. Lyddie   **Fic**
Rees, D. C. Vampire High   **Fic**
Smith, P. C. Weetamoo, heart of the Pocassets   **Fic**
Velmans, H. Isabel of the whales   **Fic**
    History—1600-1775, Colonial period
Armentrout, D. The Mayflower Compact   **974.4**
Aronson, M. John Winthrop, Oliver Cromwell, and the Land of Promise [dual biography of John Winthrop and Oliver Cromwell]   **92**
Collier, C. Pilgrims and Puritans, 1620-1676   **974.4**
Doherty, K. William Bradford   **92**
Edwards, J. The Plymouth Colony and the Pilgrim adventure in American history   **974.4**
Erickson, P. Daily life in the Pilgrim colony, 1636   **974.4**
Harness, C. The adventurous life of Myles Standish   **92**
Philbrick, N. The Mayflower and the Pilgrims' New World   **973.2**
Stille, D. R. Anne Hutchinson   **92**
    History—1600-1775, Colonial period—Fiction
Duble, K. B. The sacrifice   **Fic**

Massacre at Virginia Tech. Worth, R.   **364.1**

Mattison, Christopher
Snake   **597.96**

Matulka, Denise I.
Picture this   **011.6**

Matzigkeit, Philip
(jt. auth) Marsden, C. Sahwira   **Fic**

Maurer, Richard, 1950-
The Wright sister [biography of Katharine Wright Haskell]   **92**

Mauritania
Blauer, E. Mauritania   **966.1**

Maus. Spiegelman, A.   **940.53**

Mawson, Sir Douglas, 1882-1958
About
Bredeson, C. After the last dog died [biography of Douglas Mawson]   **92**

Max Quigley. Roy, J.   **Fic**

Maximum Ride: the angel experiment. Patterson, J.   **Fic**

Maxwell, Nicole, d. 1998
See/See also pages in the following book(s):
Atkins, J. How high can we climb?   **920**

May, Mike
Sensation and perception   **612.8**

May, Suellen
Invasive microbes   **579**

Mayall, Beth
Mermaid Park   **Fic**
(jt. auth) Farrell, J. Middle school, the real deal   **373.1**

Mayas
Harris, N. Ancient Maya   **972**
Kallen, S. A. Rigoberta Menchu, Indian rights activist   **92**
Kops, D. Palenque   **972**
Perl, L. The ancient Maya   **972**
Antiquities
Mann, E. Tikal   **972.81**
Fiction
Greene, M. Chasing the jaguar   **Fic**
Rollins, J. Jake Ransom and the Skull King's shadow   **Fic**
Voelkel, J. Middleworld   **Fic**
Folklore
Menchú, R. The secret legacy   **398.2**

Maydell, Natalie
Extraordinary women from the Muslim world   **920**

Mayell, Mark
Tragedies of space exploration   **363.1**

Mayer, Maria Goeppert- *See* Goeppert-Mayer, Maria, 1906-1972

Mayer, Robert H., 1950-
When the children marched   **323.1**

Mayflower (Ship)
Armentrout, D. The Mayflower Compact   **974.4**

The **Mayflower** and the Pilgrims' New World. Philbrick, N.   **973.2**

The **Mayflower** Compact. Armentrout, D.   **974.4**

Maynard, John, 1941-
(ed) Blake, W. William Blake [Poetry for young people series]   **821**

Maynard, Joyce, 1953-
The cloud chamber   **Fic**

The **maze** of bones. Riordan, R.   **Fic**

Mazer, Harry, 1925-
A boy at war   **Fic**
The last mission   **Fic**
My brother Abe   **Fic**
Snow bound   **Fic**

Mazer, Norma Fox, 1931-
After the rain   **Fic**
Girlhearts   **Fic**
The missing girl   **Fic**

McAlpine, Margaret
Working in music and dance   **780**
Working in the fashion industry   **746.9**
Working in the food industry   **647.9**
Working with animals   **636**
Working with children   **362.7**
Working with computers   **004**

McArdle, Paula, 1971-
(il) Shelby, A. The adventures of Molly Whuppie and other Appalachian folktales   **398.2**

McArthur, Debra
The Kansas-Nebraska Act and "Bleeding Kansas" in American history   **978.1**
Mark Twain   **92**
Raoul Wallenberg   **92**
A student's guide to Edgar Allan Poe   **813.009**

McAuliffe, Christa
About
Jeffrey, L. S. Christa McAuliffe   **92**

McCaffrey, Anne
Dragonflight   **Fic**

McCage, Crystal
(ed) Oil. See Oil   **333.8**

McCain, John S., 1936-
About
Wells, C. John McCain   **92**

McCain, Mary Maude
Dictionary for school library media specialists   **020**

McCampbell, Darlene Z., 1942-
(ed) Leaving home: stories. See Leaving home: stories   **808.8**
(comp) Who do you think you are? See Who do you think you are?   **S C**

McCarthy, Colin, 1951-
Reptile   **597.9**

McCarthy, Joseph, 1908-1957
About
Fitzgerald, B. McCarthyism   **973.921**
The McCarthy hearings   **973.921**

The **McCarthy** hearings   **973.921**

McCarthyism. Fitzgerald, B.   **973.921**

McCarty, Henry *See* Billy, the Kid

McCarty, Nick
The Iliad   **883**
Marco Polo   **92**

McGough, Roger, 1937-—*Continued*
(ed) Wicked poems. See Wicked poems
811.008

McGowan, Eileen Nixon
Stock market smart **332.6**

McGowan, Gary
(jt. auth) Hansen, J. Breaking ground, breaking silence **974.7**
(jt. auth) Hansen, J. Freedom roads: searching for the Underground Railroad **973.7**

McGowen, Tom
Air raid **940.54**
Assault from the sky **940.54**
Carrier war **940.54**

McGraw, Eloise Jarvis, 1915-2000
The moorchild **Fic**

McGraw, John Joseph, 1873-1934
Fiction
Tocher, T. Bill Pennant, Babe Ruth, and me **Fic**

McGuigan, Mary Ann, 1949-
Morning in a different place **Fic**

McHargue, Dove
(il) Serling, R. The Twilight Zone: walking distance **741.5**

McIntire, Suzanne, 1951-
(ed) American Heritage book of great American speeches for young people. See American Heritage book of great American speeches for young people **815.008**

McIntosh, Jane
Archeology **930.1**

McIntosh, Kenneth, 1959-
When religion & politics mix **201**

McIntosh, Marsha
(jt. auth) McIntosh, K. When religion & politics mix **201**

McIntyre, Thomas, 1952-
The behavior survival guide for kids **158**

McKain, Mark
(ed) Making and using the atomic bomb. See Making and using the atomic bomb **355.8**

McKay, Christopher P.
About
Turner, P. S. Life on earth—and beyond **576.8**

McKay, George
(jt. auth) McGhee, K. Encyclopedia of animals **590.3**

McKay, Hilary, 1959-
Saffy's angel **Fic**

McKean, Dave
(il) Almond, D. The savage **Fic**
(il) Gaiman, N. Coraline **Fic**
(il) Gaiman, N. The graveyard book **Fic**

McKellar, Danica
Math doesn't suck **510**

McKenzie, Nancy
Guinevere's gift **Fic**

McKeown, Adam
Julius Caesar **822.3**

McKernan, Victoria
The devil's paintbox **Fic**

Shackleton's stowaway **Fic**

McKinley, Michael, 1961-
Ice time **796.962**

McKinley, Robin
Beauty **Fic**
The blue sword **Fic**
Chalice **Fic**
The door in the hedge **S C**
Dragonhaven **Fic**
The hero and the crown **Fic**
The outlaws of Sherwood **398.2**
Rose daughter **Fic**
Water: tales of elemental spirits **S C**

McKinley, William, 1843-1901
See/See also pages in the following book(s):
St. George, J. In the line of fire **364.1**

McKinnell, Robert Gilmore
Prevention of cancer **616.99**

McKinney, Jack *See* Luceno, James, 1947-

McKinnon, Hannah Roberts
Franny Parker **Fic**

McKissack, Fredrick, 1939-
(jt. auth) McKissack, P. C. Black diamond **796.357**
(jt. auth) McKissack, P. C. Black hands, white sails **639.2**
(jt. auth) McKissack, P. C. Days of Jubilee **973.7**
(jt. auth) McKissack, P. C. Let my people go **Fic**
(jt. auth) McKissack, P. C. Rebels against slavery **326**
(jt. auth) McKissack, P. C. The royal kingdoms of Ghana, Mali, and Songhay **966.2**

McKissack, Pat *See* McKissack, Patricia C., 1944-

McKissack, Patricia C., 1944-
Black diamond **796.357**
Black hands, white sails **639.2**
The dark-thirty **S C**
Days of Jubilee **973.7**
A friendship for today **Fic**
Let my people go **Fic**
Nzinga, warrior queen of Matamba **Fic**
Porch lies **S C**
Rebels against slavery **326**
The royal kingdoms of Ghana, Mali, and Songhay **966.2**
To establish justice **342**

McKowen, Scott
(il) Pyle, H. The merry adventures of Robin Hood **398.2**
(il) Swift, J. Gulliver's travels **Fic**

McLaren, Clemence, 1938-
Inside the walls of Troy **Fic**

McLeish, Ewan, 1950-
Overcrowded world **363.9**

McMann, Lisa
Wake **Fic**

McMillan, Beverly
Oceans **551.46**

McMillan, Naomi *See* Grimes, Nikki

McMullan, Margaret
Cashay **Fic**
How I found the Strong **Fic**

Media literacy—*Continued*

Wan Guofang. TV takeover	**384.55**
Wan Guofang. Virtually true	**025.04**

Media madness. Ali, D.   **302.23**

Media violence: opposing viewpoints   **363.3**

Medical assistance

Morley, D. Healing our world   **610**

Medical botany

Kidd, J. S. Potent natural medicines   **615**

Medical care

Naden, C. J. Patients' rights   **362.1**

Fiction

Forman, G. If I stay	**Fic**
Jocelyn, M. Would you	**Fic**

Medical ethics

See also Human experimentation in medicine; Right to die

Lovegrove, R. Health	**174.2**
Stefoff, R. The right to die	**179.7**
Winkler, K. High-tech babies	**618.1**

The **medical** examiner. Allman, T.   **363.2**

Medical imaging. Sherrow, V.   **616.07**

Medical jurisprudence

Allman, T. The medical examiner	**363.2**
Hunter, W. DNA analysis	**363.2**

Medical mysteries. Auden, S.   **610**

Medicinal plants *See* Medical botany

Medicine

See also Alternative medicine; Sports medicine; Surgery; Therapeutics; Women in medicine and names of diseases and groups of diseases

Goldsmith, C. Cutting-edge medicine	**610**
Reeves, D. L. Career ideas for teens in health science	**610.69**
What can I do now?: Health care	**362.1**

Fiction

Morgan, N. Fleshmarket   **Fic**

History

Davis, L. Medicine in the American West   **610.9**

Dawson, I. Renaissance medicine	**610.9**
Townsend, J. Pox, pus & plague	**616**
Woolf, A. Death and disease	**610.9**

Law and legislation

See also Medical jurisprudence

Physiological effect

See Pharmacology

Research

Auden, S. Medical mysteries	**610**
Dendy, L. A. Guinea pig scientists	**616**
Piddock, C. Outbreak	**614.4**

Medicine, Veterinary *See* Veterinary medicine

Medicine in the American West. Davis, L.   **610.9**

Médicis, Catherine de, Queen, consort of Henry II, King of France, 1519-1589 *See* Catherine de Médicis, Queen, consort of Henry II, King of France, 1519-1589

The **medieval & early modern world** [series]

Des Forges, R. V. The Asian world, 600-1500   **950**

Huff, T. E. An age of science and revolutions, 1600-1800	**909.08**
Wiesner, M. E. An age of voyages, 1350-1600	**909.08**

Medieval art

Martin, A. Knights & castles   **940.1**

Medieval church history *See* Church history—600-1500, Middle Ages

Medieval civilization

Adams, S. The Kingfisher atlas of the medieval world	**909.07**
Barter, J. A medieval knight	**940.1**
Chrisp, P. Town and country life	**940.1**
Chrisp, P. Warfare	**355**
Corbishley, M. The Middle Ages	**940.1**
Exploring the Middle Ages	**909.07**
Gravett, C. Knight	**940.1**
Hanel, R. Knights	**940.1**
Hart, A. Knights & castles	**940.1**
Haywood, J. Medieval Europe	**940.1**
Hinds, K. The castle [Life in the Middle Ages series]	**940.1**
Hinds, K. The city [Life in the Middle Ages series]	**940.1**
Hinds, K. The city [Life in the Medieval Muslim world series]	**909.07**
Hinds, K. The countryside [Life in the Middle Ages series]	**940.1**
Hinds, K. The countryside [Life in the Medieval Muslim world series]	**909.07**
Hinds, K. Everyday life in medieval Europe	**940.1**
Hinds, K. Faith	**297**
Hinds, K. Medieval England	**942.03**
Hinds, K. The palace	**909.07**
Kallen, S. A. A medieval merchant	**940.1**
Knight, J. Middle ages: almanac	**909.07**
Knight, J. Middle ages: biographies	**920**
Langley, A. Medieval life	**940.1**
Martin, A. Knights & castles	**940.1**
Medieval world	**909.07**
Nardo, D. Lords, ladies, peasants, and knights	**940.1**
Ramen, F. Albucasis (Abu al-Qasim al-Zahrawi)	**92**
Ross, S. Monarchs	**940.1**
Service, A. 1200	**909.07**
Woolf, A. Death and disease	**610.9**
Woolf, A. Education	**940.1**

Medieval England. Hinds, K.   **942.03**

Medieval Europe. Haywood, J.   **940.1**

A **medieval** knight. Barter, J.   **940.1**

Medieval life. Langley, A.   **940.1**

A **medieval** merchant. Kallen, S. A.   **940.1**

Medieval realms [series]

Chrisp, P. Town and country life	**940.1**
Chrisp, P. Warfare	**355**
Ross, S. Monarchs	**940.1**
Woolf, A. Death and disease	**610.9**
Woolf, A. Education	**940.1**

Medieval world   **909.07**

Medina, Meg, 1963-

Milagros   **Fic**

Menchú, Rigoberta—*Continued*
About
Kallen, S. A. Rigoberta Menchu, Indian rights
   activist   **92**
See/See also pages in the following book(s):
Krull, K. Lives of extraordinary women   **920**

Mendel, Gregor, 1822-1884
About
Edelson, E. Gregor Mendel, and the roots of ge-
   netics   **92**
Klare, R. Gregor Mendel   **92**
See/See also pages in the following book(s):
Gardner, R. Genetics and evolution science fair
   projects   **576**
Phelan, G. Double helix   **572.8**

Mendel, Johann Gregor *See* Mendel, Gregor,
   1822-1884

Mendell, David
Obama. See Thomson, S. L. Obama   **92**

Mendoza, Patrick M.
Extraordinary people in extraordinary times
    920

Mendrinos, Roxanne Baxter
Using educational technology with at-risk students   **027.8**

Menhard, Francha Roffe
The facts about amphetamines   **362.29**
The facts about inhalants   **362.29**
The facts about ritalin   **615**
Teen consumer smarts   **332.024**

Meningitis
Klosterman, L. Meningitis   **616.8**
Routh, K. Meningitis   **616.8**

Menon, Sujatha
Discover snakes   **597.96**

Menstruation
Gravelle, K. The period book   **612.6**
Jukes, M. Growing up: it's a girl thing
    612.6
See/See also pages in the following book(s):
Jukes, M. It's a girl thing   **305.23**
Fiction
Don't cramp my style   **S C**

Mental health
Mental health information for teens   **616.89**
A student's guide to mental health & wellness
    616.89
Szabo, R. Behind happy faces   **616.89**
Mental health information for teens   **616.89**

Mental illness
   See also Personality disorders
Kent, D. Snake pits, talking cures, & magic bul-
   lets   **616.89**
Mental illness: opposing viewpoints   **362.2**
Stewart, G. People with mental illness
    616.89
A student's guide to mental health & wellness
    616.89
Szabo, R. Behind happy faces   **616.89**
Fiction
Barkley, B. Jars of glass   **Fic**
Griffin, A. Where I want to be   **Fic**
Halpern, J. Get well soon   **Fic**
Holmes, E. A. Tracktown summer   **Fic**

Leavitt, M. Heck, superhero   **Fic**
McNish, C. Angel   **Fic**
Moore, P. Caught in the act   **Fic**
Sones, S. Stop pretending   **Fic**
Whelan, G. The locked garden   **Fic**
Mental illness: opposing viewpoints   **362.2**

Mental retardation
Libal, A. My name is not Slow   **362.3**

Mental telepathy *See* Telepathy

Mental tests *See* Psychological tests

Mentally handicapped
Fiction
Lowry, L. The silent boy   **Fic**
Martin, A. M. A corner of the universe   **Fic**
Nolan, H. A face in every window   **Fic**
Nuzum, K. A. A small white scar   **Fic**
Wood, J. R. The man who loved clowns
    Fic

Mentally handicapped children
Fiction
Byars, B. C. The summer of the swans   **Fic**

Mentally ill
Fiction
Fensham, E. Helicopter man   **Fic**
Lowenstein, S. C. Waiting for Eugene   **Fic**
Mitchard, J. Now you see her   **Fic**
Russo, M. A portrait of Pia   **Fic**
Trueman, T. Inside out   **Fic**
White, R. Memories of Summer   **Fic**
Institutional care
   See also Psychiatric hospitals

Mentoring
Fiction
McMullan, M. Cashay   **Fic**

Menzel, Peter
What the world eats   **641.3**

Merali, Alim, 1984-
Talk the talk   **808.53**

Mercado, Nancy E., 1975-
(ed) Baseball crazy: ten short stories that cover
   all the bases. See Baseball crazy: ten short
   stories that cover all the bases   **S C**
(ed) Every man for himself. See Every man for
   himself   **S C**
(ed) Tripping over the lunch lady and other
   school stories. See Tripping over the lunch
   lady and other school stories   **S C**

Mercator, Gerardus, 1512-1594
About
Heinrichs, A. Gerardus Mercator   **92**

Mercer, Bobby, 1961-
(jt. auth) Newcomb, R. Smash it! crash it!
   launch it!   **507.8**

The **merchant** of Venice. Hinds, G.   **741.5**

Merchants
Kallen, S. A. A medieval merchant   **940.1**

Mercury (Planet)
Spangenburg, R. A look at Mercury   **523.4**

Mercury Project *See* Project Mercury

Mercy killing *See* Euthanasia

Meret, Sasha
(il) Feiler, B. S. Walking the Bible   **222**

Mexican Americans—Fiction—*Continued*

Cisneros, S. The house on Mango Street **Fic**
De la Peña, M. Mexican whiteboy **Fic**
Estevis, A. Chicken Foot Farm **Fic**
Estevis, A. Down Garrapata road **S C**
Greene, M. Chasing the jaguar **Fic**
Jiménez, F. Breaking through **Fic**
Jiménez, F. The circuit: stories from the life of a migrant child **Fic**
Jiménez, F. Reaching out **Fic**
Johnston, T. Any small goodness **Fic**
Lachtman, O. D. The truth about Las Mariposas **Fic**
Lopez, D. Confetti girl **Fic**
López, L. Call me Henri **Fic**
Nails, J. Next to Mexico **Fic**
Rice, D. Crazy loco **S C**
Ryan, P. M. Esperanza rising **Fic**
Saenz, B. A. He forgot to say good-bye **Fic**
Saldaña, R. The whole sky full of stars **Fic**
Sanchez, A. So hard to say **Fic**
Sitomer, A. L. The secret story of Sonia Rodriguez **Fic**
Soto, G. The afterlife **Fic**
Soto, G. Baseball in April, and other stories **S C**
Soto, G. Buried onions **Fic**
Soto, G. Help wanted **S C**
Soto, G. Local news **S C**
Volponi, P. Homestretch **Fic**

Poetry
Herrera, J. F. Laughing out loud, I fly **811**
Soto, G. Canto familiar **811**
Soto, G. A fire in my hands **811**
Soto, G. A natural man **811**

Mexican art
Lewis, E. Mexican art & culture **709.72**

Mexican art & culture. Lewis, E. **709.72**

Mexican artists *See* Artists, Mexican

Mexican literature
Collections
The Tree is older than you are **860.8**

The **Mexican** Revolution. Stein, R. C. **972**

Mexican War, 1846-1848
Bardhan-Quallen, S. The Mexican-American War **973.6**
Carey, C. W. The Mexican War **973.6**
Collier, C. Hispanic America, Texas, and the Mexican War, 1835-1850 **973.6**
Feldman, R. T. The Mexican-American War **973.6**
Worth, R. The Texas war of independence: the 1800s **976.4**

Mexican whiteboy. De la Peña, M. **Fic**

Mexicans
Fiction
Hobbs, W. Crossing the wire **Fic**
Jaramillo, A. La linea **Fic**
United States
See also Mexican Americans
The **Mexicans** **305.8**

Mexico
Délano, P. When I was a boy Neruda called me Policarpo **92**

Gruber, B. Mexico **972**
Hamilton, J. Mexico in pictures **972**
Junior Worldmark encyclopedia of the Mexican states **972**
Reilly, M.-J. Mexico **972**
Stein, R. C. Mexico **972**
Antiquities
Harris, N. Ancient Maya **972**
Kops, D. Palenque **972**
Civilization
Bingham, J. The Aztec empire **972**
Fiction
Landman, T. I am Apache **Fic**
Resau, L. Red glass **Fic**
Resau, L. What the moon saw **Fic**
Steinbeck, J. The pearl **Fic**
History
Lourie, P. On the Texas trail of Cabeza de Vaca **92**
Mattern, J. Celebrate Cinco de Mayo **394.26**
Serrano, F. The poet king of Tezcoco [biography of Nezahualcóyotl] **92**
Stein, R. C. Benito Juarez and the French intervention **92**
Stein, R. C. Cortes and the Spanish Conquest **972**
Stein, R. C. The Mexican Revolution **972**
Stein, R. C. The Mexican War of Independence **972**
Social life and customs
Lewis, E. Mexican art & culture **709.72**
Mattern, J. Celebrate Cinco de Mayo **394.26**

Mexico in pictures. Hamilton, J. **972**

Meyer, Carolyn
Beware, Princess Elizabeth **Fic**
Duchessina **Fic**
The true adventures of Charley Darwin **Fic**

Meyer, Don
(ed) The sibling slam book. See The sibling slam book **306.8**

Meyer, Kai, 1969-
The water mirror **Fic**

Meyer, L. A., 1942-
Bloody Jack **Fic**

Meyer, Stephenie, 1973-
Twilight **Fic**

Meyers-Rice, Barry *See* Rice, Barry A.

Meyerson, Golda *See* Meir, Golda, 1898-1978

Mezinski, Pierre, 1950-
Drugs explained **362.29**

Miami (Fla.)
Fiction
Gantos, J. Jack on the tracks **Fic**

Mice
Fiction
Conly, J. L. Racso and the rats of NIMH **Fic**
Hoeye, M. Time stops for no mouse **Fic**
Jacques, B. Redwall **Fic**
Milway, A. The mousehunter **Fic**
O'Brien, R. C. Mrs. Frisby and the rats of NIMH **Fic**
Graphic novels
Glass, B. J. L. The mice templar, volume one: the prophecy **741.5**

Mice—Graphic novels—*Continued*
Jacques, B. Redwall: the graphic novel
741.5

The **mice** templar, volume one: the prophecy.
Glass, B. J. L.   **741.5**

Michael, Jan, 1947-
City boy   **Fic**

Michael, Livi, 1960-
City of dogs   **Fic**

Michael, Pamela
(ed) River of words. See River of words
808.81

Michael, Scott W.
(jt. auth) Wood, K. The 101 best tropical fishes
639.34

Michael L. Printz award
Gillespie, J. T. The Newbery/Printz companion
028.5

Michaelis, Antonia, 1979-
Tiger moon   **Fic**

Michaels, Alexandra
(il) Baker, D. Jazzy jewelry   **745.594**

Michaels, Rune
Genesis Alpha   **Fic**
The reminder   **Fic**

Michaels, Ski *See* Pellowski, Michael, 1949-

Micheaux, Oscar, 1884-1951
See/See also pages in the following book(s):
Haskins, J. African American entrepreneurs
920

Michelangelo Buonarroti, 1475-1564
About
Stanley, D. Michelangelo   **92**
Wilkinson, P. Michelangelo   **92**

Michigan
Fiction
Day, K. No cream puffs   **Fic**
Ford, J. C. The morgue and me **Fic**
Strickland, B. The sign of the sinister sorcerer
Fic
Whelan, G. The locked garden   **Fic**
White, R. Memories of Summer   **Fic**

Micklos, John, 1956-
Unsolved: what really happened to Amelia Earhart? **92**

Microbes *See* Bacteria

Microbiology
See also Biotechnology
Rainis, K. G. Cell and microbe science fair projects using microscopes, mold, and more
571.6

Microorganisms
See also Bacteria
Farrell, J. Invisible allies   **579**
Latta, S. L. The good, the bad, the slimy
579
May, S. Invasive microbes   **579**
Stefoff, R. The Moneran kingdom **579**
Walker, R. Microscopic life   **579**

Microquests [series]
Johnson, R. L. Amazing DNA   **572.8**
Johnson, R. L. Powerful plant cells **581.7**

Johnson, R. L. Ultra-organized cell systems
612

Microscopes
Kramer, S. Hidden worlds: looking through a scientist's microscope **502.8**
Levine, S. The ultimate guide to your microscope **502.8**
Petersen, C. The microscope   **502.8**
Stefoff, R. Microscopes and telescopes **502.8**
Yount, L. Antoni van Leeuwenhoek **92**

Microscopes and telescopes. Stefoff, R. **502.8**

Microscopic life. Walker, R. **579**

Microsoft Corporation
Aronson, M. Bill Gates   **92**
Lesinski, J. M. Bill Gates   **92**

Microsoft Excel (Computer program) *See* Excel (Computer program)

The **midbrain**. Morgan, M.   **612.8**

Middle Ages
See also Church history—600-1500, Middle Ages; Europe—History—476-1492; Medieval civilization; World history—13th century
Cohen, B. Canterbury tales   **821**
Corbishley, M. The Middle Ages **940.1**
Crossley-Holland, K. The world of King Arthur and his court **942.01**
Currie, S. Miracles, saints, and superstition
940.1
Davenport, J. The age of feudalism **940.1**
George, L. S. 800   **909.07**
Hart, A. Knights & castles   **940.1**
Haywood, J. Medieval Europe   **940.1**
Hinds, K. The church [Life in the Middle Ages series] **274**
Hinds, K. The city [Life in the Medieval Muslim world series] **909.07**
Hinds, K. The countryside [Life in the Medieval Muslim world series] **909.07**
Hinds, K. Everyday life in medieval Europe
940.1
Hinds, K. Faith   **297**
Hinds, K. The palace   **909.07**
Knight, J. Middle ages: almanac **909.07**
Lace, W. W. The unholy crusade **956.1**
Medieval world   **909.07**
Middle ages: primary sources   **909.07**
Nardo, D. Lords, ladies, peasants, and knights
940.1
Peters, S. T. The Black Death **614.5**
Plain, N. Eleanor of Aquitaine and the High Middle Ages **942.03**
Slavicek, L. C. The Black Death **614.5**
White, P. Exploration in the world of the Middle Ages, 500-1500 **910.4**
White, T. H. The once and future king **Fic**
Wiesner, M. E. An age of voyages, 1350-1600
909.08
Williams, M. Chaucer's Canterbury Tales
821
Zahler, D. The Black Death   **614.5**
Bibliography
Barnhouse, R. The Middle Ages in literature for youth **011.6**
Biography
Knight, J. Middle ages: biographies **920**

Middle Ages—*Continued*
Drama
Schlitz, L. A. Good masters! Sweet ladies! **940.1**
Encyclopedias
Exploring the Middle Ages **909.07**
Fiction
Avi. The Book Without Words **Fic**
Avi. Crispin: the cross of lead **Fic**
Cadnum, M. The book of the Lion **Fic**
Cadnum, M. Forbidden forest **Fic**
Cadnum, M. The king's arrow **Fic**
Crossley-Holland, K. Crossing to Paradise **Fic**
Crossley-Holland, K. The seeing stone **Fic**
Cushman, K. Catherine, called Birdy **Fic**
Cushman, K. The midwife's apprentice **Fic**
Gilman, L. A. Grail quest: the Camelot spell **Fic**
Grant, K. M. Blood red horse **Fic**
Grant, K. M. Blue flame **Fic**
Jinks, C. Babylonne **Fic**
Karr, K. Fortune's fool **Fic**
Leeds, C. The silver cup **Fic**
Moran, K. Bloodline **Fic**
Napoli, D. J. Hush **Fic**
Russell, C. Dogboy **Fic**
Spradlin, M. P. Keeper of the Grail **Fic**
Springer, N. Rowan Hood, outlaw girl of Sherwood Forest **Fic**
Stroud, J. Heroes of the valley **Fic**
Temple, F. The Ramsay scallop **Fic**

Middle ages: almanac. Knight, J. **909.07**

Middle ages: biographies. Knight, J. **920**

The **Middle** Ages in literature for youth. Barnhouse, R. **011.6**

Middle ages: primary sources **909.07**

Middle East
See also Arab countries
Feiler, B. S. Walking the Bible **222**
Gritzner, J. A. North Africa and the Middle East **956**
Kort, M. The handbook of the Middle East **956**
The Middle East **956**
Perliger, A. Middle Eastern terrorism **303.6**
Steele, P. Middle East **956**
Stewart, G. Human rights in the Middle East **323**
Woods, M. Seven natural wonders of Asia and the Middle East **508**
See/See also pages in the following book(s):
Frank, M. Understanding September 11th **973.931**
Antiquities
Podany, A. H. The ancient Near Eastern world **939**
Bibliography
Al-Hazza, T. C. Books about the Middle East **016**
Civilization
Podany, A. H. The ancient Near Eastern world **939**
Stefoff, R. The ancient Near East **939**

Fiction
Alexander, L. The golden dream of Carlo Chuchio **Fic**
Marston, E. Santa Claus in Baghdad and other stories about teens in the Arab world **S C**
Temple, F. The Beduins' gazelle **Fic**
Tunnell, M. O. Wishing moon **Fic**
Whelan, G. Parade of shadows **Fic**
History
Hampton, W. War in the Middle East **956.04**
January, B. The Arab Conquests of the Middle East **956**
Stefoff, R. The ancient Near East **939**
Poetry
Nye, N. S. 19 varieties of gazelle **811**
The Space between our footsteps **808.81**
Politics and government
Gunderson, C. G. The need for oil **338.2**
The Middle East: opposing viewpoints **956**

The **Middle** East **956**

The **Middle** East: opposing viewpoints **956**

Middle East War, 1991 *See* Persian Gulf War, 1991

Middle Eastern cooking
Batmanglij, N. Happy Nowruz **641.5**

Middle Eastern terrorism. Perliger, A. **303.6**

The **middle** of somewhere. Cheaney, J. B. **Fic**

The **middle** road: American politics, 1945-2000. Collier, C. **973.92**

Middle school confidential [series]
Fox, A. Be confident in who you are **158**

Middle school: how to deal **373.1**

Middle school is worse than meatloaf. Holm, J. L. **Fic**

Middle school reference [series]
American presidents in world history **920.003**
The Newest Americans **325.73**
Student almanac of African American history **305.8**
Student almanac of Native American history **970.004**

The **middle** school survival guide. Erlbach, A. **373.1**

Middle school, the real deal. Farrell, J. **373.1**

Middle schools
Collins, J. Motivating readers in the middle grades **028.5**
Erlbach, A. The middle school survival guide **373.1**
Farrell, J. Middle school, the real deal **373.1**
Middle school: how to deal **373.1**

Middleman, Amy B.
(ed) American Medical Association boy's guide to becoming a teen. See American Medical Assocation boy's guide to becoming a teen **613**
(ed) American Medical Association girl's guide to becoming a teen. See American Medical Association girl's guide to becoming a teen **613**

Misconduct in office
See also Political corruption
The **misfits**. Howe, J.   Fic
Misiroglu, Gina Renée
(ed) The Superhero book. See The Superhero
book   **741.5**
Mismatch. Namioka, L.   Fic
Miss Crandall's School for Young Ladies and Lit-
tle Misses of Color. Alexander, E.   **811**
Miss Spitfire. Miller, S.   Fic
The missing [series]
Haddix, M. P. Found   Fic
Missing children
See also Runaway children
Fiction
Bowler, T. Frozen fire   Fic
DiCamillo, K. The magician's elephant   Fic
Dowd, S. The London Eye mystery   Fic
Godwin, J. Falling from Grace   Fic
Hartnett, S. What the birds see   Fic
Plum-Ucci, C. The night my sister went missing
                                                            Fic
Vande Velde, V. Stolen   Fic
The **missing** girl. Mazer, N. F.   Fic
Missing link trilogy [series]
Thompson, K. Fourth World   Fic
Missing May. Rylant, C.   Fic
Missing persons
See also Runaway teenagers
Fiction
Abrahams, P. Reality check   Fic
Bradbury, J. Shift   Fic
Cantor, J. The September sisters   Fic
Doyle, M. Bewitching season   Fic
Finn, M. Anila's journey   Fic
Grant, V. Quid pro quo   Fic
Hiaasen, C. Scat   Fic
Hollyer, B. Secrets, lies and my sister Kate
                                                            Fic
Les Becquets, D. Season of ice   Fic
McDonnell, M. Torn to pieces   Fic
Miklowitz, G. D. The enemy has a face   Fic
Parkinson, S. Blue like Friday   Fic
Prévost, G. The book of time   Fic
Springer, N. The case of the missing marquess
                                                            Fic
Valentine, J. Me, the missing, and the dead
                                                            Fic
Vrettos, A. M. Sight   Fic
Weingarten, L. Wherever Nina lies   Fic
Westerfeld, S. So yesterday   Fic
Wilson, N. D. Leepike Ridge   Fic
Mission control, this is Apollo. Chaikin, A.
                                                          629.45
Mission: science [series]
Cregan, E. R. The atom   **539.7**
Cregan, E. R. Marie Curie   **92**
Herweck, D. Robert Fulton   **92**
Lee, K. F. Cells   **571.6**
Van Gorp, L. Antoine Lavoisier   **92**
Van Gorp, L. Elements   **540**
Zamosky, L. Louis Pasteur   **92**
Mission to the moon. Dyer, A.   **629.45**

Missions, Christian *See* Christian missions
Mississippi
Fiction
McMullan, M. How I found the Strong   Fic
McMullan, M. When I crossed No-Bob   Fic
Taylor, M. D. The friendship   Fic
Taylor, M. D. Let the circle be unbroken
                                            Fic
Taylor, M. D. The road to Memphis   Fic
Taylor, M. D. Roll of thunder, hear my cry
                                            Fic
Taylor, M. D. The well   Fic
Wiles, D. The Aurora County All-Stars   Fic
Poetry
Lewis, J. P. Black cat bone   **811**
Nelson, M. A wreath for Emmett Till   **811**
Race relations
Aretha, D. Freedom Summer   **323.1**
Aretha, D. The murder of Emmett Till
                                            364.1
Crowe, C. Getting away with murder: the true
story of the Emmett Till case   **364.1**
Mississippi Freedom Project
Aretha, D. Freedom Summer   **323.1**
Mississippi River
Waldman, N. Voyages   **92**
Fiction
Gray, D. E. Tomorrow, the river   Fic
Helgerson, J. Horns & wrinkles   Fic
Twain, M. The adventures of Huckleberry Finn
                                            Fic
Twain, M. The adventures of Tom Sawyer
                                            Fic
Mississippi River valley
Faber, H. La Salle   **92**
Goodman, J. E. Despite all obstacles: La Salle
and the conquest of the Mississippi   **92**
History
Harkins, S. S. The life and times of Father
Jacques Marquette   **92**
Mississippi trial, 1955. Crowe, C.   Fic
Mississippi valley *See* Mississippi River valley
Missouri
Fiction
Crocker, N. Billie Standish was here   Fic
Harness, C. Just for you to know   Fic
Katcher, B. Playing with matches   Fic
McKissack, P. C. A friendship for today
                                            Fic
Twain, M. The adventures of Huckleberry Finn
                                            Fic
Twain, M. The adventures of Tom Sawyer
                                            Fic
Mister Monday. Nix, G.   Fic
Mistik Lake. Brooks, M.   Fic
Mitchard, Jacquelyn
All we know of heaven   Fic
The midnight twins   Fic
Now you see her   Fic
Mitchell, Don, 1957-
Liftoff [biography of John Glenn]   **92**
Mitchell, Maria, 1818-1889
About
Anderson, D. Maria Mitchell, astronomer   **92**

Molloy, Michael
  Peter Raven under fire   **Fic**
Moloney, James, 1954-
  The Book of Lies   **Fic**
Momo no Tane
  Shugo chara!   **741.5**
Monaco
  King, D. C. Monaco   **944**
Monarchs *See* Kings and rulers
Monarchs. Lasky, K.   **595.7**
Monarchs. Ross, S.   **940.1**
Monarchy
  See also Empresses; Queens
  Stefoff, R. Monarchy   **321**
Monasticism and religious orders for women
  See also Nuns
Mondowney, JoAnn G.
  Hold them in your heart   **027.62**
The **Moneran** kingdom. Stefoff, R.   **579**
Monet, Claude, 1840-1926
        About
  Kallen, S. A. Claude Monet   **92**
Monet and the impressionists for kids. Sabbeth, C.   **759.05**
Money
  Cribb, J. Money   **332.4**
  Hall, A. Show me the money   **332.024**
  Kummer, P. K. Currency   **332.4**
Money-making projects for children
  Bielagus, P. G. Quick cash for teens   **658.1**
  Bochner, A. B. The new totally awesome business book for kids (and their parents)   **658**
        Fiction
  Graff, L. The life and crimes of Bernetta Wallflower   **Fic**
Mongolia
  Pang, G.-C. Mongolia   **951.7**
        Fiction
  Tschinag, G. The blue sky   **Fic**
Mongolians *See* Mongols
Mongols
  Demi. Genghis Khan   **92**
  Greenblatt, M. Genghis Khan and the Mongol Empire   **950**
  Lange, B. Genghis Khan   **92**
The **monkey** garden. Cisneros, S.
  In Growing up Latino; memoirs and stories p288-91   **810.8**
Monkey High!: vol. 1. Akira, S.   **741.5**
Monkey town. Kidd, R.   **Fic**
Monkeys
  See also Baboons
  Zabludoff, M. Monkeys   **599.8**
Monninger, Joseph
  Baby   **Fic**
  Hippie chick   **Fic**
Mono (Disease) *See* Mononucleosis
Monologues
  Actor's choice   **808.82**
  The Book of monologues for aspiring actors   **808.82**
  Great monologues for young actors   **808.82**

Millennium monologs   **812.008**
New audition scenes and monologs from contemporary playwrights   **808.82**
Schlitz, L. A. Good masters! Sweet ladies!   **940.1**
Shakespeare, W. One hundred and eleven Shakespeare monologues   **822.3**
Surface, M. H. More short scenes and monologues for middle school students   **808.82**
Surface, M. H. Short scenes and monologues for middle school actors   **808.82**
Mononucleosis
  Hoffmann, G. Mononucleosis   **616.9**
Monroe, James, 1758-1831
        About
  Naden, C. J. James Monroe   **92**
Monroe, Judy
  Cystic fibrosis   **616.3**
  The Susan B. Anthony women's voting rights trial   **324.6**
Monroe Doctrine
  Renehan, E. J. The Monroe doctrine   **327.73**
The **Monroe** doctrine. Renehan, E. J.   **327.73**
Monroy, Manuel
  (il) Délano, P. When I was a boy Neruda called me Policarpo   **92**
Monsoon summer. Perkins, M.   **Fic**
Monster. Myers, W. D.   **Fic**
Monster origami. Nguyen, D.   **736**
Monsters
  Ape-men   **001.9**
  Bardhan-Quallen, S. The real monsters   **001.9**
  Gee, J. Encyclopedia horrifica   **001.9**
  Halls, K. M. Tales of the cryptids   **001.9**
  Nguyen, D. Monster origami   **736**
        Fiction
  Coville, B. The monsters of Morley Manor   **Fic**
  McNamee, G. Bonechiller   **Fic**
  Snow, A. Here be monsters!   **Fic**
        Folklore
  Morpurgo, M. Beowulf   **398.2**
  Raven, N. Beowulf   **398.2**
  Rogasky, B. The golem   **398.2**
  Rumford, J. Beowulf   **398.2**
        Graphic novels
  Fajardo, A. E. Kid Beowulf and the blood-bound oath   **741.5**
  Hinds, G. Beowulf   **741.5**
  Petrucha, S. Beowulf   **741.5**
  Shelley, M. W. Frankenstein   **741.5**
  Storrie, P. D. Beowulf   **741.5**
  Toriyama, A. Cowa!   **741.5**
Monsters!. Stephens, J.   **741.5**
Monsters [series]
  Nardo, D. Martians   **001.9**
Monsters in art
  Stephens, J. Monsters!   **741.5**
The **monsters** of Morley Manor. Coville, B.   **Fic**
Montana
        Fiction
  Ingold, J. Hitch   **Fic**
  Larson, K. Hattie Big Sky   **Fic**

Montana—Fiction—*Continued*
  Lemna, D. When the sergeant came marching home **Fic**
  Maynard, J. The cloud chamber **Fic**
  Thomas, J. R. Blind mountain **Fic**
Montardre, Hélène
  (jt. auth) Burleigh, R. Volcanoes **551.2**
Montenegro
  King, D. C. Serbia and Montenegro **949.7**
Montes, Marisa, 1951-
  A circle of time **Fic**
Montgomery, Bernard Law *See* Montgomery of Alamein, Bernard Law Montgomery, Viscount, 1887-1976
Montgomery, L. M. (Lucy Maud), 1874-1942
  See/See also pages in the following book(s):
  Ellis, S. From reader to writer **372.6**
Montgomery, Lucy Maud *See* Montgomery, L. M. (Lucy Maud), 1874-1942
Montgomery, Sy
  Encantado **599.5**
  The man-eating tigers of Sundarbans **599.75**
  Quest for the tree kangaroo **599.2**
  Search for the golden moon bear **599.78**
  The snake scientist **597.96**
  The tarantula scientist **595.4**
Montgomery (Ala.)
  Race relations
  Aretha, D. Montgomery bus boycott **323.1**
  Freedman, R. Freedom walkers **323.1**
  Parks, R. Rosa Parks: my story **92**
  Tracy, K. The life and times of Rosa Parks **92**
  Walsh, F. The Montgomery bus boycott **323.1**
Montgomery bus boycott. Aretha, D. **323.1**
The **Montgomery** bus boycott. Walsh, F. **323.1**
Montgomery of Alamein, Bernard Law Montgomery, Viscount, 1887-1976
  See/See also pages in the following book(s):
  Ross, S. Leaders of World War II **920**
The **monthly** sky guide. Ridpath, I. **523**
Montmorency. Updale, E. **Fic**
Monumental milestones [series]
  Gibson, K. B. The Obama view **92**
  Torres, J. A. Disaster in the Indian Ocean, Tsunami 2004 **909.83**
  Tracy, K. The Clinton view **92**
  Whiting, J. The story of the attack on Pearl Harbor **940.54**
Monumental verses. Lewis, J. P. **811**
Monuments
  Poetry
  Lewis, J. P. Monumental verses **811**
Monuments, National *See* National monuments
Moon, Allan
  (il) Thomas, K. Blades, boards & scooters **796.2**
Moon
  Carlowicz, M. J. The moon **523.3**
  Dyson, M. J. Home on the moon **629.45**
  Miller, R. Earth and the moon **525**

Simon, S. The moon **523.3**
Stefoff, R. Earth and the moon **550**
  Exploration
  Dyer, A. Mission to the moon **629.45**
  Godwin, R. Project Apollo **629.45**
  Fiction
  Enderle, D. Man in the moon **Fic**
  Keehn, S. M. Magpie Gabbard and the quest for the buried moon **Fic**
  Lin, G. Where the mountain meets the moon **Fic**
Moon, Voyages to *See* Space flight to the moon
Moon & sun [series]
  Lisle, H. The Ruby Key **Fic**
The **moon** and I. Byars, B. C. **92**
Moon landing. Platt, R. **629.45**
Mooney, Bel, 1946-
  (ed) You never did learn to knock. See You never did learn to knock **S C**
Moonrunner. Thomason, M. **Fic**
Moonshine express. Norville, R. **Fic**
Moonshining
  Fiction
  Norville, R. Moonshine express **Fic**
The **moorchild**. McGraw, E. J. **Fic**
Moore, Ann
  See/See also pages in the following book(s):
  Thimmesh, C. Girls think of everything **920**
Moore, Inga
  (il) Burnett, F. H. The secret garden **Fic**
Moore, J. Stuart
  (adapter) Jacques, B. Redwall: the graphic novel **741.5**
Moore, Perry
  Hero **Fic**
Moore, Pete, 1962-
  The debate about genetic engineering **660.6**
Moore, Peter
  Caught in the act **Fic**
Moore, Peter D. (Peter Dale)
  Tundra **577.5**
  Wetlands **577.6**
Moore, Yvette
  Freedom songs **Fic**
Mora, Pat
  The desert is my mother. El desierto es mi madre **811**
  About
  Marcovitz, H. Pat Mora **92**
Moragne, Wendy
  Depression **616.85**
Moral philosophy *See* Ethics
Moran, Barbara B.
  (jt. auth) Stueart, R. D. Library and information center management **025.1**
Moran, Katy
  Bloodline **Fic**
Moran Cho *See* Cho, Margaret, 1968-
Moranville, Sharelle Byars
  Over the river **Fic**
  The Snows **Fic**

Mordan, C. B.
  (il) Dendy, L. A. Guinea pig scientists   **616**
  (il) Marrin, A. Oh, rats!   **599.35**
Mordecai, Martin
  Blue Mountain trouble   **Fic**
Morden, Simon
  The lost art   **Fic**
Mordred (Legendary character)
      Fiction
  Springer, N. I am Mordred   **Fic**
  Vande Velde, V. The book of Mordred   **Fic**
More award-winning science fair projects.
  Bochinski, J. B.   **507.8**
More bones. Olson, A. N.   **398.2**
More booktalking that works. Bromann, J.
      028.5
More Horowitz horror. Horowitz, A.   **S C**
More hot links. Wright, C. M.   **011.6**
More scary stories to tell in the dark. Schwartz,
  A.   **398.2**
More short scenes and monologues for middle
  school students. Surface, M. H.   **808.82**
More teen programs that work. Honnold, R.
      027.62
More telescope power. Matloff, G. L.   **522**
More than a game. Crowe, C.   **810.9**
More than a label. Muharrar, A.   **305.23**
More than friends. Holbrook, S.   **811**
More word histories and mysteries   **422.03**
Moreillon, Judi
  Collaborative strategies for teaching reading
  comprehension   **372.4**
Morgan, Clay
  The boy who spoke dog   **Fic**
Morgan, Jennifer, 1955-
  Cells of the nervous system   **611**
Morgan, Julian, 1958-
  Cleopatra   **92**
Morgan, Michael, 1960-
  The midbrain   **612.8**
Morgan, Nicola, 1961-
  Chicken friend   **Fic**
  Fleshmarket   **Fic**
  The highwayman's footsteps   **Fic**
Morgan, Sally
  Body doubles   **660.6**
  Focus on Pakistan   **954.91**
  From Greek atoms to quarks   **530**
  From Mendel's peas to genetic fingerprinting
      576.5
  From microscopes to stem cell research   **616**
  From sea urchins to dolly the sheep   **571.8**
  From windmills to hydrogen fuel cells
      333.79
Morgan le Fay (Legendary character)
      Fiction
  Service, P. F. Tomorrow's magic   **Fic**
  Springer, N. I am Morgan le Fay   **Fic**
Morganelli, Adrianna, 1979-
  Formula One   **796.72**
Morgenroth, Kate
  Jude   **Fic**

Morgenstern, Julie
  Organizing from the inside out for teens
      646.7
Morgenstern, Susie Hoch
  Secret letters from 0 to 10   **Fic**
Morgenstern-Colón, Jessi
  (jt. auth) Morgenstern, J. Organizing from the
  inside out for teens   **646.7**
The **morgue** and me. Ford, J. C.   **Fic**
Moriarty, Jaclyn
  The murder of Bindy Mackenzie   **Fic**
  The year of secret assignments   **Fic**
Moribito. Uehashi, N.   **Fic**
Morley, David
  Healing our world   **610**
Mormon Church *See* Church of Jesus Christ of
  Latter-day Saints
The **Mormon** Trail. Sonneborn, L.   **978**
Mormons
  Bial, R. Nauvoo   **289.3**
  Book of Mormon. The Book of Mormon
      289.3
  Bushman, C. L. Mormons in America   **289.3**
  Sonneborn, L. The Mormon Trail   **978**
      Fiction
  Heuston, K. B. The Book of Jude   **Fic**
  Smith, E. W. The way he lived   **Fic**
Mormons in America. Bushman, C. L.   **289.3**
Morning Girl. Dorris, M.   **Fic**
Morning in a different place. McGuigan, M. A.
      Fic
Morocco
  Blauer, E. Morocco   **964**
  Donovan, S. Teens in Morocco   **964**
  Seward, P. Morocco   **964**
Morphine
    See also Heroin
Morphology *See* Comparative anatomy
Morpurgo, Michael
  The amazing story of Adolphus Tips   **Fic**
  Beowulf   **398.2**
  Kensuke's kingdom   **Fic**
  The Mozart question   **Fic**
  Private Peaceful   **Fic**
  Sir Gawain and the Green Knight   **398.2**
  War horse   **Fic**
Morris, Betty J.
  Administering the school library media center
      027.8
Morris, Bruce C.
  (jt. auth) Wells, D. K. Live aware, not in fear
      158
Morris, Gerald, 1963-
  The squire's tale   **Fic**
Morris, Karyn
  The Kids Can Press jumbo book of gardening
      635
Morris, Mary, 1913-
  (jt. auth) Morris, W. Morris dictionary of word
  and phrase origins   **422.03**

Morris, Neil, 1946-
Do you know where your food comes from?
363.8
Food for sports **613.2**
Global warming **363.7**

Morris, William, 1913-1994
Morris dictionary of word and phrase origins
422.03

Morris dictionary of word and phrase origins.
Morris, W. **422.03**

Morris-Lipsman, Arlene
Presidential races **324**

Morrison, Gordon
(il) Kricher, J. C. Peterson first guide to seashores **577.7**

Morrison, M. A. (Martha A.), 1948-
Judaism **296**

Morrison, Marion
Costa Rica **972.86**
Guyana **988.1**

Morrison, Martha A. *See* Morrison, M. A. (Martha A.), 1948-

Morrison, Taylor, 1971-
The coast mappers **623.89**
Tsunami warning **551.46**
Wildfire **634.9**

Morrison, Toni, 1931-
About
Andersen, R. Toni Morrison **92**
Crayton, L. A. A student's guide to Toni Morri-
son **813.009**
Haskins, J. Toni Morrison **92**
See/See also pages in the following book(s):
Hacker, C. Nobel Prize winners **920**
Hansen, J. Women of hope **920**

Morrow, Glenn
(il) Fleischman, P. Dateline: Troy **292**

Morse, Joe, 1960-
(il) Thayer, E. L. Casey at the bat **811**

Morse, Samuel Finley Breese, 1791-1872
About
Coe, L. The telegraph **621.383**

Morse, Scott
The barefoot serpent **741.5**

Morse, Susan
(jt. auth) Swinburne, S. R. The woods scientist
591.7

Mortenson, Greg, 1957-
Three cups of tea **954.91**

Mortimer, Sean
(jt. auth) Hawk, T. Hawk **92**

Mortin, Christine *See* Morton-Shaw, Christine

Morton-Shaw, Christine
The hunt for the seventh **Fic**
The riddles of Epsilon **Fic**

Mosaics
Harris, N. Mosaics **738.5**

Moschovitis, Valerie Tomaselli- *See* Tomaselli-
Moschovitis, Valerie

Moscovich, Ivan
Big book of brain games **793.73**

Moser, Barry
Ashen sky **937**

(il) Cowboy stories. See Cowboy stories
S C
(il) Doyle, Sir A. C. The adventures of Sherlock
Holmes **S C**
(il) Hamilton, V. In the beginning; creation stories from around the world **201**
(il) Lasky, K. A brilliant streak: the making of
Mark Twain **92**
(il) Rylant, C. Appalachia **974**
(il) Scary stories. See Scary stories **S C**
(il) Twain, M. The adventures of Tom Sawyer
Fic

Moser, Diane, 1944-
(jt. auth) Spangenburg, R. Barbara McClintock
92
(jt. auth) Spangenburg, R. Civil liberties **323**
(jt. auth) Spangenburg, R. Genetic engineering
660.6
(jt. auth) Spangenburg, R. The history of science
509
(jt. auth) Spangenburg, R. The Hubble Space
Telescope **522**
(jt. auth) Spangenburg, R. A look at Mercury
523.4
(jt. auth) Spangenburg, R. Meteors, meteorites,
and meteoroids **523.5**
(jt. auth) Spangenburg, R. The sun **523.7**

Moser, Kit *See* Moser, Diane, 1944-

Moses (Biblical figure)
About
Chaikin, M. Angels sweep the desert floor
296.1

Moses, Shelia P.
The baptism **Fic**
Joseph **Fic**
The legend of Buddy Bush **Fic**

Mosher, Richard, 1949-
Zazoo **Fic**

Mosier, Elizabeth
My life as a girl **Fic**

Moslem countries *See* Islamic countries

Moslemism *See* Islam

Moslems *See* Muslims

Mosley, Shelley, 1950-
The suffragists in literature for youth **016.3**

Mosley, Walter
47 **Fic**

Mosque. Macaulay, D. **726**

Mosques
Design and construction
Macaulay, D. Mosque **726**

Mossman, Jennifer
(ed) Almanac of famous people. See Almanac
of famous people **920.003**

The **most** beautiful roof in the world. Lasky, K.
577.3

The **mostly** true adventures of Homer P. Figg.
Philbrick, W. R. **Fic**

Motels *See* Hotels and motels

Mother and child *See* Mother-child relationship

Muradi, Abdul Khaliq
See/See also pages in the following book(s):
Major, J. S. Caravan to America   920

Mural painting and decoration
     See also Mosaics

Murder *See* Homicide

The **murder** of Bindy Mackenzie. Moriarty, J.
                                                Fic

The **murder** of Emmett Till. Aretha, D.   **364.1**

Murder trials *See* Trials (Homicide)

Murdoch, David Hamilton, 1937-
     Cowboy   **978**
     North American Indian   **970.004**

Murdock, Catherine Gilbert
     Dairy Queen   Fic
     Princess Ben   Fic

Murdock, James R.
     (jt. auth) Martin, H. J., Jr. Serving lesbian, gay, bisexual, transgender, and questioning teens   **027.62**

Murie, Margaret E., 1902-2003
See/See also pages in the following book(s):
Byrnes, P. Environmental pioneers   **920**

Murie, Olaus Johan, 1889-1963
See/See also pages in the following book(s):
Byrnes, P. Environmental pioneers   **920**

Murillo, Kathy Cano- *See* Cano-Murillo, Kathy

Murphy, Bruce, 1962-
     (ed) Benet's reader's encyclopedia. See Benet's reader's encyclopedia   **803**

Murphy, Chris
     (il) Haduch, B. Go fly a bike!   **629.227**

Murphy, Claire Rudolf
     Children of Alcatraz   **979.4**
     Free radical   Fic
     Daughters of the desert. See Daughters of the desert   **220.9**

Murphy, Donald J.
     (ed) World War I. See World War I [Turning points in world history series]   **940.3**

Murphy, Glenn
     Why is snot green   **500**

Murphy, Jim, 1947-
     Across America on an emigrant train [biography of Robert Louis Stevenson]   **92**
     An American plague   **614.5**
     The boys' war   **973.7**
     Desperate journey   Fic
     Gone a-whaling   **639.2**
     The great fire   **977.3**
     The long road to Gettysburg   **973.7**
     Pick & shovel poet: the journeys of Pascal D'Angelo   **92**
     The real Benedict Arnold   **92**
     A young patriot   **973.3**

Murphy, Kelly, 1977-
     (il) Broach, E. Masterpiece   Fic

Murphy, Larry
     African-American faith in America   **200**

Murphy, Pat, 1955-
     The wild girls   Fic

Murphy, Rita
     Bird   Fic

     Looking for Lucy Buick   Fic

Murray, Jaye
     Bottled up   Fic

Murray, Kirsty, 1960-
     The secret life of Maeve Lee Kwong   Fic

Murray, Peter, 1952-
     See also Hautman, Pete, 1952-

Musa, d. 1337
See/See also pages in the following book(s):
Meltzer, M. Ten kings   **920**

Muscles
     Brynie, F. H. 101 questions about muscles to stretch your mind and flex your brain   **612.7**

Musculoskeletal system
     See also Muscles
     Gold, S. D. The musculoskeletal system and the skin   **612.7**
     Parker, S. The skeleton and muscles   **612.7**
     Parker, S. Skin, muscles, and bones   **612.7**

The **musculoskeletal** system and the skin. Gold, S. D.   **612.7**

Museums
     See also Art museums appropriate subjects with the subdivision *Museums;* and names of galleries and museums
         Fiction
     La Fevers, R. L. Theodosia and the Serpents of Chaos   Fic

Mushona (African people) *See* Shona (African people)

Mushrooms
     See also Fungi
     Lincoff, G. The Audubon Society field guide to North American mushrooms   **579.6**

Music
     Ardley, N. A young person's guide to music   **780**
     Gardner, R. Sound projects with a music lab you can build   **534**
     McAlpine, M. Working in music and dance   **780**
     Nathan, A. Meet the musicians   **780**
     Parker, S. The science of sound   **534**
         Analysis, appreciation
     See Music appreciation
         Dictionaries
     Kennedy, M. The concise Oxford dictionary of music   **780.3**
         Fiction
     Galante, C. Hershey herself   Fic
     Thompson, K. The new policeman   Fic
     Tomlinson, H. Aurelie   Fic
     What a song can do   S C
         History and criticism
     Kallen, S. A. The history of classical music   **781.6**
         Poetry
     Adoff, J. The song shoots out of my mouth   **811**
         Australia
     Underwood, D. Australia, Hawaii, and the Pacific   **780.9**

Music—*Continued*
Caribbean region
Solway, A. Latin America and the Caribbean
780.9
Europe
Allen, P. Europe **780.94**
Hawaii
Underwood, D. Australia, Hawaii, and the Pacific **780.9**
Latin America
Solway, A. Latin America and the Caribbean
780.9
Oceania
Underwood, D. Australia, Hawaii, and the Pacific **780.9**

Music, African *See* African music

Music, African American *See* African American music

Music appreciation
   See also Music—History and criticism
Ganeri, A. The young person's guide to the orchestra **784.2**

Music library [series]
Kallen, S. A. The history of classical music
781.6
Kallen, S. A. The history of country music
781.642
Kallen, S. A. The history of jazz **781.65**
Kallen, S. A. The history of rock and roll
781.66
Kallen, S. A. The instruments of music
784.19

Music throughout history [series]
Lee, L. Handel's world **92**
Malaspina, A. Chopin's world **92**
Norton, J. R. Haydn's world **92**
Viegas, J. Beethoven's world **92**

Musical instruments
Ganeri, A. The young person's guide to the orchestra **784.2**
Helsby, G. Those amazing musical instruments
784.19
Kallen, S. A. The instruments of music
784.19
Dictionaries
Baines, A. The Oxford companion to musical instruments **784.19**

Musicals
Fiction
Wood, M. My life the musical **Fic**

Musicians
   See also Composers; Conductors (Music);
Violoncellists; Women musicians
Earls, I. Young musicians in world history
920
George-Warren, H. Shake, rattle, & roll **920**
Marx, T. Steel drumming at the Apollo **785**
McNeese, T. Tito Puente **92**
Miller, C. C. Reggae poet: the story of Bob Marley **92**
Nathan, A. Meet the musicians **780**
Paprocki, S. B. Bob Marley **92**
Dictionaries
Kennedy, M. The concise Oxford dictionary of music **780.3**

Fiction
Blume, L. M. M. The rising star of Rusty Nail
Fic
Collins, P. L. Hidden voices **Fic**
Dunlap, S. E. The musician's daughter **Fic**
Going, K. L. Fat kid rules the world **Fic**
Ritter, J. H. Under the baseball moon **Fic**
Sonnenblick, J. Notes from the midnight driver
Fic
Stiefvater, M. Lament **Fic**
Yolen, J. Troll Bridge **Fic**

Musicians, African American *See* African American musicians

The **musician's** daughter. Dunlap, S. E. **Fic**

Musick, John A.
(jt. auth) McMillan, B. Oceans **551.46**

Muslim countries *See* Islamic countries

Muslim women
   See also Women in Islam
Kovarik, C. A. Interviews with Muslim women of Pakistan **954.91**
Maydell, N. Extraordinary women from the Muslim world **920**

Muslimism *See* Islam

Muslims
Oliver, M. T. Muhammad **297**
Siddiqui, H. Being Muslim **297**
Fiction
Abdel-Fattah, R. Does my head look big in this?
Fic
Abdel-Fattah, R. Ten things I hate about me
Fic
Ellis, D. Bifocal **Fic**
Jolin, P. In the name of God **Fic**
Karim, S. Skunk girl **Fic**
Stolz, J. The shadows of Ghadames **Fic**
Graphic novels
Lat. Kampung boy **741.5**
United States
Hafiz, D. The American Muslim teenager's handbook **297**
Islam in America **297**

Muslims, Black *See* Black Muslims

Musser, Susan
(ed) Can the War on Terrorism be won? See Can the War on Terrorism be won?
363.32
(ed) Media violence: opposing viewpoints. See Media violence: opposing viewpoints
363.3

Mussi, Sarah
The door of no return **Fic**

Mussolini, Benito, 1883-1945
See/See also pages in the following book(s):
Ross, S. Leaders of World War II **920**

Must love black. McClymer, K. **Fic**

Mustashrik, 1985-
(il) Appignanesi, R. Julius Caesar **822.3**

Mutants, clones, and killer corn. Seiple, S.
660.6

Mutilation, Female genital *See* Female circumcision

Mwangi, Meja
The Mzungu boy **Fic**

My 13th season. Roberts, K.   **Fic**

My almost epic summer. Griffin, A.   **Fic**

My America   **811.008**

My black me   **811.008**

My bridges of hope. Bitton-Jackson, L.   **92**

My brother Abe. Mazer, H.   **Fic**

My brother, my sister, and I. Watkins, Y. K.   **Fic**

My brother Sam is dead. Collier, J. L.   **Fic**

My brother's keeper. McCormick, P.   **Fic**

My childhood under fire. Halilbegovich, N.   **949.7**

My contract with Henry. Vaupel, R.   **Fic**

My cup runneth over. Whytock, C.   **Fic**

My dad's a punk   **S C**

My Daniel. Conrad, P.   **Fic**

My darlin' Clementine. Gregory, K.   **Fic**

My desperate love diary. Rettig, L.   **Fic**

My future career [series]

  McAlpine, M. Working in music and dance   **780**

  McAlpine, M. Working in the fashion industry   **746.9**

  McAlpine, M. Working in the food industry   **647.9**

  McAlpine, M. Working with animals   **636**

  McAlpine, M. Working with children   **362.7**

  McAlpine, M. Working with computers   **004**

My heartbeat. Freymann-Weyr, G.   **Fic**

My kind of sad. Scowen, K.   **616.85**

My last skirt. Durrant, L.   **Fic**

My letter to the world and other poems. Dickinson, E.   **811**

My life as a girl. Mosier, E.   **Fic**

My life in dog years. Paulsen, G.   **92**

My life in pink and green. Greenwald, L.   **Fic**

My life the musical. Wood, M.   **Fic**

My most excellent year. Kluger, S.   **Fic**

My mother the cheerleader. Sharenow, R.   **Fic**

My name is not Slow. Libal, A.   **362.3**

My name is Sally Little Song. Woods, B.   **Fic**

My nights at the Improv. Siebold, J.   **Fic**

My one hundred adventures. Horvath, P.   **Fic**

My season with penguins. Webb, S.   **598**

My so-called family. Sheinmel, C.   **Fic**

My swordhand is singing. Sedgwick, M.   **Fic**

My thirteenth season. See Roberts, K. My 13th season   **Fic**

Myanmar

        Fiction

  Smith, R. Elephant run   **Fic**

Mycology *See* Fungi

Myers, Anna

  Assassin   **Fic**

  Spy!   **Fic**

  Tulsa burning   **Fic**

  Wart   **Fic**

Myers, Christopher

  (il) Carroll, L. Jabberwocky   **821**

  (jt. auth) Myers, W. D. Autobiography of my dead brother   **Fic**

  (il) Myers, W. D. Harlem   **811**

Myers, Edward, 1950-

  Storyteller   **Fic**

  When will I stop hurting?   **155.9**

Myers, Jack

  On the trail of the Komodo dragon and other explorations of science in action   **590**

Myers, Walter Dean, 1937-

  145th Street   **S C**

  Amiri & Odette   **Fic**

  Antarctica   **998**

  At her majesty's request [biography of Sarah Forbes Bonetta]   **92**

  Autobiography of my dead brother   **Fic**

  Bad boy   **92**

  The Beast   **Fic**

  Dope sick   **Fic**

  Fallen angels   **Fic**

  Game   **Fic**

  The greatest: Muhammad Ali   **92**

  Harlem   **811**

  The Harlem Hellfighters   **940.4**

  Harlem summer   **Fic**

  Here in Harlem   **811**

  Hoops   **Fic**

  Monster   **Fic**

  Scorpions   **Fic**

  Slam!   **Fic**

  Street love   **Fic**

  Sunrise over Fallujah   **Fic**

  USS Constellation   **359.8**

  What they found   **S C**

        About

  Marler, M. D. Walter Dean Myers   **813.009**

  Sickels, A. Walter Dean Myers   **92**

  (jt. auth) Lawrence, J. The great migration   **759.13**

Myracle, Lauren, 1969-

  Eleven   **Fic**

  Peace, love, and baby ducks   **Fic**

  Twelve   **Fic**

MySpace (Web site)

  Anderson, T. MySpace/OurPlanet   **333.72**

Mysteries in our National Parks [series]

  Skurzynski, G. Cliff hanger   **Fic**

The **mysteries** of Beethoven's hair. Martin, R.   **92**

Mysteries of the mummy kids. Halls, K. M.   **393**

Mysteries unwrapped [series]

  Bardhan-Quallen, S. The real monsters   **001.9**

  Wetzel, C. Haunted U.S.A.   **133.1**

The mysterious & unknown [series]

  George, C. Pyramids   **909**

  Lace, W. W. The curse of King Tut   **932**

  Stewart, G. UFOs   **001.9**

The **mysterious** Benedict Society. Stewart, T. L.   **Fic**

The **mysterious** edge of the heroic world. Konigsburg, E. L.   **Fic**

The **mysterious** matter of I.M. Fine. Stanley, D.   **Fic**

The **mysterious** universe. Jackson, E. B.   **523.8**

Mystery and detective stories *See* Mystery fiction

Mystery fiction

Abbott, T. The postcard   **Fic**
Abrahams, P. Down the rabbit hole   **Fic**
Allison, J. Gilda Joyce, psychic investigator
                                                Fic
Avi. The man who was Poe   **Fic**
Balliett, B. Chasing Vermeer   **Fic**
Barrett, T. The 100-year-old secret   **Fic**
Beil, M. D. The Red Blazer Girls: the ring of
  Rocamadour   **Fic**
Bellairs, J. The curse of the blue figurine
                                                Fic
Bennett, J. Coverup   **Fic**
Berlin, E. The puzzling world of Winston Breen
                                                Fic
Blundell, J. What I saw and how I lied   **Fic**
Broach, E. Masterpiece   **Fic**
Broach, E. Shakespeare's secret   **Fic**
Bryant, J. Kaleidoscope eyes   **Fic**
Bunting, E. The man with the red bag   **Fic**
Byars, B. C. The dark stairs   **Fic**
Colfer, E. Half-Moon investigations   **Fic**
Cusick, R. T. Walk of the spirits   **Fic**
Dowd, S. The London Eye mystery   **Fic**
Doyle, Sir A. C. The adventures of Sherlock
  Holmes   **S C**
Draanen, W. v. Sammy Keyes and the hotel
  thief   **Fic**
Duncan, L. I know what you did last summer
                                                Fic
Duncan, L. Locked in time   **Fic**
Dunlap, S. E. The musician's daughter   **Fic**
Feinstein, J. Last shot   **Fic**
Ferraiolo, J. D. The big splash   **Fic**
Ford, J. C. The morgue and me   **Fic**
Grant, V. Quid pro quo   **Fic**
Greene, M. Chasing the jaguar   **Fic**
Hamilton, V. The house of Dies Drear   **Fic**
Hautman, P. Snatched   **Fic**
Hoeye, M. Time stops for no mouse   **Fic**
Hoobler, D. The ghost in the Tokaido Inn
                                                Fic
Horowitz, A. Public enemy number two   **Fic**
Ibbotson, E. The star of Kazan   **Fic**
Jinks, C. The reformed vampire support group
                                                Fic
Juby, S. Getting the girl   **Fic**
Kehret, P. Trapped!   **Fic**
Konigsburg, E. L. Silent to the bone   **Fic**
Lachtman, O. D. The truth about Las Mariposas
                                                Fic
Larson, J. C. Bringing mysteries alive for chil-
  dren and young adults   **028.5**
Lawrence, C. The thieves of Ostia   **Fic**
Lawrence, I. The seance   **Fic**
Littke, L. Lake of secrets   **Fic**
Mack, T. The fall of the Amazing Zalindas
                                                Fic
Madison, B. Lulu Dark and the summer of the
  Fox   **Fic**
Madison, B. Lulu Dark can see through walls
                                                Fic
Matthews, T. L. Danger in the dark   **Fic**
McNamee, G. Acceleration   **Fic**

Miller, K. Kiki Strike: inside the shadow city
                                                Fic
Morton-Shaw, C. The hunt for the seventh
                                                Fic
Newbery, L. Lost boy   **Fic**
Nixon, J. L. Nightmare   **Fic**
Osterlund, A. Aurelia   **Fic**
Parker, R. B. The Edenville Owls   **Fic**
Peacock, S. Eye of the crow   **Fic**
Richards, J. The chaos code   **Fic**
Runholt, S. The mystery of the third Lucretia
                                                Fic
Scrimger, R. From Charlie's point of view
                                                Fic
Selzer, A. I put a spell on you   **Fic**
Shearer, A. Canned   **Fic**
Skurzynski, G. Cliff hanger   **Fic**
Sorrells, W. Fake ID   **Fic**
Sorrells, W. First shot   **Fic**
Springer, N. The case of the missing marquess
                                                Fic
Stanley, D. The mysterious matter of I.M. Fine
                                                Fic
Staub, W. C. Lily Dale: awakening   **Fic**
Stewart, P. The curse of the night wolf   **Fic**
Strickland, B. The sign of the sinister sorcerer
                                                Fic
Vande Velde, V. Never trust a dead man
                                                Fic
Volponi, P. Rucker Park setup   **Fic**
Westerfeld, S. So yesterday   **Fic**
Wynne-Jones, T. The boy in the burning house
                                                Fic

Authorship
Farrell, T. Write your own mystery story
                                              808.3

Mystery graphic novels
Geary, R. The invisible man   **741.5**
Jaffe, M. Bad kitty volume 1: catnipped
                                              741.5
Kibuishi, K. Amulet book one: the stonekeeper
                                              741.5
Rocks, M. Detective Jermain, volume 1
                                              741.5
Watson, A. Clubbing   **741.5**

Mystery library [series]
Kallen, S. A. Shamans   **201**
Nardo, D. Atlantis   **001.9**

The **mystery** of gravity. Parker, B. R.   **531**

The **mystery** of the mammoth bones. Giblin, J.
                                                569

The **mystery** of the third Lucretia. Runholt, S.
                                                Fic

Mythical animals
   See also Animals—Folklore; Dragons; Mer-
   maids and mermen
Allen, J. Fantasy encyclopedia   **398**
Baynes, P. Questionable creatures   **398.2**
Dobrzycki, M. The art of drawing dragons
                                                743
Peffer, J. DragonArt   **743**
Fiction
Golding, J. Secret of the sirens   **Fic**
St. John, L. The white giraffe   **Fic**
Ursu, A. The shadow thieves   **Fic**

Mythmaker: the story of J.K. Rowling. Sickels, A.   **92**

Mythology

   See also Gods and goddesses; Mythical animals mythology of particular national or ethnic groups or of particular geographic areas

Glick, S. War and peace   **201**
Hamilton, V. In the beginning; creation stories from around the world   **201**
Hearne, B. G. Beauties and beasts   **398.2**
Mass, W. Gods and goddesses   **201**
World mythology   **201**

          Bibliography
Helbig, A. Myths and hero tales   **398.2**

          Dictionaries
Brewer's dictionary of phrase & fable   **803**
Myths and legends   **398**
Wilkinson, P. Illustrated dictionary of mythology   **201**

          Encyclopedias
UXL Encyclopedia of world mythology   **201.03**

          Indexes
Index to fairy tales   **398.2**

Mythology, African *See* African mythology

Mythology, Celtic *See* Celtic mythology

Mythology, Classical *See* Classical mythology

Mythology, Egyptian *See* Egyptian mythology

Mythology, Japanese *See* Japanese mythology

Mythology, Norse *See* Norse mythology

Mythology. Hamilton, E.   **292**

Mythology A to Z [series]
   Lynch, P. A. African mythology A to Z   **299.6**
   Matson, G. Celtic mythology A to Z   **299**
   Roberts, J. Chinese mythology A to Z   **299.5**

Mythology around the world [series]
   Levin, J. Japanese mythology   **299.5**
   Porterfield, J. Scandinavian mythology   **293**

Myths and hero tales. Helbig, A.   **398.2**

Myths and legends   **398**

Myths of the world [series]
   Schomp, V. The ancient Africans   **299.6**
   Schomp, V. The ancient Egyptians   **299**
   Schomp, V. The ancient Greeks   **292**
   Schomp, V. The ancient Mesopotamians   **935**
   Schomp, V. The ancient Romans   **292**
   Schomp, V. The Aztecs   **972**
   Schomp, V. The Native Americans   **970.004**
   Schomp, V. The Norsemen   **293**

N

Na, An, 1972-
   The fold   **Fic**
   A step from heaven   **Fic**
   Wait for me   **Fic**

Nacky Patcher and the curse of the dry-land boats. Kluger, J.   **Fic**

Nadeau, Robert
   See also Zanger, Mark H.

Naden, Corinne J.
   Abortion   **363.46**
   Dred Scott   **342**
   The facts about the A-Z of drugs   **615**
   James Monroe   **92**
   John Muir   **92**
   Mao Zedong and the Chinese Revolution   **92**
   Patients' rights   **362.1**
   (jt. auth) Gillespie, J. T. Classic teenplots   **011.6**
   (jt. auth) Gillespie, J. T. The Newbery/Printz companion   **028.5**

Naff, Clay Farris
   Nicotine and tobacco   **362.29**
   (ed) Evolution. See Evolution [Exploring science and medical discoveries series]   **576.8**

Nagasaki (Japan)
          Bombardment, 1945
   Bodden, V. The bombing of Hiroshima and Nagasaki   **940.54**

Nagatomo, Haruno
   Draw your own Manga   **741.5**

Nagel, Rob
   Body by design   **612**
   Space exploration, Almanac   **629.4**
   (ed) U.X.L encyclopedia of science. See U.X.L encyclopedia of science   **503**

Nagle, Jeanne M.
   Living green   **333.72**

Nahum, Andrew
   Flying machine   **629.133**

Naidoo, Beverley
   Burn my heart   **Fic**
   Journey to Jo'burg   **Fic**
   The other side of truth   **Fic**
   Out of bounds: seven stories of conflict and hope   **S C**
   Web of lies   **Fic**

Naifeh, Ted
   Courtney Crumrin and the night things   **741.5**
   (jt. auth) Black, H. The Good Neighbors; book one: Kin   **741.5**

Nailling, Lee, 1917-
          About
   Warren, A. Orphan train rider   **362.7**

Nails, Jennifer
   Next to Mexico   **Fic**

Nair, Charissa M.
   (jt. auth) Seah, A. Vietnam   **959.704**

Nakahama, Manjirō, 1827-1898
          About
   Blumberg, R. Shipwrecked!: the true adventures of a Japanese boy [biography of Manjiro Nakahama]   **92**

Nakajo, Hisaya
   Sugar Princess volume 1: skating to win   **741.5**

Nakaya, Andrea C.
   (ed) Civil liberties. See Civil liberties   **342**
   (ed) Civil liberties and war. See Civil liberties and war   **323**

Nakaya, Andrea C.—*Continued*
(ed) Terminal illness: opposing viewpoints. See
Terminal illness: opposing viewpoints
362.1

Nakaya, Andrea C., 1976-
Energy alternatives 333.79

Nakayama, David, 1978-
(il) Benjamin, P. Hulk: misunderstood monster
741.5

Name that style. Raczka, B. 709

Names

See also Geographic names

Names and naming in young adult literature.
Nilsen, A. P. 813.009

Namibia

Fiction
Gilman, D. The devil's breath Fic

Namioka, Lensey
Mismatch Fic
An ocean apart, a world away Fic
Ties that bind, ties that break Fic

Nance, Andrew
Daemon Hall Fic

Nanji, Shenaaz, 1954-
Child of dandelions Fic

Nanotechnology
Johnson, R. L. Nanotechnology 620

Napoleon I, Emperor of the French, 1769-1821
About
Burleigh, R. Napoleon 92
Greenblatt, M. Napoleon Bonaparte and Imperial
France 944.05

Napoleon Bonaparte and Imperial France.
Greenblatt, M. 944.05

Napoleonic Wars See France—History—1799-
1815

Napoli, Donna Jo, 1948-
Alligator bayou Fic
Beast Fic
Bound Fic
Fire in the hills Fic
The great god Pan Fic
Hush Fic
The king of Mulberry Street Fic
The smile Fic
Stones in water Fic
Zel Fic

Napton, Robert Place
(jt. auth) Brooks, T. Dark wraith of Shannara
741.5

Narcotic traffic See Drug traffic

Narcotics

See also Cocaine; Heroin; Marijuana
Breguet, A. Vicodin, OxyContin, and other pain
relievers 362.29

Narcotics and crime See Drugs and crime

Narcotics and teenagers See Teenagers—Drug
use

Narcotics and youth See Youth—Drug use

Nardo, Don, 1947-
Ancient Alexandria 932

Ancient Rome [History of weapons and warfare
series] 937
Artistry in stone 932
Arts and literature in ancient Mesopotamia
700
Arts, leisure, and entertainment 937
Arts, leisure, and sport in ancient Egypt 932
The Atlantic slave trade 326
Atlantis 001.9
The Civil War 973.7
Climate crisis 363.7
Cure quest 616
DNA evidence 614
Force and motion 531
From founding to fall: a history of Rome
937
Great Elizabethan playwrights 920
The Greenhaven encyclopedia of Greek and Ro-
man mythology 292
Julius Caesar 92
King Arthur 942.01
Lords, ladies, peasants, and knights 940.1
Martians 001.9
Tycho Brahe 92
Understanding Frankenstein 823.009
Vaccines 615
Words of the ancient Romans 937
(ed) Julius Caesar. See Julius Caesar [essays
about] 92

Narragansett Indians
Fiction
Bruchac, J. Whisper in the dark Fic

Narrations See Monologues

NASCAR See National Association for Stock Car
Auto Racing

NASCAR. Buckley, J., Jr. 796.72

NASCAR. Eagen, R. 796.72

Nascimento, Edson Arantes do See Pelé, 1940-

Nash, Gary B.
Landmarks of the American Revolution
973.3

Nathan, Amy
Count on us 355
Meet the dancers 920
Meet the musicians 780
Yankee doodle gals 940.54

Nathan Fox [series]
Brittney, L. Dangerous times Fic

Nation. Pratchett, T. Fic

A **Nation** challenged 973.931

Nation of Islam See Black Muslims

National anthems of the world 782.42

National Association for Stock Car Auto Racing
Buckley, J., Jr. NASCAR 796.72
Caldwell, D. Speed show 796.72
Eagen, R. NASCAR 796.72
Kelley, K. C. Hottest NASCAR machines
796.72

National Audubon Society field guide to fishes,
North America. Gilbert, C. R. 597

The **National** Audubon Society field guide to
North American birds, Eastern region. Bull, J.
L. 598

National Audubon Society field guide to North American birds, Western region. Udvardy, M. D. F. **598**

National Audubon Society field guide to North American mammals. Whitaker, J. O., Jr. **599**

National Audubon Society field guide to North American wildflowers: eastern region. Thieret, J. W. **582.13**

National Audubon Society field guide to North American wildflowers, western region. Spellenberg, R. **582.13**

National Council for the Social Studies
Notable social studies trade books for young people. See Notable social studies trade books for young people **016.3**

National Council of Teachers of English
A Jar of tiny stars: poems by NCTE award-winning poets. See A Jar of tiny stars: poems by NCTE award-winning poets **811.008**

National Council of Teachers of English. Committee on the Junior High and Middle School Booklist
Your reading. See Your reading **011.6**

National debts *See* Public debts

National emblems
Bateman, T. Red, white, blue, and Uncle who? **929.9**

National Football League
The Child's World encyclopedia of the NFL **796.332**

National Geographic Bee. Cunha, S. F. **910**

National Geographic dinosaurs. Barrett, P. M. **567.9**

National Geographic investigates [series]
Auden, S. Medical mysteries **610**
Ball, J. A. Ancient China **931**
Croy, A. Ancient Pueblo **978**
Deckker, Z. Ancient Rome **937**
Green, J. Ancient Celts **936**
Gruber, B. Ancient Inca **985**
Gruber, B. Ancient Iraq **935**
Harris, N. Ancient Maya **972**
McGee, M. Ancient Greece **938**
Piddock, C. Outbreak **614.4**
Pobst, S. Animals on the edge **578.68**
Rubalcaba, J. Ancient Egypt **932**
Sherrow, V. Ancient Africa **939**
Simpson, K. Extreme weather **551.6**
Simpson, K. Genetics **576.5**

National Geographic prehistoric mammals. Turner, A. **569**

National Geographic Society (U.S.)
Allen, T. B. Remember Pearl Harbor **940.54**
Barrett, P. M. National Geographic dinosaurs **567.9**
Bausum, A. Dragon bones and dinosaur eggs: a photobiography of Roy Chapman Andrews **92**
Bausum, A. Our country's presidents **920**
Deckker, Z. Portugal **946.9**
Every human has rights. See Every human has rights **323**

Longfellow, H. W. Hiawatha and Megissogwon **811**
Phillips, C. Sweden **948.5**
Pollack, P. Ski **796.93**
Shields, S. D. Turkey **956.1**
Sloan, C. Bury the dead **393**
Sloan, C. The human story **599.93**
Sloan, C. Supercroc and the origin of crocodiles **567.9**

National Geographic student atlas of the world **912**

National Geographic United States atlas for young explorers **912**

National Institutes of Health (U.S.)
Mintzer, R. The National Institutes of Health **362.1**

National monuments
Bateman, T. Red, white, blue, and Uncle who? **929.9**

National Museum of the American Indian (U.S.)
Do all Indians live in tipis? See Do all Indians live in tipis? **970.004**

National parks and reserves
See also National monuments
Alaska
See also Arctic National Wildlife Refuge (Alaska)
United States
Graham, A. Great Smoky Mountains National Park **976.8**
Jankowski, S. Everglades National Park **975.9**
Jankowski, S. Olympic National Park **979.7**
Reed, J. Cape Hatteras National Seashore **975.6**

National resources *See* Natural resources

National Science Teachers Association
Outstanding science trade books for students K-12. See Outstanding science trade books for students K-12 **016.5**

National security
Campbell, G. A. A vulnerable America **363.3**
Freedman, J. America debates privacy versus security **323.44**
Kallen, S. A. National security **355**
Miller, D. A. The Patriot Act **345**
Torr, J. D. The Patriot Act **345**
See/See also pages in the following book(s):
Weapons of mass destruction: opposing viewpoints **358**

National socialism
Altman, L. J. Hitler's rise to power and the Holocaust **943.086**
Bartoletti, S. C. Hitler Youth **943.086**
Cartlidge, C. Life of a Nazi soldier **940.54**
Living in Nazi Germany **943.086**
Rice, E. Adolf Hitler and Nazi Germany **92**
Fiction
Bartoletti, S. C. The boy who dared **Fic**
Chotjewitz, D. Daniel half human **Fic**
Wolf, J. M. Someone named Eva **Fic**

National songs
National anthems of the world **782.42**

National Transportation Safety Board (U.S.) *See* United States. National Transportation Safety Board

The **National** Transportation Safety Board. Mintzer, R.   **363.1**

National Wildlife Federation field guide to insects and spiders & related species of North America. Evans, A. V.   **595.7**

Nationalism
    Tames, R. Nationalism   **320.5**

Nationalist China *See* Taiwan

Nations in transition [series]
    Kort, M. Russia   **947**
    Otfinoski, S. Afghanistan   **958.1**
    Otfinoski, S. Ukraine   **947.7**

Native American art
    January, B. Native American art & culture   **709.7**
    January, B. Native Americans   **709.7**

Native American art & culture. January, B.   **709.7**

Native American crafts of the Northeast and Southeast. Corwin, J. H.   **745.5**

Native American religion. Martin, J.   **299.7**

Native American religions. Hartz, P.   **299.7**

Native American women
Dictionaries
    Sonneborn, L. A to Z of American Indian women   **920.003**

Native Americans
    See also Taino Indians names of Native American peoples and linguistic families
    Bial, R. Lifeways [series]   **970.004**
    Collier, C. Clash of cultures, prehistory-1638   **970.004**
    Corwin, J. H. Native American crafts of the Northeast and Southeast   **745.5**
    Do all Indians live in tipis?   **970.004**
    Goble, P. All our relatives   **970.004**
    January, B. Native American art & culture   **709.7**
    January, B. Native Americans   **709.7**
    Katz, W. L. Black Indians   **305.8**
    Keoke, E. D. American Indian contributions to the world   **970.004**
    King, D. C. First people   **970.004**
    Murdoch, D. H. North American Indian   **970.004**
    Philbrick, N. The Mayflower and the Pilgrims' New World   **973.2**
    Philip, N. The great circle   **970.004**
    Schomp, V. The Native Americans   **970.004**
    Trottier, M. Native crafts   **745.5**
    Weber, E. N. R. Rattlesnake Mesa   **92**
Biography
    American Indian biographies   **920.003**
    Bruchac, J. Jim Thorpe   **92**
    Freedman, R. Indian chiefs   **920**
Civil rights
    Gold, S. D. Worcester v. Georgia   **342**
    Johnson, T. R. Red power   **323.1**
    Kallen, S. A. Rigoberta Menchu, Indian rights activist   **92**

Encyclopedias
    Waldman, C. Encyclopedia of Native American tribes   **970.004**
Fiction
    Alexie, S. The absolutely true diary of a part-time Indian   **Fic**
    Bruchac, J. Hidden roots   **Fic**
    Dorris, M. Sees Behind Trees   **Fic**
    Helgerson, J. Crows & cards   **Fic**
    Lisle, J. T. The crying rocks   **Fic**
    Moccasin thunder   **S C**
    O'Dell, S. Island of the Blue Dolphins   **Fic**
    O'Dell, S. Streams to the river, river to the sea   **Fic**
    O'Dell, S. Zia   **Fic**
    Olsen, S. The girl with a baby   **Fic**
    Olsen, S. White girl   **Fic**
    Smelcer, J. E. The trap   **Fic**
    Smith, C. L. Rain is not my Indian name   **Fic**
    Smith, P. C. Weetamoo, heart of the Pocassets   **Fic**
    Speare, E. G. The sign of the beaver   **Fic**
    Talking leaves   **S C**
    Yee, P. Learning to fly   **Fic**
Folklore
    American Indian myths and legends   **398.2**
    Brown, D. A. Dee Brown's folktales of the Native American   **398.2**
    Curry, J. L. Hold up the sky: and other Native American tales from Texas and the Southern Plains   **398.2**
    Delacre, L. Golden tales   **398.2**
    Tingle, T. Spirits dark and light   **398.2**
Government relations
    Stewart, M. The Indian Removal Act   **973.5**
History
    Edwards, J. The history of the American Indians and the reservation   **970.004**
    Student almanac of Native American history   **970.004**
Poetry
    Dancing teepees: poems of American Indian youth   **897**
    Longfellow, H. W. Hiawatha and Megissogwon   **811**
Religion
    American Indian myths and legends   **398.2**
    Hartz, P. Native American religions   **299.7**
    Martin, J. Native American religion   **299.7**
Wars
    See also Black Hawk War, 1832; United States—History—1755-1763, French and Indian War
    Brown, D. A. Bury my heart at Wounded Knee   **970.004**
    Custer, E. B. The diary of Elizabeth Bacon Custer   **973.8**
    Dolan, E. F. The American Indian wars   **970.004**
    Ehrlich, A. Wounded Knee: an Indian history of the American West   **970.004**
    Marker, S. Plains Indian wars   **973.5**
Wars—Encyclopedias
    Encyclopedia of Native American wars and warfare   **970.004**

Native Americans—*Continued*

Central America

See also Mayas

Great Plains

Collier, C. Indians, cowboys, and farmers and the battle for the Great Plains, 1865-1910 **978**

January, B. Little Bighorn, June 25, 1876 **973.8**

Marker, S. Plains Indian wars **973.5**

Patent, D. H. The buffalo and the Indians **978**

Terry, M. B. H. Daily life in a Plains Indian village, 1868 **970.004**

Mexico

See also Aztecs; Mayas

South America

See also Guayaki Indians; Incas

West (U.S.)

Brown, D. A. Bury my heart at Wounded Knee **970.004**

Ehrlich, A. Wounded Knee: an Indian history of the American West **970.004**

West Indies

See also Taino Indians

Native Americans in art

Reich, S. Painting the wild frontier: the art and adventures of George Catlin **92**

Native crafts. Trottier, M. **745.5**

Native son: the story of Richard Wright. Hart, J. **92**

Natural childbirth

See also Midwives

Natural disasters

See also Environmental degradation; Storms; Tsunamis

Barnard, B. Dangerous planet **363.34**

Day, T. DK guide to savage Earth **550**

Engelbert, P. Dangerous planet **363.34**

Langley, A. Hurricanes, tsunamis, and other natural disasters **363.34**

Fiction

Pfeffer, S. B. The dead & the gone **Fic**

Pfeffer, S. B. Life as we knew it **Fic**

Natural foods

Dunn-Georgiou, E. Everything you need to know about organic foods **641.3**

Miller, D. A. Organic foods **641.3**

Natural foods industry

Miller, D. A. Organic foods **641.3**

Natural gardening *See* Organic gardening

Natural history

Calhoun, Y. Plant and animal science fair projects **570**

Kelsey, E. Strange new species **578**

Matsen, B. Go wild in New York City **974.7**

Quinlan, S. E. The case of the monkeys that fell from the trees **577.3**

Fiction

Meyer, C. The true adventures of Charley Darwin **Fic**

Africa

Woods, M. Seven natural wonders of Africa **508**

Asia

Woods, M. Seven natural wonders of Asia and the Middle East **508**

Australia

Woods, M. Seven natural wonders of Australia and Oceania **508**

Central America

Woods, M. Seven natural wonders of Central and South America **508**

Europe

Woods, M. Seven natural wonders of Europe **508**

Florida

Lynch, W. The Everglades **508**

Middle East

Woods, M. Seven natural wonders of Asia and the Middle East **508**

New York (State)

Weber, S. Two in the wilderness **508**

North America

Woods, M. Seven natural wonders of North America **508**

Rocky Mountains

Lynch, W. Rocky Mountains **577.4**

South America

Woods, M. Seven natural wonders of Central and South America **508**

Natural History Museum (London, England)

Symes, R. F. Eyewitness rocks & minerals **549**

Natural law *See* Ethics

A **natural** man. Soto, G. **811**

Natural monuments

Dumont-Le Cornec, E. Wonders of the world **910**

Natural resources

See also Conservation of natural resources; Energy resources; Forests and forestry; Mines and mineral resources

Management

Global resources: opposing viewpoints **333.71**

Ravilious, K. Power **179**

Natural resources [series]

Casper, J. K. Agriculture **630**

Casper, J. K. Animals **590**

Casper, J. K. Energy **333.79**

Casper, J. K. Forests **333.75**

Casper, J. K. Lands **333.73**

Casper, J. K. Minerals **549**

Casper, J. K. Plants **580**

Casper, J. K. Water and atmosphere **553.7**

Natural selection

See also Biological invasions; Evolution

Natural theology

See also Intelligent design theory

Natural writer: a story about Marjorie Kinnan Rawlings. Cook, J. **92**

Naturalists

Anderson, M. J. Carl Linnaeus **92**

Anderson, M. J. Charles Darwin **92**

Neanderthals
La Pierre, Y. Neandertals **599.93**

Near East *See* Middle East

Nebraska
Fiction
Conrad, P. My Daniel **Fic**
McNeal, L. The decoding of Lana Morris
Fic

Nebulae, Extragalactic *See* Galaxies

Necessary noise: stories about our families as they
really are **S C**

The **Neddiad**. Pinkwater, D. M. **Fic**

The **need** for oil. Gunderson, C. G. **338.2**

Need to know library [series]
Dunn-Georgiou, E. Everything you need to
know about organic foods **641.3**
Kaminker, L. Everything you need to know
about being adopted **362.7**
Kreiner, A. Everything you need to know about
creating your own support system **158**
Wiloch, T. Everything you need to know about
protecting yourself and others from abduction
613.6

Needham, Tom
Albert Pujols **92**

Neely, Keith, 1943-
(il) Krasner, S. Play ball like the hall of famers
796.357

**Nefertiti, Queen, consort of Akhenaton, King of
Egypt, 14th cent. B.C.**
About
Lange, B. Nefertiti **92**

Neff, Henry H., 1973-
The hound of Rowan **Fic**

Negotiation
See also Conflict management

The **Negro** almanac. See The African American
almanac **305.8**

Neighborhood odes. Soto, G. **811**

Neimark, Anne E., 1935-
Johnny Cash **92**

Nelson, Annika
(il) Soto, G. Canto familiar **811**

Nelson, Blake, 1960-
New rules of high school **Fic**
Paranoid Park **Fic**
They came from below **Fic**

Nelson, Gaylord
See/See also pages in the following book(s):
Byrnes, P. Environmental pioneers **920**

Nelson, Horatio Nelson, Viscount, 1758-1805
Fiction
Bell, T. Nick of time **Fic**

Nelson, Lisa W.
(jt. auth) Agenbroad, L. D. Mammoths **569**

Nelson, Marilyn, 1946-
Carver, a life in poems **811**
Fortune's bones **811**
A wreath for Emmett Till **811**
(jt. auth) Alexander, E. Miss Crandall's School
for Young Ladies and Little Misses of Color
811
(jt. auth) Hegamin, T. Pemba's song **Fic**

Nelson, Michael, 1949-
(ed) The presidency A to Z. See The presidency
A to Z **352.23**

Nelson, Nina
Bringing the boy home **Fic**

Nelson, Pete
Left for dead **940.54**

Nelson, Richard E.
The power to prevent suicide **362.28**

Nelson, Scott Reynolds
Ain't nothing but a man [biography of John
William Henry] **92**

Nelson, Theresa, 1948-
Ruby electric **Fic**

Nemeth, Sally
The heights, the depths, and everything in between **Fic**

Nepal
Burbank, J. Nepal **954.96**
Yackley-Franken, N. Teens in Nepal **954.96**

Neptune (Planet)
Stefoff, R. Neptune **523.4**
Tabak, J. A look at Neptune **523.4**

Neptune's children. Dobkin, B. **Fic**

Neri, Greg
Chess rumble **Fic**

Neruda, Pablo, 1904-1973
About
Délano, P. When I was a boy Neruda called me
Policarpo **92**
Goodnough, D. Pablo Neruda **92**

Nervous system
See also Spinal cord
Morgan, J. Cells of the nervous system **611**
Parker, S. Brain, nerves, and senses **612.8**
Simon, S. The brain **612.8**
Viegas, J. The revolution in healing the brain
612.8

Diseases
See also Epilepsy; Huntington's chorea;
Meningitis; Multiple sclerosis; Tourette syn-
drome

Ness, Patrick, 1971-
The knife of never letting go **Fic**

Netherlands
Seward, P. Netherlands **949.2**
Fiction
Cullen, L. I am Rembrandt's daughter **Fic**
Duble, K. B. Quest **Fic**
Peet, M. Tamar **Fic**
History—1940-1945, German occupation
Frank, A. The diary of a young girl: the defini-
tive edition **92**
Reiss, J. The upstairs room **92**
Rol, R. v. d. Anne Frank, beyond the diary
92
Wukovits, J. F. Anne Frank **92**
History—1940-1945, German occupation—Fiction
Polak, M. What world is left **Fic**

Netscape Communications Corporation
Ehrenhaft, D. Marc Andreessen **92**

Nettleton, Pamela Hill, 1955-
William Shakespeare **822.3**

Networks, Computer *See* Computer networks

Networks, Information *See* Information networks

Netzley, Patricia D.
Civil War **973.7**
The Greenhaven encyclopedia of ancient Egypt **932**

Neumeier, Rachel
The City in the Lake **Fic**

The **neurobiology** of addiction. Stoehr, J. D. **616.86**

Neurology *See* Nervous system

Neuroses
See also Anxiety; Obsessive-compulsive disorder

Neutrality
See also Intervention (International law)

Never to forget: the Jews of the Holocaust. Meltzer, M. **940.53**

Never trust a dead man. Vande Velde, V. **Fic**

Nevermore. Lange, K. E. **92**

New Amsterdam Theatre (New York, N.Y.)
Amendola, D. A day at the New Amsterdam Theatre **792.6**

New audition scenes and monologs from contemporary playwrights **808.82**

New blood. McPhee, P. **Fic**

The **new** book of popular science **503**

New boy. Houston, J. **Fic**

The **New** Cassell's German dictionary. See Cassell's German-English, English-German dictionary **433**

The **new** dictionary of cultural literacy. Hirsch, E. D. **031**

New directions for library service to young adults **027.62**

New elements [biography of Marie Curie] Yannuzzi, D. A. **92**

New England
Fiction
Alcott, L. M. Little women **Fic**

New England
History
Johnson, C. D. Daily life in colonial New England **974**
History—1600-1775, Colonial period
Mandell, D. R. King Philip's war **973.2**

New found land. Wolf, A. **Fic**

New genetics. Kidd, J. S. **576.5**

New Globe (London, England) *See* Shakespeare's Globe (London, England)

New Guinea
Montgomery, S. Quest for the tree kangaroo **599.2**

New Hampshire
Fiction
Emerson, K. Carlos is gonna get it **Fic**
Monninger, J. Baby **Fic**
Schmidt, G. First boy **Fic**

The **new immigrants** [series]
Choi, A. S. Korean Americans **305.8**
Horst, H. A. Jamaican Americans **305.8**

Radzilowski, J. Ukrainian Americans **305.8**
Rangaswamy, P. Indian Americans **305.8**
Schroeder, M. J. Mexican Americans **305.8**
Sonneborn, L. Vietnamese Americans **305.8**
Sterngass, J. Filipino Americans **305.8**

New Jersey
Fiction
Bauer, A. C. E. No castles here **Fic**
Bryant, J. Kaleidoscope eyes **Fic**
Green, T. Football hero **Fic**
Holm, J. L. Penny from heaven **Fic**
Lecesne, J. Absolute brightness **Fic**
Mayall, B. Mermaid Park **Fic**
Ostow, M. So punk rock (and other ways to disappoint your mother) **Fic**
Schumacher, J. The book of one hundred truths **Fic**
Vivian, S. Same difference **Fic**

The **new** Jerusalem Bible. Bible **220.5**

New London Globe (England) *See* Shakespeare's Globe (London, England)

New Mexico
Fiction
Davies, J. Where the ground meets the sky **Fic**
Klages, E. The green glass sea **Fic**
Thurlo, A. The spirit line **Fic**

New Orleans (La.)
Fiction
Antieau, K. Ruby's imagine **Fic**
Blume, L. M. M. Tennyson **Fic**
Sharenow, R. My mother the cheerleader **Fic**
Tiernan, C. A chalice of wind **Fic**
Volponi, P. Hurricane song **Fic**

The **new** policeman. Thompson, K. **Fic**

The **New** Republic (1763-1815). Stanley, G. E. **973.2**

New rules of high school. Nelson, B. **Fic**

New technology [series]
Graham, I. Military technology **355**

New Testament miracles. Connolly, S. **226**

The **new** totally awesome business book for kids (and their parents). Bochner, A. B. **658**

The **new** totally awesome money book for kids (and their parents). Bochner, A. B. **332.024**

The **new** way things work. Macaulay, D. **600**

The **new** weapons of the world encyclopedia **623.4**

New Year
Batmanglij, N. Happy Nowruz **641.5**

New Year, Chinese *See* Chinese New Year

New York (N.Y.)
See also Lower East Side (New York, N.Y.)
Matsen, B. Go wild in New York City **974.7**
Antiquities
Hansen, J. Breaking ground, breaking silence **974.7**
Fiction
Anderson, L. H. Chains **Fic**

Nicaragua—*Continued*
Politics and government
Kallen, S. A. The aftermath of the Sandinista
Revolution   **972.85**

Nicholas Copernicus and the founding of modern
astronomy. Goble, T.   **92**

Nicholls, Calvin
(il) Martin, R. The world before this one
398.2

Nicholls, Sally, 1983-
Ways to live forever   **Fic**

Nichols, Beverly
Managing curriculum and assessment. See Managing curriculum and assessment   **375**

Nichols, Terry Lynn
See/See also pages in the following book(s):
Sherrow, V. The Oklahoma City bombing
364.1

Nichols, Travis
Punk rock etiquette   **781.66**

Nicholson, Dorinda Makanaõnalani
Remember World War II   **940.53**

Nicholson, John, 1757-1800
See/See also pages in the following book(s):
Aaseng, N. Business builders in real estate
920

Nicholson, Lois, 1949-
Dian Fossey   **92**

Nicholson, William
Seeker   **Fic**

Nick of time. Bell, T.   **Fic**

Nickles, Nina
(il) Things I have to tell you. See Things I have
to tell you   **810.8**

Nicky Deuce. Schirripa, S. R.   **Fic**

Nicola, Christos
(jt. auth) Taylor, P. L. The secret of Priest's
Grotto   **940.53**

Nicotine. Price, S.   **616.86**

Nicotine and tobacco. Naff, C. F.   **362.29**

Niehaus, Theodore F.
A field guide to Pacific states wildflowers
582.13

Nielsen, Susin
Word nerd   **Fic**

Nieuwenhuizen, Agnes
Right book, right time   **011.6**

Nigeria
Giles, B. Nigeria   **966.9**
Levy, P. Nigeria   **966.9**
Walker, I. Nigeria   **966.9**
Fiction
Naidoo, B. The other side of truth   **Fic**

Nigg, Joe
How to raise and keep a dragon   **Fic**
Wonder beasts   **398**

Night
Fiction
Up all night   **S C**

Night hoops. Deuker, C.   **Fic**

The **night** I freed John Brown. Cummings, J. M.
Fic

Night is gone, day is still coming   **808.8**

The **night** journey. Lasky, K.   **Fic**

The **night** my sister went missing. Plum-Ucci, C.
Fic

Night of the howling dogs. Salisbury, G.   **Fic**

Night road. Jenkins, A. M.   **Fic**

The **night** tourist. Marsh, K.   **Fic**

Nightjohn. Paulsen, G.   **Fic**

Nightmare. Nixon, J. L.   **Fic**

Nightsong. Cadnum, M.   **Fic**

NightWatch: a practical guide to viewing the universe   **520**

NIH *See* National Institutes of Health (U.S.)

The **Nile**. Bowden, R.   **962**

The **Nile**. Heinrichs, A.   **962**

Nile River
Bowden, R. The Nile   **962**
Heinrichs, A. The Nile   **962**

Nile River valley
Bowden, R. The Nile   **962**
Heinrichs, A. The Nile   **962**

Nilsen, Alleen Pace
Literature for today's young adults   **028.5**
Names and naming in young adult literature
813.009

Nilsen, Don L. F. (Don Lee Fred)
(jt. auth) Nilsen, A. P. Names and naming in
young adult literature   **813.009**

Nimmo, Jenny, 1944-
Midnight for Charlie Bone   **Fic**
The snow spider   **Fic**

Nimr, Sonia
(jt. auth) Laird, E. A little piece of ground
Fic

Nine eleven: the book of help. See 911: the book
of help   **810.8**

The **nine** pound hammer. Bemis, J. C.   **Fic**

Nineteen eighty-four. Orwell, G.   **Fic**

Nineteen-eighty - Two thousand: the twentieth
century. See 1980-2000: the twentieth century
909.82

Nineteen-forty - Nineteen-sixty: the twentieth century. See 1940-1960: the twentieth century
909.82

Nineteen hundred - Nineteen-forty: the twentieth
century. See 1900-1920: the twentieth century
909.82

Nineteen-sixty - Nineteen-eighty: the twentieth
century. See 1960-1980: the twentieth century
909.82

Nineteen-twenty - Nineteen-forty: the twentieth
century. See 1920-1940: the twentieth century
909.82

Nineteen varieties of gazelle. See Nye, N. S. 19
varieties of gazelle   **811**

Ninth book of junior authors and illustrators
920.003

Nix, Garth, 1963-
Across the wall   **S C**
Mister Monday   **Fic**
Sabriel   **Fic**
Shade's children   **Fic**

North across the border. Perl, L.   **305.8**

North Africa
> Gritzner, J. A. North Africa and the Middle East   **956**

North Africa and the Middle East. Gritzner, J. A.   **956**

North America
> Desaulniers, K. L. Northern America   **970**
> Woods, M. Seven natural wonders of North America   **508**
>> **Natural history**
>> *See* Natural history—North America

North American Indian. Murdoch, D. H.   **970.004**

North American Indians *See* Native Americans

North by night. Ayres, K.   **Fic**

North Carolina
> **Fiction**
> Barkley, B. Scrambled eggs at midnight   **Fic**
> Dowell, F. O. Dovey Coe   **Fic**
> Hicks, B. Get real   **Fic**
> Hostetter, J. Blue   **Fic**
> Hostetter, J. Comfort   **Fic**
> Krisher, T. Fallout   **Fic**
> Madden, K. Gentle's Holler   **Fic**
> Moses, S. P. The baptism   **Fic**
> Moses, S. P. The legend of Buddy Bush   **Fic**
> O'Connor, B. Greetings from nowhere   **Fic**
>> **Race relations**
>> Tillage, L. Leon's story   **92**

North Dakota
> Manning, P. L. Dinomummy   **567.9**
> **Fiction**
> Spooner, M. Last Child   **Fic**

North Korea *See* Korea (North)

North of beautiful. Headley, J. C.   **Fic**

North Pole
> *See also* Arctic regions
> Calvert, P. Robert E. Peary   **92**
> Johnson, D. Onward [biography of Matthew Henson]   **92**
> Olmstead, K. A. Matthew Henson   **92**
> Revkin, A. The North Pole was here   **998**

The **North** Pole was here. Revkin, A.   **998**

Northern America. Desaulniers, K. L.   **970**

Northern Ireland
> **Fiction**
> Dowd, S. Bog child   **Fic**

Northern lights. See Pullman, P. The golden compass   **Fic**

Northern Lights young novels [series]
> Aspin, D. Ordinary miracles   **S C**

Northern Rhodesia *See* Zambia

Northmen *See* Vikings

Northwest, Pacific *See* Pacific Northwest

Northwest Passage
> Warrick, K. C. The perilous search for the fabled Northwest Passage in American history   **910.4**

Norton, James R.
> Haydn's world   **92**

Norville, Rod
> Moonshine express   **Fic**

Norway
> Kagda, S. Norway   **948.1**
> **Fiction**
> Casanova, M. The klipfish code   **Fic**
> Haig, M. Samuel Blink and the forbidden forest   **Fic**

Nory Ryan's song. Giff, P. R.   **Fic**

Not like you. Davis, D.   **Fic**

Not the end of the world. McCaughrean, G.   **Fic**

Notable Americans [series]
> Barron, R. Richard Nixon   **92**
> Young, J. C. Dwight D. Eisenhower   **92**

Notable mathematicians   **920.003**

Notable social studies trade books for young people   **016.3**

Notable women scientists   **920.003**

Notes from a liar and her dog. Choldenko, G.   **Fic**

Notes from the midnight driver. Sonnenblick, J.   **Fic**

Nothing but the truth. Avi   **Fic**

Nothing here but stones. Oswald, N.   **Fic**

Nouvian, Claire
> (ed) The Deep. See The Deep   **591.7**

Nova Scotia
> **Fiction**
> Kositsky, L. Claire by moonlight   **Fic**

Novels in verse
> Applegate, K. Home of the brave   **Fic**
> Bingham, K. Shark girl   **Fic**
> Bryant, J. Kaleidoscope eyes   **Fic**
> Bryant, J. Ringside, 1925   **Fic**
> Burg, A. E. All the broken pieces   **Fic**
> Chaltas, T. Because I am furniture   **Fic**
> Engle, M. The surrender tree   **Fic**
> Engle, M. Tropical secrets   **Fic**
> Fehler, G. Beanball   **Fic**
> Ford, C. Scout   **Fic**
> Frost, H. The braid   **Fic**
> Frost, H. Diamond Willow   **Fic**
> Fullerton, A. Walking on glass   **Fic**
> Grimes, N. Dark sons   **Fic**
> Hemphill, S. Things left unsaid   **Fic**
> Hesse, K. Out of the dust   **Fic**
> Hesse, K. Witness   **Fic**
> LeZotte, A. C. T4   **Fic**
> Myers, W. D. Amiri & Odette   **Fic**
> Myers, W. D. Street love   **Fic**
> Schroeder, L. I heart you, you haunt me   **Fic**
> Smith, H. A. Keeping the night watch   **Fic**
> Smith, H. A. The way a door closes   **Fic**
> Smith, K. The geography of girlhood   **Fic**
> Turner, A. W. Hard hit   **Fic**
> Wayland, A. H. Girl coming in for a landing   **Fic**
> Weatherford, C. B. Becoming Billie Holiday   **Fic**
> Weston, R. P. Zorgamazoo   **Fic**
> Wolff, V. E. Make lemonade   **Fic**
> Woodson, J. Locomotion   **Fic**

Occupations—*Continued*

Schwager, T. Cool women, hot jobs . . . and how you can go for it, too! **650.14**

United States. Bureau of Labor Statistics. Occupational outlook handbook 2008-2009 **331.7**

Young person's occupational outlook handbook **331.7**

Ocean

See also Seashore

Carson, R. The sea around us **551.46**
Day, T. Oceans **551.46**
Desonie, D. Oceans **551.46**
McMillan, B. Oceans **551.46**
Olmstead, K. A. Jacques Cousteau **92**
Young, K. R. Across the wide ocean **623.89**

Fiction

Banghart, T. What the sea wants **Fic**

An **ocean** apart, a world away. Namioka, L. **Fic**

Ocean bottom

Aleshire, P. Ocean ridges and trenches **551.46**

Gowell, E. T. Fountains of life **577.7**
Lindop, L. Venturing the deep sea **551.46**
Mallory, K. Diving to a deep-sea volcano **551.46**
Matsen, B. The incredible record-setting deep-sea dive of the bathysphere **551.46**

Ocean currents

See also El Niño Current

Burns, L. G. Tracking trash **551.46**

Ocean ridges and trenches. Aleshire, P. **551.46**

Ocean sciences *See* Marine sciences

Ocean travel

Paulsen, G. Caught by the sea **92**

Ocean waves

See also Tsunamis

Ocean wildlife. Vogel, C. G. **591.7**

Oceania

Lawlor, L. Magnificent voyage **910.4**
Leppman, E. J. Australia and the Pacific **994**

Oceanography

Day, T. Oceans **551.46**
Desonie, D. Oceans **551.46**
Olmstead, K. A. Jacques Cousteau **92**
Walker, P. The open ocean **578.7**

Ochoa, Annette Piña

(ed) Night is gone, day is still coming. See Night is gone, day is still coming **808.8**

Ochoa, Ellen, 1958-

About

Paige, J. Ellen Ochoa **92**

Ochoa, George

Atlas of Hispanic-American history **305.8**
The Wilson chronology of ideas **909**
The Wilson chronology of science and technology **502**
(ed) American history on file. See American history on file **973**

O'Connell, Diane

People person [biography of Marta Tienda] **92**

Strong force [biography of Shirley Ann Jackson] **92**

O'Connell, Tyne

True love, the sphinx, and other unsolvable riddles **Fic**

O'Conner, Patricia T.

Woe is I Jr **428**

O'Connor, Barbara

Barefoot dancer: the story of Isadora Duncan **92**

Fame and glory in Freedom, Georgia **Fic**
Greetings from nowhere **Fic**
How to steal a dog **Fic**
Leonardo da Vinci **92**

O'Connor, George

(il) Simmons, M. Alien feast **Fic**

O'Connor, Jane, 1947-

The emperor's silent army **931**
(jt. auth) Gore, A., Jr. An inconvenient truth **363.7**

Octavian *See* Augustus, Emperor of Rome, 63 B.C.-14 A.D.

O'Day, Anita, 1919-2006

See/See also pages in the following book(s):

Orgill, R. Shout, sister, shout! **920**

Odd man out. Ellis, S. **Fic**

Oddballs. Sleator, W. **S C**

Oddest of all. Coville, B. **S C**

Oddities *See* Curiosities and wonders

Oddly Normal. Frampton, O. **741.5**

O'Dell, Kathleen

Agnes Parker . . . girl in progress **Fic**

O'Dell, Katie

Library materials and services for teen girls **027.62**

O'Dell, Scott, 1898-1989

Island of the Blue Dolphins **Fic**
Sing down the moon **Fic**
Streams to the river, river to the sea **Fic**
Thunder rolling in the mountains **Fic**
Zia **Fic**

About

Marcovitz, H. Scott O'Dell **92**

O'Donnell, Kerri, 1972-

The gold rush **979.4**

O'Donnell, Liam, 1970-

Wild ride: a graphic guide adventure **741.5**

O'Donnell, Rosie

Rosie O'Donnell's crafty U **745.5**

Odysseus (Greek mythology)

Lister, R. The odyssey **883**
McCaughrean, G. Odysseus **292**
Osborne, M. P. The gray-eyed goddess **883**
Osborne, M. P. The land of the dead **883**
Osborne, M. P. The one-eyed giant **883**
Osborne, M. P. Return to Ithaca **883**

See/See also pages in the following book(s):

Hamilton, E. Mythology **292**

Fiction

Geras, A. Ithaka **Fic**

Orphans—Fiction—*Continued*

Gardner, S. The red necklace **Fic**
Garland, S. The silent storm **Fic**
George, J. D. Dragon slippers **Fic**
Golding, J. The diamond of Drury Lane **Fic**
Haig, M. Samuel Blink and the forbidden forest **Fic**
Heneghan, J. The magician's apprentice **Fic**
Heuston, K. B. The Shakeress **Fic**
Hobbs, W. Jason's gold **Fic**
Hopkinson, D. Into the firestorm **Fic**
Horowitz, A. Stormbreaker **Fic**
Hurst, C. O. Through the lock **Fic**
Jacques, B. Castaways of the Flying Dutchman **Fic**
Jarvis, R. The Whitby witches **Fic**
Jinks, C. Babylonne **Fic**
Key, W. Alabama moon **Fic**
Kluger, J. Nacky Patcher and the curse of the dry-land boats **Fic**
Koertge, R. Strays **Fic**
Koja, K. Headlong **Fic**
LaFaye, A. Stella stands alone **Fic**
Landman, T. I am Apache **Fic**
Larson, K. Hattie Big Sky **Fic**
Lawlor, L. Dead reckoning **Fic**
Levine, G. C. Dave at night **Fic**
Lisle, J. T. The crying rocks **Fic**
Maguire, G. What-the-Dickens **Fic**
Matthews, L. S. Lexi **Fic**
Mazer, N. F. Girlhearts **Fic**
McDowell, M. T. Carolina Harmony **Fic**
McKernan, V. The devil's paintbox **Fic**
McNab, A. Traitor **Fic**
Meyer, C. Duchessina **Fic**
Meyer, K. The water mirror **Fic**
Meyer, L. A. Bloody Jack **Fic**
Michael, J. City boy **Fic**
Moloney, J. The Book of Lies **Fic**
Morgan, C. The boy who spoke dog **Fic**
Mosher, R. Zazoo **Fic**
Myers, A. Spy! **Fic**
Orenstein, D. G. The secret twin **Fic**
Petrucha, S. Teen, Inc. **Fic**
Philbrick, W. R. The mostly true adventures of Homer P. Figg **Fic**
Potter, E. Slob **Fic**
Ravel, E. The saver **Fic**
Resau, L. Red glass **Fic**
Ritter, J. H. The desperado who stole baseball **Fic**
Russell, C. Dogboy **Fic**
Schlitz, L. A. A drowned maiden's hair **Fic**
Schwabach, K. A pickpocket's tale **Fic**
Schwartz, E. Stealing home **Fic**
Seidler, T. Brainboy and the Deathmaster **Fic**
Selfors, S. Fortune's magic farm **Fic**
Selznick, B. The invention of Hugo Cabret **Fic**
Simmons, M. Alien feast **Fic**
Spinelli, J. Maniac Magee **Fic**
St. Crow, L. Strange angels **Fic**
St. John, L. The white giraffe **Fic**
Strickland, B. The sign of the sinister sorcerer **Fic**
Torrey, M. Voyage of midnight **Fic**

Tunnell, M. O. Wishing moon **Fic**
Whelan, G. Listening for lions **Fic**
White, R. Way Down Deep **Fic**
Woodruff, E. Fearless **Fic**
Woodson, J. Peace, Locomotion **Fic**
Yancey, R. The extraordinary adventures of Alfred Kropp **Fic**

Graphic novels

Geary, R. Great expectations **741.5**

Orr, Tamra
Alan Shepard **92**
Bangladesh **954.92**
Extraordinary essays **808.4**
Qatar **953.6**
Saint Lucia **972.98**
Slovenia **949.7**
Test tube babies **618.1**
Turkey **956.1**
Violence in our schools **371.7**
When the mirror lies **616.85**
Great Hispanic-Americans. See Great Hispanic-Americans **920**

Ortiz, Alfonso, 1939-1997
(ed) American Indian myths and legends. See American Indian myths and legends **398.2**

Ortiz Cofer, Judith, 1952-
Call me Maria **Fic**

Orwell, George, 1903-1950
Animal farm **Fic**
Nineteen eighty-four **Fic**
About
Means, A. L. A student's guide to George Orwell **828**

Orwell's luck. Jennings, R. W. **Fic**

Oryx multicultural folktale series
Hearne, B. G. Beauties and beasts **398.2**

Osa, Nancy
Cuba 15 **Fic**

Osama bin Laden
About
Landau, E. Osama bin Laden **92**
See/See also pages in the following book(s):
Frank, M. Understanding September 11th **973.931**

Osborn, Elinor, 1939-
Project UltraSwan **598**

Osborne, Linda Barrett, 1949-
Traveling the freedom road **973.7**

Osborne, Mary Pope, 1949-
The gray-eyed goddess **883**
The land of the dead **883**
The one-eyed giant **883**
One world, many religions **200**
Return to Ithaca **883**
Standing in the light **Fic**

Osburn, Jennifer, 1983-
(jt. auth) Selfridge, B. A teen's guide to creating Web pages and blogs **006.7**

O'Shea, Maria
Kuwait **953.67**

Osteoporosis
Hoffmann, G. Osteoporosis **616.7**

Osterlund, Anne
Aurelia **Fic**

Out of the dust. Hesse, K. **Fic**

Out of the shadows. Waldman, N. **92**

Out of this world [series]

Spangenburg, R. The Hubble Space Telescope **522**

Spangenburg, R. A look at Mercury **523.4**

Spangenburg, R. Meteors, meteorites, and meteoroids **523.5**

Tabak, J. A look at earth **550**

Tabak, J. A look at Neptune **523.4**

Tocci, S. A look at Uranus **523.4**

Out-of-this-world astronomy. Rhatigan, J. **520**

Outbreak. Friedlander, M. P. **614.4**

Outbreak. Piddock, C. **614.4**

The **outcasts**. Matthews, L. S. **Fic**

The **outcasts** of 19 Schuyler Place. Konigsburg, E. L. **Fic**

Outdoor life

See also Camping

Paulsen, G. Woodsong **796.5**

Weber, S. Two in the wilderness **508**

Outdoor life [series]

Fitzgerald, R. Essential fishing for teens **799.1**

Outdoor survival *See* Wilderness survival

Outer space

Colonies

See Space colonies

Exploration

See also Space probes

Carlisle, R. P. Exploring space **629.4**

Carson, M. K. Exploring the solar system **523.2**

Chaikin, A. Space **629.4**

Jedicke, P. Great moments in space exploration **629.4**

Miller, R. Space exploration **629.4**

Nagel, R. Space exploration, Almanac **629.4**

Saari, P. Space exploration, Biographies **629.45**

Solway, A. Can we travel to the stars? **629.45**

Stott, C. Space exploration **629.4**

Outer space travel *See* Interplanetary voyages

Outlaws. Blackwood, G. L. **364.1**

Outlaws, mobsters & crooks. MacNee, M. J. **920.003**

The **outlaws** of Sherwood. McKinley, R. **398.2**

Outman, Elisabeth M., 1951-

(jt. auth) Outman, J. L. Industrial Revolution: almanac **330.9**

(jt. auth) Outman, J. L. Industrial Revolution: biographies **920**

(jt. auth) Outman, J. L. Industrial Revolution: primary sources **330.9**

Outman, James L., 1946-

Industrial Revolution: almanac **330.9**

Industrial Revolution: biographies **920**

Industrial Revolution: primary sources **330.9**

Outside and inside mummies. Markle, S. **393**

Outside beauty. Kadohata, C. **Fic**

Outside rules **S C**

The **outsiders**. Hinton, S. E. **Fic**

Outsourcing

Ching, J. Outsourcing U.S. jobs **331.1**

Outsourcing U.S. jobs. Ching, J. **331.1**

Outstanding science trade books for students K-12 **016.5**

Over a thousand hills I walk with you. Jansen, H. **Fic**

Over sea, under stone. Cooper, S. **Fic**

Over the mountains. Collier, M. **557**

Over the river. Moranville, S. B. **Fic**

Overcoming adversity [series]

Chippendale, L. A. Triumph of the imagination: the story of writer J.K. Rowling **92**

Overcrowded world. McLeish, E. **363.9**

Overland journeys to the Pacific

See also West (U.S.)—Exploration

Calabro, M. The perilous journey of the Donner Party **978**

Harness, C. The tragic tale of Narcissa Whitman and a faithful history of the Oregon Trail **92**

Olson, T. How to get rich on the Oregon Trail **978**

Fiction

Lawlor, L. He will go fearless **Fic**

McKernan, V. The devil's paintbox **Fic**

Overpopulation

McLeish, E. Overcrowded world **363.9**

Overview series

Miller, D. A. Hurricane Katrina **363.34**

Overweight. Heller, T. **613.2**

Ovsyanikov, Nikita

Polar bears **599.78**

Owen, David, 1939-

Police lab **363.2**

Owen, James A.

Here, there be dragons **Fic**

Owens, Tom, 1960-

Collecting baseball memorabilia **796.357**

The **owl** and the pussycat. Lear, E. **821**

Owl in love. Kindl, P. **Fic**

Owls

Sattler, H. R. The book of North American owls **598**

Warhol, T. Owls **598**

Fiction

Hiaasen, C. Hoot **Fic**

Kindl, P. Owl in love **Fic**

Poetry

Lear, E. The owl and the pussycat **821**

Owning it **S C**

Ox, house, stick. Robb, D. **411**

Oxford atlas of the world **912**

The **Oxford** book of American poetry **811.008**

The **Oxford** book of children's verse in America **811.008**

The **Oxford** book of story poems **808.81**

The **Oxford** book of twentieth-century English verse **821.008**

Paige, Satchel, 1906-1982
Graphic novels
Sturm, J. Satchel Paige   **741.5**

Pain
   See also Headache
Hains, B. C. Pain   **616**

Pain relievers *See* Analgesics

The **Pain** tree, and other teenage angst-ridden poetry   **811.008**

Painful history of crime [series]
   Townsend, J. Crime through time   **364**
   Townsend, J. Prisons and prisoners   **365**
   Townsend, J. Punishment and pain   **364.6**

Painful history of medicine [series]
   Townsend, J. Pills, powders & potions   **615**
   Townsend, J. Pox, pus & plague   **616**
   Townsend, J. Scalpels, stitches & scars   **617**

Painkillers and tranquilizers. Durham, M.   **615**

Paint
   See/See also pages in the following book(s):
Knapp, B. J. Materials science   **620.1**

Paint me like I am   **811.008**

The **painted** wall and other strange tales. Bedard, M.   **398.2**

Painters
   See also Artists

Painting
   D'Harcourt, C. Masterpieces up close   **759**
   Dickins, R. The Usborne art treasury   **701**
   Raczka, B. Unlikely pairs   **750**
   See/See also pages in the following book(s):
Luxbacher, I. The jumbo book of art   **702.8**

Painting, Chinese *See* Chinese painting

Painting, French *See* French painting

Painting, Italian *See* Italian painting

Painting the black. Deuker, C.   **Fic**

Painting the picture. Bodden, V.   **808.3**

Painting the wild frontier: the art and adventures of George Catlin. Reich, S.   **92**

Pakistan
   Kovarik, C. A. Interviews with Muslim women of Pakistan   **954.91**
   Morgan, S. Focus on Pakistan   **954.91**
   Mortenson, G. Three cups of tea   **954.91**
Fiction
   D'Adamo, F. Iqbal   **Fic**
   Qamar, A. Beneath my mother's feet   **Fic**
   Staples, S. F. Shabanu   **Fic**
   Staples, S. F. Under the Persimmon tree   **Fic**

Pakistani Americans
Fiction
   Karim, S. Skunk girl   **Fic**
   Perkins, M. First daughter: extreme American makeover   **Fic**

The **palace.** Hinds, K.   **909.07**

Paladino, Variny
   (jt. auth) Blatt, J. The teen girl's gotta-have-it guide to money   **332.024**

Palen, Debbie
   (il) Gravelle, K. The period book   **612.6**

Palenque. Kops, D.   **972**

Palenque site (Mexico)
   Kops, D. Palenque   **972**

Paleo bugs. Bradley, T. J.   **560**

Paleo sharks. Bradley, T. J.   **567**

Paleontology *See* Fossils

Palestine
   Wingate, K. The Intifadas   **956.95**
Civilization
   Sherman, J. Your travel guide to ancient Israel   **933**
Fiction
   Carter, A. The shepherd's granddaughter   **Fic**
   Laird, E. A little piece of ground   **Fic**

Palestine problem, 1917- *See* Israel-Arab conflicts; Jewish-Arab relations

Palestinian Arabs
   Barakat, I. Tasting the sky   **92**
   Ellis, D. Three wishes   **956.94**
   Headlam, G. Yasser Arafat   **92**
   Israel: opposing viewpoints   **956.94**
   Rosaler, M. Hamas: Palestinian terrorists   **956.94**

The **Palestinians** and the disputed territories   **956.04**

Paley, Sasha
   Huge   **Fic**

Palmer, Martin
   (jt. auth) Breuilly, E. Festivals of the world   **394.26**

Palmer, Martin, 1953-
   (jt. auth) Breuilly, E. Religions of the world   **200**

Palms to the ground. Stolls, A.   **Fic**

Palser, Barb
   Hurricane Katrina   **363.34**

Pan (Greek deity)
Fiction
   Napoli, D. J. The great god Pan   **Fic**

Pan-Americanism
   See also Monroe Doctrine

Panama
   Hassig, S. M. Panama   **972.87**

Panama Canal
   DuTemple, L. A. The Panama Canal   **972.87**
   See/See also pages in the following book(s):
Aaseng, N. Construction: building the impossible   **624**

Panchyk, Richard, 1970-
   American folk art for kids   **745**
   Franklin Delano Roosevelt for kids   **92**
   Galileo for kids   **92**
   The keys to American history   **973**
   Our Supreme Court   **347**
   (jt. auth) Levy, M. Engineering the city   **624**

Panda *See* Giant panda

Panda rescue. Bortolotti, D.   **599.78**

Pandemics. Miller, D. A.   **614.4**

Pandora (Legendary character)
Fiction
   Hennesy, C. Pandora gets jealous   **Fic**

Pandora gets jealous. Hennesy, C.   **Fic**

Pang, Guek-Cheng, 1950-
Canada   **971**
Grenada   **972.98**
Mongolia   **951.7**
(jt. auth) Layton, L. Singapore   **959.57**

Panic disorders
Connolly, S. Anxiety disorders   **616.85**
Levin, J. Anxiety and panic attacks   **616.85**
Miller, A. R. Living with anxiety disorders
    616.85
Schutz, S. I don't want to be crazy   **92**

Pantheon (Rome, Italy)
DuTemple, L. A. The Pantheon   **726**

Pantheon fairy tale & folklore library [series]
African folktales   **398.2**

Paolini, Christopher
Eragon   **Fic**

Papacy
See also Popes

Papademetriou, Lisa
Drop   **Fic**
M or F?   **Fic**

Paper
See/See also pages in the following book(s):
Knapp, B. J. Materials science   **620.1**

Paper crafts
See also Origami
Collins, J. M. Fantastic flight   **745.592**
Collins, J. M. The gliding flight   **745.592**
Diehn, G. Making books that fly, fold, wrap,
hide, pop up, twist, and turn   **745.54**
Harbo, C. L. The kids' guide to paper airplanes
    745.592
Henry, S. Paper folding   **736**
Prins, M. D. Paper galaxy   **745.54**

Paper folding. Henry, S.   **736**

Paper galaxy. Prins, M. D.   **745.54**

Papillomaviruses
Parks, P. J. HPV   **362.1**

Paprocki, Sherry Beck
Bob Marley   **92**

Papua New Guinea
Gascoigne, I. Papua New Guinea   **995.3**

Paquette, Penny Hutchins
Learning disabilities   **371.9**

Parachute troops
McGowen, T. Assault from the sky   **940.54**

Parade of shadows. Whelan, G.   **Fic**

Paraguay
Jermyn, L. Paraguay   **989.2**
See/See also pages in the following book(s):
Batten, M. Anthropologist: scientist of the peo-
ple   **301**

Paranoid Park. Nelson, B.   **Fic**

Paranormal phenomena: opposing viewpoints
    133

Parapsychology
See also Extrasensory perception; Occult-
ism
Allen, J. Unexplained   **001.9**
Blackwood, G. L. Extraordinary events and odd-
ball occurrences   **001.9**

Paranormal phenomena: opposing viewpoints
    133
      Fiction
Hegamin, T. Pemba's song   **Fic**
Ryan, A. K. Vibes   **Fic**
Vrettos, A. M. Sight   **Fic**

Parasites
See also Symbiosis
Fleisher, P. Parasites   **578.6**

A **parcel** of patterns. Paton Walsh, J.   **Fic**

Pardes, Bronwen
Doing it right   **613.9**

Paredes, Angel García de *See* García de Paredes,
Angel

Parent and child *See* Parent-child relationship

Parent-child relationship
See also Children of alcoholics; Children of
immigrants; Mother-child relationship
Snow, J. E. How it feels to have a gay or lesbi-
an parent   **306.8**
      Fiction
Cleary, B. Dear Mr. Henshaw   **Fic**
Danziger, P. The Divorce Express   **Fic**
Voigt, C. A solitary blue   **Fic**

Parenting
Trapani, M. Reality check   **306.8**

Parents
See also Gay parents

Parents, Single *See* Single parent family

Paris (France)
      Fiction
Morgenstern, S. H. Secret letters from 0 to 10
    Fic
Selznick, B. The invention of Hugo Cabret
    Fic

Park, Barbara, 1947-
The graduation of Jake Moon   **Fic**

Park, Linda Sue, 1960-
Archer's quest   **Fic**
Keeping score   **Fic**
Project Mulberry   **Fic**
A single shard   **Fic**
When my name was Keoko   **Fic**

Parker, Barry R.
The mystery of gravity   **531**

Parker, Buzz
(il) Reger, R. Emily the Strange: the lost days
    Fic

Parker, Charlie, 1920-1955
See/See also pages in the following book(s):
Mour, S. I. American jazz musicians   **920**

Parker, Ely Samuel, 1828-1895
See/See also pages in the following book(s):
Brown, D. A. Bury my heart at Wounded Knee
    970.004
Ehrlich, A. Wounded Knee: an Indian history of
the American West   **970.004**

Parker, Jeff, 1966-
The avengers: heroes assembled   **741.5**

Parker, Marjorie Hodgson
David and the Mighty Eighth   **Fic**

Physical fitness—*Continued*

Purperhart, H. Yoga exercises for teens **613.7**

Shryer, D. Peak performance **617.1**

Vedral, J. L. Toning for teens **613.7**

Physical geography

Taylor, B. Understanding landforms **551.4**

Physically handicapped

See also Blind; Deaf

Bankston, J. Stephen Hawking **92**

Thornton, D. Physical disabilities **362.4**

Fiction

Konigsburg, E. L. The view from Saturday **Fic**

Physicians

See also Surgeons; Women physicians

Ramen, F. Albucasis (Abu al-Qasim al-Zahrawi) **92**

Rodriguez, A. M. Edward Jenner **92**

Stevenson, R. L. The strange case of Dr. Jekyll and Mr. Hyde **Fic**

Yount, L. William Harvey **92**

Fiction

Morgan, N. Fleshmarket **Fic**

Stewart, P. The curse of the night wolf **Fic**

Torrey, M. Voyage of midnight **Fic**

Whelan, G. Listening for lions **Fic**

Physicists

Allman, T. J. Robert Oppenheimer **92**

Bankston, J. Stephen Hawking **92**

Bernstein, J. Albert Einstein and the frontiers of physics **92**

Borzendowski, J. Marie Curie **92**

Cooper, D. Enrico Fermi and the revolutions in modern physics **92**

Delano, M. F. Genius [biography of Albert Einstein] **92**

Ferry, J. Maria Goeppert Mayer **92**

Goldenstern, J. Albert Einstein **92**

Hamilton, J. Lise Meitner **92**

Henderson, H. Nuclear physics **539.7**

Lassieur, A. Albert Einstein **92**

MacLeod, E. Albert Einstein **92**

O'Connell, D. Strong force [biography of Shirley Ann Jackson] **92**

Pasachoff, N. E. Ernest Rutherford **92**

Scherer, G. J. Robert Oppenheimer **92**

Sullivan, A. M. Albert Einstein **92**

Physics

See also Nuclear physics

Balmer, A. J. Doc Fizzix mousetrap racers **629.22**

The Facts on File physics handbook **530**

Farndon, J. Experimenting with physics **530**

Gardner, R. Bicycle science projects **531**

Gardner, R. Physics projects with a light box you can build **530**

Gardner, R. Science projects about physics in the home **530**

Green, D. Physics **530**

Hakim, J. The story of science: Newton at the center **509**

Hammond, R. Can you feel the force? **530**

Townsend, J. Foolish physics **530**

Fiction

Reisman, M. Simon Bloom, the gravity keeper **Fic**

Physics. Green, D. **530**

Physics! best science projects [series]

Gardner, R. Light, sound, and waves science fair projects **507.8**

Physics projects with a light box you can build. Gardner, R. **530**

Physiology

See also Human body; Immune system

Calabresi, L. Human body **612**

Human physiology on file **612**

Nagel, R. Body by design **612**

Redd, N. A. Body drama **612**

Pianists

Lang, L. Lang Lang **92**

Reich, S. Clara Schumann **92**

Fiction

Blume, L. M. M. The rising star of Rusty Nail **Fic**

Fogelin, A. The big nothing **Fic**

Picasso, Pablo, 1881-1973

About

Hodge, S. Pablo Picasso **92**

McNeese, T. Pablo Picasso **92**

Scarborough, K. Pablo Picasso **92**

Pick & shovel poet: the journeys of Pascal D'Angelo. Murphy, J. **92**

Pickering, William H., 1910-2004

See/See also pages in the following book(s):

Richie, J. Space flight **920**

Picketing *See* Strikes

A **pickpocket's** tale. Schwabach, K. **Fic**

Pickthall, Marmaduke, 1875-1936

(tr) Koran. The meaning of the glorious Koran **297.1**

Picture books for children

Artist to artist **741.6**

Bibliography

Matulka, D. I. Picture this **011.6**

Picture dictionaries

Corbeil, J.-C. The Firefly Spanish/English junior visual dictionary **463**

Shapiro, N. The Oxford picture dictionary, English-Korean **495.7**

A **picture** history of great buildings. Clements, G. **720.9**

Picture perfect. Love, D. A. **Fic**

Picture that! [series]

Chapman, C. Battles & weapons: exploring history through art **355**

Galford, E. The trail West **978**

Martin, A. Knights & castles **940.1**

Picture this. Matulka, D. I. **011.6**

Picture writing

See also Hieroglyphics

Liungman, C. G. Dictionary of symbols **302.2**

Pictures of Hollis Woods. Giff, P. R. **Fic**

Picturing Lincoln. Sullivan, G. **92**

Plants—*Continued*

Gardner, R. Science projects about plants
    580.7

Gibson, J. P. Plant diversity   **580**
Hopkins, W. G. Plant biotechnology   **630**
Johnson, R. L. Powerful plant cells   **581.7**
Plant sciences   **580**
Spilsbury, R. Plant habitats   **581.7**
Spilsbury, R. Plant reproduction   **575.6**
Stefoff, R. The flowering plant division   **580**
VanCleave, J. P. Janice VanCleave's plants
    580.7
Whitehouse, P. Plants   **580.7**

Ecology

See Plant ecology

Encyclopedias

Wildlife and plants   **578**

Fiction

Pikc, A. Wings   **Fic**

Growth

Spilsbury, R. Plant growth   **571.8**

United States

Patent, D. H. Plants on the trail with Lewis and
Clark   **978**

Plants, Hallucinogenic *See* Hallucinogens

Plants, Industrial *See* Factories

Plants on the trail with Lewis and Clark. Patent,
D. H.   **978**

Plastic surgery

Fiction

Na, A. The fold   **Fic**
Williams, L. E. Slant   **Fic**

Plastics

Finkelstein, N. H. Plastics   **620.1**
Goodstein, M. Plastics and polymers science fair
projects   **507.8**
See/See also pages in the following book(s):
Knapp, B. J. Materials science   **620.1**

Plastics and polymers science fair projects.
Goodstein, M.   **507.8**

Plate tectonics

Gallant, R. A. Dance of the continents
    551.1
Gallant, R. A. Plates   **551.1**
Hanson, E. A. Canyons   **551.4**
Silverstein, A. Plate tectonics   **551.1**
Stille, D. R. Plate tectonics   **551.1**

Plates. Gallant, R. A.   **551.1**

Plath, Sylvia

Poetry

Hemphill, S. Your own, Sylvia   **811**

Platkin, Charles Stuart

Lighten up   **613.2**

Platt, Richard, 1953-

Crime scene   **363.2**
Forensics   **363.2**
Moon landing   **629.45**
Shipwreck   **910.4**
They wore what?!   **391**

Play ball like the hall of famers. Krasner, S.
    796.357

Play ball like the pros. Krasner, S.   **796.357**

Play-by-play mountain biking. King, A.   **796.6**

Play direction (Theater) *See* Theater—Production
and direction

Play me. Ruby, L.   **Fic**

Play production *See* Theater—Production and direction

Play writing *See* Motion picture plays—Technique

Playing with matches. Katcher, B.   **Fic**

Playmates, Imaginary *See* Imaginary playmates

Plays *See* Drama—Collections; One act plays

Playwrights *See* Dramatists

Plessy, Homer
About
Anderson, W. Plessy v. Ferguson   **342**
Axelrod-Contrada, J. Plessy v. Ferguson   **342**

Plessy v. Ferguson. Anderson, W.   **342**

Plessy v. Ferguson. Axelrod-Contrada, J.   **342**

Pliny, the Younger, ca. 61-ca. 112
Epistularum libri VI.; Adaptation. See Moser, B.
Ashen sky   **937**

Plisson, Philip
Lighthouses   **387.1**

Plum-Ucci, Carol, 1957-
Celebrate Diwali   **294.5**
The night my sister went missing   **Fic**

Plummer, Louise
Finding Daddy   **Fic**

Pluralism (Social sciences) *See* Multiculturalism

Pluto (Planet)
Tyson, N. D. G. The Pluto files   **523.4**

The **Pluto** files. Tyson, N. D. G.   **523.4**

The **Plymouth** Colony and the Pilgrim adventure
in American history. Edwards, J.   **974.4**

Pneumonia
Silverstein, A. The flu and pneumonia update
    616.2

Pobst, Sandy, 1959-
Animals on the edge   **578.68**

Pocho. Villarreal, J. A.
In Growing up Latino; memoirs and stories
p165-92   **810.8**

Pocket babies and other amazing marsupials. Collard, S. B., III   **599.2**

Pocket space guide [series]
Godwin, R. Project Apollo   **629.45**

A **pod** of killer whales. León, V.   **599.5**

Podany, Amanda H.
The ancient Near Eastern world   **939**
(ed) The world in ancient times. See The world
in ancient times   **930**

Podcasting
Braun, L. W. Listen up!   **371.3**
Fontichiaro, K. Podcasting at school   **371.3**

Podcasting at school. Fontichiaro, K.   **371.3**

Podell, Janet
Old worlds to new   **920.003**
(ed) Facts about the presidents. See Facts about
the presidents   **920**
(jt. auth) Kane, J. N. Famous first facts
    031.02

Poe, Edgar Allan, 1809-1849
Edgar Allan Poe   **S C**

Poe, Edgar Allan, 1809-1849—*Continued*

Edgar Allan Poe's tales of mystery and madness
S C

The raven **811**
The raven and other poems **741.5**
Tales of terror **S C**

About

Binns, T. B. Edgar Allan Poe **92**
Lange, K. E. Nevermore **92**
McArthur, D. A student's guide to Edgar Allan Poe **813.009**
Meltzer, M. Edgar Allan Poe **92**

Adaptations

Poe, E. A. The raven and other poems **741.5**

Fiction

Avi. The man who was Poe **Fic**
A **Poem** of her own **811.008**
Poems from homeroom. Appelt, K. **811**
The **poet** slave of Cuba. Engle, M. **92**

Poetics

Appelt, K. Poems from homeroom **811**
Fandel, J. Puns, allusions, and other word secrets **808.1**
Fandel, J. Rhyme, meter, and other word music **808.1**
Fletcher, R. Poetry matters **808.1**
The Place my words are looking for **811.008**
Poetry from A to Z **808.1**
Prelutsky, J. Pizza, pigs, and poetry **808.1**
Seeing the blue between **808.1**
Wolf, A. Immersed in verse **808.1**

Poetry

> *See also* African poetry; American poetry; Animals—Poetry; Chinese poetry; English poetry; Native Americans—Poetry; Persian poetry and types of poetry; subjects with the subdivision *Poetry*

Janeczko, P. B. Worlds afire **811**

Bibliography

Leeper, A. Poetry in literature for youth **016.8**

By individual authors

Adoff, J. The song shoots out of my mouth **811**
Angelou, M. Maya Angelou **811**
Appelt, K. Poems from homeroom **811**
Bernier-Grand, C. T. Diego **811**
Bernier-Grand, C. T. Frida **811**
Borus, A. A student's guide to Emily Dickinson **811.009**
Cohen, B. Canterbury tales **821**
Dickinson, E. My letter to the world and other poems **811**
Fleischman, P. Big talk **811**
Frost, R. Robert Frost **811**
Grandits, J. Blue lipstick **811**
Grandits, J. Technically, it's not my fault **811**
Grover, L. A. Loose threads **811**
Harley, A. African acrostics **811**
Hemphill, S. Your own, Sylvia **811**
Herrera, J. F. Laughing out loud, I fly **811**
Homer. The Iliad **883**

Homer. The Odyssey **883**
Hopkins, L. B. Been to yesterdays: poems of a life **811**
Hovey, K. Ancient voices **811**
Kirk, C. A. A student's guide to Robert Frost **811.009**
Lawson, J. Black stars in a white night sky **811**
Lear, E. The owl and the pussycat **821**
Lewis, J. P. The brothers' war **811**
Lewis, J. P. Countdown to summer **811**
Longfellow, H. W. Henry Wadsworth Longfellow **811**
Longfellow, H. W. Hiawatha and Megissogwon **811**
Mora, P. The desert is my mother. El desierto es mi madre **811**
Nelson, M. Fortune's bones **811**
Noyes, A. The highwayman **821**
Nye, N. S. A maze me **811**
Nye, N. S. Honeybee **811**
Soto, G. A fire in my hands **811**
Spires, E. I heard God talking to me **811**
Tennyson, A. T., Baron. The Lady of Shalott **821**
Thayer, E. L. Casey at the bat **811**
Weatherford, C. B. Remember the bridge **811**
Williams, M. Chaucer's Canterbury Tales **821**
Williams, W. C. William Carlos Williams **811**
Young, E. Beyond the great mountains **811**

Collections

The Body eclectic **808.81**
Classic poetry **821.008**
A foot in the mouth **808.81**
I feel a little jumpy around you **808.81**
I wouldn't thank you for a valentine **808.81**
It's a woman's world **808.81**
Light-gathering poems **808.81**
The Oxford book of story poems **808.81**
The Oxford book of war poetry **808.81**
Revenge and forgiveness **808.81**
River of words **808.81**
Side by side **808.81**
The Space between our footsteps **808.81**
Step lightly **808.81**
War and the pity of war **808.81**
What have you lost? **808.81**

Fiction

Carney, J. The adventures of Michael MacInnes **Fic**
Creech, S. Love that dog **Fic**
Kephart, B. Undercover **Fic**

Indexes

Index to children's poetry **808.81**
Index to poetry for children and young people **808.81**

Study and teaching

Hopkins, L. B. Pass the poetry, please! **372.6**

Poetry for young people [series]

Angelou, M. Maya Angelou **811**
Blake, W. William Blake **821**

Police brutality: opposing viewpoints   **363.2**

Police lab. Owen, D.   **363.2**

Poliomyelitis

Peters, S. T. The battle against polio   **614.5**
Fiction
Durbin, W. The Winter War   **Fic**

Hostetter, J. Blue   **Fic**

Hostetter, J. Comfort   **Fic**

Poliomyelitis vaccine

De la Bédoyère, G. The first polio vaccine   **615**

Sherrow, V. Jonas Salk   **92**

Tocci, S. Jonas Salk   **92**

Polish Americans
Fiction
Cushman, K. Rodzina   **Fic**

Sternberg, L. The case against my brother   **Fic**

Political action committees *See* Lobbying

Political activists

Brave Bird, M. Lakota woman   **92**

Pioneers of human rights   **920**
Fiction
Nye, N. S. Going going   **Fic**

Political advocacy for school librarians. Schuckett, S.   **027.8**

Political campaigns *See* Politics

Political corruption

Miller, D. A. Political corruption   **364.1**
Fiction
Singer, N. Gem X   **Fic**

Political corruption. Miller, D. A.   **364.1**

Political crimes and offenses

See also Bombings; Political corruption

Political defectors *See* Defectors

Political leaders. Uschan, M. V.   **920**

Political parties

See also Third parties (United States politics)

Political profiles [series]

Sapet, K. Al Gore   **92**

Sapet, K. Barack Obama   **92**

Sapet, K. Ted Kennedy   **92**

Sharp, A. L. Rudy Giuliani   **92**

Shichtman, S. H. Nancy Pelosi   **92**

Wells, C. Hillary Clinton   **92**

Wells, C. John McCain   **92**

Young, J. C. Arnold Schwarzenegger   **92**

Political refugees

See also Defectors

Political science

Countries of the world and their leaders yearbook   **910.3**

The statesman's yearbook 2009   **310.5**

Political systems of the world [series]

Fleming, T. Socialism   **320.5**

Fridell, R. Dictatorship   **321.9**

Lansford, T. Communism   **335.4**

Lansford, T. Democracy   **321.8**

Perl, L. Theocracy   **321**

Stefoff, R. Monarchy   **321**

Politicians

See also Women politicians

Aronson, M. Robert F. Kennedy   **92**

Countries of the world and their leaders yearbook   **910.3**
United States
Kennedy, J. F. Profiles in courage   **920**

Sharp, A. L. Rudy Giuliani   **92**

Politics

See also Political science

Marzilli, A. Election reform   **324.6**

See/See also pages in the following book(s):

Mass media: opposing viewpoints   **302.23**
Fiction
Fitzgerald, D. Soccer chick rules   **Fic**

Gephart, D. As if being 12 3/4 isn't bad enough, my mother is running for president!   **Fic**

Perkins, M. First daughter: extreme American makeover   **Fic**

White, E. E. The President's daughter   **Fic**

Politics, Practical *See* Politics

Politics and religion *See* Religion and politics

The **politics** of slavery. Altman, L. J.   **326**

Pollack, Pam

Ski   **796.93**

Pollak, Barbara

(il) Haab, S. Dangles and bangles   **745.5**

Pollet, Alison

Nobody was here   **Fic**

Pollock, Steve

Ecology   **577**

Pollution

See also Air pollution; Environmental protection; Marine pollution; Water pollution

Bryan, N. Love Canal   **363.7**

Burns, L. G. Tracking trash   **551.46**

The Environment: opposing viewpoints   **363.7**

Gifford, C. Pollution   **363.7**

Hirschmann, K. Pollution   **363.7**

Pollution: opposing viewpoints   **363.7**
Fiction
Petrucha, S. Teen, Inc.   **Fic**

Pollution control industry

See also Recycling

Pollution: opposing viewpoints   **363.7**

Polo, Marco, 1254-1323?
About
Childress, D. Marco Polo's journey to China   **92**

Demi. Marco Polo   **92**

Freedman, R. The adventures of Marco Polo   **92**

McCarty, N. Marco Polo   **92**

Otfinoski, S. Marco Polo   **92**

Polygamy
Fiction
Williams, C. L. The chosen one   **Fic**

Polymers

Goodstein, M. Plastics and polymers science fair projects   **507.8**

Pomeroy, George M.
(jt. auth) Benhart, J. E. South Asia   954
Pompeii (Extinct city)
Connolly, P. Pompeii   937
Deem, J. M. Bodies from the ash   937
Moser, B. Ashen sky   937
Sonneborn, L. Pompeii   937
Fiction
Lasky, K. The last girls of Pompeii   Fic
Pompeii. Sonneborn, L.   937
Ponce de Leon, Juan, 1460?-1521
About
Otfinoski, S. Juan Ponce de Leon   92
See/See also pages in the following book(s):
Fritz, J. Around the world in a hundred years
    910.4
Pond ecology
Josephs, D. Lakes, ponds, and temporary pools
    577.6
Sayre, A. P. Lake and pond   577.6
Pony express
Fiction
Wilson, D. L. Black storm comin'   Fic
Poor
Bial, R. Tenement   974.7
Hopkinson, D. Shutting out the sky   974.7
Senker, C. Poverty   362.5
United States
Inner-city poverty   362.5
Kowalski, K. M. Poverty in America   362.5
Poverty   362.5
Poor is just a starting place. Wyatt, L. J.   Fic
Pop art
Demilly, C. Pop art   709.04
Greenberg, J. Andy Warhol   92
Rubin, S. G. Andy Warhol   92
Rubin, S. G. Whaam!: the art & life of Roy
    Lichtenstein   92
Spilsbury, R. Pop art   709.04
Pop art. Demilly, C.   709.04
Pop-up books
Chu, M. Birdscapes   598
Fischer, C. In the beginning: the art of Genesis
    222
Ganeri, A. Alive   612
Platt, R. Moon landing   629.45
Reinhart, M. Star Wars: a pop-up guide to the
    galaxy   791.43
Sabuda, R. Dinosaurs   567.9
Sabuda, R. Mega beasts   569
Sabuda, R. Sharks and other sea monsters
    560
Popes
Behnke, A. Pope John Paul II   92
Renehan, E. J. Pope John Paul II   92
Popular authors series
Bostrom, K. L. Winning authors   920
Popular contemporary writers   920.003
Popular culture
Nardo, D. Martians   001.9
United States
Bowling, beatniks, and bell-bottoms   306
Popular mechanics for kids [series]
Thomas, K. Blades, boards & scooters   796.2

Popular music
See also Blues music; Country music; Rap
    music; Rock music
Orgill, R. Shout, sister, shout!   920
Popular series fiction for middle school and teen
    readers. Thomas, R. L.   016.8
Popularity
Fiction
Hurley, T. Ghostgirl   Fic
Juby, S. Getting the girl   Fic
McNish, C. Angel   Fic
Ziegler, J. How not to be popular   Fic
Population
See also Baby boom generation
Andryszewski, T. Walking the earth   304.8
Mason, P. Population   363.9
Population explosion *See* Overpopulation
Porcellino, John
Thoreau at Walden   818
Porch lies. McKissack, P. C.   S C
Porcupine. Tilly, M.   Fic
The **porcupine** year. Erdrich, L.   Fic
Pordes, Laurence
(il) Brookfield, K. Book   070.5
Pornography
See also Obscenity (Law)
Pornography: opposing viewpoints   363.4
See/See also pages in the following book(s):
Mass media: opposing viewpoints   302.23
Pornography: opposing viewpoints   363.4
Porter, David, 1960-
Winning weight training for girls   613.7
Porter, Tracey
Billy Creekmore   Fic
Porter, William Sydney *See* Henry, O., 1862-
    1910
Porterfield, Jason
Doping   362.29
The Lincoln-Douglas senatorial debates of 1858
    973.7
Scandinavian mythology   293
Porterfield, Kay Marie
(jt. auth) Keoke, E. D. American Indian contri-
    butions to the world   970.004
Portland (Or.)
Fiction
Sternberg, L. The case against my brother
    Fic
Portocarrero, Louis Vera- *See* Vera-Portocarrero,
    Louis
A **portrait** of Pia. Russo, M.   Fic
Portraits of African-American heroes. Bolden, T.
    920
Portraits of Black Americans [series]
Bohannon, L. F. Freedom cannot rest   92
Miller, C. C. A. Philip Randolph and the Afri-
    can American labor movement   92
Portraits of Jewish American heroes. Drucker, M.
    920
Portugal
Deckker, Z. Portugal   946.9
Heale, J. Portugal   946.9

Positively ADD. Corman, C. A.   **616.85**

A **posse** of princesses. Smith, S.   **Fic**

Possessions, Lost and found *See* Lost and found possessions

The **possibilities** of sainthood. Freitas, D.   **Fic**

Post, Peggy, 1945-
  Emily Post's table manners for kids   **395**
  Emily Post's The guide to good manners for kids   **395**
  (jt. auth) Senning, C. P. Teen manners   **395**

Post-traumatic stress disorder
  Connolly, S. Anxiety disorders   **616.85**
  Miller, A. R. Living with anxiety disorders   **616.85**
           Fiction
  Paulsen, G. Soldier's heart   **Fic**

Postage stamps
           Catalogs
  Postal Service guide to U.S. stamps   **769.56**
  Scott standard postage stamp catalogue   **769.56**

Postal Service guide to U.S. stamps   **769.56**

The **postcard**. Abbott, T.   **Fic**

Postimpressionism (Art)
  Bingham, J. Post-Impressionism   **759.05**

Postlethwaite, Mark, 1964-
  (il) Parker, M. H. David and the Mighty Eighth   **Fic**

Potent natural medicines. Kidd, J. S.   **615**

Potter, Beatrix, 1866-1943
  See/See also pages in the following book(s):
  Ellis, S. From reader to writer   **372.6**

Potter, Ellen, 1963-
  Slob   **Fic**

Pottery
           Fiction
  Park, L. S. A single shard   **Fic**

Pough, Frederick H., 1906-2006
  A field guide to rocks and minerals   **549**

Pouy, Jean-Bernard, 1946-
  The big book of dummies, rebels and other geniuses   **920**

Poverty
    See also Poor
  Chambers, C. Living as a child laborer   **331.3**
  Inner-city poverty   **362.5**
  Kowalski, K. M. Poverty in America   **362.5**
  Mason, P. Poverty   **362.5**
  Poverty   **362.5**
  Poverty: opposing viewpoints   **339.4**
  Senker, C. Poverty   **362.5**
           Fiction
  Avi. Traitor's gate   **Fic**
  Brown, D. The train jumper   **Fic**
  Cullen, L. I am Rembrandt's daughter   **Fic**
  Madden, K. Gentle's Holler   **Fic**
  Morgan, N. Fleshmarket   **Fic**
  Newton, R. Runner   **Fic**
  Qamar, A. Beneath my mother's feet   **Fic**
  Steinbeck, J. The pearl   **Fic**
  Strasser, T. If I grow up   **Fic**
  Wolff, V. E. Make lemonade   **Fic**

Wyatt, L. J. Poor is just a starting place   **Fic**

Poverty   **362.5**

Poverty in America. Kowalski, K. M.   **362.5**

Poverty: opposing viewpoints   **339.4**

Povey, Karen D., 1962-
  Energy alternatives   **333.79**

Pow, Tom, 1950-
  The pack   **Fic**

Powder monkey. Dowswell, P.   **Fic**

Powell, Anton
  Ancient Greece   **938**

Powell, Ben
  Skateboarding skills   **796.22**

Powell, Colin L., 1937-
           About
  Finlayson, R. Colin Powell   **92**
  Shichtman, S. H. Colin Powell   **92**

Powell, Jillian
  Alcohol and drug abuse   **362.29**
  Self-harm and suicide   **616.85**

Powell, Randy
  Swiss mist   **Fic**
  Three clams and an oyster   **Fic**

Powell, Ransom J., 1849-1899
           Fiction
  Wisler, G. C. Red Cap   **Fic**

Power, Rebecca, 1975-
  (jt. auth) Brown, M. E. Exhibits in libraries   **021.7**

Power (Mechanics)
    See also Electric power; Wind power
  Farndon, J. Energy   **531**

Power (Social sciences)
    See also Elite (Social sciences)

Power. Ravilious, K.   **179**

The **power** of one [biography of Daisy Bates] Fradin, J. B.   **92**

The **power** of reading. Krashen, S. D.   **028.5**

Power research tools. Valenza, J. K.   **001.4**

Power resources *See* Energy resources

The **power** to prevent suicide. Nelson, R. E.   **362.28**

Power tools. See Valenza, J. K. Power tools recharged   **027.8**

Power tools recharged. Valenza, J. K.   **027.8**

Powerful plant cells. Johnson, R. L.   **581.7**

Powerful words. Hudson, W.   **808.8**

PowerMath [series]
  Levy, J. Breaking the code with cryptography   **652**

Powers, Ron
  (jt. auth) Bradley, J. Flags of our fathers   **940.54**

Powhatan Indians
           Fiction
  Carbone, E. L. Blood on the river   **Fic**

POWs *See* Prisoners of war

Pox, pus & plague. Townsend, J.   **616**

Poynter, Margaret
  The Leakeys   **92**

Prejudices—Fiction—*Continued*
Taylor, M. D. The gold Cadillac | **Fic**
Uchida, Y. A jar of dreams | **Fic**
Venkatraman, P. Climbing the stairs | **Fic**
Volponi, P. Homestretch | **Fic**
Waters, D. Generation dead | **Fic**
Williams, L. E. Slant | **Fic**
Wiseman, E. Puppet | **Fic**
Yee, P. Learning to fly | **Fic**
Yep, L. The traitor | **Fic**

Preller, James, 1961-
Six innings | **Fic**

Prelutsky, Jack
Pizza, pigs, and poetry | **808.1**
(ed) The Random House book of poetry for children. See The Random House book of poetry for children | **811.008**

Premiers *See* Prime ministers

Prescription pain relievers. Olive, M. F. | **615**

Preservation of wildlife *See* Wildlife conservation

Preserve our planet [series]
Delano, M. F. Earth in the hot seat | **363.7**

The **presidency** A to Z | **352.23**

The **president** is shot!. Holzer, H. | **973.7**

Presidential losers. Goldman, D. J. | **920**

Presidential races. Morris-Lipsman, A. | **324**

Presidents
See also Vice-presidents
Abrams, D. Nicolas Sarkozy | **92**
Fiction
Cabot, M. All-American girl | **Fic**
Schmidt, G. First boy | **Fic**
United States
Abramson, J. Obama | **92**
Adams, J. John Adams the writer | **92**
Adler, D. A. George Washington | **92**
Allen, M. G. Calvin Coolidge | **92**
Allen, T. B. George Washington, spymaster | **92**
American presidents in world history | **920.003**
Aronson, B. Abraham Lincoln | **92**
Aronson, B. Richard M. Nixon | **92**
Aronson, B. Ulysses S. Grant | **92**
Barron, R. Richard Nixon | **92**
Bausum, A. Our country's presidents | **920**
Brill, M. T. Barack Obama | **92**
Burgan, M. John F. Kennedy | **92**
Cooper, I. Jack: the early years of John F. Kennedy | **92**
Cooper, M. L. Theodore Roosevelt | **92**
Davis, W. Barack Obama | **92**
Denenberg, B. Lincoln shot! | **92**
Dolan, E. F. George Washington | **92**
Elish, D. Franklin Delano Roosevelt | **92**
Elish, D. James Madison | **92**
Elish, D. Theodore Roosevelt | **92**
Facts about the presidents | **920**
Fleming, C. The Lincolns | **92**
Freedman, R. Franklin Delano Roosevelt | **92**
Freedman, R. Lincoln: a photobiography | **92**
Fritz, J. Bully for you, Teddy Roosevelt! | **92**
Gold, S. D. Lyndon B. Johnson | **92**
Gottfried, T. Millard Fillmore | **92**

Harness, C. The remarkable, rough-riding life of Theodore Roosevelt and the rise of empire America | **92**
Heiligman, D. High hopes [biography of John F. Kennedy] | **92**
Holford, D. M. Herbert Hoover | **92**
Kraft, B. H. Theodore Roosevelt | **92**
Krull, K. Lives of the presidents | **920**
Lincoln, A. Abraham Lincoln the writer | **92**
Lukes, B. L. Woodrow Wilson and the Progressive Era | **92**
Malone, M. James Madison | **92**
Mara, W. John Adams | **92**
Marrin, A. The great adventure: Theodore Roosevelt and the rise of modern America | **92**
Marrin, A. Old Hickory [biography of Andrew Jackson] | **92**
Miller, B. M. George Washington for kids | **92**
Naden, C. J. James Monroe | **92**
Obama, B. Dreams from my father | **92**
Panchyk, R. Franklin Delano Roosevelt for kids | **92**
Rubel, D. Scholastic encyclopedia of the presidents and their times | **920**
Sandler, M. W. Lincoln through the lens | **92**
Sapet, K. Barack Obama | **92**
Sapp, R. Ulysses S. Grant and the road to Appomattox | **92**
Schuman, M. Barack Obama | **92**
Severance, J. B. Thomas Jefferson | **92**
Sommer, S. John F. Kennedy | **92**
Stanley, G. E. America in today's world (1969-2004) | **973.92**
Sullivan, G. Picturing Lincoln | **92**
Sutherland, J. Ronald Reagan | **92**
Thomson, S. L. Obama | **92**
Wagner, H. L. Barack Obama | **92**
Waldman, N. Voyages | **92**
Whitelaw, N. Thomas Jefferson | **92**
Young, J. C. Dwight D. Eisenhower | **92**
United States—Assassination
St. George, J. In the line of fire | **364.1**
United States—Election
Goldman, D. J. Presidential losers | **920**
Goodman, S. See how they run | **324**
Morris-Lipsman, A. Presidential races | **324**
Wagner, H. L. How the president is elected | **324**
United States—Election—2000
The Election of 2000 and the administration of George W. Bush | **324**
Sergis, D. K. Bush v. Gore | **342**
United States—Election—2008
Gibson, K. B. The Obama view | **92**
Tracy, K. The Clinton view | **92**
United States—Encyclopedias
The presidency A to Z | **352.23**
United States—Spouses
See Presidents' spouses—United States
Venezuela
Levin, J. Hugo Chávez | **92**
Young, J. C. Hugo Chavez | **92**

Presidents and their times [series]
Aronson, B. Abraham Lincoln | **92**
Aronson, B. Richard M. Nixon | **92**

Psychical research *See* Parapsychology

Psychoactive drugs *See* Psychotropic drugs

Psychogenetics *See* Behavior genetics

Psychokinesis
Graphic novels
Clugston, C. Queen Bee   **741.5**

Psychological disorders [series]
Connolly, S. Anxiety disorders   **616.85**
Salomon, R. Suicide   **616.85**
Veague, H. B. Schizophrenia   **616.89**

Psychological tests
Kincher, J. Psychology for kids vol. 1: 40 fun tests that help you learn about yourself
    150

Psychologists
See also Psychiatrists

Psychology
See also Adolescent psychology; Behaviorism
Gardner, R. Health science projects about psychology   **150**
Kincher, J. Psychology for kids vol. 2: 40 fun experiments that help you learn about others
    150
A student's guide to mental health & wellness
    616.89

Psychology for kids vol. 1: 40 fun tests that help you learn about yourself. Kincher, J.   **150**

Psychology for kids vol. 2: 40 fun experiments that help you learn about others. Kincher, J.
    150

Psychology of learning
See also Reading comprehension
Hudmon, A. Learning and memory   **153.1**

Psychopharmaceuticals *See* Psychotropic drugs

Psychotherapy
Fiction
Giles, G. Right behind you   **Fic**
Juby, S. Alice, I think   **Fic**
Stolls, A. Palms to the ground   **Fic**

Psychotropic drugs
See also Antidepressants; Cocaine; Hallucinogens
Durham, M. Painkillers and tranquilizers
    615
Esherick, J. The FDA and psychiatric drugs

PTSD *See* Post-traumatic stress disorder

Pu-i *See* Pu Yi, 1906-1967

Pu Songling
(jt. auth) Bedard, M. The painted wall and other strange tales   **398.2**

Pu Yi, 1906-1967
See/See also pages in the following book(s):
Cotter, C. Kids who rule   **920**

Puberty
American Medical Assocation boy's guide to becoming a teen   **613**
American Medical Association girl's guide to becoming a teen   **613**
Bailey, J. Sex, puberty, and all that stuff
    612.6
Dunham, K. The girl's body book   **613**

Madaras, L. The "what's happening to my body?" book for boys   **613.9**
Madaras, L. The "what's happening to my body?" book for girls   **613.9**
Movsessian, S. Puberty girl   **612.6**
Price, G. Puberty boy   **612.6**
Redd, N. A. Body drama   **612**
Teen dreams   **612.6**

Puberty boy. Price, G.   **612.6**

Puberty girl. Movsessian, S.   **612.6**

Public debts
Garlake, T. Global debt   **336.3**

Public Education Information Network
The Information-powered school. See The Information-powered school   **027.8**

Public enemy number two. Horowitz, A.   **Fic**

Public figures *See* Celebrities

Public health
See also Epidemiology
Foley, R. World health   **362.1**

Public housing
Fiction
McDonald, J. Twists and turns   **Fic**

Public lands
See also National parks and reserves

Public libraries
Jones, P. Do it right!   **027.62**
McClure, C. R. Public libraries and internet service roles   **025.04**
Miller, E. G. W. Library board strategic guide
    025.1
Simpson, M. S. Bringing classes into the public library   **027.62**
Vogel, J. A library story   **727**
Cultural programs
See Cultural programs

Public libraries and internet service roles. McClure, C. R.   **025.04**

Public relations
Libraries
See Libraries—Public relations

Public relations for school library media programs. Flowers, H. F.   **021.7**

Public school safety. Hester, J. P.   **371.7**

Public schools
Pipkin, G. At the schoolhouse gate   **373.1**

Public schools and religion *See* Religion in the public schools

Public speaking
Merali, A. Talk the talk   **808.53**
Ryan, M. Extraordinary oral presentations
    808.5

Public utilities
See/See also pages in the following book(s):
Macaulay, D. Underground   **624**

Public welfare
See also Food relief
Inner-city poverty   **362.5**

Publishers and publishing
Botzakis, S. Pretty in print   **050**
Dunn, J. A teen's guide to getting published
    808

Pyle, Howard, 1853-1911—*Continued*
The story of the Grail and the passing of Arthur
398.2
Pyle, Robert Michael
The Audubon Society field guide to North American butterflies **595.7**
Pyramids
Filer, J. Pyramids **932**
George, C. Pyramids **909**
Macaulay, D. Pyramid **726**
Nardo, D. Artistry in stone **932**
See/See also pages in the following book(s):
Aaseng, N. Construction: building the impossible **624**

Q

Qaeda (Organization) *See* Al Qaeda (Organization)
Qamar, Amjed
Beneath my mother's feet **Fic**
Qatar
Orr, T. Qatar **953.6**
Qi Shu Fang *See* Qi Shufang
Qi Shufang
See/See also pages in the following book(s):
Major, J. S. Caravan to America **920**
Qin Shi Huang, Emperor of China *See* Ch'in Shih-huang, Emperor of China, 259-210 B.C.
Quakers *See* Society of Friends
Quaking. Erskine, K. **Fic**
Qualey, Marsha, 1953-
Just like that **Fic**
Quallen, Sudipta Bardhan- *See* Bardhan-Quallen, Sudipta
Qualls, Sean
(il) Hudson, W. Powerful words **808.8**
Quant, Mary, 1934-
See/See also pages in the following book(s):
Kent, J. Business builders in fashion **920**
The **quantum** July. King, R. **Fic**
Quantum theory
Hakim, J. The story of science: Einstein adds a new dimension **509**
Willett, E. The basics of quantum physics **539**
Fiction
King, R. The quantum July **Fic**
The **Queen** of Air and Darkness. White, T. H.
In White, T. H. The once and future king **Fic**
Queens
See also Empresses names of queens and countries with the subdivision *Kings and rulers*
Adams, S. Elizabeth I **92**
Kramer, A. Eleanor of Aquitaine **92**
Lange, B. Nefertiti **92**
Lucks, N. Queen of Sheba **92**
Meltzer, M. Ten queens **920**
Morgan, J. Cleopatra **92**
Plain, N. Eleanor of Aquitaine and the High Middle Ages **942.03**

Sapet, K. Cleopatra **92**
Stanley, D. Cleopatra **92**
Stanley, D. Good Queen Bess: the story of Elizabeth I of England **92**
Thomas, J. R. Behind the mask: the life of Queen Elizabeth I **92**
Weatherly, M. Elizabeth I **92**
Fiction
Meyer, C. Duchessina **Fic**
Queens (New York, N.Y.)
Fiction
Woodson, J. After Tupac and D Foster **Fic**
The **queen's** own fool. Yolen, J. **Fic**
Quek, Lynette, 1977-
(jt. auth) Falconer, K. Peru **985**
(jt. auth) Hassig, S. M. Panama **972.87**
Quest. Duble, K. B. **Fic**
Quest for the tree kangaroo. Montgomery, S. **599.2**
Questionable creatures. Baynes, P. **398.2**
Questions and answers
The Nobel book of answers **001.4**
Questors. Lennon, J. **Fic**
Quick cash for teens. Bielagus, P. G. **658.1**
Quick starts for kids! [series]
Check, L. Create your own candles **745.5**
Quicksand pony. Lester, A. **Fic**
Quicksilver. Spinner, S. **Fic**
Quid pro quo. Grant, V. **Fic**
Quilt of states. Yorinks, A. **973**
Quinceañera (Social custom)
Fiction
Alegría, M. Estrella's quinceanera **Fic**
Quinlan, Susan E., 1954-
The case of the monkeys that fell from the trees **577.3**
Quinn, Spencer *See* Abrahams, Peter, 1947-
Quit-smoking programs *See* Smoking cessation programs
Quiver. Spinner, S. **Fic**
Quotations
Bartlett, J. Bartlett's familiar quotations **808.88**

R

Raabe, Michelle
Hemophilia **616.1**
Raatma, Lucia
Safety for babysitters **649**
Safety in your neighborhood **613.6**
Safety on the Internet **025.04**
Rabatti, Alessandro
(il) Bos, S. Super structures **720**
Rabbits
Fiction
Adams, R. Watership Down **Fic**
Jennings, R. W. Orwell's luck **Fic**
Zuckerman, L. A taste for rabbit **Fic**
Rabies
Klosterman, L. Rabies **616.9**

Racially mixed people—Fiction—*Continued*
Taylor, M. D. The land   **Fic**
Wilson, D. L. Black storm comin'   **Fic**
     Graphic novels
Tamaki, M. Emiko superstar   **741.5**
Racing. Gifford, C.   **796.72**
Racing to freedom [series]
Hart, A. Gabriel's horses   **Fic**
Racism

   See also Race discrimination; White supremacy movements
Aronson, M. Race: a history beyond black and white   **305.8**
Crowe, C. Getting away with murder: the true story of the Emmett Till case   **364.1**
Gay, K. Cultural diversity   **305.8**
Racism: an opposing viewpoints guide   **305.8**
Racism: an opposing viewpoints guide   **305.8**
Rackers, Mark
(ed) The Arab-Israeli conflict. See The Arab-Israeli conflict   **956.04**
Racso and the rats of NIMH. Conly, J. L.   **Fic**
Racz, Michael
(il) Mann, E. The Roman Colosseum   **937**
Raczka, Bob
Name that style   **709**
Unlikely pairs   **750**
Radical reads. Bodart, J. R.   **028.5**
Radical reptiles. Miller, S. S.   **597.9**
Radio
     Fiction
Fleischman, P. Seek   **Fic**
     History
Zannos, S. Guglielmo Marconi and the story of radio waves   **92**
Radio journalism *See* Broadcast journalism
Radio stations
     Graphic novels
Fisher, J. S. WJHC: on the air!   **741.5**
Radioactive waste disposal
Scarborough, K. Nuclear waste   **363.7**
Radioactivity
Jerome, K. B. Atomic universe   **539.7**
Radzilowski, John, 1965-
Ukrainian Americans   **305.8**
Raffaelle, Gerda-Ann
(ed) Benson, S. Korean War: almanac and primary sources   **951.9**
Rafferty, Trisha
(il) I wouldn't thank you for a valentine. See I wouldn't thank you for a valentine   **808.81**
Rafting (Sports)
George, C. White-water rafting   **797.1**
     Fiction
Woods, R. The hero   **Fic**
The **rag** and bone shop. Cormier, R.   **Fic**
Rage *See* Anger
Raicht, Mike
(jt. auth) Dezago, T. Spider-man: Spidey strikes back Vol. 1 digest   **741.5**

Railroad engineering
Barter, J. A worker on the transcontinental railroad   **331.7**
Railroads
Zimmermann, K. R. All aboard!   **385**
See/See also pages in the following book(s):
Collier, C. Indians, cowboys, and farmers and the battle for the Great Plains, 1865-1910   **978**
     Fiction
Slayton, F. C. When the whistle blows   **Fic**
Yep, L. Dragon's gate   **Fic**
     History
Barter, J. A worker on the transcontinental railroad   **331.7**
Landau, E. The transcontinental railroad   **385.09**
Laughlin, R. The Pullman strike of 1894   **331.8**
Meltzer, M. Hear that train whistle blow!   **385.09**
Murphy, J. Across America on an emigrant train [biography of Robert Louis Stevenson]   **92**
Nelson, S. R. Ain't nothing but a man [biography of John William Henry]   **92**
Renehan, E. J. The Transcontinental Railroad   **385.09**
     United States
Perl, L. To the Golden Mountain   **305.8**
Rain
   See also Droughts
Gardner, R. Science project ideas about rain   **551.57**
     Fiction
Scaletta, K. Mudville   **Fic**
Rain forest animals
Kenyon, L. Rainforest bird rescue   **598**
Rain forest ecology
Castner, J. L. Layers of life   **577.3**
Castner, J. L. Partners and rivals   **577.3**
Greenaway, T. Jungle   **577.3**
Jackson, K. Rain forests   **577.3**
Jackson, T. Tropical forests   **577.3**
Lasky, K. The most beautiful roof in the world   **577.3**
Quinlan, S. E. The case of the monkeys that fell from the trees   **577.3**
Sobol, R. Breakfast in the rainforest   **599.8**
Tocci, S. Life in the tropical forests   **577.3**
Rain forests
Jackson, K. Rain forests   **577.3**
Vogt, R. C. Rain forests   **577.3**
Welsbacher, A. Protecting Earth's rain forests   **577.3**
     Fiction
Nelson, N. Bringing the boy home   **Fic**
Rain is not my Indian name. Smith, C. L.   **Fic**
The **rainbow** people. Yep, L.   **398.2**
Rainey, Ma, 1886-1939
   See/See also pages in the following book(s):
Orgill, R. Shout, sister, shout!   **920**
Rainfall *See* Rain
Rainforest bird rescue. Kenyon, L.   **598**
Rainis, Kenneth G.
Blood & DNA evidence   **363.2**

Rainis, Kenneth G.—*Continued*
Cell and microbe science fair projects using microscopes, mold, and more **571.6**
Fingerprints **363.2**
Forgery **363.2**
Hair, clothing and tire track evidence **363.2**

Rainmaker. Jackson, A. **Fic**

Raintree fusion [series]
Hall, M. Skin deep **612.7**

Raising voices. Sima, J. **027.62**

Rajendra, Rudi
(jt. auth) Rajendra, V. Iran **955**

Rajendra, Sundran, 1967-
(jt. auth) Rajendra, V. Australia **994**

Rajendra, Vijeya, 1936-
Australia **994**
Iran **955**

Rajtar, Steve, 1951-
United States holidays and observances **394.26**

Ralegh, Walter *See* Raleigh, Sir Walter, 1552?-1618

Raleigh, Sir Walter, 1552?-1618
About
Aronson, M. Sir Walter Ralegh and the quest for El Dorado **92**

Ralph Masiello's ancient Egypt drawing book. Masiello, R. **743**

Ralph Masiello's dragon drawing book. Masiello, R. **743**

Ramadan
Jeffrey, L. S. Celebrate Ramadan **297.3**

The **Ramayana** and Hinduism. Ganeri, A. **294.5**

Ramen, Fred
Albucasis (Abu al-Qasim al-Zahrawi) **92**
A historical atlas of Iran **955**

Rameses II, King of Egypt *See* Ramses II, King of Egypt

Rampersad, Arnold
(ed) Hughes, L. Langston Hughes **811**

The **Ramsay** scallop. Temple, F. **Fic**

Ramses II, King of Egypt
About
Fitzgerald, S. J. Ramses II **92**

Ranch life
Freedman, R. In the days of the vaqueros **636.2**
Steele, C. Cattle ranching in the American West **978**
Fiction
Amateau, G. A certain strain of peculiar **Fic**
Estevis, A. Chicken Foot Farm **Fic**
Parry, R. Heart of a shepherd **Fic**
Steinbeck, J. The red pony **Fic**
Waters, Z. C. Blood moon rider **Fic**

Ranchers, homesteaders, and traders. Doherty, K. **920**

Randall, David, 1972-
Clovermead **Fic**

Randall, Ron
(il) Jolley, D. Guan Yu **741.5**

(il) Storrie, P. D. Beowulf **741.5**

Randolph, Asa Philip, 1889-1979
About
Miller, C. C. A. Philip Randolph and the African American labor movement **92**
See/See also pages in the following book(s):
Streissguth, T. Legendary labor leaders **920**

Random House American Sign Language dictionary. See Costello, E. Random House Webster's American Sign Language dictionary: unabridged **419**

The **Random** House book of poetry for children **811.008**

Random House Webster's American Sign Language dictionary: unabridged. Costello, E. **419**

Random House Webster's unabridged dictionary **423**

Rangaswamy, Padma, 1945-
Indian Americans **305.8**

Ranger's apprentice [series]
Flanagan, J. The ruins of Gorlan **Fic**

Rankin, Jeannette, 1880-1973
About
Woelfle, G. Jeannette Rankin **92**
See/See also pages in the following book(s):
Krull, K. Lives of extraordinary women **920**
Mendoza, P. M. Extraordinary people in extraordinary times **920**

Rankin, Virginia
The thoughtful researcher **027.62**

Ransford, Sandy
The Kingfisher illustrated horse & pony encyclopedia **636.1**

Ransome, Arthur, 1884-1967
See/See also pages in the following book(s):
Ellis, S. From reader to writer **372.6**

Ransome, James
(il) McKissack, P. C. Let my people go **Fic**

Rap music
Sanna, E. Hip hop: a short history **781.66**
Fiction
McDonald, J. Harlem Hustle **Fic**

Rape
See also Date rape
Bode, J. Voices of rape **362.88**
Kaminker, L. Everything you need to know about dealing with sexual assault **364.1**
Strong at the heart **362.7**
Fiction
Anderson, L. H. Speak **Fic**
Crocker, N. Billie Standish was here **Fic**
Lynch, C. Inexcusable **Fic**
Peck, R. Are you in the house alone? **Fic**
Shaw, S. Safe **Fic**

Rapp, Valerie
Protecting Earth's air quality **363.7**
Protecting Earth's land **333.72**

Rappaport, Doreen, 1939-
John's secret dreams [biography of John Lennon] **92**
United no more! **973.7**

Rapparlie, Leslie
(jt. auth) Wurdinger, S. D. Kayaking **797.1**

Rapparlie, Leslie—*Continued*
(jt. auth) Wurdinger, S. D. Rock climbing
796.52

Rappoport, Ken
Lebron James   92

Raptor! a kid's guide to birds of prey. Laubach, C. M.   598

Rapunzel and other magic fairy tales   398.2

Rapunzel's revenge. Hale, S.   741.5

Rare animals
See also Endangered species
McGavin, G. Endangered   578.68
Mills, A. Animals like us   333.95

Rare plants
See also Endangered species

Rasamandala Das
Hinduism   294.5

Raschka, Christopher
(il) Best shorts. See Best shorts   S C
(il) A foot in the mouth. See A foot in the mouth   808.81
(il) A kick in the head. See A kick in the head   811.008
(il) A Poke in the I. See A Poke in the I   811.008

Rasmussen, R. Kent
(ed) Encyclopedia of American government. See Encyclopedia of American government   320.03

Rasputin, Grigoriĭ Efimovich, 1871-1916
About
Goldberg, E. A. Grigory Rasputin   92

The Ratbridge chronicles [series]
Snow, A. Here be monsters!   Fic

Ratliff, Gerald Lee
(ed) Millennium monologs. See Millennium monologs   812.008

Rats
Marrin, A. Oh, rats!   599.35
McNicholas, J. Rats   636.9
Fiction
Conly, J. L. Racso and the rats of NIMH   Fic
Jonell, L. Emmy and the incredible shrinking rat   Fic
O'Brien, R. C. Mrs. Frisby and the rats of NIMH   Fic
Pratchett, T. The amazing Maurice and his educated rodents   Fic

Rattlesnake Mesa. Weber, E. N. R.   92

The raucous royals. Beccia, C.   920

Rauf, Don
Computer game designer   794.8
(jt. auth) Reeves, D. L. Career ideas for teens in architecture and construction   624

Rauzon, Mark J.
Hummingbirds   598
Vultures   598

Ravel, Edeet
The saver   Fic

Raven, Nicky
Beowulf   398.2

The **raven**. Poe, E. A.   811

Raven. Whitlock, D.   Fic

The **raven** and other poems. Poe, E. A.   741.5

Ravens
Fiction
George, J. C. Charlie's raven   Fic

Raven's gate. Horowitz, A.   Fic

Ravilious, Kate
Power   179

Rawlings, Marjorie Kinnan, 1896-1953
The yearling   Fic
About
Cook, J. Natural writer: a story about Marjorie Kinnan Rawlings   92

Rawlins, Carol
The Colorado River   979.1

Rawls, Wilson, 1913-1984
Where the red fern grows   Fic

Rawls, Woodrow Wilson *See* Rawls, Wilson, 1913-1984

Ray, Delia
Ghost girl   Fic
Singing hands   Fic

Ray, Rachael
About
Abrams, D. Rachael Ray   92

Ray, Virginia Lawrence
School wide book events   027.8

Ray Charles and the birth of soul. Woog, A.   92

Rays (Fishes)
Fiction
Medina, M. Milagros   Fic

Rayyan, Omar
(il) Howe, P. Waggit's tale   Fic

Re-Gifters. Carey, M.   741.5

Reaching for sun. Zimmer, T. V.   Fic

Reaching out. Jiménez, F.   Fic

Reaching reluctant young adult readers. Sullivan, E. T.   028.5

Read all about it!   808.8

The **read-aloud** handbook. Trelease, J.   028.5

A **reader's** guide to Amy Tan's The joy luck club. Loos, P.   813.009

A **reader's** guide to Chinua Achebe's Things fall apart. Shea, G.   823.009

A **reader's** guide to Lorraine Hansberry's A raisin in the sun. Loos, P.   812.009

A **reader's** guide to Richard Wright's Black boy. Hinds, M. J.   813.009

Readers' theater
Black, A. N. Readers theatre for middle school boys   812

Readers theatre [series]
Black, A. N. Readers theatre for middle school boys   812

Reading
Bouchard, D. The gift of reading   372.4
Into focus   028.1
Kajder, S. B. Bringing the outside in   028.5
Krashen, S. D. The power of reading   028.5

Reference books—*Continued*

Thomas, R. L. Popular series fiction for middle school and teen readers **016.8**

Timelines of history **902**

U.X.L encyclopedia of biomes **577.8**

U.X.L encyclopedia of science **503**

United States. Bureau of Labor Statistics. Occupational outlook handbook 2008-2009 **331.7**

United States. Bureau of the Census. Statistical abstract of the United States, 2008 **317.3**

UXL Encyclopedia of world mythology **201.03**

Waldman, C. Encyclopedia of Native American tribes **970.004**

Walker, B. J. Developing Christian fiction collections for children and adults **025.2**

Walter, V. A. War & peace **016.3**

Weather almanac **551.6**

Webster's third new international dictionary of the English language, unabridged **423**

Wee, P. H. World War II in literature for youth **016.9**

Wildlife and plants **578**

Wilkinson, P. Illustrated dictionary of mythology **201**

The Wilson chronology of Asia and the Pacific **950**

Word histories and mysteries **422.03**

The world almanac and book of facts, 2008 **031.02**

World authors, 1995-2000 **920.003**

The World Book encyclopedia **031**

The World Book student discovery science encyclopedia **503**

World Book's encyclopedia of flags **929.9**

World Book's human body works **612**

The world in ancient times **930**

Wright, C. M. More hot links **011.6**

York, S. Ethnic book awards **011.6**

Young Adult Library Services Association. The official YALSA awards guidebook **011.6**

Young person's occupational outlook handbook **331.7**

Yount, L. A to Z of women in science and math **920.003**

Your reading **011.6**

Bibliography

Recommended reference books for small and medium-sized libraries and media centers **011**

Reviews

Recommended reference books for small and medium-sized libraries and media centers **011**

Reference services (Libraries)

Lanning, S. Essential reference services for to-day's school media specialists **025.5**

Reflections on a gift of watermelon pickle—and other modern verse **811.008**

Reform movements in American history [series]

Malaspina, A. The ethnic and group identity movements **323.1**

McNeese, T. The abolitionist movement **973.7**

Reformation

See also World history—16th century

Hinds, K. The church [Life in the Renaissance series] **274**

Renaissance & Reformation: almanac **940.2**

Renaissance & Reformation: primary sources **940.2**

Reformation, exploration, and empire **909**

The **reformed** vampire support group. Jinks, C. **Fic**

Reformers

Boomhower, R. E. Fighting for equality **92**

Refugees

Dalton, D. Living in a refugee camp **305.23**

Ellis, D. Children of war **956.7**

Howard, H. Living as a refugee in America **305.23**

Making it home **305.23**

Fiction

Applegate, K. Home of the brave **Fic**

Cooney, C. B. Diamonds in the shadow **Fic**

Engle, M. Tropical secrets **Fic**

Give me shelter **S C**

Mead, A. Dawn and dusk **Fic**

Naidoo, B. The other side of truth **Fic**

Naidoo, B. Web of lies **Fic**

Pausewang, G. Dark hours **Fic**

Whelan, G. Goodbye, Vietnam **Fic**

Refugees, Cuban *See* Cuban refugees

Refugees, Jewish *See* Jewish refugees

Refuse and refuse disposal

See also Radioactive waste disposal; Recycling

Bowden, R. Waste **363.7**

Wilcox, C. Earth-friendly waste management **363.7**

Regarding the sink. Klise, K. **Fic**

Reger, Rob

Emily the Strange: the lost days **Fic**

Reggae music

Miller, C. C. Reggae poet: the story of Bob Marley **92**

Paprocki, S. B. Bob Marley **92**

Reggae poet: the story of Bob Marley. Miller, C. C. **92**

Rehwoldt, Sheri Bell- *See* Bell-Rehwoldt, Sheri, 1962-

Reich, Susanna, 1954-

Clara Schumann **92**

Painting the wild frontier: the art and adventures of George Catlin **92**

Reichman, Henry, 1947-

Censorship and selection **025.2**

Reichmann, Paul

See/See also pages in the following book(s):

Aaseng, N. Business builders in real estate **920**

Reid, Rob

Something funny happened at the library **027.62**

Reid, Suzanne Elizabeth

Virginia Euwer Wolff **813.009**

Rites and ceremonies
Beker, J. The big night out   **646.7**

Rits. Jongman, M.   **Fic**

Ritschel, John
The kickboxing handbook   **796.8**

Ritter, John H., 1951-
The boy who saved baseball   **Fic**
Choosing up sides   **Fic**
The desperado who stole baseball   **Fic**
Under the baseball moon   **Fic**

Ritual *See* Rites and ceremonies

River and stream. Sayre, A. P.   **577.6**

The **river** between us. Peck, R.   **Fic**

River ecology
Castner, J. L. River life   **577.6**
Sayre, A. P. River and stream   **577.6**

River journey [series]
Bowden, R. The Nile   **962**

River life. Castner, J. L.   **577.6**

River of dreams. Talbott, H.   **974.7**

River of words   **808.81**

River roads west. Roop, P.   **386**

River song. Hollyer, B.   **Fic**

Rivera, Diego, 1886-1957
About
Hillstrom, K. Diego Rivera   **92**
Litwin, L. B. Diego Rivera   **92**
Sabbeth, C. Frida Kahlo and Diego Rivera: their lives and ideas   **92**
Poetry
Bernier-Grand, C. T. Diego   **811**

Rivera, Frida Kahlo *See* Kahlo, Frida, 1907-1954

Rivera, Tomás
On the road to Texas: Pete Fonseca
In Growing up Latino; memoirs and stories p147-54   **810.8**

Rivers
See also Amazon River; Colorado River (Colo.-Mexico); Hudson River (N.Y. and N.J.); Mekong River; Mississippi River; Nile River
Burnham, L. Rivers   **551.48**
Roop, P. River roads west   **386**

Rivers of North America [series]
Harris, T. The Mackenzie River   **971**

Rizal, José, 1861-1896
About
Arruda, S. M. Freedom's martyr [biography of Jose Rizal]   **92**

Rizzo, Margaret
(jt. auth) Jweid, R. Building character through literature   **028.5**
(jt. auth) Jweid, R. The library-classroom partnership   **027.8**

Roach, David A.
(ed) The Superhero book. See The Superhero book   **741.5**

Roach (Insect) *See* Cockroaches

The **road** to Communism. Gottfried, T.   **947**

The **road** to Memphis. Taylor, M. D.   **Fic**

The **road** to Paris. Grimes, N.   **Fic**

The **road** to there. Ross, V.   **912**

Roanoke. Miller, L.   **975.6**

Roanoke Island (N.C.)
History
Miller, L. Roanoke   **975.6**

The **roar.** Clayton, E.   **Fic**

The **Roaring** twenties   **973.91**

The **roaring** twenties almanac and primary sources. Howes, K. K.   **973.91**

The **roaring** twenties biographies. Howes, K. K.   **920**

The roaring twenties reference library [series]
Howes, K. K. The roaring twenties almanac and primary sources   **973.91**
Howes, K. K. The roaring twenties biographies   **920**

Robb, Don
Ox, house, stick   **411**

Robbers and outlaws *See* Thieves

Robbi, Alfa
(il) Farr, J. eV: vol. 1   **741.5**

Robbie reader. Gardening for kids [series]
Harkins, S. S. Design your own butterfly garden   **638**

Robbins, Chandler S., 1918-
Birds of North America   **598**

Robbins, Gerald
Azerbaijan   **947.5**

Robbins, Louise E.
Louis Pasteur   **92**

Robbins, Michael W.
(jt. auth) Art, H. W. Woodswalk   **508**

Robbins, Ruth
(il) Le Guin, U. K. A wizard of Earthsea   **Fic**

Robbins, Trina, 1938-
Go girl!. Vol. 1, The time team   **741.5**

The **robe** of skulls. French, V.   **Fic**

Robert I, King of Scotland, 1274-1329
Fiction
Yolen, J. Girl in a cage   **Fic**

Robert F. Kennedy Jr.'s American heroes [series]
Kennedy, R. F. Robert Smalls   **92**

Robert Frost. Frost, R.   **811**

Robert Fulton and the development of the steamboat. Pierce, M. A.   **92**

Robert Louis Stevenson's Strange case of Dr. Jekyll and Mr. Hyde. Grant, A.   **741.5**

Robert Mugabe's Zimbabwe. Arnold, J. R.   **92**

Robert the Bruce *See* Robert I, King of Scotland, 1274-1329

Roberts, Alison Marion *See* Roberts, Marion, 1966-

Roberts, David, 1970-
(il) Priestley, C. Uncle Montague's tales of terror   **S C**

Roberts, J. M. (John Morris), 1928-2003
The illustrated history of the world   **909**

Roberts, Jennifer Tolbert, 1947-
The ancient Greek world

Rosenbloom, Fiona
You are so not invited to my bat mitzvah!   **Fic**

Rosenthal, Beth, 1964-
(ed) Bullying. See Bullying   302.3

Rosenthal, Joe, 1911-2006
About
Bradley, J. Flags of our fathers   940.54

Rosenwald, Laurie, 1955-
All the wrong people have self esteem
646.7

Rosetta stone
Giblin, J. The riddle of the Rosetta Stone
493

Rosh, Mair
(jt. auth) DuBois, J. Israel   956.94

Rosie and Mrs. America. Gourley, C.   305.4

Rosie O'Donnell's crafty U. O'Donnell, R.
745.5

Rosie the riveter. Colman, P.   331.4

Rosinsky, Natalie M. (Natalie Myra)
Write your own biography   808
Write your own fairy tale   808.3
Write your own graphic novel   741.5
Write your own myth   808.3
Write your own tall tale   808.3

Rosmarin, Ike, 1915-
South Africa   968

Rosner, Marc Alan
Science fair success using the Internet   507.8

Ross, Edmund Gibson, 1826-1907
See/See also pages in the following book(s):
Kennedy, J. F. Profiles in courage   920

Ross, Jeffrey Ian
Will terrorism end?   303.6

Ross, Kathy, 1948-
Earth-friendly crafts   745.5

Ross, Stewart
Leaders of World War II   920
Monarchs   940.1
The technology of World War I   940.3
The United Nations   341.23
(jt. auth) Biesty, S. Egypt in spectacular cross-
section   932

Ross, Tony, 1938-
(il) Shields, C. D. English, fresh squeezed!
811

Ross, Val
The road to there   912
You can't read this   028

Ross-Stroud, Catherine
Janet McDonald   813.009

Rossi, Ann
Bright ideas   609

Rosteck, Mary Kay
(ed) People of the Holocaust. See People of the
Holocaust   920.003
(jt. auth) Schmittroth, L. American Revolution:
biographies   920

Rosten, Carrie
Chloe Leiberman (sometimes Wong)   **Fic**

Roth, Rita
The story road to literacy   372.6

Roth, Roger
(il) Armstrong, J. The American story   973

Roth, Susan L.
(il) Tillage, L. Leon's story   92

Roth, Terri
About
Carson, M. K. Emi and the rhino scientist
599.66

Rotman, Jeffrey L.
(il) Cerullo, M. M. The truth about great white
sharks   597

Roughnecks. Cochran, T.   **Fic**

Routes of science [series]
Day, T. Genetics   576.5
Woodford, C. Electricity   537

Routh, Kristina, 1961-
Down syndrome   616.85
Epilepsy
Meningitis   616.8

Rover. French, J.   **Fic**

Rowan Hood, outlaw girl of Sherwood Forest.
Springer, N.   **Fic**

Rowland-Warne, L.
Costume   391

Rowling, J. K.
Harry Potter and the Sorcerer's Stone   **Fic**
The tales of Beedle the Bard   **S C**
About
Chippendale, L. A. Triumph of the imagination:
the story of writer J.K. Rowling   92
Harmin, K. L. J. K. Rowling   92
Sickels, A. Mythmaker: the story of J.K.
Rowling   92

Roy, James, 1968-
Max Quigley   **Fic**

Roy, Jennifer Rozines
Depression   616.85
Yellow star   **Fic**

Royal diaries [series]
Gregory, K. Eleanor: crown jewel of Aquitaine
Fic
Lasky, K. Elizabeth I   **Fic**
Lasky, K. Jahanara, Princess of Princesses
Fic
Lasky, K. Mary, Queen of Scots, queen without
a country   **Fic**
McKissack, P. C. Nzinga, warrior queen of
Matamba   **Fic**
Smith, P. C. Weetamoo, heart of the Pocassets
Fic

The **royal** kingdoms of Ghana, Mali, and Songhay.
McKissack, P. C.   966.2

Royalty *See* Kings and rulers; Princes; Princesses;
Queens

Ruanda *See* Rwanda

Rubalcaba, Jill
Ancient Egypt   932
(jt. auth) Cline, E. H. The ancient Egyptian
world   932
(jt. auth) Robertshaw, P. The early human world
599.93

Rubber houses. Yeomans, E.   **Fic**

Running the dogs. Cochran, T.   **Fic**

Runyon, Brent
The burn journals   **92**
Surface tension   **Fic**

Rural life *See* Country life; Farm life

Ruschmann, Paul
Legalizing marijuana   **345**

Rushton, Rosie
Friends, enemies   **Fic**

Russell, Carrie
(ed) Complete copyright. See Complete copy-right   **346.04**

Russell, Christopher, 1947-
Dogboy   **Fic**

Russell, Harriet, 1977-
(jt. auth) Weinstein, B. D. Is it still cheating if I don't get caught   **170**

Russell, Henry, 1954-
Germany   **943**
Russia   **947**

Russell, Lillian, 1861-1922
Fiction
Peck, R. Fair weather   **Fic**

Russell, P. Craig, 1951-
Coraline [graphic novel]   **741.5**
(il) Smith, C. R. The mighty 12   **292**

Russell, Patricia Yates, 1937-
(jt. auth) Garcha, R. The world of Islam in literature for youth   **016.3058**

Russia
See also Russia (Federation); Soviet Union
McCray, T. R. Russia and the former Soviet republics   **947**
Russell, H. Russia   **947**
Torchinskiĭ, O. Russia   **947**
Fiction
Durbin, W. The darkest evening   **Fic**
Holub, J. An innocent soldier   **Fic**
Lasky, K. Broken song   **Fic**
Lasky, K. The night journey   **Fic**
History
Goldberg, E. A. Grigory Rasputin   **92**
Vincent, Z. Catherine the Great   **92**
Kings and rulers
Vincent, Z. Catherine the Great   **92**

Russia (Federation)
See also Russia; Soviet Union
Kort, M. Russia   **947**
Politics and government
Shields, C. J. Vladimir Putin   **92**
Streissguth, T. Vladimir Putin   **92**

Russia and the former Soviet republics. McCray, T. R.   **947**

Russian Americans
Fiction
Blume, L. M. M. The rising star of Rusty Nail   **Fic**
Hesse, K. Brooklyn Bridge   **Fic**

Russian Empire *See* Russia

Russian revolution *See* Soviet Union—History—1917-1921, Revolution

Russo, Marisabina, 1950-
A portrait of Pia   **Fic**

Russo-Finnish War, 1939-1940
Fiction
Durbin, W. The Winter War   **Fic**

Russon, Anne E.
Orangutans: wizards of the rainforest   **599.8**

Rustin, Bayard, 1910-1987
About
Brimner, L. D. We are one: the story of Bayard Rustin   **92**
Miller, C. C. No easy answers [biography of Bayard Rustin]   **92**

Ruth, Babe, 1895-1948
About
Hampton, W. Babe Ruth   **92**
Fiction
Tocher, T. Bill Pennant, Babe Ruth, and me   **Fic**

Ruth, George Herman *See* Ruth, Babe, 1895-1948

Ruth, Greg
(il) Mack, T. The fall of the Amazing Zalindas   **Fic**

Rutherford, Ernest, 1871-1937
About
Pasachoff, N. E. Ernest Rutherford   **92**
See/See also pages in the following book(s):
Henderson, H. Nuclear physics   **539.7**

Rutka's notebook. Laskier, R.   **940.53**

Rutkoski, Marie
The Cabinet of Wonders   **Fic**

Rwanda
King, D. C. Rwanda   **967.571**
Koopmans, A. Rwanda   **967.571**
Fiction
Jansen, H. Over a thousand hills I walk with you   **Fic**

Ryan, Amy Kathleen
Vibes   **Fic**

Ryan, Margaret, 1950-
Extraordinary oral presentations   **808.5**

Ryan, Nellie
(il) Jeffrie, S. The girls' book of glamour   **646.7**

Ryan, Pam Muñoz
Esperanza rising   **Fic**

Ryan, Patrick, 1965-
Saints of Augustine   **Fic**

Ryback, Carol
Hurricanes   **551.55**

Rybolt, Thomas R.
Environmental science fair projects   **577**

Ryden, Hope
Wildflowers around the year   **582.13**

Rylant, Cynthia
Appalachia   **974**
The beautiful stories of life   **292**
A fine white dust   **Fic**
Missing May   **Fic**
Something permanent   **811**

S

Saab, Carl Y.
The hindbrain   **612.8**
The spinal cord   **612.8**

Saari, Aaron Maurice
(ed) Renaissance & Reformation: almanac. See
Renaissance & Reformation: almanac
    940.2
(ed) Renaissance & Reformation: biographies.
See Renaissance & Reformation: biographies
    920
(ed) Renaissance & Reformation: primary
sources. See Renaissance & Reformation: primary sources   **940.2**

Saari, Peggy
Colonial America: almanac   **973.2**
Colonial America: primary sources   **973.2**
Space exploration, Biographies   **629.45**
Space exploration, Primary sources   **629.4**
(ed) Explorers & discoverers. See Explorers &
discoverers   **920.003**
(ed) Renaissance & Reformation: almanac. See
Renaissance & Reformation: almanac
    940.2
(ed) Renaissance & Reformation: biographies.
See Renaissance & Reformation: biographies
    920
(ed) Renaissance & Reformation: primary
sources. See Renaissance & Reformation: primary sources   **940.2**
(ed) Scientists: their lives and works. See Scientists: their lives and works   **920.003**

Sabbeth, Carol, 1957-
Frida Kahlo and Diego Rivera: their lives and
ideas   **92**
Monet and the impressionists for kids
    759.05

Sabin vaccine See Poliomyelitis vaccine

Sabriel. Nix, G.   **Fic**

Sabuda, Robert
Dinosaurs   **567.9**
Mega beasts   **569**
Sharks and other sea monsters   **560**

Sac Indians See Sauk Indians

Sacagawea, b. 1786
About
St. George, J. Sacagawea   **92**
Fiction
O'Dell, S. Streams to the river, river to the sea
    Fic

Sacagawea. Crosby, M. T.   **92**

Sacajawea See Sacagawea, b. 1786

Sachar, Louis, 1954-
Holes   **Fic**
Small steps   **Fic**
About
Greene, M. Louis Sachar   **92**

Sachs, Marilyn, 1927-
Lost in America   **Fic**

Sacred art See Christian art

Sacred places. Yolen, J.   **811**

Sacred texts [series]
Brown, A. The Bible and Christianity   **220**
Ganeri, A. The Ramayana and Hinduism
    294.5

The **sacrifice**. Duble, K. B.   **Fic**

Saenz, Benjamin Alire
He forgot to say good-bye   **Fic**

Safe. Shaw, S.   **Fic**

Safe house. Heneghan, J.   **Fic**

Safety devices
See also Accidents—Prevention

Safety education
Allman, T. Internet predators   **364.1**
Child and youth security sourcebook   **362.7**
Orndorff, J. Terrorists, tornadoes, and tsunamis
    613.6
Raatma, L. Safety for babysitters   **649**
Raatma, L. Safety in your neighborhood
    613.6
Raatma, L. Safety on the Internet   **025.04**
Wiloch, T. Everything you need to know about
protecting yourself and others from abduction
    613.6

Safety for babysitters. Raatma, L.   **649**

Safety in your neighborhood. Raatma, L.
    613.6

Safety measures See Accidents—Prevention

Safety on the Internet. Raatma, L.   **025.04**

Saffy's angel. McKay, H.   **Fic**

Safire, William
(comp) Lend me your ears. See Lend me your
ears   **808.85**

Saga. Kostick, C.   **Fic**

Sage, Angie
Magyk   **Fic**

Sahara Desert
Heinrichs, A. The Sahara   **966**
Fiction
Okorafor, N. The shadow speaker   **Fic**

Sahwira. Marsden, C.   **Fic**

Saign, Geoffrey, 1955-
The African cats   **599.75**
The great apes   **599.8**

Sailing
Fiction
Creech, S. The Wanderer   **Fic**
Herlong, M. The great wide sea   **Fic**
Stevenson, R. H. Dead in the water   **Fic**

Sailors' life See Seafaring life

Saint-Exupéry, Antoine de, 1900-1944
The little prince   **Fic**

**Saint-Georges, Joseph Boulogne, chevalier de,
1745-1799**
About
Brewster, H. The other Mozart [biography of
Joseph Bologne Saint-Georges]   **92**

Saint Louis (Mo.)
Fiction
Helgerson, J. Crows & cards   **Fic**

Saint Lucia
Orr, T. Saint Lucia   **972.98**

Saint Petersburg (Russia)
    Siege, 1941-1944—Fiction
    Whelan, G. Burying the sun   **Fic**
Saints

    See also Christian saints
      Fiction
    Freitas, D. The possibilities of sainthood   **Fic**
Saints among the animals. Zarin, C.   **920**
Saints of Augustine. Ryan, P.   **Fic**
Saito, Manabu
    (il) Venning, F. D. Wildflowers of North America   **582.13**
Sakai, Stan
    Usagi Yojimbo, Vol. 18   **741.5**
Sakolsky, Josh
    Copernicus and modern astronomy   **92**
Sakura, Kenichi
    Dragon drive. Vol. 1, D-break   **741.5**
Sakyamuni *See* Gautama Buddha
Saladin, Sultan of Egypt and Syria, 1137-1193
      About
    Crompton, S. The Third Crusade   **956**
    Geyer, F. Saladin   **92**
    Stanley, D. Saladin: noble prince of Islam   **92**
Saladin: noble prince of Islam. Stanley, D.   **92**
Salariya, David
    (jt. auth) Malam, J. Super structures   **624**
Saldaña, René
    The whole sky full of stars   **Fic**
Salem (Mass.)
      Fiction
    Hearn, J. The minister's daughter   **Fic**
    Hightman, J. Spirit   **Fic**
Salisbury, Graham, 1944-
    Eyes of the emperor   **Fic**
    House of the red fish   **Fic**
    Lord of the deep   **Fic**
    Night of the howling dogs   **Fic**
    Under the blood-red sun   **Fic**
      About
    Gill, D. M. Graham Salisbury   **92**
Salk, Jonas, 1914-1995
      About
    Sherrow, V. Jonas Salk   **92**
    Tocci, S. Jonas Salk   **92**
Salk vaccine *See* Poliomyelitis vaccine
Salmansohn, Pete, 1947-
    Saving birds   **333.95**
Salmonella infections *See* Salmonellosis
Salmonellosis
    Brands, D. A. Salmonella   **615.9**
Salomon, Ron
    Suicide   **616.85**
Salsa stories. Delacre, L.   **S C**
Salt marshes
    Wechsler, D. Marvels in the muck   **578.7**
Salting the ocean   **811.008**
Salvadori, Mario George, 1907-1997
    Math games for middle school   **510.7**
    (jt. auth) Levy, M. Earthquakes, volcanoes, and tsunamis   **551.2**

Salvage
    Wilcox, C. Recycling   **363.7**
Salzman, Jack
    African-American culture and history. See African-American culture and history   **305.8**
Sam Stern's get cooking. Stern, S.   **641.5**
Same difference. Vivian, S.   **Fic**
Same-sex marriage
    Andryszewski, T. Same-sex marriage   **306.8**
Same-sex marriage. Andryszewski, T.   **306.8**
The **same** stuff as stars. Paterson, K.   **Fic**
Sami (European people)
    Robinson, D. B. The Sami of Northern Europe   **948**
The **Sami** of Northern Europe. Robinson, D. B.   **948**
Sammy Keyes and the hotel thief. Draanen, W. v.   **Fic**
Samora, John
    (il) Cano-Murillo, K. The crafty diva's lifestyle makeover   **745.5**
Sampson, Deborah, 1760-1827
      Fiction
    Klass, S. S. Soldier's secret   **Fic**
Samuel Blink and the forbidden forest. Haig, M.   **Fic**
Samuels, Barbara G.
    (ed) Into focus. See Into focus   **028.1**
Samuels, Charlie, 1961-
    Iraq   **956.7**
Samurai
    Hanel, R. Samurai   **952**
    Turnbull, S. R. Real samurai   **952**
      Fiction
    Bradford, C. Young samurai   **Fic**
    Matthews, A. The way of the warrior   **Fic**
    Snow, M. Sisters of the sword   **Fic**
Samurai shortstop. Gratz, A.   **Fic**
San Antonio (Tex.)
      Fiction
    Nye, N. S. Going going   **Fic**
San Francisco (Calif.)
      Fiction
    Doctorow, C. Little brother   **Fic**
    Hopkinson, D. Into the firestorm   **Fic**
    Lavender, W. Aftershocks   **Fic**
    Scott, M. The alchemyst   **Fic**
    Snyder, Z. K. The magic nation thing   **Fic**
    Yep, L. Dragonwings   **Fic**
San Nicolas Island (Calif.)
      Fiction
    O'Dell, S. Island of the Blue Dolphins   **Fic**
San Souci, Robert, 1946-
    Cut from the same cloth   **398.2**
    Double-dare to be scared: another thirteen chilling tales   **S C**
    A terrifying taste of short & shivery   **398.2**
    Triple-dare to be scared   **S C**
    (jt. auth) Ouimet, D. Dare to be scared   **S C**
Sanchez, Alex, 1957-
    So hard to say   **Fic**

The **saver**. Ravel, E. **Fic**
Saving birds. Salmansohn, P. **333.95**
Saving endangered species [series]
  Feinstein, S. The chimpanzee **599.8**
Saving Juliet. Selfors, S. **Fic**
Saving manatees. Swinburne, S. R. **599.5**
Saving our living earth [series]
  Fridell, R. Earth-friendly energy **333.79**
  Fridell, R. Protecting Earth's water supply
    363.7
  Johnson, R. L. Understanding global warming
    363.7
  Rapp, V. Protecting Earth's air quality **363.7**
  Rapp, V. Protecting Earth's land **333.72**
  Welsbacher, A. Earth-friendly design **745.2**
  Welsbacher, A. Protecting Earth's rain forests
    577.3
  Wilcox, C. Earth-friendly waste management
    363.7
Saving the American wilderness. Malaspina, A.
  333.72
Saving the buffalo. Marrin, A. **599.64**
Savvy. Law, I. **Fic**
Sawa, Maureen
  (jt. auth) Edmonston, L.-P. Car smarts
    629.222
Sawinski, Diane M.
  (ed) Hillstrom, K. Vietnam War: biographies
    920
Sawvel, Patty Jo, 1958-
  (ed) Student drug testing. See Student drug test-
    ing **371.7**
Sawyer, Kem Knapp
  The underground railroad in American history
    326
Say it with music. Furstinger, N. **92**
Sayago, Mauricio Trenard, 1963-
  (il) Hayes, J. Dance, Nana, dance **398.2**
Sayre, April Pulley
  Lake and pond **577.6**
  River and stream **577.6**
  Secrets of sound **591.59**
  Taiga **577.3**
Sayre, Henry M., 1948-
  Cave paintings to Picasso **709**
Scales, Pat R.
  Teaching banned books **323.44**
Scaletta, Kurtis, 1968-
  Mudville **Fic**
Scalpels, stitches & scars. Townsend, J. **617**
Scams!. Schroeder, A. **364.1**
Scandiffio, Laura
  Evil masters **920**
Scandinavia
Civilization
  Porterfield, J. Scandinavian mythology **293**
  Schomp, V. The Norsemen **293**
Scandinavian civilization See Scandinavia—Civi-
  lization
Scandinavian mythology. Porterfield, J. **293**
Scandinavians
  See also Vikings

Scarborough, Kate
  Nuclear waste **363.7**
  Pablo Picasso **92**
Scarecrow studies in young adult literature [se-
  ries]
  Aronson, M. Beyond the pale **810.9**
  Bilz, R. L. Life is tough **028.5**
  Cart, M. The heart has its reasons **813.009**
  Crowe, C. More than a game **810.9**
  Gallo, D. R. Richard Peck **813.009**
  Gill, D. M. Graham Salisbury **92**
  Glenn, W. J. Sarah Dessen **813.009**
  Hinton, K. Angela Johnson **813.009**
  Hinton, K. Sharon M. Draper **813.009**
  Hogan, W. Humor in young adult literature
    813.009
  Latham, D. David Almond **823.009**
  Nilsen, A. P. Names and naming in young adult
    literature **813.009**
  Reid, S. E. Virginia Euwer Wolff **813.009**
  Ross-Stroud, C. Janet McDonald **813.009**
  Stover, L. T. Jacqueline Woodson **813.009**
  Tighe, M. A. Sharon Creech **813.009**
  Tyson, E. S. Orson Scott Card **813.009**
Scarlett. Cassidy, C. **Fic**
Scary stories **S C**
Scary stories 3. Schwartz, A. **398.2**
Scary stories to tell in the dark. Schwartz, A.
  398.2
Scat. Hiaasen, C. **Fic**
Scenarios *See* Motion picture plays
Schaap, Phil, 1951-
  (jt. auth) Marsalis, W. Jazz A-B-Z **781.65**
Schacter, Bernice Zeldin, 1943-2008
  Genetics in the news **576.5**
Schall, Lucy
  Booktalks and beyond **028.5**
  Teen genre connections **028.5**
Schaller, George B.
About
  Turner, P. S. A life in the wild [biography of
    George Schaller] **92**
Schanzer, Rosalyn
  What Darwin saw **92**
Schecter, Ellen
  The family Haggadah **296.4**
Scheduling the heavens [biography of Edmond
  Halley] Fox, M. V. **92**
Schenck, Charles
About
  Alonso, K. Schenck v. United States **342**
  Icenoggle, J. Schenck v. United States and the
    freedom of speech debate **342**
Schenck v. United States. Alonso, K. **342**
Schenck v. United States and the freedom of
  speech debate. Icenoggle, J. **342**
Scherer, Glenn
  J. Robert Oppenheimer **92**
The **Schernoff** discoveries. Paulsen, G. **Fic**
Scheuer, Philip
  (il) Haduch, B. Science fair success secrets
    507.8

Schindler, Oskar, 1908-1974
See/See also pages in the following book(s):
Lyman, D. Holocaust rescuers   920

Schirripa, Steven R.
Nicky Deuce   Fic

Schizophrenia
Veague, H. B. Schizophrenia   616.89
Fiction
Atwater-Rhodes, A. Persistence of memory
Fic
Trueman, T. Inside out   Fic

Schlaepfer, Gloria G.
Butterflies   595.7
Elephants   599.67
The Louisiana Purchase   973.4

Schlager, Neil, 1966-
(ed) Alternative energy. See Alternative energy
333.79

Schlein, Lonnie, 1949-
(ed) A Nation challenged. See A Nation challenged
973.931

Schlesinger, Arthur M., 1917-
(ed) The Election of 2000 and the administration of George W. Bush. See The Election of 2000 and the administration of George W. Bush   324

Schlissel, Lillian
Black frontiers   978

Schlitz, Laura Amy
A drowned maiden's hair   Fic
Good masters! Sweet ladies!   940.1

Schlosser, Eric
Chew on this   394.1

Schmemann, Serge
When the wall came down   943

Schmidt, C. A.
Useful fools   Fic

Schmidt, Gary
First boy   Fic

Schmidt, Gary D.
Lizzie Bright and the Buckminster boy   Fic
Trouble   Fic
The Wednesday wars   Fic
(ed) Frost, R. Robert Frost   811

Schmittroth, Linda
American Revolution: biographies   920
(comp) American Revolution: primary sources. See American Revolution: primary sources
973.3
(jt. auth) Bigelow, B. C. American Revolution: almanac   973.3
(ed) People of the Holocaust. See People of the Holocaust   920.003

Schnare, Mary Kay W., 1945-
(jt. auth) Job, A. G. The school library media specialist as manager   027.8

Schoell, William
Remarkable journeys: the story of Jules Verne
92

Schoenherr, Ian
(il) Jacques, B. Castaways of the Flying Dutchman   Fic

Schoenherr, John, 1935-
(il) George, J. C. Julie of the wolves   Fic

Scholastic achievement *See* Academic achievement

Scholastic atlas of the United States. Rubel, D.
912

Scholastic children's encyclopedia   031

Scholastic choices [series]
Winchester, E. Sisters and brothers   306.8

Scholastic classics [series]
Stevenson, R. L. Kidnapped   Fic

Scholastic dictionary of idioms. Terban, M.
423

Scholastic dictionary of spelling. Terban, M.
428

Scholastic dictionary of synonyms, antonyms, and homonyms   423

Scholastic encyclopedia of thc presidents and their times. Rubel, D.   920

Scholastic guides [series]
Janeczko, P. B. Writing winning reports and essays   808

Schomp, Virginia, 1953-
1500   909.08
American voices from the Vietnam era
973.923
American voices from the women's movement
305.4
The ancient Africans   299.6
The ancient Chinese   931
The ancient Egyptians   299
The ancient Greeks   292
Ancient India   934
Ancient Mesopotamia   935
The ancient Mesopotamians   935
The ancient Romans   292
The Aztecs   972
The Italian Renaissance   945
Japan in the days of the samurai   952
Marching toward freedom   305.8
The Native Americans   970.004
The Norsemen   293
The Vikings   948
(jt. auth) Haskins, J. The rise of Jim Crow
305.8
(jt. auth) Johnson, D. The Harlem Renaissance
700
(jt. auth) Jordan, A. D. The Civil War
973.7
(jt. auth) Jordan, A. D. Slavery and resistance
326
(jt. auth) McClaurin, I. The civil rights movement   323.1
(jt. auth) McClaurin, I. Facing the future
305.8
(jt. auth) Sharp, S. P. The slave trade and the middle passage   326
(jt. auth) Stroud, B. The Reconstruction era
973.8

Schon, Isabel
The best of Latino heritage 1996-2002   011.6

School desegregation and the story of the Little Rock Nine. Miller, M.   379

School discipline
Beaudoin, M.-N. Responding to the culture of bullying and disrespect   371.5

School library management   **025.1**

The **school** library media facilities planner. Hart, T. L.   **027.8**

The **school** library media manager. Woolls, E. B.   **027.8**

The **school** library media specialist as manager. Job, A. G.   **027.8**

School media centers *See* Instructional materials centers

School of American Ballet
    Schorer, S. Put your best foot forward   **792.8**

School prayer. Andryszewski, T.   **344**

School reform and the school library media specialist. Hughes-Hassell, S.   **027.8**

School science projects *See* Science projects

School stories
    Abdel-Fattah, R. Does my head look big in this?   **Fic**
    Abdel-Fattah, R. Ten things I hate about me   **Fic**
    Abrahams, P. Reality check   **Fic**
    Alender, K. Bad girls don't die   **Fic**
    Alexie, S. The absolutely true diary of a part-time Indian   **Fic**
    Anderson, L. H. Speak   **Fic**
    Appelt, K. Kissing Tennessee and other stories from the Stardust Dance   **S C**
    Asher, J. Thirteen reasons why   **Fic**
    Atkins, C. Alt ed   **Fic**
    Avi. Nothing but the truth   **Fic**
    Ayres, K. Macaroni boy   **Fic**
    Barnes, J. L. The Squad: perfect cover   **Fic**
    Baskin, N. R. Anything but typical   **Fic**
    Basye, D. E. Heck   **Fic**
    Bauer, J. Peeled   **Fic**
    Beil, M. D. The Red Blazer Girls: the ring of Rocamadour   **Fic**
    Bennett, C. A heart divided
    Birney, B. G. The princess and the Peabodys   **Fic**
    Bloor, E. London calling   **Fic**
    Bonk, J. J. Dustin Grubbs   **Fic**
    Bradley, K. B. Leap of faith   **Fic**
    Brande, R. Evolution, me, & other freaks of nature   **Fic**
    Brewer, H. The chronicles of Vladimir Tod: eighth grade bites   **Fic**
    Brown, J. R. 13   **Fic**
    Budhos, M. T. Ask me no questions   **Fic**
    Bunting, E. Spying on Miss Müller   **Fic**
    Burton, R. Leaving Jetty Road   **Fic**
    Butler, D. H. The truth about Truman School   **Fic**
    Byars, B. C. The burning questions of Bingo Brown   **Fic**
    Cabot, M. How to be popular   **Fic**
    Carney, J. The adventures of Michael MacInnes   **Fic**
    Carter, A. R. Love, football, and other contact sports   **S C**
    Carvell, M. Sweetgrass basket   **Fic**
    Carvell, M. Who will tell my brother?   **Fic**
    Chaltas, T. Because I am furniture   **Fic**
    Cheva, C. She's so money   **Fic**
    Cirrone, D. Prom kings and drama queens   **Fic**
    Cleary, B. Dear Mr. Henshaw   **Fic**
    Cohen, T. The invisible rules of the Zoë Lama   **Fic**
    Comerford, L. B. Rissa Bartholomew's declaration of independence   **Fic**
    Cooney, C. B. Code orange   **Fic**
    Coy, J. Box out   **Fic**
    Coy, J. Crackback   **Fic**
    Crabtree, J. Discovering pig magic   **Fic**
    Crawford, B. Carter finally gets it   **Fic**
    Creech, S. Bloomability   **Fic**
    Creech, S. Love that dog   **Fic**
    Crutcher, C. Deadline   **Fic**
    Crutcher, C. Ironman   **Fic**
    Crutcher, C. Whale talk   **Fic**
    Cushman, K. The loud silence of Francine Green   **Fic**
    Danziger, P. The cat ate my gymsuit   **Fic**
    De la Cruz, M. Fresh off the boat   **Fic**
    De Lint, C. The blue girl   **Fic**
    Dee, B. Solving Zoe   **Fic**
    Deriso, C. H. Talia Talk   **Fic**
    Deuker, C. Gym candy   **Fic**
    Deuker, C. High heat   **Fic**
    Deuker, C. Painting the black   **Fic**
    Donofrio, B. Thank you, Lucky Stars   **Fic**
    Dowell, F. O. The kind of friends we used to be   **Fic**
    Draanen, W. v. Confessions of a serial kisser   **Fic**
    Draper, S. M. The Battle of Jericho   **Fic**
    Draper, S. M. Fire from the rock   **Fic**
    Duncan, L. Killing Mr. Griffin   **Fic**
    Easton, K. White magic   **Fic**
    Ellis, A. D. This is what I did   **Fic**
    Ellis, D. Bifocal   **Fic**
    Emerson, K. Carlos is gonna get it   **Fic**
    Erskine, K. Quaking   **Fic**
    Fehler, G. Beanball   **Fic**
    Ferraiolo, J. D. The big splash   **Fic**
    Fitzgerald, D. Soccer chick rules   **Fic**
    Flake, S. G. The broken bike boy and the Queen of 33rd Street   **Fic**
    Flake, S. G. The skin I'm in   **Fic**
    Fleischman, P. A fate totally worse than death   **Fic**
    Flinn, A. Breaking point   **Fic**
    Forester, V. The girl who could fly   **Fic**
    Fredericks, M. Crunch time   **Fic**
    Fredericks, M. Head games   **Fic**
    Fredericks, M. Love   **Fic**
    Freitas, D. The possibilities of sainthood   **Fic**
    Gantos, J. Jack on the tracks   **Fic**
    Gantos, J. Joey Pigza swallowed the key   **Fic**
    Garden, N. Endgame   **Fic**
    George, M. Looks   **Fic**
    Gephart, D. As if being 12 3/4 isn't bad enough, my mother is running for president!   **Fic**
    Goldschmidt, J. The secret blog of Raisin Rodriguez   **Fic**
    Gorman, C. Games   **Fic**
    Graff, L. The life and crimes of Bernetta Wallflower   **Fic**

School stories—*Continued*

Grant, V. Pigboy	Fic
Gratz, A. Samurai shortstop	Fic
Gray, C. Evernight	Fic
Green, T. Baseball great	Fic
Grimes, N. Bronx masquerade	Fic
Halpin, B. Forever changes	Fic
Halpin, B. How ya like me now	Fic
Han, J. Shug	Fic
Hernandez, D. No more us for you	Fic
Hershey, M. 10 lucky things that have happened to me since I nearly got hit by lightning	Fic
Holm, J. L. Middle school is worse than meatloaf	Fic
Houston, J. New boy	Fic
Howe, J. The misfits	Fic
Hughes, P. Open ice	Fic
Hurley, T. Ghostgirl	Fic
Ibbotson, E. The dragonfly pool	Fic
James, B. Zombie blondes	Fic
Jenkins, A. M. Repossessed	Fic
Jinks, C. Evil genius	Fic
Johnson, M. The Bermudez Triangle	Fic
Johnson, M. Devilish	Fic
Jones, T. L. Standing against the wind	Fic
Jonsberg, B. Dreamrider	Fic
Juby, S. Getting the girl	Fic
Kantor, M. Confessions of a not it girl	Fic
Karasyov, C. Bittersweet sixteen	Fic
Karim, S. Skunk girl	Fic
Katcher, B. Playing with matches	Fic
Kephart, B. Undercover	Fic
Kimmel, E. C. Spin the bottle	Fic
Kinney, J. Diary of a wimpy kid: Greg Heffley's journal	Fic
Klass, D. Dark angel	Fic
Klass, D. Home of the Braves	Fic
Kline, L. W. Write before your eyes	Fic
Klinger, S. The Kingdom of Strange	Fic
Klise, K. Regarding the sink	Fic
Koertge, R. Stoner & Spaz	Fic
Koja, K. Buddha Boy	Fic
Koja, K. Headlong	Fic
Koja, K. Kissing the bee	Fic
Konigsburg, E. L. The view from Saturday	Fic
Korman, G. Jake, reinvented	Fic
Korman, G. No more dead dogs	Fic
Korman, G. Schooled	Fic
Koss, A. G. Poison Ivy	Fic
Kuhlman, E. The last invisible boy	Fic
Kwasney, M. D. Itch	Fic
LaFleur, S. M. Love, Aubrey	Fic
Langston, L. The trouble with Cupid	Fic
LaRochelle, D. Absolutely, positively not	Fic
Laser, M. Cheater	Fic
Lekich, J. King of the Lost and Found	Fic
Levine, G. C. The wish	Fic
Levy, E. Seventh grade tango	Fic
Limb, S. Zoe and Chloe: on the prowl	Fic
Lockhart, E. The disreputable history of Frankie Landau-Banks	Fic
Lockhart, E. Dramarama	Fic
Lopez, D. Confetti girl	Fic
López, L. Call me Henri	Fic

Love, D. A. Defying the diva	Fic
Love, D. A. Picture perfect	Fic
Lubar, D. Sleeping freshmen never lie	Fic
Luddy, K. Spelldown	Fic
Lyga, B. The astonishing adventures of Fanboy & Goth Girl	Fic
Lyga, B. Hero-type	Fic
Lynch, C. Inexcusable	Fic
Mackey, W. K. Throwing like a girl	Fic
Mackler, C. The earth, my butt, and other big, round things	Fic
Margolis, L. Boys are dogs	Fic
Mass, W. Heaven looks a lot like the mall	Fic
Mass, W. A mango-shaped space	Fic
Matthews, L. S. The outcasts	Fic
Maynard, J. The cloud chamber	Fic
McDaniel, L. Hit and run	Fic
McMann, L. Wake	Fic
McNish, C. Angel	Fic
McPhee, P. New blood	Fic
Meminger, N. Shine, coconut moon	Fic
Meyer, S. Twilight	Fic
Mikaelsen, B. Ghost of Spirit Bear	Fic
Mills, C. Alex Ryan, stop that!	Fic
Morgenstern, S. H. Secret letters from 0 to 10	Fic
Moriarty, J. The murder of Bindy Mackenzie	Fic
Moriarty, J. The year of secret assignments	Fic
Murphy, P. The wild girls	Fic
Myers, W. D. Game	Fic
Myers, W. D. Slam!	Fic
Nails, J. Next to Mexico	Fic
Naylor, P. R. Cricket man	Fic
Naylor, P. R. Faith, hope, and Ivy June	Fic
Naylor, P. R. Reluctantly Alice	Fic
Neff, H. H. The hound of Rowan	Fic
Nelson, B. New rules of high school	Fic
Nimmo, J. Midnight for Charlie Bone	Fic
Nixon, J. L. Laugh till you cry	Fic
Oates, J. C. Big Mouth & Ugly Girl	Fic
O'Connell, T. True love, the sphinx, and other unsolvable riddles	Fic
O'Connor, B. Fame and glory in Freedom, Georgia	Fic
O'Dell, K. Agnes Parker . . . girl in progress	Fic
Ostow, M. So punk rock (and other ways to disappoint your mother)	Fic
Padian, M. Brett McCarthy: work in progress	Fic
Paulsen, G. The Schernoff discoveries	Fic
Pearsall, S. All of the above	Fic
Perez, M. Dead is the new black	Fic
Peters, J. A. Define "normal"	Fic
Petrucha, S. The Rule of Won	Fic
Pixley, M. Freak	Fic
Pollet, A. Nobody was here	Fic
Prose, F. After	Fic
Prose, F. Touch	Fic
Ray, D. Ghost girl	Fic
Rees, D. C. Vampire High	Fic
Rosten, C. Chloe Leiberman (sometimes Wong)	Fic
Ryan, A. K. Vibes	Fic

Schram, Peninnah, 1934-
(ed) Oberman, S. Solomon and the ant
398.2

Schreck, Karen Halvorsen, 1962-
Dream journal **Fic**

Schreiber, Ellen
Vampire kisses **Fic**
Vampire kisses: blood relatives **741.5**

Schroeder, Andreas, 1946-
Scams! **364.1**

Schroeder, Becky
See/See also pages in the following book(s):
Thimmesh, C. Girls think of everything **920**

Schroeder, Fred E. H.
(jt. auth) Cole, D. J. Encyclopedia of modern
everyday inventions **609**

Schroeder, Lisa
I heart you, you haunt me **Fic**

Schroeder, Michael J.
Mexican Americans **305.8**

Schroeder, Patricia Miller- *See* Miller-Schroeder,
Patricia

Schroeder, Peter W., 1942-
Six million paper clips **940.53**

Schroeder-Hildebrand, Dagmar, 1943-
(jt. auth) Schroeder, P. W. Six million paper
clips **940.53**

Schuckett, Sandy
Political advocacy for school librarians
027.8

Schudel, Matt
(jt. auth) Schulke, F. Witness to our times
92

Schuerger, Michele, 1961-
(jt. auth) Schwager, T. Cool women, hot jobs
. . . and how you can go for it, too!
650.14

Schulke, Flip
Witness to our times **92**

Schultz, Ashlee
(il) Dreier, D. L. Electrical circuits **537**

Schultz-Jones, Barbara
An automation primer for school library media
centers and small libraries **027.8**

Schulz, Carol D., 1948-
(jt. auth) Soumerai, E. N. A voice from the
Holocaust **940.53**

Schumacher, Julie
The book of one hundred truths **Fic**
The chain letter **Fic**

Schumacher, Julie, 1958-
Black box **Fic**

Schumacher, Thomas L.
How does the show go on? **792**

Schumaker, Ward
(il) Zeiler, F. A kid's guide to giving **361.2**

Schuman, Michael, 1953-
Barack Obama **92**
Frederick Douglass **92**

Schumann, Clara, 1819-1896
About
Reich, S. Clara Schumann **92**

Schur, Joan Brodsky
(ed) The Arabs. See The Arabs **305.8**

Schutz, Samantha, 1978-
I don't want to be crazy **92**

The **Schwa** was here. Shusterman, N. **Fic**

Schwabach, Karen
The Hope Chest **Fic**
A pickpocket's tale **Fic**

Schwabacher, Martin
Bees **595.7**
Jupiter **523.4**

Schwager, Tina, 1964-
Cool women, hot jobs . . . and how you can go
for it, too! **650.14**

Schwalb, Edith
About
Kacer, K. Hiding Edith **940.53**

Schwartz, Alvin, 1927-1992
More scary stories to tell in the dark **398.2**
Scary stories 3 **398.2**
Scary stories to tell in the dark **398.2**

Schwartz, Ellen, 1949-
I'm a vegetarian **613.2**
Stealing home **Fic**

Schwartz, Howard, 1945-
The day the Rabbi disappeared: Jewish holiday
tales of magic **398.2**
(jt. auth) Olson, A. N. Ask the bones: scary stories from around the world **398.2**
(jt. auth) Olson, A. N. More bones **398.2**

Schwartz, Tina P., 1969-
Organ transplants **617.9**

Schwartz, Virginia Frances, 1950-
4 kids in 5E & 1 crazy year **Fic**
Send one angel down **Fic**

Schwarzenegger, Arnold
About
Young, J. C. Arnold Schwarzenegger **92**

Schyffert, Bea Uusma
The man who went to the far side of the moon:
the story of Apollo 11 astronaut Michael Collins **92**

Science
See also Computer science
Bazin, M. Math and science across cultures
510
Gribbin, M. The science of Philip Pullman's His
Dark Materials **823.009**
Murphy, G. Why is snot green **500**
Sussman, A. Dr. Art's guide to science **500**
Thimmesh, C. The sky's the limit **500**
Wollard, K. How come? in the neighborhood
500
Bibliography
Outstanding science trade books for students
K-12 **016.5**
Dictionaries
The American Heritage science dictionary
503
American Heritage student science dictionary **503**
Encyclopedias
Britannica illustrated science library **503**
Growing up with science **503**
The new book of popular science **503**

Science fiction—*Continued*

Hulme, J. The glitch in sleep	Fic
Johansen, K. V. The Cassandra Virus	Fic
Keaney, B. The hollow people	Fic
Klass, D. Firestorm	Fic
Le Guin, U. K. A wizard of Earthsea	Fic
Link, K. Pretty monsters	S C
Lowry, L. Gathering blue	Fic
Lowry, L. The giver	Fic
Lynch, C. Cyberia	Fic
Lyon, S. The gift moves	Fic
Malley, G. The Declaration	Fic
McNaughton, J. The secret under my skin	Fic
Moore, P. Hero	Fic
Morden, S. The lost art	Fic
Ness, P. The knife of never letting go	Fic
Nix, G. Shade's children	Fic
Ó Guilín, P. The inferior	Fic
O'Brien, R. C. Z for Zachariah	Fic
Okorafor, N. The shadow speaker	Fic
Park, L. S. Archer's quest	Fic
Patterson, J. Maximum Ride: the angel experiment	Fic
Paulsen, G. The Transall saga	Fic
Pearson, M. The adoration of Jenna Fox	Fic
Pfeffer, S. B. The dead & the gone	Fic
Pfeffer, S. B. Life as we knew it	Fic
Pow, T. The pack	Fic
Prévost, G. The book of time	Fic
Rabin, S. Black powder	Fic
Reeve, P. Starcross	Fic
Reisman, M. Simon Bloom, the gravity keeper	Fic
Rex, A. The true meaning of Smekday	Fic
Sargent, P. Farseed	Fic
Seidler, T. Brainboy and the Deathmaster	Fic
Service, P. F. Tomorrow's magic	Fic
Shusterman, N. Unwind	Fic
Simmons, M. Alien feast	Fic
Singer, N. Gem X	Fic
Skurzynski, G. The Virtual War	Fic
Sleator, W. The duplicate	Fic
Sleator, W. House of stairs	Fic
Sleator, W. Interstellar pig	Fic
Sleator, W. Singularity	Fic
Sorrells, W. Erratum	Fic
The Starry rift	S C
Stewart, T. L. The mysterious Benedict Society	Fic
Thompson, K. Fourth World	Fic
Vande Velde, V. Heir apparent	Fic
Vaupel, R. Rules of the universe by Austin W. Hale	Fic
Verne, J. 20,000 leagues under the sea	Fic
Voake, S. The dreamwalker's child	Fic
Voake, S. The web of fire	Fic
Ward, D. Escape the mask	Fic
Wells, H. G. The war of the worlds	Fic
Werlin, N. Double helix	Fic
Westerfeld, S. Uglies	Fic
White, A. Surviving Antarctica	Fic
Wild, K. Fight game	Fic
Winterson, J. Tanglewreck	Fic
Wooding, C. The storm thief	Fic

Authorship
Farrell, T. Write your own science fiction story **808.3**

Bibliography
Fichtelberg, S. Encountering enchantment **016.8**

Dictionaries
Brave new words **813.009**

Graphic novels
Farr, J. eV: vol. 1 **741.5**
Huddleston, C. Decoy **741.5**

Science fiction graphic novels
Anderson, E. A. PX! Book one: a girl and her panda **741.5**
Blackman, H. Star Wars: Clone wars adventures, Vol. 1 **741.5**
Flight explorer **741.5**
Geary, R. The invisible man **741.5**

Science for every kid series
VanCleave, J. P. Janice VanCleave's energy for every kid **531**
VanCleave, J. P. Janice VanCleave's engineering for every kid **507.8**

Science in art
Bingham, J. Science & technology **704.9**

Science in focus [series]
Woodford, C. Digital technology **621.381**

Science news flash [series]
Schacter, B. Z. Genetics in the news **576.5**

Science news for kids [series]
Sohn, E. The environment **363.7**

The **science** of air. Parker, S. **533**

The **science** of health [series]
Bauchner, E. What do I have to lose? **613.2**
Esherick, J. Dying for acceptance **616.86**
Hovius, C. The best you can be **613.7**
Libal, A. Can I change the way I look? **613**

The **science** of Philip Pullman's His Dark Materials. Gribbin, M. **823.009**

Science of saving animals [series]
Thomas, P. Big cat conservation **333.95**
Thomas, P. Bird alert **333.95**

The **science** of sound. Parker, S. **534**

The **science** of water. Parker, S. **532**

Science on the edge [series]
Bledsoe, K. E. Genetically engineered foods **664**
Lindop, L. Cave sleuths **551.4**
Lindop, L. Chasing tornadoes **551.55**
Lindop, L. Probing volcanoes **551.2**
Lindop, L. Venturing the deep sea **551.46**
Margulies, P. Artificial intelligence **006.3**
Orr, T. Test tube babies **618.1**

Science project ideas [series]
Gardner, R. Science project ideas about rain **551.57**
Gardner, R. Science project ideas about trees **582.16**

Science project ideas about kitchen chemistry. Gardner, R. **540.7**

Science project ideas about rain. Gardner, R. **551.57**

Science project ideas about trees. Gardner, R.
582.16

Science projects
Bardhan-Quallen, S. Last-minute science fair projects 507.8
Bochinski, J. B. The complete handbook of science fair projects 507.8
Bochinski, J. B. More award-winning science fair projects 507.8
Bonnet, R. L. 46 science fair projects for the evil genius 507.8
Calhoun, Y. Earth science fair projects using rocks, minerals, magnets, mud, and more 550
Calhoun, Y. Plant and animal science fair projects 570
Gardner, R. Astronomy projects with an observatory you can build 522
Gardner, R. Bicycle science projects 531
Gardner, R. Chemistry science fair projects using acids, bases, metals, salts, and inorganic stuff 540
Gardner, R. Chemistry science fair projects using french fries, gumdrops, soap, and other organic stuff 547
Gardner, R. Easy genius science projects with light 537
Gardner, R. Forces and motion science fair projects 531
Gardner, R. Forensic science projects with a crime lab you can build 363.2
Gardner, R. Genetics and evolution science fair projects 576
Gardner, R. Health science projects about psychology 150
Gardner, R. Light, sound, and waves science fair projects 507.8
Gardner, R. Meteorology projects with a weather station you can build 551.5
Gardner, R. Physics projects with a light box you can build 530
Gardner, R. Planet Earth science fair projects using the moon, stars, beach balls, frisbees, and other far-out stuff 507.8
Gardner, R. Science project ideas about kitchen chemistry 540.7
Gardner, R. Science project ideas about rain 551.57
Gardner, R. Science project ideas about trees 582.16
Gardner, R. Science projects about physics in the home 530
Gardner, R. Science projects about plants 580.7
Gardner, R. Science projects about the environment and ecology 363.7
Gardner, R. Sound projects with a music lab you can build 534
Goodstein, M. Plastics and polymers science fair projects 507.8
Haduch, B. Science fair success secrets 507.8
Harris, E. S. Crime scene science fair projects 363.2
Harris, E. S. Save the Earth science experiments 507.8

Oxlade, C. Chemistry 540.7
Rainis, K. G. Cell and microbe science fair projects using microscopes, mold, and more 571.6
Reilly, K. M. Planet Earth 363.7
Rompella, N. Ecosystems 577
Rosner, M. A. Science fair success using the Internet 507.8
Rybolt, T. R. Environmental science fair projects 577
Science activities for *all* students 507.8
VanCleave, J. P. Janice VanCleave's A+ projects in astronomy 520
VanCleave, J. P. Janice VanCleave's A+ projects in earth science 550
VanCleave, J. P. Janice VanCleave's energy for every kid 531
VanCleave, J. P. Janice VanCleave's engineering for every kid 507.8
VanCleave, J. P. Janice VanCleave's guide to more of the best science fair projects 507.8
VanCleave, J. P. Janice VanCleave's plants 580.7
VanCleave, J. P. Janice VanCleave's solar system 523.2
Walker, P. Ecosystem science fair projects using worms, leaves, crickets, and other stuff 577
Whitehouse, P. Plants 580.7

Science projects [Enslow series]
Gardner, R. Health science projects about psychology 150
Gardner, R. Science projects about physics in the home 530
Gardner, R. Science projects about plants 580.7
Gardner, R. Science projects about temperature and heat 536
Gardner, R. Science projects about the environment and ecology 363.7

Science projects [Raintree series]
Oxlade, C. Chemistry 540.7

Science projects about physics in the home. Gardner, R. 530
Science projects about plants. Gardner, R. 580.7
Science projects about temperature and heat. Gardner, R. 536
Science projects about the environment and ecology. Gardner, R. 363.7

Science quest [series]
Jerome, K. B. Atomic universe 539.7
Phelan, G. Double helix 572.8
Phelan, G. Invisible force 531
Phelan, G. Killing germs, saving lives 615
Science warriors. Collard, S. B., III 578.6

Scientific American [series]
Bell, T. E. Earth's journey through space 525
Jedicke, P. Great inventions of the 20th century 609
Jedicke, P. Great moments in space exploration 629.4

Short stories—*Continued*

Gothic!	**S C**
Half-human	**S C**
Hearne, B. G. The canine connection: stories about dogs and people	**S C**
Hearne, B. G. Hauntings, and other tales of danger, love, and sometimes loss	**S C**
Heyman, A. The big book of horror	**S C**
Holt, K. W. Part of me	**S C**
Horowitz, A. Horowitz horror	**S C**
Horowitz, A. More Horowitz horror	**S C**
Jacques, B. The Ribbajack & other curious yarns	**S C**
Join in	**S C**
Kimmel, E. A. The jar of fools: eight Hanukkah stories from Chelm	**S C**
Kipling, R. The jungle book: the Mowgli stories	**S C**
Lanagan, M. White time	**S C**
Lay-ups and long shots	**S C**
Leaving home: stories	**808.8**
Lester, J. Long journey home: stories from black history	**S C**
Levithan, D. How they met, and other stories	**S C**
Link, K. Pretty monsters	**S C**
Love is hell	**S C**
Magic in the mirrorstone	**S C**
Make me over	**S C**
Marston, E. Santa Claus in Baghdad and other stories about teens in the Arab world	**S C**
McKinley, R. The door in the hedge	**S C**
McKinley, R. Water: tales of elemental spirits	**S C**
McKissack, P. C. The dark-thirty	**S C**
McKissack, P. C. Porch lies	**S C**
McRobbie, D. A whole lot of Wayne	**S C**
Moccasin thunder	**S C**
My dad's a punk	**S C**
Myers, W. D. 145th Street	**S C**
Myers, W. D. What they found	**S C**
Naidoo, B. Out of bounds: seven stories of conflict and hope	**S C**
Necessary noise: stories about our families as they really are	**S C**
Nix, G. Across the wall	**S C**
No such thing as the real world	**S C**
Noyes, D. The ghosts of Kerfol	**S C**
On the fringe	**S C**
Once upon a cuento	**S C**
Outside rules	**S C**
Owning it	**S C**
Paterson, K. Angels and other strangers	**S C**
Peck, R. Past perfect, present tense: new and collected stories	**S C**
Places I never meant to be	**S C**
Poe, E. A. Edgar Allan Poe	**S C**
Poe, E. A. Edgar Allan Poe's tales of mystery and madness	**S C**
Poe, E. A. Tales of terror	**S C**
Priestley, C. Uncle Montague's tales of terror	**S C**
The restless dead	**S C**
Rice, D. Crazy loco	**S C**
Rowling, J. K. The tales of Beedle the Bard	**S C**
San Souci, R. Dare to be scared	**S C**

San Souci, R. Double-dare to be scared: another thirteen chilling tales	**S C**
San Souci, R. Triple-dare to be scared	**S C**
Scary stories	**S C**
Shattered: stories of children and war	**S C**
Shelf life: stories by the book	**S C**
Shining on	**S C**
Shusterman, N. Darkness creeping	**S C**
Sideshow	**S C**
Sleator, W. Oddballs	**S C**
Smith, C. R. Winning words	**S C**
Somehow tenderness survives	**S C**
Soto, G. Baseball in April, and other stories	**S C**
Soto, G. Help wanted	**S C**
Soto, G. Local news	**S C**
Spinelli, J. The library card	**S C**
Sports shorts	**S C**
The Starry rift	**S C**
Swan sister	**S C**
Talking leaves	**S C**
Tan, S. Tales from outer suburbia	**S C**
This is PUSH	**S C**
Tripping over the lunch lady and other school stories	**S C**
Troll's eye view	**S C**
Twain, M. Mark Twain	**S C**
Twice told	**S C**
Ultimate sports	**S C**
Up all night	**S C**
Vande Velde, V. All Hallows' Eve	**S C**
Vande Velde, V. Being dead	**S C**
Vande Velde, V. Tales from the Brothers Grimm and the Sisters Weird	**S C**
Visions: nineteen short stories by outstanding writers for young adults	**S C**
Voices in first person	**S C**
Wallace, R. Losing is not an option: stories	**S C**
What a song can do	**S C**
What are you afraid of?	**S C**
Who do you think you are?	**S C**
Yee, P. Tales from Gold Mountain	**S C**
You never did learn to knock	**S C**
Young warriors	**S C**

Short story

Otfinoski, S. Extraordinary short story writing	**808.3**

Shoshoni Indians

Crosby, M. T. Sacagawea	**92**
St. George, J. Sacagawea	**92**

See/See also pages in the following book(s):

Freedman, R. Indian chiefs	**920**

The **Shotokan** karate bible. Martin, A. P. **796.8**

Should drilling be permitted in the Arctic National Wildlife Refuge? **333.95**

Shout, sister, shout!. Orgill, R. **920**

Show me the money. Hall, A. **332.024**

Shreve, Susan Richards

Under the Watson's porch	**Fic**

Shrimps

See/See also pages in the following book(s):

Lassieur, A. Crabs, lobsters, and shrimps	**595.3**

Shroder, John F., 1939-
(jt. auth) Gritzner, J. A. Afghanistan   **958.1**
Shrublands. Burnie, D.   **577.3**
Shrubs
Petrides, G. A. A field guide to trees and shrubs
   582.16
Shryer, Donna
Body fuel   **613.2**
Peak performance   **617.1**
Shug. Han, J.   **Fic**
Shugo chara!. Momo no Tane   **741.5**
Shulman, Mark, 1962-
Attack of the killer video book   **778.59**
Shulman, Polly
Enthusiasm   **Fic**
Shurgin, Ann H., 1952-
(ed) Junior Worldmark encyclopedia of world
   holidays. See Junior Worldmark encyclopedia
   of world holidays   **394.26**
Shurtleff, Robert *See* Sampson, Deborah, 1760-
1827
Shusterman, Neal
Antsy does time   **Fic**
Darkness creeping   **S C**
Downsiders   **Fic**
Full tilt   **Fic**
The Schwa was here   **Fic**
Unwind   **Fic**
Shute, Carolyn
(ed) Best shorts. See Best shorts   **S C**
Shuter, Jane, 1955-
Ancient China   **931**
The camp system   **940.53**
Resistance to the Nazis   **943.086**
Shutting out the sky. Hopkinson, D.   **974.7**
Shuttles, Space *See* Space shuttles
Siamese twins
Fiction
Orenstein, D. G. The secret twin   **Fic**
Siberell, Anne
Bravo! brava! a night at the opera   **792.5**
Siberia. Halam, A.   **Fic**
The **sibling** slam book   **306.8**
Siblings
See also Twins
The sibling slam book   **306.8**
Winchester, E. Sisters and brothers   **306.8**
Fiction
Aguiar, N. The lost island of Tamarind   **Fic**
Barkley, B. Jars of glass   **Fic**
Basye, D. E. Heck   **Fic**
Beaty, A. Cicada summer   **Fic**
Bemis, J. C. The nine pound hammer   **Fic**
Berlin, E. The puzzling world of Winston Breen
   Fic
Blume, J. Here's to you, Rachel Robinson
   Fic
Byars, B. C. The summer of the swans   **Fic**
Charlton-Trujillo, e. E. Feels like home   **Fic**
Cheaney, J. B. The middle of somewhere
   Fic
Choldenko, G. Al Capone does my shirts
   Fic

Cleaver, V. Where the lillies bloom   **Fic**
Cooney, C. B. If the witness lied   **Fic**
Creech, S. The Castle Corona   **Fic**
Dekker, J. C. Scum   **Fic**
DiCamillo, K. The magician's elephant   **Fic**
Dowd, S. The London Eye mystery   **Fic**
Draper, S. M. Forged by fire   **Fic**
Durrant, L. Imperfections   **Fic**
Enderle, D. Man in the moon   **Fic**
Freymann-Weyr, G. My heartbeat   **Fic**
Gates, S. Beyond the billboard   **Fic**
Gregory, N. I'll sing you one-o   **Fic**
Grimes, N. The road to Paris   **Fic**
Hahn, M. D. Hear the wind blow   **Fic**
Haig, M. Samuel Blink and the forbidden forest
   Fic
Holt, S. The Devouring   **Fic**
Horvath, P. My one hundred adventures   **Fic**
Hughes, C. Dirty magic   **Fic**
Hyde, C. R. The year of my miraculous reap-
   pearance   **Fic**
Jaramillo, A. La linea   **Fic**
Joseph, L. The color of my words   **Fic**
King, R. The quantum July   **Fic**
Klise, K. Letters from camp   **Fic**
Konigsburg, E. L. Silent to the bone   **Fic**
Landman, T. I am Apache   **Fic**
Leal, A. H. Also known as Harper   **Fic**
Lemna, D. When the sergeant came marching
   home   **Fic**
Lisle, H. The Ruby Key   **Fic**
Lord, C. Rules   **Fic**
Lurie, A. Brothers, boyfriends & other criminal
   minds   **Fic**
MacCullough, C. Drawing the ocean   **Fic**
McDaniel, L. Breathless   **Fic**
McKernan, V. The devil's paintbox   **Fic**
McNicoll, S. Last chance for Paris   **Fic**
Mordecai, M. Blue Mountain trouble   **Fic**
Nelson, T. Ruby electric   **Fic**
O'Connor, B. How to steal a dog   **Fic**
Peck, D. The lost cities   **Fic**
Peterson, W. Triskellion   **Fic**
Potter, E. Slob   **Fic**
Rodman, M. A. Jimmy's stars   **Fic**
Rollins, J. Jake Ransom and the Skull King's
   shadow   **Fic**
Russo, M. A portrait of Pia   **Fic**
Scott, M. The alchemyst   **Fic**
Sheinmel, C. My so-called family   **Fic**
Spinelli, J. Smiles to go   **Fic**
Sweeney, J. The guardian   **Fic**
Voigt, C. Dicey's song   **Fic**
Voigt, C. Homecoming   **Fic**
Vrettos, A. M. Skin   **Fic**
Wait, L. Wintering well   **Fic**
Warner, S. It's only temporary   **Fic**
Werlin, N. The rules of survival   **Fic**
Whelan, G. The Disappeared   **Fic**
Williams, M. The golden hour   **Fic**
Woodson, J. Peace, Locomotion   **Fic**
Yeomans, E. Rubber houses   **Fic**
Sick
See also Terminally ill

Solar energy
 Hirschmann, K. Solar energy **333.79**
 Walker, N. Harnessing power from the sun
  621.47

Solar radiation
 See also Greenhouse effect

Solar system
 Aguilar, D. A. 11 planets **523.4**
 Aguilar, D. A. Planets, stars, and galaxies
  520
 Bell, T. E. Earth's journey through space
  525
 Benson, M. Beyond **523.2**
 Carson, M. K. Exploring the solar system
  523.2
 Croswell, K. Ten worlds **523.4**
 VanCleave, J. P. Janice VanCleave's solar system **523.2**

Solbert, Ronni
 (il) Merrill, J. The pushcart war **Fic**

Soldier boys. Hughes, D. **Fic**

Soldier X. Wulffson, D. L. **Fic**

Soldiers
 See also Women soldiers
  Fiction
 Dowell, F. O. Shooting the moon **Fic**
 Durbin, W. The Winter War **Fic**
 Hughes, D. Soldier boys **Fic**
 Klass, S. S. Soldier's secret **Fic**
 Levine, A. Freefall **Fic**
 Rodman, M. A. Jimmy's stars **Fic**
 Shinn, S. General Winston's daughter **Fic**
  Rome
 Beller, S. P. Roman legions on the march
  937
  United States
 Beller, S. P. Battling in the Pacific **940.54**
 Beller, S. P. Billy Yank and Johnny Reb
  973.7
 Beller, S. P. The doughboys over there
  940.4
 Smithson, R. Ghosts of war **956.7**
 Stewart, G. Life of a soldier in Washington's army **973.3**
 Uschan, M. V. The cavalry during the Civil War
  973.7

Soldier's courage: the story of Stephen Crane. Lukes, B. L. **92**

Soldier's heart. Paulsen, G. **Fic**

Soldiers on the battlefront [series]
 Beller, S. P. Battling in the Pacific **940.54**
 Beller, S. P. Billy Yank and Johnny Reb
  973.7
 Beller, S. P. The doughboys over there
  940.4
 Beller, S. P. Roman legions on the march
  937

Soldier's secret. Klass, S. S. **Fic**

Solheim, James
 It's disgusting—and we ate it! **641.3**

Solids, liquids, and gases. Farndon, J. **530.4**

A **solitary** blue. Voigt, C. **Fic**

Solitude
 Crist, J. J. What to do when you're sad & lonely **158**
 Perrier, P. Flying solo **158**

Solomon, Debra
 (il) Wollard, K. How come? in the neighborhood **500**

Solomon and the ant. Oberman, S. **398.2**

Soltan, Rita
 Reading raps **027.62**

Solvent abuse
 Menhard, F. R. The facts about inhalants
  362.29

Solving Zoe. Dee, B. **Fic**

Solway, Andrew
 Africa **780.9**
 Can we travel to the stars? **629.45**
 Exploring forces and motion **531**
 Latin America and the Caribbean **780.9**
 Modern dance **792.8**
 What's inside a black hole? **523.1**
 (jt. auth) Biesty, S. Rome: in spectacular cross section **937**

Somalia
 Hassig, S. M. Somalia **967.73**

Somehow tenderness survives **S C**

Someone like summer. Kerr, M. E. **Fic**

Someone named Eva. Wolf, J. M. **Fic**

Somerlott, Robert, 1928-
 The Little Rock school desegregation crisis in American history **379**

Somervill, Barbara A., 1948-
 Brown v. Board of Education **344**
 Clara Barton **92**
 The human body **612**
 Our living world **577**
 Pierre-Auguste Renoir **92**

Something about America. Testa, M. **811**

Something about the author **920.003**

Something about the author: autobiography series
  920.003

Something funny happened at the library. Reid, R.
  027.62

Something out of nothing [biography of Marie Curie] McClafferty, C. K. **92**

Something permanent. Rylant, C. **811**

Something wicked this way comes. Bradbury, R.
  Fic

Sommer, Shelley
 John F. Kennedy **92**

Sommers, Michael A., 1966-
 Avi **92**
 Chris Crutcher **92**

Somper, Justin
 Vampirates: demons of the ocean **Fic**

Son, John
 Finding my hat **Fic**

Son of the mob. Korman, G. **Fic**

Sones, Sonya
 Stop pretending **Fic**
 What my girlfriend doesn't know **Fic**
 What my mother doesn't know **Fic**

Spy technology. Fridell, R.   327.12

Spying *See* Espionage

Spying on Miss Müller. Bunting, E.   Fic

The Squad: perfect cover. Barnes, J. L.   Fic

Squashed. Bauer, J.   Fic

Squires, Claire, 1972-
    Philip Pullman, master storyteller   823.009

The squire's tale. Morris, G.   Fic

Squire's tales [series]
    Morris, G. The squire's tale   Fic

Sri Lanka
    Wanasundera, N. P. Sri Lanka   954.93

Srinivasan, Radhika
    India   954

St. Anthony, Jane
    Grace above all   Fic
    The summer Sherman loved me   Fic

St. Antoine, Sara, 1966-
    (ed) The Great North American prairie. See The Great North American prairie   810.8

St. Crow, Lili, 1976-
    Strange angels   Fic

St. George, Judith, 1931-
    The duel: the parallel lives of Alexander Hamilton and Aaron Burr   92
    In the line of fire   364.1
    Sacagawea   92

St. John, Lauren, 1966-
    The white giraffe   Fic

St. Louis (Mo.) *See* Saint Louis (Mo.)

St. Petersburg (Russia) *See* Saint Petersburg (Russia)

Stacey, Gill
    London   942.1

Staeger, Rob
    Ancient mathematicians   920

Stafford, James, 1963-
    The European Union: facts and figures   940

Stafford, Marie Peary *See* Peary, Marie Ahnighito, 1893-1978

Stahler, David, Jr.
    Doppelganger   Fic
    A gathering of shades   Fic

Stalin, Joseph, 1879-1953
    About
    Gottfried, T. The Stalinist empire   947.084
    See/See also pages in the following book(s):
    Ross, S. Leaders of World War II   920
    Uschan, M. V. Political leaders   920

The Stalinist empire. Gottfried, T.   947.084

Stallworthy, Jon
    (ed) The Oxford book of war poetry. See The Oxford book of war poetry   808.81

Stamina, Physical *See* Physical fitness

Stamping art. Boonyadhistarn, T.   761

Stamps, Postage *See* Postage stamps

Stand tall. Bauer, J.   Fic

Standard catalog for high school libraries. See Senior high core collection   011.6

Standard cataloging for school and public libraries. Intner, S. S.   025.3

Standard hero behavior. Anderson, J. D.   Fic

Standard Oil Co. (Ohio)
    See also Standard Oil Company

Standard Oil Company
    See/See also pages in the following book(s):
    Segall, G. John D. Rockefeller   92

Standing against the wind. Jones, T. L.   Fic

Standing Bear, Ponca Chief, 1829?-1908
    See/See also pages in the following book(s):
    Brown, D. A. Bury my heart at Wounded Knee   970.004

Standing in the light. Osborne, M. P.   Fic

Standish, Myles, 1584?-1656
    About
    Harness, C. The adventurous life of Myles Standish   92

Stanford, Eleanor
    (ed) Interracial America: opposing viewpoints. See Interracial America: opposing viewpoints   305.8

Stanley, Diane, 1943-
    Bard of Avon: the story of William Shakespeare   822.3
    Bella at midnight   Fic
    Cleopatra   92
    Good Queen Bess: the story of Elizabeth I of England   92
    Joan of Arc   92
    Michelangelo   92
    The mysterious matter of I.M. Fine   Fic
    Saladin: noble prince of Islam   92

Stanley, George Edward, 1942-
    America in today's world (1969-2004)   973.92
    An emerging world power (1900-1929)   973.91
    The European settlement of North America (1492-1763)   973.2
    The New Republic (1763-1815)   973.2

Stanley, Henry M. (Henry Morton), 1841-1904
    Fiction
    Karr, K. Born for adventure   Fic

Stanley, Jerry, 1941-
    Children of the Dust Bowl   371.9

Stanton, Elizabeth Cady, 1815-1902
    About
    Sigerman, H. Elizabeth Cady Stanton   92

Stanton, Tom
    Hank Aaron and the home run that changed America   92

Staples, Suzanne Fisher
    Dangerous skies   Fic
    Shabanu   Fic
    Shiva's fire   Fic
    Under the Persimmon tree   Fic

The star guide. Kerrod, R.   523.8

The star of Kazan. Ibbotson, E.   Fic

Star Wars: a pop-up guide to the galaxy. Reinhart, M.   791.43

Star Wars: Clone wars adventures, Vol. 1. Blackman, H.   741.5

Stories for young people [series]
Poe, E. A. Edgar Allan Poe   **S C**
Twain, M. Mark Twain   **S C**
Stories from Adam and Eve to Ezekiel. Lottridge, C. B.   **220.9**
Stories from the Billabong. Marshall, J. V.   **398.2**
Stories from the life of Jesus. Lottridge, C. B.   **232.9**
Stories from where we live [series]
The Great North American prairie   **810.8**
Stories in art [series]
Harris, N. Mosaics   **738.5**
Stories without words
Tan, S. The arrival   **741.5**
Stork, Francisco X.
Marcelo in the real world   **Fic**
STORM: The Infinity Code. Young, E. L.   **Fic**
The **storm** thief. Wooding, C.   **Fic**
Stormbreaker. Horowitz, A.   **Fic**
Stormbreaker: the graphic novel. Horowitz, A.   **741.5**

Storms
> *See also* Dust storms; Hurricanes; Tornadoes

Harris, C. Wild weather   **551.55**
Stewart, M. Blizzards and winter storms   **551.55**
Treaster, J. B. Hurricane force   **551.55**
Fiction
Maguire, G. What-the-Dickens   **Fic**
Storrie, Paul D.
Beowulf   **741.5**
(jt. auth) Beechen, A. Justice League Unlimited: the ties that bind   **741.5**
The **story** of King Arthur and his knights. Pyle, H.   **398.2**
The story of Mexico [series]
Stein, R. C. Benito Juarez and the French intervention   **92**
Stein, R. C. Cortes and the Spanish Conquest   **972**
Stein, R. C. The Mexican Revolution   **972**
Stein, R. C. The Mexican War of Independence   **972**
The **story** of my life. Keller, H.   **92**
Story of science [series]
Gallant, R. A. Dance of the continents   **551.1**
Gallant, R. A. The wonders of biodiversity   **333.95**
Hakim, J. The story of science: Aristotle leads the way   **509**
Hakim, J. The story of science: Einstein adds a new dimension   **509**
Hakim, J. The story of science: Newton at the center   **509**
Parker, B. R. The mystery of gravity   **531**
Reed, G. Eyes on the universe   **520**
The **story** of science: Aristotle leads the way. Hakim, J.   **509**
The **story** of science: Einstein adds a new dimension. Hakim, J.   **509**

The **story** of science: Newton at the center. Hakim, J.   **509**
The **story** of the attack on Pearl Harbor. Whiting, J.   **940.54**
The **story** of the champions of the Round Table. Pyle, H.   **398.2**
The **story** of writing. Donoughue, C.   **411**
Story painter: the life of Jacob Lawrence. Duggleby, J.   **92**
The **story** road to literacy. Roth, R.   **372.6**
Story theater *See* Readers' theater
Storyteller. Myers, E.   **Fic**
Storytelling
Hamilton, M. Children tell stories   **372.6**
Pellowski, A. The storytelling handbook   **372.6**
Reid, R. Something funny happened at the library   **027.62**
Sima, J. Raising voices   **027.62**
Fiction
Beck, I. The secret history of Tom Trueheart   **Fic**
Blubaugh, P. Serendipity Market   **Fic**
Kladstrup, K. The book of story beginnings   **Fic**
Maguire, G. What-the-Dickens   **Fic**
Michaelis, A. Tiger moon   **Fic**
Myers, E. Storyteller   **Fic**
Priestley, C. Uncle Montague's tales of terror   **S C**
Wooding, C. Poison   **Fic**
The **storytelling** handbook. Pellowski, A.   **372.6**
Stotan!. Crutcher, C.   **Fic**
Stott, Carole
Space exploration   **629.4**
Stout, Harry S.
(ed) Braude, A. Women and American religion   **200.9**
(ed) Noll, M. A. Protestants in America   **280**
Stover, Lois T.
Jacqueline Woodson   **813.009**
Stowe, Harriet Beecher, 1811-1896
About
Fritz, J. Harriet Beecher Stowe and the Beecher preachers   **92**
Stowe, Harriet Elizabeth *See* Stowe, Harriet Beecher, 1811-1896
Stower, Adam
(il) Johnson, J. The secret country   **Fic**
Strahan, Jonathan
(ed) The Starry rift. See The Starry rift   **S C**
Strain (Psychology) *See* Stress (Psychology)
Strange angels. St. Crow, L.   **Fic**
The **strange** case of Dr. Jekyll and Mr. Hyde. Stevenson, R. L.   **Fic**
Strange happenings. Avi   **S C**
Strange relations. Levitin, S.   **Fic**
Stranger with my face. Duncan, L.   **Fic**
Strapp, James
Science and technology   **609**

Strasser, Todd, 1950-
Boot camp   Fic
Can't get there from here   Fic
If I grow up   Fic
Strategies for evaluation. Wilson, D.   370.15
Stratigraphic geology
Gallant, R. A. History   551.7
Stratton, Allan
Chanda's secrets   Fic
Straub, Deborah Gillan
(ed) U.X.L Asian American voices. See U.X.L
Asian American voices   815.008
Strauss, Levi, 1829-1902
See/See also pages in the following book(s):
Kent, J. Business builders in fashion   920
Stravaganza: city of masks. Hoffman, M.   Fic
Stray. Goldblatt, S.   Fic
Straydog. Koja, K.   Fic
Strays. Koertge, R.   Fic
Strays like us. Peck, R.   Fic
Streams to the river, river to the sea. O'Dell, S.
       Fic
Street gangs *See* Gangs
Street love. Myers, W. D.   Fic
Street people *See* Homeless persons
A **street** through time. Millard, A.   936
Streiffert, Kristi
(jt. auth) Kott, J. Nicaragua   972.85
Streissguth, Thomas
Brazil in pictures   981
Clay v. United States and how Muhammad Ali
fought the draft   343
Legendary labor leaders   920
Media bias   302.23
Vladimir Putin   92
(ed) Custer's last stand. See Custer's last stand
       973.8
(ed) The Rise of the Soviet Union. See The
Rise of the Soviet Union   947.084
The **strength** of these arms. Bial, R.   326
Stress (Psychology)
     See also Anxiety; Post-traumatic stress dis-
order
Bingham, J. Stress and depression   616.85
Evans-Martin, F. Emotion and stress   612.8
Fox, A. Too stressed to think?   158
Hyde, M. O. Stress 101   616.85
Reber, D. Chill   613
Wells, D. K. Live aware, not in fear   158
Stress 101. Hyde, M. O.   616.85
Stress and depression. Bingham, J.   616.85
Strickland, Brad
The sign of the sinister sorcerer   Fic
Strike a pose. Birkemoe, K.   613.7
Strikes
Baker, J. The Bread and Roses strike of 1912
       331.8
Bartoletti, S. C. Kids on strike!   331.8
Laughlin, R. The Ludlow massacre of 1913-14
       331.8
Laughlin, R. The Pullman strike of 1894
       331.8

Whitelaw, N. The Homestead Steel Strike of
1892   331.8
       Fiction
Haddix, M. P. Uprising   Fic
Paterson, K. Bread and roses, too   Fic
Stripling, Barbara K.
(ed) Curriculum connections through the library.
See Curriculum connections through the li-
brary   027.8
Strong at the heart   362.7
Strong force [biography of Shirley Ann Jackson]
O'Connell, D.   92
A **strong** right arm: the story of Mamie "Peanut"
Johnson. Green, M. Y.   92
Strong stuff. Harris, J.   398.2
Strother, Scott
The adventurous book of outdoor games
       796
Stroud, Bettye, 1939-
The Reconstruction era   973.8
Stroud, Jonathan, 1970-
The Amulet of Samarkand   Fic
Heroes of the valley   Fic
Structural engineering
Bos, S. Super structures   720
Malam, J. Super structures   624
Struggling to become American. Doak, R. S.
       305.8
Stuart-Clark, Christopher
(ed) The Oxford book of story poems. See The
Oxford book of story poems   808.81
Stuck in neutral. Trueman, T.   Fic
Stuck in the middle   741.5
Stuckenschneider, Dan
(il) Tomecek, S. What a great idea!   609
Student almanac of African American history
       305.8
Student almanac of Native American history
       970.004
Student Atlas   912
Student cheating *See* Cheating (Education)
Student dishonesty *See* Cheating (Education)
Student drug testing   371.7
Student movement *See* Youth movement
Student success and library media programs. Far-
mer, L. S. J.   027.8
Students
     See also High school students
       Civil rights
Student drug testing   371.7
       Law and legislation
Gold, S. D. Vernonia School District v. Acton
       344
Kowalski, K. M. The Earls case and the student
drug testing debate   344
Phillips, T. A. Hazelwood v. Kuhlmeier and the
school newspaper censorship debate   342
A **student's** guide to Arthur Miller. Dunkleberger,
A.   812.009
A **Student's** guide to biotechnology   660.6
A **student's** guide to Edgar Allan Poe. McArthur,
D.   813.009

A **student's** guide to Emily Dickinson. Borus, A. **811.009**

A **student's** guide to Ernest Hemingway. Pingelton, T. J. **813.009**

A **student's** guide to George Orwell. Means, A. L. **828**

A **student's** guide to Herman Melville. Diorio, M. A. L. **813.009**

A **student's** guide to Mark Twain. Diorio, M. A. L. **813.009**

A **student's** guide to mental health & wellness **616.89**

A **student's** guide to Robert Frost. Kirk, C. A. **811.009**

A **student's** guide to Toni Morrison. Crayton, L. A. **813.009**

Students on strike. Stokes, J. **379**

Study, Method of See Study skills

Study skills
Fox, J. S. Get organized without losing it **371.3**

Stueart, Robert D.
Library and information center management **025.1**

Sturgis, Alexander
Optical illusions in art **750.1**

Sturm, James, 1965-
Satchel Paige **741.5**

Sturtevant, Katherine, 1950-
A true and faithful narrative **Fic**

Stuve-Bodeen, Stephanie See Bodeen, S. A., 1965-

Stuyvesant High School (New York, N.Y.)
With their eyes **812.008**

Suarez, Ana Veciana- See Veciana-Suarez, Ana

Sub-Saharan Africa
Oppong, J. R. Africa South of the Sahara **967**

Subject catalogs
Subject guide to Books in print **015.73**
Subject guide to Children's books in print **015.73**

Subject guide to Books in print **015.73**

Subject guide to Children's books in print **015.73**

Subject headings
Sears list of subject headings **025.4**

Submarine exploration See Underwater exploration

Submarine geology
Erickson, J. Marine geology **551.46**

Submarines
Lefkowitz, A. S. Bushnell's submarine **973.3**
Stefoff, R. Submarines **623.82**
Walker, S. M. Secrets of a Civil War submarine **973.7**
Fiction
Carlson, D. Attack of the Turtle **Fic**
Verne, J. 20,000 leagues under the sea **Fic**

Substance abuse See Drug abuse

Suburban life
Fiction
Tan, S. Tales from outer suburbia **S C**

Subways
DuTemple, L. A. The New York subways **388.4**
Sandler, M. W. Secret subway **388.4**
See/See also pages in the following book(s):
Macaulay, D. Underground **624**
Fiction
Shusterman, N. Downsiders **Fic**

Success
See also Academic achievement
Bachel, B. K. What do you really want? **153.8**
Rimm, S. B. See Jane win for girls **305.23**

Suciu, Peter
(jt. auth) Gerardi, D. Careers in the computer game industry **794.8**

Suck it up. Meehl, B. **Fic**

Suckerpunch. Hernandez, D. **Fic**

Sudan
Dalton, D. Living in a refugee camp **305.23**
Levy, P. Sudan **962.4**
History—Darfur conflict, 2003-
Xavier, J. Darfur **962.4**

Suellentrop, Tricia, 1970-
(jt. auth) Gorman, M. Connecting young adults and libraries **027.62**

Suffrage
See also African Americans—Suffrage; Women—Suffrage
Connolly, S. The right to vote **324.6**
Declare yourself **323**

The **suffragists** in literature for youth. Mosley, S. **016.3**

Sugar Princess volume 1: skating to win. Nakajo, H. **741.5**

Sugihara, Chiune See Sugihara, Sempo, 1900-1986

Sugihara, Sempo, 1900-1986
See/See also pages in the following book(s):
Lyman, D. Holocaust rescuers **920**

Suicide
Nelson, R. E. The power to prevent suicide **362.28**
Powell, J. Self-harm and suicide **616.85**
Runyon, B. The burn journals **92**
Salomon, R. Suicide **616.85**
Stefoff, R. The right to die **179.7**
Suicide: opposing viewpoints **362.28**
Fiction
Asher, J. Thirteen reasons why **Fic**
Cohn, R. You know where to find me **Fic**
Ford, M. T. Suicide notes **Fic**
Foxlee, K. The anatomy of wings **Fic**
Fullerton, A. Walking on glass **Fic**
Hemphill, S. Things left unsaid **Fic**
Heneghan, J. Payback **Fic**
Maynard, J. The cloud chamber **Fic**
McClintock, N. Dooley takes the fall **Fic**
McDaniel, L. Breathless **Fic**
Miller, M. B. Aimee **Fic**
Trueman, T. Inside out **Fic**

The **swan** maiden. Tomlinson, H.   **Fic**
Swan sister   **S C**
Swan, Vol. 1. Ariyoshi, K.   **741.5**
Swans
  Osborn, E. Project UltraSwan   **598**
Swanson, James L.
  Chasing Lincoln's killer   **92**
Swanson, Julie A., 1964-
  Going for the record   **Fic**
Sweat and blood. Skurzynski, G.   **331.8**
Sweden
  Gan, D. Sweden   **948.5**
  Phillips, C. Sweden   **948.5**
         Fiction
  Mankell, H. A bridge to the stars   **Fic**
Sweeney, Joyce, 1955-
  The guardian   **Fic**
Sweeney, Mary Ellen
  (jt. auth) Wood, K. The 101 best tropical fishes
         639.34
Sweet, Melissa
  (il) Thimmesh, C. Girls think of everything
         920
  (il) Thimmesh, C. The sky's the limit   **500**
Sweet!. Love, A.   **641.8**
The **sweet,** terrible, glorious year I truly, completely lost it. Shanahan, L.   **Fic**
Sweet Thang. Whittenberg, A.   **Fic**
Sweet victory: Lance Armstrong's incredible journey. Stewart, M.   **92**
Sweetblood. Hautman, P.   **Fic**
Sweetgrass basket. Carvell, M.   **Fic**
Sweethearts. Zarr, S.   **Fic**
Swerling, Lisa
  (il) MacLeod, J. How nearly everything was invented . . . by the Brainwaves   **609**
Swett, Sarah
  Kids weaving   **746.41**
Swift, Jonathan, 1667-1745
  Gulliver's travels   **Fic**
Swifter, higher, stronger. Macy, S.   **796.48**
Swim the fly. Calame, D.   **Fic**
Swimming
  Timblin, S. Swimming   **797.2**
         Fiction
  Calame, D. Swim the fly   **Fic**
  Crutcher, C. Staying fat for Sarah Byrnes
         Fic
  Crutcher, C. Stotan!   **Fic**
  Crutcher, C. Whale talk   **Fic**
  Mayall, B. Mermaid Park   **Fic**
Swimming to America. Mead, A.   **Fic**
Swimming upstream. George, K. O.   **811**
Swimming with hammerhead sharks. Mallory, K.   **597**
Swinburne, Stephen R.
  Once a wolf   **333.95**
  Saving manatees   **599.5**
  The woods scientist   **591.7**
Swindlers. Blackwood, G. L.   **364.1**

Swindlers and swindling
  Blackwood, G. L. Swindlers   **364.1**
  Schroeder, A. Scams!   **364.1**
         Fiction
  Avi. The seer of shadows   **Fic**
  Barker, M. P. A difficult boy   **Fic**
  De Guzman, M. The bamboozlers   **Fic**
  Graff, L. The life and crimes of Bernetta Wallflower   **Fic**
  Heneghan, J. The magician's apprentice   **Fic**
  Jocelyn, M. How it happened in Peach Hill
         Fic
  LaFaye, A. Stella stands alone   **Fic**
Swish. Stewart, M.   **796.323**
Swisher, Clarice, 1933-
  Women of the roaring twenties   **305.4**
Swiss mist. Powell, R.   **Fic**
Swissler, Becky
  Winning lacrosse for girls   **796.34**
Switch. Snow, C.   **Fic**
Switched. Wollman, J.   **Fic**
Switzerland
  Levy, P. Switzerland   **949.4**
         Fiction
  Creech, S. Bloomability   **Fic**
Sword. Chen, D.   **Fic**
The **sword** in the stone. White, T. H.
  In White, T. H. The once and future king
         Fic
Sword song. Sutcliff, R.   **Fic**
Sylvie and the songman. Binding, T.   **Fic**
Symbiosis
  Silverstein, A. Symbiosis   **577.8**
Symbolism of numbers
    See also Numbers
Symbols *See* Signs and symbols
Symes, R. F.
  Crystal & gem   **548**
  Eyewitness rocks & minerals   **549**
Symons, Ann K.
  Protecting the right to read   **025.2**
Synesthesia
         Fiction
  Mass, W. A mango-shaped space   **Fic**
  Parkinson, S. Blue like Friday   **Fic**
Syphilis
  Uschan, M. V. Forty years of medical racism
         174.2
Syria
  South, C. Syria   **956.91**
         Fiction
  Jolin, P. In the name of God   **Fic**
Szabo, Ross
  Behind happy faces   **616.89**
Szeptycki, Andreas *See* Sheptyts´kyĭ, Andriĭ, 1865-1944
Szuc, Jeff
  (il) Scowen, K. My kind of sad   **616.85**

Teens in Cuba. Donovan, S.   **972.91**

Teens in Finland. Skog, J.   **948.97**

Teens in Ghana. Weatherly, M.   **966.7**

Teens in Iran. Seidman, D.   **955**

Teens in Morocco. Donovan, S.   **964**

Teens in Nepal. Yackley-Franken, N.   **954.96**

Teens in Peru. Donovan, S.   **985**

Teens in South Africa. Seidman, D.   **968**

Teens in the Philippines. Skog, J.   **959.9**

Teens in Turkey. Lilly, A.   **956.1**

Teens, technology, and literacy; or, Why bad grammar isn't always bad. Braun, L. W.   **373.1**

Teens @ the library series
Braun, L. W. Hooking teens with the Net   **025.04**
Bromann, J. Booktalking that works   **028.5**
Bromann, J. More booktalking that works   **028.5**
Doyle, M. 101+ great ideas for teen library Web sites   **027.62**
Honnold, R. 101+ teen programs that work   **027.62**
Honnold, R. More teen programs that work   **027.62**
Honnold, R. The teen reader's advisor   **028.5**
Hubert, J. Reading rants   **011.6**
Jones, P. Do it right!   **027.62**
Miller, S. Developing and promoting graphic novel collections   **025.2**
Mondowney, J. G. Hold them in your heart   **027.62**

Teitelbaum, Michael, 1953-
Baseball   **796.357**

Telecommunication
> *See also* Computer networks; Electronic mail systems

Henderson, H. Communications and broadcasting   **384**

Telegraph
Coe, L. The telegraph   **621.383**
Zannos, S. Guglielmo Marconi and the story of radio waves   **92**

Telekinesis *See* Psychokinesis

Telemarking *See* Skiing

Telepathy
Fiction
Mitchard, J. The midnight twins   **Fic**
Ness, P. The knife of never letting go   **Fic**

Telephone
Kummer, P. K. The telephone   **621.385**
Stefoff, R. The telephone   **621.385**

Teleprocessing networks *See* Computer networks

Telereference *See* Information networks

Telescopes
> *See also* Hubble Space Telescope

Matloff, G. L. More telescope power   **522**
Stefoff, R. Microscopes and telescopes   **502.8**

Television
Otfinoski, S. Television   **621.388**
See/See also pages in the following book(s):
Mass media: opposing viewpoints   **302.23**

Equipment and supplies
> *See also* Video recording
Fiction
Atinsky, S. Tyler on prime time   **Fic**
Van Etten, D. Likely story   **Fic**

Television actors *See* Actors

Television and children
See/See also pages in the following book(s):
Mass media: opposing viewpoints   **302.23**

Television broadcasting
Wan Guofang. TV takeover   **384.55**

Television broadcasting of news
Garner, J. We interrupt this broadcast   **070.1**
Reeves, D. L. TV journalist   **070.4**

Television industry *See* Television broadcasting

Television journalism *See* Broadcast journalism

Television programs
Fiction
Collins, Y. The Black Sheep   **Fic**
Deriso, C. H. Talia Talk   **Fic**

Telgen, Diane
Brown v. Board of Education   **344**

Tell all the children our story. Bolden, T.   **305.8**

Tell the world   **811.008**

Telling the tale. Bodden, V.   **808.3**

Temerson, Catherine
(jt. auth) Stolz, J. The shadows of Ghadames   **Fic**

Temko, Florence
Origami holiday decorations for Christmas, Hanukkah, and Kwanzaa   **736**

Temperance
> *See also* Drinking of alcoholic beverages; Prohibition

Temperate forests. Allaby, M.   **577.3**

Temperate grasslands. Hoare, B.   **577.4**

Temperature
Gardner, R. Science projects about temperature and heat   **536**
Sullivan, N. Temperature   **536**

Temping fate. Friesner, E. M.   **Fic**

Temple, Charles A., 1947-
Children's books in children's hands. See Children's books in children's hands   **028.5**

Temple, Frances, 1945-1995
The Beduins' gazelle   **Fic**
The Ramsay scallop   **Fic**

Temple, Kathryn
Drawing   **741.2**

Temples
DuTemple, L. A. The Pantheon   **726**

Tempo change. Hall, B.   **Fic**

Ten kings. Meltzer, M.   **920**

Ten kings & queens who changed the world. See Gifford, C. 10 kings & queens who changed the world   **920**

Ten lucky things that have happened to me since I nearly got hit by lightning. See Hershey, M. 10 lucky things that have happened to me since I nearly got hit by lightning   **Fic**

Ten Mile River. Griffin, P.   **Fic**

The **thirteen** colonies [series]. Doherty, C. A. **973.2**

Thirteen reasons why. Asher, J. **Fic**

Thirteenth century *See* World history—13th century

The **thirteenth** child. Wrede, P. C. **Fic**

Thirty days to finding and keeping sassy sidekicks and BFFs. See Hantman, C. 30 days to finding and keeping sassy sidekicks and BFFs **158**

Thirty days to getting over the dork you used to call your boyfriend. See Hantman, C. 30 days to getting over the dork you used to call your boyfriend **158**

Thirty three things every girl should know. See 33 things every girl should know **810.8**

Thirty three things every girl should know about women's history. See 33 things every girl should know about women's history **305.4**

This is PUSH **S C**

This is what I did. Ellis, A. D. **Fic**

This land was made for you and me: the life and songs of Woody Guthrie. Partridge, E. **92**

This our dark country. Reef, C. **966.62**

Thisdale, François, 1964-
(il) Pinsker, M. In the days of sand and stars **296.1**

Thomas, Jane Resh, 1936-
Behind the mask: the life of Queen Elizabeth I **92**
Blind mountain **Fic**

Thomas, Joyce Carol
The skull talks back and other haunting tales **398.2**
(ed) Linda Brown, you are not alone. See Linda Brown, you are not alone **323.1**

Thomas, Keltie
Bear rescue **599.78**
Blades, boards & scooters **796.2**
How basketball works **796.323**

Thomas, Peggy
Big cat conservation **333.95**
Bird alert **333.95**

Thomas, Rebecca L.
Popular series fiction for middle school and teen readers **016.8**

Thomas, Valerie
See/See also pages in the following book(s):
Thimmesh, C. Girls think of everything **920**

Thomas, Velma Maia
Lest we forget **326**

Thomas, Vickie, 1950-
(jt. auth) Closter, K. Fiction, food, and fun **028.5**

Thomas Edison for kids. Carlson, L. M. **92**

Thomason, Mark
Moonrunner **Fic**

Thompson, Bill, III, 1962-
The young birder's guide to birds of eastern North America **598**

Thompson, Cliff
(ed) Current biography yearbook, 2008. See Current biography yearbook, 2008 **920.003**
(ed) World authors, 1995-2000. See World authors, 1995-2000 **920.003**

Thompson, Jeffrey, 1970-
(jt. auth) Longfellow, H. W. Hiawatha and Megissogwon **811**

Thompson, John, 1940-
(il) Lewis, J. P. Freedom like sunlight **811**

Thompson, Kate
Fourth World **Fic**
The new policeman **Fic**

Thompson, Sharon Elaine, 1952-
Built for speed **599.75**

Thoms, Annie
(ed) With their eyes. See With their eyes **812.008**

Thomson, Melissa
Women of the Renaissance **940.2**
(jt. auth) Dean, R. Teen prostitution **362.7**

Thomson, Sarah L.
Obama **92**
The secret of the Rose **Fic**
(jt. auth) Mortenson, G. Three cups of tea **954.91**

Thoreau, Henry David, 1817-1862
About
Meltzer, M. Henry David Thoreau **92**
Fiction
Hausman, G. A mind with wings **Fic**
Vaupel, R. My contract with Henry **Fic**
Graphic novels
Porcellino, J. Thoreau at Walden **818**

Thoreau at Walden. Porcellino, J. **818**

Thorne-Thomsen, Kathleen
Greene & Greene for kids [biography of Charlie & Henry Greene] **92**

Thornspell. Lowe, H. **Fic**

Thornton, Denise, 1949-
Physical disabilities **362.4**

Thorpe, James Francis *See* Thorpe, Jim, 1888-1953

Thorpe, Jim, 1888-1953
About
Bruchac, J. Jim Thorpe **92**

Those amazing musical instruments. Helsby, G. **784.19**

Those courageous women of the Civil War. Zeinert, K. **973.7**

Thought and thinking
See also Perception

The **thought** of high windows. Kositsky, L. **Fic**

Thought transference *See* Telepathy

The **thoughtful** researcher. Rankin, V. **027.62**

A **thousand** never evers. Burg, S. **Fic**

A **thousand** peaks. Liu Siyu **895.1**

Threatened species *See* Endangered species

Three across. Finkelstein, N. H. **629.13**

Three clams and an oyster. Powell, R. **Fic**

Three cups of tea. Mortenson, G. **954.91**
Three hundred B.C. See Service, P. F. 300 B.C. **930**
Three little words. Rhodes-Courter, A. M. **92**
The three musketeers. Dumas, A. **Fic**
Three wishes. Ellis, D. **956.94**
Through artists' eyes [series]
  Bingham, J. Emotion & relationships **704.9**
  Bingham, J. Landscape & the environment **704.9**
  Bingham, J. Science & technology **704.9**
  Bingham, J. Society & class **704.9**
Through the eyes of your ancestors. Taylor, M. **929**
Through the lock. Hurst, C. O. **Fic**
Through the looking-glass. Baker, K. **741.5**
Throwing like a girl. Mackey, W. K. **Fic**
Thunder lizards. See Miller, S. Dinosaurs: how to draw thunder lizards and other prehistoric beasts **743**
Thunder rolling in the mountains. O'Dell, S. **Fic**
Thurlo, Aimée
  The spirit line **Fic**
Thurlo, David
  (jt. auth) Thurlo, A. The spirit line **Fic**
Tibet (China)
  Demi. The Dalai Lama **92**
  Kimmel, E. C. Boy on the lion throne [biography of the Dalai Lama] **92**
  Kummer, P. K. Tibet **951**
  Levy, P. Tibet **951**
  Sís, P. Tibet **951**
Tick-borne diseases
  Colligan, L. H. Tick-borne illnesses **616.9**
Tick-borne illnesses. Colligan, L. H. **616.9**
Ticks
  See also Lyme disease
Tidal waves, Seismic *See* Tsunamis
Tienda, Marta
  About
  O'Connell, D. People person [biography of Marta Tienda] **92**
Tiernan, Cate, 1961-
  A chalice of wind **Fic**
Ties that bind, ties that break. Namioka, L. **Fic**
Tiffany, Grace, 1958-
  Ariel **Fic**
Tiffany, Sean
  (jt. auth) Maddox, J. Free throw **Fic**
Tigelaar, Liz
  Pretty tough **Fic**
Tiger, Caroline
  Isamu Noguchi **92**
  Margaret Cho **92**
Tiger eyes. Blume, J. **Fic**
Tiger moon. Michaelis, A. **Fic**
Tiger rescue. Bortolotti, D. **333.95**
Tiger Woods. Roberts, J. **92**

Tigers
  Bortolotti, D. Tiger rescue **333.95**
  Montgomery, S. The man-eating tigers of Sundarbans **599.75**
  Fiction
  Michaelis, A. Tiger moon **Fic**
Tighe, Mary Ann
  Sharon Creech **813.009**
Tikal. Mann, E. **972.81**
Tilden, Thomasine E. Lewis, 1958-
  Help! What's eating my flesh? **614.4**
Till, Emmett
  About
  Aretha, D. The murder of Emmett Till **364.1**
  Crowe, C. Getting away with murder: the true story of the Emmett Till case **364.1**
  Fiction
  Crowe, C. Mississippi trial, 1955 **Fic**
  Poetry
  Nelson, M. A wreath for Emmett Till **811**
Tillage, Leon, 1936-
  Leon's story **92**
Tilley, Debbie
  (jt. auth) George, K. O. Swimming upstream **811**
  (il) Jukes, M. Growing up: it's a girl thing **612.6**
  (il) Jukes, M. It's a girl thing **305.23**
Tilly, Meg
  Porcupine **Fic**
Tilton, Rafael, 1929-
  Henry Ford **92**
Tim, defender of the Earth!. Enthoven, S. **Fic**
Timblin, Stephen
  Swimming **797.2**
Time
  See also Night
  Collier, J. L. Clocks **681.1**
  Farndon, J. Time **529**
  Sullivan, N. Time **529**
  Fiction
  McNamee, E. The Navigator **Fic**
  Peck, D. Drift House: the first voyage **Fic**
  Peck, D. The lost cities **Fic**
Time and space *See* Space and time
Time bomb. Hinton, N. **Fic**
Time management
  Fox, J. S. Get organized without losing it **371.3**
  Morgenstern, J. Organizing from the inside out for teens **646.7**
Time of the eagle. Jordan, S. **Fic**
Time quest book [series]
  Beattie, O. Buried in ice **998**
Time stops for no mouse. Hoeye, M. **Fic**
Time travel
  Fiction
  Cockcroft, J. Counter clockwise **Fic**
  Mason, T. The last synapsid **Fic**
Time travel guide [series]
  Bingham, J. The Aztec empire **972**
  Bingham, J. The Inca empire **985**

The **tough** guide to Fantasyland. Jones, D. W.   **828**

Tough times. Meltzer, M.   **Fic**

Toupin, Laurie, 1963-
Freshwater habitats   **577.6**
Life in the temperate grasslands   **577.4**
Savannas   **577.4**

Tourette syndrome
Brill, M. T. Tourette syndrome   **616.8**

Touro Synagogue (Newport, R.I.)
Fisher, L. E. To bigotry, no sanction   **296**

Toussaint, Pierre, 1766-1853
See/See also pages in the following book(s):
Haskins, J. African American entrepreneurs   **920**

Toussaint Louverture, 1743?-1803
About
Rockwell, A. F. Open the door to liberty!: a biography of Toussaint L'Ouverture   **92**

Town and country life. Chrisp, P.   **940.1**

Town Boy. Lat   **741.5**

Town planning *See* City planning

Townesend, Frances Eliza Hodgson Burnett *See* Burnett, Frances Hodgson, 1849-1924

Townley, Rod
Sky   **Fic**

Towns *See* Cities and towns

Townsend, John, 1955-
Crazy chemistry   **540**
Crime through time   **364**
Foolish physics   **530**
Pills, powders & potions   **615**
Pox, pus & plague   **616**
Predicting the effects of climate change   **363.7**
Prisons and prisoners   **365**
Punishment and pain   **364.6**
Scalpels, stitches & scars   **617**

Townsend, Wendy
Lizard love   **Fic**

Toxic substances *See* Poisons and poisoning

Toys
Haden, C. Creepy cute crochet   **746.43**
Rigsby, M. Amazing rubber band cars   **745.592**
Rimoli, A. P. Amigurumi world   **746.43**
Snow, T. Tiny yarn animals   **746.43**

Track athletics
See also Running
Hotchkiss, R. The matchless six   **796.48**
Housewright, E. Winning track and field for girls   **796.42**
Manley, C. B. Competitive track and field for girls   **796.42**
Fiction
Wallace, R. One good punch   **Fic**

Tracking and trailing
Johnson, J. Animal tracks & signs   **590**

Tracking trash. Burns, L. G.   **551.46**

Tracktown summer. Holmes, E. A.   **Fic**

Tracy, Kathleen
The Clinton view   **92**
The life and times of Rosa Parks   **92**

Trade routes
Major, J. S. The Silk Route   **950**

Trade unions *See* Labor unions

Trades *See* Occupations

Traffic accidents
See also Drunk driving
Crash   **617.1**
Mintzer, R. The National Transportation Safety Board   **363.1**
Fiction
Bruchac, J. Whisper in the dark   **Fic**
Frank, E. R. Wrecked   **Fic**
Jocelyn, M. Would you   **Fic**
Johnson, P. What happened   **Fic**
McDaniel, L. Hit and run   **Fic**
McGhee, A. All rivers flow to the sea   **Fic**
Mitchard, J. All we know of heaven   **Fic**
Newbery, L. Lost boy   **Fic**
Schmidt, G. D. Trouble   **Fic**

Trafficking in drugs *See* Drug traffic

Tragedies of space exploration. Mayell, M.   **363.1**

The **tragic** history of the Japanese-American internment camps. Kent, D.   **940.53**

The **tragic** tale of Narcissa Whitman and a faithful history of the Oregon Trail. Harness, C.   **92**

The **Trail** of Tears. Elish, D.   **970.004**

The **trail** West. Galford, E.   **978**

Trailblazer biography [series]
Brill, M. T. Marshall "Major" Taylor   **92**
Harrah, M. Blind Boone   **92**
Havelin, K. Victoria Woodhull   **92**
Johnson, R. L. Ernest Shackleton   **92**
Manheimer, A. S. Martin Luther King Jr   **92**
Márquez, H. Roberto Clemente   **92**
Norgren, J. Belva Lockwood   **92**
O'Connor, B. Leonardo da Vinci   **92**

Trailblazers. Katz, B.   **811**

Trailblazers [series]
Hart, P. S. Up in the air: the story of Bessie Coleman   **92**
O'Connor, B. Barefoot dancer: the story of Isadora Duncan   **92**

Trailblazers of the modern world [series]
Burgan, M. John F. Kennedy   **92**
Macdonald, F. Winston Churchill   **92**

Trailing *See* Tracking and trailing

The **train** jumper. Brown, D.   **Fic**

Training, Occupational *See* Occupational training

Trains, Railroad *See* Railroads

Traitor. McNab, A.   **Fic**

Traitor. Pausewang, G.   **Fic**

The **traitor.** Yep, L.   **Fic**

The **Traitor** King. Mitchell, T.   **Fic**

Traitor: the case of Benedict Arnold. Fritz, J.   **92**

Traitor's gate. Avi   **Fic**

Traitors' Gate and other doorways to the past. Eamer, C.   **909**

The **trial** of the police officers in the shooting death of Amadou Diallo. Fireside, B. J.

The **trial** of the Scottsboro boys. Aretha, D. 345

Trials
Aaseng, N. You are the juror 345
Aretha, D. The trial of the Scottsboro boys 345
Crewe, S. The Scottsboro case 345
Fireside, B. J. The trial of the police officers in the shooting death of Amadou Diallo
Jarrow, G. The printer's trial 345
Margulies, P. The devil on trial 345
Pellowski, M. The terrorist trial of the 1993 bombing of the World Trade Center 974.7
Sergis, D. K. Cipollone v. Liggett Group 346.03
Sorensen, L. The Scottsboro Boys Trial 345
Fiction
Myers, W. D. Monster **Fic**

Trials (Homicide)
Crowe, C. Getting away with murder: the true story of the Emmett Till case 364.1
Pellowski, M. The O.J. Simpson murder trial 345

Trials (Murder) *See* Trials (Homicide)

Triangle histories, Revolutionary War [series]
Ingram, S. King George III 92

Triangle Shirtwaist Company, Inc.
Getzinger, D. The Triangle Shirtwaist Factory fire 974.7
Houle, M. M. Triangle Shirtwaist Factory fire 974.7
Fiction
Auch, M. J. Ashes of roses **Fic**
Davies, J. Lost **Fic**
Haddix, M. P. Uprising **Fic**
Lieurance, S. The locket **Fic**
The **Triangle** Shirtwaist Factory fire. Getzinger, D. 974.7
Triangle Shirtwaist Factory fire. Houle, M. M. 974.7

Triathlon
Fiction
Crutcher, C. Ironman **Fic**

Tricks
See also Magic tricks

Trickster's choice. Pierce, T. **Fic**

Triple-dare to be scared. San Souci, R. **S C**

Tripping over the lunch lady and other school stories **S C**

Triskellion. Peterson, W. **Fic**

Triumph of the imagination: the story of writer J.K. Rowling. Chippendale, L. A. 92

Triumphs and struggles for Latino civil rights. Cruz, B. · 323.1

Trivia *See* Curiosities and wonders

Trojan War
Fleischman, P. Dateline: Troy 292
McCarty, N. The Iliad 883
See/See also pages in the following book(s):
Hamilton, E. Mythology 292

Fiction
Geras, A. Ithaka **Fic**
Geras, A. Troy **Fic**
Troll Bridge. Yolen, J. **Fic**
Troll Fell. Langrish, K. **Fic**
Trolls
Fiction
French, V. The robe of skulls **Fic**
Helgerson, J. Horns & wrinkles **Fic**
Langrish, K. Troll Fell **Fic**
Pike, A. Wings **Fic**
Troll's eye view **S C**
Trondheim, Lewis
Tiny Tyrant 741.5
(jt. auth) Sfar, J. Dungeon Vol. 1: Duck Heart 741.5
Tropical fish
Wood, K. The 101 best tropical fishes 639.34
Tropical forests. Jackson, T. 577.3
Tropical rain forests *See* Rain forests
Tropical secrets. Engle, M. **Fic**
Tropics
Gritzner, C. F. The tropics 910
The **tropics**. Gritzner, C. F. 910
Trottier, Maxine
Native crafts 745.5
Sister to the wolf **Fic**
Trouble. Schmidt, G. D. **Fic**
The **trouble** begins at 8: a life of Mark Twain in the wild, wild West. Fleischman, S. 92
The **trouble** with Cupid. Langston, L. **Fic**
Troy. Geras, A. **Fic**
Trucks
Fiction
Merrill, J. The pushcart war **Fic**
Trudeau, Noah Andre, 1949-
Like men of war 973.7
The **true** adventures of Charley Darwin. Meyer, C. **Fic**
A **true** and faithful narrative. Sturtevant, K. **Fic**
True confessions of a heartless girl. Brooks, M. **Fic**
True love, the sphinx, and other unsolvable riddles. O'Connell, T. **Fic**
The **true** meaning of Smekday. Rex, A. **Fic**
True stories from the edge [series]
Schroeder, A. Scams! 364.1
True talents. Lubar, D. **Fic**
Trueit, Trudi Strain
ADHD 616.85
Earthquakes 551.2
Fossils 560
Gunpowder 623.4
Keeping a journal 808
Rocks, gems, and minerals 552
Surviving divorce 306.89
Volcanoes 551.2
Trueman, Terry
7 days at the hot corner **Fic**

Twilight zone (Television program)
Graphic novels
Serling, R. The twilight zone: the after hours
741.5
Serling, R. The Twilight Zone: walking distance
741.5
The **twilight** zone: the after hours. Serling, R.
741.5
The **Twilight** Zone: walking distance. Serling, R.
741.5

Twins
Fiction
Barber, T. Go long!   **Fic**
Binder, M. The brothers Schlemiel   **Fic**
Bodeen, S. A. The Compound   **Fic**
Clayton, E. The roar   **Fic**
Doyle, M. Bewitching season   **Fic**
Duncan, L. Stranger with my face   **Fic**
Gates, S. Beyond the billboard   **Fic**
Gregory, N. I'll sing you one-o   **Fic**
Heuston, K. B. The Book of Jude   **Fic**
Higgins, J. Sure fire   **Fic**
Kelly, T. Finn's going   **Fic**
MacCullough, C. Drawing the ocean   **Fic**
Matthews, L. S. Lexi   **Fic**
McClymer, K. Must love black   **Fic**
McNicoll, S. Last chance for Paris   **Fic**
Mitchard, J. The midnight twins   **Fic**
Mordecai, M. Blue Mountain trouble   **Fic**
Moses, S. P. The baptism   **Fic**
Mourlevat, J.-C. The pull of the ocean   **Fic**
Nuzum, K. A. A small white scar   **Fic**
Orenstein, D. G. The secret twin   **Fic**
Paterson, K. Jacob have I loved   **Fic**
Peterson, W. Triskellion   **Fic**
Scott, M. The alchemyst   **Fic**
Sleator, W. Singularity   **Fic**
Smith, R. Cryptid hunters   **Fic**
Somper, J. Vampirates: demons of the ocean
Fic
Tiernan, C. A chalice of wind   **Fic**
Wrede, P. C. The thirteenth child   **Fic**
Zink, M. Prophecy of the sisters   **Fic**
Twists and turns. McDonald, J.   **Fic**
Two girls of Gettysburg. Klein, L. M.   **Fic**
Two hot dogs with everything. Haven, P. **Fic**
Two in the wilderness. Weber, S.   **508**
Two novels: Baby; Journey. MacLachlan, P.
Fic
Two thousand and one: a space odyssey. See
Clarke, A. C. 2001: a space odyssey **Fic**
Twomey, Cathleen
Beachmont letters   **Fic**
Tyge See Brahe, Tycho, 1546-1601
Tyler on prime time. Atinsky, S.   **Fic**
Tym, Kate
Coping with your emotions   **152.4**
School survival   **371.8**
Typhoons
See also Hurricanes
Ceban, B. J. Hurricanes, typhoons, and cyclones
551.55

Encyclopedias
Longshore, D. Encyclopedia of hurricanes, ty-
phoons, and cyclones   **551.55**
Typography See Printing
Tyson, Edith S.
Orson Scott Card   **813.009**
Tyson, Neil De Grasse
The Pluto files   **523.4**
Tz'u-hsi, Empress dowager of China, 1835-1908
See/See also pages in the following book(s):
Krull, K. Lives of extraordinary women   **920**

U

U.F.O.'s See Unidentified flying objects
The **U.S.** Air Force and military careers. Camelo,
W.   **358.4**
The **U.S. Armed Forces and military careers**
[series]
Camelo, W. The U.S. Air Force and military ca-
reers   **358.4**
Gray, J. S. The U.S. Coast Guard and military
careers   **359.9**
Kiland, T. B. The U.S. Navy and military ca-
reers   **359**
Rice, E. The U.S. Army and military careers
355.3
Stein, R. C. The U.S. Marine Corps and military
careers   **359.9**
The **U.S.** Army and military careers. Rice, E.
355.3
The **U.S.** Coast Guard and military careers. Gray,
J. S.   **359.9**
The **U.S. government: how it works** [series]
Cox, V. The history of the third parties
324.2
Wagner, H. L. How the president is elected
324
The **U.S.** Marine Corps and military careers. Stein,
R. C.   **359.9**
The **U.S.** Navy and military careers. Kiland, T. B.
359
U.S.S.R. See Soviet Union
U.S. Space Camp (Huntsville, Ala.)
Goodman, S. Ultimate field trip 5   **629.45**
U.S. v. Eichman. Fridell, R.   **342**
U.S. v. Nixon. Stefoff, R.   **342**
U.X.L Asian American voices   **815.008**
U.X.L encyclopedia of biomes   **577.8**
U.X.L encyclopedia of science   **503**
Ucci, Carol Plum- See Plum-Ucci, Carol, 1957-
Uchida, Yoshiko, 1921-1992
A jar of dreams   **Fic**
Journey to Topaz   **Fic**
Udvardy, Miklos D. F., 1919-1998
National Audubon Society field guide to North
American birds, Western region   **598**
Uehashi, Nahoko, 1962-
Moribito   **Fic**
UFOs See Unidentified flying objects
UFOs. Stewart, G.   **001.9**

Uganda
   Barlas, R. Uganda   **967.6**
   Sobol, R. Breakfast in the rainforest   **599.8**
     Fiction
   Nanji, S. Child of dandelions   **Fic**

Uglies. Westerfeld, S.   **Fic**

Uh huh!: the story of Ray Charles. Duggleby, J.
    92

Uhlman, Tom
   (il) Carson, M. K. Emi and the rhino scientist
    599.66

Ukraine
   Bassis, V. Ukraine   **947.7**
   Cooper, C. W. Ukraine   **947.7**
   Kummer, P. K. Ukraine   **947.7**
   Otfinoski, S. Ukraine   **947.7**
   Siegal, A. Memories of Babi   **92**

Ukrainian Americans
   Radzilowski, J. Ukrainian Americans   **305.8**

The ultimate 10. Natural disasters [series]
   Prokos, A. Tornadoes   **551.55**
   Ryback, C. Hurricanes   **551.55**
   Stewart, M. Blizzards and winter storms
    551.55

Ultimate field trip 5. Goodman, S.   **629.45**

The **ultimate** guide to your microscope. Levine, S.
    502.8

Ultimate sports   **S C**

The **ultimate** teen book guide   **028.1**

The **ultimate** weapon. Sullivan, E. T.   **355.8**

Ultimate X-men. See Sanderson, P. X-men: the
   ultimate guide   **741.5**

Ultra-organized cell systems. Johnson, R. L.
    612

Uluru, Australia's Aboriginal heart. Arnold, C.
    994

Uluru-Kata Tjuta National Park (Australia)
   Arnold, C. Uluru, Australia's Aboriginal heart
    994

Ulysses S. Grant and the road to Appomattox.
   Sapp, R.   **92**

UN See United Nations

Unbuilding. Macaulay, D.   **690**

Uncharted, unexplored, and unexplained [series]
   Conley, K. A. Joseph Priestley and the discovery of oxygen   **92**
   Zannos, S. Guglielmo Marconi and the story of
   radio waves   **92**

Uncle Montague's tales of terror. Priestley, C.
    S C

Uncle Remus, the complete tales. Lester, J.
    398.2

Uncle Shelby See Silverstein, Shel

Uncles
     Fiction
   Appelbaum, S. The Hollow Bettle   **Fic**
   Avi. Hard gold   **Fic**
   Bunce, E. C. A curse dark as gold   **Fic**
   Carmichael, C. Wild things   **Fic**
   Herrera, J. F. Cinnamon girl   **Fic**
   Horvath, P. The Corps of the Bare-Boned Plane
    Fic

   Horvath, P. ,Everything on a waffle   **Fic**
   Jones, D. W. House of many ways   **Fic**
   Jongman, M. Rits   **Fic**
   Martin, A. M. A corner of the universe   **Fic**
   Martin, N. Flight of the Fisherbird   **Fic**
   Matthews, K. Flying lessons   **Fic**
   Moore, Y. Freedom songs   **Fic**
   Napoli, D. J. Alligator bayou   **Fic**
   Oaks, J. A. Why I fight   **Fic**
   Peck, D. Drift House: the first voyage   **Fic**
   Peck, D. The lost cities   **Fic**
   Priestley, C. Uncle Montague's tales of terror
    S C
   Ravel, E. The saver   **Fic**
   Rinaldi, A. The Ever-After Bird   **Fic**
   Schirripa, S. R. Nicky Deuce   **Fic**
   Shafer, A. The mailbox   **Fic**
   Strickland, B. The sign of the sinister sorcerer
    Fic
   Torrey, M. Voyage of midnight   **Fic**
   Wood, J. R. The man who loved clowns
    Fic
   Woodworth, C. Double-click for trouble   **Fic**

Uncommon champions. Kaminsky, M.   **920**

Uncommon Faith. Krisher, T.   **Fic**

Under a war-torn sky. Elliott, L.   **Fic**

Under our skin. Birdseye, D. H.   **305.8**

Under siege!. Warren, A.   **973.7**

Under the baseball moon. Ritter, J. H.   **Fic**

Under the blood-red sun. Salisbury, G.   **Fic**

Under the ice. Conlan, K.   **578.7**

Under the Persimmon tree. Staples, S. F.   **Fic**

Under the sea origami. Nguyen, D.   **736**

Under the Watson's porch. Shreve, S. R.   **Fic**

Undercover. Kephart, B.   **Fic**

Underdeveloped areas See Developing countries

Underground. Ferris, J.   **Fic**

Underground. Macaulay, D.   **624**

Underground railroad
   Allen, T. B. Harriet Tubman, secret agent
    92
   Bial, R. The Underground Railroad   **326**
   Eskridge, A. E. Slave uprisings and runaways
    326
   Fradin, D. B. Bound for the North Star   **326**
   Hansen, J. Freedom roads: searching for the Un-
   derground Railroad   **973.7**
   Katz, W. L. Black pioneers   **920**
   Landau, E. Fleeing to freedom on the Under-
   ground Railroad   **973.7**
   Sawyer, K. K. The underground railroad in
   American history   **326**
   Stein, R. C. Escaping slavery on the Under-
   ground Railroad   **973.7**
     Fiction
   Ayres, K. North by night   **Fic**
   Carbone, E. L. Stealing freedom   **Fic**
   Ferris, J. Underground   **Fic**
   Rinaldi, A. The Ever-After Bird   **Fic**
   Vande Velde, V. There's a dead person follow-
   ing my sister around   **Fic**
   Wisler, G. C. Caleb's choice   **Fic**
   Woodruff, E. Dear Austin   **Fic**

Ute Indians
Fiction
Hobbs, W. Bearstone   **Fic**
Wyss, T. H. Bear dancer   **Fic**

Utomo, Gabhor
(il) Currier, K. S. Kai's journey to Gold Mountain   **Fic**

Utopias
Fiction
Booraem, E. The unnameables   **Fic**
Huxley, A. Brave new world   **Fic**

UXL encyclopedia of U.S. history. Benson, S.   **973.03**

UXL Encyclopedia of world mythology   **201.03**

Uzbekistan
Knowlton, M. Uzbekistan   **958.7**

V

V.C.R.'s *See* Video recording

V.D. *See* Sexually transmitted diseases

Vaca, Alvar Nuñez Cabeza de *See* Nuñez Cabeza de Vaca, Alvar, 16th cent.

The **vacation**. Horvath, P.   **Fic**

Vacations
Fiction
Han, J. The summer I turned pretty   **Fic**
Harrington, J. Four things my geeky-jock-of-a-best-friend must do in Europe   **Fic**
Horvath, P. The vacation   **Fic**
Runyon, B. Surface tension   **Fic**
St. Anthony, J. Grace above all   **Fic**
Stein, T. High dive   **Fic**

Vaccination
Collier, J. L. Vaccines   **615**
Nardo, D. Vaccines   **615**
Phelan, G. Killing germs, saving lives   **615**
See/See also pages in the following book(s):
Epidemics: opposing viewpoints   **614.4**

Vaccines. Collier, J. L.   **615**

Vaccines. Nardo, D.   **615**

Vagabonds *See* Tramps

Vagrants *See* Tramps

Vail, Rachel
Lucky   **Fic**
You, maybe   **Fic**

Valdez (Ship) *See* Exxon Valdez (Ship)

Valentine, Jenny
Broken soup   **Fic**
Me, the missing, and the dead   **Fic**

Valentine, Rebecca
(jt. auth) Benson, S. UXL encyclopedia of U.S. history   **973.03**

Valenza, Joyce Kasman
Power research tools   **001.4**
Power tools recharged   **027.8**

Valley Forge (Pa.)
History
Allen, T. B. Remember Valley Forge   **973.3**
Freedman, R. Washington at Valley Forge   **973.3**

Valley of the Kings. Smith, S. T.   **932**

Valli, Clayton
(ed) The Gallaudet dictionary of American Sign Language. See The Gallaudet dictionary of American Sign Language   **419**

Valliant, Doris
Bangladesh   **954.92**

Values
Robinson, S. Jackie's nine   **170**

Vampirates: demons of the ocean. Somper, J.   **Fic**

Vampire High. Rees, D. C.   **Fic**

Vampire kisses. Schreiber, E.   **Fic**

Vampire kisses: blood relatives. Schreiber, E.   **741.5**

Vampires
Gee, J. Encyclopedia horrifica   **001.9**
Stefoff, R. Vampires, zombies, and shape-shifters   **398**
Fiction
Atwater-Rhodes, A. Persistence of memory   **Fic**
Brewer, H. The chronicles of Vladimir Tod: eighth grade bites   **Fic**
Cary, K. Bloodline   **Fic**
Fantaskey, B. Jessica's guide to dating on the dark side   **Fic**
Gray, C. Evernight   **Fic**
Jenkins, A. M. Night road   **Fic**
Jinks, C. The reformed vampire support group   **Fic**
Klause, A. C. The silver kiss   **Fic**
Meehl, B. Suck it up   **Fic**
Meyer, S. Twilight   **Fic**
Rees, D. C. Vampire High   **Fic**
Schreiber, E. Vampire kisses   **Fic**
Sedgwick, M. My swordhand is singing   **Fic**
Somper, J. Vampirates: demons of the ocean   **Fic**
St. Crow, L. Strange angels   **Fic**
Graphic novels
Schreiber, E. Vampire kisses: blood relatives   **741.5**

Vampires, zombies, and shape-shifters. Stefoff, R.   **398**

Van Beethoven, Ludwig *See* Beethoven, Ludwig van, 1770-1827

Van de Ruit, John, 1975-
Spud   **Fic**

Van der Gaag, Nikki *See* Gaag, Nikki van der

Van der Meer, Jan *See* Vermeer, Johannes, 1632-1675

Van Deusen, Jean Donham, 1946-
Enhancing teaching and learning   **027.8**

Van Diepen, Allison, 1977-
Snitch   **Fic**

Van Draanen, Wendelin *See* Draanen, Wendelin van

Van Etten, David
Likely story   **Fic**

Van Gogh, Vincent *See* Gogh, Vincent van, 1853-1890

Van Gorp, Lynn
Antoine Lavoisier   **92**

Ventriloquism

Fiction

De Guzman, M. Finding Stinko **Fic**

Fleischman, S. The entertainer and the dybbuk
  Fic

Venturing the deep sea. Lindop, L. **551.46**

Venus & Serena. Williams, V. **92**

Vera-Portocarrero, Louis
  Brain facts **612.8**

Verbal abuse *See* Invective

Verbal learning

  See also Reading comprehension

Verdick, Elizabeth
  (ed) Cobain, B. When nothing matters anymore
  616.85
  (ed) Crump, M. No B.O.! **613**

Verhoeven, Rian
  (jt. auth) Rol, R. v. d. Anne Frank, beyond the
  diary **92**

Vermeer, Johannes, 1632-1675

Fiction

Balliett, B. Chasing Vermeer **Fic**

Vermeer van Delft, Jan *See* Vermeer, Johannes,
  1632-1675

Vermont

Fiction

Alvarez, J. How Tía Lola came to visit/stay
  Fic
Alvarez, J. Return to sender **Fic**
Anderson, M. T. The Game of Sunken Places
  Fic
Gould, P. L. Write naked **Fic**
Hesse, K. Witness **Fic**
James, B. Zombie blondes **Fic**
LaFleur, S. M. Love, Aubrey **Fic**
Murphy, R. Bird **Fic**
Paterson, K. Jip **Fic**
Paterson, K. Preacher's boy **Fic**
Peck, R. N. A day no pigs would die **Fic**
Stahler, D., Jr. A gathering of shades **Fic**
Wilson, N. H. Mountain pose **Fic**
Winthrop, E. Counting on Grace **Fic**

Verne, Jules, 1828-1905
  20,000 leagues under the sea **Fic**

About

Schoell, W. Remarkable journeys: the story of
  Jules Verne **92**

Adaptations

Macdonald, F. Journey to the Center of the
  Earth **741.5**

Verniero, Joan
  (jt. auth) Rappaport, D. United no more!
  973.7

Vernon, Ursula
  Nurk **Fic**

Vernonia School District 47J (Or.)
  Gold, S. D. Vernonia School District v. Acton
  344

Vernonia School District v. Acton. Gold, S. D.
  344

Verplancke, Klaas, 1964-
  (il) Perrier, P. Flying solo **158**

Verrillo, Erica F.
  Elissa's quest **Fic**

Vertebrates
  Holmes, T. The first vertebrates **567**
  Silverstein, A. Vertebrates **596**

A **very** fine line. Johnston, J. **Fic**

The **very** ordered existence of Merilee Marvelous.
  Crowley, S. **Fic**

Vescia, Monique
  (jt. auth) Rauf, D. Computer game designer
  794.8

Vespucci, Amerigo, 1451-1512
  See/See also pages in the following book(s):
  Fritz, J. Around the world in a hundred years
  910.4

Vess, Charles
  (il) The Coyote Road. See The Coyote Road
  808.8
  (il) The Green Man: tales from the mythic forest. See The Green Man: tales from the mythic forest **808.8**

Veterans

Fiction

Williams, S. Bull rider **Fic**

Veterinary medicine
  Jackson, D. M. ER vets **636.089**

Fiction

Wilson, D. L. Firehorse **Fic**

Vibes. Ryan, A. K. **Fic**

Vice-presidents

United States

Sapet, K. Al Gore **92**

Vicksburg (Miss.)

Siege, 1863

Warren, A. Under siege! **973.7**

Vicodin, OxyContin, and other pain relievers.
  Breguet, A. **362.29**

Victims and victims' rights. Faherty, S. **362.88**

Victims of crimes

  See also Abused women
  Faherty, S. Victims and victims' rights
  362.88

Victoria, Queen of Great Britain, 1819-1901
  See/See also pages in the following book(s):
  Krull, K. Lives of extraordinary women **920**
  Myers, W. D. At her majesty's request [biogra-
  phy of Sarah Forbes Bonetta] **92**

Video cassette recorders and recording *See* Video recording

Video games
  Parks, P. J. Video games **794.8**

Fiction

Kostick, C. Epic **Fic**
Kostick, C. Saga **Fic**
Michaels, R. Genesis Alpha **Fic**
Seidler, T. Brainboy and the Deathmaster
  Fic

Graphic novels

Sakura, K. Dragon drive. Vol. 1, D-break
  741.5

Video recording
  Shaner, P. A. Digital filmmaking for teens
  778.5

Voake, Steve—_Continued_
The web of fire   **Fic**

Vocabulary
L is for lollygag   **428**

Vocational education
Unger, H. G. But what if I don't want to go to college?   **331.7**

Vocational guidance
Camelo, W. The U.S. Air Force and military careers   **358.4**
Career discovery encyclopedia   **331.7**
Encyclopedia of careers and vocational guidance   **331.7**
Gerardi, D. Careers in the computer game industry   **794.8**
Gray, J. S. The U.S. Coast Guard and military careers   **359.9**
Green, D. H. Dream job profiles   **650.1**
Kiland, T. B. The U.S. Navy and military careers   **359**
McAlpine, M. Working in music and dance   **780**
McAlpine, M. Working in the fashion industry   **746.9**
McAlpine, M. Working in the food industry   **647.9**
McAlpine, M. Working with animals   **636**
McAlpine, M. Working with children   **362.7**
McAlpine, M. Working with computers   **004**
McNamee, G. Careers in renewable energy   **333.79**
Nichols, T. Punk rock etiquette   **781.66**
Rauf, D. Computer game designer   **794.8**
Reber, D. In their shoes   **331.4**
Reeves, D. L. Career ideas for teens in architecture and construction   **624**
Reeves, D. L. Career ideas for teens in education and training   **331.7**
Reeves, D. L. Career ideas for teens in health science   **610.69**
Reeves, D. L. TV journalist   **070.4**
Rice, E. The U.S. Army and military careers   **355.3**
Schwager, T. Cool women, hot jobs . . . and how you can go for it, too!   **650.14**
Stein, R. C. The U.S. Marine Corps and military careers   **359.9**
Unger, H. G. But what if I don't want to go to college?   **331.7**
United States. Bureau of Labor Statistics. Occupational outlook handbook 2008-2009   **331.7**
What can I do now?: Health care   **362.1**
Young person's occupational outlook handbook   **331.7**

Vocational training _See_ Occupational training

Vocations _See_ Occupations

Voelkel, J.
Middleworld   **Fic**

Voelkel, P.
(jt. auth) Voelkel, J. Middleworld   **Fic**

Vogel, Carole Garbuny
Human impact   **333.91**
Ocean wildlife   **591.7**

Vogel, Jennifer
A library story   **727**

Vögelein. Irwin, J.   **741.5**

Vogt, Gregory
The atmosphere   **551.5**
Disasters in space exploration   **363.1**
Earth's core and mantle   **551.1**
The lithosphere   **551.1**

Vogt, Richard Carl
Rain forests   **577.3**

Voice from afar. Johnston, T.   **811**

A **voice** from the Holocaust. Soumerai, E. N.   **940.53**

The **voice** that challenged a nation [biography of Marian Anderson] Freedman, R.   **92**

Voices from colonial America [series]   **973.2**

Voices from slavery's past. Cloud Tapper, S.   **326**

Voices from the fields. Atkin, S. B.   **331.5**

Voices in first person   **S C**

Voices in poetry [series]
Angelou, M. Maya Angelou   **811**

Voices of rape. Bode, J.   **362.88**

Voices of twentieth century conflict [series]
Soumerai, E. N. A voice from the Holocaust   **940.53**

Voigt, Cynthia
Bad girls in love   **Fic**
Dicey's song   **Fic**
Homecoming   **Fic**
Izzy, willy-nilly   **Fic**
A solitary blue   **Fic**

Volavková, Hana
(ed) —I never saw another butterfly—. See —I never saw another butterfly—   **741.9**

Volcanic eruptions, earthquakes, and tsunamis. McCollum, S.   **551.2**

Volcanoes
Burleigh, R. Volcanoes   **551.2**
Fradin, J. B. Volcanoes   **551.2**
Grace, C. O. Forces of nature   **551.2**
Levy, M. Earthquakes, volcanoes, and tsunamis   **551.2**
Lindop, L. Probing volcanoes   **551.2**
McCollum, S. Volcanic eruptions, earthquakes, and tsunamis   **551.2**
Trueit, T. S. Volcanoes   **551.2**
Winchester, S. The day the world exploded   **551.2**

See/See also pages in the following book(s):
Day, T. DK guide to savage Earth   **550**
          Fiction
Dickinson, P. Tears of the salamander   **Fic**

Volleyball
Manley, C. B. Competitive volleyball for girls   **796.325**

Vollmar, Rob
The castaways   **741.5**

Volpe, Lane E., 1976-
(ed) Battered women. See Battered women   **362.82**

Volponi, Paul
Black and white   **Fic**

Walsh, Marissa, 1972-
(ed) Does this book make me look fat? See
Does this book make me look fat? **S C**
Walsh, Tina Cash- See Cash-Walsh, Tina, 1960-
Walsingham, Sir Francis, 1530?-1590
Fiction
Brittney, L. Dangerous times **Fic**
Walt Disney Company
Finch, C. The art of Walt Disney **791.43**
Walt Disney Productions
See also Walt Disney Company
Peet, B. Bill Peet: an autobiography **92**
Walt Disney World (Fla.)
Fiction
Barkley, B. Dream factory **Fic**
Walter, Virginia A.
War & peace **016.3**
Walter Wick's optical tricks. Wick, W.
152.14
Walters, Eric, 1957-
Sketches **Fic**
Splat! **Fic**
(jt. auth) Ellis, D. Bifocal **Fic**
Waltham, A. C. (Antony Clive), 1942-
Great caves of the world **551.4**
Waltham, Antony Clive See Waltham, A. C. (Antony Clive), 1942-
Waltham, Tony See Waltham, A. C. (Antony Clive), 1942-
Waltman, Kevin
Learning the game **Fic**
Wampanoag Indians
Mandell, D. R. King Philip's war **973.2**
Wan Guofang
TV takeover **384.55**
Virtually true **025.04**
Wanasundera, Nanda P., 1932-
Sri Lanka **954.93**
Wand, Kelly
(ed) Ape-men. See Ape-men **001.9**
The **wand** in the word **813.009**
The **Wanderer**. Creech, S. **Fic**
Wang, Vera
About
Krohn, K. E. Vera Wang **92**
Todd, A. M. Vera Wang **92**
See/See also pages in the following book(s):
Kent, J. Business builders in fashion **920**
Wangu, Madhu Bazaz
Buddhism **294.3**
Hinduism **294.5**
Waniek, Marilyn Nelson See Nelson, Marilyn, 1946-
Wansbrough, Henry, 1934-
(ed) Bible. The new Jerusalem Bible **220.5**
Want fries with that? Ingram, S. **613.2**
Wanting Mor. Khan, R. **Fic**
War
See also Intervention (International law)
Brownlie, A. Why do people fight wars?
355
Glick, S. War and peace **201**

Gottfried, T. The fight for peace **303.6**
Sullivan, G. Journalists at risk **070.4**
War: opposing viewpoints **355**
Bibliography
Crew, H. S. Women engaged in war in literature for youth **016.3**
Walter, V. A. War & peace **016.3**
Fiction
See War stories
Graphic novels
Hama, L. The battle of Iwo Jima **940.54**
Watson, A. Princess at midnight **741.5**
Public opinion
Civil liberties and war **323**
Religious aspects
Is Islam a religion of war or peace? **297**
War, Space See Space warfare
War & peace. Walter, V. A. **016.3**
War and children See Children and war
War and conflict in the Middle East [series]
Wingate, K. The Intifadas **956.95**
War and peace. Glick, S. **201**
War and religion See War—Religious aspects
War and the pity of war **808.81**
The **war** at Ellsmere. Hicks, F. E. **741.5**
War comes to Willy Freeman. Collier, J. L.
Fic
War crime trials
See also Nuremberg Trial of Major German War Criminals, 1945-1946
War horse. Morpurgo, M. **Fic**
War in art
Chapman, C. Battles & weapons: exploring history through art **355**
War in the Middle East. Hampton, W. **956.04**
War of 1812
Childress, D. The War of 1812 **973.5**
Edelman, R. The War of 1812 **973.5**
Greenblatt, M. War of 1812 **973.5**
Warrick, K. C. The War of 1812 **973.5**
The **war** of the worlds. Wells, H. G. **Fic**
The **war** on drugs: opposing viewpoints **363.4**
War on terrorism
Can the War on Terrorism be won? **363.32**
Miller, D. A. The Patriot Act **345**
Torr, J. D. The Patriot Act **345**
See/See also pages in the following book(s):
Kops, D. Racial profiling **363.2**
War on terrorism [series]
Hamilton, J. Weapons of war **623.4**
Wheeler, J. C. September 11, 2001: the day that changed America **973.931**
War: opposing viewpoints **355**
War poetry
America at war **811.008**
Johnston, T. Voice from afar **811**
The Oxford book of war poetry **808.81**
War and the pity of war **808.81**
War relief
Morley, D. Healing our world **610**
War stories
Aguiar, N. The lost island of Tamarind **Fic**

War stories—*Continued*

Holub, J. An innocent soldier   **Fic**
Jinks, C. Babylonne   **Fic**
Jones, A. F. Warrior princess   **Fic**
Mankell, H. Secrets in the fire   **Fic**
Marsden, J. Tomorrow, when the war began   **Fic**
Mason, P. Camel rider   **Fic**
Moran, K. Bloodline   **Fic**
Pratchett, T. Only you can save mankind   **Fic**
Schmidt, C. A. Useful fools   **Fic**
Shattered: stories of children and war   **S C**
Shinn, S. General Winston's daughter   **Fic**

War-torn Bosnia   **949.7**

War, women, and the news. Gourley, C.   **070.4**

Warburton, Lianne
Amphetamines and other stimulants   **362.29**

Ward, Brian R.
Epidemic   **614.4**

Ward, David, 1967-
Escape the mask   **Fic**

Ward, David J. (David John)
Exploring Mars   **523.4**
Materials science   **620.1**

Ward, Elaine M.
Old Testament women   **221.9**

Ward, Paul, 1959-
Bears of the world   **599.78**

Wardlaw, Lee, 1955-
101 ways to bug your teacher   **Fic**

Warfare. Chrisp, P.   **355**

Warhol, Andy, 1928?-1987
About
Greenberg, J. Andy Warhol   **92**
Rubin, S. G. Andy Warhol   **92**

Warhol, Tom
Chaparral and scrub   **577.3**
Desert   **577.5**
Eagles   **598**
Forest   **577.3**
Grassland   **577.4**
Hawks   **598**
Owls   **598**
Tundra   **577.5**
Water   **577.6**

Warne, L. Rowland- *See* Rowland-Warne, L.

Warner, Penny
Signing fun   **419**

Warner, Sally
It's only temporary   **Fic**

Warren, Andrea
Escape from Saigon [biography of Matt Steiner]   **92**
Orphan train rider   **362.7**
Surviving Hitler   **940.53**
Under siege!   **973.7**
We rode the orphan trains   **362.7**

Warren, Holly George- *See* George-Warren, Holly

Warrick, Karen Clemens
Hannibal   **92**

John Muir: crusader for the wilderness   **92**
The perilous search for the fabled Northwest Passage in American history   **910.4**
The War of 1812   **973.5**

Warrick, Leanne
Hair trix for cool chix   **646.7**

The **warrior** heir. Chima, C. W.   **Fic**

Warrior princess. Jones, A. F.   **Fic**

Warriors [series]
Hunter, E. Into the wild   **Fic**
Hunter, E. The lost warrior   **741.5**

Warriors: power of three [series]
Hunter, E. The sight   **Fic**

Warriors: the new prophecy [series]
Hunter, E. Midnight   **Fic**

Warriors: Tiger & Sasha #1: into the woods. Hunter, E.   **741.5**

Wart. Myers, A.   **Fic**

Warwick, Ellen
Everywear   **745.5**
Injeanuity   **746**
(jt. auth) Roderick, S. Centsibility   **332.024**

Washakie, Shoshone Chief, 1797-1900
See/See also pages in the following book(s):
Freedman, R. Indian chiefs   **920**

Washington, Booker T., 1856-1915
Up from slavery   **92**

Washington, George, 1732-1799
About
Adler, D. A. George Washington   **92**
Allen, T. B. George Washington, spymaster   **92**
Allen, T. B. Remember Valley Forge   **973.3**
Dolan, E. F. George Washington   **92**
Freedman, R. Washington at Valley Forge   **973.3**
Miller, B. M. George Washington for kids   **92**

Washington (D.C.)
Fiction
Cohn, R. You know where to find me   **Fic**
Ehrenberg, P. Ethan, suspended   **Fic**
White, E. E. The President's daughter   **Fic**
Social life and customs
Jones, L. Mrs. Lincoln's dressmaker: the unlikely friendship of Elizabeth Keckley and Mary Todd Lincoln   **92**

Washington (State)
Fiction
Caletti, D. The fortunes of Indigo Skye   **Fic**
Deuker, C. Gym candy   **Fic**
Holm, J. L. Boston Jane: an adventure   **Fic**
Holm, J. L. Our only May Amelia   **Fic**
Kehret, P. The ghost's grave   **Fic**
Martin, N. Flight of the Fisherbird   **Fic**
Meyer, S. Twilight   **Fic**
Mochizuki, K. Beacon Hill boys   **Fic**
Powell, R. Swiss mist   **Fic**

Washington at Valley Forge. Freedman, R.   **973.3**

Wasow, Omar, 1970-
See/See also pages in the following book(s):
Haskins, J. African American entrepreneurs   **920**

Women

See also Abused women; Widows and women of particular racial or ethnic groups, e.g. *African American women;* and women in various occupations and professions

Bibliography

Crew, H. S. Women engaged in war in literature for youth   **016.3**

Biography

Atkins, J. How high can we climb?   **920**
Butts, E. She dared   **920**
Chin-Lee, C. Amelia to Zora   **920**
Colman, P. Adventurous women   **920**
Gourse, L. Sophisticated ladies   **920**
Hacker, C. Nobel Prize winners   **920**
Kallen, S. A. Women of the civil rights movement   **323.1**
Kimmel, E. C. Ladies first   **920**
Maydell, N. Extraordinary women from the Muslim world   **920**

Civil rights

See Women's rights

Employment

Colman, P. Rosie the riveter   **331.4**
Reber, D. In their shoes   **331.4**
Schwager, T. Cool women, hot jobs . . . and how you can go for it, too!   **650.14**

Folklore

San Souci, R. Cut from the same cloth   **398.2**
Tchana, K. H. The serpent slayer: and other stories of strong women   **398.2**

Health and hygiene

Waters, S. Seeing the gynecologist   **618.1**
See/See also pages in the following book(s):
Jukes, M. It's a girl thing   **305.23**

History

Encyclopedia of women in the Renaissance   **940.2**
Thomson, M. Women of the Renaissance   **940.2**

Political activity

See also Women politicians

Religious life

Braude, A. Women and American religion   **200.9**

Social conditions

Coppens, L. M. What American women did, 1789-1920   **305.4**
Macdonald, F. Women in 19th-century Europe   **305.4**

Suffrage

Bausum, A. With courage and cloth   **305.4**
Monroe, J. The Susan B. Anthony women's voting rights trial   **324.6**

Suffrage—Bibliography

Mosley, S. The suffragists in literature for youth   **016.3**

Suffrage—Fiction

Schwabach, K. The Hope Chest   **Fic**

Arab countries

Esherick, J. Women in the Arab world   **305.4**

Egypt

Sharp, A. W. Women of Ancient Egypt   **932**

Europe

Encyclopedia of women in the Renaissance   **940.2**
Macdonald, F. Women in 19th-century Europe   **305.4**

India

Woog, A. Jyotirmayee Mohapatra   **92**

India—Fiction

Whelan, G. Homeless bird   **Fic**

Middle East

Harik, R. M. Women in the Middle East   **305.4**

United States

Hartman, H. Girlwonder   **305.23**

United States—History

33 things every girl should know about women's history   **305.4**
Bausum, A. With courage and cloth   **305.4**
Coppens, L. M. What American women did, 1789-1920   **305.4**
Cullen-DuPont, K. Encyclopedia of women's history in America   **305.4**
Gourley, C. Flappers and the new American woman   **305.4**
Gourley, C. Gibson girls and suffragists   **305.4**
Gourley, C. Gidgets and women warriors   **305.4**
Gourley, C. Rosie and Mrs. America   **305.4**
Matthews, G. American women's history   **305.4**
Miller, B. M. Good women of a well-blessed land   **305.4**
Schomp, V. American voices from the women's movement   **305.4**
Swisher, C. Women of the roaring twenties   **305.4**
Zeinert, K. Those courageous women of the Civil War   **973.7**

Women, Hispanic American See Hispanic American women

Women adventurers [series]
Anema, D. Ynes Mexia, botanist and adventurer   **92**

Women air pilots

Blair, M. W. The roaring 20   **797.5**
Gherman, B. Anne Morrow Lindbergh   **92**
Hart, P. S. Up in the air: the story of Bessie Coleman   **92**
Langley, W. Women of the wind   **920**
Micklos, J. Unsolved: what really happened to Amelia Earhart?   **92**
Nathan, A. Yankee doodle gals   **940.54**

Fiction

Smith, S. L. Flygirl   **Fic**

Women Airforce Service Pilots (U.S.)

Fiction

Smith, S. L. Flygirl   **Fic**

Women and American religion. Braude, A.   **200.9**

Women architects

Lashnits, T. Maya Lin   **92**

Women artists

Debon, N. Four pictures by Emily Carr   **92**
Hillstrom, L. Frida Kahlo   **92**

Woods, Bob—Continued

Hottest muscle cars	629.222
Hottest sports cars	629.222
(jt. auth) Mueller, M. Corvette	629.222

Woods, Brenda

Emako Blue	Fic
My name is Sally Little Song	Fic

Woods, Eldrick See Woods, Tiger, 1975-

Woods, Granville, 1856-1910

See/See also pages in the following book(s):

Haskins, J. African American entrepreneurs
920

Woods, Mary B., 1946-

(jt. auth) Woods, M. Seven natural wonders of Africa	508
(jt. auth) Woods, M. Seven natural wonders of Asia and the Middle East	508
(jt. auth) Woods, M. Seven natural wonders of Australia and Oceania	508
(jt. auth) Woods, M. Seven natural wonders of Central and South America	508
(jt. auth) Woods, M. Seven natural wonders of Europe	508
(jt. auth) Woods, M. Seven natural wonders of North America	508
(jt. auth) Woods, M. Seven wonders of Ancient Asia	950

Woods, Michael, 1946-

Seven natural wonders of Africa	508
Seven natural wonders of Asia and the Middle East	508
Seven natural wonders of Australia and Oceania	508
Seven natural wonders of Central and South America	508
Seven natural wonders of Europe	508
Seven natural wonders of North America	508
Seven wonders of Ancient Asia	950

Woods, Ron

The hero	Fic

Woods, Thomas E., Jr., 1972

(ed) Exploring American history: from colonial times to 1877. See Exploring American history: from colonial times to 1877 **973.03**

Woods, Tiger, 1975-

About

Roberts, J. Tiger Woods	92

Woods See Forests and forestry

Woods and forests. Martin, P. A. F. **577.3**

The **woods** scientist. Swinburne, S. R. **591.7**

Woodside, Martin

Thomas A. Edison	92

Woodson, Jacqueline

After Tupac and D Foster	Fic
Feathers	Fic
From the notebooks of Melanin Sun	Fic
Hush	Fic
If you come softly	Fic
Lena	Fic
Locomotion	Fic
Peace, Locomotion	Fic

About

Hinton, K. Jacqueline Woodson	92

Stover, L. T. Jacqueline Woodson	813.009

Woodson, Sarah Jane

See/See also pages in the following book(s):

Katz, W. L. Black pioneers	920

Woodsong. Paulsen, G. **796.5**

Woodswalk. Art, H. W. **508**

Woodward, John, 1954-

Water	553.7
(jt. auth) Malam, J. Dinosaur atlas	567.9

Woodward, John, 1958-

(ed) Conserving the environment. See Conserving the environment **333.7**

(ed) Israel: opposing viewpoints. See Israel: opposing viewpoints **956.94**

Woodwork

Fiction

Giff, P. R. Eleven	Fic

Woodworth, Chris, 1957-

Double-click for trouble	Fic
When Ratboy lived next door	Fic

Woog, Adam, 1953-

Fidel Castro	92
Jennifer Lopez	92
Jyotirmayee Mohapatra	92
Ray Charles and the birth of soul	92

Woolf, Alex

Death and disease	610.9
Education	940.1
Why are people terrorists?	303.6

Woolley, John T. (John Turner), 1950-

(ed) The presidency A to Z. See The presidency A to Z **352.23**

Woolls, Blanche See Woolls, E. Blanche

Woolls, E. Blanche

The school library media manager	027.8
(ed) The Whole school library handbook. See The Whole school library handbook	027.8

Wooster, Robert, 1956-

(ed) Encyclopedia of Native American wars and warfare. See Encyclopedia of Native American wars and warfare **970.004**

Wooten, Sara McIntosh

Frida Kahlo	92
Robert Frost	92

Worcester, Samuel Austin, 1798-1859

About

Gold, S. D. Worcester v. Georgia	342

Worcester v. Georgia. Gold, S. D. **342**

Word games

See also Scrabble (Game)

Cleary, B. P. The laugh stand	817

Word histories and mysteries **422.03**

Word nerd. Nielsen, S. **Fic**

Words See Vocabulary

The **words** of Martin Luther King, Jr. King, M. L., Jr. **323.1**

Words of the ancient Romans. Nardo, D. **937**

Words with wings **811.008**

Wordsworth, William, 1770-1850

William Wordsworth	821

Wright, David K., 1943-
Cuba   972.91
Paul Robeson   92

Wright, Frank Lloyd, 1867-1959
About
Adkins, J. Frank Lloyd Wright   92

Wright, John W., 1941-
(ed) The New York Times 2008 almanac. See
The New York Times 2008 almanac
    031.02

Wright, Joseph P., 1939-
(jt. auth) Salvadori, M. G. Math games for middle school   510.7

Wright, Katharine *See* Haskell, Katharine Wright,
1874-1929

Wright, Orville, 1871-1948
About
Carson, M. K. The Wright Brothers for kids
    629.13
Collins, M. Airborne: a photobiography of Wilbur and Orville Wright   92
Crompton, S. The Wright brothers   92
Dixon-Engel, T. The Wright brothers   92
Freedman, R. The Wright brothers: how they invented the airplane   92
Maurer, R. The Wright sister [biography of Katharine Wright Haskell]   92

Wright, Richard, 1908-1960
About
Hinds, M. J. A reader's guide to Richard Wright's Black boy   813.009
Levy, D. Richard Wright   92

Wright, Wilbur, 1867-1912
About
Carson, M. K. The Wright Brothers for kids
    629.13
Collins, M. Airborne: a photobiography of Wilbur and Orville Wright   92
Crompton, S. The Wright brothers   92
Dixon-Engel, T. The Wright brothers   92
Freedman, R. The Wright brothers: how they invented the airplane   92
Maurer, R. The Wright sister [biography of Katharine Wright Haskell]   92
The **Wright** brothers. Crompton, S.   92
The **Wright** brothers. Dixon-Engel, T.   92
The **Wright** Brothers for kids. Carson, M. K.
    629.13
The **Wright** brothers: how they invented the airplane. Freedman, R.   92
The **Wright** sister [biography of Katharine Wright Haskell] Maurer, R.   92

Wrigley, Chris
Winston Churchill: a biographical companion
    92

Wringer. Spinelli, J.   Fic
A **wrinkle** in time. L'Engle, M.   Fic
Write before your eyes. Kline, L. W.   Fic
Write grants, get money. Anderson, C.   025.1
Write naked. Gould, P. L.   Fic

Write your own [series]
Gilbert, S. Write your own article   808

Rosinsky, N. M. Write your own biography
    808
Rosinsky, N. M. Write your own fairy tale
    808.3
Rosinsky, N. M. Write your own graphic novel
    741.5
Rosinsky, N. M. Write your own myth
    808.3
Rosinsky, N. M. Write your own tall tale
    808.3
Write your own article. Gilbert, S.   808
Write your own biography. Rosinsky, N. M.
    808
Write your own fairy tale. Rosinsky, N. M.
    808.3
Write your own fantasy story. Farrell, T.
    808.3
Write your own graphic novel. Rosinsky, N. M.
    741.5
Write your own mystery story. Farrell, T.
    808.3
Write your own myth. Rosinsky, N. M.   808.3
Write your own science fiction story. Farrell, T.
    808.3
Write your own tall tale. Rosinsky, N. M.
    808.3

Writers *See* Authors
Writers and their works [series]
Andersen, R. Arthur Miller   92
Andersen, R. Toni Morrison   92
Boon, K. A. F. Scott Fitzgerald   92
McArthur, D. Mark Twain   92
Reiff, R. H. Charlotte Brontë   92
Wallace, M. O. Langston Hughes   92
A **writer's** story. Bauer, M. D.   92
Writing
See also Calligraphy; Picture writing
History
Donoughue, C. The story of writing   411
Robb, D. Ox, house, stick   411
Writing (Authorship) *See* Authorship; Creative writing; Journalism
Writing is my business. Caravantes, P.   92
Writing magic. Levine, G. C.   808.3
Writing the critical essay [series]
Cloning   176
Global warming   363.7
Racism: an opposing viewpoints guide   305.8
Terrorism   363.32
Writing winning reports and essays. Janeczko, P. B.   808
Writings of teenagers *See* Teenagers' writings
Written in bone. Walker, S. M.   614
Wu, Janice, 1981-
(jt. auth) Moiz, A. Taiwan   951.2
Wu-ti *See* Han Wu-ti, Emperor of China, 156-87 B.C.
Wudi *See* Han Wu-ti, Emperor of China, 156-87 B.C.
Wukovits, John F., 1944-
Anne Frank   92

Yeomans, Ellen, 1962-
Rubber houses   **Fic**

Yep, Laurence
Dragon road   **Fic**
Dragon's gate   **Fic**
Dragonwings   **Fic**
Hiroshima   **Fic**
The lost garden   **92**
The rainbow people   **398.2**
The traitor   **Fic**
About
Marcovitz, H. Laurence Yep   **92**
(ed) American dragons: twenty-five Asian American voices. See American dragons: twenty-five Asian American voices   **810.8**

Yeshi Dorjee
See/See also pages in the following book(s):
Major, J. S. Caravan to America   **920**

Yeti
Ape-men   **001.9**

The **Yggyssey**. Pinkwater, D. M.   **Fic**

Ynes Mexia, botanist and adventurer. Anema, D.   **92**

Yoder, Carolyn P., 1953-
(ed) Adams, J. John Adams the writer   **92**

Yoga
Birkemoe, K. Strike a pose   **613.7**
Purperhart, H. Yoga exercises for teens   **613.7**

Yoga exercises for teens. Purperhart, H.   **613.7**

Yohalem, Eve
Escape under the forever sky   **Fic**

Yokota, Junko
Children's books in children's hands. See Children's books in children's hands   **028.5**

Yolen, Jane
Apple for the teacher   **782.42**
Briar Rose   **Fic**
Dragon's blood   **Fic**
Girl in a cage   **Fic**
Mightier than the sword   **398.2**
Passager   **Fic**
Pay the piper   **Fic**
The queen's own fool   **Fic**
The Rogues   **Fic**
Sacred places   **811**
Sea queens   **920**
Troll Bridge   **Fic**
About
Carpan, C. Jane Yolen   **92**

Yom Kippur War, 1973 *See* Israel-Arab War, 1973

Yong, Teo Chuu
(jt. auth) Shelley, R. Japan   **952**

Yoo, Paula
Good enough   **Fic**

Yorinks, Adrienne
Quilt of states   **973**

York, ca. 1775-ca. 1815
About
Blumberg, R. York's adventures with Lewis and Clark   **978**

York, Sherry, 1947-
Children's and young adult literature by Latino writers   **028.5**
Ethnic book awards   **011.6**

York's adventures with Lewis and Clark. Blumberg, R.   **978**

Yoshina, Joan M.
(jt. auth) Harada, V. H. Assessing learning   **027.8**
(jt. auth) Harada, V. H. Inquiry learning through librarian-teacher partnerships   **371.1**

You are so not invited to my bat mitzvah!. Rosenbloom, F.   **Fic**
You are the juror. Aaseng, N.   **345**
You can't read this. Ross, V.   **028**
You hear me?   **810.8**
You know where to find me. Cohn, R.   **Fic**
You, maybe. Vail, R.   **Fic**
You never did learn to knock   **S C**

Young, Abe Louise
(ed) Hip deep. See Hip deep   **808.8**

Young, E. L.
STORM: The Infinity Code   **Fic**

Young, Ed
Beyond the great mountains   **811**
(il) Grimes, N. Tai chi morning   **811**

Young, Emma, 1973-
Israel   **956.94**

Young, Jeff C., 1948-
Arnold Schwarzenegger   **92**
Cesar Chavez   **92**
Dwight D. Eisenhower   **92**
Hugo Chavez   **92**

Young, Karen Romano, 1959-
Across the wide ocean   **623.89**

Young, Kim J.
Ethnobotany   **581.6**

Young, Marilyn Blatt
The Vietnam War: a history in documents   **959.704**

Young, Mitchell
(ed) Racial discrimination. See Racial discrimination   **342**

Young, Robyn V.
(ed) Notable mathematicians. See Notable mathematicians   **920.003**

Young, Roxyanne
(jt. auth) Halls, K. M. Tales of the cryptids   **001.9**

Young, Serinity
Richard Francis Burton   **92**

Young actors series
Shakespeare, W. One hundred and eleven Shakespeare monologues   **822.3**
Surface, M. H. More short scenes and monologues for middle school students   **808.82**
Surface, M. H. Short scenes and monologues for middle school actors   **808.82**

Young Adult Library Services Association
Best books for young adults. See Best books for young adults   **028.1**

Your government—how it works—*Continued*
Mintzer, R. The National Transportation Safety Board   **363.1**

Your name in print. Harper, E.   **808**

Your own, Sylvia. Hemphill, S.   **811**

Your reading   **011.6**

Your travel guide to ancient Israel. Sherman, J.   **933**

You're smarter than you think. Armstrong, T.   **153.9**

Youth
> *See also* Teenagers

Engle, D. PeaceJam   **303.6**
Hoose, P. M. We were there, too!   **973**

Alcohol use
> *See also* Teenagers—Alcohol use

Books and reading
Collins, J. Motivating readers in the middle grades   **028.5**

Drug use
> *See also* Teenagers—Drug use

Student drug testing   **371.7**

Employment
> *See also* Summer employment; Teenagers—Employment

Fiction
Leaving home: stories   **808.8**

Health and hygiene
Child and youth security sourcebook   **362.7**
Crump, M. No B.O.!   **613**

Law and legislation
Jacobs, T. A. What are my rights?   **346**

Political activity
Declare yourself   **323**

Religious life
> *See also* Teenagers—Religious life

Sexual behavior
Pregnancy   **362.7**

Iran
Seidman, D. Teens in Iran   **955**

United States
> *See also* Teenagers—United States

Youth movement
Hill, L. C. America dreaming   **303.4**

Youth violence   **364.36**

Youth with special needs [series]
Brinkerhoff, S. Why can't I learn like everyone else?   **371.9**
Esherick, J. The journey toward recovery   **616.8**
Libal, A. My name is not Slow   **362.3**

Yu Chun, 1966-
Little Green   **951.05**

Yucht, Alice H.
Flip it!   **025.5**

Yue, Charlotte
The wigwam and the longhouse   **970.004**

Yue, David
(jt. auth) Yue, C. The wigwam and the long-house   **970.004**

Yuen, Charles
(il) Lagasse, E. Emeril's there's a chef in my family!   **641.5**
(il) Lagasse, E. Emeril's there's a chef in my world!   **641.5**

Yugoslav War, 1991-1995
Halilbegovich, N. My childhood under fire   **949.7**
O'Grady, S. F. Basher five-two   **949.7**
War-torn Bosnia   **949.7**

Yugoslavia
> *See also* Bosnia and Hercegovina; Croatia; Serbia

History—Civil War, 1991-1995
See Yugoslav War, 1991-1995

Yukon Territory

History
> *See also* Klondike River valley (Yukon)—Gold discoveries

Poetry
Service, R. W. The cremation of Sam McGee   **811**

Z

Z for Zachariah. O'Brien, R. C.   **Fic**

Zabludoff, Marc
Beetles   **595.7**
The insect class   **595.7**
Monkeys   **599.8**
The protoctist kingdom   **579**
The reptile class   **597.9**
Spiders   **595.4**

Zacharias, Gary
(ed) 1900-1920: the twentieth century. See 1900-1920: the twentieth century   **909.82**

Zaharias, Babe Didrikson, 1911-1956
About
Freedman, R. Babe Didrikson Zaharias   **92**

Zahensky, Barbara A.
Diet fads   **613.2**

Zahler, Diane
The Black Death   **614.5**

Zahrah the Windseeker. Okorafor, N.   **Fic**

Zallinger, Jean
(il) Sattler, H. R. The book of North American owls   **598**

Zambia
Holmes, T. Zambia   **968.94**

Zamora, Pedro, 1972-1994
About
Winick, J. Pedro and me   **362.1**

Zamosky, Lisa
Louis Pasteur   **92**

Zanger, Mark H.
The American ethnic cookbook for students   **641.5**

Zannos, Susan
Guglielmo Marconi and the story of radio waves   **92**